2025
STANDARD POSTAGE STAMP CATALOGUE

ONE HUNDRED AND EIGHTY-FIRST EDITION IN SIX VOLUMES

Volume 3B
H-I

EDITOR-IN-CHIEF	Jay Bigalke
EDITOR-AT-LARGE	Donna Houseman
CONTRIBUTING EDITOR	Charles Snee
EDITOR EMERITUS	James E. Kloetzel
SENIOR EDITOR /NEW ISSUES AND VALUING	Martin J. Frankevicz
ASSOCIATE EDITOR	David Hartwig
CATALOGUE COORDINATOR	Eric Wiessinger
SENIOR GRAPHIC DESIGNER	Cinda McAlexander
SALES DIRECTOR	David Pistello
SALES DIRECTOR	Eric Roth
SALES DIRECTOR	Brenda Wyen
SALES REPRESENTATIVE	Julie Dahlstrom

Released June 2024
Includes New Stamp Listings through the April 2024 *Scott Stamp Monthly* Catalogue Update

Copyright© 2024 by

AMOS MEDIA

1660 Campbell Road, Suite A, Sidney, OH 45365
Publishers of *Linn's Stamp News, Scott Stamp Monthly, Coin World* and *Coin World Monthly*.

Scott catalog editorial team contact information
scottstamp.com | scottcatalogueeditorial@amosmedia.com

Scott catalog customer service contact information
amosadvantage.com | cuserv@amosmedia.com | 800-572-6885 | Monday-Thursday 9 a.m. to 5 p.m.; Friday 9 a.m. to noon, Eastern Standard Time

Table of contents

Letter from the editor	Vol. 3A, 3A
2025 Volume 3A-3B catalogue number additions, deletions and changes	3A
Common design types	4A
Acknowledgments	Vol. 3A, 4A
Information on philatelic societies	Vol. 3A, 5A
Expertizing services	Vol. 3A, 9A
Information on catalogue values, grade and condition	Vol. 3A, 10A
Grading illustrations	Vol. 3A, 11A
Gum chart	Vol. 3A, 13A
Understanding the listings	Vol. 3A, 14A
Catalogue listing policy	Vol. 3A, 16A
Special notices	Vol. 3A, 17A
Abbreviations	Vol. 3A, 17A
Basic stamp information	Vol. 3A, 19A
Currency conversion	24A
Terminology	Vol. 3A, 26A
Pronunciation symbols	Vol. 3A, 28A
The British Commonwealth of Nations	Vol. 3A, 30A
Colonies, former colonies, offices, territories controlled by parent states	Vol. 3A, 32A
Dies of British Colonial stamps referred to in the catalogue	Vol. 3A, 33A
British Colonial and Crown Agents watermarks	Vol. 3A, 34A
Countries of the World H-I	**1**
Index and Identifier	**731**
Index to advertisers	742
Dealer directory yellow pages	743

See the following volumes for other country listings:
Volume 1A: United States, United Nations, Abu Dhabi-Australia; Volume 1B: Austria-B
Volume 2A: C-Cur; Volume 2B: Cyp-F
Volume 3A: G
Volume 4A: J-L; Volume 4B: M
Volume 5A: N-Phil; Volume 5B: Pit-Sam
Volume 6A: San-Tete; Volume 6B: Thai-Z

Scott Catalogue Mission Statement

The Scott Catalogue Team exists to serve the recreational, educational and commercial hobby needs of stamp collectors and dealers.
We strive to set the industry standard for philatelic information and products by developing and providing goods that help collectors identify, value, organize and present their collections.
Quality customer service is, and will continue to be, our highest priority.
We aspire toward achieving total customer satisfaction.

Copyright Notice

The contents of this book are owned exclusively by Amos Media Co. and all rights thereto are reserved under the Pan American and Universal Copyright Conventions.

Copyright ©2024 by Amos Media Co., Sidney, Ohio. Printed in U.S.A.

COPYRIGHT NOTE
Permission is hereby given for the use of material in this book and covered by copyright if:
 (a) The material is used in advertising matter, circulars or price lists for the purpose of offering stamps for sale or purchase at the prices listed therein; and
 (b) Such use is incidental to the business of buying and selling stamps and is limited in scope and length, i.e., it does not cover a substantial portion of the total number of stamps issued by any country or of any special category of stamps of any country; and
 (c) Such material is not used as part of any catalogue, stamp album or computerized or other system based upon the Scott catalogue numbers, or in any updated valuations of stamps not offered for sale or purchase; and
 (d) Such use is not competitive with the business of the copyright owner; and
 (e) Such use is for editorial purposes in publications in the form of articles and commentary, except for computer software or the serialization of books in such publications, for which separate written permission is required.
Any use of the material in this book which does not satisfy all the foregoing conditions is forbidden in any form unless permission in each instance is given in writing by the copyright owner.

Trademark Notice

The terms SCOTT, SCOTT'S, SCOTT CATALOGUE NUMBERING SYSTEM, SCOTT CATALOGUE NUMBER, SCOTT NUMBER and abbreviations thereof, are trademarks of Amos Media Co., used to identify its publications and its copyrighted system for identifying and classifying postage stamps for dealers and collectors. These trademarks are to be used only with the prior consent of Amos Media Co.

No part of this work may be reproduced in any form or by any means, electronic or mechanical, including photocopying, without permission in writing from Amos Media Co., P.O. Box 4129, Sidney, OH 45365-4129.

ISBN 978-0-89487-726-1

Library of Congress Card No. 2-3301

Vols. 3A-3B number additions, deletions and changes

| Number in 2024 Catalogue | Number in 2025 Catalogue |
|---|---|//

Great Britain
4326a 4328a

Guyana
1027a .... deleted
1036a .... deleted
1046a .... deleted
1052a .... deleted
1054a .... deleted
1084a .... deleted
1091a .... deleted
1094a .... deleted
1106a .... deleted
1108a .... deleted

Honduras
new C1a

Ireland
new 201a
390a .... deleted
391a .... deleted
new 392c
new 700a
new 869a

COMMON DESIGN TYPES

Pictured in this section are issues where one illustration has been used for a number of countries in the Catalogue. Not included in this section are overprinted stamps or those issues which are illustrated in each country. Because the location of Never Hinged breakpoints varies from country to country, some of the values in the listings below will be for unused stamps that were previously hinged.

EUROPA
Europa, 1956

The design symbolizing the cooperation among the six countries comprising the Coal and Steel Community is illustrated in each country.

Belgium	496-497
France	805-806
Germany	748-749
Italy	715-716
Luxembourg	318-320
Netherlands	368-369

Nos. 496-497 (2)	9.00	.50
Nos. 805-806 (2)	5.25	1.00
Nos. 748-749 (2)	7.40	1.10
Nos. 715-716 (2)	9.25	1.25
Nos. 318-320 (3)	65.50	42.00
Nos. 368-369 (2)	25.75	1.50
Set total (13) Stamps	122.15	47.35

Europa, 1958

"E" and Dove — CD1

European Postal Union at the service of European integration.

1958, Sept. 13

Belgium	527-528
France	889-890
Germany	790-791
Italy	750-751
Luxembourg	341-343
Netherlands	375-376
Saar	317-318

Nos. 527-528 (2)	3.75	.60
Nos. 889-890 (2)	1.65	.55
Nos. 790-791 (2)	2.95	.60
Nos. 750-751 (2)	1.05	.60
Nos. 341-343 (3)	1.35	.90
Nos. 375-376 (2)	1.25	.75
Nos. 317-318 (2)	1.05	2.30
Set total (15) Stamps	13.05	6.30

Europa, 1959

6-Link Enless Chain — CD2

1959, Sept. 19

Belgium	536-537
France	929-930
Germany	805-806
Italy	791-792
Luxembourg	354-355
Netherlands	379-380

Nos. 536-537 (2)	1.55	.60
Nos. 929-930 (2)	1.40	.80
Nos. 805-806 (2)	1.35	.60
Nos. 791-792 (2)	.80	.90
Nos. 354-355 (2)	2.65	1.00
Nos. 379-380 (2)	2.10	1.85
Set total (12) Stamps	9.85	5.35

Europa, 1960

19-Spoke Wheel CD3

First anniverary of the establishment of C.E.P.T. (Conference Europeenne des Administrations des Postes et des Telecommunications.) The spokes symbolize the 19 founding members of the Conference.

1960, Sept.

Belgium	553-554
Denmark	379
Finland	376-377
France	970-971
Germany	818-820
Great Britain	377-378
Greece	688
Iceland	327-328
Ireland	175-176
Italy	809-810
Luxembourg	374-375
Netherlands	385-386
Norway	387
Portugal	866-867
Spain	941-942
Sweden	562-563
Switzerland	400-401
Turkey	1493-1494

Nos. 553-554 (2)	1.25	.55
No. 379 (1)	.55	.50
Nos. 376-377 (2)	1.80	1.40
Nos. 970-971 (2)	.50	.50
Nos. 818-820 (3)	1.90	1.35
Nos. 377-378 (2)	7.00	2.75
No. 688 (1)	4.25	1.75
Nos. 327-328 (2)	1.30	1.85
Nos. 175-176 (2)	13.25	16.00
Nos. 809-810 (2)	.50	.50
Nos. 374-375 (2)	1.00	.80
Nos. 385-386 (2)	2.00	2.00
No. 387 (1)	1.00	.80
Nos. 866-867 (2)	3.05	1.75
Nos. 941-942 (2)	1.50	.75
Nos. 562-563 (2)	1.05	.55
Nos. 400-401 (2)	1.75	.75
Nos. 1493-1494 (2)	2.10	1.35
Set total (34) Stamps	45.75	35.90

Europa, 1961

19 Doves Flying as One — CD4

The 19 doves represent the 19 members of the Conference of European Postal and Telecommunications Administrations C.E.P.T.

1961-62

Belgium	572-573
Cyprus	201-203
France	1005-1006
Germany	844-845
Great Britain	382-384
Greece	718-719
Iceland	340-341
Italy	845-846
Luxembourg	382-383
Netherlands	387-388
Spain	1010-1011
Switzerland	410-411
Turkey	1518-1520

Nos. 572-573 (2)	.75	.50
Nos. 201-203 (3)	.90	.75
Nos. 1005-1006 (2)	.50	.50
Nos. 844-845 (2)	.60	.75
Nos. 382-384 (3)	.75	.75
Nos. 718-719 (2)	.80	.50
Nos. 340-341 (2)	1.10	1.60
Nos. 845-846 (2)	.50	.50
Nos. 382-383 (2)	.55	.55
Nos. 387-388 (2)	.50	.50
Nos. 1010-1011 (2)	.60	.50
Nos. 410-411 (2)	1.90	.60
Nos. 1518-1520 (3)	1.55	.90
Set total (29) Stamps	11.00	8.90

Europa, 1962

Young Tree with 19 Leaves CD5

The 19 leaves represent the 19 original members of C.E.P.T.

1962-63

Belgium	582-583
Cyprus	219-221
France	1045-1046
Germany	852-853
Greece	739-740
Iceland	348-349
Ireland	184-185
Italy	860-861
Luxembourg	386-387
Netherlands	394-395
Norway	414-415
Switzerland	416-417
Turkey	1553-1555

Nos. 582-583 (2)	.65	.65
Nos. 219-221 (3)	21.35	6.75
Nos. 1045-1046 (2)	.60	.50
Nos. 852-853 (2)	.65	.75
Nos. 739-740 (2)	2.00	1.15
Nos. 348-349 (2)	.85	.85
Nos. 184-185 (2)	1.45	2.75
Nos. 860-861 (2)	1.00	.55
Nos. 386-387 (2)	.75	.55
Nos. 394-395 (2)	1.35	.90
Nos. 414-415 (2)	1.75	1.70
Nos. 416-417 (2)	1.65	1.00
Nos. 1553-1555 (3)	2.05	1.10
Set total (28) Stamps	36.10	19.20

Europa, 1963

Stylized Links, Symbolizing Unity — CD6

1963, Sept.

Belgium	598-599
Cyprus	229-231
Finland	419
France	1074-1075
Germany	867-868
Greece	768-769
Iceland	357-358
Ireland	188-189
Italy	880-881
Luxembourg	403-404
Netherlands	416-417
Norway	441-442
Switzerland	429
Turkey	1602-1603

Nos. 598-599 (2)	1.60	.55
Nos. 229-231 (3)	18.30	8.65
No. 419 (1)	1.25	.55
Nos. 1074-1075 (2)	.60	.50
Nos. 867-868 (2)	.50	.55
Nos. 768-769 (2)	4.65	1.65
Nos. 357-358 (2)	1.20	1.20
Nos. 188-189 (2)	2.75	3.25
Nos. 880-881 (2)	.50	.50
Nos. 403-404 (2)	.75	.55
Nos. 416-417 (2)	1.30	1.00
Nos. 441-442 (2)	2.60	2.40
No. 429 (1)	.90	.60
Nos. 1602-1603 (2)	1.20	.50
Set total (27) Stamps	38.10	22.45

Europa, 1964

Symbolic Daisy — CD7

5th anniversary of the establishment of C.E.P.T. The 22 petals of the flower symbolize the 22 members of the Conference.

1964, Sept.

Austria	738
Belgium	614-615
Cyprus	244-246
France	1109-1110
Germany	897-898
Greece	801-802
Iceland	367-368
Ireland	196-197
Italy	894-895
Luxembourg	411-412
Monaco	590-591
Netherlands	428-429
Norway	458
Portugal	931-933
Spain	1262-1263
Switzerland	438-439
Turkey	1628-1629

No. 738 (1)	1.10	.25
Nos. 614-615 (2)	1.40	.60
Nos. 244-246 (3)	10.95	5.00
Nos. 1109-1110 (2)	.50	.50
Nos. 897-898 (2)	.50	.50
Nos. 801-802 (2)	4.15	1.55
Nos. 367-368 (2)	1.40	1.15
Nos. 196-197 (2)	4.50	4.25
Nos. 894-895 (2)	.50	.50
Nos. 411-412 (2)	.75	.55
Nos. 590-591 (2)	2.50	.70
Nos. 428-429 (2)	.75	.60
No. 458 (1)	3.50	3.50
Nos. 931-933 (3)	10.00	2.00
Nos. 1262-1263 (2)	1.15	.80
Nos. 438-439 (2)	1.65	.50
Nos. 1628-1629 (2)	2.00	.80
Set total (34) Stamps	47.30	23.75

Europa, 1965

Leaves and "Fruit" CD8

1965

Belgium	636-637
Cyprus	262-264
Finland	437
France	1131-1132
Germany	934-935
Greece	833-834
Iceland	375-376
Ireland	204-205
Italy	915-916
Luxembourg	432-433
Monaco	616-617
Netherlands	438-439
Norway	475-476
Portugal	958-960
Switzerland	469
Turkey	1665-1666

Nos. 636-637 (2)	.50	.50
Nos. 262-264 (3)	10.80	7.45
No. 437 (1)	1.25	.55
Nos. 1131-1132 (2)	.70	.55
Nos. 934-935 (2)	.50	.50
Nos. 833-834 (2)	2.25	1.15
Nos. 375-376 (2)	2.50	1.75
Nos. 204-205 (2)	5.75	4.60
Nos. 915-916 (2)	.50	.50
Nos. 432-433 (2)	.75	.55
Nos. 616-617 (2)	3.25	1.65
Nos. 438-439 (2)	.55	.55
Nos. 475-476 (2)	2.40	1.90
Nos. 958-960 (3)	16.00	2.75
No. 469 (1)	1.15	.50
Nos. 1665-1666 (2)	2.00	1.25
Set total (32) Stamps	50.85	26.65

Europa, 1966

Symbolic Sailboat — CD9

1966, Sept.

Andorra, French	172
Belgium	675-676
Cyprus	275-277
France	1163-1164
Germany	963-964

COMMON DESIGN TYPES

Greece	862-863
Iceland	384-385
Ireland	216-217
Italy	942-943
Liechtenstein	415
Luxembourg	440-441
Monaco	639-640
Netherlands	441-442
Norway	496-497
Portugal	980-982
Switzerland	477-478
Turkey	1718-1719

No. 172 (1)	3.00	3.00
Nos. 675-676 (2)	.80	.50
Nos. 275-277 (3)	3.10	3.25
Nos. 1163-1164 (2)	.55	.50
Nos. 963-964 (2)	.50	.55
Nos. 862-863 (2)	2.10	1.05
Nos. 384-385 (2)	4.50	3.50
Nos. 216-217 (2)	2.35	3.75
Nos. 942-943 (2)	.50	.50
No. 415 (1)	.40	.35
Nos. 440-441 (2)	.70	.55
Nos. 639-640 (2)	2.00	.65
Nos. 441-442 (2)	.85	.50
Nos. 496-497 (2)	2.35	2.15
Nos. 980-982 (3)	15.90	2.25
Nos. 477-478 (2)	1.40	.60
Nos. 1718-1719 (2)	3.35	1.75
Set total (34) Stamps	44.35	25.40

Europa, 1967

Cogwheels
CD10

1967

Andorra, French	174-175
Belgium	688-689
Cyprus	297-299
France	1178-1179
Germany	969-970
Greece	891-892
Iceland	389-390
Ireland	232-233
Italy	951-952
Liechtenstein	420
Luxembourg	449-450
Monaco	669-670
Netherlands	444-447
Norway	504-505
Portugal	994-996
Spain	1465-1466
Switzerland	482
Turkey	B120-B121

Nos. 174-175 (2)	10.75	6.25
Nos. 688-689 (2)	1.05	.55
Nos. 297-299 (3)	2.55	2.90
Nos. 1178-1179 (2)	.55	.50
Nos. 969-970 (2)	.55	.55
Nos. 891-892 (2)	3.05	.85
Nos. 389-390 (2)	3.00	2.00
Nos. 232-233 (2)	2.25	2.30
Nos. 951-952 (2)	.60	.50
No. 420 (1)	.45	.40
Nos. 449-450 (2)	1.00	.70
Nos. 669-670 (2)	2.75	.70
Nos. 444-447 (4)	2.70	2.05
Nos. 504-505 (2)	2.00	1.80
Nos. 994-996 (3)	16.10	1.85
Nos. 1465-1466 (2)	.50	.50
No. 482 (1)	.60	.30
Nos. B120-B121 (2)	2.50	2.00
Set total (38) Stamps	52.95	26.70

Europa, 1968

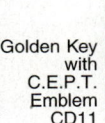

Golden Key
with
C.E.P.T.
Emblem
CD11

1968

Andorra, French	182-183
Belgium	705-706
Cyprus	314-316
France	1209-1210
Germany	983-984
Greece	916-917
Iceland	395-396
Ireland	242-243
Italy	979-980
Liechtenstein	442
Luxembourg	466-467
Monaco	689-691
Netherlands	452-453
Portugal	1019-1021
San Marino	687
Spain	1526
Switzerland	488
Turkey	1775-1776

Nos. 182-183 (2)	16.50	10.00
Nos. 705-706 (2)	1.25	.50
Nos. 314-316 (3)	1.70	2.90
Nos. 1209-1210 (2)	.85	.55
Nos. 983-984 (2)	.50	.55
Nos. 916-917 (2)	3.10	1.45
Nos. 395-396 (2)	3.00	2.20
Nos. 242-243 (2)	2.50	1.70
Nos. 979-980 (2)	.50	.50
No. 442 (1)	.45	.40
Nos. 466-467 (2)	.80	.70
Nos. 689-691 (3)	5.40	.95
Nos. 452-453 (2)	1.05	.70
Nos. 1019-1021 (3)	15.90	2.10
No. 687 (1)	.55	.35
No. 1526 (1)	.25	.25
No. 488 (1)	.40	.25
Nos. 1775-1776 (2)	2.50	1.25
Set total (35) Stamps	57.20	27.30

Europa, 1969

"EUROPA"
and "CEPT"
CD12

Tenth anniversary of C.E.P.T.

1969

Andorra, French	188-189
Austria	837
Belgium	718-719
Cyprus	326-328
Denmark	458
Finland	483
France	1245-1246
Germany	996-997
Great Britain	585
Greece	947-948
Iceland	406-407
Ireland	270-271
Italy	1000-1001
Liechtenstein	453
Luxembourg	475-476
Monaco	722-724
Netherlands	475-476
Norway	533-534
Portugal	1038-1040
San Marino	701-702
Spain	1567
Sweden	814-816
Switzerland	500-501
Turkey	1799-1800
Vatican	470-472
Yugoslavia	1003-1004

Nos. 188-189 (2)	18.50	12.00
No. 837 (1)	.55	.25
Nos. 718-719 (2)	.75	.50
Nos. 326-328 (3)	1.60	2.70
No. 458 (1)	.75	.75
No. 483 (1)	2.50	.60
Nos. 1245-1246 (2)	.55	.50
Nos. 996-997 (2)	.70	.55
No. 585 (1)	.25	.25
Nos. 947-948 (2)	4.00	1.25
Nos. 406-407 (2)	4.20	2.40
Nos. 270-271 (2)	2.00	2.00
Nos. 1000-1001 (2)	.50	.50
No. 453 (1)	.45	.45
Nos. 475-476 (2)	.95	.50
Nos. 722-724 (3)	10.50	2.00
Nos. 475-476 (2)	1.35	1.00
Nos. 533-534 (2)	2.20	1.95
Nos. 1038-1040 (3)	17.75	2.40
Nos. 701-702 (2)	.90	.90
No. 1567 (1)	.25	.25
Nos. 814-816 (3)	4.00	2.85
Nos. 500-501 (2)	1.85	1.00
Nos. 1799-1800 (2)	2.50	1.65
Nos. 470-472 (3)	.75	.75
Nos. 1003-1004 (2)	4.00	4.00
Set total (51) Stamps	84.30	43.90

Europa, 1970

Interwoven
Threads
CD13

1970

Andorra, French	196-197
Belgium	741-742
Cyprus	340-342
France	1271-1272
Germany	1018-1019
Greece	985, 987
Iceland	420-421
Ireland	279-281
Italy	1013-1014
Liechtenstein	470
Luxembourg	489-490
Monaco	768-770
Netherlands	483-484
Portugal	1060-1062
San Marino	729-730
Spain	1607
Switzerland	515-516
Turkey	1848-1849
Yugoslavia	1024-1025

Nos. 196-197 (2)	20.00	8.50
Nos. 741-742 (2)	1.10	.55
Nos. 340-342 (3)	1.70	2.75
Nos. 1271-1272 (2)	.65	.50
Nos. 1018-1019 (2)	.60	.50
Nos. 985, 987 (2)	6.35	1.60
Nos. 420-421 (2)	6.00	4.00
Nos. 279-281 (3)	2.55	2.50
Nos. 1013-1014 (2)	.50	.50
No. 470 (1)	.45	.45
Nos. 489-490 (2)	.80	.55
Nos. 768-770 (3)	6.35	2.10
Nos. 483-484 (2)	1.30	1.15
Nos. 1060-1062 (3)	18.95	2.35
Nos. 729-730 (2)	.90	.55
No. 1607 (1)	.25	.25
Nos. 515-516 (2)	1.85	.70
Nos. 1848-1849 (2)	2.50	1.50
Nos. 1024-1025 (2)	.80	.80
Set total (40) Stamps	73.60	31.80

Europa, 1971

"Fraternity,
Cooperation,
Common
Effort"
CD14

1971

Andorra, French	205-206
Belgium	803-804
Cyprus	365-367
Finland	504
France	1304
Germany	1064-1065
Greece	1029-1030
Iceland	429-430
Ireland	305-306
Italy	1038-1039
Liechtenstein	485
Luxembourg	500-501
Malta	425-427
Monaco	797-799
Netherlands	488-489
Portugal	1094-1096
San Marino	749-750
Spain	1675-1676
Switzerland	531-532
Turkey	1876-1877
Yugoslavia	1052-1053

Nos. 205-206 (2)	20.00	7.75
Nos. 803-804 (2)	1.30	.55
Nos. 365-367 (3)	1.80	2.75
No. 504 (1)	2.50	.50
No. 1304 (1)	.45	.40
Nos. 1064-1065 (2)	.60	.50
Nos. 1029-1030 (2)	4.00	1.80
Nos. 429-430 (2)	5.00	3.75
Nos. 305-306 (2)	2.45	1.50
Nos. 1038-1039 (2)	.65	.50
No. 485 (1)	.45	.45
Nos. 500-501 (2)	1.00	.65
Nos. 425-427 (3)	.80	.80
Nos. 797-799 (3)	15.00	2.80
Nos. 488-489 (2)	1.20	.95
Nos. 1094-1096 (3)	16.15	1.75
Nos. 749-750 (2)	.65	.55
Nos. 1675-1676 (2)	.75	.55
Nos. 531-532 (2)	1.85	.65
Nos. 1876-1877 (2)	2.50	1.25
Nos. 1052-1053 (2)	.50	.50
Set total (43) Stamps	79.60	30.90

Europa, 1972

Sparkles, Symbolic
of Communications
CD15

1972

Andorra, French	210-211
Andorra, Spanish	62
Belgium	825-826
Cyprus	380-382
Finland	512-513
France	1341
Germany	1089-1090
Greece	1049-1050
Iceland	439-440
Ireland	316-317
Italy	1065-1066
Liechtenstein	504
Luxembourg	512-513
Malta	450-453
Monaco	831-832
Netherlands	494-495
Portugal	1141-1143
San Marino	771-772
Spain	1718
Switzerland	544-545
Turkey	1907-1908
Yugoslavia	1100-1101

Nos. 210-211 (2)	21.00	7.00
No. 62 (1)	60.00	60.00
Nos. 825-826 (2)	.95	.55
Nos. 380-382 (3)	2.45	3.25
Nos. 512-513 (2)	4.00	1.00
No. 1341 (1)	.50	.35
Nos. 1089-1090 (2)	1.10	.50
Nos. 1049-1050 (2)	2.00	1.55
Nos. 439-440 (2)	2.90	2.65
Nos. 316-317 (2)	5.25	3.05
Nos. 1065-1066 (2)	.55	.50
No. 504 (1)	.45	.45
Nos. 512-513 (2)	.95	.65
Nos. 450-453 (4)	1.05	1.40
Nos. 831-832 (2)	5.00	1.40
Nos. 494-495 (2)	1.20	.90
Nos. 1141-1143 (3)	15.85	1.50
Nos. 771-772 (2)	.70	.50
No. 1718 (1)	.50	.40
Nos. 544-545 (2)	1.65	.60
Nos. 1907-1908 (2)	4.00	2.00
Nos. 1100-1101 (2)	1.20	1.20
Set total (44) Stamps	133.25	91.40

Europa, 1973

Post Horn
and Arrows
CD16

1973

Andorra, French	219-220
Andorra, Spanish	76
Belgium	839-840
Cyprus	396-398
Finland	526
France	1367
Germany	1114-1115
Greece	1090-1092
Iceland	447-448
Ireland	329-330
Italy	1108-1109
Liechtenstein	528-529
Luxembourg	523-524
Malta	469-471
Monaco	866-867
Netherlands	504-505
Norway	604-605
Portugal	1'70-1172
San Marino	802-803
Spain	1753
Switzerland	580-581
Turkey	1935-1936
Yugoslavia	1138-1139

Nos. 219-220 (2)	20.00	11.00
No. 76 (1)	1.25	.85
Nos. 839-840 (2)	1.00	.65
Nos. 396-398 (3)	1.80	2.40
No. 526 (1)	1.25	.55
No. 1367 (1)	1.25	.75
Nos. 1114-1115 (2)	.85	.50
Nos. 1090-1092 (3)	2.10	1.40
Nos. 447-448 (2)	6.65	3.35

COMMON DESIGN TYPES

Nos. 329-330 (2)	3.95	2.00
Nos. 1108-1109 (2)	.50	.50
Nos. 528-529 (2)	.60	.60
Nos. 523-524 (2)	.90	.75
Nos. 469-471 (3)	.90	1.20
Nos. 866-867 (2)	15.00	2.40
Nos. 504-505 (2)	1.20	.95
Nos. 604-605 (2)	4.00	1.80
Nos. 1170-1172 (3)	24.95	2.15
Nos. 802-803 (2)	1.00	.60
No. 1753 (1)	.35	.25
Nos. 580-581 (2)	1.55	.60
Nos. 1935-1936 (2)	4.15	2.25
Nos. 1138-1139 (2)	1.15	1.10
Set total (46) Stamps	96.35	38.60

Europa, 2000

CD17

2000

Albania	2621-2622
Andorra, French	522
Andorra, Spanish	262
Armenia	610-611
Austria	1814
Azerbaijan	698-699
Belarus	350
Belgium	1818
Bosnia & Herzegovina (Moslem)	358
Bosnia & Herzegovina (Serb)	111-112
Croatia	428-429
Cyprus	959
Czech Republic	3120
Denmark	1189
Estonia	394
Faroe Islands	376
Finland	1129
Aland Islands	166
France	2771
Georgia	228-229
Germany	2086-2087
Gibraltar	837-840
Great Britain (Jersey)	935-936
Great Britain (Isle of Man)	883
Greece	1959
Greenland	363
Hungary	3699-3700
Iceland	910
Ireland	1230-1231
Italy	2349
Latvia	504
Liechtenstein	1178
Lithuania	668
Luxembourg	1035
Macedonia	187
Malta	1011-1012
Moldova	355
Monaco	2161-2162
Poland	3519
Portugal	2358
Portugal (Azores)	455
Portugal (Madeira)	208
Romania	4370
Russia	6589
San Marino	1480
Slovakia	355
Slovenia	424
Spain	3036
Sweden	2394
Switzerland	1074
Turkey	2762
Turkish Rep. of Northern Cyprus	500
Ukraine	379
Vatican City	1152

Nos. 2621-2622 (2)	9.50	9.50
No. 522 (1)	2.00	1.00
No. 262 (1)	1.75	.80
Nos. 610-611 (2)	4.75	4.75
No. 1814 (1)	1.25	1.25
Nos. 698-699 (2)	6.00	6.00
No. 350 (1)	1.75	1.75
No. 1818 (1)	1.40	.60
No. 358 (1)	4.75	4.75
Nos. 111-112 (2)	110.00	110.00
Nos. 428-429 (2)	6.25	6.25
No. 959 (1)	2.10	1.40
No. 3120 (1)	1.20	.40
No. 1189 (1)	3.50	2.25
No. 394 (1)	1.25	1.25
No. 376 (1)	2.40	2.40
No. 1129 (1)	2.00	.60
No. 166 (1)	1.10	1.20
No. 2771 (1)	1.25	.40
Nos. 228-229 (2)	9.00	9.00
Nos. 2086-2087 (2)	4.35	2.10
Nos. 837-840 (4)	4.20	5.30
Nos. 935-936 (2)	2.40	2.40
No. 883 (1)	1.75	1.75
No. 363 (1)	1.90	1.90
Nos. 3699-3700 (2)	4.50	3.00
No. 910 (1)	1.60	1.60
Nos. 1230-1231 (2)	2.60	2.60
No. 2349 (1)	1.50	.40
No. 504 (1)	5.00	2.40
No. 1178 (1)	2.25	1.75
No. 668 (1)	1.50	1.50
No. 1035 (1)	1.40	.85
No. 187 (1)	3.00	3.00
Nos. 1011-1012 (2)	4.35	4.35
No. 355 (1)	3.50	3.50
Nos. 2161-2162 (2)	2.80	1.40
No. 3519 (1)	1.25	.75
No. 2358 (1)	1.95	.65
No. 455 (1)	2.00	.50
No. 208 (1)	2.25	.50
No. 4370 (1)	2.50	1.25
No. 6589 (1)	4.00	.85
No. 1480 (1)	1.00	1.00
No. 355 (1)	1.60	.80
No. 424 (1)	3.25	3.25
No. 3036 (1)	1.00	.40
No. 2394 (1)	3.00	1.50
No. 1074 (1)	2.10	1.05
No. 2762 (1)	2.75	2.00
No. 500 (1)	2.50	2.50
No. 379 (1)	4.50	3.00
No. 1152 (1)	1.75	1.75
Set total (68) Stamps	259.20	227.10

The Gibraltar stamps are similar to the stamp illustrated, but none have the design shown above. All other sets listed above include at least one stamp with the design shown, but some include stamps with entirely different designs. Bulgaria Nos. 4131-4132, Guernsey Nos. 802-803 and Yugoslavia Nos. 2485-2486 are Europa stamps with completely different designs.

PORTUGAL & COLONIES
Vasco da Gama

Fleet Departing CD20

Fleet Arriving at Calicut — CD21

Embarking at Rastello CD22

Muse of History CD23

San Gabriel, da Gama and Camoens CD24

Archangel Gabriel, the Patron Saint CD25

Flagship San Gabriel — CD26

Vasco da Gama — CD27

Fourth centenary of Vasco da Gama's discovery of the route to India.

1898

Azores	93-100
Macao	67-74
Madeira	37-44
Portugal	147-154
Port. Africa	1-8
Port. Congo	75-98
Port. India	189-196
St. Thomas & Prince Islands	170-193
Timor	45-52

Nos. 93-100 (8)	113.50	73.50
Nos. 67-74 (8)	250.25	170.25
Nos. 37-44 (8)	60.55	37.25
Nos. 147-154 (8)	249.05	84.90
Nos. 1-8 (8)	44.00	29.25
Nos. 75-98 (24)	78.50	64.65
Nos. 189-196 (8)	25.25	15.50
Nos. 170-193 (24)	60.40	44.75
Nos. 45-52 (8)	33.50	23.25
Set total (104) Stamps	915.00	543.30

Pombal
POSTAL TAX
POSTAL TAX DUES

Marquis de Pombal — CD28

Planning Reconstruction of Lisbon, 1755 — CD29

Pombal Monument, Lisbon — CD30

Sebastiao Jose de Carvalho e Mello, Marquis de Pombal (1699-1782), statesman, rebuilt Lisbon after earthquake of 1755. Tax was for the erection of Pombal monument. Obligatory on all mail on certain days throughout the year. Postal Tax Dues are inscribed "Multa."

1925

Angola	RA1-RA3, RAJ1-RAJ3
Azores	RA9-RA11, RAJ2-RAJ4
Cape Verde	RA1-RA3, RAJ1-RAJ3
Macao	RA1-RA3, RAJ1-RAJ3
Madeira	RA1-RA3, RAJ1-RAJ3
Mozambique	RA1-RA3, RAJ1-RAJ3
Nyassa	RA1-RA3, RAJ1-RAJ3
Portugal	RA11-RA13, RAJ2-RAJ4
Port. Guinea	RA1-RA3, RAJ1-RAJ3
Port. India	RA1-RA3, RAJ1-RAJ3
St. Thomas & Prince Islands	RA1-RA3, RAJ1-RAJ3
Timor	RA1-RA3, RAJ1-RAJ3

Nos. RA1-RA3,RAJ1-RAJ3 (6)	6.60	5.40
Nos. RA9-RA11,RAJ2-RAJ4 (6)	6.60	6.60
Nos. RA1-RA3,RAJ1-RAJ3 (6)	7.80	7.65
Nos. RA1-RA3,RAJ1-RAJ3 (6)	36.50	17.25
Nos. RA1-RA3,RAJ1-RAJ3 (6)	7.95	14.70
Nos. RA1-RA3,RAJ1-RAJ3 (6)	3.75	3.60
Nos. RA1-RA3,RAJ1-RAJ3 (6)	85.50	76.50
Nos. RA11-RA13,RAJ2-RAJ4 (6)	8.75	8.55
Nos. RA1-RA3,RAJ1-RAJ3 (6)	5.85	5.40
Nos. RA1-RA3,RAJ1-RAJ3 (6)	4.05	4.05
Nos. RA1-RA3,RAJ1-RAJ3 (6)	4.95	3.45
Nos. RA1-RA3,RAJ1-RAJ3 (6)	3.90	3.45
Set total (72) Stamps	182.20	156.60

Vasco da Gama CD34

Mousinho de Albuquerque CD35

Dam CD36

Prince Henry the Navigator CD37

Affonso de Albuquerque CD38

Plane over Globe CD39

1938-39

Angola	274-291, C1-C9
Cape Verde	234-251, C1-C9
Macao	289-305, C7-C15
Mozambique	270-287, C1-C9
Port. Guinea	233-250, C1-C9
Port. India	439-453, C1-C8
St. Thomas & Prince Islands	302-319, 323-340, C1-C18
Timor	223-239, C1-C9

Nos. 274-291,C1-C9 (27)	121.45	20.95
Nos. 234-251,C1-C9 (27)	122.40	38.30
Nos. 289-305,C7-C15 (26)	889.60	338.55
Nos. 270-287,C1-C9 (27)	95.71	15.95
Nos. 233-250,C1-C9 (27)	130.20	49.15
Nos. 439-453,C1-C8 (23)	98.15	34.70
Nos. 302-319,323-340,C1-C18 (54)	468.30	263.80
Nos. 223-239,C1-C9 (26)	213.85	104.90
Set total (237) Stamps	2,140.	866.30

Lady of Fatima

Our Lady of the Rosary, Fatima, Portugal — CD40

1948-49

Angola	315-318
Cape Verde	266
Macao	336
Mozambique	325-328
Port. Guinea	271
Port. India	480
St. Thomas & Prince Islands	351
Timor	254

Nos. 315-318 (4)	68.00	20.60
No. 266 (1)	8.50	9.00
No. 336 (1)	90.00	30.00
Nos. 325-328 (4)	73.25	27.50
No. 271 (1)	6.50	6.00
No. 480 (1)	4.50	4.75
No. 351 (1)	8.50	7.00
No. 254 (1)	6.00	12.50
Set total (14) Stamps	265.25	117.35

A souvenir sheet of 9 stamps was issued in 1951 to mark the extension of the 1950 Holy Year. The sheet contains: Angola No. 316, Cape Verde No. 266, Macao No. 336, Mozambique No. 325, Portuguese Guinea No. 271, Portuguese India Nos. 480, 485, St. Thomas & Prince Islands No. 351, Timor No. 254. The sheet also contains a portrait of Pope Pius XII and is inscribed "Encerramento do

COMMON DESIGN TYPES

Ano Santo, Fatima 1951." It was sold for 11 escudos.

Holy Year

Church Bells and Dove
CD41

Angel Holding Candelabra
CD42

Holy Year, 1950.

1950-51

Angola	331-332
Cape Verde	268-269
Macao	339-340
Mozambique	330-331
Port. Guinea	273-274
Port. India	490-491, 496-503
St. Thomas & Prince Islands	353-354
Timor	258-259

Nos. 331-332 (2)	7.60	1.35
Nos. 268-269 (2)	7.35	4.75
Nos. 339-340 (2)	110.00	34.00
Nos. 330-331 (2)	3.00	1.60
Nos. 273-274 (2)	8.50	5.05
Nos. 490-491,496-503 (10)	14.50	7.30
Nos. 353-354 (2)	10.50	7.25
Nos. 258-259 (2)	8.75	5.00
Set total (24) Stamps	170.20	66.30

A souvenir sheet of 8 stamps was issued in 1951 to mark the extension of the Holy Year. The sheet contains: Angola No. 331, Cape Verde No. 269, Macao No. 340, Mozambique No. 331, Portuguese Guinea No. 275, Portuguese India No. 490, St. Thomas & Prince Islands No. 354, Timor No. 258, some with colors changed. The sheet contains doves and is inscribed 'Encerramento do Ano Santo, Fatima 1951.' It was sold for 17 escudos.

Holy Year Conclusion

Our Lady of Fatima — CD43

Conclusion of Holy Year. Sheets contain alternate vertical rows of stamps and labels bearing quotation from Pope Pius XII, different for each colony.

1951

Angola	357
Cape Verde	270
Macao	352
Mozambique	356
Port. Guinea	275
Port. India	506
St. Thomas & Prince Islands	355
Timor	270

No. 357 (1)	4.50	1.60
No. 270 (1)	1.75	1.25
No. 352 (1)	110.00	23.00
No. 356 (1)	3.25	1.75
No. 275 (1)	2.00	1.00
No. 506 (1)	2.50	1.60
No. 355 (1)	3.50	2.75
No. 270 (1)	3.75	2.75
Set total (8) Stamps	131.25	35.70

Medical Congress

CD44

First National Congress of Tropical Medicine, Lisbon, 1952. Each stamp has a different design.

1952

Angola	358
Cape Verde	287
Macao	364
Mozambique	359
Port. Guinea	276
Port. India	516
St. Thomas & Prince Islands	356
Timor	271

No. 358 (1)	1.35	.45
No. 287 (1)	.95	.75
No. 364 (1)	20.00	7.00
No. 359 (1)	1.90	.90
No. 276 (1)	.75	.65
No. 516 (1)	7.50	3.25
No. 356 (1)	.75	.30
No. 271 (1)	2.00	1.60
Set total (8) Stamps	35.20	14.90

Postage Due Stamps

CD45

1952

Angola	J37-J42
Cape Verde	J31-J36
Macao	J53-J58
Mozambique	J51-J56
Port. Guinea	J40-J45
Port. India	J47-J52
St. Thomas & Prince Islands	J52-J57
Timor	J31-J36

Nos. J37-J42 (6)	3.15	2.95
Nos. J31-J36 (6)	2.80	2.30
Nos. J53-J58 (6)	27.80	12.05
Nos. J51-J56 (6)	2.40	1.95
Nos. J40-J45 (6)	2.70	2.55
Nos. J47-J52 (6)	6.10	6.10
Nos. J52-J57 (6)	2.85	2.70
Nos. J31-J36 (6)	4.00	2.35
Set total (48) Stamps	51.80	32.95

Sao Paulo

Father Manuel da Nobrega and View of Sao Paulo — CD46

Founding of Sao Paulo, Brazil, 400th anniv.

1954

Angola	385
Cape Verde	297
Macao	382
Mozambique	395
Port. Guinea	291
Port. India	530
St. Thomas & Prince Islands	369
Timor	279

No. 385 (1)	.80	.30
No. 297 (1)	.95	.80
No. 382 (1)	30.00	6.00
No. 395 (1)	.75	.30
No. 291 (1)	.50	.35
No. 530 (1)	1.00	.55
No. 369 (1)	.70	.50
No. 279 (1)	2.00	1.40
Set total (8) Stamps	36.70	10.20

Tropical Medicine Congress

CD47

Sixth International Congress for Tropical Medicine and Malaria, Lisbon, Sept. 1958. Each stamp shows a different plant.

1958

Angola	409
Cape Verde	303
Macao	392
Mozambique	404
Port. Guinea	295
Port. India	569
St. Thomas & Prince Islands	371
Timor	289

No. 409 (1)	3.50	1.00
No. 303 (1)	6.75	3.25
No. 392 (1)	13.00	6.00
No. 404 (1)	3.50	1.50
No. 295 (1)	4.50	2.00
No. 569 (1)	1.75	.75
No. 371 (1)	2.75	2.00
No. 289 (1)	5.50	4.25
Set total (8) Stamps	41.25	20.75

Sports

CD48

Each stamp shows a different sport.

1962

Angola	433-438
Cape Verde	320-325
Macao	394-399
Mozambique	424-429
Port. Guinea	299-304
St. Thomas & Prince Islands	374-379
Timor	313-318

Nos. 433-438 (6)	5.55	3.20
Nos. 320-325 (6)	16.05	7.40
Nos. 394-399 (6)	129.85	28.95
Nos. 424-429 (6)	6.55	2.45
Nos. 299-304 (6)	6.00	3.00
Nos. 374-379 (6)	6.80	3.20
Nos. 313-318 (6)	11.65	5.90
Set total (42) Stamps	182.45	54.10

Anti-Malaria

Anopheles Funestus and Malaria Eradication Symbol — CD49

World Health Organization drive to eradicate malaria.

1962

Angola	439
Cape Verde	326
Macao	400
Mozambique	430
Port. Guinea	305
St. Thomas & Prince Islands	380
Timor	319

No. 439 (1)	2.25	.90
No. 326 (1)	1.90	1.60
No. 400 (1)	12.00	4.00
No. 430 (1)	2.00	.50
No. 305 (1)	1.50	.60
No. 380 (1)	2.25	1.25
No. 319 (1)	2.25	1.40
Set total (7) Stamps	24.15	10.25

Airline Anniversary

Map of Africa, Super Constellation and Jet Liner — CD50

Tenth anniversary of Transportes Aereos Portugueses (TAP).

1963

Angola	490
Cape Verde	327
Mozambique	434
Port. Guinea	318
St. Thomas & Prince Islands	381

No. 490 (1)	1.35	.35
No. 327 (1)	1.50	1.10
No. 434 (1)	.55	.25
No. 318 (1)	1.25	.60
No. 381 (1)	.80	.50
Set total (5) Stamps	5.45	2.80

National Overseas Bank

Antonio Teixeira de Sousa — CD51

Centenary of the National Overseas Bank of Portugal.

1964, May 16

Angola	509
Cape Verde	328
Port. Guinea	319
St. Thomas & Prince Islands	382
Timor	320

No. 509 (1)	.90	.45
No. 328 (1)	1.50	1.30
No. 319 (1)	.95	.60
No. 382 (1)	.95	.65
No. 320 (1)	1.50	1.30
Set total (5) Stamps	5.80	4.15

ITU

ITU Emblem and the Archangel Gabriel — CD52

International Communications Union, Cent.

1965, May 17

Angola	511
Cape Verde	329
Macao	402
Mozambique	464
Port. Guinea	320
St. Thomas & Prince Islands	383
Timor	321

No. 511 (1)	1.25	.65
No. 329 (1)	2.90	2.25
No. 402 (1)	9.00	3.00
No. 464 (1)	.65	.25
No. 320 (1)	2.50	1.00
No. 383 (1)	2.00	1.00
No. 321 (1)	2.20	1.40
Set total (7) Stamps	20.50	9.55

National Revolution

CD53

40th anniv. of the National Revolution. Different buildings on each stamp.

1966, May 28

Angola	525
Cape Verde	338
Macao	403
Mozambique	465
Port. Guinea	329
St. Thomas & Prince Islands	392
Timor	322

No. 525 (1)	.50	.25
No. 338 (1)	.85	.75
No. 403 (1)	9.00	3.75
No. 465 (1)	.65	.30
No. 329 (1)	.85	.65
No. 392 (1)	.80	.50
No. 322 (1)	2.40	1.40
Set total (7) Stamps	15.05	7.60

Navy Club

CD54

COMMON DESIGN TYPES

Centenary of Portugal's Navy Club. Each stamp has a different design.

1967, Jan. 31

Angola	527-528
Cape Verde	339-340
Macao	412-413
Mozambique	478-479
Port. Guinea	330-331
St. Thomas & Prince Islands	393-394
Timor	323-324

Nos. 527-528 (2)	2.35	1.20
Nos. 339-340 (2)	2.70	2.30
Nos. 412-413 (2)	18.00	4.70
Nos. 478-479 (2)	1.75	.65
Nos. 330-331 (2)	1.65	.65
Nos. 393-394 (2)	3.30	1.30
Nos. 323-324 (2)	4.25	2.40
Set total (14) Stamps	34.00	13.45

Admiral Coutinho

CD55

Centenary of the birth of Admiral Carlos Viegas Gago Coutinho (1869-1959), explorer and aviation pioneer. Each stamp has a different design.

1969, Feb. 17

Angola	547
Cape Verde	355
Macao	417
Mozambique	484
Port. Guinea	335
St. Thomas & Prince Islands	397
Timor	335

No. 547 (1)	.85	.35
No. 355 (1)	.60	.25
No. 417 (1)	7.50	2.25
No. 484 (1)	.30	.25
No. 335 (1)	.50	.25
No. 397 (1)	.70	.35
No. 335 (1)	2.50	1.40
Set total (7) Stamps	12.95	5.10

Administration Reform

Luiz Augusto Rebello da Silva — CD56

Centenary of the administration reforms of the overseas territories.

1969, Sept. 25

Angola	549
Cape Verde	357
Macao	419
Mozambique	491
Port. Guinea	337
St. Thomas & Prince Islands	399
Timor	338

No. 549 (1)	.30	.25
No. 357 (1)	.65	.40
No. 419 (1)	12.50	2.00
No. 491 (1)	.30	.25
No. 337 (1)	.35	.25
No. 399 (1)	.60	.45
No. 338 (1)	1.40	.70
Set total (7) Stamps	16.10	4.30

Marshal Carmona

CD57

Birth centenary of Marshal Antonio Oscar Carmona de Fragoso (1869-1951), President of Portugal. Each stamp has a different design.

1970, Nov. 15

Angola	563
Cape Verde	359
Macao	422
Mozambique	493
Port. Guinea	340
St. Thomas & Prince Islands	403
Timor	341

No. 563 (1)	.45	.25
No. 359 (1)	.70	.50
No. 422 (1)	5.00	1.75
No. 493 (1)	.40	.25
No. 340 (1)	.45	.25
No. 403 (1)	.90	.40
No. 341 (1)	1.00	.50
Set total (7) Stamps	8.90	3.90

Olympic Games

CD59

20th Olympic Games, Munich, Aug. 26-Sept. 11. Each stamp shows a different sport.

1972, June 20

Angola	569
Cape Verde	361
Macao	426
Mozambique	504
Port. Guinea	342
St. Thomas & Prince Islands	408
Timor	343

No. 569 (1)	.65	.25
No. 361 (1)	.85	.40
No. 426 (1)	2.50	1.50
No. 504 (1)	.30	.25
No. 342 (1)	.95	.25
No. 408 (1)	.60	.25
No. 343 (1)	1.60	.80
Set total (7) Stamps	7.45	3.70

Lisbon-Rio de Janeiro Flight

CD60

50th anniversary of the Lisbon to Rio de Janeiro flight by Arturo de Sacadura and Coutinho, March 30-June 5, 1922. Each stamp shows a different stage of the flight.

1972, Sept. 20

Angola	570
Cape Verde	362
Macao	427
Mozambique	505
Port. Guinea	343
St. Thomas & Prince Islands	409
Timor	344

No. 570 (1)	.35	.25
No. 362 (1)	.85	.40
No. 427 (1)	40.00	12.00
No. 505 (1)	.30	.25
No. 343 (1)	.35	.25
No. 409 (1)	.50	.25
No. 344 (1)	1.25	.90
Set total (7) Stamps	43.60	14.30

WMO Centenary

WMO Emblem — CD61

Centenary of international meteorological cooperation.

1973, Dec. 15

Angola	571
Cape Verde	363
Macao	429
Mozambique	509
Port. Guinea	344
St. Thomas & Prince Islands	410
Timor	345

No. 571 (1)	.45	.25
No. 363 (1)	.85	.40
No. 429 (1)	15.00	2.50
No. 509 (1)	.40	.25
No. 344 (1)	.55	.40
No. 410 (1)	.80	.50
No. 345 (1)	3.75	2.75
Set total (7) Stamps	21.80	7.05

FRENCH COMMUNITY

Upper Volta can be found under Burkina Faso in Vol. 1
Madagascar can be found under Malagasy in Vol. 3

Colonial Exposition

People of French Empire CD70

Women's Heads CD71

France Showing Way to Civilization CD72

"Colonial Commerce" CD73

International Colonial Exposition, Paris.

1931

Cameroun	213-216
Chad	60-63
Dahomey	97-100
Fr. Guiana	152-155
Fr. Guinea	116-119
Fr. India	100-103
Fr. Polynesia	76-79
Fr. Sudan	102-105
Gabon	120-123
Guadeloupe	138-141
Indo-China	140-142
Ivory Coast	92-95
Madagascar	169-172
Martinique	129-132
Mauritania	65-68
Middle Congo	61-64
New Caledonia	176-179
Niger	73-76
Reunion	122-125
St. Pierre & Miquelon	132-135
Senegal	138-141
Somali Coast	135-138
Togo	254-257
Ubangi-Shari	82-85
Upper Volta	66-69
Wallis & Futuna Isls.	85-88

Nos. 213-216 (4)	23.00	18.25
Nos. 60-63 (4)	22.00	22.00
Nos. 97-100 (4)	26.00	26.00
Nos. 152-155 (4)	22.00	22.00
Nos. 116-119 (4)	19.75	19.75
Nos. 100-103 (4)	18.00	18.00
Nos. 76-79 (4)	30.00	30.00
Nos. 102-105 (4)	19.00	19.00
Nos. 120-123 (4)	17.50	17.50
Nos. 138-141 (4)	19.00	19.00
Nos. 140-142 (4)	12.00	11.50
Nos. 92-95 (4)	22.50	22.50
Nos. 169-172 (4)	9.25	6.50
Nos. 129-132 (4)	21.00	21.00
Nos. 65-68 (4)	22.00	22.00
Nos. 61-64 (4)	20.00	18.50
Nos. 176-179 (4)	24.00	24.00
Nos. 73-76 (4)	20.50	20.50
Nos. 122-125 (4)	22.00	22.00
Nos. 132-135 (4)	24.00	24.00
Nos. 138-141 (4)	20.00	20.00
Nos. 135-138 (4)	22.00	22.00
Nos. 254-257 (4)	22.00	22.00
Nos. 82-85 (4)	21.00	21.00
Nos. 66-69 (4)	19.00	19.00
Nos. 85-88 (4)	31.00	35.00
Set total (103) Stamps	548.50	543.00

Paris International Exposition
Colonial Arts Exposition

"Colonial Resources"
CD74   CD77

Overseas Commerce CD75

Exposition Building and Women CD76

"France and the Empire" CD78

Cultural Treasures of the Colonies CD79

Souvenir sheets contain one imperf. stamp.

1937

Cameroun	217-222A
Dahomey	101-107
Fr. Equatorial Africa	27-32, 73
Fr. Guiana	162-168
Fr. Guinea	120-126
Fr. India	104-110
Fr. Polynesia	117-123
Fr. Sudan	106-112
Guadeloupe	148-154
Indo-China	193-199
Inini	41
Ivory Coast	152-158
Kwangchowan	132
Madagascar	191-197
Martinique	179-185
Mauritania	69-75
New Caledonia	208-214
Niger	77-83
Reunion	167-173
St. Pierre & Miquelon	165-171
Senegal	172-178
Somali Coast	139-145
Togo	258-264
Wallis & Futuna Isls.	89

Nos. 217-222A (7)	18.80	20.30
Nos. 101-107 (7)	23.60	27.60
Nos. 27-32, 73 (7)	28.10	32.10
Nos. 162-168 (7)	22.50	24.50
Nos. 120-126 (7)	24.00	28.00
Nos. 104-110 (7)	21.15	36.50
Nos. 117-123 (7)	58.50	75.00
Nos. 106-112 (7)	23.60	27.60
Nos. 148-154 (7)	19.55	21.05
Nos. 193-199 (7)	17.70	19.70
No. 41 (1)	21.00	27.50
Nos. 152-158 (7)	22.20	26.20
No. 132 (1)	9.25	11.00
Nos. 191-197 (7)	19.25	21.75
Nos. 179-185 (7)	19.95	21.70
Nos. 69-75 (7)	20.50	24.50
Nos. 208-214 (7)	39.00	50.50
Nos. 73-83 (11)	40.60	45.10
Nos. 167-173 (7)	21.70	23.20
Nos. 165-171 (7)	49.60	64.00
Nos. 172-178 (7)	21.00	23.80
Nos. 139-145 (7)	25.60	32.60
Nos. 258-264 (7)	20.40	20.40
No. 89 (1)	19.00	37.50
Set total (154) Stamps	606.55	742.10

COMMON DESIGN TYPES

Curie

Pierre and Marie Curie
CD80

40th anniversary of the discovery of radium. The surtax was for the benefit of the Intl. Union for the Control of Cancer.

1938

Cameroun	B1
Cuba	B1-B2
Dahomey	B2
France	B76
Fr. Equatorial Africa	B1
Fr. Guiana	B3
Fr. Guinea	B2
Fr. India	B6
Fr. Polynesia	B5
Fr. Sudan	B1
Guadeloupe	B3
Indo-China	B14
Ivory Coast	B2
Madagascar	B2
Martinique	B2
Mauritania	B3
New Caledonia	B4
Niger	B1
Reunion	B4
St. Pierre & Miquelon	B3
Senegal	B3
Somali Coast	B2
Togo	B1

No. B1 (1)	10.00	10.00
Nos. B1-B2 (2)	12.00	3.35
No. B2 (1)	9.50	9.50
No. B76 (1)	21.00	12.50
No. B1 (1)	24.00	24.00
No. B3 (1)	13.50	13.50
No. B2 (1)	8.75	8.75
No. B6 (1)	10.00	10.00
No. B5 (1)	20.00	20.00
No. B1 (1)	12.50	12.50
No. B3 (1)	11.00	10.50
No. B14 (1)	12.00	12.00
No. B2 (1)	11.00	7.50
No. B2 (1)	11.00	11.00
No. B2 (1)	13.00	13.00
No. B3 (1)	7.75	7.75
No. B4 (1)	16.50	17.50
No. B1 (1)	16.50	16.50
No. B4 (1)	14.00	14.00
No. B3 (1)	21.00	22.50
No. B3 (1)	10.50	10.50
No. B2 (1)	7.75	7.75
No. B1 (1)	20.00	20.00
Set total (24) Stamps	313.25	294.60

Caillie

Rene Caillie and Map of Northwestern Africa — CD81

Death centenary of Rene Caillie (1799-1838), French explorer. All three denominations exist with colony name omitted.

1939

Dahomey	108-110
Fr. Guinea	161-163
Fr. Sudan	113-115
Ivory Coast	160-162
Mauritania	109-111
Niger	84-86
Senegal	188-190
Togo	265-267

Nos. 108-110 (3)	1.20	3.60
Nos. 161-163 (3)	1.20	3.20
Nos. 113-115 (3)	1.20	3.20
Nos. 160-162 (3)	1.05	2.55
Nos. 109-111 (3)	1.05	3.80
Nos. 84-86 (3)	2.35	2.35
Nos. 188-190 (3)	1.05	2.90
Nos. 265-267 (3)	1.05	3.30
Set total (24) Stamps	10.15	24.90

New York World's Fair

Natives and New York Skyline
CD82

1939

Cameroun	223-224
Dahomey	111-112
Fr. Equatorial Africa	78-79
Fr. Guiana	169-170
Fr. Guinea	164-165
Fr. India	111-112
Fr. Polynesia	124-125
Fr. Sudan	116-117
Guadeloupe	155-156
Indo-China	203-204
Inini	42-43
Ivory Coast	163-164
Kwangchowan	133-134
Madagascar	209-210
Martinique	186-187
Mauritania	112-113
New Caledonia	215-216
Niger	87-88
Reunion	174-175
St. Pierre & Miquelon	205-206
Senegal	191-192
Somali Coast	179-180
Togo	268-269
Wallis & Futuna Isls.	90-91

Nos. 223-224 (2)	2.80	2.40
Nos. 111-112 (2)	1.60	3.20
Nos. 78-79 (2)	1.60	3.20
Nos. 169-170 (2)	2.60	2.60
Nos. 164-165 (2)	1.60	3.20
Nos. 111-112 (2)	3.00	8.00
Nos. 124-125 (2)	4.80	4.80
Nos. 116-117 (2)	1.60	3.20
Nos. 155-156 (2)	2.50	2.50
Nos. 203-204 (2)	2.05	2.05
Nos. 42-43 (2)	7.50	9.00
Nos. 163-164 (2)	1.50	3.00
Nos. 133-134 (2)	2.50	2.50
Nos. 209-210 (2)	1.50	2.50
Nos. 186-187 (2)	2.35	2.35
Nos. 112-113 (2)	1.40	2.80
Nos. 215-216 (2)	3.35	3.35
Nos. 87-88 (2)	1.60	2.80
Nos. 174-175 (2)	2.80	2.80
Nos. 205-206 (2)	4.80	6.00
Nos. 191-192 (2)	1.40	2.80
Nos. 179-180 (2)	1.40	2.80
Nos. 268-269 (2)	1.40	2.80
Nos. 90-91 (2)	5.00	6.00
Set total (48) Stamps	62.65	86.65

French Revolution

Storming of the Bastille
CD83

French Revolution, 150th anniv. The surtax was for the defense of the colonies.

1939

Cameroun	B2-B6
Dahomey	B3-B7
Fr. Equatorial Africa	B4-B8, CB1
Fr. Guiana	B4-B8, CB1
Fr. Guinea	B3-B7
Fr. India	B7-B11
Fr. Polynesia	B6-B10, CB1
Fr. Sudan	B2-B6
Guadeloupe	B4-B8
Indo-China	B15-B19, CB1
Inini	B1-B5
Ivory Coast	B3-B7
Kwangchowan	B1-B5
Madagascar	B3-B7, CB1
Martinique	B3-B7
Mauritania	B4-B8
New Caledonia	B5-B9, CB1
Niger	B2-B6
Reunion	B5-B9, CB1
St. Pierre & Miquelon	B4-B8
Senegal	B4-B8, CB1
Somali Coast	B3-B7
Togo	B2-B6
Wallis & Futuna Isls.	B1-B5

Nos. B2-B6 (5)	60.00	60.00
Nos. B3-B7 (5)	47.50	47.50
Nos. B4-B8,CB1 (6)	120.00	120.00
Nos. B4-B8,CB1 (6)	79.50	79.50
Nos. B3-B7 (5)	47.50	47.50
Nos. B7-B11 (5)	28.75	32.50
Nos. B6-B10,CB1 (6)	122.50	122.50
Nos. B2-B6 (5)	50.00	50.00
Nos. B4-B8 (5)	50.00	50.00
Nos. B15-B19,CB1 (6)	85.00	85.00
Nos. B1-B5 (5)	80.00	100.00
Nos. B3-B7 (5)	43.75	43.75
Nos. B1-B5 (5)	46.25	46.25
Nos. B3-B7,CB1 (6)	65.50	65.50
Nos. B3-B7 (5)	52.50	52.50
Nos. B4-B8 (5)	42.50	42.50
Nos. B5-B9,CB1 (6)	101.50	101.50
Nos. B2-B6 (5)	60.00	60.00
Nos. B5-B9,CB1 (6)	87.50	87.50
Nos. B4-B8 (5)	67.50	72.50
Nos. B4-B8,CB1 (6)	56.50	56.50
Nos. B3-B7 (5)	45.00	45.00
Nos. B2-B6 (5)	42.50	42.50
Nos. B1-B5 (5)	80.00	110.00
Set total (128) Stamps	1,562.	1,621.

Plane over Coastal Area
CD85

All five denominations exist with colony name omitted.

1940

Dahomey	C1-C5
Fr. Guinea	C1-C5
Fr. Sudan	C1-C5
Ivory Coast	C1-C5
Mauritania	C1-C5
Niger	C1-C5
Senegal	C12-C16
Togo	C1-C5

Nos. C1-C5 (5)	4.00	4.00
Nos. C1-C5 (5)	4.00	4.00
Nos. C1-C5 (5)	4.00	4.00
Nos. C1-C5 (5)	3.80	3.80
Nos. C1-C5 (5)	3.50	3.50
Nos. C1-C5 (5)	3.50	3.50
Nos. C12-C16 (5)	3.50	3.50
Nos. C1-C5 (5)	3.15	3.15
Set total (40) Stamps	29.45	29.45

Defense of the Empire

Colonial Infantryman — CD86

1941

Cameroun	B13B
Dahomey	B13
Fr. Equatorial Africa	B8B
Fr. Guiana	B10
Fr. Guinea	B13
Fr. India	B13
Fr. Polynesia	B12
Fr. Sudan	B12
Guadeloupe	B10
Indo-China	B19B
Inini	B7
Ivory Coast	B13
Kwangchowan	B7
Madagascar	B9
Martinique	B9
Mauritania	B14
New Caledonia	B11
Niger	B12
Reunion	B11
St. Pierre & Miquelon	B8B
Senegal	B14
Somali Coast	B10B
Togo	B10B
Wallis & Futuna Isls.	B7

No. B13B (1)	1.60	
No. B13 (1)	1.20	
No. B8B (1)	3.50	
No. B10 (1)	1.40	
No. B13 (1)	1.40	
No. B13 (1)	1.25	
No. B12 (1)	3.50	
No. B12 (1)	1.40	
No. B10 (1)	1.00	
No. B19B (1)	3.00	
No. B7 (1)	1.75	
No. B13 (1)	1.25	
No. B7 (1)	.85	
No. B9 (1)	1.50	
No. B9 (1)	1.40	
No. B14 (1)	.95	
No. B12 (1)	1.40	
No. B11 (1)	1.60	
No. B8B (1)	4.50	
No. B14 (1)	1.25	
No. B9 (1)	1.60	
No. B10B (1)	1.10	
No. B7 (1)	1.05	
Set total (23) Stamps	40.15	

Each of the CD86 stamps listed above is part of a set of three stamps. The designs of the other two stamps in the set vary from country to country. Only the values of the Common Design stamps are listed here.

Colonial Education Fund

CD86a

1942

Cameroun	CB3
Dahomey	CB4
Fr. Equatorial Africa	CB5
Fr. Guiana	CB4
Fr. Guinea	CB4
Fr. India	CB4
Fr. Polynesia	CB4
Fr. Sudan	CB4
Guadeloupe	CB3
Indo-China	CB5
Inini	CB3
Ivory Coast	CB4
Kwangchowan	CB4
Malagasy	CB5
Martinique	CB3
Mauritania	CB5
New Caledonia	CB4
Niger	CB4
Reunion	CB4
St. Pierre & Miquelon	CB3
Senegal	CB5
Somali Coast	CB3
Togo	CB3
Wallis & Futuna	CB3

No. CB3 (1)	1.10	
No. CB4 (1)	.80	5.50
No. CB5 (1)	.80	
No. CB4 (1)	1.10	
No. CB4 (1)	.40	5.50
No. CB3 (1)	.90	
No. CB4 (1)	2.00	
No. CB4 (1)	.40	5.50
No. CB5 (1)	1.10	
No. CB3 (1)	2.00	
No. CB3 (1)	1.25	
No. CB4 (1)	1.00	5.50
No. CB4 (1)	1.00	
No. CB5 (1)	.65	
No. CB3 (1)	1.00	
No. CB4 (1)	.80	
No. CB4 (1)	2.25	
No. CB4 (1)	.35	
No. CB4 (1)	.90	
No. CB3 (1)	7.00	
No. CB5 (1)	.80	6.50
No. CB3 (1)	.70	
No. CB3 (1)	.35	
No. CB3 (1)	2.00	
Set total (24) Stamps	30.65	28.50

Cross of Lorraine & Four-motor Plane
CD87

1941-5

Cameroun	C1-C7
Fr. Equatorial Africa	C17-C23
Fr. Guiana	C9-C10
Fr. India	C1-C6
Fr. Polynesia	C3-C9
Fr. West Africa	C1-C3
Guadeloupe	C1-C2
Madagascar	C37-C43

COMMON DESIGN TYPES

Martinique	C1-C2
New Caledonia	C7-C13
Reunion	C18-C24
St. Pierre & Miquelon	C1-C7
Somali Coast	C1-C7

Nos. C1-C7 (7)	6.30	6.30
Nos. C17-C23 (7)	10.40	6.35
Nos. C9-C10 (2)	3.80	3.10
Nos. C1-C6 (6)	9.30	15.00
Nos. C3-C9 (7)	13.75	10.00
Nos. C1-C3 (3)	9.50	3.90
Nos. C1-C2 (2)	3.75	2.50
Nos. C37-C43 (7)	5.60	3.80
Nos. C1-C2 (2)	3.00	1.60
Nos. C7-C13 (7)	8.85	7.30
Nos. C18-C24 (7)	7.05	5.00
Nos. C1-C7 (7)	11.60	9.40
Nos. C1-C7 (7)	13.95	11.10
Set total (71) Stamps	106.85	85.35

Somali Coast stamps are inscribed "Djibouti."

Transport Plane CD88

Caravan and Plane CD89

1942

Dahomey	C6-C13
Fr. Guinea	C6-C13
Fr. Sudan	C6-C13
Ivory Coast	C6-C13
Mauritania	C6-C13
Niger	C6-C13
Senegal	C17-C25
Togo	C6-C13

Nos. C6-C13 (8)	7.15
Nos. C6-C13 (8)	5.75
Nos. C6-C13 (8)	8.00
Nos. C6-C13 (8)	11.15
Nos. C6-C13 (8)	9.75
Nos. C6-C13 (8)	6.20
Nos. C17-C25 (9)	9.45
Nos. C6-C13 (8)	6.75
Set total (65) Stamps	64.20

Red Cross

Marianne CD90

The surtax was for the French Red Cross and national relief.

1944

Cameroun	B28
Fr. Equatorial Africa	B38
Fr. Guiana	B12
Fr. India	B14
Fr. Polynesia	B13
Fr. West Africa	B1
Guadeloupe	B12
Madagascar	B15
Martinique	B11
New Caledonia	B13
Reunion	B15
St. Pierre & Miquelon	B13
Somali Coast	B13
Wallis & Futuna Isls.	B9

No. B28 (1)	2.00	1.60
No. B38 (1)	1.60	1.20
No. B12 (1)	1.75	1.25
No. B14 (1)	1.50	1.25
No. B13 (1)	2.00	1.60
No. B1 (1)	6.50	4.75
No. B12 (1)	1.40	1.00
No. B15 (1)	.90	.90
No. B11 (1)	1.20	1.20
No. B13 (1)	1.50	1.50
No. B15 (1)	1.60	1.10
No. B13 (1)	2.60	2.60
No. B13 (1)	1.75	2.00
No. B9 (1)	3.00	3.00
Set total (14) Stamps	29.30	24.95

Eboue

CD91

Felix Eboue, first French colonial administrator to proclaim resistance to Germany after French surrender in World War II.

1945

Cameroun	296-297
Fr. Equatorial Africa	156-157
Fr. Guiana	171-172
Fr. India	210-211
Fr. Polynesia	150-151
Fr. West Africa	15-16
Guadeloupe	187-188
Madagascar	259-260
Martinique	196-197
New Caledonia	274-275
Reunion	238-239
St. Pierre & Miquelon	322-323
Somali Coast	238-239

Nos. 296-297 (2)	2.40	1.95
Nos. 156-157 (2)	2.55	2.00
Nos. 171-172 (2)	2.45	2.00
Nos. 210-211 (2)	2.20	1.95
Nos. 150-151 (2)	3.60	2.85
Nos. 15-16 (2)	2.40	2.40
Nos. 187-188 (2)	2.05	1.60
Nos. 259-260 (2)	2.00	1.45
Nos. 196-197 (2)	2.05	1.55
Nos. 274-275 (2)	3.40	3.00
Nos. 238-239 (2)	2.40	2.00
Nos. 322-323 (2)	4.40	3.45
Nos. 238-239 (2)	2.45	2.10
Set total (26) Stamps	34.35	28.30

Victory

Victory — CD92

European victory of the Allied Nations in World War II.

1946, May 8

Cameroun	C8
Fr. Equatorial Africa	C24
Fr. Guiana	C11
Fr. India	C7
Fr. Polynesia	C10
Fr. West Africa	C4
Guadeloupe	C3
Indo-China	C19
Madagascar	C44
Martinique	C3
New Caledonia	C14
Reunion	C25
St. Pierre & Miquelon	C8
Somali Coast	C8
Wallis & Futuna Isls.	C1

No. C8 (1)	1.60	1.20
No. C24 (1)	1.60	1.25
No. C11 (1)	1.75	1.25
No. C7 (1)	1.00	4.00
No. C10 (1)	2.75	2.00
No. C4 (1)	1.60	1.20
No. C3 (1)	1.25	1.00
No. C19 (1)	1.00	.55
No. C44 (1)	1.00	.35
No. C3 (1)	1.30	1.00
No. C14 (1)	1.50	1.25
No. C25 (1)	1.10	.90
No. C8 (1)	2.10	2.10
No. C8 (1)	1.75	1.40
No. C1 (1)	2.25	1.90
Set total (15) Stamps	23.55	21.35

Chad to Rhine

Leclerc's Departure from Chad — CD93

Battle at Cufra Oasis — CD94

Tanks in Action, Mareth — CD95

Normandy Invasion — CD96

Entering Paris — CD97

Liberation of Strasbourg — CD98

"Chad to the Rhine" march, 1942-44, by Gen. Jacques Leclerc's column, later French 2nd Armored Division.

1946, June 6

Cameroun	C9-C14
Fr. Equatorial Africa	C25-C30
Fr. Guiana	C12-C17
Fr. India	C8-C13
Fr. Polynesia	C11-C16
Fr. West Africa	C5-C10
Guadeloupe	C4-C9
Indo-China	C20-C25
Madagascar	C45-C50
Martinique	C4-C9
New Caledonia	C15-C20
Reunion	C26-C31
St. Pierre & Miquelon	C9-C14
Somali Coast	C9-C14
Wallis & Futuna Isls.	C2-C7

Nos. C9-C14 (6)	12.05	9.70
Nos. C25-C30 (6)	14.70	10.80
Nos. C12-C17 (6)	12.65	10.35
Nos. C8-C13 (6)	12.80	15.00
Nos. C11-C16 (6)	17.55	13.40
Nos. C5-C10 (6)	16.05	11.95
Nos. C4-C9 (6)	12.00	9.60
Nos. C20-C25 (6)	6.40	6.40
Nos. C45-C50 (6)	10.30	8.40
Nos. C4-C9 (6)	8.85	7.30
Nos. C15-C20 (6)	13.40	11.90
Nos. C26-C31 (6)	10.25	6.55
Nos. C9-C14 (6)	17.30	14.35
Nos. C9-C14 (6)	18.10	12.65
Nos. C2-C7 (6)	13.75	10.45
Set total (90) Stamps	196.15	158.80

UPU

French Colonials, Globe and Plane — CD99

Universal Postal Union, 75th anniv.

1949, July 4

Cameroun	C29
Fr. Equatorial Africa	C34
Fr. India	C17
Fr. Polynesia	C20
Fr. West Africa	C15
Indo-China	C26
Madagascar	C55
New Caledonia	C24
St. Pierre & Miquelon	C18
Somali Coast	C18
Togo	C18
Wallis & Futuna Isls.	C10

No. C29 (1)	8.00	4.75
No. C34 (1)	16.00	12.00
No. C17 (1)	11.50	8.75
No. C20 (1)	20.00	15.00
No. C15 (1)	12.00	8.75
No. C26 (1)	4.75	4.00
No. C55 (1)	4.00	2.75
No. C24 (1)	7.50	5.00
No. C18 (1)	20.00	12.00
No. C18 (1)	14.00	10.50
No. C18 (1)	8.50	7.00
No. C10 (1)	11.00	8.25
Set total (12) Stamps	137.25	98.75

Tropical Medicine

Doctor Treating Infant CD100

The surtax was for charitable work.

1950

Cameroun	B29
Fr. Equatorial Africa	B39
Fr. India	B15
Fr. Polynesia	B14
Fr. West Africa	B3
Madagascar	B17
New Caledonia	B14
St. Pierre & Miquelon	B14
Somali Coast	B14
Togo	B11

No. B29 (1)	7.25	5.50
No. B39 (1)	7.25	5.50
No. B15 (1)	6.00	4.00
No. B14 (1)	10.50	8.00
No. B3 (1)	9.50	7.25
No. B17 (1)	5.50	5.50
No. B14 (1)	6.75	5.25
No. B14 (1)	16.00	15.00
No. B14 (1)	7.75	6.25
No. B11 (1)	5.00	3.50
Set total (10) Stamps	81.50	65.75

Military Medal

Medal, Early Marine and Colonial Soldier — CD101

Centenary of the creation of the French Military Medal.

1952

Cameroun	322
Comoro Isls.	39
Fr. Equatorial Africa	186

COMMON DESIGN TYPES

Fr. India	233
Fr. Polynesia	179
Fr. West Africa	57
Madagascar	286
New Caledonia	295
St. Pierre & Miquelon	345
Somali Coast	267
Togo	327
Wallis & Futuna Isls.	149

No. 322 (1)	7.25	3.25
No. 39 (1)	45.00	37.50
No. 186 (1)	8.00	5.50
No. 233 (1)	5.50	7.00
No. 179 (1)	13.50	10.00
No. 57 (1)	8.75	6.50
No. 286 (1)	3.75	2.50
No. 295 (1)	6.50	6.00
No. 345 (1)	16.00	15.00
No. 267 (1)	9.00	8.00
No. 327 (1)	5.50	4.75
No. 149 (1)	7.25	7.25
Set total (12) Stamps	136.00	113.25

Liberation

Allied Landing, Victory Sign and Cross of Lorraine — CD102

Liberation of France, 10th anniv.

1954, June 6

Cameroun	C32
Comoro Isls.	C4
Fr. Equatorial Africa	C38
Fr. India	C18
Fr. Polynesia	C22
Fr. West Africa	C17
Madagascar	C57
New Caledonia	C25
St. Pierre & Miquelon	C19
Somali Coast	C19
Togo	C19
Wallis & Futuna Isls.	C11

No. C32 (1)	7.25	4.75
No. C4 (1)	32.50	19.00
No. C38 (1)	12.00	8.00
No. C18 (1)	11.00	8.00
No. C22 (1)	10.00	8.00
No. C17 (1)	12.00	5.50
No. C57 (1)	3.25	2.00
No. C25 (1)	7.50	5.00
No. C19 (1)	19.00	12.00
No. C19 (1)	10.50	8.50
No. C19 (1)	7.00	5.50
No. C11 (1)	11.00	8.25
Set total (12) Stamps	143.00	94.50

FIDES

Plowmen CD103

Efforts of FIDES, the Economic and Social Development Fund for Overseas Possessions (Fonds d' Investissement pour le Developpement Economique et Social). Each stamp has a different design.

1956

Cameroun	326-329
Comoro Isls.	43
Fr. Equatorial Africa	189-192
Fr. Polynesia	181
Fr. West Africa	65-72
Madagascar	292-295
New Caledonia	303
St. Pierre & Miquelon	350
Somali Coast	268-269
Togo	331

Nos. 326-329 (4)	6.90	3.20
No. 43 (1)	2.25	1.60
Nos. 189-192 (4)	3.20	1.65
No. 181 (1)	4.00	2.00
Nos. 65-72 (8)	16.00	6.35
Nos. 292-295 (4)	2.25	1.20
No. 303 (1)	1.90	1.10
No. 350 (1)	6.00	4.00
Nos. 268-269 (2)	5.35	3.15
No. 331 (1)	4.25	2.10
Set total (27) Stamps	52.10	26.35

Flower

CD104

Each stamp shows a different flower.

1958-9

Cameroun	333
Comoro Isls.	45
Fr. Equatorial Africa	200-201
Fr. Polynesia	192
Fr. So. & Antarctic Terr.	11
Fr. West Africa	79-83
Madagascar	301-302
New Caledonia	304-305
St. Pierre & Miquelon	357
Somali Coast	270
Togo	348-349
Wallis & Futuna Isls.	152

No. 333 (1)	1.60	.80
No. 45 (1)	5.25	4.25
Nos. 200-201 (2)	3.60	1.60
No. 192 (1)	6.50	4.00
No. 11 (1)	8.75	7.50
Nos. 79-83 (5)	10.45	5.60
Nos. 301-302 (2)	1.60	.60
Nos. 304-305 (2)	8.00	3.00
No. 357 (1)	4.50	2.25
No. 270 (1)	4.25	1.40
Nos. 348-349 (2)	1.10	.50
No. 152 (1)	3.25	3.25
Set total (20) Stamps	58.85	34.75

Human Rights

Sun, Dove and U.N. Emblem CD105

10th anniversary of the signing of the Universal Declaration of Human Rights.

1958

Comoro Isls.	44
Fr. Equatorial Africa	202
Fr. Polynesia	191
Fr. West Africa	85
Madagascar	300
New Caledonia	306
St. Pierre & Miquelon	356
Somali Coast	274
Wallis & Futuna Isls.	153

No. 44 (1)	9.00	9.00
No. 202 (1)	2.40	1.25
No. 191 (1)	13.00	8.75
No. 85 (1)	2.40	2.00
No. 300 (1)	.80	.40
No. 306 (1)	2.00	1.50
No. 356 (1)	3.50	2.50
No. 274 (1)	3.50	2.10
No. 153 (1)	4.50	4.50
Set total (9) Stamps	41.10	32.00

C.C.T.A.

CD106

Commission for Technical Cooperation in Africa south of the Sahara, 10th anniv.

1960

Cameroun	339
Cent. Africa	3
Chad	66
Congo, P.R.	90
Dahomey	138
Gabon	150
Ivory Coast	180
Madagascar	317
Mali	9
Mauritania	117
Niger	104
Upper Volta	89

No. 339 (1)	1.60	.75
No. 3 (1)	1.60	.75
No. 66 (1)	1.75	.50
No. 90 (1)	1.00	1.00
No. 138 (1)	.50	.25
No. 150 (1)	1.25	1.10
No. 180 (1)	1.10	.50
No. 317 (1)	.60	.30
No. 9 (1)	1.20	.50
No. 117 (1)	.75	.40
No. 104 (1)	.85	.45
No. 89 (1)	.65	.40
Set total (12) Stamps	12.85	6.90

Air Afrique, 1961

Modern and Ancient Africa, Map and Planes — CD107

Founding of Air Afrique (African Airlines).

1961-62

Cameroun	C37
Cent. Africa	C5
Chad	C7
Congo, P.R.	C5
Dahomey	C17
Gabon	C5
Ivory Coast	C18
Mauritania	C17
Niger	C22
Senegal	C31
Upper Volta	C4

No. C37 (1)	1.00	.50
No. C5 (1)	1.00	.65
No. C7 (1)	1.00	.25
No. C5 (1)	1.75	.90
No. C17 (1)	.80	.40
No. C5 (1)	11.00	6.00
No. C18 (1)	2.00	1.25
No. C17 (1)	2.40	1.25
No. C22 (1)	1.75	.90
No. C31 (1)	.80	.30
No. C4 (1)	3.50	1.75
Set total (11) Stamps	27.00	14.15

Anti-Malaria

CD108

World Health Organization drive to eradicate malaria.

1962, Apr. 7

Cameroun	B36
Cent. Africa	B1
Chad	B1
Comoro Isls.	B1
Congo, P.R.	B3
Dahomey	B15
Gabon	B4
Ivory Coast	B15
Madagascar	B19
Mali	B1
Mauritania	B16
Niger	B14
Senegal	B16
Somali Coast	B15
Upper Volta	B1

No. B36 (1)	1.00	.45
No. B1 (1)	1.40	1.40
No. B1 (1)	1.00	.70
No. B1 (1)	3.50	3.50
No. B3 (1)	1.40	1.00
No. B15 (1)	.75	.75
No. B4 (1)	1.00	1.00
No. B15 (1)	1.25	1.25
No. B19 (1)	.75	.50
No. B1 (1)	1.25	.60
No. B16 (1)	.50	.50
No. B14 (1)	.75	.75
No. B16 (1)	1.10	.65
No. B15 (1)	7.00	7.00
No. B1 (1)	.75	.70
Set total (15) Stamps	23.40	20.55

Abidjan Games

CD109

Abidjan Games, Ivory Coast, Dec. 24-31, 1961. Each stamp shows a different sport.

1962

Cent. Africa	19-20, C6
Chad	83-84, C8
Congo, P.R.	103-104, C7
Gabon	163-164, C6
Niger	109-111
Upper Volta	103-105

Nos. 19-20,C6 (3)	4.15	2.85
Nos. 83-84,C8 (3)	5.80	1.55
Nos. 103-104,C7 (3)	3.85	1.80
Nos. 163-164, C6 (3)	5.00	3.00
Nos. 109-111 (3)	2.60	1.25
Nos. 103-105 (3)	2.80	1.75
Set total (18) Stamps	24.20	12.20

African and Malagasy Union

Flag of Union CD110

First anniversary of the Union.

1962, Sept. 8

Cameroun	373
Cent. Africa	21
Chad	85
Congo, P.R.	105
Dahomey	155
Gabon	165
Ivory Coast	198
Madagascar	332
Mauritania	170
Niger	112
Senegal	211
Upper Volta	106

No. 373 (1)	2.00	.75
No. 21 (1)	1.25	.75
No. 85 (1)	1.25	.25
No. 105 (1)	1.50	.50
No. 155 (1)	1.25	.90
No. 165 (1)	1.60	1.25
No. 198 (1)	2.10	.75
No. 332 (1)	.80	.80
No. 170 (1)	.75	.50
No. 112 (1)	.80	.50
No. 211 (1)	.80	.50
No. 106 (1)	1.10	.75
Set total (12) Stamps	15.20	8.20

Telstar

Telstar and Globe Showing Andover and Pleumeur-Bodou — CD111

First television connection of the United States and Europe through the Telstar satellite, July 11-12, 1962.

1962-63

Andorra, French	154
Comoro Isls.	C7
Fr. Polynesia	C29
Fr. So. & Antarctic Terr.	C5
New Caledonia	C33
St. Pierre & Miquelon	C26
Somali Coast	C31
Wallis & Futuna Isls.	C17

No. 154 (1)	2.00	1.60
No. C7 (1)	4.50	2.75
No. C29 (1)	11.50	8.00

COMMON DESIGN TYPES

No. C5 (1)	29.00	21.00
No. C33 (1)	25.00	18.50
No. C26 (1)	7.25	4.50
No. C31 (1)	1.00	1.00
No. C17 (1)	3.75	3.75
Set total (8) Stamps	84.00	61.10

Freedom From Hunger

World Map and Wheat Emblem
CD112

U.N. Food and Agriculture Organization's "Freedom from Hunger" campaign.

1963, Mar. 21

Cameroun	B37-B38
Cent. Africa	B2
Chad	B2
Congo, P.R.	B4
Dahomey	B16
Gabon	B5
Ivory Coast	B16
Madagascar	B21
Mauritania	B17
Niger	B15
Senegal	B17
Upper Volta	B2

Nos. B37-B38 (2)	2.25	.75
No. B2 (1)	1.25	1.25
No. B2 (1)	1.10	.50
No. B4 (1)	1.40	1.00
No. B16 (1)	.80	.80
No. B5 (1)	1.00	1.00
No. B16 (1)	1.50	1.50
No. B21 (1)	.60	.45
No. B17 (1)	.60	.60
No. B15 (1)	.75	.75
No. B17 (1)	.80	.50
No. B2 (1)	.75	.70
Set total (13) Stamps	12.80	9.80

Red Cross Centenary

CD113

Centenary of the International Red Cross.

1963, Sept. 2

Comoro Isls.	55
Fr. Polynesia	205
New Caledonia	328
St. Pierre & Miquelon	367
Somali Coast	297
Wallis & Futuna Isls.	165

No. 55 (1)	7.50	6.00
No. 205 (1)	15.00	12.00
No. 328 (1)	8.00	6.75
No. 367 (1)	12.00	5.50
No. 297 (1)	6.25	6.25
No. 165 (1)	4.00	4.00
Set total (6) Stamps	52.75	40.50

African Postal Union, 1963

UAMPT Emblem, Radio Masts, Plane and Mail
CD114

Establishment of the African and Malagasy Posts and Telecommunications Union.

1963, Sept. 8

Cameroun	C47
Cent. Africa	C10
Chad	C9
Congo, P.R.	C13
Dahomey	C19
Gabon	C13
Ivory Coast	C25
Madagascar	C75
Mauritania	C22
Niger	C27
Rwanda	36
Senegal	C32
Upper Volta	C9

No. C47 (1)	2.25	1.00
No. C10 (1)	1.90	.90
No. C9 (1)	1.80	.60
No. C13 (1)	1.40	.75
No. C19 (1)	.75	.25
No. C13 (1)	1.90	.80
No. C25 (1)	2.50	1.50
No. C75 (1)	1.25	.80
No. C22 (1)	1.50	.60
No. C27 (1)	1.25	.60
No. 36 (1)	1.10	.75
No. C32 (1)	1.75	.50
No. C9 (1)	1.50	.75
Set total (13) Stamps	20.85	9.80

Air Afrique, 1963

Symbols of Flight — CD115

First anniversary of Air Afrique and inauguration of DC-8 service.

1963, Nov. 19

Cameroun	C48
Chad	C10
Congo, P.R.	C14
Gabon	C18
Ivory Coast	C26
Mauritania	C26
Niger	C35
Senegal	C33

No. C48 (1)	1.25	.40
No. C10 (1)	1.80	.60
No. C14 (1)	1.60	.60
No. C18 (1)	1.25	.65
No. C26 (1)	1.00	.50
No. C26 (1)	.70	.25
No. C35 (1)	1.00	.55
No. C33 (1)	2.00	.65
Set total (8) Stamps	10.60	4.20

Europafrica

Europe and Africa Linked — CD116

Signing of an economic agreement between the European Economic Community and the African and Malagasy Union, Yaounde, Cameroun, July 20, 1963.

1963-64

Cameroun	402
Cent. Africa	C12
Chad	C11
Congo, P.R.	C16
Gabon	C19
Ivory Coast	217
Niger	C43
Upper Volta	C11

No. 402 (1)	2.25	.60
No. C12 (1)	2.50	1.75
No. C11 (1)	1.60	.50
No. C16 (1)	1.60	1.00
No. C19 (1)	1.25	.75
No. 217 (1)	1.10	.35
No. C43 (1)	.85	.50
No. C11 (1)	1.50	.80
Set total (8) Stamps	12.65	6.25

Human Rights

Scales of Justice and Globe
CD117

15th anniversary of the Universal Declaration of Human Rights.

1963, Dec. 10

Comoro Isls.	56
Fr. Polynesia	206
New Caledonia	329
St. Pierre & Miquelon	368
Somali Coast	300
Wallis & Futuna Isls.	166

No. 56 (1)	7.50	6.00
No. 205 (1)	15.00	12.00
No. 329 (1)	7.00	6.00
No. 368 (1)	7.00	3.50
No. 300 (1)	8.50	8.50
No. 166 (1)	7.00	7.00
Set total (6) Stamps	52.00	43.00

PHILATEC

Stamp Album, Champs Elysees Palace and Horses of Marly
CD118

Intl. Philatelic and Postal Techniques Exhibition, Paris, June 5-21, 1964.

1963-64

Comoro Isls.	60
France	1078
Fr. Polynesia	207
New Caledonia	341
St. Pierre & Miquelon	369
Somali Coast	301
Wallis & Futuna Isls.	167

No. 60 (1)	4.00	3.50
No. 1078 (1)	.25	.25
No. 206 (1)	15.00	10.00
No. 341 (1)	6.50	6.50
No. 369 (1)	11.00	8.00
No. 301 (1)	7.75	7.75
No. 167 (1)	3.00	3.00
Set total (7) Stamps	47.50	39.00

Cooperation

CD119

Cooperation between France and the French-speaking countries of Africa and Madagascar.

1964

Cameroun	409-410
Cent. Africa	39
Chad	103
Congo, P.R.	121
Dahomey	193
France	1111
Gabon	175
Ivory Coast	221
Madagascar	360
Mauritania	181
Niger	143
Senegal	236
Togo	495

Nos. 409-410 (2)	2.50	.50
No. 39 (1)	.90	.50
No. 103 (1)	1.00	.25
No. 121 (1)	.90	.35
No. 193 (1)	.80	.35
No. 1111 (1)	.25	.25
No. 175 (1)	.90	.60
No. 221 (1)	1.10	.35
No. 360 (1)	.60	.25
No. 181 (1)	.60	.35
No. 143 (1)	.80	.40
No. 236 (1)	1.60	.85
No. 495 (1)	.70	.25
Set total (14) Stamps	12.65	5.25

ITU

Telegraph, Syncom Satellite and ITU Emblem
CD120

Intl. Telecommunication Union, Cent.

1965, May 17

Comoro Isls.	C14
Fr. Polynesia	C33
Fr. So. & Antarctic Terr.	C8
New Caledonia	C40
New Hebrides	124-125
St. Pierre & Miquelon	C29
Somali Coast	C36
Wallis & Futuna Isls.	C20

No. C14 (1)	18.00	9.00
No. C33 (1)	80.00	52.50
No. C8 (1)	200.00	160.00
No. C40 (1)	10.00	8.00
Nos. 124-125 (2)	32.25	27.25
No. C29 (1)	24.00	11.50
No. C36 (1)	15.00	9.00
No. C20 (1)	16.00	16.00
Set total (9) Stamps	395.25	293.25

French Satellite A-1

Diamant Rocket and Launching Installation — CD121

Launching of France's first satellite, Nov. 26, 1965.

1965-66

Comoro Isls.	C16a
France	1138a
Reunion	359a
Fr. Polynesia	C41a
Fr. So. & Antarctic Terr.	C10a
New Caledonia	C45a
St. Pierre & Miquelon	C31a
Somali Coast	C40a
Wallis & Futuna Isls.	C23a

No. C16a (1)	9.00	9.00
No. 1138a (1)	.65	.65
No. 359a (1)	3.50	3.00
No. C41a (1)	14.00	14.00
No. C10a (1)	29.00	24.00
No. C45a (1)	7.00	7.00
No. C31a (1)	14.50	14.50
No. C40a (1)	7.00	7.00
No. C23a (1)	8.50	8.50
Set total (9) Stamps	93.15	87.65

French Satellite D-1

D-1 Satellite in Orbit — CD122

Launching of the D-1 satellite at Hammaguir, Algeria, Feb. 17, 1966.

1966

Comoro Isls.	C17
France	1148

COMMON DESIGN TYPES

Fr. Polynesia	C42
Fr. So. & Antarctic Terr.	C11
New Caledonia	C46
St. Pierre & Miquelon	C32
Somali Coast	C49
Wallis & Futuna Isls.	C24

No. C17 (1)	4.00	4.00
No. 1148 (1)	.25	.25
No. C42 (1)	7.00	4.75
No. C11 (1)	57.50	40.00
No. C46 (1)	2.25	2.00
No. C32 (1)	9.00	6.00
No. C49 (1)	4.25	2.75
No. C24 (1)	3.50	3.50
Set total (8) Stamps	87.75	63.25

Air Afrique, 1966

Planes and Air Afrique Emblem — CD123

Introduction of DC-8F planes by Air Afrique.

1966

Cameroun	C79
Cent. Africa	C35
Chad	C26
Congo, P.R.	C42
Dahomey	C42
Gabon	C47
Ivory Coast	C32
Mauritania	C57
Niger	C63
Senegal	C47
Togo	C54
Upper Volta	C31

No. C79 (1)	.80	.25
No. C35 (1)	1.00	.50
No. C26 (1)	.85	.25
No. C42 (1)	1.00	.25
No. C42 (1)	.75	.25
No. C47 (1)	.90	.35
No. C32 (1)	1.00	.60
No. C57 (1)	.60	.30
No. C63 (1)	.70	.35
No. C47 (1)	.80	.30
No. C54 (1)	.80	.25
No. C31 (1)	.75	.50
Set total (12) Stamps	9.95	4.15

African Postal Union, 1967

Telecommunications Symbols and Map of Africa — CD124

Fifth anniversary of the establishment of the African and Malagasy Union of Posts and Telecommunications, UAMPT.

1967

Cameroun	C90
Cent. Africa	C46
Chad	C37
Congo, P.R.	C57
Dahomey	C61
Gabon	C58
Ivory Coast	C34
Madagascar	C85
Mauritania	C65
Niger	C75
Rwanda	C1-C3
Senegal	C60
Togo	C81
Upper Volta	C50

No. C90 (1)	2.40	.65
No. C46 (1)	2.25	.85
No. C37 (1)	2.00	.60
No. C57 (1)	1.60	.60
No. C61 (1)	1.75	.95
No. C58 (1)	2.00	.85
No. C34 (1)	3.50	1.50
No. C85 (1)	1.25	.60
No. C65 (1)	1.25	.60
No. C75 (1)	1.40	.60

Nos. C1-C3 (3)	2.05	1.25
No. C60 (1)	1.75	.50
No. C81 (1)	1.90	.30
No. C50 (1)	1.80	.70
Set total (16) Stamps	26.90	10.55

Monetary Union

Gold Token of the Ashantis, 17-18th Centuries — CD125

West African Monetary Union, 5th anniv.

1967, Nov. 4

Dahomey	244
Ivory Coast	259
Mauritania	238
Niger	204
Senegal	294
Togo	623
Upper Volta	181

No. 244 (1)	.65	.65
No. 259 (1)	.85	.40
No. 238 (1)	.45	.25
No. 204 (1)	.55	.25
No. 294 (1)	.60	.25
No. 623 (1)	.60	.25
No. 181 (1)	.65	.35
Set total (7) Stamps	4.35	2.40

WHO Anniversary

Sun, Flowers and WHO Emblem CD126

World Health Organization, 20th anniv.

1968, May 4

Afars & Issas	317
Comoro Isls.	73
Fr. Polynesia	241-242
Fr. So. & Antarctic Terr.	31
New Caledonia	367
St. Pierre & Miquelon	377
Wallis & Futuna Isls.	169

No. 317 (1)	3.00	3.00
No. 73 (1)	2.40	1.75
Nos. 241-242 (2)	22.00	12.75
No. 31 (1)	62.50	47.50
No. 367 (1)	4.00	2.25
No. 377 (1)	12.00	9.00
No. 169 (1)	5.75	5.75
Set total (8) Stamps	111.65	82.00

Human Rights Year

Human Rights Flame — CD127

1968, Aug. 10

Afars & Issas	322-323
Comoro Isls.	76
Fr. Polynesia	243-244
Fr. So. & Antarctic Terr.	32
New Caledonia	369
St. Pierre & Miquelon	382
Wallis & Futuna Isls.	170

Nos. 322-323 (2)	6.75	4.00
No. 76 (1)	3.25	3.25
Nos. 243-244 (2)	24.00	14.00
No. 32 (1)	55.00	47.50
No. 369 (1)	2.75	1.50
No. 382 (1)	8.00	5.50
No. 170 (1)	3.25	3.25
Set total (9) Stamps	103.00	79.00

2nd PHILEXAFRIQUE

CD128

Opening of PHILEXAFRIQUE, Abidjan, Feb. 14. Each stamp shows a local scene and stamp.

1969, Feb. 14

Cameroun	C118
Cent. Africa	C65
Chad	C48
Congo, P.R.	C77
Dahomey	C94
Gabon	C82
Ivory Coast	C38-C40
Madagascar	C92
Mali	C65
Mauritania	C80
Niger	C104
Senegal	C68
Togo	C104
Upper Volta	C62

No. C118 (1)	3.25	1.25
No. C65 (1)	1.75	1.75
No. C48 (1)	2.40	1.00
No. C77 (1)	2.00	1.75
No. C94 (1)	2.25	2.25
No. C82 (1)	2.00	2.00
Nos. C38-C40 (3)	14.50	14.50
No. C92 (1)	1.75	.85
No. C65 (1)	1.75	1.00
No. C80 (1)	1.90	.75
No. C104 (1)	3.00	1.90
No. C68 (1)	2.00	1.40
No. C104 (1)	2.25	.45
No. C62 (1)	4.00	3.25
Set total (16) Stamps	44.80	34.10

Concorde

Concorde in Flight CD129

First flight of the prototype Concorde supersonic plane at Toulouse, Mar. 1, 1969.

1969

Afars & Issas	C56
Comoro Isls.	C29
France	C42
Fr. Polynesia	C50
Fr. So. & Antarctic Terr.	C18
New Caledonia	C63
St. Pierre & Miquelon	C40
Wallis & Futuna Isls.	C30

No. C56 (1)	26.00	16.00
No. C29 (1)	18.00	12.00
No. C42 (1)	.75	.35
No. C50 (1)	55.00	35.00
No. C18 (1)	55.00	37.50
No. C63 (1)	27.50	20.00
No. C40 (1)	32.50	11.00
No. C30 (1)	15.00	10.00
Set total (8) Stamps	229.75	141.85

Development Bank

Bank Emblem — CD130

African Development Bank, fifth anniv.

1969

Cameroun	499
Chad	217
Congo, P.R.	181-182

Ivory Coast	281
Mali	127-128
Mauritania	267
Niger	220
Senegal	317-318
Upper Volta	201

No. 499 (1)	.80	.25
No. 217 (1)	.90	.25
Nos. 181-182 (2)	1.00	.50
No. 281 (1)	.70	.40
Nos. 127-128 (2)	1.00	.50
No. 267 (1)	.60	.25
No. 220 (1)	.70	.30
Nos. 317-318 (2)	1.55	.50
No. 201 (1)	.65	.30
Set total (12) Stamps	7.90	3.25

ILO

ILO Headquarters, Geneva, and Emblem — CD131

Intl. Labor Organization, 50th anniv.

1969-70

Afars & Issas	337
Comoro Isls.	83
Fr. Polynesia	251-252
Fr. So. & Antarctic Terr.	35
New Caledonia	379
St. Pierre & Miquelon	396
Wallis & Futuna Isls.	172

No. 337 (1)	2.75	2.00
No. 83 (1)	1.25	.75
Nos. 251-252 (2)	24.00	12.50
No. 35 (1)	15.00	10.00
No. 379 (1)	2.25	1.10
No. 396 (1)	10.00	5.50
No. 172 (1)	2.75	2.75
Set total (8) Stamps	58.00	34.60

ASECNA

Map of Africa, Plane and Airport CD132

10th anniversary of the Agency for the Security of Aerial Navigation in Africa and Madagascar (ASECNA, Agence pour la Securite de la Navigation Aerienne en Afrique et a Madagascar).

1969-70

Cameroun	500
Cent. Africa	119
Chad	222
Congo, P.R.	197
Dahomey	269
Gabon	260
Ivory Coast	287
Mali	130
Niger	221
Senegal	321
Upper Volta	204

No. 500 (1)	2.00	.60
No. 119 (1)	2.00	.80
No. 222 (1)	1.00	.25
No. 197 (1)	2.00	.40
No. 269 (1)	.90	.55
No. 260 (1)	1.75	.75
No. 287 (1)	.90	.40
No. 130 (1)	.90	.40
No. 221 (1)	1.40	.70
No. 321 (1)	1.60	1.00
No. 204 (1)	1.75	1.00
Set total (11) Stamps	16.20	6.35

U.P.U. Headquarters

CD133

New Universal Postal Union headquarters, Bern, Switzerland.

COMMON DESIGN TYPES

1970

Afars & Issas	342
Algeria	443
Cameroun	503-504
Cent. Africa	125
Chad	225
Comoro Isls.	84
Congo, P.R.	216
Fr. Polynesia	261-262
Fr. So. & Antarctic Terr.	36
Gabon	258
Ivory Coast	295
Madagascar	444
Mali	134-135
Mauritania	283
New Caledonia	382
Niger	231-232
St. Pierre & Miquelon	397-398
Senegal	328-329
Tunisia	535
Wallis & Futuna Isls.	173

No. 342 (1)	2.50	1.40
No. 443 (1)	1.10	.40
Nos. 503-504 (2)	2.60	.55
No. 125 (1)	1.75	.70
No. 225 (1)	1.20	.25
No. 84 (1)	5.50	2.00
No. 216 (1)	1.00	.25
Nos. 261-262 (2)	20.00	10.00
No. 36 (1)	40.00	27.50
No. 258 (1)	.90	.55
No. 295 (1)	1.10	.50
No. 444 (1)	.55	.25
Nos. 134-135 (2)	1.05	.50
No. 283 (1)	.60	.30
No. 382 (1)	3.00	1.50
Nos. 231-232 (2)	1.50	.60
Nos. 397-398 (2)	34.00	16.25
Nos. 328-329 (2)	1.55	.55
No. 535 (1)	.60	.25
No. 173 (1)	3.25	3.25
Set total (26) Stamps	123.75	67.55

De Gaulle

CD134

First anniversary of the death of Charles de Gaulle, (1890-1970), President of France.

1971-72

Afars & Issas	356-357
Comoro Isls.	104-105
France	1325a
Fr. Polynesia	270-271
Fr. So. & Antarctic Terr.	52-53
New Caledonia	393-394
Reunion	380a
St. Pierre & Miquelon	417-418
Wallis & Futuna Isls.	177-178

Nos. 356-357 (2)	12.50	7.50
Nos. 104-105 (2)	9.00	5.75
No. 1325a (1)	3.00	2.50
Nos. 270-271 (2)	51.50	29.50
Ncs. 52-53 (2)	40.00	29.50
Nos. 393-394 (2)	23.00	11.75
No. 380a (1)	9.25	8.00
Nos. 417-418 (2)	56.50	31.00
Nos. 177-178 (2)	20.00	16.25
Set total (16) Stamps	224.75	141.75

African Postal Union, 1971

UAMPT Building, Brazzaville, Congo — CD135

10th anniversary of the establishment of the African and Malagasy Posts and Telecommunications Union, UAMPT. Each stamp has a different native design.

1971, Nov. 13

Cameroun	C177
Cent. Africa	C89
Chad	C94
Congo, P.R.	C136
Dahomey	C146
Gabon	C120
Ivory Coast	C47
Mauritania	C113
Niger	C164
Rwanda	C8
Senegal	C105
Togo	C166
Upper Volta	C97

No. C177 (1)	2.00	.50
No. C89 (1)	2.25	.85
No. C94 (1)	1.50	.50
No. C136 (1)	1.60	.75
No. C146 (1)	1.75	.80
No. C120 (1)	1.75	.70
No. C47 (1)	2.00	1.00
No. C113 (1)	1.10	.65
No. C164 (1)	1.25	.60
No. C8 (1)	2.75	2.50
No. C105 (1)	1.60	.50
No. C166 (1)	1.25	.40
No. C97 (1)	1.50	.70
Set total (13) Stamps	22.30	10.45

West African Monetary Union

African Couple, City, Village and Commemorative Coin — CD136

West African Monetary Union, 10th anniv.

1972, Nov. 2

Dahomey	300
Ivory Coast	331
Mauritania	299
Niger	258
Senegal	374
Togo	825
Upper Volta	280

No. 300 (1)	.65	.25
No. 331 (1)	1.00	.50
No. 299 (1)	.75	.25
No. 258 (1)	.65	.30
No. 374 (1)	.50	.30
No. 825 (1)	.60	.25
No. 280 (1)	.60	.25
Set total (7) Stamps	4.75	2.10

African Postal Union, 1973

Telecommunications Symbols and Map of Africa — CD137

11th anniversary of the African and Malagasy Posts and Telecommunications Union (UAMPT).

1973, Sept. 12

Cameroun	574
Cent. Africa	194
Chad	294
Congo, P.R.	289
Dahomey	311
Gabon	320
Ivory Coast	361
Madagascar	500
Mauritania	304
Niger	287
Rwanda	540
Senegal	393
Togo	849
Upper Volta	297

No. 574 (1)	1.75	.40
No. 194 (1)	1.25	.75
No. 294 (1)	1.75	.40
No. 289 (1)	1.60	.50
No. 311 (1)	1.25	.55
No. 320 (1)	1.40	.75
No. 361 (1)	2.50	1.00
No. 500 (1)	1.10	.35
No. 304 (1)	1.10	.40
No. 287 (1)	.90	.60
No. 540 (1)	3.00	2.00
No. 393 (1)	1.60	.50
No. 849 (1)	1.00	.35
No. 297 (1)	1.25	.70
Set total (14) Stamps	21.45	9.25

Philexafrique II — Essen

CD138

CD139

Designs: Indigenous fauna, local and German stamps. Types CD138-CD139 printed horizontally and vertically se-tenant in sheets of 10 (2x5). Label between horizontal pairs alternately commemoratives Philexafrique II, Libreville, Gabon, June 1978, and 2nd International Stamp Fair, Essen, Germany, Nov. 1-5.

1978-1979

Benin	C286a
Central Africa	C201a
Chad	C239a
Congo Republic	C246a
Djibouti	C122a
Gabon	C216a
Ivory Coast	C65a
Mali	C357a
Mauritania	C186a
Niger	C292a
Rwanda	C13a
Senegal	C147a
Togo	C364a

No. C286a (1)	9.00	8.50
No. C201a (1)	7.50	7.50
No. C239a (1)	7.50	4.00
No. C246a (1)	7.00	7.00
No. C122a (1)	6.50	6.50
No. C216a (1)	6.50	4.00
No. C65a (1)	9.00	9.00
No. C357a (1)	5.00	3.00
No. C186a (1)	5.50	5.00
No. C292a (1)	6.00	6.00
No. C13a (1)	4.00	4.00
No. C147a (1)	10.00	4.00
No. C364a (1)	3.00	1.50
Set total (13) Stamps	86.50	70.00

BRITISH COMMONWEALTH OF NATIONS

The listings follow established trade practices when these issues are offered as units by dealers. The Peace issue, for example, includes only one stamp from the Indian state of Hyderabad. The U.P.U. issue includes the Egypt set. Pairs are included for those varieties issued with bilingual designs se-tenant.

Silver Jubilee

Windsor Castle and King George V CD301

Reign of King George V, 25th anniv.

1935

Antigua	77-80
Ascension	33-36
Bahamas	92-95
Barbados	186-189
Basutoland	11-14
Bechuanaland Protectorate	117-120
Bermuda	100-103
British Guiana	223-226
British Honduras	108-111
Cayman Islands	81-84
Ceylon	260-263
Cyprus	136-139
Dominica	90-93
Falkland Islands	77-80
Fiji	110-113
Gambia	125-128
Gibraltar	100-103
Gilbert & Ellice Islands	33-36
Gold Coast	108-111
Grenada	124-127
Hong Kong	147-150
Jamaica	109-112
Kenya, Uganda, Tanzania	42-45
Leeward Islands	96-99
Malta	184-187
Mauritius	204-207
Montserrat	85-88
Newfoundland	226-229
Nigeria	34-37
Northern Rhodesia	18-21
Nyasaland Protectorate	47-50
St. Helena	111-114
St. Kitts-Nevis	72-75
St. Lucia	91-94
St. Vincent	134-137
Seychelles	118-121
Sierra Leone	166-169
Solomon Islands	60-63
Somaliland Protectorate	77-80
Straits Settlements	213-216
Swaziland	20-23
Trinidad & Tobago	43-46
Turks & Caicos Islands	71-74
Virgin Islands	69-72

The following have different designs but are included in the omnibus set:

Great Britain	226-229
Offices in Morocco (Sp. Curr.)	67-70
Offices in Morocco (Br. Curr.)	226-229
Offices in Morocco (Fr. Curr.)	422-425
Offices in Morocco (Tangier)	508-510
Australia	152-154
Canada	211-216
Cook Islands	98-100
India	142-148
Nauru	31-34
New Guinea	46-47
New Zealand	199-201
Niue	67-69
Papua	114-117
Samoa	163-165
South Africa	68-71
Southern Rhodesia	33-36
South-West Africa	121-124

Nos. 77-80 (4)	20.25	23.25
Nos. 33-36 (4)	58.50	127.50
Nos. 92-95 (4)	25.00	46.00
Nos. 186-189 (4)	30.00	50.30
Nos. 11-14 (4)	11.60	21.25
Nos. 117-120 (4)	15.75	36.00
Nos. 100-103 (4)	16.80	58.50
Nos. 223-226 (4)	22.35	35.50
Nos. 108-111 (4)	15.25	16.35
Nos. 81-84 (4)	21.60	24.50
Nos. 260-263 (4)	10.40	21.60
Nos. 136-139 (4)	39.75	34.40
Nos. 90-93 (4)	18.85	19.85
Nos. 77-80 (4)	55.00	14.75
Nos. 110-113 (4)	20.25	34.00
Nos. 125-128 (4)	13.05	25.25
Nos. 100-103 (4)	28.75	42.75
Nos. 33-36 (4)	36.80	67.00
Nos. 108-111 (4)	25.75	78.10
Nos. 124-127 (4)	16.70	40.60
Nos. 147-150 (4)	73.75	20.75
Nos. 109-112 (4)	24.20	50.50
Nos. 42-45 (4)	10.25	11.75
Nos. 96-99 (4)	35.75	49.60
Nos. 184-187 (4)	22.00	33.70
Nos. 204-207 (4)	44.60	58.25
Nos. 85-88 (4)	10.25	30.25
Nos. 226-229 (4)	17.50	12.05
Nos. 34-37 (4)	17.50	73.00
Nos. 18-21 (4)	17.00	15.00
Nos. 47-50 (4)	43.50	82.50
Nos. 111-114 (4)	31.15	36.50
Nos. 72-75 (4)	11.80	18.65
Nos. 91-94 (4)	16.00	20.80
Nos. 134-137 (4)	9.45	21.25
Nos. 118-121 (4)	15.75	40.00
Nos. 166-169 (4)	23.60	50.35
Nos. 60-63 (4)	29.00	38.00
Nos. 77-80 (4)	17.00	48.25
Nos. 213-216 (4)	15.00	25.10
Nos. 20-23 (4)	6.80	18.25
Nos. 43-46 (4)	18.60	37.50
Nos. 71-74 (4)	9.90	14.50
Nos. 69-72 (4)	25.00	55.25
Nos. 226-229 (4)	5.15	9.90

COMMON DESIGN TYPES 15A

Nos. 67-70 (4)	13.60	30.70
Nos. 226-229 (4)	16.30	56.00
Nos. 422-425 (4)	9.35	3.95
Nos. 508-510 (3)	26.00	33.50
Nos. 152-154 (3)	49.50	45.35
Nos. 211-216 (6)	23.85	13.35
Nos. 98-100 (3)	9.65	12.00
Nos. 142-148 (7)	28.85	14.00
Nos. 31-34 (4)	12.35	13.15
Nos. 46-47 (2)	4.35	1.70
Nos. 199-201 (3)	23.00	28.50
Nos. 67-69 (3)	19.25	31.00
Nos. 114-117 (4)	9.20	17.50
Nos. 163-165 (3)	4.40	6.50
Nos. 68-71 (4)	57.50	153.00
Nos. 33-36 (4)	27.75	45.25
Nos. 121-124 (4)	13.00	36.10
Set total (245) Stamps	1,401.	2,231.

Coronation

Queen Elizabeth and King George VI
CD302

1937

Aden	13-15
Antigua	81-83
Ascension	37-39
Bahamas	97-99
Barbados	190-192
Basutoland	15-17
Bechuanaland Protectorate	121-123
Bermuda	115-117
British Guiana	227-229
British Honduras	112-114
Cayman Islands	97-99
Ceylon	275-277
Cyprus	140-142
Dominica	94-96
Falkland Islands	81-83
Fiji	114-116
Gambia	129-131
Gibraltar	104-106
Gilbert & Ellice Islands	37-39
Gold Coast	112-114
Grenada	128-130
Hong Kong	151-153
Jamaica	113-115
Kenya, Uganda, Tanzania	60-62
Leeward Islands	100-102
Malta	188-190
Mauritius	208-210
Montserrat	89-91
Newfoundland	230-232
Nigeria	50-52
Northern Rhodesia	22-24
Nyasaland Protectorate	51-53
St. Helena	115-117
St. Kitts-Nevis	76-78
St. Lucia	107-109
St. Vincent	138-140
Seychelles	122-124
Sierra Leone	170-172
Solomon Islands	64-66
Somaliland Protectorate	81-83
Straits Settlements	235-237
Swaziland	24-26
Trinidad & Tobago	47-49
Turks & Caicos Islands	75-77
Virgin Islands	73-75

The following have different designs but are included in the omnibus set:

Great Britain	234
Offices in Morocco (Sp. Curr.)	82
Offices in Morocco (Fr. Curr.)	439
Offices in Morocco (Tangier)	514
Canada	237
Cook Islands	109-111
Nauru	35-38
Newfoundland	233-243
New Guinea	48-51
New Zealand	223-225
Niue	70-72
Papua	118-121
South Africa	74-78
Southern Rhodesia	38-41
South-West Africa	125-132

Nos. 13-15 (3)	2.70	5.65
Nos. 81-83 (3)	1.85	8.00
Nos. 37-39 (3)	2.75	2.75
Nos. 97-99 (3)	1.05	3.05
Nos. 190-192 (3)	1.10	1.95
Nos. 15-17 (3)	1.15	3.00
Nos. 121-123 (3)	.95	3.35
Nos. 115-117 (3)	1.25	5.00
Nos. 227-229 (3)	1.50	3.05
Nos. 112-114 (3)	1.20	2.40
Nos. 97-99 (3)	1.10	2.70
Nos. 275-277 (3)	8.25	10.35

Nos. 140-142 (3)	3.75	6.50
Nos. 94-96 (3)	.85	2.40
Nos. 81-83 (3)	2.90	2.30
Nos. 114-116 (3)	1.35	5.75
Nos. 129-131 (3)	.95	3.95
Nos. 104-106 (3)	2.25	6.45
Nos. 37-39 (3)	.85	2.15
Nos. 112-114 (3)	3.10	10.00
Nos. 128-130 (3)	1.00	.85
Nos. 151-153 (3)	17.00	17.75
Nos. 113-115 (3)	1.25	1.25
Nos. 60-62 (3)	1.25	2.35
Nos. 100-102 (3)	1.55	4.00
Nos. 188-190 (3)	1.25	1.60
Nos. 208-210 (3)	1.75	3.50
Nos. 89-91 (3)	1.00	3.35
Nos. 230-232 (3)	7.00	2.80
Nos. 50-52 (3)	3.25	8.50
Nos. 22-24 (3)	.95	2.25
Nos. 51-53 (3)	1.05	1.30
Nos. 115-117 (3)	1.45	2.05
Nos. 76-78 (3)	.95	2.15
Nos. 107-109 (3)	1.05	2.05
Nos. 138-140 (3)	.80	4.75
Nos. 122-124 (3)	1.20	1.90
Nos. 170-172 (3)	1.95	5.65
Nos. 64-66 (3)	.90	2.00
Nos. 81-83 (3)	1.10	3.50
Nos. 235-237 (3)	3.25	1.60
Nos. 24-26 (3)	.75	2.70
Nos. 47-49 (3)	1.10	3.20
Nos. 75-77 (3)	1.25	.95
Nos. 73-75 (3)	2.20	6.90
No. 234 (1)	.30	.25
No. 82 (1)	.80	.60
No. 439 (1)	.50	.25
No. 514 (1)	1.25	.50
No. 237 (1)	.35	.25
Nos. 109-111 (3)	.85	.80
Nos. 35-38 (4)	1.25	5.50
Nos. 233-243 (11)	41.90	30.40
Nos. 48-51 (4)	1.40	7.90
Nos. 223-225 (3)	1.75	2.25
Nos. 70-72 (3)	.90	2.05
Nos. 118-121 (4)	1.60	5.25
Nos. 74-78 (5)	7.60	9.35
Nos. 38-41 (4)	3.55	15.50
Nos. 125-132 (8)	5.00	8.40
Set total (189) Stamps	166.10	268.90

Peace

King George VI and Parliament Buildings, London
CD303

Return to peace at the close of World War II.

1945-46

Aden	28-29
Antigua	96-97
Ascension	50-51
Bahamas	130-131
Barbados	207-208
Bermuda	131-132
British Guiana	242-243
British Honduras	127-128
Cayman Islands	112-113
Ceylon	293-294
Cyprus	156-157
Dominica	112-113
Falkland Islands	97-98
Falkland Islands Dep.	1L9-1L10
Fiji	137-138
Gambia	144-145
Gibraltar	119-120
Gilbert & Ellice Islands	52-53
Gold Coast	128-129
Grenada	143-144
Jamaica	136-137
Kenya, Uganda, Tanzania	90-91
Leeward Islands	116-117
Malta	206-207
Mauritius	223-224
Montserrat	104-105
Nigeria	71-72
Northern Rhodesia	46-47
Nyasaland Protectorate	82-83
Pitcairn Islands	9-10
St. Helena	128-129
St. Kitts-Nevis	91-92
St. Lucia	127-128
St. Vincent	152-153
Seychelles	149-150
Sierra Leone	186-187
Solomon Islands	80-81
Somaliland Protectorate	108-109
Trinidad & Tobago	62-63
Turks & Caicos Islands	90-91
Virgin Islands	88-89

The following have different designs but are included in the omnibus set:

Great Britain	264-265
Offices in Morocco (Tangier)	523-524
Aden	
Kathiri State of Seiyun	12-13
Qu'aiti State of Shihr and Mukalla	12-13
Australia	200-202
Basutoland	29-31
Bechuanaland Protectorate	137-139
Burma	66-69
Cook Islands	127-130
Hong Kong	174-175
India	195-198
Hyderabad	51-53
New Zealand	247-257
Niue	90-93
Pakistan-Bahawalpur	O16
Samoa	191-194
South Africa	100-102
Southern Rhodesia	67-70
South-West Africa	153-155
Swaziland	38-40
Zanzibar	222-223

Nos. 28-29 (2)	.95	2.50
Nos. 96-97 (2)	.50	.80
Nos. 50-51 (2)	.80	2.00
Nos. 130-131 (2)	.50	1.40
Nos. 207-208 (2)	.50	1.10
Nos. 131-132 (2)	.55	.55
Nos. 242-243 (2)	1.05	1.40
Nos. 127-128 (2)	.50	.50
Nos. 112-113 (2)	.80	.80
Nos. 293-294 (2)	.60	2.10
Nos. 156-157 (2)	.90	.70
Nos. 112-113 (2)	.50	.50
Nos. 97-98 (2)	.90	1.35
Nos. 1L9-1L10 (2)	1.30	1.00
Nos. 137-138 (2)	.75	1.75
Nos. 144-145 (2)	.60	.95
Nos. 119-120 (2)	.75	1.00
Nos. 52-53 (2)	.50	1.10
Nos. 128-129 (2)	1.85	3.75
Nos. 143-144 (2)	.50	.95
Nos. 136-137 (2)	2.00	13.50
Nos. 90-91 (2)	.65	.85
Nos. 116-117 (2)	.50	1.50
Nos. 206-207 (2)	.65	2.00
Nos. 223-224 (2)	.50	1.05
Nos. 104-105 (2)	.50	.50
Nos. 71-72 (2)	.70	2.75
Nos. 46-47 (2)	1.25	2.00
Nos. 82-83 (2)	.55	.60
Nos. 9-10 (2)	1.40	.60
Nos. 128-129 (2)	.65	.70
Nos. 91-92 (2)	.50	.50
Nos. 127-128 (2)	.50	.60
Nos. 152-153 (2)	.50	.50
Nos. 149-150 (2)	.55	.50
Nos. 186-187 (2)	.50	.50
Nos. 80-81 (2)	.50	1.50
Nos. 108-109 (2)	.70	.50
Nos. 62-63 (2)	.75	1.85
Nos. 90-91 (2)	.50	.50
Nos. 88-89 (2)	.50	.50
Nos. 264-265 (2)	.50	.50
Nos. 523-524 (2)	2.00	2.55
Nos. 12-13 (2)	.50	.90
Nos. 12-13 (2)	.50	1.25
Nos. 200-202 (3)	1.60	1.25
Nos. 29-31 (3)	2.10	2.60
Nos. 137-139 (3)	2.05	4.75
Nos. 66-69 (4)	1.50	1.25
Nos. 127-130 (4)	2.00	1.85
Nos. 174-175 (2)	6.75	2.75
Nos. 195-198 (4)	5.60	5.50
Nos. 51-53 (3)	1.50	1.70
Nos. 247-257 (11)	3.35	3.65
Nos. 90-93 (4)	1.70	2.20
No. O16 (1)	15.00	10.00
Nos. 191-194 (4)	2.05	1.00
Nos. 100-102 (3)	1.00	3.25
Nos. 67-70 (4)	1.40	1.75
Nos. 153-155 (3)	1.85	3.25
Nos. 38-40 (3)	2.40	5.50
Nos. 222-223 (2)	.65	1.00
Set total (151) Stamps	86.15	118.15

Silver Wedding

King George VI and Queen Elizabeth
CD304   CD305

1948-49

Aden	30-31
Kathiri State of Seiyun	14-15
Qu'aiti State of Shihr and Mukalla	14-15

Antigua	98-99
Ascension	52-53
Bahamas	148-149
Barbados	210-211
Basutoland	39-40
Bechuanaland Protectorate	147-148
Bermuda	133-134
British Guiana	244-245
British Honduras	129-130
Cayman Islands	116-117
Cyprus	158-159
Dominica	114-115
Falkland Islands	99-100
Falkland Islands Dep.	1L11-1L12
Fiji	139-140
Gambia	146-147
Gibraltar	121-122
Gilbert & Ellice Islands	54-55
Gold Coast	142-143
Grenada	145-146
Hong Kong	178-179
Jamaica	138-139
Kenya, Uganda, Tanzania	92-93
Leeward Islands	118-119
Malaya	
Johore	128-129
Kedah	55-56
Kelantan	44-45
Malacca	1-2
Negri Sembilan	36-37
Pahang	44-45
Penang	1-2
Perak	99-100
Perlis	1-2
Selangor	74-75
Trengganu	47-48
Malta	223-224
Mauritius	229-230
Montserrat	106-107
Nigeria	73-74
North Borneo	238-239
Northern Rhodesia	48-49
Nyasaland Protectorate	85-86
Pitcairn Islands	11-12
St. Helena	130-131
St. Kitts-Nevis	93-94
St. Lucia	129-130
St. Vincent	154-155
Sarawak	174-175
Seychelles	151-152
Sierra Leone	188-189
Singapore	21-22
Solomon Islands	82-83
Somaliland Protectorate	110-111
Swaziland	48-49
Trinidad & Tobago	64-65
Turks & Caicos Islands	92-93
Virgin Islands	90-91
Zanzibar	224-225

The following have different designs but are included in the omnibus set:

Great Britain	267-268
Offices in Morocco (Sp. Curr.)	93-94
Offices in Morocco (Tangier)	525-526
Bahrain	62-63
Kuwait	82-83
Oman	25-26
South Africa	106
South-West Africa	159

Nos. 30-31 (2)	40.40	56.50
Nos. 14-15 (2)	17.85	16.00
Nos. 14-15 (2)	18.55	12.50
Nos. 98-99 (2)	13.55	15.75
Nos. 52-53 (2)	55.55	50.45
Nos. 148-149 (2)	45.25	40.30
Nos. 210-211 (2)	18.55	13.55
Nos. 39-40 (2)	52.80	55.25
Nos. 147-148 (2)	42.85	47.75
Nos. 133-134 (2)	47.75	55.25
Nos. 244-245 (2)	24.25	28.45
Nos. 129-130 (2)	25.25	53.20
Nos. 116-117 (2)	25.25	33.50
Nos. 158-159 (2)	58.50	78.05
Nos. 114-115 (2)	25.25	32.75
Nos. 99-100 (2)	112.10	76.10
Nos. 1L11-1L12 (2)	4.25	6.00
Nos. 139-140 (2)	18.20	11.50
Nos. 146-147 (2)	21.30	21.25
Nos. 121-122 (2)	61.00	78.00
Nos. 54-55 (2)	14.25	26.25
Nos. 142-143 (2)	35.25	48.20
Nos. 145-146 (2)	21.75	21.75
Nos. 178-179 (2)	329.00	106.75
Nos. 138-139 (2)	30.35	71.85
Nos. 92-93 (2)	51.00	68.00
Nos. 118-119 (2)	7.00	8.25
Nos. 128-129 (2)	29.25	53.25
Nos. 55-56 (2)	35.25	50.25
Nos. 44-45 (2)	35.75	62.75
Nos. 1-2 (2)	35.40	49.75
Nos. 36-37 (2)	28.10	38.20
Nos. 44-45 (2)	28.00	38.05
Nos. 1-2 (2)	40.50	37.80

COMMON DESIGN TYPES

16A

Nos. 99-100 (2)	27.80	37.75
Nos. 1-2 (2)	33.50	58.00
Nos. 74-75 (2)	30.25	25.30
Nos. 47-48 (2)	32.75	61.75
Nos. 223-224 (2)	40.55	45.25
Nos. 229-230 (2)	19.25	45.25
Nos. 106-107 (2)	8.75	17.25
Nos. 73-74 (2)	17.85	22.80
Nos. 238-239 (2)	35.30	45.75
Nos. 48-49 (2)	100.30	90.25
Nos. 85-86 (2)	18.25	35.25
Nos. 11-12 (2)	44.50	54.00
Nos. 130-131 (2)	32.80	42.80
Nos. 93-94 (2)	13.25	10.50
Nos. 129-130 (2)	22.25	40.25
Nos. 154-155 (2)	27.75	30.25
Nos. 174-175 (2)	52.80	67.80
Nos. 151-152 (2)	16.25	48.25
Nos. 188-189 (2)	25.25	29.75
Nos. 21-22 (2)	116.00	45.40
Nos. 82-83 (2)	13.40	13.40
Nos. 110-111 (2)	8.40	8.75
Nos. 48-49 (2)	40.30	47.75
Nos. 64-65 (2)	31.80	50.25
Nos. 92-93 (2)	16.25	22.75
Nos. 90-91 (2)	16.25	22.25
Nos. 224-225 (2)	29.60	38.00
Nos. 267-268 (2)	30.40	25.25
Nos. 93-94 (2)	17.10	25.75
Nos. 525-526 (2)	22.90	32.75
Nos. 62-63 (2)	38.50	58.00
Nos. 82-83 (2)	69.50	45.50
Nos. 25-26 (2)	41.00	42.50
No. 106 (1)	.80	1.00
No. 159 (1)	1.10	.35
Set total (136) Stamps	2,542.	2,754.

U.P.U.

Mercury and Symbols of Communications — CD306

Plane, Ship and Hemispheres — CD307

Mercury Scattering Letters over Globe CD308

U.P.U. Monument, Bern CD309

Universal Postal Union, 75th anniversary.

1949

Aden	32-35
Kathiri State of Seiyun	16-19
Qu'aiti State of Shihr and Mukalla	16-19
Antigua	100-103
Ascension	57-60
Bahamas	150-153
Barbados	212-215
Basutoland	41-44
Bechuanaland Protectorate	149-152
Bermuda	138-141
British Guiana	246-249
British Honduras	137-140
Brunei	79-82
Cayman Islands	118-121
Cyprus	160-163
Dominica	116-119
Falkland Islands	103-106
Falkland Islands Dep.	1L14-1L17
Fiji	141-144
Gambia	148-151
Gibraltar	123-126
Gilbert & Ellice Islands	56-59
Gold Coast	144-147
Grenada	147-150
Hong Kong	180-183
Jamaica	142-145
Kenya, Uganda, Tanzania	94-97
Leeward Islands	126-129
Malaya	
Johore	151-154
Kedah	57-60
Kelantan	46-49
Malacca	18-21
Negri Sembilan	59-62
Pahang	46-49
Penang	23-26
Perak	101-104
Perlis	3-6
Selangor	76-79
Trengganu	49-52
Malta	225-228
Mauritius	231-234
Montserrat	108-111
New Hebrides, British	62-65
New Hebrides, French	79-82
Nigeria	75-78
North Borneo	240-243
Northern Rhodesia	50-53
Nyasaland Protectorate	87-90
Pitcairn Islands	13-16
St. Helena	132-135
St. Kitts-Nevis	95-98
St. Lucia	131-134
St. Vincent	170-173
Sarawak	176-179
Seychelles	153-156
Sierra Leone	190-193
Singapore	23-26
Solomon Islands	84-87
Somaliland Protectorate	112-115
Southern Rhodesia	71-72
Swaziland	50-53
Tonga	87-90
Trinidad & Tobago	66-69
Turks & Caicos Islands	101-104
Virgin Islands	92-95
Zanzibar	226-229

The following have different designs but are included in the omnibus set:

Great Britain	276-279
Offices in Morocco (Tangier)	546-549
Australia	223
Bahrain	68-71
Burma	116-121
Ceylon	304-306
Egypt	281-283
India	223-226
Kuwait	89-92
Oman	31-34
Pakistan-Bahawalpur	26-29, O25-O28
South Africa	109-111
South-West Africa	160-162

Nos. 32-35 (4)	5.85	8.45
Nos. 16-19 (4)	2.75	16.00
Nos. 16-19 (4)	2.60	8.00
Nos. 100-103 (4)	3.60	7.70
Nos. 57-60 (4)	11.10	9.00
Nos. 150-153 (4)	5.35	9.30
Nos. 212-215 (4)	4.40	14.85
Nos. 41-44 (4)	4.75	10.00
Nos. 149-152 (4)	3.35	7.25
Nos. 138-141 (4)	4.75	6.15
Nos. 246-249 (4)	2.75	4.20
Nos. 137-140 (4)	3.30	6.35
Nos. 79-82 (4)	9.50	8.45
Nos. 118-121 (4)	3.60	7.25
Nos. 160-163 (4)	4.60	10.70
Nos. 116-119 (4)	2.30	5.65
Nos. 103-106 (4)	14.00	17.10
Nos. 1L14-1L17 (4)	14.60	14.50
Nos. 141-144 (4)	3.35	15.75
Nos. 148-151 (4)	2.75	7.10
Nos. 123-126 (4)	5.90	8.75
Nos. 56-59 (4)	4.30	13.00
Nos. 144-147 (4)	2.55	10.35
Nos. 147-150 (4)	2.15	3.55
Nos. 180-183 (4)	66.75	19.95
Nos. 142-145 (4)	2.50	2.45
Nos. 94-97 (4)	2.90	4.00
Nos. 126-129 (4)	3.05	9.60
Nos. 151-154 (4)	4.70	8.90
Nos. 57-60 (4)	4.80	12.00
Nos. 46-49 (4)	4.25	12.65
Nos. 18-21 (4)	4.25	17.30
Nos. 59-62 (4)	3.50	10.75
Nos. 46-49 (4)	3.00	7.25
Nos. 23-26 (4)	5.10	11.75
Nos. 101-104 (4)	3.65	10.75
Nos. 3-6 (4)	3.95	14.25
Nos. 76-79 (4)	4.90	12.30
Nos. 49-52 (4)	5.55	12.25
Nos. 225-228 (4)	4.50	4.85
Nos. 231-234 (4)	3.70	7.05
Nos. 108-111 (4)	3.30	4.35
Nos. 62-65 (4)	1.60	4.25
Nos. 79-82 (4)	15.40	22.00
Nos. 75-78 (4)	2.80	9.25
Nos. 240-243 (4)	7.15	6.50
Nos. 50-53 (4)	5.00	6.50
Nos. 87-90 (4)	4.55	6.60
Nos. 13-16 (4)	15.05	14.25
Nos. 132-135 (4)	4.85	7.10
Nos. 95-98 (4)	4.35	5.55
Nos. 131-134 (4)	2.55	3.85
Nos. 170-173 (4)	2.20	5.05
Nos. 176-179 (4)	13.40	13.35
Nos. 153-156 (4)	3.00	5.15
Nos. 190-193 (4)	2.90	9.15
Nos. 23-26 (4)	19.00	13.70
Nos. 84-87 (4)	4.05	4.90
Nos. 112-115 (4)	3.95	9.95
Nos. 71-72 (4)	1.95	2.25
Nos. 50-53 (4)	2.80	4.65
Nos. 87-90 (4)	3.00	5.25
Nos. 66-69 (4)	3.55	6.80
Nos. 101-104 (4)	3.05	8.90
Nos. 92-95 (4)	2.60	5.90
Nos. 226-229 (4)	4.95	13.50
Nos. 276-279 (4)	1.35	1.00
Nos. 546-549 (4)	2.60	16.00
No. 223 (1)	.40	.40
Nos. 68-71 (4)	4.75	16.50
Nos. 116-121 (6)	7.30	5.35
Nos. 304-306 (3)	3.35	4.25
Nos. 281-283 (3)	5.75	2.70
Nos. 223-226 (4)	27.25	10.50
Nos. 89-92 (4)	6.10	10.25
Nos. 31-34 (4)	8.00	17.50
Nos. 26-29, O25-O28 (8)	2.40	44.00
Nos. 109-111 (3)	2.00	2.70
Nos. 160-162 (3)	3.00	5.50
Set total (313) Stamps	466.45	742.80

University

Arms of University College CD310

Alice, Princess of Athlone CD311

1948 opening of University College of the West Indies at Jamaica.

1951

Antigua	104-105
Barbados	228-229
British Guiana	250-251
British Honduras	141-142
Dominica	120-121
Grenada	164-165
Jamaica	146-147
Leeward Islands	130-131
Montserrat	112-113
St. Kitts-Nevis	105-106
St. Lucia	149-150
St. Vincent	174-175
Trinidad & Tobago	70-71
Virgin Islands	96-97

Nos. 104-105 (2)	1.35	3.75
Nos. 228-229 (2)	1.75	2.65
Nos. 250-251 (2)	1.10	1.25
Nos. 141-142 (2)	1.40	2.20
Nos. 120-121 (2)	1.40	1.75
Nos. 164-165 (2)	1.20	1.60
Nos. 146-147 (2)	1.05	.70
Nos. 130-131 (2)	1.35	4.00
Nos. 112-113 (2)	.85	2.00
Nos. 105-106 (2)	1.40	2.25
Nos. 149-150 (2)	1.40	1.50
Nos. 174-175 (2)	1.00	2.15
Nos. 70-71 (2)	1.00	4.20
Nos. 96-97 (2)	1.50	3.75
Set total (28) Stamps	17.75	33.75

Coronation

Queen Elizabeth II — CD312

1953

Aden	47
Kathiri State of Seiyun	28
Qu'aiti State of Shihr and Mukalla	28
Antigua	106
Ascension	61
Bahamas	157
Barbados	234
Basutoland	45
Bechuanaland Protectorate	153
Bermuda	142
British Guiana	252
British Honduras	143
Cayman Islands	150
Cyprus	167
Dominica	141
Falkland Islands	121
Falkland Islands Dependencies	1L18
Fiji	145
Gambia	152
Gibraltar	131
Gilbert & Ellice Islands	60
Gold Coast	160
Grenada	170
Hong Kong	184
Jamaica	153
Kenya, Uganda, Tanzania	101
Leeward Islands	132
Malaya	
Johore	155
Kedah	82
Kelantan	71
Malacca	27
Negri Sembilan	63
Pahang	71
Penang	27
Perak	126
Perlis	28
Selangor	101
Trengganu	74
Malta	241
Mauritius	250
Montserrat	127
New Hebrides, British	77
Nigeria	79
North Borneo	260
Northern Rhodesia	60
Nyasaland Protectorate	96
Pitcairn Islands	19
St. Helena	139
St. Kitts-Nevis	119
St. Lucia	156
St. Vincent	185
Sarawak	196
Seychelles	172
Sierra Leone	194
Singapore	27
Solomon Islands	88
Somaliland Protectorate	127
Swaziland	54
Trinidad & Tobago	84
Tristan da Cunha	13
Turks & Caicos Islands	118
Virgin Islands	114

The following have different designs but are included in the omnibus set:

Great Britain	313-316
Offices in Morocco (Tangier)	579-582
Australia	259-261
Bahrain	92-95
Canada	330
Ceylon	317
Cook Islands	145-146
Kuwait	113-116
New Zealand	280-284
Niue	104-105
Oman	52-55
Samoa	214-215
South Africa	192
Southern Rhodesia	80
South-West Africa	244-248
Tokelau Islands	4

No. 47 (1)	1.25	1.25
No. 28 (1)	.75	1.50
No. 28 (1)	1.10	.60
No. 106 (1)	.40	.75
No. 61 (1)	1.25	2.75
No. 157 (1)	1.40	.75
No. 234 (1)	1.00	.25
No. 45 (1)	.50	.60
No. 153 (1)	.50	.35
No. 142 (1)	.85	.50
No. 252 (1)	.45	.25
No. 143 (1)	.60	.40
No. 150 (1)	.40	1.75
No. 167 (1)	2.75	.25
No. 141 (1)	.40	.40
No. 121 (1)	.90	1.50
No. 1L18 (1)	1.80	1.40
No. 145 (1)	1.00	.60
No. 152 (1)	.50	.50
No. 131 (1)	.80	2.20
No. 60 (1)	.65	2.25
No. 160 (1)	1.00	

COMMON DESIGN TYPES

17A

No. 170 (1)	.30	.25
No. 184 (1)	3.00	.30
No. 153 (1)	.70	.25
No. 101 (1)	.40	.25
No. 132 (1)	1.00	2.25
No. 155 (1)	1.40	.30
No. 82 (1)	2.25	.60
No. 71 (1)	1.60	1.60
No. 27 (1)	1.10	1.50
No. 63 (1)	1.40	.65
No. 71 (1)	2.25	.25
No. 27 (1)	1.75	.30
No. 126 (1)	1.60	.25
No. 28 (1)	1.75	4.00
No. 101 (1)	1.75	.25
No. 74 (1)	1.50	1.00
No. 241 (1)	.50	.25
No. 250 (1)	1.10	.25
No. 127 (1)	.60	.45
No. 77 (1)	.75	.60
No. 79 (1)	.40	.25
No. 260 (1)	1.75	1.00
No. 60 (1)	.70	.25
No. 96 (1)	.75	.75
No. 19 (1)	2.00	3.50
No. 139 (1)	1.25	1.25
No. 119 (1)	.35	.25
No. 156 (1)	.70	.35
No. 185 (1)	.50	.30
No. 196 (1)	1.75	1.75
No. 172 (1)	.80	.80
No. 194 (1)	.40	.40
No. 27 (1)	2.50	.40
No. 88 (1)	1.00	1.00
No. 127 (1)	.40	.25
No. 54 (1)	.30	.25
No. 84 (1)	.30	.25
No. 13 (1)	1.00	1.75
No. 118 (1)	.40	1.10
No. 114 (1)	.40	1.00
Nos. 313-316 (4)	11.40	4.05
Nos. 579-582 (4)	10.90	5.30
Nos. 259-261 (3)	3.60	2.75
Nos. 92-95 (4)	15.25	12.75
No. 330 (1)	.30	.25
No. 317 (1)	1.40	.25
Nos. 145-146 (2)	2.65	2.65
Nos. 113-116 (4)	16.00	8.50
Nos. 280-284 (5)	3.30	4.55
Nos. 104-105 (2)	2.25	1.50
Nos. 52-55 (4)	14.25	6.50
Nos. 214-215 (2)	2.50	.80
No. 192 (1)	.45	.30
No. 80 (1)	7.25	7.25
Nos. 244-248 (5)	3.00	2.35
No. 4 (1)	2.75	2.75
Set total (106) Stamps	161.85	115.95

Separate designs for each country for the visit of Queen Elizabeth II and the Duke of Edinburgh.

Royal Visit 1953
1953

Aden		62
Australia		267-269
Bermuda		163
Ceylon		318
Fiji		146
Gibraltar		146
Jamaica		154
Kenya, Uganda, Tanzania		102
Malta		242
New Zealand		286-287

No. 62 (1)	.65	4.00
Nos. 267-269 (3)	2.75	2.05
No. 163 (1)	.50	.25
No. 318 (1)	1.00	.25
No. 146 (1)	.65	.35
No. 146 (1)	.75	.25
No. 154 (1)	.50	.25
No. 102 (1)	.50	.25
No. 242 (1)	.35	.25
Nos. 286-287 (2)	.50	.50
Set total (13) Stamps	8.15	8.40

West Indies Federation

Map of the Caribbean CD313

Federation of the West Indies, April 22, 1958.

1958

Antigua		122-124
Barbados		248-250
Dominica		161-163
Grenada		184-186
Jamaica		175-177
Montserrat		143-145
St. Kitts-Nevis		136-138
St. Lucia		170-172
St. Vincent		198-200
Trinidad & Tobago		86-88

Nos. 122-124 (3)	5.80	3.80
Nos. 248-250 (3)	1.60	2.90
Nos. 161-163 (3)	1.95	1.85
Nos. 184-186 (3)	1.50	1.20
Nos. 175-177 (3)	2.65	3.45
Nos. 143-145 (3)	2.35	1.35
Nos. 136-138 (3)	3.00	3.10
Nos. 170-172 (3)	2.05	2.80
Nos. 198-200 (3)	1.50	1.75
Nos. 86-88 (3)	2.40	2.35
Set total (30) Stamps	24.80	24.55

Freedom from Hunger

Protein Food CD314

U.N. Food and Agricultural Organization's "Freedom from Hunger" campaign.

1963

Aden		65
Antigua		133
Ascension		89
Bahamas		180
Basutoland		83
Bechuanaland Protectorate		194
Bermuda		192
British Guiana		271
British Honduras		179
Brunei		100
Cayman Islands		168
Dominica		181
Falkland Islands		146
Fiji		198
Gambia		172
Gibraltar		161
Gilbert & Ellice Islands		76
Grenada		190
Hong Kong		218
Malta		291
Mauritius		270
Montserrat		150
New Hebrides, British		93
North Borneo		296
Pitcairn Islands		35
St. Helena		173
St. Lucia		179
St. Vincent		201
Sarawak		212
Seychelles		213
Solomon Islands		109
Swaziland		108
Tonga		127
Tristan da Cunha		68
Turks & Caicos Islands		138
Virgin Islands		140
Zanzibar		280

No. 65 (1)	1.50	1.75
No. 133 (1)	.35	.35
No. 89 (1)	1.00	.50
No. 180 (1)	.65	.65
No. 83 (1)	.50	.25
No. 194 (1)	.50	.50
No. 192 (1)	1.00	.50
No. 271 (1)	.45	.25
No. 179 (1)	.60	.25
No. 100 (1)	3.25	2.25
No. 168 (1)	.55	.30
No. 181 (1)	.30	.30
No. 146 (1)	10.50	2.50
No. 198 (1)	3.50	2.25
No. 172 (1)	.50	.25
No. 161 (1)	4.00	2.25
No. 76 (1)	1.40	.40
No. 190 (1)	.30	.25
No. 218 (1)	37.50	5.00
No. 291 (1)	2.00	2.00
No. 270 (1)	.45	.25
No. 150 (1)	.55	.35
No. 93 (1)	.60	.25
No. 296 (1)	1.90	.75
No. 35 (1)	3.50	1.50
No. 173 (1)	2.25	1.10
No. 179 (1)	.40	.40
No. 201 (1)	.90	.50
No. 212 (1)	1.60	1.00
No. 213 (1)	.85	.35
No. 109 (1)	3.00	.85
No. 108 (1)	.50	.50
No. 127 (1)	.60	.35
No. 68 (1)	.75	.35
No. 138 (1)	.30	.25
No. 140 (1)	.50	.50
No. 280 (1)	1.50	.80
Set total (37) Stamps	90.50	32.80

Red Cross Centenary

Red Cross and Elizabeth II CD315

1963

Antigua		134-135
Ascension		90-91
Bahamas		183-184
Basutoland		84-85
Bechuanaland Protectorate		195-196
Bermuda		193-194
British Guiana		272-273
British Honduras		180-181
Cayman Islands		169-170
Dominica		182-183
Falkland Islands		147-148
Fiji		203-204
Gambia		173-174
Gibraltar		162-163
Gilbert & Ellice Islands		77-78
Grenada		191-192
Hong Kong		219-220
Jamaica		203-204
Malta		292-293
Mauritius		271-272
Montserrat		151-152
New Hebrides, British		94-95
Pitcairn Islands		36-37
St. Helena		174-175
St. Kitts-Nevis		143-144
St. Lucia		180-181
St. Vincent		202-203
Seychelles		214-215
Solomon Islands		110-111
South Arabia		1-2
Swaziland		109-110
Tonga		134-135
Tristan da Cunha		69-70
Turks & Caicos Islands		139-140
Virgin Islands		141-142

Nos. 134-135 (2)	1.00	2.00
Nos. 90-91 (2)	6.75	3.35
Nos. 183-184 (2)	2.30	2.80
Nos. 84-85 (2)	1.20	.90
Nos. 195-196 (2)	.95	.85
Nos. 193-194 (2)	3.00	2.80
Nos. 272-273 (2)	.85	.60
Nos. 180-181 (2)	1.00	2.50
Nos. 169-170 (2)	1.10	3.00
Nos. 182-183 (2)	.70	1.05
Nos. 147-148 (2)	18.00	5.50
Nos. 203-204 (2)	3.25	2.80
Nos. 173-174 (2)	.80	1.00
Nos. 162-163 (2)	6.25	5.40
Nos. 77-78 (2)	2.00	3.50
Nos. 191-192 (2)	.80	.50
Nos. 219-220 (2)	18.75	7.35
Nos. 203-204 (2)	.75	1.65
Nos. 292-293 (2)	2.50	4.75
Nos. 271-272 (2)	.85	.50
Nos. 151-152 (2)	1.00	.75
Nos. 94-95 (2)	1.00	.50
Nos. 36-37 (2)	2.50	4.00
Nos. 174-175 (2)	1.70	2.30
Nos. 143-144 (2)	.90	.90
Nos. 180-181 (2)	1.25	1.25
Nos. 202-203 (2)	.90	.90
Nos. 214-215 (2)	1.00	1.50
Nos. 110-111 (2)	1.25	1.15
Nos. 1-2 (2)	1.25	1.25
Nos. 109-110 (2)	1.10	1.10
Nos. 134-135 (2)	1.00	1.25
Nos. 69-70 (2)	1.15	.80
Nos. 139-140 (2)	.55	1.00
Nos. 141-142 (2)	.80	1.25
Set total (70) Stamps	90.15	72.70

Shakespeare

Shakespeare Memorial Theatre, Stratford-on-Avon — CD316

400th anniversary of the birth of William Shakespeare.

1964

Antigua		151
Bahamas		201
Bechuanaland Protectorate		197
Cayman Islands		171
Dominica		184
Falkland Islands		149
Gambia		192
Gibraltar		164
Montserrat		153
St. Lucia		196
Turks & Caicos Islands		141
Virgin Islands		143

No. 151 (1)	.35	.25
No. 201 (1)	.60	.35
No. 197 (1)	.35	.35
No. 171 (1)	.35	.30
No. 184 (1)	.35	.35
No. 149 (1)	1.60	.50
No. 192 (1)	.35	.25
No. 164 (1)	.55	.25
No. 153 (1)	.35	.25
No. 196 (1)	.45	.25
No. 141 (1)	.30	.25
No. 143 (1)	.45	.45
Set total (12) Stamps	6.05	3.80

ITU

ITU Emblem CD317

Intl. Telecommunication Union, cent.

1965

Antigua		153-154
Ascension		92-93
Bahamas		219-220
Barbados		265-266
Basutoland		101-102
Bechuanaland Protectorate		202-203
Bermuda		196-197
British Guiana		293-294
British Honduras		187-188
Brunei		116-117
Cayman Islands		172-173
Dominica		185-186
Falkland Islands		154-155
Fiji		211-212
Gibraltar		167-168
Gilbert & Ellice Islands		87-88
Grenada		205-206
Hong Kong		221-222
Mauritius		291-292
Montserrat		157-158
New Hebrides, British		108-109
Pitcairn Islands		52-53
St. Helena		180-181
St. Kitts-Nevis		163-164
St. Lucia		197-198
St. Vincent		224-225
Seychelles		218-219
Solomon Islands		126-127
Swaziland		115-116
Tristan da Cunha		85-86
Turks & Caicos Islands		142-143
Virgin Islands		159-160

Nos. 153-154 (2)	1.45	1.35
Nos. 92-93 (2)	1.90	1.30
Nos. 219-220 (2)	1.35	1.50
Nos. 265-266 (2)	1.50	1.25
Nos. 101-102 (2)	.85	.65
Nos. 202-203 (2)	1.10	.75
Nos. 196-197 (2)	2.15	2.25
Nos. 293-294 (2)	.50	.50
Nos. 187-188 (2)	.75	.75
Nos. 116-117 (2)	1.75	1.75
Nos. 172-173 (2)	1.00	.85
Nos. 185-186 (2)	.55	.55
Nos. 154-155 (2)	6.75	3.15
Nos. 211-212 (2)	2.00	1.05
Nos. 167-168 (2)	6.40	5.95
Nos. 87-88 (2)	.85	.60
Nos. 205-206 (2)	.50	.50
Nos. 221-222 (2)	10.50	4.75
Nos. 291-292 (2)	1.10	.50
Nos. 157-158 (2)	1.05	1.15
Nos. 108-109 (2)	.65	.50
Nos. 52-53 (2)	1.65	1.90
Nos. 180-181 (2)	.80	.60
Nos. 163-164 (2)	.60	.60
Nos. 197-198 (2)	1.25	1.25
Nos. 224-225 (2)	.80	.90
Nos. 218-219 (2)	.75	.60
Nos. 126-127 (2)	.70	.55
Nos. 115-116 (2)	.70	.70
Nos. 85-86 (2)	1.00	.65
Nos. 142-143 (2)	.50	.50
Nos. 159-160 (2)	.85	.85
Set total (64) Stamps	54.25	40.70

COMMON DESIGN TYPES

Intl. Cooperation Year

ICY Emblem CD318

1965

Antigua	155-156
Ascension	94-95
Bahamas	222-223
Basutoland	103-104
Bechuanaland Protectorate	204-205
Bermuda	199-200
British Guiana	295-296
British Honduras	189-190
Brunei	118-119
Cayman Islands	174-175
Dominica	187-188
Falkland Islands	156-157
Fiji	213-214
Gibraltar	169-170
Gilbert & Ellice Islands	104-105
Grenada	207-208
Hong Kong	223-224
Mauritius	293-294
Montserrat	176-177
New Hebrides, British	110-111
New Hebrides, French	126-127
Pitcairn Islands	54-55
St. Helena	182-183
St. Kitts-Nevis	165-166
St. Lucia	199-200
Seychelles	220-221
Solomon Islands	143-144
South Arabia	17-18
Swaziland	117-118
Tristan da Cunha	87-88
Turks & Caicos Islands	144-145
Virgin Islands	161-162

Nos. 155-156 (2)	.55	.50
Nos. 94-95 (2)	1.30	1.40
Nos. 222-223 (2)	.65	1.90
Nos. 103-104 (2)	.75	.85
Nos. 204-205 (2)	.85	1.00
Nos. 199-200 (2)	2.05	1.25
Nos. 295-296 (2)	.55	.50
Nos. 189-190 (2)	.60	.55
Nos. 118-119 (2)	.85	.85
Nos. 174-175 (2)	1.00	.75
Nos. 187-188 (2)	.55	.55
Nos. 156-157 (2)	6.00	1.65
Nos. 213-214 (2)	1.95	1.25
Nos. 169-170 (2)	1.30	2.75
Nos. 104-105 (2)	.85	.60
Nos. 207-208 (2)	.50	.50
Nos. 223-224 (2)	11.00	3.50
Nos. 293-294 (2)	.65	.50
Nos. 176-177 (2)	.80	.65
Nos. 110-111 (2)	.50	.50
Nos. 126-127 (2)	12.00	12.00
Nos. 54-55 (2)	1.60	1.85
Nos. 182-183 (2)	.95	.50
Nos. 165-166 (2)	.80	.60
Nos. 199-200 (2)	.55	.55
Nos. 220-221 (2)	.80	.60
Nos. 143-144 (2)	.70	.60
Nos. 17-18 (2)	1.20	.50
Nos. 117-118 (2)	.75	.75
Nos. 87-88 (2)	1.05	.65
Nos. 144-145 (2)	.50	.50
Nos. 161-162 (2)	.65	.50
Set total (64) Stamps	54.80	41.60

Churchill Memorial

Winston Churchill and St. Paul's, London, During Air Attack
CD319

1966

Antigua	157-160
Ascension	96-99
Bahamas	224-227
Barbados	281-284
Basutoland	105-108
Bechuanaland Protectorate	206-209
Bermuda	201-204
British Antarctic Territory	16-19
British Honduras	191-194
Brunei	120-123
Cayman Islands	176-179
Dominica	189-192
Falkland Islands	158-161
Fiji	215-218
Gibraltar	171-174
Gilbert & Ellice Islands	106-109
Grenada	209-212
Hong Kong	225-228
Mauritius	295-298
Montserrat	178-181
New Hebrides, British	112-115
New Hebrides, French	128-131
Pitcairn Islands	56-59
St. Helena	184-187
St. Kitts-Nevis	167-170
St. Lucia	201-204
St. Vincent	241-244
Seychelles	222-225
Solomon Islands	145-148
South Arabia	19-22
Swaziland	119-122
Tristan da Cunha	89-92
Turks & Caicos Islands	146-149
Virgin Islands	163-166

Nos. 157-160 (4)	3.05	3.05
Nos. 96-99 (4)	10.00	6.40
Nos. 224-227 (4)	2.30	3.20
Nos. 281-284 (4)	3.00	4.95
Nos. 105-108 (4)	2.80	3.25
Nos. 206-209 (4)	2.50	2.50
Nos. 201-204 (4)	4.00	4.75
Nos. 16-19 (4)	41.20	18.00
Nos. 191-194 (4)	2.45	1.30
Nos. 120-123 (4)	7.65	6.55
Nos. 176-179 (4)	3.10	3.65
Nos. 189-192 (4)	1.15	1.15
Nos. 158-161 (4)	12.75	9.55
Nos. 215-218 (4)	4.40	3.00
Nos. 171-174 (4)	4.75	5.30
Nos. 106-109 (4)	1.50	1.30
Nos. 209-212 (4)	1.10	1.10
Nos. 225-228 (4)	52.50	11.40
Nos. 295-298 (4)	3.70	3.75
Nos. 178-181 (4)	1.60	1.55
Nos. 112-115 (4)	2.30	1.00
Nos. 128-131 (4)	8.35	8.35
Nos. 56-59 (4)	4.45	6.10
Nos. 184-187 (4)	1.85	1.95
Nos. 167-170 (4)	1.50	1.70
Nos. 201-204 (4)	1.50	1.50
Nos. 241-244 (4)	1.50	1.75
Nos. 222-225 (4)	3.20	4.35
Nos. 145-148 (4)	1.50	1.60
Nos. 19-22 (4)	2.95	2.20
Nos. 119-122 (4)	1.70	2.55
Nos. 89-92 (4)	5.95	2.70
Nos. 146-149 (4)	1.60	1.75
Nos. 163-166 (4)	1.90	1.90
Set total (136) Stamps	205.75	135.10

Royal Visit, 1966

Queen Elizabeth II and Prince Philip
CD320

Caribbean visit, Feb. 4 - Mar. 6, 1966.

1966

Antigua	161-162
Bahamas	228-229
Barbados	285-286
British Guiana	299-300
Cayman Islands	180-181
Dominica	193-194
Grenada	213-214
Montserrat	182-183
St. Kitts-Nevis	171-172
St. Lucia	205-206
St. Vincent	245-246
Turks & Caicos Islands	150-151
Virgin Islands	167-168

Nos. 161-162 (2)	3.50	2.60
Nos. 228-229 (2)	3.05	3.05
Nos. 285-286 (2)	3.00	2.00
Nos. 299-300 (2)	2.35	.85
Nos. 180-181 (2)	3.45	1.80
Nos. 193-194 (2)	3.00	.60
Nos. 213-214 (2)	.80	.50
Nos. 182-183 (2)	2.00	1.00
Nos. 171-172 (2)	.90	.75
Nos. 205-206 (2)	1.50	1.35
Nos. 245-246 (2)	2.75	1.35
Nos. 150-151 (2)	1.00	.50
Nos. 167-168 (2)	1.75	1.75
Set total (26) Stamps	29.05	18.10

World Cup Soccer

Soccer Player and Jules Rimet Cup
CD321

World Cup Soccer Championship, Wembley, England, July 11-30.

1966

Antigua	163-164
Ascension	100-101
Bahamas	245-246
Bermuda	205-206
Brunei	124-125
Cayman Islands	182-183
Dominica	195-196
Fiji	219-220
Gibraltar	175-176
Gilbert & Ellice Islands	125-126
Grenada	230-231
New Hebrides, British	116-117
New Hebrides, French	132-133
Pitcairn Islands	60-61
St. Helena	188-189
St. Kitts-Nevis	173-174
St. Lucia	207-208
Seychelles	226-227
Solomon Islands	167-168
South Arabia	23-24
Tristan da Cunha	93-94

Nos. 163-164 (2)	.80	.85
Nos. 100-101 (2)	2.50	2.00
Nos. 245-246 (2)	.65	.65
Nos. 205-206 (2)	1.75	1.75
Nos. 124-125 (2)	1.30	1.25
Nos. 182-183 (2)	.75	.65
Nos. 195-196 (2)	1.20	.75
Nos. 219-220 (2)	1.70	.60
Nos. 175-176 (2)	2.00	3.55
Nos. 125-126 (2)	.70	.60
Nos. 230-231 (2)	.65	.95
Nos. 116-117 (2)	1.00	1.00
Nos. 132-133 (2)	7.00	7.00
Nos. 60-61 (2)	2.00	2.00
Nos. 188-189 (2)	1.25	.60
Nos. 173-174 (2)	.85	.60
Nos. 207-208 (2)	1.15	.90
Nos. 226-227 (2)	.85	.75
Nos. 167-168 (2)	1.10	1.10
Nos. 23-24 (2)	1.90	.55
Nos. 93-94 (2)	1.25	.80
Set total (42) Stamps	32.35	29.10

WHO Headquarters

World Health Organization Headquarters, Geneva — CD322

1966

Antigua	165-166
Ascension	102-103
Bahamas	247-248
Brunei	126-127
Cayman Islands	184-185
Dominica	197-198
Fiji	224-225
Gibraltar	180-181
Gilbert & Ellice Islands	127-128
Grenada	232-233
Hong Kong	229-230
Montserrat	184-185
New Hebrides, British	118-119
New Hebrides, French	134-135
Pitcairn Islands	62-63
St. Helena	190-191
St. Kitts-Nevis	177-178
St. Lucia	209-210
St. Vincent	247-248
Seychelles	228-229
Solomon Islands	169-170
South Arabia	25-26
Tristan da Cunha	99-100

Nos. 165-166 (2)	1.15	.55
Nos. 102-103 (2)	6.60	3.35
Nos. 247-248 (2)	.80	.80
Nos. 126-127 (2)	1.35	1.35
Nos. 184-185 (2)	2.25	1.20
Nos. 197-198 (2)	.75	.75
Nos. 224-225 (2)	4.70	3.30
Nos. 180-181 (2)	6.50	6.75
Nos. 127-128 (2)	.80	.70
Nos. 232-233 (2)	.80	.80
Nos. 229-230 (2)	11.25	2.30
Nos. 184-185 (2)	1.00	1.00
Nos. 118-119 (2)	.75	.50
Nos. 134-135 (2)	8.50	8.50
Nos. 62-63 (2)	5.50	7.00
Nos. 190-191 (2)	3.50	1.50
Nos. 177-178 (2)	.60	.60
Nos. 209-210 (2)	.80	.80
Nos. 247-248 (2)	1.15	1.05
Nos. 228-229 (2)	1.25	.65
Nos. 169-170 (2)	.95	.80

Nos. 25-26 (2)	2.10	.70
Nos. 99-100 (2)	1.90	1.25
Set total (46) Stamps	64.95	45.90

UNESCO Anniversary

"Education" — CD323

"Science" (Wheat ears & flask enclosing globe). "Culture" (lyre & columns). 20th anniversary of the UNESCO.

1966-67

Antigua	183-185
Ascension	108-110
Bahamas	249-251
Barbados	287-289
Bermuda	207-209
Brunei	128-130
Cayman Islands	186-188
Dominica	199-201
Gibraltar	183-185
Gilbert & Ellice Islands	129-131
Grenada	234-236
Hong Kong	231-233
Mauritius	299-301
Montserrat	186-188
New Hebrides, British	120-122
New Hebrides, French	136-138
Pitcairn Islands	64-66
St. Helena	192-194
St. Kitts-Nevis	179-181
St. Lucia	211-213
St. Vincent	249-251
Seychelles	230-232
Solomon Islands	171-173
South Arabia	27-29
Swaziland	123-125
Tristan da Cunha	101-103
Turks & Caicos Islands	155-157
Virgin Islands	176-178

Nos. 183-185 (3)	1.90	2.50
Nos. 108-110 (3)	11.00	5.80
Nos. 249-251 (3)	2.35	2.15
Nos. 287-289 (3)	2.35	2.15
Nos. 207-209 (3)	3.80	3.90
Nos. 128-130 (3)	4.65	5.40
Nos. 186-188 (3)	2.50	1.50
Nos. 199-201 (3)	1.60	.75
Nos. 183-185 (3)	6.50	3.25
Nos. 129-131 (3)	2.50	2.45
Nos. 234-236 (3)	1.10	1.20
Nos. 231-233 (3)	49.50	24.00
Nos. 299-301 (3)	2.10	1.50
Nos. 186-188 (3)	2.40	2.40
Nos. 120-122 (3)	1.90	1.90
Nos. 136-138 (3)	7.75	7.75
Nos. 64-66 (3)	4.05	4.00
Nos. 192-194 (3)	5.25	3.65
Nos. 179-181 (3)	.90	.90
Nos. 211-213 (3)	1.15	1.15
Nos. 249-251 (3)	2.30	1.35
Nos. 230-232 (3)	2.40	2.40
Nos. 171-173 (3)	2.00	1.50
Nos. 27-29 (3)	5.50	5.50
Nos. 123-125 (3)	1.40	1.40
Nos. 101-103 (3)	2.00	1.40
Nos. 155-157 (3)	1.15	1.20
Nos. 176-178 (3)	1.40	1.30
Set total (84) Stamps	133.40	94.55

Silver Wedding, 1972

Queen Elizabeth II and Prince Philip — CD324

Designs: borders differ for each country.

1972

Anguilla	161-162
Antigua	295-296
Ascension	164-165
Bahamas	344-345
Bermuda	296-297
British Antarctic Territory	43-44
British Honduras	306-307
British Indian Ocean Territory	48-49

COMMON DESIGN TYPES

Brunei	186-187
Cayman Islands	304-305
Dominica	352-353
Falkland Islands	223-224
Fiji	328-329
Gibraltar	292-293
Gilbert & Ellice Islands	206-207
Grenada	466-467
Hong Kong	271-272
Montserrat	286-287
New Hebrides, British	169-170
New Hebrides, French	188-189
Pitcairn Islands	127-128
St. Helena	271-272
St. Kitts-Nevis	257-258
St. Lucia	328-329
St. Vincent	344-345
Seychelles	309-310
Solomon Islands	248-249
South Georgia	35-36
Tristan da Cunha	178-179
Turks & Caicos Islands	257-258
Virgin Islands	241-242

Nos. 161-162 (2)	1.10	1.50
Nos. 295-296 (2)	.50	.50
Nos. 164-165 (2)	.70	.70
Nos. 344-345 (2)	.60	.60
Nos. 296-297 (2)	.50	.65
Nos. 43-44 (2)	6.50	5.65
Nos. 306-307 (2)	.80	.80
Nos. 48-49 (2)	2.00	1.80
Nos. 186-187 (2)	.70	.70
Nos. 304-305 (2)	.75	.75
Nos. 352-353 (2)	.65	.65
Nos. 223-224 (2)	1.00	1.15
Nos. 328-329 (2)	.70	.70
Nos. 292-293 (2)	.60	.50
Nos. 206-207 (2)	.50	.50
Nos. 466-467 (2)	.70	.70
Nos. 271-272 (2)	1.70	1.50
Nos. 286-287 (2)	.50	.50
Nos. 169-170 (2)	.50	.50
Nos. 188-189 (2)	1.25	1.25
Nos. 127-128 (2)	.90	.85
Nos. 271-272 (2)	.60	1.20
Nos. 257-258 (2)	.65	.50
Nos. 328-329 (2)	.75	.75
Nos. 344-345 (2)	.55	.55
Nos. 309-310 (2)	.90	.90
Nos. 248-249 (2)	.50	.50
Nos. 35-36 (2)	1.40	1.40
Nos. 178-179 (2)	.70	.70
Nos. 257-258 (2)	.50	.50
Nos. 241-242 (2)	.50	.50
Set total (62) Stamps	30.20	29.15

Princess Anne's Wedding

Princess Anne and Mark Phillips — CD325

Wedding of Princess Anne and Mark Phillips, Nov. 14, 1973.

1973

Anguilla	179-180
Ascension	177-178
Belize	325-326
Bermuda	302-303
British Antarctic Territory	60-61
Cayman Islands	320-321
Falkland Islands	225-226
Gibraltar	305-306
Gilbert & Ellice Islands	216-217
Hong Kong	289-290
Montserrat	300-301
Pitcairn Islands	135-136
St. Helena	277-278
St. Kitts-Nevis	274-275
St. Lucia	349-350
St. Vincent	358-359
St. Vincent Grenadines	1-2
Seychelles	311-312
Solomon Islands	259-260
South Georgia	37-38
Tristan da Cunha	189-190
Turks & Caicos Islands	286-287
Virgin Islands	260-261

Nos. 179-180 (2)	.55	.55
Nos. 177-178 (2)	.60	.60
Nos. 325-326 (2)	1.10	.50
Nos. 302-303 (2)	.50	.50
Nos. 60-61 (2)	1.10	1.10
Nos. 320-321 (2)	.50	.50
Nos. 225-226 (2)	.70	.60
Nos. 305-306 (2)	.60	.50
Nos. 216-217 (2)	.50	.50
Nos. 289-290 (2)	2.65	2.00
Nos. 300-301 (2)	.55	.55
Nos. 135-136 (2)	.70	.60
Nos. 277-278 (2)	.50	.50
Nos. 274-275 (2)	.50	.50
Nos. 349-350 (2)	.50	.50
Nos. 358-359 (2)	.50	.50
Nos. 1-2 (2)	.50	.50
Nos. 311-312 (2)	.65	.65
Nos. 259-260 (2)	.70	.70
Nos. 37-38 (2)	.75	.75
Nos. 189-190 (2)	.50	.50
Nos. 286-287 (2)	.50	.50
Nos. 260-261 (2)	.50	.50
Set total (46) Stamps	16.15	14.60

Elizabeth II Coronation Anniv.

CD326   CD327

CD328

Designs: Royal and local beasts in heraldic form and simulated stonework. Portrait of Elizabeth II by Peter Grugeon. 25th anniversary of coronation of Queen Elizabeth II.

1978

Ascension	229
Barbados	474
Belize	397
British Antarctic Territory	71
Cayman Islands	404
Christmas Island	87
Falkland Islands	275
Fiji	384
Gambia	380
Gilbert Islands	312
Mauritius	464
New Hebrides, British	258
New Hebrides, French	278
St. Helena	317
St. Kitts-Nevis	354
Samoa	472
Solomon Islands	368
South Georgia	51
Swaziland	302
Tristan da Cunha	238
Virgin Islands	337

No. 229 (1)	2.00	2.00
No. 474 (1)	1.35	1.35
No. 397 (1)	4.50	5.00
No. 71 (1)	6.00	6.00
No. 404 (1)	2.00	2.00
No. 87 (1)	3.50	4.00
No. 275 (1)	4.00	5.50
No. 384 (1)	1.75	1.75
No. 380 (1)	1.50	1.50
No. 312 (1)	1.25	1.25
No. 464 (1)	2.10	2.10
No. 258 (1)	1.75	1.75
No. 278 (1)	3.50	3.50
No. 317 (1)	1.75	1.75
No. 354 (1)	1.00	1.00
No. 472 (1)	2.10	2.10
No. 368 (1)	2.50	2.50
No. 51 (1)	3.00	3.00
No. 302 (1)	1.60	1.60
No. 238 (1)	1.50	1.50
No. 337 (1)	1.80	1.80
Set total (21) Stamps	50.45	52.95

Queen Mother Elizabeth's 80th Birthday

CD330

Designs: Photographs of Queen Mother Elizabeth. Falkland Islands issued in sheets of 50; others in sheets of 9.

1980

Ascension	261
Bermuda	401
Cayman Islands	443
Falkland Islands	305
Gambia	412
Gibraltar	393
Hong Kong	364
Pitcairn Islands	193
St. Helena	341
Samoa	532
Solomon Islands	426
Tristan da Cunha	277

No. 261 (1)	.40	.40
No. 401 (1)	.45	.75
No. 443 (1)	.40	.40
No. 305 (1)	.40	.40
No. 412 (1)	.40	.50
No. 393 (1)	.30	.25
No. 364 (1)	1.10	1.25
No. 193 (1)	.60	.60
No. 341 (1)	.50	.50
No. 532 (1)	.55	.55
No. 426 (1)	.50	.50
No. 277 (1)	.45	.45
Set total (12) Stamps	6.05	6.55

Royal Wedding, 1981

Prince Charles and Lady Diana — CD331   CD331a

Wedding of Charles, Prince of Wales, and Lady Diana Spencer, St. Paul's Cathedral, London, July 29, 1981.

1981

Antigua	623-627
Ascension	294-296
Barbados	547-549
Barbuda	497-501
Bermuda	412-414
Brunei	268-270
Cayman Islands	471-473
Dominica	701-705
Falkland Islands	324-326
Falkland Islands Dep.	1L59-1L61
Fiji	442-444
Gambia	426-428
Ghana	759-764
Grenada	1051-1055
Grenada Grenadines	440-443
Hong Kong	373-375
Jamaica	500-503
Lesotho	335-337
Maldive Islands	906-909
Mauritius	520-522
Norfolk Island	280-282
Pitcairn Islands	206-208
St. Helena	353-355
St. Lucia	543-549
Samoa	558-560
Sierra Leone	509-518
Solomon Islands	450-452
Swaziland	382-384
Tristan da Cunha	294-296
Turks & Caicos Islands	486-489
Caicos Island	8-11
Uganda	314-317
Vanuatu	308-310
Virgin Islands	406-408

Nos. 623-627 (5)	6.55	2.55
Nos. 294-296 (3)	1.00	1.00
Nos. 547-549 (3)	.90	.90
Nos. 497-501 (5)	10.95	10.95
Nos. 412-414 (3)	2.00	2.00
Nos. 268-270 (3)	2.15	4.50
Nos. 471-473 (3)	1.20	1.30
Nos. 701-705 (5)	8.35	2.35
Nos. 324-326 (3)	1.65	1.70
Nos. 1L59-1L61 (3)	1.45	1.45
Nos. 442-444 (3)	1.35	1.35
Nos. 426-428 (3)	.90	.80
Nos. 759-764 (6)	6.20	6.20
Nos. 1051-1055 (5)	9.85	1.85
Nos. 440-443 (4)	2.35	2.35
Nos. 373-375 (3)	3.10	2.85
Nos. 500-503 (4)	1.45	1.35
Nos. 335-337 (3)	.90	.90
Nos. 906-909 (4)	1.55	1.55
Nos. 520-522 (3)	2.15	2.15
Nos. 280-282 (3)	1.75	1.75
Nos. 206-208 (3)	1.20	1.10
Nos. 353-355 (3)	.85	.85
Nos. 543-549 (5)	7.00	7.00
Nos. 558-560 (3)	.85	.85
Nos. 509-518 (10)	15.50	15.50
Nos. 450-452 (3)	1.25	1.25
Nos. 382-384 (3)	1.30	1.25
Nos. 294-296 (3)	.90	.90
Nos. 486-489 (4)	2.20	2.20
Nos. 8-11 (4)	5.00	5.00
Nos. 314-317 (4)	3.10	3.00
Nos. 308-310 (3)	1.15	1.15
Nos. 406-408 (3)	1.10	1.10
Set total (131) Stamps	109.15	92.95

Princess Diana

CD332

CD333

Designs: Photographs and portrait of Princess Diana, wedding or honeymoon photographs, royal residences, arms of issuing country. Portrait photograph by Clive Friend. Souvenir sheet margins show family tree, various people related to the princess. 21st birthday of Princess Diana of Wales, July 1.

1982

Antigua	663-666
Ascension	313-316
Bahamas	510-513
Barbados	585-588
Barbuda	544-547
British Antarctic Territory	92-95
Cayman Islands	486-489
Dominica	773-776
Falkland Islands	348-351
Falkland Islands Dep.	1L72-1L75
Fiji	470-473
Gambia	447-450
Grenada	1101A-1105
Grenada Grenadines	485-491
Lesotho	372-375
Maldive Islands	952-955
Mauritius	548-551
Pitcairn Islands	213-216
St. Helena	372-375
St. Lucia	591-594
Sierra Leone	531-534
Solomon Islands	471-474
Swaziland	406-409
Tristan da Cunha	310-313
Turks and Caicos Islands	531-534
Virgin Islands	430-433

Nos. 663-666 (4)	8.25	7.35
Nos. 313-316 (4)	3.50	3.50
Nos. 510-513 (4)	6.00	3.85
Nos. 585-588 (4)	3.40	3.25
Nos. 544-547 (4)	9.75	7.70
Nos. 92-95 (4)	4.25	3.45
Nos. 486-489 (4)	4.75	2.70
Nos. 773-776 (4)	7.05	7.05
Nos. 348-351 (4)	2.95	2.95
Nos. 1L72-1L75 (4)	2.50	2.60
Nos. 470-473 (4)	3.25	2.95
Nos. 447-450 (4)	2.90	2.85
Nos. 1101A-1105 (7)	16.05	15.55

COMMON DESIGN TYPES

20A

Nos. 485-491 (7)	17.65	17.65
Nos. 372-375 (4)	4.00	4.00
Nos. 952-955 (4)	5.50	3.90
Nos. 548-551 (4)	5.00	5.00
Nos. 213-216 (4)	1.90	1.85
Nos. 372-375 (4)	2.00	2.00
Nos. 591-594 (4)	8.70	8.70
Nos. 531-534 (4)	7.20	7.20
Nos. 471-474 (4)	2.90	2.90
Nos. 406-409 (4)	3.85	2.25
Nos. 310-313 (4)	3.65	1.45
Nos. 486-489 (4)	2.20	2.20
Nos. 430-433 (4)	3.00	3.00
Set total (110) Stamps	142.15	127.85

250th anniv. of first edition of Lloyd's List (shipping news publication) & of Lloyd's marine insurance.

CD335

Designs: First page of early edition of the list; historical ships, modern transportation or harbor scenes.

1984

Ascension	351-354
Bahamas	555-558
Barbados	627-630
Cayes of Belize	10-13
Cayman Islands	522-526
Falkland Islands	404-407
Fiji	509-512
Gambia	519-522
Mauritius	587-590
Nauru	280-283
St. Helena	412-415
Samoa	624-627
Seychelles	538-541
Solomon Islands	521-524
Vanuatu	368-371
Virgin Islands	466-469

Nos. 351-354 (4)	2.90	2.55
Nos. 555-558 (4)	4.15	2.95
Nos. 627-630 (4)	6.10	5.15
Nos. 10-13 (4)	4.85	4.85
Nos. 522-526 (5)	9.30	8.45
Nos. 404-407 (4)	3.50	3.65
Nos. 509-512 (4)	5.30	4.90
Nos. 519-522 (4)	4.20	4.30
Nos. 587-590 (4)	9.40	9.40
Nos. 280-283 (4)	2.40	2.35
Nos. 412-415 (4)	2.40	2.40
Nos. 624-627 (4)	2.55	2.35
Nos. 538-541 (4)	5.00	5.00
Nos. 521-524 (4)	4.65	3.95
Nos. 368-371 (4)	1.85	1.85
Nos. 466-469 (4)	4.25	4.25
Set total (65) Stamps	72.80	68.35

Queen Mother 85th Birthday

CD336

Designs: Photographs tracing the life of the Queen Mother, Elizabeth. The high value in each set pictures the same photograph taken of the Queen Mother holding the infant Prince Henry.

1985

Ascension	372-376
Bahamas	580-584
Barbados	660-664
Bermuda	469-473
Falkland Islands	420-424
Falkland Islands Dep.	1L92-1L96
Fiji	531-535
Hong Kong	447-450
Jamaica	599-603
Mauritius	604-608
Norfolk Island	364-368
Pitcairn Islands	253-257
St. Helena	428-432
Samoa	649-653
Seychelles	567-571
Zil Elwannyen Sesel	101-105
Solomon Islands	543-547
Swaziland	476-480
Tristan da Cunha	372-376
Vanuatu	392-396

Nos. 372-376 (5)	4.65	4.65
Nos. 580-584 (5)	7.70	6.45
Nos. 660-664 (5)	8.00	6.70
Nos. 469-473 (5)	9.40	9.40
Nos. 420-424 (5)	7.35	6.65
Nos. 1L92-1L96 (5)	8.00	8.00
Nos. 531-535 (5)	6.15	6.15
Nos. 447-450 (4)	9.50	8.50
Nos. 599-603 (5)	6.15	7.00
Nos. 604-608 (5)	11.30	11.30
Nos. 364-368 (5)	5.00	5.00
Nos. 253-257 (5)	5.30	5.95
Nos. 428-432 (5)	5.25	5.25
Nos. 649-653 (5)	8.40	7.55
Nos. 567-571 (5)	8.70	8.70
Nos. 101-105 (5)	6.60	6.60
Nos. 543-547 (5)	3.95	3.95
Nos. 476-480 (5)	7.75	7.25
Nos. 372-376 (5)	5.40	5.40
Nos. 392-396 (5)	5.25	5.25
Set total (99) Stamps	139.80	135.70

Queen Elizabeth II, 60th Birthday

CD337

1986, April 21

Ascension	389-393
Bahamas	592-596
Barbados	675-679
Bermuda	499-503
Cayman Islands	555-559
Falkland Islands	441-445
Fiji	544-548
Hong Kong	465-469
Jamaica	620-624
Kiribati	470-474
Mauritius	629-633
Papua New Guinea	640-644
Pitcairn Islands	270-274
St. Helena	451-455
Samoa	670-674
Seychelles	592-596
Zil Elwannyen Sesel	114-118
Solomon Islands	562-566
South Georgia	101-105
Swaziland	490-494
Tristan da Cunha	388-392
Vanuatu	414-418
Zambia	343-347

Nos. 389-393 (5)	2.80	3.30
Nos. 592-596 (5)	2.75	3.70
Nos. 675-679 (5)	3.25	3.10
Nos. 499-503 (5)	4.65	5.15
Nos. 555-559 (5)	4.55	5.60
Nos. 441-445 (5)	3.95	4.95
Nos. 544-548 (5)	3.00	3.00
Nos. 465-469 (5)	8.75	6.75
Nos. 620-624 (5)	2.75	2.70
Nos. 470-474 (5)	2.25	2.10
Nos. 629-633 (5)	3.50	3.50
Nos. 640-644 (5)	4.10	4.10
Nos. 270-274 (5)	2.80	2.70
Nos. 451-455 (5)	2.50	3.05
Nos. 670-674 (5)	2.55	2.55
Nos. 592-596 (5)	2.70	2.70
Nos. 114-118 (5)	2.15	2.15
Nos. 562-566 (5)	2.90	2.90
Nos. 101-105 (5)	3.30	3.65
Nos. 490-494 (5)	2.15	2.15
Nos. 388-392 (5)	3.00	3.00
Nos. 414-418 (5)	3.10	3.10
Nos. 343-347 (5)	1.65	1.60
Set total (115) Stamps	75.10	77.50

Royal Wedding

Marriage of Prince Andrew and Sarah Ferguson
CD338

1986, July 23

Ascension	399-400
Bahamas	602-603
Barbados	687-688
Cayman Islands	560-561
Jamaica	629-630
Pitcairn Islands	275-276
St. Helena	460-461
St. Kitts	181-182
Seychelles	602-603
Zil Elwannyen Sesel	119-120
Solomon Islands	567-568
Tristan da Cunha	397-398
Zambia	348-349

Nos. 399-400 (2)	1.60	1.60
Nos. 602-603 (2)	2.75	2.75
Nos. 687-688 (2)	2.00	1.25
Nos. 560-561 (2)	1.70	2.35
Nos. 629-630 (2)	1.35	1.35
Nos. 275-276 (2)	2.40	2.40
Nos. 460-461 (2)	1.05	1.05
Nos. 181-182 (2)	1.50	2.25
Nos. 602-603 (2)	2.50	2.50
Nos. 119-120 (2)	2.30	2.30
Nos. 567-568 (2)	1.00	1.00
Nos. 397-398 (2)	1.40	1.40
Nos. 348-349 (2)	1.10	1.30
Set total (26) Stamps	22.65	23.50

Queen Elizabeth II, 60th Birthday

Queen Elizabeth II & Prince Philip, 1947 Wedding Portrait — CD339

Designs: Photographs tracing the life of Queen Elizabeth II.

1986

Anguilla	674-677
Antigua	925-928
Barbuda	783-786
Dominica	950-953
Gambia	611-614
Grenada	1371-1374
Grenada Grenadines	749-752
Lesotho	531-534
Maldive Islands	1172-1175
Sierra Leone	760-763
Uganda	495-498

Nos. 674-677 (4)	8.00	8.00
Nos. 925-928 (4)	5.50	6.20
Nos. 783-786 (4)	23.15	23.15
Nos. 950-953 (4)	7.25	7.25
Nos. 611-614 (4)	8.25	7.90
Nos. 1371-1374 (4)	6.80	6.80
Nos. 749-752 (4)	6.75	6.75
Nos. 531-534 (4)	5.25	5.25
Nos. 1172-1175 (4)	6.25	6.25
Nos. 760-763 (4)	5.25	5.25
Nos. 495-498 (4)	8.50	8.50
Set total (44) Stamps	90.95	91.30

Royal Wedding, 1986

CD340

Designs: Photographs of Prince Andrew and Sarah Ferguson during courtship, engagement and marriage.

1986

Antigua	939-942
Barbuda	809-812
Dominica	970-973
Gambia	635-638
Grenada	1385-1388
Grenada Grenadines	758-761
Lesotho	545-548
Maldive Islands	1181-1184
Sierra Leone	769-772
Uganda	510-513

Nos. 939-942 (4)	7.00	8.75
Nos. 809-812 (4)	14.55	14.55
Nos. 970-973 (4)	7.25	7.25
Nos. 635-638 (4)	7.80	7.80
Nos. 1385-1388 (4)	8.30	8.30
Nos. 758-761 (4)	9.00	9.00
Nos. 545-548 (4)	7.45	7.45
Nos. 1181-1184 (4)	8.45	8.45
Nos. 769-772 (4)	5.35	5.35
Nos. 510-513 (4)	9.25	10.00
Set total (40) Stamps	84.40	86.90

Lloyds of London, 300th Anniv.

CD341

Designs: 17th century aspects of Lloyds, representations of each country's individual connections with Lloyds and publicized disasters insured by the organization.

1986

Ascension	454-457
Bahamas	655-658
Barbados	731-734
Bermuda	541-544
Falkland Islands	481-484
Liberia	1101-1104
Malawi	534-537
Nevis	571-574
St. Helena	501-504
St. Lucia	923-926
Seychelles	649-652
Zil Elwannyen Sesel	146-149
Solomon Islands	627-630
South Georgia	131-134
Trinidad & Tobago	484-487
Tristan da Cunha	439-442
Vanuatu	485-488

Nos. 454-457 (4)	5.00	5.00
Nos. 655-658 (4)	8.90	4.95
Nos. 731-734 (4)	12.50	8.35
Nos. 541-544 (4)	8.00	6.60
Nos. 481-484 (4)	5.45	3.85
Nos. 1101-1104 (4)	4.25	4.25
Nos. 534-537 (4)	11.00	7.85
Nos. 571-574 (4)	8.35	8.35
Nos. 501-504 (4)	8.70	7.15
Nos. 923-926 (4)	8.80	8.80
Nos. 649-652 (4)	12.85	12.85
Nos. 146-149 (4)	11.25	11.25
Nos. 627-630 (4)	7.00	4.45
Nos. 131-134 (4)	6.30	3.70
Nos. 484-487 (4)	10.25	6.35
Nos. 439-442 (4)	7.60	7.60
Nos. 485-488 (4)	4.85	4.85
Set total (68) Stamps	141.05	116.20

Moon Landing, 20th Anniv.

CD342

Designs: Equipment, crew photographs, spacecraft, official emblems and report profiles created for the Apollo Missions. Two stamps in each set are square in format rather than like the stamp shown; see individual country listings for more information.

1989

Ascension	468-472
Bahamas	674-678
Belize	916-920
Kiribati	517-521
Liberia	1125-1129
Nevis	586-590
St. Kitts	248-252
Samoa	760-764
Seychelles	676-680
Zil Elwannyen Sesel	154-158
Solomon Islands	643-647
Vanuatu	507-511

Nos. 468-472 (5)	9.40	8.60
Nos. 674-678 (5)	23.00	19.70
Nos. 916-920 (5)	29.25	21.60
Nos. 517-521 (5)	12.50	12.50
Nos. 1125-1129 (5)	8.50	8.50
Nos. 586-590 (5)	7.50	7.50

COMMON DESIGN TYPES

Nos. 248-252 (5)	8.00	8.25
Nos. 760-764 (5)	9.85	9.30
Nos. 676-680 (5)	16.05	16.05
Nos. 154-158 (5)	26.85	26.85
Nos. 643-647 (5)	9.00	6.75
Nos. 507-511 (5)	8.60	8.60
Set total (60) Stamps	168.50	154.20

Queen Mother, 90th Birthday

CD343   CD344

Designs: Portraits of Queen Elizabeth, the Queen Mother. See individual country listings for more information.

1990

Ascension	491-492
Bahamas	698-699
Barbados	782-783
British Antarctic Territory	170-171
British Indian Ocean Territory	106-107
Cayman Islands	622-623
Falkland Islands	524-525
Kenya	527-528
Kiribati	555-556
Liberia	1145-1146
Pitcairn Islands	336-337
St. Helena	532-533
St. Lucia	969-970
Seychelles	710-711
Zil Elwannyen Sesel	171-172
Solomon Islands	671-672
South Georgia	143-144
Swaziland	565-566
Tristan da Cunha	480-481

Nos. 491-492 (2)	4.75	4.75
Nos. 698-699 (2)	5.25	5.25
Nos. 782-783 (2)	4.00	3.70
Nos. 170-171 (2)	6.00	6.00
Nos. 106-107 (2)	18.00	18.50
Nos. 622-623 (2)	4.00	5.50
Nos. 524-525 (2)	4.75	4.75
Nos. 527-528 (2)	6.05	6.05
Nos. 555-556 (2)	4.75	4.75
Nos. 1145-1146 (2)	3.25	3.25
Nos. 336-337 (2)	4.25	4.25
Nos. 532-533 (2)	5.25	5.25
Nos. 969-970 (2)	4.60	4.60
Nos. 710-711 (2)	6.60	6.60
Nos. 171-172 (2)	8.25	8.25
Nos. 671-672 (2)	5.00	5.30
Nos. 143-144 (2)	5.50	6.50
Nos. 565-566 (2)	4.10	4.10
Nos. 480-481 (2)	5.60	5.60
Set total (38) Stamps	109.95	112.95

Queen Elizabeth II, 65th Birthday, and Prince Philip, 70th Birthday

CD345

CD346

Designs: Portraits of Queen Elizabeth II and Prince Philip differ for each country. Printed in sheets of 10 + 5 labels (3 different) between. Stamps alternate, producing 5 different triptychs.

1991

Ascension	506a
Bahamas	731a
Belize	970a
Bermuda	618a
Kiribati	572a
Mauritius	734a
Pitcairn Islands	349a
St. Helena	555a
St. Kitts	319a
Samoa	791a
Seychelles	724a
Zil Elwannyen Sesel	178a
Solomon Islands	689a
South Georgia	150a
Swaziland	587a
Vanuatu	541a

No. 506a (1)	3.50	3.75
No. 731a (1)	4.00	4.00
No. 970a (1)	4.25	4.25
No. 618a (1)	3.50	4.00
No. 572a (1)	4.00	4.00
No. 734a (1)	4.00	4.00
No. 349a (1)	3.25	3.25
No. 555a (1)	2.75	2.75
No. 319a (1)	3.00	3.00
No. 791a (1)	3.75	3.75
No. 724a (1)	5.00	5.00
No. 178a (1)	6.25	6.25
No. 689a (1)	3.75	3.75
No. 150a (1)	4.75	7.00
No. 587a (1)	4.00	4.00
No. 541a (1)	2.50	2.50
Set total (16) Stamps	62.25	65.25

Royal Family Birthday, Anniversary

CD347

Queen Elizabeth II, 65th birthday, Charles and Diana, 10th wedding anniversary: Various photographs of Queen Elizabeth II, Prince Philip, Prince Charles, Princess Diana and their sons William and Henry.

1991

Antigua	1446-1455
Barbuda	1229-1238
Dominica	1328-1337
Gambia	1080-1089
Grenada	2006-2015
Grenada Grenadines	1331-1340
Guyana	2440-2451
Lesotho	871-875
Maldive Islands	1533-1542
Nevis	666-675
St. Vincent	1485-1494
St. Vincent Grenadines	769-778
Sierra Leone	1387-1396
Turks & Caicos Islands	913-922
Uganda	918-927

Nos. 1446-1455 (10)	21.70	20.05
Nos. 1229-1238 (10)	125.00	119.50
Nos. 1328-1337 (10)	30.20	30.20
Nos. 1080-1089 (10)	24.65	24.40
Nos. 2006-2015 (10)	25.45	22.10
Nos. 1331-1340 (10)	23.85	23.35
Nos. 2440-2451 (12)	21.40	21.15
Nos. 871-875 (5)	13.55	13.55
Nos. 1533-1542 (10)	28.10	28.10
Nos. 666-675 (10)	23.65	23.65
Nos. 1485-1494 (10)	26.75	25.90
Nos. 769-778 (10)	25.40	25.40
Nos. 1387-1396 (10)	26.35	26.35
Nos. 913-922 (10)	27.50	25.30
Nos. 918-927 (10)	17.65	17.65
Set total (147) Stamps	461.20	446.65

Queen Elizabeth II's Accession to the Throne, 40th Anniv.

CD348

Various photographs of Queen Elizabeth II with local Scenes.

1992

Antigua	1513-1518
Barbuda	1306-1311
Dominica	1414-1419
Gambia	1172-1177
Grenada	2047-2052
Grenada Grenadines	1368-1373
Lesotho	881-885
Maldive Islands	1637-1642
Nevis	702-707
St. Vincent	1582-1587
St. Vincent Grenadines	829-834
Sierra Leone	1482-1487
Turks and Caicos Islands	978-987
Uganda	990-995
Virgin Islands	742-746

Nos. 1513-1518 (6)	15.00	15.10
Nos. 1306-1311 (6)	125.25	83.65
Nos. 1414-1419 (6)	12.50	12.50
Nos. 1172-1177 (6)	15.00	14.85
Nos. 2047-2052 (6)	15.95	15.95
Nos. 1368-1373 (6)	17.00	15.35
Nos. 881-885 (5)	11.90	11.90
Nos. 1637-1642 (6)	17.55	17.55
Nos. 702-707 (6)	13.55	13.55
Nos. 1582-1587 (6)	14.40	14.40
Nos. 829-834 (6)	19.65	19.65
Nos. 1482-1487 (6)	22.50	22.50
Nos. 913-922 (10)	27.50	25.30
Nos. 990-995 (6)	19.50	19.50
Nos. 742-746 (5)	15.50	15.50
Set total (92) Stamps	362.75	317.25

CD349

1992

Ascension	531-535
Bahamas	744-748
Bermuda	623-627
British Indian Ocean Territory	119-123
Cayman Islands	648-652
Falkland Islands	549-553
Gibraltar	605-609
Hong Kong	619-623
Kenya	563-567
Kiribati	582-586
Pitcairn Islands	362-366
St. Helena	570-574
St. Kitts	332-336
Samoa	805-809
Seychelles	734-738
Zil Elwannyen Sesel	183-187
Solomon Islands	708-712
South Georgia	157-161
Tristan da Cunha	508-512
Vanuatu	555-559
Zambia	561-565

Nos. 531-535 (5)	6.10	6.10
Nos. 744-748 (5)	6.90	4.70
Nos. 623-627 (5)	7.40	7.55
Nos. 119-123 (5)	22.75	19.25
Nos. 648-652 (5)	7.60	6.60
Nos. 549-553 (5)	5.95	5.90
Nos. 605-609 (5)	3.55	3.85
Nos. 619-623 (5)	5.10	5.25
Nos. 563-567 (5)	7.80	7.75
Nos. 582-586 (5)	3.85	3.85
Nos. 362-366 (5)	5.35	5.35
Nos. 570-574 (5)	5.70	5.70
Nos. 332-336 (5)	6.60	5.50
Nos. 805-809 (5)	7.85	5.90
Nos. 734-738 (5)	10.55	10.55
Nos. 183-187 (5)	9.40	9.40
Nos. 708-712 (5)	5.00	5.30
Nos. 157-161 (5)	5.60	5.90
Nos. 508-512 (5)	8.75	8.30
Nos. 555-559 (5)	3.10	3.10
Nos. 561-565 (5)	5.20	5.15
Set total (105) Stamps	150.10	140.95

Royal Air Force, 75th Anniversary

CD350

1993

Ascension	557-561
Bahamas	771-775
Barbados	842-846
Belize	1003-1008
Bermuda	648-651
British Indian Ocean Territory	136-140
Falkland Is.	573-577
Fiji	687-691
Montserrat	830-834
St. Kitts	351-355

Nos. 557-561 (5)	15.60	14.60
Nos. 771-775 (5)	24.65	21.45
Nos. 842-846 (5)	14.15	12.85
Nos. 1003-1008 (6)	21.15	16.50
Nos. 648-651 (4)	9.65	10.45
Nos. 136-140 (5)	16.10	16.10
Nos. 573-577 (5)	10.85	10.85
Nos. 687-691 (5)	17.75	17.40
Nos. 830-834 (5)	14.10	14.10
Nos. 351-355 (5)	22.80	23.55
Set total (50) Stamps	166.80	157.85

Royal Air Force, 80th Anniv.

Design CD350 Re-inscribed

1998

Ascension	697-701
Bahamas	907-911
British Indian Ocean Terr	198-202
Cayman Islands	754-758
Fiji	814-818
Gibraltar	755-759
Samoa	957-961
Turks & Caicos Islands	1258-1265
Tuvalu	763-767
Virgin Islands	879-883

Nos. 697-701 (5)	16.10	16.10
Nos. 907-911 (5)	13.60	12.65
Nos. 136-140 (5)	16.10	16.10
Nos. 754-758 (5)	15.25	15.25
Nos. 814-818 (5)	14.00	12.75
Nos. 755-759 (5)	7.85	9.00
Nos. 957-961 (5)	15.70	14.90
Nos. 1258-1265 (2)	27.50	27.50
Nos. 763-767 (5)	7.75	7.75
Nos. 879-883 (5)	15.00	15.00
Set total (47) Stamps	148.85	147.00

End of World War II, 50th Anniv.

CD351

CD352

1995

Ascension	613-617
Bahamas	824-828
Barbados	891-895
Belize	1047-1050
British Indian Ocean Territory	163-167
Cayman Islands	704-708
Falkland Islands	634-638
Fiji	720-724
Kiribati	662-668
Liberia	1175-1179
Mauritius	803-805
St. Helena	646-654
St. Kitts	389-393
St. Lucia	1018-1022
Samoa	890-894
Solomon Islands	799-803
South Georgia	198-200
Tristan da Cunha	562-566

Nos. 613-617 (5)	21.50	21.50

22A COMMON DESIGN TYPES

Nos. 824-828 (5)	22.00	18.70
Nos. 891-895 (5)	14.20	11.90
Nos. 1047-1050 (4)	8.25	5.90
Nos. 163-167 (5)	16.25	16.25
Nos. 704-708 (5)	17.65	13.95
Nos. 634-638 (5)	18.65	17.15
Nos. 720-724 (5)	17.50	14.50
Nos. 662-668 (7)	12.55	12.55
Nos. 1175-1179 (5)	15.25	11.15
Nos. 803-805 (3)	7.50	7.50
Nos. 646-654 (9)	26.10	26.10
Nos. 389-393 (5)	16.40	16.40
Nos. 1018-1022 (5)	12.25	10.15
Nos. 890-894 (5)	15.25	14.50
Nos. 799-803 (5)	14.75	14.75
Nos. 198-200 (3)	14.50	15.50
Nos. 562-566 (5)	20.10	20.10
Set total (91) Stamps	290.65	268.55

UN, 50th Anniv.

CD353

1995

Bahamas	839-842
Barbados	901-904
Belize	1055-1058
Jamaica	847-851
Liberia	1187-1190
Mauritius	813-816
Pitcairn Islands	436-439
St. Kitts	398-401
St. Lucia	1023-1026
Samoa	900-903
Tristan da Cunha	568-571
Virgin Islands	807-810

Nos. 839-842 (4)	7.15	6.40
Nos. 901-904 (4)	7.00	5.75
Nos. 1055-1058 (4)	6.80	4.70
Nos. 847-851 (5)	5.40	5.45
Nos. 1187-1190 (4)	10.90	10.90
Nos. 813-816 (4)	4.55	4.55
Nos. 436-439 (4)	8.15	8.15
Nos. 398-401 (4)	6.15	7.15
Nos. 1023-1026 (4)	7.50	7.25
Nos. 900-903 (4)	9.35	8.20
Nos. 568-571 (4)	13.50	13.50
Nos. 807-810 (4)	7.45	7.45
Set total (49) Stamps	93.90	89.45

Queen Elizabeth, 70th Birthday

CD354

1996

Ascension	632-635
British Antarctic Territory	240-243
British Indian Ocean Territory	176-180
Falkland Islands	653-657
Pitcairn Islands	446-449
St. Helena	672-676
Samoa	912-916
Tokelau	223-227
Tristan da Cunha	576-579
Virgin Islands	824-828

Nos. 632-635 (4)	5.30	5.30
Nos. 240-243 (4)	9.45	8.15
Nos. 176-180 (5)	11.50	11.50
Nos. 653-657 (5)	13.55	11.20
Nos. 446-449 (4)	8.60	8.60
Nos. 672-676 (5)	12.45	12.70
Nos. 912-916 (5)	10.50	10.50
Nos. 223-227 (5)	10.50	10.50
Nos. 576-579 (4)	8.35	8.35
Nos. 824-828 (5)	11.30	11.30
Set total (46) Stamps	101.50	98.10

Diana, Princess of Wales (1961-97)

CD355

1998

Ascension	696
Bahamas	901A-902
Barbados	950
Belize	1091
Bermuda	753
Botswana	659-663
British Antarctic Territory	258
British Indian Ocean Terr.	197
Cayman Islands	752A-753
Falkland Islands	694
Fiji	819-820
Gibraltar	754
Kiribati	719A-720
Namibia	909
Niue	706
Norfolk Island	644-645
Papua New Guinea	937
Pitcairn Islands	487
St. Helena	711
St. Kitts	437A-438
Samoa	955A-956
Seychelles	802
Solomon Islands	866-867
South Georgia	220
Tokelau	252B-253
Tonga	980
Niuafo'ou	201
Tristan da Cunha	618
Tuvalu	762
Vanuatu	718A-719
Virgin Islands	878

No. 696 (1)	5.25	5.25
Nos. 901A-902 (2)	5.30	5.30
No. 950 (1)	6.25	6.25
No. 1091 (1)	10.00	10.00
No. 753 (1)	5.00	5.00
Nos. 659-663 (5)	8.25	8.80
No. 258 (1)	5.50	5.50
No. 197 (1)	5.50	5.50
Nos. 752A-753 (3)	7.40	7.40
No. 694 (1)	5.00	5.00
Nos. 819-820 (2)	5.25	5.25
No. 754 (1)	1.10	3.25
Nos. 719A-720 (2)	4.60	4.60
No. 909 (1)	1.75	1.75
No. 706 (1)	5.50	5.50
Nos. 644-645 (2)	5.60	5.60
No. 937 (1)	6.25	6.25
No. 487 (1)	4.75	4.75
No. 711 (1)	4.25	4.25
Nos. 437A-438 (2)	5.15	5.15
Nos. 955A-956 (2)	7.00	7.00
No. 802 (1)	6.25	6.25
Nos. 866-867 (2)	5.40	5.40
No. 220 (1)	4.50	5.00
Nos. 252B-253 (2)	6.00	6.00
No. 980 (1)	4.00	4.00
No. 201 (1)	6.50	6.50
No. 618 (1)	5.00	5.00
No. 762 (1)	3.50	3.50
Nos. 718A-719 (2)	8.00	8.00
No. 878 (1)	4.50	4.50
Set total (46) Stamps	168.30	171.50

Wedding of Prince Edward and Sophie Rhys-Jones

CD356

1999

Ascension	729-730
Cayman Islands	775-776
Falkland Islands	729-730
Pitcairn Islands	505-506
St. Helena	733-734
Samoa	971-972
Tristan da Cunha	636-637
Virgin Islands	908-909

Nos. 729-730 (2)	4.50	4.50
Nos. 775-776 (2)	4.95	4.95
Nos. 729-730 (2)	14.00	14.00
Nos. 505-506 (2)	7.00	7.00
Nos. 733-734 (2)	5.00	5.00
Nos. 971-972 (2)	5.00	5.00
Nos. 636-637 (2)	7.50	7.50
Nos. 908-909 (2)	7.50	7.50
Set total (16) Stamps	55.45	55.45

1st Manned Moon Landing, 30th Anniv.

CD357

1999

Ascension	731-735
Bahamas	942-946
Barbados	967-971
Bermuda	778
Cayman Islands	777-781
Fiji	853-857
Jamaica	889-893
Kiribati	746-750
Nauru	465-469
St. Kitts	460-464
Samoa	973-977
Solomon Islands	875-879
Tuvalu	800-804
Virgin Islands	910-914

Nos. 731-735 (5)	12.80	12.80
Nos. 942-946 (5)	14.10	14.10
Nos. 967-971 (5)	9.45	8.25
No. 778 (1)	9.00	9.00
Nos. 777-781 (5)	9.25	9.25
Nos. 853-857 (5)	9.25	8.45
Nos. 889-893 (5)	8.30	7.18
Nos. 746-750 (5)	8.60	8.60
Nos. 465-469 (5)	7.55	7.10
Nos. 460-464 (5)	11.35	11.65
Nos. 973-977 (5)	12.60	12.45
Nos. 875-879 (5)	7.50	7.50
Nos. 800-804 (5)	6.75	6.75
Nos. 910-914 (5)	11.75	11.75
Set total (66) Stamps	138.25	134.83

Queen Mother's Century

CD358

1999

Ascension	736-740
Bahamas	951-955
Cayman Islands	782-786
Falkland Islands	734-738
Fiji	858-862
Norfolk Island	688-692
St. Helena	740-744
Samoa	978-982
Solomon Islands	880-884
South Georgia	231-235
Tristan da Cunha	638-642
Tuvalu	805-809

Nos. 736-740 (5)	15.50	15.50
Nos. 951-955 (5)	13.75	12.65
Nos. 782-786 (5)	8.35	8.35
Nos. 734-738 (5)	30.00	28.25
Nos. 858-862 (5)	12.80	13.25
Nos. 688-692 (5)	9.50	9.50
Nos. 740-744 (5)	16.15	16.15
Nos. 978-982 (5)	12.50	12.10
Nos. 880-884 (5)	7.50	7.00
Nos. 231-235 (5)	29.75	30.00
Nos. 638-642 (5)	18.00	18.00
Nos. 805-809 (5)	7.00	7.00
Set total (60) Stamps	180.80	177.75

Prince William, 18th Birthday

CD359

2000

Ascension	755-759
Cayman Islands	797-801
Falkland Islands	762-766
Fiji	889-893
South Georgia	257-261
Tristan da Cunha	664-668
Virgin Islands	925-929

Nos. 755-759 (5)	15.50	15.50
Nos. 797-801 (5)	11.15	10.90
Nos. 762-766 (5)	24.60	22.50
Nos. 889-893 (5)	12.90	12.90
Nos. 257-261 (5)	29.00	28.75
Nos. 664-668 (5)	21.50	21.50
Nos. 925-929 (5)	14.50	14.50
Set total (35) Stamps	129.15	126.55

Reign of Queen Elizabeth II, 50th Anniv.

CD360

2002

Ascension	790-794
Bahamas	1033-1037
Barbados	1019-1023
Belize	1152-1156
Bermuda	822-826
British Antarctic Territory	307-311
British Indian Ocean Territory	239-243
Cayman Islands	844-848
Falkland Islands	804-808
Gibraltar	896-900
Jamaica	952-956
Nauru	491-495
Norfolk Island	758-762
Papua New Guinea	1019-1023
Pitcairn Islands	552
St. Helena	788-792
St. Lucia	1146-1150
Solomon Islands	931-935
South Georgia	274-278
Swaziland	706-710
Tokelau	302-306
Tonga	1059
Niuafo'ou	239
Tristan da Cunha	706-710
Virgin Islands	967-971

Nos. 790-794 (5)	14.10	14.10
Nos. 1033-1037 (5)	15.25	15.25
Nos. 1019-1023 (5)	12.90	12.90
Nos. 1152-1156 (5)	17.10	15.10
Nos. 822-826 (5)	18.00	18.00
Nos. 307-311 (5)	23.00	23.00
Nos. 239-243 (5)	19.40	19.40
Nos. 844-848 (5)	13.25	13.25
Nos. 804-808 (5)	23.00	22.00
Nos. 896-900 (5)	4.50	6.50
Nos. 952-956 (5)	16.65	16.65
Nos. 491-495 (5)	17.75	17.75
Nos. 758-762 (5)	15.90	15.90
Nos. 1019-1023 (5)	14.50	14.50
No. 552 (1)	8.50	8.50
Nos. 788-792 (5)	19.75	19.75
Nos. 1146-1150 (5)	12.25	12.25
Nos. 931-935 (5)	12.40	12.40
Nos. 274-278 (5)	28.00	28.50
Nos. 706-710 (5)	12.50	12.50
Nos. 302-306 (5)	14.50	14.50
No. 1059 (1)	8.00	8.00
No. 239 (1)	8.75	8.75
Nos. 706-710 (5)	18.50	18.50
Nos. 967-971 (5)	16.50	16.50
Set total (113) Stamps	384.95	384.45

COMMON DESIGN TYPES

Queen Mother Elizabeth (1900-2002)

CD361

2002

Ascension	799-801
Bahamas	1044-1046
Bermuda	834-836
British Antarctic Territory	312-314
British Indian Ocean Territory	245-247
Cayman Islands	857-861
Falkland Islands	812-816
Nauru	499-501
Pitcairn Islands	561-565
St. Helena	808-812
St. Lucia	1155-1159
Seychelles	830
Solomon Islands	945-947
South Georgia	281-285
Tokelau	312-314
Tristan da Cunha	715-717
Virgin Islands	979-983

Nos. 799-801 (3)	8.85	8.85
Nos. 1044-1046 (3)	9.10	9.10
Nos. 834-836 (3)	12.25	12.25
Nos. 312-314 (3)	18.75	18.75
Nos. 245-247 (3)	17.35	17.35
Nos. 857-861 (5)	15.00	15.00
Nos. 812-816 (5)	28.50	28.50
Nos. 499-501 (3)	14.00	14.00
Nos. 561-565 (5)	15.25	15.25
Nos. 808-812 (5)	12.00	12.00
Nos. 1155-1159 (5)	12.00	12.00
No. 830 (1)	6.50	6.50
Nos. 945-947 (3)	9.25	9.25
Nos. 281-285 (5)	19.50	19.50
Nos. 312-314 (3)	11.85	11.85
Nos. 715-717 (3)	16.25	16.25
Nos. 979-983 (5)	23.50	23.50
Set total (63) Stamps	249.90	249.90

Head of Queen Elizabeth II

CD362

2003

Ascension	822
Bermuda	865
British Antarctic Territory	322
British Indian Ocean Territory	261
Cayman Islands	878
Falkland Islands	828
St. Helena	820
South Georgia	294
Tristan da Cunha	731
Virgin Islands	1003

No. 822 (1)	12.50	12.50
No. 865 (1)	50.00	50.00
No. 322 (1)	9.50	9.50
No. 261 (1)	11.00	11.00
No. 878 (1)	14.00	14.00
No. 828 (1)	9.00	9.00
No. 820 (1)	9.00	9.00
No. 294 (1)	8.50	8.50
No. 731 (1)	10.00	10.00
No. 1003 (1)	10.00	10.00
Set total (10) Stamps	143.50	143.50

Coronation of Queen Elizabeth II, 50th Anniv.

CD363

2003

Ascension	823-825
Bahamas	1073-1075
Bermuda	866-868
British Antarctic Territory	323-325
British Indian Ocean Territory	262-264
Cayman Islands	879-881
Jamaica	970-972
Kiribati	825-827
Pitcairn Islands	577-581
St. Helena	821-823
St. Lucia	1171-1173
Tokelau	320-322
Tristan da Cunha	732-734
Virgin Islands	1004-1006

Nos. 823-825 (3)	12.50	12.50
Nos. 1073-1075 (3)	13.00	13.00
Nos. 866-868 (2)	14.25	14.25
Nos. 323-325 (3)	23.00	23.00
Nos. 262-264 (3)	28.00	28.00
Nos. 879-881 (3)	19.25	19.25
Nos. 970-972 (3)	10.00	10.00
Nos. 825-827 (3)	13.00	13.00
Nos. 577-581 (5)	14.40	14.40
Nos. 821-823 (3)	7.25	7.25
Nos. 1171-1173 (3)	8.75	8.75
Nos. 320-322 (3)	17.25	17.25
Nos. 732-734 (3)	16.75	16.75
Nos. 1004-1006 (3)	25.00	25.00
Set total (43) Stamps	222.40	222.40

Prince William, 21st Birthday

 CD364

2003

Ascension	826
British Indian Ocean Territory	265
Cayman Islands	882-884
Falkland Islands	829
South Georgia	295
Tokelau	323
Tristan da Cunha	735
Virgin Islands	1007-1009

No. 826 (1)	7.25	7.25
No. 265 (1)	8.00	8.00
Nos. 882-884 (3)	6.95	6.95
No. 829 (1)	13.50	13.50
No. 295 (1)	8.50	8.50
No. 323 (1)	7.25	7.25
No. 735 (1)	6.00	6.00
Nos. 1007-1009 (3)	10.00	10.00
Set total (12) Stamps	67.45	67.45

Currency conversion

Country	Dollar	Pound	S Franc	Yen	HK $	Euro	Cdn $	Aus $
Australia	1.5341	1.9443	1.7770	0.0104	0.1962	1.6590	1.1409	—
Canada	1.3446	1.7041	1.5575	0.0091	0.1719	1.4541	—	0.8765
European Union	0.9247	1.1720	1.0711	0.0063	0.1182	—	0.6877	0.6028
Hong Kong	7.8200	9.9110	9.0583	0.0532	—	8.4568	5.8159	5.0975
Japan	147.06	186.38	170.35	—	18.806	159.04	109.37	95.861
Switzerland	0.8633	1.0941	—	0.0059	0.1104	0.9336	0.6420	0.5627
United Kingdom	0.7890	—	0.9140	0.0054	0.1009	0.8533	0.5868	0.5143
United States	—	1.2674	1.1583	0.0068	0.1279	1.0814	0.7437	0.6518

Country	Currency	U.S. $ Equiv.
Haiti	gourde	.0076
Honduras	lempira	.0405
Hong Kong	dollar	.1279
Hungary	forint	.0028
Iceland	krona	.0073
India	rupee	.0121
Indonesia	rupiah	.0001
Iran	rial	.0001
Iraq	dinar	.0008
Ireland	euro	1.0814
Israel	shekel	.2737
Italy	euro	1.0814
Ivory Coast	CFA franc	.0016

Source: xe.com, Feb. 1, 2024. Figures reflect values as of Feb. 1, 2024.

HAITI

'hā-tē

LOCATION — Western part of Hispaniola
GOVT. — Republic
AREA — 10,714 sq. mi.
POP. — 11,400,000 (2020 est.)
CAPITAL — Port-au-Prince

100 Centimes = 1 Piaster (1906)
100 Centimes = 1 Gourde

Catalogue values for unused stamps in this country are for Never Hinged items, beginning with Scott 370 in the regular postage section, Scott B2 in the semi-postal section, Scott C33 in the air post section, Scott CB9 in the air post semi-postal section, Scott CO6 in the air post official section, Scott CQ1 in the air post parcel post seciton, Scott E1 in the special delivery section, Scott J21 in the postage due section, Scott Q1 in the parcel post section, Scott RA1 in the postal tax section, and Scott RAC1 in the air post postal tax section.

ISSUES OF THE REPUBLIC
Watermark

Wmk. 131 — RH

Liberty Head — A1

On A3 (Nos. 18, 19) there are crossed lines of dots on face. On A4 the "5" is 3mm wide, on A1 2½mm wide.

1881   Unwmk.   Typo.   Imperf.

1	A1	1c vermilion, *yelsh*	10.00	5.50
2	A1	2c violet, *pale lil*	12.00	5.50
3	A1	3c gray bister, *pale bis*	22.50	8.00
4	A1	5c yel green, *grnsh*	35.00	16.00
5	A1	7c deep blue, *grysh*	24.00	4.00
6	A1	20c red brown, *yelsh*	85.00	30.00
		Nos. 1-6 (6)	188.50	69.00
		Set, never hinged	384.00	

Nos. 1-6 were printed from plate I, Nos. 7-13 from plates II and III.

1882   Perf. 13½

7	A1	1c dp ver, *dp yelsh* ('83)	6.25	2.10
a.		Vert. pair imperf. btwn.	200.00	250.00
8	A1	2c dp purple, *pale lil* ('83)	12.00	3.25
a.		2c dark violet, *white* ('84)	13.00	6.50
b.		As "a," vert. pair, imperf between	175.00	250.00
c.		As "b," horiz. pair, imperf between	175.00	250.00
d.		2c red violet, *pale lilac* ('85)	8.00	2.60
e.		As "d," vert. pair, imperf between		275.00
f.		As "d," horiz. pair, imperf between	175.00	275.00
9	A1	3c gray bister, *pale bis*	12.50	3.25
10	A1	5c blue grn, *grnsh*	9.00	1.60
a.		5c yellow green, *greenish* ('85)	8.50	1.40
b.		5c deep green, *greenish* ('85)	8.50	1.40
c.		As "b," horiz. pair, imperf between	190.00	275.00
11	A1	7c deep blue, *grysh* ('85)	11.50	2.10
a.		Horiz. pair, imperf. between	150.00	250.00
12	A1	7c ultra, *grysh* ('85)	17.50	3.25
		Vert. pair, imperf. between	150.00	250.00
13	A1	20c pale brn, *yelsh* ('86)	17.50	4.50
a.		Vert. pair, imperf between	175.00	275.00
b.		20c red brown, *yellowish* ('84)	21.00	8.00
c.		As "b," vert. pair, imperf between	150.00	300.00
d.		As "b," horiz. pair, imperf between	150.00	300.00
		Nos. 7-13 (7)	86.25	20.05
		Set, never hinged	189.00	

Stamps perf. 14, 16 are postal forgeries.

A3   A4

1886-87   Perf. 13½

18	A3	1c vermilion, *yelsh*	5.75	2.00
a.		Horiz. pair, imperf. vert.	175.00	175.00
b.		Horiz. pair, imperf. between	200.00	190.00
19	A3	2c dk violet, *lilac*	42.50	7.00
20	A4	5c green ('87)	20.00	2.75
		Nos. 18-20 (3)	68.25	11.75
		Set, never hinged	137.00	

General Louis Etienne
Félicité Salomon — A5

1887   Engr.   Perf. 14

21	A5	1c lake	.40	.30
22	A5	2c violet	1.00	.70
23	A5	3c blue	.70	.45
24	A5	5c green	60.00	.55
a.		Double impression	2,500.	
		Nos. 21-24 (4)	62.10	2.00
		Set, never hinged	89.00	

Imperfs. of Nos. 21-24 are plate proofs. Value per pair, $50.

Nos. 21-22 are known overprinted "R:S:" and postally used. Neither is known unused. Overprint is of a provisional or revolutionary government.

No. 23 Handstamp Surcharged in Red

1890

25	A5	2c on 3c blue	3.50	3.00
		Never hinged	15.00	
a.		Inverted surcharge	30.00	40.00
b.		Double surcharge	30.00	40.00
c.		Double surcharge, one inverted	—	37.50
d.		Pair, one without surcharge	100.00	

Missing letters are frequently found. This applies to succeeding surcharged issues.

Coat of Arms — A7

1891   Perf. 13¼

26	A7	1c violet	1.00	.30
27	A7	2c blue	1.50	.30
28	A7	3c gray lilac	2.00	.45
a.		3c slate	1.75	.55
29	A7	5c orange	5.50	.50
30	A7	7c red	25.00	2.75
		Nos. 26-30 (5)	35.00	4.30
		Set, never hinged	85.25	

Nos. 26-30 exist imperf. These are plate proofs. Value of unused pairs, each $100.
The 2c, 3c and 7c exist imperf. vertically. Value, each $75.

No. 28 Surcharged Like No. 25 in Red

1892

31	A7	2c on 3c gray lilac	3.00	2.00
		Never hinged	10.00	
a.		2c on 3c slate	3.50	2.25
b.		Inverted surcharge	24.00	
c.		Double surcharge	32.50	
d.		Pair, one without surcharge	32.50	

Coat of Arms (Leaves Drooping) — A9

1892-95   Engr., Litho. (20c)   Perf. 14

32	A9	1c lilac	.40	.25
b.		Double impression	700.00	
33	A9	2c deep blue	.50	.25
34	A9	3c gray	.70	.45
35	A9	5c orange	2.75	.50
36	A9	7c red	.50	.25
a.		Imperf., pair	30.00	
37	A9	20c brown	1.40	1.00
		Nos. 32-37 (6)	6.25	2.70
		Set, never hinged	15.75	

Nos. 32, 33, 35 exist in horiz. pairs, imperf. vert., Nos. 33, 35, in vert. pairs, imperf. horiz. No. 32 exists imperf. It is a proof.

1896   Engr.   Perf. 13½

38	A9	1c light blue	.55	.70
39	A9	2c red brown	.65	1.20
40	A9	3c lilac brown	.55	1.20
41	A9	5c slate green	.65	1.20
42	A9	7c dark gray	.90	1.75
43	A9	20c orange	1.10	2.25
		Nos. 38-43 (6)	4.40	8.30
		Set, never hinged	27.50	

Nos. 32-37 are 23¾mm high, Nos. 38-43 23¼mm to 23½mm. The "C" is closed on Nos. 32-37, open on Nos. 38-43. Other differences exist. The stamps of the two issues may be readily distinguished by their colors and perfs. Nos. 38-43 exist imperf. and in horiz. pairs, imperf. vert. The 1c, 3c, 5c, 7c exist in vert. pairs, imperf. horiz. or imperf. between. The 5c, 7c exist in horiz. pairs, imperf. between. Value of unused pairs, $9 and up.

Nos. 37, 43 Surcharged Like No. 25 in Red

1898

44	A9	2c on 20c brown	3.00	6.00
		Never hinged	10.00	
a.		Inverted surcharge	30.00	
b.		Double surcharge	35.00	
45	A9	2c on 20c orange	1.75	1.40
		Never hinged	6.00	
a.		Inverted surcharge	22.50	
b.		Double surcharge	32.50	
c.		Double surcharge, one inverted	40.00	

No. 45 exists in various part perf. varieties.

Coat of Arms — A11

1898   Wmk. 131   Perf. 11

46	A11	1c ultra	2.50	5.00
47	A11	2c brown carmine	.55	.40
48	A11	3c dull violet	2.50	5.00
49	A11	5c dark green	.55	.40
a.		Double impression	700.00	
50	A11	7c gray	5.00	10.00
51	A11	20c orange	10.00	20.00
		Nos. 46-51 (6)	21.10	40.80
		Set, never hinged	42.00	

Nos. 46-51 exist imperforate. They are plate proofs. Value, pair $30-$40 each.

Pres. T. Augustin Simon Sam — A12   Coat of Arms A13

1898-99   Unwmk.   Perf. 12

52	A12	1c ultra	.25	.25
53	A13	1c yel green ('99)	.25	.25
54	A13	2c deep orange	.25	.25
55	A13	2c car lake ('99)	.25	.25
56	A13	3c green	.25	.25
57	A13	4c red	.25	.25
58	A13	5c red brown	.25	.25
59	A13	5c pale blue ('99)	.25	.25
60	A12	7c gray	.25	.25
61	A13	8c carmine	.25	.25
62	A13	10c orange red	.25	.25
63	A13	15c olive green	.60	.45
64	A12	20c black	.60	.45
65	A12	50c rose brown	1.00	.50
66	A12	1g red violet	2.25	2.00
		Nos. 52-66 (15)	7.20	6.15
		Set, never hinged	21.66	

Nos. 52-66 imperf are color plate proofs.
For overprints see Nos. 67-81, 110-124, 169, 247-248.

Stamps of 1898-99 Handstamped in Black

1902

67	A12	1c ultra	.60	1.50
a.		Inverted overprint	4.50	
b.		Pair, one without overprint	50.00	
68	A13	1c yellow green	.45	.30
a.		Inverted overprint	4.50	
b.		Double overprint	30.00	
c.		Pair, one without overprint	60.00	
69	A12	2c deep orange	.80	1.50
a.		Inverted overprint	5.00	
b.		Double overprint	10.00	
c.		Pair, one without overprint	50.00	
70	A13	2c carmine lake	.45	.30
a.		Inverted overprint	10.00	
b.		Double overprint	6.00	
71	A12	3c green	.45	.45
a.		Inverted overprint	4.00	
72	A13	4c red	.60	.90
a.		Inverted overprint	4.00	
b.		Double overprint	6.00	
c.		Pair, one without overprint	100.00	
73	A12	5c red brown	1.25	6.00
a.		Inverted overprint	6.50	
74	A13	5c pale blue	.45	.45
a.		Inverted overprint	4.50	
b.		Double overprint	20.00	
75	A12	7c gray	.95	.95
a.		Inverted overprint	5.00	
b.		Double overprint	6.00	
76	A13	8c carmine	.95	8.50
a.		Inverted overprint	6.00	
b.		Double overprint	6.00	
77	A13	10c orange red	.95	1.50
a.		Inverted overprint	7.00	
b.		Double overprint	6.00	
78	A13	15c olive green	5.00	7.00
a.		Inverted overprint	20.00	
b.		Double overprint	10.00	
79	A12	20c black	5.00	6.00
a.		Inverted overprint	14.00	
b.		Double overprint	16.00	
80	A12	50c rose brown	17.50	37.50
a.		Inverted overprint	50.00	
81	A12	1g red violet	25.00	60.00
a.		Inverted overprint	130.00	
b.		Pair, one without overprint	150.00	
		Nos. 67-81 (15)	60.40	132.85

Many forgeries exist of this overprint. Specialists have called into question the existence of the double-overprint errors listed for this set except Nos. 68b and 74b. The editors would like to see documented evidence of the existence of Nos. 67b, 69b, 70b, 72b, 75b, 76b, 77b, 78b, 79b and 81b.
Scott editors are interested in information on the existence of Nos. 70b, 72b, 74b, 75b, 76b, 77b, 78b and 81b.

Centenary of Independence Issues

Coat of Arms — A14

Francois-Dominique Toussaint L'Ouverture — A15

Emperor Jean Jacques Dessalines A16   Pres. Alexandre Sabes Pétion A17

1903, Dec. 31   Engr.   Perf. 13¼, 14

82	A14	1c green	.35	.35

Center Engr., Frame Litho.

83	A15	2c rose & blk	1.25	3.00
84	A15	5c dull blue & blk	1.25	3.00
85	A16	7c plum & blk	1.25	3.00
86	A16	10c yellow & blk	1.25	3.00
87	A17	20c slate & blk	1.25	3.00
88	A17	50c olive & blk	1.25	3.00
		Nos. 82-88 (7)	7.85	18.35

Nos. 82 to 88 exist imperforate.
Nos. 83-88 exist with centers inverted. Some are known with head omitted.
Forgeries exist both perforated and imperf and constitute the great majority of Nos. 83-88 offered in the marketplace. Stamps perforated 13½ are forgeries. Many forgeries exist with heads lithographed instead of engraved. Genuine examples can be recognized by a backslash, under "CENTIMES" tablet between letters "M" and "E" of "CENTIMES."

HAITI

Same Handstamped in Blue

1904
89	A14	1c green	.50	1.50
90	A15	2c rose & blk	.50	1.50
91	A15	5c dull blue & blk	.50	1.50
92	A16	7c plum & blk	.50	1.50
93	A16	10c yellow & blk	.50	1.50
94	A17	20c slate & blk	.50	1.50
95	A17	50c olive & blk	.50	1.50
		Nos. 89-95 (7)	3.50	10.50

Two dies were used for the handstamped overprint on Nos. 89-95. Letters and figures are larger on one than on the other.

Pres. Pierre Nord-Alexis — A18

1904 Engr. Perf. 13¼, 14
96	A18	1c green	.35	.35
97	A18	2c carmine	.35	.35
98	A18	5c dark blue	.35	.35
99	A18	10c orange brown	.35	.35
100	A18	20c orange	.35	.35
101	A18	50c claret	.35	.35
a.		Tête bêche pair	500.00	
		Nos. 96-101 (6)	2.10	2.10

Used values are for c-t-o's. Postally used examples are worth considerably more.

Nos. 96-101 exist imperforate. Value, set $10.

This issue, and the overprints and surcharges, exist in horiz. pairs, imperf. vert., and in vert. pairs, imperf. horiz.

For overprints and surcharges see Nos. 102-109, 150-161, 170-176, 217-218, 235-238, 240-242, 302-303.

Forgeries of Nos. 96, 101, 101a exist.

Some specialists believe No. 101a is a proof. Research is ongoing.

Reprints or very accurate imitations of this issue exist, including No. 101a. Some are printed in very bright colors on very white paper and are found both perforated and imperforate. The original stamps are perf. 13¼ or 14, the reprints (forgeries) perf. 13½, as well as numerous other perforations, including compound perfs.

Same Handstamped in Blue like Nos. 89-95

1904
102	A18	1c green	.60	1.50
103	A18	2c carmine	.60	1.50
104	A18	5c dark blue	.60	1.50
105	A18	10c orange brown	.60	1.50
106	A18	20c orange	.60	1.50
107	A18	50c claret	.60	1.50
		Nos. 102-107 (6)	3.60	9.00

The note after No. 95 applies also to Nos. 102-107. All values exist imperf.

Forgeries exist.

Regular Issue of 1904 Handstamp Surcharged in Black

Nos. 52-66 Handstamped in Red

1906, Feb. 20
108	A18	1c on 20c orange	.35	.25
a.		1c on 50c claret	1,400.	1,150.
109	A18	2c on 50c claret	.35	.25

No. 108a is known only with inverted surcharge.

Forgeries exist.

1906
110	A12	1c ultra	1.40	.95
a.		Inverted overprint	5.00	
111	A13	1c yellow green	.75	.75
a.		Inverted overprint		
112	A12	2c deep orange	2.50	2.25
a.		Inverted overprint	5.00	25.00
113	A13	2c carmine lake	1.50	1.25
a.		Inverted overprint	5.00	
114	A12	3c green	1.50	1.25
a.		Inverted overprint	5.00	10.00
115	A13	4c red	5.75	4.50
a.		Pair, one without overprint	225.00	
116	A12	5c red brown	7.00	5.50
a.		Inverted overprint	12.00	
117	A13	5c pale blue	1.10	.60
a.		Inverted overprint	5.00	
118	A12	7c gray	5.00	4.50
a.		Inverted overprint	22.50	
119	A13	8c carmine	1.10	1.00
a.		Inverted overprint	6.00	
b.		Double overprint	70.00	
c.		Pair, one without overprint	115.00	
120	A13	10c orange red	2.00	1.25
a.		Inverted overprint	7.00	
b.		Pair, one without overprint	150.00	—
121	A13	15c olive green	2.50	1.25
a.		Inverted overprint	18.00	
122	A12	20c black	5.75	4.50
123	A12	50c rose brown	5.50	3.50
a.		Inverted overprint	50.00	
124	A12	1g red violet	15.00	10.00
a.		Inverted overprint	125.00	
		Nos. 110-124 (15)	58.35	43.05

The ink used in this overprint is fugitive and will bleed in water.

Forgeries of this overprint are plentiful.

Coat of Arms A19   President Nord-Alexis A20

Market at Port-au-Prince A21   Sans Souci Palace A22

Independence Palace at Gonaives A23   Entrance to Catholic College at Port-au-Prince A24

Monastery and Church at Port-au-Prince A25   Seat of Government at Port-au-Prince A26

Presidential Palace at Port-au-Prince — A27

For Foreign Postage (centimes de piastre)

1906-13 Perf. 12
125	A19	1c de p green	.35	.25
126	A20	2c de p ver	.45	.25
127	A21	3c de p brown	.60	.25
128	A21	3c de p org yel ('11)	6.00	7.00
129	A22	4c de p car lake	.60	.35
130	A22	4c de p lt ol grn ('13)	25.00	27.00
131	A20	5c de p dk blue	2.50	.30
132	A23	7c de p gray	1.75	.85
133	A23	7c de p org red ('13)	65.00	67.50
134	A24	8c de p car rose	1.75	.80
135	A24	8c de p ol grn ('13)	55.00	45.00
136	A25	10c de p org red	1.25	.30
137	A25	10c de p red brn ('13)	27.50	24.00
138	A26	15c de p sl grn	2.25	.90
139	A26	15c dp p yel ('13)	20.00	13.00
140	A20	20c de p blue grn	2.25	.90
141	A19	50c de p red	3.25	2.25
142	A19	50c de p org yel ('13)	20.00	13.00
143	A27	1p claret	7.25	4.50
144	A27	1p red ('13)	13.00	12.00
		Nos. 125-144 (20)	255.75	220.40

All 1906 values exist imperf. These are plate proofs.

For overprints and surcharges see Nos. 177-195, 213-216, 239, 245, 249-260, 263, 265-277, 279-284, 286-301, 304.

Nord-Alexis A28   Coat of Arms A29

For Domestic Postage (centimes de gourde)

1906-10
145	A28	1c de g blue	.35	.25
146	A29	2c de g org yel	.45	.25
147	A29	2c de g lemon ('10)	.65	.25
148	A28	3c de g slate	.40	.25
149	A29	7c de g green	1.25	.45
		Nos. 145-149 (5)	3.10	1.45

For overprints see Nos. 196-197.

Regular Issue of 1904 Handstamp Surcharged in Red like Nos. 108-109

1907
150	A18	1c on 5c dk bl	.40	.35
151	A18	1c on 20c org	.40	.25
152	A18	2c on 10c orn brn	.40	.40
153	A18	2c on 50c claret	.50	.40

Black Surcharge
154	A18	1c on 5c dk bl	.50	.40
155	A18	1c on 10c orn brn	.50	.25
156	A18	2c on 20c org	.40	.40

Brown Surcharge
157	A18	1c on 5c dk bl	1.75	1.50
158	A18	1c on 10c org brn	1.75	1.50
159	A18	2c on 20c org	6.00	5.00
160	A18	2c on 50c claret	30.00	25.00

Violet Surcharge
161	A18	1c on 20c org	150.00	

The handstamps are found sideways, diagonal, inverted and double.

Forgeries exist.

A30   President Antoine T. Simon — A31

For Foreign Postage

1910
162	A30	2c de p rose red & blk	.65	.50
163	A30	5c de p bl & blk	13.00	17.00
164	A30	20c de p yel grn & blk	15.00	16.00

For Domestic Postage
165	A31	1c de g lake & blk	.30	.25
		Nos. 162-165 (4)	28.95	17.75

For overprint and surcharges see Nos. 198, 262, 278, 285.

A32   A33

Pres. Cincinnatus Leconte — A34

1912
166	A32	1c de g car lake	.40	.40
167	A33	2c de g dp org	.50	.40

For Foreign Postage
168	A34	5c de p dp blue	.90	.40
		Nos. 166-168 (3)	1.80	1.20

For overprints see Nos. 199-201.

Stamps of Preceding Issues Handstamped Vertically

1914 On No. 61
169	A13	8c carmine	20.00	13.00

On Nos. 96-101
170	A18	1c green	47.50	35.00
171	A18	2c carmine	47.50	35.00
172	A18	5c dk blue	.75	.50
173	A18	10c orange brn	.75	.50
174	A18	20c orange	1.25	.60
175	A18	50c claret	3.00	1.50
		Nos. 170-175 (6)	100.75	73.10

Perforation varieties of Nos. 172-175 exist.

No. 175 overprinted "T. M." is a revenue stamp. The letters are the initials of "Timbre Mobile."

On No. 107
176	A18	50c claret	10,000.	13,000.

Horizontally on Stamps of 1906-13
177	A19	1c de p green	.55	.45
178	A20	2c de p ver	.75	.45
179	A21	3c de p brown	1.25	.65
180	A21	3c de p org yel	.55	.45
181	A22	4c de p car lake	1.25	.65
182	A22	4c de p lt ol grn	3.00	1.60
183	A23	7c de p gray	2.75	2.75
184	A23	7c de p org red	7.25	6.75
185	A24	8c de p car rose	5.00	4.50
186	A24	8c de p ol grn	9.25	9.00
187	A25	10c de p org red	1.50	.65
188	A25	10c de p red brn	4.00	2.50
189	A26	15c de p sl grn	4.25	3.75
190	A26	15c de p yellow	3.00	1.60
191	A20	20c de p bl grn	3.75	1.40
192	A19	50c de p red	6.50	6.00
193	A19	50c de p org yel	11.00	10.00
194	A27	1p claret	6.50	6.00
195	A27	1p red	12.00	11.00
196	A29	2c de g lemon	.55	.45
197	A28	3c de g slate	.55	.45
		Nos. 177-197 (21)	85.20	71.05

On No. 164
198	A30	20c de p yel grn & blk	3.75	3.50

Vertically on Nos. 166-168
199	A32	1c de g car lake	.50	.40
200	A33	2c de g dp org	.65	.50
201	A34	5c de g dp blue	1.10	.40
		Nos. 199-201 (3)	2.25	1.30

Two handstamps were used for the overprints on Nos. 169-201. They may be distinguished by the short and long foot of the "L" of "GL" and the position of the first "1" in "1914" with regard to the period above it. Both handstamps are found on all but Nos. 176, 294, 295, 306, 308.

Handstamp Surcharged

On Nos. 141 and 143
213	A19	1c de p on 50c de p red	.50	.40
214	A27	1c de p on 1p claret	.65	.50

On Nos. 142 and 144
215	A19	1c de p on 50c de p org yel	.65	.50
216	A27	1c de p on 1p red	.65	.50

Handstamp Surcharged

On Nos. 100 and 101
217	A18	7c on 20c orange	.50	.25
218	A18	7c on 50c claret	.45	.25

The initials on the preceding handstamps are those of Gen. Oreste Zamor; the date is that of his triumphal entry into Port-au-Prince.

Pres. Oreste Zamor

HAITI

Coat of Arms

Pres. Tancrède Auguste

Owing to the theft of a large quantity of this 1914 issue, while in transit from the printers, the stamps were never placed on sale at post offices. A few stamps have been canceled through carelessness orf favor. Value, set of 10, $8.50.

Preceding Issues Handstamp Surcharged in Carmine or Blue

1915-16 **On Nos. 98-101**
235	A18 1c on 5c dk bl (C)	2.00	2.25
236	A18 1c on 10c org brn	.60	.75
237	A18 1c on 20c orange	.60	.75
238	A18 1c on 50c claret	.60	.75

On No. 132
239	A23 1c on 7c de p gray (C)	.60	.75

On Nos. 106-107
240	A18 1c on 20c orange	1.50	1.50
241	A18 1c on 50c claret	3.50	1.50
242	A18 1c on 50c cl (C)	125.00	150.00
	Nos. 235-242 (8)	134.40	158.25

Nos. 240-242 are known with two types of the "Post Paye" overprint. No. 237 with red surcharge and any stamps with violet surcharge are unofficial.

Values for Nos. 245-308 are for examples with the boxed "Gourde" surcharge partially on the stamp. Examples upon which this surcharge is fully present on the stamp command substantial premiums.

No. 143 Handstamp Surcharged in Red

1917-19
245	A27 2c on 1p claret	.50	.50

Stamps of 1906-14 Handstamp Surcharged in Various Colors

1c, 5c

On Nos. 123-124
247	A12 1c on 50c (R)	90.00	47.50
248	A12 1c on 1g (R)	90.00	47.50

On #127, 129, 134, 136, 138, 140-141
249	A22 1c on 4c de p (Br)	.65	.75
250	A25 1c on 10c de p (Bl)	.65	.75
252	A20 1c on 20c de p (R)	.65	.75
253	A20 1c on 20c de p (Bk)	.65	.75
254	A19 1c on 50c de p (R)	.65	.75
255	A19 1c on 50c de p (Bk)	.65	.75
256	A21 2c on 3c de p (R)	.65	.75
257	A24 2c on 8c de p (R)	.65	.75
258	A24 2c on 8c de p (Bk)	.65	.75
259	A26 2c on 15c de p (R)	.65	.75
260	A20 2c on 20c de p (R)	.65	.75
	Nos. 249-260 (11)	7.15	8.25

The 1c on 10c de p stamp in black is actually a blue ink which bled into the stamps.

On Nos. 164, 128
262	A30 1c on 20c de p (Bk)	3.75	3.50
263	A21 2c on 3c de p (R)	.60	.75

On #130, 133, 135, 137, 139, 142, 144
265	A22 1c on 4c de p (R)	.70	.85
266	A23 1c on 7c de p (Br)	.70	.85
267	A26 1c on 15c de p (R)	.70	.85
268	A19 1c on 50c de p (Bk)	2.25	2.75
269	A27 1c on 1p (Bk)	2.25	2.75
270	A24 2c on 8c de p (R)	.70	.85
271	A25 2c on 10c de p (Br)	.70	.85
272	A26 2c on 10c de p (R)	.70	.85
274	A25 5c on 10c de p (Bk)	.70	.85
275	A26 5c on 15c de p (R)	5.50	6.75
	Nos. 265-275 (10)	14.90	18.20

"O. Z." Stamps of 1914 Handstamp Surcharged in Red or Brown

276	A26 1c on 15c de p sl grn	.70	.85
277	A20 1c on 20c de p bl grn	.70	.85
278	A30 1c on 20c de p yel grn & blk	.70	.85
279	A27 1c on 1p claret (Br)	.70	.85
280	A27 1c on 1p claret	2.25	2.75
281	A27 5c on 1p red (Br)	.70	.85
	Nos. 276-281 (6)	5.75	7.00

Srchd. in Violet, Green, Red, Magenta or Black 1 ct and 2 cts as in 1917-19 and

1919-20

282	A22 2c on 4c de p car lake (V)	.70	.85
283	A24 2c on 8c de p car rose (G)	.70	.85
284	A24 2c on 8c de p ol grn (R)	.70	.85
285	A30 2c on 20c de p yel grn & blk (R)	.85	1.10
286	A19 2c on 50c de p red (G)	.70	.85
288	A19 2c on 50c de p red (R)	.70	.85
289	A19 2c on 50c de p org yel (R)	.70	.85
290	A27 2c on 1p claret (R)	3.50	4.00
291	A27 2c on 1p red (R)	2.25	2.75
292	A21 3c on 3c de p brn (R)	.70	.85
293	A23 3c on 7c de p org red (R)	.70	.85
294	A21 5c on 3c de p brn (R)	.70	.85
295	A21 5c on 3c de p org yel (R)	2.25	2.75
296	A22 5c on 4c de p car lake (R)	.70	.85
297	A22 5c on 4c de p ol grn (R)	.70	.85
298	A23 5c on 7c de p gray (V)	.70	.85
299	A23 5c on 7c de p org red (V)	.70	.85
300	A25 5c on 10c de p org red (V)	.70	.85
301	A26 5c on 15c de p yel (M)	.70	.85
	Nos. 282-301 (19)	19.35	23.35

Nos. 217 and 218 Handstamp Surcharged with New Value in Magenta

302	A18 5c on 7c on 20c orange	.60	.75
303	A18 5c on 7c on 50c claret	3.50	4.00

No. 187 Handstamp Surcharged in Magenta

304	A25 5c de p on 10c de p	.60	.75

Postage Due Stamps of 1906-14 Handstamp Surcharged in Black or Magenta (#308)

On Stamp of 1906
305	D2 5c on 50c ol gray	15.00	15.00

On Stamp of 1914
306	D2 5c on 10c violet	.60	.75
307	D2 5c on 50c olive gray	.60	.75
308	D2 5c on 50c ol gray (M)	2.50	2.00
	Nos. 305-308 (4)	18.70	18.50

Nos. 299 with red surcharge and 306-307 with violet are trial colors or essays.

Allegory of Agriculture A40

Allegory of Commerce A41

1920, Apr. Engr. Perf. 12
310	A40 3c deep orange	.40	.40
311	A40 5c green	.40	.40
312	A41 10c vermilion	.50	.40
313	A41 15c violet	.50	.40
314	A41 25c deep blue	.65	.50
	Nos. 310-314 (5)	2.45	2.10
	Set, never hinged	18.50	

Nos. 311-313 overprinted "T. M." are revenue stamps. The letters are the initials of "Timbre Mobile."

President Louis J. Borno A42

Christophe's Citadel A43

Old Map of West Indies A44

Borno A45

National Capitol — A46

1924, Sept. 3
315	A42 5c deep green	.40	.25
316	A43 10c carmine	.40	.25
317	A44 20c blue	.90	.40
318	A45 50c orange & blk	.90	.40
319	A46 1g olive green	1.60	.50
	Nos. 315-319 (5)	4.20	1.80
	Set, never hinged	25.00	

For surcharges see Nos. 359, C4A.

Coffee Beans and Flowers A47

1928, Feb. 6
320	A47 35c deep green	3.75	.60

For surcharge see No. 337.

Pres. Louis Borno — A48

1929, Nov. 4
321	A48 10c carmine rose	.50	.40

Signing of the "Frontier" treaty between Haiti and the Dominican Republic.

Presidents Salomon and Vincent — A49

Pres. Sténio Vincent — A50

1931, Oct. 16
322	A49 5c deep green	1.30	.50
323	A50 10c carmine rose	1.30	.50

50th anniv. of Haiti's joining the UPU.

President Vincent A52

Aqueduct at Port-au-Prince A53

Fort National — A54

Christophe's Chapel at Milot — A56

Palace of Sans Souci — A55

King's Gallery Citadel — A57

Vallières Battery — A58

1933-40
325	A52 3c orange	.30	.25
326	A52 3c dp ol grn ('39)	.30	.25
327	A53 5c green	.30	.25
a.	5c emerald ('38)	.30	.25
b.	5c bright green ('39)	.30	.25
c.	5c brown olive ('40)	.50	.25
329	A54 10c rose car	.50	.25
a.	10c vermilion	.65	.25
330	A54 10c red brn ('40)	.50	.25
331	A55 25c blue	.90	.25
332	A56 50c brown	2.50	.55
333	A57 1g dark green	2.50	.55
334	A58 2.50g olive bister	4.50	.90
	Nos. 325-334 (9)	12.30	3.50
	Set, never hinged	70.00	

For surcharges see Nos. 357-358, 360.

Alexandre Dumas, His Father and Son — A59

1935, Dec. 29 Litho. Perf. 11½
335	A59 10c rose pink & choc	.90	.40
336	A59 25c blue & chocolate	1.60	.50
	Nos. 335-336,C10 (3)	7.00	3.40
	Set, never hinged	70.00	

Visit of a delegation from France to Haiti. No. 335 exists imperf and in horiz. pair, imperf. between. No. 336 exists as pair, imperf horiz.

HAITI

No. 320 Surcharged in Red

1939, Jan. 24   *Perf. 12*
337 A47 25c on 35c dp grn .90 .40

Statue of Liberty, Map of Haiti and Flags of American Republics — A60

1941, June 30   *Engr.*   *Perf. 12*
338 A60 10c rose carmine 1.00 .50
339 A60 25c dark blue .90 .40
    Nos. 338-339,C12-C13 (4) 8.40 2.40
    Set, never hinged 25.00

3rd Inter-American Caribbean Conf., held at Port-au-Prince.

Patroness of Haiti, Map and Coat of Arms — A61

1942, Dec. 8   Size: 26x36¼mm
340 A61 3c dull violet .40 .25
341 A61 5c brt green .50 .25
342 A61 10c rose car .50 .25
343 A61 15c orange .65 .50
344 A61 20c brown .65 .50
345 A61 25c deep blue 1.40 .50
346 A61 50c red orange 1.75 .70
347 A61 2.50g olive black 4.75 1.10

Size: 32x45mm
348 A61 5g purple 14.00 9.00
    Nos. 340-348,C14-C18 (14) 30.30 15.10
    Set, never hinged 80.00

Issued in honor of Our Lady of Perpetual Help, patroness of Haiti.
For surcharges see Nos. 355-356.

Adm. Hammerton Killick and Destruction of "La Crête-à-Pierrot" — A62

1943, Sept. 6
349 A62 3c orange .40 .25
350 A62 5c turq green .50 .40
351 A62 10c carmine rose .50 .40
352 A62 25c deep blue .65 .40
353 A62 50c olive 1.40 .50
354 A62 5g brown black 5.75 3.00
    Nos. 349-354,C22-C23 (8) 11.45 6.95
    Set, never hinged 40.00

Nos. 343 and 345 Surcharged with New Value and Bars in Red

1944, July 19
355 A61 10c on 15c orange .40 .25
356 A61 10c on 25c dp blue .40 .25
    Set, never hinged 10.00

Nos. 319, 326 and 334 Surcharged with New Values and Bars in Red

1944-45
357 A52 2c on 3c dp ol grn .30 .25
358 A52 5c on 3c dp ol grn .40 .40
359 A46 10c on 1g ol grn .50 .40
   a. Surcharged "01.0" 1.50 3.00
360 A58 20c on 2.50g ol bis .50 .40
    Nos. 357-360 (4) 1.70 1.45
    Set, never hinged 20.00

Nurse and Wounded Soldier on Battlefield — A63

1945, Feb. 20   Cross in Rose
361 A63 3c gray black .25 .25
362 A63 5c dk blue grn .25 .25
363 A63 10c red orange .30 .25
364 A63 20c black brn .30 .25
365 A63 25c deep blue .40 .25
366 A63 35c orange .50 .25
367 A63 50c car rose .50 .25
368 A63 1g olive green .90 .40
369 A63 2.50g pale violet 2.50 .50
    Nos. 361-369,C25-C32 (17) 18.75 7.55
    Set, never hinged 80.00

Issued to honor the Intl. Red Cross. 20c, 1g, 2.50g, Aug. 14. Others, Feb. 20.
For overprints and surcharges see Nos. 456-457, C153-C160.

Catalogue values for unused stamps in this section, from this point to the end of the section, are for Never Hinged items.

Col. François Capois — A64

1946, July 18   *Unwmk.*   *Engr.*   *Perf. 12*
370 A64 3c red orange .25 .25
371 A64 5c Prus green .25 .25
372 A64 10c red .25 .25
373 A64 20c olive black .25 .25
374 A64 25c deep blue .30 .25
375 A64 35c orange .40 .25
376 A64 50c red brown .50 .40
377 A64 1g olive brown .50 .40
378 A64 2.50g gray 1.30 .50
    Nos. 370-378,C35-C42 (17) 9.60 6.15

For surcharges see Nos. 383, 392, C43-C45, C49-C51, C61-C62. For overprint see Nos. 483, Q4.

Jean Jacques Dessalines — A65

1947-54
379 A65 3c orange yel .25 .25
380 A65 5c green .25 .25
380A A65 5c dp vio ('54) .65 .25
381 A65 10c carmine rose .25 .25
382 A65 25c deep blue .40 .25
    Nos. 379-382,C46 (6) 2.20 1.50

No. 375 Surcharged with New Value and Rectangular Block in Black

1948
383 A64 10c on 35c orange .40 .25

Arms of Port-au-Prince A66

Engraved and Lithographed
1950, Feb. 12   *Perf. 12½*
384 A66 10c multicolored .40 .25
    Nos. 384,C47-C48 (3) 2.20 1.25

200th anniv. (in 1949) of the founding of Port-au-Prince.

Nos. RA10-RA12 and RA16 Surcharged or Overprinted in Black

1950, Oct. 4   *Unwmk.*   *Perf. 12*
385 PT2 3c on 5c ol gray .25 .25
386 PT2 5c green .40 .25
387 PT2 10c on 5c car rose .40 .25
388 PT2 20c on 5c blue .50 .50
    Nos. 385-388,C49-C51 (7) 4.30 3.55

75th anniv. (in 1949) of the UPU.
Exist with inverted or double surcharge and 10c on 5c green.

Cacao — A67

1951, Sept. 3   *Photo.*   *Perf. 12½*
389 A67 5c dark green .40 .25
    Nos. 389,C52-C54 (4) 27.15 4.75

Pres. Paul E. Magloire and Day Nursery, Saline — A68

Design: 10c, Applying asphalt.

1953, May 4   *Engr.*   *Perf. 12*
390 A68 5c green .25 .25
391 A68 10c rose carmine .30 .25
    Nos. 390-391,C57-C60 (6) 3.80 2.35

No. 375 Surcharged in Black

1953, Apr. 7
392 A64 50c on 35c orange .50 .40

Gen. Pierre Dominique Toussaint L'Ouverture, 1743-1803, liberator.

J. J. Dessalines and Paul E. Magloire A69

Alexandre Sabes Pétion A70

Battle of Vertieres — A71

Design: No. 395, Larmartiniere. No. 396, Boisrond-Tonnerre. No. 397, Toussaint L'Ouverture. No. 399, Capois. No. 401, Marie Jeanne and Lamartiniere leading attack.

1954, Jan. 1   *Photo.*   *Perf. 11½*
Portraits in Black
393 A69 3c blue gray .25 .25
394 A70 5c yellow green .30 .25
395 A70 5c yellow green .30 .25
396 A70 5c yellow green .40 .30
397 A70 5c yellow green .30 .25
398 A69 10c crimson .30 .25
399 A70 15c rose lilac .40 .25

Perf. 12½
400 A71 25c dark gray .40 .25
401 A71 25c deep orange .40 .25
    Nos. 393-401 (9) 3.05 2.30
    Nos. 393-401,C63-C70,C71-C74 (21) 14.90 10.65

150th anniv. of Haitian independence.
See Nos. C95-C96.

Mme. Yolette Magloire — A72

1954, Jan. 1   *Perf. 11½*
402 A72 10c orange .30 .25
403 A72 10c blue .30 .25
    Nos. 402-403,C75-C80 (8) 6.75 5.20

Henri Christophe, Paul Magloire and Citadel A73

Tomb and Arms of Henri Christophe A74

Perf. 13½x13
1954, Dec. 6   *Litho.*   *Unwmk.*
404 A73 10c carmine .25 .25

Perf. 13
405 A74 10c red, blk & car .30 .25
    Nos. 404-405,C81-C90 (12) 15.10 8.85

Restoration of Christophe's Citadel.

J. J. Dessalines — A75

1955-57   *Photo.*   *Perf. 11½*
406 A75 3c ocher & blk .25 .25
407 A75 5c pale vio & blk ('56) .25 .25
408 A75 10c rose & blk .25 .25
   a. 10c salmon pink & black ('57) .25 .25
409 A75 25c chalky bl & blk ('56) .30 .25
   a. 25c blue & black ('57) .30 .25
    Nos. 406-409,C93-C94 (6) 1.55 1.50

For surcharges, see Nos. 454-455.

Pres. Magloire and Dessalines Memorial, Gonaives — A76

1955, Aug. 1
410 A76 10c deep blue & blk .40 .25
411 A76 10c crimson & blk .40 .25
    Nos. 410-411,C97-C98 (4) 2.10 1.00

21st anniv. of the new Haitian army.
Nos. 410-411 were printed in a single sheet of 20 (5x4). The two upper rows are of No. 410, the two lower No. 411, providing five se-tenant pairs. Value 85 cents.

Flamingo A77

Mallard A78

1956, Apr. 14   *Photo.*   *Perf. 11½*
Granite Paper
412 A77 10c blue & ultra 2.25 .30
413 A78 25c dk grn & bluish grn 3.25 .45
    Nos. 412-413,C99-C104 (8) 43.40 6.80

Immanuel Kant — A79

HAITI

1956, July 19 **Perf. 12**
Granite Paper
414 A79 10c brt ultra .30 .25
  Nos. 414,C105-C107 (4) 2.45 1.40
10th anniv. of the 1st Inter-American Philosophical Congress.

Zim Waterfall — A80

1957, Dec. 16 **Unwmk.** **Perf. 11½**
Granite Paper
415 A80 10c orange & blue .50 .25
  Nos. 415,C108-C111 (5) 5.90 3.00
For surcharge & overprint see Nos. CB49, CQ2.

J. J. Dessalines and Dessalines Memorial, Gonaives — A81

1958, July 1 **Photo.**
416 A81 5c yel grn & blk .25 .25
Bicentenary of birth of J. J. Dessalines.
See Nos. 470-471, C112, C170. For overprints see Nos. 480-482, C183-C184, CQ1, Q1-Q3.

"Atomium" A82

View of Brussels Exposition A83

Perf. 13x13½, 13½x13
1958, July 22 **Litho.** **Unwmk.**
417 A82 50c brown .40 .25
418 A83 75c brt green .40 .25
419 A82 1g purple .75 .25
420 A83 1.50g red orange .75 .40
  Nos. 417-420,C113-C114 (6) 5.05 2.50
Issued for the Universal and International Exposition at Brussels.
For surcharges see Nos. B2-B3, CB9.

Sylvio Cator — A84

1958, Aug. 16 **Photo.** **Perf. 11½**
Granite Paper
421 A84 5c green .25 .25
422 A84 10c brown .25 .25
423 A84 20c lilac .25 .25
  Nos. 421-423,C115-C118 (7) 4.15 2.50
30th anniversary of the world championship record broad jump of Sylvio Cator.

U. S. Satellite — A85

Designs: 20c, Emperor penguins. 50c, Modern observatory. 1g, Ocean exploration.

1958, Oct. 8 **Perf. 14x13½**
424 A85 10c brt bl & brn red .40 .25
425 A85 20c black & dp org 1.50 .50
426 A85 50c grn & rose brn 1.00 .30
427 A85 1g black & blue 1.05 .30
  Nos. 424-427,C119-C121 (7) 11.45 2.75
Issued for the International Geophysical Year 1957-58.

President François Duvalier — A86

Engraved and Lithographed
1958, Oct. 22 **Unwmk.** **Perf. 11½**
Commemorative Inscription in Ultramarine
428 A86 10c blk & dp pink .30 .25
429 A86 50c blk & lt grn .40 .25
430 A86 1g blk & brick red 1.25 .75
431 A86 5g blk & sal 2.40 1.50
  Nos. 428-431,C122-C125 (8) 10.90 6.50
1st anniv. of the inauguration of Pres. Dr. François Duvalier. See note on souvenir sheets after No. C125.

1958 Nov. 20
Without Commemorative Inscription
432 A86 5c blk & lt vio bl .25 .25
433 A86 10c blk & dp pink .25 .25
434 A86 20c blk & yel .25 .25
435 A86 50c blk & lt grn .30 .25
436 A86 1g blk & brick red .50 .40
437 A86 1.50g blk & orange .65 .50
438 A86 2.50g blk & gray vio .90 .50
439 A86 5g blk & sal 1.60 1.10
  Nos. 432-439,C126-C132 (15) 13.35 8.15
For surcharges see Nos. B13, B22-B24.

Map of Haiti — A87

1958, Dec. 5 **Photo.** **Perf. 11½**
Granite Paper
440 A87 10c rose pink .50 .25
441 A87 25c green .55 .25
  Nos. 440-441,C133-C135 (5) 3.00 1.40
Tribute to the UN. See No. C135a. For overprints and surcharges see Nos. 442-443, B4-B5, CB11-CB12.

Nos. 440-441 Overprinted
Overprint reads "10th ANNIVERSARY OF THE / UNIVERSAL DECLARATION / OF HUMAN RIGHTS" in: a, English; b, French; c, Spanish; d, Portuguese.

1959, Jan. 28
442 Block of 4 .45 .35
  a.-d. A87 10c any single .30 .25
443 Block of 4 1.15 .70
  a.-d. A87 25c any single .30 .25
  Nos. 442-443,C136-C138 (5) 18.85 14.55
10th anniv. of the signing of the Universal Declaration of Human Rights.

Pope Pius XII and Children — A88

50c, Pope praying. 2g, Pope on throne.

1959, Feb. 28 **Photo.** **Perf. 14x13½**
444 A88 10c vio bl & ol .25 .25
445 A88 50c green & dp brn .40 .25
446 A88 2g dp claret & dk brn .90 .50
  Nos. 444-446,C139-C141 (6) 3.45 2.05
Issued in memory of Pope Pius XII.
For surcharges see Nos. B6-B8.

Abraham Lincoln — A89

1959, May 12 **Photo.** **Perf. 12**
447 A89 50c lt bl & deep claret .40 .25
  Nos. 447,C142-C144 (4) 2.50 1.55
Sesquicentennial of the birth of Abraham Lincoln. Imperf. pairs exist.
For surcharges see No. B9, CB16-CB18.

Chicago's Skyline and Dessables House — A90

Jean Baptiste Dessables and Map of American Midwest, c. 1791 — A91

Design: 50c, Discus thrower and flag of Haiti.

1959, Aug. 27 **Unwmk.** **Perf. 14**
448 A90 25c blk brn & lt bl .40 .25
449 A90 50c multicolored .50 .40
450 A91 75c brown & blue .65 .50
  Nos. 448-450,C145-C147 (6) 4.70 2.30
3rd Pan American Games, Chicago, 8/27-9/7.
For surcharges see Nos. B10-B12, CB19-CB21.

No. 449 Overprinted

1960, Feb. 29
451 A90 50c multicolored 1.60 1.20
  Nos. 451,C148-C150 (4) 7.65 7.25
8th Olympic Winter Games, Squaw Valley, Calif., Feb. 18-29, 1960.

Uprooted Oak Emblem and Hands — A92

1960, Apr. 7 **Litho.** **Perf. 12½x13**
452 A92 10c salmon & grn .25 .25
453 A92 50c violet & mag .40 .25
  Nos. 452-453,C151-C152 (4) 1.55 1.15
World Refugee Year, July 1, 1959-June 30, 1960. See Nos. 489-490, C191-C192. For surcharges see Nos. B14-B17, B28-B29, CB24-CB27, CB45-CB46.

No. 406 Surcharged with New Values
1960, Apr. 27 **Photo.** **Perf. 11½**
454 A75 5c on 3c ocher & blk .25 .25
455 A75 10c on 3c ocher & blk .35 .25

No. 369 Surcharged or Overprinted in Red: "28eme ANNIVERSAIRE"
1960, May 8 **Engr.** **Perf. 12**
Cross in Rose
456 A63 1g on 2.50g pale vio .90 .50
457 A63 2.50g pale violet 1.40 1.00
  Nos. 456-457,C153-C160 (10) 7.30 5.35
28th anniversary of the Haitian Red Cross.

Claudinette Fouchard, Miss Haiti, Sugar Queen — A93

Sugar Queen and: 20c, Sugar harvest. 50c, Beach. 1g, Sugar plantation.

Perf. 11½
1960, May 30 **Photo.** **Unwmk.**
Granite Paper
458 A93 10c ol bis & vio .25 .25
459 A93 20c red brn & blk .30 .25
460 A93 50c brt bl & brn .75 .25
461 A93 1g green & brn 1.75 .25
  Nos. 458-461,C161-C162 (6) 6.20 1.75
Haitian sugar industry.

Melbourne Stadium and Olympic Flame — A94

Designs: 20c, Discus thrower and Rome stadium. 50c, Pierre de Coubertin and victors, Melbourne, 1956. 1g, Athens stadium, 1896.

1960, Aug. 18 **Photo.** **Perf. 12**
462 A94 10c black & org .25 .25
463 A94 20c dk blue & crim .25 .25
464 A94 50c green & ocher .65 .25
465 A94 1g dk brn & grnsh bl .80 .65
  Nos. 462-465,C163-C165 (7) 5.60 2.50
Olympic Victors, Athens, 1896, 17th Olympic Games, Rome, Aug. 25-Sept. 11.
For surcharges see Nos. B18-B19, CB28-CB29.

Occide Jeanty and Score from "1804" — A95

20c, Occide Jeanty and National Capitol.

1960, Oct. 19 **Perf. 14x14½**
466 A95 10c orange & red lilac .25 .25
467 A95 20c blue & red lilac .35 .25
468 A95 50c green & sepia .50 .40
  Nos. 466-468,C166-C167 (5) 2.35 1.40
Cent. of the birth of Occide Jeanty, composer. Printed in sheets of 12 (3x4) with commemorative inscription and opening bars of "1804," Jeanty's military march, in top margin.

UN Headquarters, NYC — A96

1960, Nov. 25 **Engr.** **Perf. 10½**
469 A96 1g green & blk .50 .40
  Nos. 469,C168-C169 (3) 1.40 1.05
15th anniv. of the UN.
No. 469 exists with center inverted.
For surcharges see Nos. B20-B21, CB30-CB31, CB35-CB36.

Dessalines Type of 1958
Perf. 11½
1960, Nov. 5 **Unwmk.** **Photo.**
Granite Paper
470 A81 10c red org & blk .25 .25
471 A81 25c ultra & blk .35 .25
  Nos. 470-471,C170 (3) .85 .75

Alexandre Dumas Père and Musketeer — A97

HAITI

5c, Map of Haiti & birthplace of General Alexandre Dumas, horiz. 50c, Alexandre Dumas, father & son, French & Haitian flags, horiz.

1961, Feb. 10   *Perf. 11½*
Granite Paper

472	A97	5c lt blue & choc	.25	.25
473	A97	10c rose, blk & sep	.25	.25
474	A97	50c dk blue & crim	.40	.25
		Nos. 472-474,C177-C179 (6)	3.35	1.60

Gen. Dumas (Alexandre Davy de la Pailleterie), born in Jeremie, Haiti, and his son and grandson, French authors.

Three Pirates — A98

Tourist publicity: 5c, Map of Tortuga. 15c, Pirates. 20c, Privateer in battle. 50c, Pirate with cutlass in rigging.

1961, Apr. 4   *Litho.*   *Perf. 12*

475	A98	5c blue & yel	.30	.25
476	A98	10c lake & yel	.30	.25
477	A98	15c ol grn & org	.30	.25
478	A98	20c choc & org	.35	.25
479	A98	50c vio bl & yel	.45	.25
		Nos. 475-479,C180-C182 (8)	3.50	2.15

For surcharges and overprints see Nos. 484-485, C186-C187.

Nos. 416, 470-471 and 378 Overprinted: "Dr. F. Duvalier / Président / 22 Mai 1961"

1961, May 22   *Photo.*   *Perf. 11½*

480	A81	5c yel grn & blk	.25	.25
481	A81	10c red org & blk	.25	.25
482	A81	25c ultra & blk	.25	.25

Engr.   *Perf. 12*

483	A64	2.50g gray	1.10	.60
		Nos. 480-483,C183-C185 (7)	2.75	2.25

Re-election of Pres. François Duvalier.

No. 475 Surcharged: "EXPLORATION SPATIALE JOHN GLENN," Capsule

1962, May 10   *Litho.*

484	A98	50c on 5c bl & yel	.50	.40
485	A98	1.50g on 5c bl & yel	1.40	1.00
		Nos. 484-485,C186-C187 (4)	3.80	2.80

U.S. achievement in space exploration and for the 1st orbital flight of a US astronaut, Lt. Col. John H. Glenn, Jr., Feb. 20, 1962.

Malaria Eradication Emblem — A99

Design: 10c, Triangle pointing down.

Unwmk.

1962, May 30   *Litho.*   *Perf. 12*

486	A99	5c crimson & dp bl	.25	.25
487	A99	10c red brn & emer	.25	.25
488	A99	50c blue & crimson	.40	.25
		Nos. 486-488,C188-C190 (6)	2.05	1.65

WHO drive to eradicate malaria. Sheets of 12 with marginal inscription.
For surcharges see Nos. B25-B27, CB42-CB44.

WRY Type of 1960 Dated "1962"

1962, June 22   *Perf. 12½x13*

489	A92	10c lt blue & org	.25	.25
490	A92	50c rose lil & ol grn	.40	.40
		Nos. 489-490,C191-C192 (4)	1.40	1.30

Issued to publicize the plight of refugees. For souvenir sheet see note after Nos. C191-C192.

Haitian Scout Emblem — A100

5c, 50c, Scout giving Scout sign. 10c, Lord and Lady Baden-Powell, horiz.

Perf. 14x14½, 14½x14

1962, Aug. 6   *Photo.*

491	A100	3c blk, ocher & pur	.25	.25
492	A100	5c cit, red brn & blk	.25	.25
493	A100	10c ocher, blk & grn	.25	.25
494	A100	25c maroon, ol & bl	.25	.25
495	A100	50c violet, grn & red	.40	.25
		Nos. 491-495,C193-C195 (8)	2.80	2.30

22nd anniv. of the Haitian Boy Scouts.
For surcharges and overprints see Nos. B31-B34, C196-C199.

TIMBRE MOBILE, etc.

From 1970 through 1979 postage and airmail stamps were overprinted for use as revenue stamps. The overprints used were: "TIMBRE MOBILE," "TIMBRE DE SOLIDARITE," "SOLIDARITE," "TIMBRE SOLIDARITE," "OBLIGATION PELIGRE."

Space Needle, Space Capsule and Globe — A101

1962, Nov. 19   *Litho.*   *Perf. 12½*

496	A101	10c red brn & lt bl	.25	.25
497	A101	20c vio bl & pink	.25	.25
498	A101	50c emerald & yel	.40	.25
499	A101	1g car & lt grn	.50	.40
		Nos. 496-499,C200-C202 (7)	3.10	2.20

"Century 21" International Exposition, Seattle, Wash., Apr. 21-Oct. 21.
For overprints see Nos. 503-504, C206-C207.

Plan of Duvalier Ville and Stamp of 1904 — A102

1962, Dec. 10   *Photo.*   *Perf. 14x14½*

500	A102	5c vio, yel & blk	.25	.25
501	A102	10c car rose, yel & blk	.25	.25
502	A102	25c bl gray, yel & blk	.35	.25
		Nos. 500-502,C203-C205 (6)	3.25	1.90

Issued to publicize Duvalier Ville.
For surcharge see No. B30.

Nos. 498-499 with Vertical Overprint in Black or Claret

1963, Jan. 23   *Litho.*   *Perf. 12½*

503	A101	50c emerald & yel	.65	.40
a.		Claret overprint, horiz.	.65	.40
504	A101	1g car & lt grn	1.40	.50
a.		Claret overprint, horiz.	1.40	.50
		Nos. 503-504,C206-C207 (4)	5.20	2.60
		Nos. 503a-504a,C206a-C207a (4)	5.20	2.60

"Peaceful Uses of Outer Space." The black vertical overprint has no outside frame lines and no broken shading lines around capsule. Nos. 503a and 504a were issued Feb. 20.

Symbolic Harvest — A103

1963, July 12   *Photo.*   *Perf. 13x14*

505	A103	10c orange & blk	.25	.25
506	A103	20c bluish grn & blk	.25	.25
		Nos. 505-506,C208-C209 (4)	1.40	1.15

FAO "Freedom from Hunger" campaign.

J. J. Dessalines — A104

1963, Oct. 17   *Perf. 14x14½*

507	A104	5c tan & ver	.25	.25
508	A104	10c yellow & blue	.25	.25
		Nos. 507-508,C214-C215 (4)	1.00	1.00

For overprints see Nos. 509, C216-C217.

No. 508 Overprinted: "FETE DES MERES / 1964"

1964, July 22

509	A104	10c yellow & blue	.25	.25
		Nos. 509,C216-C218 (3)	1.65	1.15

Issued for Mother's Day, 1964.

Weight Lifter — A105

Design: 50c, Hurdler.

1964, Nov. 12   *Photo.*   *Perf. 11½*
Granite Paper

510	A105	10c lt bl & dk brn	.25	.25
511	A105	25c salmon & dk brn	.25	.25
512	A105	50c pale rose lil & dk brn	.40	.25
		Nos. 510-512,C223-C226 (7)	2.85	2.15

18th Olympic Games, Tokyo, Oct. 10-25. Printed in sheets of 50 (10x5), with map of Japan in background extending over 27 stamps.
For surcharges see Nos. B35-B37, CB51-CB54.

Madonna of Haiti and International Airport, Port-au-Prince — A106

1964, Dec. 15   *Perf. 14½x14*

513	A106	10c org yel & blk	.25	.25
514	A106	25c bl grn & blk	.25	.25
515	A106	50c brt yel grn & blk	.40	.25
516	A106	1g vermilion & blk	.50	.40
		Nos. 513-516,C227-C229 (7)	3.85	2.45

Nos. 513-516 Overprinted in Black

1965, Feb. 11

517	A106	10c org, yel & blk	.25	.25
518	A106	25c blue grn & blk	.25	.25
519	A106	50c brt yel grn & blk	.40	.25
520	A106	1g vermilion & blk	.50	.40
		Nos. 517-520,C230-C232 (7)	3.45	2.50

Unisphere, NY World's Fair — A107

20c, "Rocket Thrower" by Donald De Lue.

1965, Mar. 22   *Photo.*   *Perf. 13½*

521	A107	10c grn, yel ol & dk red	.25	.25
522	A107	20c plum & orange	.25	.25
523	A107	50c dk brn, dk red, yel & grn	.40	.25
		Nos. 521-523,C233-C235 (6)	4.20	3.30

New York World's Fair, 1964-65.

Merchantmen — A108

1965, May 13   *Unwmk.*   *Perf. 11½*

524	A108	10c blk, lt grn & red	.25	.25
525	A108	50c blk, lt bl & red	.40	.25
		Nos. 524-525,C236-C237 (4)	1.80	1.50

The merchant marine.

ITU Emblem, Old and New Communication Equipment — A109

1965, Aug. 16   *Litho.*   *Perf. 13½*

526	A109	10c gray & multi	.25	.25
527	A109	25c multicolored	.40	.25
528	A109	50c multicolored	.50	.25
		Nos. 526-528,C242-C245 (7)	4.55	2.50

Cent. of the ITU.
For overprints see Nos. 537-539, C255-C256.

Statue of Our Lady of the Assumption — A110

Designs: 5c, Cathedral of Port-au-Prince, horiz. 10c, High altar.

Perf. 14x13, 13x14

1965, Nov. 19   *Photo.*
Size: 39x29mm, 29x39mm

529	A110	5c multicolored	.25	.25
530	A110	10c multicolored	.25	.25
531	A110	25c multicolored	.30	.25
		Nos. 529-531,C246-C248 (6)	4.60	3.65

200th anniv. of the Metropolitan Cathedral of Port-au-Prince.

Passionflower — A111

Flowers: 5c, 15c, American elder. 10c, Okra.

1965, Dec. 20   *Photo.*   *Perf. 11½*
Granite Paper

532	A111	3c dk vio, lt vio bl & grn	.30	.25
533	A111	5c grn, lt bl & yel	.30	.25
534	A111	10c multicolored	.30	.25
a.		"0.10" omitted		
535	A111	15c grn, pink & yel	.80	.25
536	A111	50c dk vio, yel & grn	1.50	1.10
		Nos. 532-536,C249-C254 (11)	16.70	7.15

For surcharges see Nos. 566, B38-B40, CB55-CB56.

HAITI

**Nos. 526-528 Overprinted in Red:
"20e. Anniversaire / UNESCO"**

1965, Aug. 27   Litho.   Perf. 13½
537 A109 10c gray & multi   .30   .25
538 A109 25c yel brn & multi   .35   .35
539 A109 50c pale grn & multi   .70   .70
  Nos. 537-539,C255-C256 (5)   5.35 2.65
  20th anniversary of UNESCO.

Amulet
A112

Ceremonial Stool
A113

Perf. 14x½x14, 14x14½
1966, Mar. 14   Photo.   Unwmk.
540 A112 5c grnsh bl, blk & yel   .25   .25
541 A113 10c multi   .25   .25
542 A112 50c scar, yel & blk   .40   .25
  Nos. 540-542,C257-C259 (6)   3.45 2.35
  For overprints and surcharges see Nos. 543, 567-570, C257-C258, C260-C261, C280-C281.

**No. 541 Overprinted in Red
"Hommage / a Hailé Sélassiéler / 24-25 Avril 1966"**

1966, Apr. 24
543 A113 10c multi   .30   .25
  Nos. 543,C260-C262 (4)   2.35 1.70
  Visit of Emperor Haile Selassie of Ethiopia, Apr. 24-25.

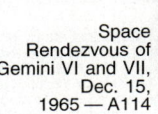
Space Rendezvous of Gemini VI and VII, Dec. 15, 1965 — A114

1966, May 3   Perf. 13½
544 A114 5c vio bl, brn & lt bl   .25   .25
545 A114 10c pur, brn & lt bl   .25   .25
546 A114 25c grn, brn & lt bl   .30   .25
547 A114 50c dk red, brn & lt bl .40   .25
  Nos. 544-547,C263-C265 (7)   2.75 2.15
  Walter M. Schirra, Thomas P. Stafford, Frank A. Borman, James A. Lovell and Gemini VI.
  For overprint see No. 584.

Soccer Ball within Wreath and Pres. Duvalier
A115

Design: 10c, 50c, Soccer player within wreath and Duvalier.

Lithographed and Photogravure
1966, June 16   Perf. 13x13½
**Portrait in Black; Gold Inscription;
Green Commemorative Inscription
in Two Lines**
548 A115 5c pale sal & grn   .25   .25
549 A115 10c lt ultra & grn   .25   .25
550 A115 15c lt grn & grn   .25   .25
551 A115 50c pale lil rose & grn .40   .25

**Green Commemorative Inscription
in 3 Lines; Gold Inscription Omitted**
552 A115 5c pale sal & grn   .25   .25
553 A115 10c lt ultra & grn   .25   .25
554 A115 15c lt grn & grn   .25   .25
555 A115 50c pale lil rose & grn .40   .25
  Nos. 548-555,C266-C269 (12) 4.40 3.65
  Caribbean Soccer Festival, June 10-22. Nos. 548-551 also for the Natl. Soccer Championships, May 8-22.
  For surcharges and overprint see Nos. 578-579, C288, CB57.

"ABC," Boy and Girl — A116

10c, Scout symbols. 25c, Television set, book and communications satellite, horiz.

Perf. 14x13½, 13½x14
1966, Oct. 18   Litho. & Engr.
556 A116 5c grn, sal pink & brn   .25   .25
557 A116 10c red brn, lt brn & blk .25   .25
558 A116 25c grn, bl & dk vio   .25   .25
  Nos. 556-558,C270-C272 (6)   2.30 1.90
  Issued to publicize education through literacy, Scouting and by audio-visual means.

Dr. Albert Schweitzer, Maps of Alsace and Gabon — A117

Designs: 10c, Dr. Schweitzer and pipe organ. 20c, Dr. Schweitzer and Albert Schweitzer Hospital, Deschapelles, Haiti.

Perf. 12½x13
1967, Apr. 20   Unwmk.
559 A117 5c pale lil & multi   .25   .25
560 A117 10c buff & multi   .25   .25
561 A117 20c gray & multi   .40   .25
  Nos. 559-561,C273-C276 (7)   3.45 2.75
  Issued in memory of Dr. Albert Schweitzer (1875-1965), medical missionary to Gabon, theologian and musician.

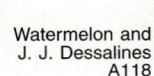
Watermelon and J. J. Dessalines A118

1967, July 4   Photo.   Perf. 12½
562 A118 5c shown   .25   .25
563 A118 10c Cabbage   .25   .25
564 A118 20c Tangerine   1.25   .25
565 A118 50c Chayote   2.00   .25
  Nos. 562-565,C277-C279 (7) 11.25 5.75

No. 532 Surcharged

1967, Aug. 21   Photo.   Perf. 11½
566 A111 50c on 3c multi   .30   .25
  Nos. 566,B38-B40,CB55-CB56 (6) 2.25 1.90
  12th Boy Scout World Jamboree, Farragut State Park, Idaho, Aug. 1-9.

Nos. 540-542 Overprinted and Surcharged

Perf. 14½x14, 14x14½
1967, Aug. 30   Photo.
567 A112 5c grnsh bl, blk & yel   .25   .25
568 A113 10c multi   .25   .25
569 A112 50c scar, yel & blk   .25   .25
570 A112 1g on 5c multi   .50   .40
  Nos. 567-570,C280-C281 (6)   2.60 2.10
  EXPO '67 Intl. Exhibition, Montreal, 4/28-10/27.

Pres. Duvalier and Brush Turkey — A119

1967, Sept. 22   Photo.   Perf. 14x13
571 A119 5c car rose & gold   .25   .25
572 A119 10c ultra & gold   .25   .25
573 A119 25c dk red brn & gold   .25   .25
574 A119 50c dp red lil & gold   .40   .25
  Nos. 571-574,C282-C284 (7)   3.40 2.60
  10th anniversary of Duvalier revolution.

Writing Hands — A120

Designs: 10c, Scout emblem and Scouts, vert. 25c, Audio-visual teaching of algebra.

1967, Dec. 11   Litho.   Perf. 11½
575 A120 5c multicolored   .25   .25
576 A120 10c multicolored   .25   .25
577 A120 25c dk grn, lt bl & yel .25   .25
  Nos. 575-577,C285-C287 (6)   2.15 1.90
  Issued to publicize the importance of education.
  For surcharges see Nos. CB58-CB60.

Nos. 552 and 554 Surcharged

Lithographed and Photogravure
1968, Jan. 18   Perf. 13x13½
578 A115 50c on 15c   .85   .25
579 A115 1g on 5c   1.00   .85
  Nos. 578-579,C288,CB57 (4)   4.60
  19th Olympic Games, Mexico City, Oct. 12-27.
  The 1968 date is missing on 2 stamps in every sheet of 50.

Caiman Woods, by Raoul Dupoux — A121

**1968, Apr. 22   Photo.   Perf. 12
Size: 36x26mm**
580 A121 5c multi   .25   .25
581 A121 10c rose red & multi   .25   .25
582 A121 25c multi   .25   .25
583 A121 50c dl lil & multi   .40   .25
  Nos. 580-583,C289-C295 (11) 6.60 5.00
  Caiman Woods ceremony during the Slaves' Rebellion, Aug. 14, 1791.

No. 547 Overprinted

1968, Apr. 19   Photo.   Perf. 13½
584 A114 50c dk red, brn & lt bl .90   .80
  Nos. 584,C296-C298 (4)   5.40 2.90
  10th Winter Olympic Games, Grenoble, France, Feb. 6-18, 1968.

Monument to the Unknown Maroon — A122

**1968, May 22   Perf. 11½
Granite Paper**
585 A122 5c bl & blk   .25   .25
586 A122 10c rose brn & blk   .25   .25
587 A122 20c vio & blk   .25   .25
588 A122 25c lt ultra & blk   .25   .25
589 A122 50c brt bl grn & blk   .40   .25
  Nos. 585-589,C299-C301 (8)   3.10 2.40
  Unveiling of the monument to the Unknown Maroon, Port-au-Prince.
  For surcharges see Nos. 610 and C324-C325.

Palm Tree and Provincial Coats of Arms — A123

Madonna, Papal Arms and Arms of Haiti — A124

Design: 25c, Cathedral, arms of Pope Paul VI and arms of Haiti.

Perf. 13x14, 12½x13½
1968, Aug. 16   Photo.
590 A123 5c grn & multi   .25   .25
591 A124 10c grn & multi   .25   .25
592 A124 25c multi   .25   .25
  Nos. 590-592,C302-C305 (7)   3.70 3.00
  Consecration of the Bishopric of Haiti, 10/28/66.

Air Terminal, Port-au-Prince A125

**1968, Sept. 22   Photo.   Perf. 11½
Portrait in Black**
593 A125 5c brn & lt ultra   .25   .25
594 A125 10c brn & lt bl   .25   .25
595 A125 25c brn & pale lil   .25   .25
  Nos. 593-595,C306-C308 (6)   2.70 2.30
  Inauguration of the Francois Duvalier Airport in Port-au-Prince.

Slave Breaking Chains, Map of Haiti, Torch, Conch — A126

1968, Oct. 28   Litho.   Perf. 14½x14
596 A126 5c brn, lt bl & brt pink .25   .25
597 A126 10c brn, lt ol & brt pink .25 .25
598 A126 25c brn, bis & brt pink .25   .25
  Nos. 596-598,C310-C313 (7)   3.10 2.50
  Slaves' Rebellion, of 1791.

Children Learning to Read — A127

10c, Children watching television. 50c, Hands setting volleyball and sports medal.

1968, Nov. 14   Perf. 11½
599 A127 5c multi   .25   .25
600 A127 10c multi   .25   .25
601 A127 50c multi   .40   .25
  Nos. 599-601,C314-C316 (6)   2.45 1.90
  Issued to publicize education through literacy, audio-visual means and sport.
  For surcharges see Nos. B41-B42, CB61-CB62.

HAITI

Winston Churchill — A128

Churchill: 5c, as painter. 10c, as Knight of the Garter. 15c, and soldiers at Normandy. 20c, and early seaplane. 25c, and Queen Elizabeth II. 50c, and Big Ben, London.

1968, Dec. 23   Photo.   *Perf. 13*
602	A128	3c gold & multi	.25	.25
603	A128	5c gold & multi	.25	.25
604	A128	10c gold & multi	.25	.25
605	A128	15c gold & multi	.25	.25
606	A128	20c gold & multi	.25	.25
607	A128	25c gold & multi	.25	.25
608	A128	50c gold & multi	.40	.25
	Nos. 602-608,C319-C322 (11)		4.25	3.50

Exist imperf. For surcharge see No. 828.

1968 Winter Olympics, Grenoble — A128a

Designs: 5c, 1.50g, Peggy Fleming, US, figure skating. 10c, Harold Groenningen, Norway, cross-country skiing. 20c, Belousova & Protopopov, USSR, pairs figure skating. 25c, Toini Gustafsson, Sweden, cross country skiing. 50c, Eugenio Monti, Italy, 4-man bobsled. 2g, Erhard Keller, Germany, speed skating. 4g, Jean-Claude Killy, France, downhill skiing.

1968, Nov. 11   Litho.   *Perf. 14x13½*
609	A128a	5c brt bl & multi	.25	.25
609A	A128a	10c bl grn & multi	.25	.25
609B	A128a	20c brt rose & multi	.25	.25
609C	A128a	25c sky bl & multi	.25	.25
609D	A128a	50c ol bis & multi	.45	.30
609E	A128a	1.50g vio & multi	1.10	.65

Size: 36x65mm
Perf. 12x12½
609F	A128a	2g emer grn & multi	2.25	2.25
	Nos. 609-609F (7)		4.80	4.20

Souvenir Sheet
609G	A128a	4g brn & multi	20.00	20.00

No. 609G contains one 36x65mm stamp. Nos. 609F-609G are airmail. No. 609G exists imperf. with green, brown and blue margin.

No. 589 Surcharged

1969, Feb. 21   Photo.   *Perf. 11½*
610	A122	70c on 50c	.50	.40
	Nos. 610,C324-C325 (3)		1.80	1.30

Blue-headed Euphonia — A129

Birds of Haiti: 10c, Hispaniolan trogon. 20c, Palm chat. 25c, Stripe-headed tanager. 50c, Like 5c.

1969, Feb. 26   *Perf. 13½*
611	A129	5c lt grn & multi	2.00	.50
612	A129	10c yel & multi	2.00	.50
613	A129	20c cream & multi	2.25	.50
614	A129	25c lil & multi	2.50	.60
615	A129	50c lt gray & multi	3.50	.60
	Nos. 611-615,C326-C329 (9)		28.50	9.45

For overprints see Nos. C344A-C344D.

Olympic Marathon Winners, 1896-1968 — A130

Designs: Games location, date, winner, country and time over various stamp designs. Souvenir sheets do not show location, date, country or time.

1969, May 16   *Perf. 12½x12*
Size: 66x35mm (Nos. 616, 616C, 616F, 616N)
616	A130	5c like Greece #124	.25	.25
616A	A130	10c like France #124	.25	.25
616B	A130	15c US #327	.25	.25
616C	A130	20c like Great Britain #142	.50	.40
616D	A130	20c Sweden #68	.50	.40
616E	A130	25c Belgium #B49	.80	.40
616F	A130	25c like France #198	.80	.40
616G	A130	25c Netherlands #B30	.80	.40
616H	A130	30c US #718	.90	.40
616I	A130	50c Germany #B86	1.40	1.00
616J	A130	60c Great Britain #274	1.75	1.00
616K	A130	75c like Finland #B110	2.50	2.00
616L	A130	75c like Australia #277	2.50	2.00
616M	A130	90c Italy #799	2.75	2.00
616N	A130	1g like Japan #822	3.75	3.00
616O	A130	1.25g like Mexico #C328	5.00	4.00
	Nos. 616-616O (16)		24.70	18.15

Souvenir Sheets
616P	A130	1.50g US #718, diff.	16.00	16.00

Imperf
616Q	A130	1.50g Germany #B86, diff.	16.00	16.00

Nos. 616H-616O are airmail. Nos. 616P-616Q contain one 66x35mm stamp. A 2g souvenir sheet exists, perf. & imperf. Value, each $9.

Power Lines and Light Bulb — A131

1969, May 22   Litho.   *Perf. 13x13½*
617	A131	20c lilac & blue	.25	.25

Issued to publicize the Duvalier Hydroelectric Station. See Nos. C338-C340.

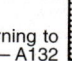

Learning to Write — A132

Designs: 10c, children playing, vert. 50c, Peace poster on educational television, vert.

1969, Aug. 12   Litho.   *Perf. 13½*
618	A132	5c multi	.25	.25
619	A132	10c multi	.25	.25
620	A132	50c multi	.25	.25
	Nos. 618-620,C342-C344 (6)		2.35	1.90

Issued to publicize national education.

ILO Emblem — A133

1969, Sept. 22   *Perf. 14*
621	A133	5c bl grn & blk	.25	.25
622	A133	10c brn & blk	.25	.25
623	A133	20c vio bl & blk	.25	.25
	Nos. 621-623,C345-C347 (6)		3.10	1.95

50th anniv. of the ILO.

Apollo Space Missions — A133a

Designs: 10c, Apollo 7 rendezvous of command module, third stage. 15c, Apollo 7, preparation for re-entry. 20c, Apollo 8, separation of third stage. 25c, Apollo 8, mid-course correction. 70c, Apollo 8, approaching moon. 1g, Apollo 8, orbiting moon, Christmas 1968, vert. 1.25, Apollo 8, leaving moon. 1.50g, Apollo 8, crew, vert. 1.75g, 2g, Apollo 11, first lunar landing.

1969, Oct. 6   *Perf. 12x12½*
624	A133a	10c brt rose & multi	.25	.25
624A	A133a	15c vio & multi	.25	.25
624B	A133a	20c ver & multi	.25	.25
624C	A133a	25c emer grn & multi	.25	.25
624D	A133a	70c brt bl & multi	.25	.25
624E	A133a	1g bl & multi	.55	.30
624F	A133a	1.25g dk bl & multi	.65	.40
624G	A133a	1.50g dp rose lil & multi	.80	.50

Souvenir Sheets
624H	A133a	1.75g grn & multi	12.00	12.00
624I	A133a	2g sky bl & multi	12.00	12.00
	Nos. 624-624I (10)		27.25	26.45

Nos. 624D-624I are airmail. Nos. 624-624I exist imperf. in different colors.

Papilio Zonaria — A134

Butterflies: 20c, Zerene cesonia cynops. 25c, Papilio machaonides.

1969, Nov. 14   Photo.   *Perf. 13½*
625	A134	10c pink & multi	2.25	.75
626	A134	20c gray & multi	4.00	3.00
627	A134	25c lt bl & multi	6.00	3.00
	Nos. 625-627,C348-C350 (6)		52.25	19.75

Martin Luther King, Jr. — A135

1970, Jan. 12   Litho.   *Perf. 12½x13½*
628	A135	10c bis, red & blk	.25	.25
629	A135	20c grnsh bl, red & blk	.25	.25
630	A135	25c brt rose, red & blk	.25	.25
	Nos. 628-630,C351-C353 (6)		3.20	2.45

Martin Luther King, Jr. (1929-1968), American civil rights leader.

Laeliopsis Dominguensis — A136

Haitian Orchids: 20c, Oncidium Haitiense. 25c, Oncidium calochilum.

1970, Apr. 3   Litho.   *Perf. 13x12½*
631	A136	10c yel, lil & blk	.30	.25
632	A136	20c lt bl grn, yel & brn	2.25	2.00
633	A136	25c bl & multi	2.75	2.00
	Nos. 631-633,C354-C356 (6)		16.80	10.50

UPU Monument and Map of Haiti — A137

Designs: 25c, Propeller and UPU emblem, vert. 50c, Globe and doves.

1970, June 23   Photo.   *Perf. 11½*
634	A137	10c blk, brt grn & ol bis	.25	.25
635	A137	25c blk, brt rose & ol bis	.25	.25
636	A137	50c blk & bl	.35	.25
	Nos. 634-636,C357-C359 (6)		2.80	2.10

16th Cong. of the UPU, Tokyo, Oct. 1-Nov. 16, 1970.
For overprints see Nos. 640, C360-C362.

Map of Haiti, Dam and Generator — A138

Design: 25c, Map of Haiti, Dam and Pylon.

1970   Litho.   *Perf. 14x13½*
637	A138	20c lt grn & multi	.25	.25
638	A138	25c lt bl & multi	.25	.25

François Duvalier Central Hydroelectric Plant. For surcharges see Nos. B43-B44, RA40-RA41.

Apollo 12 — A138a

No. 639, Lift-off. No. 639A, 2nd stage ignition. No. 639B, Docking preparations. No. 639C, Heading for moon. No. 639E, Lunar exploration. No. 639F, Landing on Moon. No. 639G, Lift-off from Moon. No. 639H, 3rd stage separation. No. 639I, Lunar module, crew. No. 639J, Lunar orbital activities. No. 639K, Leaving Moon orbit. No. 639L, In Earth orbit. No. 639M, Re-entry. No. 639N, Landing at sea. No. 639O, Docking with lunar module.

1970, Sept. 7   *Perf. 13½x14*
639	A138a	5c multi	.25	.25
639A	A138a	10c multi	.25	.25
639B	A138a	15c multi	.35	.25
639C	A138a	20c multi	.35	.25
639D	A138a	25c like 639B	.45	.25
639E	A138a	25c multi	.25	.25
639F	A138a	30c multi	.65	.25
639G	A138a	30c multi	.45	.25
639H	A138a	40c multi	.90	.35
639I	A138a	40c multi	.55	.25
639J	A138a	50c multi	1.10	.80
639K	A138a	50c multi	.65	.35
639L	A138a	75c multi	1.10	.75
639M	A138a	1g multi	1.50	1.25
639N	A138a	1.25g multi	2.25	1.50
639O	A138a	1.50g multi	2.40	2.00
	Nos. 639-639O (16)		13.35	9.25

Nos. 639E, 639G, 639I, 639K-639O are airmail. Nos. 639-639O exist imperf. with brighter colors. Value, unused $16.
For overprints see Nos. 656-656O.

No. 636 Overprinted in Red with UN Emblem and: "XXVe ANNIVERSAIRE / O.N.U."

1970, Dec. 14   Photo.   *Perf. 11½*
640	A137	50c blk & bl	.75	.25
	Nos. 640,C360-C362 (4)		2.70	1.60

UN, 25th anniv.

Fort Nativity, Drawing by Columbus — A139

HAITI

1970, Dec. 22

| 641 | A139 | 3c dk brn & buff | .25 | .25 |
| 642 | A139 | 5c dk grn & pale grn | .30 | .25 |

Christmas 1970.

Ascension, by Castera Bazile — A140

Paintings: 5c, Man with Turban, by Rembrandt. 20c, Iris in a Vase, by Van Gogh. 50c, Baptism of Christ, by Castera Bazile. No. 647, Young Mother Sewing, by Mary Cassatt. No. 648, The Card Players, by Cezanne.

Size: 20x40mm

1971, Apr. 29 Litho. *Perf. 12x12½*

| 643 | A140 | 5c multi | .25 | .25 |
| 644 | A140 | 10c multi | .25 | .25 |

Perf. 13x12½

Size: 25x37mm

| 645 | A140 | 20c multi | .25 | .25 |

Perf. 12x12½

Size: 20x40mm

| 646 | A140 | 50c multi | .50 | .25 |

Nos. 643-646,C366-C368 (7) 3.65 2.70

Souvenir Sheets
Imperf

| 647 | A140 | 3g multi | 5.00 | 5.00 |
| 648 | A140 | 3g multi | 5.00 | 5.00 |

No. 647 contains one stamp, size: 20x40mm, No. 648 size: 25x37mm.
Nos. 643-646,C366-C368 exist imperf in changed colors.

Soccer Ball — A141

Design: No. 651, 1g, 5g, Jules Rimet cup.

1971, June 14 Photo. *Perf. 11½*

649	A141	5c salmon & blk	.25	.25
650	A141	50c tan & blk	.50	.35
651	A141	50c rose pink, blk & gold	.50	.35
652	A141	1g lil, blk & gold	.65	.45
653	A141	1.50g gray & blk	.80	.55
654	A141	5g gray, blk & gold	2.40	1.60

Nos. 649-654 (6) 5.10 3.55

Souvenir Sheet
Imperf

655		Sheet of 2	12.00	8.50
a.		A141 70c light violet & black	4.00	3.00
b.		A141 1g light green, blue & gold	4.00	3.00

9th World Soccer Championships for the Jules Rimet Cup, Mexico City, May 30-June 21, 1970. The surface tint of the sheets of 50 (10x5) of Nos. 649-654 includes a map of Brazil covering 26 stamps. Positions 27, 37 and 38 inscribed "Brasilia," "Santos," "Rio de Janeiro" respectively. On soccer ball design the 4 corner stamps are inscribed "Pele."

Nos. 655a and 655b have portions of map of Brazil in background; No. 655a inscribed "Pele" and "Santos," No. 655b "Brasilia."

Nos. 639-639O Ovptd. in Gold or Red

1971, Mar. 15

656	A138a	5c multi (G)	.25	.25
656A	A138a	10c multi (G)	.25	.25
656B	A138a	15c multi (G)	.25	.25
656C	A138a	20c multi (G)	.35	.25
656D	A138a	25c multi (R)	.45	.25
656E	A138a	25c multi (R)	.25	.25
656F	A138a	30c multi (R)	.65	.25
656G	A138a	30c multi (R)	.45	.25
656H	A138a	40c multi (R)	.90	.35
656I	A138a	40c multi (R)	.55	.35
656J	A138a	50c multi (R)	1.10	.35
656K	A138a	50c multi (R)	.65	.35
656L	A138a	75c multi (R)	1.10	.40
656M	A138a	1g multi (R)	1.50	.50
656N	A138a	1.25g multi (R)	2.25	.75
656O	A138a	1.50g multi (R)	2.40	.75

Nos. 656-656O (16) 13.35 5.80

Nos. 656E, 656G, 656I, 656K-656O are airmail.
Nos. 656-656O exist imperf. overprinted in silver. Value, unused $16.

J. J. Dessalines — A142

1972, Apr. 28 Photo. *Perf. 11½*

657	A142	5c grn & blk	.25	.25
658	A142	10c brt bl & blk	.25	.25
659	A142	25c org & blk	.25	.25

Nos. 657-659,C378-C379 (5) 2.20 1.65

See Nos. 697-700, C448-C458, 727, C490-C493, C513-C514. For surcharges see Nos. 692, 705-709, 724-726, C438, C512.

"Sun" and EXPO '70 Emblem — A143

1972, Oct. 27 Photo. *Perf. 11½*

| 660 | A143 | 10c ocher, yel & grn | .25 | .25 |
| 661 | A143 | 25c ocher, yel & lake | .25 | .25 |

Nos. 660-661,C387-C390 (6) 3.00 2.10

EXPO '70 International Exposition, Osaka, Japan, Mar. 15-Sept. 13, 1970.

Gold Medalists, 1972 Summer Olympics, Munich — A143a

Designs: 5c, L. Linsenhoff, dressage, W. Ruska, judo. 10c, S. Kato, gymnastics, S.Gould, women's swimming. 20c, M. Peters, women's pentathlon, K. Keino, steeplechase. 25c, L. Viren, 5000, 10,000m races, R. Milburn, 110m hurdles. No. 662D, D. Morelon, cycling, J. Akii-Bua, 400m hurdles. No. 662E, R. Williams, long jump. 75c, G. Mancinelli, equestrian. 1.50g, W. Nordwig, pole vault. 2.50c, K. Wolferman, javelin. 5g, M. Spitz, swimming.

1972, Dec. 29 *Perf. 13½*

662	A143a	5c multicolored	.25	.25
662A	A143a	10c multicolored	.25	.25
662B	A143a	20c multicolored	.25	.25
662C	A143a	25c multicolored	.25	.25
662D	A143a	50c multicolored	.25	.25
662E	A143a	50c multicolored	.70	.25
662F	A143a	75c multicolored	1.00	.25
662G	A143a	1.50g multicolored	1.50	.70
662H	A143a	2.50g multicolored	3.00	1.10
662I	A143a	5g multicolored	5.75	1.60

Nos. 662-662I (10) 13.20 5.15

Nos. 662E-662I are airmail.

Basket Vendors — A144

Designs: 80c, 2.50g, Postal bus.

1973, Jan. Photo. *Perf. 11½*

665	A144	50c blk & multi	.35	.25
666	A144	80c blk & multi	.45	.35
667	A144	1.50g blk & multi	.70	.45
668	A144	2.50g blk & multi	1.50	.80

Nos. 665-668 (4) 3.00 1.85

20th anniv. of Caribbean Travel Assoc.

Space Exploration

A set of 12 stamps for US-USSR space exploration, the same overprinted for the centenary of the UPU and 3 overprinted in silver for Apollo 17 exist but we have no evidence that they were printed with the approval of the Haitian postal authorities. Value, $10 and $6, respectively.

Micromelo Undata — A145

Marine life: 10c, Nemaster rubiginosa. 25c, Cyerce cristallina. 50c, Desmophyllum riisei, horiz.

1973, Sept. 4 Litho. *Perf. 14*

669	A145	5c shown	.25	.25
670	A145	10c multicolored	.25	.25
671	A145	25c multicolored	.50	.25
672	A145	50c multicolored	1.00	.25

Nos. 669-672,C395-C398 (8) 8.90 2.20

For surcharge see No. C439.

Gramma Loreto A146

50c, Acanthurus coeruleus.

1973 *Perf. 13½*

| 673 | A146 | 10c shown | .60 | .25 |
| 674 | A146 | 50c multicolored | .80 | .50 |

Nos. 673-674,C399-C402 (6) 8.75 4.55

For surcharges see Nos. 693, C440.

Soccer Stadium — A147

Design: 20c, Haiti No. 654.

1973, Nov. 29 *Perf. 14x13*

| 675 | A147 | 10c bis, blk & emer | .25 | .25 |
| 676 | A147 | 20c rose lil, blk & tan | .25 | .25 |

Nos. 675-676,C407-C410 (6) 5.50 3.80

Caribbean countries preliminary games of the World Soccer Championships, Munich, 1974.

Jean Jacques Dessalines — A148

1974, Apr. 22 Photo. *Perf. 14*

677	A148	10c lt bl & emer	.25	.25
678	A148	20c rose & blk	.25	.25
679	A148	25c yel & vio	.25	.25

Nos. 677-679,C411-C414 (7) 3.05 2.35

For surcharges see Nos. 694, C443.

Nicolaus Copernicus — A149

Design: 10c, Symbol of heliocentric system.

1974, May 24 Litho. *Perf. 14x13½*

| 680 | A149 | 10c multi | .25 | .25 |
| 681 | A149 | 25c brt grn & multi | .25 | .25 |

Nos. 680-681,C415-C419 (7) 3.15 2.35

For overprint and surcharges see Nos. 695, C444, C460-C463.

Pres. Jean-Claude Duvalier — A151

1974 Photo. *Perf. 14x13½*

689	A151	10c grn & gold	.25	.25
690	A151	20c car rose & gold	.30	.25
691	A151	50c bl & gold	.40	.25

Nos. 689-691,C421-C426 (9) 7.40 4.60

For surcharge and overprints see Nos. C445, C487-C489.

Audubon Birds

In 1975 or later various sets of bird paintings by Audubon were produced by government employees without official authorization. They were not sold by the Haiti post office and were not valid for postage. The first set consisted of 23 values and was sold in 1975. A second set containing some of the original stamps and some new stamps appeared unannounced several years later. More sets may have been printed as there are 75 different stamps. These consist of 5 denominations each for the 15 designs.

Perf and imperf souvenir sheets picturing Audubon were also produced.

Nos. 659, 673 and 679-680 Surcharged with New Value and Bar
Perf. 11½, 13½, 14, 14x13½

1976 Photo.; Litho.

692	A142	80c on 25c	.55	.35
693	A146	80c on 10c	.55	.35
694	A148	80c on 25c	.55	.35
695	A149	80c on 10c	.55	.35

Nos. 692-695 (4) 2.20 1.40

Haiti No. C11 and Bicentennial Emblem A152

1976, Apr. 22 Photo. *Perf. 11½*
Granite Paper

| 696 | A152 | 10c multi | .25 | .25 |

Nos. 696,C434-C437 (5) 4.70 3.30

American Bicentennial.

Dessalines Type of 1972

1977 Photo. *Perf. 11½*

697	A142	10c rose & blk	.25	.25
698	A142	20c lemon & blk	.25	.25
699	A142	50c vio & blk	.35	.25
700	A142	50c tan & blk	.35	.25

Nos. 697-700 (4) 1.20 1.00

Dessalines Type of 1972 Surcharged in Black or Red

1978 Photo. *Perf. 11½*

705	A142	1g on 20c (#698)	.65	.35
706	A142	1g on 1.75g (#C454)	.65	.35
707	A142	1.25g on 75c (#C448)	.65	.35
708	A142	1.25g on 1.50g (#C453)	.65	.35
709	A142	1.25g on 1.50g (#C453; R)	.65	.35

Nos. 705-709 (5) 3.25 1.75

Rectangular bar obliterates old denomination on Nos. 705-709 and "Par Avion" on Nos. 706-709.

J. C. Duvalier Earth Telecommunications Station — A153

Designs: 20c, Video telephone. 50c, Alexander Graham Bell, vert.

HAITI

1978, June 19   Litho.   Perf. 13½
710	A153	10c multi	.25	.25
711	A153	20c multi	.25	.25
712	A153	50c multi	.35	.25

Nos. 710-712,C466-C468 (6)   2.70   2.10

Centenary of first telephone call by Alexander Graham Bell, Mar. 10, 1876.

Athletes' Inaugural Parade — A154

1978, Sept. 4   Litho.   Perf. 13½x13
713	A154	5c shown	.25	.25
714	A154	25c Bicyclists	.25	.25
715	A154	50c Pole Vault	.40	.25

Nos. 713-715,C469-C471 (6)   6.60   4.10

21st Olympic Games, Montreal, 7/17-8/1/76.

Mother Nursing Child — A155

1979, Jan. 15   Photo.   Perf. 14x14½
716	A155	25c multi	.25	.25

Nos. 716,C472-C473 (3)   1.60   1.15

Inter-American Children's Inst., 50th anniv.

Mother Feeding Child — A156

1979, May 11   Photo.   Perf. 11½
717	A156	25c multi	.25	.25
718	A156	50c multi	.35	.25

Nos. 717-718,C474-C476 (5)   3.60   2.55

30th anniversary of CARE (Cooperative for American Relief Everywhere).

Human Rights Emblem — A157

1979, July 20   Litho.   Perf. 14
719	A157	25c multi	.30	.25

Nos. 719,C477-C479 (4)   3.30   2.30

30th anniversary of declaration of human rights.

Anti-Apartheid Year Emblem, Antenor Firmin, "On the Equality of Human Races" — A158

1979, Nov. 22   Photo.   Perf. 12x11½
720	A158	50c tan & black	.50	.25

Nos. 720,C480-C482 (4)   4.35   2.30

Anti-Apartheid Year (1978).

Children Playing, IYC Emblem — A159

1979, Dec. 19   Photo.   Perf. 12
721	A159	10c multi	.25	.25
722	A159	25c multi	.25	.25
723	A159	50c multi	.40	.25

Nos. 721-723,C483-C486 (7)   8.50   4.65

International Year of the Child.

Nos. C379, C449, C454 Surcharged

1980   Photo.   Perf. 11½   Granite Paper
724	A142	1g on 2.50g lil & blk	.55	.45
725	A142	1.25g on 80c emer & blk	.65	.55
726	A142	1.25g on 1.75g rose & blk	.65	.55

Nos. 724-726 (3)   1.85   1.55

Dessalines Type of 1972

1980, Aug. 27   Photo.   Perf. 11½   Granite Paper
727	A142	25c org yel & blk	.30	.25

Nos. 727,C490-C493 (5)   5.10   3.70

Henry Christophe Citadel — A160

1980, Dec. 2   Litho.   Perf. 12½x12
728	A160	5c shown	.25	.25
729	A160	25c Sans Souci Palace	.25	.25
730	A160	50c Vallieres market	.35	.25

Nos. 728-730,C494-C498 (8)   5.60   4.25

World Tourism Conf., Manila, Sept. 27.
For surcharges see Nos. 738, C511.

Soccer Players, World Cup, Flag of Uruguay (1930 Champion) — A161

1980, Dec. 30   Litho.   Perf. 14
731	A161	10c shown	.25	.25
732	A161	20c Italy, 1934	.25	.25
733	A161	25c Italy, 1938	.25	.25

Nos. 731-733,C499-C506 (11)   10.25   6.90

World Cup Soccer Championship, 50th anniv.
For surcharges see Nos. 741, 829.

Going to Church, by Gregoire Etienne — A162

Paintings: 5c, Woman with Birds and Flowers, by Hector Hyppolite, vert. 20c, Street Market, by Petion Savain. 25c, Market Vendors, by Michele Manuel.

1981, May 12   Photo.   Perf. 11½
734	A162	5c multi	.25	.25
735	A162	10c multi	.25	.25
736	A162	20c multi	.25	.25
737	A162	25c multi	.25	.25

Nos. 734-737,C507-C510 (8)   5.65   4.25

For surcharges see Nos. 739-740.

Nos. 728, 734-735, 732 Surcharged
Perf. 12½x12, 14, 11½

1981, Dec. 30   Litho., Photo.
738	A160	1.25g on 5c multi	.65	.55
739	A162	1.25g on 5c multi	.65	.55
740	A162	1.25g on 10c multi	.65	.55
741	A161	1.25g on 20c multi	.65	.55

Nos. 738-741,C511-C512 (6)   4.45   3.60

10th Anniv. of Pres. Duvalier Reforms — A163

1982, June 21   Photo.   Perf. 11½x12   Granite Paper
742	A163	25c yel grn & blk	.25	.25
743	A163	50c olive & blk	.35	.25
744	A163	1g rose & blk	.55	.45
745	A163	1.25g bl & blk	.65	.55
746	A163	2g org red & blk	1.10	.85
747	A163	5g org & blk	2.40	1.60

Nos. 742-747 (6)   5.30   3.95

Nos. 742, 744-746 Overprinted in Blue: "1957-1982 / 25 ANS DE REVOLUTION"

1982, Nov. 29   Photo.   Perf. 11½x12   Granite Paper
748	A163	25c yel grn & blk	.25	.25
749	A163	1g rose & blk	.55	.45
750	A163	1.25g blue & blk	.65	.55
751	A163	2g org red & blk	1.10	.85

Nos. 748-751 (4)   2.55   2.10

25th anniv. of revolution.

Scouting Year — A164

5c, Building campfire. 10c, Baden-Powell, vert. 25c, Boat building.

Perf. 13½x14, 14x13½

1983, Feb. 26   Litho.
752	A164	5c multi	.25	.25
753	A164	10c multi	.25	.25
754	A164	25c multi	.25	.25
755	A164	50c like 10c	.50	.25
756	A164	75c like 25c	1.25	.25
757	A164	1g like 5c	1.50	.30
758	A164	1.25g like 25c	2.00	.35
759	A164	2g like 10c	2.75	.60

Nos. 752-759 (8)   8.75   2.50

Nos. 756-759 airmail.
For surcharge see No. 827.

Patroness of Haiti — A165

1983, Mar. 9   Litho.   Perf. 14
760	A165	10c multi	.25	.25
761	A165	20c multi	.25	.25
762	A165	25c multi	.25	.25
763	A165	50c multi	.25	.25
764	A165	75c multi	.35	.25
765	A165	1g multi	.60	.25
766	A165	1.25g multi	.70	.30
767	A165	1.50g multi	1.00	.35
768	A165	1.75g multi	1.40	.40
769	A165	2g multi	1.75	.50
770	A165	5g multi	2.75	1.00
a.	Souvenir sheet, 116x90mm		37.50	37.50
j.	Souvenir sheet, 90x116mm		37.50	37.50

Nos. 760-770 (11)   9.55   4.05

Centenary of the Miracle of Our Lady of Perpetual Help. Nos. 764-770 airmail.
For surcharge see No. 875.

UPU Admission, 100th Anniv. — A165a

10c, L.F. Salomon, J.C. Duvalier. 25c, No. 1, UPU emblem.

1983, June 10   Litho.   Perf. 15x14
770B	A165a	5c shown	.50	.25
770C	A165a	10c multi	.50	.25
770D	A165a	25c multi	.50	.25
770E	A165a	50c like 5c	.50	.25
770F	A165a	75c like 10c	.60	.25
770G	A165a	1g like 5c	.80	.25
770H	A165a	1.25g like 25c	1.00	.30
770I	A165a	2g like 25c	1.60	.40

Nos. 770B-770I (8)   6.00   2.20

Nos. 770F-770I airmail.
For surcharge see No. 825.

1982 World Cup — A166

Games and scores: 5c, Argentina, Belgium. 10c, Northern Ireland, Yugoslavia. 20c, England, France. 25c, Spain, Northern Ireland. 50c, Italy (champion). 1g, Brazil, Scotland. 1.25g, Northern Ireland, France. 1.50g, Poland, Cameroun. 2g, Italy, Germany. 2.50g, Argentina, Brazil.

Nos. 776-780 airmail, horiz.

1983, Nov. 22   Litho.   Perf. 14
771	A166	5c multicolored	.25	.25
772	A166	10c multicolored	.25	.25
773	A166	20c multicolored	.25	.25
774	A166	25c multicolored	.25	.25
775	A166	50c multicolored	.35	.25
776	A166	1g multicolored	.55	.45
777	A166	1.25g multicolored	.65	.55
778	A166	1.50g multicolored	.95	.65
779	A166	2g multicolored	1.10	.85
780	A166	2.50g multicolored	1.40	1.10

Nos. 771-780 (10)   6.00   4.85

For surcharge see No. 826.

Haiti Postage Stamp Centenary A167

1984, Feb. 28   Litho.   Perf. 14½
781	A167	5c #1	.30	.25
782	A167	10c #2	.30	.25
783	A167	25c #3	.30	.25
784	A167	50c #5	.30	.25
785	A167	75c Liberty, Salomon	.45	.25
786	A167	1g Liberty, Salomon	.60	.35
787	A167	1.25g Liberty, Duvalier	.70	.40
788	A167	2g Liberty, Duvalier	1.10	.75

Nos. 781-788 (8)   4.05   2.75

Nos. 785-788 airmail.
For surcharge see No. 826A.

A168

25c, Broadcasting equipment, horiz. 1g, Drum. 2g, Globe.

1984, May 30   Photo.   Perf. 11½   Granite Paper
789	A168	25c multicolored	.25	.25
790	A168	50c like 25c	.35	.25
791	A168	1g multicolored	.55	.45
792	A168	1.25g like 1g	.65	.55
793	A168	2g multicolored	1.10	.85
794	A168	2.50g like 2g	1.40	1.10

Nos. 789-794 (6)   4.30   3.45

World Communications Year.

A169

5c, Javelin, running, pole vault, horiz. 25c, Hurdles, horiz. 1g, Long jump.

1984, July 27   Granite Paper
795	A169	5c multicolored	.25	.25
796	A169	10c like 5c	.25	.25
797	A169	25c multicolored	.25	.25
798	A169	50c like 25c	.75	.25
799	A169	1g multicolored	1.25	
800	A169	1.25g like 1g	1.75	1.25
801	A169	2g like 1g	2.40	1.75

Nos. 795-801 (7)   6.90   4.95

Souvenir Sheet
802	A169	2.50g like 1g	15.00	10.00

1984 Summer Olympics. No. 802 exists imperf. Value $15.
For surcharge see No. 874.

HAITI

Arrival of Europeans in America, 500th Anniv. — A170

The Unknown Indian, detail or full perspective of statue. Nos. 807-809 are vert. and airmail.

1984, Dec. 5		Litho.	Perf. 14	
803	A170	5c multi	.55	.45
804	A170	10c multi	.55	.45
805	A170	25c multi	.55	.45
806	A170	50c multi	.90	.60
807	A170	1g multi	1.10	.60
808	A170	1.25g multi	1.75	.90
809	A170	2g multi	6.00	3.00
a.		Souvenir sheet of #806, 809	16.00	16.00
		Nos. 803-809 (7)	11.40	6.45

For surcharge see No. 881.

Simon Bolivar and Alexander Petion — A171

Designs: 25c, 1.25g, 7.50g, Portraits reversed. 50c, 4.50g, Bolivar, flags of Grand Colombian Confederation member nations.

1985, Aug. 30			Perf. 13½x14	
810	A171	5c multi	.30	.25
811	A171	25c multi	.30	.25
812	A171	50c multi	.35	.25
813	A171	1g multi	.55	.30
814	A171	1.25g multi	.60	.45
815	A171	2g multi	1.10	.85
816	A171	7.50g multi	3.25	3.75
		Nos. 810-816 (7)	6.45	6.10

Souvenir Sheet
Imperf

| 817 | A171 | 4.50g multi | 3.50 | 2.50 |

Nos. 813-817 airmail.
For surcharge see No. 876.

Arrival of Europeans in America, 500th Anniv. — A172

Designs: 10c, 25c, 50c, Henri, cacique of Bahoruco, hero of the Spanish period, 1492-1625. 1g, 1.25g, 2g, Henri in tropical forest.

1986, Apr. 11		Litho.	Perf. 14	
818	A172	10c multi	1.00	.35
819	A172	25c multi	1.00	.35
820	A172	50c multi	1.00	.35
821	A172	1g multi	1.75	.45
822	A172	1.25g multi	2.50	.50
823	A172	2g multi	3.75	.75
		Nos. 818-823 (6)	11.00	2.75

Nos. 821-823 are airmail. A 3g souvenir sheet exists picturing Henri in tropical forest. Value $16.
For surcharge see No. 883.

Nos. 770B, 771, 781, 756, C322, C500 Surcharged

1986, Apr. 18				
825	A165a	25c on 5c No. 770B	.30	.25
826	A166	25c on 5c No. 771	.30	.25
826A	A167	25c on 5c No. 781	115.00	100.00
827	A164	25c on 75c No. 756	.30	.25
828	A128	25c on 1.50g No. C322	.30	.25
829	A161	25c on 75c No. C500	.30	.25
		Nos. 825-829 (6)	116.50	101.25

Intl. Youth Year — A173

1986, May 20		Litho.	Perf. 14x15	
830	A173	10c Afforestation	.25	.25
831	A173	25c IYY emblem	.25	.25
832	A173	50c Girl Guides	.35	.25
833	A173	1g like 10c	.55	.45
834	A173	1.25g like 25c	.65	.55
835	A173	2g like 50c	1.10	.85
		Nos. 830-835 (6)	3.15	2.60

Souvenir Sheet

| 836 | A173 | 3g multi | 12.50 | 12.50 |

Nos. 833-836 are airmail.
For surcharge see No. 873.

UNESCO, 40th Anniv. (in 1986) — A174

1987, May 29		Photo.	Perf. 11½
		Granite Paper	
837	A174	10c multi	.25 .25
838	A174	25c multi	.25 .25
839	A174	50c multi	.35 .25
840	A174	1g multi	.55 .45
841	A174	1.25g multi	.70 .55
842	A174	2.50g multi	1.40 1.10
		Nos. 837-842 (6)	3.50 2.85

Souvenir Sheet
Granite Paper

| 843 | A174 | 2g multi | 3.00 3.00 |

Nos. 840-842 are airmail.
For surcharge see No. 882.

Charlemagne Peralte, Resistance Leader — A175

1988, Oct. 18		Litho.	Perf. 14
844	A175	25c multi	.25 .25
845	A175	50c multi	.35 .25
846	A175	1g multi	.55 .45
847	A175	2g multi	1.10 .85
a.		Souvenir sheet of 1	7.50 7.50
848	A175	3g multi	1.75 1.40
		Nos. 844-848 (5)	4.00 3.20

Nos. 846-848, 847a are airmail.

Slave Rebellion, 200th Anniv. — A176

Design: 1g, 2g, 3g, Slaves around fire, vert.

1991, Aug. 22		Litho.	Perf. 12x11½
849	A176	25c brt grn & multi	.60 .30
850	A176	50c pink & multi	1.00 .50

Perf. 11½x12

851	A176	1g blue & multi	2.00 1.00
852	A176	2g yellow & multi	4.00 2.00
a.		Souv. sheet of 2, #850 & 852	27.50 27.50
853	A176	3g buff & multi	7.50 3.50
		Nos. 849-853 (5)	15.10 7.30

Nos. 851-853 are airmail.

Discovery of America, 500th Anniv. — A177

Designs: 25c, 50c, Ships at anchor, men coming ashore, native. 1g, 2g, 3g, Ships, beached long boats, vert.

1993, July 30		Litho.	Perf. 11½
854	A177	25c green & multi	.65 .35
855	A177	50c yellow & multi	1.00 .40
856	A177	1g blue & multi	1.60 .75
857	A177	2g pink & multi	3.25 1.25
a.		Souvenir sheet of 2, #856-857	500.00 500.00
858	A177	3g org yel & multi	6.75 3.75
		Nos. 854-858 (5)	13.25 6.50

Nos. 856-858, 857a are airmail.

25th Genl. Assembly of the Organization of American States — A178

Designs: 50c, 75c, 7.50g, Emblem, map of Haiti. 1g, 2g, 3g, 5g, Emblems, map of North, South America, vert.

Perf. 14x12½, 12½x14

1995, June 25			Litho.	
859	A178	50c violet & multi	.40	.25
860	A178	75c green & multi	.60	.30
861	A178	1g gray bl & multi	.75	.45
862	A178	2g lil rose & multi	1.50	.85
863	A178	3g green & multi	2.00	1.40
864	A178	5g violet & multi	3.25	1.90
		Nos. 859-864 (6)	8.50	5.15

Souvenir Sheet
Imperf

| 865 | A178 | 7.50g grn bl & multi | 10.00 10.00 |

UN, 50th Anniv. — A179

Designs: 50c, 75c, Dove holding UN, Haitian flags. 1g, 2g, 3g, 5g, Haitian, UN flags, dove carrying olive branch.

1995, Nov. 24		Litho.	Perf. 12x11½
866	A179	50c blue & multi	.65 .30
867	A179	75c lilac & multi	.85 .40
868	A179	1g apple grn & multi	1.50 .60
869	A179	2g yellow & multi	2.75 1.00
870	A179	3g org brn & multi	4.00 1.50
871	A179	5g bl grn & multi	6.00 3.00
		Nos. 866-871 (6)	15.75 6.80

Souvenir Sheet

| 872 | A179 | 5g multicolored | 17.50 16.50 |

Nos. 868-872 are airmail.

Nos. 766, 800, 814, 834 Surcharged

1996		Perfs., Etc., as Before	
873	A173	1g on 1.25g #834	.75 .60
874	A169	2g on 1.25g #800	1.50 1.00
875	A165	2g on 1.25g #766	2.25 1.50
876	A171	3g on 1.25g #814	2.50 1.50
		Nos. 873-876 (4)	7.00 4.60

Size and location of surcharge varies. Nos. 873, 875-876 are airmail.

1996 Summer Olympic Games, Atlanta — A180

1996, Aug. 2		Litho.	Perf. 14
877	A180	3g Hurdler	.75 .45
878	A180	10g Athlete up close	2.50 1.60

Volleyball Federation, 1996 Summer Olympics, Atlanta — A181

No. 879: a, 50c, Three players in yellow shirts. b, 75c, Three players in red shirts. c, 1g, Two players in white shirts, torch. d, 2g, Players in yellow, in red. 15g, Player in red.

1996, Aug. 2				
879	A181	Sheet of 4, #a.-d.	17.50	17.50

Souvenir Sheet

| 880 | A181 | 15g multicolored | 17.50 17.50 |

Volleyball, cent. (No. 880).

Nos. 803, 818, 837 Surcharged

1996, Nov.		Litho.	Perfs. as Before
881	A170	1g on 5c #803	.75 .60
882	A174	4g on 10c #837	3.00 2.00
883	A172	6g on 10c #818	4.00 3.00
		Nos. 881-883 (3)	7.75 5.60

Size and location of surcharge varies.

Christmas — A182

Paintings: 2g, The Virgin and Infant, by Jacopo Bellini. 3g, Adoration of the Shepherds, by Strozzi. 6g, Virgin and the Infant, by Giovanni Bellini. 10g, Virgin and the Infant, by Francesco Mazzola. No. 888, Adoration of the Magi, by Gentile da Fabriano.
No. 889 The Nativity, by Jan de Beer, horiz.

1996, Dec. 16		Litho.	Perf. 13½x14
884	A182	2g multicolored	1.00 .30
885	A182	3g multicolored	1.75 .60
886	A182	6g multicolored	3.50 1.25
887	A182	10g multicolored	5.00 1.50
888	A182	25g multicolored	8.75 7.00
		Nos. 884-888 (5)	20.00 10.65

Souvenir Sheet
Perf. 14x13½

| 889 | A182 | 25g multicolored | 10.00 10.00 |

UNICEF, 50th Anniv. A183

1997, Jan. 28			Perf. 14
890	A183	4g green & multi	1.75 .75
891	A183	5g pink & multi	2.25 1.00
892	A183	6g blue & multi	3.00 1.50
893	A183	10g brown & multi	4.75 2.00
894	A183	20g bister & multi	9.00 3.50
		Nos. 890-894 (5)	16.00 8.75

Souvenir Sheet

| 895 | A183 | 25g like #890-894, vert. | 20.00 25.00 |

Nos. 890-894 were each issued in sheets of 6.

Grimm's Fairy Tales — A184

No. 896, No. 902a, 2g, Sleeping Beauty. No. 897, No. 902b, 3g, Snow White. No. 898, No. 902c, 4g, Prince awakening Sleeping Beauty. No. 899, No. 902d, 6g, Old man sleeping from "The Drink of Life." No. 900, No. 902e, 10g, Cinderella. No. 901, No. 902f, 20g, Old man awakened after taking drink.
No. 903, Cottage of the Seven Dwarfs, horiz.

1998, Jan. 5		Litho.	Perf. 13½
896	A184	2g multicolored	1.50 1.50
897	A184	3g multicolored	2.00 2.00
898	A184	4g multicolored	2.50 2.50
899	A184	6g multicolored	4.00 4.00
900	A184	10g multicolored	7.00 7.00
901	A184	20g multicolored	14.00 14.00
		Nos. 896-901 (6)	31.00 31.00

HAITI

Size: 38x50mm
Perf. 14
902 A184 Sheet of 6, #a.-f. 36.50 35.00

Souvenir Sheet
903 A184 25g multicolored 29.50 27.50

Abstract paintings — A185

2g, "Coconut on Pastel Stairs," by Luce Turnier. 3g, "Ogou," by Rose Marie Desruisseau. 5g, "Lantern," by Hilda Williams. 6g, Woman using artist's brush and palette. 15g, Fish, flower and geometric design with faces, snakes by Philippe Dodard.

1998, Oct. 30	Litho.	Perf. 12½
904 A185	2g multicolored	3.00 1.50
905 A185	3g multicolored	5.00 2.00
906 A185	5g multicolored	7.00 2.75
907 A185	6g multicolored	12.00 4.00
Nos. 904-907 (4)		10.25

Souvenir Sheet
Perf. 13
908 A185 15g multicolored 42.50 35.00

Tourism. Nos. 904-907 exist in imperf. souvenir sheet of 4. No. 908 contains one 28x36mm stamp.

Birds — A186

Designs: 2g, Priotelus roseigaster. 4g, Xenoligea mantana. 10g, Phoenicophilus poliocephalus. 20g, Phoenicopterus ruber.

1999, Aug. 27	Litho.	Perf. 14
909 A186	2g multicolored	.75 .75
910 A186	4g multicolored	1.50 1.50
911 A186	10g multicolored	4.00 4.00
912 A186	20g multicolored	7.00 7.00
a. Souv. sheet, #909-912		15.00 15.00
Nos. 909-912 (4)		13.25 14.25

Nos. 911-912 are airmail.

Worldwide Fund for Nature — A187

No. 913: a, 2g, Hyla vasta. b, 4g, Head of Hyla vasta. c, 2g, Cyclura ricordii. d, 4g, Head of Cyclura ricordii.

1999, Aug. 27	Litho.	Perf. 14
913 A187	Block of 4, #a.-d.	6.00 3.00

Issued in sheets of 16 (4x4) and 8 (2x4).

Souvenir Sheet

Protection of Natural Resources — A188

1999	Litho.	Perf. 13¾
914 A188	20g multicolored	12.50 17.50

A188a Christmas A188b

1999	Photo.	Perf. 11¾

Panel Color
914A A188a	1g Prussian blue	.75 .75
914B A188a	3g red brown	1.00 1.00
914C A188a	5g dark blue	2.50 2.50
914D A188b	10g dk purple	4.00 4.00
914E A188b	15g red	5.00 5.00
914F A188b	20g blue	7.50 7.50
g. Souvenir sheet, #915A-915F		25.00 25.00
Nos. 914A-914F (6)		14.45 14.45

Nos. 914D-914F are airmail.

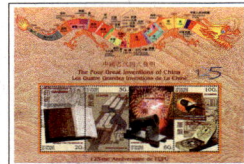

Chinese Inventions — A189

No. 915, 2g, Movable type. No. 916, 3g, Paper. No. 917, 6g, Gunpowder, cannon. No. 918, 10g, Compass.

1999, Dec. 20	Litho.	Perf. 13¾
915-918	Set of 4	30.00 30.00
a. A189 Souv. sheet, #915-918		20.00 20.00

UPU, 125th anniv.
No. 918a exists imperf. Value, $40.

Tourism — A190

Designs: 2g, Pirogue. 3g, Smiling girl. 4g, Zim Pond, vert. 5g, Ardadins Island, vert. 6g, Gingerbread House. 10g, National Palace. 20g, Peligre Reservoir, vert.

Perf. 14¼x14½, 14½x14¼
2000, June 5	Litho.	
919-925 A190	Set of 7	11.00 11.00
a. Souv. sheet, #919-925 + label		15.00 20.00

Souvenir Sheet
926 A190 25g Boat "Pays," vert. 15.00 20.00

1801 Constitution, Bicent. — A191

Designs: 1g, 2g, 5g, 10g, 25g, 50g, Toussaint L'Ouverture and 1801 Constitution. No. 933: a, Toussaint L'Ouverture. b, 1801 Constitution.

2001	Litho.	Perf. 13¾x13¼
927 A191	1g multi	.90 .50
928 A191	2g multi	.90 .50
929 A191	5g multi	.90 .50
930 A191	10g multi	3.75 1.25
931 A191	25g multi	7.25 2.25
932 A191	50g multi	14.50 3.75
Nos. 927-932 (6)		28.20 8.75

Souvenir Sheet
Perf. 12¾
933 A191 25g Sheet of 2, #a-b 70.00 70.00

Nos. 929-932 are airmail. No. 933 contains two 25x29mm stamps.

Toussaint L'Ouverture (c. 1743-1803) A192

Background color: 1g, Green. 2g, Brown. 3g, Yellow green. 5g, Red brown. 6g, blue. 10g, Violet.

2003, Apr. 7	Litho.	Perf. 13
934-939 A192	Set of 6	32.50 32.50

Souvenir Sheet
Imperf
940 A192 15g multi 110.00 110.00

Pope John Paul II and Pope Benedict XVI Stamps

In 2005 a set of 8 face-different stamps with the image of John Paul II and 8 face different stamps with the image of Benedict XVI were printed without official authorization. They were printed in sheetlets numbered 1-40, with either three or six stamps per sheet. Selvage of various sheets containing the same stamps bear text in either French, English, Latin, Polish, Italian or Spanish. They were not sold by the Haiti post office and were not valid for postage.

The following items inscribed "Republic of Haiti" have been declared "illegal" by Haitian postal authorities:

Sheets of six 8g stamps depicting Pope John Paul II, and Pope Benedict XVI.

Sheets of six 10g stamps depicting Pope John Paul II, and Pope Benedict XVI.

Sheets of six 15g stamps depicting Pope John Paul II, and Pope Benedict XVI.

Sheet of three 20g stamps depicting Pope John Paul II.

Sheet of three 30g stamps depicting Pope John Paul II.

Sheets of two 25g stamps depicting Pope Benedict XVI (2 different).

A sheet of seven stamps of various denominations and two labels and a sheet of eight 25g stamp and one label commemorating the Jan. 12, 2010 Haiti earthquake have been determined to be bogus issues.

SEMI-POSTAL STAMPS

Pierre de Coubertin — SP1

Engraved & Litho. (flag)
1939, Oct. 3	Unwmk.	Perf. 12
B1 SP1	10c + 10c multi	27.50 27.50
Nos. B1,CB1-CB2 (3)		77.50 77.50

Pierre de Coubertin, organizer of the modern Olympic Games. The surtax was used to build a Sports Stadium at Port-au-Prince.

Catalogue values for unused stamps in this section, from this point to the end of the section, are for Never Hinged items.

Nos. 419-420 Surcharged in Deep Carmine

Perf. 13x13½, 13½x13
1958, Aug. 30	Litho.	Unwmk.
B2 A82	1g + 50c purple	2.50 2.40
B3 A83	1.50g + 50c red org	2.50 2.40
Nos. B2-B3,CB9 (3)		7.50 7.20

The surtax was for the Red Cross. Overprint arranged horizontally on No. B3.

Nos. 440-441 Srchd. in Red

1959, Apr. 7	Photo.	Perf. 11½

Granite Paper
| B4 A87 | 10c + 25c rose pink | .40 .25 |
| B5 A87 | 25c + 25c green | .40 .35 |

Nos. 444-446 Surcharged Like Nos. B2-B3 in Red
Perf. 14x13½
B6 A88	10c + 50c vio bl & ol	.75 .50
B7 A88	50c + 50c grn & dp brn	.75 .60
B8 A88	2g + 50c dp cl & dk brn	1.25 1.00
Nos. B6-B8,CB10-CB15 (9)		7.65 7.00

The surtax was for the Red Cross.

No. 447 Surcharged Diagonally

Nos. 448-450 Surcharged in Dark Carmine

1959, Oct. 30		Perf. 14
B10 A90	25c + 75c blk brn & lt bl	.65 .60
B11 A90	50c + 75c multi	.90 .60
B12 A91	75c + 75c brn & bl	.90 .60
Nos. B10-B12,CB19-CB21 (6)		5.45 4.80

The surtax was for Haitian athletes. On No. B12, surcharge lines are spaced to total depth of 16mm.

No. 436 Surcharged in Red: "Hommage a l'UNICEF +G. 0,50"
Engraved and Lithographed
1960, Feb. 2		Perf. 11½
B13 A86	1g + 50c blk & brick red	.90 .90
Nos. B13,CB22-CB23 (3)		3.65 3.65

UNICEF.

Unwmk.
1959, July 23	Photo.	Perf. 12
B9 A89	50c + 20c lt bl & dp cl	.85 .85
Nos. B9,CB16-CB18 (4)		4.05 4.05

Issued for the World Refugee Year, July 1, 1959-June 30, 1960.

HAITI

Nos. 452-453 Surcharged with Additional Value and Overprinted "ALPHABETISATION" in Red or Black

Perf. 12½x13

1960, July 12	Litho.		Unwmk.	
B14	A92	10c + 20c sal & grn (R)	.35	.25
B15	A92	10c + 30c sal & grn	.40	.25
B16	A92	50c + 20c vio & mag (R)	.40	.40
B17	A92	50c + 30c vio & mag	.55	.50
Nos. B14-B17, CB24-CB27 (8)			4.55	3.70

Olympic Games Issue
Nos. 464-465 Surcharged with Additional Value

1960, Sept. 9	Photo.		Perf. 12	
B18	A94	50c + 25c grn & ocher	.40	.25
B19	A94	1g + 25c dk brn & grnsh bl	.50	.40
Nos. B18-B19, CB28-CB29 (4)			1.95	1.45

No. 469 Surcharged: "UNICEF +25 centimes"

1961, Jan. 14	Engr.		Perf. 10½	
B20	A96	1g + 25c grn & blk	.50	.40
Nos. B20, CB30-CB31 (3)			1.55	1.20

UNICEF.

No. 469 Surcharged: "OMS SNEM +20 CENTIMES"

1961, Dec. 11				
B21	A96	1g + 20c grn & blk	.55	.50
Nos. B21, CB35-CB36 (3)			4.40	4.35

Haiti's participation in the UN malaria eradication drive.

Nos. 434, 436 and 438 Surcharged in Black or Red

(Surcharge arranged to fit shape of stamp.)

1961-62	Engr. & Litho.		Perf. 11½	
B22	A86	20c + 25c blk & yel	.30	.25
B23	A86	1g + 50c blk & brick red (R) ('62)	.50	.50
B24	A86	2.50g + 50c blk & gray vio (R) ('62)	.90	.60
Nos. B22-B24, CB37-CB41 (8)			5.55	5.20

The surtax was for the benefit of the urban rehabilitation program in Duvalier Ville.

Nos. 486-488 Surcharged: "+25 centimes"

1962, Sept. 13	Litho.		Perf. 12	
B25	A99	5c + 25c crim & dp bl	.30	.25
B26	A99	10c + 25c red brn & emer	.30	.25
B27	A99	50c + 25c bl & crim	.40	.25
Nos. B25-B27, CB42-CB44 (6)			2.15	1.65

Nos. 489-490 Surcharged in Red: "+0.20"

1962	Unwmk.		Perf. 12½x13	
B28	A92	10c + 20c bl & grn	.30	.25
B29	A92	50c + 20c rose lil & ol grn	.40	.40
Nos. B28-B29, CB45-CB46 (4)			1.60	1.45

No. 502 Surcharged: "ALPHABETISATION" and "+0,10"

1963, Mar. 15	Photo.		Perf. 14x14½	
B30	A102	25c + 10c bl gray, yel & blk	.25	.25
Nos. B30, CB47-CB48 (3)			1.15	.90

Nos. 491-494 Surcharged and Overprinted in Black or Red

Overprint includes Olympic Emblem and: "JEUX OLYMPIQUES / D'HIVER / INNSBRUCK 1964".

Perf. 14x14½, 14½x14

1964, July 27			Unwmk.	
B31	A100	5c + 10c on 3c (R)	.60	.40
B32	A100	50c + 10c on 5c	.60	.40
B33	A100	50c + 10c on 10c (R)	.60	.40
B34	A100	50c + 10c on 25c	.60	.40
Nos. B31-B34, CB49 (5)			3.30	2.40

9th Winter Olympic Games, Innsbruck, Austria, Jan. 20-Feb. 9, 1964. The 10c surtax went for charitable purposes.

Nos. 510-512 Surcharged: "+ 5c." in Black

1965, Mar. 15	Photo.		Perf. 11½	
	Granite Paper			
B35	A105	10c + 5c lt bl & dk brn	.25	.25
B36	A105	25c + 5c sal & dk brn	.30	.25
B37	A105	50c + 5c pale rose lil & dk brn	.50	.40
Nos. B35-B37, CB51-CB54 (7)			3.15	2.45

Nos. B35-B37 and CB51-CB54 also exist with this surcharge (without period after "c") in red. They also exist with a similar black surcharge which lacks the period and is in a thinner, lighter type face.

Nos. 533 and 535-536 Surcharged and Overprinted with Haitian Scout Emblem and "12e Jamboree / Mondial 1967" Like Regular Issue

1967, Aug. 21	Photo.		Perf. 11½	
B38	A111	10c + 10c on 5c multi	.25	.25
B39	A111	15c + 10c multi	.25	.25
B40	A111	50c + 10c multi	.30	.25
Nos. B38-B40, CB55-CB56 (5)			1.85	1.50

12th Boy Scout World Jamboree, Farragut State Park, Idaho, Aug. 1-9. The surcharge on No. B38 includes 2 bars through old denomination.

Nos. 600-601 Surcharged in Red

Surcharge includes new value, Red Cross and: "50ème. Anniversaire / de la Ligue des / Sociétés de la / Croix Rouge".

1969, June 25	Litho.		Perf. 11½	
B41	A127	10c + 10c multi	.25	.25
B42	A127	50c + 20c multi	.50	.40
Nos. B41-B42, CB61-CB62 (4)			2.15	1.55

50th anniv. of the League of Red Cross Societies.

Nos. 637-638 Surcharged with New Value and: "INAUGURATION / 22-7-71"

1971, Aug. 3	Litho.		Perf. 14x13½	
B43	A138	20c + 50c multi	.45	.35
B44	A138	25c + 1.50g multi	.80	.45

Inauguration of the François Duvalier Central Hydroelectric Plant, July 22, 1971.

AIR POST STAMPS

Plane over Port-au-Prince — AP1

1929-30	Unwmk.		Engr.	Perf. 12	
C1	AP1	25c dp grn ('30)		.50	.40
C2	AP1	50c dp vio		.65	.40
C3	AP1	75c red brn ('30)		1.75	1.25
C4	AP1	1g dp ultra		1.90	1.60
Nos. C1-C4 (4)				4.80	3.65

No. 317 Surcharged in Red

1933, July 6
C4A A44 60c on 20c blue 75.00 80.00

Non-stop flight of Capt. J. Errol Boyd and Robert G. Lyon from New York to Port-au-Prince.

Plane over Christophe's Citadel — AP2

1933-40
C5	AP2	50c org brn	5.25	1.00
C6	AP2	50c ol grn ('35)	4.00	1.00
C7	AP2	50c car rose ('37)	3.50	2.00
C8	AP2	50c blk ('38)	2.00	1.00
C8A	AP2	60c choc ('40)	1.10	.50
C9	AP2	1g ultra	1.75	.50
Nos. C5-C9 (6)			17.60	6.00

For surcharge see No. C24.

Dumas Type of Regular Issue

1935, Dec. 29	Litho.	Perf. 11½
C10	A59	60c brt vio & choc	4.50	2.50

Visit of delegation from France to Haiti.

Arms of Haiti and Portrait of George Washington — AP4

1938, Aug. 29		Engr.	Perf. 12
C11	AP4	60c deep blue	.70	.40

150th anniv. of the US Constitution.

Caribbean Conference Type of Regular Issue

1941, June 30			
C12	A60	60c olive	3.25	.85
C13	A60	1.25g purple	3.25	.65

Madonna Type of Regular Issue

1942, Dec. 8			Perf. 12
C14	A61	10c dk olive	.40	.25
C15	A61	25c brt ultra	.50	.40
C16	A61	50c turq grn	.90	.40
C17	A61	60c rose car	1.40	.50
C18	A61	1.25g black	2.50	.50
Nos. C14-C18 (5)			5.70	2.05

Souvenir Sheets

C19	A61	Sheet of 2, #C14, C16	5.00	5.00
a.		Imperf	25.00	25.00
C20	A61	Sheet of 2, #C15, C17	5.00	5.00
a.		Imperf	25.00	25.00
C21	A61	Sheet of 1, #C18	5.00	5.00
a.		Imperf	25.00	25.00

Our Lady of Perpetual Help, patroness of Haiti.

Killick Type of Regular Issue

1943, Sept. 6			
C22	A62	60c purple	.65	.40
C23	A62	1.25g black	1.60	1.60

No. C8A Surcharged with New Value and Bars in Red

1944, Nov. 25			
C24	AP2	10c on 60c choc	.50	.25
a.		Bars at right vertical	2.40	
b.		Double surcharge	75.00	

Red Cross Type of Regular Issue

1945		Cross in Rose	
C25	A63	20c yel org	.40	.25
C26	A63	25c brt ultra	.40	.25
C27	A63	50c ol blk	.40	.25
C28	A63	60c dl vio	.50	.25
C29	A63	1g yellow	1.40	.40
C30	A63	1.25g carmine	1.25	.40
C31	A63	1.35g green	1.25	.60
C32	A63	5g black	7.25	2.50
Nos. C25-C32 (8)			12.85	4.90

Issue dates: 1g, Aug. 14; others, Feb. 20. For surcharges see Nos. C153-C160.

> Catalogue values for unused stamps in this section, from this point to the end of the section, are for Never Hinged items.

Franklin D. Roosevelt — AP11

1946, Feb. 5	Unwmk.		Perf. 12
C33	AP11	20c black	.40	.25
C34	AP11	60c black	.50	.25

Capois Type of Regular Issue

1946, July 18			Engr.
C35	A64	20c car rose	.25	.25
C36	A64	25c dk grn	.25	.25
C37	A64	50c orange	.25	.25
C38	A64	60c purple	.40	.25
C39	A64	1g gray blk	.50	.25
C40	A64	1.25g red vio	.75	.40
C41	A64	1.35g black	.80	.50
C42	A64	5g rose car	2.40	1.20
Nos. C35-C42 (8)			5.60	3.35

For surcharges see Nos. C43-C45, C49-C51, C61-C62.

Nos. C37 and C41 Surcharged with New Value and Bar or Block in Red or Black

1947-48				
C43	A64	5c on 1.35g (R) ('48)	.60	.40
C44	A64	30c on 50c	.50	.40
C45	A64	30c on 1.35g (R)	.50	.40
Nos. C43-C45 (3)			1.60	1.20

Dessalines Type of 1947-54 Regular Issue

1947, Oct. 17			Engr.
C46	A65	20c chocolate	.40	.25

Christopher Columbus and Fleet — AP14

Pres. Dumarsais Estimé and Exposition Buildings — AP15

1950, Feb. 12			Perf. 12½
C47	AP14	30c ultra & gray	.90	.50
C48	AP15	1g black	.90	.50

200th anniversary (in 1949) of the founding of Port-au-Prince.

Nos. C36, C39 and C41 Surcharged or Overprinted in Carmine

1950, Oct. 4			Perf. 12
C49	A64	30c on 25c dk grn	.40	.30
a.		30c on 1g gray black	100.00	
C50	A64	1g gray blk	.60	.50
a.		"P" of overprint omitted	70.00	60.00
C51	A64	1.50g on 1.35g blk	1.75	1.50
Nos. C49-C51 (3)			2.75	2.30

75th anniv. (in 1949) of the UPU.

Bananas — AP16
Coffee — AP17
Sisal — AP18

1951, Sept. 3	Photo.		Perf. 12½
C52	AP16	30c dp org	2.25	.40
C53	AP17	80c dk grn & sal pink	5.50	.60
C54	AP18	5g gray	19.00	3.50
Nos. C52-C54 (3)			26.75	4.50

For surcharge see No. C218.

Isabella I — AP19

1951, Oct. 12			Perf. 13
C55	AP19	15c brown	.30	.25
C56	AP19	30c dull blue	.40	.40

Queen Isabella I of Spain, 500th birth anniv.

Type of Regular Issue

20c, Cap Haitien Roadstead. 30c, Workers' housing, St. Martin. 1.50g, Restored cathedral. 2.50g, School lunchroom.

HAITI

1953, May 4   Engr.   *Perf. 12*

C57	A68	20c dp bl	.25	.25
C58	A68	30c red brn	.40	.25
C59	A68	1.50g gray blk	.85	.50
C60	A68	2.50g violet	1.75	.85
		Nos. C57-C60 (4)	3.25	1.85

Nos. C38 and C41 Surcharged in Black

1953, May 18

C61	A64	50c on 60c pur	.40	.25
a.		Double surcharge	225.00	225.00
C62	A64	50c on 1.35g blk	.40	.25
a.		Double surcharge	200.00	200.00

150th anniv. of the adoption of the natl. flag.
Scott editors are seeking information on the existence of No. C62a unused.

Dessalines and Magloire Type and

Henri Christophe — AP21

No. C64, Toussaint L'Ouverture. No. C65, Dessalines. No. C66, Petion. No. C67, Bois-rond-Tonerre. No. C68, Petion. No. C69, Lamartiniere.

1954, Jan. 1   Photo.   *Perf. 11½*

C63	AP21	50c shown	.50	.25
C64	AP21	50c multicolored	.50	.25
C65	AP21	50c multicolored	.50	.25
C66	AP21	50c multicolored	.50	.25
C67	AP21	50c multicolored	.50	.25
C68	AP21	1g multicolored	.80	.50
C69	AP21	1.50g multicolored	1.50	1.00
C70	A69	7.50g multicolored	5.50	5.00
		Nos. C63-C70 (8)	10.30	7.75

See Nos. C95-C96.

Marie Jeanne and Lamartinière Leading Attack — AP23

Design: Nos. C73, C74, Battle of Vertieres.

1954, Jan. 1   *Perf. 12½*

C71	AP23	50c black	.40	.25
C72	AP23	50c carmine	.40	.25
C73	AP23	50c ultra	.40	.25
C74	AP23	50c sal pink	.40	.25
		Nos. C71-C74 (4)	1.60	1.00

150th anniv. of Haitian independence.

Mme. Magloire Type of Regular Issue

1954, Jan. 1   *Perf. 11½*

C75	A72	20c red org	.25	.25
C76	A72	50c brown	.40	.40
C77	A72	1g grn	.50	.40
C78	A72	1.50g crimson	.75	.50
C79	A72	2.50g bl grn	1.25	.90
C80	A72	5g gray	3.00	2.25
		Nos. C75-C80 (6)	6.15	4.70

Christophe Types of Regular Issue

1954, Dec. 6   Litho.   *Perf. 13½x13*

Portraits in Black

C81	A73	50c orange	.40	.25
C82	A73	1g blue	.80	.50
C83	A73	1.50g green	1.10	.65
C84	A73	2.50g gray	1.75	.90
C85	A73	5g rose car	3.25	1.90

Perf. 13

Flag in Black and Carmine

C86	A74	50c orange	.40	.25
C87	A74	1g dp bl	.75	.45
C88	A74	1.50g bl grn	1.10	.65
C89	A74	2.50g grey	1.75	.90
C90	A74	5g red org	3.25	1.90
		Nos. C81-C90 (10)	14.55	8.35

Fort Nativity, Drawing by Christopher Columbus — AP27

1954, Dec. 14   Engr.   *Perf. 12*

| C91 | AP27 | 50c dk rose car | .65 | .50 |
| C92 | AP27 | 50c dk gray | .65 | .50 |

Dessalines Type of 1955-57 Issue

Perf. 11½

1955, July 14   Unwmk.   Photo.

| C93 | A75 | 20c org & blk | .25 | .25 |
| C94 | A75 | 20c yel grn & blk | .25 | .25 |

For overprint see No. C183a.

Portrait Type of 1954
Dates omitted

Design: J. J. Dessalines.

1955, July 19   Portrait in Black

| C95 | AP21 | 50c gray | .40 | .25 |
| C96 | AP21 | 50c blue | .40 | .25 |

Dessalines Memorial Type of Regular Issue

1955, Aug. 1

| C97 | A76 | 1.50g gray & blk | .65 | .25 |
| C98 | A76 | 1.50g grn & blk | .65 | .25 |

Types of 1956 Regular Issue and

Car and Coastal View — AP30

Designs: No. C100, 75c, Plane, steamship and Haiti map. 1g, Car and coastal view. 2.50g, Flamingo. 5g, Mallard.

1956, Apr. 14   Unwmk.   *Perf. 11½*

Granite Paper

C99	AP30	50c hn brn & lt bl	.70	.25
C100	AP30	50c blk & gray	.45	.25
C101	AP30	75c dp grn & bl grn	.95	.50
C102	AP30	1g ol grn & lt bl	.80	.30
C103	A77	2.50g dp org & org	14.00	1.75
C104	A78	5g red & buff	21.00	3.00
		Nos. C99-C104 (6)	37.90	6.05

For overprint see No. C185.

Kant Type of Regular Issue

1956, July 19   Photo.   *Perf. 12*

Granite Paper

C105	A79	50c chestnut	.40	.25
C106	A79	75c dp yel grn	.50	.25
C107	A79	1.50g dp magenta	1.25	.50
a.		Miniature sheet of 3	8.00	5.00
		Nos. C105-C107 (3)	2.15	1.15

No. C107a exists both perf. and imperf. Each sheet contains Nos. C105, C106 and a 1.25g gray black of same design.

Waterfall Type of Regular Issue

1957, Dec. 16   *Perf. 11½*

Granite Paper

C108	A80	50c grn & grnsh bl	.50	.25
C109	A80	1.50g ol grn & grnsh bl	.90	.40
C110	A80	2.50g dk bl & brt bl	1.25	.60
C111	A80	5g bluish blk & saph	2.75	1.50
		Nos. C108-C111 (4)	5.40	2.75

For surcharge and overprint see Nos. CB49, CQ2.

Dessalines Type of Regular Issue

1958, July 2

| C112 | A81 | 50c org & blk | .65 | .40 |

For overprints see Nos. C184, CQ1.

Brussels Fair Types of Regular Issue, 1958

Perf. 13x13½, 13½x13

1958, July 22   Litho.   Unwmk.

C113	A82	2.50g pale car rose	1.25	.50
C114	A83	5g bright blue	1.50	.85
a.		Souv. sheet of 2, #C113-C114, imperf.	5.50	5.00

For surcharge see No. CB9.

Sylvio Cator — AP33

1958, Aug. 16   Photo.   *Perf. 11½*

Granite Paper

C115	AP33	50c green	.25	.25
C116	AP33	50c blk brn	.25	.25
C117	AP33	1g org brn	.50	.40
C118	AP33	5g gray	2.40	.85
		Nos. C115-C118 (4)	3.40	1.75

30th anniversary of the world championship record broad jump of Sylvio Cator.

IGY Type of Regular Issue, 1958

Designs: 50c, US Satellite. 1.50g, Emperor penguins. 2g, Modern observatory.

1958, Oct. 8   *Perf. 14x13½*

C119	A85	50c dp ultra & brn red	1.00	.25
C120	A85	1.50g brn & crim	3.75	.75
C121	A85	2g dk bl & crim	2.75	.40
a.		Souv. sheet of 4, #427, C119-C121, imperf.	8.00	7.50
		Nos. C119-C121 (3)	7.50	1.40

President François Duvalier — AP34

Commemorative Inscription in Ultramarine
Engraved and Lithographed

1958, Oct. 22   Unwmk.   *Perf. 11½*

C122	AP34	50c blk & rose	1.00	.25
C123	AP34	2.50g blk & ocher	1.40	.60
C124	AP34	5g blk & rose lil	1.90	1.25
C125	AP34	7.50g blk & lt bl grn	3.00	2.00
		Nos. C122-C125 (4)	7.30	4.10

See note after No. 431.
Souvenir sheets of 3 exist, perf. and imperf., containing one each of Nos. C124-C125 and No. 431. Sheets measure 132x77mm. with marginal inscription in ultramarine. Value, $6.25 each.
For surcharges see Nos. CB37-CB39.

Same Without Commemorative Inscription

1958, Nov. 20

C126	AP34	50c blk & rose	.40	.25
C127	AP34	1g blk & vio	.50	.25
C128	AP34	1.50g blk & pale brn	.75	.40
C129	AP34	2g blk & rose pink	1.00	.40
C130	AP34	2.50g blk & ocher	1.00	.50
C131	AP34	5g blk & rose lil	2.00	1.25
C132	AP34	7.50g blk & lt bl grn	3.00	1.60
		Nos. C126-C132 (7)	8.65	4.65

For surcharges see Nos. CB22-CB23, CB40-CB41.

Type of Regular Issue and

Flags of Haiti and UN — AP35

Perf. 11½

1958, Dec. 5   Unwmk.   Photo.

Granite Paper

C133	AP35	50c pink, car & ultra	.60	.25
C134	A87	75c brt bl	.60	.25
C135	A87	1g brown	.75	.40
a.		Souv. sheet of 2, #C133, C135, imperf.	3.50	3.50
		Nos. C133-C135 (3)	1.95	.90

For surcharges see Nos. CB10-CB12.

Nos. C133-C135 Overprinted

Overprint reads "10th ANNIVERSARY OF THE UNIVERSAL DECLARATION OF HUMAN RIGHTS" in: a, English; b, French; c, Spanish; d, Portuguese.

1959, Jan. 28

C136		Block of 4	3.50	2.75
a.-d.		AP35 50c any single	.75	.60
C137		Block of 4	4.75	3.75
a.-d.		A87 75c any single	1.00	.80
C138		Block of 4	9.00	7.00
a.-d.		A87 1g any single	1.95	1.50
		Nos. C136-C138 (3)	17.25	13.50

Pope Pius XII — AP36

1.50g, Pope praying. 2.50g, Pope on throne.

1959, Feb. 28   Photo.   *Perf. 14x13½*

C139	AP36	50c grn & lil	.25	.25
C140	AP36	1.50g ol & red brn	.65	.40
C141	AP36	2.50g pur & dk bl	1.00	.40
		Nos. C139-C141 (3)	1.90	1.05

Issued in memory of Pope Pius XII.
For surcharges see Nos. CB13-CB15.

Lincoln Type of Regular Issue, 1959

Designs: Various Portraits of Lincoln.

1959, May 12   *Perf. 12*

C142	A89	1g lt grn & chnt	.50	.40
C143	A89	2g pale lem & sl grn	.75	.50
C144	A89	2.50g buff & vio bl	.85	.40
a.		Min. sheet of 4, #447, C142-C144, imperf.	3.00	2.75
		Nos. C142-C144 (3)	2.10	1.30

Imperf. pairs exist.
For surcharges see Nos. CB16-CB18.

Pan American Games Types of Regular Issue

Designs: 50c, Jean Baptiste Dessables and map of American Midwest, c. 1791. 1g, Chicago's skyline and Dessables house. 1.50g, Discus thrower and flag of Haiti.

1959, Aug. 27   Unwmk.   *Perf. 14*

Photo.

C145	A91	50c hn brn & aqua	.75	.25
C146	A90	1g lil & aqua	1.00	.40
C147	A90	1.50g multi	1.40	.50
		Nos. C145-C147 (3)	3.15	1.15

For surcharges see Nos. CB19-CB21.

Nos. C145-C147 Overprinted like No. 451

1960, Feb. 29

C148	A91	50c hn brn & aqua	1.40	1.40
C149	A90	1g lil & aqua	1.90	1.90
C150	A90	1.50g multi	2.75	2.75
		Nos. C148-C150 (3)	6.05	6.05

WRY Type of Regular Issue, 1960

1960, Apr. 7   Litho.   *Perf. 12½x13*

C151	A92	50c bl & blk	.40	.40
C152	A92	1g lt grn & mar	.50	.40
a.		Souv. sheet of 4, #452-453, C151-C152, imperf.	6.50	6.00

See Nos. C191-C192. For surcharges see Nos. CB24-CB27, CB45-CB46.

Nos. C31, C28 and 369 Surcharged or Overprinted in Red: "28ème ANNIVERSAIRE"

1960, May 8   Engr.   *Perf. 12*

Cross in Rose

C153	A63	20c on 1.35g grn	.40	.25
C154	A63	50c on 60c dl vio	.65	.40
C155	A63	50c on 1.35g grn	.40	.40
C156	A63	50c on 2.50g pale vio	.40	.40
C157	A63	60c dl vio	.40	.40
C158	A63	1g on 1.35g grn	.70	.50
C159	A63	1.35g green	.65	.50
C160	A63	2g on 1.35g grn	1.40	1.00
		Nos. C153-C160 (8)	5.00	3.85

28th anniv. of the Haitian Red Cross. Additional overprint "Avion" on No. C156.

Sugar Type of Regular Issue

Miss Fouchard &: 50c, Harvest. 2.50g, Beach.

Perf. 11½

1960, May 30   Unwmk.   Photo.

Granite Paper

| C161 | A93 | 50c lil rose & brn | .90 | .25 |
| C162 | A93 | 2.50g ultra & brn | 2.25 | .50 |

Olympic Type of Regular Issue

Designs: 50c, Pierre de Coubertin, Melbourne stadium and Olympic Flame. 1.50g, Discus thrower and Rome stadium. 2.50g, Victors' parade, Athens, 1896, and Melbourne, 1956.

HAITI

1960, Aug. 18   *Perf. 12*
C163 A94 50c mar & bis .65 .25
C164 A94 1.50g rose car & yel grn 1.40 .40
C165 A94 2.50g sl grn & mag 1.60 .45
  a. Souv. sheet of 2, #465, C165, imperf. 5.50 5.50
  Nos. C163-C165 (3) 3.65 1.10

For surcharges see Nos. CB28-CB29.

Jeanty Type of Regular Issue
50c, Occide Jeanty and score from "1804."
1.50g, Occide Jeanty and National Capitol.

1960, Oct. 19   *Perf. 14x14½*
C166 A95 50c yel & bl .50 .25
C167 A95 1.50g lil rose & sl grn .75 .25

Printed in sheets of 12 (3x4) with inscription and opening bars of "1804," Jeanty's military march, in top margin.

UN Type of Regular Issue, 1960
1960, Nov. 25   *Engr.*   *Perf. 10½*
C168 A96 50c red org & blk .40 .25
C169 A96 1.50g dk bl & blk .50 .40
  a. Souv. sheet of 3, #469, C168-C169, imperf. 3.25 3.25

For surcharges see Nos. CB30-CB31, CB35-CB36.

Nos. C168-C169 exist with centers inverted.

Dessalines Type of Regular Issue
1960, Nov. 5   *Photo.*   *Perf. 11½*
    Granite Paper
C170 A81 20c gray & blk .25 .25

For overprint see No. C183.

Sud-Caravelle Jet Airliner and Orchid AP37

Designs: 50c, Boeing 707 jet airliner, facing left, and Kittyhawk. 1g, Sud-Caravelle jet airliner and Orchid. 1.50g, Boeing 707 jet airliner and air post stamp of 1933.

1960, Dec. 17   *Photo.*   *Unwmk.*
    Granite Paper
C171 AP37 20c dp ultra & car .25 .25
C172 AP37 50c rose brn & grn .50 .25
C173 AP37 50c brt grnsh bl & ol grn .50 .25
C174 AP37 50c gray & grn .50 .25
C175 AP37 1g gray ol & ver 1.60 .25
C176 AP37 1.50g brt pink & dk bl 1.25 .30
  a. Souv. sheet of 3, #C174-C176, imperf. 4.00 4.00
  Nos. C171-C176 (6) 4.60 1.55

Issued for Aviation Week, Dec. 17-23.

Nos. C172-C174 are dated 17 Decembre 1903.

For overprints and surcharges see Nos. CB32-CB34, CO1-CO5.

Dumas Type of Regular Issue
Designs: 50c, The Three Musketeers and Dumas père, horiz 1g, The Lady of the Camellias and Dumas fils. 1.50g, The Count of Monte Cristo and Dumas père.

1961, Feb. 10   *Photo.*   *Perf. 11½*
    Granite Paper
C177 A97 50c brt bl & blk .60 .25
C178 A97 1g blk & red .75 .35
C179 A97 1.50g brt grn & bl blk 1.10 .35
  Nos. C177-C179 (3) 2.45 .85

Type of Regular Issue, 1961
Tourist publicity: 20c, Privateer in Battle. 50c, Pirate with cutlass in rigging. 1g, Map of Tortuga.

1961, Apr. 4   *Litho.*   *Perf. 12*
C180 A98 20c dk bl & yel .50 .25
C181 A98 50c brt pur & org .75 .25
C182 A98 1g Prus grn & yel .55 .40
  Nos. C180-C182 (3) 1.80 .90

For overprint and surcharge see Nos. C186-C187.

Nos. C170, C112 and C101 Overprinted: "Dr. F. Duvalier Président 22 Mai 1961"
1961, May 22   *Photo.*   *Perf. 11½*
C183 A81 20c gray & blk .25 .25
  a. On No. C93

C184 A81 50c org & blk .25 .25
C185 AP30 75c dp grn & bl grn .40 .40
  Nos. C183-C185 (3) .90 .90

Re-election of Pres. Francois Duvalier.

No. C182 Overprinted or Surcharged
Overprint or Surcharge includes Capsule and: "EXPLORATION SPATIALE JOHN GLENN".

1962, May 10   *Litho.*   *Perf. 12*
C186 A98 1g Prus grn & yel .50 .40
C187 A98 2g on 1g Prus grn & yel 1.40 1.00

See note after No. 485.

Malaria Type of Regular Issue
Designs: 20c, 1g, Triangle pointing down. 50c, Triangle pointing up.

1962, May 30   *Unwmk.*
C188 A99 20c lilac & red .25 .25
C189 A99 50c emer & rose car .40 .25
C190 A99 1g org & dk vio .50 .40
  a. Souv. sheet of 3 3.00 3.00
  Nos. C188-C190 (3) 1.15 .90

Sheets of 12 with marginal inscription.
No. C190a contains stamps similar to Nos. 488 and C189-C190 in changed colors and imperf. Issued July 16.
A similar sheet without the "Contribution..." inscription was issued May 30.

For surcharges see Nos. CB42-CB44.

WRY Type of 1960 Dated "1962"
1962, June 22   *Perf. 12½x13*
C191 A92 50c lt bl & red brn .35 .25
C192 A92 1g bister & blk .40 .40

A souvenir sheet exists containing one each of Nos. 489-490, C191-C192, imperf. Value, $5.50.

For surcharges see Nos. CB45-CB46.

Boy Scout Type of 1962
Designs: 20c, Scout giving Scout sign. 50c, Haitian Scout emblem. 1.50g, Lord and Lady Baden-Powell, horiz.

Perf. 14x14½, 14½x14

1962, Aug. 6   *Photo.*   *Unwmk.*
C193 A100 20c multi .25 .25
C194 A100 50c multi .50 .40
C195 A100 1.50g multi .65 .40
  Nos. C193-C195 (3) 1.40 1.05

A souvenir sheet contains one each of Nos. C194-C195 imperf. Value, $5.50.
A similar sheet inscribed in gold, "Epreuves De Luxe," was issued Dec. 10. Value $3.

Nos. 495 and C193-C195 Overprinted: "AÉROPORT INTERNATIONAL 1962"
1962, Oct. 26   *Perf. 14x14½, 14½x14*
C196 A100 20c multi, #C193 .25 .25
C197 A100 50c multi, #495 .40 .25
C198 A100 50c multi, #C194 .40 .25
C199 A100 1.50g multi, #C195 .60 .40
  Nos. C196-C199 (4) 1.65 1.15

Proceeds from the sale of Nos. C196-C199 were for the construction of new airport at Port-au-Prince. The overprint on No. C197 has "Poste Aérienne" added.

Seattle Fair Type of 1962
Design: Denomination at left, "Avion" at right.

1962, Nov. 19   *Litho.*   *Perf. 12½*
C200 A101 50c blk & pale lil .40 .25
C201 A101 1g org brn & gray .60 .40
C202 A101 1.50g red lil & org .70 .40
  Nos. C200-C202 (3) 1.70 1.05

An imperf. sheet of two exists containing one each of Nos. C201-C202 with simulated gray perforations. Size: 133x82mm. Value, $5.50.

Street in Duvalier Ville and Stamp of 1881 — AP38

1962, Dec. 10   *Photo.*   *Perf. 14x14½*
    Stamp in Dark Brown
C203 AP38 50c orange .50 .25
C204 AP38 1g blue .90 .40
C205 AP38 1.50g green 1.00 .50
  Nos. C203-C205 (3) 2.40 1.15

Issued to publicize Duvalier Ville.

For surcharges see Nos. CB47-CB48.

Nos. C201-C202 Overprinted Vertically in Black or Claret

1963, Jan. 23   *Litho.*   *Perf. 12½*
C206 A101 1g org brn & gray 1.40 .60
  a. Claret overprint, horiz. 1.40 .60
C207 A101 1.50g red lil & org 1.75 1.10
  a. Claret overprint, horiz. 1.75 1.10

"Peaceful Uses of Outer Space." The black vertical overprint has no outside frame lines and no broken shading lines around capsule. Nos. C206a and C207a were issued Feb. 20.

Hunger Type of Regular Issue

Perf. 13x14
1963, July 12   *Unwmk.*   *Photo.*
C208 A103 50c lil rose & blk .40 .25
C209 A103 1g lt ol grn & blk .50 .40

Dag Hammarskjold and UN Emblem AP39

Lithographed and Photogravure
1963, Sept. 28   *Perf. 13½x14*
    Portrait in Slate
C210 AP39 20c buff & brn .25 .25
C211 AP39 50c lt bl & car .40 .25
  a. Souvenir sheet of 2 3.50 3.50
C212 AP39 1g pink & bl .40 .25
C213 AP39 1.50g gray & grn .65 .50
  Nos. C210-C213 (4) 1.70 1.25

Dag Hammarskjold, Sec. Gen. of the UN, 1953-61. Printed in sheets of 25 (5x5) with map of Sweden extending over 9 stamps in second and third vertical rows. No. C211a contains 2 imperf. stamps: 50c blue and carmine and 1.50g ocher and brown with map of southern Sweden in background.

For overprints see Nos. C219-C222, C238-C241, CB50.

Dessalines Type of Regular Issue, 1963
1963, Oct. 17   *Photo.*   *Perf. 14x14½*
C214 A104 50c bl & lil rose .25 .25
C215 A104 50c org & grn .25 .25

Nos. C214-C215 and C53 Overprinted in Black or Red: "FETE DES MERES / 1964"
1964, July 22   *Perf. 14x14½, 12½*
C216 A104 50c bl & lil rose .40 .25
C217 A104 50c org & grn .40 .25
C218 AP17 1.50g on 80c dk grn & sal pink (R) .60 .40
  a. Inverted surcharge 20.00
  Nos. C216-C218 (3) 1.40 .90

Issued for Mother's Day, 1964.

Nos. C210-C213 Overprinted in Red

Lithographed and Engraved
1964, Oct. 2   *Perf. 13½x14*
    Portrait in Slate
C219 AP39 20c buff & brn .40 .25
C220 AP39 50c lt bl & car .40 .25
C221 AP39 1g pink & bl .60 .40
C222 AP39 1.50g gray & grn .70 .50
  Nos. C219-C222, CB50 (5) 3.50 2.65

Cent. (in 1963) of the Intl. Red Cross.

Olympic Type of Regular Issue
No. C223, Weight lifter. Nos. C224-C226, Hurdler.

1964, Nov. 12   *Photo.*   *Perf. 11½*
    Granite Paper
C223 A105 50c pale lil & dk brn .40 .25
C224 A105 50c pale grn & dk brn .40 .25
C225 A105 75c buff & dk brn .50 .40
C226 A105 1.50g gray & dk brn .65 .50
  a. Souv. sheet of 4 2.60 2.50
  Nos. C223-C226 (4) 1.95 1.40

Printed in sheets of 50 (10x5), with map of Japan in background extending over 27 stamps.

No. C226a contains four imperf. stamps similar to Nos. C223-C226 in changed colors and imperf. and with map of Tokyo area in background.

For surcharges see Nos. CB51-CB54.

Airport Type of Regular Issue, 1964
1964, Dec. 15   *Perf. 14½x14*
C227 A106 50c org & blk .40 .25
C228 A106 1.50g brt lil rose & blk .65 .45
C229 A106 2.50g lt vio & blk 1.40 .60
  Nos. C227-C229 (3) 2.45 1.30

Same Overprinted "1965"
1965, Feb. 11   *Photo.*
C230 A106 50c org & blk .40 .25
C231 A106 1.50g brt lil rose & blk .65 .40
C232 A106 2.50g lt vio & blk 1.00 .70
  Nos. C230-C232 (3) 2.05 1.35

World's Fair Type of Regular Issue, 1965
Designs: 50c, 5g, "Rocket Thrower" by Donald De Lue. 5g, Unisphere, NY World's Fair.

1965, Mar. 22   *Unwmk.*   *Perf. 13½*
C233 A107 50c dp bl & org .40 .25
C234 A107 1.50g gray & org .50 .40
C235 A107 5g multi 2.40 1.90
  Nos. C233-C235 (3) 3.30 2.55

Merchant Marine Type of Regular Issue, 1965
1965, May 13   *Photo.*   *Perf. 11½*
C236 A108 50c blk, lt grnsh bl & red .40 .25
C237 A108 1.50g blk, lt vio & red .75 .50

Nos. C210-C213 Overprinted

Lithographed and Photogravure
1965, June 26   *Perf. 13½x14*
    Portrait in Slate
C238 AP39 20c buff & brn .25 .25
C239 AP39 50c lt bl & car .40 .25
C240 AP39 1g pink & bl .50 .40
C241 AP39 1.50g gray & grn .65 .50
  Nos. C238-C241 (4) 1.80 1.40

20th anniversary of the United Nations.

ITU Type of Regular Issue

Perf. 13½
1965, Aug. 16   *Unwmk.*   *Litho.*
C242 A109 50c multi .40 .25
C243 A109 1g multi .50 .40
C244 A109 1.50g bl & multi 1.00 .50
C245 A109 2g pink & multi 1.50 .60
  Nos. C242-C245 (4) 3.40 1.75

A souvenir sheet, released in 1966, contains 50c and 2g stamps resembling Nos. C242 and C245, with simulated perforations. Value $15.

For overprints see Nos. C255-C256.

HAITI

Cathedral Type of Regular Issue, 1965
Designs: 50c, Cathedral, Port-au-Prince, horiz. 1g, High Altar. 7.50g, Statue of Our Lady of the Assumption.

Perf. 14x13, 13x14

1965, Nov. 19   Photo.

Size: 39x29mm, 29x39mm

C246	A110	50c multi	.40	.25
C247	A110	1g multi	.65	.40

Size: 38x52mm

C248	A110	7.50g multi	2.75	2.25
		Nos. C246-C248 (3)	3.80	2.90

Flower Type of Regular Issue
No. C249, 5g, Passionflower. Nos. C250, C252, Okra. Nos. C251, C253, American elder.

1965, Dec. 20   Photo.   **Perf. 11½**
Granite Paper

C249	A111	50c dk vio, yel & grn	1.25	.25
C250	A111	50c multi	1.25	.25
C251	A111	50c grn, gray & yel	1.25	.25
C252	A111	1.50g multi	2.00	1.40
C253	A111	1.50g grn, tan & yel	2.00	1.40
C254	A111	5g dk vio, yel grn & grn	5.75	1.50
		Nos. C249-C254 (6)	13.50	5.05

For surcharges see Nos. CB55-CB56.

Nos. C242-C243 Overprinted in Red: "20e. Anniversaire / UNESCO"

1965, Aug. 27   Litho.   **Perf. 13½**

C255	A109	50c lt vio & multi	1.40	.50
C256	A109	1g citron & multi	2.60	.85

20th anniversary of UNESCO. The souvenir sheet noted below No. C245 was also overprinted "20e. Anniversaire / UNESCO" in red. Value, $20.

Culture Types of Regular Issue and

Modern Painting AP40

Designs: 50c, Ceremonial stool. 1.50g, Amulet.

Perf. 14x14½, 14½x14, 14

1966, Mar. 14   Photo.   Unwmk.

C257	A113	50c lil, brn & brnz	.40	.25
C258	A112	1.50g brt rose lil, yel & blk	.65	.50
C259	AP40	2.50g multi	1.50	.85
		Nos. C257-C259 (3)	2.55	1.60

For overprints and surcharge see Nos. C260-C262, C280-C281.

Nos. C257-C259 Overprinted in Black or Red: "Hommage / a Hailé Sélassié Ier / 24-25 Avril 1966"

1966, Apr. 24

C260	A113	50c (R)	.40	.25
C261	A112	1.50g (vert. ovpt.)	.65	.50
C262	AP40	2.50g (R)	1.00	.70
		Nos. C260-C262 (3)	2.05	1.45

See note after No. 543.

Walter M. Schirra, Thomas P. Stafford, Frank A. Borman, James A. Lovell and Gemini VI and VII — AP41

1966, May 3   **Perf. 13½**

C263	AP41	50c vio bl, brn & lt bl	.40	.25
C264	AP41	1g grn, brn & lt bl	.50	.40
C265	AP41	1.50g car, brn & bl	.65	.50
		Nos. C263-C265 (3)	1.55	1.15

See No. 547.
For overprints see Nos. C296-C298.

Soccer Type of Regular Issue Portrait in Black; Gold Inscription; Green Commemorative Inscription in Two Lines
Designs: 50c, Pres. Duvalier and soccer ball within wreath. 1.50g, President Duvalier and soccer player within wreath.

Lithographed and Photogravure

1966, June 16   **Perf. 13x13½**

C266	A115	50c lt ol grn & plum	.40	.25
C267	A115	1.50g rose & plum	.65	.50

Green Commemorative Inscription in 3 Lines; Gold Inscription Omitted

C268	A115	50c lt ol grn & plum	.40	.40
C269	A115	1.50g rose & plum	.65	.50
		Nos. C266-C269 (4)	2.10	1.65

Caribbean Soccer Festival, June 10-22. No. C266-C267 also for the National Soccer Championships, May 8-22.
For overprint and surcharge see Nos. C288, CB57.

Education Type of Regular Issue
Designs: 50c, "ABC", boy and girl. 1g, Scout symbols. 1.50g, Television set, book and communications satellite, horiz.

Perf. 14x13½, 13½x14
Litho. and Engraved

1966, Oct. 18

C270	A116	50c grn, yel & brn	.40	.25
C271	A116	1g dk brn, org & blk	.50	.40
C272	A116	1.50g brn, bl grn & dk bl	.65	.50
		Nos. C270-C272 (3)	1.55	1.15

Schweitzer Type of Regular Issue
Designs (Schweitzer and): 50c, 1g, Albert Schweitzer Hospital, Deschapelles, Haiti. 1.50g, Maps of Alsace and Gabon. 2g, Pipe organ.

Perf. 12½x13

1967, Apr. 20   Photo.   Unwmk.

C273	A117	50c multi	.50	.40
C274	A117	1g multi	.50	.40
C275	A117	1.50g lt bl & multi	.65	.50
C276	A117	2g multi	.90	.70
		Nos. C273-C276 (4)	2.55	2.00

Fruit-Vegetable Type of Regular Issue, 1967

1967, July 4   Photo.   **Perf. 12½**

C277	A118	50c Watermelon	2.00	.25
C278	A118	1g Cabbage	2.50	2.00
C279	A118	1.50g Tangerine	3.00	2.50
		Nos. C277-C279 (3)	7.50	4.75

No. C258 Overprinted or Surcharged Like EXPO '67 Regular Issue

1967, Aug. 30   Photo.   **Perf. 14½x14**

C280	A112	1.50g multi	.60	.40
C281	A112	2g on 1.50g multi	.75	.55

Issued to commemorate EXPO '67 International Exhibition, Montreal, Apr. 28-Oct. 27.

Duvalier Type of Regular Issue, 1967

1967, Sept. 22   Photo.   **Perf. 14x13**

C282	A119	1g brt grn & gold	.50	.40
C283	A119	1.50g vio & gold	.65	.50
C284	A119	2g org & gold	1.10	.70
		Nos. C282-C284 (3)	2.25	1.60

Education Type of Regular Issue, 1967
50c, Writing hands. 1g, Scout emblem and Scouts, vert. 1.50g, Audio-visual teaching of algebra.

1967, Dec. 11   Litho.   **Perf. 11½**

C285	A120	50c multi	.25	.25
C286	A120	1g multi	.50	.40
C287	A120	1.50g multi	.65	.50
		Nos. C285-C287 (3)	1.40	1.15

For surcharges see Nos. CB58-CB60.

No. C269 Overprinted

Lithographed and Photogravure
1968, Jan. 18   **Perf. 13x13½**

C288	A115	1.50g rose & plum	1.40	1.00

See note after No. 579.

Caiman Woods Type of Regular Issue

1968, Apr. 22   Photo.   **Perf. 12**
Size: 36x26mm

C289	A121	50c multi	.40	.25
C290	A121	1g multi	.50	.40

Perf. 12½x13½
Size: 49x36mm

C291	A121	50c multi	.40	.25
C292	A121	1g multi	.50	.40
C293	A121	1.50g multi	.75	.60
C294	A121	2g gray & multi	.90	.70
C295	A121	5g multi	2.00	1.40
		Nos. C289-C295 (7)	5.45	4.00

Nos. C263-C265 Overprinted

1968, Apr. 19   **Perf. 13½**

C296	AP41	50c multi	.70	.40
C297	AP41	1g multi	1.40	.60
C298	AP41	1.50g multi	2.40	1.10
		Nos. C296-C298 (3)	4.50	2.10

See note after No. 584.

Monument Type of Regular Issue
1968, May 22   **Perf. 11½**
Granite Paper

C299	A122	50c ol bis & blk	.40	.25
C300	A122	1g brt rose & blk	.50	.40
C301	A122	1.50g org & blk	.80	.50
		Nos. C299-C301 (3)	1.70	1.15

For surcharges see Nos. C324-C325.

Types of Regular Bishopric Issue
50c, Palm tree & provincial coats of arms. 1g, 2.50g, Madonna, papal arms & arms of Haiti. 1.50g, Cathedral, arms of Pope Paul VI & arms of Haiti.

Perf. 13x14, 12½x13½

1968, Aug. 16   Photo.

C302	A123	50c lil & multi	.40	.25
C303	A124	1g multi	.50	.40
C304	A124	1.50g multi	.65	.50
C305	A124	2.50g multi	1.40	1.10
		Nos. C302-C305 (4)	2.95	2.25

Airport Type of Regular Issue
50c, 1.50g, 2.50g, Front view of air terminal.

1968, Sept. 22   Photo.   **Perf. 11½**
Portrait in Black

C306	A125	50c rose lake & pale vio	.40	.25
C307	A125	1.50g rose lake & bl	.65	.50
C308	A125	2.50g rose lake & lt grnsh bl	.90	.80
		Nos. C306-C308 (3)	1.95	1.55

Pres. François Duvalier AP42

Embossed & Typo. on Gold Foil
1968, Sept. 22   **Die Cut Perf. 14**

C309	AP42	30g black & red	40.00	50.00

Freed Slaves' Type of Regular Issue
1968, Oct. 28   Litho.   **Perf. 14½x14**

C310	A126	50c brn, lil & brt pink	.40	.25
C311	A126	1g brn, yel grn & brt pink	.50	.40
C312	A126	1.50g brn, lt vio bl & brt pink	.65	.50
C313	A126	2g brn, lt grn & brt pink	.80	.60
		Nos. C310-C313 (4)	2.35	1.75

Education Type of Regular Issue, 1968
50c, 1.50g, Children watching television. 1g, Hands throwing ball, and sports medal.

1968, Nov. 14   **Perf. 11½**

C314	A127	50c multi	.40	.25
C315	A127	1g multi	.50	.40
C316	A127	1.50g multi	.65	.50
		Nos. C314-C316 (3)	1.55	1.15

For surcharges see Nos. CB61-CB62.

Jan Boesman and his Balloon — AP43

1968, Nov. 28   Litho.   **Perf. 13½**

C317	AP43	70c lt yel grn & sepia	.65	.50
C318	AP43	1.75g grnsh bl & sepia	1.40	1.00

Dr. Jan Boesman's balloon flight, Mexico City, Nov. 1968.

Miniature Sheet

Cachet of May 2, 1925 Flight — AP44

Black Cachets, Magenta Inscriptions and Rose Lilac Background

1968, Nov. 28   Litho.   **Perf. 13½x14**

C318A	AP44	Sheet of 12	16.50	16.50
b.		70c 2 Mai 1925	.70	.80
c.		70c 2 Septembre 1925	.70	.80
d.		70c 28 Mars 1927	.70	.80
f.		70c 12 Juillet 1927	.70	.80
f.		70c 13 Septembre 1927	.70	.80
g.		70c 6 Fevrier 1928	.70	.80

Galiffet 1784 balloon flight and pioneer flights of the 1920's. No. C318A contains 2 each of Nos. C318b-C318g. The background of the sheet shows in white outlines a balloon and the inscription "BALLON GALIFFET 1784." The design of each stamp shows a different airmail cachet, date of a special flight and part of the white background design.

Churchill Type of Regular Issue
Churchill: 50c, and early seaplane. 75c, and soldiers at Normandy. 1g, and Queen Elizabeth II. 1.50g, and Big Ben, London. 3g, and coat of arms, horiz.

1968, Dec. 23   Photo.   **Perf. 13**

C319	A128	50c gold & multi	.40	.25
C320	A128	75c gold & multi	.50	.40
C321	A128	1g gold & multi	.65	.50
C322	A128	1.50g gold & multi	.80	.60
		Nos. C319-C322 (4)	2.35	1.75

Souvenir Sheet
Perf. 12½x13, Imperf.

C323		3g sil, blk & red	6.00	6.00

Nos. C319-C322 exist imperf. Value, $6. No. C323 contains one horizontal stamp. For surcharge, see No. C515. size: 38x25½mm.

Nos. C299-C300 Surcharged

1969, Feb. 21   Photo.   **Perf. 11½**

C324	A122	70c on 50c	.80	.40
C325	A122	1.75g on 1g	.80	.50

Bird Type of Regular Issue
Birds of Haiti: 50c, Hispaniolan trogon. 1g, Black-cowled oriole. 1.50g, Stripe-headed tanager. 2g, Striated woodpecker.

HAITI

1969, Feb. 26 — *Perf. 13½*
C326	A129	50c multi	3.00 .85
C327	A129	1g lt bl & multi	3.75 1.40
C328	A129	1.50g multi	4.50 2.00
C329	A129	2g gray & multi	5.00 2.50
	Nos. C326-C329 (4)		16.25 6.75

For overprints see Nos. C344A-C344D.

Electric Power Type of 1969
1969, May 22 — *Litho.* *Perf. 13x13½*
C338	A131	20c dk bl & lil	.25 .25
C339	A131	25c grn & rose red	.25 .25
C340	A131	25c rose red & grn	.25 .25
	Nos. C338-C340 (3)		.75 .75

Education Type of 1969
Designs: 50c, Peace poster on educational television, vert. 1g, Learning to write. 1.50g, Playing children, vert.

1969, Aug. 12 — *Litho.* *Perf. 13½*
C342	A132	50c multi	.30 .25
C343	A132	1g multi	.50 .40
C344	A132	1.50g multi	.80 .50
	Nos. C342-C344 (3)		1.60 1.15

Nos. C326-C329 Overprinted

1969, Aug. 29 — *Photo.* *Perf. 13½*
C344A	A129	50c multi	1.25 1.25
C344B	A129	1g lt bl & multi	2.40 2.40
C344C	A129	1.50g multi	4.50 4.50
C344D	A129	2g gray & multi	5.75 5.75
	Nos. C344A-C344D (4)		13.90 13.90

ILO Type of Regular Issue
1969, Sept. 22 — *Perf. 14*
C345	A133	25c red & blk	.30 .25
C346	A133	70c org & blk	.65 .25
C347	A133	1.75g brt pur & blk	1.40 .70
	Nos. C345-C347 (3)		2.35 1.20

Butterfly Type of Regular Issue
50c, Danaus eresimus kaempfferi. 1.50g, Anaea marthesia nemesis. 2g, Prepona antimache.

1969, Nov. 14 — *Photo.* *Perf. 13½*
C348	A134	50c multi	7.00 3.00
C349	A134	1.50g multi	13.00 4.00
C350	A134	2g yel & multi	20.00 6.00
	Nos. C348-C350 (3)		40.00 13.00

King Type of Regular Issue
1970, Jan. 12 — *Litho.* *Perf. 12½x13½*
C351	A135	50c emer, red & blk	.45 .25
C352	A135	1g brick red, red & blk	.80 .60
C353	A135	1.50g brt bl, red & blk	1.20 .85
	Nos. C351-C353 (3)		2.45 1.70

Orchid Type of Regular Issue
Haitian Orchids: 50c, Tetramicra elegans. 1.50g, Epidendrum truncatum. 2g, Oncidium desertorum.

1970, Apr. 3 — *Litho.* *Perf. 13x12½*
C354	A136	50c buff, brn & mag	2.25 .25
C355	A136	1.50g multi	3.75 2.50
C356	A136	2g lilac & multi	5.50 3.50
	Nos. C354-C356 (3)		11.50 6.25

UPU Type of Regular Issue
Designs: 50c, Globe and doves. 1.50g, Propeller and UPU emblem, vert. 2g, UPU Monument and map of Haiti.

1970, June 23 — *Photo.* *Perf. 11½*
C357	A137	50c blk & vio	.35 .25
C358	A137	1.50g multi	.65 .45
C359	A137	2g multi	.95 .65
a.	Souvenir sheet of 3, #C357-C359, imperf.		2.50 2.25
	Nos. C357-C359 (3)		1.95 1.35

Nos. C357-C359a Overprinted in Red with UN Emblem and: "XXVe ANNIVERSAIRE / O.N.U."

1970, Dec. 14 — *Photo.* *Perf. 11½*
C360	A137	50c blk & vio	.35 .25
C361	A137	1.50g multi	.65 .45
C362	A137	2g multi	.95 .65
a.	Souvenir sheet of 3		3.50 3.00
	Nos. C360-C362 (3)		1.95 1.35

United Nations, 25th anniversary.

Haitian Nativity — AP45

1970, Dec. 22
C363	AP45	1.50g sepia & multi	.65 .45
C364	AP45	1.50g ultra & multi	.65 .45
C365	AP45	2g multi	1.10 .65
	Nos. C363-C365 (3)		2.40 1.55

Christmas 1970.

Painting Type of Regular Issue
Paintings: 50c, Nativity, by Rigaud Benoit. 1g, Head of a Negro, by Rubens. 1.50g, Ascension, by Castera Bazile (like No. 648).

1971, Apr. 29 — *Litho.* *Perf. 12x12½*
Size: 20x40mm
C366	A140	50c multi	.50 .25
C367	A140	1g multi	.80 .65
C368	A140	1.50g multi	1.10 .80
	Nos. C366-C368 (3)		2.40 1.70

Nos. C366-C368 exist imperf in changed colors.

Balloon and Haiti No. C2 — AP46

1971, Dec. 22 — *Photo.* *Perf. 11½*
C369	AP46	20c bl, red org & blk	.30 .25
C370	AP46	50c ultra, red org & blk	.50 .25
C371	AP46	1g org & blk	1.25 .35
C372	AP46	1.50g lil rose & blk	1.90 .45
	Nos. C369-C372 (4)		3.95 1.30

Souvenir Sheet
Imperf
C373	AP46	50c brt grn & multi	9.00 4.50

40th anniv. (in 1969) of air post service in Haiti.

For overprints see Nos. C374-C377, C380-C386.

Nos. C369-C372 Overprinted

1972, Mar. 17 — *Perf. 11½*
C374	AP46	20c multi	.25 .25
C375	AP46	50c multi	.35 .35
C376	AP46	1g org & blk	.55 .55
C377	AP46	1.50g lil rose & blk	.65 .55
	Nos. C374-C377 (4)		1.80 1.60

14th INTERPEX, NYC, Mar. 17-19.

Dessalines Type of Regular Issue
1972, Apr. 28 — *Photo.* *Perf. 11½*
C378	A142	50c yel grn & blk	.35 .25
C379	A142	2.50g lil & blk	1.10 .65

For surcharge see No. C438.

Nos. C369-C372 Overprinted

1972, May 4
C380	AP46	20c multi	.25 .25
C381	AP46	50c multi	.35 .25
C382	AP46	1g org & blk	.45 .35
C383	AP46	1.50g lil rose & blk	.65 .45
	Nos. C380-C383 (4)		1.70 1.30

HAIPEX, 5th Congress.

Nos. C370-C372 Overprinted

1972, July
C384	AP46	50c multi	.35 .25
C385	AP46	1g org & blk	.45 .35
C386	AP46	1.50g lil rose & blk	.65 .45
	Nos. C384-C386 (3)		1.45 1.05

Belgica '72, International Philatelic Exhibition, Brussels, June 24-July 9.

Tower of the Sun, EXPO '70 Emblem — AP47

1972, Oct. 27
C387	AP47	50c bl, lake & dk bl	.35 .25
C388	AP47	1g bl, lake & red	.45 .35
C389	AP47	1.50g bl, lake & brn	.65 .45
C390	AP47	2.50g bl, lake & grn	.95 .55
	Nos. C387-C390 (4)		2.50 1.60

EXPO '70 International Exposition, Osaka, Japan, Mar. 15-Sept. 13, 1970.
For surcharges see Nos. C447-C447A.

Souvenir Sheets

1972 Summer Olympics, Munich — AP47a

Designs: 2.50g, Israeli delegation, opening ceremony in Munich Stadium. 5g, Assassinated Israeli athlete David Berger.

1973 — *Perf. 13½*
C390A	AP47a	2.50g multi	2.00 2.00
C390B	AP47a	5g multi	2.25 1.50

No. C390B contains one 22½x34mm stamp.

Headquarters and Map of Americas — AP48

1973, May 11 — *Litho.* *Perf. 14½*
C391	AP48	50c dk bl & multi	.35 .25
C392	AP48	80c multi	.50 .35
C393	AP48	1.50g vio & multi	.60 .45
C394	AP48	2g brn & multi	.85 .55
	Nos. C391-C394 (4)		2.30 1.60

70th anniversary (in 1972) of the Panamerican Health Organization.

Marine Life Type of Regular Issue
50c, Platypodia spectabilis, horiz. 85c, Goniaster tessellatus. 1.50g, Stephanocyathus diadema, horiz. 2g, Phyllangia americana.

1973, Sept. 4 — *Perf. 14*
C395	A145	50c multicolored	1.00 .25
C396	A145	85c multicolored	1.40 .25
C397	A145	1.50g multicolored	2.00 .30
C398	A145	2g multicolored	2.50 .40
	Nos. C395-C398 (4)		6.90 1.20

For surcharge see No. C439.

Fish Type of Regular Issue
Tropical fish: 50c, Gramma melacara. 85c, Holacanthus tricolor. 1.50g, Liopropoma rubre. 5g, Clepticus parrai.

1973 — *Perf. 13½*
C399	A146	50c multicolored	.75 .50
C400	A146	85c multicolored	.85 .65
C401	A146	1.50g multicolored	1.50 .75
C402	A146	5g multicolored	4.25 1.90
	Nos. C399-C402 (4)		7.35 3.80

For surcharge see No. C440.

Haitian Flag — AP49

Nos. C404, C405, Haitian flag and coat of arms. No. C406, Flag and Pres. Jean-Claude Duvalier.

1973, Nov. 18 — *Perf. 14½x14*
Size: 35x22½mm
C403	AP49	80c blk & red	.45 .35
C404	AP49	80c red & blk	.45 .35

Perf. 14x13½
Size: 42x27mm
C405	AP49	1.85g blk & red	.95 .65
C406	AP49	1.85g red & blk	.95 .65
	Nos. C403-C406 (4)		2.80 2.00

For overprints and surcharges see Nos. C427-C428, C432-C433, C441-C442.

Soccer Type of Regular Issue
50c, 80c, Soccer Stadium. 1.75g, 10g, Haiti #654.

1973, Nov. 29 — *Perf. 14x13*
C407	A147	50c multi	.35 .25
C408	A147	80c multi	.45 .35
C409	A147	1.75g multi	.95 .45
C410	A147	10g multi	3.25 2.25
	Nos. C407-C410 (4)		5.00 3.30

Dessalines Type of 1974
1974, Apr. 22 — *Photo.* *Perf. 14*
C411	A148	50c brn & grnsh bl	.35 .25
C412	A148	80c gray & brn	.45 .35
C413	A148	1g lt grn & mar	.55 .45
C414	A148	1.75g lil & ol brn	.95 .55
	Nos. C411-C414 (4)		2.30 1.60

For surcharge see No. C443.

Copernicus Type of 1974
Designs: No. C415, 80c, 1.50g, 1.75g, Symbol of heliocentric system. No. C416, 1g, 2.50g, Nicolaus Copernicus.

1974, May 24 — *Litho.* *Perf. 14x13½*
C415	A149	50c org & multi	.35 .25
C416	A149	50c yel & multi	.35 .25
C417	A149	80c multi	.45 .35
C418	A149	1g multi	.55 .45
C419	A149	1.75g brn & multi	.95 .55
	Nos. C415-C419 (5)		2.65 1.85

Souvenir Sheet
Imperf
C420		Sheet of 2	2.50 2.50
a.	A149 1.50g light green & multi		.90 .90
b.	A149 2.50g deep orange & multi		1.40 1.40

For overprint and surcharges see Nos. C444, C460-C463.

Pres. Duvalier Type of 1974
1974 — *Photo.* *Perf. 14x13½*
C421	A151	50c vio brn & gold	.35 .25
C422	A151	80c rose red & gold	.45 .35
C423	A151	1g red lil & gold	.65 .45
C424	A151	1.50g Prus bl & gold	1.00 .65
C425	A151	1.75g brt vio & gold	1.25 .65
C426	A151	5g ol grn & gold	2.75 1.50
	Nos. C421-C426 (6)		6.45 3.85

For surcharge and overprints see Nos. C445, C487-C489.

Nos. C405-C406 Surcharged in Violet Blue

1975, July 15 — *Litho.* *Perf. 14x13½*
C427	AP49	80c on 1.85g, #C405	1.50 1.50
C428	AP49	80c on 1.85g, #C406	1.50 1.50

HAITI

Nos. C405-C406 Overprinted in Blue

1975, July 15 Litho. *Perf. 14x13½*
C432	AP49	1.85g blk & red	.95	.65
C433	AP49	1.85g red & blk	.95	.65

Centenary of Universal Postal Union. "100 ANS" in 2 lines on No. C433.

Names of Haitian Participants at Siege of Savannah
AP50

1976, Apr. 22 Photo. *Perf. 11½*
Granite Paper
C434	AP50	50c multi	.35	.25
C435	AP50	80c multi	.55	.35
C436	AP50	1.50g multi	.80	.55
C437	AP50	7.50g multi	2.75	1.90
	Nos. C434-C437 (4)		4.45	3.05

American Bicentennial.

Stamps of 1972-74 Surcharged with New Value and Bar in Black or Violet Blue
Photogravure; Lithographed

1976 *Perf. 11½, 13½, 14x13½, 14*
C438	A142	80c on 2.50g, #C379	.55	.35
C439	A145	80c on 85c, #C396	.55	.35
C440	A146	80c on 85c, #C400	.55	.35
C441	AP49	80c on 1.85g, #C405	.55	.35
C442	AP49	80c on 1.85g, #C406	.55	.35
C443	A148	80c on 1.75g, #C414 (VB)	.55	.35
C444	A149	80c on 1.75g, #C419 (VB)	.55	.35
C445	A151	80c on 1.75g, #C425	.55	.35
C446	AP50	80c on 1.50g, #C436	.55	.35
C447	AP47	80c on 1.50g, #C389	.55	.35
C447A	AP47	80c on 2.50g, #C390	.55	.35
	Nos. C438-C447A (11)		6.05	3.85

Black surcharge of Nos. C441-C442 differs from the violet blue surcharge of Nos. C427-C428 in type face, arrangement of denomination and bar, and size of bar (10x6mm).

Dessalines Type of 1972
1976-77 Photo. *Perf. 11½*
Granite Paper
C448	A142	75c yel & blk	.35	.25
C449	A142	80c emer & blk	.35	.25
C450	A142	1g bl & blk	.45	.35
C451	A142	1g red brn & blk	.55	.45
C452	A142	1.25g yel grn & blk	.45	.35
C453	A142	1.50g bl gray & blk	.45	.35
C454	A142	1.75g rose & blk	.55	.45
C455	A142	2g ol & blk	.65	.55
C457	A142	5g bl grn & blk	1.75	1.10
C458	A142	10g ocher & blk	3.50	2.10
	Nos. C448-C458 (10)		9.05	6.40

Issued: 75c, 80c, No. C451, 1,75g, 5g, 10g, 1977.

Nos. C415-C416, C418-C419 Overprinted or Surcharged in Black, Dark Blue or Green

1977, July 6 Litho. *Perf. 14x13½*
C460	A149	1g (Bk)	.45	.35
C461	A149	1.25g on 50c (DB)	.55	.45
C462	A149	1.25g on 50c (G)	.55	.45
C463	A149	1.25g on 85c (Bk)	.55	.45
	Nos. C460-C463 (4)		2.10	1.70

Charles A. Lindbergh's solo transatlantic flight from NY to Paris, 50th anniv.

Telephone Type of 1978
Designs: 1g, Telstar over globe. 1.25g, Duvalier Earth Telecommunications Station. 2g, Wall telephone, 1890, vert.

1978, June 19 Litho. *Perf. 13½*
C466	A153	1g multi	.45	.35
C467	A153	1.25g multi	.55	.45
C468	A153	2g multi	.85	.55
	Nos. C466-C468 (3)		1.85	1.35

Olympic Games Type of 1978
Montreal Olympic Games' Emblem. 1.25g, Equestrian. 2.50g, Basketball. 5g, Yachting.

1978, Sept. 4 Litho. *Perf. 13½x13*
C469	A154	1.25g multi	.70	.60
C470	A154	2.50g multi	1.50	1.20
C471	A154	5g multi	3.50	1.50
	Nos. C469-C471 (3)		5.70	3.35

Children's Institute Type, 1979
Designs: 1.25g, Mother nursing child. 2g, Nurse giving injection.

1979, Jan. 15 Photo. *Perf. 14x14½*
C472	A155	1.25g multi	.55	.35
C473	A155	2g multi	.80	.55

Haitians Spinning Cotton, CARE Workshop — **AP51**

1979, May 11 Photo. *Perf. 11½*
C474	AP51	1g multi	.65	.55
C475	AP51	1.25g multi	.95	.65
C476	AP51	2g multi	1.40	.85
	Nos. C474-C476 (3)		3.00	2.05

30th anniversary of CARE.

Human Rights Type of 1979
1979, July 20 Litho. *Perf. 14*
C477	A157	1g multi	.65	.55
C478	A157	1.25g multi	.95	.65
C479	A157	2g multi	1.40	.85
	Nos. C477-C479 (3)		3.00	2.05

Anti-Apartheid Year Type of 1979
1979, Nov. 22 Photo. *Perf. 12x11½*
C480	A158	1g yel grn & blk	1.00	.55
C481	A158	1.25g bl & blk	1.10	.65
C482	A158	2g gray olive	1.75	.85
	Nos. C480-C482 (3)		3.85	2.05

IYC Type of 1979
1979, Dec. 19 Photo. *Perf. 12*
C483	A159	1g multi	.65	.55
C484	A159	1.25g multi	.95	.65
C485	A159	2.50g multi	2.50	1.10
C486	A159	5g multi	3.50	1.60
	Nos. C483-C486 (4)		7.60	3.90

Nos. C421, C424-C425 Overprinted

1980, May 17 Photo. *Perf. 14x13½*
C487	A151	50c multi	.35	.25
C488	A151	1.50g multi	.95	.45
C489	A151	1.75g multi	1.20	.55
	Nos. C487-C489 (3)		2.50	1.25

Wedding of Pres. Duvalier, May 27.

Dessalines Type of 1972
1980, Aug. 27 Photo. *Perf. 11½*
Granite Paper
C490	A142	2g gray vio & blk	.55	.45
C491	A142	1.25g sal pink & blk	.65	.55
C492	A142	2g pale grn & blk	1.20	.85
C493	A142	5g lt bl & blk	2.40	1.60
	Nos. C490-C493 (4)		4.80	3.45

For surcharge see No. C512.

Tourism Type
1980, Dec. 2 Litho. *Perf. 12½x12*
C494	A160	1g like #728	.55	.45
C495	A160	1.25g like #729	.65	.55
C496	A160	1.50g Carnival dancers	.95	.55
C497	A160	2g Vendors	1.20	.85
C498	A160	2.50g like #C497	1.40	1.10
	Nos. C494-C498 (5)		4.75	3.50

For surcharge see No. C511.

Soccer Type of 1980
50c, Uruguay, 1950. 75c, Germany, 1954. 1g, Brazil, 1958. 1.25g, Brazil, 1962. 1.50g, Gt. Britain, 1966. 1.75g, Brazil, 1970. 2g, Germany, 1974. 5g, Argentina, 1978.

1980, Dec. 30 Litho. *Perf. 14*
C499	A161	50c multi	.35	.25
C500	A161	75c multi	.45	.35
C501	A161	1g multi	.65	.45
C502	A161	1.25g multi	.80	.55
C503	A161	1.50g multi	1.10	.65
C504	A161	1.75g multi	1.25	.85
C505	A161	2g multi	1.40	.95
C506	A161	5g multi	3.50	2.10
	Nos. C499-C506 (8)		9.50	6.15

Painting Type of 1981
1981, May 12 Photo. *Perf. 11½*
C507	A162	50c like #734	.35	.25
C508	A162	1.25g like #735	.65	.55
C509	A162	2g like #736	1.25	.85
C510	A162	5g like #737	2.40	1.60
	Nos. C507-C510 (4)		4.65	3.25

Nos. C496, C493 Surcharged
Perf. 12½x12, 11½

1981, Dec. 30 Litho., Photo.
C511	A160	1.25g on 1.50g multi	.65	.55
C512	A142	2g on 5g multi	1.20	.85

Dessalines Type of 1972
1982, Jan. 25 Photo. *Perf. 11½*
Granite Paper
C513	A142	1.25g lt brn & blk	.65	.55
C514	A142	2g lilac & blk	1.20	.85

No. C320 Surcharged

2000? Photo. *Perf. 13*
C515	A128	3g on 75c #C320	—	—

The existence of No. C515 is questioned by experts. Editors are interested in seeing any examples of this stamp.

AIR POST SEMI-POSTAL STAMPS

Coubertin Semipostal Type of 1939
Unwmk.

1939, Oct. 3 Engr. *Perf. 12*
CB1	SP1	60c + 40c multi	25.00	25.00
CB2	SP1	1.25g + 60c multi	25.00	25.00

Mosquito and National Sanatorium
SPAP2

1949, July 22 Cross in Carmine
CB3	SPAP2	20c + 20c sep	11.00	6.00
CB4	SPAP2	30c + 30c dp grn	11.00	6.00
CB5	SPAP2	45c + 45c lt red brn	11.00	6.00
CB6	SPAP2	80c + 80c pur	11.00	6.00
CB7	SPAP2	1.25g + 1.25g car rose	11.00	6.00
a.	Souvenir sheet		40.00	40.00
CB8	SPAP2	1.75g + 1.75g bl	11.00	6.00
a.	Souvenir sheet			
	Nos. CB3-CB8 (6)		66.00	36.00

The surtax was used for fighting tuberculosis and malaria.

Catalogue values for unused stamps in this section, from this point to the end of the section, are for Never Hinged items.

No. C113 Surcharged in Deep Carmine

1958, Aug. 30 Litho. *Perf. 13x13½*
CB9	A82	2.50g + 50c	2.50	2.40

The surtax was for the Red Cross.

Similar Surcharge in Red on One Line on Nos. C133-C135

1959, Apr. 7 Photo. *Perf. 11½*
Granite Paper
CB10	AP35	50c + 25c pink, car & ultra	.40	.40
CB11	A87	75c + 25c brt bl	.50	.50
CB12	A87	1g + 25c brn	.75	.75

Nos. C139-C141 Surcharged Like No. CB9 in Red
CB13	AP36	50c + 50c grn & lil	1.00	1.00
CB14	AP36	1.50g + 50c ol & red brn	1.00	1.00
CB15	AP36	2.50g + 50c pur & dk bl	1.25	1.25
	Nos. CB10-CB15 (6)		4.90	4.90

Surtax for the Red Cross.

Nos. C142-C144 Surcharged Diagonally

1959, July 23 Unwmk. *Perf. 12*
CB16	A89	1g + 20c	1.00	1.00
CB17	A89	2g + 20c	1.10	1.10
CB18	A89	2.50g + 20c	1.10	1.10
	Nos. CB16-CB18 (3)		3.20	3.20

World Refugee Year, July 1, 1959-June 30, 1960. A similar surcharge of 50c was applied horizontally to stamps in No. C144a. Value $25.

C145-C147 Surcharged in Dark Carmine

1959, Oct. 30 Photo. *Perf. 14*
CB19	A91	50c + 75c hn brn & aqua	1.00	1.00
CB20	A90	1g + 75c lil & aqua	1.00	1.00
CB21	A90	1.50g + 75c multi	1.00	1.00
	Nos. CB19-CB21 (3)		3.00	3.00

The surtax was for Haitian athletes. On No. CB19, surcharge lines are spaced to total depth of 16mm.

Nos. C129-C130 Surcharged in Red: "Hommage a l'UNICEF +G. 0,50" Engraved and Lithographed

1960, Feb. 2 *Perf. 11½*
CB22	AP34	2g + 50c	1.00	1.00
CB23	AP34	2.50g + 50c	1.75	1.75

Issued to honor UNICEF.

Nos. C151-C152 Surcharged and Overprinted: "ALPHABETISATION" in Red or Black.

1960, July 12 Litho. *Perf. 12½x13*
CB24	A92	50c + 20c (R)	.40	.40
CB25	A92	50c + 30c	.65	.65
CB26	A92	1g + 20c (R)	.90	.75
CB27	A92	1g + 30c	.90	.75
	Nos. CB24-CB27 (4)		2.85	2.45

HAITI

Olympic Games Issue
Nos. C163-C164 Surcharged
1960, Sept. 9   Photo.   *Perf. 12*

CB28	A94	50c + 25c	.40	.25
CB29	A94	1.50g + 25c	.65	.55

Nos. C168-C169 Surcharged:
"UNICEF +25 centimes"
1961, Jan. 14   Engr.   *Perf. 10½*

CB30	A96	50c + 25c red org & blk	.40	.25
CB31	A96	1.50g + 25c dk bl & blk	.65	.55

Nos. C171, C175-C176 Surcharged

1961, Sept. 30   Photo.   *Perf. 11½*

CB32	AP37	20c + 25c	.40	.30
CB33	AP37	1g + 25c	.50	.40
CB34	AP37	1.50g + 25c	.60	.60
		Nos. CB32-CB34 (3)	1.50	1.30

Issued to commemorate the 18th Boy Scout World Conference, Lisbon, Sept. 19-24, 1961. The surtax was for the Red Cross. Additional proceeds from the sale of Nos. CB32-CB34 benefited the Port-au-Prince airport project.

The same surcharge was also applied to No. C176a. Value $3.

Nos. C168-C169 Surcharged:
"OMS SNEM +20 CENTIMES"
1961, Dec. 11   Engr.   *Perf. 10½*

CB35	A96	50c + 20c	1.60	1.60
CB36	A96	1.50g + 20c	2.25	2.25

Issued to publicize Haiti's participation in the UN malaria eradication drive.

Nos. C123, C126-C127 and C131-C132 Surcharged in Black or Red

Engraved and Lithographed
1961-62   *Perf. 11½*

CB37	AP34	50c + 25c	.25	.25
CB38	AP34	1g + 50c	.35	.35
CB39	AP34	2.50g + 50c (R) ('62)	.65	.65
CB40	AP34	5g + 50c	1.10	1.10
CB41	AP34	7.50g + 50c (R) ('62)	1.50	1.50
		Nos. CB37-CB41 (5)	3.85	3.85

The surtax was for the benefit of the urban rehabilitation program in Duvalier Ville.

Nos. C188-C190 Surcharged: "+25 centimes"
1962, Sept. 13   Litho.   *Perf. 12*

CB42	A99	20c + 25c	.25	.25
CB43	A99	50c + 25c	.40	.25
CB44	A99	1g + 25c	.50	.40
		Nos. CB42-CB44 (3)	1.15	.80

Nos. C191-C192 Surcharged in Red: "+0.20"
1962   *Perf. 12½x13*

CB45	A92	50c + 20c	.40	.40
CB46	A92	1g + 20c	.50	.50

Nos. C203 and C205 Surcharged: "ALPHABETISATION" and "+0, 10"
1963, Mar. 15   Photo.   *Perf. 14x14½*

CB47	AP38	50c + 10c	.40	.25
CB48	AP38	1.50g + 10c	.50	.40

No. C110 Surcharged in Red

Surcharge includes Olympic Emblem and: "JEUX OLYMPIQUES / D'HIVER / INNSBRUCK 1964".

1964, July 27   Photo.   *Perf. 11½*

CB49	A80	2.50g + 50c + 10c	.90	.80

See note after No. B34. The 50c+10c surtax went for charity.

No. C213 Surcharged in Red

Engraved and Photogravure
1964, Oct. 2   *Perf. 13½x14*

CB50	AP39	2.50g + 1.25g on 1.50g	1.40	1.25

Issued to commemorate the centenary (in 1963) of the International Red Cross.

Nos. C223-C226 Surcharged: "+ 5c."
1965, Mar. 15   Photo.   *Perf. 11½*

CB51	A105	50c + 5c pale lil & dk brn	.40	.25
CB52	A105	50c + 5c pale grn & dk brn	.40	.25
CB53	A105	75c + 5c buff & dk brn	.40	.25
CB54	A105	1.50g + 5c gray & dk brn	.80	.65
		Nos. CB51-CB54 (4)	2.10	1.45

The souvenir sheet No. C226a was surcharged "+25c." Value, $8. See note following No. B37.

Nos. C251 and C253 Surcharged and Overprinted

Overprint includes Haitian Scout Emblem and "12e Jamboree / Mondial 1967" Like Regular Issue.

1967, Aug. 21   Photo.   *Perf. 11½*

CB55	A111	50c + 10c multi	.50	.40
CB56	A111	1.50g + 50c multi	.65	.50

See note after No. B40.

No. C269 Surcharged Like Regular Issue
Lithographed and Photogravure
1968, Jan. 18   *Perf. 13x13½*

CB57	A115	2.50g + 1.25g on 1.50g	3.25	2.50
a.		Double surcharge	15.00	
b.		Inverted surcharge	25.00	

See note after No. 579.

Nos. C285-C287 Surcharged "CULTURE + 10"
1968, July 4   Litho.   *Perf. 11½*

CB58	A120	50c + 10c multi	.40	.25
CB59	A120	1g + 10c multi	.50	.40
CB60	A120	1.50g + 10c multi	.65	.50
		Nos. CB58-CB60 (3)	1.55	1.15

Nos. C314 and C316 Surcharged in Red

Surcharge includes Red Cross and: "50ème. Anniversaire / de la Ligue des / Sociétés de la / Croix Rouge".

1969, June 25   Litho.   *Perf. 11½*

CB61	A127	50c + 20c multi	.50	.40
CB62	A127	1.50g + 25c multi	.90	.50

League of Red Cross Societies, 50th anniv.

AIR POST OFFICIAL STAMPS

Nos. C172-C176 and C176a Overprinted: "OFFICIEL"
Perf. 11½
1961, Mar.   Unwmk.   Photo.

CO1	AP37	50c rose brn & grn		.60
CO2	AP37	50c brt grnsh bl & ol grn		.60
CO3	AP37	50c gray & grn		.60
CO4	AP37	1g gray ol & ver		.85
CO5	AP37	1.50g brt pink & dk bl		1.40
a.		Sheet of 3		3.75
		Nos. CO1-CO5 (5)		4.05

Nos. CO1-CO5a only available canceled.

Catalogue values for unused stamps in this section, from this point to the end of the section, are for Never Hinged items.

Jean Jacques Dessalines — OA1

1962, Mar. 7   Photo.   *Perf. 14x14½*
Size: 20½x38mm

CO6	OA1	50c dk bl & sepia	.50	.40
CO7	OA1	1g lt bl & maroon	.80	.50
CO8	OA1	1.50g bister & bl	1.00	.70

Size: 30x40mm

CO9	OA1	5g rose & ol grn	2.75	2.40
		Nos. CO6-CO9 (4)	5.05	4.00

Inscription at bottom of No. CO9 is in 2 lines.

AIR POST PARCEL POST STAMPS

Catalogue values for unused stamps in this section are for Never Hinged items.

Nos. C112 and C111 Overprinted in Red

Perf. 11½
1960, Nov. 21   Unwmk.   Photo.

CQ1	A81	50c orange & black	.50	.40
CQ2	A80	5g bluish blk & saph	3.50	2.60

Type of Parcel Post Stamps, 1961
Inscribed "Poste Aerienne"
1961, Mar. 24   *Perf. 14*

CQ3	PP1	2.50g yel grn & mar	2.00	1.40
CQ4	PP1	5g org & green	2.50	1.60

SPECIAL DELIVERY STAMP

The catalogue value for the unused stamp in this section is for Never Hinged.

Postal Administration Building — SD1

Unwmk.
1953, May 4   Engr.   *Perf. 12*

E1	SD1	25c vermilion	.70	.50

POSTAGE DUE STAMPS

D1

1898, Aug.   Unwmk.   Engr.   *Perf. 12*

J1	D1	2c black	1.00	.75
J2	D1	5c red brown	1.50	1.00
J3	D1	10c brown orange	2.00	1.50
J4	D1	50c slate	3.00	2.50
		Nos. J1-J4 (4)	7.50	5.75

For overprints see Nos. J5-J9, J14-J16.

Stamps of 1898 Handstamped like Nos. 67-81
1902   **Black Overprint**

J5	D1	2c black	2.50	1.50
J6	D1	5c red brown	2.50	1.50
J7	D1	10c brown orange	2.50	1.50
J8	D1	50c slate	12.00	7.00

Red Overprint

J9	D1	2c black	3.50	3.50
		Nos. J5-J9 (5)	23.00	15.00

D2

1906

J10	D2	2c dull red	1.50	1.00
J11	D2	5c ultra	2.75	2.50
J12	D2	10c violet	2.75	2.50
J13	D2	50c olive gray	11.50	7.50
		Nos. J10-J13 (4)	18.50	13.50

For surcharges and overprints see Nos. 305-308, J17-J20.

Preceding Issues Handstamped like Nos. 169-201
1914   **On Stamps of 1898**

J14	D1	5c red brown	1.50	1.10
J15	D1	10c brown orange	1.50	1.10
J16	D1	50c slate	6.00	5.50
		Nos. J14-J16 (3)	9.00	7.70

On Stamps of 1906

J17	D2	2c dull red	1.25	1.00
J18	D2	5c ultra	2.25	2.25
J19	D2	10c violet	7.50	5.50
J20	D2	50c olive gray	45.00	45.00
		Nos. J17-J20 (4)	56.00	53.75

The note after No. 201 applies to Nos. J14-J20 also.

Nos. J14-J20 exist with inverted overprint.

Catalogue values for unused stamps in this section, from this point to the end of the section, are for Never Hinged items.

Unpaid Letter — D3

1951, July   Litho.   *Perf. 11½*

J21	D3	10c carmine	.25	.25
J22	D3	20c red brown	.25	.25
J23	D3	40c green	.40	.40
J24	D3	50c orange yellow	.50	.50
		Nos. J21-J24 (4)	1.40	1.40

PARCEL POST STAMPS

Catalogue values for unused stamps in this section are for Never Hinged items.

Nos. 416, 470-471 and 378 Overprinted in Red

Photogravure, Engraved
Perf. 11½, 12
1960, Nov. 21   Unwmk.

Q1	A81	5c yel grn & blk	.25	.25
Q2	A81	10c red org & blk	.25	.25
Q3	A81	25c ultra & black	.40	.25
Q4	A64	2.50g gray	2.75	2.40
		Nos. Q1-Q4 (4)	3.65	3.15

Coat of Arms — PP1

Unwmk.
1961, Mar. 24   Photo.   *Perf. 14*

Q5	PP1	50c bister & purple	.50	.40
Q6	PP1	1g pink & dark blue	.80	.50

See Nos. CQ3-CQ4.

HAITI — HATAY

POSTAL TAX STAMPS

Catalogue values for unused stamps in this section are for Never Hinged items.

Haitian Woman, War Invalids and Ruined Buildings — PT1

1944, Aug. 16   Engr.   Perf. 12
Unwmk.

RA1	PT1 5c dull purple	1.40	.60
RA2	PT1 5c dark blue	1.40	.60
RA3	PT1 5c olive green	1.40	.60
RA4	PT1 5c black	1.40	.60

1945, Dec. 17

RA5	PT1 5c dark green	1.40	.60
RA6	PT1 5c sepia	1.40	.60
RA7	PT1 5c red brown	1.40	.60
RA8	PT1 5c rose carmine	1.40	.60
	Nos. RA1-RA8 (8)	11.20	4.80

The proceeds from the sale of Nos. RA1 to RA8 were for United Nations Relief.

George Washington, J.J. Dessalines and Simón Bolívar — PT2

1949, Sept. 20

RA9	PT2 5c red brown	.50	.40
RA10	PT2 5c olive gray	.50	.40
RA11	PT2 5c blue	.50	.40
RA12	PT2 5c green	.50	.40
RA13	PT2 5c violet	.50	.40
RA14	PT2 5c black	.50	.40
RA15	PT2 5c orange	.50	.40
RA16	PT2 5c carmine rose	.50	.40
	Nos. RA9-RA16 (8)	4.00	3.20

Bicentenary of Port-au-Prince.
For overprint and surcharges see #385-388.

Helicopter Inspection of Hurricane Damage — PT3

1955, Jan. 3   Photo.   Perf. 11½

RA17	PT3 10c bright green	.25	.25
RA18	PT3 10c bright blue	.25	.25
RA19	PT3 10c gray black	.25	.25
RA20	PT3 10c orange	.25	.25
RA21	PT3 20c rose carmine	.35	.25
RA22	PT3 20c deep green	.35	.25
	Nos. RA17-RA22 (6)	1.70	1.50

Helicopter — PT4

1955, May 3

RA23	PT4 10c black, *gray*	.25	.25
RA24	PT4 20c violet blue, *blue*	.25	.25

The surface tint of the sheets of 50, (10x5) of Nos. RA23-RA24, RAC1-RAC2 includes a map of Haiti's southern peninsula which extends over the three center rows of stamps.
The tax was for reconstruction.
See Nos. RAC1-RAC2.

PT5

1959-60   Unwmk.   Photo.   Perf. 11½
Size: 38x22½mm

RA25	PT5 5c green	.30	.25
RA26	PT5 5c black ('60)	.30	.25
RA27	PT5 10c red	.60	.25
	Nos. RA25-RA27 (3)	1.20	.75

1960-61   Size: 28x17mm

RA28	PT5 5c green	.30	.25
RA29	PT5 10c red	.30	.25
RA30	PT5 10c blue ('61)	.30	.25
	Nos. RA28-RA30 (3)	.90	.75

PT6

1963, Sept.   Perf. 14½x14
Size: 13½x21mm

RA31	PT6 10c red orange	.25	.25
RA32	PT6 10c bright blue	.25	.25
RA33	PT6 10c olive	.25	.25
	Nos. RA31-RA33,RAC6-RAC8 (6)	1.50	1.50

1966-69   Photo.   Perf. 14x14½
Size: 17x25mm

RA34	PT6 10c bright green	.25	.25
RA35	PT6 10c violet	.25	.25
RA36	PT6 10c violet blue	.25	.25
RA37	PT6 10c brown ('69)	.25	.25
	Nos. RA34-RA37,RAC9-RAC15 (11)	2.75	2.75

Nos. RA25-RA37 represent a tax for a literacy campaign.
See Nos. RA42-RA45, RAC20-RAC22.

Duvalier de Peligre Hydroelectric Works — PT7

1970-72

RA38	PT7 20c violet & olive	.25	.25
RA39	PT7 20c ultra & blk ('72)	.25	.25

See Nos. RA46, RAC16-RAC19, RAC23.

**Nos. 637-638 Surcharged:
"ALPHABETISATION +10"**

1971, Dec. 23   Litho.   Perf. 14x13½

RA40	A138 20c + 10c multi	.35	.25
a.	Inverted surcharge	2.00	
RA41	A138 25c + 10c multi	.35	.25

Tax was for the literacy campaign.

"CA" Type of 1963

1972-74   Photo.   Perf. 14x14½
Size: 17x25mm

RA42	PT6 5c violet blue	.25	.25
RA43	PT6 5c deep carmine	.25	.25
RA44	PT6 5c ultra ('74)	.25	.25
RA45	PT6 5c carmine rose ('74)	.25	.25
	Nos. RA42-RA45 (4)	1.00	1.00

Tax was for literacy campaign.

Hydroelectric Type of 1970

1980   Photo.   Perf. 14x14½

RA46	PT7 25c choc & green	.25	.25

AIR POST POSTAL TAX STAMPS

Catalogue values for unused stamps in this section are for Never Hinged items.

Helicopter Type of 1955

1955   Unwmk.   Photo.   Perf. 11½

RAC1	PT4 10c red brn, *pale sal*	.35	.25
RAC2	PT4 20c rose pink, *pink*	.40	.25

See note after No. RA24.

Type of Postal Tax Stamps, 1960-61

1959   Size: 28x17mm

RAC3	PT5 5c yellow	.30	.25
RAC4	PT5 10c dull salmon	.30	.25
RAC5	PT5 10c blue	.30	.25
	Nos. RAC3-RAC5 (3)	.90	.75

Type of Postal Tax Stamps, 1963

1963, Sept.   Perf. 14½x14
Size: 13½x21mm

RAC6	PT6 10c dark gray	.25	.25
RAC7	PT6 10c violet	.25	.25
RAC8	PT6 10c brown	.60	.60
	Nos. RAC6-RAC8 (3)		

1966-69   Size: 17x25mm   Perf. 14x14½

RAC9	PT6 10c orange	.25	.25
RAC10	PT6 10c sky blue	.25	.25
RAC11	PT6 10c yellow ('69)	.25	.25
RAC12	PT6 10c carmine ('69)	.25	.25
RAC13	PT6 10c gray grn ('69)	.25	.25
RAC14	PT6 10c lilac ('69)	.25	.25
RAC15	PT6 10c dp claret ('69)	.25	.25
	Nos. RAC9-RAC15 (7)	1.40	1.40

Nos. RAC3-RAC15, RAC20-RAC21 represent a tax for a literacy campaign.

Hydroelectric Type of 1970

1970-74

RAC16	PT7 20c tan & slate	.25	.25
RAC17	PT7 20c brt bl & dl vio	.25	.25
RAC18	PT7 25c sal & bluish blk ('74)	.25	.25
RAC19	PT7 25c yel ol & bluish blk ('74)	.25	.25
	Nos. RAC16-RAC19 (4)	1.00	1.00

"CA" Type of 1963

1973   Photo.   Perf. 14x14½
Size: 17x26mm

RAC20	PT6 10c brn & blue	.35	.25
RAC21	PT6 10c brn & green	.35	.25
RAC22	PT6 10c brn & orange	.35	.25
	Nos. RAC20-RAC22 (3)	1.05	.75

Hydroelectric Power Type of 1970

1979(?)   Photo.   Perf. 14x14½

RAC23	PT7 25c blue & vio brn	.25	.25

HATAY

hä-'tī

LOCATION — Northwest of Syria, bordering on Mediterranean Sea
GOVT. — Semi-independent republic
AREA — 10,000 sq. mi. (approx.)
POP. — 273,350 (1939)
CAPITAL — Antioch

Alexandretta, a semi-autonomous district of Syria under French mandate, was renamed Hatay in 1938 and transferred to Turkey in 1939.

100 Santims = 1 Kurush
40 Paras = 1 Kurush (1939)

Stamps of Turkey, 1931-38, Surcharged in Black

On A77   On A78

1939   Unwmk.   Perf. 11½x12

1	A77 10s on 20pa dp org	1.75	.35
a.	"Sent" instead of "Sant"	140.00	27.50
2	A78 25s on 1ku dk sl grn	2.25	.50
a.	Small "25"	15.00	2.00
3	A78 50s on 2ku dk vio	2.00	.35
a.	Small "50"	7.00	2.50
4	A77 75s on 2½ku green	1.75	.40
5	A78 1ku on 4ku slate	10.00	4.25
6	A78 1ku on 5ku rose red	5.50	1.40
7	A78 1½ku on 3ku brn org	3.50	1.25
8	A78 2½ku on 4ku slate	4.00	1.00
9	A78 5ku on 8ku brt blue	6.00	1.25
10	A77 12½ku on 20ku ol grn	7.00	2.00
11	A77 20ku on 25ku Prus bl	15.00	7.25
	Nos. 1-11 (11)	58.75	20.00
	Set, never hinged	114.00	

Map of Hatay — A1

Lions of Antioch — A2

Flag of Hatay — A3

Post Office — A4

1939   Unwmk.   Typo.   Perf. 12

12	A1 10p orange & aqua	2.50	.75
13	A1 30p lt vio & aqua	2.50	.75
14	A1 1½ku olive & aqua	2.50	.75
15	A2 2½ku turq grn	3.00	1.00
16	A2 3ku light blue	3.00	1.00
17	A2 5ku chocolate	3.50	1.00
18	A3 6ku brt blue & car	3.75	1.25
19	A3 7½ku dp grn & car	4.25	1.40
20	A3 10ku violet & car	5.00	1.40
21	A3 12½ku dk blue & car	4.50	1.50
22	A4 17½ku brown car	8.00	3.00
23	A4 25ku olive brn	9.00	3.50
24	A4 50ku slate blue	18.00	8.75
	Nos. 12-24 (13)	69.50	26.05
	Set, never hinged	137.00	

Stamps of 1939 Overprinted in Black

1939

25	A1 10p orange & aqua	2.00	.90
a.	Overprint reading up	37.50	
26	A1 30p lt vio & aqua	2.00	.90
27	A1 1½ku ol & aqua	2.75	1.00
28	A2 2½ku turq grn	2.75	1.00
29	A2 3ku light blue	3.00	1.00
30	A2 5ku chocolate	3.75	1.40
a.	Overprint inverted	37.50	
31	A3 6ku brt bl & car	4.00	1.40
32	A3 7½ku dp grn & car	4.50	2.25
33	A3 12ku vio & car	4.25	1.50
34	A3 12½ku dk bl & car	4.75	1.50
35	A4 17½ku brn car	6.00	2.50
a.	Overprint inverted	37.50	
36	A4 25ku olive brn	10.00	4.75
37	A4 50ku slate blue	21.00	11.00
	Nos. 25-37 (13)	70.75	31.10
	Set, never hinged	124.00	

The overprint reads "Date of annexation to the Turkish Republic, June 30, 1939."
On Nos. 25-27, the overprint reads down.
On Nos. 28-37, it is horizontal.

POSTAGE DUE STAMPS

Postage Due Stamps of Turkey, 1936, Surcharged or Overprinted in Black

1939   Unwmk.   Perf. 11½

J1	D6 1ku on 2ku lt bl	4.25	1.00
J2	D6 3ku on 3ku bright violet	4.75	1.75
J3	D6 4ku on 5ku Prus bl	5.00	2.00
J4	D6 5ku on 12ku brt rose	5.50	2.00
J5	D6 12ku bright rose	60.00	42.50
	Nos. J1-J5 (5)	79.50	49.25
	Set, never hinged	137.00	

Castle at Antioch — D1

1939   Typo.   Perf. 12

J6	D1 1ku red orange	5.00	2.00
J7	D1 3ku dk olive brown	5.75	2.25
J8	D1 4ku turqoise green	6.25	2.50
J9	D1 5ku slate black	7.25	3.00
	Nos. J6-J9 (4)	24.25	9.75
	Set, never hinged	43.00	

HATAY — HELIGOLAND — HONDURAS

Nos. J6-J9 Overprinted in Black like Nos. 25-37

1939
J10	D1	1ku red orange	4.75	2.00
J11	D1	3ku dk olive brown	5.75	2.25
J12	D1	4ku turqoise green	6.00	2.50
J13	D1	5ku slate black	8.25	3.50
a.		Overprint inverted	45.00	
		Nos. J10-J13 (4)	24.75	10.25
		Set, never hinged	44.00	

HELIGOLAND

ˈhe-lə-gō-ˌland

LOCATION — An island in the North Sea near the northern coast of Germany
GOVT. — Former British Possession
AREA — ¼ sq. mi.
POP. — 2,307 (1900)

Great Britain ceded Heligoland to Germany in 1890. It became part of Schleswig-Holstein province. Stamps of Heligoland were superseded by those of the German Empire.

16 Schillings = 1 Mark
100 Pfennig = 1 Mark = 1 Schilling (1875)

REPRINTS

Most Heligoland issues were extensively reprinted between 1875 and 1895, and these comprise the great majority of Heligoland stamps in the marketplace. Such reprints sell for much less than the originals, usually for $1-$2 each. All stamps on surfaced paper with glossy white gum, and small hole perforations are reprints from Leipzig. All stamps perforated 14 are reprints from Hamburg. Reprints from Berlin are discussed after each listing. Expertization of Heligoland issues is strongly recommended by the editors.

Some Heligoland issues were officially reprinted for the Philatelic Archive in Bonn. A few have become available to the public and are exceedingly scarce.

Queen Victoria
A1 A2
A2a A3

Type I Type II
Type III

Type I: Curl below chignon is rounded
Type II: Curl resembles an upside-down question mark
Type III: Curl is hooked
All stamps with a different head type from the listing are reprints.

Typo., Head Embossed

1867-68 Unwmk. Rouletted 10
1	A1	½sch bl grn & rose, I	315.00	900.00
1A	A2	½sch bl grn & rose, II	725.00	1,500.
2	A1	1sch rose & dp grn	170.00	175.00
3	A3	2sch rose & pale grn, I	12.50	50.00
4	A3	6sch gray grn & rose, I	16.00	350.00

All genuine stamps have a ridge that appears as a very faint gray line near the rouletting, best viewed under angled light. The ridge must be visible on at least one margin. Reprints lack the ridge. The 2sch and 6sch perforated exist only as reprints.

1869-71 Perf. 13½x14¼
Thick Soft Paper
5	A2	½sch ol grn & car rose, II	112.50	145.00
6	A2a	1sch red & yel grn, III	160.00	270.00

Berlin reprints have comparatively poor printing quality. The thin frame line inside the text is broken and often merges with the thick frame line.

A4

1873 Thick Quadrille Paper
7	A4	¼sch pale rose & pale grn, I	30.00	2,000.
a.		¼sch dp carmine & pale yel grn	250.00	2,000.
8	A4	½sch yel grn & rose, I	100.00	3,000.
9	A2	½sch brt grn & rose, I	115.00	265.00
10	A4	¾sch gray grn & pale rose, I	45.00	2,000.
11	A2a	1sch rose & yel grn, III	185.00	225.00
12	A4	1½sch grn & rose, I	60.00	250.00

Reprints are never on quadrille paper.

1874 Thin Wove Paper
13	A4	¼sch rose & yel grn, I		16.00

Berlin reprints are head type 2.

A5 A6
A7

1875 Wove Paper
14	A5	1pf dk rose & dk grn, II	10.00	500.00
15	A5	2pf yel grn & dk rose, II	12.00	800.00
16	A6	5pf dk rose & dk grn, II	19.50	21.50
17	A6	10pf blue grn & red, II	10.00	35.00
a.		10pf yel green & dark rose	100.00	22.50
		No gum	45.00	
b.		10pf lt green & pink red	125.00	22.50
18	A7	25pf rose & dk grn, II	17.00	27.50
a.		25pf dk rose & dk green	17.00	27.50
19	A7	50pf grn & brick red, II	18.00	75.00
a.		50pf dl grn & dk rose	55.00	32.50

Under UV the red in Berlin reprints glows orange. Originals remain dull.
There are no reprints of Nos. 16-19.

Coat of Arms — A8

1876-88 Typo.
20	A8	3pf dp grn & dl red	250.00	1,350.
a.		3pf green & bright red ('77)	160.00	900.00
21	A8	20pf ver & brt yel grn ('88)	12.00	27.50
		No gum	45.00	
b.		20pf lila rose & grn ('82)	215.00	110.00
c.		20pf salmon & yel grn ('85)	375.00	57.50
d.		20pf vio car & yel grn ('76)	215.00	110.00
e.		20pf lila rose & dk grn ('80)	210.00	115.00

The coat-of-arms on Nos. 20, 21 and subvarieties is printed in three colors: varying shades of yellow, red and green.
The 3pf has been reprinted. Reprints usually have a paler red. However some Berlin reprints are the same shade as the originals. Expertizing is strongly recommended.

A9 A10

1879 Typo.
22	A9	1m dp grn & car	200.00	195.00
a.		1m blue green & salmon	175.00	195.00
b.		1m dark green & ver	65.00	
23	A10	5m blue grn & sal	165.00	1,100.

Perf. 11½
24	A9	1m dp grn & car	1,500.	—
25	A10	5m bl grn & rose red	1,500.	
a.		Horiz. pair, imperf. vert.	6,000.	

Nos. 13, 22b, 24 and 25 were never placed in use. Forged cancellations of Nos. 1-23 are plentiful.
Heligoland stamps were replaced by those of the German Empire in 1890.

HONDURAS

hän-ˈdur-əs

LOCATION — Central America, between Guatemala on the north and Nicaragua on the south
GOVT. — Republic
AREA — 43,277 sq. mi.
POP. — 9,910,000 (2020 est.)
CAPITAL — Tegucigalpa

8 Reales = 1 Peso
100 Centavos = 1 Peso (1878)
100 Centavos = 1 Lempira (1933)

Catalogue values for unused stamps in this country are for Never Hinged items, beginning with Scott 344 in the regular postage section, Scott B1 in the semi-postal section, Scott C144 in the airpost section, Scott CB5 in the airpost semi-postal section, Scott CE3 in the airpost special delivery section, Scott CO110 in the airpost official section, and Scott RA6 in the postal tax section.

Values for unused stamps are for examples with original gum as defined in the catalogue introduction. Very fine examples of the locally printed Nos. 95-110, 127, 140, 151-210C, and 218-279 will have margins clear of the perforations but will be noticeably off center.

Watermark

Wmk. 209 — Multiple Ovals

Coat of Arms — A1

1865, Dec. Unwmk. Litho. Imperf.
1	A1	2r black, green	.65	250.00
2	A1	2r black, pink	.65	250.00

Comayagua

Tegucigalpa

Medio real = ½ real
Un real = 1 real
Dos reales = 2 reales

Comayagua Issue
1877, May Red Surcharge
3	A1	½r on 2r blk, grn	70.00

Blue Surcharge
5	A1	2r on 2r blk, grn	150.00	—
6	A1	2r on 2r blk, pink	475.00	—

Black Surcharge
7	A1	1r on 2r blk, grn	150.00	
8	A1	2r on 2r blk, grn	800.00	
9	A1	2r on 2r blk, pink	500.00	500.00

No. 5 may exist only as the base for No. 13a.

Tegucigalpa Issue
1877, July Black Surcharge
13	A1	1r on 2r blk, grn	15.00	35.00
a.		Surcharged on #5	1000.	
14	A1	1r on 2r blk, pink	80.00	80.00
16	A1	2r on 2r blk, pink	100.00	

Blue Surcharge
18	A1	½r on 2r blk, grn	80.00	
19	A1	½r on 2r blk, pink	25.00	
20	A1	1r on 2r blk, grn	35.00	
23	A1	2r on 2r blk, pink	15.00	25.00

Red Surcharge
24	A1	½r on 2r blk, grn	15.00	35.00
25	A1	½r on 2r blk, pink	60.00	60.00

Only the stamps valued or dashed used are known to have been postally used. Nos. 3 and 7 may have been postally used, but to date no examples are recorded used. The other listed stamps were sold as remainders. No covers bearing Nos. 3 to 25 are known.
The blue surcharges range from light blue to violet black. The black surcharge has no tinge of blue. The red surcharges range from light to dark carmine. Some exist double or inverted, but genuine errors are rare. Normal cancel is a blue or black 7-bar killer. Target cancels on Nos. 1-24 are forgeries. Surcharges and cancels have been extensively forged.

Regular Issue

President Francisco Morazán — A4

Printed by National Bank Note Co. of N.Y.
Thin, hard paper, colorless gum
Various Frames

1878, July Engr. Perf. 12
30	A4	1c violet	.50	.50
31	A4	2c brown	.50	.50
32	A4	½r black	5.00	.50
33	A4	1r green	25.00	.50
34	A4	2r deep blue	3.00	6.00
35	A4	4r vermilion	5.00	10.00
36	A4	1p orange	6.00	25.00
		Nos. 30-36 (7)	45.00	42.00

Various counterfeit cancellations exist on Nos. 30-36. Most used copies of Nos. 35-36 offered are actually 35a-36a with fake or favor cancels.

Printed by American Bank Note Co. of N.Y.
Re-Issue Soft paper, yellowish gum
Various Frames

1889
30a	A4	1c deep violet	10.00	10.00
31a	A4	2c red brown	.25	.25
32a	A4	½r black	.25	.25
33a	A4	1r blue green	.25	.25
34a	A4	2r ultramarine	5.00	5.00

HONDURAS

35a	A4	4r scarlet vermilion	.25	.25
36a	A4	1p orange yellow	.25	.25
		Nos. 30a-36a (7)	16.25	

Although Nos. 30a-36a were not intended for postal use, they were valid, and genuine cancels are known on Nos. 31a-34a.

Arms of Honduras — A5

1890, Jan. 6

40	A5	1c yellow green	.30	.30
41	A5	2c red	.30	.30
42	A5	5c blue	.30	.30
43	A5	10c orange	.35	.40
44	A5	20c ocher	.35	.40
45	A5	25c rose red	.35	.40
46	A5	30c purple	.50	.60
47	A5	40c dark blue	.50	.80
48	A5	50c brown	.55	.80
49	A5	75c blue green	.55	2.00
50	A5	1p carmine	.70	2.25
		Nos. 40-50 (11)	4.75	8.55

The tablets and numerals of Nos. 40 to 50 differ for each denomination.
For overprints see Nos. O1-O11.

Used values of Nos. 1-110 are for stamps with genuine cancellations applied while the stamps were valid. Various counterfeit cancellations exist.

A6

President Luis Bográn — A7

1891, July 31

51	A6	1c dark blue	.30	.30
52	A6	2c yellow brown	.30	.30
53	A6	5c blue green	.30	.30
54	A6	10c vermilion	.30	.30
55	A6	20c brown red	.30	.30
56	A6	25c carmine	.40	.55
57	A6	30c slate	.40	.55
58	A6	40c blue green	.40	.55
59	A6	50c black brown	.50	.80
60	A6	75c purple	.50	1.25
61	A6	1p brown	.75	1.60
62	A7	2p brn & black	2.25	5.00
a.		Head inverted	225.00	
63	A7	5p pur & black	2.00	5.75
a.		Head inverted	125.00	
64	A7	10p green & blk	2.00	5.75
a.		Head inverted	125.00	
		Nos. 51-64 (14)	10.70	23.30

Nos. 62, 64 exist with papermakers watermark.
For overprints see Nos. O12-O22.

Columbus Sighting Honduran Coast — A8

1892, July 31

65	A8	1c slate	.40	.45
66	A8	2c deep blue	.40	.45
67	A8	5c yellow green	.40	.45
68	A8	10c blue green	.40	.45
69	A8	20c red	.40	.45
70	A8	25c orange brown	.50	.55
71	A8	30c ultramarine	.50	.60
72	A8	40c orange	.50	.90
73	A8	50c brown	.65	.85
74	A8	75c lake	.75	1.25
75	A8	1p purple	.75	1.40
		Nos. 65-75 (11)	5.65	7.80

Discovery of America by Christopher Columbus, 400th anniv.

General Trinidad Cabanas — A9

1893, Aug.

76	A9	1c green	.25	1.50
77	A9	2c scarlet	.25	1.50
78	A9	5c dark blue	.25	1.50
79	A9	10c orange brn	.25	1.50
80	A9	20c brown red	.25	1.50
81	A9	25c dark blue	.30	1.50
82	A9	30c red orange	.50	1.50
83	A9	40c black	.50	1.50
84	A9	50c olive brn	.50	1.50
85	A9	75c purple	.75	1.50
86	A9	1p deep magenta	.75	1.75
		Nos. 76-86 (11)	4.55	16.75

"Justice" — A10

1895, Feb. 15

87	A10	1c vermilion	.30	.30
88	A10	2c deep blue	.30	.30
89	A10	5c slate	.35	.50
90	A10	10c brown rose	.45	.50
91	A10	20c violet	.45	.50
92	A10	30c deep violet	.45	.85
93	A10	50c olive brown	.55	1.25
94	A10	1p dark green	.60	1.60
		Nos. 87-94 (8)	3.45	5.80

The tablets and numerals of Nos. 76-94 differ for each denomination.

President Celio Arias — A11

1896, Jan. 1 Litho. Perf. 11½

95	A11	1c dark blue	.30	.35
96	A11	2c yellow brn	.30	.35
97	A11	5c purple	1.10	.30
a.		5c red violet	.60	1.10
98	A11	10c vermilion	.40	.40
a.		10c red	4.50	4.50
99	A11	20c emerald	.75	.50
a.		20c deep green		
100	A11	30c ultramarine	.65	.70
101	A11	50c rose	.90	1.00
102	A11	1p black brown	1.25	1.50
		Nos. 95-102 (8)	5.65	5.10

Counterfeits are plentiful. Nos. 95-102 exist imperf. between horiz. or vertically.
Originals of Nos. 95 to 102 are on both thin, semi-transparent paper and opaque paper; reprints are on thicker, opaque paper and usually have a black cancellation "HONDURAS" between horizontal bars.

Railroad Train — A12

1898, Aug. 1

103	A12	1c brown	.50	.25
104	A12	2c rose	.50	.25
105	A12	5c dull ultra	1.00	.25
b.		5c red violet (error)	1.50	.70
106	A12	6c red violet	.90	.25
b.		6c dull rose	1.60	.75
107	A12	10c dark blue	1.00	.30
108	A12	20c dull orange	1.25	.75
109	A12	50c orange red	2.00	1.25
110	A12	1p blue green	4.00	3.00
		Nos. 103-110 (8)	11.15	6.30

Excellent counterfeits of Nos. 103-110 exist.
For overprints see Nos. O23-O27.

Laid Paper

103a	A12	1c	1.00	.70
104a	A12	2c	1.25	.70
105a	A12	5c	1.60	.70
106a	A12	6c	1.60	.75
107a	A12	10c	1.60	1.00
		Nos. 103a-107a (5)	7.05	3.85

General Santos Guardiola — A13

1903, Jan. 1 Engr. Perf. 12

111	A13	1c yellow grn	.35	.25
112	A13	2c carmine rose	.35	.30
113	A13	5c blue	.35	.30
114	A13	6c dk violet	.35	.30
115	A13	10c brown	.40	.30
116	A13	20c dull ultra	.45	.40
117	A13	50c vermilion	1.25	1.10
118	A13	1p orange	1.25	1.10
		Nos. 111-118 (8)	4.75	4.05

"PERMITASE" handstamped on stamps of 1896-1903 was applied as a control mark by the isolated Pacific Coast post office of Amapala to prevent use of stolen stamps.

President José Medina — A14

1907, Jan. 1 Perf. 14

119	A14	1c dark green	.25	.25
120	A14	2c scarlet	.25	.25
120A	A14	2c carmine	9.00	5.50
121	A14	5c blue	.30	.30
122	A14	6c purple	.35	.30
a.		6c dark violet	.80	.60
123	A14	10c gray brown	.40	.35
124	A14	20c ultra	.90	.85
a.		20c blue violet	110.00	110.00
125	A14	50c deep lake	1.10	1.10
126	A14	1p orange	1.50	1.50
a.		1p orange yellow		—
		Nos. 119-126 (9)	14.05	10.40

All values of the above set exist imperforate, imperforate horizontally and in horizontal pairs, imperforate between. No. 124a imperf is worth only 10% of the listed perforated variety.
For surcharges see Nos. 128-130.

1909 Typo. Perf. 11½

127	A14	1c green	1.25	1.00
a.		Imperf., pair	4.00	4.00
b.		Printed on both sides	7.50	10.00

The 1909 issue is roughly typographed in imitation of the 1907 design. It exists pin perf. 8, 13, etc.

No. 124 Handstamp Surcharged in Black, Green or Red

1910, Nov. Perf. 14

128	A14	1c on 20c ultra	8.50	6.00
129	A14	5c on 20c ultra (G)	8.50	6.00
130	A14	10c on 20c ultra (R)	8.50	6.00
		Nos. 128-130 (3)	25.50	18.00

As is usual with handstamped surcharges inverts and double exist.

Honduran Scene — A15

1911, Jan. Litho. Perf. 14, 12 (1p)

131	A15	1c violet	.35	.25
132	A15	2c green	.35	.25
a.		Perf. 12	5.00	1.25
133	A15	5c carmine	.40	.25
a.		Perf. 12	8.00	3.50
134	A15	6c ultramarine	.50	.30
135	A15	10c blue	.60	.40
136	A15	20c yellow	.60	.50
137	A15	50c brown	2.00	1.75
138	A15	1p olive green	2.50	2.00
		Nos. 131-138 (8)	7.30	5.70

For overprints and surcharges see Nos. 139, 141-147, O28-O47.

No. 132a Overprinted in Red

1911, Sept. 19 Perf. 12

139	A15	2c green	20.00	18.00
a.		Inverted overprint	24.00	22.50

90th anniversary of Independence.
Counterfeit overprints on perf. 14 stamps exist.

President Manuel Bonilla — A16

1912, Feb. 1 Typo. Perf. 11½

140	A16	1c orange red	12.00	12.00

Election of Pres. Manuel Bonilla.

Stamps of 1911 Surcharged in Black, Red or Blue

a   b

1913 Litho. Perf. 14

141	A15(a)	2c on 1c violet	1.25	.75
a.		Double surcharge		3.25
b.		Inverted surcharge	4.50	
c.		Double surch., one invtd.	6.75	
d.		Red surcharge	40.00	40.00
142	A15(b)	2c on 1c violet	7.00	5.75
a.		Inverted surcharge	14.00	
143	A15(b)	2c on 10c blue	2.75	2.25
a.		Double surcharge		
b.		Inverted surcharge	5.75	5.75
144	A15(b)	2c on 20c yellow	7.00	6.75
145	A15(b)	5c on 1c violet	2.50	.75
146	A15(b)	5c on 10c bl (Bl)	2.75	1.50
147	A15(b)	6c on 1c violet	2.75	2.25
		Nos. 141-147 (7)	26.00	20.00

Counterfeit surcharges exist.

Terencio Sierra A17   **Bonilla A18**

ONE CENTAVO:
Type I — Solid border at sides below numerals.
Type II — Border of light and dark stripes.

1913-14 Typo. Perf. 11½

151	A17	1c dark brn, I	.40	.35
a.		1c brown, type II	.75	.45
152	A17	2c carmine	.40	.35
153	A18	5c blue	.70	.35
154	A18	5c ultra ('14)	.70	.35
155	A18	6c gray vio	.85	.35
156	A18	6c purple ('14)	.70	.35
a.		6c red lilac	.60	.40
157	A17	10c blue	1.25	1.00
158	A17	10c brown ('14)	2.10	.65
159	A17	20c brown	1.75	1.00
160	A18	50c rose	3.50	2.60
161	A18	1p gray green	3.75	2.90
		Nos. 151-161 (11)	16.10	10.25

For overprints and surcharges see Nos. 162-173, O48-O57.

Surcharged in Black or Carmine

1914

162	A17	1c on 2c carmine	.80	.75
163	A17	5c on 2c carmine	1.40	.90
164	A18	5c on 6c gray vio	2.25	2.00
165	A17	10c on 2c carmine	2.25	2.00
166	A18	10c on 6c gray vio	2.25	2.00
a.		Double surcharge	10.00	
167	A18	10c on 6c gray vio (C)	2.25	2.00
168	A18	10c on 50c rose	7.00	5.00
		Nos. 162-168 (7)	18.20	14.65

HONDURAS

No. 158 Surcharged

1915
173 A17 5c on 10c dk brn ... 2.50 1.75

Ulua Bridge A19

Bonilla Theater A20

1915-16 — Typo.
174	A19	1c chocolate	.25	.25
175	A19	2c carmine	.25	.25
a.		Tête bêche pair	1.00	1.00
176	A20	5c bright blue	.25	.25
177	A20	6c deep purple	.35	.25
178	A20	10c dull blue	.75	.25
179	A19	20c red brown	1.25	1.00
a.		Tête bêche pair	4.00	4.00
180	A20	50c red	1.50	1.50
181	A20	1p yellow grn	2.50	2.50
		Nos. 174-181 (8)	7.10	6.25

For overprints & surcharges see Nos. 183, 231-232, 237, 239-240, 285, 292, C1-C13, C25, C28, C31, C36, C57, CO21, CO30-CO32, CO42, O58-O65.

Imperf., Pairs
174a	A19	1c	2.00	2.00
175b	A19	2c	2.00	2.00
176a	A20	5c	3.50	
178a	A19	10c	3.50	
179b	A19	20c	5.25	
180b	A20	50c	7.00	
181a	A20	1p	8.75	8.75

Francisco Bertrand — A21

1916, Feb. 1
182 A21 1c orange ... 2.00 2.00
Election of Pres. Francisco Bertrand.
Unauthorized reprints exist.

Official Stamp No. O60 Overprinted

1918
183 A20 5c bright blue ... 2.00 1.50
a. Inverted overprint ... 5.00 5.00

Statue to Francisco Morazán — A22

1919 — Typo.
184	A22	1c brown	.40	.35
a.		Printed on both sides	2.00	
b.		Imperf., pair		.70
185	A22	2c carmine	.40	.35
186	A22	5c lilac rose	.40	.35
187	A22	6c brt purple	.40	.35
188	A22	10c dull blue	.40	.35
189	A22	15c light blue	1.25	.35
190	A22	15c dark violet	1.00	.35
191	A22	20c orange brn	1.60	.40
a.		20c gray brown	10.00	.40
b.		Imperf., pair	2.75	
192	A22	50c light brown	6.50	2.50
a.		Imperf. pair	15.00	20.00
193	A22	1p yellow green	12.00	20.00
a.		Imperf., pair	20.00	20.00
b.		Printed on both sides	9.00	
c.		Tête bêche pair	15.00	
		Nos. 184-193 (10)	24.35	25.35

See note on handstamp following No. 217.
Unauthorized reprints exist.
For overprints and surcharges see Nos. 201-210C, 230, 233, 235-236, 238, 241-243, 287, 289, C58, C61, CO23, CO25, CO33, CO36-CO38, CO39, CO40, O66-O74.

"Dawn of Peace" — A23

1920, Feb. 1 — Size: 27x21mm
194	A23	2c rose	2.50	2.50
a.		Tête bêche pair	15.00	12.50
b.		Imperf., pair	20.00	12.50

Size: 51x40mm
195	A23	2c gold	10.00	10.00
196	A23	2c silver	10.00	10.00
197	A23	2c bronze	10.00	10.00
198	A23	2c red	12.00	12.00
		Nos. 194-198 (5)	44.50	44.50

Assumption of power by Gen. Rafael Lopez Gutierrez.
Nos. 195-198 exist imperf.
Unauthorized reprints of Nos. 195-198 exist.

Type of 1919, Dated "1920"

1921
201 A22 6c dark violet ... 10.00 5.00
a. Tête bêche pair ... 15.00
b. Imperf., pair ... 15.00
Unauthorized reprints exist.

No. 185 Surcharged in Antique Letters

1922
202	A22	6c on 2c carmine	.40	.40
a.		"ALE" for "VALE"	2.00	2.00
b.		Comma after "CTS"	2.00	2.00
c.		Without period after "CTS"	2.00	2.00
d.		"CT" for "CTS"	2.00	2.00
e.		Double surcharge	4.25	
f.		Inverted surcharge		4.25

Stamps of 1919 Surcharged in Roman Figures and Antique Letters in Green

1923
203	A22	10c on 1c brown	1.50	1.50
204	A22	50c on 2c carmine	2.00	2.00
a.		Inverted surcharge	10.00	10.00
b.		"HABILTADO"	6.00	6.00

Surcharged in Black or Violet Blue

205	A22	1p on 5c lil rose (Bk)	3.50	3.50
a.		"PSEO"	20.00	20.00
b.		Inverted surcharge	20.00	20.00
206	A22	1p on 5c lil rose (VB)	20.00	20.00
a.		"PSEO"	70.00	

On Nos. 205-206, "Habilitado Vale" is in Antique letters, "Un Peso" in Roman.

No. 185 Surcharged in Roman Letters in Green

207 A22 6c on 2c carmine ... 3.50 2.75

Nos. 184-185 Surcharged in Roman Letters in Green

208	A22	10c on 1c brown	1.75	1.25
a.		"DIES"	6.00	
b.		"DEIZ"	6.00	
c.		"DEIZ CAS"	6.00	
d.		"TTS" for "CTS"	6.00	
e.		"HABILTADO"	6.00	
f.		"HABILITAD"	6.00	
g.		"HABILITA"	6.00	
h.		Inverted surcharge	30.00	
209	A22	50c on 2c carmine	3.75	2.75
a.		"CAT" for "CTA"	10.00	
b.		"TCA" for "CTA"	10.00	
c.		"TTS" for "CTS"	10.00	
d.		"CAS" for "CTS"	10.00	
e.		"HABILTADO"	10.00	

Surcharge on No. 209 is found in two spacings between value and HABILTADO: 5mm (illustrated) and 1½mm.

No. 186 Surcharged in Antique Letters in Black

210 A22 1p on 5c lil rose ... 25.00 25.00
a. "PFSO" ... 75.00

In the surcharges on Nos. 202 to 210 there are various wrong font, inverted and omitted letters.

No. 184 Surcharged in Large Antique Letters in Green

210C A22 10c on 1c brown ... 15.00 15.00
d. "DIFZ" ... 55.00 55.00

Dionisio de Herrera — A24

1924, June — Litho. Perf. 11, 11½
211	A24	1c olive green	.30	.25
212	A24	2c deep rose	.35	.25
213	A24	6c red violet	.40	.25
214	A24	10c blue	.40	.25
215	A24	20c yellow brn	.80	.35
216	A24	50c vermilion	1.75	1.10
217	A24	1p emerald	4.00	2.75
		Nos. 211-217 (7)	8.00	5.20

Dated 1923.
In 1924 a facsimile of the signatures of Santiago Herrera and Francisco Caceres, covering four stamps, was handstamped in violet to prevent the use of stamps that had been stolen during a revolution.
Imperfs exist.
For overprints and surcharges see Nos. 280-281, 290-291, C14-C24, C26-C27, C29-C30, C32-C35, C56, C60, C73-C76, CO1-CO5, CO22, CO24, CO28-CO29, CO34-CO35, CO38A, CO39A, CO41, CO43, O75-O81.

Pres. Miguel Paz Baraona — A25

1925, Feb. 1 — Typo. Perf. 11½
218	A25	1c dull blue	2.00	2.00
a.		1c dark blue	2.00	2.00
219	A25	1c car rose	5.00	5.00
a.		1c brown carmine	5.00	5.00
220	A25	1c olive brn	14.00	14.00
a.		1c orange brown	14.00	14.00
b.		1c dark brown	14.00	14.00
c.		1c black brown	14.00	14.00
221	A25	1c buff	12.00	12.00
222	A25	1c red	60.00	60.00
223	A25	1c green	40.00	40.00
		Nos. 218-223 (6)	133.00	133.00

Imperf
225	A25	1c dull blue	5.50	5.50
a.		1c dark blue	5.50	5.50
226	A25	1c car rose	8.75	8.75
a.		1c brown carmine	8.75	8.75
227	A25	1c olive brn	20.00	20.00
a.		1c orange brown	13.25	13.25
b.		1c deep brown	13.25	13.25
c.		1c black brown	8.75	8.75
228	A25	1c buff	8.75	8.75
229	A25	1c red	60.00	60.00
229A	A25	1c green	27.50	27.50
		Nos. 225-229A (6)	130.50	130.50

Inauguration of President Baraona.
Counterfeits and unauthorized reprints exist.

No. 187 Overprinted in Black and Red

1926, June — Perf. 11½
230 A22 6c brt purple ... 1.50 1.25
Many varieties of this two-part overprint exist: one or both inverted or double, and various combinations. Value, each $10.

Nos. 177 and 187 Overprinted in Black or Red

1926
231	A20	6c deep pur (Bk)	2.00	2.00
a.		Inverted overprint	5.50	5.50
b.		Double overprint	5.50	5.50
232	A20	6c deep pur (R)	2.50	2.50
a.		Double overprint	5.00	5.00
233	A22	6c lilac (Bk)	.60	.60
a.		6c violet	.75	.75
b.		Inverted overprint	5.00	5.00
c.		Double overprint	5.00	5.00
d.		Double ovpt., one inverted	5.00	5.00
e.		"192"	7.50	7.50
f.		Double ovpt., both inverted	7.50	7.50

No. 230 Overprinted

235	A22	6c violet	20.00	20.00
a.		"1926" inverted	20.00	20.00
b.		"Habilitado" triple, one invtd.	20.00	20.00

No. 188 Surcharged in Red or Black

236	A22	6c on 10c blue (R)	.50	.40
c.		Double surcharge	5.00	4.00
d.		Without bar		
e.		Inverted surcharge	4.00	3.50
f.		"Vale" omitted		
g.		"6cts" omitted		
h.		"cts" omitted		
k.		Black surcharge	55.00	55.00

Nos. 175 and 185 Overprinted in Green

237	A19	2c carmine	.40	.40
a.		Tête bêche pair	4.00	4.00
b.		Double overprint	2.00	1.40
c.		"HARILITADO"	2.00	1.40
d.		"1926" only	2.75	2.75
e.		Double overprint, one inverted	2.75	2.75
f.		"1926" omitted	3.50	3.50
g.		Triple overprint, two inverted	5.25	5.25
h.		Double on face, one on back	5.25	5.25
238	A22	2c carmine	.40	.40
a.		"HARILITADO"	1.00	1.00
b.		Double overprint	1.40	1.40
c.		Inverted overprint	2.00	2.00

No. 177 Overprinted in Red

1927 — Large Numerals, 12x5mm
239 A20 6c deep purple ... 25.00 25.00
a. "1926" over "1927" ... 35.00 35.00
b. Invtd. ovpt. on face of stamp, normal ovpt. on back ... 30.00

No. 179 Surcharged

1927
240 A19 6c on 20c brown ... .75 .75
Tête bêche pair ... 2.75 2.75
c. Interted surcharge ... 2.50 2.50
d. Double surcharge ... 8.50 8.50

Nos. 8 and 10 in the setting have no period after "cts" and No. 50 has the "t" of "cts" inverted.

HONDURAS

Nos. 189-191 Surcharged

241	A22	6c on 15c blue	35.00	27.50
a.		"c" of "cts" omitted		
242	A22	6c on 15c vio	.70	.70
a.		Double surcharge	1.75	1.75
b.		Double surch., one invtd.	2.00	2.00
c.		"L" of "Vale" omitted		
243	A22	6c on 20c yel brn	.60	.60
a.		6c on 20c deep brown		
b.		"6" omitted	1.75	1.75
c.		"Vale" and "cts" omitted	3.50	3.50
		Nos. 240-243 (4)	37.05	29.55

On Nos. 242 and 243 stamps Nos. 12, 16 and 43 in the setting have no period after "cts" and No. 34 often lacks the "s." On No. 243 the "c" of "cts" is missing on stamp No. 38. On No. 241 occur the varieties "ct" or "ts" for "cts." and no period.

Southern Highway — A26
Ruins of Copán — A27
Pine Tree — A28
Presidential Palace — A29
Ponciano Leiva — A30
Pres. M.A. Soto — A31
Lempira — A32
Map of Honduras — A33
President Juan Lindo — A34
Statue of Columbus — A35

1927-29   Typo.   Wmk. 209

244	A26	1c ultramarine	.30	.25
a.		1c blue	.40	.40
245	A27	2c carmine	.30	.25
246	A28	5c dull violet	.30	.25
247	A28	5c bl gray ('29)	25.00	7.00
248	A29	6c blue black	.75	.50
a.		6c gray black	.75	.50
249	A29	6c dark bl ('29)	.40	.25
a.		6c light blue	.40	.40
250	A30	10c blue	.70	.25
251	A31	15c deep blue	1.00	.50
252	A32	20c dark blue	1.25	.60
253	A33	30c dark brown	1.50	1.00
254	A34	50c light blue	2.50	1.50
255	A35	1p red	5.00	2.50
		Nos. 244-255 (12)	39.00	14.85

In 1929 a quantity of imperforate sheets of No. 249 were stolen from the Litografia Nacional. Some of them were perforated by sewing machine and a few copies were passed through the post. To prevent the use of stolen stamps of the 1927-29 issues they were declared invalid and the stock on hand was overprinted "1929 a 1930."

For overprints and surcharges see Nos. 259-278, CO19-CO20B.

Pres. Vicente Mejia Colindres and Vice-Pres. Rafael Diaz Chávez — A36
President Mejia Colindres — A37

1929, Feb. 25

256	A36	1c dk carmine	3.00	3.00
257	A37	2c emerald	3.00	3.00

Installation of Pres. Vicente Mejia Colindres. Printed in sheets of ten.

Nos. 256 and 257 were surreptitiously printed in transposed colors. They were not regularly issued.

Stamps of 1927-29 Overprinted in Various Colors

1929, Oct.

259	A26	1c blue (R)	.25	.25
a.		1c ultramarine (R)	.50	.40
b.		Double overprint	2.50	1.75
c.		As "a," double overprint	2.50	1.75
260	A26	1c blue (Bk)	6.50	6.50
a.		1c ultramarine (Bk)		
261	A27	2c car (R Br)	3.50	3.50
a.		Double overprint		
262	A27	2c car (Bl Gr)	1.00	1.00
a.		Double overprint		
263	A27	2c car (Bk)	1.00	.50
264	A27	2c car (V)	.50	.25
a.		Double overprint		
b.		Double ovpt., one inverted		
265	A27	2c org red (V)	1.50	
266	A28	5c dl vio (R)	.40	.30
a.		Double overprint (R+V)	1.00	.75
267	A28	5c bl gray (R)		
a.		Double overprint (R+Bk)	2.50	2.00
269	A29	6c gray blk (R)	6.00	6.00
a.		Double overprint		
272	A29	6c dk blue (R)	.40	.25
a.		6c light blue (R)	.40	.40
b.		Double overprint	2.00	2.00
c.		Double overprint (R+V)		
273	A30	10c blue (R)	.40	.25
a.		Double overprint	2.50	1.75
274	A31	15c dp blue (R)	.50	.25
a.		Double overprint	3.50	2.50
275	A32	20c dark bl (R)	.50	.35
276	A33	30c dark brn (R)	.75	.60
a.		Double overprint	3.50	2.50
277	A34	50c light bl (R)	2.00	1.00
278	A35	1p red (V)	5.00	2.50
		Nos. 259-278 (17)	27.70	20.25

Nos. 259-278 exist in numerous shades. There are also various shades of the red and violet overprints. The overprint may be found reading upwards, downwards, inverted, double, triple, tête bêche or combinations. Status of both 6c stamps with overprint in black is questioned.

Herrera Monument — A38

1929, Dec. 10

279	A38	1c on 6c lilac rose	.70	.70
a.		"1992" for "1929"		
b.		"9192" for "1929"		
c.		Surcharge reading down	8.00	
d.		Dbl. surch., one reading down		

Dated 1924-1928 in lower corners of stamp. Varieties include "1992" reading down and pairs with one surcharge reading down, double or with "1992."

No. 214 Surcharged in Red

Perf. 11, 11½

1930, Mar. 26   Unwmk.

280	A24	1c on 10c blue	.40	.40
a.		"1093" for "1930"	1.40	
b.		"tsc" for "cts"	1.40	
281	A24	2c on 10c blue	.40	.40
a.		"tsc" for "cts"		
b.		"Vale 2" omitted	2.00	

Official Stamps of 1929 Overprinted in Red or Violet

1930, Mar.   Wmk. 209   Perf. 11½

282	O1	1c blue (R)	.50	.50
a.		Double overprint	2.00	2.00
284	O1	2c carmine (V)	.90	.90

Stamps of 1915-26 Overprinted in Blue

On No. 174

1930, July 19   Unwmk.

285	A19	1c chocolate	.40	.40
a.		Double overprint	1.00	1.00
b.		Inverted overprint	1.40	1.40
c.		Dbl. ovpt., one inverted	1.40	1.40

On No. 184

287	A22	1c brown	21.00	21.00
b.		Double overprint		
c.		Inverted overprint		

On No. 204

289	A22	50c on 2c carmine	100.00	100.00
b.		Inverted surcharge		

On Nos. 211 and 212

290	A24	1c olive green	.40	.40
a.		Double overprint	1.75	1.75
b.		Inverted overprint	1.75	1.75
c.		On No. O75	12.00	
291	A24	2c carmine rose	.40	.40
a.		Double overprint	1.75	1.75
b.		Inverted overprint	1.75	1.75

On No. 237

292	A19	2c car (G & Bl)	100.00	100.00

From Title Page of Government Gazette, First Issue — A39

1930, Aug. 11   Typo.   Wmk. 209

295	A39	2c orange	2.00	2.00
296	A39	2c ultramarine	2.00	2.00
297	A39	2c red	2.00	2.00
		Nos. 295-297 (3)	6.00	6.00

Publication of the 1st newspaper in Honduras, cent. The stamps were on sale and available for postage on Aug. 11th, 1930, only. Not more than 5 examples of each color could be purchased by an applicant.

Nos. 295-297 exist imperf. and part-perforate. Unauthorized reprints exist.

For surcharges see Nos. CO15-CO18A.

Paz Baraona — A40
Manuel Bonilla — A41
Lake Yojoa — A42
View of Palace at Tegucigalpa — A43
City of Amapala — A44
Mayan Stele at Copán — A45

Christopher Columbus — A46
Discovery of America — A47
Loarque Bridge — A48

Unwmk.

1931, Jan. 2   Engr.   Perf. 12

298	A40	1c black brown	.75	.25
299	A41	2c carmine rose	.75	.25
300	A42	5c dull violet	1.00	.25
301	A43	6c deep green	1.00	.25
302	A44	10c brown	1.50	.25
303	A45	15c dark blue	2.00	.25
304	A46	20c black	3.50	.40
305	A47	50c olive green	4.50	1.50
306	A48	1p slate black	9.00	2.50
		Nos. 298-306 (9)	24.00	5.95

Regular Issue of 1931 Overprinted in Black or Various Colors

1931

307	A40	1c black brown	.40	.30
308	A41	2c carmine rose	.60	.30
309	A45	15c dark blue	1.00	.30
310	A46	20c black	2.50	.40

Overprinted

311	A42	5c dull violet	.50	.30
312	A43	6c deep green	.50	.30
315	A44	10c brown	1.50	.35
316	A47	50c olive green	8.00	5.00
317	A48	1p slate black	10.00	7.50
		Nos. 307-317 (9)	25.00	14.75
		Nos. 307-317,C51-C55 (14)	50.00	35.75

The overprint is a control mark. It stands for "Tribunal Superior de Cuentas" (Superior Tribunal of Accounts).

Overprint varieties include: inverted; double; double, one or both inverted; on back; pair, one without overprint; differing colors (6c exists with overprint in orange, yellow and red).

President Carías and Vice-President Williams — A49

1933, Apr. 29

318	A49	2c carmine rose	.50	.50
319	A49	6c deep green	.75	.75
320	A49	10c deep blue	1.00	1.00
321	A49	15c red orange	1.25	1.25
		Nos. 318-321 (4)	3.50	3.50

Inauguration of Pres. Tiburcio Carias Andino and Vice-Pres. Abraham Williams, Feb. 1, 1933.

Columbus' Fleet and Flag of the Race — A50

Wmk. 209

1933, Aug. 3   Typo.   Perf. 11½

322	A50	2c ultramarine	1.00	.65
323	A50	6c yellow	1.00	.65
324	A50	10c lemon	1.40	.85

Perf. 12

325	A50	15c violet	2.00	1.50
326	A50	50c red	4.00	3.50
327	A50	1 l emerald	7.00	7.00
		Nos. 322-327 (6)	16.40	14.15

"Day of the Race," an annual holiday throughout Spanish-American countries. Also

HONDURAS

for the 441st anniv. of the sailing of Columbus to the New World, Aug. 3, 1492.

Masonic Temple, Tegucigalpa — A51

Designs: 2c, President Carias. 5c, Flag. 6c, Tomás Estrada Palma.

Unwmk.
1935, Jan. 12	Engr.		Perf. 12	
328	A51	1c green	.40	.40
329	A51	2c carmine	.40	.40
330	A51	5c dark blue	.40	.40
331	A51	6c black brown	.40	.40
a.	Vert. pair, imperf. btwn.		20.00	20.00
Nos. 328-331 (4)			1.60	1.60
Nos. 328-331,C77-C83 (11)			15.20	7.20

Gen. Carías Bridge — A55

1937, June 4				
332	A55	6c car & ol green	.90	.40
333	A55	21c grn & violet	1.50	.65
334	A55	46c orange & brn	2.10	1.50
335	A55	55c ultra & black	3.00	2.40
Nos. 332-335 (4)			7.50	4.95

Prolongation of the Presidential term to Jan. 19, 1943.

Seal of Honduras — A56

Central District Palace — A57

Designs: 3c, Map of Honduras. 5c, Bridge of Choluteca. 8c, Flag.

1939, Mar. 1			Perf. 12½	
336	A56	1c orange yellow	.40	.40
337	A57	2c red orange	.40	.40
338	A57	3c carmine	.40	.40
339	A57	5c orange	.40	.40
340	A56	8c dark blue	.50	.40
Nos. 336-340 (5)			2.10	2.00
Nos. 336-340,C89-C98 (15)			15.95	9.65

Nos. 336-340 exist imperf.
For overprints see Nos. 342-343.

Nos. 336 and 337 Overprinted in Green

1944			Perf. 12½	
342	A56	1c orange yellow	.30	.30
a.	Inverted overprint		5.00	5.00
343	A57	2c red orange	1.25	.75
a.	Inverted overprint		5.00	5.00

Catalogue values for unused stamps in this section, from this point to the end of the section, are for Never Hinged items.

International Peace Movement — A58

1984, Feb. 15	Litho.		Perf. 12	
344	A58	78c multi	.95	.65
345	A58	85c multi	1.00	.30
346	A58	95c multi	1.10	.35
347	A58	1.50 l multi	1.90	.55
348	A58	2 l multi	2.40	.70
349	A58	5 l multi	6.00	1.75
Nos. 344-349 (6)			13.35	4.30

Central American Aeronautics Corp., 25th Anniv. — A59

Designs: 2c, Edward Warner Award issued by the Intl. Civil Aviation Organization, vert. 5c, Corp. emblem, flags of Guatemala, Honduras, El Salvador, Costa Rica and Panama. 60c, Transmission tower, plane. 75c, Corp. emblem, vert. 1 l, 1.50 l, Emblem, flags, diff.

1987, Feb. 26	Litho.		Perf. 12	
350	A59	2c multi	.40	.40
351	A59	5c multi	.40	.40
352	A59	60c multi	1.00	.60
353	A59	75c multi	1.30	.65
354	A59	1 l multi	1.75	.90
Nos. 350-354 (5)			4.85	2.95

Souvenir Sheet
| 355 | A59 | 1.50 l multi | 3.25 | 3.00 |

Housing Institute (INVA), 30th Anniv. — A60

1987, Oct. 9	Litho.		Perf. 13½	
356	A60	5c shown	.50	.40
357	A60	95c Map, emblem, text	1.60	.40

EXFILHON '88 — A61

1988, Sept. 11	Litho.		Imperf.	
358	A61	3 l dl red brn & brt ultra	4.75	4.50

1988 Summer Olympics, Seoul — A62

1988, Sept. 30	Litho.		Imperf.	
359	A62	4 l multi	5.75	5.50
Nos. 359,C772-C773 (3)			8.75	8.00

Luis Bogran Technical Institute, Cent. — A63

85c, Cogwheel, map, flag of Honduras.

1990, Sept. 28	Litho.		Perf. 10½	
360	A63	20c multicolored	.50	.40
361	A63	85c multicolored	1.75	.40

Size: 114x82mm
Imperf
| 362 | A63 | 2 l like #360 | 2.25 | 2.00 |
| Nos. 360-362 (3) | | | 4.50 | 2.80 |

Nos. 360-361 are airmail.

America Issue — A64

UPAE emblem, land and seascapes showing produce and fish.

1990, Oct. 31	Litho.		Perf. 13½	
363	A64	20c multi, vert.	1.00	.80
364	A64	1 l multicolored	1.90	1.60

1992 Winter Olympics, Albertville — A65

3 l, Cross-country skiing.

1992, Feb. 17				
365	A65	50c shown	1.25	.50
366	A65	3 l multicolored	2.10	2.40

A66

Mother's Day (Paintings): 20c, Saleswoman, by Manuel Rodriguez. 50c, The Grandmother and Baby, by Rodriguez. 5 l, Saleswomen, by Maury Flores.

1992, May 21	Litho.		Perf. 13½	
367	A66	20c shown	.45	.40
368	A66	50c multicolored	.75	.40
369	A66	5 l multicolored	3.75	3.50
Nos. 367-369 (3)			4.95	4.30

Butterflies — A67

Designs: 25c, Melitaeinae chlosyne janais. 85c, Heliconiinae agrilus vanillae. 3 l, Morphinae morpho granadensis. 5 l, Heliconiinae dryadula phalusa.

1992, June 22				
370	A67	25c multicolored	.55	.50
371	A67	85c multicolored	1.40	1.25
372	A67	3 l multicolored	3.00	4.50

Size: 108x76mm
Imperf
| 373 | A67 | 5 l multicolored | 6.25 | 6.00 |
| Nos. 370-373 (4) | | | 11.20 | 12.25 |

1992 Summer Olympics, Barcelona — A68

1992, Mar. 16	Litho.		Perf. 13½	
374	A68	20c Running	.50	.40
375	A68	50c Tennis	1.00	.40
376	A68	85c Soccer	1.60	.40
Nos. 374-376 (3)			3.10	1.20

Japanese Overseas Cooperation Volunteers in Honduras, 20th Anniv. — A69

Designs: 1.40 l, Volunteers working on Japanese letter, vert. 4.30 l, Folding screen showing Mayan Gods. 5.40 l, Men, women of Honduras in traditional costumes, volunteer.

1995, Sept. 20	Litho.		Perf. 13½	
377	A69	1.40 l multicolored	.50	.40
378	A69	4.30 l multicolored	1.50	1.40
379	A69	5.40 l multicolored	2.00	1.90
Nos. 377-379 (3)			4.00	3.70

Nos. 378-379 are airmail.

Birds — A70

Designs: 1.40 l, Buteo jamaicensis. 1.50 l, Ramphastos sulfuratus. 2 l, Dendrocygna autumnalis. 2.15 l, Micrastur semitorquatus. 3 l, Polyporus plancus. 5.40 l, 10 l, Sarcoramphus papa.

1997, Apr. 29	Litho.		Perf. 13½	
380	A70	1.40 l multicolored	1.40	1.30
381	A70	1.50 l multicolored	1.60	1.40
382	A70	2 l multicolored	1.90	1.70
383	A70	2.15 l multicolored	2.25	2.00
a.	Pair, #382, 383		5.50	5.00
384	A70	3 l multicolored	3.00	2.75
a.	Pair, #380, 384		5.50	5.00
385	A70	5.40 l multicolored	4.75	4.25
a.	Pair, #381, 385		7.75	7.00
Nos. 380-385 (6)			14.90	13.40

Size: 50x73mm
Imperf
| 386 | A70 | 20 l multicolored | 7.75 | 7.00 |

Nos. 380-385 were printed in panes of 30 (5x6), with one value comprising the top three rows and another the bottom three rows. Thus, each pane contains five setenant pairs.
No. 386 is airmail.

No. RA8 Surcharged in Gold

1999, June 25	Litho.		Perf. 13½	
387	PT6	2.60 l on 1c	1.25	.35
388	PT6	7.85 l on 1c	3.90	.95
389	PT6	10.65 l on 1c	5.00	1.25
390	PT6	11.55 l on 1c	5.50	1.40
391	PT6	12.45 l on 1c	6.00	1.50
392	PT6	13.85 l on 1c	6.75	1.75
Nos. 387-392 (6)			28.40	7.20

For surcharges, see C1199//C1206.

Inauguration of Pres. Juan Orlando Hernández — A71

Designs: No. 393, 50 l, Honduras coat of arms. No. 394, 50 l, Isla Conejo, horiz. 100 l, Pres. Hernández wearing sash, flag of Honduras. 150 l, Pres. Hernánadez, with arm raised, horiz. 200 l, Pres. Hernández wearing sash, waving.

2014, June 4	Litho.		Perf. 13½	
393-397	A71	Set of 5	65.00	65.00

A72

Independence, 200th Anniv. — A73

Designs: 2 l, Obverse and reverse of 1824 Central American Republic coin. 5 l, Mallol Bridge, Tegucigalpa. 10 l, Cabildo de Comayagua. 30 l, Act of Independence.

HONDURAS

No. 402 — Tegucigalpa landmarks: a, 5 l, Metropolis Towers (41x30mm). b, 5 l, Civic Government Center (41x30mm). c, 5 l, Centenary Obelisk (41x30mm). d, 5 l, St. Michael the Archangel statue (41x30mm). e, 100 l, Signing of the Act of Independence (82x60mm).

	2021	Litho.		Perf. 13¼
398-401	A72	Set of 4	4.00	4.00

Miniature Sheet

| 402 | A73 | Sheet of 5, #a-e | 10.00 | 10.00 |

Issued: Nos. 398-401, 9/28; No. 402, 9/29. No. 402e has a row of perforations running horizontally through the middle of the stamp and a column running vertically through the middle of the stamp, with the vertical perforations running through the country name on the lower left and lower right quadrants. No. 402 exists imperforate.

Cooperation Between Honduras and Germany, 60th Anniv. — A74

Designs: No. 403, 5 l, AEG turbine, Francisco Morazán Hydroelectric Power Plant. No. 404, 5 l, Children reading books. 10 l, Environmental protection. 50 l, Suyapa Radio School.

2021, Oct. 28	Litho.		Perf. 13¼
403-406	A74	Set of 4	6.00	6.00

Miniature Sheet

Honduras National Railroad — A75

No. 407: a, 10 l, 1903 National Railroad postmark (41x30mm). b, 10 l, Undated Standard Fruit Company postmark (41x30mm). c, 10 l, 1927 Tela Railroad Company postmark (41x30mm). d, 10 l, 1929 Truxillo Railroad Company postmark (41x30mm). e, 20 l, National Railroad train crossing the Bermejo River (81x56mm).

Perf. 13¼ (#407a-407d), 13¼ at bottom (#407e)

2021, Nov. 9		Litho.		
407	A75	Sheet of 5, #a-e	5.00	5.00

San Juan, Puerto Rico, 500th Anniv. — A76

Designs: No. 408, 5 l, 1521 town charter. No. 409, 5 l, 1519 map of San Juan area, horiz. 10 l, Engraving of San Juan in 1616, by Arnoldus Montanus, horiz. 25 l, San José Church, horiz.

2021, Nov. 19	Litho.		Perf. 13¼
408-411	A76	Set of 4	3.75	3.75
408a		Inscribed ". . . donde se funda. . ."	—	—

No. 408 is inscribed ". . . donde de funda. . ."

SEMI-POSTAL STAMPS

Catalogue values for unused stamps in this section are for Never Hinged items.

Indigenous Musical Instruments SP1

No. B1: a, Garífuna drum. b, Flutes. c, Toltec drum. d, Hornpipe. e, Maya drum. f, Conch shell.

2000, Apr. 7	Litho.		Perf. 13¼
B1	Sheet of 6, "Pro filatelia" in black	23.00	18.00
a.-f.	SP1 10 l + 1 l Any single	3.25	2.50
g.	As #B1, "Pro filatelia" in gold	21.50	17.50

See Nos. C1073, C1209.

AIR POST STAMPS

Regular Issue of 1915-16 Overprinted in Black, Blue or Red

1925		Unwmk.		Perf. 11½
C1	A20	5c lt blue (Bk)	87.50	87.50
a.		Inverted overprint	200.00	
C2	A20	5c lt blue (Bl)	300.00	300.00
a.		Inverted overprint	400.00	
b.		Vertical overprint	600.00	
c.		Double overprint	800.00	
C3	A20	5c lt blue (R)	7,250.	

Value for No. C3 is for an example without gum.

C4	A19	10c dk blue (R)	175.00	
a.		Inverted overprint	325.00	
b.		Overprint tête bêche, pair	800.00	
C5	A19	10c dk blue (Bl)	1,100.	
C6	A19	20c red brn (Bk)	175.00	175.00
a.		Inverted overprint	250.00	
b.		Tête bêche pair	400.00	
c.		Overprint tête bêche, pair	725.00	
d.		"AFRO"	1,400.	
e.		Double overprint	600.00	
C7	A19	20c red brn (Bl)	700.00	350.00
a.		Inverted overprint	700.00	
b.		Tête bêche pair	1,000	
c.		Vertical overprint	900.00	
C8	A20	50c red (Bk)	450.00	300.00
a.		Inverted overprint	550.00	
b.		Overprint tête bêche, pair	900.00	
C9	A20	1p yel grn (Bk)	600.00	600.00

Surcharged in Black or Blue

C10	A19	25c on 1c choc	125.00	125.00
a.		Inverted surcharge	700.00	
C11	A20	25c on 5c lt bl (Bl)	225.00	225.00
a.		Inverted surcharge	700.00	
b.		Double inverted surcharge	675.00	
C12	A19	25c on 10c dk bl	125,000.	
C13	A19	25c on 20c brn (Bl)	200.00	200.00
a.		Inverted surcharge	325.00	
b.		Tête bêche pair	450.00	

Counterfeits of Nos. C1-C13 are plentiful.

Monoplane and Lisandro Garay — AP1

1929, June 5	Engr.		Perf. 12
C13C	AP1	50c carmine	2.25	1.75

For overprints and surcharges, see Nos. CB1-CB4.

No. 216 Surcharged in Blue

1929			Perf. 11, 11½
C14	A24	25c on 50c ver	5.00	3.50

In the surcharges on Nos. C14 to C40 there are various wrong font and defective letters and numerals, also periods omitted.

Nos. 215-217 Surcharged in Green, Black or Red

1929, Oct.			
C15	A24	5c on 20c yel brn (G)	1.40	1.40
a.		Double surcharge (R+G)	45.00	
C16	A24	10c on 50c ver (Bk)	2.25	1.90
C17	A24	15c on 1p emer (R)	3.50	3.50
		Nos. C15-C17 (3)	7.15	6.80

Nos. 214 and 216 Surcharged Vertically in Red or Black

1929, Dec. 10			
C18	A24(a)	5c on 10c bl (R)	.60	.60
C19	A24(b)	20c on 50c ver	1.00	1.00
a.		"1299" for "1929"	190.00	
b.		"cts. cts." for "cts. oro."	190.00	
c.		"r" of "Aereo" omitted	2.00	
d.		Horiz. pair, imperf. btwn.	20.00	

Nos. 214, 215 and 180 Surcharged in Various Colors

1930, Feb.			
C20	A24	5c on 10c (R)	.50	.50
a.		"1930" reading down	3.50	
b.		"1903" for "1930"	3.50	
c.		Surcharge reading down	10.00	
d.		Double surcharge	14.00	
e.		Dbl. surch., one downward	14.00	
C21	A24	5c on 10c (Y)	450.00	450.00
C22	A24	5c on 10c (Bl)	125.00	125.00
C23	A24	10c on 20c (Bk)	.75	.75
a.		"0" for "10"	3.50	
b.		Double surcharge	8.75	
c.		Dbl. surch., one downward	12.00	
d.		Horiz. pair, imperf. btwn.	70.00	
C24	A24	10c on 20c (V)	750.00	750.00
a.		"0" for "10"	1,600.	
C25	A20	25c on 50c (Bk)	.95	.95
a.		"Internaoicnal"	3.50	
b.		"o" for "oro"	3.50	
c.		Inverted surcharge	17.50	
d.		As "a," invtd. srch.	175.00	
e.		As "b," invtd. srch.	175.00	

Surcharge on Nos. C20-C24 are vertical.

Nos. 214, 215 and 180 Surcharged

1930, Apr. 1			
C26	A24	5c on 10c blue	.50	.50
a.		Double surcharge	9.50	
b.		"Servicioa"	3.50	
C27	A24	15c on 20c yel brn	.55	.55
a.		Double surcharge	7.00	
C28	A20	20c on 50c red, srch. reading down	.95	.95
a.		Surcharge reading up	7.00	
		Nos. C26-C28 (3)	2.00	2.00

Nos. C22 and C23 Surcharged Vertically in Red

1930			
C29	A24	10c on 5c on 20c (Bl+R)	.90	.90
a.		"1930" reading down	9.00	9.00
b.		"1903" for "1930"	9.00	9.00
c.		Red surcharge, reading down	14.00	
C30	A24	10c on 10c on 20c (Bk+R)	87.50	87.50
a.		"0" for "10"	190.00	

No. 181 Surcharged as No. C25 and Re-surcharged

C31	A20	50c on 25c on 1p grn	4.25	4.25
a.		"Internaoicnal"	7.00	
b.		"o" for "oro"	7.00	
c.		25c surcharge inverted	17.50	17.50
d.		50c surcharge inverted	17.50	17.50
e.		As "a" and "c"		
f.		As "a" and "d"		
g.		As "b" and "c"		
h.		As "b" and "d"		
		Nos. C29-C31 (3)	92.65	92.65

No. 215 Surcharged in Dark Blue

1930, May 22			
C32	A24	5c on 20c yel brn	1.25	1.00
a.		Double surcharge	5.25	5.25
b.		Horiz. pair, imperf. btwn.	60.00	200.00
c.		Vertical pair, imperf. between	20.00	40.00

Nos. O78-O80 Surcharged in Various Colors

1930			
C33	A24	5c on 10c (R)	450.00	350.00
a.		"1930" reading down	1,500.	
b.		"1903" for "1930"	1,500.	
C34	A24	5c on 20c (Bl)	400.00	400.00
C35	A24	25c on 50c (Bk)	225.00	225.00
a.		55c on 50c vermilion	325.00	325.00

No. C35 exists with inverted surcharge.

No. O64 Surcharged like No. C28

C36	A20	20c on 50c red, surcharge reading down	350.00	350.00
a.		Surcharge reading up	350.00	350.00
b.		Dbl. srch., reading down	350.00	350.00
c.		Dbl. srch., reading up	350.00	350.00

No. O87 Overprinted

1930, Feb. 21	Wmk. 209		Perf. 11½
C37	O1	50c yel, grn & blue	1.40	1.25
a.		"Internacioanl"	5.25	
b.		"Iuternacional"	5.25	
c.		Double overprint	5.25	

Nos. O86-O88 Overprinted in Various Colors

1930, May 23			
C38	O1	20c dark blue (R)	1.10	.85
a.		Double overprint	8.75	
b.		Triple overprint	12.00	
C39	O1	50c org, grn & bl (Bk)	1.10	.90
C40	O1	1p buff (Bl)	1.40	1.25
a.		Double overprint	10.50	
		Nos. C38-C40 (3)	3.60	3.00

National Palace — AP3

		Unwmk.		
1930, Oct. 1		Engr.		Perf. 12
C41	AP3	5c yel orange	.65	.30
C42	AP3	10c carmine	1.00	.60
C43	AP3	15c green	1.30	.75
C44	AP3	20c dull violet	1.60	.60
C45	AP3	1p light brown	5.25	4.00
		Nos. C41-C45 (5)	9.80	6.25

Overprinted in Various Colors

1931			Perf. 12
C51	AP3	5c yel orange (R)	2.00	1.50
C52	AP3	10c carmine (Bk)	3.00	2.50
C53	AP3	15c green (Br)	5.00	4.00

HONDURAS

C54	AP3 20c dull vio (O)	5.00	4.25
C55	AP3 1p lt brown (G)	10.00	8.75
	Nos. C51-C55 (5)	25.00	21.00

See note after No. 317.

Stamps of Various Issues Surcharged in Blue or Black (#C59)

1931, Oct.   On No. 215   Perf. 11½

C56	A24 15c on 20c yel brn	3.50	2.75
a.	Horiz. pair, imperf. btwn.	42.50	
b.	Green surcharge	20.00	20.00

On No. O64

C57	A20 15c on 50c red	4.25	3.50
a.	Inverted surcharge	10.50	10.50

On No. O72

C58	A22 15c on 20c brn	4.25	4.25
a.	Vert. pair, imperf. between	12.00	

On Nos. C57 and C58 the word "OFICIAL" is canceled by two bars.

On No. O88
Wmk. 209

C59	O1 15c on 1p buff	4.25	4.25
a.	Vert. pair, imperf. horiz.	25.00	25.00
b.	"Sevricio"	14.00	14.00

The varieties "Vaie" for "Vale," "aereo" with circumflex accent on the first "e" and "Interior" with initial capital "I" are found on Nos. C56, C58-C59. No. C57 is known with initial capital in "Interior."

A similar surcharge, in slightly larger letters and with many minor varieties, exists on Nos. 215, O63, O64 and O73. The authenticity of this surcharge is questioned.

Nos. 215, O73, O87-O88 Surcharged in Green, Red or Black

1931, Nov.   Unwmk.

C60	A24 15c on 20c (G)	3.50	2.75
a.	Inverted surcharge	6.25	
b.	"XI" omitted	6.25	
c.	"X" for "XI"	6.25	
d.	"PI" for "XI"	6.25	
C61	A22 15c on 50c (R)	3.50	2.75
a.	"XI" omitted	6.75	
b.	"PI" for "XI"	6.75	
c.	Double surcharge	20.00	20.00

On No. C61 the word "OFICIAL" is not barred out.

Wmk. 209

C62	O1 15c on 50c (Bk)	2.75	2.50
a.	"1391" for "1931"	10.50	10.50
b.	Double surcharge	8.75	8.75
C63	O1 15c on 1p (Bk)	2.50	2.25
a.	"1391" for "1931"	12.50	
b.	Surcharged on both sides	7.00	

Nos. O76-O78 Surcharged in Black or Red

1932   Unwmk.   Perf. 11, 11½

C73	A24 15c on 2c	.80	.80
a.	Double surcharge	5.50	
b.	Inverted surcharge	4.25	
c.	"Ae" of "Aero" omitted	1.00	
d.	On No. 212 (no "Official")		
C74	A24 15c on 6c	.80	.80
a.	Double surcharge	3.50	
b.	Horiz. pair, imperf. btwn.	17.50	
c.	"Aer" omitted	10.00	10.00
d.	"A" omitted	1.00	
e.	Inverted surcharge	3.50	3.50
C75	A24 15c on 10c (R)	.80	.80
a.	Double surcharge	5.50	
b.	Inverted surcharge	3.50	
c.	"r" of "Aereo" omitted	1.00	

Same Surcharge on No. 214 in Red

C76	A24 15c on 10c dp bl	150.00	100.00

There are various broken and missing letters in the setting.
A similar surcharge with slightly larger letters exists.

Post Office and National Palace — AP4

View of Tegucigalpa AP5

Designs: 15c, Map of Honduras. 20c, Mayol Bridge. 40c, View of Tegucigalpa. 50c, Owl. 1 l, Coat of Arms.

1935, Jan. 10   Perf. 12

C77	AP4 8c blue	.25	.25
C78	AP5 10c gray	.25	.25
C79	AP5 15c olive gray	.40	.25
C80	AP5 20c dull green	.50	.25
C81	AP5 40c brown	.70	.25
C82	AP4 50c yellow	8.25	1.60
C83	AP4 1 l green	3.25	2.75
	Nos. C77-C83 (7)	13.55	5.35

Flags of US and Honduras AP11

Engr. & Litho.
1937, Sept. 17   Unwmk.

C84	AP11 46c multicolored	3.00	1.40

US Constitution, 150th anniv.

Comayagua Cathedral AP12

Founding of Comayagua AP13

Alonzo Cáceres and Pres. Carías AP14

Lintel of Royal Palace — AP15

1937, Dec. 7   Engr.

C85	AP12 2c copper red	.25	.25
C86	AP13 8c dark blue	.35	.25
C87	AP14 15c slate black	.70	.70
C88	AP15 50c dark brown	4.25	2.75
	Nos. C85-C88 (4)	5.55	3.95

City of Comayagua founding, 400th anniv.
For surcharges see Nos. C144-C146.

Mayan Stele at Copán — AP16

Mayan Temple, Copán — AP17

Designs: 15c, President Carias. 30c, José C. de Valle. 40c, Presidential House. 46c, Lempira. 55c, Church of Our Lady of Suyapa. 66c, J. T. Reyes. 1 l, Hospital at Choluteca. 2 l, Ramón Rosa.

1939, Mar. 1   Perf. 12½

C89	AP16 10c orange brn	.25	.25
C90	AP16 15c grnsh blue	.30	.25
C91	AP17 21c gray	.50	.25
C92	AP16 30c dk blue grn	.55	.25
C93	AP17 40c dull violet	1.00	.65
C94	AP16 46c dk gray brn	1.00	.65
C95	AP16 55c green	1.25	1.00
a.	Imperf., pair	22.50	
C96	AP16 66c black	1.75	1.25
C97	AP16 1 l olive grn	3.00	1.00
C98	AP16 2 l henna red	4.25	2.50
	Nos. C89-C98 (10)	13.80	7.45

For surcharges see Nos. C118-C119, C147-C152.

Souvenir Sheets

AP26

14c, Francisco Morazan. 16c, George Washington. 30c, J. C. de Valle. 40c, Simon Bolivar.

1940, Apr. 13   Engr.   Perf. 12
Centers of Stamps Lithographed

C99	AP26 Sheet of 4	10.00	10.00
a.	14c black, yellow, ultra & rose	1.40	1.40
b.	16c black, yellow, ultra & rose	1.75	1.75
c.	30c black, yellow, ultra & rose	2.40	2.40
d.	40c black, yellow, ultra & rose	2.75	2.75

Imperf

C100	AP26 Sheet of 4	16.00	16.00
a.	14c black, yellow, ultra & rose	2.25	2.25
b.	16c black, yellow, ultra & rose	2.75	2.75
c.	30c black, yellow, ultra & rose	4.00	4.00
d.	40c black, yellow, ultra & rose	4.50	4.50

Pan American Union, 50th anniv.
For overprints see Nos. C153-C154, C187.

Air Post Official Stamps of 1939 Overprinted in Red

1940, Oct. 12   Perf. 12½

C101	OA2 2c dp bl & green	.25	.25
C102	OA2 5c dp blue & org	.25	.25
C103	OA2 8c deep bl & brn	.30	.30
C104	OA2 15c dp blue & car	.50	.50
C105	OA2 46c dp bl & ol grn	.80	.80
C106	OA2 50c dp bl & vio	.90	.90
C107	OA2 1 l dp bl & red brn	3.75	3.75
C108	OA2 2 l dp bl & red org	7.50	7.50
	Nos. C101-C108 (8)	14.25	14.25

Erection and dedication of the Columbus Memorial Lighthouse.

Air Post Official Stamps of 1939 Overprinted in Black

1941, Aug. 2

C109	OA2 5c deep bl & org	3.00	.40
C110	OA2 8c dp blue & brn	5.00	.40
a.	Overprint inverted	225.00	

Nos. CO44, CO47-CO51 Surcharged in Black

1941, Oct. 28

C111	OA2 3c on 2c	.40	.25
C112	OA2 8c on 2c	.50	.50
C113	OA2 8c on 15c	.50	.50
C114	OA2 8c on 46c	.60	.60
C115	OA2 8c on 50c	.75	.50
C116	OA2 8c on 1 l	1.25	.70
C117	OA2 8c on 2 l	2.00	1.50
	Nos. C111-C117 (7)	6.00	4.30

Once in each sheet a large "h" occurs in "ocho."

Nos. C90, C94 Surcharged in Red

1942, July 14

C118	AP16 8c on 15c	.70	.40
a.	"Cerreo"	2.00	2.00
b.	Double surcharge	25.00	25.00
c.	As "a," double surcharge	175.00	
C119	AP16 16c on 46c	.70	.40
a.	"Cerreo"	2.00	2.00

Plaque AP27

Morazán's Tomb, San Salvador AP28

Designs: 5c, Battle of La Trinidad. 8c, Morazán's birthplace. 14c black. 21c, Church where Morazán was baptized. 1 l, Arms of Central American Federation. 2 l, Gen. Francisco Morazán.

1942, Sept. 15   Perf. 12

C120	AP27 2c red orange	.25	.25
C121	AP27 5c turq green	.25	.25
C122	AP27 8c sepia	.25	.25
C123	AP28 14c black	.40	.30
C124	AP27 16c olive gray	.25	.25
C125	AP27 21c light blue	1.00	.65
C126	AP27 1 l brt ultra	3.00	2.25
C127	AP28 2 l dl ol brn	7.50	7.25
	Nos. C120-C127 (8)	12.90	11.45

Gen. Francisco Morazan (1799-1842).
For surcharges see Nos. C349-C350.

Coat of Arms — AP35

Cattle AP36

Bananas AP37

Pine Tree — AP38

Tobacco Plant — AP39

Orchid — AP40

Coco Palm — AP41

Map of Honduras — AP42

Designs: 2c, Flag. 8c, Rosario. 16c, Sugar cane. 30c, Oranges. 40c, Wheat. 1 l, Corn. 2 l, Map of Americas.

1943, Sept. 14   Perf. 12½

C128	AP35 1c light grn	.30	.25
C129	AP35 2c blue	.30	.25
C130	AP36 5c green	.35	.25
C131	AP37 6c dark bl grn	.30	.25
C132	AP36 8c lilac	.35	.25
C133	AP38 10c lilac brn	.35	.25
C134	AP39 15c dp claret	.40	.25
C135	AP38 16c dark red	.40	.25
C136	AP40 21c deep blue	.90	.25
C137	AP39 30c org brown	.70	.25
C138	AP40 40c red orange	.70	.25
C139	AP41 55c black	1.30	.60

HONDURAS

C140	AP41	1 l dark olive		2.00	1.40
C141	AP37	2 l brown red		6.25	4.00
C142	AP42	5 l orange		15.00	13.00
a.		Vert. pair, imperf. btwn.		150.00	
		Nos. C128-C142 (15)		29.60	21.75

Pan-American School of Agriculture — AP50

1944, Oct. 12   *Perf. 12*

C143	AP50	21c dk blue grn	.40	.40

Inauguration of the Pan-American School of Agriculture, Tegucigalpa.

Catalogue values for unused stamps in this section, from this point to the end of the section, are for Never Hinged items.

Air Post Stamps of 1937-39 Surcharged in Red or Green

1945, Mar. 13   *Perf. 11, 12½*

C144	AP15	1c on 50c dk brn	.30	.25
C145	AP12	2c on 2c cop red	.30	.25
C146	AP14	8c on 15c sl blk	.30	.25
C147	AP16	10c on 10c org brown (G)	.50	.30
C148	AP16	15c on 15c grnsh blue (G)	.35	.25
C149	AP17	30c on 21c gray (G)	5.25	3.00
C150	AP17	40c on 40c dull violet (G)	2.60	1.25
C151	AP16	1 l on 46c dk gray brown (G)	2.60	1.75
C152	AP16	2 l on 66c blk (G)	5.00	3.00
		Nos. C144-C152 (9)	17.20	10.30

Nos. C99 and C100 Overprinted in Red
Souvenir Sheets

1945, Oct. 1   *Perf. 12*

C153	AP26	Sheet of 4	5.00	4.00

Imperf

| C154 | AP26 | Sheet of 4 | 7.50 | 6.50 |

Allied Nations' victory and Germany's unconditional surrender, May 8, 1945.

Seal of Honduras AP51

Arms of Gracias and Trujillo AP52

Franklin D. Roosevelt ("F.D.R." under Column) AP53

Arms of San Miguel de Heredia de Tegucigalpa AP54

Designs (Coats of Arms): 5c, Comayagua and San Jorge de Olancho. 15c, Province of Honduras and San Juan de Puerto Caballas. 21c, Comayagua and Tencoa. 1 l, Jerez de la Frontera de Choluteca and San Pedro de Zula.

Perf. 12½

1946, Oct. 15   Unwmk.   Engr.

C155	AP51	1c red	.30	.25
a.		Vert. pair, imperf. between	17.50	
b.		Imperf., pair	70.00	
C156	AP52	2c red orange	.30	.25
a.		Imperf., pair	70.00	
C157	AP52	5c violet	.50	.25
C158	AP53	8c brown	1.90	.50
a.		Horiz. pair, imperf. btwn.	70.00	
C159	AP52	15c sepia	.95	.25
C160	AP52	21c deep blue	1.00	.30
a.		Horiz. pair, imperf. btwn.	15.00	
b.		Imperf., pair	70.00	
C161	AP52	1 l green	3.75	1.25
C162	AP54	2 l dark grn	5.75	2.00
		Nos. C155-C162 (8)	14.45	5.05

No. C158 commemorates the death of Franklin D. Roosevelt and the Allied victory over Japan in World War II.

Type AP53 Redrawn ("Franklin D. Roosevelt" under Column) — AP59

1947, Oct.   *Perf. 12½*

C163	AP59	8c brown	.75	.40
a.		Vert. pair, imperf. between	87.50	
b.		Horiz. pair, imperf. btwn.	175.00	
c.		Perf. 12x6	175.00	

Map, Ancient Monuments and Conference Badge — AP60

1947, Oct. 20   *Perf. 11x12½*
Various Frames

C164	AP60	16c green	.45	.25
C165	AP60	22c orange yel	.35	.25
C166	AP60	40c orange	.70	.35
C167	AP60	1 l deep blue	1.20	.90
C168	AP60	2 l lilac	4.50	3.50
C169	AP60	5 l brown	11.50	8.00
		Nos. C164-C169 (6)	18.70	13.25

1st Intl. Archeological Conf. of the Caribbean.
For overprints and surcharges see Nos. C181-C186, C351, C353-C354, C379, C544.

Flag and Arms of Honduras AP61

Juan Manuel Galvez AP62

J. M. Galvez, Gen. Tiburcio Carias A. and Julio Lozano — AP63

National Stadium — AP64

Designs: 5c, 15c, Julio Lozano. 9c, Juan Manuel Galvez. 40c, Custom House. 1 l, Recinto Hall. 2 l, Gen. Tiburcio Carias A. 5 l, Galvez and Lozano.
Various frames inscribed: "Conmemorativa de la Sucesion Presidencial para el Periodo de 1949-1955."

1949, Sept. 17   Engr.   *Perf. 12*

C170	AP61	1c deep blue	.30	.25
C171	AP62	2c rose car	.30	.25
C172	AP62	5c deep blue	.30	.25
C173	AP62	9c sepia	.30	.25
C174	AP62	15c red brown	.30	.25
C175	AP63	21c gray black	.50	.25
C176	AP64	30c olive gray	.70	.25
C177	AP64	40c slate gray	1.00	.25
C178	AP61	1 l red brown	1.60	.40
C179	AP61	2 l violet	3.75	1.50
C180	AP64	5 l rose car	10.75	5.50
		Nos. C170-C180 (11)	19.80	9.40

Presidential succession for the 1949-1955 term.

For overprints and surcharges see Nos. C188-C197, C206-C208, C346, C355, C419-C420, C478, C545.

Nos. C164-C169 Overprinted in Carmine

1951, Feb. 26   *Perf. 11x12½*

C181	AP60	16c green	.50	.40
a.		Inverted overprint	45.00	45.00
C182	AP60	22c orange yel	.65	.55
a.		Inverted overprint	45.00	
C183	AP60	40c orange	.65	.55
C184	AP60	1 l deep blue	2.10	1.75
C185	AP60	2 l lilac	3.90	3.25
a.		Inverted overprint	60.00	
C186	AP60	5 l brown	33.50	29.00
		Nos. C181-C186 (6)	41.30	35.50

Souvenir Sheets
Same Overprint in Carmine on Nos. C99 and C100
Perf. 12

C187	AP26	Sheet of 4	9.00	4.75
a.		Imperf.	400.00	250.00

UPU, 75th anniv. (in 1949).

Nos. C170 to C179 Overprinted in Carmine

1951, Feb. 27   *Perf. 12*

C188	AP61	1c deep blue	.30	.25
C189	AP62	2c rose car	.30	.25
C190	AP62	5c deep blue	.30	.25
C191	AP62	9c sepia	.30	.25
C192	AP62	15c red brown	.30	.25
C193	AP63	21c gray black	.50	.25
C194	AP64	30c olive gray	.70	.30
C195	AP64	40c slate gray	1.10	.60
C196	AP61	1 l red brown	2.75	1.50
C197	AP62	2 l violet	8.75	5.00
		Nos. C188-C197 (10)	15.10	8.90

Founding of Central Bank, July 1, 1950.

Discovery of America — AP65

Queen Isabella I — AP66

2c, 1 l, Columbus at court. 8c, Surrender of Granada. 30c, Queen Isabella offering her jewels.

Perf. 13½x14, 14x13½
1952, Oct. 11   Engr.   Unwmk.

C198	AP65	1c red org & indigo	.40	.25
C199	AP65	2c bl & red brn	.40	.25
C200	AP65	8c dk grn & dk brn	.40	.25
C201	AP66	16c dk bl & blk	.70	.25
C202	AP65	30c pur & dk grn	1.20	.70
C203	AP65	1 l dp car & blk	3.00	1.40
C204	AP65	2 l brn & vio	7.50	3.50
C205	AP66	5 l rose lil & ol	16.00	8.75
		Nos. C198-C205 (8)	29.60	15.35

500th birth anniv. of Isabella I of Spain.
For overprints and surcharges see Nos. C209-C221, C377-C378, C404-C406, C489, CO52-CO59.

No. C175 Surcharged in Carmine

1953, May 13   *Perf. 12*

C206	AP63	5c on 21c gray blk	.40	.40
C207	AP63	8c on 21c gray blk	.80	.50
C208	AP63	16c on 21c gray blk	1.30	.40
		Nos. C206-C208 (3)	2.50	1.20

Nos. CO52-CO54 Surcharged "HABILITADO 1953" and New Value in Red

1953, Dec. 8   *Perf. 13½x14, 14x13½*

C209	AP65	10c on 1c	.30	.25
a.		Inverted surcharge	50.00	50.00
C210	AP65	12c on 1c	.30	.25
C211	AP65	15c on 2c	.35	.25
C212	AP65	20c on 2c	.55	.30
C213	AP65	24c on 2c	.55	.30
a.		Inverted surcharge	50.00	50.00
C214	AP65	25c on 2c	.55	.30
C215	AP65	30c on 8c	.65	.30
C216	AP65	35c on 8c	.75	.45
C217	AP65	50c on 8c	.90	.45
C218	AP65	60c on 8c	1.10	.90

Same Overprint on Nos. CO57-CO59

C219	AP65	1 l dk grn & dk brown	3.25	2.25
C220	AP65	2 l bl & red brn	7.25	5.25
C221	AP66	5 l red org & blk	17.50	13.00
a.		Date inverted	150.00	
		Nos. C209-C221 (13)	34.00	24.50

Flags of UN and Honduras AP67

2c, UN emblem. 3c, UN building. 5c, Shield. 15c, Juan Manuel Galvez. 30c, UNICEF. 1 l, UNRRA. 2 l, UNESCO. 5 l, FAO.

Engraved; Center of 1c Litho.
1953, Dec. 18   *Perf. 12½*
Frames in Black

C222	AP67	1c ultra & vio bl	.30	.25
C223	AP67	2c blue	.30	.25
C224	AP67	3c rose lilac	.30	.25
C225	AP67	5c green	.30	.25
C226	AP67	15c red brown	.40	.25
C227	AP67	30c brown	.90	.55
C228	AP67	1 l dp carmine	7.00	4.50
C229	AP67	2 l orange	9.25	6.25
C230	AP67	5 l blue green	20.00	15.00
		Nos. C222-C230 (9)	38.75	27.50

Issued to honor the United Nations.
For overprints and surcharges see Nos. C231-C249, C331-C335, C472, C490, CO60-CO68.

Nos. CO60-CO66 Overprinted in Red

1955, Feb. 23   Unwmk.   *Perf. 12½*
Frames in Black

C231	AP67	1c ultra & vio bl	.30	.30
C232	AP67	2c dp blue grn	.30	.30
C233	AP67	3c orange	.30	.30
C234	AP67	5c dp carmine	.30	.30
C235	AP67	15c dk brown	.45	.40
C236	AP67	30c purple	1.25	1.10
C237	AP67	1 l olive gray	20.00	15.00

Overprint exists inverted on 1c, 3c.

Nos. C231 to C233 Surcharged in Black

C238	AP67	8c on 1c	.25	.25
C239	AP67	10c on 2c	.25	.25
C240	AP67	12c on 3c	.25	.25
		Nos. C231-C240 (10)	23.65	18.45

50th anniv. of the founding of Rotary International (Nos. C231-C240).

Nos. CO60-CO63, C226-C230 Overprinted

HONDURAS

1956, July 14   Unwmk.   *Perf. 12½*
Frames in Black

C241	AP67	1c ultra & vio bl	.30	.25
C242	AP67	2c dp bl grn	.30	.25
C243	AP67	3c orange	.30	.25
C244	AP67	5c dp car	.35	.25
C245	AP67	15c red brn	.40	.30
C246	AP67	30c brown	.60	.40
C247	AP67	1 l dp car	4.25	2.75
C248	AP67	2 l orange	6.25	4.75
C249	AP67	5 l bl grn	16.00	14.00
	Nos. C241-C249 (9)		28.75	23.20

10th anniv. of UN (in 1955). The red "OFICIAL" overprint was not obliterated.
The "ONU" overprint exists inverted on 1c, 3c, 5c and 1-lempira.

Basilica of Suyapa — AP68
Pres. Julio Lozano Diaz — AP69

3c, Southern Highway. 4c, Genoveva Guardiola de Estrada Palma. 5c, Maria Josefa Lastiri de Morazan. 8c, Landscape and cornucopia (5-Year Plan). 10c, National Stadium. 12c, US School. 15c, Central Bank. 20c, Legislative Palace. 25c, Development Bank (projected). 30c, Toncontin Airport. 40c, Juan Ramon Molina Bridge. 50c, Peace Monument. 60c, Treasury Palace. 1 l, Blood bank. 2 l, Communications Building. 5 l, Presidential Palace.

Engraved; #C255 Litho.
1956, Oct. 3   *Perf. 13x12½, 12½x13*

C250	AP68	1c black & vio bl	.30	.25
C251	AP69	2c black & dk bl	.30	.25
C252	AP68	3c black & brown	.30	.25
C253	AP69	4c black & lilac	.30	.25
C254	AP68	5c black & dk red	.30	.25
C255	AP68	8c brown & multi	.30	.25
C256	AP68	10c black & emer	.30	.25
C257	AP68	12c black & green	.30	.25
C258	AP68	15c dk red & blk	.35	.25
C259	AP68	20c black & ultra	.35	.25
C260	AP68	24c black & lil	.45	.25
C261	AP68	25c black & green	.50	.25
C262	AP68	30c blk & car rose	.50	.25
C263	AP68	40c blk & red brn	.60	.25
C264	AP68	50c blk & bl grn	.75	.35
C265	AP68	60c blk & org	1.00	.45
C266	AP68	1 l blk & rose vio	2.50	1.00
C267	AP69	2 l black & mag	4.50	2.25
C268	AP69	5 l blk & brn car	11.00	5.00
	Nos. C250-C268 (19)		24.90	12.55

Issued to publicize the Five-Year Plan.
For overprints and surcharges see Nos. C414-C418, C491-C493, C537-C538, C542, C550.
Types AP68 and AP69 in different colors, overprinted "OFICIAL," see Nos. CO69-CO87.

Flag of Honduras — AP70

Designs: 2c, 8c, Monument and mountains. 10c, 15c, 1 l, Lempira. 30c, 2 l, Coat of arms.

1957, Oct. 21   Litho.   *Perf. 13*
Frames in Black

C269	AP70	1c buff & ultra	.35	.25
C270	AP70	2c org, pur & emer	.35	.25
C271	AP70	5c pink & ultra	.35	.25
C272	AP70	8c org, vio & ol	.35	.25
C273	AP70	10c violet & brown	.35	.25
C274	AP70	12c lt grn & ultra	.35	.25
C275	AP70	15c green & brown	.40	.25
C276	AP70	30c pink & slate	.60	.25
C277	AP70	1 l blue & brown	2.50	1.50
C278	AP70	2 l lt grn & slate	5.00	3.00
	Nos. C269-C278 (10)		10.60	6.30

First anniv. of the October revolution.
For overprints and surcharge, see Nos. C551, CO88-CO97.

Control marks were handstamped in violet on many current stamps in July and August, 1958, following fire and theft of stamps at Tegucigalpa in April.
All post offices were ordered to honor only stamps overprinted with the facsimile signature of their departmental revenue administrator. Honduras has 18 departments.

Flags of Honduras and US — AP71

1958, Oct. 2   Engr.   *Perf. 12*
Flags in National Colors

C279	AP71	1c light blue	.30	.25
C280	AP71	2c red	.30	.25
C281	AP71	5c green	.30	.25
C282	AP71	10c brown	.30	.25
C283	AP71	20c orange	.50	.25
C284	AP71	30c deep rose	.50	.25
C285	AP71	50c gray	.70	.40
C286	AP71	1 l orange yel	1.50	1.00
C287	AP71	2 l gray olive	2.90	2.00
C288	AP71	5 l vio blue	6.50	4.00
	Nos. C279-C288 (10)		13.80	8.90

Honduras Institute of Inter-American Culture. The proceeds were intended for the Binational Center, Tegucigalpa.
For overprints see Nos. C320-C324.

Abraham Lincoln — AP72
Lincoln's Birthplace — AP73

Designs: 3c, 50c, Gettysburg Address. 5c, 1 l, Freeing the slaves. 10c, 2 l, Assassination. 12c, 5 l, Memorial, Washington.

1959, Feb. 12   Unwmk.   *Perf. 13½*
Flags in National Colors

C289	AP72	1c dp green	.30	.25
C290	AP73	2c dark blue	.30	.25
C291	AP73	3c purple	.30	.25
C292	AP73	5c dk carmine	.30	.25
C293	AP73	10c black	.45	.25
C294	AP73	12c dark brown	.45	.25
C295	AP72	15c red orange	.50	.25
C296	AP73	25c dull pur	.75	.40
C297	AP73	50c ultra	.90	.65
C298	AP73	1 l red brown	1.90	1.40
C299	AP73	2 l gray olive	3.00	1.75
C300	AP73	5 l ocher	6.75	5.00
a.	Miniature sheet		11.50	10.00
	Nos. C289-C300 (12)		15.90	10.95

Birth sesquicentennial of Abraham Lincoln.
No. C300a contains one each of the 1c, 3c, 10c, 25c, 1 l and 5 l, imperf.
For overprints and surcharges see Nos. C316-C319, C325-C330, C345, C347-C348, C352, C356-C364, C494-C495, C539-C541, C552-C553.
Types AP72 and AP73 in different colors, overprinted "OFICIAL," see Nos. CO98-CO109.

Constitution — AP74

Designs: 2c, 12c, Inauguration of Pres. Villeda Morales, horiz. 3c, 25c, Pres. Ramon Villeda Morales. 5c, 50c, Allegory of Second Republic (Torch and olive branches).

Engr.; Seal Litho. on 1c, 10c
1959, Dec. 21   *Perf. 13½*

C301	AP74	1c red brn, car & ultra	.40	.40
C302	AP74	2c bister brn	.40	.40
C303	AP74	3c ultra	.40	.40
C304	AP74	5c orange	.40	.40
C305	AP74	10c dl grn, car & ultra	.40	.40
C306	AP74	12c rose red	.50	.40
C307	AP74	25c dull lilac	1.25	.40
C308	AP74	50c dark blue	2.10	.40
	Nos. C301-C308 (8)		5.85	3.20

Second Republic of Honduras, 2nd anniv.
For surcharge see No. C543.

King Alfonso XIII and Map — AP75

Designs: 2c, 1906 award of King Alfonso XIII of Spain. 5c, Arbitration commission delivering its award, 1907. 10c, Intl. Court of Justice. 20c, Verdict of the Court, 1960. 50c, Pres. Morales, Foreign Minister Puerto and map. 1 l, Pres. Davila and Pres. Morales.

1961, Nov. 18   Engr.   *Perf. 14½x14*

C309	AP75	1c dark blue	.35	.25
C310	AP75	2c magenta	.35	.25
C311	AP75	5c deep green	.35	.25
C312	AP75	10c brn orange	.35	.25
C313	AP75	20c vermilion	.60	.35
C314	AP75	50c brown	1.50	.55
C315	AP75	1 l vio black	2.25	1.00
	Nos. C309-C315 (7)		5.75	2.90

Judgment of the Intl. Court of Justice at The Hague, Nov. 18, 1960, returning a disputed territory to Honduras from Nicaragua.

Nos. C295-C297 and CO105 Surcharged

L 0.06

1964, Apr. 7   *Perf. 13½*
Flags in National Colors

C316	AP72	6c on 15c red org	.40	.40
C317	AP73	8c on 25c dull pur	.40	.40
C318	AP73	10c on 50c ultra	.50	.40
C319	AP73	20c on 25c black	1.10	.40
	Nos. C316-C319 (4)		2.40	1.60

The red "OFICIAL" overprint on No. C319 was not obliterated.
See Nos. C345-C355, C419-C421.

Nos. C279-C281, C284 and C287 Overprinted: "FAO / Lucha Contra / el Hambre"

1964, Mar. 23   Unwmk.   *Perf. 12*
Flags in National Colors

C320	AP71	1c light blue	.40	.40
C321	AP71	2c red	.40	.40
C322	AP71	5c green	.40	.40
C323	AP71	30c deep rose	1.60	.75
C324	AP71	2 l gray olive	8.50	5.50
	Nos. C320-C324 (5)		11.30	7.45

FAO "Freedom from Hunger Campaign" (1963).

Nos. CO98-CO101, CO104 and CO106 Overprinted in Blue or Black

Overprint reads: "IN MEMORIAM / JOHN F. KENNEDY / 22 NOVEMBRE 1963"

1964, May 29   *Perf. 13½*
Flags in National Colors

C325	AP72	1c ocher (Bl)	.30	.30
C326	AP73	2c gray ol (Bl)	.30	.30
C327	AP73	3c red brn (Bl)	.40	.30
C328	AP73	5c ultra (Bk)	.55	.30
C329	AP72	15c dk brn (Bl)	2.25	1.25
C330	AP73	50c dk car (Bl)	11.50	6.25
	Nos. C325-C330 (6)		15.30	8.70

Pres. John F. Kennedy (1917-63). The red "OFICIAL" overprint was not obliterated. The same overprint was applied to the stamps in miniature sheet No. C300a and seal of Honduras and Alliance for Progress emblem added in margin. Value $105.

Nos. C222-C224, C226 and CO67 Overprinted with Olympic Rings and "1964"

Engr.; Center of 1c Litho.
1964, July 23   *Perf. 12½*
Frames in Black

C331	AP67	1c ultra & vio bl	.30	.30
C332	AP67	2c blue	.30	.30
C333	AP67	3c rose lilac	.30	.30
C334	AP67	15c red brown	.60	.50
C335	AP67	2 l lilac rose	7.25	6.25
	Nos. C331-C335 (5)		8.75	7.65

18th Olympic Games, Tokyo, Oct. 10-25. The red "OFICIAL" overprint on No. C335 was not obliterated.
The same overprint was applied to the 6 stamps in No. CO108a, with additional rings and "1964" in margins of souvenir sheet. Value $52.50.

View of Copan — AP76

Designs: 2c, 12c, Stone marker from Copan. 5c, 1 l, Mayan ball player (stone). 8c, 2 l, Olympic Stadium, Tokyo.

Unwmk.
1964, Nov. 27   Photo.   *Perf. 14*
Black Design and Inscription

C336	AP76	1c yellow grn	.35	.30
C337	AP76	2c pale rose lil	.35	.30
C338	AP76	5c light ultra	.35	.30
C339	AP76	8c bluish green	.35	.30
C340	AP76	10c buff	.55	.30
C341	AP76	12c lemon	.85	.35
C342	AP76	1 l light ocher	2.25	1.25
C343	AP76	2 l pale ol grn	5.75	3.50
C344	AP76	3 l rose	3.00	4.00
	Nos. C336-C344 (9)		13.80	10.60

18th Olympic Games, Tokyo, Oct. 10-25. Perf. and imperf. souvenir sheets of four exist containing one each of Nos. C338-C339, C341 and C344. Size: 129x110mm. Values: perf $42.50; imperf $52.50.
For overprints, see Nos. CO111-CO119.

Nos. C292, C174, CO106, CO104, C124-C125, C165, CO105, C167-C168 and C178 Surcharged

L. 0.12

1964-65

C345	AP73	4c on 5c dk car, bl & red	.45	.40
C346	AP62	10c on 15c red brn	.45	.40
C347	AP73	10c on 50c dk car, bl & red	.45	.40
C348	AP72	12c on 15c dk brn, bl & red	.50	.40
C349	AP27	12c on 16c ol gray	.50	.40
C350	AP27	12c on 21c lt blue	.50	.40
C351	AP60	12c on 22c org yel	.50	.40
C352	AP73	12c on 25c blk, bl & red	.50	.40
C353	AP60	30c on 1 l dp blue	.85	.40
C354	AP60	40c on 2 l lilac ('65)	1.20	.40
C355	AP61	40c on 1 l red brn ('65)	1.20	.40
	Nos. C345-C355 (11)		7.10	4.40

The red "OFICIAL" overprint on Nos. C347-C348 and C352 was not obliterated.

Nos. C289, CO99, C291-C292, C295-C296, CO106 and C299-C300 Overprinted in Black or Green

Overprint reads: "Toma de Posesión / General / Oswaldo López A. / Junio 6, 1965"

1965, June 6   Engr.   *Perf. 13½*
Flags in National Colors

C356	AP72	1c dp green	.30	.25
C357	AP73	2c gray ol (G)	.30	.25
C358	AP73	3c purple (G)	.30	.25
C359	AP73	5c dk car (G)	.30	.25
C360	AP72	15c red orange	.40	.35
C361	AP73	25c dull pur (G)	.55	.50
C362	AP73	50c dk car (G)	1.10	1.00
C363	AP73	2 l gray olive (G)	4.50	4.00
C364	AP73	5 l ocher (G)	10.75	9.50
	Nos. C356-C364 (9)		18.50	16.35

Inauguration of Gen. Oswaldo López Arellano as president. The red "OFICIAL" overprint on Nos. C357 and C362 was not obliterated.

Ambulance and Maltese Cross — AP77

Designs (Maltese Cross and): 5c, Hospital of Knights of Malta. 12c, Patients treated in village. 1 l, Map of Honduras.

1965, Aug. 30   Litho.   *Perf. 12x11*

C365	AP77	1c ultra	.50	.25
C366	AP77	5c dark green	.55	.30
C367	AP77	12c dark brown	.75	.50
C368	AP77	1 l brown	3.00	1.90
	Nos. C365-C368 (4)		4.80	2.95

Knights of Malta; campaign against leprosy.

HONDURAS

Father Manuel de Jesus Subirana — AP78

Designs: 1c, Jicaque Indian. 2c, Preaching to the Indians. 10c, Msgr. Juan de Jesus Zepeda. 7c, Pope Pius IX. 20c, Tomb of Father Subirana, Yore. 1 l, Mission church. 2 l, Jicaque mother and child.

Perf. 13½x14

1965, July 27		Litho.		Unwmk.	
C369	AP78	1c multicolored		.30	.30
C370	AP78	2c multicolored		.30	.30
C371	AP78	8c multicolored		.30	.30
C372	AP78	10c multicolored		.30	.30
C373	AP78	12c multicolored		.30	.30
C374	AP78	20c multicolored		.55	.30
C375	AP78	1 l multicolored		2.50	1.50
C376	AP78	2 l multicolored		5.00	3.00
a.	Souv. sheet of 4, #C371, C373, C375-C376			21.00	20.00
	Nos. C369-C376 (8)			9.55	6.30

Centenary (in 1964) of the death of Father Manuel de Jesus Subirana (1807-64), Spanish missionary to the Central American Indians.
For overprints and surcharges see Nos. C380-C386, C407-C413, C487-C488, C554.

Nos. C198-C199, C168 Overprinted

Overprint reads: "IN MEMORIAM / Sir Winston Churchill / 1874-1965."

1965, Dec. 20		Engr.		Perf. 13½x14	
C377	AP65	1c red org & indigo		.35	.30
C378	AP65	2c blue & red brn		.90	.80
C379	AP60	2 l lilac		7.25	7.00
	Nos. C377-C379 (3)			8.50	8.10

Sir Winston Spencer Churchill (1874-1965), statesman and World War II leader.

Nos. C369-C375 Overprinted

1966, Mar. 10		Litho.		Perf. 13½x14	
C380	AP78	1c multicolored		.45	.25
C381	AP78	2c multicolored		.45	.25
C382	AP78	8c multicolored		.45	.25
C383	AP78	10c multicolored		.45	.25
C384	AP78	12c multicolored		.50	.25
C385	AP78	20c multicolored		.60	.35
C386	AP78	1 l multicolored		5.00	3.25
	Nos. C380-C386 (7)			7.90	4.85

Visit of Pope Paul VI to the UN, New York City, Oct. 4, 1965.

Stamp of 1866, #1 — AP79

Tomas Estrada Palma — AP80

Post Office, Tegucigalpa — AP81

Designs: 2c, Air post stamp of 1925, #C1. 5c, Locomotive. 6c, 19th cent. mail transport with mules. 7c, 19th cent. mail room. 8c, Sir Rowland Hill. 9c, Modern mail truck. 10c, Gen. Oswaldo Lopez Arellano. 12c, Postal emblem. 15c, Heinrich von Stephan. 20c, Mail plane. 30c, Flag of Honduras. 40c, Coat of Arms. 1 l, UPU monument, Bern. 2 l, José Maria Medina.

Perf. 14½x14, 14x14½

1966, May 31		Litho.		Unwmk.	
C387	AP79	1c gold, blk & grnsh gray		.35	.25
C388	AP79	2c org, blk & lt bl		.35	.25
C389	AP80	3c brt rose, gold & dp plum		.35	.25
C390	AP81	4c bl, gold & blk		.35	.25
C391	AP81	5c pink, gold & blk		1.00	.25
C392	AP81	6c lil, gold & blk		.35	.25
C393	AP81	7c lt bl grn, gold & black		.35	.25
C394	AP80	8c lt bl, gold & blk		.35	.25
C395	AP81	9c lt ultra, gold & black		.35	.25
C396	AP80	10c cit, gold & blk		.35	.25
C397	AP79	12c gold, blk, yel & emerald		.35	.25
C398	AP81	15c brt pink, gold & dp claret		.55	.40
C399	AP81	20c org, gold & blk		.60	.45
C400	AP79	30c gold & bl		.75	.55
C401	AP79	40c multi		1.20	.80
C402	AP79	1 l emer, gold & dk green		2.75	1.50
C403	AP80	2 l gray, gold & black		5.75	4.25
a.	Souv. sheet of 6, #C387-C388, C396-C397, C402-C403			8.00	6.75
	Nos. C387-C403 (17)			16.10	10.70

Centenary of the first Honduran postage stamp. No. C403a exists perf. and imperf. See No. CE3. For surcharges see Nos. C473-C474, C479, C486, C496.

Nos. CO53, C201, C204 Overprinted

Overprint reads: "CAMPEONATO DE FOOTBALL Copa Mundial 1966 Inglaterra-Alemania Wembley, Julio 30"

Perf. 13½x14, 14x13½

1966, Nov. 25				Engr.	
C404	AP65	2c brown & vio		.35	.25
C405	AP66	16c dk bl & blk		.40	.30
C406	AP65	2 l brn & vio		9.00	8.50
	Nos. C404-C406 (3)			9.75	9.05

Final game between England and Germany in the World Soccer Cup Championship, Wembley, July 30, 1966. The overprint on the 2c and 2 l is in 5 lines, it is in 8 lines on the 16c. There is no hyphen between "Inglaterra" and "Alemania" on the 16c.

Nos. C369-C371 and C373-C376 Overprinted in Red

Overprint reads: "CONMEMORATIVA / del XX Aniversario / ONU 1966".

1967, Jan. 31		Litho.		Perf. 13½x14	
C407	AP78	1c multicolored		.30	.25
C408	AP78	2c multicolored		.30	.25
C409	AP78	8c multicolored		.40	.30
C410	AP78	12c multicolored		.60	.40
C411	AP78	20c multicolored		.80	.55
C412	AP78	1 l multicolored		1.80	1.50
C413	AP78	2 l multicolored		4.25	3.25
	Nos. C407-C413 (7)			8.45	6.50

UN, 20th anniversary.

Nos. C250, C252, C258, C261 and C267 Overprinted in Red

Overprint reads: "Siméon Cañas y Villacorta / Libertador de los esclavos / en Centro America / 1767-1967"

1967, Feb. 27				Engr.	
C414	AP68	1c blk & vio bl		.40	.40
C415	AP68	3c blk & brown		.40	.40
C416	AP68	15c dk red & blk		.45	.40
C417	AP68	25c blk & grn		1.25	.80
C418	AP69	2 l blk & mag		3.50	2.60
	Nos. C414-C418 (5)			6.00	4.60

Birth bicentenary of Father José Siméon Canas y Villacorta, D.D. (1767-1838), emancipator of the Central American slaves. The overprint is in 6 lines on the 2 l, in 4 lines on all others.

Nos. C178-C179 and CE2 Surcharged

1967

C419	AP61	10c on 1 l	.65	.40
C420	AP62	10c on 2 l	.65	.40
C421	APSD1	10c on 20c	.65	.40
	Nos. C419-C421 (3)		1.95	1.20

José Cecilio del Valle, Honduras — AP82

Designs: 12c, Ruben Dario, Nicaragua. 14c, Batres Montufar, Guatemala. 20c, Francisco Antonio Gavidia, El Salvador. 30c, Juan Mora Fernandez, Costa Rica. 40c, Federation Emblem with map of Americas. 50c, Map of Central America.

1967, Aug. 4		Litho.		Perf. 13	
C422	AP82	11c gold, dp ultra & blk		.40	.25
C423	AP82	12c lt bl, yel & blk		.40	.25
C424	AP82	14c sil, grn & blk		.40	.25
C425	AP82	20c pink, grn & blk		.40	.25
C426	AP82	30c bluish lil, yel & black		.65	.35
C427	AP82	40c pur, lt bl & gold		1.10	.70
C428	AP82	50c lem, grn & car rose		1.10	.70
	Nos. C422-C428 (7)			4.45	2.75

Founding of the Federation of Central American Journalists.
For surcharges see Nos. C475-C476.

Olympic Rings, Flags of Mexico and Honduras — AP83

Olympic Rings and Winners of 1964 Olympics: 2c, Like 1c. 5c, Italian flag and boxers. 10c, French flag and women skiers. 12c, German flag and equestrian team. 50c, British flag and women runners. 1 l, US flag and runners (Bob Hayes).

1968, Mar. 4		Litho.		Perf. 14x13½	
C429	AP83	1c gold & multi		.30	.25
C430	AP83	2c gold & multi		.30	.25
C431	AP83	5c gold & multi		.30	.25
C432	AP83	10c gold & multi		.35	.25
C433	AP83	12c gold & multi		.55	.25
C434	AP83	50c gold & multi		3.75	3.25
C435	AP83	1 l gold & multi		7.25	6.25
	Nos. C429-C435 (7)			12.80	10.75

19th Olympic Games, Mexico City, Oct. 12-27.
Exist imperf. Value $45.
Perf. and imperf. souvenir sheets of 2 exist containing 20c and 40c stamps in design of 1c. Values: perf $9; imperf $17.
For surcharge see No. C499.

John F. Kennedy, Rocket at Cape Kennedy — AP84

ITU Emblem and: 2c, Radar and telephone. 3c, Radar and television set. 5c, Radar and globe showing Central America. 8c, Communications satellite. 10c, 20c, like 1c.

1968, Nov. 28				Perf. 14x13½	
C436	AP84	1c vio & multi		.25	.25
C437	AP84	2c sil & multi		.25	.25
C438	AP84	3c multicolored		.35	.35
C439	AP84	5c org & multi		.40	.40
C440	AP84	8c multicolored		.50	.50
C441	AP84	10c olive & multi		.55	.55
C442	AP84	20c multicolored		.70	.70
	Nos. C436-C442 (7)			3.00	3.00

ITU, cent. A 30c in design of 2c, a 1 l in design of 5c and a 1.50 l in design of 1c exist; also two souvenir sheets, one containing 10c, 50c and 75c, the other one 1.50 l.
For overprints see Nos. C446-C453.

Nos. C436, C441-C442 Overprinted: "In Memoriam / Robert F. Kennedy / 1925-1968"

1968, Dec. 23					
C446	AP84	1c vio & multi		.25	.25
C447	AP84	10c olive & multi		.50	.50
C448	AP84	20c multicolored		.80	.80
	Nos. C446-C448 (3)			1.55	1.55

In memory of Robert F. Kennedy. Same overprint was also applied to a 1.50 l and to a souvenir sheet containing one 1.50 l. Value, souvenir sheet $6.

Nos. C437-C440 Overprinted in Blue or Red with Olympic Rings and: "Medalias de Oro / Mexico 1968"

1969, Mar. 3					
C450	AP84	2c multi (Bl)		.50	.50
C451	AP84	3c multi (Bl)		1.00	1.00
C452	AP84	5c multi (Bl)		1.50	1.50
C453	AP84	8c multi (R)		2.00	2.00
	Nos. C450-C453 (4)			5.00	5.00

Gold medal winners in 19th Olympic Games, Mexico City. The same red overprint was also applied to a 30c and a 1 l. The souvenir sheet of 3 noted after No. C442 exists with this overprint in black. Value, souvenir sheet $6.

Rocket Blast-off — AP85

Designs: 10c, Close-up view of moon. 12c, Spacecraft, horiz. 20c, Astronaut and module on moon, horiz. 24c, Lunar landing module.

Perf. 14½x13½, 13½x14

1969, Oct. 29					
C454	AP85	5c multicolored		.25	.25
C455	AP85	10c multicolored		.30	.30
C456	AP85	12c multicolored		.40	.40
C457	AP85	20c multicolored		.50	.50
C458	AP85	24c multicolored		1.00	1.00
	Nos. C454-C458 (5)			2.45	2.45

Man's first landing on the moon, July 20, 1969. A 30c showing re-entry of capsule, a 1 l in design of 20c and a 1.50 l in design of 24c exist. Two souvenir sheets exist, one containing Nos. C454-C455 and 1.50 l, and the other No. C456, 30c and 1 l.
For the safe return of Apollo 13, overprints were applied in 1970 to Nos. C454-C458, the 3 unlisted denominations and the 2 souvenir sheets. Value of 2 souvenir sheets $20.
For overprints and surcharges see Nos. C500-C504, C555.

Nos. C224, C393, C395, C422, C424, CE2 and C178 Surcharged

1970, Feb. 20				Engr.; Litho.	
C472	AP67	4c on 3c blk & rose lil		.50	.40
C473	AP81	5c on 7c multi		.50	.40
C474	AP81	10c on 9c multi		.65	.40
C475	AP82	10c on 11c multi		.65	.40
C476	AP82	12c on 14c multi		.75	.40
C477	APSD1	12c on 20c blk & red		.75	.40
C478	AP61	12c on 1 l red brn		.75	.40
	Nos. C472-C478 (7)			4.55	2.80

No. CE3 Overprinted "HABILITADO"

1970		Litho.		Perf. 14x14½	
C479	AP81	20c bis brn, brn & gold		1.00	.40

Julio Adolfo Sanhueza — AP86

Emblems, Map and Flag of Honduras — AP87

Designs: 8c, Rigoberto Ordoñez Rodriguez. 12c, Forest Fire Brigade emblem (with map of Honduras) and emblems of fire fighters, FAO and Alliance for Progress, horiz. 1 l, Flags of Honduras, UN and US, Arms of Honduras and emblems as on 12c.

Perf. 14½x14, 14x14½

1970, Aug. 15		Litho.			
C480	AP86	5c gold, emer & ind		.35	.30
C481	AP86	8c gold, org brn & indigo		.50	.40
C482	AP87	12c bl & multi		.60	.40
C483	AP87	20c yel & multi		.85	.40
C484	AP87	1 l gray & multi		4.25	4.00
a.	Souvenir sheet of 5			10.50	9.00
	Nos. C480-C484 (5)			6.55	5.50

Campaign against forest fires and in memory of the men who lost their lives fighting forest fires. No. C484a contains 5 imperf. stamps with simulated perforations and without gum similar to Nos. C480-C484. Sold for 1.45 l.
For surcharges see Nos. C497-C498.

HONDURAS

Hotel Honduras Maya — AP88

1970, Oct. 24   Litho.   Perf. 14

C485	AP88	12c sky blue & blk	.65	.40

Hotel Honduras Maya, Tegucigalpa, opening.

Stamps of 1952-1968 Srchd.

1971   Litho.; Engr.

C486	AP79	4c on 1c (#C387)	.25	.25
C487	AP78	5c on 1c (#C369)	.30	.25
C488	AP78	8c on 2c (#C370)	.65	.30
C489	AP65	10c on 2c (#C199)	.80	.40
C490	AP67	10c on 3c (#C224)	.80	.40
a.		Inverted surcharge	.80	
C491	AP68	10c on 3c (#C252)	.80	.40
C492	AP68	10c on 3c (#CO71)	.80	.40
C493	AP69	10c on 2c (#C251)	.80	.40
C494	AP73	10c on 2c (#CO99)	.80	.40
C495	AP73	10c on 3c (#CO100)	.80	.40
C496	AP80	10c on 3c (#C389)	.80	.40
C497	AP87	15c on 12c (#C482)	1.00	.55
C498	AP87	30c on 12c (#C482)	1.25	.80
C499	AP83	40c on 50c (#C434)	2.10	1.60
C500	AP85	40c on 24c (#C458)	2.10	1.60
		Nos. C486-C500 (15)	14.05	8.55

Red "OFICIAL" overprint was not obliterated on Nos. C492, C494-C495.

No. C491 exists with inverted surcharge.

Nos. C454, C456-C458 Ovptd. & Srchd.

Perf. 14½x13½, 13½x14½

1972, May 15   Litho.

C501	AP85	5c multi	2.00	.50
C502	AP85	12c multi	3.25	1.25
C503	AP85	1 l on 20c multi	7.25	3.25
C504	AP85	2 l on 24c multi	13.00	6.50
		Nos. C501-C504 (4)	25.50	11.50

Masonic Grand Lodge of Honduras, 50th anniv. Overprint varies to fit stamp shape.

Soldier's Bay, Guanaja — AP89

5c, Taps, vert. 6c, Yojoa Lake. 7c, Banana Carrier, by Roberto Aguilar, vert. 8c, Military parade. 9c, Orchid, national flower, vert. 12c, Soldier with machine gun. 15c, Sunset over beach. 20c, Litter bearers. 30c, Landscape, by Antonio Velasquez. 40c, Ruins of Copan. 50c, Girl from Huacal, by Pablo Zelaya Sierra. 1 l, Trujillo Bay. 2 l, Orchid, national flower, vert.

1972, May 19   Perf. 13

C505	AP89	4c shown	.45	.25
C506	AP89	5c multi	.45	.25
C507	AP89	6c multi	.45	.25
C508	AP89	7c multi	.45	.25
C509	AP89	8c multi	.45	.25
C510	AP89	9c multi	.45	.25
C511	AP89	10c like 9c, vert.	.45	.25
C512	AP89	12c multi	.45	.25
C513	AP89	15c multi	.55	.25
C514	AP89	20c multi	.55	.25
C515	AP89	30c multi	.90	.25
C516	AP89	40c multi	1.30	.40
a.		Souv. sheet of 4, #C508, C513, C515-C516	3.25	3.25
C517	AP89	50c multi	1.40	.35
a.		Souv. sheet of 4, #C506-C507, C514, C517	3.25	3.25
C518	AP89	1 l multi	2.25	1.00
a.		Souv. sheet of 4, #C505, C509, C512, C518	4.25	4.25
C519	AP89	2 l multi	7.25	3.00
a.		Souv. sheet of 3, #C510-C511, C519, CE4	11.00	11.00
		Nos. C505-C519, CE4 (16)	19.05	7.85

Sesquicentennial of independence (stamps inscribed 1970).

For surcharge see No. CE5.

Sister Maria Rosa and Child — AP90

Designs: 15c, SOS Children's Village emblem, horiz. 30c, Father José Trinidad Reyes. 40c, Kennedy Center, first SOS village in Central America, horiz. 1 l, Boy.

Perf. 13½x13, 13x13½

1972, Nov. 10   Photo.

C520	AP90	10c grn, gold & brn	.35	.25
C521	AP90	15c grn, gold & brn	.35	.25
C522	AP90	30c grn, gold & brn	.55	.25
C523	AP90	40c grn, gold & brn	.70	.25
C524	AP90	1 l grn, gold & brn	2.75	1.50
		Nos. C520-C524 (5)	4.70	2.50

Children's Villages in Honduras (Intl. SOS movement to save homeless children).

For overprints and surcharges see Nos. C531, C534-C536, C546-C549, C556, C560-C561.

Map of Honduras and Society Emblem — AP91

Design: 12c, Map of Honduras, emblems of National Geographic Institute and Interamerican Geodesic Service.

1973, Mar. 27   Litho.   Perf. 13

C525	AP91	10c multicolored	.75	.40
C526	AP91	12c multicolored	.95	.40

25th anniv. of Natl. Cartographic Service (10c) and of joint cartographic work (12c).

For overprints and surcharges see Nos. C532-C533, C557-C558.

Juan Ramón Molina — AP92

Designs: 8c, Illustration from Molina's book "Habitante de la Osa." 1 l, Illustration from "Tierras Mares y Cielos." 2 l, "UNESCO."

1973, Apr. 17   Litho.   Perf. 13½

C527	AP92	8c brn org, blk & red brn	.30	.25
C528	AP92	20c brt bl & multi	.80	.25
C529	AP92	1 l green & multi	1.90	1.00
C530	AP92	2 l org & multi	4.00	2.75
a.		Sheet of 4	7.00	7.00
		Nos. C527-C530 (4)	7.00	4.25

Molina (1875-1908), poet, and 25th anniv. (in 1971) of UNESCO. No. C530a contains 4 stamps similar to Nos. C527-C530. Exists perf. & imperf.

For surcharge see No. C559.

Nos. C520-C523, C525-C526 Overprinted in Red or Black

Overprint reads: "Censos de Población y Vivienda, marzo 1974. 1974, Año Mundial de Población"

Perf. 13½x13, 13x13½, 13

1973, Dec. 28   Photo; Litho.

C531	AP90	10c multi (R)	.50	.40
C532	AP91	10c multi (B)	.50	.40
C533	AP91	12c multi (B)	.50	.40
C534	AP90	15c multi (R)	.50	.40
C535	AP90	30c multi (R)	.80	.40
C536	AP90	40c multi (R)	1.10	.40
		Nos. C531-C536 (6)	3.90	2.40

1974 population and housing census; World Population Year. The overprint is in 7 lines on vertical stamps, in 5 lines on horizontal.

Issues of 1947-59 Surcharged in Red or Black

Perf. 13x12½, 13½, 11x12½, 12

1974, June 28   Engr.

C537	AP68	2c on 1c (#C250) (R)	.25	.25
C538	AP68	2c on 1c (#CO69)	.35	.25
C539	AP72	2c on 1c (#C289)	.35	.25
C540	AP72	2c on 1c (#CO98)	.35	.25
C541	AP72	3c on 1c (#C289)	.35	.25
C542	AP68	3c on 1c (#C250) (R)	.35	.25
C543	AP74	1 l on 50c (#C308)	1.95	1.40
C544	AP60	1 l on 2 l (#C168)	1.95	1.40
C545	AP62	1 l on 1 l (#C179) (R)	1.95	1.40
		Nos. C537-C545 (9)	7.95	5.70

Red "OFICIAL" overprint was not obliterated on Nos. C538 and C540.

Nos. C520-C523 Ovptd. in Bright Green

Overprint reads: "1949-1974 SOS Kinderdorfer International Honduras-Austria"

1974, July 25   Photo.

C546	AP90	10c grn, gold & brn	.60	.40
C547	AP90	15c grn, gold & brn	.60	.40
C548	AP90	30c grn, gold & brn	.60	.40
C549	AP90	40c grn, gold & brn	.80	.40
		Nos. C546-C549 (4)	2.60	1.60

25th anniversary of Children's Villages in Honduras. Overprint in 6 lines on 10c and 30c, in 4 lines on 15c and 40c.

Stamps of 1956-73 Surcharged

1975, Feb. 24   Litho.; Engr.

C550	AP68	16c on 1c (#C250)	.35	.30
C551	AP70	16c on 1c (#C269)	.35	.30
C552	AP72	16c on 1c (#C289)	.35	.30
C553	AP72	16c on 1c (#CO98)	.35	.30
C554	AP78	16c on 1c (#C369)	.45	.30
C555	AP85	16c on 12c (#C456)	.60	.30
C556	AP90	18c on 10c (#C520)	.35	.30
C557	AP91	18c on 10c (#C525)	.35	.30
C558	AP91	18c on 12c (#C526)	.35	.30
C559	AP92	18c on 8c (#C527)	.35	.30
C560	AP90	50c on 30c (#C522)	1.10	.50
C561	AP90	1 l on 30c (#C522)	1.90	.90
		Nos. C550-C561, CE5 (13)	9.85	5.25

Denominations not obliterated on Nos. C551, C553-C558, C560-C561; "OFICIAL" overprint not obliterated on No. C553.

For surcharges, see Nos. C1197, C1198, C1200.

Flags of Germany and Austria — AP93

Designs (Flags): 2c, Belgium & Denmark. 3c, Spain & France. 4c, Hungary & Russia. 5c, Great Britain & Italy. 10c, Norway & Sweden. 12c, Honduras. 15c, US & Switzerland. 20c, Greece & Portugal. 30c, Romania & Serbia. 1 l, Egypt & Netherlands. 2 l, Luxembourg & Turkey.

1975, June 18   Litho.   Perf. 13

Gold & Multicolored; Colors Listed are for Shields

C562	AP93	1c lilac	.35	.25
C563	AP93	2c gold	.35	.25
C564	AP93	3c rose gray	.35	.25
C565	AP93	4c light blue	.35	.25
C566	AP93	5c yellow	.35	.25
C567	AP93	10c gray	.35	.25
C568	AP93	12c lilac rose	.35	.25
C569	AP93	15c bluish green	.45	.35
C570	AP93	20c bright blue	.55	.40
C571	AP93	30c pink	1.00	.75
C572	AP93	1 l salmon	2.40	1.75
C573	AP93	2 l yellow green	5.00	3.75
		Nos. C562-C573 (12)	11.85	8.75

Souvenir Sheet

C574	AP93	Sheet of 12	20.00	20.00

UPU, cent. (in 1974). No. C574 contains 12 stamps similar to Nos. C562-C573 with shields in different colors.

Humuya Youth Center and Mrs. Arellano — AP94

Designs (Portrait of First Lady, Gloria de Lopez Arellano, IWY Emblem): 16c, Jalteva Youth Center. 18c, Mrs. Arellano (diff. portrait) and IWY emblem. 30c, El Carmen de San Pedro Sula Youth Center. 55c, Flag of National Social Welfare Organization, vert. 1 l, La Isla sports and recreational facilities. 2 l, Women's Social Center.

1976, Mar. 5   Litho.   Perf. 13½

C575	AP94	8c sal & multi	.35	.25
C576	AP94	16c yel & multi	.35	.25
C577	AP94	18c pink & multi	.35	.25
C578	AP94	30c org & multi	.60	.45
C579	AP94	55c multicolored	.95	.70
C580	AP94	1 l multicolored	2.10	1.50
C581	AP94	2 l multicolored	3.75	2.75
		Nos. C575-C581 (7)	8.45	6.15

International Women's Year (1975).

For surcharges see Nos. C736-C737, C781, C798, C886, C887, C919, C1203.

"CARE" and Globe — AP95

Designs: 1c, 16c, 30c, 55c, 1 l, Care package and globe, vert. Others like 5c.

1976, May 24   Litho.   Perf. 13½

C582	AP95	1c blk & lt blue	.40	.25
C583	AP95	5c rose brn & blk	.40	.25
C584	AP95	16c black & org	.40	.25
C585	AP95	18c lemon & blk	.40	.25
C586	AP95	30c blk & blue	.60	.35
C587	AP95	50c yel grn & blk	.85	.50
C588	AP95	55c blk & buff	.85	.50
C589	AP95	70c brt rose & blk	1.20	.70
C590	AP95	1 l blk & lt grn	2.10	1.25
C591	AP95	2 l ocher & blk	4.25	2.40
		Nos. C582-C591 (10)	11.45	6.70

20th anniversary of CARE in Honduras.

For surcharges see Nos. C735, C738, C788, C888, C922, C1105.

Fawn in Burnt-out Forest — AP96

Forest Protection: 16c, COHDEFOR emblem (Corporacion Hondureña de Desarrollo Forestal). 18c, Forest, horiz. 30c, 2 l, Live and burning trees. 50c, like 10c. 70c, Emblem. 1 l, Young forest, horiz.

1976, May 28   Litho.   Perf. 13½

C592	AP96	10c multicolored	.35	.25
C593	AP96	16c multicolored	.35	.25
C594	AP96	18c multicolored	.35	.25
C595	AP96	30c grn & multi	.75	.25
C596	AP96	50c multicolored	1.10	.30
C597	AP96	70c brn & multi	1.50	.40
C598	AP96	1 l yel & multi	3.00	.75
C599	AP96	2 l vio & multi	5.25	3.50
		Nos. C592-C599, CE6 (9)	14.15	6.50

For surcharges see Nos. C784, C787, C917, C1100.

"Sons of Liberty" — AP97

American Bicentennial: 2c, Raising flag of "Liberty and Union." 3c, Bunker Hill flag. 4c, Washington's Cruisers' flag. 5c, 1st Navy Jack. 6c, Flag of Honduras over Presidential Palace, Tegucigalpa. 18c, US flag over Capitol. 55c, Grand Union flag. 2 l, Bennington flag. 3 l, Betsy Ross and her flag.

1976, Aug. 29   Litho.   Perf. 12

C601	AP97	1c multicolored	.35	.30
C602	AP97	2c multicolored	.35	.30
C603	AP97	3c multicolored	.35	.30
C604	AP97	4c multicolored	.35	.30
C605	AP97	5c multicolored	.35	.30
C606	AP97	6c multicolored	.35	.30
C607	AP97	18c multicolored	.45	.40
C608	AP97	55c multicolored	1.10	.85
a.		Souv. sheet of 4, #C603, C606-C608	3.50	3.50

HONDURAS

C609	AP97	2 l multicolored	2.40	2.40
a.		Souv. sheet of 3, #C601, C604, C609	6.75	6.75
C610	AP97	3 l multicolored	7.00	7.00
a.		Souv. sheet of 3, #C602, C605, C610	8.25	8.25
	Nos. C601-C610 (10)		13.05	12.45

For surcharges see Nos. C883-C884, C885, C889, C1102.

King Juan Carlos of Spain — AP98

Designs: 16c, Queen Sophia. 30c, Queen Sophia and King Juan Carlos. 2 l, Arms of Honduras and Spain, horiz.

1977, Sept. 13 Litho. Perf. 14

C611	AP98	16c multicolored	.35	.25
C612	AP98	18c multicolored	.35	.25
C613	AP98	30c multicolored	.40	.25
C614	AP98	2 l multicolored	2.75	2.10
	Nos. C611-C614 (4)		3.85	2.85

Visit of King and Queen of Spain.
For surcharges see Nos. C890, C918, C1107.

Mayan Steles, Exhibition Emblems — AP99

Designs: 18c, Giant head. 30c, Statue. 55c, Sun god. 1.50 l, Mayan pelota court.

1978, Apr. 28 Litho. Perf. 12

C615	AP99	15c multi	.30	.30
C616	AP99	18c multi	.65	.55
C617	AP99	30c multi	1.00	.85
C618	AP99	55c multi	2.00	1.80

Imperf

C619	AP99	1.50 l multi	4.50	4.00
	Nos. C615-C619 (5)		8.45	7.20

Honduras '78 Philatelic Exhibition.
For overprints and surcharges see Nos. C642-C645, C786, C920, C924, CB6.

Del Valle's Birthplace AP100

Designs: 14c, La Merced Church, Choluteca, where del Valle was baptized. 15c, Baptismal font, vert. 20c, Del Valle reading independence acts. 25c, Portrait, documents, map of Central America. 40c, Portrait, vert. 1 l, Monument, Central Park, Choluteca, vert. 3 l, Bust, vert.

1978, Apr. 11 Litho. Perf. 14

C620	AP100	8c multicolored	.30	.25
C621	AP100	14c multicolored	.30	.25
C622	AP100	15c multicolored	.30	.25
C623	AP100	20c multicolored	.30	.25
C624	AP100	25c multicolored	.40	.30
C625	AP100	40c multicolored	.50	.40
C626	AP100	1 l multicolored	1.60	1.25
C627	AP100	3 l multicolored	5.00	4.00
	Nos. C620-C627 (8)		8.70	6.95

Bicentenary of the birth of José Cecilio del Valle (1780-1834), Central American patriot and statesman.
For surcharges see Nos. C739, C793, C795, C886A, C1098.

Rural Health Center — AP101

Designs: 6c, Child at water pump. 10c, Los Laureles Dam, Tegucigalpa. 20c, Rural aqueduct. 40c, Teaching hospital, Tegucigalpa. 2 l, Parents and child. 3 l, National vaccination campaign. 5 l, Panamerican Health Organization Building, Washington, DC.

1978, May 10 Litho. Perf. 14

C628	AP101	5c multicolored	.35	.30
C629	AP101	6c multicolored	.35	.30
C630	AP101	10c multicolored	.35	.30
C631	AP101	20c multicolored	.35	.30
C632	AP101	40c multicolored	.60	.50
C633	AP101	2 l multicolored	2.50	2.10
C634	AP101	3 l multicolored	4.00	3.45
C635	AP101	5 l multicolored	5.75	5.00
	Nos. C628-C635 (8)		14.25	12.05

75th anniv. of Panamerican Health Organization (in 1977).
For surcharges see Nos. C783, C783A.

Luis Landa and his "Botanica" AP102

Designs (Luis Landa and): 16c, Map of Honduras showing St. Ignacio. 18c, Medals received by Landa. 30c, Landa's birthplace in St. Ignacio. 2 l, Brassavola (orchid), national flower. 3 l, Women's Normal School.

1978, Aug. 29 Photo. Perf. 13x13½

C636	AP102	14c multicolored	.35	.35
C637	AP102	16c multicolored	.35	.35
C638	AP102	18c multicolored	.35	.35
C639	AP102	30c multicolored	.40	.35
C640	AP102	2 l multicolored	4.00	1.60
C641	AP102	3 l multicolored	5.00	6.00
	Nos. C636-C641 (6)		10.45	9.00

Prof. Luis Landa (1875-1975), botanist.
For surcharges see Nos. C740, C794, C888A, C923, C1099.

Nos. C615-C618 Overprinted in Red
Overprint includes Argentina '78 Soccer Cup Emblem and: "Argentina Campeon / Holanda Sub-Campeon / XI Campeonato Mundial / de Football".

1978, Sept. 6 Litho. Perf. 12

C642	AP99	15c multicolored	.35	.35
C643	AP99	18c multicolored	.50	.35
C644	AP99	30c multicolored	.65	.50
C645	AP99	55c multicolored	1.50	.80
	Nos. C642-C645 (4)		3.00	2.00

Argentina's victory in World Cup Soccer Championship. Same overprint was applied to No. C619. Value $45.
For surcharges, see No. C924.

Central University and Coat of Arms AP103

Designs show for each denomination a 19th century print and a contemporary photograph of same area (except 1.50 l, 5 l): No. C647, University City. 8c, Manuel Bonilla Theater. No. C650, Court House, vert. No. C651, North Boulevard highway intersection, vert. No. C652, Natl. Palace. No. C653, Presidential Palace. 20c, Hospital. 40c, Cathedral of Tegucigalpa. 50c, View of Tegucigalpa. 1.50 l, Aerial view of Tegucigalpa. No. C660, Arms of San Miguel de Tegucigalpa, 18th cent., vert. No. C661, Pres. Marco Aurelio Soto (1846-1908) (painting), vert.

1978, Sept. 29

C646	AP103	6c black & brn	.30	.25
C647	AP103	6c multicolored	.30	.25
a.		Pair, #C646-C647	.30	.25
C648	AP103	8c black & brn	.30	.25
C649	AP103	8c multicolored	.30	.25
a.		Pair, #C648-C649	.30	.25
C650	AP103	10c black & brn	.30	.25
C651	AP103	10c multicolored	.30	.25
a.		Pair, #C650-C651	.35	.30
C652	AP103	16c black & brn	.30	.25
C653	AP103	16c multicolored	.30	.25
a.		Pair, #C652-C653	.60	.50
C654	AP103	20c black & brn	.35	.30
C655	AP103	20c multicolored	.35	.30
a.		Pair, #C654-C655	.75	.75
C656	AP103	40c black & brn	.90	.75
C657	AP103	40c multicolored	.90	.75
a.		Pair, #C656-C657	1.90	1.90
C658	AP103	50c black & brn	1.20	1.00
C659	AP103	50c multicolored	1.20	1.00
a.		Pair, #C658-C659	2.50	2.50
C660	AP103	5 l black & brn	8.00	6.75
C661	AP103	5 l multicolored	8.00	6.75
a.		Pair, #C660-C661	17.00	17.00
	Nos. C646-C661 (16)		23.30	19.60

Souvenir Sheet

C662	AP103	1.50 l multi	2.75	2.75

400th anniv. of the founding of Tegucigalpa. In the listing the first number is for the 19th cent. design, the second for the 20th cent. design.
For overprints and surcharges see Nos. C724-C725, C740A-C746, C766-C769, C779-C780, C1094-C1095, C1103-C1104.

Goalkeeper AP104

Designs: Various soccer scenes.

1978, Nov. 26 Litho. Perf. 12

C663	AP104	15c multi, vert.	.30	.25
C664	AP104	30c multi	.40	.30
C665	AP104	55c multi, vert.	.75	.60
C666	AP104	1 l multi	1.75	1.40
C667	AP104	2 l multi	3.00	2.50
	Nos. C663-C667 (5)		6.20	5.05

7th Youth Soccer Championship, Nov. 26.
For surcharge see No. C797.

UPU Emblem AP105

2c, Postal emblem of Honduras. 25c, Dr. Ramon Rosa, vert. 50c, Pres. Marco Aurelio Soto, vert.

1979, Apr. 1 Litho. Perf. 12

C668	AP105	2c multicolored	.55	.40
C669	AP105	15c multicolored	.55	.40
C670	AP105	25c multicolored	.55	.40
C671	AP105	50c multicolored	.95	.40
	Nos. C668-C671 (4)		2.60	1.60

Centenary of Honduras joining UPU.

Rotary Emblem and "50" — AP106

1979, Apr. 26 Litho. Perf. 14

C672	AP106	3c multi	.35	.25
C673	AP106	5c multi	.35	.25
C674	AP106	50c multi	.70	.50
C675	AP106	2 l multi	2.40	1.75
	Nos. C672-C675 (4)		3.80	2.75

Rotary Intl. of Honduras, 50th anniv.
For surcharge see No. C884A, C1096.

Map of Caratasca Lagoon — AP107

Designs: 10c, Fort San Fernando de Omoa. 24c, Institute anniversary emblem, vert. 5 l, Map of Santanilla islands.

1979, Sept. 15 Litho. Perf. 13½

C676	AP107	5c multi	.30	.25
C677	AP107	10c multi	.30	.25
C678	AP107	24c multi	.30	.25
C679	AP107	5 l multi	4.75	4.00
	Nos. C676-C679 (4)		5.65	4.75

Panamerican Institute of History and Geography, 50th anniversary.
For surcharge see No. C891.

General Post Office, 1979 AP108

UPU Membership Cent.: 3 l, Post Office, 19th cent.

1980, Feb. 20 Litho. Perf. 12

C680	AP108	24c multi	.50	.25
C681	AP108	3 l multi	3.00	2.75

For surcharge see No. C925.

Workers in the Field, IYC Emblem AP109

5c, Landscape, vert. 15c, Sitting boy, vert. 20c, IYC emblem, vert. 30c, Beach scene. 1 l, UNICEF and IYC emblems, vert.

1980, Dec. 9 Litho. Perf. 14½

C682	AP109	1c shown	.65	.40
C683	AP109	5c multicolored	.65	.40
C684	AP109	15c multicolored	.65	.40
C685	AP109	20c multicolored	.65	.40
C686	AP109	30c multicolored	.65	.40
	Nos. C682-C686 (5)		3.25	2.00

Souvenir Sheet

C687	AP109	1 l multicolored	1.75	1.75

International Year of the Child (1979).

Maltese Cross, Hill — AP110

2c, Penny Black. 5c, Honduras type A1. 10c, Honduras type A1. 15c, Postal emblem. 20c, Flags of Honduras, Gt. Britain.
1 l, Honduras #C402.

1980, Dec. 17

C688	AP110	1c shown	.65	.40
C689	AP110	2c multicolored	.65	.40
C690	AP110	5c multicolored	.65	.40
C691	AP110	10c multicolored	.65	.40

Size: 47x34mm

C692	AP110	15c multicolored	.65	.40
C693	AP110	20c multicolored	.65	.40
	Nos. C688-C693 (6)		3.90	2.40

Souvenir Sheet

C694	AP110	1 l multicolored	2.75	2.50

Sir Rowland Hill (1795-1879), originator of penny postage. No. C694 contains one stamp 47x34mm.

Intibucana Mother and Child — AP111

Inter-American Women's Commission, 50th Anniv.: 2c, Visitacion Padilla, Honduras Section founder. 10c, Maria Trinidad del Cid, Section member. 1 l, Emblem, horiz.

1981, June 15 Litho. Perf. 14½

C695	AP111	2c multicolored	.65	.40
C696	AP111	10c multicolored	.65	.40
C697	AP111	40c multicolored	.65	.40
C698	AP111	1 l multicolored	.65	.40
	Nos. C695-C698 (4)		2.60	1.60

Bernardo O'Higgins, by Jose Gil de Castro — AP112

HONDURAS

Paintings of O'Higgins: 16c, Liberation of Chile, by Cosme San Martin, horiz. 20c, Portrait of Ambrosio O'Higgins (father). 1 l, Abdication of Office, by Antonio Caro, horiz.

1981, June 29
C699	AP112	16c multicolored	.40	.35
C700	AP112	20c multicolored	.40	.35
C701	AP112	30c multicolored	.40	.35
C702	AP112	1 l multicolored	1.50	.70
		Nos. C699-C702 (4)	2.70	1.75

For surcharges see Nos. C785, C888B, C1106.

CONCACAF 81 Soccer Cup — AP113

1981, Dec. 30 Litho. Perf. 14
C703	AP113	20c Emblem	.70	.60
C704	AP113	50c Player	1.40	1.25
C705	AP113	70c Flags	2.25	1.80
C706	AP113	1 l Stadium	3.25	2.75
		Nos. C703-C706 (4)	7.60	6.40

Souvenir Sheet
| C707 | AP113 | 1.50 l like #C703 | 2.50 | 2.25 |

For overprint see No. C797.

50th Anniv. of Air Force (1981) — AP114

Designs: 3c, Curtiss CT-32 Condor. 15c, North American NA-16. 25c, Chance Vought F4U-5. 65c, Douglas C47. 1 l Cessna A37-B. 2 l, Super Mystere SMB-11. 1.55 l, Helicopter.

1983, Jan. 14 Litho. Perf. 12
C708	AP114	3c multi	.35	.25
C709	AP114	15c multi	.35	.25
C710	AP114	25c multi	.45	.35
C711	AP114	65c multi	.85	.65
C712	AP114	1 l multi	1.30	1.00
C713	AP114	2 l multi	2.60	2.00
		Nos. C708-C713 (6)	5.90	4.50

Souvenir Sheet
| C714 | AP114 | 1.55 l multi | 4.25 | .40 |

For surcharges see Nos. C884B, C1097.

UPU Executive Council Membership, 3rd Anniv. — AP115

16c, UPU monument. 18c, 18th UPU Congress emblem. 30c, Natl. Postal Service emblem. 55c, Rio de Janeiro. 2 l, Dove on globe.

1983, Jan. 14
C715	AP115	16c multicolored	.35	.25
C716	AP115	18c multicolored	.35	.25
C717	AP115	30c multicolored	.50	.35
C718	AP115	55c multicolored	.70	.50
C719	AP115	2 l multicolored	2.75	2.00
		Nos. C715-C719 (5)	4.65	3.35

Souvenir Sheet
| C720 | AP115 | 1 l like 2 l | 2.75 | 2.50 |

For surcharges see Nos. C921, C1204.

Natl. Library and Archives Centenary (1980) — AP116

1983, Feb. 11 Litho. Perf. 12
| C721 | AP116 | 9c Library | .40 | .40 |
| C722 | AP116 | 1 l Books | 1.50 | .40 |

For surcharge see No. C1101.

Intl. Year of the Disabled (1979) — AP117

1983, Feb. 11
| C723 | AP117 | 25c Emblem | .65 | .40 |

No. C657a Ovptd. in Red
"CONMEMORATIVA DE LA VISITA / DE SS. JUAN PABLO II / 8 de marzo de 1983"

1983, Mar. 8
C724	AP103	40c blk & brn	3.25	2.50
C725	AP103	40c multicolored	3.25	2.50
a.		Pair, #C724-C725	7.00	5.00

Visit of Pope John Paul II.

Literacy Campaign (1980) — AP118

40c, Hands, open book. 1.50 l, People holding books.

1983, May 18 Litho. Perf. 12
| C726 | AP118 | 40c multi | .65 | .50 |
| C727 | AP118 | 1.50 l multi | 2.60 | 2.25 |

World Food Day, Oct. 16, 1981 — AP119

65c, Produce, emblem.

1983, May 18
| C728 | AP119 | 65c multicolored | 1.25 | 1.00 |

20th Anniv. of Inter-American Development Bank (1980) — AP120

1 l, Comayagua River Bridge. 2 l, Luis Bogran Technical Institute of Physics.

1983, June 17 Litho. Perf. 12
| C729 | AP120 | 1 l multi | 1.75 | 1.50 |
| C730 | AP120 | 2 l multi | 3.00 | 2.75 |

2nd Anniv. of Return to Constitutional Government — AP121

1984, Jan. 27 Litho. Perf. 12
C731		20c Arms, text	.65	.40
C732		20c Pres. Suazo Cordova	.65	.40
a.	AP121	Pair, #C731-C732	1.30	.80

La Gaceta Newspaper Sesquicentenary (1980) — AP122

1984, May 25 Litho. Perf. 12
| C733 | AP122 | 10c multicolored | .80 | .50 |
| C734 | AP122 | 20c multicolored | .80 | .55 |

Nos. C582, C575-C576 Surcharged

1985, June 26 Litho. Perf. 13½
C735	AP95	5c on 1c #C582	.40	.25
C736	AP94	10c on 8c #C575	.40	.25
C737	AP94	20c on 16c #C576	.40	.25
C738	AP95	1 l on 1c #C582	1.90	1.00
		Nos. C735-C738 (4)	3.10	1.75

Nos. C621, C636, C647a Surcharged
Litho., Photo. (No. C740)

1986, Aug. 21 Perfs. as before
C739	AP100	50c on 14c #C621	1.00	.70
C740	AP102	60c on 14c #C636	1.20	.90
C740A	AP103	85c on 6c #C646	1.75	1.60
C740B	AP103	85c on 6c #C647	1.75	1.60
c.		Pair, #C740A-C740B	3.50	3.00
C741	AP103	95c on 6c #C646	2.00	1.75
C742	AP103	95c on 6c #C647	2.00	1.75
a.		Pair, #C741-C742	4.00	3.50
		Nos. C739-C742 (6)	9.70	8.30

Black bar obliterating old values on Nos. C739-C740 also cover "aéreo."

Nos. C656-C657 Overprinted in Red

No. C743

No. C744

No. C745

No. C746

1986, Sept. 12 Litho. Perf. 12
C743	AP103	40c No. C656	.65	.40
C744	AP103	40c No. C657	.65	.40
C745	AP103	40c No. C657	.65	.40
C746	AP103	40c No. C656	.65	.40
a.		Block of 4, #C743-C746	3.00	2.00

AP123

San Fernando de Omoa Castle — AP124

20c, Phulapanzak Falls. 78c, Bahia Isls. beach. 85c, Bahia Isls. cove. 95c, Yojoa Lake. 1 l, Woman painting pottery.

Perf. 13½x14, 14x13½

1986, Nov. 10 Litho.
C747	AP123	20c multi, vert.	.30	.25
C748	AP123	78c multi	1.40	.55
C749	AP123	85c multi	1.60	.55
C750	AP123	95c multi, vert.	1.75	.65
C751	AP123	1 l multi, vert.	1.50	.70

Size: 84x59mm
Imperf

| C752 | AP124 | 1.50 l multi | 3.00 | 2.75 |
| | | Nos. C747-C752 (6) | 9.55 | 5.45 |

For overprint see No. C782.

AP125

National flag, Pres. Jose Azcona Hoyo.

1987, Feb. 2 Litho. Perf. 13½
| C753 | AP125 | 20c grn & multi | .45 | .40 |
| C754 | AP125 | 85c red & multi | 1.80 | 1.30 |

Democratic government, 1st anniv.

Flora — AP126

10c, Eupatorium cyrillinelsonii. 20c, Salvia ernesti-vargasii. 95c, Robinsonella erasmisosae.

1987, July 8 Litho. Perf. 13½x14
C755	AP126	10c multicolored	.35	.35
C756	AP126	20c multicolored	.60	.60
C757	AP126	95c multicolored	1.90	1.20
		Nos. C755-C757 (3)	2.85	2.15

Birds — AP127

50c, Eumomota superciliosa. 60c, Ramphastos sulfuratus. 85c, Amazona autumnalis.

1987, Sept. 10 Litho. Perf. 13½x14
C758	AP127	50c multicolored	2.40	2.25
C759	AP127	60c multicolored	2.75	2.50
C760	AP127	85c multicolored	4.50	4.25
		Nos. C758-C760 (3)	9.65	9.00

AP128

1987, Dec. 10 Litho. Perf. 13½
| C761 | AP128 | 1 l blk, brt yel & dark red | 1.90 | 1.60 |

Natl. Autonomous University of Honduras, 30th anniv.

AP129

1987, Dec. 23 Litho. Perf. 13½
| C762 | AP129 | 20c red & dk ultra | .75 | .50 |

Natl. Red Cross, 50th anniv.

AP130

1988, Jan. 27 Litho. Perf. 13½
| C763 | AP130 | 95c brt blue & org yel | 1.30 | 1.10 |

17th regional meeting of Lions Intl.

HONDURAS

Atlantida Bank, 75th Anniv. — AP131

Main offices: 10c, La Ceiba, Atlantida, 1913. 85c, Tegucigalpa, 1988.

1988, Feb. 10
C764	AP131	10c multi	.50	.30
C765	AP131	85c mutli	1.50	.50
a.	Souv. sheet of 2, #358-359, imperf.		2.10	1.60

No. C765a sold for 1 l.

No. C649a Surcharged

1988, June 9   Litho.   *Perf. 12*
C766	AP103	20c on 8c #C648	1.20	.90
C767	AP103	20c on 8c #C649	1.20	.90
a.	Pair, #C766-C767		2.75	2.00

No. C647a Surcharged

1988, July 8   Litho.   *Perf. 12*
C768	AP103	5c on 6c #C646	.40	.30
C769	AP103	5c on 6c #C647	.40	.30
a.	Pair, #C768-C769		1.10	.80

Postman AP132

Tegucigalpa Postmark on Stampless Cover, 1789 AP133

1988, Sept. 11   Litho.   *Perf. 13½*
C770	AP132	85c dull red brn	1.60	1.50
C771	AP133	2 l dull red brn & ver	3.50	3.00

EXFILHON '88.

Summer Olympics Type of 1988

85c, Running, vert. 1 l, Baseball, soccer, basketball.

1988, Sept. 30   Litho.   *Perf. 13½*

Size: 28x33mm
C772	A62	85c multi	1.40	1.20

Size: 36x27mm
C773	A62	1 l multi	1.60	1.30

Discovery of America, 500th Anniv. (in 1992) — AP134

Pre-Colombian pottery artifacts: 10c, Footed vase, vert. 25c, Bowl. 30c, Footed bowl. 50c, Pitcher, vert. 1 l, Rectangular footed bowl.

1988   Litho.   *Perf. 13½*
C774	AP134	10c multicolored	.70	.60
C775	AP134	25c multicolored	1.75	1.50
C776	AP134	30c multicolored	2.10	2.00
C777	AP134	50c multicolored	3.50	3.00
	Nos. C774-C777 (4)		8.05	7.10

Size: 115x83mm
Imperf
C778	AP134	1 l multicolored	4.25	4.00

Nos. C653a and C576 Surcharged

1988   Litho.   *Perf. 12, 13½*
C779	AP103	10c on 16c #C652	.40	.30
C780	AP103	10c on 16c #C653	.40	.30
a.	Pair, #C779-C780		1.00	.80
C781	AP94	50c on 16c #C576	1.20	.50
	Nos. C779-C781 (3)		2.00	1.10

Nos. C779-C780 exist with double surcharge.
Issued: 10c, Apr. 7, 50c, May 25.

No. C752 Overprinted

1989, July 14   Litho.   *Imperf*
C782	AP124	1.50 l multi	3.00	2.75

French revolution, bicent.

Nos. C629 and C593 Surcharged

I

II

1989   Litho.   *Perf. 14, 13½*
C783	AP101	15c on 6c, I	1.75	.75
C783A	AP101	15c on 6c, II	2.25	.75
C784	AP96	1 l on 16c	2.75	3.50
	Nos. C783-C784 (3)		6.75	5.00

Issue date: 1 l, June 15.

Nos. C699 and C616 Surcharged

1989, Dec. 15   Litho.   *Perf. 14½, 12*
C785	AP112	20c on 16c #C699	1.20	.75
C786	AP99	95c on 18c #C616	3.00	2.90

No. C786 exists with inverted surcharge.
Issued: No. C785, 12/15; No. C786, 12/28.

Nos. C594 and C585 Surcharged with New Denomination and "IV Juegos / Olimpicos / Centroamericanos"

1990, Jan. 12   *Perf. 13½*
C787	AP96	75c on 18c #C594 (S)	1.50	1.25
C788	AP95	85c on 18c #C585	1.75	1.50

No. C787 exists with double and inverted surcharge.

World Wildlife Fund — AP135

Various Mono ateles: No. C790, Adult, young. No. C791, Adult hanging, diff. No. C792, Adult, young, diff.

1990, Apr. 18   Litho.   *Perf. 13½*
C789	AP135	10c shown	8.50	8.00
C790	AP135	10c multi	8.50	8.00
C791	AP135	20c multi	12.00	11.00
C792	AP135	20c multi	13.00	12.00
	Nos. C789-C792 (4)		42.00	39.00

No. C621 Surcharged

1990, Feb. 8   Litho.   *Perf. 14*
C793	AP100	20c on 14c multi	.65	.40

Nos. C621 and C636 Surcharged "50 Aniversario / IHCI / 1939-1989"

1990, Mar. 29
C794	AP102	20c on 14c No. C636	.60	.30
C795	AP100	1 l on 14c No. C621	1.30	.90

No. C665 Surcharged

1990, June 14   Litho.   *Perf. 12*
C796	AP104	1 l on 55c multi	1.25	1.00

World Cup Soccer Championships, Italy.

No. C707 Ovptd. in Margin

Overprint includes Character Trademark and: "CAMPEONATO MUNDIAL DE FUTBOL Italia '90".

Souvenir Sheet

1990, June 14   *Perf. 14*
C797	AP113	1.50 l multi	1.75	1.50

No. C577 Surcharged in Black

1990, Feb. 22   Litho.   *Perf. 13½*
C798	AP94	20c on 18c multi	.75	.50

FAO, 45th Anniv. — AP136

1990, Oct. 16   Litho.   *Perf. 13½*
C799	AP136	95c yel, blk, bl, grn	1.25	1.00

17th Interamerican Congress of Industry and Construction AP137

20c, Map, vert. 1 l, Jose Cecilio Del Valle Palace.

1990, Nov. 21   Litho.   *Perf. 13½*
C800	AP137	20c multi	.40	.35
C801	AP137	1 l multi	1.10	.65

AP138

Christmas — AP139

95c, Madonna and Child, vert. 3 l, Poinsettia.

1990, Nov. 30   Litho.   *Perf. 13½*
C802	AP138	20c shown	1.00	.75
C803	AP138	95c multicolored	1.50	1.25

Size: 112x82mm
Imperf
C804	AP139	3 l multicolored	3.00	2.75
	Nos. C802-C804 (3)		5.50	4.75

Salesian Order in Honduras, 80th Anniv. — AP140

75c, St. John Bosco. 1 l, Natl. Youth Sanctuary.

1990, Dec. 28   Litho.   *Perf. 13½*
C805	AP140	75c multi	.80	.60
C806	AP140	1 l multi	1.10	.80

Pres. Rafael Leonardo Callejas — AP141

1991, Jan. 31
C807	AP141	30c Taking oath	.60	.45
C808	AP141	2 l Portrait	1.75	1.40

Moths and Butterflies AP142

85c, Strymon melinus. 90c, Diorina sp. 1.50 l, Hyalophora cecropia. 5 l, Papilio polixenes.

1991, Feb. 28   Litho.   *Perf. 13½*
C809	AP142	85c multi	2.00	1.85
C810	AP142	90c multi	2.50	2.25
C811	AP142	1.50 l multi	3.75	3.50

Size: 114x82mm
Imperf
C812	AP142	5 l multi	7.00	6.75
	Nos. C809-C812 (4)		15.25	14.35

Notary Day — AP143

1991, May 22   Litho.   *Perf. 13½*
C813	AP143	50c multicolored	1.65	1.40

Rafael Heliodoro Valle, Birth Cent. — AP144

1991, July 26   Litho.   *Perf. 13½*
C815	AP144	2 l pale pink & blk	1.90	1.65

Churches AP145

Discovery of America, 500th Anniv. emblem and: 30c, Church of St. Manuel of Colohete, Gracias. 95c, Church of Our Lady of Mercy, Gracias. 1 l, Comayagua Cathedral.

1991, Aug. 30   Litho.   *Perf. 13½*
C816	AP145	30c multicolored	.35	.35
C817	AP145	95c multicolored	1.00	.60
C818	AP145	1 l multicolored	1.25	1.00
	Nos. C816-C818 (3)		2.60	1.95

HONDURAS

Latin American Institute, 25th Anniv. — AP146

1991, June 20
C819 AP146 1 l multicolored   .95   .70

Flowers — AP147

30c, Rhyncholaelia glauca. 50c, Oncidium splendidum, vert. 95c, Laelia anceps, vert. 1.50 l, Cattleya skinneri.

1991, Apr. 30
C820 AP147   30c multicolored   .55   .40
C821 AP147   50c multicolored   .75   .55
C822 AP147   95c multicolored   1.00   .75
C823 AP147 1.50 l multicolored 1.80 1.40
Nos. C820-C823 (4)   4.10 3.10

Espamer '91, Buenos Aires — AP148

1991, July 1
C824 AP148 2 l multicolored   2.50 2.25

Size: 101x82mm
Imperf
C825 AP148 5 l like #C824   5.75 5.50
Discovery of America, 500th anniv. (in 1992).

11th Pan American Games, Havana — AP149

30c, Equestrian. 85c, Judo. 95c, Men's swimming. 5 l, Women's swimming.

1991, Aug. 8
C826 AP149 30c multicolored   .35   .35
C827 AP149 85c multicolored   .90   .60
C828 AP149 95c multicolored   1.10   .75

Size: 114x83mm
Imperf
C829 AP149 5 l multicolored   4.50 4.25
Nos. C826-C829 (4)   6.85 5.95

Pre-Columbian Culture — AP150

UPAEP emblem, artifacts and: 25c, ears of corn. 40c, ear of corn, map. 1.50 l, map.

1991, Sept. 30   Litho.   Perf. 13½
C830 AP150 25c multicolored   .35   .35
C831 AP150 40c multicolored   1.00   .75
C832 AP150 1.50 l multicolored 1.90 1.50
Nos. C830-C832 (3)   3.25 2.60

4th Intl. Congress on Control of Insect Pests — AP151

Designs: 30c, Tactics to control pests. 75c, Integration of science. 1 l, Cooperation between farmers and scientists. 5 l, Pests and biological controls.

1991, Nov. 22
C833 AP151 30c multicolored   .50   .40
C834 AP151 75c multicolored   1.30 1.10
C835 AP151 1 l multicolored   2.50 2.10

Size: 115x83mm
Imperf
C836 AP151 5 l multicolored   4.25 3.90
Nos. C833-C836 (4)   8.55 7.50

America Issue — AP152

90c, Sighting land. 1 l, Columbus' ships. 2 l, Ship, map, birds.

1992, Jan. 27   Litho.   Perf. 13½
C837 AP152 90c multicolored   .95   .75
C838 AP152 1 l multicolored   1.00   .85
C839 AP152 2 l multicolored   2.00 1.60
Nos. C837-C839 (3)   3.95 3.20

Christmas — AP153

2 l, Poinsettias in rooster vase.

1991, Dec. 19
C840 AP153 1 l shown   1.20   .80
C841 AP153 2 l multicolored   1.75 1.60

Honduran Savings Insurance Company, 75th Anniv. — AP154

1992, Jan. 17
C842 AP154 85c multicolored   .95   .75
C843 AP154 1 l Priest saying mass 1.50 1.25

Size: 115x83mm
Imperf
C844 AP154 5 l like #C842   4.75 4.50
Nos. C842-C844 (3)   7.20 6.50

First mass in New World, 490th anniv. (No. C843). Taking possession of new continent, 490th anniv. (Nos. C842, C844).

Pres. Rafael Leonardo Callejas, 2nd Year in Office — AP155

Callejas with: 20c, Italian president Francesco Cossiga. 2 l, Pope John Paul II.

1992, Jan. 27   Litho.   Perf. 13½
C845 AP155 20c black & purple   .55   .45
C846 AP155 2 l black & multi   2.90 2.50

Flowers — AP156

20c, Bougainvillea glabra. 30c, Canna indica. 75c, Epiphyllum. 95c, Sobralia macrantha.

1992, July 25   Litho.   Perf. 13½
C847 AP156 20c multicolored   .50   .40
C848 AP156 30c multicolored   .55   .45
C849 AP156 75c multicolored   1.50 1.20
C850 AP156 95c multicolored   2.50 2.00
Nos. C847-C850 (4)   5.05 4.05

Gen. Francisco Morazan Hydroelectric Complex AP157

1992, Aug. 17
C851 AP157 85c Dam face, vert. .85   .75
C852 AP157 4 l Rear of dam   .90   .65

AP158

1992, Aug. 24
C853 AP158 95c black & multi   .90   .65
C854 AP158 95c multicolored   .90   .65
Intl. Conference on Agriculture, 50th anniv.

AP159

Gen. Francisco Morazan (1792-1842): 5c, Morazan mounted on horseback. 10c, Statue of Morazan. 50c, Watch and sword, horiz. 95c, Portrait of Josefa Lastiri de Morazan. 5 l, Portrait of Morazan in uniform.

1992, Sept. 18   Litho.   Perf. 13½
C855 AP159 5c blk, purple blk   .45   .30
C856 AP159 10c multicolored   .50   .35
C857 AP159 50c multicolored   .65   .45
C858 AP159 95c multicolored   1.75 1.20

Size: 76x108mm
Imperf
C859 AP159 5 l multicolored   4.25 4.00
Nos. C855-C859 (5)   7.60 6.30

Children's Day — AP160

Paintings of children: 25c, Musicians. 95c, Boy, dog standing in doorway. 2 l, Flower girl.

1992, Sept. 7
C860 AP160 25c multicolored   .35   .35
C861 AP160 95c multicolored   .80   .60
C862 AP160 2 l multicolored   1.60 1.25
Nos. C860-C862 (3)   2.75 2.20

Intl. Conference on Nutrition AP161

1992, Sept. 30   Litho.   Perf. 13½
C863 AP161 1.05 l multicolored 1.05   .80

Pan-American Agricultural School, 50th Anniv. — AP162

20c, Bee keepers. 85c, Woman, goats. 1 l, Plowing. 2 l, Man with tool, vert.

1992, Oct. 9
C864 AP162 20c multicolored   .35   .35
C865 AP162 85c multicolored   .75   .50
C866 AP162 1 l multicolored   1.00   .65
C867 AP162 2 l multicolored   2.10 1.30
Nos. C864-C867 (4)   4.20 2.80

Exfilhon '92 — AP163

Birds: 1.50 l, F. triquilidos. 2.45 l, Ara macao. 5 l, Quetzal pharomachrus mocinno.

1992, Oct. 2
C868 AP163 1.50 l multicolored 2.25 2.00
C869 AP163 2.45 l multicolored 3.25 3.00

Size: 76x108mm
Imperf
C870 AP163 5 l multicolored   8.00 7.75
Nos. C868-C870 (3)   13.50 12.75
Discovery of America, 500th anniv.

America Issue — AP164

UPAEP emblem and: 35c, Native settlement. 5 l, Explorers meeting natives in boats.

1992, Oct. 30   Litho.   Perf. 13½
C871 AP164 35c multicolored   .35   .35
C872 AP164 5 l multicolored   4.00 3.50
Printed on both thick and thin paper.

Discovery of America, 500th Anniv. — AP165

Details from First Mass, by Roque Zelaya: 95c, Ships off-shore. 1 l, Holding services with natives, horiz. 2 l, Natives, countryside, temples, horiz.

1992, Oct. 30
C873 AP165 95c multicolored   .75   .60
C874 AP165 1 l multicolored   .95   .65
C875 AP165 2 l multicolored   2.10 1.65
Nos. C873-C875 (3)   3.80 2.90

City of El Progreso, Cent. — AP166

1992, Oct. 17
C876 AP166 1.55 l multicolored 2.00 1.75

First Road Conservation Congress of Panama and Central America — AP167

85c, Bulldozer on highway.

1992, Nov. 16   Perf. 13½
C878 AP167 20c shown   .50   .35
C879 AP167 85c multicolored   .85   .50

Pan-American Health Organization, 90th Anniv. — AP168

1992, Nov. 27
C880 AP168 3.95 l multicolored 2.50 2.25

Christmas AP169

Paintings by Roque Zelaya: 20c, Crowd watching people climb pole in front of church, vert. 85c, Nativity scene.

1992, Nov. 24
C881 AP169 20c multicolored   .50   .40
C882 AP169 85c multicolored   1.00   .60

HONDURAS

No. C601 Surcharged

Nos. C606-C607 Surcharged

Nos. C584, C612, C637 Surcharged

Nos. C672, C678, C708 Surcharged

Nos. C575-C576, C603, C620, C699 Surcharged

1992-93
Perfs. and Printing Methods as Before

C883	AP97	20c on 1c #C601	.65	.45
C884	AP97	20c on 3c #C603	.85	.55
C884A	AP106	20c on 3c #C672	.85	.55
C884B	AP114	20c on 3c #C708	.60	.40
C885	AP97	20c on 6c #C606	.60	.40
C886	AP94	20c on 8c #C575	.60	.40
C886A	AP100	20c on 8c #C620	.35	.35
C887	AP94	50c on 16c #C576	.60	.35
C888	AP95	50c on 16c #C584	.60	.35
C888A	AP102	50c on 16c #C637	.60	.35
C888B	AP112	50c on 16c #C699	.60	.35
C889	AP97	85c on 18c #C607	.85	.55
C890	AP98	85c on 18c #C612	.95	.65
C891	AP107	85c on 24c #C678	.95	.65
		Nos. C883-C891 (14)	9.65	6.35

Size and location of surcharge varies.

Issued: No. C883, 12/18/92; No. C889, 1/22/93; No. C885, 3/8/93; No. C888A, 9/7/93; No. C888, 9/13/93; No. C890, 9/24/93; No. C891, 10/1/93; No. C884A, 10/5/93; No. C884B, 10/8/93; Nos. C884, C886A, 10/21/93; No. C886, 10/29/93; Nos. C887, C888B, 11/3/93.

Intl. Court of Justice Decision on Border Dispute Between Honduras & El Salvador
AP170

Designs: 90c, Pres. of El Salvador and Pres. Callejas of Honduras, vert. 1.05 l, Country flags, map of Honduras and El Salvador.

1993, Feb. 24   Litho.   Perf. 13½
C893	AP170	90c multicolored	.70	.50
C894	AP170	1.05 l multicolored	.95	.65

Third year of Pres. Callejas' term.

Mother's Day — AP171

Paintings of a mother and child, by Sandra Pendrey: 50c, Red blanket. 95c, Green blanket.

1993, May 5   Litho.   Perf. 13½
C895	AP171	50c multi	.55	.40
C896	AP171	95c multi	1.60	1.25

Endangered Animals — AP172

85c, Manatee, horiz. 2.45 l, Puma, horiz. 10 l, Jaguar.

1993, May 14   Perf. 13½
C897	AP172	85c multi	.80	.75
C898	AP172	2.45 l multi	1.90	1.75
C899	AP172	10 l multi	7.00	6.50
		Nos. C897-C899 (3)	9.70	9.00

Natl. Symbols — AP173

25c, Ara macao. 95c, Odocoileus virginianus.

1993, June 25   Litho.   Perf. 13½
C900	AP173	25c multi	1.75	1.50
C901	AP173	95c multi	2.25	2.00

First Brazilian Postage Stamps, 150th Anniv. — AP174

1993, Sept. 10   Litho.   Perf. 13½
C902	AP174	20c Brazil No. 1	.45	.30
C903	AP174	50c Brazil No. 2	.65	.40
C904	AP174	95c Brazil No. 3	.90	.50
		Nos. C902-C904 (3)	2.00	1.20

Departments in Honduras AP175

Various scenes, department name: No. C905a, Atlantida. b, Colon. c, Cortes. d, Choluteca. e, El Paraiso. f, Francisco Morazan.
No. C906a, Comayagua. b, Copan. c, Intibuca. d, Islas de la Bahia. e, Lempira. f, Ocotepeque.
No. C907a, La Paz. b, Olancho. c, Santa Barbara. d, Valle. e, Yoro. f, Gracias a Dios.

1993, Sept. 20   Litho.   Perf. 13½
C905	AP175	20c Strip of 6, #a.-f.	2.90	2.25
C906	AP175	50c Strip of 6, #a.-f.	4.90	3.75
C907	AP175	1.50 l Strip of 6, #a.-f.	11.50	8.75
		Nos. C905-C907 (3)	19.30	14.75

No. C906 is vert.

Endangered Birds — AP176

20c, Spizaetus ornatus. 80c, Cairina moschata, horiz. 2 l, Harpia harpija, horiz.

1993, Oct. 11   Litho.   Perf. 13½
C908	AP176	20c multicolored	.65	.55
C909	AP176	80c multicolored	1.50	1.30
C910	AP176	2 l multicolored	3.00	2.50
		Nos. C908-C910 (3)	5.15	4.35

UN Development Program — AP177

1993, Oct. 19
C911	AP177	95c multicolored	.75	.50

Christmas — AP178

1993, Nov. 5
C912	AP178	20c Church	.40	.35
C913	AP178	85c Woman, flowers	.80	.45

Nos. C577, C585, C593, C611, C616, C638, C643, C680, C716 Surcharged

1993
Perfs. and Printing Methods as Before
C917	AP96	50c on 16c #C593	.45	.30
C918	AP98	50c on 16c #C611	.45	.30
C919	AP94	50c on 18c #C577	.45	.30
C920	AP99	50c on 18c #C616	.45	.30
C921	AP115	50c on 18c #C716	.85	.55
C922	AP95	85c on 18c #C585	.85	.55
C923	AP102	85c on 18c #C638	.85	.55
C924	AP99	85c on 18c #C643	.85	.55
C925	AP108	85c on 24c #C680	.85	.55
		Nos. C917-C925 (9)	6.05	3.95

Size and location of surcharge varies.

Issued: Nos. C917-C918, 11/12; Nos. C920, C924, 11/23; Nos. C921, C925, 11/30; Nos. C922-C923, 12/3; No. C919, 12/10.

Fish — AP179

20c, Pomacanthus arcuatus. 85c, Holacanthus ciliaris. 3 l, Chaetodon striatus.

1993, Dec. 7   Litho.   Perf. 13½
C931	AP179	20c multicolored	.35	.30
C932	AP179	85c multicolored	.95	.80
C933	AP179	3 l multicolored	3.00	2.50
		Nos. C931-C933 (3)	4.30	3.60

Famous Men — AP180

25c, Ramon Rosa. 65c, Jesus Aguilar Paz. 85c, Augusto C. Coello.

1993, Nov. 17
C934	AP180	25c multicolored	.50	.40
C935	AP180	65c multicolored	.60	.40
C936	AP180	85c multicolored	.65	.40
		Nos. C934-C936 (3)	1.75	1.20

Pres. Rafael Leonardo Callejas, 4th Year in Office — AP181

95c, Wife, Norma, planting tree, vert.

1994, Jan. 21   Litho.   Perf. 13½
C937	AP181	95c multicolored	.75	.50
C938	AP181	1 l multicolored	1.00	.75

AP182

1994, Mar. 8   Litho.   Perf. 13½
C939	AP182	1 l multicolored	1.05	.80

Intl. Year of the Family.

AP183

1994, Oct. 24   Litho.   Perf. 13½
C940	AP183	1 l multicolored	1.05	.80

Intl. Conference on Peace and Development in Central America, Tegucigalpa.

Christmas — AP184

Paintings by Gelasio Gimenez: 95c, Madonna and Child. 1 l, Holy Family.

1994, Dec. 15   Litho.   Perf. 13½
C941	AP184	95c multicolored	1.30	1.10
C942	AP184	1 l multicolored	1.40	1.10

UN, 50th Anniv. — AP185

Designs: 1 l, The Sowing: Ecological Family, by Elisa Dulcey. 2 l, Family Scene, by Delmer Mejia. 3 l, UN emblem, "50."

1995, Jan. 17
C943	AP185	1 l multicolored	.95	.75
C944	AP185	2 l multicolored	1.30	1.10
C945	AP185	3 l multicolored	2.00	1.65
		Nos. C943-C945 (3)	4.25	3.50

Pres. Carlos Roberto Reina, 1st Anniv. of Taking Office — AP186

Designs: 80c, Beside flag, vert. 1 l, Summit meeting of area presidents & vice presidents.

1995, Jan. 27
C946	AP186	80c multicolored	.50	.30
C947	AP186	95c multicolored	.65	.30
C948	AP186	1 l multicolored	.75	.55
		Nos. C946-C948 (3)	1.90	1.15

America Issue — AP187

Postal vehicles.

1995, Feb. 28   Litho.   Perf. 13½
C949	AP187	1.50 l Van	1.25	1.00
C950	AP187	2 l Motorcycle	1.50	1.25

HONDURAS

Miniature Sheet

Mushrooms — AP188

1 l: a, Marasmius cohaerens. b, Lepista nuda. c, Polyporus pargamenus. d, Fomes. e, Paneolus sphinctrinus. f, Hygrophorus aurantiaca.
1.50 l, vert: g, Psathyrella. h, Amanita rubescens. i, Boletellus russelli. j, Boletus frostii. k, Marasmius spegazzinii. l, Fomes annosus.
2 l, vert: m, Craterellus cornucopioides. n, Amanita. o, Auricularia delicata. p, Psllocybe cubensis. q, Clavariadelphus pistilaris. r, Boletus regius.
2.50 l: s, Scleroderma aurantium. t, Amanita praegraveolens. u, Cantharellus cibarius. v, Geastrum triplex. w, Russula emetica. x, Boletus pinicola.
3 l: y, Fomes versicolor. z, Cantharellus pupurascens. aa, Lyophyllum decastes. ab, Pleurotus ostreatus. ac, Boletus ananas. ad, Amanita caesarea.

1995, Apr. 7
C951 AP188 Sheet of 30, #a.-ad.   47.50   40.00

FAO, 50th Anniv. — AP189

1995, May 25   Litho.   Perf. 13½
C952 AP189 3 l multicolored   1.50   1.25

CARE, 50th Anniv. — AP190

Designs: 1.40 l, Family, farm. No. C954, Orchid, wildlife, couple working in soil. No. C955, Couple in vegetable garden.

1995, Aug. 4   Litho.   Perf. 13½
C953 AP190 1.40 l multicolored   .85   .75
C954 AP190 5.40 l multicolored   2.75   2.40
C955 AP190 5.40 l multicolored   2.75   2.40
    Nos. C953-C955 (3)   6.35   5.55

El Puente Archaeological Park — AP191

1995, Aug. 8   Imperf.
C956 AP191 20 l multicolored   9.25   9.00

America Issue — AP192

1.40 l, Kinosternon scorpioides. 4.54 l, Alpinia purpurata, vert. 10 l, Polyborus plancus, vert.

1995, Oct. 10   Litho.   Perf. 13½
C957 AP192 1.40 l multicolored   .85   .75
C958 AP192 4.54 l multicolored   2.00   1.85
C959 AP192 10 l multicolored   4.25   3.75
    Nos. C957-C959 (3)   7.10   6.35

Reptiles and Amphibians AP193

No. C960, Iguana iguana. No. C961, Agalychnis.

1995, Nov. 10   Litho.   Perf. 13
C960 AP193 5.40 l multicolored   2.35   2.10
C961 AP193 5.40 l multicolored   2.35   2.10

Christmas AP194

1.40 l, Bell, vert. 5.40 l, Nativity figurines. 6.90 l, Carved deer, vert.

1995, Dec. 4   Litho.   Perf. 13½
C962 AP194 1.40 l multi   .55   .50
C963 AP194 5.40 l multi   2.60   2.25
C964 AP194 6.90 l multi   2.90   2.50
    Nos. C962-C964 (3)   6.05   5.25

Integration System of Central America — AP195

1.40 l, Map of Central America, Tegucigalpa Protocol, 1991. 4.30 l, Functions listed, 1993. 5.40 l, 17th Summit of Presidents of Central America.

1996, Feb. 19   Litho.   Perf. 13½
C965 AP195 1.40 l multicolored   .60   .50
C966 AP195 4.30 l multicolored   1.90   1.60
C967 AP195 5.40 l multicolored   2.40   2.00
    Nos. C965-C967 (3)   4.90   4.10

UN Fight Against Drug Trafficking and Abuse, 10th Anniv. — AP196

Designs: 1.40 l, Stylized picture of minds on drugs. 5.40 l, Person with butterfly for brain, vert. 10 l, Musical score, "Viva la Vida."

1996, May 3
C968 AP196 1.40 l multicolored   .45   .40
C969 AP196 5.40 l multicolored   2.00   1.75
C970 AP196 10 l multicolored   3.25   2.75
    Nos. C968-C970 (3)   5.70   4.90

Arrival of the Garifunas in Honduras, Bicent. — AP197

Designs: 1.40 l, Headdress, vert. 5.40 l, Dancers, men playing drums. 10 l, Drums.

1996, June 13   Litho.   Perf. 13½
C971 AP197 1.40 l multicolored   .45   .40
C972 AP197 5.40 l multicolored   1.75   1.50
C973 AP197 10 l multicolored   3.25   2.75
    Nos. C971-C973 (3)   5.45   4.65

EXFILHON '96, 7th Philatelic Exhibition AP198

No. C974, Steam locomotive. No. C975, Passenger railcar.

1996, July 12   Litho.   Perf. 13½
C974 AP198 5.40 l multi   2.75   2.50
C975 AP198 5.40 l multi   2.75   2.50
     73x52mm
     Imperf
C976 AP198 20 l +2 l like #C974   11.00   10.50
    Nos. C974-C976 (3)   16.50   15.50

6th Central American Games — AP199

1996, Aug. 30   Litho.   Perf. 13½
C977 AP199 4.30 l Soccer   1.75   1.50
C978 AP199 4.54 l Volleyball   1.75   1.50
C979 AP199 l Mascot, vert.   1.75   1.50
    Nos. C977-C979 (3)   5.25   4.50

Scouting in Honduras, 75th Anniv. — AP200

1996, Oct. 25   Litho.   Perf. 13½
C980 AP200 2.15 l Emblems   .60   .50
C981 AP200 5.40 l Emblem, vert.   1.65   1.40
C982 AP200 6.90 l Scout feeding deer, vert.   2.50   2.10
    Nos. C980-C982 (3)   4.75   4.00

Christmas AP201

Poinsettia and: 1.40 l, Candles. 5.40 l, Candles, vert.

1996, Dec. 23   Litho.   Perf. 13½
C983 AP201 1.40 l multicolored   .80   .65
C984 AP201 3 l shown   1.50   1.25
C985 AP201 5.40 l multicolored   2.40   2.10
    Nos. C983-C985 (3)   4.70   4.00

Traditional Costumes — AP202

America issue: 4.55 l, Man in costume. 5.40 l, Woman in costume. 10 l, Couple in costumes.

1997, Jan. 17   Litho.   Perf. 13½
C986 AP202 4.55 l multicolored   1.25   1.10
C987 AP202 5.40 l multicolored   1.60   1.40
C988 AP202 10 l multicolored   4.00   3.50
    Nos. C986-C988 (3)   6.85   6.00

Honduras Plan, 20th Anniv., Intl. Plan, 60th Anniv. — AP203

Children's paintings: 1.40 l, Outdoor scene, children swimming, vert. 5.40 l, Girl standing beside lake, fish. 9.70 l, People working between buildings.

1997, Feb. 7   Litho.   Perf. 13½
C989 AP203 1.40 l multicolored   .60   .50
C990 AP203 5.40 l multicolored   1.75   1.50
C991 AP203 9.70 l multicolored   3.25   3.00
    Nos. C989-C991 (3)   5.60   5.00

Heinrich von Stephan (1831-97) — AP205

1997, May 9   Litho.   Perf. 13½
C995 AP205 5.40 l multicolored   1.75   1.50

World Population Day — AP206

Designs: 6.90 l, Child's drawing of people outside, trees, houses.

1997, July 11   Litho.   Perf. 13½
C996 AP206 3.40 l shown   .85   .75
C997 AP206 6.90 l multicolored   2.90   2.50

Butterflies AP207

Designs: 1 l, Rothchildia forbesi. 1.40 l, Parides photinus. 2.15 l, Morpho peleides. 3 l, Eurytides marcellus. 4.30 l, Parides iphidamas. 5.40 l, Danaus plexippus. 20 l+2 l, Hamadryas arinome.

1997, July 31
C998 AP207 1 l multi   .60   .50
C999 AP207 1.40 l multi   .60   .50
C1000 AP207 2.15 l multi   1.10   .90
C1001 AP207 3 l multi   1.50   1.25
C1002 AP207 4.30 l multi   1.90   1.60
C1003 AP207 5.40 l multi   2.75   2.25
     Imperf
     Size: 80x53mm
C1004 AP207 20 l +2 l multi   7.75   7.50
    Nos. C998-C1004 (7)   16.20   14.50
For surcharge see No. C1175.

St. Teresa of Jesus, Death Cent. — AP208

1997, Aug. 20   Litho.   Perf. 13½
C1005 AP208 1.40 l shown   1.00   .60
C1006 AP208 5.40 l Portrait, diff.   2.10   2.00

Astronomical Observatory — AP209

Designs: 5.40 l, Statue of Father Jose Trinidad Reyes. 10 l, Woman with book leading child up steps.

1997, Sept. 19   Litho.   Perf. 13½
C1007 AP209 1.40 l multicolored   .50   .50
C1008 AP209 5.40 l multicolored   1.50   1.20
C1009 AP209 10 l multicolored   2.60   2.25
    Nos. C1007-C1009 (3)   4.60   3.95

Alma Mater Foundation, 150th anniv., Autonomous University, 40th anniv.

Alcoholics Anonymous in Honduras, 37th anniv. — AP210

1997, Oct. 27
C1010 AP210 5.40 l multicolored   2.25   2.00

Diana, Princess of Wales (1961-97) AP211

1.40 l, Portrait, vert. 5.40 l, Diana dressed to walk through mine field, warning sign. 20 l, Mother Teresa, Princess Diana.

1997, Oct. 15
C1011 AP211 1.40 l multi   .50   .40
C1012 AP211 5.40 l multi   2.00   1.60
     Size: 51x78mm
     Imperf
C1013 AP211 20 l multi   6.25   6.00
    Nos. C1011-C1013 (3)   8.75   8.00

HONDURAS

Christmas — AP212

1.40 l, Christ of Picacho. 5.40 l, Virgin of Suyapa.

1997, Dec. 2		Litho.		Perf. 13½	
C1014	AP212	1.40 l	multi	.50	.40
C1015	AP212	5.40 l	multi	2.00	1.20

Mascot — AP213

C1016: a, Basketball. b, At bat, baseball. c, Soccer. d, Racquetball. e, Spiking volleyball. f, Setting volleyball. g, Bowling. h, Table tennis. i, Rings over map of Central America. j, Pitching, baseball.

No. C1017: a, Kicking, karate. b, Chopping, karate. c, Bowing, karate. d, Wrestling. e, Weight lifting. f, Boxing. g, Body building. h, Fencing. i, Program cover. j, Shooting.

No. C1018: a, Riding bicycle. b, Riding bicycle by shoreline. c, Swimming. d, Water polo. e, Hurdles. f, Gymnastics. g, Riding horse. h, Tennis. i, Program cover with mascot. j, Chess.

1997			Sheets of 10	
C1016	AP213	1.40 l	#a.-j.	7.00	5.00
C1017	AP213	1.50 l	#a.-j.	8.00	5.50
C1018	AP213	2.15 l	#a.-j.	10.00	7.00

6th Central American Games, San Pedro Sula.

Fish — AP214

1.40 l, Cichlasoma dovii. 2 l, Cichlasoma spilurum. 3 l, Cichlasoma spilurum facing right. 5.40 l, Astyanay fasciatus.

1997		Litho.		Perf. 13½	
C1019	AP214	1.40 l	multicolored	.60	.50
C1020	AP214	2 l	multicolored	.90	.75
C1021	AP214	3 l	multicolored	1.40	1.20
C1022	AP214	5.40 l	multicolored	2.60	2.10
	Nos. C1019-C1022 (4)			5.50	4.55

Marine Life, Islas de la Bahía (Bay Islands) — AP215

Designs: a, Balistes vetula. b, Haemudon plumieri. c, Pomacanthus paru. d, Juvenile halichoeres garnoti. e, Pomacanthus arcuatus. f, Holacanthus ciliaris. g, Diver's face, pseud opterogorgia. h, Diver's oxygen tanks, pseud opterogorgia. i, Dendrogya cylindrus. j, Holocentrus adscensionis. k, Dendrogya cylindrus, diff. l, Stegastes fuscus. m, Gorgonia mariae. n, Pillar coral. o, Pomacanthus arcuatus, diff. p, Holocentrus adscensionis, diff. q, Eusmilia fastigiata. r, Scarus coelestinus. s, Pillar coral, diff. t, Lachnolaimus masimus.

1998, Mar. 13		Litho.		Perf. 13½	
		Sheet of 20			
C1023	AP215	2.50 l	#a.-t.	26.50	21.50

Bancahsa, 50th anniv. Exists imperf. Value, $35.

America Issue — AP216

No. C1024, Post Office headquarters. No. C1025, Postman on motorcycle.

1998, May 29		Litho.		Perf. 13½	
C1024	AP216	5.40 l	multi	1.90	1.60
C1025	AP216	5.40 l	multi	1.90	1.60

Maya Artifacts — AP217

Designs: 1 l, Large carving on temple. 1.40 l, Stele of Mayan king. 2.15 l, Large stelae. 5.40 l, Small ornamental carving. 20 l, Maya Ruins, Copán.

1998, June 19		Litho.		Perf. 13½	
C1026	AP217	1 l	multi	.35	.30
C1027	AP217	1.40 l	multi	.65	.55
C1028	AP217	2.15 l	multi	2.40	2.10
C1029	AP217	5.40 l	multi	2.50	2.10

Size: 78x52mm
Imperf

C1030	AP217	20 l	multi	6.75	6.50
	Nos. C1026-C1030 (5)			12.65	11.55

1998 World Cup Soccer Championships, France — AP218

No. C1032, Players, vert. No. C1033: a, Stadium, Tegucigalpa. b, St. Denis Stadium, France.

1998, July 3		Litho.		Perf. 13½	
C1031	AP218	5.40 l	shown	1.25	1.00
C1032	AP218	10 l	multi	4.25	4.00

Imperf

| C1033 | AP218 | 10 l | Pair, #a.-b. | 8.75 | 8.50 |

No. C1033 contains two 53x42mm stamps. No. C1033 also issued rouletted between the stamps; value the same.

Reptiles — AP219

Designs: 1.40 l, Green iguana. 2 l, Rattlesnake. 3 l, Two iguanas. 5.40 l, Coral snake. 20 l + 2 l, Marine turtle.

1998, July 31		Litho.		Perf. 13½	
C1034	AP219	1.40 l	multi	.60	.40
C1035	AP219	2 l	multi	1.00	.75
C1036	AP219	3 l	multi	1.25	.95
C1037	AP219	5.40 l	multi	2.40	1.90

Size: 77x52mm
Imperf

C1038	AP219	20 l +2 l	multi	2.40	1.90
	Nos. C1034-C1038 (5)			7.65	5.90

Christmas AP220

Designs: 3 l, Girl taking ornament from bird, vert. 5.40 l, Christ Child asleep on bed of holly, dove, stars. 10 l, Boy with lantern leading donkey, cabin in the snow, vert.

1998, Dec. 8		Litho.		Perf. 13½	
C1039	AP220	3 l	multicolored	.80	.70
C1040	AP220	5.40 l	multicolored	1.50	1.25
C1041	AP220	10 l	multicolored	2.60	2.25
	Nos. C1039-C1041 (3)			4.90	4.20

Pres. Carlos Roberto Flores, 1st Anniv. of Taking Office — AP221

Designs: 5.40 l, Pres. and Mrs. Flores, Pope John Paul II. 10 l, Portrait of Pres., Mrs. Flores, vert.

1999, Jan. 27		Litho.		Perf. 13½	
C1042	AP221	5.40 l	multicolored	1.60	1.40
C1043	AP221	10 l	multicolored	2.40	2.10

Hurricane Mitch — AP222

No. C1044: a, Men working to clean up. b, Helicopter distributing aid. c, Vehicles under water, North Zone. d, Tipper Gore, Mary de Flores cleaning. e, Working to save banana crop. f, Destruction of Tegucigalpa. g, Cars, buses, trucks blocked by rock slide. h, Destruction of Comayagüela. i, Streets of Comayagüela. j, Oriental Zone. k, Loading debris, help from Mexico. l, Streets of Limpieza. m, Pres. Flores with Pres. Chirac of France. n, Business district of Comayagüela. o, Flooding, Tegucigalpa. p, Car in street, Comayagüela.

No. C1045: a, Central Zone. b, South Zone. c, Prince Felipe de Borbon, Mary de Flores. d, Small child crying. e, Cleaning up debris, Comayagüela. f, Families, man carrying baby, North Zone. g, Two men looking at destruction of building, Tegucigalpa. h, Man, child, woman wading in water, North Zone. i, Destruction in rural area. j, Cars piled up, concrete abutment along roadway. k, Cars, buildings along roadway. l, Mexican troops, airplane. m, Boys swimming. n, Pres. & Mrs. Flores, Hillary Clinton. o, People walking over rubble and debris, South Zone. p, Pres. Flores, former US Pres. George Bush.

1999, Feb. 19			Rouletted	
		Sheets of 16		
C1044	AP222	5.40 l	#a.-p.	26.50	22.50
C1045	AP222	5.40 l	#a.-p.	26.50	22.50

For surcharges, see Nos. C1207, C1208.

Famous Honduran Women — AP223

America Issue: 2.60 l, Maria del Pilar Salinas (b. 1914), scholar. 7.30 l, Clementina Suarez (1902-91), poet, writer. 10.65 l, Mary Flake de Flores, first lady of Honduras.

1999, Apr. 20		Litho.		Perf. 13½	
C1046	AP223	2.60 l	multi	.95	.85
C1047	AP223	7.30 l	multi	2.10	1.85
C1048	AP223	10.65 l	multi	3.00	2.60
	Nos. C1046-C1048 (3)			6.05	5.30

Dated 1998.

Mother's Day — AP224

Designs: 20 l, Police officer Orellana breastfeeding baby, vert. 30 l, Paphiopedilum urbanianum. 50 l, Miltoniopsis vexillaria.

1999, May 14		Litho.		Perf. 13½	
C1049	AP224	20 l	multicolored	4.65	4.50
C1050	AP224	30 l	multicolored	6.75	6.50
C1051	AP224	50 l	multicolored	11.00	10.75
	Nos. C1049-C1051 (3)			22.40	21.75

Endangered Birds — AP225

No. C1052, 5 l: a, Sarcorampohus papa. b, Leucopternis albicollis. c, Harpia harpyja. d, Pulsatrix perspicallata. e, Spizaetus ornatus. f, Pharomarchrus mocinno. g, Aulacorhynchus prasinus. h, Amazilia luciae. i, Ara macao. j, Centurus pygmaeus.

3 l: k, Aratinga canicularis. l, Amazona albifrons. m, Amazona auropalliata. n, Amazona autumnalis. o, Eurypyga helias. p, Crax rubra. q, Brotogeris jugularis. r, Pionus senilis. s, Aratinga rubritorques. t, Tinamus major.

No. C1053: a, Jaberu mycteria. b, Chondrohierax uncinatus. c, Pharomachrus mocinno. d, Ramphastos sulfuratus.

1999, July 8				
C1052	AP225		Sheeet of 20, #a.-t.	32.50 27.50
C1053	AP225	10 l	Sheet of 4, #a.-d.	11.00 10.00

Banco Sogerin, 30th anniv.

Inter-American Development Bank, 40th Anniv. — AP226

1999, Nov. 22		Litho.		Perf. 13½	
C1054	AP226	18.30 l	multi	4.25	4.00

For surcharge see No. C1249.

Blessed Josemaría Escrivá de Balaguer (1902-75), Founder of Opus Dei — AP227

1999, Nov. 29					
C1055	AP227	2.60 l	multi	.95	.85
C1056	AP227	16.40 l	multi	3.90	3.50

Millennium AP228

Designs: 2 l, Salvador Moncada, discoverer of nitric oxide in blood, vert. 8.65 l, Albert Einstein, vert. 10 l, Wilhelm Röntgen, vert. 14.95 l, George Stephenson and locomotive "Rocket."

1999, Oct. 18					
C1057	AP228	2 l	multi	1.25	1.15
C1058	AP228	8.65 l	multi	2.25	2.00
C1059	AP228	10 l	multi	2.75	2.50
C1060	AP228	14.95 l	multi	4.40	4.00
	Nos. C1057-C1060 (4)			10.65	9.65

National Congress, 175th Anniv. — AP229

Designs: 4.30, Statue of Francisco Morazán. 10 l, Congress President Rafael Pineda Ponce, Congress Building.

1999, Dec. 17		Litho.		Perf. 13¼	
C1061	AP229	4.30 l	multi	1.25	1.00
C1062	AP229	10 l	multi	3.50	2.25

HONDURAS

AP230

Holy Year
2000 — AP231

Holy Year Emblem and: 4 l, Pope John Paul II, people. 4.30 l, St. Peter. 6.90 l, Jesus, Jerusalem, horiz. 7.30 l, John Paul II, crowd, horiz. 10 l, John Paul II giving blessing. 14 l, Pres. Carlos Roberto Flores, John Paul II.

2000, Jan. 1		Litho.		Perf. 13¼
C1063	AP230	4 l multi	3.65	3.50
C1064	AP230	4.30 l shown	26.00	20.00
C1065	AP230	6.90 l multi	5.75	5.50
C1066	AP230	7.30 l multi	6.25	6.00
C1067	AP230	10 l multi	15.50	16.00
C1068	AP231	14 l shown	9.50	9.25

Nos. C1064, C1068 Redrawn

C1069	AP230	4.30 l multi	3.65	3.50
C1070	AP230	14 l multi	10.50	10.00
		Nos. C1063-C1070 (8)	80.80	73.75

No. C1067 issued in sheets of 6, with picture of John Paul II in selvage. No. C1069 has "HONDURAS" in yellow; No. C1064 in white. No. C1070 has "HONDURAS" at right, reading up; No. C1068 at top.

2nd Anniv. of Inauguration of Pres. Flores — AP232

Pres. Flores and: 10 l, Conference delegates. 10.65 l, Mario Hung Pacheco.

2000, Jan. 27				
C1071	AP232	10 l multi	3.25	3.00
C1072	AP232	10.65 l multi	3.75	3.50

Musical Instruments Type of Semi-postals of 2000

No. 1073, vert.: a, 1.40 l, Marimba, denomination at L. b, 1.40 l, Marimba, denomination at L. c, 1.40 l, Ayotl. d, 10 l, Maya drum. e, 10 l, Teponaxtle. f, 2.60 l, Maracas. g, 2.60 l, Güiro. h, 2.60 l, Chinchín. i, 2.60 l, Raspador. j, 2.60 l, Horse's jawbone. k, 3 l, Green zoomorphic whistle. l, 3 l, Aztec drum. m, 3 l, One-tone zoomorphic whistle. n, 3 l, Two-tone zoomorphic whistle. o, 3 l, Tun. p, 4 l, Gourd. q, 4 l, Deer hide drum. r, 4 l, Guacalitos. s, 4 l, Five musicians, marimba. t, 4 l, Four musicians, marimba.

2000, Apr. 7		Litho.	Perf. 13¼
C1073	SP1	Sheet of 20, #a-t	32.00 27.00

Paintings of Pablo Zelaya Sierra — AP233

No. C1074: a, 2 l, Green City (building and tree). b, 2 l, Old Woman With Rosary. c, 2 l, Rural Women (women with jars). d, 2 l, Woman With Green Robe. e, 2 l, City. f, 1.40 l, Shoulders of a Man. g, 1.40 l, Goat. h, 1.40 l, Spanish City. i, 1.40 l, Woman With Chignon. j, 1.40 l, Woman With Calabash. k, 2.60 l, Goat and Birds. l, 2.60 l, Tree Trunks. m, 2.60 l, Nuns. n, 2.60 l, Archers. o, 2.60 l, Moon and Boats. p, 2.60 l, Bust. q, 10 l, Still-life. r, 10 l, Composition With Books. s, 2.60 l, Landscape. t, 2.60 l, Head, Fan and Book.

2000, July 1			
C1074	AP233	Sheet of 20, #a-t	32.50 27.50

Airmail Anniv. Type of Semi-postals

Designs: 7.30 l, #C12. 10 l, Thomas Canfield Pounds, owner of Central American Airline, vert. 10.65 l, Pres. Rafael López Gutiérrez, signer of first airmail contract, vert.

2000, July 7		Size: 35x25mm		
C1075	SP2	7.30 l multi	1.80	1.60
		Size: 25x35mm		
C1076	SP2	10 l multi	2.50	2.25
C1077	SP2	10.65 l multi	2.75	2.40
		Nos. C1075-C1077 (3)	7.05	6.25

America Issue, A New Millennium Without Arms — AP234

Designs: 10 l, Sobralia macrantha, No guns. 10.65 l, Peace dove, No soldiers. 14 l, Train, No bombs, no more terrorism, horiz.

2000, July 28		Litho.	Perf. 13¼
C1078-C1080	AP234	Set of 3	9.75 9.00

2000 Summer Olympics, Sydney AP235

Designs: 2.60 l, Soccer players Ivan Guerrero, Mario Chirinos. 10.65 l, Swimmer Ramon Valle, vert. 12.45 l, Runner Gina Coello. No. C1084: a, 4.30 l, Swimmer. b, 4.30 l, Soccer player Danilo Turcios. c, 10.65 l, Runner Pedro Ventura. d, 12.45 l, Soccer player David Suazo.

2000, Sept. 13			
C1081-C1083	AP235	Set of 3	11.75 11.00
		Souvenir Sheet	
C1084	AP235	Sheet of 4, #a-d	30.00 28.00

No. C1084 exists imperf. Value, $37.50.

Intl. Voluntarism Year — AP236

Emblem, people and: 2.60 l, White-crowned parrot. 10.65 l, Telipogon ampliflorus.

2000, Dec. 5			
C1085-C1086	AP236	Set of 2	4.00 3.50

Christmas AP237

Designs: 2.60 l, Madonna and child. 7.30 l, Nativity, vert. 14 l, Carpet painter.

2000, Dec. 18			
C1087-C1089	AP237	Set of 3	6.00 5.25

America Issue, Birds — AP238

Designs: 2.60 l, Amazona auropalliata caribea. 4.30 l, Columbina passerina, horiz. 10.65 l, Ara macao. 20 l, Aguila harpia.

2001, Feb. 16		Litho.	Perf. 13¼
C1090-C1093	AP238	Set of 4	10.00 10.00

Nos. C584, C593, C606, C611, C646-C647, C652-C653, C699 Surcharged — c

Nos. C620, C672, C708, C721 Surcharged — d

No. C637 Surcharged — e

Methods and Perfs. as Before

2001

C1094	AP103(c)	2 l on 16c #C652	.50	.40
C1095	AP103(c)	2 l on 16c #C653	.50	.40
a.		Pair, #C1094-C1095	1.00	.80
C1096	AP106(d)	2.60 l on 3c #C672	.65	.55
C1097	AP114(d)	2.60 l on 3c #C708	.65	.55
C1098	AP100(d)	2.60 l on 8c #C620	.65	.55
C1099	AP102(e)	2.60 l on 16c #C637	.65	.55
C1100	AP96(c)	3 l on 16c #C593	.80	.65
C1101	AP116(d)	4 l on 9c #C721	1.00	.80
C1102	AP97(c)	4.30 l on 6c #C606	1.10	.90
C1103	AP103(c)	7.30 l on 6c #C646	1.75	1.45
C1104	AP103(c)	7.30 l on 6c #C647	1.75	1.45
a.		Pair, #C1103-C1104	3.50	3.50
C1105	AP95(c)	10 l on 16c #C584	2.40	2.00
C1106	AP112(c)	10.65 l on 16c #C699	2.50	2.10
C1107	AP98(c)	14 l on 16c #C611	4.25	3.50
		Nos. C1094-C1107 (14)	19.15	15.85

Size and location of surcharge varies. Issued: Nos. C1096-C1099, 3/26; others, 4/3.

Oscar Cardinal Rodriguez — AP239

No. C1108: a, 2.60 l, With father, 1946. b, 2.60 l, In Sanctuary of Our Lady of Suyapa. c, 2.60 l, As seminarian, 1964. d, 2.60 l, Installation as archbishop. e, 2.60 l, Ordination, 1960. f, 2.60 l, At Vatican, Feb. 21, 2001. g, 2.60 l, At mass in Guatemala, 1970. h, 2.60 l, Standing behind Honduran flag. i, 2.60 l, With Pope John Paul II, 1993. j, 2.60 l, Returning to Honduras as Cardinal. k, 2.60 l, Giving address as Cardinal, Mar. 10, 2001. l, 10.65 l, With Pope and woman, 1993. m, 10.65 l, Papal audience, Feb. 23, 2001. n, 10.65 l, Celebration of the Eucharist. o, 10.65 l, Kneeling before Pope, 1993. p, 10.65 l, Installation as Cardinal, Feb. 21, 2001. q, 15 l, Installation as Cardinal, St. Peter's Square.

2001, May 9		Litho.	Perf. 13¼
C1108	AP239	Sheet of 17, #a-q	38.00 34.00

Stamp sizes: Nos. C1108a-C1108j, 29x40mm; C1108k-C1108p, 49x40mm; C1108q, 163x131mm. No. C1108 exists imperf. Value $38.

Banco de Occidente, S.A., 50th Anniv. — AP240

Mayan ceramics: a, 2 l, Flower pot. b, 2 l, Anthropomorphic jar. c, 2 l, Anthropomorphic cover. d, 2 l, Cylindrical vase. e, 2 l, Censer tripod. f, 3 l, Scribe. g, 3 l, Cylindrical jar with anthropomorphic figures. h, 3 l, Three-part container. i, 3 l, Ceramic face. j, 3 l, Anthropomorphic jar, diff. k, 5 l, Three-legged vessel. l, 5 l, Pot with handles. m, 5 l, Censer. n, 5 l, Anthropomorphic cover. o, 5 l, Anthropomorphic jar, diff. p, 6.90 l, Pot with handles, diff. q, 6.90 l, Anthropomorphic cover, diff. r, 6.90 l, Anthropomorphic jar, diff. s, 6.90 l, Red cylindrical container. t, 6.90 l, Decorated container.

2001, Sept. 1		Litho.	Perf. 13¼
C1109	AP240	Sheet of 20, #a-t	36.00 31.00

UN High Commissioner for Refugees, 50th Anniv. — AP241

Designs: 2.60 l, Refugee and child, vert. 10.65 l, Refugees running.

2001

C1110-C1111	AP241	Set of 2	5.00 4.50

Souvenir Sheet

Juan Ramon Molina Bridge AP242

No. C1112: a, 2.60 l, Aerial view from end. b, 10 l, Close-up view from side. c, 10.65 l, Aerial view from side. d, 13.65 l, Side view showing river.

2001, Dec. 20		Litho.	Rouletted 6½
C1112	AP242	Sheet of 4, #a-d	17.00 16.00

Stamp sizes: No. C1112b, 152x93mm; others, 40x30mm.

America Issue — Wildlife — AP243

Designs: 10 l, Bird, Yojoa Lake. 10.65 l, Iguana, Cisne Islands. 20 l, Chrysina quetzalcoatli, Morpho sp., Pulaphanzhak Cataracts.

2002, Jan. 31			Perf. 13¼
C1113-C1115	AP243	Set of 3	14.25 13.50

HONDURAS

Pan-American Health Organization, Cent. — AP244

2002, Apr. 7
C1116 AP244 10 l multi 3.75 3.50

Miguel R. Pastor, Central District Mayor AP245

Central District emblem and: a, 1.40 l, Cathedral of San Miguel, statues, birds (57x35mm). b, 1.40 l, Chimpanzee throwing banana peel in trash can (57x35mm). c, 1.40 l, Municipal building (57x35mm). d, 2.60 l, Mayor Pastor, flags (27x35mm). e, 2.60 l, Mayor Pastor under tree (27x35mm). f, 2.60 l, Mayor Pastor with old woman (27x35mm). g, 2.60 l, Mayor Pastor with crowd (27x35mm). h, 2.60 l, Mayor Pastor planting seedling (27x35mm). i, 2.60 l, Mayor Pastor and family (27x35mm). j, 10 l, Municipal council (57x35mm). k, 10 l, Mayor with guests (57x35mm). l, 10.65 l, Cathedral of San Miguel, statues, birds (114x75mm).

2002, June 13 Litho. Perf. 13¼
C1117 AP245 Sheet of 12, #a-l 22.00 19.00

Souvenir Sheet

Discovery of Honduras, 500th Anniv. — AP246

No. C1118: a, 10.65 l, Boat on shore, jungle. b, 12.45 l, Natives on shore. c, 13.65 l, Spaniards coming ashore. d, 20 l, Spanish ship.

2002, Aug. 14
C1118 AP246 Sheet of 4, #a-d 11.00 10.00
Exfilhon 2002.

Souvenir Sheet

Christianity in Honduras, 500th Anniv. — AP247

No. C1119: a, 2.60 l, Natives and cross. b, 3 l, Santa Barbara Trujillo Fort. c, 10 l, 400 Years of History, by Mario Castillo. d, 10 l, Spaniards on shore, ships at sea.

2002, Aug. 14
C1119 AP247 Sheet of 4, #a-d 7.00 6.00
America issue.

Banco del Pais, 10th Anniv. — AP248

2002, Sept. 5 Litho. Perf. 13¼
C1120 AP248 2 l multi .40 .35
 a. Block of 10 3.75 3.75
C1121 AP248 2.60 l multi .80 .65
 a. Block of 10 7.00 7.00
C1122 AP248 10 l multi 2.50 2.10
 a. Sheet of 30 69.00 69.00
C1123 AP248 10.65 l multi 3.00 2.50
 a. Sheet of 30 80.00 80.00
Nos. C1120-C1123 (4) 6.70 5.60

Backgrounds of Nos. C1120-C1123 show a flag on a staff and clouds in the blocks and the flag on the sheets, giving each stamp a different background.

Orchids — AP249

Designs: 1.40 l, Vanilla planifolia. 2.60 l, Lycaste viriginalis. 3 l, Coelia bella. 4.30 l, Chysis laevis. 8.65 l, Myrmecophila bryslana. 10 l, Rhyncolaelia digbyana. 20 l, Mormodes aromatica.

2002, Sept. 25 Litho. Perf. 13¼
C1124-C1129 AP249 Set of 6 9.50 8.00

Size: 96x66mm
Imperf
C1130 AP249 20 l multi 6.50 6.25

for surcharges see Nos. C1241, C1243, C1252-C1253.

Christmas AP250

Designs: 2.60 l, Creche scene. 10.65 l, Holy Family. 14 l, People at recreation of nativity scene.

2002, Nov. 25
C1131-C1133 AP250 Set of 3 5.50 4.75

National Children's Foundation AP251

Designs: 2.60 l, Children. 10 l, Elderly people. 10.65 l, Symbols of Honduras, vert.

2002, Dec. 6
C1134-C1136 AP251 Set of 3 5.00 4.25

Insects AP252

No. C1137: a, 2 l, Chrysina spectabilis. b, 2 l, Chrysina strasseni. c, 2 l, Viridimicus omoaensis. d, 2 l, Hoplopyga liturata. e, 2.60 l, Chrysina cusuquensis. f, 2.60 l, Calomacraspis haroldi. g, 2.60 l, Pelidnota strigosa. h, 2.60 l, Odontocheila tawahka. i, 3 l, Chrysina cavei. j, 3 l, Chrysina pastori. n, 4 l, Platycoelia humeralis. o, 4 l, Phanaeus eximius. p, 4 l, Acanthoderes cavei. q, 10.65 l, Chrysina quetzalcoatli. r, 10.65 l, Cyclocephala abrelata. s, 10.65 l, Aegithus rufipennis. t, 10.65 l, Callipogon barbatum.
No. C1138 — Chrysina spp.: a, Eggs. b, Larva. b, Pupa.

2003, Feb. 20
C1137 AP252 Sheet of 20, #a-t 27.00 22.00

Souvenir Sheet

C1138 AP252 10 l Sheet of 3, #a-c 7.50 6.75

Banco Atlantida, 90th anniv. (No. C1137).

World Food Program — AP253

Designs: 2.60 l, Children with food. 6.90 l, Child with food. 10.65 l, Child with bowl and spoon.

2003, May 15
C1139-C1141 AP253 Set of 3 5.00 4.25
For surcharge see No. C1196.

Souvenir Sheet

Pontificate of John Paul II, 25th Anniv., and 20th Anniv. of Visit to Honduras — AP254

No. C1142: a, 13.65 l, Pope giving blessing. b, 14.55 l, Pope at airport. c, 15.45 l, Pope with staff. d, 16.65 l, Pope with rosary beads.

2003, Oct. 10 Perf. 10½
C1142 AP254 Sheet of 4, #a-d 13.00 12.00
For surcharges, See Nos. C1299-C1300.

Regional Sanitary Agricultural Organization, 50th Anniv. — AP255

Designs: 2.60 l, Eggs, sliced meat. 10 l, Eye, map of Central America, corn. 10.65 l, Emblem, map of Central America. 14 l, Vegetables. 20 l, Corn, tomato, fish.

2003, Oct. 24 Perf. 13¼
C1143-C1147 AP255 Set of 5 12.25 11.00

Bridges Built by Japan AP256

No. C1148: a, 3 l, Ilama Bridge, Santa Bárbara. b, 3 l, Sol Naciente Bridge, Choluteca. c, 4.30 l, Río Hondo Bridge, Francisco Morazán. d, 4.30 l, El Chile Bridge, Central District. e, 4.30 l, Iztoca Bridge, Choluteca. f, 10 l, La Democracia Bridge, near El Progreso. g, 10 l, Guasaule Bridge, Honduras-Nicaragua border. 20 l, Juan Ramón Molina Bridge, Tegucigalpa (168x109mm).

2003, Nov. 25 Litho. Perf. 13¼
C1148 AP256 Sheet of 7, #a-h + label 13.75 12.00

Telethon Honduras AP257

Telethon emblem and: 1.40 l, Flag on staff. 2.60 l, Hand, flag in light blue. 7.30 l, Hand, flag in dark blue. 10 l, Map.

2003, Dec. 4
C1149-C1152 AP257 Set of 4 5.25 4.25
For surcharges see Nos. C1244-C1245, C1247.

Christmas — AP258

Designs: 10.65 l, Angel. 14 l, Holy Family in manger.

2003, Dec. 8
C1153-C1154 AP258 Set of 2 5.00 4.50

Souvenir Sheet

Endangered Birds — AP259

No. C1155: a, 10 l, Arantinga strenua. b, 10.65 l, Falco deiroleucus. c, 14 l, Spizaetus melanoleucos. d, 20 l, Amazona xantholora.

2004, May 13
C1155 AP259 Sheet of 4, #a-d 12.00 11.00
Exfilhon 2004.

Endangered Animals — AP260

Designs: 85c, Pecari tajacu. 1.40 l, Mazama americana. 2 l, Tamandua mexicana, vert. 2.60 l, Felis concolor. No. C1160, Tamandua mexicana, vert. No. C1161, Felis concolor. No. C1162, Mazama americana. No. C1163, Bradypus variegatus. 4.30 l, Pecari tajacu. 7.85 l, Agalychinis challidryas, vert. 10.65 l, Bradypus variegatus. 14.95 l, Agalchinis challidryas, vert.
No. C1168, vert.: a, Mono titi. b, Cebus capucinus. c, Ateles geoffroyi. d, Alouatta palliata.

2004, May 24 Litho. Perf. 13¼
C1156 AP260 85c multi .40 .35
C1157 AP260 1.40 l multi .40 .35
C1158 AP260 2 l multi .65 .55
C1159 AP260 2.60 l multi .70 .60
C1160 AP260 3 l multi .90 .75
C1161 AP260 3 l multi .90 .75
C1162 AP260 4 l multi .95 .80
C1163 AP260 4 l multi .95 .80
C1164 AP260 4.30 l multi 1.00 .85
C1165 AP260 7.85 l multi 2.10 1.75
C1166 AP260 10.65 l multi 3.25 2.75
C1167 AP260 14.95 l multi 4.75 4.00
Nos. C1156-C1167 (12) 16.95 14.30
C1168 AP260 10 l Sheet of 4, #a-d 9.50 8.50

Nos. C1156-C1158, C1161, C1163, and C1165 were each printed in souvenir sheets of 4.
For surcharges see Nos. C1239-C1240, C1242, C1254-C1255.

Shells — AP261

Designs: Nos. C1169, C1174f, Voluta polypleura. Nos. C1170, C1174d, Strombus gallus. Nos. C1171, C1174a, Charonia variegata, Terebra taurina. Nos. C1172, C1174e, Spondylus americanus. Nos. C1173, C1174c, Strombus raninus. No. C1174b, Man blowing conch shell.

HONDURAS

2004, July 19 Litho. Perf. 13¼
C1169 AP261 85c multi .45 .35
C1170 AP261 1.40 l multi .65 .55
C1171 AP261 2 l multi .90 .75
C1172 AP261 2.60 l multi 1.25 1.00
C1173 AP261 10.65 l multi 3.25 2.75
Nos. C1169-C1173 (5) 6.50 5.40

Miniature Sheet
C1174 Sheet of 6 14.00 12.50
a.-b. AP261 4 l Either single .85 .75
c.-d. AP261 5 l Either single 1.00 .95
e.-f. AP261 20 l Either single 4.00 3.75

For surcharges see Nos. C1246, C1248, C1250-C1251.

No. C1004 Surcharged in Red

2004, Aug. 13 Litho. Imperf.
C1175 AP207 50 l on 20 l+2 l multi 9.50 9.25

Miniature Sheet

Banco Ficohsa, Sponsor of National Soccer Team — AP262

No. C1176: a, 4.30 l, Players, Honduras flag. b, 10.65 l, Team. c, 14 l, Saúl Martínez, David Suazo. d, 20 l, Amado Guevara.

2004, Sept. 3 Litho. Perf. 13¼
C1176 AP262 Sheet of 4, #a-d 8.50 7.50

Christmas — AP263

Designs: 2.60 l, Flight into Egypt. 7.85 l, Santa Claus on ornament. 10.65 l, Three Kings. 20 l, Holy Family.

2004, Nov. 23 Litho. Perf. 13¼
C1177-C1180 AP263 Set of 4 9.50 8.50
C1178a Sheet of 4 #C1178 8.50 7.50

For surcharges see Nos. C1224-C1227.

AP264

National Unity — AP265

2005, Feb. 3
C1181 AP264 10 l multi 1.50 1.25
C1182 AP265 20 l multi 2.75 2.50

Rotary International, Cent. — AP266

Rotary International emblem and: 2.60 l, Rafael Díaz Chávez, Paul Harris and Jorge Fidel Durón. 5 l, "100 años," vert. 8 l, Globe and arrows. 10.65 l, Map of Honduras, PolioPlus emblem. 14 l, Mayan sculpture.

2005, Feb. 23
C1183-C1187 AP266 Set of 5 7.75 6.50

Pope John Paul II (1920-2005) — AP267

Pope: 10 l, Wearing white vestments. 15 l, Wearing colored vestments. 20 l, Holding crucifix.

2005, Apr. 15 Litho. Perf. 13¼
C1188-C1189 AP267 Set of 2 4.25 3.75

Souvenir Sheet
C1190 Sheet of 2 #C1190a 6.25 5.75
a. AP267 20 l multi, 29x42mm 3.00 2.75

Honduran Medical Review, 75th Anniv. — AP268

Designs: 3 l, House. 5 l, Bird. 12 l, Jaguar. 30 l, Flowers.
No. C1195: a, Macaws. b, Macaw in banana tree. c, Rooster. d, Turkeys and hens.

2005, May 18
C1191-C1194 AP268 Set of 4 8.50 7.50

Souvenir Sheet
C1195 AP268 25 l Sheet of 4, #a-d 15.00 14.00

Nos. 390-392, B1, C550, C552, C553, C576, C715, C1044-C1045, C1140 and RA8 Surcharged

"X" Obliterators — f
Box Obliterator and "Aereo" — g

Box Obliterator — h

Methods and Perfs as Before
2005, June 3
C1196 AP253(f) 3 l on 6.90 l #C1140 .40 .35
C1197 AP72(f) 5 l on 16c on 1c #C552 .70 .65
C1198 AP72(f) 5 l on 16c on 1c #C553 .70 .65
C1199 PT6(g) 10 l on 13.85 l on 1c #392 1.40 1.30
C1200 AP68(f) 14 l on 16c on 1c #C550 1.90 1.75
C1201 PT6(g) 20 l on 13.85 l on 1c #392 2.60 2.40
C1202 PT6(g) 25 l on 11.55 l on 1c #390 3.50 3.25
C1203 AP94(f) 30 l on 16c #C576 4.00 3.75
C1204 AP115(f) 35 l on 16c #C715 4.90 4.50
C1205 PT6(g) 40 l on 11.55 l on 1c #390 5.40 5.00
C1206 PT6(g) 50 l on 12.45 l on 1c #391 7.00 6.50
Nos. C1196-C1206 (11) 32.50 30.10

Sheets
C1207 Sheet of 16 (#C1044) 23.50 19.50
a.-p. AP222(h) 8 l on 5.40 l any single 1.40 1.20
C1208 Sheet of 16 (#C1045) 23.50 19.50
a.-p. AP222(h) 8 l on 5.40 l any single 1.40 1.20
C1209 Sheet of 6 (#B1) 13.50 12.00
a.-f. SP1(f) 15 l on 10 l +1 l any single 2.25 2.00
g. As No. C1209, no. On No. B1g 13.50 12.00

Size, location and font of surcharges and obliterators vary on types "f" and "h."

Honduras — Japan Diplomatic Relations, 70th Anniv. — AP269

Designs: 8 l, Actors in play. 15 l, Emblem of Japanese-Central American Year. 30 l, National Congress, Japanese Princess Sayako.
No. C1213: a, Japanese ceramics. b, Flowers. c, Mayan ceramics. d, Mount Fuji, Japan and Pico Bonito National Park, Honduras.

2005, Aug. 9 Litho. Perf. 13¼
C1210-C1212 AP269 Set of 3 8.50 7.75

Souvenir Sheet
C1213 AP269 25 l Sheet of 4, #a-d 15.00 14.00

Gen. José Trinidad Cabañas (1805-71) — AP270

Cabañas: 3 l, With green panel at bottom. 8 l, With university buildings, horiz. 15 l, In oval frame.

2005, Sept. 12
C1214-C1216 AP270 Set of 3 4.25 4.00

Honduras, Water Capital — AP271

Water droplet and: 30 l, Heart, butterfly, Sanaa and Ras-hon emblems. 50 l, Heart.

2005, Sept. 28
C1217 AP271 30 l multi 4.50 4.25
C1218 AP271 50 l multi 9.50 9.25

Souvenir Sheet

America Issue — Endangered Mushrooms — AP272

No. C1219: a, 20 l, Hygrophorus marzuolus. b, 25 l, Lactarius deliciosus. c, 30 l, Boletus pinophilus. d, 50 l, Gyromitra esculenta.

2005
C1219 AP272 Sheet of 4, #a-d 19.00 18.00

AP273

Mail Transport — AP274

Designs: 5 l, Charles Lindbergh, PAA emblem. 25 l, Postal rail car, 1920. 30 l, First Honduran postal car, 1914. 50 l, Sikorsky S-38 airplane, PAA emblem, horiz.

2005, Dec. 6 Litho. Perf. 13¼
C1220 AP273 5 l multi .85 .80
C1221 AP274 25 l multi 4.00 3.75
C1222 AP274 30 l multi 5.25 4.75
Nos. C1220-C1222 (3) 10.10 9.30

Imperf
Size: 89x64mm
C1223 AP273 50 l multi 7.00 6.75

Nos. C1177-C1179 Surcharged

2005 Litho. Perf. 13¼
C1224 AP263 3 l on 2.60 l #C1177 .40 .40
C1225 AP263 15 l on 7.85 l #C1178 2.10 2.10
C1226 AP263 25 l on 7.85 l #C1178 4.00 4.00
C1227 AP263 50 l on 10.65 l #C1179 8.00 7.50
Nos. C1224-C1227 (4) 14.50 14.00

No. C1226 has a thick wavy line obliterator and was issued in sheets of four.

2006 Winter Olympics, Turin — AP275

Skier and: 20 l, Turin Olympics emblem, Olympic rings. 50 l, Olympic rings.

2006, Jan. 24
C1228-C1229 AP275 Set of 2 10.00 9.50

Forgiveness of Honduran Debts by Foreign Nations — AP276

Designs: 14 l, Structure 4, Copán Ruins. 15 l, Flags of nations forgiving debts. 30 l, Honduras Pres. Ricardo Maduro, vert.

2006, Jan. 26
C1230-C1232 AP276 Set of 3 14.25 13.50

Cortés Chamber of Commerce and Industry, 75th Anniv. — AP277

Anniversary and Chamber of Commerce emblem and: 20 l, Gears. 35 l, The Forger, sculpture by J. Zelaya, horiz. 50 l, El Industrial, mural by A. Martínez.

2006
C1233-C1235 AP277 Set of 3 16.25 15.50

HONDURAS

Diplomatic Relations Between Honduras and Brazil, Cent. — AP278

Designs: 20 l, Flags of Honduras and Brazil. 30 l, Baron of Rio Branco (1845-1912) Brazilian diplomat, vert.

2006 Litho. Perf. 13¼
C1236-C1237 AP278 Set of 2   8.00 7.50

Miniature Sheet

Honduran Friendship With Japan — AP279

No. C1238: a, 10 l, Children learning about Chagas disease. b, 15 l, Teacher and children. c, 20 l, Japanese naval vessels and flag. d, 25 l, Sailors in dress uniforms.

2006
C1238 AP279 Sheet of 4, #a-d   11.50 10.50

Nos. C1054, C1124-C1125, C1127-C1128, C1149-C1151, C1159, C1162, C1164, C1166-C1167, C1169-C1170, C1172-C1173 Surcharged

Methods and Perfs As Before

2007 ?
C1239	AP260	2 l on 2.60 l #C1159	.65	.50
C1240	AP260	2 l on 4 l #C1162	.65	.50
C1241	AP249	2 l on 8.65 l #C1128	.65	.50
C1242	AP260	2 l on 10.65 l #C1166	.65	.50
C1243	AP249	3 l on 1.40 l #C1124	.90	.70
C1244	AP257	3 l on 1.40 l #C1149	.90	.70
C1245	AP257	3 l on 2.60 l #C1150	.90	.70
C1246	AP261	3 l on 2.60 l #C1172	.90	.70
C1247	AP257	3 l on 7.30 l #C1151	.90	.70
C1248	AP261	3 l on 10.65 l #C1173	.90	.70
C1249	AP226	3 l on 18.30 l #C1054	.90	.70
C1250	AP261	5 l on 85c #C1169	1.40	1.05
C1251	AP261	5 l on 1.40 l #C1170	1.40	1.05
C1252	AP249	5 l on 2.60 l #C1125	1.40	1.05
C1253	AP249	5 l on 4.30 l #C1127	1.40	1.05
C1254	AP260	5 l on 4.30 l #C1164	1.40	1.05
C1255	AP260	5 l on 14.95 l #C1167	1.40	1.05

Nos. C1239-C1255 (17)   17.30 13.20

Constitution, 25th Anniv. — AP280

Designs: 5 l, Leaders of the Legislative, Executive and Judicial branches of government. 10 l, 1824 Constituent Assembly Building. 15 l, Presidential House, 1922-91, vert. 20 l, Legislative Building.

2007 Litho. Perf. 13¼
C1256-C1259 AP280 Set of 4   9.00 8.00

Miniature Sheet

Central Bank of Honduras, 50th Anniv. — AP281

No. C1260 — Central Bank of Honduras emblem and paintings: a, 5 l, Holocausto, by César Rendón. b, 10 l, La Novia, by Miguel Angel Ruiz Matute. c, 15 l, Ayer, Hoy y Mañana, by Felipe Bouchard. d, 20 l, Paisaje de Tegucigalpa, by Mario Castillo. e, 25 l, Dinamismo, by Benigno Gómez. f, 30 l, Guitarras en Descanso, by Dante Lazzaroni.

2007
C1260 AP281 Sheet of 6, #a-f   17.50 16.00

Adjudication of "Four Cardinal Points" Police Torture Case AP282

2007, Oct. 18 Litho. Perf. 13¼
C1261 AP282 50 l multi   14.50 14.50
Printed in sheets of 2.

Miniature Sheets

Launch of Sputnik I, 50th Anniv. AP283

No. C1262: a, 25 l, Sputnik launch vehicle, pale blue background (30x40mm). b, 35 l, Sputnik I, yellow background (30x40mm). c, 50 l, Sputnik orbiting Earth, pale green background (60x40mm).

No. C1263: a, 25 l, As #C1262a, pale green background. b, 35 l, As #C1262b, pale blue background. c, 50 l, As #C1262c, yellow background.

2007, Nov. 30
C1262 AP283 Sheet of 3, #a-c   14.00 13.50
C1263 AP283 Sheet of 3, #a-c   24.00 23.00

Miniature Sheet

Paintings by Gaye-Darléne Bidart de Satulsky — AP284

No. C1264: a, 3 l, Medusa de las Islas. b, 3 l, Nido de Amor. c, 3 l, Guitarrista Isleño. d, 5 l, "M" Hombre Cruz. e, 5 l, Amor a Martillazos. f, 5 l, Sor María Rosa. g, 5 l, Isleña,

Luna y Mar. h, 5 l, Clementina Suárez. i, 5 l, La Naranjera.

2008
C1264 AP284 Sheet of 9, #a-i   12.00 9.75

Miniature Sheet

America Issue AP285

No. C1265: a, 2 l, Factory workers and sewing machine. b, 3 l, Energy savings mascot. c, 5 l, School children. d, 10 l, Children in native costumes.

2008
C1265 AP285 Sheet of 4, #a-d   5.00 4.00

2008 Summer Olympics, Beijing — AP286

Designs: 3 l, Olympic torch. No. C1267, 5 l, Judo. No. C1268, 5 l, Runners. 25 l, Soccer.

2008, July 30
C1266-C1269 AP286 Set of 4   7.50 6.50

Juan Ramón Molina (1875-1908), Poet — AP287

Designs: 10 l, Molina, mermaid and ship. 25 l, Molina.

2008, Oct. 30
C1270-C1271 AP287 Set of 2   7.50 5.50

Miniature Sheet

Treaty of Amity, Commerce and Navigation Between Honduras and Mexico, Cent. — AP288

No. C1272: a, 5 l, Sailor and ship. b, 10 l, Hands, flags and maps. c, 15 l, Handshake, double helix of flags, horiz. d, 20 l, Flags and "100 Años de Amistad." e, 25 l, "100" and colors of flags, horiz. f, 50 l, Parrot and eagle, horiz.

2008 Litho. Perf. 13¼
C1272 AP288 Sheet of 6, #a-f + 3 labels   21.00 19.50

España Normal School, Villa Ahumada, 58th Anniv. — AP289

Designs: 2 l, School. 5 l, School emblem.

2009, Aug. 28 Litho. Perf. 13¼
C1273-C1274 AP289 Set of 2   1.75 1.25

America Issue — AP290

Traditional toys and games: 3 l, Hopscotch. 10 l, Kite. 20 l, Top. 50 l, Children playing soccer, jumping rope and flying kite.

2009, Aug. 28
C1275-C1278 AP290 Set of 4   13.75 12.00

President's House — AP291

Dove, Map of Honduras — AP292

Interim President Roberto Micheletti Baín — AP293

2009, Dec. 3
C1279 AP291 3 l multi   .55 .50
C1280 AP292 15 l multi   2.50 2.25
C1281 AP293 20 l multi   3.50 3.00
Nos. C1279-C1281 (3)   6.55 5.75

2010 World Cup Soccer Championships, South Africa — AP294

Designs: 5 l, Child playing soccer. 20 l, Honduras soccer team. 25 l, Emblem of Honduras soccer team.

2009, Dec. 3
C1282-C1284 AP294 Set of 3   8.50 7.75

2010 World Cup Soccer Championships, South Africa — AP295

2010 World Cup emblem, Ficohsa Bank emblem, stadium and flag of: 3 l, Chile. 5 l, Switzerland. 14 l, Spain.
No. C1288, vert.: a, 2010 World Cup emblem, World Cup trophy. b, 2010 World Cup emblem.

2010, May Litho. Perf. 13¼
C1285-C1287 AP295 Set of 3   4.50 3.75

Souvenir Sheet
C1288 AP295 20 l Sheet of 2, #a-b   6.50 6.00

America Issue, National Symbols AP296

Designs: 5 l, Flag and coat of arms of Honduras. 25 l, Odocoileus virginianus. 50 l, Ara macao.

2010, Nov.
C1289-C1291 AP296 Set of 3   14.25 13.50

Maria Auxiliadora Institute, Cent. — AP297

HONDURAS

Designs: 10 l, Virgin Mary and Jesus, "100" with hearts replacing zeroes. 50 l, Virgin Mary and Jesus.

2010, Nov.
C1292-C1293 AP297 Set of 2 10.50 10.00

Christmas — AP298

Designs: 3 l, Angel and lamb. 20 l, Adoration of the Magi. 50 l, Locomotive with Christmas decorations, horiz.

2010, Nov. **Perf. 13¼**
C1294-C1295 AP298 Set of 2 4.00 3.50
Imperf
Size: 90x63mm
C1296 AP298 50 l multi 7.00 6.75

Postal Union of the Americas, Spain and Portugal (UPAEP), Cent. — AP299

Designs: 5 l, Mayan sculpture. 25 l, Yum Kax, Mayan agricultural deity.

2011, Mar. 23 **Perf. 13½x13¼**
C1297-C1298 AP299 Set of 2 5.25 4.75

No. C1142 Surcharged

Method and Perf. As Before
2011, May 2
C1299 Sheet of 4 13.00 12.00
  a. AP254 5 l on 13.65 l #C1142a 2.00 2.00
  b. AP254 5 l on 14.55 l #C1142b 2.00 2.00
  c. AP254 10 l on 15.45 l #C1142c 3.00 3.00
  d. AP254 10 l on 16.65 l #C1142d 3.00 3.00
C1300 Sheet of 4 24.00 23.00
  a. AP254 15 l on 13.65 l #C1142a 4.00 4.00
  b. AP254 15 l on 14.55 l #C1142b 4.00 4.00
  c. AP254 20 l on 15.45 l #C1142c 6.00 6.00
  d. AP254 20 l on 16.65 l #C1142d 6.00 6.00

Inscribed across the stamps of the sheet is the text "Beato Juan Pablo 01/05/2011" on No. C1299 and "Beatificacion 01/05/2011" on No. C1300.

AP300

Diplomatic Relations Between Honduras and South Korea, 50th Anniv. — AP301

Designs: 5 l, Presidents and flags of Honduras and South Korea.
No. C1302: a, Korean vase. b, Mayan calendar. c, Korean statue of Buddha. d, Honduran bowl. e, Korean sundial. f, Mayan stele.

2012, Apr. 25 **Litho.** **Perf. 13¼**
C1301 AP300 5 l multi 1.50 1.25
Miniature Sheet
C1302 AP301 2 l Sheet of 6, #a-f 8.00 6.50

National Library and Archives, 132nd Anniv. — AP302

Designs: 2 l, Pres. Porfirio Lobo Sosa, Tulio Mariano Gonzales, Minister of Sport, Culture and Art.
No. C1304: a, 8 l, Pres. Marco A. Soto (1846-1908). b, 8 l, Old Mint Building (National Library). c, 8 l, Old Presidential House (National Archives). d, 12 l, Antonio R. Vallejo (1844-1914), founder of National Library and Archives. e, 12 l, Ramón Rosa (1848-93), governmental minister. f, 12 l, Juan Ramón Molina (1875-1908), writer.

2012, Oct. 10
C1303 AP302 2 l multi .90 .65
Miniature Sheet
C1304 AP302 Sheet of 6, #a-f, + 3 labels 10.75 9.25

Blanca Jeannette Kawas (1946-95), Murdered Environmental Activist — AP303

Designs: No. C1305, 20 l, Kawas. No. C1306, 20 l, Kawas, vert.
No. C1307 — Scenes from Blanca Jeannette Kawas National Park: a, 15 l, Beach, denomination in white. b, 15 l, Beach, denomination in black. c, 15 l, Birds on boat. d, 25 l, Buildings on shore. e, 25 l, Aerial view of cove. f, 25 l, River shore and forest.

2013, Feb. 8
C1305-C1306 AP303 Set of 2 5.75 5.25
Miniature Sheet
C1307 AP303 Sheet of 6, #a-f, + 3 labels 17.00 15.50

Wildlife Conservation AP304

Designs: No. C1308, 5 l, Río Cangrejal. No. C1309, 5 l, Iguana iguana. 8 l, Amanita caesarea, vert. No. C1311, 10 l, Isla de El Tigre. No. C1312, 10 l, Bothriechis schlegelii. 15 l, Athene cunicularia. 30 l, Siproeta stelenes. 50 l, Amazilia luciae.

2014, June **Litho.** **Perf. 13½**
C1308-C1315 AP304 Set of 8 18.00 16.00

Christmas AP305

Designs: 5 l, Ribbon and star. 25 l, Angel, lamb and Holy Family, vert. 30 l, Candles and poinsettias, vert.

2014, Oct. 15 **Litho.** **Perf. 13½**
C1316-C1318 AP305 Set of 3 7.75 7.00

Convention on the Rights of the Child, 25th Anniv. — AP306

Designs: 2 l, Child, facing left. 5 l, Clock face. 10 l, Child, facing right chin on knees. 15 l, Child, head on knees with hand up. 35 l, Child, facing forward. 40 l, Whole clock.

2014, Nov. 25 **Litho.** **Perf. 13½**
C1319-C1324 AP306 Set of 6 14.00 12.00

Alfredo Hawit Banegas, 2011-2012 President of CONCACAF, and CONCACAF Emblem — AP307

2014, Dec. 1 **Litho.** **Perf. 13½**
C1325 AP307 10 l multi 1.45 1.20

San Fernando de Omoa Fortress — AP308

Designs: 5 l, Coat of Arms of King Ferdinand VI. 10 l, King Ferdinand VI of Spain. 25 l, Fortress, horiz. 50 l, Ship and fortress, horiz.

2015, Jan. 20 **Litho.** **Perf. 13½**
C1326-C1329 AP308 Set of 4 12.50 11.50

Cooperation Between Japan and Central American Integration System Countries AP309

Designs: No. C1330, 2 l, Emblem, flag of Japan, schools and children. No. C1331, 2 l, Emblem, flag of Japan, Japanese volunteer with baby. No. C1332, 5 l, Emblem, flag of Japan, public works projects. No. C1333, 5 l, Emblem, flags of Japan and Honduras, Japanese and Honduran foods. No. C1334, 10 l, Flags of Japan and Honduras, Friendship Bridge. No. C1335, 10 l, Flags of Japan and Honduras, El Puente Archaeological Park. 15 l, Emblem, flags of Japan and Honduras, judokas. 50 l, Emblem.

2015, Feb. 9 **Litho.** **Perf. 13½**
C1330-C1337 AP309 Set of 8 13.50 11.50

Environmental Protection — AP310

Designs: No. C1338, 5 l, Miner at El Mochito mine. No. C1339, 5 l, Cuero y Salado Wildlife Refuge. No. C1340, 5 l, Light bulb. No. C1341, 5 l, Amazilia luciae. No. C1342, 10 l, Jepidochelys olivacea. No. C1343, 10 l, Stream in Nombre de Dios National Park. No. C1344, 10 l, Forest in Merendón Mountains. No. C1345, 10 l, Sky and forest in Merendón Mountains.

2015, Apr. 10 **Litho.** **Perf. 13½**
C1338-C1345 AP310 Set of 8 9.50 7.50

No. C1342 is misspelled "Jepidochelys" on the stamp. The proper genus is "Lepidochelys."

Peruvian People and Places — AP311

Designs: No. C1346, 5 l, César Vallejo (1892-1938), poet. No. C1347, 5 l, Chabuca Granda (1920-83), singer. No. C1348, 5 l, Enrique Zileri (1931-2014), magazine publisher, vert. No. C1349, 10 l, Machu Picchu, vert. No. C1350, 10 l, Andrés Townsend (1915-94), novelist and politician, vert. 15 l, Túpac Amaru II (1738-81), leader of indigenous people's uprising, vert. 25 l, José Luis Bustamante y Rivero (1894-1989), president of Peru, vert. 35 l, Miguel Grau (1834-79), Peruvian admiral, vert.

2015, May 29 **Litho.** **Perf. 13¼**
C1346-C1353 AP311 Set of 8 15.00 15.00

AP312

Interamerican Commission on Sustainable Development — AP313

Designs: No. C1354, Wind generators. No. C1355, Reservoir. 10 l, Farmers in field. 25 l, Shell.

2015 **Litho.** **Perf. 13¼**
C1354 AP312 5 l multi .80 .65
C1355 AP312 5 l multi .80 .65
C1356 AP312 10 l multi 1.50 1.30
C1357 AP313 25 l multi 4.00 4.00
Nos. C1354-C1357 (4) 7.10 6.60

AP314

Knights of the Holy Sepulchre in Tegucigalpa, 50th Anniv. — AP315

Designs: No. C1358, Religious procession. No. C1359, Crucifixion icon. No. C1360, Religious procession, diff. No. C1361, Knights wearing suits. No. C1362, Head of Jesus icon. 15 l, Religious procession and crowd. 25 l, Emblem.

2016, Apr. 15 **Litho.** **Perf. 13¼**
C1358 AP314 5 l multi .65 .60
C1359 AP315 5 l multi .65 .60
C1360 AP314 10 l multi 1.40 1.10
C1361 AP314 10 l multi 1.40 1.10
C1362 AP315 10 l multi 1.40 1.10
C1363 AP315 15 l multi 2.10 1.80
C1364 AP315 25 l multi 3.50 2.90
Nos. C1358-C1364 (7) 11.10 9.20

Honduran Postal Service — AP316

Designs: 2 l, Honducor emblem, post office interior. No. C1366, 5 l, EMS Honduras emblem. No. C1367, 5 l, Honducor emblem, post office and mail delivery vehicle. No. C1368, 10 l, Honducor emblem. No. C1369, 10 l, ExportaFácil emblem. 15 l, Honducor emblem, post office, mail delivery vehicle and postal worker delivering package.

2016, Apr. 26 **Litho.** **Perf. 13¼**
C1365-C1370 AP316 Set of 6 7.00 5.50

HONDURAS

Tourism — AP317

Tourism emblem and: No. C1371, 5 l, Sculpture of head, Ciudad Blanca. No. C1372, 5 l, Fisherman, Lago de Yojoa. No. C1373, 5 l, Cacao pods. No. C1374, 5 l, Coffee berries. No. C1375, 5 l, Pico Bonito zip line, vert. No. C1376, 10 l, Church, Comayagua. No. C1377, 10 l, Los Naranjos Park, vert. No. C1378, 10 l, Person near Pulhapanzak Waterfall, vert. No. C1379, 10 l, "Somos tierra, somos mar, somos gente, somos corazón, somos Hondureños," vert. No. C1380, 15 l, Turtle in water, Guanaja Island. No. C1381, 15 l, Emblem for Kaha Kamasa archaeological site, Ciudad Blanca, vert. 25 l, Sculpture, Copán archaeological site.

2016, June 28   Litho.   Perf. 13¼
C1371-C1382 AP317 Set of 12 18.00 15.00

Honduras Bar Association, Cent. — AP318

2016, Aug. 9   Litho.   Perf. 13¼
C1383 AP318 25 l blk & ochre 3.00 2.75

Arts and Culture — AP319

Sports — AP319a

University Emblem and National Pedagogical University Emblem — AP319b

National Pedagogical University Building — AP319c

President Morazán (1792-1842), Book and Butterflies — AP319d

Morazán, Hands, Flag of Honduras — AP319e

2016, Nov. 4   Litho.   Perf. 13¼
C1384	AP319	10 l multi	1.80 1.60
C1385	AP319a	10 l multi	1.80 1.60
C1386	AP319b	10 l multi	1.80 1.60
C1387	AP319c	15 l multi	1.80 1.60
C1388	AP319d	15 l multi	1.80 1.60
C1389	AP319e	25 l multi	1.80 1.60

Nos. C1384-C1389 (6) 10.80 9.60

Francisco Morazán University, 60th Anniv.

AP320

AP321

Archdiocese of Tegucigalpa, Cent. — AP322

Designs: No. C1390, Religious procession with statue of Virgin Mary. No. C1391, President of the Republic of China in Cathedral with Archbishop and others. No. C1392, Religious procession with statue of Crucifixion. No. C1393, Bishops of Tegucigalpa from 1916-2016, vert. No. C1394, Oscar Cardinal Rodríguez and Pope Francis, vert. No. C1395, Virgin of Suyapa, 270th anniv. of discovery, vert. 15 l, Basilica of Our Lady of Suyapa. 25 l, Cathedral retable depicting St. Michael, vert. 50 l, Angel, Basilica, chalice and host.

2017, Apr. 8   Litho.   Perf. 13¼
C1390	AP320	5 l multi	.65 .60
C1391	AP320	5 l multi	.65 .60
C1392	AP320	5 l multi	.65 .60
C1393	AP320	10 l multi	1.25 1.10
C1394	AP320	10 l multi	1.25 1.10
C1395	AP321	10 l multi	1.25 1.10
C1396	AP320	15 l multi	2.10 1.80
C1397	AP320	25 l multi	3.25 2.90
C1398	AP322	50 l multi	6.50 5.50

Nos. C1390-C1398 (9) 17.55 15.30

Bonn Challenge — AP323

Designs: 10 l, Motagua River and Bonn Challenge emblem. 25 l, Bonn Challenge emblem.

2017, June 7   Litho.   Perf. 13½
C1399-C1400 AP323 Set of 2 5.25 4.75

National Electrical Power Company, 60th Anniv. — AP324

Designs: 2 l, Patuca III Power Plant. No. C1402, 5 l, San Nicolas Substation. No. C1403, 5 l, Cañaveral Hydroelectric Project. 8 l, Amarateca Substation. No. C1405, 10 l, 60th anniversary emblem and building. No. C1406, 10 l, Worker fixing street lamp, vert. No. C1407, 10 l, Workers fixing transmission lines, vert. 15 l, El Cajón Dam. 25 l, People examining fluorescent light bulb. 50 l, 60th anniversary emblem, wind generators, houses, transmission towers.

2017, July 28   Litho.   Perf. 13½
C1401-C1410 AP324 Set of 10 18.50 16.00

Plan International AP325

Plan International emblem and: No. C1411, 10 l, "Plan. . . Mi Orgullo, Mi Compromiso" (Plan, My Pride, My Committment). No. C1412, 10 l, Children reading. No. C1413, 10 l, Children with soccer ball. No. C1414, 15 l, "Basta de Bullying" (Enough of Bullying). No. C1415, 15 l, Young girl. No. 1416, 25 l, "40 Aniversario" (40th Anniversary). No. C1417, 25 l, Hummingbird and map of Honduras. 35 l, Drawing of girl.

2017, Sept. 27   Litho.   Perf. 13½
C1411-C1418 AP325 Set of 8 17.00 15.00

Tegucigalpa — AP326

No. C1419: a, 10 l, Cabildo Municipal (municipal council chamber). b, 10 l, Los Dolores Church. c, 10 l, Tegucigalpa skyline. d, 10 l, Paseo Liquidámbar. e, 10 l, Spiral exit ramp. f, 10 l, Street during Holy Week. g, 10 l, Carnaval. h, 15 l, Highway and ramp. i, 15 l, Santa Semana (Street during Holy Week). j, 35 l, Toncontín Airport (121x91mm).

Rouletted 5¼, Rouletted 5¼ at Bottom (35 l)

2017, Oct. 10   Litho.
C1419 AP326 Sheet of 10, #a-j 18.50 16.00

Honduran Postal Service, 140th Anniv. — AP327

Designs: 25 l, Mail box. 50 l, Bicycle.

2018, Mar. 6   Litho.   Perf. 13½
C1420-C1421 AP327 Set of 2 10.00 9.50

Dated 2017. America Issue (No. C1421).

America Issue — AP328

Domesticated animals: 5 l, Felis silvestris catus. 30 l, Trachemys scripta, horiz. 100 l, Canis lupus familiaris, horiz.

2018, Sept. 28   Litho.   Perf. 13¼
C1422-C1424 AP328 Set of 3 15.00 14.00

President José Trinidad Cabañas Fiallos (1805-71) — AP329

2018, Dec. 7   Litho.   Perf. 13¼
C1425 AP329 50 l multi 5.50 5.25

America Issue — AP330

Traditional foods: No. C1426, 5 l, Rosquillas en miel (honey donuts). No. C1427, 5 l, Nacatamales. 25 l, Sopa de tortas de pescado (fish cake soup).

2019, July 25   Litho.   Perf. 13¼
C1426-C1428 AP330 Set of 3 4.50 3.75

Río Plátano Biosphere AP331

Designs: No. C1429, 5 l, Garifuna girl. No. C1430, 5 l, Agalychnis callidryas. No. C1431, 5 l, Panthera onca. 30 l, Río Plátano.

2019, Sept. 24   Litho.   Perf. 13½
C1429-C1432 AP331 Set of 4 5.25 4.25

Institute of Forest Conservation, 11th anniv.

SOS Children's Villages in Honduras, 50th Anniv. — AP332

Children's art: No. C1433, 5 l, House, by María José Orellano. No. C1434, 5 l, House and palm tree, by Selvin Carranza. 10 l, SOS Children's Villages 50th anniversary emblem, by Katherin Trochez, vert. 30 l, People at village, by Dania Fernández.

2020, Apr. 21   Litho.   Perf. 13¼
C1433-C1436 AP332 Set of 4 7.50 6.50

AIR POST SEMI-POSTAL STAMPS

No. C13C Surcharged in Black

Unwmk.

1929, June 5   Engr.   Perf. 12
CB1	AP1	50c + 5c carmine	.65 .30
CB2	AP1	50c + 10c carmine	.70 .35
CB3	AP1	50c + 15c carmine	.95 .55
CB4	AP1	50c + 20c carmine	1.40 .75

Nos. CB1-CB4 (4) 3.70 1.95

Catalogue values for unused stamps in this section, from this point to the end of the section, are for Never Hinged items.

Souvenir Sheet

Airmail Pilot Sumner B. Morgan and Airplane SP2

2000, July 7
CB5 SP2 50 l + 5 l multi 18.50 18.00

First airmail flight in Honduras, 75th anniv., EXFILHON 2000. See Nos. C1075-C1077.

No. C619 Surcharged With New Value in Black and 2000 Sydney Olympics Emblem in Red

2000, Sept. 13   Litho.   Imperf.
CB6 AP99 48.50 l +1.50 l multi 25.00 24.00

AIR POST SPECIAL DELIVERY STAMPS

No. CO52 Surcharged in Red

Perf. 13½x14
1953, Dec. 8   Engr.   Unwmk.
CE1 AP65 20c on 1c 3.00 1.50

HONDURAS

Transport Plane — APSD1

1956, Oct. 3   Perf. 13x12½
CE2   APSD1   20c black & red   .80   .50

Surcharges on No. CE2 (see Nos. C421, C477) eliminate its special delivery character.

> Catalogue values for unused stamps in this section, from this point to the end of the section, are for Never Hinged items.

Stamp Centenary Type of Air Post Issue

Design: 20c, Mailman on motorcycle.

1966, May 31   Litho.   Perf. 14x14½
CE3   AP81   20c bis brn, brn & gold   1.25   .50

Centenary (in 1965) of the first Honduran postage stamp.
The "HABILITADO" overprint on No. CE3 (see No. C479) eliminates its special delivery character.

Independence Type of Air Post Issue

1972, May 19   Litho.   Perf. 13
CE4   AP89   20c Corsair plane   1.25   .35

No. CE4 Surcharged

1975
CE5   AP89   60c on 20c   3.00   .85

Forest Protection Type of Air Post

1976, May 28   Litho.   Perf. 13½
CE6   AP96   60c Stag in forest   1.50   .55

AIR POST OFFICIAL STAMPS

Official Stamps Nos. O78 to O81 Overprinted in Red, Green or Black

1930   Perf. 11, 11½
CO1	A24	10c deep blue (R)	1.25	1.25
CO2	A24	20c yellow brown	1.25	1.25
a.		Vert. pair, imperf. btwn.	14.00	
CO3	A24	50c vermilion (Bk)	1.40	1.40
CO4	A24	1p emerald (R)	1.25	1.25
		Nos. CO1-CO4 (4)	5.15	5.15

No. O77 Surcharged in Green

CO5   A24   5c on 6c red vio   1.00   1.00
    a.   "1910" for "1930"   2.75   2.75
    b.   "1920" for "1930"   2.75   2.75

The overprint exists in other colors and on other denominations but the status of these is questioned.

Official Stamps of 1931 Overprinted

1931   Unwmk.   Perf. 12
CO6	O2	1c ultra	.35	.35
CO7	O2	2c black brown	.85	.85
CO8	O2	5c olive gray	1.00	1.00
CO9	O2	6c orange red	1.00	1.00
a.		Inverted overprint	24.00	24.00
CO10	O2	10c dark green	1.25	1.25
CO11	O2	15c olive brown	2.00	1.75
a.		Inverted overprint	20.00	20.00
CO12	O2	20c red brown	2.00	1.75
CO13	O2	50c gray violet	1.40	1.40
CO14	O2	1p deep orange	2.00	1.75
		Nos. CO6-CO14 (9)	11.85	11.10

In the setting of the overprint there are numerous errors in the spelling and punctuation, letters omitted and similar varieties.

This set is known with blue overprint. A similar overprint is known in larger type, but its status has not been fully determined.

Postage Stamps of 1918-30 Surcharged Type "a" or Type "b" (#CO22-CO23) in Green, Black, Red and Blue

1933   Wmk. 209, Unwmk.
CO15	A39	20c on 2c #295 (G)	3.25	3.25
CO16	A39	20c on 2c #296	3.25	3.25
CO17	A39	20c on 2c #297 (G)	3.25	3.25
CO17A	A39	40c on 2c #295	2.00	2.00
CO18	A39	40c on 2c #297 (G)	7.00	7.00
CO18A	A39	40c on 2c #297	4.25	4.25
CO19	A28	40c on 5c #246	4.25	4.25
CO19A	A28	40c on 5c #247	7.00	7.00
CO20	A28	40c on 5c #266	15.00	15.00
CO20A	A28	40c on 5c #267	9.00	9.00
CO20B	A28	40c on 5c #267 (R)	14.00	14.00
CO21	A20	70c on 5c #183	3.00	3.00
CO22	A24	70c on 10c #214 (R)	3.25	3.25
CO23	A22	1 l on 20c #191 (Bl)	3.25	3.25
CO24	A24	1 l on 50c #216 (Bl)	14.00	14.00
CO25	A22	1.20 l on 1p #193 (Bl)	1.00	1.00
		Nos. CO15-CO25 (16)	96.75	96.75

Official Stamps of 1915-29 Surcharged Type "a" or Type "b" (#CO28-CO29, CO33-CO41, CO43) in Black, Red, Green, Orange, Carmine or Blue

CO26	O1	40c on 5c #O84 (Bk)	1.00	1.00
CO27	O1	40c on 5c #O84 (R)	25.00	25.00
CO28	A24	60c on 6c #O77 (Bk)	.70	.70
CO29	A24	60c on 6c #O77 (G)	25.00	25.00
CO30	A20	70c on 5c #O60 (Bk)	5.25	5.25
CO31	A19	70c on 10c #O62 (R)	9.00	9.00
CO32	A19	70c on 10c #O62 (Bk)	7.75	7.75
CO33	A22	70c on 10c #O70 (R)	4.50	4.00
CO34	A24	70c on 10c #O78 (O)	3.50	3.50
CO35	A24	70c on 10c #O78 (C)	4.50	4.50
CO36	A22	70c on 15c #O71 (R)	87.50	87.50
CO37	A22	90c on 10c #O70 (R)	5.25	5.25
CO38	A22	90c on 15c #O71 (R)	8.00	8.00
CO38A	A24	1 l on 2c #O76	1.40	1.40
CO39	A22	1 l on 20c #O72	2.50	2.50
CO39A	A24	1 l on 20c #O79	3.75	3.75
CO40	A22	1 l on 50c #O73	1.90	1.90
CO41	A24	1 l on 50c #O80	4.25	4.25
CO42	A20	1.20 l on 1p #O65	9.00	7.00
CO43	A24	1.20 l on 1p #O81	3.00	3.00
		Nos. CO26-CO43 (20)	212.75	210.25

Varieties of foregoing surcharges exist.

Merchant Flag and Seal of Honduras — OA2

1939, Feb. 27   Unwmk.   Perf. 12½
CO44	OA2	2c dp blue & grn	.25	.25
CO45	OA2	5c dp blue & org	.25	.25
CO46	OA2	8c dp blue & brn	.25	.25
CO47	OA2	15c dp blue & car	.30	.25
CO48	OA2	46c dp blue & ol grn	.40	.30
CO49	OA2	50c dp blue & vio	.50	.30
CO50	OA2	1 l dp blue & red brn	1.75	1.25
CO51	OA2	2 l dp blue & red org	3.75	2.25
		Nos. CO44-CO51 (8)	7.45	5.10

For overprints and surcharges see Nos. C101-C117.

Types of Air Post Stamps of 1952 Ovptd. in Red

Perf. 13½x14, 14x13½
1952   Engr.   Unwmk.
CO52	AP65	1c rose lil & ol	.25	.25
CO53	AP65	2c brown & vio	.25	.25
CO54	AP65	8c dp car & blk	.25	.25
CO55	AP66	16c pur & dk grn	.25	.25
CO56	AP65	30c dk bl & blk	.50	.50
CO57	AP65	1 l dk grn & dk brown	1.75	1.75
CO58	AP65	2 l bl & red brn	3.50	3.50
CO59	AP66	5 l red org & blk	8.50	8.50
		Nos. CO52-CO59 (8)	15.25	15.25

Queen Isabella I of Spain, 500th birth anniv.
For overprints and surcharge, see Nos. CE1, CO110.

No. C222 and Types of Air Post Stamps of 1953 Overprinted in Red

Engraved; Center of 1c Litho.
1953, Dec. 18   Perf. 12½
Frames in Black
CO60	AP67	1c ultra & vio bl	.25	.25
CO61	AP97	2c dp blue grn	.25	.25
CO62	AP67	3c orange	.25	.25
CO63	AP67	5c dp carmine	.25	.25
CO64	AP67	15c dk brown	.25	.25
CO65	AP67	30c purple	.45	.35
CO66	AP67	1 l olive gray	4.00	2.25
CO67	AP67	2 l lilac rose	5.00	3.00
CO68	AP67	5 l ultra	11.50	7.00
		Nos. CO60-CO68 (9)	22.20	13.85

Issued to honor the United Nations.

Types of Air Post Stamps Overprinted in Red

Engraved; 8c Lithographed
1956, Oct. 3   Perf. 13x12½
CO69	AP68	1c blk & brn car	.25	.25
CO70	AP69	2c black & mag	.25	.25
CO71	AP68	3c blk & rose vio	.25	.25
CO72	AP69	4c black & org	.25	.25
CO73	AP69	5c black & bl grn	.25	.25
CO74	AP68	8c violet & multi	.25	.25
CO75	AP68	10c blk & red brn	.25	.25
CO76	AP68	12c blk & car rose	.25	.25
CO77	AP68	15c carmine & blk	.25	.25
CO78	AP68	20c blk & ol brn	.25	.25
CO79	AP69	24c black & blue	.25	.25
CO80	AP69	25c blk & rose vio	.25	.25
CO81	AP68	30c black & grn	.25	.25
CO82	AP68	40c blk & red org	.25	.25
CO83	AP69	50c blk & brn red	.30	.30
CO84	AP68	60c blk & rose vio	.40	.40
CO85	AP69	1 l black & brn	1.40	1.10
CO86	AP69	2 l black & dk bl	2.75	2.25
CO87	AP69	5 l black & vio bl	5.75	5.25
		Nos. CO69-CO87 (19)	14.10	12.80

Nos. C269-C278 Overprinted Vertically in Red (Horizontally on Nos. CO89 and CO91)

1957, Oct. 21   Litho.   Perf. 13
Frames in Black
CO88	AP70	1c buff & aqua	.25	.25
CO89	AP70	2c org, pur & emer	.25	.25
CO90	AP70	5c pink & ultra	.25	.25
a.		Inverted overprint		
CO91	AP70	8c orange, vio & ol	.25	.25
CO92	AP70	10c violet & brn	.25	.25
CO93	AP70	12c lt grn & ultra	.25	.25
CO94	AP70	15c green & brn	.25	.25
CO95	AP70	30c pink & sl	.55	.25
CO96	AP70	1 l blue & brn	1.40	1.00
CO97	AP70	2 l lt grn & sl	2.75	2.25
		Nos. CO88-CO97 (10)	6.45	5.25

Types of Lincoln Air Post Stamps 1959 Overprinted in Red

1959   Engr.   Perf. 13½
Flags in National Colors
CO98	AP72	1c ocher	.25	.25
CO99	AP73	2c gray olive	.25	.25
a.		Inverted overprint		
CO100	AP73	3c red brown	.25	.25
CO101	AP73	5c ultra	.25	.25
CO102	AP73	10c dull purple	.25	.25
a.		Overprint omitted		
CO103	AP73	12c red orange	.25	.25
CO104	AP72	15c dark brown	.25	.25
CO105	AP73	25c black	.25	.25
CO106	AP73	50c dark car	.30	.25
CO107	AP73	1 l purple	.75	.65
CO108	AP73	2 l dark blue	1.40	1.10
a.		Min. sheet of 6, 2c, 5c, 12c, 15c, 50c, 2 l, imperf.	3.00	3.00
CO109	AP73	5 l green	4.50	3.75
		Nos. CO98-CO109 (12)	8.95	7.75

> Catalogue values for unused stamps in this section, from this point to the end of the section, are for Never Hinged items.

No. CO55 Overprinted: "IN MEMORIAM / Sir Winston / Churchill / 1874-1965"

1965, Dec. 20   Perf. 14x13½
CO110   AP66   16c purple & dk grn   1.00   1.00

See note after No. C379.

Nos. C336-C344 Ovptd. in Red

1965   Photo.   Perf. 14
Black Design and Inscription
CO111	AP76	1c yellow green	.30	.25
CO112	AP76	2c pale rose lil	.30	.25
CO113	AP76	5c light ultra	.30	.25
CO114	AP76	8c bluish grn	.30	.25
CO115	AP76	10c buff	.35	.30
CO116	AP76	12c lemon	.40	.35
CO117	AP76	1 l light ocher	4.25	4.00
CO118	AP76	2 l pale ol grn	9.50	8.75
CO119	AP76	3 l rose	12.00	11.00
		Nos. CO111-CO119 (9)	27.70	25.40

OFFICIAL STAMPS

Type of Regular Issue of 1890 Overprinted in Red

1890   Unwmk.   Perf. 12
O1	A5	1c pale yellow	.40
O2	A5	2c pale yellow	.40
O3	A5	5c pale yellow	.40
O4	A5	10c pale yellow	.40
O5	A5	20c pale yellow	.40
O6	A5	25c pale yellow	.40
O7	A5	30c pale yellow	.40
O8	A5	40c pale yellow	.40
O9	A5	50c pale yellow	.40
O10	A5	75c pale yellow	.40
O11	A5	1p pale yellow	.40
		Nos. O1-O11 (11)	4.40

Type of Regular Issue of 1891 Overprinted in Red

1891
O12	A6	1c yellow	.40
O13	A6	2c yellow	.40
O14	A6	5c yellow	.40
O15	A6	10c yellow	.40
O16	A6	20c yellow	.40
O17	A6	25c yellow	.40
O18	A6	30c yellow	.40
O19	A6	40c yellow	.40
O20	A6	50c yellow	.40

HONDURAS

O21 A6 75c yellow .40
O22 A6 1p yellow .40
 Nos. O12-O22 (11) 4.40

Nos. O1 to O22 were never placed in use. Cancellations were applied to remainders. They exist with overprint inverted, double, triple and omitted; also, imperf. and part perf.

Regular Issue of 1898 Overprinted

1898-99 Perf. 11½
O23 A12 5c lilac .45
O24 A12 10c dark bl .85
O25 A12 20c dull org 1.30
O26 A12 50c org red 2.50
O27 A12 1p blue grn 3.25
 Nos. O23-O27 (5) 8.35

Counterfeits of basic stamps and of overprint exist.

Regular Issue of 1911 Overprinted

1911-15 Perf. 12, 14
Carmine Overprint
O28 A15 1c violet 1.50 .65
 a. Inverted overprint 2.40 2.40
 b. Double overprint 2.00
O29 A15 6c dull ultra 2.50 2.00
 a. Inverted overprint 2.75 2.75
O30 A15 10c blue 1.50 1.25
 a. "OFICAIL" 2.50
 b. Double overprint 3.50
O31 A15 20c yellow 15.00 12.00
O32 A15 50c brown 8.00 7.00
O33 A15 1p ol grn 12.00 10.00
 Nos. O28-O33 (6) 40.50 32.90

Black Overprint
O34 A15 2c green 1.00 .70
 a. "CIFICIAL" 5.00
O35 A15 5c carmine 1.50 1.00
 Perf. 12 7.50 5.00
O36 A15 6c ultra 4.50 4.50
O37 A15 10c blue 4.00 4.00
O38 A15 20c yellow 5.00 5.00
O39 A15 50c brown 5.50 4.00
 Nos. O34-O39 (6) 21.50 19.20

Counterfeits of overprint of Nos. O28-O39 exist.

With Additional Surcharge

1913-14
O40 A15 1c on 5c car 1.75 1.50
O41 A15 2c on 5c car 2.00 1.50
O42 A15 10c on 1c vio 4.00 3.50
 a. "OFICIAL" inverted 7.50
O43 A15 20c on 1c vio 3.00 2.50
 Nos. O40-O43 (4) 10.75 9.00

On No. O40 the surcharge reads "1 cent." Nos. O40-O43 exist with double surcharge.

No. O43 Surcharged Vertically in Black, Yellow or Maroon

1914
O44 A15 10c on 20c on 1c 20.00 20.00
 a. Maroon surcharge 20.00 20.00
O45 A15 10c on 20c on 1c (Y) 40.00 40.00

No. O35 Surcharged

1915
O46 A15 10c on 5c car 20.00 20.00

No. O39 Surcharged

O47 A15 20c on 50c brn 5.00 5.00

Regular Issues of 1913-14 Overprinted in Red or Black

1915 Perf. 11½
O48 A17 1c brn (R) .40 .40
 a. "OFICAIL" 5.00
O49 A17 2c car (Bk) .40 .40
 a. "OFICAIL" 5.00
 b. Double overprint 4.00
O50 A18 5c ultra (Bk) .45 .45
 a. "OFIC" 4.00
O51 A18 5c ultra (R) 1.00 1.00
 a. "OFIC"
 b. "OFICIAIL" 5.00
O52 A18 6c pur (Bk) 1.50 1.50
 a. 6c red lil (Bk)
O53 A17 10c brn (Bk) 1.25 1.25
O54 A17 20c brn (Bk) 3.00 3.00
O55 A17 20c brn (R) 3.00 3.00
 a. Double overprint (R+Bk) 10.00
 b. "OFICIAIL" 5.00
O56 A18 50c rose (Bk) 6.00 6.00
 Nos. O48-O56 (9) 17.00 17.00

The 10c blue has the overprint "OFICIAL" in different type from the other stamps of the series. It is stated that forty stamps were overprinted for the Postmaster General but the stamp was never put in use or on sale at the post office.

No. 152 Surcharged

O57 A17 1c on 2c car 2.00 2.00
 a. "0.10" for "0.01" 4.25 4.25
 b. "0.20" for "0.01" 4.25 4.25
 c. Double surcharge 8.50 8.50
 d. As "a," double surcharge 77.50
 e. As "b," double surcharge 77.50

Regular Issue of 1915-16 Overprinted in Black or Red

1915-16
O58 A19 1c choc (Bk) .50 .50
O59 A19 2c car (Bk) .50 .50
 a. Tête bêche pair 1.25 1.25
 b. Double overprint 2.00
 c. Double overprint, one inverted 2.00
 d. "b" and "c" in tête bêche pair
O60 A20 5c brt blue (R) .60 .60
 a. Inverted overprint 3.00
O61 A20 6c deep pur (R) .80 .80
 a. Black overprint 3.00
 b. Inverted overprint 2.00 2.00
O62 A19 10c dl bl (R) .80 .80
O63 A19 20c red brn (Bk) 1.20 1.20
 a. Tête bêche pair 2.50
O64 A20 50c red (Bk) 3.50 3.50
O65 A20 1p yel grn (C) 7.50 7.50
 Nos. O58-O65 (8) 15.40 15.40

The 6c, 10c and 1p exist imperf.

Regular Issue of 1919 Overprinted

1921
O66 A22 1c brown 2.25 2.25
 a. Inverted overprint 3.00 3.00
O67 A22 2c carmine 6.50 6.50
 a. Inverted overprint 3.00 3.00
O68 A22 5c lilac rose 6.50 6.50
 a. Inverted overprint 3.00
O69 A22 6c brt vio .50 .50
 a. Inverted overprint
O70 A22 10c dull blue .60 .60
 a. Double overprint
O71 A22 15c light blue .70 .70
 a. Inverted overprint 2.00
 b. Double ovpt., one inverted 4.00
O72 A22 20c brown 1.00 1.00
O73 A22 50c light brown 1.50 1.50
O74 A22 1p yellow green 3.00 3.00
 Nos. O66-O74 (9) 22.55 22.55

Regular Issue of 1924 Overprinted

1924 Perf. 11, 11½
O75 A24 1c olive brn .25 .25
O76 A24 2c deep rose .25 .25
O77 A24 6c red vio .30 .30
O78 A24 10c deep bl .45 .45
O79 A24 20c yel brn .60 .60
O80 A24 50c vermilion 1.25 1.25
O81 A24 1p emerald 2.00 2.00
 Nos. O75-O81 (7) 5.10 5.10

J. C. del Valle — O1

Designs: 2c, J. R. Molina. 5c, Coffee tree. 10c, J. T. Reyes. 20c, Tegucigalpa Cathedral. 50c, San Lorenzo Creek. 1p, Radio station.

1929 Litho. Wmk. 209 Perf. 11½
O82 O1 1c blue .25 .25
O83 O1 2c carmine .25 .25
 a. 2c rose .25 .25
O84 O1 5c purple .35 .35
O85 O1 10c emerald .50 .35
O86 O1 20c dk bl .60 .60
O87 O1 50c org, grn & bl 1.00 1.00
O88 O1 1p buff 1.75 1.75
 Nos. O82-O88 (7) 4.70 4.55

Nos. O82-O88 exist imperf.

For overprints and surcharges see Nos. 282, 284, C37-C40, C59, C62-C63, CO26-CO27.

View of Tegucigalpa — O2

1931 Unwmk. Engr. Perf. 12
O89 O2 1c ultra .30 .25
O90 O2 2c black brn .30 .25
O91 O2 5c olive gray .35 .25
O92 O2 6c orange red .40 .30
O93 O2 10c dark green .50 .35
O94 O2 15c olive brn .65 .40
O95 O2 20c red brown .75 .50
O96 O2 50c gray vio 1.00 .65
O97 O2 1p dp orange 1.75 1.75
 Nos. O89-O97 (9) 6.00 4.70

For overprints see Nos. CO6-CO14, O98-O105.

Official Stamps of 1931 Overprinted in Black

1936-37
O98 O2 1c ultra .25 .25
O99 O2 2c black brn .25 .25
 a. Inverted overprint 10.00
O100 O2 5c olive gray .30 .30
O101 O2 6c red orange .40 .40
O102 O2 10c dark green .40 .40
O103 O2 15c olive brown .50 .50
 a. Inverted overprint 5.00
O104 O2 20c red brown 1.00 1.00
 a. "1938-1935"
O105 O2 50c gray violet 4.00 3.00
 Nos. O98-O105 (8) 7.10 6.10

Double overprints exist on 1c and 2c. No. O97 with this overprint is fraudulent.

POSTAL TAX STAMPS

Red Cross — PT1

Engr.; Cross Litho.
1941, Aug. 1 Unwmk. Perf. 12
RA1 PT1 1c blue & carmine .40 .40

Obligatory on all domestic or foreign mail, the tax to be used by the Honduran Red Cross.

Francisco Morazán — PT2

1941, Aug. 1 Engr.
RA2 PT2 1c copper brown .40 .40

Francisco Morazan, 100th anniv. of death.

Mother and Child — PT3

1945 Engr.; Cross Litho.
RA3 PT3 1c ol brn, car & bl .40 .40

The tax was for the Honduran Red Cross.

Similar to Type of 1945 Large Red Cross

1950
RA4 PT3 1c olive brn & red .40 .40

The tax was for the Honduran Red Cross.

Henri Dunant — PT4

1959 Perf. 13x13½
RA5 PT4 1c blue & red .40 .40

The tax was for the Red Cross.

Catalogue values for unused stamps in this section, from this point to the end of the section, are for Never Hinged items.

Henri Dunant — PT5

No. RA7, as PT5, but redrawn; country name panel at bottom, value at right, "El poder ..." at top.

1964, Dec. 15 Litho. Perf. 11
RA6 PT5 1c brt grn & red .65 .40
RA7 PT5 1c brown & red .65 .40

The tax was for the Red Cross.

Nurse and Patient — PT6

1969, June Litho. Perf. 13½
RA8 PT6 1c light blue & red 1.25 .40

The tax was for the Red Cross.

For surcharges see Nos. 387-391, C1199, C1201-C1202, C1205-C1206.

HONG KONG

ˈhäŋˌkäŋ

LOCATION — A peninsula and island in southeast China at the mouth of the Canton River
GOVT. — Special Administrative Area of China (PRC) (as of 7/1/97)
AREA — 426 sq. mi.
POP. — 7,500,000 (2020 est.)
CAPITAL — Victoria

100 Cents = 1 Dollar

Catalogue values for unused stamps in this country are for Never Hinged items, beginning with Scott 174 in the regular postage section, Scott B1 in the semi-postal section and Scott J13 in the postage due section.

Watermark

Wmk. 340

Values for unused stamps are for examples with original gum as defined in the catalogue introduction. Very fine examples of Nos. 1-25, 29-48, 61-66d and 69-70a will have perforations touching the design on at least one side due to the narrow spacing of the stamps on the plates. Stamps with perfs clear of the design on all four sides are scarce and will command higher prices.

Queen Victoria — A1

Unwmk.

1862, Dec. 8   Typo.   Perf. 14

1	A1	2c pale brown	650.00	140.00
a.		2c deep brown	850.00	200.00
2	A1	8c buff	850.00	105.00
3	A1	12c blue	775.00	75.00
4	A1	18c lilac	750.00	70.00
5	A1	24c green	1,650.	140.00
6	A1	48c rose	3,250.	450.00
7	A1	96c gray	4,750.	525.00

1863-80   Wmk. 1

8	A1	2c brn ('65)	160.00	10.00
a.		2c deep brown ('64)	400.00	40.00
9	A1	2c dull rose ('80)	325.00	47.50
a.		2c rose	350.00	47.50
10	A1	4c slate	155.00	11.25
a.		4c greenish grey	425.00	60.00
b.		4c bluish slate	575.00	30.00
11	A1	5c ultra ('80)	950.00	70.00
12	A1	6c lilac	525.00	26.00
a.		6c violet	775.00	26.50
13	A1	8c org buff ('65)	725.00	15.00
a.		8c bright orange	600.00	19.00
b.		8c brownish orange	600.00	19.00
14	A1	10c violet ('80)	1,075.	25.00
15	A1	12c light blue	42.00	11.25
a.		12c light greenish blue	1,300.	47.50
b.		12c deep blue	350.00	16.50
16	A1	16c yel ('77)	2,400.	82.50
17	A1	18c lilac ('66)	8,250.	375.00
18	A1	24c grn ('65)	775.00	14.50
a.		24c deep green	1,550.	40.00
19	A1	30c vermilion	1,325.	19.00
20	A1	30c violet ('71)	325.00	7.00
21	A1	48c rose car	1,325.	45.00
22	A1	48c brn ('80)	1,800.	145.00
23	A1	96c bis ('65)	95,000.	950.00
24	A1	96c gray ('66)	1,900.	90.00

Imperfs. are plate proofs.

1874   Perf. 12½

25	A1	4c slate	14,000.	325.00

See Nos. 36-48. For surcharges or overprints on stamps of type A1 see Nos. 29-35B, 51-56, 61-66, 69-70.

A2

A3

A4

1874   Engr.   Wmk. 1   Perf. 15½x15

26	A2	$2 sage green	500.00	82.50
27	A3	$3 violet	475.00	65.00
28	A4	$10 rose	10,250.	950.00

Nos. 26-28 are revenues which were used postally. Used values are for postally canceled examples. Black "Paid All" cancels are fiscal usage.
See Nos. 57-59. For surcharges see Nos. 50, 67. For type surcharged see No. 60.

Nos. 17 and 20 Surcharged in Black

1876   Perf. 14

29	A1	16c on 18c lilac	3,000.	190.00
30	A1	28c on 30c violet	2,400.	65.00

Stamps of 1863-80 Surcharged in Black

1879-80

31	A1	5c on 8c org ('80)	1,300.	140.00
a.		Inverted surcharge		25,000.
b.		Double surcharge		25,000.
32	A1	5c on 18c lilac	1,200.	90.00
33	A1	10c on 12c pale blue	1,300.	65.00
a.		10c on 12c blue	2,000.	125.00
b.		Double surcharge		60,000.
34	A1	10c on 16c yellow	5,000.	190.00
a.		Inverted surcharge		110,000.
b.		Double surcharge		90,000.
35	A1	10c on 24c grn ('80)	1,750.	120.00

Most examples of No. 31a are damaged.

Nos. 16-17 Surcharged in Black

No. 35B Surcharged in Black

1879

35A	A5	3c on 16c on card	650.	2,200.
		Stamp off card		525.00
35B	A5	5c on 18c on card	650.	2,600.
		Stamp off card		575.
35C	A6	3c on 5c on 18c on card	10,500.	12,000.
		Stamp off card	9,500.	10,500.

Nos. 35A-35C were sold affixed to postal cards. Most used examples are found off card so values are given for these.

Type of 1862

1882-1902   Wmk. 2   Perf. 14

36b	A1	2c carmine ('84)	65.00	3.50
37	A1	2c green ('00)	35.00	1.05
38	A1	4c slate ('96)	47.50	4.75
39	A1	4c car rose ('00)	26.00	1.05
40	A1	5c ultramarine	65.00	1.00
41	A1	5c yellow ('00)	37.50	13.00
42	A1	10c lilac	1,200.	27.50
43	A1	10c green	215.00	2.50
		10c blue green	2,250.	47.50
44	A1	10c vio, red ('91)	52.50	2.00
45	A1	10c ultra ('00)	60.00	3.25
46	A1	12c blue ('02)	60.00	82.50
47	A1	30c gray grn ('91)	140.00	32.50
a.		30c yellow green	190.00	52.50
48	A1	30c brown ('01)	77.50	35.00
a.		Pair, imperf.		2,000.
		Nos. 36b-48 (13)	2,081.	210.10

No. 47 has fugitive ink. Both colors will turn dull green upon soaking.
The 2c rose, perf 12, is a proof.

No. 28 Surcharged in Black

1880   Wmk. 1   Perf. 15½x15

50	A4	12c on $10 rose	1,100.	400.00

Surcharged in Black

1885-91   Wmk. 2   Perf. 14

51	A1	20c on 30c ver	235.00	10.00
a.		Double surcharge		
52	A1	20c on 30c gray grn ('91)	100.00	140.00
a.		20c on 30c yellow green	150.00	160.00
53	A1	50c on 48c brown	500.00	60.00
54	A1	50c on 48c lil ('91)	300.00	300.00
55	A1	$1 on 96c ol gray	950.00	110.00
56	A1	$1 on 96c vio, red ('91)	750.00	325.00

For overprints see Nos. 61-63.

Types of 1874 and

A7

1890-1902   Wmk. 2   Perf. 14

56A	A7	2c dull purple	240.00	60.00

Wmk. 1

57	A2	$2 gray green	525.00	325.00
58	A3	$3 lilac ('02)	825.00	650.00
59	A4	$10 gray grn ('92)	14,000.	13,000.
		Fiscal cancellation		500.00

Due to a shortage of 2c postage stamps, No. 56A was authorized for postal use December 24-30, 1890.
Fake postmarks are known on No. 59. Beware also of fiscal cancels altered to resemble postal cancels.
For surcharge see No. 68.

Type of 1874 Surcharged in Black

1891, Jan. 1   Wmk. 2

60	A4	$5 on $10 vio, red	525.00	140.00

Nos. 36b, 44 Overprinted

a   b

1891, Jan. 1

60A	A1	2c carmine (a)	1,200.	450.00
60B	A1	2c carmine (b)	775.00	240.00
a.		Inverted overprint		10,750.
60C	A1	10c vio, red (a)	2,250.	525.00

Nos. 60A-60C were overprinted for use as fiscal stamps, "S.O." denoting "Stamp Office" and "S.D." denoting "Stamp Duty." They were authorized for postal use Jan. 1, 1891-1893. Examples of No. 60A with "O" changed to "D" in manuscript are known.
Forged overprints are often encountered. Expertization is required.

Nos. 52, 54 and 56 Handstamped with Chinese characters

g   h

i

61	A1 (g)	20c on 30c yellow green	65.00	17.50
a.		20c on 30c dull green	40.00	16.00
b.		"20 CENTS" double	30,000.	30,000.
62	A1 (h)	50c on 48c	100.00	6.50
63	A1 (i)	$1 on 96c	525.00	27.50
a.		Chinese inscriptions both sides		950.00

No. 61 may be found with Chinese character 2mm, 2½mm or 3mm high.
The handstamped Chinese surcharges on Nos. 61-63 exist in several varieties including inverted, double, triple, misplaced, omitted and (on No. 63) on both front and back.

HONG KONG

Nos. 43 and 20 Surcharged

1891
64	A1	7c on 10c green	110.00	12.00
a.		Double surcharge	8,250.	1,500.
b.		Antique "t" in "cents"	825.00	190.00
c.		Small "t" in "cents"	800.00	185.00
		On cover		—

Wmk. 1
65	A1	14c on 30c violet	270.00	100.00

Beware of faked varieties.

No. 36 Overprinted in Black

1891, Jan. 22 **Wmk. 2**
66	A1	2c rose	550.00	150.00
a.		Double overprint	21,500.	16,750.
b.		"U" of "JUBILEE" shorter	950.00	240.00
c.		"J" of "JUBILEE" shorter	950.00	240.00
d.		Tall "K" in "KONG"	1,550.	550.00
g.		"1841" omitted		7,500.

50th anniversary of the colony.
Beware of faked varieties. Value for 66a are for doubling clearly seperated & visible. Overprint nearly over each other are valued much less. No. 66g is from a shift of a single row or 12 of the overprint.

No. 26 Surcharged (Chinese Handstamped)

1897, Sept. **Wmk. 1** **Perf. 15½x15**
67	A2	$1 on $2 sage green	260.00	150.00
a.		Without Chinese surcharges	5,000.	3,500.
b.		Diagonal Chinese surcharge omitted	26,000.	

On No. 57 **Perf. 14**
68	A2	$1 on $2 gray green	325.00	175.00
a.		Without Chinese surcharges	2,400.	2,000.
b.		Diagonal Chinese surcharge omitted	47,500.	
c.		Vertical Chinese surcharge omitted Handstamped "SPECIMEN"	175.00	

Handstamp Surcharged in Black

1898 **Wmk. 2**
69	A1	10c on 30c gray grn	95.00	120.00
a.		Large Chinese surcharge	1,200.	1,200.
b.		Without Chinese surcharge	700.00	2,100.
70	A1	$1 on 96c black	300.00	30.00
a.		Without Chinese surcharge Overprinted "SPECIMEN"	3,750. 625.00	4,750.

The Chinese surcharge is added separately. See notes below Nos. 61-63. The small Chinese surcharge is illustrated.

King Edward VII — A10

1903 **Wmk. 2**
71	A10	1c brown & lilac	3.50	.60
72	A10	2c gray green	28.00	3.50
73	A10	4c violet, red	35.00	.45
74	A10	5c org & gray grn	30.00	13.00
75	A10	8c vio & blk	81.00	2.50
76	A10	10c ultra & lil, bl	82.50	1.75
77	A10	12c red vio & gray grn, yel	19.00	8.25
78	A10	20c org brn & blk	77.50	8.25
79	A10	30c blk & gray grn	77.50	33.00
80	A10	50c red vio & gray grn	77.50	82.50
81	A10	$1 ol grn & lil	155.00	35.00
82	A10	$2 scar & black	450.00	450.00
83	A10	$3 dp bl & blk	525.00	500.00
84	A10	$5 blue grn & lil	775.00	700.00
85	A10	$10 org & blk, bl	1,650.	550.00
		Nos. 71-85 (15)	4,007.	2,389.

1904-11 **Wmk. 3**
Ordinary or Chalky Paper
86	A10	1c brown ('10)	13.00	1.25
a.		Booklet pane of 4		
87	A10	2c gray green	34.50	3.25
88	A10	2c deep green	57.50	2.00
a.		Booklet pane of 4		
b.		Booklet pane of 12		
89	A10	4c violet, red	33.00	.45
90	A10	4c carmine	26.00	.60
a.		Booklet pane of 4		
91	A10	5c org & gray grn	90.00	26.00
a.		Chalky paper ('06)	30.00	8.25
92	A10	6c red vio & org ('07)	57.50	11.00
93	A10	8c vio & blk ('07)	26.00	2.50
94	A10	10c ultra & lil, bl	47.50	1.75
95	A10	10c ultramarine	77.50	.60
96	A10	12c red vio & gray grn, yel ('07)	26.00	10.75
97	A10	20c org brn & blk	82.50	5.50
a.		Chalky paper ('06)	77.50	5.00
98	A10	20c ol grn & vio ('11)	65.00	57.50
99	A10	30c blk & gray grn	82.50	47.50
a.		Chalky paper ('06)	82.50	28.50
100	A10	30c org & vio ('11)	77.50	60.00
101	A10	50c red vio & gray green	130.00	21.50
a.		Chalky paper ('06)	110.00	27.50
102	A10	50c blk, grn ('11)	60.00	25.00
103	A10	$1 ol grn & lil	240.00	60.00
a.		Chalky paper ('06)	215.00	60.00
104	A10	$2 scar & black	540.00	200.00
a.		Chalky paper ('06)	420.00	165.00
105	A10	$2 blk & car ('10)	475.00	500.00
106	A10	$3 dp bl & blk	450.00	420.00
107	A10	$5 bl grn & lil	650.00	550.00
108	A10	$10 org & blk, bl	2,250.	1,750.
a.		Chalky paper ('06)	2,400.	1,400.
		Nos. 86-108 (23)	5,591.	3,757.

Nos. 86, 88, 90, 94 and 95 are on ordinary paper only. Nos. 92, 93, 96, 98, 100, 102, 105, 106 and 107 are on chalky paper and the others of the issue are on both papers.
The 4c, 5c, 8c, 12c 20c, 50c, $2 and $5 denominations of type A10 are expressed in colored letters or numerals and letters on a colorless background.

King George V
A11 A12

A13 A14

A15

Two Types of 25c:
I: A short vertical stroke crosses the bottom of the top Chinese character in the left label.
II: The vertical stroke is absent from the character.

1912-14 **Ordinary Paper**
109	A11	1c brown	9.00	.65
a.		Booklet pane of 12		
110	A11	2c deep green	24.00	.35
a.		Booklet pane of 12		
111	A12	4c carmine	16.75	.35
a.		Booklet pane of 4		
112	A13	6c orange	10.00	3.75
113	A12	8c gray	45.00	13.00
114	A11	10c ultramarine	42.00	.35

Chalky Paper
115	A14	12c vio, yel	19.00	20.00
116	A14	20c ol grn & vio	24.00	2.00
117	A15	25c red vio & dl vio (I) ('14)	60.00	57.50
118	A13	30c org & violet	52.50	10.75
119	A14	50c black, bl grn, white back	47.50	5.25
a.		50c black, emerald, emerald back	47.50	13.00
b.		50c black, bl grn, ol back	1,675.	40.00
c.		50c black, emer, ol back	57.50	10.00
120	A11	$1 blue & vio, bl	90.00	7.50
121	A14	$2 black & red	240.00	45.00
122	A13	$3 vio & green	350.00	155.00
123	A14	$5 red & grn, grn	850.00	525.00
a.		$5 red & grn, bl grn, ol back	1,425.	500.00
124	A13	$10 blk & vio, red	700.00	130.00
		Nos. 109-124 (16)	2,580.	1,021.

For overprints see British Offices in China Nos. 1-27.

1914, May **Surface-colored Paper**
125	A14	12c violet, yel	17.50	18.00
126	A14	50c black, green	30.00	3.50
127	A14	$5 red & grn, grn	700.00	400.00
		Nos. 125-127 (3)	747.50	421.50

Stamp of 1912-14 Redrawn (Type II)

1919, Aug. **Chalky Paper**
128	A15	25c red vio & dl vio	275.00	80.00

Types of 1912-14 Issue

1921-37 **Ordinary Paper** **Wmk. 4**
129	A11	1c brown	4.00	.45
130	A11	2c deep green	8.25	1.20
131	A11	2c gray ('37)	30.00	16.75
132	A12	3c gray ('31)	17.50	2.40
133	A12	4c rose red	9.50	.80
134	A12	5c violet ('31)	28.75	.35
135	A12	8c gray	31.00	52.50
136	A12	8c orange	9.50	3.25
137	A11	10c ultramarine	17.50	.35

Chalky Paper
138	A14	12c vio ('33)	31.00	6.00
139	A14	20c ol grn & dl vio	16.75	.35
140	A15	25c red vio & dl vio, redrawn	12.00	3.75
141	A13	30c yel & violet	16.75	3.75
142	A14	50c blk, emerald	42.00	.35
143	A11	$1 ultra & vio, bl	60.00	1.50
144	A14	$2 black & red	165.00	14.00
145	A13	$3 dl vio & grn ('26)	240.00	90.00
146	A14	$5 red & grn, emer ('25)	600.00	100.00
		Nos. 129-146 (18)	1,340.	297.75

Common Design Types pictured following the introduction.

Silver Jubilee Issue
Common Design Type

1935, May 6 **Engr.** **Perf. 11x12**
147	CD301	3c black & ultra	4.75	4.00
148	CD301	5c indigo & grn	10.00	3.25
149	CD301	10c ultra & brn	21.00	1.50
150	CD301	20c brn vio & ind	38.00	12.00
		Nos. 147-150 (4)	73.75	20.75
		Set, never hinged	135.00	

Coronation Issue
Common Design Type

1937, May 12 **Perf. 11x11½**
151	CD302	4c deep green	2.50	7.75
152	CD302	15c dark carmine	6.25	3.50
153	CD302	25c deep ultra	8.25	6.50
		Nos. 151-153 (3)	17.00	17.75
		Set, never hinged	24.00	

King George VI — A16

1938-52 **Typo.** **Perf. 14**
Ordinary Paper
154	A16	1c brown	1.00	7.50
a.		Double printed	10,000.	
155	A16	2c gray	1.00	1.20
156	A16	4c orange	5.00	7.50
157	A16	5c green	.60	.80
157B	A16	8c brn red ('41)	1.00	4.00
c.		Imperf., pair	60,000.	
158	A16	10c violet	10.00	1.75
		10c red lil ('47)	20.00	.30
159	A16	15c carmine	1.00	.35
159A	A16	20c gray ('46)	2.00	.35
159B	A16	20c rose red ('48)	7.00	.35
160	A16	25c ultramarine	14.50	5.50
160A	A16	25c gray ol ('46)	4.25	5.50
161	A16	30c olive bister	75.00	4.50
161B	A16	30c lt ultra ('46)	3.50	.25
162B	A16	50c red vio	17.00	3.00

Chalky Paper
162	A16	50c brt red violet	6.00	.25
b.		Ordinary paper	17.00	3.00
162C	A16	80c lilac rose ('48)	3.25	1.25
163	A16	$1 lilac & ultra	4.25	5.00
a.		Ordinary paper	11.00	38.00
163B	A16	$1 dp org & grn ('46)	26.00	2.25
c.		Ordinary paper	13.50	.35
164	A16	$2 dp org & grn	40.00	52.50
164A	A16	$2 vio & red ('46)	27.50	1.20
b.		Ordinary paper	25.00	13.00
165	A16	$5 lilac & red	35.00	65.00
165A	A16	$5 grn & vio ('46)	60.00	6.00
b.		Ordinary paper	25.00	30.00
166	A16	$10 grn & vio	350.00	165.00
166A	A16	$10 vio & ultra ('46)	100.00	26.00
b.		Ordinary paper	70.00	7.50
		Nos. 154-166A (23)	776.45	364.00
		Set, never hinged	1,300.	350.00

Coarse Impressions
Ordinary Rough-Surfaced Paper
1941-46 **Perf. 14½x14**
155a	A16	2c gray	.90	8.25
156a	A16	4c orange ('46)	2.50	4.00
157a	A16	5c green	1.75	6.50
158a	A16	10c violet	4.75	.25
161a	A16	30c dull olive bister	14.00	16.50
162a	A16	50c red lilac	15.00	1.60
		Nos. 155a-162a (6)	38.90	37.10
		Set, never hinged	92.50	

A17

1938, Jan. 11 **Wmk. 4**
167	A17	5c green	60.00	20.00

No. 167 is a revenue stamp officially authorized to be sold and used for postal purposes. Used Jan. 11-20, 1938. The used price is for the stamp on cover. CTO covers exist.

Street Scene A18

Hong Kong Bank A22

Liner and Junk — A19

University of Hong Kong — A20

Harbor — A21

China Clipper and Seaplane — A23

Perf. 13½x13, 13x13½
1941, Feb. 26 **Engr.** **Wmk. 4**
168	A18	2c sepia & org	4.00	3.25
169	A19	4c rose car & vio	4.75	6.00
170	A20	5c yel grn & blk	1.75	.60
171	A21	15c red & black	4.75	3.50
172	A22	25c dp blue & dk brn	9.50	11.00
173	A23	$1 brn org & blue	25.00	15.00
		Nos. 168-173 (6)	49.75	39.35
		Set, never hinged	105.00	

Centenary of British rule.

Catalogue values for unused stamps in this section, from this point to the end of the section, are for Never Hinged items.

HONG KONG

Peace Issue

Phoenix Rising from Flames — A24

1946, Aug. 29		Perf. 13x12½	
174	A24 30c car & dp blue	3.00	2.00
175	A24 $1 car & brown	3.75	.75
	Set, hinged	4.00	

Return to peace after WWII.

Silver Wedding Issue
Common Design Types

Perf. 14x14½
1948, Dec. 22	Photo.	Wmk. 4	
178	CD304 10c purple	4.00	1.75

Engr.; Name Typo.
Perf. 11½x11
| 179 | CD305 $10 rose car | 325.00 | 105.00 |
| | Set, hinged | 225.00 | |

UPU Issue
Common Design Types
Engr.; Name Typo. on 20c & 30c

1949, Oct. 10		Perf. 13½, 11x11½	
180	CD306 10c violet	4.75	1.20
181	CD307 20c deep car	15.00	7.00
182	CD308 30c indigo	12.00	7.00
183	CD309 80c red violet	35.00	4.75
	Nos. 180-183 (4)	66.75	19.95
	Set, hinged	66.75	

Coronation Issue
Common Design Type

1953, June 2	Engr.	Perf. 13½x13	
184	CD312 10c pur & blk	3.00	.30
	Hinged	2.25	

Elizabeth II — A25

1954-60	Typo.	Perf. 13½x14	
185	A25 5c orange	1.60	.25
a.	Imperf., pair	2,250.	
186	A25 10c violet	2.00	.25
187	A25 15c green	4.00	3.25
188	A25 20c brown	5.50	.30
189	A25 25c rose red	5.00	4.75
190	A25 30c gray	4.50	.25
191	A25 40c blue	5.25	.40
192	A25 50c red violet	6.00	.25
193	A25 65c lt gray ('60)	20.00	17.50
194	A25 $1 org & green	8.50	.25
195	A25 $1.30 bl & ver ('60)	27.50	2.75
196	A25 $2 violet & red	14.00	.90
197	A25 $5 green & vio	85.00	4.00
198	A25 $10 violet & ultra	70.00	13.00
	Nos. 185-198 (14)	258.85	48.10
	Set, hinged	110.00	

Nos. 185-187 are on ordinary paper; Nos. 188-198 on chalky paper. No. 191 exists as imperf, but is a printer's trial. Value, $600.

Arms of University — A26

Perf. 11½x12
1961, Sept. 11	Photo.	Wmk. 314	
199	A26 $1 bl, blk, red, grn & gold	6.00	1.75
a.	Gold omitted	3,000.	

University of Hong Kong, 50th anniv.

Queen Victoria Statue, Victoria Park, Hong Kong — A27

1962, May 4		Perf. 14	
200	A27 10c car rose & black	.60	.25
201	A27 20c blue & black	1.75	2.00
202	A27 50c bister & black	4.25	.45
	Nos. 200-202 (3)	6.60	2.70

1st postage stamps of Hong Kong, cent.

Queen Elizabeth II — A28

Wmk. 314 Upright
1962, Oct. 4	Photo.	Perf. 14½x14	

Size: 17x21mm
203	A28 5c red orange	.85	.50
a.	Booklet pane of 4	4.00	
204	A28 10c purple	1.60	.25
a.	Booklet pane of 4	7.50	
205	A28 15c green	4.00	1.90
206	A28 20c red brown	1.75	.25
a.	Booklet pane of 4	14.00	
207	A28 25c lilac rose	3.75	4.25
208	A28 30c dark blue	2.75	.25
209	A28 40c Prus green	5.25	.65
210	A28 50c crimson	1.90	.30
a.	Booklet pane of 4	25.00	
211	A28 65c ultramarine	19.00	2.00
212	A28 $1 dark brown	25.00	.40

Perf. 14x14½
Size: 25½x30½mm
Portrait in Natural Colors
213	A28 $1.30 sky blue	4.00	.25
a.	Ocher (sash) omitted	70.00	
b.	Yellow omitted	70.00	
214	A28 $2 fawn	7.00	1.00
a.	Yellow and ocher (sash) omitted	275.00	
b.	Yellow omitted	70.00	
c.	Ocher (sash) omitted	70.00	
215	A28 $5 orange	15.00	1.50
a.	Ocher (sash) omitted	50.00	
216	A28 $10 green	25.00	2.50
a.	Ocher (sash) omitted	175.00	
b.	Pale yellow and ocher (sash) omitted	275.00	
217	A28 $20 violet blue	70.00	27.50
a.	Ocher (sash) omitted	325.00	
	Nos. 203-217 (15)	186.85	43.50

1966-72	Wmk. 314 Sideways		
203b	A28 5c ('67)	.55	1.00
204b	A28 10c ('67)	.65	.75
204c	As No. 204b, imperf. horiz. pair	1,250.00	
205a	A28 15c ('67)	1.75	5.00
206b	A28 20c	2.00	2.50
207a	A28 25c ('67)	3.00	6.00
208a	A28 30c ('70)	12.50	8.00
209a	A28 40c ('67)	4.00	3.50
210b	A28 50c ('67)	2.50	1.50
211a	A28 65c ('67)	6.50	12.50
212a	A28 $1 ('67)	17.50	1.75
213c	A28 $1.30 ('72)	15.00	3.00
213d	As No. 213c, Pale yellow omitted	70.00	
214c	A28 $2 ('71)	25.00	3.25
214d	As No. 214c, Pale yellow omitted	75.00	
215b	A28 $5 ('71)	75.00	32.50
215c	As No. 215b, Pale yellow omitted	170.00	
217a	A28 $20 ('72)	175.00	90.00
	Nos. 203b-217a (14)	340.95	171.25

Most of the A28 type issue were reissued in 1971-73 on glazed paper. These are all valued higher than the listed stamps.

Freedom from Hunger Issue
Common Design Type

1963, June 4	Photo.	Wmk. 314	
218	CD314 $1.30 green	37.50	5.00

Red Cross Centenary Issue
Common Design Type

1963, Sept. 2	Litho.	Perf. 13	
219	CD315 10c black & red	3.75	.35
220	CD315 $1.30 ultra & red	15.00	7.00

ITU Issue
Common Design Type

1965, May 17		Perf. 11x11½	
221	CD317 10c red lil & yel	2.00	.25
222	CD317 $1.30 apple grn & turq blue	8.50	4.50

Intl. Cooperation Year Issue
Common Design Type

1965, Oct. 25		Perf. 14½	
223	CD318 10c blue grn & cl	2.50	.25
224	CD318 $1.30 lt violet & grn	8.50	3.25

Churchill Memorial Issue
Common Design Type

1966, Jan. 24	Photo.	Perf. 14	

Design in Black, Gold and Carmine Rose
225	CD319 10c bright blue	2.75	.25
226	CD319 50c green	3.25	.40
227	CD319 $1.30 brown	17.50	3.25
228	CD319 $2 violet	29.00	7.50
	Nos. 225-228 (4)	52.50	11.40

WHO Headquarters Issue
Common Design Type

1966, Sept. 20	Litho.	Perf. 14	
229	CD322 10c multicolored	2.25	.30
230	CD322 50c multicolored	9.00	2.00

UNESCO Anniversary Issue
Common Design Type

1966, Dec. 1	Litho.	Perf. 14	
231	CD323 10c "Education"	2.00	.25
232	CD323 50c "Science"	10.00	1.25
233	CD323 $2 "Culture"	37.50	22.50
	Nos. 231-233 (3)	49.50	24.00

Three Rams' Heads — A29

Lunar New Year: $1.30, Three rams.

1967, Jan. 17	Photo.	Perf. 14	
234	A29 10c red, citron & grn	2.00	.60
235	A29 $1.30 red, cit & brt grn	17.00	8.00

Outline of Telephone with Map of South East Asia and Australia — A30

1967, Mar. 30	Photo.	Perf. 12½	
236	A30 $1.30 dk red & blue	7.50	1.75

Completion of the Hong Kong-Malaysia link of the South East Asia Commonwealth Cable, SEACOM.

Monkeys — A31

Lunar New Year: $1.30, Two monkey families.

1968, Jan. 23	Wmk. 314	Perf. 14	
237	A31 10c crim, blk & gold	2.25	.50
238	A31 $1.30 crim, blk & gold	15.00	7.00

Liner and New Sea Terminal — A32

Seacraft: 20c, Pleasure launch and sailing cruiser. 40c, Vehicle ferry. 50c, Passenger ferry. $1, Sampan. $1.30, Junk.

Perf. 13x12½
1968, Apr. 24	Litho.	Unwmk.	
239	A32 10c multicolored	1.65	.25
a.	Dull org. & new blue omitted	3,500.	
240	A32 20c sky blue, bis & black	2.50	1.65
241	A32 40c org, rose lil & black	7.00	11.25
242	A32 50c brt red, emer & black	5.25	1.65
a.	Green omitted	1,600.	
243	A32 $1 yel, cop red & black	9.00	6.75
244	A32 $1.30 dk bl, brt pink & black	24.50	8.25
	Nos. 239-244 (6)	49.90	29.80

Bauhinia Blakeana — A33

Perf. 14x14½
1968, Sept. 25	Photo.	Wmk. 314	
245	A33 65c shown	8.50	.50
	Wmkd. sideways ('72)	75.00	50.00
246	A33 $1 Coat of Arms	8.50	.40
a.	Wmkd. sideways ('71)	10.00	2.50

Human Rights Flame and "Lamp of Life" — A34

1968, Nov. 20	Litho.	Perf. 13½	
247	A34 10c green, org & blk	1.25	.50
248	A34 50c magenta, yel & blk	2.50	3.00

International Human Rights Year.

Cock — A35

Design: $1.30, Cock, vert.

Perf. 13x13½, 13½x13
1969, Feb. 11	Photo.	Unwmk.	
249	A35 10c brn, blk, org & red	4.00	1.25
a.	Red omitted	400.00	
250	A35 $1.30 ocher, blk, org & red	40.00	9.50

Lunar New Year, Feb. 17, 1969.

Chinese University Seal — A36

1969, Aug. 26	Unwmk.	Perf. 13	
251	A36 40c multicolored	3.00	2.75

Chinese University of Hong Kong, founded 1963.

Radar, Globe and Satellite — A37

Perf. 14x14½
1969, Sept. 24	Photo.	Wmk. 314	
252	A37 $1 scar, blk, sil & bl	6.50	2.50

Opening of the satellite earth station (connected through the Indian Ocean satellite Intelsat III) on Stanley Peninsula, Hong Kong.

Chow — A38

Lunar New Year (Year of the Dog): $1.30, Chow, horiz.

1970, Jan. 28		Perf. 14	
253	A38 10c black & multi	3.50	.80
254	A38 $1.30 green & multi	47.50	12.50

Emblem — A39

25c, Emblem and Chinese junks, horiz.

Perf. 13½x13, 13x13½
1970, Mar. 14	Litho.	Wmk. 314	
255	A39 15c multicolored	2.00	.75
256	A39 25c multicolored	2.00	1.50

EXPO '70 Intl. Exposition, Osaka, Japan, Mar. 15-Sept. 13.

HONG KONG

"A Compassionate Ship on the Bitter Sea" — A40

1970, Apr. 9   Photo.   Perf. 14
257 A40 10c yel green & multi   1.00   .30
258 A40 50c scarlet & multi   3.25   1.50
Centenary of the Tung Wah Group of Hospitals (including schools and various charitable organizations).

A.P.Y. Emblem — A41

1970, Aug. 5   Litho.   Wmk. 314
259 A41 10c yellow & multi   2.00   1.00
Issued for Asian Productivity Year.

Boar — A42

     Perf. 13x13½
1971, Jan. 20   Photo.   Unwmk.
260 A42 10c yel grn, gold & black   2.10   1.25
261 A42 $1.30 vio, gold & blk   23.00   6.00
Lunar New Year.

Scout Emblem and "60" — A43

     Perf. 14x14½
1971, July 23   Litho.   Wmk. 314
262 A43 10c red, yel & blk   .80   .25
263 A43 50c blue, emer & blk   3.25   1.50
264 A43 $2 vio, lil rose & blk   16.50   9.00
Nos. 262-264 (3)   20.55   10.25
60th anniversary of Hong Kong Boy Scouts.

Festival Emblem A44   Symbolic Flower A45

Festival of Hong Kong: 50c, Dancers, horiz.

1971, Nov. 2   Perf. 14
265 A44 10c lilac & orange   1.25   .25
     Perf. 14½
266 A45 50c lilac & multi   3.25   .90
267 A45 $1 lilac & multi   8.50   6.00
Nos. 265-267 (3)   13.00   7.15

Rats — A46

     Perf. 13½x13
1972, Feb. 8   Photo.   Unwmk.
268 A46 10c blk, red & gold   3.00   .50
269 A46 $1.30 blk, gold & red   33.00   6.00
Lunar New Year.

Cross Harbor Tunnel Entrance A47

     Perf. 14x14½
1972, Oct. 20   Litho.   Wmk. 314
270 A47 $1 multicolored   5.75   1.75
Inauguration of Cross Harbor Tunnel linking Victoria and Kowloon.

Silver Wedding Issue, 1972
Common Design Type
Design: Queen Elizabeth II, Prince Philip, phoenix and dragon.

1972, Nov. 20   Photo.   Perf. 14x14½
271 CD324 10c citron & multi   .60   .25
272 CD324 50c gray & multi   1.10   1.25

Ox — A48

1973, Feb. 3   Perf. 14
273 A48 10c dk brown & red   2.75   .50
274 A48 $1.30 dk brn, yel & org   8.00   5.75

Elizabeth II — A49

Wmk. 314 Upright; Sideways (15c, 30c, 40c)
1973, June 12   Photo.   Perf. 14½x14
Size: 20x24mm
275 A49 10c orange   .85   .50
   d. Watermark sideways (coil)   1.50   1.50
276 A49 15c olive green   7.00   7.50
277 A49 20c bright purple   1.75   .30
278 A49 25c deep brown   8.00   7.50
279 A49 30c ultramarine   .90   .50
280 A49 40c blue green   2.75   2.75
281 A49 50c red   1.25   .50
282 A49 65c dp bister   12.50   11.50
283 A49 $1 dk slate green   2.00   .65
     Perf. 14x14½
Wmk. 314 Sideways
Size: 28x32mm
284 A49 $1.30 dk pur & yel   6.00   .75
285 A49 $2 dp brn & lt grn   7.50   1.00
286 A49 $5 dk vio bl & rose   10.00   3.00
Photo. & Embossed
287 A49 $10 dk sl green & pink   12.00   8.00
288 A49 $20 black & rose   21.00   18.50
Nos. 275-288 (14)   93.50   62.95
No. 281, 286 exists imperforate.

1975-78   Wmk. 373   Perf. 14½x14
Size: 20x24mm
275a A49 10c orange   .50   .30
   c. Booklet pane of 4 ('76)   2.00
276a A49 15c olive green   13.50   11.00
   c. Booklet pane of 4   70.00
277a A49 20c bright purple   .50   .25
   c. Booklet pane of 4 ('76)   2.00
278a A49 25c deep brown   16.00   15.00
279a A49 30c ultramarine   .75   .70
280a A49 40c blue green   1.00   1.75
281a A49 50c red   2.50   .75
   c. Complete booklet, 2 #275c, 276c, 2 #277c, 281c   11.00
     90.00
282a A49 65c deep bister   18.00   11.00
283a A49 $1 dark slate green   2.50   .75
     Perf. 14x14½
Size: 28x32mm
284a A49 $1.30 dark purple & yel   2.25   .45
285a A49 $2 dp brn & lt grn   2.75   1.10
286a A49 $5 dk vio bl & rose ('78)   4.25   2.00
287a A49 $10 dk sl grn & pink ('78)   4.75   6.00
288a A49 $20 black & rose ('78)   7.25   2.00
     Nos. 275a-288a (14)   76.50   62.05
No. 288a exists imperf. Value, pair $750.
See Nos. 314-327.

Princess Anne's Wedding Issue
Common Design Type
Wmk. 314
1973, Nov. 14   Litho.   Perf. 14
289 CD325 50c ocher & multi   .65   .25
290 CD325 $2 lilac & multi   2.00   1.75

Chinese Character "Hong" — A50

Designs: 50c, "Kong." $1, "Festival."
1973, Nov. 23   Litho.   Perf. 14½x14
291 A50 10c red & green   .50   .25
292 A50 50c plum & red   1.50   .90
293 A50 $1 emerald & plum   3.75   3.00
Nos. 291-293 (3)   5.75   4.15
Festival of Hong Kong 1973.

Tiger — A51

Lunar New Year: $1.30, Tiger, vert.
     Perf. 14½x14, 14x14½
1974, Jan. 8   Wmk. 314
294 A51 10c green & multi   3.00   .50
295 A51 $1.30 lilac & multi   13.00   12.00

Chinese Opera Mask — A52

Designs: Chinese opera masks.
1974, Feb. 1   Photo.   Perf. 12x12½
296 A52 10c black, red & org   .55   .25
297 A52 $1 multicolored   5.00   3.75
298 A52 $2 black, org & gold   10.00   8.00
   a. Souvenir sheet of 3, #296-298, perf. 14x13   60.00   50.00
Nos. 296-298 (3)   15.55   12.00
Hong Kong Arts Festival.

Carrier Pigeons — A53

Cent. of UPU: 50c, Symbolic globe in envelope. $2, Hands holding letters.
1974, Oct. 9   Litho.   Perf. 14
299 A53 10c blue, grn & blk   .50   .25
   a. Unwatermarked   35.00
300 A53 50c magenta & multi   2.00   .40
301 A53 $2 violet & multi   4.25   3.00
Nos. 299-301 (3)   6.75   3.65

Rabbit — A54

Lunar New Year: $1.30, Two rabbits.
1975, Feb. 5   Wmk. 314   Perf. 14
302 A54 10c silver & red   1.25   .50
   a. Unwatermarked   1.40   1.00
303 A54 $1.30 gold & green   6.75   6.75
   a. Unwatermarked   7.50   9.50

Queen Elizabeth II, Prince Philip, Hong Kong Arms — A55

     Wmk. 373
1975, Apr. 30   Litho.   Perf. 13½
304 A55 $1.30 blue & multi   3.25   1.90
305 A55 $2 yellow & multi   4.50   4.25
Royal Visit 1975.

Mid-Autumn Festival — A56

Abstract Designs: $1, Dragon Boat Festival (boats). $2, Tin Hau Festival (ships with flags).
1975, July 31   Unwmk.   Perf. 14
306 A56 50c rose lil & multi   2.75   .75
307 A56 $1 brt grn & multi   10.00   2.50
308 A56 $2 orange & multi   27.50   9.00
   a. Souv. sheet of 3, #306-308   110.00   55.00
Nos. 306-308 (3)   40.25   12.25
Hong Kong Festivals, 1975.

Brown Laughing Thrush — A57

Birds: $1.30, Chinese bulbul. $2, Black-capped kingfisher.
1975, Oct. 29   Litho.   Wmk. 373
309 A57 50c lt blue & multi   2.50   .75
310 A57 $1.30 pink & multi   9.00   5.50
311 A57 $2 yellow & multi   17.50   10.00
Nos. 309-311 (3)   29.00   16.25

Dragon — A58

Lunar New Year: $1.30, like 20c, pattern reversed.
1976, Jan. 21   Litho.   Perf. 14½
312 A58 20c gold, pur & lilac   1.10   .45
313 A58 $1.30 gold, red & grn   6.75   2.75

Queen Elizabeth Type of 1973
Wmk. 373 (#320-323), Unwmkd.
1976-81   Photo.   Perf. 14½x14
Size: 20x24mm
314 A49 10c orange   24.00   10.00
316 A49 20c bright purple   3.50   1.25
318 A49 30c ultramarine   8.00   2.25
320 A49 60c lt violet ('77)   1.75   2.50
321 A49 70c yellow ('77)   1.75   .75
322 A49 80c brt mag ('77)   2.25   3.25
323 A49 90c sepia ('81)   9.00   2.75
Size: 28x32mm
     Perf. 14x14½
324 A49 $2 dp brn & lt grn   10.50   4.00
325 A49 $5 dk vio bl & rose   17.00   7.50
Photo. & Embossed
326 A49 $10 dk sl grn & pink   90.00   42.50
327 A49 $20 black & rose   175.00   65.00
Nos. 314-327 (11)   342.75   141.75
No. 316, 318 exist imperforate.

"60" and Girl Guides Emblem — A59

$1.30, "60", tents and Girl Guides emblem.
1976, Apr. 23   Wmk. 314   Perf. 14½
328 A59 20c silver & multi   1.00   .25
329 A59 $1.30 silver & multi   5.50   4.00
60th anniv. of Hong Kong Girl Guides.

HONG KONG

"Postal Services" (in Chinese) — A60

Designs: $1.30, General Post Office, 1911-1976. $2, New G.P.O., 1976.

1976, Aug. 11   Litho.   Wmk. 373
330 A60 20c gray, grn & blk   .75   .25
331 A60 $1.30 gray, red & black 3.50 1.50
332 A60 $2 gray, yel & black   6.00 4.00
    Nos. 330-332 (3)   10.25 5.75
Opening of new GPO building.

Snake — A61

Lunar New Year: $1.30, Snake & branch face left.

1977, Jan. 6   Perf. 13½
333 A61 20c multicolored   .75   .25
334 A61 $1.30 multicolored   4.75 3.50

Queen Dotting Eye of Dragon, 1975 Visit — A62

20c, Presentation of the orb. $2, Orb, vert.

1977, Feb. 7   Litho.
335 A62 20c multicolored   .55   .25
336 A62 $1.30 multicolored   1.35   .85
337 A62 $2 multicolored   1.75 1.50
    Nos. 335-337 (3)   3.65 2.60
25th anniv. of the reign of Elizabeth II.

Streetcars — A63

Designs: 60c, Star ferryboat. $1.30, Funicular railway. $2, Junk and sampan.

1977, June 30   Wmk. 373   Perf. 13½
338 A63 20c multicolored   .60   .25
339 A63 60c multicolored   1.50 2.00
340 A63 $1.30 multicolored   2.75 2.00
341 A63 $2 multicolored   3.25 3.50
    Nos. 338-341 (4)   8.10 7.75
Tourist publicity.

Buttercup Orchid — A64

$1.30, Lady's-slipper. $2, Susan orchid.

1977, Oct. 12   Litho.   Perf. 14
342 A64 20c blue & multi   1.50   .30
343 A64 $1.30 yellow & multi 4.00 1.75
344 A64 $2 green & multi   7.00 4.50
    Nos. 342-344 (3)   12.50 6.55

Horse and Chinese Character "Ma" — A65

1978, Jan. 26   Litho.   Perf. 14½
345 A65 20c multicolored   .75   .25
346 A65 $1.30 multicolored   4.00 4.00
Lunar New Year.

Elizabeth II — A66

1978, June 2   Litho.   Perf. 14x14½
347 A66 20c carmine & dk blue   .45   .25
348 A66 $1.30 dk blue & carmine 1.60 1.75
25th anniv. of coronation of Elizabeth II.

Boy and Girl — A67

Design: $1.30, Ring-around-a-rosy.

1978, Nov. 8   Wmk. 373   Perf. 14½
349 A67 20c multicolored   .30   .25
350 A67 $1.30 multicolored   1.50 2.00
Centenary of Po Leung Kuk, society for help and education of orphans and poor children.

Electronics A68

Industries: $1.30, Toy (bear and drum). $2, Garment (mannequins).

1979, Jan. 9   Litho.   Perf. 14½
351 A68 20c multicolored   .30   .25
352 A68 $1.30 multicolored   1.00 1.60
353 A68 $2 multicolored   1.10 2.00
    Nos. 351-353 (3)   2.40 3.85

Precis Orithya — A69

Butterflies: $1, Graphium sarpedon. $1.30, Heliophorus epicles phoenicoparyphus. $2, Danaus genutia.

1979, June 20   Photo.   Unwmk.
354 A69 20c multicolored   .90   .25
355 A69 $1 multicolored   1.60   .65
356 A69 $1.30 multicolored   1.75 1.50
357 A69 $2 multicolored   2.00 3.25
    Nos. 354-357 (4)   6.25 5.65

Cross Section of Station — A70

Mass Transit Railroad: $1.30, Front, rear and side views of train. $2, Map of routes.

1979, Oct. 1   Litho.   Perf. 13½
358 A70 20c multicolored   .50   .25
359 A70 $1.30 multicolored   1.60   .55
360 A70 $2 multicolored   2.10 2.50
    Nos. 358-360 (3)   4.20 3.30

Ching Chung Koon Temple, Tuen Mun — A71

Rural Architecture: 20c, Tsui Shing Lau Pagoda, Sheung Cheung Wai, vert. $1.30, Village house, Sai O.

Perf. 13x13½, 13½x13
1980, May 14   Litho.   Wmk. 373
361 A71 20c multicolored   .35   .25
362 A71 $1.30 multicolored   1.25 1.00
363 A71 $2 multicolored   1.60 2.00
    Nos. 361-363 (3)   3.20 3.25

Queen Mother Elizabeth Birthday Issue
Common Design Type
1980, Aug. 4   Litho.   Perf. 14
364 CD330 $1.30 multicolored 1.10 1.25

Botanical Gardens — A72

1980, Nov. 12   Litho.   Perf. 13½
365 A72 20c shown   .30   .25
366 A72 $1 Ocean Park   .65   .35
367 A72 $1.30 Kowloon Park   .75   .75
368 A72 $2 Country Park   1.40 2.00
    Nos. 365-368 (4)   3.10 3.35

Epinephelus Akaara — A73

$1, Nemipterus virgatus. $1.30, Choerodon azurio. $2, Scarus ghobban.

1981, Jan. 28   Litho.   Perf. 13½
369 A73 20c shown   .30   .25
370 A73 $1 multicolored   .65   .45
371 A73 $1.30 multicolored   .80   .60
372 A73 $2 multicolored   1.25 2.00
    Nos. 369-372 (4)   3.00 3.30

Royal Wedding Issue
Common Design Type
1981, July 29   Photo.   Perf. 14
373 CD331 20c Bouquet   .30   .25
374 CD331 $1.30 Charles   .55   .35
375 CD331 $5 Couple   2.25 2.25
    Nos. 373-375 (3)   3.10 2.85

Public Housing Development — A74

Various public housing developments.

1981, Oct. 14   Litho.   Perf. 13½
376 A74 20c multicolored   .30   .25
377 A74 $1 multicolored   .70   .40
378 A74 $1.30 multicolored   1.00   .65
379 A74 $2 multicolored   1.25 1.75
  a. Souvenir sheet of 4, #376-379 6.00 6.00
    Nos. 376-379 (4)   3.25 3.05

Port of Hong Kong — A75

Various views of Port of Hong Kong.

1982, Jan. 12   Litho.   Perf. 14½
380 A75 20c multicolored   .60   .25
381 A75 $1 multicolored   1.60 1.10
382 A75 $1.30 multicolored   1.75 1.60
383 A75 $2 multicolored   2.10 2.50
    Nos. 380-383 (4)   6.05 5.45

Five-banded Civet — A76

$1, Pangolin. $1.30, Chinese porcupine. $5, Barking deer.

1982, May 4   Litho.   Perf. 14½
384 A76 20c shown   .30   .25
385 A76 $1 multicolored   .60   .45
386 A76 $1.30 multicolored   1.10   .85
387 A76 $5 multicolored   3.00 3.25
    Nos. 384-387 (4)   5.00 4.80

Queen Elizabeth II
A77   A78

Perf. 14½x14
1982, Aug. 30   Photo.   Wmk. 373
388 A77 10c yellow & dk red   .80   .60
389 A77 20c blue vio & vio   1.00 1.00
390 A77 30c orange & pur   1.50   .30
391 A77 40c lt blue & red   1.50   .30
392 A77 50c pale grn & brn   1.50   .30
393 A77 60c gray & brt mag   2.75 2.00
394 A77 70c brt org & dk grn   2.75   .90
395 A77 80c gray ol & brn ol   2.75 3.00
396 A77 90c grnsh bl & grn   4.50   .60
397 A77 $1 brt pink & brn org   2.50   .30
398 A77 $1.30 rose vio & dk bl 4.00   .30
399 A77 $2 buff & blue   6.50 1.00

Photo. & Embossed
Perf. 14x14½
400 A78 $5 lemon & lake   8.00 2.50
401 A78 $10 brn & blk brn   9.00 5.00
402 A78 $20 lt blue & lake   15.00 14.00
403 A78 $50 gray & lake   36.00 29.00
    Nos. 388-403 (16)   100.05 61.10
Nos. 388 and 397 also issued in coils.

1985-87   Unwmk.
388a A77 10c   .75 1.50
389a A77 20c   20.00 16.00
391a A77 40c   1.00 1.00
392a A77 50c   1.00   .30
393a A77 60c   1.60 1.10
394a A77 70c   3.50 1.00
395a A77 80c   3.75 3.50
396a A77 90c   4.75   .75
397a A77 $1   1.90   .40
398b A77 $1.30   2.50   .45
398A A77 $1.70 brt yel grn & dp bl 4.50 1.50
399a A77 $2   4.00 1.50
400a A78 $5   10.00 3.75
401a A78 $10   10.00 5.00
402a A78 $20   11.00 7.50
403a A78 $50   32.50 26.00
    Nos. 388a-403a (16)   112.75 71.25
Issued: $1.30, 6/13/86; $1.70, 9/2/86; 20c, 6/87; others, 10/10/85.
Nos. 394, 398A exists imperforate.

3rd Far East and South Pacific Games for the Disabled — A79

1982, Oct. 31   Litho.   Wmk. 373
Perf. 14x14½
404 A79 30c Table tennis   .50   .25
405 A79 $1 Racing   .90 1.00
406 A79 $1.30 Basketball   2.60 1.75
407 A79 $5 Archery   4.25 6.00
    Nos. 404-407 (4)   8.25 9.00

Performing Arts — A80

1983, Jan. 26   Litho.   Perf. 14½x14
408 A80 30c Dancing   .50   .25
409 A80 $1.30 Theater   1.75 1.25
410 A80 $5 Music   4.50 5.00
    Nos. 408-410 (3)   6.75 6.50

A81

1983, Mar. 14   Perf. 14½x13½
411 A81 30c Aerial view   .75   .25
412 A81 $1 Liverpool Bay   1.75 1.10
413 A81 $1.30 Flag   2.00 1.25

HONG KONG

414	A81	$5 Queen Elizabeth II	4.50	6.25
		Nos. 411-414 (4)	9.00	8.85
		Commonwealth Day.		

Views by Night — A82

30c, Victoria Harbor. $1, Space Museum. $1.30, Chinese New Year Fireworks. $5, Jumbo Restaurant.

1983, Aug. 17   Litho.   Perf. 14½

415	A82	30c multicolored	1.50	.60
416	A82	$1 multicolored	3.50	1.75
417	A82	$1.30 multicolored	4.50	2.25
a.		Silver omitted		275.00
418	A82	$5 multicolored	14.50	11.00
		Nos. 415-418 (4)	24.00	15.60

Royal Observatory Centenary A83

40c, Technical facilities. $1, Wind measurement. $1.30, Temperature measurement. $5, Earthquake measurement.

1983, Nov. 23   Litho.   Perf. 14½

419	A83	40c multicolored	.80	.30
420	A83	$1 multicolored	2.25	1.50
421	A83	$1.30 multicolored	2.50	1.50
422	A83	$5 multicolored	7.75	8.00
		Nos. 419-422 (4)	13.30	11.30

Training Plane, Dorado — A84

$1, Hong Kong Clipper seaplane. $1.30, Jumbo jet, Kai Tak Airport. $5, Baldwin Brothers balloon, vert.

1984, Mar. 7   Wmk. 373   Perf. 13½

423	A84	40c not shown	1.80	.30
424	A84	$1 multicolored	2.25	1.50
425	A84	$1.30 multicolored	2.75	1.50
426	A84	$5 multicolored	7.75	9.75
		Nos. 423-426 (4)	14.55	13.05

Map of Hong Kong, 19th Cent. — A85

Various maps.

1984, June 21   Litho.   Perf. 14

427	A85	40c multicolored	1.10	.35
428	A85	$1 multicolored	1.75	1.40
429	A85	$1.30 multicolored	2.75	2.00
430	A85	$5 multicolored	10.00	12.00
		Nos. 427-430 (4)	15.60	15.75

Chinese Lanterns — A86

1984, Sept. 6   Litho.   Perf. 13½x13

431	A86	40c Rooster	1.25	.50
432	A86	$1 Bull	3.00	1.75
433	A86	$1.30 Butterfly	4.00	2.00
434	A86	$5 Fish	10.00	12.00
		Nos. 431-434 (4)	18.25	16.25

Jockey Club Centenary A87

40c, Supporting health care. $1, Supporting disabled. $1.30, Supporting the arts. $5, Supporting Ocean Park.

1984, Nov. 21   Litho.   Perf. 14½

435	A87	40c multicolored	1.35	.40
436	A87	$1 multicolored	2.75	1.75
437	A87	$1.30 multicolored	3.50	2.00
438	A87	$5 multicolored	8.00	11.00
a.		Souvenir sheet of 4, #435-438	27.50	27.50
		Nos. 435-438 (4)	15.60	15.15

Historic Buildings — A88

40c, Hung Sing Temple. $1, St. John's Cathedral. $1.30, Old Supreme Court Building. $5, Wan Chai Post Office.

Perf. 13½

1985, Mar. 14   Unwmk.   Litho.

439	A88	40c multicolored	.95	.30
440	A88	$1 multicolored	1.90	1.60
441	A88	$1.30 multicolored	2.40	1.75
442	A88	$5 multicolored	6.75	8.50
		Nos. 439-442 (4)	12.00	12.15

Intl. Dragon Boat Festival — A89

Perf. 13½x13

1985, June 19   Wmk. 373   Litho.

443	A89	40c multicolored	.60	.30
444	A89	$1 multicolored	2.00	1.50
445	A89	$1.30 multicolored	3.25	1.75
446	A89	$5 multicolored	10.00	11.00
a.		Strip of 4, #443-446	30.00	30.00
b.		Souvenir sheet of 4, #443-446, perf. 13x12½	30.00	30.00
		Nos. 443-446 (4)	15.85	14.55

Nos. 443-446 when placed together form a continuous design.

Queen Mother 85th Birthday Issue
Common Design Type

40c, At Glamis Castle, age 9. $1, On balcony with Princes William and Charles. $1.30, Photograph by Cecil Beaton,1980. $5, Holding Prince Henry.

1985, Aug. 7   Litho.   Perf. 14½x14

447	CD336	40c multicolored	.65	.25
448	CD336	$1 multicolored	1.60	1.25
449	CD336	$1.30 multicolored	2.00	1.25
450	CD336	$5 multicolored	5.25	5.75
		Nos. 447-450 (4)	9.50	8.50

Indigenous Flowers — A90

40c, Melastoma. 50c, Chinese lily. 60c, Grantham's camellia. $1.30, Narcissus. $1.70, Bauhinia. $5, Chinese New Year flower.

1985, Sept. 25   Litho.   Perf. 13½

451	A90	40c multicolored	1.75	.30
452	A90	50c multicolored	2.00	.50
453	A90	60c multicolored	2.50	1.50
454	A90	$1.30 multicolored	3.50	1.50
455	A90	$1.70 multicolored	3.75	1.75
456	A90	$5 multicolored	7.25	11.00
		Nos. 451-456 (6)	20.75	16.55

See No. 898.

Modern Architecture A91

50c, Hong Kong Academy for Performing Arts. $1.30, Exchange Square, vert. $1.70, Hong Kong Bank Hdqtrs., vert. $5, Hong Kong Coliseum.

1985, Nov. 27   Perf. 15

457	A91	50c multicolored	.65	.25
458	A91	$1.30 multicolored	1.25	.80
459	A91	$1.70 multicolored	1.90	1.00
460	A91	$5 multicolored	6.00	6.00
		Nos. 457-460 (4)	9.80	8.05

Halley's Comet — A92

50c, Comet, solar system. $1.30, Edmond Halley. $1.70, Hong Kong, trajectory. $5, Comet, Earth.

1986, Feb. 26   Litho.   Perf. 13½x13

461	A92	50c multi	1.35	.25
462	A92	$1.30 multi	2.00	1.25
463	A92	$1.70 multi	3.25	1.50
464	A92	$5 multicolored	9.00	10.00
a.		Souvenir sheet of 4, #461-464	28.00	28.00
		Nos. 461-464 (4)	15.60	13.00

Queen Elizabeth II 60th Birthday
Common Design Type

Designs: 50c, At the wedding of Cecillia Bowes-Lyon, Brompton Parish Church, 1939. $1, Most Noble Order of the Garter, service at St. George's Chapel, Windsor Castle, 1977. $1.30, State visit, 1975. $1.70, Queen Mother's 80th birthday celebration, Royal Lodge, Windsor, 1980. $5, Visiting Crown Agents' offices, 1983.

1986, Apr. 21   Perf. 14½

465	CD337	50c scar, blk & sil	.45	.25
466	CD337	$1 ultra & multi	1.00	.35
467	CD337	$1.30 green & multi	1.35	.50
468	CD337	$1.70 violet & multi	1.45	.65
469	CD337	$5 rose vio & multi	4.50	5.00
		Nos. 465-469 (5)	8.75	6.75

EXPO '86, Vancouver A93

50c, Transportation. $1.30, Finance. $1.70, Trade. $5, Communications.

1986, July 18   Litho.   Perf. 13½

470	A93	50c multicolored	.90	.30
471	A93	$1.30 multicolored	1.60	1.00
472	A93	$1.70 multicolored	2.50	1.50
473	A93	$5 multicolored	6.75	8.00
		Nos. 470-473 (4)	11.75	10.80

Fishing Vessels — A94

Designs: 50c, Hand-liner sampan. $1.30, Stern trawler. $1.70, Long liner junk. $5, Junk trawler.

1986, Sept. 24   Litho.

474	A94	50c multicolored	.80	.25
475	A94	$1.30 multicolored	1.60	1.00
476	A94	$1.70 multicolored	3.25	1.25
477	A94	$5 multicolored	6.75	8.00
		Nos. 474-477 (4)	12.40	10.50

19th Cent. Paintings — A95

50c, Possibly, Second puan khequa, by Spoilum. $1.30, Chinese woman, artist unknown. $1.70, Self-portrait at age 52, by Kwan Kiu Chin. $5, Possibly, Wife of a merchant, by George Chinnery.

1986, Dec. 9   Litho.   Perf. 14

478	A95	50c multicolored	.45	.25
479	A95	$1.30 multicolored	1.45	1.25
480	A95	$1.70 multicolored	1.75	1.50
481	A95	$5 multicolored	4.75	6.25
		Nos. 478-481 (4)	8.40	9.25

New Year (Year of the Hare) — A96

Embroideries of various rabbits.

1987, Jan. 21   Litho.   Perf. 13½x14

482	A96	50c multicolored	.90	.35
483	A96	$1.30 multicolored	1.45	1.25
484	A96	$1.70 multicolored	1.75	1.25
485	A96	$5 multicolored	6.25	6.50
a.		Souvenir sheet of 4, #482-485	40.00	40.00
		Nos. 482-485 (4)	10.35	9.30

19th Century Paintings in the Hong Kong Museum of Art and Shanghai Banking Corp. — A97

Scenes: 50c, A Village Square, Hong Kong Island, 1838, by Auguste Borget (1809-1877). $1.30, Boat Dwellers in Kowloon Bay, 1838, by Borget. $1.70, Flagstaff House, Lt. Governor D'Aguilar's Residence, 1846, by Murdoch Bruce. $5, A View of Wellington Street, late 19th century, by C. Andrasi.

1987, Apr. 23   Litho.   Perf. 14

486	A97	50c multicolored	.90	.25
487	A97	$1.30 multicolored	2.25	1.40
488	A97	$1.70 multicolored	2.75	1.50
489	A97	$5 multicolored	8.00	10.50
		Nos. 486-489 (4)	13.90	13.65

Elizabeth II, Hong Kong Waterfront A98

Queen, Natl. Landmarks A99

Type I — Darker Shading Under Chin

Type II — Lighter Shading Under Chin

Designs: $5, Tsim Shah Tsui, Kowloon. $10, Victoria Harbor. $20, Legislative Council Building. $50, Government House.

Type I

1987, July 13   Litho.   Perf. 14½x14
No date inscription below design

490	A98	10c yel grn, gray & blk	.80	.90
491	A98	40c bluish grn, lt yel & blk	1.75	2.25
492	A98	50c brn org, buff & blk	1.00	.30
493	A98	60c lt blue, pale rose & blk	2.25	1.25
494	A98	70c vio, pale rose & blk	2.00	1.00
495	A98	80c brt rose lil, lt blue & blk	2.75	2.10
496	A98	90c pink, pale beige & blk	2.75	1.00
497	A98	$1 brt lem & blk	2.25	.70
498	A98	$1.30 rose clar, brt yel grn & blk	3.00	.80
499	A98	$1.70 lt blue & blk	3.00	.80
500	A98	$2 yel grn, cream & blk	3.00	1.40

Perf. 14

501	A99	$5 grn, lt grn & blk	3.00	2.25
502	A99	$10 brn, yel brn & blk	8.50	5.25
503	A99	$20 rose vio, lil & blk	13.00	12.00
504	A99	$50 sep, gray & blk	20.00	28.00
		Nos. 490-504 (15)	69.05	60.00

Type II
No date inscription below design
1988, Sept. 1

490a	A98	10c	.75	.60
491a	A98	40c	1.75	1.75
492a	A98	50c	1.50	.55
493a	A98	60c	1.75	1.10
494a	A98	70c	2.00	.80
495a	A98	80c	2.00	2.25
496a	A98	90c	2.25	1.00
497a	A98	$1	8.50	1.75
498a	A98	$1.30	3.50	1.25
499a	A98	$1.70	9.00	2.00
500a	A98	$2	3.50	1.10
501a	A99	$5	5.00	2.50
502a	A99	$10	13.00	5.50

HONG KONG

503a	A99	$20	18.00	12.00
504a	A99	$50	37.50	20.00
	Nos. 490a-504a (15)		110.00	54.15

See Nos. 532-533, 592-593, 629.

1989, Aug. 1   Inscribed "1989"

490b	A98	10c	1.00	1.25
491b	A98	40c	2.75	2.75
492b	A98	50c	1.25	.90
493b	A98	60c	1.75	.30
494b	A98	70c	2.50	2.25
495b	A98	80c	2.00	1.60
496b	A98	90c	1.75	1.25
497b	A98	$1	2.25	.90
498b	A98	$1.30	4.00	2.50
500b	A98	$2	2.50	.60
501b	A99	$5	7.00	2.00
502b	A99	$10	10.00	6.00
503b	A99	$20	14.00	12.00
504b	A99	$50	21.00	22.50
	Nos. 490b-504b (14)		73.75	56.80

1990   Inscribed "1990"

490c	A98	10c	1.00	1.25
491c	A98	40c	2.75	2.75
492c	A98	50c	1.25	.90
493c	A98	60c	1.75	.30
494c	A98	70c	2.50	2.25
495c	A98	80c	2.00	1.60
496c	A98	90c	1.75	1.25
497c	A98	$1	2.25	.90
498c	A98	$1.30	4.00	2.50
500c	A98	$2	2.50	.60
501c	A99	$5	7.00	2.00
502c	A99	$10	10.00	6.00
e.	Souv. sheet of 1		110.00	
503c	A99	$20	14.00	12.00
504c	A99	$50	21.00	22.50
	Nos. 490c-504c (14)		73.75	56.80

No. 502e was issued in conjunction with the New Zealand 1990 World Stamp Exhibition with NZ 1990 inscriptions and related design in the sheet selvage.

No. 502e issued 8/24.

1991   Inscribed "1991"

490d	A98	10c	1.10	1.25
492d	A98	50c	2.00	.90
493d	A98	60c	2.50	.30
494d	A98	70c	3.25	2.25
495d	A98	80c	3.25	1.60
496d	A98	90c	2.40	1.25
497d	A98	$1	3.25	.90
499d	A98	$1.70	3.50	4.50
500d	A98	$2	3.50	.60
501d	A99	$5	8.75	2.00
502d	A99	$10	12.00	6.50
f.	Souv. sheet of 1, PHI-LANIPPON selvage		47.50	27.50
g.	As "f," Olympics selvage		22.50	17.50
503d	A99	$20	20.00	12.00
504d	A99	$50	20.00	22.50
	Nos. 490d-504d (13)		85.50	56.55

Nos. 502f-502g were were issued to commemorate Hong Kong's participation in PHI-LANIPPON '91 and the sponsorship of the 1992 Olympics Games by the Hong Kong Post Office, respectively. The selvage of each sheets bears a distinctive design and inscriptions. See No. 629.

Issued: No. 502f, 11/16; 502g, 12/4.

Nethersole Hospital, Cent. — A100

50c, Hospital, 1887. $1.30, Patients, staff. $1.70, Technology, 1987. $5, Treatment.

1987, Sept. 8   Perf. 14½

505	A100	50c multicolored	1.25	.25
506	A100	$1.30 multicolored	2.75	1.40
507	A100	$1.70 multicolored	3.25	1.50
508	A100	$5 multicolored	9.00	9.00
	Nos. 505-508 (4)		16.25	12.15

Natl. Flag A101

Map of Hong Kong A101a

Coil Stamps

1987, July 13   Perf. 15x14
No date inscription below design

509	A101	10c shown	1.75	2.25
a.	Inscribed "1989"		1.50	1.50
b.	Inscribed "1990"		1.50	1.50
c.	Inscribed "1991"		1.50	1.50
510	A101a	50c blk, dl ol & lake	2.00	2.75
a.	Inscribed "1989"		1.50	1.50

Issued: Nos. 509a, 510a, 8/1/89.
See Nos. 611-614.

Folk Costumes A102

1987, Nov. 18   Perf. 13½

511	A102	50c multicolored	.60	.25
512	A102	$1.30 multi, diff.	1.60	1.10
513	A102	$1.70 multi, diff.	1.75	1.40
514	A102	$5 multi, diff.	5.75	6.75
	Nos. 511-514 (4)		9.70	9.50

New Year (Year of the Dragon) A103

1988, Jan. 27   Litho.   Perf. 13½

515	A103	50c multicolored	.80	.30
516	A103	$1.30 multi, diff.	2.00	.90
517	A103	$1.70 multi, diff.	2.25	1.35
518	A103	$5 multi, diff.	4.50	5.00
a.	Souv. sheet of 4, #515-518		18.00	18.00
	Nos. 515-518 (4)		9.55	7.55

See No. 838e.

Indigenous Birds — A104

50c, White-breasted kingfisher. $1.30, Fukien niltava. $1.70, Black kite. $5, Pied kingfisher.

1988, Apr. 20   Perf. 13½x14

519	A104	50c multicolored	1.10	.30
520	A104	$1.30 multi, diff.	2.25	1.25
521	A104	$1.70 multi, diff.	2.45	1.50
522	A104	$5 multi, diff.	5.75	6.50
	Nos. 519-522 (4)		11.55	9.55

Indigenous Trees — A105

50c, Chinese banyan. $1.30, Bauhinia blakeana. $1.70, Cotton tree. $5, Schima.

1988, June 16   Litho.   Perf. 13½

523	A105	50c multicolored	.30	.25
524	A105	$1.30 multicolored	1.00	.65
525	A105	$1.70 multicolored	1.25	.75
526	A105	$5 multicolored	3.50	4.75
a.	Souv. sheet of 4, #523-526		16.00	12.00
	Nos. 523-526 (4)		6.05	6.40

See No. 923. See note after No. 940.

Peak Tramway, Victoria, Cent. — A106

Various views of Hong Kong and the tram line.

1988, Aug. 4   Litho.   Perf. 15

527	A106	50c multicolored	.50	.25
528	A106	$1.30 multi, diff.	1.00	1.00
529	A106	$1.70 multi, diff.	1.10	1.25
530	A106	$5 multi, diff.	3.50	4.75
a.	Souvenir sheet of 4, #527-530		12.00	12.00
	Nos. 527-530 (4)		6.10	7.25

Catholic Cathedral, Caine Road, Cent. — A107

1988, Sept. 30   Litho.   Perf. 14

531	A107	60c multicolored	1.60	1.60

Queen and Waterfront Type of 1987 Type II

1988, Sept. 1   Litho.   Perf. 14½x14
No date inscription below design

532	A98	$1.40 multicolored	4.00	3.00
a.	Inscribed "1989"		4.00	1.10
b.	Inscribed "1990"		4.00	1.10
533	A98	$1.80 multicolored	4.50	1.50
a.	Inscribed "1989"		4.50	.75
b.	Inscribed "1990"		4.50	.75
c.	Inscribed "1991"		4.50	.75

Issued: No. 532a, 533a, 8/1/89; 532b, 533b, 1990; No. 533c, 4/2/91.

New Year (Year of the Snake) — A108

1989, Jan. 18   Litho.   Perf. 13½x14

534	A108	60c multicolored	.75	.25
535	A108	$1.40 multi, diff.	1.75	.70
536	A108	$1.80 multi, diff.	2.00	.90
a.	Bklt. pane, 5 each #534, 536		14.00	
537	A108	$5 multi, diff.	5.50	6.75
a.	Souv. sheet of 4, #534-537		16.50	11.50
	Nos. 534-537 (4)		10.00	8.60

See No. 838g.

Cheung Chau Bun Festival — A109

60c, Girl, doll. $1.40, Girl. $1.80, Festival paper god. $5, Bun tower gate.

1989, May 4   Unwmk.   Perf. 13½

538	A109	60c multicolored	.60	.25
539	A109	$1.40 multi, diff.	1.25	.80
540	A109	$1.80 multi, diff.	1.75	.90
541	A109	$5 multi, diff.	4.50	5.50
	Nos. 538-541 (4)		8.10	7.45

Modern Art — A110

60c, Twin, sculpture by Cheung Yee (b. 1936). $1.40, Figures, painted by Luis Chan (b. 1905). $1.80, Lotus, sculpture by Van Lau (b. 1933). $5, Zen, painted by Lui Shou-kwan (1919-1975).

1989, July 19   Perf. 12x13

542	A110	60c multicolored	.60	.25
543	A110	$1.40 multi, diff.	1.35	.80
544	A110	$1.80 multi, diff.	1.75	.95
545	A110	$5 multi, diff.	3.50	4.50
	Nos. 542-545 (4)		7.20	6.50

Hong Kong People — A111

Designs: 60c, Youth holding autumn festival decoration, lunar year festival dragon. $1.40, Shadow boxer, horse racing. $1.80, Office and construction workers. $5, Two women, two men (ethnic multiplicity).

1989, Sept. 6   Perf. 13x14½

546	A111	60c multicolored	.70	.25
547	A111	$1.40 multicolored	2.10	.80
548	A111	$1.80 multicolored	2.25	.90
549	A111	$5 multicolored	4.75	7.50
	Nos. 546-549 (4)		9.80	9.45

See No. 762.

Construction Projects — A112

60c, University of Science and Technology. 70c, Cultural center. $1.30, Eastern Harbor Crossing. $1.40, Bank of China. $1.80, Convention center. $5, Light rail transit.

1989, Oct. 5   Unwmk.   Perf. 13

550	A112	60c multicolored	.55	.25
551	A112	70c multicolored	.60	.40
552	A112	$1.30 multicolored	1.10	1.10
553	A112	$1.40 multicolored	1.25	.80
554	A112	$1.80 multicolored	1.40	1.10
555	A112	$5 multicolored	6.50	8.00
	Nos. 550-555 (6)		11.40	11.65

Visit of the Prince and Princess of Wales — A113

Portraits and view of Hong Kong: 60c, Charles and Diana. $1.40, Diana. $1.80, Charles. $5, Couple wearing formal attire.

1989, Nov. 8   Wmk. 340   Perf. 14½

556	A113	60c multicolored	1.50	.30
557	A113	$1.40 multicolored	2.50	1.10
558	A113	$1.80 multicolored	1.75	1.10
559	A113	$5 multicolored	7.50	7.50
a.	Souvenir sheet of 1		16.50	13.50
	Nos. 556-559 (4)		13.25	10.00

New Year 1990 (Year of the Horse) — A114

     Perf. 13½x12½

1990, Jan. 23   Unwmk.

560	A114	60c multicolored	.80	.35
561	A114	$1.40 multi, diff.	1.90	1.25
562	A114	$1.80 multi, diff.	2.10	1.25
a.	Bklt. pane, 3 each 60c, $1.80		8.75	
	Complete booklet, 2 #562a		17.50	
563	A114	$5 multi, diff.	6.50	9.50
a.	Souvenir sheet of 4, #560-563		18.00	13.00
	Nos. 560-563 (4)		11.30	12.35

Examples of No. 562a ovptd. with marginal inscription were released on May 3 to publicize Stamp World London '90.
See No. 838k.

Intl. Cuisine — A115

1990, Apr. 26   Litho.   Perf. 12½x13

564	A115	60c Chinese	.65	.25
565	A115	70c Indian	.65	.50
566	A115	$1.30 Chinese, diff.	1.10	1.25
567	A115	$1.40 Thai	1.10	.70
568	A115	$1.80 Japanese	1.40	1.00
569	A115	$5 French	4.75	7.50
	Nos. 564-569 (6)		9.65	11.20

HONG KONG

Pollutants — A116

Wmk. 340

1990, June 5	Litho.		Perf. 14½	
570	A116	60c Air	.45	.25
571	A116	$1.40 Noise	.95	.70
572	A116	$1.80 Water	1.60	.70
573	A116	$5 Land	3.50	3.75
	Nos. 570-573 (4)		6.50	5.40

World Environment Day.

Electrification of Hong Kong, Cent. — A117

Views of Hong Kong and streetlights.

1990, Oct. 2	Litho.		Perf. 14½	
574	A117	60c 1890	.60	.25
575	A117	$1.40 1940	1.25	.90
576	A117	$1.80 1960	1.40	.90
577	A117	$5 1980	3.00	4.25
a.	Souvenir sheet of 2, #575, 577		6.75	6.75
	Complete booklet, 4 #577a		27.50	
	Nos. 574-577 (4)		6.25	6.30

Christmas A118

60c, Dove, holly. $1.40, Skyline, snowman. $1.80, Santa Claus' hat, skyscraper. $2, Children, Santa Claus. $5, Candy cane, skyline.

1990, Nov. 8				
578	A118	50c shown	.30	.25
579	A118	60c multicolored	.35	.25
580	A118	$1.40 multicolored	.90	.45
581	A118	$1.80 multicolored	1.00	.55
582	A118	$2 multicolored	1.45	1.40
583	A118	$5 multicolored	3.50	5.50
	Nos. 578-583 (6)		7.50	8.40

New Year 1991 (Year of the Sheep) — A119

Different embroidered rams.

1991, Jan. 24	Litho.	Perf. 13½x12½		
584	A119	60c multicolored	.40	.25
585	A119	$1.40 multicolored	.95	.60
586	A119	$1.80 multicolored	1.10	.75
a.	Bklt. pane, 3 each #584, 586		6.50	
	Complete booklet, 2 #586a		13.00	
587	A119	$5 multicolored	3.50	5.25
a.	Souv. sheet of 4, #584-587		9.00	9.00
	Nos. 584-587 (4)		5.95	6.85

See No. 838j.

Education — A120

80c, Kindergarten. $1.80, Primary & secondary. $2.30, Vocational. $5, Tertiary.

	Perf. 13½x13			
1991, Apr. 18	Litho.	Unwmk.		
588	A120	80c multicolored	.40	.25
589	A120	$1.80 multicolored	1.25	.70
590	A120	$2.30 multicolored	1.50	1.25
591	A120	$5 multicolored	4.00	5.25
	Nos. 588-591 (4)		7.15	7.45

Queen and Waterfront Type of 1987 Type II

1991, Apr. 2	Litho.	Perf. 14½x14		
592	A98	$1.20 multicolored	3.00	3.50
593	A98	$2.30 multicolored	3.00	3.50

Transportation — A121

80c, Rickshaw. 90c, Bus. $1.70, Ferry. $1.80, Tram. $2.30, Mass transit railway. $5, Hydrofoil.

1991, June 6	Unwmk.	Perf. 14		
594	A121	80c multicolored	.45	.30
595	A121	90c multicolored	.75	.60
596	A121	$1.70 multicolored	1.25	1.00
597	A121	$1.80 multicolored	1.50	.80
598	A121	$2.30 multicolored	2.25	2.00
599	A121	$5 multicolored	4.00	6.00
	Nos. 594-599 (6)		10.20	10.70

A122

Royal postboxes with contemporary envelopes: 80c, Stamp of Type A1, Queen Victoria. $1.70, Stamps of Type A10, King Edward VII. $1.80, #149, King George V. $2.30, Stamps of Type A16, King George VI. $5, $10, Stamps of Type A98, Queen Elizabeth II.

1991, Aug. 25	Litho.	Perf. 14		
600	A122	80c multicolored	.60	.30
601	A122	$1.70 multicolored	1.25	1.00
602	A122	$1.75 multicolored	1.75	.80
603	A122	$2.30 multicolored	1.50	1.75
604	A122	$5 multicolored	4.00	7.00
	Nos. 600-604 (5)		9.10	10.85

Souvenir Sheet

| 605 | A122 | $10 multicolored | 14.00 | 16.00 |

Hong Kong Post Office, 150th anniv. See No. 792.

Historic Landmarks — A123

80c, Bronze Buddha. $1.70, Peak Pavilion. $1.80, Clock Tower. $2.30, Catholic Cathedral. $5, Wong Tai Sin Temple.

1991, Oct. 24				
606	A123	80c mag & blk	.65	.25
607	A123	$1.70 brt grn & blk	1.10	.55
608	A123	$1.80 brt pur & blk	1.75	.60
609	A123	$2.30 brt blue & blk	1.25	.75
610	A123	$5 brt org & blk	4.25	6.75
	Nos. 606-610 (5)		9.00	8.90

Map of Hong Kong Type

1992, Mar. 26	Photo.	Perf. 14½x14		

Coil Stamps
Color of Map

611	A101a	80c red lilac	1.50	3.25
612	A101a	90c blue	1.50	2.90
613	A101a	$1.80 brt yel grn	2.00	2.75
614	A101a	$2.30 red brown	2.25	3.75
	Nos. 611-614 (4)		7.25	11.75

Inscribed 1991.

New Year 1992 (Year of the Monkey) A125

Various embroidery designs of monkeys.

1992, Jan. 22	Litho.	Perf. 14½		
615	A125	80c multicolored	.35	.25
616	A125	$1.80 multicolored	.90	.60
617	A125	$2.30 multicolored	1.50	1.50
a.	Bklt. pane, 3 ea #615, 617		6.25	
	Complete booklet, 2 #617a		14.00	
618	A125	$5 multicolored	3.50	6.50
a.	Sheet of 4, #615-618		12.00	12.00
	Nos. 615-618 (4)		6.25	8.85

See No. 838i.

Queen Elizabeth II's Accession to the Throne, 40th Anniv.
Common Design Type

1992, Feb. 11	Litho.	Unwmk.	Perf. 14	
619	CD349	80c multicolored	.35	.25
620	CD349	$1.70 multicolored	.60	.50
621	CD349	$1.80 multicolored	.65	.40
622	CD349	$2.30 multicolored	1.00	1.00
623	CD349	$5 multicolored	2.50	3.00
	Nos. 619-623 (5)		5.10	5.25

1992 Summer Olympics, Barcelona A126

80c, Running. $1.80, Swimming and javelin. $2.30, Cycling. $5, High jump.

1992, Apr. 2	Litho.	Perf. 14½		

Black Inscription

624	A126	80c multi	.40	.25
625	A126	$1.80 multi	1.00	.70
626	A126	$2.30 multi	1.50	1.50
627	A126	$5 multi	2.75	4.50
	Nos. 624-627 (4)		5.65	6.95

Souvenir Sheet

628	Sheet of 4		8.00	8.00
a.	A126 80c red inscription		.25	.25
b.	A126 $1.80 green inscription		.65	.65
c.	A126 $2.30 blue inscription		1.05	1.05
d.	A126 $5 orange yellow inscription		1.90	1.90
e.	Sheet of 4 with inscription in margin		5.75	5.75

Issue date: No. 628e, July 25. New inscription on No. 628e sheet margin reads "To Commemorate the Opening of the 1992 Summer Olympic Games 25 July 1992" in English and Chinese.

Queen and Landmarks Type of 1987
Souvenir Sheet

	Perf. 14			
1992, May 22	Litho.	Type II		
629	A99	$10 lt violet & black	6.50	6.50

World Columbian Stamp Expo '92.

A127

	Perf. 15x14			
1992-97	Photo.	Unwmk.		

Color of Chinese Inscription

630	A127	10c pink	.35	.40
630A	A127	20c black	1.00	1.50
631	A127	50c red orange	.35	.30
632	A127	60c blue	2.00	1.50
633	A127	70c red lilac	2.00	1.25
634	A127	80c rose	.45	.45
635	A127	90c gray green	.45	.50
636	A127	$1 org brn	.45	.25
637	A127	$1.10 carmine	2.00	1.25
638	A127	$1.20 violet	.55	.35
639	A127	$1.30 dark blue	2.25	1.10
640	A127	$1.40 apple green	1.75	1.00
641	A127	$1.50 brown	2.00	1.50
642	A127	$1.60 green	1.75	1.00
643	A127	$1.70 ultramarine	1.25	.90
644	A127	$1.80 rose lilac	1.50	.55
645	A127	$1.90 green	1.50	1.25
646	A127	$2 blue green	1.75	.55
647	A127	$2.10 claret	2.50	2.75
648	A127	$2.30 gray	2.50	.70
649	A127	$2.40 dark blue	3.00	2.00
650	A127	$2.50 olive green	1.75	2.00
a.	Sheet of 6, 2 #647, 4 #650		12.00	
d.	Booklet pane, 2 #647, 4 #650		12.00	
651	A127	$2.60 dark brown	2.25	2.00
651A	A127	$3.10 salmon	2.00	1.00
l.	Sheet of 6, 2 #642, 4 #651A		11.50	
o.	Booklet pane, 2 #642, 4 #651A		11.50	
651B	A127	$5 bright green	3.00	2.00
k.	Souvenir sheet of 1		7.00	5.00
m.	Sheet of 6, 4 #639, 2 #651B		15.00	
n.	Booklet pane, 4 #639, 2 #651B		15.00	
p.	Souvenir booklet, #650d, 651Ao, 651Bn		38.50	

Size: 25x30mm
Perf. 14½x14

651C	A127	$10 brown	5.00	2.50
h.	Souvenir sheet of 1		5.00	6.00
651D	A127	$20 orange red	7.00	4.25
651E	A127	$50 gray	14.00	10.50
	Nos. 630-651E (28)		66.35	45.20

Issued: 20c, $1.30, $1.90, $2.40, 11/1/93; No. 651Bk, 2/18/94; No. 651Ch, 8/16/94; $1.10, $1.50, $2.10, $2.60, 6/1/95; $1.40, $1.60, $2.50, $3.10, 9/2/96; No. 651Bp, 2/14/97; others, 6/16/92.

10c, 50c, 80c, 90c, $1, $1.20, $1.30, $1.50, $1.60, $1.80, $1.90, $2.10, $2.30, $2.40, $2.50, $2.60, $3.10 also issued in coils. These have numbers on the back of every fifth stamp. No. 651 issued for Hong Kong '94; No. 651Ch for Conference of Commonwealth Postal Administrations.

Nos. 650a, 651Al, 651Bm are 130x85mm. Nos. 650d, 651Ao, 651Bn are 180x130mm and are rouletted at left.

See Nos. 656, 677-678, 683, 688, 724, 729, 738, 743, 756-757.

1993-96	Litho.	Perf. 15x14		
636a			1.00	1.00
b.	As "a," bklt. pane of 10		10.00	
638a			1.00	1.00
b.	As "a," bklt. pane of 10		10.00	
	Complete booklet, #638b		10.00	
639a	A127	$1.30 multi	.65	.65
b.	As "a," bklt. pane of 10		6.50	
645a	A127	$1.90 multi	1.25	1.25
b.	As "a," bklt. pane of 10		12.50	
647a	A127	$2.10 multi	1.25	1.25
b.	As "a," bklt. pane of 10		12.50	
	Complete booklet, #647b		12.50	
649a	A127	$2.40 multi	1.25	1.25
b.	As "a," bklt. pane of 10		12.50	
650b	A127	$2.50 Litho.	1.25	1.25
c.	As "b," booklet pane of 10		12.50	
651f	A127	$2.60 Litho.	1.25	1.25
g.	As "f," bklt. pane of 10		12.50	
	Complete booklet, #651g		12.50	
651Ai	A127	$3.10 Litho.	1.25	1.25
j.	As "i," booklet pane of 10		12.50	
	Nos. 636a-651Ai (9)		10.15	10.15

Chinese characters on Nos. 636a, 638a, 645a, 647a, 649a, 651f are lighter in shade and contrast less with the background color than characters on Nos. 636, 638, 645, 647, 649, 651.

Issued: No. 636a, 12/14/93; Nos. 645a, 649a, 12/28/93; Nos. 638a, 647a, 651f, 6/1/95; Nos. 639a, 650a, 651Ai, 9/2/96.

Stamp Collecting A128

Stamps and: 80c, Perforation gauge, #559, 586a. $1.80, Canceler, #66, stamp tongs. $2.30, Magnifying glass, #174, 180, 181. $5, Watermark detector, Type A1.

1992, July 15	Litho.	Perf. 14½		
652	A128	80c multicolored	.35	.25
653	A128	$1.80 multicolored	.75	.65
654	A128	$2.30 multicolored	1.10	1.10
655	A128	$5 multicolored	2.25	3.50
	Nos. 652-655 (4)		4.45	5.50

See note after No. 940.

Queen Type of 1992
Souvenir Sheet
Perf. 14½x14

1992, Sept. 1	Photo.	Unwmk.		

Background Color

| 656 | A127 | $10 blue | 6.00 | 6.00 |

Kuala Lumpur Philatelic Exhibition '92. Size of stamp: 25x30mm.

Chinese Opera — A129

80c, Principal male role. $1.80, Martial role. $2.30, Principal female role. $5, Comic role.

1992, Sept. 24	Litho.	Perf. 13½		
657	A129	80c multicolored	1.10	.30
658	A129	$1.80 multicolored	1.90	1.50
659	A129	$2.30 multicolored	2.25	2.25
660	A129	$5 multicolored	4.25	8.00
	Nos. 657-660 (4)		9.50	12.05

HONG KONG

Greetings Stamps — A130

1992, Nov. 19   Litho.   Perf. 14½
661	A130	80c Hearts	.35	.25
662	A130	$1.80 Stars	.70	.50
663	A130	$2.30 Presents	.80	.80
664	A130	$5 Balloons	1.90	3.00
a.	Bklt. pane of 6, #662-664, 3 #661		6.50	5.00
	Complete booklet, 2 #664a		13.00	
	Nos. 661-664 (4)		3.75	4.55

New Year 1993 (Year of the Rooster) A131

Various embroidery designs of a rooster.

1993, Jan. 7   Litho.   Perf. 13½
665	A131	80c multicolored	.30	.25
666	A131	$1.80 multicolored	.70	.50
667	A131	$2.30 multicolored	1.10	1.10
a.	Bklt. pane, 3 ea #665, 667		5.00	
	Complete booklet, 2 #667a		10.00	
668	A131	$5 multicolored	2.75	3.75
a.	Souvenir sheet of 4, #665-668		7.50	7.50
	Nos. 665-668 (4)		4.85	5.60

See No. 838h.

Chinese String Instruments — A132

1993, Apr. 14   Litho.   Perf. 14½
669	A132	80c Pipa	.45	.25
670	A132	$1.80 Erhu	.80	.70
671	A132	$2.30 Ruan	1.25	1.10
672	A132	$5 Gehu	2.50	3.25
	Nos. 669-672 (4)		5.00	5.30

Coronation of Queen Elizabeth II, 40th Anniv. — A133

Different views of Hong Kong with portraits of Queen that appear on Types A25, A28, A49 and A127.

1993, June 3   Litho.   Perf. 14
673	A133	80c multicolored	.40	.25
674	A133	$1.80 multicolored	.80	.80
675	A133	$2.30 multicolored	1.10	1.10
676	A133	$5 multicolored	2.75	3.75
	Nos. 673-676 (4)		5.05	5.85

Queen Type of 1992
Souvenir Sheets

1993, July 6   Litho.   Perf. 14½x14
Background Color
677	A127	$10 brown	7.00	7.00

1993, Aug. 12   Background Color
678	A127	$10 bright blue	6.50	6.50

Hong Kong '94 Stamp Exhibition. Nos. 677-678 contain a 25x30mm stamp.

No. 678 exists with gold, silver or red overprints with the Hong Kong Philatelic Society emblem and Chinese characters. These sheets were sold only at various philatelic exhibitions.

Science and Technology A134

Designs: 80c, Education, Hong Kong University of Science and Technology. $1.80, Public presentation, Hong Kong Science Museum. $2.30, Achievement recognition, Governor's Award. $5, World class telecommunications, telecommunications industry.

1993, Sept. 8   Perf. 14½
679	A134	80c multicolored	.30	.25
680	A134	$1.80 multicolored	.60	.40
681	A134	$2.30 multicolored	.80	.80
682	A134	$5 multicolored	1.90	3.00
	Nos. 679-682 (4)		3.60	4.45

Queen Type of 1992
Souvenir Sheet

1993, Oct. 5   Litho.   Perf. 14½x14
Background Color
683	A127	$10 bright green	4.25	4.25

Bangkok '93 Stamp Exhibition. No. 683 contains one 25x30mm stamp.

Goldfish A135

$1, Red calico egg-fish. $1.90, Red cap oranda. $2.40, Red & white fringetail. $5, Black & gold dragon-eye.

1993, Nov. 17   Litho.   Perf. 14½
684	A135	$1 multicolored	.50	.35
685	A135	$1.90 multicolored	.80	.50
686	A135	$2.40 multicolored	1.25	1.10
687	A135	$5 multicolored	3.25	5.00
a.	Souvenir sheet of 4, #684-687		10.00	10.00
	Nos. 684-687 (4)		5.80	6.95

Queen Type of 1992
Perf. 15x14

1994, Jan. 27   Photo.   Wmk. 373
688		Souvenir booklet	22.50	22.50
a.	A127 Sheet of #630, 5 #646		7.25	7.25
b.	A127 Sheet of #643, 5 #644		7.25	7.25
c.	A127 Sheet of 5 #636, #651B		7.25	7.25

First Hong Kong stamps, 130th anniv. No. 688 sold for $38.

Year of the Dog — A136

Various embroidery designs of dogs.

1994, Jan. 27   Litho.   Perf. 14½
689	A136	$1 multicolored	.35	.25
690	A136	$1.90 multicolored	.75	.50
691	A136	$2.40 multicolored	1.00	.80
a.	Bklt. pane, 3 ea #689, 691		6.00	
	Complete booklet, 2 #691a		12.00	
692	A136	$5 multicolored	2.25	4.50
a.	Souvenir sheet of 4, #689-692		10.00	10.00
	Nos. 689-692 (4)		4.35	6.05

See No. 838f.

Royal Hong Kong Police Force, 150th Anniv. — A137

Designs: $1, Traffic policeman, woman. $1.20, Marine policeman. $1.90, Male, female officers of 1950. $2, Policeman holding M-16. $2.40, Policemen, 1906, pre-1920. $5, Policemen, 1900.

1994, May 4   Litho.   Perf. 13½
693	A137	$1 multicolored	.35	.30
694	A137	$1.20 multicolored	.45	.50
695	A137	$1.90 multicolored	.65	.50
696	A137	$2 multicolored	1.00	.80
697	A137	$2.40 multicolored	1.50	1.25
698	A137	$5 multicolored	3.25	4.00
	Nos. 693-698 (6)		7.20	7.35

Traditional Chinese Festivals — A138

Designs: $1, Dragon Boat Festival. $1.90, Lunar New Year. $2.40, Seven Sisters Festival. $5, Mid-Autumn Festival.

1994, June 8   Litho.   Perf. 14
699	A138	$1 multicolored	.35	.25
700	A138	$1.90 multicolored	.75	.65
701	A138	$2.40 multicolored	1.25	1.10
702	A138	$5 multicolored	2.25	4.00
	Nos. 699-702 (4)		4.60	6.00

XV Commonwealth Games, Victoria, BC, Canada — A139

Unwmk.

1994, Aug. 25   Litho.   Perf. 14
703	A139	$1 Swimming	.30	.25
704	A139	$1.90 Lawn bowling	.90	.50
705	A139	$2.40 Gymnastics	1.10	.80
706	A139	$5 Weight lifting	1.75	3.00
	Nos. 703-706 (4)		4.05	4.55

Dr. James Legge (1815-97), Religious Leader, Translator A140

1994, Oct. 5   Litho.   Perf. 14
707	A140	$1 multicolored	1.00	1.00

Corals — A141

1994, Nov. 17   Litho.   Perf. 14
708	A141	$1 Alcyonium	.30	.25
709	A141	$1.90 Zoanthus	.50	.45
710	A141	$2.40 Tubastrea	.65	.50
711	A141	$5 Platygyra	1.50	2.75
a.	Souv. sheet of 4, #708-711		6.50	6.50
	Nos. 708-711 (4)		2.95	4.00

See No. 916.

New Year 1995 (Year of the Boar) — A142

Various embroidery designs of pigs.

1995, Jan. 17   Litho.   Perf. 14½
712	A142	$1 multicolored	.40	.35
713	A142	$1.90 multicolored	.85	.65
714	A142	$2.40 multicolored	1.10	.75
a.	Bklt. pane, 3 each #712, 714		6.00	
	Complete booklet, 2 #714a		12.00	
715	A142	$5 multicolored	2.25	3.50
a.	Souvenir sheet of 4, #712-715		7.50	7.50
	Nos. 712-715 (4)		4.60	5.25

See No. 838d.

Intl. Sporting Events — A143

Designs: $1, Hong Kong Rugby Sevens. $1.90, China Sea Race. $2.40, Intl. Dragon Boat Races. $5, Hong Kong Intl. Horse Races.

1995, Mar. 22   Litho.   Perf. 14½
716	A143	$1 multicolored	.50	.25
717	A143	$1.90 multicolored	.80	.80
718	A143	$2.40 multicolored	1.25	1.25
719	A143	$5 multicolored	2.50	3.75
	Nos. 716-719 (4)		5.05	6.05

Traditional Buildings A144

Litho. & Engr.

1995, May 24   Perf. 13½
720	A144	$1 Tsui Shing Lau	.40	.25
721	A144	$1.90 Sam Tung UK	.75	.45
722	A144	$2.40 Lo Wai	.85	.50
723	A144	$5 Man Shek Tong	2.00	3.00
	Nos. 720-723 (4)		4.00	4.20

Queen Type of 1992
Souvenir Sheet

1995, Aug. 25   Litho.   Perf. 14
Background Color
724	A127	$10 carmine	5.50	5.50
a.	Yellow omitted		175.00	

Singapore '95 World Stamp Exhibition. No. 724 contains one 25x30mm stamp.

Royal Hong Kong Regiment (1854-1995) A145

$1.20, Modern Regimental Badge, vert. $2.10, Current flag. $2.60, Former flag. $5, Royal Hong Kong Defense Force, 1951 soldier's badge, vert.

1995, Aug. 16   Litho.   Perf. 14½
725	A145	$1.20 multicolored	.50	.30
726	A145	$2.10 multicolored	.60	.50
727	A145	$2.60 multicolored	.80	.80
728	A145	$5 multicolored	2.00	3.00
	Nos. 725-728 (4)		3.90	4.60

Queen Type of 1992
Souvenir Sheet

1995, Oct. 9   Litho.   Perf. 14
Background Color
729	A127	$10 brown	6.25	7.00

End of World War II, 50th anniv. No. 729 contains one 25x30mm stamp.

Hong Kong Movie Stars — A146

$1.20, Bruce Lee. $2.10, Leung Sing-Por. $2.60, Yam Kim-Fai. $5, Lin Dai.

1995, Nov. 15   Litho.   Perf. 13½
730	A146	$1.20 multi	1.75	.80
731	A146	$2.10 multi	2.75	1.25
732	A146	$2.60 multi	3.75	2.00
733	A146	$5 multi	5.50	5.50
	Nos. 730-733 (4)		13.75	9.55

New Year 1996 (Year of the Rat) — A147

Various embroidery designs of rats.

1996, Jan. 31   Litho.   Perf. 13½
734	A147	$1.20 multicolored	.30	.30
735	A147	$2.10 multicolored	.55	.55
736	A147	$2.60 multicolored	.70	.70
a.	Bklt. pane, 3 ea #734, 736		3.75	
	Complete booklet, 2 #736a		7.50	
737	A147	$5 multicolored	1.50	1.50
a.	Souvenir sheet of 4, #734-737		5.00	5.00
	Nos. 734-737 (4)		3.05	3.05

See No. 838a.

Queen Type of 1992
Souvenir Sheet
Unwmk.

1996, Feb. 23   Litho.   Perf. 14
738	A127	$10 org & grn	7.00	7.00

Hong Kong '97 Stamp Exhibition. No. 738 contains one 25x30mm stamp.

1996 Summer Olympics, Atlanta — A148

HONG KONG

1996, Mar. 20   Litho.   Perf. 13½

739	A148	$1.20 Gymnastics	.30	.30
740	A148	$2.10 Diving	.70	.70
741	A148	$2.60 Running	.90	.90
742	A148	$5 Basketball	1.60	2.75
	Nos. 739-742 (4)		3.50	4.65

Souvenir Sheet

742A Sheet of 4, #742b-742e   4.00 4.00
  f. As #742A, different sheet margin   4.75 4.75

No. 742Af shows Olympic gold medal at top of sheet margin.

Nos. 748-751 have denominations in color and Olympic rings in gold. Nos. 739-742 have denominations in black, Olympic rings in different colors. No. 742Ab-742Ae have gold Olympic rings.

No. 742f issued 7/19/96.

Queen Type of 1992
Souvenir Sheet
Unwmk.

1996, May 18   Litho.   Perf. 14

743 A127 $10 brt grn & bl vio   4.00 4.00

Hong Kong '97 Stamp Exhibition. No. 743 contains one 25x30mm stamp.

Archaeological Finds — A149

$1.20, Painted pottery basin. $2.10, Stone "Yue". $2.60, Stone "GE". $5, Pottery tripod.

1996, June 26   Litho.   Perf. 13½

744	A149	$1.20 multicolored	.40	.30
745	A149	$2.10 multicolored	.55	.55
746	A149	$2.60 multicolored	.80	.90
747	A149	$5 multicolored	1.50	2.25
	Nos. 744-747 (4)		3.25	4.00

1996 Summer Olympic Games Type
1996, July 19   Litho.   Perf. 14x14½
Color of Denomination

748	A148	$1.20 like #739, red	.35	.25
749	A148	$2.10 like #740, blue	.40	.50
750	A148	$2.60 like #741, green	.75	.85
751	A148	$5 like #742, org	1.50	2.50
	Nos. 748-751 (4)		3.00	4.10

Nos. 748-751 have denominations in color and Olympic rings in gold. Nos. 739-742 have denommninations in black, Olympic rings in different colors.

Mountains in Hong Kong A150

$1.30, Pat Sing Leng. $2.50, Ma On Shan. $3.10, Lion Rock, vert. $5, Lantau Peak, vert.

Unwmk.
1996, Sept. 24   Litho.   13½x14

752 A150 $1.30 multicolored   .50 .45

Perf. 14x14½, 14½x14

753 A150 $2.50 multi   1.00 1.00
754 A150 $3.10 multi   1.25 1.25

Perf. 14x13½

755 A150 $5 multi   1.90 3.75
  Nos. 752-755 (4)   4.65 6.45

No. 753 is 40x36mm, No. 754 36x40mm.
See Nos. 899, 905.

Queen Type of 1992
Souvenir Sheets

1996   Photo.   Unwmk.   Perf. 14

756 A127 $10 red & grn   3.25
757 A127 $10 brn & dk brn   3.75

Issued: No. 756, 10/16; No. 757, 10/29. Visit Hong Kong '97 Stamp Exhibition (No. 756). 1996 Summer Olympic Games, Atlanta (No. 757). Nos. 756-757 each contain one 25x30mm stamp.

Urban Heritage A151

Designs: $1.30, Main building, University of Hong Kong, 1912. $2.50, Western Market,

1906. $3.10, Old Pathological Institute, 1905. $5, Flagstaff House, 1846.

Litho. & Engr.
1996, Nov. 20   Perf. 13½

758	A151	$1.30 multicolored	.40	.60
759	A151	$2.50 multicolored	.70	.80
760	A151	$3.10 multicolored	.80	.90
761	A151	$5 multicolored	1.35	2.00
	Nos. 758-761 (4)		3.25	4.30

Hong Kong People Type of 1989
Souvenir Sheet

1997, Jan.   Photo.   Perf. 13x13½

762 A111 $5 like No. 549   1.90 1.90

No. 762 contains one 23x33mm stamp that has darker colors and a different perf. than No. 549.

Panoramic Views of Hong Kong Skyline — A152

Nos. 763-775: Various daytime views from harbor.
Nos. 776-778, Various nighttime views from harbor.

Perf. 13½x13
1997, Jan. 26   Litho.   Unwmk.
Background Color

763	A152	10c pink	.30	.25
764	A152	20c vermilion	.30	.35
765	A152	50c orange	.30	.35
766	A152	$1 orange yellow	.30	.25
767	A152	$1.20 olive	.30	.30
768	A152	$1.30 apple green	.35	.35
a.	Booklet pane of 10		3.50	
	Complete booklet, #768a		3.50	
769	A152	$1.40 green	.30	.40
770	A152	$1.60 blue green	.35	.45
771	A152	$2 green blue	.50	.50
772	A152	$2.10 blue	.50	.60
773	A152	$2.50 purple	.55	.90
a.	Booklet pane of 10		5.50	
	Complete booklet, #773a		5.50	
774	A152	$3.10 rose	.70	.70
a.	Booklet pane of 10		7.00	
	Complete booklet, #774a		7.00	
c.	Sheet of 4, #771-774		2.50	2.50
775	A152	$5 orange	1.25	1.25
a.	Sheet of 13, #763-775		5.75	5.75

Size: 28x33mm
Perf. 14x13½

776	A152	$10 blue	2.50	2.50
a.	Souv. sheet of 1 (Series #4)		8.00	
b.	Souv. sheet of 1 (Series #5)		8.00	
c.	Souv. sheet of 1 (Series #12)		3.00	3.00
d.	Souv. sheet of 1, perf14x13¼ (Sheet #14)		2.60	2.60
777	A152	$20 bl, pur & rose	5.25	5.25
778	A152	$50 purple & rose	13.00	13.00
a.	Sheet of 3, #776-778		22.00	
	Nos. 763-778 (16)		26.75	27.30

Hong Kong '97 (Nos. 776a-776b). 1996 Atlanta Paralympic Games (No. 776c). 13th Asian Games, Bangkok, Thailand (No. 774c). China 1999 World Philatelic Exhibition (No. 776d).

Perforations are alternating small and large holes.

Nos. 775a and 778a are continuous designs.

Issued: No. 776a, 2/12; No. 776b, 2/16; No. 774c, 3/27/99; No. 776d, 8/21/99.
See note after No. 940.
No. 776a exists imperforate.
No. 776a exists with the exhibition logo at upper right omitted.

Coil Stamps
Photo.   Perf. 14½x14

763a	A152	10c	.30	.50
765a	A152	50c	.30	.70
768b	A152	$1.30	.45	.70
770a	A152	$1.60	.50	.70
773b	A152	$2.50	.80	.75
774b	A152	$3.10	1.00	1.25
	Nos. 763a-774b (6)		3.35	4.60

These have numbers on back of every fifth stamp.
Perforations are the same size.

New Year 1997 (Year of the Ox) — A153

Various designs of oxen.

Perf. 14½
1997, Feb. 27   Litho.   Unwmk.
Background Color

780	A153	$1.30 pink	.30	.30
781	A153	$2.50 orange yellow	.65	.65
782	A153	$3.10 green	.80	.80
a.	Booklet pane, 3 each #780a, 782b		6.00	
	Complete booklet, 2 #782a		12.00	
783	A153	$5 blue	1.25	1.75
a.	Souvenir sheet of 4, #780-783		4.50	4.50
	Nos. 780-783 (4)		3.00	3.50

See Nos. 838b, 838c.

Perf. 13½

780a	A153	$1.30	.50	.50
781a	A153	$2.50	.90	.90
782b	A153	$3.10	1.10	1.10
783b	A153	$5	1.75	2.25
c.	Souvenir sheet of 4, #780a-781a, 782b-783b		4.50	4.50

Migratory Birds — A154

$1.30, Yellow-breasted bunting. $2.50, Great knot. $3.10, Falcated teal. $5, Black-faced spoonbill.

Perf. 13½
1997, Apr. 27   Unwmk.   Photo.

784	A154	$1.30 multicolored	.30	.30
785	A154	$2.50 multicolored	.65	.65
786	A154	$3.10 multicolored	.80	.80
787	A154	$5 multicolored	1.25	1.75
	Nos. 784-787 (4)		3.00	3.50

Landmarks A155

$1.30, Hong Kong Stadium. $2.50, The Peak Tower. $3.10, Hong Kong Convention & Exhibition Center. $5, The Lantau Link (bridge).

1997, May 18   Litho.   Perf. 13½

788	A155	$1.30 multicolored	.30	.30
789	A155	$2.50 multicolored	.75	.75
790	A155	$3.10 multicolored	1.00	1.00
791	A155	$5 multicolored	1.75	2.25
a.	Souvenir sheet of 4		2.25	2.25
	Nos. 788-791 (4)		3.80	4.30

Opening of the Lantau Link (bridge) (No. 791a).
Nos. 788-791 and 791a also exist perf 14x14½. Values are the same.
No. 791a exists imperforate.

Royal Postbox Type of 1991
Souvenir Sheet

1997, June 30   Litho.   Perf. 11½

792 A122 $5 like No. 604   1.75 1.75

No. 792 contains one 19x29mm stamp.

Special Administrative Region of People's Republic of China

First Issue Under Chinese Administration — A156

Sights and symbols of Hong Kong: $1.30, Chinese architecture. $1.60, Modern buildings, methods of transportation. $2.50, Skyscrapers, Hong Kong Convention & Exhibition Center. $2.60, Cargo ship entering port. $3.10, Chinese junks, dolphins jumping in water. $5, Hibiscus flower.

1997, July 1   Litho.   Perf. 12x12½

793	A156	$1.30 multicolored	.35	.35
794	A156	$1.60 multicolored	.40	.40
795	A156	$2.50 multicolored	.65	.65
796	A156	$2.60 multicolored	.70	.70
797	A156	$3.10 multicolored	.80	.80
798	A156	$5 multicolored	1.25	1.25
a.	Souvenir sheet of 1		1.25	1.25
	Nos. 793-798 (6)		4.15	4.15

1997 World Bank Group/Intl. Monetary Fund Annual Meetings A157

Designs: $1.30, Finance, banking. $2.50, Investment, stock exchange. $3.10, Trade, telecommunications. $5, Infrastructure, transport.

Perf. 14½
1997, Sept. 21   Litho.   Unwmk.

799	A157	$1.30 multicolored	.35	.35
800	A157	$2.50 multicolored	.70	.70
801	A157	$3.10 multicolored	.90	.90
802	A157	$5 multicolored	1.40	1.40
	Nos. 799-802 (4)		3.35	3.35

Shells — A158

1997, Nov. 9   Photo.   Perf. 13½

803	A158	$1.30 Clam	.40	.40
804	A158	$2.50 Cowrie	.70	.70
805	A158	$3.10 Cone	.90	.90
806	A158	$5 Murex	1.40	1.40
	Nos. 803-806 (4)		3.40	3.40

New Year 1998 (Year of the Tiger) — A159

Various embroidery designs of tigers.

1998, Jan. 4   Litho.   Perf. 13½

807	A159	$1.30 multicolored	.35	.35
808	A159	$2.50 multicolored	.75	.75
809	A159	$3.10 multicolored	.95	.95
a.	Bklt. pane, 6 ea #807, 809		9.00	
	Complete booklet, #809a		10.00	
810	A159	$5 multicolored	1.50	1.50
a.	Souvenir sheet #807-810		4.75	4.75
	Nos. 807-810 (4)		3.55	3.55

See No. 838.

Star Ferry, Cent. — A160

Star Ferry during: $1.30, 1900's. $2.50, 1910's-1920's. $3.10, 1920's-1950's. $5, Mid-1950's on.

1998, Apr. 26   Photo.   Perf. 13½

811	A160	$1.30 multicolored	.40	.40
812	A160	$2.50 multicolored	.85	.85
813	A160	$3.10 multicolored	1.05	1.05
814	A160	$5 multicolored	1.60	1.60
	Nos. 811-814 (4)		3.90	3.90

Nos. 811-814 also exist perf 14½ from a booklet of one each sold only at "Australia '99" International Stamp Exhibition for $25.

Souvenir Sheet

The Closing of Kai Tak Airport — A161

1998, July 5   Photo.   Perf. 13½

815 A161 $5 multicolored   2.25 2.25

New Hong Kong Airport — A162

$1.30, Passengers on terminal's moving sidewalks. $1.60, Couple entering Automated

HONG KONG

People Mover. $2.50, Airport Railway, Tsing Ma Bridge. $2.60, Terminal building, Airmail Center. $3.10, Aircraft gates. $5, Terminal departure level.

1998, July 5   Perf. 14
816	A162	$1.30 multicolored	.40	.40
817	A162	$1.60 multicolored	.45	.45
818	A162	$2.50 multicolored	.70	.70
819	A162	$2.60 multicolored	.80	.80
820	A162	$3.10 multicolored	.90	.90
821	A162	$5 multicolored	1.40	1.40
a.		Souvenir sheet of 1	2.00	2.00
b.		Block of 6, #816-821	5.25	5.25
		Nos. 816-821 (6)	4.65	4.65

See note after No. 940.

A163

Scouting in Hong Kong: Rope tied in various knots, different scouting divisions: $1.30, Grasshopper Scouts, Cub Scouts. $2.50, Tower, tents, Boy Scouts, Girl Scouts. $3.10, Helicopter, sailboats, Venture Scouts. $5, City buildings, Rover Scouts, adult leaders.

Unwmk.
1998, July 26   Litho.   Perf. 14
822	A163	$1.30 multicolored	.40	.40
823	A163	$2.50 multicolored	.70	.70
824	A163	$3.10 multicolored	1.00	1.00
825	A163	$5 multicolored	1.50	1.50
		Nos. 822-825 (4)	3.60	3.60

A164

Hong Kong designs.

1998, Sept. 20   Litho.   Perf. 13½
826	A164	$1.30 Graphic	.50	.40
827	A164	$2.50 Product	.90	.90
828	A164	$3.10 Interior	1.15	.95
829	A164	$5 Fashion	1.70	1.40
		Nos. 826-829 (4)	4.25	3.50

Kites — A165

1998, Nov. 15   Litho.   Perf. 13½
830	A165	$1.30 Dragonfly	.40	.40
831	A165	$2.50 Dragon	.85	.85
832	A165	$3.10 Butterfly	1.10	1.10
833	A165	$5 Goldfish	1.60	1.60
a.		Souvenir sheet, #830-833	4.00	4.00
		Nos. 830-833 (4)	3.95	3.95

A166

New Year 1999 (Year of the Rabbit): White rabbit with flower designs in various positions.

1999, Jan. 31   Photo.   Perf. 14x13¼
834	A166	$1.30 yel org & multi	.40	.40
a.		Scratched panel		.40
		Sheet of 10		
835	A166	$2.50 green & multi	.75	.75
a.		Scratched panel		
		Sheet of 10	7.50	
836	A166	$3.10 orange & multi	.90	.90
a.		Scratched panel		.40
		Sheet of 10	9.25	
837	A166	$5 red lilac & multi	1.45	1.45
a.		Scratched panel		.40
		Sheet of 10	14.50	
		Nos. 834-837 (4)	3.50	3.50

Nos. 834-837 are printed with a layering of gold "scratch off" ink, which, when removed, reveals a Chinese greeting.

New Year Types of 1987-98

1999, Feb. 21   Litho.   Perf. 13½
Sheet of 12

Designs: a, Like #734. b, Like #780. c, Like #783. d, Like #712. e Like 515. f, LIke #691. g, Like #534. h, Like #668. i, Like #615. j, Like #584. k, Like #560. #a.-k. have 4 Chinese characters at UL instead of crown and ER.

838		$1.30 #a.-k, #807 + label	7.75	7.75

Design in label and sheet selvage is engraved.

Intl. Year of Older Persons — A167

$1.30, Calligraphy. $2.50, Bird raising. $3.10, Playing Go. $5, Voluntary services.

Perf. 14½
1999, Mar. 14   Litho.   Unwmk.
839	A167	$1.30 multicolored	.40	.40
840	A167	$2.50 multicolored	.75	.75
841	A167	$3.10 multicolored	.90	.90
842	A167	$5 multicolored	1.45	1.45
		Nos. 839-842 (4)	3.50	3.50

Souvenir Sheet
Giant Pandas in Hong Kong A168

1999, Apr. 25   Litho.   Perf. 14¼
843	A168	$10 multicolored	4.00	4.00

No. 843 contains one circular stamp 38mm in diameter.

Public Transport A169

1999, May 23
844	A169	$1.30 Bus	.45	.45
845	A169	$2.40 Minibus	.90	.90
846	A169	$2.50 Tram	.95	.95
847	A169	$2.60 Taxi	1.00	1.00
848	A169	$3.10 Airport express	1.15	1.15
		Nos. 844-848 (5)	4.45	4.45

Hong Kong and Singapore Tourism — A170

Designs: $1.20, Hong Kong Harbor. $1.30, Singapore Skyline. $2.50, Giant Buddha, Hong Kong. $2.60, Merlion, Sentosa Island, Singapore. $5, Hong Kong street scene. $5, Bugis Junction, Singapore.

Perf. 13¼
1999, July 1   Litho.   Unwmk.
849	A170	$1.20 multicolored	.35	.35
850	A170	$1.30 multicolored	.40	.40
851	A170	$2.50 multicolored	.70	.70
852	A170	$2.60 multicolored	.70	.70
853	A170	$3.10 multicolored	.85	.85
854	A170	$5 multicolored	1.75	1.75
a.		Souvenir sheet #849-854	4.75	4.75
		Nos. 849-854 (6)	4.75	4.75

See Singapore Nos. 896-902.

People's Republic of China, 50th Anniv. — A171

Designs: $1.30, Flags of People's Republic and Hong Kong Special Administrative District. $2.50 Bauhinia blakeana flower, Hong Kong skyline. $3.10, Dragon dance. $5, Fireworks.

Perf. 14¼ Syncopated
1999, Oct. 1   Photo.
Granite Paper
855	A171	$1.30 multicolored	.50	.50
856	A171	$2.50 multicolored	1.00	1.00
857	A171	$3.10 multicolored	1.10	1.10
858	A171	$5 multicolored	1.90	1.90
a.		Block or strip of 4, #855-858	4.50	4.50

Issued in sheets of 4 blocks or strips and individually in sheets of 20.

Landmarks — A172

10c, Museum of Tea Ware. 20c, St. John's Cathedral. 50c, Legislative Council building. $1, Tai Fu Tai. $1.20, Wong Tai Sin Temple. $1.30, Victoria Harbor. $1.40, Hong Kong Railway Museum. $1.60, Tsim Sha Tsui Clock Tower. $2, Happy Valley Racecourse. $2.10, Kowloon-Canton Railway. $2.50, Chi Lin Nunnery. $3.10, Buddha at Po Lin Monastery. $5, Aw Boon Haw Gardens. $10, Tsing Ma Bridge. $20, Hong Kong Convention & Exhibition Center. $50, Hong Kong Intl. Airport.

Perf. 13x13¾ Syncopated
1999, Oct. 18   Photo.
Granite Paper
859	A172	10c blue & multi	.30	.25
a.		Booklet pane of 1	.35	
860	A172	20c blue & multi	.30	.25
a.		Booklet pane of 1	.35	
861	A172	50c blue & multi	.30	.25
a.		Booklet pane of 1	.35	
862	A172	$1 blue & multi	.30	.25
a.		Booklet pane of 1	.60	
863	A172	$1.20 blue & multi	.35	.30
a.		Booklet pane of 1	.70	
864	A172	$1.30 blue & multi	.40	.35
a.		Booklet pane of 1	.80	
865	A172	$1.40 blue & multi	.40	.35
a.		Booklet pane of 1	.80	
b.		Booklet pane of 10	4.00	
		Booklet, #865b	4.00	
866	A172	$1.60 blue & multi	.45	.40
a.		Booklet pane of 1	.90	
867	A172	$2 blue & multi	.55	.50
a.		Booklet pane of 1	1.10	
868	A172	$2.10 blue & multi	.60	.55
a.		Booklet pane of 1	1.20	
869	A172	$2.50 blue & multi	.65	.60
a.		Booklet pane of 1	1.30	
870	A172	$3.10 blue & multi	.85	.75
a.		Booklet pane of 1	1.75	
871	A172	$5 blue & multi	1.50	1.25
a.		Booklet pane of 1	3.00	
		Souv. booklet, #859a-871a	14.00	
b.		Sheet of 13, #859-871	6.00	6.00
c.		Souvenir sheet of 1 (Definitive #4)	1.50	1.50
d.		Souv. sheet of 1 (Definitive #6)	1.50	1.50

Size: 26x32mm
Perf. 13¼
872	A172	$10 blue & multi	2.75	2.50
a.		Souv. sheet of 1 (Definitive #1)	2.75	2.75
b.		Souv. sheet of 1 (Exhibition #1)	4.00	4.00
c.		Souv. sheet of 1 (Exhibition #2)	2.75	2.75
d.		Souv. sheet of 1 (Definitive #2)	2.75	2.75
e.		Souv. sheet of 1 (Definitive #5)	2.75	2.75
873	A172	$20 blue & multi	5.50	5.00
874	A172	$50 blue & multi	14.00	12.50
a.		Sheet of 3, #872-874	22.00	22.00
		Nos. 859-874 (16)	29.20	26.05

Coil Stamps
Perf. 15x13½ Syncopated
Size: 18x22mm
874B	A172	10c blue & multi	.60	.40
874C	A172	50c blue & multi	.60	.40
874D	A172	$1.30 blue & multi	.90	.55
874E	A172	$1.60 blue & multi	1.00	.65
874F	A172	$2.50 blue & multi	1.50	.95
874G	A172	$3.10 blue & multi	1.90	1.20
		Nos. 874B-874G (6)	6.50	4.15

Nos. 872a-872b are Syncopated perf 14x14¼. No. 872c is Syncopated perf 13¼x13. No. 872d is Syncopated perf 14x14½. No. 872e is Syncopated perf 13¼x13.

Issued: No. 872a, 1/31/00; No. 872b, 2/10/00; No. 872c, 4/15/00; No. 872d, 12/2/00; No. 871c, 4/21/01; No. 872e, 8/1/01; Nos. 874B-874E, 874G, 10/18/99; No. 874F, 10/18/99; No. 871d, 1/19/02. No. 865b, 4/1/02.
See note after No. 940.
See also Nos. 917, 965-973, 991-993, 1083.

Chinese White Dolphin — A173

Various views of dolphin.

1999, Nov. 14   Litho.   Perf. 14½
Granite Paper
875	A173	$1.30 green & multi	.60	.60
876	A173	$2.50 bl grn & multi	1.00	1.00
877	A173	$3.10 blue & multi	1.25	1.25
878	A173	$5 pur & multi	1.75	1.75

Souvenir Sheet
879		Sheet of 4, #a.-d.	4.75	4.75

Nos. 875-878 have Worldwide Fund for Nature (WWF) emblem; Nos. 879a-879d do not.
See No. 900.

Souvenir Sheet
Millennium — A174

No. 880: a, Dragon boat races, skyline. b, Bridge, birds.

Perf. 14¼ Syncopated
1999, Dec. 31   Photo.
Granite Paper
880	A174	$5 Sheet of 2, #a.-b.	6.00	6.00

New Millennium Children's Stamp Design Contest Winners A175

Designs: $1.30, Scales. $2.50, Children planting tree on planet. $3.10, Planets. $5, Inhabited planets, space shuttle, rocket.

2000, Jan. 1   Granite Paper
881	A175	$1.30 multi	.45	.45
882	A175	$2.50 multi	.85	.85
883	A175	$3.10 multi	.95	.95
884	A175	$5 multi	1.75	1.75
		Nos. 881-884 (4)	4.00	4.00

Victoria Harbor — A176

Litho. & Embossed with Foil Application
2000, Jan. 1   Perf. 13¼
885	A176	$50 gold & multi	22.50	22.50

HONG KONG

New Year 2000 (Year of the Dragon) — A177

Various dragons.

Perf. 14¼ Syncopated
2000, Jan. 23   Litho.
Granite Paper

886	A177	$1.30 multi	.40	.40
887	A177	$2.50 multi	.75	.75
888	A177	$3.10 multi	.85	.85
889	A177	$5 multi	1.45	1.45
a.		Souvenir sheet of 1, imperf.	15.00	15.00
b.		Souvenir sheet, #886-889	4.00	4.00
		Nos. 886-889 (4)	3.45	3.45

See Nos. 1030a, 1431a, 1479a, 1480a.

Museums and Libraries — A178

Designs: $1.30, Heritage Museum. $2.50, Central Library. $3.10, Museum of Coastal Defense. $5 Museum of History.

Perf. 14½x14¼
2000, Mar. 26   Photo.
Granite Paper

890	A178	$1.30 multi	.60	.35
891	A178	$2.50 multi	1.30	.95
892	A178	$3.10 multi	1.25	1.00
893	A178	$5 multi	2.25	2.25
a.		Block, #890-893	8.00	8.00
		Nos. 890-893 (4)	5.40	4.55

Nos. 890-893 issued in sheets of 24. No. 893a issued only in sheet containing 4 blocks.

Red Cross — A179

Designs: $1.30, Blood transfusion. $2.50, Special education. $3.10, Disaster relief. $5, Voluntary service.

Perf. 14¼ Syncopated
2000, May 7   Photo.
Granite Paper

894	A179	$1.30 multi	.45	.45
895	A179	$2.50 multi	.85	.85
896	A179	$3.10 multi	.95	.95
897	A179	$5 multi	1.75	1.75
a.		Souvenir sheet, #894-897	4.25	4.25
		Nos. 894-897 (4)	4.00	4.00

Flower Type of 1989, Mountain Type of 1996 Inscribed "Hong Kong, China," and Dolphin Type of 1999
Perf. 14¼ Syncopated
2000, June 17   Photo.
Granite Paper

898	A90	$5 Booklet pane of 1, like #455	4.50	4.50
899	A150	$5 Booklet pane of 1, like #755	4.50	4.50
900	A173	$5 Booklet pane of 1, like #879d	4.50	4.50
		Booklet, #898-900	13.50	

Hong Kong 2001 Stamp Exhibition. Booklet sold for $35.

Insects — A180

Designs: $1.30, Pyrops candelarius. $2.50, Macromidia ellenae. $3.10, Troides helena spilotia. $5, Chiridopsis bowringi.

Perf. 13½x13¼ Syncopated
2000, July 16   Litho.
Granite Paper

| 901-904 | A180 | Set of 4 | 4.50 | 4.50 |
| 904a | | Souvenir sheet, #901-904 | 4.50 | 4.50 |

Mountain Type of 1996 Inscribed "Hong Kong, China"
Souvenir Sheet
Perf. 13¼ Syncopated
2000, Aug. 12   Photo.
Granite Paper

| 905 | A150 | $10 Like #754 | 4.50 | 4.00 |

Hong Kong 2001 Stamp Exhibition.

2000 Summer Olympics, Sydney — A181

Designs: $1.30, Cycling, badminton. $2.50, Table tennis, running. $3.10, Judo, rowing. $5, Swimming, sailboarding.

Perf. 14¼ Syncopated
2000, Aug. 27   Litho.
Granite Paper

| 906-909 | A181 | Set of 4 | 4.50 | 3.75 |

Birds — A182

2000, Sept. 30   Photo.
Granite Paper

910		Booklet pane of 2		4.50
a.	A182	$1.30 Yellow-breasted bunting	1.50	1.50
b.	A182	$2.50 Great knot	3.00	3.00
911		Booklet pane of 2		6.50
a.	A182	$3.10 Falcated teal	2.50	2.50
b.	A182	$5 Black-faced spoonbill	4.00	4.00
		Booklet, #910-911	11.00	

Booklet containing Nos. 910-911 sold for $25.

Chinese General Chamber of Commerce, Cent. — A183

Designs: $1.30, Hong Kong in 1900. $2.50, Headquarters buildings. $3.10, People reading notice for distribution of relief funds. $5, Hand with computer mouse, currency symbols.

Perf. 13¾ Syncopated
2000, Oct. 22   Litho.
Granite Paper

| 912-915 | A183 | Set of 4 | 4.50 | 3.75 |

Coral Type of 1994 Inscribed "Hong Kong, China"
Souvenir Sheet
Perf. 13¼ Syncopated
2000, Nov. 25   Photo.
Granite Paper

| 916 | A141 | $10 Like #709 | 5.00 | 4.00 |

Landmarks Type of 1999
Souvenir Sheet
Litho. & Holography
2000, Dec. 31

| 917 | A172 | $20 Like #873 | 8.00 | 8.00 |

Soaking in water may affect hologram.

New Year 2001 (Year of the Snake) — A184

Various snakes. Denominations: $1.30, $2.50, $3.10, $5.

Perf. 14½ Sync.
2001, Jan. 1   Photo.

918-921	A184	Set of 4	4.50	4.00
921a		Souvenir sheet of 1, imperf.	2.75	2.50
921b		Souvenir sheet, #918-921	4.75	4.75

See Nos. 1030b, 1431b, 1479b, 1480b.

Souvenir Sheet

Opening of Hong Kong 2001 Stamp Exhibition — A185

No. 922: a, Year of the Dragon. b, Year of the Snake.

Litho. & Embossed with Foil Application
2001, Feb. 1   Perf. 13¼

| 922 | A185 | $50 Sheet of 2, #a-b | 45.00 | 45.00 |

Indiginous Trees Type of 1988 Inscribed "Hong Kong, China"
2001   Photo.   *Perf. 14¼ Syncopated*
Granite Paper

923	A105	$5 multi, sheetlet #5	2.25	2.25
a.		Sheetlet #6	2.25	2.25
b.		Sheetlet #7	2.25	2.25
c.		Sheetlet #8	2.25	2.25

Issued: No. 923, 2/2; No. 923a, 2/3; No. 923b, 2/4; No. 923c, 2/5. No. 923b with gold overprint in margin reading "To commemorate the FIAP Day of HONG KONG 2001 Stamp Exhibition on 4th February, 2001" is a private emission.

See note after No. 940 for unsyncopated stamp.

Greetings A186

Designs: $1.30, Maple leaves. $1.60, Swans. $2.50, Chicks. $2.60, Cherry blossoms. $3.10, Bamboo. $5, Snow-covered plant.

Stamps + Labels
2001, Feb. 1   Photo.
Granite Paper

| 924-929 | A186 | Set of 6 | 5.75 | 4.75 |

See note after Nos. 934-937.

Hong Kong Water Supply, 150th Anniv. — A187

Designs: $1.30, Tai Tam Tuk Reservoir. $2.50, Plover Cove Reservoir. $3.10, Pipelines. $5, Beakers, chemical symbols.

2001, Mar. 18   Litho. & Embossed
Granite Paper

| 930-933 | A187 | Set of 4 | 5.00 | 4.00 |
| 933a | | Block of 4, #930-933 | 6.00 | 6.00 |

Movie Stars — A188

Designs: $1.30, Ng Cho-fan (1911-93) and Pak Yin (1920-87). $2.50, Sun Ma Si-tsang (1916-97) and Tang Bik-wan (1926-91). $3.10, Cheung Wood-yau (1910-85) and Wong Man-lei (1913-98). $5, Mak Bing-wing (1915-84) and Fung Wong-nui (1925-92).

2001, Apr. 8   Litho.
Granite Paper

| 934-937 | A188 | Set of 4 | 4.25 | 3.25 |
| 937a | | Block of 4, #934-937 | 4.50 | 4.50 |

Values are for stamps with surrounding selvage.

On June 12, 2001 Hong Kong sold for $120 limited numbers of a sheet containing 18 examples of the $1.30 stamp, No. 924. The 18 labels to the right of the stamps on this sheet differ from those found on examples of No. 924 sold on the stamp's original date of issue, and the 18 labels to the left of the stamps depict Chinese celebrities.

Dragon Boat Races — A189

Dragon boats and: No. 938, $5, Sydney Opera House. No. 939, Hong Kong Convention and Exhibition Center.

2001, June 25   Litho.   Perf. 14x14½
Granite Paper

| 938-939 | A189 | Set of 2 | 3.75 | 2.75 |
| 939a | | Souvenir sheet, #938-939 | 3.75 | 3.75 |

See Australia Nos. 1977-1978.

Emblem of 2008 Summer Olympics, Beijing — A190

2001, July 14   Photo.   Perf. 13x13¼

| 940 | A190 | $1.30 multi + label | 1.25 | 1.25 |

No. 940 printed in sheets of 12 stamp + label pairs with one large central label. See People's Republic of China No. 3119, Macao No. 1067. No. 940 with different label is from People's Republic of China No. 3119a.

On July 21, 2001 Hong Kong sold a booklet containing stamps with a face value of $12.40 for $30. The stamps are the Indigenous Trees type of 1988 with the inscription "Hong Kong, China." The first pane in the booklet contained $1.30 and $2.50 stamps, and those on the second pane contained $3.10 and $5 stamps.

On Aug. 25, 2001 Hong Kong sold a booklet containing stamps with a face value of $30 for $65. The first pane in the booklet contained four stamps with a face value of $1.80 of the Stamp Collecting type of 1992 with the inscription "Hong Kong, China." The second pane contained two $3.10 perf. 13½x13 stamps on granite paper of type A152, and two $3.10 perf. 13¾ syncopated stamps on granite paper of type A172. The third pane contained four $2.60 perf. 14¼ stamps on granite paper of type A162.

HONG KONG

Tea Culture — A191

Various tea services and background colors of: $1.30, Lilac. $2.50, Orange brown. $3.10, Bright orange. $5, Green.

Perf. 14¼x14½ Syncopated
2001, Sept. 9   Litho.
944-947   A191   Set of 4   4.25   3.75

Herbs — A192

Designs: $1.30, Centella asiatica. $2.50, Lobelia chinensis. $3.10, Gardenia jasminoides. $5, Scutellaria indica.

Perf. 14½ Syncopated
2001, Oct. 7   Granite Paper   Litho.
948-951   A192   Set of 4   4.25   3.75

Children's Stamp Coloring Contest — A193

Designs: $1.30, Bear. $2.50, Penguin. $3.10, Flower. $5, Bee.

Granite Paper
Die Cut Perf. 13¾x13¼ Sync.
2001, Nov. 18   Self-Adhesive
952-955   A193   Set of 4   5.00   4.00
   955a   Souvenir sheet, #952-955   5.00   5.00

New Year 2002 (Year of the Horse) — A194

Various horses. Denominations: $1.30, $2.50, $3.10, $5.

2002, Jan. 13   **Perf. 14½ Syncopated**
Granite Paper
956-959   A194   Set of 4   4.25   3.75
   959a   Souvenir sheet of 1, imperf.   2.50   2.50
   959b   Souvenir sheet, #956-959   4.75   4.75
See Nos. 1030c, 1431c, 1479c, 1480c.

Souvenir Sheet

New Year 2002 (Year of the Horse) A195

No. 960: a, Snake. b, Horse.

Litho. & Embossed with Foil Application
2002, Feb. 9   **Perf. 13¼**
960   A195 $50 Sheet of 2, #a-b   42.50   42.50

Works of Art — A196

Details from: $1.30, Lines in Motion, by Chui Tze-hung. $2.50, Volume and Time, by Hon Chi-fun. $3.10, Bright Sun, by Aries Lee. $5, Midsummer, by Irene Chou.

Perf. 14½ Syncopated
2002, Feb. 24   Granite Paper   Litho.
961-964   A196   Set of 4   4.50   3.50

Landmarks Type of 1999

Designs: $1.40, Hong Kong Railway Museum. $1.80, Hong Kong Stadium. $1.90, Western Market. $2.40, Kwun Yam statue, Repulse Bay. $3, Peak Tower. $13, Hong Kong Cultural Center.

Perf. 13x13¾ Syncopated
2002, Apr. 1   Granite Paper   Photo.
965   A172 $1.80 blue & multi   .50   .50
966   A172 $1.90 blue & multi   .55   .55
967   A172 $2.40 blue & multi   .65   .65
  a.   Booklet pane of 10   6.50   —
     Complete booklet, #967a   6.50
968   A172 $3 blue & multi   .85   .85
  a.   Booklet pane of 10   8.50
     Complete booklet, #968a   8.50

Size: 26x32mm
Perf. 13¼ Syncopated
969   A172 $13 blue & multi   4.00   4.00
   Nos. 965-969 (5)   6.55   6.55

Coil Stamps
Size: 18x22mm
Perf. 14¾x13¼ Syncopated
970   A172 $1.40 blue & multi   .75   .50
971   A172 $1.80 blue & multi   .75   .80
972   A172 $2.40 blue & multi   1.25   1.00
973   A172 $3 blue & multi   1.60   1.50
   Nos. 970-973 (4)   4.35   3.80

Cyberindustry in Hong Kong — A197

Designs: $1.40, Innovation. $2.40, Connectivity. $3, Trend. $5, Strength.

Perf. 13¾ Syncopated
2002, Apr. 14   Granite Paper   Litho.
974-977   A197   Set of 4   4.00   3.50
   977a   Block of 4, #974-977   4.50   4.50

A booklet of two panes, one containing one each of Nos. 974 and 976, and another containing one each of Nos. 975 and 977, sold for $30. Value, $11.

2002 World Cup Soccer Championships, Japan and Korea — A198

No. 978: a, Goalie. b, Crowd and players.

Perf. 12 Syncopated
2002, May 16   Photo.
978   Horiz. pair, with central label   2.00   2.00
  a.-b.   A198 $1.40 Either single   1.00   1.00

No. 978 was printed in sheets of 5 pairs and five different labels.
A souvenir sheet containing Nos. 978a-978b, People's Republic of China No. 3198, and Macao Nos. 1091a-1091b exists. Value, $45.

Corals — A199

Designs: $1.40, North Atlantic pink tree, Pacific orange cup, and North Pacific horn corals. $2.40, North Atlantic giant orange tree, and Black corals. $3, Dendronepthea gigantea and Dendronepthea corals. $5, Tubastrea and Echinogorgia corals.

Perf. 13¾x14 Syncopated
2002, May 19   Litho.
Granite Paper
979-982   A199   Set of 4   4.50   4.00
   982a   Souvenir sheet, #979-982   5.00   5.00

On May 10, 2003, Hong Kong sold a booklet with a face value of $11.80 for $25. The first pane contains Nos. 979-980 perf 13¼x13. The second pane contains Nos. 981-982, perf 13¼x13.
See Canada Nos. 1948-1951.

Beijing — Kowloon Through Trains — A200

Train and: $1.40, Hong Kong commercial buildings. $2.40, Wuhan-Changjiang Bridge, Wuchang. $3, Shaolin Monastery Pagodas, Zhengzhou. $5, Temple of Heaven, Beijing.

2002, June 9   **Perf. 14¼ Syncopated**
Granite Paper
983-986   A200   Set of 4   4.25   3.75
   986a   Horiz. strip of 4, #983-986   5.00   5.00

Hong Kong Special Administrative Region, 5th Anniv. — A201

Designs: $1.40, White dolphins, corals. $2.40, Students, bauhinia flowers. $3, Flying cranes, Hong Kong International Airport. $5, Flags of Hong Kong and People's Republic of China, fireworks over skyline.

2002, July 1   Granite Paper
987-990   A201   Set of 4   4.50   4.00
   990a   Souvenir sheet, #987-990   4.50   4.50

Landmarks Type of 1999 with Pink Denomination and Country Name
Souvenir Sheet
Design: Tsing Ma Bridge.

Perf. 13¼ Syncopated
2002, July 27   Photo.
Granite Paper
991   A172 $10 pink & multi   4.25   3.75
Philakorea 2002.

Landmarks Type of 1999 With Olive Green Denomination and Country Name
Souvenir Sheet
Design: Tsing Ma Bridge.

Perf. 13¼ Syncopated
2002, Aug. 24   Photo.
Granite Paper
992   A172 $10 ol green & multi   4.50   4.00
Amphilex 2002 Intl. Stamp Exhibition, Amsterdam.

Landmarks Type of 1999 With Buff Background
Souvenir Sheet
Design: Tsing Ma Bridge.

2002, Sept. 7
993   A172 $10 blue, buff & multi   4.50   4.00

Rocks — A202

Designs: $1.40, Ping Chau (siltstone). $2.40, Port Island (conglomerate). $3, Po Pin Chau (tuff). $5, Lamma Island (granite).

Perf. 13¼x12¾
2002, Sept. 15   Litho.
994-997   A202   Set of 4   4.75   4.25
   997a   Souvenir sheet #994-997   4.75   4.75

Portions of the designs were applied by a thermographic process, producing a shiny, raised effect.

Eastern and Western Cultures — A203

Designs: 10c, Radar screen, luopan. 20c, Calculator, abacus. 50c, Incense coil, stained glass window. $1, Chair, Chinese bed. $1.40, Dim sum, loaves of bread. $1.80, Silverware, chopsticks and spoon. $1.90, Canned drinks, tea caddies. $2, Western and Eastern wedding cakes. $2.40, Erhu, violin. $2.50, Letter boxes, internet. $3, Sailboats, dragon boat. $5, Tiled roof, glass wall. $10, Ballet, Chinese opera. $13, Chess, Xiangqi. $20, Christmas decorations, lanterns. $50, Eastern and Western sculptures.

Perf. 13¼x13 Syncopated
2002, Oct. 14   Photo.
Granite Paper
998   A203   10c multi   .30   .25
999   A203   20c multi   .30   .25
1000   A203   50c multi   .30   .25
1001   A203 $1 multi   .35   .35
1002   A203 $1.40 multi   .45   .40
  a.   Booklet pane of 10   4.50
     Complete booklet, #1002a   4.50
1003   A203 $1.80 multi   .60   .50
  a.   Booklet pane of 10 ('03)   6.00   —
     Complete booklet, #1003a   6.00
1004   A203 $1.90 multi   .65   .50
1005   A203 $2 multi   .65   .50
1006   A203 $2.40 multi   .75   .55
  a.   Booklet pane of 10   7.50
     Complete booklet, #1006a   7.50
1007   A203 $2.50 multi   .80   .60
1008   A203 $3 multi   .90   .80
  a.   Booklet pane of 10   9.00
     Complete booklet, #1008a   9.00
1009   A203 $5 multi   1.75   1.25
  a.   Souvenir sheet, #998-1009   8.00   8.00
  b.   Booklet pane, #998-1009   8.00
     Complete booklet, #1009b   8.00

Size: 40x24mm
Perf. 14¾ Syncopated
1010   A203 $10 multi   3.00   1.40
1011   A203 $13 multi   3.75   1.75
1012   A203 $20 multi   7.00   3.00
1013   A203 $50 multi   16.00   7.00
  a.   Souvenir sheet #1010-1013   30.00   30.00
   Nos. 998-1013 (16)   37.55   19.85

Coil Stamps
Size: 22x19mm
Perf. 13¼x14¾ Syncopated
1014   A203 $1.40 multi   1.60   1.00
1015   A203 $1.80 multi   2.00   1.40
1016   A203 $2.40 multi   3.00   2.00
1017   A203 $3 multi   4.00   3.00
   Nos. 1014-1017 (4)   10.60   7.40

No. 1003a issued 10/7/04.

Christmas — A204

Designs: $1.40, Christmas tree. $2.40, Ornament. $3, Snowman. $5, Bell.

Photo. with Hologram Applied
Perf. 13½ Syncopated
2002, Nov. 24   Granite Paper
1018-1021   A204   Set of 4   4.50   4.00
   1021a   Block or strip of 4, #1018-1021   4.75   4.75

Perforations within the stamp outline the designs.

Hong Kong Disneyland — A205

Designs: $1.40, Main Street. $2.40, Fantasyland. $3, Adventureland. $5, Tomorrowland.

HONG KONG

Perf. 13¾ Syncopated
2003, Jan. 12   Litho. & Embossed
Granite Paper

1022-1025	A205	Set of 4	5.00	4.50
1025a		Souvenir sheet, #1022-1025	5.50	5.50

New Year 2003 (Year of the Ram) — A206

Various rams: $1.40, $2.40, $3, $5.

Perf. 14¼ Syncopated
2003, Jan. 19   Litho.
Granite Paper

1026-1029	A206	Set of 4	4.75	4.25
1029a		Souvenir sheet of 1, imperf.	3.00	3.00
1029b		Souvenir sheet, #1026-1029	4.75	4.75

See Nos. 1030d, 1431d, 1479d, 1480d.

New Year Types of 2000-03
2003, Jan. 19   Litho.   Perf. 12¾x13¼
Flocked Paper

1030		Block of 4	15.00	15.00
a.	A177	$10 Like #888	3.75	3.75
b.	A184	$10 Like #920	3.75	3.75
c.	A194	$10 Like #957	3.75	3.75
d.	A206	$10 Like #1029	3.75	3.75

Souvenir Sheet

New Year 2003 (Year of the Ram) A207

No. 1031: a, Horse. b, Ram.

Litho. & Embossed with Foil Application
2003, Jan. 19   Perf. 13¼

1031	A207	$50 Sheet of 2, #a-b	42.50	42.50

Traditional Trades and Handicrafts A208

Designs: $1.40, Letter writing. $1.80, Bird cage making, vert. $2.40, Qipao tailoring. $2.50, Hairdressing, vert. $3, Dough figurine making, vert. $5, Olive selling.

Perf. 13½x14 Syncopated, 13½ Syncopated (vert. stamps)
2003, Mar. 13   Litho.
Granite Paper

1032-1037	A208	Set of 6	6.00	5.00
1037a		Souvenir sheet, #1032-1037	6.00	6.00

Souvenir Sheet

Hong Kong 2004 Stamp Expo A209

2003, Apr. 8   Perf. 13¼ Syncopated
Granite Paper

1038	A209	$10 multi	4.50	4.00

Souvenir Sheet

Master-of-Nets Garden, Suzhou — A210

2003, June 27   Granite Paper

1039	A210	$10 multi	4.50	4.00

See No. 1456f.

Miniature Landscapes A211

Plants: $1.40, Fukien tea. $2.40, Hedge sageretia. $3, Fire-thorn, vert. $5, Chinese hackberry, vert.

Perf. 13¾x12¾ Syncopated, 12¾x13¾ Syncopated
2003, July 17   Photo.
Granite Paper

1040-1043	A211	Set of 4	4.50	4.00

Aquarium Fish — A212

Various fish: $1.40, $2.40, $3, $5.

2003, Aug. 7   Perf. 14¼ Syncopated
Granite Paper
With Fish-Shaped Holes in Paper

1044-1047	A212	Set of 4	5.00	4.25
1047a		Block of 4, #1044-1047	5.50	5.50

A213

Heartwarming A214

Perf. 13¾ Syncopated
2003, Sept. 10   Litho.
Inscribed "Local Mail Postage"
Granite Paper

1048	A213	($1.40) multi	.60	.50
1049	A214	($1.40) multi	.60	.50
a.		Sheet of 16 + 17 labels ('04)	19.50	19.50

Inscribed "Air Mail Postage"

1050	A213	($3) multi	1.60	1.10
1051	A214	($3) multi	1.60	1.10
a.		Sheet, 4 each #1048-1051, + 17 labels	18.00	18.00
		Nos. 1048-1051 (4)	4.40	3.20

No. 1049a issued 10/7/04. No. 1049a sold for $50 and has a 2004 Olympic Games theme on the labels. A similar sheet issued in 2005 with labels having a Lions Club Convention theme, was sold for $108 in conjunction with other items, and was not available separately.

See Nos. 1594-1597.

Birds — A215

Designs: $1.40, Pied avocet. $2.40, Horned grebe. $3, Black-throated diver. $5, Great crested grebe.

Perf. 12½ Syncopated
2003, Oct. 4   Litho. & Engr.
Granite Paper

1052-1055	A215	Set of 4	4.50	4.00
1055a		Booklet pane, #1052-1055	5.25	—
		Complete booklet, 2 #1055a	20.00	

See Sweden No. 2469.

Souvenir Sheet

Hong Kong 2004 Stamp Expo A216

Perf. 13¼ Syncopated
2003, Oct. 14   Litho.
Granite Paper

1056	A216	$10 multi	4.75	4.75
1056a		Sheet, 2 each #1038, 1056, + 2 labels	32.50	32.50

No. 1056a was issued 1/30/04 and sold for $80. Labels could be personalized.

Percussion Instruments — A217

Designs: $1.40, Drum. $2.40, Clappers. $3, Cymbals. $5, Gongs. $13, Chimes.

Perf. 13½x13¼ Syncopated
2003, Nov. 6   Photo.

1057-1060	A217	Set of 4	4.00	3.50

Souvenir Sheet
Perf. 13¾x13¼ Syncopated

1061	A217	$13 multi	4.50	4.00

No. 1061 contains one 35x45mm stamp.

Launch of First Manned Chinese Spacecraft — A218

No. 1062: a, Astronaut, Shenzhou spacecraft. b, Rocket lift-off.

2003, Oct. 16   Photo.   Perf. 13x13¼

1062	A218	$1.40 Pair, #a-b	2.00	2.00

A booklet containing No. 1062, People's Republic of China No. 3314 and Macao No. 1128a exists. The booklet sold for a premium over face value.

UNESCO World Heritage Sites in People's Republic of China — A219

Designs: $1.40, Potala Palace, vert. (27x75mm). $1.80, Imperial Palace of the Ming and Qing Dynasties. $2.40, Mausoleum of the First Qin Emperor. $2.50, Mount Huangshan, vert. $3, Old Town of Lijiang, vert. $5, Jiuzhaigou Valley (75x27mm).

Perf. 13¼ Syncopated
2003, Nov. 25   Litho.
Granite Paper

1063	A219	$1.40 multi	.60	.55
a.		Perf. 13¼x13¼x13 Syncopated	.60	.55

Perf. 13x13¼ Syncopated

1064	A219	$1.80 multi	.75	.70
a.		Perf. 13x13¼x12½x13 Syncopated	.75	.70

1065	A219	$2.40 multi	.90	.85
a.		Perf. 12½x13¼ Syncopated	.90	.85

Perf. 13 Syncopated

1066	A219	$2.50 multi	1.05	.90
a.		Perf. 13x13x13¼ Syncopated	1.05	.90
b.		Perf. 13¼x13x13x13 Syncopated	1.05	.90
c.		Perf. 13¼x13x13¼x13¼ Syncopated	1.05	.90
1067	A219	$3 multi	1.25	1.10
a.		Perf. 12½x13x13 Syncopated	1.25	1.10

Perf. 13x12¾ Syncopated

1068	A219	$5 multi	2.00	1.75
a.		Perf. 13x12¾x13 and 13¼x13 Syncopated	2.00	1.75
b.		Perf. 13 Syncopated	2.00	1.75
c.		Miniature sheet (see note below)	22.50	22.50
		Nos. 1063-1068 (6)	6.55	5.85

No. 1068c contains one each of Nos. 1063, 1064, 1065, 1066a, 1066b, 1066c, 1067a, 1068b and two each of Nos. 1063, 1064a, 1065a, 1067 and 1068a. Perfs for the minor varieties are for the measurement that comprises the longest part of each side, as the sides of some stamps have sections with varying perf measurements. Approximately one half of the bottom row of perfs on No. 1068a is perf. 13 while the other half is perf. 13¼.

Development of Public Housing — A220

Various buildings.

Perf. 13¼x13 Syncopated
2003, Dec. 11   Photo.
Granite Paper

1069	A220	$1.40 org & multi	.60	.45
a.		Tete-beche pair	1.20	.90
1070	A220	$2.40 yel & multi	.85	.70
a.		Tete-beche pair	1.75	1.40
1071	A220	$3 pur & multi	1.50	.95
a.		Tete-beche pair	3.00	1.90
1072	A220	$5 red & multi	2.25	1.50
a.		Tete-beche pair	4.50	3.00
		Nos. 1069-1072 (4)	5.20	3.60

New Year 2004 (Year of the Monkey) — A221

Various monkeys: $1.40, $2.40, $3, $5.

Perf. 13½x13¼ Syncopated
2004, Jan. 4   Litho.
Granite Paper

1073-1076	A221	Set of 4	4.00	4.00
1076a		Souvenir sheet of 1, imperf.	2.25	2.25
1076b		Souvenir sheet, #1073-1076	4.00	4.00

See Nos. 1253a, 1431e, 1479e, 1480e.

Souvenir Sheet

New Year 2004 (Year of the Monkey) A222

No. 1077: a, Ram. b, Monkey.

Litho. & Embossed with Foil Application
2004, Jan. 4   Perf. 13¼

1077	A222	$50 Sheet of 2, #a-b	35.00	35.00

HONG KONG

Souvenir Sheets

New Year Puddings and Greeting A223

New Year Puddings With Two Greetings — A224

New Year Parade A225

Jade A226

Fire Dragon Dance A227

No. 1079: a, Same Chinese text as on No. 1078 when viewed from directly above (top character with long curved line at bottom). b, Text different from that on No. 1078 when viewed from directly above.

2004 Litho. Perf. 13¼ Syncopated
Granite Paper

1078	A223	$10 multi	4.00	4.00
1079	A224	$10 Sheet of 2, #a-b	5.00	5.00
1080	A225	$10 multi	4.00	4.00
1081	A226	$10 multi	4.00	4.00
1082	A227	$10 multi	4.00	4.00
	Nos. 1078-1082 (5)		21.00	21.00

2004 Hong Kong Stamp Expo. Issued: Nos. 1078-1079, 1/30; No. 1080, 1/31; No. 1081, 2/1; No. 1082, 2/2.

Nos. 1079a and 1079b show the same two Chinese texts, but the texts appear different depending on the angle at which one views the stamps. Under magnification it can be seen that the two Chinese texts are printed differently to achieve this effect.

Landmarks Type of 1999 With Red Violet Denomination and Country Name

No. 1083: a, Museum of Tea Ware. b, St. John's Cathedral. c, Legislative Council Building. d, Tai Fu Tai. e, Wong Tai Sin Temple. f, Victoria Harbor. g, Hong Kong Railway Museum. h, Tsim Sha Tsui Clock Tower. i, Hong Kong Stadium. j, Western Market. k, Happy Valley Racecourse. l, Kowloon-Canton Railway. m, Repulse Bay. n, Chi Lin Nunnery. o, Peak Tower. p, Buddha at Po Lin Monastery. q, Aw Boon Haw Gardens. r, Tsing Ma Bridge. s, Hong Kong Cultural Center. t, Hong Kong Convention and Exhibition Center. u, Hong Kong Intl. Airport.

Perf. 13x13¾ Syncopated
2004, Feb. 3   Photo.
Granite Paper

1083		Sheet of 21	10.00	10.00
a.-u.	A172 $1.40 Any single, red vio & multi (23x27mm)		.45	.45

2004 Hong Kong Stamp Expo.

Rugby Sevens — A228

Perf. 13¼x14¼ Syncopated
2004, Feb. 25   Litho.
Granite Paper

1084-1087	A228	Set of 4	4.25	4.25
1087a		Block of 4, #1084-1087	5.25	5.25

No. 1087a printed in sheets of four blocks.

Children's Games and Activities A229

Designs: $1.40, Scissors, Paper, Stone. $2.40, Chinese chess. $3, Blowing bubbles. $5, Hopscotch.

2004, Apr. 7   Granite Paper

1088-1091	A229	Set of 4	4.00	3.50
1091a		Block of 4, #1088-1091	4.00	4.00

No. 1091a printed in sheets of four blocks.

Souvenir Sheet

Chen Clan Academy A230

Perf. 13½x13¼ Syncopated
2004, May 6

1092	A230	$10 multi	4.00	3.50

See No. 1456g.

Trams in Hong Kong, Cent. — A231

Various trams and tickets: $1.40, Green ticket. $2.40, Brown ticket. $3, Blue ticket. No. 1096, $5, Yellow ticket. No. 1097, Olive ticket.

2004, May 27   Granite Paper

1093-1096	A231	Set of 4	4.00	3.50
1096a		Souvenir sheet, #1093-1096	4.00	4.00

Souvenir Sheet

1097	A231	$5 multi	1.60	1.60

People's Liberation Army Forces of Hong Kong — A232

Inscriptions: $1.40, The Powerful and Civilized Military Force. $1.80, Social Services. $2.40, Open Day. $2.50, Army. $3, Navy. $5, Air Force.

Perf. 13¼x14 Syncopated
2004, June 30   Litho.
Granite Paper

1098	A232	$1.40 multi	.45	.45
a.		Booklet pane of 4	2.60	
1099	A232	$1.80 multi	.65	.65
a.		Booklet pane of 4	3.25	
1100	A232	$2.40 multi	.80	.80
a.		Booklet pane of 4	4.25	
1101	A232	$2.50 multi	.85	.85
a.		Booklet pane of 4	4.75	
1102	A232	$3 multi	1.05	1.05
a.		Booklet pane of 4	5.50	
1103	A232	$5 multi	1.60	1.60
a.		Booklet pane of 4	8.50	
	Complete booklet, #1098a-1103a		29.00	
	Nos. 1098-1103 (6)		5.40	5.40

Complete booklet sold for $85.

Relay Race A233

Diving A234

Volleyball A235

Cycling A236

Badminton — A237

No. 1104: a, Runners in blocks. b, Runners. c, Runner taking baton. d, Runner at finish.
No. 1105: a, Diver on board. b, Diver with legs tucked in. c, Diver with arms and legs extended. d, Diver entering water.
No. 1106: a, Player making save. b, Player leaping to get ball. c, Player striking ball above net. d, Player trying to block ball.
No. 1107: a, Cyclists, denomination at left. b, Cyclist at right, denomination at left. c, Cyclists, denomination at right. d, Cyclist with arms extended.
No. 1108: a, Bird above head, racquet at shoulder level. b, Bird at shoulder level, racquet at knee level. c, Bird and racquet above head. d, Player with face covered by arm.

Perf. 13½x13¼ Syncopated
2004, July 20   Granite Paper

1104	A233	$1.40 Horiz. strip of 4, #a-d	1.75	1.75
1105	A234	$1.40 Horiz. strip of 4, #a-d	1.75	1.75
1106	A235	$1.40 Horiz. strip of 4, #a-d	1.75	1.75
1107	A236	$1.40 Horiz. strip of 4, #a-d	1.75	1.75
1108	A237	$1.40 Horiz. strip of 4, #a-d	1.75	1.75
e.		Miniature sheet, #1104-1108	8.75	8.75

Souvenir Sheet

2004 Summer Olympics, Athens — A238

No. 1109: a, Runner without clothes. b, Runner with clothes.

2004, Aug. 13   Granite Paper

1109	A238	$5 Sheet of 2, #a-b	4.00	4.00

Deng Xiaoping (1904-97), Chinese Leader — A239

No. 1110: a, Saluting flags. b, Watching fireworks.
$10, Three photographs.

2004, Aug. 22   Perf. 13x13¼

1110	A239	$1.40 Horiz. pair, #a-b	1.00	1.00

Souvenir Sheet

1111	A239	$10 multi	4.25	4.25

Hong Kong Currency A240

Obverse and reverse of: $1.40, 1863 one mil bronze coin. $2.40, 1866 twenty cent silver coin. $3, 1935 one dollar banknotes. No. 1115, $5, 1997 one thousand dollar gold coin commemorating establishment of Special Administrative Region.
No. 1116, $5, 1993 ten dollar coin.

Perf. 13¼x14 Syncopated
2004, Sept. 2   Granite Paper

1112-1115	A240	Set of 4	4.25	4.25
1115a		Miniature sheet, #1112-1115	4.25	4.25

Souvenir Sheet

1116	A240	$5 multi	2.50	2.50

Pearl River Delta Region Development A241

Designs: $1.40, Men and bridge. $2.40, Men and crane. $3, Tourist attractions. $5, Men and buildings.

2004, Oct. 19   Granite Paper

1117-1120	A241	Set of 4	4.00	4.00
1120a		Block of 4, #1117-1120	4.75	4.75

No. 1120a printed in sheets of 4 blocks.

Mushrooms — A242

Designs: $1.40, Straw mushrooms. $2.40, Red-orange mushrooms. $3, Violet marasmius. No. 1124, $5, Lingzhi mushrooms. No. 1125, Hexagon fungi.

Perf. 13½x13¼ Syncopated
2004, Nov. 23   Granite Paper

1121-1124	A242	Set of 4	4.25	4.25
1124a		Souvenir sheet, #1121-1124	4.25	4.25

Souvenir Sheet

1125	A242	$5 multi	3.75	3.75

Letters of the Alphabet A243

Nos. 1126 and 1127 — Upper half of letters made with common household items: a, Clothespin. b, Scissors. c, Lamp. d, Plastic cap for glue bottle. e, Steaming rack. f, Caliper with ruler. g, Bolt of padlock. h, Bamboo ladder. i, Flashlight. j, Toilet brush. k, Stapler. l, Sock. m, Draftsman's triangle. n, Nail clippers. o, Rubber band. p, Strainer. q, Link from chain. r, Sunglasses. s, Clothes hanger. t, Wooden broom. u, Sandals. v, Compass. w, Corkscrew. x, Faucet. y, Fork. z, Paint roller.

Perf. 13¼x13 Syncopated
2005, Jan. 4   Litho.
Granite Paper (#1126)

1126	A243	Sheet of 30 (see footnote)	13.00	13.00
a.-z.		$1.40 Any single	.45	.45

HONG KONG

Self-Adhesive
Serpentine Die Cut 12½ Syncopated

1127	A243	Sheet of 30 (see footnote)	14.00	
a.-z.		$1.40 Any single	.45	.45

Each sheet contains one of each letter and an additional example of a, e, i and o stamps. Covers were prepared in 2006 with se-tenant strips spelling "KUNG," "HEI," "FAT" and "CHOY," which are not found in No. 1126.

New Year 2005 (Year of the Rooster) — A244

Various roosters with background colors of: $1.40, Orange. $2.40, Green. $3, Dark red. $5, Blue.

2005, Jan. 30 Perf. 14¼ Syncopated
Granite Paper

1128-1131	A244	Set of 4	10.00	10.00
1128a		Dated "2011," perf. 13½x13¼ syncopated (1431)	.50	.50
1131a		Souvenir sheet of 1, imperf.	7.50	7.50
1131b		Souvenir sheet, #1128-1131	10.00	10.00

Issued: No. 1128a, 1/22/11. See Nos. 1253b, 1479f, 1480f.

Souvenir Sheet

New Year 2005 (Year of the Rooster) A245

No. 1132: a, Monkey. b, Rooster.

Litho. & Embossed With Foil Application

2005, Jan. 30 Perf. 13¼

1132	A245	$50 Sheet of 2, #a-b	50.00	50.00

Fairy Tales by Hans Christian Andersen (1805-75) — A246

Designs: $1.40, The Ugly Duckling. $2.40, The Little Mermaid. $3, The Little Match Girl. $5, The Emperor's New Clothes.

Perf. 13¾ Syncopated
2005, Mar. 22 Litho. & Embossed
Granite Paper

1133-1136	A246	Set of 4	10.00	10.00
1133a		Souvenir sheet of 4	6.50	6.50
1134a		Souvenir sheet of 4	11.00	11.00
1135a		Souvenir sheet of 4	14.75	14.75
1136a		Souvenir sheet of 4	24.00	24.00

Souvenir Sheet

Hong Kong Skyline, Sydney Opera House A247

Perf. 13½ Syncopated
2005, Apr. 21 Litho.
Granite Paper

1137	A247	$10 multi	4.00	4.00

Pacific Explorer 2005 World Stamp Expo, Sydney.

Goldfish A248

Designs: $1.40, Variegated pearl-scale. $2.40, Red and white swallow-tail. $3, Pale bronze egg-phoenix. No. 1141, $5, Blue wenyu.
No. 1142, $5, Red and white dragon-eye.

Perf. 13¼x14 Syncopated
2005, May 12 Granite Paper

1138-1141	A248	Set of 4	4.25	4.25
1141a		Souvenir sheet, #1138-1141	4.25	4.25

Souvenir Sheet

1142	A248	$5 multi	9.00	9.00

No. 1142 contains one 45x35mm stamp.

Maritime Expeditions of Zheng He, 600th Anniv. — A249

No. 1143 — Ships and: a, Zheng He (1371-1433), explorer. b, Giraffe, ceramics. c, Compass wheel.
$10, Zheng He on ship.

2005, June 28 Perf. 13x13¼

1143		Horiz. strip of 3	2.10	2.10
a.-c.	A249	$1.40 Any single	.70	.70

Souvenir Sheet
Perf. 13¼

1144	A249	$10 multi	5.00	5.00

No. 1144 contains one 50x30mm stamp.

Creative Industries A250

Designs: $1.40, Circles, squares and triangles (advertising). $2.40, Numerals, letters and symbols (computer and digital industries). $3, Vertical and horizontal lines (broadcasting industries). $5, Curved brushstrokes (arts and crafts).

Perf. 14x14¼ Syncopated
2005, July 21 Litho.
Granite Paper

1145-1148	A250	Set of 4	4.50	4.50
1148a		Block of 4 with selvage, #1145-1148	4.50	4.50
1148b		Booklet pane, 2 #1148a	9.00	
		Complete booklet, 2 #1148b	18.00	

Each block of 4 in the booklet has a different arrangement. Rouletting separates the blocks within each booklet pane.

Great Inventions of Ancient China — A251

Designs: $1.40, Compass. $2.40, Printing. $3, Gunpowder. $5, Papermaking.

Perf. 13¼x14¼ Syncopated
2005, Aug. 18

1149-1152	A251	Set of 4	4.25	4.25
1152a		Miniature sheet, 4 each #1149-1152	17.00	17.00

Opening of Hong Kong Disneyland — A252

Designs: $1.40, Mickey and Minnie Mouse. $2.40, Dumbo. $3, Simba and Nala. No. 1156, $5, Pluto.
Nos. 1157, 1158, Mickey Mouse.

Perf. 13¾x13½ Syncopated
2005, Sept. 12 Litho.
Granite Paper (#1153-1157)

1153-1156	A252	Set of 4	5.00	5.00
1156a		Souvenir sheet, #1153-1156	5.00	5.00

Souvenir Sheets

1157	A252	$5 multi	4.00	4.00

Litho. & Embossed with Foil Application

1158	A252	$50 gold & multi	24.50	24.50

Souvenir Sheet

Qiantang Tidal Bore A253

Perf. 13¼ Syncopated
2005, Sept. 16 Litho.

1159	A253	$10 multi	5.00	5.00

See No. 1456a.

Fishing Villages A254

Designs: $1.40, Tai O, Hong Kong. $2.40, Aldeia da Carrasqueira, Portugal. $3, Tai O, diff. $5, Aldeia da Carrasqueira, diff.

Perf. 14¼x14 Syncopated
2005, Oct. 18

1160-1163	A254	Set of 4	4.50	4.50
1163a		Miniature sheet, 4 each #1160-1163	18.00	18.00

See Portugal Nos. 2767-2768.
No. 1163a was printed in sheets of eight pairs.

Popular Singers — A255

Designs: $1.40, Wong Ka Kui. $1.80, Danny Chan. $2.40, Roman Tam. $3, Leslie Cheung. $5, Anita Mui.

Perf. 13½x13¼ Syncopated
2005, Nov. 8 Granite Paper

1164-1168	A255	Set of 5	5.00	5.00

Because of concerns about the licensing of the images of the singers in foreign countries, the philatelic bureau did not make Nos. 1164-1168 available by mail order to foreign customers. The stamps were freely available to any purchasers over the counter.

New Year 2006 (Year of the Dog) — A256

Designs: $1.40, Golden retriever. $2.40, Pekingese. $3, German shepherd. $5, Beagle.

Perf. 13½x13¼ Syncopated
2006, Jan. 15 Litho.
Granite Paper

1169-1172	A256	Set of 4	4.00	4.00
1172a		Souvenir sheet of #1172, imperf.	2.75	2.75
1172b		Souvenir sheet, #1169-1172	5.00	5.00

See Nos. 1253c, 1431f, 1479g, 1480g.

Souvenir Sheet

New Year 2006 (Year of the Dog) A257

No. 1173: a, Rooster. b, Dog.

Litho. & Embossed with Foil Application
2006, Jan. 15 Perf. 13½x13¼

1173	A257	$50 Sheet of 2, #a-b	40.00	40.00

Chinese Lanterns A258

No. 1174: a, $1.40, Lotus Fairy lantern. $1.80, Narcissus lantern. $2.40, Peacock lantern.
$5, Boys holding Dragon lantern.

Perf. 12¾x13¼ Syncopated
2006, Feb. 12 Litho.
Granite Paper (#1174)

1174	A258	Horiz. strip of 3, #a-c	2.75	2.75

Souvenir Sheet
Perf. 13¼ Syncopated

1175	A258	$5 multi	3.00	3.00

No. 1175 contains one 35x46mm stamp.

Teddy Bears in Costumes — A259

Teddy bears in various costumes.

Perf. 13¾ Syncopated
2006, Mar. 30 Granite Paper

1176	A259	$1.40 multi	.50	.50
1177	A259	$1.80 multi	.75	.75
a.		Booklet pane, #1176-1177	2.00	
1178	A259	$2.40 multi	.85	.85
1179	A259	$2.50 multi	.90	.90
a.		Booklet pane, #1178-1179	3.00	
1180	A259	$3 multi	1.15	1.15
1181	A259	$5 multi	1.80	1.80
a.		Booklet pane, #1180-1181, 1179a, 1181a	4.75	
		Complete booklet, #1177a, 1179a, 1181a		9.75
b.		Souvenir sheet, #1176-1181, + central label	6.00	6.00
		Nos. 1176-1181 (6)	5.95	5.95

Complete booklet sold for $30.

Souvenir Sheet

Gongbei Rock, Mount Taishan A260

2006, May 4 Perf. 14¼ Syncopated
Granite Paper

1182	A260	$10 multi	4.25	4.25

See No. 1456i.

Souvenir Sheet

Washington 2006 World Philatelic Exhibition — A261

HONG KONG

Perf. 13¼x12¾ Syncopated
2006, May 27   **Granite Paper**
1183 A261 $10 multi   3.75 3.75

Chinese Idioms — A262

Idioms: $1.40, Respect makes successful marriage. $2.40, Reading is always rewarding. $3, Prepare for success. $5, All in the same boat.

Perf. 13¾ Syncopated
2006, June 15   **Granite Paper**
1184-1187 A262 Set of 4   4.00 4.00
1187a   Souvenir sheet, #1184-1187 5.00 5.00

Attractions in Hong Kong's Districts — A263

Designs: No. 1188, $1.40, Central Police Station Historical Compound, Peak Tram, International Finance Center, Central and Western District. No. 1189, $1.40, Victoria Park, Island Eastern Corridor, Hong Kong Museum of Coastal Defense, Eastern District. No. 1190, $1.40, Floating restaurant, Murray House, Ocean Park, Southern District. No. 1191, $1.40, Hong Kong Convention and Exhibition Center, Old Wan Chai Post Office, Lovers' Rock, Wan Chai District. No. 1192, $1.40, Hong Kong Cultural Center, Temple Street, Yuen Po Bird Garden, Yau Tsim Mong District. No. 1193, $1.40, Wong Tai Sin Temple, Lion Rock, Chi Lin Nunnery, Wong Tai Sin District. No. 1194, $1.40, Lei Yue Mun Seafood Bazaar, buildings, Child-giving Rocks, Kwun Tong District. No. 1195, $1.40, Computer shopping center, Lingnan Garden, Festival Walk, Sham Shui Po District. No. 1196, $1.40, Kowloon Walled City Park, Wonderful Worlds of Whampoa, Sung Wong Toi, Kowloon City District. No. 1197, $1.40, Seafood Street, Tai Long Wan, Lions Nature Education Center Shell House, Sai Kung District. No. 1198, $1.40, Lantau Link View Point, Kwai Chung Container Terminals, Tsing Ma Bridge, Kwai Tsing District. No. 1199, $1.40, Lookout Tower, Lam Tsuen Wishing Tree, Tai Po Waterfront Park, Tai Po District. No. 1200, $1.40, Fung Ying Seen Koon, Chung Ying Street, Pak Hok Lam, North District. No. 1201, $1.40, Sam Tung Uk Museum, Yuen Yuen Institute, Tai Mo Shan Country Park, Tsuen Wan District. No. 1202, $1.40, Amah Rock, Shing Mun River Promenade, Che Kung Temple, Sha Tin District. No. 1203, $1.40, Hong Kong Gold Coast, Ching Chung Koon, Tsing Shan Monastery, Tuen Mun District. No. 1204, $1.40, Mai Po Nature Reserve, birds over farm, Chinese cakes, Yuen Long District. No. 1205, $1.40, Tian Tan Buddha, Cheung Chau Bun Festival, Tai O, Islands District.

2006, July 18   Perf. 13½ Syncopated
Granite Paper
1188-1205 A263 Set of 18   8.00 8.00
1205a   Souvenir sheet, #1188-1205 8.00 8.00

Fireworks A264

Designs: No. 1206, $5, No. 1208a, $50, Fireworks over Hong Kong Harbor. No. 1207, $5, No. 1208b, $50, Fireworks over Prater Ferris Wheel, Vienna, Austria.

2006, Aug. 22 **Litho.** **Perf. 14**
1206-1207 A264 Set of 2   3.00 3.00

Souvenir Sheet
Photo. With Glass Beads Affixed
1208 A264 $50 Sheet of 2, #a-
             b   35.00 35.00
   c. Sheet, Austria #2060b,
       Hong Kong #1208a   40.00 40.00
See Austria No. 2060.
No. 1208c sold for €12.40 in Austria and for $120 in Hong Kong, and is identical to Austria No. 2060c.

Intl. Day of Peace — A265

Chinese characters and: $1.40, Flower and "Love." $1.80, Origami crane and "Peace." $2.40, Four-leaf clover and "Hope." $3, Tree and "Caring." $5, Earth and "Harmony."

Perf. 13½x13¼ Syncopated
2006, Sept. 21   **Litho.**
Granite Paper
1209-1213 A265 Set of 5   4.50 4.50
1213a   Souvenir sheet, #1209-1213 4.50 4.50

Government Vehicles A266

Designs: $1.40, Correctional Services security bus. $1.80, Customs Department X-ray scanning vehicle. $2.40, Fire Department hydraulic platform pumper truck. $2.50, Government Flying Service Super Puma helicopter. $3, Police Department traffic patrol motorcycle. $5, Immigration Department launch.

Perf. 13¼x14½ Syncopated
2006, Oct. 19   **Litho.**
Granite Paper
1214-1219 A266 Set of 6   5.50 5.50
1219a   Sheet, 3 each #1214-1219 16.50 16.50

Dr. Sun Yat-sen (1866-1925), Republic of China President A267

Photographs from: $1.40, 1883. $2.40, 1912. $3, 1916. No. 1223, $5, 1922. No. 1224, $5, 1924 (hands visible).

Perf. 13¼x13 Syncopated
2006, Nov. 12   **Granite Paper**
1220-1223 A267 Set of 4   4.25 4.25
Souvenir Sheet
1224 A267 $5 multi   3.00 3.00
A booklet containing two panes, one containing Nos. 1220-1221, and one containing Nos. 1222-1223 sold for $25.

Heartwarming — A268

No. 1225, Hearts. No. 1226, Bottles. No. 1227, Flowers. No. 1228, Drink glasses.

Perf. 13½ Syncopated
2006, Nov. 28   **Granite Paper**
Inscribed "Local Mail Postage"
1225 A268 ($1.40) multi   .40   .40
   a. Sheet of 8 + 8 labels   3.25 3.25
1226 A268 ($1.40) multi   .40   .40
   a. Sheet of 20 + 21 labels   12.50 12.50
Inscribed "Air Mail Postage"
1227 A268 ($3) multi   .90   .90
1228 A268 ($3) multi   .90   .90
   a. Sheet, 5 each #1225-1228,
       + 21 labels   13.00 13.00
   b. Sheet of 20 + 21 labels   27.50 27.50
Nos. 1225-1228 (4)   2.60 2.60
Issued: Nos. 1226, 1228b, 5/2/08; No. 1225a, 2/14/12. Labels on Nos. 1225a, 1226a and 1228b could not be personalized. Nos. 1226a and 1228b sold as a set for $154.
No. 1225a is impregnated with a rose scent.

Birds — A269

Designs: 10c, White-bellied sea eagle. 20c, Collared scops owl. 50c, Scarlet minivet. $1, Common kingfisher. $1.40, Fork-tailed sunbird. $1.80, Roseate tern. $1.90, Black-faced spoonbill. $2, Little egret. $2.40, Greater painted snipe. $2.50, Barn swallow. $3, Red-whiskered bulbul. $5, Long-tailed shrike. $10, White wagtail. $13, Northern shoveler. $20, Common magpie. $50, Dalmatian pelican.

Perf. 13x13¾ Syncopated
2006, Dec. 31   **Photo.**
Granite Paper
Size: 22x26mm
1229 A269 10c multi   .25   .25
1230 A269 20c multi   .25   .25
1231 A269 50c multi   .25   .25
1232 A269 $1 multi   .25   .25
1233 A269 $1.40 multi   .35   .35
   a. Booklet pane of 10   3.50
       Complete booklet, #1233a   3.50
1234 A269 $1.80 multi   .45   .45
   a. Booklet pane of 10   4.50
       Complete booklet, #1234a   4.50
1235 A269 $1.90 multi   .50   .50
1236 A269 $2 multi   .55   .55
1237 A269 $2.40 multi   .60   .60
   a. Booklet pane of 10   6.00
       Complete booklet, #1237a   6.00
1238 A269 $2.50 multi   .65   .65
1239 A269 $3 multi   .80   .80
   a. Booklet pane of 10   8.00
       Complete booklet, #1239a   8.00
1240 A269 $5 multi   1.40 1.40
   a. Miniature sheet, #1229-1240 6.25 6.25
   b. Booklet pane, #1229-1240   6.25
       Complete booklet, #1240b   6.25
Size: 25x30mm
Perf. 13½x13¼ Syncopated
1241 A269 $10 multi   2.60 2.60
   a. Souvenir sheet of 1   2.60 2.60
1242 A269 $13 multi   3.50 3.50
1243 A269 $20 multi   5.25 5.25
1244 A269 $50 multi   13.00 13.00
   a. Souvenir sheet, #1241-1244 25.00 25.00
Nos. 1229-1244 (16)   30.65 30.65
Coil Stamps
Size: 17x21mm
Perf. 14¾x13½ Syncopated
1245 A269 $1.40 multi   .60   .60
1246 A269 $1.80 multi   .70   .70
1247 A269 $2.40 multi   .95   .95
1248 A269 $3 multi   1.25 1.25
Nos. 1245-1248 (4)   3.50 3.50
Nos. 1241-1244 have microperforations around denominations.
Issued: No. 1241a, 9/21/10.

New Year 2007 (Year of the Pig) — A270

Various pigs with background colors of: $1.40, Brown. $2.40, Orange red. $3, Green. $5, Rose.

2007, Feb. 4 Perf. 13½ Syncopated
Granite Paper
1249-1252 A270 Set of 4   3.25 3.25
1249a   Dated "2011," perf. 13½x13¼
           syncopated (1431)   .35   .35
1252a   Souvenir sheet of #1252, im-
           perf.   2.00 2.00
1252b   Souvenir sheet, #1249-1252 3.75 3.75
Issued: No. 1249a, 1/22/11. See Nos. 1253d, 1479h, 1480h.

New Year Types of 2004-07
2007, Feb. 4 **Litho.** Perf. 13x13½
Flocked Paper
1253 Block of 4   11.00 11.00
   a. A221 $10 Like #1075   2.75 2.75
   b. A244 $10 Like #1128   2.75 2.75
   c. A256 $10 Like #1170   2.75 2.75
   d. A270 $10 Like #1251   2.75 2.75

Souvenir Sheet

New Year 2007 (Year of the Pig) A271

Litho. & Embossed With Foil Application
2007, Feb. 4   Perf. 13¼
1254 A271 $50 Sheet of 2, #a-
             b   27.50 27.50

Scouting, Cent. — A272

Designs: $1.40, Campfire, Lord Robert Baden-Powell. $2.40, Hong Kong Scouting emblem, compass. $3, Backpack, knot. $5, Scouts, tent.

Litho. With Foil Application
Perf. 13¼x14¼ Syncopated
2007, Mar. 1   **Granite Paper**
1255-1258 A272 Set of 4   3.50 3.50
1258a   Souvenir sheet, #1255-1258 4.25 4.25

Children's Games and Puzzles — A273

Designs: $1.40, Find the difference between the two rabbits. $1.80, Color in the dotted areas. $2.40, Maze. $2.50, Follow lines to hunt for Easter Eggs. $3, Find the ten rabbits. $5, Look for a star.

Perf. 13¾ Syncopated
2007, Mar. 22   **Litho.**
Granite Paper
1259-1264 A273 Set of 6   4.50 4.50
1264a   Souvenir sheet, #1259-1264 4.50 4.50
A booklet containing three panes, containing Nos. 1259-1260, 1261-1262, and 1263-1264 respectively, sold for $36.

Souvenir Sheet

Stone Forest, Shilin A274

Perf. 13¼x14¼ Syncopated
2007, May 3   **Granite Paper**
1265 A274 $10 multi   3.00 3.00
See No. 1456h.

Chinese Martial Arts — A275

Designs: $1.40, Southern Lion Dance. $2.40, Nanquan. $3, Northern Lion Dance. $5, Beitui.

Litho. with Foil Application
2007, May 22
1266-1269 A275 Set of 4   3.25 3.25
1269a   Souvenir sheet, #1266-1269 3.25 3.25

Butterflies — A276

Designs: $1.40, Faunis eumeus. $1.80, Prioneris philonome. $2.40, Polyura nepenthes. $3, Tajuria maculata. $5, Acraea issoria.

No. 1254: a, Beagle. b, Pig and piglet.

HONG KONG

Perf. 13½ Syncopated
2007, June 14   Litho.
Granite Paper
1270-1274 A276 Set of 5   3.75   3.75

A booklet containing two panes, one containing Nos. 1270-1272 and the other containing Nos. 1273-1274, sold for $38.

Return of Hong Kong to China, 10th Anniv. — A277

Perf. 13x12¾ Syncopated
2007, July 1   Photo.
1275 A277 $1.40 multi   .80   .80

A souvenir sheet containing No. 1275 and People's Republic of China Nos. 3594-3596 sold for $12.95.

A278

Hong Kong Special Administrative Region, 10th Anniv. — A279

Designs: $1.40, Ten children with joined hands. $1.80, Banner on Hong Kong Heritage Museum. $2.40, Vehicles on Tsing Ma Bridge. $2.50, Ten birds over Hong Kong Wetland Park. $3, Two International Finance Center Building and Moon. $5, Fireworks over Hong Kong.

No. 1282: a, "7" over Bank of China Tower, fireworks over Cheung Kong Center. b, Fireworks over smaller buildings. c, Fireworks over smaller buildings, Two International Finance Center Building at right.

Perf. 13½x14¼ Syncopated
2007, July 1   Granite Paper   Litho.
1276-1281 A278 Set of 6   4.75   4.75

Litho. With Foil Application and Hologram
Perf. 13½
1282 A279 $10 Sheet of 3, #a-c   8.25   8.25

Souvenir Sheet

Bangkok 2007 Asian International Stamp Exhibition — A280

Perf. 13½x14¼ Syncopated
2007, Aug. 3   Litho.
Granite Paper
1283 A280 $10 multi   3.00   3.00

Civic Education A281

Designs: $1.40, Human rights. $2.40, Rule of law. $3, Social participation. $5, Corporate citizenship.

2007, Aug. 23   Perf. 13 Syncopated
Granite Paper
1284-1287 A281 Set of 4   3.25   3.25
  1287a   Miniature sheet, 4 each #1284-1287   15.00   15.00

Declared Monuments A282

Designs: $1.40, Tin Hau Temple, Causeway Bay. $1.80, Old Wan Chai Post Office. $2.40, Former Central Police Station Compound. $2.50, Former Yamen Building of Kowloon Walled City. $3, Kun Lung Gate Tower, Lung Yeuk Tau. $5, Tang Lung Chau Lighthouse.

Litho. & Engr.
2007, Sept. 20   Perf. 14x13¼
Granite Paper
1288-1293 A282 Set of 6   4.50   4.50
  1293a   Miniature sheet, #1288-1293   4.50   4.50

Christmas — A283

Designs: $1.40, Stocking. $2.40, Gingerbread man-shaped egg tart. $3, Bell decorated with neon lights. $5, Snowman with Chinese vest.

2007, Oct. 11   Litho.   Perf. 13x13½
Granite Paper
1294-1297 A283 Set of 4   3.25   3.25

Woodwork A284

Designs: No. 1298, $5, Zitan armchair with dragon design, China, denomination at left. No. 1299, $5, Modern Finnish bowls, denomination at right.

Perf. 13½x14¼ Syncopated
2007, Nov. 2   Granite Paper
1298-1299 A284 Set of 2   3.00   3.00
  1299a   Souvenir sheet, #1298-1299   3.25   3.25

See Finland No. 1298.

Heartwarming — A285

Designs: No. 1300, Birds and flowers. No. 1301, Firecrackers. No. 1302, Gifts and balloons. No. 1303, Slippers.

Perf. 13½ Syncopated
2007, Dec. 28   Litho.
Granite Paper
Inscribed "Local Mail Postage"
1300 A285 ($1.40) multi   .40   .40
1301 A285 ($1.40) multi   .40   .40
Inscribed "Air Mail Postage"
1302 A285 ($3) multi   1.00   1.00
1303 A285 ($3) multi   1.00   1.00
  a.   Sheet, 5 each #1300-1303 + 21 labels   14.00   14.00

New Year 2008 (Year of the Rat) — A286

Various rats with background colors of: $1.40, Blue. $2.40, Green. $3, Orange red. $5, Brown.

Perf. 13½x13¼ Syncopated
2008, Jan. 26   Litho.
Granite Paper
1304-1307 A286 Set of 4   4.00   4.00
  1304a   Dated "2011" (1431)   .45   .45
  1307a   Souvenir sheet of #1307, imperf.   2.40   2.40
  1307b   Souvenir sheet, #1304-1307   4.50   4.50

Issued: No. 1304a, 1/22/11. See Nos. 1432a, 1479i, 1480i.

Souvenir Sheet

New Year 2008 (Year of the Rat) A287

No. 1308: a, Pig. b, Rat.

Litho. & Embossed With Foil Application
2008, Jan. 26   Perf. 13¼
1308 A287 $50 Sheet of 2, #a-b   30.00   30.00

Souvenir Sheet

Huanglong — A288

Perf. 14¼ Syncopated
2008, Feb. 28   Litho.
Granite Paper
1309 A288 $10 multi   3.00   3.00

See No. 1456d.

Flowers A289

Designs: $1.40, Chinese hibiscus. $1.80, Tree cotton. $2.40, Allamandas. $2.50, Azaleas. $3, Lotus. $5, Morning glories.

Perf. 13½x13¼ Syncopated
2008, Mar. 14   Granite Paper
1310-1315 A289 Set of 6   6.00   6.00
  1315a   Souvenir sheet, #1310-1315   6.00   6.00

Paper Folding Art — A290

Designs: $1.40, Bauhinia blossoms. $1.80, Bear, horiz. $2.40, Lunar New Year decorations. $2.50, Lotus flowers and rainbow, horiz. $3, Koalas, monkey with banana. $5, Christmas party scene, horiz.

Perf. 14¼x13½, 13½x14¼ Syncopated
2008, May 22
1316-1321 A290 Set of 6   6.00   6.00
  1321a   Souvenir sheet, #1316-1321   6.00   6.00

Jellyfish — A291

Designs: $1.40, Flower hat jellyfish. $1.80, Octopus jellyfish, horiz. $2.40, Brown sea nettle. $2.50, Moon jellyfish, horiz. $3, Lion's mane jellyfish. $5, Pacific sea nettle.

Perf. 14¼ Syncopated
2008, June 12   Litho.
Granite Paper
1322-1327 A291 Set of 6   6.25   6.25
  1327a   Souvenir sheet, #1322-1327   6.25   6.25

Stamps have a glow-in-the-dark coating on the jellyfish illustrations. A booklet containing panes of Nos. 1322-1323, 1324-1325, and 1326-1327, sold for $36.

Giant Pandas — A292

Designs: $1.40, Ying Ying, Le Le, and hearts. $2.40, Ying Ying and leaves. $3, Le Le and panda heads. $5, Ying Ying, Le Le, and circles.

2008, July 1   Perf. 13¾ Syncopated
Granite Paper
1328-1331 A292 Set of 4   5.00   5.00
  1331a   Sheet, 2 each # 1328-1331, + 4 labels   10.00   10.00

Hong Kong, Venue for 2008 Summer Olympic Equestrian Events — A293

Designs: $1.40, Horse and rider jumping fence. $2.40, Dressage. $3, Horse and rider jumping over water obstacle. $5, Horse and rider at medal stand.

Perf. 13¼x14 Syncopated
2008, Aug. 9   Granite Paper
1332-1335 A293 Set of 4   4.00   4.00
  1335a   Souvenir sheet, #1332-1335   4.00   4.00

Souvenir Sheet

Praga 2008 World Stamp Exhibition — A294

Perf. 13¼x14¼ Syncopated
2008, Sept. 12   Litho.
Granite Paper
1336 A294 $10 multi   3.75   3.75

Big Head Buddha Mask, Hong Kong — A295

Chwibari Mask, Korea — A296

Perf. 13¼x14 Syncopated
2008, Nov. 6   Granite Paper
1337 A295 $5 multi   2.00   2.00
1338 A296 $5 multi   2.00   2.00
  a.   Souvenir sheet, #1337-1338   4.00   4.00

See South Korea No. 2299.

The Judiciary — A297

HONG KONG

Designs: $1.40, Statue of Justice. $2.40, Court of Final Appeal. $3, Judicial robes for various courts. $5, Chief Justice's mace.

Perf. 13¾ Syncopated
2008, Nov. 27   **Granite Paper**
1339-1342   A297   Set of 4   4.25   4.25
1342a   Souvenir sheet, #1339-1342   4.25   4.25

New Year 2009 (Year of the Ox) — A298

Various oxen with background colors of: $1.40, Purple. $2.40, Brown. $3, Green. $5, Blue.

Perf. 13½ x 13¼ Syncopated
2009, Jan. 17   Litho.
Granite Paper
1343-1346   A298   Set of 4   4.25   4.25
1346a   Souvenir sheet of #1346, imperf.   2.00   2.00
1346b   Souvenir sheet #1343-1346   4.25   4.25
See Nos. 1431g, 1432b, 1479j, 1480j.

Souvenir Sheet

New Year 2009 (Year of the Ox) A299

No. 1347: a, Rat. b, Ox.

Litho. & Embossed With Foil Application
2009, Jan. 17   Perf. 13¼
1347   A299 $50 Sheet of 2, #a-b   40.00   40.00

Souvenir Sheet

Mount Tianshan A300

Perf. 14¼ Syncopated
2009, Feb. 24   Litho.
Granite Paper
1348   A300 $10 multi   4.00   4.00
See No. 1456c.

Souvenir Sheet

Peony and Bauhinia Flowers A301

2009, Apr. 7   **Perf. 13¼ Syncopated**
Granite Paper
1349   A301 $5 multi   1.75   1.75
China 2009 World Stamp Exhibition, Luoyang.

Souvenir Sheet

Tangram Figure A302

2009, May 14   **Perf. 13¼**
Granite Paper
1350   A302 $50 multi + 2 labels   15.00   15.00
Hong Kong 2009 Intl. Stamp Exhibition.

Items in Hong Kong Museums — A303

Designs: $1.40, Poem by Wang Duo, Hong Kong Museum of Art. $1.80, Landscape, painting by Wang Yuanqi, Hong Kong Museum of Art. $2.40, Calligraphy by Wang Xizhi, Art Museum of the Chinese University of Hong Kong. $2.50, Bird in Moonlight, painting by Gao Qifeng, Hong Kong Heritage Museum. $3, Flower and Butterfly, fan painting by Ju Lian, Hong Kong Heritage Museum, horiz. (50x30mm). $5, Drawing by Gu Huai, University Museum and Art Gallery of the University of Hong Kong, horiz. (50x30mm).

Perf. 13½ x 13¼ Syncopated
2009, May 16   **Granite Paper**
1351-1356   A303   Set of 6   5.25   5.25
1356a   Souvenir sheet, #1351-1356   5.75   5.75

Heartwarming — A304

Designs: No. 1357, Flowers. No. 1358, Lion. No. 1359, Birthday hats. No. 1360, Butterflies and heart.

Perf. 13½ Syncopated
2009, June 25   **Granite Paper**
Inscribed "Local Mail Postage"
1357   A304   ($1.40) multi   .90   .90
1358   A304   ($1.40) multi   .90   .90
Inscribed "Air Mail Postage"
1359   A304   ($3) multi   2.00   2.00
1360   A304   ($3) multi   2.00   2.00
    a.   Sheet of 12, 3 each #1357-1360, + 12 labels   17.50   17.50
    Nos. 1357-1360 (4)   5.80   5.80
Labels on No. 1360a could not be personalized.

Customs and Excise Service, Cent. — A305

Designs: $1.40, Officer with drug-sniffing dog and baggage inspectors of 1960s. $2.40, Mobile x-ray vehicle scanner and Sheng Shui Customs Station, 1935. $3, Patrol boats. $5, Officers raising flag.

Perf. 13¼ x 13 Syncopated
2009, Sept. 17   Litho.
Granite Paper
1361-1364   A305   Set of 4   4.00   4.00
1364a   Souvenir sheet, #1361-1364   4.00   4.00
A booklet containing two panes, one with Nos. 1361-1362, and the other with Nos. 1363-1364, sold for $36.

A306

People's Republic of China, 60th Anniv. A307

Designs: $1.40, Cogwheels, Victoria Harbor, Hong Kong and Tiananmen Square, Beijing. $1.80, Flag of People's Republic of China, Forever Blooming Bauhinia statue, Hong Kong. $2.40, Dove, Olympic Stadium, Beijing. $2.50, Shenzhou-7 on launch pad. $3, Doves, Temple of Heaven. $5, Dragon, Great Wall of China.

No. 1371: a, Emblem of People's Republic of China, Tiananmen Square. b, Emblem of Hong Kong, Hong Kong skyline at night.

2009, Oct. 1   **Perf. 13¼**
Granite Paper (A306)
1365-1370   A306   Set of 6   5.75   5.75
1370a   Souvenir sheet, #1365-1370   6.25   6.25

Souvenir Sheet
Perf. 13
1371   A307 $5 Sheet of 2, #a-b   4.50   4.50

Soccer — A308

Soccer player from: $1.40, Hong Kong. $2.40, Hong Kong, diff. $3, Brazil. $5, Brazil, diff.

Perf. 13¼ x 14¼ Syncopated
2009, Nov. 5   **Granite Paper**
1372-1375   A308   Set of 4   4.00   4.00
1375a   Souvenir sheet, #1372-1375   4.00   4.00
See Brazil No. 3114.

2009 East Asia Games, Hong Kong — A309

Designs: No. 1376, $1.40, Judo, rowing and rugby. No. 1377, $1.40, Wushu, track, badminton and shooting. No. 1378, $2.40, Squash, basketball, field hockey and swimming. No. 1379, $2.40, Cycling, weight lifting and tennis. No. 1380, $3, Bowling, windsurfing, soccer and taekwondo. No. 1381, $3, Dancing, table tennis, volleyball and billiards.

Litho. With Foil Application
2009, Dec. 5   **Perf. 14¼ Syncopated**
Granite Paper
1376-1381   A309   Set of 6   4.50   4.50
1381a   Souvenir sheet, #1376-1381   4.50   4.50

Stonecutters Bridge — A310

Designs: $1.40, View of bridge tower from water level. $2.40, Aerial view of bridge, horiz. $3, View of bridge from water level, horiz. $5, Aerial view of bridge tower.

Perf. 14½ x 14 Syncopated, 14x14½ Syncopated
2009, Dec. 17   Litho.
Granite Paper
1382-1385   A310   Set of 4   4.50   4.50
1385a   Souvenir sheet, #1382-1385   4.50   4.50

New Year 2010 (Year of the Tiger) — A311

Various tigers with background colors of: $1.40, Red. $2.40, Green. $3, Blue. $5, Orange.

Perf. 13½ x 13¼ Syncopated
2010, Feb. 6   **Granite Paper**
1386-1389   A311   Set of 4   4.50   4.50
1386a   Dated "2011" (1431)   .50   .50
1389a   Souvenir sheet of #1389, imperf.   1.90   1.90
1389b   Souvenir sheet, #1386-1389   4.50   4.50
Issued: No. 1386a, 1/22/11. See Nos. 1432c, 1479k, 1480k.

Souvenir Sheet

New Year 2010 (Year of the Tiger) A312

Litho. & Embossed With Foil Application
2010, Feb. 6   **Perf. 13¾**
1390   A312 $50 Sheet of 2, #a-b   27.50   27.50

Souvenir Sheet

Fujian Tulou UNESCO World Heritage Site — A313

Perf. 13¼ Syncopated
2010, Mar. 18   Litho.
Granite Paper
1391   A313 $10 multi   4.00   4.00
See No. 1456e.

Expo 2010, Shanghai A314

Designs: $1.40, Dragon dance. $2.40, Hong Kong on green leaf. $3, Tsing Ma Bridge, Hong Kong. $5, Smart Card chip, head, Hong Kong skyline.

2010, Apr. 27   **Perf. 13¼ Syncopated**
Granite Paper
1392-1395   A314   Set of 4   3.50   3.50
1395a   Souvenir sheet, #1392-1395   3.50   3.50
No. 1395a was printed in sheet containing four souvenir sheets.

Souvenir Sheet

London 2010 Intl. Philatelic Exhibition — A315

2010, May 8   Litho.   **Granite Paper**
1396   A315 $10 multi   3.25   3.25

Hong Kong Street Scenes — A316

Designs: No. 1397, $1.40, Pottinger Street. No. 1398, $1.40, Nathan Road. No. 1399, $2.40, Hollywood Road. No. 1400, $2.40, Temple Street. No. 1401, $3, Des Voeux Road West. No. 1402, $3, Stanley Market.

HONG KONG

Perf. 13¾ Syncopated
2010, June 24   Granite Paper
1397-1402   A316   Set of 6   4.00   4.00
    1402a   Souvenir sheet, #1397-1402   4.00   4.00

Intl. Year of Biodiversity — A317

Designs: $1.40, Macropodus hongkongensis. $2.40, Liuixalus romeri. $3, Sinopora hongkongensis. $5, Fukienogomphus choifongae.

Perf. 13¼x14¼ Syncopated
2010, July 15   Granite Paper   Litho.
1403-1406   A317   Set of 4   4.00   4.00
    1406a   Souvenir sheet, #1403-1406   4.50   4.50

Railways in Hong Kong, Cent. — A318

Designs: $1.40, Steam train, Hong Kong Railway Museum. $1.80, Diesel train, clock tower of Kowloon-Canton Railway Terminus. $2.40, Electric train, Hung Hom Terminus. $2.50, Mass Transit Railway train, International Finance Center. $3, Kowloon-Guangzhou through train, Mass Transit Railway Hung Hom Station. $5, Airport Express train, aerial view of Hong Kong International Airport.

$20, Steam train, Hong Kong Railway Museum, diff.

Perf. 13½x13¼ Syncopated
2010, Sept. 28   Granite Paper   Litho.
1407-1412   A318   Set of 6   4.50   4.50
    1412a   Souvenir sheet, #1407-1412   4.50   4.50

Souvenir Sheet
Litho. With Three-Dimensional Plastic Affixed
1413   A318 $20 multi   6.25   6.25

No. 1413 contains one 37x51mm stamp.
A booklet containing three panes, containing Nos. 1407-1408, 1409-1410, and 1411-1412 respectively, sold for $36.

Winning Entries in Children's Stamp Design Contest — A319

Designs: $1.40, "Harbor of Hong Kong." $2.40, "Beautiful Hong Kong." $3, "Hong Kong is Fun." $5, "City Beat."

Perf. 13¼x13½ Syncopated
2010, Oct. 21   Granite Paper   Litho.
1414-1417   A319   Set of 4   3.50   3.50
    1417a   Souvenir sheet, #1414-1417   3.50   3.50

Renovation of Old Neighborhoods — A320

Designs: $1.40, Rehabilitation. $2.40, Revitalization. $3, Preservation. $5, Redevelopment.

Perf. 13¾ Syncopated
2010, Nov. 16   Granite Paper
1418-1421   A320   Set of 4   3.50   3.50
    1421a   Souvenir sheet, #1418-1421   3.50   3.50

Lighthouses — A321

Map and: $1.40, Cape D'Aguilar Lighthouse. $1.80, Old Green Island Lighthouse. $2.40, New Green Island Lighthouse. $3, Tang Lung Chau Lighthouse. $5, Waglan Lighthouse.

Perf. 13½x13¼ Syncopated
2010, Dec. 29   Granite Paper   Litho.
1422-1426   A321   Set of 5   4.00   4.00
    1426a   Souvenir sheet of 5, #1422-1426   4.00   4.00

New Year 2011 (Year of the Rabbit) — A322

Various rabbits with background color of: $1.40, Green. $2.40, Blue. $3, Brown. $5, Red.

Perf. 13½x13¼ Syncopated
2011, Jan. 22   Granite Paper
1427-1430   A322   Set of 4   3.75   3.75
    1430a   Souvenir sheet of #1430, imperf.   1.60   1.60
    1430b   Souvenir sheet of 4, #1427-1430   3.75   3.75

See Nos. 1432d, 1479l, 1480l.

New Year Types of 2000-11
Perf. 13½x13¼ Syncopated
2011, Jan. 22   Granite Paper   Litho.
1431   Sheet of 12, #1128a, 1249a, 1304a, 1386a, 1427, 1431a-1431g   6.00   6.00
   a.   A177 $1.40 Dragon   .50   .50
   b.   A184 $1.40 Snake   .50   .50
   c.   A194 $1.40 Horse   .50   .50
   d.   A206 $1.40 Ram (like #1028)   .50   .50
   e.   A221 $1.40 Monkey (like #1076)   .50   .50
   f.   A256 $1.40 Dog (like #1170)   .50   .50
   g.   A298 $1.40 Ox (like #1344)   .50   .50

Flocked Paper
Perf. 13½x13¼
1432   Block of 4   13.00   13.00
   a.   A286 $10 Rat   3.25   3.25
   b.   A298 $10 Ox   3.25   3.25
   c.   A311 $10 Tiger   3.25   3.25
   d.   A322 $10 Rabbit   3.25   3.25

Souvenir Sheet

New Year 2011 (Year of the Rabbit) A323

No. 1433: a, Tiger. b, Rabbit.

Litho. & Embossed With Foil Application
2011, Jan. 22   Perf. 13¾
1433   A323 $50 Sheet of 2, #a-b   32.50   32.50

Souvenir Sheet

Powered Flight in Hong Kong, Cent. — A324

No. 1434: a, Drawing of first aircraft. b, Photograph of first flight.

Perf. 13¼ Syncopated
2011, Mar. 18   Granite Paper   Litho.
1434   A324 $3 Sheet of 2, #a-b   1.75   1.75

Volunteerism — A326

Designs: $1.40, Leaf, child's notebook page. $2.40, Volunteer recruitment web page. $3, E-mail message, children. No. 1438, $5, Written reminder on calendar page.

Perf. 13½x13¼ Syncopated
2011, Mar. 29   Granite Paper
1435-1438   A325   Set of 4   3.50   3.50

Souvenir Sheet
Perf.
1439   A326 $5 shown   1.50   1.50

Green Living — A327

Growing plant and: $1.40, Water faucet, Earth in water droplet. $2.40, Cloud, tree, Earth. $3, Fluorescent lightbulb, Earth under lampshade. No. 1443, $5, Recycling emblem, recyclable items, Earth.
No. 1444, $5, Growing plant on Earth.

2011, Apr. 14   **Perf. 13¾ Syncopated**
         Granite Paper
1440-1443   A327   Set of 4   3.50   3.50

Souvenir Sheet
1444   A327 $5 multi   1.50   1.50

Hong Kong General Chamber of Commerce, 150th Anniv. — A328

Designs: $1.40, Old Hong Kong Club Building. $2.40, Wharf. $3, Handshake, Good Citizen Award Certificate. $5, Chamber of Commerce members in China near train, 1978.

2011, May 26   Litho.
         Granite Paper
1445-1448   A328   Set of 4   3.25   3.25
    1448a   Souvenir sheet of 4, #1445-1448   3.25   3.25

Chinese Idioms — A329

Idioms: Nos. 1449, 1454a, $1.40, Mutual help in hard times. Nos. 1450, 1454b, $1.80, Water drops wear away rocks. Nos. 1451, 1454c, $2.40, Practice makes perfect. Nos. 1452, 1454d, $3, Save to give. Nos. 1453, 1454e, $5, As deft as a master butcher.

Perf. 13¼x14¼ Syncopated
2011, June 28   Granite Paper
Multicolored Designs
1449-1453   A329   Set of 5   3.50   3.50
Stamp Designs With Gray Areas
1454   A329   Sheet of 5, #a-e   3.50   3.50

No. 1454 was sold with a sheet of multicolored self-adhesive stickers that could be placed over corresponding gray areas on the souvenir sheet. Value for No. 1454 is for sheet without stickers attached.

Souvenir Sheet

Dunhuang Grottoes — A330

Perf. 13½x13¼ Syncopated
2011, Aug. 2   Granite Paper
1455   A330 $10 multi   2.60   2.60
     See No. 1456b.

Chinese Scenery Types of 2003-11
Miniature Sheet
Perf. 13¼x13½ Syncopated, 13¼ Syncopated (#1456a), 13½x13¼ Syncopated (#1456b, 1456i), 13¼x13 Syncopated (#1456d)
2011, Aug. 2   Litho.
         Granite Paper
1456   Sheet of 9   6.25   6.25
   a.   A253 $2.40 Qiantang Bore   .65   .65
   b.   A330 $2.40 Dunhuang Grottoes   .65   .65
   c.   A300 $2.40 Mount Tianshan   .65   .65
   d.   A288 $2.40 Huanglong   .65   .65
   e.   A313 $2.40 Fujian Tulou   .65   .65
   f.   A210 $2.40 Master-of-Nets Garden   .65   .65
   g.   A230 $2.40 Chen Clan Academy   .65   .65
   h.   A274 $2.40 Shilin   .65   .65
   i.   A260 $2.40 Mount Taishan   .65   .65

Souvenir Sheet

Hong Kong Postal Service, 170th Anniv. A331

Litho. & Embossed With Foil Application
Perf. 13½ Syncopated
2011, Aug. 25   Granite Paper
1457   A331 $10 multi   2.60   2.60

University of Hong Kong, Cent. — A332

University crest and: $1.40, Main Building, 1910, and golden trowel. $1.80, Main Building, 1912, and University Bazaar poster. $2.40, Union Building, 1919, Main Building, and statue of Dr. Sun Yat-sen. $2.50, Main Building, 1946, and mace. $3, Main Building and West Gate, 1940s, and inkstand. No. 1463, $5, Courtyard and Main Building, 2011, University arms. No. 1464, $5, Letters patent, vert.

Perf. 13¼x13 Syncopated
2011, Sept. 5   Litho.
         Granite Paper
1458-1463   A332   Set of 6   4.25   4.25

Souvenir Sheet
Perf. 13¾x14¼ Syncopated
1464   A332 $5 multi   1.40   1.40

A booklet containing two panes, containing Nos. 1458-1460 and 1461-1463, respectively, sold for $45.

HONG KONG

Chinese Revolution, Cent. — A333

Designs: $1.40, Monument to the 72 Martyrs of Huanghuagang. $2.40, Wuchang Uprising. $3, Revolution leaders Cai Yuanpei, Zhang Taiyan, Huang Xing and Song Jiaoren. No. 1468, $5, Dr. Sun Yat-sen assuming office of Provisional President.
No. 1469, $5, horiz. — Dr. Sun Yat-sen and: a, Central School. b, Proclamation of the Three Principles of the People.

Perf. 13½x13¼ Syncopated
2011, Oct. 10   Granite Paper
1465-1468   A333   Set of 4   3.25   3.25

Souvenir Sheet
Perf. 13¼x13 Syncopated
1469   A333 $5 Sheet of 2, #a-b   2.75   2.75

Handicrafts — A334

Artisan creating: No. 1470, $5, Dough figurines, Hong Kong. No. 1471, $5, Painted Easter egg, Romania.

Perf. 13¼ Syncopated
2011, Nov. 24   Granite Paper
1470-1471   A334   Set of 2   2.60   2.60
1471a   Souvenir sheet of 2, #1470-1471   2.60   2.60

See Romania Nos. 5311-5312.

Items in Hong Kong Museums — A335

Designs: $1.40, Forehead headdress used in opera, The Sounds of Battle. $1.80, Qipao, 1920s-1930s. $2.40, Silver-footed bowl decorated in repousse, horiz. $2.50, Sequined reversible palace costume, horiz. $3, Green glazed barrel for herbal tea, horiz. $5, Traditional baby carrier with head support, horiz.

Perf. 13¾x14¼ Syncopated, 14¼x13¾ Syncopated
2011, Dec. 6   Granite Paper
1472-1477   A335   Set of 6   4.25   4.25
1477a   Souvenir sheet of 6, #1472-1477   4.25   4.25

Souvenir Sheet

Tamar Development Project — A336

Perf. 13¼ Syncopated
2011, Dec. 15   Litho.
           Granite Paper
1478   A336 $10 multi   3.00   3.00

New Year Types of 2000-11

No. 1479: a, Dragon, green background. b, Snake, orange brown background. c, Horse, red background. d, Ram, dull red background. e, Monkey, blue green background. f, Rooster, blue background. g, Dog, green background. h, Pig, dull red background. i, Rat, blue background. j, Ox, red brown background. k, Tiger, blue green background. l, Rabbit, orange brown background.

No. 1480: a, Dragon, blue background. b, Snake, red background. c, Horse, green background. d, Ram, orange brown background. e, Monkey, green background. f, Rooster, orange background. g, Dog, red violet background. h, Pigs, red brown background. i, Rat, brown background. j, Ox, lilac background. k, Tiger, green background. l, Rabbit, dull green background.

Perf. 13½x13¼ Syncopated
2012, Jan. 14   Litho.
     Granite Paper
Animals in Silver and Gold
1479   Sheet of 12   7.00   7.00
  a.   A177 $1.40 multi   .55   .55
  b.   A184 $1.40 multi   .55   .55
  c.   A194 $1.40 multi   .55   .55
  d.   A206 $1.40 multi   .55   .55
  e.   A221 $1.40 multi   .55   .55
  f.   A244 $1.40 multi   .55   .55
  g.   A256 $1.40 multi   .55   .55
  h.   A270 $1.40 multi   .55   .55
  i.   A286 $1.40 multi   .55   .55
  j.   A298 $1.40 multi   .55   .55
  k.   A311 $1.40 multi   .55   .55
  l.   A322 $1.40 multi   .55   .55
1480   Sheet of 12   7.00   7.00
  a.   A177 $1.40 multi   .55   .55
  b.   A184 $1.40 multi   .55   .55
  c.   A194 $1.40 multi   .55   .55
  d.   A206 $1.40 multi   .55   .55
  e.   A221 $1.40 multi   .55   .55
  f.   A244 $1.40 multi   .55   .55
  g.   A256 $1.40 multi   .55   .55
  h.   A270 $1.40 multi   .55   .55
  i.   A286 $1.40 multi   .55   .55
  j.   A298 $1.40 multi   .55   .55
  k.   A311 $1.40 multi   .55   .55
  l.   A322 $1.40 multi   .55   .55

Souvenir Sheet

New Year 2012 (Year of the Dragon) A337

No. 1481: a, Rabbit. b, Dragon.

Litho. & Embossed With Foil Application
2012, Jan. 14   Perf. 14x13¾
1481   A337 $50 Sheet of 2, #a-b   27.50   27.50

New Year 2012 (Year of the Dragon) A338

Various dragons with background colors of: $1.40, Orange. $2.40, Red violet. $3, Purple. $5, Green.
$10, Dragon, red background. $50, Dragon, multicolored background.

Litho. With Foil Application
2012, Jan. 14   Perf. 13¼ Syncopated
           Granite Paper
1482-1485   A338   Set of 4   3.50   3.50

Souvenir Sheets
1486   A338 $10 multi   3.00   3.00

Litho.
Silk-faced Paper
1487   A338 $50 multi   15.00   15.00

Nos. 1487 and 1488 each contain one 45x45mm stamp. See Nos. 1700a, 2281-2284.

Queen's College, 150th Anniv. — A339

2012, Mar. 27   Perf.
1488   Sheet of 4   10.50   10.50
  a.   A339 $10 Litho., text at top in tan, denomination in black, glitter on shield frame   2.60   2.60
  b.   A339 $10 Litho., text at top in claret, denomination in tan, lacquer on part of design   2.60   2.60
  c.   A339 $10 Litho. & embossed, text at top in tan, denomination in black   2.60   2.60
  d.   A339 $10 Litho. & embossed with foil application, denomination and building in gold   2.60   2.60

Souvenir Sheet
1489   A339 $10 Text at top in tan, denomination in black   2.60   2.60

Art — A340

Designs: $1.40, Douglas Castle, painting by unknown Chinese artist. $2.40, Crab, sculpture by Cheung Yee. $3, The Racecourse - Amateur Jockeys Close to a Carriage, painting by Edgar Degas. $5, The Horse, sculpture by Raymond Duchamp-Villon.

Perf. 13 Syncopated
2012, May 3   Litho.
     Granite Paper
1490-1493   A340   Set of 4   3.00   3.00
1493a   Souvenir sheet of 4, #1490-1493   3.00   3.00

See France Nos. 4201-4205.

Festivals — A341

Designs: $1.40, Tin Hau Festival. $2.40, Kwun Yum Festival. $3, Birthday of the Buddha. No. 1497, $5, Tuen Ng Festival.
No. 1498, $5, Mid-autumn Festival.

Perf. 13¾x14 Syncopated
2012, May 22   Granite Paper
1494-1497   A341   Set of 4   3.00   3.00

Souvenir Sheet
1498   A341 $5 multi   1.40   1.40

Working Dogs — A342

Designs: $1.40, Beagle (quarantine detector dog) and emblem of Agriculture, Fisheries and Conservation Department. $1.80, German shepherd (correctional services dog) and emblem of Correctional Services Department. $2.40, English Springer spaniel (customs detector dog) and emblem of Customs and Excise Department. $2.50, Labrador retriever (fire investigation dog) and emblem of Fire Services Department. $3, Labrador retriever (quarantine detector dog) and emblem of Food and Environmental Hygiene Department. No. 1504, $5, Malinois (police dog) and emblem of Police Force.
No. 1505, Beagle, German shepherd, English Springer spaniel, Labrador retrievers, and Malinois.

Perf. 13½x14¼ Syncopated
2012, June 6   Granite Paper
1499-1504   A342   Set of 6   4.25   4.25

Souvenir Sheet
Perf. 13¼x13 Syncopated
1505   A342 $5 multi   1.40   1.40

No. 1505 contains one 100x40mm stamp. A booklet containing panes of Nos. 1499-1500, 1501-1502, and 1503-1504, respectively, sold for $45.

Souvenir Sheet

Hong Kong Special Administrative Region, 15th Anniv. — A343

No. 1506 — Various Hong Kong landmarks and panel in: a, Blue. b, Yellow. c, Green.

Perf. 13½x13 Syncopated
2012, June 25   Granite Paper
1506   A343 $5 Sheet of 3, #a-c   4.00   4.00

On June 19, 2012, Hong Kong issued the stamps pictured above, having franking values of $1.40 and $3 respectively. The stamps were each printed in sheets of 12 + 12 non-personalizable labels depicting various infants. The sheets sold for $40 and $66 respectively. Sheets with other non-personalizable label designs were made available later.

2012 Summer Olympics, London — A344

Designs: $1.40, Windsurfing, rowing, "2." $2.40, Badminton, archery, "0." $3, Table tennis, cycling, "1." $5, Swimming, track, "2."

2012, July 27   **Perf. 13¾ Syncopated**
1507-1510   A344   Set of 4   3.00   3.00
1510a   Souvenir sheet of 4, #1507-1510   3.00   3.00

Delicacies A345

Designs: $1.40, Egg tart and milk tea. $2.40, Wontons. $3, Roast goose. $5, Crab.

Perf. 14¼x14 Syncopated
2012, Aug. 30   Granite Paper
1511-1514   A345   Set of 4   3.00   3.00
1514a   Souvenir sheet of 4, #1511-1514   3.00   3.00

Souvenir Sheet

Great Wall of China A346

Granite Paper
Perf. 13¼x14 Syncopated
Litho. & Silk-screened
2012, Sept. 17
1515   A346 $10 multi   2.60   2.60

See No. 2191a.

Signs of the Zodiac — A347

Designs: Nos. 1516, 1528, Capricorn. Nos. 1517, 1529, Aquarius. Nos. 1518, 1530, Pisces. Nos. 1519, 1531, Aries. Nos. 1520, 1532, Taurus. Nos. 1521, 1533, Gemini. Nos. 1522, 1534, Cancer. Nos. 1523, 1535, Leo. Nos. 1524, 1536, Virgo. Nos. 1525, 1537, Libra. Nos. 1526, 1538, Scorpio. Nos. 1527, 1539, Sagittarius.

Granite Paper (#1516-1527)

HONG KONG

Perf. 14 Syncopated
2012, Nov. 1			Litho.	
1516	A347	$1.40 multi	.35	.35
1517	A347	$1.40 multi	.35	.35
1518	A347	$1.40 multi	.35	.35
1519	A347	$1.40 multi	.35	.35
1520	A347	$1.40 multi	.35	.35
1521	A347	$1.40 multi	.35	.35
1522	A347	$1.40 multi	.35	.35
1523	A347	$1.40 multi	.35	.35
1524	A347	$1.40 multi	.35	.35
1525	A347	$1.40 multi	.35	.35
1526	A347	$1.40 multi	.35	.35
1527	A347	$1.40 multi	.35	.35
a.	Souvenir sheet of 12, #1516-1527		4.25	4.25
	Nos. 1516-1527 (12)		4.20	4.20

Self-Adhesive
Die Cut Perf. 14 Syncopated
1528	A347	$1.40 multi	.35	.35
1529	A347	$1.40 multi	.35	.35
1530	A347	$1.40 multi	.35	.35
1531	A347	$1.40 multi	.35	.35
1532	A347	$1.40 multi	.35	.35
1533	A347	$1.40 multi	.35	.35
1534	A347	$1.40 multi	.35	.35
1535	A347	$1.40 multi	.35	.35
1536	A347	$1.40 multi	.35	.35
1537	A347	$1.40 multi	.35	.35
1538	A347	$1.40 multi	.35	.35
1539	A347	$1.40 multi	.35	.35
a.	Vert. coil strip of 12, #1528-1539		4.25	
b.	Booklet pane of 12, #1528-1539		4.25	
	Nos. 1528-1539 (12)		4.20	4.20

A sheet containing Nos. 1516-1527 + 12 non-personalizable labels sold for $40. Sheets containing eight stamps of any of Nos. 1516-1527 + eight non-personalizable labels sold for $30 each.

Insects — A348

Designs: $1.40, Spittle bug. $1.80, Flower mantid. $2.40, Mangrove China-mark moth. $2.50, White dragontail butterfly. $3, Four-spot midget damselfly. $5, Hong Kong bent-winged firefly.

Perf. 13¼x14 Syncopated
2012, Nov. 22		Granite Paper		
1540-1545	A348	Set of 6	4.25	4.25
1545a		Souvenir sheet of 6, #1540-1545	4.25	4.25

Hong Kong Postage Stamps, 150th Anniv. — A349

Designs: $1.40, Hong Kong #1, quill and inkwell. $1.80, Hong Kong #2, fountain pen. $2.40, Hong Kong #3, ball-point pen. $2.50, Hong Kong #4, typewriter. $3, Hong Kong #5, computer keyboard. $5, Hong Kong #6, quick response code. $10, Hong Kong #7, bar code, horiz.

Granite Paper
2012, Dec. 8	Perf. 13¾ Syncopated			
1546-1551	A349	Set of 6	4.25	4.25
1548a		Booklet pane of 3, #1546-1548	2.75	—
1551a		Booklet pane of 3, #1549-1551	5.25	—

Souvenir Sheet
Perf. 13½ Syncopated
1552	A349	$10 multi	2.60	2.60
a.	Booklet pane of 1	5.00		
	Complete booklet, #1548a, 1551a, 1552a	13.00		

No. 1552 contains one 67x24mm stamp. Complete booklet sold for $50.

New Year 2013 (Year of the Snake) — A350

Designs: $1.40, Paper-cutting of snake. $2.40, Painting of snake. $3, Seal carvings depicting snake and Chinese character for snake. $5, Jade carving of snake.

No. 1557: a, Dragon and clouds, green background. b, Snake. No. 1558, Snake, hexagons with Chinese characters. No. 1559, Snake, no hexagons.

Perf. 13¼x14 Syncopated
2013, Jan. 26			Litho.	
1553-1556	A350	Set of 4	3.00	3.00

Litho. With Foil Application (#1557a, 1558), Litho. With Metal Affixed (#1557b)
Perf. 13¼ Syncopated
1557	A350	$50 Sheet of 2, #a-b	26.00	26.00

Souvenir Sheets
1558	A350	$10 multi	2.60	2.60

Litho.
On Silk-faced Paper
1559	A350	$50 multi	13.00	13.00

Nos. 1558 and 1559 each contain one 45x45mm stamp. See Nos. 1700b, 2281-2284.

On Dec. 8, 2012, Hong Kong issued the stamp pictured above, having franking values of $1.40. The stamp was printed in sheets of 12 + 12 non-personalizable labels depicting various items. The sheet sold for $40. A similar stamp, having the franking value of $3, and depicting the same items found on No. 1550, was printed in sheets of 8 + 8 non-personalizable labels. The sheet sold for $55.

On Feb. 12, 2013, Hong Kong issued the stamps pictured above, having franking values of $1.40 and $3 respectively. The stamps were each printed in sheets of 12 + 12 non-personalizable labels depicting various flowers. The sheets sold for $40 and $66 respectively. A sheet of the $1.40 value with other non-personalizable label designs was made available later.

International Red Cross, 150th Anniv. — A351

Designs: $1.40, Airplane, Red Cross worker with person. $2.40, Red Cross tent, worker bandaging arm. $3, Red Cross worker talking to people. $5, World map, worker carrying supplies.

Perf. 13¾ Syncopated
2013, Feb. 28		Granite Paper		
1560-1563	A351	Set of 4	3.00	3.00
1563a		Souvenir sheet of 4, #1560-1563	3.00	3.00

Children and Pets — A352

Children and: $1.40, Dog. $1.80, Cat. $2.40, Tortoise. $2.50, Guinea pig. $3, Rabbit. $5, Hamster.

2013, Mar. 28			Litho.	
1564-1569	A352	Set of 6	4.25	4.25
1569a		Souvenir sheet of 6, #1564-1569	4.25	4.25

On Mar. 28, 2013, Hong Kong issued the stamps pictured above, having franking values of $1.40 and $3 respectively. The stamps were each printed in sheets of 8 + 8 non-personalizable labels depicting children and dogs or children and rabbits. The sheets sold for $30 and $55 respectively.

Revitalization of Historic Buildings A353

Designs: $1.40, YHA Mei Ho House Youth Hostel. $1.80, Yuen Yuen Institute "Fong Yuen Study Hall." $2.40, Jao Tsung-I Academy. $2.50, Hong Kong Baptist University School of Chinese Medicine - Lui Seng Chun. $3, Tai O Heritage Hotel. $5, SCAD Hong Kong.

Perf. 13¼x14¼ Syncopated
2013, May 7		Granite Paper		
1570-1575	A353	Set of 6	4.25	4.25
1575a		Souvenir sheet of 6, #1570-1575	4.25	4.25

A booklet containing panes of Nos. 1570-1571, 1572-1573, and 1574-1575, respectively sold for $45.

Souvenir Sheets

Kai Tak Cruise Terminal A354

Perf. 13¼x13 Syncopated
2013, June 11		Granite Paper	Litho.	
1576	A354	$10 multi	3.00	3.00

Litho. With Foil Application
1577	A354	$20 multi	5.25	5.25

Chinese and Western Wedding Customs — A355

Designs: $1.40, Chinese bride and groom in traditional outfits bowing. $1.80, Western bride in gown and groom in tuxedo exchanging vows. $2.40, Items in Chinese wedding gift presentation. $2.50, Western wedding cake. $3, Chinese bride and groom, dragon and phoenix. $5, Western bride and groom, wedding bells, flowered archway. $10, Chinese and Western couples, bangles depicting dragon and phoenix, wedding rings, horiz.

Perf. 13¾x13¼ Syncopated
2013, July 23		Granite Paper	Litho.	
1578-1583	A355	Set of 6	4.25	4.25

Souvenir Sheet
Perf. 13¼x13 Syncopated
1584	A355	$10 multi	2.60	2.60

No. 1584 contains one 100x40mm stamp.

On July 23, 2013, Hong Kong issued the stamps pictured above, having franking values of $1.40 and $5 respectively. The stamps were each printed in sheets of 8 + 8 with non-personalizable labels depicting various wedding items. The sheets sold for $30 and $55 respectively.

Souvenir Sheet

Old Town of Lijiang UNESCO World Heritage Site, People's Republic of China — A356

Perf. 14 Syncopated
Litho. & Embossed
Granite Paper
2013, Aug. 22				
1585	A356	$10 multi	2.60	2.60

See No. 2191i.

Buses — A357

Designs: $1.40, 1947 Tilling Stevens bus. $1.80, 1949 Daimler A bus. $2.40, 1975 Albion Coach. $2.50, 1988 Leyland Olympian 11m bus. $3, 1995 Volvo Olympian 11m bus. No. 1591, $5, 1997 Dennis Trident bus. No. 1592, $5, Euro V bus, horiz. $20, Euro V bus, diff. horiz.

Perf. 13½x13¼ Syncopated
2013, Sept. 24		Granite Paper	Litho.	
1586-1591	A357	Set of 6	4.25	4.25

Souvenir Sheets
Perf. 13¾x14 Syncopated
1592	A357	$5 multi	1.40	1.40

Litho. With Three-Dimensional Plastic Affixed
Perf. 13¾x14 Syncopated
1593	A357	$20 multi	5.25	5.25

Nos. 1592 and 1593 each contain one 100x40mm stamp. A booklet containing panes of Nos. 1586-1588, 1589-1591 and 1592, respectively, sold for $50.

HONG KONG

Heartwarming Types of 2003 Redrawn Removing White Chinese Characters and "Heartwarming" and

A358   A359

Size: 30x30mm
Granite Paper
Perf. 13¼ Syncopated
2013, Oct. 1   Litho.
Inscribed "Local Mail Postage"
1594	A214	($1.70) multi	.45	.45
a.	Booklet pane of 10		4.50	
	Complete booklet, #1594a		4.50	

Inscribed "Air Mail Postage"
1595	A213	($3.70) multi	.95	.95
a.	Booklet pane of 10		9.50	
	Complete booklet, #1595a		9.50	

Coil Stamps
Inscribed "Local Mail Postage"
Perf. 15x14 Syncopated
| 1596 | A358 | ($1.70) multi | .45 | .45 |
| 1597 | A359 | ($3.70) multi | .95 | .95 |

Works of Handicapped Artists — A360

Designs: $1.70, Thanksgiving, painting by Chan Tung Mui. $2.90, Always By Your Side, photograph by Cheng Kai Man. $3.70, The Vitality of Hong Kong, painting, by Ko Nam. $5, How Are You, painting by Liu Tung Mui.

Perf. 13¼x14¼ Syncopated
Litho. & Thermography
2013, Oct. 15   **Granite Paper**
| 1598-1601 | A360 | Set of 4 | 4.00 | 4.00 |
| 1601a | | Souvenir sheet of 4, #1598-1601 | 4.00 | 4.00 |

New Technologies — A361

Designs: $1.70, Green technology. $2.20, Information and communication technology. $2.90, Chinese medicine. $3.10, Biotechnology. $3.70, Nanotechnology and advanced materials. $5, Radio frequency identification.

Perf. 14x14¼ Syncopated
2013, Nov. 19   Litho.
Granite Paper
| 1602-1607 | A361 | Set of 6 | 4.75 | 4.75 |
| 1607a | | Souvenir sheet of 6, #1602-1607 | 4.75 | 4.75 |

Hong Kong Legislative Council — A362

Designs: $1.70, New Legislative Council Complex. $2.90, Old Legislative Council Building. $3.70, Chamber in New Legislative Council Complex. $5, President's Chair in Old Legislative Council Building.

Perf. 13½x13¼ Syncopated
2013, Dec. 5   Litho.
Granite Paper
| 1608-1611 | A362 | Set of 4 | 4.00 | 4.00 |
| 1611a | | Souvenir sheet of 4, #1608-1611 | 4.00 | 4.00 |

New Year 2014 (Year of the Horse) — A363

Designs: $1.70, Horse made of fabric. $2.90, Wood carving of horse. $3.70, Metal sculpture of horse. $5, Lacquer ware horse.
No. 1616: a, Snake. b, Horse.
$10, Horse (with gold emblem at right). No. 1618, Horse (without gold emblem at right).

Perf. 13¼x14¼ Syncopated
2014, Jan. 11   Litho.
Granite Paper
| 1612-1615 | A363 | Set of 4 | 3.50 | 3.50 |

Litho. With Foil Application (#1616a), Litho. With Metal Affixed (#1616b)
Perf. 13¼x12¾ Syncopated
| 1616 | A363 | $50 Sheet of 2, #a-b | 26.00 | 26.00 |

Souvenir Sheets
Litho. With Foil Application
Perf. 13¼ Syncopated
| 1617 | A363 | $10 multi | 2.60 | 2.60 |

Litho.
On Silk-Faced Granite Paper
| 1618 | A363 | $50 multi | 13.00 | 13.00 |

Nos. 1617-1618 each contain one 45x45mm stamp. Imperforate examples of No. 1617 with silver lines replacing the perforations were given away as gifts to standing order customers and are not valid for postage. See Nos. 1700c, 2281-2284.

On Jan. 11, 2014, Hong Kong issued the stamps pictured above, having franking values of $1.70 and $3.70 respectively. The stamps were each printed in sheets of 12 + 12 non-personalizable labels depicting various images. The sheets sold for $42 and $70 respectively.

Heartwarming — A364

Designs: No. 1619, Champagne flutes. No. 1620, Birthday cake and candle. No. 1621, Flower held by man and woman. No. 1622, People watching fireworks. No. 1623, Birthday party decorations, gifts, birthday cake and candle. No. 1624, Family, balloons and hearts.

Litho. With Foil Application
2014, Jan. 23   *Perf. 13¼ Syncopated*
Granite Paper
Inscribed "Local Mail Postage"
1619	A364	($1.70) multi	.45	.45
1620	A364	($1.70) multi	.45	.45
1621	A364	($1.70) multi	.45	.45

Inscribed "Air Mail Postage"
1622	A364	($3.70) multi	.95	.95
1623	A364	($3.70) multi	.95	.95
1624	A364	($3.70) multi	.95	.95
a.	Sheet of 12, 2 each #1619-1624, + 12 labels		8.50	8.50
	Nos. 1619-1624 (6)		4.20	4.20

Dinosaurs — A365

Designs: $1.70, Daxiatitan binglingi. $2.20, Microraptor gui. $2.90, Lufengosaurus magnus. $3.10, Tuojiangosaurus multispinus. $3.70, Protoceratops andrewsi. $5, Yangchuanosaurus shangyouensis.

Perf. 13½x13¼ Syncopated
2014, Feb. 20   Litho.
Granite Paper
| 1625-1630 | A365 | Set of 6 | 4.75 | 4.75 |
| 1630a | | Souvenir sheet of 6, #1625-1630 | 4.75 | 4.75 |

A booklet containing panes of Nos. 1625-1626, 1627-1628 and 1629-1630, respectively sold for $48.

Weather Phenomena A366

Designs: $1.70, Rainbow. $2.20, Frost. $2.90, Cloud. $3.10, Lightning. $3.70, Fog. No. 1636, $5, Rain.
Nos. 1637, $5, 1638, $20, Typhoon.

Perf. 13¾ Syncopated
2014, Mar. 27   Litho.
Granite Paper
| 1631-1636 | A366 | Set of 6 | 4.75 | 4.75 |

Souvenir Sheets
Perf. 13¼ Syncopated
| 1637 | A366 | $5 multi | 1.40 | 1.40 |

Litho. With Three-Dimensional Plastic Affixed
| 1638 | A366 | $20 multi | 5.25 | 5.25 |

Nos. 1637 and 1638 each contain one 45x45mm stamp. A booklet containing panes of Nos. 1631-1633 and 1634-1636 repsectively sold for $53.

Old General Post Office Building A367

Litho., Sheet Margin Litho. With Foil Application
Perf. 14x13¾ Syncopated
2014, Apr. 29   **Granite Paper**
| 1639 | A367 | $20 multi | 5.25 | 5.25 |

No. 1639 was also sold in a commemorative booklet that sold for $60. The sheet in that booklet was placed in a stamp mount. Values are for sheets without booklet.

International Day of Families — A368

Clasped hands and words at lower right: $1.70, Filial piety. $2.90, Love. $3.70, Harmony. $5, Care.

Perf. 13½x13¼ Syncopated
2014, May 15   Litho.
Granite Paper
| 1640-1643 | A368 | Set of 4 | 3.50 | 3.50 |
| 1643a | | Souvenir sheet of 4, #1640-1643 | 3.50 | 3.50 |

Paintings by Wu Guanzhong (1919-2010) — A369

Designs: $1.70, Victoria Harbour, 2002. $2.20, Memories of Home, 1991. $2.90, Waterway, 1997, vert. (30x45mm). $3.10, Faces Unchanged, 2001, vert. (30x45mm). $3.70, Two Swallows, 1981. $5, The Farthest Corner of the World, 2009, vert. (30x45mm). $10, At Rest, 2010.

Perf. 13¼x13½ Syncopated, 13¼ Syncopated (Vert. Stamps)
2014, June 17   Litho.
Granite Paper
| 1644-1649 | A369 | Set of 6 | 4.75 | 4.75 |

Souvenir Sheet
Perf. 13¼x13
| 1650 | A369 | $10 multi | 2.60 | 2.60 |

No. 1650 contains one 130x68mm stamp.

Earth Features — A370

Designs: 10c, North Ninepin Island. 20c, Basalt Island. 50c, Tai Long Wan. $1, Po Pin Chau. $1.70, High Island Reservoir East Dam. $2, Port Island. $2.20, Wong Chuk Kok Tsui. $2.30, Bride's Pool. $2.90, Lan Kwo Shui. $3.10, Lung Lok Shui. $3.70, Kang Lau Shek. $5, Ap Chau. $10, Sharp Island. $15.50, High Island. $20, Lai Chi Chong. $50, Pak Sha Tau Tsui.

Perf. 12¾x13¾ Syncopated
2014, July 24   Litho.
Granite Paper (#1651-1670)
Size: 25x29mm
1651	A370	10c multi	.25	.25
1652	A370	20c multi	.25	.25
1653	A370	50c multi	.25	.25
1654	A370	$1 multi	.25	.25
1655	A370	$1.70 multi	.45	.45
1656	A370	$2 multi	.50	.50
1657	A370	$2.20 multi	.55	.55
1658	A370	$2.30 multi	.60	.60
1659	A370	$2.90 multi	.75	.75
1660	A370	$3.10 multi	.80	.80
1661	A370	$3.70 multi	.95	.95
1662	A370	$5 multi	1.40	1.40
a.		Souvenir sheet of 12, #1651-1662	7.00	7.00

Size: 29x34mm
Perf. 13¼x13 Syncopated
1663	A370	$10 multi	2.60	2.60
1664	A370	$15.50 multi	4.00	4.00
1665	A370	$20 multi	5.25	5.25
1666	A370	$50 multi	13.00	13.00
a.		Souvenir sheet of 4, #1663-1666	25.00	25.00
	Nos. 1651-1666 (16)		31.85	31.85

Coil Stamps
Size: 20x24mm
Perf. 14¾x13¾ Syncopated
1667	A370	$1.70 multi	.45	.45
1668	A370	$2.20 multi	.55	.55
1669	A370	$2.90 multi	.75	.75
1670	A370	$3.70 multi	.95	.95
	Nos. 1667-1670 (4)		2.70	2.70

Booklet Stamps
Self-Adhesive
Size: 25x29mm
Die Cut Perf. 12¾x13¾ Syncopated
1671	A370	$1.70 multi	.45	.45
a.	Booklet pane of 10		4.50	
1672	A370	$2.20 multi	.55	.55
a.	Booklet pane of 10		5.50	
1673	A370	$2.90 multi	.75	.75
a.	Booklet pane of 10		7.50	
1674	A370	$3.70 multi	.95	.95
a.	Booklet pane of 10		9.50	
	Nos. 1671-1674 (4)		2.70	2.70

Nos. 1662-1666 have microperforations in the denominations. See Nos. 1897-1905.

Cantonese Opera Costumes — A371

Designs: $1.70, Great Han costume. $2.20, Gown with sloping collar. $2.90, Dress for young ladies. $3.10, Military uniform for soldiers. $3.70, Python ceremonial robe. $5, Gown with a vertical collar.
$10, Joint investiture, horiz.

HONG KONG

Perf. 13½x13¼ Syncopated
2014, Aug. 21   Litho.
Granite Paper
1675-1680   A371   Set of 6   5.00   5.00

Souvenir Sheet
Perf. 13¾x14
1681   A371 $10 multi   2.60   2.60

No. 1681 contains one 100x40mm stamp.

Souvenir Sheet

Hong Kong 2015 Intl. Stamp Exhibition — A372

Litho. With Foil Application
Perf. 13½x13¼ Syncopated
2014, Sept. 18   Granite Paper
1682   A372 $20 multi   5.25   5.25
 a.   With 2015 copyright date (#1750a)   5.50   5.50

Issued: No. 1682a, 11/23/15.

Local Foods of Hong Kong and Malaysia — A373

Flower and: $1.70, Egg waffle. $2.90, Nasi lemak. $3.70, Poon choi. $5, Satay.

Perf. 13½x13¼ Syncopated
2014, Oct. 9   Granite Paper   Litho.
1683-1686   A373   Set of 4   3.50   3.50
 1686a   Souvenir sheet of 4, #1683-1686   3.50   3.50

See Malaysia Nos. 1510-1513.

Christmas — A374

Designs: Nos. 1687, 1691, $1.70, Santa Claus and reindeer. Nos. 1688, 1692, $2.90, Reindeer. Nos. 1689, 1693, $3.70, Snowman and birds. Nos. 1690, 1694, $5, Angel and snowmen.

Perf. 13½ Syncopated
2014, Nov. 4   Litho.
Granite Paper (#1687-1690)
1687-1690   A374   Set of 4   3.50   3.50
 1690a   Souvenir sheet of 4, #1687-1690   3.50   3.50

Self-Adhesive
Die Cut Perf. 13½ Syncopated
1691-1694   A374   Set of 4   3.50   3.50
 1694a   Souvenir sheet of 4, #1691-1694   3.50

On Dec. 4, 2014, Hong Kong issued the stamps pictured above, having franking values of $1.70 and $3.70 respectively. The stamps were each printed in sheets of 8 + 8 non-personalizable labels depicting various Christmas images. The sheets sold for $32 and $60 respectively.

Souvenir Sheet

China Danxia UNESCO World Heritage Site — A375

Perf. 13½x13¼ Syncopated
Litho. & Silk-Screened
2014, Dec. 4   Granite Paper
1695   A375 $10 multi   2.60   2.60

See No. 2191h.

New Year Types of 2012-14 and

New Year 2015 (Year of the Ram) — A376

Designs: $1.70, Celadon ram figurine. $2.90, Gold glazed ceramic ram. $3.70, Clay ram. $5, Jade ram.
No. 1700: a, Like #1483. b, Like #1554. c, Like #1612. d, Like #1699.
No. 1701, Cloisonné ram (gold emblem at right). No. 1702, Cloisonné ram (without gold emblem at right).
No. 1703: a, Horse. b, Ram.

Perf. 13¼ Syncopated
2015, Jan. 24   Litho.
Granite Paper
1696-1699   A376   Set of 4   3.50   3.50

Litho. & Embossed With Foil Application
1700   Block of 4   10.50   10.50
 a.   A338 $10 multi   2.60   2.60
 b.   A350 $10 multi   2.60   2.60
 c.   A363 $10 multi   2.60   2.60
 d.   A376 $10 multi   2.60   2.60

Souvenir Sheets
1701   A376 $10 multi   2.60   2.60

Litho.
Silk-Faced Granite Paper
1702   A376 $50 multi   13.00   13.00

Litho. With Foil Application (#1703a), Litho. With Metal Affixed (#1703b)
Granite Paper
1703   A376 $50 Sheet of 2, #a-b   26.00   26.00

Nos. 1701-1702 each contain one 45x45mm stamp. See Nos. 2281-2284.

On Jan. 24, 2015, Hong Kong issued the stamps pictured above, having franking values of $1.70 and $3.70 respectively. The stamps were each printed in sheets of 12 + 12 non-personalizable labels. The sheets sold for $42 and $70 respectively.

Hearts — A377

Heart-shaped items: No. 1704, Lollipop. No. 1705, Decorated cake. No. 1706, Eggs on slice of bread. No. 1707, Four-leaf clovers. No. 1708, Party balloons. No. 1709, Photograph frame.

Perf. 13¼ Syncopated
2015, Feb. 12   Litho. & Embossed
Granite Paper
Inscribed "Local Mail Postage"
1704   A377   ($1.70) multi   .45   .45
1705   A377   ($1.70) multi   .45   .45
1706   A377   ($1.70) multi   .45   .45

Inscribed "Air Mail Postage"
1707   A377   ($3.70) multi   .95   .95
1708   A377   ($3.70) multi   .95   .95
1709   A377   ($3.70) multi   .95   .95
 a.   Souvenir sheet of 12, 2 each #1704-1709, + 12 labels   8.50   8.50
 Nos. 1704-1709 (6)   4.20   4.20

Astronomical Phenomena — A378

Designs: $1.70, Solar eclipse. $2.20, Meteor shower. $2.90, Comet. $3.10, Variation in Saturn's ring tilt. $3.70, Sunspot. $5, Moon-planet conjunction. $10, $20, Lunar Eclipse.

Perf. 13¾x14 Syncopated
2015, Mar. 17   Litho.
Granite Paper
1710-1715   A378   Set of 6   5.00   5.00
 1715a   Horiz. strip of 6, #1710-1715   5.00   5.00

Souvenir Sheets
Perf. 14x13¾ Syncopated
1716   A378 $10 multi   2.60   2.60

Litho. With Foil Application
1717   A378 $20 multi   5.25   5.25

A booklet containing panes of Nos. 1710-1712, 1713-1715 and 1716, respectively sold for $60.

Promulgation of the Basic Law, 25th Anniv. — A379

Flags of People's Republic of China and Hong Kong, people and: $1.70, Legislators, government officials and buildings. $2.90, Shenzhen Bay Bridge. $3.70, Return of Hong Kong Monument, Forever Blooming Bauhinia sculpture. $5, Spiral Lookout Tower, Tai Po.

Perf. 13¼x13½ Syncopated
2015, Apr. 2   Litho.
Granite Paper
1718-1721   A379   Set of 4   3.50   3.50
 1721a   Souvenir sheet of 4, #1718-1721   3.50   3.50

Sports — A380

Designs: $1.70, Cycling. $2.20, Table tennis. $2.90, Soccer. $3.10, Track. $3.70, Badminton. $5, Swimming.

Perf. 13½x13¼ Syncopated
2015, Apr. 23   Litho.
Granite Paper
1722-1727   A380   Set of 6   5.00   5.00
 1727a   Souvenir sheet of 6, #1722-1727   5.00   5.00

Governmental Ships — A381

Designs: $1.70, Customs and Excise Department Sector Patrol Launch. $2.20, Department of Health Port Quarantine Launch. $2.90, Environmental Protection Department Marine Monitoring Vessel. $3.10, Fire Services Department Fireboat. $3.70, Police Force Training Launch. $5, Marine Department Hydrographic Survey Launch. $10, Sector Patrol Launch, Port Quarantine Launch, Marine Monitoring Vessel, Fireboat, Training Launch and Hydrographic Survey Launch.

Perf. 13¼x14¼ Syncopated
2015, May 21   Litho.
Granite Paper
1728-1733   A381   Set of 6   5.00   5.00
 1733a   Souvenir sheet of 18, 3 each #1728-1733   15.00   15.00

Souvenir Sheet
Perf. 14 Syncopated
1734   A381 $10 multi   3.00   3.00

No. 1734 contains one 75x40mm stamp. A booklet containing panes of Nos. 1728-1729, 1730-1731 and 1732-1733, respectively sold for $50.

Souvenir Sheet

Honghe Hani Rice Terrace UNESCO World Heritage Site — A382

Perf. 13¾x13½ Syncopated
2015, June 18   Litho. & Embossed
Granite Paper
1735   A382 $10 multi   2.60   2.60

See No. 2191b.

Chinese and Foreign Folklore — A383

Designs: Nos. 1736, 1742a, $1.70, The Old Man Who Moved Mountains. Nos. 1737, 1742b, $2.20, The Tortoise and the Hare. Nos. 1738, 1742c, $2.90, The Little Engine That Could. Nos. 1739, 1742d, $3.10, The Wild Swans. Nos. 1740, 1742e, $3.70, The Three Little Pigs. Nos. 1741, 1742f, $5, The Parable of the Pipeline.

Perf. 13¾ Syncopated
2015, July 16   Litho.
Granite Paper (#1736-1741)
1736-1741   A383   Set of 6   5.00   5.00
 1741a   Souvenir sheet of 6, #1736-1741   5.00   5.00

Self-Adhesive
Die Cut Perf. 13¼ Syncopated
1742   A383   Sheet of 6, #a-f   5.00   5.00

Souvenir Sheet

End of World War II, 70th Anniv. A384

HONG KONG

Perf. 14 Syncopated
2015, Sept. 2   Litho.
Granite Paper
| 1743 | A384 | $10 multi | 2.60 | 2.60 |

Souvenir Sheet

Relocation of Court of Final Appeal — A385

Perf. 14 Syncopated
Litho. & Embossed
2015, Sept. 30   **Granite Paper**
| 1744 | A385 | $10 multi | 2.60 | 2.60 |

World Post Day — A386

Shadow pigeons made of hands, various cancels and map of: $1.70, Oceania. $2.90, Indian Ocean and East Africa. $3.70, East Asia. $5, Europe.

Perf. 13¼x14¼ Syncopated
2015, Oct. 9   Litho.
Granite Paper
| 1745-1748 | A386 | Set of 4 | 3.50 | 3.50 |
| 1748a | | Souvenir sheet of 4, #1745-1748 | 3.50 | 3.50 |

Souvenir Sheets

A387

Hong Kong 2015 Intl. Stamp Exhibition — A388

Litho. With Foil Application
2015   *Perf. 13½x13¼ Syncopated*
Granite Paper
1749	A387	$20 multi	5.25	5.25
1750	A388	$20 multi	5.25	5.25
a.		Booklet pane of 3, #1682a, 1749, 1750	16.50	—
		Complete booklet, #1750a	16.50	

Issued: No. 1749, 11/20; Nos. 1750, 1750a, 11/23. The edges of the souvenir sheet margins on Nos. 1749 and 1750 are perf. 6½ syncopated. The perforations around the souvenir sheet margins of items in the booklet are perf. 13¼ syncopated. Complete booklet sold for $65.

Ancient Chinese Scientists A389

Designs: $1.70, Zhang Heng (78-139), and seismoscope. $2.90, Zu Chongzhi (429-500), and calculation of pi. $3.70, Guo Shoujing (1231-1316), and simplified armilla. $5, Li Shizhen (1518-93), and Compendium of Materia Medica.

Perf. 13½x13¼ Syncopated
2015, Dec. 8   Litho.
Granite Paper
| 1751-1754 | A389 | Set of 4 | 3.50 | 3.50 |
| 1754a | | Souvenir sheet of 4, #1751-1754 | 3.50 | 3.50 |

New Year 2016 (Year of the Monkey) A390

Designs: $1.70, Monkey holding peach. $2.90, Monkey. $3.70, Silver monkey. $5, Beijing Opera Sun Wukong monkey mask. $10, Monkey holding peach, diff.
No. 1760, Like $10.
No. 1761: a, Ram. b, Monkey.

Perf. 13¼x14¼ Syncopated
2016, Jan. 16   Litho.
Granite Paper
| 1755-1758 | A390 | Set of 4 | 3.50 | 3.50 |

Souvenir Sheets
Litho. With Foil Application
Perf. 13¼ Syncopated
| 1759 | A390 | $10 multi | 2.60 | 2.60 |

Litho.
Silk-Faced Granite Paper
| 1760 | A390 | $50 multi | 13.00 | 13.00 |

Litho. With Foil Application (#1761a), Litho. with Metal Affixed (#1761b)
Granite Paper
| 1761 | A390 | $50 Sheet of 2, #a-b | 26.00 | 26.00 |

Nos. 1759-1760 each contain one 45x45mm stamp. See Nos. 1984a, 2281-2284.

On Jan. 16, 2016, Hong Kong issued the stamps pictured above, having franking values of $1.70 and $3.70 respectively. The stamps were each printed in sheets of 12 + 12 non-personalizable labels. The sheets sold for $42 and $70 respectively.

Hong Kong Girl Guides, Cent. — A391

Designs: $1.70, First Aid, AIDS Knowledge, Environmental Protection and Community Health badges, girl wearing current Girl Guides uniform. $2.90, Against Corruption, Book Lover, Friendship and Thrift badges, girl wearing Brownie uniform of 1970s. $3.70, Orienteering, Country Walking, Basic Survival and Star Gazing badges, girl wearing Sea Ranger's uniform from 1940s-1970s. $5, Artist, Signaller, Craft and Knotter badges, girl wearing Brownie uniform from 1920s-1930s.

Perf. 13¼ Syncopated
2016, Feb. 22   Litho.
Granite Paper
| 1762-1765 | A391 | Set of 4 | 3.50 | 3.50 |
| 1765a | | Souvenir sheet of 4, #1762-1765, perf. 13¼x14¼ syncopated | 3.50 | 3.50 |

Syncopation on No. 1765a differs from that on Nos. 1762-1765. A booklet containing panes of Nos. 1762-1763 and 1764-1765 respectively sold for $45.

Public Architecture A392

Designs: $1.70, Hong Kong Museum of Coastal Defense. $2.70, Victoria Park Swimming Pool. $2.90, Sai Kung Waterfront Park. $3.10, Ping Shan Tin Shui Wai Leisure and Cultural Building. $3.70, Hong Kong Wetland Park. $5, Electrical and Mechanical Services Department Headquarters.

Perf. 13¼ Syncopated
2016, Mar. 31   Litho.
Granite Paper
| 1766-1771 | A392 | Set of 6 | 4.75 | 4.75 |
| 1771a | | Souvenir sheet of 6, #1766-1771 | 4.75 | 4.75 |

St. John Ambulance Brigade, Cent. — A393

Designs: $1.70, Ambulance, medic treating child. $2.90, Medic treating fallen runner. $3.70, Dentistry for wheelchair-bound patient. $5, First aid training for teenagers.

Perf. 13¼x13½ Syncopated
2016, Apr. 14   Litho.
Granite Paper
| 1772-1775 | A393 | Set of 4 | 3.50 | 3.50 |
| 1775a | | Souvenir sheet of 4, #1772-1775 | 3.50 | 3.50 |

A booklet containing panes of Nos. 1772-1773 and 1774-1775 respectively sold for $45.

Souvenir Sheet

Grand Canal World Heritage Site, People's Republic of China A394

Perf. 14 Syncopated
2016, May 10   **Litho. & Embossed**
Granite Paper
| 1776 | A394 | $10 multi | 2.60 | 2.60 |

See No. 2191g.

Toys Made in Hong Kong From 1940s-1960s A395

Designs: $1.70, Plastic hammer. $2.20, Paper dolls. $2.90, Water pistol. $3.10, Miniature plastic swords. $3.70, Yellow plastic ducks. $5, Tin frog.

Perf. 13¼x14¼ Syncopated
2016, June 8   Litho.
Granite Paper
| 1777-1782 | A395 | Set of 6 | 4.75 | 4.75 |
| 1782a | | Miniature sheet of 18, 3 each #1777-1782 | 14.50 | 14.50 |

Souvenir Sheet

Ceva's Theorem A396

2016, July 6   Litho.   Perf.
Granite Paper
| 1783 | A396 | $10 multi | 2.60 | 2.60 |

57th International Mathematical Olympiad, Hong Kong.
No. 1783 exists imperforate.

2016 Summer Olympics, Rio de Janeiro — A397

Designs: $1.70, Track and cycling. $2.90, Table tennis and badminton. $3.70, Windsurfing and swimming. $5, Golf and rugby.

Litho. With Foil Application
2016, Aug. 5   *Perf. 13¾ Syncopated*
Granite Paper
| 1784-1787 | A397 | Set of 4 | 3.50 | 3.50 |
| 1787a | | Souvenir sheet of 4, #1784-1787 | 3.50 | 3.50 |

Tribute to Teachers — A398

Designs: $1.70, Hearts and open book. $2.90, Teacher and students. $3.70, Trophy. $5, Teacher and student. $10, Mortarboard and books.

Perf. 13½x13¼ Syncopated
2016, Sept. 6   Litho.
Granite Paper
| 1788-1791 | A398 | Set of 4 | 3.50 | 3.50 |

Souvenir Sheet
| 1792 | A398 | $10 multi | 2.60 | 2.60 |

Lantau Trail — A399

Designs and trail segment: Nos. 1793, 1805, $1.70, Mui Wo Ferry Pier (Mui Wo to Nam Shan). Nos. 1794, 1806, $1.70, Stone chalets (Nam Shan to Pak Kung Au). Nos. 1795, 1807, $1.70, Lantau Peak (Pak Kung Au to Ngong Ping). Nos. 1796, 1808, $1.70, Wisdom Path and Statue of Buddha (Ngong Ping to Sham Wat Road). Nos. 1797, 1809, $1.70, Kneecap Peak (Sham Wat Road to Man Cheung Po). Nos. 1798, 1810, $1.70, Tai O fishing village (Man Cheung Po to Tai O). Nos. 1799, 1811, $1.70, Fan Lau Fort (Tai O to Kau Ling Chung). Nos. 1800, 1812, $1.70, Lantau South Obelisk (Kau Ling Chung to Shek Pik). Nos. 1801, 1813, $1.70, Shek Pik Reservoir (Shek Pik to Shui Hau). Nos. 1802, 1814, $1.70, Shui Hau Wan (Shui Hau to Tung Chung Road). Nos. 1803, 1815, $1.70, Waterfall (Tung Chunng Road to Pui O). Nos. 1804, 1816, $1.70, Pui O Beach, Sunset Peak, Lin Fa Shan (Pui O to Mui Wo).

Perf. 13¼ Syncopated
2016, Oct. 13   Litho.
Granite Paper
| 1793-1804 | A399 | Set of 12 | 5.25 | 5.25 |
| 1804a | | Souvenir sheet of 12, #1793-1804 | 5.25 | 5.25 |

Booklet Stamps
Self-Adhesive
Die Cut Perf. 13¼ Syncopated
Litho.
| 1805-1816 | A399 | Set of 12 | 5.25 | 5.25 |
| 1816a | | Booklet pane of 12, #1805-1816 | | 5.25 |

Sun Yat-sen (1866-1925), President of the Republic of China — A400

Sun Yat-sen and: $1.70, Government Central School. $2.90, Alice Memorial Hospital and College of Medicine, vert. $3.70, Hong Kong Hotel, vert. $5, Main Building of University of Hong Kong.

HONG KONG

Perf. 13¼ Syncopated
2016, Nov. 12 Litho.
Granite Paper
1817-1820 A400 Set of 4 3.50 3.50
1820a Souvenir sheet of 4, #1817-1820 3.50 3.50

A booklet containing panes of Nos. 1817-1818 and 1819-1820 respectively sold for $45.

Pencil Drawings by Kong Kai-Ming — A401

Designs: $1.70, Airport Tunnel, Hung Hom. $2.20, Argyle Street, Mong Kok. $2.90, Kwun Tong MTR Station. $3.10, Wan Chai Tram Depot. $3.70, Canton Road. $5, Zoroastrian Church, Causeway Bay. $10, Aberdeen.

Perf. 13½ Syncopated
2016, Dec. 6 Litho. & Engr.
Granite Paper
1821-1826 A401 Set of 6 4.75 4.75
Souvenir Sheet
Perf. 13½x13¾
1827 A401 $10 multi 2.60 2.60

No. 1827 contains one 60x43mm stamp.

New Year 2017 (Year of the Rooster) A402

Designs: $1.70, Rooster made of fabric. $2.90, Tin rooster. $3.70, Rooster made of seashells. $5, Silver rooster.
$10, Embroidered rooster, diff.
No. 1833, Like $10.
No. 1834: a, Monkey. b, Rooster.

Perf. 13¼x14¼ Syncopated
2017, Jan. 7 Litho.
Granite Paper
1828-1831 A402 Set of 4 3.50 3.50
Souvenir Sheets
Litho. With Foil Application
Perf. 13¼ Syncopated
1832 A402 $10 multi 2.60 2.60
Litho.
Silk-Faced Granite Paper
1833 A402 $50 multi 13.00 13.00
Litho. With Foil Application (#1834a), Litho. with Metal Affixed (#1834b)
Granite Paper
1834 A402 $50 Sheet of 2, #a-b 26.00 26.00

Nos. 1832-1833 each contain one 45x45mm stamp. See Nos. 1984b, 2281-2284.

On Jan. 7, 2017, Hong Kong issued the stamps pictured above, having franking values of $1.70 and $3.70 respectively. The stamps were each printed in sheets of 12 + 12 non-personalizable labels. The sheets sold for $42 and $70 respectively.

Souvenir Sheet

Kaiping Diaolou and Villages UNESCO World Heritage Site — A403

Perf. 13x13¼ Syncopated
2017, Feb. 16 Litho. & Embossed
Granite Paper
1835 A403 $10 multi 2.60 2.60
See No. 2191f.

Revitalization of Historic Buildings A404

Designs: $1.70, Viva Blue House. $2.20, Oi! Arts Center. $2.90, Green Hub. $3.10, Stone Houses Family Garden. $3.70, PMQ. $5, Mallory Street Revitalization Project.

Litho. With Foil Application
Perf. 13¼x14¼ Syncopated
2017, Apr. 25 **Granite Paper**
1836-1841 A404 Set of 6 4.75 4.75
1841a Souvenir sheet of 6, #1836-1841 4.75 4.75

A booklet containing panes of Nos. 1836-1837, 1838-1839 and 1840-1841, respectively sold for $50.

Outdoor Activities — A405

Inscriptions: $1.70, Picnic and barbecue. $2.20, Cycling. $2.90, Visiting heritage sites. $3.10, Beach fun. $3.70, Hiking. $5, Outdoor photography.

Perf. 13½x13¼ Syncopated
2017, May 2 Litho.
Granite Paper
1842-1847 A405 Set of 6 4.75 4.75
1847a Souvenir sheet of 6, #1842-1847 4.75 4.75

Numbered Typhoon Signals, Cent. — A406

Inscriptions: $1.70, Standby signal No. 1. $2.20, Strong wind signal No. 3. $2.90, Gale or storm signal No. 8. $3.70, Increasing gale or storm signal No. 9. $5, Hurricane signal No. 10.
$10, Hoisting of hurricane signal No. 10, horiz.

Perf. 13½x13¼ Syncopated
Litho. & Silk-Screened
2017, June 13 **Granite Paper**
1848-1852 A406 Set of 5 4.00 4.00
Souvenir Sheet
Perf. 14¼x14 Syncopated
1853 A406 $10 multi 2.60 2.60

A booklet containing panes of Nos. 1848-1850 and 1851-1852, respectively sold for $48. No. 1853 contains one 63x34mm stamp.

Souvenir Sheet

Stationing of People's Liberation Army in Hong Kong, 20th Anniv. — A407

Perf. 14¼x14 Syncopated
2017, June 20 Litho.
Granite Paper
1854 A407 $10 multi 2.60 2.60

Return of Hong Kong to People's Republic of China, 20th Anniv. — A408

Perf. 13 Syncopated
2017, July 1 Photo.
1855 A408 $1.70 multi .45 .45

See People's Republic of China Nos. 4455-4457.

Hong Kong Special Administrative Region, 20th Anniv. — A409

Designs: $1.70, Buildings and flags of Hong Kong and People's Republic of China. $2.90, Athletes, violinist, dancer and actors. $3.70, Buildings and doves. $5, People releasing balloons.

Litho. With Foil Application
Perf. 14x13¼ Syncopated
2017, July 1 **Granite Paper**
1856-1859 A409 Set of 4 3.50 3.50
1859a Souvenir sheet of 4, #1856-1859 3.50 3.50

Five Senses — A410

Designs: $1.70, Hearing. $2.20, Sight. $2.90, Smell. $3.70, Taste. $5, Touch.
$10, Children experiencing the five senses, horiz.

Litho. & Thermography ($1.70, $5), Litho.
Perf. 13¾ Syncopated
2017, July 18 **Granite Paper**
1860-1864 A410 Set of 5 4.00 4.00
1864a Souvenir sheet of 15, 3 each #1860-1864 12.00 12.00
Souvenir Sheet
Perf. 14¼x14 Syncopated
1865 A410 $10 multi 2.60 2.60

No. 1861 has a circular die cut hole punched out to simulate camera lens. No. 1862 is impregnated with a peach scent. No. 1863 has vanilla-flavored gum. No. 1865 contains one 105x60mm stamp.

Rare Flora — A411

Designs: $1.70, Ilex graciliflora. $2.90, Bulbophyllum bicolor. $3.70, Begonia hongkongensis. $5, Illicium angustisepalum.

Perf. 13¾ Syncopated
2017, Aug. 17 Litho.
Granite Paper
1866-1869 A411 Set of 4 3.50 3.50
1869a Souvenir sheet of 4, #1866-1869 3.50 3.50

Paintings and Calligraphy by Jao Tsung-I (1917-2018) — A412

Designs: $1.70, Pine Trees in Huangshan. $2.20, Pine Trees and Arhat. $2.90, Five Character Couplet in Official Script. $3.10, Victoria Peak After the Rain. $3.70, Avalokitesvara After the Style of Tang Dynasty. $5, Calligraphy in Bronze Script.
$10, Four-screen Lotus Set, horiz.

Perf. 14¼x14 Syncopated
2017, Sept. 5 Litho.
Granite Paper
1870-1875 A412 Set of 6 4.75 4.75
1875a Souvenir sheet of 12, 2 each #1870-1875 9.50 9.50
Souvenir Sheet
Perf. 14x14¼ Syncopated
1876 A412 $10 multi 2.60 2.60

No. 1876 contains one 75x65mm stamp.

Shopping Areas — A413

Designs: $1.70, Goldfish Market. $2.20, Chinese Medicine Street. $2.90, Jade Market. $3.10, Kitchenware Street. $3.70, Flower Market. $5, Yau Ma Tei Wholesale Fruit Market.

Perf. 13¼x12¾ Syncopated
2017, Sept. 19 Litho.
Granite Paper
1877-1882 A413 Set of 6 4.75 4.75
1882a Souvenir sheet of 6, #1877-1882 4.75 4.75

Qipaos — A414

Qipao from: $1.70, 1920s. $2.20, 1930s. $2.90, 1940s. $3.10, 1950s. $3.70, 1960s. $5, 1970s.
$10, $20, Contemporary qipao.

Perf. 13½x13¼ Syncopated
2017, Oct. 17 Litho.
Granite Paper (#1883-1889)
1883-1888 A414 Set of 6 4.75 4.75
1888a Souvenir sheet of 18, 3 each #1883-1888 14.50 14.50
Souvenir Sheet
Perf. 12¾x13
1889 A414 $10 multi 2.60 2.60
On Taffeta-Faced Paper
1890 A414 $20 multi 5.25 5.25

Nos. 1889-1890 each contain one 35x78mm stamp. A booklet containing panes of Nos. 1883-1885, 1886-1888, and 1889, respectively sold for $60.

HONG KONG

Bamboo Carvings — A415

Designs: $1.70, Cricket cage, by Xu Subai, 1959. $2.20, Lingzhi fungus and narcissus, c. 1723-35 (50x30mm). $2.90, Brushpot, 18th cent. (50x30mm). $3.10, Incense holder, 17th-18th cent. (50x30mm). $3.70, Water container, c. 1662-1722 (50x30mm). $5, Jar, c. 1736-95 (50x30mm).

Perf. 13½x13¼ Syncopated
2017, Nov. 14   Litho. & Embossed
Granite Paper

1891-1896	A415	Set of 6	4.75	4.75
1896a		Souvenir sheet of 6, #1891-1896	4.75	4.75

Earth Features Type of 2014

Designs: $2, Port Island. $2.60, Ma Shi Chau. $3.40, Yan Chau. $4.90, Fa Shan.

Perf. 12¾x13¼ Syncopated
2018, Jan. 1   Litho.
Granite Paper (#1897-1902)

1897	A370	$2 multi	.70	.70
1898	A370	$3.40 multi	.90	.90
1899	A370	$4.90 multi	1.25	1.25
		Nos. 1897-1899 (3)	2.85	2.85

Coil Stamps
Size:20x24mm
Perf. 14¾x13¾

1900	A370	$2 multi	.55	.55
1901	A370	$2.60 multi	.70	.70
1902	A370	$4.90 multi	1.25	1.25
		Nos. 1900-1902 (3)	2.50	2.50

Booklet Stamps
Self-Adhesive
Size: 25x29mm
Die Cut Perf. 12¾x13¾ Syncopated

1903	A370	$2 multi	.55	.55
a.		Booklet pane of 10	5.50	
1904	A370	$2.60 multi	.70	.70
a.		Booklet pane of 10	7.00	
1905	A370	$4.90 multi	1.25	1.25
a.		Booklet pane of 10	12.50	
		Nos. 1903-1905 (3)	2.50	2.50

New Year 2018 (Year of the Dog) — A416

Designs: $2, Porcelain dog. $3.70, Jade dog. $4.90, Ceramic dog. $5, Dog made of seashells.
No. 1910: a, Rooster. b, Dog.
$10, Porcelain dog (with gold emblem at right). No. 1912, Porcelain dog (without gold emblem at right).

Perf. 13¼x14¼ Syncopated
2018, Jan. 27   Litho.
Granite Paper

| 1906-1909 | A416 | Set of 4 | 4.00 | 4.00 |

Litho. With Foil Application (#1910a), Litho. With Metal Affixed (#1910b)
Perf. 13¼x12¾ Syncopated

| 1910 | A416 | $50 Sheet of 2, #a-b | 26.00 | 26.00 |

Souvenir Sheets
Litho. With Foil Application
Perf. 13¼ Syncopated

| 1911 | A416 | $10 gold & multi | 2.60 | 2.60 |

Litho.
On Silk-Faced Granite Paper

| 1912 | A416 | $50 multi | 13.00 | 13.00 |

Nos. 1911-1912 each contain one 45x45mm stamp. See Nos. 1984c, 2281-2284.

On Jan. 27, 2018, Hong Kong issued the stamps pictured above, having franking values of $2 and $3.70, respectively. The stamps were each printed in sheets of 12 + 12 non-personalizable labels depicting various images. The sheets sold for $46 and $85, respectively.

Festive Customs — A417

Inscriptions: $2, Putting Up Spring Festival Scrolls. $2.60, Throwing Wishing Placards. $3.40, Offering First Incense in Chinese New Year. $3.70, Spinning Wheels of Fortune. $4.90, Drawing Chinese Fortune Sticks. $5, Unicorn Dance.

Litho. With Silver Foil Application
Perf. 13½x13¾ Syncopated
2018, Feb. 27   Granite Paper

| 1913-1918 | A417 | Set of 6 | 5.50 | 5.50 |
| 1918a | | Souvenir sheet of 6, #1913-1918 | 5.50 | 5.50 |

Hong Kong at Night A418

Designs: $2, Intersection of Apliu and Kweilin Streets, Sham Shui Po. $3.70, Street view of Central Hong Kong. $4.90, Monster Building housing complex, Quarry Bay. $5, Tian Tan Buddha.

Perf. 14½ Syncopated
2018, Mar. 22   Litho.
Granite Paper

| 1919-1922 | A418 | Set of 4 | 4.00 | 4.00 |
| 1922a | | Souvenir sheet of 4, #1919-1922 | 4.00 | 4.00 |

Hong Kong Fire Services Department, 150th Anniv. A419

Designs: $2, Pump Escape truck. $2.60, Mobile Command Unit. $3.40, Ambulance. $3.70, Major Pump. $4.90, Mobile Command Unit, diff. $5, Ambulance, diff.
$10, Uniforms of firefighters from 19th century to present.

Perf. 14 Syncopated
2018, May 8   Litho.
Granite Paper

| 1923-1928 | A419 | Set of 6 | 5.50 | 5.50 |

Souvenir Sheet
Perf. 13¼ Syncopated

| 1929 | A419 | $10 multi | 2.60 | 2.60 |

No. 1929 contains one 130x30mm stamp. A booklet containing panes of Nos. 1923 and 1926, 1924 and 1927, and 1925 and 1928, respectively sold for $53.

Inclusive Communication — A420

Person, English, Chinese and Braille words for: $2, Friend. $2.60, Good morning. $3.40, Hello. $3.70, Keep it up. $4.90, Love. $5, Thank you.
$20, Woman using sign language, vert.

Litho. & Thermography
2018, June 7   *Perf. 13¼ Syncopated*
Granite Paper

| 1930-1935 | A420 | Set of 6 | 5.50 | 5.50 |

Litho. With Plastic Lenticular Lens Affixed
Perf. 13½x13¾ Syncopated

| 1936 | A420 | $20 multi | 5.25 | 5.25 |

No. 1936 contains one 28x45mm stamp.

Numerals and Mathematical Symbols — A421

Designs: No. 1937, $2, "0." No. 1938, $2, "1." No. 1939, $2, "2." No. 1940, $2, "3." No. 1941, $2, "4." No. 1942, $2, "5." No. 1943, $2, "6." No. 1944, $2, "7." No. 1945, $2, "8." No. 1946, $2, "9." No. 1947, $2, Plus sign No. 1948, $2, Minus sign. No. 1949, $2, Multiplication sign. No. 1950, $2, Division sign. No. 1951, $2, Percent sign. No. 1952, $2, Equal sign.

Perf. 13¼ Syncopated
2018, July 17   Litho.
Granite Paper

| 1937-1952 | A421 | Set of 16 | 8.25 | 8.25 |
| 1952a | | Souvenir sheet of 16, #1937-1952 | 8.25 | 8.25 |

Souvenir Sheet
Temple of Heaven, Beijing A422

Perf. 13¼x13 Syncopated
2018, Aug. 10   Litho. & Embossed
Granite Paper

| 1953 | A422 | $10 multi | 2.60 | 2.60 |

See No. 2191d.

Guangzhou-Shenzhen-Hong Kong Express Rail Link — A423

Outline of train and attractions from: $2, Guangzhou. $3.70, Shenzhen. $4.90, Hong Kong. $5, Hong Kong, diff.

Perf. 14¼x14 Syncopated
2018, Sept. 17   Litho.
Granite Paper

| 1954-1957 | A423 | Set of 4 | 4.00 | 4.00 |
| 1957a | | Souvenir sheet of 4, #1954-1957 | 4.00 | 4.00 |

Souvenir Sheet
Lotus and Bauhinia Blakeana Flowers A424

Perf. 13¼ Syncopated
2018, Sept. 21   Litho.
Granite Paper

| 1958 | A424 | $10 multi | 2.60 | 2.60 |

Macao 2018 Asian International Stamp Exhibition.

Cantonese Opera — A425

Scenes from: $2, The Story of Princess Changping. $2.60, The Moon Pavilion. $3.40, Lord Guan Gong Releasing Lady Diao Chan. $3.70, The Princess in Distress. $4.90, Butterfly Lovers. $5, Lady Zhaojun Departing for the Frontier.

Perf. 14x13½ Syncopated
2018, Oct. 9   Litho.
Granite Paper

| 1959-1964 | A425 | Set of 6 | 5.50 | 5.50 |
| 1964a | | Block of 6, #1959-1964 | 5.50 | 5.50 |

No. 1964a was printed in sheets containing two blocks. A booklet containing panes of Nos. 1959-1960, 1961-1962 and 1963-1964, respectively sold for $53.

Opening of Hong Kong-Zhuhai-Macao Bridge — A426

Structures and: $2, H. $3.70, Z. $4.90, M. $5, B.
$10, Network of lines, horiz.

Perf. 13¾ Syncopated
2018, Oct. 30   Litho.
Granite Paper

| 1965-1968 | A426 | Set of 4 | 4.00 | 4.00 |

Souvenir Sheet
Perf. 12 Syncopated

| 1969 | A426 | $10 multi | 2.60 | 2.60 |

No. 1969 contains one 100x40mm stamp.

Miniature Sheet

Opening of Hong-Kong-Zhuhai-Macao Bridge — A427

No. 1970: a, $2, Qingzhou Navigational Channel Bridge, city skyline. b, $3.70, East Artificial Island. c, $4, Tunnel.

Perf. 13 Syncopated (Hong Kong and Macao stamps), 13¼ Syncopated (People's Republic of China stamps)
2018, Oct. 30   Photo.

| 1970 | A427 | Sheet of 9, #1970a-1970c, People's Republic of China #4584-4586, Macao #1542a-1542c | 10.50 | 10.50 |

No. 1970 sold for $40 and 40p in Macao, and is identical to Macao #1542d.

HONG KONG

Souvenir Sheet

Ying Wa College, 200th Anniv, A428

Perf. 14¼x13¾ Syncopated
2018, Nov. 9   Litho.
Granite Paper

1971	A428	$10 multi + 5 labels	2.60	2.60

Characters From Novels by Jin Yong (1924-2018) — A429

Designs: $2, Guo Jing and Huang Rong from *The Eagle-shooting Heroes*. $2.60, Chen Jialuo from *The Book and the Sword*. $3.40, Linghu Chong and Ren Yingying from *The Smiling Proud Wanderer*. $3.70, Zhang Wuji from *The Heaven Sword and the Dragong Sabre*. $4.90, Yang Guo and Xiaolongnü from *The Giant Eagle and its Companion*. $5, Wei Xiaobao and Kangxi from *The Deer and the Cauldron*.
$10, Qiao Feng, Xu Zhu, and Duan Yu from *The Demi-gods and Semi-devils*.
Nos. 1979a-1979ad: Various images of Zhang Wu Ji in Tai Chi poses.

Perf. 13¾x13½ Syncopated
2018, Dec. 6   Litho.
Granite Paper

1972-1977	A429	Set of 6	5.50	5.50

Souvenir Sheet
Perf. 13¾ Syncopated
1978	A429	$10 multi	2.60	2.60

Perf. 13¼x14 Syncopated
1979		Booklet of 30	18.00	
a.-ad.	A429	$2 Any booklet pane	.60	—

No. 1978 contains one 45x70mm stamp. No. 1979, a booklet bound by string that sold for $70, contains 30 different booklet panes, each containing one 45x70mm stamp. The panes in the booklet are arranged so that when the pages are riffled the image of Zhang Wu Ji appears to go through a series of Tai Chi moves, and the yin-yang emblem in the pane margins rotates. There is no marking on any of the stamps or booklet pane margins that indicate its placement in the booklet.

New Year Types of 2016-2018 and

New Year 2019 (Year of the Pig) — A430

Designs: $2, Fabric pig. $3.70, Carved wooden pigs. $4.90, Ceramic pig. $5, Jade pig.
No. 1984: a, Monkey holding peach. b, Rooster made of sea shells. c, Dog made of sea shells. d, Ceramic pig.
No. 1985: a, Dog. b, Pig.
$10, Pig and piglets (with gold emblem at right). No. 1987, Pig and piglets (without gold emblem at right).

Perf. 13¼x14¼ Syncopated
2019, Jan. 12   Litho.
Granite Paper

1980-1983	A430	Set of 4	4.00	4.00

Litho. & Embossed With Foil Application
Perf. 13¼x13¾ Syncopated
1984		Block of 4	10.50	10.50
a.	A390	$10 multi	2.60	2.60
b.	A402	$10 multi	2.60	2.60
c.	A416	$10 multi	2.60	2.60
d.	A430	$10 multi	2.60	2.60

Litho. With Foil Application (#1985a), Litho. With Metal Affixed (#1985b)
Perf. 13¼x12¼ Syncopated
1985	A430	$50 Sheet of 2, #a-		
		b	25.50	25.50

Souvenir Sheets
Litho. With Foil Application
Perf. 13¼ Syncopated
1986	A430	$10 gold & multi	2.60	2.60

Litho.
On Silk-Faced Granite Paper
1987	A430	$50 multi	13.00	13.00

Nos. 1986-1987 each contain one 45x45mm stamp. See Nos. 2281-2284.

On Jan. 12, 2019, Hong Kong issued the stamps pictured above, having franking values of $2 and $3.70, respectively. The stamps were each printed in sheets of 12 + 12 non-personalizable labels depicting various images. The sheets sold for $46 and $85, respectively.

Government Flying Service — A431

Designs: $2, Air ambulance. $2.60, Inshore search and rescue. $3.40, Offshore search and rescue. $3.70, Fire fighting. $4.90, Aerial survey. $5, Internal security.
$10, Government Flying Service helicopter and airplane over Hong Kong.

Perf. 13¼x14¼ Syncopated
2019, Feb. 28   Litho.
Granite Paper

1988-1993	A431	Set of 6	5.50	5.50
1993a		Souvenir sheet of 12, 2 each #1988-1993	11.00	11.00

Souvenir Sheet
Perf. 13½ Syncopated
1994	A431	$10 multi	2.60	2.60

No. 1994 contains one 108x38mm stamp. A booklet containing panes of Nos. 1988-1989, 1990-1991, 1992-1993 and 1994, respectively, sold for $63.

Souvenir Sheets

Xiqu Center A432

Perf. 14x13½ Syncopated
2019, Mar. 19   Litho.
Granite Paper

1995	A432	$10 multi	2.60	2.60

Litho. & Embossed With Foil Application
1996	A432	$20 sil & multi	5.25	5.25

Pok Oi Hospital, Cent. — A433

Inscription: $2, Chinese & Western Medicine Services. $3.70, Education Services. $4.90, Elderly Services. $5, Youth & Family Services.

Perf. 13½x13¼ Syncopated
2019, Apr. 2   Litho.
Granite Paper

1997-2000	A433	Set of 4	4.00	4.00
2000a		Souvenir sheet of 4, #1997-2000	4.00	4.00

A booklet containing panes of Nos. 1997-1998 and 1999-2000 sold for $48.

Hong Kong Police Force — A434

Inscription: $2, Boundary Security. $2.60, Crime Investigation and Detection. $3.40, Cultural Diversity and Equal Opportunity. $3.70, Police Training. $4.90, International Collaboration. $5, Traffic Management.
$10, Police officers and Emergency Unit vehicle.

Perf. 13¼x14¼ Syncopated
2019, Apr. 30   Litho.
Granite Paper

2001-2006	A434	Set of 6	5.50	5.50

Souvenir Sheet
Perf. 12x11¾ Syncopated
2007	A434	$10 multi	2.60	2.60

No. 2007 contains one 60x40mm stamp. A booklet containing panes of Nos. 2001-2002, 2003-2004, and 2005-2006, respectively, sold for $53.

Souvenir Sheet

China 2019 World Stamp Exhibition, Wuhan, People's Republic of China — A435

Perf. 13¼ Syncopated
2019, June 11   Litho.
Granite Paper

2008	A435	$10 multi	2.60	2.60

Stars and Jars A436

Hearts in Envelope A437

Rose and Hearts A438

Fireworks A439

Disco Balls A440

Diamonds A441

Perf. 12 Syncopated
2019, June 11   Litho.
Granite Paper
Inscribed "Local Mail Postage"

2009	A436	($2) multi	.55	.55
2010	A437	($2) multi	.55	.55
2011	A438	($2) multi	.55	.55
2012	A439	($2) multi	.55	.55

Litho. With Holographic Foil Application
Inscribed "Air Mail Postage"

2013	A440	($4.90) multi	1.25	1.25
2014	A441	($4.90) multi	1.25	1.25
a.		Block of 6, #2009-2014, + 6 labels	4.75	4.75
		Nos. 2009-2014 (6)	4.70	4.70

Marine Life — A442

Designs: $2, Various fish. $2.60, Jellyfish and fish. $3.40, Fish, dolphin and sea turtle. $3.70, Fish and coral. $4.90, Seahorse, fish and coral. $5, Fish, sea cucumber and coral.

Perf. 13¼ Syncopated
2019, July 16   Litho.
Granite Paper

2015	A442	$2 multi	.50	.50
a.		Miniature sheet of 4	2.00	2.00
2016	A442	$2.60 multi	.65	.65
a.		Miniature sheet of 4	2.60	2.60
2017	A442	$3.40 multi	.90	.90
a.		Miniature sheet of 4	3.75	3.75
2018	A442	$3.70 multi	.95	.95
a.		Miniature sheet of 4	4.00	4.00
2019	A442	$4.90 multi	1.25	1.25
a.		Miniature sheet of 4	5.00	5.00
2020	A442	$5 multi	1.40	1.40
a.		Miniature sheet of 4	5.75	5.75
b.		Souvenir sheet of 6, #2015-2020	5.75	5.75
		Nos. 2015-2020 (6)	5.65	5.65

Souvenir Sheet

Zuojiang Huashan Rock Art UNESCO World Heritage Site — A443

Perf. 13½x13¼ Syncopated
2019, Aug. 13   Litho. & Embossed
Granite Paper

2021	A443	$10 multi	2.60	2.60

See No. 2191e.

Souvenir Sheet

Map of Guangdong-Hong Kong-Macao Greater Bay Area — A444

Perf. 14x13½ Syncopated
2019, Sept. 26   Litho.
Granite Paper

2022	A444	$10 multi	2.60	2.60

A445

HONG KONG

A446

A447

A448

People's Republic of China, 70th Anniv. A449

Perf. 13¼x14 Syncopated
2019, Oct. 1   Litho.
Granite Paper
2023	A445	$2 multi	.50	.50
2024	A446	$3.70 multi	.95	.95
2025	A447	$4.90 multi	1.25	1.25
2026	A448	$5 multi	1.40	1.40
a.	Souvenir sheet of 4, #2023-2026		4.25	4.25
	Nos. 2023-2026 (4)		4.10	4.10

Souvenir Sheet
Perf. 13x13½ Syncopated
| 2027 | A449 | $10 multi | 2.60 | 2.60 |

Sections of the MacLehose Trail — A450

Hiking trail section: No. 2028, $2, Pak Tam Chung to Long Ke. No. 2029, $2, Long Ke to Pak Tam Au. No. 2030, $2, Pak Tam Au to Kei Ling Ha. No. 2031, $2, Kei Ling Ha to Tate's Cairn. No. 2032, $2, Tate's Cairn to Tai Po Road. No. 2033, $2, Tai Po Road to Shing Mun. No. 2034, $2, Shing Mun to Lead Mine Pass. No. 2035, $2, Lead Mine Pass to Route Twisk. No. 2036, $2, Route Twisk to Tin Fu Tsai. No. 2037, $2, Tin Fu Tsai to Tuen Mun.

Perf. 13¼x14¼ Syncopated
Litho. & Silk-Screened
2019, Oct. 24
Granite Paper
| 2028-2037 | A450 | Set of 10 | 5.25 | 5.25 |
| 2037a | | Souvenir sheet of 10, #2028-2037 | 5.25 | 5.25 |

Nos. 2028-2037 and 2037a have laser-cut holes in the vignette.

Mr. Chin, Old Master Q, Big Potato on Unicycles A451

Miss Chen and Old Master Q A452

Old Master Q at His Fortune Telling Table A453

Old Master Q in Superhero Costume A454

Old Master Q, Big Potato, Mr. Chin Dining A455

Mr. Chin, Big Potato, Old Master Q Eating From Hot Pot A456

Old Master Q, Big Potato, Mr. Chin Under Umbrella A457

Old Master Q at Butcher's Stall A458

Characters Seated — A459

Litho., Litho. & Embossed ($20)
Perf. 13½x13 Syncopated
2019, Dec. 5
Printing on Reverse (#2038-2045)
Granite Paper
2038	A451	$2 multi	.55	.55
2039	A452	$2 multi	.55	.55
2040	A453	$2 multi	.55	.55
2041	A454	$2 multi	.55	.55
2042	A455	$2 multi	.55	.55
2043	A456	$2 multi	.55	.55
2044	A457	$2 multi	.55	.55
2045	A458	$2 multi	.55	.55
	Nos. 2038-2045 (8)		4.40	4.40

Souvenir Sheets
Perf. 13½x13¼ Syncopated
| 2046 | A459 | $10 multi | 2.60 | 2.60 |
| 2047 | A459 | $20 multi | 5.25 | 5.25 |

Coil Stamps
Self-Adhesive
Die Cut Perf. 13½x13¼ Syncopated
2048	A451	$2 multi	.55	.55
2049	A452	$2 multi	.55	.55
2050	A453	$2 multi	.55	.55
2051	A454	$2 multi	.55	.55
2052	A455	$2 multi	.55	.55
2053	A456	$2 multi	.55	.55
2054	A457	$2 multi	.55	.55
2055	A458	$2 multi	.55	.55
a.	Vert. strip of 8, 2048-2055		4.50	
	Nos. 2048-2055 (8)		4.40	4.40

Characters from "Old Master Q," comic strip by Alphonso Wong (1925-2017).

New Year 2020 (Year of the Rat) — A460

Designs: $2, Clay rat. $3.70, Embroidered rat. $4.90, Ceramic rat. $5, Glass rat.
No. 2060: a, Pig. b, Rat.
$10, Rat facing left (with red metallic emblem at left). No. 2062, Rat facing left (without red metallic emblem at left).

Perf. 13½x13¼ Syncopated
2020, Jan. 11   Litho.
Granite Paper
| 2056-2059 | A460 | Set of 4 | 4.00 | 4.00 |

Litho. (#2060a), Litho. With Metal Affixed (#2060b)
| 2060 | A460 | $50 Sheet of 2, #a-b | 26.00 | 26.00 |

Souvenir Sheets
Litho. With Foil Application
Perf. 13¼ Syncopated
| 2061 | A460 | $10 multi | 2.60 | 2.60 |

Litho.
On Silk-Faced Granite Paper
| 2062 | A460 | $50 multi | 13.00 | 13.00 |

Nos. 2061-2062 each contain one 45x45mm stamp. See Nos. 2281-2284.

On Jan. 11, 2020, Hong Kong issued the stamps pictured above, having franking values of $2 and $4.90, respectively. The stamps were each printed in sheets of 12 + 12 non-personalizable labels depicting various images. The sheets sold for $63 and $99, respectively.

Spring Showers A461

Spring Commences A462

Vernal Equinox A463

Insects Waken A464

Corn Rain A465

Bright and Clear A466

Perf. 13x13¼ Syncopated
2020, Feb. 4   Litho.
Granite Paper
2063	A461	$2 multi	.55	.55
2064	A462	$2 multi	.55	.55
2065	A463	$2 multi	.55	.55
2066	A464	$2 multi	.55	.55
2067	A465	$2 multi	.55	.55
2068	A466	$2 multi	.55	.55
a.	Souvenir sheet of 6, #2063-2068		3.50	3.50
	Nos. 2063-2068 (6)		3.30	3.30

Values for Nos. 2063-2068 are for stamps with flanking selvage.

Hong Kong Young Women's Christian Association, Cent. — A467

Inscriptions: $2, Women & Family Services. $3.70, Youth & Community Services. $4.90, Education & Employment Services. $5, Elderly Services.

Perf. 14x14¼ Syncopated
2020, Mar. 10   Litho.
Granite Paper
| 2069-2072 | A467 | Set of 4 | 4.00 | 4.00 |
| 2072a | | Souvenir sheet of 4, #2069-2072 | 4.00 | 4.00 |

A booklet containing two panes, one with Nos. 2069-2070 and the other with Nos. 2071-2072, sold for $48.

Board Games — A468

Designs: $2, Chinese chess. $2.60, Jungle. $3.40, Aeroplane chess game. $3.70, Chess. $4.90, Chinese checkers. $5, Go.

Perf. 14x13¾ Syncopated
2020, Apr. 21   Litho.
| 2073-2078 | A468 | Set of 6 | 5.75 | 5.75 |
| 2078a | | Souvenir sheet of 6, #2073-2078, perf. 13¼ syncopated, + 3 labels | 5.75 | 5.75 |

Art From the Chih Lo Lou Collection A469

Designs: $2, Landscapes Depicting Poems of Huang Yanlu, by Shitao (1642-1707). $2.60, Gathering Fungus, by Lu Zhi (1496-1576) (42x44mm). $3.40, Miscellaneous Subject, by Chen Zi (1634-1711). $3.70, Left third of Peach Blossom Retreat, by Tang Yin (1470-1523) (42x44mm). $4.90, Center third of Peach Blossom Retreat (42x44mm). $5, Right third of Peach Blossom Retreat (42x44mm). $10, $20, Splashed-color Landscape, by Zhang Daqian (1899-1983).

Perf. 13 Syncopated
2020, May 21   Litho.
Granite Paper
| 2079-2084 | A469 | Set of 6 | 5.75 | 5.75 |
| 2084a | | Souvenir sheet of 12, 2 each #2079-2084 | 11.50 | 11.50 |

Souvenir Sheets
| 2085 | A469 | $10 multi | 2.60 | 2.60 |

On Cotton-faced Paper
| 2086 | A469 | $20 multi | 5.25 | 5.25 |

Nos. 2085-2086 each contain one 60x85mm stamp.

HONG KONG

Souvenir Sheet

Qinghai Hoh Xil UNESCO World Heritage Site — A470

Litho., Litho. & Embossed Sheet Margin
Perf. 13. Vert. Syncopated
2020, June 23
Granite Paper

| 2087 | A470 | $10 multi | 2.60 | 2.60 |

See No. 2191c.

Ocean Park Hong Kong Theme Park — A471

Designs: $2, Indo-Pacific bottlenose dolphins. $2.60, Toco toucan. $3.40, Sichuan golden snub-nosed monkeys. $3.70, Meerkats. $4.90, Giant panda. $5, King penguins. $10, Aerial view of Ocean Park Hong Kong.

Perf. 13½x13¾ Syncopated
2020, Aug. 18   Litho.
Granite Paper

| 2088-2093 | A471 | Set of 6 | 5.75 | 5.75 |
| 2093a | | Souvenir sheet of 12, 2 each #2088-2093 | 11.50 | 11.50 |

Souvenir Sheet
Perf. 13¾x13½ Syncopated

| 2094 | A471 | $10 multi | 2.60 | 2.60 |

No. 2094 contains one 91x29mm stamp.

Souvenir Sheet

Buildings of Hong Kong International Legal Hub — A472

Perf. 14¾x14 Syncopated
2020, Sept. 17   Litho.
Granite Paper

| 2095 | A472 | $10 multi | 2.60 | 2.60 |

Views of Victoria Harbor From 1962 and 2020 — A473

Photographs from 1962 and 2020 from various viewpoints: $2, $3.70, $4.90, $5.

Perf. 13¼x13¾ Syncopated
2020, Sept. 29   Litho.
Granite Paper

2096-2099	A473	Set of 4	4.00	4.00
2099a		Horiz. strip of 4, #2096-2099	4.00	4.00
2099b		Souvenir sheet of 4, #2096-2099	4.00	4.00

A474

A475

Characters From *Storm Riders* Comics — A476

Various characters: $2, $2.60, $3.40, $3.70, $4.90, $5.

Perf. 14¼x13½ Syncopated
2020, Oct. 29   Litho.
Granite Paper

| 2100-2105 | A474 | Set of 6 | 5.75 | 5.75 |

Souvenir Sheets
Perf. 14¼ Syncopated

| 2106 | A475 | $10 multi | 2.60 | 2.60 |

Litho. With Foil Application

| 2107 | A476 | $20 gold & multi | 5.25 | 5.25 |

Bruce Lee (1940-73), Martial Artist and Actor — A477

Various photographs of Lee and inscription: $2, Jeet Kune Do. $2.60, The Big Boss. $3.40, Fist of Fury. $3.70, The Way of the Dragon. $4.90, Game of Death. $5, Philosophy. $10, $20, Lee and Chinese characters.

Perf. 13¾x14 Syncopated
2020, Nov. 27   Litho.
Granite Paper

| 2108-2113 | A477 | Set of 6 | 5.50 | 5.50 |
| 2113a | | Souvenir sheet of 12, 2 each #2108-2113 | 11.00 | 11.00 |

Souvenir Sheets
Perf. 14¼ Syncopated

| 2114 | A477 | $10 multi | 2.60 | 2.60 |

Litho. & Embossed With Foil Application

| 2115 | A477 | $20 gold & multi | 5.25 | 5.25 |

Christmas A478

Designs: Nos. 2116, 2120, $2, Santa Claus at table with Chinese foods. Nos. 2117, 2121, $3.70, Santa Claus and reindeer on swings. Nos. 2118, 2122, $4.90, Santa Claus, man and gingerbread men performing tai chi. Nos. 2119, 2123, $5, Santa Claus, snowman and gingerbread men on trolley.

Litho. With Foil Application
Perf. 13¾x13½ Syncopated
2020, Dec. 4
Granite Paper (Nos. 2116-2119)

| 2116-2119 | A478 | Set of 4 | 4.00 | 4.00 |
| 2119a | | Souvenir sheet of 4, #2116-2119 | 4.00 | 4.00 |

Self-Adhesive
Die Cut Perf. 13¼ Syncopated

| 2120-2123 | A478 | Set of 4 | 4.00 | 4.00 |
| 2123a | | Souvenir sheet of 4, #2120-2123 | 4.00 | 4.00 |

Souvenir Sheets

Campaign Against COVID-19 Pandemic — A480

Perf. 13¼ Syncopated
2020, Dec. 29   Litho.
Granite Paper

| 2124 | A479 | $10 multi | 2.60 | 2.60 |
| 2125 | A480 | $10 multi | 2.60 | 2.60 |

New Year 2021 (Year of the Ox) — A481

Various oxen and flowers with background colors of: $2, Magenta. $3.70, Green. $4.90, Red and orange. $5, Violet and lilac.
No. 2130: a, Rat. b, Ox.
$10, Ox facing right (with red metallic emblem at left). No. 2132, Ox facing right (without red metallic emblem at left).

Perf. 14¼ Syncopated
2021, Jan. 28   Litho.
Granite Paper

| 2126-2129 | A481 | Set of 4 | 4.00 | 4.00 |

Litho. With Foil Application (#2130a), Litho. With Metal Affixed (#2130b)
Perf. 13¼x13½ Syncopated

| 2130 | A481 | $50 Sheet of 2, #a-b | 26.00 | 26.00 |

Souvenir Sheets
Litho. With Foil Application
Perf. 13¼ Syncopated

| 2131 | A481 | $10 multi | 2.60 | 2.60 |

Litho.
On Silk-Faced Granite Paper

| 2132 | A481 | $50 multi | 13.00 | 13.00 |

Nos. 2131-2132 each contain one 45x45mm stamp. See Nos. 2281-2284.

On Jan. 28, 2021, Hong Kong issued the stamps pictured above, having franking values of $2 and $4.90, respectively. The stamps were each printed in sheets of 12 + 12 non-personalizable labels depicting various images. The sheets sold for $63 and $99, respectively.

Traditonal Dances — A482

Designs: $2, Lion dancer. $3.70, Pixiu dancer. $4.90, Unicorn dancer. $5, Dragon dancer.
Tai Hang Fire Dragon dancers of Mid-autumn Festival with background color of: $10, Purple, horiz. $20, Yellow brown, horiz.

Perf. 13½ Syncopated
2021, Feb. 23
Granite Paper   Litho.

| 2133-2136 | A482 | Set of 4 | 4.00 | 4.00 |
| 2136a | | Souvenir sheet of 8, 2 each #2133-2136, perf. 14¼ syncopated | 8.00 | 8.00 |

Souvenir Sheets
Perf. 14¼ Syncopated

| 2137 | A482 | $10 multi | 2.60 | 2.60 |

Litho. With Foil Application

| 2138 | A482 | $20 gold & multi | 5.25 | 5.25 |

Nos. 2137-2138 each contain one 113x48mm stamp.

Scenes From *Romance of the Three Kingdoms*, by Luo Guanzhong (c. 1330-c. 1400) — A483

Inscriptions: $2, The Oath of the Peach Garden. $2.60, A Notion of Heroes over Warm Wine. $3.40, Escorting Sisters-in law over a Thousand Miles. $3.70, Three Visits to the Thatched Cottage. $4.90, Zhao Yun Saving the Young Lord. $5, Empty Fort Stratagem. $10, The Arrow Through the Halberd. $20, Borrowing Arrows with Straw Boats.

Perf. 14x13½ Syncopated
2021, Mar. 16   Litho.
Granite Paper

| 2139-2144 | A483 | Set of 6 | 5.50 | 5.50 |

Souvenir Sheets
Perf. 14¼ Syncopated

| 2145 | A483 | $10 multi | 2.60 | 2.60 |

Litho. & Embossed

| 2146 | A483 | $20 multi | 5.25 | 5.25 |

Nos. 2145-2146 each contain one 86x78mm triangular stamp.

Snack Foods — A484

Designs: $2, Fishballs. $2.60, Candy and coconut wrap. $3.40, Stuffed three treasures. $3.70, Buttered pineapple bun. $4.90, Stewed skewers. $5, Peanut candy.
$10, Steamed rice rolls.

Perf. 13½ Syncopated
2021, Apr. 22   Litho. & Embossed
Granite Paper

| 2147-2152 | A484 | Set of 6 | 5.50 | 5.50 |
| 2152a | | Souvenir sheet of 12, 2 each #2147-2152 | 11.00 | 11.00 |

Souvenir Sheet
Perf. 14 Syncopated

| 2153 | A484 | $10 multi | 2.60 | 2.60 |

No. 2153 contains one 42x70mm stamp.

HONG KONG

19th Century China Trade Paintings A485

Paintings by unknown artists: $2, Queen's Road Looking East From Canton Bazaar. $2.60, Cake Shop, Canton, vert. $3.40, Porcelain Shop, Canton, vert. $3.70, Production of Ceramics: Packing in Barrels. $4.90, New China Street. $5, Production of Silk: Spinning Silk Threads.
$10, The Studio of Tingqua. $20, Packing of Tea, vert.

Perf. 14x13½ Syncopated
2021, May 25 Litho.
Granite Paper

2154	A485	$2 multi	.50	.50
2155	A485	$2.60 multi	.70	.70
a.		Perf. 13½ Syncopated	.70	.70
2156	A485	$3.40 multi	.90	.90
a.		Perf. 13½ Syncopated	.90	.90
2157	A485	$3.70 multi	.95	.95
2158	A485	$4.90 multi	1.25	1.25
2159	A485	$5 multi	1.30	1.30
a.		Souvenir sheet of 12, 2 each #2154, 2155a, 2156a, 2157-2159	11.50	11.50
		Nos. 2154-2159 (6)	5.60	5.60

Souvenir Sheets
Perf. 14 Syncopated

2160	A485	$10 multi	2.60	2.60

Litho. & Embossed
Perf. 14¼x14

2161	A485	$20 multi	5.25	5.25

No. 2160 contains one 73x52mm stamp. No. 2161 contains one 48x66mm stamp.

Hong Kong Society for the Prevention of Cruelty to Animals, Cent. — A486

Society emblem and: $2, Dog. $2.60, Hamster. $3.40, Turtle. $3.70, Rabbit. $4.90, Cat. $5, Cockatiel.

Perf. 13½x14 Syncopated
2021, June 22 Litho.
Granite Paper

2162-2167	A486	Set of 6	5.50	5.50
2167a		Souvenir sheet of 6, #2162-2167	5.50	5.50

Chinese Communist Party, Cent. — A487

Centenary emblem and: $2, Building, flag and boat. $3.70, Gate of Heavenly Peace, Beijing. $4.90, City skyline. $5, High-speed train and satellite.
$10, Centenary emblem and fireworks, vert.

Perf. 13½x13 Syncopated
2021, July 1 Litho.

2168-2171	A487	Set of 4	4.00	4.00

Souvenir Sheet
Perf. 13¼x13 Syncopated

2172	A487	$10 multi	2.60	2.60

2020 Summer Olympics, Tokyo — A488

Designs: $2, Table tennis. $3.70, Windsurfing. $4.90, Cycling. $5, Swimming.

Litho. With Foil Application
Perf. 13½x14 Syncopated
2021, July 23
Granite Paper

2173-2176	A488	Set of 4	4.00	4.00
2176a		Souvenir sheet of 4, #2173-2176	4.00	4.00

The 2020 Summer Olympics were postponed until 2021 because of the COVID-19 pandemic.

Hong Kong Postal Service, 180th Anniv. — A489

Designs: $2, Boat, postman on bicycle, half of Hong Kong postmark. $2.60, Half of Hong Kong postmark, postal worker delivering mail, woman and child, barcode. $3.40, Barcode, postal workers sorting mail, half of "@" symbol. $3.70, Half of "@" symbol, post office, mail vans, mailbox, postal worker moving parcels with handcart, half of QR code. $4.90, Half of QR code, woman holding letter, man holding parcel, postal kiosk, vending machine and half of stylized globe symbol. $5, Half of stylized globe symbol and arrow, parcels, postal carts and postal worker.

Perf. 13¾ Syncopated
2021, Aug. 25 Litho.
Granite Paper

2177-2182	A489	Set of 6	5.50	5.50
2182a		Souvenir sheet of 6, #2177-2182	5.50	5.50

Characters From *Feel 100%* Comic Books — A490

Unnamed characters: $2, Male. $2.60, Male, diff. $3.40, Female. $3.70, Female, diff. $4.90, Male and female. $5, Male and female, diff.
$10, Two male and one female characters, horiz. $20, Male and female characters, horiz.

Perf. 13½ Syncopated
2021, Sept. 16 Litho.
Granite Paper

2183-2188	A490	Set of 6	5.50	5.50

Souvenir Sheets

2189	A490	$10 multi	2.60	2.60
2190	A490	$20 multi	5.25	5.25

Nos. 2189-2190 each contain one 56x45mm stamp.

UNESCO World Heritage Sites Types of 2011-20 and South China Karst UNESCO World Heritage Site — A491

Perf. 13¼x13½ Syncopated (#2191a, 2191d), 13¼ Syncopated (#2191b, 2191h), 13x13¼ Syncopated (#2191e, 2191f, 2191g, 2191i), 13½x13 Syncopated (#2191j), Perf. x13¼ Syncopated (#2191c)
2021, Oct. 12 Litho.
Granite Paper

2191		Sheet of 10	7.00	7.00
a.	A346	$2.60 Great Wall of China	.70	.70
b.	A382	$2.60 Honghe Hani Rice Terrace	.70	.70
c.	A470	$2.60 Qinghai Hoh Xil	.70	.70
d.	A422	$2.60 Temple of Heaven	.70	.70
e.		$2.60 Zuojiang Huashan Rock Art	.70	.70
f.	A403	$2.60 Kaiping Diaolou and Villages	.70	.70
g.	A394	$2.60 Grand Canal	.70	.70
h.	A375	$2.60 China Danxia	.70	.70
i.	A356	$2.60 Old Town of Lijiang	.70	.70
j.	A491	$2.60 South China Karst	.70	.70

Souvenir Sheet
Litho. & Embossed
Perf. 14¼x14 Syncopated

2192	A491	$10 multi	2.60	2.60

Miniature Sheet

Sports in Which Hong Kong Athletes Won Medals at 2020 Summer Olympics A492

No. 2193: a, Fencing. b, Swimming. c, Table tennis. d, Karate. e, Track cycling.

Perf. 13½ Syncopated
2021, Oct. 28 Litho.

2193	A492	Sheet of 5	13.00	13.00
a.-e.		$10 Any single	2.60	2.60

The 2020 Summer Olympics were postponed until 2021 because of the COVID-19 pandemic.

Flowers A493

Designs: $2, Camellia hongkongensis. $2.60, Rhododendron hongkongense. $3.40, Lysimachia alpestris. $3.70, Thismia hongkongensis, vert. $4.90, Carpinus insularis, vert. $5, Impatiens hongkongensis.

Perf. 13½ Syncopated
2021, Nov. 16 Litho.
Granite Paper

2194-2199	A493	Set of 6	5.50	5.50
2199a		Souvenir sheet of 6, #2194-2199	5.50	5.50

Movie Scene Locations in Hong Kong A494

Designs: $2, Kau U Fong. $3.70, Monster Building. $4.90, Two International Finance Center. $5, Jumbo Floating Restaurant.

Perf. 14 Syncopated
2021, Dec. 2 Litho.
Granite Paper

2200-2203	A494	Set of 4	4.00	4.00
2203a		Souvenir sheet of 4, #2200-2203	4.00	4.00

Souvenir Sheet

Achievements of Hong Kong Athletes at 2020 Paralympics, Tokyo — A495

No. 2204 — Sports in which Hong Kong athletes medaled: a, Table tennis. b, Bocce. c, Badminton.

Perf. 13¼ Syncopated
2021, Dec. 9 Litho.

2204	A495	Sheet of 3	7.75	7.75
a.-c.		$10 Any single	2.50	2.50

The 2020 Paralympics were postponed until 2021 because of the COVID-19 pandemic.

New Year 2022 (Year of the Tiger) — A496

Various tigers and flowers with background colors of: $2, Cerise and salmon. $3.70, Tan and olive green. $4.90, Yellow and orange. $5, Greenish blue and blue green.
No. 2209: a, Ox. b, Tiger.

$10, Tiger facing left (with gold emblem at lower right). No. 2211, Tiger facing left (without gold emblem at lower right).

Perf. 13¼x13 Syncopated
2022, Jan. 18 Litho.
Granite Paper

2205-2208	A496	Set of 4	4.00	4.00

Litho. With Foil Application (#2209a), Litho. With Metal Affixed (#2209b)
Perf. 13¼x13½ Syncopated

2209	A496	$50 Sheet of 2, #a-b	26.00	26.00

Souvenir Sheets
Litho. With Foil Application
Perf. 13¼ Syncopated

2210	A496	$10 gold & multi	2.60	2.60

Litho.
On Silk-Faced Granite Paper

2211	A496	$50 multi	13.00	13.00

Nos. 2210-2211 each contain one 45x45mm stamp. See Nos. 2281-2284.

On Jan. 18, 2022, Hong Kong issued the stamps pictured above, having franking values of $2 and $4.90, respectively. The stamps were each printed in sheets of 12 + 12 non-personalizable labels depicting various images. The sheets sold for $46 and $85, respectively, but only 2 sheets were allowed to be sold to each customer.

2022 Winter Olympics, Beijing — A497

Designs: $2, Skiing. $3.70, Ice hockey. $4.90, Figure skating. $5, Speed skating.

Perf. 13¼x13½ Syncopated
2022, Feb. 4 Litho.
Granite Paper

2212-2215	A497	Set of 4	4.00	4.00
2215a		Souvenir sheet of 4, #2212-2215	4.00	4.00

Guangdong-Hong Kong-Macao Greater Bay Area Development — A498

Development area: No. 2216, $2, Hong Kong. No. 2217, $2, Macao. No. 2218, $2, Guangzhou. No. 2219, $2, Shenzhen. No. 2220, $2, Zhuhai. No. 2221, $2, Foshan. No. 2222, $2, Huizhou. No. 2223, $2, Dongguan. No. 2224, $2, Zhongshan. No. 2225, $2, Jiangmen. No. 2226, $2, Zhaoqing.

Perf. 13¾ Syncopated
2022, Feb. 18 Litho.
Granite Paper

2216-2226	A498	Set of 11	5.75	5.75
2226a		Souvenir sheet of 11, #2216-2226	5.75	5.75

Local Snacks A500

HONG KONG

Designs: $2, Egg tart, coconut tart. $2.60, Faux shark's fin soup, fish and lettuce soup. $3.40, French toast, Hong Kong waffle. $3.70, Ding ding candy, dragon's beard candy. $4.90, Iced gem biscuit, sachima. $5, Banana roll, black sesame roll.
$10, Aeroplane olives, Siu mai and Stinky tofu.

Perf. 14x14¼ Syncopated
2022, May 26   Litho. & Embossed
Granite Paper

| 2228-2233 | A500 | Set of 6 | 5.50 | 5.50 |

Perf. 14¼ Syncopated
Souvenir Sheet

| 2234 | A500 | $10 multi | | 2.60 | 2.60 |

No. 2234 contains one 112x71mm stamp.

Souvenir Sheet

Ta Kung Pao Building A501

Perf. 13¼ Syncopated
2022, June 17   Litho.

| 2235 | A501 | $10 multi | | 2.60 | 2.60 |

Ta Kung Pao newspaper, 120th anniv.

Two Ladies by a Moon Gate, Qing Dynasty A502

Dish With Narcissus, Yuan Dynasty — A503

Cup in the Shape of a Raft with Seated Figure, Yuan Dynasty — A504

Mirror with Polo Players, Tang Dynasty A505

Zhao Mengfu, Mounted Official, Yuan Dynasty — A506

Headrest in the Shape of a Reclining Boy, Northern Song Dynasty A507

Cup and Tray with Flowers, Qing Dynasty A508

Jar with Fish and Aquatic Plants, Ming Dynasty A509

Perf. 13½x13¼ Syncopated, 13¼x13½ Syncopated
2022, June 30   Litho.
Granite Paper

2236	A502	$2 multi	.50	.50
2237	A503	$2.60 multi	.70	.70
2238	A504	$3.40 multi	.90	.90
2239	A505	$3.70 multi	.95	.95
2240	A506	$4.90 multi	1.25	1.25
2241	A507	$5 multi	1.30	1.30
		Nos. 2236-2241 (6)	5.60	5.60

Souvenir Sheets
Perf. 14 Syncopated

| 2242 | A508 | $10 multi | 2.60 | 2.60 |

Litho. & Embossed

| 2243 | A509 | $20 multi | 5.25 | 5.25 |

Items in Hong Kong Palace Museum.

Hong Kong Special Administrative Region, 25th Anniv. — A510

Designs: $2, Soldiers at flag ceremony. $3.70, Legislative Council chamber. $4.90, Qianhai Shenzhen-Hong Kong Youth Innovation and Entrepreneur Hub. $5, Children at flag ceremony.

Litho. With Foil Application
Perf. 13½x14½ Syncopated
2022, July 1
Granite Paper

| 2244-2247 | A510 | Set of 4 | 3.50 | 3.50 |
| 2247a | | Souvenir sheet of 4, #2244-2247 | 3.50 | 3.50 |

Souvenir Sheet

Stationing of Chinese People's Liberation Army in Hong Kong, 25th Anniv. — A511

Litho. With Foil Application
Perf. 14¾x13¼ Syncopated
2022, July 1

| 2248 | A511 | $20 multi | 5.25 | 5.25 |

Fruits — A512

Designs: $2, Oranges. $2.60, Watermelons. $3.40, Guavas. $3.70, Lychees. $4.90, Bananas. $5, Papayas.
$10, Oranges, guavas, watermelons, papayas, bananas and lychees.

Perf. 13½x13¼ Syncopated
2022, Aug. 18   Litho. & Embossed

| 2249-2254 | A512 | Set of 6 | 5.50 | 5.50 |

Souvenir Sheet
Perf. 13½x14 Syncopated

| 2255 | A512 | $10 multi | 2.60 | 2.60 |

No. 2255 contains one 90x70mm stamp.

Hong Kong Cheongsam Making Technique A513

Perf. 13¼x13¾ Syncopated
2022, Sept. 22   Litho.
Granite Paper

| 2256-2259 | A513 | Set of 4 | 4.00 | 4.00 |

Souvenir Sheets

| 2260 | A513 | $10 multi | 2.60 | 2.60 |

Litho, Sheet Margin Litho. & Embossed

| 2261 | A513 | $20 multi | 5.25 | 5.25 |

Dinosaurs A514

Designs: $2.20, Tyrannosaurus rex. $2.80, Spinosaurus. $3.70, Triceratops. $4, Diplodocus. $5.40, Brachiosaurus. $5.50, Allosaurus and Hesperosaurus.

Perf. 13½x13¼ Syncopated
2022, Nov. 15   Litho. & Embossed
Granite Paper

| 2262-2267 | A514 | Set of 6 | 6.00 | 6.00 |
| 2267a | | Souvenir sheet of 6, #2262-2267 | 6.00 | 6.00 |

Miss 13 Dots, Comic Strip by Lee Wai Chun (c. 1929-2020) — A515

Miss 13 Dots, "13" and Chinese symbol in various fabric patterns.

Perf. 13½x14 Syncopated
2022, Dec. 6   Litho.
Granite Paper (Nos. 2268-2275)

2268	A515	$2.20 multi	.55	.55
2269	A515	$2.80 multi	.70	.70
2270	A515	$3.70 multi	.95	.95
2271	A515	$4 multi	1.00	1.00
2272	A515	$5.40 multi	1.40	1.40
2273	A515	$5.50 multi	1.40	1.40
		Nos. 2268-2273 (6)	6.00	6.00

Souvenir Sheets
Perf. 13¼ Syncopated

| 2274 | A515 | $10 multi | 2.60 | 2.60 |

Perf.

| 2275 | A515 | $20 multi | 5.25 | 5.25 |

Die Cut Perf. 13¼ Syncopated
Self-Adhesive

2276		Sheet of 6	12.00	
a.	A515	$2.20 Like #2268	1.10	1.10
b.	A515	$2.80 Like #2269	1.40	1.40
c.	A515	$3.70 Like #2270	1.90	1.90
d.	A515	$4 Like #2271	2.00	2.00
e.	A515	$5.40 Like #2272	2.75	2.75
f.	A515	$5.50 Like #2273	2.75	2.75

No. 2274 contains one 49x75mm oval stamp. No. 2275 contains one 65mm diameter stamp. No. 2276 sold for $47.

New Year Types of 2012-22 and

New Year 2023 (Year of the Rabbit) — A516

Rabbit and flower with: $2.20, Orange and pink background. $4, Yellow green and dark green background. $5.40, Blue and purple background. $5.50, Yellow orange and orange background.
No. 2286: a, Tiger. b, Rabbit.
Nos. 2287, 2288, Rabbit.

Perf. 13¼x13 Syncopated
2023, Jan. 10   Litho.
Granite Paper

2277	A516	$2.20 multi	.55	.55
a.		Perf. 13¼x14¼ Syncopated	.55	.55
2278	A516	$4 multi	1.00	1.00
a.		Perf. 13¼x14¼ Syncopated	1.00	1.00
2279	A516	$5.40 multi	1.40	1.40
a.		Perf. 13¼x14¼ Syncopated	1.40	1.40
2280	A516	$5.50 multi	1.40	1.40
a.		Perf. 13¼x14¼ Syncopated	1.40	1.40
		Nos. 2277-2280 (4)	4.35	4.35

Perf. 13¼x14¼ Syncopated

2281		Sheet of 12, #2277a, 2281a-2281k, + central label	6.75	6.75
a.	A338	$2.20 Like #1482	.55	.55
b.	A350	$2.20 Like #1553	.55	.55
c.	A363	$2.20 Like #1612	.55	.55
d.	A376	$2.20 Like #1696	.55	.55
e.	A390	$2.20 Like #1755	.55	.55
f.	A402	$2.20 Like #1828	.55	.55
g.	A416	$2.20 Like #1906	.55	.55
h.	A430	$2.30 Like #1980	.55	.55
i.	A460	$2.30 Like #2056	.55	.55
j.	A481	$2.30 Like #2126	.55	.55
k.	A496	$2.30 Like #2205	.55	.55
2282		Sheet of 12, #2278a, 2282a-2282k, + central label	12.00	12.00
a.	A338	$4 Like #1483	1.00	1.00
b.	A350	$4 Like #1554	1.00	1.00
c.	A363	$4 Like #1613	1.00	1.00
d.	A376	$4 Like #1697	1.00	1.00
e.	A390	$4 Like #1756	1.00	1.00
f.	A402	$4 Like #1829	1.00	1.00
g.	A416	$4 Like #1907	1.00	1.00
h.	A430	$4 Like #1981	1.00	1.00
i.	A460	$4 Like #2057	1.00	1.00
j.	A481	$4 Like #2127	1.00	1.00
k.	A496	$4 Like #2206	1.00	1.00
2283		Sheet of 12, #2279a, 2283a-2283k, + central label	17.00	17.00
a.	A338	$5.40 Like #1484	1.40	1.40
b.	A350	$5.40 Like #1555	1.40	1.40
c.	A363	$5.40 Like #1614	1.40	1.40
d.	A376	$5.40 Like #1698	1.40	1.40
e.	A390	$5.40 Like #1757	1.40	1.40
f.	A402	$5.40 Like #1830	1.40	1.40
g.	A416	$5.40 Like #1908	1.40	1.40
h.	A430	$5.40 Like #1982	1.40	1.40
i.	A460	$5.40 Like #2058	1.40	1.40
j.	A481	$5.40 Like #2128	1.40	1.40
k.	A496	$5.40 Like #2207	1.40	1.40
2284		Sheet of 12, #2280a, 2284a-2284k, + central label	17.00	17.00
a.	A338	$5.50 Like #1485	1.40	1.40
b.	A350	$5.50 Like #1556	1.40	1.40
c.	A363	$5.50 Like #1615	1.40	1.40
d.	A376	$5.50 Like #1699	1.40	1.40
e.	A390	$5.50 Like #1758	1.40	1.40
f.	A402	$5.50 Like #1831	1.40	1.40
g.	A416	$5.50 Like #1909	1.40	1.40
h.	A430	$5.50 Like #1983	1.40	1.40
i.	A460	$5.50 Like #2059	1.40	1.40
j.	A481	$5.50 Like #2129	1.40	1.40
k.	A496	$5.50 Like #2208	1.40	1.40
		Nos. 2281-2284 (4)	52.75	52.75

HONG KONG

Litho. & Embossed With Foil Application

2285		Block of 4	10.50	10.50
a.	A460	$10 Rat	2.60	2.60
b.	A481	$10 Ox	2.60	2.60
c.	A496	$10 Tiger	2.60	2.60
d.	A516	$10 Rabbit	2.60	2.60

Souvenir Sheets
Litho. With Foil Application (#2286a), Litho. With Metal Affixed (#2286b)

2286	A516	$50 Sheet of 2, #a-b	26.00	26.00

Litho. With Foil Application
Perf. 13¼ Syncopated

2287	A516	$10 multi	2.60	2.60

Litho.
On Silk-Faced Granite Paper

2288	A516	$50 multi	13.00	13.00

Nos. 2287-2288 each contain one 45x45mm stamp.

On Jan. 10, 2023, Hong Kong issued the stamps pictured above, having franking values of $2.20 and $5.40, respectively. The stamps were each printed in sheets of 12 + 12 non-personalizable labels depicting various images. The sheets sold for $49 and $91, respectively, but only five sheets were allowed to be sold to each customer.

Trees — A517

Trees: $2.20, Yellow pui. $4, Jacaranda. $5.40, Bald cypress. $5.50, Bell-flower cherry.

Perf. 13½x13 Syncopated
2023, Feb. 14 *Litho.*
Granite Paper

2289-2292	A517	Set of 4	4.50	4.50
2292a		Souvenir sheet of 4, #2289-2292	4.50	4.50

Hong Kong Museum of Art's Jingguanlou Collection — A518

Designs: $2.20, Mountain Ranges from the Front, by Zhu Qizhan (1892-1996). $2.80, Towering Peaks, by Xie Zhiliu (1910-97). $3.70, Wintry Mountains, by Zhu Qizhan. $4, Birds and Bamboo, by Xie Zhiliu and Chen Peiqiu (1922-2020). $5.40, Jiangnan in March, by Zhu Qizhan. $5.50, Landscape and Calligraphy, by Chen Peiqiu.
$10, Cicada Resting on a Red Leaf, by Chen Peiqiu, horiz. $20, Valleys in Mountains, by Xie Zhiliu, horiz.

Perf. 13½x14½ Syncopated
2023, Mar. 23 *Litho.*
Granite Paper

2293-2298	A518	Set of 6	6.00	6.00

Souvenir Sheets

2299	A518	$10 multi	2.60	2.60

On Silk-Faced Granite Paper

2300	A518	$20 multi	5.25	5.25

Nos. 2299 and 2300 each contain one 63x44mm stamp.

Health Care Workers — A519

Designs: $2.20, Doctors and Chinese medical practitioners. $4, Nurses. $5.40, Other healthcare professionals. $5.50, Care-related supporting staff.
$10, Various healthcare workers, horiz.

Perf. 13½x13¼ Syncopated
2023, Apr. 18 *Litho.*
Granite Paper

2301-2304	A519	Set of 4	4.50	4.50

Souvenir Sheet
Perf. 13½ Syncopated

2305	A519	$10 multi	2.60	2.60

No. 2305 contains one 80x60mm stamp.

Corn Forms A520
Summer Commences A521
Summer Solstice A522
Corn on Ear A523
Great Heat A524
Moderate Heat A525

Perf. 13x13¼ Syncopated
2023, May 4 *Litho.*
Granite Paper

2306	A520	$2.20 multi	.55	.55
2307	A521	$2.20 multi	.55	.55
2308	A522	$2.20 multi	.55	.55
2309	A523	$2.20 multi	.55	.55
2310	A524	$2.20 multi	.55	.55
2311	A525	$2.20 multi	.55	.55
a.		Souvenir sheet of 6, #2306-2311	3.30	3.30
		Nos. 2306-2311 (6)	3.30	3.30

Values for Nos. 2306-2311 are for stamps with flanking selvage.

Toys of the 1970s and 1980s — A526

Designs: $2.20, Peace and Happiness chess. $2.80, Spinning top. $3.70, Alloy toy train. $4, Rocket. $5.40, Stove and pots from play house. $5.50, Robot.

Perf. 13½x13 Syncopated
2023, June 13 *Litho.*
Granite Paper

2312-2317	A526	Set of 6	6.00	6.00

Milk Tea Making Techniques — A527

Designs: $2.20, Pouring loose tea into strainer. $4, Tea brewing in pot on stove. $5.40, Pouring brewed tea into strainer. $5.50, Pouring tea into tea cup.
$10, Kettles, hot plate, strainer, milk cans, tea cups, saucers, sugar bowl and bag of loose tea, horiz. $20, Processes for making milk tea, horiz.

Perf. 13½x13¾ Syncopated
2023, July 25 *Litho.*
Granite Paper

2318-2321	A527	Set of 4	4.50	4.50

Souvenir Sheets
Perf. 14¼ Syncopated

2322	A527	$10 multi	2.60	2.60

Litho. & Embossed

2323	A527	$20 multi	5.25	5.25

Nos. 2322 and 2323 each contain one 112x48mm stamp.

Hong Kong Landmarks — A529

Designs: $2.20, Hong Kong Cultural Center. $2.80, Hong Kong Museum of Art. $3.70, M+ Art Museum. $4, Hong Kong Palace Museum. $5.40, Xiqu Center. $5.50, Hong Kong City Hall.
$10, Courtyard and exterior of JC Contemporary Art Museum, Tai Kwun.

Perf. 13½x14 Syncopated
2023, Aug. 22 *Litho.*
Granite Paper

2324-2329	A528	Set of 6	6.00	6.00

Souvenir Sheet
Perf.

2330	A529	$10 multi	2.60	2.60

Vegetables — A531

Designs: $2.20, Carrots. $2.80, Corn. $3.70, Radishes. $4, Flowering Chinese cabbage. $5.40, Sweet potatoes. $5.50, Chinese white cabbage.
$10, Basket containing beetroot, eggplants, tomatoes, carrots, lettuce and cauliflower.

Perf. 13½x13¾ Syncopated
2023, Sept. 21 *Litho.*
Granite Paper

2332-2337	A531	Set of 6	6.00	6.00

Souvenir Sheet
Perf. 13½ Syncopated

2338	A531	$10 multi	2.60	2.60

No. 2338 contains one 60x60mm stamp.

Trains A533

Train from: Nos. 2347, 2355, $2.20, East Rail Line. Nos. 2348, 2356, $2.80, Tuen Ma Line. Nos. 2349, 2357, $3.70, South Island Line. Nos. 2350, 2358, $4, Kwun Tong Line. Nos. 2351, 2359, $5.40, Tseung Kwan O Line. Nos. 2352, 2360, $5.50, Tung Chung Line.
$10, Airport Express train. $20, Hong Kong Section High Speed Rail train.

Perf. 13½x13 Syncopated
2023, Nov. 23 *Litho.*
Granite Paper (Nos. 2347-2354)

2347-2352	A533	Set of 6	6.00	6.00

Souvenir Sheets
Perf. 13¼ Syncopated

2353	A533	$10 multi	2.60	2.60

Litho. & Embossed

2354	A533	$20 multi	5.25	5.25

Self-Adhesive
Die Cut Perf. 13¼x13¾ Syncopated

2355-2360	A533	Set of 6	6.00	6.00

Nos. 2353 and 2354 each contain one 80x45mm stamp. Nos. 2355-2360 were each printed in sheets of 4.

SEMI-POSTAL STAMPS

Catalogue values for unused stamps in this section are for Never Hinged items.

Community Chest of Hong Kong — SP1

No. B1, Girl. No. B2, Elderly woman. No. B3, Blind youth. No. B4, Mother and child.

1988, Nov. 30 *Litho.* *Perf. 14½*

B1	SP1	60c +10c multi	.50	.90
B2	SP1	$1.40 +20c multi	.60	1.00
B3	SP1	$1.80 +30c multi	1.40	1.50
B4	SP1	$5 +$1 multi	3.50	4.00
		Nos. B1-B4 (4)	6.00	7.40

Surtax for the social welfare organization.

POSTAGE DUE STAMPS

Scales Showing Letter Overweight — D1

1923, Dec. *Typo.* *Wmk. 4* *Perf. 14*

J1	D1	1c yellow brown	4.00	.90
a.		Chalky paper	.35	1.20
J2	D1	2c green	55.00	14.00
J3	D1	4c red	60.00	9.00
J4	D1	6c orange	45.00	17.00
J5	D1	10c ultramarine	35.00	10.50
		Nos. J1-J5 (5)	199.00	51.90
		Set, never hinged	360.00	

No. J1a issued Mar. 21, 1956.

1938-47 *Perf. 14*

J6	D1	2c gray	1.75	12.00
J7	D1	4c orange yellow	4.00	3.25
J8	D1	6c carmine	4.00	6.50
J9	D1	8c fawn ('46)	2.25	45.00
J10	D1	10c violet	19.00	.55
J11	D1	20c black ('46)	2.40	2.00
J12	D1	50c blue ('47)	45.00	21.00
		Nos. J6-J12 (7)	78.40	90.30
		Set, never hinged	150.00	

Nos. J6-J7 and J10 exist on both ordinary and chalky paper. The value shown is for the cheaper variety.

HONG KONG — HORTA — HUNGARY

For later issues with the same design, see Scott *Standard Postage Stamp Catalogue.*

Catalogue values for unused stamps in this section, from this point to the end of the section, are for Never Hinged items.

Wmk. 314 Sideways
1965-69   *Perf. 14*
Chalk-surfaced Paper

J13	D1	4c orange yellow	3.75	37.50
J14	D1	5c orange ver ('69)	2.50	5.25
a.		5c carmine, wmk. upright ('67)	3.50	5.00
J15	D1	10c purple ('67)	3.75	8.50
J16	D1	20c black	6.00	3.25
J17	D1	50c dark blue	37.50	8.00
a.		Wmk. upright ('70)	50.00	11.50
		Nos. J13-J17 (5)	53.50	62.50

Size of 5c, 21x18mm.; others, 22x18mm.

Wmk. 314 Upright
1972-74   *Perf. 13½x14*
Glazed Ordinary Paper

J18	D1	5c red brown ('74)	3.00	6.00

Perf. 14x14½

J19	D1	10c lilac	7.00	5.00
J20	D1	20c black	8.50	7.00
J21	D1	50c dull blue	6.00	11.00
		Nos. J18-J21 (4)	24.50	29.00

1978   *Wmk. 373*

J22	D1	10c lilac	1.00	6.00
f.		Chalk-surfaced paper	1.00	2.25
J22A	D1	20c black	1.50	7.50
g.		Chalk-surfaced paper	1.75	2.50
J22B	D1	50c dull blue	1.50	6.00
h.		Chalk-surfaced paper	1.75	4.00
J22C	D1	$1 yellow	14.00	14.00
i.		Chalk-surfaced paper	1.50	4.25
		Nos. J22-J22C (4)	18.00	33.50

Size of $1, 20½x17mm; others, 22x18mm. Issued: Nos. J22-J22C, 3/19; J22f-J22i, 12/15.

1986, Jan. 11   Unwmk.
Chalk-surfaced Paper

J22D	D1	50c dull blue	2.25	5.75
J22E	D1	$1 yellow	3.00	8.00

D2

Perf. 14x15
1986, Mar. 25   Litho.   Unwmk.

J23	D2	10c light green	.30	.70
J24	D2	20c dark red brown	.30	.70
J25	D2	50c lilac	.30	.25
J26	D2	$1 light orange	.30	.90
J27	D2	$5 grayish blue	.75	1.75
J28	D2	$10 rose red	1.50	3.50
		Nos. J23-J28 (6)	3.45	7.20

D3

Perf. 14x14¾
2004, Sept. 23   Litho.   Unwmk.

J29	D3	10c dark blue	.30	.50
J30	D3	20c blue	.30	.60
J31	D3	50c orange	.30	.25
J32	D3	$1 pink	.55	.75
J33	D3	$5 olive green	1.50	1.75
J34	D3	$10 cerise	8.00	3.50
		Nos. J29-J34 (6)	10.95	7.25

OCCUPATION STAMPS
Issued under Japanese Occupation

Japan No. 325 Surcharged in Black

Japan No. 259 Surcharged in Black

Japan No. 261 Surcharged in Black

Wmk. 257
1945, Apr.   Typo.   *Perf. 13*

N1	A144	1½y on 1s org brn	47.50	37.50
N2	A84	3y on 2s ver	17.50	32.50
N3	A86	5y on 5s brn lake	1,050.	190.00
		Nos. N1-N3 (3)	1,115.	260.00

No. N1 has eleven characters.

HORTA
ˈhȯr-tə

LOCATION — An administrative district of the Azores, consisting of the islands of Pico, Fayal, Flores and Corvo
GOVT. — A district of the Republic of Portugal
AREA — 305 sq. mi.
POP. — 49,000 (approx.)
CAPITAL — Horta

1000 Reis = 1 Milreis

King Carlos — A1

Enamel-surfaced Paper
1892-93   Typo.   Unwmk.   *Perf. 12½*

1	A1	5r yellow	4.50	3.25
2	A1	10r reddish violet	4.50	3.25
3	A1	15r chocolate	4.50	3.25
4	A1	20r lavender	5.75	5.00
6	A1	50r blue	12.50	5.75
7	A1	75r carmine	15.50	8.50
8	A1	80r yellow green	19.00	17.00
10	A1	150r car, *rose* ('93)	95.00	80.00
11	A1	200r dk bl, *bl* ('93)	95.00	80.00
12	A1	300r dk bl, *sal* ('93)	95.00	80.00
		Nos. 1-12 (12)	444.75	343.20
		Set, never hinged	660.00	

Bisects of No. 1 were used in Aug. 1894. Value, on newsprint, $30.

Perf. 13½

1a	A1	5r yellow	4.50	3.25
2a	A1	10r reddish violet	5.50	4.50
3a	A1	15r chocolate	6.75	6.25
4a	A1	20r lavender	8.00	6.00
6a	A1	50r blue	19.00	9.75
9	A1	100r brn, *yel* ('93)	85.00	55.00
10a	A1	150r car, *rose*	95.00	80.00
11a	A1	200r dk bl, *bl*	95.00	80.00
12a	A1	300r dk bl, *sal*	95.00	80.00

Perf. 11½

1b	A1	5r yellow	40.00	30.00
5	A1	25r dp grn	8.50	2.20

Chalk-surfaced Paper
Perf. 13½

1c	A1	5r yellow	10.00	4.25
5a	A1	25r dp grn	10.00	7.50
7c	A1	75r carmine	14.50	9.50

Perf. 11½

5b	A1	25r dp grn	17.50	7.50

A2

King Carlos — A2a

1897-1905   *Perf. 11½*
Name and Value in Black; Nos. 25 and 34 in Red

13	A2	2½r gray	.95	.50
14	A2	5r orange	.95	.50
15	A2	10r lt green	.95	.50
16	A2	15r brown	12.50	9.50
17	A2	15r gray grn ('99)	2.50	1.75
18	A2	20r gray violet	2.40	2.00
19	A2	25r sea green	4.25	1.60
20	A2	25r car rose ('99)	2.50	1.20
21	A2	50r blue	5.00	2.20
22	A2	50r ultra ('05)	21.00	17.00
23	A2	65r slate blue ('98)	1.70	1.40
24	A2	75r rose	4.50	2.20
25	A2a	75r brn, *yel* ('05)	20.00	17.50
26	A2	80r violet	2.70	1.60
27	A2	100r dk blue, *bl*	4.75	1.70
28	A2	115r org brn, *pink* ('98)	3.50	2.50
29	A2	130r gray brn, *buff* ('98)	3.50	2.50
30	A2	150r lt brn, *buff*	3.00	1.60
31	A2	180r sl, *pnksh* ('98)	3.50	2.50
32	A2	200r red vio, *pale lil*	9.50	7.75
33	A2	300r dk blue, *rose*	17.00	12.00
34	A2a	500r blk & red, *bl*	22.00	20.00
		Nos. 13-34 (22)	148.65	110.00
		Set, never hinged	207.00	

Stamps of Portugal replaced those of Horta.

HUNGARY
ˈhəŋ-gə-ˌrē

LOCATION — Central Europe
GOVT. — Republic
AREA — 35,911 sq. mi.
POP. — 9,660,000 (2020 est.)
CAPITAL — Budapest

Prior to World War I, Hungary together with Austria comprised the Austro-Hungarian Empire. The Hungarian post became independent on May 1, 1867. During 1850-1871 stamps listed under Austria were also used in Hungary. Copies showing clear Hungarian cancels sell for substantially more.

100 Krajczár (Kreuzer) = 1 Forint 100 Fillér = 1 Korona (1900) 100 Fillér = 1 Pengö (1926) 100 Fillér = 1 Forint (1946)

Catalogue values for unused stamps in this country are for Never Hinged items, beginning with Scott 503 in the regular postage section, Scott B92 in the semi-postal section, Scott C35 in the airpost section, Scott CB1 in the airpost semi-postal section, Scott F1 in the registration section, Scott J130 in the postage due section, and Scott Q9 in the parcel post section.

Watermarks

Wmk. 91 — "ZEITUNGS-MARKEN" in Double-lined Capitals across the Sheet

Wmk. 106 — Multiple Star

Wmk. 132 — kr in Oval

Wmk. 133 — Four Double Crosses

Wmk. 135 — Crown in Oval or Circle, Sideways

Wmk. 136

Wmk. 136a

Wmk. 137 — Double Cross

Wmk. 210 — Double Cross on Pyramid

Wmk. 266 — Double Barred Cross, Wreath and Crown

Wmk. 283 — Double Barred Cross on Shield, Multiple

Watermarks 132, 135, 136 and 136a can be found normal, reversed, inverted, or reversed and inverted.

HUNGARY

Values for unused stamps are for examples with original gum as defined in the catalogue introduction. Very fine examples of Nos. 1-12 will have perforations touching the framelines on one or two sides due to imperfect perforating methods. Stamps with perfs clear on all four sides are very scarce and will command substantial premiums.

Issues of the Monarchy

Franz Josef I — A1

1871	**Unwmk.**	**Litho.**	**Perf.**	**9½**
1	A1	2k orange	325.00	110.00
a.		2k yellow	1,200.	325.00
2	A1	3k lt green	1,000.	750.00
3	A1	5k rose	375.00	25.00
a.		5k brick red	900.00	75.00
4	A1	10k blue	1,000.	140.00
a.		10k pale blue	2,400.	450.00
5	A1	15k yellow brn	1,100.	150.00
6	A1	25k violet	1,000.	60.00
a.		25k bright violet	1,500.	350.00

The first printing of No. 1, in dark yellow, was not issued because of spots on the King's face. A few stamps were used at Pest in 1873. Value, $3,000.

1871-72				**Engr.**
7	A1	2k orange	40.00	7.50
a.		2k yellow	175.00	17.50
b.		Bisect on cover		
8	A1	3k green	125.00	30.00
a.		3k blue green	150.00	35.00
9	A1	5k rose	110.00	1.50
a.		5k brick red	200.00	9.00
10	A1	10k deep blue	300.00	20.00
11	A1	15k brown	400.00	30.00
a.		15k copper brown		1,500.
b.		15k black brown	950.00	100.00
12	A1	25k lilac	200.00	60.00
		Nos. 7-12 (6)	1,175.	149.00

Reprints are perf. 11½ and watermarked "kr" in oval. Value, set $225.

Crown of St. Stephen — A2

1874-76				**Perf. 13**
13	A2	2k red violet	25.00	2.00
a.		2k violet	50.00	2.50
14	A2	3k yellow green	30.00	2.00
a.		3k blue green	37.50	2.50
15	A2	5k red	10.00	.50
a.		5k brick red	45.00	1.50
b.		5k lilac red	15.00	.75
c.		5k rose	10.00	.40
16	A2	10k blue	35.00	.75
17	A2	20k grnsh gray	600.00	9.00
a.		20k gray	750.00	10.00
		Nos. 13-17 (5)	700.00	14.25

				Perf. 11½
13b	A2	2k red violet	45.00	5.00
c.		2k violet	—	6.00
d.		2k rose lilac	75.00	4.50
e.		2k gray blue	60.00	3.75
14b	A2	3k yellow green	50.00	4.00
c.		3k blue green	60.00	5.00
15d	A2	5k red	60.00	1.00
e.		5k rose	50.00	.75
16a	A2	10k blue	75.00	5.00
17b	A2	20k gray	700.00	45.00

				Perf. 13x11½
13f	A2	2k red violet	180.00	30.00
g.		2k rose lilac	200.00	30.00
14d	A2	3k yellow green	125.00	4.50
15f	A2	5k lilac red	250.00	12.00
g.		5k rose	300.00	15.00
16b	A2	10k blue	250.00	6.00
17c	A2	20k gray	800.00	50.00

				Perf. 11½x13
13h	A2	2k red violet	60.00	5.00
i.		2k rose lilac	100.00	4.00
j.		2k gray blue	75.00	3.75
15h	A2	5k red	75.00	1.00
17d	A2	20k gray	—	100.00

				Perf. 9½
14e	A2	3k green	7,500.	2,500.

All examples of the 5k perf 9½ are counterfeit.

1881	**Wmk. 132**			**Perf. 11½**
18	A2	2k lilac	3.50	.40
a.		2k violet	3.50	.40
b.		2k gray blue	4.50	.50
19	A2	3k blue green	3.50	.40
a.		3k yellow green	4.50	.60
20	A2	5k rose	2.50	.25
21	A2	10k blue	6.00	.40
a.		10k pale blue	7.00	.60

22	A2	20k gray	4.50	.65
a.		20k greenish gray	5.00	.75
		Nos. 18-22 (5)	20.00	2.10

				Perf. 13
18c	A2	2k violet	150.00	20.00
d.		2k gray blue	120.00	10.00
19b	A2	3k blue green	90.00	4.00
c.		3k yellow green	100.00	5.50
20a	A2	5k rose	120.00	4.00
21b	A2	10k blue	75.00	5.00
22b	A2	20k gray	350.00	15.00

				Perf. 13x11½
18e	A2	2k violet	—	40.00
19d	A2	3k blue green	160.00	6.00
e.		3k yellow green		8.00
20b	A2	5k rose		15.00
21c	A2	10k blue		8.00
22c	A2	20k gray		12.50

				Perf. 11½x13
18f	A2	2k violet	200.00	9.00
g.		2k gray blue	180.00	6.00
19f	A2	3k blue green		60.00
g.		3k yellow green		75.00
20c	A2	5k rose	150.00	1.00
21d	A2	10k blue		1.75
22d	A2	20k gray		40.00

				Perf. 12x11½
18h	A2	2k lilac	1.00	.25
i.		2k violet	15.00	1.20
19h	A2	3k blue green	1.00	.25
20d	A2	5k rose	2.50	.25
21e	A2	10k blue	3.00	.25
22e	A2	20k gray	300.00	7.50

Crown of St. Stephen — A3

Design A3 has an overall burelage of colored vertical lines. Compare with design N3.

1888-98	**Typo.**			**Perf. 12x11¾**
		Numerals in Black		
22A	A3	1k black, one plate	1.25	.30
c.		"1" printed separately	15.00	3.00
23	A3	2k red violet	1.50	.50
24	A3	3k green	1.75	.40
25	A3	5k rose	2.00	.25
a.		"5" double, inverted	1,750.	
26	A3	8k orange	6.00	.60
a.		"8" double	150.00	
27	A3	10k blue	5.00	1.25
28	A3	12k brown & green	12.50	1.00
29	A3	15k claret & blue	10.00	.40
30	A3	20k gray	7.50	2.00
31	A3	24k brn vio & red	22.50	1.25
32	A3	30k ol grn & brn	25.00	.35
33	A3	50k red & org	40.00	1.50

Numerals in Red

34	A3	1fo gray bl & sil	175.00	2.25
		Nos. 22A-34 (13)	310.00	12.05

				Perf. 11½
22i	A3	1k black, one plate	1.00	.40
j.		"1" printed separately	500.00	125.00
23i	A3	2k red violet	600.00	50.00
24i	A3	3k green	60.00	20.00
25i	A3	5k rose	60.00	20.00
26i	A3	8k orange	10.00	.75
27i	A3	10k blue	1,750.	750.00
28i	A3	12k brown & green	12.50	2.00
29i	A3	15k claret & blue	14.00	.40
30i	A3	20k gray	2,000.	900.00
31i	A3	24k brn vio & red	25.00	2.00
32i	A3	30k ol grn & brn	275.00	.50
33i	A3	50k red & org	40.00	3.00
34i	A3	1fo gray blue & sil	190.00	3.00
35	A3	3fo lilac brn & gold	25.00	12.00

1898-99				**Perf. 12x11½**
		Numerals in Black		
		Wmk. 135 (Oval)		
35A	A3	1k black	1.50	.50
36	A3	2k violet	6.00	.50
37	A3	3k green	4.00	.60
38	A3	5k rose	5.00	.40
39	A3	8k orange	17.50	4.00
40	A3	10k blue	5.00	1.00
41	A3	12k red brn & grn	75.00	9.00
42	A3	15k rose & blue	5.00	.75
43	A3	20k gray	35.00	2.00
44	A3	24k vio brn & red	6.00	4.75
45	A3	30k ol grn & brn	40.00	1.50
46	A3	50k dull red & org	100.00	15.00
		Nos. 35A-46 (12)	300.00	40.00

				Perf. 11½
35Ab	A3	1k black	40.00	7.50
36a	A3	2k violet	125.00	20.00
37a	A3	3k green	100.00	15.00
38a	A3	5k rose	140.00	15.00
39a	A3	8k orange	250.00	120.00
40a	A3	10k blue	150.00	60.00
41a	A3	12k red brn & grn	375.00	100.00
42a	A3	15k rose & blue	250.00	60.00
43a	A3	20k gray	375.00	75.00
44a	A3	24k vio brn & red	450.00	200.00
45a	A3	30k ol grn & brn	250.00	60.00
46a	A3	50k dull red & org	200.00	250.00

Wmk. 135 (Circle)

				Perf. 12x11½
35Ac	A3	1k black	14.00	2.50
36b	A3	2k violet	7.50	1.50
37b	A3	3k green	8.50	2.00
38b	A3	5k rose	10.00	1.00
39b	A3	8k orange	50.00	25.00

40b	A3	10k blue	75.00	4.00
41b	A3	12k red brn & grn	60.00	30.00
42b	A3	15k rose & blue	250.00	4.00
43b	A3	20k gray	5.00	6.00
44b	A3	24k vio brn & red	1,250.	45.00
45b	A3	30k ol grn & brn	5.00	4.00
46b	A3	50k dull red & org	15.00	35.00

				Perf. 11½
35Ad	A3	1k black	50.00	15.00
36c	A3	2k violet	200.00	25.00
37c	A3	3k green	200.00	40.00
38c	A3	5k rose	100.00	19.00
39c	A3	8k orange	80.00	12.50
40c	A3	10k blue	450.00	80.00
41c	A3	12k red brn & grn	750.00	300.00
42c	A3	15k rose & blue	450.00	200.00
43c	A3	20k gray	1,500.	350.00
44c	A3	24k vio brn & red	2,250.	600.00
45c	A3	30k ol grn & brn	750.00	150.00
46c	A3	50k dull red & org	500.00	400.00

In the watermark with circles, a four-pointed star and "VI" appear four times in the sheet in the large spaces between the intersecting circles. The paper with the circular watermark is often yellowish and thinner than that with the oval watermark.

"Turul" and Crown of St. Stephen — A4

Franz Josef I Wearing Hungarian Crown — A5

1900-04	**Wmk. 135**			**Perf. 12x11½**
		Numerals in Black		
47	A4	1f gray	.75	.30
a.		1f dull lilac	.75	.30
48	A4	2f olive yel	1.00	.75
49	A4	3f orange	.75	.25
50	A4	4f violet	1.00	.25
a.		Booklet pane of 6	60.00	
51	A4	5f emerald	2.50	.25
a.		Booklet pane of 6	35.00	
52	A4	6f claret	1.50	.60
a.		6f violet brown	2.50	.50
53	A4	6f bister ('01)	20.00	1.20
54	A4	6f olive grn ('02)	7.50	.50
55	A4	10f carmine	4.00	.25
a.		Booklet pane of 6	35.00	
56	A4	12f violet ('04)	2.00	1.25
57	A4	20f brown ('01)	4.00	.60
58	A4	25f blue	5.00	.60
a.		Booklet pane of 6	60.00	
59	A4	30f orange brn	24.00	.25
60	A4	35f red vio ('01)	14.00	1.00
a.		Booklet pane of 6	100.00	
61	A4	50f lake	12.00	1.00
62	A4	60f green	45.00	.30
63	A5	1k brown red	37.50	.75
64	A5	2k gray blue ('01)	600.00	22.50
65	A5	3k sea green	90.00	3.75
66	A5	5k vio brown ('01)	125.00	40.00
		Nos. 47-66 (20)	997.50	76.35

The watermark on Nos. 47 to 66 is always the circular form of Wmk. 135 described in the note following No. 46.

Pairs imperf between of Nos. 47-49, 51 were favor prints made for an influential Budapest collector. Value, $90 each.

For overprints & surcharges see Nos. B35-B52, 2N1-2N3, 6N1-6N6, 6NB127N1-7N6, 7NB1, 10N1.

				Perf. 11½
47b	A4	1f gray	350.00	80.00
48a	A4	2f olive yel	350.00	60.00
49a	A4	3f orange	100.00	20.00
50b	A4	4f violet	225.00	12.50
51b	A4	5f emerald	50.00	3.75
52b	A4	6f claret	—	60.00
53a	A4	6f bister ('01)	—	110.00
54a	A4	6f olive grn ('02)	—	300.00
55b	A4	10f carmine	400.00	25.00
56a	A4	12f violet ('04)	250.00	80.00
57a	A4	20f brown ('01)	—	150.00
58b	A4	25f blue	—	75.00
59a	A4	30f orange brn	—	125.00
60b	A4	35f red vio ('01)	—	275.00
61a	A4	50f lake	400.00	75.00
62a	A4	60f green	600.00	150.00
63a	A5	1k brown red	175.00	15.00
64a	A5	2k gray blue	—	600.00
65a	A5	3k sea green		4,000.
66a	A5	5k vio brown ('01)		1,000.

1908-13	**Wmk. 136**			**Perf. 15**
67	A4	1f slate	.30	.25
68	A4	2f olive yellow	.25	.25
69	A4	3f orange	.30	.25
70	A4	5f emerald	.30	.25
c.		Booklet pane of 6	100.00	
71	A4	6f olive green	.30	.25
72	A4	10f carmine	.40	.25
c.		Booklet pane of 6	100.00	
73	A4	12f violet	.40	.25
74	A4	16f gray green ('13)	.50	.50
75	A4	20f dark brown	7.50	.25
76	A4	25f blue	6.25	.25
77	A4	30f orange brown	7.50	.25
78	A4	35f red violet	10.00	.25
79	A4	50f lake	3.00	.30
80	A4	60f green	9.00	.25
81	A5	1k brown red	12.50	.25
82	A5	2k gray blue	90.00	.30
83	A5	5k violet brown	125.00	9.00
		Nos. 67-83 (17)	273.50	13.45

Nos. 67-73, 75-83 exist imperf. Value, set $1,000.

1904-05	**Wmk. 136a**			**Perf. 12x11½**
67a	A4	1f slate	2.50	2.50
68a	A4	2f olive yellow	5.00	2.50
69a	A4	3f orange	2.00	.40
70a	A4	5f emerald	4.00	.25
71a	A4	6f olive green	2.50	.40
72a	A4	10f carmine	7.50	.25
73a	A4	12f violet	4.00	3.00
75a	A4	20f dark brown	20.00	1.00
76a	A4	25f blue	40.00	1.00
77a	A4	30f orange brown	9.00	.40
78a	A4	35f red violet	22.50	.40
79a	A4	50f lake	15.00	4.00
c.		50f magenta	1.00	10.00
80a	A4	60f green	250.00	.40
81a	A5	1k brown red	250.00	.75
82a	A5	2k gray blue	900.00	50.00
c.		Perf. 11½	2,000.	150.00
83a	A5	5k violet brown	240.00	75.00
		Nos. 67a-83a (16)	1,774.	140.05

HUNGARY, ROMANIA, RUSSIA & WORLDWIDE

Extensive Stock of Mint & Used

Request our free 68-page price list

ALMAZ CO. Dept. VH
P.O. Box 100-812 • Vanderveer Station
Brooklyn, NY 11210
Phone/Fax (718) 241-6360
AlmazStamps@aol.com

HUNGARY

1906 — Perf. 15

67b	A4	1f slate		2.50	.50
68b	A4	2f olive yellow		1.75	.25
69b	A4	3f orange		2.25	.25
70b	A4	5f emerald		2.00	.25
71b	A4	6f olive green		2.00	.25
72b	A4	10f carmine		2.50	.25
73b	A4	12f violet		4.00	.25
75b	A4	20f dark brown		10.00	.30
76b	A4	25f blue		8.00	.30
77b	A4	30f orange brown		10.00	.25
78b	A4	35f red violet		50.00	.25
79b	A4	50f lake		5.00	1.00
80b	A4	60f green		62.50	.25
81b	A5	1k brown red		60.00	.60
82b	A5	2k gray blue		225.00	8.00

Nos. 67b-82b (15) 447.50 12.95

1913-16 — Wmk. 137 Vert. — Perf. 15

84	A4	1f slate		.25	.25
85	A4	2f olive yellow		.25	.25
86	A4	3f orange		.25	.25
87	A4	5f emerald		.50	.25
88	A4	6f olive green		.25	.25
89	A4	10f carmine		.25	.25
90	A4	12f violet, yel		.30	.25
91	A4	16f gray green		.35	.90
92	A4	20f dark brown		1.00	.25
93	A4	25f ultra		1.20	.25
94	A4	30f orange brown		.90	.25
95	A4	35f red violet		.90	.25
96	A4	50f lake, blue		.30	.25
a.		Cliché of 35f in plate of 50f		325.00	—
97	A4	60f green		5.75	2.00
98	A4	60f green, salmon		.80	.30
99	A4	70f red brn, grn ('16)		.25	.25
100	A4	80f dull violet ('16)		.25	.25
101	A5	1k dull red		2.50	.25
102	A5	2k dull blue		4.25	.25
103	A5	5k violet brown		20.00	5.00

Nos. 84-103 (20) 40.50 12.20

Nos. 89-97, 99-103 exist imperf. Value, set $1,200.

For overprints and surcharges see Nos. 2N1-2N3, 6N1-6N6, 6NB12, 7N1-7N6, 7NB1, 10N1.

Wmk. 137 Horiz.

84a	A4	1f slate		.75	.60
85a	A4	2f olive yellow		2.00	.40
87a	A4	5f emerald		.50	.25
88a	A4	6f olive green		1.00	.25
89a	A4	10f carmine		1.00	.25
90a	A4	12f violet, yellow		2.00	.25
92a	A4	20f dark brown		6.25	.25
94a	A4	30f orange brown		50.00	.25
95a	A4	35f red violet		200.00	.25
96b	A4	50f lake, blue		15.00	6.25
97a	A4	60f green		4.25	1.75
98a	A4	60f green, salmon		1.50	.25
101a	A5	1k dull red		16.00	.40
102a	A5	2k dull blue		100.00	1.00

Nos. 84a-102a (14) 400.25 12.25

A5a

Wmk. 137 Vert.

1916, July 1 — Perf. 15

103A	A5a	10f violet brown		.30	.30

Although issued as a postal savings stamp, No. 103A was also valid for postage. Used value is for postal usage.

Exists imperf. Value $10.

For overprints and surcharges see Nos. 2N59, 5N23, 6N50, 8N13, 10N42.

Queen Zita — A6

Charles IV — A7

1916, Dec. 30

104	A6	10f violet		.60	.60
105	A7	15f red		.60	.60

Coronation of King Charles IV and Queen Zita on Dec. 30, 1916.

Exist imperf. Value, set $24.

During 1921-24 the two center rows of panes of various stamps then current were punched with three holes forming a triangle. These were sold at post offices. Collectors and dealers who wanted the stamps unpunched would have to purchase them through the philatelic agency at a 10% advance over face value.

Harvesting (White Numerals) — A8

1916

106	A8	10f rose		.75	.25
107	A8	15f violet		.75	.25

Exist imperf. Value, set $15.

For overprints and surcharges see Nos. B56-B57, 2N4-2N5, 5N1.

Harvesting Wheat A9

Parliament Building at Budapest A10

1916-18 — Wmk. 137 Vert. — Perf. 15

108	A9	2f brown orange		.25	.25
109	A9	3f red lilac		.25	.25
110	A9	4f slate gray ('18)		.25	.25
111	A9	5f green		.25	.25
112	A9	6f grnsh blue		.25	.25
113	A9	10f rose red		1.40	.25
114	A9	15f violet		.25	.25
115	A9	20f gray brown		.25	.25
116	A9	25f dull blue		.30	.25
117	A9	35f brown		.25	.25
118	A9	40f olive green		.25	.25

Perf. 14

119	A10	50f red vio & lil		.25	.25
120	A10	75f brt bl & pale bl		.25	.25
121	A10	80f grn & pale grn		.25	.25
122	A10	1k red brn & claret		.25	.25
123	A10	2k ol brn & bister		.25	.25
124	A10	3k dk vio & indigo		.60	.25
125	A10	5k dk brn & lt brn		.25	.25
126	A10	10k vio brn & vio		1.20	.25

Nos. 108-126 (19) 7.60 4.75

Nos. 108-126 exist imperf. Value, set $100.

See Nos. 335-377, 388-396. For overprints and surcharges see Nos. 153-167, C1-C5, J76-J99, 1N1-1N21, 1N26-1N30, 1N33, 1N36-1N39, 2N6-2N27, 2N33-2N38, 2N41, 2N43-2N48, 4N1-4N4, 5N2-5N17, 6N7-6N24, 6N29-6N39, 7N7-7N30, 7N38, 7N41-7N42, 8N1-8N4, 9N1-9N2, 9N4, 10N2-10N16, 10N25-10N29, 10N31, 10N33-10N41, 11N1-15, 11N20-24, 11N27, 11N30, 11N32-33.

Charles IV A11

Queen Zita A12

1918 — Wmk. 137 Vert. — Perf. 15

127	A11	10f scarlet		.30	.25
128	A11	15f deep violet		.45	.60
129	A11	20f dark brown		.30	.25
130	A11	25f brt blue		.30	.25
131	A12	40f olive green		.35	.30
132	A12	50f lilac		.35	.30

Nos. 127-132 (6) 2.05 1.95

Exist imperf. Value, set $35.

For overprints see Nos. 168-173, 1N32, 1N34-1N35, 2N28-2N32, 2N39-2N40, 2N42, 2N49-2N51, 5N18-5N22, 6N25-6N28, 6N40-6N43, 7N31-7N37, 7N39-7N40, 8N5, 9N3, 10N17-10N21, 10N30, 10N32, 11N16-19, 11N25-26, 11N28-29, 11N31.

Issues of the Republic

Hungarian Stamps of 1916-18 Overprinted in Black

1918-19 — Wmk. 137 — Perf. 15, 14

On Stamps of 1916-18

153	A9	2f brown orange		.25	.25
154	A9	3f red lilac		.25	.25
155	A9	4f slate gray		.25	.25
156	A9	5f green		.25	.25
157	A9	6f grnsh blue		.25	.25
158	A9	10f rose red		.25	.25
159	A9	20f gray brown		.25	.25
162	A9	40f olive green		.25	.25
163	A10	1k red brn & claret		.25	.25
164	A10	2k ol brn & bis		.25	.25
165	A10	3k dk violet & ind		.40	1.00
166	A10	5k dk brn & lt brn		2.00	5.00
167	A10	10k vio brn & vio		.65	1.50

On Stamps of 1918

168	A11	10f scarlet		.25	.25
169	A11	15f deep violet		.25	.25
170	A11	20f dark brown		.25	.25
171	A11	25f brt blue		.25	.25
172	A12	40f olive green		.30	.60
173	A12	50f lilac		.25	.25

Nos. 153-173 (19) 7.10 11.90

Nos. 153-164 exist imperf. Value, set $90.
Nos. 153-162, 168-173 exist with overprint inverted. Value, each $6.

A13

A14

1919-20 — Perf. 15

174	A13	2f brown orange		.25	.25
176	A13	4f slate gray		.25	.25
177	A13	5f yellow grn		.25	.25
178	A13	6f grnsh blue		.25	.25
179	A13	10f red		.25	.25
180	A13	15f violet		.25	.25
181	A13	20f dark brown		.25	.25
182	A13	20f green ('20)		.25	.25
183	A13	25f dull blue		.25	.25
184	A13	40f olive green		.25	.25
185	A13	40f rose red ('20)		.25	.25
186	A13	45f orange		.25	.25

Perf. 14

187	A14	50f brn vio & pale vio		.25	.25
188	A14	60f brown & bl ('20)		.25	.25
189	A14	95f dk bl & bl		.25	.25
190	A14	1k red brn		.25	.25
191	A14	1k dk bl & dull bl ('20)		.25	.25
192	A14	1.20k dk grn & grn		.25	.25
193	A14	1.40k yellow green		.25	.25
194	A14	2k ol brn & bis		.25	.25
195	A14	3k dk vio & ind		.25	.25
196	A14	5k dk brn & brn		.25	.85
197	A14	10k vio brn & red vio		.50	.75

Nos. 174-197 (23) 6.00 6.85

The 3f red lilac, type A13, was never regularly issued without overprint (Nos. 204 and 312). In 1923 a small quantity was sold by the Government at public auction. Value $3.

For overprints see Nos. 203-222, 306-330, 1N40, 2N52-2N58, 6N44-6N49, 8N6-8N12, 10N22-10N24, 11N34-35.

Nos. 174, 177-179, 181-197 exist imperf. Value set $60.

Issues of the Soviet Republic

Karl Marx — A15

Sándor Petőfi — A16

Ignác Martinovics A17

György Dózsa A18

Friedrich Engels — A19

1919, June 12 Litho. — Wmk. 137 Horiz. — Perf. 12½x12

198	A15	20f rose & brown		.40	.40
199	A16	45f brn org & dk grn		.40	.40
200	A17	60f blue gray & brn		4.00	4.00
201	A18	75f claret & vio brn		4.00	4.00
202	A19	80f olive db & blk brn		4.00	4.00

Nos. 198-202 (5) 12.80 12.80

Used values are for favor cancels.
Exist imperf. Value, Set $150.

Wmk. Vertical

198a	A15	20f		7.50	7.50
199a	A16	45f		7.50	7.50
200a	A17	60f		7.50	7.50
201a	A18	75f		7.50	7.50
202a	A19	80f		25.00	25.00

Nos. 198a-202a (5) 55.00

Nos. 198a-202a were not used postally. Used examples are favor canceled.

Stamps of 1919 Overprinted in Red

1919, July 21 Typo. — Perf. 15

203	A13	2f brown orange		.25	.25
204	A13	3f red lilac		.25	.25
205	A13	4f slate gray		.25	.25
206	A13	5f yellow green		.25	.25
207	A13	6f grnsh blue		.25	.25
208	A13	10f red		.25	.25
209	A13	15f violet		.25	.25
210	A13	20f dark brown		.25	.25
211	A13	25f dull blue		.25	.25
212	A13	40f olive green		.25	.25
213	A13	45f orange		.25	.25

Overprinted in Red

Perf. 14

214	A14	50f brn vio & pale vio		.25	.30
215	A14	95f dk blue & blue		.25	.30
216	A14	1k red brown		.25	.30
217	A14	1.20k dk grn & grn		.25	.40
218	A14	1.40k yellow green		.25	.40
219	A14	2k ol brn & bister		.40	1.25
220	A14	3k dk vio & ind		.65	1.00
221	A14	5k dk brn & brn		.50	.80
222	A14	10k vio brn & red vio		.75	1.75

Nos. 203-222 (20) 6.30 9.25

"Magyar Tanacsköztársaság" on Nos. 198 to 222 means "Hungarian Soviet Republic."

Nos. 203-218, 221-222 exist imperf. Value, set $125.

Issues of the Kingdom

Stamps of 1919 Overprinted in Black

1919, Nov. 16

306	A13	5f green		.65	1.00
307	A13	10f rose red		.65	1.00
308	A13	15f violet		.65	1.00
309	A13	20f gray brown		.65	1.00
310	A13	25f dull blue		.65	1.00

Nos. 306-310 (5) 3.25 5.00

Issued to commemorate the Romanian evacuation. The overprint reads: "Entry of the National Army-November 16, 1919."

Forged overprints exist.

Nos. 203 to 213 Overprinted in Black

1920, Jan. 26 — Perf. 15

311	A13	2f brown orange		1.25	1.60
312	A13	3f red lilac		.25	.30
313	A13	4f slate gray		1.25	1.60
314	A13	5f yellow green		.25	.25
315	A13	6f blue green		.25	.40
316	A13	10f red		.25	.25
317	A13	15f violet		.25	.25
318	A13	20f dark brown		.25	.25
319	A13	25f dull blue		.25	.30
320	A13	40f olive green		1.50	2.00
321	A13	45f orange		1.50	2.00

HUNGARY

Nos. 214 to 222 Overprinted in Black

Perf. 14

322	A14	50f brn vio & pale vio	1.50	2.00
323	A14	95f dk bl & bl	1.50	2.00
324	A14	1k red brown	1.50	2.00
325	A14	1.20k dk grn & grn	1.50	2.50
326	A14	1.40k yellow green	1.50	2.50
327	A14	2k ol brn & bis	8.50	17.50
328	A14	3k dk vio & ind	8.50	17.50
329	A14	5k dk brn & brn	.25	.50
330	A14	10k vio brn & red vio	8.50	17.50
		Nos. 311-330 (20)	40.50	73.20

Counterfeit overprints exist.

Types of 1916-18 Issue Denomination Tablets Without Inner Frame on Nos. 350 to 363

1920-24		Wmk. 137	Perf. 15	
335	A9	5f brown orange	.25	.25
336	A9	10f red violet	.25	.25
337	A9	40f rose red	.25	.25
338	A9	50f yellow green	.25	.25
339	A9	50f blue vio ('22)	.25	.25
340	A9	60f black	.25	.25
341	A9	1k green ('22)	.25	.25
342	A9	1½k brown vio ('22)	.25	.25
343	A9	2k grnsh blue ('22)	.25	.25
344	A9	2½k dp green ('22)	.25	.25
345	A9	3k brown org ('22)	.25	.25
346	A9	4k lt red ('22)	.25	.25
347	A9	4½k dull violet ('22)	.25	.25
348	A9	5k dp brn ('22)	.25	.25
349	A9	6k dark blue ('22)	.25	.25
350	A9	10k brown ('23)	.25	.25
351	A9	15k slate ('23)	.25	.25
352	A9	20k red vio ('23)	.25	.25
353	A9	25k orange ('23)	.25	.25
354	A9	40k gray grn ('23)	.25	.25
355	A9	50k dark blue ('23)	.25	.25
356	A9	100k claret ('23)	.25	.25
357	A9	150k dk grn ('23)	.30	.25
358	A9	200k green ('23)	.30	.25
359	A9	300k rose red ('24)	.80	.30
360	A9	350k violet ('23)	1.50	.30
361	A9	500k dark gray ('24)	2.50	.30
362	A9	600k olive bis ('24)	2.50	.30
363	A9	800k org yel ('24)	2.50	.30

Perf. 14

364	A10	2.50k bl & gray bl	.25	.25
365	A10	3.50k gray	.25	.25
366	A10	10k brown ('22)	.50	.25
367	A10	15k dk gray ('22)	.25	.25
368	A10	20k red vio ('22)	.25	.25
369	A10	25k orange ('22)	.25	.25
370	A10	30k claret ('22)	.75	.25
371	A10	40k gray grn ('22)	.75	.25
372	A10	50k dp blue ('22)	.75	.25
373	A10	100k yel brn ('22)	.75	.25
374	A10	400k turq bl ('23)	.75	.30
375	A10	500k brt vio ('23)	1.10	.25
376	A10	1000k lilac ('24)	1.50	.25
377	A10	2000k car ('24)	2.00	.60
		Nos. 335-377 (43)	26.00	11.40

Nos. 372 to 377 have colored numerals.
Nos. 335-338, 340, 350-365, 368, 370, 372-377 exist imperf. Value, set $200.

Madonna and Child — A23

1921-25		Typo.	Perf. 12	
378	A23	50k dk brn & bl	.25	.25
379	A23	100k ol bis & yel brn	.40	.35

Wmk. 133

380	A23	200k dk bl & ultra	.40	.25
381	A23	500k vio brn & vio	.75	.40
382	A23	1000k vio & red vio	1.00	.35
383	A23	2000k grnsh bl & vio	1.75	.50
384	A23	2500k ol brn & buff	2.00	.25
385	A23	3000k brn red & vio	2.00	.25
386	A23	5000k dk grn & yel grn	2.00	.25
a.		Center inverted	16,000.	12,000.

387	A23	10000k gray vio & pale bl	2.00	.25
		Nos. 378-387 (10)	12.55	3.10

Nos. 380-387 exist imperf. Value, set of 8 $175.
Issue dates: 50k, 100k, Feb. 27, 1921; 2500k, 10,000k, 1925; others, 1923.

Types of 1916-18 Denomination Tablets Without Inner Frame on Nos. 388-394

1924		Wmk. 133	Perf. 15	
388	A9	100k claret	.40	.25
389	A9	200k yellow grn	.25	.25
390	A9	300k rose red	.30	.35
391	A9	400k deep blue	.30	.35
392	A9	500k dark gray	.40	.25
393	A9	600k olive bister	.45	.25
a.		"800" in upper right corner	110.00	260.00
394	A9	800k org yel	.50	.25

Perf. 14½x14

395	A10	1000k lilac	1.50	.25
396	A10	2000k carmine	2.00	.25
		Nos. 388-396 (9)	6.10	2.45

Nos. 395 and 396 have colored numerals.
Exist imperf. Value, set $37.50.

Maurus Jókai (1825-1904), Novelist — A24

1925, Feb. 1		Unwmk.	Perf. 12	
400	A24	1000k dp grn & blk brn	1.75	3.25
401	A24	2000k lt brn & blk brn	.80	1.00
402	A24	2500k dk bl & blk brn	1.75	3.25
		Nos. 400-402 (3)	4.30	7.50

Exist imperf. Value, set $90.

Crown of St. Stephen A25

Matthias Cathedral A26

Palace at Budapest — A27

Perf. 14x14¼, 15

1926-27		Wmk. 133	Litho.	
403	A25	1f dk gray	.45	.25
404	A25	2f lt blue	.55	.25
405	A25	3f orange	.55	.25
406	A25	4f violet	.65	.25
407	A25	6f lt green	.90	.25
408	A25	8f lilac rose	1.60	.25

Typo.

409	A26	10f deep blue	2.75	.25
410	A26	16f dark violet	2.25	.25
411	A26	20f carmine	2.75	.25
412	A26	25f lt brown	2.75	.25

Perf. 14¼x14

413	A27	32f dp vio & brt vio	4.25	.25
414	A27	40f dk blue & blue	5.00	.25
		Nos. 403-414 (12)	24.45	3.00

See Nos. 428-436. For surcharges see Nos. 450-456, 466-467.
Nos. 403-414, 418-421 exist imperf. Value, set $250.

Madonna and Child — A28

1926-27		Engr.	Perf. 14	
415	A28	1p violet	15.00	.65
416	A28	2p red	17.50	.85
417	A28	5p blue ('27)	17.50	4.00
		Nos. 415-417 (3)	50.00	5.50

Exist imperf. Value, set $400.

Palace at Budapest — A29

1926-27		Typo.	Perf. 14x14¼	
418	A29	30f blue grn ('27)	4.00	.25
419	A29	46f ultra ('27)	5.25	.30
420	A29	50f brown blk ('27)	6.00	.25
421	A29	70f scarlet	9.75	.25
		Nos. 418-421 (4)	25.00	1.05

For surcharge see No. 480.

St. Stephen — A30

1928-29		Engr.	Perf. 15	
422	A30	8f yellow grn	.65	.30
423	A30	8f rose lake ('29)	.65	.30
424	A30	16f orange red	.85	.30
425	A30	16f violet ('29)	.85	.30
426	A30	32f ultra	2.50	4.00
427	A30	32f bister ('29)	2.50	4.00
		Nos. 422-427 (6)	8.00	9.20

890th death anniversary of St. Stephen, the first king of Hungary.
Exist imperf. Value, set $300.

Types of 1926-27 Issue Perf. 14x14¼, 15

1928-30		Typo.	Wmk. 210	
428	A25	1f black	.25	.25
429	A25	2f blue	.35	.25
430	A25	3f orange	.35	.25
431	A25	4f violet	.45	.25
432	A25	6f blue grn	.60	.25
433	A25	8f lilac rose	1.25	.25
434	A26	10f dp blue ('30)	4.50	.25
435	A26	16f violet	1.50	.25
436	A26	20f dull red	1.25	.25
		Nos. 428-436 (9)	10.50	2.25

On Nos. 428-433 the numerals have thicker strokes than on the same values of the 1926-27 issue.
Exist imperf. Value, set $110.

Palace at Budapest — A31

Type A31 resembles A27 but the steamer is nearer the right of the design. A31, A29 & A27 are similar but the frame borders are different.

1928-31			Perf. 14¼x14	
437	A31	30f lt grn ('31)	4.00	.25
438	A31	32f red violet	4.00	.25
439	A31	40f deep blue	5.00	.25
440	A31	46f apple green	4.50	.25
441	A31	50f ocher ('31)	4.50	.25
		Nos. 437-441 (5)	22.00	1.25

Exist imperf. Value, set $110.

Admiral Nicholas Horthy — A32

1930, Mar. 1		Litho.	Perf. 15	
445	A32	8f myrtle green	.75	.25
446	A32	16f purple	1.00	.25
447	A32	20f carmine	6.00	1.10
448	A32	32f olive brown	4.00	1.25
449	A32	40f dull blue	7.00	.50
		Nos. 445-449 (5)	18.75	3.35

10th anniv. of the election of Adm. Nicholas Horthy as Regent, Mar. 1, 1920.
Exist imperf. Value, set $200.

Stamps of 1926-28 Surcharged

1931, Jan. 1			Perf. 14¼, 15	
450	A25	2f on 3f orange	.50	.40
451	A25	6f on 8f magenta	.50	.25
a.		Perf. 14x14¼	30.00	30.00
452	A26	10f on 16f violet	.50	.25

Wmk. 133

453	A25	2f on 3f orange	2.50	5.00
a.		Perf. 14x14¼	3.00	6.00
454	A25	6f on 8f magenta	2.00	4.00
a.		Perf. 14x14¼	50.00	100.00
455	A26	10f on 16f dk vio	1.75	3.50
a.		Perf. 14x14¼	2.00	4.00
456	A26	10f on 25f lt brn	1.25	2.50
a.		Perf. 14x14¼	1.25	2.25
		Nos. 450-456 (7)	9.00	15.90

For surcharges see Nos. 466-467.

St. Elizabeth A33

Ministering to Children A34

Wmk. 210

1932, Apr. 21		Photo.	Perf. 15	
458	A33	10f ultra	.75	.25
459	A33	20f scarlet	.75	.25

Perf. 14

460	A34	32f deep violet	1.50	2.50
461	A34	40f deep blue	2.00	1.00
		Nos. 458-461 (4)	5.00	4.00

700th anniv. of the death of St. Elizabeth of Hungary.
Exist imperf. Value, set $100.

Hungaria Stamp Exchange

Eastern Europe Dealer

Hungary • Balkans • Baltics
Croatia • Czech • Greece
Poland • Romania • Russia
Slovakia • Ukraine
and more...

(888) 868-8293

www.hungarianstamps.com

HUNGARY

Madonna, Patroness of Hungary — A35

1932, June 1 — Perf. 12
462	A35	1p yellow grn	30.00	.25
463	A35	2p carmine	30.00	.40
464	A35	5p deep blue	42.50	3.00
465	A35	10p olive bister	42.50	22.50
		Nos. 462-465 (4)	145.00	26.15

Exist imperf. Value, set $1,000.

Nos. 451 and 454 Surcharged

1932, June 14 — Wmk. 210 — Perf. 15
466	A25	2f on 6f on 8f mag	.30	.25

Wmk. 133
467	A25	2f on 6f on 8f mag	50.00	100.00

Imre Madách — A36

Designs: 2f, Janos Arany. 4f, Dr. Ignaz Semmelweis. 6f, Baron Lorand Eotvos. 10f, Count Stephen Szechenyi. 16f, Ferenc Deak. 20f, Franz Liszt. 30f, Louis Kossuth. 32f, Stephen Tisza. 40f, Mihaly Munkacsy. 50f, Alexander Csoma. 70f, Farkas Bolyai.

1932 — Wmk. 210 — Perf. 15
468	A36	1f slate violet	.25	.25
469	A36	2f orange	.25	.25
470	A36	4f ultra	.25	.25
471	A36	6f yellow grn	.25	.25
472	A36	10f Prus green	.35	.25
473	A36	16f dull violet	.35	.25
474	A36	20f deep rose	.45	.25
475	A36	30f brown	.50	.25
476	A36	32f brown vio	.90	.25
477	A36	40f dull blue	.90	.25
478	A36	50f deep green	1.10	.50
479	A36	70f cerise	1.50	.35
		Nos. 468-479 (12)	7.05	3.35
		Set, never hinged	11.50	

Issued in honor of famous Hungarians.
Exist imperf. Value, set $125.
See Nos. 509-510.

No. 421 Surcharged

1933, Apr. 15 — Wmk. 133 — Perf. 14
480	A29	10f on 70f scarlet	2.50	.40
		Never hinged	5.00	

Leaping Stag and Double Cross — A47

1933, July 10 — Wmk. 210 — Photo. — Perf. 15
481	A47	10f dk green	.75	.80
482	A47	16f violet brn	2.00	2.50
483	A47	20f car lake	1.50	1.25
484	A47	32f yellow	5.00	6.00
485	A47	40f deep blue	5.00	4.00
		Nos. 481-485 (5)	14.25	14.55
		Set, never hinged	27.50	

Boy Scout Jamboree at Gödöllö, Hungary, July 20 - Aug. 20, 1933.
Exists imperf. Value, set $150.

Souvenir Sheet

Franz Liszt A48

1934, May 6 — Perf. 15
486	A48	20f lake	70.00	90.00
		Never hinged	140.00	

2nd Hungarian Phil. Exhib., Budapest, and Jubilee of the 1st Hungarian Phil. Soc. Sold for 90f, including entrance fee. Size: 64x76mm.
Exists imperf. Value, set $2,500.

Francis II Rákóczy (1676-1735), Prince of Transylvania — A49

1935, Apr. 8 — Perf. 12
487	A49	10f yellow green	.90	.50
488	A49	16f brt violet	5.00	3.75
489	A49	20f dark carmine	2.00	1.50
490	A49	32f brown lake	7.00	7.25
491	A49	40f blue	8.50	8.50
		Nos. 487-491 (5)	23.40	21.50
		Set, never hinged	42.50	

Exists imperf. Value, set $400.

Cardinal Pázmány A50

Signing the Charter A51

1935, Sept. 25
492	A50	6f dull green	1.10	1.00
493	A51	10f dark green	.25	.25
494	A50	16f slate violet	1.50	1.60
495	A50	20f magenta	.25	.25
496	A51	32f deep claret	2.50	3.25
497	A51	40f dark blue	2.00	3.25
		Nos. 492-497 (6)	7.60	9.75
		Set, never hinged	15.00	

Tercentenary of the founding of the University of Budapest by Peter Cardinal Pázmány.
Exists imperf. Value, set $400.

Ancient City and Fortress of Buda — A52

Guardian Angel over Buda — A53

Shield of Buda, Cannon and Massed Flags — A54

First Hungarian Soldier to Enter Buda — A55

1936, Sept. 2 — Perf. 11½x12½
498	A52	10f dark green	.40	.25
499	A53	16f deep violet	2.50	3.50
500	A54	20f car lake	.40	.25
501	A55	32f dark brown	2.50	3.25
502	A52	40f deep blue	2.50	3.25
		Nos. 498-502 (5)	8.30	10.50
		Set, never hinged	16.00	

250th anniv. of the recapture of Budapest from the Turks.

Exists imperf. Value, set $400.

Catalogue values for unused stamps in this section, from this point to the end of the section, are for Never Hinged items.

Budapest International Fair — A56

1937, Feb. 22 — Perf. 12
503	A56	2f deep orange	.25	.25
504	A56	6f yellow green	.40	.25
505	A56	10f myrtle green	.55	.25
506	A56	20f deep cerise	1.25	.40
507	A56	32f dark violet	2.00	.55
508	A56	40f ultra	1.60	.80
		Nos. 503-508 (6)	6.05	2.50

Exist imperf. Value, set $250.

Portrait Type of 1932

5f, Ferenc Kolcsey. 25f, Mihaly Vorosmarty.

1937, May 5 — Perf. 15
509	A36	5f brown orange	.80	.25
510	A36	25f olive green	1.60	.25

Exist imperf. Value, set $400.

Pope Sylvester II, Archbishop Astrik — A59

Designs: 2f, 16f, Stephen the Church builder. 4f, 20f, St. Stephen enthroned. 5f, 25f, Sts. Gerhardt, Emerich, Stephen. 6f, 30f, St. Stephen offering holy crown to Virgin Mary. 10f, same as 1f. 32f, 50f, Portrait of St. Stephen. 40f, Madonna and Child. 70f, Crown of St. Stephen.
See designs A75-A77 for smaller stamps of designs similar to Nos. 521-524, but with slanted "MAGYAR KIR POSTA."

1938, Jan. 1 — Perf. 12
511	A59	1f deep violet	.35	.25
512	A59	2f olive brown	.35	.25
513	A59	4f brt blue	.75	.25
514	A59	5f magenta	1.10	.25
515	A59	6f dp yel grn	1.40	.25
516	A59	10f red orange	1.10	.25
517	A59	16f gray violet	1.75	.55
518	A59	20f car lake	1.10	.25
519	A59	25f dark green	1.40	.80
520	A59	30f olive bister	2.25	.25
521	A59	32f dp claret, buff	1.75	1.50
522	A59	40f Prus green	.25	.25
523	A59	50f rose vio, grnsh	2.50	.25
524	A59	70f ol grn, bluish	4.00	.55
		Nos. 511-524 (14)	22.05	5.90

900th anniv. of the death of St. Stephen.
Exists imperf. Value, set $400.
For overprints see Nos. 535-536.

Admiral Horthy — A67

1938, Jan. 1 — Perf. 12½x12
525	A67	1p peacock green	2.50	.25
526	A67	2p brown	3.00	.35
527	A67	5p sapphire blue	3.75	1.90
		Nos. 525-527 (3)	9.25	2.50

Exist imperf. Value, set $475.

Souvenir Sheet

St. Stephen A68

1938, May 22 — Wmk. 210 — Perf. 12
528	A68	20f carmine lake	32.50	25.00

3rd Hungarian Phil. Exhib., Budapest. Sheet sold only at exhibition with 1p ticket.
Exists imperf. Value, set $4,500.

College of Debrecen A69

Three Students A71

George Marothy — A73

10f, 18th cent. view of College. 20f, 19th cent. view of College. 40f, Stephen Hatvani.

Perf. 12x12½, 12½x12
1938, Sept. 24 — Wmk. 210
529	A69	6f deep green	.35	.25
530	A69	10f brown	.35	.25
531	A71	16f brown car	.35	.30
532	A69	20f crimson	.35	.30
533	A73	32f slate green	.90	.50
534	A73	40f brt blue	.90	.50
		Nos. 529-534 (6)	3.20	2.10

Founding of Debrecen College, 400th anniv.
Exists imperf. Value, set $300.

Types of 1938 Overprinted in Blue (#535) or Carmine (#536)

a b

1938 — Perf. 12
535	A59(a)	20f sal pink	1.75	1.50
536	A59(b)	70f brn, grnsh	1.75	1.50
a.		Overprint omitted	12,500.	7,500.

Restoration of the territory ceded by Czechoslovakia.
Exists imperf. Value $135.
Forgeries exist of No. 536a.

Crown of St. Stephen A75

St. Stephen A76

Madonna, Patroness of Hungary A77

Coronation Church, Budapest A78

HUNGARY

Reformed Church, Debrecen — A79
Cathedral, Esztergom — A80
Deák Square Evangelical Church, Budapest — A81
Cathedral of Kassa — A82

Wmk. 210
1939, June 1   Photo.   Perf. 15
537	A75	1f brown car	.25	.25
538	A75	2f Prus green	.25	.25
539	A75	4f ocher	.25	.25
540	A75	5f brown violet	.25	.25
541	A75	6f yellow green	.25	.25
542	A75	10f bister brn	.25	.25
543	A75	16f rose violet	.25	.25
544	A76	20f rose red	.25	.25
545	A77	25f blue gray	.25	.25

Perf. 12
546	A78	30f red violet	.25	.25
547	A79	32f brown	.25	.25
548	A80	40f greenish blue	.25	.25
549	A81	50f olive	.25	.25
550	A82	70f henna brown	.25	.25
		Nos. 537-550 (14)	3.50	3.50

See Nos. 521-524, 578-596. For overprints see Nos. 559-560.
Exists imperf. Value, set $275.

Girl Scout Sign and Olive Branch — A83

6f, Scout lily, Hungary's shield, Crown of St. Stephen. 10f, Girls in Scout hat & national headdress. 20f, Dove & Scout emblems.

1939, July 20   Photo.   Perf. 12
551	A83	2f brown orange	.40	.35
552	A83	6f green	.40	.35
553	A83	10f brown	.75	.40
554	A83	20f lilac rose	1.00	.80
		Nos. 551-554 (4)	2.55	1.95

Girl Scout Jamboree at Gödöllö.
Exists imperf. Value, set $300.

Admiral Horthy at Szeged, 1919 — A87
Admiral Nicholas Horthy — A88
Cathedral of Kassa and Angel Ringing "Bell of Liberty" — A89

1940, Mar. 1
555	A87	6f green	.25	.25
556	A88	10f ol blk & ol bis	.25	.25
557	A89	20f brt rose brown	.75	.45
		Nos. 555-557 (3)	1.25	.95

20th anniversary of the election of Admiral Horthy as Regent of Hungary.
Exists imperf. Value, set $100.

Crown of St. Stephen — A90

1940, Sept. 5
| 558 | A90 | 10f dk green & yellow | .35 | .35 |

Issued in commemoration of the recovery of northeastern Transylvania from Romania.
Exists imperf. Value $25.

Nos. 542, 544 Overprinted in Red or Black

1941, Apr. 21   Perf. 15
559	A75	10f bister brn (R)	.30	.25
560	A76	20f rose red (Bk)	.30	.25

Return of the Bacska territory from Yugoslavia.
Exist imperf. Value, set $50.

Admiral Nicholas Horthy — A92

Wmk. 210
1941, June 18   Photo.   Perf. 12
570	A92	1p dk green & buff	.30	.25
571	A92	2p dk brown & buff	.50	.40
572	A92	5p dk rose vio & buff	2.00	.80
		Nos. 570-572 (3)	2.80	1.45

Exist imperf. Value, set $75.
See Nos. 597-599.

Count Stephen Széchenyi — A93
Count Széchenyi and Royal Academy of Science — A94
Representation of the Narrows of Kazán — A95
Chain Bridge, Budapest — A96
Mercury, Train and Boat — A97

1941, Sept. 21
573	A93	10f dk olive grn	.40	.40
574	A94	16f olive brown	.40	.40
575	A95	20f carmine lake	.40	.40
576	A96	32f red orange	.40	.40
577	A97	40f royal blue	1.00	.40
		Nos. 573-577 (5)	2.60	2.00

Count Stephen Szechenyi (1791-1860).
Exist imperf. Value, set $200.

Types of 1939
Perf. 12x12½, 12½x12, 15
1941-43   Wmk. 266
578	A75	1f rose lake ('42)	.30	.25
579	A75	3f dark brown	.30	.25
580	A75	5f violet gray ('42)	.30	.25
581	A75	6f lt green ('42)	.30	.25
582	A75	8f slate grn	.30	.25
583	A75	10f olive brn ('42)	.30	.25
584	A75	12f red orange	.30	.25
585	A76	20f rose red ('42)	.30	.25
586	A76	24f brown violet	.30	.25
587	A78	30f lilac ('42)	.30	.25
588	A82	30f rose red ('43)	.30	.25
589	A80	40f blue green ('42)	.30	.25
590	A79	40f gray black ('43)	.30	.25
591	A81	50f olive grn ('42)	.30	.25
592	A80	50f brt blue ('43)	.30	.25
593	A82	70f copper red ('42)	.30	.25
594	A81	70f gray green ('43)	.30	.25
595	A77	80f brown bister	.30	.25
596	A78	80f bister brn ('43)	.30	.25
		Nos. 578-596 (19)	5.70	4.75

Exist imperf. Value, set $350.

Horthy Type of 1941
Perf. 12x12½
1941, Dec. 18   Wmk. 266
597	A92	1p dk green & buff	.30	.25
598	A92	2p dk brown & buff	.30	.25
599	A92	5p dk rose vio & buff	.30	.25
		Nos. 597-599 (3)	.90	.75

Exist imperf. Value, set $60.

Stephen Horthy — A98

1942, Oct. 15   Perf. 12
| 600 | A98 | 20f black | .40 | .40 |

Death of Stephen Horthy (1904-42), son of Regent Nicholas Horthy, who died in a plane crash.
Exists imperf. Value $65.

Árpád A99
Crown of St. Stephen A109

Portraits: 2f, King Ladislaus I. 3f, Miklós Toldi. 4f, János Hunyadi. 5f, Paul Kinizsi. 6f, Count Miklós Zrinyi. 8f, Francis II Rákóczy. 10f, Count Andrew Hadik. 12f, Arthur Görgei. 18f, 24f, Virgin Mary, Patroness of Hungary.

1943-45   Perf. 15
601	A99	1f grnsh black	.30	.25
602	A99	2f red orange	.30	.25
603	A99	3f ultra	.30	.25
604	A99	4f brown	.30	.25
605	A99	5f vermilion	.30	.25
606	A99	6f slate blue	.30	.25
607	A99	8f dk ol grn	.30	.25
608	A99	10f brown	.30	.25
609	A99	12f dp blue grn	.30	.25
610	A99	18f dk gray	.30	.25
611	A109	20f chestnut brn	.30	.25
612	A99	24f rose violet	.30	.25
613	A109	30f brt carmine	.30	.25
614	A109	50f blue	.30	.25
615	A109	80f yellow brn	.30	.25
616	A109	1p green	.30	.25
616A	A109	2p brown ('45)	.30	.40
616B	A109	5p dk red violet ('45)	.30	.40
		Nos. 601-616B (18)	5.40	5.20

Exist imperf. Value, set $150.
For overprints and surcharges see Nos. 631-658, 660-661, 664, 666-669, 671-672, 674-677, 679, 680, 682, 685-689, 691-698, 801-803, 805-806, 810-815, F2, Q2-Q3, Q7.

Message to the Shepherds — A110

20f, Nativity. 30f, Adoration of the Magi.

1943, Dec. 1   Perf. 12x12½
617	A110	4f dark green	.30	.25
618	A110	20f dull blue	.30	.25
619	A110	30f brown orange	.30	.25
		Nos. 617-619 (3)	.90	.75

Exist imperf. Value, set $150.

St. Margaret — A113

1944, Jan. 19   Perf. 15
| 620 | A113 | 30f deep carmine | .40 | .40 |

Canonization of St. Margaret of Hungary.
Exists imperf. Value $40.
For surcharges see Nos. 662, 673A.

Kossuth with Family A114
Lajos Kossuth A117
Honvéd Drummer — A115

Design: 30f, Kossuth orating.

1944, Mar. 20   Perf. 12½x12, 12x12½
621	A114	4f yellow brown	.30	.25
622	A115	20f dk olive grn	.30	.25
623	A115	30f henna brown	.30	.25
624	A117	50f slate blue	.30	.25
		Nos. 621-624 (4)	1.20	1.00

Louis (Lajos) Kossuth (1802-94).
Exist imperf. Value, set $200.
For surcharges see Nos. B175-B178.

St. Elizabeth — A118

Portraits: 24f, St. Margaret. 30f, Elizabeth Szilágyi. 50f, Dorothy Kanuizsai. 70f, Susanna Lóránttfy. 80f, Ilona Zrinyi.

1944, Aug. 1   Perf. 15
625	A118	20f brn olive	.30	.25
626	A118	24f rose violet	.30	.25
627	A118	30f copper red	.30	.25
628	A118	50f dark blue	.30	.25
629	A118	70f orange red	.30	.25
630	A118	80f brown car	.30	.25
		Nos. 625-630 (6)	1.80	1.50

Exist imperf. Value, set $120.
For overprints and surcharges see Nos. 659, 663, 665, 670, 673, 678, 681, 683-684, 690, 804, 807-809, F1, F3, Q1, Q4-Q6, Q8.

Issues of the Republic

Types of Hungary, 1943 Surcharged in Carmine

1945, May 1   Wmk. 266
Blue Surface-tinted Paper
631	A99	10f on 1f grnsh blk	1.50	1.50
632	A99	20f on 3f ultra	1.50	1.50
633	A99	30f on 4f brown	1.50	1.50
634	A99	40f on 6f slate bl	1.50	1.50
635	A99	50f on 8f dk ol grn	1.50	1.50
636	A99	1p on 10f brown	1.50	1.50
637	A99	150f on 12f dp bl grn	1.50	1.50
638	A99	2p on 18f dk gray	1.50	1.50
639	A109	3p on 20f chnt brn	1.50	1.50
640	A109	5p on 24f rose vio	1.50	1.50
641	A109	6p on 50f blue	1.50	1.50
642	A109	10p on 80f yel brn	1.50	1.50
643	A109	20p on 1p green	1.50	1.50

Yellow Surface-tinted Paper
644	A99	10f on 1f grnsh blk	1.50	1.50
645	A99	20f on 3f ultra	1.50	1.50
646	A99	30f on 4f brown	1.50	1.50
647	A99	40f on 6f slate bl	1.50	1.50
648	A99	50f on 8f dk ol grn	1.50	1.50
649	A99	1p on 10f brown	1.50	1.50
650	A99	150f on 12f dp bl grn	1.50	1.50
651	A99	2p on 18f dk gray	1.50	1.50
652	A109	3p on 20f chnt brn	1.50	1.50
653	A109	5p on 24f rose vio	1.50	1.50
654	A109	6p on 50f blue	1.50	1.50
655	A109	10p on 80f yel brn	1.50	1.50
656	A109	20p on 1p green	1.50	1.50
		Nos. 631-656 (26)	39.00	39.00

Hungary's liberation.

HUNGARY

Types of Hungary, 1943-45, Surcharged in Carmine or Black

1945		Blue Surface-tinted Paper
657	A99	10f on 4f brn (C)	.30	.25
658	A99	10f on 10f brn (C)	.30	.45
659	A118	20f on 20f ol (C)	.30	.25
660	A99	28f on 5f ver	.30	.25
661	A109	30f on 30f brt car	.30	.25
662	A113	30f on 30f dp car	.30	.25
663	A118	30f on 30f cop red	.30	.25
664	A99	40f on 10f brown	.30	.25
665	A118	1p on 70f org red	.30	.25
666	A109	1p on 80f yel brn (C)	.30	.25
667	A99	2p on 4f brown	.30	.25
668	A109	2p on 2p brn (C)	.30	.25
669	A99	4p on 30f brt car	.30	.25
670	A118	8p on 20f olive	.30	.25
671	A99	10p on 2f red org	5.50	5.50
672	A109	10p on 80f yel brn	.30	.25
673	A118	20p on 30f cop red	.30	.25

Same Surcharge with Thinner Unshaded Numerals of Value

| 673A | A113 | 300p on 30f dp car | .30 | .25 |

Surcharged as Nos. 657-673 Yellow Surface-tinted Paper

674	A99	10f on 12f dp bl grn (C)	.30	.25
675	A99	20f on 1f grnsh blk (C)	.30	.25
676	A99	20f on 18f dk gray (C)	.30	.25
a.		Double surcharge		
677	A99	40f on 24f rose vio (C)	.30	.25
678	A118	40f on 24f rose vio	.30	.25
679	A109	42f on 20f chnt brn (C)	.30	.25
680	A109	50f on 50f bl (C)	.30	.25
681	A118	50f on 50f dk bl (C)	.30	.25
682	A99	60f on 8f dk ol grn (C)	.30	.25
683	A118	60f on 24f rose vio	.30	.25
684	A118	80f on 20f brn car (C)	.30	.25
685	A109	1p on 20f chnt brn	.30	.25
686	A109	1p on 1p grn (C)	.30	.25
687	A99	150f on 6f sl bl (C)	1.50	1.50
688	A99	1.60p on 12f dp bl grn	.30	.25
689	A99	3p on 3f ultra (C)	.30	.25
690	A118	3p on 50f dk bl	.30	.25
691	A99	5p on 8f dk ol grn	.30	.25
692	A109	5p on 5p dk red vio (C)	.30	.25
693	A109	6p on 50f blue	.30	.25
694	A109	7p on 1p grn	.30	.25
695	A99	9p on 1f grnsh blk	.30	.25

Same Surcharge with Thinner, Unshaded Numerals of Value

696	A99	40p on 8f dk ol grn	.30	.25
697	A99	60p on 18f dk gray	.30	.25
698	A99	100p on 12f dp bl grn	.30	.25
Nos. 657-698 (43)			19.30	17.45

Various shades and errors of overprint exist on Nos. 657-698.
These surface-tinted stamps exist without surcharge, but were not so issued.

Mining — A124

Designs: 1.60p, Manufacturing. 2p, Railroading. 3p, Construction. 5p, Agriculture. 8p, Communications. 10p, Architecture. 20p, Writing.

Wmk. 266
1945, Sept. 11 — **Photo.** — **Perf. 12**

700	A124	40f gray black	5.50	6.50
701	A124	1.60p olive bis	5.50	6.50
702	A124	2p slate green	5.50	6.50
703	A124	3p dark purple	5.50	6.50
704	A124	5p dark red	5.50	6.50
705	A124	8p brown	5.50	6.50
706	A124	10p deep claret	5.50	6.50
707	A124	20p slate blue	5.50	6.50
Nos. 700-707 (8)			44.00	52.00

World Trade Union Conf., Paris, Sept. 25 to Oct. 10, 1945.
Exist imperf. Value, set $500.

"Reconstruction" A132

1945-46

708	A132	12p brown olive	.30	.25
709	A132	20p brt green	.30	.25
710	A132	24p orange brn	.30	.25
711	A132	30p gray black	.30	.25
712	A132	40p olive green	.30	.25
713	A132	60p red orange	.30	.25
714	A132	100p orange yel	.30	.25
715	A132	120p brt ultra	.30	.25
716	A132	140p brt red	.30	.25
717	A132	200p olive brn	.30	.25
718	A132	240p brt blue	.30	.25
719	A132	300p dk carmine	.30	.25
720	A132	500p dull green	.30	.25
721	A132	1000p red violet	.30	.25
722	A132	3000p brt red ('46)	.30	.25
Nos. 708-722 (15)			4.50	3.75

Nos. 708-721 exist tête bêche. Value: $16.
Exist imperf. Value, set $175.

"Liberation" — A133

1946, Feb. 12

| 723 | A133 | 3ez p dark red | .30 | .25 |
| 724 | A133 | 15ez p ultra | .30 | .25 |

Exist imperf. Value, set $50.

Postrider — A134

Photo.; Values Typo.
1946 — **Perf. 15**

725	A134	4ez p brown org	.30	.25
726	A134	10ez p brt red	.30	.25
727	A134	15ez p ultra	.30	.25
728	A134	20ez p dk brown	.30	.25
729	A134	30ez p red violet	.30	.25
730	A134	50ez p gray black	.30	.25
731	A134	80ez p brt ultra	.30	.25
732	A134	100ez p rose car	.30	.25
733	A134	160ez p gray green	.30	.25
734	A134	200ez p yellow grn	.30	.25
735	A134	500ez p red	.30	.25
736	A134	640ez p olive bis	.30	.25
737	A134	800ez p rose violet	.30	.25
Nos. 725-737 (13)			3.90	3.25

Exist imperf. Value, set $60.

Abbreviations:
Ez (Ezer) = Thousand
Mil (Milpengo) = Million
Mlrd (Milliard) = Billion
Bil (Billio-pengo) = Trillion

Arms of Hungary — A135

1946 — Wmk. 210

738	A135	1mil p vermilion	.30	.25
a.	"1" in center omitted		600.00	
739	A135	2mil p ultra	.30	.25
740	A135	3mil p brown	.30	.25
741	A135	4mil p slate gray	.30	.25
742	A135	5mil p rose violet	.30	.25
743	A135	10mil p green	.30	.25
744	A135	20mil p carmine	.30	.25
745	A135	50mil p olive	.30	.25

Arms and Post Horn
A136   A137

746	A136	100mil p henna brn	.30	.25
747	A136	200mil p henna brn	.30	.25
748	A136	500mil p henna brn	.30	.25
749	A136	1000mil p henna brn	.30	.25
750	A136	2000mil p henna brn	.30	.25
751	A136	3000mil p henna brn	.30	.25
752	A136	5000mil p henna brn	.30	.25
753	A136	10,000mil p henna brn	.30	.25
754	A136	20,000mil p henna brn	.30	.25
755	A136	30,000mil p henna brn	.30	.25
756	A136	50,000mil p henna brn	.30	.25

Denomination in Carmine

757	A137	100mlrd p olive	.30	.25
758	A137	200mlrd p olive	.30	.25
759	A137	500mlrd p olive	.30	.25

Dove and Letter — A138

Denomination in Carmine

760	A138	1bil p grnsh blk	.30	.25
761	A138	2bil p grnsh blk	.30	.25
763	A138	5bil p grnsh blk	.30	.25
764	A138	10bil p grnsh blk	.30	.25
765	A138	20bil p grnsh blk	.30	.25
766	A138	50bil p grnsh blk	.30	.25
767	A138	100bil p grnsh blk	.30	.25
768	A138	200bil p grnsh blk	.30	.25
769	A138	500bil p grnsh blk	.30	.25
770	A138	1000bil p grnsh blk	.30	.25
771	A138	10,000bil p grnsh blk	.30	.25
772	A138	50,000bil p grnsh blk	.30	.25
773	A138	100,000bil p grnsh blk	.30	.25
774	A138	500,000bil p grnsh blk	.30	.25

Denomination in Black

775	A137	5ez ap green	.30	.25
776	A137	10ez ap green	.30	.25
777	A137	20ez ap green	.30	.25
778	A137	50ez ap green	.30	.25
779	A137	80ez ap green	.30	.25
780	A137	100ez ap green	.30	.25
781	A137	200ez ap green	.30	.25
782	A137	500ez ap green	.30	.25
783	A137	1mil ap vermilion	.30	.25
784	A137	5mil ap vermilion	.30	.25
Nos. 738-784 (46)			13.80	11.50

Denominations are expressed in "ado" or "tax" pengos.
Nos. 738-784 exist imperf. Value, set $400.

Early Steam Locomotive — A139

Designs: 20,000ap, Recent steam locomotive. 30,000ap, Electric locomotive. 40,000ap, Diesel locomotive.

1946, July 15 — **Wmk. 266** — **Perf. 12**

785	A139	10,000ap vio brn	3.75	3.75
786	A139	20,000ap dk blue	3.75	3.75
787	A139	30,000ap dp yel grn	3.75	3.75
788	A139	40,000ap rose car	3.75	3.75
b.	"40,000 ap" omitted		2,000.	
Nos. 785-788 (4)			15.00	15.00

Centenary of Hungarian railways.
Exist imperf. Value, set $700.

Industry A143

Agriculture A144

1946 — **Wmk. 210** — **Photo.** — **Perf. 15**

788A	A143	8f henna brn	.30	.25
789	A143	10f henna brn	.30	.25
790	A143	12f henna brn	.30	.25
791	A143	20f henna brn	.30	.25
792	A143	30f henna brn	.30	.25
793	A143	40f henna brn	.30	.25
794	A143	60f henna brn	.30	.25
795	A144	1fo dp yel grn	.40	.25
796	A144	1.40fo dp yel grn	.40	.25
797	A144	2fo dp yel grn	1.15	.25
798	A144	3fo dp yel grn	3.75	.25
799	A144	5fo dp yel grn	1.15	.25
800	A144	10fo dp yel grn	2.25	.25
Nos. 788A-800 (13)			11.20	3.25

For surcharges see Nos. Q9-Q11.
Exist imperf. Value, set $175.

Stamps and Types of 1943-45 Ovptd. in Carmine or Black to Show Class of Postage for which Valid

a   b

"Any." or "Nyomtatv." = Printed Matter.
"Hl" or "Helyi levél" = Local Letter.
"Hlp." or "Helyi lev.-lap" = Local Postcard.
"Tl." or "Távolsági levél" = Domestic Letter.
"Tlp." or "Távolsági lev.-lap" = Domestic Postcard.

1946 — **Wmk. 266**

801	A99(a)	"Any 1." on 1f (#601;C)	.30	.25
802	A99(a)	"Any 2." on 1f (#601;C)	.30	.25
803	A99(b)	"Nyomtatv. 20gr" on 60f on 8f (#682;Bk + C)	.30	.25
804	A118(a)	"Hl. 1" on 50f (#628;C)	.30	.25
805	A99(a)	"Hl. 2" on 40f on 10f (#664;C + Bk)	.30	.25
806	A99(b)	"Helyi levél" on 10f brn, bl (Bk)	.30	.25
807	A118(a)	"Hlp.1" on 8p on 20f (#670;C + Bk)	.30	.25
808	A118(a)	"Hlp.2." on 8p on 20f (#670;C + Bk)	.30	.25
809	A118(b)	"Helyi lev.-lap" on 20f ol, bl (C)	.30	.25
810	A99(a)	"Tl.1" on 10f (#608;Bk)	.30	.25
811	A99(a)	"Tl.2." on 10f on 4f (#657;Bk + C)	.30	.25
812	A99(b)	"Tavolsagi level" on 18f (#610;C)	.30	.25
813	A99(a)	"Tlp.1." on 4f (#604;Bk)	.30	.25
814	A99(a)	"Tlp.2." on 4f (#604;Bk)	.30	.25
815	A99(b)	"Tavolsagi lev.-lap" on 4f (#604;Bk)	.30	.25
Nos. 801-815 (15)			4.50	3.75

Nos. 806, 809 not issued without overprint.

György Dózsa — A145

Designs: 10f, Antal Budai-Nagy. 12f, Tamas Esze. 20f, Ignac Martinovics. 30f, Janos Batsanyi. 40f, Lajos Kossuth. 60f, Mihaly Tancsics. 1fo, Sandor Petőfi. 2fo, Andreas Ady. 4fo, Jozsef Attila.

1947, Mar. 15 — **Photo.** — **Wmk. 210**

816	A145	8f rose brown	.30	.25
817	A145	10f deep ultra	.30	.25
818	A145	12f deep brown	.30	.25
819	A145	20f dk yel grn	.30	.25
820	A145	30f dk ol bis	.55	.25
821	A145	40f brown car	.55	.25
822	A145	60f cerise	.75	.25
823	A145	1fo dp grnsh bl	.75	.25
824	A145	2fo dk violet	1.50	.25
825	A145	4fo grnsh black	2.40	.25
Nos. 816-825 (10)			7.70	2.50

Exist imperf. Value, set $250.

Peace and Agriculture — A155

1947, Sept. 22 — **Perf. 12**

| 826 | A155 | 60f bright red | .45 | .25 |
| a. | "60f." omitted | | 1,500. | |

Peace treaty.
Exists imperf. Value, set $300.

Postal Savings Emblem — A156

60f, Postal Savings Bank, Budapest.

1947, Oct. 31

| 827 | A156 | 40f rose brown | .50 | .25 |
| 828 | A156 | 60f brt rose car | .50 | .25 |

Savings Day, Oct. 31, 1947.
Exist imperf. Value, set $125.

Hungarian Flag — A157

1848 Printing Press — A158

HUGARY

Barred Window and Dove — A159

1848 Shako, Sword and Trumpet — A160

"On your feet Hungarian, the Homeland is Calling!" A161

Arms of Hungary A162

Perf. 12½x12, 12x12½

1948		Wmk. 283	Photo.
829	A157	8f dk rose red	.30 .25
830	A158	10f ultra	.30 .25
831	A159	12f copper brn	.30 .25
832	A160	20f deep green	.30 .25
833	A161	30f olive brown	.30 .25
834	A157	40f dk vio brn	.30 .25
835	A161	60f carmine lake	.75 .25
a.		Printed on both sides	1,100.
836	A162	1fo brt ultra	.75 .25
837	A162	2fo red brown	1.65 .25
838	A162	3fo green	2.25 .25
839	A162	4fo scarlet	3.75 .25
		Nos. 829-839 (11)	10.95 2.75

Cent. of the beginning of Hungary's war for independence.
No. 834 is inscribed "Kossuth," No. 835 "Petöfi."
Exist imperf. Value, set $300.

Baron Lorand Eötvös — A163

1948, July 27

840	A163	60f deep red	1.15 .35

Roland Eötvös, physicist, birth cent.
Exists imperf. Value $130.

Hungarian Workers — A164

1948, Oct. 17   Wmk. 283   Perf. 12

841	A164	30f dk carmine rose	.75 .50
a.		Sheet of 4	32.50 32.50

The 17th Trade Union Congress, Budapest, October 1948. No. 841a was sold for 2 forint.
Exist imperf. Value: single $25; sheet of 4 $2,000.

Marx Stamp of 1919 and Crowd Carrying Flags — A165

Petöfi Stamp of 1919 and Flags — A166

1949, Mar. 19   Flags in Carmine

842	A165	40f brown	.50 .40
843	A166	60f olive gray	.50 .40

1st Hungarian Soviet Republic, 30th anniv.
Exist imperf. Value, set $50.

Workers of the Five Continents and Flag — A167

1949, June 29   Perf. 12x12½   Flag in Red

844	A167	30f yellow brown	2.75 2.25
845	A167	40f brown violet	2.75 2.25
846	A167	60f lilac rose	2.75 2.25
847	A167	1fo violet blue	2.75 2.25
		Nos. 844-847 (4)	11.00 9.00

2nd Congress of the World Federation of Trade Unions, Milan, 1949.
Exist imperf. Value, set $125.

Sándor Petöfi — A168

Perf. 12½x12
1949, July 31   Engr.   Unwmk.

848	A168	40f claret	.50 .25
849	A168	60f dark red	.40 .25
850	A168	1fo deep blue	.50 .25
		Nos. 848-850 (3)	1.40 .75

Cent. of the death of Sándor Petöfi, poet.
Exist imperf. Value, set $30.
See Nos. 867-869.

Youth of Three Races — A169

Perf. 12½x12
1949, Aug. 14   Photo.   Wmk. 283

851	A169	20f dk violet brn	.90 .90
a.		20f blue green	3.75 3.75
852	A169	30f blue green	1.15 1.15
a.		30f violet brown	3.75 3.75
853	A169	40f olive bister	1.50 1.50
a.		40f ultramarine	3.75 3.75
854	A169	60f rose pink	1.15 1.15
855	A169	1fo ultra	1.95 1.95
a.		1fo olive bister	3.75 3.75
b.		Souv. sheet of 5, #851a-853a, 854, 855a	27.50 27.50
		Nos. 851-855 (5)	6.65 6.65

World Festival of Youth and Students, Budapest, Aug. 14-28, 1949.
Exist imperf. Value, set $100. No. 855b imperf, $2,000.

Arms of Hungarian People's Republic — A170

Arms in Bister, Carmine, Blue and Green

1949   Wmk. 283

856	A170	20f green	1.25 .50
a.		Unwatermarked	1.75 .80
857	A170	60f carmine	1.25 .30
a.		Unwatermarked	1.10 .30
858	A170	1fo blue	2.50 1.10
a.		Unwatermarked	1.25 .30
		Nos. 856-858 (3)	5.00 1.90

Adoption of the Hungarian People's Republic constitution.
Nos. 856-858 exist imperf. Value, set $175.
Nos. 856a-858a also exist imperf. Value, set $200.
Nos. 856-858 exist with papermaker's watermark. These sell for the same.

Symbols of the UPU — A171

1949, Nov. 1   Perf. 12x12½

859	A171	60f rose red	.50 .50
a.		Booklet pane of 6	10.00
860	A171	1fo blue	.50 .50
a.		Booklet pane of 6	14.00
		Nos. 859-860,C63 (3)	2.00 2.00

75th anniv. of the UPU.
Nos. 859 and 860 exist imperf. and stamps from 859a and 860a in horiz. pairs, imperf. between. Values: set $15; pairs, imperf between $10.
See No. C63, C81.

Chain Bridge — A172

1949, Nov. 20   Wmk. 283

861	A172	40f blue green	.50 .30
862	A172	60f red brown	.50 .35
863	A172	1fo blue	.50 .35
		Nos. 861-863,C64-C65 (5)	4.00 2.60

Cent. of the opening of the Chain Bridge at Budapest to traffic.
Exist imperf. Value, set $12.
For souvenir sheet see No. C66.

Joseph V. Stalin — A173

Perf. 12½x12
1949, Dec. 21   Engr.   Unwmk.

864	A173	60f dark red	.75 .25
865	A173	1fo deep blue	1.15 .40
866	A173	2fo brown	1.50 .90
		Nos. 864-866 (3)	3.40 1.55

70th anniv. of the birth of Joseph V. Stalin.
Exist imperf. Value, set $15.
See Nos. 1034-1035.

Petöfi Type of 1949
1950, Feb. 5   Perf. 12½x12

867	A168	40f brown	.60 .35
868	A168	60f dark carmine	.40 .25
869	A168	1fo dark green	.40 .25
		Nos. 867-869 (3)	1.40 .85

Exist imperf. Value, set $30.

Philatelic Museum, Budapest A174

Perf. 12x12½
1950, Mar. 12   Photo.   Wmk. 283

870	A174	60f gray & brown	7.50 6.00

20th anniv. of the establishment of the Hungarian PO Phil. Museum.
Exists imperf. Value $90.
See No. C68.

Coal Mining — A175

Designs: 10f, Heavy industry. 12f, Power production. 20f, Textile industry. 30f, "Cultured workers." 40f, Mechanized agriculture. 60f, Village cooperative. 1fo, Train. 1.70fo, "Holiday." 2fo, Defense. 3fo, Shipping. 4fo, Livestock. 5fo, Engineering. 10fo, Sports.

1950   Wmk. 283

871	A175	8f gray	.75 .25
872	A175	10f claret	.75 .25
873	A175	12f orange ver	1.15 .25
874	A175	20f blue green	.75 .25
875	A175	30f rose violet	1.15 .25
876	A175	40f sepia	1.15 .25
877	A175	60f red	1.50 .25
878	A175	1fo gray brn, yel & lil	3.75 .25
879	A175	1.70fo dk grn & yel	9.00 .25
880	A175	2fo vio brn & cr	5.50 .25
881	A175	3fo slate & cream	9.00 .25
882	A175	4fo blk brn & sal	40.00 .25
883	A175	5fo rose vio & yel	18.75 .30
884	A175	10fo dk brn & yel	55.00 6.00
		Nos. 871-884 (14)	148.20 10.30
		Hinged set	80.00

Issued to publicize Hungary's Five Year Plan.
Exist imperf. Value, set $450.
See Nos. 945-958.

Citizens Welcoming Liberators A176

1950, Apr. 4   Unwmk.   Perf. 12

885	A176	40f gray black	1.15 .35
886	A176	60f rose brown	.75 .25
887	A176	1fo deep blue	.75 .25
888	A176	2fo brown	1.15 .35
		Nos. 885-888 (4)	3.80 1.20

Fifth anniversary of Hungary's liberation.
Exist imperf. Value, set $50.

Chess Players — A177

Design: 1fo, Iron Workers Union building and chess emblem.

1950, Apr. 9   Wmk. 106

889	A177	60f deep magenta	1.90 .40
890	A177	1fo deep blue	3.75 .75
		Nos. 889-890,C69 (3)	11.15 3.05

World Chess Championship Matches, Budapest.
Exist imperf. Value, set (3) $200.

Workers Symbolizing International Proletariat A178

Design: 60f, Blast furnace, tractor, workers holding Maypole.

1950, May 1

891	A178	40f orange brown	1.95 .35
892	A178	60f rose carmine	.90 .25
893	A178	1fo deep blue	1.65 .50
		Nos. 891-893 (3)	4.50 1.10

Issued to publicize Labor Day, May 1, 1950.
Exist imperf. Value, set $75.

Liberty, Cogwheel, Dove and Globes — A179

Design: 60f, Three workers and flag.

Inscribed: "1950. V. 10.-24."

1950, May 10   Photo.   Perf. 12x12½

894	A179	40f olive green	1.50 .35
895	A179	1fo 60f dark carmine	.75 .25
		Nos. 894-895,C70 (3)	3.75 1.15

Meeting of the World Federation of Trade Unions, Budapest, May 1950.
Exist imperf. Value, set $70.

Doctor Inspecting Baby's Bath — A180

Children's Day: 30f, Physical Culture. 40f, Education. 60f, Boys' Camp. 1.70fo, Model plane building.

1950, June 4   Wmk. 106

896	A180	20f gray & brn	1.50 1.25
897	A180	30f brn & rose lake	.60 .25

HUNGARY

898	A180	40f indigo & dk grn		.60	.25
899	A180	60f SZABAD		.60	.25
a.		UTANPOTLASUNK		750.00	450.00
900	A180	1.70fo dp grn & gray		1.25	.75
		Nos. 896-900 (5)		4.55	2.75

Exist imperf. Value, set $60.

Youths Marching on Globe A181

Working Man and Woman A182

30f, Foundry worker. 60f, Workers on Mt. Gellert. 1.70fo, Worker, peasant & student; flags.
Inscribed: Budapest 1950. VI. 17-18.

Perf. 12x12½, 12½x12

1950, June 17

901	A181	20f dark green	.90	.40
902	A181	30f deep red org	.30	.25
903	A182	40f dark brown	.30	.25
904	A182	60f dark claret	.90	.25
905	A182	1.70fo dark olive grn	1.65	.45
		Nos. 901-905 (5)	3.75	1.60

Issued to publicize the First Congress of the Working Youth, Budapest, June 17-18, 1950.
Exist imperf. Value, set $60.

Peonies — A183

Designs: 40f, Anemones. 60f, Pheasant's-eye. 1fo, Geraniums. 1.70fo, Bluebells.

Engraved and Lithographed
Perf. 12½x12

1950, Aug. 20 Unwmk.

906	A183	30f rose brn, rose pink & grn	1.15	.30
907	A183	40f dk green, lil & yel	1.15	.30
908	A183	60f red brn, yel & grn	1.90	.30
909	A183	1fo pur, red & grn	3.75	1.25
910	A183	1.70fo dk violet & grn	3.75	1.00
		Nos. 906-910 (5)	11.70	3.15

Exist imperf. Value, set $60.

Miner — A184

Designs: 60f, High speed lathe. 1fo, Prefabricated building construction.

Perf. 12x12½

1950, Oct. 7 Photo. Wmk. 106

911	A184	40f brown	1.00	.35
912	A184	60f carmine rose	1.25	.25
913	A184	1fo brt blue	2.25	.25
		Nos. 911-913 (3)	4.50	.85

2nd National Exhibition of Inventions.
Exist imperf. Value, set $35.

Gen. Josef Bem and Battle at Piski — A185

Perf. 12½x12

1950, Dec. 10 Engr. Unwmk.

914	A185	40f dark brown	.90	.40
915	A185	60f deep carmine	.90	.40
916	A185	1fo deep blue	1.85	.60
		Nos. 914-916 (3)	3.65	1.30

Gen. Josef Bem, death centenary.
Exist imperf. Value, set $25.

See No. C80.

Signing Petition A186

Peace Demonstrator Holding Dove A187

1fo, Mother and Children with soldier.

Wmk. 106

1950, Nov. 23 Photo. *Perf. 12*

917	A186	40f ultra & red brn	9.75	7.50
918	A187	60f red org & dk grn	2.25	1.50
919	A186	1fo ol grn & dk brn	9.75	7.50
		Nos. 917-919 (3)	21.75	16.50

Exist imperf. Value, set $65.

Women Swimmers — A188

Designs: 20f, Vaulting. 1fo, Mountain climbing. 1.70fo, Basketball. 2fo, Motorcycling.

1950, Dec. 2 *Perf. 12½*

920	A188	10f blue & gray	.30	.25
921	A188	20f sal & dk brn	.30	.25
922	A188	1fo olive & grn	.75	.25
923	A188	1.70fo ver & brn car	.90	.25
924	A188	2fo salmon & pur	2.25	.30
		Nos. 920-924,C82-C86 (10)	11.30	5.00

Exist imperf. Value, set (10) $100.

Canceled to Order
The government stamp agency started about 1950 to sell canceled sets of new issues. Values in the second ("used") column are for these canceled-to-order stamps. Postally used stamps are worth more.
The practice was to end Apr. 1, 1991.

A189

Worker, Peasant, Soldier and Party Flag — A190

60f, Matthias Rakosi & allegory. 1fo, House of Parliament, columns of workers & banner.
Inscribed: "Budapest * 1951 * Februar 24."

1951, Feb. 24 *Perf. 12½x12, 12x12½*

925	A189	10f yellow green	.40	.25
926	A190	30f brown	.45	.25
927	A190	60f carmine rose	.75	.25
928	A189	1fo blue	1.25	.75
		Nos. 925-928 (4)	2.85	1.50

2nd Congress of the Hungarian Workers' Party.
Exist imperf. Value, set $40.

Mare and Foal — A191

Designs: 30f, Sow and shoats. 40f, Ram and ewe. 60f, Cow and calf.

1951, Apr. 5 *Perf. 12x12½*

929	A191	10f ol bis & rose brn	.30	.25
930	A191	30f rose brn & ol bis	.40	.25
931	A191	40f dk green & brn	.45	.25
932	A191	60f brown org & brn	.60	.25
		Nos. 929-932,C87-C90 (8)	10.80	4.35

Issued to encourage increased livestock production.
Exist imperf. Value, set (8) $75.

Flags of Russia and Hungary A192

Russian Technician Teaching Hungarians A193

1951, Apr. 4 *Perf. 12½x12, 12x12½*

| 933 | A192 | 60f brnsh carmine | .40 | .25 |
| 934 | A193 | 1fo dull violet | .75 | .40 |

Issued to publicize the "Month of Friendship" between Hungary and Russia, 1951.
Exist imperf. Value, set $30.

Worker Holding Olive Branch and Mallet A194

Workers Carrying Flags A195

1fo, Workers approaching Place of Heroes.

Perf. 12½x12, 12x12½

1951, May 1 Photo. Wmk. 106

935	A194	40f brown	.75	.75
936	A195	60f scarlet	.75	.75
937	A194	1fo blue	.75	.45
		Nos. 935-937 (3)	2.25	1.95

Issued to publicize Labor Day, May 1, 1951.
Exist imperf. Value, set $30.

Leo Frankel A196

Paris Street Fighting, 1871 A197

1951, May 20

| 938 | A196 | 60f dark brown | .75 | .25 |
| 939 | A197 | 1fo blue & red | 1.15 | .40 |

80th anniv. of the Commune of Paris.
Exist imperf. Value, set $28.

Children of Various Races — A198

Designs: 40f, Boy and girl at play. 50f, Street car and Girl Pioneer. 60f, Chemistry students. 1.70fo, Pioneer bugler.
Inscribed: "Nemzetkozi Gyermeknap 1951"

1951, June 3 *Perf. 12½x12*

940	A198	30f dark brown	.40	.25
941	A198	40f green	.55	.25
942	A198	50f brown red	.55	.25
943	A198	60f plum	.75	.35
944	A198	1.70fo blue	1.15	1.00
		Nos. 940-944 (5)	3.40	2.10

International Day of Children, 6/3/51.
Exist imperf. Value, set $40.

5-Year-Plan Type of 1950
Designs as before.

1951-52 Wmk. 106 *Perf. 12½x12*

945	A175	8f gray	.75	.25
946	A175	10f claret	.30	.25
947	A175	12f orange ver	.30	.25
948	A175	20f blue green	.30	.25
949	A175	30f rose violet	.40	.25
950	A175	40f sepia	.90	.25
951	A175	60f red	.90	.25
952	A175	1fo gray brn, yel & lil	1.15	.25
953	A175	1.70fo dk grn & yel	1.90	.25
954	A175	2fo vio brn & cr	2.25	.25
955	A175	3fo slate & cream	2.40	.25
956	A175	4fo blk brn & sal	2.65	.30
957	A175	5fo rose vio & yel ('52)	4.50	.60
958	A175	10fo dk brn & yel ('52)	5.75	1.90
		Nos. 945-958 (14)	24.45	5.55

Maxim Gorky — A199

Perf. 12½x12

1951, June 17 Engr. Unwmk.

959	A199	60f copper red	.40	.25
960	A199	1fo deep blue	.25	.25
961	A199	2fo rose violet	1.10	.60
		Nos. 959-961 (3)	1.75	1.10

15th anniversary of the death of Gorky.
Exist imperf. Value, set $25.

Budapest Buildings

Railroad Workshop A200

Building in Lehel Street A201

Suburban Bus Terminal A202

Rakosi House of Culture A203

George Kilian Street School A204

Central Construction Headquarters A205

Design Size: 22x18mm

1951 Wmk. 106 Photo. *Perf. 15*

962	A200	20f green	.55	.25
963	A201	30f red orange	.55	.25
964	A202	40f brown	.55	.25
965	A203	60f red	.75	.25
966	A204	1fo blue	1.00	.25
967	A205	3fo deep plum	3.00	.25
		Nos. 962-967 (6)	6.40	1.50

Exist imperf. Value, set $100.
See Nos. 1004-1011, 1048-1056C.

1958 **Design Size: 21x17mm**

962a	A200	20f green	.55	.25
963a	A201	30f red orange	.55	.25
964a	A202	40f brown	.55	.25
965a	A203	60f red	.75	.25
966a	A204	1fo blue	1.00	.25
967a	A205	3fo deep plum	3.00	.25
		Nos. 962a-967a (6)	6.40	1.50

Tractor Manufacture A206

30f, Fluoroscope examination. 40f, Checking lathework. 60f, Woman tractor operator.

1951, Aug. 20 *Perf. 12½x12*

968	A206	20f black brown	.25	.25
969	A206	30f deep blue	.25	.25
970	A206	40f crimson rose	.55	.25
971	A206	60f red brown	.60	.25
		Nos. 968-971,C91-C93 (7)	4.55	2.35

The successful conclusion of the first year under Hungary's 5-year plan.
Exist imperf. Value, set $50.

HUNGARY

Soldiers of the People's Army — A207

1951, Sept. 29
972 A207 1fo brown   1.25 .25
Issued to publicize Army Day, Sept. 29, 1951. See No. C94.
Exist imperf. Value (with C94) $30.

Stamp of 1871, Portrait Replaced by Postmark — A208

Perf. 12½x12
1951, Sept. 12 Engr. Unwmk.
973 A208 60f olive green   2.25 1.50
Nos. 973,B207-B208 (3)   26.25 21.00
80th anniv. of Hungary's 1st postage stamp. See Nos. C95, CB13-CB14.
Exist imperf. Value, set (3) $60.

Cornflower — A209

40f, Lily of the Valley. 60f, Tulip. 1fo, Poppy. 1.70fo, Cowslip.

1951, Nov. 4   Engr. & Litho.
974 A209 30f shown   .40 .25
975 A209 40f multi   1.35 .75
976 A209 60f multi   .90 .25
977 A209 1fo multi   1.50 .25
978 A209 1.70fo multi   3.00 .30
Nos. 974-978 (5)   7.15 1.80
Exist imperf. Value, set $40.

Storming of the Winter Palace — A210

Designs: 60f, Lenin speaking to soldiers. 1fo, Lenin and Stalin.

Perf. 12x12½
1951, Nov. 7   Photo.   Wmk. 106
979 A210 40f gray green   .90 .25
980 A210 60f deep blue   .75 .30
981 A210 1fo rose lake   .90 .50
Nos. 979-981 (3)   2.55 1.05
34th anniversary of the Russian Revolution.
Exist imperf. Value, set $40.

Marchers Passing Stalin Monument A211

1951, Dec. 16   Wmk. 106
982 A211 60f henna brown   1.35 .60
983 A211 1fo deep blue   1.35 .60
Joseph V. Stalin, 72nd birthday.
Exist imperf. Value, set $30.

Grand Theater, Moscow — A212

Views of Moscow: 1fo, Lenin Mausoleum. 1.60fo, Kremlin.

1952, Feb. 20   Perf. 12
984 A212 60f ol grn & rose brn   .65 .25
985 A212 1fo lil rose & ol brn   1.00 .35
986 A212 1.60fo red brn & ol   2.00 .55
Nos. 984-986 (3)   3.65 1.15
Hungarian-Soviet Friendship Month.
Exist imperf. Value, set $30.

Rakosi and Farmers A213

Matyas Rakosi A214

Design: 2fo, Rakosi and Workers.

Perf. 12x12½, 12x12
1952, Mar. 9   Engr.   Unwmk.
987 A213 60f deep plum   .80 .25
988 A213 1fo dk red brown   .90 .25
989 A213 2fo dp violet blue   1.90 .55
Nos. 987-989 (3)   3.60 1.05
60th anniv. of the birth of Matyas Rakosi, communist leader.
Exist imperf. Value, set $30.

Lajos Kossuth and Speech at Debrecen — A215

Designs: 30f, Sándor Petőfi. 50f, Gen. Josef Bem. 60f, Mihaly Tancsics. 1fo, Gen. János Damjanich. 1.50fo, Gen. Jozsef Nagysandor.

1952, Mar. 15   Perf. 12x12½
990 A215 20f green   .30 .25
991 A215 30f rose violet   .30 .25
992 A215 50f grnsh blk   .30 .25
993 A215 60f brown car   .35 .25
994 A215 1fo blue   1.00 .25
995 A215 1.50fo redsh brown   1.10 .45
Nos. 990-995 (6)   3.35 1.70
Heroes of the 1848 revolution.
Exist imperf. Value, set $32.50.
Nos. 990-995 also exist perf. 12. Value, set $300.

No. B204 Surcharged in Black with Bars Obliterating Inscription and Surtax
Perf. 12½x12
1952, Apr. 27   Photo.   Wmk. 283
996 SP121 60f magenta   35.00 35.00
Budapest Philatelic Exhibition. Counterfeits exist.

Girl Drummer Leading Parade — A216

Designs: 60f, Workers and soldier. 1fo, Worker, flag-encircled globe and dove.

Perf. 12x12½
1952, May 1   Photo.   Wmk. 106
997 A216 40f dk grn & dull red   1.50 .50
998 A216 60f dk red brn & dull red   1.00 .25
999 A216 1fo sepia & dull red   1.50 .30
Nos. 997-999 (3)   4.00 1.05
Issued to publicize Labor Day, May 1, 1952.
Exist imperf. Value, set $50.

Runner A217

Designs: 40f, Swimmer. 60f, Fencer. 1fo, Woman gymnast.

1952, May 26   Perf. 11
1000 A217 30f dark red brown   .55 .25
1001 A217 40f deep green   .55 .25
1002 A217 60f deep lilac rose   .90 .25
1003 A217 1fo deep blue   1.50 .50
Nos. 1000-1003,C107-C108 (6)   7.55 3.35
Issued to publicize Hungary's participation in the Olympic Games, Helsinki, 1952.
Exist imperf. Value, set (6) $60.

Building Types of 1951

Buildings: 8f, School, Stalinvarost. 10f, Szekesfehervar Station. 12f, Building, Ujpest. 50f, Metal works, Inotai. 70f, Grain elevator, Hajdunanas. 80f, Tiszalok dam. 4fo, Miners' union headquarters. 5fo, Workers' apartments, Ujpest.

Design Size: 22x18mm
1952   Wmk. 106   Perf. 15
1004 A202 8f green   .45 .25
1005 A200 10f purple   .45 .25
1006 A202 12f carmine   .45 .25
1007 A202 50f gray blue   .65 .25
1008 A202 70f yellow brn   1.15 .25
1009 A200 80f maroon   1.15 .25
1010 A202 4fo olive grn   2.40 .25
1011 A202 5fo gray black   3.75 .25
Nos. 1004-1011 (8)   10.45 2.00
Exist imperf. Value, set $140.

Design Size: 21x17mm
1958
1004a A202 8f green   .80 .25
1005a A200 10f purple   .80 .25
1006a A202 12f carmine   .80 .25
1007a A202 50f gray blue   1.15 .25
1008a A202 70f yellow brn   2.00 .25
1009a A200 80f maroon   2.00 .25
1010a A202 4fo olive grn   4.25 .25
1011a A202 5fo gray black   6.50 .25
Nos. 1004a-1011a (8)   18.30 2.00

Approaching Train — A218

Railroad Day: 1fo, Railroad Construction.

1952, Aug. 10   Perf. 12x12½
1012 A218 60f red brown   .90 .35
1013 A218 1fo deep olive grn   1.25 .40
Exist imperf. Value, set $30.

Coal Excavator — A219

Miners' Day: 1fo, Coal breaker.

1952, Sept. 7
1014 A219 60f brown   .90 .25
1015 A219 1fo dark green   1.25 .30
Exist imperf. Value, set $25.

Lajos Kossuth — A220

Design: 60f, Kossuth statue.

1952, Sept. 19   Perf. 12½x12
1016 A220 40f ol brn, *pink*   .90 .25
1017 A220 60f black brn, *bl*   .40 .25
1018 A220 1fo purple, *citron*   .90 .55
Nos. 1016-1018 (3)   2.20 1.05
150th anniv. of the birth of Lajos Kossuth.
Exist imperf. Value, set $40.

Janos Hunyadi — A221

Portraits: 30f, Gyorgy Dozsa. 40f, Miklos Zrinyi. 60f, Ilona Zriuyi. 1fo, Bottyan Vak. 1.50fo, Aurel Stromfeld.

1952, Sept. 28   Engr.   Unwmk.
1019 A221 20f purple   .30 .25
1020 A221 30f dark green   .30 .25
1021 A221 40f indigo   .30 .25
1022 A221 60f dk violet brn   .55 .25
1023 A221 1fo dk blue grn   .80 .25
1024 A221 1.50fo dark brown   1.90 1.00
Nos. 1019-1024 (6)   4.15 2.25
Army Day, Sept. 28, 1952.
Exist imperf. Value, set $50.

Lenin and Conference at Smolny Palace — A222

Designs: 60f, Stalin and Cavalry Attack. 1fo, Marx, Engels, Lenin and Stalin.

1952, Nov. 7   Wmk. 106
Portraits in Olive Gray
1025 A222 40f deep claret   1.75 .50
1026 A222 60f gray   1.25 .25
1027 A222 1fo rose red   2.00 .35
Nos. 1025-1027 (3)   5.00 1.10
Russian Revolution, 35th anniversary.
Exist imperf. Value, set $50.

Peasant Woman Holding Wheat — A223

Peace Meeting — A224

Perf. 12½x12, 12x12½
1952, Nov. 22
1028 A223 60f brn red, *citron*   .75 .25
1029 A224 1fo brown, *blue*   .75 .35
Third Hungarian Peace Congress, 1952.
Exist imperf. Value, set $25.

Subway Construction A225

Design: 1fo, Station and map.

1953, Jan. 19   Photo.   Perf. 12x12½
1030 A225 60f dk slate green   1.15 .40
1031 A225 1fo brown red   1.15 .55
Completion of the Budapest subway extension.
Exist imperf. Value, set $25.

Tank and Flag — A226

60f, Map of Central Europe and Soldier.

1953, Feb. 18
1032 A226 40f dark car rose   1.15 .25
1033 A226 60f chocolate   1.15 .45
Battle of Stalingrad, 10th anniversary.
Exist imperf. Value, set $30.

Stalin — A227

Two types of No. 1035. Type I: "MAGYAR POSTA" on solid background. Type II: "MAGYAR POSTA" on background of vertical lines.

HUNGARY

1953   Perf. 12x11½   Engr.   Wmk. 106
1034 A227 60f pur blk   .50   .35

Souvenir Sheet
1035 A227 2fo pur blk, Type II   20.00   20.00
   a. Type I   450.00   225.00

Death of Joseph Stalin (1879-1953).
Exist imperf. Values: 60f $20; No. 1035 $150; No. 1035a $450.
Issue dates: No. 1034, Mar. 27; No. 1035, Mar. 9.

Workers' Rest Home, Galyateto — A228

Designs: 40f, Home at Mecsek. 50f, Parad Mineral Baths. 60f, Home at Kekes. 70f, Balatonfured Mineral Baths.

1953, Apr.   Photo.   Perf. 12x12½
1036 A228 30f fawn   .30   .25
1037 A228 40f deep blue   .30   .25
1038 A228 50f dk olive bis   .30   .25
1039 A228 60f dp yellow grn   .30   .25
1040 A228 70f scarlet   .40   .25
   Nos. 1036-1040,C121-C122 (7)   2.60   1.75

Exist imperf. Value, set (7) $60.

Young Workers with Red Flags — A229

1953, May 1   Perf. 12½x12
1041 A229 60f brn & red, yel   .75   .25

Issued to publicize Labor Day, May 1, 1953.
Exist imperf. Value $25.

Karl Marx — A230

1953, May 1   Engr.   Perf. 11½x12
1042 A230 1fo black, pink   .75   .25
   a. Perf 12½x12   60.00   18.75

70th anniv. of the death of Karl Marx. See No. 1898.
Exist imperf. Value $30.

Insurgents in the Forest — A231

30f, Drummer & fighters. 40f, Battle scene. 60f, Cavalry attack. 1fo, Francis Rákóczy II.

1953, June 14   Photo.   Perf. 11
1043 A231 20f dk ol grn & org red, grnsh   .75   .25
1044 A231 30f vio brn & red org   .90   .25
1045 A231 40f gray bl & red org, pink   1.15   .25
1046 A231 60f dk ol brn & org, yel   1.90   .55
1047 A231 1fo dk red brn & org red, yel   2.60   .75
   Nos. 1043-1047 (5)   7.30   2.05

250th anniv. of the insurrection of 1703.
Exist imperf. Value $45.

Building Types of 1951

Buildings: 8f, Day Nursery, Ozd. 10f, Medical research institute, Szombathely. 12f, Apartments, Komlo. 20f, Department store, Ujpest. 30f, Brick factory, Maly. 40f, Metropolitan hospital. 50f, Sports building, Stalinvaros. 60f, Post office, Csepel. 70f, Blast furnace, Diosgyor. 1.20fo, Agricultural school, Ajkacsinger Valley. 1.70fo, Iron Works School, Csepel. 2fo, Optical works house of culture.

Design Size: 22x18mm
1953   Wmk. 106   Perf. 15
1048 A204 8f olive green   .30   .25
1049 A204 10f purple   .40   .25
1050 A205 12f rose car   .75   .25
1051 A204 20f dark green   .75   .25
1052 A204 30f orange   .75   .25
1053 A204 40f dark brown   1.15   .25
1054 A205 50f blue violet   1.15   .25
1055 A205 60f rose red   1.15   .25
1056 A204 70f yel brn   1.50   .25
1056A A205 1.20fo red   1.75   .25
1056B A204 1.70fo blue   1.30   .25
1056C A204 2fo green   1.30   .25
   Nos. 1048-1056C (12)   12.25   3.00

Exist imperf. Value, set $175.

Design Size: 21x17mm
1958
1048a A204 8f olive green   .30   .25
1049a A204 10f purple   .40   .25
1050a A205 12f rose car   .75   .25
1051a A204 20f dark green   .75   .25
1052a A204 30f orange   .75   .25
1053a A204 40f dark brown   1.15   .25
1054a A205 50f blue violet   1.15   .25
1055a A205 60f rose red   1.15   .25
1056a A204 70f yel brn   1.50   .25
1056Aa A205 1.20fo red   1.75   .25
1056Ba A204 1.70fo blue   1.30   .25
1056Ca A204 2fo green   1.30   .25
   Nos. 1048a-1056Ca (12)   12.25   3.00

Exist imperf. Value, set $150.

Bicycling A232

1953, Aug. 20   Perf. 11
1057 A232 20f shown   .30   .25
1058 A232 30f Swimming   .30   .25
1059 A232 40f Calisthenics   .30   .25
1060 A232 50f Discus   .30   .25
1061 A232 60f Wrestling   .30   .25
   Nos. 1057-1061,C123-C127 (10)   8.00   4.30

Opening of the People's Stadium, Budapest.
Exist imperf. Value, set (10) $75.

Kazar Costume — A233

Provincial Costumes: 30f, Ersekcsanad. 40f, Kalocsa. 60f, Sioagard. 1fo, Sarkoz. 1.70fo, Boldog. 2fo, Orhalom. 2.50fo, Hosszuheteny.

1953, Sept. 12   Engr.   Perf. 12
1062 A233 20f blue green   1.10   .35
1063 A233 30f chocolate   1.50   .35
1064 A233 40f ultra   1.90   .35
1065 A233 60f red   2.65   1.50
1066 A233 1fo grnsh blue   3.00   1.50
1067 A233 1.70fo brt green   3.75   2.25
1068 A233 2fo car rose   6.00   2.25
1069 A233 2.50fo purple   10.00   4.25
   Nos. 1062-1069 (8)   29.90   12.80

Exist imperf. Value, set $100.
See No. 1189.

Lenin — A234

Designs: 60f, Lenin and Stalin at meeting. 1fo, Lenin, facing left.

1954, Jan. 21   Wmk. 106   Perf. 12
1073 A234 40f dk blue grn   1.50   .75
1074 A234 60f black brown   2.00   .25
1075 A234 1fo dk car rose   3.00   .65
   Nos. 1073-1075 (3)   6.50   1.65

30th anniversary, death of Lenin.

Exist imperf. Value, set $65.

Worker Reading — A235   **Revolutionary and Red Flag — A236**

Design: 1fo, Soldier.

1954, Mar. 21   Photo.
1076 A235 40f gray blue & red   1.50   .25
1077 A236 60f brown & red   3.75   .50
1078 A235 1fo gray & red   5.25   .80
   Nos. 1076-1078 (3)   10.50   1.55

35th anniversary of the "First Hungarian Communist Republic."
Exist imperf. Value, set $60.

Blood Test — A237

Designs: 40f, Mother receiving newborn baby. 60f, Medical examination of baby.

1954, Mar. 8   Perf. 12
1079 A237 30f brt blue   .25   .25
1080 A237 40f brown bister   .45   .25
1081 A237 60f purple   .55   .25
   Nos. 1079-1081,C146-C148 (6)   5.40   2.35

Exist imperf. Value, set $55.

Maypole — A238

Design: 60f, Flag bearer.

1954, May 1   Perf. 12½x12
1082 A238 40f olive   .40   .25
1083 A238 60f orange red   .40   .25

Issued to publicize Labor Day, May 1, 1954.
Exist imperf. Value, set $25.

Farm Woman with Fruit — A239

1954, May 24   Perf. 12
1084 A239 60f red orange   .60   .25

3rd Congress of the Hungarian Workers Party, Budapest, May 24, 1954.
Exists imperf. Value, set $25.

Natl. Museum, Budapest — A240

Designs: 60f, Arms of People's Republic. 1fo, Dome of Parliament Building.

1954, Aug. 20   Perf. 12½x12
1085 A240 40f brt blue   1.20   .75
1086 A240 60f redsh brown   1.10   .45
1087 A240 1fo dark brown   1.20   .60
   Nos. 1085-1087 (3)   3.50   1.80

People's Republic Constitution, 5th anniv.
Exist imperf. Value, set $45.

Peppers — A241

Fruit: 50f, Tomatoes. 60f, Grapes. 80f, Apricots. 1fo, Apples. 1.20fo, Plums. 1.50fo, Cherries. 2fo, Peaches.

1954, Sept. 11   Engr., Litho.
Fruit in Natural Colors
1088 A241 40f gray blue   .35   .25
1089 A241 50f plum   .35   .25
1090 A241 60f gray blue   .35   .25
1091 A241 80f chocolate   .35   .25
1092 A241 1fo rose violet   .75   .25
1093 A241 1.20fo dull blue   1.15   .25
1094 A241 1.50fo plum   1.90   .75
1095 A241 2fo gray blue   3.75   .40
   Nos. 1088-1095 (8)   8.95   2.65

National agricultural fair.
Exist imperf. Value, set $50.

Maurus Jokai — A242

1954, Oct. 17   Engr.
1096 A242 60f dk brown olive   1.00   .25
1097 A242 1fo deep claret   2.00   .75

50th anniv. of the death of Maurus Jokai, writer.
Exist imperf. Value, set $25.
No. 1097 in violet blue is from the souvenir sheet, No. C157.

Janos Apaczai Csere — A243

Scientists: 10f, Csoma Sandor Korosi. 12f, Anyos Jedlik. 20f, Ignaz Semmelweis. 30f, Janos Irinyi. 40f, Frigyes Koranyi. 50f, Armin Vambery. 60f, Karoly Than. 1fo, Otto Herman. 1.70fo, Tivadar Puskas. 2fo, Endre Hogyes.

1954, Dec. 5   Photo.   Perf. 12x12½
1098 A243 8f dk vio brn, yel   .30   .25
1099 A243 10f brn, car, pink   .30   .25
1100 A243 12f gray, bl   .30   .25
1101 A243 20f brn, yel   .30   .25
1102 A243 30f vio bl, pink   .30   .25
1103 A243 40f dk grn, yel   .30   .25
1104 A243 50f red brn, pale grn   .30   .25
1105 A243 60f blue, pink   .30   .25
1106 A243 1fo olive   .75   .25
1107 A243 1.70fo rose brn, yel   1.15   .25
1108 A243 2fo blue green   2.25   .25
   Nos. 1098-1108 (11)   6.55   2.75

Exist imperf. Value, set $45.

Readers in Industrial Library A244   **Industry A245**

1fo, Agriculture. 2fo, Liberation monument.

1955, Apr. 4   Perf. 12½x12, 12x12½
1109 A244 40f dk car & ol brn   .55   .35
1110 A245 60f dk green & red   .55   .25
1111 A245 1fo choc & grn   .90   .25
1112 A244 2fo blue grn & brn   1.25   .35
   Nos. 1109-1112 (4)   3.25   1.20

10th anniversary of Hungary's liberation.
Exist imperf. Value, set $35.

HUNGARY

Date, Flags, Grain Elevator and Tractor — A246

1955, May 1 Perf. 12x12½
1113 A246 1fo rose carmine .60 .25
Labor Day, May 1, 1955.
Exist imperf. Value, set $20.

Government Printing Plant — A247

1955, May 28 Wmk. 106
1114 A247 60f gray grn & hn brn .60 .25
Centenary of the establishment of the government printing plant.
Exist imperf. Value, set $20.

Young Citizens and Hungarian Flag — A248

1955, June 15 Perf. 12
1115 A248 1fo red brown .60 .25
Issued to publicize the second national congress of the Hungarian Youth Organization.
Exist imperf. Value, set $20.

Truck Farmer — A249

10f, Fisherman. 12f, Bricklayer. 20f, Radio assembler. 30f, Woman potter. 40f, Railwayman & train. 50f, Clerk & scales. 60f, Postman emptying mail box. 70f, Cattle & herdsman. 80f, Textile worker. 1fo, Riveter. 1.20fo, Carpenter. 1.40fo, Streetcar conductor. 1.70fo, Herdsman & pigs. 2fo, Welder. 2.60fo, Woman tractor driver. 3fo, Herdsman in national costume & horse. 4fo, Bus driver. 5fo, Lineman. 10fo, Coal miner.

1955 Wmk. 106 Perf. 12x12½
1116 A249 8f chestnut .30 .25
1117 A249 10f Prus green .30 .25
1118 A249 12f red orange .30 .25
1119 A249 20f olive green .40 .25
1120 A249 30f dark red .35 .25
1121 A249 40f brown .40 .25
1122 A249 50f violet bl .40 .25
1123 A249 60f brown red .50 .25
1124 A249 70f olive .80 .25
1125 A249 80f purple .50 .25
1126 A249 1fo blue 1.00 .25
1127 A249 1.20fo olive bis 1.20 .25
1128 A249 1.40fo deep green 1.00 .25
1129 A249 1.70fo purple 1.00 .25
1130 A249 2fo rose brown 1.00 .25
1131 A249 2.60fo vermilion 1.50 .25
1132 A249 3fo green 2.25 .25
1133 A249 4fo peacock blue 2.00 .25
1134 A249 5fo orange brown 2.00 .25
1135 A249 10fo violet 1.75 .25
Nos. 1116-1135 (20) 18.95 5.00
Exist imperf. Value, set $175.
For surcharges see Nos. B211-B216.

Postrider Blowing Horn — A250

1955, June 25 Perf. 12½x12
1136 A250 1fo rose violet .50 .25
Hungarian Postal Museum, 25th anniv.
Exists tete-beche. Value: 2½ times the value of a single.
Exists imperf. Value $25.

Mihaly Csokonai Vitez — A251

1fo, Mihaly Vorosmarty. 2fo, Attila József.

1955, July 28 Perf. 12
1137 A251 60f olive black .75 .25
1138 A251 1fo dark blue .75 .35
1139 A251 2fo rose brown .75 .55
Nos. 1137-1139 (3) 2.25 1.15
Issued to honor three Hungarian poets.
Exist imperf. Value $35.

Bela Bartok — A252

1955, Oct. 9
1140 A252 60f light brown .75 .25
Nos. 1140,C168-C169 (3) 6.25 3.50
10th anniversary of the death of Bela Bartok, composer.
Exist imperf. Value, set (3) $40.

Diesel Train — A253

Designs: 60f, Bus. 80f, Motorcycle. 1fo, Truck. 1.20fo, Steam locomotive. 1.50fo, Dump truck. 2fo, Freighter.

1955, Dec. 20 Perf. 14½
1141 A253 40f grn & vio brn .35 .25
1142 A253 60f dp grn & ol .45 .25
1143 A253 80f ol grn & brn .65 .25
1144 A253 1fo ocher & grn .65 .25
1145 A253 1.20fo salmon & blk 1.15 .25
1146 A253 1.50fo grnsh blk & red brn 1.30 .25
1147 A253 2fo aqua & brown 1.65 .55
Nos. 1141-1147 (7) 6.20 2.05
Exist imperf. Value, set $75.

Puli (Sheepdog) — A254

Puli and Steer — A255 **Hungarian Pointer — A256**

Hungarian Dogs: 60f, Pumi (sheepdog). 1fo, Retriever with fowl. 1.20fo, Kuvasz (sheepdog). 1.50fo, Komondor (sheepdog) and cottage. 2fo, Komondor (head).

Perf. 11x13 (A254), 12
1956, Mar. 17 Engr. & Litho.
1148 A254 40f yel, blk & red .30 .25
1149 A255 50f blue, bis & blk .30 .25
1150 A254 60f yel grn, blk & red .30 .25
1151 A256 80f bluish grn, ocher & blk .30 .30
1152 A256 1fo turq, ocher & blk .40 .25
1153 A254 1.20fo salmon, blk & chnt .75 .25
1154 A254 1.50fo ultra, blk & buff 1.75 .35
1155 A254 2fo cerise, blk & chnt 2.50 .55
Nos. 1148-1155 (8) 6.60 2.45
Exist imperf. Value, set $45.

Pioneer Emblem — A257

Perf. 12x12½
1956, June 2 Photo. Wmk. 106
1156 A257 1fo red .40 .25
1157 A257 1fo gray .40 .25
Pioneer movement, 10th anniversary.
Exist imperf. Value, set $27.50.

Janos Hunyadi Statue — A258

1956, Aug. 12 Perf. 12
1158 A258 1fo brown, yelsh .60 .35
500th anniv. of the defeat of the Turks at the battle of Pecs under Janos Hunyadi.
Printed in sheets of 50 with alternate vertical rows inverted and center row of perforation omitted, providing 25 tête bêche pairs, of which 5 are imperf. between. Values for tete-beche pairs: unused $1.50; used $1.15. Values for tete-beche pairs, imperf between: unused $3; used $1.50.
Exists imperf. Value $35. Tête bêche pair also exists imperf. Value, $100.

Miner — A259

1956, Sept. 2
1159 A259 1fo dark blue .50 .25
Issued in honor of Miners' Day 1956.
Exists imperf. Value $15.

Kayak Racer — A260

Sports: 30f, Horse jumping hurdle. 40f, Fencing. 60f, Women hurdlers. 1fo, Soccer. 1.50fo, Weight lifting. 2fo, Gymnastics. 3fo, Basketball.

1956, Sept. 25 Wmk. 106 Perf. 11
Figures in Brown Olive
1160 A260 20f lt blue .30 .25
1161 A260 30f lt olive grn .30 .25
1162 A260 40f deep orange .30 .25
1163 A260 60f bluish grn .30 .25
1164 A260 1fo vermilion .35 .25
1165 A260 1.50fo blue violet .65 .25
1166 A260 2fo emerald .80 .25
1167 A260 3fo rose lilac 1.40 .30
Nos. 1160-1167 (8) 4.40 2.05
16th Olympic Games at Melbourne, Nov. 22-Dec. 8, 1956.
Exist imperf. Value, set $75.

Franz Liszt — A261

Portrait: No. 1169, Frederic Chopin facing left.

1956, Oct. 7 Photo. Perf. 12x12½
1168 A261 1fo violet blue 1.75 1.75
1169 A261 1fo magenta 1.75 1.75
a. Pair, #1168-1169 3.50 3.50
29th Day of the Stamp. Sold only at the Philatelic Exhibition together with entrance ticket for 4fo.

Exist imperf. Value, pair $25.

Janos Arany — A262

1957, Sept. 15 Wmk. 106 Perf. 12
1170 A262 2fo bright blue .60 .25
75th anniv. of the death of Janos Arany, poet.
Exists imperf. Value $10.

Arms of Hungary — A263

1957, Oct. 1
1171 A263 60f brt red .75 .25
1172 A263 1fo dp yellow grn .75 .25
Exists imperf. Value, set $17.50.

Trade Union Congress Emblem — A264

1957, Oct. 4
1173 A264 1fo dk carmine .35 .25
4th Intl. Trade Union Cong., Leipzig, 10/4-15.
Exists imperf. Value $10.

Dove and Colors of Communist Countries A265

Design: 1fo, Lenin.

1957, Nov. 7 Litho. Perf. 12
1174 A265 60f gray, blk & multi .30 .25
  a. Perf 11 .30 .25
1175 A265 1fo ol bis & indigo .45 .35
  a. Perf 11 .55 .25
Russian Revolution, 40th anniversary.
Exist imperf. Value, set $17.50.

Komarom Tumbler Pigeons — A266

Pigeons: 40f, Two short-beaked Budapest pigeons. 60f, Giant domestic pigeon. 1fo, Three Szeged pigeons. 2fo, Two Hungarian fantails.

Perf. 12x12½
1957-58 Photo. Wmk. 106
1176 A266 30f yel grn, cl & ocher .25 .25
1177 A266 40f ocher & blk .25 .25
1178 A266 60f blue & gray .25 .25
1179 A266 1fo gray & red brn .25 .25
1180 A266 2fo brt pink & gray .60 .40
Nos. 1176-1180,C175 (6) 2.50 1.65
Intl. Pigeon Exhibition, Budapest, 12/14-16.
Exist imperf. Value, set (6) $60.
Issued: 30f, 1/12/58; others, 12/14/57.

Television Station — A267

HUNGARY

1958, Feb. 22   Engr.   Perf. 11
1181 A267 2fo rose violet   .90   .45
  a.   Perf. 12   2.70 2.70

Souvenir Sheet
1182 A267 2fo green   47.50 47.50

Issued to publicize the television industry. No. 1182 sold for 25fo.
Exist imperf. Values: single $12.50; souvenir sheet $125.

Mother and Child — A268

Designs: 30f, Old man feeding pigeons. 40f, School boys. 60f, "Working ants and fiddling grasshopper." 1fo, Honeycomb and bee. 2fo, Handing over money.

1958, Mar. 9   Photo.   Perf. 12
1183 A268 20f yel grn & ol gray   .30   .25
1184 A268 30f lt olive & mar   .30   .25
1185 A268 40f yel bis & brn   .50   .25
1186 A268 60f rose car & grnsh
              blk   .50   .25
1187 A268 1fo ol gray & dk brn   .75   .25
1188 A268 2fo org & ol gray   1.25   .35
      Nos. 1183-1188 (6)   3.60 1.60

Issued to publicize the value of savings and insurance.
Exist imperf. Value, set $27.50.

Kazar Costume Type of 1953
Souvenir Sheet
1958, Apr. 17   Engr.   Perf. 12
1189 A233 10fo magenta   18.75 18.75

Issued for the Universal and International Exposition at Brussels.
Exists imperf. Value $40.

Arms of Hungary — A269

1958, May 23   Litho.   Wmk. 106
Arms in Original Colors
1190 A269 60f lt red brn & red   .30   .25
1191 A269 1fo gray grn & grn   .50   .25
1192 A269 2fo gray & dk brn   .80   .25
      Nos. 1190-1192 (3)   1.60   .75

1st anniv. of the law amending the constitution.
Exist imperf. Value, set $14.

Youth Holding Book A270

1958, June 14   Photo.   Perf. 12½x12
1193 A270 1fo brown carmine   .60   .50

5th Hungarian Youth Festival at Keszthely. Printed with alternating label, inscribed: V. IFJUSAGI TALAKOZO KESZTHELY 1958.
Exists imperf. Value, with label $15.

Post Horn and Town Hall, Prague — A271

1958, June 30
1194 A271 60f green   .50   .25
  a.   Pair, #1194, C184   .90   .60

Conference of Postal Ministers of Communist Countries at Prague, June 30-July 8.
Exists imperf. Value, in pair with No. C184 imperf, value $15.

Dolomite Flax A272

Hungarian Thistles — A273

30f, Kitaibelia vitifolia. 60f, Crocuses. 1fo, Hellebore. 2fo, Lilies. 2.50fo, Pinks. 3fo, Dog roses.

Perf. 11x13, 12½x12 (A273)
1958, Aug. 12   Photo.   Wmk. 106
1195 A272 20f red vio & yel   .30   .25
1196 A272 30f blue, yel &
              grn   .30   .25
1197 A273 40f brown & bis   .30   .25
1198 A273 60f bl grn & pink   .30   .25
1199 A273 1fo rose car &
              yel grn   .50   .25
1200 A273 2fo grn & yel   .90   .25
1201 A272 2.50fo vio bl & pink   1.05   .25
1202 A272 3fo green & pink   1.80   .60
  a.   Souv. sheet of 4, perf. 12 30.00 30.00
      Nos. 1195-1202 (8)   5.45 2.35

No. 1202a and a similar imperf. sheet were issued for the International Philatelic Congress at Brussels, Sept. 15-17, 1958. They contain the triangular 20f, 30f, 2.50fo and 3fo stamps printed in different colors. Sheets measure 111x111mm. and are printed on unwatermarked, linen-finish paper. Background of stamps, marginal inscriptions and ornaments in green. No. 1202a also exists perf. 11. Value, $50.
Exist imperf. Value, set $75. Value of 1202a imperf, $50.

Paddle, Ball and Olive Branch — A274

Designs: 30f, Table tennis player, vert. 40f, Wrestlers, vert. 60f, Wrestlers, horiz. 1fo, Water polo player, vert. 2.50fo, High dive, vert. 3fo, Swimmer.

1958, Aug. 30   Wmk. 106   Perf. 12
1203 A274 20f rose red,
              pnksh   .30   .25
1204 A274 30f olive, *grnsh*   .30   .25
1205 A274 40f mag, *yel*   .30   .25
1206 A274 60f brown, *bluish*   .40   .25
1207 A274 1fo ultra, *bluish*   .45   .25
1208 A274 2.50fo dk red, *yel*   1.10   .30
1209 A274 3fo grnsh bl, *grnsh* 1.40   .50
      Nos. 1203-1209 (7)   4.25 2.05

Intl. Wrestling and European Swimming and Table Tennis Championships, held at Budapest.
Exist imperf. Value, set $32.50.

Red Flag — A275

Design: 2fo, Hand holding newspaper.

1958, Nov. 21   Perf. 12½x12
1210 A275 1fo brown & red   .25   .25
1211 A275 2fo dk gray bl & red   .55   .25

40th anniversary of the founding of the Hungarian Communist Party and newspaper.
Exist imperf. Value, set $11.

Satellite, Sputnik and American Rocket — A276

Designs: 10f, Eötvös Torsion Balance and Globe. 20f, Deep sea exploration. 30f, Icebergs, penguins and polar light. 40f, Soviet Antarctic camp and map of Pole. 60f, "Rocket" approaching moon. 1fo, Sun and observatory.

1959, Mar. 14   Perf. 12x12½
Size: 32x21mm
1212 A276 10f car rose & sepia   .30   .25
1213 A276 20f brt blue & gray   .30   .25
1214 A276 30f dk slate grn & bis .35   .25

Perf. 12
Size: 35x26mm
1215 A276 40f slate bl & lt bl   .40   .25

Perf. 15
Size: 58x21mm
1216 A276 60f Prus bl & lemon   .50   .25

Perf. 12
Size: 35x26mm
1217 A276 1fo scarlet & yel   .60   .30
1218 A276 5fo brn & red brn   1.50   .80
      Nos. 1212-1218 (7)   3.95 2.35

Intl. Geophysical Year. See No. 1262.
Exist imperf. Value, set $35.

"Revolution" — A277

1959, Mar. 21   Perf. 12½x12
1219 A277 20f vio brn & red   .25   .25
1220 A277 60f blue & red   .25   .25
1221 A277 1fo brown & red   .60   .25
      Nos. 1219-1221 (3)   1.10   .75

40th anniv. of the proclamation of the Hungarian Soviet Republic.
Exist imperf. Value, set $12.50.

Rose A278

1959, May 1   Photo.   Perf. 11
1222 A278 60f lilac, dp car & grn .40   .25
1223 A278 1fo lt brn, dl red &
              grn   .60   .25

Issued for Labor Day, May 1, 1959.
Exist imperf. Value, set $15.

Early Locomotive A279

Designs: 30f, Diesel coach. 40f, Early semaphore, vert. 60f, Csonka automobile. 1fo, Icarus bus. 2fo, First Lake Balaton steamboat. 2.50fo, Stagecoach.

1959, May 26   Litho.   Perf. 14½x15
1224 A279 20f multi   .30   .25
1225 A279 30f multi   .30   .25
1226 A279 40f multi   .30   .25
1227 A279 60f multi   .30   .25
1228 A279 1fo multi   .30   .25
1229 A279 2fo multi   .30   .25
1230 A279 2.50fo multi   1.25   .30
      Nos. 1224-1230,C201 (8)   5.05 3.05

Transport Museum, Budapest.
Exist imperf. Value, set (8) $45.

Perf. 10½x11½
1959, May 29   Wmk. 106
1231 A279 2.50fo multi   2.25 2.25

Designer's name on No. 1231. Printed in sheets of four with four labels to commemorate the congress of the International Federation for Philately in Hamburg. Value $15.
Exist imperf. Values: pair with label $15; sheetlet $120.

Post Horn and World Map A280

1959, June 1   Photo.   Perf. 12
1232 A280 1fo cerise   .60   .30

Postal Ministers Conference, Berlin. Printed in sheets of 25 stamps with 25 alternating gray labels showing East Berlin Opera House.
Exists imperf. Value: in pair with label, $15.

Great Cormorant — A281

Birds: 20f, Little egret and nest. 30f, Purple heron and nest. 40f, Great egret. 60f, White spoonbill. 1fo, Gray heron. 2fo, Squacco heron and nest. 3fo, Glossy ibis.

1959, June 14
1233 A281 10f green & indigo   .30   .25
1234 A281 20f gray bl & ol grn   .30   .25
1235 A281 30f org, grnsh blk &
              vio   .30   .25
1236 A281 40f dark grn & gray   .30   .25
1237 A281 60f dp cl & pale rose   .35   .25
1238 A281 1fo dp bl grn & blk   .50   .25
1239 A281 2fo dp orange & gray   .85   .30
1240 A281 3fo bister & brn lake 1.50   .70
      Nos. 1233-1240 (8)   4.40 2.50

Exist imperf. Value, set $45.

Warrior, 10th Century — A282

Designs: 20f, Warrior, 15th century. 30f, Soldier, 18th century. 40f, Soldier, 19th century. 60f, Cavalry man, 19th century. 1fo, Fencer, assault. 1.40fo, Fencer on guard. 3fo, Swordsman saluting.

1959, July 11
1241 A282 10f gray & blue   .30   .25
1242 A282 20f gray & dull yel   .30   .25
1243 A282 30f gray & gray vio   .30   .25
1244 A282 40f gray & ver   .30   .25
1245 A282 60f gray & rose lil   .30   .25
1246 A282 1fo ind & lt bl grn   .30   .25
1247 A282 1.40fo orange & blk   .60   .25
1248 A282 3fo blk & ol grn   .90   .70
      Nos. 1241-1248 (8)   3.30 2.45

24th World Fencing Championships, Budapest.
Exist imperf. Value, set $25.

Sailboat, Lake Balaton — A283

40f, Vintager & lake, horiz. 60f, Bathers. 1.20fo, Fishermen. 2fo, Summer guests & ship.

1959, July 11   Photo.   Wmk. 106
1249 A283 30f blue   .30   .25
1250 A283 40f carmine rose   .30   .25
1251 A283 60f dp red brown   .30   .25
1252 A283 1.20fo violet   .30   .25
1253 A283 2fo red org, *yel*   .60   .50
      Nos. 1249-1253,C202-C205 (9) 3.20 2.55

Issued to publicize Lake Balaton and the opening of the Summer University.
Exist imperf. Value, set (9) $35.

HUNGARY

Haydn's Monogram — A284

Esterhazy Palace — A285

Haydn and Schiller Monograms — A286

Design: 1fo, Joseph Haydn and score.

1959, Sept. 20   Wmk. 106   Perf. 12

1254	A284	40f dp claret & yel	.30	.25
1255	A285	60f Prus bl, gray & yel	.75	.75
1256	A284	1fo dk vio, lt brn & org	.65	.25

Designs: 40f, Schiller's monogram. 60f, Pegasus rearing from flames. 1fo, Friedrich von Schiller.

1257	A284	40f olive grn & org	.30	.25
1258	A285	60f violet bl & lil	.40	.25
1259	A284	1fo dp cl & org brn	.80	.25
		Nos. 1254-1259 (6)	3.20	2.00

Souvenir Sheet
Imperf

1260	A286	Sheet of 2	12.50	12.50
a.		3fo magenta	2.50	2.50
b.		3fo green	2.50	2.60

150th anniv. of the death of Joseph Haydn, Austrian composer, Nos. 1254-1256; 200th anniv. of the birth of Friedrich von Schiller, German poet and dramatist, Nos. 1257-1259; No. 1260 honors both Haydn and Schiller.
Nos. 1254-1259 exist imperf. Value, set $45.

Shepherd — A287

1959, Sept. 25   Engr.   Perf. 12

1261	A287	2fo deep claret	1.20	1.20
a.		With ticket	1.75	1.75

Day of the Stamp and Natl. Stamp Exhib. Issued in sheets of 8 with alternating ticket. The 4fo sale price marked on the ticket was the admission fee to the Natl. Stamp Exhib.
Exist imperf. Values: single $6; single with ticket $12.50.

Type of 1959 Overprinted in Red

1959, Sept. 24   Photo.   Perf. 15

1262	A276	60f dull bl & lem	.50	.25
a.		Overprint omitted	3,000.	

Landing of Lunik 2 on moon, Sept. 14.
Exists imperf. Value $7.50.

Handing over Letter — A288

1959, Oct. 4   Litho.   Perf. 12

1263	A288	60f multicolored	.50	.25

Intl. Letter Writing Week, Oct. 4-10.
Exists imperf. Value $10.

Szamuely and Lenin — A289

Designs: 40f, Aleksander Pushkin. 60pf, Vladimir V. Mayakovsky. 1fo, Hands holding peace flag.

1959, Nov. 14   Photo.   Wmk. 106

1264	A289	20f dk red & bister	.30	.25
1265	A289	40f brn & rose lil, bluish	.30	.25
1266	A289	60f dk blue & bis	.30	.25
1267	A289	1fo bl, car, buff, red & grn	.45	.25
		Nos. 1264-1267 (4)	1.35	1.05

Soviet Stamp Exhibition, Budapest.
Exists imperf. Value $15.

European Swallowtail — A290

Butterflies: 30f, Arctia hebe, horiz. 40f, Lysandra hylas, horiz. 60f, Apatura ilia.

Perf. 11½x12, 12x11½
1959, Nov. 20
Butterflies in Natural Colors

1268	A290	20f blk & yel grn	.30	.25
1269	A290	30f lt blue & blk	.30	.25
1270	A290	40f dk gray & org brn	.35	.25
1271	A290	60f dk gray & dl yel	.75	.25
		Nos. 1268-1271,C206-C208 (7)	6.45	2.35

Exist imperf. Value, set (7) $75.

Worker with Banner — A291

Design: 1fo, Congress flag.

1959, Nov. 30   Perf. 14½

1272	A291	60f brown, grn & red	.30	.25
1273	A291	1fo brn, red, red & grn	.30	.25

Issued to commemorate the 7th Congress of the Hungarian Socialist Workers' Party.
Exist imperf. Value, set $15.

Teacher Reading Fairy Tales — A292

Fairy Tales: 30f, Sleeping Beauty. 40f, Matt, the Goose Boy. 60f, The Cricket and the Ant. 1fo, Mashenka and the Three Bears. 2fo, Hansel and Gretel. 2.50fo, Pied Piper. 3fo, Little Red Riding Hood.

1959, Dec. 15   Litho.   Perf. 11½
Designs in Black

1274	A292	20f gray & multi	.30	.25
1275	A292	30f brt pink	.30	.25
1276	A292	40f lt blue grn	.30	.25
1277	A292	60f lt blue	.45	.25
1278	A292	1fo yellow	.75	.25
1279	A292	2fo brt yellow grn	.75	.25
1280	A292	2.50fo orange	1.10	.40
1281	A292	3fo crimson	1.10	.60
		Nos. 1274-1281 (8)	5.05	2.50

Exist imperf. Value, set $20.

Sumeg Castle — A293

Castles: 20fr, Tata. 30f, Diosgyor. 60f, Saros-Patak. 70f, Nagyvazsony. 1.40fo, Siklos. 1.70fo, Somlo. 3fo, Csesznek, vert. 5fo, Koszeg, vert. 10fo, Sarvar, vert.

Wmk. 106
1960, Feb. 1   Photo.   Perf. 14½
Size: 21x17½mm

1282	A293	8f purple	.30	.25
1283	A293	20f dk yel grn	.30	.25
1284	A293	30f orange brn	.30	.25
1285	A293	60f rose red	.30	.25
1286	A293	70f emerald	.30	.25

Perf. 12x11½, 11½x12
Size: 28x21mm, 21x28mm

1287	A293	1.40fo ultra	.30	.25
1288	A293	1.70fo dl vio, "Somlo"	.30	.25
b.		"Somlyo"	.70	.25
1289	A293	3fo red brown	1.00	.25
1290	A293	5fo yellow green	1.40	.25
1291	A293	10fo car rose	3.00	.25
		Nos. 1282-1291 (10)	7.50	2.50

Exist imperf. Value, set $75.

Tinted Paper
Perf. 14½
Size: 21x17½mm

1282a	A293	8f pur, bluish	.30	.25
1283a	A293	20f dk yel grn, grnsh	.30	.25
1284a	A293	30f org brn, yel	.30	.25
1285a	A293	60f rose red, pnksh	.30	.25
1286a	A293	70f emer, bluish	.30	.25

Perf. 12x11½
Size: 28x21mm

1287a	A293	1.40fo ultra, bluish	.60	.25
1288a	A293	1.70fo dull vio, bluish	1.50	.25
		Nos. 1282a-1288a (7)	3.60	1.75

Exist imperf. Value, set $22.50.
See Nos. 1356-1365, 1644-1646.

Halas Lace — A294

Designs: Various Halas lace patterns.

Sizes: 20f, 60f, 1fo, 3fo: 27x37mm
30f, 40f, 1.50fo, 2fo: 37½x43½mm

Wmk. 106
1960, Feb. 15   Litho.   Perf. 11½
Inscriptions in Orange

1292	A294	20f brown black	.30	.25
1293	A294	30f violet	.30	.25
1294	A294	40f Prus blue	.30	.25
1295	A294	60f dark brown	.30	.25
1296	A294	1fo dark green	.50	.25
1297	A294	1.50fo green	.60	.30
1298	A294	2fo dark blue	1.10	.45
1299	A294	3fo dk carmine	2.00	.75
		Nos. 1292-1299 (8)	5.40	2.75

Exist imperf. Value, set $25.
See Nos. 1570-1577.

Inscriptions in Orange
1960, Sept. 3   Souvenir Sheet

1300	A294	Sheet of 4 + 4 labels	15.00	15.00
a.		3fo brown olive	3.00	3.00
b.		3fo bright violet	3.00	3.00
c.		3fo emerald	3.00	3.00
d.		3fo bright blue	3.00	3.00

Fédération Internationale de Philatélie Congress, Warsaw, Sept. 3-11. No. 1300 contains 4 stamps and 4 alternating labels, printed in colors of adjoining stamps.
Exists imperf. Value $100.

Cross-country Skier — A295

Sports: 40f, Ice hockey player. 60f, Ski jumper. 80f, Woman speed skater. 1fo, Downhill skier. 1.20fo, Woman figure skater.

1960, Feb. 29   Photo.   Perf. 11½x12
Inscriptions and Figures in Bister

1301	A295	30f deep blue	.30	.25
1302	A295	40f brt green	.30	.25
1303	A295	60f scarlet	.30	.25
1304	A295	80f purple	.30	.25
1305	A295	1fo brt grnsh blue	.60	.25
1306	A295	1.20fo brown red	.70	.30
		Nos. 1301-1306,B217 (7)	3.75	1.90

8th Olympic Winter Games, Squaw Valley, Calif., Feb. 18-29, 1960.
Exists imperf. Value $17.50.

Clara Zetkin — A296

Portraits: No. 1308, Kato Haman. No. 1309, Lajos Tüköry. No. 1310, Giuseppe Garibaldi. No. 1311, István Türr. No. 1312, Ottó Herman. No. 1313, Ludwig van Beethoven. No. 1314, Ferenc Mora. No. 1315, Istvan Toth Bucsoki. No. 1316, Donat Banki. No. 1317, Abraham G. Pattantyus. No. 1318, Ignaz Semmelweis. No. 1319, Frédéric Joliot-Curie. No. 1320, Ferenc Erkel. No. 1321, Janos Bolyai. No. 1322, Lenin.

1960   Photo.   Perf. 10½

1307	A296	60f lt red brn	.30	.25

Engr.

1308	A296	60f pale purple	.30	.25
1309	A296	60f rose red	.30	.25
1310	A296	60f violet	.30	.25
1311	A296	60f blue green	.30	.25
1312	A296	60f blue	.30	.25
1313	A296	60f gray brown	.30	.25
1314	A296	60f salmon pink	.30	.25
1315	A296	60f gray	.30	.25
1316	A296	60f rose lilac	.30	.25
1317	A296	60f green	.30	.25
1318	A296	60f violet blue	.30	.25
1319	A296	60f brown	.30	.25
1320	A296	60f rose brown	.30	.25
1321	A296	60f grnsh blue	.30	.25
1322	A296	60f dull red	.30	.25
		Nos. 1307-1322 (16)	4.80	4.00

Nos. 1307-1308 commemorate International Women's Day, Mar. 8.
Exists imperf. Value $55.

Flower and Quill — A297

1960, Apr. 2   Photo.   Wmk. 106   Perf. 12

1323	A297	2fo brn, yel & grn	1.10	1.10
a.		With ticket	1.35	1.35

Issued for the stamp show of the National Federation of Hungarian Philatelists. The olive green 4fo ticket pictures the Federation's headquarters and served as entrance ticket to the show. Printed in sheets of 35 stamps and 35 tickets.
Exists imperf. Value, stamp + ticket, $15.

Soviet Capt. Ostapenko Statue — A298

Designs: 60f, Youth holding flag, horiz.

Perf. 12½x11½, 11½x12½
1960, Apr. 4

1324	A298	40f dp carmine & brn	.30	.25
1325	A298	60f red brn, red & grn	.50	.25

Hungary's liberation from the Nazis, 15th anniv.
Exist imperf. Value, set $10.

HUNGARY

Boxers — A299

Sports: 10f, Rowers. 30f, Archer. 40f, Discus thrower. 50f, Girls playing ball. 60f, Javelin thrower. 1fo, Rider. 1.40fo, Wrestlers. 1.70fo, Swordsmen. 3fo, Hungarian Olympic emblem.

1960, Aug. 21   **Perf. 11½x12**
Designs in Ocher and Black

1326	A299	10f blue	.30	.25
1327	A299	20f salmon	.30	.25
1328	A299	30f lt violet	.30	.25
1329	A299	40f yellow	.30	.25
1330	A299	50f deep pink	.30	.25
1331	A299	60f gray	.30	.25
1332	A299	1fo pale brn vio	.30	.25
1333	A299	1.40fo lt violet bl	.30	.25
1334	A299	1.70fo ocher	.35	.25
1335	A299	3fo multi	.80	.50

Nos. 1326-1335,B218 (11)   4.55   3.00

17th Olympic Games, Rome, 8/25-9/11.
Exist imperf. Value, set $17.50.

Souvenir Sheet

Romulus and Remus Statue and Olympic Flame — A300

1960, Aug. 21
1336   A300   10fo multicolored   18.00   18.00

Winter and Summer Olympic Games, 1960.
Exists imperf. Value $40.

Woman of Mezokovesd Writing Letter — A301

1960, Oct. 15   **Photo.**   **Wmk. 106**
  Perf. 11½x12
1337   A301   2fo multicolored   1.00   1.00
     a. With ticket   1.25   1.25

Day of the Stamp and Natl. Stamp Exhib. Issued in sheets of 8 with alternating ticket. The 4fo sale price marked on the ticket was the admission fee to the Natl. Stamp Exhib.
Exists imperf. Value, stamp + ticket, $12.50.

The Turnip, Russian Fairy Tale — A302

Fairy Tales: 30f, Snow White and the Seven Dwarfs. 40f, The Miller, His Son and the Donkey. 60f, Puss in Boots. 80f, The Fox and the Raven. 1fo, The Maple-Wood Pipe. 1.70fo, The Fox and the Stork. 2fo, Momotaro (Japanese).

1960, Dec. 1   **Perf. 11½x12**

1338	A302	20f multi	.30	.25
1339	A302	30f multi	.30	.25
1340	A302	40f multi	.30	.25
1341	A302	60f multi	.30	.25
1342	A302	80f multi	.30	.25
1343	A302	1fo multi	.35	.25
1344	A302	1.70fo multi	.65	.25
1345	A302	2fo multi	1.00	.25

Nos. 1338-1345 (8)   3.50   2.00

Exist imperf. Value, set $65.

Brown Bear — A303

Animals: 20f, Kangaroo. 30f, Bison. 60f, Elephants. 80fr, Tiger with cubs. 1fo, Ibex. 1.40fo, Polar bear. 2fo, Zebra and young. 2.60fo, Bison cow with calf. 3fo, Main entrance to Budapest Zoological Gardens. 30f, 60f, 80f, 1.40fo, 2fo, 2.60fo are horizontal.

1961, Feb. 24   **Perf. 11½x12**

1346	A303	20f orange & blk	.30	.25
1347	A303	30f yel grn & blk brn	.30	.25
1348	A303	40f org brn & brn	.30	.25
1349	A303	60f lil rose & gray	.30	.25
1350	A303	80f gray & yel	.30	.25
1351	A303	1fo blue grn & brn	.30	.25
1352	A303	1.40fo grnsh bl, gray & blk	.60	.25
1353	A303	2fo pink & black	.50	.25
1354	A303	2.60fo brt vio & brn	1.00	.40
1355	A303	3fo multicolored	1.40	.75

Nos. 1346-1355 (10)   5.30   3.15

Issued for the Budapest Zoo.
Exist imperf. Value, set $65.

Castle Type of 1960

10f, Kisvárda. 12f, Szigliget. 40f, Simon Tornya. 50f, Füzér. 80f, Egervár. 1fo, Vitány. 1.20fo, Sirok. 2fo, Boldogkö. 2.60fo, Hollókö. 4fo, Eger.

1961, Mar. 3   **Photo.**   **Perf. 14½**
  Size: 21x17½mm

1356	A293	10f orange brn	.30	.25
1357	A293	12f violet blue	.30	.25
1358	A293	40f brt green	.30	.25
1359	A293	50f brown	.30	.25
1360	A293	80f dull claret	.30	.25

Perf. 12x11½
Size: 28x21mm

1361	A293	1fo brt blue	.30	.25
1362	A293	1.20fo rose violet	.30	.25
1363	A293	2fo olive bister	.40	.25
1364	A293	2.60fo dull blue	.60	.25
1365	A293	4fo brt violet	.75	.25

Nos. 1356-1365 (10)   3.85   2.50

Exist imperf. Value, set $37.50.

Child Chasing Butterfly — A304

40f, Man on operating table. 60f, Ambulance & stretcher. 1fo, Traffic light & scooter. 1.70fo, Syringe. 4fo, Emblem of Health Information Service (torch & serpent).

1961, Mar. 17   **Litho.**   **Perf. 10½**
Cross in Red
Size: 18x18mm

1366	A304	30f org brn & blk	.30	.25
1367	A304	40f bl grn, bl & sepia	.30	.25

Size: 25x30mm

1368	A304	60f multi	.30	.25
1369	A304	1fo multi	.30	.25
1370	A304	1.70fo multi	.30	.25
1371	A304	4fo gray & yel grn	.60	.50

Nos. 1366-1371 (6)   2.10   1.75

Health Information Service.
Exist imperf. Value, set $20.

Ferenc Rozsa, Journalist — A305

Portraits: No. 1373, Gyorgy Kilian. No. 1374, Jozsef Rippl-Ronai. No. 1375, Sandor Latinka. No. 1376, Maté Zalka. No. 1377, Jozsef Katona.

1961   **Wmk. 106, Unwmk.**
  Photo.   **Perf. 12**

1372	A305	1fo red brown	.30	.25
1373	A305	1fo greenish blue	.30	.25
1374	A305	1fo rose brown	.30	.25
1375	A305	1fo olive bister	.30	.25
1376	A305	1fo olive green	.30	.25
1377	A305	1fo maroon	.30	.25

Nos. 1372-1377 (6)   1.80   1.50

Press Day (No. 1372); the inauguration of the Gyorgy Kilian Sports Movement (No. 1373); birth cent. of Jozsef Rippl-Ronai, painter (No. 1374); Sandor Latinka, revolutionary leader, 75th death anniv. (No. 1375); Mate Zalka, author and revolutionist (No. 1376); Jozsef Katona, dramatist (No. 1377).
Nos. 1374, 1375, 1377 are unwmkd. Others in this set have wmk. 106.
Exist imperf. Value, set $30.

Yuri A. Gagarin and Vostok 1 — A306

Design: 1fo, Launching Vostok 1.

Perf. 11½x12
1961, Apr. 25   **Wmk. 106**

1381	A306	1fo dk bl & bis brn	.75	.50
1382	A306	2fo dp ultra & bis brn	2.25	1.25

1st man in space, Yuri A. Gagarin, 4/12/61.
Exist imperf. Value, set $60.

Roses — A307

Design: 2fo, as 1fo, design reversed.

1961, Apr. 29   **Perf. 12½x11½**

1383	A307	1fo grn & dp car	.30	.25
1384	A307	2fo grn & dp car	.80	.25
	a.	Pair, #1383-1384	1.50	.30

Issued for May Day, 1961.
Exist imperf. Value, No. 1384a $20.

"Venus" and Moon — A308

Designs: Various Stages of Rocket.

1961, May 24   **Wmk. 106**   **Perf. 15**

1385	A308	40f grnsh bl, bis & blk	.30	.25
1386	A308	60f brt bl, bis & blk	.50	.25
1387	A308	80f ultra & blk	.55	.25

Perf. 11½x11
1388	A308	2fo violet & yel	1.50	1.25

Nos. 1385-1388 (4)   2.85   2.00

Soviet launching of the Venus space probe, Feb. 12, 1961. Exist imperf. Value, set $25. No. 1388 was also printed in sheets of four, perf. and imperf. Size: 130x76mm. Value: perf $12.50; imperf $85.

Warsaw Mermaid, Letter and Sea, Air and Land Transport A309

Mermaid and: 60f, Television screen and antenna. 1fo, Radio.

1961, June 19   **Photo.**   **Perf. 13½**

1389	A309	40f red org & blk	.30	.25
1390	A309	60f lilac & blk	.30	.25
1391	A309	1fo brt blue & blk	.60	.25

Nos. 1389-1391 (3)   1.20   .75

Conference of Postal Ministers of Communist Countries held at Warsaw.
Exist imperf. Value, set $8.

Flag and Parliament A310

Designs: 1.70fo, Orchid. 2.60fo, Small tortoise-shell butterfly. 3fo, Goldfinch.

1961, June 23   **Perf. 11**
Background in Silver

1392	A310	1fo grn, red & blk	.40	.35
1393	A310	1.70fo red & multi	.50	.45
1394	A310	2.60fo purple & multi	.75	.75
1395	A310	3fo blue & multi	1.00	1.00

1961, Aug. 19
Background in Gold

1396	A310	1fo green & blk	.35	.30
1397	A310	1.70fo red & multi	.50	.40
1398	A310	2.60fo purple & multi	.75	.75
1399	A310	3fo blue & multi	1.00	1.00

Nos. 1392-1399 (8)   5.25   5.00

Issued to publicize the International Stamp Exhibition, Budapest, Sept. 23-Oct. 3, 1961. Nos. 1392-1399 each printed in sheets of 4. In gold background issue the top left inscription is changed on 1fo and 3fo.
Exist imperf. Values: set $35; sheetlet set $200.

George Stephenson A311

Winged Wheel, Steering Wheel and Road A312

Design: 2fo, Jenö Landler.

Perf. 12½x11½
1961, July 4   **Photo.**   **Wmk. 106**

1400	A311	60f yellow olive	.30	.25
1401	A312	1fo blue & bister	.30	.25
1402	A311	2fo yellow brown	.50	.35

Nos. 1400-1402 (3)   1.10   .85

Conference of Transport Ministers of Communist Countries held at Budapest.
Exist imperf. Value, set $10.

Soccer — A313

1961, July 8   **Unwmk.**   **Perf. 14½**

1403	A313	40f shown	.30	.25
1404	A313	60f Wrestlers	.30	.25
1405	A313	1fo Gymnast	.30	.25

Nos. 1403-1405 (3)   .90   .75

50th anniv. of the Steel Workers Sport Club (VASAS). See No. B219.
Exist imperf. Value, set of 4 (with B219) $12.50.

Galloping Horses — A314

40f, Hurdle Jump. 60f, Two trotters. 1fo, Three trotters. 1.70fo, Mares & foals. 2fo, Race horse "Baka." 3fo, Race horse "Kincsem."

1961, July 22

1406	A314	30f multi	.30	.25
1407	A314	40f multi	.30	.25
1408	A314	60f multi	.35	.25
1409	A314	1fo multi	.35	.25
1410	A314	1.70fo multi	.50	.25
1411	A314	2fo multi	1.40	.30
1412	A314	3fo multi	1.60	.75

Nos. 1406-1412 (7)   4.80   2.20

Exist imperf. Value, set $25.

HUNGARY

Keyboard, Music and Liszt Silhouette — A315

Liszt Monument, Budapest — A316

Designs: 2fo, Academy of Music, Budapest, and bar of music. 10fo, Franz Liszt.

1961, Oct. 2		Unwmk.		Perf. 12
1413	A315	60f gold & blk	.30	.25
1414	A316	1fo dark gray	.30	.25
1415	A315	2fo dk bl & gray grn	.75	.40
		Nos. 1413-1415 (3)	1.35	.90
		Souvenir Sheet		
1416	A316	10fo multi	8.00	8.00

150th anniv. of the birth, and the 75th anniv. of the death of Franz Liszt, composer.
Exist imperf. Value: set $14; souvenir sheet $25.

Lenin — A317

1961, Oct. 22			Perf. 11½
1417	A317	1fo deep brown	.40 .25

22nd Congress of the Communist Party of the USSR, Oct. 17-31.
Exist imperf. Value $5.

Monk's Hood — A318

30f, Centaury. 40f, Blue iris. 60f, Thorn apple. 1fo, Purple hollyhock. 1.70fo, Hop. 2fo, Poppy. 3fo, Mullein.

Wmk. 106

1961, Nov. 4		Photo.	Perf. 12
1418	A318	20f shown	.30 .25
1419	A318	30f multi	.30 .25
1420	A318	40f multi	.30 .25
1421	A318	60f multi	.30 .25
1422	A318	1fo multi	.30 .25
1423	A318	1.70fo multi	.30 .25
1424	A318	2fo multi	.60 .30
1425	A318	3fo multi	.90 .60
		Nos. 1418-1425 (8)	3.30 2.40

Exist imperf. Value, set $32.50.

Nightingale — A319

Birds: 40f, Great titmouse. 60f, Chaffinch, horiz. 1fo, Eurasian jay. 1.20fo, Golden oriole, horiz. 1.50fo, European blackbird, horiz. 2fo, Yellowhammer, 3fo, Lapwing, horiz.

1961, Dec. 18		Unwmk.	Perf. 12
1426	A319	30f multi	.30 .25
1427	A319	40f multi	.30 .25
1428	A319	60f multi	.30 .25
1429	A319	1fo multi	.30 .25
1430	A319	1.20fo multi	.30 .25
1431	A319	1.50fo multi	.45 .25
1432	A319	2fo multi	.55 .25
1433	A319	3fo multi	.75 .25
		Nos. 1426-1433 (8)	3.25 2.00

Exist imperf. Value, set $25.

Mihaly Karolyi — A320

1962, Mar. 18			
1434	A320	1fo black	.25 .25

Mihaly Karolyi, (1875-1955), Prime Minister of Hungarian Republic (1918-19).
Exists imperf. Value $4.

1962, Mar. 29

Portrait: No. 1435, Ferenc Berkes.

1435	A320	1fo red brown	.25 .25

Fifth Congress of the Hungarian Cooperative Movement, and to honor Ferenc Berkes, revolutionary. See Nos. 1457, 1459.
Exists imperf. Value $4.

Map of Europe, Train Signals and Emblem — A321

1962, May 2			Photo.
1436	A321	1fo blue green	.25 .25

14th Intl. Esperanto Cong. of Railway Men.
Exists imperf. Value $2.

Xiphophorus Helleri — A322

Tropical Fish: 30f, Macropodus opercularis. 40f, Lebistes reticulatus. 60f, Betta splendens. 80f, Puntius tetrazona. 1fo, Pterophyllum scalare. 1.20fo, Mesogonistius chaetodon. 1.50fo, Aphyosemion australe. 2fo, Hyphessobrycon innesi. 3fo, Symphysodon aequifasciata haraldi.

1962, May 5			Perf. 11½x12
Fish in Natural Colors, Black Inscriptions			
1437	A322	20f blue	.30 .25
1438	A322	30f citron	.30 .25
1439	A322	40f lt blue	.30 .25
1440	A322	60f lt yellow grn	.30 .25
1441	A322	80f blue green	.30 .25
1442	A322	1fo brt bl grn	.30 .25
1443	A322	1.20fo blue green	.30 .25
1444	A322	1.50fo grnsh blue	.55 .25
a.		"1962" twice in design	10.00 10.00
1445	A322	2fo green	.70 .25
1446	A322	3fo gray grn & yel	1.50 1.00
		Nos. 1437-1446 (10)	4.85 3.25

On No. 1444a, the year date appears both to the left and below the value inscription. On No. 1444, it appears only to the left of the value.
Exist imperf. Value, set $50.

Globe, Soccer Ball and Flags of Colombia and Uruguay — A323

Goalkeeper — A324

Flags of: 40f, USSR and Yugoslavia. 60f, Switzerland and Chile. 1fo, Germany and Italy. 1.70fo, Argentina and Bulgaria. 3fo, Brazil and Mexico.

1962, May 21		Unwmk. Photo.	Perf. 11
Flags in National Colors			
1447	A323	30f rose & bis	.30 .25
1448	A323	40f pale grn & bis	.30 .25
1449	A323	60f pale lil & bis	.30 .25
1450	A323	1fo blue & bis	.35 .25
1451	A323	1.70fo ocher & bis	.50 .25
1452	A323	3fo pink & blue bis	.75 .25
		Nos. 1447-1452, B224, C209A (8)	4.60 2.20
		Souvenir Sheet	**Perf. 12**
1453	A324	10fo multicolored	7.00 7.00

World Cup Soccer Championship, Chile, May 30-June 17.
Exist imperf. Value: set (8) $20; souvenir sheet $25.

Type of 1961 and

Johann Gutenberg — A325

No. 1456, Miklós Misztófalusi Kis, Hungarian printer (1650-1702). No. 1457, Jozsef Pach. No. 1458, András Cházár. No. 1459, Dr. Ferenc Hutyra. No. 1460, Gábor Egressy & National Theater.

1962		Unwmk. Photo.	Perf. 12
1455	A325	1fo blue black	.30 .25
1456	A325	1fo red brown	.30 .25
1457	A320	1fo blue	.30 .25
1458	A325	1fo violet	.30 .25
1459	A320	1fo deep blue	.30 .25
1460	A325	1fo rose red	.40 .25
		Nos. 1455-1460 (6)	1.90 1.50

Cent. of Printers' and Papermakers' Union (Nos. 1455-1456). 75th anniv. of founding, by Joszef Pech, of Hungarian Hydroelectric Service (No. 1457). András Cházár, founder of Hungarian deaf-mute education (No. 1458). Dr. Ferenc Hutyra, founder of Hungarian veterinary medicine (No. 1459). 125th anniv. of National Theater (No. 1460).
Exist imperf. Value, set $20.

Malaria Eradication Emblem — A327

1962, June 25			Perf. 15
1461	A327	2.50fo lemon & blk	.75 .50
a.		2.50fo grn & blk, sheet of 4, perf. 11	4.00 3.75

WHO drive to eradicate malaria.
Imperfs exist. Values: single (lemon) $5; single (green) $7.50; green sheetlet of 4 $35.
Imperf. sheets with control numbers exist.

Sword-into-Plowshare Statue, United Nations, NY — A328

1962, July 7			Perf. 12
1462	A328	1fo brown	.25 .25

World Congress for Peace and Disarmament, Moscow, July 9-14.
Exists imperf. Value $1.25.

Floribunda Rose — A329

Festival Emblem — A330

1962			Perf. 12½x11½
Various Roses in Natural Colors			
1465	A329	20f orange brn	.30 .25
1466	A329	40f slate grn	.30 .25
1467	A329	60f violet	.30 .25
1468	A329	80f rose red	.30 .25
1469	A329	1fo dark green	.30 .25
1470	A329	1.20fo orange	.60 .25
1471	A329	2fo dk blue grn	1.10 .25
1472	A330	3fo multi	.30 1.25
		Nos. 1465-1472 (8)	3.50 3.00

No. 1472 was issued for the 8th World Youth Festival, Helsinki, July 28-Aug. 6.
Exist imperf. Value, set $37.50.

Weight Lifter — A331

1962, Sept. 16			Perf. 12
1473	A331	1fo copper red	.40 .25

European Weight Lifting Championships.
Exists imperf. Value $2.50.

Oil Derrick and Primitive Oil Well — A332

			Perf. 12x11½
1962, Oct. 8		Unwmk. Photo.	
1474	A332	1fo green	.30 .25

25th anniv. of the Hungarian oil industry.
Exists imperf. Value $0.75.

Racing Motorcyclist — A333

Designs: 30f, Stunt racing. 40f, Uphill race. 60f, Cyclist in curve. 1fo, Start. 1.20fo, Speed racing. 1.70fo, Motorcyclist with sidecar. 2fo, Motor scooter. 3fo, Racing car.

1962, Dec. 28			Perf. 11
1475	A333	20f multi	.30 .25
1476	A333	30f multi	.30 .25
1477	A333	40f multi	.30 .25
1478	A333	60f multi	.30 .25
1479	A333	1fo multi	.40 .25
1480	A333	1.20fo multi	.45 .25
1481	A333	1.70fo multi	.75 .25

HUNGARY

1482	A333	2fo multi	.85	.25
1483	A333	3fo multi	1.00	.25

Nos. 1475-1483 (9)   4.65   2.25

Exist imperf. Value, set $25.

Ice Skater — A334

Designs: 20f-3fo, Various figure skating and ice dancing positions. 20f, 3fo horiz. 10fo, Figure skater and flags of participating nations.

Perf. 12x11½, 11½x12

1963, Feb. 5		Photo.	Unwmk.	
1484	A334	20f multi	.30	.25
1485	A334	40f multi	.30	.25
1486	A334	60f multi	.30	.25
1487	A334	1fo multi	.35	.25
1488	A334	1.40fo multi	.50	.25
1489	A334	2fo multi	.60	.25
1490	A334	3fo multi	1.25	.60

Nos. 1484-1490 (7)   3.60   2.10

Souvenir Sheet
Perf. 11½x12

| 1491 | A334 | 10fo multi | 4.50 | 4.50 |

European Figure Skating and Ice Dancing Championships, Budapest, Feb. 5-10.
Exist imperf. Value: set $20; souvenir sheet $80.

János Batsányi (1763-1845) — A335

No. 1493, Helicon Monument. No. 1494, Actors before Szeged Cathedral. No. 1495, Leo Weiner, composer. No. 1496, Ferenc Entz, horticulturist. No. 1497, Ivan Markovits, inventor of Hungarian shorthand, 1863. No. 1498, Dr. Frigyes Koranyi. No. 1499, Ferenc Erkel (1810-93), composer. No. 1500, Geza Gardonyi (1863-1922), writer of Hungarian historical novels for youth. No. 1501, Pierre de Coubertin, Frenchman, reviver of Olympic Games. No. 1502, Jozsef Eötvös, author, philosopher, educator. No. 1503, Budapest Industrial Fair emblem. No. 1504, Stagecoach and Arc de Triomphe, Paris. No. 1505, Hungary map and power lines. No. 1506, Roses.

1963		Unwmk.	Perf. 11	
1492	A335	40f dk car rose	.30	.25
1493	A335	40f blue	.30	.25
1494	A335	40f violet blue	.30	.25
1495	A335	40f olive	.30	.25
1496	A335	40f emerald	.30	.25
1497	A335	40f dark blue	.30	.25
1498	A335	60f dull violet	.30	.25
1499	A335	60f bister brn	.30	.25
1500	A335	60f gray green	.30	.25
1501	A335	60f red brown	.30	.25
1502	A335	60f lilac	.30	.25
1503	A335	1fo purple	.30	.25
1504	A335	1fo rose red	.30	.25
1505	A335	1fo gray	.30	.25
1506	A335	2fo multi	.30	.25

Nos. 1492-1506 (15)   4.50   3.75

No. 1493, 10th Youth Festival, Keszthely. No. 1494, Outdoor plays, Szeged. No. 1495, Budapest Music Competition. No. 1496, Cent. of professional horticultural training. No. 1498, 50th anniv. of the death of Prof. Koranyi, pioneer in fight against tuberculosis. No. 1499, Erkel Memorial Festival, Gyula. No. 1501, 10th anniv. of the People's Stadium, Budapest. No. 1502, 150th anniv. of birth of Jozsef Eötvös, organizer of modern public education in Hungary. No. 1504, Paris Postal Conf., 1863. No. 1505, Rural electrification. No. 1506, 5th Natl. Rose Show.
Exist imperf. Value, set $50.

Ship and Chain Bridge, Budapest A336

Bus and Parliament A337

20f, Trolley. 30f, Sightseeing bus & Natl. Museum. 40f, Bus & trailer. 50f, Railroad tank car. 60f, Trolley bus. 70f, Railroad mail car. 80f, Motorcycle messenger. No. 1516, Mail plane, vert. No. 1517, Television transmitter, Miskolc, vert. 1.40fo, Mobile post office. 1.70fo, Diesel locomotive. 2fo, Mobile radio transmitter & stadium. 2.50fo, Tourist bus. 2.60fo, Passenger train. 3fo, P.O. parcel conveyor. 4fo, Television transmitters, Pecs, vert. 5fo, Hydraulic lift truck & mail car. 6fo, Woman teletypist. 8fo, Map of Budapest & automatic dial phone. 10fo, Girl pioneer & woman letter carrier.

1963-64		Photo.	Perf. 11	
1507	A336	10f brt blue	.30	.25
1508	A336	20f dp yellow grn	.30	.25
1509	A336	30f violet	.30	.25
1510	A336	40f orange	.30	.25
1511	A336	50f brown	.30	.25
1512	A336	60f crimson	.30	.25
1513	A336	70f olive gray	.30	.25
1514	A336	80f red brn ('64)	.30	.25

Perf. 12x11½, 11½x12

1515	A337	1fo rose claret	.30	.25
1516	A337	1.20fo orange brn	.80	.60
1517	A337	1.20fo dp vio ('64)	.30	.25
1518	A337	1.40fo dp yel grn	.30	.25
1519	A337	1.70fo maroon	.30	.25
1520	A337	2fo grnsh blue	.30	.25
1521	A337	2.50fo lilac	.30	.25
1522	A337	2.60fo olive	.30	.25
1523	A337	3fo dk blue ('64)	.30	.25
1524	A337	4fo blue ('64)	.30	.25
1525	A337	5fo ol brn ('64)	.40	.25
1526	A337	6fo dk ol bis ('64)	.50	.25
1527	A337	8fo red lilac ('64)	.85	.25
1528	A337	10fo emerald ('64)	1.00	.75

Nos. 1507-1528 (22)   8.65   6.35

Size of 20f, 60f: 20½-21x16¾-17mm.
Minute inscription in lower margin includes year date, number of stamp in set and designer's name (Bokros F. or Legrady S.).
Exist imperf. Value, set $60.
See Nos. 1983-1983B, 2201-2204.

Size: 21½x16½mm

1965-67		Coil Stamps	Perf. 14	
1508a	A336	20f deep yellow green	.35	.25
1512a	A336	60f crimson ('67)	.35	.25

Black control number on back of every 3rd stamp.

Motorboat — A338

Girl, Steamer and Castle — A339

Design: 60f, Sailboat.

1963, July 13			Perf. 11	
1529	A338	20f sl grn, red & blk	.30	.25
1530	A339	40f multicolored	.30	.25
1531	A338	60f bl, blk, brn & org	.30	.25

Nos. 1529-1531 (3)   .90   .75

Centenary of the summer resort Siofok.
Exist imperf. Value, set $20.

Child with Towel and Toothbrush — A340

Designs: 40f, Child with medicines. 60f, Girls of 3 races. 1fo, Girl and heart. 1.40fo, Boys of 3 races. 2fo, Medical examination of child. 3fo, Hands shielding plants.

1963, July 27			Perf. 12x11½	
1532	A340	30f multi	.30	.25
1533	A340	40f multi	.30	.25
1534	A340	60f multi	.30	.25
1535	A340	1fo multi	.30	.25
1536	A340	1.40fo multi	.30	.25
1537	A340	2fo multi	.75	.25
1538	A340	3fo multi	.75	.25

Nos. 1532-1538 (7)   2.55   1.75

Centenary of the International Red Cross.
Exist imperf. Value, set $17.50.

Karancsság Woman — A341

Provincial Costumes: 30f, Kapuvár man. 40f, Debrecen woman. 60f, Hortobágy man. 1fo, Csököly woman. 1.70fo, Dunántul man. 2fo, Buják woman. 2.50fo, Alföld man. 3fo, Mezökövesd bride.

1963, Aug. 18		Engr.	Perf. 11½	
1539	A341	20f claret	.30	.25
1540	A341	30f green	.30	.25
1541	A341	40f brown	.30	.25
1542	A341	60f brt blue	.30	.25
1543	A341	1fo brown red	.35	.25
1544	A341	1.70fo purple	.40	.25
1545	A341	2fo dk blue grn	.50	.25
1546	A341	2.50fo dk carmine	.60	.35
1547	A341	3fo violet blue	1.25	.60

Nos. 1539-1547 (9)   4.30   2.70

Popular Art Exhibition in Budapest.
Exist imperf. Value, set $40.

Slalom and 1964 Olympic Emblem — A342

Sports: 60f, Downhill skiing. 70f, Ski jump. 80f, Biathlon. 1fo, Figure skating pair. 2fo, Ice hockey. 2.60fo, Speed ice skating. 10fo, Skier and mountains, vert.

1963-64		Photo.	Perf. 12	

1964 Olympic Emblem in Black and Red

1548	A342	40f yel grn & bis	.30	.25
1549	A342	60f violet & bis	.30	.25
1550	A342	70f ultra & bis	.30	.25
1551	A342	80f emer & bis	.30	.25
1552	A342	1fo brn org & bis	.30	.25
1553	A342	2fo brt blue & bis	.30	.25
1554	A342	2.60fo rose lake & bis	.50	.25

Nos. 1548-1554, B234 (8)   3.30   2.00

Souvenir Sheet
Perf. 11½x12

| 1555 | A342 | 10fo grnsh bl, red & brn ('64) | 3.00 | 3.00 |

9th Winter Olympic Games, Innsbruck, Austria, Jan. 29-Feb. 9, 1964.
Exist imperf. Value: set (8) $20; souvenir sheet $20.

Four-Leaf Clover — A343

Good Luck Symbols: 20f, Calendar and mistletoe, horiz. 30f, Chimneysweep and clover. 60f, Top hat, pig and clover. 1fo, Clown with balloon and clover, horiz. 2fo, Lanterns, mask and clover.

Perf. 12x11½, 11½x12

1963, Dec. 12		Photo.	Unwmk.	

Sizes: 28x22mm (20f, 1fo);
22x28mm (40f);
28x39mm (30f, 60f, 2fo)

1556	A343	20f multi	.30	.25
1557	A343	30f multi	.30	.25
1558	A343	40f multi	.30	.25
1559	A343	60f multi	.30	.25
1560	A343	1fo multi	.30	.25
1561	A343	2fo multi	.30	.25

Nos. 1556-1561, B235-B236 (8)   2.50   2.00

New Year 1964.
Exist imperf. Value, set $12.50.
The 20f and 40f issued in booklet panes of 10, perf. and imperf.; sold for 2 times and 1½ times face respectively.

Moon Rocket — A344

U.S. & USSR Spacecraft: 40f, Venus space probe. 60f, Vostok I, horiz. 1fo, Friendship 7. 1.70fo, Vostok III & IV. 2fo, Telstar 1 & 2, horiz. 2.60fo, Mars I. 3fo, Radar, rockets and satellites, horiz.

1964, Jan. 8		Perf. 11½x12, 12x11½		
1562	A344	30f grn, yel & brnz	.30	.25
1563	A344	40f pur, bl & sil	.30	.25
1564	A344	60f bl, blk, yel, sil & red	.30	.25
1565	A344	1fo dk brn, red & sil	.30	.25
1566	A344	1.70fo vio bl, blk, tan & red	.30	.25
1567	A344	2fo sl grn, yel & sil	.40	.25
1568	A344	2.60fo dp bl, yel & brnz	.50	.25
1569	A344	3fo dp vio, lt bl & sil	.60	.25

Nos. 1562-1569 (8)   3.00   2.00

Achievements in space research.
Exist imperf. Value, set $15.

Lace Type of 1960

Various Halas Lace Designs.
Sizes: 20f, 2.60fo: 38x28mm. 30f, 40f, 60f, 1fo, 1.40fo, 2fo: 38x45mm.

Engr. & Litho.

1964, Feb. 28			Perf. 11½	
1570	A294	20f emerald & blk	.30	.25
1571	A294	30f dull yel & blk	.30	.25
1572	A294	40f deep rose & blk	.30	.25
1573	A294	60f olive & blk	.30	.25
1574	A294	1fo red org & blk	.35	.25
1575	A294	1.40fo blue & blk	.45	.25
1576	A294	2fo bluish grn & blk	.55	.25
1577	A294	2.60fo lt vio & blk	.85	.25

Nos. 1570-1577 (8)   3.40   2.00

Exist imperf. Value, set $35.

Special Anniversaries-Events Issue

Imre Madach (1823-64) A345

Shakespeare A346

Karl Marx and Membership Card of International Working Men's Association A347

Michelangelo — A348

HUNGARY

Lajos Kossuth and György Dózsa — A349

Budapest Fair Buildings — A350

No. 1579, Ervin Szabo. No. 1580, Writer Andras Fay (1786-1864). No. 1581, Aggtelek Cave scene. No. 1582, Excavating bauxite. No. 1584, Equestrian statue, Szekesfehervar. No. 1585, Bowler. No. 1586, Waterfall and forest. No. 1587, Architect Miklos Ybl (1814-91) and Budapest Opera. No. 1590, Armor, saber, sword & foil. No. 1592, Galileo Galilei. No. 1593, Women basketball players. No. 1595, Two runners breaking tape.

Perf. 11½x12, 12x11½, 11

1964   Photo.   Unwmk.
Inscribed: "ÉVFORDULÓK-ESEMÉNYEK"

1578	A345	60f brt purple	.30	.25
1579	A345	60f olive	.30	.25
1580	A345	60f olive grn	.30	.25
1581	A346	60f bluish grn	.30	.25
1582	A346	60f Prus blue	.30	.25
1583	A347	60f rose red	.30	.25
1584	A346	60f slate blue	.30	.25
1585	A345	1fo car rose	.30	.25
a.		With Olympic rings bottom tab	1.00	1.00
1586	A346	1fo dull blue grn	.30	.25
1587	A348	1fo orange brn	.30	.25
1588	A349	1fo ultra	.30	.25
1589	A350	1fo brt green	.30	.25
1590	A345	2fo yellow brn	.30	.25
1591	A346	2fo magenta	.30	.25
1592	A346	2fo red brown	.30	.25
1593	A346	2fo brt blue	.30	.25
1594	A348	2fo gray brown	.30	.25
1595	A348	2fo brown red	.30	.25
		Nos. 1578-1595 (18)	5.40	4.50

No. 1579, Municipal libraries, 60th anniv., and librarian Szabo (1877-1918). No. 1582, Bauxite mining in Hungary, 30th year. No. 1583, Cent. of 1st Socialist Intl. No. 1584, King Alba Day in Székesfehérvár. No. 1585, 1st European Bowling Championship, Budapest. No. 1586, Cong. of Natl. Forestry Federation. No. 1588, City of Cegléd, 600th anniv. No. 1589, Opening of 1964 Budapest Intl. Fair. No. 1590, Hungarian Youth Fencing Association, 50th anniv. Nos. 1591-1592, Shakespeare and Galileo, 400th birth anniversaries. No. 1593, 9th European Women's Basketball Championship. No. 1594, Michelangelo's 400th death anniv. No. 1595, 50th anniv. of 1st Hungarian-Swedish athletic meet.
Exists imperf. Value, set $100. No. 1585a imperf value $150.

Eleanor Roosevelt — A351

Design, horiz.: a, d, Portrait at right. b, c, Portrait at left.

1964, Apr. 27   Perf. 12½

1596	A351	2fo gray, black & buff	.35	.25

Miniature Sheet
Perf. 11

1597		Sheet of 4	2.00	2.00
a.		A351 2fo dp claret, brn & blk	.45	.45
b.		A351 2fo dk bl, brn & blk	.45	.45
c.		A351 2fo grn, brn & blk	.45	.45
d.		A351 2fo olive, brn & blk	.45	.45

Exist imperf. Value: single $4.50; souvenir sheet $20.

Fencing A352

Sport: 40f, Women's gymnastics. 60f, Soccer. 80f, Equestrian. 1fo, Running. 1.40fo, Weight lifting. 1.70fo, Gymnast on rings. 2fo, Hammer throw and javelin. 2.50fo, Boxing.

1964, June 12   Photo.   Perf. 11
Multicolored Design and Inscription

1598	A352	30f lt ver	.30	.25
1599	A352	40f blue	.30	.25
1600	A352	60f emerald	.30	.25
1601	A352	80f tan	.30	.25
1602	A352	1fo yellow	.30	.25
1603	A352	1.40fo bis brn	.30	.25
1604	A352	1.70fo bluish gray	.30	.25
1605	A352	2fo gray grn	.30	.25
1606	A352	2.50fo vio gray	.35	.25
		Nos. 1598-1606,B237 (10)	3.35	2.50

18th Olympic Games, Tokyo, Oct. 10-25.
Exist imperf. Value, set (10) $20.

Elberta Peaches — A353

Peaches: 40h, Blossoms (J. H. Hale). 60h, Magyar Kajszi. 1fo, Mandula Kajszi. 1.50fo, Borsi Rozsa. 1.70fo, Blossoms (Alexander). 2fo, Champion. 3fo, Mayflower.

1964, July 24   Perf. 11½

1607	A353	40f multi	.30	.25
1608	A353	60f multi	.30	.25
1609	A353	1fo multi	.30	.25
1610	A353	1.50fo multi	.30	.25
1611	A353	1.70fo multi	.30	.25
1612	A353	2fo multi	.30	.25
1613	A353	2.60fo multi	.45	.30
1614	A353	3fo multi	.65	.30
		Nos. 1607-1614 (8)	2.90	2.10

National Peach Exhibition, Szeged.
Exist imperf. Value, set $30.

Crossing Street in Safety Zone A354

60f, "Watch out for Children" (child & ball). 1fo, "Look before Crossing" (mother & child).

1964, Sept. 27   Perf. 11

1615	A354	20f multicolored	.30	.25
1616	A354	60f multicolored	.30	.25
1617	A354	1fo lilac & multi	.35	.25
		Nos. 1615-1617 (3)	.95	.75

Issued to publicize traffic safety.
Exist imperf. Value, set $9.

Souvenir Sheet

Voskhod 1 and Globe — A355

1964, Nov. 6   Perf. 12x11½

1618	A355	10fo multicolored	3.50	3.50

Russian space flight of Vladimir M. Komarov, Boris B. Yegorov and Konstantine Feoktistov.
Exists imperf. Value $22.50.

Arpad Bridge — A356

Danube Bridges, Budapest: 30f, Margaret Bridge. 60f, Chain Bridge. 1fo, Elizabeth Bridge. 1.50fo, Freedom Bridge. 2fo, Petőfi Bridge. 2.50fo, Railroad Bridge.

1964, Nov. 21   Photo.   Perf. 11x11½

1619	A356	20f multi	.30	.25
1620	A356	30f multi	.30	.25
1621	A356	60f multi	.30	.25
1622	A356	1fo multi	.30	.25
1623	A356	1.50fo multi	.35	.25
1624	A356	2fo multi	.50	.25
1625	A356	2.50fo multi	1.00	.25
		Nos. 1619-1625 (7)	3.05	1.75

Opening of the reconstructed Elizabeth Bridge. See No. C250.
Exist imperf. Value, set $60.

Ring-necked Pheasant and Hunting Rifle — A357

Designs: 30f, Wild boar. 40f, Gray partridges. 60f, Varying hare. 80f, Fallow deer. 1fo, Mouflon. 1.70fo, Red deer. 2fo, Great bustard. 2.50fo, Roebuck and roe deer. 3fo, Emblem of National Federation of Hungarian Hunters (antlers).

1964, Dec. 30   Photo.   Perf. 12x11½

1626	A357	20f multi	.30	.25
1627	A357	30f multi	.30	.25
1628	A357	40f multi	.30	.25
1629	A357	60f multi	.30	.25
1630	A357	80f multi	.30	.25
1631	A357	1fo multi	.30	.25
1632	A357	1.70fo multi	.30	.25
1633	A357	2fo multi	.30	.25
1634	A357	2.50fo multi	.50	.25
1635	A357	3fo multi	1.00	.25
		Nos. 1626-1635 (10)	3.90	2.50

Exist imperf. Value, set $15.

Castle Type of 1960

3fo, Czesznek, vert. 4fo, Eger. 5fo, Koszeg, vert.

1964   Perf. 11½x12, 12x11½
Size: 21x28mm, 28x21mm

1644	A293	3fo red brown	1.00	.25
1645	A293	4fo brt violet	1.50	.25
1646	A293	5fo yellow grn	1.50	.25
		Nos. 1644-1646 (3)	4.00	.75

Equestrian, Gold and Bronze Medals — A358

Medals: 30f, Women's gymnastics, silver & bronze. 50f, Small-bore rifle, gold & bronze. 60f, Water polo, gold. 70f, Shot put, bronze. 80f, Soccer, gold. 1fo, Weight lifting, 1 bronze, 2 silver. 1.20fo, Canoeing, silver. 1.40fo, Hammer throw, silver. 1.50fo, Wrestling, 2 gold. 1.70fo, Javelin, 2 silver. 3fo, Fencing, 4 gold.

1965, Feb. 20   Perf. 12
Medals in Gold, Silver or Bronze

1647	A358	20f lt ol grn & dk brn	.30	.25
1648	A358	30f vio & dk brn	.30	.25
1649	A358	50f olive & dk brn	.30	.25
1650	A358	60f lt bl & red brn	.30	.25
1651	A358	70f lt gray & red brn	.30	.25
1652	A358	80f yel grn & dk brn	.30	.25
1653	A358	1fo lil, vio & red brn	.30	.25
1654	A358	1.20fo lt bl, ultra & red brn	.30	.25
1655	A358	1.40fo gray & red brn	.30	.25
1656	A358	1.50fo tan, lt brn & red brn	.60	.25
1657	A358	1.70fo pink & red brn	.75	.25
1658	A358	3fo grnsh blue & brn	1.00	.25
		Nos. 1647-1658 (12)	5.05	3.00

Victories by the Hungarian team in the 1964 Olympic Games, Tokyo, Oct. 10-25.
Exist imperf. Value, set $20.

Arctic Exploration — A359

Designs: 30f, Radar tracking rocket, ionosphere research. 60f, Rocket and earth with reflecting layer diagrams, atmospheric research. 80f, Telescope and map of Milky Way, radio astronomy. 1.50fo, Earth, compass rose and needle, earth magnetism. 1.70fo, Weather balloon and lightning, meteorology. 2fo, Aurora australis and penguins, arctic research. 2.50fo, Satellite, earth and planets, space research. 3fo, IQSY emblem and world map. 10fo, Sun with flares and corona, snow crystals and rain.

Perf. 11½x12
1965, Mar. 25   Photo.   Unwmk.

1659	A359	20f blue, org & blk	.30	.25
1660	A359	30f gray, blk & ember	.30	.25
1661	A359	60f lilac, blk & yel	.30	.25
1662	A359	80f lt grn, yel & blk	.30	.25
1663	A359	1.50fo lemon, bl & blk	.30	.25
1664	A359	1.70fo blue, pink & blk	.30	.25
1665	A359	2fo ultra, sal & blk	.30	.25
1666	A359	2.50fo org brn, yel & blk	.50	.25
1667	A359	3fo lt bl, cit & blk	.60	.25
		Nos. 1659-1667 (9)	3.20	2.25

Souvenir Sheet

1668	A359	10fo ultra, org & blk	1.50	1.50

Intl. Quiet Sun Year, 1964-65.
Exist imperf. Value: set $20; souvenir sheet $32.50.

Chrysanthemums — A360

30f, Peonies. 50f, Carnations. 60f, Roses. 1.40fo, Lilies. 1.70fo, Anemones. 2fo, Gladioli. 2.50fo, Tulips. 3fo, Mixed flower bouquet.

1965, Apr. 4
Flowers in Natural Colors

1669	A360	20f gold & gray	.30	.25
1670	A360	30f gold & gray	.30	.25
1671	A360	50f gold & gray	.30	.25
1672	A360	60f gold & gray	.30	.25
1673	A360	1.40fo gold & gray	.30	.25
1674	A360	1.70fo gold & gray	.30	.25
1675	A360	2fo gold & gray	.30	.25
1676	A360	2.50fo gold & gray	.35	.25
1677	A360	3fo gold & gray	.60	.25
		Nos. 1669-1677 (9)	3.05	2.25

20th anniversary of liberation from the Nazis.
Exist imperf. Value, set $15.

"Head of a Combatant" by Leonardo da Vinci — A361

Perf. 11½x12
1965, May 4   Photo.   Unwmk.

1678	A361	60f bister & org brn	.30	.25

Issued to publicize the First International Renaissance Conference, Budapest.
Exists imperf. Value $9.

HUNGARY

Nikolayev, Tereshkova and View of Budapest — A362

1965, May 10   Perf. 11
1679 A362 1fo dull blue & brn .40 .25
Visit of the Russian astronauts Andrian G. Nikolayev and Valentina Tereshkova (Mr. & Mrs. Nikolayev) to Budapest.
Exists imperf. Value $7.50.

ITU Emblem, Old and New Communication Equipment — A363

1965, May 17
1680 A363 60f violet blue .30 .25
Cent. of the ITU.
Exists imperf. Value $7.

Souvenir Sheet

Austrian WIPA Stamp of 1933 — A363a

1965, June 4   Photo.   Perf. 11
1681 A363a Sheet of 2 + 2 labels 2.50 2.50
   a. 2fo gray & deep ultra 1.10 1.10
1965 Vienna Intl. Phil. Exhib. WIPA, 6/4-13.
Exists imperf. Value $20.

Marx and Lenin, Crowds with Flags — A364

1965, June 15   Perf. 11½x12
1682 A364 60f red, blk & yel .30 .25
6th Conference of Ministers of Post of Socialist Countries, Peking, June 21-July 15.
Exists imperf. Value $9.

ICY Emblem and Pulley — A365

1965, June 25
1683 A365 2fo dark red .30 .25
   a. Min. sheet of 4, perf. 11 1.25 1.25
Intl. Cooperation Year, 1965. No. 1683a contains rose red, olive, Prussian green and violet stamps.
Exists imperf. Value: single $6; sheetlet of 4 $20.

Musical Clown — A366

Circus Acts: 20f, Equestrians. 40f, Elephant. 50f, Seal balancing ball. 60f, Lions. 1fo, Wildcat jumping through burning hoops. 1.50fo,

Black leopards. 2.50fo, Juggler. 3fo, Leopard and dogs. 4fo, Bear on bicycle.

1965, July 26   Photo.   Perf. 11½x12
1684 A366 20f multi .30 .25
1685 A366 30f multi .30 .25
1686 A366 40f multi .30 .25
1687 A366 50f multi .30 .25
1688 A366 60f multi .30 .25
1689 A366 1fo multi .30 .25
1690 A366 1.50fo multi .30 .25
1691 A366 2.50fo multi .35 .25
1692 A366 3fo multi .40 .25
1693 A366 4fo multi .50 .40
Nos. 1684-1693 (10) 3.35 2.65
Exist imperf. Value, set $20.

Dr. Semmelweis — A367

1965, Aug. 20   Photo.   Unwmk.
1694 A367 60f red brown .25 .25
Dr. Ignaz Philipp Semmelweis (1818-1865), discoverer of the cause of puerperal fever and introduced antisepsis into obstetrics.
Exists imperf. Value $6.

Runner A368

Sport: 30f, Swimmer at start. 50f, Woman diver. 60f, Gymnastics. 80f, Tennis. 1.70fo, Fencing. 2fo, Volleyball. 2.50fo, Basketball. 4fo, Water polo. 10fo, People's Stadium, Budapest, horiz.

1965, Aug. 20   Perf. 11
Size: 38x38mm
1695 A368 20f multi .30 .25
1696 A368 30f blue & red brn .30 .25
1697 A368 50f bl grn, blk & red brn .30 .25
1698 A368 60f vio, blk & red brn .30 .25
1699 A368 80f tan, ol & red brn .30 .25
1700 A368 1.70fo multi .30 .25
1701 A368 2fo multi .30 .25
1702 A368 2.50fo gray, blk & red brn .30 .25
1703 A368 4fo bl, red brn & blk .60 .25
Nos. 1695-1703 (9) 3.00 2.25

Souvenir Sheet
Perf. 12x11½
1704 A368 10fo bis, red brn & gray 2.25 2.25
Intl. College Championships, "Universiade," Budapest. No. 1704 contains one 38x28mm stamp.
Exist imperf. Value: set $15; souvenir sheet $22.50.

Hemispheres and Warsaw Mermaid A369

1965, Oct. 8   Photo.   Perf. 12x11½
1705 A369 60f brt blue .30 .25
Sixth Congress of the World Federation of Trade Unions, Warsaw.
Exists imperf. Value $6.

Phyllocactus Hybridus — A370

Flowers from Botanical Gardens: 30f, Cattleya Warszewiczii (orchid). 60f, Rebutia calliantha. 70f, Paphiopedilum hybridium. 80f, Opuntia cactus. 1fo, Laelia elegans (orchid). 1.50fo, Christmas cactus. 2fo, Bird-of-paradise flower. 2.50fo, Lithops Weberi. 3fo, Victoria water lily.

1965, Oct. 11   Perf. 11½x12
1706 A370 20f gray & multi .30 .25
1707 A370 30f gray & multi .30 .25
1708 A370 60f gray & multi .30 .25
1709 A370 70f gray & multi .30 .25
1710 A370 80f gray & multi .30 .25
1711 A370 1fo gray & multi .30 .25
1712 A370 1.50fo gray & multi .30 .25
1713 A370 2fo gray & multi .30 .25
1714 A370 2.50fo gray & multi .50 .25
1715 A370 3fo gray & multi 1.00 .25
Nos. 1706-1715 (10) 3.90 2.50
Exist imperf. Value, set $22.

"The Black Stallion" — A371

Tales from the Arabian Nights: 30f, Shahriar and Scheherazade. 50f, Sinbad's Fifth Voyage (ship). 60f, Aladdin, or The Wonderful Lamp. 80f, Harun al-Rashid. 1fo, The Flying Carpet. 1.70fo, The Fisherman and the Genie. 2fo, Ali Baba and the Forty Thieves. 3fo, Sinbad's Second Voyage (flying bird).

1965, Dec. 15   Litho.   Perf. 11½
1716 A371 20f multi .30 .25
1717 A371 30f multi .30 .25
1718 A371 50f multi .30 .25
1719 A371 60f multi .30 .25
1720 A371 80f multi .30 .25
1721 A371 1fo multi .30 .25
1722 A371 1.70fo multi .30 .25
1723 A371 2fo multi .50 .25
1724 A371 3fo multi 1.00 .25
Nos. 1716-1724 (9) 3.60 2.25
Exist imperf. Value $17.50.

Congress Emblem — A372

1965, Dec. 9   Photo.   Perf. 11½x12
1725 A372 2fo dark blue .30 .25
Fifth Congress of the International Federation of Resistance Fighters (FIR), Budapest.
Exists imperf. Value $1.50.

Callimorpha Dominula — A373

1966, Feb. 1   Photo.   Perf. 11½x12
Various Butterflies in Natural Colors; Black Inscription
1726 A373 20f lt aqua .30 .25
1727 A373 60f pale violet .30 .25
1728 A373 70f tan .30 .25
1729 A373 80f lt ultra .30 .25
1730 A373 1fo gray .30 .25
1731 A373 1.50fo emerald .30 .25
1732 A373 2fo dull rose .30 .25

1733 A373 2.50fo bister .50 .25
1734 A373 3fo blue .75 .25
Nos. 1726-1734 (9) 3.35 2.25
Exist imperf. Value, set $30.

Lal Bahadur Shastri — A374

Designs: 60f, Bela Kun. 2fo, Istvan Széchenyi and Chain Bridge.

Lithographed; Photogravure (#1736)
1966   Perf. 11½x12, 12x11½
1735 A374 60f red & black .30 .25
1736 A374 1fo brt violet .30 .25
1737 A374 2fo dull yel, buff & sepia .30 .25
Nos. 1735-1737 (3) .90 .75
Kun (1886-1939), communist labor leader; Shastri (1904-66), Indian Prime Minister; Count Istvan Széchenyi (1791-1860), statesman.
Exist imperf. Value, set $12.
See Nos. 1764-1765, 1769-1770.

Luna 9 — A375

Design: 3fo, Luna 9 sending signals from moon to earth, horiz.

1966, Mar. 12   Photo.   Perf. 12
1738 A375 2fo violet, blk & yel .30 .25
1739 A375 3fo lt ultra, blk & yel .30 .25
1st soft landing on the moon by the Russian satellite Luna 9, Feb. 3, 1966.
Exist imperf. Value, set $12.

Crocus — A376

Flowers: 30f, Cyclamen. 60f, Ligularia sibirica. 1.40fo, Lilium bulbiferum. 1.50fo, Snake's head. 3fo, Snapdragon and emblem of Hungarian Nature Preservation Society.

Flowers in Natural Colors
1966, Mar. 12   Perf. 11
1740 A376 20f brown .30 .25
1741 A376 30f aqua .30 .25
1742 A376 60f rose claret .30 .25
1743 A376 1.40fo gray .30 .25
1744 A376 1.50fo ultra .45 .25
1745 A376 3fo mag & sepia .65 .25
Nos. 1740-1745 (6) 2.30 1.50
Exist imperf. Value, set $20.

Birds in Natural Colors

Designs: 20f, Barn swallows. 30f, Long-tailed tits. 60f, Red crossbill and pine cone. 1.40fo, Middle spotted woodpecker. 1.50fo, Hoopoe feeding young. 3fo, Forest preserve, lapwing and emblem of National Forest Preservation Society.

1966, Apr. 16
1746 A376 20f brt green .30 .25
1747 A376 30f vermilion .30 .25
1748 A376 60f brt green .30 .25
1749 A376 1.40fo vio blue .50 .25

HUNGARY

1750 A376 1.50fo blue .60 .25
1751 A376 3fo brn, mag & grn 1.10 .40
    Nos. 1746-1751 (6) 3.10 1.65

Nos. 1740-1751 issued to promote protection of wild flowers and birds.
Exist imperf. Value, set $30.

Locomotive, 1847; Monoplane, 1912; Autobus, 1911; Steamer, 1853, and Budapest Railroad Station, 1846 — A377

Designs: 2fo, Transportation, 1966: electric locomotive V.43; turboprop airliner IL-18; Ikarusz autobus; Diesel passenger ship, and Budapest South Railroad Station.

1966, Apr. 2   Photo.   Perf. 12
1752 A377 1fo yel, brn & grn .30 .25
1753 A377 2fo pale grn, bl & brn .30 .25

Re-opening of the Transport Museum, Budapest.
Exist imperf. Value, set $15.

Bronze Order of Labor — A378

Decorations: 30f, Silver Order of Labor. 50f, Banner Order, third class. 60f, Gold Order of Labor. 70f, Banner Order, second class. 1fo, Red Banner Order of Labor. 1.20fo, Banner Order, first class. 2fo, Order of Merit. 2.50fo, Hero of Socialist Labor. Sizes: 20f, 30f, 60f, 1fo, 2fo, 2.50fo: 19½x38mm. 50f: 21x29mm. 70f, 25x31mm. 1.20fo: 28x38mm.

1966, Apr. 2   Unwmk.   Perf. 11
Decorations in Original Colors
1754 A378 20f dp ultra .30 .25
1755 A378 30f lt brown .30 .25
1756 A378 50f blue green .30 .25
1757 A378 60f violet .30 .25
1758 A378 70f carmine .30 .25
1759 A378 1fo violet bl .30 .25
1760 A378 1.20fo brt blue .30 .25
1761 A378 2fo olive .30 .25
1762 A378 2.50fo dull blue .30 .25
    Nos. 1754-1762 (9) 2.70 2.25

Exist imperf. Value, set $12.50.

Portrait Type of 1966 and

Dubna Nuclear Research Institute — A379

WHO Headquarters, Geneva — A380

Designs: No. 1764, Pioneer girl. No. 1765, Tamás Esze (1666-1708), military hero. No. 1767, Old view of Buda and UNESCO emblem. No. 1768, Horse-drawn fire pump and emblem of Sopron Fire Brigade. No. 1769, Miklos Zrinyi (1508-66), hero of Turkish Wars. No. 1770, Sandor Koranyi (1866-1944), physician and scientist.

1966   Litho.   Perf. 11½x12
1763 A379 60f blue grn & blk .30 .25
1764 A374 60f multicolored .30 .25
1765 A374 60f brt bl & blk .30 .25
1766 A380 2fo lt ultra & blk .30 .25
1767 A380 2fo lt blue & pur .30 .25
1768 A380 2fo orange & blk .30 .25
1769 A374 2fo ol bis & brn .30 .25
1770 A374 2fo multicolored .30 .25
    Nos. 1763-1770 (8) 2.40 2.00

No. 1763, 10th anniv. of the United Institute for Nuclear Research, Dubna, USSR; No.

1764, 20th anniv. of Pioneer Movement; No. 1766, Inauguration of the WHO Headquarters, Geneva; No. 1767, 20th anniv. of UNESCO and 72nd session of Executive Council, Budapest, May 30-31; No. 1768, Cent. of Volunteer Fire Brigade.
Exist imperf. Value, set $50.

Hungarian Soccer Player and Soccer Field — A381

Designs (Views of Soccer play): 30f, Montevideo 1930 (Uruguay 4, Argentina 2). 60f, Rome 1934 (Italy 2, Czechoslovakia 1). 1fo, Paris 1938 (Italy 4, Hungary 2). 1.40fo, Helsinki 1952 (Hungary 2, Germany 1). 1.70fo, Rio de Janeiro 1950 (Uruguay 2, Brazil 1). 1.70fo, Bern 1954 (Germany 3, Hungary 2). 2fo, Stockholm 1958 (Brazil 5, Sweden 2). 2.50fo, Santiago 1962 (Brazil 3, Czechoslovakia 1).

Souvenir Sheet
1966, May 16   Photo.   Perf. 11½x12
1771 A381 10fo multi 2.50 2.50

Exists imperf. Value $30.

Jules Rimet, Cup and Soccer Ball A382

1966, June 6   Perf. 12x11½
1772 A382 20f blue & multi .30 .25
1773 A382 30f orange & multi .30 .25
1774 A382 60f multi .30 .25
1775 A382 1fo multi .30 .25
1776 A382 1.40fo multi .30 .25
1777 A382 1.70fo multi .30 .25
1778 A382 2fo multi .30 .25
1779 A382 2.50fo multi .60 .25
    Nos. 1772-1779, B258 (9) 3.45 2.50

World Cup Soccer Championship, Wembley, England, July 11-30.
Exist imperf. Value, set (9) $22.75.

European Red Fox — A383

Hunting Trophies: 60f, Wild boar. 70f, Wildcat. 80f, Roebuck. 1.50fo, Red deer. 2.50fo, Fallow deer. 3fo, Mouflon.

1966, July 4   Photo.   Perf. 11½x12
Animals in Natural Colors
1780 A383 20f gray & lt brn .30 .25
1781 A383 60f buff & gray .30 .25
1782 A383 70f lt bl & gray .30 .25
1783 A383 80f pale grn & yel bis .30 .25
1784 A383 1.50fo pale lem & brn .30 .25
1785 A383 2.50fo gray & brn .30 .25
1786 A383 3fo pale pink & gray .60 .25
    Nos. 1780-1786 (7) 2.40 1.75

The 80f and 1.50fo were issued with and without alternating labels, which show date and place when trophy was taken; the 2.50fo was issued only with labels, 20f, 60f, 70f and 3fo without labels only.
Nos. 1780-1786 exist imperf. Value, set $25.

Discus Thrower and Matthias Cathedral A384

30f, High jump & Agriculture Museum. 40f, Javelin (women's) & Parliament. 50f, Hammer throw, Mt. Gellert & Liberty Bridge. 60f, Broad jump & view of Buda. 1fo, Shot put & Chain Bridge. 2fo, Pole vault & Stadium. 3fo, Long distance runners & Millenium Monument.

1966, Aug. 30   Photo.   Perf. 12x11½
1787 A384 20f grn, brn & org .30 .25
1788 A384 30f multi .30 .25
1789 A384 40f multi .30 .25
1790 A384 50f multi .30 .25
1791 A384 60f multi .30 .25
1792 A384 1fo multi .30 .25
1793 A384 2fo multi .50 .25
1794 A384 3fo multi .75 .25
    Nos. 1787-1794 (8) 3.05 2.00

8th European Athletic Championships, Budapest, Aug. 30-Sept. 4. See No. C261.
Exist imperf. Value, set $18.

Girl in the Forest by Miklos Barabas — A385

Paintings: 1fo, Mrs. Istvan Bitto by Miklos Barabas (1810-98). 1.50fo, Hunyadi's Farewell by Gyula Benczur (1844-1920). 1.70fo, Reading Woman by Gyula Benczur, horiz. 2fo, Woman with Fagots by Mihaly Munkacsi (1844-1900). 2.50fo, Yawning Boy by Mihaly Munkacsi. 3fo, Lady in Violet by Pal Szinyei Merse (1845-1920). 10fo, Picnic in May by Pal Szinyei Merse, horiz.

1966, Dec. 9   Perf. 12½
Gold Frame
1795 A385 60f multi .30 .25
1796 A385 1fo multi .30 .25
1797 A385 1.50fo multi .35 .25
1798 A385 1.70fo multi .35 .25
1799 A385 2fo multi .35 .25
1800 A385 2.50fo multi .35 .40
1801 A385 3fo multi .75 .50
    Nos. 1795-1801 (7) 2.75 2.15

Souvenir Sheet
1802 A385 10fo multi 4.00 4.00

Issued to honor Hungarian painters. Size of stamp in No. 1802: 56x51mm.
Exist imperf. Value: set $20; souvenir sheet $30.

Vostoks 3 and 4 A386

Space Craft: 60f, Gemini 6 and 7. 80f, Vostoks 5 and 6. 1fo, Gemini 9 and target rocket. 1.50fo, Alexei Leonov walking in space. 2fo, Edward White walking in space. 2.50fo, Voskhod. 3fo, Gemini 11 docking Agena target.

1966, Dec. 29   Perf. 11
1803 A386 20f multi .30 .25
1804 A386 60f multi .30 .25
1805 A386 80f multi .30 .25
1806 A386 1fo multi .30 .25
1807 A386 1.50fo multi .30 .25
1808 A386 2fo multi .30 .25
1809 A386 2.50fo multi .50 .25
1810 A386 3fo multi .75 .25
    Nos. 1803-1810 (8) 3.05 2.00

American and Russian twin space flights.
Exist imperf. Value, set $17.

Pal Kitaibel and Kitaibelia Vitifolia — A387

Flowers of the Carpathian Basin: 60f, Dentaria glandulosa. 1fo, Edraianthus tenuifolius. 1.50fo, Althaea pallida. 2fo, Centaurea mollis. 2.50fo, Sternbergia colchiciflora. 3fo, Iris Hungarica.

1967, Feb. 7   Photo.   Perf. 11½x12
Flowers in Natural Colors
1811 A387 20f rose, blk & gold .30 .25
1812 A387 60f green .30 .25
1813 A387 1fo violet gray .30 .25
1814 A387 1.50fo blue .30 .25
1815 A387 2fo light olive .30 .25
1816 A387 2.50fo gray grn .45 .25
1817 A387 3fo yellow grn .75 .25
    Nos. 1811-1817 (7) 2.70 1.75

Pal Kitaibel (1757-1817), botanist, chemist and physician.
Exist imperf. Value, set $18.

Militiaman — A388

1967, Feb. 18   Photo.   Perf. 11½x12
1818 A388 2fo blue gray .30 .25

Workers' Militia, 10th anniversary.
Exists imperf. Value $3.

Mme. Du Barry and Louis XV, by Gyula Benczur (1844-1920) A390

Painting: 10fo, Milton dictating "Paradise Lost" to his daughters, by Soma Orlai Petrics.

Souvenir Sheet
1967, May 6   Photo.   Perf. 12½
1819 A390 10fo multi 3.00 3.00

Exists imperf. Value $20.

1967, June 22   Gold Frame
Paintings: 60f, Franz Liszt by Mihaly Munkacsi (1844-1900). 1fo, Samuel Lanyi, self-portrait, 1840. 1.50fo, Lady in Fur-lined Jacket by Jozsef Borsos (1821-83). 1.70fo, The Lovers, by Pal Szinyei Merse (1845-1920). 2fo, Portrait of Szidonia Deak, 1861, by Alajos Gyorgyi (1821-63). 2.50fo, National Guardsman, 1848, by Jozsef Borsos.

1820 A390 60f multi .30 .25
1821 A390 1fo multi .30 .25
1822 A390 1.50fo multi .30 .25
1823 A390 1.70fo multi, horiz. .30 .25
1824 A390 2fo multi .35 .25
1825 A390 2.50fo multi .45 .25
1826 A390 3fo multi .75 .25
    Nos. 1820-1826 (7) 2.75 1.75

Issued to honor Hungarian painters. No. 1819 commemorates AMPHILEX 67 and the F.I.P. Congress, Amsterdam, May 11-21. No. 1819 contains one 56x50mm stamp.
Exist imperf. Value, set $15.
See Nos. 1863-1870, 1900-1907, 1940-1947.

Map of Hungary, Tourist Year Emblem, Plane, Train, Car and Ship — A391

1967, May 6   Perf. 12x11½
1827 A391 1fo brt blue & blk .30 .25

International Tourist Year, 1967.
Exists imperf. Value $6.

HUNGARY

S.S. Ferencz Deak, Schönbüchel Castle, Austrian Flag — A392

Designs: 60f, Diesel hydrobus, Bratislava Castle and Czechoslovak flag. 1fo, Diesel ship Hunyadi, Buda Castle and Hungarian flag. 1.50fo, Diesel tug Szekszard, Golubac Fortress and Yugoslav flag. 1.70fo, Towboat Miskolc, Vidin Fortress and Bulgarian flag. 2fo, Cargo ship Tihany, Galati shipyard and Romanian flag. 2.50fo, Hydrofoil Siraly I, Izmail Harbor and Russian flag.

1967, June 1   Perf. 11½x12
Flags in National Colors

1828	A392	30f lt blue grn	.30	.25
1829	A392	60f orange brn	.40	.25
1830	A392	1fo grnsh blue	.60	.25
1831	A392	1.50fo lt green	1.00	.25
1832	A392	1.70fo blue	1.75	.40
1833	A392	2fo rose lilac	2.00	.60
1834	A392	2.50fo lt olive grn	3.00	.75
		Nos. 1828-1834 (7)	9.05	2.75

25th session of the Danube Commission.
Exists imperf. Value, set $125.

Poodle A393   **Collie A394**

1fo, Hungarian pointer. 1.40fo, Fox terriers. 2fo, Pumi, Hungarian sheep dog. 3fo, German shepherd. 4fo, Puli, Hungarian sheep dog.

1967, July 7   Litho.   Perf. 12

1835	A393	30f multi	.30	.25
1836	A394	60f multi	.30	.25
1837	A393	1fo multi	.30	.25
1838	A393	1.40fo multi	.30	.25
1839	A393	2fo multi	.35	.25
1840	A393	3fo multi	.60	.25
1841	A393	4fo multi	.95	.25
		Nos. 1835-1841 (7)	3.10	1.75

Exist imperf. Value, set $40.

Sterlets — A395

Fish: 60f, Pike perch. 1fo, Carp. 1.70fo, European catfish. 2fo, Pike. 2.50fo, Rapfin.

1967, Aug. 22   Photo.   Perf. 12x11½

1842	A395	20f multi	.30	.25
1843	A395	60f bister & multi	.30	.25
1844	A395	1fo multi	.30	.25
1845	A395	1.70fo multi	.30	.25
1846	A395	2fo green & multi	.30	.25
1847	A395	2.50fo gray & multi	.75	.25
		Nos. 1842-1847,B263 (7)	3.15	1.75

14th Cong. of the Intl. Federation of Anglers (C.I.P.S.), Dunaujvaros, Aug. 20-28.
Exists imperf. Value, set $20.

Prince Igor, by Aleksandr Borodin — A396

Opera Scenes: 30f, Freischütz, by Karl Maria von Weber. 40f, The Magic Flute, by Mozart. 60f, Prince Bluebeard's Castle, by Bela Bartok. 80f, Carmen, by Bizet, vert. Don Carlos, by Verdi, vert. 1.70fo, Tannhäuser, by Wagner, vert. 3fo, Laszlo Hunyadi, by Ferenc Erkel, vert.

1967, Sept. 26   Photo.   Perf. 12

1848	A396	20f multi	.30	.25
1849	A396	30f multi	.30	.25
1850	A396	40f multi	.30	.25
1851	A396	60f multi	.30	.25
1852	A396	80f multi	.30	.25
1853	A396	1fo multi	.30	.25
1854	A396	1.70fo multi	.45	.30
1855	A396	3fo multi	1.00	.70
		Nos. 1848-1855 (8)	3.25	2.50

Exist imperf. Value, set $15.

Teacher, Students and Stone from Pecs University, 14th Century — A397

1967, Oct. 9   Photo.   Perf. 11½x12
1856   A397   2fo gold & dp grn   .40   .25

600th anniv. of higher education in Hungary; University of Pecs was founded in 1367.
Exists imperf. Value $3.50.

Eötvös University, and Symbols of Law and Justice — A398

1967, Oct. 12   Perf. 12x11½
1857   A398   2fo slate   .40   .25

300th anniv. of the School of Political Science and Law at the Lorand Eötvös University, Budapest.
Exists imperf. Value $7.50.

Lenin as Teacher, by Sandor Legrady — A399

Paintings by Sandor Legrady: 1fo, Lenin. 3fo, Lenin, Revolutionaries.

1967, Oct. 31   Perf. 12½

1858	A399	60f gold & multi	.30	.25
1859	A399	1fo gold & multi	.30	.25
1860	A399	3fo gold & multi	.40	.25
		Nos. 1858-1860 (3)	1.00	.75

50th anniv. of the Russian October Revolution.
Exist imperf. Value, set $8.

Venera 4 Landing on Venus A400

1967, Nov. 6   Perf. 12
1861   A400   5fo gold & multi   .85   .65

Landing of the Russian automatic space station Venera 4 on the planet Venus.
Exists imperf. Value $9.

Souvenir Sheet

19th Century Mail Coach and Post Horn — A401

Photogravure; Gold Impressed
1967, Nov. 21   Perf. 12½
1862   A401   10f multicolored   2.00   2.00

Hungarian Postal Administration, cent.
Exists imperf. Value $25.

Painting Type of 1967

Paintings: 60f, Brother and Sister by Adolf Fenyes (1867-1945). 1fo, Wrestling Boys by Oszkar Glatz (1872-1958). 1.50fo, "October" by Karoly Ferenczy (1862-1917). 1.70fo, Women at the River Bank by Istvan Szönyi (1894-1960), horiz. 2fo, Godfather's Breakfast by Istvan Csok (1865-1961). 2.50fo, "Eviction Notice" by Gyula Derkovits (1894-1934). 3fo, Self-portrait by M. T. Csontvary Kosztka (1853-1919). 10fo, The Apple Pickers by Bela Uitz (1887-).

1967, Dec. 21   Photo.   Perf. 12½

1863	A390	60f multi	.30	.25
1864	A390	1fo multi	.30	.25
1865	A390	1.50fo multi	.30	.25
1866	A390	1.70fo multi	.30	.25
1867	A390	2fo multi	.30	.25
1868	A390	2.50fo multi	.40	.25
1869	A390	3fo multi	.70	.25
		Nos. 1863-1869 (7)	2.60	1.75

Miniature Sheet
1870   A390   10fo multi   1.50   1.50

Issued to honor Hungarian painters.
Exists imperf. Value: set $15; souvenir sheet $22.

Biathlon A402

Sport (Olympic Rings and): 60f, Figure skating, pair. 1fo, Bobsledding. 1.40fo, Slalom. 1.70fo, Women's figure skating. 2fo, Speed skating. 3fo, Ski jump. 10fo, Ice hockey.

1967, Dec. 30   Photo.   Perf. 12½
Souvenir Sheet
1871   A402   10fo lilac & multi   1.50   1.50

Exists imperf. Value $18.

1968, Jan. 29   Perf. 11

1872	A402	30f multi	.30	.25
1873	A402	60f multi	.30	.25
1874	A402	1fo multi	.30	.25
1875	A402	1.40fo rose & multi	.30	.25
1876	A402	1.70fo multi	.30	.25
1877	A402	2fo multi	.30	.25
1878	A402	3fo ol & multi	.50	.25
		Nos. 1872-1878,B264 (8)	3.00	2.05

10th Winter Olympic Games, Grenoble, France, Feb. 6-18. No. 1871 contains one 43x43mm stamp.
Exist imperf. Value, set (8) $15.

A403

Design: 2fo, Kando Statue, Miskolc, Kando Locomotive and Map of Hungary.

1968, Mar. 30   Photo.   Perf. 11½x12
1879   A403   2fo dark blue   .40   .25

Kalman Kando (1869-1931), engineer, inventor of Kando locomotive.
Exists imperf. Value $4.

Domestic Cat — A404

60f, Cream Persian. 1fo, Smoky Persian. 1.20fo, Domestic kitten. 1.50fo, White Persian. 2fo, Brown-striped Persian. 2.50fo, Siamese. 5fo, Blue Persian.

1968, Mar. 30   Perf. 11

1880	A404	20f shown	.25	.25
1881	A404	60f multi	.25	.25
1882	A404	1fo multi	.25	.25
1883	A404	1.20fo multi	.25	.25
1884	A404	1.50fo multi	.30	.25
1885	A404	2fo multi	.30	.25
1886	A404	2.50fo multi	.60	.25
1887	A404	5fo multi	1.25	.55
		Nos. 1880-1887 (8)	3.45	2.30

Exist imperf. Value, set $20.

Zoltan Kodaly, by Sandor Légrády — A405

1968, Apr. 17   Photo.   Perf. 12½
1888   A405   5fo gold & multi   1.00   .75

Kodaly (1882-1967), composer & musicologist.
Exists imperf. Value $6.

White Storks — A406

Birds: 50f, Golden orioles. 60f, Imperial eagle. 1fo, Red-footed falcons. 1.20fo, Scops owl. 1.50fo, Great bustard. 2fo, European bee-eaters. 2.50fo, Graylag goose.

1968, Apr. 25
Birds in Natural Colors

1889	A406	20f ver & lt ultra	.25	.25
1890	A406	50f ver & gray	.25	.25
1891	A406	60f ver & lt bl	.25	.25
1892	A406	1fo ver & yel grn	.25	.25
1893	A406	1.20fo ver & brt grn	.25	.25
1894	A406	1.50fo ver & lt vio	.25	.25
1895	A406	2fo ver & pale lil	.55	.30
1896	A406	2.50fo ver & bl grn	1.10	.50
		Nos. 1889-1896 (8)	3.15	2.30

International Bird Preservation Congress.
Exists imperf. Value, set $25.

City Hall, Kecskemét — A407

1968, Apr. 25   Perf. 12x11½
1897   A407   2fo brown orange   .30   .25

600th anniversary of Kecskemét.
Exists imperf. Value $4.

Marx Type of 1953
1968, May 5   Engr.   Perf. 12
1898   A230   1fo claret   .30   .25

Karl Marx (1818-1883).
Exists imperf. Value $5.

Student and Agricultural College — A408

1968, May 24   Photo.   Perf. 12x11½
1899   A408   2fo dk olive green   .30   .25

150th anniv. of the founding of the Agricultural College at Mosonmagyarovár.
Exists imperf. Value $2.

HUNGARY

Painting Type of 1967
Paintings: 40f, Girl with Pitcher, by Goya (1746-1828). 60f, Head of an Apostle, by El Greco (c. 1541-1614). 1fo, Boy with Apple Basket and Dogs, by Pedro Nunez (1639-1700), horiz. 1.50fo, Mary Magdalene, by El Greco. 2.50fo, The Breakfast, by Velazquez (1599-1660), horiz. 4fo, The Virgin from The Holy Family, by El Greco. 5fo, The Knife Grinder, by Goya. 10fo, Portrait of a Girl, by Palma Vecchio (1480-1528).

1968, May 30 Perf. 12½
1900	A390	40f multi	.30	.25
1901	A390	60f multi	.30	.25
1902	A390	1fo multi	.30	.25
1903	A390	1.50fo multi	.30	.25
1904	A390	2.50fo multi	.50	.25
1905	A390	4fo multi	.65	.25
1906	A390	5fo multi	.75	.35
	Nos. 1900-1906 (7)		3.10	1.85

Souvenir Sheet
1907	A390	10fo multi	1.50	1.50

Issued to publicize art treasures in the Budapest Museum of Fine Arts and to publicize an art exhibition.
Exist imperf. Values: set of 7, $17.50; souvenir sheet $22.50.

Lake Balaton at Badacsony — A409

Views on Lake Balaton: 40f like 20f. 60f, Tihanyi Peninsula. 1fo, Sailboats at Almadi. 2fo, Szigliget Bay.

1968-69 Litho. Perf. 12
1908	A409	20f multi	.30	.25
1908A	A409	40f multi ('69)	.30	.25
b.	Bklt. pane, #1909, 1911, 2 each #1908A, 1910		.75	
c.	Bklt. pane, #1909-1911, 3 #1908A		.75	
d.	Bklt. pane, #1911, 3 #1908A, 2 #1909		.75	
1909	A409	60f multi	.30	.25
1910	A409	1fo multi	.30	.25
1911	A409	2fo multi	.30	.25
	Nos. 1908-1911 (5)		1.50	1.25

Exist imperf. Value, set $12.50.

Locomotive, Type 424 — A410

1968, July 14 Photo. Perf. 12x11½
1912	A410	2fo gold, lt bl & slate	.60	.25

Centenary of the Hungarian State Railroad.
Exists imperf. Value $6.

Horses Grazing — A411

Designs: 40f, Horses in storm. 60f, Horse race on the steppe. 80f, Horsedrawn sleigh. 1fo, Four-in-hand and rainbow. 1.40fo, Farm wagon drawn by 7 horses. 2fo, One rider driving five horses. 2.50fo, Campfire on the range. 4fo, Coach with 5 horses.

1968, July 25 Perf. 11
1913	A411	30f multi	.30	.25
1914	A411	40f multi	.30	.25
1915	A411	60f multi	.30	.25
1916	A411	80f multi	.30	.25
1917	A411	1fo multi	.30	.25
1918	A411	1.40fo multi	.30	.25
1919	A411	2fo multi	.30	.25
1920	A411	2.50fo multi	.40	.25
1921	A411	4fo multi	.50	.25
	Nos. 1913-1921 (9)		3.00	2.25

Horse breeding on the Hungarian steppe (Puszta).
Exist imperf. Value, set $40.

Mihály Tompa (1817-68), Poet — A412

1968, July 30 Photo. Perf. 12x11½
1922	A412	60f blue black	.30	.25

Exists imperf. Value $4.

Festival Emblem, Bulgarian and Hungarian National Costumes — A413

1968, Aug. 3 Litho. Perf. 12
1923	A413	60f multicolored	.30	.25

Issued to publicize the 9th Youth Festival for Peace and Friendship, Sofia, Bulgaria.
Exists imperf. Value $5.

Souvenir Sheet

Runners and Aztec Calendar Stone — A414

1968, Aug. 21 Photo. Perf. 12½
1924	A414	10fo multicolored	1.50	1.50

19th Olympic Games, Mexico City, 10/12-27.
Exists imperf. Value $20.

Scientific Society Emblem — A415

Perf. 12½x11½
1968, Oct. 11 Photo.
1925	A415	2fo brt blue & blk	.30	.25

Society for the Popularization of Scientific Knowledge.
Exists imperf. Value $2.50.

Hesperis — A416

Garden Flowers: 60f, Pansy. 80f, Zinnias. 1fo, Morning-glory. 1.40fo, Petunia. 1.50fo, Portulaca. 2fo, Michaelmas daisies. 2.50fo, Dahlia.

1968, Oct. 29 Perf. 11½x12
Flowers in Natural Colors
1926	A416	20f gray	.30	.25
1927	A416	60f lt green	.30	.25
1928	A416	80f bluish lilac	.30	.25
1929	A416	1fo buff	.30	.25
1930	A416	1.40fo lt grnsh bl	.30	.25
1931	A416	1.50fo lt blue	.30	.25
1932	A416	2fo pale pink	.30	.25
1933	A416	2.50fo lt blue	.60	.40
	Nos. 1926-1933 (8)		2.70	2.15

Exist imperf. Value, set $25.

Pioneers Saluting Communist Party — A417

Children's Paintings: 60f, Four pioneers holding banner saluting Communist Party. 1fo, Pioneer camp.

1968, Nov. 16 Photo. Perf. 12x11½
1934	A417	40f buff & multi	.30	.25
1935	A417	60f buff & multi	.30	.25
1936	A417	1fo buff & multi	.30	.25
	Nos. 1934-1936 (3)		.90	.75

50th anniv. of the Communist Party of Hungary. The designs are from a competition among elementary school children.
Exist imperf. Value, set $7.50.

Workers, Monument by Z. Olcsai-Kiss — A418

Design: 1fo, "Workers of the World Unite!" poster by N. Por, vert.

Perf. 11½x12, 12x11½
1968, Nov. 24 Photo.
1937	A418	1fo gold, red, & blk	.30	.25
1938	A418	2fo gold & multi	.30	.25

Communist Party of Hungary, 50th anniv.
Exist imperf. Value, set $18.

Human Rights Flame — A419

1968, Dec. 10 Perf. 12½x11½
1939	A419	1fo dark red brown	.30	.25

International Human Rights Year.
Exists imperf. Value $1.50.

Painting Type of 1967
Italian Paintings: 40f, Esterhazy Madonna, by Raphael. 60f, The Annunciation, by Bernardo Strozzi. 1fo, Portrait of a Young Man, by Raphael. 1.50fo, The Three Graces, by Battista Naldini. 2.50fo, Portrait of a Man, by Sebastiano del Piombo. 4fo, The Doge Marcantonio Trevisani, by Titian. 5fo, Venus, Cupid and Jealousy, by Angelo Bronzino. 10fo, Bathsheba Bathing, by Sebastiano Ricci, horiz.

1968, Dec. 10 Photo. Perf. 12½
1940	A390	40f multi	.30	.25
1941	A390	60f multi	.30	.25
1942	A390	1fo multi	.30	.25
1943	A390	1.50fo multi	.30	.25
1944	A390	2.50fo multi	.30	.25
1945	A390	4fo multi	.60	.25
1946	A390	5fo multi	.80	.35
	Nos. 1940-1946 (7)		2.90	1.85

Miniature Sheet
Perf. 11
1947	A390	10fo multi	2.00	2.00

Issued to publicize art treasures in the Budapest Museum of Fine Arts. No. 1947 contains one stamp size of stamp: 62x45mm.
Exist imperf. Value: set $15; souvenir sheet $22.

1869 and 1969 Emblems of Athenaeum Press — A420

1969, Jan. 27 Perf. 12½x11½
1948	A420	2fo gold, gray, lt bl &	.30	.25

Centenary of Athenaeum Press, Budapest.
Exists imperf. Value $2.50.

Endre Ady (1877-1919), Lyric Poet — A421

1969, Jan. 27 Perf. 11½x12
1949	A421	1fo multicolored	.30	.25

Exists imperf. Value $3.

Olympic Medal and Women's Javelin — A422

Olympic Medal and: 60f, Canadian singles (canoeing). 1fo, Soccer. 1.20fo, Hammer throw. 2fo, Fencing. 3fo, Greco-Roman Wrestling. 4fo, Kayak single. 5fo, Equestrian. 10fo, Head of Mercury by Praxiteles and Olympic torch.

1969, Mar. 7 Photo. Perf. 12
1950	A422	40f multi	.30	.25
1951	A422	60f multi	.30	.25
1952	A422	1fo multi	.30	.25
1953	A422	1.20fo multi	.30	.25
1954	A422	2fo multi	.30	.25
1955	A422	3fo multi	.30	.25
1956	A422	4fo multi	.70	.25
1957	A422	5fo multi	.75	.25
	Nos. 1950-1957 (8)		3.25	2.00

Souvenir Sheet
Litho. Perf. 11½
1958	A422	10fo multi	2.00	2.00

Victories won by the Hungarian team in the 1968 Olympic Games, Mexico City, Oct. 12-27, 1968. No. 1958 contains one 45x33mm stamp.
Exist imperf. Value: set $15; souvenir sheet $22.

1919 Revolutionary Poster — A423

Revolutionary Posters: 60f, Lenin. 1fo, Man breaking chains. 2fo, Industrial worker looking at family and farm. 3fo, Militia recruiter. 10fo, Shouting revolutionist with red banner, horiz.

1969, Mar. 21 Photo. Perf. 11½x12
Gold Frame
1960	A423	40f red & black	.30	.25
1961	A423	60f red & black	.30	.25
1962	A423	1fo red & black	.30	.25
1963	A423	2fo black, gray & red	.30	.25
1964	A423	3fo multicolored	.35	.25
	Nos. 1960-1964 (5)		1.55	1.25

Souvenir Sheet
Perf. 12½
1965	A423	10fo red, gray & blk	1.25	1.25

50th anniv. of the proclamation of the Hungarian Soviet Republic.
Exist imperf. Values: set $8; souvenir sheet $15.
The 60f red lilac with 4-line black printing on back was given away by the Hungarian PO. Value $1, mint or canceled.
No. 1965 contains one 51x38½mm stamp.

Jersey Tiger — A424

HUNGARY

Butterflies and Moths: 60f, Eyed hawk moth. 80f, Painted lady. 1fo, Tiger moth. 1.20fo, Small fire moth. 2fo, Large blue. 3fo, Belted oak egger. 4fo, Peacock.

1969, Apr. 15   Litho.   Perf. 12
1966	A424	40f shown	.30	.25
1967	A424	60f multi	.30	.25
1968	A424	80f multi	.30	.25
1969	A424	1fo multi	.30	.25
1970	A424	1.20fo multi	.30	.25
1971	A424	2fo multi	.35	.25
1972	A424	3fo multi	.65	.25
1973	A424	4fo multi	.90	.25

Nos. 1966-1973 (8)   3.40 2.00

Exist imperf. Value, set $25.

ILO Emblem — A426

1969, May 22   Photo.   Perf. 12x11½
| 1974 | A426 | 1fo car lake & lake | .30 | .25 |

50th anniv. of the ILO.
Exist imperf. Value $4.

Black Pigs, by Paul Gauguin — A427

French Paintings: 60f, These Women, by Toulouse-Lautrec, horiz. 1fo, Venus in the Clouds, by Simon Vouet. 2fo, Lady with Fan, by Edouard Manet, horiz. 3fo, La Petra Camara (dancer), by Théodore Chassériau. 4fo, The Cowherd, by Constant Troyon, horiz. 5fo, The Wrestlers, by Gustave Courbet. 10fo, Pomona, by Nicolas Fouché.

1969, May 28   Photo.   Perf. 12½
1975	A427	40f multicolored	.30	.25
1976	A427	60f multicolored	.30	.25
1977	A427	1fo multicolored	.30	.25
1978	A427	2fo multicolored	.30	.25
1979	A427	3fo multicolored	.50	.25
1980	A427	4fo multicolored	.80	.25
1981	A427	5fo multicolored	.80	.25

Nos. 1975-1981 (7)   3.30 1.75

Miniature Sheet
| 1982 | A427 | 10fo multicolored | 2.00 | 2.00 |

Art treasures in the Budapest Museum of Fine Arts. No. 1982 contains one 40x62mm stamp.
Exist imperf. Value: set $17.50; souvenir sheet $17.50.

Hotel Budapest A428

Budapest Post Office 100 A429

1969-70   Photo.   Perf. 11
| 1983 | A428 | 1fo brown | .30 | .25 |

Coil Stamps
Perf. 14
| 1983A | A429 | 40f gray | .30 | .25 |
| 1983B | A428 | 1fo brown | .30 | .25 |

Issued: No. 1983, May, 1969, Nos. 1983A-1983B, 8/3/70. No. 1983 exists imperf. Value $7.50. Nos. 1983A-1983B have black control number on back of every 5th stamp.

Arms and Buildings of Vac — A430

Towns of the Danube Bend: 1fo, Szentendre. 1.20fo, Visegrad. 3fo, Esztergom.

1969, June 9   Litho.   Perf. 12
1984	A430	40f multi	.30	.25
a.	Bklt. pane, #1985, 1987, 4 #1984		2.75	
b.	Bklt. pane, #1986, 3 #1984, 2 #1985		2.75	
1985	A430	1fo multi	.30	.25
1986	A430	1.20fo multi	.30	.25
1987	A430	3fo multi	.30	.25

Nos. 1984-1987 (4)   1.20 1.00

Stamps in booklet panes Nos. 1984a-1984b come in two arrangements.
Exist imperf. Value, set $7.

"PAX" and Men Holding Hands — A431

1969, June 17   Photo.   Perf. 11½x12
| 1988 | A431 | 1fo lt bl, dk bl & gold | .30 | .25 |

20th anniversary of Peace Movement.
Exists imperf. Value $1.75.

The Scholar, by Rembrandt — A432

1969, Sept. 15   Perf. 11½x12
| 1989 | A432 | 1fo sepia | .40 | .25 |

Issued to publicize the 22nd International Congress of Art Historians, Budapest.
Exists imperf. Value $2.75.

Fossilized Zelkova Leaves — A433

Designs: 60f, Greenockit calcite sphalerite crystals. 1fo, Fossilized fish, clupea hungarica. 1.20fo, Quartz crystals. 2fo, Ammonite. 3fo, Copper. 4fo, Fossilized turtle, placochelys placodonta. 5fo, Cuprite crystals.

1969, Sept. 21   Photo.
1990	A433	40f red, gray & sep	.30	.25
1991	A433	60f violet, yel & blk	.30	.25
1992	A433	1fo blue, tan & brn	.30	.25
1993	A433	1.20fo emer, gray & lil	.30	.25
1994	A433	2fo ol, tan & brn	.30	.25
1995	A433	3fo org, brt & dk grn	.30	.25
1996	A433	4fo dull blk grn, brn & blk	.55	.25
1997	A433	5fo multicolored	.90	.25

Nos. 1990-1997 (8)   3.25 2.00

Centenary of the Hungarian State Institute of Geology.
Exists imperf. Value, set $30.

Steeplechase A434

Designs: 60f, Fencing. 1fo, Pistol shooting. 2fo, Swimmers at start. 3fo, Relay race. 5fo, Pentathlon.

1969, Sept. 15   Photo.   Perf. 12x11½
1998	A434	40f blue & multi	.30	.25
1999	A434	60f multi	.30	.25
2000	A434	1fo multi	.30	.25
2001	A434	2fo violet & multi	.30	.25
2002	A434	3fo lemon & multi	.50	.25
2003	A434	5fo bluish grn, gold & dk red	.50	.25

Nos. 1998-2003 (6)   2.20 1.50

Hungarian Pentathlon Championships.
Exists imperf. Value, set $15.

First Hungarian Postal Card — A435

1969, Oct. 1
| 2004 | A435 | 60f ver & ocher | .30 | .25 |

Centenary of the postal card. Hungary and Austria both issued cards in 1869.
Exists imperf. Value $1.50.

Mahatma Gandhi — A436

1969, Oct. 1   Perf. 11½x12
| 2005 | A436 | 5fo green & multi | .75 | .50 |

Mohandas K. Gandhi (1869-1948), leader in India's fight for independence.
Exists imperf. Value $6.

World Trade Union Emblem — A437

1969, Oct. 17   Photo.   Perf. 12x11½
| 2006 | A437 | 2fo fawn & dk blue | .30 | .25 |

Issued to publicize the 7th Congress of the World Federation of Trade Unions.
Exists imperf. Value $1.75.

Janos Balogh Nagy, Self-portrait — A438

1969, Oct. 17   Perf. 11½x12
| 2007 | A438 | 5fo gold & multi | .75 | .50 |

Janos Balogh Nagy (1874-1919), painter.
Exists imperf. Value $6.

St. John the Evangelist, by Anthony Van Dyck — A439

Dutch Paintings: 60f, Three Fruit Pickers (by Pieter de Molyn?). 1fo, Boy Lighting Pipe, by Hendrick Terbrugghen. 2fo, The Feast, by Jan Steen. 3fo, Woman Reading Letter, by Pieter de Hooch. 4fo, The Fiddler, by Dirk Hals. 5fo, Portrait of Jan Asselyn, by Frans Hals. 10fo, Mucius Scaevola before Porsena, by Rubens and Van Dyck.

1969-70   Photo.   Perf. 12½
2008	A439	40f multi	.30	.25
2009	A439	60f multi	.30	.25
2010	A439	1fo multi	.30	.25
2011	A439	2fo multi	.30	.25
2012	A439	3fo multi	.40	.25
2013	A439	4fo multi	.50	.25
2014	A439	5fo multi	1.00	.25

Nos. 2008-2014 (7)   3.10 1.75

Miniature Sheet
| 2015 | A439 | 10fo multi | 1.75 | 1.75 |

Treasures in the Museum of Fine Arts, Budapest and the Museum in Eger.
Exist imperf. Value: set $15; souvenir sheet $35.
Issued: 40f-5fo, 12/2/69; 10fo, 1/70.

Kiskunfelegyhaza Circling Pigeon — A440

1969, Dec. 12   Perf. 11½x12
| 2016 | A440 | 1fo multicolored | .30 | .25 |

Issued to publicize the International Pigeon Show, Budapest, Dec. 1969.
Exists imperf. Value $4.

Subway A441

1970, Apr. 3   Photo.   Perf. 12
| 2017 | A441 | 1fo blk, lt grn & ultra | .40 | .25 |

Opening of new Budapest subway.
Exists imperf. Value $15.

Souvenir Sheet

Panoramic View of Budapest 1945 and 1970, and Soviet Cenotaph — A442

1970, Apr. 3   Perf. 12x11½
2018	A442	Sheet of 2	1.75	1.75
a.	5fo "1945"	.65	.65
b.	5fo "1970"	.65	.65

25th anniv. of the liberation of Budapest.
Exists imperf. Value $25.

Cloud Formation, Satellite, Earth and Receiving Station — A443

1970, Apr. 8   Litho.   Perf. 12
| 2019 | A443 | 1fo dk bl, yel & blk | .30 | .25 |

Centenary of the Hungarian Meteorological Service.
Exists imperf. Value $3.50.

Lenin Statue, Budapest — A444

Design: 2fo, Lenin portrait.

1970, Apr. 22   Photo.   Perf. 11
| 2020 | A444 | 1fo gold & multi | .30 | .25 |
| 2021 | A444 | 2fo gold & multi | .30 | .25 |

Lenin (1870-1924), Russian communist leader.
Exist imperf. Value, set $4.50.

Franz Lehar and "Giuditta" Music A445

1970, Apr. 30   Photo.   Perf. 12
| 2022 | A445 | 2fo multicolored | .30 | .25 |

Franz Lehar (1870-1948), composer.

HUNGARY

Exists imperf. Value $4.

Samson and Delilah, by Michele Rocca — A446

Paintings: 60f, Joseph Telling Dream, by Giovanni Battista Langetti. 1fo, Clio, by Pierre Mignard. 1.50fo, Venus and Satyr, by Sebastiano Ricci, horiz. 2.50fo, Andromeda, by Francesco Furini. 4fo, Venus, Adonis and Cupid, by Luca Giordano. 5fo, Allegorical Feast, by Corrado Giaquinto. 10fo, Diana and Callisto, by Abraham Janssens, horiz.

1970, June 2	Photo.	Perf. 12½		
2023	A446	40f gold & multi	.30	.25
2024	A446	60f gold & multi	.30	.25
2025	A446	1fo gold & multi	.30	.25
2026	A446	1.50fo gold & multi	.30	.25
2027	A446	2.50fo gold & multi	.30	.25
2028	A446	4fo gold & multi	.60	.25
2029	A446	5fo gold & multi	.75	.30
Nos. 2023-2029 (7)			2.85	1.80

Miniature Sheet
Perf. 11
2030 A446 10fo gold & multi 2.00 2.00

No. 2030 contains one 63x46mm horizontal stamp.
Exist imperf. Values: set $12.50; souvenir sheet $7.50.

Beethoven Statue, by Janos Pasztor, at Martonvasar — A447

1970, June 27	Litho.	Perf. 12		
2031	A447	1fo plum, gray grn & org yel	.30	.25

Ludwig van Beethoven, composer. The music in the design is from his Sonatina No. 1.
Exists imperf. Value $6.

Foundryman — A448

1970, July 28	Litho.	Perf. 12		
2032	A448	1fo multicolored	.30	.25

200th anniversary of the first Hungarian steel foundry at Diosgyor, now the Lenin Metallurgical Works.
Exists imperf. Value $2.75.

King Stephen I — A449

1970, Aug. 19	Photo.	Perf. 11½x12		
2033	A449	3fo multicolored	.75	.30

Millenary of the birth of Saint Stephen, first King of Hungary.
Exists imperf. Value $4.

Women's Four on Lake Tata and Tata Castle — A450

1970, Aug. 19	Litho.	Perf. 12		
2034	A450	1fo multicolored	.35	.25

17th European Women's Rowing Championships, Lake Tata.
Exists imperf. Value $5.

Mother Giving Bread to her Children, FAO Emblem A451

1970, Sept. 21	Litho.	Perf. 12		
2035	A451	1fo lt blue & multi	.30	.25

7th European Regional Cong. of the UNFAO, Budapest, Sept. 21-25.
Exists imperf. Value $7.50.

Boxing and Olympic Rings — A452

Designs (Olympic Rings and): 60f, Canoeing. 1fo, Fencing. 1.50fo, Water polo. 2fo, Woman gymnast. 2.50fo, Hammer throwing. 3fo, Wrestling. 5fo, Swimming, butterfly stroke.

1970, Sept. 26	Photo.	Perf. 11		
2036	A452	40f lilac & multi	.30	.25
2037	A452	60f sky blue & multi	.30	.25
2038	A452	1fo orange & multi	.30	.25
2039	A452	1.50fo multi	.30	.25
2040	A452	2fo multi	.30	.25
2041	A452	2.50fo multi	.30	.25
2042	A452	3fo multi	.40	.25
2043	A452	5fo multi	.60	.25
Nos. 2036-2043 (8)			2.80	2.00

75th anniv. of the Hungarian Olympic Committee. The 5fo also publicizes the 1972 Olympic Games in Munich.
Exist imperf. Value, set $15.

Flame and Family — A453

1970, Sept. 28	Litho.	Perf. 12		
2044	A453	1fo ultra, org & emer	.30	.25

5th Education Congress, Budapest.
Exists imperf. Value $7.50.

Chalice, by Benedek Suky, 1440 — A454

Hungarian Goldsmiths' Art: 60f, Altar burette, 1500. 1fo, Nadasdy goblet, 16th century. 1.50fo, Coconut goblet, 1600. 2fo, Silver tankard, by Mihaly Toldalaghy, 1623. 2.50fo, Communion cup of Gyorgy Rakoczy I, 1670. 3fo, Tankard, 1690. 4fo, Bell-flower cup, 1710.

1970, Oct.	Photo.	Perf. 12		
2045	A454	40f gold & multi	.30	.25
2046	A454	60f gold & multi	.30	.25
2047	A454	1fo gold & multi	.30	.25
2048	A454	1.50fo gold & multi	.30	.25
2049	A454	2fo gold & multi	.30	.25
2050	A454	2.50fo gold & multi	.30	.25
2051	A454	3fo gold & multi	.50	.25
2052	A454	4fo gold & multi	.60	.25
Nos. 2045-2052 (8)			2.90	2.00

Exist imperf. Value, set $12.50.

Virgin and Child, by Giampietrino A455

Paintings from Christian Museum, Esztergom: 60f, "Love" (woman with 3 children), by Gregorio Lazzarini. 1fo, Legend of St. Catherine, by Master of Bat. 1.50fo, Adoration of the Shepherds, by Francesco Fontebasso, horiz. 2.50fo, Adoration of the Kings, by Master of Aranyosmarot. 4fo, Temptation of St. Anthony the Hermit, by Jan de Cock. 5fo, St. Sebastian, by Marco Palmezzano. 10fo, Lady with the Unicorn, by Painter of Lombardy.

1970, Dec. 7	Photo.	Perf. 12½		
2053	A455	40f silver & multi	.30	.25
2054	A455	60f silver & multi	.30	.25
2055	A455	1fo silver & multi	.30	.25
2056	A455	1.50fo silver & multi	.30	.25
2057	A455	2.50fo silver & multi	.40	.25
2058	A455	4fo silver & multi	.65	.25
2059	A455	5fo silver & multi	.90	.40
Nos. 2053-2059 (7)			3.15	1.90

Souvenir Sheet
2060 A455 10fo silver & multi 2.00 2.00

No. 2060 contains one 50½x56mm stamp.
Exist imperf. Values: set $15; souvenir sheet $17.50.

Monument to Hungarian Martyrs, by A. Makrisz — A456

1970, Dec. 30	Photo.	Perf. 12x11½		
2061	A456	1fo ultra & sepia	.30	.25

The 25th anniversary of the liberation of the concentration camps at Auschwitz, Mauthausen and Dachau.
Exists imperf. Value $1.

"Souvenir Sheets"
Beginning in 1971, the government stamp agency, as well as a number of other state sanctioned organizations, have created souvenir sheets that do not have postal validity. These are not listed in this catalogue.

Marseillaise, by Francois Rude — A457

1971, Mar. 18	Litho.	Perf. 12		
2062	A457	3fo bister & green	.30	.25

Centenary of the Paris Commune.
Exists imperf. Value $3.25.

Béla Bartók (1881-1945), Composer — A458

1971
| 2063 | A458 | 1fo gray & dk car | .30 | .25 |
| 2064 | A458 | 1fo gray & green | .30 | .25 |

Issued: No. 2063, Mar. 25; No. 2064, Apr. 17.
Exist imperf. Value, set $6.50.

Győr Castle, 1594 — A459

1971, Mar. 27				
2065	A459	2fo lt blue & multi	.30	.25

700th anniversary of Győr.
Exists imperf. Value $3.25.

Bison Hunt A460

Designs: 60f, Wild boar hunt. 80f, Deer hunt. 1fo, Falconry. 1.20fo, Felled stag and dogs. 2fo, Bustards. 3fo, Net fishing. 4fo, Angling.

1971, May	Photo.	Perf. 12		
2066	A460	40f ver & multi	.30	.25
2067	A460	60f plum & multi	.30	.25
2068	A460	80f multi	.30	.25
2069	A460	1fo lilac & multi	.30	.25
2070	A460	1.20fo multi	.30	.25
2071	A460	2fo multi	.30	.25
2072	A460	3fo multi	.40	.30
2073	A460	4fo green & multi	.55	.40
Nos. 2066-2073 (8)			2.75	2.20

World Hunting Exhibition, Budapest, Aug. 27-30. See No. C313.
Exist imperf. Value, set $20.

Souvenir Sheet

Portrait of a Man, by Dürer — A461

1971, May 21		Perf. 12½		
2074	A461	10fo gold & multi	2.00	2.00

Albrecht Dürer (1471-1528), German painter and etcher.
Exists imperf. Value $15.

Carnation and Pioneers' Emblem A462

1971, June 5	Photo.	Perf. 12		
2075	A462	1fo dark red & multi	.75	.25

Hungarian Pioneers' Organization, 25th anniv.
Exists imperf. Value $7.50.

Design: No. 2064, András L. Achim (1871-1911), peasant leader.

HUNGARY

FIR Emblem, Resistance Fighters — A463

1971, July 3
2076 A463 1fo brown & multi   .30   .25

International Federation of Resistance Fighters (FIR), 20th anniversary.
Exists imperf. Value $4.

Walking in Garden, Tokyo School — A464

Japanese Prints from Museum of East Asian Art, Budapest: 60f, Geisha in Boat, by Yeishi (1756-1829). 1fo, Woman with Scroll, by Yeishi. 1.50fo, Courtesans, by Kiyonaga (1752-1815). 2fo, Awabi Fisher Women, by Utamaro (1753-1806). 2.50fo, Seated Courtesan, by Harunobu (1725-1770). 3fo, Peasant Woman Carrying Fagots, by Hokusai (1760-1849). 4fo, Women and Girls Walking, by Yeishi.

1971, July 9   Perf. 12½
2077 A464 40f gold & multi   .30   .25
2078 A464 60f gold & multi   .30   .25
2079 A464 1fo gold & multi   .30   .25
2080 A464 1.50fo gold & multi .30   .25
2081 A464 2fo gold & multi   .30   .25
2082 A464 2.50fo gold & multi .30   .25
2083 A464 3fo gold & multi   .50   .25
2084 A464 4fo gold & multi   .65   .45
   Nos. 2077-2084 (8)   2.95 2.10

Exist imperf. Value, set $15.

Locomotive, Map of Rail System and Danube — A465

1971, July 15   Litho.   Perf. 12
2086 A465 1fo multi   .30   .25

125th anniversary of first Hungarian railroad between Pest and Vac.
Exists imperf. Value $15.

Griffin Holding Ink Balls — A466

1971, Sept. 11   Photo.   Perf. 12x11½
2087 A466 1fo multicolored   .30   .25

Centenary of stamp printing in Hungary. Printed se-tenant with 2 labels showing printing presses of 1871 and 1971 and Hungary Nos. P1 and 1171. Value unused, $1.
Exists imperf. Value, strip $5.

OIJ Emblem and Printed Page — A467

1971, Sept. 21   Perf. 11½x12
2088 A467 1fo dk bl, bl & gold .30   .25

25th anniversary of the International Organization of Journalists (OIJ).
Exists imperf. Value $2.

Josef Jacob Winterl and Barren Strawberry — A468

Plants: 60f, Bromeliaceae. 80f, Titanopsis calcarea. 1fo, Periwinkle. 1.20fo, Gymnocalycium. 2fo, White water lily. 3fo, Iris arenaria. 5fo, Peony.

1971, Oct. 29   Litho.   Perf. 12
2089 A468 40f lt vio & multi   .30   .25
2090 A468 60f sl blue & multi   .30   .25
2091 A468 80f multi   .30   .25
2092 A468 1fo multi   .30   .25
2093 A468 1.20fo lilac & multi .30   .25
2094 A468 2fo gray & multi   .30   .25
2095 A468 3fo multi   .40   .25
2096 A468 5fo multi   .50   .25
   Nos. 2089-2096 (8)   2.70 2.00

Bicentenary of Budapest Botanical Gardens.
Exist imperf. Value, set $17.50.

Galloping — A469

Equestrian Sports: 60f, Trotting. 80f, Horses fording river. 1fo, Jumping. 1.20fo, Start. 2fo, Polo. 3fo, Steeplechase. 5fo, Dressage.

1971, Nov. 22   Photo.   Perf. 12
2097 A469 40f blue & multi   .30   .25
2098 A469 60f ocher & multi   .30   .25
2099 A469 80f olive & multi   .30   .25
2100 A469 1fo red & multi   .30   .25
2101 A469 1.20fo multi   .30   .25
2102 A469 2fo multi   .30   .25
2103 A469 3fo violet & multi   .40   .25
2104 A469 5fo blue & multi   .50   .25
   Nos. 2097-2104 (8)   2.70 2.00

Exist imperf. Value, set $22.50.

Beheading of Heathen Chief Koppany — A470

Designs: 60f, Samuel Aba pursuing King Peter. 1fo, Basarad's victory over King Charles Robert. 1.50fo, Strife between King Salomon and Prince Geza. 2.50fo, Founding of Obuda Church by King Stephen I and Queen Gisela. 4fo, Reconciliation of King Koloman and his brother Almos. 5fo, Oradea Church built by King Ladislas I. 10fo, Funeral of Prince Emeric and blinding of Vazul.

1971, Dec. 10   Litho.
2105 A470 40f buff & multi   .30   .25
2106 A470 60f buff & multi   .30   .25
2107 A470 1fo buff & multi   .30   .25
2108 A470 1.50fo buff & multi   .30   .25
2109 A470 2.50fo buff & multi   .30   .25
2110 A470 4fo buff & multi   .50   .25
2111 A470 5fo buff & multi   .75   .30
   Nos. 2105-2111 (7)   2.75 1.80

Miniature Sheet
Perf. 11½
2112 A470 10fo buff & multi   2.00 2.00

History of Hungary, from miniatures from Illuminated Chronicle of King Louis the Great, c. 1370. No. 2112 contains one stamp (size 44½x52mm).
Exist imperf. Value: set $12.50; souvenir sheet $20.

Equality Year Emblem — A471

1971, Dec. 30   Litho.   Perf. 12
2113 A471 1fo bister & multi   .30   .25

Intl. Year Against Racial Discrimination.
Exists imperf. Value $3.50.

Ice Hockey and Sapporo '72 Emblem — A472

Sport and Sapporo '72 Emblem: 60f, Men's slalom. 80f, Women's figure skating. 1fo, Ski jump. 1.20fo, Long-distance skiing. 2fo, Men's figure skating. 3fo, Bobsledding. 4fo, Biathlon. 10fo, Buddha.

1971, Dec. 30   Perf. 12
2114 A472 40f black & multi   .30   .25
2115 A472 60f black & multi   .30   .25
2116 A472 80f black & multi   .30   .25
2117 A472 1fo black & multi   .30   .25
2118 A472 1.20fo black & multi .30   .25
2119 A472 2fo black & multi   .30   .25
2120 A472 3fo black & multi   .30   .25
2121 A472 4fo black & multi   .50   .25
   Nos. 2114-2121 (8)   2.60 2.00

Souvenir Sheet
Perf. 11½
2122 A472 10fo gold & multi   2.00 2.00

11th Winter Olympic Games, Sapporo, Japan, Feb. 3-13, 1972. No. 2122 contains one 86x48mm stamp.
Exist imperf. Value: set $15; souvenir sheet $20.

Hungarian Locomotive — A473

Locomotives: 60f, Germany. 80f, Italy. 1fo, Soviet Union. 1.20fo, Japan. 2fo, Great Britain. 4fo, Austria. 5fo, France.

1972, Feb. 23   Photo.   Perf. 12x11½
2123 A473 40f multi   .30   .25
2124 A473 60f ocher & multi   .30   .25
2125 A473 80f multi   .30   .25
2126 A473 1fo olive & multi   .30   .25
2127 A473 1.20fo ultra & multi .30   .25
2128 A473 2fo ver & multi   .30   .25
2129 A473 4fo multi   .75   .25
2130 A473 5fo multi   1.00   .45
   Nos. 2123-2130 (8)   3.55 2.20

Exist imperf. Value, set $27.50.

Janus Pannonius, by Andrea Mantegna — A474

1972, Mar. 27   Litho.   Perf. 12
2131 A474 1fo gold & multi   .30   .25

Janus Pannonius (Johannes Czezmiczei, 1434-1472), humanist and poet.
Exists imperf. Value $2.50.

Mariner 9 — A475

Design: No. 2133, Mars 2 and 3 spacecraft.

1972, Mar. 30   Photo.   Perf. 11½x12
2132 A475 2fo dk blue & multi   .35   .35
2133 A475 2fo multi   .35   .35
   a. Strip #2132-2133 + label 1.40 1.40

Exploration of Mars by Mariner 9 (US), and Mars 2 and 3 (USSR). Issued in sheets containing 4 each of Nos. 2132-2133 and 4 labels inscribed in Hungarian, Russian and English.
Exist imperf. Values: strip $5, sheetlet $25.

13th Century Church Portal — A476

1972, Apr. 11
2134 A476 3fo greenish black   .30   .25

Centenary of the Society for the Protection of Historic Monuments.
Exists imperf. Value $5.

Hungarian Greyhound A477

Hounds: 60f, Afghan hound (head). 80f, Irish wolfhound. 1.20fo, Borzoi. 2fo, Running greyhound. 4fo, Whippet. 6fo, Afghan hound.

1972, Apr. 14   Litho.   Perf. 12
2135 A477 40f multi   .30   .25
2136 A477 60f brown & multi   .30   .25
2137 A477 80f multi   .30   .25
2138 A477 1.20fo multi   .30   .25
2139 A477 2fo multi   .30   .25
2140 A477 4fo multi   .70   .25
2141 A477 6fo multi   1.00   .30
   Nos. 2135-2141 (7)   3.20 1.80

Exist imperf. Value, set $25.

József Imre, Emil Grósz, László Blaskovics (Ophthalmologists) — A478

Design: 2fo, Allvar Gullstrand, V. P. Filatov, Jules Gonin, ophthalmologists.

1972, Apr. 17
2142 A478 1fo red, brn & blk   .50   .25
2143 A478 2fo blue, brn & blk   .75   .35

First European Ophthalmologists' Congress, Budapest.
Exist imperf. Value, set $12.50.

Girl Reading and UNESCO Emblem — A479

1972, May 27   Photo.   Perf. 11½x12
2144 A479 1fo multicolored   .30   .25

International Book Year 1971.
Exists imperf. Value $3.50.

HUNGARY

Roses — A480

1972, June 1
2145 A480 1fo multicolored .30 .25
15th Rose Exhibition, Budapest.
Exists imperf. Value $10.

George Dimitrov — A481

1972, June 18 *Litho. Perf. 12*
2146 A481 3fo black & multi .30 .25
90th anniversary, birth of George Dimitrov (1882-1949), communist leader.
Exists imperf. Value $3.50.

Souvenir Sheet

St. Martin and the Beggar, Stained-glass Window — A482

1972, June 20 *Perf. 10½*
2147 A482 10fo multi 2.00 2.00
Belgica 72, International Philatelic Exhibition, Brussels, June 24-July 9.
Exists imperf. Value $20.

Gyorgy Dozsa (1474-1514), Peasant Leader — A483

1972, June 25 *Photo. Perf. 11½x12*
2148 A483 1fo red & multi .30 .25
Exists imperf. Value $3.50.

Olympic Rings, Soccer A484

Designs (Olympic Rings and): 60f, Water polo. 80f, Javelin, women's. 1fo, Kayak, women's. 1.20fo, Boxing. 2fo, Gymnastics, women's. 5fo, Fencing.

1972, July 15 *Perf. 11*
2149 A484 40f multi .30 .25
2150 A484 60f multi .30 .25
2151 A484 80f multi .30 .25
2152 A484 1fo lilac & multi .30 .25
2153 A484 1.20fo blue & multi .30 .25
2154 A484 2fo multi .40 .25
2155 A484 5fo green & multi .75 .25
Nos. 2149-2155,B299 (8) 3.15 2.00
20th Olympic Games, Munich, Aug. 26-Sept. 11. See No. C325.
Exist imperf. Value, set $17.50.

Prince Geza Selecting Site of Székesfehérvár — A485

Designs: 60f, St. Stephen, first King of Hungary. 80f, Knights (country's defense). 1.20fo, King Stephen dictating to scribe (legal organization). 2fo, Sculptor at work (education). 4fo, Merchants before king (foreign relations). 6fo, View of castle and town of Székesfehérvár, 10th century. 10fo, King Andreas II presenting Golden Bull to noblemen.

1972, Aug. 20 *Photo. Perf. 12*
2156 A485 40f slate & multi .30 .25
2157 A485 60f multi .30 .25
2158 A485 80f lilac & multi .30 .25
2159 A485 1.20fo multi .30 .25
2160 A485 2fo bister & multi .40 .25
2161 A485 4fo blue & multi .55 .25
2162 A485 6fo purple & multi .75 .25
Nos. 2156-2162 (7) 2.90 1.75

Souvenir Sheet
Perf. 12½
2163 A485 10fo black & multi 2.00 2.00
Millennium of the town of Székesfehérvár; 750th anniv. of the Golden Bull granting rights to lesser nobility.
Different printings of Nos. 2157 and 2160 have the year date at the lower left and lower right.
No. 2163 contains one 94x45mm stamp.
Exist imperf. Value: set $15; souvenir sheet $15.

Parliament, Budapest — A486

Design: 6fo, Session room of Parliament.

1972, Aug. 20 *Litho.*
2164 A486 5fo dk blue & multi .60 .25
2165 A486 6fo multicolored .75 .25
Constitution of 1949.
Exist imperf. Value, set $11.

Eger, 17th Century View, and Bottle of Bull's Blood A487

Design: 2fo, Contemporary view of Tokay and bottle of Tokay Aszu.

1972, Aug. 21 *Litho. Perf. 12*
2166 A487 1fo buff & multi .30 .25
2167 A487 2fo green & multi .65 .25
1st World Wine Exhibition, Budapest, Aug. 1972.
Exist imperf. Value, set $5.

Georgikon Emblems, Grain, Potato Flower — A488

1972, Sept. 3
2168 A488 1fo multi .30 .25
175th anniv. of the founding of the Georgikon at Keszthely, the 1st scientific agricultural academy.
Exists imperf. Value $4.

Vase with Bird — A489

Herend Porcelain: 60f, Covered candy dish. 80f, Vase with flowers and butterflies. 1fo, Plate with Mexican landscape. 1.20fo, Covered dish. 2fo, Teapot, cup and saucer. 4fo, Plate with flowers. 5fo, Baroque vase showing Herend factory.

1972, Sept. 15
Sizes: 23x46mm (40f, 80f, 2fo, 5fo); 33x36mm, others
2169 A489 40f gray & multi .30 .25
2170 A489 60f ocher & multi .30 .25
2171 A489 80f multi .30 .25
2172 A489 1fo multi .30 .25
2173 A489 1.20fo green & multi .30 .25
2174 A489 2fo multi .30 .25
2175 A489 4fo red & multi .50 .30
2176 A489 5fo multi .70 .50
Nos. 2169-2176 (8) 3.00 2.30
Herend china factory, founded 1839.
Exist imperf. Value, set $15.

UIC Emblem and M-62 Diesel Locomotive A490

1972, Sept. 19 *Photo. Perf. 11½x12*
2177 A490 1fo dark red .30 .25
50th anniversary of International Railroad Union Congress, Budapest, Sept. 19.
Exist imperf. Value $15.

"25" and Graph — A491

1972, Sept. 26 *Perf. 11½x12*
2178 A491 1fo yellow & brown .30 .25
Planned national economy, 25th anniv.
Exist imperf. Value $5.

Budapest, 1972 — A492

No. 2179, View of Obuda, 1872. No. 2181, Buda, 1872. No. 2183, Pest, 1872. Nos. 2182, 2184, Budapest, 1972.

1972, Sept. 26 *Perf. 12x11½*
2179 A492 1fo Prus bl & rose car .30 .25
2180 A492 1fo rose car & Prus bl .30 .25
 a. Pair, #2179-2180 .40 .25
2181 A492 2fo ocher & olive .30 .25
2182 A492 2fo olive & ocher .30 .25
 a. Pair, #2181-2182 .40 .35
2183 A492 3fo green & lt brn .30 .25
2184 A492 3fo lt brown & grn .30 .25
 a. Pair, #2183-2184 .60 .50
Nos. 2179-2184 (6) 1.80 1.50
Centenary of unification of Obuda, Buda and Pest into Budapest.
Exist imperf. Value, set in pairs $20.

Ear and Congress Emblem — A493

1972, Oct. 3 *Perf. 11½x12*
2185 A493 1fo brown, yel & blk .30 .25
11th Intl. Audiology Cong., Budapest.
Exists imperf. Value $6.

Flora Martos — A494

Portrait: No. 2187, Miklós Radnóti.

1972 *Photo. Perf. 11½x12*
2186 A494 1fo green & multi .30 .25
2187 A494 1fo brown & multi .30 .25
Flora Martos (1897-1938), Hungarian labor leader, & Miklós Radnóti (1909-44), poet.
Exist imperf. Value, set $6.
Issued: No. 2186, Nov. 5; No. 2187, Nov. 11.

Muses, by Jozsef Rippl-Ronai A495

Stained-glass Windows, 19th-20th Centuries: 60f, 16th century scribe, by Ferenc Sebesteny. 1fo, Flight into Egypt, by Karoly Lotz and Bertalan Székely. 1.50fo, Prince Arpad's Messenger, by Jenő Percz. 2.50fo, Nativity, by Lili Sztehlo. 4fo, Prince Arpad and Leaders, by Karoly Kernstock. 5fo, King Matthias and Jester, by Jenő Haranghy.

1972, Nov. 15 *Perf. 12*
2188 A495 40f multi .30 .25
2189 A495 60f multi .30 .25
2190 A495 1fo multi .30 .25
2191 A495 1.50fo multi .30 .25
2192 A495 2.50fo multi .30 .25
2193 A495 4fo multi .50 .25
2194 A495 5fo multi .75 .25
Nos. 2188-2194 (7) 2.75 1.75
Exist imperf. Value, set $15.

Weaver, Cloth and Cogwheel A496

1972, Nov. 27 *Litho. Perf. 12*
2195 A496 1fo silver & multi .30 .25
Opening of Museum of Textile Techniques, Budapest.
Exists imperf. Value $6.

Main Square, Szarvas — A497

1fo, Modern buildings, Salgotarjan.

HUNGARY

1972, Dec. 16   **Litho.**   *Perf. 11*
2196	A497	40f brown & orange	.30	.25
2197	A497	1fo dk & lt blue	.30	.25

Exist imperf. Value, set $15.

Vineyard, Tokaj — A498

3fo, Tokaj and vineyard. 4fo, Esztergom Cathedral. 7fo, Town Hall, Kaposvar. 20fo, Veszprem.

1973   *Perf. 12x11½*
2198	A498	3fo dk & lt green	.30	.25
2199	A498	4fo red brn & org	.30	.25
2200	A498	7fo blue vio & lil	.50	.25
2200A	A498	20fo multicolored	2.00	.40
		Nos. 2196-2200A (6)	3.70	1.65

Exist imperf. Value, set $40.
See Nos. 2330-2335. Issued: No. 2198, 5/25; 2200, 5/29; 2199, 8/18; and 2200A, 11/30.

Type of 1963-64 Coil Stamps
Designs as before.

1972, Oct. 30   **Photo.**   *Perf. 14*
Size: 21½x17½mm, 17½x21½mm
2201	A336	2fo blue green	.30	.25
2202	A336	3fo dark blue	.30	.25
2203	A336	4fo blue, vert.	.40	.25
2204	A336	6fo bister	.60	.25
		Nos. 2201-2204 (4)	1.60	1.00

Black control number on back of every 5th stamp.
Minute inscription centered in lower margin: "Legrady Sandor."

Arms of Soviet Union — A498a

1972, Dec. 30   **Photo.**   *Perf. 11½x12*
2205	A498a	1fo multicolored	.30	.25

50th anniversary of Soviet Union.
Exists imperf. Value $9.

Petőfi Speaking at Pilvax Cafe — A499

2fo, Portrait. 3fo, Petőfi on horseback, 1848-49.

1972, Dec. 30   **Engr.**   *Perf. 12*
2206	A499	1fo rose carmine	.30	.25
2207	A499	2fo violet	.30	.25
2208	A499	3fo Prus green	.40	.25
		Nos. 2206-2208 (3)	1.00	.75

Sesquicentennial of the birth of Sandor Petőfi (1823-49), poet and revolutionary.
Exist imperf. Value, set $5.

Postal Zone Map of Hungary and Letter-carrying Crow — A500

1973, Jan. 2   **Litho.**   *Perf. 12*
2209	A500	1fo red & black	.30	.25

Introduction of postal code system.
Exists imperf. Value $6.

Imre Madách (1823-64), Poet and Dramatist — A501

1973, Jan. 20   **Photo.**   *Perf. 11½x12*
2210	A501	1fo multicolored	.30	.25

Exists imperf. Value $6.

Busho Mask — A502

Designs: Various Busho masks.

1973, Feb. 17   **Litho.**   *Perf. 12*
2211	A502	40f bistre brn & multi	.30	.25
2212	A502	60f turq grn & multi	.30	.25
2213	A502	80f lilac & multi	.30	.25
2214	A502	1.20fo ol grn & multi	.30	.25
2215	A502	2fo dl mauve & multi	.30	.25
2216	A502	4fo turq grn & multi	.50	.25
2217	A502	6fo lilac & multi	.75	.25
		Nos. 2211-2217 (7)	2.75	1.75

Busho Walk at Mohacs, ancient ceremony to drive out winter.
Exist imperf. Value, set $15.

Nicolaus Copernicus — A503

1973, Feb. 19   **Engr.**   *Perf. 12*
2218	A503	3fo bright ultra	.75	.50

Printed with alternating label showing heliocentric system and view of Torun.
Exists imperf. Value $15.

Vascular System and WHO Emblem — A504

1973, Apr. 16   **Photo.**   *Perf. 12*
2219	A504	1fo sl grn & brn red	.30	.25

25th anniv. of WHO.
Exists imperf. Value $5.

Tank, Rocket, Radar, Plane, Ship and Soldier — A505

1973, May 9   **Litho.**   *Perf. 12*
2220	A505	3fo blue & multi	.35	.25

Philatelic Exhibition of Military Stamp Collectors of Warsaw Treaty Member States. No. 2220 was printed with alternating label showing flags of Warsaw Treaty members.
Exists imperf. Value $7.50.

Hungary No. 1396 and IBRA '73 Emblem A506

No. 2222, No. 1397, POLSKA '73. No. 2223, No. 1398, IBRA '73. No. 2224, No. 1399, POLSKA. No. 2225, No. B293a, IBRA. No. 2226, No. B293b, POLSKA. No. 2227, No. B293c, IBRA. No. 2228, No. B293d, POLSKA.

1973, May 11   **Litho.**   *Perf. 12*
2221	A506	40f shown	.30	.25
2222	A506	60f multi	.30	.25
2223	A506	80f multi	.30	.25
2224	A506	1fo multi	.30	.25
2225	A506	1.20fo multi	.30	.25
2226	A506	2fo multi	.30	.25
2227	A506	4fo multi	.30	.25
2228	A506	5fo multi	.50	.30
		Nos. 2221-2228 (8)	2.60	2.05

Publicity for IBRA '73 International Philatelic Exhibition, Munich, May 11-20; and POLSKA '73, Poznan, Aug. 15-Sept. 2. See No. C345.
Exist imperf. Value, set $15.

Typesetting, from "Orbis Pictus," by Comenius — A507

3fo, Printer & wooden screw press, woodcut from Hungarian translation of Gospels.

1973, June 5   **Photo.**   *Perf. 11½x12*
2229	A507	1fo black & gold	.30	.25
2230	A507	3fo black & gold	.40	.25

500th anniv. of book printing in Hungary.
Exist imperf. Value $5.75.

Storm over Hortobagy Puszta, by Csontvary — A508

Paintings: 60f, Mary's Well, Nazareth. 1fo, Carriage Ride by Moonlight in Athens, vert. 1.50fo, Pilgrimage to Cedars of Lebanon, vert. 2.50fo, The Lonely Cedar. 4fo, Waterfall at Jajce. 5fo, Ruins of Greek Theater at Taormina. 10fo, Horseback Riders on Shore.

1973, June 18   *Perf. 12½*
2231	A508	40f gold & multi	.30	.25
2232	A508	60f gold & multi	.30	.25
2233	A508	1fo gold & multi	.30	.25
2234	A508	1.50fo gold & multi	.30	.25
2235	A508	2.50fo gold & multi	.30	.25
2236	A508	4fo gold & multi	.40	.25
2237	A508	5fo gold & multi	.50	1.00
		Nos. 2231-2237 (7)	2.40	2.50

Souvenir Sheet
2238	A508	10fo gold & multi	2.00	2.00

Paintings by Tivadar Kosztka Csontvary (1853-1919). No. 2238 contains one stamp (size: 90x43mm).
Exist imperf. Value: set $15; souvenir sheet $20.

Hands Holding Map of Europe — A509

1973, July 3   **Photo.**   *Perf. 11½x12*
2239	A509	2.50fo blk & gldn brn	1.25	1.25
a.		Sheetlet of 4 + 2 labels	4.00	6.00

Conference for European Security and Cooperation. Helsinki, July 1973. No. 2239 was printed in a sheetlet of 4 stamps and 2 blue labels showing conference sites.
Exists imperf. Value, sheetlet $60.

Flowers — A510

1973, Aug. 4
2240	A510	40f Provence roses	.30	.25
2241	A510	60f Cyclamen	.30	.25
2242	A510	80f Lungwort	.30	.25
2243	A510	1.20fo English daisies	.30	.25
2244	A510	2fo Buttercups	.30	.25
2245	A510	4fo Violets	.50	.25
2246	A510	6fo Poppies	.75	.25
		Nos. 2240-2246 (7)	2.75	1.75

Exist imperf. Value, set $20.

"Let's be Friends in Traffic" — A511

Designs: 60f, "Not even one drink." 1fo, "Light your bicycle."

1973, Aug. 18   **Photo.**   *Perf. 12x11½*
2247	A511	40f green & orange	.30	.25
2248	A511	60f purple & orange	.30	.25
2249	A511	1fo indigo & orange	.30	.25
		Nos. 2247-2249 (3)	.90	.75

To publicize traffic rules.
Exist imperf. Value $7.50.

Adoration of the Kings — A512

Paintings: 60f, Angels playing violin and lute. 1fo, Adoration of the Kings. 1.50fo, Annunciation. 2.50fo, Angels playing organ and harp. 4fo, Visitation of Mary. 5fo, Legend of St. Catherine of Alexandria. 10fo, Nativity.

1973, Nov. 3   **Photo.**   *Perf. 12½*
2250	A512	40f gold & multi	.30	.25
2251	A512	60f gold & multi	.30	.25
2252	A512	1fo gold & multi	.30	.25
2253	A512	1.50fo gold & multi	.30	.25
2254	A512	2.50fo gold & multi	.30	.25
2255	A512	4fo gold & multi	.35	.25
2256	A512	5fo gold & multi	.50	.25
		Nos. 2250-2256 (7)	2.35	1.75

Souvenir Sheet
Perf. 11
2257	A512	10fo gold & multi	2.00	2.00

Paintings by Hungarian anonymous early masters from the Christian Museum at Esztergom. No. 2257 contains one 49x74mm stamp.
Exist imperf. Value: set $15; souvenir sheet $20.

Mihaly Csokonai Vitez — A513

1973, Nov. 17   **Photo.**   *Perf. 11½x12*
2258	A513	2fo bister & multi	.35	.25

Mihaly Csokonai Vitez (1773-1805), poet.
Exists imperf. Value $4.

HUNGARY

José Marti and Cuban Flag — A514

1973, Nov. 30
2259 A514 1fo dk brn, red & bl .30 .25

Marti (1853-95), Cuban natl. hero and poet.
Exists imperf. Value $3.

Barnabas Pesti (1920-44), Member of Hungarian Underground Communist Party — A515

1973, Nov. 30
2260 A515 1fo blue, brn & buff .30 .25

Exists imperf. Value $3.

Women's Double Kayak A516

Designs: 60f, Water polo. 80f, Men's single kayak. 1.20fo, Butterfly stroke. 2fo, Men's fours kayak. 4fo, Men's single canoe. 6fo, Men's double canoe.

1973, Dec. 29 Litho. Perf. 12x11
2261 A516 40f red & multi .30 .25
2262 A516 60f blue & multi .30 .25
2263 A516 80f multicolored .30 .25
2264 A516 1.20fo green & multi .30 .25
2265 A516 2fo car & multi .30 .25
2266 A516 4fo violet & multi .30 .25
2267 A516 6fo multicolored .50 .25
Nos. 2261-2267 (7) 2.30 1.75

Hungarian victories in water sports at Tampere and Belgrade.
Exist imperf. Value, set $14.00.

Souvenir Sheet

Map of Europe — A517

1974, Jan. 15 Photo. Perf. 12x11½
2268 A517 Sheet of 2 + label 3.00 3.00
  a. 5fo multicolored .80 .80

European Peace Conference (Arab-Israeli War), Geneva, Jan. 1974.
Exists imperf. Value $75.

Lenin A518

1974, Jan. 21 Photo. Perf. 11½x12
2269 A518 2fo gold, dull bl & brn .40 .25

50th anniv. of the death of Lenin (1870-1924).
Exists imperf. Value $3.

Jozsef Boczor, Imre Békés, Tamás Elek — A519

1974, Feb. 21 Perf. 12½
2270 A519 3fo brown & multi .40 .25

30th anniversary of the death in France of Hungarian resistance fighters.
Exists imperf. Value $5.

Comecon Building, Moscow and Flags — A520

1974, Feb. 26 Photo. Perf. 12x11½
2271 A520 1fo multicolored .30 .25

25th anniversary of the Council of Mutual Economic Assistance.
Exists imperf. Value $6.

Bank Emblem, Coins and Banknote — A521

1974, Mar. 1 Perf. 11½x12
2272 A521 1fo lt green & multi .30 .25

25th anniversary of the State Savings Bank.
Exists imperf. Value $3.50.

Spacecraft on Way to Mars A522

Designs: 60f, Mars 2 over Mars. 80f, Mariner 4. 1fo, Mars and Mt. Palomar Observatory. 1.20fo, Soft landing of Mars 3. 5fo, Mariner 9 with Mars satellites Phobos and Deimos.

1974, Mar. 11 Photo. Perf. 12½
2273 A522 40f gold & multi .30 .25
2274 A522 60f silver & multi .30 .25
2275 A522 80f gold & multi .30 .25
2276 A522 1fo silver & multi .30 .25
2277 A522 1.20fo gold & multi .30 .25
2278 A522 5fo silver & multi .75 .25
Nos. 2273-2278,C347 (7) 3.00 1.75

Exploration of Mars. See No. C348.
Exist imperf. Value, set (7) $22.50.

Salvador Allende (1908-73), Pres. of Chile — A523

1974, Mar. 27 Photo. Perf. 11½x12
2279 A523 1fo black & multi .40 .25

Exists imperf. Value $3.

Mona Lisa, by Leonardo da Vinci — A524

1974, Apr. 19 Perf. 12½
2280 A524 4fo gold & multi 4.75 4.50

Exists imperf. Value $20. Exhibition of the Mona Lisa in Asia.
Printed in sheets of 6 stamps and 6 labels with commemorative inscription. Value, $45.
Exist imperf. Value: single with labels $20; sheetlet $135.

Souvenir Sheet

Issue of 1874 and Flowers — A525

a, Mallow. b, Aster. c, Daisy. d, Columbine.

1974, May 11 Litho. Perf. 11½
2281 A525 Sheet of 4 1.50 1.50
  a.-d. 2.50fo any single .30 .30

Centenary of the first issue inscribed "Magyar Posta" (Hungarian Post).
Exists imperf. Value, sheet of 4 $20.

Carrier Pigeon, World Map, UPU Emblem — A526

1974, May 22 Litho. Perf. 12
2282 A526 40f shown .30 .25
2283 A526 60f Mail coach .30 .25
2284 A526 80f Old mail automobile .30 .25
2285 A526 1.20fo Balloon post .35 .25
2286 A526 2fo Mail train .40 .25
2287 A526 5fo Mail bus .50 .25
Nos. 2282-2287,C349 (7) 2.90 1.75

Centenary of the Universal Postal Union.
Exist imperf. Value, set $20.

Dove of Basel, Switzerland No. 3L1, 1845 A527

1974, June 7 Photo. Perf. 11½x12
2288 A527 3fo gold & multi .75 .75

INTERNABA 1974 Philatelic Exhibition, Basel, June 7-16. No. 2288 issued in sheets of 3 stamps and 3 labels showing Internaba 1974 emblem. Size: 104x125mm.
Exist imperf. Values: single $6; sheet $19.

Chess Players, from 13th Century Manuscript — A528

Designs: 60f, Chess players, 15th century English woodcut. 80f, Royal chess party, 15th century Italian chess book. 1.20fo, Chess players, 17th century copper engraving by Selenus. 2fo, Farkas Kempelen's chess playing machine, 1769. 4fo, Hungarian Grand Master Geza Maroczy (1870-1951). 6fo, View of Nice and emblem of 1974 Chess Olympiad.

1974, June 6 Litho. Perf. 12
2289 A528 40f multi .30 .25
2290 A528 60f multi .30 .25
2291 A528 80f multi .30 .25
2292 A528 1.20fo multi .30 .25
2293 A528 2fo multi .60 .25
2294 A528 4fo multi .75 .30
2295 A528 6fo multi .85 .50
Nos. 2289-2295 (7) 3.40 2.05

50th anniv. of Intl. Chess Federation and 21st Chess Olympiad, Nice, June 6-30.
Exist imperf. Value, set $80.

Souvenir Sheet

Cogwheel Railroad — A529

Designs: a, Passenger train, 1874. b, Freight train, 1874. c, Electric train, 1929-73. d, Twin motor train, 1973.

1974, June 25 Litho. Perf. 12
2296 A529 Sheet of 4 3.00 3.00
  a.-d. 2.50fo, any single .40 .40

Cent. of Budapest's cogwheel railroad.
Exist imperf. Value, sheet $30.

Congress Emblem (Globe and Parliament) A530

1974, Aug. 18 Photo. Perf. 12
2297 A530 2fo silver, dk & lt bl .40 .25

4th World Congress of Economists, Budapest, Aug. 19-24.
Exists imperf. Value $4.

Bathing Woman, by Károly Lotz — A531

Paintings of Nudes: 60f, Awakening, by Károly Brocky. 1fo, Venus and Cupid, by Brocky, horiz. 1.50fo, After the Bath, by Lotz. 2.50fo, Resting Woman, by Istvan Csok, horiz. 4fo, After the Bath, by Bertalan Szekely. 5fo, "Devotion," by Erzsebet Korb. 10fo, Lark, by Pál Szinyei Merse.

1974, Aug. Perf. 12½
2298 A531 40f gold & multi .30 .25
2299 A531 60f gold & multi .30 .25
2300 A531 1fo gold & multi .30 .25
2301 A531 1.50fo gold & multi .30 .25
2302 A531 2.50fo gold & multi .50 .25
2303 A531 4fo gold & multi .60 .25
2304 A531 5fo gold & multi .75 .30
Nos. 2298-2304 (7) 3.05 1.80

Souvenir Sheet
Perf. 11
2305 A531 10fo gold & multi 2.50 2.50

No. 2305 contains one stamp (45x70mm).
Exist imperf. Value: set $15; souvenir sheet $20.

HUNGARY

Mimi, by Béla Czóbel — A532

1974, Sept. 4
2306 A532 1fo multicolored .50 .25
91st birthday of Béla Czóbel, Hungarian painter.
Exists imperf. Value $3.25.

Intersputnik Tracking Station A533

High Voltage Line "Peace" and Pipe Line "Friendship" A534

Perf. 11½x12, 12x11½
1974, Sept. 5 Litho.
2307 A533 1fo blue & violet .30 .25
2308 A534 3fo multicolored .60 .25
Technical assistance and cooperation between Hungary and USSR, 25th anniv.
Exist imperf. Value, set $6.

Pablo Neruda — A535

1974, Sept. 11 Photo. *Perf. 11½x12*
2309 A535 1fo multicolored .40 .25
Pablo Neruda (Neftali Ricar do Reyes, 1904-1973), Chilean poet.
Exists imperf. Value $3.

Sweden No. 1 and Lion from Royal Palace, Stockholm — A536

1974, Sept. 21 *Perf. 12x11½*
2310 A536 3fo ultra, yel grn & gold .85 .85
Stockholmia 74 Intl. Philatelic Exhibition, Stockholm, Sept. 21-29. No. 2310 issued in sheets of 3 stamps and 3 labels showing Stockholmia emblem. White margin inscribed "UPU" multiple in white. Size: 126x104mm. Value $6.50.
Exists imperf. Value: single $7.50; sheetlet $22.50.

Tank Battle and Soldier with Anti-tank Grenade A537

1974, Sept. 28 Litho. *Perf. 12*
2311 A537 1fo gold, orange & blk .30 .25
Nos. 2311,C351-C352 (3) .95 .75
Army Day.
Exist imperf. Value, set (3) $9.50.

Segner and Segner Crater on Moon — A538

1974, Oct. 5
2312 A538 3fo multicolored .75 .35
270th anniversary of the birth of Janos Andras Segner, naturalist. No. 2312 printed se-tenant with label arranged checkerwise in sheet. Label shows Segner wheel.
Exists imperf. Value, with label $6.75.

Rhyparia Purpurata A539

Lepidoptera: 60f, Melanargia galathea. 80f, Parnassius Apollo. 1fo, Celerio euphorbia. 1.20fo, Catocala fraxini. 5fo, Apatura iris. 6fo, Palaeochrysophanus hyppothoe.

1974, Nov. 11 Photo. *Perf. 12½*
2313 A539 40f multicolored .30 .25
2314 A539 60f violet & multi .30 .25
2315 A539 80f multicolored .30 .25
2316 A539 1fo brown & multi .30 .25
2317 A539 1.20fo blue & multi .30 .25
2318 A539 5fo purple & multi .75 .30
2319 A539 6fo multicolored 1.00 .40
Nos. 2313-2319 (7) 3.25 1.95
Exist imperf. Value, set $30.

Motherhood — A540

1974, Dec. 24 Litho. *Perf. 12*
2320 A540 1fo lt blue, blk & yel brn .30 .25
Exists imperf. Value $3.50.

Robert Kreutz — A541

1974, Dec. 24
2321 A541 1fo shown .30 .25
2322 A541 1fo István Pataki .30 .25
30th death anniv. of anti-fascist martyrs Kreutz (1923-44) and Pataki (1914-44).
Exist imperf. Value, set $5.

Puppy — A542

Young Animals: 60f, Siamese kittens, horiz. 80f, Rabbit. 1.20fo, Foal, horiz. 2fo, Lamb. 4fo, Calf, horiz. 6fo, Piglet.

1974, Dec. 30
2323 A542 40f lt blue & multi .30 .25
2324 A542 60f multicolored .30 .25
2325 A542 80f olive & multi .30 .25
2326 A542 1.20fo green & multi .30 .25
2327 A542 2fo brown & multi .30 .25
2328 A542 4fo orange & multi .50 .25
2329 A542 6fo violet & multi .60 .50
Nos. 2323-2329 (7) 2.60 2.00
Exist imperf. Value, set $25.
See Nos. 2403-2409.

Building Type of 1972
4fo, Szentendre. 5fo, View of Szolnok across Tisza River. 6fo, Skyscraper, Dunaújváros. 8fo, Church and city hall, Vac. 10fo, City Hall, Kiskunfélegyháza. 50fo, Church (Turkish Mosque), Hunyadi Statue & TV tower, Pecs.

1974-80 Litho. *Perf. 12x11½*
2330 A498 4fo red brn & pink .30 .25
2331 A498 5fo dk blue & ultra .30 .25
2332 A498 6fo dk brn & org .75 .25
2333 A498 8fo dk & brt grn .50 .25
2334 A498 10fo brown & yel .50 .25
2335 A498 50fo multi 4.00 1.00
Nos. 2330-2335 (6) 6.35 2.25
Exist imperf. Value, set $30.
Issued: 8fo, 12/7; 10fo, 50fo, 12/30; 5fo, 3/8/75; 6fo, 6/10/75; 4fo, 6/20/80.

Hospital, Lambarene — A544

60f, Dr. Schweitzer, patient & microscope. 80f, Patient arriving by boat. 1.20fo, Hospital supplies arriving by ship. 2fo, Globe, Red Cross, carrier pigeons. 4fo, Nobel Peace Prize medal. 6fo, Portrait & signature of Dr. Schweitzer, organ pipes & "J. S. Bach."

1975, Jan. 14 Photo. *Perf. 12*
2340 A544 40f gold & multi .30 .25
2341 A544 60f gold & multi .30 .25
2342 A544 80f gold & multi .30 .25
2343 A544 1.20fo gold & multi .30 .25
2344 A544 2fo gold & multi .30 .25
2345 A544 4fo gold & multi .50 .25
2346 A544 6fo lil & multi .75 .25
Nos. 2340-2346 (7) 2.60 1.75
Dr. Albert Schweitzer (1875-1965), medical missionary and musician, birth centenary.
Exist imperf. Value, set $15.

Farkas Bolyai — A545

1975, Feb. 7 Litho. *Perf. 11½x12*
2347 A545 1fo gray & red brown .30 .25
Bolyai (1775-1856), mathematician.
Exists imperf. Value $4.50.

Mihály Károlyi — A546

1975, Mar. 4 Litho. *Perf. 12*
2348 A546 1fo lt blue & brown .30 .25
Birth centenary of Count Mihály Károlyi (1875-1955), prime minister, 1918-1919.
Exists imperf. Value $4.

Woman, IWY Emblem — A547

1975, Mar. 8 *Perf. 12x11½*
2349 A547 1fo aqua & black .30 .25
International Women's Year 1975.
Exists imperf. Value $4.

"Let us Build up the Railroads" — A548

Posters: 60f, "Bread starts here." 2fo, "Hungarian Communist Party-a Party of Action." 4fo, "Heavy Industry-secure base of Three-year Plan." 5fo, "Our common interest-a developed socialist society."

1975, Mar. 17 Photo. *Perf. 11*
2350 A548 40f red & multi .30 .25
2351 A548 60f red & multi .30 .25
2352 A548 2fo red & multi .30 .25
2353 A548 4fo red & multi .40 .25
2354 A548 5fo red & multi .50 .25
Nos. 2350-2354 (5) 1.80 1.25
Hungary's liberation from Fascism, 30th anniv.
Exist imperf. Value, set $15.

Arrow, 1915, Pagoda and Mt. Fuji — A549

Antique Cars: 60f, Swift, 1911. Big Ben and Tower of London. 80f, Model T Ford, 1908, Capitol and Statue of Liberty. 1fo, Mercedes, 1901, Towers of Stuttgart. 1.20fo, Panhard Levassor, 1912, Arc de Triomphe and Eiffel Tower. 5fo, Csonka, 1906, Fishermen's Bastion and Chain Bridge. 6fo, Emblems of Hungarian Automobile Club, Alliance Internationale de Tourisme and Federation Internationale de l'Automobile.

1975, Mar. 27 Litho. *Perf. 12*
2355 A549 40f lt blue & multi .30 .25
2356 A549 60f lt green & multi .30 .25
2357 A549 80f pink & multi .30 .25
2358 A549 1fo lilac & multi .30 .25
2359 A549 1.20fo orange & multi .30 .25
2360 A549 5fo ultra & multi .65 .25
2361 A549 6fo lilac rose & multi 1.00 .40
Nos. 2355-2361 (7) 3.15 1.90
Hungarian Automobile Club, 75th anniv.
Exist imperf. Value, set $13.50.

The Creation of Adam, by Michelangelo — A550

1975, Apr. 23 Photo. *Perf. 12½*
2362 A550 10fo gold & multi 3.00 3.00
Michelangelo Buonarroti (1475-1564), Italian painter, sculptor and architect.
Exists imperf. Value $22.50.

Academy of Science — A551

Designs: 2fo, Dates "1975 1825." 3fo, Count Istvan Szechenyi.

1975, May 5 Litho. *Perf. 12*
2363 A551 1fo green & multi .30 .25
2364 A551 2fo green & multi .30 .25
2365 A551 3fo green & multi .50 .30
Nos. 2363-2365 (3) 1.10 .80
Sesquicentennial of Academy of Science, Budapest, founded by Count Istvan Szechenyi.
Exists imperf. Value, set $9.50.

HUNGARY

Emblem of 1980 Olympics and Proposed Moscow Stadium — A553

1975, May 8   Photo.   Perf. 11½x12
2366 A553 5fo lt blue & multi   1.00 1.00
Socfilex 75 Intl. Philatelic Exhibition, Moscow, 5/8-18. No. 2366 issued in sheets of 3 stamps and 3 labels showing Socfilex 75 emblem (War Memorial, Berlin-Treptow).
Exists imperf. Value: single with label $6.50; sheetlet $22.50.

France No. 1100 and Venus of Milo — A554

1975, June 3   Photo.   Perf. 11½x12
2367 A554 5fo lilac & multi   1.00 1.00
ARPHILA 75 International Philatelic Exhibition, Paris, June 6-16. No. 2367 issued in sheets of 3 stamps and 3 labels showing ARPHILA 75 emblem.
Exists imperf. Value: single with label $7; sheetlet $22.50.

Early Transformer, Kando Locomotive, 1902, Pylon — A555

1975, June 10   Litho.   Perf. 12
2368 A555 1fo multicolored   .40 .25
Hungarian Electrotechnical Association, 75th anniversary.
Exists imperf. Value $9.50.

Epée, Saber, Foil and Globe — A556

1975, July 11
2369 A556 1fo multicolored   .40 .25
32nd World Fencing Championships, Budapest, July 11-20.
Exists imperf. Value $5.50.

Souvenir Sheet

Whale Pavilion, Oceanexpo 75 — A557

1975, July 21   Photo.   Perf. 12½
2370 A557 10fo gold & multi   2.00 2.00
Oceanexpo 75, International Exhibition, Okinawa, July 20, 1975-Jan. 1976.
Exists imperf. Value $30.

Dr. Agoston Zimmermann (1875-1963), Veterinarian — A558

1975, Sept. 4   Litho.   Perf. 12
2371 A558 1fo brown & blue   .30 .25
Exists imperf. Value $5.00.

Symbolic of 14 Cognate Languages — A559

1975, Sept. 9
2372 A559 1fo gold & multi   .30 .25
International Finno-Ugrian Congress.
Exists imperf. Value $6.

Voters — A560

Design: No. 2374, Map of Hungary with electoral districts.

1975, Oct. 1
2373 A560 1fo multicolored   .30 .25
2374 A560 1fo multicolored   .30 .25
Hungarian Council System, 25th anniv.
Exist imperf. Value, set $5.

Fish and Waves (Ocean Pollution) — A561

Designs: 60f, Skeleton hand reaching for rose in water glass. 80f, Fish gasping for raindrop. 1fo, Carnation wilting in polluted soil. 1.20fo, Bird dying in polluted air. 5fo, Sick human lung and smokestack. 6fo, "Stop Pollution" (raised hand protecting globe from skeleton hand).

1975, Oct. 16   Litho.   Perf. 11½
2375 A561 40f multi   .30 .25
2376 A561 60f multi   .30 .25
2377 A561 80f multi   .30 .25
2378 A561 1fo multi   .30 .25
2379 A561 1.20fo multi   .30 .25
2380 A561 5fo multi   .50 .25
2381 A561 6fo multi   .65 .25
     Nos. 2375-2381 (7)   2.65 1.75
Environmental Protection.
Exist imperf. Value, set $15.

Mariska Gárdos (1885-1973) — A562

Portraits: No. 2383, Imre Mező (1905-56). No. 2384, Imre Tarr (1900-37).

1975, Nov. 4   Litho.   Perf. 12
2382 A562 1fo black & red org   .30 .25
2383 A562 1fo black & red org   .30 .25
2384 A562 1fo black & red org   .30 .25
     Nos. 2382-2384 (3)   .90 .75
Famous Hungarians, birth anniversaries.

Exist imperf. Value, set $8.50.

Treble Clef, Organ and Orchestra — A563

1975, Nov. 14
2385 A563 1fo multicolored   .30 .25
Franz Liszt Musical Academy, centenary.
Exists imperf. Value $8.

Szigetcsep Icon — A564

Virgin and Child, 18th Century Icons: 60f, Graboc. 1fo, Esztergom. 1.50fo, Vatoped. 2.50fo, Tottos. 4fo, Gyor. 5fo, Kazan.

1975, Nov. 25   Photo.   Perf. 12½
2386 A564 40f gold & multi   .30 .25
2387 A564 60f gold & multi   .30 .25
2388 A564 1fo gold & multi   .30 .25
2389 A564 1.50fo gold & multi   .30 .25
2390 A564 2.50fo gold & multi   .35 .25
2391 A564 4fo gold & multi   .65 .25
2392 A564 5fo gold & multi   .65 .35
     Nos. 2386-2392 (7)   2.85 1.85
Exist imperf. Value, set $13.50.

Members' Flags, Radar, Mother and Child — A565

1975, Dec. 15   Litho.   Perf. 12
2393 A565 1fo multicolored   .30 .25
20th anniversary of the signing of the Warsaw Treaty (Bulgaria, Czechoslovakia, German Democratic Rep., Hungary, Poland, Romania, USSR).
Exists imperf. Value $4.50.

Ice Hockey, Winter Olympics' Emblem — A566

Designs (Emblem and): 60f, Slalom. 80f, Ski race. 1.20fo, Ski jump. 2fo, Speed skating. 4fo, Cross-country skiing. 6fo, Bobsled. 10fo, Figure skating, pair.

1975, Dec. 29   Photo.   Perf. 12x11½
2394 A566 40f silver & multi   .30 .25
2395 A566 60f silver & multi   .30 .25
2396 A566 80f silver & multi   .30 .25
2397 A566 1.20fo silver & multi   .30 .25
2398 A566 2fo silver & multi   .30 .25
2399 A566 4fo silver & multi   .50 .25
2400 A566 6fo silver & multi   .70 .25
     Nos. 2394-2400 (7)   2.70 1.75

Souvenir Sheet
Perf. 12½
2401 A566 10fo silver & multi   2.00 2.00
12th Winter Olympic Games, Innsbruck, Austria, Feb. 4-15, 1976. No. 2401 contains one stamp (59x36mm).
Exist imperf. Value: set $22.50; souvenir sheet $20.

"P," 5-pengö and 500-pengö Notes — A567

1976, Jan. 16   Litho.   Perf. 12
2402 A567 1fo multicolored   .30 .25
Hungarian Bank Note Co., 50th anniversary.
Exists imperf. Value $7.50.

Animal Type of 1974
Young Animals: 40f, Wild boars, horiz. 60f, Squirrels. 80f, Lynx, horiz. 1.20fo, Wolves. 2fo, Foxes, horiz. 4fo, Bears. 6fo, Lions, horiz.

1976, Jan. 26
2403 A542 40f multi   .30 .25
2404 A542 60f blue & multi   .30 .25
2405 A542 80f multi   .30 .25
2406 A542 1.20fo multi   .30 .25
2407 A542 2fo violet & multi   .30 .25
2408 A542 4fo yellow & multi   .50 .25
2409 A542 6fo multi   .70 .25
     Nos. 2403-2409 (7)   2.70 1.75
Exist imperf. Value, set $25.

A.G. Bell, Telephone, Molniya I and Radar — A568

1976, Mar. 10   Litho.   Perf. 11½x12
2410 A568 3fo multicolored   .60 .60
Centenary of first telephone call by Alexander Graham Bell, Mar. 10, 1876. Issued in sheets of 4.
Exists imperf. Value: single $4; sheetlet $15.

Battle of Kuruc-Labantz — A569

Paintings: 60f, Meeting of Rakoczi and Tamas Esze, by Endre Veszpremi. 1fo, Diet of Onod, by Mor Than. 2fo, Camp of the Kurucs. 3fo, Ilona Zrinyi (Rakoczi's mother), vert. 4fo, Kuruc officers, vert. 5fo, Prince Francis II Rakoczy, by Adam Manyoki, vert. Painters of 40f, 2fo, 3fo, 4fo, are unknown.

1976, Mar. 27   Photo.   Perf. 12½
2411 A569 40f gold & multi   .30 .25
2412 A569 60f gold & multi   .30 .25
2413 A569 1fo gold & multi   .30 .25
2414 A569 2fo gold & multi   .50 .25
2415 A569 3fo gold & multi   1.00 .25
2416 A569 4fo gold & multi   1.25 .25
2417 A569 5fo gold & multi   1.50 .40
     Nos. 2411-2417 (7)   5.15 1.90
Francis II Rakoczy (1676-1735), leader of Hungarian Protestant insurrection, 300th birth anniversary.
Exist imperf. Value, set $15.

Standard Meter, Hungarian Meter Act — A570

2fo, Istvan Krusper, his vacuum balance, standard kilogram. 3fo, Interferometer & rocket.

HUNGARY

1976, Apr. 5   **Perf. 11½x12**
2418	A570	1fo multicolored	.30	.25
2419	A570	2fo multicolored	.30	.25
2420	A570	3fo multicolored	.50	.25
		Nos. 2418-2420 (3)	1.10	.75

Introduction of metric system in Hungary, cent.
Exist imperf. Value, set $11.

US No. 1353 and Independence Hall, Philadelphia — A571

Photogravure and Foil Embossed
1976, May 29   **Perf. 11½x12**
| 2421 | A571 | 5fo blue & multi | 1.00 | 1.00 |

Interphil 76 International Philatelic Exhibition, Philadelphia, Pa., May 29-June 6. No. 2421 issued in sheets of 3 stamps and 3 labels showing bells. Size: 115x125mm.
Exists imperf. Value: single with label $5.50; sheetlet $25.

"30" and Various Pioneer Activities A572

1976, June 5   **Litho.**   **Perf. 12**
| 2422 | A570 | 1fo multicolored | .40 | .25 |

Hungarian Pioneers, 30th anniversary.
Exists imperf. Value $12.50.

Trucks, Safety Devices, Trade Union Emblem A573

1976, June   **Perf. 12½**
| 2423 | A573 | 1fo multicolored | .30 | .25 |

Labor safety.
Exists imperf. Value $3.

Intelstat 4, Montreal Olympic Emblem, Canadian Flag — A574

Designs: 60f, Equestrian. 1fo, Butterfly stroke. 2fo, One-man kayak. 3fo, Fencing. 4fo, Javelin. 5fo, Athlete on vaulting horse.

1976, June 29 Photo.   **Perf. 11½x12**
2424	A574	40f dk blue & multi	.30	.25
2425	A574	60f slate grn & multi	.30	.25
2426	A574	1fo blue & multi	.30	.25
2427	A574	2fo green & multi	.30	.25
2428	A574	3fo brown & multi	.30	.25
2429	A574	4fo bister & multi	.30	.25
2430	A574	5fo maroon & multi	.50	.25
		Nos. 2424-2430 (7)	2.30	1.75

21st Olympic Games, Montreal, Canada, July 17-Aug. 1. See No. C365.
Exist imperf. Value, set $14.

Denmark No. 2 and Mermaid, Copenhagen — A575

1976, Aug. 19 Photo.   **Perf. 11½x12**
| 2431 | A575 | 3fo multicolored | .85 | .85 |

HAFNIA 76 Intl. Phil. Exhib., Copenhagen, Aug. 20-29. No. 2431 issued in sheets of 3 stamps and 3 labels showing HAFNIA emblem.
Exists imperf. Value: single with label $6; sheetlet $17.50.

Souvenir Sheet

Discovery of Body of Lajos II, by Bertalan Székely — A576

1976, Aug. 27   **Photo.**   **Perf. 12½**
| 2432 | A576 | 20fo multicolored | 2.00 | 2.00 |

450th anniversary of the Battle of Mohacs against the Turks.
Exists imperf. Value $20.

Flora, by Titian — A577

1976, Aug. 27
| 2433 | A577 | 4fo gold & multi | .60 | .25 |

Titian (1477-1576), Venetian painter.
Exists imperf. Value $12.50.

Hussar, Herend China — A578

1976, Sept. 28   **Litho.**   **Perf. 12**
| 2434 | A578 | 4fo multicolored | .60 | .25 |

Herend China manufacture, sesqui.
Exists imperf. Value $5.

Daniel Berzsenyi (1776-1836), Poet — A579

1976, Sept. 28
| 2435 | A579 | 2fo black, gold & yel | .30 | .25 |

Exists imperf. Value $2.

Pal Gyulai (1826-1909), Poet and Historian — A580

1976, Sept. 28
| 2436 | A580 | 2fo orange & black | .30 | .25 |

Exists imperf. Value $4.

Tuscany No. 1 and Emblem A581

1976, Oct. 13   **Photo.**   **Perf. 11½x12**
| 2437 | A581 | 5fo orange & multi | 1.75 | 1.75 |

ITALIA 76 International Philatelic Exhibition, Milan, Oct. 14-24. No. 2437 issued in sheets of 3 stamps and 3 labels showing Italia 76 emblem. Size: 106x127mm.
Exists imperf. Value: single with label $8; sheetlet $25.

Jozsef Madzsar, M.D. — A582

Labor leaders: No. 2439, Ignac Bogar (1876-1933), secretary of printers' union. No. 2440, Rudolf Golub (1901-44), miner.

1976, Nov. 4   **Litho.**   **Perf. 12**
2438	A582	1fo deep brown & red	.30	.25
2439	A582	1fo deep brown & red	.30	.25
2440	A582	1fo deep brown & red	.30	.25
		Nos. 2438-2440 (3)	.90	.75

Exist imperf. Value, set $9.

Science and Culture House, Georgian Dancer, Hungarian and USSR Flags — A583

1976, Nov. 4   **Perf. 12½x12**
| 2441 | A583 | 1fo multicolored | .30 | .25 |

House of Soviet Science and Culture, Budapest, 2nd anniversary.
Exists imperf. Value $6.

Koranyi Sanitarium and Statue — A584

1976, Nov. 11   **Perf. 12**
| 2442 | A584 | 2fo multicolored | .35 | .25 |

Koranyi TB Sanitarium, founded by Dr. Frigyes Koranyi, 75th anniversary.
Exists imperf. Value $2.50.

Locomotive, 1875, Enese Station — A585

Designs: 60f, Steam engine No. 17, 1885, Rabatamasi Station. 1fo, Railbus, 1925, Fertoszentmiklos Station. 2fo, Express steam engine, Kapuvar Station. 3fo, Engine and trailer, 1926, Gyor Station. 4fo, Eight-wheel express engine, 1934, and Fertoboz Station. 5fo, Raba-Balaton engine, Sopron Station.

1976, Nov. 26   **Litho.**   **Perf. 12**
2443	A585	40f multicolored	.30	.25
2444	A585	60f multicolored	.30	.25
2445	A585	1fo multicolored	.30	.25
2446	A585	2fo multicolored	.30	.25
2447	A585	3fo multicolored	.50	.25
2448	A585	4fo multicolored	.70	.25
2449	A585	5fo multicolored	.90	.25
		Nos. 2443-2449 (7)	3.30	1.75

Gyor-Sopron Railroad, centenary.
Exist imperf. Value, set $25.

Poplar, Oak, Pine and Map of Hungary — A586

1976, Dec. 14
| 2450 | A586 | 1fo multicolored | .30 | .25 |

Millionth hectare of reforestation.
Exists imperf. Value $10.

Weight Lifting and Wrestling, Silver Medals A587

60f, Kayak, men's single & women's double. 1fo, Horse vaulting. 4fo, Women's fencing. 6fo, Javelin. 20fo, Water polo.

1976, Dec. 14   **Photo.**   **Perf. 11½x12**
2451	A587	40f multicolored	.30	.25
2452	A587	60f multicolored	.30	.25
2453	A587	1fo multicolored	.30	.25
2454	A587	4fo multicolored	.50	.25
2455	A587	6fo multicolored	.90	.40
		Nos. 2451-2455 (5)	2.30	1.40

Souvenir Sheet
Perf. 12½x11½
| 2456 | A587 | 20fo multicolored | 2.00 | 2.00 |

Hungarian medalists in 21st Olympic Games.
Exist imperf. Value: set $20; souvenir sheet $20.

Spoonbills A588

Birds: 60f, White storks. 1fo, Purple herons. 2fo, Great bustard. 3fo, Common cranes. 4fo, White wagtails. 5fo, Garganey teals.

1977, Jan. 3   **Litho.**   **Perf. 12**
2457	A588	40f multicolored	.30	.25
2458	A588	60f multicolored	.30	.25
2459	A588	1fo multicolored	.30	.25
2460	A588	2fo multicolored	.30	.25
2461	A588	3fo multicolored	.45	.25
2462	A588	4fo multicolored	.90	.25
2463	A588	5fo multicolored	1.10	.40
		Nos. 2457-2463 (7)	3.65	1.90

Birds from Hortobagy National Park.
Exist imperf. Value, set $20.

1976 World Champion Imre Abonyi Driving Four-in-hand A589

Designs: 60f, Omnibus on Boulevard, 1870. 1fo, One-horse cab at Budapest Railroad Station, 1890. 2fo, Mail coach, Buda to Vienna route. 3fo, Covered wagon of Hajduszoboszlo. 4fo, Hungarian coach, by Jeremias Schemel, 1563. 5fo, Post chaise, from a Lübeck wood panel, 1430.

1977, Jan. 31   **Litho.**   **Perf. 12x11½**
2464	A589	40f multicolored	.30	.25
2465	A589	60f multicolored	.30	.25
2466	A589	1fo multicolored	.30	.25

HUNGARY

2467	A589	2fo multicolored	.30	.25
2468	A589	3fo multicolored	.30	.25
2469	A589	4fo multicolored	.50	.25
2470	A589	5fo multicolored	.70	.25

Nos. 2464-2470 (7)   2.70   1.75

History of the coach.
Exist imperf. Value, set $20.

Peacock — A590

Birds: 60f, Green peacock. 1fo, Congo peacock. 3fo, Argus pheasant. 4fo, Impeyan pheasant. 6fo, Peacock pheasant.

1977, Feb. 22   Litho.   Perf. 12

2471	A590	40f multicolored	.30	.25
2472	A590	60f multicolored	.30	.25
2473	A590	1fo multicolored	.30	.25
2474	A590	3fo multicolored	.40	.25
2475	A590	4fo multicolored	.60	.25
2476	A590	6fo multicolored	.90	.25

Nos. 2471-2476 (6)   2.80   1.50

Exist imperf. Value, set $20.

Newspaper Front Page, Factories — A591

1977, Mar. 3   Litho.   Perf. 12

2477   A591   1fo gold, black & ver   .30   .25

Nepszava newspaper, centenary.
Exists imperf. Value $5.

Flowers, by Mihaly Munkacsy A592

Flowers, by Hungarian Painters: 60f, Jakab Bogdany. 1fo, Istvan Csok, horiz. 2fo, Janos Halapy. 3fo, Jozsef Rippl-Ronai, horiz. 4fo, Janos Tornyai. 5fo, Jozsef Koszta.

1977, Mar. 18   Photo.   Perf. 12½

2478	A592	40f gold & multi	.30	.25
2479	A592	60f gold & multi	.30	.25
2480	A592	1fo gold & multi	.30	.25
2481	A592	2fo gold & multi	.30	.25
2482	A592	3fo gold & multi	.40	.25
2483	A592	4fo gold & multi	.50	.25
2484	A592	5fo gold & multi	.75	.25

Nos. 2478-2484 (7)   2.85   1.75

Exist imperf. Value, set $15.

Newton and Double Convex Lens — A593

1977, Mar. 31   Litho.   Perf. 12

2485   A593   3fo tan & multi   .60   .60

Isaac Newton (1643-1727), natural philosopher and mathematician, 250th death anniversary. No. 2485 issued in sheets of 4 stamps and 4 blue and black labels showing illustration from Newton's "Principia Mathematica," and Soviet space rocket.
Exists imperf. Value: single with label $5; sheetlet $25.

Janos Vajda (1827-97), Poet — A594

1977, May 2   Litho.   Perf. 12

2486   A594   1fo green, cream & blk   .30   .25

Exists imperf. Value $3.25.

Netherlands No. 1 and Tulips A595

1977, May 23   Photo.   Perf. 11½x12

2487   A595   3fo multicolored   .80   .80

AMPHILEX '77, Intl. Stamp Exhib., Amsterdam, May 26-June 5. Issued in sheets of 3 stamps + 3 labels showing Amphilex poster. Value, $5.
Exist imperf. Value: single with label $7; sheetlet $22.50.

Scene from "Wedding at Nagyrede" — A596

1977, June 14   Litho.   Perf. 12

2488   A596   3fo multicolored   .75   .25

State Folk Ensemble, 25th anniversary.
Exists imperf. Value $4.50.

Souvenir Sheet

Bath of Bathsheba, by Rubens — A597

1977, June 14   Photo.   Perf. 11

2489   A597   20fo multicolored   5.00   5.00

Peter Paul Rubens (1577-1640), Flemish painter.
Exists imperf. Value $45.

Medieval View of Sopron, Fidelity Tower, Arms — A598

1977, June 25   Litho.   Perf. 12x11½

2490   A598   1fo multicolored   1.25   1.25

700th anniv. of Sopron. Printed se-tenant with label showing European Architectural Heritage medal awarded Sopron in 1975.
Exists imperf. Value, single with label $15.

Race Horse Kincsem A599

1977, July 16   Litho.   Perf. 12

2491   A599   1fo multicolored   1.00   .90

Sesquicentennial of horse racing in Hungary. Printed se-tenant with label showing portrait of Count Istvan Szechenyi and vignette from his 1827 book "Rules of Horse Racing in Hungary."
Exists imperf. Value, single with label $15.

German Democratic Republic No. 370 — A600

1977, Aug. 18   Photo.   Perf. 12x11½

2492   A600   3fo multicolored   .85   .85

SOZPHILEX 77 Philatelic Exhibition, Berlin, Aug. 19-28. No. 2492 issued in sheets of 3 stamps and 3 labels showing SOZPHILEX emblem.
Exist imperf. Value: single with label $5; sheetlet $15.

Scythian Iron Bell, 6th Century B.C. — A601

Panel, Crown of Emperor Constantin Monomakhos — A602

Designs: No. 2494, Bronze candlestick in shape of winged woman, 12th-13th centuries. No. 2495, Centaur carrying child, copper aquamanile, 12th century. No. 2496, Gold figure of Christ, from 11th century Crucifix. Designs show art treasures from Hungarian National Museum, founded 1802.

1977, Sept. 3   Perf. 12

2493	A601	2fo multicolored	.50	.50
2494	A601	2fo multicolored	.50	.50
2495	A601	2fo multicolored	.50	.50
2496	A601	2fo multicolored	.50	.50

  a.   Horiz. strip of 4, #2493-2496   2.00   2.00

Souvenir Sheet

2497   A602   10fo multicolored   2.00   2.00

50th Stamp Day.
Exist imperf. Value: strip of 4 $20; souvenir sheet $17.50.

Sputnik — A603

Spacecraft: 60f, Skylab. 1fo, Soyuz-Salyut 5. 3fo, Luna 24. 4fo, Mars 3. 6fo, Viking.

1977, Sept. 20

2498	A603	40f multicolored	.30	.25
2499	A603	60f multicolored	.30	.25
2500	A603	1fo multicolored	.30	.25
2501	A603	3fo multicolored	.40	.25
2502	A603	4fo multicolored	.65	.25
2503	A603	6fo multicolored	.90	.25

Nos. 2498-2503 (6)   2.85   1.50

Space explorations, from Sputnik to Viking. See No. C375.
Exist imperf. Value, set $20.

Janos Szanto Kovacs (1852-1908), Agrarian Movement Pioneer — A604

Ervin Szabo (1877-1918), Revolutionary Workers' Movement Pioneer — A605

1977, Nov. 4   Litho.   Perf. 12

2504	A604	1fo red & black	.30	.25
2505	A605	1fo red & black	.30	.25

Exist imperf. Value, set $5.

Monument to Hungarian October Revolutionists, Omsk — A606

1977, Nov. 4

2506   A606   1fo black & red   .30   .25

60th anniv. of Russian October Revolution.
Exists imperf. Value $3.75.

Hands and Feet Bathed in Thermal Spring — A607

1977, Nov. 1

2507   A607   1fo multicolored   .30   .25

World Rheumatism Year.
Exists imperf. Value $15.

Endre Ady — A608

1977, Nov. 22   Engr.   Perf. 12

2508   A608   1fo violet blue   .30   .25

Endre Ady (1877-1919), lyric poet. Issued in sheets of 4.
Exists imperf. Value $7.50. Sheetlet $25.

Lesser Panda — A609

Designs: 60f, Giant panda. 1fo, Asiatic black bear. 4fo, Polar bear. 6fo, Brown bear.

1977, Dec. 16   Litho.   Perf. 11½x12

2509	A609	40f yellow & multi	.30	.25
2510	A609	60f yellow & multi	.30	.25
2511	A609	1fo yellow & multi	.30	.25

HUNGARY

2512	A609	4fo yellow & multi	.55	.25
2513	A609	6fo yellow & multi	1.00	.25
		Nos. 2509-2513 (5)	2.45	1.25

Exist imperf. Value $30.

Souvenir Sheet

Flags and Ships along Intercontinental Waterway — A610

Flags: a, Austria. b, Bulgaria. c, Czechoslovakia. d, France. e, Luxembourg. f, Yugoslavia. g, Hungary. h, Fed. Rep. of Germany. i, Romania. j, Switzerland. k, USSR.

1977, Dec. 28   Litho.   Perf. 12

2514	A610	Sheet of 11	3.50	3.50
a.-k.		2fo, any single	.45	.45

European Intercontinental Waterway: Danube, Main and Rhine.
Exists imperf. Value $67.50.

Lancer, 17th Century — A611

Hussars: 60f, Kuruts, 1710. 1fo, Baranya, 1762. 2fo, Palatine officer, 1809. 4fo, Sandor, 1848. 6fo, Trumpeter, 5th Honved Regiment, 1900.

1978, Jan.   Litho.   Perf. 11½x12

2515	A611	40f lilac & multi	.30	.25
2516	A611	60f yel grn & multi	.30	.25
2517	A611	1fo red & multi	.30	.25
2518	A611	2fo dull bl & multi	.30	.25
2519	A611	4fo olive bis & multi	.40	.25
2520	A611	6fo gray & multi	1.00	.25
		Nos. 2515-2520 (6)	2.60	1.50

Exist imperf. Value, set $25.

School of Arts and Crafts — A612

1978, Mar. 31   Litho.   Perf. 12

| 2521 | A612 | 1fo multicolored | .30 | .25 |

School of Arts and Crafts, 200th anniv.
Exists imperf. Value $5.

Soccer Players, Flags of West Germany and Poland — A613

Designs (Various Soccer Scenes and Flags): No. 2523, Hungary and Argentina. No. 2524, France and Italy. No. 2525, Tunisia and Mexico. No. 2526, Sweden and Brazil. No. 2527, Spain and Austria. No. 2528, Peru and Scotland. No. 2529, Iran and Netherlands. Flags represent first round of contestants. 20fo, Argentina '78 emblem.

1978, May 25   Litho.   Perf. 12

2522	A613	2fo multicolored	.30	.25
2523	A613	2fo multicolored	.30	.25
2524	A613	2fo multicolored	.30	.25
2525	A613	2fo multicolored	.30	.25
2526	A613	2fo multicolored	.30	.25
2527	A613	2fo multicolored	.30	.25
2528	A613	2fo multicolored	.35	.25
2529	A613	2fo multicolored	.35	.25
		Nos. 2522-2529 (8)	2.50	2.00

Souvenir Sheet
Perf. 11½

| 2530 | A613 | 20fo multicolored | 2.50 | 2.50 |

Argentina '78 11th World Cup Soccer Championships, Argentina, June 2-25.
Exist imperf. Values: set $15; souvenir sheet $17.50.

Vase, Star and Glass Blower's Tube — A614

1978, May 20   Litho.   Perf. 12

| 2531 | A614 | 1fo multicolored | .30 | .25 |

Ajka Glass Works, centenary.
Exist imperf. Value $6.

Canada No. 1 and Trillium A615

1978, June 2

| 2532 | A615 | 3fo multicolored | .75 | .75 |

CAPEX '78, Canadian International Philatelic Exhibition, Toronto, Ont., June 9-18. Issued in sheets of 3 stamps and 3 labels showing CAPEX '78 emblem.
Exists imperf. Value: single with label $5; sheetlet $15.

Souvenir Sheets

Explorers and Their Ships — A616

No. 2533: a, Leif Ericson. b, Columbus. c, Vasco da Gama. d, Magellan. No. 2534: a, Drake. b, Hudson. c, Cook. d, Peary.

1978, June 10   Litho.   Perf. 12x11½

2533	A616	Sheet of 4	3.25	3.00
a.-d.		2fo, any single	.70	.70
2534	A616	Sheet of 4	3.25	3.00
a.-d.		2fo, any single	.70	.70

Exist imperf. Value: set of 2 sheets $75.

Diesel Train, Pioneer's Kerchief — A617

1978, June 10   Perf. 12

| 2535 | A617 | 1fo multicolored | .30 | .25 |

30th anniversary of Pioneer Railroad.
Exists imperf. Value $4.

Congress Emblem as Flower — A618

Design: No. 2537, Congress emblem, "Cuba" and map of Cuba.

1978, June 27

2536	A618	1fo multi	.30	.25
2537	A618	1fo multi	.30	.25
a.		Pair, #2536-2537	.50	.50

11th World Youth Festival, Havana.
Exist imperf. Value $17.50.

WHO Emblem, Stylized Body and Heart — A619

1978, Aug. 21   Litho.   Perf. 12

| 2538 | A619 | 1fo multicolored | .30 | .25 |

Drive against hypertension.
Exists imperf. Value $7.50.

Clenched Fist, Dove and Olive Branch — A620

1978, Sept. 1   Litho.   Perf. 12

| 2539 | A620 | 1fo gray, red & black | .30 | .25 |

Publication of review "Peace and Socialism," 20th anniversary.
Exists imperf. Value $7.50.

Train, Telephone, Space Communication A621

1978, Sept. 25   Litho.   Perf. 12

| 2540 | A621 | 1fo multicolored | .30 | .25 |

20th anniv. of Organization for Communication Cooperation of Socialist Countries.
Exists imperf. Value $7.50.

"Toshiba" Automatic Letter Sorting Machine A622

1978, Sept. 15   Litho.   Perf. 11½x12

| 2541 | A622 | 1fo multicolored | .30 | .25 |

Introduction of automatic letter sorting. No. 2541 printed with se-tenant label showing bird holding letter.
Exists imperf. Value: single with label $10.

Eros Offering Grapes, Villa Hercules — A623

Roman Mosaics Found in Hungary: No. 2543, Tiger (Villa Hercules, Budapest). No. 2544, Bird eating berries (Balacapuszta). No. 2545, Dolphin (Aquincum). 10fo, Hercules aiming at Centaur fleeing with Deianeira (Villa Hercules).

Photogravure and Engraved
1978, Sept. 16   Perf. 11½

2542	A623	2fo multicolored	1.25	1.25
2543	A623	2fo multicolored	1.25	1.25
2544	A623	2fo multicolored	1.25	1.25
2545	A623	2fo multicolored	1.25	1.25
		Nos. 2542-2545 (4)	5.00	5.00

Souvenir Sheet

| 2546 | A623 | 10fo multicolored | 3.00 | 3.00 |

Stamp Day. No. 2546 contains one stamp (52x35mm).
Exist imperf. Value: set $70; souvenir sheet $125.

Count Imre Thököly — A624

1978, Oct. 2   Photo.   Perf. 12½

| 2547 | A624 | 1fo black & yellow | .30 | .25 |

300th anniv. of Hungary's independence movement, led by Imre Thököly (1657-1705).
Exists imperf. Value $7.50.

Souvenir Sheet

Hungarian Crown Jewels — A625

1978, Oct. 10

| 2548 | A625 | 20fo gold & multi | 3.00 | 3.00 |

Return of Crown Jewels from US, 1/6/78.
Exists imperf. Value $30.

"The Red Coach" — A626

1978, Oct. 20   Litho.   Perf. 12

| 2549 | A626 | 3fo red & black | .45 | .25 |

Gyula Krudy, 1878-1933, novelist.
Exists imperf. Value $10.

St. Ladislas I Reliquary, Györ Cathedral — A627

1978, Nov. 15   Perf. 11½x12½

| 2550 | A627 | 1fo multicolored | .30 | .25 |

Ladislas I (1040-1095), 900th anniversary of accession to throne of Hungary.
Exists imperf. Value $12.50.

Miklos Jurisics Statue, Köszeg A628

1978, Nov. 15   Perf. 12

| 2551 | A628 | 1fo multicolored | .30 | .25 |

650th anniversary of founding of Köszeg.
Exists imperf. Value $8.

Samu Czaban and Gizella Berzeviczy A629

HUNGARY

Photogravure and Engraved
1978, Nov. 24   Perf. 11½x12
2552   A629   1fo brown, buff & red   .30   .25

Samu Czaban (1878-1942) and Gizella Berzeviczy (1878-1954), Communist teachers during Soviet Republic (1918-1919).
Exists imperf. Value $5.

Communist Party Emblem — A630

1978, Nov. 24   Litho.   Perf. 12
2553   A630   1fo gray, red & blk   .30   .25

Hungarian Communist Party, 60th anniv.
Exists imperf. Value $9.

Woman Cutting Bread — A631

Ceramics by Margit Kovacs (1902-1976): 2fo, Woman with pitcher. 3fo, Potter.

1978, Nov. 30   Litho.   Perf. 11½x12
2554   A631   1fo multicolored   .30   .25
2555   A631   2fo multicolored   .30   .25
2556   A631   3fo multicolored   .50   .25
    Nos. 2554-2556 (3)   1.10   .75

Exist imperf. Value, set $20.

Virgin and Child, by Dürer — A632

Dürer Paintings: 60f, Adoration of the Kings, horiz. 1fo, Self-portrait, 1500. 2fo, St. George. 3fo, Nativity, horiz. 4fo, St. Eustatius. 5fo, The Four Apostles. 20fo, Dancing Peasant Couple, 1514 (etching).

1979, Jan. 8   Photo.   Perf. 12½
2557   A632   40f gold & multi   .30   .25
2558   A632   60f gold & multi   .30   .25
2559   A632   1fo gold & multi   .30   .25
2560   A632   2fo gold & multi   .30   .25
2561   A632   3fo gold & multi   .35   .25
2562   A632   4fo gold & multi   .50   .25
2563   A632   5fo gold & multi   .75   .25
    Nos. 2557-2563 (7)   2.80   1.75

Souvenir Sheet
Litho.
2564   A632   20fo buff & brown   2.50   2.50

Albrecht Dürer (1471-1528), German painter and engraver.
Exist imperf. Value: set $15; souvenir sheet $32.50.

Human Rights Flame — A633

1979, Feb. 8   Litho.   Perf. 11½x12
2565   A633   1fo dk & lt blue   .75   .75

Universal Declaration of Human Rights, 30th anniversary. No. 2565 issued in sheets of 12 stamps (3x4) and 4 labels. Alternating horizontal rows inverted.

Exists imperf. Value $5. Strip of 3 $15, Sheetlet $60.

Child at Play — A634

IYC Emblem and: No. 2567, Family. No. 2568, 3 children (international friendship).

1979, Feb. 26   Perf. 12
2566   A634   1fo multicolored   .50   .50
2567   A634   1fo multicolored   .50   .50
2568   A634   1fo multicolored   4.00   3.00
    Nos. 2566-2568 (3)   5.00   4.00

Exist imperf. Value, set $22.50.

Soldiers of the Red Army, by Bela Uitz — A635

1979, Mar. 21   Litho.   Perf. 12
2569   A635   1fo silver, blk & red   .30   .25

60th anniv. of Hungarian Soviet Republic.
Exists imperf. Value $3.

Calvinist Church, Nyirbator — A636

1979, Mar. 28   Perf. 11
2570   A636   1fo brown & yellow   .30   .25

700th anniv. of Nyirbator. See No. 2601.
Exists imperf. Value $16.

Chessmen, Gold Cup, Flag — A637

1979, Apr. 12   Litho.   Perf. 12
2571   A637   3fo multicolored   .85   .75

Hungarian victories in 23rd Chess Olympiad, Buenos Aires, 1978.
Exists imperf. Value $8.

Alexander Nevsky Cathedral, Sofia, Bulgaria No. 1 — A638

1979, May 18   Litho.   Perf. 11½x12
2572   A638   3fo multicolored   .65   .65

Philaserdica '79 Philatelic Exhibition, Sofia, Bulgaria, May 18-27. No. 2572 issued in sheets of 3 stamps and 3 labels showing Philaserdica emblem and arms of Sofia.
Exist imperf. Value: single with label $8; sheetlet $17.50.

Stephenson's Rocket, 1829, IVA '79 Emblem — A639

Railroad Development: 60f, Siemens' first electric locomotive, 1879. 1fo, "Pioneer," Chicago & Northwestern Railroad, 1836. 2fo, Orient Express, 1883. 3fo, Trans-Siberian train, 1898. 4fo, Express train on Tokaido line, 1964. 5fo, Transrapid-O5 train, exhibited 1979. 20fo, Map of European railroad network.

1979, June 8   Litho.   Perf. 12x11½
2573   A639   40f multi   .30   .25
2574   A639   60f multi   .30   .25
2575   A639   1fo multi   .30   .25
2576   A639   2fo multi   .30   .25
2577   A639   3fo multi   .45   .25
2578   A639   4fo multi   .50   .25
2579   A639   5fo multi   .75   .40
    Nos. 2573-2579 (7)   2.90   1.90

Souvenir Sheet
Perf. 12½x11½
2580   A639   20fo multi   2.00   2.00

Intl. Transportation Exhibition (IVA '79), Hamburg. No. 2580 contains one 47x32mm stamp.
Exist imperf. Value: set $25; souvenir sheet $35.

Natural Gas Pipeline and Compressor — A640

2fo, Lenin power station & dam, Dnieprepetrovsk & pylon. 3fo, Comecon Building, Moscow, & star symbolizing 10 member states.

1979, June 26   Perf. 11½x12
2581   A640   1fo multi   .30   .25
2582   A640   2fo multi   .30   .25
2583   A640   3fo multi   .35   .25
    Nos. 2581-2583 (3)   .95   .75

30th anniversary of the Council of Mutual Economic Assistance, Comecon.
Exist imperf. Value, set $8.

Zsigmond Moricz (1879-1942), Writer, by Jozsef Ripple-Ronai A641

1979, June 29   Perf. 12
2584   A641   1fo multi   .30   .25

Exists imperf. Value $3.

Town Hall, Helsinki, Finnish Flag, Moscow '80 Emblem — A642

Designs (Moscow '80 Emblem and): 60f, Colosseum, Rome, Italian flag. 1fo, Asakusa Temple, Tokyo, Japanese flag. 2fo, Mexico City Cathedral, Mexican flag. 3fo, Our Lady's Church, Munich, German flag. 4fo, Skyscrapers, Montreal, Canadian flag. 5fo, Lomonosov University, Misha the bear and Soviet flag.

1979, July 31   Perf. 12x11½
2585   A642   40f multi   .30   .25
2586   A642   60f multi   .30   .25
2587   A642   1fo multi   .30   .25
2588   A642   2fo multi   .30   .25
2589   A642   3fo multi   .30   .25
2590   A642   4fo multi   .40   .25
2591   A642   5fo multi   .70   .25
    Nos. 2585-2591 (7)   2.60   1.75

Pre-Olympic Year.
Exist imperf. Value, set $20.

Boy with Horse and Greyhounds, by Janos Vaszary — A643

Paintings of Horses: 60f, Coach and Five, by Karoly Lotz. 1fo, Boys on Horseback, by Celesztin Pallya. 2fo, Farewell, by Lotz. 3fo, Horse Market, by Pallya. 4fo, Wanderer, by

Bela Ivanyi-Grunwald. 5fo, Ready for the Hunt, by Karoly Sterio.

1979, Aug. 11   Photo.   Perf. 12½
2592   A643   40f multi   .30   .25
2593   A643   60f multi   .30   .25
2594   A643   1fo multi   .30   .25
2595   A643   2fo multi   .30   .25
2596   A643   3fo multi   .40   .25
2597   A643   4fo multi   .50   .25
2598   A643   5fo multi   .75   .40
    Nos. 2592-2598 (7)   2.85   1.90

Exist imperf. Value, set $20.

Sturgeons, Map of Danube, "Calypso" A644

1979, Aug. 11
2599   A644   3fo multi   .50   .25

Environmental protection of rivers and seas.
Exists imperf. Value $6.

Pentathlon — A645

1979, Aug. 11   Litho.   Perf. 12
2600   A645   2fo multi   .50   .25

Pentathlon World Championship, Budapest, Aug. 12-18.
Exists imperf. Value $10.

Architecture Type of 1979

Design: Vasvar Public Health Center.

1979, Aug. 15   Litho.   Perf. 11
2601   A636   40f grn & blk   .30   .25

700th anniversary of Vasvar.
Exists imperf. Value $15.

Denarius of Stephen I, 1000-1038, Reverse — A646

Hungarian Coins: 2fo, Copper coin of Bela III, 1172-1196. 3fo, Golden groat of King Louis the Great, 1342-1382. 4fo, Golden forint of Matthias I, 1458-1490. 5fo, Silver gulden of Wladislaw II, 1490-1516.

Engraved and Photogravure
1979, Sept. 3   Perf. 12x11½
2602   A646   1fo multi   .30   .25
2603   A646   2fo multi   .30   .25
2604   A646   3fo multi   .35   .25
2605   A646   4fo multi   .50   .25
2606   A646   5fo multi   .30   .50
    Nos. 2602-2606 (5)   1.75   1.50

9th International Numismatic Congress, Berne, Switzerland.
Exist imperf. Value, set $11.

Souvenir Sheet

Unofficial Stamp, 1848 A647

1979, Sept. 15   Litho.   Perf. 12
2607   A647   10fo dk brown, blk & red   2.00   2.00

Stamp Day.
Exists imperf. Value $20.

HUNGARY

Souvenir Sheet

Gyor-Sopron-Ebenfurt rail service, cent. — A648

Designs: a, Elbel Locomotive. b, Type 424 steam engine. c, "War Locomotive." d, Hydraulic diesel locomotive.

1979, Oct. 19   Litho.   *Perf. 12*
| 2608 | A648 | Sheet of 4 | 2.50 | 2.50 |
| a.-d. | A648 | 5fo any single | .50 | .50 |

Exists imperf. Value $27.50

Vega-Chess, by Victor Vasarely — A649

1979, Oct. 29
| 2609 | A649 | 1fo multi | .30 | .25 |

Exists imperf. Value $3.50.

International Savings Day — A650

1979, Oct. 29   Litho.   *Perf. 12*
| 2610 | A650 | 1fo multi | .30 | .25 |

Exists imperf. Value $3.

Otter — A651

Wildlife Protection: 60f, Wild cat. 1fo, Pine marten. 2fo, Eurasian badger. 4fo, Polecat. 6fo, Beech marten.

1979, Nov. 20
2611	A651	40f multi	.30	.25
2612	A651	60f multi	.30	.25
2613	A651	1fo multi	.30	.25
2614	A651	2fo multi	.30	.25
2615	A651	4fo multi	.50	.25
2616	A651	6fo multi	1.00	.25
	Nos. 2611-2616 (6)		2.70	1.50

Exist imperf. Value, set $25.

Tom Thumb, IYC Emblem — A652

IYC Emblem and Fairy Tale Scenes: 60f, The Ugly Duckling. 1fo, The Fisherman and the Goldfish. 2fo, Cinderella. 3fo, Gulliver's Travels. 4fo, The Little Pigs and the Wolf. 5fo, Janos the Knight. 20fo, The Fairy Ilona.

1979, Dec. 29   Litho.   *Perf. 12x11½*
2617	A652	40f multi	.30	.25
2618	A652	60f multi	.30	.25
2619	A652	1fo multi	.30	.25
2620	A652	2fo multi	.35	.25
2621	A652	3fo multi	.50	.30
2622	A652	4fo multi	.65	.25
2623	A652	5fo multi	1.00	.25
	Nos. 2617-2623 (7)		3.40	1.80

Souvenir Sheet
| 2624 | A652 | 20fo multi | 2.00 | 2.00 |

Exist imperf. Value: set $22.50; souvenir sheet $22.50.

Trichodes Apairius and Yarrow — A653

Insects Pollinating Flowers: 60f, Bumblebee and blanketflower. 1fo, Red admiral butterfly and daisy. 2fo, Cetonia aurata and rose. 4fo, Graphosoma lineatum and petroselinum hortense. 6fo, Chlorophorus varius and thistle.

1980, Jan. 25   Litho.   *Perf. 12*
2625	A653	40f multi	.30	.25
2626	A653	60f multi	.30	.25
2627	A653	1fo multi	.30	.25
2628	A653	2fo multi	.30	.25
2629	A653	4fo multi	.50	.25
2630	A653	6fo multi	.90	.25
	Nos. 2625-2630 (6)		2.60	1.50

Exist imperf. Value, set $25.

Hanging Gardens of Semiramis, 6th Century B.C., Map showing Babylon — A654

Seven Wonders of the Ancient World (and Map): 60f, Temple of Artemis, Ephesus, 6th century B.C. 1fo, Zeus, by Phidias, Olympia. 2fo, Tomb of Maussolos, Halikarnassos, 3rd century B.C. 3fo, Colossos of Rhodes. 4fo, Pharos Lighthouse, Alexandria, 3rd century B.C. 5fo, Pyramids, 26th-24th centuries B.C.

1980, Feb. 29   Litho.   *Perf. 12x11½*
2631	A654	40f multi	.30	.25
2632	A654	60f multi	.30	.25
2633	A654	1fo multi	.30	.25
2634	A654	2fo multi	.30	.25
2635	A654	3fo multi	.40	.25
2636	A654	4fo multi	.60	.25
2637	A654	5fo multi	.85	.25
	Nos. 2631-2637 (7)		3.05	1.75

Exist imperf. Value, set $16.

Tihany Benedictine Abbey and Deed — A655

1980, Mar. 19   Litho.   *Perf. 12*
| 2638 | A655 | 1fo multi | .30 | .25 |

Benedictine Abbey, Tihany, 925th anniversary of deed (oldest document in Hungarian). Exists imperf. Value $12.50.

Gabor Bethlen, Copperplate Print — A656

1980, Mar. 19
| 2639 | A656 | 1fo multi | .30 | .25 |

Gabor Bethlen (1580-1629), Prince of Transylvania (1613-29) and King of Hungary (1620-29).

Exists imperf. Value $10.

Easter Casket of Garamszentbenedek, 15th Century (Restoration) — A657

1980, Mar. 19
2640	A657	1fo shown	.30	.25
2641	A657	2fo Three Marys	.30	.25
2642	A657	3fo Apostle James	.30	.35
2643	A657	4fo Thaddeus	.50	.50
2644	A657	5fo Andrew	.65	.65
	Nos. 2640-2644 (5)		2.05	2.00

Exist imperf. Value, set $12.50.

Liberation from Fascism, 35th Anniversary — A658

1980, March 24   Litho.   *Perf. 12*
| 2645 | A658 | 1fr multi | .30 | .25 |

Exists imperf. Value $8.

Jozsef Attila, Poet and Lyricist — A659

1980, Apr. 11
| 2646 | A659 | 1fo rose car & olive | .30 | .25 |

Exists imperf. Value $7.50. See No. 2675.

Hungarian Postal Museum, 50th anniv. A660

1980, Apr. 28   *Perf. 11½x12*
| 2647 | A660 | 1fo multi | .90 | .90 |

Features Hungary No. 386a. Exists imperf. Value $20.

Two Pence Blue, Mounted Guardsman, London 1980 Emblem A661

1980, Apr. 30   *Perf. 11½x12*
| 2648 | A661 | 3fo multi | .50 | .50 |

London 1980 International Stamp Exhibition, May 6-14. No. 2648 issued in sheets of 3 stamps and 3 labels showing London 1980 emblem and arms of city. Size: 104x125mm. Exists imperf. Value: single with label $7.50; sheetlet $15.

Norway No. B51, Mother with Child, by Gustav Vigeland A662

1980, June 9   Litho.   *Perf. 11½x12*
| 2649 | A662 | 3fo multi | .60 | .60 |

NORWEX '80 Stamp Exhibition, Oslo, June 13-22. No. 2649 issued in sheets of 3 stamps and 3 labels showing NORWEX emblem. Size: 108x125mm.
Exists imperf. Value: single with label $5; sheetlet $15.

Margit Kaffka (1880-1918), Writer — A663

1980, June 9   *Perf. 12*
| 2650 | A663 | 1fo blk & pur, cr | .30 | .25 |

Exists imperf. Value $10.

Zoltan Schönherz (1905-42), Antifascist Martyr — A664

1980, July 25   Litho.
| 2652 | A664 | 1fo multi | .30 | .25 |

Exists imperf. Value $4.

Dr. Endre Hogyes and Congress Emblem — A665

1980, July 25
| 2653 | A665 | 1fo multi | .30 | .25 |

28th International Congress of Physiological Sciences, Budapest, Dr. Hogyes (1847-1906) first described equilibrium reflex-curve and modified Pasteur's rabies vaccine.
Exists imperf. Value $7.50.

Decanter, c. 1850 — A666

1980, Sept. 13   Litho.   *Perf. 12*
2654	A666	1fo shown	.30	.25
2655	A666	2fo Decorated glass	.30	.25
2656	A666	3fo Stem glass	.50	.25
	Nos. 2654-2656 (3)		1.10	.85

Souvenir Sheet
| 2657 | A666 | 10fo Pecs glass | 1.75 | 1.75 |

53rd Stamp Day.
Exist imperf. Value: set $17.50; souvenir sheet $20.

HUNGARY

Bertalan Por, Self-portrait — A667

1980, Nov. 4   **Litho.**   **Perf. 12**
2658 A667 1fo Artist (1880-1964)   .30   .25
Exists imperf. Value $7.50.

Graylag Goose — A668

60f, Black-crowned night heron. 1fo, Shoveler. 2fo, Chlidonias leucopterus. 4fo, Great crested grebe. 6fo, Black-necked stilt. 20fo, Great white heron.

1980, Nov. 11   **Perf. 11½x12**
2659 A668 40f shown   .30   .25
2660 A668 60f multicolored   .30   .25
2661 A668 1fo multicolored   .30   .25
2662 A668 2fo multicolored   .30   .25
2663 A668 4fo multicolored   .60   .25
2664 A668 6fo multicolored   1.00   .25
    Nos. 2659-2664 (6)   2.80 1.50

Souvenir Sheet
2665 A668 20fo multicolored   2.75 2.75
European Nature Protection Year. No. 2665 contains one stamp (37x59mm).
Exist imperf. Value: set $22.50; souvenir sheet $25.

Souvenir Sheet

Dove on Map of Europe A669

1980, Nov. 11   **Perf. 12½x11½**
2666 A669 20fo multi   1.50 1.50
European Security and Cooperation Conference, Madrid.
Exists imperf. Value $25.

Johannes Kepler and Model of his Theory — A670

1980, Nov. 21   **Litho.**   **Perf. 12**
2667 A670 1fo multi   .30   .25
Johannes Kepler (1571-1630), German astronomer, 350th anniversary of death. No. 2667 printed se-tenant with label showing rocket and satellites orbiting earth.
Exists imperf. Value, single with label $20.

Karoly Kisfaludy (1788-1830), Poet and Dramatist — A671

1980, Nov. 21
2668 A671 1fo brn red & dull brn   .30   .25
Exists imperf. Value $10.

UN Headquarters, New York — A672

UN membership, 25th anniversary: 60f, Geneva headquarters. 1fo, Vienna headquarters. 2fo, UN & Hungary flags. 4fo, UN, Hungary arms. 6fo, World map.

Photogravure and Engraved
1980, Dec. 12   **Perf. 11½x12**
2669 A672 40f shown   .30   .25
2670 A672 60f multicolored   .30   .25
2671 A672 1fo multicolored   .30   .25
2672 A672 2fo multicolored   .30   .25
2673 A672 4fo multicolored   .40   .25
2674 A672 6fo multicolored   1.00   .35
    Nos. 2669-2674 (6)   2.60 1.60
Exist imperf. Value, set $20.

Attila Type of 1980
Ferenc Erdei (1910-71), economist & statesman.

1980, Dec. 23   **Litho.**   **Perf. 12**
2675 A659 1fo dk green & brown   .30   .25
Exists imperf. Value $7.50.

Bela Szanto — A674

1981, Jan. 31   **Litho.**   **Perf. 12**
2676 A674 1fo multi   .30   .25
Bela Szanto (1881-1951), labor movement leader.
Exists imperf. Value $7.50.
See Nos. 2698, 2724, 2767.

Count Lajos Batthyany — A675

1981, Feb. 14
2677 A675 1fo multi   .30   .25
Count Lajos Batthyany (1806-1849), prime minister, later executed.
Exists imperf. Value $7.50.

A677

Design: a, Bela Bartok (1881-1945), Composer. b, Cantata Profana illustration.

1981, Mar. 25   **Litho.**   **Perf. 12½**
2685 A677 Sheet of 2   2.50 2.50
a.-b.   10fo any single   1.25 1.25
Exists imperf. Value $20.

Telephone Exchange System Cent. — A678

1981, Apr. 29   **Litho.**   **Perf. 12**
2686 A678 2fo multi   .40   .25
Exists imperf. Value $10.

Belling Stag — A679

1981, Apr. 29
2687 A679 2fo multi   .30   .25
Exists imperf. Value $10.

Flag of the House of Arpad, 11th Cent. — A680

60f, Hunyadi family, 15th cent. 1fo, Gabor Bethlen, 1600. 2fo, Ferenc Rakoczi II, 1716. 4fo, Honved, 1848. 6fo, Troop flag, 1919.

1981, Apr. 29
2688 A680 40f shown   .30   .25
2689 A680 60f multicolored   .30   .25
2690 A680 1fo multicolored   .30   .25
2691 A680 2fo multicolored   .30   .25
2692 A680 4fo multicolored   .60   .25
2693 A680 6fo multicolored   .80   .25
    Nos. 2688-2693 (6)   2.60 1.50
Exist imperf. Value, set $20.

Red Cross and Ambulance Vehicles — A681

Map of Europe and J. Henry Dunant (Red Cross Founder) A682

1981, May 4
2694 A681 2fo multi   .40   .25

Souvenir Sheet
Perf. 12½x11½
2695 A682 20fo multi   1.50 1.50
Hungarian Red Cross cent. (2fo); 3rd European Red Cross Conf., Budapest, May 4-7 (20fo).
Exist imperf. Value: single $4; souvenir sheet $22.50.

Souvenir Sheet

1933 WIPA Exhibition Seals — A683

1981, May 15   **Perf. 12x12½**
2696 A683 Sheet of 4   2.00 2.00
a.-d.   5fo any single   .50   .50
WIPA 1981 Phil. Exhib., Vienna, May 22-31.
Exists imperf. Value $20.

Stephenson and his Nonpareil — A684

1981, June 12   **Litho.**   **Perf. 12**
2697 A684 2fo multi   .40   .25
George Stephenson (1781-1848), British railroad engineer, birth bicentenary.
Exists imperf. Value $10.

Famous Hungarians Type
Bela Vago (1881-1939), anti-fascist martyr.

1981, Aug. 7   **Litho.**   **Perf. 12**
2698 A674 2fo ocher & brn ol   .40   .25
Exists imperf. Value $5.

Alexander Fleming (1881-1955), Discoverer of Penicillin — A686

1981, Aug. 7
2699 A686 2fo multi   .40   .25
Exists imperf. Value $10.

Bridal Chest — A687

Bridal chests: 1fo, Szentgal, 18th cent. 2fo, Hodmezovasar-hely, 19th cent. 10fo, Bacs County, 17th cent.

1981, Sept. 12   **Litho.**   **Perf. 12**
2700 A687 1fo multicolored   .30   .25
2701 A687 2fo multicolored   .50   .25

Souvenir Sheet
2702 A687 10fo multicolored   1.75 1.75
54th Stamp Day. No. 2702 contains one stamp (44x25mm).
Exist imperf. Values: Nos. 2700-2701 $12.50; No. 2702 $20.

Calvinist College, Papa, 450th Anniv. — A688

1981, Oct. 3   **Litho.**   **Perf. 12**
2703 A688 2fo multi   .40   .25
Exists imperf. Value $5.

World Food Day — A689

1981, Oct. 16
2704 A689 2fo multi   .40   .25
Exists imperf. Value $6.

Passenger Ship Rakoczi, 1964, No. 1834 — A690

Sidewheelers and Hungarian stamps: No. 2705, Franz I, #1828. No. 2706, Arpad, #1829. No. 2707, Szechenyi, #1830. No. 2708, Grof Szechenyi Istvan, #1831. No. 2709, Sofia, #1832. No. 2710, Felszabadulas, #1833. No. 2712, Hydrofoil Solyom, #1830.

HUNGARY

1981, Nov. 25   *Perf. 12x11½*
2705	A690	1fo multicolored	.30	.25
2706	A690	1fo multicolored	.30	.25
2707	A690	2fo multicolored	.30	.25
2708	A690	2fo multicolored	.30	.25
2709	A690	4fo multicolored	.30	.25
2710	A690	6fo multicolored	.40	.40
2711	A690	8fo shown	.75	.75
		Nos. 2705-2711 (7)	2.65	2.40

Souvenir Sheet
Perf. 13
| 2712 | A690 | 20fo multicolored | 1.75 | 1.75 |

European Danube Commission, 125th anniv.
Exist imperf. Value: set $20; souvenir sheet $20.

Souvenir Sheet

Natl. Costumes — A691

Perf. 12½x11½
1981, Nov. 18   *Litho.*
2713	A691	Sheet of 4	2.00	1.90
a.		1fo Slovakian	.30	.25
b.		2fo German	.40	.35
c.		3fo Croatian	.60	.60
d.		4fo Romanian	.80	.75

Exists imperf. Value $20.

Christmas 1981 — A692

Sculptures: 1fo, Mary Nursing the Infant Jesus, by Margit Kovacs. 2fo, Madonna of Csurgo.

1981, Dec. 4   *Perf. 12½x11½*
| 2714 | A692 | 1fo multi | .30 | .25 |
| 2715 | A692 | 2fo multi | .40 | .25 |

Exist imperf. Value, set $15.

Pen Pals, by Norman Rockwell — A693

Norman Rockwell Illustrations: No. 2717, Courting Under the Clock at Midnight. No. 2718, Maiden Voyage. No. 2719, Threading the Needle.

1981, Dec. 29   *Perf. 11½x12*
2716	A693	1fo shown	.30	.25
2717	A693	2fo multicolored	.30	.25
2718	A693	2fo multicolored	.30	.25
2719	A693	4fo multicolored	.40	.25
		Nos. 2716-2719, C435-C437 (7)	3.20	2.90

Exist imperf. Value, set (7) $17.50.

Souvenir Sheet

La Toilette, by Pablo Picasso (1881-1973) — A694

1981, Dec. 29   *Litho.*   *Perf. 11½*
| 2720 | A694 | 20fo multicolored | 2.50 | 2.50 |

Exists imperf. Value $50.

25th Anniv. of Worker's Militia — A695

1982, Jan. 26   *Litho.*   *Perf. 12*
| 2721 | A695 | 1fo Shooting practice | .30 | .25 |
| 2722 | A695 | 4fo Members, 3 generations | .50 | .25 |

Exist imperf. Value, set $12.50.

10th World Trade Union Congress — A696

1982, Feb. 12   *Litho.*   *Perf. 12x11½*
| 2723 | A696 | 2fo multicolored | .30 | .25 |

Exists imperf. Value $5.

Famous Hungarians Type

Gyula Alpári (1882-1944), anti-fascist martyr.

1982, Mar. 24   *Perf. 12*
| 2724 | A674 | 2fo multicolored | .30 | .25 |

Exists imperf. Value $5.

Robert Koch — A698

1982, Mar. 24   *Litho.*   *Perf. 12*
| 2725 | A698 | 2fo multicolored | .30 | .25 |

TB Bacillus centenary.
Exists imperf. Value $10.

1982 World Cup A699

Designs: Hungary in competition with other World Cup teams.
No. 2733: a, Barcelona Stadium. b, Madrid Stadium.

1982, Apr. 16   *Perf. 11*
2726	A699	1fo Egypt, 1934	.30	.25
2727	A699	1fo Italy, 1938	.30	.25
2728	A699	2fo Germany, 1954	.30	.25
2729	A699	2fo Mexico, 1958	.30	.25
2730	A699	4fo England, 1962	.45	.25
2731	A699	6fo Brazil, 1966	.70	.25
2732	A699	8fo Argentina, 1978	.90	.25
		Nos. 2726-2732 (7)	3.25	1.75

Souvenir Sheet
| 2733 | | Sheet of 2 | 2.00 | 2.00 |
| a.-b. | A699 | 10fo any single | .95 | .95 |

No. 2733 contains 44x44mm stamps.
Exist imperf. Value: set $17; souvenir sheet $20.

European Table Tennis Championship, Budapest, Apr. 17-25 — A700

1982, Apr. 16   *Litho.*   *Perf. 11½x12*
| 2734 | A700 | 2fo multi | .40 | .25 |

Exists imperf. Value $4.

Roses — A701

1982, Apr. 30   *Perf. 12*
2735	A701	1fo Pascali	.30	.25
2736	A701	1fo Michele Meilland	.30	.25
2737	A701	2fo Diorama	.30	.25
2738	A701	2fo Wendy Cussons	.30	.25
2739	A701	3fo Blue Moon	.40	.25
2740	A701	3fo Invitation	.40	.25
2741	A701	4fo Tropicana	.80	.25
		Nos. 2735-2741 (7)	2.80	1.75

Souvenir Sheet
| 2742 | A701 | 10fo Bouquet | 2.50 | 2.50 |

No. 2742 contains one stamp (34x59mm, perf. 11).
Exist imperf. Value: set $22.50; souvenir sheet $30.

25 Years of Space Travel — A702

No. 2743, Columbia shuttle, 1981. No. 2744, Armstrong, Apollo 11, 1969. No. 2745, A. Leonov, Voskhod 2, 1965. No. 2746, Yuri Gagarin, Vostok. No. 2747, Laika, Sputnik 2, 1957. No. 2748, Sputnik I, 1957. No. 2749, Space researcher K.E. Tsiolkovsky.

1982, May 18   *Photo.*   *Perf. 11½*
2743	A702	1fo multicolored	.30	.25
2744	A702	1fo multicolored	.30	.25
2745	A702	2fo multicolored	.30	.25
2746	A702	2fo multicolored	.30	.25
2747	A702	4fo multicolored	.40	.25
2748	A702	4fo multicolored	.40	.25
2749	A702	6fo multicolored	.90	.25
		Nos. 2743-2749 (7)	2.90	1.75

Exist imperf. Value, set $15.

A703

1982, May 7   *Litho.*   *Perf. 12*
| 2750 | A703 | 2fo multi | .30 | .25 |

George Dimitrov (1882-1947), 1st prime minister of Bulgaria. SOZPHILEX '82 Stamp Exhib., Sofia, Bulgaria, May. No. 2750 se-tenant with label showing Bulgarian 1300th anniv. emblems.
Exists imperf. Value, with label $10.

Diosgyor paper mill, bicent. — A704

1982, May 27   *Litho.*   *Perf. 12x11½*
| 2751 | A704 | 2fo multi | .30 | .25 |

Exists imperf. Value $5.

First Rubik's Cube World Championship, Budapest, June 5 — A705

1982, June 4   *Perf. 11½x12*
| 2752 | A705 | 2fo multi | .30 | .25 |

Exists imperf. Value $9.

Souvenir Sheet

George Washington, by F. Kemmelmeyer — A706

Washington's 250th Birth Anniv.: a, Michael Kovats de Fabricy (1724-1779), Cavalry Commandant, by Sandor Finta.

1982, July 2   *Litho.*   *Perf. 11*
| 2753 | A706 | Sheet of 2 | 2.00 | 2.00 |
| a.-b. | | 5fo any single | .60 | .60 |

Exists imperf. Value $17.50.

World Hematology Congress, Budapest — A707

1982, July 30   *Perf. 12½x11½*
| 2754 | A707 | 2fo multi | .30 | .25 |

Exists imperf. Value $3.

Zirc Abbey, 800th Anniv. — A708

1982, Aug. 19   *Perf. 11½x12*
| 2755 | A708 | 2fo multi | .30 | .25 |

Exists imperf. Value $7.50.

KNER Printing Office, Gyoma, Centenary — A709

1982, Sept. 23   *Litho.*   *Perf. 12x11½*
| 2756 | A709 | 2fo Emblem | .30 | .25 |

Exists imperf. Value $7.50.

HUGARY

AGROFILA '82 Intl. Agricultural Stamp Exhibition, Godollo — A710

1982, Sept. 24   *Perf. 11½x12*
2757   A710   5fo Map   .75   .75

Issued in sheets of 3 stamps and 3 labels showing Godollo Agricultural University, emblem. Size: 109x127mm. Value, $5.
Exist imperf. Value: single with label $7.50; sheetlet $20.

Public Transportation Sesquicentennial — A711

1982, Oct. 6   *Litho.*   *Perf. 12x11½*
2758   A711   2fo multi   .40   .25
Exists imperf. Value $15.

Vuk and a Bird — A712

Scenes from Vuk the Fox Cub, Cartoon by Attila Dargay.

1982, Nov. 11   *Perf. 12½*
2759   A712   1fo shown   .30   .25
2760   A712   1fo Dogs   .30   .25
2761   A712   2fo Rooster   .30   .25
2762   A712   2fo Owl   .30   .25
2763   A712   4fo Geese   .50   .25
2764   A712   6fo Frog   .70   .25
2765   A712   8fo Master fox   1.00   .40
    Nos. 2759-2765 (7)   3.40   1.90
Exist imperf. Value, set $25.

Engineering Education Bicentenary — A713

2fo, Budapest Polytechnical University.

1982, Oct. 13   *Perf. 12*
2766   A713   2fo multicolored   .30   .25
Exists imperf. Value $7.50.

Famous Hungarians Type

Gyorgy Boloni (1882-1959), writer and journalist.

1982, Oct. 29
2767   A674   2fo multi   .30   .25
Exists imperf. Value $7.50.

October Revolution, 65th Anniv. — A715

1982, Nov. 5   *Litho.*   *Perf. 11½x12*
2768   A715   5fo Lenin   .60   .25
Exists imperf. Value $12.50.

Works of Art in Hungarian Chapel, Vatican — A716

Designs: No. 2769, St. Stephen, first King of Hungary (1001-1038). No. 2770, Pope Sylvester II making donation to St. Stephen. No. 2771, Pope Callixtus III ordering noon victory bell ringing by St. John of Capistrano, 1456. No. 2772, Pope Paul VI showing Cardinal Lekai location of Hungarian Chapel. No. 2773, Pope John Paul II consecrating chapel, 1980. No. 2774, Madonna and Child. Nos. 2769, 2774 sculptures by Imre Varga; others by Amerigo Tot. Nos. 2770-2773, size 37x18mm, in continuous design in block of 4 between Nos. 2769 and 2774.

1982, Nov. 30   *Perf. 12x11½*
2769   A716   2fo multi   .30   .30
2770   A716   2fo multi   .30   .30
2771   A716   2fo multi   .30   .30
2772   A716   2fo multi   .30   .30
2773   A716   2fo multi   .30   .30
2774   A716   2fo multi   .30   .30
   a.   Block of 6, #2769-2774   1.80   1.80
Exist imperf. Value, block $12.50.

Souvenir Sheet

Zoltan Kodaly (1882-1967), Composer — A717

1982, Dec. 16   *Perf. 11½*
2775   A717   20fo multi   2.00   2.00
Exists imperf. Value $20.

A718

    Perf. 12½x11½
1982, Dec. 16   *Litho.*
2776   A718   2fo multi   .40   .25
New Year 1983.
Exists imperf. Value $10.

A719

Design: Johann Wolfgang Goethe (1749-1832), German poet, by Heinrich Kolbe.

1982, Dec. 29   *Perf. 11½x12½*
Souvenir Sheet
2777   A719   20fo multi   2.00   2.00
Exists imperf. Value $27.50.

10th Anniv. of Postal Code — A720

1983, Jan. 24   *Perf. 11½x12*
2778   A720   2fo multi   .30   .25
Exists imperf. Value $7.50.

3rd Budapest Spring Festival, Mar. 18-27 — A721

2fo, Ship of Peace, by Engre Szasz.

1983, Mar. 18   *Litho.*   *Perf. 12x11½*
2779   A721   2fo multicolored   .30   .25
Exists imperf. Value $3.

Gyula Juhasz (1883-1937), Poet — A722

1983, Apr. 15   *Perf. 12*
2780   A722   2fo multi   .30   .25
Exists imperf. Value $7.50.

City of Szentgotthard, 800th Anniv. — A723

2fo, Monastery, seal, 1489.

1983, May 4   *Litho.*   *Perf. 11½*
2781   A723   2fo multicolored   .30   .25
Exists imperf. Value $7.50.

Malomto Lake, Tapolca — A724

1983, May 17   *Perf. 11½x12*
2782   A724   5fo multi   .80   .80

TEMBAL '83 Intl. Topical Stamp Exhibition, Basel, May 21-29. Issued in sheets of 3 stamps and 3 labels.
Exists imperf. Value: single with label $7.50; sheetlet $15.

Souvenir Sheet

5th Interparliamentary Union Conference on European Cooperation, Budapest, May 30-June 5 — A725

20fo, Budapest Parliament.

1983, May 30   *Litho.*   *Perf. 12½*
2783   A725   20fo multi   1.50   1.50
Exists imperf. Value $17.50.

Jeno Hamburger (1883-1936) — A726

1983, May 31   *Perf. 12*
2784   A726   2fo multi   .30   .25
Exists imperf. Value $7.50.

Lady with Unicorn, by Raphael (1483-1517) — A727

Paintings: No. 2786, Joan of Aragon. No. 2787, Granduca Madonna. No. 2788, Madonna and Child with St. John. 4fo, La Muta. 6fo, La Valeta. 8fo, La Fornarina. 20fo, Esterhazy Madonna.

    Perf. 11½x12½
1983, June 29   *Litho.*
2785   A727   1fo multi   .30   .25
2786   A727   1fo multi   .30   .25
2787   A727   2fo multi   .30   .25
2788   A727   2fo multi   .30   .25
2789   A727   4fo multi   .30   .25
2790   A727   6fo multi   .50   .25
2791   A727   8fo multi   .85   .25
    Nos. 2785-2791 (7)   2.85   1.75

Souvenir Sheet
2792   A727   20fo multi   2.00   2.00

No. 2792 contains one stamp (24x37mm).
Exist imperf. Value: set $17.50; souvenir sheet $17.50.

Simon Bolivar (1783-1830) — A728

1983, July 22   *Litho.*   *Perf. 12*
2793   A728   2fo multi   .30   .25
Exists imperf. Value $7.50.

Istvan Vagi (1883-1940), Anti-fascist Martyr — A729

1983, July 22   *Perf. 11½x12½*
2794   A729   2fo multi   .30   .25
Exists imperf. Value $7.50.

68th World Esperanto Congress, Budapest, July 30-Aug. 6 — A730

1983, July 29   *Perf. 12*
2795   A730   2fo multi   .30   .25
Exists imperf. Value $7.50.

HUNGARY

Souvenir Sheet

Martin Luther (1483-1546) — A731

1983, Aug. 12   *Perf. 12½*
2796 A731 20fo multi   2.00   2.00
Exists imperf. Value $20.

Birds — A732

Designs: Protected birds of prey and World Wildlife Fund emblem.

1983, Aug. 18   *Perf. 11½x12*
2797 A732 1fo Aquila heliaca   .30   .25
2798 A732 1fo Aquila pomarina   .30   .25
2799 A732 2fo Haliaetus albicilla   .30   .25
2800 A732 2fo Falco vespertinus   .30   .25
2801 A732 4fo Falco cherrug   .50   .25
2802 A732 6fo Buteo lagopus   .85   .40
2803 A732 8fo Buteo buteo   1.10   .50
   Nos. 2797-2803 (7)   3.65   2.15
Exist imperf. Value, set $30.

29th Intl. Apicultural Congress, Budapest, Aug. 25-31 — A733

1fo, Bee collecting pollen.

1983, Aug. 25   *Perf. 12*
2804 A733 1fo multi   .30   .25
Exists imperf. Value $7.50.

Fruit, by Bela Czobel (1883-1976) A734

1983, Sept. 15   *Litho.*   *Perf. 12x11½*
2805 A734 2fo multi   .30   .25
Exists imperf. Value $7.50.

World Communications Year — A735

No. 2806, Telecommunications, Earth Satellite. No. 2807, Intersputnik Earth Station. 2fo, TMM-81 Telephone Service. 3fo, Intelligent Terminal System. 5fo, OCR Optical Reading Instrument. 8fo, Teletext. 20fo, Molniya Communications Satellite.

1983, Oct. 7   *Litho.*   *Perf. 11½x12*
2806 A735 1fo multi   .30   .25
2807 A735 1fo multi   .30   .25
2808 A735 2fo multi   .30   .25
2809 A735 3fo multi   .30   .25
2810 A735 5fo multi   .50   .25
2811 A735 8fo multi   1.00   .25
   Nos. 2806-2811 (6)   2.70   1.50

Souvenir Sheet
Perf. 12x12½
2812 A735 20fo multi   2.00   2.00
Exist imperf. Value: set $15; souvenir sheet $20.

34th Intl. Astronautical Federation Congress — A736

1983, Oct. 10   *Photo.*   *Perf. 12*
2813 A736 2fo multi   .30   .25
Exists imperf. Value $7.50.

SOZPHILEX 83, Moscow — A737

1983, Oct. 14   *Litho.*   *Perf. 12*
2814 A737 2fo Kremlin   .35   .35
Issued in sheets of 3 stamps and 3 labels showing emblem. Size: 101x133mm.
Exists imperf. Value: single with label $5; sheetlet $16.

Mihaly Babits (1883-1941), Poet and Translator — A738

1983, Nov. 25
2815 A738 2fo multi   .30   .25
Exists imperf. Value $7.50.

Souvenir Sheet

European Security and Cooperation Conference, Madrid — A739

Perf. 12½x11½
1983, Nov. 10   *Litho.*
2816 A739 20fo multi   2.00   2.00
Exists imperf. Value $17.50.

1984 Winter Olympics, Sarajevo — A740

Designs: Ice dancers representing the seven phases of a figure cut: No. 2817, Emblem upper right. No. 2818, Emblem upper left. No. 2819, Arms extended. No. 2820, Arms bent. No. 2821, Man looking down. No. 2822, Girl looking up.

1983, Dec. 22   *Litho.*   *Perf. 12x12½*
2817 A740 1fo multicolored   .30   .25
2818 A740 1fo multicolored   .30   .25
2819 A740 2fo multicolored   .30   .25
2820 A740 2fo multicolored   .30   .25
2821 A740 4fo multicolored   .40   .25
2822 A740 4fo multicolored   .40   .25
2823 A740 6fo multicolored   .50   .25
   a. Strip of 7, #2817-2823   2.25   1.25

Souvenir Sheet
Perf. 12½
2824 A740 20fo multicolored   2.00   2.00
No. 2824 contains one 49x39mm stamp.
Exist imperf. Value: strip $15; souvenir sheet $20.

Christmas — A741

Designs: 1fo, Madonna with Rose, Kassa, 1500. 2fo, Altar piece, Csikmenasag, 1543.

1983, Dec. 13   *Litho.*   *Perf. 11½x12*
2825 A741 1fo multi   .30   .25
2826 A741 2fo multi   .30   .25
Exist imperf. Value, set $12.50.

Resorts and Spas — A742

1fo, Zanka, Lake Balaton. 2fo, Hajduszoboszlo. 5fo, Heviz.

1983, Dec. 18
2827 A742 1fo multicolored   .30   .25
2828 A742 2fo multicolored   .30   .25
2829 A742 5fo multicolored   .45   .25
   Nos. 2827-2829 (3)   1.05   .75
Exist imperf. Value, set $15.

Virgin with Six Saints, by Giovanni Battista Tiepolo — A743

Rest During Flight into Egypt, by Giovanni Domenico Tiepolo A744

Paintings Stolen and Later Recovered, Museum of Fine Arts, Budapest: b, Esterhazy Madonna, by Raphael. c, Portrait of Giorgione, 16th cent. d, Portrait of a Woman, by Tintoretto. e, Pietro Bempo, by Raphael. f, Portrait of a Man, by Tintoretto.

1984, Feb. 16   *Perf. 12½x12*
2839 Sheet of 7   2.50   2.50
   a.-f. A743 2fo multi   .30
   g. A744 8fo multi   .75
Exists imperf. Value $35.

Energy Conservation — A745

1984, Mar. 30   *Litho.*   *Perf. 11½x12*
2840 A745 1fo multi   .30   .25
Exists imperf. Value $5.

A746

Design: 2fo, Sandor Korosi Csoma (1784-1842), Master of Tibetan Philology.

1984, Mar. 30   *Perf. 11½x12½*
2841 A746 2fo multi   .35   .25
Stamps with silver inscription and with back inscription "Gift of the Hungarian Post" issued to members of Natl. Fed. of Hungarian Philatelists. Value $.65.
Exists imperf. Value $10.

Miniature Sheet

No. 1900 — A747

Designs: b, No. 1346. c, No. 1259.

1984, Apr. 20   *Litho.*   *Perf. 12x11½*
2842 A747 Sheet of 3 + 3 labels   2.00   2.00
   a.-c. 4fo multi   .60
Espana '84; Ausipex '84; Philatelia '84.
Exists imperf. Value $20.

Post-Roman Archaeological Discoveries A748

No. 2843, Round gold disc hair ornaments, Rakamaz. No. 2844, Saber belt plates, Szolnok-Strazsahalom and Galgocz. No. 2845, Silver disc hair ornaments, Sarospatak. No. 2846, Swords. 4fo, Silver and gold bowl, Ketpo. 6fo, Bone walking stick handles, Hajdudorog and Szabadbattyan. 8fo, Ivory saddle bow, Izsak; bit, stirrups, Muszka.

1984, May 15   *Perf. 12*
2843 A748 1fo dk brn & tan   .30   .25
2844 A748 1fo dk brn & tan   .30   .25
2845 A748 2fo dk brn & tan   .30   .25
2846 A748 2fo dk brn & tan   .30   .25
2847 A748 4fo dk brn & tan   .30   .25
2848 A748 6fo dk brn & tan   .50   .25
2849 A748 8fo dk brn & tan   .75   .25
   Nos. 2843-2849 (7)   2.75   1.75
Exist imperf. Value, set $15.

View of Cracow — A749

1984, May 21   *Litho.*   *Perf. 12½x11½*
2850 A749 2fo multi   .30   .25
Permanent Committee of Posts and Telecommunications, 25th Session, Cracow.
Exists imperf. Value $7.50.

Butterflies — A750

No. 2851, Epihille dilecta. No. 2852, Agra sara. No. 2853, Morpho cypris. No. 2854, Ancylusis formossissima. No. 2855, Danaus chrysippus. No. 2856, Catagramma cynosura. No. 2857, Ornithoptera paradisea.

1984, June 7   *Perf. 11½x12*
2851 A750 1fo multicolored   .30   .25
2852 A750 1fo multicolored   .30   .25
2853 A750 2fo multicolored   .30   .25
2854 A750 2fo multicolored   .30   .25
2855 A750 4fo multicolored   .50   .25

HUNGARY

| 2856 | A750 | 6fo multicolored | .65 | .25 |
| 2857 | A750 | 8fo multicolored | .90 | .25 |

Nos. 2851-2857 (7) 3.25 1.75
Exist imperf. Value, set $30.

A751

Archer, by Kisfaludy Strobl (1884-1975).

1984, July 26 Litho. Perf. 12½x11½

| 2858 | A751 | 2fo cream, red brn | .30 | .25 |

Exists imperf. Value $8.

A752

1984, July 26

| 2859 | A752 | 2fo gold, blk, red brn | .30 | .25 |

Akos Hevesi (1884-1937), revolutionary. See Nos. 2884-2885, 2910, 2915, 2962.
Exists imperf. Value $7.50.

Kepes Ujsag Peace Festival — A753

1984, Aug. 3 Litho. Perf. 12½x11½

| 2860 | A753 | 2fo Map, building | .30 | .25 |

Exists imperf. Value $4.

Aerobatic Championship — A754

2fo, Plane, map.

1984, Aug. 14

| 2861 | A754 | 2fo multicolored | .30 | .25 |

Exists imperf. Value $9.

Horse Team World Championship, Szilvasvarad, Aug. 17-20 — A755

2fo, Horse-drawn wagon.

1984, Aug. 17 Perf. 12

| 2862 | A755 | 2fo multicolored | .30 | .25 |

Exists imperf. Value $10.

Budapest Riverside Hotels — A756

No. 2863, Atrium Hyatt. No. 2864, Duna Intercontinental. No. 2865, Forum. No. 2866, Thermal Hotel, Margaret Island. No. 2867, Hilton. No. 2868, Gellert. No. 2869, Hilton, diff.

1984, Oct. 4

2863	A756	1fo multicolored	.30	.25
2864	A756	2fo multicolored	.30	.25
2865	A756	4fo multicolored	.30	.25
2866	A756	4fo multicolored	.30	.25
2867	A756	5fo multicolored	.40	.25
2868	A756	8fo multicolored	.70	.25

Nos. 2863-2868 (6) 2.30 1.50

Souvenir Sheet

| 2869 | A756 | 20fo multicolored | 2.00 | 2.00 |

Exist imperf. Value: set $15; souvenir sheet $20.

14th Conference of Postal Ministers, Budapest — A757

2fo, Building, post horn.

1984, Sept. 10 Perf. 12½x11½

| 2870 | A757 | 2fo multi | .30 | .25 |

Exists imperf. Value $7.50.

57th Stamp Day — A758

1fo, Four-handled vase, Zsolnay. 2fo, Platter, vert. 10fo, #19 on cover.

1984, Sept. 21 Perf. 12

| 2871 | A758 | 1fo multi | .30 | .25 |
| 2872 | A758 | 2fo multi | .35 | .25 |

Souvenir Sheet

| 2872A | A758 | 10fo multi | 1.50 | 1.50 |

No. 2872A contains one stamp (44x27mm, perf. 11).
Exist imperf. Value: set $12.50; souvenir sheet $20.

Edible Mushrooms A759

No. 2873, Boletus edulis. No. 2874, Marasmius oreades. No. 2875, Morchella esculenta. No. 2876, Agaricus campester. No. 2877, Macrolepiota procera. No. 2878, Cantharellus cibarius. No. 2879, Armillariella mellea.

Photogravure and Engraved

1984, Oct. 16 Perf. 12x11½

2873	A759	1fo multicolored	.30	.25
2874	A759	1fo multicolored	.30	.25
2875	A759	2fo multicolored	.40	.25
2876	A759	2fo multicolored	.40	.25
2877	A759	3fo multicolored	.60	.25
2878	A759	3fo multicolored	.60	.25
2879	A759	4fo multicolored	.85	.25

Nos. 2873-2879 (7) 3.45 1.75
Exist imperf. Value, set $30.

Budapest Opera House Centenary A760

1fo, Fresco by Mor Than. 2fo, Hallway. 5fo, Auditorium. 20fo, Building.

1984, Sept. 27 Perf. 12x11½

2880	A760	1fo multi	.25	.25
2881	A760	2fo multi	.25	.25
2882	A760	5fo multi	.50	.25

Nos. 2880-2882 (3) 1.00 .75

Souvenir Sheet

| 2883 | A760 | 20fo multi | 2.00 | 2.00 |

No. 2883 contains one stamp (49x40mm, perf. 12½).
Exist imperf. Value: set $12.50; souvenir sheet $20.

Famous Hungarians Type of 1984

No. 2884, Bela Balazs, writer (1884-1949); No. 2885, Kato Haman, labor leader (1884-1936).

1984, Dec. 3 Litho. Perf. 12½x11½

| 2884 | A752 | 2fo multi | .30 | .25 |
| 2885 | A752 | 2fo multi | .30 | .25 |

Exist imperf. Value, set $12.50.

Madonna and Child, Trensceny — A763

1984, Dec. 17 Litho. Perf. 11½x12

| 2886 | A763 | 1fo multi | .30 | .25 |

Exists imperf. Value $3.

Owls — A764

Photogravure and Engraved

1984, Dec. 28 Perf. 12½x11½

2887	A764	1fo Athene Noctua	.30	.25
2888	A764	1fo Tyto alba	.30	.25
2889	A764	2fo Strix aluco	.30	.25
2890	A764	2fo Asio otus	.30	.25
2891	A764	4fo Nyctea scadiaca	.45	.25
2892	A764	6fo Strix uralensis	.75	.25
2893	A764	8fo Bubo bubo	.90	.25

Nos. 2887-2893 (7) 3.30 1.75
Exist imperf. Value, set $35.

Torah Crown, Buda — A765

19th Cent. Art from Jewish Museum, Budapest: No. 2895, Chalice, Moscow. No. 2896, Torah shield, Vienna. No. 2897, Chalice, Warsaw. No. 2898, Container, Augsburg. No. 2899, Candlestick holder, Warsaw. No. 2900, Money box, Pest.

1984, Dec. 21 Litho. Perf. 12

2894	A765	1fo shown	.30	.25
2895	A765	1fo multicolored	.30	.25
2896	A765	2fo multicolored	.30	.25
2897	A765	2fo multicolored	.30	.25
2898	A765	4fo multicolored	.30	.25
2899	A765	6fo multicolored	.40	.25
2900	A765	8fo multicolored	.70	.25

Nos. 2894-2900 (7) 2.60 1.75
Exist imperf. Value, set $20.

Souvenir Sheet

Hungarian Olympic Committee, 90th Anniv. — A766

1985, Jan. 2 Photo. Perf. 12x12½

| 2901 | A766 | 20fo Long jump | 2.00 | 2.00 |

Exists imperf. Value $20.

Novi Sad, Yugoslavia A767

Danube Bridges: No. 2903, Baja. No. 2904, Arpad Bridge, Budapest. No. 2905, Bratislava, Czechoslovakia. 4fo, Reichsbrucke, Vienna. 6fo, Linz, Austria. 8fo, Regensburg, Federal Rep. of Germany. 20fo, Elizabeth Bridge, Budapest, and map.

1985, Feb. 12 Litho. Perf. 12x11½

2902	A767	1fo multi	.30	.25
2903	A767	1fo multi	.30	.25
2904	A767	2fo multi	.30	.25
2905	A767	2fo multi	.30	.25
2906	A767	4fo multi	.30	.25
2907	A767	6fo multi	.50	.25
2908	A767	8fo multi	.75	.25

Nos. 2902-2908 (7) 2.75 1.75

Souvenir Sheet Perf. 12½

| 2909 | A767 | 20fo multi | 2.00 | 2.00 |

Exist imperf. Value: set $30; souvenir sheet $20.
For surcharge, see No. 4333.

Famous Hungarians Type of 1984

Design: Laszlo Rudas (1885-1950), communist philosopher.

1985, Feb. 21 Perf. 12½x11½

| 2910 | A752 | 2fo gold & brn | .30 | .25 |

Exists imperf. Value $7.50.

Intl. Women's Day, 75th Anniv. — A769

1985, Mar. 5 Photo. Perf. 11½x12½

| 2911 | A769 | 2fo gold & multi | .30 | .25 |

Exists imperf. Value $8.

OLYMPHILEX '85, Lausanne — A770

1985, Mar. 14 Litho. Perf. 11½x12

| 2912 | A770 | 4fo No. B81 | .50 | .25 |
| 2913 | A770 | 5fo No. B82 | .50 | .25 |

Exist imperf. Value, set $17.50.

Souvenir Sheet

Liberation of Hungary From German Occupation Forces, 40th Anniv. — A771

Design: Liberty Bridge, Budapest and silhouette of the Liberation Monument on Gellert Hill illuminated by fireworks.

1985, Mar. 28 Perf. 12½

| 2914 | A771 | 20fo multi | 2.00 | 2.00 |

Exists imperf. Value $20.

HUNGARY

Famous Hungarians Type of 1984
Design: Gyorgy Lukacs (1885-1971) communist philosopher, educator.

1985, Apr. 12		Perf. 12½x11½
2915 A752 2fo gold & brn	.30	.25

Exists imperf. Value $7.50.

Totfalusi Bible, 300th Anniv. — A773

1985, Apr. 25		Perf. 12
2916 A773 2fo gold & black	.30	.25

1st Bible printed in Hungarian by Nicolas Totfalusi Kis (1650-1702), publisher, in 1685.
Exists imperf. Value $12.

Lorand Eotvos Univ., 350th Anniv. — A774

Design: Archbishop Peter Pazmany (1570-1637), founder.

1985, May 14		
2917 A774 2fo magenta & gray	.30	.25

No. 2917 printed se-tenant with label picturing obverse and reverse of university commemorative medal.
Exists imperf. Value, with label $7.50.

A775

1985, May 25		
2918 A775 2fo multi	.30	.25

26th European Boxing Championships, Budapest.
Exists imperf. Value $3.50.

Intl. Youth Year — A776

1985, May 29		Perf. 11½x12
2919 A776 1fo Girl's soccer	.30	.25
2920 A776 2fo Windsurfing	.30	.25
2921 A776 2fo Aerobic exercise	.30	.25
2922 A776 4fo Karate	.35	.25
2923 A776 4fo Go-kart racing	.35	.25
2924 A776 5fo Hang gliding	.50	.25
2925 A776 6fo Skateboarding	.50	.25
Nos. 2919-2925 (7)	2.60	1.75

Exist imperf. Value, set $25.

Electro-magnetic High-speed Railway — A777

EXPO '85, Tsukuba, Japan: futuristic technology: 4fo, Fuyo (robot) Theater.

1985, May 29		Perf. 12x11½
2926 A777 2fo shown	.30	.25
2927 A777 4fo multicolored	.50	.25

Exist imperf. Value, set $17.50.

Audubon Birth Bicentenary — A778

Audubon illustrations: No. 2928, Colaptes cafer. No. 2929, Bombycilla garrulus. No. 2930, Dryocopus pileatus. No. 2931, Icterus galbula.

1985, June 19		Perf. 12
2928 A778 2fo multicolored	.30	.25
2929 A778 2fo multicolored	.30	.25
2930 A778 2fo multicolored	.30	.25
2931 A778 4fo multicolored	.55	.25
Nos. 2928-2931,C446-C447 (6)	2.90	1.50

Exist imperf. Value, set (6) $40.

Mezohegyes Stud Farm, Bicent. — A779

Horses: No. 2932, Nonius-36, 1883, a dark chestnut. No. 2933, Furioso-23, 1889, a light chestnut. No. 2934, Gidran-1, 1935, a blond breed. No. 2935, Ramses-3, 1960, gray sporting horse. No. 2936, Krozus-1, 1970, chestnut sporting horse.

1985, June 28		
2932 A779 1fo multi	.30	.25
2933 A779 2fo multi	.30	.25
2934 A779 4fo multi	.55	.25
2935 A779 5fo multi	.55	.25
2936 A779 6fo multi	.85	.25
Nos. 2932-2936 (5)	2.55	1.25

Exist imperf. Value, set $25.

Prevention of Nuclear War — A780

Design: Illustration of a damaged globe and hands, by Imre Varga (b. 1923), 1973 Kossuth prize-winner.

1985, June 28		Perf. 11½x12
2937 A780 2fo multi	.30	.25

Intl. Physician's Movement for the Prevention of Nuclear War, 5th Congress.
Exists imperf. Value $4.75.

European Music Year — A781

Composers and instruments: 1fo, George Frideric Handel (1685-1759), kettle drum, horn. 2fo, Johann Sebastian Bach (1685-1750), Thomas Church organ. No. 2940, Luigi Cherubini (1760-1842), harp, bass viol, baryton. No. 2941, Frederic Chopin (1810-1849), piano, 1817. 5fo, Gustav Mahler (1860-1911), pardessus de viole, kettle drum, double horn. 6fo, Erkel Ferenc (1810-1893), bass tuba, violin.

1985, July 10		Perf. 11
2938 A781 1fo multi	.30	.25
2939 A781 2fo multi	.30	.25
2940 A781 4fo multi	.30	.25
2941 A781 4fo multi	.30	.25
2942 A781 5fo multi	.50	.25
2943 A781 6fo multi	.60	.25
Nos. 2938-2943 (6)	2.30	1.50

Exist imperf. Value, set $17.50.

Souvenir Sheet

12th World Youth Festival, Moscow A782

20fo, Emblem, Red Square.

1985, July 22		Perf. 12½
2944 A782 20fo multi	1.50	1.50

Exists imperf. Value $27.50.

Souvenir Sheet

Helsinki Agreement, 10th Anniv. — A783

20fo, Finlandia Hall, Helsinki.

1985, Aug. 1		Perf. 11
2945 A783 20fo multi	2.00	2.00

Exists imperf. Value $27.50.

World Tourism Day — A784

2fo, Key, globe, heart.

1985, Sept. 27		Perf. 12½x11½ Litho.
2946 A784 2fo multi	.30	.25

Exists imperf. Value $7.50.

COMNET '85 — A785

4fo, Computer terminal.

1985, Oct. 1		Perf. 11½
2947 A785 4fo multi	.35	.30

3rd Computer Sciences Conference, Budapest, Oct. 1-4.
Exists imperf. Value $7.50.

Souvenir Sheet

Danube River, Budapest Bridges — A786

1985, Oct. 15		Perf. 12
2948 A786 20fo multi	2.00	2.00

European Security and Cooperation Conference and Cultural Forum, Budapest, Oct. 15-Nov. 25. Exists inscribed "Kuturalis Forum Resztvevoi Tiszteletere" in gold on front and "Gift of the Hungarian Post" on back. Not valid for postage.
Exists imperf. Value $25.

16-17th Century Ceramics — A787

1fo, Faience water jar and dispenser, 1609. 2fo, Tankard, 1670. 10fo, Hexagonal medicine jar, 1774.

1985, Oct. 18		Perf. 12½x11½
2949 A787 1fo multi	.30	.25
2950 A787 2fo multi	.35	.25

Souvenir Sheet

| 2951 A787 10fo multi | 1.50 | 1.50 |

EUROPHILEX '85, Oct. 14-31.
Exist imperf. Value: set $12.50; souvenir sheet $20.

Italy No. 799, view of Rome — A788

1985, Oct. 21		Perf. 12x11½
2952 A788 5fo multi	.75	.75

Italia '85, Rome, Oct. 25-Nov. 3. Issued in sheets of 3 stamps and 3 labels showing emblem.
Exists imperf. Value: single with label $7; sheetlet $17.50.

UN, 40th Anniv. — A789

4fo, Dove, globe, emblem.

1985, Oct. 24		Perf. 11½x12
2953 A789 4fo multicolored	.35	.25

Exists imperf. Value $9.

Indigenous Lilies — A790

No. 2954, Lilium bulbiferum. No. 2955, Lilium martagon. No. 2956, Erythronium denscanis. No. 2957, Fritillaria meleagris. No. 2958, Lilium tigrinum. No. 2959, Hemerocallis lilio-asphodelus. No. 2960, Bulbocodium vernum.

Photogravure and Engraved

1985, Oct. 28		Perf. 12½x11½
2954 A790 1fo multicolored	.30	.25
2955 A790 2fo multicolored	.30	.25
2956 A790 3fo multicolored	.30	.25
2957 A790 4fo multicolored	.40	.25
2958 A790 4fo multicolored	.40	.25
2959 A790 5fo multicolored	.50	.25
2960 A790 6fo multicolored	.75	.25
Nos. 2954-2960 (7)	2.95	1.75

Exists imperf. Value, set $20.

HUNGARY

Christmas 1985 — A791

1985, Nov. 6   Litho.   Perf. 13½x13
2961 A791 2fo Youths caroling   .30   .25
Exists imperf. Value $10.

Famous Hungarians Type of 1984
Design: Istvan Ries (1885-1950), Minister of Justice (1949), labor movement.

1985, Nov. 11   Perf. 12½x11½
2962 A752 2fo gold & ol brn   .30   .25
Exists imperf. Value $7.50.

Motorcycle Centenary A793

No. 2963, Fantic Sprinter, 1984. No. 2964, Suzuki Katana GSX, 1983. No. 2965, Harley-Davidson Duo-Glide, 1960. No. 2966, Rudge-Whitworth, 1935. No. 2967, BMW R47, 1927. No. 2968, NSU, 1910. No. 2969, Daimler, 1885.

Photogravure & Engraved
1985, Dec. 28   Perf. 11½x12
2963 A793 1fo multicolored   .30   .25
2964 A793 2fo multicolored   .30   .25
2965 A793 2fo multicolored   .30   .25
2966 A793 4fo multicolored   .35   .25
2967 A793 4fo multicolored   .35   .25
2968 A793 5fo multicolored   .50   .25
2969 A793 6fo multicolored   .75   .25
Nos. 2963-2969 (7)   2.85 1.75
Exist imperf. Value, set $22.50.

Bela Kun (1886-1939), Communist Party Founder — A794

1986, Feb. 20   Perf. 12½x11½   Litho.
2970 A794 4fo multi   .35   .25
Exist imperf. Value $7.50.

Souvenir Sheet

US Shuttle Challenger — A795

1986, Feb. 21   Perf. 11½
2971 A795 20fo multi   2.50 2.50
Memorial to the US astronauts who died when the Challenger exploded during takeoff, Jan. 28.
Exist imperf. Value $20.

Halley's Comet — A796

No. 2972, US ICE satellite, dinosaurs. No. 2973, USSR Vega and Bayeaux tapestry detail, 1066, France. No. 2974, Japanese Suisei and German engraving, 1507. No. 2975, European Space Agency Giotto and The Three Magi, tapestry by Giotto. No. 2976, USSR Astron and Apianis constellation, 1531. No. 2977, US space shuttle and Edmond Halley.

Perf. 11½x13½
1986, Feb. 14   Litho.
2972 A796 2fo multi   .30   .25
2973 A796 2fo multi   .30   .25
2974 A796 2fo multi   .30   .25
2975 A796 4fo multi   .50   .25
2976 A796 4fo multi   .50   .25
2977 A796 6fo multi   .75   .25
Nos. 2972-2977 (6)   2.65 1.50
Exist imperf. Value, set $25.

Seeing-eye Dog, Red Cross — A797

Perf. 12½x11½
1986, Mar. 20   Litho.
2978 A797 4fo multi   .35   .25
Assistance for the blind.
Exists imperf. Value $25.

Soccer Players in Blue and Red Uniforms — A798

1986, Apr. 2   Perf. 11
Color of Uniforms
2979 A798 2fo shown   .30   .25
2980 A798 2fo blue & green   .30   .25
2981 A798 4fo red & black   .55   .25
2982 A798 4fo yellow & red   .55   .25
2983 A798 4fo yellow & green   .55   .25
2984 A798 6fo orange & white   .75   .25
Nos. 2979-2984 (6)   3.00 1.50

Souvenir Sheet
Perf. 12½
2985 A798 20fo Victors   1.50 1.50
1986 World Cup Soccer Championships, Mexico. No. 2979 contains one stamp (size: 41x32mm). Also exists with added inscription "In honor of the winner . . ." and red control number. Value $90.
Exist imperf. Value: set $20; souvenir sheet $20.

Buda Castle Cable Railway Station Reopening — A799

1986, Apr. 30   Perf. 11½x12
2986 A799 2fo org, brn & pale yel   .35   .25
Exists imperf. Value $8.50.

Souvenir Sheet

A800

AMERIPEX '86, Chicago, May 22-June 1: a, Yankee doodle rose. b, America rose. c, George Washington, statue by Gyula Bezeredy (1858-1935), Budapest.

1986, Apr. 30   Perf. 12½x11½
2987 A800   Sheet of 3   2.00 2.00
a.-b.   5fo any single   .50   .50
c.   10fo multi   1.00 1.00
Size of No. 2987c: 27x74mm.
Exists imperf. Value $25.

Folk Dolls — A801

1986, May 6   Perf. 11½x12
2988 A801 4fo multi   .35   .25
Hungary Days in Tokyo.
Exists imperf. Value $12.

Andras Fay (1786-1864), Author, Politician — A802

Lithographed and Engraved
1986, May 29   Perf. 12
2989 A802 4fo beige & fawn   .35   .35
Printed se-tenant with label picturing First Hungarian Savings Bank Union, founded by Fay.
Exists imperf. Value, with label $7.50.

Automobile, Cent. — A803

No. 2990, 1961 Ferrari Tipo 156, 1985 race car. No. 2991, 1932 Alfa Romeo Tipo B, 1984 race car. No. 2992, 1936 Volkswagen, 1986 Porsche 959. No. 2993, 1902 Renault 14CV, 1985 Renault 5 GT Turbo. No. 2994, 1899 Fiat 3½, 1985 Fiat Ritmo. 6fo, 1886 Daimler, 1986 Mercedes-Benz 230SE.

1986, July 24   Litho.   Perf. 12
2990 A803 2fo multi   .30   .25
2991 A803 2fo multi   .30   .25
2992 A803 2fo multi   .30   .25
2993 A803 4fo multi   .55   .25
2994 A803 4fo multi   .55   .25
2995 A803 6fo multi   .75   .25
Nos. 2990-2995 (6)   2.75 1.50
Exists imperf. Value, set $25.

Wasa, 1628, Warship A804

1986, Aug. 15   Litho.   Perf. 11½x12
2996 A804 2fo multi   .55   .55
STOCKHOLMIA '86, 8/28-9/7. Printed se-tenant with label (size: 27x34mm) picturing exhibition emblem. Printed in sheets of 3.
Exists imperf. Value: single with label $6; sheetlet $20.

14th Intl. Cancer Congress, Budapest — A805

Design: Moritz Kaposi (1837-1902), Austrian cancer researcher.

1986, Aug. 21   Perf. 12½x11½
2997 A805 4fo multicolored   .35   .25
Exists imperf. Value $9.

Recapture of Buda Castle, by Gyula Benzcur (1844-1920) — A806

1986, Sept. 2   Perf. 12
2998 A806 4fo multicolored   .35   .25
Recapture of Buda from the Turks, 300th anniv.
Exists imperf. Value $10.

Tranquility A807

Hope A808

Stamp Day: Paintings by Endre Szasz.

1986, Sept. 5
2999 A807 2fo shown   .40   .25
3000 A807 2fo Confidence   .40   .25

Souvenir Sheet
Perf. 11½
3001 A808 10fo shown   1.50 1.50
Exist imperf. Value: set $17.50; souvenir sheet $25.

5th Intl. Conference on Oriental Carpets, Vienna and Budapest — A809

4fo, Anatolia crivelli, 15th cent.

1986, Sept. 17   Litho.   Perf. 11
3002 A809 4fo multi   .35   .25
Exists imperf. Value $9.

Franz Liszt, Composer A810

1986, Oct. 21   Engr.   Perf. 12
3003 A810 4fo grayish green   .35   .25
Exists imperf. Value $10.

Intl. Peace Year A811

1986, Oct. 24   Litho.
3004 A811 4fo multicolored   .50   .50
No. 3004 printed se-tenant with label.
Exists imperf. Value, with label $13.50.

HUNGARY

Souvenir Sheet

Hofburg Palace, Vienna, and Map — A812

1986, Nov. 4   *Perf. 11*
3005   A812   20fo multicolored   2.00   2.00
European Security and Cooperation Conference, Vienna.
Exists imperf. Value $25.

Fruits — A813

Photogravure & Engraved
1986, Nov. 25   *Perf. 12x11½*
3006   A813   2fo Sour cherries   .30   .25
3007   A813   2fo Apricots   .30   .25
3008   A813   4fo Peaches   .50   .25
3009   A813   4fo Raspberries   .50   .25
3010   A813   4fo Apples   .50   .25
3011   A813   6fo Grapes   1.00   .35
Nos. 3006-3011 (6)   3.10   1.60
Exist imperf. Value, set $25.

Natl. Heroes — A814

Designs: No. 3012, Jozseph Pogany (1886-1939), journalist, martyr. No. 3013, Ferenc Munnich (1886-1967), prime minister, 1958-61.

1986   *Litho.*   *Perf. 12½x11½*
3012   A814   4fo multi   .35   .25
3013   A814   4fo multi   .35   .25
Issued: No. 3012, Nov. 6; No. 3013, Nov. 14.
Exist imperf. Value, set $15.

World Communist Youth Fed., 12th Congress — A815

1986, Nov. 21   *Perf. 12*
3014   A815   4fo multi   .35   .25
Exist imperf. Value $7.50.

Castles — A816

2fo, Forgach, Szecseny. 3fo, Savoya, Rackeve. 4fo, Batthyany, Kormend. 5fo, Szechenyi, Nagycenk. 6fo, Rudnyanszky, Nagyteteny. 7fo, Esterhazy, Papa. 8fo, Szapary, Buk. 10fo, Festetics, Keszthely. 12fo, Dory Castle, Mihalyi. 20fo, Brunswick, Martonvasar. 30fo, De la Motte, Nosvaj. 40fo, L'Huillier-Coborg, Edeleny. 50fo, Teleki-Degenfeld, Szirak. 70fo, Magochy, Pacin. 100fo, Eszterhazy, Fertod.

Perf. 12x11½, 11½x12½ (7fo)
1986-91   *Litho.*
3015   A816   2fo multi   .30   .25
3016   A816   3fo multi   .30   .25
3017   A816   4fo multi   .30   .25
3018   A816   5fo multi   .30   .25
3019   A816   6fo multi   .35   .25
3020   A816   7fo multi   .50   .30
3021   A816   8fo multi   .50   .50
3022   A816   10fo multi   .85   .40
3023   A816   12fo multi   .90   .50
3024   A816   20fo multi   1.75   .75
3025   A816   30fo multi   2.25   1.10
3026   A816   40fo multi   3.00   1.60
3027   A816   50fo multi   4.00   1.90
3028   A816   70fo multi   5.00   2.75
3029   A816   100fo multi   8.00   4.00
Nos. 3015-3029 (15)   28.30   14.85
The 7fo, 12fo are inscribed "Magyarorszag."
Issued: 2fo-6fo, 8fo, 11/28; 10fo, 20fo-30fo, 100fo, 5/28/87; 40fo-70fo, 7/30/87; 7fo, 6/27/91; 12fo, 9/6/91.
Exist imperf. Value, set $125.
For overprint see No. 3320.

Festetics Castle, Keszthely — A816a

1989-92   *Litho. & Engr.*   *Perf. 12*
3030   A816a   10fo brn blk & yel ochre   .75   .25
    Litho.
3031   A816a   15fo lt grn & brn   .60   .45
The 15fo is inscribed "Magyarorszag."
Issued: 10fo, Feb. 28; 15fo, Mar. 27, 1992.
No. 3030 exist imperf. Value $5.

Wildlife Conservation A817

No. 3035, Felis silvestris. No. 3036, Lutra lutra. No. 3037, Mustela erminea. No. 3038, Sciurus vulgaris. No. 3039, Erinaceus concolor. No. 3040, Emys orbicularis.

1986, Dec. 5   *Perf. 12*
3035   A817   2fo multi   .30   .25
3036   A817   2fo multi   .30   .25
3037   A817   3fo multi   .30   .25
3038   A817   4fo multi   .50   .25
3039   A817   4fo multi   .50   .25
3040   A817   6fo multi   .75   .25
Nos. 3035-3040 (6)   2.65   1.50
Exist imperf. Value, set $25.

Portraits of Hungarian Kings in the Historical Portrait Gallery — A818

King and reign: No. 3041, St. Steven, 997-1038. No. 3042, Geza I, 1074-1077. No. 3043, St. Ladislas, 1077-1095. No. 3044, Bela III, 1172-1196. No. 3045, Bela IV, 1235-1270.

1986, Dec. 10   *Perf. 11½x12*
3041   A818   2fo multi   .30   .25
3042   A818   2fo multi   .30   .25
3043   A818   4fo multi   .45   .25
3044   A818   4fo multi   .45   .25
3045   A818   6fo multi   .60   .25
Nos. 3041-3045 (5)   2.10   1.25
Exist imperf. Value, set $25.
See Nos. 3120-3122.

Fungi — A819

No. 3046, Amanita phalloides. No. 3047, Inocybe patouillardi. No. 3048, Amanita muscaria. No. 3049, Omphalotus olearius. No. 3050, Amanita pantherina. No. 3051, Gyromitra esculenta.

Lithographed and Engraved
1986, Dec. 30   *Perf. 11½*
3046   A819   2fo multicolored   .30   .25
3047   A819   2fo multicolored   .30   .25
3048   A819   2fo multicolored   .30   .25
3049   A819   4fo multicolored   .55   .30
3050   A819   4fo multicolored   .55   .30
3051   A819   6fo multicolored   .80   .40
Nos. 3046-3051 (6)   2.80   1.75
Exist imperf. Value, set $40.

Saltwater Fish — A820

No. 3052, Colisa fasciata. No. 3053, Pseudotropheus zebra. No. 3054, Iriatherina werneri. No. 3055, Aphyosemion multicolor. No. 3056, Papiliochromis ramirezi. No. 3057, Hyphessobrycon erythrostigma.

1987, Jan. 15   *Photo.*   *Perf. 11½*
3052   A820   2fo multicolored   .30   .25
3053   A820   2fo multicolored   .30   .25
3054   A820   2fo multicolored   .30   .25
3055   A820   4fo multicolored   .40   .25
3056   A820   4fo multicolored   .40   .25
3057   A820   6fo multicolored   .60   .25
Nos. 3052-3057 (6)   2.30   1.50
Exist imperf. Value, set $30.

Seated Woman, 1918, by Bela Uitz (1887-1972), Painter — A821

1987, Mar. 6   *Litho.*   *Perf. 12*
3058   A821   4fo multicolored   .30   .25
Exists imperf. Value $7.50.

Abstract, 1960, by Lajos Kassak (1887-1967) — A822

1987, Mar. 20
3059   A822   4fo black & red   .30   .25
Exists imperf. Value $7.50.

Medical Pioneers — A823

Designs: 2fo, Hippocrates (460-377 B.C.), Greek physician. No. 3061, Avicenna or Ibn Sina (A.D. 980-1037), Islamic pharmacist, diagnostician. No. 3062, Ambroise Pare (1510-1590), French surgeon. No. 3063, William Harvey (1578-1657), English physician, anatomist. 6fo, Ignaz Semmelweis (1818-1865), Hungarian obstetrician.

1987, Mar. 31
3060   A823   2fo black & dk red brn   .30   .25
3061   A823   4fo black & dk grn   .45   .25
3062   A823   4fo black & steel bl   .45   .25
3063   A823   4fo black & olive blk   .45   .25
3064   A823   6fo black & grn blk   .70   .25
Nos. 3060-3064 (5)   2.35   1.25
Exist imperf. Value, set $25.

Neolithic and Copper Age Artifacts — A824

Designs: 2fo, Urn, Hodmezovasarhely. No. 3066, Altar, Szeged. No. 3067, Deity, Szegvar-Tuzkoves. 5fo, Vase, Center.

1987, Apr. 15   *Litho.*   *Perf. 12*
3065   A824   2fo pale bl grn & sep   .30   .25
3066   A824   4fo buff & sepia   .50   .25
3067   A824   4fo pale org & sepia   .50   .25
3068   A824   5fo pale yel grn & sep   .60   .25
Nos. 3065-3068 (4)   1.90   1.00
Exists imperf. Value, set $25.

Souvenir Sheet

Esztergom Cathedral Treasury Reopening A825

20fo, Calvary of King Matthias.

1987, Apr. 28   *Perf. 11*
3069   A825   20fo multi   1.75   1.75
No. 3069 margin pictures the Horn Chalice of King Sigismund, Rhineland, 1408 (UL), Crozier of Archbishop Miklos Olah, Hungary, c. 1490 (UR), Monstrance of Imre Eszterhazy, by Gaspar Meichl, Vienna, 1728 (LL), and the Chalice of Matthias, Hungary, c. 1480.
Exists imperf. Value $25.

Hungarian First Aid Assoc., Cent. — A826

4fo, Ambulances, 1887-1987.

1987, May 5   *Perf. 11½x12*
3070   A826   4fo multicolored   .30   .25
Exists imperf. Value $9.50.

Souvenir Sheet

CAPEX '87, Toronto — A827

Stamp exhibitions: b, OLYMPHILEX '87, Rome. c, HAFNIA '87, Copenhagen.

1987, May 20   *Litho.*   *Perf. 11*
3071   A827   Sheet of 3 + 3 labels   1.75   1.75
    a.-c.   5fo any single   .50   .50
Exists imperf. Value $17.50.

HUNGARY

Jozsef Marek (1886-1952), Veterinarian — A828

1987, May 25   Perf. 12x11½
3072 A828 4fo multicolored .30 .25
Veterinary education, bicent.
Exists imperf. Value $7.50.

Teleki's African Expedition, Cent. — A829

1987, June 10
3073 A829 4fo multicolored .30 .25
Samuel Teleki (1845-1916), explorer.
Exists imperf. Value $7.50.

Woodcut by Abraham von Werdt, 18th Cent. — A830

Litho. & Engr.
1987, June 25   Perf. 12
3074 A830 4fo beige & sepia .30 .25
Hungarian Printing, Paper and Press Workers' Union, 125th anniv.
Exists imperf. Value $10.

Antarctic Research, 75th Anniv. — A831

Helicopter Landing, Mirnij Research Station — A832

Map, explorer and scene: No. 3075, James Cook (1728-1779) and ship. No. 3076, Fabian von Bellingshausen (1778-1852) and seals. No. 3077, Ernest H. Shackleton (1874-1922) and penguins. No. 3078, Roald Amundsen (1872-1928) discovering South Pole, dog team. No. 3079, Robert F. Scott (1868-1912) and ship. No. 3080, Richard E. Byrd (1888-1957) and Floyd Bennett monoplane.

1987, June 30   Litho.
3075 A831 2fo multi .30 .25
3076 A831 2fo multi .30 .25
3077 A831 3fo multi .30 .25
3078 A831 4fo multi .45 .25
3079 A831 4fo multi .45 .25
3080 A831 6fo multi .60 .25
    Nos. 3075-3080 (6) 2.40 1.50
Souvenir Sheet
Perf. 11½
3081 A832 20fo multi 3.50 3.50
Exist imperf. Value: set $25; souvenir sheet $40.

Railway Officers Training Institute, Cent. — A833

1987, Sept. 4   Litho.   Perf. 11½x12
3082 A833 4fo blue & black .30 .25
Exists imperf. Value $12.50.

Stamp Day, 60th Anniv. — A834

Masonry of the medieval Buda Castle: 2fo, Flowers, dolphin. 4fo, Arms of King Matthias. 10fo, "ONDIDIT/GENEROSVM" inscribed on capital.

Litho. & Engr.
1987, Sept. 18   Perf. 12
3083 A834 2fo lt blue & dk blue .30 .25
3084 A834 4fo lt grn & dk grn .50 .50
Souvenir Sheet
Perf. 11
3085 A834 10fo multicolored 1.50 1.50
Exist imperf. Value: set $12.50; souvenir sheet $25.

A835

1987, Sept. 30   Litho.   Perf. 12
3086 A835 4fo multi .80 .80
    a. Se-tenant with label .85 .85
No 3086 printed in sheet of 50 and in sheet of 25 plus 25 labels picturing 13th cent. church at Gyongyospata which houses the altar.
Exists imperf. Value $10; with label $20.

Orchids — A836 / A837

No. 3087, Cypripedium calceolus. No. 3088, Orchis purpurea. No. 3089, Himantoglossum hircinum. No. 3090, Ophrys scolopax cornuta. No. 3091, Cephalanthera rubra. No. 3092, Epipactis atrorubens.

1987, Oct. 29   Litho.   Perf. 11
3087 A836 2fo multicolored .30 .25
3088 A836 2fo multicolored .30 .25
3089 A836 4fo multicolored .35 .25
3090 A836 4fo multicolored .35 .25
3091 A836 5fo multicolored .50 .25
3092 A836 6fo multicolored .65 .25
    Nos. 3087-3092 (6) 2.45 1.50
Miniature Sheet
3093 A837 20fo shown 2.50 2.50
Exist imperf. Value: set $30; souvenir sheet $35.

1988 Winter Olympics, Calgary — A838

No. 3094, Speed skating. No. 3095, Cross-country skiing. No. 3096, Biathlon. No. 3097, Ice hockey. No. 3098, 4-Man bobsled. No. 3099, Ski-jumping. No. 3100, Slalom.

1987, Nov. 24
3094 A838 2fo multicolored .35 .25
3095 A838 2fo multicolored .35 .25
3096 A838 4fo multicolored .40 .25
3097 A838 4fo multicolored .40 .25
3098 A838 4fo multicolored .40 .25
3099 A838 6fo multicolored .65 .25
    Nos. 3094-3099 (6) 2.55 1.50
Souvenir Sheet
3100 A838 20fo multicolored 2.00 2.00
Exist imperf. Value: set $20; souvenir sheet $20.

Souvenir Sheet

U.S.-Soviet Summit, Dec. 7-10 — A839

1987, Dec. 7   Perf. 12
3101 A839 20fo Shaking hands 2.00 2.00
Meeting of Gen. Secretary Gorbachev and Pres. Reagan to discuss and sign nuclear arms reduction treaty.
Exists imperf. Value $20.

Fairy Tales — A840

Designs: No. 3102, The White Crane, from Japan. No. 3103, The Fox and the Crow, Aesop's Fables. No. 3104, The Tortoise and the Hare, Aesop's Fables. No. 3105, The Ugly Duckling, by Hans Christian Andersen. No. 3106, The Steadfast Tin Soldier, by Andersen.

1987, Dec. 11
3102 A840 2fo multi .30 .25
3103 A840 2fo multi .30 .25
3104 A840 4fo multi .50 .25
3105 A840 4fo multi .50 .25
3106 A840 6fo multi .75 .25
    Nos. 3102-3106 (5) 2.35 1.25
Exist imperf. Value, set $22.50.

Count Ferdinand von Zeppelin (1838-1917), Designer of Dirigibles — A841

No. 3107, LZ-2, 1905. No. 3108, LZ-4, 1908. No. 3109, LZ-10, Schwaben, 1911. No. 3110, LZ-127, Graf Zeppelin, 1928.

1988, Jan. 29   Litho.   Perf. 12
3107 A841 2fo blue .40 .25
3108 A841 4fo brown .50 .25
3109 A841 4fo lilac .50 .25
3110 A841 8fo green .70 .25
    Nos. 3107-3110 (4) 2.10 1.00
Exist imperf. Value, set $20.

1988 World Figure Skating Championships, Budapest — A842

Various athletes wearing period costumes: No. 3111, Male, 20th cent. No. 3112, Male, (cap), 19th cent. No. 3113, Male (hat), 18th cent. No. 3114, Woman, c. 1930. No. 3115, Woman (contemporary). No. 3116, Pair. No. 3117, Death spiral.

1988, Feb. 29   Photo.   Perf. 11½
3111 A842 2fo multicolored .30 .25
3112 A842 2fo multicolored .30 .25
3113 A842 4fo multicolored .40 .25
3114 A842 4fo multicolored .40 .25
3115 A842 5fo multicolored .50 .25
3116 A842 6fo multicolored .50 .25
    Nos. 3111-3116 (6) 2.40 1.50
Souvenir Sheet
Perf. 12x11½
3117 A842 20fo multicolored 1.75 1.75
No. 3117 contains one 37x52mm stamp.
Exist imperf. Value: set $15; souvenir sheet $20.

Illes Monus (1888-1944), Party Leader — A843

1988, Mar. 11   Litho.   Perf. 11½x12
3118 A843 4fo multi .30 .25
Exists imperf. Value $7.50.
See Nos. 3152, 3160.

Miniature Sheet

Postmaster's Coat, Hat and Post Horn, 18th Cent. — A844

1988, Mar. 18   Litho.   Perf. 13
3119 A844 4fo + 4 labels .85 .85
Intl. stamp exhibitions, 1988. No. 3119 contains 4 labels picturing exhibition emblems: JUVALUX '88, Luxembourg, Mar. 29-Apr. 4 (UL), SYDPEX '88, Sydney, Australia, July 30-Aug.7 (UR), FINLANDIA '88, Helsinki, Finland, June 1-12 (LR), and PRAGA '88, Prague, Czechoslovakia, Aug. 26-Sept. 4 (LL).
Exists imperf. Value $25.

King Type of 1986

Portraits of Hungarian kings in the Historical Portrait Gallery. King and reign: 2fo, Charles Robert (1308-1342). 4fo, Louis I (1342-1382). 6fo, Sigismund (1387-1437).

1988, Mar. 31   Perf. 11½x12
3120 A818 2fo pale grn, sep & red .30 .25
3121 A818 4fo pale ultra, sep & red .40 .25
3122 A818 6fo pale vio, sep & red .60 .25
    Nos. 3120-3122 (3) 1.30 .75
Exists imperf. Value, set $25.

1988 Summer Olympics, Seoul — A845

1988, Apr. 20   Litho.   Perf. 13½x13
3123 A845 2fo Rowing .30 .25
3124 A845 4fo Hurdling .40 .25
3125 A845 4fo Fencing .40 .25
3126 A845 6fo Boxing .75 .25
    Nos. 3123-3126 (4) 1.85 1.00

HUNGARY

Souvenir Sheet
Perf. 12½
3127 A845 20fo Tennis ... 2.00 2.00
Exist imperf. Value: set $20; souvenir sheet $25.

Computer Animation — A846

Design: Graphic from the computer-animated film *Dilemma*, 1972, by graphic artist Janos Kass (b. 1927) and cartoon film director John Halas (b. 1912).

1988, May 12 — **Perf. 12**
3128 A846 4fo black, pur & ver ... .30 .25
Exists imperf. Value $10.

Eurocheck Congress, June 10, Budapest — A847

1988, June 10 — **Litho.** — **Perf. 12**
3129 A847 4fo multicolored ... .30 .25
Eurocheck as legal tender, 20th anniv.
Exists imperf. Value $8.

Sovereign of the Seas — A848

No. 3131, Santa Maria. No. 3132, Mayflower. No. 3133, Jylland. No. 3134, St. Jupat.

1988, June 30
3130 A848 2fo shown ... .30 .25
3131 A848 2fo multicolored ... .30 .25
3132 A848 2fo multicolored ... .30 .25
3133 A848 4fo multicolored ... .55 .25
3134 A848 6fo multicolored ... .80 .25
Nos. 3130-3134 (5) ... 2.25 1.25
Exist imperf. Value, set $25.

Fight Drug Abuse — A849

1988, July 7 — **Litho.** — **Perf. 12**
3135 A849 4fo multicolored ... .30 .25
Exists imperf. Value $10.

Ducks — A850

No. 3136, Anas crecca. No. 3137, Bucephala clangula. No. 3138, Anas penelope. No. 3139, Netta rufina. No. 3140, Anas strepera. No. 3141, Anas platyrhynchos.

1988, July 29 — **Litho.** — **Perf. 13x13½**
3136 A850 2fo multicolored ... .30 .25
3137 A850 2fo multicolored ... .30 .25
3138 A850 4fo multicolored ... .65 .25
  a. Pane of 10 #3136 + 10 #3138 with gutter btwn. ... 12.00
    Complete booklet, #3138a, with text and cover in either English or German ... 12.00
3139 A850 4fo multicolored ... .65 .25
3140 A850 6fo multicolored ... 1.10 .25
Nos. 3136-3140 (5) ... 3.00 1.25

Souvenir Sheet
Perf. 12½x11½
3141 A850 20fo multicolored ... 4.75 4.75
No. 3141 contains one 52x37mm stamp.
Exist imperf. Value: set $35; souvenir sheet $30.
For surcharges see Nos. 3199-3200.

Antique Toys — A851

No. 3142, Train. No. 3143, See-saw. No. 3144, Pecking chickens. No. 3145, String-manipulated soldier.

1988, Aug. 12 — **Perf. 12**
3142 A851 2fo multi ... .30 .25
3143 A851 2fo multi ... .30 .25
3144 A851 4fo +2fo multi ... .75 .25
3145 A851 5fo multi ... .50 .25
Nos. 3142-3145 (4) ... 1.85 1.00
Surtax for youth philately programs.
Exist imperf. Value, set $25.

Calvinist College, Debrecen, 450th Anniv. — A852

1988, Aug. 16 — **Litho.** — **Perf. 13½x13**
3146 A852 4fo multi ... .30 .25
Exists imperf. Value $7.50.

A853

1988, Aug. 30 — **Perf. 12**
3147 A853 4fo multi ... .30 .25
58th American Society of Travel Agents World Congress, Oct. 23-29, Budapest.
Exists imperf. Value $7.50.

P.O. Officials Training School, Cent. — A854

1988, Sept. 9 — **Litho.** — **Perf. 12**
3148 A854 4fo Badge on collar ... .30 .25
Exists imperf. Value $7.50.

Gabor Baross (1848-1892), Minister of Commerce and Communication — A855

Portrait and: 2fo, Postal Savings Bank, Budapest, emblem and postal savings stamp. 4fo, Telephone and telegraph apparatus, registration label and cancellations. 10fo, East Railway Station, Budapest.

1988, Sept. 16
3149 A855 2fo multi ... .30 .25
3150 A855 4fo multi ... .50 .50

Souvenir Sheet
Perf. 11½
3151 A855 10fo multi ... 2.25 2.00
No. 3151 contains one 50x29mm stamp.
Exist imperf. Value: set $12.50; souvenir sheet $35.

Famous Hungarians Type of 1988
Gyula Lengyel (1888-1941), political writer.

1988, Oct. 7 — **Perf. 11½x12**
3152 A843 4fo multi ... .30 .25
Exists imperf. Value $7.50.

Christmas — A857

Perf. 12½x11½
1988, Nov. 10 — **Litho.**
3153 A857 2fo multi ... .30 .25
Exists imperf. Value $7.50.

Nobel Prize Winners — A858

Designs: No. 3154, Richard Adolf Zsigmondy (1865-1929), Germany, chemistry (1925). No. 3155, Robert Barany (1876-1936), Austria, medicine (1914). No. 3156, Georg von Hevesy (1885-1966), Hungary, chemistry (1943). No. 3157, Albert Szent-Gyorgyi (1893-1986), Hungary-US, medicine (1937). No. 3158, Georg von Bekesy (1899-1972), US, medicine (1961). 6fo, Denis Gabor (1900-1979), Great Britain, physics (1971).

Litho. & Engr.
1988, Nov. 30 — **Perf. 12**
3154 A858 2fo red brown ... .30 .25
3155 A858 2fo green ... .30 .25
3156 A858 2fo deep claret ... .30 .25
3157 A858 4fo rose lake ... .30 .25
3158 A858 4fo steel blue ... .30 .25
3159 A858 6fo sepia ... .55 .25
Nos. 3154-3159 (6) ... 2.05 1.50
Exist imperf. Value, set $27.50.

Famous Hungarians Type of 1988
Arpad Szakasits (1888-1965), party leader.

1988, Dec. 6 — **Perf. 11½x12**
3160 A843 4fo multicolored ... .30 .25
Exists imperf. Value $7.50.

Souvenir Sheet
Medals Won by Hungarian Athletes at the 1988 Seoul Olympic Games — A860

1988, Dec. 19 — **Litho.** — **Perf. 12**
3161 A860 20fo multicolored ... 2.00 2.00
Exists imperf. Value $20.

Silver and Cast Iron — A861

No. 3162, Teapot, Pest, 1846. No. 3163, Coffee pot, Buda, 18th cent. No. 3164, Sugar bowl, Pest, 1822. No. 3165, Cast iron plate, Romania, 1850.

1988, Dec. 28 — **Litho. & Engr.**
3162 A861 2fo multicolored ... .30 .25
3163 A861 2fo multicolored ... .30 .25
3164 A861 4fo multicolored ... .60 .25
3165 A861 5fo multicolored ... .75 .25
Nos. 3162-3165 (4) ... 1.95 1.00
Exist imperf. Value, set $15.

Postal Savings Bank Inauguration — A862

1989, Jan. 20 — **Litho.** — **Perf. 12x11½**
3166 A862 5fo royal blue, blk & silver ... .30 .25
Exists imperf. Value $4.

Kalman Wallisch (1889-1934), Labor Leader — A863

1989, Feb. 28 — **Litho.** — **Perf. 12**
3167 A863 3fo dk red & brt bl ... .30 .25
Exists imperf. Value $3.75.
See No. 3170.

A864

1989, Mar. 3 — **Perf. 13x13½**
3168 A864 3fo multicolored ... .30 .25
World Indoor Sports Championships, Budapest, Mar. 3-5.
Exists imperf. Value $10.

Souvenir Sheet

Interparliamentary Union Cent. and 81st Session, Budapest, Mar. 13-18 — A865

a, Parliament, Big Ben & Tower Bridge, London. b, Parliament & Chain Bridge, Budapest.

1989, Mar. 13 — **Litho.** — **Perf. 11**
3169 A865 Sheet of 2 ... 2.25 2.25
  a.-b. 10fo any single ... 1.00 1.00
Exists with red inscriptions and control number. Value $75.
Exists imperf. Value $25.

Famous Hungarians Type of 1989
Janos Gyetvai (1889-1967), journalist, diplomat.

1989, Apr. 7 — **Litho.** — **Perf. 12**
3170 A863 3fo dark red & brt grn ... .30 .25
Exists imperf. Value $3.75.

Stud Farm at Babolna, 200th Anniv. — A867

HUNGARY

Horses: a, O Bajan. b, Meneskari Csikos. c, Gazal II.

1989, May 18		Litho.	Perf. 12	
3171	A867	Strip of 3	1.10	1.10
a.-c.		3fo any single	.35	.35

Exists imperf. Value, strip $10.

ART '89, May 23-27, Budapest — A868

1989, May 23			Perf. 12x11½	
3172	A868	5fo multi	.30	.25

Exhibition for disabled artists.
Exists imperf. Value $7.50.

Flower Arrangements — A869

1989, May 31			Perf. 12	
3173	A869	2fo multi, vert.	.30	.25
3174	A869	3fo multi, vert.	.30	.25
3175	A869	3fo shown	.30	.30
3176	A869	5fo multi, diff.	.50	.50
3177	A869	10fo multi, vert.	1.00	1.00
		Nos. 3173-3177 (5)	2.40	2.35

Exist imperf. Value, set $15.

French Revolution, Bicent. — A870

1989, June 1			Perf. 12	
3178	A870	5fo brt blue, blk & red	.30	.25

Souvenir Sheet
Perf. 11½

| 3179 | A870 | 20fo like 5fo | 2.00 | 2.00 |

No. 3179 contains one 50x30mm stamp.
Exist imperf. Value: single $12.50; souvenir sheet $22.50.

Medieval Church of the Csolts Near Veszto — A871

1989, June 15		Litho.	Perf. 12	
3180	A871	3fo multi	.30	.25

Exists imperf. Value $7.50.

Photography, 150th Anniv. — A872

1989, June 15				
3181	A872	5fo multi	.30	.25

Exists imperf. Value $4.

Old Mills — A873

Designs: 2fo, Water mill, Turistvandi, 18th cent. 3fo, Horse-driven mill, Szarvas, 1836. 5fo, Windmill, Kiskunhalas, 18th cent. 10fo, Water wheel on the Drava River.

1989, June 20				
3182	A873	2fo multi	.30	.25
3183	A873	3fo multi	.30	.25
3184	A873	5fo multi	.40	.25
3185	A873	10fo multi	.90	.25
		Nos. 3182-3185 (4)	1.90	1.00

Exist imperf. Value, set $12.

Souvenir Sheet

1st Moon Landing, 20th Anniv. — A874

1989, July 12		Litho.	Perf. 12½	
3186	A874	20fo multi	2.25	2.25

Exists imperf. Value $20.

Gliders A875

1989, July 20			Perf. 12	
3187	A875	3fo Futar	.30	.25
3188	A875	5fo Cimbora	.45	.25

17th Intl. Old Timers Rally, Budakeszi Airport, and 60th anniv. of glider flying in Hungary.
Exist imperf. Value, set $8.50.

Reptiles — A876

Designs: 2fo, Lacerta agilis. 3fo, Lacerta viridis. No. 3191, Vipera rakosiensis. No. 3192, Natrix natrix. 10fr, Emys orbicularis.

1989, July 26			Perf. 11	
3189	A876	2fo multicolored	.30	.25
3190	A876	3fo multicolored	.30	.25
3191	A876	5fo multicolored	.30	.25
3192	A876	5fo multicolored	.45	.25
3193	A876	10fo multicolored	.90	.25
		Nos. 3189-3193 (5)	2.25	1.25

Exist imperf. Value, set $40.

31st Modern Pentathlon World Championships, Aug. 30-Sept. 4, Budapest A877

1989, July 31			Perf. 13½x13	
3194	A877	5fo multi	.30	.25

Exists imperf. Value $4.

Caves — A878

10th World Speleology Congress, Aug. 13-20, Sofia: 3fo, Baradla. 5fo, Szemlohegy. 10fo, Anna. 12fo, Lake Cave of Tapolca.

1989, Aug. 14		Litho.	Perf. 11	
3195	A878	3fo multi	.30	.25
3196	A878	5fo multi	.35	.25
3197	A878	10fo multi	.75	.25
3198	A878	12fo multi	.90	.25
		Nos. 3195-3198 (4)	2.30	1.00

Exist imperf. Value, set $25.

Nos. 3136 and 3138 Surcharged

No. 3199

No. 3200

1989, Aug. 14			Perf. 13x13½	
3199	A850	3fo on 2fo #3136	.75	.25
3200	A850	5fo on 4fo #3138	.75	.35
a.		Pane of 10 #3199 + pane of 10 #3200 with gutter between	15.00	
		Complete booklet, #3200a, with text and cover in either English or German	26.00	

A879

1989, Aug. 24			Perf. 12	
3201	A879	5fo multi	.60	.25

Third World Two-in-Hand Carriage-driving Championships, Balatonfenyves, Aug. 24-27.
Exists imperf. Value $7.50.

A880

Nurses: 5fo, Zsuzsanna Kossuth (1820-1854) and emblem. 10fo, Florence Nightingale (1820-1910) and medal awarded in her name by the Red Cross.

1989, Sept. 8		Litho.	Perf. 12	
3202	A880	5fo multi	.35	.30
3203	A880	10fo multi	.75	.60

Stamp Day. See No. B341.
Exist imperf. Value, set $11.50.

Pro-Philatelia 1989 — A881

1989, Oct. 10		Litho.	Imperf.	
3204	A881	50fo #2665, C426, 2742, 3005, B233	6.25	5.75

Dismantling of the Electronic Surveillance System (Iron Curtain) on the Hungary-Austria Border — A882

1989, Oct. 30			Perf. 11	
3205	A882	5fo multi	1.00	.50

Exists imperf. Value $6.

Conquest of Hungary, by Mor Than — A883

1989, Oct. 31				
3206	A883	5fo multi	.50	.25

Arpad, chief who founded the 1st Magyar dynasty of Hungary in 889.
Exists imperf. Value $7.50.

Christmas — A884

1989, Nov. 10		Litho.	Perf. 11½x12	
3207	A884	3fo Flight to Egypt	.50	.25

Exists imperf. Value $3.50.

Jawaharlal Nehru — A885

Litho. & Engr.

1989, Nov. 14			Perf. 12	
3208	A885	3fo buff & rose brn	.60	.25

Jawaharlal Nehru, 1st prime minister of independent India.
Exists imperf. Value $9.50.

Modern Art (Paintings) — A886

3fo, Mike, by Dezso Korniss. 5fo, Sunrise, by Lajos Kassak. 10fo, Grotesque Burial, by Endre Balint. 12fo, Memory of Toys, by Tihamer Gyarmathy.

1989, Dec. 18		Litho.	Perf. 12	
3209	A886	3fo multicolored	.30	.25
3210	A886	5fo multicolored	.50	.25
3211	A886	10fo multicolored	1.00	.25
3212	A886	12fo multicolored	1.20	.25
		Nos. 3209-3212 (4)	3.00	1.00

Exist imperf. Value, set $20.

Medical Pioneers — A887

No. 3213, Galen (129-c.199), Greek physician. No. 3214, Paracelsus (1493-1541), German alchemist. 4fo, Andreas Vesalius (1514-

HUNGARY

64), Belgian anatomist. 6fo, Rudolf Virchow (1821-1902), German pathologist. 10fo, Ivan Petrovich Pavlov (1849-1936), Russian physiologist.

1989, Dec. 29   Engr.   Perf. 12
3213	A887	3fo olive gray	.30	.25
3214	A887	3fo brown	.30	.25
3215	A887	4fo black	.40	.25
3216	A887	6fo intense black	.60	.25
3217	A887	10fo brown violet	1.00	.25
		Nos. 3213-3217 (5)	2.60	1.25

Exist imperf. Value, set $20.

Hungarian Savings Bank, 150th Anniv. — A888

1990, Jan. 11   Litho.
| 3218 | A888 | 5fo multicolored | .35 | .25 |

Exists imperf. Value $4.

A889

1990, Jan. 15   Perf. 12
| 3219 | A889 | 5fo brown & sepia | .35 | .25 |

Singer Sewing Machine, 25th anniv.
Exists imperf. Value $4.50.

A890

3fo, Telephone, Budapest Exchange. 5fo, Mailbox and main p.o., Budapest, c. 1900.

1990, Jan. 29
| 3220 | A890 | 3fo multicolored | .30 | .25 |
| 3221 | A890 | 5fo multicolored | .30 | .25 |

Coil Stamps
Size: 17x22mm
Perf. 14
Photo.
3222	A890	3fo multi	.30	.25
3223	A890	5fo shown	.30	.25
		Nos. 3220-3223 (4)	1.20	1.00

Nos. 3220-3221 inscribed "Pj 1989." Nos. 3222-3223 inscribed "1989."
Nos. 3220-3221 exist imperf. Value, set $10.

A891

Protected bird species: No. 3224, Alcedo atthis. No. 3225, Pyrrhula pyrrhula. No. 3226, Dendrocopos syriacus. No. 3227, Upupa epops. No. 3228, Merops apiaster. 10fo, Coracias garrulus.

1990, Feb. 20   Litho.   Perf. 11½x12
3224	A891	3fo multicolored	.30	.25
3225	A891	3fo multicolored	.30	.25
3226	A891	3fo multicolored	.30	.25
3227	A891	5fo multicolored	.55	.25
3228	A891	5fo multicolored	.55	.25
3229	A891	10fo multicolored	1.00	.25
		Nos. 3224-3229 (6)	3.00	1.50

Exist imperf. Value, set $37.50.

A892

Flowers of the continents (Africa): No. 3230, Leucadendron. No. 3231, Protea compacta. No. 3232, Leucadendron spissifolium. No. 3233, Protea barbigera. No. 3234, Protea lepidocarpodendron. 10fr, Protea cynaroides. 20fo, Montage of African flowers.

1990, Mar. 14   Litho.   Perf. 12
3230	A892	3fo multicolored	.30	.25
3231	A892	3fo multicolored	.30	.25
3232	A892	3fo multicolored	.30	.25
3233	A892	5fo multicolored	.55	.25
3234	A892	5fo multicolored	.55	.25
3235	A892	10fo multicolored	1.00	.25
		Nos. 3230-3235 (6)	3.00	1.50

Souvenir Sheet
Perf. 12½x12
| 3236 | A892 | 20fo multicolored | 3.00 | 3.00 |

No. 3236 contains one 27x38mm stamp.
See Nos. 3278-3283, 3371-3375, 3377-3381, 3451-3455.
Exist imperf. Value: set $20; souvenir sheet $20.

A893

Portraits of Hungarian kings in the Historical Portrait Gallery. King and reign: No. 3237, Janos Hunyadi (c. 1407-1409). No. 3238, Matthias Hunyadi (1443-1490).

1990, Apr. 6   Litho.   Perf. 11½x12
3237	A893	5fo multicolored	.35	.25
3238	A893	5fo multicolored	.35	.25
	a.	Pair, #3237-3238	.70	.25

Exist imperf. Value, pair $8.

Souvenir Sheet

A894

Litho. & Engr.
1990, Apr. 17   Perf. 12½x12
| 3239 | A894 | 20fo black & buff | 2.75 | 2.75 |

Penny Black 150th anniv., Stamp World London '90.
Exists imperf. Value $20.

Karoli Bible, 400th Anniv. — A895

1990, Apr. 24   Litho.
| 3240 | A895 | 8fo Gaspar Karoli | 1.00 | 1.00 |

No. 3240 printed se-tenant with label picturing Bible frontispiece.
Exists imperf. Value, with label $7.50.

1990 World Cup Soccer Championships, Italy — A896

Various athletes.

1990, Apr. 27   Perf. 11½x12
3241	A896	3fo Dribble	.30	.25
3242	A896	5fo Heading the ball	.45	.25
3243	A896	5fo Kick	.45	.25
3244	A896	8fo Goal attempt	.70	.25
3245	A896	8fo Dribble, diff.	.70	.25
3246	A896	10fo Dribble, diff.	.90	.25
		Nos. 3241-3246 (6)	3.50	1.50

Souvenir Sheet
Perf. 12½
| 3247 | A896 | 20fo Dribble, diff. | 2.25 | 2.25 |

No. 3247 contains one 32x42mm stamp.
Exist imperf. Value: set $20; souvenir sheet $20.

Kelemen Mikes (1690-1761), Writer — A897

1990, May 31   Litho.   Perf. 13½x13
| 3248 | A897 | 8fo black & gold | .75 | .25 |

Exists imperf. Value $5.

Noemi and Beni Ferenczy, Birth Cent. — A898

Designs: 3fo, Painting by Noemi Ferenczy. 5fo, Sculpture by Beni Ferenczy.

1990, June 18   Litho.   Perf. 12
| 3249 | A898 | 3fo multicolored | .40 | .25 |
| 3250 | A898 | 5fo multicolored | .65 | .25 |

Exist imperf. Value, set $7.50.

Ferenc Kazinczy (1759-1831), Hungarian Language Reformer — A899

1990, July 18   Litho.   Perf. 12
| 3251 | A899 | 8fo multicolored | .50 | .25 |

Exists imperf. Value $5.

Ferenc Kolcsey (1790-1838), Poet — A900

1990, Aug. 3
| 3252 | A900 | 8fo multicolored | .50 | .25 |

Exists imperf. Value $5.50.

New Coat of Arms — A901

1990, Aug. 17   Litho.   Perf. 13½x13
| 3253 | A901 | 8fo multicolored | .50 | .25 |

Souvenir Sheet
Perf. 11
| 3254 | A901 | 20fo multicolored | 5.00 | 5.00 |

No. 3254 contains one 34x50mm stamp. A souvenir sheet like No. 3254 was released with a hologram as the stamp. The sheet exists with black or red control numbers on the reverse. Values: with black numbers $175; with red numbers $300.
Exist imperf. Value: single $10; souvenir sheet $30.

Grapes and Wine Producing Areas — A902

Grapes and Growing Area: 3fo, Cabernet franc, Hajos-Vaskut. 5fo, Cabernet sauvignon, Villany-Siklos. No. 3257, Italian Riesling, Badacsony. No. 3258, Kadarka, Szekszard. No. 3259, Leanyka, Eger. 10fo, Furmint, Tokaj-Hegyalja.

1990, Aug. 31   Perf. 13x13½
3255	A902	3fo multicolored	.30	.25
3256	A902	5fo multicolored	.35	.25
3257	A902	8fo multicolored	.50	.25
3258	A902	8fo multicolored	.50	.25
3259	A902	8fo multicolored	.50	.25
3260	A902	10fo multicolored	.70	.25
		Nos. 3255-3260 (6)	2.85	1.50

Exist imperf. Value, set $35.
See Nos. 3580-3582, 3656-3657, 3704-3705, 3773-3774, 3832-3833, 3938-3939, 4037-4039.

Paintings by Endre Szasz — A903

1990, Oct. 12   Litho.   Perf. 12
| 3261 | A903 | 8fo Feast | .50 | .35 |
| 3262 | A903 | 12fo Message | .85 | .65 |

Stamp Day. See No. B344.
Exist imperf. Value, set $15.

Prehistoric Animals — A904

1990, Nov. 16   Litho.   Perf. 12
3263	A904	3fo Tarbosaurus	.30	.25
3264	A904	5fo Brontosaurus	.35	.25
3265	A904	5fo Stegosaurus	.50	.25
3266	A904	5fo Dimorphodon	.50	.25
3267	A904	8fo Platybelodon	.50	.25
3268	A904	10fo Mammoth	.70	.25
		Nos. 3263-3268 (6)	2.85	1.50

Exist imperf. Value, set $40.

Intl. Literacy Year — A905

1990, Nov. 21   Perf. 13x13½
| 3269 | A905 | 10fo multicolored | .75 | .25 |

Exist imperf. Value $10.

Budapest Stamp Museum, 60th Anniv. A906

1990, Nov. 23   Perf. 12½
| 3270 | A906 | 5fo brn red & grn | .35 | .25 |

Exist imperf. Value $4.50.

HUNGARY

Souvenir Sheet

Thurn & Taxis Postal System, 500th Anniv. — A907

1990, Nov. 30   **Litho.**   **Perf. 12½x12**
3271   A907   50fo multicolored   7.50   7.50

Antique Clocks — A908

No. 3272, Travelling clock, 1576. No. 3273, Table clock, 1643. No. 3274, Mantel clock, 1790. No. 3275, Table clock, 1814.

1990, Dec. 14   **Perf. 12**
3272   A908   3fo multicolored   .30   .25
3273   A908   4fo multicolored   .40   .25
3274   A908   5fo multicolored   .40   .25
3275   A908   10fo multicolored   .90   .25
   Nos. 3272-3275 (4)   2.00   1.00

Exist imperf. Value, set $17.50.

Madonna with Child by Botticelli — A909

1990, Dec. 14   **Perf. 12½x11½**
3276   A909   5fo multicolored   .35   .25

Exists imperf. Value $4.50.

Lorand Eotvos (1848-1919) and Torsion Pendulum — A910

1991, Jan. 31   **Litho.**   **Perf. 11**
3277   A910   12fo multicolored   .75   .25

Exists imperf. Value $7.50.

Flowers of the Continents Type

Flowers of the Americas: No. 3278, Mandevilla splendens. No. 3279, Lobelia cardinalis. No. 3280, Cobaea scandens. No. 3281, Steriphoma paradoxa. No. 3282, Beloperone guttata.
No. 3283, Flowers of the Americas.

1991, Feb. 28   **Litho.**   **Perf. 12**
3278   A892   5fo multicolored   .30   .25
3279   A892   7fo multicolored   .30   .25
3280   A892   7fo multicolored   .30   .25
3281   A892   12fo multicolored   .45   .25
3282   A892   15fo multicolored   .50   .25
   Nos. 3278-3282 (5)   1.85   1.25

Souvenir Sheet
Perf. 11
3283   A892   20fo multicolored   2.50   2.50

No. 3283 contains one 27x44mm stamp.
Exist imperf. Value: set $35; souvenir sheet $40.

Post Office, Budapest — A911

Designs: 7fo, Post Office, Pecs.

1991, Mar. 22   **Perf. 11½x12½**   **Litho.**
3284   A911   5fo multicolored   3.50   3.50
3285   A911   7fo multicolored   4.50   4.50
   a.   Pair, #3284-3285   8.00   8.00

Admission to CEPT.
Exist imperf. Value, pair $25.

Europa — A912

12fo, Ulysses probe. 30fo, Cassini-Huygens probe.

1991, Apr.   **Litho.**   **Perf. 12½**
3286   A912   12fo multi   1.00   .75
3287   A912   30fo multi   2.75   1.75

Exist imperf. Value, set $30.

Budapest Zoological and Botanical Gardens, 125th Anniv. — A913

1991, May 15   **Perf. 13½x13**
3288   A913   7fo Gorilla   .30   .25
3289   A913   12fo Rhinoceros   .40   .25
3290   A913   12fo Toucan   .40   .25
3291   A913   12fo Polar bear   .40   .25
3292   A913   20fo Orchid   .75   .25
   Nos. 3288-3292 (5)   2.25   1.55

Exist imperf. Value, set $40.

A914

1991, May 24   **Litho.**   **Perf. 12**
3293   A914   12fo multi   .60   .60

Count Pal Teleki (1879-1941), politician.
Exists imperf. Value $5.

A915

1991, June 13   **Perf. 13x13½**
3294   A915   12fo multicolored   .60   .60

44th World Fencing Championships, Budapest.
Exists imperf. Value $6.

Images of the Virgin and Child in Hungarian Shrines — A916

Designs: 7fo, Mariapocs. No. 3296, Mariagyud. No. 3297, Celldomolk. No. 3298, Mariaremete. 20fo, Esztergom.

1991, June 17   **Perf. 12½**
3295   A916   7fo multicolored   .30   .25
3296   A916   12fo multicolored   .40   .25
3297   A916   12fo multicolored   .40   .25
3298   A916   12fo multicolored   .40   .25
3299   A916   20fo multicolored   .75   .55
   Nos. 3295-3299 (5)   2.25   1.55

Compare with design A927.
Exist imperf. Value, set $17.50.

Souvenir Sheet

Visit of Pope John Paul II, Aug. 16-20, 1991 — A917

Litho. & Engr.
1991, July 15   **Perf. 12**
3300   A917   50fo multicolored   3.25   3.25

Exists imperf. Value $32.50.

Karoly Marko (1791-1860), Painter — A918

1991, June 17   **Perf. 12**
3301   A918   12fo multicolored   .60   .50

Exists imperf. Value $6.

Basketball, Cent. — A919

1991, June 27   **Litho.**   **Perf. 12**
3302   A919   10fo multicolored   .60   .50

Exists imperf. Value $6.

Otto Lilienthal's First Glider Flight, Cent. — A920

Aircraft of aviation pioneers: 7fo, Otto Lilienthal. 12fo, Wright Brothers. 20fo, Alberto Santos-Dumont. 30fo, Aladar Zselyi.

1991, June 27
3303   A920   7fo multi   .30   .25
3304   A920   12fo multi   .35   .30
3305   A920   20fo multi   .60   .50
3306   A920   30fo multi   1.00   .75
   Nos. 3303-3306 (4)   2.25   1.80

Exist imperf. Value, set $20.

3rd Intl. Hungarian Philological Congress — A921

1991, Aug. 12   **Litho.**   **Perf. 13½x13**
3307   A921   12fo multicolored   .60   .50

Exists imperf. Value $6.

A922

1991, Sept. 6   **Engr.**   **Perf. 12**
3308   A922   12fo dark red   .60   .50

Count Istvan Szechenyi (1791-1860), founder of Academy of Sciences.
Exists imperf. Value $6.

A923

Wolfgang Amadeus Mozart (1756-91).

1991, Sept. 6   **Litho.**
3309   A923   12fo As child   1.00   .70
3310   A923   20fo As adult   1.70   1.30

Souvenir Sheet
3311   A923   30fo +15fo, in red coat   4.00   4.00

Stamp Day. No. 3311 contains one 30x40mm stamp.
Exist imperf. Value: set $22.50; souvenir sheet $60.

Telecom '91 — A924

1991, Sept. 30   **Litho.**   **Perf. 12**
3312   A924   12fo multicolored   .60   .50

6th World Forum and Exposition on Telecommunications, Geneva, Switzerland. Exists imperf. Value $10.

A925

1991, Oct. 30   **Litho.**   **Perf. 13½x13**
3313   A925   12fo multicolored   .60   .60

Sovereign Order of the Knights of Malta.
Exists imperf. Value, set $6.

A926

Early explorers and Discovery of America, 500th anniv. (in 1992): 7fo, Sebastian Cabot, Labrador Peninsula, Nova Scotia. No. 3315, Amerigo Vespucci, South American region. No. 3316, Hernando Cortez, Mexico. 15fo, Ferdinand Magellan, Straits of Magellan. 20fo, Francisco Pizarro, Peru, Andes Mountain region. 30fo, Christopher Columbus and coat of arms.

1991, Oct. 30   **Perf. 12**
3314   A926   7fo multicolored   .30   .25
3315   A926   12fo multicolored   .35   .25
3316   A926   12fo multicolored   .35   .25
3317   A926   15fo multicolored   .50   .35
3318   A926   20fo multicolored   .75   .60
   Nos. 3314-3318 (5)   2.25   1.70

Souvenir Sheet
3319   A926   30fo multicolored   3.00   3.00

No. 3319 contains one 26x37mm stamp.

HUNGARY

Exist imperf. Value: set $20; souvenir sheet $60.

No. 3023 Overprinted in Brown

1991, Oct. 22	Litho.	Perf. 12x11½
3320 A816 12fo multicolored	1.25	.75

Anniversary of Hungarian revolution, 1956.

Christmas — A927

Images of the Virgin and Child from: 7fo, Mariapocs. 12fo, Mariaremete.

1991, Nov. 20	Perf. 13½x13
3322 A927 7fo multicolored	.35 .35
3323 A927 12fo multicolored	.50 .50

Nos. 3322-3323 issued in sheets of 20 plus 20 labels.

A928

1991, Nov. 20	Perf. 12
3324 A928 12fo multicolored	.60 .50

Fight for human rights. Exist imperf. Value $10.

A929

7fo, Cross-country skiing. 12fo, Slalom skiing. 15fo, Four-man bobsled. 20fo, Ski jump. 30fo, Hockey.
No. 3330, Pairs figure skating.

1991, Dec. 6	Perf. 13½x13
3325 A929 7fo multicolored	.30 .25
3326 A929 12fo multicolored	.55 .30
3327 A929 15fo multicolored	.50 .40
3328 A929 20fo multicolored	.60 .50
3329 A929 30fo multicolored	1.00 .85
Nos. 3325-3329 (5)	2.95 2.30

Souvenir Sheet
Perf. 12½x11½
3330 A929 30fo multicolored 2.50 2.50

1992 Winter Olympics, Albertville. Exist imperf. Value: set $20; souvenir sheet $20.

Souvenir Sheet

First Hungarian Postage Stamp, 120th Anniv. — A930

1991, Dec. 20	Litho.	Perf. 12x12½
3331 A930 50fo No. 6	3.00 3.00

Piarist Order in Hungary, 350th Anniv. — A931

1992, Jan. 22	Perf. 13½x13
3332 A931 10fo multicolored	.45 .40

World Heritage Village of Holloko — A932

1992, Jan. 22	Perf. 12
3333 A932 15fo multicolored	1.15 .90

1992 Summer Olympics, Barcelona A933

1992, Feb. 26	Litho.	Perf. 13½x13
3334 A933 7fo Swimming	.75 .60
3335 A933 9fo Cycling	1.15 .75
3336 A933 10fo Gymnastics	1.15 .90
3337 A933 15fo Running	1.90 1.50
Nos. 3334-3337 (4)	4.95 3.75

Discovery of America, 500th Anniv. — A934

Expo '92, Seville: No. 3338, Map shaped as Indian, Columbus' fleet. No. 3339, Face-shaped map of ocean, sailing ship. No. 3340, Map shaped as European face, ship. No. 3341, Map, square, protractor, compass.

1992, Mar. 27	Litho.	Perf. 12
3338 A934 10fo multicolored	.75 .60
3339 A934 10fo multicolored	.75 .60
3340 A934 15fo multicolored	1.00 .75
3341 A934 15fo multicolored	1.00 .75
Nos. 3338-3341 (4)	3.50 2.70

A935

Design: 15fo, Jozsef Cardinal Mindszenty (1892-1975), Leader of Hungarian Catholic Church.

1992, Mar. 27	Perf. 12½x11½
3342 A935 15fo red, brn & buff	.90 .75

A936

1992, Mar. 27	Perf. 13½x13
3343 A936 15fo multicolored	.90 .75

Jan Amos Komensky (Comenius), writer, 400th birth anniv.

Maya Indian Sculpture — A937

40fo, Indian sculpture, diff.

1992, Apr. 14	Litho.	Perf. 13½x13
3344 A937 15fo multicolored	1.00 .75
3345 A937 40fo multicolored	2.75 2.25

Europa. Discovery of America, 500th anniversary.

European Gymnastics Championships, Budapest A938

1992, May 15	Litho.	Perf. 12
3346 A938 15fo multicolored	.90 .75

A939

1992, June 26	Litho.	Perf. 13½x13
3347 A939 15fo multicolored	1.00 1.00

St. Margaret, 750th Anniv. (in 1991). No. 3347 printed with se-tenant label.

A940

Protected birds: 9fo, Falco cherrug. 10fo, Hieraaetus pennatus. 15fo, Circaetus gallicus. 40fo, Milvus milvus.

1992, June 26	Perf. 13x13½
3348 A940 9fo multicolored	.40 .25
3349 A940 10fo multicolored	.60 .25
3350 A940 15fo multicolored	.85 .50
3351 A940 40fo multicolored	1.60 1.00
Nos. 3348-3351 (4)	3.45 2.00

Raoul Wallenberg, Swedish Diplomat, 80th Anniv. of Birth — A941

1992, July 30	Litho.	Perf. 12
3352 A941 15fo gray & red	1.50 .45

Theodore von Karman (1881-1963), Physicist and Aeronautical Engineer A942

Design: 40fo, John von Neumann (1903-1957), mathematician.

1992, Aug. 3	Litho.	Perf. 12x11½
3353 A942 15fo multicolored	.45 .25
3354 A942 40fo multicolored	1.90 .70

3rd World Congress of Hungarians — A943

1992, Aug. 3	Perf. 13½x13
3355 A943 15fo multicolored	.80 .35

Telecom '92 — A945

1992, Oct. 6	Litho.	Perf. 12½x11½
3360 A945 15fo multicolored	.60 .45

Stamp Day — A946

No. 3361, Coat of arms, vert. No. 3363, like #3362, inscribed "65. Belyegnap".
No. 3364, Postilion.

1992, Sept. 4	Perf. 12
3361 A946 10fo +5fo multi	.75 .60
3362 A946 15fo shown	.85 .75
3363 A946 15fo +5fo multi	1.15 .90
Nos. 3361-3363 (3)	2.75 2.25

Souvenir Sheet
3364 A946 50fo +20fo multi 2.70 2.70

Eurofilex '92 (Nos. 3361, 3363-3364). Nos. 3361, 3363 printed with se-tenant label. No. 3364 contains one 40x30mm stamp.

Famous Men — A947

Designs: 10fo, Stephen Bathory (1533-1586), Prince of Transylvania and King of Poland. 15fo, Stephen Bocskay (1557-1606), Prince of Transylvania. 40fo, Gabriel Bethlen (1580-1629), Prince of Transylvania and King of Hungary.

1992, Oct. 28	Litho.	Perf. 12
3365 A947 10fo multicolored	.40 .25
3366 A947 15fo multicolored	.70 .30
3367 A947 40fo multicolored	1.25 .85
Nos. 3365-3367 (3)	2.35 1.40

Postal Uniforms — A948

Designs: 10fo, Postrider, 1703-1711. 15fo, Letter carrier, 1874.

1992, Nov. 20	Perf. 13½x13
3368 A948 10fo multicolored	.65 .30
3369 A948 15fo multicolored	1.00 .50

Christmas — A949

Litho. & Engr.

1992, Nov. 20	Perf. 12
3370 A949 15fo blue & black	.70 .70

Flowers of the Continents Type of 1990

Flowers of Australia: 9fo, Clianthus formosus. 10fo, Leschenaultia biloba. 15fo, Anigosanthos manglesii. 40fo, Comesperma ericinum. 50fo, Bouquet of flowers.

1992, Nov. 20	Litho.
3371 A892 9fo multicolored	.35 .25
3372 A892 10fo multicolored	.55 .50
3373 A892 15fo multicolored	.75 .50
3374 A892 40fo multicolored	1.75 1.25
Nos. 3371-3374 (4)	3.40 2.40

HUNGARY

Souvenir Sheet
Perf. 12½

| 3375 | A892 | 50fo multicolored | 3.75 | 3.75 |

No. 3375 contains one 32x41mm stamp.

1992 European Chess Championships A950

1992, Oct. 28 — *Perf. 11*
| 3376 | A950 | 15fo multicolored | 1.25 | 1.05 |

Flowers of the Continents Type of 1990

Flowers of Asia: No. 3377, Dendrobium densiflorum. No. 3378, Arachnis flos-aeris. No. 3379, Lilium speciosum. No. 3380, Meconopsis aculeata. 50fo, Bouquet of flowers.

1993, Jan. 27 — *Litho.* *Perf. 13½x13*
3377	A892	10fo multicolored	.35	.25
3378	A892	10fo multicolored	.35	.25
3379	A892	15fo multicolored	.75	.50
3380	A892	15fo multicolored	.75	.50
Nos. 3377-3380 (4)			2.20	1.50

Souvenir Sheet
Perf. 12½
| 3381 | A892 | 50fo multicolored | 7.50 | 7.50 |

No. 3381 contains one 32x41mm stamp.

Scythian Archaeological Artifacts — A951

1993, Feb. 25 — *Litho.* *Perf. 13½x13*
| 3382 | A951 | 10fo Horse standing | .50 | .25 |
| 3383 | A951 | 17fo Horse lying down | 1.00 | .25 |

Hungarian Rowing Association, Cent. — A952

1993, Feb. 25 — *Litho.* *Perf. 12*
| 3384 | A952 | 17fo multicolored | .75 | .25 |

Missale Romanum of Matthias Corvinus (Matyas Hunyadi, King of Hungary) — A953

Design: 40fo, Illuminated page.

1993, Mar. 12 — *Litho.* *Perf. 12*
| 3385 | A953 | 15fo multicolored | 1.05 | .40 |

Souvenir Sheet
| 3386 | A953 | 40fo multicolored | 3.50 | 3.50 |

No. 3386 contains one 60x38mm stamp.
See Belgium Nos. 1474, 1476.

Motocross World Championships A954

1993, May 5 — *Litho.* *Perf. 11½x12*
| 3387 | A954 | 17fo multicolored | .60 | .25 |

Europa — A955

Buildings designed by Imre Makovecz: 17fo, Roman Catholic Church, Paks. 45fo, Hungarian Pavilion, Expo '92, Seville.

1993, May 5 — *Perf. 13x13½*
| 3388 | A955 | 17fo multicolored | .75 | .60 |
| 3389 | A955 | 45fo multicolored | 2.25 | 1.65 |

Heliocentric Solar System, Copernicus A956

1993, May 5 — *Perf. 12*
| 3390 | A956 | 17fo multicolored | .45 | .25 |

Polska '93. No. 3390 issued in sheets of 8 + 4 labels.

Edible Mushrooms — A957

10fo, Ramaria botrytis. 17fo, Craterellus cornucopioides. 45fo, Amanita caesarea.

1993, June 18 — *Litho.* *Perf. 13½x13*
3391	A957	10fo multicolored	.30	.25
3392	A957	17fo multicolored	.45	.35
3393	A957	45fo multicolored	1.50	1.05
Nos. 3391-3393 (3)			2.25	1.65

St. Christopher, by Albrecht Durer — A958

1993, June 18 — *Perf. 12*
| 3394 | A958 | 17fo sil, blk & buff | .45 | .25 |

Year of the Elderly.

City of Mohacs, 900th Anniv. — A959

1993, June 18 — *Perf. 13½x13*
| 3395 | A959 | 17fo buff, mar & red brn | .45 | .25 |

Hungarian State Railways, 125th Anniv. — A960

1993, June 18 — *Perf. 13x13½*
| 3396 | A960 | 17fo lt blue & blue | .55 | .25 |

Comedians — A961

1993, July 28 — *Litho.* *Perf. 12*
| 3397 | A961 | 17fo Kalman Latabar | .55 | .25 |
| 3398 | A961 | 30fo Charlie Chaplin | 1.00 | .75 |

Butterflies — A962

10fo, Limenitis populi. 17fo, Aricia artaxerxes. 30fo, Plebejides pylaon.

1993, July 28 — *Perf. 13½x13*
3399	A962	10fo multicolored	.30	.25
3400	A962	17fo multicolored	.70	.25
3401	A962	30fo multicolored	1.25	.65
Nos. 3399-3401 (3)			2.25	1.15

Souvenir Sheet

Helsinki Conference on European Security and Cooperation, 20th Anniv. — A963

1993, July 28 — *Perf. 12*
| 3402 | A963 | 50fo multicolored | 3.00 | 3.00 |

Intl. Solar Energy Society Congress, Budapest — A964

Perf. 12½x11½

1993, Aug. 23 — *Litho.*
| 3403 | A964 | 17fo multicolored | .65 | .25 |

No. 3403 printed se-tenant with label.

Writers — A965

Designs: No. 3404, Laszlo Nemeth (1901-75). No. 3405, Dezso Szabo (1879-1945). No. 3406, Antal Szerb (1901-45).

1993, Aug. 23 — *Perf. 12*
3404	A965	17fo blue	.50	.25
3405	A965	17fo blue	.50	.25
3406	A965	17fo blue	.50	.25
Nos. 3404-3406 (3)			1.50	.75

School of Agronomy, Pannon Agricultural Univ., 175th Anniv. — A966

1993, Nov. 11 — *Litho.* *Perf. 12*
| 3407 | A966 | 17fo multicolored | .60 | .30 |

Ships — A967

10fo, Steamer with sails. 30fo, Battleship.

1993, Oct. 27 — *Perf. 13x13½*
3408	A967	10fo multicolored	.35	.25
3409	A967	30fo multicolored	1.00	.50
a.	Pair, #3408-3409		1.60	.70

Prehistoric Man — A968

1993, Oct. 27 — *Perf. 13½x13*
| 3410 | A968 | 17fo Skull fragment | .55 | .30 |
| 3411 | A968 | 30fo Stone tool | 1.00 | .50 |

Souvenir Sheet

Roman Roads — A969

1993, Oct. 27 — *Perf. 11*
| 3412 | A969 | 50fo multicolored | 3.25 | 3.25 |

Christmas — A970

Altarpiece: 10fo, Virgin and Christ Child, Cathedral of Szekesfehervar, by F. A. Hillebrant.

1993, Nov. 24 — *Perf. 13½x13*
| 3413 | A970 | 10fo multicolored | .35 | .25 |

Sights of Budapest — A971

Designs: 17fo, Szechenyi Chain Bridge. 30fo, Opera House. 45fo, Matthias Church, vert.

Photo. & Engr.

1993, Dec. 16 — *Perf. 12*
3414	A971	17fo lt grn & dk grn	1.10	.55
3415	A971	30fo lt mag & dk mag	1.75	1.00
3416	A971	45fo lt brn & dk brn	2.75	1.70
Nos. 3414-3416 (3)			5.60	3.25

Expo '96.

József Antall (1932-93) — A972

1993, Dec. 30 — *Litho.* *Perf. 11*
| 3417 | A972 | 19fo multicolored | .80 | .40 |
| a. | Souvenir sheet of 1 | | 1.80 | 1.80 |

For surcharge, see No. 4167.

ICAO, 50th Anniv. — A973

1994, Jan. 13 — *Perf. 13x13½*
| 3418 | A973 | 56fo multicolored | 1.65 | .95 |

HUNGARY

1994 Winter Olympics, Lillehammer — A974

1994, Jan. 13 — Perf. 12
3419 A974 12fo Downhill skiing .40 .25
3420 A974 19fo Ice hockey .70 .30

Easter — A975

Design: Golgotha, by Mihaly Munkacsy.

1994, Feb. 17 Litho. Perf. 11½x12
3421 A975 12fo multicolored .50 .25

A976

Artists: 12fo, Gyula Benczur (1844-1920). 19fo, Mihaly Munkacsy (1844-1900).

1994, Feb. 17
3422 A976 12fo multicolored .40 .25
3423 A976 19fo multicolored .65 .30

Lajos Kossuth (1802-94) — A977

1994, Feb. 17
3424 A977 19fo multicolored .65 .30

Gen. Joseph Bem (1794-1850) — A978

1994, Mar. 10 Perf. 12
3425 A978 19fo multicolored .75 .30

Otis Tarda — A979

World Wildlife Fund: No. 3426, Female, male with feathers ruffled in mating dance. No. 3427, Nestlings, female on nest. No. 3428, Nestlings, female standing. No. 3429, Three flying.

1994, Mar. 14
3426 A979 10fo multicolored .40 .35
3427 A979 10fo multicolored .40 .35
3428 A979 10fo multicolored .40 .35
3429 A979 10fo multicolored .40 .35
  a. Block of 4, #3426-3429 1.65 1.50

A980

Europa: 19fo, Sailing steamer Tegetthoff, Franz-Joseph Land, Julius Payer (1842-1915), Austrian explorer. 50fo, Mark Aurel Stein (1862-1943), explorer, archeologist, geographer, Asian scenes.

1994, Apr. 1 Litho. Perf. 13x13½
3430 A980 19fo multicolored 1.15 .75
3431 A980 50fo multicolored 1.90 1.50

Austro-Hungarian Arctic Expedition, 120th anniv. (No. 3430).

A981

No. 3432, Baron Miklos Josika (1794-1865), Novelist. No. 3433, Balint Balassi (1551-94), poet.

1994, May 19 Litho. Perf. 12
3432 A981 19fo gray .55 .30
3433 A981 19fo rose lake .55 .30

Creation of Magyar Hungary, 1100th Anniv. (in 1996) — A982

Designs: No. 3434, Two soldiers on horseback. No. 3435, Soldier on white horse, others in background with flags. No. 3436, Soldier on black horse, others in background. No. 3437, Man with staff, oxen pulling carts. No. 3438, Oxen pulling royal cart. No. 3439, Man with staff on shoulder, oxen with packs. No. 3440, Minstrels, bard celebrating. No. 3441, Soldiers preparing to sacrifice white horse. No. 3442, Shaman before fire, headsman.

1994-96
3434 A982 19fo multicolored .75 .65
3435 A982 19fo multicolored .75 .65
3436 A982 19fo multicolored .75 .65
  a. Strip of 3, #3434-3436 2.50 2.20
3437 A982 22fo multicolored .75 .65
3438 A982 22fo multicolored .75 .65
3439 A982 22fo multicolored .75 .65
  a. Strip of 3, #3437-3439 2.50 2.20
3440 A982 24fo multicolored .75 .65
3441 A982 24fo multicolored .75 .65
3442 A982 24fo multicolored .75 .65
  a. Strip of 3, #3440-3442 2.50 2.20
  Nos. 3434-3442 (9) 6.75 5.85

Souvenir Sheet
3442B A982 195fo multicolored 14.00 14.00

Nos. 3436a, 3439a, 3442a are continuous design. No. 3436a sold for 59fo.
Nos. 3435, 3438, 3441 are 60x40mm.
No. 3442B contains one each of Nos. 3436a, 3439a, 3442a.
Issued: Nos. 3434-3436, 5/19/94; Nos. 3437-3439, 2/23/95; Nos. 3440-3442, 2/29/96, No. 3442B, 4/18/96.

Intl. Olympic Committee, Cent. — A985

Designs: 12fo, 1896, 1992 medals. No. 3444, Flag, runners, Olympic flame. No. 3445, Athens Stadium, 1896. 35fo, Pierre de Coubertin (1863-1937), first president.

1994, June 16 Litho. Perf. 12½
3443 A985 12fo multicolored .30 .25
3444 A985 19fo multicolored .45 .30
3445 A985 19fo multicolored .45 .30
3446 A985 35fo multicolored .85 .60
  Nos. 3443-3446 (4) 2.05 1.45

1994 World Cup Soccer Championships, US — A986

US flag, soccer players and: No. 3447, Elvis Presley. No. 3448, Marilyn Monroe. No. 3449, John Wayne.

1994, June 16 Perf. 12
3447 A986 19fo multicolored .45 .30
3448 A986 19fo multicolored .45 .30
3449 A986 35fo multicolored .75 .60
  Nos. 3447-3449 (3) 1.65 1.20

Intl. Year of the Family — A987

1994, July 21 Litho. Perf. 11
3450 A987 19fo multicolored .65 .30

Flowers of the Continents Type of 1990

Flowers of Europe: 12fo, Leucojum aestivum. 19fo, Helianthemum nummularium. 35fo, Eryngium alpinum. 50fo, Thlaspi rotundifolium. 100fo, Bouquet of European flowers.

1994, Aug. 18 Litho. Perf. 11½x12
3451 A892 12fo multicolored .30 .25
3452 A892 19fo multicolored .45 .35
3453 A892 35fo multicolored .75 .60
3454 A892 50fo multicolored 1.15 .85
  Nos. 3451-3454 (4) 2.65 2.05

Souvenir Sheet Perf. 12½
3455 A892 100fo multicolored 3.50 3.50

No. 3455 contains one 32x41mm stamp.

UPU, 120th Anniv. — A988

UPU emblem and: 19fo, Heinrich Von Stephan (1831-97). 35fo, Mihaly Gervay (1819-96).
No. 3458: a, Von Stephan, vert. b, Gervay, vert.

1994, Sept. 9 Litho. Perf. 12
3456 A988 19fo multicolored .45 .35
3457 A988 35fo multicolored .75 .60

Souvenir Sheet of 2
3458 A988 50fo +25fo, #a.-b. 3.50 3.50

Stamp Day, 67th anniv.
No. 3458 with printing in the margin on the back of the sheet, "140 éves az Egyetemes Postaegyesület / A Magyar Posta köszönt a bélyeg-elofizetoket!", was given as a gift to standing order customers in 2014.

Folk Designs — A989

Various ornate designs.

1994-96 Litho. Perf. 11½x12
3459 A989 1fo bl vio & blk .30 .25
3460 A989 2fo multi .30 .25
3461 A989 3fo multi .30 .25
3461A A989 9fo multi .30 .25
3462 A989 11fo multi .30 .25
3463 A989 12fo multi .30 .25
3463A A989 13fo grn, red & blk .30 .25
3464 A989 14fo multi .30 .25
3465 A989 16fo bl, red & blk .30 .25
3466 A989 17fo red & blk .30 .25
3467 A989 19fo multi .30 .25
3468 A989 22fo multi .35 .25
3469 A989 24fo multi .35 .25
3470 A989 32fo multi .60 .35
3471 A989 35fo multi .75 .60
3472 A989 38fo multi .65 .30
3473 A989 40fo multi .90 .75
3474 A989 50fo multi 1.50 1.00
3475 A989 75fo multi 1.05 .75
3476 A989 80fo multi 1.30 .90
3477 A989 300fo multi 3.75 2.25
3478 A989 500fo multi 8.00 3.75
  Nos. 3459-3478 (22) 22.50 13.90

Issued: 11fo, 12fo, 19fo, 32fo, 35fo, 40fo, 50fo, 10/10/94; 1fo, 1/10/95; 2fo, 3fo, 9fo, 14fo, 22fo, 38fo, 4/3/95; 13fo, 16fo, 17fo, 24fo, 75fo, 80fo, 7/1/96.
See Nos. 3561, 3615, 3630, 3644-3646, 3649-3650. For surcharge see No. 3583.

Summit Meeting of the Conference for European Security & Cooperation — A990

1994, Oct. 10 Litho. Perf. 12
3479 A990 100fo Budapest 3.25 3.25

Holocaust, 50th Anniv. — A991

1994, Oct. 20
3480 A991 19fo multicolored .60 .45

Buildings in Budapest A992

No. 3481, Vajdahunyadvar Castle. No. 3482, Nemzeti Museum. No. 3483, Muszaki Palace.

1994, Nov. 17 Engr.
3481 A992 19fo violet .45 .30
3482 A992 19fo green .45 .30
3483 A992 19fo brown .45 .30
  Nos. 3481-3483 (3) 1.35 .90

Christmas — A993

1994, Nov. 17 Litho.
3484 A993 12fo shown .35 .25
3485 A993 35fo Flight into Egypt .75 .60

Hungarian Shipping Co., Cent. — A994

Design: 22fo, Early steamer Francis Joseph I, cargo ship Baross.

1995, Jan. 24 Litho. Perf. 13
3486 A994 22fo multicolored .65 .30

Easter — A995

1995, Mar. 7 Perf. 12
3487 A995 14fo black & lilac .45 .25

Hungarian Shipping A996

Designs: 14fo, Tug-wheeled steamship, map of first navigable section of the Tisza, view of Szeged. 60fo, Pal Vasarhelyi, Tisza survey ship, surveyor.

1995, Mar. 7 Perf. 13
3488 A996 14fo multicolored .30 .25
3489 A996 60fo multicolored 1.20 1.00

HUNGARY

1995, Apr. 7   *Perf. 12*
3490 A997 22fo multicolored   .65   .30
Natl. Meteorological Service, 125th anniv.

FAO, 50th Anniv. — A998

1995, Apr. 7
3491 A998 22fo multicolored   .80   .30

European Nature Conservation Year — A999

No. 3492, Crane, frog, flowers. No. 3493, Squirrel, insect. No. 3494, Bird, berries, flowers. No. 3495, Butterfly, hedgehog, flowers.

1995, May 9   *Litho.*   *Perf. 13½x13*
3492 A999 14fo multicolored   .55   .45
3493 A999 14fo multicolored   .55   .45
3494 A999 14fo multicolored   .55   .45
3495 A999 14fo multicolored   .55   .45
   a. Strip of 4, #3492-3495   2.25   1.80

Peace & Liberty — A1000

1995, May 9
3496 A1000 22fo multicolored   1.50   1.15
Europa.

Hungarian Olympic Committee, Cent. — A1001

22fo, Diver, Pierre de Coubertin. 60fo, Javelin. 100fo, Fencing.

1995, June 12   *Litho.*   *Perf. 12*
3497 A1001 22fo multicolored   .60   .30
3498 A1001 60fo multicolored   1.35   .80
3499 A1001 100fo multicolored   2.25   1.40
   Nos. 3497-3499 (3)   4.20   2.50

St. Ladislas I (1040?-1095) — A1002

1995, June 12
3500 A1002 22fo multicolored   .75   .30

Laszlo Almasy, Sahara Researcher, Birth Cent. — A1003

1995, Aug. 22   *Litho.*   *Perf. 13x13½*
3501 A1003 22fo multicolored   .75   .30

Odon Lechner, Architect, 150th Birth Anniv. A1004

Design: 22fo, Museum of Applied Arts, Lechner.

1995, Aug. 22   *Litho. & Engr.*   *Perf. 12*
3502 A1004 22fo multicolored   .75   .30

Contemporary Paintings — A1005

No. 3503, Abstract, by Laszlo Moholy-Nagy (1895-1946). No. 3504, Woman with a violin, by Aurel Bernath (1895-1982).

1995, Sept. 18   *Litho.*
3503 A1005 22fo multicolored   .75   .30
3504 A1005 22fo multicolored   .75   .30

Eotvos College, Cent. — A1006

60fo, Eotvos College, Josef Eotvos (1813-71), statesman, writer, educational leader.

1995, Sept. 18
3505 A1006 60fo red brn, blk   1.60   .60

Stamp Day — A1007

Designs: 22fo, Horse-drawn mail chaise. 40fo, Jet, map. 100fo + 30fo, Man, boys looking at stamp album, vert.

1995, Sept. 29   *Litho.*   *Perf. 13½x13*
3506 A1007 22fo multicolored   .35   .30
3507 A1007 40fo multicolored   .75   .55

Souvenir Sheet
Perf. 12x12½
3508 A1007 100fo +30fo multi   3.00   3.00

Buildings of Budapest A1008

No. 3509, Nyugati Palyaudvar. No. 3510, Vigado.

1995, Oct. 24   *Engr.*   *Perf. 12*
3509 A1008 22fo dark olive brn   .80   .60
3510 A1008 22fo deep claret   .80   .60

UN, 50th Anniv. — A1009

1995, Oct. 24   *Litho.*   *Perf. 11*
3511 A1009 60fo multicolored   1.15   .80

Christmas — A1010

Children's designs: 14fo, Spark thrower. 60fo, The Three Magi.

1995, Nov. 16   *Perf. 12*
3512 A1010 14fo multicolored   .30   .25
3513 A1010 60fo multicolored   1.05   .90

Nobel Prize Fund Established, Cent. — A1011

1995, Nov. 16
3514 A1011 100fo Medals   2.40   1.90
No. 3514 is printed se-tenant with label.

St. Elizabeth of Hungary Bathing Lepers — A1012

1995, Nov. 16   *Perf. 13*
3515 A1012 22fo multicolored   .60   .60
No. 3515 is printed se-tenant with label.

A1013

Archaeological Finds from Karos: a, Gold and silver saber. b, Badge.

1996, Mar. 14   *Litho.*   *Perf. 13½x13*
3516 A1013 24fo #a.-b. + 2 labels   1.50   1.50

Souvenir Sheet

Pannonhalma, Benedictine Monastery, 1000th Anniv. — A1014

1996, Mar. 21   *Engr.*   *Perf. 12*
3517 A1014 100fo deep violet   3.50   3.50
Sheet margin is litho. and multicolored.

1996 Summer Olympics, Atlanta — A1015

1996, Apr. 18   *Litho.*   *Perf. 11½x12*
3518 A1015 24fo Swimming   .35   .30
3519 A1015 50fo Tennis   .75   .60
3520 A1015 75fo Kayak   .90   .85
   Nos. 3518-3520 (3)   2.00   1.75

National Productivity — A1016

1996, Apr. 18   *Litho.*   *Perf. 12*
3521 A1016 24fo multicolored   .45   .30

Natl. Writers Assoc., Cent. — A1017

1996, Apr. 18   *Perf. 12x11½*
3522 A1017 50fo multicolored   .85   .75

Budapest Subway, Cent. — A1018

1996, May 2   *Perf. 12*
3523 A1018 24fo multicolored   .45   .30

Famous Women A1019

Europa: 24fo, Queen Gizella. 75fo, Bavarian Princess Elisabeth Wittelsbach.

1996, May 2   *Litho.*   *Perf. 12*
3524 A1019 24fo multicolored   .75   .60
3525 A1019 75fo multicolored   1.90   1.40

Pannonhalma, Benedictine Monastery, 1000th Anniv. — A1020

Designs: 17fo, Entrance to cathedral. 24fo, Monks in northern wing.

1996, June 21   *Engr.*   *Perf. 12*
3526 A1020 17fo red brown   .45   .40
3527 A1020 24fo dark blue   .65   .45
See Nos. 3536-3537.

Intl. Anti-Drug Day — A1021

1996, June 21   *Litho.*   *Perf. 14*
3528 A1021 24fo multicolored   .65   .30

HUNGARY

Hungarian Developers of Technolgy — A1022

Inventor, invention: 24fo, Denes Mihaly (1894-1953), Telehor. 50fo, Jozsef Biro Laszlo (1899-1985), mass-produced ball-point pen. 75fo, Zoltan Bay (1900-92), lunar radar set.

1996, June 21		Perf. 12x11½		
3529	A1022	24fo multicolored	.30	.25
3530	A1022	50fo multicolored	.65	.55
3531	A1022	75fo multicolored	1.05	.75
	Nos. 3529-3531 (3)		2.00	1.55

Hungarian Railways, 150th Anniv. — A1023

Designs: 17fo, 303-Series steam tender locomotive. No. 3533, 325-Series locomotive. No. 3534, "Pest," steam locomotive made by Cokerill and Co.

1996, July 12		Perf. 13½x13		
3532	A1023	17fo multicolored	.55	.45
3533	A1023	24fo multicolored	.70	.55
3534	A1023	24fo multicolored	1.50	.55
	Nos. 3532-3534 (3)		2.75	1.55

Second European Congress of Mathematicians — A1024

1996, July 12			Perf. 12	
3535	A1024	24fo multicolored	.65	.30

Pannonhalma, Benedictine Monastery, Type of 1996

Designs: 17fo, Refectory. 24fo, Main library.

1996, Aug. 12		Engr.	Perf. 12	
3536	A1020	17fo dark brown	.55	.30
3537	A1020	24fo dark green	.80	.30

Nature Expo '96 — A1025

No. 3538, Egretta alba. No. 3539, Iris sibirica. No. 3540, Lynx lynx. No. 3541, Ropalopus ungaricus.

1996, Aug. 12		Litho.	Perf. 12x11½	
3538	A1025	13fo multi	.30	.25
3539	A1025	13fo multi	.30	.25
3540	A1025	13fo multi	.30	.25
3541	A1025	13fo multi	.30	.25
a.	Block of 4, #3538-3541		2.00	2.00

A1026

1996, Aug. 12			Perf. 12	
3542	A1026	24fo No. 4	1.00	.25

Hungarian postage stamps, 125th anniv. Issued in miniature sheets of 6 stamps in two columns of 3 separated by a column of labels. Values, stamp plus label $1.50, miniature sheet $7.50.

A1027

Stamp Day, Budapest '96: 17fo, Prince Arpad, people from 14th cent. "Vienna Picture Chronicle," man stirring liquid in pot. 24fo, Prince on horseback, archer.
150fo+50fo, #601, first page from "The Deeds of Hungarians."

1996, Aug. 12		Litho.	Perf. 11½x12	
3543	A1027	17fo multicolored	.55	.30
3544	A1027	24fo multicolored	.80	.30

Souvenir Sheet
Perf. 12x12½

| 3545 | A1027 | 150fo +50fo multi | 4.50 | 4.50 |

Steamships on Lake Balaton, 150th Anniv. — A1028

Steamer Kisfaludy.

1996, Sept. 17		Litho.	Perf. 12	
3548	A1028	17fo multicolored	.60	.25

Hungarian Revolution, 40th Anniv. — A1029

Newspaper clippings and: 13fo, People marching. 16fo, Troops on back of truck. 17fo, Two men with guns. 24fo, Imre Nagy addressing people.
40fo, Nagy Cabinet.

1996, Oct. 23		Litho.	Perf. 12	
3549	A1029	13fo multicolored	.35	.25
3550	A1029	16fo multicolored	.40	.25
3551	A1029	17fo multicolored	.40	.25
3552	A1029	24fo multicolored	.60	.25
	Nos. 3549-3552 (4)		1.75	1.00

Souvenir Sheet

| 3553 | A1029 | 40fo multicolored | 4.00 | 4.90 |

Souvenir Sheet

1996 Summer Olympic Games, Atlanta A1030

1996, Oct. 22				
3554	A1030	150fo multicolored	4.50	.25

A1036

1996, Nov. 14		Litho.	Perf. 11½x12	
3555	A1036	24fo multicolored		.45

Miklos Wesselenyi (1796-1850), writer.

A1037

1996, Nov. 14			Perf. 13½x13	
3556	A1037	24fo multicolored	.45	.45

UNICEF, 50th anniv.

Christmas A1038

Paintings: 17fo, Mary with Infant Jesus and Two Angels, by Matteo di Giovanni. 24fo, Adoration of the Kings, by unknown painter of Salsburg.

1996, Nov. 14			Perf. 12	
3557	A1038	17fo multicolored	.35	.25
3558	A1038	24fo multicolored	.65	.25

Hungarian Literature A1039

Designs: No. 3559, Scenes from "The Umbrella of St. Peter," Kalman Mikszath (1847-1910). No. 3560, Scenes of men and dogs from "Abel in the Vast Trackless Forest" and "Matthias the Ice-breaker," Aron Tamasi (1897-1966).

1997, Jan. 16		Litho.	Perf. 12x11½	
3559	A1039	17fo multicolored	.35	.25
3560	A1039	27fo multicolored	.35	.25

Folk Art Type of 1994

1997, Mar. 26			Perf. 11½x12	
3561	A989	27fo multicolored	.45	.25

Coat of Arms of Budapest and Counties — A1040

No. 3562: a, Hajdú-Bihar. b, Baranya. c, Bács-Kiskun. d, Békés. e, Borsod-Abaúj-Zemplén.
No. 3563: a, Fejér. b, Győr-Moson-Sopron. c, Heves. d, Jász-Nagykun-Szolnok. e, Komárom-Esztergom. f, Nógrád.
No. 3564: a, Pest. b, Somogy. c, Tolna. d, Vas. e, Veszprém. f, Zala.
No. 3565: a, Budapest. b, Csongrád. c, Szaboics-Szatmár-Bereg.

1997, Mar. 26			Perf. 11½x12	
3562	A1040	27fo Sheet of 5, #a.-e. + label	6.00	3.25
3563	A1040	27fo Sheet of 6, #a.-f.	6.25	5.50
3564	A1040	27fo Sheet of 6, #a.-f.	6.25	5.50
3564G	A1040	27fo Hajdu-Bihar	5.00	5.00

Size: 51x33mm

| 3565 | A1040 | 27fo Sheet of 3, #a.-c. | 4.00 | 1.75 |

No. 3564G is 51x33mm and has the same design as No. 3562a which has a se-tenant label, but lacks the perforations separating these items. Nos. 3262a-3262e, 3563a-3563f, 3564a-3564f, 3565a-3565c were also printed in individual sheets. Value, set of singles (20): mint $7.50; used $6.

A1041

Youth Stamps A1042

Designs: 20fo, Scouting emblem, tents, sailboat, waterfall. 27fo+10fo, Knights on horseback from "Toldi," by Janos Arany.

1997, Apr. 23			Perf. 12	
3566	A1041	20fo multicolored	.50	.35
3567	A1042	27fo +10fo multi	.50	.35

A1043

1997, Apr. 23			Perf. 13½x13	
3568	A1043	90fo multicolored	1.15	.80

World Meeting of Custom Directors.

A1044

1997, Apr. 23		Engr.	Perf. 12	
3569	A1044	80fo deep violet	4.00	3.75

St. Adalbert (956-997). See Germany No. 1964, Poland No. 3307, Czech Republic No. 3012, Vatican City No. 1040.

Stories and Legends A1045

Europa: 27fo, Hunters on horseback shooting bow and arrow at deer. 90fo, Preparing body in sarcophagus of Prince Geza.

1997, May 5		Litho.	Perf. 13x13½	
3570	A1045	27fo multicolored	.75	.55
3571	A1045	90fo multicolored	1.50	1.35

African Animals — A1046

16fo, Oryx gazella. No. 3573, Equus burchelli. No. 3574, Diceros bicornis. 27fo, Panthera leo.
90fo, Loxodonta africana.

1997, May 5			Perf. 12	
3572	A1046	16fo multicolored	.30	.25
3573	A1046	20fo multicolored	.60	.25
3574	A1046	20fo multicolored	.60	.25
3575	A1046	27fo multicolored	1.00	.30
	Nos. 3572-3575 (4)		2.50	1.05

Souvenir Sheet

| 3576 | A1046 | 90fo multicolored | 4.50 | 4.50 |

A1047

1997, June 8		Litho.	Perf. 12	
3577	A1047	90fo multicolored	1.60	.70

Polish Queen Jadwiga (1373-99).

HUNGARY

A1048

World Congress on Stress, Budapest: Janos (Hans) Selye (1907-82), founder of theory of stress, face of person under stress.

1997, July 1
3578 A1048 90fo multicolored   1.75   .70

Indigenous Fish — A1049

Designs: a, Gymnocephalus schraetzer. b, Cottus gobio. c, Alburnoides bipunctatus. d, Cobitis taenia.

1997, June 6   Litho.   Perf. 13x13½
3579 A1049 20fo Strip of 4, #a.-d.   1.75 1.75

Grapes and Wine Producing Areas Type of 1990

Grapes and growing area: No. 3580, Nemes kadarka, Great Kiskoros. No. 3581, Teitfürtü ezerjo, Mor. No. 3582, Harslevelu, Gyongyos.

1997, Aug. 12   Litho.   Perf. 13x13½
3580 A902 27fo multicolored   .45 .35
3581 A902 27fo multicolored   .45 .35
3582 A902 27fo multicolored   .45 .35
    Nos. 3580-3582 (3)   1.35 1.05

No. 3469 Surcharged in Red

1997, July 10   Litho.   Perf. 11½x12
3583 A989 60fo on 24fo multi   1.00 .45

Christmas A1050

20fo, Holy family. 27fo, Adoration of the Magi.

1997, Oct. 31   Litho.   Perf. 13x13½
3584 A1050 20fo multicolored   .30 .30
3585 A1050 27fo multicolored   .50 .50

World Weight Lifting Championships, Thailand — A1051

1997, Nov. 12   Perf. 12
3586 A1051 90fo multicolored   1.15 1.15

Zsigmond Szechenyi, African Explorer — A1052

1998, Jan. 22   Litho.   Perf. 12
3587 A1052 60fo multicolored   .75 .60

Natl. Anthem by Ferenc Kolcsey, 175th Anniv. — A1053

1998, Jan. 22
3588 A1053 75fo multicolored   1.60 .55

1998 Winter Olympic Games, Nagano — A1054

1998, Jan. 22   Perf. 13½x13
3589 A1054 30fo Downhill skiing   .75 .30
3590 A1054 100fo Snowboarding   1.25 .85

Valentine's Day — A1055

1998, Feb. 11   Perf. 11½x12
3591 A1055 24fo multicolored   .65 .40

A1056

1998, Feb. 11   Perf. 12
3592 A1056 50fo multicolored   1.25 .60
Leo Szilard (1898-1964), physicist.

A1057

Balint Postas (Post Office Mascot) in front of printed material: 23fo, Holding letter. 24fo, Bowing. 30fo, Standing straight with arms outstretched. 65fo, Flying.

1998, Feb. 11   Perf. 11½x12
3593 A1057 23fo multicolored   .30 .25
3594 A1057 24fo multicolored   .30 .25
3595 A1057 30fo multicolored   .30 .25
3596 A1057 65fo multicolored   .75 .65
   Nos. 3593-3596 (4)   1.65 1.40

A1058

Easter — A1059

1998, Mar. 13   Litho.   Perf. 13½x13
3597 A1058 24fo Stylized egg   .55 .25
     Perf. 11
3598 A1059 30fo Christ's resurrection   .65 .25

1848-49 Revolution, War of Independence, 150th Anniv. — A1060

23fo, Sandor Petofi (1823-49), poet, handwriting, tricolor. 24fo, Mihaly Tancsics, writer & politician, ink well. 30fo, Lajos Kossuth (1802-94), seal.

1998, Mar. 13   Perf. 12
3599 A1060 23fo multicolored   .30 .25
3600 A1060 24fo multicolored   .30 .25
3601 A1060 30fo multicolored   .30 .30
   Nos. 3599-3601 (3)   .90 .80
     See Nos. 3640-3643.

Art Nouveau A1061

Ceramics: 20fo, Vase with relief design of young girl picking flowers, 1899. 24fo, Flower holder with peacock-eyed butterflies, 1901. 30fo, Vase with tulip stems, 1899. 95fo, Round container with legs, 1912.

1998, Mar. 31   Litho.   Perf. 12
3602 A1061 20fo multi, vert.   .30 .25
    Complete booklet, 10 #3602   2.25
3603 A1061 24fo multi   .30 .25
    Complete booklet, 10 #3603   2.70
3604 A1061 30fo multi, vert.   .30 .25
    Complete booklet, 10 #3604   3.50
3605 A1061 95fo multi   1.15 .70
   Nos. 3602-3605 (4)   2.05 1.45

Postal Regulation, 250th Anniv. A1062

Designs: 24fo+10fo, Courier of 1748, detail of postal route connecting counties of Zala and Gyor. 30fo+10fo, Mounted courier, blowing post horn, script of regulation. 150fo, Horse-drawn postal coach, detail of postal route.

1998, Apr. 10
3606 A1062 24fo +10fo multi   .60 .50
3607 A1062 30fo +10fo multi   .60 .50
     Souvenir Sheet
3608 A1062 150fo multicolored   3.50 3.50
     Stamp Day.

Animals of the Americas A1063

23fo, Bison bison. No. 3610, Ursus horribilis. No. 3611, Alligator mississippiensis. 30fo, Leopardus pardalis. 150fo, Loddigesia mirabilis.

1998, Apr. 30
3609 A1063 23fo multicolored   .40 .35
3610 A1063 24fo multicolored   .40 .35
3611 A1063 24fo multicolored   .40 .35
3612 A1063 30fo multicolored   1.60 .35
   Nos. 3609-3612 (4)   2.80 1.40
     Souvenir Sheet
3613 A1063 150fo multicolored   3.00 3.00

Gyorgy Jendrassik, Engineer, Birth Cent. — A1064

1998, May 4   Engr.
3614 A1064 100fo dark blue   1.20 .75

Folk Designs Type of 1994
1998, June 5   Litho.   Perf. 11½x12
3615 A989 5fo multicolored   .40 .25

1998 Canoe-Kayak World Championships, Szeged — A1065

1998, June 5   Perf. 12
3616 A1065 30fo multicolored   .50 .25

1998 World Cup Soccer Championships, France — A1066

Different soccer players.

1998, June 5
3617 A1066 30fo multicolored   .30 .30
3618 A1066 110fo multicolored   1.20 1.05
  a. Pair, 3617-3618   1.90 1.50

1998 European Track & Field Championships, Budapest — A1067

1998, June 5   Perf. 12x11
3619 A1067 24fo Hurdles   .30 .25
3620 A1067 65fo Pole vault   .60 .55
3621 A1067 80fo Hammer throw   1.00 .75
   Nos. 3619-3621 (3)   1.90 1.55

Gabor Baross (1848-92), Postal Administrator A1068

1998, June 5   Perf. 12
3622 A1068 60fo multicolored   .90 .60

A1069

1998, July 31   Litho.   Perf. 12
3623 A1069 24fo multicolored   .60 .25
    Complete booklet, 10 #3623   3.50
Széchenyi Hill Children's Railway, 50th anniv.

A1070

1998, July 31   Perf. 12x11½
3624 A1070 65fo multicolored   1.25 .50
World Congress of Computer Technology, Budapest.

Natl. Holidays — A1071

Europa: 50fo, Sculptures, Festival of the 1956 Revolution, Proclamation of the Republic, 1989, October 23. 60fo, Sheaf of grain, Natl. arms, National Day, August 20.

1998, Aug. 19   Litho.   Perf. 12
3625 A1071 50fo multicolored   1.50 .65
3626 A1071 60fo multicolored   2.25 .85

133

HUNGARY

1998, Aug. 19
3627 A1072 100fo multicolored 1.20 .70
World Federation of Hungarians, 60th Anniv.

National Parks — A1073

Various flora, fauna, explorer of given region: 24fo, Dr. Miklós Udvardy, Hortobágy Natl. Park. 70fo, Ádám Boros, Kiskunság Natl. Park.

1998, Oct. 6   Litho.   Perf. 12
3628 A1073 24fo multicolored .30 .25
3629 A1073 70fo multicolored 1.25 .70
See Nos. 3654-3655, 3689-3690, 3745-3747, 3689-3690, 4072.

Folk Designs Type of 1994
1998   Litho.   Perf. 11½x12
3630 A989 200fo multicolored 3.25 2.25

Christmas — A1074

Designs: 20fo, Painting, "Visit of the Shepherds," by Agnolo Bronzino (1503-72). 24fo, Artwork, "Mary Upon the Throne with the Infant," by Carlo Crivelli (1430?-94?), vert.

1998, Oct. 30   Perf. 12x11½, 11½x12
3631 A1074 20fo multicolored .40 .25
   Complete booklet, 10 #3631 3.75
3632 A1074 24fo multicolored .45 .25
   Complete booklet, 10 #3632 6.50
See No. 3676.

Easter — A1075

1999, Feb. 11   Litho.   Perf. 12
3633 A1075 27fo Decorated eggs .35 .25
3634 A1075 32fo Shroud of Turin .45 .25
No. 3634 is 38x53mm.

Intl. Year of the Elderly — A1076

1999, Feb. 11   Perf. 12½x13½
3635 A1076 32fo multicolored .60 .40

Sailing Ships — A1077

32fo, Novara. 79fo, Phoenix. 110fo, Galley, 15th cent.

1999, Feb. 11   Perf. 12
3636 A1077 32fo multi .30 .25
3637 A1077 79fo multi .75 .55
3638 A1077 110fo multi 1.20 .75
   Nos. 3636-3638 (3) 2.25 1.55

Souvenir Sheet

Total Solar Eclipse, Aug. 11 — A1078

1999, Feb. 11
3639 A1078 1999fo multi 20.00 20.00
No. 3639 contains a holographic image. Soaking in water may affect the hologram.

Revolution of 1848-49 Type of 1998
24fo, Sword, Artúr Görgey (1818-1916), general. 27fo, Military decoration, Lajos Batthyány (1806-49), premier of 1st Hungarian ministry. 32fo, Military decoration, Jósef Bem (1794-1850), Polish General who joined Hungarian army. 100fo, Battle scene.

1999, Mar. 12
3640 A1060 24fo multicolored .40 .40
3641 A1060 27fo multicolored .40 .40
3642 A1060 32fo multicolored .40 .40
   Nos. 3640-3642 (3) 1.20 1.20

Souvenir Sheet
3643 A1060 100fo multicolored 3.00 3.00
No. 3643 contains one 45x28mm stamp.

Folk Designs Type of 1994
1999   Litho.   Perf. 12½
3644 A989 24fo multicolored .50 .25
3645 A989 65fo red & black 1.00 .55
3646 A989 90fo multicolored 1.50 .90
   Nos. 3644-3646 (3) 3.00 1.70
Nos. 3644-3646 are inscribed "1999."

Entrance into NATO — A1079

1999, Mar. 12   Litho.   Perf. 12x11½
3647 A1079 110fo multicolored 1.50 1.50

Souvenir Sheet

1999 Modern Pentathlon World Championships, Budapest — A1080

1999, Mar. 24   Perf. 12½
3648 A1080 100fo multicolored 2.00 2.00

Folk Designs Type of 1994
Various ornate designs.

1999, Apr. 19   Litho.   Perf. 11½x12
3649 A989 79fo multicolored .80 .50
3650 A989 100fo multicolored 1.20 .70

A1081

1999, May 3   Perf. 12
3651 A1081 50fo slate & bister .60 .30
Ferenc Pápai Páriz (1649-1716).

A1082

1999, May 3
3652 A1082 100fo multicolored 1.00 .65
Ferencvárosi Torna Sport Club, cent.

World Science Conference A1082a

1999, May 3   Litho.   Perf. 11½x12½
3652A A1082a 65fo multicolored .70 .60

Council of Europe, 50th Anniv. — A1083

1999, May 4   Perf. 13x13¼
3653 A1083 50fo multicolored 1.25 1.25

National Parks Type of 1998
Europa: 27fo, Aggteleki National Park. 32fo, Bükki National Park.

1999, May 6   Perf. 12
3654 A1073 27fo multicolored 3.00 1.40
3655 A1073 32fo multicolored 3.50 1.60

Grapes and Wine Producing Areas Type of 1990
Grapes, growing area and: 24fo, Castle ruins, Somló region. 27fo, 17th cent. view of Sopron.

1999, May 6   Litho.   Perf. 12¼x12½
3656 A902 24fo multi, horiz. .30 .25
3657 A902 27fo multi, horiz. .30 .30

Animals of Asia — A1085

Designs: 27fo, Tigris regalis. 32fo, Ailuropodus melanoleucus. 52fo, Panthera pardus. 79fo, Pongo pygmaeus. 100fo, Aix galericulata.

1999, May 6   Perf. 12
3658 A1085 27fo multicolored .40 .40
3659 A1085 32fo multicolored .40 .40
3660 A1085 52fo multicolored .65 .60
3661 A1085 79fo multicolored .80 .80
   Nos. 3658-3661 (4) 2.25 2.20

Souvenir Sheet
3662 A1085 100fo multicolored 3.50 3.50
No. 3662 contains one 50x30mm stamp.

Queen Maria Theresa's Introduction of Mail Coach Service, 250th Anniv. — A1086

Stamp Day: 32fo+15fo, Decree by Maria Theresa, coach, street. 52fo+20fo, People entering coach, woman with letters, portion of decree.
150fo, Horse-drawn coach arriving a station.

1999, May 21   Litho.   Perf. 12½x12¼
3663 A1086 32fo +15fo multi .60 .50
3664 A1086 52fo +20fo multi .80 .70

Souvenir Sheet
3665 A1086 150fo multicolored 2.50 2.50
No. 3665 contains one 32x42mm stamp.

Red Poppy — A1087
32fo, Stalkless gentian.

1999, July 7   Litho.   Perf. 12x11½
3666 A1087 27fo shown .35 .35
3667 A1087 32fo multi .45 .45
Compare with types A1644-A1645. See Nos. 3805-3806.

George Cukor (1899-1983), Film Director — A1088

1999, July 7   Litho.   Perf. 12
3668 A1088 50fo multicolored .70 .50

UPU, 125th Anniv. — A1089

1999, Aug. 13   Litho.   Perf. 12
3669 A1089 32fo multicolored .50 .50
Issued in sheets of 3. Value $1.50.

Frankfurt Book Fair A1090

1999, Sept. 9   Litho.   Perf. 12
3670 A1090 40fo multicolored .60 .60

Antique Furniture — A1091

Designs: 10fo, Chair, 17th cent, vert. 20fo, Chair by Károly Lingel, 1915, vert. 50fo, Chair by Pál Esterházy, vert. 70fo, Upholstered chair, vert. 100fo, Couch by Lajos Kozma.

   Perf. 11½x12, 12x11½
1999, Oct. 7   Litho.
3671 A1091 10fo bister & dk brn .30 .25
3672 A1091 20fo grn & dk grn .30 .25
3673 A1091 50fo blue & dk bl .30 .25
3674 A1091 70fo red & dk red .75 .40
3675 A1091 100fo brn & dk brn .95 .75
   Nos. 3671-3675 (5) 2.60 1.90
Nos. 3671-3673, 3675 exist dated "2001."
See Nos. 3711-3721, 3737-3743, 3790-3791, 3821-3823, 3960-3965, 4154, 4184.

Bronzino Christmas Painting Type of 1998 and

Magi A1092

Madonna and Child, Stained Glass by Miksa Róth A1093

1999, Oct. 15   Perf. 12x11½, 11½x12
3676 A1074 24fo multi .45 .25
   Complete booklet, 10 #3676 6.00
3677 A1092 27fo multi .45 .25
   Complete booklet, 10 #3677 6.00
3678 A1093 32fo multi .45 .25
   Complete booklet, 10 #3678 6.00
   Nos. 3676-3678 (3) 1.35 .75

HUNGARY

Jenö Wigner (1902-95), Winner of 1963 Nobel Physics Prize — A1094

1999, Nov. 3			Perf. 12	
3679	A1094	32fo blue	.45	.45

Souvenir Sheet

Chain Bridge, 150th Anniv. — A1095

1999, Nov. 3				
3680	A1095	150fo multi	2.25	2.25

Hungarian Millennium — A1096

Designs: 28fo, 30fo, Coronation scepter. 34fo, 40fo, Millennium flag.

2000		Litho.	Perf. 12x11½	
3681	A1096	28fo multi	.35	.25
3682	A1096	30fo multi	.40	.25
3683	A1096	34fo multi	.45	.25
3684	A1096	40fo multi	.60	.35
	Nos. 3681-3684 (4)		1.80	1.10

Coronation of Stephen I, Hungarian conversion to Christianity, 1000th anniv.
Issued: 30fo, 40fo, 1/1; 28fo, 34fo, 2/24.
No. 3681 exists dated 2001.
See No. 3744.

Souvenir Sheet

Famous Hungarians — A1097

No. 3685: a, 30fo, Miklós Misztófalusi Kis (1650-1702), scientist. b, 40fo, Anyos Jedlik (1800-95), physicist. c, 50fo, Jeno Kvassay (1850-1919), engineer. d, 80fo, Jeno Barcsay (1900-88), painter.

2000, Jan. 11			Perf. 11½x12	
3685	A1097	Sheet of 4, #a.-d.	3.75	3.75

Souvenir Sheet

Literary and Theatrical Personalities — A1098

No. 3686: a, Mihály Vörösmarty (1800-55), dramatist. b, Mari Jászai (1850-1926), actress. c, Sándor Márai (1900-89), writer. d, Lujza Blaha (1850-1926), actress. e, Lorinc Szabó (1900-57), writer.

2000, Feb. 24			Perf. 12	
3686	A1098	50fo Sheet of 5, #a.-e.	3.75	3.75

A1099

Easter — A1100

2000, Mar. 20				
3687	A1099	26fo multi	.30	.30
3688	A1100	28fo multi	.30	.30

National Parks Type of 1998

Designs: 29fo, Bluethroat, Siberian iris, ornithologist György Breuer (1887-1955), Ferto-Hanság Park. 34fo, Black stork, fritillary, scientist Pál Kitaibel (1757-1817), Duna-Dráva Park.

2000, Mar. 20		Litho.	Perf. 12	
3689	A1073	29fo multi	.50	.40
	Complete booklet, 10 #36892		4.00	
3690	A1073	34fo multi	.50	.40
	Complete booklet, 10 #3690		4.00	

Ferihegy Airport, 50th Anniv. — A1101

2000, May 3			Perf. 12x11½	
3691	A1101	136fo multi	1.20	.90

István Türr (1825-1908) and Canal Boat — A1102

2000, May 9			Perf. 12	
3692	A1102	80fo multi	1.10	.90

Expo 2000, Hanover.

Australian Wildlife — A1103

2000, May 9				
3693	A1103	26fo shown	.30	.25
3694	A1103	28fo Opossum	.30	.25
3695	A1103	83fo Koala	.75	.45
3696	A1103	90fo Red kangaroo	.85	.75
	Nos. 3693-3696 (4)		2.20	1.70

Souvenir Sheet

3697	A1103	110fo Platypus	2.25	2.25

Souvenir Sheet

Millennium — A1104

Litho., Hologram in Margin

2000, June 30				
3698	A1104	2000fo multi	19.00	19.00

Soaking in water may affect the hologram.

Europa, 2000
Common Design Type and

A1105

Stamp Day — A1106

2000, May 9			Litho.	
3699	A1105	34fo multi	2.00	1.20
3700	CD17	54fo multi	2.50	1.80

26fo, Queen Gisela in coronation gown. 28fo, King Stephen I in coronation gown.

2000, May 18				
3701	A1106	26fo multi	.35	.35
3702	A1106	28fo multi	.35	.35

Austria No. 4 and Bisect — A1107

2000, May 18				
3703	A1107	110fo multi	1.25	.95

WIPA 2000 Philatelic Exhibition, Vienna.

Grapes and Wine Producing Areas Type of 1990

Grapes and: 29fo, Winery building, Balatonfüred-Csopak region, horiz. 34fo, Storage containers, Aszár-Neszmély region, horiz.

2000, May 25			Perf. 13¼x13	
3704	A902	29fo multi	.35	.35
3705	A902	34fo multi	.45	.45

Houses of Worship — A1108

Designs: No. 3706, 30fo, Abbey Church, Ják. No. 3707, 30fo, Reformed Church, Tákos. No. 3708, 30fo, St. Antal's Church, Eger. No. 3709, 30fo, Deák Evangelical Church, Budapest. 120fo, Dohany Synagogue, Budapest.

2000		Litho.	Perf. 12	
3706-3710	A1108	Set of 5	2.50	2.50

Issued: 120fo, 9/19; others 6/30. See Israel No. 1416.

Furniture Type of 1999

Designs: 2fo, Wooden chair, 1838, vert. 3fo, 19th cent. chair, vert. 4fo, Chair by Géza Maróti, 1900, vert. 5fo, Chair by Odon Farago, 1900, vert. 6fo, Chair by Márton Kovács, 1893, vert. 9fo, 18th cent. chair from Dunapataj, vert. 26fo, 1850 chair, vert. 29fo, 19th cent. chair with animal designs, vert. 30fo, Chair by Károly Nagy, 1935, vert. 80fo, 1840-50 chair, vert. 90fo, Chair by Lajos Kozma, 1928, vert.

2000			Perf. 11½x12	
3711-3721	A1091	Set of 11	3.00	2.75

Issued: 2fo, 3fo, 9fo, 26fo, 30fo, 6/30; others, 10/9.

Hungarian Aviation, 90th Anniv. — A1109

2000, Aug. 18			Perf. 12¾x12¼	
3722	A1109	120fo multi	1.75	1.50

Souvenir Sheets

Hungarian History — A1110

No. 3723: a, King with orb, knights. b, St. Laszlo with sword. c, St. Elizabeth, Mongol invasion. d, King Sigismund, knight on horseback. e, Janos Hunuyadi and Janos Kapisztran.
No. 3724: a, King Matthias. b, Crucifixion scene, Miklos Zrinyi. c, Trumpeter on horseback, battle scenes. d, Gabor Bethlen (in black hat). e, Peer Parmany, university.

2000, Aug. 18			Perf. 12	
3723	A1110	Sheet of 5	5.00	3.50
a.-e.		50fo Any single	.70	.35
3724	A1110	Sheet of 5	5.00	3.50
a.-e.		50fo Any single	.70	.35

See Nos. 3770-3771.

A1111 A1112

Christmas — A1113

2000, Oct. 16			Perf. 12¼x11½	
3725	A1111	26fo shown	.35	.35
			Perf. 13¼x13	
3726	A1112	28fo shown	.45	.35
	Booklet, 10 #3726		4.00	
3727	A1112	29fo Christmas tree	.45	.35
			Perf. 12	
3728	A1113	34fo multi	.45	.45
	Booklet, 10 #3728		4.00	
	Nos. 3725-3728 (4)		1.70	1.50

European Convention on Human Rights, 50th Anniv. A1114

2000, Nov. 3			Perf. 12½	
3729	A1114	50fo multicolored	.90	.90

2000 Summer Olympics, Sydney — A1115

Sports and total of medals won: 30fo, Shooting, three bronzes. 40fo, Weight lifting, six silvers. 80fo, Men's rings, eight golds. 120fo, Rowing, total count.

2000, Nov. 22			Perf. 12	
3730-3732	A1115	Set of 3	1.50	1.50

Souvenir Sheet

3733	A1115	120fo multi	2.25	2.25

European Language Year — A1116

2001, Jan. 15		Litho.	Perf. 13x13¼	
3734	A1116	100fo multi	1.25	1.25

Souvenir Sheet

Greetings — A1117

No. 3735: a, Bugler on pig. b, Man, woman, flower. c, Baby in cradle. d, Clown. e, Mother and child.

2001, Feb. 9			Perf. 11½x12	
3735	A1117	36fo Sheet of 5, #a-f	2.50	2.50

World Speed Skating Championships, Budapest A1118

2001, Feb. 9		Litho.	Perf. 13	
3736	A1118	140fo multi	1.50	1.35

Furniture Type of 1999

Designs: 1fo, Three-legged stool, by János Vincze, 1910, vert. 7fo, 1853 chair, vert. 8fo,

HUNGARY

19th cent. chair, vert. 31fo, Like No. 3717, vert. 40fo, Armchair by Ignác Alpár, 1896, vert. 60fo, Armchair by Ferenc Steindl, 1840, vert. 200fo, Settee by Sebestyén Vogel, 1810.

2001		Perf. 11½x12, 12x11½
3737-3743	A1091 Set of 7	4.00 3.00

Issued: 31fo, 3/5; others, 2/9.

Hungarian Millennium Type of 2000

2001, Mar. 5		Perf. 12x11½
3744	A1096 36fo Millennium flag	.60 .35

National Parks Type of 1998

Designs: 28fo, Balaton. 36fo, Körös-maros. 70fo, Duna-Ipoly.

2001, Mar. 5		Perf. 12
3745-3747	A1073 Set of 3	1.50 1.35

Easter — A1119

2001, Mar. 5		Perf. 13
3748	A1119 28fo multi	.50 .25

Locomotives A1120

Designs: 31fo, Mk. 48. 36fo, 490. 100fo, 394. 150fo, C50.

2001, Apr. 13		Perf. 13¼x13
3749-3752	A1120 Set of 4	3.25 2.75

Esztergom Archbishopric, 1000th Anniv. — A1121

2001, Apr. 18		Perf. 12
3753	A1121 124fo multi	1.35 1.15

Organizations — A1122

No. 3754: a, 70fo, Emblems of European and Mediterranean Plant Protection Organization and Intl. Plant Protection Convention. b, 80fo, UN High Commissioner for Refugees, 50th anniv.

2001, Apr. 18		Perf. 13¼x13
3754	A1122 Horiz. pair, #a-b	1.25 1.25

Europa — A1123

Designs: 36fo, Open chest with water. 90fo, Split globe with water.

2001, May 9		Perf. 12
3755-3756	A1123 Set of 2	2.00 1.90

Animals A1124

Designs: 28fo, Phoca hispida. 36fo, Canis lupus. 70fo, Testudo hermanni. 90fo, Alcedo atthis ispida. 200fo, Cervus elaphus.

2001, May 9		Perf. 12
3757-3760	A1124 Set of 4	2.50 2.50

Souvenir Sheet

| 3761 | A1124 200fo multi | 3.00 3.00 |

A1125

Stamp Day A1126

Designs: 36fo, #N2. 90fo, #2. 200fo+40fo, Pigeon Post, by Miklos Barabás.

2001, May 25		Perf. 12¼x11½
3762-3763	A1125 Set of 2	1.35 1.15
a.	Sheet, 6 each #3762-3763	9.00 9.00

Souvenir Sheet Perf. 12½

| 3764 | A1126 200fo +40fo multi | 3.00 3.00 |

European Water Polo Championships A1127

2001, June 14		Perf. 13½x13
3765	A1127 150fo multi	1.50 1.35

Intl. Scouting Conference A1128

2001, June 21		Perf. 12
3766	A1128 150fo multi	1.50 1.50

World Youth Track and Field Championships, Debrecen A1129

2001, July 12	Litho.	Perf. 13x13¼
3767	A1129 140fo multi	1.50 1.35

Artist's Colony, Gödöllö, Cent. — A1130

Fészek Arts Club, Cent. A1131

2001, July 12		Perf. 12
3768	A1130 100fo multi	1.15 .90
3769	A1131 150fo blue & blk	1.50 1.35

Hungarian History Type of 2000

Souvenir Sheets

No. 3770: a, Prince Francis II Rákóczy, swordsman on horseback, Ilona Zrinyi. b, Rider from Royal Horse Guard, Castle at Munkács, Queen Maria Theresa. c, Count Stephen Széchenyi, Chain Bridge. d, Lajos Kossuth, Artúr Görgey with sword on horseback, battle scene. e, Poet János Arany, Parliament building.

No. 3771: a, World War I soldier on horseback, outline map of Hungary and lost parts of empire, Hungarian people. b, Albert Szent-Gyorgi and chemistry equipment. c, Chain Bridge, World War II soldiers, Bishop Vilmos Apor. d, Pictures of 1956 revolution, Polish-Hungarian Solidarity banner. e, Barbed wire, children representing Hungary's future, Hungarian millennium flag.

2001, Aug. 15			
3770	A1110	Sheet of 5	5.00 5.00
a.-e.	50fo Any single		1.00 1.00
3771	A1110	Sheet of 5	5.00 5.00
a.-e.	50fo Any single		1.00 1.00

Souvenir Sheet

Crown of St. Stephen A1132

2001, Aug. 15	Litho. & Embossed	Perf. 13x12¾
3772	A1132 2001fo multi	20.00 20.00

Grapes and Wine Producing Areas Type of 1990

Grapes and: 60fo, Pannonhalma Abbey, Pannonhalma-Sokoróalja region, horiz. 70fo, Spherical observatory and Red Chapel, Balatonboglár, horiz.

2001, Aug. 17	Litho.	Perf. 13¼x13
3773-3774	A902 Set of 2	1.50 .75

Attempt To Create World's Largest Stamp Mosaic — A1133

2001, Oct. 9		Perf. 12
3775	A1133 10fo multi	.30 .25

Maria Valeria Bridge Reconstruction A1134

2001, Oct. 11		Perf. 13¼x13
3776	A1134 36fo multi	.50 .50

See Slovakia No. 388.

Christmas — A1135

2001, Oct. 16		Perf. 12
3777	A1135 36fo multi	.50 .25

State Printers, 150th Anniv. — A1136

2001, Nov. 23	Litho.	Perf. 13¼x13
3778	A1136 150fo multi	1.65 1.50

2002 Winter Olympics, Salt Lake City A1137

2002, Feb. 8	Litho.	Perf. 12
3779	A1137 160fo multi	1.65 1.50

Souvenir Sheet

History of the Bicycle A1138

No. 3780: a, Large-wheeled bicycle and rider, c. 1880. b, Tricycle, early 1900s. c, Károly Iszer (1860-1929), Budapest Sport Club chairman and bicycle. d, Tandem bicycle.

2002, Feb. 20		Perf. 11½x12¼
3780	A1138 40fo Sheet of 4, #a-d	2.50 2.50

Souvenir Sheet

Hungarian — Ottoman Battles of 1552 — A1139

No. 3781: a, 50fo, Siege of Eger Castle (25x30mm). b, 50fo, Battle of Temesvár (25x30mm). c, 100fo+50fo, Battle of Drégely Castle (40x30mm).

2002, Feb. 20		Perf. 12
3781	A1139 Sheet of 3, #a-c	3.00 3.00

Easter — A1140

2002, Mar. 14		Perf. 11½x12¼
3782	A1140 30fo multi	.35 .25

Airplanes Designed by Hungarians A1141

Designs: 180fo, Libelle, by János adorján, 1910. 190fo, Magyar Lloyd, by Tibor Melczer, 1914.

2002, Mar. 14		Perf. 12½
3783-3784	A1141 Set of 2	3.50 2.00

See Nos. 3831-3832, 3968-3969.

Famous Hungarians A1142

Designs: 33fo, Lajos Kossuth (1802-94), leader of Hungarian independence movement. 134fo, János Bolyai (1802-60), mathematician. 150fo, Gyula Illyés (1902-83), writer.

2002, Mar. 14		Perf. 13x13½
3785-3787	A1142 Set of 3	3.25 2.40

HUNGARY

Souvenir Sheet

Parliament Building, Cent. — A1143

2002, Mar. 14		*Perf. 11½x12¼*
3788	A1143 500fo multi	5.00 5.00

Souvenir Sheet

Opening of National Theater A1144

2002, Mar. 14		
3789	A1144 500fo multi	5.00 5.00

Furniture Type of 1999

Designs: 33fo, Chair, 1809, vert. 134fo, Theater armchair, 1900.

2002, Mar. 14	*Perf. 11½x12, 12x11½*
3790-3791 A1091	Set of 2 2.50 1.00

Environmental Protection A1145

2002, Mar. 14		*Perf. 12*
3792	A1145 158fo multi	1.50 .80

Souvenir Sheet

Founding of Hungarian National Museum and National Széchényi Library, Bicent. — A1146

No. 3793: a, Mihály Apafi psalter, 1686. b, Illuminated letter from Graduale Pars II. c, Standard of the Civil Guard of Pest, 1848. d, Basin for holy water, 12th cent.

2002, Apr. 29		
3793	A1146 150fo Sheet of 4, #a-d	6.00 6.00

Halas Lace, Cent. A1147

Designs: 100fo, Tablecloth with Two Deer, by Mrs. Béla Bazala, 1916. 110fo, Swan Tablecloth, by Ernő Stepanek, 1930. 140fo, Jancsi and Iluska, by Antal Tar, 1935.

Litho. & Embossed

2002, May 3		*Perf. 12*
3794-3796 A1147	Set of 3	3.50 3.00

Europa — A1148

2002, May 9	Litho.	*Perf. 11*
3797	A1148 62fo multi	1.30 1.30

2002 World Cup Soccer Championships, Japan and Korea — A1149

2002, May 9		*Perf. 13x13½*
3798	A1149 160fo multi + label	1.65 1.50

Fauna — A1150

Designs: 30fo, Felis sylvestris. 38fo, Podarcis taurica. 110fo, Garrulus glandarius. 160fo, Rosalia alpina. 500fo, Acipenser ruthenus.

2002, May 9		*Perf. 12*
3799-3802 A1150	Set of 4	3.50 3.00

Souvenir Sheet

| 3803 | A1150 500fo multi | 5.00 5.00 |

Greetings — A1151

No. 3804: a, Etesd meg! b, Megszülettem! c, Sok boldogságot! d, Ontözd meg! e, Ennyire szeretlek!

Serpentine Die Cut 12¼x12¾	
2002, June 24	*Self-Adhesive*
3804 Booklet pane of 5	2.25
a.-e. A1151 38fo Any single	.35 .25

Flower Type of 1999

Designs: 30fo, Red poppy. 38fo, Stalkless gentian.

2002, June 24		*Perf. 12¼x11½*
3805-3806 A1087	Set of 2	.75 .45

Art — A1152

Designs: 62fo, Kodobálók, by Károly Ferenczy. 188fo, Táncosno, sculpture by Ferenc Megyessy, vert.

	Perf. 12¾x12¼, 12¼x12¾
2002, June 24	
3807-3808 A1152	Set of 2 2.50 2.25

UNESCO World Heritage Sites — A1153

Designs: 100fo, Budapest. 150fo, Hollóko. 180fo, Caves of Aggtelek Karst, horiz.

2002, June 24		*Perf. 12*
3809-3811 A1153	Set of 3	4.00 3.25

See Nos. 3881-3882, 4073.

Kalocsa Archbishopric, 1000th Anniv. — A1154

2002, Aug. 1	Litho.	*Perf. 13¼x12½*
3812	A1154 150fo multi	1.50 .75

Medical Congresses A1155

No. 3813: a, 100fo, 38th European Diabetes Association Congress. b, 150fo, 16th European Arm and Shoulder Surgeons Congress.

2002, Aug. 23		*Perf. 13x13¼*
3813	A1155 Vert. pair, #a-b	2.00 2.00

Printed in sheets of two pairs. Value $5.

Ceramics by Margit Kovács A1156

No. 3814: a, 33fo, Madonna and Child, 1938. b, 38fo, Mother and Children, 1953. 400fo+200fo, St. George, 1936.

2002, Oct. 3		*Perf. 13¼x13*
3814	A1156 Pair, #a-b	.60 .60

Souvenir Sheet
Perf. 12¼x11½

| 3815 | A1156 400fo +200fo multi | 6.00 6.00 |

Stamp Day. No. 3814 printed in sheets of two pairs. Value $1.75. No. 3815 contains one 25x36mm stamp.

Christmas A1157

Designs: 30fo, Adoration of the Magi. 38fo, Bethlehem.

Litho. with Foil Application

2002, Oct. 30		*Perf. 12*
3816-3817 A1157	Set of 2	1.25 .75

See No. 4006.

World Gymnastics Championships, Debrecen — A1158

2002, Nov. 20	Litho.	*Perf. 13x13¼*
3818	A1158 160fo multi	1.40 1.25

Hungarian and Turkish Buildings — A1159

Designs: 40fo, Rakoczi House, Tekirdag, Turkey. 110fo, Gazi Kassim Pasha Mosque, Pécs, Hungary.

2002, Dec. 2	Litho.	*Perf. 13½x13¼*
3819-3820 A1159	Set of 2	1.50 1.25

See Turkey No. 2844.

Furniture Type of 1999

Designs: 32fo, Wooden chair with carved back, 19th cent., vert. 35fo, Armchair, 18th cent., vert. 65fo, Armchair with carved back, 1920, vert.

2003, Jan. 30		*Perf. 11½x12¼*
3821-3823 A1091	Set of 3	1.75 .70

Scientists A1160

Designs: 32fo, John von Neumann (1903-57), mathematician, and computer pioneer. 40fo, Rezső Soó (1903-80), botanist. 60fo, Károly Zipernowsky (1853-1942), electrical engineer.

2003, Feb. 12		*Perf. 13x13¼*
3824 A1160	32fo multicolored	.30 .25
3825 A1160	40fo multicolored	.45 .35
3826 A1160	60fo multicolored	.60 .55
Nos. 3824-3826 (3)		1.35 1.15

Souvenir Sheet

Herend Porcelain A1161

No. 3827: a, Platter with floral design, Frankenthal coffee set. b, Vase with floral design, coffee set. c, Vase with ram's head handles. d, Shell-shaped bowl, pitcher.

2003, Feb. 12		*Perf. 12*
3827	A1161 150fo Sheet of 4, #a-d	4.50 4.50

Defeat of Royal Hungarian Army, 60th Anniv. A1162

2003, Feb. 15		*Perf. 12¼x12½*
3828	A1162 40fo multi	.60 .25

Easter — A1163

2003, Mar. 14		
3829	A1163 32fo multi	.50 .25

Nemzeti Sport, Cent. A1164

2003, Mar. 14		*Perf. 13x13¼*
3830	A1164 150fo multi + label	1.50 1.35

Airplanes Type of 2002

Designs: 142fo, Gerle 13, by Antal Bánhidi, 1933. 160fo, L-2 Róma, by Árpád Lampich, 1925.

2003, Mar. 20		*Perf. 12½*
3831-3832 A1141	Set of 2	2.75 2.10

Hotels A1165

Designs: 110fo, Rogner Hotel, Héviz. 120fo, Hélia Hotel, Budapest.

2003, Mar. 20		
3833-3834 A1165	Set of 2	2.50 1.75

See Nos. 3883-3884.

Souvenir Sheet

Extreme Sports A1166

HUNGARY

No. 3835: a, 100fo, BMX cycling. b, 100fo, Snowboarding. c, 100fo, Parachuting. d, 100fo+50fo, Kayaking.

2003, Mar. 20		Perf. 12	
3835	A1166	Sheet of 4, #a-d	4.50 4.50

Greetings — A1167

No. 3836: a, Church. b, Two flowers. c, One flower. d, Easter eggs. e, Candles in window, Christmas tree.

Serpentine Die Cut 12¾

2003, Mar. 20		Self-Adhesive	
3836		Booklet pane of 5	2.00
a.-e.	A1167	40fo Any single	.40 .25

Souvenir Sheet

Space Shuttle Columbia — A1168

2003, Apr. 9		Perf. 12	
3837	A1168	500fo multi	4.75 4.75

World Ice Hockey Championships, Budapest — A1169

2003, Apr. 10		Perf. 13x13¼	
3838	A1169	110fo multi + label	1.10 .80

Budapest Sports Arena — A1170

2003, Apr. 10			
3839	A1170	120fo multi + label	1.25 .85

Souvenir Sheet

Ratification of European Union Accession Treaty — A1171

2003, Apr. 14		Perf. 12	
3840	A1171	500fo multi	5.00 5.00

Policeman on Motorcycle and Emergency Phone Number — A1172

2003, Apr. 24			
3841	A1172	65fo multi	.75 .60

Stamp Day — A1173

Designs: 35fo, Statue of woman with legs crossed. 40fo, Statue of woman with hand on chin. 400fo+100fo, Fountain.

2003, May 6		Perf. 13¼x13	
3842-3843	A1173	Set of 2	.90 .75

Souvenir Sheet
Perf. 12¾x13

| 3844 | A1173 | 400fo +100fo multi | 5.00 5.00 |

No. 3844 contains one 31x40mm stamp.

Souvenir Sheet

Uprising Against Hapsburgs of Ferenc Rákóczi II, 400th Anniv. — A1174

No. 3845: a, Swords and scabbards. b, Coins. c, Banner, pipes and drums. d, Guns.

2003, May 6		Perf. 12	
3845	A1174	120fo Sheet of 4, #a-d	4.25 4.25

Europa — A1175

2003, May 9			
3846	A1175	65fo multi	1.15 1.15

Fauna — A1176

Designs: 35fo, Mustela eversmanni. 40fo, Calandrella brachydactyla. 100fo, Hyla arborea. 110fo, Misgurnus fossilis. 500fo, Eresus cinnabarinus.

2003, May 9			
3847-3850	A1176	Set of 4	4.00 1.75

Souvenir Sheet

| 3851 | A1176 | 500fo multi | 4.75 4.75 |

Grapes and Wine Producing Areas Type of 1990

Grapes: 60fo, Bükkalja region, horiz. 130fo, Balaton-felvidéki region, horiz.

2003, June 6		Perf. 13¼x12½	
3852-3853	A902	Set of 2	1.60 1.60

Souvenir Sheet

Robe of St. László A1177

2003, June 13		Perf. 12	
3854	A1177	300fo multi	3.50 3.50

Art — A1178

Designs: 32fo, Sculpture by Imre Varga, vert. 60fo, Mostar Bridge, by Tivadar Csontváry Kosztka.

Perf. 12½x13¼, 13¼x12½

2003, July 18			
3855-3856	A1178	Set of 2	1.00 .85

Souvenir Sheet

Sports History A1179

No. 3857: a, Ferenc Puskás Stadium Budapest, 50th anniv. b, Hungary vs. England soccer match, 50th anniv.

2003, July 18		Perf. 11½x12¼	
3857	A1179	250fo Sheet of 2, #a-b	4.50 4.50

European Union Membership — A1180

2003		Litho.	Perf. 12x11½
3858	A1180	115fo shown	.95 .60
3859	A1180	130fo Clock at 11:35	1.05 .70

Issued: 115fo, 9/16; 130fo, 10/18. See Nos. 3877-3878.

Nutrition — A1181

2003, Sept. 16		Perf. 12	
3860	A1181	120fo multi	1.15 .90

European Automobile-free Day — A1182

2003, Sept. 16			
3861	A1182	150fo multi	1.50 .90

Reszo Soó (1903-80), Botanist — A1183

2003, Sept. 23			
3862	A1183	44fo multi	.45 .25

Book Printing A1184

Designs: No. 3863, 44fo, Hungarian Illuminated Chronicle, 1358. No. 3864, 44fo, Ritual of Zhou, China.

2003, Sept. 30			
3863-3864	A1184	Set of 2	.90 .75

See People's Republic of China Nos. 3309-3310.

Souvenir Sheet

Ferenc Deák (1803-76), Statesman — A1185

2003, Oct. 18			
3865	A1185	500fo multi	5.00 5.00

Christmas — A1186

Designs: 35fo, Reindeer. 44fo, Angels, Christmas tree, houses.

2003, Oct. 31		Perf. 11½x12	
3866-3867	A1186	Set of 2	.90 .75

Souvenir Sheet

World Science Forum, Budapest — A1187

2003, Nov. 7		Litho.	Perf. 12
3868	A1187	500fo multi	5.00 5.00

Locomotives Type of 2001

Designs: 120fo, Muki Diesel locomotive, Kemence Forest Railway. 150fo, Rezét steam locomotive, Gemenc Forest Railway.

2004, Feb. 4		Perf. 13¼x13	
3869-3870	A1120	Set of 2	2.70 2.70

Famous Men — A1188

Designs: 40fo, Bálint Balassi (1554-94), poet. 44fo, József Bajza (1804-58), poet. 80fo, János András Segner (1704-77), physicist.

2004, Feb. 4		Perf. 13	
3871-3873	A1188	Set of 3	1.65 1.25

Souvenir Sheet

Dogs A1189

No. 3874: a, 100fo, Puli. b, 100fo, Hungarian greyhound. c, 100fo, Mudi. d, 100fo+50fo, Vizsla.

2004, Feb. 19		Perf. 12	
3874	A1189	Sheet of 4, #a-d	4.50 4.50

Surtax on No. 3874d for youth philately.

Souvenir Sheet

Festivals A1190

No. 3875: a, Busójárás Carnival. b, Virágkarnevál (Flower Carnival). c, Borfesztivál (Wine Festival). d, Fesztiválok Karneválok (Festivals and Carnivals).

2004, Feb. 19			
3875	A1190	60fo Sheet of 4, #a-d	3.25 3.25

European Ministerial Conference on the Information Society — A1191

HUNGARY

No. 3876 — Color of panel and "e:" a, Red violet. b, Dark blue. c, Lt. green. d, Light orange.

2004, Feb. 26		Perf. 13¼x13		
3876	A1191	40fo Block of 4, #a-d	2.25	2.25

European Union Membership (Clock) Type of 2003

2004			Perf. 12x11½	
3877	A1180	100fo Clock at 11:48	1.25	.50
3878	A1180	190fo Clock at 11:57	2.25	.90

Issued: 100fo, 3/5; 190fo, 4/19.

Tenth World Indoor Track and Field Championships, Budapest — A1192

2004, Mar. 5			Perf. 13x13¼	
3879	A1192	120fo multi	1.20	1.00

Easter — A1193

2004, Mar. 18			Litho.	
3880	A1193	48fo multi	.50	.25

World Heritage Sites Type of 2002

Designs: 150fo, Abbey of Pannonhalma. 170fo, Hortobágy National Park, horiz.

2004, Mar. 18			Perf. 12	
3881-3882	A1153	Set of 2	2.70	2.40

Hotels Type of 2003

Designs: 120fo, Bük Thermal and Sports Hotel, Bükfürdo. 150fo, Aqua-Sol Hotel, Hajdúszoboszló.

2004, Mar. 18				
3883-3884	A1165	Set of 2	2.70	2.40

Holocaust, 60th Anniv. — A1194

2004, Apr. 16			Perf. 13x13¼	
3885	A1194	160fo multi	1.50	1.35

Zsolnay Porcelain, 150th Anniv. — A1195

No. 3886: a, Vase with handles. b, Small vase, vessel with horse and rider top. c, Vase. d, Mocha set.

2004, Apr. 20		Litho.	Perf. 12	
3886	A1195	160fo Sheet of 4, #a-d	5.50	5.50

Police Boat and Emergency Phone Number — A1196

2004, Apr. 23		Litho.	Perf. 13x13¼	
3887	A1196	48fo multi	.50	.35

Souvenir Sheet

Admission to European Union — A1197

2004, Apr. 30			Perf. 12	
3888	A1197	500fo multi	5.25	5.25

Expansion of the European Union — A1198

No. 3889: a, 120fo, Stars and flowers. b, 150fo, Stars, map of Europe, flags of nations entering European Union.

2004, May 1			Litho.	
3889	A1198	Horiz. pair, #a-b	2.75	2.75

European Parliament Elections — A1199

2004, May 7			Perf. 12½x13½	
3890	A1199	150fo multi	1.50	1.50

Europa — A1200

2004, May 7			Perf. 12	
3891	A1200	160fo multi	1.75	1.75

Fauna — A1201

Designs: 48fo, Nannospalax leucodon. 65fo, Panurus biarmicus. 90fo, Ablepharus kitaibelii fitzingeri. 120fo, Huso huso. 500fo, Anthaxia hungarica.

2004, May 7				
3892-3895	A1201	Set of 4	3.25	2.50

Souvenir Sheet

3896	A1201	500fo multi	5.00	5.00

Stamp Day — A1202

Designs: 48fo, Walls and Doors, sculpture by Erzsébet Schaár. 65fo, Translucent Red Circle, painting by Tihamér Gyarmathy. 400fo+200fo, The Wasp King, painting by Béla Kondor.

2004, May 7		Litho.	Perf. 12¼x12¾	
3897-3898	A1202	Set of 2	1.60	1.35

Souvenir Sheet Perf. 12¾x12¼

3899	A1202	400fo +200fo multi	5.75	5.75

No. 3899 contains one 41x31mm stamp.

FIFA (Fédération Internationale de Football Association), Cent. — A1203

2004, May 21		Litho.	Perf. 13¼x13	
3900	A1203	100fo multi	1.25	.75

Central European Catholics' Day — A1204

No. 3901: a, Basilica, Mariazell, Austria. b, Statue of Madonna, Mariazell. c, Statue of Madonna and Child, Mariazell. d, Statue of Madonna, Celldömölk, Hungary. e, Framed painting of Madonna and Child, Mariazell. f, Statue of Mary of Kiscell, Obuda Parish, Hungary.

2004, May 21		Litho.	Perf. 11½x12	
3901	A1204	100fo Sheet of 6, #a-f	5.75	5.75

Information Technology A1205

2004, June 28			Perf. 13x13¼	
3902	A1205	120fo multi	1.15	.90

Theodor Herzl (1860-1904), Zionist Leader — A1206

2004, July 6		Litho.	Perf. 12	
3903	A1206	150fo multi	1.50	1.50

See Austria No. 1960, Israel No. 1566.

2004 Summer Olympics, Athens A1207

Designs: 90fo, Canoeing. 130fo, Volleyball. 150fo, Running.

2004, July 13				
3904-3906	A1207	Set of 3	3.50	2.75

A1208

A1209

A1210

A1211

A1212

A1213

A1214

Folkloriada Festival — A1215

2004, Aug. 12				
3907		Block of 10 + 10 labels	7.50	7.50
a.	A1208	65fo dark blue	.75	.40
b.	A1208	65fo orange	.75	.40
c.	A1209	65fo orange brown	.75	.40
d.	A1209	65fo purple	.75	.40
e.	A1210	65fo carmine	.75	.40
f.	A1211	65fo orange brown	.75	.40
g.	A1212	65fo orange brown	.75	.40
h.	A1213	65fo Prussian blue	.75	.40
i.	A1214	65fo green	.75	.40
j.	A1215	65fo orange brown	.75	.40
k.		Sheet, #3907	24.50	24.50

No. 3907k has labels that could be personalized. The personalized sheet sold for 1600fo.

Chess History — A1216

No. 3908 — Beginning of text, square color, piece (if any): a, A sakkjáték, tan, black rook. b, A magyaroknak, brown. c, A magyar történelem, tan, black bishop. d, A magyar sakkirodalom, brown, black king. e, A XVIII. században, tan, black queen. f, Az elso, brown. g, Az 1839-ben, tan, black knight. h, A XIX. század, brown, black rook. i, A magyar sakkfeladványszerok, brown, black pawn. j, Három, a XIX. század, tan, black pawn. k, Maróczy Géza, brown, black pawn. l, Két kiváló, tan, black pawn. m, A levelezési, brown, black bishop. n, A sakkélet, tan, black pawn. o, A férfi országos, brown, black pawn. p, A II. világháború tan után sokáig, black pawn. q, A nol sakkozás, tan. r, 1958-ban már, brown. s, A sakkozók, tan, black knight. t, 1951-ben indult, brown. u, A XX. századnak, tan. v, A II. világháború utá feladvány, brown. w, A XX. században, tan. x, A XX. század elején, brown. y, A világ sakkéletét, brown. z, A két világháború között, tan. aa, A háború után, brown. ab, A férfi sakkolimpián, tan. ac, A nemzetek közti, brown, black pawn. ad, 1957-ben a hollandiai, tan. ae, A nol sakkolimpiákon, brown. af, A XIX. és XX. században, tan. ag, Sakkirodalom nélkül, tan. ah, A XX. század magyar, brown. ai, A széles sakkozó, tan, white bishop. aj, A Magyar Sakkszövetség, brown. ak, Barcza Gedeon, tan, white pawn. al, Szábo László, brown. am, Portisch Lajos, tan. an, Adorján András, brown. ao, Sax Gyula, brown. ap, Ribli Zoltán, tan. aq, Lékó Péter, brown. ar, Almási Zoltán, tan. as, Bilek, István, brown. at, A két világháború közti, tan, white knight. au, Az olimpiákon többször, brown. av, Sok kiváló magyar, tan. aw, Polgár Zsuzsa, tan, white pawn. ax, Polgár Judit, brown, white pawn. ay, Polgár Zsófia, tan, white pawn. az, Lángos Józsa, brown, white pawn. ba, Veroci Zsuzsa, tan. bb, Ivánka Mária, brown, white pawn. bc, Mádl Ildikó, tan, white pawn. bd, Országos bajnoki, brown, white pawn. be, Sakkozásunk a XXI. századot, brown, white rook. bf, A sakkozással, tan, white knight. bg, A magyar sakkozás, brown, white queen. bh, Minden összefoglaló, tan, white king. bi, A jelen munkában, brown, white queen. bj, Elek Ferenc, tan. bk, Katkó (Regos) Imre, brown. bl, Gróf Pongrácz Arnold, tan, white rook.

2004, Sept. 24				
3908		Sheet of 64	33.75	33.75
a.-bl.	A1216	50fo Any single	.60	.40

HUNGARY

Souvenir Sheet

Admission to European Union — A1217

No. 3909 — Large stars and time of small clock: a, 11:20. b, 11:35. c, 11:48. d, 11:57.

2004, Oct. 8   *Perf. 12x11½*
3909 A1217 100fo Sheet of 4, #a-d   3.50 3.50

Istvan Bocskay (1557-1606), Leader of 1604-06 Rebellion — A1218

2004, Nov. 11   *Litho.*   *Perf. 11½x12*
3910 A1218 120fo multi   1.25 1.05

Intl. Organization of Supreme Audit Institutions, 18th Congress, Budapest — A1219

2004, Oct. 11   *Perf. 11¼*
3911 A1219 150fo multi   1.35 1.35

Christmas Type of 2002 and

A1220
A1221
A1222
A1223
A1224
A1225
A1226
A1227
A1228
A1229
A1230
A1231
A1232
A1233
A1234

Christmas — A1235

No. 3915: Various Christmas cookies.

Litho. With Foil Application
2004   *Perf. 12*
3912 A1157 48fo Bethlehem   .50 .25

Litho.
Perf. 11¼
3913   Sheet of 20 + 20 labels   20.00 20.00
   a. A1220 48fo multi + label   .55 .40
   b. A1221 48fo multi + label   .55 .40
   c. A1222 48fo multi + label   .55 .40
   d. A1223 48fo multi + label   .55 .40
   e. A1224 48fo multi + label   .55 .40
   f. A1225 48fo multi + label   .55 .40
3914   Sheet of 20 + 20 labels   20.00 20.00
   a. A1226 48fo multi + label   .55 .40
   b. A1227 48fo multi + label   .55 .40
   c. A1228 48fo multi + label   .55 .40
   d. A1229 48fo multi + label   .55 .40
   e. A1230 48fo multi + label   .55 .40
   f. A1231 48fo multi + label   .55 .40
   g. A1232 48fo multi + label   .55 .40
   h. A1233 48fo multi + label   .55 .40
   i. A1234 48fo multi + label   .55 .40
3915 A1235 48fo Sheet of 20, #a-t, + 20 labels   24.00 24.00

Issued: No. 3912, 10/28; Nos. 3913-3915, 11/3.

No. 3913 contains 5 No. 3913b, 3 No. 3913c, 4 each Nos. 3913a, 3913e, 2 each Nos. 3913d, 3913f. Background colors on some stamps differ slightly.

No. 3914 contains Nos. 3914d, 3914e, 4 each Nos. 3914a, 3914b, 2 each Nos. 3914c, 3914f, 3914g, 3914h, 3914i.

Nos. 3913-3915 could be personalized, with each sheet selling for 2000fo.

Sándor Körösi Csoma (1784-1842), Philologist and Sir Marc Aurel Stein (1862-1943), Archaeologist A1236

2004, Nov. 3   *Litho.*   *Perf. 13x13¼*
3916 A1236 80fo multi   .90 .75

Natura 2000 — A1237

2004, Dec. 3   *Perf. 11½x12*
3917 A1237 100fo multi   1.05 .90

Zodiac A1238

No. 3918: a, Capricorn (goat). b, Aquarius (water bearer). c, Pisces (fish). d, Aries (ram). e, Taurus (bull). f, Gemini (twins). g, Cancer (crab). h, Leo (lion). i, Virgo (virgin). j, Libra (scales). k, Scorpio (scorpion). l, Sagittarius (archer).

2005, Jan. 3   *Litho.*   *Perf. 11¼*
3918 A1238 50fo Sheet of 12, #a-l   7.50 7.50
   m. Sheet of 20 #3918a + 20 labels   22.00 —
   n. Sheet of 20 #3918b + 20 labels   22.00 —
   o. Sheet of 20 #3918c + 20 labels   22.00 —
   p. Sheet of 20 #3918d + 20 labels   22.00 —
   q. Sheet of 20 #3918e + 20 labels   22.00 —
   r. Sheet of 20 #3918f + 20 labels   22.00 —
   s. Sheet of 20 #3918g + 20 labels   22.00 —
   t. Sheet of 20 #3918h + 20 labels   22.00 —
   u. Sheet of 20 #3918i + 20 labels   22.00 —
   v. Sheet of 20 #3918j + 20 labels   22.00 —
   w. Sheet of 20 #3918k + 20 labels   22.00 —
   x. Sheet of 20 #3918l + 20 labels   22.00 —

Nos. 3918m-3918x each sold for 2100fo and had labels that could be personalized.

Rotary International, Cent. — A1239

2005, Feb. 4   *Perf. 13¼x13*
3919 A1239 130fo multi   1.25 1.10

Souvenir Sheet

Cats A1240

No. 3920: a, 100fo, Siamese, silhouette of cat sitting. b, 100fo, Maine Coon cat, silhouette of cat with arched back and thin tail. c, 100fo, Persian, silhouette of cat with large tail. d, 100fo+50fo, Domestic cat, silhouette of cat walking.

2005, Feb. 4   *Perf. 12x11½*
3920 A1240 Sheet of 4, #a-d   4.75 4.75

Easter — A1241

2005, Feb. 21   *Perf. 12*
3921 A1241 50fo multi   .55 .25

Intl. Weight Lifting Federation, Cent. — A1242

2005, Mar. 3   *Perf. 12¼x12½*
3922 A1242 170fo multi   1.65 1.35

Sándor Iharos (1930-96), Runner — A1243

2005, Mar. 10   *Perf. 13x13¼*
3923 A1243 90fo multi   1.00 .75

Souvenir Sheet

Opening of Palace of Arts, Budapest — A1244

2005, Mar. 10   *Perf. 12*
3924 A1244 500fo multi   5.00 5.00

World Theater Day — A1245

2005, Mar. 21   *Perf. 11¼*
3925 A1245 50fo multi   .80 .25
See No. 4198.

Compass and Map of Hungary A1246

No. 3926: a, Compass at right, map of western Hungary. b, Compass at left, map of eastern Hungary.

2005, Apr. 1   *Litho.*   *Perf. 11¼*
3926 A1246 50fo Pair, #a-b, + 2 labels   1.25 1.25
   c. Sheet of 20, 10 each #3926a-3926b, + 20 labels   18.75 —

No. 3926c sold for 2100fo. Labels on sheets of 3926 and 3926c could be personalized. Compare with No. 4054.

Writers — A1247

HUNGARY

Designs: 90fo, Jeno Rejto (1905-43), novelist, playwright. 140fo, Attila József (1905-37), poet.

2005, Apr. 11   Litho.   Perf. 13x13¼
3927-3928   A1247   Set of 2   2.25   1.85

Police Helicopter and Emergency Phone Number — A1248

2005, Apr. 22   Perf. 13x13¼
3929   A1248   85fo multi   .90   .45

End of World War II, 60th Anniv. — A1249

2005, May 6   Perf. 13
3930   A1249   150fo multi   1.25   1.25

Farm Animals — A1250

Designs: 50fo, Hungarian gray bull. 70fo, Hungarian spotted cow. 100fo, Hortobágy Racka sheep. 110fo, Cigája sheep. 500fo, Mangalica pigs.

2005, May 9   Perf. 13x13¼
3931-3934   A1250   Set of 4   3.75   2.75
     Souvenir Sheet
3935   A1250   500fo multi   4.75   4.75
No. 3935 contains one 41x32mm stamp.

Souvenir Sheet

Europa — A1251

No. 3936 — Plate of Chicken Paprika and Dumplings with: a, Flowers at UR. b, Flowers at UL.

2005, May 9   Perf. 12
3936   A1251   160fo Sheet, 2 each #a-b   6.00   6.00
The top and bottom rows of stamps in the sheet are tete-beche.

Souvenir Sheet

Pope John Paul II (1920-2005) — A1252

2005, May 18
3937   A1252   500fo multi   4.50   4.50

Grapes and Wine Producing Areas Type of 1990

Designs: 120fo, Pintes grapes, Zala region, horiz. 140fo, Kunleány grapes, Csongrád region, horiz.

2005, May 25   Perf. 13¼x12½
3938-3939   A902   Set of 2   2.50   2.25

Church, Ják, and Ornament From Cluny Abbey, France — A1253

2005, May 25   Perf. 13x13¼
3940   A1253   110fo multi   1.15   1.00

Souvenir Sheet

Consecration of St. Stephen's Basilica, Budapest, Cent. — A1254

2005, May 25   Perf. 12¾x13
3941   A1254   500fo multi   4.50   4.50

Miniature Sheet

Budapest Tourist Attractions — A1255

No. 3942: a, Hallway and exhibits, Postal Museum. b, #386a and die of vignette, Stamp Museum, horiz. c, Agriculture Museum, Vajdahunyad Castle. d, Ethnographic Museum, horiz. e, Sándor Palace, horiz.

Perf. 11½x12, 12x11½ (horiz. stamps)
2005, May 25
3942   A1255   100fo Sheet of 5, #a-e, + 5 labels   4.75   4.75

First Hungarian in Space, 25th Anniv. — A1256

2005, May 26   Perf. 12½
3943   A1256   130fo multi   1.25   1.15

A1257

Formula I Auto Racing in Hungary, 20th Anniv. (in 2006) — A1258

Designs: Nos. 3944, 3947, Hungaroring Race Track. No. 3945, Car No. 12. No. 3946, Driver in red car.

2005   Litho.   Perf. 11¼
3944   A1257   50fo multi + label   .75   .75
     Perf. 13x13¼
3945   A1258   50fo multi   .55   .45
3946   A1258   90fo multi   .90   .75
     Souvenir Sheet
     Perf. 13x12¾
3947   A1258   500fo +200fo multi   5.50   5.50

78th Stamp Day (Nos. 3945-3947). Issued: Nos. 3944, 3947, 7/18; Nos. 3945-3946, 6/17. Labels on No. 3944 could be personalized.

Souvenir Sheet

Enameled Pictures on St. Stephen's Crown — A1259

No. 3948: a, 100fo, St. Thomas (20x26mm). b, 100fo, King Géza I (in square panel with black lettering) (20x26mm). c, 100fo, Byzantine Emperor Michael Ducas (in arched panel with red lettering) (20x26mm). d, 100fo, Byzantine Emperor Constantine (in square panel with red lettering) (20x26mm). e, 100fo, Jesus Christ (in arched panel with no lettering) (20x26mm). f, 500fo, St. Stephen's Crown (30x36mm).

2005, Aug. 19   Litho.   Perf. 12x11½
3948   A1259   Sheet of 6, #a-f   9.00   9.00

First Hungarian Mail Vehicle, Cent. — A1260

2005, Sept. 15   Perf. 11¼x11
3949   A1260   50fo multi   .50   .25

Trash Recycling A1261

2005, Sept. 15   Perf. 13x13¼
3950   A1261   140fo multi   1.35   1.15

World Wrestling Championships, Budapest — A1262

2005, Sept. 26   Perf. 13
3951   A1262   150fo multi   1.45   1.25

Ferenc Farkas (1905-2000), Composer A1263

2005, Sept. 30   Perf. 13x13¼
3952   A1263   100fo multi   1.00   .85

World Science Forum, Budapest — A1264

2005, Sept. 30
3953   A1264   120fo multi   1.75   .60
See No. 4052.

Hungarian University of Craft and Design, 125th Anniv. — A1265

2005, Oct. 19   Perf. 12
3954   A1265   90fo multi   1.60   1.05

The Three Magi A1266   Christmas A1267

No. 3956: a, Candle. b, Apple. c, Heart-shaped ornament. d, Teddy bear.

Litho. with Foil Application
2005, Oct. 19   Perf. 12¾x12¼
3955   A1266   50fo blue   .55   .25
     Self-Adhesive
     Litho.
     Serpentine Die Cut 12¾
3956   Booklet pane of 4   2.00
a.-d.   A1267   50fo Any single   .50   .25

House of the Future — A1268

2005, Dec. 16   Litho.   Perf. 12
3957   A1268   100fo multi   1.05   .75

Hungarian News Agency, 125th Anniv. — A1269

2006, Jan. 6   Litho.   Perf. 12x11½
3958   A1269   90fo multi   1.00   .75

2006 Winter Olympics, Turin — A1270

2006, Feb. 10   Perf. 13¼
3959   A1270   200fo multi   2.00   2.00

Furniture Type of 1999

Designs: 52fo, Like #3790, vert. 75fo, Chair with heart carved in back, 1893, vert. 212fo, Like #3791. 300fo, Settee, 18th cent. 500fo, Rococo settee, c. 1880. 1000fo, Vassily chair, by Marcel Breuer, 1925.

2006   Perf. 11½x12¼
3960   A1091   52fo bl & dk bl   .45   .45
3961   A1091   75fo org brn & brn   .70   .70
     Perf. 12¼x11½
3962   A1091   212fo grn & dk grn   1.90   1.90
     Perf. 12¾x12¼
3963   A1091   300fo red & dk red   3.00   1.90
3964   A1091   500fo bl & dk bl   4.50   3.50
3965   A1091   1000fo ol & dk ol   9.00   6.75
Nos. 3960-3965 (6)   19.55   15.20
Issued: 52fo, 75fo, 212fo, 3/16; others, 5/19.

World Heritage Sites — A1271

HUNGARY

Designs: 52fo, Early Christian Necropolis, Pecs. 90fo, Ferto-Neuseidler Lake Cultural Landscape, horiz.

2006, Mar. 16			Perf. 12
3966-3967	A1271	Set of 2	1.25 1.00

Airplanes Type of 2002

Designs: 120fo, Boeing 767-200ER. 140fo, Lockheed Sirius 8A.

2006, Mar. 16			
3968-3969	A1141	Set of 2	2.25 2.10

Easter — A1272

2006, Mar. 22			
3970	A1272	52fo multi	.50 .25

Union of European Football Associations Congress, Budapest — A1273

2006, Mar. 22			Perf. 13x13¼
3971	A1273	170fo multi	1.50 1.25

Sándor Légrády (1906-87), Stamp Designer, and Vignette of Unissued Stamp — A1274

2006, Mar. 30	Litho.		Perf. 12x11½
3972	A1274	75fo multi	1.00 .70

Ilona Sasváriné-Paulik (1954-99), Paralymic Athlete — A1275

2006, Mar. 30			Perf. 13x13¼
3973	A1275	185fo multi	1.65 1.40

László Detre (1906-74), Astronomer A1276

2006, Mar. 30			Perf. 12
3974	A1276	212fo multi	1.90 1.50

Wi-fi Technology A1277

2006, Mar. 30			Perf. 13x13¼
3975	A1277	240fo multi	2.10 1.80

Orchid A1278

Rose A1279

Lily A1280

Tulip A1281

Gerbera Daisy A1282

Rose A1283

Rose A1284

Rose A1285

Butterfly and Wedding Rings A1286

Butterfly and Rose A1287

Daisy and Rubber Duck A1288

Daisy and Blue Booties A1289

Daisy and Pink Booties A1290

Daisy and Rattle A1291

Rose A1292

Clematis A1293

2006		Litho.	Perf. 11¼
3976		Vert. strip of 5 + 5 labels	9.00 9.00
a.	A1278	52fo multi + label	.60 .60
b.	A1279	52fo multi + label	.60 .60
c.	A1280	52fo multi + label	.60 .60
d.	A1281	52fo multi + label	.60 .60
e.	A1282	52fo multi + label	.60 .60
		Sheet, 4 each #3976a-3976e	45.00 45.00
3977		Strip of 3 + 3 labels	9.00 9.00
a.	A1283	52fo multi + label	.60 .60
b.	A1284	52fo multi + label	.60 .60
c.	A1285	52fo multi + label	.60 .60
		Sheet, 7 each #3977a-3977b, 6 #3977c	20.00 20.00
3978		Pair + 2 labels	9.00 9.00
a.	A1286	52fo multi + label	.60 .60
b.	A1287	52fo multi + label	.60 .60
		Sheet, 10 each #3978a-3978b	20.00 20.00
3979		Block or strip of 4 + 4 labels	9.00 9.00
a.	A1288	52fo multi + label	.60 .60
b.	A1289	52fo multi + label	.60 .60
c.	A1290	52fo multi + label	.60 .60
d.	A1291	52fo multi + label	.60 .60
		Sheet, 3 each #3979b-3979c, 7 each #3977a, 3977d	55.00 —
3980		Pair + 2 labels	15.00 15.00
a.	A1292	90fo multi + label	.75 .75
b.	A1293	90fo multi + label	.75 .75
		Sheet, 10 each #3980a-3980b	60.00 60.00
		Nos. 3976-3980 (5)	51.00 51.00

Issued: Nos. 3976, 3977, 5/4, others, 5/19. Background colors of stamps in full sheets varies. Labels could be personalized for an additional fee.
Compare with Nos. 4092, 4199, 4298.

Battle of Belgrade, 550th Anniv. A1294

2006, May 9			Perf. 13½x12½
3981	A1294	120fo multi	1.05 .95

2006 World Cup Soccer Championships, Germany A1295

2006, May 9			Perf. 13x13¼
3982	A1295	170fo multi	2.00 2.00

Europa — A1296

2006, May 9			Perf. 12
3983	A1296	190fo multi	1.75 1.60

Printed in sheets of 4, with each stamp rotated 90 degrees to create circle of faces. Value $7.50.

Horses — A1297

Breeds: 75fo, Shagya Arab. 90fo, Furioso (Mezohegyes halfbreed). 140fo, Gidran. 160fo, Nonius.
No. 3988: a, Huçul. b, Lippizaner. c, Kibér halfbreed.

2006, May 9			
3984-3987	A1297	Set of 4	4.00 3.50
		Souvenir Sheet	
3988	A1297	200fo Sheet of 3, #a-c	5.50 5.50

Margin of No. 3988 is embossed.

Composers A1298

Designs: No. 3989, 90fo, George Enescu (1881-1955), and Romanian flag. No. 3990, 90fo, Béla Bartók (1881-1945) and Hungarian flag.

2006, June 8			Perf. 13x13¼
3989-3990	A1298	Set of 2	1.50 1.35

See Romania No. 4838.

Miskolc Intl. Opera Festival — A1299

2006, June 15			Perf. 13¼x13
3991	A1299	190fo multi	1.65 1.50

Souvenir Sheet

Budapest Museum of Fine Arts, Cent. — A1300

No. 3992: a, Esterházy Madonna, by Raphael. b, Mary Magdalene, by El Greco. c, Equestrian statue, by Leonardo da Vinci, horiz. d, Three Fishing Boats, by Claude Monet, horiz.

2006, June 23		Litho.	Perf. 12
3992	A1300	200fo Sheet of 4, #a-d	6.50 6.50

The Four Virtues, Frescoes From Castle Museum, Esztergom — A1301

Iconostasis, Szentendre Cathedral — A1302

No. 3993: a, Bölcsesség and Mértékletesség. b, Allhatatosság and Igazságosság.

2006, June 23			Perf. 13¼x13
3993	A1301	52fo Horiz. pair, #a-b	1.00 1.00
		Souvenir Sheet	
		Perf. 12	
3994	A1302	400fo +200fo multi	5.25 5.25

Stamp Day.

Emblem of Border Guard and Falcon — A1303

2006, June 27			Perf. 12
3995	A1303	170fo multi	1.50 1.35

European Swimming Championships, Budapest A1304

Designs: 90fo, Synchronized swimmers and diver. 180fo, Swimmers and fish.

2006, July 27			Perf. 13x13¼
3996-3997	A1304	Set of 2	2.40 2.00

Contemporary Art — A1305

HUGARY

Designs: 120fo, Child with Model Aircraft, by László Fehér. 140fo, Circle Dance, sculpture by István Haraszty, vert. 160fo, Aequilibrium, tapestry by Zsuzsa Péreli, vert.

2006, July 27   Perf. 13x13¼, 13¼x13
3998-4000   A1305   Set of 3   3.60   3.00

Hungaroring Race Track, 20th Anniv. — A1306

2006, Aug. 3   Perf. 13x13¼
4001   A1306   75fo multi   1.00   .70

Souvenir Sheet
Budapest Zoo, 140th Anniv. — A1307

2006, Aug. 9   Litho.   Perf. 12
4002   A1307   500fo multi   4.75   4.50

Souvenir Sheet
Consecration of Esztergom Basilica, 150th Anniv. — A1308

2006, Aug. 18
4003   A1308   500fo multi   4.50   4.50

Miniature Sheet
Enamel Paintings on St. Stephen's Crown — A1309

No. 4004: a, St. John (scsiohs inscription at top). b, St. Andrew (scsandreas) c, St. Peter (scspetrvs). d, God. e, St. Paul (scspavlus). f, St. Philip (scsphilipvs). g, St. Jacob (scsiacobvs).

Litho. (Foil Application on Sheet Margin)
2006, Aug. 18   Perf. 12x11½
4004   A1309   100fo Sheet of 7, #a-g   6.00   6.00

Souvenir Sheet
1956 Revolution, 50th Anniv. — A1310

2006, Oct. 20   Litho.   Perf. 13x12¾
4005   A1310   500fo multi   4.75   4.75

No. 4005 has a die cut hole in the middle of the flag.

Christmas Type of 2002
52fo, Adoration of the Magi.

Litho. With Foil Application
2006, Oct. 27   Perf. 12
4006   A1157   52fo multi   .45   .25

Souvenir Sheet
1956 Melbourne Summer Olympics, 50th Anniv. — A1311

2006, Nov. 13   Litho.   Perf. 12
4007   A1311   500fo László Papp   4.75   4.75

Hungarian Red Cross, 125th Anniv. — A1312

2006, Nov. 24   Perf. 12¼x11½
4008   A1312   100fo multi   .90   .75

Launch of Sputnik 1 and Sputnik 2, 50th Anniv. A1313

2007, Feb. 6   Litho.   Perf. 12
4009   A1313   350fo multi   3.00   3.00

Easter — A1314

2007, Feb. 9   Perf. 12¼x12¾
4010   A1314   62fo multi   .55   .55

Famous Men A1315

Designs: 107fo, János Ferencsik (1907-84), conductor. 135fo, Count Lajos Batthyány (1807-49), prime minister.

2007, Feb. 9   Perf. 12
4011-4012   A1315   Set of 2   2.10   1.80

Rural Life — A1316

Designs: 62fo, Man with bottle and woman with glass. 95fo, Girl with flowers and birds. 242fo, Man cooking fish over fire.

2007, Feb. 9   Perf. 12¼x11½
4013-4015   A1316   Set of 3   4.00   2.10

Customs and Finance Guards, 140th Anniv. — A1317

2007, Mar. 10   Perf. 12
4016   A1317   180fo multi   1.50   1.50

Diets — A1318

Designs: 210fo, Prince John Sigismund of Transylvania and Torda Church. 230fo, Prince Ferenc Rákóczi II and Marosvásárhely Castle

2007, Apr. 10   Perf. 13¼x12½
4017-4018   A1318   Set of 2   3.75   3.75

Diet of Torda, 450th anniv.; Diet of Marosvásárhely, 300th anniv.

Souvenir Sheet
The Boys of Paul Street, Novel by Ferenc Molnár (1878-1952) — A1319

No. 4019: a, 160fo, Molnar. b, 160fo, Posted handbill. c, 160fo+30fo, Boy in red shirt. d, 160fo+30fo, Boy in green shirt.

2007, Apr. 10   Perf. 12
4019   A1319   Sheet of 4, #a-d   5.75   5.75

A1320, A1321, A1322, A1323, A1324, A1325, A1326, A1327, A1328, A1329, A1330

A1331

Graduation A1332

No. 4020: a, Two hot air balloons. b, Graduate pulled by balloon, arch of books, diploma, hot air balloon. c, Graduation cap, hot air balloon, graduate. d, Three graduates, hot air balloon. e, Hot air balloon, graduate pulled by balloon, two graduates standing on books. f, Graduate on path, graduate holding portfolio. g, Diploma, two graduates standing on books. h, Diploma on path, bottom half of graduate at upper right. i, Three graduates on path. j, Arch of books, diploma, inkwell, quill pen, path. k, Two graduates on path. l, Inkwell, quill pen, three books. m, Graduate with magnifying glass, path. n, Graduate with magnifying glass. o, Diploma on path, legs of two graduates, path. p, Graduate carrying portfolio, diploma on arch of books. q, Arch of books, diploma, inkwell, quill pen. r, Arch of books, diploma. s, Inkwell, quill pen, graduate. t, Diploma on path, graduate at right, legs of graduate at top.

2007, Apr. 16   Litho.   Perf. 11¼
4020   A1320   (62fo) Sheet of 20, #a-t, + 20 labels   20.00   20.00
4021   Block of 8 + 8 labels   10.00   10.00
a.   A1321 (62fo) multi + label   .75   .75
b.   A1322 (62fo) multi + label   .75   .75
c.   A1323 (62fo) multi + label   .75   .75
d.   A1324 (62fo) multi + label   .75   .75
e.   A1325 (62fo) multi + label   .75   .75
f.   A1326 (62fo) multi + label   .75   .75
g.   A1327 (62fo) multi + label   .75   .75
h.   A1328 (62fo) multi + label   .75   .75
Sheet, 3 each #4021a-4021d, 2 each #4021e-4021h, + 20 labels   20.00   20.00
4022   Pair + 2 labels   2.50   2.50
a.   A1329 (62fo) multi + label   .75   .75
b.   A1330 (62fo) multi + label   .75   .75
Sheet, 10 each #4022a-4022b, + 20 labels   20.00   20.00
4023   Pair + 2 labels   2.50   2.50
a.   A1331 (95fo) multi + label   1.20   1.20
b.   A1332 (95fo) multi + label   1.20   1.20
Sheet, 10 each #4023a-4023b, + 20 labels   21.00   21.00

Labels on Nos. 4020-4023 could be personalized for an additional fee.

Stamp Day — A1333

Designs: 62fo, St. Elizabeth of Hungary (1207-31) caring for the sick. 95fo, St. Elizabeth caring for poor. 500fo+200fo, St. Emeric (1007-31) praying.

2007, Apr. 27   Litho.   Perf. 13
4024-4025   A1333   Set of 2   1.20   1.20

Souvenir Sheet
  Perf. 13x12¾
4026   A1333   500fo +200fo multi   5.00   5.00

No. 4026 contains one 40x32mm stamp.

Television Broadcasting in Hungary, 50th Anniv. — A1334

2007, May 9   Perf. 13x13½
4027   A1334   160fo multi   1.15   1.15

Souvenir Sheet
Europa A1335

No. 4028: a, Scouts in canoe. b, Scouts and Brownsea Island commemorative stone.

HUNGARY

2007, May 9 — Perf. 12
4028 A1335 210fo Sheet, 2 each #a-b 4.50 4.50
Scouting, cent.

Dogs — A1336

Designs: 62fo, Komondor. 150fo, Transylvanian hound. 180fo, Kuvasz. 240fo, Pumis. 600fo, Hungarian vizsla.

2007, May 9 — Perf. 13x13½
4029-4032 A1336 Set of 4 5.00 5.00
Souvenir Sheet
Perf. 12
4033 A1336 600fo multi 4.75 4.75

11th Intl. Cave Rescue Conference, Aggtelek-Jósvafo — A1337

2007, May 15 Litho. Perf. 12
4034 A1337 200fo multi 1.45 1.45

Academy of Music Building, Budapest, Cent. — A1338

2007, May 18
4035 A1338 250fo multi 1.65 1.65

Souvenir Sheet

National Gallery, 50th Anniv. A1339

No. 4036: a, The Mystical Betrothal of St. Catherine, c. 1490. b, View of Rome, by Károly Markó the Elder, 1835. c, October, by Károly Ferenczy, 1903. d, Picnic in May, by Pál Szinyei Merse, 1873, horiz.

2007, May 23 Perf. 12
4036 A1339 150fo Sheet of 4, #a-d 4.00 3.75

Grapes and Wine Producing Areas Type of 1990

Designs: 95fo, Cirfandli grapes, Pecs region. 140fo, Ezerfürtü grapes, Etyek-Buda region. 260fo, Zenit grapes, Tolna region.

2007, May 25 Perf. 12½x13¼
4037-4039 A902 Set of 3 3.40 3.40

Emblem of Border Guard and German Shepherd A1340

2007, June 27 Litho. Perf. 12
4040 A1340 107fo multi 1.00 .60

Personalized Stamp Types of 2004-05 Redrawn With "Belföld" Instead of Denomination and

Pens A1341

A1342
A1343
A1344
A1345
A1346
A1347
A1348
A1349
A1350

Doorknockers — A1351

Chain Bridge, Budapest A1352

Parliament, Budapest A1353

Buda Castle, Budapest A1354

Heroes Square, Budapest A1355

Fisherman's Bastion, Budapest — A1356

No. 4043: a, Quill pen, open inkwell, ink spots, green background. b, Brown fountain pen with point on flourish of "M," brown background. c, Open and closed black and gold fountain pens, green background. d, Black and gold fountain pen with point on flourish of "M," green background. e, Ball-point pen, pen point at LL, pink background. f, Cap of black and gold pen, green background. g, Brown fountain head with flat circular tip on nib, open inkwell, brown background. h, Black and gold pen with pen point at UL, pink background. i, Black and gold fountain pen, pen point at LR, green background. j, Ball-point pen, pen point at LR, pink background. k, Fountain pen and quill, green background. l, Fountain pen, pen point at LR, brown background. m, Brown fountain pen, inkwell, brown background. n, Inkwell, quill, fountain pen, ink spots, green background. o, Plunger and clip of black ball-point pen, pink background. p, Quills, quill pen, ink spots, green background. q, Closed inkwell, pen nib, quill, ink spots, green background. r, Two fountain pens, brown background. s, Black and gold fountain pen and cap, green background. t, Tip of ball-point pen with point on flourish of "M," pink background.

2007 Litho. Perf. 11¼
4041 Sheet of 20 + 20 labels 20.00 20.00
a. A1220 (62fo) multi + label 1.00 .80
b. A1221 (62fo) multi + label 1.00 .80
c. A1222 (62fo) multi + label 1.00 .80
d. A1223 (62fo) multi + label 1.00 .80
e. A1224 (62fo) multi + label 1.00 .80
f. A1225 (62fo) multi + label 1.00 .80
4042 Block or horiz. strip of 4 + 4 labels 10.00 10.00
a. A1288 (62fo) multi + label 2.50 2.50
b. A1289 (62fo) multi + label 2.50 2.50
c. A1290 (62fo) multi + label 2.50 2.50
d. A1291 (62fo) multi + label 2.50 2.50
Sheet of 20, 7 each #4042a, 4042d, 3 each #4042b, 4042c, + 20 labels 20.00 20.00
4043 A1341 Sheet of 20 + 20 labels 20.00 20.00
a.-t. (62fo) Any single + label 1.00 .80
4044 Block of 10 + 10 labels 10.00 10.00
a. A1342 (62fo) multi + label 1.00 .80
b. A1343 (62fo) multi + label 1.00 .80
c. A1344 (62fo) multi + label 1.00 .80
d. A1345 (62fo) multi + label 1.00 .80
e. A1346 (62fo) multi + label 1.00 .80
f. A1347 (62fo) multi + label 1.00 .80
g. A1348 (62fo) multi + label 1.00 .80
h. A1349 (62fo) multi + label 1.00 .80
i. A1350 (62fo) multi + label 1.00 .80
j. A1351 (62fo) multi + label 1.00 .80
Sheet of 20, 2 each #4044a-4044j, + 20 labels 20.00 20.00
4045 Vert. strip of 5 + 5 labels 5.00 5.00
a. A1352 (62fo) multi + label 1.00 .80
b. A1353 (62fo) multi + label 1.00 .80
c. A1354 (62fo) multi + label 1.00 .80
d. A1355 (62fo) multi + label 1.00 .80
e. A1356 (62fo) multi + label 1.00 .80
Sheet of 20, 4 each #4045a-4045e, + 20 labels 20.00 20.00
Nos. 4041-4045 (5) 65.00 65.00

Issued: No. 4041, 9/27; others, 7/16.
No. 4041 contains 4 each Nos. 4041a, 4041e, 2 each Nos. 4041d, 4041f, 5 No. 4041b and 3 No. 4041c. Background colors on some stamps differ slightly. Labels could be personalized for an additional fee.

Zoltán Kodály (1882-1967), Composer A1357

2007, July 16 Perf. 13x13¼
4046 A1357 200fo multi 1.35 1.25

Hungarian University Sports Federation, Cent. — A1358

2007, July 30 Perf. 11½x12
4047 A1358 360fo multi 3.25 3.25

Dolomite Flax A1359

Pasque Flower A1360

Booklet Stamps
Serpentine Die Cut 10¾x10½
2007, Aug. 1 Self-Adhesive
4048 A1359 (230fo) multi 1.80 1.80
a. Booklet pane of 4 + 4 etiquettes 7.25
4049 A1360 (260fo) multi 2.20 2.20
a. Booklet pane of 4 + 4 etiquettes 8.75

Souvenir Sheet

Enamel Paintings on St. Stephen's Crown — A1361

No. 4050: a, St. Cosmas (light blue robe). b, St. George (holding spear and shield). c, Archangel Michael (holding staff).

Litho. (Litho. With Foil Application in Sheet Margin)
2007, Aug. 17 Perf. 12x11½
4050 A1361 300fo Sheet of 3, #a-c 6.50 6.50

János Selye (1907-82), Stress Researcher A1362

Perf. 13¼x12¾
2007, Aug. 23 Litho.
4051 A1362 400fo multi 2.75 2.75
Second World Stress Conference, Budapest.

World Science Forum Type of 2005 Redrawn
2007, Sept. 27 Perf. 13x13¼
4052 A1264 230fo multi 2.00 2.00

Christmas — A1363

No. 4053: a, Annunciation. b, Holy Family and Shepherds. c, Adoration of the Magi.

2007, Oct. 19 Perf. 12
4053 A1363 62fo Horiz. strip of 3, #a-c 2.00 2.00

Compass and Map Type of 2005 Redrawn With "Belföld" Instead of Denomination

No. 4054: a, Compass at right, map of western Hungary. b, Compass at left, map of eastern Hungary.

HUNGARY

2008, Feb. 8	Litho.	Perf. 11¼
4054	A1246 (70fo) Pair, #a-b, + 2 labels	.90 .75
	Sheet of 18 #4054a, 17 #4054b, + 35 labels	15.00 —

Labels could be personalized.

Easter — A1364

2008, Feb. 27		Perf. 12
4055	A1364 70fo multi	.80 .80

King Matthias, 550th Anniv. of Election — A1365

King Matthias, arms and: 70fo, Fountain. 100fo, Castle and horses. 600fo+200fo, King and Queen on throne.

2008, Mar. 13		
4056-4057	A1365 Set of 2	1.75 1.75

Souvenir Sheet

| 4058 | A1365 600fo +200fo multi | 6.00 6.00 |

Stamp Day. No. 4058 contains one 40x30mm stamp.

General Károly Knezich (1808-49) — A1366

2008, Mar. 14		Perf. 13x12½
4059	A1366 380fo multi	2.75 2.75

Miniature Sheet

Transportation — A1367

No. 4060: a, 150fo, Automobile. b, 150fo, Ship. c, 150fo+30fo, Train. d, 150fo+30fo, Airplane.

2008, Mar. 14		Perf. 12
4060	A1367 Sheet of 4, #a-d	4.75 4.75

Romany Dancer and Musicians — A1368

German Dancer and Accordion — A1369

2008		Perf. 13½x13
4061	A1368 260fo multi	2.00 1.75
4062	A1369 275fo multi	2.00 1.75

Hungarian ethnic minorities. Issued: 260fo, 4/8; 275fo, 5/9.

2008 Summer Olympics, Beijing — A1370

Designs: 70fo, Water polo. 100fo, Wrestling. 170fo, Fencing.

2008, Apr. 16		Perf. 13x13¼
4063-4065	A1370 Set of 3	3.50 3.50

Miniature Sheet

Europa — A1371

No. 4066: a, 100fo, Letter in envelope, capital "A." b, 230fo, Pen nib.

2008, May 9		Perf. 12
4066	A1371 Sheet, 2 each #a-b	4.00 4.00

Stamps on bottom row are tete-beche in relation to the top row.

Indigenous Animals — A1372

Designs: 145fo, Hungarian giant rabbit. 150fo, Hungarian domestic goat. 170fo, Cikta sheep. 310fo, Hungarian donkey. 600fo, Water buffalo.

2008, May 9		
4067-4070	A1372 Set of 4	5.50 5.50

Souvenir Sheet

| 4071 | A1372 600fo multi | 4.75 4.75 |

National Parks Type of 1998

Design: Orség National Park.

2008, May 16		
4072	A1073 220fo multi	1.65 1.65

UNESCO World Heritage Sites Type of 2002

Design: Tokaj Wine Region.

2008, May 16		
4073	A1153 290fo multi	2.00 2.00

UEFA Euro 2008 Soccer Championships, Austria and Switzerland — A1373

2008, May 16		Perf. 13½x13
4074	A1373 250fo multi	1.80 1.80

Vacation Vouchers, 10th Anniv. — A1374

2008, May 20		Perf. 12x11½
4075	A1374 70fo multi	.55 .45

A1375, A1376, A1377, A1378, A1379

Philavillage — A1380

2008	Perf. 12, 13¼x13 (#4077)
4076	A1375 100fo multi 1.40 .75
4077	A1376 100fo multi 1.40 .75
4078	A1377 100fo multi 1.40 .75
4079	A1378 100fo multi 1.40 .75
4080	A1379 100fo multi 1.40 .75
4081	A1380 100fo multi 1.40 .75
	Nos. 4076-4081 (6) 8.40 4.50

Issued: Nos. 4076-4077, 6/6; Nos. 4078-4079, 6/20; Nos. 4080-4081, 7/10. Stamps also served as game pieces for Philavillage board game.

A1381, A1382, A1383, A1384, A1385

Philavillage — A1386

2008	Litho.	Perf. 12
4082	A1381 100fo multi	.80 .80
4083	A1382 100fo multi	.80 .80

	Perf. 13x13¼, 13¼x13 (#4086)
4084	A1383 100fo multi .80 .80
4085	A1384 100fo multi .80 .80
4086	A1385 100fo multi .80 .80
4087	A1386 100fo multi .80 .80
	Nos. 4082-4087 (6) 4.80 4.80

Issued: Nos. 4082-4083, 9/2; Nos. 4084-4085, 10/9; Nos. 4086-4087, 11/5. Stamps also served as game pieces for Philavillage board game.

Hungarian Illuminated Chronicle, 650th Anniv. — A1387

Litho. & Embossed With Foil Application

2008, June 20		Perf. 12
4088	A1387 400fo multi	3.00 3.00

Souvenir Sheet

Debrecen and Veszprém Zoos, 50th Anniv. — A1388

No. 4089: a, Giraffes, cranes, hippopotamus, camel (Debrecen). b, Camel, crane, lion, zebra, rhinoceros, flamingo (Veszprém).

2008, Aug. 14	Litho.	Perf. 12
4089	A1388 260fo Sheet of 2, #a-b	4.00 4.00

Souvenir Sheet

Enamel Paintings on St. Stephen's Crown — A1389

No. 4090: a, Archangel Gabriel (holding staff). b, St. Demeter (with shield and spear). c, St. Damian (with beard).

Litho. (Litho. With Foil Application in Sheet Margin)

2008, Aug. 19		Perf. 12x11½
4090	A1389 300fo Sheet of 3, #a-c	6.25 6.25

Miklós Zrinyi (1508-66), Military Leader — A1390

2008, Sept. 5	Litho.	Perf. 13x13¼
4091	A1390 190fo multi	1.45 1.45

Flowers Types of 2006 Redrawn With "Belföld" Instead of Denomination

2008, Sept. 2	Litho.	Perf. 11¼
4092	Vert. strip of 5 + 5 labels	6.00 6.00
a.	A1278 (70fo) multi + label	1.20 1.20
b.	A1279 (70fo) multi + label	1.20 1.20
c.	A1280 (70fo) multi + label	1.20 1.20
d.	A1281 (70fo) multi + label	1.20 1.20
e.	A1282 (70fo) multi + label	1.20 1.20
	Sheet, 4 each #4092a-4092e, + 20 labels	11.00 —

Background colors of stamps in full sheets varies. Labels could be personalized for an additional fee.

Archangel Gabriel, Sculpture by György Zala (1858-1937) — A1391

2008, Sept. 25	Litho.	Perf. 13¼x13
4093	A1391 200fo multi	1.50 1.50

Synagogues — A1392

HUNGARY

Designs: 200fo, Synagogue, Szeged. 250fo, Synagogue of the Jewish Theological Seminary, Budapest.

2008, Sept. 25 — Perf. 12½x13¼
4094-4095 A1392 Set of 2   3.25 3.25

Cat A1393
Bear A1394
Rabbit A1395
Lion A1396
Giraffe A1397

2008, Oct. 9 — Perf. 11¼
4096 Vert. strip of 5 + 5 labels   4.25 4.25
  a. A1393 (70fo) multi   .85 .85
  b. A1394 (70fo) multi   .85 .85
  c. A1395 (70fo) multi   .85 .85
  d. A1396 (70fo) multi   .85 .85
  e. A1397 (70fo) multi   .85 .85
     Sheet, 4 each #4096a-4096e, + 20 labels   11.00 11.00

Labels on No. 4096 could be personalized for an additional fee.

Souvenir Sheet

Ferenc Puskás (1927-2006), Player on 1952 Hungarian Olympic Soccer Team — A1398

2008, Oct. 28 — Perf. 12
4097 A1398 600fo multi   4.75 4.75

Christmas — A1399

Art by György Konecsni (1908-70): 70fo, Nativity. 100fo, Adoration of the Magi.

2008, Oct. 28 — Perf. 12¼x11½
4098-4099 A1399 Set of 2   1.25 .85

Edward Teller (1908-2003), Nuclear Physicist A1400

2008, Nov. 3 — Perf. 13x13¼
4100 A1400 250fo multi   1.80 1.80

Ludovika Academy, 200th Anniv. — A1401

2008, Nov. 5 — Perf. 13¼x13
4101 A1401 300fo multi   3.00 3.00

Crocus A1402
Scilla A1403

2009, Feb. 24 — Litho. — Perf. 11½x12
4102 A1402 (75fo) multi   .55 .55
4103 A1403 (100fo) multi   .75 .75

Self-Adhesive
Serpentine Die Cut 10x10¼
4104 A1402 (75fo) multi   .55 .55
     Nos. 4102-4104 (3)   1.85 1.85

Easter — A1404

2009, Feb. 24 — Perf. 12x12½
4105 A1404 75fo multi   .60 .60

Franciscan Order, 800th Anniv. A1405

2009, Feb. 24 — Perf. 12
4106 A1405 100fo multi   .85 .40

1909 Flights of Louis Blériot, Cent. A1406

No. 4107: a, Flight across English Channel. b, Flight at Kisrákoson, Hungary.

2009, Mar. 12
4107 A1406 105fo Horiz. pair, #a-b, + central label   1.50 1.50

Souvenir Sheet

Budapest Research Reactor, 50th Anniv. — A1407

2009, Mar. 25 — Perf. 11¼
4108 A1407 1000fo multi   7.50 7.50

Preservation of Polar Regions and Glaciers — A1408

Designs: Nos. 4109, 4113, 75fo, Ursus maritimus and walruses. Nos. 4110, 4114, 130fo, Ovibos moschatus. Nos. 4111, 4115, 145fo, Uncia uncia. Nos. 4112, 4116, 275fo, Aptenodytes patagonicus.
No. 4117: a, Ursus maritimus. b, Alopex lagopus.

2009, Mar. 27 — Litho. — Perf. 12½x12
4109-4112 A1408 Set of 4   4.00 4.00

Litho. & Silk-screened
4113-4116 A1408 Set of 4   5.00 5.00

Souvenir Sheet
4117 A1408 260fo Sheet of 2, #a-b   5.00 5.00

Portions of the designs of Nos. 4113-4117 that were applied by the silk-screen process have a silvery shine when viewed at an angle.

Joseph Haydn (1732-1809), Composer A1409

2009, Apr. 2 — Litho. — Perf. 13x13¼
4118 A1409 300fo red & black   2.25 1.65

Locomotives A1410

Designs: 75fo, Mk48 Diesel locomotive. 100fo, C 50 Diesel locomotive. 125fo, MD 40 Diesel locomotive. 275fo, Morgó steam locomotive.

2009, Apr. 2 — Perf. 13¼x13
4119-4122 A1410 Set of 4   4.25 4.25

Souvenir Sheet

Ferenc Kazinczy (1759-1831), Writer — A1411

2009, Apr. 2 — Perf. 13x12¾
4123 A1411 600fo multi   4.75 4.75

Miniature Sheet

Elek Benedek (1859-1929), Fable Writer and Translator — A1412

No. 4124: a, 100fo, Arabian man, chicken and bees. b, 100fo, Three pigs. c, 100fo+50fo, Cat in king's robes. d, 100fo+50fo, Benedek.

2009, Apr. 2 — Perf. 12x12½
4124 A1412 Sheet of 4, #a-d   4.75 3.75

Miklós Radnóti (1909-44), Poet — A1413

2009, May 5 — Perf. 13¼x13
4125 A1413 280fo multi   2.10 2.10

Souvenir Sheet

Europa A1414

No. 4126: a, 100fo, Galileo Galilei and Galileo space probe. b, 230fo, Planets.

2009, May 8 — Perf. 12
4126 A1414 Sheet, 2 each #a-b   3.75 3.75
Intl. Year of Astronomy.

John Calvin (1509-64), Theologian and Religious Reformer — A1415

2009, May 22 — Perf. 13¼x13
4127 A1415 200fo multi   1.50 1.50

Donát Bánki (1859-1922), Inventor of Carburetor A1416

2009, June 5 — Perf.
4128 A1416 300fo multi   2.25 2.25

Visegrád, 1000th Anniv. — A1417

Designs: 75fo, Column and entableture. 100fo, Solomon Tower, octagonal column, carved head. 600fo+200fo, Summer Palace, fountain, monument, Madonna and Child.

2009, June 5 — Perf. 13x13¼
4129-4130 A1417 Set of 2   1.35 1.35

Souvenir Sheet
4131 A1417 600fo +200fo multi   5.75 5.75
Stamp Day.

Discovery of Statue of Virgin Mary, Máriabesnyo, 250th Anniv. — A1418

2009, Aug. 14 — Perf. 13¼x12
4132 A1418 200fo multi   1.50 1.50

Bishopric of Pécs, 1000th Anniv. A1419

2009, Aug. 19 — Perf. 12
4133 A1419 100fo multi   .75 .55

Furniture Type of 1999
Design like No. 3791.

2009, Sept. 4 — Litho. — Perf. 12¼x11½
4134 A1091 230fo blue green   1.90 1.60

Building, Pecs A1420

Calvary Hill, Pecs A1421

HUNGARY

City Hall, Szechenyi Square, Pecs A1422

Sts. Peter and Paul Cathedral, Pecs A1423

Building, Pecs A1424

Hungarian Academy of Sciences, Sculpture, Pecs A1425

Synagogue, Pecs — A1426

Sts. Peter and Paul Cathedral, Pecs A1427

Door Knocker and Handle, Pecs A1428

Klimó Library, Pecs A1429

National Theater, Pecs A1430

Zsolnay Fountain, Pecs A1431

Roof, Pecs A1432

Street, Pecs A1433

Necropolis, Pecs A1434

Post Office Roof, Pecs A1435

Mosque, Pecs A1436

Barbican, Pecs A1437

Mosque and Minaret, Pecs A1438

Sculpture, Pecs A1439

2009, Sept. 4   Litho.   Perf. 11¼
4135   Sheet of 20 + 20 labels   16.00 16.00
 a. A1420 (75fo) multi + label   .80   .80
 b. A1421 (75fo) multi + label   .80   .80
 c. A1422 (75fo) multi + label   .80   .80
 d. A1423 (75fo) multi + label   .80   .80
 e. A1424 (75fo) multi + label   .80   .80
 f. A1425 (75fo) multi + label   .80   .80
 g. A1426 (75fo) multi + label   .80   .80
 h. A1427 (75fo) multi + label   .80   .80
 i. A1428 (75fo) multi + label   .80   .80
 j. A1429 (75fo) multi + label   .80   .80
 k. A1430 (75fo) multi + label   .80   .80
 l. A1431 (75fo) multi + label   .80   .80
 m. A1432 (75fo) multi + label   .80   .80
 n. A1433 (75fo) multi + label   .80   .80
 o. A1434 (75fo) multi + label   .80   .80
 p. A1435 (75fo) multi + label   .80   .80
 q. A1436 (75fo) multi + label   .80   .80
 r. A1437 (75fo) multi + label   .80   .80
 s. A1438 (75fo) multi + label   .80   .80
 t. A1439 (75fo) multi + label   .80   .80
Labels could be personalized for an additional fee.

Opening of Border Between Austria and Hungary, 20th Anniv. — A1440

2009, Sept. 10   Litho.   Perf. 12
4136 A1440 210fo multi   1.80 1.80
See Austria No. 2219, Germany No. 2548.

Rainbow, by Jòzsef Egry (1883-1951) A1441

2009, Sept. 10   Perf. 13¼x12½
4137 A1441 275fo multi   2.00 2.00

Louis Braille (1809-52), Educator of the Blind — A1442

Litho. & Embossed
2009, Oct. 15   Perf. 13¼x13
4138 A1442 200fo multi   1.50 1.50

A1443

Christmas — A1444

2009, Oct. 15   Litho.   Perf. 12
4139 A1443 75fo multi   .60   .40
   Perf. 12x11½
4140 A1444 100fo blue & yel org   .75   .50
   Miniature Sheet

Hungarian-Japanese Jubilee Year — A1445

No. 4141: a, Hungarian flask. b, Mount Fuji, horiz. c, Jar from Japanese tea service. d, Matyo folk embroidery, Hungary. e, Elizabeth Bridge, Hungary, horiz. f, Crane and leaves fabric pattern from Japanese kimono.

2009, Oct. 16   Perf. 12
4141 A1445 260fo Sheet of 6, #a-f   12.50 12.50
See Japan No. 3167.

Ajka Crystal A1446

2009, Oct. 28
4142 A1446 300fo multi   2.25 2.25

World Science Forum, Budapest — A1447

2009, Nov. 5   Perf. 13x13¼
4143 A1447 100fo multi   .75   .75

Filaclub Characters A1448

No. 4144: a, Bogi Fila. b, Levi Fila. c, Pötyi Fila.

2009, Dec. 4
4144   Horiz. strip of 3   .70   .70
 a.-c. A1448 20fo Any single   .30   .25
Promotion of children's philately.

Hassan Jakovali Mosque, Pecs — A1449

Calvary Hill, Pecs — A1450

National Theater, Pecs — A1451

Hungarian Academy of Sciences, Pecs — A1452

Barbican, Pecs — A1453

Synagogue, Pecs — A1454

Statue of St. Francis of Assisi, by György Bársony, Pecs — A1455

Interior of National Theater, Pecs — A1456

Statue of Janus Pannonius, by Sándor Rétfalvi, Pecs — A1457

County Hall, Pecs — A1458

Post Office, Pecs — A1459

St. Peter and Paul Cathedral, Pecs — A1460

St. Peter and Paul Cathedral, Pecs — A1461

Statue of the Holy Trinity, by György Kiss, Pecs — A1462

Mosque of Pasha Gazi Kasim, Pecs — A1463

University Gate, Pecs — A1464

Necropolis, Pecs — A1465

Zsolnay Fountain, Pecs — A1466

Klimó Library, Pecs — A1467

Statue of Tivadar Csontváry Kosztka, Zsolnay Vase, Pecs — A1468

Reformed Church, Pecs — A1469

Tettye Ruins, Pecs — A1470

HUNGARY

Lutheran Church, Pecs — A1471

City Hall, Pecs — A1472

Symbol Sculpture, by Victor Vasarely, Pecs — A1473

2010, Jan. 10	Litho.	Perf. 12
4145	Sheet of 25	24.00 24.00
a.	A1449 (75fo) multi	.60 .60
b.	A1450 (75fo) multi	.60 .60
c.	A1451 (75fo) multi	.60 .60
d.	A1452 (75fo) multi	.60 .60
e.	A1453 (75fo) multi	.60 .60
f.	A1454 (75fo) multi	.60 .60
g.	A1455 (75fo) multi	.60 .60
h.	A1456 (75fo) multi	.60 .60
i.	A1457 (75fo) multi	.60 .60
j.	A1458 (75fo) multi	.60 .60
k.	A1459 (75fo) multi	.60 .60
l.	A1460 (75fo) multi	.60 .60
m.	A1461 (75fo) multi	.60 .60
n.	A1462 (75fo) multi	.60 .60
o.	A1463 (75fo) multi	.60 .60
p.	A1464 (75fo) multi	.60 .60
q.	A1465 (75fo) multi	.60 .60
r.	A1466 (75fo) multi	.60 .60
s.	A1467 (75fo) multi	.60 .60
t.	A1468 (75fo) multi	.60 .60
u.	A1469 (75fo) multi	.60 .60
v.	A1470 (75fo) multi	.60 .60
w.	A1471 (75fo) multi	.60 .60
x.	A1472 (75fo) multi	.60 .60
y.	A1473 (75fo) multi	.60 .60

Pecs, 2010 European Cultural Capital.

2010 Winter Olympics, Vancouver A1474

2010, Feb. 5		
4146	A1474 260fo multi	2.60 2.60

Izidor Kner (1860-1935), Publisher A1475

2010, Feb. 5		Perf. 12x13¼
4147	A1475 295fo multi	2.25 2.25

Budapest Landmarks A1476

Designs: 295fo, Tympanum of Humanities Building, Loránd Eötvös University, Budapest. 400fo, Elisabeth Tower, Budapest.

2010, Feb. 19		Perf. 12½x12
4148-4149	A1476 Set of 2	4.75 4.75

Loránd Eötvös University, 375th anniv., Elisabeth Tower, cent.

Easter — A1477

2010, Mar. 1		
4150	A1477 80fo multi	.60 .40

Republican Guard Regiment, 250th Anniv. — A1478

2010, Mar. 1		Perf. 13x13¼
4151	A1478 320fo multi	2.40 2.40

Souvenir Sheet

Ferenc Erkel (1810-93), Composer — A1479

2010, Mar. 26		Perf. 12
4152	A1479 500fo multi	4.75 4.75

Stamp Day — A1480

Sites in Sopron: 80fo, Saint Ursula's Church, Church of the Virgin Mary. 105fo, Sculptur of the Virgin Mary, Gates of Faith, horiz.
500fo+200fo, Statue of the Holy Trinity.

2010, Mar. 26		Perf. 12x12½, 12½x12
4153-4154	A1480 Set of 2	1.35 1.35

Souvenir Sheet

| 4155 | A1480 500fo +200fo multi | 5.00 5.00 |

Surtax on No. 4155 for Natl. Association of Hungarian Stamp Collectors.

Hungarian Documents on Paper, 700th Anniv. — A1481

2010, Apr. 8		Perf. 13x13¼
4156	A1481 140fo multi	1.10 1.10

Chronicle of the Ways of the Hungarians, by Gáspár Heltai (c. 1510-74), Writer — A1482

2010, Apr. 8		Perf. 13¼x13
4157	A1482 240fo multi	1.75 1.75

Expo 2010, Shanghai A1483

Gömböc in various positions with stamps numbered in lower left: Nos. 4158a, 4158ae, 1. Nos. 4158b, 4158af, 2. Nos. 4158c, 4158ag, 3. Nos. 4158d, 4158ah, 2 squared (4). Nos. 4158e, 4158ai, 5. Nos. 4158f, 4158aj, 2*3 (6). Nos. 4158g, 4158ak, 7. Nos. 4158h, 4158al, 2 cubed (8). Nos. 4158i, 4158am, 3 squared (9). Nos. 4158j, 4158an, 2*5 (10). Nos. 4158k, 4158ao, 11. Nos. 4158l, 4158ap, 2 squared * 3 (12). Nos. 4158m, 4158aq, 13. Nos. 4158n, 4158ar, 2*7 (14). Nos. 4158o, 4158as, 3*5 (15). Nos. 4158p, 4158at, 2 to the fourth power (16). Nos. 4158q, 4158au, 17. Nos. 4158r, 4158av, 2*9 (18). Nos. 4158s, 4158aw, 19. Nos. 4158t, 4158ax, 2 squared * 5 (20). Nos. 4158u, 4158ay, 3*7 (21). Nos. 4158v, 4158az, 2*11 (22). Nos. 4158w, 4158ba, 23. Nos. 4158x, 4158bb, 2 cubed * 3 (24). Nos. 4158y, 4158bc, 5 squared (25). Nos. 4158z, 4158bd, 2*13 (26). Nos. 4158aa, 4158be, 3 cubed (27). Nos. 4158ab, 4158bf, 2 squared * 7 (28). Nos. 4158ac, 4158bg, 29. Nos. 4158ad, 4158bh, 2*3*5 (30).

2010, Apr. 30	Litho.	Perf. 12
4158	Sheet of 30	25.00 25.00
a.-ad.	A1483 100fo Any single	.85 .85
ae.-bh.	A1483 100fo Any booklet single, perf. 12 horiz. at top	.85 .85
	Complete booklet, #4158ae-4158bh	22.50

Miniature Sheet

The Tragedy of Man, Play by Imre Madách, 150th Anniv. A1484

No. 4159 — Scenes from play: a, 105fo, Adam and Eve in Garden of Eden (denomination in white). b, 105fo, Men and women in London (denomination in black). c, 105fo+50fo, Men and women in Rome (denomination at bottom in white). d, 105fo+50fo, Woman in Prague (denomination at top in white).

2010, May 3		Perf. 13x13¼
4159	A1484 Sheet of 4, #a-d	4.00 4.00

Surtax for supporting youth stamp collecting.

2010 World Cup Soccer Championships, South Africa — A1485

2010, May 7		Perf. 11
4160	A1485 325fo multi	2.40 2.40

Intl. Year of Biodiversity A1486

Designs: 80fo, Spermophilus citellus. 110fo, Phyllomorpha lacinata. 215fo, Parus caeruleus. 350fo, Vipera ursinii rakosiensis. 500fo, Iris aphylla ssp. hungarica.

2010, May 7		Perf. 12½x12
4161-4164	A1486 Set of 4	5.50 5.50

Souvenir Sheet
Perf. 12

| 4165 | A1486 500fo multi | 4.00 4.00 |

Miniature Sheet

Europa A1487

No. 4166 — Vackor the Bear: a, Holding plant. b, Picking fruit.

2010, May 7		Perf. 12
4166	A1487 150fo Sheet, 2 each #a-b	3.75 3.75

No. 3417a Surcharged in Red

Method and Perf. As Before

2010, June 18		
4167	A972 200fo on 19fo multi (R)	6.50 6.50

Election of Prime Minister József Antall, 20th anniv.

Frédéric Chopin (1810-49), Composer A1488

2010, June 18	Litho.	Perf. 12½
4168	A1488 240fo multi	1.80 1.80

Self-Portrait of Miklós Barabás (1810-98) — A1489

2010, June 18		Perf. 12½x13¼
4169	A1489 365fo multi	2.75 2.75

World Triathlon Championships, Budapest A1490

2010, July 2	Litho.	Perf. 13x13¼
4170	A1490 280fo multi	2.10 2.10

European Swimming League Championships, Budapest and Lake Balaton — A1491

2010, July 2		Perf. 13¼x13
4171	A1491 300fo multi	2.00 2.00

25th Hungarian Formula 1 Grand Prix — A1492

2010, July 30		Perf. 12
4172	A1492 230fo multi	2.10 2.10

Synagogues — A1493

Designs: 110fo, Nagykoros Synagogue. 175fo, New Synagogue, Szolnok.

2010, Sept. 6		Perf. 12½x13¼
4173-4174	A1493 Set of 2	2.10 2.10

Hungarian Gymnastics Federation, 125th Anniv. — A1494

2010, Sept. 24	Litho.	Perf. 12x12½
4175	A1494 140fo multi	1.05 1.05

HUGARY

Christmas — A1495

Designs: 80fo, Madonna and Child. 105fo, Angels making music, horiz.

Litho. With Foil Application
2010, Oct. 28   Perf. 12
4176-4177 A1495 Set of 2   1.45 1.45

Embroidery A1496

Designs: 80fo, Termeh embroidery designs, Yazd, Iran. 240fo, Jazgyian embroidery designs, Hungary.

2010, Nov. 10   Litho.   Perf. 12½x12
4178-4179 A1496 Set of 2   2.25 2.25
See Iran No. 3027.

Souvenir Sheet

Rudolf Kárpáti (1920-99), Fencing Gold Medalist at 1960 Summer Olympics — A1497

2010, Dec. 10   Perf. 12
4180 A1497 500fo multi   4.75 4.75

Sándor Püski (1911-2009), Book Publisher — A1498

2011, Feb. 4   Litho.   Perf. 12x12½
4181 A1498 270fo multi   2.00 2.00

Hungarian Presidency of the Council of the European Union A1499

2011, Feb. 7   Perf. 12
4182 A1499 90fo multi   .75 .75

Visegrád Group, 20th Anniv. — A1500

2011, Feb. 15
4183 A1500 240fo multi   1.80 1.80
See Czech Republic No. 3490, Poland No. 4001, Slovakia No. 611.

Furniture Type of 1999
Design like No. 3738.

2011, Mar. 1   Litho.   Perf. 11½x12¼
4184 A1091 225fo green   1.75 1.60

Hungarian Golgotha, Textile Art by Erzsébet Szekeres — A1501

2011, Mar. 1   Perf. 12
4185 A1501 90fo multi   .70 .45
Easter.

Tourist Attractions A1502

Designs: 160fo, Pauline Piarist Church, Sátoraljaújhely. 220fo, Royal Palace of Gödöllő.

2011, Mar. 4   Perf. 12½x12
4186-4187 A1502 Set of 2   2.85 1.75

Vasas Sport Club, Cent. — A1503

2011, Mar. 16
4188 A1503 315fo multi   2.40 2.40

Entertainers A1504

Designs: 250fo, Rodolfo (Rezso Gács) (1911-87), magician. 340fo, Lajos Básti (1911-77), actor. 370fo, Manyi Kiss (1911-71), actress.

2011, Mar. 28   Perf. 12
4189-4191 A1504 Set of 3   7.00 7.00

Stamp Day — A1505

Buildings in Balatonfüred: 90fo, Anna Grand Hotel. 115fo, Heart Hospital. 600fo+200fo, Vaszary Villa.

2011, Apr. 8   Perf. 12x12½
4192-4193 A1505 Set of 2   1.50 1.50
Souvenir Sheet
4194 A1505 600fo +200fo   5.50 5.50
Balatonfüred, 800th anniv. Surtax on No. 4194 is for National Federation of Hungarian Philatelists.

Miniature Sheet

City Park, Budapest — A1506

No. 4195: a, 160fo, Buildings and animals of Budapest Zoo and Botanical Garden. b, 160fo, Vajdahunyad Castle. c, 160fo+50fo, Amusement Park. d, 160fo+50fo, Ice rink.

2011, Apr. 8   Perf. 12
4195 A1506 Sheet of 4, #a-d   5.50 5.50
Surtax on Nos. 5195c-4195d for youth philately.

Souvenir Sheet

First Manned Space Flight, 50th Anniv. A1507

2011, Apr. 12   Perf. 12x12½
4196 A1507 600fo multi   4.75 4.75

Souvenir Sheet

Crown of St. Stephen A1508

Litho. & Embossed With Foil Application
2011, Apr. 25   Perf. 13x12¾
4197 A1508 2011fo multi   15.00 15.00
 a. As #4197, with inscriptions added in sheet margin   25.00 25.00

Enactment of new Fundamental Law for Hungary. A souvenir sheet with red serial number and affixed glass crystals sold for 5000fo. A souvenir sheet like No. 4197a, with red serial number, affixed glass crystals and inscriptions of "Ötéves Magyarsrszág Alaptörvénye" and "2016. Aprilis 25." was released in limited quantities in 2016 and sold for 5990fo.
Issued: No. 4197a, 4/25/16. Sheet margin of No. 4197a has black serial number and added inscriptions of "Ötéves Magyarsrszág Alaptörvénye" and "2016. Aprilis 25."

World Theater Day Type of 2005 and Butterfly Types of 2006 Redrawn With "Belföld" Instead of Denomination

2011, Apr. 26   Litho.   Perf. 11¼
4198 A1245 (90fo) multi + label   1.00 1.00
 Sheet of 20 + 20 labels   13.50 13.50
4199 Pair + 2 labels   2.00 2.00
 a. A1286 (90fo) multi + label   1.00 .50
 b. A1287 (90fo) multi + label   1.00 .50
 Sheet of 20, 10 each #4199a-4199b + 20 labels   13.50 13.50

Labels on Nos. 4198-4199 could be personalized for an extra fee.

Fruit and Blossoms — A1509

Designs: 145fo, Apples. 310fo, Pears.

2011, May 6   Perf. 12
4200-4201 A1509 Set of 2   3.25 3.25
See Nos. 4238-4239, 4322-4323.

Butterflies A1510

Designs: 80fo, Apatura metis. 105fo, Melanargia russiae. 255fo, Arctia caja. 370fo, Proserpinus proserpina. 600fo, Lycaena dispar.

2011, May 6   Perf. 13x13¼
4202-4205 A1510 Set of 4   6.00 4.95
Souvenir Sheet
Perf. 13x12¾
4206 A1510 600fo multi   4.50 4.50
No. 4206 contains one 40x32mm stamp.

Miniature Sheet

Europa A1511

No. 4207: a, Orség area forest in summer. b, Forest in Visegrád Mountains in winter.

2011, May 6   Perf. 12
4207 A1511 200fo Sheet of 4, 2 each #a-b   4.50 4.50
Intl. Year of Forests.

Paintings — A1512

Designs: 195fo, Small Girl with Geranium, by József Koszta (1861-1949). 345fo, Female Profile, Zorka, by József Rippi-Rónai (1861-1927).

2011, May 18   Perf. 13½x13
4208-4209 A1512 Set of 2   4.00 4.00

Items in Hungarian Museums A1513

Various items from and building for: 280fo, Rákóczi Museum, Sárospatak. 385fo, Várpalota Museum of Chemistry.

2011, May 18   Perf. 12
4210-4211 A1513 Set of 2   4.50 4.50

Pannon Philharmonic Orchestra, Pécs, 200th Anniv. — A1514

2011, June 2   Litho.
4212 A1514 330fo multi   2.50 2.50

Budapest Spas — A1515

Spa and statue at: 240fo, Lukács Spa. 250fo, Gellért Spa.

2011, July 7   Perf. 12½x12
4213-4214 A1515 Set of 2   3.50 3.50

István Bibó (1911-79), Politician — A1516

2011, Aug. 5   Perf. 12x12½
4215 A1516 345fo multi   2.50 2.50

HUNGARY

Souvenir Sheet

Franz Liszt (1811-86), Composer — A1517

2011, Aug. 19			Perf. 12¾x13
4216	A1517	600fo multi	4.50 4.50

Christmas A1518

2011, Oct. 27			Perf. 12
4217-4218	A1518	Set of 2	1.50 .95

Creche scenes and Catholic churches in: 90fo, Nagykarácsony. 115fo, Vörs.

Litho. With Foil Application

Bell and Christmas Ornament A1519

Christmas Ornament and Gift Box A1520

2011, Oct. 27		Litho.	Perf. 11¼
4219		Pair + 2 labels	1.35 1.35
a.	A1519 (90fo) multi + label		.65 .40
b.	A1520 (90fo) multi + label		.65 .40
	Sheet of 20, 10 each #4219a-4219b + 20 labels		13.50 13.50

Labels on Nos. 4219 could be personalized for an extra fee.

World Science Forum, Budapest A1521

2011, Nov. 3		Litho.	Perf. 13x13¼
4220	A1521	270fo multi	2.75 2.75

St. Martin of Tours (c. 316-97) — A1522

2011, Nov. 11			Perf. 12
4221	A1522	160fo multi	1.20 1.20

Morning Sunshine, by Károly Ferenczy (1862-1917) A1523

2012, Feb. 8			Perf. 12
4222	A1523	420fo multi	2.75 2.75

Greek Orthodox Diocese of Hajdúdorog, Cent. — A1524

2012, Feb. 17			Perf. 13¼x12½
4223	A1524	380fo multi	2.50 2.50

Easter — A1525

2012, Feb. 24			Perf. 12¼x12¾
4224	A1525	105fo multi	.70 .35

University Centenaries A1526

Buildings at: 180fo, Tivadar Puskás Technical School of Telecommunications, Budapest. 270fo, University of Debrecen, Debrecen.

2012, Mar. 22			Perf. 12½x12
4225-4226	A1526	Set of 2	2.75 1.60

Budapest Baths — A1527

Designs: 235fo, Király Baths. 260fo, Rudas Baths.

2012, Mar. 22			
4227-4228	A1527	Set of 2	3.00 2.25

Performing Artists — A1528

Designs: 395fo, Zoltán Várkonyi (1912-79), actor and director. 425fo, Katalin Karády (1910-90), actress and singer.

2012, Mar. 27			
4229-4230	A1528	Set of 2	5.00 5.00

Launch of Masat 1, First Hungarian Satellite — A1529

2012, Apr. 12			Perf. 13¼x13
4231	A1529	310fo multi	2.00 2.00

Souvenir Sheet

Sinking of the Titanic, Cent. — A1530

No. 4232: a, Two aft smokestacks (denomination at UL). b, Two fore smokestacks (denomination at UR).

Litho. & Embossed

2012, Apr. 13			Perf. 12
4232	A1530	800fo Sheet of 2, #a-b	11.00 11.00

Miniature Sheet

Hungarian Scout Association, Cent. — A1531

No. 4233: a, 105fo, Scouts, emblem of 1933 International Jamboree, Gödöllö. b, 105fo, Scout praying at cross, Scout sign. c, 105fo+50fo, Leaf, Scouts putting up tent. d, 105fo+50fo, Scout trefoil, Scouts bandaging boy's leg.

2012, Apr. 20		Litho.	Perf. 13¼x13
4233	A1531	Sheet of 4, #a-d	3.50 3.50

Surtax on Nos. 4233c-4233d for youth philately.

Protected Birds — A1532

Designs: 80fo, Aquila heliaca. 140fo, Haliaeetus albicilla. 180fo, Falco vespertinus. 345fo, Falco cherrug.

2012, May 4			Perf. 13x13¼
4234-4237	A1532	Set of 4	4.75 4.75

See No. 4246.

Fruit and Blossoms Type of 2011

Designs: 185fo, Sour cherries. 230fo, Rose apricots.

2012, May 9			Perf. 12
4238-4239	A1509	Set of 2	2.75 2.75

Miniature Sheet

Europa A1533

No. 4240: a, Peppers and grapes. b, Items in Library of Abbey of Pannonhalma.

2012, May 9			Perf. 12½x12
4240	A1533	235fo Sheet of 4, 2 each #a-b	3.00 3.00

Raoul Wallenberg (1912-47), Swedish Diplomat Who Saved Jews in World War II — A1534

2012, May 10			Perf. 12
4241	A1534	340fo multi	2.25 2.25

See Sweden No. 2693.

"Belföld" A1535

2012, May 14			Perf. 11
4242	A1535	(175fo) green + label	.85 .75
		Sheet of 28+28 labels	28.50 21.00

Labels could be personalized for an additional fee. The label shown is one of a number of generic labels produced.

Solidarity Between Generations A1536

2012, May 17			Perf. 12½x12
4243	A1536	200fo multi	1.25 .65

Souvenir Sheet

Smokehouses and Pottery — A1537

No. 4244: a, Felsöszönok, Hungary smokehouse at left, pitcher, two lidded jars. b, Filovci, Slovenia smokehouse at right, jug, colander.

2012, May 25			
4244	A1537	260fo Sheet of 2, #a-b	3.25 3.25

See Slovenia No. 948.

2012 European Soccer Championships, Poland and Ukraine — A1538

2012, June 8			Perf. 12
4245	A1538	270fo multi	1.75 1.75

Protected Birds Type of 2012
Souvenir Sheet

2012, June 15			Perf. 12½x12
4246	A1532	500fo Buteo buteo	4.00 4.00

Battle of Rozgony, 700th Anniv. — A1539

2012, June 15			Perf. 12x12½
4247	A1539	370fo multi	2.50 2.50

2012 Summer Olympics, London A1540

Designs: 315fo, Swimming. 360fo, Kayaking.

2012, June 22			Perf. 12
4248-4249	A1540	Set of 2	4.25 4.25

A1541

HUNGARY

Stamp Day — A1542

Designs: 80fo, Kalocsa embroidery. 130fo, Peppers, Paprika Museum, Kaposi. 600fo+200fo, Chalice.

2012, July 6		Perf. 12
4250-4251	A1541 Set of 2	2.25 2.25

Souvenir Sheet
Perf. 12¾x13

| 4252 | A1542 600fo +200fo multi | 5.75 5.75 |

Surtax on No. 4252 is for National Federation of Hungarian Philatelists.

Miniature Sheet

Famous Men — A1543

No. 4253: a, Istvan Orkény (1912-79), writer. b, Sir Georg Solti (1912-97), conductor. c, Géza Ottlik (1912-90), writer. d, János Szentágothai (1912-94), anatomist.

2012, July 6		Perf. 12x12½
4253	A1543 105fo Sheet of 4, #a-d	2.75 2.75

Synagogues — A1544

Synagogue in: 300fo, Baja. 400fo, Kiskunhalas.

2012, Sept. 4		Perf. 12
4254-4255	A1544 Set of 2	4.75 4.75

Sixth World Congress of Finno-Ugric People, Siofók — A1545

2012, Sept. 5		Perf. 12½x12
4256	A1545 290fo multi	2.25 2.25

Miniature Sheet

Parliament Building, 110th Anniv. — A1546

No. 4257: a, Statues, panel in tan at right. b, Speaker's dais and coats of arms, panel in brown at bottom. c, Speaker's chair, panel in gray green at right. d, Decorative arches, panel in gray green at bottom. e, Wall sculpture of horse and rider, panel in tan at bottom. f, Chamber, panel in gray at right. g, Coat of arms, panel in beige at right. h, Chamber, panel in brown at bottom.

2012, Oct. 8		Perf. 13¼
4257	A1546 Sheet of 8 + central label	10.00 10.00
a.-h.	200fo Any single	1.20 1.20

An embossed sheet with a lacquered finish was printed in a limited edition and sold for 3200fo.

Christmas A1547

Litho. With Foil Application

2012, Oct. 26		Perf. 12
4258	A1547 130fo multi	.90 .90

No. 4258 was printed in sheets of 4.

Souvenir Sheet

Benedictine Abey, Tihany — A1548

2012, Oct. 26	Litho.	Perf. 12x12½
4259	A1548 600fo multi	4.75 4.75

Souvenir Sheet

Miklos Prison, Kosice, Slovakia A1549

2013, Jan. 25		Perf. 12
4260	A1549 600fo multi	3.50 3.50

Kosice, 2013 European Capital of Culture.

József Galamb (1881-1955), Mechanical Engineer, and Ford Model Ts — A1550

2013, Feb. 5		
4261	A1550 145fo multi	1.00 1.00

Dr. Miklós Ujvárosi (1913-81), Botanist — A1551

2013, Feb. 5		Perf. 12½x12
4262	A1551 395fo multi	2.50 2.50

Composers A1552

Designs: 165fo, Richard Wagner (1813-83). 325fo, Giuseppe Verdi (1813-1901).

2013, Mar. 5		Perf. 13x13¼
4263-4264	A1552 Set of 2	3.00 3.00

A1553, A1554, A1555, A1556, A1557, A1558, A1559, A1560, A1561, A1562, A1563, A1564, A1565, A1566

2013, Mar. 5	Litho.	Perf. 12¼x12¾
4265	Horiz. pair	1.50 .75
a.	A1553 85fo multi	.75 .35
b.	A1554 85fo multi	.75 .35
4266	Horiz. pair	1.90 1.00
a.	A1555 110fo multi	.95 .50
b.	A1556 110fo multi	.95 .50
4267	Sheet of 12	12.50 12.50
a.	A1553 85fo multi	.75 .35
b.	A1554 85fo multi	.75 .35
c.	A1557 85fo multi	.75 .35
d.	A1558 85fo multi	.75 .35
e.	A1559 85fo multi	.75 .35
f.	A1560 85fo multi	.75 .35
g.	A1561 85fo multi	.75 .35
h.	A1562 85fo multi	.75 .35
i.	A1563 85fo multi	.75 .35
j.	A1564 85fo multi	.75 .35
k.	A1565 85fo multi	.75 .35
l.	A1566 85fo multi	.75 .35

Easter. Nos. 4265a and 4265b have lithographed dots in rows with the red dots on the white portions of the eggs near the side being large. Nos. 4267a and 4267b were printed with stochastic lithography, with red dots that are smaller, and appearing to be randomly placed rather than in rows.

Tourist Attractions A1567

Designs: 85fo, Szeged Cathedral. 195fo, Water Tower, Margaret Island, vert. 325fo, Springhouse, Orfu, vert.

2013		Perf. 12½x12, 12x12½
4268-4270	A1567 Set of 3	3.50 3.50

Issued: 85fo, 325fo, 5/3; 195fo, 3/5.

European Judo Championships, Budapest A1568

2013, Apr. 2		Perf. 13x13¼
4271	A1568 360fo multi	2.25 2.25

Széchenyi Thermal Baths — A1569

Buildings, baths and: 145fo, Statue of nude woman. 165fo, Mosaic of nude woman.

2013, Apr. 2		Perf. 12½x12
4272-4273	A1569 Set of 2	1.90 2.90

Mammals A1570

Designs: 110fo, Mustela erminea. 140fo, Sorex minutus. 230fo, Lynx lynx. 390fo, Myotis myotis. 600fo, Erinaceus roumanicus.

2013, Apr. 9	Litho.	Perf. 12
4274-4277	A1570 Set of 4	4.75 4.75

Souvenir Sheet

| 4278 | A1570 600fo multi | 3.75 3.75 |

Stamp Day — A1571

Attractions in Székesfehérvár: 85fo, Bishops Fountain, Statue of St. Astrik of Pannonhalma. 110fo, City Hall, Statue of Justice, horiz. 500fo+200fo, Cistercian Church.

2013, Apr. 26	Perf. 13¼x13, 13x13¼
4279-4280	A1571 Set of 2 1.25 1.25

Souvenir Sheet
Perf. 12¾x13

| 4281 | A1571 500fo +200fo multi | 4.75 4.75 |

No. 4281 contains one 32x40mm stamp. Surtax on No. 4281 is for National Federation of Hungarian Philatelists.

Miniature Sheet

Europa A1572

No. 4282: a, 1914 Csonka parcel delivery van. b, Modern Ford postal van.

2013, May 3		Perf. 13x13¼
4282	A1572 235fo Sheet of 4, 2 each #a-b	5.00 5.00

Items in Hungarian Museums A1573

Designs: 250fo, Calcite crystals, Calcite Crystal Museum, Fertorákos. 400fo, Lamps, Lamp Museum, Zsámbék.

2013, May 3		
4283-4284	A1573 Set of 2	4.25 4.25

Nos. 4283-4284 were printed in sheets of 4. The designs, when viewed through red and blue glasses, become three-dimensional.

Locomotives A1574

HUNGARY

Designs: 195fo, V43 Szili electric locomotive. 445fo, M61 Nohab Diesel-electric locomotive.

2013, June 5		Perf. 12
4285-4286	A1574 Set of 2	4.75 4.75

Souvenir Sheet
Fabric Designs Depicting Peacocks — A1575

No. 4287 — Peacock from: a, Hungarian embroidered pillow cover (white background). b, Azeri woven horse blanket (tan background).

2013, June 15		Perf. 13x13¼
4287	A1575 300fo Sheet of 2, #a-b	3.75 3.75

See Azerbaijan No. 1028.

Miniature Sheet
Sándor Weöres (1913-89), Writer — A1576

No. 4288: a, 110fo, Writer. b, 110fo, Frog playing flute. c, 110fo+50fo, Upside-down girl. d, 110fo+50fo, Castle.

2013, June 20		Perf. 12x12½
4288	A1576 Sheet of 4, #a-d	3.50 3.50

Surtax for support of youth philately.

World Fencing Championships, Budapest — A1577

2013, July 4		Perf. 11
4289	A1577 300fo multi + label	2.00 2.00

Hungarian Skiing Association, Cent. — A1578

	Serpentine Die Cut 10x10¼
2013, July 15	Self-Adhesive
4290 A1578 500fo multi	3.00 3.00

World Wrestling Championships, Budapest A1579

2013, Aug. 2		Perf. 13¼x12½
4291	A1579 360fo multi	2.25 2.25

Géza Gárdonyi (1863-1922), Writer — A1580

2013, Aug. 14		Perf. 12½x13¼
4292	A1580 425fo multi	2.75 2.75

Souvenir Sheet
Saints A1581

No. 4293 — Paintings from Cathedral of St. Martin, Spisska Kapitula, Slovakia: a, St. Laszlo, denomination at LR. b, St. Imre (Emeric), denomination at UL. c, St. Stephen, denomination at bottom center.

2013, Aug. 14	Litho.	Perf. 12
4293	A1581 600fo Sheet of 3, #a-c	13.50 13.50
d.	As #4293, litho. with foil application	15.00 15.00

A lithographed green monocolored sheet of type A1581 that was not valid for postage was sold together with Nos. 4293 and 4293d in a package costing 4100fo.

Miniature Sheet
Dome Hall of Parliament Building — A1582

No. 4294: a, Main staircases. b, Scepter. c, Dome, denomination at UR. d, Dome, diff., denomination at UL. e, Glass windows at UL. f, Glass windows at UR. g, Soldiers at display of Hungarian crown. h, Statues atop pillars.

2013, Sept. 3	Litho.	Perf. 13¼
4294	A1582 Sheet of 8 + central label	12.50 12.50
a.-h.	250fo Any single	1.50 1.50

Woman Gathering a Bundle of Hay on a Collective Farm, Photograph by Robert Capa (1913-54) — A1583

2013, Oct. 2		Perf. 12
4295	A1583 310fo multi	2.00 2.00

The Source of Art, Painting by Aladár Körösfői-Kriesch (1863-1920) A1584

2013, Oct. 2		Perf. 13¼x12½
4296	A1584 315fo multi	2.00 2.00

Souvenir Sheet
Budapest Water Summit — A1585

2013, Oct. 4		Perf. 13¼x13
4297	A1585 365fo multi	3.50 3.50

Rose A1586
Rose A1587
Rose A1588

2013, Oct. 8	Litho.	Perf. 11¼
4298	Strip of 3 + 3 labels	3.00 3.00
a.	A1586 (110fo) multi + label	1.00 1.00
b.	A1587 (110fo) multi + label	1.00 1.00
c.	A1588 (110fo) multi + label	1.00 1.00
	Sheet, 7 each #4298a, 4298c, 6 #4298b	20.00 20.00

Labels could be personalized for an additional fee. Compare with No. 3977.

MTK Sports Club, 125th Anniv. — A1589

2013, Nov. 5	Litho.	Perf. 13¼x13
4299	A1589 400fo blue & dk bl	2.50 2.50

Christmas — A1590

Decorated gingerbread cookies in shape of: 85fo, Christmas tree. 110fo, Star of Bethlehem, horiz. 140fo, Angel.

2013, Nov. 5	Litho.	Die Cut
	Self-Adhesive	
4300	A1590 85fo multi	.60 .60
a.	Booklet pane of 5	3.00
4301	A1590 110fo multi	.75 .75
a.	Booklet pane of 5	3.75
4302	A1590 140fo multi	.90 .90
a.	Booklet pane of 5	4.50
	Nos. 4300-4302 (3)	2.25 2.25

Miniature Sheet
New Year 2014 (Year of the Horse) A1591

No. 4303 — Horse: a, Galloping, head at right. b, Galloping, head at left. c, Grooming itself. d, Grazing.

2014, Jan. 6	Litho.	Perf. 12½x12¼
4303	A1591 110fo Sheet of 4, #a-d	3.25 3.25

Hungarian Maltese Charity, 25th Anniv. — A1592

2014, Feb. 4	Litho. & Embossed	Perf. 12
4304	A1592 300fo multi	1.90 1.90

Souvenir Sheet
Beatified Hungarians — A1593

No. 4305: a, Blessed Zoltán Lajos Meszlényi (1892-1951), bishop of Esztergom. b, Blessed Istvan Sándor (1914-53), monk. c, Blessed Szilárd Bogdánffy (1911-53), clandestine bishop of Oradea, Romania.

2014, Feb. 25	Litho.	Perf. 12
4305	A1593 400fo Sheet of 3, #a-c	7.00 7.00
d.	As No. 4305, litho. with foil application	11.00 11.00

A lithographed blue monocolored sheet of type A1593 that was not valid for postage was only sold together with Nos. 4305 and 4305d in a package that sold for 3990fo.

Miniature Sheet
Baby Animals Recently Born at the Budapest Zoo — A1594

No. 4306: a, Sempala, the giraffe (zsiraf). b, Sid, the two-toes sloth (kétujjú lajhár. c, Jakab, the Barbary sheep (sörényes juh). d, Moira, the orangutan. e, Bangita, the blackbuck (Indiai antilop). f, Maszat, the prairie dog (prérikutya). g, Mazsola, the ground cuscus (földi kuszkusz). h, Rozi, the meerkat (szurikata). i, Gizmó, the ring-tailed lemur (gyurusfarkú maki). j, Skipper, the African penguin (pápaszemes pingvin). k, Kiran, the Asiatic lion (Perzsa oroszlán). l, Willow, the common wombat (csupaszorrú vombat).

2014, Mar. 4	Litho.	Perf. 12
4306	A1594 115fo Sheet of 12, #a-l	8.50 8.50

Klári Tolnay (1914-98), Actress A1595

Annie Fischer (1914-95), Pianist A1596

2014, Mar. 5	Litho.	Perf. 12x12½
4307	A1595 260fo multi	1.50 1.50
4308	A1596 285fo multi	1.65 1.65

Nos. 4307-4308 were each printed in sheets of 4.

A1597

HUNGARY

Easter — A1598

No. 4310 — Stations of the Cross in Roman numerals: a, I. b, II. c, III. d, IV. e, V. f, VI. g, VII. h, VIII. i, IX. j, X. k, XI. l, XII. m, XIII. n, XIV. o, XV.

Litho. With Foil Application
2014, Mar. 28   Perf. 12
4309 A1597 115fo multi   .75   .75

Miniature Sheet
4310 A1598 90fo Sheet of 15,
              #a-o   11.00 11.00

Souvenir Sheet

Wenckheim Palace, Szabadkigyós, Designed by Miklós Ybl (1814-91) — A1599

2014, Apr. 4   Litho.   Perf. 12x12½
4311 A1599 1000fo multi   7.75   7.75

Stamp Day — A1600

Buildings in Debrecen: 115fo, Kölcsey Center. 145fo, Small Reformed Church, vert. 600fo+200fo, Great Reformed Church, vert.

Perf. 13x13¼, 13¼x13
2014, Apr. 25   Litho.
4312-4313 A1600 Set of 2   1.75   1.75

Souvenir Sheet
Perf. 12¾x13
4314 A1600 600fo +200fo multi 5.00   5.00

Examples of No. 4314 with a red serial number and a quartz crystal affixed to the sheet margin were printed in limited quantities

Souvenir Sheet

Canonization of Popes John XXIII and John Paul II — A1601

No. 4315: a, Pope John XXIII. b, Pope John Paul II.

2014, Apr. 27   Litho.   Perf. 12x12½
4315 A1601 250fo Sheet of 2,
              #a-b   3.25   3.25

Hands of Holocaust Survivor Holding Uprooted Plant — A1602

2014, Apr. 28   Litho.   Perf. 13¼x13
4316 A1602 375fo multi   2.50   2.50

Jewish Ghetto Decrees, 70th anniv. (start of Holocaust for Hungarian Jews).

Béni Egressy (1814-51), Composer — A1603

2014, May 9   Litho.   Perf. 12
4317 A1603 200fo multi   1.25   1.25

No. 4317 was printed in sheets of 4.

Miniature Sheet

Europa A1604

No. 4318: a, Hurdy-gurdy (gardon). b, Mouth harp (doromb).

2014, May 9   Litho.   Perf. 11½x12
4318 A1604 250fo Sheet of 4, 2
              each #a-b   3.50   3.50

2014 World Cup Soccer Championships, Brazil — A1605

2014, June 4   Litho.   Perf. 11½x12
4319 A1605 145fo multi   .95   .95

Tripartitum, Compilation of Hungarian Law, by István Werboczy, 500th Anniv. — A1606

2014, July 4   Litho.   Perf. 13¼x13
4320 A1606 330fo multi   2.00   2.00

No. 4320 was printed in sheets of 4.

World War I, Cent. — A1607

2014, July 28   Litho.   Perf. 13¼x13
4321 A1607 440fo multi   2.75   2.75

Fruit and Blossoms Type of 2011
Designs: 245fo, Plums. 260fo, Strawberries.

2014, Aug. 6   Litho.   Perf. 14¼
4322-4323 A1509 Set of 2   3.00   3.00

Souvenir Sheet

Repatriation of the Sevso Treasure — A1608

No. 4324: a, Plate with central design of hunters (30x45mm). b, Plate with central geometric design, Dionysius ewer, basin (60x50mm). c, Basin, ewer with geometric design, container (30x45mm).

Litho. & Embossed With Foil Application
2014, Aug. 25   Perf. 12
4324 A1608 1000fo Sheet of 3,
              #a-c   19.00 19.00

Imperforate examples of No. 4324 are from a limited printing.

Synagogues A1609

Designs: 285fo, Miskolc Synagogue. 330fo, Mád Synagogue.

2014, Sept. 2   Litho.   Perf. 12
4325-4326 A1609 Set of 2   3.75   3.75

Nos. 4325-4326 each were printed in sheets of 4.

Insects — A1610

Designs: 90fo, Dendroleon pantherinus. 115fo, Mantispa styriaca. 405fo, Carabus auronitens. 445fo, Stilbum cyanurum. 600fo, Aeshna viridis.

Litho., Litho. With Foil Application (#4329-4330)
2014, Sept. 9   Perf. 12
4327-4330 A1610 Set of 4   6.50   6.50

Souvenir Sheet
4331 A1610 600fo multi   4.00   4.00

Miniature Sheet

Motorcycles — A1611

No. 4332: a, 1932 Csepel WM98. b, 1942 Mátra 100. c, 1948 Csepel Túra 100. d, 1953 Csepel 250. e, 1953 Csepel 125 T. f, 1957 Pannonia TLT. g, 1961 Danuvia 125. h, 1961 Berva. i, 1963 Danuvia Moto-cross. j, 1964 Pannonia T5 Export. k, 1969 Pannonia P10H. l, 1969, Pannonia P20.

2014, Sept. 9   Litho.   Perf. 12½x12
4332 A1611 90fo Sheet of 12,
              #a-l   6.75   6.75

No. 2909 Surcharged
Souvenir Sheet

Method and Perf. As Before
2014, Sept. 22
4333 A767 300fo on 20fo #2909 3.75   3.75

Seat of Danube Commission in Budapest, 60th anniv.

Miniature Sheet

Speaker's Reception Halls in House of Parliament — A1612

No. 4334: a, Blue sofa and chairs, table, fireplace. b, Wooden cabinet. c, Mantelpiece clock. d, Circle in diamond wall decoration. e, Framed wall decoration. f, Triangular cabinet top. g, Columns and arches wall decoration. h, Red sofa and chairs, table.

2014, Oct. 3   Litho.   Perf. 13¼
4334 A1612 200fo Sheet of 8,
              #a-h, +
              central label   10.00 10.00

2014 European Women's Handball Championships, Hungary and Croatia — A1613

2014, Nov. 6   Litho.   Perf. 13x13¼
4335 A1613 145fo multi   .95   .95

Railway Wheel Assembly A1614

2014, Nov. 6   Litho.   Perf. 11½x12¼
4336 A1614 200fo multi   1.25   1.25

Abrahám Ganz (1814-67), foundry owner, patent holder for casting railway wheels.

Christmas — A1615

2014, Nov. 18   Litho.   Perf. 14
4337 A1615 145fo multi   .95   .95

HUNGARY

34th Racing Pigeon Olympiad, Budapest — A1616

Racing pigeon: 115fo, First Lady and Heroes' Square. 145fo, Mr. Villám and Fishermen's Bastion.
No. 4340: a, Jr. Villám and Liberty Statue. b, Release of pigeons, horiz.

2015, Jan. 16	Litho.		Perf. 14
4338-4339	A1616	Set of 2	1.65 1.65

Souvenir Sheet
Perf. 13½x13, 13x13½

4340	A1616	450fo Sheet of 2,
		#a-b 5.50 5.50

UNICEF in Hungary, 40th Anniv. — A1617

2015, Feb. 5	Litho.		Perf. 11¼
4341	A1617	500fo multi	3.25 3.25

Third World Conference on Disaster Risk Reduction, Sendai City, Japan A1618

2015, Feb. 19	Litho.		Perf. 14
4342	A1618	330fo multi	2.00 2.00

Miniature Sheet

New Year 2015 (Year of the Goat) A1619

No. 4343 — Goat with background color of: a, Buff. b, Dark blue.

Perf. 11½x12¼

2015, Feb. 19		Litho.
4343	A1619	285fo Sheet of 4, 2 each #a-b 4.00 4.00

Nos. 4343a and 4343b are tete-beche within the sheet.

Easter A1620

No. 4344 — Easter egg with: a, Maroon background. b, Cream background.

2015, Mar. 5	Litho.		Perf. 11½x12
4344	A1620	115fo Horiz. pair,
		#a-b 1.75 1.75

Bánk Bán, Play by József Katona, 200th Anniv. — A1621

2015, Mar. 19	Litho.		Perf. 14
4345	A1621	275fo multi	1.80 1.80

The Gypsy Princess, Operetta by Imre Kálmán, Cent. — A1622

2015, Mar. 19	Litho.		Perf. 14
4346	A1622	375fo multi	2.50 2.50

Zita Szeleczky (1915-99), Actress — A1623

2015, Apr. 10	Litho.		Perf. 12½x12
4347	A1623	150fo multi	1.00 1.00

No. 4347 was printed in sheets of 4.

Use of M62 Locomotive, 50th Anniv. — A1624

2015, Apr. 16	Litho.		Perf. 13x13¼
4348	A1624	420fo multi	2.90 2.90

Scheduled Bus Service in Budapest, Cent. A1625

2015, Apr. 16	Litho.		Perf. 14x13¾
4349	A1625	475fo multi	3.00 3.00

Frank Sinatra (1915-98), Singer A1626

2015, May 8	Litho.		Perf. 12
4350	A1626	200fo multi	1.30 1.30

No. 4350 was printed in sheets of 4, with adjacent stamps rotated 90 degrees.

Edith Piaf (1915-63), Singer — A1627

2015, May 8	Litho.		Perf. 12x12½
4351	A1627	325fo multi	2.10 2.10

No. 4351 was printed in sheets of 4.

Europa A1628

No. 4352 — Toys: a, Dolls, hussar on horseback, castle. b, Dolls, blacksmith and horse-drawn cart.

2015, May 8	Litho.		Perf. 12½x12
4352	A1628	285fo Horiz. pair,
		#a-b 4.00 4.00

No. 4352 was printed in sheets containing 2 pairs.

2015 European Women's Basketball Championships, Hungary and Romania — A1629

2015, June 4	Litho.		Perf. 13¼x13
4353	A1629	390fo multi	2.50 2.50

Souvenir Sheet

Pax, Mosaic by Miksa Roth (1865-1944) — A1630

2015, June 4	Litho.		Perf. 13¼x13
4354	A1630	1000fo multi	9.00 9.00

Examples of No. 4354 with green serial number, imperforate with red serial number, and a monochrome design, were printed in limited quantities.

Ujpest Torna Egylet Sports Club, 130th Anniv. — A1631

2015, June 19	Litho.		Perf. 13¼x13
4355	A1631	400fo multi	2.50 2.50

Stamp Day — A1632

Buildings in Tata: 115fo, Bell Tower. 145fo, Tata Castle.
600fo+300fo, Statue of St. John the Baptist, Old Lake, Jószef Eötvös High School.

2015, June 26	Litho.		Perf. 12x12½
4356-4357	A1632	Set of 2	1.65 1.65

Souvenir Sheet

| 4358 | A1632 | 600fo +300fo multi | 5.75 5.75 |

Surtax on No. 4358 is for promotion of philately.

Items in Hungarian Museums A1633

Designs: 200fo, Chest, pottery jug, Flóris Rómer (1815-89), founder of Museum of Art and History, Gyor. 270fo, Ceramic items from Zsolnay Collection of the Janus Pannonius Museum, Pécs.

2015, July 3	Litho.		Perf. 12½x12
4359-4360	A1633	Set of 2	3.00 3.00

Nos. 4359-4360 were each printed in sheets of 4.

Vigadó Concert Hall, Budapest, 150th Anniv. — A1634

2015, July 24	Litho.		Perf. 14x13¾
4361	A1634	285fo multi	1.85 1.85

Flowers — A1635

Designs: 115fo, Iris bucharica. 215fo, Paeonia suffruticosa.

2015, Aug. 7	Litho.		Perf. 14
4362-4363	A1635	Set of 2	2.15 2.15

Souvenir Sheet

St. Astrik Offering Crown to St. Stephen and Queen Gisela A1636

2015, Aug. 7	Litho.		Perf. 12
4364	A1636	600fo multi	4.50 4.50
a.		As #4364, litho. with foil application	6.75 6.75

A lithographed sheet with the vignette in brown that was not valid for postage was printed in limited quantities and only sold together with Nos. 4364 and 4364a in a package that sold for 2790fo.

Albert Einstein's General Theory of Relativity, Cent. — A1637

2015, Sept. 7	Litho.		Perf. 13¼x12½
4365	A1637	285fo multi	1.85 1.85

Kálmán Széll (1843-1915), Prime Minister — A1638

2015, Oct. 1	Litho.		Perf. 14
4366	A1638	145fo multi	.95 .95

Miniature Sheet

Hunting Hall and Delegation Room in House of Parliament — A1639

No. 4367: a, Hunting Hall (dining room) with windows at right. b, Painting of Buda and Attila fighting bison, clock and doors. c, Chandelier and arches. d, Doors. e, Door under arch. f, Stained-glass window depicting dragons. g, Painting of coronation of Franz Joseph I. h, Tables in meeting room.

HUNGARY

2015, Oct. 1   Litho.   *Perf. 12*
4367   A1639   250fo   Sheet of 8, #a-h, + central label   12.00   12.00

International Telecommunication Union, 150th Anniv. — A1640

2015, Oct. 12   Litho.   *Perf. 11*
4368   A1640   375fo   multi + label   2.25   2.25

2015 ITU Conference, Budapest.

Hungarian Academy of Sciences, 150th Anniv. — A1641

2015, Nov. 10   Engr.   *Perf. 12½x12*
4369   A1641   500fo   brown   3.00   3.00

Miniature Sheet

Space Achievements — A1642

No. 4370: a, Drawing of Soviet space capsule, cosmonaut in blue space suit spacewalking. b, New Horizons space probe, denomination at LL. c, Drawing of dog in space helmet, bone, space capsule. d, Astronaut Edward White spacewalking. e, Cosmonaut Alexei Leonov spacewalking. f, Drawing of rocket, antenna on planet. g, Dawn space probe, denomination at UL. h, Drawing of monkey in space helmet.

2015, Nov. 10   Litho.   *Perf. 14*
4370   A1642   115fo   Sheet of 8, #a-h   6.25   6.25

Christmas — A1643

Serpentine Die Cut 10¼x10
2015, Nov. 10   Litho.
Self-Adhesive
4371   A1643   (115fo)   multi   .75   .75

Litho. With Foil Application
Serpentine Die Cut 10x9½
4372   A1643   (115fo)   multi   .95   .95

No. 4372 was printed in sheets of 4.

Stalkless Gentian A1644

Red Poppy A1645

2016, Jan. 22   Litho.   *Perf. 12x11½*
4373   A1644   (305fo)   multi   1.70   1.70
4374   A1645   (355fo)   multi   2.30   2.30

Dated 2015. Compare with type A1087.

István Tömörkény (1866-1917), Writer — A1646

2016, Jan. 22   Litho.   *Perf. 12x12½*
4375   A1646   340fo   multi   2.10   2.10

Miniature Sheet

New Year 2016 (Year of the Monkey) A1647

No. 4376 — Color of monkey: a, Black. b, Red.

2016, Feb. 8   Litho.   *Perf. 12*
4376   A1647   300fo   Sheet of 4, 2 each #a-b   4.50   4.50

Nos. 4376a and 4376b are tete-beche within the sheet.

Easter — A1648

2016, Mar. 4   Litho.   *Perf. 14*
4377   A1648   115fo   multi   .70   .70

József Simándy (1916-97), Opera Singer — A1649

2016, Mar. 4   Litho.   *Perf. 12½x12*
4378   A1649   150fo   multi   .75   .75

St. Martin of Tours (316-97) — A1650

Litho. With Foil Application
2016, Mar. 18   *Perf. 14*
4379   A1650   115fo   multi   .75   .75

Count István Széchenyi (1791-1860) Statesman — A1651

2016, Apr. 8   Litho.   *Perf. 12x12½*
4380   A1651   225fo   multi   1.40   1.40

Europa — A1652

2016, May 6   Litho.   *Perf. 12½x12*
4381   A1652   305fo   multi   1.85   1.85

Think Green Issue.

Stamp Day — A1653

Attractions in Szombathely: 115fo, Funerary stele of the Sempronius family, Roman Emperor Constantius Chlorus proclaiming law in Savaria (Szombathely). 145fo, Holy Trinity statue, chancel of Szombathely Cathedral. 600fo+300fo, St. Martin of Tours, capital of Roman column, horiz.

2016, May 6   Litho.   *Perf. 14*
4382-4383   A1653   Set of 2   1.60   1.60
Souvenir Sheet
Perf. 14x13½
4384   A1653   600fo +300fo   multi   5.75   5.75

Hungarian Interchurch Aid, 25th Anniv. — A1654

Litho. & Embossed
2016, May 17   *Perf. 14*
4385   A1654   145fo   blue & orange   .95   .95

2016 European Soccer Championships, France — A1655

2016, June 3   Litho.   *Perf. 12½x12*
4386   A1655   340fo   multi   2.00   2.00

Items in Hungarian Museums A1656

Designs: 355fo, Chess pieces, Chess Museum, Heves. 395fo, Pipes, Pipe Museum, Ibafa.

2016, June 3   Litho.   *Perf. 12*
4387-4388   A1656   Set of 2   4.50   4.50

Nos. 4387-4388 comes in sheets of 4.

Geological Treasures A1657

Designs: 115fo, Daphnogene polymorpha fossil. 145fo, Raskya vetusta fossil. 600fo, Glyptostrobus europaeus fossil.

2016, June 8   Litho.   *Perf. 12½x12*
4389-4390   A1657   Set of 2   1.60   1.60
Souvenir Sheet
4391   A1657   600fo   multi   3.75   3.75

Miniature Sheet

Exterior Details of House of Parliament — A1658

No. 4392: a, Tower and upper stories, sky at top, light chestnut panel at left. b, Dome, lavender gray panel at right. c, Tower, bridge in background, greenish slate panel at left. d, Dome, brownish gray panel at left. e, Tower and rooftop, ochre panel at right. f, Gargoyles and root spires, light chestnut panel at left. g, Statues on pillars, light olive gray panel at right. h, Statues on pillars, roof, light red brown panel at right.

2016, June 8   Litho.   *Perf. 12*
4392   A1658   200fo   Sheet of 8, #a-h, + central label   9.75   9.75

Jan Jessinius (1566-1621), Physician and Professor of Anatomy — A1659

Photo. & Engr.
2016, June 22   *Perf. 11¼x11¾*
4393   A1659   280fo   multi + label   1.75   1.75

See Czech Republic No. 3677, Poland No. 4232, Slovakia No. 743.

Miniature Sheet

Fire Fighting A1660

No. 4394: a, 150fo, Károly Koszeghi-Mártony (1783-1848), inventor of compressed air breathing system, fire wagon. b, 150fo, Count Odön Széchenyi (1839-1922), chief officer of Budapest Fire Brigade, fire wagon. c, 150fo+75fo, Kornél Szilvay (1890-1957), inventor of dry fire extinguisher, fire truck. d, 150fo+75fo, Fire fighter and Heros Aquadux-X 4000 fire truck.

2016, June 22   Litho.   *Perf. 12*
4394   A1660   Sheet of 4, #a-d   4.75   4.75

Surtax for youth philately.

2016 Summer Olympics, Rio de Janeiro — A1661

Designs: 115fo, Swimming. 355fo, Kayaking.

2016, July 7   Litho.   *Perf. 12½x12*
4395-4396   A1661   Set of 2   2.90   2.90

First Horse Tramway in Pest, 150th Anniv. — A1662

2016, July 8   Litho.   *Perf. 13¼x13*
4397   A1662   200fo   multi   1.50   1.50

Introduction of M40 Locomotive in Hungary, 50th Anniv. — A1663

2016, July 8   Litho.   *Perf. 12*
4398   A1663   260fo   multi   1.70   1.70

Miniature Sheet

Baby Animals Recently Born at the Budapest Zoo — A1664

No. 4399: a, Rudi, the African forest buffalo (vörös kafferbivaly). b, Adolf, the Javan surili (Javai langur). c, Ócsi, the northern bald ibis (tarvarjú). d, Bulan, the Visayan warty pig (Cebu-szigeti disznó). e, Panka, the greater rhea (nandu). f, Batty, the Lyle's flying fox (Lyle-repülökutya). g, Gátor, the Dalmatian pelican (borzas gödény). h, Evita, the mhorr gazelle (mhorr gazella). i, Nefriti, the night monkey (éji majom). j, Lóránt, the red-fronted macaw (vörösfülü ara). k, Dalma, the dhole

HUNGARY

(ázsiai vadkutya). l, Kia, the eyelash viper (schlegel-lándzsakígyó).

2016, Aug. 9   **Litho.**   **Perf. 12**
4399 A1664 115fo Sheet of 12, #a-l   9.50   9.50

Souvenir Sheet
Budapest Zoo, 150th Anniv. — A1665

2016, Aug. 9   **Litho.**   **Perf. 13¼x13**
4400 A1665 1000fo multi   9.50   9.50

Examples of No. 4400 with a green serial number, and imperforate with a red serial number were printed in limited quantities.

Souvenir Sheet
Hungarian Royalty — A1666

No. 4401: a, Blessed King Charles IV (1887-1922) (26x33mm). b, Crown of St. Stephen, orb, scepter and sword (35x41mm). c, Queen Zita (1892-1989) (26x33mm).

Perf. 11½x12, 13 (#4401b)
2016, Aug. 17   **Litho.**
4401 A1666 200fo Sheet of 3, #a-c   4.50   4.50
   d. As No. 4401, litho. & embossed with foil application   4.50   4.50

Coronation of King Charles IV, cent. A lithographed black monocolor sheet of type A1666 that was not valid for postage was sold together with Nos 4401 and 4401d in a package costing 3990fo.

Souvenir Sheet
Battle of Szigetvár, 450th Anniv. — A1667

No. 4402: a, Zrinski's Charge from the Szigetvár Fortress, by Bertalan Székely. b, Szigetvár coat of arms.

Perf. 13¼x13x13¼x14
2016, Sept. 5   **Litho.**
4402 A1667 300fo Sheet of 2, #a-b   3.75   3.75

See Croatia No. 1004.

Souvenir Sheet
Leaders of the Battle of Szigetvár A1668

No. 4403: a, Nikola Zrinski (1508-66). b, Suleiman the Magnificent (1495-1566).

Perf. 13¼x13x13¼x14
2016, Sept. 5   **Litho.**
4403 A1668 300fo Sheet of 2, #a-b   3.75   3.75

See Turkey No. 3522.

Ulmus Minor — A1669

2016, Sept. 8   **Litho.**   **Perf. 12x12½**
4404 A1669 115fo multi   .75   .75

Károly Simonyi (1916-2001), Physicist and Electrical Engineer — A1670

2016, Oct. 5   **Litho.**   **Perf. 12½x12**
4405 A1670 400fo multi   2.40   2.40

Souvenir Sheet
Revolution of 1956, 60th Anniv. — A1671

2016, Oct. 21   **Litho.**   **Perf.**
4406 A1671 800fo multi   4.75   4.75

Royal Wedding Garments — A1672

No. 4407 — Garment of: a, King Louis II, brown purple denomination. b, Queen Mary, red denomination.

2016, Nov. 8   **Litho.**   **Perf. 12½x12**
4407 A1672 250fo Pair, #a-b   2.95   2.95

Printed in sheets containing two each Nos. 4407a-4407b.

Souvenir Sheet
City With Various European Landmarks — A1673

2016, Nov. 8   **Litho.**   **Perf. 12¼**
4408 A1673 600fo multi   3.50   3.50

Christmas — A1674

Die Cut Perf. 11½
2016, Nov. 8   **Typo.**
Self-Adhesive
4409 A1674 (115fo) blue & org yel   .80   .80
4410 A1674 (115fo) blue & gold   .80   .80

No. 4409 has four die cut diagonal lines in the vignette. No. 4410 was printed in vertical strips of 5.

Souvenir Sheet
Budapest Water Summit — A1675

2016, Nov. 21   **Litho.**   **Perf. 13¼x13**
4411 A1675 400fo multi   2.50   2.50

New Year 2017 (Year of the Rooster) A1676

No. 4412: a, Gold rooster. b, Blue rooster.

Litho. With Foil Application
2017, Jan. 27   **Perf. 11½x12**
4412 A1676 335fo Pair, #a-b   4.00   4.00

Printed in sheets containing two each Nos. 4412a-4412b.

Dove and Barbed Wire — A1677

2017, Feb. 1   **Litho.**   **Perf. 14**
4413 A1677 360fo multi   2.15   2.15

Remembrance of victims of Soviet Gulag and GUPVI labor camps.

Regiomontanus (1436-76), Astronomer, and Frontispiece of *Epitome of the Almagest* — A1678

2017, Feb. 3   **Litho.**   **Perf. 13¾**
4414 A1678 235fo multi   1.45   1.45

Arrival of Regiomontanus in Hungary, 550th anniv.

Easter — A1679

Die Cut Perf. 11½
2017, Mar. 6   **Litho.**
Self-Adhesive
4415 A1679 120fo multi   .70   .70

Claudio Monteverdi (1567-1643), Composer A1680

2017, Mar. 6   **Litho.**   **Perf. 12**
4416 A1680 210fo multi   1.30   1.30

No. 4416 was printed in sheets of 4.

Zoltán Fábri (1917-94), Film Director — A1681

2017, Mar. 6   **Litho.**   **Perf. 12**
4417 A1681 300fo multi   1.80   1.80

No. 4417 was printed in sheets of 4, with each stamp rotated 90 degrees from each adjacent stamp.

Lions Club International, Cent. — A1682

2017, Apr. 3   **Litho.**   **Perf. 14**
4418 A1682 120fo multi   .75   .75

No. 4418 was printed in sheets of 10.

Zoltán Kodály (1882-1967), Composer — A1683

2017, Apr. 3   **Litho.**   **Perf. 11½x12**
4419 A1683 155fo multi   1.25   1.25

No. 4419 was printed in sheets of 4.

2017 World Aquatics Championships, Budapest and Lake Balaton — A1684

2017, Apr. 5   **Litho.**   **Perf. 14**
4420 A1684 435fo multi   2.75   2.75

Protestant Reformation, 500th Anniv. — A1685

Designs: 290fo, Statue of Gáspár Károli (c. 1530-91), translator of Bible into Hungarian, printing press, Bible, alpha, omega and quill pen. 445fo, Reformed College of Debrecen, Lamb of God, horiz. 800fo, Martin Luther nailing 95 Theses to church door, Sacred Heart.

2017, Apr. 20   **Litho.**   **Perf. 14**
4421-4422 A1685 Set of 2   4.50   4.50

Souvenir Sheet
Perf. 13¼x13
4423 A1685 800fo multi   5.00   5.00

Hungarian Postal Service, 150th Anniv. — A1686

Designs: 5fo, Handstamps used from 1867-1945. 10fo, Horse-drawn parcel delivery cart used from 1867-1958. 30fo, Mail box, 1894. 100fo, Post office sign used from 1875-1945. 200fo, Postman's cap, 1895. 300fo, Posthorn, 19th cent.

Die Cut Perf. 11½
2017, May 4   **Typo.**
Self-Adhesive
4424 A1686 5fo multi   .30   .25
4425 A1686 10fo multi   .30   .25
4426 A1686 30fo multi   .30   .25
   100fo multi   .75   .75

HUNGARY

4428 A1686 200fo multi 1.25 1.25
4429 A1686 300fo multi 1.95 1.95
Nos. 4424-4429 (6) 4.85 4.70
See Nos. 4464-4469, 4509-4514, 4548-4553, 4590-4593, F5.

Miniature Sheet
Postal Transportation — A1687

No. 4430: a, Horse-drawn parcel delivery cart. b, Postman with János Csonka motorized tricycle. c, Postmen on Cespel bicycles. d, Postal rail car, postman on Danuvia motorcycle. e, Barkas mail van and airplane. f, Nissan ENV 200 electric mail van.

2017, May 4 Litho. Perf. 14
4430 A1687 120fo Sheet of 6, #a-f 4.25 4.25
Hungarian Postal Service, 150th anniv.

Nagybánya Landscape with the Gutin Mountains, by Béla Iványi Grünwald (1867-1940) — A1688

2017, May 5 Litho. Perf. 12
4431 A1688 375fo multi 2.30 2.30
No. 4431 was printed in sheets of 4.

Europa — A1689

No. 4432: a, Andrássy Castle, Tiszadob. b, Nádasdy Castle, Nádasdladány.

2017, May 5 Litho. Perf. 12
4432 A1689 335fo Pair, #a-b 4.25 4.25
Printed in sheets containing two pairs.

Souvenir Sheet
Holy Roman Empress Maria Theresa (1717-80) — A1690

2017, May 12 Litho. Perf. 13¼x13
4433 A1690 495fo multi 3.00 3.00
See Austria No. 2677, Croatia No. 1038, Slovenia No. 1219, Ukraine No. 1093.

Hungarian Stamps, 150th Anniv. — A1691

No. 4434: a, Unissued stamp designed for independent Hungary in 1848. b, Austria #27. c, Hungary #3. d, Hungary #14.

2017, June 1 Litho. Perf. 12
4434 Vert. strip of 4 6.75 6.75
a.-d. A1691 275fo Any single 1.70 1.70
Printed in sheets containing two strips.

Owls — A1692

Designs: 200fo, Tyto alba. 360fo, Strix aluco. 390fo, Asio otus. 410fo, Athene noctua. 600fo, Otus scops.

2017, July 3 Litho. Perf. 14
4435-4438 A1692 Set of 4 8.50 8.50
Souvenir Sheet
4439 A1692 600fo multi 3.75 3.75

Miniature Sheet
János Arany (1817-82), Writer — A1693

No. 4440 — Illustrations by Mihály Zichy of scenes from ballads by Arany: a, 120fo, The Hero of Bor (Bor Vitéz). b, The Bards of Wales (A Walesi Bárdok). c, 120fo+75fo, Mistress Agnes (Agnes Asszony). d, 120fo+75fo, The Mother of King Matthias (Mátyás Anyja).

2017, July 10 Litho. Perf. 13x13¼
4440 A1693 Sheet of 4, #a-d 4.00 4.00
Surtax for youth philately.

Souvenir Sheet
1867 Stamps of the Austro-Hungarian Empire — A1694

No. 4441: a, 120fo, Austria #29. b, 450fo, Austria #33.

2017, Aug. 25 Litho. Perf. 13¼x13
4441 A1694 Sheet of 2, #a-b 3.75 3.75
See Austria No. 2690.

"Belföld" A1695

2017, Sept. 1 Litho. Perf. 11
4442 A1695 (120fo) gold + label .95 .95
Labels could be personalized for an additional fee. The label shown is one of a number of generic labels produced.

Miniature Sheet
Old Eastern European Automobiles — A1696

No. 4443: a, Warszawa 220, Poland. b, Moszkvics 407, Russia. c, GAZ-12 ZIM, Russia. d, Trabant P 50, German Democratic Republic. e, Tatra 2-603, Czechoslovakia. f, Wartburg 311, German Democratic Republic.

Litho. & Embossed
2017, Sept. 1 Perf. 12
4443 A1696 120fo Sheet of 6, #a-f 4.75 4.75

Daughters of King Béla IV — A1697

No. 4444: a, St. Margaret (1242-70). b, St. Kinga (1224-92). c, Blessed Yolanda (c. 1235-98).

2017, Sept. 1 Litho. Perf. 13¼x13
4444 A1697 400fo Sheet of 3, #a-c 7.75 7.75
d. As #4444, litho. & embossed with foil application 20.00 20.00

A lithographed orange and black sheet of type A1697 that was not valid for postage was sold with Nos. 4444 and 4444d in a package costing 3990fo.

Synagogues — A1698

Designs: 210fo, Gyor Synagogue. 235fo, Pécs, Synagogue, horiz.

Perf. 13x13¼, 13¼x13
2017, Sept. 5 Litho.
4445-4446 A1698 Set of 2 2.90 2.90

Flórián Albert (1941-2011), Soccer Player, and Recipient of 1967 Ballon d'Or Trophy — A1699

2017, Sept. 15 Litho. Perf. 14
4447 A1699 300fo multi 1.85 1.85

Magda Szabó (1917-2007), Writer — A1700

Litho. & Embossed
2017, Oct. 5 Perf. 14
4448 A1700 435fo multi 2.75 2.75

Stamp Day — A1701

Designs: 120fo, Archduke Joseph Karl (1833-1905) and Military Merit Cross with war decoration. 155fo, 1890 shako and 1904 saber, vert. 550fo+300fo, Stefánia Palace, Budapest.

2017, Nov. 3 Litho. Perf. 14
4449-4450 A1701 Set of 2 1.75 1.75
Souvenir Sheet
4451 A1701 500fo +300fo multi 5.00 5.00

Christmas — A1702

Die Cut Perf. 11½
2017, Nov. 3 Typo.
Self-Adhesive
4452 A1702 (120fo) gold & black .90 .90
Typo. With Foil Application
4453 A1702 (120fo) gold & black .90 .90
On No. 4453, the gold is more reflective of light than No. 4452.
No. 4453 is printed in miniature sheets of 5 + label.

Statue From Piarist Secondary School, Budapest A1703

2017, Nov. 15 Litho. Perf. 14
4454 A1703 200fo multi 1.25 1.25
Piarist Secondary School, 300th anniv.

Postcrossing — A1704

2018, Feb. 2 Litho. Perf. 12
4455 A1704 120fo multi .75 .75
No. 4455 was printed in sheets of 4.

2018 Winter Olympics, PyeongChang, South Korea — A1705

2018, Feb. 2 Litho. Perf. 13¼x13
4456 A1705 445fo multi 2.75 2.75

New Year 2018 (Year of the Dog) A1706

No. 4457 — Dog with background color of: a, Light blue. b, Scarlet.

2018, Feb. 6 Litho. Perf. 12
4457 A1706 400fo Pair, #a-b 6.50 6.50
Printed in sheets containing two each Nos. 4457a-4457b.

Easter — A1707

Die Cut Perf. 11½
2018, Mar. 2 Typo.
Self-Adhesive
4458 A1707 (120fo) multi .75 .75

Ingmar Bergman (1918-2007), Film Director — A1708

2018, Mar. 2 Litho. Perf. 14
4459 A1708 305fo blk & neon org 1.90 1.90

HUNGARY

Leonard Bernstein (1918-90), Conductor — A1709

2018, Mar. 2	Litho.		Perf. 14
4460	A1709	370fo multi	2.40 2.40

Characters From *Bluebeard's Castle*, Opera by Béla Bartók (1881-1945) — A1710

No. 4461: a, 200fo, Bluebeard. b, 250fo, Judith.

2018, Mar. 2	Litho.	Perf. 12¼x11¼
4461	A1710	Pair, #a-b	2.95 2.95

Premiere of *Bluebeard's Castle*, cent. Printed in sheets containing two each Nos. 4461a-4461b.

17th Century Wedding Costumes — A1711

No. 4462: a, Man's dolman, denomination at UR. b, Women's skirt and bodice, denomination at UL.

2018, Apr. 3	Litho.		Perf. 12
4462	A1711	210fo Pair, #a-b	2.75 2.75

Printed in sheets containing two each Nos. 4462a-4462b.

Miniature Sheet

Roma Heroes of 1956 Uprising A1712

No. 4463: a, Gyula Dandos (1938-57), leader of Revolutionary Students' Council. b, István Fátyol (1934-2004), Terézváros group leader. c, Sándor Csányi (1929-59), freedom fighter. d, Mátyás Kolompár (1924-57), freedom fighter. e, György Cziffra (1921-94), pianist. f, Károly Strausz (1928-86), Soroksár freedom fighter. g, József Kóte Sörös (1927-59), freedom fighter. h, Gábor Dilinko (1929-2014), freedom fighter. i, Erszébet Hrozova (1938-2013), nurse for wounded freedom fighters. j, Ilona Szabó (c. 1939-56), freedom fighter.

2018, Apr. 5	Litho.		Perf. 14
4463	A1712	100fo Sheet of 10, #a-j	6.50 6.50

Hungarian Postal Service, 150th Anniv. Type of 2017

Designs: 20fo, Postbox, 1902. 40fo, Decorative crest, 1896. 50fo, Collar and button of clerk's uniform, c. 1900. 60fo, Balance scale and set of weights, 1910. 90fo, Motorized mail tricycle built by János Csonka, 1900. 500fo, Mail vehicle built by Csonka, 1905.

Die Cut Perf. 11½

2018, May 2		Typo.
Self-Adhesive		
4464	A1686	20fo multi	.30 .30
4465	A1686	40fo multi	.30 .30
4466	A1686	50fo multi	.30 .30
4467	A1686	60fo multi	.40 .40
4468	A1686	90fo multi	.60 .60
4469	A1686	500fo multi	3.25 3.25
	Nos. 4464-4469 (6)		5.15 5.15

Ferenc Dávid's Address to the 1568 Diet of Torda, by Aladar Körösfoi-Kreisch (1863-1920) — A1713

2018, May 2	Litho.		Perf. 12
4470	A1713	450fo multi	2.90 2.90

Diet of Torda, 450th anniv.

Europa A1714

No. 4471: a, Megyeri Bridge. b, Köröshegy Valley Bridge.

2018, May 2	Litho.		Perf. 12
4471	A1714	345fo Pair, #a-b	5.00 5.00

Printed in sheets containing two each Nos. 4471a-4471b.

Souvenir Sheet

Lavandula Angustifolia — A1715

2018, May 2	Litho.		Perf. 14
4472	A1715	1000fo multi	6.25 6.25

An example of No. 4472 with green serial numbers, an imperforate example with red serial numbers, and perforated and imperforate examples with lavender serial numbers and a scratch-and-sniff coating with a lavender scent were printed in limited quantities and sold in a set together with No. 4472 for 20,000fo.

Miniature Sheet

Messier Objects A1716

No. 4473: a, 155fo, Pleaides (M45). b, 155fo, Crab Nebula (M1). c, 155fo+75fo, Orion Nebula (M42). d, 155fo+75fo, Ring Nebula (M57).

2018, May 2	Litho.		Perf. 14
4473	A1716	Sheet of 4, #a-d	5.00 5.00

Surtax for youth philately.

Souvenir Sheet

Year of Families A1717

2018, May 24	Litho.		Perf. 12x12½
4474	A1717	500fo multi	3.25 3.25

2018 World Cup Soccer Championships, Russia — A1718

2018, May 25	Litho.		Perf. 14
4475	A1718	385fo multi	2.50 2.50

Items in Hungarian Museums A1719

Designs: 345fo, Portrait of Jósa András (1834-1918), by János Zahoray, sculpture of Hungarian Hussar, metal ornament, Jósa András Museum, Nyíregyháza. 415fo, Dyeing tub, textile pattern wood blocks, Museum of Blue Dyeing, Pápa.

2018, June 1	Litho.		Perf. 12
4476-4477	A1719	Set of 2	4.75 4.75

Nos. 4476 and 4477 were each printed in sheets of 4.

Cities — A1720

Designs: No. 4478, 200fo, Cultural Center and Library, Sárospatak. No. 4479, 200fo, Nádasdy Castle, Sárvár. No. 4480, 200fo, Water tower, Siófok.

2018, June 1	Litho.	Perf. 13¼x13
4478-4480	A1720	Set of 3	3.75 3.75

Souvenir Sheet

Sinking of the SMS Saint Stephen, Cent. A1721

2018, June 29	Litho.	Perf. 13¼x13
4481	A1721	800fo multi	6.00 6.00

Stamp Day — A1722

Attractions in Nagykörös: 120fo, János Arany Reformed Church Secondary Vocational School and College, statue of Bor-Kalán, by Imre Varga. 155fo, Postal Palace, Statue of Lajos Kossuth, vert. 500fo+300fo, Town Hall, vert.

2018, June 29	Litho.		Perf. 14
4482-4483	A1722	Set of 2	1.75 1.75

Souvenir Sheet
Litho., Sheet Margin Litho & Embossed
Perf. 13¼x13

4484	A1722	500fo +300fo multi	4.50 4.50

Pregnant Woman and Hands Being Washed — A1723

2018, June 30	Litho.		Perf. 14
4485	A1723	415fo multi	2.50 2.50

Ignaz Semmelweis (1818-65), obstetrician, gynecologist and proponent of antiseptic medical procedures.

Worldwide Fund for Nature (WWF) — A1724

Designs: 210fo, Ailuropoda melanoleuca. 320fo, Loxodonta africana. 330fo, Ursus maritimus. 485fo, Pongo pygmaeus.

2018, July 2		Perf. 14½
4486-4489	A1724	Set of 4	8.50 8.50

Souvenir Sheet

Hungarian State Railways, 150th Anniv. — A1725

No. 4490: a, H-START 5341 060-2. b, H-START 415 062.

2018, July 6	Litho.	Perf. 13x13¼
4490	A1725	250fo Sheet of 2, #a-b	4.75 4.75

Souvenir Sheet

Hungarian Saints — A1726

No. 4491: a, St. Andrew Zorard (Szent Zoerard András, c. 980-c. 1009). b, St. Benedict of Szkalka (Szent Benedek, c. 10th cent. -c. 1012). c, St. Maurus of Pécs (Boldog Mór, c. 1000-c. 1075).

2018, Aug. 1	Litho.		Perf. 12
4491	A1726	300fo Sheet of 3, #a-c	6.50 6.50
d.		As #4491, litho. on reflective paper	6.50 6.50

A lithographed black monocolor sheet of type A1726 that was not valid for postage was sold together with Nos 4491 and 4491d in a package costing 3990fo.

Miniature Sheet

Castles A1727

No. 4492: a, Bishop's Castle, Sümeg. b, Széczenyi Castle, Nagycenk. c, Károlyi Castle, Fehérvárcsurgó. d, Sándor-Metternich Castle, Bajna. e, Festetics Castle, Dég. f, Esterházy Castle, Tata. g, Kamalduli Hermitage, Majk. h, Károlyi Castle, Füzérradvány.

2018, Sept. 3	Litho.	Perf. 13x13¼
4492	A1727	155fo Sheet of 8, #a-h	8.00 8.00

HUNGARY

Miniature Sheet

Dinosaurs — A1728

No. 4493: a, Ajkaceratops kozmai. b, Pneumatoraptor fodori. c, Bakonydraco galaczi. d, Hungarosaurus tormai. e, Iharkutosuchus makadii. f, Pannoniasaurus inexpectatus.

2018, Sept. 3   Litho.   Perf. 14
4493 A1728 120fo Sheet of 6, #a-f   4.75 4.75

Agriculture and Food Science Faculty of István Széchenyi University, Mosonmagyaróvár, Bicent. — A1729

2018, Oct. 2   Litho.   Perf. 14
4494 A1729 530fo multi   3.50 3.50

Miniature Sheet

Heroes of World War I — A1730

No. 4495: a, Baron Sándor Szurmay. b, Dr. Lajos Ördögh. c, Baron Sándor Proff. d, János Cucor. e, Béla Fábry. f, Károly Kratochwill. g, Frigyes Scheip. h, Tamás Prigl. i, Olivér Perczel. j, Tibor Kemény.

2018, Oct. 25   Litho.   Perf. 12x12½
4495 A1730 60fo Sheet of 10, #a-j   4.25 4.25

Christmas — A1731

Die Cut Perf. 11½
2018, Nov. 5   Typo.
Self-Adhesive
White Snowflakes
4496 A1731 (120fo) multi   .85 .85
Silver Snowflakes
4497 A1731 (120fo) multi   .85 .85

New Year 2019 (Year of the Pig) — A1732

No. 4498: a, White pig. b, Red pig.

2019, Jan. 25   Litho.   Perf. 12
4498 A1732 435fo Pair, #a-b   5.25 5.25

Printed in sheets containing two each Nos. 4498a-4498b.

Mohandas K. Gandhi (1869-1948), Indian Nationalist Leader — A1733

2019, Feb. 21   Litho.   Perf. 12x12½
4499 A1733 370fo multi   2.40 2.40

Printed in sheets of 4.

The Resurrection, by El Greco (1541-1614) — A1734

Die Cut Perf. 11½
2019, Mar. 11   Typo.
Self-Adhesive
4500 A1734 (120fo) multi   .75 .75
Easter.

Sir Edmund Hillary (1919-2008), and Tenzing Norgay (1914-86), First Men to Ascend Mount Everest — A1735

2019, Mar. 11   Litho.   Perf. 14
4501 A1735 445fo multi   2.75 2.75

Film Actors — A1736

Designs: 335fo, Ferenc Bessenyei (1919-2004). 350fo, Juci Komlós (1919-2011). 400fo, Miklós Gábor (1919-98).

2019, Mar. 11   Litho.   Perf. 14
4502-4504 A1736 Set of 3   6.50 6.50

Souvenir Sheet

Renovation of Romanesque Hall of the Museum of Fine Arts, Budapest — A1737

2019, Mar. 11   Litho.   Perf. 13½x13
4505 A1737 800fo multi   5.00 5.00

Imperforate examples of No. 4505 with red serial numbers were printed in limited quantities.

Experimental Color Television Transmissions, 50th Anniv. — A1738

2019, Apr. 5   Litho.   Perf. 14
4506 A1738 375fo multi   2.25 2.25

Captain Nemo, Character from Novels by Jules Verne (1828-1905) — A1739

No. 4507: a, 120fo, The Nautilus. b, 120fo, Three divers at shipwreck. c, 120fo+75fo, Ship. d, 120fo+75fo, Marine life.

2019, Apr. 5   Litho.   Perf. 14
4507 A1739 Block of 4, #a-d   4.00 4.00

Surtax for youth philately.

Loránd Eötvös (1848-1919), Physicist — A1740

2019, Apr. 8   Litho.   Perf. 14
4508 A1740 475fo multi   3.00 3.00

Hungarian Postal Service, 150th Anniv. Type of 2017

Designs: 70fo, String holder, 1920. 80fo, Horse blanket, 1920. 400fo, Parcel scale, 1940. 600fo, Stamp vending machines, 1910. 700fo, Scout postbox, 1933. 1000fo, Rába AF bus, 1929-34.

Die Cut Perf. 11½
2019, May 9   Typo.
Self-Adhesive
4509 A1686 70fo multi   .45 .45
4510 A1686 80fo multi   .50 .50
4511 A1686 400fo multi   2.40 2.40
4512 A1686 600fo multi   3.75 3.75
4513 A1686 700fo multi   4.50 4.50
4514 A1686 1000fo multi   6.00 6.00
Nos. 4509-4514 (6)   17.60 17.60

Europa A1741

No. 4515: a, Ardea alba. b, Ciconia ciconia.

2019, May 9   Litho.   Perf. 12
4515 A1741 400fo Pair #a-b   5.25 5.25

Printed in sheets containing two each Nos. 4515a-4515b.

Cities — A1742

Designs: No. 4516, 215fo, Church of St. Anne and statue by Pál Pátzay, Kapuvár. No. 4517, 215fo, Zsigmond Szentpétery Cultural Center and Theater and Fountain by Lajos Biró, Mátészalka,

2019, May 9   Litho.   Perf. 13¼x13
4516-4517 A1742 Set of 2   2.75 2.75

Miniature Sheet

Zrínyi 2026 Defense and Army Development Program — A1743

No. 4518: a, Airbus A319. b, Jet fighters. c, Mi-24 helicopter. d, MRZR 4 personnel transport. e, Guns. f, Ships.

2019, May 9   Litho.   Perf. 11¼x12¼
4518 A1743 120fo Sheet of 6, #a-f   5.00 5.00

Souvenir Sheet

First Postal Cards, 150th Anniv. A1744

No. 4519: a, Postal card with Poprad postmark and Locse receiving mark. b, Postal card with Buda postmark.

2019, May 9   Litho.   Perf. 13x12¾
4519 A1744 500fo Sheet of 2, #a-b   6.25 6.25

Mihály Gervay (1819-96), first postmaster general of Hungarian postal service.

Hungarian Royal Geological Institute, 150th Anniv. — A1745

2019, June 3   Litho.   Perf. 13¼x13
4520 A1745 235fo multi   1.50 1.50

Dmitri Mendeleev (1834-1907), Formulator of Periodic Table of Elements A1746

2019, June 3   Litho.   Perf. 14
4521 A1746 510fo multi   3.25 3.25

Periodic Table, 150th anniv.

2019 Canoe Sprint World Championships, Szeged — A1747

2019, June 3   Litho.   Perf. 14
4522 A1747 545fo multi   3.50 3.50

Souvenir Sheet

Hungarian Parliament in Inter-Parliamentary Union, 130th Anniv. — A1748

No. 4523: a, Hungarian Parliament Building (Országház). b, Headquarters of Inter-Parliamentary Union, Geneva.

2019, June 4   Litho.   Perf. 14
4523 A1748 300fo Sheet of 2, #a-b   4.00 4.00

2019 Modern Pentathlon World Championships, Budapest — A1749

2019, July 8   Litho.   Perf. 14
4524 A1749 470fo multi   3.00 3.00

Souvenir Sheet

First Man on the Moon, 50th Anniv. A1750

2019, July 8   Litho.   Perf. 14
4525 A1750 550fo multi   3.50 3.50

HUNGARY

Miniature Sheet

Working Dogs — A1751

No. 4526: a, German shepherd narcotics detection dog named Kuruc. b, German shepherd rescue dog named Mancs. c, Hungarian viszla arson detection dog named Szikra. d, Wire-haired fox terrier explosives detection dog named Zeusz.

2019, July 8	Litho.		Perf. 12
4526	A1751	215fo Sheet of 4, #a-d	6.00 6.00

Souvenir Sheet

Silver Items From Sevso Treasure — A1752

No. 4527: a, Achilles Plate and amphora (30x45mm). b, Hippolytus Set (ewer and buckets), Meleager Plate (60x50mm). c, Animal ewer (30x45mm).

Litho. & Embossed With Foil Application

2019, July 8			Perf. 12
4527	A1752	1000fo Sheet of 3, #a-c	19.00 19.00

Souvenir Sheet

Martyrs of Kassa — A1753

No. 4528: a, St. Melchior (Menyhért) Grodziecki (c. 1584-1619). b, St. Marko Krizan (1588-1619). c, St. István Pongrácz (1582-1619).

2019, Aug. 1	Litho.		Perf. 11½x12
4528	A1753	300fo Sheet of 3, #a-c	6.25 6.25

Miniature Sheet

Castles A1754

No. 4529: a, Sirok Castle, Sirok. b, Kinizsi Castle, Nagyvázsony. c, Eger Castle, Eger. d, Szigetvár Castle, Szigetvár. e, Rákóczi Castle, Sárospatak. f, Pipó Castle, Ozora. g, Visegrád Castle, Visegrád. h, Csesznek Castle, Csesznek.

2019, Sept. 2	Litho.		Perf. 13x13½
4529	A1754	120fo Sheet of 8, #a-h	6.00 6.00

Souvenir Sheet

Characters From *Süsü the Dragon* Children's Television Show — A1755

No. 4530: a, Chancellor and Nurse. b, Süsü, vert. c, Prince and princesses.

Perf. 13x13¼, 13¼x13

2019, Sept. 2			Litho.
4530	A1755	200fo Sheet of 3, #a-c	4.00 4.00

Stamp Day — A1756

Designs: 120fo, László Csány (1790-1849), Minister of Public Works and Transport, and János Jeszenák (1800-49), politician. 160fo, Zsigmond Perényi (1783-1849), politician, and Imre Szacsvay (1818-49), politician. 500fo+300fo, Lajos Batthyány (1807-49), Prime Minister.

2019, Oct. 4	Litho.		Perf. 14
4531-4532	A1756	Set of 2	1.80 1.80

Souvenir Sheet

| 4533 | A1756 | 500fo +300fo multi | 4.75 4.75 |

Martyrs of the 1848-49 Hungarian Revolution and War of Independence.

Souvenir Sheet

2019 Budapest Water Summit — A1757

2019, Oct. 7	Litho.		Perf. 12
4534	A1757	400fo multi	2.50 2.50

Miniature Sheet

Diplomatic Relations Between Hungary and Japan, 150th Anniv. — A1758

No. 4535: a, Hungarian Parliament Building. b, Mount Fuji. c, White and yellow chamomile flowers. d, Pink and white cherry blossoms. e, Hungarian woman in traditional costume of Kalocsa. f, Japanese woman wearing kimono. g, Pot of Hungarian goulash. h, Sushi. i, Puli (black dog). j, Akita (white and brown dog).

2019, Oct. 15	Litho.		Perf. 13¼x13
4535	A1758	60fo Sheet of 10, #a-j	4.25 4.25

See Japan No. 4347.

Christmas — A1759

Die Cut Perf. 11½

2019, Nov. 5			Typo.
		Color of Star	
4536	A1759	(120fo) olive green	.80 .80
4537	A1759	(120fo) gold	.80 .80

Miniature Sheet

Freedom From Communist Rule, 30th Anniv. — A1760

No. 4538: a, Dénes Csengey (1953-91), writer. b, Sándor Csoóri (1930-2016), poet. c, István Csurka (1934-2012), poet. d, Gábor Karátson (1935-2015), painter. e, Dr. György Krassó (1932-91), journalist. f, András Süto (1927-2006), writer. g, Dr. György Szabad (1924-2015), historian. h, Kata Beke (1936-2009), writer.

2019, Dec. 16	Litho.		Perf. 14
4538	A1760	90fo Sheet of 8, #a-h	5.00 5.00

34th European Water Polo Championships, Budapest — A1761

2020, Jan. 10	Litho.		Perf. 14
4539	A1761	500fo multi	3.25 3.25

Miniature Sheet

New Year 2020 (Year of the Rat) A1762

No. 4540: a, Head of rat, white background. b, Rat, red background.

2020, Feb. 6	Litho.		Perf. 12
4540	A1762	400fo Sheet of 4, 2 each #a-b	10.50 10.50

Nos. 4540a and 4540b are tete-beche within the sheet.

Clothing of the Hungarian Nobility — A1763

No. 4541: a, Man's lambskin-trimmed coat and embroidered trousers. b, Women's silk dress.

2020, Feb. 12	Litho.		Perf. 14
4541	A1763	300fo Pair, #a-b	4.00 4.00

Printed in sheets containing two each Nos. 4541a-4541b.

Easter — A1764

Die Cut Perf. 11½

2020, Mar. 4			Typo.
		Self-Adhesive	
4542	A1764	(135fo) multi	.85 .85

Circumnavigation by Ferdinand Magellan's Expedition, 500th Anniv. — A1765

2020, Mar. 4	Litho.		Perf. 14
4543	A1765	405fo multi	2.60 2.60

Ludwig van Beethoven (1770-1827), Composer — A1766

2020, Mar. 4	Litho.		Perf. 14
4544	A1766	520fo multi	3.25 3.25

Miniature Sheet

Prehistoric Animals — A1767

No. 4545: a, Hungarobatrachus szukacsi. b, Mochlodon vorosi. c, Bauxitornis mindszentyae. d, Atractosteus. e, Foxemys trabanti. f, Doratodon carcharidens.

2020, Mar. 4	Litho.		Perf. 12
4545	A1767	200fo Sheet of 6, #a-f	7.75 7.75

Ferenc Zenthe (1920-2006), Actor — A1768

2020, Apr. 2	Litho.		Perf. 14
4546	A1768	385fo multi	2.25 2.25

HUGARY

Miklós Zrínyi (1620-64), Ban of Croatia and Writer — A1769

2020, Apr. 2 Litho. *Perf. 14*
4547 A1769 390fo multi 2.40 2.40

Hungarian Postal Service, 150th Anniv. Type of 2017

Designs: 25fo, Postcode guides, 1973. 225fo, Mail bag, 1975. 350fo, Postal worker's cap, 1983. 450fo, Rural letterboxes, 1971. 800fo, Stamp vending machine, 1962. 900fo, 1970 Robur mail van.

Die Cut Perf. 11½
2020, May 4 Typo.
Self-Adhesive
4548	A1686	25fo multi	.30	.30
4549	A1686	225fo multi	1.50	1.50
4550	A1686	350fo multi	2.25	2.25
4551	A1686	450fo multi	3.00	3.00
4552	A1686	800fo multi	5.25	5.25
4553	A1686	900fo multi	5.75	5.75
Nos. 4548-4553 (6)			18.05	18.05

Hungarian Meterological Service, 150th Anniv. — A1770

2020, May 4 Litho. *Perf. 14*
4554 A1770 515fo multi 3.25 3.25

Count Ödön Széchenyo (1839-1922), Commander of Budapest Fire Brigade, and 1864 Fire Fighting Manual A1771

St. Florian (250-304), Patron Saint of Firefighters, and 1871 Fire Training Exercise A1772

2020, May 4 Litho. *Perf. 14*
4555 A1771 125fo multi .70 .70
4556 A1772 135fo multi .80 .80

Europa A1773

No. 4557: a, The Butcher's Post Progressing Through Hungary in 1680, brass sign to summon meetings of butchers, denomination in brown red. b, Diligence Crossing the Hortobágy Plain, horn, denomination in deep green.

2020, May 4 Litho. *Perf. 11½x12*
4557 A1773 650fo Pair, #a-b 8.00 8.00

Printed in sheets containing two each Nos. 4557a-4557b.

Souvenir Sheet

St. John Paul II (1920-2005) — A1774

2020, May 4 Litho. *Perf. 14*
4558 A1774 1500fo multi 9.75 9.75

Zugliget Chairlift, Budapest, 50th Anniv. — A1775

2020, May 11 Litho. *Perf. 14*
4559 A1775 540fo multi 3.50 3.50

Buda Castle Funicular, 150th Anniv. — A1776

2020, May 11 Litho. *Perf. 14*
4560 A1776 590fo multi 3.75 3.75

Miniature Sheet

First Hungarian in Space, 40th Anniv. — A1777

No. 4561: a, 135fo, Yuri Gagarin Cosmonaut Training Center, Star City, Russia. b, 135fo, Cosmonaut and Soyuz 35 capsule. c, 135fo+75fo, Launch of Soyuz 36. d, 135fo+75fo, Salyut 6 Space Station in orbit.

2020, June 3 Litho. *Perf. 14*
4561 A1777 Sheet of 4, #a-d 4.50 4.50

Buildings A1778

Designs: 275fo, District Court Building, Dombóvár. 435fo, Kisvárda Castle, Kisvárda. 570fo, Church of St. Stephen, Százhalombatta.

2020, July 6 Litho. *Perf. 13¼x13*
4562-4564 A1778 Set of 3 8.00 8.00

Flora and Fauna — A1779

No. 4565: a, Trypocopris vernalis. b, Echinacea purpurea. c, Acer tataricum. d, Sander lucioperca.

2020, Aug. 5 Litho. *Perf. 14*
4565 Horiz. strip of 4 4.75 4.75
a.-d. A1779 185fo Any single 1.20 1.20

Souvenir Sheet

Record With Emblem of Rock Band, Omega A1780

2020, Aug. 5 Litho. *Perf.*
4566 A1780 800fo multi 5.00 5.00

Souvenir Sheet

Famous Religious Figures Named Elizabeth A1781

No. 4567: a, Blessed Elizabeth the Widow (c. 1255-c. 1320). b, St. Elizabeth of Portugal (1271-1336). c, Blessed Elizabeth of Hungary (c. 1292-c. 1338).

2020, Aug. 5 Litho. *Perf. 12*
4567 A1781 400fo Sheet of 3, #a-c 7.50 7.50

Souvenir Sheet

Year of National Unity A1782

2020, Sept. 29 Litho. *Perf. 14*
4568 A1782 1000fo multi 6.25 6.25

Lacquered lines running along contoured lines of vaulted dome.

Stamp Day — A1783

Designs: 135fo, Various essays for Hungarian stamps created by Ferenc Helbing (1870-1958). 185fo, Different essays. 500fo+300fo, Helbing.

2020, Oct. 9 Litho. *Perf. 14*
4569-4570 A1783 Set of 2 2.00 2.00
Souvenir Sheet
4571 A1783 500fo +300fo multi 5.00 5.00

Surtax on No. 4571 for organized philately.

Souvenir Sheet

Hungarian Olympic Committee, 125th Anniv. — A1784

2020, Oct. 9 Litho. *Perf. 14*
4572 A1784 710fo multi 4.50 4.50

Miniature Sheet

Castles A1785

No. 4573: a, Tisza Castle, Geszt. b, Forgách-Lipthay Castle, Szécsény. c, Festetics Castle, Keszthely. d, Zichy Castle, Várpalota.

e, Wenckheim Castle, Szabadkígyós. f, Becsky-Kossuth Mansion, Komlódtótfalu. g, Nádasdy Castle, Nádasdladány. h, Andrássy Castle, Tiszadob.

2020, Oct. 9 Litho. *Perf. 13x13¼*
4573 A1785 100fo Sheet of 8, #a-h 5.25 5.25

Diplomatic Relations Between Hungary and Singapore, 50th Anniv. — A1786

No. 4574: a, Széczenyi Chain Bridge, Budapest. b, Cavenagh Bridge, Singapore.

2020, Oct. 22 Litho. *Perf. 14*
4574 A1786 300fo Sheet of 2, #a-b 3.75 3.75

See Singapore Nos. 2045-2046.

Madonna and Sleeping Child, by Giovanni Battista Salvi (1609-85) — A1787

Die Cut Perf. 11½
2020, Oct. 22 Typo.
Self-Adhesive
4575 A1787 (135fo) multi .85 .85
With Lacquer Lines Added along Edges of Virgin and Child
4576 A1787 (135fo) multi .85 .85

Souvenir Sheet

Characters from Animated Cartoon, *Frakk, the Cat's Nightmare* — A1788

No. 4577: a, Uncle Charles and Aunt Irma. b, Frakk in dog house, vert. c, Cats Lucretia and Serena, vert.

Perf. 13x13¼ (#4577a), 14 (#4577b, 4577c)
2020, Nov. 4 Litho.
4577 A1788 200fo Sheet of 3, #a-c 3.75 3.75

Souvenir Sheet

Puskás Arena, Budapest, 1st Anniv. — A1789

2020, Nov. 20 Litho. *Perf. 14*
4578 A1789 800fo multi 5.00 5.00

Miniature Sheet

Free Elections in Hungary, 30th Anniv. A1790

No. 4579: a, Dr. József Antall (1932-93), Prime Minister. b, Dr. István Balsai (1947-2020), Minister of Justice. c, Hungarian Parliament chamber. d, Dr. Lajos Für (1930-2013), Minister of Defense. e, Jeno Gerbovits (1925-2011), Minister of Compensation. f, Sándor Gyoriványi (1927-2007), Minister of Labor. g,

HUNGARY

Dr. Balázs Horváth (1942-2006), Interior Minister. h, Dr. Ferenc Mádl (1931-2011), Minister of Education and second President. i, Ferenc József Nagy (1923-2019), Minister of Agriculture. j, Ferenc Rabár (1929-99), Minister of Finance.

2020, Dec. 16   Litho.   Perf. 14
4579 A1790 90fo Sheet of 10, #a-j   6.00 6.00

New Year 2021 (Year of the Ox) — A1791

No. 4580: a, White ox. b, Yellow ox.

2021, Feb. 8   Litho.   Perf. 14
4580 A1791 390fo Pair, #a-b   5.25 5.25

Printed in sheets containing two each Nos. 4580a-4580b.

St. Norbert of Xanten (c. 1075-1134), Founder of Premonstratensian Order of Canons Regular — A1792

2021, Feb. 10   Litho.   Perf. 12¼
4581 A1792 500fo multi   3.25 3.25

Canons Regular of Prémontré, 900th anniv.

Visegrád Group, 30th Anniv. — A1793

2021, Feb. 15   Litho.   Perf. 13x13¼
4582 A1793 600fo multi   3.75 3.75

See Czech Republic No. 3860, Poland No. 4528, and Slovakia No. 870.

Risen Christ, by Alvaro Pirez (c. 1411-c. 1434) — A1794

Die Cut Perf. 11½
2021, Mar. 8   Typo.
Self-Adhesive
4583 A1794 (145fo) multi   .85 .85

Easter.

Dominican Order in Hungary, 800th Anniv. — A1795

2021, Mar. 8   Litho.   Perf. 14
4584 A1795 540fo multi   3.50 3.50

József Romhányi (1921-83), Writer — A1796

2021, Mar. 8   Litho.   Perf. 14
4585 A1796 430fo multi   2.75 2.75

Rhinoceros, Woodcut by Albrecht Dürer (1471-1528) A1797

2021, Mar. 8   Litho.   Perf. 13¼x13
4586 A1797 660fo multi   4.25 4.25

Miniature Sheet

Fables by Jean de La Fontaine (1621-95) — A1798

No. 4587: a, 145fo, The Two Bulls and the Frog. b, 145fo, The Ant and the Grasshopper. c, 145fo+75fo, The Town Mouse and the Country Mouse. d, 145fo+75fo, The Wolf and the Stork.

2021, Mar. 8   Litho.   Perf. 13x13¼
4587 A1798 Sheet of 4, #a-d   4.75 4.75

Surtax for youth philately.

2021 European Aquatics Championships, Budapest A1799

2021, Mar. 29   Litho.   Perf. 14
4588 A1799 185fo multi   1.20 1.20

Miklós Jancsó (1921-2014), Film Director and Screenwriter A1800

2021, Apr. 8   Litho.   Perf. 14
4589 A1800 685fo multi   4.25 4.25

Electrically-Assisted Postal Bicycle, 2019 — A1801

Electric Three-Wheeled Delivery Vehicle, 2018 — A1802

Mail Truck, 2019 A1803

Mailbox, 2004 A1804

Die Cut Perf. 11½
2021, May 5   Typo.
Self-Adhesive
4590 A1801 (145fo) multi   .95 .95
4591 A1802 (200fo) multi   1.25 1.25
4592 A1803 (570fo) multi   3.50 3.50
4593 A1804 (660fo) multi   4.25 4.25
    Nos. 4590-4593 (4)   9.95 9.95

Hungarian Postal Service, 150th anniv.

Endangered Animals — A1805

No. 4594: a, Saxicola rubicola. b, Mustela eversmanii.

2021, May 5   Litho.   Perf. 12
4594 A1805 715fo Vert. pair, #a-b   9.00 9.00

Europa. No. 4594 was printed in sheets containing two pairs.

Souvenir Sheet

Bombus Terrestris Pollinating Flower — A1806

2021, May 5   Litho.   Perf. 14
4595 A1806 1000fo multi   6.25 6.25

Hungarian Chairmanship of the European Council — A1807

2021, May 18   Litho.   Perf. 14
4596 A1807 570fo multi   3.75 3.75

A1808

Stamp Day A1809

Designs: 145fo, Hungary #2226. 200fo, Hungary #2227. 500fo+300fo, Headquarters of the National Federation of Hungarian Philatelists, Budapest.

2021, May 28   Litho.   Perf. 14
4597-4598 A1808 Set of 2   2.20 2.20
Souvenir Sheet
4599 A1809 500fo +300fo multi   5.00 5.00

Souvenir Sheet

First Hungarian Stamps, 150th Anniv. — A1810

No. 4600: a, Hungary #5. b, Hungary #11.

2021, May 28   Litho.   Perf. 12¾x13
4600 A1810 950fo Sheet of 2, #a-b   12.00 12.00

Souvenir Sheet

Puskás Arena, Budapest — A1811

2021, June 4   Litho.   Perf. 13x13¼
4601 A1811 800fo multi   7.00 7.00

2020 European Soccer Championships. The championships were postponed until 2021 because of the COVID-19 pandemic.

Souvenir Sheet

Swimmer A1812

2021, June 4   Litho.   Perf. 13x13¼
4602 A1812 780fo multi   5.00 5.00

2020 Summer Olympics, Tokyo. The Olympics were postponed until 2021 because of the COVID-19 pandemic.

Completion of Renovations to Rákóczi Palace, Borsa, Slovakia — A1813

2021, June 19   Litho.   Perf. 14
4603 A1813 570fo multi   3.50 3.50

Buildings A1814

Designs: No. 4604, 195fo, Round Church, Balatonfüred. No. 4605, 195fo, Premonstratensian Abbey, Csorna. No. 4606, 195fo, City Hall, Gyor. No. 4607, 195fo, Sports Hall, Nagyatád.

2021, July 5   Litho.   Perf. 13¼x13
4604-4607 A1814 Set of 4   5.00 5.00

Souvenir Sheet

Lokomotiv GT, Rock Band, 50th Anniv. — A1815

2021, July 5   Litho.   Perf.
4608 A1815 800fo multi   5.00 5.00

Souvenir Sheet

Firewatch Tower, Sopron — A1816

2021, July 5   Litho.   Perf. 14
4609 A1816 1000fo multi   6.25 6.25

Plebiscite of Sopron to decide whether to remain in Hungary, cent.

HUNGARY

2021 European Four-in-Hand Horse Driving Championships, Budapest — A1817

2021, Aug. 4   Litho.   Perf. 14
4610   A1817   445fo   multi   3.00   3.00

Souvenir Sheet

52nd International Eucharistic Congress, Budapest — A1818

2021, Sept. 1   Litho.   Perf. 14
4611   A1818   900fo   multi   5.75   5.75

Miniature Sheet

Castles — A1819

No. 4612: a, Diósgyor Castle, Miskolc. b, Sümeg Castle, Sümeg. c, Szád Castle, Szögliget. d, Kisvárda Castle, Kisvárda. e, City wall and museum quarter, Sopron. f, Mosonmagyaróvár Castle, Mosonmagyaróvár. g, Somló Castle, Doba. h, Füzér Castle, Füzér.

2021, Sept. 2   Litho.   Perf. 13x13¼
4612   A1819   200fo Sheet of 8, #a-h   10.00   10.00

Souvenir Sheet

Kukori and Kotkoda, Television Cartoon Series — A1820

No. 4613: a, Hápogi the Duck. b, Kotkoda the Hen. c, Kukori the Rooster.

2021, Sept. 2   Litho.   Perf. 14
4613   A1820   200fo Sheet of 3, #a-c   3.75   3.75

János Pilinszky (1921-81), Poet — A1821

2021, Sept. 14   Litho.   Perf. 14
4614   A1821   485fo   multi   3.00   3.00

A1822

One With Nature World Hunting and Nature Exhibition, Budapest — A1823

No. 4615: a, Ovis aries. b, Sus scrofa. c, Anas platyrhynchos. d, Lepus europaeus, Perdix perdix and Phasianus colchicus. e, Dama dama. f, Cervus elaphus. g, Capreolus capreolus. h, Hungarian wirehaired viszla.

1500fo, Zsigmond Széczenyi (1898-1967), hunter, Kálmán Kittenberger (1881-1958), biologist, and István Fekete (1900-70), writer.

2021, Sept. 25   Litho.   Perf. 14
4615   A1822   Block of 8   16.00   16.00
   a.-b.   145fo Either single   .95   .95
   c.-d.   200fo Either single   1.30   1.30
   e.-f.   425fo Either single   2.75   2.75
   g.-h.   460fo Either single   3.00   3.00

Souvenir Sheet
Perf. 13x13¼
4616   A1823   1500fo   multi   9.25   9.25

Evergreen Branches and Cone — A1824

Die Cut Perf. 11½
2021, Oct. 25   Typo.   Self-Adhesive
4617   A1824   (145fo) multi   .95   .95

With Gold Snowflakes Printed Over Evergreen Branches
4618   A1824   (145fo) multi   .95   .95

Christmas. No. 4618 was printed in strips of 5 + etiquette and has a scratch-and-sniff coating with a pine scent.

Souvenir Sheet

Planet Budapest 2021 Sustainability Expo and Summit, Budapest — A1825

2021, Nov. 8   Litho.   Perf. 12½
4619   A1825   500fo   multi   3.25   3.25

Souvenir Sheet

Crown of St. Stephen — A1826

2022, Jan. 10   Litho.   Perf. 14
4620   A1826   2010fo multi   11.00   11.00
   a.   Imperforate   13.00   13.00

Enactment of new Fundamental Law for Hungary, 10th anniv. No. 4620a has red serial numbers.

Souvenir Sheet

New Year 2022 (Year of the Tiger) — A1827

2022, Jan. 25   Litho.   Perf. 12x11½
4621   A1827   780fo Sheet of 2 #4621a   8.50   8.50
   a.   Single stamp   4.25   4.25

Souvenir Sheet

2022 Winter Olympics, Beijing — A1828

2022, Feb. 4   Litho.   Perf. 14
4622   A1828   1000fo black & blue   5.50   5.50

Arpád Göncz (1922-2015), President of Hungary — A1829

2022, Feb. 10   Litho.   Perf. 14
4623   A1829   430fo   multi   2.30   2.30

Hunfilex 2022 World Stamp Championships, Budapest — A1830

No. 4624 — Fisherman's Bastion, Budapest at: a, Right (denomination at UR). b, Left (denomination at UL).

2022, Mar. 4   Litho.   Perf. 13½
4624   A1830   325fo Horiz. pair, #a-b   3.50   3.50

Miniature Sheet

Illustrations of John the Valiant, by Almos Jaschik — A1831

No. 4625: a, 145fo, John on flying horse. b, 145fo, John on horse on cliff looking at fairies. c, 145fo+75fo, John as shepherd boy. d, 145fo+75fo, John on shoulder of giant.

2022, Mar. 4   Litho.   Perf. 13½
4625   A1831   Sheet of 4, #a-d   4.00   4.00

Sándor Petofi (1823-49), writer of poem "John the Valiant."

Miniature Sheet

Museum of Ethnography, Budapest, 150th Anniv. — A1832

No. 4626: a, Chest with flower decoration and 1872 date. b, Guild jar. c, Earthenware canteen. d, Chest with tulip decoration.

2022, Mar. 4   Litho.   Perf. 12½x12
4626   A1832   200fo Sheet of 4. #a-d   4.50   4.50

Easter — A1833

Die Cut Perf. 11½
2022, Mar. 11   Typo.   Self-Adhesive
4627   A1833   (145fo) multi   .75   .75

Conversion of St. Ignatius of Loyola (1491-1556), 500th Anniv. — A1834

2022, Mar. 11   Litho.   Perf. 14
4628   A1834   685fo   multi   3.75   3.75

Souvenir Sheet

Discovery of the Tomb of King Tutankhamun, Cent. — A1835

2022, Mar. 11   Litho.   Perf. 12
4629   A1835   900fo   multi   5.00   5.00

A1836

Stamp Day — A1837

No. 4630 — Stamps designed by József Vertel (1922-93): a, 145fo, Hungary #1058, B220-B221, and #862 in altered colors. b, 200fo, Hungary #3253, B222-B223, B316c. 550fo+300fo, Vertel designing stamp.

2022, Mar. 31   Litho.   Perf. 14
4630   A1836   Horiz. pair, #a-b   1.70   1.70

Souvenir Sheet
Perf. 13½x13
4631   A1837   550fo +300fo multi   4.25   4.25

Surtax on No. 4631 for supporting organized stamp collecting in Hungary.

Souvenir Sheet

Emblem of National Federation of Hungarian Philatelists — A1838

2022, Mar. 31   Litho.   Perf.
4632   A1838   1600fo multi   8.00   8.00

Hunphilex 2022 World Stamp Championships, Budapest, and National Federation of Hungarian Philatelists, cent.

Roald Amundsen (1872-1928), Polar Explorer — A1839

2022, Apr. 1   Litho.   Perf. 14
4633   A1839   570fo   multi   2.75   2.75

HUNGARY

Louis Pasteur (1822-95), Microbiologist — A1840

2022, Apr. 1		Litho.		Perf. 14
4634	A1840	660fo multi	3.25	3.25

Hungarian Poultry Breeds — A1841

No. 4635: a, White Transylvanian naked-necked chickens. b, Speckled Transylvanian naked-necked chickens. c, Black Transylvanian naked-necked chickens.

2022, May 2		Litho.		Perf. 14
4635	A1841	305fo Strip of 3, #a-c	4.75	4.75

Europa A1842

No. 4636 — The Legend of the White Horse: a, King Arpád on throne sending out emissaries with white horse. b, Prince Svatopluk receiving white horse in exchange for water, soil and grain.

2022, May 2		Litho.		Perf. 11
4636	A1842	715fo Horiz. pair, #a-b	6.50	6.50

Printed in sheets containing two pairs.

European Botanic Gardens Congress, Budapest A1843

Cypress Knees, National Botanic Garden of the Ecological Research Center, Vácrátót — A1844

Lotus Flowers, Botanical Garden of the University of Szeged, Füvészkert A1845

Amazonian Water Lily, Loránd Eötvös University Botanical Garden, Budapest A1846

Rhododendrons, Jeli Arborétum, Kám — A1847

2022, May 16		Litho.		Perf. 13x13¼
4637	A1843	330fo multi	1.60	1.60
4638		Horiz. strip of 4	6.50	6.50
a.		A1844 330fo multi	1.60	1.60
b.		A1845 330fo multi	1.60	1.60
c.		A1846 330fo multi	1.60	1.60
d.		A1847 330fo multi	1.60	1.60

Souvenir Sheet

S.M.S. Leitha Monitor, 150th Anniv. A1848

2022, May 17		Litho.		Perf. 12
4639	A1848	1150fo multi	5.75	5.75

Gyor-Sopron-Ebenfurt Railway, 150th Anniv. — A1849

2022, June 10		Litho.		Perf. 13x13¼
4640	A1849	715fo multi	3.50	3.50

Souvenir Sheet

Proclamation of the Golden Bull of King Andrew II, 800th Anniv. — A1850

No. 4641: a, Noblemen and obverse of golden pendant seal of bull depicting King Andrew II on throne. b, Andrew II: The Proclamation of the Golden Bull, fresco by Béla Kontuly (1904-83). c, Noblemen, horse, ship and reverse of golden pendant seal of bull depicting coat of arms of King Andrew II.

2022, June 24		Litho.		Perf. 12
4641	A1850	400fo Sheet of 3, #a-c	6.00	6.00

Gedeon Richter (1872-1944), Pharmacist, and his Pharmaceutical Factory, Budapest A1851

2022, July 1		Litho.		Perf. 13x13¼
4642	A1851	630fo multi	3.00	3.00

Count Menyhért Lónyay (1822-84), Prime Minister — A1852

2022, July 1		Litho.		Perf. 13¼x13
4643	A1852	780fo multi	3.75	3.75

Malert Airlines, Cent. — A1853

2022, Sept. 2		Litho.		Perf. 13¼x13
4644	A1853	795fo multi	4.00	4.00

Souvenir Sheet

Founding of Rock Band Lord, 50th Anniv. A1854

2022, Sept. 2		Litho.		Perf.
4645	A1854	1000fo multi	5.00	5.00

Souvenir Sheet

Characters From *Mazsola and Tádé* Animated Films — A1855

No. 4646: a, Mazsola the Pig and door of Pumpkin House. b, Manócska the Elf and window of Pumpkin House. c, Tádé the Guinea Pig.

2022, Sept. 2		Litho.		Perf. 12x12½
4646	A1855	200fo Sheet of 3, #a-c	2.75	2.75

Tibor Benedek (1972-2020), Water Polo Player and Coach — A1856

2022, Oct. 12		Litho.		Perf. 14
4647	A1856	640fo multi	3.25	3.25

Miniature Sheet

Coats of Arms of the Kings of the House of Arpád A1857

No. 4648 — Arms of: a, King Emeric (1174-1204), ruler from 1196-1204. b, King Andrew II (1177-1235), ruler from 1205-35. c, King Béla IV (1206-70), ruler from 1235-70. d, King Stephen V (1239-72), ruler from 1270-72. e, King Ladislaus IV (1262-90), ruler from 1272-90. f, King Andrew III (1265-1301), ruler from 1290-1301.

2022, Oct. 25		Litho.		Perf. 12½x12
4648	A1857	300fo Sheet of 6, #a-f	8.75	8.75

The Holy Night, Painting by Carlo Maratta (1625-1713) — A1858

Die Cut Perf. 11½

2022, Oct. 25 **Typo.**
Self-Adhesive
4649 A1858 (160fo) dull gold & multi   .80 .90

Typo. With Foil Application
4650 A1858 (160fo) bright gold & multi   .80 .90

Christmas.

Miniature Sheet

New Year 2023 (Year of the Rabbit) A1859

No. 4651 — Color of rabbit: a, White. b, Blue.

2023, Jan. 16		Litho.		Perf. 12½x12
4651	A1859	500fo Sheet of 4, 2 each #a-b	11.50	5.75

Nos. 4651a and 4651b are tete-beche within the sheet.

Souvenir Sheet

House of Music Hungary, Budapest, 1st Anniv. — A1860

2023, Jan. 23		Litho.		Perf.
4652	A1860	950fo multi	5.50	2.75

The Resurrection of Christ, by Bartolomé Esteban Murillo (1618-82) — A1861

Die Cut Perf. 11½
2023, Feb. 20 **Typo.**
Self-Adhesive
4653 A1861 (175fo) multi   1.00 .50

Easter.

Count Gyula Andrássy (1823-90), Prime Minister of Hungary — A1862

2023, Mar. 3		Litho.		Perf. 13¼x13
4654	A1862	525fo multi	3.00	1.50

Canonization of St. Thomas Aquinas (1225-74), 500th Anniv. — A1863

2023, Mar. 3		Litho.		Perf. 13¼x13
4655	A1863	715fo multi	4.25	2.10

Fruit and Their Blossoms — A1864

Fruit and blossoms of: 700fo, Bereczki quince. 810fo, Giant Badascony cherry.

2023, Mar. 3		Litho.		Perf. 14¼
4656-4657	A1864	Set of 2	8.75	4.50

Souvenir Sheet

P. Mobil Rock Band, 50th Anniv. A1865

2023, Mar. 3		Litho.		Perf.
4658	A1865	1050fo multi	6.00	3.00

Imperforate examples of No. 4658 with red serial numbers were printed in limited quantities.

HUNGARY

165

Captain James Cook (1728-79), and His Ship HMS Resolution — A1866

2023, Apr. 4   Litho.   Perf. 13x13¼
4659 A1866 720fo multi   4.25 2.10
First crossing of the Antarctic Circle, by Cook, 250th anniv.

White Hungarian Hen and Rooster — A1867

Speckled Hungarian Hen and Rooster — A1868

Yellow Hungarian Hen and Rooster — A1869

Partridge-Colored Hungarian Hen and Rooster — A1870

2023, Apr. 4   Litho.   Perf. 13x13¼
4660   Horiz. strip of 4   6.00 3.00
  a. A1867 250fo multi   1.50   .75
  b. A1868 250fo multi   1.50   .75
  c. A1869 250fo multi   1.50   .75
  d. A1870 250fo multi   1.50   .75

Miniature Sheet

Locomotives — A1871

No. 4661: a, 175fo, Front of steam locomotive. b, 175fo, Electric locomotive facing right. c, 175fo+75fo, Steam locomotive No. 2032. d, 175fo+75fo, Electric locomotive with pantograph facing left.

2023, Apr. 4   Litho.   Perf. 12
4661 A1871   Sheet of 4, #a-d   5.00 2.50
First Hungarian steam locomotive, 150th anniv.; first electric locomotives in Hungary, cent. Surtax for youth philately.

Mihály Csokonai Vitéz (1773-1805), Poet — A1872

2023, May 9   Litho.   Perf. 13x13¼
4662 A1872 545fo multi   3.25 1.60

19th Century Clothing A1873

No. 4663: a, Man's dolman, trousers and boots, 1840, and map of Sáros County. b, Woman's dress, 1845, Valero Silk Factory.

2023, May 9   Litho.   Perf. 12
4663 A1873 270fo Pair, #a-b   3.25 1.60
Printed in sheets containing two pairs.

Child Embracing Dove A1874

Interlocking Hands A1875

2023, May 9   Litho.   Perf. 12
4664   Sheet of 4, 2 each
             #a-b   21.00 10.50
  a. A1874 875fo multi   5.25 2.60
  b. A1875 875fo multi   5.25 2.60
Europa.

2023 World Track and Field Championships, Budapest A1876

2023, May 12   Litho.   Perf. 13x13¼
4665 A1876 960fo multi   5.50 2.75

Souvenir Sheet

TV Teddy, Puppet Character in *The Bedtime Story* Television Series — A1877

No. 4666 — TV Teddy: a, Brushing his teeth. b, With his doll. c, Asleep with his doll.

2023, June 8   Litho.   Perf. 12
4666 A1877 250fo Sheet of 3,
             #a-c   4.50 2.25

National Archives of Hungary, 300th Anniv. A1878

No. 4667: a, Text of Law 45 of 1723 establishing Archives, seal of Palatine Lajos Batthyány (1696-1765), half of wax impression of seal. b, Archives building, half of wax impression of seal.

2023, June 19   Litho.   Perf. 13¼x13
4667 A1878   Horiz. pair   7.25 3.75
  a. 525fo multi   3.00 1.50
  b. 715fo multi   4.25 2.10

Stamp Day — A1879

Tourist attractions of Tata: 175fo, Summer house of Count Miklós Esterházy (1775-1856) and its English Garden. 250fo, Exaltation of the Holy Cross parish church and Tata buildings. 550fo+300fo, Painting depicting Esterházy by Joseph Hickel (1736-1807) in Esterházy Palace, vert.

2023, June 30   Litho.   Perf. 13x13¼
4668-4669 A1879 Set of 2   2.50 1.25
Souvenir Sheet
Perf. 14
4670 A1879 550fo +300fo multi   5.00 5.00
Surtax on No. 4670 for National Federation of Hungarian Philatelists.

Map of Hungarian Postal Districts — A1880

Die Cut Perf. 11½
2023, July 7   Typo.
Self-Adhesive
4671 A1880 (210fo) multi   1.25   .60
Hungarian postal codes, 50th anniv.

Milk Chocolate Piece of Candy — A1881

Dark Chocolate Piece of Candy — A1882

2023, July 7   Typo.   Die Cut
Self-Adhesive
4672   Pair   3.50 1.75
  a. A1881 300fo multi   1.75   .85
  b. A1882 300fo multi   1.75   .85
Szerencs Chocolate Factory, cent.

A1883
A1884
A1885
A1886
A1887
A1888
A1889
A1890

Veszprém-Balaton Region, 2023 European Capital of Culture — A1891

2023, Aug. 2   Litho.   Perf. 12½x12
4673   Miniature sheet of 8 10.00 5.00
  a. A1883 (210fo) multi   1.25 .60
  b. A1884 (210fo) multi   1.25 .60
  c. A1885 (210fo) multi   1.25 .60
  d. A1886 (210fo) multi   1.25 .60
  e. A1887 (210fo) multi   1.25 .60
  f. A1888 (210fo) multi   1.25 .60
  g. A1889 (210fo) multi   1.25 .60
  h. A1890 (210fo) multi   1.25 .60

Souvenir Sheet
4674 A1891 1250fo multi   7.00 3.50
Imperforate examples of No. 4674 with a red serial number were printed in limited quantities.

Renovation of Basilica of the Assumption of the Blessed Virgin Mary and St. Adalbert, Esztergom A1892

2023, Aug. 18   Litho.   Perf. 13x13¼
4675 A1892 700fo multi   4.00 2.00

Souvenir Sheet

Creation of Budapest, 150th Anniv. — A1893

2023, Aug. 18   Litho.   Perf. 12½x12
4676 A1893 500fo multi   2.75 1.40

Souvenir Sheet

St. Stephen (c. 975-1038), First King of Hungary — A1894

2023, Aug. 18   Litho.   Perf. 12
4677 A1894 1500fo multi   8.50 4.25
Examples of No. 4677 with a different perforation and green serial number and imperforate examples with a red serial number were printed in limited quantities. These items and No. 4677 were sold for 20,000fo in a set, along with a monochrome print of No. 4677 that was not valid for postage.

Coronation Mantle — A1895

Gold Scythian Figurine Depicting Stag Found at Zöldhalompuszta A1896

Cover Plate for Belt Bag from Tiszabesdéd A1897

Monomachos Crown — A1898

HUNGARY

Piano Owned by Ludwig van Beethoven and Franz Liszt — A1899

Funeral Crown from Margaret Island — A1900

2023, Aug. 30   Litho.   Perf. 12½x12
4678   Sheet of 6   12.00   6.00
a.   A1895 350fo multi   2.00   1.00
b.   A1896 350fo multi   2.00   1.00
c.   A1897 350fo multi   2.00   1.00
d.   A1898 350fo multi   2.00   1.00
e.   A1899 350fo multi   2.00   1.00
f.   A1900 350fo multi   2.00   1.00

Treasures from the Hungarian National Museum. An imperforate example of No. 4678 with a red serial number was produced in limited quantities. A set containing that imperforate sheet, an example of No. 4678, and a monochrome example of No. 4678 that was not valid for postage sold for 7990fo.

Souvenir Sheet

Ferenc Deák (1803-76), Minister of Justice — A1901

2023, Oct. 17   Litho.   Perf. 12x12½
4679   A1901 1400fo multi   7.75   4.00

Buildings, Heart, Evergreen Trees — A1902

Die Cut Perf. 11½x12
2023, Oct. 17   Self-Adhesive   Typo.
4680   A1902 (210fo) multi   1.25   .60

Christmas.

Souvenir Sheet

Grand Palace, Royal Barge, Bangkok, and Buda Castle, Budapest — A1903

2023, Nov. 29   Litho.   Perf. 13x14
4682   A1903 2000fo multi   11.50   5.75

Diplomatic relations between Hungary and Thailand, 50th anniv.

New Year 2024 (Year of the Dragon) A1904

No. 4683 — Dragon with background color of: a. White. b. Red.

2024, Feb. 1   Litho.   Perf. 11
4683   A1904 975fo Pair, #a-b   11.00   5.50

Printed in sheets containing two each Nos. 4683a-4683b.

SEMI-POSTAL STAMPS

Issues of the Monarchy

"Turul" and St. Stephen's Crown SP1

Franz Josef I Wearing Hungarian Crown SP2

Wmk. Double Cross (137)
1913, Nov. 20   Typo.   Perf. 14
B1   SP1   1f slate   .30   .25
B2   SP1   2f olive yellow   .30   .25
B3   SP1   3f orange   .30   .25
B4   SP1   5f emerald   .30   .25
B5   SP1   6f olive green   .30   .25
B6   SP1   10f carmine   .45   .25
B7   SP1   12f violet, yellow   .35   .25
B8   SP1   16f gray green   .50   .25
B9   SP1   20f dark brown   2.10   .40
B10   SP1   25f ultra   1.25   .25
B11   SP1   30f org brn   1.40   .25
B12   SP1   35f red violet   1.40   .25
B13   SP1   50f lake, blue   2.75   .60
B14   SP1   60f grn, sal   2.25   .50
B15   SP2   1k dull red   17.50   2.00
B16   SP2   2k dull blue   55.00   40.00
B17   SP2   5k violet brown   21.00   30.00
 Nos. B1-B17 (17)   107.45   76.25

Nos. B1-B17 were sold at an advance of 2f over face value, as indicated by the label at bottom. The surtax was to aid flood victims.
For overprints see Nos. 5NB1-5NB10, 6NB1-6NB11.
Exist imperf. Value, set $1,000.

Semi-Postal Stamps of 1913 Surcharged in Red, Green or Brown

a   b

1914
B18   SP1(a)   1f slate   .30   .25
B19   SP1(a)   2f olive yel   .30   .25
B20   SP1(a)   3f orange   .30   .25
B21   SP1(a)   5f emerald   .30   .25
B22   SP1(a)   6f olive green   .30   .25
B23   SP1(a)   10f carmine (G)   .30   .25
B24   SP1(a)   12f violet, yel   .30   .25
B25   SP1(a)   16f gray green   .30   .25
B26   SP1(a)   20f dark brown   .70   .25
B27   SP1(a)   25f ultra   .70   .25
B28   SP1(a)   30f orange brn   .85   .25
B29   SP1(a)   35f red violet   1.40   .25
B30   SP1(a)   50f lake, bl   1.10   .50
B31   SP1(a)   60f grn, sal   1.50   .25
B32   SP2(b)   1k dull red (Br)   45.00   25.00
B33   SP2(b)   2k dull blue   28.00   26.00
B34   SP2(b)   5k violet brn   22.50   25.00
 Nos. B18-B34 (17)   104.15   80.05

Exist imperf. Value, set $800.

Regular Issue of 1913 Surcharged in Red or Green

c   d

1915, Jan. 1
B35   A4(c)   1f slate   .25   .25
B36   A4(c)   2f olive yel   .25   .25
B37   A4(c)   3f orange   .25   .25
B38   A4(c)   5f emerald   .25   .25
B39   A4(c)   6f olive grn   .25   .25
B40   A4(c)   10f carmine (G)   .25   .25
B41   A4(c)   12f violet, yel   .25   .25
B42   A4(c)   16f gray green   .25   .25
B43   A4(c)   20f dark brown   .25   .25
B44   A4(c)   25f ultra   .25   .25
B45   A4(c)   30f orange brn   .25   .25
B46   A4(c)   35f red violet   .45   .25
B47   A4(c)   50f lake, bl   .65   .25
 a.   On No. 96a   5,000.
B48   A4(c)   60f green, salmon   .80   .30
B49   A5(d)   1k dull red   1.10   3.00
B50   A5(d)   2k dull blue   3.00   7.50
B51   A5(d)   5k violet brown   9.50   17.50

Surcharged as Type "c" but in Smaller Letters

B52   A4   60f green, salmon   2.25   1.25
 Nos. B35-B52 (18)   20.65   32.80

Nos. B18-B52 were sold at an advance of 2f over face value. The surtax to aid war widows and orphans.
Exist imperf. Value, set $200.

Soldiers Fighting
SP3   SP4

Eagle with Sword — SP5

1916-17   Perf. 15
B53   SP3   10f + 2f rose red   .25   .30
B54   SP4   15f + 2f dull violet   .25   .30
B55   SP5   40f + 2f brn car ('17)   .25   .40
 Nos. B53-B55 (3)   .75   1.00

Exist imperf. Value, set $20.
For overprints and surcharge see Nos. B58-B60. 1NB1-1NB3, 2NB1-2NB6, 4NJ1, 5NB11-5NB13, 6NB13-6NB15, 7NB2-7NB3, 9NB1, 10NB1-10NB4, 11NB1-B4.

Nos. 106-107 Surcharged in Red

1917, Sept. 15
B56   A8   10f + 1k rose   .55   .55
B57   A8   15f + 1k violet   .55   .55

Nos. B56 and B57 were issued in connection with the War Exhibition of Archduke Josef.

Issues of the Republic

Semi-Postal Stamps of 1916-17 Overprinted in Black

1918
B58   SP3   10f + 2f rose red   .25   .25
B59   SP4   15f + 2f dull violet   .25   .25
B60   SP5   40f + 2f brown car   .25   .25
 Nos. B58-B60 (3)   .75   .75

Nos. B58-B60 exist with inverted overprint.
Exist imperf. Value, set $12.50.

Postally used examples of Nos. B69-B174 sell for more.

Issues of the Kingdom

Released Prisoner Walking Home — SP7

Prisoners of War — SP8

Homecoming of Soldier — SP9

Wmk. 137 Vert. or. Horiz.
1920, Mar. 10   Perf. 12
B69a   SP7   40f + 1k dull red   .50   6.00
B70a   SP8   60f + 2k gray brown   2.00   3.75
B71   SP9   1k + 5k dk blue   .75   1.50
 Set, never hinged   7.00

The surtax was used to help prisoners of war return home from Siberia.
Exist imperf. Value, set $75.

Statue of Petőfi
SP10

Griffin
SP11

Sándor Petőfi
SP12

Petőfi Dying
SP13

Petőfi Addressing People — SP14

1923, Jan. 23   Perf. 14 (10k, 40k), 12
B72   SP10   10k slate green   .35   .60
B73   SP11   15k dull blue   .75   1.10
B74   SP12   25k gray brown   .35   .60
B75   SP13   40k brown violet   1.10   1.50
B76   SP14   50k violet brown   1.10   1.50
 Nos. B72-B76 (5)   3.65   5.30
 Set, never hinged   7.50

Birth centenary of the Hungarian poet Sándor Petőfi. The stamps were on sale at double face value, for a limited time and in restricted quantities, after which the remainders were given to a charitable organization.
Exist imperf. Value, set $60.

Child with Symbols of Peace
SP15

Mother and Infant
SP16

Instruction in Archery — SP17

Wmk. 133
1924, Apr. 8   Engr.   Perf. 12
B77   SP15   300k dark blue   1.50   3.00
 a.   Perf. 11½   35.00   30.00
B78   SP16   500k black brown   1.50   3.00
B79   SP17   1000k black green   1.50   3.50
 Nos. B77-B79 (3)   4.50   9.50
 Set, never hinged   12.00

Each stamp has on the back an inscription stating that it was sold at a premium of 100 per cent over the face value.
Exist imperf. Value, set $90.

Parade of Athletes
SP18

Skiing
SP19

Skating
SP20

Diving
SP21

HUNGARY

Fencing SP22
Scouts Camping SP23
Soccer SP24
Hurdling SP25

Perf. 12, 12½ and Compound
1925   Typo.   Unwmk.
B80	SP18	100k bl grn & brn	2.25	2.00
B81	SP19	200k lt brn & myr grn	2.90	2.50
B82	SP20	300k dark blue	3.50	3.50
B83	SP21	400k dp bl & dp grn	3.80	3.50
B84	SP22	500k pur brn	7.50	10.00
B85	SP23	1000k red brown	6.25	7.00
B86	SP24	2000k brown violet	7.50	7.50
B87	SP25	2500k olive brown	7.50	9.00
		Nos. B80-B87 (8)	41.20	45.00
		Set, never hinged		75.00

These stamps were sold at double face value, plus a premium of 10 per cent on orders sent by mail. They did not serve any postal need and were issued solely to raise funds to aid athletic associations. An inscription regarding the 100 per cent premium is printed on the back of each stamp.

Exist imperf. Value, set $450.

St. Emerich SP26
Sts. Stephen and Gisela SP27
St. Ladislaus SP28
Sts. Gerhardt and Emerich SP29

1930, May 15   Wmk. 210   Perf. 14
B88	SP26	8f + 2f deep green	.45	.40
B89	SP27	16f + 4f brt violet	.65	.60
B90	SP28	20f + 4f deep rose	1.90	1.50
B91	SP29	32f + 8f ultra	2.50	1.50
		Nos. B88-B91 (4)	5.50	4.00
		Set, never hinged		11.00

900th anniv. of the death of St. Emerich, son of Stephen I, king, saint and martyr.
Exist imperf. Value, set $100.

> Catalogue values for unused stamps in this section, from this point to the end of the section, are for Never Hinged items.

St. Ladislaus SP30
Holy Sacrament SP31

SP32

1938 May 16   Photo.   Perf. 12
B92	SP30	16f + 16f dull slate bl	2.25	2.25
B93	SP31	20f + 20f dk car	2.25	2.25

Souvenir Sheet
B94	SP32	Sheet of 7	45.00	40.00
a.		6f + 6f St. Stephen	4.00	3.00
b.		10f + 10f St. Emerich	4.00	3.00
c.		16f + 16f slate blue (B92)	4.00	3.00
d.		20f + 20f dark carmine (B93)	4.00	3.00
e.		32f + 32f St. Elizabeth	4.00	3.00
f.		40f + 40f St. Maurice	4.00	3.00
g.		50f + 50f St. Margaret	4.00	3.00

Printed in sheets measuring 136½x155mm.
Nos. B94c and B94d are slightly smaller than B92 and B93.
Eucharistic Cong. in Budapest, May, 1938.
Exist imperf. Value: set $125; souvenir sheet $3,750.

St. Stephen, Victorious Warrior — SP33
St. Stephen, Offering Crown — SP34

SP35

1938, Aug. 12   Perf. 12
B95	SP33	10f + 10f violet brn	3.00	3.00
B96	SP34	20f + 20f red org	3.00	3.00

Souvenir Sheet
B97	SP35	Sheet of 7	32.50	20.00
a.		6f + 6f St. Stephen the Missionary	3.25	2.00
b.		10f + 10f violet brown (B95)	3.25	2.00
c.		16f + 16f Seated Upon Throne	3.25	2.00
d.		20f + 20f red orange (B96)	3.25	2.00
e.		32f + 32f Receives Bishops and Monks	3.25	2.00
f.		40f + 40f St. Gisela, St. Stephen and St. Emerich	3.25	2.00
g.		50f + 50f St. Stephen on Bier	3.25	2.00

Death of St. Stephen, 900th anniversary.
No. B97 is on brownish paper, Nos. B95-B96 on white.
Nos. B95-B97 exist imperf. Values: Nos. B95-B96 $150; No. B97 $4,500.

Statue Symbolizing Recovered Territories SP36
Castle of Munkács SP37
Admiral Horthy Entering Komárom SP38
Cathedral of Kassa SP39

Girl Offering Flowers to Soldier — SP40

1939, Jan. 16
B98	SP36	6f + 3f myrtle grn	.75	.50
B99	SP37	10f + 5f olive grn	.50	.40
B100	SP38	20f + 10f dark red	.50	.40
B101	SP39	30f + 15f grnsh blue	1.10	.75
B102	SP40	40f + 20f dk bl gray	1.50	.75
		Nos. B98-B102 (5)	4.35	2.80

The surtax was for the aid of "Hungary for Hungarians" patriotic movement.
Exist imperf. Value, set $175.

Memorial Tablets SP41
Gáspár Károlyi, Translator of the Bible into Hungarian SP42
Albert Molnár de Szenci, Translator of the Psalms SP43
Prince Gabriel Bethlen SP44
Susanna Lórántffy — SP45

Perf. 12x12½, 12½x12
1939   Photo.   Wmk. 210
B103	SP41	6f + 3f green	.90	.50
B104	SP42	10f + 5f claret	.90	.50
B105	SP43	20f + 10f cop red	1.50	1.00
B106	SP44	32f + 16f bister	1.50	1.50
B107	SP45	40f + 20f chalky blue	1.75	1.75
		Nos. B103-B107 (5)	6.55	5.25

Souvenir Sheets
Perf. 12
B108	SP44	32f olive & vio brn	30.00	15.00

Imperf
B109	SP44	32f bl grn, cop red & gold	30.00	15.00

National Protestant Day. The surtax was used to erect an Intl. Protestant Institute.
The souvenir sheets sold for 1.32p each.
Nos. B103-B108 exist imperf. Values: Nos. B103-B107 $350; No. B108 $4,000.
Issue dates: Nos. B103-B107, Oct. 2. Nos. B108-B109, Oct. 27.

Boy Scout Flying Kite SP47
Allegory of Flight SP48
Archangel Gabriel from Millennium Monument, Budapest, and Planes — SP49

1940, Jan. 1   Perf. 12½x12
B110	SP47	6f + 6f yellow grn	.50	.50
B111	SP48	10f + 10f chocolate	.95	.90
B112	SP49	20f + 20f copper red	1.25	1.25
		Nos. B110-B112 (3)	2.70	2.65

The surtax was used for the Horthy National Aviation Fund.
Exist imperf. Value, set $150.

Souvenir Sheet
SP50

Wmk. 210
1940, May 6   Photo.   Perf. 12
B113	SP50	20f + 1p dk blue grn	6.00	6.00

Exist imperf. Value $4,500.

Soldier Protecting Family from Floods — SP51

1940, May
B114	SP51	10f + 2f gray brown	.40	.25
B115	SP51	20f + 4f orange red	.40	.25
B116	SP51	20f + 50f red brown	1.25	1.25
		Nos. B114-B116 (3)	2.05	1.75

The surtax on Nos. B113-B116 was used to aid flood victims.
Exist imperf. Value, set $200.

Hunyadi Coat of Arms SP52
King Matthias SP54
Hunyadi Castle — SP53
Equestrian Statue of King Matthias — SP55

Corvin Codex — SP56

HUNGARY

Equestrian Statue of King Matthias — SP57

1940   Perf. 12½x12, 12x12½
B117	SP52	6f + 3f blue grn	.50 .40
B118	SP53	10f + 5f gldn brn	.50 .40
B119	SP54	16f + 8f dk ol bis	.60 .40
B120	SP55	20f + 10f brick red	.60 .40
B121	SP56	32f + 16f dk gray	.75 .75
	Nos. B117-B121 (5)		2.95 2.35

Souvenir Sheet
B122	SP57	20f + 1p dk bl grn & pale grn	7.50 7.50

King Matthias (1440-1490) at Kolozsvar, Transylvania. The surtax was used for war relief.
Nos. B117-B122 exist imperf. Values: Nos. B117-B121 $250; No. B122 $4,500.
Issued: Nos. B117-B121, July 1. No. B122, Nov. 7.

Hungarian Soldier — SP58

20f+50f, Virgin Mary and Szekley, symbolizing the return of transylvania. 32f+50f, Szekley Mother Offering Infant Son to the Fatherland.

1940, Dec. 2   Photo.   Perf. 12½x12
B123	SP58	10f + 50f dk blue grn	.90 .90
B124	SP58	20f + 50f brown car	1.00 1.00
B125	SP58	32f + 50f yellow brn	1.25 1.25
	Nos. B123-B125 (3)		3.15 3.15

Occupation of Transylvania. The surtax was for the Pro-Transylvania movement.
Exist imperf. Value, set $225.

Symbol for Drama SP61   Symbol for Sculpture SP62

Symbols: 16f+16f, Art. 20f+20f, Literature.

1940, Dec. 15   Perf. 12x12½, 12½x12
B126	SP61	6f + 6f dark green	1.25 1.25
B127	SP62	10f + 10f olive bis	1.25 1.25
B128	SP62	16f + 16f dk violet	1.25 1.25
B129	SP61	20f + 20f fawn	1.25 1.25
	Nos. B126-B129 (4)		5.00 5.00

Souvenir Sheet

1941, Jan. 5   Imperf.
B130		Sheet of 4	6.00 6.00
a.		SP61 6f + 6f olive brown	1.25 1.25
b.		SP62 10f + 10f henna brown	1.25 1.25
c.		SP62 16f + 16f dk blue green	1.25 1.25
d.		SP61 20f + 20f rose violet	1.25 1.25

Surtax on Nos. B126-B130 was used for the Pension and Assistance Institution for Artists.
Nos. B126-B129 exist imperf. Value, set $70.

Winged Head of Pilot — SP66

Designs: 10f+10f, Boy Scout with model plane. 20f+20f, Glider in flight. 32f+32f, Our Lady of Loreto, patroness of Hungarian pilots.

1941, Mar. 24   Perf. 12x12½
B131	SP66	6f + 6f grn olive	.55 .50
B132	SP66	10f + 10f dp claret	.55 .50
B133	SP66	20f + 20f org ver	.65 .60
B134	SP66	32f + 32f turq blue	1.60 1.50
	Nos. B131-B134 (4)		3.35 3.10

The surtax was used to finance civilian and army pilot training through the Horthy National Aviation Fund.
Exist imperf. Value, set $175.

Infantry — SP70

12f+18f, Heavy artillery. 20f+30f, Plane and tanks. 40f+60f, Cavalryman and cyclist.

1941, Dec. 1   Photo.   Wmk. 266
Inscribed: "Honvedeink Karacsonyara 1941"
B135	SP70	8f + 12f dk green	.50 .40
B136	SP70	12f + 18f olive grn	.50 .40
B137	SP70	20f + 30f slate	.60 .40
B138	SP70	40f + 60f red brown	.60 .40
	Nos. B135-B138 (4)		2.20 1.60

The surtax was for the benefit of the Army.
Exist imperf. Value, set $200.

Soldier and Emblem — SP74

1941, Dec. 1
B139	SP74	20f + 40f dark red	2.25 2.25

The surtax was for the soldiers' Christmas.
Exists imperf. Value $70.

Aviator and Plane SP75   Planes and Ghostly Band of Old Chiefs SP76

Plane and Archer SP77   Aviators and Plane SP78

1942, Mar. 15   Perf. 12½x12, 12x12½
B140	SP75	8f + 8f dark green	.80 .80
B141	SP76	12f + 12f sapphire	.80 .80
B142	SP77	20f + 20f brown	.80 .80
B143	SP78	30f + 30f dark red	.80 .80
	Nos. B140-B143 (4)		3.20 3.20

The surtax aided the Horthy National Aviation Fund.
Exist imperf. Value, set $175.

Blood Transfusion — SP79

Designs: 8f+32f, Bandaging wounded soldier. 12f+50f, Radio and carrier pigeons. 20f+1p, Widows and orphans.

1942, Sept. 1   Perf. 12½x12
B144	SP79	3f + 18f dk ol & red	1.25 1.25
B145	SP79	8f + 32f dp brn & red	1.25 1.25
B146	SP79	12f + 50f dp cl & red	1.25 1.25
B147	SP79	20f + 1p slate bl & red	1.25 1.25
	Nos. B144-B147 (4)		5.00 5.00

The surtax aided the Hungarian Red Cross. Sheets of 10. Value, set $85.
Exist imperf. Value, set $250.

Widow of Stephen Horthy SP83   Red Cross Nurse Aiding Soldier SP84

Magdalene Horthy Mother of Stephen Horthy — SP85

1942, Dec. 1   Perf. 13, Imperf.
B148	SP83	6f + 1p vio bl & red	2.50 2.50
a.		Sheet of 4	25.00 25.00
B149	SP84	8f + 1p dk ol grn & red	2.50 2.50
a.		Sheet of 4	25.00 25.00
B150	SP85	20f + 1p dk red brn & red	2.50 2.50
a.		Sheet of 4	25.00 25.00
	Nos. B148-B150 (3)		7.50 7.50

The surtax aided the Hungarian Red Cross.

King Ladislaus I SP86   SP87

1942, Dec. 21   Wmk. 266   Perf. 12
B151	SP86	6f + 6f olive gray	.55 .50
B152	SP87	8f + 8f green	.55 .50
B153	SP86	12f + 12f dull violet	.55 .50
B154	SP87	20f + 20f Prus green	.55 .50
B155	SP86	24f + 24f brown	.55 .50
B156	SP87	30f + 30f rose car	.55 .50
	Nos. B151-B156 (6)		3.30 3.00

900th anniv. of the birth of St. Ladislaus (1040-95), the 700th anniv. of the beginning of the country's reconstruction by King Béla IV (1206-70) and the 600th anniv. of the accession of King Lajos the Great (1326-82).
The surtax aided war invalids and their families.
Exist imperf. Value, set $275.

Archer on Horseback SP92   Knight with Sword and Shield SP93

Old Magyar Arms — SP94

Designs: 3f+1f, 4f+1f, Warrior with shield and battle ax. 12f+2f, Knight with lance. 20f+2f, Musketeer. 40f+4f, Hussar. 50f+6f, Artilleryman.

1943
B157	SP92	1f + 1f dk gray	.30 .25
B158	SP93	3f + 1f dull violet	.30 .25
B159	SP93	4f + 1f lake	.30 .25
B160	SP93	8f + 2f green	.30 .25
B161	SP92	12f + 2f bister brn	.30 .25
B162	SP93	20f + 2f dp claret	.30 .25
B163	SP92	40f + 4f gray vio	.30 .25
B164	SP93	50f + 6f org brn	.30 .25
B165	SP94	70f + 8f slate blue	.30 .25
	Nos. B157-B165 (9)		2.70 2.25

The surtax aided war invalids.
Exist imperf. Value, set $225.

Model Glider SP101   Gliders SP102

White-tailed Sea Eagle and Planes SP103   ME-109E Fighter and Gliders SP104

1943, July 17
B166	SP101	8f + 8f green	.80 .55
B167	SP102	12f + 12f royal blue	.80 .55
B168	SP103	20f + 20f chestnut	.80 .55
B169	SP104	30f + 30f rose car	.80 .55
	Nos. B166-B169 (4)		3.20 2.20

The surtax aided the Horthy National Aviation Fund.
Exist imperf. Value, set $200.

Stephen Horthy — SP105

1943, Aug. 16
B170	SP105	30f + 20f dp rose vio	.45 .25

The surtax aided the Horthy National Aviation Fund.
Exists imperf. Value $50.

Nurse and Soldier — SP106

Designs: 30f+30f, Soldier, nurse, mother and child. 50f+50f, Nurse keeping lamp alight. 70f+70f, Wounded soldier and tree shoot.

1944, Mar. 1   Cross in Red
B171	SP106	20f + 20f brown	.50 .40
B172	SP106	30f + 30f henna	.50 .40
B173	SP106	50f + 50f brown vio	.55 .40
B174	SP106	70f + 70f Prus blue	.55 .40
	Nos. B171-B174 (4)		2.10 1.60

The surtax aided the Hungarian Red Cross.
Exist imperf. Value, set $250.

Issues of the Republic
Types of 1944 Surcharged in Red or Black

a   b

1945, July 23   Wmk. 266   Perf. 12
B175	A115(a)	3p + 9p on 20f dk ol grn, yel	.90 .70
B176	A114(b)	4p + 12p on 4f yel brn, bl (Bk)	.90 .70
B177	A117(b)	8p + 24p on 50f sl bl, yel	.90 .70
B178	A115(a)	10p + 30p on 30f hn brn, bl	.90 .70
	Nos. B175-B178 (4)		3.60 2.80

The surtax was for the Peoples Universities. "Béke" means "peace".

HUNGARY

Imre Sallai and Sandor Fürst — SP110

Designs: 3p+3p, L. Kabok and Illes Monus. 4p+4p, Ferenc Rozsa and Zoltan Schonerz. 6p+6p, Anna Koltai and Mrs. Paul Knurr. 10p+10p, George Sarkozi and Imre Nagy. 15p+15p, Vilmos Tartsay and Jeno Nagy. 20p+20p, Janos Kiss and Andreas Bajcsy-Zsilinszky. 40p+40p, Endre Sagvari and Otto Hoffmann.

1945, Oct. 6   Photo.
B179	SP110	2p + 2p yel brn	1.50	1.50
B180	SP110	3p + 3p dp red	1.50	1.50
B181	SP110	4p + 4p dk pur	1.50	1.50
B182	SP110	6p + 6p dk yel grn	1.50	1.50
B183	SP110	10p + 10p dp car	1.50	1.50
B184	SP110	15p + 15p dk sl	1.50	1.50
B185	SP110	20p + 20p dk brn	1.50	1.50
B186	SP110	40p + 40p dp bl	1.50	1.50
	Nos. B179-B186 (8)		12.00	12.00

The surtax was for child welfare.
Exist imperf. Value, set $150.

Andreas Bajcsy-Zsilinszky and Eagle — SP111

1945, May 27
B187	SP111	1p + 1p dk brn vio	.75	.75

1st anniv. of the death of Andreas Bajcsy-Zsilinszky, hanged by the Nazis for anti-fascist activities.
Exists imperf. Value $110.

Lion with Broken Shackles — SP112

1946, May 1
B188	SP112	500ez p + 500ez p	2.00	1.50
B189	SP112	1mil p + 1mil p	2.00	1.50
B190	SP112	1.5mil p + 1.5mil p	2.00	1.50
B191	SP112	2mil p + 2mil p	2.00	1.50
	Nos. B188-B191 (4)		8.00	6.00

75th anniv. of Hungary's 1st postage stamp. The surtax was for the benefit of postal employees.
Exist imperf. Value, set $135.

"Agriculture" Holding Wheat — SP113

1946, Sept. 7   Photo.
B192	SP113	30f + 60f dp yel grn	4.25	4.75
B193	SP113	60f + 1.20fo rose brn	4.25	4.75
B194	SP113	1fo + 2fo dp blue	4.25	4.75
	Nos. B192-B194 (3)		12.75	14.25

1st Agricultural Congress and Exhibition.
Exist imperf. Value, set $275.

Physician with Syringe — SP114

Designs: 12f+50f, Physician examining X-ray picture. 20f+50f, Nurse and child. 60f+50f, Prisoner of war starting home.

Perf. 12½x12

1947, May 16   Wmk. 210
B195	SP114	8f + 50f ultra	3.25	4.50
B196	SP114	12f + 50f choc	3.25	4.50
B197	SP114	20f + 50f dk grn	3.25	4.50
B198	SP114	60f + 50f dk red	.40	.40
	Nos. B195-B198 (4)		10.15	13.90

The surtax was for charitable purposes.
Exist imperf. Value, set $325.

Franklin D. Roosevelt and Freedom of Speech Allegory — SP115

Pres. F. D. Roosevelt and Allegory: 12f+12f, Freedom of Religion. 20f+20f, Freedom from Want. 30f+30f, Freedom from Fear.

1947, June 11   Photo.   *Perf. 12x12½*
Portrait in Sepia
B198A	SP115	8f + 8f dk red	3.75	4.00
B198B	SP115	12f + 12f dp grn	3.75	4.00
B198C	SP115	20f + 20f brown	3.75	4.00
B198D	SP115	30f + 30f blue	3.75	4.00
	Nos. B198A-B198D,CB1-CB1C (8)		30.00	32.00

Exist imperf. Value, set $250.
Nos. B198A-B198D and CB1-CB1C were also printed in sheets of 4 of each denomination (size: 117x96mm). Value, set of 8, $350. Exist imperf. Value $450.
A souvenir sheet exists, containing one each of Nos. B198A-B198D with border inscriptions and decorations in brown. Size: 161x122mm. Value $75. Also printed in tête-bêche souvenir sheets of 4. Value $800. Exists imperf. Value $250.

Lenin — SP118

Designs: 60f+60f, Soviet Cenotaph, Budapest. 1fo+1fo, Joseph V. Stalin.

1947, Oct. 29   Photo.   Wmk. 283
B199	SP118	40f + 40f ol grn & org brn	4.50	4.50
B200	SP118	60f + 60f red & sl bl	2.00	2.00
B201	SP118	1fo + 1fo vio & brn blk	4.50	4.50
	Nos. B199-B201 (3)		11.00	11.00

The surtax was for the Hungarian-Soviet Cultural Association.
Exist imperf. Value, set $625.

XVI Century Mail Coach — SP119

1947, Dec. 21   *Perf. 12x12½*
B202	SP119	30f (+ 50f) hn brn	7.50	6.50
	Sheet of 4		42.50	50.00

Stamp Day. The surtax paid admission to a philatelic exhibition in any of eight Hungarian towns, where the stamps were sold.
No. B202 exists imperf. Values: single $500; sheetlet of 4 $2,750.

Globe and Carrier Pigeon — SP120

1948, Oct. 17   *Perf. 12½x12*
B203	SP120	30f (+ 1fo) grnsh bl	4.50	4.50
	Sheet of 4		40.00	40.00

5th Natl. Hungarian Stamp Exhib., Budapest. Each stamp sold for 1.30 forint, which included admission to the exhibition.
Exists imperf. Value: single $325; sheetlet $1,625.

Woman Worker — SP121

1949, Mar. 8
B204	SP121	60f + 60f magenta	2.25	2.25

Intl. Woman's Day, Mar. 8, 1949. The surtax was for the Democratic Alliance of Hungarian Women.
Exists imperf. Value $50.

Aleksander S. Pushkin — SP122

1949, June 6   Photo.
B205	SP122	1fo + 1fo car lake	8.00	7.50

Souvenir Sheet
Perf. 12½x12, Imperf
B206	SP123	1fo + 1fo red vio & car lake	13.00	13.00

150th anniversary of the birth of Aleksander S. Pushkin. The surtax was for the Hungarian-Russian Culture Society.
No. B205 exists imperf. Value $425.

IMPERFORATE STAMPS

Through 1991, most semi-postal stamps were also issued imperforate. Where these items form part of a larger set with regular issues, values for imperfs will be included in that of the sets to which they belong, footnoted in the Regular Issues section. For Nos. B207-B345, values for imperfs will be given only for those items not included in sets with regular issues.

1st Stamp Type
Perf. 12½x12

1951, Oct. 6   Engr.   Unwmk.
B207	A208	1fo + 1fo red	11.25	8.25
B208	A208	2fo + 2fo blue	12.75	11.25

Exists imperf.

Postwoman Delivering Mail — SP124

1953, Nov. 1   Wmk. 106   *Perf. 12*
B209	SP124	1fo + 1fo blue grn	3.75	1.75
B210	SP124	2fo + 2fo rose vio	3.75	1.75

Stamp Day, Nov. 1, 1953.
Exist imperf. Value, set $35.

Stamps of 1955 Surcharged in Red or Lake

1957, Jan. 31   Photo.   *Perf. 12x12½*
B211	A249	20f + 20f olive grn	.30	.25
B212	A249	30f + 30f dk red (L)	.30	.25
a.	Red (cross) inverted		450.00	
B213	A249	40f + 40f brown	.30	.25
B214	A249	60f + 60f brn red (L)	.35	.30
B215	A249	1fo + 1fo blue	.75	.50
B216	A249	2fo + 2fo rose brn	1.25	.90
	Nos. B211-B216 (6)		3.25	2.45

The surtax was for the Hungarian Red Cross.
Exist imperf. Value, set $40.

Winter Olympic Type of 1960

Design: Olympic Games emblem.

Perf. 11½x12

1960, Feb. 29   Wmk. 106
B217	A295	2fo + 1fo multi	1.25	.35

Exists imperf.

Olympic Type of 1960

Design: 2fo+1fo, Romulus and Remus.

Perf. 11½x12

1960, Aug. 21   Photo.   Wmk. 106
B218	A299	2fo + 1fo multi	1.00	.25

Exists imperf.

Sport Club Type of 1961

Sport: 2fo+1fo, Sailboats.

1961, July 8   Unwmk.   *Perf. 14½*
B219	A313	2fo + 1fo multi	.40	.25

Exists imperf.

St. Margaret's Island and Danube SP125

Views of Budapest: No. B221, Fishermen's Bastion. No. B222, Coronation Church and Chain Bridge. No. B223, Mount Gellert.

Unwmk.

1961, Sept. 24   Photo.   *Perf. 12*
B220	SP125	2fo + 1fo multi	1.00	.75
B221	SP125	2fo + 1fo multi	1.00	.75
B222	SP125	2fo + 1fo multi	1.00	.75
B223	SP125	2fo + 1fo multi	1.00	.75
a.	Horiz. strip of 4, #B220-B223		4.00	3.00

Stamp Day, 1961, and Budapest Intl. Stamp Exhibition.
No. B223a has a continuous design.
Exist imperf. Value, strip $22.50.
Miniature presentation sheets, perf. and imperf., contain one each of Nos. B220-B223; size: 204x66½mm. Value for both sheets, $1,000.

Soccer Type of Regular Issue, 1962

Design: Flags of Spain and Czechoslovakia.

1962, May 21   *Perf. 11*
Flags in Original Colors
B224	A323	4fo + 1fo lt grn & bis	1.50	.40

Exists imperf.

Austrian Stamp of 1850 with Pesth Postmark — SP126

Stamps: No. B226, #201. No. B227, #C164. No. B228, #C208.

Lithographed and Engraved
1962, Sept. 22   Unwmk.   *Perf. 11*
Design and Inscription in Dark Brown
B225	SP126	2fo + 1fo yellow	.75	.65
B226	SP126	2fo + 1fo pale pink	.75	.65
B227	SP126	2fo + 1fo pale blue	.75	.65

169

HUNGARY

B228 SP126 2fo + 1fo pale yel grn .75 .65
  a. Horiz. strip of 4, #B225-B228 4.50 4.50
  b. Souv. sheet of 4, #B225-B228 6.00 6.00

35th Stamp Day and 10th anniv. of Mabeosz, the Hungarian Phil. Fed.
Exist imperf. Value: strip $15; souvenir sheet $32.50.

Emblem, Cup and Soccer Ball — SP127

1962, Nov. 18   *Photo.*   *Perf. 11½x12*
B229 SP127 2fo + 1fo multi .50 .40

Winning of the "Coupe de l'Europe Centrale" by the Steel Workers Sport Club (VASAS) in the Central European Soccer Championships.
Exists imperf. Value $2.75.

Stamp Day — SP128

No. B230, Hyacinth. No. B231, Narcissus. No. B232, Chrysanthemum. No. B233, Tiger lily.

1963, Oct. 24   *Perf. 11½x12*
    Size: 32x43mm
B230 SP128 2fo + 1fo multi .50 .45
B231 SP128 2fo + 1fo multi .50 .45
B232 SP128 2fo + 1fo multi .50 .45
B233 SP128 2fo + 1fo multi .50 .45
  a. Horiz. strip of 4, #B230-B233 3.00 2.75
  b. Min. sheet of 4, #B230-B233 3.00 3.00

No. B233b contains 25x32mm stamps, perf. 11.
Exist imperf. Value: strip $7.50; miniature sheet $35.

Winter Olympic Type of 1963
Design: 4fo+1fo, Bobsledding.

1963, Nov. 11   *Perf. 12*
B234 A342 4fo + 1fo grnsh bl & bis 1.00 .25
    Exists imperf.

New Year Type of Regular Issue
Good Luck Symbols: 2.50fo+1.20fo, Horseshoe, mistletoe and clover. 3fo+1.50fo, Pigs, clover and balloon, horiz.

    Perf. 12x11½, 11½x12
1963, Dec. 12   *Photo.*   *Unwmk.*
   Sizes: 28x39mm (#B235); 28x22mm (#B206)
B235 A343 2.50fo + 1.20fo multi .30 .25
B236 A343 3fo + 1.50fo multi .40 .25

The surtax was for the modernization of the Hungarian Postal and Philatelic Museum.
Exist imperf.

Olympic Type of Regular Issue
Design: 3fo+1fo, Water polo.

1964, June 12   *Perf. 11*
B237 A352 3fo + 1fo multi .60 .25
    Exists imperf.

Exhibition Hall — SP129

1964, July 23   *Photo.*
B238 SP129 3fo + 1.50fo blk, red org & gray .60 .25

Tennis Exhibition, Budapest Sports Museum.
Exists imperf. Value $8.

Twirling Woman Gymnast — SP130

No. B239, Lilac. No. B240, Mallards. No. B241, Gymnast. No. B242, Rocket & globe.

1964, Sept. 4   *Perf. 11½x12*
    Size: 27x38mm
B239 SP130 2fo + 1fo multi .65 .65
B240 SP130 2fo + 1fo multi .65 .65
B241 SP130 2fo + 1fo multi .65 .65
B242 SP130 2fo + 1fo multi .65 .65
  a. Horiz. strip of 4, #B239-B242 2.50 2.50
  b. Souv. sheet of 4, #B239-B242 2.50 2.50

37th Stamp Day and Intl. Topical Stamp Exhib., IMEX. No. B242b contains 4 20x28mm stamps, perf. 11.
Exist imperf. Value: strip $17.50; souvenir sheet $32.50.

13th Century Tennis — SP131

History of Tennis: 40f+10f, Indoor tennis, 16th century. 60f+10f, Tennis, 18th century. 70f+30f, Tennis court and castle. 80f+40f, Tennis court, Fontainebleau (buildings). 1fo+50f, Tennis, 17th century. 1.50fo+50f, W. C. Wingfield, Wimbledon champion 1877, and Wimbledon Cup. 1.70fo+50f, Davis Cup, 1900. 2fo+1fo, Bela Kehrling (1891-1937), Hungarian champion.

Lithographed and Engraved
1965, June 15   *Unwmk.*   *Perf. 12*
B243 SP131 30f + 10f mar, dl org .30 .25
B244 SP131 40f + 10f blk, pale lil .30 .25
B245 SP131 60f + 10f grn, ol .30 .25
B246 SP131 70f + 30f lil, brt grn .30 .25
B247 SP131 80f + 40f dk bl, lt vio .30 .25
B248 SP131 1fo + 50f grn, yel .30 .25
B249 SP131 1.50fo + 50f sep, lt ol grn .30 .25
B250 SP131 1.70fo + 50f ind, lt bl .40 .25
B251 SP131 2fo + 1fo dk red, lt grn .50 .25
    Nos. B243-B251 (9) 3.00 2.25
Exist imperf. Value, set $15.

Flood Scene — SP132

10fo+5fo, Relief commemorating 1838 flood.

1965, Aug. 14   *Photo.*   *Perf. 12x11½*
B252 SP132 1fo + 50f org brn & bl .30 .30

Souvenir Sheet
B253 SP132 10fo + 5fo gldn brn & buff 1.50 1.50

Surtax for aid to 1965 flood victims.
Exist imperf. Value: No. B252 $6; No. B253 $20.

Geranium Stamp of 1950 (No. 909) — SP133

Stamp Day: No. B255, #120. No. B256, #1489. No. B257, #1382.

    Perf. 12x11½
1965, Oct. 30   *Photo.*   *Unwmk.*
   Stamps in Original Colors
B254 SP133 2fo + 1fo gray & dk bl .50 .50
B255 SP133 2fo + 1fo gray & red .50 .50
B256 SP133 2fo + 1fo gray & ocher .50 .50
B257 SP133 2fo + 1fo gray & vio .50 .50
  a. Horiz. strip of 4, #B254-B257 2.25 2.25
  b. Souv. sheet of 4, #B254-B257 2.75 2.75

No. B257b contains 32x23mm stamps, perf. 11.
Exist imperf. Value: No. B257a $10; No. B257b $25.

Soccer Type of Regular Issue
Design: 3f0+1fo, Championship emblem and map of Great Britain showing cities where matches were held.

1966, June 6   *Photo.*   *Perf. 12x11½*
B258 A382 3fo + 1fo multi .75 .50

Exists imperf.

Woman Archer and Danube at Visegrad SP134

Stamp Day: No. B260, Gloria Hungariae grapes and Lake Balaton. No. B261, Red poppies and ruins of Diosgyor Castle. No. B262, Russian space dogs Ugolek and Veterok.

1966, Sept. 16   *Photo.*   *Perf. 12x11½*
B259 SP134 2fo + 50f multi .60 .60
B260 SP134 2fo + 50f multi .60 .60
B261 SP134 2fo + 50f multi .60 .60
B262 SP134 2fo + 50f multi .60 .60
  a. Horiz. strip of 4, #B259-B262 2.75 2.75
  b. Souv. sheet of 4, #B259-B262 2.75 2.75

No. B262b contains 4 29x21mm stamps, perf. 11.
Exist imperf. Value: B262a $20; B262b $30.

Anglers, C.I.P.S. Emblem and View of Danube SP135

1967, Aug. 22   *Photo.*   *Perf. 12x11½*
B263 SP135 2fo + 1fo multi .90 .25

See note after No. 1847.
Exists imperf.

Olympic Type of Regular Issue
Indoor stadium & Winter Olympics emblem.

1968, Jan. 29   *Photo.*   *Perf. 11*
B264 A402 4fo + 1fo multi .70 .30

Exists imperf.

Jug, Western Hungary, 1618 — SP136

Hungarian Earthenware: No. B266, Tiszafüred vase, 1847. No. B267, Toby jug, 1848. No. B268, Decorative Baja plate, 1870. No. B269a, Jug, Northern Hungary, 1672. No. B269b, Decorative Mezőcsat plate, 1843. No. B269c, Decorative Moragy plate, 1860. No. B269d, Pitcher, Debrecen, 1793.

1968, Oct. 5   *Litho.*   *Perf. 12*
B265 SP136 1fo + 50f ultra & multi .50 .50
B266 SP136 1fo + 50f sky bl & multi .50 .50
B267 SP136 1fo + 50f sepia & multi .50 .50
B268 SP136 1fo + 50f yel brn & multi .50 .50
    Nos. B265-B268 (4) 2.00 2.00

Miniature Sheet
B269   Sheet of 4 2.75 2.50
  a. SP136 2fo + 50f ultra & multi .45 .40
  b. SP136 2fo + 50f yel brn & multi .45 .40
  c. SP136 2fo + 50f olive & multi .45 .40
  d. SP136 2fo + 50f brt rose & multi .45 .40

Issued for 41st Stamp Day. No. B269 contains 4 25x36mm stamps. See Nos. B271-B275.
Exist imperf. Value: Nos. B265-B268 $15; No. B269 $15.

Suspension Bridge, Buda Castle and Arms of Budapest SP137

Lithographed and Engraved
1969, May 22   *Perf. 12*
B270 SP137 5fo + 2fo sep, pale yel & gray 1.00 1.00

Budapest 71 Philatelic Exposition.
Exists imperf. Value $7.50.

Folk Art Type of 1968
Hungarian Wood Carvings: No. B271, Stirrup cup from Okorag, 1880. No. B272, Jar with flower decorations from Felsötiszavidek, 1898. No. B273, Round jug, Somogyharsagy, 1935. No. B274, Two-legged jug, Alföld, 1740. No. B275a, Carved panel (farm couple), Csorna, 1879. No. B275b, Tankard, Okany, 1914. No. B275c, Round jar with soldiers, Sellye, 1899. No. B275d, Square box with 2 women, Lengyeltoti, 1880.

1969, Sept. 13   *Litho.*   *Perf. 12*
B271 SP136 1fo + 50f rose cl & multi .60 .45
B272 SP136 1fo + 50f dp bis & multi .60 .45
B273 SP136 1fo + 50f bl & multi .60 .45
B274 SP136 1fo + 50f lt bl grn & multi .60 .45
    Nos. B271-B274 (4) 2.40 1.80

Miniature Sheet
B275   Sheet of 4 2.00 2.00
  a. SP136 2fo + 50f ultra & multi .45 .35
  b. SP136 2fo + 50f brn org & multi .45 .35
  c. SP136 2fo + 50f lt brn & multi .45 .35
  d. SP136 2fo + 50f bl grn & multi .45 .35

Issued for the 42nd Stamp Day. No. B275 contains 4 stamps (size: 25x36mm).
Exists imperf. Value: B271-B274 $15; B275 $15.

Fishermen's Bastion, Coronation Church and Chain Bridge — SP138

Designs: No. B277, Parliament and Elizabeth Bridge. No. B278, Castle and Margaret Bridge.

1970, Mar. 7   *Litho.*   *Perf. 12*
B276 SP138 2fo + 1fo gldn brn & multi .45 .45
B277 SP138 2fo + 1fo bl & multi .45 .45
B278 SP138 2fo + 1fo lt vio & multi .45 .45
    Nos. B276-B278 (3) 1.35 1.35

Budapest 71 Philatelic Exhibition, commemorating the centenary of Hungarian postage stamps.
Exist imperf. Value, set $15.

King Matthias I Corvinus — SP139

Initials and Paintings from Bibliotheca Corvina: No. B280, Letter "A." No. B281, Letter "N." No. B282, Letter "O." No. B283a, Ransanus Speaking before King Matthias. No. B283b, Scholar and letter "Q." No. B283c, Portrait of Appianus and letter "C." No. B283d, King David and letter "A."

HUNGARY

1970, Aug. 22 Photo. Perf. 11½x12
B279	SP139	1fo + 50f multi	.40	.40
B280	SP139	1fo + 50f multi	.40	.40
B281	SP139	1fo + 50f multi	.40	.40
B282	SP139	1fo + 50f multi	.40	.40
	Nos. B279-B282 (4)		1.60	1.60

Miniature Sheet
B283		Sheet of 4	2.00	2.00
a.-d.	SP139 2fo + 50f, any single		.50	.45

Issued for the 43rd Stamp Day. No. B283 contains 4 stamps (size: 22½x32mm).
Exist imperf. Value: B279-B282 $12.50; B283 $20.

View of Buda, 1470 — SP140

No. B285, Buda, 1600. No. B286, Buda and Pest, about 1638. No. B287, Buda and Pest, 1770. No. B288a, Buda, 1777. No. B288b, Buda, 1850. No. B288c, Buda, 1895. No. B288d, Budapest, 1970.

1971, Feb. 26 Litho. Perf. 12
B284	SP140	2fo + 1fo blk & yel	.45	.45
B285	SP140	2fo + 1fo blk & pink	.45	.45
B286	SP140	2fo + 1fo blk & pale grn	.45	.45
B287	SP140	2fo + 1fo blk & pale sal	.45	.45
	Nos. B284-B287 (4)		1.80	1.80

Souvenir Sheet Perf. 10½
B288		Sheet of 4	1.50	1.50
a.	SP140 2fo + 1fo blk & pale sal		.30	.30
b.	SP140 2fo + 1fo blk & pale grn		.30	.30
c.	SP140 2fo + 1fo blk & lilac		.30	.30
d.	SP140 2fo + 1fo blk & pink		.30	.30

Budapest 71 Intl. Stamp Exhib. for the cent. of Hungarian postage stamps, Budapest, Sept. 4-12. No. B288 contains 4 stamps, size: 39½x18mm.
Exist imperf. Value: Nos. B284-B287 $12.50; No. B288 $15.

Iris and #P1 — SP141

Designs: No. B290, Daisy and #199. No. B291, Poppy and #391. No. B292, Rose and #B128. No. B293a, Carnations and #B200. No. B293b, Dahlia and #1068. No. B293c, Tulips and #C196. No. B293d, Anemones and #C251.

1971, Sept. 4 Photo. Perf. 12x11½
B289	SP141	2fo + 1fo sil & multi	.60	.60
B290	SP141	2fo + 1fo sil & multi	.60	.60
B291	SP141	2fo + 1fo sil & multi	.60	.60
B292	SP141	2fo + 1fo sil & multi	.60	.60
	Nos. B289-B292 (4)		2.40	2.40

Souvenir Sheet Perf. 11½
B293		Sheet of 4	2.00	2.00
a.-d.	SP141 2fo + 1fo, any single		.35	.35

Cent. of 1st Hungarian postage stamps and in connection with Budapest 71 Intl. Stamp Exhib., Sept. 4-12.
Exist imperf. Value: Nos. B289-B292 $16; No. B293 $20.

Miskólcz Postmark, 1818-43 — SP142

Postmarks: No. B295, Szegedin, 1827-48. No. B296, Esztergom, 1848-51. No. B297, Budapest 1971 Exhibition. No. B298a, Paar family signet, 1593. No. B298b, Courier letter, 1708. No. B298c, First well-known Hungarian postmark "V. TOKAI," 1752. No. B298d, Letter, 1705.

1972, May Perf. 12x11½
B294	SP142	2fo + 1fo blue & blk	.50	.50
B295	SP142	2fo + 1fo yel & blk	.50	.50
B296	SP142	2fo + 1fo yel grn & blk	.50	.50
B297	SP142	2fo + 1fo ver & multi	.50	.50
	Nos. B294-B297 (4)		2.00	2.00

Souvenir Sheet
B298		Sheet of 4	2.00	2.00
a.	SP142 2fo + 1fo yel grn & multi		.40	.40
b.	SP142 2fo + 1fo brn & multi		.40	.40
c.	SP142 2fo + 1fo ultra & multi		.40	.40
d.	SP142 2fo + 1fo red & multi		.40	.40

9th Congress of National Federation of Hungarian Philatelists (Mabeosz). No. B298 contains 4 stamps (size: 32x23mm).
Exist imperf. Value: Nos. B294-B297 $12.50; No. B298 $17.50.

Olympic Type of Regular Issue
Design: Wrestling and Olympic rings.

1972, July 15 Photo. Perf. 11
B299	A484	3fo + 1fo multi	.50	.25

Exists imperf.

Historic Mail Box, Telephone and Molniya Satellite — SP143

Design: No. B301, Post horn, Tokai postmark, and Nos. 183, 1802, 1809.

1972, Oct. 27 Perf. 12
B300	SP143	4fo + 2fo grn & multi	.80	.70
B301	SP143	4fo + 2fo bl & multi	.80	.70

Reopening of the Post and Philatelic Museums, Budapest.
Exist imperf. Value, set $15.

Bird on Silver Disk, 10th Century — SP144

Treasures from Hungarian Natl. Museum. No. B303, Ring with serpent's head, 11th cent. No. B304, Lovers, belt buckle, 12th cent. No. B305, Flower, belt buckle, 15th cent. No. B306a, Opal pendant, 16th cent. No. B306b, Jeweled belt buckle, 18th cent. No. B306c, Flower pin, 17th cent. No. B306d, Rosette pendant, 17th cent.

1973, Sept. 22 Litho. Perf. 12
B302	SP144	2fo + 50f brn & multi	.65	.65
B303	SP144	2fo + 50f brt rose lil & multi	.65	.65
B304	SP144	2fo + 50f dk bl & multi	.65	.65
B305	SP144	2fo + 50f mul-ti	.65	.65
	Nos. B302-B305 (4)		2.60	2.60

Souvenir Sheet
B306		Sheet of 4	2.50	2.50
a.	SP144 2fo + 50f brown & multi		.35	.35
b.	SP144 2fo + 50f car & multi		.35	.35
c.	SP144 2fo + 50f ol grn & multi		.35	.35
d.	SP144 2fo + 50f brt bl & multi		.35	.35

46th Stamp Day. No. B306 contains 4 stamps (size: 25x35mm).
Exist imperf. Value: Nos. B302-B305 $12.50; No. B306 $15.

Gothic Wall Fountain — SP145

Visegrad Castle and Bas-reliefs — SP146

Designs: No. B308, Wellhead, Anjou period. No. B309, Twin lion-head wall fountain. B310, Fountain with Hercules riding dolphin. No. B311a, Raven panel. No. B311b, Visegrad Madonna. B311c, Lion panel. No. B311d, Visegrad Castle. Designs show artworks from Visegrad Palace of King Matthias Corvinus I, 15th century.

1975, Sept. 13 Litho. Perf. 12
Multicolored and:
B307	SP145	2fo + 1fo green	.75	.75
B308	SP145	2fo + 1fo ver	.75	.75
B309	SP145	2fo + 1fo blue	.75	.75
B310	SP145	2fo + 1fo lilac	.75	.75
a.	Horizontal strip of 4		3.00	3.00

Souvenir Sheet
B311	SP146	Sheet of 4	2.00	2.00
a.	2fo + 1fo 21x32mm		.35	.35
b.	2fo + 1fo 47x32mm		.35	.35
c.	2fo + 1fo 21x32mm		.35	.35
d.	2fo + 1fo 99x32mm		.35	.35

European Architectural Heritage Year 1975 and 48th Stamp Day.
Exist imperf. Value: Nos. B307-B310 $85; No. B311 $75.

Knight — SP147

Gothic Sculptures, Buda Castle — SP148

Gothic sculptures from Buda Castle: No. B313, Armor-bearer. No. B314, Apostle. No. B315, Bishop.

1976 Photo. Perf. 12
B312	SP147	2.50 + 1fo shown	.50	.50
B313	SP147	2.50 + 1fo multi	.50	.50
B314	SP147	2.50 + 1fo multi	.50	.50
B315	SP147	2.50 + 1fo multi	.50	.50
a.	Horizontal strip of 4, #B312-B315		2.25	2.25

Souvenir Sheet
Designs: a, Man with hat. b, Woman with wimple. c, Man with cloth cap. d, Man with fur hat.
B316	SP148	Sheet of 4	1.75	1.75
a.-d.	2.50 + 1fo any single		.30	.30

49th Stamp Day.
No. B316 issued in connection with 10th Congress of National Federation of Hungarian Philatelists (Mabeosz).
Exist imperf. Value: Nos. B312-B315 $13; No. B316 $20.
Issued: No. B316, 5/22; Nos. B312-B315, 9/4.

Young Runners — SP149

1977, Apr. 2 Litho. Perf. 12
B317	SP149	3fo + 1.50fo multi	.75	.50

Sports promotion among young people.
Exists imperf. Value $5.

Young Man and Woman, Profiles — SP150

1978, Apr. 1 Litho. Perf. 12
B318	SP150	3fo + 1.50fo multi	1.25	1.25

Hungarian Communist Youth Movement, 60th anniversary.
Exists imperf. Value $10.

"Generations," by Gyula Derkovits — SP151

1978, May 6 Litho. Perf. 12
B319	SP151	3fo + 1.50fo multi	.75	.75

Szocfilex '78, Szombathely. No. B319 printed in sheets of 3 stamps and 3 labels showing Szocfilex emblem.
Exists imperf. Value: single $7.50; sheetlet $15.

Girl Reading Book, by Ferenc Kovacs — SP152

1979, Mar. 31 Litho. Perf. 12
B320	SP152	3fo + 1.50fo blk & ultra	.45	.45

Surtax was for Junior Stamp Exhibition, Bekescsaba.
Exists imperf. Value $7.50.

Watch Symbolizing Environmental Protection — SP153

1980, Apr. 3 Litho. Perf. 12
B321	SP153	3fo + 1.50fo multi	.50	.50

Surtax was for Junior Stamp Exhibition, Dunaujvaros.
Exists imperf. Value $5.

HUGARY

International Year of the Disabled — SP154
1981, May 15 Litho. *Perf. 12*
B322 SP154 2fo + 1fo multi .30 .25
Exists imperf. Value $6.

Youths and Factory — SP155
1981, May 29 *Perf. 12x11½*
B323 SP155 4fo + 2fo multi .80 .80
Young Communist League, 10th Congress, Budapest, May 29-31.
Exists imperf. Value $7.

European Junior Tennis Cup, July 25-Aug. 1 — SP156
1982, Apr. 2 Litho. *Perf. 12x11½*
B324 SP156 4fo + 2fo multi .80 .80
Exists imperf. Value $5.

Souvenir Sheet
SP157
Perf. 12½x11½
1982, June 11 Litho.
B325 SP157 20fo +10fo multi 2.00 2.00
PHILEXFRANCE '82 Stamp Exhibition, Paris, June 11-21.
Exists imperf. Value $15.

55th Stamp Day — SP158
Budapest Architecture and Statues: No. B326, Fishermen's Bastion, Janos Hunyadi (1403-1456). No. B327, Parliament, Ferenc Rakoczi the Second (1676-1735).
1982, Sept. 10 *Perf. 12*
B326 SP158 4fo + 2fo multi .75 .75
B327 SP158 4fo + 2fo shown .75 .75
Exist imperf. Value, set $15.

Souvenir Sheet
Parliament, Chain Bridge, Buda Castle, Budapest — SP159
1982, Sept. 10 *Perf. 11½*
B328 SP159 20fo + 10fo multi 2.00 2.00
European Security and Cooperation Conference, 10th anniv.
Exists imperf. Value $24.

21st Junior Stamp Exhibition, Baja, Mar. 31-Apr. 9 — SP160
1983, Mar. 31 Litho. *Perf. 12x11½*
B329 SP160 4fo + 2fo multi .75 .75
Surtax was for show.
Exists imperf. Value $10.

56th Natl. Stamp Day — SP161
Budapest Architecture (19th Cent. Engravings by) — Rudolph Alt, H. Luders (No. B331): No. B330, Old Natl. Theater. No. B331, Municipal Concert Hall. No. B332, Holy Trinity Square.
1983, Sept. 9 Litho. *Perf. 12*
B330 SP161 4fo + 2fo multi .85 .85
B331 SP161 4fo + 2fo multi .85 .85
Souvenir Sheet
Lithographed and Engraved
Perf. 11
B332 SP161 20fo + 10fo multi 2.00 2.00
No. B332 contains one stamp (28x45mm).
Exist imperf. Value: Nos. B330-B331 $15; No. B332 $20.

Mother & Child — SP162
1984, Apr. 2 Litho. *Perf. 12½x11½*
B333 SP162 4fo + 2fo multi .75 .75
Surtax was for children's foundation.
Exists imperf. Value $10.

SP163
Little Red Riding Hood, by the Brothers Grimm.
1985, Apr. 2 Litho. *Perf. 11½x12*
B334 SP163 4fo + 2fo multi 1.00 .75
Jacob (1785-1863) and Wilhelm (1786-1859) Grimm, fabulists and philologists.
Exists imperf. Value $8.

Natl. SOS Children's Village Assoc., 3rd Anniv. — SP164
1985, Dec. 10 Litho. *Perf. 11*
B335 SP164 4fo + 2fo multi .85 .85
Surtax for natl. SOS Children's Village.
Exists imperf. Value $7.

Natl. Young Pioneers Org., 40th Anniv. — SP165
1986, May 30 *Perf. 11½x12½*
B336 SP165 4fo + 2fo multi .75 .75
Exists imperf. Value $7.50.

Souvenir Sheet
Budapest Natl. Theater — SP166
Lithographed and Engraved
1986, Oct. 10 *Perf. 11*
B337 SP166 20fo + 10fo tan, brn & buff 2.00 2.00
Surtax benefited natl. theater construction.
Exists imperf. Value $20.

Natl. Communist Youth League, 30th Anniv. — SP167
1987, Mar. 20 *Perf. 13½x13*
B338 SP167 4fo + 2fo multi .75 .75
Exists imperf. Value $7.50.

Souvenir Sheet
SOCFILEX '88, Aug. 12-21, Kecskemet — SP168
1988, Mar. 10 Litho. *Perf. 11½*
B339 SP168 20fo +10fo multi 2.50 2.50
Surtax for SOCFILEX '88.
Exists imperf. Value $20.

Sky High Tree, a Tapestry by Erzsebet Szekeres SP169
1989, Apr. 12 Litho. *Perf. 12*
B340 SP169 5fo +2fo multi .75 .75
Surtax to promote youth philately.

Exist imperf. Value, set $10.

Souvenir Sheet
Battle of Solferino, by Carlo Bossoli — SP170
1989, Sept. 8 Litho. *Perf. 10½*
B341 SP170 20fo +10fo multi 3.25 3.25
Stamp Day.
Exists imperf. Value $35.

Souvenir Sheet
Martyrs of Arad, Arad, Romania, 1849 — SP171
1989, Oct. 6 *Perf. 11½x12½*
B342 SP171 20fo +10fo multi 2.50 2.50
Surtax to fund production of another statue.
Exists imperf. Value $20.

Teacher's Training High School, Sarospatak Municipal Arms — SP172
1990, Mar. 30 Litho. *Perf. 12x11½*
B343 SP172 8fo +4fo multi 1.00 1.00
28th Youth Stamp Exhib., Sarospatak, Apr. 6-22.
Exists imperf. Value $7.50.

Souvenir Sheet
Yesterday, by Endre Szasz — SP173
1990, Oct. 12 Litho. *Perf. 12*
B344 SP173 20fo +10fo multi 3.00 3.00
Stamp Day. Surtax for National Federation of Hungarian Philatelists.
Exists imperf. Value $20.

Tapestry, Peter and the Wolf, by Gabriella Hajnal SP174
1991, Apr. 30 Litho. *Perf. 12*
B345 SP174 12fo +6fo multi .75 .75
Surtax to promote youth philately.
Exists imperf. Value $7.

HUNGARY

Children's Drawings — SP175

Designs: 9fo + 4fo, Girl holding flower, vert. 10fo + 4fo, Child standing beneath sun. 15fo + 4fo, Boy wearing crown, vert.

1992, May 15　　Litho.　　Perf. 12
B346　SP175　9fo +4fo multi　　.55　.45
B347　SP175　10fo +4fo multi　　.55　.45
B348　SP175　15fo +4fo multi　　.75　.60
Nos. B346-B348 (3)　　　　1.85　1.50
Surtax for children's welfare.

Souvenir Sheet

1992 Summer Olympics, Barcelona — SP176

1992, Sept. 4　　Litho.　　Perf. 12
B349　SP176　50fo +20fo multi　　3.75　3.75

Textile Art, by Erzsebet Szekeres — SP177

No. B350, Outdoor scene. No. B351, Tree of life.

1993, Apr. 14　　Litho.　　Perf. 12
B350　SP177　10fo +5fo multi　　.75　.60
B351　SP177　17fo +8fo multi　　1.20　1.05

Stamp Day — SP178

Stamp designers, stamps: 10fo + 5fo, Zoltan Nagy (1916-1987), #1062. 17fo + 5fo, Sandor Legrady (1906-1987), #523. 50fo + 20fo, Ferenc Helbing (1870-1959), #465.

1993, Sept. 10　　Litho.　　Perf. 12
B352　SP178　10fo +5fo multi　　.75　.50
B353　SP178　17fo +5fo multi　　1.00　.80

Souvenir Sheet
B354　SP178　50fo +20fo multi　　3.25　3.25
No. B354 contains one 35x27mm stamp.

The Little Prince, by Antoine de Saint-Exupery — SP179

1994, Apr. 1　　Litho.　　Perf. 13½x13
B355　SP179　19fo +5fo multi　　1.00　1.00
Surtax for children's welfare.

Poem, "John the Hero," 150th Anniv. — SP180

1995, Apr. 7　　Litho.　　Perf. 12
B356　SP180　22fo +10fo multi　　1.00　.60
Surtax to promote youth philately.

Olympiafila '95, Budapest — SP181

No. B357, Yellow rings. No. B358, Purple rings.

1995, June 12　　Litho.　　Perf. 11
B357　SP181　22fo +11fo multi　　.85　.65
B358　SP181　22fo +11fo multi　　.85　.65
　a.　Pair, #B357-B358　　　1.95　1.95
No. B358a also sold in a strip of 3 pairs in a booklet.

World Festival of Puppet Players, Budapest — SP182

Laszlo Vitez puppet and ghost puppet.

1996, June 21　　Litho.　　Perf. 12
B359　SP182　24fo +10fo multi　　1.00　.75

Oder River Flood of 1997 — SP183

No. B360, Flower in water.

1997, Sept. 12　　Litho.　　Perf. 12
B360　SP183　27fo +100fo multi　　1.50　1.50
Surtax is for aid to flood victims.

Stamp Day — SP184

Early postman using: 27fo + 5fo, Motorized tricycle. 55fo + 5fo, Experimental registered letter-receiving machine, vert. 90fo + 30fo, Postal van.

1997, Sept. 19
B361　SP184　27fo +5fo multi　　.50　.50
B362　SP184　55fo +5fo multi　　1.00　1.00

Souvenir Sheet
B363　SP184　90fo +30fo multi　　5.00　5.00

Souvenir Sheet

Revolution of 1848 — SP185

Design: Seven members of movement, newspaper *Nemzeti dal*.

1998, Mar. 13　　Litho.　　Perf. 12
B364　SP185　150fo +50fo multi　　3.00　3.00
Surtax to promote youth philately.

Youth Stamp SP186

1999, Mar. 12　　Litho.　　Perf. 12
B365　SP186　52fo +25fo multi　　1.00　.80

István Fekete (1900-70), Writer — SP187

2000, Jan. 11　　Litho.　　Perf. 12
B366　SP187　60fo +30fo multi　　1.25　1.00
Surtax for youth philately.

Hunphilex 2000 Stamp Exhibition, Budapest SP188

2000, Jan. 11
B367　SP188　200fo +100fo multi　　3.00　2.75
Surtax to support stamp exhibition.

Souvenir Sheet

Hunphilex 2000 Stamp Exhibition, Budapest — SP189

No. B368, Coronation robe.

2000, Aug. 18　　Litho.　　Perf. 12
B368　SP189　200fo +100fo multi　　3.75　3.75
　a.　Sheet of 2　　　　7.50　7.50

Star Over Eger, by Geza Gardonyi — SP190

2001, Jan. 15　　Litho.　　Perf. 13¼x13
B369　SP190　60fo +30fo multi　　1.15　1.15
Surtax for youth philately.

Campaign Against Breast Cancer — SP191

2005, Sept. 29　　Litho.　　Perf. 12
B370　SP191　90fo +50fo multi　　1.35　1.15

Victory in First Grand Prix Race by Ferenc Szisz (1873-1944) SP192

2006, May 9　　Litho.　　Perf. 13x13¼
B371　SP192　120fo +50fo multi　　1.50　1.50

Smile, by Zita Zagyi — SP193

2008, May 20　　Litho.　　Perf. 13x13¼
B372　SP193　100fo +50fo multi　　1.15　1.15
Design was a winner in a children's art contest. Surtax for Hungarian Ambulance Service.

Togetherness SP194

2009, Aug. 31
B373　SP194　75fo +50fo multi　　1.25　1.25
Surtax for Crisis Foundation.

Hungarian Red Cross — SP195

2010, Mar. 1　　Litho.　　Perf. 12¼x12¾
B374　SP195　105fo +55fo multi　　1.20　1.20
Surtax for Red Cross.

Interlocking Hands — SP196

2010, Nov. 24　　Litho.　　Perf. 13x13¼
B375　SP196　(80fo) +100fo multi　　1.40　1.40
Surtax for victims of Hungarian Red Sludge disaster of Oct. 4, 2010.

Child and Heart — SP197

2011, Mar. 1　　Litho.　　Perf. 12½x12
B376　SP197　(90fo) +50fo multi　　1.05　.85
Surtax for Intl. Children's Safety Service. For overprint, see No. B379.

Souvenir Sheet

William Shakespeare (1564-1616), Writer — SP198

No. B377 — Characters from *Hamlet*: a, Queen Gertrude. b, Hamlet.

2014, Apr. 25　　Litho.　　Perf. 13¼
B377　SP198　200fo +50fo Sheet of 2, #a-b　　3.25　3.25
Surtax for youth philately.

HUNGARY

Souvenir Sheet

Publication of Poem *Matyi, the Goose Boy*, by Mihály Fazekas, 200th Anniv. — SP199

2015, Mar. 24   Litho.   Perf. 14x13½
B378   SP199   400fo +150fo multi   4.50   4.50
Surtax for youth philately.

No. B376 Overprinted in Green

2015, May 29   Litho.   Perf. 12½x12
B379   SP197   (115fo) +50fo multi   1.25   1.25
Intl. Children's Safety Service, 25th anniv.

Hunfilex 2022 International Philatelic Exhibition, Budapest — SP200

No. B380 — Széchenyi Chain Bridge, Budapest, with denomination at: a, UR. b, UL.

2021, Apr. 8   Litho.   Perf. 13½
B380   SP200   200fo +200fo Horiz.
              pair, #a-b   5.00   5.00
Surtax for defraying the costs of Hunfilex 2022.

AIR POST STAMPS

Issues of the Monarchy

Nos. 120, 123 Surcharged in Red or Blue

Wmk. 137
1918, July 4   Typo.   Perf. 14
C1   A10   1k 50f on 75f (R)   12.00   15.00
C2   A10   4k 50f on 2k (Bl)   12.00   15.00
Counterfeits exist.
Exist imperf. Value, set $350.

No. 126 Surcharged

1920, Nov. 7
C3   A10   3k on 10k (G)   1.20   2.00
C4   A10   8k on 10k (R)   1.20   2.00
C5   A10   12k on 10k (Bl) 1.20   2.00
     Nos. C3-C5 (3)   3.60   6.00
Set, never hinged   7.50

Icarus — AP3

1924-25   Perf. 14
C6   AP3   100k red brn & red   1.25   2.50
C7   AP3   500k bl grn & yel
              grn   1.25   2.50
C8   AP3   1000k bis brn & brn   1.25   2.50
C9   AP3   2000k dk bl & lt bl   1.25   2.50

Wmk. 133
C10 AP3   5000k dl vio & brt
              vio   2.00   2.50
C11 AP3   10000k red & dl vio   2.00   4.00
     Nos. C6-C11 (6)   9.00   16.50
Set, never hinged   20.00
Issue dates: 100k-2000k, 4/11/24. Others, 4/20/25.
Exist imperf. Value, set $100.
Forgeries exist.
For surcharges see Nos. J112-J116.

Mythical "Turul" AP4

"Turul" Carrying Messenger AP5

1927-30   Engr.   Perf. 14
C12 AP4   4f orange ('30)   .25   .40
C13 AP4   12f deep green   .45   .40
C14 AP4   16f red brown   .45   .40
C15 AP4   20f carmine   .45   .40
C16 AP4   32f brown vio   1.75   1.20
C17 AP4   40f dp ultra   1.40   .80
C18 AP5   50f claret   1.40   .80
C19 AP5   72f olive grn   1.90   1.20
C20 AP5   80f dp violet   1.90   1.20
C21 AP5   1p emerald ('30)   2.25   .90
C22 AP5   2p red ('30)   4.50   3.00
C23 AP5   5p dk blue ('30)   16.50 27.50
     Nos. C12-C23 (12)   33.20 37.80
Set, never hinged   66.50
Exist imperf. Value, set $250.

"Turul" Carrying Messenger — AP6

1931, Mar. 27   Overprinted
C24 AP6   1p orange (Bk)   40.00 65.00
C25 AP6   2p dull vio (G)   40.00 65.00
Set, never hinged   160.00
Exist imperf. Value, set $450.

Monoplane over Danube Valley AP7

Worker Welcoming Plane, Double Cross and Sun Rays AP8

Spirit of Flight on Plane Wing AP9

"Flight" Holding Propeller AP10

Wmk. 210
1933, June 20   Photo.   Perf. 15
C26 AP7   10f blue green   1.40   .40
C27 AP7   16f purple   1.40   .40
     Perf. 12½x12
C28 AP8   20f carmine   3.25   .75
C29 AP8   40f blue   2.75   1.25
C30 AP9   48f gray black   6.50   2.00
C31 AP9   72f bister brn   14.00   3.00
C32 AP10 1p yellow grn   17.50   3.00

C33 AP10 2p violet brn   35.00 18.00
C34 AP10 5p dk gray   60.00 150.00
     Nos. C26-C34 (9)   141.80 178.80
Set, never hinged   285.00
Exist imperf. Value, set $2,600.

Catalogue values for unused stamps in this section, from this point to the end of the section, are for Never Hinged items.

Fokker F VII over Mail Coach AP11

Plane over Parliament AP12

Airplane — AP13

1936, May 8   Perf. 12x12½
C35 AP11 10f brt green   .80   .40
C36 AP11 20f crimson   .80   .40
C37 AP11 36f brown   .90   .40
C38 AP12 40f brt blue   .90   .40
C39 AP12 52f red org   3.25   .85
C40 AP12 60f brt violet   20.00   2.00
C41 AP12 80f dk sl grn   4.00   .60
C42 AP13 1p dk yel grn   4.75   .55
C43 AP13 2p brown car   7.50   2.00
C44 AP13 5p dark blue   24.00 19.50
     Nos. C35-C44 (10)   66.90 27.10
Set, hinged   27.50
Exist imperf. Value, set $675.

Issues of the Republic

Loyalty Tower, Sopron — AP14

Designs: 20f, Cathedral of Esztergom. 50f, Liberty Bridge, Budapest. 70f, Palace Hotel, Lillafüred. 1fo, Vajdahunyad Castle, Budapest. 1.40fo, Visegrád Fortress on the Danube. 3fo, Lake Balaton. 5fo, Parliament Building, Budapest.

Perf. 12½x12
1947, Mar. 5   Photo.   Wmk. 210
C45 AP14 10f rose lake   .30   .45
C46 AP14 20f gray green   .30   .45
C47 AP14 50f copper brn   .30   .45
C48 AP14 70f olive grn   .40   .45
C49 AP14 1fo gray blue   1.20   .45
C50 AP14 1.40fo brown   1.20   .45
C51 AP14 3fo green   1.20   .55
C52 AP14 5fo rose violet   4.75   .55
     Nos. C45-C52 (8)   9.65   3.80
Exist imperf. Value, set $250.

Johannes Gutenberg and Printing Press — AP22

Designs: 2f, Columbus. 4f, Robert Fulton. 5f, George Stephenson. 6f, David Schwarz and Ferdinand von Zeppelin. 8f, Thomas A. Edison. 10f, Louis Bleriot. 12f, Roald Amundsen. 30f, Kalman Kando. 40f, Alexander S. Popov.

Perf. 12½x12
1948, May 15   Wmk. 283
C53 AP22 1f orange red   .30   .25
C54 AP22 2f dp magenta   .30   .25
C55 AP22 4f blue   .30   .25
C56 AP22 5f orange brn   .30   .25
C57 AP22 6f green   .30   .25
C58 AP22 8f dp red vio   .30   .25
C59 AP22 10f brown   .40   .40
C60 AP22 12f blue grn   .40   .40
C61 AP22 30f brown rose   1.50   1.50
C62 AP22 40f blue violet   1.90   1.90
     Nos. C53-C62 (10)   6.00   5.70
Explorers and inventors.
Exist imperf. Value, set $90.

See Nos. CB3-CB12.

IMPERFORATE STAMPS

Through 1991, most air post stamps were also issued imperforate. Where these items form part of a larger set with regular issues, values for imperfs will be included in that of the sets to which they belong, footnoted in the Regular Issues section. For Nos. C63-C452, values for imperfs will be given only for those items not included in sets with regular issues.

UPU Type

1949, Nov. 1
C63 A171 2fo orange brn   1.00   1.00
   a.   Booklet pane of 6 37.50
75th anniv. of the UPU. See No. C81.
Exists imperf.

Chain Bridge Type and

Symbols of Labor AP25

1949, Nov. 20
C64 A172 1.60fo scarlet   1.25   .80
C65 A172 2fo olive   1.25   .80

Souvenir Sheet
Perf. 12½x12
C66 AP25 50fo car lake   350.00 225.00
Opening of the Chain Bridge, Budapest, cent.
No. C66 exists imperf. Value $5,500.

Postman and Mail Carrying Vehicles — AP26

1949, Dec. 11   Perf. 12
C67 AP26 50f lilac gray   5.50   5.50
     Sheet of 4   37.50 37.50
Stamp Day, 1949.
Exists imperf. Value: single $100; sheet $525.

Plane, Globe, Stamps and Stagecoach AP27

1950, Mar. 12   Perf. 12x12½
C68 AP27 2fo red brn & yel   9.00   7.50
20th anniv. of the establishment of the Hungarian Post Office Philatelic Museum.
Exists imperf. Value $50.

Chess Emblem, Globe and Plane — AP28

1950, Apr. 9   Wmk. 106   Perf. 12
C69 AP28 1.60fo brown   5.50   1.90
World Chess Championship Matches, Budapest.
Exists imperf.

HUNGARY

Globes, Parliament Building and Chain Bridge — AP29

1950, May 16   *Perf. 12x12½*
C70   AP29   1fo red brown   1.50   .55

Meeting of the World Federation of Trade Unions, Budapest, May 1950.
Exists imperf.

Statue of Liberty and View of Budapest — AP30

Designs: 30f, Crane and apartment house. 70f, Steel mill. 1fo, Stalinyec tractor. 1.60fo, Steamship. 2fo, Reaping-threshing machine. 3fo, Passenger train. 5fo, Matyas Rakosi Steel Mill, Csepel. 10fo, Budaörs Airport.

Perf. 12½x12
1950, Oct. 29   *Engr.*   *Unwmk.*
C71   AP30   20f claret   .30   .25
C72   AP30   30f blue vio   .30   .25
C73   AP30   70f violet brn   .40   .25
C74   AP30   1fo yellow brn   .40   .25
C75   AP30   1.60fo ultra   .75   .25
C76   AP30   2fo red org   .90   .25
C77   AP30   3fo olive blk   1.15   .25
C78   AP30   5fo gray blue   1.65   .25
C79   AP30   10fo chestnut   5.50   .25
   Nos. C71-C79 (9)   11.35   2.25

See Nos. C167 and C172.
Exist imperf. Value, set $100.

Bem Type
Souvenir Sheet
1950, Dec. 10   *Engr.*   *Imperf.*
C80   A185   2fo deep plum   37.50   37.50

Stamp Day and Budapest Stamp Exhibition.

UPU Type of 1949
Perf. 12x12½, Imperf.
1950, July 2   *Photo.*   *Wmk. 106*
C81   A171   3fo dk car & dk brn   40.00   40.00
   Sheet of 4   375.00   400.00

Exists imperf. Value: single $65; sheet of 4 $400.

Sports Type

Designs: 30f, Volleyball. 40f, Javelin-throwing. 60f, Sports badge. 70f, Soccer. 3fo, Glider meet.

1950, Dec. 2
C82   A188   30f lilac & magenta   .40   .25
C83   A188   40f olive & indigo   .75   .25
C84   A188   60f ol, dk brn & org red   .90   .40
C85   A188   70f gray & dk brn   1.50   .55
C86   A188   3fo buff & dk brn   3.25   2.25
   Nos. C82-C86 (5)   6.80   3.70

Exist imperf.

Livestock Type
1951, Apr. 5   *Photo.*   *Perf. 12x12½*
C87   A191   20f Mare & foal   .30   .30
C88   A191   70f Sow & shoats   .75   .40
C89   A191   1fo Ram & ewe   2.75   .75
C90   A191   1.60fo Cow & calf   5.25   1.90
   Nos. C87-C90 (4)   9.05   3.35

Exist imperf.

Telegraph Linemen — AP34

Designs: 1fo, Workers on vacation. 2fo, Air view of Stalin Bridge.

1951, Aug. 20
C91   AP34   70f henna brown   .75   .30
C92   AP34   1fo blue green   .90   .35
C93   AP34   2fo deep plum   1.25   .70
   Nos. C91-C93 (3)   2.90   1.35

Successful conclusion of the 1st year under Hungary's 5-year plan.

Exist imperf.

Tank Column — AP35

1951, Sept. 29   *Perf. 12½x12*
C94   AP35   60f deep blue   .75   .25

Army Day, Sept. 29, 1951.
Exists imperf.

1st Stamp Type
Souvenir Sheet
1951, Oct. 6   *Engr.*   *Unwmk.*
C95   A208   60f olive green   45.00   45.00

Stamp exhibition to commemorate the 80th anniv. of Hungary's 1st postage stamp.
Exists imperf. Value $200.
Twelve hundred copies in rose lilac, perf. and imperf., were presented to exhibitors and members of the arranging committee of the exhibition. Value, each $1,600.

Avocet AP37

Hungarian Birds: 30f, White stork. 40f, Golden oriole. 50f, Kentish plover. 60f, Black-winged stilt. 70f, Lesser gray shrike. 80f, Great bustard. 1fo, Redfooted falcon. 1.40fo, European bee-eater. 1.60fo, Glossy ibis. 2.50fo, Great white egret.

Perf. 13x11
1952, Mar. 16   *Photo.*   *Wmk. 106*
Birds in Natural Colors
C96   AP37   20f emer, *grnsh*   .30   .25
C97   AP37   30f sage grn, *grysh*   .30   .25
C98   AP37   40f brown, *cr*   .30   .25
C99   AP37   50f orange, *cr*   .40   .25
C100   AP37   60f dp car   .60   .25
C101   AP37   70f red org, *cr*   .70   .25
C102   AP37   80f olive, *cr*   1.00   .25
C103   AP37   1fo dp blue, *bluish*   1.20   .25
C104   AP37   1.40fo gray, *grysh*   1.50   .45
C105   AP37   1.60fo org brn, *cr*   1.70   .75
C106   AP37   2.50fo rose vio, *cr*   3.00   1.15
   Nos. C96-C106 (11)   11.00   4.35

Exist imperf. Value, set $100.

Olympic Games Type

Designs: 1.70fo, hammer thrower; 2fo, Stadium, Budapest.

1952, May 26   *Perf. 11*
C107   A217   1.70fo dp red orange   1.80   1.05
C108   A217   2fo olive brown   2.25   1.05

Issued to publicize Hungary's participation in the Olympic Games, Helsinki, 1952.
Exists imperf.

Leonardo da Vinci — AP39

1952, June 15   *Perf. 12½x12*
C109   AP39   1.60fo shown   .90   .55
C110   AP39   2fo Victor Hugo   1.50   .90

Exist imperf. Value, set $35.

AP40   **AP41**

20f, Red squirrel. 30f, Hedgehog. 40f, Hare. 50f, Beech marten. 60f, Otter. 70f, Red fox.

80f, Fallow deer. 1fo, Roe deer. 1.50fo, Boar. 2fo, Red deer.

1953, Mar. 4   *Perf. 12x12½*
C111   AP40   20f multi   .30   .25
C112   AP41   30f multi   .30   .25
C113   AP41   40f multi   .40   .25
C114   AP41   50f multi   .60   .30
C115   AP41   60f multi   .80   .45
C116   AP41   70f multi   1.00   .50
C117   AP40   80f multi   1.25   .75
C118   AP41   1fo multi   1.50   .90
C119   AP41   1.50fo multi   3.00   1.25
C120   AP40   2fo multi   3.75   1.50
   Nos. C111-C120 (10)   12.90   6.40

Exist imperf. Value, set $60.

Type of Regular Issue

Designs: 1fo, Children at Balaton Lake. 1.50fo, Workers' Home at Lillafured.

1953, Apr. 19   *Perf. 12*
C121   A228   1fo brt grnsh blue   .45   .25
C122   A228   1.50fo dp red lilac   .55   .25

Exist imperf.

People's Stadium Type
1953, Aug. 20   *Perf. 11*
C123   A232   80f Water polo   .30   .25
C124   A232   1fo Boxing   .40   .25
C125   A232   2fo Soccer   .90   .35
C126   A232   3fo Track   1.90   .55
C127   A232   5fo Stadium   3.00   1.65
   Nos. C123-C127 (5)   6.50   3.05

Exist imperf.

No. C125 Overprinted in Black

1953, Dec. 3
C128   A232   2fo green & brown   21.00   15.00

Hungary's success in the soccer matches at Wembley, England, Nov. 25, 1953. Counterfeits exist.
Exists imperf. Value $250.

Janos Bihari and Scene from Verbunkos — AP44

Portraits: 40f, Ferenc Erkel. 60f, Franz Liszt. 70f, Mihaly Mosonyi. 80f, Karl Goldmark. 1fo, Bela Bartok. 2fo, Zoltan Kodaly.

1953, Dec. 5   *Photo.*   *Perf. 12*
Frames and Portraits in Brown
C129   AP44   30f blue gray   .35   .25
C130   AP44   40f orange   .35   .25
C131   AP44   60f green   .55   .25
C132   AP44   70f red   .45   .30
C133   AP44   80f gray blue   .50   .40
C134   AP44   1fo olive bis   1.00   .60
C135   AP44   2fo violet   1.50   1.25
   Nos. C129-C135 (7)   4.70   3.30

Hungarian composers.
Exists imperf. Value, set $40.

Carrot Beetle AP45   **May (or June) Beetle AP46**

Designs: Various beetles. 60f, Bee.

Perf. 12½x12, 12x12½
1954, Feb. 6   *Wmk. 106*
C136   AP45   30f dp org & dk brn   .50   .35
C137   AP46   40f grn & dk brn   .50   .35
C138   AP46   50f rose brn & blk   .70   .35
C139   AP46   60f vio, dk brn & yel   .80   .35
C140   AP45   80f grnsh gray, pur & rose   1.10   .35
C141   AP45   1fo ocher & blk   1.30   .75
C142   AP46   1.20fo dl grn & dk brn   1.50   .75
C143   AP46   1.50fo ol brn & dk brn   2.20   .75
C144   AP46   2fo hn brn & dk brn   2.60   1.15
C145   AP45   3fo bl grn & dk brn   3.75   1.90
   Nos. C136-C145 (10)   14.95   7.05

Exists imperf. Value, set $75.

Lunchtime at the Nursery — AP47

Designs: 1.50fo, Mother taking child from doctor. 2fo, Nurse and children.

1954, Mar. 8   *Perf. 12*
C146   AP47   1fo olive green   .75   .25
C147   AP47   1.50fo red brown   1.15   .45
C148   AP47   2fo red brown   2.25   .90
   Nos. C146-C148 (3)   4.15   1.60

Exist imperf.

Model Glider Construction — AP48

Boy Flying Model Glider — AP49

Designs: 60f, Gliders. 80f, Pilot leaving plane. 1fo, Parachutists. 1.20fo, Biplane. 1.50fo, Plane over Danube. 2fo, Jet planes.

1954, June 25   *Perf. 11*
C149   AP48   40f brn, ol & dk bl gray   .30   .25
C150   AP49   50f gray & red brn   .40   .25
C151   AP48   60f red brn & dk bl gray   .40   .25
C152   AP49   80f violet & sep   .45   .25
C153   AP48   1fo brn & dk bl gray   .65   .25
C154   AP49   1.20fo olive & sep   1.00   .25
C155   AP48   1.50fo cl & dk bl gray   1.25   .50
C156   AP49   2fo blue & dk brn   1.90   .50
   Nos. C149-C156 (8)   6.35   2.50

Exist imperf. Value, set $50.

Jokai Type
Souvenir Sheet
1954, Oct. 17   *Engr.*   *Perf. 12½x12*
C157   A242   1fo violet blue   32.50   32.50

Stamp Day. Exists imperforate. Value $75.

Children on Sled — AP51   **Skaters — AP52**

50f, Ski racer. 60f, Ice yacht. 80f, Ice hockey. 1fo, Ski jumper. 1.50fo, Downhill ski racer. 2fo, Man and woman exhibition-skating.

HUNGARY

		1955	Photo.	Perf. 12
C158	AP51	40f multi	.55	.25
C159	AP52	50f multi	.35	.25
C160	AP51	60f multi	.35	.25
C161	AP52	80f multi	.45	.25
C162	AP51	1fo multi	1.10	.30
C163	AP52	1.20fo multi	1.10	.30
C164	AP51	1.50fo multi	2.75	.60
C165	AP52	2fo multi	3.25	.50
		Nos. C158-C165 (8)	9.90	2.70

Exist imperf. Value, set $75.
Issued: 1.20fo, 2fo, Jan. 27; others Feb. 26.

Government Printing Plant Type
Souvenir Sheet
1955, May 28 — *Perf. 12x12½*
C166 A247 5fo hn brn & gray grn 25.00 25.00

Cent. of the establishment of the government printing plant.
Exists imperf. Value $110.

No. C78 Printed on Aluminum Foil
Perf. 12½x12
1955, Oct. 5 — *Engr.* — *Unwmk.*
C167 AP30 5fo gray blue 12.50 12.50

Intl. Cong. of the Light Metal Industry and for 20 years of aluminum production in Hungary.
Exists imperf. Value $60.

Bartok Type
Wmk. 106
1955, Oct. 9 — *Photo.* — *Perf. 12*
C168 A252 1fo gray green 2.00 1.25
C169 A252 1fo violet brn 3.50 2.00
  a. With ticket 7.50 7.50

10th anniv. of the death of Bela Bartok, composer. No. C169a was issued for the Day of the Stamp, Oct. 16, 1955. The 5fo sales price, marked on the attached ticket, was the admission fee to any one of 14 simultaneous stamp shows.
Exist imperf. Value, set with ticket, $100.

"Esperanto" AP55

Lazarus Ludwig Zamenhof AP56

1957, June 8
C170 AP55 60f red brown .40 .25
C171 AP56 1fo dark green .50 .30

10th anniversary of the death of L. L. Zamenhof, inventor of Esperanto.
Exist imperf. Value $30.

Type of 1950
Design: 20fo, Budaörs Airport.

Perf. 12½x12
1957, July 18 — *Engr.* — *Unwmk.*
C172 AP30 20fo dk slate grn 8.75 5.50
  Punched 3 holes 11.00 11.00

A few days after issuance, stocks of No. C172 were punched with three holes and used on domestic surface mail.
Exist imperf. Value $60.

Courier and Fort Buda — AP57

Design: No. C174, Plane over Budapest.

Wmk. 106
1957, Oct. 13 — *Photo.* — *Perf. 12*
C173 AP57 1fo ol bis & brn, *buff* 1.00 1.00
C174 AP57 1fo ol bis & dp cl, *buff* 1.00 1.00
  a. Strip of #C173-C174 + label 2.25 2.25

Stamp Day, Oct. 20th. The triptych sold for 6fo.
Exists imperf. Value, strip $20.

Type of Regular Pigeon Issue
Design: 3fo, Two carrier pigeons.

1957, Dec. 14 — *Perf. 12x12½*
C175 A266 3fo red, grn, gray & blk .90 .25

Exists imperf.

Hungarian Pavilion, Brussels AP58

Designs: 40f, Map, lake and local products. 60f, Parliament. 1fo, Chain Bridge, Budapest. 1.40fo, Arms of Hungary and Belgium. 2fo, Fountain, Brussels, vert. 3fo, City Hall, Brussels vert. 5fo, Exposition emblem.

Perf. 14½x15
1958, Apr. 17 — *Litho.* — *Wmk. 106*
C176 AP58 20f red org & red brn .30 .25
C177 AP58 40f lt blue & brn .30 .25
C178 AP58 60f crimson & sep .30 .25
C179 AP58 1fo bis & red brn .30 .25
C180 AP58 1.40fo dull vio & multi .40 .25
C181 AP58 2fo gldn brn & dk brn .40 .25
C182 AP58 3fo bl grn & sep 1.50 .40
C183 AP58 5fo gray ol, blk, red, bl & yel 1.90 .60
  Nos. C176-C183 (8) 5.40 2.50

Universal and Intl. Exposition at Brussels.
Exist imperf. Value, set $17.50.

View of Prague and Morse Code — AP59

1958, June 30 — *Photo.* — *Perf. 12x12½*
C184 AP59 1fo rose brown .45 .25

See No. 1194a for se-tenant pair.
Conference of Postal Ministers of Communist Countries at Prague, June 30-July 8.
Exists imperf.

Post Horn, Pigeon and Pen — AP60

No. C185, Stamp under magnifying glass.

1958, Oct. 25 — *Wmk. 106* — *Perf. 12*
C185 AP60 1fo dp car & bis .80 .80
C186 AP60 1fo yel grn & bis .80 .80
  a. Strip, #C185-C186 + label 1.90 1.90

Natl. Stamp Exhib., Budapest, 10/25-11/2.
No. C185 inscribed: "XXXI Belyegnap 1958."
Exist imperf. Value, strip $25.

1958, Oct. 26

Designs: 60f, as No. C186. 1fo, Ship, plane, locomotive and pen surrounding letter.
C187 AP60 60f dp plum & grysh buff .50 .25
C188 AP60 1fo bl & grysh buff .70 .25

Issued for Letter Writing Week.
Exist imperf. Value, set $40.

Plane over Heroes' Square Budapest — AP61

Design: 5fo, Plane over Tower of Sopron.

Perf. 12½x12
1958, Nov. 1 — *Engr.* — *Wmk. 106*
C189 AP61 3fo gray, rose vio & red .50 .35
C190 AP61 5fo gry, dk bl & red 1.00 .55

40th anniv. of Hungarian air post stamps.
Exist imperf. Value, set $17.50.

Same Without Commemorative Inscription
Plane over: 20f, Szeged. 30f, Sarospatak. 70f, Gyor. 1fo, Budapest, Opera House. 1.60fo, Veszprém. 2fo, Budapest, Chain Bridge. 3fo, Sopron. 5fo, Heroes' Square, Budapest. 10fo, Budapest, Academy of Science and Parliament. 20fo, Budapest.

1958, Dec. 31 — *Engr.* — *Wmk. 106*
Yellow Paper and Vermilion Inscriptions
C191 AP61 20f green .30 .25
C192 AP61 30f violet .30 .25
C193 AP61 70f brown vio .30 .25
C194 AP61 1fo blue .30 .25
C195 AP61 1.60fo purple .30 .25
C196 AP61 2fo Prus green .30 .25
C197 AP61 3fo brown .35 .25
C198 AP61 5fo olive green .60 .25
C199 AP61 10fo dark blue 1.50 .35
C200 AP61 20fo brown 3.50 .75
  Nos. C191-C200 (10) 7.75 3.10

Exist imperf. Value, set $50.

Transport Type of Regular Issue
Design: 3fo, Early plane.

1959, May — *Litho.* — *Perf. 14½x15*
C201 A279 3fo dl lil, blk, yel & brn 2.00 1.25

Exist imperf.

Tihany — AP62

Designs: 70f, Ship. 1fo, Heviz and water lily. 1.70fo, Sailboat and fisherman statue.

1959, July 15 — *Photo.* — *Perf. 11½x12*
C202 AP62 20f brt green .30 .25
C203 AP62 70f brt blue .30 .25
C204 AP62 1fo ultra & car rose .30 .25
C205 AP62 1.70fo red brn, *yel* .50 .30
  Nos. C202-C205 (4) 1.40 1.05

Issued to publicize Lake Balaton and the opening of the Summer University.
Exist imperf.

Moth-Butterfly Type of 1959
Butterflies: 1fo, Lycaena virgaureae. 2fo, Acherontia atropos, horiz. 3fo, Red admiral.

Perf. 11½x12, 12x11½
1959, Nov. 20 — *Wmk. 106*
Butterflies in Natural Colors
C206 A290 1fo black & lt bl grn .75 .25
C207 A290 2fo black & lilac 1.50 .35
C208 A290 3fo dk gray & emer 2.50 .75
  Nos. C206-C208 (3) 4.75 1.35

Exist imperf.

Souvenir Sheet
Rockets in Orbit, Gagarin, Titov & Glenn — AP63

Perf. 11, Imperf.
1962, Mar. 29 — *Unwmk.*
C209 AP63 10fo multi 14.00 14.00

Cosmonants Yuri A. Gagarin and Gherman Titov, USSR and astronaut John H. Glenn, Jr., US.
Exists imperf. Value $30.

Soccer Type of 1962
Flags of Hungary and Great Britain.

1962, May 21 — *Photo.* — *Perf. 11*
Flags in National Colors
C209A A323 2fo greenish bister .60 .30

Exists imperf.

Glider and Lilienthal's 1898 Design — AP64

Designs: 30f, Icarus and Aero Club emblem. 60f, Light monoplane and 1912 aerobatic plane. 80f, Airship GZ-1 and Montgolfier balloon. 1fo, IL-18 Malev and Wright 1903 plane. 1.40fo, Stunt plane and Nyesterov's 1913 plane. 2fo, Helicopter and Asboth's 1929 helicopter. 3fo, Supersonic bomber and Zhukovski's turbomotor. 4fo, Space rocket and Tsiolkovsky's rocket.

1962, July 19 — *Unwmk.* — *Perf. 15*
C210 AP64 30f blue & dull yel .30 .25
C211 AP64 40f yel grn & ultra .30 .25
C212 AP64 60f ultra & ver .30 .25
C213 AP64 80f grnsh bl & sil .30 .25
C214 AP64 1fo lilac, sil & bl .30 .25
C215 AP64 1.40fo blue & org .30 .25
C216 AP64 2fo bluish grn & brn .30 .25
C217 AP64 3fo vio, sil & bl .50 .25
C218 AP64 4fo grn, sil & blk .80 .35
  Nos. C210-C218 (9) 3.40 2.35

Issued to show flight development: "From Icarus to the Space Rocket."
Exist imperf. Value, set $12.50.

AP65

Design: 1fo, Earth, TV Screens and Rockets. 2fo, Andrian G. Nikolayev, Pavel R. Popovich and rockets.

1962, Sept. 4 — *Perf. 12*
C219 1fo dk bl & org brn .35 .25
C220 2fo dk bl & org brn .75 .25
  a. AP65 Pair, #C219-C220 1.10 1.10

First group space flight of Vostoks 3 and 4, Aug. 11-15, 1962. Printed in alternating horizontal rows.
Exist imperf. Value $16.

John H. Glenn, Jr. — AP66

Astronauts: 40f, Yuri A. Gagarin. 60f, Gherman Titov. 1.40fo, Scott Carpenter. 1.70fo, Andrian G. Nikolayev. 2.60fo, Pavel R. Popovich. 3fo, Walter Schirra.

1962, Oct. 27 — *Perf. 12x11½*
Portraits in Bister
C221 AP66 40f purple .30 .25
C222 AP66 60f dark green .30 .25
C223 AP66 1fo dk bl grn .30 .25
C224 AP66 1.40fo dark brown .30 .25
C225 AP66 1.70fo deep blue .30 .25
C226 AP66 2.60fo violet .65 .30
C227 AP66 3fo red brown 1.10 .45
  Nos. C221-C227 (7) 3.25 2.00

Issued to honor the first seven astronauts and in connection with the Astronautical Congress in Paris.
Exist imperf. Value, set $15.

Eagle Owl — AP67

Birds: 40f, Osprey. 60f, Marsh harrier. 80f, Booted eagle. 1fo, African fish eagle. 2fo, Lammergeier. 3fo, Golden eagle. 4fo, Kestrel.

HUNGARY

1962, Nov. 18　Litho.　Perf. 11½

C228	AP67	30f yel grn & blk	.30	.25
C229	AP67	40f org yel & blk	.30	.25
C230	AP67	60f bister & blk	.30	.25
C231	AP67	80f lt grn & blk	.30	.25
C232	AP67	1fo ol bis & blk	.30	.25
C233	AP67	2fo bluish grn & blk	.35	.25
C234	AP67	3fo lt vio & blk	.65	.30
C235	AP67	4fo dp org & blk	1.25	.50
		Nos. C228-C235 (8)	3.75	2.30

Exist imperf. Value, set $40.

Radio Mast and Albania No. 623 — AP68

Designs (Communication symbols and rocket stamps of various countries): 30f, Bulgaria #C77, vert. 40f, Czechoslovakia #1108. 50f, Communist China #380. 60f, North Korea. 80f, Poland #875. 1fo, Hungary #1386. 1.20fo, Mongolia #189, vert. 1.40fo, DDR #580. 1.70fo, Romania #1200. 2fo, Russia #2456, vert. 2.60fo, North Viet Nam.

Perf. 12x11½, 11½x12

1963, May 9　Photo.　Unwmk.
Stamp Reproductions in Original Colors

C236	AP68	20f olive green	.30	.25
C237	AP68	30f rose lake	.30	.25
C238	AP68	40f violet	.30	.25
C239	AP68	50f brt blue	.30	.25
C240	AP68	60f orange brn	.30	.25
C241	AP68	80f ultra	.30	.25
C242	AP68	1fo dull red brn	.30	.25
C243	AP68	1.20fo aqua	.30	.25
C244	AP68	1.40fo olive	.30	.25
C245	AP68	1.70fo brown olive	.30	.25
C246	AP68	2fo rose lilac	.30	.25
C247	AP68	2.60fo bluish green	.40	.25
		Nos. C236-C247 (12)	3.70	3.00

5th Conference of Postal Ministers of Communist Countries, Budapest.
Exist imperf. Value, set $20.

Souvenir Sheet

Globe and Spaceships — AP69

Perf. 11½x12, Imperf.

1963, July 13　Photo.　Unwmk.

C248	AP69	10fo dk & lt blue	6.00	6.00

Space flights of Valeri Bykovski, June 14-19, and Valentina Tereshkova, 1st woman cosmonaut, June 16-19, 1963.
Exists imperf. Value $25.

Souvenir Sheet

Mt. Fuji and Stadium AP70

1964, Sept. 22　Photo.　Perf. 11½x12

C249	AP70	10fo multi	3.50	3.50

18th Olympic Games, Tokyo, Oct. 10-24.
Exists imperf. Value $20.

Bridge Type of 1964
Souvenir Sheet

Design: Elizabeth Bridge.

1964, Nov. 21　Photo.　Perf. 11

C250	A356	10fo silver & dp grn	3.50	3.50

No. C250 contains one 59x20mm stamp.
Exists imperf. Value $100.

Lt. Col. Alexei Leonov in Space — AP71

Design: 2fo, Col. Pavel Belyayev, Lt. Col. Alexei Leonov and Voskhod 2.

1965, Apr. 17　Photo.　Perf. 11½x12

C251	AP71	1fo violet & gray	.30	.25
C252	AP71	2fo rose claret & ocher	.75	.60

Space flight of Voskhod 2 and of Lt. Col. Alexei Leonov, the first man floating in space.
Exists imperf. Value, set $15.

Mariner IV (USA) — AP72

New achievements in space research: 30f, San Marco satellite, Italy. 40f, Molniya satellite, USSR. 60f, Moon rocket, 1965, USSR. 1fo, Shapir rocket, France. 2.50fo, Zond III satellite, USSR. 3fo, Syncom III satellite, US. 10fo, Rocket sending off satellites, horiz.

1965, Dec. 31　Photo.　Perf. 11

C253	AP72	20f ultra, blk & org yel		
C254	AP72	30f brn, vio & yel	.30	.25
C255	AP72	40f vio, brn & pink	.30	.25
C256	AP72	60f lt pur, blk & org yel	.30	.25
C257	AP72	1fo red lil, blk & buff	.30	.25
C258	AP72	2.50fo rose cl, blk & gray	.60	.25
C259	AP72	3fo bl grn, blk & bis	1.00	.25
		Nos. C253-C259 (7)	3.10	1.75

1965, Dec. 20　Souvenir Sheet

C260	AP72	10fo brt bl, yel & dk ol	2.50	2.50

Exist imperf. Value: Nos. C253-C259 $20; No. C260 $25.

Sport Type of Regular Issue
Souvenir Sheet

10fo, Women hurdlers and Ferihegy airport.

1966, Sept. 4　Photo.　Perf. 12x11½

C261	A384	10fo brt bl, brn & red	2.00	2.00

Exists imperf. Value $20.

Plane over Helsinki — AP73

Plane over Cities Served by Hungarian Airlines: 50f, Athens. 1fo, Beirut. 1.10fo, Frankfort on the Main. 1.20fo, Cairo. 1.50fo, Copenhagen. 2fo, London. 2.50fo, Moscow. 3fo, Paris. 4fo, Prague. 5fo, Rome. 10fo, Damascus. 20fo, Budapest.

1966-67　Photo.　Perf. 12x11½

C262	AP73	20f brown org	.30	.25
C263	AP73	50f brown	.30	.25
C264	AP73	1fo blue	.30	.25
C265	AP73	1.10fo black	.30	.25
C266	AP73	1.20fo orange	.30	.25
C267	AP73	1.50fo blue grn	.30	.25
C268	AP73	2fo brt blue	.30	.25
C269	AP73	2.50fo brt red	.30	.25
C270	AP73	3fo yel grn	.40	.25
C271	AP73	4fo brown red	.40	.25
C272	AP73	5fo brt pur	.30	.25
C273	AP73	10fo violet bl ('67)	.30	.25
C274	AP73	20fo gray ol ('67)	.40	.25
		Nos. C262-C274 (13)	4.20	3.25

Exist imperf. Value, set $90.
See No. C276.

Souvenir Sheet

Icarus Falling AP73a

1968, May 11　Photo.　Perf. 11

C275	AP73a	10fo multicolored	1.50	1.50

In memory of the astronauts Edward H. White, US, Vladimir M. Komarov and Yuri A. Gagarin, USSR.
Exists imperf. Value $20.

Type of 1966-67 without "Legiposta" Inscription

Design: 2.60fo, Malev Airlines jet over St. Stephen's Cathedral, Vienna.

1968, July 4　Photo.　Perf. 12x11½

C276	AP73	2.60fo violet	.50	.25

50th anniv. of regular airmail service between Budapest and Vienna.
Exists imperf. Value $15.00.

Women Swimmers and Aztec Calendar Stone — AP74

Aztec Calendar Stone, Olympic Rings and: 60f, Soccer. 80f, Wrestling. 1fo, Canoeing. 1.40fo, Gymnast on rings. 3fo, Fencing. 4fo, Javelin.

1968, Aug. 21　Photo.　Perf. 12

C277	AP74	20f brt bl & multi	.30	.25
C278	AP74	60f green & multi	.30	.25
C279	AP74	80f car rose & multi	.30	.25
C280	AP74	1fo grnsh bl & multi	.30	.25
C281	AP74	1.40fo violet & multi	.30	.25
C282	AP74	3fo brt lilac & multi	.50	.25
C283	AP74	4fo green & multi	.75	.25
		Nos. C277-C283,CB31 (8)	3.05	2.00

Issued to publicize the 19th Olympic Games, Mexico City, Oct. 12-27.

Exist imperf. Value, set (8) $20.

Souvenir Sheet

Apollo 8 Trip Around the Moon — AP75

1969, Feb.　Photo.　Perf. 12½

C284	AP75	10fo multi	2.00	2.00

Man's 1st flight around the moon, Dec. 21-27, 1968.
Exists imperf. Value $20.

Soyuz 4 and 5, and Men in Space — AP76

Design: No. C286, Soyuz 4 and 5.

1969, Mar. 21　Photo.　Perf. 12x11½

C285	AP76	2fo multi	.35	.35
C286	AP76	2fo dk bl, lt bl & red	.35	.35
a.		Strip, # C285-C286 + label	.75	

First team flights of Russian spacecraft Soyuz 4 and 5, Jan. 16, 1969.
Exist imperf. Value, strip $4.50.

Journey to the Moon, by Jules Verne AP77

Designs: 60f, Tsiolkovski's space station. 1fo, Luna 1. 1.50fo, Ranger 7. 2fo, Luna 9 landing on moon. 2.50fo, Apollo 8 in orbit around moon. 3fo, Soyuz 4 and 5 docking in space. 4fo, Lunar landing module landing on moon. 10fo, Apollo 11 astronauts on moon and lunar landing module.

1969　Photo.　Perf. 12x11½

C287	AP77	40f multi	.30	.25
C288	AP77	60f multi	.30	.25
C289	AP77	1fo multi	.30	.25
C290	AP77	1.50fo multi	.30	.25
C291	AP77	2fo multi	.30	.25
C292	AP77	2.50fo multi	.30	.25
C293	AP77	3fo multi	.50	.25
C294	AP77	4fo multi	.75	.25
		Nos. C287-C294 (8)	3.05	2.00

Souvenir Sheet
Perf. 11

C295	AP77	10fo multi	3.50	3.50

Moon landing issue. See note after Algeria No. 427.
No. C295 contains one 74x49mm stamp. Issued: Nos. C287-C294, 11/1; No. C295, 8/15.
Exist imperf. Value: Nos. C287-C294 $15; No. C295 $30.

Daimler, 1886 AP78

Automobiles: 60f, Peugeot, 1894. 1fo, Benz, 1901. 1.50fo, Cudell mail truck, 1902. 2fo, Rolls Royce, 1908. 2.50fo, Model T Ford, 1908. 3fo, Vermorel, 1912. 4fo, Csonka mail car, 1912.

1970, Feb. 28　Photo.　Perf. 12

C296	AP78	40f ocher & multi	.30	.25
C297	AP78	60f multi	.30	.25
C298	AP78	1fo red & multi	.30	.25
C299	AP78	1.50fo bl & multi	.30	.25
C300	AP78	2fo multi	.30	.25
C301	AP78	2.50fo vio & multi	.30	.25

HUNGARY

| C302 | AP78 | 3fo multi | .40 | .30 |
| C303 | AP78 | 4fo multi | .70 | .50 |

Nos. C296-C303 (8) 2.90 2.30
Exist imperf. Value, set $20.

American Astronauts on Moon — AP79

No. C305, Soyuz 6, 7 and 8 in space.

1970, Mar. 20   **Photo.**   **Perf. 11**
| C304 | AP79 | 3fo blue & multi | .50 | .50 |
| C305 | AP79 | 3fo car rose & multi | .50 | .50 |

Landing of Apollo 12 on the moon, Nov. 14, 1969, and group flight of Russian spacecraft Soyuz 6, 7 & 8, Oct. 11-13, 1969.
Nos. C304-C305 issued in sheets of 4. Size: 112½x78mm.
Exist imperf. Value: set $10; sheets of 4 $40.

"Rain at Foot of Fujiyama," by Hokusai, and Pavilion AP80

3fo, Sun Tower, Peace Bell and globe.

1970, Apr. 30   **Photo.**   **Perf. 12½**
| C306 | AP80 | 2fo multi | .50 | .50 |
| C307 | AP80 | 3fo multi | .75 | .75 |

Issued to publicize EXPO '70 International Exhibition, Osaka, Japan, Mar. 15-Sept. 13.
Exist imperf. Value, set $8.50.

Miniature Sheets

Phases of Apollo 13 Moon Flight AP81

Vignettes of No. C308: Apollo 13 over moon; return to earth; capsule with parachutes; capsule floating, aircraft carrier and helicopter.
Vignettes of No. C309: Soyuz 9 on way to launching pad; launching of Soyuz 9 capsule in orbit; cosmonauts Andrian Nikolayev and Vitaly Sevastyanov.
Vignettes of No. C310: Luna 16 approaching moon; module on moon; landing; nose cone on ground.
Vignettes of No. C311: Lunokhod 1 on moon; trajectories of Luna 17 around earth and moon.

1970-71   **Litho.**   **Perf. 11½**
| C308 | AP81 | Sheet of 4 | 2.00 2.00 |

Photo.
C309	AP81	Sheet of 4	2.00 2.00
C310	AP81	Sheet of 4 ('71)	2.00 2.00
C311	AP81	Sheet of 4 ('71)	2.00 2.00

Nos. C308-C311 were valid for postage only as full sheets. Each contains four 2.50fo vignettes.
No. C308 for the aborted moon flight and safe return of Apollo 13, 4/11-17/70.
No. C309 for the 424-hour flight of Soyuz 9, 6/1-9.
No. C310 for Luna 16, the unmanned, automated moon mission, 9/12-24/70.
No. C311 for Luna 17, unmanned, automated moon mission, 11/10-17/70.
Exist imperf. Value, set $70.
Issued: No. C308, 6/10; No. C309, 9/4; No. C310, 1/15; No. C311 3/8.

Souvenir Sheet

American Astronauts on Moon — AP82

1971, Mar. 31   **Perf. 12½**
| C312 | AP82 | 10fo multi | 1.75 1.75 |

Apollo 14 moon landing, 1/31-2/9/71.
Exists imperf. Value $20.
See Nos. C315, C326-C328.

Hunting Type of Regular Issue
Souvenir Sheet

Design: 10fo, Red deer group.

1971, Aug. 27   **Photo.**   **Perf. 11**
| C313 | A460 | 10fo multi | 3.00 2.50 |

No. C313 contains one 70x45mm stamp.
Exists imperf. Value $35.

Souvenir Sheet

Astronauts Volkov, Dobrovolsky and Patsayev — AP83

1971, Oct. 4   **Photo.**   **Perf. 12½**
| C314 | AP83 | 10fo multi | 1.50 1.50 |

In memory of the Russian astronauts Vladislav N. Volkov, Lt. Col. Georgi T. Dobrovolsky and Victor I. Patsayev, who died during the Soyuz 11 space mission, June 6-30, 1971.
Exists imperf. Value $15.

Apollo 14 Type of 1971
Souvenir Sheet

10fo, American Lunar Rover on moon.

1972, Jan. 20   **Photo.**   **Perf. 12½**
| C315 | AP82 | 10fo multi | 2.00 2.00 |

Apollo 15 moon mission, 7/26-8/7/71.
Exists imperf. Value $15.

Soccer and Hungarian Flag AP84

Various Scenes from Soccer and Natl. Flags of: 60f, Romania. 80f, DDR. 1fo, Great Britain. 1.20fo, Yugoslavia. 2fo, USSR. 4fo, Italy. 5fo, Belgium.

1972, Apr. 29
C316	AP84	40f gold & multi	.30	.25
C317	AP84	60f gold & multi	.30	.25
C318	AP84	80f gold & multi	.30	.25
C319	AP84	1fo gold & multi	.30	.25
C320	AP84	1.20fo gold & multi	.30	.25
C321	AP84	2fo gold & multi	.30	.25
C322	AP84	4fo gold & multi	.85	.25
C323	AP84	5fo gold & multi	1.00	.50
a.		Sheet of 8, #C316-C323	3.25 3.25

Nos. C316-C323 (8) 3.65 2.25
European Soccer Championships for the Henri Delaunay Cup.
Exist imperf. Value: set $15; sheet $30.
Nos. C316-C321 were later issued individually in sheets of 20 and in partly changed colors.

Souvenir Sheet

Olympic Rings and Globe — AP85

1972, June 10   **Photo.**   **Perf. 12½**
| C324 | AP85 | 10fo multi | 4.00 4.00 |

20th Olympic Games, Munich, 8/26-9/11.
Exists imperf. Value $70.

Olympic Type of Regular Issue
Souvenir Sheet

Design: Equestrian and Olympic Rings.

1972, July 15   **Photo.**   **Perf. 12½**
| C325 | A484 | 10fo multi | 2.00 2.00 |

20th Olympic Games, Munich, Aug. 26-Sept. 11. No. C325 contains one 43x43mm stamp.
Exists imperf. Value $20.

Apollo 14 Type of 1971
Souvenir Sheets

Design: 10fo, Astronaut in space, Apollo 16 capsule and badge.

1972, Oct. 10   **Photo.**   **Perf. 12½**
| C326 | AP82 | 10fo blue & multi | 2.00 2.00 |

Apollo 16 US moon mission, 4/15-27/72.
Exists imperf. Value $12.50.

1973, Jan. 15

Design: Astronaut exploring moon, vert.
| C327 | AP82 | 10fo blue & multi | 2.50 2.50 |

Apollo 17 US moon mission, Dec. 7-19, 1972. No. C327 contains one vertical stamp.
Exists imperf. Value $20.

1973, Mar. 12   **Photo.**   **Perf. 12½**
| C328 | AP82 | 10fo Venera 8 | 2.00 2.00 |

Venera 8 USSR space mission, Mar. 27-July 22, 1972.
Exists imperf. Value $17.50.

Equestrian (Pentathlon), Olympic Rings and Medal — AP86

Designs (Olympic Rings and Medals): 60f, Weight lifting. 1fo, Canoeing. 1.20fo, Swimming, women's. 1.80fo, Boxing. 4fo, Wrestling. 6fo, Fencing. 10fo, Allegorical figure lighting flame, vert.

1973, Mar. 31
C329	AP86	40f multi	.30	.25
C330	AP86	60f multi	.30	.25
C331	AP86	1fo blue & multi	.30	.25
C332	AP86	1.20fo multi	.30	.25
C333	AP86	1.80fo multi	.30	.25
C334	AP86	4fo multi	.50	.25
C335	AP86	6fo multi	.60	.25

Nos. C329-C335 (7) 2.60 1.75

Souvenir Sheet
Perf. 11
| C336 | AP86 | 10fo blue & multi | 3.75 3.75 |

Hungarian medalists at 20th Olympic Games. No. C336 contains one 44x71mm stamp.
Exist imperf. Value: Nos. C329-C335 $15; No. C336 $50.

Wrens — AP87

60f, Rock thrush. 80f, Robins. 1fo, Firecrests. 1.20fo, Linnets. 2fo, Blue titmice. 4fo, White-spotted blue throat. 5fo, Gray wagtails.

1973, Apr. 16   **Litho.**   **Perf. 12**
C337	AP87	40f shown	.30	.25
C338	AP87	60f multi	.30	.25
C339	AP87	80f multi	.30	.25
C340	AP87	1fo multi	.30	.25
C341	AP87	1.20fo multi	.30	.25
C342	AP87	2fo multi	.35	.25
C343	AP87	4fo multi	.60	.25
C344	AP87	5fo multi	.75	.25

Nos. C337-C344 (8) 3.20 2.00
Exist imperf. Value $7.50.

Exhibition Type of Regular Issue
Souvenir Sheet

10fo, Bavaria #1 with mill wheel cancellation; Munich City Hall, TV Tower and Olympic tent.

1973, May 11   **Litho.**   **Perf. 11**
| C345 | A506 | 10fo multi | 2.00 2.00 |

No. C345 contains one 83x45mm stamp.
Exists imperf. Value $20.

Souvenir Sheet

Skylab over Earth AP88

1973, Oct. 16   **Photo.**   **Perf. 12½**
| C346 | AP88 | 10fo dk bl, lt bl & yel | 2.25 2.25 |

First US manned space station.
Exists imperf. Value $15.

Space Type of Regular Issue

Designs: 6fo, Mars "canals" and Giovanni V. Schiaparelli. 10fo, Mars 7 spacecraft.

1974, Mar. 11   **Photo.**   **Perf. 12½**
| C347 | A522 | 6fo gold & multi | .75 | .25 |

Souvenir Sheet
| C348 | A522 | 10fo gold & multi | 2.00 2.00 |

Exist imperf. Value, souvenir sheet $17.50.

UPU Type of 1974

Designs: a, Mail coach. b, Old mail automobile. c, Jet. d, Apollo 15.

1974, May 22   **Litho.**   **Perf. 12**
| C349 | A526 | 6fo UPU emblem and TU-154 jet | .75 | .25 |

Souvenir Sheet
| C350 | | Sheet of 4 | 2.00 2.00 |
| a.-d. | | A526 2.50fo, any single | .30 | .30 |

No. C350 has bister UPU emblem in center where 4 stamps meet.
Exist imperf. Value, souvenir sheet $35.

Army Day Type of 1974

Designs: 2fo, Ground-to-air missiles, vert. 3fo, Parachutist, helicopter, supersonic jets.

1974, Sept. 28   **Litho.**   **Perf. 12**
| C351 | A537 | 2fo gold, emer & blk | .30 | .25 |
| C352 | A537 | 3fo gold, emer & blk | .35 | .25 |

Exist imperf.

Carrier Pigeon, Elizabeth Bridge, Mt. Gellert AP89

1975, Feb. 7   **Litho.**   **Perf. 12**
| C353 | AP89 | 3fo multi | .75 | .75 |

Carrier Pigeons' Olympics, Budapest, Feb. 7-9. No. C353 printed checkerwise with black and violet coupon showing Pigeon Olympics emblem.
Exists imperf. Value $13.50.

HUNGARY

Sputnik 2, Apollo-Soyuz Emblem — AP90

Spacecraft and Apollo-Soyuz Emblem: 60f, Mercury-Atlas 5. 80f, Lunokhod I on moon. 1.20fo, Lunar rover, Apollo 15 mission. 2fo, Soyuz take-off, Baikonur. 4fo, Apollo take-off, Cape Kennedy. 6fo, Apollo-Soyuz link-up. 10fo, Apollo, Soyuz, American and Russian flags over earth, horiz.

1975, July 7	Photo.	Perf. 12x11½
C354 AP90	40f silver & multi	.30 .25
C355 AP90	60f silver & multi	.30 .25
C356 AP90	80f silver & multi	.30 .25
C357 AP90	1.20fo silver & multi	.30 .25
C358 AP90	2fo silver & multi	.30 .25
C359 AP90	4fo silver & multi	.45 .25
C360 AP90	6fo silver & multi	.75 .25
Nos. C354-C360 (7)		2.70 1.75

Souvenir Sheet
Perf. 12½

C361 AP90 10fo blue & multi 2.00 2.00

Apollo Soyuz space test project (Russo-American cooperation), launching July 15; link-up July 17. No. C361 contains one 59x38mm stamp.
Exist imperf. Value: Nos. C354-C360 $25; No. C361 $22.50.

Souvenir Sheet

Map of Europe and Cogwheels — AP91

1975, July 30	Litho.	Perf. 12½
C362 AP91	10fo multi	2.00 2.00

European Security and Cooperation Conference, Helsinki, July 30-Aug. 1.
Exists imperf. Value $40.

Souvenir Sheet

Hungary Nos. 1585, 1382, 2239, 2280, C81 — AP92

1975, Sept. 9	Photo.	Perf. 12½
C363 AP92	10fo multi	2.00 2.00

30 years of stamps.
Exists imperf. Value $20.
A similar souvenir sheet with blue margin, no denomination and no postal validity was released for the 25th anniversary of Filatelica Hungarica.

Souvenir Sheet

Paintings by Károly Lotz and János Halápi AP93

1976, Mar. 19	Photo.	Perf. 12½
C364 AP93	Sheet of 2	2.00 2.00
a.	5fo Horses in Storm	.80 .80
b.	5fo Morning at Tihany	.80 .80

Tourist publicity. Nos. C364a and C364b are imperf. between.
Exists imperf. Value $27.50.

Souvenir Sheet

Montreal Olympic Stadium — AP94

1976, June 29	Litho.	Perf. 12½
C365 AP94	20fo red, gray & blk	3.50 3.50

21st Olympic Games, Montreal, Canada, July 17-Aug. 1.
Exists imperf. Value $27.50.

US Mars Mission — AP95

60f, Viking in space. 1fo, Viking on Mars. 2fo, Venus, rocket take-off. 3fo, Venera 9 in space. 4fo, Venera 10, separation in space. 5fo, Venera on Venus. 20fo, Viking 1 landing on Mars, vert.

1976, Nov. 11	Photo.	Perf. 11
C366 AP95	40f silver & multi	.30 .25
C367 AP95	60f silver & multi	.30 .25
C368 AP95	1fo silver & multi	.30 .25
C369 AP95	2fo silver & multi	.30 .25
C370 AP95	3fo silver & multi	.30 .25
C371 AP95	4fo silver & multi	.50 .25
C372 AP95	5fo silver & multi	.60 .25
Nos. C366-C372 (7)		2.60 1.75

Souvenir Sheet
Perf. 12½

C373 AP95 20fo black & multi 2.25 2.25

US-USSR space missions. No. C373 contains one stamp (size: 41x64mm).
Exist imperf. Value: Nos. C366-C372 $20; No. C373 $20.

Hungary No. CB33 AP96

1977, May 2	Litho.	Perf. 11½x12
C374 AP96	3fo multi	.85 .85

European stamp exhibitions. Issued in sheets of 3 stamps and 3 labels. Labels show exhibition emblems respectively: 125th anniversary of Brunswick stamps, Brunswick, May 5-8; Regiofil XII, Lugano, June 17-19; centenary of San Marino Stamps, Riccione, Aug. 27-29.
Exists imperf. Value: single $10; sheetlet $22.50.

Space Type 1977
Souvenir Sheet

Design: 20fo, Viking on Mars.

1977, Sept. 20	Litho.	Perf. 11½
C375 A603	20fo multi	2.00 2.00

Exists imperf. Value $20.

Souvenir Sheet

"EUROPA," Map and Dove — AP97

1977, Oct. 3		Perf. 12½
C376 AP97	20fo multi	1.50 1.50

European Security Conference, Belgrade, Oct.-Nov.
Exists imperf. Value $20.

TU-154, Malev over Europe — AP98

Planes, Airlines, Maps: 1.20fo, DC-8, Swissair, Southeast Asia. 2fo, IL-62, CSA, North Africa. 2.40fo, A 300B Airbus, Lufthansa, Northwest Europe. 4fo, Boeing 747, Pan Am, North America. 5fo, TU-144, Aeroflot, Northern Europe. 10fo, Concorde, Air France, South America. 20fo, IL-86, Aeroflot, Northeast Asia.

1977, Oct. 26	Litho.	Perf. 11½x12
Size: 32x21mm		
C377 AP98	60f orange & blk	.30 .25
C378 AP98	1.20fo violet & blk	.30 .25
C379 AP98	2fo yellow & blk	.30 .25
C380 AP98	2.40fo bl grn & blk	.30 .25
C381 AP98	4fo ultra & blk	.30 .25
C382 AP98	5fo dp rose & blk	.30 .25
C383 AP98	10fo blue & blk	.75 .25
Perf. 12x11½		
Size: 37½x29mm		
C384 AP98	20fo green & blk	1.75 .25
Nos. C377-C384 (8)		4.30 2.00

Exist imperf. Value, set $27.50.

Montgolfier Brothers and Balloon, 1783 AP99

Designs: 60f, David Schwarz and airship, 1850. 1fo, Alberto Santos-Dumont and airship flying around Eiffel Tower, 1901. 2fo, Konstantin E. Tsiolkovsky, airship and Kremlin, 1857. 3fo, Roald Amundsen, airship Norge, Polar bears and map, 1872. 4fo, Hugo Eckener, Graf Zeppelin over Mt. Fuji, 1930. 5fo, Count Ferdinand von Zeppelin, Graf Zeppelin over Chicago, 1932. 20fo, Graf Zeppelin over Budapest, 1931.

1977, Nov. 1	Photo.	Perf. 12x11½
C385 AP99	40f gold & multi	.30 .25
C386 AP99	60f gold & multi	.30 .25
C387 AP99	1fo gold & multi	.30 .25
C388 AP99	2fo gold & multi	.30 .25
C389 AP99	3fo gold & multi	.40 .25
C390 AP99	4fo gold & multi	.50 .25
C391 AP99	5fo gold & multi	.90 .25
Nos. C385-C391 (7)		3.00 1.75

Souvenir Sheet
Perf. 12½

C392 AP99 20fo silver & multi 2.00 2.00

History of airships. No. C392 contains one 60x36mm stamp.
Exist imperf. Value: Nos. C385-C391 $15; No. C392 $25.

Moon Station AP100

Science Fiction Paintings by Pal Varga: 60f, Moon settlement. 1fo, Spaceship near Phobos. 2fo, Exploration of asteroids. 3fo, Spaceship in gravitational field of Mars. 4fo, Spaceship and rings of Saturn. 5fo, Spaceship landing on 3rd Jupiter moon.

1978, Mar. 10	Litho.	Perf. 11
C393 AP100	40f multi	.30 .25
C394 AP100	60f multi	.30 .25
C395 AP100	1fo multi	.30 .25
C396 AP100	2fo multi	.30 .25
C397 AP100	3fo multi	.30 .25
C398 AP100	4fo multi	.50 .25
C399 AP100	5fo multi	.60 .25
Nos. C393-C399 (7)		2.60 1.75

Exist imperf. Value, set $13.50.

Louis Bleriot and La Manche AP101

60f, J. Alcock & R. W. Brown, Vickers Vimy, 1919. 1fo, A. C. Read, Navy Curtiss NC-4, 1919. 2fo, H. Köhl, G. Hünefeld, J. Fitzmaurice, Junkers W33, 1928. 3fo, A. Johnson, J. Mollison, Gipsy Moth, 1930. 4fo, G. Endresz, S. Magyar, Lockheed Sirius, 1931. 5fo, W. Gronau, Dornier WAL, 1932. 20fo, Wilbur & Orville Wright & their plane.

1978, May 10	Litho.	Perf. 12
C400 AP101	40f multi	.30 .25
C401 AP101	60f multi	.30 .25
C402 AP101	1fo multi	.30 .25
C403 AP101	2fo multi	.30 .25
C404 AP101	3fo multi	.40 .25
C405 AP101	4fo multi	.50 .25
C406 AP101	5fo multi	.75 .25
Nos. C400-C406 (7)		2.85 1.75

Souvenir Sheet

C407 AP101 20fo multi 2.00 2.00

75th anniv. of 1st powered flight by Wright brothers. No. C407 contains one 75x25mm stamp.
Exist imperf. Value: Nos. C400-C406 $20; No. C407 $25.

Souvenir Sheet

Jules Verne and "Voyage from Earth to Moon" — AP102

1978, Aug. 21		Perf. 12½x11½
C408 AP102	20fo multi	2.00 2.00

Jules Verne (1828-1905), French science fiction writer.
Exists imperf. Value $15.

Vladimir Remek Postmarking Mail on Board Salyut 6 — AP103

1978, Sept. 1	Photo.	Perf. 11½x12
C409 AP103	3fo multi	.75 .75

PRAGA '78 International Philatelic Exhibition, Prague, Sept. 8-17. Issued in sheets of 3 stamps and 3 labels, showing PRAGA '78 emblem and Golden Tower, Prague. FISA emblems in margin.
Exists imperf. Value: single $6; sheetlet $15.

Ski Jump AP104

HUNGARY

Lake Placid '80 Emblem and: 60f, 20fo, Figure skating, diff. 1fo, Downhill skiing. 2fo, Ice hockey. 4fo, Bobsledding. 6fo, Cross-country skiing.

1979, Dec. 15	Litho.		Perf. 12	
C410	AP104	40f multi	.30	.25
C411	AP104	60f multi	.30	.25
C412	AP104	1fo multi	.30	.25
C413	AP104	2fo multi	.50	.25
C414	AP104	4fo multi	.75	.30
C415	AP104	6fo multi	1.00	.55
	Nos. C410-C415 (6)		3.15	1.85

Souvenir Sheet

| C416 | AP104 | 20fo multi | 1.50 | 1.50 |

13th Winter Olympic Games, Lake Placid, NY, Feb. 12-24, 1980.
Exist imperf. Value: Nos. C410-C415 $20; No. C416 $25.

Soviet and Hungarian Cosmonauts — AP105

1980, May 27	Litho.		Perf. 11½x12	
C417	AP105	5fo multi	.75	.25

Intercosmos cooperative space program.
Exists imperf. Value $20.

Women's Handball, Moscow '80 Emblem, Olympic Rings — AP106

1980, June 16	Photo.		Perf. 11½x12	
C418	AP106	40f shown	.30	.25
C419	AP106	60f Double kayak	.30	.25
C420	AP106	1fo Running	.30	.25
C421	AP106	2fo Gymnast	.30	.25
C422	AP106	3fo Equestrian	.30	.25
C423	AP106	4fo Wrestling	.55	.25
C424	AP106	5fo Water polo	.65	.25
	Nos. C418-C424 (7)		2.70	1.75

Souvenir Sheet

| C425 | AP106 | 20fo Torch bearers | 2.00 | 2.00 |

22nd Summer Olympic Games, Moscow, July 19-Aug. 3.
See No. C427.
Exist imperf. Value: Nos. C418-C424 $20; No. C425 $17.50.

Souvenir Sheet

Cosmonauts Bertalan Farkes and Valery Kubasov, Salyut 6-Soyuz 35 and 36 — AP107

1980, July 12	Litho.		Perf. 12½	
C426	AP107	20fo multi	2.50	2.50

Intercosmos cooperative space program (USSR-Hungary).
Exists imperf. Value $25.

Olympic Type of 1980
Souvenir Sheet

20fo, Greek Frieze and gold medal.

1980, Sept. 26	Litho.		Perf. 12½	
C427	AP106	20fo multi	2.00	2.00

Olympic Champions.
Exists imperf. Value $20.

Kalman Kittenberger (1881-1958), Zoologist and Explorer — AP108

40f, Cheetah. 60f, Lion. 1fo, Leopard. 2fo, Rhinoceros. 3fo, Antelope. 4fo, African elephant.

1981, Mar. 6	Photo.		Perf. 11½	
C427A	AP108	40f multi	.30	.25
C427B	AP108	60f multi	.30	.25
C427C	AP108	1fo multi	.30	.25
C427D	AP108	2fo multi	.30	.25
C427E	AP108	3fo multi	.30	.25
C427F	AP108	4fo multi	.50	.25
C427G	AP108	5fo shown	1.15	.35
	Nos. C427A-C427G (7)		3.15	1.85

Exist imperf. Value, set $20.

Graf Zeppelin over Tokyo, First Worldwide Flight, Aug. 7-Sept. 4, 1929 — AP109

Graf Zeppelin Flights (Zeppelin and): 2fo, Icebreaker Malygin, Polar flight, July 24-31, 1931. 3fo, Nine Arch Bridge, Hortobagy, Hungary, Mar. 28-30, 1931. 4fo, Holsten Tor, Lubeck, Baltic Sea, May 12-15, 1931. 5fo, Tower Bridge, England, Aug. 18-20, 1931. 6fo, Federal Palace, Chicago World's Fair, 50th crossing of Atlantic, Oct. 14-Nov. 2, 1933. 7fo, Lucerne, first flight across Switzerland, Sept. 26, 1929.

	Perf. 12½x11½			
1981, Mar. 16			Litho.	
C428	AP109	1fo multi	.30	.25
C429	AP109	2fo multi	.30	.25
C430	AP109	3fo multi	.30	.25
C431	AP109	4fo multi	.40	.25
C432	AP109	5fo multi	.50	.25
C433	AP109	6fo multi	.50	.25
C434	AP109	7fo multi	.75	.35
	Nos. C428-C434 (7)		3.05	1.85

LURABA '81, First Aviation and Space Philatelic Exhibition, Lucerne, Switzerland, Mar. 20-29. No. C434 se-tenant with label showing exhibition emblem.
Exist imperf. Value, set $15.

Illustrator Type of 1981

Illustrations by A. Lesznai: 4fo, At the End of the Village. 5fo, Dance. 6fo, Sunday.

1981, Dec. 29	Litho.		Perf. 11½x12	
C435	A693	4fo multicolored	.40	.40
C436	A693	5fo multicolored	.50	.50
C437	A693	6fo multicolored	1.00	1.00
	Nos. C435-C437 (3)		1.90	1.90

Exist imperf.

Manned Flight Bicentenary — AP110

Various hot air balloons.

1983, Apr. 5	Litho.		Perf. 12x11½	
C438	AP110	1fo 1811	.30	.25
C439	AP110	1fo 1896	.30	.25
C440	AP110	2fo 1904	.30	.25
C441	AP110	2fo 1977	.30	.25
C442	AP110	4fo 1981	.40	.25
C443	AP110	4fo 1982	.40	.25
C444	AP110	5fo 1981	.75	.25
	Nos. C438-C444 (7)		2.75	1.75

Souvenir Sheet
Perf. 12½

| C445 | AP110 | 20fo 1983 | 2.25 | 2.25 |

No. C445 contains one 39x49mm stamp.
Exist imperf. Value: Nos. C438-C444 $25; No. C445 $32.50.

Audubon Type of 1985

4fo, Colaptes auratus. 6fo, Richmondena cardinalis.

1985, June 19	Litho.		Perf. 12	
C446	A778	4fo multi	.60	.25
C447	A778	6fo multi	.85	.25

Exist imperf.

Aircraft — AP111

1fo, Lloyd CII. 2fo, Brandenburg Cl. 4fo, UFAG Cl. 10fo, Gerle 13. 12fo, WM 13.

1988, Aug. 31	Litho.		Perf. 11	
C448	AP111	1fo multi	.30	.25
C449	AP111	2fo multi	.30	.25
C450	AP111	4fo multi	.30	.25
C451	AP111	10fo multi	.60	.25
C452	AP111	12fo multi	.75	.25
	Nos. C448-C452 (5)		2.25	1.25

Exist imperf. Value, set $30.

AIR POST SEMI-POSTAL STAMPS

> Catalogue values for unused stamps in this section are for Never Hinged items.

Roosevelt Type of Semipostal Stamps, 1947

F. D. Roosevelt, Plane and Place: 10f+10f, Casablanca. 20f+20f, Tehran. 50f+50f, Yalta (map). 70f+70f, Hyde Park.

1947, June 11	Photo.	Wmk. 210
Portrait in Sepia		
CB1	SP115 10f + 10f red vio	3.75 4.00
CB1A	SP115 20f + 20f brn ol	3.75 4.00
CB1B	SP115 50f + 50f vio	3.75 4.00
CB1C	SP115 70f + 70f blk	3.75 4.00
	Nos. CB1-CB1C (4)	15.00 16.00

Exist imperf.
A souvenir sheet contains one each of Nos. CB1-CB1C with border inscriptions and decorations in gray. Size: 161x122mm. Value $75. Exists imperf. Value $135.
See note below Nos. B198A-B198D.

Souvenir Sheet

Chain Bridge, Budapest — SPAP1

	Perf. 12x12½	
1948, May 15	Photo.	Wmk. 283
CB1D	SPAP1 2fo + 18fo brn car	100.00 100.00

Exists imperf. Value $1,750.

Souvenir Sheet

Chain Bridge SPAP2

1948, Oct. 16
CB2 SPAP2 3fo + 18fo dp grnsh bl   100.00 100.00

Exists imperf. Value $1,750.

Type of Air Post Stamps of 1948
Portraits at Right

Writers: 1f, William Shakespeare. 2f, Francois Voltaire. 4f, Johann Wolfgang von Goethe. 5f, Lord Byron. 6f, Victor Hugo. 8f, Edgar Allen Poe. 10f, Sandor Petőfi. 12f, Mark Twain. 30f, Count Leo Tolstoy. 40f, Maxim Gorky.

1948, Oct. 16			Photo.	
CB3	AP22	1f dp ultra	.30	.25
CB4	AP22	2f rose carmine	.30	.25
CB5	AP22	4f dp yellow grn	.30	.25
CB6	AP22	5f dp rose lilac	.30	.25
CB7	AP22	6f deep blue	.30	.25
CB8	AP22	8f olive brn	.30	.25
CB9	AP22	10f red	.35	.40
CB10	AP22	12f deep violet	.35	.40
CB11	AP22	30f orange brn	1.35	1.25
CB12	AP22	40f sepia	1.65	1.50
	Nos. CB3-CB12 (10)		5.50	5.05

Sold at a 50 per cent increase over face, half of which aided reconstruction of the Chain Bridge and the other half the hospital for postal employees.
Exist imperf. Value, set $100.

1st Stamp Type
Souvenir Sheets
Perf. 12½x12

1951, Sept. 12		Engr.	Unwmk.
CB13	A208	1fo + 1fo red	45.00 45.00
CB14	A208	2fo + 2fo blue	45.00 45.00

Exist imperf. Value, each $175.

Children Inspecting Stamp Album — SPAP3

2fo+2fo, Children at stamp exhibition.

Perf. 12x12½

1952, Oct. 12	Photo.	Wmk. 106
CB15	SPAP3 1fo + 1fo blue	7.50 7.50
CB16	SPAP3 2fo + 2fo brn red	7.50 7.50

Stamp week, Oct. 11-19, 1952.
Exist imperf. Value, set $80.

Globe and Mailbox — SPAP4

Designs: 1fo+50f, Mobile post office. 2fo+1fo, Telegraph pole. 3fo+1.50fo, Radio. 5fo+2.50fo, Telephone. 10fo+5fo, Post horn.

1957, June 20		Perf. 12x12½, 12	
Cross in Red			
Size: 32x21mm			
CB17	SPAP4 60f + 30f bis brn	.35	.25
CB18	SPAP4 1fo + 50f lilac	.35	.25
CB19	SPAP4 2fo + 1fo org ver	.75	.25
CB20	SPAP4 3fo + 1.50fo blue	1.15	.45
CB21	SPAP4 5fo + 2.50fo gray	2.25	.75
Size: 46x31mm			
CB22	SPAP4 10fo + 5fo pale grn	4.50	1.20
	Nos. CB17-CB22 (6)	9.35	3.30

The surtax was for the benefit of hospitals for postal and telegraph employees.
Exist imperf. Value, set $70.

Parachute of Fausztusz Verancsics, 1617 — SPAP5

History of Hungarian Aviation: No. CB24, Balloon of David Schwarz, 1897. No. CB25, Monoplane of Ernö Horvath, 1911. No. CB26, PKZ-2 helicopter, 1918.

Engraved and Lithographed

1967, May 6		Perf. 10½	
CB23	SPAP5 2fo + 1fo sep & yel	.50	.50
CB24	SPAP5 2fo + 1fo sep & lt bl	.50	.50
CB25	SPAP5 2fo + 1fo sep & lt grn	.50	.50

HUNGARY

CB26 SPAP5 2fo + 1fo sep & pink .50 .50
   a. Horiz. strip of 4, #CB23-CB26 2.75 2.75
   b. Souv. sheet of 4, #CB23-CB26 3.00 2.75

"AEROFILA 67" International Airmail Exhibition, Budapest, Sept. 3-10.
Exist imperf. Value: strip $12.50; souvenir sheet $35.

1967, Sept. 3

Aviation, 1967: No. CB27, Parachutist. No. CB28, Helicopter Mi-1. No. CB29, TU-154 jet. No. CB30, Space station Luna 12.

CB27 SPAP5 2fo + 1fo slate & lt grn .50 .50
CB28 SPAP5 2fo + 1fo slate & buff .50 .50
CB29 SPAP5 2fo + 1fo slate & yel .50 .50
CB30 SPAP5 2fo + 1fo slate & pink .50 .50
   a. Horiz. strip of 4, #CB27-CB30 2.00 2.00
   b. Souv. sheet of 4, #CB27-CB30 2.50 2.50

Issued to commemorate (in connection with AEROFILA 67) the 7th Congress of FISA (Fédération Internationale des Sociétés Aérophilatéliques) and the 40th Stamp Day.
Exist imperf. Value: strip $15; souvenir sheet $30.

Olympic Games Airmail Type

Design: 2fo+1fo, Equestrian.

1968, Aug. 21   Photo.   Perf. 12
CB31 AP74 2fo + 1fo multi .30 .25
Exists imperf.

1st Hungarian Airmail Letter, 1918, Plane — SPAP6

Designs: No. CB33, Letter, 1931, and Zeppelin. No. CB34, Balloon post letter, 1967, and balloon. No. CB35, Letter, 1969, and helicopter.
No. CB36: a, #C1. b, #C7. c, #C305. d, #C312.

1974, Oct. 19   Litho.   Perf. 12
CB32 SPAP6 2fo + 1fo multi .75 .75
CB33 SPAP6 2fo + 1fo multi .75 .75
   a. Pair, #CB32-CB33 1.60 1.60
CB34 SPAP6 2fo + 1fo multi .75 .75
CB35 SPAP6 2fo + 1fo multi .75 .75
   a. Pair, #CB34-CB35 1.60 1.60
Nos. CB32-CB35 (4) 3.00 3.00

Souvenir Sheet

CB36 Sheet of 4 2.50 2.50
   a.-d. SPAP6 2fo+1fo any single .40 .40

AEROFILA, International Airmail Exhibition, Budapest, Oct. 19-27.
No. CB36 contains 4 35x25mm stamps.
Exist imperf. Value: set of 2 pairs $15; souvenir sheet $12.50.

SPECIAL DELIVERY STAMPS

Issue of the Monarchy

SD1

1916   Typo.   Wmk. 137   Perf. 15
E1 SD1 2f gray green & red .30 .25
Exists imperf. Value $7.50.
For overprints and surcharges see Nos. 1NE1, 2NE1, 4N5, 5NE1, 6NE1, 7NE1, 8NE1, 10NE1, 11NE1, 11NJ7-J8.

Issues of the Republic

Special Delivery Stamp of 1916 Overprinted

1919
E2 SD1 2f gray green & red .30 .75
Exists imperf. Value $12.50.

General Issue

SD2

1919
E3 SD2 2f gray green & red .30 .75
Exists imperf. Value $10.

REGISTRATION STAMPS

Catalogue values for unused stamps in this section are for Never Hinged items.

Nos. 625, 609 and 626 Overprinted in Carmine

a   b

"Ajl." or "Ajánlás" = Registered Letter.

1946   Wmk. 266   Perf. 15
F1 A118(a) "Ajl.1." on 20f .30 .25
   a. "Ajl.1." 50.00
F2 A99(a) "Ajl.2." on 12f .30 .25
F3 A118(b) "Ajánlás" on 24f .30 .25
Nos. F1-F3 (3) .90 .75

Hellebore — R1

2011, May 2   Litho.   Perf. 12¼x12¾
F4 R1 (315fo) multi 3.50 1.75

Illuminated Postal Service Sign, 1993 — R2

Die Cut Perf. 11½
2021, May 5   Self-Adhesive   Typo.
F5 R2 (630fo) multi 4.50 2.25
Hungarian Postal Service, 150th anniv.

POSTAGE DUE STAMPS

Issues of the Monarchy

D1

Perf. 11½, 11¾x12
1903   Typo.   Wmk. 135
J1 D1 1f green & blk 1.50 .30
J2 D1 2f green & blk 4.50 .90
J3 D1 5f green & blk 15.00 4.00
J4 D1 6f green & blk 12.00 3.50
J5 D1 10f green & blk 75.00 1.75
J6 D1 12f green & blk 4.50 1.50
J7 D1 20f green & blk 20.00 .90
J8 D1 50f green & blk 15.00 7.50
J9 D1 100f green & blk 3.00 .60
Nos. J1-J9 (9) 150.50 20.95

See Nos. J10-J26, J28-J43. For overprints and surcharges see Nos. J27, J44-J50, 1NJ1-1NJ5, 2NJ1-2NJ16, 4NJ2-4NJ3, 5NJ1-5NJ8, 6NJ1-6NJ9, 7NJ1-7NJ4, 9NJ1-9NJ3, 10NJ1-10NJ6, 11NJ1-J6.

1908-09   Wmk. 136   Perf. 15
J10 D1 1f green & black .75 .50
J11 D1 2f green & black 1.00 .50
J12 D1 5f green & black 2.50 .75
J13 D1 6f green & black 1.50 .50
J14 D1 10f green & black 1.50 .50
J15 D1 12f green & black 1.25 .50
J16 D1 20f green & black 10.00 .50
   c. Center inverted 9,000. 9,000.
J17 D1 50f green & black 1.75 .75
Nos. J10-J17 (8) 20.25 4.50

1905   Wmk. 136a   Perf. 11½x12
J12a D1 5f green & black 175.00 70.00
J13a D1 6f green & black 14.00 7.50
J14a D1 10f green & black 175.00 5.00
J15a D1 12f green & black 25.00 16.00
J17a D1 50f green & black 6.00 2.50
J18 D1 100f green & black 5.00

1906   Perf. 15
J11b D1 2f green & black 3.50 3.50
J12b D1 5f green & black 2.50 2.00
J13b D1 6f green & black 2.50 2.00
J14b D1 10f green & black 15.00 .60
J15b D1 12f green & black .75 .60
J16b D1 20f green & black 25.00 .60
   d. Center inverted 9,000. 9,000.
J17b D1 50f green & black 1.00 1.00
Nos. J11b-J17b (7) 50.25 10.30

1914   Wmk. 137 Horiz.   Perf. 15
J19 D1 1f green & black .35 .25
J20 D1 2f green & black .25 .25
J21 D1 5f green & black .40 .40
J22 D1 6f green & black .80 .60
J23 D1 10f green & black .90 .70
J24 D1 12f green & black .40 .25
J25 D1 20f green & black .35 .25
J26 D1 50f green & black .70 .25
Nos. J19-J26 (8) 4.15 2.95

1914   Wmk. 137 Vert.
J20a D1 2f green & black 57.50 57.50
J21a D1 5f green & black 4.50 4.50
J22a D1 6f green & black 9.00 7.50
J25a D1 20f green & black 2,250. 900.00
J26a D1 50f green & black 2.50 2.50

During 1921-24, a number of Postage Due stamps were punched with three holes prior to sale. See note following No. 105 in the Regular Postage section.

No. J9 Surcharged in Red

1915   Wmk. 135
J27 D1 20f on 100f grn & blk .30 1.50
   a. On No. J18, Wmk. 136a 15.00 32.50

1915-22   Wmk. 137
J28 D1 1f green & red .25 .25
J29 D1 2f green & red .25 .25
J30 D1 5f green & red .35 .25
J31 D1 6f green & red .25 .25
J32 D1 10f green & red .25 .25
J33 D1 12f green & red .25 .25
J34 D1 15f green & red .35 .50
J35 D1 20f green & red .25 .25
J36 D1 30f green & red .25 .25
J37 D1 40f green & red ('20) .25 .25
J38 D1 50f green & red ('20) .25 .25
   a. Center inverted 60.00
J39 D1 120f green & red ('20) .25 .25
J40 D1 200f green & red ('20) .25 .25
J41 D1 2k green & red ('22) .25 .90
J42 D1 5k green & red ('22) .25 .25
J43 D1 50k green & red ('22) .50 .30
Nos. J28-J43 (16) 4.45 4.95

Issues of the Republic

Postage Due Stamps of 1914-18 Overprinted in Black

1918-19   On Issue of 1914
J44 D1 50f green & black 3.00 5.50

On Stamps and Type of 1915-18
J45 D1 2f green & red .25 .75
J46 D1 3f green & red .25 .75
   a. "KOZTARSASAG" omitted 650.00
J47 D1 10f green & red .25 .75
J48 D1 20f green & red .25 .75
J49 D1 40f green & red .25 .75
   a. Inverted overprint 60.00 60.00
J50 D1 50f green & red .25 .75
   a. Center and overprint inverted 75.00 75.00
Nos. J44-J50 (7) 4.50 10.00

Issues of the Kingdom

D3

1919-20   Typo.
J65 D3 2f green & black .25 .50
   a. Inverted center 2,200.
J66 D3 3f green & black .25 .50
J67 D3 20f green & black .25 .50
J68 D3 40f green & black .25 .50
J69 D3 50f green & black .25 .50
Nos. J65-J69 (5) 1.25 2.50

Postage Due Stamps of this type have been overprinted "Magyar Tancskztarsasag" but have not been reported as having been issued without the additional overprint "heads of wheat."
For overprints see Nos. J70-J75.

Additional Overprint in Black

1920
J70 D3 2f green & black .85 1.50
J71 D3 3f green & black .85 1.50
J72 D3 10f green & black 1.40 2.50
J73 D3 20f green & black .85 1.50
J74 D3 40f green & black .85 1.50
J75 D3 50f green & black .85 1.50
Nos. J70-J75 (6) 5.65 10.00

Postage Issues Surcharged

a   b

c

1921-25   Red Surcharge
J76 A9(a) 100f on 15f violet .25 .25
J77 A9(a) 500f on 15f violet .25 .25
J78 A9(b) 2½k on 10f red vio .25 .25
J79 A9(b) 3k on 15f violet .25 .25
J80 A9(c) 6k on 1½k violet .25 1.50
J81 A9(b) 9k on 40f ol grn .25 .25
J82 A9(b) 10k on 2½k green .25 1.25
J83 A9(b) 12k on 60f blk brn .25 .25
J84 A9(c) 15k on 1½k vio .25 .25
J85 A9(c) 20k on 2½k grn .25 1.10
J86 A9(c) 25k on 1½k vio .25 .25
J87 A9(c) 30k on 1½k vio .25 .25
J88 A9(c) 40k on 2½k grn .25 1.25
J89 A9(c) 50k on 1½k vio .25 .25
J90 A9(c) 100k on 4½k dl vio .25 .25
J91 A9(c) 200k on 4½k dl vio .25 .25
J92 A9(c) 300k on 4½k dl vio .25 .25
J93 A9(c) 500k on 2k green
   bl .60 .25
J94 A9(c) 500k on 3k org brn 2.10 .30
J95 A9(c) 1000k on 2k grnsh
   bl 1.20 .25
J96 A9(c) 1000k on 3k org brn 1.75 .25
J97 A9(c) 2000k on 2k grnsh
   bl 1.20 .40
J98 A9(c) 2000k on 3k org brn 2.10 .35
J99 A9(c) 5000k on 5k brown .90 1.75
Nos. J76-J99 (24) 14.10 11.90

Year of issue: 6k, 15k, 25k, 30k, 50k, 1922. 10k, 20k, 40k, 100k - No. J93, Nos. J95, J97, 1923. 5,000k, 1924. Nos. J94, J96, J98, 1925. Others, 1921.

D6

Perf. 14x14½, 15
1926   Wmk. 133   Litho.
J100 D6 1f rose red .25 .25
J101 D6 2f rose red .25 .25
J102 D6 3f rose red .30 .60
J103 D6 4f rose red .25 .25
J104 D6 5f rose red 1.75 2.50

HUNGARY

J105	D6	8f rose red	.25	.25
J106	D6	10f rose red	1.25	.25
J107	D6	16f rose red	.30	.25
J108	D6	32f rose red	.50	.25
J109	D6	40f rose red	.75	.25
J110	D6	50f rose red	.90	.40
J111	D6	80f rose red	1.25	.65
		Nos. J100-J111 (12)	8.00	6.15

Exist imperf. Value, set $100.
See Nos. J117-J123. For surcharges see Nos. J124-J129.

Nos. C7-C11 Surcharged in Red or Green

1926   Wmk. 137   Perf. 14
J112	AP3	1f on 500k (R)	.25	.30
J113	AP3	2f on 1000k (G)	.25	.30
J114	AP3	3f on 2000k (R)	.25	.30

Wmk. 133
J115	AP3	5f on 5000k (G)	.65	1.50
J116	AP3	10f on 10000k (G)	.50	1.10
		Nos. J112-J116 (5)	1.90	3.50

Type of 1926 Issue
1928-32   Wmk. 210   Perf. 15
J117	D6	2f rose red	.25	.25
J118	D6	4f rose red ('32)	.25	.25
J119	D6	8f rose red	.25	.25
J120	D6	10f rose red	.25	.25
J121	D6	16f rose red	.35	.25
J122	D6	20f rose red	.60	.25
J123	D6	40f rose red	.50	.25
		Nos. J117-J123 (7)	2.45	1.75

Exist imperf. Value, set $60.

Postage Due Stamps of 1926 Surcharged in Black

1931-33   Wmk. 133
J124	D6	4f on 5f rose red	.25	.25
J125	D6	10f on 16f rose red	1.50	3.75
J126	D6	10f on 80f rose red ('33)	.35	.25
J127	D6	12f on 32f rose red ('33)	.35	.25
J128	D6	20f on 32f rose red	.35	.25
		Nos. J124-J128 (5)	2.75	4.80

Surcharged on No. J121
1931   Wmk. 210   Perf. 15
J129	D6	10f on 16f rose red	.85	1.25

Catalogue values for unused stamps in this section, from this point to the end of the section, are for Never Hinged items.

Figure of Value — D7

1934   Photo.   Wmk. 210
J130	D7	2f ultra	.25	.25
J131	D7	4f ultra	.25	.25
J132	D7	6f ultra	.25	.25
J133	D7	8f ultra	.25	.25
J134	D7	10f ultra	.25	.25
J135	D7	12f ultra	.25	.25
J136	D7	16f ultra	.25	.25
J137	D7	20f ultra	.40	.25
J138	D7	40f ultra	.60	.25
J139	D7	80f ultra	2.00	.50
		Nos. J130-J139 (10)	4.75	2.75

Exist imperf. Value, set $60.

Coat of Arms and Post Horn — D8

1941
J140	D8	2f brown red	.30	.25
J141	D8	4f brown red	.30	.25
J142	D8	4f brown red	.30	.25
J143	D8	6f brown red	.30	.25
J144	D8	8f brown red	.30	.25
J145	D8	10f brown red	.30	.25
J146	D8	12f brown red	.30	.25
J147	D8	16f brown red	.30	.25
J148	D8	20f brown red	.30	.25
J150	D8	40f brown red	.30	.25
		Nos. J140-J150 (9)	2.70	2.25

Exist imperf. Value, set $25.

1941-44   Wmk. 266
J151	D8	2f brown red	.30	.25
J152	D8	3f brown red	.30	.25
J153	D8	4f brown red	.30	.25
J154	D8	6f brown red	.30	.25
J155	D8	8f brown red	.30	.25
J156	D8	10f brown red	.30	.25
J157	D8	12f brown red	.30	.25
J158	D8	16f brown red	.30	.25
J159	D8	18f brown red ('44)	.30	.25
J160	D8	20f brown red	.30	.25
J161	D8	24f brown red	.30	.25
J162	D8	30f brown red ('44)	.30	.25
J163	D8	36f brown red ('44)	.30	.25
J164	D8	40f brown red	.30	.25
J165	D8	50f brown red	.30	.25
J166	D8	60f brown red ('44)	.30	.25
		Nos. J151-J166 (16)	4.80	4.00

Exist imperf. Value, set $30.
For surcharges see Nos. J167-J185.

Issues of the Republic

Types of Hungary Postage Due Stamps, 1941-44, Surcharged in Carmine

1945   Wmk. 266   Photo.   Perf. 15
Blue Surface-tinted Paper
J167	D8	10f on 2f brn red	.30	.25
J168	D8	10f on 3f brn red	.30	.25
J169	D8	20f on 4f brn red	.30	.25
J170	D8	20f on 6f brn red	.40	.40
J171	D8	20f on 8f brn red	.30	.25
J172	D8	40f on 12f brn red	.30	.25
J173	D8	40f on 16f brn red	.30	.25
J174	D8	40f on 18f brn red	.30	.25
J175	D8	60f on 24f brn red	.30	.25
J176	D8	80f on 30f brn red	.30	.25
J177	D8	90f on 36f brn red	.30	.25
J178	D8	1p on 10f brn red	.30	.25
J179	D8	1p on 40f brn red	.30	.25
J180	D8	2p on 20f brn red	.30	.25
J181	D8	2p on 50f brn red	.30	.25
J182	D8	2p on 60f brn red	.30	.25

Surcharged in Black, Thicker Type
J183	D8	10p on 3f brn red	.30	.25
J184	D8	12p on 8f brn red	.30	.25
J185	D8	20p on 24f brn red	.30	.25
		Nos. J167-J185 (19)	5.80	4.90

D9

1946-50   Wmk. 210   Perf. 15
Numerals in Deep Magenta
J186	D9	4f magenta	.35	.25
J187	D9	10f magenta	.85	.25
J188	D9	10f magenta	.35	.25
J189	D9	30f magenta	.35	.25
J190	D9	40f magenta	.50	.25
J191	D9	50f mag ('50)	1.50	.25
J192	D9	60f magenta	1.00	.25
J193	D9	1.20fo magenta	1.50	.25
J194	D9	2fo magenta	2.50	.25
		Nos. J186-J194 (9)	8.90	2.25

1951   Wmk. 106
Numerals in Deep Magenta
J194A	D9	4f magenta	.30	.25
J194B	D9	10f magenta	.30	.25
J194C	D9	20f magenta	.65	.25
j.		"fiellr"	35.00	7.50
J194D	D9	30f magenta	.80	.25
J194E	D9	40f magenta	.30	.25
J194F	D9	50f magenta	.55	.25
J194G	D9	60f magenta	.45	.25
J194H	D9	1.20fo magenta	1.90	.25
J194I	D9	2fo magenta	1.60	.25
		Nos. J194A-J194I (9)	6.85	2.25

Nos. J194A-J194I are found in both large format (about 18x22mm) and small about 17x21mm).

Revenue Stamps with Blue Surcharge — D10
Paper with Vertical Lines in Green

1951   Unwmk.   Typo.   Perf. 14½x15
J195	D10	8f dark brown	.30	.25
J196	D10	10f dark brown	.30	.25
J197	D10	12f dark brown	.30	.25
		Nos. J195-J197 (3)	.90	.75

D11

1951   Wmk. 106   Photo.   Perf. 14½
J198	D11	4f brown	.30	.25
J199	D11	6f brown	.30	.25
J200	D11	8f brown	.30	.25
J201	D11	10f brown	.30	.25
J202	D11	14f brown	.30	.25
J203	D11	20f brown	.30	.25
J204	D11	30f brown	.30	.25
J205	D11	40f brown	.30	.25
J206	D11	50f brown	.30	.25
J207	D11	60f brown	.30	.25
J208	D11	1.20fo brown	.30	.25
J209	D11	2fo brown	.30	.25
		Nos. J198-J209 (12)	3.60	3.00

Exist imperf. Value, set $30.

D12

Photo., Numeral Typo. in Black
1953   Numerals 3mm High
J210	D12	4f dull green	.30	.25
J211	D12	6f dull green	.30	.25
J212	D12	8f dull green	.30	.25
J213	D12	10f dull green	.30	.25
J214	D12	12f dull green	.30	.25
J215	D12	14f dull green	.30	.25
J216	D12	16f dull green	.30	.25
J217	D12	20f dull green	.30	.25
J218	D12	24f dull green	.30	.25
J219	D12	30f dull green	.30	.25
J220	D12	36f dull green	.30	.25
J221	D12	40f dull green	.30	.25
J222	D12	50f dull green	.30	.25
J223	D12	60f dull green	.30	.25
J224	D12	70f dull green	.30	.25
J225	D12	80f dull green	.30	.25

Numerals 4½mm High
J226	D12	1.20fo dull green	.30	.25
J227	D12	2fo dull green	.30	.25
a.		Small "2" (3mm high)	1.10	.90
		Nos. J210-J227 (18)	5.40	4.50

1st Hungarian postage due stamp, 50th anniv.
Exist imperf. Value, set $100.

D13

Photo., Numeral Typo. in Black on Nos. J228-J243
1958   Wmk. 106   Perf. 14½
Size: 21x16½mm
J228	D13	4f red	.30	.25
J229	D13	6f red	.30	.25
J230	D13	8f red	.30	.25
J231	D13	10f red	.30	.25
J232	D13	12f red	.30	.25
J233	D13	14f red	.30	.25
J234	D13	16f red	.30	.25
J235	D13	20f red	.30	.25
J236	D13	24f red	.30	.25
J237	D13	30f red	.30	.25
J238	D13	36f red	.30	.25
J239	D13	40f red	.30	.25
J240	D13	50f red	.30	.25
J241	D13	60f red	.30	.25
J242	D13	70f red	.30	.25
J243	D13	80f red	.30	.25

Perf. 12
Size: 31x21mm
J244	D13	1.20fo dk red brn	.30	.25
J245	D13	2fo dk red brn	.30	.25
		Nos. J228-J245 (18)	5.40	4.50

Exist imperf. Value, set $15.

Photo., Numeral Typo. in Black on Nos. J246-J261
1965-69   Unwmk.   Perf. 11½
Size: 21x16½mm
J246	D13	4f red	.30	.25
J247	D13	6f red	.30	.25
J248	D13	8f red	.30	.25
J249	D13	10f red	.30	.25
J250	D13	12f red	.30	.25
J251	D13	14f red	.30	.25
J252	D13	16f red	.30	.25
J253	D13	20f red	.30	.25
J254	D13	24f red	.30	.25
J255	D13	30f red	.30	.25
J256	D13	36f red	.30	.25
J257	D13	40f red	.30	.25
J258	D13	50f red	.30	.25
J259	D13	60f red	.30	.25
J260	D13	70f red	.30	.25
J261	D13	80f red	.30	.25

Perf. 11½x12
Size: 31x21mm
J262	D13	1fo dk red brn ('69)	.30	.25
J263	D13	1.20fo dk red brn	.30	.25
J264	D13	2fo dk red brn	.30	.25
J265	D13	4fo dk red brn ('69)	.30	.25
		Nos. J246-J265 (20)	6.00	5.00

Mail Plane and Truck — D14

Designs: 20f, Money order canceling machine. 40f, Scales in self-service P.O. 80f, Automat for registering parcels. 1fo, Keypunch operator. 1.20fo, Mail plane and truck. 2fo, Diesel mail train. 3fo, Mailman on motorcycle with sidecar. 4fo, Rural mail delivery. 8fo, Automatic letter sorting machine. 10fo, Postman riding motorcycle.

1973-85   Photo.   Perf. 11
Size: 21x18mm
J266	D14	20f brown & ver	.30	.25
J267	D14	40f dl bl & ver	.30	.25
J268	D14	80f violet & ver	.30	.25
J269	D14	1fo ol grn & ver	.30	.25

Perf. 12x11½
Size: 28x22mm
J270	D14	1.20fo green & ver	.30	.25
J271	D14	2fo lilac & ver	.30	.25
J272	D14	3fo brt blue & ver	.30	.25
J273	D14	4fo org brn & ver	.35	.25
J274	D14	8fo dp mag & dk red	.65	.25
J275	D14	10fo grn & dk red	.75	.25
		Nos. J266-J275 (10)	3.85	2.50

Issued: 20f-4fo, 12/1973; 8fo, 10fo, 12/16/85.

Postal History — D15

Designs: Excerpt from 18th cent. letter, innovations in letter carrying: 1fo, Foot messenger, 16th cent. 4fo, Post rider, 17th cent. 6fo, Horse-drawn mail coach, 18th cent. 8fo, Railroad mail car, 19th cent. 10fo, Mail truck, 20th cent. 20fo, Airplane, 20th cent.

1987, Dec. 10   Litho.   Perf. 12
J276	D15	1fo multicolored	.30	.25
J277	D15	4fo multicolored	.30	.25
J278	D15	6fo multicolored	.30	.25
J279	D15	8fo multicolored	.30	.25
J280	D15	10fo multicolored	.50	.25
J281	D15	20fo multicolored	1.00	.25
		Nos. J276-J281 (6)	2.70	1.50

OFFICIAL STAMPS

During 1921-24, a number of Official stamps were punched with three holes prior to sale. See note following No. 105 in the Regular Postage section.

O1

1921-23   Wmk. 137   Typo.   Perf. 15
O1	O1	10f brn vio & blk	.25	.25
O2	O1	20f ol brn & blk	.25	.25
a.		"HIVATALOS" inverted		10,000.
O3	O1	60f blk brn & blk	.25	.25
O4	O1	100f dl rose & blk	.25	.25
O5	O1	250f bl & blk	.25	.25
O6	O1	350f gray & blk	.25	.25
O7	O1	500f lt brn & blk	.25	.25
O8	O1	1000f lil brn & blk	.25	.25
O9	O1	5k brn ('23)	.25	.25
O10	O1	10k choc ('23)	.25	.25
O11	O1	15k gray blk ('23)	.25	.25
O12	O1	25k org ('23)	.25	.25

HUNGARY

O13	O1	50k brn & red ('22)	.25 .25
O14	O1	100k bis & red ('22)	.25 .25
O15	O1	150k grn & red ('23)	.25 .25
O16	O1	300k dl red & red ('23)	.25 .25
O17	O1	350k vio & red ('23)	.25 .25
O18	O1	500k org & red ('22)	.30 .25
O19	O1	600k ol bis & red ('23)	.30 .25
O20	O1	1000k bl & red ('22)	1.20 1.00
		Nos. O1-O20 (20)	6.60 5.35

Counterfeits of No. O2a exist.

Stamps of 1921 Surcharged in Red

1922
| O21 | O1 | 15k on 20f ol brn & blk | .25 .25 |
| O22 | O1 | 25k on 60f blk brn & blk | .25 .25 |

Stamps of 1921 Overprinted in Red

1923
| O23 | O1 | 350k gray & blk | .25 .25 |

With Additional Surcharge of New Value in Red

O24	O1	150k on 100f dl rose & blk	.30 .25
O25	O1	2000k on 250f bl & blk	1.50 .60
		Nos. O23-O25 (3)	2.05 .90

Three-Hole Punch

1923-24 Paper with Gray Moiré on Face
O26	O1	500k org & red ('23)	2.10 .25
O27	O1	1000k bl & red ('23)	2.10 .25
O28	O1	3000k vio & red ('24)	2.10 1.25
O29	O1	5000k bl & red ('24)	2.40 1.50
		Nos. O26-O29 (4)	8.70 3.25

1924 Wmk. 133
| O30 | O1 | 500k orange & red | 1.40 1.00 |
| O31 | O1 | 1000k blue & red | 1.40 1.00 |

NEWSPAPER STAMPS

Issues of the Monarchy

St. Stephen's Crown and Post Horn
N1   N2

Litho. (#P1), Typo. (#P2)

1871-72 Unwmk. Imperf.
P1	N1	(1k) ver red	50.00 20.00
P2	N2	(1k) rose red ('72)	20.00 6.00
a.		(1k) vermilion	10.00 2.00
b.		Printed on both sides	

Reprints of No. P2 are watermarked. Value, $450.

Letter with Crown and Post Horn — N3

1874
| P3 | N3 | 1k orange | 4.50 .35 |

1881 Wmk. "kr" in Oval (132)
P4	N3	1k orange	1.25 .25
a.		1k lemon yellow	16.00 4.50
b.		Printed on both sides	

1898 Wmk. 135
| P5 | N3 | 1k orange | 1.25 .30 |

See watermark note after No. 46.

N5

1900 Wmk. Crown in Circle (135)
| P6 | N5 | (2f) red orange | .75 .25 |

1905 Wmk. Crown (136a)
| P7 | N5 | (2f) red orange | 1.25 .35 |
| a. | | Wmk. 136 ('08) | 1.00 .25 |

1914-22 Wmk. Double Cross (137)
P8	N5	(2f) orange	.35 .50
a.		Wmk. horiz.	4.50 3.75
P9	N5	(10f) deep blue ('20)	.40 .25
P10	N5	(20f) lilac ('22)	.40 .25
		Nos. P8-P10 (3)	1.15 1.00

For overprints and surcharges see Nos. 1NJ6-1NJ10, 1NP1, 2NP1, 5NP1, 6NP1, 8NP1, 10NP1, 11NP1.

NEWSPAPER TAX STAMPS

Issues of the Monarchy

NT1   NT2

Wmk. 91; Unwmk. from 1871

1868 Typo. Imperf.
PR1	NT1	1k blue	4.00 1.00
a.		Pair, one sideways	
PR2	NT2	2k brown	20.00 10.00
a.		2k red brown	275.00 47.50

NT3

1868
| PR2B | NT3 | 1k blue | 50,000. 11,000. |

No. PR2B was issued for the Military Border District only. All used stamps are precanceled (newspaper text printed on the stamp). A similar 2k was not issued.

1889-90 Wmk. "kr" in Oval (132)
| PR3 | NT1 | 1k blue | 2.00 .80 |
| PR4 | NT2 | 2k brown | 5.50 5.00 |

1898 Wmk. Crown in Oval (135)
| PR5 | NT1 | 1k blue | 6.00 7.50 |

These stamps did not pay postage, but represented a fiscal tax collected by the postal authorities on newspapers.
Nos. PR3 and PR5 have a tall "k" in "kr."

PARCEL POST STAMPS

Nos. 629, 613, 612, 615, 630, 667 and Type of 1943-45 Overprinted in Black or Carmine

a   b

"Cs." or "Csomag"=Parcel

1946 Wmk. 266 Perf. 15
Q1	A118	"Cs. 5-1." on 70f #629	.30 .25
Q2	A109	"Cs. 5-1." on 30f #613	17.25 17.25
Q3	A99	"Cs. 5-2." on 24f #612	.30 .25
Q4	A118	"Cs. 10-1." on 70f #629	.30 .25
Q5	A118	"Cs. 10-1." on 80f #615	30.00 30.00
Q6	A118	"Cs. 10-2." on 80f #630	.30 .25
Q7	A99	"Csomag 5kg." on 2p on 4f #667 (C+Bk)	.30 .25
Q8	A118	"Csomag 10kg." on 30f copper red, bl	.30 .25
		Nos. Q1-Q8 (8)	49.05 48.75

No. Q8 was not issued without overprint.

Catalogue values for unused stamps in this section, from this point to the end of the section, are for Never Hinged items.

No. 796 Surcharged with New Value in Red or Black

1954 Wmk. 210
Q9	A144	1.70fo on 1.40fo	1.15 1.15
Q10	A144	2fo on 1.40fo (Bk)	1.50 .35
Q11	A144	3fo on 1.40fo	1.15 1.15
		Nos. Q9-Q11 (3)	3.80 1.85
		Set, hinged	1.80

OCCUPATION STAMPS

Issued under French Occupation

ARAD ISSUE

The overprints on this issue have been extensively forged. Even the inexpensive values are difficult to find with genuine overprints. Values are for genuine overprints. Collectors should be aware that stamps sold "as is" are likely to be forgeries, and unexpertized collections should be assumed to consist of mostly forged stamps. Education plus working with knowledgeable dealers is mandatory in this collecting area. More valuable stamps should be expertized.

Stamps of Hungary Overprinted in Red or Blue

On Issue of 1916-18

1919 Wmk. 137 Perf. 15, 14
1N1	A9	2f brn org (R)	1.60 1.60
1N2	A9	3f red lil (R)	.75 .75
1N3	A9	5f green (R)	20.00 20.00
1N4	A9	6f grnsh bl (R)	1.90 1.90
a.		Inverted overprint	30.00 30.00
1N5	A9	10f rose red	4.00 4.00
1N6	A9	15f violet (R)	1.75 1.75
a.		Double overprint	50.00 50.00
1N7	A9	20f gray brn (R)	50.00 50.00
1N8	A9	35f brown (R)	65.00 65.00
1N9	A9	40f ol grn (R)	37.50 37.50
1N10	A10	50f red vio & lil	6.00 6.00
1N11	A10	75f brt bl & pale bl	2.00 2.00
1N12	A10	80f grn & pale grn	2.75 2.75
1N13	A10	1k red brn & cl	15.00 15.00
1N14	A10	2k ol brn & bis	3.00 3.00
a.		Inverted overprint	50.00 50.00
1N15	A10	3k dk vio & ind	17.50 17.50
1N16	A10	5k dk brn & lt brn	13.50 13.50
1N17	A10	10k vio brn & vio	70.00 70.00
		Nos. 1N1-1N17 (17)	312.25 312.25

With Additional Surcharges

a   b

c   d

1N18	A9	(a) 45f on 2f brn org	8.00 8.00
1N19	A9	(b) 45f on 2f brn org	8.00 8.00
1N20	A9	(c) 50f on 3f red lil	8.00 8.00
1N21	A9	(d) 50f on 3f red lil	8.00 8.00
		Nos. 1N18-1N21 (4)	32.00 32.00

Overprinted On Issue of 1918

1N22	A11	10f scarlet (Bl)	60.00 60.00
1N23	A11	20f dk brn	.90 .90
1N24	A11	25f brt bl	2.40 2.40
a.		Inverted overprint	30.00 30.00
1N25	A12	40f ol grn	3.25 3.25
		Nos. 1N22-1N25 (4)	66.55 66.55

Ovptd. On Issue of 1918-19, Overprinted "Koztarsasag"

1N26	A9	2f brn org	2.00 2.00
a.		Inverted overprint	50.00 50.00
1N27	A9	4f slate gray	2.00 2.00
1N28	A9	5f green	.60 .60
1N29	A9	6f grnsh bl	12.00 12.00
a.		Inverted overprint	30.00 30.00
1N30	A9	10f rose red (Bl)	60.00 60.00
1N31	A9	20f gray brn	15.00 15.00
1N32	A11	25f brt bl	2.75 2.75
a.		Inverted overprint	30.00 30.00
1N33	A9	40f ol grn	2.00 2.00
1N34	A12	40f ol grn	60.00 60.00
a.		Inverted overprint	125.00 125.00
1N35	A12	50f lilac	8.00 8.00
1N36	A10	1k red brn & cl (Bl)	3.25 3.25
1N37	A10	3k dk vio & ind (Bl)	15.00 15.00
		Nos. 1N26-1N37 (12)	182.60 182.60

No. 1N36 With Additional Surcharge

e

f

| 1N38 | A10 | (e) 10k on 1k | 13.50 13.50 |
| 1N39 | A10 | (f) 10k on 1k | 13.50 13.50 |

On Issue of 1919 Inscribed "MAGYAR POSTA"

| 1N40 | A13 | 5f red (R) | 55.00 55.00 |
| 1N41 | A13 | 10f red (Bl) | 6.50 6.50 |

SEMI-POSTAL STAMPS

Hungarian Semi-Postal Stamps of 1916-17 Overprinted "Occupation francaise" in Blue or Red

1919 Wmk. 137 Perf. 15
1NB1	SP3	10f + 2f rose red	65.00 65.00
1NB2	SP4	15f + 2f dl vio (R)	9.50 9.50
1NB3	SP5	40f + 2f brn car	12.50 12.50
		Nos. 1NB1-1NB3 (3)	87.00 87.00

SPECIAL DELIVERY STAMP

Hungarian Special Delivery Stamp of 1916 Overprinted "Occupation francaise"

1919 Wmk. 137 Perf. 15
| 1NE1 | SD1 | 2f gray green & red | .60 .60 |

POSTAGE DUE STAMPS

Hungarian Postage Due Stamps of 1915 Overprinted "Occupation francaise"

1919 Wmk. 137 Perf. 15
1NJ1	D1	2f green & red	7.50 7.50
1NJ2	D1	10f green & red	4.00 4.00
1NJ3	D1	12f green & red	32.50 32.50
1NJ4	D1	15f green & red	42.50 42.50
1NJ5	D1	20f green & red	3.00 3.00

Hungarian Newspaper Stamp of 1914 Surcharged

1NJ6	N5	12f on 2f orange	8.00 8.00
1NJ7	N5	15f on 2f orange	8.00 8.00
1NJ8	N5	30f on 2f orange	8.00 8.00
a.		Double surcharge	50.00 50.00
1NJ9	N5	50f on 2f orange	8.00 8.00
1NJ10	N5	100f on 2f orange	8.00 8.00
		Nos. 1NJ1-1NJ10 (10)	129.50 129.50

183

HUNGARY

NEWSPAPER STAMP

Hungarian Newspaper Stamp of 1914 Overprinted "Occupation francaise"

			1919	Wmk. 137	Imperf.
1NP1	N5	(2f) orange		1.25	1.25

ISSUED UNDER ROMANIAN OCCUPATION

FIRST DEBRECEN ISSUE

The overprints on this issue have been extensively forged. Even the inexpensive values are difficult to find with genuine overprints. The more extensive note before No. 1N1 also applies to Nos. 2N1-2NP16.

Hungarian Stamps of 1913-19 Overprinted in Blue, Red or Black

1919 Wmk. 137 Perf. 15, 14½x14

On Stamps of 1913

2N1	A4	2f ol yel	90.00	90.00
2N2	A4	3f orange	125.00	125.00
2N3	A4	6f ol grn (R)	50.00	50.00

On Stamps of 1916

| 2N4 | A8 | 10f rose | 75.00 | 75.00 |
| 2N5 | A8 | 15f violet (Bk) | 65.00 | 65.00 |

On Stamps of 1916-18

2N6	A9	2f brown org	1.50	1.50
2N7	A9	3f red lilac	.70	.70
2N8	A9	5f green	4.75	4.75
2N9	A9	6f grnsh bl (R)	1.60	1.60
2N10	A9	15f violet (Bk)	.80	.80
a.		Red overprint	75.00	75.00
2N11	A9	20f gray brn	125.00	125.00
2N12	A9	25f dull bl (Bk)	4.50	4.50
2N13	A9	35f brown	60.00	60.00
2N14	A9	40f olive grn	3.75	3.75
2N15	A10	50f red vio & lil	8.25	8.25
2N16	A10	75f brt bl & pale bl (Bk)	2.00	2.00
2N17	A10	80f grn & pale grn (R)	3.50	3.50
2N18	A10	1k red brn & cl	4.75	4.75
2N19	A10	2k ol brn & bis (Bk)	1.75	1.75
2N20	A10	3k dk vio & ind (R)	30.00	30.00
a.		Blue overprint	65.00	65.00
b.		Black overprint	250.00	250.00
2N21	A10	5k dk brn & lt brn (Bk)	27.50	27.50
2N22	A10	10k vio brn & vio	160.00	160.00

With New Value Added

2N23	A9	35f on 3f red lil	2.00	2.00
2N24	A9	45f on 2f brn org	2.00	2.00
2N25	A10	3k on 75f brt bl & pale bl (Bk)	4.00	4.00
2N26	A10	5k on 75f brt bl & pale bl (R)	3.75	3.75
2N27	A10	10k on 80f grn & pale grn (R)	3.50	3.50

On Stamps of 1918

2N28	A11	10f scarlet	60.00	60.00
2N28A	A11	15f violet (R)	75.00	75.00
		Black overprint	125.00	125.00
2N29	A11	20f dk brn (R)	6.25	6.25
a.		Black overprint	30.00	30.00
b.		Blue overprint	75.00	75.00
2N30	A11	25f brt blue	7.00	7.00
a.		Black overprint	75.00	75.00
2N31	A12	40f ol grn	3.00	3.00
2N32	A12	50f lilac	50.00	50.00

On Stamps of 1918-19, Overprinted "Koztarsasag"

2N33	A9	2f brn org	3.00	3.00
2N34	A9	3f red lilac	65.00	65.00
2N35	A9	4f sl gray (R)	1.75	1.75
2N36	A9	5f green	.65	.65
2N37	A9	6f grnsh bl (R)	30.00	30.00
2N38	A9	10f rose red	37.50	37.50
2N39	A11	10f scarlet	25.00	25.00
2N40	A11	15f dp vio (Bk)	45.00	45.00
a.		Red overprint	125.00	125.00
2N41	A9	20f gray brn	3.25	3.25
2N42	A11	20f dk brn (Bk)	37.50	37.50
b.		Red overprint	50.00	50.00
2N43	A9	40f olive grn	1.75	1.75
2N44	A10	1k red brn & cl	2.75	2.75
2N45	A10	2k ol brn & bis (Bk)	60.00	60.00
a.		Blue overprint	125.00	125.00
2N46	A10	3k dk vio & ind (R)	9.75	9.75
a.		Blue overprint	60.00	60.00
b.		Black overprint	200.00	200.00
2N47	A10	5k dk & lt brn (Bk)	225.00	225.00
2N48	A10	10k vio brn & vio	500.00	500.00
2N49	A11	25f brt bl (R)	3.25	3.25
a.		Black overprint	25.00	25.00
2N50	A12	40f olive grn	125.00	125.00
2N51	A12	50f lilac	2.25	2.25

On Stamps of 1919

2N52	A13	5f green	.50	.50
2N53	A13	6f grnsh bl (Bk)	22.50	22.50
2N54	A13	10f red	.25	.25
2N55	A13	20f dk brown	.25	.25
2N56	A13	25f dl bl (Bk)	1.25	1.25
2N56A	A13	40f ol grn	125.00	125.00
2N57	A13	45f orange	15.00	15.00
2N57A	A14	95f dk bl & bl	125.00	125.00
2N57B	A14	1.20k dk grn & grn	125.00	125.00
2N57C	A14	1.40k yel grn	125.00	125.00

No. 2N58

| 2N58 | A14 | 5k dk brn & brn | 3,000. | 3,000. |

No. 2N58 is handstamped. Counterfeits exist. Expertization is required.

On No. 103A

| 2N59 | A5a | 10f violet brn (R) | 50.00 | 50.00 |

On No. 208

| 2N60 | A13 | 10f red | 75.00 | 75.00 |
| Nos. 2N1-2N57,2N59-2N60 (61) | | | 2,530. | 2,530. |

SEMI-POSTAL STAMPS

Hungary Nos. B36, B37 Overprinted like Regular Issues in Blue

1919 Wmk. 137 Perf. 14

| 2NB1 | A4(c) | 2f olive yellow | 125.00 | 125.00 |
| 2NB1A | A4(c) | 3f orange | 125.00 | 125.00 |

Same Overprint in Blue or Black on Hungary Nos. B53--B55

1919 Wmk. 137 Perf. 15

2NB1B	SP3	10f + 2f rose red	4.00	4.00
2NB2	SP4	15f + 2f dl vio (Bk)	17.00	17.00
2NB3	SP5	40f + 2f brn car	11.00	11.00
Nos. 2NB1B-2NB3 (3)			32.00	32.00

Same Overprint on Hungary Nos. B58-B60 (with "Köztarsasag")

1919

2NB4	SP3	10f + 2f rose red	42.50	42.50
2NB5	SP4	15f + 2f dl vio (Bk)	75.00	75.00
2NB6	SP5	40f + 2f brn car	32.50	32.50
Nos. 2NB4-2NB6 (3)			150.00	150.00

SPECIAL DELIVERY STAMP

Hungarian Special Delivery Stamp of 1916 Overprinted like Regular Issues

1919 Wmk. 137 Perf. 15

| 2NE1 | SD1 | 2f gray grn & red (Bl) | 3.00 | 3.00 |

POSTAGE DUE STAMPS

Hungarian Postage Due Stamps of 1914-19 Overprinted in Black like Regular Issues

1919 Wmk. 137 Perf. 15

On Stamp of 1914

| 2NJ1 | D1 | 50f grn & blk | 125.00 | 125.00 |

On Stamps of 1915

2NJ2	D1	1f green & red	62.50	62.50
2NJ3	D1	2f green & red	2.00	2.00
2NJ4	D1	5f green & red	225.00	225.00
2NJ5	D1	6f green & red	125.00	125.00
2NJ6	D1	10f green & red	.80	.80
2NJ7	D1	12f green & red	125.00	125.00
2NJ8	D1	15f green & red	20.00	20.00
2NJ9	D1	20f green & red	4.50	4.50
2NJ10	D1	30f green & red	13.50	13.50

On Stamps of 1918-19, Overprinted "Koztarsasag"

2NJ11	D1	2f green & red	25.00	25.00
2NJ12	D1	3f green & red	30.00	30.00
2NJ13	D1	10f green & red	30.00	30.00
2NJ14	D1	20f green & red	30.00	30.00
2NJ15	D1	40f green & red	30.00	30.00
2NJ16	D1	50f green & red	30.00	30.00
Nos. 2NJ1-2NJ16 (16)			878.30	878.30
Nos. 2NJ1-2NJ13,2NJ15-2NJ16 (15)				848.30

NEWSPAPER STAMP

Hungarian Newspaper Stamp of 1914 Overprinted like Regular Issues

1919 Wmk. 137 Imperf.

2NP1	N5	(2f) orange (Bl)	.55	.55
a.		Inverted overprint	50.00	50.00
b.		Double overprint	125.00	125.00

SECOND DEBRECEN ISSUE

Complete forgeries exist of this issue and are often found in large multiples or even complete sheets. Values are for genuine stamps.

Mythical "Turul" OS5

Throwing Lariat OS6

Hungarian Peasant — OS7

1920 Unwmk. Typo. Perf. 11½

3N1	OS5	2f lt brown	2.25	2.25
3N2	OS5	3f red brown	2.25	2.25
3N3	OS5	4f gray	2.25	2.25
3N4	OS5	5f lt green	.50	.50
3N5	OS5	6f slate	2.25	2.25
3N6	OS5	10f scarlet	.50	.50
3N7	OS5	15f dk violet	3.00	3.00
3N8	OS5	20f dk brown	.60	.60
3N9	OS5	25f ultra	1.25	1.25
3N10	OS6	30f buff	.65	.65
3N11	OS6	35f claret	1.25	1.25
3N12	OS6	40f olive grn	.75	.75
3N13	OS6	45f salmon	1.00	1.00
3N14	OS6	50f pale vio	.75	.75
3N15	OS6	60f yellow grn	.90	.90
3N16	OS6	75f Prus blue	.75	.75
3N17	OS7	80f gray grn	.85	.85
3N18	OS7	1k brown red	3.00	3.00
3N19	OS7	2k chocolate	3.00	3.00
3N20	OS7	3k brown vio	2.25	2.25
3N21	OS7	5k bister brn	2.25	2.25
3N22	OS7	10k dull vio	2.25	2.25
Nos. 3N1-3N22 (22)			34.50	34.50

Thick, Glazed Paper

3N23	OS5	2f lt brown	3.00	3.00
3N24	OS5	3f red brown	3.00	3.00
3N25	OS5	4f gray	3.00	3.00
3N26	OS5	5f lt green	3.00	3.00
3N27	OS5	6f slate	3.00	3.00
3N28	OS5	10f scarlet	.75	.75
3N29	OS5	15f dk vio	3.00	3.00
3N30	OS5	20f dk brown	1.00	1.00
3N31	OS7	80f gray grn	1.50	1.50
3N32	OS7	1k brown red	4.00	4.00
3N33	OS7	1.20k orange	8.00	8.00
3N34	OS7	2k chocolate	4.50	4.50
Nos. 3N23-3N34 (12)			37.75	37.75

SEMI-POSTAL STAMPS

Carrying Wounded — SP1

1920 Unwmk. Typo. Perf. 11½

3NB1	SP1	20f green	1.25	1.25
3NB2	SP1	50f gray brn	2.25	2.25
3NB3	SP1	1k blue green	2.25	2.25
3NB4	SP1	2k dk green	2.25	2.25

Colored Paper

3NB5	SP1	20f green, bl	3.00	3.00
3NB6	SP1	50f brn, rose	3.00	3.00
3NB7	SP1	1k dk grn, grn	3.00	3.00
Nos. 3NB1-3NB7 (7)			17.00	17.00

POSTAGE DUE STAMPS

D1

1920 Typo. Perf. 15

3NJ1	D1	5f blue green	1.50	1.50
3NJ2	D1	10f blue green	1.50	1.50
3NJ3	D1	20f blue green	.75	.75
3NJ4	D1	30f blue green	.75	.75
3NJ5	D1	40f blue green	1.25	1.25
Nos. 3NJ1-3NJ5 (5)			5.75	5.75

TEMESVAR ISSUE

Issued under Romanian Occupation

Forgeries exist of the inverted and color error surcharges.

Hungary Nos. 108, 155, 109, 111, E1 Surcharged

1919 Wmk. 137 Perf. 15

4N1	A9	30f on 2f brn org (Bl)	.40	.40
a.		Red surcharge	2.00	2.00
b.		Inverted surcharge (R)	25.00	25.00
4N2	A9	1k on 4f sl gray (R)	.30	.30
4N3	A9	150f on 3f red lil (Bk)	.25	.25
4N4	A9	150f on 5f grn (Bk)	.40	.40
4N5	SD1	3k on 2f gray grn & red (Bk)	2.00	2.00
a.		Blue surcharge	.80	.80
Nos. 4N1-4N5 (5)			3.35	3.35

POSTAGE DUE STAMPS

D1   D2

HUNGARY

1919	Wmk. 137		Perf. 15
4NJ1	D1 40f on 15f + 2f vio (Bk)	.50	.50
a.	Red surcharge	2.00	2.00
4NJ2	D2 60f on 2f grn & red (Bk)	2.50	2.50
a.	Red surcharge	8.00	8.00
4NJ3	D2 60f on 10f grn & red (Bk)	1.25	1.25
a.	Red surcharge	4.00	4.00
	Nos. 4NJ1-4NJ3 (3)	4.25	4.25

FIRST TRANSYLVANIA ISSUE

Issued under Romanian Occupation

The scarcer values of this issue have been extensively forged. Genuine common values are more easily found.

Issued in Kolozsvar (Cluj)

Hungarian Stamps of 1916-18 Overprinted

1919	Wmk. 137		Perf. 15, 14
	On Stamp of 1916, White Numerals		
5N1	A8 15b violet	4.75	4.75
	On Stamps of 1916-18		
5N2	A9 2b brown org	.25	.25
5N3	A9 3b red lilac	.25	.25
5N4	A9 5b green	.25	.25
5N5	A9 6b grnsh blue	.40	.40
5N5A	A9 10b rose red	60.00	60.00
5N6	A9 15b violet	.25	.25
5N7	A9 25b dull blue	.25	.25
5N8	A9 35b brown	.25	.25
5N9	A9 40b olive grn	.50	.50
5N10	A10 50b red vio & lil	1.00	1.00
5N11	A10 75b brt bl & pale bl	.30	.30
5N12	A10 80b grn & pale grn	.25	.25
5N13	A10 1 l red brn & cl	.25	.25
5N14	A10 2 l ol brn & bis	.60	.60
5N15	A10 3 l dk vio & ind	3.50	3.50
5N16	A10 5 l dk brn & lt brn	2.50	2.50
5N17	A10 10 l vio brn & vio	3.00	3.00
	On Stamps of 1918		
5N18	A11 10b scarlet	40.00	40.00
5N19	A11 15b dp violet	20.00	20.00
5N20	A11 20b dk brown	.25	.25
a.	Gold overprint	75.00	75.00
b.	Silver overprint	75.00	75.00
5N21	A11 25b brt blue	.65	.65
5N22	A12 40b olive grn	.30	.30
	On No. 103A		
5N23	A5a 10b violet brn	.35	.35
	Nos. 5N1-5N23 (24)	140.10	140.10

SEMI-POSTAL STAMPS

Hungarian Semi-Postal Stamps of 1913-17 Overprinted like Regular Issues
On Issue of 1913

1919	Wmk. 137		Perf. 14
5NB1	SP1 1 l on 1f slate	27.50	27.50
5NB2	SP1 1 l on 2f ol yel	70.00	70.00
5NB3	SP1 1 l on 3f org	37.50	37.50
5NB4	SP1 1 l on 5f emer	3.25	3.25
5NB5	SP1 1 l on 10f car	4.50	4.50
5NB6	SP1 1 l on 12f vio, yel	16.00	16.00
5NB7	SP1 1 l on 16f gray grn	6.25	6.25
5NB8	SP1 1 l on 25f ultra	60.00	60.00
5NB9	SP1 1 l on 35f red vio	10.00	10.00
5NB10	SP2 1 l on 1k dl red	60.00	60.00
	On Issue of 1916-17		
	Perf. 15		
5NB11	SP3 10b + 2b rose red	.25	.25
5NB12	SP4 15b + 2b dull vio	.25	.25
5NB13	SP5 40b + 2b brn car	.25	.25
	Nos. 5NB1-5NB13 (13)	295.75	295.75

SPECIAL DELIVERY STAMP

Hungarian Special Delivery Stamp of 1916 Overprinted like Regular Issues

1919	Wmk. 137		Perf. 15
5NE1	SD1 2b gray grn & red	.30	.30

POSTAGE DUE STAMPS

Hungarian Postage Due Stamps of 1914-18 Overprinted like Regular Issues
On Stamp of 1914

1919	Wmk. 137		Perf. 15
5NJ1	D1 50b green & blk	13.00	13.00
	On Stamps of 1915		
5NJ2	D1 1b green & red	350.00	350.00
5NJ3	D1 2b green & red	.70	.70
5NJ4	D1 5b green & red	60.00	60.00
5NJ5	D1 10b green & red	.45	.45
5NJ6	D1 15b green & red	20.00	20.00
5NJ7	D1 20b green & red	.40	.40
5NJ8	D1 30b green & red	30.00	30.00
	Nos. 5NJ1-5NJ8 (8)	474.55	474.55

NEWSPAPER STAMP

Hungarian Newspaper Stamp of 1914 Overprinted like Regular Issues

1919	Wmk. 137		Imperf.
5NP1	N5 2b orange	3.75	3.75

SECOND TRANSYLVANIA ISSUE

The scarcer values of this issue have been extensively forged. Genuine common values are more easily found.

Issued in Nagyvarad (Oradea)

Hungarian Stamps of 1916-19 Overprinted

1919	Wmk. 137		Perf. 15, 14
	On Stamps of 1913-16		
6N1	A4 2b olive yel	7.00	7.00
6N2	A4 3b orange	13.00	13.00
6N3	A4 6b olive grn	1.75	1.75
6N4	A4 16b gray grn	37.50	37.50
6N5	A4 50b lake, bl	1.75	1.75
6N6	A4 70b red brn & grn	26.00	26.00
	On Stamp of 1916 (White Numerals)		
6N6A	A8 15b violet	125.00	125.00
	On Stamps of 1916-18		
6N7	A9 2b brown org	.25	.25
6N8	A9 3b red lilac	.25	.25
6N9	A9 5b green	.30	.30
6N10	A9 6b grnsh blue	1.60	1.60
6N11	A9 10b rose red	2.10	2.10
6N12	A9 15b violet	.25	.25
6N13	A9 20b gray brn	20.00	20.00
6N14	A9 25b dull blue	.30	.30
6N15	A9 35b brown	.45	.45
6N16	A9 40b olive grn	.30	.30
6N17	A10 50b red vio & lil	.60	.60
6N18	A10 75b brt bl & pale bl	.25	.25
6N19	A10 80b grn & pale grn	.30	.30
6N20	A10 1 l red brn & cl	.75	.75
6N21	A10 2 l ol brn & bis	.75	.75
6N22	A10 3 l dk vio & ind	6.50	6.50
6N23	A10 5 l dk brn & lt brn	3.25	3.25
6N24	A10 10 l vio brn & vio	1.50	1.50
	On Stamps of 1918		
6N25	A11 10b scarlet	3.25	3.25
6N26	A11 20b dk brown	.25	.25
6N27	A11 25b brt blue	.75	.75
6N28	A12 40b olive grn	1.10	1.10
	On Stamps of 1918-19, Overprinted "Koztarsasag"		
6N29	A9 2b brown org	4.00	4.00
6N30	A9 3b red lilac	.25	.25
6N31	A9 4b slate gray	.25	.25
6N32	A9 5b green	.50	.50
6N33	A9 6b grnsh bl	3.00	3.00
6N34	A9 10b rose red	17.50	17.50
6N35	A9 20b gray brn	2.50	2.50
6N36	A9 40b olive grn	.50	.50
6N37	A10 1 l red brn & cl	.25	.25
6N38	A10 3 l dk vio & ind	.75	.75
6N39	A10 5 l dk brn & lt brn	4.50	4.50
6N40	A11 10b scarlet	75.00	75.00
6N41	A11 20b dk brown	4.50	4.50
6N42	A11 25b brt blue	1.25	1.25
6N43	A12 50b lilac	.25	.25
	On Stamps of 1919 Inscribed "MAGYAR POSTA"		
6N44	A13 5b yellow grn	.25	.25
6N45	A13 10b red	.25	.25
6N46	A13 20b dk brown	.40	.40
6N47	A13 25b dull blue	2.00	2.00
6N48	A13 40b olive grn	.65	.65
6N49	A14 5 l dk brn & lt brn	6.50	6.50
	On No. 103A		
6N50	A5a 10b violet brn	.85	.85
	Nos. 6N1-6N50 (51)	382.45	382.45

SEMI-POSTAL STAMPS

Hungarian Semi-Postal Stamps of 1913-17 Overprinted like Regular Issues
On Stamps of 1913

1919	Wmk. 137		Perf. 14
6NB1	SP1 1 l on 1f slate	2.25	2.25
6NB2	SP1 1 l on 2f olive yel	8.50	8.50
6NB3	SP1 1 l on 3f orange	2.75	2.75
6NB4	SP1 1 l on 5f emerald	.25	.25
6NB5	SP1 1 l on 6f olive grn	2.25	2.25
6NB6	SP1 1 l on 10f carmine	.30	.30
6NB7	SP1 1 l on 12f vio, yel	60.00	60.00
6NB8	SP1 1 l on 16f gray grn	2.50	2.50
6NB9	SP1 1 l on 20f dk brn	11.00	11.00
6NB10	SP1 1 l on 25f ultra	7.50	7.50
6NB11	SP1 1 l on 35f red vio	7.75	7.75
	On Stamp of 1915		
	Wmk. 135		Perf. 11½
6NB12	A4 5b emerald	20.00	20.00
	On Stamps of 1916-17		
	Wmk. 137		Perf. 15
6NB13	SP3 10b + 2b rose red	1.25	1.25
6NB14	SP4 15b + 2b dull vio	.45	.45
6NB15	SP5 40b + 2b brn car	.25	.25
	Nos. 6NB1-6NB15 (15)	127.00	127.00

SPECIAL DELIVERY STAMP

Hungarian Special Delivery Stamp of 1916 Overprinted like Regular Issues

1919	Wmk. 137		Perf. 15
6NE1	SD1 2b gray grn & red	.40	.40

POSTAGE DUE STAMPS

Hungarian Postage Due Stamps of 1915 Overprinted like Regular Issues

1919	Wmk. 137		Perf. 15
6NJ1	D1 1b green & red	30.00	30.00
6NJ2	D1 2b green & red	.25	.25
6NJ3	D1 5b green & red	9.75	9.75
6NJ4	D1 6b green & red	6.75	6.75
6NJ5	D1 10b green & red	.25	.25
6NJ6	D1 12b green & red	1.50	1.50
6NJ7	D1 15b green & red	1.50	1.50
6NJ8	D1 20b green & red	.25	.25
6NJ9	D1 30b green & red	1.60	1.60
	Nos. 6NJ1-6NJ9 (9)	51.85	51.85

On Hungary No. J27
Perf. 11½x12
Wmk. 135

6NJ10	D1 20b on 100b grn & blk	350.00	350.00

NEWSPAPER STAMP

Hungarian Newspaper Stamp of 1914 Overprinted like Regular Issues

1919	Wmk. 137		Imperf.
6NP1	N5 2b orange	.45	.45

FIRST BARANYA ISSUE

Issued under Serbian Occupation

The scarcer values of this issue have been extensively forged. Genuine common values are more easily found.

Hungarian Stamps of 1913-18 Overprinted in Black or Red

On A4, A9, A11, A12   On A10

1919	Wmk. 137		Perf. 15
	On Issue of 1913-16		
7N1	A4 6f olive grn (R)	.90	.90
7N2	A4 50f lake, bl	.25	.25
7N3	A4 60f grn, salmon	.75	.75
7N4	A4 70f red brn & grn (R)	2.00	2.00
7N5	A4 70f red brn & grn (Bk)	.25	.25
7N6	A4 80f dl vio (R)	3.25	3.25
	On Issue of 1916-18		
7N7	A9 2f brown org (Bk)	4.25	4.25
7N8	A9 2f brown org (R)	.25	.25
7N9	A9 3f red lilac (Bk)	.25	.25
7N10	A9 3f red lilac (R)	.80	.80
7N11	A9 5f green (Bk)	.80	.80
7N12	A9 5f green (R)	.25	.25
7N13	A9 6f grnsh bl (Bk)	1.75	1.75
7N14	A9 6f grnsh bl (R)	2.00	2.00
7N15	A9 15f violet	.35	.35
7N16	A9 20f gray brn	20.00	20.00
7N17	A9 25f dull blue	3.50	3.50
7N18	A9 35f brown	5.75	5.75
7N19	A9 40f olive grn	20.00	20.00
7N20	A10 50f red vio & lil	2.00	2.00
7N21	A10 75f brt bl & pale bl	.40	.40
7N22	A10 80f grn & pale grn	.65	.65
7N23	A10 1k red brn & cl	.55	.55
7N24	A10 2k ol brn & bis	.65	.65
7N25	A10 3k dk vio & ind	.65	.65
7N26	A10 5k dk brn & lt brn	1.25	1.25
7N27	A10 10k vio brn & vio	4.00	4.00
7N28	A9 45f on 2f brn org	.35	.35
7N29	A9 45f on 5f green	.25	.25
7N30	A9 45f on 15f violet	.25	.25
	On Issue of 1918		
7N31	A11 10f scarlet (Bk)	.25	.25
7N32	A11 20f dk brn (Bk)	.25	.25
7N34	A11 25f dp blue (Bk)	1.90	1.90
7N35	A11 25f dp blue (R)	1.10	1.10
7N36	A12 40f olive grn (Bk)	4.50	4.50
7N37	A12 40f olive grn (R)	30.00	30.00
	On Issue of 1918-19 (Koztarsasag)		
7N38	A9 2f brown org (Bk)	3.50	3.50
7N39	A12 40f ol grn (Bk)	125.00	125.00
7N40	A12 40f ol grn (R)	20.00	20.00
	With New Value Added		
7N41	A9 45f on 2f brn org (Bk)	2.00	2.00
7N42	A9 45f on 2f brn org (R)	.45	.45

The overprints were set in groups of 25. In each group two stamps have the figures "1" of "1919" with serifs.

SEMI-POSTAL STAMPS

Hungarian Semi-Postal Stamps Overprinted Regular Issue First Type On Stamp of 1915

1919	Wmk. 137		Perf. 15
7NB1	A4 50f + 2f lake, bl	16.00	16.00
	On Stamps of 1916		
7NB2	SP3 10f + 2f rose red	.30	.30
7NB3	SP4 15f + 2f dull vio	.40	.40
	Nos. 7NB1-7NB3 (3)	16.70	16.70

HUNGARY

SPECIAL DELIVERY STAMP

1919		Wmk. 137	Perf. 15
7NE1	SD1	105f on 2f gray grn & red	1.25 1.25

POSTAGE DUE STAMPS

Overprinted or Surcharged on Hungary Nos. J29, J32, J35

1919		Wmk. 137	Perf. 15
7NJ1	D1	2f green & red	3.75 3.75
7NJ2	D1	10f green & red	1.25 1.25
7NJ3	D1	20f green & red	1.60 1.60

With New Value Added

7NJ4	D1	40f on 2f grn & red	1.50 1.50
		Nos. 7NJ1-7NJ4 (4)	8.10 8.10

SECOND BARANYA ISSUE

The scarcer values of this issue have been extensively forged. Genuine common values are more easily found.

Hungarian Stamps of 1916-19 Surcharged in Black and Red

1919

On Stamps of 1916-18

8N1	A9	20f on 2f brn org	4.25 4.25
8N2	A9	50f on 5f green	2.00 2.00
8N3	A9	150f on 15f violet	2.00 2.00
8N4	A10	200f on 75f brt bl & pale bl	.75 .75

On Stamp of 1918-19, Overprinted "Koztarsasag"

8N5	A11	150f on 15f dp vio	.50 .50

On Stamps of 1919

8N6	A13	20f on 2f brn org	.35 .35
8N7	A13	50f on 6f grnsh bl	.70 .70
8N8	A13	50f on 5f yel grn	.25 .25
8N9	A13	100f on 25f dull bl	.25 .25
8N10	A13	100f on 40f ol grn	.25 .25
8N11	A13	100f on 45f orange	1.10 1.10
8N12	A13	150f on 20f dk brn	1.40 1.40

On No. 103A

8N13	A5a	10f on 10f vio brn	.75 .75
		Nos. 8N1-8N13 (13)	14.55 14.55

SPECIAL DELIVERY STAMP

Hungarian Special Delivery Stamp of 1916 Surcharged like Regular Issues

1919		Wmk. 137	Perf. 15
8NE1	SD1	10f on 2f gray grn & red	.65 .65

NEWSPAPER STAMP

Hungarian Newspaper Stamp of 1914 Surcharged like Regular Issues

1919		Wmk. 137	Imperf.
8NP1	N5	10f on 2f orange	.80 .80

TEMESVAR ISSUES

Issued under Serbian Occupation

Forgeries exist of the inverted and color error surcharges.

Hungarian Stamps of 1916-18 Surcharged in Black, Blue or Brown

a b

1919

9N1	A9(a)	10f on 2f brn org (Bl)	.25 .25
a.		Black surcharge	15.00 15.00
9N2	A9(b)	30f on 2f brn org	.25 .25
a.		Inverted surcharge	75.00 75.00
9N3	A11(b)	50f on 20f dk brn (Bl)	.25 .25
a.		Inverted surcharge	
9N4	A9(b)	1k 50f on 15f vio	.30 .30
a.		Brown surcharge	.75 .75
b.		Double surcharge (Bk)	50.00 50.00
		Nos. 9N1-9N4 (4)	1.05 1.05

SEMI-POSTAL STAMP

Hungarian Semi-Postal Stamp of 1916 Surcharged in Blue

1919		Wmk. 137	Perf. 15
9NB1	SP3	45f on 10f + 2f rose red	.25 .25

POSTAGE DUE STAMPS

Hungarian Postage Due Stamps of 1915 Surcharged

1919		Wmk. 137	Perf. 15
9NJ1	D1	40f on 2f grn & red	.80 .80
9NJ2	D1	60f on 2f grn & red	.80 .80
9NJ3	D1	100f on 2f grn & red	.80 .80
		Nos. 9NJ1-9NJ3 (3)	2.40 2.40

BANAT, BACSKA ISSUE

Issued under Serbian Occupation

Postal authorities at Temesvar applied these overprints. The stamps were available for postage, but were chiefly used to pay postal employees' salaries.

The overprints on this issue have been extensively forged. Even the inexpensive values are difficult to find with genuine overprints. The more extensive note before 1N1 also applies to Nos. 10N1-10NP1.

Hungarian Stamps of 1913-19 Overprinted in Black or Red

a b

1919

Type "a" on Stamp of 1913

10N1	A4	50f lake, blue	4.00 4.00

Type "a" on Stamps of 1916-18

10N2	A9	2f brown org	4.00 4.00
10N3	A9	3f red lilac	4.00 4.00
10N4	A9	5f green	4.00 4.00
10N5	A9	6f grnsh blue	4.00 4.00
10N6	A9	15f violet	4.00 4.00
10N7	A9	35f brown	35.00 35.00

Type "b"

10N8	A10	50f red vio & lil (R)	30.00 30.00
10N9	A10	75f brt bl & pale bl	4.00 4.00
10N10	A10	80f grn & pale grn	4.00 4.00
a.		Red overprint	37.50 37.50
10N11	A10	1k red brn & cl	4.00 4.00
10N12	A10	2k ol brn & bis	4.00 4.00
a.		Red overprint	37.50 37.50
10N14	A10	3k dk vio & ind	65.00 65.00
10N15	A10	5k dk brn & lt brn	4.00 4.00
10N16	A10	10k vio brn & vio	4.00 4.00

Type "a" on Stamps of 1918

10N17	A11	10f scarlet	4.00 4.00
10N18	A11	20f dk brown	4.00 4.00
10N19	A11	25f brt blue	4.00 4.00
10N20	A12	40f olive grn	4.00 4.00
10N21	A12	50f lilac	4.00 4.00

Type "a" on Stamps of 1919 Inscribed "Magyar Posta"

10N22	A13	10f red	30.00 30.00
10N23	A13	20f dk brown	30.00 30.00
10N24	A13	25f dull blue	37.50 37.50

Type "a" on Stamps of 1918-19 Overprinted "Koztarsasag"

10N25	A9	4f slate gray	3.50 3.50
10N26	A9	4f sl gray (R)	42.50 42.50
10N27	A9	5f green	4.00 4.00
10N28	A9	6f grnsh blue	4.00 4.00
10N29	A9	10f rose red	30.00 30.00
10N30	A11	15f dp violet	30.00 30.00
10N31	A9	20f gray brn	30.00 30.00
10N32	A11	25f brt blue	30.00 30.00
10N33	A9	40f olive grn	3.50 3.50
10N34	A9	40f ol grn (R)	32.50 32.50

Type "b"

10N35	A10	1k red brn & cl	4.00 4.00
10N36	A10	2k ol brn & bis	30.00 30.00
10N37	A10	3k dk vio & ind	30.00 30.00
10N38	A10	5k dk brn & lt brn	30.00 30.00
10N39	A10	10k vio brn & vio	30.00 30.00

Type "a" on Temesvár Issue

10N40	A9	10f on 2f brn org (Bl & Bk)	4.00 4.00
10N41	A9	1k50f on 15f vio	4.00 4.00

10N42	A5a	50f on 10f vio brn	4.00 4.00
a.		Red overprint	75.00 75.00
		Nos. 10N1-10N42 (41)	641.50 641.50

SEMI-POSTAL STAMPS

Semi-Postal Stamps of 1916-17 Overprinted Type "a" in Black

1919

10NB1	SP3	10f + 2f rose red	4.00 4.00
10NB2	SP4	15f + 2f dull vio	4.00 4.00
10NB3	SP5	40f + 2f brn car	4.00 4.00

Same Overprint on Temesvar Issue

10NB4	SP3	45f on 10f + 2f rose red (Bl & Bk)	4.00 4.00
		Nos. 10NB1-10NB4 (4)	16.00 16.00

SPECIAL DELIVERY STAMP

Hungary No. E1 Surcharged in Black

1919

10NE1	SD1	30f on 2f gray grn & red	4.00 4.00
a.		Red overprint	75.00 75.00

POSTAGE DUE STAMPS

Postage Due Stamps of 1914-15 Overprinted Type "a" in Black

1919

10NJ1	D1	2f green & red	4.00 4.00
10NJ2	D1	10f green & red	4.00 4.00
10NJ3	D1	15f green & red	32.50 32.50
10NJ4	D1	20f green & red	4.00 4.00
10NJ5	D1	30f green & red	30.00 30.00
10NJ6	D1	50f green & blk	30.00 30.00
		Nos. 10NJ1-10NJ6 (6)	104.50 104.50

NEWSPAPER STAMP

Stamp of 1914 Overprinted Type "a" in Black

1919

10NP1	N5	(2f) orange	4.00 4.00

SZEGED ISSUE

The "Hungarian National Government, Szeged, 1919," as the overprint reads, was an anti-Bolshevist government which opposed the Soviet Republic then in control at Budapest.

The overprints on this issue have been extensively forged. Even the inexpensive stamps are difficult to find with genuine overprints. The more extensive note before No. 1N1 also applies to Szeged Nos. 11N1-11NP1.

Hungary Stamps of 1916-19 Overprinted in Green, Red and Blue

On Stamps of 1916-18

1919			Perf. 15, 14
11N1	A9	2f brn org (G)	2.25 2.25
11N2	A9	3f red lilac (G)	.75 .75
11N3	A9	5f green	2.75 2.75
11N4	A9	6f grnsh blue	32.50 32.50
11N5	A9	15f violet	3.50 3.50
11N6	A10	50f red vio & lil	19.00 19.00
11N7	A10	75f brt bl & pale bl	4.25 4.25
11N8	A10	80f grn & pale grn	18.00 18.00
11N9	A10	1k red brn & cl (G)	2.25 2.25
11N10	A10	2k ol brn & bis	4.75 4.75
11N11	A10	3k dk vio & ind	7.25 7.25
11N12	A10	5k dk brn & lt brn	60.00 60.00
11N13	A10	10k vio brn & vio	60.00 60.00

With New Value Added

11N14	A9	45f on 3f red lil (R & G)	.80 .80
11N15	A10	10k on 1k red brn & cl (Bl & G)	8.00 8.00

On Stamps of 1918

11N16	A11	10f scarlet (G)	2.50 2.50
11N17	A11	20f dk brown	.60 .60
11N18	A11	25f brt blue	22.50 22.50
11N19	A12	40f olive grn	11.00 11.00

On Stamps of 1918-19 Overprinted "Koztarsasag"

11N20	A9	3f red lil (G)	42.50 42.50
11N21	A9	4f slate gray	11.00 11.00
11N22	A9	5f green	25.00 25.00
11N23	A9	6f grnsh blue	15.00 15.00
11N24	A9	10f rose red	32.50 32.50
11N25	A11	10f scarlet)	30.00 30.00
11N26	A11	15f dp violet	10.00 10.00
11N27	A9	20f gray brown	50.00 50.00
11N28	A11	20f dk brown	65.00 65.00
11N29	A11	25f brt blue	20.00 20.00
11N30	A9	40f olive	2.25 2.25
11N31	A12	50f lilac	1.75 1.75
11N32	A10	3k dk vio & ind	37.50 37.50

With New Value Added

11N33	A9	20f on 2f brn org (R & G)	.80 .80

On Stamps of 1919 Inscribed "Magyar Posta"

11N34	A13	20f dk brown	60.00 60.00
11N35	A13	25f dull blue	1.75 1.75
		Nos. 11N1-11N35 (35)	667.70 667.70

HUNGARY — ICELAND

SEMI-POSTAL STAMPS

Szeged Overprint on Semi-Postal Stamps of 1916-17 in Green or Red

1919
11NB1	SP3	10f + 2f rose red (G)		.85	.85
11NB2	SP4	15f + 2f dl vio (R)		3.75	3.75
11NB3	SP5	40f + 2f brn car (G)		10.00	10.00

With Additional Overprint "Koztarsasag"

11NB4	SP5	40f + 2f brn car (Bk & G)	15.00	15.00
		Nos. 11NB1-11NB4 (4)	29.60	29.60

SPECIAL DELIVERY STAMP

Szeged Overprint on Special Delivery Stamp of 1916 in Red

1919
11NE1	SD1	2f gray grn & red	11.00	11.00

POSTAGE DUE STAMPS

Szeged Overprint on Stamps of 1915-18 in Red

1919
11NJ1	D1	2f green & red	3.00	3.00
11NJ2	D1	6f green & red	9.75	9.75
11NJ3	D1	10f green & red	3.75	3.75
11NJ4	D1	12f green & red	4.75	4.75
11NJ5	D1	20f green & red	6.00	6.00
11NJ6	D1	30f green & red	9.00	9.00

Surcharged in Red

11NJ7	SD1	50f on 2f gray grn & red	2.75	2.75
11NJ8	SD1	100f on 2f gray grn & red	2.75	2.75
		Nos. 11NJ1-11NJ8 (8)	41.75	41.75

NEWSPAPER STAMP

Szeged Overprint on Stamp of 1914 in Green

1919   Wmk. 137   Imperf.
11NP1	N5	(2f) orange	.85	.85

ICELAND

ˈīs-lənd

LOCATION — Island in the North Atlantic Ocean, east of Greenland
GOVT. — Republic
AREA — 39,758 sq. mi.
POP. — 341,000 (2020 est.)
CAPITAL — Reykjavik

Iceland became a republic on June 17, 1944. Formerly this country was united with Denmark under the government of King Christian X who, as a ruling sovereign of both countries, was assigned the dual title of king of each. Although the two countries were temporarily united in certain affairs beyond the king's person, both were acknowledged as sovereign states.

96 Skillings = 1 Rigsdaler
100 Aurar (singular "Eyrir") = 1 Krona (1876)

Catalogue values for unused stamps in this country are for Never Hinged items, beginning with Scott 246 in the regular postage section, Scott B7 in the semi-postal section and Scott C21 in the air post section.

Watermarks

Wmk. 112 — Crown
Wmk. 113 — Crown
Wmk. 47 — Multiple Rosette
Wmk. 114 — Multiple Crosses
Wmk. 409 — State Shield
Wmk. 410 — State Arms

Values for unused stamps are for examples with original gum as defined in the catalogue introduction. Very fine examples of Nos. 1-33A and O1-O12 will have centering with perforations clear of the framelines but with design noticeably off center, and Nos. 1-7 and O1-O3 additionally will have some irregular or shorter perforations. Well centered stamps are quite scarce and will command higher prices.

A1

1873   **Perf. 14x13½**   **Typo.**   **Wmk. 112**
1	A1	2s	ultra	1,050.	2,150.
a.			Imperf.		625.
2	A1	4s	dark car	175.	1,050.
a.			Imperf.		625.
3	A1	8s	brown	325.	1,200.
a.			Imperf.		350.
4	A1	16s	yellow	1,450.	2,600.
a.			Imperf.		400.

Perf. 12½
5	A1	3s	gray	475.	1,450.
a.			Imperf.		750.
6	A1	4s	carmine	1,400.	2,250.
7	A1	16s	yellow		140. 650.00

False and favor cancellations are often found on Nos. 1-7. Values are considerably less than those shown.

A2

1876
8	A2	5a	grayish ultra	475.00	950.00

Perf. 14x13½
9	A2	5a	ultra	425.00	900.00
a.			Imperf.	2,450.	
10	A2	6a	gray	150.00	32.50
11	A2	10a	carmine	225.00	8.00
a.			Imperf.	625.00	750.00
12	A2	16a	brown	140.00	75.00
13	A2	20a	dark violet	35.00	500.00
a.			20a light violet	1,100.	500.
14	A2	40a	green	100.00	225.00

Perforations of No. 8 are always very rough. Clean-perforated examples are either reperforated Nos. 8 or 9 stamps, are No. 16 reperforated and color changed, or No. 24 with changed color. Examples of No. 9 that are not ultramarine are either faded or color changed by sunlight, color-changed No. 16, or are color changed and reperfed No. 24 stamps

Fake and favor cancellations are almost always found on No. 13, and value is considerably less than that shown.

Beware of unused color-faded examples of No. 13 described as No. 13a. Expertization is recommended.

Small "3" — A3

1882-98
15	A3	3a	orange	62.50	27.50
16	A2	5a	green	67.50	14.00
17	A2	20a	blue	325.00	50.00
a.			20a ultramarine	800.00	275.00
18	A2	40a	red violet	65.00	45.00
a.			Perf. 13 ('98)	5,000.	
19	A2	50a	bl & car ('92)	90.00	100.00
20	A2	100a	brn & vio ('92)	95.00	140.00
			Nos. 15-20 (6)	705.00	376.50

The small "3" is thin and measures about 3.2 millimeters high. The large "3" is thick and bold, and measures about 3.8 mm high. (See No. 22).
See note after No. 68.

Large "3" — A3a

Small 3
Large 3

1896-1901   **Perf. 13**
21	A3	3a	orange yellow ('97)	125.00	12.00
22	A3a	3a	orange yellow ('01)	9.00	24.00
23	A2	4a	rose & gray ('99)	18.00	20.00
24	A2	5a	green	4.00	3.00
25	A2	6a	gray ('97)	17.50	19.00
26	A2	10a	carmine ('97)	17.00	3.00
27	A2	16a	brown	75.00	110.00
28	A2	20a	dull blue ('98)	45.00	40.00
a.			20a dull ultramarine	575.00	45.00
29	A2	25a	yel brn & bl ('00)	22.50	32.50
30	A2	50a	bl & car ('98)	450.00	

See note after No. 68.
For surcharges see Nos. 31-33A, 45-68.

Black and Red Surcharge

Large "prir"

1897   **Perf. 13**
31	A2	3a on 5a green		875.	650.
a.		Perf. 14x13½			3,900.
b.		Inverted surcharge		1,400.	1,200.
c.		As "a," inverted surcharge		—	

Large "prir" is 6.1mm to 6.3mm wide by 3.5mm tall.

Small "prir"

32	A2	3a on 5a green		700.	575.
a.		Inverted surcharge		1,250.	1,050.
b.		Perf. 14x13½		—	
c.		In vert. pair with #31		2,000.	1,500.
d.		As "b," in vert. pair with #31a		—	

All 5 known unused examples of No. 32b lack gum.
Small "prir" is 5.5mm to 5.6mm wide by 3.1mm tall.

Black Surcharge

Large "prir"

33	A2	3a on 5a green		1,000.	750.
b.		Inverted surcharge		1,500.	1,250.

Large "prir" is 6.1mm to 6.3mm wide by 3.5mm tall.

Small "prir"

33A	A2	3a on 5a green		1,100.	750.
c.		Inverted surcharge		1,800.	1,500.

Excellent counterfeits are known.
Small "prir" is 5.5mm to 5.6mm wide by 3.1mm tall.

ICELAND

King Christian IX — A4

1902-04   Wmk. 113   Perf. 13

34	A4	3a orange	6.00	4.00
35	A4	4a gray & rose	3.50	1.40
36	A4	5a yel green	42.50	1.20
37	A4	6a gray brown	22.50	11.00
38	A4	10a car rose	6.50	1.10
39	A4	16a chocolate	8.50	12.00
40	A4	20a deep blue	3.00	4.50
a.		Inscribed "PJONUSTA"	95.00	160.00
41	A4	25a brn & grn	4.00	7.00
42	A4	40a violet	4.25	7.00
43	A4	50a gray & bl blk	6.25	25.00
44	A4	1k sl bl & yel brn	6.50	10.50
44A	A4	2k olive brn & brt blue ('04)	27.00	77.50
44B	A4	5k org brn & slate blue ('04)	140.00	240.00
		Nos. 34-44B (13)	280.50	402.20

For surcharge see No. 142.

Stamps of 1882-1901 Overprinted

1902-03   Wmk. 112   Perf. 13
Red Overprint

45	A2	5a green	1.40	10.50
a.		Inverted overprint	80.00	105.00
b.		"I" before Gildi omitted	175.00	250.00
c.		'03-'03	750.00	
d.		'02-'03	625.00	850.00
e.		Pair, one without overprint	175.00	
46	A2	6a gray	1.20	10.50
a.		Double overprint	140.00	
b.		Inverted overprint	80.00	
c.		'03-'03	525.00	
d.		'02-'03	525.00	
e.		Pair, one with invtd. ovpt.	400.00	
f.		Pair, one without overprint	225.00	
g.		As "f," inverted	400.00	
47	A2	20a dull blue	1.20	12.50
a.		Inverted overprint	85.00	110.00
b.		"I" before Gildi omitted	175.00	
c.		'02-'03	1,500.	
48	A2	25a yel brn & bl	1.20	19.00
a.		Inverted overprint	75.00	85.00
b.		'03-'03	450.00	
c.		'02-'03	450.00	675.00
d.		Double overprint	175.00	

Black Overprint

49	A3	3a orange	240.00	525.00
b.		Inverted overprint	375.00	850.00
c.		"I" before Gildi omitted	575.00	
d.		'03-'03	625.00	
e.		'02-'03	625.00	
50	A3a	3a yellow	1.40	2.50
a.		Double overprint	400.00	
b.		Inverted overprint	85.00	105.00
c.		"I" before Gildi omitted	625.00	
d.		'02-'03	750.00	
51	A2	4a rose & gray	40.00	57.50
a.		Double overprint	525.00	
b.		Inverted overprint	120.00	
c.		Dbl. ovpt., one invtd.	400.00	
d.		"I" before Gildi omitted	290.00	
e.		'03-'03	525.00	700.00
f.		'02-'03	525.00	
g.		Pair, one with invtd. ovpt.	400.00	
52	A2	5a green	350.00	925.00
a.		Inverted overprint	400.00	975.00
b.		Pair, one without overprint	510.00	
c.		As "b", inverted	625.00	
53	A2	6a gray	750.00	1,150.
a.		Inverted overprint	800.00	
b.		Pair, one without overprint	800.00	
c.		Double overprint	1,150.	
54	A2	10a carmine	1.40	12.50
a.		Inverted overprint	75.00	110.00
b.		Pair, one without overprint	210.00	
55	A2	16a brown	26.00	40.00
a.		"I" before Gildi omitted	175.00	
c.		'03-'03	350.00	
d.		'02-'03	700.00	
			625.00	
56	A2	20a dull blue	10,000.	
a.		Inverted overprint	9,600.	
57	A2	25a yel brn & bl	10,500.	
a.		Inverted overprint	14,500.	
58	A2	40a red vio	1.20	40.00
a.		Inverted overprint	90.00	
59	A2	50a bl & car	3.50	70.00
a.		Double overprint	250.00	
b.		'02-'03	850.00	
c.		'03-'03	850.00	

Perf. 14x13½
Red Overprint

60	A2	5a green	2,100.	—
a.		'03-'03	45,500.	
b.		'02-'03		
61	A2	6a gray	2,100.	—
a.		'02-'03		
62	A2	20a blue	5,750.	—
b.		'02-'03		

Black Overprint

63	A3	3a orange	1,350.	2,100.
a.		Inverted overprint	1,750.	
b.		'03-'03	2,500.	
c.		'02-'03	2,750.	
64	A2	10a carmine	9,750.	—
65	A2	16a brown	1,500.	2,100.
a.		Inverted overprint	1,900.	
b.		'03-'03	2,300.	
d.		'02-'03	22,000.	
65C	A2	20a dull blue	9,100.	
a.		Inverted overprint	15,500.	
66	A2	40a red vio	21.00	105.00
a.		Inverted overprint	250.00	
b.		'03-'03	525.00	
c.		'02-'03	525.00	
67	A2	50a bl & car	55.00	140.00
a.		Inverted overprint	350.00	
b.		'03-'03	475.00	
c.		'02-'03	475.00	800.00
d.		As "c," inverted		
68	A2	100a brn & vio	60.00	80.00
a.		Inverted overprint	210.00	
b.		'02-'03	575.00	800.00
c.		'03-'03	850.00	

"I GILDI" means "valid."

In 1904 18 stamps were reprinted for distribution through the Universal Postal Union. A total of 104 sets of 18 were left without overprint. A larger quantity of stamps was further overprinted 'I GILDI'. The reprints are perf. 13 and have watermark type 113. Reprints without overprint resemble Nos. 18a, 20 (perf. 14x13½), 22-29, 30, O9 (perf. 14x13½), O10-O12A, and O28 (perf. 14x13½). The 18 stamps with overprint resemble Nos. 45-48, 50-51, 54-55, 58-59, 68 (perf. 14x13½), O20-O24, O28 (perf. 14x13½), O30 (perf. 14x13½).
Value: $85 each never hinged, $60 each unused. Centering of reprints ranges from fine to fine-very fine. Value: $180 each never hinged, $130 each unused, except Nos. 18a, O11A, O12A ($425 each never hinged, $300 each unused). Very fine examples are rare and command higher prices.

Kings Christian IX and Frederik VIII — A5

Typo., Center Engr.
1907-08   Wmk. 113   Perf. 13

71	A5	1e yel grn & red	1.75	1.40
72	A5	3a yel brn & ocher	4.75	1.75
73	A5	4a gray & red	3.00	1.75
74	A5	5a green	95.00	1.40
75	A5	6a gray & gray brn	60.00	4.00
76	A5	10a scarlet	150.00	1.60
77	A5	15a red & green	7.50	1.25
78	A5	16a brown	9.75	40.00
79	A5	20a blue	8.00	5.75
80	A5	25a bis brn & grn	7.00	12.00
81	A5	40a claret & vio	7.00	15.00
82	A5	50a gray & vio	7.00	15.00
83	A5	1k blue & brn	32.50	70.00
84	A5	2k dk brn & dk grn	37.50	80.00
85	A5	5k brn & slate	175.00	350.00
		Nos. 71-85 (15)	605.75	600.90
		Set, never hinged	1,800.	

See Nos. 99-107.
For surcharges and overprints see Nos. 130-138, 143, C2, O69.

Jon Sigurdsson — A6

1911   Typo. and Embossed

86	A6	1e olive green	2.50	2.00
87	A6	3a light brown	5.00	15.00
88	A6	4a ultramarine	2.00	1.75
89	A6	6a gray	15.00	26.00
90	A6	15a violet	15.00	2.00
91	A6	25a orange	35.00	50.00
		Nos. 86-91 (6)	74.50	96.75
		Set, never hinged	190.00	

Sigurdsson (1811-79), statesman and author.
For surcharge see No. 149.

Frederik VIII — A7

1912, Feb. 17

92	A7	5a green	35.00	13.00
93	A7	10a red	35.00	13.00
94	A7	20a pale blue	50.00	18.00
95	A7	50a claret	12.50	35.00
96	A7	1k yellow	35.00	75.00
97	A7	2k rose	37.50	75.00
98	A7	5k brown	160.00	225.00
		Nos. 92-98 (7)	365.00	454.00
		Set, never hinged	825.00	

For surcharges and overprints see Nos. 140-141, O50-O51.

Revenue cancellations consisting of "TOLLUR" boxed in frame are found on stamps used to pay the tax on parcel post packages entering Iceland.

Type of 1907-08
Typo., Center Engr.
1915-18   Wmk. 114   Perf. 14x14½

99	A5	1e yel grn & red	10.00	18.00
		Revenue cancellation		25.00
100	A5	3a bister brn	4.25	3.00
101	A5	4a gray & red	4.25	9.50
102	A5	5a green	100.00	1.40
103	A5	6a gray & gray brn	24.00	130.00
104	A5	10a scarlet	3.50	1.25
107	A5	20a blue	240.00	24.00
		Nos. 99-107 (7)	386.00	187.15
		Set, never hinged	1,150.	

Christian X — A8

1920-22   Typo.

108	A8	1e yel grn & red	1.25	1.25
		Revenue cancellation		9.50
109	A8	3a bister brn	9.00	18.00
		Revenue cancellation		9.50
110	A8	4a gray & red	6.00	2.60
		Revenue cancellation		9.50
111	A8	5a green	2.25	2.25
		Revenue cancellation		18.00
112	A8	5a ol green ('22)	5.75	1.75
		Revenue cancellation		7.25
113	A8	6a dark gray	16.00	9.00
		Revenue cancellation		14.00
114	A8	8a dark brown	9.00	2.50
		Revenue cancellation		12.00
115	A8	10a red	3.00	12.00
		Revenue cancellation		24.00
116	A8	10a green ('21)	4.00	2.00
		Revenue cancellation		10.00
117	A8	15a violet	42.50	1.40
		Revenue cancellation		9.50
118	A8	20a deep blue	3.00	19.00
		Revenue cancellation		24.00
119	A8	20a choc ('22)	65.00	1.75
		Revenue cancellation		9.50
120	A8	25a brown & grn	18.00	2.00
		Revenue cancellation		9.50
121	A8	25a red ('21)	18.00	60.00
		Revenue cancellation		4.25
122	A8	30a red & green	52.50	3.50
		Revenue cancellation		4.25
123	A8	40a claret	42.50	3.50
		Revenue cancellation		9.50
124	A8	40a dk bl ('21)	90.00	14.50
		Revenue cancellation		11.00
125	A8	50a dk gray & cl	190.00	12.00
		Revenue cancellation		14.50
126	A8	1k dp bl & dk brn	110.00	1.75
		Revenue cancellation		1.75
127	A8	2k ol brn & myr green	240.00	35.00
		Revenue cancellation		3.50
128	A8	5k brn & ind	60.00	18.00
		Revenue cancellation		3.50
		Nos. 108-128 (21)	987.75	223.75
		Set, never hinged	4,400.	

See Nos. 176-187, 202.
For surcharges and overprints see Nos. 139, 150, C1, C9-C14, O52, O70-O71.

A9   A10   A11

1921-25   Wmk. 113   Perf. 13

130	A9	5a on 16a brown	4.25	30.00
		Revenue cancellation		35.00
131	A11	5a on 16a brown	2.50	9.00
		Revenue cancellation		24.00
132	A10	20a on 25a brn & green	8.25	9.00
a.		Double surcharge		
133	A11	20a on 25a bis brn & green	4.75	9.00
134	A9	20a on 40a violet	8.25	20.00
135	A11	20a on 40a cl & vio	15.00	24.00
		Revenue cancellation		18.00
137	A9	30a on 50a gray & bl blk ('25)	35.00	37.50
		Revenue cancellation		18.00
138	A9	50a on 5k org brn & sl bl ('25)	65.00	52.50
		Revenue cancellation		21.00
		Nos. 130-138 (8)	143.00	191.00
		Set, never hinged	480.00	

No. 111 Surcharged

1922   Wmk. 114   Perf. 14x14½

139	A8	10a on 5a green	8.00	3.50
		Revenue cancellation		35.00

Nos. 95-96, 44A, 85 Surcharged

1924-30   Wmk. 113   Perf. 13

140	A7	10k on 50a ('25)	300.00	450.00
		Revenue cancellation		35.00
141	A7	10k on 1k	400.00	650.00
		Revenue cancellation		75.00
142	A4	10k on 2k ('29)	80.00	32.50
		Revenue cancellation		11.00
143	A5	10k on 5k ('30)	475.00	600.00
		Revenue cancellation		35.00
		Nos. 140-143 (4)	1,255.	1,733.
		Set, never hinged	3,000.	

Landing the Mail — A12

Designs: 7a, 50a, Landing the mail. 10a, 35a, View of Reykjavik. 20a, Museum building.

Perf. 14x15
1925, Sept. 12   Typo.   Wmk. 114

144	A12	7a yel green	42.50	7.50
		Revenue cancellation		6.00
145	A12	10a dp bl & brn	42.50	.85
		Revenue cancellation		6.00
146	A12	20a vermilion	42.50	.85
		Revenue cancellation		4.75
147	A12	35a deep blue	72.50	9.50
		Revenue cancellation		3.50
148	A12	50a yel grn & brn	72.50	1.75
		Revenue cancellation		1.75
		Nos. 144-148 (5)	272.50	20.45
		Set, never hinged	850.00	

No. 91 Surcharged

1925   Wmk. 113   Perf. 13

149	A6	2k on 25a orange	160.00	140.00
		Revenue cancellation		18.00

No. 124 Surcharged in Red

1926

150	A8	1k on 40a dark blue	150.00	35.00
		Revenue cancellation		24.00

Parliament Building — A15

Designs: 5a, Viking ship in storm. 7a, Parliament meeting place, 1690. 10a, Viking funeral. 15a, Vikings naming land. 20a, The dash for Thing. 25a, Gathering wood. 30a, Thingvalla Lake. 35a, Iceland woman in national costume. 40a, Iceland flag. 50a, First Althing, 930 A.D. 1k, Map of Iceland. 2k, Winter-bound

ICELAND

home. 5k, Woman spinning. 10k, Viking Sacrifice to Thor.

Perf. 12½x12
1930, Jan. 1   Litho.   Unwmk.

152	A15	3a dull vio & gray vio	3.00	9.50
153	A15	5a dk bl & sl grn	3.00	9.50
154	A15	7a grn & gray grn	2.50	9.50
155	A15	10a dk vio & lilac	9.00	18.00
156	A15	15a dp ultra & bl gray	1.75	11.00
157	A15	20a rose red & sal	42.50	85.00
a.		Double impression	350.00	
158	A15	25a dk brn & lt brn	7.50	15.00
159	A15	30a dk grn & sl grn	6.00	14.50
160	A15	35a ultra & bl gray	6.00	14.50
161	A15	40a dk ultra, red & slate grn	6.00	14.50
162	A15	50a red brn & cinn	60.00	150.00
163	A15	1k ol grn & gray green	55.00	150.00
164	A15	2k turq bl & gray green	60.00	175.00
165	A15	5k org & yellow	42.50	140.00
166	A15	10k mag & dl rose	42.50	140.00
		Nos. 152-166 (15)	347.25	956.00
		Set, never hinged	850.00	

Millenary of the "Althing," the Icelandic Parliament, oldest in the world.
Imperfs were privately printed.
For overprints see Nos. O53-O67.
Nos. 152-166 exist with "TOLLUR" revenue cancellations, but regulations did not permit their use as revenues.
Beware of fakes.

Gullfoss (Golden Falls) — A30

1931-32   Unwmk.   Engr.   Perf. 14

170	A30	5a gray	14.00	1.10
		Revenue cancellation		1.75
171	A30	20a red	12.00	.25
		Revenue cancellation		6.00
172	A30	35a ultramarine	24.00	16.00
		Revenue cancellation		1.75
173	A30	60a red lil ('32)	15.00	1.50
		Revenue cancellation		1.75
174	A30	65a red brn ('32)	2.50	1.25
		Revenue cancellation		1.75
175	A30	75a grnsh bl ('32)	95.00	32.50
		Revenue cancellation		5.00
		Nos. 170-175 (6)	162.50	52.60
		Set, never hinged	460.00	

Issued: 5a-35a, Dec. 15; 60a-75a, May 30.

Type of 1920 Christian X Issue Redrawn
Perf. 14x14½

1931-33   Typo.   Wmk. 114

176	A8	1e yel grn & red	1.00	1.75
		Revenue cancellation		3.00
177	A8	3a bister brown	15.00	15.00
		Revenue cancellation		8.50
178	A8	4a gray & red	2.50	2.50
		Revenue cancellation		7.25
179	A8	6a dark gray	1.75	5.00
		Revenue cancellation		7.25
180	A8	7a yel grn ('33)	.65	1.75
		Revenue cancellation		9.50
181	A8	10a chocolate	140.00	1.40
		Revenue cancellation		7.25
182	A8	25a brn & green	17.50	4.25
		Revenue cancellation		3.50
183	A8	30a red & green	30.00	7.00
		Revenue cancellation		8.50
184	A8	40a claret	240.00	21.00
		Revenue cancellation		12.00
185	A8	1k dk bl & lt brn	42.50	7.50
		Revenue cancellation		3.50
186	A8	2k choc & dk grn	240.00	82.50
		Revenue cancellation		8.50
187	A8	10k yel grn & blk	250.00	210.00
		Revenue cancellation		18.00
		Nos. 176-187 (12)	980.90	359.65
		Set, never hinged	4,300.	

On the redrawn stamps the horizontal lines of the portrait and the oval are closer together than on the 1920 stamps and are crossed by many fine vertical lines.
See No. 202.
No. 183 was perforated on a different perforating machine than the other stamps in the set. The stamp is roughly perforated with small-hole perfs.

Dynjandi Falls A31

Mount Hekla A32

Perf. 12½
1935, June 28   Engr.   Unwmk.

193	A31	10a blue	18.00	.25
		Never hinged	90.00	
		Revenue cancellation		24.00
194	A32	1k greenish gray	32.50	.25
		Never hinged	160.00	
		Revenue cancellation		6.00

Matthias Jochumsson — A33

1935, Nov. 11

195	A33	3a gray green	.60	4.25
		Revenue cancellation		4.25
196	A33	5a gray	12.00	1.40
		Revenue cancellation		18.00
197	A33	7a yel green	18.00	2.40
		Revenue cancellation		7.25
198	A33	35a blue	.50	1.40
		Revenue cancellation		9.50
		Nos. 195-198 (4)	31.10	9.45
		Set, never hinged	115.00	

Birth cent. of Matthias Jochumsson, poet.
For surcharges see Nos. 212, 236.

King Christian X — A34

1937, May 14   Perf. 13x12½

199	A34	10a green	1.80	26.00
		Revenue cancellation		24.00
200	A34	30a brown	1.80	10.50
		Revenue cancellation		24.00
201	A34	40a claret	1.80	10.50
		Revenue cancellation		24.00
		Nos. 199-201 (3)	5.40	47.00
		Set, never hinged	12.00	

Reign of Christian X, 25th anniv.

Christian X Type of 1931-33
1937   Unwmk.   Typo.   Perf. 11½

202	A8	1e yel grn & red	.80	2.50
		Never hinged	2.40	
		Revenue cancellation		4.75

Geyser A35   A36

1938-47   Engr.   Perf. 14

203	A35	15a dp rose vio	5.00	12.00
		Revenue cancellation		24.00
a.		Imperf., pair	1,300.	
		Never hinged	1,650.	
204	A35	20a rose red	22.00	.25
		Revenue cancellation		18.00
205	A35	35a ultra	.60	1.20
		Revenue cancellation		24.00
206	A36	40a dk brn ('39)	12.00	30.00
207	A36	45a brt ultra ('40)	.75	1.20
208	A36	50a dk slate grn	21.00	1.20
		Revenue cancellation		24.00
208A	A36	60a brt ultra ('43)	5.50	1.20
c.		Perf. 11½ ('47)	2.60	12.00
		Never hinged (#208Ac)	7.50	
208B	A36	1k indigo ('45)	10.50	.50
d.		Perf. 11½ ('47)	2.60	12.00
		Never hinged (#208Bd)	7.50	
		Nos. 203-208B (8)	77.35	47.55
		Set, never hinged	215.00	

University of Iceland — A37

1938, Dec. 1   Perf. 13½

209	A37	25a dark grn	6.50	16.00
210	A37	30a brown	6.50	16.00
211	A37	40a brt red vio	6.50	16.00
		Nos. 209-211 (3)	19.50	48.00
		Set, never hinged	37.50	

20th anniversary of independence.

No. 198 Surcharged with New Value
1939, Mar. 17   Perf. 12½

212	A33	5a on 35a blue	.80	1.60
		Never hinged	1.60	
a.		Double surcharge	250.00	
		Never hinged	525.00	

Trylon and Perisphere A38

Leif Ericsson's Ship and Route to America A39

Statue of Thorfinn Karlsefni — A40

1939   Engr.   Perf. 14

213	A38	20a crimson	3.50	7.00
214	A39	35a bright ultra	4.00	9.00
215	A40	45a bright green	4.25	12.00
216	A40	2k dark gray	52.50	150.00
		Nos. 213-216 (4)	64.25	178.00
		Set, never hinged	110.00	

New York World's Fair.
For overprints see Nos. 232-235.

Codfish A41   **Herring A42**

Flag of Iceland — A43

1939-45   Engr.   Perf. 14, 14x13½

217	A41	1e Prussian blue	.45	4.50
a.		Perf. 14x13½	1.75	5.75
218	A42	3a dark violet	.45	1.25
a.		Perf. 14x13½	2.40	8.50
219	A41	5a dark brown	.45	.45
c.		Perf. 14x13½	2.75	1.75
220	A42	7a dark green	4.75	10.50
221	A42	10a green ('40)	35.00	1.25
b.		Perf. 14x13½	55.00	.60
		Never hinged	180.00	
222	A42	10a slate gray ('45)	.25	.25
223	A42	12a dk grn ('43)	.45	.90
224	A41	25a brt red ('40)	29.00	.60
b.		Perf. 14x13½	57.50	3.00
		Never hinged (#224b)	190.00	
225	A41	25a hn brn ('45)	1.25	.45
226	A42	35a carmine ('43)	.60	.70
227	A41	50a dk bl grn ('43)	.70	.25

Typo.
228	A43	10a car & ultra	2.50	1.75

Nos. 217-228: Some values are known with "TOLLUR" revenue cancellations, but these are favor cancels. Use of "TOLLUR" cancels ceased Dec. 1, 1938.

	Nos. 217-228 (12)	75.85	22.85
	Set, never hinged	250.00	

Statue of Thorfinn Karlsefni — A44

1939-45   Engr.   Perf. 14

229	A44	2k dark gray	3.00	.50
230	A44	5k dk brn ('43)	24.00	.60
231	A44	10k brn yel ('45)	12.00	2.50
		Nos. 229-231 (3)	39.00	3.60
		Set, never hinged	92.50	

1947   Perf. 11½

229a	A44	2k	8.00	1.75
230a	A44	5k	30.00	2.40
231a	A44	10k	12.00	45.00
		Nos. 229a-231a (3)	50.00	49.15
		Set, never hinged	160.00	

New York World's Fair Issue of 1939 Overprinted "1940" in Black
1940, May 11   Perf. 14

232	A38	20a crimson	8.00	30.00
233	A39	35a bright ultra	8.00	30.00
234	A40	45a bright green	8.00	30.00
235	A40	2k dark gray	100.00	540.00
		Nos. 232-235 (4)	124.00	630.00
		Set, never hinged	240.00	

No. 195 Surcharged in Red
1941, Mar. 6   Perf. 12½

236	A33	25a on 3a gray green	1.00	1.60
		Never hinged	1.60	

Statue of Snorri Sturluson — A45

1941, Nov. 17   Engr.   Perf. 14

237	A45	25a rose red	1.20	2.40
238	A45	50a deep ultra	1.75	5.25
239	A45	1k dk olive grn	1.75	5.25
		Nos. 237-239 (3)	4.70	12.90
		Set, never hinged	8.50	

Snorri Sturluson, writer and historian, 700th death anniv.

Republic

Jon Sigurdsson — A46

1944, June 17   Perf. 14x13½

240	A46	10a gray black	.50	1.00
241	A46	25a dk red brn	.50	1.00
242	A46	50a slate grn	.50	1.00
243	A46	1k blue black	.75	1.00
244	A46	5k henna	1.75	12.50
245	A46	10k golden brn	30.00	100.00
		Nos. 240-245 (6)	34.00	116.50
		Set, never hinged	100.00	

Founding of Republic of Iceland, June 17, 1944.

Catalogue values for unused stamps in this section, from this point to the end of the section, are for Never Hinged items.

A47   **A48**

Eruption of Hekla Volcano: 35a, 60a, Close view of Hekla.

Unwmk.
1948, Dec. 3   Engr.   Perf. 14

246	A47	12a dark vio brn	.25	.60
247	A48	25a green	1.75	.25
248	A47	35a carmine rose	.50	.35
249	A47	50a brown	2.50	.25
250	A47	60a brt ultra	8.25	4.75
251	A48	1k orange brown	12.00	.25
252	A48	10k violet black	60.00	.50
		Nos. 246-252 (7)	85.25	6.95
		Set, hinged	40.00	

For surcharge see No. 283.

Pack Train and UPU Monument, Bern — A49

UPU, 75th Anniv.: 35a, Reykjavik. 60a, Map. 2k, Thingvellir Road.

ICELAND

1949, Oct. 9
253	A49	25a dark green	.25	.60
254	A49	35a deep carmine	.25	.60
255	A49	60a blue	.60	1.40
256	A49	2k orange red	1.60	1.50
		Nos. 253-256 (4)	2.70	4.10

Trawler — A50

Designs: 20a, 75a, 1k, Tractor plowing. 60a, 5k, Flock of sheep. 5a, 90a, 2k, Vestmannaeyjar harbor.

1950-54 *Perf. 13*
257	A50	5a dk brn ('54)	.25	.25
258	A50	10a gray	.50	.60
259	A50	20a brown	.50	.60
260	A50	25a car ('54)	.25	.25
261	A50	60a green	17.50	24.00
262	A50	75a red org ('52)	.70	.25
263	A50	90a carmine	.70	.70
264	A50	1k chocolate	7.75	.25
265	A50	1.25k red vio ('52)	24.00	.45
266	A50	1.50k deep ultra	16.00	.60
267	A50	2k purple	30.00	.45
268	A50	5k dark grn	45.00	1.50
		Nos. 257-268 (12)	143.15	29.90
		Set, hinged	50.00	

For surcharges see Nos. B12-B13.

Jon Arason — A51

1950, Nov. 7 *Perf. 14*
269	A51	1.80k carmine	3.50	4.25
270	A51	3.30k green	2.50	3.50

Bishop Jon Arason, 400th anniv. of death.

Mail Delivery, 1776 — A52

Design: 3k, Airmail, 1951.

1951, May 13
271	A52	2k deep ultra	3.00	3.00
272	A52	3k dark purple	4.25	4.25

175th anniv. of Iceland's postal service.

Parliament Building — A53

1952, Apr. 1 *Perf. 13x12½*
273	A53	25k gray black	190.00	17.50
		Hinged	80.00	

Sveinn Björnsson — A54

1952, Sept. 1 *Perf. 13½*
274	A54	1.25k deep blue	3.00	.25
275	A54	2.20k deep green	.75	4.75
276	A54	5k indigo	10.00	1.75
277	A54	10k brown red	45.00	30.00
		Nos. 274-277 (4)	58.75	36.75

Sveinn Björnsson, 1st President of Iceland.

Reykjabok — A55

Designs: 70a, Lettering manuscript. 1k, Corner of 15th century manuscript, "Stjorn." 1.75k, Reykjabok. 10k, Corner from law manuscript.

1953, Oct. 1 *Perf. 13½x13*
278	A55	10a black	.25	.25
279	A55	70a green	.25	.25
280	A55	1k carmine	.50	.25
281	A55	1.75k blue	30.00	1.75
282	A55	10k orange brn	13.00	1.40
		Nos. 278-282 (5)	44.00	3.90

No. 248 Surcharged With New Value and Bars in Black

1954, Mar. 31 *Perf. 14*
283	A47	5a on 35a car rose	.30	.30
a.		Bars omitted	210.00	
b.		Inverted surcharge	240.00	

Hannes Hafstein — A56

Portraits: 2.45k, in oval. 5k, fullface.

1954, June 1 *Engr. Perf. 13*
284	A56	1.25k deep blue	4.75	.70
285	A56	2.45k dark green	24.00	35.00
286	A56	5k carmine	26.00	3.00
		Nos. 284-286 (3)	54.75	38.70

Appointment of the first native minister to Denmark, 50th anniv.

Icelandic Wrestling — A57

1955, Aug. 9 *Unwmk. Perf. 14*
287	A57	75a shown	.30	.25
288	A57	1.25k Diving	.60	.30

See Nos. 300-301.

Skoga Falls — A58

Ellidaar Power Plant — A59

Waterfalls: 60a, Goda. 2kr, Detti. 5kr, Gull. Electric Power Plants: 1.50kr, Sogs. 2.45kr, Andakilsar. 3kr, Laxar.

Perf. 11½, 13½x14 (A59)

1956, Apr. 4 *Unwmk.*
289	A58	15a vio blue	.25	.25
290	A59	50a dull green	.30	.25
291	A59	60a brown	3.50	4.75
292	A59	1.50k violet	32.50	.25
293	A59	2k sepia	1.75	.60
294	A59	2.45k gray black	7.00	11.00
295	A59	3k dark blue	6.00	1.20
296	A58	5k dark green	14.50	2.25
		Nos. 289-296 (8)	65.80	20.55

Telegraph-Telephone Emblem and Map — A60

1956, Sept. 29 *Engr. Perf. 13*
297	A60	2.30k ultramarine	.30	1.20

Telegraph and Telephone service in Iceland, 50th anniv.

Northern Countries Issue

Whooper Swans — A60a

1956, Oct. 30 *Perf. 12½*
298	A60a	1.50k rose red	.60	1.10
299	A60a	1.75k ultramarine	9.50	12.00

To emphasize the bonds among Denmark, Finland, Iceland, Norway and Sweden.

Sports Type of 1955

1.50k, Icelandic wrestling. 1.75k, Diving.

1957, Apr. 1 *Engr. Perf. 14*
300	A57	1.50k carmine	1.40	.25
301	A57	1.75k ultramarine	.70	.25

Type of 1952 Air Post Stamps, Plane Omitted

Glaciers: 2k, Snaefellsjokull. 3k, Eiriksjokull. 10k, Oraefajokull.

1957, May 8 *Perf. 13½x14*
302	AP16	2k green	4.75	.30
303	AP16	3k dark blue	5.25	.30
304	AP16	10k reddish brn	7.25	.45
		Nos. 302-304 (3)	17.25	1.05

Bessastadir, President's Residence — A61

1957, Aug. 1 *Engr. Unwmk.*
305	A61	25k gray blk	25.00	5.00

Evergreen and Volcanoes — A62

1957, Sept. 4 *Perf. 13½x13*
306	A62	35a shown	.25	.25
307	A62	70a Birch	.25	.25

Issued to publicize a reforestation program.

Jonas Hallgrimsson — A63

1957, Nov 16
308	A63	5k grn & blk	1.75	.60

150th birth anniv. of Jonas Hallgrimsson, poet.

Willow Herb — A64

1958, July 8 *Litho. Unwmk.*
309	A64	1k shown	.25	.50
310	A64	2.50k Wild pansy	.50	.50

Icelandic Pony — A65

1958, Sept. 27 *Engr.*
311	A65	10a gray black	.25	.25
312	A65	2.25k brown	.60	.30

See No. 324.

Flag — A66

Perf. 13½x14

1958, Dec. 1 *Litho. Unwmk.*
Size: 17½x21mm
313	A66	3.50k brt ultra & red	2.50	.75

Size: 23x26½mm
314	A66	50k brt ultra & red	7.00	7.00

40th anniversary of Icelandic flag.

Old Icelandic Government Building — A67

1958, Dec. 9 *Photo. Perf. 11½*
315	A67	2k deep green	.50	.50
316	A67	4k deep brown	.60	.60

See Nos. 333-334.

Jon Thorkelsson Teaching — A68

1959, May 5 *Engr. Perf. 13½*
317	A68	2k green	.60	.70
318	A68	3k dull purple	.85	.95

Death bicentenary of Jon Thorkelsson, headmaster of Skaholt.

Sockeye Salmon A69

Eider Ducks A70

Design: 25k, Gyrfalcon.

1959-60 *Engr. Perf. 14*
319	A69	25a dark blue	.25	.25
320	A70	90a chestnut & blk	.30	.25
321	A70	2k olive grn & blk	.60	.25
322	A69	5k gray green	10.00	1.40

Litho.
323	A70	25k dl pur, gray & yel	15.00	16.00
		Nos. 319-323 (5)	26.15	18.15

Issued: 25k, Mar. 1, 1960; others, Nov. 25.

Pony Type of 1958

1960, Apr. 7 *Engr. Perf. 13½x13*
324	A65	1k dark carmine	.70	.30

"The Outlaw" by Einar Jonsson — A71

1960, Apr. 7 *Perf. 14*
325	A71	2.50k reddish brn	.30	.30
326	A71	4.50k ultramarine	.80	1.20

World Refugee Year, 7/1/59-6/30/60.

Common Design Types pictured following the introduction.

Europa Issue, 1960
Common Design Type

1960, Sept. 18 *Photo. Perf. 11½*
Size: 32½x22mm
327	CD3	3k grn & lt grn	.65	.45
328	CD3	5.50k dk bl & lt bl	.65	1.40

Wild Geranium — A72

Flowers: 50a, Bellflower. 2.50k, Dandelion. 3.50k, Buttercup.

1960-62 *Photo. Perf. 11½*
329	A72	50a gray grn, grn & violet ('62)	.25	.25
330	A72	1.20k sep, vio & grn	.25	.25
331	A72	2.50k brn, yel & grn	.25	.25
332	A72	3.50k dl bl, yel & green ('62)	.60	.60
		Nos. 329-332 (4)	1.35	1.35

See Nos. 363-366, 393-394.

Building Type of 1958

1961, Apr. 11 *Unwmk. Perf. 11½*
333	A67	1.50k deep blue	.30	.25
334	A67	3k dark carmine	.30	.25

ICELAND

Jon Sigurdsson — A73

Typographed and Embossed
1961, June 17   *Perf. 12½x14*
335   A73   50a crimson   .25   .25
336   A73   3k dark blue   1.50   1.25
337   A73   5k deep plum   .60   .55
     Nos. 335-337 (3)   2.35   2.05

Jon Sigurdsson (1811-1879), statesman and scholar.

Reykjavik — A74

1961, Aug. 18   *Photo.*   *Perf. 11½*
338   A74   2.50k blue & grn   .60   .30
339   A74   4.50k lilac & vio bl   1.00   .50

Municipal charter of Reykjavik, 175th anniv.

Europa Issue, 1961
Common Design Type
1961, Sept. 18   *Size: 32x22½mm*
340   CD4   5.50k multicolored   .55   .80
341   CD4   6k multicolored   .55   .80

Benedikt Sveinsson A75   University of Iceland A76

Design: 1.40k, Björn M. Olsen.

1961, Oct. 6   *Photo.*   *Perf. 11½*
342   A75   1k red brown   .25   .25
343   A75   1.40k ultramarine   .25   .25
344   A76   10k green   1.40   .60
   a.   Souv. sheet of 3, #342-344, imperf.   1.00   2.25
     Nos. 342-344 (3)   1.90   1.10

50th anniv. of the University of Iceland; Benedikt Sveinsson (1827-1899), statesman; and Björn M. Olsen (1850-1919), first rector.

Production Institute — A77

New Buildings: 4k, Fishing Research Institute. 6k, Farm Bureau.

1962, July 6   *Unwmk.*   *Perf. 11½*
345   A77   2.50k ultramarine   .30   .25
346   A77   4k dull green   .50   .25
347   A77   6k brown   .60   .30
     Nos. 345-347 (3)   1.40   .80

Europa Issue, 1962
Common Design Type
1962, Sept. 17   *Size: 32½x22½mm*
348   CD5   5.50k yel, lt grn & brn   .25   .25
349   CD5   6.50k lt grn, grn & brn   .60   .60

Map Showing Submarine Telephone Cable — A78

1962, Nov. 20   *Granite Paper*
350   A78   5k multicolored   1.10   .60
351   A78   7k grn, lt bl & red   .60   .45

Inauguration of the submarine telephone cable from Newfoundland, via Greenland and Iceland to Scotland.

Sigurdur Gudmundsson, Self-portrait — A79

5.50k, Knight slaying dragon, Romanesque door from Valthjofsstad Church, ca. 1200 A.D.

1963, Feb. 20   *Photo.*   *Perf. 11½*
352   A79   4k bis brn & choc   .60   .45
353   A79   5.50k gray ol & brn   .45   .45

National Museum of Iceland, cent., and its first curator, Sigurdur Gudmundsson.

Herring Boat — A80

1963, Mar. 21
354   A80   5k multicolored   .80   .30
355   A80   7.50k multicolored   .25   .25

FAO "Freedom from Hunger" campaign.

View of Akureyri — A81

1963, July 2   *Unwmk.*   *Perf. 11½*
356   A81   3k gray green   .25   .50

Europa Issue, 1963
Common Design Type
1963, Sept. 16   *Size: 32½x23mm*
357   CD6   6k org brn & yel   .60   .60
358   CD6   7k blue & yellow   .60   .60

M.S. Gullfoss — A82

1964, Jan. 17   *Photo.*   *Perf. 11½*
359   A82   10k ultra, blk & gray   2.40   1.75
   a.   Accent on 2nd "E" omitted   35.00   47.50

Iceland Steamship Company, 50th anniv.

Scout Emblem and "Be Prepared" — A83

1964, Apr. 24
360   A83   3.50k multicolored   .60   .45
361   A83   4.50k multicolored   .60   .45

Issued to honor the Boy Scouts.

Icelandic Coat of Arms — A84

1964, June 17   *Perf. 11½*
362   A84   25k multicolored   3.00   2.50

20th anniversary, Republic of Iceland.

Flower Type of 1960-62

Flowers: 50a, Eight-petal dryas. 1k, Crowfoot (Ranunculus glacialis). 1.50k, Buck bean. 2k, Clover (trifolium repens).

Flowers in Natural Colors

1964, July 15
363   A72   50a vio bl & lt vio bl   .30   .25
364   A72   1k gray & dk gray   .30   .25
365   A72   1.50k brn & pale brn   .30   .25
366   A72   2k ol & pale olive   .30   .25
     Nos. 363-366 (4)   1.20   1.00

Europa Issue, 1964
Common Design Type
1964, Sept. 14   *Photo.*   *Perf. 11½*
Granite Paper
Size: 22½x33mm
367   CD7   4.50k golden brn, yel & Prus grn   .70   .45
368   CD7   9k bl, yel & dk brn   .70   .70

Jumper — A85

1964, Oct. 20   *Unwmk.*   *Perf. 11½*
369   A85   10k lt grn & blk   1.25   .90

18th Olympic Games, Tokyo, Oct. 10-25.

ITU Emblem — A86

1965, May 17   *Photo.*   *Perf. 11½*
370   A86   4.50k green   .95   .60
371   A86   7.50k bright ultra   .25   .25

ITU, centenary.

Surtsey Island, April 1964 — A87

1.50k, Underwater volcanic eruption, Nov. 1963, vert. 3.50k, Surtsey, Sept. 1964.

1965, June 23   *Unwmk.*   *Perf. 11½*
372   A87   1.50k bl, bis & blk   .70   .70
373   A87   2k multicolored   .70   .70
374   A87   3.50k bl, blk & red   .85   .70
     Nos. 372-374 (3)   2.25   2.10

Emergence of a new volcanic island off the southern coast of Iceland.

Europa Issue, 1965
Common Design Type
1965, Sept. 27   *Photo.*   *Perf. 11½*
Size: 33x22½mm
375   CD8   5k tan, brn & brt grn   1.50   1.00
376   CD8   8k brt grn, brn & yel green   1.00   .75

Einar Benediktsson — A88

Engr. & Litho.
1965, Nov. 16   *Perf. 14*
377   A88   10k brt blue & brn   3.50   4.75

Einar Benediktsson, poet (1864-1940).

White-tailed Sea Eagle A89   National Costume A90

1965-66   *Photo.*   *Perf. 11½*
378   A89   50k multicolored   12.00   12.00
379   A90   100k multicolored   10.00   9.00

Issued: No. 378, 4/26/66; No. 379, 12/3/65.

West Iceland — A91

1966, Aug. 4   *Photo.*   *Perf. 11½*
380   A91   2.50k shown   .35   .45
381   A91   4k North Iceland   .65   .45
382   A91   5k East Iceland   .90   .45
383   A91   6.50k South Iceland   .70   .45
     Nos. 380-383 (4)   2.60   1.80

Europa Issue, 1966
Common Design Type
1966, Sept. 26   *Photo.*   *Perf. 11½*
Size: 22½x33mm
384   CD9   7k grnsh bl, lt bl & red   2.25   1.75
385   CD9   8k brn, buff & red   2.25   1.75

Literary Society Emblem — A92

1966, Nov. 18   *Engr.*   *Perf. 11½*
386   A92   4k ultramarine   .30   .30
387   A92   10k vermilion   .85   .60

Icelandic Literary Society, 150th anniv.

Common Loon — A93

1967, Mar. 16   *Photo.*   *Perf. 11½*
388   A93   20k multicolored   6.00   6.00

Europa Issue, 1967
Common Design Type
1967, May 2   *Photo.*   *Perf. 11½*
Size: 22½x33mm
389   CD10   7k yel, brn & dk bl   1.50   1.00
390   CD10   8k emer, gray & dk bl   1.50   1.00

Old and New Maps of Iceland and North America — A94

1967, June 8   *Photo.*   *Perf. 11½*
391   A94   10k blk, tan & lt bl   .30   .45

EXPO '67 Intl. Exhibition, Montreal, Apr. 28-Oct. 27, 1967. The old map, drawn about 1590 by Sigurdur Stefansson, is at the Royal Library, Copenhagen.

Symbols of Trade, Fishing, Husbandry and Industry — A95

1967, Sept. 14   *Photo.*   *Perf. 11½*
392   A95   5k dk bl, yel & emerald   .30   .25

Icelandic Chamber of Commerce, 50th anniv.

Flower Type of 1960-62

Flowers: 50a, Saxifraga oppositifolia. 2.50k, Orchis maculata.

1968, Jan. 17   *Photo.*   *Perf. 11½*
Flowers in Natural Colors
393   A72   50a green & dk brn   .25   .25
394   A72   2.50k dk brn, yel & grn   .30   .30

Europa Issue, 1968
Common Design Type
1968, Apr. 29   *Photo.*   *Perf. 11½*
Size: 33½x23mm
395   CD11   9.50k dl yel, car rose & blk   1.75   1.20
396   CD11   10k brt yel grn, blk & org   1.25   1.00

ICELAND

Right-hand Driving — A96

1968, May 21   Photo.   Perf. 11½
397 A96 4k yellow & brn   .30 .25
398 A96 5k lt reddish brn   .30 .25
Introduction of right-hand driving in Iceland, May 26, 1968.

Fridrik Fridriksson, by Sigurjón Olafsson — A97

1968, Sept. 5   Photo.   Perf. 11½
399 A97 10k sky bl & dk gray   .45 .60
Rev. Fridrik Fridriksson (1868-1961), founder of the YMCA in Reykjavik and writer.

Reading Room, National Library — A98

1968, Oct. 30   Photo.   Perf. 11½
Granite Paper
400 A98 5k yellow & brn   .25 .25
401 A98 20k lt bl & dp ultra   1.25 1.25
Natl. Library, Reykjavik, sesquicentennial.

Prime Minister Jon Magnusson (1859-1926) — A99

1968, Dec. 12   Granite Paper
402 A99 4k carmine lake   .35 .25
403 A99 50k dark brown   3.50 4.50
50th anniversary of independence.

Nordic Cooperation Issue

Five Ancient Ships — A99a

1969, Feb. 28   Engr.   Perf. 12½
404 A99a 6.50k vermilion   .60 .45
405 A99a 10k bright blue   .70 .60
50th anniv. of the Nordic Society and centenary of postal cooperation among the northern countries. The design is taken from a coin found at the site of Birka, an ancient Swedish town. See also Denmark Nos. 454-455, Finland No. 481, Norway Nos. 523-524, and Sweden Nos. 808-810.

Europa Issue, 1969
Common Design Type

1969, Apr. 28   Photo.   Perf. 11½
Size: 32½x23mm
406 CD12 13k pink & multi   3.75 2.00
407 CD12 14.50k yel & multi   .45 .40

Flag of Iceland and Rising Sun — A100

1969, June 17   Photo.   Perf. 11½
408 A100 25k gray, gold, vio bl & red   1.00 .60
409 A100 100k lt bl, gold, vio bl & red 6.00 6.00
25th anniversary, Republic of Iceland.

Boeing 727 — A101

Design: 12k, Rolls Royce 400.

1969, Sept. 3   Photo.   Perf. 11½
410 A101 9.50k dk bl & sky bl   .60 .70
411 A101 12k dk bl & ultra   .60 .70
50th anniversary of Icelandic aviation.

Snaefellsjökull Mountain — A102

1970, Jan. 6   Photo.   Perf. 11½
412 A102 1k shown   .25 .25
413 A102 4k Laxfoss   .35 .35
414 A102 5k Hattver, vert.   .45 .35
415 A102 20k Fjardargill, vert. 1.75 .75
Nos. 412-415 (4)   2.80 1.70

First Meeting of Icelandic Supreme Court — A103

1970, Feb. 16   Photo.   Perf. 11½
416 A103 6.50k multicolored   .30 .25
Icelandic Supreme Court, 50th anniv.

Column from "Skarosbók," 1363 (Law Book) — A104

Icelandic Manuscripts: 15k, Preface to "Flateyjarbók" (History of Norwegian Kings), 1387-1394. 30k, Initial from "Flateyjarbók" showing Harald Fairhair cutting fetters of Dofri.

1970, Mar. 20   Photo.   Perf. 11½
417 A104 5k multicolored   .25 .25
418 A104 15k multicolored   .70 .70
419 A104 30k multicolored   1.25 1.25
Nos. 417-419 (3)   2.20 2.20

Europa Issue, 1970
Common Design Type

1970, May 4   Photo.   Perf. 11½
Size: 32x22mm
420 CD13 9k brn & yellow   2.50 1.50
421 CD13 25k brt grn & bister 3.50 2.50

Nurse A105

Grimur Thomsen A106

The Rest, by Thorarinn B. Thorlaksson A107

1970, June 19   Photo.   Perf. 11½
422 A105 7k ultra & lt bl   .45 .25
423 A106 10k ind & lt grnsh bl .35 .45
424 A107 50k gold & multi   1.75 1.60
Nos. 422-424 (3)   2.55 2.30
50th anniv. (in 1969) of the Icelandic Nursing Association (No. 422); 150th birth anniv. of Grimur Thomsen (1820-1896), poet (No. 423); Intl. Arts Festival, Reykjavik, June 1970 (No. 424).

Saxifraga Oppositifolia A108

Lakagigar A109

1970, Aug. 25   Photo.   Perf. 11½
425 A108 3k multicolored   .30 .30
426 A109 15k multicolored   1.20 1.20
European Nature Conservation Year.

UN Emblem and Map of Iceland — A110

1970, Oct. 23   Photo.   Perf. 11½
427 A110 12k multicolored   .60 .70
25th anniversary of United Nations.

"Flight," by Asgrimur Jonsson — A111

1971, Mar. 26   Photo.   Perf. 11½
428 A111 10k multicolored   .85 .85
Joint northern campaign for the benefit of refugees.

Europa Issue, 1971
Common Design Type

1971, May 3   Photo.   Perf. 11½
Size: 33x22mm
429 CD14 7k rose cl, yel & blk 2.25 1.75
430 CD14 15k ultra, yel & blk   2.75 2.00

Postal Checking Service Emblem — A112

1971, June 22   Photo.   Perf. 11½
431 A112 5k vio bl & lt blue   .25 .25
432 A112 7k dk grn & yel grn   .30 .25
Introduction of Postal Checking Service, Apr. 30, 1971.

Tryggvi Gunnarsson — A113

Design: 30k, Patriotic Society emblem.

1971, Aug. 19   Photo.   Perf. 11½
433 A113 30k lt bl & vio blk   1.40 .95
434 A113 100k gray & vio blk   6.00 6.00
Icelandic Patriotic Society, cent.; Tryggvi Gunnarsson (1835-1917), founder and president.

Haddock Freezing Plant — A114

Fish Industry: 7k, Cod fishing. 20k, Shrimp canning plant.

1971, Nov. 18
435 A114 5k multicolored   .25 .25
436 A114 7k multicolored   .25 .25
437 A114 20k green & multi   1.20 .70
Nos. 435-437 (3)   1.70 1.20

Herdubreid Mountain A115

Engr. & Litho.
1972, Mar. 9   Perf. 14
438 A115 250k blue & multi   .60 .30

Europa Issue 1972
Common Design Type
1972, May 2   Photo.   Perf. 11½
Size: 22x32mm
439 CD15 9k lt vio & multi   1.00 .90
440 CD15 13k yel grn & multi   1.90 1.75

"United Municipalities" A116

1972, June 14   Photo.   Perf. 11½
441 A116 16k multicolored   .25 .50
Legislation for local government, cent.

Chessboard, World Map, Rook — A117

1972, July 2   Litho.   Perf. 13
442 A117 15k lt ol & multi   .45 .45
World Chess Championship, Reykjavik, July-Sept. 1972.

Hothouse Tomatoes A118

Designs: 12k, Steam valve and natural steam. 40k, Hothouse roses.

1972, Aug. 23   Photo.   Perf. 11½
443 A118 8k Prus bl & multi   .25 .25
444 A118 12k green & multi   .25 .25
445 A118 40k dk pur & multi   1.40 1.20
Nos. 443-445 (3)   1.90 1.70
Hothouse gardening in Iceland, using natural steam and hot springs.

Iceland and the Continental Shelf — A119

1972, Sept. 27   Litho.   Perf. 13
446 A119 9k blue & multi   .25 .50
To publicize Iceland's offshore fishing rights.

Europa Issue 1973
Common Design Type
1973, Apr. 30   Photo.   Perf. 11½
Size: 32½x22mm
447 CD16 13k vio & multi   5.75 2.75
448 CD16 25k olive & multi   .90 .60

Iceland No. 1 and Messenger A120

Designs (First Issue of Iceland and): 15k, No. 5 and pony train. 20k, No. 2 and mailboat "Esja". 40k, No. 3 and mail truck. 80k, No. 4 and Beech-18 mail plane.

Litho. & Engr.
1973, May 23   Perf. 13x13½
449 A120 10k dl bl, blk & ultra .30 .30
450 A120 15k grn, blk & gray   .25 .25
451 A120 20k maroon, blk & car .25 .25

ICELAND

452 A120 40k vio, blk & brn .25 .25
453 A120 80k olive, blk & yel 1.40 1.00
Nos. 449-453 (5) 2.45 2.05

Centenary of Iceland's first postage stamps.

Nordic Cooperation Issue

Nordic House, Reykjavik — A120a

1973, June 26   Engr.   Perf. 12½
454 A120a 9k multicolored .45 .25
455 A120a 10k multicolored 1.40 1.10

A century of postal cooperation among Denmark, Finland, Iceland, Norway and Sweden, and in connection with the Nordic Postal Conference, Reykjavik.

A121

Designs: 13k, 15k, Ásgeir Ásgeirsson, (1894-1972), President of Iceland 1952-1968.

Perf. 13x13½   Wmk. 409   Engr.
456 A121 13k carmine .45 .25
457 A121 15k blue .25 .25

Islandia 73 Emblem — A122

20k, Islandia 73 emblem; diff. arrangement.

Perf. 11½
1973, Aug. 31   Photo.   Unwmk.
458 A122 17k gray & multi .45 .45
459 A122 20k brn, ocher & yel .30 .45

Islandia 73 Philatelic Exhibition, Reykjavik, Aug. 31-Sept. 9.

Man and WMO Emblem — A123

1973, Nov. 14   Photo.   Perf. 12½
460 A123 50k silver & multi .70 .60

Intl. meteorological cooperation, cent.

The Settlement, Tapestry by Vigdis Kristjansdottir — A124

Designs: 13k, Establishment of Althing, painting by Johannes Johannesson, horiz. 15k, Gudbrandur Thorlakkson, Bishop of Holar 1571-1627. 17k, Age of Sturlungar (Fighting Vikings), drawing by Thorvaldur Skulason. 20k, Stained glass window honoring Hallgrimur Petursson (1614-74), hymn writer. 25k, Illumination from Book of Flatey, 14th century. 30k, Conversion to Christianity (altarpiece, Skalholt), mosaic by Nina Tryggvadottir. 40k, Wood carving (family and plants), 18th century. 60k, Curing the Catch, cement bas-relief. 70k, Age of Writing (Saemundur Riding Seal), sculpture by Asmundur Sveinsson. 100k, Virgin and Child with Angels, embroidered antependium, Stafafell Church, 14th century, horiz.

1974   Photo.   Perf. 11½
461 A124 10k multicolored .25 .25
462 A124 13k multicolored .25 .25
463 A124 15k multicolored .25 .25
464 A124 17k multicolored .35 .25
465 A124 20k multicolored .35 .25
466 A124 25k multicolored .25 .25
467 A124 30k multicolored 1.00 .70
468 A124 40k multicolored 1.15 .90
469 A124 60k multicolored 1.15 1.15
470 A124 70k multicolored 1.15 1.00
471 A124 100k multicolored 1.50 .70
Nos. 461-471 (11) 7.65 5.95

1100th anniv. of settlement of Iceland.
Issued: 10k, 13k, 30k, 70k, 3/12; 17k, 25k, 100k, 6/11; 15k, 20k, 40k, 60k, 7/16.

Horseback Rider, Wood, 17th Century — A125

Europa: 20k, "Through the Sound Barrier," contemporary bronze by Asmundur Sveinsson.

1974, Apr. 29   Photo.   Perf. 11½
472 A125 13k brn red & multi .30 .30
473 A125 20k gray & multi 1.00 1.00

Clerk Selling Stamps, UPU Emblem — A126

Design: 20k, Mailman delivering mail.

1974, Oct. 9   Photo.   Perf. 11½
474 A126 17k ocher & multi .30 .30
475 A126 20k olive & multi .30 .30

Centenary of Universal Postal Union.

Volcanic Eruption, Heimaey, Jan. 23, 1973 — A127

Design: 25k, Volcanic eruption, night view.

1975, Jan. 23   Photo.   Perf. 11½
476 A127 20k multicolored .70 .45
477 A127 25k multicolored .30 .30

Europa Issue

Bird, by Thorvaldur Skulason A128

Sun Queen, by Johannes S. Kjarval A129

1975, May 12   Photo.   Perf. 11½
478 A128 18k multicolored .35 .35
479 A129 23k gold & multi 1.10 .70

Stephan G. Stephansson — A130

1975, Aug. 1   Engr.   Perf. 13
480 A130 27k green & brn .60 .30

Stephan G. Stephansson (1853-1927), Icelandic poet and settler in North America; centenary of Icelandic emigration to North America.

Petursson, by Hjalti Thorsteinsson A131

Einar Jonsson, Self-portrait A132

23k, Arni Magnusson, by Hjalti Thorsteinsson. 30k, Jon Eiriksson, sculpture by Olafur Olafsson.

1975, Sept. 18   Engr.   Perf. 13
481 A131 18k sl grn & indigo .25 .60
482 A131 23k Prussian blue .25 .25
483 A131 30k deep magenta .25 .25
484 A132 50k indigo .50 .25
Nos. 481-484 (4) 1.25 1.35

Famous Icelanders: Hallgrimur Petursson (1614-1674), minister and religious poet; Arni Magnusson (1663-1730), historian, registrar and manuscript collector; Jon Eiriksson (1728-1787), professor of law and cabinet member; Einar Jonsson (1874-1954), sculptor, painter and writer.

Red Cross — A133

1975, Oct. 15   Photo.   Perf. 11½x12
485 A133 23k multicolored .45 .45

Icelandic Red Cross, 50th anniversary.

Abstract Painting, by Nina Tryggvadottir — A134

1975, Oct. 15   Perf. 12x12½
486 A134 100k multicolored 1.25 .60

International Women's Year 1975.

Thorvaldsen Statue, by Thorvaldsen — A135

1975, Nov. 19   Photo.   Perf. 11½
487 A135 27k lt vio & multi .80 .45

Centenary of Thorvaldsen Society, a charity honoring Bertel Thorvaldsen (1768-1844), sculptor.

Saplings Growing in Bare Landscape — A136

1975, Nov. 19   Perf. 12x11½
488 A136 35k multicolored .60 .45

Reforestation.

Lang Glacier, by Asgrimur Jonsson — A137

1976, Mar. 18   Photo.   Perf. 11½
489 A137 150k gold & multi 1.75 1.50

Asgrimur Jonsson (1876-1958), painter.

Wooden Bowl — A138

Europa: 45k, Spinning wheel, vert.

1976, May 3   Photo.   Perf. 11½
490 A138 35k ver & multi 1.25 .90
491 A138 45k blue & multi 1.25 1.25

No. 9 with First Day Cancel — A139

1976, Sept. 22   Photo.   Perf. 11½   Granite Paper
492 A139 30k bis, blk & gray bl .30 .45

Centenary of aurar stamps.

Decree Establishing Postal Service — A140

45k, Conclusion of Decree with signatures.

1976, Sept. 22   Engr.   Perf. 13
493 A140 35k dark brown .45 .30
494 A140 45k dark blue .70 .45

Iceland's Postal Service, bicentenary.

Federation Emblem, People — A141

1976, Dec. 2   Photo.   Perf. 12½   Granite Paper
495 A141 100k multicolored 1.10 .70

Icelandic Federation of Labor, 60th anniv.

Five Water Lilies — A142

Photo. & Engr.   Perf. 12½
1977, Feb. 2
496 A142 35k brt grn & multi .80 .60
497 A142 45k ultra & multi .80 .60

Nordic countries cooperation for protection of the environment and 25th Session of Nordic Council, Helsinki, Feb. 19.

Ofaerufoss, Eldgja — A143

Europa: 85k, Kirkjufell Mountain, seen from Grundarfjord.

1977, May 2   Photo.   Perf. 12
498 A143 45k multicolored 3.25 .90
499 A143 85k multicolored 1.25 .35

193

ICELAND

Harlequin Duck — A144

1977, June 14   **Photo.**   *Perf. 11½*
500 A144 40k multicolored   .55   .45
Wetlands conservation, European campaign.

Society Emblem — A145

1977, June 14
501 A145 60k vio bl & ultra   .75   .65
Federation of Icelandic Cooperative Societies, 75th anniversary.

Hot Springs, Therapeutic Bath, Emblem — A146

1977, Nov. 16   **Photo.**   *Perf. 11½*
502 A146 90k multicolored   .65   .55
World Rheumatism Year.

Stone Marker — A147

1977, Dec. 12   **Engr.**   *Perf. 11½*
503 A147 45k dark blue   .90   .65
Touring Club of Iceland, 50th anniversary.

Thorvaldur Thoroddsen, (1855-1921), Geologist, Scientist and Writer — A148

Design: 60k, Briet Bjarnhedinsdottir (1856-1940), Founder of Icelandic Women's Association and Reykjavik city councillor.

1977, Dec. 12   **Engr.**   *Perf. 11½*
504 A148 50k brn & slate grn   .25   .25
505 A148 60k grn & vio brn   .80   .60

Bailiff's Residence, Videy Island, 1752 — A149

Europa: 120k, Husavik Church, 1906.

1978, May 2   **Photo.**   *Perf. 11½*
506 A149 80k multicolored   1.40   .60
507 A149 120k multi, vert.   3.00   .80

Alexander Johannesson, Junkers Planes — A150

100k, Fokker Friendship plane over mountains.

1978, June 21   **Photo.**   *Perf. 12½*
508 A150 60k multicolored   .55   .30
509 A150 100k multicolored   .55   .55
50th anniv. of domestic flights in Iceland.

Skeioara River Bridge — A151

1978, Aug. 17   **Photo.**   *Perf. 11½*
510 A151 70k multicolored   .30   .30

Lava Near Mt. Hekla, by Jon Stefansson A152

1978, Nov. 16   **Photo.**   *Perf. 12*
511 A152 1000k multicolored   4.00   3.50
Jon Stefansson (1881-1962), Icelandic painter.

Ship to Shore Rescue — A153

1978, Dec. 1   **Engr.**   *Perf. 13*
512 A153 60k black   .30   .30
National Life Saving Assoc., 50th anniv.

Halldor Hermannsson (1878-1958), Historian, Librarian — A154

1978, Dec. 1
513 A154 150k indigo   .55   .45

Lighthouse — A155

1978, Dec. 1   **Photo.**   *Perf. 11½*
514 A155 90k multicolored   .55   .45
Centenary of Icelandic lighthouses.

Telephone, c. 1900 — A156

Europa: 190k, Post horn and satchel.

1979, Apr. 30   **Photo.**   *Perf. 11½*
515 A156 110k multicolored   1.75   .45
516 A156 190k multicolored   2.90   .70

Jon Sigurdsson and Ingibjorg Einarsdottir A157

1979, Nov. 1   **Engr.**   *Perf. 13x12½*
517 A157 150k black   .60   .60
Jon Sigurdsson (1811-1879), Icelandic statesman and leader in independence movement.

Excerpt from Olafs Saga Helga — A158

1979, Nov. 1   **Photo.**   *Perf. 11½*
518 A158 200k multicolored   .80   .55
Snorri Sturluson (1178-1241), Icelandic historian and writer.

Children with Flowers ICY Emblem — A159

1979, Sept. 12
519 A159 140k multicolored   .80   .55
International Year of the Child.

A160

Icelandic Arms, before 1904 and 1904-1919.

1979, Sept. 12
520 A160 500k multicolored   1.40   .90
Home rule, 75th anniversary.

A161

Designs: 80k, Ingibjorg H. Bjarnason (1867-1941). 100k, Bjarni Thorsteinsson (1861-1938), composer. 120k, Petur Gudjohnsen (1812-77), organist. 130k, Sveinbjorn Sveinbjornson (1847-1927), composer. 170k, Torfhildur Holm (1845-1918), poet.

1979   **Engr.**   *Perf. 13*
521 A161   80k rose violet   .25   .25
522 A161 100k black   .25   .25
523 A161 120k rose carmine   .25   .25
524 A161 130k sepia   .45   .45
525 A161 170k carmine rose   .55   .45
   Nos. 521-525 (5)   1.75   1.65
Issued: 80k, 170k, Aug. 3; others, Dec. 12.

Canis Familiaris — A162

Design: 90k, Alopex lagopus.

1980, Jan. 24
526 A162 10k black   .25   .25
527 A162 90k sepia   .25   .25
See Nos. 534-536, 543-545, 552, 553, 556-558, 610-612.

Jon Sveinsson Nonni (1857-1944), Writer — A163

Europa: 250k, Gunnar Gunnarsson (1889-1975), writer.

1980, Apr. 28   **Photo.**   *Perf. 11½*
Granite Paper
528 A163 140k dl rose & blk   .90   .45
529 A163 250k tan & blk   1.25   .70

Mountain Ash Branch and Berries — A164

1980, July 8   **Photo.**   *Perf. 12½*
530 A164 120k multicolored   .35   .35
Year of the Tree.

Laugardalur Sports Complex, Reykjavik — A165

1980, July 8   **Engr.**   *Perf. 13x12½*
531 A165 300k slate green   .70   .55
1980 Olympic Games.

Carved and Painted Cabinet Door, 18th Cent. — A166

Nordic Cooperation: 180k, Embroidered cushion, 19th cent.

1980, Sept. 9   **Photo.**   *Perf. 11½*
Granite Paper
532 A166 150k multicolored   .60   .45
533 A166 180k multicolored   .70   .55

Animal Type of 1980

Designs: 160k, Sebastes marinus. 170k, Fratercula arctica. 190k, Phoca vitulina.

1980, Oct. 16   **Engr.**   *Perf. 13*
534 A162 160k rose violet   .85   .25
535 A162 170k black   .95   .25
536 A162 190k dark brown   .25   .25
   Nos. 534-536 (3)   2.05   1.10

Radio Receiver, 1930 — A168

1980, Nov. 20   **Photo.**   *Perf. 12½*
Granite Paper
537 A168 400k multicolored   1.10   .45
State Broadcasting Service, 50th anniv.

University Hospital, 50th Anniversary A169

1980, Nov. 20   *Perf. 11½*
538 A169 200k multicolored   .45   .45

A170

Design: 170a, Magnus Stephensen (1762-1833), Chief Justice. 190a, Finnur Magnusson (1781-1847), Privy Archives keeper.

1981, Feb. 24   **Engr.**   *Perf. 13*
539 A170 170a bright ultra   .55   .45
540 A170 190a olive green   .55   .45

Europa Issue

Europa — A171

ICELAND

180a, Luftur the Sorcerer. 220a, Sea witch.

1981, May 4	Photo.		Perf. 11½
Granite Paper			
541	A171	180a multicolored	1.25 .80
542	A171	220a multicolored	1.25 .80

Animal Type of 1980
Designs: 50a, Troglodytes troglodytes. 100a, Pluvialis apricaria. 200a, Corvus corax.

1981, Aug. 20	Engr.		Perf. 13
543	A162	50a brown	.25 .25
544	A162	100a blue	.25 .25
545	A162	200a black	.25 .25
		Nos. 543-545 (3)	.75 .75

Intl. Year of the Disabled — A173

1981, Sept. 29	Photo.		Perf. 11½
546	A173	200a multicolored	.30 .25

Skyggnir Earth Satellite Station, First Anniv. — A174

1981, Sept. 29	Photo.		Perf. 11½
547	A174	500a multicolored	1.25 .60

Hauling the Line, by Gunnlaugur Scheving (1904-1972) A175

1981, Oct. 21	Photo.		Perf. 11½
548	A175	5000a multi	5.75 3.50

Christian Missionary Work in Iceland Millennium — A176

1981, Nov. 24	Engr.		Perf. 13
549	A176	200a dark violet	.35 .35

Christmas — A177

1981, Nov. 24	Photo.		Perf. 12½
Granite Paper			
550	A177	200a Leaf bread	.70 .70
551	A177	250a Leaf bread, diff.	.70 .55

Animal Type of 1980
Designs: 20a, Buccinum undatum, vert. 600a, Chlamys islandica.

1982, Mar. 23	Engr.		Perf. 13
552	A162	20a copper brn	.25 .25
553	A162	600a vio brown	.90 .45

Europa Issue

First Norse Settlement, 874 — A179

450a, Discovery of North America, 1000.

1982, May 3	Photo.		Perf. 11½
Granite Paper			
554	A179	350a shown	5.25 1.25
555	A179	450a multi	5.25 1.25

Animal Type of 1980
Designs: 300a, Ovis aries, vert. 400a, Bos taurus, vert. 500a, Felis catus, vert.

1982, June 3	Engr.		Perf. 13
556	A162	300a brown	.80 .45
557	A162	400a lake	.60 .35
558	A162	500a gray	.25 .25
		Nos. 556-558 (3)	1.65 1.05

Kaupfelag Thingeyinga Cooperative Society Centenary A181

1982, June 3			
559	A181	1000a black & red	.90 .45

Man Riding Iceland Pony — A182

1982, July 1	Photo.		Perf. 11½
Granite Paper			
560	A182	700a multicolored	.80 .35

Centenary of School of Agriculture, Holar — A183

1982, July 1		Granite Paper	
561	A183	1500a multi	1.25 .70

Mount Herdubreid, by Isleifur Konradsson (1889-1972) A184

1982, Sept. 8	Photo.		Perf. 11½
Granite Paper			
562	A184	800a multicolored	.70 .55

UN World Assembly on Aging, 7/26-8/6.

Borbjorg Sveinsdottir (1828-1903) — A185

1982, Sept. 8	Engr.		Perf. 13
563	A185	900a red brown	.55 .45

Borbjorg Sveinsdottir (1828-1903), midwife and Univ. founder.

Souvenir Sheet

NORDIA '84 — A186

	Photo. & Engr.		Perf. 13½
1982, Oct. 7			
564	A186	Sheet of 2	5.00 5.00
a.		400a Reynistaour Monastery seal	2.50 2.50
b.		800a Bingeyrar	2.50 2.50

NORDIA '84 Intl. Stamp Exhibition, Reykjavik, July 3-8, 1984. Sold for 18k. See No. 581.

Christmas — A187

Score from The Night was Such a Splendid One.

1982, Nov. 16	Photo.		Perf. 11½
Granite Paper			
565	A187	3k Birds	.90 .55
566	A187	3.50k Bells	1.00 .55

Caltha Palustris — A188

8k, Lychnis alpina. 10k, Potentilla palustris. 20k, Myosotis scorpioides.

1983, Feb. 10		Photo.	
	Granite Paper		
567	A188	7.50k shown	.55 .55
568	A188	8k multicolored	.90 .55
569	A188	10k multicolored	1.25 .55
570	A188	20k multicolored	2.50 .90
		Nos. 567-570 (4)	5.20 2.55

See Nos. 586-587, 593-594, 602-605, 663-664.

Nordic Cooperation A189

1983, Mar. 24		Granite Paper	
571	A189	4.50k Mt. Sulur	1.20 .75
572	A189	5k Urrida Falls	1.20 .75

Europa Issue

Thermal Energy Projects — A190

1983, May 5		Granite Paper	
573	A190	5k shown	3.00 1.40
574	A190	5.50k multi, diff.	22.50 2.00

Fishing Industry — A191

1983, June 8	Engr.		Perf. 13x12½
575	A191	11k Fishing boats	.30 .30
576	A191	13k Fishermen	1.40 .80

Bicentenary of Skaftareldar Volcanic Eruption — A192

15k, Volcano, by Finnur Jonsson.

1983, June 8	Photo.		Perf. 11½
Granite Paper			
577	A192	15k multicolored	.75 .55

Skiing — A193

1983, Sept. 8	Photo.		Perf. 11½
578	A193	12k shown	.85 .55
579	A193	14k Running	1.00 .75

World Communications Year — A194

1983, Sept. 8			Perf. 12½
580	A194	30k multi	2.40 1.25

NORDIA '84 Type of 1982
Souvenir Sheet

Bishops' Seals: 8k, Magnus Eyjolfsson of Skalholt, 1477-90. 12k, Ogmundur Palsson of Skalhot, 1521-40.

	Photo. & Engr.		Perf. 13½
1983, Oct. 6			
581		Sheet of 2	6.50 6.50
a.	A186	8k violet blue & black	3.25 3.25
b.	A186	12k pale green & black	3.25 3.25

Sold for 30k.

Christmas — A195

1983, Nov. 10	Photo.		Perf. 11½
Granite Paper			
582	A195	6k Virgin and Child	.90 .55
583	A195	6.50k Angel	.90 .55

Pres. Kristjan Eldjarn (1916-82) — A196

			Perf. 14x13½
1983, Dec. 6	Engr.		Wmk. 410
584	A196	6.50k brn carmine	.90 .70
585	A196	7k dark blue	.35 .25

Flower Type of 1983
6k, Rosa pimpinellifolia. 25k, Potentilla anserium.

			Perf. 11½
1984, Mar. 1	Photo.		Unwmk.
Granite Paper			
586	A188	6k multicolored	.90 .45
587	A188	25k multicolored	1.25 .45

Europa 1959-84 — A197

1984, May 3			
588	A197	6.50k grnsh bl & blk	2.40 .75
589	A197	7.50k rose & black	1.25 .75

Souvenir Sheet

A198

Design: Abraham Ortelius' map of Northern Europe, 1570.

	Photo. & Engr.		Perf. 14x13½
1984, June 6			
590	A198	40k multi	15.00 15.00

NORDIA '84 Intl. Stamp Exhibition, Reykjavik, July 3-8. Sold for 60k.

A199

ICELAND

1984, June 17   Photo.   Perf. 11½
Granite Paper
591 A199 50k Flags   5.75 3.00
40th Anniv. of Republic.

Good Templars Headquarters, Akureyri — A200

1984, July 18   Engr.   Perf. 13
592 A200 10k green   .70   .45
Order of the Good Templars, centenary in Iceland, temperance org.

Flower Type of 1983
6.50k, Loiseleuria procumbens. 7.50k, Arctostaphylos uva-ursi.

1984, Sept. 11   Photo.   Perf. 11½
Granite Paper
593 A188 6.50k multicolored   .55   .30
594 A188 7.50k multicolored   .55   .30

Christmas — A201

1984, Nov. 29   Photo.
595 A201 600a multicolored   .65   .30
596 A201 650a multicolored   .65   .45
600a, Madonna and Child. 650a, Angel, Christmas rose.

Gudbrand's Bible, 400th Anniv. — A202

1984, Nov. 29   Engr.   Perf. 12½x13
597 A202 6.50k Text   .65   .30
598 A202 7.50k Illustration   .45   .70
First Icelandic Bible.

Confederation of Employers, 50th Anniv. — A203

1984, Nov. 9   Photo.   Perf. 12x12½
Granite Paper
599 A203 30k Building blocks   1.40 1.25

Bjorn Bjarnarson (1853-1918) — A204

40k, New gallery building, horiz.

1984, Nov. 9   Photo.   Perf. 11½
Granite Paper
600 A204 12k shown   .60   .60
601 A204 40k multicolored   2.10 1.25
Natl. Gallery centenary.

Flower Type of 1983

1985, Mar. 20   Photo.   Perf. 11½
Granite Paper
602 A188   8k Rubus saxatilis   .90   .35
603 A188   9k Veronica fruticans .90   .35
604 A188 16k Lathyrus japonicus 2.50   .45
605 A188 17k Draba alpina   .70   .55
    Nos. 602-605 (4)   5.00 1.80

Music Year Emblem, Woman Playing the Langspil — A205

Europa: 7.50k, Man playing the Icelandic violin.

1985, May 3   Photo.   Perf. 11½
Granite Paper
606 A205 6.50k multicolored   3.00   .75
607 A205 7.50k multicolored   3.00   .95

Natl. Horticulture Soc., Cent. — A206

1985, June 20   Photo.   Perf. 12
608 A206 20k Sorbus intermedia 1.00   .55

Intl. Youth Year — A207

1985, June 20   Photo.   Perf. 11½
609 A207 25k Icelandic girl   1.25   .95

Animal Type of 1980
Designs: 700a, Todarodes sagittatus. 800a, Hyas araneus. 900a, Tealia felina.

1985, Sept. 10   Engr.   Perf. 13
610 A162 700a brn carmine   .25   .30
611 A162 800a dk brown   .35   .25
612 A162 900a carmine   1.25   .45
    Nos. 610-612 (3)   1.85 1.00

Hannes Stephensen (1799-1856), Cleric, Politician, Translator — A209

Famous men: 30k, Jon Gudmudsson (1807-1875), editor, politician.

1985, Sept. 10   Engr.
613 A209 13k dp magenta   .65   .45
614 A209 30k deep violet   1.60   .75

Yearning to Fly, by Johannes S. Kjarval (1885-1972), Reykjavik Natl. Museum — A210

1985, Oct. 15   Photo.   Perf. 12x11½
615 A210 100k multi   5.75 4.75

A211

Abstract ice crystal paintings, by Snorri Sveinn Fridriksson (b. 1934).

1985, Nov. 14   Photo.   Perf. 11½
616 A211 8k Crucifix   .80   .35
617 A211 9k Pine Trees   .80   .55
Christmas.

Birds — A212

1986, Mar. 19   Photo.   Perf. 11½
Granite Paper
618 A212   6k Motacilla alba   .25   .25
619 A212 10k Anas acuta   1.75   .60
620 A212 12k Falco columbarius 1.25   .60
621 A212 15k Alca torda   .70   .45
    Nos. 618-621 (4)   3.95 1.90
See Nos. 642-645, 665-666, 671-672, 686-687, 721-722.

Europa Issue

Natl. Parks — A213

1986, May 5
622 A213 10k Skaftafell   11.00 1.10
623 A213 12k Jokulsargljufur   4.75 1.40

Nordic Cooperation Issue — A214

Sister towns: 10k, Stykkishólmur. 12k, Seydisfjördur.

1986, May 27   Perf. 11½
624 A214 10k multicolored   1.20   .80
625 A214 12k multicolored   1.20   .80

Natl. Bank, Cent. — A215

13k, Headquarters, Reykjavik. 250k, Banknote reverse, 1928.

1986, July 1   Engr.   Perf. 14
626 A215   13k black   .90   .70
627 A215 250k red brn   9.00 9.00

Reykjavik Bicent. — A216

10k, City seal, 1815. 12k, View from bank, illustration, 1856. 13k, Laugardalur hot water brook. 40k, City Theater.

1986, Aug. 18   Engr.   Perf. 13½x14
628 A216 10k red   .70   .35
629 A216 12k brown   .70   .35
630 A216 13k green   .70   .55
631 A216 40k blue   1.75 1.40
    Nos. 628-631 (4)   3.85 2.65

Introduction of the Telephone in Iceland, 80th Anniv. — A217

10k, Morse receiver, 1906. 20k, Handset, microchip, 1986.

1986, Sept. 29   Photo.   Perf. 11½
Granite Paper
632 A217 10k multicolored   .45   .35
633 A217 20k multicolored   1.10   .60

Souvenir Sheet

Hvita River Crossing, Loa, 1836, by Auguste Mayer — A218

Photo. & Engr.
1986, Oct. 9   Perf. 14
634 A218 20k bluish black   5.25 5.25
Stamp Day. Sold for 30k to benefit philatelic organizations. See Nos. 646, 667.

Christmas — A219

Paintings by Bjoerg Thorsteinsdottir: 10k, Christmas at Peace. 12k, Christmas Night.

1986, Nov. 13   Photo.   Perf. 12
635 A219 10k multicolored   1.00   .45
636 A219 12k multicolored   .45   .45

Olafsvik Trading Station, 300th Anniv. — A220

50k, Merchantman Svanur, 1777.

1987, Mar. 26   Engr.   Perf. 14x13½
637 A220 50k bluish black   2.50 1.25

Keflavik Intl. Airport Terminal Inauguration A221

1987, Apr. 14   Photo.   Perf. 12x11½
638 A221 100k multi   4.50 1.75

Europa Issue

A222

Designs: Stained Glass Windows by Leifur Breidfjoerd, Fossvogur Cemetery Chapel: 12k, Christ carrying the cross. 15k, Soldiers, peace dove.

1987, May 4   Photo.   Perf. 12x11½
639 A222 12k multicolored   2.00   .70
640 A222 15k multicolored   2.00   .70

Rasmus Christian Rask (1787-1832), Danish Linguist — A223

1987, June 10   Engr.   Perf. 13½
641 A223 20k black   .90   .70
Preservation of the Icelandic language.

Bird Type of 1986
13k, Asio flammeus. 40k, Turdus iliacus. 70k, Haematopus ostralegus. 90k, Anas platyrhynchos.

1987, Sept. 16   Photo.   Perf. 11½
Granite Paper
642 A212 13k multicolored   1.25   .45
643 A212 40k multicolored   2.00   .60
644 A212 70k multicolored   2.75   .95
645 A212 90k multicolored   4.50 1.50
    Nos. 642-645 (4)   10.50 3.50

Stamp Day Type of 1986
Souvenir Sheet

Trading Station of Djupivogur in 1836, by Auguste Mayer.

1987, Oct. 9   Engr.   Perf. 13½x14
646 A218 30k black   5.50 5.50
Stamp Day. Sold for 45k to benefit the Stamp and Postal History Fund.

ICELAND

Dental Protection — A226

1987, Oct. 9   Photo.   Perf. 11½x12
Granite Paper
647   A226   12k multicolored   .55   .45

Eagle — A227

Guardian Spirits of the North, East, South and West.

Perf. 13 on 3 sides
1987, Oct. 9   Engr.
Booklet Stamps
648   A227   13k shown   .60   .60
649   A227   13k Dragon   .60   .60
650   A227   13k Bull   .60   .60
651   A227   13k Giant   .60   .60
   a.   Block of 4, #648-651   2.50   2.50
   b.   Bklt. pane of 12, 3 #651a   7.50   —

Legend of Heimskringla, the story of the Norse kings. Haraldur Gormsson, king of Denmark, deterred from invading Iceland after hearing of the guardian spirits.
See Nos. 656-659, 677, 688-695.

Christmas — A228

1987, Oct. 21   Photo.   Perf. 11½x12
652   A228   13k Fir branch   .65   .25
653   A228   17k Candle flame   .65   .45

Steinn Steinarr (1908-1958) A229

Poets: 21k, David Stefansson (1895-1964).

1988, Feb. 25   Photo.   Perf. 12
654   A229   16k multi   .80   .35
655   A229   21k multi   .80   .65

Guardian Spirit Type of 1987
Perf. 13 on 3 sides
1988, May 2   Engr.
Booklet Stamps
656   A227   16k Eagle   .60   .60
657   A227   16k Dragon   .60   .60
658   A227   16k Bull   .60   .60
659   A227   16k Giant   .60   .60
   a.   Block of 4, #656-659   2.50   2.50
   b.   Bklt. pane of 12, 3 #659a   7.50   —

Europa Issue

Modern Communication A230

16k, Data transmission system. 21k, Facsimile machine.

1988, May 2   Photo.   Perf. 12x11½
660   A230   16k multicolored   1.00   .60
661   A230   21k multicolored   4.25   2.00

1988 Summer Olympics, Seoul — A231

1988, June 9   Photo.   Perf. 12
Granite Paper
662   A231   18k Handball   .70   .60

Flower Type of 1983
1988, June 9   Perf. 11½
Granite Paper
663   A188   10k Vicia cracca   .55   .30
664   A188   50k Thymus praecox   3.00   .80

Bird Type of 1986
1988, Sept. 21   Photo.   Perf. 11½
Granite Paper
665   A212   5k Limosa limosa   .45   .25
666   A212   30k Clangula hyemalis   1.75   .80

Stamp Day Type of 1986
Souvenir Sheet
Nupsstadur Farm, Fljotshverfi, 1836, by Auguste Mayer.
1988, Oct. 9   Engr.   Perf. 14
667   A218   40k black   4.75   4.75
Stamp Day. Sold for 60k to benefit the Stamp and Postal History Fund.

WHO, 40th Anniv. — A234

1988, Nov. 3   Photo.   Perf. 11½x12
Granite Paper
668   A234   19k multicolored   .80   .45

Christmas — A235

1988, Nov. 3   Perf. 11½
Granite Paper
669   A235   19k Fisherman at sea   1.00   .30
670   A235   24k Ship, buoy   1.25   1.25

Bird Type of 1986
19k, Phalaropus lobatus. 100k, Plectrophenax nivalis.
1989, Feb. 2   Photo.
671   A212   19k multicolored   1.00   .35
672   A212   100k multicolored   5.25   1.40

Women's Folk Costumes — A236

1989, Apr. 20   Photo.   Perf. 11½x12
Granite Paper
673   A236   21k Peysufot   1.75   .70
674   A236   26k Upphlutur   1.75   .90
Nordic cooperation.

Europa 1989 — A237

Children's games.

1989, May 30   Photo.   Perf. 11½
Granite Paper
675   A237   21k Sailing toy boats   5.25   1.25
676   A237   26k Hoop, stick pony   5.25   1.25

Guardian Spirit Type of 1987
1989, June 27   Engr.   Perf. 13
677   A227   500k Dragon   17.00   7.00

Landscapes A238

35k, Mt. Skeggi, Arnarfjord. 45k, Thermal spring, Namaskard.

1989, Sept. 20   Photo.   Perf. 11½
Granite Paper
678   A238   35k multicolored   1.40   .55
679   A238   45k multicolored   1.75   .55
See Nos. 713-714, 728, 737.

Agricultural College at Hvanneyri, Cent. — A239

1989, Sept. 20   Engr.   Perf. 14
680   A239   50k multi   1.40   1.00

Souvenir Sheet

NORDIA '91 A240

Detail of *A Chart and Description of Northern Routes and Wonders to Be Found in the Nordic Countries*, 1539, by Olaus Magnus (1490-1557).

1989, Oct. 9   Perf. 12½
681   A240   Sheet of 3   9.50   9.50
   a.-c.   30k any single   3.00   3.00
Stamp Day. Sold for 130k to benefit the exhibition.
See Nos. 715, 740.

Natural History Soc., Cent. — A241

Flowers or fish and: 21k, Stefan Stefansson (1863-1921), botanist and founder. 26k, Bjarni Saemundsson (1867-1940), chairman.

1989, Nov. 9   Photo.   Perf. 11½
Granite Paper
682   A241   21k multi   .85   .85
683   A241   26k multi   .90   .90

Christmas — A242

Paintings like stained-glass windows by Johannes Johannesson (b. 1921): 21k, Madonna and Child. 26k, Three Wise Men.

1989, Nov. 9   Granite Paper
684   A242   21k multi   1.20   .35
685   A242   26k multi   1.20   1.10

Bird Type of 1986
21k, Anas penelope. 80k, Anser brachyrhynchus.
1990, Feb. 15   Granite Paper
686   A212   21k multicolored   1.75   .70
687   A212   80k multicolored   4.00   1.60

Guardian Spirit Type of 1987
Perf. 13 on 3 Sides
1990, Feb. 15   Engr.
688   A227   5k Eagle   .25   .25
689   A227   5k Dragon   .25   .25
690   A227   5k Bull   .25   .25
691   A227   5k Giant   .25   .25
   a.   Block of 4, #688-691   1.00   1.00
692   A227   21k Eagle   .60   .60
693   A227   21k Dragon   .60   .60
694   A227   21k Bull   .60   .60
695   A227   21k Giant   .60   .60
   a.   Block of 4, #692-695   2.50   2.50
   b.   Block of 8, #688-695   5.00   5.00
   c.   Bklt. pane, 2 each #691a, 695a   7.50   7.50

Famous Women — A243

No. 696, Gudrun Larusdottir (1880-1938), author and politician, by Halldor Petursson. No. 697, Ragnhildur Petursdottir (1880-1961), educator, by Asgrimur Jonsson.

1990, Mar. 22   Litho.   Perf. 13½x14
696   A243   21k multicolored   .70   .60
697   A243   21k multicolored   .70   .60

Europa 1990 — A244

Old and new post offices in Reykjavik and letter scales.

1990, May 7   Photo.   Perf. 12x11½
Granite Paper
698   A244   21k 1915   3.75   .90
699   A244   40k 1989   3.75   2.00

Sports — A245

No. 700, Archery. No. 701, Soccer. No. 706, Golf. No. 707, Icelandic wrestling. No. 708, Volleyball. No. 709, Skiing. No. 710, Running. No. 711, Team handball. No. 711A, Swimming. No. 711B, Weight lifting.

1990-94   Litho.   Perf. 13x14½
700   A245   21k multicolored   .80   .55
701   A245   21k multicolored   .80   .55
706   A245   26k multicolored   .80   .60
707   A245   26k multicolored   .90   .60

Perf. 13½x14½
Photo.
708   A245   30k multicolored   1.25   .70
709   A245   30k multicolored   1.25   .70
710   A245   30k multicolored   1.00   .55
711   A245   30k multicolored   1.00   .55

Litho.
Perf. 14x14½
711A   A245   30k multicolored   1.00   .45
711B   A245   30k multicolored   1.00   .45
    Nos. 700-711B (10)   9.80   5.70

Issued: Nos. 700-701, 6/28; Nos. 706-707, 8/14/91; Nos. 708-709, 2/20/92; Nos. 710-711, 3/10/93; Nos. 711A-711B, 2/25/94.

European Tourism Year — A246

1990, Sept. 6   Litho.   Perf. 13½
712   A246   30k multicolored   .95   .60

Landscape Type of 1989
1990, Sept. 6   Photo.   Perf.
713   A238   25k Hvitserkur   1.20   .60
714   A238   200k Lomagnupur   6.75   2.25

NORDIA '91 Map Type of 1989
Souvenir Sheet
Detail of 1539 Map by Olaus Magnus: a, Dania. b, Gothia. c, Gotlandia.
Perf. 12x12½
1990, Oct. 9   Lith & Engr.
715   A240   Sheet of 3   12.50   12.50
   a.-c.   40k any single   4.00   4.00
Stamp Day. Sold for 170k to benefit the exhibition.

ICELAND

Christmas — A247

1990, Nov. 8   *Perf. 13½x13*
716 A247 25k shown   1.40   .55
717 A247 30k Carolers   1.40   .95

Bird Type of 1986
1991, Feb. 7   *Photo.*   *Perf. 11½*
Granite Paper
721 A212 25k Podiceps auritus   1.25   .45
722 A212 100k Sula bassana   5.75   1.20

Landscape Type of 1989
1991, Mar. 7   *Photo.*   *Perf. 11½*
Granite Paper
728 A238 10k Vestrahorn   .55   .30
737 A238 300k Kverkfjoll   10.00   3.50

Europa — A248

1991, Apr. 29   *Litho.*   *Perf. 14*
738 A248 26k Weather map   7.00   1.00
739 A248 47k Solar panels   3.50   2.00

NORDIA '91 Map Type of 1989
Souvenir Sheet
Detail of 1539 Map by Olaus Magnus: a, Iceland's west coast. b, Islandia. c, Mare Glacial.

Litho. & Engr.
1991, May 23   *Perf. 12½*
740 A240 Sheet of 3   14.00   14.00
a.-c.   50k any single   4.50   4.50
Sold for 215k to benefit the exhibition.

Jokulsarlon Lagoon — A249

Design: 31k, Strokkur hot spring.

1991, May 23   *Litho.*   *Perf. 15x14*
741 A249 26k multicolored   1.75   .80
742 A249 31k multicolored   1.75   .90

Ragnar Jonsson (1904-1984), Patron of the Arts — A250

70k, Pall Isolfsson (1893-1974), musician, vert.

1991, Aug. 14   *Litho.*   *Perf. 14*
743 A250 60k multicolored   1.75   1.20
744 A250 70k multicolored   2.50   1.40

Ships — A251

Designs: a, Soloven, schooner, 1840. b, Arcturus, steamer with sails, 1858. c, Gullfoss, steamer, 1915. d, Esja II, diesel ship, 1939.

1991, Oct. 9   *Litho.*   *Perf. 14*
745   Block or strip of 4   27.50   27.50
a.-d.   A251 30k any single   3.50   1.75
e.   A251 Bklt. pane, 2 #745   55.00
Issued in sheet of 8. No. 745e is distinguished from sheet of 8 by rouletted selvage at left.
See Nos. 803-806.

College of Navigation, Reykjavik, Cent. — A252

1991, Oct. 9   *Perf. 13½*
746 A252 50k multicolored   1.50   1.25

Christmas — A253

Paintings by Eirikur Smith (b. 1925): 30k, Christmas star. 35k, Star over winter landscape.

1991, Nov. 7   *Litho.*   *Perf. 13½*
747 A253 30k multicolored   1.20   .45
748 A253 35k multicolored   1.20   .90

Europa — A254

Map and: No. 749, Viking longboat of Leif Eriksson. No. 750, Sailing ship of Columbus.

1992, Apr. 6   *Litho.*   *Perf. 13½x14*
749 A254 55k multicolored   5.00   2.25
750 A254 55k multicolored   5.00   2.25

Souvenir Sheet
751 A254   Sheet of 2, #749-750   13.50   8.00
First landing in the Americas by Leif Erikson (No. 749). Discovery of America by Christopher Columbus, 500th anniv. (No. 750).
Stamps on No. 751 printed in continuous design. Nos. 749-750 have borders.

Export Trade and Commerce — A255

Designs: 35k, Fishing boat, fish.

1992, June 16   *Litho.*   *Perf. 13½*
752 A255 30k multicolored   1.25   .45
753 A255 35k multicolored   1.25   .90

Bridges — A256

1992, Oct. 9   *Litho.*   *Perf. 13½*
754 A256 5k Fnjoska, 1908   .25   .25
755 A256 250k Olfusa, 1891   8.50   5.75
See Nos. 766-767.

Mail Trucks — A257

No. 756, Mail transport car RE 231, 1933. No. 757, Ford bus, 1946. No. 758, Ford Model TT truck, 1920-26. No. 759, Citroen snowmobile, 1929.

1992, Oct. 9   *Perf. 14*
756 A257 30k shown   2.40   1.20
757 A257 30k multicolored   2.40   1.20
758 A257 30k multicolored   2.40   1.20
759 A257 30k multicolored   2.40   1.20
a.   Block or strip of 4, #756-759   9.75   9.75
b.   Bklt. pane, 2 ea #756-759   30.00
Issued in sheets of 8. No. 759b has rouletted selvage at left.
See Nos. 820-823.

Christmas — A258

Paintings by Bragi Asgeirsson: 35k, Sun over mountains.

1992, Nov. 9   *Litho.*   *Perf. 13½x13*
760 A258 30k shown   1.25   .45
761 A258 35k multicolored   1.25   1.25

Falco Rusticolus — A259

5k, Adult, two young. 10k, Adult feeding. 20k, Adult, head up. 35k, Adult.

1992, Dec. 3   *Photo.*   *Perf. 11½*
Granite Paper
762 A259 5k multi   2.30   .55
763 A259 10k multi   2.90   1.20
764 A259 20k multi   2.90   1.40
765 A259 35k multi   2.90   2.40
Nos. 762-765 (4)   11.00   5.55

Bridges Type of 1992

90k, Hvita, 1928. 150k, Jokulsa a Fjollum, 1947.

1993, Mar. 10   *Litho.*   *Perf. 13½x13*
766 A256 90k multi   2.75   1.60
767 A256 150k multi   5.00   2.25

Nordica '93 — A260

Designs: 30k, The Blue Lagoon therapeutic bathing area, hot water plant, Svartsengi. 35k, Perlan hot water storage tanks, restaurant.

1993, Apr. 26   *Litho.*   *Perf. 13½x13*
768 A260 30k multicolored   1.25   .65
769 A260 35k multicolored   1.40   1.25

Sculptures — A261

Europa: 35k, Sailing, by Jon Gunnar Arnason. 55k, Hatching of the Jet, by Magnus Tomasson.

1993, Apr. 26   *Perf. 13x13½*
770 A261 35k multicolored   1.75   1.25
771 A261 55k multicolored   2.90   2.50

Souvenir Sheet

Italian Group Flight, 60th Anniv. A262

1993, Oct. 9   *Litho.*   *Perf. 13½*
772 A262 Sheet of 3, #a.-c.   7.00   7.00
a.   10k #C12   .60   .60
b.   50k #C13   2.40   2.40
c.   100k #C14   4.00   4.00
No. 772 sold for 200k.

Seaplanes A263

No. 773, Junkers F-13 (D463). No. 774, Waco YKS-7 (TF-ORN). No. 775, Grumman G-21A/JRF-5 (RVK). No. 776, PBY-5 Catalina (TF-ISP).

1993, Oct. 9   *Perf. 14*
773 A263 30k multicolored   2.50   1.00
774 A263 30k multicolored   2.50   1.00
775 A263 30k multicolored   2.50   1.00
776 A263 30k multicolored   2.50   1.00
a.   Block or strip of 4, #773-776   10.00   10.00
b.   Bklt. pane, 2 ea #773-776   22.50
No. 776b is distinguished from sheet of 8 by rouletted selvage at left.
Issued in sheet of 8.
See Nos. 838-841.

Christmas — A264

30k, Adoration of the Magi. 35k, Virgin and Child.

1993, Nov. 8   *Litho.*   *Perf. 12½*
777 A264 30k multicolored   1.25   .55
778 A264 35k multicolored   1.25   1.25

Intl. Year of the Family — A265

1994, Feb. 25   *Litho.*   *Perf. 13½x13*
779 A265 40k multicolored   1.25   .70

Voyages of St. Brendan (484-577) A266

Europa: 35k, St. Brendan, Irish monks sailing past volcano. 55k, St. Brendan on island with sheep, monks in boat.

1994, Apr. 18   *Litho.*   *Perf. 14½x14*
780 A266 35k multicolored   2.50   1.10
   Booklet, 10 #780   25.00
781 A266 55k multicolored   2.75   1.40
   Booklet, 10 #781   27.50
a.   Miniature sheet of 2, #780-781   5.75   4.25
See Ireland Nos. 923-924; Faroe Islands Nos. 264-265.

Icelandic Art and Culture — A267

No. 782, Music. No. 783, Crafts. No. 784, Film making. No. 785, Ballet, modern dance. No. 786, Theatre.

1994, May 25   *Litho.*   *Perf. 13½x13*
782 A267 30k multicolored   1.00   .70
783 A267 30k multicolored   1.00   .70
784 A267 30k multicolored   1.00   .70
785 A267 30k multicolored   1.00   .70
786 A267 30k multicolored   1.00   .70
Nos. 782-786 (5)   5.00   3.50
Independence, 50th anniv.

Gisli Sveinsson (1880-1959), Politician — A268

1994, June 14   *Perf. 14*
787 A268 30k multicolored   1.00   .60
Proclamation of new constitution, 50th anniv.

ICELAND

Souvenir Sheet
Republic of Iceland, 50th Anniv. — A269

Presidents of Iceland: a, Sveinn Bjornsson (1881-1952). b, Asgeir Asgeirsson (1894-1972). c, Kristjan Eldjarn (1916-82). d, Vigdis Finnbogadottir (b. 1930).

1994, June 17	Photo.	Perf. 11½
Granite Paper		
788 A269 Sheet of 4, #a.-d.	7.00	7.00
a.-d. 50k any single	1.75	1.75

Souvenir Sheet
Stamp Day — A270

Designs: a, Boy, girl with stamp album. b, Nos. 672, 713, portions of other Icelandic stamps. c, Girl, elderly man looking at globe.

1994, Oct. 7	Litho.	Perf. 13½
789 A270 Sheet of 3	7.00	7.00
a. 30k multicolored	1.75	1.75
b. 35k multicolored	1.75	1.75
c. 100k multicolored	3.50	3.50

No. 789 sold for 200k for the benefit of the Stamp and Postal History Fund.

Christmas — A271

1994, Nov. 9	Litho.	Perf. 14½
790 A271 30k Woman, stars	1.00	.45
791 A271 35k Man, stars	1.25	1.25

ICAO, 50th Anniv. — A272

1994, Nov. 9		Perf. 13½x14
792 A272 100k multicolored	3.50	2.00

A273

1995, Mar. 14	Litho.	Perf. 13
793 A273 35k multicolored	1.25	.80

Salvation Army in Iceland, cent.

A274

1995, Mar. 14		
794 A274 90k multicolored	4.25	1.75

Town of Seydisfjordur, cent.

1995 Men's Team Handball World Championships, Iceland — A275

Federation emblem, handball and: No. 795, Geyser, landscape. No. 796, Silhouette of building, landscape. No. 797, Volcano, lake. No. 798, Inlet, sunlight on water.

1995, Mar. 14	Litho.	Perf. 14
795 A275 35k multicolored	1.75	1.10
796 A275 35k multicolored	1.75	1.10
797 A275 35k multicolored	1.75	1.10
798 A275 35k multicolored	1.75	1.10
a. Block or strip of 4, #795-798	7.25	7.00
b. Booklet pane, 2 #798a	17.50	
Complete booklet, #798b	17.50	

Nos. 795-798 issued in sheets of 8 containing 2 each. No. 798b is separated from booklet by rouletted selvage at left, and sold for 480k in the complete booklet.

Norden 1995 — A276

Designs: 30k, Turf farmhouses, church. 35k, Volcano, Fjallsjokull glacier.

1995, May 5	Litho.	Perf. 13½x13
799 A276 30k multicolored	.80	.40
Booklet, 10 #799	9.00	
800 A276 35k multicolored	1.40	1.00

Spell-Broken, by Einar Jonsson (1874-1954) — A277

1995, May 5		Perf. 13x13½
801 A277 35k brown & multi	1.10	1.00
Booklet, 10 #801	12.60	
802 A277 55k blue & multi	2.00	1.75
Booklet, 10 #802	20.00	

Europa.

Ship Type of 1991

No. 803, SS Laura. No. 804, MS Dronning Alexandrine. No. 805, MS Laxfoss. No. 806, MS Godafoss III.

1995, June 30	Litho.	Perf. 14
803 A251 30k multi	1.20	.90
804 A251 30k multi	1.20	.90
805 A251 30k multi	1.20	.90
806 A251 30k multi	1.20	.90
a. Block or strip of 4, #803-806	5.00	4.50
b. Bklt. pane, 2 ea #803-806	10.00	
Prestige booklet, #806b	16.00	

No. 806b is distinguished from sheet of 8 by rouletted selvage at left. Issued in sheets of 8. Prestige booklet sold for 400k.

Luxembourg-Reykjavik, Iceland Air Route, 40th Anniv. — A278

1995, Sept. 18	Litho.	Perf. 13½
807 A278 35k multicolored	1.25	1.10

See Luxembourg No. 936.

Birds — A279

25k, Acanthis flammea. 250k, Gallinago gallinago.

1995, Sept. 18		Perf. 13½
808 A279 25k multicolored	.80	.65
809 A279 250k multicolored	8.50	6.00

Souvenir Sheet
Nordia '96, Reykjavik — A280

1995, Oct. 9		Perf. 13½x14
810 A280 Sheet of 2, #a.-b.	7.00	7.00
a. 10k multicolored	2.50	2.50
b. 150k multicolored	4.50	4.50

See No. 830.

Christmas — A281

1995, Nov. 8	Litho.	Perf. 13½
811 A281 30k Snowman, woman	1.00	.60
812 A281 35k Three trees	1.10	.90

UN, 50th Anniv. — A282

1995, Nov. 8		Perf. 13x13½
813 A282 100k multicolored	3.25	2.50

Water Birds — A283

Designs: 20k, Phalacrocorax carbo. 40k, Bucephala islandica.

1996, Feb. 7	Litho.	Perf. 13½
814 A283 20k multicolored	.60	.45
815 A283 40k multicolored	1.25	1.00

See Nos. 834-835.

Paintings — A284

100k, Seamen in a Boat, by Gunnlaugur Scheving (1904-72). 200k, At the Washing Springs, by Kristín Jónsdóttir (1888-1959).

1996, Feb. 7		
816 A284 100k multicolored	3.00	2.40
817 A284 200k multicolored	5.25	4.50

Famous Women — A285

Europa: 35k, Halldóra Bjarnadóttir (1873-1981), educator. 55k, Olafía Jóhannsdóttir (1863-1924), representative of women's rights, temperance affairs.

1996, Apr. 18	Litho.	Perf. 14½
818 A285 35k multicolored	1.25	.80
Booklet, 10 #818	12.50	
819 A285 55k multicolored	1.45	1.25
Booklet, 10 #819	14.50	

Postal Vehicle Type of 1992

Designs: No. 820, 1931 Buick. No. 821, 1933 Studebaker bus with destination sign, Reykjavík Municipal Bus Service. No. 822, Orange 1937 Ford bus, Iceland Motor Coach Service. No. 823, Red 1946 REO bus, Post and Telecommunications.

1996, May 13	Litho.	Perf. 14
820 A257 35k multicolored	1.25	1.25
821 A257 35k multicolored	1.25	1.25
822 A257 35k multicolored	1.25	1.25
823 A257 35k multicolored	1.25	1.25
a. Block or strip of 4, #820-823	5.00	5.00
b. Bklt. pane, 2 ea #820-823	10.00	10.00
Souvenir booklet, #823b	12.00	

No. 823a issued in sheets of 8 stamps. No. 823b has rouletted selvage at left.

1996 Summer Olympic Games, Atlanta — A286

1996, June 25	Litho.	Perf. 12½
824 A286 5k Running	.25	.25
825 A286 25k Javelin	.70	.50
826 A286 45k Long jump	1.40	1.10
827 A286 65k Shot put	2.10	1.50
Nos. 824-827 (4)	4.45	3.25

Order of the Sisters of St. Joseph in Iceland, Cent. — A287

1996, Sept. 17	Litho.	Perf. 14½x13
828 A287 65k multicolored	1.75	1.75

Reykjavik School, 150th Anniv. — A288

1996, Sept. 17		Perf. 12½x13
829 A288 150k multicolored	4.25	3.50

Nordia '96 Type of 1995

Design: Godafoss Waterfalls, Skjalfandafljot River.

1996, Oct. 9	Litho.	Perf. 13½x14
830 A280 Sheet of 3, #a.-c.	10.50	10.50
a. 45k multicolored	3.50	3.50
b. 65k multicolored	3.50	3.50
c. 90k multicolored	3.50	3.50

Reykjavik Cathedral, Bicent. — A289

1996, Nov. 5		Perf. 14
831 A289 45k multicolored	1.40	1.10

Christmas — A290

Artifacts from Natl. Museum of Iceland: 35k, Figurine of Madonna and Child carved from walrus tusk. 45k, Pax showing Nativity.

1996, Nov. 5		Perf. 13½
832 A290 35k multicolored	1.10	.60
a. Booklet pane of 10	11.00	
Booklet, #832a	11.00	
833 A290 45k multicolored	1.40	1.25

Bird Type of 1996

10k, Mergus serrator. 500k, Anas crecca.

1997, Apr. 2	Litho.	Perf. 13½
834 A283 10k multicolored	.45	.35
835 A283 500k multicolored	14.00	12.00

ICELAND

Paintings A291

150k, Song of Iceland, by Svavar Guthnason. 200k, The Harbor, by Thorvaldur Skúlason.

1997, Mar. 6   Litho.   *Perf. 14*
| 836 | A291 | 150k multicolored | 4.75 | 4.00 |
| 837 | A291 | 200k multicolored | 5.75 | 4.50 |

Airplane Type of 1993

No. 838, De Havilland DH-89A (TF-ISM). No. 839, Stinson SR 8B Reliant (TF-RVB). No. 840, Douglas DC-3 (TF-ISH). No. 841, De Havilland DHC-6 Twin Otter (TF-REG).

1997, Apr. 15   Litho.   *Perf. 14*
838	A263	35k multicolored	1.25	1.25
839	A263	35k multicolored	1.25	1.25
840	A263	35k multicolored	1.25	1.25
841	A263	35k multicolored	1.25	1.25
a.		Block or strip of 4, #838-841	5.00	5.00
b.		Booklet pane, 2 each #838-841	10.00	
		Booklet, #841b	10.00	

Issued in sheet of 8.
No. 841b has rouletted selvage at left.

European Games — A292

1997, May 13   Litho.   *Perf. 14½*
| 842 | A292 | 35k Hurdles | 1.10 | .70 |
| 843 | A292 | 45k Sailing | 1.40 | 1.10 |

Europa — A293

Stories and legends by Asgrimur Jonsson: 45k, Couple on galloping horse. 65k, Old woman reaching for children.

1997, May 13   *Perf. 13½*
844	A293	45k multicolored	1.60	1.25
		Complete booklet of 10	16.00	
845	A293	65k multicolored	2.50	1.75
		Complete booklet of 10	25.00	

Union of Graphic Workers, Cent. — A294

1997, Sept. 3   Litho.   *Perf. 13½*
| 846 | A294 | 90k multicolored | 2.75 | 2.25 |

Reykjavik Theater, Cent. — A295

1997, Sept. 3   *Perf. 13½x14*
| 847 | A295 | 100k multicolored | 2.75 | 2.25 |

Stamp Day A296

Icelandic row boats: a, Gideon, eight-oared lugger, 1836. b, Breidafjördur double-ended transport, 1904. c, Engey, six-oared craft, 1912.

1997, Oct. 9   Litho.   *Perf. 15*
848	A296	Sheet of 3	10.00	10.00
a.		35k multicolored	2.25	2.25
b.		100k multicolored	3.50	3.50
c.		65k multicolored	4.00	4.00

Christmas — A297

1997, Nov. 5   Litho.   *Perf. 13½x13*
849	A297	35k Magi	1.00	.60
a.		Booklet pane of 10	10.00	
		Booklet, #849a	10.00	
850	A297	45k Nativity	1.40	.90

Rural Postman — A298

Litho. & Engr.
1997, Nov. 5   *Perf. 13½*
| 851 | A298 | 50k multicolored | 1.50 | 1.25 |

1998 Winter Olympic Games, Nagano — A299

1998, Jan. 22   Litho.   *Perf. 13½*
| 852 | A299 | 35k Downhill skier | 1.00 | .70 |
| 853 | A299 | 45k Cross country skier | 1.40 | 1.25 |

Nordic Stamps — A300

1998, Mar. 5   Litho.   *Perf. 13½x13*
| 854 | A300 | 35k Sailboats | 1.25 | .70 |
| 855 | A300 | 45k Power boats | 1.75 | 1.40 |

Fish — A301

5k, Cyclopterus lumpus. 10k, Gadus morhua. 60k, Raja batis. 300k, Anarhicus lupus.

1998, Apr. 16
856	A301	5k multicolored	.45	.45
857	A301	10k multicolored	.45	.45
858	A301	60k multicolored	2.25	2.25
859	A301	300k multicolored	8.50	8.50
a.		Min. sheet of 4, #856-859	11.00	11.00
		Nos. 856-859 (4)	11.65	11.65

Intl. Year of the Ocean (No. 859a). See Nos. 871-872, 915-916, 928-929.

National Holidays and Festivals — A302

Independence Day, June 17th: 45k, Children standing at attention, flag. 65k, Monument, parade.

1998, May 12   Litho.   *Perf. 14½*
860	A302	45k multicolored	1.50	1.00
		Complete booklet, 10 #860	15.00	
861	A302	65k multicolored	2.10	1.50
		Complete booklet, 10 #861	21.00	

Europa.

Minerals — A303

1998, Sept. 3   Litho.   *Perf. 13½*
| 862 | A303 | 35k Stilbite | 1.20 | .90 |
| 863 | A303 | 45k Scolecite | 1.40 | 1.10 |

See Nos. 885-886.

Leprosy Hospital, Laugarnes — A304

1998, Sept. 3   *Perf. 13½x14*
| 864 | A304 | 70k multicolored | 2.00 | 1.60 |

First Icelandic Postage Stamp, 125th Anniv. — A305

1998, Oct. 9   Litho.   *Perf. 13½*
| 865 | A305 | 35k multicolored | 1.20 | .80 |

Agricultural Tools — A306

1998, Oct. 9   *Perf. 15*
866	A306	Sheet of 3	7.50	7.50
a.		35k Turf scythe	1.75	1.75
b.		65k Hay mower	2.50	2.50
c.		100k Manure mincer	3.25	3.25

Stamp Day.

Christmas, Children's Drawings — A307

35k, Black cat, homes, mountains. 45k, Angels, Christmas tree, moon and stars.

1998, Nov. 5   Litho.   *Perf. 13x13½*
867	A307	35k multicolored	1.10	.90
a.		Booklet pane of 10	11.00	
		Complete booklet, #867a	11.00	
868	A307	45k multicolored	1.25	1.10

Universal Declaration of Human Rights, 50th Anniv. — A308

1998, Nov. 5   *Perf. 14½*
| 869 | A308 | 50k multicolored | 1.60 | 1.60 |

Jón Leifs (1899-1968), Composer — A309

1999, Jan. 22   Litho.   *Perf. 14½*
| 870 | A309 | 35k multicolored | 1.25 | 1.25 |

Fish Type of 1998

35k, Pleuronectez platessa. 55k, Clupea harengus.

1999, Jan. 22   *Perf. 14½x15*
| 871 | A301 | 35k multicolored | 1.40 | .90 |
| 872 | A301 | 55k multicolored | 1.60 | 1.60 |

Marine Mammals A311

Designs: 35k, Orcinus orca. 45k, Physeter macrocephalus. 65k, Balaenoptera musculus. 85k, Phocoena phocoena.

1999, Mar. 4   *Perf. 14½*
873	A311	35k multicolored	1.40	.90
874	A311	45k multicolored	1.75	1.10
875	A311	65k multicolored	2.25	1.90
876	A311	85k multicolored	3.00	2.40
a.		Sheet of 4, #873-876	8.40	8.40
		Nos. 873-876 (4)	8.40	6.30

See Nos. 911-914, 945-948. For surcharge see No. 944.

Locomotive — A312

Perf. 13 on 2 or 3 Sides
1999, Apr. 15   **Booklet Stamps**
877	A312	25k green & multi	3.50	3.50
878	A312	50k brown & multi	1.25	1.25
a.		Booklet pane, 1 #877, 3 #878	7.50	
		Complete booklet, #878a	7.50	
879	A312	75k Ship	2.50	2.50
a.		Booklet pane of 4	10.00	
		Complete booklet, #879a	10.00	
		Nos. 877-879 (3)	7.25	7.25

See Nos. 908-909.

Council of Europe, 50th Anniv. — A313

1999, Apr.15   *Perf. 13x13½*
| 880 | A313 | 35k multicolored | 1.20 | .90 |

Mushrooms — A314

35k, Suillus grevillei. 75k, Agaricus campestris.

1999, May 20   Litho.   *Perf. 14½*
| 881 | A314 | 35k multicolored | 1.10 | 1.10 |
| 882 | A314 | 75k multicolored | 2.25 | 2.25 |

See Nos. 898-899, 957-958, 1021-1022, 1087-1088.

National Parks — A315

1999, May 20   *Perf. 13¼*
883	A315	50k Skutustadagigar	1.40	1.40
a.		Booklet pane of 10	14.00	
		Complete booklet, #883a	14.00	
884	A315	75k Vid Arnarstapa	2.50	2.00
a.		Booklet pane of 10	25.00	
		Complete booklet, #884a	26.00	

Europa.

Minerals Type of 1998

1999, Sept. 9   Litho.   *Perf. 14¾*
| 885 | A303 | 40k Calcite | 1.25 | 1.25 |
| 886 | A303 | 50k Heulandite | 1.75 | 1.75 |

Nature Conservation — A316

1999, Sept. 9   Litho.   *Perf. 14¼*
887	A316	35k "Hreinar"	1.25	1.25
888	A316	35k "Markviss"	1.25	1.25
889	A316	35k "Hreint"	1.25	1.25
890	A316	35k "Endurheimt"	1.25	1.25
891	A316	35k "Eflum"	1.25	1.25
a.		Strip of 5, #887-891	6.00	6.00

Reykjavik, European Cultural City for 2000 — A317

35k, Facescape, by Erro. 50k, Book, violin, palette, masks, camera, computer.

1999, Oct. 7   Litho.   *Perf. 13¼*
| 892 | A317 | 35k multi | 1.10 | .90 |
| 893 | A317 | 50k multi | 1.50 | 1.50 |

ICELAND

Souvenir Sheet

View of Skagafjordur, by Carl Emil Baagoe — A318

1999, Oct. 7		Perf. 13¼x13
894 A318 200k olive & black		9.00 9.00

Stamp Day. No. 894 sold for 250k.

Children's Art — A319

1999, Nov. 4	Litho.	Perf. 13
895 A319 35k multi		1.00 1.00

Christmas — A320

No. 896, Elf: a, With walking stick. b, Jumping over rock. c, Waving. d, Licking spoon. e, With hand in cauldron. f, With cup. g, At door. h, With ladle and barrel. i, With sausages. j, At window.
No. 897, Elf: a, Looking up. b, With ham. c, With candles.

1999, Nov. 4		
896 Strip of 10		12.50 12.50
a.-j. A320 35k any single		1.25 1.25
k. Booklet pane, #896a-896j		12.50
Complete booklet, #896k		12.50
897 Strip of 3		5.25 5.25
a.-c. A320 50k any single		1.75 1.75

See Nos. 924-926.
Nos. 896a-896k and 897a-897c were also released in a sheet of 15 undenominated labels made available as a gift to buyers of the stamps.

Mushroom Type of 1999

Designs: 40k, Cantharellus cibarius. 50k, Coprinus comatus.

2000, Feb. 4	Litho.	Perf. 13
898 A314 40k multi		1.25 1.25
a. Booklet pane of 10		12.50
Complete booklet, #898a		12.50
899 A314 50k multi		1.75 1.75

A321

Christianity in Iceland, 1000th Anniv. — A322

2000, Feb. 4		Perf. 13¼x13¾
900 A321 40k multi		1.25 1.25

Souvenir Sheet

Perf. 13¼x13

901 A322 40k multi	1.25 1.25

See Vatican City No. 1151.

Discovery of Vinland, 1000th Anniv. — A323

Designs: 40k, Viking with shield, globe. 50k, Viking ship sailing. 75k, Viking ship at shore. 90k, Viking without shield, globe.

2000, Mar. 16	Litho. & Engr.	Perf. 12½x13
902 A323 40k multi		1.25 1.25
903 A323 50k multi		1.75 1.75
904 A323 75k multi		2.25 2.25
905 A323 90k multi		2.75 2.75
a. Souvenir sheet, #902-905		8.00 8.00
Nos. 902-905 (4)		8.00 8.00

Millennium — A324

Designs: 40k, Head, quill pen. 50k, Man, genealogical chart, circuit board.

2000, Apr. 27	Litho.	Perf. 13x13¼
906 A324 40k multi		1.10 1.10
907 A324 50k multi		1.40 1.40

Locomotive Type of 1999

Perf. 13 on 2 or 3 sides

2000, Apr. 27	Litho.	
Booklet Stamps		
908 A312 50k Steam roller		1.50 1.50
a. Booklet pane of 4		6.00
Booklet, #908a		6.00
909 A312 75k Fire pumper		2.25 2.25
a. Booklet pane of 4		9.00
Booklet, #909a		9.00

Europa, 2000
Common Design Type

2000, May 18	Litho.	Perf. 13¼x13
910 CD17 50k multi		1.60 1.60
a. Booklet pane of 10		16.00
Booklet, #910a		16.00

Marine Mammals Type of 1999

Designs: 5k, Hyperoodon ampullatus. 40k, Lagenorhynchus acutus. 50k, Megaptera novaeangliae. 75k, Balaenoptera acutorostrata.

2000, May 18		Perf. 14½
911 A311 5k multi		.25 .25
912 A311 40k multi		1.40 1.40
913 A311 50k multi		1.75 1.75
914 A311 75k multi		2.50 2.50
Nos. 911-914 (4)		5.90 5.90

Fish Type of 1998

Designs: 10k, Melanogrammus aeglefinus. 250k, Mallotus villosus.

2000, Sept. 14	Litho.	Perf. 13
915-916 A301 Set of 2		9.50 9.50

Flowers — A325

Designs: 40k, Viola x wittrockiana. 50k, Petunia x hybrida.

2000, Sept. 14		Perf. 13
917-918 A325 Set of 2		2.50 2.50

See Nos. 931-932, 968-969, 982-983, 1005-1006.

Butterflies — A326

Designs: 40k, Chloroclysta citrata. 50k, Cerapteryx graminis.

2000, Oct. 9		Perf. 14x14½
919-920 A326 Set of 2		2.75 2.75

Souvenir Sheet

Stamp Day A327

2000, Oct. 9	Litho. & Engr.	Perf. 13¼
921 A327 200k multi		9.00 9.00

No. 921 sold for 250k.

Ancient Architecture A328

Various buildings. Denominations: 45k, 75k.

2000, Nov. 9	Litho.	Perf. 14
922-923 A328 Set of 2		4.00 4.00

Christmas Type of 1999

Designs: 40k, Elf grasping walking stick. 50k, Female elf carrying bag.

2000, Nov. 9		Perf. 13
924 A320 40k multi		1.25 1.00
a. Perf. 12¾x13¼		1.50 1.50
b. Booklet pane, 4 #924a		6.00
c. Booklet pane, 6 #924a		9.00
Booklet, #924b, 924c		15.00
925 A320 50k multi		1.60 1.25

Souvenir Sheet

926 Sheet of 2		2.90 2.25
a. A320 40k As #924, 26x40mm		1.25 .95
b. A320 50k As #925, 26x40mm		1.60 1.25

Coast Guard, 75th Anniv. — A329

2001, Jan. 18	Litho.	Perf. 13
927 A329 (40k) multi		1.50 1.50
a. Booklet pane of 10		15.00
Booklet, #927a		15.00

Fish Type of 1998

Designs: 55k, Reinhardtius hippoglossoides. 80k, Pollachius virens.

2001, Jan. 18		
928-929 A301 Set of 2		4.00 4.00

UN High Commissioner for Refugees, 50th Anniv. — A330

2001, Mar. 8		Perf. 13¼x13
930 A330 50k multi		1.50 1.25

Flower Type of 2000

Designs: 55k, Calendula officinalis. 65k, Dorotheanthus bellidiformis.

2001, Mar. 8		Perf. 13
931-932 A325 Set of 2		3.75 3.25

Icelandic Sheepdog — A331

Dog's coat: 40k, Brown. 80k, Black.

2001, Apr. 18		Perf. 14¼
933-934 A331 Set of 2		4.00 3.25

Airplanes — A332

Designs: 55k: TF-OGN (biplane). 80k, Klemm TF-SUX (monoplane).

Perf. 13½x12¾ on 2 or 3 Sides

2001, Apr. 18	**Booklet Stamps**	
935 A332 55k multi		1.75 1.40
a. Booklet pane of 4		7.00
Booklet, #935a		7.00
936 A332 80k multi		2.50 2.25
a. Booklet pane of 4		10.00
Booklet, #936a		10.00

Europa — A333

Designs: 55k, Head, waterfall. 80k, Hand, wave.

2001, May 17		Perf. 13
937 A333 55k multi		1.60 1.50
a. Booklet pane of 10		16.00
Booklet, #937a		17.00
938 A333 80k multi		2.40 2.00
a. Booklet pane of 10		24.00
Booklet, #938a		26.00

Horses — A334

Designs: 40k, Fet. 50k, Tölt. 55k, Brokk. 60k, Skeidh. 80k, Stökk.

2001, May 17		Perf. 13x13¼
939-943 A334 Set of 5		8.75 8.75

No. 873 Surcharged in Red

2001, July 10	Litho.	Perf. 14½
944 A311 (53k) on 35k multi		1.75 1.75

Marine Mammals Type of 1999

Designs: 5k, Lagenorhynchus albirostris. 40k, Balaenoptera physalus. 80k, Balaenoptera borealis. 100k, Globicephala melas.

2001, Sept. 6	Litho.	Perf. 14½
945 A311 5k multi		.30 .30
946 A311 40k multi		1.25 1.25
947 A311 80k multi		2.50 2.50
948 A311 100k multi		3.25 3.25
Nos. 945-948 (4)		7.30 7.30

Islands — A335

Designs: 40k, Grimsey. 55k, Papey.

2001, Oct. 9	Litho.	Perf. 13¼x13
949-950 A335 Set of 2		2.75 2.50

See Nos. 975-976, 1001-1002, 1033-1034, 1158-1159.

Souvenir Sheet

Esja Mountain A336

2001, Oct. 9		Perf. 13¼
951 A336 250k multi		9.00 9.00

Stamp Day.

Birds — A337

ICELAND

Designs: 42k, Oenanthe oenanthe. 250k, Charadrius hiaticula.

2001, Nov. 8		Perf. 13¼x13
952-953 A337	Set of 2	10.00 10.00

Christmas — A338

Churches: (42k), Brautarholt. 55k, Vidhmyri.

2001, Nov. 8			
954 A338	(42k) multi	1.25	1.25
a.	Booklet pane of 6	7.50	—
	Booklet, #954a, 4 #954	12.50	
955 A338	55k multi	1.60	1.40

First Motorboat in Iceland, Cent. — A339

2002, Jan. 17	Litho.	Perf. 13x13½
956 A339	60k multi	1.90 1.90

Mushroom Type of 1999

Designs: (40k), Leccinum scabrum. 85k, Hydnum repandum.

2002, Jan. 17		Perf. 13¼x12¾
957-958 A314	Set of 2	3.75 3.75
	Booklet, 10 #957	14.00

No. 957 is inscribed "Bref 20g."

Intl. Year of Mountains — A340

2002, Mar. 7	Litho.	Perf. 13
959 A340	(42k) multi	1.50 1.50

Halldór Laxness (1902-98), 1955 Nobel Literature Laureate — A341

2002, Mar. 7	Litho.	Perf. 13x13¼
960 A341	100k multi	3.50 3.50
a.	Souvenir sheet of 1	3.75 3.75

Examples of No. 960a with Nobel Prize medal in margin printed in gold foil and embossed sold for 1700k. Value, $110.

Lighthouses — A342

Perf. 12¾x13¼ on 2 or 3 Sides

2002, Apr. 18		Booklet Stamps
961 A342	60k Grótta	1.75 1.60
a.	Booklet pane of 4	7.00 —
	Complete booklet, #961a	7.00
962 A342	85k Kögur	2.50 2.25
a.	Booklet pane of 4	10.00 —
	Complete booklet, #962a	10.00

Fyssa, by Rúrí A343

Spenna, by Hafsteinn Austmann A344

2002, Apr. 18	Litho.	Perf. 14½x14¾
963 A343	(42k) multi	1.25 1.10
964 A344	60k multi	1.75 1.50

Nordic Council, 50th anniv. (No. 963).

Sesselja Sigmundsdóttir (1902-74), Advocate for Mentally Handicapped A345

2002, May 9		
965 A345	45k multi	1.25 1.10

Europa — A346

2002, May 9		Perf. 13
966 A346	60k multi	1.75 1.25
a.	Booklet pane of 10	17.50
	Booklet, #966a	19.00
967 A346	85k multi	2.50 1.50
a.	Booklet pane of 10	25.00
	Booklet, #967a	26.00

Designs: 60k, Acrobats, juggling clown. 85k, Head on stick, lion jumping through ring of fire.

Flowers Type of 2000

Designs: 10k, Lobelia erinus. 200k, Centaurea cyanus.

2002, Sept. 5	Litho.	Perf. 14¾x14½
968-969 A325	Set of 2	7.00 7.00

Fish of Lake Thingvallavatn A347

Designs: (45k), Salvelinus alpinus (Murta). (55k), Salmo trutta, vert. 60k, Salvelinus alpinus (Sílableikja). 90k, Salvelinus alpinus (Kuthungableikja). 200k, Salvelinus alpinus (Dvergbleikja).

Perf. 13¼x12¾, 12¾x13¼ (#971)

2002, Sept. 5			
970 A347	(45k) multi	1.50	1.50
a.	Perf. 13¼x12½;13¼x13	1.50	1.50
971 A347	(55k) multi	2.50	2.50
a.	Perf. 13¼x12½;13¼x13¼x13:12½	2.50	2.50
972 A347	60k multi	2.00	2.00
a.	Perf. 13¼x13	2.00	2.00
973 A347	90k multi	2.75	2.75
a.	Perf. 13¼x13	2.75	2.75
974 A347	200k multi	6.00	6.00
a.	Perf. 13¼x13	6.00	6.00
b.	Booklet pane, #970a-974a	27.50	
	Complete booklet, #974b	27.50	
	Nos. 970-974 (5)	14.75	14.75

Nos. 970-974 were issued both in sheet format, perf 13¼x12¾ or 12¾x13¼ (No. 971), and in booklet pane format (Nos. 970a-974a), with small differences in the gauge of the stamps' perforations.

Islands Type of 2001

Designs: 45k, Vigur. 55k, Flatey.

2002, Oct. 9		Perf. 14
975-976 A335	Set of 2	2.75 2.75

Souvenir Sheet

Sudurgata, Reykjavik — A348

2002, Oct. 9		Perf. 14½x14¾
977 A348	250k multi	9.00 9.00

Stamp Day.

Birds — A349

Designs: 50k, Tringa totanus. 85k, Phalaropus fulicarius.

2002, Nov. 7		Perf. 13¼x13
978-979 A349	Set of 2	4.00 4.00

See Nos. 997-998, 1029-1030, 1059-1060.

Christmas — A350

Designs: 45k, Gifts and ornaments. 60k, Gifts.

2002, Nov. 7		Perf. 13
980 A350	45k multi	1.25 1.25
a.	Booklet pane of 10	12.50
	Booklet, #980a	12.50
981 A350	60k multi	1.75 1.75

Flower Type of 2000

Designs: 45k, Phlox drummondii. 60k, Gazania x hybrida.

2003, Jan. 16		Perf. 13
982 A325	45k multi	1.25 1.25
a.	Booklet pane of 10	12.50
	Booklet, #982a	12.50
983 A325	60k multi	1.75 1.75

Icelandic Police Force, Bicent. — A351

Designs: 45k, Police officers, 2003. 55k, Policeman, 1803.

2003, Jan. 16		
984-985 A351	Set of 2	2.90 2.90

Icelandic Cattle — A352

Designs: 45k, Bull. 85k, Cow.

2003, Mar. 13	Litho.	Perf. 13x13¼
986-987 A352	Set of 2	3.75 3.75

Souvenir Sheet

Nordia 2003 Philatelic Exhibition, Reykjavik — A353

Litho. & Engr.

2003, Mar. 13		Perf. 14
988 A353	250k multi	9.00 9.00

No. 988 sold for 300k.

Free Church, Reykjavik, Cent. — A354

2003, Apr. 23	Litho.	Perf. 13
989 A354	200k multi	6.50 6.50

Ferries — A355

No. 990: a, Saefari. b, Saevar.
No. 991: a, Herjólfur. b, Baldur.

Perf. 13 on 2 or 3 Sides

2003, Apr. 23		Booklet Stamps
990	Pair	2.75 2.75
a.-b.	A355 45k Either single	1.35 1.35
c.	Booklet pane, 2 #990	5.50 —
	Complete booklet, #990c	5.50
991	Pair	3.75 3.75
a.-b.	A355 60k Either single	1.75 1.75
c.	Booklet pane, 2 #991	7.50 —
	Complete booklet, #991c	7.50

Icelandic Chickens — A356

2003, May 22		Perf. 13¼
992 A356	45k multi	1.25 1.25

Europa — A357

Poster art.

2003, May 22		Perf. 13½
993 A357	60k red & multi	1.75 1.25
a.	Booklet pane of 10, perf. 13½ on 3 sides	17.50 —
	Complete booklet, #993a	19.00
994 A357	85k green & multi	2.50 1.75
a.	Booklet pane of 10, perf. 13½ on 3 sides	25.00 —
	Complete booklet, #994a	26.00

Friendship — A358

2003, Sept. 4		Perf. 14¼x14½
995 A358	45k multi	1.25 1.25

First Census, 300th Anniv. — A359

2003, Sept. 4		Perf. 13
996 A359	60k multi	1.75 1.75

Bird Type of 2002

Designs: 70k, Anthus pratensis. 250k, Numenius phaeopus.

2003, Sept. 4		Perf. 13¼x13
997-998 A349	Set of 2	10.00 10.00

Rangifer Tarandus — A360

2003, Oct. 9	Litho.	Perf. 13
999 A360	45k multi	1.25 1.25

Souvenir Sheet

Quonset Hut A361

2003, Oct. 9		
1000 A361	250k multi	8.25 8.25

Stamp Day.

ICELAND

Islands Type of 2001

Designs: 85k, Heimaey. 200k, Hrísey.

2003, Nov. 6		Perf. 13¼x13
1001-1002 A335	Set of 2	8.50 8.50

Christmas — A362

Designs: 45k, Girl placing ornament on Christmas tree. 60k, Boy lighting candle.

2003, Nov. 6		Perf. 14¼
1003-1004 A362	Set of 2	3.00 3.00
a.	Booklet pane of 10, #1003	12.50
	Booklet, #1003a	12.50

Flowers Type of 2000

Designs: 50k, Tagetes patula. 55k, Begonia x tuberhybrida.

2004, Jan. 15	Litho.	Perf. 13
1005-1006 A325	Set of 2	3.25 3.25

Hannes Hafstein (1861-1922), Politician, Poet — A363

2004, Jan. 15		Perf. 13¼x13½
1007 A363	150k multi	4.50 4.50
a.	Souvenir sheet of 1	4.50 4.50

Icelandic home rule, cent.

Trawler "Coot," Cent. — A364

2004, Mar. 11	Litho.	Perf. 13¼
1008 A364	50k multi	1.40 1.40

Geothermal Energy — A365

Designs: 50k, Snorralaug hot water pool. 55k, Valve on geodesic dome, steam cloud, vert. (29x47mm). 60k, Steam pipes. 90k, Turbine. 250k, Map of Iceland showing geothermal zones, vert. (29x47mm).

Perf. 13x13¼, 13¼ (55k, 250k)

2004, Mar. 11		
1009 A365	50k multi	1.25 1.25
a.	Perf. 13¼	4.00 4.00
1010 A365	55k multi	1.40 1.40
1011 A365	60k multi	1.50 1.50
a.	Perf. 13¼	5.00 5.00
1012 A365	90k multi	2.75 2.75
a.	Perf. 13¼	7.00 7.00
1013 A365	250k multi	6.50 6.50
a.	Booklet pane, #1009a, 1010, 1011a, 1012a, 1013	25.00 —
	Complete booklet, #1013a	25.00
	Nos. 1009-1013 (5)	13.40 13.40

Complete booklet sold for 750k.
Nos. 1009a, 1011a and 1012a only come from the booklet pane No. 1013a.

Souvenir Sheet

Norse Mythology — A366

No. 1014: a, God Odin and bird. b, Odin's horse, Sleipnir, and bird.

2004, Mar. 26		Perf. 13
1014 A366	Sheet of 2	3.50 3.50
a.	50k multi	1.50 1.50
b.	60k multi	2.00 2.00

Automobiles A367

No. 1015: a, 1956 Ford Fairlane Victoria. b, 1954 Pobeta.
No. 1016: a, 1955 Chevrolet Bel Air. b, 1952 Volkswagen.

Perf. 13 on 2 or 3 Sides

2004, Apr. 15		Booklet Stamps
1015	Pair	6.50 6.50
a.-b.	A367 60k Either single	3.25 3.25
c.	Booklet pane, 2 #1015	13.00
	Complete booklet, #1015c	13.00
1016	Pair	9.50 9.50
a.-b.	A367 85k Either single	4.75 4.75
c.	Booklet pane, 2 #1016	19.00
	Complete booklet, #1016c	19.00

Herring Industry, Cent. — A368

2004, May 19		Perf. 13¼
1017 A368	65k multi	2.00 2.00

Hringurin Women's Society, Cent. — A369

2004, May 19		Perf. 13x13¼
1018 A369	100k violet blue	3.00 3.00

Europa — A370

2004, May 19		Perf. 13
1019 A370	65k Cyclists	1.75 1.75
a.	Booklet pane of 10	17.50
	Complete booklet, #1019a	17.50
1020 A370	90k Cars in snow	2.75 2.75
a.	Booklet pane of 10	27.50
	Complete booklet, #1020a	27.50

Mushrooms Type of 1999

Designs: 50k, Amanita vaginata. 60k, Camarophyllus pratensis.

2004, Sept. 2	Litho.	Perf. 13
1021-1022 A314	Set of 2	3.75 3.75

Reykdal Power Station, Cent. — A371

2004, Sept. 2		Perf. 13¼
1023 A371	50k multi	1.50 1.50

First Automobile in Iceland, Cent. — A372

2004, Sept. 2		
1024 A372	100k multi	3.00 3.00

French Hospital, Fáskrúthsfirthi, Cent. — A373

	Litho. & Engr.	
2004, Oct. 8		Perf. 13¾
1025 A373	60k multi	1.60 1.60

Souvenir Sheet

Brúarhlöth — A374

2004, Oct. 8	Litho.	Perf. 13
1026 A374	250k multi	8.00 8.00

Stamp Day.

Insects — A375

Designs: 50k, Nebria gyllenhali. 70k, Bombus lucorum.

2004, Oct. 8		
1027-1028 A375	Set of 2	4.00 4.00

See Nos. 1043-1044, 1089-1090, 1121-1122, 1161-1161.

Bird Type of 2002

Designs: 55k, Calidris maritima. 75k, Calidris alpina.

2004, Nov. 4	Litho.	Perf. 13¼x13
1029-1030 A349	Set of 2	4.00 4.00

Christmas A376

Designs: 45k, Ptarmigan in snow. 65k, Reindeer in snow.

2004, Nov. 4		
1031-1032 A376	Set of 2	3.50 3.50
1031a	Booklet pane of 10 #1031	14.00
	Complete booklet, #1031a	14.00

Islands Type of 2001

Designs: 5k, Vithey. 90k, Flatey.

2005, Jan. 13	Litho.	Perf. 14
1033-1034 A335	Set of 2	3.00 3.00

Organized Forestation, Cent. — A377

2005, Jan. 13		
1035 A377	45k multi	1.25 1.25

See Nos. 1101-1102, 1154-1155.

Souvenir Sheet

National Museum Artifacts A378

	Litho. & Embossed	
2005, Jan. 13		Perf. 13½x13
1036 A378	Sheet of 2 + central label	8.00 8.00
a.	100k multi	3.50 3.50
b.	150k multi	4.50 4.50

Mice — A379

Designs: 45k, Apodemus sylvaticus. 125k, Mus musculus.

2005, Mar. 10		Perf. 13½x12¾
1037-1038 A379	Set of 2	5.00 5.00

Flowers — A380

Designs: No. 1039, 50k, Roses. No. 1040, 50k, African daisies. No. 1041, 50k, Red calla lilies. 70k, Tulip.

2005, Mar. 10		Perf. 13¼
1039-1042 A380	Set of 4	7.50 7.50
1042a	Booklet pane, 2 each #1039-1042	15.00 —

Nos. 1039-1042 each printed in sheets of 10, with each stamp in the sheet having a different background swirl pattern. Stamps of the same kind in the booklet pane have the same swirl pattern, which is the same as one found on the sheet.

Insects Type of 2004

Designs: 50k, Araneus diadematus (spider). 70k, Musca domestica.

2005, Apr. 14		Perf. 13¼x13
1043-1044 A375	Set of 2	4.00 4.00

Fishing Boats — A381

No. 1045: a, Vörthur ThH4. b, Karl VE47.
No. 1046: a, Saedís IS67. b, Guthbjörg NK74.

Perf. 13 on 2 or 3 Sides

2005, Apr. 14		Booklet Stamps
1045	Pair	4.50 4.50
a.-b.	A381 70k Either single	2.25 2.25
c.	Booklet pane, 2 #1045	9.00
	Complete booklet, #1045c	9.00
1046	Pair	6.00 6.00
a.-b.	A381 95k Either single	3.00 3.00
c.	Booklet pane, 2 #1045	12.00
	Complete booklet, #1045c	12.00

Bridges, Cent. — A382

Designs: 50k, Sogith Bridge. 95k, Lagarfljót Bridge. 165k, Jökulsá Bridge.

2005, May 26	Litho.	Perf. 13¼x13½
1047-1049 A382	Set of 3	10.50 10.50

Europa — A383

ICELAND

Fork, knife and: 70k, Fish dish, gutted fish, waterfall. 90k, Meat dish, hanging meat, flowers.

2005, May 26		Perf. 13½
1050 A383 70k multi		2.10 2.10
a. Booklet pane of 10		21.00
Complete booklet, #1050a		21.00
1051 A383 90k multi		2.75 2.75
a. Booklet pane of 10		27.50
Complete booklet, #1050a		27.50

Salmon Fishermen and Fishing Flies — A384

Designs; 50k, Fisherman on Laxái Kjós River, Raud Frances fly. 60k, Fishermen in boat on Laxá i Athaldal River, Laxá Bla fly, vert.

Perf. 13¾x13½, 13½x13¾		
2005, Sept. 1		Litho.
1052-1053 A384 Set of 2		3.25 3.25

Berries — A385

Designs: 65k, Vaccinium uliginosum. 90k, Fragaria vesca.

2005, Sept. 1		Perf. 14
1054 A385 65k multi		1.75 1.75
a. Tete-beche pair		3.50 3.50
1055 A385 90k multi		2.50 2.50
a. Tete-beche pair		5.00 5.00

See Nos. 1082-1083, 1116-1117.

Motorcycles A386

2005, Oct. 7		Perf. 13¼x13½
1056 A386 50k multi		1.40 1.40

First motorcycle in Iceland, cent.

Commercial College of Iceland, Cent. — A387

2005, Oct. 7		Perf. 13½x14¼
1057 A387 70k multi		2.00 2.00

Souvenir Sheet

Aerial View of Reykjavik Rooftops — A388

2005, Oct. 7		Perf. 13¼
1058 A388 200k multi		6.50 6.50

Stamp Day.

Birds Type of 2002

Designs: 60k, Anser anser. 105k, Sturnus vulgaris.

2005, Nov. 3		Perf. 14
1059-1060 A349 Set of 2		4.50 4.50

Christmas A389

2005, Nov. 3		Perf. 13½
1061 A389 50k Apple		1.40 1.40
a. White border at top or bottom, perf. 13½ on 2 or 3 sides		1.40 1.40
b. Booklet pane of 10 #1061a		14.00
Complete booklet, #1061b		14.00
1062 A389 70k Christmas tree		2.10 2.10

No. 1061 is impregnated with an apple and cinnamon scent; No. 1062 with a pine scent.

National Flower Dryas Octopetala — A390

2006, Feb. 2	Litho.	Perf. 13¾
1063 A390 50k multi		1.40 1.40

Rock and Roll Music, 50th Anniv. — A391

2006, Feb. 2		
1064 A391 60k multi		1.60 1.60

Arrival in Iceland of Refugees of Hungarian Uprising, 50th Anniv. — A392

2006, Feb. 2		Perf. 13½x13¾
1065 A392 70k multi		2.00 2.00

Souvenir Sheet

Europa Stamps, 50th Anniv. A393

No. 1066: a, #407. b, #395.

2006, Feb. 2		Perf. 14¼x14
1066 A393 150k Sheet of 2, #a-b		9.50 9.50

Motion Pictures in Iceland, Cent. — A394

Designs: 50k, Early theater, projector and program. 95k, Projector reel, actor and actress. 160k, Actor in mask, clapboard, bag of popcorn, cameraman on location.

		Perf. 13¾x13½
2006, Mar. 29		Litho.
1067-1069 A394 Set of 3		9.00 9.00

Souvenir Sheet

Mythical Beings of Nordic Folklore A395

2006, Mar. 29		Perf. 13¼x13
1070 A395 95k multi		3.00 3.00

General Purpose Vehicles — A396

No. 1071: a, 1951 Land Rover. b, 1946 Willys. No. 1072: a, 1965 Austin Gypsy. b, 1955 GAZ-69.

Perf. 13 on 2 or 3 Sides		
2006, Mar. 29	Booklet Stamps	
1071 Pair		4.00 4.00
a.-b. A396 70k Either single		2.00 2.00
c. Booklet pane, 2 #1071		8.00
Complete booklet, #1071c		8.00
1072 Pair		5.00 5.00
a.-b. A396 90k Either single		2.50 2.50
c. Booklet pane, 2 #1072		10.00
Complete booklet, #1072c		10.00

A397 Europa — A398

2006, May 18		Perf. 13¼x13¾
1073 A397 75k blk & red		2.00 2.00
		Perf. 13¾x13¼
1074 A398 95k blue & blk		2.75 2.75

Booklet Stamps
Self-Adhesive
Serpentine Die Cut 11¾x12¼

1075 A397 75k blk & red		2.00 2.00
a. Booklet pane of 10		20.00

Serpentine Die Cut 12¼x11¾

1076 A398 95k blue & blk		2.75 2.75
a. Booklet pane of 10		27.50

Waterfalls A399

Designs: 55k, Faxi. 65k, Oxaráfoss, vert. (29x47mm). 75k, Glymur, vert. (29x47mm). 95k, Hjálparfoss. 220k, Skeifárfoss.

2006, May 18		Perf. 13¼
1077-1081 A399 Set of 5		14.50 14.50
1081a Booklet pane, #1077-1081, perf. 13½		21.00
Complete booklet, #1081a		21.00

Booklet containing No. 1081a sold for 750k.

Berries Type of 2005

Designs: 75k, Empetrum nigrum. 130k, Rubus saxatilis.

2006, Sept. 21		Perf. 13¼x13¾
1082 A385 75k multi		1.90 1.90
a. Tete-beche pair		3.75 3.75
1083 A385 130k multi		3.50 3.50
a. Tete-beche pair		7.00 7.00

Iceland's First Olympic Medal, 50th Anniv. A400

Litho. & Embossed

2006, Sept. 21		Perf. 13¼
1084 A400 55k multi		1.40 1.40

First Telephone Service in Iceland, Cent. — A401

2006, Sept. 21	Litho.	Perf. 14
1085 A401 65k multi		1.75 1.75

Souvenir Sheet

Icelandic Wrestling Tournament, Cent. — A402

Litho. & Embossed

2006, Sept. 21		Perf. 13¼x14
1086 A402 200k multi		6.00 6.00

Stamp Day.

Mushrooms Type of 1999

Designs: 70k, Xerocomus subtomentosus. 95k, Kuehneromyces mutabilis.

2006, Nov. 2	Litho.	Perf. 13¾x13¼
1087-1088 A314 Set of 2		4.50 4.50

Insects Type of 2004

Designs: 65k, Dolichovespula norwegica. 110k, Coccinella undecimpunctata.

2006, Nov. 2	Litho.	Perf. 13¾x14¼
1089-1090 A375 Set of 2		4.50 4.50

Christmas — A403

Designs: Nos. 1091, 1093, Angel, denomination at LL. 75k, Heart. No. 1094, Angel, denomination at LR.

2006, Nov. 2		Perf. 13½x13¾
1091 A403 55k multi		1.75 1.75
1092 A403 75k multi		1.75 1.75

Self-Adhesive
Booklet Stamps
Serpentine Die Cut 9½x9¾

1093 A403 55k multi		1.75 1.75
1094 A403 75k multi		1.75 1.75
a. Booklet pane, 5 each #1093-1094		20.00
Nos. 1091-1094 (4)		7.00 7.00

Women's Rights in Iceland, Cent. A404

		Perf. 13½x13¼
2007, Feb. 15		Litho.
1095 A404 60k multi		1.60 1.60

Fishing Trawler Jón Forseti, Cent. — A405

2007, Feb. 15		Perf. 13¾x13½
1096 A405 65k multi		1.75 1.75

Geothermal Energy — A406

2007, Feb. 15		Perf. 14
1097 A406 75k multi		2.00 2.00

West Nordic Council, 10th anniv.

Souvenir Sheet

Intl. Polar Year A407

2007, Feb. 15		Perf. 14x13½
1098 A407 Sheet of 2		4.75 4.75
a. 75k Volcano		2.00 2.00
b. 95k Ice cap mapping equipment		2.75 2.75

ICELAND

Youth Organization of Iceland, Cent. — A408

2007, Apr. 20		Perf. 14
1099	A408 70k multi	2.00 2.00

National Archives, 125th Anniv. — A409

2007, Apr. 20		Perf. 12½
1100	A409 80k multi	2.25 2.25
a.	Tete-beche pair, with tabs	7.00 7.00

Organized Forestry in Iceland, Cent. — A410

Various tree branches with frame color of: 10k, Olive green. 60k, Rose carmine.

2007, Apr. 20		Perf. 14
1101-1102	A410 Set of 2	3.50 3.50
1101a	Perf. 13½x14	.90 .90
1102a	Perf. 13½x14	5.25 5.25

Issued: 1101a, 1102a, 11/6/08.

Cargo Boats — A411

No. 1103: a, Hamrafell. b, Tröllafoss.
No. 1104: a, Langjökull. b, Akranes.

		Perf. 13 on 2 or 3 Sides
2007, Apr. 20		Booklet Stamps
1103	Pair	4.50 4.50
a.-b.	A411 80k Either single	2.25 2.25
c.	Booklet pane, 2 #1103	9.00 —
	Complete booklet, #1103c	9.00
1104	Pair	5.75 5.75
a.-b.	A411 105k Either single	2.75 2.75
c.	Booklet pane, 2 #1104	11.00 —
	Complete booklet, #1104c	11.00

Glaciers — A412

Designs: 5k, Breithamerkurjökull. 60k, Eystri Hagafellsjökull and Langjökull, vert. 80k, Mulajökull and Hofsjökull. 110k, Snaefellsjökull. 300k, Hvannadalshnúkur and Oraefajökull (70x30mm).

2007, May 24		Perf. 14x13¼
1105-1109	A412 Set of 5	16.00 16.00
1109a	Booklet pane, #1105-1109	25.00
	Complete booklet, #1109a	25.00

No. 1109a sold for 750k.

Europa — A413

Designs: 80k, Scouting fleur-de-lis. 105k, Scouting clover emblem.

2007, May 24		Perf. 13¼
1110	A413 80k multi	2.25 2.25
1111	A413 105k multi	2.75 2.75

Booklet Stamps
Self-Adhesive
Die Cut

1112	A413 80k multi	2.25 2.25
a.	Booklet pane of 10	22.50 22.50
1113	A413 105k multi	2.25 2.25
a.	Booklet pane of 10	22.50
	Nos. 1110-1113 (4)	9.50 9.50

Scouting, cent.

Soil Conservation Service, Cent. — A414

		Perf. 13¾x14¼
2007, May 24		Photo.
1114	A414 (60k) multi	1.75 1.75

Self-Adhesive
Serpentine Die Cut 12

| 1115 | A414 (60k) multi | 1.75 1.75 |

No. 1114 was printed in a sheet of 10, No. 1115 was printed in a folded sheet of 50.

Berries Type of 2005

Designs: 120k, Vaccinium myrtillus. 145k, Cornus suecica.

2007, Sept. 20	Litho.	Perf. 14
1116	A385 120k multi	3.00 3.00
a.	Tete-beche pair	9.00 9.00
1117	A385 145k multi	4.00 4.00
a.	Tete-beche pair	12.00 12.00

New Bible Translation A415

Litho. With Foil Application

2007, Sept. 20		Perf. 13½
1118	A415 60k multi	1.75 1.75

Souvenir Sheet

Royal Visit, Cent. A416

Litho. & Engr.

2007, Sept. 20		Perf. 13x13¼
1119	A416 250k multi	7.00 7.00

Jökulsá Canyon and Selfoss Waterfall A417

No. 1120: a, Jökulsá Canyon (45x29mm). b, Selfoss Waterfall (30x29mm).

2007, Oct. 1	Litho.	Perf. 13¼x13¾
1120	A417 Horiz. pair	5.00 5.00
a.	80k multi	2.25 2.25
b.	105k multi	2.75 2.75

Insects Type of 2004

Designs: 70k, Prionocera turcica. 190k, Euceraphis punctipennis.

2007, Nov. 8	Litho.	Perf. 14
1121-1122	A375 Set of 2	6.75 6.75

Jónas Hallgrímsson (1807-45), Poet — A418

2007, Nov. 8	Engr.	Perf. 12¾x13
1123	A418 65k brown	1.60 1.60

Kleppur Psychiatric Hospital, Cent. — A419

2007, Nov. 8	Litho.	Perf. 13¼
1124	A419 80k multi	2.25 2.25

Christmas — A420

Various cut patterns in Icelandic leaf bread: 60k, 80k.

2007, Nov. 8	Serpentine Die Cut
	Self-Adhesive
1125	A420 60k red & multi	1.75 1.75
a.	Booklet pane of 10	17.50
1126	A420 80k grn & multi	2.25 2.25

Teachers' College of Iceland, Cent. A421

2008, Feb. 14	Litho.	Perf. 14x13¼
1127	A421 85k multi	2.25 2.25

Kisses — A422

Lines from poem by Erla Thorsteindottir and people kissing with photograph colors in: No. 1128, 65k, Blue. No. 1129, 65k, Sepia. 75k, Green. 85k, Red violet.

2008, Feb. 14		
1128-1131	A422 Set of 4	8.00 8.00

Agricultural Tools — A423

No. 1132: a, Ferguson tractor. b, International Harvester TD6 bulldozer.
No. 1133: a, Horse-drawn plow. b, Lanz turfkiller.

2008, Mar. 27	Litho.	Perf. 13¼
	Booklet Stamps	
1132	Pair	4.50 4.50
a.-b.	A423 85k Either single	2.25 2.25
c.	Booklet pane, 2 #1132	9.00
	Complete booklet, #1132c	9.00
1133	Pair	6.00 6.00
a.-b.	A423 110k Either single	3.00 3.00
c.	Booklet pane, 2 #1133	12.00
	Complete booklet, #1133c	12.00

Embroidery A424

Designs: 65k, Refilsaumur. 85k, Augnsaumur. 110k, Krosssaumur.

2008, Mar. 27		Perf. 14
1134-1136	A424 Set of 3	7.50 7.50

Souvenir Sheet

Snaefellsnes — A425

2008, Mar. 27		Perf. 14x13¼
1137	A425 120k multi	3.00 3.00

Personalized Stamp — A426

Serpentine Die Cut 10 Syncopated

2008, May 8	Self-Adhesive	Litho.
1138	A426 (75k) multi	2.00 2.00

The vignette of the stamp shown above is the generic image for the issue, which was available at face value. Other images with the stamp frame shown are personalized stamps which sold for 3120k for a sheet of 24 stamps.

Geothermal Space Heating, Cent. — A427

2008, May 8		Perf. 14x13½
1139	A427 75k multi	2.00 2.00

Hafnarfjördhur, Cent. — A428

2008, May 8		Perf. 13x12½
1140	A428 80k multi	2.00 2.00

Icelandic Industrial Design — A429

Designs: 65k, Proprio Foot prosthetic foot. 120k, Marel OptiCut volumetric portioning and meat cutting machine. 155k, Wish fly fishing reel. 200k, Gavia submarine.

2008, May 8		Perf. 12½x13
1141-1144	A429 Set of 4	13.50 13.50
1141a	Tête-bêche pair	3.25 3.25
1142a	Tête-bêche pair	5.75 5.75
1143a	Tête-bêche pair	6.75 6.75

Europa — A430

Letter folded into: 85k, Boat. 110k, Airplane.

2008, May 8		Perf. 14
1145	A430 85k multi	2.25 2.25
1146	A430 110k multi	2.75 2.75

ICELAND

Booklet Stamps
Self-Adhesive
Serpentine Die Cut 9½x10

1147	A430 85k multi	2.25	2.25
a.	Booklet pane of 10	22.50	
1148	A430 110k multi	2.75	2.75
a.	Booklet pane of 10	27.50	

Knight and Final Position of 1958 Chess Match Between Fridhrik Olafsson and Bobby Fischer — A431

2008, Sept. 18   *Litho.*   *Perf. 13¼*
1149   A431   80k multi   1.60   1.60

First Cod War, 50th Anniv. — A432

2008, Sept. 18   *Perf. 13¼x13*
1150   A432   90k multi   1.75   1.75

For surcharge, see No. 1278.

Aegagropila Linnaei — A433

2008, Sept. 18   *Perf. 13¼x13¾*
1151   A433   140k multi   2.75   2.75

Souvenir Sheet

Intl. Year of Planet Earth — A434

2008, Sept. 18
1152   A434   215k multi   4.00   4.00

Stamp Day.

Peace Tower, Videy — A435

2008, Oct. 9   *Litho.*   *Perf. 13¼*
1153   A435   120k multi + label   2.40   2.40

Parts of the design were printed with a glow-in-the-dark ink.

Forestry Type of 2005 Redrawn and

Forestry in Vaglaskógur, Cent. — A436

2008, Nov. 6   *Litho.*   *Perf. 13½x14*

1154	A436 400k multi	8.00	8.00
1155	Booklet pane of 4, #1101a, 1102a, 1154, 1155a	55.00	55.00
a.	A377 45k multi, denomination as "45" only	14.00	28.00
	Complete booklet, #1155	55.00	55.00

No. 1155 sold for 800k.

Christmas — A437

Winning designs in children's stamp art contest: 70k, Christmas goblin Stiff-legs, by Heidhar Jökull Hafsteinsson. 90k, Christmas Cat, by Konrádh Kárason Thormar.

Serpentine Die Cut 12½
2008, Nov. 6   **Self-Adhesive**

1156	A437 70k multi	1.50	1.50
a.	Booket pane of 10	15.00	
1157	A437 90k multi	1.75	1.75

Vertical pairs in booklet pane are tete-beche.

Islands Type of 2001

Designs: 75k, Hjörsey. 90k, Málmey.

2009, Jan. 29   *Litho.*   *Perf. 14*
1158-1159   A335   Set of 2   3.25   3.25

Insects Type of 2004

Designs: 80k, Psychodidae. 120k, Gnaphosidae (spider).

2009, Jan. 29
1160-1161   A375   Set of 2   4.00   4.00

Souvenir Sheet

Intl. Polar Year — A438

No. 1162 — Map of ice cover of: a, 100k, North Pole, Northern Greenland. b, 130k, Iceland, Eastern Greenland.

Litho. & Photo.
2009, Jan. 29   *Perf. 13x13½*
1162   A438   Sheet of 2, #a-b   4.50   4.50

Parts of the design were printed with a thermographic ink that disappeared when warmed.

Civil Aviation in Iceland, 90th Anniv. — A439

No. 1163: a, Avro 504K. b, Waco ZKS-7.
No. 1164: a, Boeing 757. b, Fokker 50.

Perf. 14¼ Horiz.
2009, Mar. 19   *Litho.*

Booklet Stamps

1163	Vert. pair	3.75	3.75
a.-b.	A439 90k Either single	1.75	1.75
c.	Booklet pane, 2 #1163	7.00	—
	Complete booklet, #1163c	7.00	
1164	Vert. pair	5.75	5.75
a.-b.	A439 120k Either single	2.75	2.75
c.	Booklet pane, 2 #1164	11.00	—
	Complete booklet, #1164c	11.00	

Miniature Sheet

Legendary Creatures from Folktales — A440

No. 1165: a, Hrosshvalur. b, Skoffín. c, Múshveli. d, Raudhkembingur. e, Selamódhir. f, Ofuguggi. g, Saeneyti. h, Skeljaskrímsli. i, Urdharkötur. j, Fjörulalli.

2009, Mar. 19   *Perf. 13¼*
1165   A440   80k Sheet of 10, #a-j   17.00   17.00

Reykjavik Water Works, Cent. — A441

2009, May 7   *Litho.*   *Perf. 12½*
1166   A441   10k multi   .30   .30

Iceland Youth Organization National Tournaments, Cent. — A442

2009, May 7   *Perf. 13¼*
1167   A442   105k multi   2.25   2.25

Skrúdhur Garden, Cent. — A443

2009, May 7   *Perf. 12½*
1168   A443   140k multi   3.00   3.00

Europa — A444

Designs: 105k, Sun and shadows at different times. 140k, Observatory.

2009, May 7   *Perf. 13¼*

1169	A444 105k multi	2.25	2.25
1170	A444 140k multi	3.00	3.00

Booklet Stamps
Self-Adhesive
Serpentine Die Cut 9¾x10

1171	A444 105k multi	2.25	2.25
a.	Booklet pane of 10	22.50	
1172	A444 140k multi	3.00	3.00
a.	Booklet pane of 10	30.00	

Intl. Year of Astronomy.

Souvenir Sheet

Nordia 2009 Philatelic Exhibition, Hafnarfjördhur — A445

2009, May 7   *Perf. 13*
1173   A445   190k multi   4.50   4.50

Icelandic Sheep — A446

Shepherds and sheep in: 95k, Open pasture. 160k, Pen, vert.

Perf. 12½x13, 13x12½
2009, Sept. 16
1174-1175   A446   Set of 2   5.00   5.00

Skaftafell, Vatnajökull National Park — A447

No. 1176 — Denomination at: a, UL (45x30mm). b, UR (30x30mm).

2009, Sept. 16   *Perf. 13½x14*
1176   A447   120k Horiz. pair, #a-b   4.75   4.75

Souvenir Sheet

National Center for Cultural Heritage, Cent. — A448

2009, Sept. 16   *Perf. 13*
1177   A448   150k multi   3.50   3.50

Stamp Day.

Birds — A449

Designs: 110k, Uria lomvia. 130k, Larus hyperboreus.

2009, Nov. 5   *Perf. 13x13¼*
1178-1179   A449   Set of 2   4.75   4.75

Thingvellir Church, 150th Anniv. — A450

2009, Nov. 5
1180   A450   190k multi   4.00   4.00

Christmas — A451

ICELAND

Stained-glass windows: (70k), The Sermon on the Mount, by Gudmundur Einarsson. 120k, Holy Mother of God, by Finnur Jónsson.

2009, Nov. 5   *Die Cut Perf. 13½*
Self-Adhesive

1181	A451	(70k) multi	1.75	1.75
a.		Booklet pane of 10	17.50	
1182	A451	120k multi	2.40	2.40

Seals — A452

Designs: 5k, Phoca vitulina. 220k, Phoca groenlandica.

2010, Jan. 28   *Litho.*   *Perf. 13¼x13¾*

1183-1184	A452	Set of 2	3.50	3.50

Home Furnishings — A453

Designs: 75k, Hanger tree, designed by Katrin Olina Pétursdóttir and Michael Young. 140k, Tango chair, designed by Sigurdhur Gústafsson. 155k, MGO 180 dining room table, designed by Gudhrún M. Olafsdóttir and Oddgeir Thórdharson, horiz. 165k, Dimon sofa, designed by Erla Sólveig Oskarsdóttir.

Perf. 13¼x12½, 12½x13¼

2010, Jan. 28

1185-1188	A453	Set of 4	7.50	7.50
1185a		Tête-bêche pair	2.40	2.40
1186a		Tête-bêche pair	4.50	4.50
1187a		Tête-bêche pair	5.00	5.00
1188a		Tête-bêche pair	5.25	5.25

Wood and Bone Carvings — A454

Designs: 10k, Door of Valthjófsstadhir. Nos. 1190, 1192, (75k), Judge's drinking horn. 200k, Play in Leaves, sculpture by Sigrídhur Jóna Kristjánsdóttir.

2010, Mar. 18   *Perf. 14x13¼, 13¼x14*

1189-1191	A454	Set of 3	4.50	4.50

Self-Adhesive
Serpentine Die Cut 12
Size: 32x27mm

1192	A454	(75k) multi	1.25	1.25

Fishing Trawlers A455

No. 1193: a, Bjarni Riddari GK 1. b, Ingólfur Arnarson RE 201.
No. 1194: a, Sólborg IS 260. b, Hardhbakur EA 3.

2010, Mar. 18   *Perf. 14 Horiz.*
Booklet Stamps

1193	A455	Vert. pair	2.50	2.50
a.-b.		75k Either single	1.25	1.25
c.		Booklet pane, 2 #1193	5.00	
		Complete booklet, #1193c	5.00	
1194	A455	Vert. pair	5.25	5.25
a.-b.		165k Either single	2.60	2.60
c.		Booklet pane, 2 #1194	10.50	
		Complete booklet, #1194c	10.50	

Souvenir Sheet

Life by the Sea A456

No. 1195: a, Man rolling herring barrel. b, Women filling herring barrels, fish.

2010, Mar. 18   *Perf. 13¼x14*

1195	A456	75k Sheet of 2, #a-b	2.50	2.50

Europa — A457

Illustrations from children's books: 165k, The Fate of the Gods, by Ingunn Asdísardóttir and Kristin Ragna Gunnarsdóttir. 220k, Good Evening, by Aslaug Jónsdóttir.

2010, May 6   *Litho.*   *Perf. 13¾x14*

1196	A457	165k multi	2.60	2.60
1197	A457	220k multi	3.50	3.50

Booklet Stamps
Self-Adhesive
Die Cut Perf. 13¼

1198	A457	165k multi	2.60	2.60
a.		Booklet pane of 10	26.00	
1199	A457	220k multi	3.50	3.50
a.		Booklet pane of 10	35.00	

Garden Parks — A458

Designs: 90k, Jónsgardhur, Isafjödhur. 130k, Hellisgerdhi, Hafnarfjödhur. 285k, Skalla-grímsgardhur, Borgarnes, horiz.

Perf. 13¼x13¾, 13¾x13¼

2010, May 6

1200-1202	A458	Set of 3	7.00	7.00

A460   **Personalized Stamps — A461**

Serpentine Die Cut 10 Syncopated
2010, May 6   **Self-Adhesive**

1203	A460	(165k) silver & blue	2.50	2.50
1204	A461	(220k) bronze & brn	3.00	3.00

The vignettes shown above of Nos. 1203-1204 are generic images. The vignette portion of the stamp could be personalized.

Souvenir Sheet

Iceland Pavilion, Expo 2010, Shanghai — A462

2010, May 6   *Perf. 13x12½x12¾x13*

1205	A462	130k multi	2.25	2.25

A463   **A464**

2010 Eruption of Eyjafjallajökull Volcano — A465

Litho. & Silk-screened
2010, July 22   *Perf. 13¼*

1206	A463	(75k) multi	1.25	1.25
1207	A464	(165k) multi	2.50	2.50
1208	A465	(220k) multi	3.00	3.00
		Nos. 1206-1208 (3)	6.75	6.75

Volcanic ash from the eruption was added to the ink used on the silk-screened parts of Nos. 1206-1208.

Vífilsstadhir Sanatorium, Cent. — A466

Perf. 13½x13¼

2010, Sept. 16   *Litho.*

1209	A466	(90k) multi	2.25	2.25

2010 Youth Olympics, Singapore — A467

2010, Sept. 16   *Perf. 13x12½*

1210	A467	165k multi	2.50	2.50

Gas Lighting In Reykjavik, 150th Anniv. — A468

2010, Sept. 16   *Perf. 13*

1211	A468	450k multi	6.25	6.25

Souvenir Sheet

Intl. Year of Biodiversity — A469

No. 1212: a, Hawk, wolf, rodent. b, Fish, duck.

2010, Sept. 16   *Perf. 13¼*

1212	A469	90k Sheet of 2, #a-b	3.00	3.00

Visir Newspaper, Cent. — A470

2010, Nov. 4   *Litho.*   *Perf. 13*

1213	A470	140k drab & blk	2.25	2.25

Foss, by Isleifur Konrádhsson A471

Skeggjadhur Madhur og Blómaflúr, by Sölvi Helgason A472

Breidhfirskur Víkingur, by Sigurlaug Jónasdóttir A473

Fiskar, by Karl Einarsson Dunganon A474

2010, Nov. 4

1214	A471	(75k) multi	1.25	1.25
1215	A472	(90k) multi	1.40	1.40
1216	A473	(165k) multi	2.60	2.60
1217	A474	(220k) multi	3.25	3.25
		Nos. 1214-1217 (4)	8.50	8.50

A booklet containing single stamps of Nos. 1214-1217 in mounts sold for 1,550k.

Wreath and Dove A475

Wreath and Two Doves A476

2010, Nov. 4   *Die Cut Perf. 13¾*
Self-Adhesive

1218	A475	(75k) multi	1.25	.90
a.		Booklet pane of 10	17.50	
1219	A476	(165k) multi	2.60	2.60

Halichoerus Grypus A477

Phoca Hispida A478

2011, Jan. 27   *Litho.*   *Perf. 13¼x13¾*

1220	A477	(90k) multi	3.00	3.00
1221	A478	(220k) multi	1.75	1.75

Branta Leucopsis A479

Melanitta Nigra — A480

Anser Albifrons A481

207

ICELAND

Anas Strepera
A482

2011, Jan. 27
1222	A479	(75k) multi	1.75	1.75
1223	A480	(75k) multi	1.75	1.75
1224	A481	(165k) multi	2.75	2.75
1225	A482	(165k) multi	2.75	2.75
	Nos. 1222-1225 (4)		8.50	8.50

Worldwide Fund for Nature (WWF).

Motor Sports — A483

No. 1226 — Inscriptions: a, Mótokross. b, Rally.
No. 1227 — Inscriptions: a, Torfaera. b, Kvartmíla.

2011, Mar. 17   Litho.   Perf. 14 Horiz.
Booklet Stamps
1226	A483	Vert. pair	2.50	2.50
a.-b.		(75k) Either single	1.25	1.25
c.		Booklet pane, 2 #1226	5.00	
		Complete booklet, #1226c	5.00	—
1227		Vert. pair	5.50	5.50
a.-b.		(165k) Either single	2.75	2.75
c.		Booklet pane, 2 #1227	11.00	
		Complete booklet, #1227c	11.00	—

Langanes Lighthouse A484

Stokknes Lighthouse A485

Die Cut Perf. 13¼ at Bottom
2011, Mar. 17   Self-Adhesive
1228	A484	(75k) multi	1.75	1.75

Die Cut Perf. 13¼ at Right
1229	A485	(165k) multi	2.75	2.75

Tree Rings and Table — A486

Leaf and Curved Arrows — A487

Litho. With Foil Application
2011, Mar. 17   Perf. 13¾x14
1230	A486	(165k) multi	2.50	2.50
1231	A487	(220k) multi	3.50	3.50

Booklet Stamps
Self-Adhesive
Die Cut Perf. 13¼
1232	A486	(165k) multi	2.60	2.60
a.		Booklet pane of 10	26.00	
1233	A487	(220k) multi	3.50	3.50
a.		Booklet pane of 10	35.00	

Europa, Intl. Year of Forests.

University of Iceland, Cent. — A488

2011, May 4   Litho.   Perf. 12½x13
1234	A488	(75k) multi	1.25	1.25

Melavöllur Stadium, Reykjavik, Cent. — A489

2011, May 4   Perf. 13¼
1235	A489	(130k) multi	2.25	1.75

Austurvöllur Park, Reykjavik A490

Parliament Park, Reykjavik A491

2011, May 4   Perf. 13¼x12½
1236	A490	(90k) multi	1.75	1.75
1237	A491	(285k) multi	4.00	4.00

Miniature Sheet

Opening of Harpa Reykjavik Concert Hall and Conference Center — A492

No. 1238 — Portions of building facade in colors of: a, Black and blue green. b, Black and gray with country name on white area. c, Black and gray with country name on gray area. d, Black and pink. e, Black and yellow green. Stamps are polygonal and various sizes.

2011, May 4   Litho. & Engr.   Die Cut
Self-Adhesive
1238	A492	Sheet of 5	8.50	8.50
a.-e.		(75k) Any single	1.75	1.75

Pres. Jón Sigurdhsson (1811-79) — A493

Sigurdhsson as: Nos. 1239, 1241a, Young man. No. 1240, Old man.

2011, June 17   Litho.   Perf. 13
1239	A493	(75k) multi	1.25	1.25
1240	A493	1000k multi, year date 2¼mm wide	14.00	14.00
a.		Year date 2½mm wide	14.00	14.00

Souvenir Sheet
1241		Sheet of 2, #1240a, 1241a	17.50	17.50
a.	A493	100k multi	1.60	1.60

Wetlands Conservation — A494

2011, Sept. 15   Perf. 13¼
1242	A494	(90k) multi	1.25	1.25

Amnesty International, 50th Anniv. — A495

2011, Sept. 15   Perf. 13½x14
1243	A495	(285k) yel & blk	4.00	4.00

Snaefell Glacier National Park A496

No. 1244: a, Mountain (45x29mm). b, Mountain, diff. (30x29mm).

2011, Sept. 15   Perf. 13¼x13¾
1244	A496	Horiz. pair	4.00	4.00
a.-b.		(165k) Either single	2.00	2.00

Souvenir Sheet

Fishing Boat at Húsavik A497

2011, Sept. 15   Perf. 13x13¼
1245	A497	(165k) multi	2.00	2.00

See Malta No. 1438.

Souvenir Sheet

Saga of Burnt Niall A498

No. 1246: a, Flying horseman carrying torch. b, Burning of Niall and family. c, Swordsman raising sword, dead swordsman.

2011, Sept. 15   Perf. 12½
1246	A498	Sheet of 3	6.75	6.75
a.-c.		(110k) Any single	2.25	2.25

Sólarlag vidh Tjörnina, by Thórarinn B. Thorláksson A499

Botnssúlur, by Asgrímur Jónsson — A500

Utreidharfólk, by Jón Stefánsson A501

Fornar Slódhir, by Jóhannes Kjarval — A502

2011, Nov. 3   Litho.   Perf. 13x13¼
1247	A499	(90k) multi	1.75	1.75
1248	A500	(110k) multi	2.25	2.25
1249	A501	(165k) multi	2.75	2.75
1250	A502	(220k) multi	2.75	2.75
	Nos. 1247-1250 (4)		9.50	9.50

A503

Christmas — A504

Die Cut Perf. 13¾x13½
2011, Nov. 3   Litho. & Embossed
Self-Adhesive
1251	A503	(90k) multi	1.25	.90
a.		Booklet pane of 10	12.50	
1252	A504	(165k) multi	2.25	2.25

National Olympic and Sports Association, Cent. — A505

2012, Jan. 26   Litho.   Perf. 13¼x13¾
1253	A505	(97k) multi	1.25	1.25

Landmannalaugar A506

Lake Hnausapollur A507

2012, Jan. 26   Perf. 13¾
1254	A506	(175k) multi	2.75	2.75
1255	A507	(230k) multi	2.75	2.75

Silver Chalice, 15th Cent. A508

Silver Headdress, by Sigurdhar Gudhmundsson A509

Silver Bowl, by Pétur Tryggvi Hjálmarsson A510

Silver Chalice, 15th Cent. A511

ICELAND

2012, Jan. 26   Perf. 13¼x14, 14x13¼
1256	A508	(97k) multi	1.25	1.25
1257	A509	(175k) multi	1.25	1.25
1258	A510	(230k) multi	3.00	3.00
	Nos. 1256-1258 (3)		5.50	5.50

Self-Adhesive
Serpentine Die Cut 12
1259	A511	(97k) multi	1.25	1.25

Shoes and Socks Designed by Hugrún Dögg Arnadóttir and Magni Thorsteinsson — A512

Dress Designed by Steinunn Sigurdardottir — A513

Wool Sweater Designed by Bergthora Gudnadottir — A514

Coat Designed by 66 Degrees North A515

2012, Mar. 22   Perf. 12½x13
1260	A512	(97k) multi	1.25	1.25
1261	A513	(110k) multi	1.75	1.75
1262	A514	(175k) multi	2.75	2.75
1263	A515	(230k) multi	2.75	2.75
	Nos. 1260-1263 (4)		8.50	8.50

Waterfall — A516

Aluminum A517

Geothermal Energy — A518

Tomatoes — A519

Booklet Stamps
Serpentine Die Cut 13¼
2012, Mar. 22   Self-Adhesive
1264	A516	(75k) multi	1.25	1.25
1265	A517	(75k) multi	1.25	1.25
a.	Booklet pane of 4, 2 each #1264-1265		5.00	
1266	A518	(175k) multi	2.75	2.75
1267	A519	(175k) multi	2.75	2.75
a.	Booklet pane of 4, 2 each #1266-1267		11.00	
	Nos. 1264-1267 (4)		8.00	8.00

Green energy.

Souvenir Sheet

Sea Rescue A520

2012, Mar. 22   Perf. 14¼x14¾
1268	A520	(155k) multi	3.50	3.50

Akureyri, 150th Anniv. — A521

2012, May 3   Perf. 14x13½
1269	A521	(75k) multi	1.25	1.25
a.	With period after "08"		1.25	1.25

No. 1269 is missing period after "08".
Issued: No. 1269a, 7/2.

Scouting in Iceland, Cent. — A522

2012, May 3   Perf. 13¾
1270	A522	(75k) multi	1.25	1.25

2012 Summer Olympics, London — A523

2012, May 3   Perf. 14x13½
1271	A523	(580k) multi	8.00	8.00

Akureyri Park, Akureyri A524

Hallargardhur Park, Reykjavik A525

2012, May 3   Perf. 13¼
1272	A524	(225k) multi	4.00	4.00
1273	A525	(300k) multi	4.00	4.00

Geyser A526

Aurora Borealis A527

2012, May 3   Serpentine Die Cut 18
Self-Adhesive
1274	A526	(175k) multi	3.00	3.00
1275	A527	(230k) multi	3.00	3.00

Booklet Stamps
Serpentine Die Cut 18 on 3 Sides
1276	A526	(175k) multi	3.00	3.00
a.	Booklet pane of 10		30.00	
1277	A527	(230k) multi	3.00	3.00
a.	Booklet pane of 10		30.00	

Europa.

No. 1150 Surcharged

Method and Perf. As Before
2012, July 2
1278	A432	(103k) on 90k #1150	1.90	1.90

Russula Xerampelina A528

2012, July 2   Litho.   Perf. 13¼x12¾
1279	A528	(103k) multi	1.25	1.25

Cystophora Cristata A529

Odobenus Rosmarus A530

2012, Sept. 13   Perf. 13¼x13¾
1280	A529	(475k) multi	4.00	4.00
1281	A530	(480k) multi	7.00	7.00

Engey Lighthouse A531

Kálfshamar Lighthouse A532

Die Cut Perf. 13¼ at Bottom
2012, Sept. 13   Self-Adhesive
1282	A531	(103k) multi	1.75	1.75

Die Cut Perf. 13¼ at Right
1283	A532	(175k) multi	3.00	3.00

Souvenir Sheet

Archaeological Excavations at Skriduklaustur — A533

2012, Sept. 13   Perf. 14x13¼
1284	A533	(565k) multi	7.00	7.00

Consecration of Skriduklaustur Church, 500th anniv.

Boletus Edulis — A534

2012, Nov. 1   Perf. 13¼x12¾
1285	A534	(103k) multi	1.25	1.25

Dapri Prinsinn, by Gudhmundur Thorsteinsson A535

Uppstilling, by Kristín Jónsdóttir — A536

Frá Vestmannaeyjum, by Júlíana Sveinsdóttir A537

Móðhurást, Sculpture by Nína Saemundsson A538

2012, Nov. 1   Perf. 14x13¼
1286	A535	(120k) multi	1.75	1.75
1287	A536	(125k) multi	2.25	2.25
1288	A537	(175k) multi	2.75	2.75

Perf. 13¼x14
1289	A538	(230k) multi	2.75	2.75
	Nos. 1286-1289 (4)		9.50	9.50

A539

Christmas A540

Self-Adhesive
Litho. With Foil Application
2012, Nov. 1   Die Cut Perf. 13½
1290	A539	(120k) multi	1.25	.90
a.	Booklet pane of 10		12.50	
1291	A540	(175k) multi	2.25	2.25

Intl. Year of Water Cooperation — A541

2013, Jan. 24   Litho.   Perf. 13¾x13½
1292	A541	(103k) multi	1.25	1.25

Aldeyjarfoss A542

Hafursey A543

2013, Jan. 24   Perf. 13¾
1293	A542	(175k) multi	2.75	2.75
1294	A543	(230k) multi	2.75	2.75

National Museum, 150th Anniv. — A544

Self-Adhesive
2013, Jan. 24   Perf. 13½
1295	A544	(125k) rose & blue	2.25	2.25

ICELAND

Puffin, by Sigurdur Oddsson
A545

Sofa, by Ragnar Freyr Pálsson
A546

An All Icelandic Hot Dog, by Rán Flygenring
A547

Horses, by Sigurdur Eggertsson
A548

2013, Mar. 14		Perf. 13¼x14
1296	A545 (120k) multi	1.25 1.25
1297	A546 (155k) multi	2.75 2.75
1298	A547 (300k) multi	4.00 4.00
1299	A548 (475k) multi	4.00 4.00
	Nos. 1296-1299 (4)	12.00 12.00

A549

Motor Vehicles — A550

Designs: No. 1300, 1931 Ford AA truck. No. 1301, 1942-43 Chevrolet dual purpose vehicle. No. 1302, 1957 Mercedes-Benz bus. No. 1303, 1955, Bedford fire engine.

2013, Mar. 14		Die Cut Perf. 13¼
	Booklet Stamps	
	Self-Adhesive	
1300	A549 (103k) multi	1.25 1.25
1301	A549 (103k) multi	1.25 1.25
a.	Booklet pane of 4, 2 each #1300-1301	5.00
1302	A550 (175k) multi	2.75 2.75
1303	A550 (175k) multi	2.75 2.75
a.	Booklet pane of 4, 2 each #1302-1303	11.00
	Nos. 1300-1303 (4)	8.00 8.00

Reykjavik Gay Pride Parade
A551

Never Been South Music Festival, Ísafjörður
A552

Great Fish Day — A553

Smelter Music Festival, Borganfjordur Eystri — A554

Vestmannaeyjar National Holiday — A555

2013, May 2		Perf. 13¾x14¼
	Self-Adhesive	
1304	A551 (103k) multi	1.25 1.25
1305	A552 (103k) multi	1.25 1.25
1306	A553 (120k) multi	1.25 1.25
1307	A554 (120k) multi	1.25 1.25
1308	A555 (120k) multi	1.25 1.25
	Nos. 1304-1308 (5)	6.25 6.25

2012 Ford Transit Mail Van — A556

2010 Man TGS Mail Truck — A557

2013, May 2		Serpentine Die Cut 13½
	Self-Adhesive	
1309	A556 (175k) multi	2.75 2.75
1310	A557 (230k) multi	2.75 2.75
	Booklet Stamps	
	Serpentine Die Cut 13½ on 3 Sides	
1311	A556 (175k) multi	2.75 2.75
a.	Booklet pane of 10	27.50
1312	A557 (230k) multi	2.75 2.75
a.	Booklet pane of 10	27.50

Europa.

Aurora Borealis
A558

No. 1313 — Various depictions of Aurora Borealis with: a, Brown orange sky over country name. b, White area over "til." c, Brown orange sky over "50g til." d, Light sky over "rópu" and country name.

2013, May 2		Die Cut Perf. 14½
	Self-Adhesive	
1313	A558 Sheet of 4	11.00 11.00
a.-d.	(175k) Any single	2.75 2.75

Nordia 2013 Stamp Exhibition, Gardhabaer.

Capra Hircus — A559

2013, Sept. 12		Perf. 13¼
1314	A559 (175k) multi	2.75 2.75

Emergence of Surtsey Island, 50th Anniv. — A560

2013, Sept. 12		Perf. 13¼x13
1315	A560 (565k) multi	7.00 7.00

Vattarnes Lighthouse
A561

Skardhsfjara Lighthouse
A562

	Die Cut Perf. 15 at Bottom	
2013, Sept. 12		Self-Adhesive
1316	A561 (120k) multi	1.75 1.75
	Die Cut Perf. 15 at Right	
1317	A562 (300k) multi	4.00 4.00

Stamp Day
A563

No. 1318: a, Hólar Cathedral (two separate buildings). b, Skalholt Cathedral (one building).

2013, Sept. 12		Die Cut Perf. 9
	Self-Adhesive	
1318	A563 Sheet of 2	7.00 7.00
a.-b.	(225k) Either single	3.50 3.50

Morgunbladhidh Newspaper, Cent. — A564

2013, Oct. 31	Litho.	Perf. 13¾x13½
1319	A564 (120k) gray & blk	1.50 1.50

Cleft in Thingvellir Lava Fieldi, by Eggert M. Laxdal (1897-1951)
A565

Stjarna's Bones, by Finnur Jónsson (1892-1993)
A566

Sulphur Waves at Landmannlaugar, by Gudhmundur Einarsson from Midhdalur (1895-1963)
A567

Herdhubreidh Mountain, by Sveinn Thórarinsson (1899-1977)
A568

2013, Oct. 31	Litho.	Perf. 13x13½
1320	A565 (103k) multi	1.40 1.40
1321	A566 (225k) multi	3.50 3.50
1322	A567 (580k) multi	8.00 8.00
1323	A568 (955k) multi	8.00 8.00
	Nos. 1320-1323 (4)	20.90 20.90

A569

A570

Details from Stained-Glass Windows, Hallgrimskirkja, Reykjavik — A571

	Serpentine Die Cut 9¾ Vert.	
2013, Oct. 31		Litho.
	Self-Adhesive	
1324	A569 (103k) multi	1.25 1.25
1325	A570 (120k) multi	1.75 1.25
1326	A571 (175k) multi	3.00 3.00
	Nos. 1324-1326 (3)	6.00 5.50

Christmas.

Protection for Haliaeetus Albicilla, Cent. — A572

2014, Jan. 16	Litho.	Die Cut
	Self-Adhesive	
1327	A572 (103k) multi	1.50 1.50

Statistics Iceland, Cent. — A573

2014, Jan. 16	Litho.	Perf. 13¼x13
1328	A573 (120k) multi	1.75 1.25

Icelandic Steamship Company, Cent. — A574

2014, Jan. 16	Litho.	Perf. 14xx13¼
1329	A574 (175k) multi	3.00 3.00

Sjálfberg
A575

Kvlár Glacier
A576

2014, Jan. 16	Litho.	Perf. 13¼
1330	A575 (175k) multi	3.00 3.00
1331	A576 (230k) multi	3.00 3.00

Stoneharp, Invented by Páll Gudmundsson — A577

Electromagnetic Harp, Invented by Ulfur Hansson — A578

	Serpentine Die Cut 10 Vert.	
2014, Mar. 27		Litho.
	Self-Adhesive	
1332	A577 (175k) multi	3.00 3.00
1333	A578 (230k) multi	3.00 3.00

Europa.

Swimming Pool, Hofsós
A579

Akureyri Park Café — A580

Borgarfjörðhur High School
A581

ICELAND

Footbridge Over Hringbraut
A582

2014, Mar. 27   Litho.   Perf. 13½
1334	A579	(112k) multi	1.40	1.40
1335	A580	(130k) multi	1.75	1.75
1336	A581	(155k) multi	2.40	2.40
1337	A582	(175k) multi	3.00	3.00
	Nos. 1334-1337 (4)		8.55	8.55

Souvenir Sheet

Container Ship — A583

2014, Mar. 27   Litho.   Perf. 13½
| 1338 | A583 | (155k) multi | 3.50 | 3.50 |

Pavilion Park, Reykjavik A584

Klambratún, Reykjavik A585

2014, May 8   Litho.   Perf. 13¼x13¾
| 1339 | A584 | (130k) multi | 1.75 | 1.75 |
| 1340 | A585 | (135k) multi | 2.40 | 2.40 |

Lobster Festival, Höfn A586

Herring Adventure, Siglufjördhur A587

Night of Lights, Reykjanesbaer A588

Danish Days, Stykkisholmur A589

Culture Night, Reykjavik — A590

2014, May 8   Litho.   Perf. 13¾x14¼
Self-Adhesive
1341	A586	(112k) multi	1.50	1.50
1342	A587	(112k) multi	1.75	1.75
1343	A588	(130k) multi	3.00	3.00
1344	A589	(175k) multi	3.00	3.00
1345	A590	(230k) multi	3.00	3.00
	Nos. 1341-1345 (5)		12.25	12.25

A591
Fishing Vessels — A592

Designs: No. 1346, Bardhi NK 120. No. 1347, Stálvík SI 1. No. 1348, Orvar HU 21. No. 1349, Breki VE 61.

Die Cut Perf. 13¼
2014, May 8   Litho.
Booklet Stamps
Self-Adhesive
1346	A591	(112k) multi	1.50	1.50
1347	A591	(112k) multi	1.50	1.50
a.	Booklet pane of 4, 2 each #1346-1347		6.00	
1348	A592	(175k) multi	3.00	3.00
1349	A592	(175k) multi	3.00	3.00
a.	Booklet pane of 4, 2 each #1348-1349		12.00	
	Nos. 1346-1349 (4)		9.00	9.00

Valdemar's Law of Zealand, 13th Cent. — A593

Njáls Saga, c. 1350 — A594

Litho. & Engr.
2014, Aug. 28   Perf. 13x12¾
1350		Sheet of 2	5.00	5.00
a.	A593	(145k) multi	1.75	1.75
b.	A594	(180k) multi	3.00	3.00

Self-Adhesive
Die Cut Perf. 13¼x13½
| 1351 | A593 | (145k) multi | 1.75 | 1.75 |
| 1352 | A594 | (180k) multi | 3.00 | 3.00 |

See Denmark Nos. 1691-1693.

Sturla Thórdharson (1214-84), Chieftain and Poet — A595

2014, Sept. 11   Litho.   Perf. 13¼
| 1353 | A595 | (310k) multi | 4.00 | 4.00 |

Dyrhólaey Lighthouse A596

Akranes Lighthouse A597

Die Cut Perf. 13¼ at Bottom
2014, Sept. 11
Self-Adhesive
| 1354 | A596 | (125k) multi | 1.75 | 1.75 |

Die Cut Perf. 13¼ at Right
| 1355 | A597 | (240k) multi | 3.00 | 3.00 |

Two Girls with a Doll, by Snorri Arinbjarnar (1901-58) — A598

Búdhin, by Gunnlaugur Scheving (1904-72) A599

Síldarstúlka, by Gunnlaugur Blöndal (1893-1962) A600

Skip vidh Bryggju, by Thorvaldur Skúlason (1906-84) — A601

Perf. 13x13¼, 13¼x13
2014, Nov. 6   Litho.
1356	A598	(125k) multi	1.50	1.50
1357	A599	(145k) multi	1.75	1.75
1358	A600	(180k) multi	3.00	3.00
1359	A601	(630k) multi	9.50	9.50
	Nos. 1356-1359 (4)		15.75	15.75

Nativity A602

Annunciation A603

Adoration of the Magi — A604

Litho. & Thermography
2014, Nov. 6   Die Cut Perf. 14
Self-Adhesive
1360	A602	(125k) lilac & blk	1.50	1.25
a.	Booklet pane of 10		15.00	
1361	A603	(145k) green & blk	1.75	1.25
1362	A604	(180k) sil & blk	3.00	3.00
	Nos. 1360-1362 (3)		6.25	5.50

Christmas.

Bicycles in Iceland, 125th Anniv. — A605

2015, Feb. 19   Litho.
Serpentine Die Cut
Self-Adhesive
| 1363 | A605 | (125k) multi | 1.50 | 1.25 |

Iceland Airwaves Music Festival — A606

2015, Feb. 19   Litho.   Perf. 13¼
| 1364 | A606 | (180k) multi | 2.75 | 2.75 |

Gatastakkur A607

Eldhraun Lava Field A608

2015, Feb. 19   Litho.   Perf. 13¼
| 1365 | A607 | (180k) multi | 2.75 | 2.75 |
| 1366 | A608 | (240k) multi | 2.75 | 2.75 |

Silver Necklace by Asthór Helgason A609

Silver Ring by Gudhbjörg K. Ingvarsdóttir A610

Silver Necklace by Helga Osk Einarsdóttir A611

Brooch by Helga R. Mogensen A612

Perf. 12½x13, 13x12½
2015, Feb. 19   Litho.
1367	A609	(145k) multi	1.75	1.75
1368	A610	(165k) multi	2.50	2.50
1369	A611	(180k) multi	2.75	2.75
1370	A612	(240k) multi	3.00	3.00
	Nos. 1367-1370 (4)		10.00	10.00

Icelandic Bible Society, 200th Anniv. — A613

2015, Apr. 30   Litho.   Perf. 13¼x12¾
| 1371 | A613 | (125k) multi | 1.50 | 1.25 |

Woman Suffrage, Cent. — A614

2015, Apr. 30   Litho.   Perf. 13¼x13¾
| 1372 | A614 | (145k) multi | 1.50 | 1.25 |

16th Games of the Small States of Europe, Iceland — A615

Die Cut Perf. 15¼x14½
2015, Apr. 30   Litho.
Self-Adhesive
| 1373 | A615 | (180k) multi | 2.75 | 2.75 |

A616

Flag of Iceland, Cent. A617

2015, Apr. 30   Litho.   Perf. 13¼
| 1374 | A616 | (145k) multi | 1.75 | 1.75 |

Litho. With Foil Application
Souvenir Sheet
Perf. 13½x13
| 1375 | A617 | (630k) multi | 9.75 | 9.75 |

ICELAND

Toy Duck — A618
Toy Truck — A619

2015, Apr. 30 Litho. Perf. 13½
1376 A618 (180k) multi 2.75 2.75
1377 A619 (240k) multi 3.75 3.75

Booklet Stamps
Self-Adhesive
Die Cut Perf. 13½
1378 A618 (180k) multi 2.75 2.75
  a. Booklet pane of 10 27.50
1379 A619 (240k) multi 3.75 3.75
  a. Booklet pane of 10 37.50
Europa.

Ellidhaey Lighthouse A620
Aedhey Lighthouse A621

Die Cut Perf. 13¼ at Bottom
2015, Sept. 10 Litho.
Self-Adhesive
1380 A620 (153k) multi 2.50 2.50

Die Cut Perf. 13¼ at Right
1381 A621 (180k) multi 3.00 3.00

A622
Old Buildings — A623

Designs: No. 1382, Turf shed, Vatnsfjödhur. No. 1383, Flatey Library. No. 1384, Vigur Windmill. No. 1385, Chuch, Hof.

Die Cut Perf. 14½x14¾
2015, Sept. 10 Litho.
Booklet Stamps
Self-Adhesive
1382 A622 (132k) buff & blk 2.10 2.10
1383 A622 (132k) buff & blk 2.10 2.10
  a. Booklet pane of 4, 2 each
    #1382-1383 8.50
1384 A623 (180k) buff & blk 3.00 3.00
1385 A623 (180k) buff & blk 3.00 3.00
  a. Booklet pane of 4, 2 each
    #1384-1385 12.00
  Nos. 1382-1385 (4) 10.20 10.20

Souvenir Sheet
International Year of Soils — A624

No. 1386: a, Grass. b, Roots.

Perf. 13¾x13¼
2015, Sept. 10 Litho.
1386 A624 Sheet of 2 8.00 8.00
  a.-b. (255k) Either single 4.00 4.00

An Heitis, by Ingibjörg Stein Bjarnason (1901-77) A625

Orlagateningurínn, by Finnur Jónsson (1892-1993) A626

Composition, by Baldvin Björnsson (1879-1945) — A627

Hvítasunnudagsmorgunn, by Jóhannes Kjarval (1885-1972) — A628

2015, Nov. 5 Litho. Perf. 13¼x13
1387 A625 (132k) multi 1.40 1.25
1388 A626 (180k) multi 3.00 3.00
1389 A627 (185k) multi 3.00 3.00

Perf. 13x13¼
1390 A628 (565k) multi 7.00 3.50
  Nos. 1387-1390 (4) 14.40 10.75

Hands, Hot Drinks and Cookies — A629
People Walking on Ice — A630

Computer, Cat, Musical Notes — A631

Litho. With Foil Application
2015, Nov. 5 Die Cut Perf. 11¾x12
Self-Adhesive
1391 A629 (132k) multi 1.40 1.25
  a. Booklet pane of 10 30.00
1392 A630 (153k) multi 2.40 1.20
1393 A631 (180k) multi 2.75 2.75
  Nos. 1391-1393 (3) 6.55 5.20
Christmas.

Icelandic Federation of Labor Unions, Cent. — A632

Perf. 13¼x13½
2016, Feb. 18 Litho.
1394 A632 (137k) multi 1.50 1.25

Isafjördhur, 150th Anniv. — A633

Die Cut Perf. 13¼x13½
2016, Feb. 18 Litho.
Self-Adhesive
1395 A633 (159k) multi 1.50 1.25

Icelandic Literary Society, 200th Anniv. — A634

Die Cut Perf. 15x15¾
2016, Feb. 18 Litho.
Self-Adhesive
1396 A634 (159k) multi 1.50 1.25

Icelandic Foods — A635

Die Cut Perf. 14
2016, Feb. 18 Litho.
Self-Adhesive
1397 A635 (180k) multi 1.50 1.25

Sediments, Ceramic Art by Ólöf Erla Bjarnadóttir A636

Jökla Dinner Service, Designed by Gudhbjörg Káradóttir and Ólöf Jakobina Ernudóttir A637

Dialog, Ceramic Art by Hanna Dís Whitehead A638

Clay Pot, Designed by Bordhidh Design Team A639

Die Cut Perf. 13¼
2016, Feb. 18 Litho.
Self-Adhesive
1398 A636 (137k) multi 2.40 1.20
1399 A637 (180k) multi 2.40 1.75
1400 A638 (255k) multi 3.00 3.00
1401 A639 (490k) multi 3.00 3.00
  Nos. 1398-1401 (4) 10.80 8.95

2014 Eruption of Holuhraun Volcano — A640

Die Cut Perf. 12
2016, Apr. 28 Litho.
Self-Adhesive
1402 A640 (159k) multi 2.60 2.60

Thjofafoss Waterfall A641
Jökulsárlón Glacial Lagoon A642

2016, Apr. 28 Litho. Perf. 13¼
1403 A641 (180k) multi 3.00 3.00
1404 A642 (240k) multi 3.00 3.00

Spring Flowers A643
Butterflies in Summer A644
Snowflakes in Winter A645
Autumn Leaves A646

Die Cut Perf. 14
2016, Apr. 28 Litho.
Self-Adhesive
1405 A643 (137k) multi 1.50 1.20
1406 A644 (159k) multi 3.00 3.00
1407 A645 (310k) multi 4.25 4.25
1408 A646 (985k) multi 6.00 6.00
  Nos. 1405-1408 (4) 14.75 14.45
SEPAC Issue.

A647
Europa — A648

2016, Apr. 28 Litho. Perf. 13¼
1409 A647 (180k) multi 3.00 3.00
1410 A648 (240k) multi 3.00 3.00

Booklet Stamps
Self-Adhesive
Die Cut Perf. 15½x15
1411 A647 (180k) multi 3.00 3.00
  a. Booklet pane of 10 30.00
1412 A648 (240k) multi 3.00 3.00
  a. Booklet pane of 10 30.00
Think Green Issue.

Icelandic National Television Network, 50th Anniv. — A649

2016, Sept. 16 Litho. Die Cut
Self-Adhesive
1413 A649 (160k) multi 1.50 1.25

Actinauge Sp. — A650

Gorgonocephalus Sp. — A651

Die Cut Perf. 13½
2016, Sept. 16 Litho.
Self-Adhesive
1414 A650 (160k) multi 1.50 1.25
1415 A651 (200k) multi 3.00 1.75

Silene Acaulis A652
Silene Uniflora A653

Die Cut Perf. 14x13½
2016, Sept. 16 Litho.
Self-Adhesive
1416 A652 (180k) multi 2.40 1.75
1417 A653 (275k) multi 4.25 3.00

ICELAND

Souvenir Sheet

Wreck of the Research Ship Pourquoi-Pas? Off Iceland, 80th Anniv. — A654

Die Cut Perf. 13¼x13
2016, Sept. 16 Litho.
Self-Adhesive
1418 A654 (480k) multi 5.50 5.50

Composition, by Karl Kvaran (1924-89) A655

Abstraction, by Nina Tryggvadóttir (1913-68) A656

Á Svörtum Grunni, by Valtýr Pétursson (1919-88) A657

Málverk, by Thorvaldur Skúlason (1906-84) A658

2016, Nov. 3 Litho. *Perf. 13¼x13*
1419 A655 (175k) multi 2.50 1.25
1420 A656 (310k) multi 4.25 4.25
1421 A657 (480k) multi 5.50 5.50
1422 A658 (490k) multi 4.25 4.25
     Nos. 1419-1422 (4)   16.50 15.25

Star of Bethlehem Sweater Design A659

Candle Sweater Design A660

Christmas Ornament Sweater Design — A661

Die Cut Perf. 13½
2016, Nov. 3 Litho.
Self-Adhesive
1423 A659 (160k) multi 1.50 1.25
   a. Booklet pane of 10   15.00
1424 A660 (175k) multi 2.50 1.25
1425 A661 (180k) multi 3.00 3.00
     Nos. 1423-1425 (3)   7.00 5.50

A662

Design: Prime Minister Jón Magnússon, Labor Minister Sigurdur Jonsson, Finance Minister Björn Kristjánsson.

Die Cut Perf. 14¾x16
2017, Feb. 16 Litho.
Self-Adhesive
1426 A662 (160k) multi 1.50 1.25
First Icelandic government, cent.

Reykjavik Craftsmen Guild, 150th Anniv. — A663

Die Cut Perf. 14
2017, Feb. 16 Litho.
Self-Adhesive
1427 A663 (160k) multi 1.50 1.25

Laekjartorg Kiosk, Reykjavik, Designed by Rögnvaldur Olafsson (1874-1917) — A664

Die Cut Perf. 13x12¼
2017, Feb. 16 Litho.
Self-Adhesive
1428 A664 (175k) multi 1.50 1.25

Scarf by Vík Prjónsdóttir A665

Felt Sound Absorber by Bryndís Bolladóttir A666

Textile Art by Ragna Fróðhadóttir A667

Spring/Summer 2016, Textile by Anita Hirlekar A668

Die Cut Perf. 13¼
2017, Feb. 16 Litho.
Self-Adhesive
1429 A665 (160k) multi 1.50 1.25
1430 A666 (175k) multi 1.50 1.25
1431 A667 (480k) multi 5.50 4.25
1432 A668 (565k) multi 7.50 3.75
     Nos. 1429-1432 (4)   16.00 10.50

Icelandic Sweater — A669

Die Cut Perf. 13¼
2017, Apr. 27 Litho.
Self-Adhesive
Flocked Paper
1433 A669 (225k) multi 3.00 3.00

Kid — A670

Kitten — A671

Die Cut Perf. 14
2017, Apr. 27 Litho.
Self-Adhesive
1434 A670 (160k) multi 1.50 1.25
1435 A671 (175k) multi 1.50 1.25

Blue Lagoon — A672

Myvatn Nature Baths — A673

Die Cut Perf. 14
2017, Apr. 27 Litho.
Self-Adhesive
1436 A672 (200k) multi 2.50 2.50
1437 A673 (250k) multi 2.50 2.50
International Year of Sustainable Tourism for Development.

Horses and Rider — A674

Glacier Tour — A675

2017, Apr. 27 Litho. *Perf. 13*
1438 A674 (225k) multi 3.00 3.00
1439 A675 (285k) multi 3.00 3.00
Tourism.

Castle in the Air A676

Snow Castle A677

Die Cut Perf. 16x15
2017, Apr. 27 Litho.
Self-Adhesive
1440 A676 (340k) multi 4.25 4.25
1441 A677 (535k) multi 4.25 4.25
Europa.

Title Page of First Icelandic Translation of the New Testament — A678

Die Cut Perf. 13½
2017, Sept. 14 Litho.
Self-Adhesive
1442 A678 (180k) multi 2.50 1.25
Protestant Reformation, 500th anniv.

Iceland Chamber of Commerce, Cent. — A679

Die Cut Perf. 14
2017, Sept. 14 Litho.
Self-Adhesive
1443 A679 (195k) multi 3.00 1.25

Acesta Excavata A680

Madrepora Oculata A681

Die Cut Perf. 13¼x13
2017, Sept. 14 Litho.
Self-Adhesive
1444 A680 (195k) multi 3.00 1.25
1445 A681 (300k) multi 3.50 2.50

Xanthoria Parietina A682

Placopis Gelida A683

Die Cut Perf. 14x13½
2017, Sept. 14 Litho.
Self-Adhesive
1446 A682 (180k) multi 2.50 1.25
1447 A683 (470k) multi 3.50 2.50

Souvenir Sheet

Stamp Day A684

2017, Sept. 14 Litho. *Perf. 13¼*
1448 A684 (630k) black 10.00 10.00
Foriegn expeditions to Iceland, 250th anniv.

Painting, by Kristján Davidhsson (1917-2013) A685

Untitled Painting by Hafsteinn Austmann A686

Composition, by Eiríkur Smith A687

Organ Fugue, Sculpture by Gerdur Helgadóttir (1928-75) A688

Perf. 13x13¼, 13¼x13
2017, Nov. 2 Litho.
1449 A685 (180k) multi 2.50 1.25
1450 A686 (195k) multi 3.00 1.25
1451 A687 (285k) multi 5.50 3.00
1452 A688 (650k) multi 6.00 6.00
     Nos. 1449-1452 (4)   17.00 11.50

Santa Claus Near Window of House A689

Santa Clauses Watching Children Carrying Christmas Tree A690

213

ICELAND

Santa Claus and Children on Sled — A691

Die Cut Perf. 14x14¼
2017, Nov. 2   Litho.
Self-Adhesive
1453 A689 (180k) multi   2.50   1.25
1454 A690 (195k) multi   3.00   1.25
1455 A691 (225k) multi   4.25   3.00
    Nos. 1453-1455 (3)   9.75   5.50
    Christmas.

National Library of Iceland, 200th Anniv. — A692

Die Cut Perf. 14x14½
2018, Feb. 15   Litho.
Self-Adhesive
1456 A692 (195k) multi   3.00   1.25

Jón Thoroddsen (1818-68), Writer A693

Die Cut Perf. 14½x14¼
2018, Feb. 15   Litho.
Self-Adhesive
1457 A693 (200k) multi   3.00   1.25

Ellidaár Estuary Footbridge A694

Jökulsá River Suspension Bridge — A695

Die Cut Perf. 14
2018, Feb. 15   Litho.
Self-Adhesive
1458 A694 (225k) multi   3.00   3.00
1459 A695 (285k) multi   4.25   3.00

Althing and Supreme Court — A696

Cabinet Building — A697

Die Cut Perf. 14
2018, Feb. 15   Litho.
Self-Adhesive
1460 A696 (180k) shown   1.50   1.25
1461 A697 (195k) shown   3.00   1.25
    Souvenir Sheet
    Stamps Inscribed "1000 grömm innanlands"
Die Cut Perf. 13½ on 5 Sides
1462   Sheet of 2   10.00   10.00
   a. A696 (480k) multi   5.00   5.00
   b. A697 (480k) multi   5.00   5.00
    Icelandic independence, cent.

Siglufjördhur, Cent. — A698

Die Cut Perf. 12½x14
2018, Apr. 26   Litho.
Self-Adhesive
1463 A698 (195k) multi   3.00   1.25

Nordic House, Reykjavik, 50th Anniv. — A699

Die Cut Perf. 13¼
2018, Apr. 26   Litho.
Self-Adhesive
1464 A699 (195k) multi   3.00   1.25

Qualification of Iceland's National Team for 2018 World Cup Soccer Championships, Russia — A700

Die Cut Perf. 14x13½
2018, Apr. 26   Litho.
Self-Adhesive
1465 A700 (195k) multi   3.00   1.25

Pelecanus Niger Cristatus, Minerals and Codfish — A701

Die Cut Perf. 14
2018, Apr. 26   Litho.
Self-Adhesive
1466 A701 (220k) multi   3.00   1.25
    Eggert Olafsson (1726-68), naturalist.

Calf — A702   Lamb — A703

Die Cut Perf. 14
2018, Apr. 26   Litho.
Self-Adhesive
1467 A702 (180k) multi   2.50   1.25
1468 A703 (195k) multi   3.00   1.25

Kayaking A704   Spelunking A705

2018, Apr. 26   Litho.   Perf. 13¼x13
1469 A704 (225k) multi   3.00   3.00
    Perf. 13x13¼
1470 A705 (285k) multi   4.25   3.00

Souvenir Sheet

Icelandic Farm, Embroidery by Thórdis Egilsdóttir (1878-1961) — A706

2018, Apr. 26   Litho.   Perf. 13¼x13
1471 A706 (630k) multi   12.50   12.50
    Nordia 2018 Philatelic Exhibition, Gardhabaer.

Bifröst University, Borgarfjördur, Cent. — A707

Die Cut Perf. 14
2018, Sept. 13   Litho.
Self-Adhesive
1472 A707 (180k) multi   3.00   1.25

Ship, Scomber Scrombus and Mallotus Villosus — A708

Die Cut Perf. 14¼x14½
2018, Sept. 13   Litho.
Self-Adhesive
1473 A708 (225k) multi   3.00   3.00

Vestrahorn A709

Die Cut Perf. 14½x14¼
2018, Sept. 13   Litho.
Self-Adhesive
1474 A709 (225k) multi   3.00   3.00

Mechanized Agriculture in Iceland, Cent. — A710

Die Cut Perf. 13¼x13½
2018, Sept. 13   Litho.
Self-Adhesive
1475 A710 (500k) multi   6.00   4.25

Mycale Lingua — A711   Laetmogone Violacea — A712

Die Cut Perf. 13¼x13½
2018, Sept. 13   Litho.
Self-Adhesive
1476 A711 (200k) multi   3.00   3.00
1477 A712 (250k) multi   4.25   3.00

Collage, by Sigurdur Gudmundsson A713

Attending, by Hreinn Fridfinnsson A714

Heart, by Jón Gunnar Arnason A715

Time and I, by Róska A716

Perf. 13x13¼, 13¼x13
2018, Nov. 1   Litho.
1478 A713 (180k) multi   3.00   1.25
1479 A714 (225k) multi   3.00   3.00
1480 A715 (285k) multi   4.25   3.00
1481 A716 (1075k) multi   7.25   7.25
    Nos. 1478-1481 (4)   17.50   14.50

Gingerbread Cookie in Shape of Christmas Tree — A717

Gingerbread Cookie in Shape of Star — A718

Die Cut Perf. 15¼x14¾
2018, Nov. 1   Litho.
Self-Adhesive
1482 A717 (180k) multi   3.00   1.25
1483 A718 (225k) multi   3.00   3.00
    Christmas. Nos. 1482-1483 are inpregnated with a gingerbread scent.

Lady of the Mountain — A719

Die Cut Perf. 13¾x14
2019, Feb. 7   Litho.
Self-Adhesive
1484 A719 (180k) multi   3.00   1.25
    Republic of Iceland, 75th anniv.

Vestmannaeyjar Municipality, Cent. — A720

Die Cut Perf. 14½x14¼
2019, Feb. 7   Litho.
Self-Adhesive
1485 A720 (180k) multi   3.00   1.25

Icelandic Postal Workers Union, Cent. — A721

ICELAND

2019, Feb. 7 — Die Cut Perf. 12 — Self-Adhesive — Litho.
1486 A721 (180k) multi 3.00 1.25

Thermal Beach, Gardhbaer — A722
Brimketill Pool Pathway — A723
Saxhóll Crater Pathway — A724
Bragginn Restaurant, Nauthólsvik — A725

2019, Feb. 7 — Die Cut Perf. 13½ — Self-Adhesive — Litho.
1487 A722 (180k) multi 3.00 1.25
1488 A723 (225k) multi 3.00 3.00
1489 A724 (285k) multi 4.25 3.00
1490 A725 (650k) multi 7.25 7.25
Nos. 1487-1490 (4) 17.50 14.50

Aerial views of landscape architecture.

Icelandic Midwives Association, Cent. — A726

2019, Apr. 11 — Die Cut Perf. 14x13½ — Self-Adhesive — Litho.
1491 A726 (180k) multi 3.00 1.25

Puppy — A727
Foal — A728

2019, Apr. 11 — Die Cut Perf. 14 — Self-Adhesive — Litho.
1492 A727 (180k) multi 3.00 1.25
1493 A728 (225k) multi 3.00 3.00

Haliaeetus Albicilla — A729
Falco Rusticolus Islandicus — A730

2019, Apr. 11 — Die Cut Perf. 13½x13¼ — Self-Adhesive — Litho.
1494 A729 (225k) multi 3.00 3.00
1495 A730 (285k) multi 4.25 3.00

Europa.

Diver in Thingvellir National Park Gorge — A731
Man Viewing Aurora Borealis — A732

2019, Apr. 11 — Litho. — Perf. 13
1496 A731 (225k) multi 3.00 3.00
1497 A732 (285k) multi 4.25 3.00

Aviation in Iceland, Cent. — A733

2019, Sept. 12 — Die Cut Perf. 14¼ — Self-Adhesive — Litho.
1498 A733 (195k) multi 3.00 3.00

Icelandic Nurse's Association, Cent. — A734

2019, Sept. 12 — Die Cut Perf. 14½x15 — Self-Adhesive — Litho.
1499 A734 (195k) multi 3.00 3.00

Legend of the Elves in Tungustapi, by Asgrimur Jónsson — A735

2019, Sept. 12 — Die Cut Perf. 14 — Self-Adhesive — Litho.
1500 A735 (230k) multi 3.75 3.75

Jón Arnason (1819-88), folklorist.

Factor's House, Nedstikaupstadhur — A736

2019, Sept. 12 — Die Cut Perf. 14 — Self-Adhesive — Litho.
1501 A736 (250k) multi 4.00 4.00

Souvenir Sheet

Icelandic Nature Day — A737

2019, Sept. 12 — Litho. — Perf. 13
1502 A737 Sheet of 2 18.00 18.00
a.-b. (550k) Either single 9.00 9.00

No. 1502 — Various plants with white panel at: a, Top. b, Bottom.

The Realm of Poseidon, by Helgi Thorgils Fridhjónsson — A738
Calda, Calda, Heit, Heitt, by Dadhi Gudhbjörnsson — A739

Sculpture by Brynhildur Thorgeirsdottir — A740
Untitled Painting by Jón Axel Björnsson — A741

2019, Oct. 31 — Perf. 13x13¼, 13¼x13 — Litho.
1503 A738 (195k) multi 3.25 3.25
1504 A739 (250k) multi 4.00 4.00
1505 A740 (315k) multi 5.25 5.25
1506 A741 (720k) multi 12.00 12.00
Nos. 1503-1506 (4) 24.50 24.50

Candle-lit Homemade Christmas Tree From Hruni — A742
Candle-lit Homemade Christmas Tree From Laugardaelir — A743

2019, Oct. 31 — Die Cut Perf. 14 — Self-Adhesive — Litho.
1507 A742 (195k) multi 3.25 3.25
1508 A743 (250k) multi 4.00 4.00

Equal Voting Rights for Icelandic Citizens, Cent. — A744

2020, May 7 — Die Cut Perf. 14x13½ — Self-Adhesive — Litho.
1509 A744 (195k) multi 3.00 3.00

Supreme Court of Iceland, Cent. — A745

2020, May 7 — Die Cut Perf. 13¼ — Self-Adhesive — Litho.
1510 A745 (195k) multi 3.00 3.00

Icelandic Meteorological Office, Cent. — A746

2020, May 7 — Die Cut Perf. 14½ — Self-Adhesive — Litho.
1511 A746 (195k) multi 3.00 3.00

Reykjavik Arts Festival, 50th Anniv. — A747

2020, May 7 — Die Cut Perf. 13x12 — Self-Adhesive — Litho.
1512 A747 (250k) multi 3.75 3.75

Iceland Membership in European Free Trade Association, 50th Anniv. — A748

2020, May 7 — Die Cut Perf. 13¼ — Self-Adhesive — Litho.
1513 A748 (550k) multi 8.25 8.25

Chick — A749
Piglet — A750

2020, May 7 — Litho. — Die Cut Perf. 14 — Self-Adhesive
1514 A749 (250k) multi 3.75 3.75
1515 A750 (315k) multi 4.75 4.75

White-water Rafting — A751
Whale Watching — A752

2020, May 7 — Litho. — Die Cut Perf. 14 — Self-Adhesive
1516 A751 (250k) multi 3.75 3.75
1517 A752 (315k) multi 4.75 4.75

Postal Route Around Iceland — A753
First Icelandic Postal Route — A754

2020, May 7 — Litho. — Die Cut Perf. 14 — Self-Adhesive
1518 A753 (250k) multi 3.75 3.75
1519 A754 (315k) multi 4.75 4.75

Europa.

Icelandic Land Commission, 250th Anniv. — A755

2020, Oct. 29 — Die Cut Perf. 13¼ — Self-Adhesive — Litho.
1520 A755 (195k) multi 2.75 2.75

Skjaldbredhur, Painting by Jón Stefánsson (1881-1962) — A756

2020, Oct. 29 — Die Cut Perf. 14¾ — Self-Adhesive — Litho.
1521 A756 (250k) multi 3.75 3.75

Mustela Vison — A757

ICELAND

Die Cut Perf. 13½x14
2020, Oct. 29   Litho.   Self-Adhesive
1522	A757	(250k) multi	3.75	3.75

Carrots A758
Beet A759

Die Cut Perf. 15¼x14½
2020, Oct. 29   Litho.   Self-Adhesive
1523	A758	(230k) multi	3.25	3.25
1524	A759	(315k) multi	4.50	4.50

A760
A761

Order of the Falcon, Cent. — A762

Die Cut Perf. 12
2020, Oct. 29   Litho.   Self-Adhesive
1525	A760	(195k) multi	2.75	2.75
1526	A761	(250k) multi	3.75	3.75
1527	A762	(315k) multi	4.50	4.50
	Nos. 1525-1527 (3)		11.00	11.00

Souvenir Sheet

Sturlung Era, 800th Anniv. A763

No. 1528 — Man with: a, Halbard. b, Sword and severed leg.

2020, Oct. 29   Litho.   Perf. 13½x13¼
1528	A763	Sheet of 2	16.00	16.00
a.-b.		(550k) Either single	8.00	8.00

Ptarmigan A764
Fox A765

Die Cut Perf. 14¼x14½
2020, Oct. 29   Litho.   Self-Adhesive
1529	A764	(195k) multi	2.75	2.75
1530	A765	(250k) multi	3.75	3.75

Christmas.

SEMI-POSTAL STAMPS

Shipwreck and Rescue by Breeches Buoy — SP1

Children Gathering Rock Plants — SP2

Old Fisherman at Shore — SP3

1933, Apr. 28   Unwmk.   Engr.   Perf. 14
B1	SP1	10a + 10a red brown	1.75	6.00
B2	SP2	20a + 20a org red	1.75	6.00
B3	SP1	35a + 25a ultra	1.75	6.00
B4	SP3	50a + 25a blue grn	1.75	6.00
	Nos. B1-B4 (4)		7.00	24.00
	Set, never hinged		14.00	

Receipts from the surtax were devoted to a special fund for use in various charitable works especially those indicated on the stamps: "Slysavarnir" (Rescue work), "Barnahaeli" (Asylum for scrofulous children), "Ellhaeli" (Asylum for the Aged).

Souvenir Sheets

King Christian X — SP4

1937, May 15   Typo.
B5	SP4	Sheet of 3	36.00	300.00
	Never hinged		90.00	
a.		15a violet	9.50	55.00
b.		25a red	9.50	55.00
c.		50a blue	9.50	55.00

Reign of Christian X, 25th anniv. Sheet sold for 2kr.

SP5

1938, Oct. 9   Photo.   Perf. 12
B6	SP5	Sheet of 3	5.00	30.00
	Never hinged		10.00	
a.		30a scarlet	1.25	12.00
b.		40a purple	1.25	12.00
c.		60a deep green	1.25	12.00

Designs: 30a, 40a, Ericsson statue, Reykjavik. 60a, Iceland's position on globe.

Leif Ericsson Day, Oct. 9, 1938.

Catalogue values for unused stamps in this section, from this point to the end of the section, are for Never Hinged items.

Ill Child SP6

Red Cross Nurse and Patient SP7

Nurse Covering Patient SP8

Elderly Couple SP9

Rescue at Sea — SP10

1949, June 8   Unwmk.   Engr.   Perf. 14
B7	SP6	10a + 10a olive grn	.85	1.40
B8	SP7	35a + 15a carmine	.85	1.40
B9	SP8	50a + 25a choc	.85	1.40
B10	SP9	60a + 25a brt ultra	.85	1.40
B11	SP10	75a + 25a slate gray	.85	1.40
	Nos. B7-B11 (5)		4.25	7.00

The surtax was for charitable purposes.

Nos. 262 and 265 Surcharged in Black

1953, Feb. 12   Unwmk.   Perf. 13
B12	A50	75a + 25a red org	1.40	5.25
B13	A50	1.25k + 25a red vio	2.40	5.25

The surtax was for flood relief in the Netherlands.

St. Thorlacus SP11

Cathedral at Skalholt SP12

1.75k+1.25k, Bishop Jon Thorkelsson Vidalin.

1956, Jan. 23   Perf. 11½
B14	SP11	75a + 25a car	.25	.25
B15	SP12	1.25k + 75a dk brn	.25	.60
B16	SP11	1.75k + 1.25k black	1.00	1.75
	Nos. B14-B16 (3)		1.50	2.60

Bishopric of Skalholt, 900th anniv. The surtax was for the rebuilding of Skalholt, former cultural center of Iceland.

Ambulance — SP13

1963, Nov. 15   Photo.   Unwmk.
B17	SP13	3k + 50a multi	.45	1.40
B18	SP13	3.50k + 50a multi	.45	1.40

Centenary of International Red Cross.

Rock Ptarmigan in Summer — SP14

Design: #B20, Rock ptarmigan in winter.

1965, Jan. 27   Photo.   Perf. 12½
Granite Paper
B19	SP14	3.50k + 50a multi	.85	2.40
B20	SP14	4.50k + 50a multi	.85	2.40

Ringed Plover's Nest — SP15

Design: 5k+50a, Rock ptarmigan's nest.

1967, Nov. 22   Photo.   Perf. 11½
B21	SP15	4k + 50a multi	.85	1.75
B22	SP15	5k + 50a multi	.85	1.75

Arctic Terns — SP16

1972, Nov. 22   Litho.   Perf. 13
B23	SP16	7k + 1k multi	.75	1.25
B24	SP16	9k + 1k multi	.75	1.25

AIR POST STAMPS

No. 115 Overprinted

Perf. 14x14½
1928, May 31   Wmk. 114
C1	A8	10a red	.85	12.00
	Never hinged		1.75	
	Revenue cancellation			—

Same Overprint on No. 82

1929, June 29   Wmk. 113   Perf. 13
C2	A5	50a gray & violet	60.00	120.00
	Never hinged		210.00	
	Revenue cancellation			—

Gyrfalcon — AP1

Perf. 12½x12
1930, Jan. 1   Litho.   Unwmk.
C3	AP1	10a dp ultra & gray blue	18.00	75.00
	Never hinged		52.50	

Imperfs were privately printed. For overprint see No. CO1.

Snaefellsjokull, Extinct Volcano — AP2

Parliament Millenary: 20a, Fishing boat. 35a, Iceland pony. 50a, Gullfoss (Golden Falls). 1k, Ingolfour Arnarson Statue.

Wmk. 47
1930, June 1   Typo.   Perf. 14
C4	AP2	15a org brn & dl bl	24.00	55.00
C5	AP2	20a bis brn & sl bl	24.00	55.00
C6	AP2	35a olive grn & brn	52.50	120.00
C7	AP2	50a dp grn & dp bl	52.50	120.00
C8	AP2	1k olive grn & dk red	52.50	120.00
	Nos. C4-C8 (5)		205.50	470.00
	Set, never hinged		510.00	

Regular Issue of 1920 Overprinted

Perf. 14x14½
1931, May 25   Wmk. 114
C9	A8	30a red & green	35.00	160.00
C10	A8	1k dp bl & dk brn	12.00	100.00
C11	A8	2k ol brn & myr grn	50.00	160.00
	Nos. C9-C11 (3)		97.00	440.00
	Set, never hinged		215.00	

ICELAND

Nos. 185, 128 and 187 Overprinted in Red

1933, June 16

C12	A8	1k dk bl & lt brn	175. 725.
		Never hinged	525.
C13	A8	5k brn & indigo	600. 1,600.
		Never hinged	1,600.
C14	A8	10k yel grn & blk	1,300. 3,000.
		Never hinged	3,350.

Excellent counterfeit overprints exist.

Visit of the Italian Flying Armada en route from Rome to Chicago; also for the payment of the charges on postal matter sent from Iceland to the US via the Italian seaplanes.

Plane over Thingvalla Lake — AP7

10a-20a, Plane over Thingvalla Lake. 25a-50a, Plane and Aurora Borealis. 1k-2k, Map of Iceland.

1934, Sept. 1   Engr.   Unwmk.   Perf. 12½x14

C15	AP7	10a blue	1.50 3.50
		Revenue cancellation	18.00
C16	AP7	20a emerald	4.25 8.50
		Revenue cancellation	8.50
a.		Perf. 14	30.00 21.00
		Revenue cancellation	50.00
C17	AP7	25a dk vio, perf. 14	11.00 19.00
		Revenue cancellation	47.50
a.		Perf. 12½x14	30.00 35.00
		Never hinged	115.00
		Revenue cancellation	47.50
C18	AP7	50a red vio, perf. 14	3.00 8.00
		Revenue cancellation	24.00
C19	AP7	1k dark brown	15.00 35.00
		Revenue cancellation	24.00
C20	AP7	2k red orange	7.25 14.50
		Revenue cancellation	24.00
		Nos. C15-C20 (6)	42.00 88.50
		Set, never hinged	150.00

Catalogue values for unused stamps in this section, from this point to the end of the section, are for Never Hinged items.

Thingvellir, Old Site of the Parliament AP10

Ísafjörður AP11

Eyjafjörður AP12

Mt. Strandatindur AP13

Mt. Thyrill AP14

Aerial View of Reykjavik AP15

1947, Aug. 18   Perf. 14

C21	AP10	15a red orange	.85 1.50
C22	AP11	30a gray black	.85 1.50
C23	AP12	75a brown red	.85 1.25
C24	AP13	1k indigo	.85 1.25
C25	AP14	2k chocolate	1.50 2.50
C26	AP15	3k dark green	1.50 2.50
		Nos. C21-C26 (6)	6.40 10.50

Snaefellsjokull AP16

Views: 2.50k, Eiriksjokull. 3.30k, Oraefajokull.

1952, May 2   Unwmk.   Perf. 13½x14

C27	AP16	1.80k slate blue	17.50 15.00
C28	AP16	2.50k green	30.00 1.25
C29	AP16	3.30k deep ultra	7.00 9.50
		Nos. C27-C29 (3)	54.50 25.75

See Nos. 302-304.

Vickers Viscount and Plane of 1919 — AP17

1959, Sept. 3   Engr.   Perf. 13½

C30	AP17	3.50k steel blue	1.00 .85
C31	AP17	4.05k green	.85 1.25

40th anniv. of air transportation in Iceland.

AIR POST OFFICIAL STAMPS

No. C3 Overprinted In Red

1930, Jan. 1   Unwmk.   Perf. 12½x12

CO1	AP1	10a dp ultra & gray blue	25.00 140.00

Imperfs were privately printed.

OFFICIAL STAMPS

For Nos. O1-O12, see note on condition before No. 1.

O1

Perf. 14x13½

1873   Typo.   Wmk. 112

O1	O1	4s green	9,000. 10,000.
a.		Imperf.	150.
O2	O1	8s red lilac	700. 725.
a.		Imperf.	600.

Perf. 12½

O3	O1	4s green	110. 400.
		Never hinged	350.00

The imperforate varieties lack gum.

No. O1 values are for stamps with perfs just touching the design on at least one side. Fake and favor cancellations are often found on Nos. O1-O37. Values are considerably less than those shown.

O2

1876-95   Perf. 14x13½

O4	O2	3a yellow ('82)	45.00 60.00
O5	O2	5a brown ('78)	9.50 17.50
a.		Imperf.	450.00
O6	O2	10a blue ('84)	85.00 16.00
a.		10a ultramarine	475.00 85.00
O7	O2	16a carmine	35.00 60.00
O8	O2	20a green	35.00 50.00
O9	O2	50a rose lilac ('95)	90.00 95.00
		Nos. O4-O9 (6)	299.50 298.50
		Set, never hinged	975.00

1896-1900   Perf. 13

O10	O2	3a yellow	15.00 35.00
O11	O2	4a gray ('00)	35.00 50.00
O11A	O2	5a brown ('98)	— —
O12	O2	10a ultra ('98)	65.00 120.00
O12A	O2	20a yel grn ('98)	— —
		Nos. O10-O12 (5)	115.00 205.00
		Set, never hinged	360.00

Nos. O11A and O12A were not regularly issued.

See note after No. O30.

For overprints see Nos. O20-O30.

O3

1902   Wmk. 113   Perf. 13

O13	O3	3a dull org & blksh brn	5.00 3.00
O14	O3	4a blk grn & blksh	5.00 2.50
O15	O3	5a org brn & blksh	4.00 5.00
O16	O3	10a ultra & blksh brn	4.00 5.00
O17	O3	16a carmine & blksh brn	4.00 20.00
O18	O3	20a lt grn & blksh brn	25.00 8.50
O19	O3	50a vio & blksh brn	8.00 12.50
		Nos. O13-O19 (7)	55.00 56.50
		Set, never hinged	200.00

Stamps of 1876-1901 Overprinted in Black

1902-03   Wmk. 112   Perf. 13

O20	O2	3a yellow	1.25 3.00
a.		"I" before Gildi omitted	175.00
b.		Inverted overprint	42.50 65.00
c.		As "a," invtd.	200.00
d.		Pair, one without ovpt.	190.00
e.		'03-'03	500.00
f.		02'-'03	500.00
O21	O2	4a gray	1.25 2.75
a.		"I" before Gildi omitted	175.00
b.		Inverted overprint	60.00 75.00
e.		'03-'03	525.00
f.		02'-'03	525.00
g.		Pair, one without ovpt.	225.00
i.		"L" only of "I GILDI" inverted	—
O22	O2	5a brown	1.00 2.75
a.		Double overprint	225.00
O23	O2	10a ultramarine	1.00 2.75
a.		"I" before Gildi omitted	275.00
b.		Inverted overprint	55.00 75.00
c.		'03-'03	425.00
d.		02'-'03	425.00
e.		"L" only of "I GILDI"	60.00 90.00
f.		As "e," inverted	425.00
g.		"IL" only of "I GILDI"	225.00 275.00
O24	O2	20a yel green	1.00 25.00
		Nos. O20-O24 (5)	5.50 36.25
		Set, never hinged	10.00

Perf. 14x13½

O25	O2	3a yellow	325.00 1,400.
a.		"02'-'03"	1,100.
b.		'03-'03	1,200.
O26	O2	5a brown	8.00 175.00
a.		Inverted overprint	90.00
b.		'03-'03	425.00
c.		02'-'03	425.00
d.		"L" only of "I GILDI" inverted	
O27	O2	10a blue	425.00 750.00
a.		"I" before Gildi omitted	825.00 850.00
b.		'03-'03	950.00
c.		02'-'03	950.00
O28	O2	16a carmine	18.00 75.00
a.		"I" before Gildi omitted	650.00
c.		Dbl. ovpt., one inverted	425.00
d.		Inverted overprint	700.00
e.		'03-'03	700.00
f.		02'-'03	700.00
O29	O2	20a yel green	35.00 95.00
a.		Inverted overprint	175.00 190.00
b.		'03-'03	500.00
c.		02'-'03	500.00
O30	O2	50a red lilac	6.00 60.00
a.		"I" before Gildi omitted	50.00 110.00
b.		Inverted overprint	190.00
		Nos. O25-O30 (6)	817.00 2,555.
		Set, never hinged	1,800.

Nos. O10-O12A, O20-O24, O28 and O30 were reprinted in 1904. They have the watermark of 1902 (type 113) and are perf. 13. Value $65 each. Without overprint $90 each.

Christian IX, Frederik VIII — O4

Engraved Center

1907-08   Wmk. 113   Perf. 13

O31	O4	3a yellow & gray	7.00 8.00
O32	O4	4a green & gray	3.50 9.00
O33	O4	5a brn org & gray	11.00 4.50
O34	O4	10a deep bl & gray	2.50 3.25
O35	O4	15a lt blue & gray	4.75 9.00
O36	O4	16a carmine & gray	4.75 30.00
O37	O4	20a yel grn & gray	20.00 6.00
O38	O4	50a violet & gray	7.00 11.00
		Nos. O31-O38 (8)	60.50 80.75
		Set, never hinged	240.00

1918   Wmk. 114   Perf. 14x14½

O39	O4	15a lt bl & gray	12.00 35.00

Christian X — O5

1920-30   Typo.

O40	O5	3a yellow & gray	5.00 4.25
		Revenue cancellation	
O41	O5	4a dp grn & gray	1.25 3.75
		Revenue cancellation	
O42	O5	5a orange & gray	1.25 1.75
		Revenue cancellation	
O43	O5	10a dk bl & gray	35.00 1.40
		Revenue cancellation	
O44	O5	15a lt blue & gray	.65 1.25
		Revenue cancellation	
O45	O5	20a yel grn & gray	50.00 4.50
		Revenue cancellation	
O46	O5	50a violet & gray	45.00 2.75
		Revenue cancellation	
O47	O5	1k car & gray	45.00 2.25
		Revenue cancellation	
O48	O5	2k bl & blk ('30)	5.00 21.00
		Revenue cancellation	
O49	O5	5k brn & blk ('30)	30.00 55.00
		Revenue cancellation	
		Nos. O40-O49 (10)	218.15 97.90
		Set, never hinged	875.00

See No. O68.

Nos. 97 and 98 Overprinted

1922, May   Wmk. 113   Perf. 13

O50	A7	2k rose, larger letters, no period	25.00 60.00
a.		Smaller letters, with period	95.00 60.00
O51	A7	5k brown	240.00 260.00

No. 115 Surcharged

1923   Wmk. 114   Perf. 14x14½

O52	A8	20a on 10a red	30.00 2.40
		Revenue cancellation	

Parliament Millenary Issue

#152-166 Overprinted in Red or Blue

1930, Jan. 1   Unwmk.   Perf. 12½x12

O53	A15	3a (R)	15.00 45.00
O54	A15	5a (R)	15.00 45.00
O55	A15	7a (R)	15.00 45.00
O56	A15	10a (Bl)	15.00 45.00
O57	A15	15a (R)	15.00 45.00
O58	A15	20a (Bl)	15.00 45.00
O59	A15	25a (Bl)	15.00 45.00
O60	A15	30a (R)	15.00 45.00
O61	A15	35a (R)	15.00 45.00
O62	A15	40a (Bl)	15.00 45.00
O63	A15	50a (Bl)	140.00 350.00
O64	A15	1k (R)	140.00 350.00
O65	A15	2k (R)	175.00 400.00
O66	A15	5k (Bl)	140.00 350.00
O67	A15	10k (Bl)	140.00 350.00
		Nos. O53-O67 (15)	885.00 2,250.
		Set, never hinged	2,250.

Type of 1920 Issue Redrawn

1931   Wmk. 114   Typo.

O68	O5	20a yel grn & gray	45.00 3.00

For differences in redrawing see note after No. 187.

No. 82 Overprinted in Black

Overprint 15mm long

1936, Dec. 7   Wmk. 113   Perf. 13

O69	A5	50a gray & vio	25.00 30.00

ICELAND — IFNI

Same Overprint on Nos. 180 and 115

Perf. 14x14½
Wmk. 114

O70	A8	7a yellow green	2.40	24.00
O71	A8	10a red	15.00	2.25
		Nos. O69-O71 (3)	42.40	56.25

IFNI
'if-nē

LOCATION — An enclave in southern Morocco on the Atlantic coast
GOVT. — Spanish possession
AREA — 580 sq. mi.
POP. — 51,517 (est. 1964)
CAPITAL — Sidi Ifni

Ifni was ceded to Spain by Morocco in 1860, but the Spanish did not occupy it until 1934. Sidi Ifni was also the administrative capital for Spanish West Africa. Spain turned Ifni back to Morocco June 30, 1969.

100 Centimos = 1 Peseta

Catalogue values for unused stamps in this country are for Never Hinged items, beginning with Scott 28 in the regular postage section, Scott B1 in the semipostal section, and Scott C38 in the airpost section.

Stamps of Spain, 1936-40, Overprinted in Red or Blue

1941-42 Unwmk. Imperf.

1	A159	1c green	5.00	4.50
		Perf. 10 to 11		
2	A160	2c org brn (Bl)	5.00	4.50
3	A161	5c gray brown	.90	.90
5	A161	10c dk car (Bl)	3.00	1.90
a.		Red overprint	17.50	8.25
6	A161	15c lt green	.90	.90
7	A166	20c brt violet	.90	.90
8	A166	25c deep claret	.90	.90
9	A166	30c blue	.90	.90
10	A166	40c Prus green	1.00	.90
11	A166	50c indigo	5.50	1.75
12	A166	70c blue	5.50	4.00
13	A166	1p gray black	5.50	4.00
14	A166	2p dull brown	67.50	95.00
15	A166	4p dl rose (Bl)	210.00	160.00
16	A166	10p light brn	700.00	475.00
		Nos. 1-16 (15)	1,013.	756.05
		Set, never hinged	1,650.	

Counterfeit overprints exist.

Nomads A1

Marksman A2

Alcazaba Fortress — A2a

1943 Litho. Perf. 12½

17	A1	1c brn & lil rose	.30	.25
18	A2	2c yel grn & sl lil	.30	.25
19	A2a	5c magenta & vio	.30	.25
20	A1	15c sl grn & grn	.30	.25
21	A2	20c vio & red brn	.30	.25
22	A1	40c rose vio & vio	.35	.30
23	A2	45c brn vio & red	.40	.35
24	A2a	75c indigo & bl	.40	.35
25	A1	1p red & brown	2.00	1.75
26	A2	3p bl vio & sl grn	3.50	2.75
27	A2a	10p blk brn & blk	35.00	27.50
		Nos. 17-27,E1 (12)	45.40	35.85
		Set, never hinged	90.00	

Size of Nos. 17-27 are 22mmx32½mm
Nos. 17-27 exist imperf. Value, set $150.

Catalogue values for unused stamps in this section, from this point to the end of the section, are for Never Hinged items.

Nomad Family — A3

1947, Feb. Perf. 10
Size: 21mmx35½mm

28	A3	50c choc & gray blk	18.00	.80

No. 28 exists imperf. Value, $50.

Stamps of Spain, 1939-48, Overprinted in Carmine

1948, Aug. 2 Perf. 9½x10½, 11, 13

29	A161	5c gray brn (#664)	4.50	.75
30	A194	15c gray green	5.00	.75
31	A167	90c dk grn (#714a)	20.00	4.25
32	A166	1p gray black	.70	.30
		Nos. 29-32 (4)	30.20	6.05

See Nos. 36 and 45.

Spain Nos. 769 and 770 Overprinted in Violet Blue or Carmine

1949, Oct. 9 Perf. 12½x13

33	A202	50c red brown (VB)	2.50	1.25
34	A202	75c violet blue (C)	2.50	1.25
		Nos. 33-34,C40 (3)	8.00	4.00

75th anniv. of the UPU.

Stamps of Spain, 1938-48, Overprinted in Blue or Carmine like Nos. 29-32

Perf. 13, 13½, 12½x13, 9½x10½

1949 Unwmk.

35	A160	2c org brn (Bl)	.30	.25
36	A161	5c gray brn (#664a)	.30	.25
37	A161	10c dk car (Bl)	.30	.25
38	A161	15c dk green (II)	.30	.25
39	A166	25c brown violet	.30	.25
40	A166	30c blue	.40	.25
41	A195	40c red brown	.40	.25
42	A195	45c car rose (Bl)	.70	.25
43	A166	50c indigo	.75	.30
44	A195	75c dk vio bl	.85	.45
45	A167	90c dk grn (#714)	.95	.60
47	A167	1.35p purple	5.00	4.50
48	A166	2p dl brn	4.75	2.75
49	A166	4p dl rose (Bl)	17.50	8.00
50	A166	10p lt brn	42.50	24.00
		Nos. 35-50 (15)	75.30	42.65

Gen. Francisco Franco and Desert Scene — A4

Perf. 12½x13

1951, July 18 Photo. Unwmk.

51	A4	50c dp org	.30	.25
52	A4	1p chocolate	2.40	1.25
53	A4	5p bl grn	25.00	12.00
		Nos. 51-53 (3)	27.70	13.50

Visit of Gen. Francisco Franco, 1950.

View of Granada and Globe — A5

1952, Dec. 10 Perf. 13x12½

54	A5	5c red org	.35	.25
55	A5	35c dk ol grn	.40	.25
56	A5	60c brown	.40	.30
		Nos. 54-56 (3)	1.15	.80

400th anniversary of the death of Leo Africanus (c. 1485-c. 1554), Arab traveler and scholar, author of "Descrittione dell' Africa."

Musician — A6

Design: 60c, Two musicians.

1953, June 1 Perf. 12½x13

57	A6	15c olive gray	.30	.25
58	A6	60c brown	.35	.30
		Nos. 57-58,B13-B14 (4)	1.30	1.10

Issued to promote child welfare.

Fish and Branched Sponges — A7

15c, Fish and jellyfish.

1953, Nov. 23

59	A7	15c dark green	.30	.25
60	A7	60c brown	.45	.30
		Nos. 59-60,B15-B16 (4)	1.40	1.10

Colonial Stamp Day, Nov. 23, 1953.

Sea Gull A8

Cactus A9

25c, 60c, 2p, 5p, Salsola vermiculata.

1954, Apr. 22 Perf. 12½x13, 13x12½

61	A8	5c red org	.25	.25
62	A9	10c olive	.25	.25
63	A9	25c brn car	.25	.25
64	A9	35c olive gray	.25	.25
65	A9	40c rose lilac	.25	.25
66	A9	60c dk brn	.25	.25
67	A8	1p brown	5.25	.70
68	A9	1.25p car rose	.25	.25
69	A9	2p darp blue	.30	.25
70	A9	4.50p olive grn	.40	.40
71	A9	5p olive blk	24.00	10.00
		Nos. 61-71 (11)	31.70	13.10

Mother and Child A10 A11

1954, June 1 Perf. 13x12½

72	A10	15c dk gray grn	.30	.25
73	A11	60c dk brn	.35	.30
		Nos. 72-73,B17-B18 (4)	1.30	1.10

Lobster — A12

Design: 60c, Hammerhead shark.

1954, Nov. 23 Perf. 12½x13

74	A12	15c olive green	.35	.25
75	A12	60c rose brown	.45	.35
		Nos. 74-75,B19-B20 (4)	1.45	1.15

Issued to publicize Colonial Stamp Day.

Farmer Plowing and Statue of "Justice" — A13

1955, June 1 Photo. Unwmk.

76	A13	50c gray olive	.35	.25
		Nos. 76,B21-B22 (3)	1.00	.85

Squirrel — A14

1955, Nov. 23

77	A14	70c yellow green	.35	.30
		Nos. 77,B23-B24 (3)	1.00	.85

Issued to publicize Colonial Stamp Day.

Senecio Antheuphorbium — A15

Design: 50c, Limoniastrum Ifniensis.

1956, June 1 Perf. 13x12½

78	A15	20c bluish green	.35	.25
79	A15	50c brown	.40	.35
		Nos. 78-79,B25-B26 (4)	1.40	1.15

Arms of Sidi Ifni and Shepherd — A16

1956, Nov. 23 Perf. 12½x13

80	A16	70c light green	.35	.25

Issued for Colonial Stamp Day.

Rock Doves — A17

1957, June 1 Photo. Perf. 13x12½

81	A17	70c yel grn & brn	.40	.35
		Nos. 81,B29-B30 (3)	1.05	.90

See No. 86.

Jackal — A18

Design: 70c, Jackal's head, vert.

Perf. 12½x13, 13x12½

1957, Nov. 23

82	A18	20c emerald & lt grn	.35	.25
83	A18	70c green & brown	.45	.35
		Nos. 82-83,B31-B32 (4)	1.45	1.15

Issued for the Day of the Stamp, 1957.
See Nos. 87, B41.

Basketball Players — A19

IFNI

Design: 70c, Cyclists.

1958, June 1			Perf. 13x12½	
84	A19	20c bluish green	.30	.25
85	A19	70c olive green	.45	.35
	Nos. 84-85,B36-B37 (4)		1.40	1.15

Types of 1957 inscribed "Pro-Infancia 1959"

Designs: 20c, Goat. 70c, Ewe and lamb.

1959, June 1			Perf. 13x12½, 12½x13	
86	A17	20c dull green	.30	.25
87	A18	70c yellow green	.40	.35
	Nos. 86-87,B41-B42 (4)		1.35	1.15

Issued to promote child welfare.

Red-legged Partridges — A20

1960, June 10			Perf. 13x12½	
88	A20	35c shown	.30	.25
89	A20	80c Camels	.40	.35
	Nos. 88-89,B46-B47 (4)		1.35	1.15

White Stork — A21

Birds: 50c, 1.50p, 5p, European goldfinches. 75c, 2p, 10p, Skylarks, vert.

1960		Unwmk.	Perf. 12½x13	
90	A21	25c violet	.25	.25
91	A21	50c olive black	.25	.25
92	A21	75c dull purple	.25	.25
93	A21	1p orange ver	.35	.25
94	A21	1.50p brt grnsh bl	.40	.25
95	A21	2p red lilac	.45	.30
96	A21	3p dark blue	.70	.35
97	A21	5p red brown	1.25	.55
98	A21	10p olive	4.25	1.40
	Nos. 90-98 (9)		8.15	3.85

Map of Ifni — A22

General Franco — A23

Design: 70c, Government palace.

	Perf. 13x12½, 12½x13			
1961, Oct. 1			Photo.	
99	A22	25c gray violet	.25	.25
100	A23	50c olive brown	.30	.25
101	A23	70c brt green	.35	.30
102	A23	1p red orange	.40	.35
	Nos. 99-102 (4)		1.30	1.15

25th anniv. of the nomination of Gen. Francisco Franco as Head of State.

Admiral Jofre Tenoria — A24

Design: 50c, Cesareo Fernandez-Duro (1830-1908), writer.

1962, July 10			Perf. 13x12½	
103	A24	25c dull violet	.25	.25
104	A24	50c deep blue grn	.30	.25
105	A24	1p orange brown	.35	.35
	Nos. 103-105 (3)		.90	.85

Mailman — A25

Stamp Day: 35c, Hands, letter and winged wheel.

1962, Nov. 23			Unwmk.	
106	A25	15c dark blue	.25	.25
107	A25	35c lilac rose	.35	.30
108	A25	1p rose brown	.40	.35
	Nos. 106-108 (3)		1.00	.90

Golden Tower, Seville — A26

1963, Jan. 29			Photo.	
109	A26	50c green	.30	.25
110	A26	1p brown orange	.40	.35

Issued for flood relief in Seville.

Butterflies — A27

Design: 50c, Butterfly and flower.

1963, July 6			Perf. 13x12½	
111	A27	25c deep blue	.30	.25
112	A27	50c light green	.35	.30
113	A27	1p carmine rose	.45	.40
	Nos. 111-113 (3)		1.10	.95

Issued for child welfare.

Child with Flowers and Arms — A28

1963, July 12			Perf. 12½x13	
114	A28	50c gray olive	.30	.25
115	A28	1p reddish brown	.40	.35

Issued for Barcelona flood relief.

Beetle (Steraspis Speciosa) — A29

Stamp Day: 50c, Grasshopper.

1964, Mar. 6			Perf. 13x12½	
116	A29	25c violet blue	.25	.25
117	A29	50c olive green	.35	.30
118	A29	1p red brown	.45	.30
	Nos. 116-118 (3)		1.05	.85

Mountain Gazelle — A30

Design: 50c, Head of roebuck.

1964, June 1			Photo.	
119	A30	25c brt violet	.25	.25
120	A30	50c slate blk	.35	.25
121	A30	1p orange red	.40	.35
	Nos. 119-121 (3)		1.00	.85

Issued for child welfare.

Bicycle Race — A31

Stamp Day: 1p, Motorcycle race.

1964, Nov. 23			Perf. 12½x13	
122	A31	50c brown	.30	.25
123	A31	1p orange ver	.35	.30
124	A31	1.50p Prus green	.40	.35
	Nos. 122-124 (3)		1.05	.90

Man A32

Two Boys in School A33

Cable Cars, Sidi Ifni — A34

Perf. 13x12½, 12½x13				
1965, Mar. 1			Photo.	Unwmk.
125	A32	50c dark green	.30	.25
126	A33	1p orange ver	.35	.30
127	A34	1.50p dark blue	.40	.35
	Nos. 125-127 (3)		1.05	.90

25 years of peace after the Spanish Civil War.

Eugaster Fernandezi A35

Insect: 1p, Halter halteratus.

1965, June 1			Photo.	Unwmk.
128	A35	50c purple	.30	.25
129	A35	1p rose red	.35	.30
130	A35	1.50p violet blue	.40	.35
	Nos. 128-130 (3)		1.05	.90

Issued for child welfare.

Eagle A36

Arms of Sidi Ifni A37

Perf. 13x12½, 12½x13				
1965, Nov. 23			Photo.	
131	A36	50c dk red brown	.25	.25
132	A37	1p orange ver	.35	.30
133	A36	1.50p grnsh blue	.40	.35
	Nos. 131-133 (3)		1.00	.90

Issued for Stamp Day 1965.

Jetliner over Sidi Ifni — A38

Design: 2.50p, Two 1934 biplanes, horiz.

Perf. 13x12½, 12½x13				
1966, June 1			Photo.	Unwmk.
134	A38	1p orange brn	.30	.25
135	A38	1.50p brt blue	.50	.40
136	A38	2.50p dull violet	2.25	2.00
	Nos. 134-136 (3)		3.05	2.70

Issued for child welfare.

Syntomis Alicia — A39

40c, 4p, Danais chrysippus (butterfly).

1966, Nov. 23			Photo.	Perf. 13
137	A39	10c green & red	.40	.25
138	A39	40c dk brn & gldn brn	.45	.30
139	A39	1.50p violet & yel	.55	.35
140	A39	4p dk pur & brt bl	.65	.40
	Nos. 137-140 (4)		2.05	1.30

Issued for Stamp Day, 1966.

Coconut Palms — A40

Designs: 40c, 4p, Cactus.

1967, June 1			Photo.	Perf. 13
141	A40	10c dp grn & brn	.25	.25
142	A40	40c Prus grn & ocher	.25	.25
143	A40	1.50p bl grn & sepia	.35	.30
144	A40	4p sepia & ocher	.45	.35
	Nos. 141-144 (4)		1.30	1.15

Issued for child welfare.

Sidi Ifni Harbor — A41

1967, Sept. 28			Photo.	Perf. 12½x13
145	A41	1.50p grn & red brn	.35	.25

Modernization of harbor installations.

Needlefish (Skipper) — A42

Fish: 1.50p, John Dory, vert. 3.50p, Gurnard (Trigla lucerna).

1967, Nov. 23			Photo.	Perf. 13
146	A42	1p blue & green	.30	.25
147	A42	1.50p vio blk & yel	.35	.25
148	A42	3.50p brt bl & scar	.45	.35
	Nos. 146-148 (3)		1.10	.85

Issued for Stamp Day 1967.

Zodiac Issue

Pisces — A43

Signs of the Zodiac: 1.50p, Capricorn. 2.50p, Sagittarius.

1968, Apr. 25			Photo.	Perf. 13
149	A43	1p brt mag, lt yel	.30	.25
150	A43	1.50p brown, pink	.35	.30
151	A43	2.50p dk vio, yel	.45	.35
	Nos. 149-151 (3)		1.10	.90

Issued for child welfare.

Mailing a Letter — A44

IFNI

Designs: 1.50p, Carrier pigeon carrying letter. 2.50p, Stamp under magnifying glass.

1968, Nov. 23   Photo.   Perf. 12½x13
152	A44	1p org yel & sl grn	.25	.25
153	A44	1.50p brt bl & vio blk	.30	.30
154	A44	2.50p emer & vio blk	.45	.35
		Nos. 152-154 (3)	1.05	.90

Issued for Stamp Day.

SEMI-POSTAL STAMPS

Catalogue values for unused stamps in this section are for Never Hinged items.

Gen. Francisco Franco — SP1

Perf. 13x12½

1950, Oct. 19   Unwmk.
B1	SP1	50c + 10c sepia	.40	.25
B2	SP1	1p + 25c blue	12.00	4.50
B3	SP1	6.50p + 1.65p dl grn	4.25	2.00
		Nos. B1-B3 (3)	16.65	6.75

The surtax was for child welfare.

Fennec — SP2

1951, Nov. 30
B4	SP2	5c + 5c brown	.30	.25
B5	SP2	10c + 5c red org	.35	.25
B6	SP2	60c + 15c olive brn	.55	.30
		Nos. B4-B6 (3)	1.20	.80

Colonial Stamp Day, Nov. 23, 1951.

Mother and Child — SP3

1952, June 1
B7	SP3	5c + 5c brn	.30	.25
B8	SP3	50c + 10c brn blk	.40	.30
B9	SP3	2p + 30c dp bl	2.25	.85
		Nos. B7-B9 (3)	2.95	1.40

The surtax was for child welfare.

Common Shag — SP4

1952, Nov. 23
B10	SP4	5c + 5c brn	.30	.25
B11	SP4	10c + 5c brn car	.30	.25
B12	SP4	60c + 15c dk grn	.50	.35
		Nos. B10-B12 (3)	1.10	.85

Colonial Stamp Day, Nov. 23, 1952.

Musician Type of Regular Issue

1953, June 1   Perf. 12½x13
B13	A6	5c + 5c as No. 57	.30	.25
B14	A6	10c + 5c as No. 58	.35	.30

The surtax was for child welfare.

Fish Type of Regular Issue

1953, Nov. 23
B15	A7	5c + 5c as No. 59	.30	.25
B16	A7	10c + 5c as No. 60	.35	.30

Colonial Stamp Day, Nov. 23, 1953.

Type of Regular Issue

1954, June 1   Perf. 13x12½
B17	A10	5c + 5c org	.30	.25
B18	A11	10c + 5c rose vio	.35	.30

The surtax was for child welfare.

Type of Regular Issue

1954, Nov. 23   Perf. 12½x13
B19	A12	5c + 5c as No. 74	.30	.25
B20	A12	10c + 5c as No. 75	.35	.30

"Dama de Elche" Protecting Caravan — SP5

1955, June 1   Photo.   Unwmk.
B21	A13	10c + 5c rose lilac	.30	.25
B22	SP5	25c + 10c violet	.35	.30

The surtax was to help Ifni people.

Squirrel Type of Regular Issue

Design: 15c+5c, Squirrel holding nut.

1955, Nov. 23
B23	A14	5c + 5c red brown	.30	.25
B24	A14	15c + 5c olive bister	.35	.30

Type of Regular Issue

1956, June 1   Perf. 13x12½
B25	A15	5c + 5c as No. 78	.30	.25
B26	A15	15c + 5c as No. 79	.35	.30

The tax was for child welfare.

Dorcas Gazelles and Arms of Spain — SP6

Design: 15c+5c, Arms of Sidi Ifni, boat and woman with drum.

1956, Nov. 23
B27	SP6	5c + 5c dark brown	.30	.25
B28	SP6	15c + 5c golden brn	.35	.30

Issued for Colonial Stamp Day.

Dove Type of Regular Issue

1957, June 1   Photo.   Perf. 13x12½
B29	A17	5c + 5c as No. 81	.30	.25
B30	A17	15c + 5c Stock doves	.35	.30

The surtax was for child welfare.

Type of Regular Issue

Perf. 12½x13, 13x12½

1957, Nov. 23   Photo.   Unwmk.
B31	A18	10c + 5c as No. 82	.30	.25
B32	A18	15c + 5c as No. 83	.35	.30

Swallows and Arms of Valencia and Sidi Ifni — SP7

1958, Mar. 6   Perf. 12½x13
B33	SP7	10c + 5c org brn	.30	.25
B34	SP7	15c + 10c bister	.35	.25
B35	SP7	50c + 10c brn olive	.40	.30
		Nos. B33-B35 (3)	1.05	.80

The surtax was to aid the victims of the Valencia flood, Oct. 1957.

Sport Type of Regular Issue, 1958

1958, June 1   Photo.   Perf. 13x12½
B36	A19	10c + 5c as No. 84	.30	.25
B37	A19	15c + 5c as No. 85	.35	.30

Guitarfish SP8   Sailboats SP9

Stamp Day: 10c+5c, Spotted dogfish.

Perf. 13x12½, 12½x13

1958, Nov. 23
B38	SP9	10c + 5c brn red	.30	.25
B39	SP8	25c + 10c dull vio	.35	.25
B40	SP9	50c + 10c olive	.40	.30
		Nos. B38-B40 (3)	1.05	.80

Type of 1957 and

Donkey and Man — SP10

Design: 10c+5c, Ewe and lamb.

Perf. 12½x13, 13x12½

1959, June 1   Photo.   Unwmk.
B41	A18	10c + 5c lt red brn	.30	.25
B42	SP10	15c + 5c golden brn	.35	.30

The surtax was for child welfare.

Soccer — SP11

Designs: 20c+5c, Soccer players. 50c+20c, Javelin thrower.

1959, Nov. 23   Perf. 13x12½
B43	SP11	10c + 5c fawn	.30	.25
B44	SP11	20c + 5c slate green	.35	.30
B45	SP11	50c + 20c olive gray	.40	.35
		Nos. B43-B45 (3)	1.05	.90

Issued for the day of the Stamp, 1959. See Nos. B52-B54.

Type of Regular Issue, 1960

1960, June 10   Perf. 13x12½
B46	A20	10c + 5c as No. 89	.30	.25
B47	A20	15c + 5c Wild boars	.35	.30

The surtax was for child welfare.

Santa Maria del Mar — SP12

Stamp Day: 20c+5c, 50c+20c, New school building, horiz.

Perf. 13x12½, 12½x13

1960, Dec. 29   Photo.
B48	SP12	10c + 5c org brn	.30	.25
B49	SP12	20c + 5c dk sl grn	.30	.25
B50	SP12	30c + 10c red brn	.35	.30
B51	SP12	50c + 20c sepia	.35	.30
		Nos. B48-B51 (4)	1.30	1.10

Type of 1959 inscribed: "Pro-Infancia 1961"

Designs: 10c+5c, 80c+20c, Pole vaulting, horiz. 25c+10c, Soccer player.

Perf. 12½x13, 13x12½

1961, June 21   Unwmk.
B52	SP11	10c + 5c rose brn	.30	.25
B53	SP11	25c + 10c gray vio	.35	.30
B54	SP11	80c + 20c dk green	.40	.30
		Nos. B52-B54 (3)	1.05	.80

The surtax was for child welfare.

Camel Rider and Truck — SP13

Stamp Day: 25c+10c, 1p+10c, Ship in Sidi Ifni harbor.

1961, Nov. 23   Perf. 12½x13
B55	SP13	10c + 5c rose brn	.30	.25
B56	SP13	25c + 10c dk pur	.30	.25
B57	SP13	30c + 10c dk red brn	.35	.30
B58	SP13	1p + 10c red org	.35	.35
		Nos. B55-B58 (4)	1.30	1.15

AIR POST STAMPS

Stamps formerly listed as Nos. C1-C29 were privately overprinted. These include 1936 stamps of Spain overprinted "VIA AEREA" and plane, and 1939 stamps of Spain, type AP30, overprinted "IFNI" or "Territorio de Ifni."

Oasis AP1   The Sanctuary AP2

1943   Unwmk.   Litho.   Perf. 12½
C30	AP2	5c cer & vio brn	.35	.25
C31	AP1	25c yel grn & ol grn	.35	.25
C32	AP2	50c ind & turq grn	.45	.35
C33	AP1	1p pur & grnsh bl	.50	.35
C34	AP2	1.40p gray grn & bl	.55	.35
C35	AP1	2p mag & red org	1.50	1.25
C36	AP2	5p brn & pur	2.25	1.75
C37	AP1	6p brt bl & gray grn	35.00	30.00
		Nos. C30-C37 (8)	40.95	34.55
		Set, never hinged		80.00

Nos. C30-C37 exist imperforate. Value, set $130.

Catalogue values for unused stamps in this section, from this point to the end of the section, are for Never Hinged items.

Type of Spain, 1939-47, Overprinted in Carmine

1947, Nov. 29
C38	AP30	5c dull yellow	2.75	.85
C39	AP30	10c dk bl green	2.75	.85

Spain No. C126 Overprinted in Carmine like Nos. 33-34

1949, Oct. 9		Perf. 12½x13
C40	A202 4p dk olive grn	3.00 1.50

75th anniv. of the UPU.

Spain, Nos. C110 and C112 to C116, Overprinted in Blue or Carmine like Nos. 29-32

1949		Perf. 10
C41	AP30 25c redsh brn (Bl)	.55 .25
C42	AP30 50c brown	.65 .25
C43	AP30 1p chalky blue	.70 .25
C44	AP30 2p lt gray grn	4.25 .85
C45	AP30 4p gray blue	11.00 4.50
C46	AP30 10p brt purple	14.50 8.75
	Nos. C41-C46 (6)	31.65 14.85

Lope Sancho de Valenzuela and Sheik — AP3

1950, Nov. 23	Photo.	Perf. 13x12½
C47	AP3 5p brown black	3.25 .85

Stamp Day, Nov. 23, 1950.

Woman Holding Dove — AP4

1951, Apr. 22	Engr.	Perf. 10
C48	AP4 5p red	20.00 8.25

500th anniversary of the birth of Queen Isabella I of Spain.
The majority of this issue are poorly centered. Values are for very fine examples.

Ferdinand the Catholic — AP5

	Perf. 13x12½	
1952, July 18	Photo.	Unwmk.
C49	AP5 5p brown	22.50 6.50

500th anniv. of the birth of Ferdinand the Catholic of Spain.

Plane and Mountain Gazelle — AP6

1953, Apr. 1

C50	AP6 60c light grn	.35 .30
C51	AP6 1.20p brn car	.40 .30
C52	AP6 1.60p lt brown	.45 .35
C53	AP6 2p deep blue	3.00 .50
C54	AP6 4p grnsh blk	1.75 .65
C55	AP6 10p brt red vio	9.25 2.00
	Nos. C50-C55 (6)	15.20 4.10

SPECIAL DELIVERY STAMPS

Inscribed: "URGENTE"

1943		Perf. 12½
E1	A3 25c slate green & car	2.25 1.60

Spain No. E20 Overprinted in Blue like Nos. 29-32

1949	Unwmk.	Perf. 10
E2	SD10 25c carmine	.35 .25

INDIA
'in-dē-ə

LOCATION — Southern, central Asia
GOVT. — Republic
AREA — 1,266,732 sq. mi.
POP. — 1,380,000,000 (2020 est.)
CAPITAL — New Delhi

On August 15, 1947, India was divided into two self-governing dominions: Pakistan and India. India became a republic in 1950.

The stamps of pre-partition India fall into three groups:
1) Issues inscribed simply "East India" (to 1881) and "India" (from 1882), for use mainly in British India proper, but available and valid throughout the country;
2) Issues as above and overprinted with one of the names of the six "Convention" states (Chamba, Faridkot, Gwalior, Jind, Nabha and Patiala) which had a postal convention with British India, for use in these states.
3) Issues of the feudatory states, over which the British India government exercised little internal control, valid for use only within the states issuing them.

12 Pies = 1 Anna
16 Annas = 1 Rupee
100 Naye Paise = 1 Rupee (1957)
100 Paise = 1 Rupee (1964)

Catalogue values for unused stamps in this country are for Never Hinged items, beginning with Scott 168 in the regular postage section, Scott C7 in the air post section, Scott M44 in the military section, Scott O113 in the official section, Scott RA1 in the postal tax section, Scott 51 in Hyderabad regular issues, Scott O54 in Hyderabad officials, Scott 49 in Jaipur regular issues, Scott O30 in Jaipur officials, Scott 39 in Soruth regular issues and Scott O19 in Soruth official
All of the values are for Never Hinged for all of the items in the sections for the International Commission in Indo-China, Jasdan, Rajasthan, and Travancore-Cochin.

Watermarks

Wmk. 36 — Crown and INDIA

Wmk. 37 — Coat of Arms in Sheet. (Reduced illustration. Watermark covers a large section of the sheet.)

Wmk. 38 — Elephant's Head

Wmk. 39 — Star

Wmk. 40

Wmk. 41 — Small Umbrella

Wmk. 42 — Urdu Characters

Wmk. 43 — Shell

Wmk. 43A — Shell

Wmk. 196 — Multiple Stars

Wmk. 211 — Urdu Characters

Wmk. 294 — Letters and Ornaments in Sheet (size reduced)

Wmk. 324 — Asoka Pillar, Multiple

Wmk. 360 — Star and GOVT INDIA

Wmk. 43 occurs only on handmade paper and exists in two types.
Type I: Five bumps or section on the right side of the shell. 15mm between shells, resulting in a watermark that is never center on the stamps. It is positioned upright or sideways.
Type II: Four bumps or sections on the right side of the shell. 11mm between shells, resulting in a watermark that is usually.
Wmk. 43A occurs only on machine-made paper and exists in two types.
Type I: 11mm between shells, resulting in a watermark that is usually centered. (1924-1939).
Type II: 15mm between shells, resulting in a watermark that is poorly centered. Occasionally, stamps appear unwatermarked due to spacing (1929-1930).

SCINDE DISTRICT POST

A1

1852, July 1		Embossed	Imperf.
A1	A1 ½a white	21,500.	2,450.
A2	A1 ½a blue	47,500.	10,750.
A3	A1 ½a red	175,000.	31,500.

Obsolete October, 1854.
Nos. A1-A3 were issued without gum. No. A3 is embossed on red wafer. It is usually found with cracks and these examples are worth somewhat less than the values given, depending on the degree of cracking.

GENERAL ISSUES

Unused stamps of India are valued with original gum as defined in the catalogue introduction except for Nos. 1-7 which are valued without gum.

East India Company

A1   A2

Queen Victoria

Die I

Die II

Die III

Die I — Lines in the chignon are not well defined, often appearing more like splotches of color. The corner "stars" are well-defined, with long and clear "rays". The band of the diadem is well-shaded with lines of color.
Die II — Chignon shows less color than in die I. There is a clear separation between the chignon and the back of the queen's head. The band of the diadem is heavily shaded. The star rays in the corner are cut short or not present.
Die III — Chignon features colored definition lines, finer than in dies I or II. The corner star rays are short, or completely missing. The band of diadem is almost entirely blank.

INDIA

1854-55 Litho.; Typo. (#5) Wmk. 37 Imperf.

1	A1	½a red	3,425.	
2	A2	½a blue, die I	220.00	40.00
a.		½a deep blue, die I	245.00	45.00
b.		Printed on both sides		39,000.
c.		Double impression		31,500.
2D	A3	½a blue, die II	185.00	127.50
2E	A3	½a blue, die III	2,900.	82.50
f.		½a greenish blue, die III ('55)		

Die I — Chignon and queen's head are partially separated by large blotch(es) of color. There are fewer lines in the chignon than in die II, sometimes almost blank.

Die II — There is a white separation of the chignon from the queen's head.

Die III — Bust of the queen is more pointed.

4	A3	1a red, die I	1,275.	77.50
a.		1a dp red, die I	1,950.	105.00
4B	A3	1a red, die II	195.00	82.50
		1a scarlet, die II	400.00	118.00
4C	A3	1a red, die III	4,150.	195.00
a.		1a dull red, die III ('55)	4,900.	245.00

5	A4	2a green	370.00	47.50
a.		Half used as 1a on cover		725,000.
b.		2a emerald	9,750.	

Head Die I — Band of diadem features large lines of color and is largely shaded.

Head Die II — Band of diadem is not as fully shaded, but lines are not short. Chignon features prominent "comma" shape towards top.

Head Die III — Band of diadem is not fully shaded, with short lines or no shading lines at all. Chignon is redrawn with lines of color. The "comma" is no longer present.

Head Die IV — Band of diadem is not fully shaded. The very top of chignon features two fingerlike lines protruding upward. "Comma" may still be partly present, but is less prominent and is sometimes fragmented.

Frame Die I — Diagonal lines at the upper right of stamp are clearly separated from inner circle. Dots in middle of letters "A" and "R" are small, sometimes vanishing.

Frame Die II — Diagonal lines at the upper right of stamp touch or merge with inner circle. Dots of middle of letters "A" and "R" are larger.

First Printing

6	A5	4a red & bl, head I, frame I	24,500.	1,075.
a.		Head inverted		425,000.
b.		Head II, frame I		
c.		Head IV, frame I		2,700.
6F	A5	4a red & bl, head III, frame II ('55)	13,750.	575.00

No. 1 was not placed in use.
Nos. 2, 4, 5 and 6 are known with unofficial perforation.
No. 5 is known with the watermark having the words "One Ana" in place of the lions and shield, with Urdu and Bengali characters. Values: $1,200 unused; $650 used.
Values are for cut-square stamps with four clear margins.
Beware of forgeries. Reprints also exist.

Nos. 9-35 are normally found with very heavy cancellations, and values are for stamps so canceled. Lightly canceled stamps are seldom seen. The same holds true for Nos. O1-O26.

Diadem includes Maltese Crosses — A7

1855-64 Unwmk. Typo. Perf. 14
Blue Glazed Paper

9	A7	4a black	1,350.	20.00
a.		Imperf., pair	16,000.	16,000.
b.		Half used as 2a on cover		20,000.
10	A7	8a rose	1,100.	20.00
a.		Imperf., pair	8,250.	—
b.		Half used as 4a on cover		112,500.

See Nos. 11-18, 20, 22-25, 31. For overprints see Nos. O1-O5, O7-O9, O16-O19, O22-O24.

1855-64 White Paper

11	A7	½a blue	160.00	6.00
a.		Imperf., pair	1,000.	3,750.
12	A7	1a brown	85.00	4.50
a.		Imperf., pair	1,800.	5,000.
b.		Vert. pair, imperf between		
c.		Half used as ½a on cover		112,500.
13	A7	2a dull rose	1,300.	50.00
a.		Imperf., pair	7,500.	5,000.
14	A7	2a yellow green	2,500.	3,150.
a.		Imperf., pair	21,500.	
15	A7	2a buff	825.00	35.00
a.		2a orange	1,350.	40.00
b.		Imperf., pair	4,750.	7,250.
c.		2a yellow ('63)	1,200.	55.00
16	A7	4a black	800.00	9.00
a.		Imperf., pair	9,000.	7,000.
b.		Diagonal half used as 2a on cover		45,000.
17	A7	4a green ('64)	3,600.	50.00
18	A7	8a rose	900.00	30.00
a.		Half used as 4a on cover		110,000.

No. 14 was not regularly issued. See note after No. 25.

Many stamps of types A7-A90 are overprinted "Service" or "On H. M. S." For these, see listings of Official stamps.

Crown Colony

Queen Victoria — A8

1860-64 Unwmk. Perf. 14

19	A8	8p lilac	85.00	7.50
a.		Diagonal half used as 4p on cover		110,000.
b.		Imperf., pair	13,500.	8,000.
19C	A8	8p lilac, *bluish*	550.00	135.00

See No. 21. For overprint see No. O6 and footnote after No. O4.

1865-67 Wmk. 38

20	A7	½a blue	24.00	1.50
a.		Imperf., pair	950.00	2,250.
21	A8	8p lilac	11.00	13.50
22	A7	1a brown	11.00	1.25
23	A7	2a brnsh org	37.50	2.75
a.		2a yellow	340.00	6.75
b.		Imperf., pair		6,500.
c.		2a orange	200.00	3.50
24	A7	4a green	1,200.	25.00
25	A7	8a rose	4,500.	85.00

No. 21 was variously surcharged locally, "NINE" or "NINE PIE," to indicate that it was being sold for 9 pies (the soldier's letter rate had been raised from 8 to 9 pies). These surcharges were made without government authorization.
Stamps of types A7 and A9 overprinted with crown and surcharged with new values were for use in Straits Settlements.

Diadem: Rows of pearls & diamonds — A11

FOUR ANNAS
Type I — Slanting line at corner of mouth extends downward only. Shading about mouth and chin. Pointed chin.

Type II — Line at corner of mouth extends both up and down. Upper lip and chin are defined by a colored line. Rounded chin.

1866-68

26	A9	4a bl grn, type I	110.00	4.25
26B	A9	4a dp bl grn, type II	32.50	3.50
27	A10	6a8p slate	80.00	27.50
a.		Imperf., pair	10,000.	
28	A11	8a rose ('68)	65.00	10.00
		Nos. 26-28 (4)	287.50	45.25

Type A11 is a redrawing of type A7. Type A7 has Maltese crosses in the diadem, while type A11 has shaded lozenges.
For overprints see Nos. O10, O20-O21, O25-O26, Gwalior Nos. 7, 12. Jind Nos. 38, 44, 48, Nabha Nos. 6, 10, Patiala Nos. 6, 10.

SIX ANNAS
Type I — "POSTAGE" 3½mm high
Type II — "POSTAGE" 2½mm high

Blue Glazed Paper
Green Overprint
Perf. 14 Vert.

1866, June 28 Wmk. 36

29	A12	6a vio, type I	1,800.	175.
a.		Inverted overprint		25,000.
30	A12	6a vio, type II	3,500.	225.

Nos. 29 and 30 were made from revenue stamps with the labels at top and bottom cut off. Most and sometimes all of the watermark was removed with the labels. Twenty different varieties of this overprint exist.
These stamps are often found with cracked surface or scuffs. Such examples sell for somewhat less.

1873-76 Wmk. 38 Perf. 14

31	A7	½a blue, redrawn	8.50	1.25
32	A13	9p lilac ('74)	20.00	16.00
33	A14	6a bister ('76)	10.00	2.25
34	A15	12a red brown ('76)	17.50	32.50
35	A16	1r slate ('74)	85.00	37.50
		Nos. 31-35 (5)	141.00	89.50
		Set, never hinged	300.00	

In the redrawn ½ anna the lines of the mouth are more deeply cut, making the lips appear fuller and more open, and the nostril is defined by a curved line.
For overprints see Chamba Nos. 15, O10, Faridkot Nos. 12, O8, Gwalior Nos. 8, 23, Jind No. 62, Nabha No. 25, Patiala Nos. 26, O16.

Victorian and Edwardian stamps overprinted "Postal Service" and new denominations were customs fee due stamps, not postage stamps.

Empire

INDIA

A postal counterfeit exists of No. 46. Examples are scarce.

No. 40a used value is for copy with postal cancellation.

See Nos. 56-58. For surcharges see Nos. 47, 53 and British East Africa No. 59. For overprints see Nos. M2-M4, M6-M9, O27-O31, Chamba Nos. 1-4, 6-10, O1-O8, Faridkot Nos. 4-10, 14, O1-O7, Gwalior Nos. 1-6, 9-11, 13-22, O1-O5, Jind, Nos. 33-37, 39-43, 45-47, 49-57, O1-O13, O15, Nabha Nos. 1-5, 7-9, 11-20, O1-O13, Patiala Nos. 1-5, 7-9, 11-21, O1-O15.

Beginning with the 1882-87 issue, higher denomination stamps exist used for telegrams. The telegraph cancellation has concentric circles. These sell for 10-15% of the postally used values.

No. 43 Surcharged

1891, Jan. 1

| 47 | A24 | 2½a on 4a6p green | 6.75 | 1.25 |

1892

| 48 | A28 | 2a6p green | 7.00 | .80 |
| 49 | A29 | 1r aniline car & grn | 35.00 | 3.00 |

See No. 59. For overprints see Nos. M5, M10, O32, Chamba Nos. 5, 11, O9, Faridkot Nos. 11, O9, Gwalior Nos. 24-25, O6, Jind Nos. 58, O14, Nabha Nos. 21, O14, Patiala Nos. 22, O18.

Queen Victoria — A30

1895, Sept. 1

50	A30	2r yel brn & rose	55.00	14.50
a.		Brn & rose	75.00	21.00
51	A30	3r green & brown	50.00	12.00
52	A30	5r violet & ultra	65.00	42.50
		Nos. 50-52 (3)	170.00	69.00
		Set, never hinged	260.00	

For overprints see Chamba Nos. 12-14, Gwalior Nos. 26-28, Jind Nos. 59-61, Nabha Nos. 22-24, Patiala Nos. 23-25.

Used high values such as Nos. 50-52, 71-76, 95-98, 124-125, as well as similar high value official issues are for postally used examples. Stamps bearing telegraph or revenue cancellations sell for much lower prices. Most telegraph cancellations on issues of Edward VII and George V can be recognized by the appearance of "T," "TEL" or "GTO" or if they contain the concentric circles of a target.

No. 36 Surcharged

1898

53	A17	¼a on ½a green	.25	.55
a.		Double surcharge	600.00	
b.		Double impression of stamp	600.00	

For Nos. 61, 81 with this overprint see Nos. 77, 105.

Queen Victoria — A31

1899

| 54 | A31 | 3p carmine rose | .45 | .25 |

For overprint see No. M1, O33, Chamba No. 15B, Faridkot No. 13, Gwalior Nos. 29, O11, Jind No. 63, Nabha No. 26, Patiala No. 27.

Type of 1882-1892 Stamps

1900

55	A31	3p gray	1.00	1.75
56	A17	½a light green	2.00	.60
57	A19	1a carmine rose	2.50	.25
58	A21	2a violet	6.00	2.75
59	A28	2a6p ultramarine	7.00	4.50
		Nos. 55-59 (5)	18.50	9.85

For overprints see Nos. M11, O34-O36, Chamba Nos. 16-19, O11-O14, Gwalior Nos. 30-34, O7-O10, Jind Nos. 64-66, Patiala Nos. 28-29, O17.

1882-87 — Wmk. 39

36	A17	½a green	8.00	.25
a.		Double impression	1,750.	2,250.
37	A18	9p rose	1.25	2.25
38	A19	1a maroon	8.25	.50
a.		1a violet brown	8.25	.60
39	A20	1a6p bis brn	1.50	1.75
40	A21	2a ultra	5.00	.55
a.		Double impression	7,750.	3,000.
41	A22	3a brown org	12.00	2.00
a.		3a orange	22.50	8.75
42	A23	4a olive green	20.00	3.00
43	A24	4a6p green	32.50	7.00
44	A25	8a red violet	30.00	2.75
a.		8a rose lilac	27.50	2.75
45	A26	12a violet, *red*	11.00	5.00
46	A27	1r gray	30.00	8.00
		Nos. 36-46 (11)	159.50	33.05
		Set, never hinged	300.00	

A 6a die essay was prepared, but no stamps were printed.

India Exclusive

Auction

We hold auctions featuring 300-500 specialized lots of India, six times a year

Buyers:
- All items are guaranteed genuine
- One of the lowest buyer's premiums in the industry
- Free live internet & phone bidding

Sellers:
- Maximum global exposure from our huge database of India-specific collectors
- Highest realization for your consignments
  - unlike most auction houses, we break your consignment down to individual lots, rather than offering them as-is
- Favorable seller terms. Cash advances can be made for larger consignments. Call us today

Introducing a new format auction!
ALL LOTS STARTING AT $1 WITH NO RESERVE

Retail

- Visit our website www.stampbay.com for a range of items. Or simply call/email us for specific items in your want-list

Private Treaty

- From everyday items, to exquisite rarities, to unique items, we are the one-stop shop for all your philatelic needs
- Our website barely scratches the surface of our vast inventory, so do not hesitate to reach out to us
- Please email us your want-list info@stampbay.com and you will be pleasantly surprised at what we can offer

stampbay
FINE INDIA STAMPS & POSTAL HISTORY
auction · retail · private treaty
www.stampbay.com

Deepak Jaiswal, CEO

PO Box 50848, Palo Alto, CA 94303, USA, Phone/WhatsApp: +1 650 387 3885, email: info@stampbay.com

INDIA

Edward VII — A32
A33
A34
A35
A36
A37
A38
A39
A40
A41
A42
A43

1902-09
60	A32	3p gray	1.25	.35
61	A33	½a green	2.25	
a.		Booklet pane of 6 ('04)	75.00	
62	A34	1a carmine rose	2.00	.25
a.		Booklet pane of 6 ('04)	175.00	
63	A35	2a violet	8.00	.55
64	A36	2a6p ultra	8.50	.75
65	A37	3a brown org	7.00	.75
66	A38	4a olive green	4.50	.90
67	A39	6a bister	13.50	5.50
68	A40	8a red violet	10.00	1.25
69	A41	12a violet, *red*	12.00	2.75
70	A42	1r car rose & grn	15.00	1.00
71	A43	2r brown & rose	62.50	5.00
72	A43	3r grn & brn ('04)	50.00	27.50
73	A43	5r vio & ultra ('04)	100.00	42.50
74	A43	10r car rose & grn ('09)	170.00	50.00
75	A43	15r ol gray & ultra ('09)	250.00	75.00
76	A43	25r ultra & org brn	2,300.	3,000.
		Telegraph cancel		300.00
		Nos. 60-75 (16)	716.50	214.30

For overprints and surcharge see Nos. M12-M20, O33, O37-O44, O47-O51, O67-O69, O73, Gwalior O12-O18.

No. 61 Surcharged Like No. 53
1905
77	A33	¼a on ½a green	.85	.25
a.		Inverted surcharge		925.00

A44
A45

1906
78	A44	½a green	4.50	.30
a.		Booklet pane of 4	45.00	
79	A45	1a carmine rose	2.50	.30
a.		Booklet pane of 4	75.00	

For overprints see Nos. O45-O46, Chamba Nos. 30-31, O22-O23, Gwalior Nos. 49-50, O19-O20, Jind Nos. 77-78, O23-O24, Nabha Nos. 37-38, O23-O24, Patiala Nos. 41-42, O27-O28.

A46
A47
A48
A49
A50
A51
A52
A53
A54
A55
George V — A56

1911-23   Wmk. 39
80	A46	3p gray	1.50	.30
a.		Booklet pane of 4	50.00	
81	A47	½a green	2.75	.25
a.		Double impression	175.00	
b.		Booklet pane of 4	45.00	
82	A48	1a carmine rose	3.00	.30
a.		Printed on both sides		
b.		Booklet pane of 4	70.00	
83	A48	1a dk brn ('22)	1.25	.40
a.		Booklet pane of 4	80.00	
84	A49	2a dull violet	4.75	.70
a.		Booklet pane of 4	80.00	
85	A50	2a6p ultramarine	2.50	3.25
86	A51	3a brown org	4.75	.30
87	A51	3a ultra ('23)	17.50	3.50
88	A52	4a olive green	9.00	1.00
89	A53	6a yel bister	5.75	2.50
90	A53	6a bister ('15)	7.00	1.60
91	A54	8a red violet	7.50	1.40
92	A55	12a claret	7.75	2.50
93	A56	1r grn & red brn	20.00	2.50
94	A56	2r brn & car rose	27.50	2.75
95	A56	5r vio & ultra	62.50	9.50
96	A56	10r car rose & grn	90.00	17.50
97	A56	15r ol grn & ultra	120.00	32.50
98	A56	25r ultra & brn org	210.00	45.00
		Nos. 80-98 (19)	605.00	127.75
		Set, never hinged	1,000.	

See Nos. 106-108, 110-111, 113-125. For surcharges and overprints see Nos. 104-105, M23-M25, M27, M29-M37, M39-M43, O52-O66, O70-O71, O74, O78-O81, O85, O87-O92, Gwalior O21-O27, O29-O32, O35-O39, O44-O45.

Nos. 93-98 also were used to pay for radio licenses, and stamps so used include "WIRELESS" in the cancel. Used values so canceled are worth 10-15% of the values shown, which are for postally used examples.

A57

1913-26
99	A57	2a6p ultramarine	3.50	.50
100	A57	2a6p brown org ('26)	7.00	5.00

See No. 112. For overprints see Nos. M28, M38, Chamba Nos. 48-49, 66, Gwalior Nos. 68-69, Jind Nos. 100, 105, Nabha No. 55.

A60
A61

1926-32   Typo.
126	A60	2a dull violet	3.00	.25
a.		Tete beche pair	15.00	55.00
b.		2a rose violet	17.50	15.00
c.		Booklet pane of 4	21.00	

"One and Half" — A58

1919
101	A58	1½a chocolate	4.00	.55
a.		Booklet pane of 4	60.00	

For overprint and surcharge see Nos. M26, O75, Chamba No. 45, Jind No. 99.

"One and a Half" — A59

1921-26
102	A59	1½a chocolate	5.50	6.75
103	A59	1½a rose ('26)	4.50	.55

See No. 109. For surcharge see No. O76-O77, Chamba Nos. 46-47, 64, Gwalior Nos. 66-67, Jind Nos. 102, 104.

Type of 1911-26 Surcharged

NINE PIES

1921
104	A48	9p on 1a rose	1.25	.75
a.		Surcharged "NINE-NINE"	95.00	160.00
b.		Surcharged "PIES-PIES"	95.00	160.00
c.		Double surcharge	200.00	225.00
e.		Booklet pane of 4	47.50	

Forgeries exist of Nos. 104a-104c.
For overprints see Chamba No. 44, Gwalior No. 64, Jind No. 98.

No. 81 Surcharged Like No. 53
1922
105	A47	¼a on ½a green	.75	.55
a.		Inverted surcharge	12.00	
b.		Pair, one without surcharge	250.00	

Types of 1911-26 Issues
1926-36   Wmk. 196
106	A46	3p slate	.45	.35
107	A47	½a green	1.75	.25
108	A48	1a dark brown	.80	.25
a.		Tete beche pair	2.75	15.00
b.		Booklet pane of 4	25.00	
109	A59	1½a car rose ('29)	2.75	.25
110	A49	2a dull violet	2.25	.25
a.		Booklet pane of 4	50.00	
111	A49	2a ver ('34)	4.25	.75
a.		Small die ('36)	7.00	.55
112	A57	2a6p buff	2.75	.30
113	A51	3a ultramarine	12.50	1.50
114	A51	3a blue ('30)	12.00	.30
115	A51	3a car rose ('32)	9.75	.30
116	A52	4a olive green	1.50	.25
117	A53	6a bister ('35)	17.50	2.25
118	A54	8a red violet	5.75	.30
119	A55	12a claret	7.50	.30
120	A56	1r grn & brn	7.00	.60
121	A56	2r brn org & car rose	22.50	.85
122	A56	5r dk vio & ultra	47.50	1.75
123	A56	10r car & grn	110.00	6.50
124	A56	15r ol grn & ultra	47.50	35.00
125	A56	25r blue & ocher	300.00	47.50
		Nos. 106-125 (20)	616.00	99.80
		Set, never hinged	975.00	

No. 111 measures 19x22½mm, while the small die, No. 111a, measures 18½x22mm.
For overprints see Nos. O78-O92, Chamba Nos. 50-59, 65, 67-69, O36-O49, Gwalior Nos. 71-84, 89, O30-O39, O44-O45, Jind Nos. 108-125, 128-129, 131-132, O36-O48, O51-O54, Nabha Nos. 51-53, 56, 58-59, 67-68, O34, O36-O37, Patiala Nos. 60-71, 77-79, O40-O50, O53-O54.

127	A60	2a vermilion ('32)	16.00	7.50
128	A61	4a olive green	8.50	.30
		Nos. 126-128 (3)	27.50	8.05

For overprints see #O82-O83, O86, Gwalior O33-O34.

Fortress of Purana Qila — A62

George V Flanked by Dominion Columns — A67

½a, War Memorial Arch. 1a, Council Building. 2a, Viceroy's House. 3a, Parliament Building.

Wmk. 196 Sideways
1931, Feb. 9   Litho.   Perf. 13½x14
129	A62	¼a brown & ol grn	2.50	5.50
130	A62	½a green & violet	1.60	.40
131	A62	1a choc & red vio	1.25	.30
132	A62	2a blue & green	1.60	1.10
133	A62	3a car & choc	4.25	2.50
134	A67	1r violet & green	21.00	60.00
		Nos. 129-134 (6)	32.20	69.80
		Set, never hinged	100.00	

Change of the seat of Government from Calcutta to New Delhi.

A68
A69
A70

Wmk. 196
1932, Apr. 22   Litho.   Perf. 14
135	A68	9p dark green	7.50	.25
136	A69	1a3p violet	1.25	.25
137	A70	3a6p deep blue	8.00	.30
		Nos. 135-137 (3)	16.75	.80

No. 135 exists both litho. and typo.
For overprints see Nos. O94, O96, O104, Chamba Nos. 61, 63, Gwalior Nos. 86, 88, O41, O43, Jind No. 130, Nabha Nos. 64, 66, Patiala Nos. O58-O59.

A71
A72

1934   Typo.
138	A71	½a green	7.50	.25
139	A72	1a dark brown	8.50	.25

For overprints see Nos. O94, O96, Chamba Nos. 60, 62, Gwalior Nos. 85, 87, O40, O42, Jind 126-127, O49-O50, Nabha 63, 65, O35, Patiala Nos. 75-76, O51-O52.

Silver Jubilee Issue

Gateway of India, Bombay — A73

Designs: 9p, Victoria Memorial, Calcutta. 1a, Rameswaram Temple, Madras. 1¼a, Jain Temple, Calcutta. 2½a, Taj Mahal, Agra. 3½a, Golden Temple, Amritsar. 8a, Pagoda, Mandalay.

Wmk. 196 Sideways
1935   Litho.   Perf. 13½x14
142	A73	½a lt green & black	1.25	.30
143	A73	9p dull green & blk	2.25	.30
144	A73	1a brown & black	4.50	.30
145	A73	1¼a violet & black	1.10	.30
146	A73	2½a brown org & blk	8.50	.80

INDIA

147	A73	3½a blue & black	5.50	9.00
148	A73	8a rose lilac & blk	5.75	3.00
		Nos. 142-148 (7)	28.85	14.00
		Set, never hinged		45.00

25th anniv. of the reign of George V.

King George VI A80 A82

Dak Runner — A81

Mail transport: 2a6p, Dak bullock cart. 3a, Dak tonga. 3a6p, Dak camel. 4a, Mail train. 6a, Mail steamer. 8a, Mail truck. 12a, 14a, Mail plane.

Perf. 13½x14 or 14x13½

1937-40		Typo.	Wmk. 196	
150	A80	3p slate	1.25	.25
151	A80	½a brown	6.00	.25
152	A80	9p green	5.00	.55
153	A80	1a carmine	.75	
a.		Tete beche pair	3.00	2.75
b.		Booklet pane of 4	10.00	
154	A81	2a scarlet	7.75	.35
155	A81	2a6p purple	.90	.30
156	A81	3a yellow green	7.75	.35
157	A81	3a6p ultramarine	6.75	.50
158	A81	4a dark brown	9.00	.30
159	A81	6a pck blue	10.00	1.10
160	A81	8a blue violet	4.50	.50
161	A81	12a car lake	11.00	1.25
161A	A81	14a rose vio ('40)	16.00	2.00
162	A82	1r brn & sl	1.75	.25
163	A82	2r dk brn & dk violet	8.30	.40
164	A82	5r dp ultra & dk grn	29.00	.60
165	A82	10r rose car & dk vio	21.00	1.00
166	A82	15r dk grn & dk brn	100.00	95.00
167	A82	25r dk vio & blue vio	160.00	28.00
		Nos. 150-167 (19)	406.90	133.20
		Set, never hinged		620.00

The King's portrait is larger on No. 161A than on other stamps of type A81.

For overprints see Nos. O97-O103, Chamba, 70-88, 101-107, O50-O54, O66-O69, Gwalior Nos. 90-96, 112-117, O46-O51, Jind Nos. 133-164, O55-O61, O72-O75, Nabha Nos. 69-90, O38-O39, O49-O51, Patiala Nos. 80-101, 115, O55-O56, O60-O62, O74-O76.

Catalogue values for unused stamps in this section, from this point to the end of the section, are for Never Hinged items.

A83 A84

A85

Perf. 13½x14

1941-43		Typo.	Wmk. 196	
168	A83	3p slate ('42)	.75	.25
169	A83	½a rose vio ('42)	1.50	.25
170	A83	9p light green	1.25	.25
171	A83	1a car rose ('43)	2.00	.25
172	A84	1a3p bister	1.25	.25
172A	A84	1½a dark pur ('42)	2.50	.25
173	A84	2a scarlet	1.75	.25
174	A84	3a violet	4.00	.25
175	A84	3½a ultramarine	1.50	.90
176	A85	4a chocolate	1.50	.25
177	A85	6a peacock blue	4.50	.25
178	A85	8a blue violet	1.50	.35
179	A85	12a carmine lake	14.00	1.00
		Nos. 168-179 (13)	38.00	4.75

Early printings of the 1½a and 3a were lithographed.

For surcharge see No. 199. For overprints see Chamba Nos. 89-100, Gwalior Nos. 100-111, 118-126, Jind Nos. 165-177, O62-O71, Nabha Nos. 100-112, Patiala Nos. 102-114.

For stamps with this overprint, or a smaller type, see Oman (Muscat).

Symbols of Victory — A86

1946, Jan. 2 Litho. Perf. 13

195	A86	9p green	.90	1.25
196	A86	1½a dull purple	.70	.35
197	A86	3½a ultramarine	1.75	2.50
198	A86	12a brown lake	2.25	1.40
		Nos. 195-198 (4)	5.60	5.50

Victory of the Allied Nations in WWII.

No. 172 Surcharged With New Value and Bars

1946, Aug. 8 Perf. 13½x14

| 199 | A84 | 3p on 1a3p bister | .35 | .25 |

Dominion of India

Asoka Pillar A87 **National Flag A88**

Four-Motor Plane — A89

Perf. 14x13½, 13½x14

1947		Litho.	Wmk. 196	
200	A87	1½a greenish blue	1.00	.30
201	A88	3½a multicolored	3.00	2.00
202	A89	12a ultramarine	4.00	2.50
		Nos. 200-202 (3)	8.00	4.80

Elevation to dominion status, Aug. 15, 1947.

Mahatma Gandhi — A90

Design: 10r, Gandhi profile.

Perf. 11½

1948, Aug. 15 Unwmk. Photo.
Size: 22x32½mm

203	A90	1½a brown	9.50	1.50
204	A90	3½a violet	19.00	6.00
205	A90	12a dark gray green	29.00	10.00

Size: 22x37mm

206	A90	10r rose brn & brn	500.00	200.00
		Nos. 203-206 (4)	557.50	217.50

Mohandas K. Gandhi, 1869-1948.
Nos. 203-206 exist with "Specimen" overprints in a limited edition presentation booklet. The stamps are affixed to gold foil pages. Value, complete booklet $13,000.
For overprints see Nos. O112A-O112D.

Ajanta Panel A91 **Konarak Horse A92**

Bodhisattva A93 **Tomb of Muhammad Adil Shah, Bijapur A95**

Sanchi Stupa A94 **Victory Tower, Chittorgarh A96**

Red Fort, Delhi — A97

Satrunjaya Temple, Palitana — A98

9p, Trimurti. 2a, Nataraja. 3½a, Bodh Gaya Temple. 4a, Bhuvanesvara. 8a, Kandarya Mahadeva Temple. 12a, Golden Temple, Amritsar. 5r, Taj Mahal. 10r, Qutb Minar.

Perf. 13½x14, 14x13½

1949, Aug. 15		Typo.	Wmk. 196	
207	A91	3p gray violet	.40	.25
208	A92	6p red brown	.40	.25
209	A93	9p green	.60	.25
210	A93	1a turquoise	.80	.25
211	A93	2a carmine	1.50	.25
212	A94	3a red orange	2.75	.25
213	A94	3½a ultramarine	2.25	7.00
214	A94	4a brown lake	7.00	.55
215	A95	6a purple	3.00	.60
216	A95	8a blue green	2.50	.25
217	A95	12a blue	10.00	.35

Litho.

218	A96	1r dk green & pur	37.50	1.50
219	A97	2r pur & rose red	27.50	.50
220	A97	5r brn car & dk grn	67.50	2.50
221	A96	10r dp bl & brn car	150.00	18.50

Perf. 13½x13

222	A98	15r dp car & dk brn	35.00	27.50
		Nos. 207-222 (16)	348.70	60.75

See Nos. 231, 235-236. For overprints see Nos. M44-M46, M48-M55 and Intl. Commission in Indo-china issues for Cambodia, Nos. 1, 3-5, Laos Nos. 1, 3-5 and Vietnam Nos. 1, 3-5.

Symbols of UPU and Asoka Pillar — A99

1949, Oct. Litho. Perf. 13½x13

223	A99	9p dull green	4.75	2.00
224	A99	2a carmine rose	4.50	2.00
225	A99	3½a ultramarine	7.00	3.00
226	A99	12a red brown	11.00	3.50
		Nos. 223-226 (4)	27.25	10.50

75th anniv. of the formation of the UPU.

Republic of India

Rejoicing Crowds — A100

Designs: 3½a, Quill pen, vert. 4a, Plow and wheat. 12a, Charkha and cloth.

Perf. 13½x13

1950, Jan. 26			Wmk. 196	
227	A100	2a carmine	5.75	.60
228	A100	3½a ultramarine	8.75	7.00
229	A100	4a purple	8.75	1.25
230	A100	12a claret	14.00	2.50
		Nos. 227-230 (4)	37.25	11.35

Type of 1949 Redrawn

Bodhisattva — A101

1950, July 15 Typo. Perf. 13½x14

| 231 | A101 | 1a turquoise | 4.50 | .90 |

For overprints see No. M47, Intl. Commission in Indo-china issues for Cambodia, No. 2, Laos, No. 2, and Vietnam, No. 2.

INDIA

Extinct Stegodon Ganesa — A102

1951, Jan. 13   *Perf. 13*
232   A102   2a dp car & blk   4.50   1.00
Geological Survey of India, cent.

Torch and Map — A103

1951, Mar. 4   *Typo.*
233   A103   2a red vio & red org   4.00   1.00
234   A103   12a dk brn & ultra   15.00   2.40
First Asian Games, New Delhi.

Temple Type of 1949

2½a, Bodh Gaya Temple. 4a, Bhuvanesvara.

Perf. 13½x14
1951, Apr. 30   *Wmk. 196*
235   A94   2½a brown lake   5.50   3.00
236   A94   4a ultramarine   11.00   .35

Kabir — A104

1a, Tulsidas, poet & saint. 2a, Meera, Rajput princess. 4a, Surdas, blind poet and saint. 4½a, Ghalib, Urdu poet. 12a, Rabindranath Tagore.

1952, Oct. 1   *Photo.*   *Perf. 14x13½*
237   A104   9p emerald   3.25   .80
238   A104   1a crimson   3.25   .35
239   A104   2a red orange   4.00   .35
240   A104   4a ultramarine   13.00   1.25
241   A104   4½a red violet   2.50   1.50
242   A104   12a brown   22.50   1.90
   Nos. 237-242 (6)   48.50   6.15

First Locomotive and Streamliner A105

1953, Apr. 16   *Perf. 14½x14*
243   A105   2a black   3.50   .45
Centenary of India's railroads.

Mt. Everest — A106

1953, Oct. 2
244   A106   2a violet   5.00   .35
245   A106   14a brown   13.50   1.75
Conquest of Mt. Everest, May 29, 1953.

Telegraph Poles of 1851 and 1951 — A107

1953, Nov. 1
246   A107   2a blue green   2.75   .35
247   A107   12a blue   19.00   .75
Centenary of the telegraph in India.

Mail Transport, 1854 — A108

Designs: 2a and 14a, Pigeon and plane. 4a, Mail transport, 1954.

1954, Oct. 1
248   A108   1a rose lilac   .40   .30
249   A108   2a rose pink   1.50   .30
250   A108   4a yellow brown   12.00   1.50
251   A108   14a blue   7.25   .45
   Nos. 248-251 (4)   21.15   2.55
Centenary of India's postage stamps.

UN Emblem and Lotus Blossom — A109

1954, Oct. 24
252   A109   2a Prussian green   1.25   .40
United Nations Day.

Forest Research Institute, Dehra Dun — A110

1954, Dec. 11
253   A110   2a ultramarine   1.25   .30
4th World Forestry Cong., Dehra Dun.

Tractor A111   **Charkha Operator A112**

Symbols of Malaria Control — A113

Designs: 6p, Power looms. 9p, Bullock irrigation pump. 1a, Damodar Valley dam. 3a, Naga woman at hand loom. 4a, Bullock team. 8a, Chittaranjan Locomotive Works. 10a, Plane over Marine Drive, Bombay. 12a, Hindustan aircraft factory. 14a, Plane over Kashmir valley. 1r, Telephone factory worker. 1r2a, Plane over Cape Comorin. 1r8a, Plane over Kanchenjunga Mountains. 2r, Rare earth factory. 5r, Sindri fertilizer factory. 10r, Steel mill.

Perf. 14x14½, 14½x14
1955, Jan. 26   *Photo.*
254   A111   3p rose lilac   .45   .25
255   A111   6p deep violet   .45   .25
256   A111   9p org brn   .60   .25
257   A111   1a dp bl grn   .60   .25
258   A112   2a blue   .45   .25
259   A112   3a blue green   .90   .25
260   A111   4a rose red   .85   .25
261   A113   6a yellow brown   2.25   .25
262   A111   8a deep blue   10.00   .25
263   A113   10a aquamarine   5.00   3.25
264   A111   12a violet blue   5.50   .25
265   A113   14a emerald   7.00   .55
266   A111   1r grnsh blk   6.00   .25
267   A113   1r2a gray   3.00   6.00
268   A113   1r8a claret   12.00   7.00
269   A111   2r carmine rose   5.50   .25
270   A111   5r brown   19.00   .70
271   A111   10r orange   20.00   5.00
   Nos. 254-271 (18)   99.55   25.50
See Nos. 316-319.

Bodhi Tree — A114   **Ornament and Bodhi Tree — A115**

1956, May 24   *Wmk. 196*   *Perf. 13*
272   A114   2a brown   2.00   .30
273   A115   14a brick red   13.00   3.75
2500th anniv. of the birth of Buddha.

Bal Gangadhar Tilak — A116

1956, July 23   *Wmk. 196*   *Photo.*
274   A116   2a orange brown   .80   .40
Birth cent. of Bal Gangadhar Tilak, independence leader.

Map of India — A117

1957-58   *Perf. 14x14½*
275   A117   1np blue green   .25   .25
276   A117   2np light brown   .25   .25
277   A117   3np brown   .25   .25
278   A117   5np emerald   5.25   .25
279   A117   6np gray   .25   .25
280   A117   8np brt green ('58)   5.00   1.00
281   A117   10np dark green   5.50   .25
282   A117   13np brt carmine   .90   .25
283   A117   15np violet ('58)   5.00   .25
284   A117   20np bright blue   .90   .25
285   A117   25np ultramarine   .95   .25
286   A117   50np orange   4.75   .25
287   A117   75np plum   2.25   .25
288   A117   90np red lilac ('58)   6.50   2.00
   Nos. 275-288 (14)   38.15   6.00

Denominations of the 8np, 15np and 90np are inscribed nP.
See Nos. 302-315. For overprints see No. M60 and Intl. Commission in Indo-China issues for Cambodia, Nos. 6-10, Laos, Nos. 6-10, and Vietnam, Nos. 6-10.

Laxmibai, Rani of Jhansi A118   **Banyan Sapling, Arch and Flames A119**

Perf. 14½x14, 13
1957, Aug. 15   *Wmk. 196*
289   A118   15np brown   .50   .35
290   A119   90np bright red violet   8.50   1.25
Centenary of the struggle for independence (Indian Mutiny).

Henri Dunant — A120

1957, Oct. 28   *Perf. 13½x13*
291   A120   15np car rose & black   .50   .30
19th Intl. Red Cross Conf., New Delhi.

Boy Eating Banana A121   **Bankura Horse A122**

Children's Day: 15np, Girl writing on tablet.

1957, Nov. 14   *Perf. 13½*
292   A121   8np rose lilac   .35   .25
293   A121   15np aquamarine   .35   .25
294   A122   90np lt orange brown   1.10   .25
   Nos. 292-294 (3)   1.80   .75

Madras University — A123

University Centenaries: No. 296, Calcutta. No. 297, Bombay, vert.

1957, Dec. 31   *Photo.*
   Size: 29½x25mm
295   A123   10np light brown   1.00   .35
296   A123   10np gray   1.00   .35
   Size: 21½x38mm
297   A123   10np violet   1.00   .35
   Nos. 295-297 (3)   3.00   1.05

J. N. Tata and Steel Works, Jamshedpur A124

1958, Mar. 1   *Perf. 14½x14*
298   A124   15np red orange   .50   .30
50th anniv. of Indian steel industry.

Dr. Dhondo Keshav Karve — A125

1958, Apr. 18   *Perf. 14x13½*
299   A125   15np orange brown   .60   .30
Cent. of the birth of Karve, educator and pioneer of women's education.

Wapiti and Hunter Planes — A126

1958, Apr. 30   *Perf. 14½x14*
300   A126   15np bright blue   1.50   .30
301   A126   90np ultramarine   2.50   2.00
25th anniv. of the Indian Air Force.

Map Type of 1957-58 and Industrial Type of 1955

1r, Telephone factory worker. 2r, Rare earth factory. 5r, Sindri fertilizer factory. 10r, Steel mill.

Perf. 14x14½
1958-63   *Photo.*   *Wmk. 324*
302   A117   1np bl grn ('60)   1.50   .75
   a. Imperf., pair   650.00
303   A117   2np light brown   .40   .25
304   A117   3np brown   .40   .25
305   A117   5np emerald   .40   .25
306   A117   6np gray ('63)   .55   3.25
307   A117   8np bright green   1.00   .25
308   A117   10np dark green   .60   .25
   a. Imperf., pair   1,000.
309   A117   13np brt car ('63)   2.50   3.75
310   A117   15np violet ('59)   1.00   .25
311   A117   20np bright blue   .85   .25
312   A117   25np ultramarine   .85   .25
313   A117   50np orange ('59)   1.25   .25
314   A117   75np plum ('59)   2.00   .30
315   A117   90np red lil ('60)   6.00   .30
316   A111   1r dk grn ('59)   5.00   .30
317   A111   2r lil rose ('59)   8.25   .30
318   A111   5r brown ('59)   10.00   .50
319   A111   10r orange ('59)   35.00   7.00
   Nos. 302-319 (18)   77.55   18.70

For overprints see Nos. M56-M59, M61, Intl. Commission in Indo-china issues for Cambodia, No. 12, Laos, Nos. 12-16, and Vietnam Nos. 11-16.

Bipin Chandra Pal — A128

1958, Nov. 7   *Perf. 13½*
320   A128   15np dull green   .60   .40
Birth cent. of Pal, early leader of India's freedom movement.

INDIA

1958, Nov. 30
Portrait: Sir Jagadis Chandra Bose.
321 A128 15np brt greenish blue .60 .40
Bose, physicist, plant physiologist, birth cent.

Nurse and Child — A129

1958, Nov. 14 Wmk. 324
322 A129 15np violet .60 .40
Children's Day, Nov. 14.

Exhibition Gate — A130

1958, Dec. 30 Perf. 14½x14
323 A130 15np claret .60 .30
India 1958 Exhibition at Kampur.

Sir Jamsetjee Jejeebhoy — A131

1959, Apr. 13 Perf. 13½
324 A131 15np brown .60 .30
Cent. of the death of Jejeebhoy, philosopher and philanthropist.

"Triumph of Labor," by D. P. Roy Chowdhary A132

1959, June 15 Perf. 14½x14
325 A132 15np dull green .60 .40
40th anniv. of the ILO.

Children Arriving at Institution — A133

Perf. 14x14½
1959, Nov. 14 Photo. Wmk. 324
326 A133 15np dull green .60 .40
  a. Imperf., pair 1,200.
Children's Day, Nov. 14.

Farmer Plowing with Bullocks — A134

1959, Dec. 30 Perf. 13
327 A134 15np gray .50 .30
World Agriculture Fair, New Delhi.

Thiruvalluvar Holding Stylus and Palmyra Leaf — A135

1960, Feb. 15 Perf. 14
328 A135 15np rose lilac .60 .40
Honoring the ancient and saintly Tamil poet, Thiruvalluvar.

Scene from Meghduta A136

Scene from Sakuntala A137

1960, June 22 Perf. 13
329 A136 15np gray .90 .30
330 A137 1.03r brown & bister 3.75 1.00
Honoring Kalidasa, 5th cent. poet and dramatist.
For surcharge see No. 371.

Subramania Bharati — A138

1960, Sept. 11 Photo. Perf. 14x13½
331 A138 15np bright blue .60 .40
Honoring the poet and statesman Subramania Bharati (1882-1921).

Dr. M. Visvesvaraya — A139

1960, Sept. 15 Perf. 13x13½
332 A139 15np car rose & brown .60 .40
Birth cent. of Visvesvaraya, engineer and statesman.

Children Playing and Studying — A140

1960, Nov. 14 Perf. 13½x13
333 A140 15np green .60 .40
Children's Day, Nov. 14.

Children and UN Emblem — A141

1960, Dec. 11 Wmk. 324
334 A141 15np olive gray & org brn .60 .40
UNICEF Day.

Tyagaraja, Indian Musician — A142

1961, Jan. 6 Photo. Perf. 14
335 A142 15np bright blue .60 .40
114th anniv. of Tyagaraja's death.

First Airmail Postmark — A143

Boeing 707 Jetliner A144

Design: 1r, Humber-Sommer biplane.
Perf. 14, 13x13½
1961, Feb. 18 Wmk. 324
336 A143 5np olive bister 2.75 .30
337 A144 15np gray & green 2.50 .30
338 A144 1r gray & claret 7.25 2.50
  Nos. 336-338 (3) 12.50 3.10
50th anniv. of the world's 1st airmail. The flight was from Allahabad to Naini, Feb. 18, 1911.

Chatrapati Sivaji Maharaj (1627-1680) — A145

1961, Apr. 17 Perf. 13x13½
339 A145 15np gray grn & brn 1.50 .50
Leader of the Maharattas in the fight against the Moguls.

Motilal Nehru — A146

1961, May 6 Perf. 14x13½
340 A146 15np orange & ol gray .60 .40
Cent. of the birth of Motilal Nehru, leader in India's fight for freedom.

Rabindranath Tagore — A147

1961, May 7 Perf. 13
341 A147 15np blue grn & org 1.10 .40
Cent. of the birth of Tagore, poet.

Radio Masts and All India Radio Emblem — A148

1961, June 8 Photo. Wmk. 324
342 A148 15np ultramarine .60 .40
25th anniv. of All India Radio.

Prafulla Chandra Ray — A149

1961, Aug. 2 Perf. 14x13½
343 A149 15np gray .60 .30
Cent. of the birth of Ray, scientist.

Vishnu Narayan Bhatkhande — A150

1961, Sept. 1 Perf. 13
344 A150 15np olive gray .60 .40
Bhatkhande (1860-1936), musician.

Boy Making Pottery — A151

1961, Nov. 14 Perf. 13½
345 A151 15np brown .60 .40
Children's Day, Nov. 14.

Gate at Fair — A152

1961, Nov. 14 Perf. 14x14½
346 A152 15np blue & carmine .60 .40
Indian Industries Fair at New Delhi.

Forest and Himalayas — A153

1961, Nov. 21 Perf. 13
347 A153 15np brown & green .60 .35
Cent. of the introduction of scientific forestry in India.

Yaksha, God of Fertility A154

Kalibangan Seal A155

1961, Dec. 14 Photo. Perf. 14
348 A154 15np orange brown 1.00 .45
349 A155 90np org brn & ol 3.75 .45
Cent. of the Archaeological Survey of India.

Madan Mohan Malaviya — A156

1961, Dec. 25 Perf. 14x13½
350 A156 15np slate .60 .40
Cent. of the birth of Malaviya, Pres. of the Indian Natl. Cong. and Vice Chancellor of Benares University.

227

INDIA

Nunmati Refinery, Gauhati — A157

1962, Jan. 1   Photo.   Perf. 13
351   A157   15np blue   .90   .40
1st Indian oil refinery at Gauhati.

Bhikaiji Cama — A158

1962, Jan. 26   Perf. 14
352   A158   15np rose lilac   .60   .40
Cent. of the birth of Madame Cama, a leader in India's fight for independence.

Village Council, Banyan Tree, Parliament and Map — A159

1962, Jan. 26   Perf. 13
353   A159   15np red lilac   .60   .40
Panchayati Raj, the system of government by village council.

Dayananda Sarasvati — A160

1962, Mar. 4   Perf. 14
354   A160   15np brown orange   .60   .40
135th anniv. of the birth of Sarasvati, reformer of the Vedic religion and founder of the Arya Samaj educational institutions.

Ganesh Shankar Vidyarthi — A161

1962, Mar. 25
355   A161   15np reddish brown   .60   .40
Vidyarthi (1890-1931), reformer of community life.

Malaria Eradication Emblem — A162

1962, Apr. 7   Perf. 13
356   A162   15np dk car rose & yel   .60   .40
WHO drive to eradicate malaria.

Dr. Rajendra Prasad — A163

1962, May 13   Perf. 13
357   A163   15np bright red lilac   .60   .40
Prasad, President of India (1950-62).

High Court, Calcutta — A164

1962   Photo.   Perf. 13½x14
358   A164   15np green   .80   .30
359   A164   15np Madras   .80   .30
360   A164   15np Bombay   .80   .30
Nos. 358-360 (3)   2.40   .90
Indian High Courts, cent. Issued: No. 358, July 1; No. 359, Aug. 8; No. 360, Aug. 14.

Ramabai Ranade — A165

1962, Aug. 15   Perf. 14
361   A165   15np brown orange   .60   .40
Ramabai Ranade (1862-1924), woman social reformer.

Indian Rhinoceros — A166

10np, Gaur. No. 363, Lesser panda, vert. 30np, Elephant, vert. 50np, Tiger. 1r, Lion.

1962-63   Wmk. 324   Perf. 14
   Size: 30x26mm
361A   A166   10np yel org & blk ('63)   1.50   1.75
362   A166   15np Prus blue & brn   .90   .30
   Perf. 13x13½, 13½x13
   Size: 25x36mm, 36x25mm
363   A166   15np grn & red brn ('63)   2.00   .60
364   A166   30np bis & sl ('63)   5.50   1.50
365   A166   50np dp grn, ocher & brn ('63)   5.75   1.00
366   A166   1r brt bl & pale brn ('63)   5.75   1.00
Nos. 361A-366 (6)   21.40   6.15

Child Reaching for Flag — A167

1962, Nov. 14   Perf. 13
367   A167   15np lt bluish grn & ver   .60   .40
Children's Day.

Eye within Lotus Blossom — A168

1962, Dec. 3   Photo.
368   A168   15np olive gray   .60   .30
16th Intl. Cong. of Ophthalmology, New Delhi, Dec. 1962.

Srinivasa Ramanujan — A169

1962, Dec. 22   Perf. 13½x14
369   A169   15np olive gray   1.00   .45
75th anniv. of the birth of Ramanujan (1887-1920), mathematician.

Swami Vivekananda — A170

1963, Jan. 17   Perf. 14x14½
370   A170   15np ol & org brn   .70   .40
Cent. of the birth of Vivekananda (1863-1902), philosopher.

No. 330 Surcharged with New Value and Two Bars

1963, Feb. 2   Perf. 13
371   A137   1r on 1.03r brn & bis   8.75   .70

Hands Reaching for "FAO" Emblem — A171

1963, Mar. 21   Photo.
372   A171   15np chalky blue   2.00   .50
UNFAO Freedom from Hunger campaign.

Henri Dunant and Centenary Emblem — A172

1963, May 8   Perf. 13
373   A172   15np gray & red   4.00   .50
Centenary of the International Red Cross. No. 373 exists with red cross omitted. Value, $25,000.

Field Artillery and Helicopter A173

Design: 1r, Soldier guarding frontier and plane dropping supplies.

1963, Aug. 15   Perf. 13½x14
374   A173   15np dull green   1.25   .30
375   A173   1r red brown   2.25   .90
Honoring the Armed Forces and the 16th anniv. of independence.

Dadabhoy Naoroji — A174

1963, Sept. 4   Perf. 13
376   A174   15np gray green   .60   .40
Honoring Dadabhoy Naoroji (1825-1917), mathematician and statesman.

Annie Besant — A175

1963, Oct. 1   Photo.   Perf. 14
377   A175   15np blue green   .60   .40
Besant (1847-1933), an English woman devoted to the cause of India's freedom, theosophist and writer. Stamp gives birth date as 1837.

School Lunch — A176

1963, Nov. 14   Wmk. 324   Perf. 14
378   A176   15np olive bister   .60   .40
Children's Day.

Eleanor Roosevelt at Spinning Wheel — A177

1963, Dec. 10   Perf. 13
379   A177   15np rose violet   .55   .35
Honoring Eleanor Roosevelt on the 15th anniv. of the Universal Declaration of Human Rights.

Gopabandhu Das (1877-1928) — A178

1964, Jan. 4   Perf. 13
380   A178   15np dull purple   .70   .40
Gopabandhu Das, social reformer.

Lakshmi, Goddess of Wealth — A179

1964, Jan. 4   Photo.
381   A179   15np dull violet blue   .60   .40
26th Intl. Cong. of Orientalists, New Delhi, Jan. 4-14.

Purandaradasa Holding Veena and Chipala — A180

1964, Jan. 14
382   A180   15np golden brown   .55   .35
400th anniv. of the death of Purandaradasa (1484-1564), musician.

Subhas Chandra Bose and INA Emblem — A181

Design: 55np, Bose addressing troops.

INDIA

1964, Jan. 23   **Perf. 13**
383   A181   15np olive   .55   .35
384   A181   55np red & black   1.25   .40
    67th anniv. of the birth of Bose, organizer of the Indian Natl. Army.

Sarojini Naidu (1879-1949) — A182

1964, Feb. 13   **Perf. 14x13½**
385   A182   15np dl lil & sl grn   .55   .35
    Mrs. Sarojini Naidu, poet, politician, governor of United Provinces.

Kasturba Gandhi — A183

1964, Feb. 22   **Photo.**   **Wmk. 324**
386   A183   15np brown orange   .55   .35
    20th anniv. of the death of Kasturba Gandhi (1869-1944), wife of Mahatma Gandhi.

Dr. Waldemar M. Haffkine (1860-1930) — A184

1964, Mar. 16   **Perf. 13**
387   A184   15np violet brown, *buff*   1.00   .40
    Haffkine, bacteriologist, who as director of Haffkine Institute introduced inoculations against cholera and plague.

Jawaharlal Nehru (1889-1964) and People — A185

1964, June 12   **Unwmk.**   **Perf. 13**
388   A185   15p grayish blue   .55   .35
    Prime Minister Jawaharlal Nehru.

Asutosh Mookerjee and High Court, Calcutta — A186

1964, June 29   **Wmk. 324**
389   A186   15p olive green & brn   .55   .35
    Cent. of the birth of Asutosh Mookerjee (1864-1924), educator, lawyer and judge.

Sri Aurobindo Ghose (1872-1950), Writer and Philosopher — A187

1964, Aug. 15   **Photo.**
390   A187   15p violet brown   .55   .35

Raja Rammohun Roy — A188

1964, Sept. 27   **Perf. 13**
391   A188   15p reddish brown   .55   .35
    Roy (1772-1833), Hindu religious reformer.

Globe, Lotus, and Calipers — A189

1964, Nov. 9   **Unwmk.**   **Photo.**
392   A189   15p carmine rose   .55   .35
    6th gen. assembly of the Intl. Organization for Standardization.

Nehru Medal and Rose — A190

1964, Nov. 14   **Perf. 13½**
393   A190   15p blue gray   .80   .40
    Children's Day. For overprints, see Nos. M62, Intl. Commission in Indo-china issues for Laos and Vietnam, No. 1.

St. Thomas Statue, Ortona, Italy — A191

1964, Dec. 2   **Unwmk.**   **Perf. 13½**
394   A191   15p rose violet   .45   .35
    Visit of Pope Paul VI, Nov. 30-Dec. 2.

Globe and Pickax — A192

1964, Dec. 14   **Wmk. 324**
395   A192   15p bright green   .55   .40
    22nd Intl. Geological Cong., New Delhi.

Jamsetji N. Tata — A193

1965, Jan. 7   **Unwmk.**   **Perf. 13**
396   A193   15p dk brown & orange   .45   .35
    125th anniv. of the birth of Tata (1839-1904), founder of India's steel industry.

Lala Lajpatrai (1865-1928), a Leader in India's Fight for Independence — A194

1965, Jan. 28   **Photo.**   **Perf. 13**
397   A194   15p brown   .45   .35

ICC Emblem and Globe — A195

1965, Feb. 8   **Litho.**
398   A195   15p dull green & car   .45   .35
    20th cong. of the Intl. Chamber of Commerce, New Delhi.

Freighter Jalausha at Visakhapatnam — A196

Perf. 14½x14
1965, Apr. 5   **Photo.**   **Wmk. 324**
399   A196   15p ultramarine   .65   .45
    National Maritime Day.

Death Centenary of Abraham Lincoln — A197

1965, Apr. 15   **Perf. 13**
400   A197   15p yellow & dk brown   .70   .40

ITU Emblem, Old and New Communication Equipment A198

1965, May 17   **Photo.**   **Perf. 14½x14**
401   A198   15p rose violet   1.50   .60
    Cent. of the ITU.

Torch and Rose — A199

1965, May 27   **Wmk. 324**   **Perf. 13**
402   A199   15p carmine & blue   .40   .35
    1st anniv. of the death of Jawaharlal Nehru.

ICY Emblem — A200

1965, June 26   **Photo.**   **Unwmk.**
403   A200   15p bister & dk green   1.25   .75
    International Cooperation Year.

Indians Raising Flag on Everest — A201

1965, Aug. 15   **Unwmk.**   **Perf. 13**
404   A201   15p plum   .50   .40
    Success of the Indian Mt. Everest Expedition, May 20, 1965.

Elephant from Konarak Temple, Orissa A202

Tea Picking A203

Woman Writing Letter, Chandella Carving, 11th Century A204

Trombay Atomic Center A205

    Designs: 2p, Vase (bidri ware). 3p, Brass lamp. 4p, Coffee berries. 5p, Family (family planning). 8p, Axis deer (chital). 10p, Electric locomotive, 1961. 20p, Gnat plane. 30p, Male and female figurines. 40p, General Post Office, Calcutta, 1868. 50p, Mangoes. 60p, Somnath Temple. 70p, Stone chariot, Hampi, Mysore. 2r, Dal Lake, Kashmir. 5r, Bhakra Dam, Punjab.

Perf. 14½x14, 14x14½
1965-68   **Photo.**   **Wmk. 324**
405   A202   2p redsh brown ('67)   .25   .50
406   A202   3p olive bis ('67)   .40   1.25
407   A203   4p orange brn ('68)   .25   1.00
408   A202   5p cerise ('67)   .25   .25
409   A202   6p gray ('66)   .25   1.60
410   A202   8p red brown ('67)   .40   2.00
411   A203   10p brt blue ('66)   .60   .25
412   A203   15p dk yel green   .50   .25
413   A203   20p plum ('67)   .50   .25
414   A202   30p brown ('67)   .25   .25
415   A203   40p brown vio ('68)   .25   .25
416   A203   50p green ('67)   .35   .25
417   A202   60p dark gray ('67)   .45   .25
418   A203   70p violet ('67)   .85   .25
419   A204   1r dp clar & red brn ('66)   1.25   .25
420   A205   2r vio & brt bl ('67)   3.75   .25
421   A205   5r brn & vio ('67)   8.00   .80
422   A205   10r green & gray   15.00   .50
    Nos. 405-422 (18)   33.55   10.40
    See Nos. 623, 666-670, 678, 680, 684-685. For overprints see Nos. RA1-RA2, Intl. Commission in Indo-china issues for Laos and Vietnam, Nos. 2-9.

1975-76   **Wmk. 360**   **Perf. 14½x14**
422A   A202   2p redsh brown   .75   1.10
423   A202   5p cerise   .85   .25
    Unwmk.
423A   A202   5p cerise ('76)   .75   .25

A206

1965, Sept. 10   **Unwmk.**   **Perf. 13**
424   A206   15p dk grn & brn   .50   .50
    Govind Ballabh Pant (1887-1961), Home Minister of India.

A207

1965, Oct. 31   **Perf. 14**
425   A207   15p gray   .50   .50
    Vallabhbhai Patel (1875-1950), Deputy Prime Minister of India.

INDIA

Chittaranjan Das (1870-1925) — A208

1965, Nov. 5   **Photo.**   **Perf. 13**
426   A208   15p brown   .50   .50

Das, freedom fighter, pres. of Indian Natl. Cong., mayor of Calcutta.

Vidyapati, 15th Cent. Poet — A209

1965, Nov. 17   **Perf. 14x14½**
427   A209   15p brown   .50   .50

Tomb of Akbar the Great, Sikandra — A210

1966, Jan. 24   **Perf. 14**
428   A210   15p dark gray   .50   .50

Pacific Area Travel Assoc. Conf., New Delhi.

Soldier, Planes and Warships — A211

1966, Jan. 26
429   A211   15p bright violet   1.00   .50

Honoring the Indian armed forces.

Lal Bahadur Shastri — A212

1966, Jan. 26   **Perf. 13**
430   A212   15p gray   .70   .50

Prime Minister Shastri (1904-66).

Kambar — A213

1966, Apr. 9   **Perf. 14x14½**
431   A213   15p green   .50   .50

Kambar, 9th century Tamil poet.

B. R. Ambedkar — A214

1966, Apr. 14   **Unwmk.**   **Perf. 14**
432   A214   15p violet brown   .50   .50

10th anniv. of the death of Dr. Bhimrao R. Ambedkar (1891-1956), lawyer and leader in social reform.

Kunwar Singh — A215

1966, Apr. 23   **Photo.**
433   A215   15p orange brown   .50   .50

Kunwar Singh (1777-1858), hero of 1857 War of Independence (1857 Mutiny).

Gopal Krishna Gokhale — A216

1966, May 9   **Unwmk.**   **Perf. 13**
434   A216   15p violet brown & yel   .50   .50

Cent. of the birth of Gokhale (1866-1915), professor of history and political economy and leader of the opposition party.

A. M. P. Dvivedi (1864-1938) — A217

1966, May 15   **Perf. 14**
435   A217   15p olive gray   .50   .50

Acharya Mahavir Prasad Dvivedi, Hindi writer.

Ranjit Singh (1780-1839) — A218

1966, June 28   **Unwmk.**   **Perf. 14**
436   A218   15p plum   .50   .50

Maharaja Ranjit Singh, ruler of Punjab.

Homi Bhabha and Atomic Reactor — A219

1966, Aug. 4   **Perf. 14½x14**
437   A219   15p brown violet   .75   .75

Dr. Homi Bhabha (1909-1966), scientist.

Rama Tirtha — A220

1966, Nov. 11   **Unwmk.**   **Perf. 13**
438   A220   15p greenish blue   .55   .55

60th anniv. of the death of Swami Rama Tirtha (1873-1906).

A221

1966, Nov. 11   **Photo.**   **Perf. 13½**
439   A221   15p dark violet blue   .50   .50

Abul Kalam Azad (1888-1958), president of the All-India Congress.

Child and Dove — A222

1966, Nov. 14   **Perf. 13**
440   A222   15p brt purple   .70   .40

Children's Day.

Allahabad High Court, Cent. — A223

1966, Nov. 25   **Perf. 14½x14**
441   A223   15p violet brown   .50   .50

Family — A224

1966, Dec. 12   **Perf. 13½x13**
442   A224   15p brown   .50   .50

Intl. Conf. for Marriage Guidance, New Delhi, and Family Planning Week.

Hockey — A225

1966, Dec. 31   **Unwmk.**   **Perf. 13**
443   A225   15p bright blue   1.25   1.00

Victory of the Indian hockey team at the 5th Asian Games, Bangkok, Dec. 19.

Grain Harvest — A226

1967, Jan. 11   **Perf. 13½**
444   A226   15p yellow green   .50   .50

1st anniv. of the death of Prime Minister Lal Bahadur Shastri, who advocated self-sufficiency in food production.

Voters — A227

1967, Jan. 13   **Photo.**
445   A227   15p light red brown   .50   .50

General elections, Feb. 1967.

Guru Dwara Shrine, Patna — A228

1967, Jan. 17   **Perf. 14**
446   A228   15p violet   .60   .60

300th anniv. of the birth of Gobind Singh (1666-1708), religious leader.

Taj Mahal — A229

1967, Mar. 19   **Perf. 14½x14**
447   A229   15p brown & orange   .60   .60

International Tourist Year.

Nandalal Bose and Garuda — A230

1967, Apr. 16   **Perf. 13½**
448   A230   15p brown   .50   .50

Nandalal Bose (1882-1966), painter.

Survey of India Emblem — A231

1967, May 1   **Unwmk.**   **Perf. 13**
449   A231   15p lilac   .70   .50

Bicentenary of Survey of India.

Basaveswara, 12th Cent. Statesman and Philosopher, at Work — A232

1967, May 11   **Perf. 13½x14**
450   A232   15p deep orange   .50   .50

Narsinh Mehta — A233

1967, May 30   **Perf. 13½**
451   A233   15p gray brown   .50   .50

Narsinh Mehta, 15th cent. poet.

Maharana Pratap — A234

1967, June 11   **Perf. 14x14½**
452   A234   15p reddish brown   .50   .50

Pratap (1540-1597), Mewar ruler.

Narayana Guru — A235

1967, Aug. 21   **Photo.**   **Perf. 14**
453   A235   15p brown   .50   .50

Narayana Guru (1855-1928), religious reformer.

INDIA

Dr. Sarvepalli Radhakrishnan — A236

1967, Sept. 5 Unwmk. *Perf. 13*
454 A236 15p dull claret .70 .40
Radhakrishnan, Pres. of India 1962-67.

Martyrs' Memorial, Patna — A237

1967, Oct. 1 Photo. *Perf. 14½x14*
455 A237 15p dark carmine .50 .50
25th anniv. of the "Quit India" revolt led by Gandhi.

Map Showing Indo-European Telegraph — A238

1967, Nov. 9 Photo. *Perf. 13½*
456 A238 15p blue & black .70 .50
Cent. of the laying of the Indo-European telegraph line.

Wrestlers — A239

1967, Nov. 12
457 A239 15p ocher & plum .70 .50
World Wrestling Championships, New Delhi, Nov. 1967.

Nehru and Naga Tribesmen — A240

1967, Dec. 4 Photo. *Perf. 13*
458 A240 15p ultramarine .50 .50

Rashbehari Basu — A241

1967, Dec. 26 *Perf. 13½*
459 A241 15p dull purple .50 .50
Basu (1886-1945), Bengali leader.

Bugle, Scout Emblem and Scout Sign — A242

1967, Dec. 27 *Perf. 14½x14*
460 A242 15p orange brown 1.25 .50
Boy Scout Movement, 60th anniv.

People Encircling the Globe and Human Rights Flame — A243

1968, Jan. 1 *Perf. 13*
461 A243 15p dark green .70 .50
Intl. Human Rights Year.

Conference Emblem and Gopuram Temple — A244

1968, Jan. 3 Photo. Unwmk.
462 A244 15p purple .70 .50
2nd Intl. Conf. on Tamil Studies, Madras.

UN Emblem, Plane and Ship — A245

1968, Feb. 1 *Perf. 14½x14*
463 A245 15p greenish blue .75 .50
UN Conference on Trade and Development, New Delhi, Feb. 1968.

Symbolic Bow and Quill Pen — A246

1968, Feb. 20 *Perf. 13½x14*
464 A246 15p ocher & sepia .50 .50
Cent. of the newspaper Amrit Bazar Patrika, Calcutta.

Maxim Gorky (1868-1936), Russian Writer — A247

1968, Mar. 28 Photo. *Perf. 14*
465 A247 15p brown violet .50 .50

Exhibition Emblem — A248

1968, Mar. 31 *Perf. 13*
466 A248 15p dark blue & org .65 .35
First Triennial Exhibition, New Delhi.

Symbolic Mail Box — A249

1968, July 1 Unwmk. *Perf. 13*
467 A249 20p vermilion & blue .60 .40
Opening of 100,000th Indian post office.

Wheat and Indian Agricultural Research Institute — A250

1968, July 15 Photo. *Perf. 13*
468 A250 20p brt grn & brn org .60 .40
India's 1968 bumper wheat crop.

Gaganendranath Tagore (1867-1938), Self-portrait — A251

1968, Sept. 17 Unwmk. *Perf. 13*
469 A251 20p ocher & deep clar .70 .50

Lakshminath Bezbaruah (1868-1938), Writer — A252

1968, Oct. 5 Photo. *Perf. 13½*
470 A252 20p sepia .50 .50

19th Olympic Games, Mexico City — A253

1968, Oct. 12 *Perf. 14½x14*
471 A253 20p blue gray & red brn .40 .30
472 A253 1r olive gray & dk brn .85 .30

Bhagat Singh (1907-1931), Revolutionary A254

1968, Oct. 19 Photo. *Perf. 13½x13*
473 A254 20p orange brown .50 .50

Bose Reading Proclamation — A255

1968, Oct. 21 *Perf. 14x14½*
474 A255 20p dark blue .50 .50
25th anniv. of the establishment of the Azad Hind (Free India) government by Subhas Chandra Bose (1897-1945), independence leader.

Sister Nivedita — A256

1968, Oct. 27
475 A256 20p blue green .60 .50
Sister Nivedita (Margaret Noble, 1867-1911), Irish-born friend of India.

Marie Curie and Patient Receiving Radiation — A257

1968, Nov. 6 *Perf. 14½x14*
476 A257 20p purple 2.50 .70
Marie Sklodowska Curie (1867-1934), discoverer of radium and polonium.

World Map — A258

1968, Dec. 1 *Perf. 13*
477 A258 20p blue 1.00 .60
21st Intl. Geographical Congress.

Interior of Cochin Synagogue — A259

Perf. 13x13½
1968, Dec. 15 Photo. Unwmk.
478 A259 20p vio bl & car rose 2.00 .75
400th anniv. of Cochin Synagogue.

Frigate Nilgiri — A260

1968, Dec. 15 *Perf. 13½x13*
479 A260 20p dull violet blue 1.75 .60
Navy Day. The Nilgiri, launched Oct. 23, 1968, was the 1st Indian warship.

Redbilled Blue Magpie — A261

Birds: 50p, Brown-fronted pied woodpecker. 1r, Slaty-headed scimitar babbler, vert. 2r, Yellow-backed sunbirds.

1968, Dec. 31 *Perf. 14½x14, 14x14½*
480 A261 20p pink & multi 1.10 .60
481 A261 50p multicolored 1.50 1.60
482 A261 1r multicolored 2.60 1.25
483 A261 2r multicolored 2.25 1.75
Nos. 480-483 (4) 7.45 5.20

Chatterjee (1838-94) — A262

1969, Jan. 1 *Perf. 13½*
484 A262 20p ultramarine .50 .50
Bankim Chandra Chatterjee, writer.

Dr. Bhagavan Das — A263

1969, Jan. 12 Photo. *Perf. 13½*
485 A263 20p red brown .50 .50
Das (1869-1958), philosopher.

Martin Luther King, Jr. (1929-1968), American Civil Rights Leader — A264

1969, Jan. 25
486 A264 20p olive gray 1.00 .40

INDIA

Mirza Ghalib — A265

1969, Feb. 17   *Perf. 14½x14*
487 A265 20p dk gray & salmon   .50   .50
Mirza Ghalib (Asad Ullah Beg Khan 1797-1869), poet who modernized the Urdu language.

Osmania University, Hyderabad, 50th Avviv. — A266

1969, Mar. 15   Photo.   *Perf. 14½x14*
488 A266 20p green   .50   .50

Rafi Ahmed Kidwai — A267

1969, Apr. 1   *Perf. 13*
489 A267 20p grayish blue   1.00   .60
Minister of communications and food, introduced around-the-clock airmail service.

ILO Emblems — A268

1969, Apr. 11   *Perf. 14½x14*
490 A268 20p orange brown   .50   .50
50th anniv. of the ILO.

Memorial Monument and Hands Strewing Flowers — A269

1969, Apr. 13   *Perf. 13½*
491 A269 20p rose carmine   .50   .50
50th anniv. of Jallianwala Bagh, Amritsar, massacre.

Nageswara Rao (1867-1938), Journalist and Congressman A270

1969, May 1   Photo.   *Perf. 13½x14*
492 A270 20p brown   .50   .50

Ardaseer Cursetjee Wadia and Ships — A271

1969, May 27   Photo.   *Perf. 14½x14*
493 A271 20p blue green   .70   .50
Wadia (1808-1877), shipbuilder.

Serampore College, 150th Anniv. — A272

1969, June 7   Photo.   *Perf. 13½*
494 A272 20p violet brown   .50   .50

Dr. Zakir Husain (1897-1969), President of India 1967-1969 — A273

1969, June 11   *Perf. 13*
495 A273 20p olive gray   .50   .50

Laxmanrao Kirloskar and Plow — A274

1969, June 20
496 A274 20p gray   .50   .50
Kirloskar (1869-1956), industrialist and social reformer, introduced the iron plow to India.

Mahatma Gandhi (1869-1948) A275

Gandhi on the Dandi March A276

20p, Gandhi and his wife Kasturba, horiz.
5r, Gandhi with spinning wheel, horiz.

1969, Oct. 2   Photo.   Unwmk.
Size: 29x25mm
Perf. 13½
497 A275 20p sepia   .80   .80
Size: 28x38mm
Perf. 13
498 A275 75p ol gray, sal & brn   1.90   .30
Size: 20x38mm
Perf. 14x14½
499 A276 1r bright blue   1.90   1.60
Size: 35½x25½mm
Perf. 13
500 A275 5r orange & sepia   6.50   5.50
Nos. 497-500 (4)   11.10   8.20

Freighter and IMCO Emblem — A277

1969, Oct. 14   *Perf. 13*
501 A277 20p ultramarine   2.50   .60
10th anniv. of the Intergovernmental Maritime Consultative Organization.

Globe and Parliament, New Delhi — A278

1969, Oct. 30   Photo.   *Perf. 14½x14*
502 A278 20p bright blue   .50   .50
57th Interparliamentary Conf., New Delhi.

Astronaut on Moon — A279

1969, Nov. 19   *Perf. 14x14½*
503 A279 20p olive brown   1.10   .50
See note after US No. C76.

Nanak Mausoleum, Talwandi, Punjab — A280

1969, Nov. 23   Photo.   *Perf. 13½*
504 A280 20p gray violet   .50   .50
500th anniv. of the birth of the Guru Nanak, Sikh leader.

Tiger and Globe — A281

1969, Nov. 24   *Perf. 14½x14*
505 A281 20p olive grn & red brn   .90   .55
Intl. Union for the Conservation of Nature and Natural Resources.

T. L. Vaswani — A282

1969, Nov. 25   *Perf. 14x14½*
506 A282 20p dark gray   .50   .50
T. L. Vaswani (1879-1966), writer and orator.

Thakkar Bapa — A283

1969, Nov. 29   *Perf. 13½*
507 A283 20p dark brown   .50   .50
Thakkar Bapa (1869-1951), statesman who worked to help the untouchables.

Globe and Telecommunications Symbols — A284

1970, Jan. 21   *Perf. 13*
508 A284 20p Prussian blue   .50   .50
12th Plenary Assembly of the Intl. Radio Consultative Committee.

C. N. Annadurai (1909-1969), Journalist — A285

1970, Feb. 2
509 A285 20p dk blue & magenta   .50   .50

Munshi Newal Kishore and Printing Plant — A286

1970, Feb. 19   Photo.   *Perf. 13x13½*
510 A286 20p dark carmine   .50   .50
Kishore (1836-1895), publisher.

Cent. of Nalanda College — A287

1970, Mar. 27   Photo.   *Perf. 14½x14*
511 A287 20p light red brown   .85   .45

Swami Shraddhanand (1856-1926), Patriot — A288

1970, Mar. 30   *Perf. 13½*
512 A288 20p orange brown   1.00   .50

Lenin — A289

1970, Apr. 22   Photo.   *Perf. 13*
513 A289 20p multicolored   .60   .35

UPU Headquarters, Bern — A290

1970, May 20
514 A290 20p black & green   .50   .50
New UPU Headquarters in Bern.

Sher Shah Suri — A291

1970, May 22   Photo.   *Perf. 13*
515 A291 20p blue green   .50   .50
Suri, 15th cent. ruler of Delhi and postal service reformer.

Vir D. Savarkar and Prison at Port Blair, Andamans A292

1970, May 28
516 A292 20p orange brown   .70   .50
V. D. Savarkar (1883-1966), patriot.

"UN" and UN Emblem — A293

1970, June 26   Photo.   *Perf. 13*
517 A293 20p blue   .80   .35
25th anniv. of the UN.

Harvest, Crane, Factory and Emblem — A294

1970, Aug. 18   *Perf. 14½x14*
518 A294 20p violet   .50   .50
Asian Productivity Year.

INDIA

Dr. Maria Montessori and Education Symbol — A295

1970, Aug. 31   Perf. 13½x13
519 A295 20p dull claret   .60   .50
Intl. Education Year and Maria Montessori (1870-1952), Italian educator and physician.

Jatindra Nath Mukherjee A296

1970, Sept. 9   Perf. 14½x14
520 A296 20p dark red brown   1.50   .50
Mukherjee (1879-1915), revolutionary leader.

Srinivasa Sastri (1869-1946) — A297

1970, Sept. 22   Photo.   Perf. 13
521 A297 20p dk brown & ocher   .60   .50
V. S. Srinivasa Sastri, statesman.

Iswar Chandra Vidyasagar — A298

1970, Sept. 26
522 A298 20p rose lilac & brown   .60   .50
Vidyasagar (1820-91), educator and writer.

Maharishi Valmiki (born c. 1400 B.C.), Poet — A299

1970, Oct. 14   Photo.   Perf. 13
523 A299 20p plum   .60   .40

Calcutta Harbor — A300

1970, Oct. 17
524 A300 20p blue   1.25   .75
Cent. of Calcutta Port Commissioners.

Jamia Millia Islamia University, 50th Anniv. — A301

1970, Oct. 29   Perf. 14½x14
525 A301 20p yellow green   .70   .60

Jamnalal Bajaj (1889-1942), Patriot — A302

1970, Nov. 4   Wmk. 324   Perf. 13
526 A302 20p sepia   .50   .40

Nurse and Patient — A303

1970, Nov. 5
527 A303 20p Prus. blue & red   .70   .60
50th anniv. of the Indian Red Cross Soc.

Sant Namdeo (1270-1350), Holy Man — A304

1970, Nov. 9   Photo.
528 A304 20p orange   .50   .50

Ludwig van Beethoven — A305

1970, Dec. 16   Unwmk.   Perf. 13
529 A305 20p dk brn & org   2.50   .80

Children with Stamp Album — A306

Design: 1r, Hands holding magnifying glass over Gandhi stamp.

1970, Dec. 23   Photo.   Perf. 13
530 A306 20p dull green & lt brn   .75   .35
531 A306 1r ocher & brown   5.00   1.25
INPEX 1970, Indian Natl. Phil. Exhib., New Delhi, Dec. 23, 1970-Jan. 6, 1971.

Girl Guide and Sign — A307

1970, Dec. 27
532 A307 20p dark brown violet   1.00   .50
Girl Guides, 60th anniv.

Hands Shielding Flame — A308

1971, Jan. 11
533 A308 20p bis brn & dp clar   .60   .40
Centenary of Indian Life Insurance.

Kashi Vidyapith, 50th Anniv. — A309

1971, Feb. 10   Perf. 14½x14
534 A309 20p black brown   .50   .40
Kashi Vidyapith University, Benares.

Charles Freer Andrews (1871-1940), British Publicist, Friend of Gandhi — A310

1971, Feb. 12   Perf. 13x13½
535 A310 20p orange brown   .60   .45

Ravidas, 15th Cent. Poet and Holy Man — A311

1971, Feb. 10   Perf. 13
536 A311 20p rose carmine   .80   .50

Acharya Narendra Deo (1889-1956), Educator, Patriot, Statesman — A312

1971, Feb. 18   Photo.   Perf. 13
537 A312 20p olive bister   .50   .50

Cent. of Indian Census — A313

1971, Mar. 10
538 A313 20p ultra & sepia   .50   .40

Ramana Maharshi (1879-1950), Holy Man — A314

1971, Apr. 14   Photo.   Perf. 13½x14
539 A314 20p ol gray & orange   .60   .50

Raja Ravi Varma (1848-1906) and His Painting, Damayanti and the Swan — A315

1971, Apr. 29   Perf. 13x13½
540 A315 20p deep yellow green   .70   .60

Dadasaheb Phalke, Movie Camera — A316

1971, Apr. 30   Perf. 13½x13
541 A316 20p violet brown   1.25   .60
Dadasaheb Phalke (1870-1944), motion picture pioneer.

Abhisarika, by Abanindranath Tagore — A317

1971, Aug. 7   Unwmk.   Perf. 14x14½
542 A317 20p dark brn & ocher   .60   .50
Tagore (1871-1951), painter.

Swami Virjanand — A318

1971, Sept. 14   Perf. 14x13½
543 A318 20p orange brown   .60   .50
Virjanand (1778-1868), scholar and sage.

Sculptures and Stairway, Persepolis Palace — A319

1971, Oct. 12   Perf. 13
544 A319 20p sepia   1.25   .80
2500th anniv. of the founding of the Persian empire by Cyrus the Great.

World Thrift Day — A320

1971, Oct. 31   Perf. 14½x14
545 A320 20p dark violet blue   .50   .40

Bodhisatva Padampani, from Ajanta Cave — A321

1971, Nov. 4   Perf. 13
546 A321 20p brown   2.25   .70
25th anniv. of UNESCO.

Girls at Work, by Geeta Gupta — A322

1971, Nov. 14   Perf. 14x14½
547 A322 20p salmon pink   .60   .50
Children's Day.

C. V. Raman — A323

1971, Nov. 21   Perf. 13
548 A323 20p brown & dp org   2.00   .75
Sir Chandrasekhara Venkata Raman (1888-1970), physicist, Nobel Prize winner.

Rabindranath Tagore, Visva-Bharati Building — A324

1971, Dec. 24   Perf. 14½x14
549 A324 20p blk brn & org brn   1.10   .50
50th anniv. of Visva-Bharati, center for Eastern cultural studies.

Indian Cricket Victories — A325

1971, Dec. 24
550 A325 20p green   2.75   1.00

INDIA

Intelsat 3 over Map of Eastern Hemisphere — A326

1972, Feb. 26   Photo.   Perf. 13½
551 A326 20p dark purple   .50   .40
Arvi Satellite Earth Station.

Plumb Line and Symbols — A327

1972, May 29   Photo.   Perf. 13
552 A327 20p bluish gray & black   .70   .50
Indian Standards Institution (ISI), 25th anniv.

Signal Panel and Route Diagram — A328

1972, June 30
553 A328 20p black & multi   2.50   1.00
Intl. Railroad Union (UIC), 50th anniv.

Hockey, Olympic Rings — A329

20th Olympic Games, Munich, Aug. 26-Sept. 11: 1.45r, "1972," Olympic rings, symbols for running, wrestling, shooting and hockey.

1972, Aug. 10   Photo.   Perf. 13
554 A329 20p dull violet   2.75   .35
555 A329 1.45r bl grn & dk red   3.00   3.00

Marchers with Flag, Parliament A330

1972, Aug. 15
556 A330 20p blue & multi   .65   .50
25th anniv. of Independence.

Armed Forces' Emblems — A331

1972, Aug. 15
557 A331 20p blue & multi   .70   .50
Honoring India's defense forces.

Symbol of Aurobindo and Sun — A332

1972, Aug. 15   Perf. 14x13½
558 A332 20p yellow & blue   .50   .50
Sri Aurobindo Ghose (1872-1950).

V.O. Chidambaram Pillai and Ship — A333

   Perf. 13½x13

1972, Sept. 5   Unwmk.
559 A333 20p bl & dk red brn   1.10   .55
V.O. Chidambaram Pillai (1872-1936), founder of steamship company, trade union leader, resistance fighter.

Vemana, 17th-18th Cent. Poet — A334

1972, Oct. 16   Wmk. 324   Perf. 14
560 A334 20p black   .60   .50

Bertrand Russell — A335

1972, Oct. 16   Unwmk.
561 A335 1.45r black   5.25   3.00
British philosopher and pacifist (1872-1970).

Bhai Vir Singh — A336

1972, Oct. 16   Perf. 13½
562 A336 20p dull purple   .80   .45
Bhai Vir Singh (1872-1957), poet and scholar.

T. Prakasam — A337

1972, Oct. 16
563 A337 20p yellow brown   .60   .50
T. Prakasam (1872-1957), national leader and lawyer.

Hand of Buddha, 9th Century Sculpture — A338

20p, Stylized Hand of Buddha as Fair emblem.

1972, Nov. 3   Wmk. 324   Perf. 13
564 A338 20p orange & black   .70   .40
565 A338 1.45r orange, blk & ind   1.75   2.50
3rd Asian Intl. Trade Fair, ASIA 72, New Delhi.

Vikram Ambalal Sarabhai, Rohini Rocket and Dove — A339

1972, Dec. 30   Unwmk.
566 A339 20p slate grn & brn   .60   .60
1st anniv. of the death of Dr. Vikram Ambalal Sarabhai (1919-1971), chairman of Natl. Committee for Space Research.

Flag of USSR and Spasski Tower — A340

1972, Dec. 30   Perf. 13
567 A340 20p red & yellow   .60   .60
50th anniv. of the Soviet Union.

INDIPEX 73 Emblem — A341

1973, Jan. 8   Photo.   Perf. 13
568 A341 1.45r black, pink & gold   1.10   1.90
Intl. Phil. Exhib., New Delhi, 11/14-23/73. See Nos. 597-599.

Wheel of Asoka, Naga (Serpent) A342

India Gate, Gnat Planes, India's Colors A343

1973, Jan. 26   Perf. 13
569 A342 20p orange & multi   .35   .35
   Perf. 14½x14
570 A343 1.45r violet & multi   2.25   2.00
Republic Day, 25th year of Independence.

Ramakrishna Paramahamsa (1836-86) — A344

1973, Feb. 18   Photo.   Perf. 13
571 A344 20p yellow brown   .60   .50
Hindu spiritual leader; Ramakrishna Mission founded by his followers.

Army Postal Service Corps Emblem — A345

1973, Mar. 1
572 A345 20p violet blue & red   .60   .60
1st anniv. of establishment of Army Postal Service Corps.

Flower, Flag, Map — A346

1973, Apr. 10   Unwmk.   Perf. 13
573 A346 20p blue & multi   .60   .60
1st anniv. of Bangladesh independence.

Kumaran Asan — A347

1973, Apr. 12
574 A347 20p brown   .60   .60
Kumaran Asan (1873-1924), Kerala social reformer and writer.

Flame and Flag of India — A348

1973, Apr. 13
575 A348 20p deep blue & multi   .60   .60
In honor of the martyrs of the massacre of Jallianwala Bagh, Apr. 13, 1919.

B. R. Ambedkar and Parliament Building — A349

1973, Apr. 14   Perf. 14½x14
576 A349 20p olive & plum   .60   .50
Bhimrao R. Ambedkar (1891-1956), lawyer, reformer of Hindu law and one of the writers of India's Constitution.

Radha-Kishangarh, by Nihal Chand, 1778 — A350

Indian Miniatures: 50p, Dancing Couple, late 17th century. 1r, Lovers on a Camel, by Nasir-ud-Din, c. 1605. 2r, Chained Elephant, by Zain-al-Abidin, 16th century.

1973, May 5   Photo.   Perf. 13½x13
577 A350 20p gold & multi   .55   .60
578 A350 50p lilac & multi   1.25   2.25
579 A350 1r ocher & multi   1.60   1.75
580 A350 2r gold & multi   2.25   3.75
Nos. 577-580 (4)   5.65   8.35

Himalayas — A351

1973, May 15   Perf. 13½x13
581 A351 20p blue   1.00   .60
15th anniv. of Indian Mountaineering Foundation.

INDIA

Air India Jet — A352

1973, June 8   Photo.   Perf. 13
582   A352   1.45r multicolored   5.50   5.50
Air India, 25 years of intl. service.

Stone Cross on St. Thomas's Mount, Madras — A353

1973, July 3
583   A353   20p gray ol & blue gray   .75   .65
1900th anniv. of the death of St. Thomas.

Michael Madhusudan Dutt — A354

1973, July 21   Photo.   Perf. 13
584   A354   20p ocher & olive   1.25   .90
Dutt (1824-1873), writer and poet.

Vishnu Dingambar Paluskar (1872-1931), Musician — A355

1973, July 21
585   A355   30p red brown   1.75   1.75

Dr. Armauer G. Hansen, Microscope, Petri Dish with Bacilli — A356

1973, July 21
586   A356   50p deep brown   2.00   2.00
Cent. of the discovery by Hansen of the Hansen bacillus, the cause of leprosy.

Nicolaus Copernicus, Heliocentric System — A357

1973, July 21
587   A357   1r vio blue & red brn   2.00   2.00
500th anniv. of the birth of Nicolaus Copernicus (1473-1543), Polish astronomer.

Allan Octavian Hume (1829-1912) — A358

1973, July 31
588   A358   20p gray   .50   .50
Hume, British civil servant and friend of India, on the 25th anniv. of independence.

Nehru and Gandhi — A359

1973, Aug. 15   Photo.   Perf. 13
589   A359   20p bl vio & red brn   .80   .50
25th anniv. of India's independence.

Romesh Chunder Dutt — A360

Ranjit Sinhji — A361

Vithalbhai Patel (1873-1933), National Leader — A362

1973, Sept. 27   Photo.   Perf. 13
590   A360   20p brown   .50   .50
591   A361   30p dark green   5.50   5.50
592   A362   50p brown   .50   .50
         Nos. 590-592 (3)   6.50   6.50
Birth anniv.: Dutt (1848-1909), economist and pres. of Natl. Cong. in 1890; Sinhji, Maharaja of Nawanagar (1872-1933), cricketer.

President's Body Guard — A363

1973, Sept. 30
593   A363   20p multicolored   1.75   .75
Bicentenary of President's Body Guard.

INTERPOL Emblem — A364

1973, Oct. 9   Photo.   Perf. 13
594   A364   20p brown   .80   .70
50th anniv. of Intl. Criminal Police Org.

Syed Ahmad Khan, Aligarh University — A365

1973, Oct. 17
595   A365   20p olive gray   .60   1.00
Khan (1817-1898), founder of Aligarh Muslim Univ.

Child's Drawing — A366

1973, Nov. 14   Photo.   Perf. 13
596   A366   20p multicolored   .50   .50
Children's Day.

Elephant with Howdah, and No. 200 A367

1973, Nov. 14
597   A367   20p Emblem   .35   .35
598   A367   1r shown   1.40   1.40
599   A367   2r Peacock, vert.   1.75   1.75
   a.   Souvenir sheet of 4   22.50   10.00
       Nos. 597-599 (3)   3.50   3.50
Intl. Phil. Exhib., INDIPEX 73, New Delhi, Nov. 14-23. No. 599a contains 4 imperf. stamps similar to Nos. 568, 597-599. The imperf. stamps from No. 599a were not valid individually.

NCC Emblem — A368

1973, Nov. 25
600   A368   20p multicolored   .60   .40
National Cadet Corps, 25th anniv.

Rajagopalachari A369

1973, Dec. 25
601   A369   20p gray olive   .60   .60
Chakravarti Rajagopalachari (1878-1972), statesman, governor general (1948-50).

Sun Mask — A370

Narasimha Mask — A371

Designs: Masks.

1974, Apr. 15   Photo.   Perf. 13
602   A370   20p shown   .55   .55
603   A370   50p Moon   .80   .80
604   A371   1r shown   1.25   1.25
605   A371   2r Ravana, horiz.   1.60   1.60
   a.   Souvenir sheet of 4, #602-605   57.50   20.00
       Nos. 602-605 (4)   4.20   4.20

300th Anniv. of the Coronation of Chatrapati Sivaji Maharaj (1627-1680), Military Leader of the Maharattas and Enlightened Ruler — A372

1974, June 2   Photo.   Perf. 13
606   A372   25p gold & multi   .60   .50

Maithili Sharan Gupta — A373

Utkal Gourab Madhusudan Das — A374

Kandukuri Veeresalingam A375

Tipu Sultan A376

No. 608, Jainarain Vyas, 1r, Max Mueller.

1974   Photo.   Perf. 13
607   A373   25p red brown   .30   .35
608   A373   25p brown   .30   .35
609   A374   25p olive gray   .30   .35
610   A375   25p red brown   .40   .45
611   A376   50p violet brown   .85   1.10
612   A376   1r brown   .95   1.10
       Nos. 607-612 (6)   3.10   3.70
Gupta (1886-1964), poet and patriot; Vyas (1899-1963), writer and member of parliament; Das (1848-1934), writer and patriot. Veeresalingam (1848-1919), reformer; Sultan (1750-99), military leader and reformer; Mueller (1823-1900), German scholar of Sanskrit and Indian culture.
Issued: Nos. 607-609, 7/3; Nos. 610-612, 7/15.

Kamala Nehru A377

1974, Aug 1   Photo.   Perf. 14½x14
613   A377   25p multicolored   .80   .80
Kamala Nehru (1899-1936), champion of India's freedom, mother of Indira Gandhi.

WPY Emblem — A378

1974, Aug. 14   Unwmk.   Perf. 13½
614   A378   25p buff & plum   .50   .40

V. V. Giri — A379

1974, Aug. 24   Perf. 13x13½
615   A379   25p green & multi   .50   .40
Vaharagiri Venkata Giri, pres. of India, 1969-74.

Type of 1965-68 and

Tiger A380

Veena A381

Design: 25p, Axis deer (chital).

INDIA

1974		Wmk. 324	Perf. 14½x14
622	A380	15p dk brn (white "15")	4.50 1.00
623	A202	25p brown	1.25 1.00
624	A381	1r black & brown	3.25 .40
		Nos. 622-624 (3)	9.00 2.40

Issue dates: 25p, Aug. 20; 15p, 1r, Oct. 1. See Nos. 671-682.

Madhubani Folk Design, UPU Emblem — A384

Designs: 25p, UPU emblem. 2r, Arrows circling globe, UPU emblem, vert.

1974, Oct. 3		Unwmk.	Perf. 13
634	A384	25p brt blue & gray	.85 .30
635	A384	1r olive & multi	1.25 .85
636	A384	2r ocher & multi	2.75 2.40
	a.	Souvenir sheet of 3, #634-636	65.00 20.00
		Nos. 634-636 (3)	4.85 3.55

Cent. of UPU.

Cent. of Mathura Museum — A385

No. 637, Flute player. No. 638, Vidyadhara with garland.

1974, Oct. 9		Photo.	Perf. 13½
637		25p red brn & mar	.60 .50
638		25p red brn & mar	.60 .50
	a.	A385 Pair, #637-638	2.00 2.00

Nicholas Konstantin Roerich, by Henry Dropsy — A387

1974, Oct. 9			Perf. 13
639	A387	1r dark gray & yellow	.80 .80

Roerich (1874-1947), Russian painter and sponsor of Roerich Peace Pact.

Pavapuri Temple, Bihar — A388

1974, Nov. 13		Photo.	Perf. 13
640	A388	25p slate	.65 .35

2500th anniv. of attainment of Nirvana by Bhagwan Mahavira, leader and preacher of Jainism.

Dancers and Musician (Child's Drawing) — A389

1974, Nov. 14			Perf. 14½x14
641	A389	25p multicolored	.80 .60

UNICEF in India.

Cat (Child's Drawing) — A390

1974, Nov. 14			Perf. 13
642	A390	25p multicolored	1.40 .50

Children's Day.

Territorial Army Emblem — A391

1974, Nov. 16			Perf. 13
643	A391	25p green, yel & black	.90 .60

Territorial Army, 25th anniv.

Cows, from Handpainted Rajasthan Cloth — A392

1974, Dec. 2			Perf. 14
644	A392	25p ocher & maroon	.60 .40

19th Intl. Dairy Cong., New Delhi, Dec. 2-6.

Symbol of Retardates and Child — A393

1974, Dec. 8		Photo.	Perf. 13½x13
645	A393	25p black & vermilion	.85 .60

Help the Retardates!

Guglielmo Marconi — A394

1974, Dec. 12			Perf. 13x13½
646	A394	2r slate	4.00 2.25

Marconi (1874-1937), Italian electrical engineer and inventor.

St. Francis Xavier's Tomb and Statue — A395

1974, Dec. 24			Perf. 13½x13
647	A395	25p multicolored	.65 .40

Showing of the body of St. Francis Xavier, Apostle to the Indies.

Saraswati, Goddess of Language and Learning, Inscription in Hindi — A396

1975, Jan. 10		Photo.	Perf. 14x14½
648	A396	25p dark red & gray	.50 .40

World Hindi Convention, Nagpur, Jan. 10-14. See No. 654.

Parliament House — A397

1975, Jan. 26			Perf. 13
649	A397	25p black, blue & silver	.70 .45

Republic of India, 25th anniv.

Table Tennis Paddle and Ball — A398

1975, Feb. 6			Perf. 13½x13
650	A398	25p black, red & olive	1.50 .55

33rd World Table Tennis Championship, Calcutta.

Woman's Hands Releasing Doves — A399

1975, Feb. 16			
651	A399	25p yellow & multi	1.10 .60

International Women's Year.

Bicentenary of Army Ordnance Corps — A400

1975, Apr. 8		Photo.	Perf. 13x13½
652	A400	25p black & vermilion	1.10 .70

Flame — A401

1975, Apr. 11			Perf. 13½x13
653	A401	25p orange & black	.60 .50

Cent. of the founding of Arya Samaj, a movement dedicated to enlightenment and progress and to a revival of Vedic Law and Aryan culture.

Saraswati Type of 1975

25p, Saraswati and inscription in Telugu.

1975, Apr. 12			Perf. 14x14½
654	A396	25p dp grn & dk gray	1.10 .45

World Telugu Conf., Hyderabad, Apr. 12-18.

Aryabhata Satellite — A402

1975, Apr. 20			Perf. 13½x13
655	A402	25p multicolored	.90 .70

Launching of 1st Indian satellite, Apr. 19, 1975.

Bluewinged Pitta — A403

1975, Apr. 28		Perf. 13½x13, 13x13½	
656	A403	25p multicolored	.95 .30
657	A403	50p multicolored	2.25 2.25
658	A403	1r multicolored	3.25 3.25
659	A403	2r multicolored	4.50 4.50
		Nos. 656-659 (4)	10.95 10.30

Birds: 50p, Black-headed oriole. 1r, Western tragopan, vert. 2r, Himalayan monal pheasant, vert.

Quotation from Ram Charit Manas — A404

1975, May 24		Photo.	Perf. 13½x13
660	A404	25p red, org & blk	.75 .35

Ram Charit Manas, Hindi poem by Goswami Tulsidas (1532-1623).

Women and YWCA Emblem — A405

1975, June 20		Photo.	Perf. 13x13½
661	A405	25p gray & multi	.70 .50

YWCA of India, cent.

Creation of Adam, by Michelangelo — A406

Design: Nos. 664-665, Creation of sun, moon and plants, by Michelangelo.

1975, June 28			Perf. 14x13½
662		50p multicolored	.65 .50
663		50p multicolored	1.25 1.00
	a.	A406 Pair #662-663	2.75 2.75
664		50p multicolored	1.25 1.00
665		50p multicolored	1.25 1.00
	b.	A406 Pair #664-665	2.75 2.75

Michelangelo Buonarroti (1475-1564), Italian sculptor, painter and architect.

Types of 1965-1974 Without Currency Designation and

Flying Crane A408

Jawaharlal Nehru A409

Mahatma Gandhi A410

Himalayas A411

Designs: 2p, Bidri vase. 5p, Family. 10p, Electric locomotive. 15p, Tiger. 20p, Wooden toy horse. 30p, Male and female figurines. No. 680, Somnath Temple. 1r, Veena. 5r, Bhakra Dam, Punjab. 10r, Trombay Atomic Center.

Three types of 25p Nehru:
Type I: Size at top, 25mm. Character before NEHRU has 2 lower points.
Type II: Smaller portrait. Size at top, 23mm. Character has 3 points.
Type III: Portrait as in type I. Size at top, 25½mm. Character has 3 points.

Perf. 14½x14, 14x14½, 14 (#674-676), 13 (#681)
Wmk. 324; 360 (# 666A, 667, 668, 670)

1975-88			Photo.
666	A202	2(p) redsh brn, wmk. 324 ('76)	1.25 2.25
666A	A202	2(p) redsh brn, wmk. 360 ('76)	1.25 2.25
667	A202	2(p) redsh brn, wmk. 360, litho. ('79)	1.25 2.25
668	A202	5(p) cerise ('76)	.75 .25

INDIA

669	A203	10(p)	brt blue ('76)	.75	.25
670	A203	10(p)	brt blue ('79)	4.00	.60
671	A380	15(p)	dk brn (brn "15")	2.00	.25
672	A408	20(p)	green	.40	.25
673	A409	25(p)	vio, I ('76)	10.00	.75
674	A409	25(p)	vio, II ('76)	6.50	.75
675	A409	25(p)	vio, III ('76)	5.00	.75
676	A410	25(p)	red brn ('76) (23x29mm)	1.25	.30
677	A410	25(p)	red brn ('78) (17x20mm)	8.00	2.25
678	A202	30(p)	brown ('79)	4.00	.50
679	A408	50(p)	violet blue	6.50	.30
680	A202	60(p)	dk gray ('76)	2.00	1.00
681	A410	60(p)	black ('88)	1.10	.25
682	A381	1(r)	blk & brn	4.25	.25
683	A411	2(r)	vio & brn	17.00	.50
684	A205	5(r)	brn & vio ('76)	2.50	.90
685	A205	10(r)	dl grn & sl ('76)	2.25	1.10
Nos. 666-685 (21)				82.00	17.95

No. 667 has a background of fine horizontal lines.
See Nos. 841-842, 844-845, 846A-846B, 916.
Size of No. 681, 17x20mm.

Irrigation Commission Emblem — A412

Unwmk.
1975, July 28   **Photo.**   **Perf. 14**
686   A412   25p multicolored   .65   .35
9th Intl. Cong. on Irrigation and Drainage, Moscow, and 25th anniv. of the Intl. Commission on Irrigation and Drainage.

"Educational Television" — A413

1975, Aug. 1   **Perf. 13x13½**
687   A413   25p multicolored   .65   .40
Inauguration of the Satellite Instructional Television Experiment (SITE).

Arunagirinathar A414

1975, Aug. 14   **Photo.**   **Perf. 13½**
688   A414   50p rose lilac   1.75   1.25
600th birth anniv. of Arunagirinathar, Advaita philosopher, saint and author of Tiruppugazh, a collection of songs.

A415

1975, Aug. 26   **Photo.**   **Perf. 13½**
689   A415   25p rose & black   .90   .50
Namibia Day. See note after UN No. 241.

A416

1975, Sept. 4
690   A416   25p slate green   .50   .50
Mir Anees (1803-1874), Urdu poet.

Chhatri at Maheshwar — A417

1975, Sept. 4   **Perf. 13x13½**
691   A417   25p red brown   .50   .50
Queen Ahilyabai Holkar (1725-1795); building shown was place of last rites.

Bharata Natyam Dance — A418

Designs: Indian traditional dances.

1975, Oct. 20   **Photo.**   **Perf. 13x13½**
692	A418	25p shown	.95	.65
693	A418	50p Orissi	1.40	.70
694	A418	75p Kathak	1.90	.90
695	A418	1r Kathakali	2.25	1.10
696	A418	1.50r Kuchipudi	2.75	1.60
697	A418	2r Manipuri	2.75	1.60
Nos. 692-697 (6)			12.00	6.55

Krishna Menon A419

Ameer Khusrau A420

Poem by Bahadur Shah Zafar — A421

Design: No. 699, Sardar Vallabhbhai Patel.

1975   **Perf. 13x13½, 13½x13**
698	A419	25p olive	1.00	.80
699	A419	25p slate	.55	.50
700	A420	50p yellow & brown	1.60	1.60
701	A421	1r black, brn & buff	2.00	1.20
Nos. 698-701 (4)			5.15	4.10

Men of India: V. K. Krishna Menon (1896-1974), founder of India League and member of Parliament; Patel (1875-1950), statesman who unified India, birth cent.; Khusrau (1253-1325), poet; Zafar (1775-1862), last Mogul emperor and poet.
Issued: Nos. 699, 10/31; others 10/24.

Parliament Annex, New Delhi — A422

1975, Oct. 28   **Perf. 14½x14**
702   A422   2r gray olive   3.25   2.50
21st Commonwealth Parliamentary Conf., New Delhi, Oct. 28-Nov. 4.

Karmavir Nabin Chandra Bardoloi (1875-1936), Writer and Gandhi Associate — A423

1975, Nov. 3   **Photo.**   **Perf. 13**
703   A423   25p reddish brown   .70   .45

Cow, Child's Painting — A424

1975, Nov. 14
704   A424   25p multicolored   1.10   .70
Children's Day.

Security Press Building — A425

1975, Dec. 13   **Photo.**   **Perf. 13**
705   A425   25p multicolored   .70   .50
India Security Press, 50th anniv.

Gurdwara Sisganj, Chandni Chawk — A426

1975, Dec. 16
706   A426   25p multicolored   .80   .50
300th anniv. of martyrdom of Tegh Bahadur (1621-75), 9th Sikh Guru; building shown was place of beheading.

Theosophical Society Emblem — A427

1975, Dec. 20
707   A427   25p multicolored   .70   .50
Centenary of Theosophical Society.

Meteorological Instruments — A428

1975, Dec. 24   **Photo.**   **Perf. 13**
708   A428   25p blue vio, blk & grn   .90   .65
Indian Meteorological Dept., cent.

Early Mail Cart — A429

Indian Bishop Mark, 1775 — A430

1975, Dec. 25
| 709 | A429 | 25p brown & black | 1.00 | .40 |
| 710 | A430 | 2r reddish brn & blk | 3.25 | 2.00 |
INPEX 75, Indian Natl. Phil. Exhib., Calcutta, Dec. 25-31.

Lalit Narayan Mishra — A431

1976, Jan. 3
711   A431   25p sepia   .75   .40
Mishra (1923-75), Minister of Railroads.

Tiger — A432

1976, Jan. 24
712   A432   25p multicolored   1.75   .90
Jim Corbett (1875-1955), conservationist.

Painted Storks — A433

1976, Feb. 10   **Photo.**   **Perf. 13**
713   A433   25p sky blue & multi   1.75   .80
Keoladeo Ghana, Bharatpur Water Bird Sanctuary.

Tank — A434

1976, Mar. 4   **Photo.**   **Perf. 13**
714   A434   25p multicolored   2.25   .45
16th Light Cavalry, senior regiment of Armoured Corps, bicentenary.

Alexander Graham Bell — A435

1976, Mar. 10   **Photo.**   **Perf. 13x13½**
715   A435   25p yellow & black   1.40   .70
Cent. of 1st telephone call by Bell, Mar. 10, 1876.

Muthuswami Dikshitar — A436

1976, Mar. 18   **Perf. 14x13½**
716   A436   25p dull violet   1.25   .55
Dikshitar (1775-1835), musician, composer.

Eye and Red Cross — A437

1976, Apr. 7   **Perf. 13½x13**
717   A437   25p dark brown & red   1.40   .70
World Health Day: "Foresight prevents blindness."

INDIA

"Industries" — A438

1976, Apr. 30   **Perf. 13x13½**   **Unwmk.**
718 A438 25p multicolored   .70   .50
Industrial development and progress.

1 F/I type, Ajmer, 1895 — A439

Locomotives: 25p, WDM 2 Diesel Locomotive, 1963. 1r, 1 WP./1, 4-6-2 Pacific type, 1963. 2r, 1 GIP No. 1, 1853.

1976, May 15   **Perf. 15x14**
719 A439 25p multicolored   1.10   .25
720 A439 50p multicolored   1.75   .80
721 A439 1r multicolored   4.00   1.90
722 A439 2r multicolored   4.75   3.00
     Nos. 719-722 (4)   11.60   5.95

Kumaraswamy Kamaraj (1903-1975), Independence Fighter — A440

1976, July 15   **Photo.**   **Perf. 13x13½**
723 A440 25p sepia   .70   .50

Target, Olympic Rings A441

Hockey A442

1976, July 17   **Perf. 14**
724 A441   25p dk blue & car   .40   .30
725 A441   1r "Team handball"   1.60   .80
726 A442 1.50r black & brt pur   2.75   1.60
727 A441 2.80r "Running"   2.75   2.75
     Nos. 724-727 (4)   7.50   5.45
21st Olympic Games, Montreal, Canada, July 17-Aug. 1.

Subhadra Kumari Chauhan — A443

1976, Aug. 6   **Photo.**   **Perf. 13x13½**
728 A443 25p grayish blue   .70   .40
Chauhan (1904-1948), Hindi poetess and member of Legislative Assembly.

Param Vir Chakra Medal — A444

1976, Aug. 15
729 A444 25p yellow & multi   .70   .40
Medal of Honor awarded for bravery to military men.

Women's University, Bombay — A445

1976, Sept. 3   **Photo.**   **Perf. 13½x14**
730 A445 25p violet   .70   .40
Indian Women's Univ., 60th anniv.

Bharatendu Harishchandra — A446

1976, Sept. 9   **Perf. 13**
731 A446 25p black brown   .70   .50
Harishchandra (1850-1885), writer, "Father of Modern Hindi."

Sarat Chandra Chatterji — A447

1976, Sept. 15   **Unwmk.**
732 A447 25p dull purple   .70   .50
Chatterji (1876-1938), writer.

Family Planning — A448

1976, Sept. 22   **Photo.**   **Perf. 14x14½**
733 A448 25p multicolored   .70   .50

Maharaja Agrasen, Coin and Brick Wall — A449

1976, Sept. 24   **Perf. 13½x13**
734 A449 25p red brown   .70   .50
Maharaja Agrasen, legendary ruler of Agra.

India Blood Donation Day — A450

1976, Oct. 1   **Perf. 13x13½**
735 A450 25p bister, car & black   1.00   .60

Wildlife Protection — A451

1976, Oct. 1   **Perf. 14x14½, 14½x14**
736 A451 25p Swamp deer   .70   .45
737 A451 50p Lion   1.90   1.10
738 A451 1r Leopard, horiz.   2.75   1.50
739 A451 2r Caracal, horiz.   3.00   2.00
     Nos. 736-739 (4)   8.35   5.05

Suryakant Tripathi "Nirala" (1896-1961), Hindi poet — A452

1976, Oct. 15   **Perf. 13**
740 A452 25p dark violet   .70   .45

Children's Day — A453

25p, Mongoose and Woman.

1976, Nov. 14   **Unwmk.**   **Perf. 14**
741 A453 25p multicolored   .70   .50

Hiralal Shastri — A454

1976, Nov. 24   **Perf. 13**
742 A454 25p red brown   .70   .50
Hiralal Shastri (1899-1974), social worker and political leader.

Hari Singh Gour — A455

1976, Nov. 26
743 A455 25p plum   .70   .50
Hari Singh Gour (1870-1949), University administrator, member Indian Legislative and Constituent Assemblies.

Airbus — A456

1976, Dec. 1   **Perf. 14½x14**
744 A456 2r multicolored   4.00   2.50
Inauguration of Indian Airlines Airbus.

Hybrid Coconut Palm — A457

1976, Dec. 27   **Photo.**   **Perf. 13x13½**
745 A457 25p multicolored   .70   .40
75th anniv. of coconut research in India.

Vande Mataram, First Stanza — A458

1976, Dec. 30   **Perf. 13**
746 A458 25p multicolored   .70   .40
Vande Mataram, national song of India, music by Bankim Chandra Chatterjee, 1896, words by Rabindranath Tagore, 1911.

Film and Globe — A459

1977, Jan. 3
747 A459 2r multicolored   3.50   1.50
6th Intl. Film Festival, New Delhi, Jan. 3-16.

Earth's Crust with Fault, Seismograph — A460

1977, Jan. 10
748 A460 2r dull purple   3.00   1.40
6th World Conference on Earthquake Engineering, New Delhi, Jan. 10-14.

Tarun Ram Phookun — A461

1977, Jan. 22   **Photo.**   **Perf. 13x13½**
749 A461 25p sepia   .70   .50
Phookun (1877-1939), lawyer, Assam political leader.

Paramahansa Yogananda — A462

1977, Mar. 7   **Photo.**   **Perf. 13½**
750 A462 25p deep orange   1.50   .70
Yogananda (1893-1952), religious leader, founder of Self-realization Society in America.

Red Cross Conference Emblem — A463

1977, Mar. 9
751 A463 2r multicolored   3.50   2.25
1st Asian Regional Red Cross Conference, New Delhi, Mar. 9-16.

Fakhruddin Ali Ahmed (1905-77) — A464

1977, Mar. 22   **Photo.**   **Perf. 13½x13**
752 A464 25p multicolored   .70   .40
Ahmed, Pres. of India, 1974-77.

Asian-Oceanic Postal Union Emblem — A465

1977, Apr, 1   **Perf. 13**
753 A465 2r silver & multi   3.25   1.75
Asian-Oceanic Postal Union, 15th anniv.

INDIA

"Loyalty" and Morarjee — A466

1977, Apr. 2   Perf. 13½x13
754 A466 25p blue   1.40 .90
Narottam Morarjee (1877-1929), founder of Scindia Steam Ship Navigation Co.

Makhanlal Chaturvedi — A467

1977, Apr. 4   Perf. 13
755 A467 25p orange brown   .70 .50
Chaturvedi (1889-1968), Hindi writer.

Mahaprabhu Vallabhacharya A468

1977, Apr. 14
756 A468 1r olive brown   .70 .50
Vallabhacharya (1479-1531), philosopher.

Federation Emblem — A469

1977, Apr. 23   Perf. 13½x13
757 A469 25p ocher & purple   .70 .50
Federation of Indian Chambers of Commerce, 50th anniv.

Protection of Environment A470

1977, June 5   Photo.   Perf. 13
758 A470 2r multicolored   3.00 .70

Council of States Chamber — A471

1977, June 21
759 A471 25p multicolored   .70 .50
Council of States, Rajya Sabha (Parliament), 25th anniv.

Lotus — A472

50p and 1r are vert.

1977, July 1   Perf. 15x14, 14x15
760 A472 25p shown   .50 .30
761 A472 50p Rhododendron   .85 .70
762 A472 1r Kadamba   1.10 1.00
763 A472 2r Gloriosa lily   1.90 1.75
   Nos. 760-763 (4)   4.35 3.75

Berliner Gramaphone A473

1977, July 20   Perf. 13½x13
764 A473 2r black & brown   3.00 1.00
Centenary of the phonograph.

Ananda Kentish Coomaraswamy (1877-1947) and Dancing Shiva — A474

1977, Aug. 22   Photo.   Perf. 13x13½
765 A474 25p multicolored   .80 .50
Coomaraswamy, art historian and critic.

Ganga Ram (1851-1927) and Hospital, New Delhi — A475

1977, Sept. 4   Perf. 14½x14
766 A475 25p rose carmine   .70 .40
Ram, social reformer and philanthropist.

Dr. Samuel Hahnemann and Cinchona — A476

1977, Oct. 6   Photo.   Perf. 13
767 A476 2r black & green   7.50 3.25
32nd Intl. Homeopathic Cong., New Delhi.

19th Century Postman A477

Lion and Palm Tree, East India Co. Essay A478

1977, Oct. 12   Perf. 13
768 A477 25p multicolored   1.00 .50
   Perf. 13½
769 A478 2r mag & gray, buff   2.75 2.25
INPEX '77 Phil. Exhib., Bangalore, 10/12-16.

Ram Manohar Lohia (1910-67), Founder of Congress Socialist Party, Sec. of Foreign Dept. — A479

1977, Oct. 12   Perf. 13x13½
770 A479 25p red brown   1.00 .50

Red Scinde Dawks, 1852 — A480

Design: 3r, Foreign mail arriving at Ballard Pier, Bombay, 1927.

1977, Oct. 19   Perf. 13½x13
771 A480 1r orange & multi   2.00 1.25
772 A480 3r orange & multi   4.00 2.50
ASIANA 77, First Asian International Philatelic Exhibition, Bangalore, Oct. 19-23.

Statue of Rani Channamma A481

1977, Oct. 23
773 A481 25p gray green   2.50 .80
Rani Channamma of Kittue (1778-1829), who fought against British rule.

Mother and Child, Khajuraho Sculpture — A482

1977, Oct. 23   Perf. 13x13½
774 A482 2r gray & sepia   3.50 2.50
15th Intl. Pediatrics Congress.

Sun and National Colors — A483

1977, Nov. 8   Photo.   Perf. 13
775 A483 25p multicolored   .65 .40
Union Public Service Commission, founded 1926.

Stylized Grain — A484

1977, Nov. 13
776 A484 25p green   .70 .45
AGRIEXPO '77, Intl. Agriculture Exhib.

Cats — A485

1r, Friends. Designs are from children's drawings.

1977, Nov. 14
777 A485 25p multicolored   .95 .45
778 A485 1r multicolored   3.00 2.25
Children's Day.

Jotirao Phooley — A486

1977, Nov. 28   Wmk. 324
779 A486 25p gray olive   .60 .40
Phooley (1827-1890), social reformer.

Senapati Bapat — A487

1977, Nov. 28
780 A487 25p brown orange   .60 .40
Senapati Bapat (Pandurang Mahadev Bapat, 1880-1967), scholar and fighter for India's independence.

Diagram of Population Growth — A488

   Perf. 13x13½
1977, Dec. 13   Unwmk.
781 A488 2r carmine & blue grn   3.75 1.25
41st Session of Intl. Statistical Institute, New Delhi, Dec. 5-15.

Kamta Prasad (1875-1947) and Hindi Grammar — A489

1977, Dec. 25   Wmk. 324   Perf. 14
782 A489 25p sepia   .70 .50
Prasad, compiler of Hindi Grammar.

Spasski Tower, Russian Flag — A490

1977, Dec. 30   Unwmk.   Perf. 13
783 A490 1r multicolored   1.10 .70
60th anniv. of Russian October revolution.

Climber Crossing Crevasse A491

Indian Flag near Summit A492

   Perf. 13½x13, 13x13½
1978, Jan. 15   Photo.
784 A491 25p multicolored   .60 .30
785 A492 1r multicolored   1.40 .55
Conquest of Kanchenjunga (Himalayas), by Indian team under Col. N. Kumar, May 31, 1977.

Tourists in Shikara on Dal Lake — A493

1978, Jan. 23   Perf. 13x13½
786 A493 1r multicolored   3.00 1.75
27th Pacific Area Travel Assoc. Conf., New Delhi, Jan. 23-26.

INDIA

Children in Library, Fair Emblem — A494

1978, Feb. 11   **Photo.**   **Perf. 13**
787 A494 1r rose brown & indigo   1.00   .65
3rd World Book Fair, New Delhi, Feb. 1978.

Mother of Pondicherry — A495

1978, Feb. 21
788 A495 25p dark & light brown   .70   .40
Mother of the Sri Aurobindo Ashram, Pondicherry (Mira Richard, 1878-1973, born in Paris).

Wheat, Globe and Genetic Helix — A496

1978, Feb. 23
789 A496 25p yel & blue grn   .70   .40
5th Intl. Wheat Genetics Symposium.

Nanalal Dalpatram Kavi — A497

               Wmk. 324
1978, Mar. 16   **Photo.**   **Perf. 13**
790 A497 25p rose brown   .70   .40
Kavi (1877-1946), Gujarati poet.

Surjya Sen (1894-1934), Patriot — A498

1978, Mar. 22
791 A498 25p ver, black & brown   .70   .40

Two Vaishnavas (Vishnu Worshippers) by Jaminy Roy — A499

Modern Indian Paintings: 50p, The Mosque, by Sailoz Mookherjea. 1r, Woman's Head, by Rabindranath Tagore. 2r, Hill Women, by Amrita Sher Gil.

        Perf. 13½x14
1978, Mar. 23   **Unwmk.**
792 A499 25p black & multi   .30   .30
793 A499 50p black & multi   .60   .60
794 A499 1r black & multi   1.25   1.25
795 A499 2r black & multi   2.25   2.25
     Nos. 792-795 (4)   4.40   4.40

Rubens, Self-portrait A500

1978, Apr. 4   **Photo.**   **Perf. 13½x13**
796 A500 2r multicolored   3.75   2.60

"The Little Tramp," Charlie Chaplin — A501

1978, Apr. 16   **Perf. 13**
797 A501 25p gold & indigo   2.75   1.00

Deendayal Upadhyaya (1916-68) — A502

1978, May 5   **Photo.**   **Perf. 13**
798 A502 25p multicolored   .70   .40
Upadhyaya, social and political reformer.

Syama Prasad Mookerjee (1901-1953) — A503

1978, July 6   **Photo.**   **Perf. 13**
799 A503 25p gray olive   .80   .40
Dr. Mookerjee, educator, member of 1st natl. government.

"Airavat," 19th Century Wood Carving A504

Kushan Gold Coin, 1st Century A505

Designs: 50p, Wish-fulfilling tree, 2nd century B.C. 2r, Dagger and knife.

1978, July 27
800 A504 25p multicolored   .60   .60
801 A504 50p multicolored   .80   .80
802 A505 1r multicolored   1.10   1.10
803 A505 2r multicolored   1.40   1.40
     Nos. 800-803 (4)   3.90   3.90
Treasures from Indian museums.

Krishna and Arjuna on Battlefield, Quotation — A506

1978, Aug. 25   **Unwmk.**   **Perf. 13**
804 A506 25p orange red & gold   .70   .40
Bhagavad Gita, part of Mahabharata Epic, the Divine Song of the Lord.

Bethune College for Women, Calcutta — A507

1978, Sept. 4
805 A507 25p green & brown   .70   .40

E. V. Ramasami — A508

1978, Sept. 17
806 A508 25p black   .70   .40
E. V. Ramasami (1879-1973), founder of Self-respect Movement, fighting caste system and social injustice.

Uday Shankar — A509

1978, Sept. 26
807 A509 25p buff & violet brown   .70   .40
Uday Shankar (1900-77), dancer.

Leo Tolstoi — A510

1978, Oct. 2
808 A510 1r multicolored   .85   .40
Tolstoi, novelist and philosopher.

Vallathol Narayana Menon — A511

1978, Oct. 15   **Photo.**   **Perf. 13**
809 A511 25p multicolored   .70   .40
Menon (1878-1958), poet.

"Two Friends" — A512

1978, Nov. 14   **Photo.**   **Perf. 13**
810 A512 25p multicolored   .70   .40
Children's Day.

Worker at Lathe — A513

1978, Nov. 17   **Perf. 13½**
811 A513 25p green   .70   .40
Small Industries Fair.

Skinner's Horse Soldiers — A514

1978, Nov. 25   **Perf. 13**
812 A514 25p multicolored   1.25   .80
175th anniv. of Skinner's Horse Regiment.

Chakravarti Rajagopalachari A515

1978, Dec. 10   **Photo.**   **Perf. 13**
813 A515 25p maroon   .70   .40
Chakravarti Rajagopalachari (1878-1972), first post-independence Governor General.

A516

1978, Dec. 10
814 A516 25p olive green   .70   .40
Mohammad Ali Jauhar (1878-1931), writer and patriot.

A517

1978, Dec. 23   **Perf. 13x14**
815 A517 1r ocher & purple   1.50   .50
Wright Brothers, Flyer, 75th anniv. of 1st powered flight.

Ravenshaw College, Orissa, Centenary A518

1978, Dec. 24   **Perf. 14**
816 A518 25p green & maroon   .70   .40

Franz Schubert (1797-1828), Austrian Composer — A519

1978, Dec. 25   **Perf. 13**
817 A519 1r multicolored   1.75   .90

Punjab Regiment, Uniforms and Crest — A520

1979, Feb. 20   **Photo.**   **Unwmk.**
818 A520 25p multicolored   2.00   1.00
Oldest Indian infantry unit.

INDIA

Bhai Parmanand (1876-1947) — A521

1979, Feb. 24
819 A521 25p violet blue .70 .40
Parmanand, writer and educator.

Gandhi and Child — A522

Design: 1r, IYC emblem.

1979, Mar. 5 Photo. Perf. 13
820 A522 25p dk brown & red .50 .40
821 A522 1r dp org & dk brn .75 .75

Albert Einstein (1879-1955), Theoretical Physicist — A523

1979, Mar. 14
822 A523 1r black 1.60 .75

Rajarshi Shahu Chhatrapati (1874-1922), Ruler of Kolhapur — A524

1979, May 1 Photo. Perf. 13x13½
823 A524 25p dull purple .70 .40

Lotus, India '80 Emblem — A525

1979, July 2 Photo. Perf. 13
824 A525 30p dp org & grn .70 .40
India '80 Phil. Exhib., New Delhi, Jan. 25-Feb. 3, 1980.

Postal Cards, 1879 and 1979 — A526

1979, July 2
825 A526 50p multicolored .70 .40

Raja Mahendra Pratap (1886-1979), Patriot — A527

1979, Aug. 15 Photo. Perf. 13
826 A527 30p olive gray .70 .40

Jatindra Nath Das (1904-1929) — A528

1979, Sept. 13
827 A528 30p dark brown .70 .40
Das, political martyr.

Early and Modern Light Bulbs — A529

1979, Oct. 21 Photo. Perf. 13
828 A529 1r rose magenta 1.00 .50
Centenary of invention of electric light.

Buddhist Text — A530

1979, Oct. 23 Perf. 14½x14
829 A530 30p brown & bister .70 .40
National Archives.

Hirakud Dam — A531

Perf. 13½x13
1979, Oct. 29 Wmk. 324
830 A531 30p brown red & dull grn .70 .40
13th Congress (Golden Jubilee) of the Intl. Commission on Large Dams, New Delhi, 10/29-11/2.

Boy and Alphabet Book — A532

1979, Nov. 10 Photo. Perf. 14½x14
831 A532 30p multicolored .70 .40
Intl. Children's Book Fair, New Delhi, 11/10-19.

Fair Emblem — A533

1979, Nov. 10 Perf. 13
832 A533 1r black & orange .70 .40
India Intl. Trade Fair, New Delhi, 11/10-12/9.

Dove, Agency Emblem — A534

1979, Dec. 4 Perf. 13½x13
833 A534 1r multicolored 1.00 .65
23rd Intl. Atomic Energy Agency Conf., New Delhi, Dec. 4-10.

Hindustan Pushpak Plane, Rohini-1 Glider — A535

1979, Dec. 10 Perf. 13½x13
834 A535 30p multicolored 1.75 1.25

Gurdwara Baoli Shrine, Goindwal — A536

1979, Dec. 21 Perf. 13x13½
835 A536 30p multicolored .70 .40
Guru Amardas (1469-1574), Sikh spiritual leader.

Types of 1975-79 and

Adult Education — A536a
Fish — A536b
Agriculture Technology — A536c
Child Nutrition — A536d
Chick and Eggs — A536e
Farm, Wheat, Tractor — A536f
Women in Rice Field — A537
Family Planning — A537a
Hybrid Cotton — A537b
Weaver — A537c
Rubber Tapping — A537d

Designs: Nos. 841, 844, 846A, Jawaharlal Nehru. Nos. 842, 845, 846B, Mahatma Gandhi.

Perf. 14x14½, 14½x14, 13 (#840B)
1979-85 Photo. Wmk. 324
836 A536a 2p violet   .80 .65
837 A536b 5p blue   .80 .65
838 A536c 15p blue grn ('80) .80 .65
839 A536d 20p hen brn ('81)   .80 .65
840 A536e 25p brown   .80 .65
840B A536f 25p brt grn ('85) 1.20 .65
841 A409   30p violet ('80)   2.00 .80
842 A410   30p red brn ('80) 5.00 .80
843 A537   30p yel green   .80 .65
844 A409   35p violet ('80)   2.00 .80
845 A410   35p red brn ('80) 2.00 .80
846 A537a 35p cerise ('80)   .80 .65
846A A409   50p violet ('83)   2.75 .65
846B A410   50p red brn ('83) 6.00 .80
847 A537b 1r brown ('80)   .80 .65
848 A537c 2r rose vio ('80) 2.00 .65
849 A537d 5r multi ('80)   4.50 .80
     Nos. 836-849 (17)   33.85 11.95
Size: Nos. 841-842, 844-845, 846A-846B, 17x20mm.
See Nos. 903, 904, 906, 915.

1979-83 Perf. 13
837a A536b 5p   .25 .25
837b A536b 5p Litho. ('82)   .60 .30
838a A536c 15p   .25 .25
839a A536d 20p   .40 .25
840a A536e 25p brown   .40 .25
843a A537   30p   .60 .25
844a A409   35p   2.25 .30
845a A410   35p   .30 .25
846c A537a 35p   .60 .25
846d A409   50p   .60 .25
846e A410   50p   .25 .25

Perf. 12½x13
847a A537b 1r   .25 .25

Perf. 13x13½, 13½x13
848a A537c 2r ('83)   .50 .25
849a A537d 5r ('83)   .80 .45
     Nos. 837a-849a (14)   8.05 3.80

People Holding Hands, UN Emblem — A538

1980, Jan. 21 Photo. Perf. 13
851 A538 1r multicolored .75 .40
UN Industrial Development Org. (INIDO), 3rd Gen. Conf., New Delhi, Jan. 21-Feb. 8.

Field Post Office, Cancels A539

Money Order Centenary A540

2-Anna Copper Coins, 1774 A541

Rowland Hill, Birthplace, Kidderminster A542

Wmk. 360, Unwmkd. (1r)
1980, Jan. 25
852 A539 30p gray olive   .55 .40
853 A540 50p brown & citron .85 .85
854 A541 1r bronze   1.10 1.00
855 A542 2r dark gray   1.10 1.00
    Nos. 852-855 (4)   3.60 3.25
INDIA '80 Intl. Stamp Exhib., New Delhi, Jan. 25-Feb. 3.

India Institution of Engineers, 60th Anniversary

Perf. 13x13½
1980, Feb. 17 Unwmk.
856 A543 30p dark blue & gold .70 .40

INDIA

Uniforms, 1780 and 1980, Arms and Ribbon — A544

1980, Feb. 26
857 A544 30p multicolored   1.40   1.00
   Madras Sappers bicentennial.

2nd Intl. Apiculture Conf., New Delhi — A545

1980, Feb. 29   *Perf. 13½*
858 A545 1r multicolored   1.60   1.00

A546

1980, Feb. 29   *Wmk. 360*
859 A546 30p bright blue   .70   .40
   4th World Book Fair, New Delhi.

A547

1980, Mar. 18   *Perf. 13x13½*
860 A547 30p blue gray   .70   .40
   Welthy Fisher (b. 1879), educator, Literacy House, Lucknow.

Darul Uloom Islamic School, Deoband — A548

1980, Mar. 21   *Perf. 13½*
861 A548 30p gray green   1.00   .50

Keshub Chunder Sen — A549

    Perf. 13x13½
1980, Apr. 15   *Photo.*   *Wmk. 360*
862 A549 30p brown   .70   .40
   Sen (1838-84), scholar, writer, journalist.

Sivaji, Raigad Fort — A550

1980, Apr. 21   *Unwmk.*
863 A550 30p multicolored   .70   .40
   Sivaji (1627-80), Indian patriot.

Narayan Malhar Joshi — A551

    Perf. 13x13½
1980, June 5   *Wmk. 360*
864 A551 30p lilac rose   .85   .50
   Joshi (1879-1955), trade union pioneer.

Ulloor S. Parameswara Iyer — A552

1980, June 6
865 A552 30p dull purple   .85   .50
   Iyer (1877-1949), poet and scholar.

Syed Mohammad Zamin Ali — A553

1980, June 25
866 A553 30p dk yellow green   .70   .40
   Ali (1880-1955), linguist and educator.

Helen Keller (1880-1968) — A554

1980, June 27
867 A554 30p orange & black   1.00   .75
   Keller, blind and deaf writer and lecturer.

High Jump, Olympic Rings — A555

1980, July 19   *Photo.*   *Perf. 13½x14*
868 A555 1r shown   .70   .25
869 A555 2.80r Equestrian   1.75   1.50
   22nd Summer Olympic Games, Moscow, July 19-Aug. 3.

Prem Chand (1880-1936) — A556

1980, July 31   *Perf. 13*
870 A556 30p red brown   .70   .40
   Pen name of Nawab Rai, writer.

Mother Teresa, Nobel Peace Prize Medallion — A557

    Perf. 13½x13
1980, Aug. 27   *Photo.*   *Wmk. 360*
871 A557 30p violet, *grayish*   2.00   1.00
   Mother Teresa, founder of Missionaries of Charity, 70th birthday.

Earl Mountbatten of Burma — A558

1980, Aug. 28   *Perf. 13x13½*
872 A558 2.80r multicolored   2.75   1.25
   Mountbatten (1900-79), 1st governor gen. of India.

Asian Table Tennis Championship — A559

1980, Sept.   *Photo.*   *Perf. 13x13½*
873 A559 30p magenta   .85   .45

Scottish Church College, Calcutta, Sesquicentennial A560

1980, Sept. 27   *Photo.*   *Perf. 13½*
874 A560 35p dull purple   .50   .40

Rajah Annamalai Chettiar (1881-1948), Banker, Founder of Annamalai University — A561

1980, Sept. 30   *Unwmk.*   *Perf. 14x15*
875 A561 35p dull purple   .50   .40

Gandhi — A562

   No. 876, Gandhi on Dandi March. No. 877, Gandhi Defying Salt Law.

1980, Oct. 2   *Perf. 15x14*
876   35p multicolored   .60   .50
877   35p multicolored   .60   .50
   a. A562 Pair, #876-877   1.60   1.60

Jayaprakash Narayan (1902-79), Independence Activist & Social Reformer — A564

1980, Oct. 8   *Wmk. 360*   *Perf. 14x15*
878 A564 35p red brown   .70   .55

Intl. Symposium on Bustards, Jaipur — A565

1980, Nov. 1   *Photo.*   *Perf. 13*
879 A565 2.30r Great Indian bustards   3.25   2.25

Hegira (Pilgrimage Year) — A566

1980, Nov. 3   *Perf. 13x13½*
880 A566 35p multicolored   .50   .40

Children's Day — A567

    Perf. 13½x13
1980, Nov. 14   *Unwmk.*
881 A567 35p multicolored   .60   .40

Dhyan Chand — A568

1980, Dec. 3   *Wmk. 360*   *Perf. 14x15*
882 A568 35p dark rose brown   1.25   1.00
   Chand (1906-1979), field hockey player.

Miner, Molten Gold — A569

    Perf. 13x13½
1980, Dec. 20   *Unwmk.*
883 A569 1r multicolored   1.75   .40
   Kolar gold fields centenary.

Mukhtar Ahmad Ansari (1880-1936), Surgeon — A570

    Perf. 14x15
1980, Dec. 25   *Wmk. 360*
884 A570 35p olive gray   .60   .40

Government Mint, Bombay, Sesquicentennial A571

    Perf. 13½x13
1980, Dec. 27   *Unwmk.*
885 A571 35p multicolored   .40   .30

Regional Bridal Outfits — A572

1980, Dec. 30   *Perf. 13x13½*
886 A572 1r Kashmir   .70   .50
887 A572 1r Bengal   .70   .50
888 A572 1r Rajasthan   .70   .50
889 A572 1r Tamilnadu   .70   .50
   Nos. 886-889 (4)   2.80   2.00

INDIA

Mazharul Haque (1866-1930), Patriot — A573

1981, Jan. 2   Wmk. 360   Perf. 14x15
890 A573 35p violet   .50 .40

St. Stephen's College Centenary A574

1981, Feb. 1   Photo.   Perf. 14x14½
891 A574 35p dull red   .50 .40

Gommateshwara Statue, Shravanabelgola A575

1981, Feb. 9   Unwmk.
892 A575 1r multicolored   .50 .40

Ganesh V. Mavalankar (1888-1956) — A576

1981, Feb. 27
893 A576 35p light red brown   .50 .40
Mavalankar, 1st speaker of parliament.

Fruit and Nuts — A576a

Trees on Hillside — A576b

Windmill — A576c

Designs: 2.25r, Cashew. 2.80r, Apples. 3.25r, Oranges.

Perf. 14½x14
1981-86   Photo.   Wmk. 324
895   A576a 2.25r multi   .75 .50
  a.   Perf. 14x14½   2.50 1.20
  b.   Perf. 13   .65 .25
896   A576a 2.80r multi   2.25 1.20
  a.   Perf. 14x14½   .40 .25
897   A576a 3.25r multi ('83)   .60 .45
  a.   Perf. 13½x13 ('85)   .30 .25
  b.   Perf. 13   1.10 .70
900   A576b 10r multi ('84)   .80 .40
  b.   Perf. 13x13½   1.25 .60
Perf. 13½x13
900A A576c 50r multi ('86)   3.50 2.00
      Nos. 895-900A (5)   7.90 4.55

Homage to Martyrs — A577

1981, Mar. 23   Unwmk.   Perf. 14x15
901 A577 35p multicolored   .50 .40

Heinrich von Stephan and UPU Emblem — A578

1981, Apr. 8   Perf. 15x14
902 A578 1r red brown & brt blue .50 .40

Types of 1975-79 and

Telecommunications — A578a

Natural Gas — A578b

Irrigation — A578c

Dairy Industry — A578d

Design: 1r, Mahatma Gandhi.
Perf. 14x14½, 14½x14, 13 (40p, 75p), 13x13½ (20r)
Wmk. 324, 360 (2p, 5p, 15p)
1981-90   Photo.
      Size: 20x17mm, 17x20mm (1r)
903 A536a 2p violet   .50 .25
904 A536b 5p blue   1.20 .25
905 A578c 10p green   1.75 .25
  a.   Perf. 13   .80 .25
906 A536c 15p blue green   .50 .25
912 A578a 40p dull red   .50 .25
914 A578d 50p dark blue   3.25 .25
  a.   Perf. 13   2.40 .25
915 A537a 75p vermilion   .50 .25
916 A410   1r orange brown   .65 .25
      Size: 32x19mm
917 A578b 20r sepia & dark blue 2.00 .70
      Nos. 903-917 (9)   10.85 2.70
Issued: 10p, 50p, 1/25/82; 40p, 10/15/88; 20r, 11/30/88; 75p, 1990; 1r, 1/30/91; others, 3/25/81.

Intl. Year of the Disabled — A579

Perf. 14½x14
1981, Apr. 20   Photo.   Unwmk.
919 A579 1r blue & black   .70 .40

Tribesman — A580

1981, May 30   Perf. 14x14½
920 A580 1r Khiamngan Naga   .60 .45
921 A580 1r Toda   .60 .45
922 A580 1r Bhil   .60 .45
923 A580 1r Dandami Maria   .60 .45
      Nos. 920-923 (4)   2.40 1.80

World Environment Day — A581

1981, June 15
924 A581 1r multicolored   .65 .40

Nilmoni Phukan (1880-1978), Writer — A582

1981, June 22
925 A582 35p red brown   .50 .40

Sanjay Gandhi (1946-1980), Politician — A583

1981, June 23   Perf. 13x13½
926 A583 35p multicolored   .70 .60

SLV-3 Take-off — A584

1981, July 18   Photo.   Perf. 14x15
927 A584 1r multicolored   .60 .40
Launching of India's 1st indigenous satellite, 1st anniv.

Mascot, Field Hockey — A585

1981, July 28   Perf. 13½x13
928 A585 1r shown   1.60 .80
929 A585 1r Emblem   1.60 .80
9th Asian Games, New Delhi, 1982.

Flame of the Forest — A586

Designs: Flowering trees.
1981, Sept. 1   Photo.   Perf. 13
930 A586 35p shown   .60 .35
931 A586 50p Crateva   1.00 1.00
932 A586 1r Golden shower   1.40 .75
933 A586 2r Bauhinia   2.00 1.60
      Nos. 930-933 (4)   5.00 3.70

World Food Day — A587

1981, Oct. 16   Photo.   Perf. 14x14½
934 A587 1r multicolored   .50 .30

Cyrestis Achates — A588

35p, Stichophthalma camadeva, horiz. 50p, Cethosia biblis, horiz. 2r, Treinopalpus imperialis.

1981, Oct. 20   Perf. 13
935 A588 35p multicolored   1.50 .50
936 A588 50p multicolored   2.50 1.50
937 A588 1r shown   3.25 1.00
938 A588 2r multicolored   4.00 4.00
      Nos. 935-938 (4)   11.25 7.00

Bellary Raghava (1880-1946), Actor — A589

1981, Oct. 31   Perf. 14½x14
939 A589 35p olive gray   1.25 .40

40th Anniv. of Mahar Regiment — A590

1981, Nov. 9   Perf. 13
940 A590 35p multicolored   1.25 .40

Children's Day — A591

1981, Nov. 14   Perf. 14x14½
941 A591 35p multicolored   1.10 .45

Rajghat Stadium — A591a

1981   Perf. 13½x13
942 A591a 1r shown   2.40 .45
943 A591a 1r Nehru Stadium   .35 .40
Asian games. Issued: No. 942, 11/19; No. 943, 12/30.

Kashi Prasad Jayaswal (1881-1937), Historian — A592

1981, Nov. 27   Perf. 14x14½
944 A592 35p chalky blue   .70 .40

Intl. Palestinian Solidarity Day — A593

1981, Nov. 29   Perf. 14½x14
945 A593 1r multicolored   3.00 .55

243

INDIA

Naval Ship Taragiri — A594

1981, Dec. 4
946 A594 35p multicolored   4.00 2.00

Henry Heras (1888-1955), Historian — A595

1981, Dec. 14   Photo.   Perf. 14½x14
947 A595 35p rose violet   .70 .40

Indian Ocean Commonwealth Submarine Telephone Cable — A596

1981, Dec. 24   Perf. 13½
948 A596 1r multicolored   3.00 .55

5th World Field Hockey Championship, Bombay — A597

1981, Dec. 29   Perf. 13½x13
949 A597 1r multicolored   1.75 .50

Telephone Service Centenary — A598

Perf. 13x13½
1982, Jan. 28   Unwmk.
950 A598 2r multicolored   .75 .40

12th Intl. Soil Science Congress, New Delhi, Feb. 8-16 — A599

1982, Feb. 8   Perf. 13½x13
951 A599 1r multicolored   .50 .30

Sir Jamsetjee Jejeebhoy School of Art, Bombay — A600

1981, Mar. 2   Photo.   Perf. 14x14½
952 A600 35p multicolored   .40 .30

Three Musicians, by Pablo Picasso (1881-1973) A601

1982, Mar. 15   Photo.   Perf. 14
953 A601 2.85r multicolored   1.60 .65

Deer, 5th Cent. Bas Relief A602

Radio Telescope, Ooty A603

Festival of India, England: No. 955, Krishna, 9th cent. bronze sculpture.

1982, Mar. 23   Perf. 14x15
954 A602 2r multicolored   .60 .60
955 A602 3.05r multicolored   .40 .40
   Perf. 13
956 A603 3.05r multicolored   .60 .50
   Nos. 954-956 (3)   1.60 1.50

TB Bacillus Centenary — A604

1982, Mar. 24   Perf. 13
957 A604 35p rose violet   2.50 1.25

Durgabai Deshmukh (1909-1981), Social Worker — A605

1982, May 9   Photo.   Perf. 14½x14
958 A605 35p blue   .80 .40

Himalayan Flowers — A606

1982, May 29   Perf. 14x14½
959 A606 35p Blue poppies   .75 .60
960 A606 1r Showy inula   2.25 .60
961 A606 2r Cobra lily   2.75 2.50
962 A606 2.85r Brahma kamal   3.25 4.25
   Nos. 959-962 (4)   9.00 7.95

Ariana Passenger Payload Experimental (APPLE) Satellite, First Anniv. — A607

1982, June 19   Perf. 13½x13
963 A607 2r multicolored   .80 .65

Bidhan Chandra Roy (1882-1962), Physician and Politician — A608

1982, July 1   Perf. 14½x14
964 A608 50p orange brown   1.25 .95

Sagar Samrat Drilling Rig — A609

1982, Aug. 14   Photo.   Perf. 13
985 A609 1r multicolored   1.50 .80

Bindu (Cosmic Spirit), by Raza — A610

Paintings; 3.05r, Between the Spider and the Lamp, 1956, by M.F. Husain.

1982, Sept. 17   Perf. 14x14½
986 A610 2r multicolored   .80 .55
987 A610 3.05r multicolored   1.60 1.00

Kashmir Stag — A611

1982, Oct. 1   Perf. 13x13½
988 A611 2.85r multicolored   2.25 2.00

50th Anniv. of Indian Air Force — A612

1982, Oct. 8   Perf. 13½x13
989 A612 1r Wapiti, MiG 25   5.00 1.75

50th Anniv. of Civil Aviation — A613

3.25r, J.R.D. Tata and his Puss Moth, 1932.

1982, Oct. 15
990 A613 3.25r multicolored   5.00 2.25

Police Memorial Day — A614

1982, Oct. 21
991 A614 50p Beat patrol   .70 .40

Post Office Savings Bank Centenary — A615

1982, Oct. 23
992 A615 50p brown   .50 .35

9th Asian Games — A616

No. 993, Wrestling, by Janaki, 17th cent. No. 993A, Archery.

1982   Perf. 13½x14
993 A616 1r multicolored   1.25 .60
993A A616 1r multicolored   2.75 .50
   Issued: No. 993, 10/30; No. 993A, 11/6.

India-USSR Troposcatter Communications Link — A617

1982, Nov. 2   Perf. 13½x13
994 A617 3.05r multicolored   .80 .50

Children's Day — A618

1982, Nov. 14   Perf. 14x15
995 A618 50p multicolored   .60 .40

9th Asian Games — A619

1982   Perf. 13
996 A619 50p Cycling   .25 .25
997 A619 2r Yachting   .40 .30
998 A619 2r Javelin   .45 .40
999 A619 2.85r Rowing   .65 .45
1000 A619 2.85r Discus   1.00 .45
1001 A619 3.25r Soccer   1.50 .65
   Nos. 996-1001 (6)   4.25 2.50
Issued: Nos. 997, 999, 11/25; others 11/19.

50th Anniv. of Indian Military Academy, Dehradun — A620

1982, Dec. 10   Perf. 13½x13
1002 A620 50p multicolored   .60 .40

Purushottamdas Tandon (1882-1962), Politician — A621

1982, Dec. 15   Perf. 13
1003 A621 50p bister   .50 .40

Darjeeling Himalayan Railway Centenary — A622

1982, Dec. 18   Perf. 13½x13
1004 A622 2.85r multicolored   6.00 5.50

Indian Railway Car — A623

Nos. 2 and 201 — A624

1982, Dec. 30   Photo.   Perf. 13, 14
1005 A623 50p multicolored   1.75 1.10
1006 A624 2r multicolored   2.75 2.75
   INPEX '82 Stamp Exhibition.

INDIA

First Anniv. of Antarctic Expedition — A625

1983, Jan. 9   Photo.   *Perf. 13½x13*
1007 A625 1r multicolored   5.00 3.25

Pres. Franklin D. Roosevelt (1882-1945) A626

1983, Jan. 30   *Perf. 13*
1008 A626 3.25r brown   .90 .75

Siberian Cranes — A627

1983, Feb. 7   *Perf. 13x13½*
1009 A627 2.85r multicolored   3.00 2.50

180th Anniv. of Jat Regiment — A628

1983, Feb. 16   *Perf. 13½x13*
1010 A628 50p Soldiers, emblem   2.50 2.00

7th Non-aligned Summit Conference A629

1983, Mar. 7
1011 A629 1r Emblem   .35 .35
1012 A629 2r Jawaharlal Nehru   .45 .45

Commonwealth Day — A630

1r, Shore Temple, Mahabalipuram. 2r, Mountains, Gomukh.

1983, Mar. 14   *Perf. 13*
1013 A630 1r multicolored   .25 .30
1014 A630 2r multicolored   .45 .45

86th Session of Intl. Olympic Committee, New Delhi, Mar. 21-28 — A631

1983, Mar. 25   Litho.   *Perf. 13½x13*
1015 A631 1r Acropolis   .50 .40

A632
St. Francis of Assisi (1182-1226), by Giovanni Collina.

1983, Apr. 4   Photo.   *Perf. 13*
1016 A632 1r brown   1.10 .55

A633

1983, May 5   Photo.   *Perf. 13x12½*
1017 A633 1r brown   2.00 .50
Karl Marx (1818-1883).

Charles Darwin (1809-1882) A634

1983, May 18   *Perf. 12½x13*
1018 A634 2r multicolored   3.50 2.25

50th Anniv. of Kanha Natl. Park — A635

1983, May 30   *Perf. 13½x13*
1019 A635 1r Barasinga stag   3.25 1.25

World Communications Year — A636

1983, July 18   Photo.   *Perf. 13*
1020 A636 1r multicolored   .60 .40

Simon Bolivar (1783-1830) A637

1983, July 24
1021 A637 2r multicolored   3.00 2.50

Quit India Resolution, Aug. 8, 1942 — A638

Meera Behn (Madeleine Slade). Disciple of Gandhi, d. 1982 — A639

Design: No. 1024, Mahadev Desai (1892-1942).

1983, Aug. 9   Photo.   *Perf. 14*
1022 A638 50p shown   1.40 1.10
   Perf. 13½x13
1023 A639 50p shown   1.40 1.10
1024 A639 50p org, green & brn   1.40 1.10
   a. Pair, #1023-1024   2.75 2.75

See Nos. 1033, 1035, 1042, 1052-1057, 1077, 1093-1094, 1103, 1107, 1109, 1122, 1137-1139, 1144, 1147-1149, 1163, 1167, 1198, 1202-1205, 1229-1231, 1238, 1243, 1257, 1268-1271, 1277.

Ram Nath Chopra (1882-1973), Pharmacologist — A640

1983, Aug. 17   *Perf. 13*
1025 A640 50p brown   .70 .55

Indian Mountaineering Foundation, 25th Anniv. — A641

2r, Nanda Devi, Himalayas.

1983, Aug. 27   *Perf. 13½*
1026 A641 2r multicolored   2.40 1.50

Bombay Natural History Soc. — A642

1983, Sept. 15   *Perf. 13x13½*
1027 A642 1r multicolored   3.50 1.25

Rock Garden, Chandigarh — A643

1983, Sept. 23   *Perf. 13x13½*
1028 A643 1r multicolored   2.00 1.25

Wildlife — A644

1r, Golden langur. 2r, Lion-tailed macaque.

1983, Oct. 1   *Perf. 13½x13*
1029 A644 1r multicolored   2.25 .75
1030 A644 2r multicolored   3.50 3.50

World Tourism, 5th General Assembly A645

1983, Oct. 3   Photo.   *Perf. 14*
1031 A645 2r Ghats of Varanasi   1.00 .50

Krishna Kanta Handique, Linguist, Sanskritist, Educator and Scholar — A646

1983, Oct. 7   Litho.   *Perf. 13*
1032 A646 50p deep gray violet   .50 .35

Famous Indians Type of 1983
Design: Hemu Kalani, revolutionary patriot.

1983, Oct. 18   Photo.   *Perf. 13½x13*
1033 A639 50p org, grn & red brn   .50 .50

Children's Day — A648

Painting: Festival, by Kashyap Premswala

1983, Nov. 14   Photo.   *Perf. 13*
1034 A648 50p multicolored   .60 .45

Famous Indians Type of 1983
Design: Acharya Vinoba Bhave (1895-1982), freedom fighter.

1983, Nov. 15   Photo.   *Perf. 13½x13*
1035 A639 50p org, grn & dull brn   .50 .50

Manned Flight Bicent. — A650

1r, 1st Indian Balloon. 2r, Montgolfier Balloon.

1983, Nov. 21   Photo.   *Perf. 13*
1036 A650 1r multicolored   1.25 .55
1037 A650 2r multicolored   1.75 1.25

Project Tiger — A651

1983, Nov. 22   Photo.   *Perf. 13*
1038 A651 2r multicolored   5.00 3.75

Commonwealth Heads of Government Meeting, New Delhi — A652

Design: 2r, Goanese Couple, 19th century.

1983, Nov. 23   Photo.   *Perf. 13*
1039 A652 1r lt brnsh blue & multi   .45 .40
1040 A652 2r pink & multi   .85 .50

Pratiksha — A653

1983, Dec. 5   Photo.   *Perf. 13*
1041 A653 1r multi   .50 .40
Nanda Lal Bose (1882-1966), artist.

Famous Indians Type of 1983
Design: Surendranath Banerjee, journalist.

1983, Dec. 28   Photo.   *Perf. 13½x13*
1042 A639 50p org, green & olive   .50 .50

INDIA

7th Light Cavalry Bicent. — A655

1984, Jan. 7
1043 A655 1r Soldier, banner 4.75 1.50

Deccan Horse Regiment, 194th Anniv. — A656

1984, Jan. 9 Perf. 13x13½
1044 A656 1r multicolored 2.50 1.50

Asiatic Society Bicentenary A657

Design: Society building, Calcutta; founder William Jones.

1984, Jan. 15 Perf. 13
1045 A657 1r brt green & dp lilac .50 .40

Postal Life Insurance Centenary — A658

1984, Feb. 1 Photo. Perf. 13x13½
1046 A658 1r Emblem .50 .40

Presidential Review of Naval Fleet — A659

1984, Feb. 3 Perf. 13½x13
1047 A659 1r Jet 4.00 2.00
1048 A659 1r Aircraft carrier 4.00 2.00
1049 A659 1r Submarine 4.00 2.00
1050 A659 1r Missile destroyer 4.00 2.00
  a. Block of 4, #1047-1050 22.50 12.00

12th Intl. Leprosy Congress, New Delhi — A660

1984, Feb. 10 Perf. 13x13½
1051 A660 1r Globe, emblem .70 .50

Famous Indians Type of 1983

No. 1052, Vasudeo Balvant Phadke (d. 1884), freedom fighter. No. 1053, Baba Kanshi Ram. No. 1054, Begum Hazrat Mahal. No. 1055, Mangal Pandey. No. 1056, Nana Sahib. No. 1057, Tatya Tope.

1984 Perf. 13½x13
1052 A639 50p org, grn & dk ol .55 .55
1053 A639 50p org, grn & brn .55 .55
1054 A639 50p org, grn, red org & gray 1.25 .80
1055 A639 50p org, grn, brn & gray 1.25 .80
1056 A639 50p org, grn, vio & gray 1.25 .80
1057 A639 50p org, grn, dk ol & gray 1.25 .80
  Nos. 1052-1057 (6) 6.10 4.30
Issued: No. 1052, 2/23. No. 1053, 4/23. Nos. 1054-1057, 5/10.

Indian-Russian Space Cooperation — A662

1984, Apr. 3 Photo. Perf. 14
1058 A662 3r Spacecraft 1.50 .85

G. D. Birla (1894-1983), Industrialist A663

Birla, Birla Institute of Technology, Pilani.

1984, June 11
1060 A663 50p sepia .70 .55

1984 Summer Olympics — A664

50p, Basketball. 1r, High jump. 2r, Gymnastics, horiz. 2.50r, Weight lifting, horiz.

Perf. 13x12½, 12½x13
1984, July 28 Photo.
1061 A664 50p multicolored 1.25 .75
1062 A664 1r multicolored 1.00 .40
1063 A664 2r multicolored 1.40 1.10
1064 A664 2.50r multicolored 1.60 1.60
  Nos. 1061-1064 (4) 5.25 3.85

Vellore Fort — A665

1984, Aug. 3 Perf. 13½x13, 13x13½
1065 A665 50p Gwalior, horiz. .85 .65
1066 A665 1r shown 1.25 .40
1067 A665 1.50r Simhagad 2.25 2.00
1068 A665 2r Jodhpur, horiz. 2.60 2.50
  Nos. 1065-1068 (4) 6.95 5.55

B.V. Paradkar, Editor — A665a

1984, Sept. 14 Photo. Perf. 13x13½
1068A A665a 50p sepia .80 .55

Dr. D.N. Wadia (1883-1969), Geologist A665b

1984, Oct. 23 Perf. 13
1068B A665b 1r multicolored 2.00 .40

Indira Gandhi A666

1984, Nov. 19 Photo. Perf. 15x14
1069 A666 50p multicolored 3.00 3.00

Children's Day — A667

1984, Nov. 14 Photo. Perf. 13
1070 A667 50p Birds in trees 1.25 .70

12th World Mining Congress — A668

1984, Nov. 20 Photo. Perf. 13
1071 A668 1r Congress emblem 2.00 .45

Dr. Rajendra Prasad (1884-1963), 1st, Pres. — A669

1984, Dec. 3 Photo. Perf. 13
1072 A669 50p multicolored 1.25 1.10

Roses — A670

1984, Dec. 23 Litho. Perf. 13
1073 A670 1.50r Mrinalini 3.25 2.50
1074 A670 2r Sugandha 3.50 2.75

Fergusson College Centenary A671

1985, Jan. 2 Photo. Perf. 13x13½
1076 A671 100p multicolored 1.00 .60

Famous Indians Type of 1983

Design: Narhar Vishnu Gadgil (1896-1966), freedom fighter.

1985, Jan. 10 Photo. Perf. 13½x13
1077 A639 50p org, grn & brn .75 .70

Artillery Regiment, 50th Anniv. — A673

1985, Jan. 15 Perf. 13½x13
1078 A673 1r Gunner, howitzer 5.50 2.00

Indira Gandhi (1917-1984) A674

2r, Addressing UN General Assembly.

1985, Jan. 31 Perf. 14
1079 A674 2r multicolored 4.00 3.25
See Nos. 1098-1099.

Minicoy Lighthouse Cent. — A675

1985, Feb. 2 Perf. 13
1080 A675 1r multicolored 5.25 1.40

Bengal Medical College, 150th Anniv. — A676

1985, Feb. 20 Perf. 13½x13
1081 A676 1r multicolored 3.50 .80

Madras Medical College, 150th Anniv. — A677

1985, Mar. 8 Perf. 13½x13
1082 A677 1r multicolored 3.50 .80

Assam Rifles, North-East Sentinels, 150th Anniv. — A679

1985, Mar. 29
1084 A679 1r multicolored 4.75 1.75

Potato Research, 50th Anniv. — A680

1985, Apr. 1 Perf. 13
1085 A680 50p brn & pale brn 2.25 1.60

Baba Jassa Singh Ahluwalia, 1718-1783, Sikh Leader — A681

1985, Apr. 4
1086 A681 50p rose violet 2.00 1.60

St. Xavier's College, 125th Anniv. — A682

1985, Apr. 12
1087 A682 1r multicolored 1.60 .70

INDIA

White-winged Wood Duck — A683

1985, May 18   *Perf. 14*
1088 A683 2r multicolored   6.50   5.50

Bougainvillea — A684

1985, June 5   *Perf. 13*
1089 A684 50p multicolored   2.00   1.75
1090 A684 1r multicolored   2.50   1.50

Statue of Didarganj Yakshi, Indian Deity A685

Yaudheya Tribal Republic Copper Coin, c. 200 B.C. A686

1985
1091 A685 1r multicolored   1.50   .50
1092 A686 2r multicolored   3.00   2.00
Festival of India, festival in France and the US for cultural exchange.
Issue dates: 1r, June 7. 2r, June 13.

Famous Indians Type of 1983
Designs: No. 1093, Jairamdas Doulatram (1891-1979), journalist and politician. No. 1094, Nellie (1909-1973) & Jatindra Mohan (d. 1933) Sengupta, political activists, horiz.

1985   *Perf. 13½x13*
1093 A639 50p org, grn & dl red brn   .75   .50
     Perf. 13x13½
1094 A639 50p org, green & fawn   .75   .50
Issued: No. 1093, 7/21; No. 1094, 7/22.

Swami Haridas (1478-1573), Philosopher — A689

1985, Sept. 19   Photo.   *Perf. 13½x13*
1095 A689 1r multicolored   2.75   1.50

Border Roads Org., 25th Anniv. A690

1985, Oct. 10   *Perf. 13x14*
1096 A690 2r multicolored   5.00   2.50

Prime Minister Nehru at Podium — A691

1985, Oct. 24   *Perf. 13x13½*
1097 A691 2r multicolored   1.50   1.10
UN, 40th anniv.

Indira Gandhi Memorial Type of 1985
2r, Gandhi addressing crowd. 3r, Portrait.

1985   *Perf. 14*
1098 A674 2r multicolored   3.50   3.50
1099 A674 3r multicolored   3.50   3.50
Issued: 2r, 10/31. 3r, 11/19.

Children's Day — A692

1985, Nov. 14   *Perf. 13½x13*
1100 A692 50p multicolored   1.25   1.00

Halley's Comet — A693

1985, Nov. 19   *Perf. 13x13½*
1101 A693 1r multicolored   2.50   1.75
Intl. Astronomical Union, 19th General Assembly, New Delhi, Nov. 19-28.

St. Stephen's Hospital, Delhi, Cent. — A694

1985, Nov. 25   *Perf. 13*
1102 A694 1r multicolored   1.25   .55

Famous Indians Type of 1983
Design: Kakasaheb Kalelkar (1885-1981), author.

1985, Dec. 2   *Perf. 13½x13*
1103 A639 50p org, grn & ol brn   .75   .50

Map of South Asia — A696

Flags of India, Pakistan, Bangladesh, Nepal, Bhutan, Sri Lanka and the Maldive Islands A697

1985, Dec. 8   *Perf. 13½x13, 14*
1104 A696 1r multicolored   2.25   .50
1105 A697 3r multicolored   3.75   3.50
South Asian Regional Cooperation, SARC.

Shyama Shastri (1762-1827), Composer — A698

1985, Dec. 21   *Perf. 13½x13*
1106 A698 1r multicolored   3.50   1.75

Famous Indians Type of 1983
Master Tara Singh (1885-1967), Sikh leader.

1985, Dec. 23   *Perf. 13½x13*
1107 A639 50p org, green & blue   .75   .50

Intl. Youth Year — A700

1985, Dec. 24
1108 A700 2r multicolored   2.25   1.75

Famous Indians Type of 1983
Design: Ravishankar Maharaj (1884-1984), freedom fighter, politician.

1985, Dec. 24   *Perf. 13½x13*
1109 A639 50p org, green & slate   .75   .50

Handel and Bach — A702

1985, Dec. 27   *Perf. 13½x13*
1110 A702 5r multicolored   7.25   4.75

Congress Presidents, 1924-1985 A703

1985, Dec. 28   *Perf. 14*
1111 Block of 4   21.00   13.00
a.-d. A703 1r any single   2.50   2.25
Indian Natl. Congress, cent. Withdrawn on day of issue for a period of two weeks.

Naval Dockyard, Bombay, 250th Anniv. — A704

1986, Jan. 11   Photo.   *Perf. 13½*
1112 A704 2.50r multicolored   5.25   4.50

INPEX '86, Jaipur, Feb. 14-19 — A705

Designs: 50p, Hawa Mahal Palace, Jaipur No. 3. 2r, Khar Desert mobile post office.

1986, Feb. 14   *Perf. 13½x13*
1113 A705 50p multicolored   2.00   .90
1114 A705 2r multicolored   3.00   2.10

Vikrant Aircraft Carrier, 25th Anniv. — A706

1986, Feb. 16   *Perf. 13½x13*
1115 A706 2r multicolored   7.50   5.00

Inaugural Airmail Flight, 75th Anniv. — A707

1986, Feb. 18   *Perf. 13½x13, 13x13½*
1116 A707 50p Biplane   3.25   2.50
     Size: 41x28mm
1117 A707 3r Jet   7.25   5.50

Sixth Triennale of the Arts, Lalit Kala Academy — A708

1986, Feb. 22   *Perf. 13x13½*
1118 A708 1r multicolored   2.00   1.25

Sri Chaitanya Mahaprabhu — A709

1986, Mar. 3   *Perf. 13*
1119 A709 2r multicolored   4.00   3.25

Mayo College, Ajmer, 111th Anniv. — A710

1986, Apr. 12   *Perf. 13½x13*
1120 A710 1r multicolored   2.25   1.25

1986 World Cup Soccer Championships, Mexico — A711

1986, May 31   Photo.   *Perf. 13*
1121 A711 5r multicolored   6.00   4.25

Famous Indians Type of 1983
Bhim Sen Sachar (1894-1978), freedom fighter.

1986, Aug. 14   Photo.   *Perf. 13½x13*
1122 A639 50p org, green & sepia   2.00   1.40

Swami Sivananda (1887-1963), Religious Author — A713

1986, Sept. 8   Photo.   *Perf. 13½x13*
1123 A713 2r multicolored   4.00   3.00

10th Asian Games — A714

1.50r, Women's volleyball. 3r, Hurdling.

1986, Sept. 16   *Perf. 13x13½*
1124 A714 1.50r multicolored   3.75   3.75
1125 A714 3r multicolored   4.00   3.50

Madras Post Office, Bicent. — A715

1986, Oct. 9   Photo.   *Perf. 13x13½*
1126 A715 5r blk & brn org   6.50   5.00

INDIA

1st Battalion of Parachutists Regiment, 225th Anniv. — A716

1986, Oct. 17
1127 A716 3r multicolored   7.00 5.00

Indian Police Force, 125th Anniv. A717

Uniforms, 1861-1986. No. 1129a has a continuous design.

1986, Oct. 21 *Perf. 13½*
1128   1.50r multicolored   5.00 5.00
1129   2r multicolored   5.00 5.00
  a. A717 Pair, #1129, 1128   12.00 12.00

Intl. Peace Year — A718

1986, Oct. 24
1130 A718 5r sage grn, blue & rose   4.50 2.25

Children's Day — A719

1986, Nov. 14 *Photo. Perf. 13x13½*
1131 A719 50p multicolored   3.25 2.10

UN, 40th Anniv. — A720

50p, Growth monitoring. 5r, Immunization.

1986, Dec. 11 *Perf. 13½x13*
1132 A720 50p multicolored   2.75 2.25
1133 A720 5r multicolored   5.50 4.75

Child Survival Campaign.

Miyan Tansen, 17th Cent. Dhrupad Singer, Playing the Surbahar — A721

1986, Dec. 12
1134 A721 1r multicolored   2.75 .80

Corbett Natl. Park, 50th Anniv. — A722

1986, Dec. 15
1135 A722 1r Elephant   4.00 1.25
1136 A722 2r Gavial   5.00 4.50

Famous Indians Type of 1983
Designs: No. 1137, Alluri Seetarama Raju (b. 1897), freedom fighter. No. 1138, Sagarmal Gopa (b. 1900), freedom fighter. No. 1139, Veer Surendra Sai (b. 1809), freedom fighter.

1986 *Perf. 13½x13*
1137 A639 50p red, grn & sepia   1.75 1.00
1138 A639 50p red, grn & sl blue   1.75 1.00
1139 A639 50p red, grn & dp red brn   1.75 1.00
  Nos. 1137-1139 (3)   5.25 3.00

Issued: No. 1137, 12/26; No. 1138, 12/29; No. 1139, 12/30.

St. Martha's Hospital, Bangalore, Cent. — A724

1986, Dec. 30 *Perf. 13½*
1140 A724 1r multicolored   3.00 2.25

Yacht Trishna — A725

1987, Jan. 10
1141 A725 6.50r multicolored   6.25 4.25

1st Indian Army circumnavigation of the world, Sept. 28, 1985 to 1987.

Africa Fund — A726

1987, Jan. 25 *Photo. Perf. 14x14½*
1142 A726 6.50r black   15.00 5.00

ICC 29th Congress, New Delhi — A727

1987, Feb. 11 *Perf. 13½*
1143 A727 5r multicolored   4.25 2.75

Famous Indians Type of 1983
Design: Hakim Ajmal Khan (1864-1927), physician, politician.

1987, Feb. 13 *Perf. 13½x13*
1144 A639 60p org, grn & brn   2.75 .40

A729

Family Planning — A730

1987, Feb. 27 *Perf. 13, 13x13½*
1145 A729 35p dark red   1.00 .70
1146 A730 60p green & dark red   3.00 .70

Famous Indians Type of 1983
Designs: No. 1147, Lala Har Dayal (1884-1939). No. 1148, Manabendra Nath Roy (1887-1954). No. 1149, T. Ramaswamy Chowdary (1887-1943).

1987 *Photo. Perf. 13½x13*
1147 A639 60p org, grn & pur   .70 .40
1148 A639 60p org, grn & red brn   .70 .40
1149 A639 60p org, grn & brt blue   .70 .40
  Nos. 1147-1149 (3)   2.10 1.20

Issued: No. 1147, 3/18; No. 1148, 3/21; No. 1149, 4/25.

SER Emblem, Blast Furnaces A732

Steam Locomotive No. 691 A733

Electric Train Crossing Bridge — A734

4r, Steam locomotive, c. 1890.

1987, Mar. 28 *Perf. 13x13½, 13½x13*
1150 A732 1r shown   .25 .25
1151 A733 1.50r shown   .65 .40
1152 A734 2r shown   1.10 .55
1153 A733 4r multicolored   1.50 .90
  Nos. 1150-1153 (4)   3.50 2.10

Southeastern Railway, cent.

Kalia Bhomora Bridge, Assam — A735

1987, Apr. 14 *Perf. 13½*
1154 A735 2r multicolored   1.00 .40

Madras Christian College, 150th Anniv. — A736

1987, Apr. 16 *Perf. 13x13½*
1155 A736 1.50r black & rose lake   .50 .40

A737

1987, May 1 *Perf. 13½*
1156 A737 1r dull brown   .60 .30

Shree Shree Ma Anandamayee (1896-1982), spiritualist.

A738

1987, May 8 *Perf. 14*
1157 A738 2r multicolored   1.40 .40

Rabindranath Tagore (1861-1941), 1913 Nobel Laureate for literature.

A739

1987, May 10 *Perf. 13½*
1158 A739 1r multicolored   1.00 .50

Garhwal Rifles and Garhwal Scouts, cent.

A740

1987, May 11
1159 A740 60p black brn & buff   1.00 .80

J. Krishnamurti (1895-1986), mystic.

7th Battalion, Mechanised Infantry Regiment, Cent. — A741

1987, June 3 *Perf. 13½x13*
1160 A741 1r multicolored   .90 .45

INDIA '89, New Delhi, Jan. 20-29, 1989 — A742

50p, Swan emblem. 5r, Hall of Nations, New Delhi.

1987, June 15
1161 A742 50p multicolored   .50 .25
  a. Bklt. pane of 4+inscribed margin ('89)   2.25
1162 A742 5r multicolored   1.50 .80
  a. Souv. sheet of 2, #1161-1162   12.00 12.00
  b. Bklt. pane of 4+inscribed margin ('89)   7.00 7.00

Inscribed 1986. No. 1162a sold for 8r.

Famous Indians Type of 1983
Kailas Nath Katju (1887-1968), Chief Minister.

1987, June 17 *Perf. 13½x13*
1163 A639 60p org, grn & yel brn   .75 .70

Sadyah-Snata, Sanghol Sculpture, c. 2000 B.C. — A744

1987, July 3
1164 A744 6.50r multicolored   2.00 .80

Festival of India in the USSR, July 3, 1987-88.

Natl. Independence, 40th Anniv. — A745

1987, Aug. 15 *Photo. Perf. 13x13½*
1165 A745 60p org, brt bl & dk grn   .50 .40

Sant Harchand Singh Longowal (1932-1985), Social Reformer — A746

1987, Aug. 20 *Perf. 13½*
1166 A746 1r multicolored   .75 .40

INDIA

Famous Indians Type of 1983

Design: S. Satyamurti (1887-1943), political reformer, martyr.

1987, Aug. 22 — Perf. 13½x13
1167 A639 60p org, green & brn .65 .35

Guru Ghasidas (1756-1837), Founder of the Saman Sect — A748

1987, Sept. 1
1168 A748 60p henna brown .90 .40

Sri Sri Thakur Anukul Chandra (1888-1969), Guru — A749

1987, Sept. 2 — Perf. 13½
1169 A749 1r multicolored .60 .40

University of Allahabad, Cent. — A750

1987, Sept. 23 — Perf. 13½x13
1170 A750 2r multicolored 1.10 .40

Phoolwalon Ki Sair — A751

2r, Pankha (embroidered apron).

1987, Oct. 1 — Perf. 13x13½
1171 A751 2r multicolored 1.10 .40

Festival of thanksgiving for fulfilled prayers.

Maharaja Chhatrasal — A752

1987, Oct. 2 — Perf. 14
1172 A752 60p henna brown .50 .35

Chhatrasal (1649-1731), military commander during the war against the Moguls.

Intl. Year of Shelter for the Homeless — A753

1987, Oct. 5 — Perf. 13½x13
1173 A753 5r multicolored 1.75 .60

Asia Regional Conference of Rotary Intl. — A754

6.50r, Polio immunization.

1987, Oct. 14
1174 A754 60p shown .60 .30
1175 A754 6.50r multicolored 2.75 .70

Service to the Blind, Cent. — A755

1987, Oct. 15
1176 A755 1r shown .75 .30
1177 A755 2r Eye donation 1.25 .40

World White Cane Day.

INDIA '89 — A756

Designs: 60p, The Iron Pillar, Quuwat-ul-Islam Mosque courtyard, 5th cent., Delhi. 1.50r, The India Gate, New Delhi, war memorial by Luytens, 1921. 5r, The Dewan-E-Khas, Hall of Private Audience, Red Fort, Delhi, c. 1648. 6.50r, Purana Qila, Old Fort, Delhi, c. 1540.

1987, Oct. 17
1178 A756 60p multicolored .25 .25
 a. Bklt. pane of 4 + inscribed margin ('89) .80
1179 A756 1.50r multicolored .50 .30
 a. Bklt. pane of 4 + inscribed margin ('89) 2.10
1180 A756 5r multicolored 1.25 .55
 a. Bklt. pane of 4 + inscribed margin ('89) 5.25
1181 A756 6.50r multicolored 2.00 .70
 a. Souv. sheet of 4, #1178-1811 22.50 22.50
 b. Bklt. pane of 4 + inscribed margin ('89) 7.75
Nos. 1178-1181 (4) 4.00 1.80

No. 1181a sold for 15r.

Tyagmurti Goswami Ganeshdutt (1889-1959), Educator, Social Activist — A757

1987, Nov. 2 — Perf. 13½
1182 A757 60p terra cotta .60 .40

Children's Day — A758

1987, Nov. 14
1183 A758 60p multicolored .50 .30

Trees — A759

1987, Nov. 19 Photo. — Perf. 13½
1184 A759 60p Chinar, vert. .85 .30
1185 A759 1.50r Pipal .95 .30
1186 A759 5r Sal, vert. 2.60 .65
1187 A759 6.50r Banyan 3.50 .90
Nos. 1184-1187 (4) 7.90 2.15

Festival of the USSR in India — A760

Votive coin based on The Worker and the Peasant Woman, by Soviet sculptor Mukhina.

1987, Nov. 21 — Perf. 14
1188 A760 5r multicolored 3.50 .60

White Tiger — A761

1987, Nov. 29 Photo. — Perf. 13½
1189 A761 1r shown 1.75 .40
1190 A761 5r Snow leopard, horiz. 5.00 .90

Rameshwari Nehru (1886-1966), Human Rights and World Peace Activist — A762

1987, Dec. 10
1191 A762 60p red brown .50 .30

Execution of Veer Narayan Singh (1795-1857), Sikh Uprising Leader — A763

1987, Dec. 10
1192 A763 60p brown .50 .30

Father Kuriakose Elias Chavara (1806-1871), Theologian Beatified by Pope John Paul II Feb. 8, 1986 — A764

1987, Dec. 20
1193 A764 60p dark brown olive .50 .30

Dr. Rajah Sir M.A. Muthiah Chettiar (1905-1984), Politician, Pro-chancellor of Annamalai University — A765

1987, Dec. 21 — Perf. 13
1194 A765 60p chalky blue black .50 .40

Sri Harmandir Sahib (Gold Temple), Amritsar, 400th Anniv. — A766

1987, Dec. 26 — Perf. 13½
1195 A766 60p multicolored 1.00 .70

Rukmini Devi (1904-1986), Dancer, Choreographer A767

1987, Dec. 27
1196 A767 60p dark red .75 .40

Dr. Hiralal (1867-1934), Historian — A768

1987, Dec. 31
1197 A768 60p dark blue .50 .40

Famous Indians Type of 1983

Design: Pandit Hriday Nath Kunzru (1887-1978), human rights activist, statesman.

1987, Dec. 31 — Perf. 13½x13
1198 A639 60p org, grn & red brn .50 .30

75th Session of the Indian Science Congress Assoc. — A770

1988, Jan. 1
1199 A770 4r multicolored 3.00 .65

Solar Energy — A771

Wmk. 324

1988, Jan. 1 Photo. — Perf. 13
1200 A771 5r dp orange & sepia 3.75 .40

13th Asia Pacific Dental Congress, New Delhi, Jan. 28-Feb. 2 — A772

1988, Jan. 28 Unwmk. — Perf. 13
1201 A772 4r multicolored 1.25 .65

Famous Indians Type of 1983

Designs: No. 1202, Mohan Lal Sukhadia (1916-1982). No. 1203, Dr. S.K. Sinha (1887-1961). No. 1204, Chandra Shekhar Azad (1906-1931). No. 1205, Govind Ballabh Pant (1887-1961).

1988 — Perf. 13½x13
1202 A639 60p org, grn & bluish blk 1.25 .60
1203 A639 60p org, grn & org brn 1.25 .60
1204 A639 60p org, grn & rose red 1.25 .60
1205 A639 60p org, grn & purple 1.25 .60
Nos. 1202-1205 (4) 5.00 2.40

Issue dates: Nos. 1202, Feb. 2; No. 1203, Feb. 4; No. 1204, Feb. 27; No. 1205, Mar. 7.

U. Tirot Sing (1800-1833), Patriot — A774

1988, Feb. 3
1206 A774 60p dull brown 1.00 .40

Kumaon Regiment 4th Battalion, Bicent. — A775

1r, Uniforms of 1788, 1947, 1988.

1988, Feb. 19 — Perf. 14
1207 A775 1r multicolored 1.10 .40

Balgandharva (1888-1967), Musician — A776

1988, Feb. 22 — Perf. 13x13½
1208 A776 60p brown 1.25 .40

INDIA

Mechanised Infantry Regiment — A777

1988, Feb. 24   *Perf. 13½x13*
1209   A777   1r multicolored   1.50   .45

A778

1988, Feb. 26   *Perf. 13*
1210   A778   60p bluish black   .60   .40

Sir B.N. Rau (1887-1953), constitutional advisor.

A779

1988, Mar. 14   Photo.   *Perf. 13x13½*
1211   A779   1r bright rose   .70   .40

Mohindra College, Patiala, founded in 1875 by Maharaja Mohinder Singh, is now part of Punjabi University.

Dr. D.V. Gundappa (1887-1975), Journalist, and Gikhala Institute of Public Affairs — A780

1988, Mar. 17   *Perf. 13½x13*
1212   A780   60p slate blue   1.00   .45

Woman Warrior Riding into Battle — A781

1988, Mar. 20   *Perf. 13x13½*
1213   A781   60p bright rose   1.40   .40

Rani Avantibai (d. 1858), heroine of the 1857 independence war.

Malayala Manorama Newspaper, Cent. — A782

1988, Mar. 23
1214   A782   1r blue & black   1.00   .40

Malayala Manorama, published in Kottayam, is the largest circulated daily newspaper in India.

Maharshi Dadhichi, Vedic Period Saint Purported to Have Introduced Fire to Man — A783

1988, Mar. 26
1215   A783   60p deep orange   .80   .40

Mohammad Iqbal (1877-1938), Poet — A784

1988, Apr. 21
1216   A784   60p carmine & gold   1.10   .50

Samarth Ramdas (1608-1682), Philosopher — A785

1988, May 1   *Perf. 13*
1217   A785   60p dk yellow green   1.00   .50

Swati Tirunal Rama Varma (1813-1846), Carnatic Composer — A786

1988, May 2   *Perf. 13x13½*
1218   A786   60p brt violet   1.00   .50

1st War of Independence, the "Indian Mutiny of 1857" — A787

Painting: Rani Laxmi Bai transformed from a queen into a warrior fighting for justice, by M.F. Husain.

1988, May 9   Photo.   *Perf. 13x13½*
1219   A787   60p multicolored   1.50   .40

Bhaurao Patil (b. 1887), Educator — A788

1988, May 9   *Perf. 13½x13*
1220   A788   60p red brown   1.00   .45

Himalayan Peaks — A789

1988, May 19
1221   A789   1.50r Broad Peak   1.60   .30
1222   A789   4r Godwin Austen   1.90   .40
1223   A789   5r Kanchenjunga   1.90   .55
1224   A789   6.50r Nandadevi   1.90   .70
    Nos. 1221-1224 (4)   7.30   1.95

Care for the Elderly — A790

1988, May 24   *Perf. 13x13½*
1225   A790   60p multicolored   .75   .40

Victoria Terminal, Bombay, Cent. — A791

1988, May 30   *Perf. 13½x13*
1226   A791   1r multicolored   2.00   .30

Lawrence School, Lovedale, 130th Anniv. — A792

1988, May 31   *Perf. 13*
1227   A792   1r dk grn & red brn   1.40   .50

World Environment Day — A793

1988, June 5   *Perf. 14*
1228   A793   60p Khejri tree   .75   .40

Famous Indians Type of 1983

No. 1229, Dr. Anugrah Narain Singh (1887-1957), statesman. No. 1230, Kuladhor Chaliha (1886-1963), political and social reformer. No. 1231, Shivprasad Gupta (1883-1944), freedom fighter.

1988   *Perf. 13½x13*
1229   A639   60p org, grn & rose vio   1.00   .40
1230   A639   60p org, grn & gray blk   1.00   .40
1231   A639   60p org, grn & dk vio   1.00   .40
    Nos. 1229-1231 (3)   3.00   1.20

Issued: No. 1229, 6/18; No. 1230, 6/19; No. 1231, 6/28.

Rani Durgawati (d. 1564), Ruler of Gondwana — A795

1988, June 24
1232   A795   60p red   1.00   .40

A796

1988, July 28   Photo.   *Perf. 13x13½*
1233   A796   60p red brown   1.10   .50

Acharya Shanti Dev (687-765), Sanskrit and Pali scholar.

A797

1988, Aug. 4
1234   A797   60p blue violet   1.00   .50

Yashwant Singh Parmar (1906-1981), administrator of Himachal Pradesh State.

Painting by M.F. Husain A798

1988, Aug. 16   Photo.   *Perf. 13x13½*
1235   60p India at upper left   1.50   1.50
1236   60p India at lower left   1.50   1.50
    a. A798 Pair, #1235-1236   5.00   5.00

Natl. Independence 40th anniv.

Durgadas Rathore (1638-1718), Guardian of King Ajit Singh — A799

1988, Aug. 26   *Litho.*
1237   A799   60p dark red brown   1.10   .40

Famous Indians Type of 1983

Design: Sarat Chandra Bose (1889-1950), politician, lawyer, publisher.

1988, Sept. 6   Photo.   *Perf. 13½x13*
1238   A639   60p org, grn & dk blue grn   1.00   .50

Gopinath Kaviraj (1887-1976), Scholar — A801

1988, Sept. 7   *Perf. 13½x13*
1239   A801   60p brown olive   1.10   .40

Hindi Language Day, Sept. 14 — A802

1988, Sept. 14   Photo.   *Perf. 13x13½*
1240   A802   60p ver & dk olive green   .75   .40

Indian Olympic Assoc. Emblem A803

Glory of Sport, Independence 40th Anniv. A804

Perf. 13½x13, 13x13½
1988, Sept. 17
1241   A803   60p deep claret   .90   .45
1242   A804   5r multicolored   4.25   1.60

Famous Indians Type of 1983

Baba Kharak (1867-1963), nationalist.

1988, Oct. 6   *Perf. 13½x13*
1243   A639   60p org, green & org brn   1.00   .45

INDIA

Jerdon's Courser — A806

1988, Oct. 7   *Perf. 13½*
1244   A806   1r multicolored   3.50   .70

The Times of India, Newspaper, 150th Anniv. — A807

1988, Nov. 3   *Perf. 13½x14*
1245   A807   1.50r black & gold   1.00   .45

INDIA '89 — A808

   Perf. 13½x13
1988, Oct. 9   *Unwmk.*   *Photo.*
1246   A808   4r Bangalore P.O.   .75   .30
   a.   Bklt. pane of 6+inscribed margin ('89)   4.50
1247   A808   5r Bombay P.O.   1.50   .35
   a.   Bklt. pane of 6+inscribed margin ('89)   9.00

Portrait of Azad by K.K. Hebbar — A809

1988, Nov. 11
1248   A809   60p multicolored   1.00   .50

Maulana Abul Kalam Azad (1888-1958), minister of education, natl. resources and scientific research.

Jawaharlal Nehru — A810

   Perf. 13x13½, 13½x13 (1r)
1988, Nov. 14
1249   A810   60p dk gray, dk org & dk grn   .65   .35
1250   A810   1r Portrait, vert.   .75   .35

Birsa, Munda Leader — A811

1988, Nov. 15   *Perf. 13½x13*
1251   A811   60p brown   1.00   .45

Bhakra Dam, 25th Anniv. — A812

1988, Dec. 15   *Perf. 14*
1252   A812   60p carmine rose   1.00   .70

INDIA '89 — A813

60p, Dead-letter cancellations, 1886. 6.50r, Traveling p.o. cancellation, 1864-69.

1988, Dec. 20   *Perf. 13½x13*
1253   A813   60p multicolored   .75   .40
   a.   Bklt. pane of 6+inscribed margin ('89)   5.00
1254   A813   6.50r multicolored   2.50   1.40
   a.   Bklt. pane of 6+inscribed margin ('89)   15.00

K.M. Munshi (1887-1971), Environmentalist, Statesmen A814

1988, Dec. 30
1255   A814   60p dark olive green   1.25   .50

Mannathu Padmanabhan (1878-1970), Social Reformer — A815

1989, Jan. 2   *Perf. 13½x13*
1256   A815   60p dull brown   .70   .40

Famous Indians Type of 1983

Hare Krushna Mahtab (1899-1987), author.

1989, Jan. 2   *Perf. 13½x13*
1257   A639   60p org, grn & blk   .70   .40

Lok Sabha Secretariat, 60th Anniv. — A817

1989, Jan. 10   *Perf. 13½x13*
1258   A817   60p dark olive green   1.00   .50

State Museum, Lucknow, 125th Anniv. — A818

60p, Goddess Durga, lion.

1989, Jan. 11   *Perf. 14*
1259   A818   60p blue & dk blue   1.00   .50

INDIA '89 — A819

60p, Youth collecting. 1.50r, Postal coach & p.o., 1842. 5r, Travancore #2. 6.50r, Philatelic journal mastheads.

1989, Jan. 20   *Perf. 13½x13*
1260   A819   60p multicolored   .25   .25
   a.   Bklt. pane of 6 + inscribed margin   .60
1261   A819   1.50r multicolored   .40   .25
   a.   Bklt. pane of 6 + inscribed margin   2.40
1262   A819   5r multicolored   1.00   .50
   a.   Bklt. pane of 6 + inscribed margin   6.00
1263   A819   6.50r multicolored   1.50   .70
   a.   Bklt. pane of 6 + inscribed margin   9.00
     Nos. 1260-1263 (4)   3.15   1.70

St. John Bosco (1815-1888), Educator — A820

1989, Jan. 31   *Perf. 13*
1264   A820   60p carmine rose   .75   .40

3rd Cavalry, 148th Anniv. — A821

1989, Feb. 8   *Perf. 13½x13*
1265   A821   60p multicolored   .90   .55

Dargah Sharif Ajmer — A822

1989, Feb. 13   *Litho.*   *Perf. 13½x13*
1266   A822   1r multicolored   1.00   .50

President's Review of the Naval Fleet — A823

1989, Feb. 15   *Perf. 14*
1267   A823   6.50r multicolored   5.25   2.00

Famous Indians Type of 1983

No. 1268, Sheikh Mohammad Abdullah. No. 1269, Balasaheb Gangadhar Kher (1888-1957), politician. No. 1270, Saifuddin Kitchlew (1888-1963), lawyer, diplomat. No. 1271, Rajkumari Amrit Kaur (d. 1964), minister of health and welfare.

1988-89   *Photo.*   *Perf. 13½x13*
1268   A639   60p org, grn & lil rose   .65   .45
1269   A639   60p org, grn & dk vio   .65   .45
1270   A639   60p org, grn & blk brn   .65   .45
1271   A639   60p org, grn & grnsh blk   .65   .45
     Nos. 1268-1271 (4)   2.60   1.80
Issue dates: No. 1268, 12/5; No. 1269, 3/8/89; Nos. 1270-1271, 4/13/89.

Freedom Fighters — A825

1989   *Perf. 13x13½*
1272   A825   60p slate   1.00   .50
1273   A825   60p dark olive   1.00   .50
Issue dates: No. 1272, 1/17; No. 1273, 3/30.

Freedom Fighters — A826

Designs: No. 1274, Shaheed Laxman Nayak (1899-1943), protest leader. No. 1275, Bishu Ram Medhi (1888-1981), politician.

1989   *Perf. 13½x13*
1274   A826   60p org, sage grn & brn   1.00   .50

Size: 24x37mm
1275   A826   60p org, sage grn & dp yel grn   1.00   .50
Issued: No. 1274, 3/29; No. 1275, 4/24. See Nos. 1292, 1299-1300, 1317, 1429, 1487.

Sydenham College, Bombay — A827

1989, Apr. 19   *Perf. 13½*
1276   A827   60p black   1.00   .50

Famous Indians Type of 1983

Design: Asaf Ali (1888-1953), patriot.

1989, May 11   *Photo.*   *Perf. 13½x13*
1277   A639   60p org, grn & sepia   .90   .50

N.S. Hardikar (1889-1975), Freedom Fighter — A829

1989, May 13   *Perf. 13x13½*
1278   A829   60p chestnut brown   1.00   .50

Sankaracharya (b. 788), Philosopher A830

1989, May 17   *Perf. 14x13½*
1279   A830   60p multicolored   1.00   .50

Punjab University, Chandigarh A831

1989, May 19   *Perf. 13½x13*
1280   A831   1r blue green & brn   .75   .45

Film Industry, 75th Anniv. — A832

1989, May 30   *Photo.*   *Perf. 14*
1281   A832   60p dk olive bis & blk   1.10   .50

Kirloskar Corporation, Cent. — A833

1989, June 20   *Photo.*   *Perf. 13½x13*
1282   A833   1r multicolored   1.00   .50

DAV Education Movement, Cent. — A834

1989, June 27   *Photo.*   *Perf. 13½x13*
1283   A834   1r multicolored   .70   .45

INDIA

Dakshin Gangotri Post Office in the Antarctic, 1988 — A835

1989, July 11   *Perf. 14*
1284 A835 1r multicolored   2.75   .70

Allahabad Bank, 125th Anniv. — A836

1989, July 19
1285 A836 60p multicolored   .80   .50

Central Reserve Police Force, 50th Anniv. — A837

1989, July 27   *Perf. 13½x13*
1286 A837 60p golden brown   1.50   .80

Military Farms, Cent. — A838

1989, Aug. 18
1287 A838 1r multicolored   1.20   .60

Kemal Ataturk (1881-1938), 1st President of Turkey — A839

1989, Aug. 30   *Perf. 13x13½*
1288 A839 5r multicolored   3.75   .80

Sarvepalli Radhakrishnan, President of India, 1962-67 — A840

1989, Sept. 11   *Photo.*   *Perf. 13x13½*
1289 A840 60p black   .60   .40

P. Subbarayan (1889-1962), Lawyer, Political Reformer — A841

1989, Sept. 30   *Perf. 13x13½*
1290 A841 60p brown orange   .60   .40

Mohun Bagan Soccer Team, Cent. — A842

1989, Sept. 23   *Photo.*   *Perf. 13x13½*
1291 A842 1r multicolored   1.25   .50

Freedom Fighter Type of 1989

Shyamji Krishna Varma (1857-1930).

1989, Oct. 4   *Photo.*   *Perf. 13x13½*
1292 A826 60p org, sage grn & dk red brn   1.00   .50

Sayaji Rao Gaekwad III (1863-1939), Maharaja of the Former State of Baroda — A843

1989, Oct. 6   *Perf. 13x13½*
1293 A843 60p black   .80   .60

Use Pin Code — A844

1989, Oct. 14   *Perf. 14*
1294 A844 60p multicolored   .90   .60

Namakkal Kavignar (1888-1972), Poet Laureate — A845

1989, Oct. 19   *Photo.*   *Perf. 13x13½*
1295 A845 60p black   .75   .60

18th Intl. Epilepsy Congress and 14th World Neurology Congress, New Delhi — A846

1989, Oct. 21   *Perf. 13½x13*
1296 A846 6.50r multicolored   3.50   1.25

Ramabai and Sharada Sadan School — A847

1989, Oct. 26
1297 A847 60p brown   .60   .40
Pandita Ramabai (1858-1920), women's rights activist, founder of mission to help destitute women and children.

Pigeon Post — A848

1989, Nov. 3
1298 A848 1r brown orange   1.00   .50

Freedom Fighter Type of 1989

No. 1299, Acharya Narendra Deo (1889-1956), democratic socialist movement founder. No. 1300, Acharya Kripalani (1888-1982), politician.

1989   *Perf. 13½x13*
1299 A826 60p org, sage grn & brn   .75   .40
1300 A826 60p org, sage grn & dp gray   .75   .40
Issue dates: No. 1299, 11/6; No. 1300, 11/11.

Jawaharlal Nehru, Birth Cent. — A849

1989, Nov. 14   *Perf. 14x15*
1301 A849 1r buff, dk red brn & sepia   1.00   .50

8th Asian Track and Field Meet, Nov. 14-19, New Delhi — A850

1989, Nov. 19   *Perf. 14x14½*
1302 A850 1r black, org & dp grn   1.25   .60

A851

1989, Nov. 20   *Perf. 13x13½*
1303 A851 60p deep brown   .60   .45
Gurunath Bewoor (b. 1888), 1st Indian appointed postmaster general.

A852

1989, Dec. 8   *Photo.*   *Perf. 13x13½*
1304 A852 60p black   .60   .45
Balkrishna Sharma Navin (1897-1960), litterateur, politician.

Bombay Art Soc., Cent. — A853

1989, Dec. 15   *Perf. 13x13½*
1305 A853 1r multicolored   .90   .60

Likh Florican — A854

1989, Dec. 20   *Perf. 13x13½*
1306 A854 2r multicolored   2.50   .85

Digboi Oil Field, 1889 — A855

1989, Dec. 29   *Perf. 14*
1307 A855 60p dark red brown   1.00   .60
Discovery of oil, Digboi, Assam, cent.

M.G. Ramachandran (1917-1987), Actor, Chief Minister — A856

1990, Jan. 17   *Perf. 13x13½*
1308 A856 60p dark red brown   1.00   .40

Extracting Silt from Sukhna Lake, Chandigarh A857

1990, Jan. 29   *Perf. 13½x13*
1309 A857 1r multicolored   .75   .45
Sukhna Shramda, society for the preservation of Sukhna Lake.

Presentation of Colors by Pres. Venkataraman to the Bombay Sappers (Corps of Engineers), Feb. 21 — A858

1990, Feb. 21   *Perf. 15x14x14*   *Photo.*
1310 A858 60p multicolored   1.50   1.25

Asian Development Bank — A859

1990, May 2   *Photo.*   *Perf. 14*
1311 A859 2r Seashell   1.25   .45

Great Britain No. 1, Simulated Cancel of India, Envelope A860

1990, May 6   *Perf. 13x13½*
1312 A860 6r multicolored   2.50   .75
Penny Black, 150th anniv.

Residence and Portrait — A861

1990, May 17   *Photo.*   *Perf. 13½x13*
1313 A861 2r red brown & green   2.50   .50
Ho Chi Minh (1890-1969), Vietnamese Communist Party leader.

A862

1990, May 29
1314 A862 1r orange brown   1.00   .50
Prime Minister Chaudhary Charan Singh (1902-1987).

A863

1990, July 30   *Photo.*   *Perf. 13x13½*
1315 A863 2r multicolored   1.00   .55
Indian peace keeping force in Sri Lanka.

INDIA

Indian Council of Agricultural Research — A864

1990, July 31   *Perf. 14*
1316   A864   2r multicolored   1.00   .50

Freedom Fighter Type of 1989
Design: Khudiram Bose (1889-1908), vert.

1990, Aug. 11   *Photo.*   *Perf. 13x13½*
Size: 26x35mm
1317   A826   1r org, grn & red brn   .60   .45

Russian Child's Drawing of India — A865

6.50r, Indian child's drawing of Red Square.

1990, Aug. 16   *Photo.*   *Perf. 14*
1318   1r multicolored   2.75   1.75
1319   6.50r multicolored   2.75   1.75
   a. A865 Pair, #1318-1319   6.50   6.50
See Russia Nos. 5925-5926.

K. Kelappan (1889-1971), Social Reformer — A866

1990, Aug. 24   *Perf. 13*
1320   A866   1r lt red brown   .65   .45

A867

1990, Sept. 5   *Perf. 13x13½*
1321   A867   1r multicolored   .75   .50
Care for young girls.

Intl. Literacy Year — A868

1990, Sept. 8   *Perf. 13½x13*
1322   A868   1r blue, brn & tan   .75   .50

A869

1990, Sept. 10   *Perf. 13x14*
1323   A869   4r blue grn & red   2.00   1.60
Safe drinking water.

A870

1990, Sept. 28   *Photo.*   *Perf. 13x13½*
1324   A870   60p rose lake   .75   .50
Sunder Lal Sharma (1881-1940), social reformer.

11th Asian Games, Beijing — A871

1990, Sept. 29
1325   A871   1r   Kabbadi   .65   .35
1326   A871   4r   Sprinting   1.90   1.75
1327   A871   4r   Cycling   1.90   1.75
1328   A871   6.50r   Archery   2.50   2.25
       Nos. 1325-1328 (4)   6.95   6.10

A.K. Gopalan (1904-1977), Political and Social Reformer — A872

1990, Oct. 1
1329   A872   1r red brown   .75   .50

5th Gurkha Rifles, 3rd and 5th Battalions — A873

1990, Oct. 1
1330   A873   2r yel brown & dk vio   2.25   1.75

Suryamall Mishran (1815-1868), Poet — A874

1990, Oct. 19
1331   A874   2r brown & yel brown   .80   .60

Children's Day — A875

Perf. 13½x13
1990, Nov. 14   *Photo.*   *Unwmk.*
1332   A875   1r multicolored   .90   .60

Border Security Force, 25th Anniv. — A876

1990, Nov. 30
1333   A876   5r multicolored   5.00   1.60

Greetings — A877

4r, Two elephants carrying riders, horiz.

Perf. 13x13½, 13½x13
1990, Dec. 17   *Photo.*
1334   A877   1r multicolored   .50   .40
1335   A877   4r multicolored   1.50   .75

Cities of India — A878

1990, Dec. 24   *Photo.*   *Perf. 13½x13*
1336   A878   4r Bikaner   .80   .65
1337   A878   5r Hyderabad   1.25   .95
1338   A878   6.50r Cuttack   1.75   1.25
      Nos. 1336-1338 (3)   3.80   2.85

Bhakta Kanakadas (1488-1578), Mystic — A879

1990, Dec. 26   *Perf. 14*
1339   A879   1r red orange   .90   .45

Dnyaneshwari, 700th Anniv. — A880

1990, Dec. 31   *Perf. 13½x13*
1340   A880   2r org red, red brown & blk   2.00   .40

Calcutta, 300th Anniv. — A881

Designs: 1r, Shaheed Minar. 6r, Sailing ships on Ganges River.

1990, Dec. 28   *Photo.*   *Unwmk.*   *Perf. 14*
1341   A881   1r multicolored   .50   .30
Size: 44x35mm
1342   A881   6r multicolored   2.00   1.50

Pandit Mohan Malaviya, Banaras Hindu University — A882

1991, Jan. 20   *Perf. 13½x13*
1343   A882   1r dk carmine rose   .60   .35
Banaras Hindu University, 75th Anniv.

Intl. Conference on Traffic Safety — A883

1991, Jan. 30   *Perf. 13½x13*
1344   A883   6.50r blue, red & blk   1.25   .80

7th Art Triennial — A884

1991, Feb. 12   *Photo.*   *Perf. 13x13½*
1345   A884   6.50r multicolored   1.00   .60

Jagannath Sunkersett — A885

1991, Feb. 15
1346   A885   2r ultra & henna brn   .80   .50
Jagannath Sunkersett (1803-1865), educator, reformer.

Tata Memorial Center, 50th Anniv. — A886

1991, Feb. 28   *Perf. 13½x13*
1347   A886   2r brown & buff   .75   .45

River Dolphin — A887

1991, Mar. 4
1348   A887   4r shown   2.25   1.75
1349   A887   6.50r Sea cow   3.00   2.40

Fight Against Drugs — A888

1991, Mar. 5   *Perf. 13x13½*
1350   A888   5r dp violet & red   7.00   2.00

World Peace — A889

1991, Mar. 7   *Photo.*   *Perf. 13x13½*
1351   A889   6.50r black & tan   1.75   .75

Indian Remote Sensing Satellite 1A — A890

1991, Mar. 18   *Perf. 14*
1352   A890   6.50r blue, red brn & blk   2.50   .70

Babu Jagjivan Ram (1908-1976), Politician — A891

1991, Apr. 5   *Photo.*   *Perf. 13½*
1353   A891   1r yellow & brown   .60   .50

INDIA

Dr. B.R. Ambedkar (1891-1956), Social Reformer — A892

1991, Apr. 14 — Perf. 13½x13
1354 A892 1r red brown & blue   .60   .50

Tribal Dances — A893

1991, Apr. 30 Photo. — Perf. 13½x13
1355 A893 2.50r Valar   .85   .50
1356 A893 4r Kayang   1.10   .60
1357 A893 5r Hozagiri   1.40   .70
1358 A893 6.50r Velakali   1.75   .85
  Nos. 1355-1358 (4)   5.10 2.65

Ariyakudi Ramanuja Iyengar (1890-1967), Musician — A894

1991, May 18
1359 A894 2r green & red brown 1.00   .65

Karpoori Thakur (1924-1988), Politician — A895

1991, May 30
1360 A895 1r red brown   .60   .50

Antarctic Treaty, 30th Anniv. — A896

1991, June 23 Photo. — Perf. 13½x13
1361 A896 5r Penguins   3.00 2.10
1362 A896 6.50r Map, penguins   3.00 2.10
  a. Pair, #1361-1362   6.50 6.50
No. 1362a printed in continuous design.

New Delhi, 60th Anniv. — A897

Views of New Delhi architecture.

1991, June 25
1363 A897 5r multicolored   3.50 1.90
1364 A897 6.50r multicolored   3.50 1.90
  a. Pair, #1363-1364   7.00 7.00
No. 1364a printed in continuous design.

Sri Ram Sharma Acharya (1911-1990), Social Reformer — A898

1991, June 27
1365 A898 1r red & blue green   .70   .50

K. Shankar Pillai (1902-1989), Cartoonist — A899

6.50r, The Big Show, vert.

1991, July 31 Photo. — Perf. 13½x13
1366 A899 4r shown   1.45 1.25
  Perf. 13x13½
1367 A899 6.50r dp purple   2.00 1.90

Sriprakash (1890-1971), Politician — A900

1991, Aug. 3 — Perf. 13½x13
1368 A900 2r yellow brown   .70   .40

Gopinath Bardoloi (1890-1950), Politician — A901

1991, Aug. 5 — Perf. 13x13½
1369 A901 1r violet   1.40   .50

Rajiv Gandhi (1944-1991), Prime Minister — A902

1991, Aug. 20 — Perf. 13
1370 A902 1r multicolored   1.40 1.00

Jain Muni Mishrimalji (1891-1984), Philosopher — A903

1991, Aug. 24 Photo. — Perf. 13½
1371 A903 1r brown   .60   .35

Mahadevi Verma (1907-1987), Writer and Poet — A904

No. 1373: Jayshankar Prasad (1890-1937), poet and dramatist.

1991, Sept. 16
1372 A904 2r black & blue   22.50 4.50
1373 A904 2r black & blue   22.50 4.50
  a. Pair, #1372-1373   90.00 20.00

37th Commonwealth Parliamentary Conference — A905

1991, Sept. 27 Photo. — Perf. 13½x13
1374 A905 6.50r dk blue & brown 1.50   .70

Greetings — A906

1991, Sept. 30 — Perf. 13x13½
1375 A906 1r Frog   1.00   .45
1376 A906 6.50r Bird   5.00   .80
  a. Pair, #1375-1376   6.00 1.75

Orchids — A907

1r, Cymbidium aloifolium. 2.50r, Paphiopedilum venustum. 3r, Aerides crispum. 4r, Cymbidium bicolour. 5r, Vanda spathulata. 6.50r, Cymbidium devonianum.

1991, Oct. 12
1377 A907 1r multicolored   .50   .30
1378 A907 2.50r multicolored   .90   .40
1379 A907 3r multicolored   1.25   .50
1380 A907 4r multicolored   1.75   .60
1381 A907 5r multicolored   2.10   .85
1382 A907 6.50r multicolored   2.75 1.25
  Nos. 1377-1382 (6)   9.25 3.90

2nd Battalion, Third Gurkha Rifles — A908

1991, Oct. 18 — Perf. 13½x13
1383 A908 4r multicolored   2.75 2.00

Kamaladevi Chattopadhyaya (1903-1988), Founder of All-India Handicrafts Board — A909

1991, Oct. 29 — Perf. 13x13½
1384 A909 1r Horsemen   .70   .30
1385 A909 6.50r Puppet   1.90 1.10

Chithira Tirunal Bala Rama Varma (1912-1991), Maharaja of Travancore — A910

1991, Nov. 7 Photo. — Perf. 13½x13
1386 A910 2r violet   2.10   .90

Children's Day — A911

1991, Nov. 14 — Perf. 13x13½
1387 A911 1r multicolored   1.00   .50

18th Cavalry, Sesquicentennial (in 1992) — A912

1991, Nov. 14 — Perf. 13½x13
1388 A912 6.50r multicolored   3.75 2.50

India Tourism Year — A913

1991, Nov. 15
1389 A913 6.50r multicolored   1.40   .95

Intl. Conference on Youth Tourism — A914

1991, Nov. 18 Photo. — Perf. 13½x13
1390 A914 6.50r multicolored   1.50 1.25

Wolfgang Amadeus Mozart, Death Bicent. — A915

1991, Dec. 5
1391 A915 6.50r multicolored   2.50 1.75

SAARC Year of Shelter — A916

1991, Dec. 7 — Perf. 13½x13
1392 A916 4r lake & bister   1.25   .75

Run for Your Heart — A917

1991, Dec. 11
1393 A917 1r black, red & gray 1.75   .70

Siddhartha With An Injured Bird — A918

1991, Dec. 28 — Perf. 13x13½
1394 A918 2r multicolored   1.50   .75

Asit Kumar Haldar (1890-1964), Painter

Yoga Exercises — A919

2r, Bhujangasana. 5r, Dhanurasana. 6.50r, Ustrasana. 10r, Utthita trikonasana.

1991, Dec. 30 Photo. — Perf. 13½x13
1395 A919 2r multicolored   .45   .30
1396 A919 5r multicolored   1.00   .35
1397 A919 6.50r multicolored   1.40   .50
1398 A919 10r multicolored   2.40   .75
  Nos. 1395-1398 (4)   5.25 1.90

Intl. Assoc. for Bridge and Structural Engineering — A920

No. 1399, Hooghly River Bridge, Madurai Temple. No. 1400, Sanchi Stupa gates, Hall of Nations.

1992, Mar. 1 Photo. — Perf. 13½x13
1399 A920 2r sal, brn & blue   11.50 1.00
1400 A920 2r sal, brn & blue   11.50 1.00
  a. Pair, #1399-1400   40.00 30.00

INDIA

Fifth Intl. Conference on Goats — A921

1992, Mar. 2   *Perf. 13x13½*
1401   A921   6r dk blue & brown   8.00   3.00

Natl. Council of YMCAs, Cent. (in 1991) — A922

1992, Feb. 21
1402   A922   1r blue & vermilion   3.00   1.00

National Archives — A923

1992, Apr. 20   *Photo.*   *Perf. 13½x13*
1403   A923   6r multicolored   12.00   2.00

Krushna Chandra Gajapathi A924

Vijay Singh Pathik, Writer A925

1992, Apr. 29   *Perf. 13½x13*
1404   A924   1r violet   1.10   .50
1405   A925   1r red brown   1.10   .50

Adventure Sports — A926

1992, Apr. 29   *Perf. 13½x13*
1406   A926   2r Hang gliding   1.00   .45
1407   A926   4r Wind surfing   2.75   .70
1408   A926   5r River rafting   4.00   1.25
1409   A926   11r Skiing   5.00   2.00
     Nos. 1406-1409 (4)   12.75   4.40

Henry Gidney (1873-1942), Physician and Politician — A927

1992, May 9   *Perf. 13½x13*
1410   A927   1r blue & black   3.50   1.00

Telecommunication Training Center, Jabalpur, 50th Anniv. — A928

1992, May 30
1411   A928   1r lemon   1.00   .70

Sardar Udham Singh (1899-1940), freedom fighter — A929

1992, July 31   *Perf. 13x13½*
1412   A929   1r black & brown   1.50   .70

1992 Summer Olympics, Barcelona — A930

1992, Aug. 8
1413   A930   1r Discus   .60   .35
1414   A930   6r Gymnastics   1.40   .85
1415   A930   8r Field hockey   3.25   1.90
1416   A930   11r Boxing   3.25   2.25
     Nos. 1413-1416 (4)   8.50   5.35

Quit India Movement, 50th Anniv. — A931

Designs: 1r, Spinning wheel, inscription. 2r, Mahatma Gandhi, inscription.

1992, Aug. 9   *Perf. 13½x13*
1417   A931   1r pink, blk & pale pink   3.25   .65
1418   A931   2r gray, blk & claret   4.25   3.00

60th Parachute Field Ambulance, 50th Anniv. — A932

1992, Aug. 10
1419   A932   1r multicolored   2.50   .90

Indian Air Force, 60th Anniv. — A933

1r, Mikoyan Gurevich Mig-29 Fighter & Ilyushin IL-76 Transport Aircraft. 10r, Mig-27 Fighter & a Westland Wapiti Biplane.

1992, Oct. 8   *Photo.*   *Perf. 13½x13*
1420   1r multicolored   14.00   1.75
1421   10r multicolored   14.00   2.75
   a.   A933 Pair, #1420-1421   50.00   25.00

Phad Painting of Dev Narayan — A934

1992, Sept. 2   *Photo.*   *Perf. 13½x14*
1422   A934   5r multicolored   4.00   .95

Sisters of Jesus and Mary, 150th Anniv. — A935

1992, Nov. 13   *Photo.*   *Perf. 13½x13*
1423   A935   1r gray & blue   1.10   .50

Children's Day — A936

1992, Nov. 14   *Perf. 13½x13*
1424   A936   1r multicolored   1.00   .50

Shri Yogiji Maharaj, Religious Leader, Birth Cent. — A937

1992, Dec. 2   *Photo.*   *Perf. 13½x13*
1425   A937   1r blue   4.00   1.50

Army Service Corps 1760-1992 A938

1992, Dec. 8   *Photo.*   *Perf. 13½x13*
1426   A938   1r multicolored   4.00   .90

Stephen Smith (1891-1951), Rocket Mail Pioneer — A939

1992, Dec. 19   *Photo.*   *Perf. 13½x13*
1427   A939   11r multicolored   4.00   1.40

State of Haryana, 25th Anniv. — A940

1992, Dec. 20
1428   A940   2r green & orange   1.40   .60

Freedom Fighter Type of 1989

Design: Madan Lal Dhingra, vert.

1992, Dec. 28   *Perf. 13x13½*
1429   A826   1r org, grn & brn   1.40   .40

Dr. Shri Shiyali Ramamrita Ranganathan (1892-1972), Mathematician and Librarian — A941

1992, Aug. 30   *Photo.*   *Perf. 13½x13*
1430   A941   1r blue   2.25   .75

Hanuman Prasad Poddar — A942

1992, Sept. 19   *Photo.*   *Perf. 13½x13*
1431   A942   1r green   2.00   .50

Pandit Ravishankar Shukla — A943

1992, Dec. 31
1432   A943   1r rose lake   1.10   .40

Birds — A944

2r, Pandion haliaetus. 6r, Falco peregrinus. 8r, Gypaetus barbatus. 11r, Aquila chrysaetos.

1992, Dec. 30
1433   A944   2r multicolored   2.50   .85
1434   A944   6r multicolored   3.50   1.25
1435   A944   8r multicolored   4.00   1.40
1436   A944   11r multicolored   4.25   1.90
     Nos. 1433-1436 (4)   14.25   5.40

William Carey, Baptist Missionary to India, Bicent. of Appointment A945

1993, Jan. 9   *Photo.*   *Perf. 13½x13*
1437   A945   6r multicolored   5.00   1.10

Fakir Mohan Senapati, Writer — A946

1993, Jan. 14   *Perf. 13x13½*
1438   A946   1r orange brown   .80   .45

Council of Scientific and Industrial Research, 50th Anniv. — A947

1993, Feb. 28   *Perf. 13½x13*
1439   A947   1r violet brown   1.00   .50

Squadron No. 1, Indian Air Force, 60th Anniv. — A948

No. 1440, Westland Wapiti Biplane. No. 1441, Paratroopers, planes, artillery.

1993, Apr. 1
1440   A948   1r multicolored   1.75   .45
1441   A948   1r multicolored   1.75   .45

Parachute Field Regiment 9, 50th anniv. (No. 1441).

Rahul Sankrityayan (1893-1963), Politician — A949

1993, Apr. 9
1442   A949   1r multicolored   1.00   .45

Mountain Locomotives A950

1r, Neral Matheran. 6r, DHR (Darjeeling). 8r, Nilgiri Mountain Railway. 11r, Kalka-Simla.

1993, Apr. 16   *Perf. 13½x13*
1443   A950   1r multicolored   1.00   .30
1444   A950   6r multicolored   2.00   1.00
1445   A950   8r multicolored   2.25   1.25
1446   A950   11r multicolored   3.25   1.60
     Nos. 1443-1446 (4)   8.50   4.15

INDIA

89th Inter-Parliamentary Union Conference, New Delhi — A951

1993, Apr. 11   Photo.   Perf. 13x13½
1447   A951   1r indigo   1.00   .45

Meerut College, Cent. (in 1992) — A952

1993, Apr. 25   Perf. 14
1448   A952   1r indigo & red brown   1.00   .60

P.C. Mahalanobis (b. 1893), Statistician A953

1993, June 29   Perf. 13x13½
1449   A953   1r olive yellow   1.50   .45

Dadabhai Naoroji's Election to House of Commons, Cent. — A957

1993, Aug. 26   Photo.   Perf. 14
1453   A957   6r blue & red brown   2.00   .80

A958

1993, Sept. 11   Perf. 13x13½
1454   A958   2r gray, red brn & org 1.75   .65
Swami Vivekananda, Chicago address, cent.

A959

Trees: 1r, Lagerstroemia speciosa. 6r, Cochlospermum religiosum. 8r, Erythrina variegata. 11r, Thespesia populnea.

1993, Oct. 9   Photo.   Perf. 13x13½
1455   A959   1r multicolored   .45   .30
1456   A959   6r multicolored   1.10   .30
1457   A959   8r multicolored   1.75   .65
1458   A959   11r multicolored   2.50   .90
       Nos. 1455-1458 (4)   5.80 2.15

Dr. Dwarkanath Kotnis — A960

1993, Dec. 9   Photo.   Perf. 13½x13
1459   A960   1r black & gray   1.00   .45

A961

1993, Nov. 14   Perf. 14
1460   A961   1r multicolored   1.00   .45
Children's Day.

A962

1993, Nov. 8   Perf. 13x13½
1461   A962   2r multicolored   1.00   .45
College of Military Engineering, Pune, 50th anniv.

A963

Design: Dr. Dwaram Venkataswamy Naidu.

1993, Nov. 8
1462   A963   1r orange brown   2.00   .45

A964

1993, July 31
1463   A964   2r multicolored   1.10   .45
Bombay Municipal Corporation Building, cent.

India Tea — A965

1993, Dec. 11   Perf. 13
1464   A965   6r green & red   3.00   .75

Papal Seminary, Pune, Cent. — A966

1993, Dec. 16   Perf. 13½x13
1465   A966   6r multicolored   10.00 1.25

Natl. Integration A967

1993, Aug. 19
1466   A967   1r orange & green   1.25   .40

Khan Abdul Ghaffar Khan — A968

1993, Aug. 9
1467   A968   1r multicolored   1.00   .35

Heart Care Festival — A969

1993, Dec. 9
1468   A969   6.50r multicolored   1.60   .80

Inpex '93 — A970

1993
1469   A970   1r shown   1.00   .40
1470   A970   2r Boats, beach   1.75   .60
       Issued: 1r, Dec. 25; 2r, Dec. 27.

Meghnad Saha (1893-1956), Astrophysicist — A971

1993, Dec. 23   Photo.   Perf. 13x13½
1471   A971   1r dark blue   1.40   .45

Dinanath Mangeshkar, Musician — A972

1993, Dec. 29   Perf. 13½x13
1472   A972   1r orange brown   1.50   .45

Nargis Dutt, Actress and Social Worker — A973

1993, Dec. 30   Perf. 13
1473   A973   1r orange brown   1.25   .45

Indian Natl. Army, 50th Anniv. — A974

1r, Netaji Subhash Bose inspecting soldiers.

1993, Dec. 31   Perf. 13½x13
1474   A974   1r multicolored   1.40   .60

Satyendra Nath Bose (1894-1974), Mathematician and Physicist — A975

1994, Jan. 1
1475   A975   1r dark rose brown   1.40   .50

A976

6r, Scene from film, Pather Panchali. 11r, Satyajit Ray (1921-92).

1994, Jan. 11   Perf. 13
1476   6r multicolored   2.50 1.60
1477   11r multicolored   3.50 1.60
   a. A976 Pair, #1476-1477   6.00 6.00
No. 1476 is 68x30mm. No. 1477a is a continuous design.

Dr. Sampurnanand A977

1994, Jan. 10   Photo.   Perf. 13½x13
1478   A977   1r multicolored   .60   .60

Dr. Shanti Swarup Bhatnagar — A978

1994, Feb. 21
1479   A978   1r dark blue   .70   .70

Eighth Triennale — A979

1994, Mar. 14
1480   A979   6r multicolored   1.50   .60

Prajapita Brahma (1876-1969), Religious Leader — A980

1994, Mar. 7   Photo.   Perf. 13½x13
1481   A980   1r multicolored   .70   .70

Sanchi Stupa — A981

Wmk. 324
1994, Apr. 4   Photo.   Perf. 13
1482   A981   5r blue green & brn   1.25   .50

ILO, 75th Anniv. — A982

1994, May 1   Unwmk.   Perf. 13½x13
1483   A982   6r multicolored   1.25   .70

United Planters Assoc. of Southern India, Cent. — A983

1994, Mar. 26   Photo.   Perf. 13x13½
1484   A983   2r multicolored   1.25   .50

Rani Rashmoni (1793-1861), Philanthropist A984

1994, Apr. 9   Perf. 13½x13
1485   A984   1r brown   1.25   .55

INDIA

Jallianwala Bagh Martyrdom, 75th Anniv. — A985

1994, Apr. 13
1486 A985 1r red & black   1.00   .50

Freedom Fighter Type of 1989
1r, Chandra Singh Garhwali (1891-1979).

1994, Apr. 23
1487 A826 1r org, sage grn & grn   1.00   .50

IPTA — A986

1994, May 25 Perf. 13
1488 A986 2r multi   1.00   .50

Small Families — A987
1r, Family of 3 in front of house.

1994 Perf. 13x12½
1489 A987 75p red brn & brn   .40   .30
1490 A987 1r green & rose   .40   .30

4th Battalion Madras Regiment, Bicent. — A988

1994, Aug. 12
1491 A988 6.50r multicolored   1.40   .85

Institute of Mental Health, Madras, Bicent. — A989

1994, Sept. 23 Photo. Perf. 13½x13
1492 A989 2r multicolored   1.50   .50

Mahatma Gandhi (1869-1948) A990

Design: 11r, Flag colors, Gandhi walking and at spinning wheel.

1994, Oct. 2 Perf. 13
1493 A990 6r multicolored   2.50 1.50
1494 A990 11r multicolored   3.50 2.50
   a.   Pair, #1493-1494   15.00 5.50
No. 1494 is 68x30mm.

16th Intl. Cancer Congress — A991

1994, Oct. 30 Photo. Perf. 13½
1495 A991 6r multicolored   1.25   .70

World Conference on Human Resource Development A992

1994, Nov. 8 Perf. 13½x13
1496 A992 6r multicolored   2.00   .65

Intl. Year of the Family — A993

1994, Nov. 20 Perf. 13x12½
1497 A993 2r multicolored   1.00   .50

Children's Day — A994

1994, Nov. 14 Perf. 13½x13
1498 A994 1r multicolored   .75   .50

J.R.D. Tata (1904-93) A995

1994, Nov. 29 Perf. 14
1499 A995 2r multicolored   1.00   .50

Calcutta School for the Blind, Cent. — A996

1994 Nov. 30 Perf. 13½x13
1500 A996 2r brown & carmine   1.00   .50

Endangered Waterbirds — A996a

Designs: 1r, Andaman teal. 6r, Eastern white stork. 8r, Black-necked crane. 11r, Pink-headed duck.

1994, Nov. 23 Perf. 13
1501   1r multicolored   20.00   6.25
1502   6r multicolored   30.00 12.50
1503   8r multicolored   30.00 13.00
1504   11r multicolored   32.50 18.00
   a. A996a Block of 4, #1501-1504   125.00 125.00
This set was withdrawn shortly after issue, when it was discovered that it was printed with water soluble ink.

Begum Akhtar A996b

1994, Dec 2 Perf. 13x13½
1504B A996b 2r multicolored   50.00 13.00
No. 1504B was withdrawn shortly after issue, when it was discovered that it was printed with water soluble ink.

Remount Veterinary Corps, 215th Anniv. — A998

1994, Dec. 14 Photo. Perf. 13x13½
1505 A998 6r multicolored   4.50 1.25

College of Engineering, Guindy, Madras, Bicent. — A999

1994, Dec. 19 Perf. 14
1506 A999 2r multicolored   1.00   .50

Baroda Museum, Vadodara A1000

Designs: 6r, Ancient artifact. 11r, Ancient artifact, man standing on pedestal.

1994, Dec. 20 Perf. 14x13½
1507   6r black & bister   9.00 4.50
1508   11r black & bister   9.00 4.50
   a. A1000 Pair, #1507-1508   20.00 20.00

Khuda Bakhsh Oriental Public Library — A1001

1994, Nov. 21 Photo. Perf. 14
1509 A1001 6r multicolored   6.50 1.60

A1002

1995, Jan. 9 Photo. Perf. 13½x13
1510 A1002 1r Chhoturam   1.25   .30

A1003

1995, Jan. 7
1511 A1003 6r multicolored   15.00   —
India Natl. Science Academy, 60th Anniv.

St. Xavier's College, Bombay, 125th Anniv. — A1005

1994, Dec. 4 Photo. Perf. 13½
1513 A1005 2r multicolored   .75   .40

General Post Office, Bombay, Bicent. A1006

1994, Dec. 28 Litho. Perf. 13½
1514 A1006 6r multicolored   8.00 3.00

Motion Pictures, Cent. — A1007

Designs: 6r, Colored film, world map. 11r, Early camera, black & white film.

1995, Jan. 11 Litho. Perf. 13
1515   6r multicolored   1.60 1.60
1516   11r multicolored   2.50 2.50
   a. A1007 Pair, #1515-1516   6.00 6.00

Oil Conservation — A1008

1995, Feb. 18 Photo. Perf. 13
1517 A1008 1r red brown & black   .70   .30

Rafi Ahmed Kidwai — A1009

1995, Feb. 18
1518 A1009 1r red brown   .60   .60

K. L. Saigal — A1010

1995, Apr. 4 Photo. Perf. 13½x13
1519 A1010 5r black & brown   2.25 1.00

King Rajaraja Chola — A1011

1995, Jan. 5 Photo. Perf. 13
1520 A1011 2r multicolored   5.50 1.10
8th Intl. Conference of Tamil Studies.

A1012

1995, Jan. 12 Photo. Perf. 13½x13
1521 A1012 2r multicolored   1.00   .45
SAARC Youth Year.

257

INDIA

A1013

1995, Jan. 15
1522 A1013 2r multicolored   5.75 1.10
Prithvi Theater, 50th anniv.

A1014

Field Marshall K.M. Cariappa (1900-93).
1995, Jan. 15
1523 A1014 2r multicolored   .55 .45

A1015

1995, Jan. 18
1524 A1015 2r multicolored   .75 .40
Tex-Styles India '95, National Textile Fair, Bombay.

A1017

UN, 50th Anniv.: 6r, Planting seedling, mother and child, child reading.
1995, June 6 **Photo.** **Perf. 13**
1526 A1017 1r multicolored   .60 .30
1527 A1017 6r multicolored   1.10 .55

R.S. Ruikar — A1018
1995, May 1 **Photo.** **Perf. 13½**
1528 A1018 1r brown violet   .75 .40

Bharti Bhavan Library, Allahabad — A1019
1995, Aug. 30 **Perf. 14**
1529 A1019 6r multicolored   1.25 .60

Asian Pacific Postal Training Center, Bangkok, 25th Anniv. — A1020
1995, Sept. 4 **Litho.** **Perf. 13½x13**
1530 A1020 10r multicolored   2.25 1.25

Headquarters Delhi Area — A1021
1995, Sept. 26 **Photo.** **Perf. 13**
1531 A1021 2r multicolored   .75 .55

Louis Pasteur (1822-95) — A1022
1995, Sept. 28
1532 A1022 5r pale yel & black   3.00 1.50

La Martiniere College, Lucknow, 150th Anniv. — A1023
1995, Oct. 1
1533 A1023 2r multicolored   .70 .40

Mahatma Gandhi (1869-1948) A1024
1995, Oct. 2
1534   1r As young man   1.25 .50
1535   2r As older man   1.25 .50
  a. A1024 Pair, #1534-1535   2.50 2.50
  b. Souvenir sheet, #1535a   11.00 11.00
See South Africa Nos. 918-919.

FAO, 50th Anniv. — A1025
1995, Oct. 16 **Perf. 13½**
1536 A1025 5r multicolored   1.40 1.00

A1026
1995, Oct. 30 **Perf. 13**
1537 A1026 1r carmine   .60 .50
P.M. Thevar (1908-63), politician.

A1027
1995, Nov. 8 **Photo.** **Perf. 13x13½**
1538 A1027 6r multicolored   2.50 1.50
Wilhelm Roentgen (1845-1923), discovery of the X-Ray, cent.

JAT Regiment, Bicent. — A1028
1995, Nov. 20 **Perf. 13**
1539 A1028 5r multicolored   2.00 1.25

Radio Communication, Cent. — A1029
1995, May 17 **Litho.** **Perf. 13½x13**
1540 A1029 5r multicolored   2.00 1.25

Dehli Development Authority — A1030
1995, May 23
1541 A1030 2r multicolored   .75 .60

Children's Day — A1031
1995, Nov. 14 **Photo.** **Perf. 13x13½**
1542 A1031 1r multicolored   .60 .50

Rajputana Rifles, 175th Anniv. — A1032
1995, Nov. 28 **Perf. 13½**
1543 A1032 5r multicolored   2.75 1.25

Communal Harmony — A1033
1995, Nov. 19 **Photo.** **Perf. 13**
1544 A1033 2r multicolored   5.00 .75

Sant Tukdoji Maharaj, Patriot, Social Worker — A1034
1995, Dec. 10
1545 A1034 1r brown   .70 .50
Dated 1993.

A1035

Design: Yellapragada Subbarow (1895-1948), biochemist.
1995, Dec. 19
1546 A1035 1r yellow brown   .70 .50

A1036

Giani Zail Singh (1916-94), Pres. of India.
1995, Dec. 25
1547 A1036 1r multicolored   .70 .50

Dome Barelvi's Mausoleum, Dargah — A1037
1995, Dec. 31 **Litho.**
1548 A1037 1r multicolored   .70 .50
Ala Hazrat Barelvi (1856-1921), religious scholar.

Cricket Players — A1038
1996, Mar. 13 **Photo.** **Perf. 14**
1549 A1038 2r Deodhar   .80 .65
1550 A1038 2r Vijay Merchant   .80 .65
1551 A1038 2r Vinoo Mankad   .80 .65
1552 A1038 2r C.K. Nayudu   .80 .65
  Nos. 1549-1552 (4)   3.20 2.60
  Dated 1995.

Homi Bhabha and Tata Institute of Fundamental Research A1039
1996, Feb. 9 **Photo.** **Perf. 13**
1553 A1039 2r multicolored   .80 .50

Kasturba Trust — A1040
1996, Feb. 22
1554 A1040 1r multicolored   .60 .35

Cardiac Surgery, Cent. — A1041
1996, Feb. 25 **Litho.**
1555 A1041 5r multicolored   2.25 .75

Miniature Paintings A1042

No. 1556, Two women picking berries from trees. No. 1557, Woman, man embracing. No. 1558, Women looking upward, men, animals. No. 1559, Ceremony, black clouds.

INDIA

1996, Mar. 13		Perf. 13½	
1556	A1042 5r multicolored	1.75	.80
1557	A1042 5r multicolored	1.75	.80
1558	A1042 5r multicolored	1.75	.80
1559	A1042 5r multicolored	1.75	.80
	Nos. 1556-1559 (4)	7.00	3.20

Pt. Kunjilal Dubey — A1043

1996, Mar. 18	Photo.	Perf. 13	
1560	A1043 1r brown	.60	.50

Himalayan Wildlife — A1044

No. 1561, Saussurea simpsoniana. No. 1562, Capra falconeri. No. 1563, Ithaginis cruentus. No. 1564, Meconopsis horridula.

1996, May 10		Litho.	
1561	A1044 5r multicolored	1.50	1.00
1562	A1044 5r multicolored	1.50	1.00
1563	A1044 5r multicolored	1.50	1.00
1564	A1044 5r multicolored	1.50	1.00
a.	Souv. sheet of 4, #1561-1564	7.25	7.25
	Nos. 1561-1564 (4)	6.00	4.00

No. 1564a sold for 30r. Stamps in No. 1564a do not have "1996."

Morarji Desai — A1045

1996, Apr. 10	Photo.	Perf. 13x13½	
1565	A1045 1r carmine	.90	.35

SKCG College — A1047

1996, May 25		Photo.	
1567	A1047 1r lt brn & dk brn	1.25	.65

Muhammad Ismail Sahib — A1048

1996, June 5		Perf. 13x13½	
1568	A1048 1r claret	.80	.65

1996 Summer Olympic Games, Atlanta — A1049

1996, June 25			
1569	A1049 5r Olympic stadium	1.50	.55
1570	A1049 5r Torch	1.50	.55

A1050

1996, July 19		Perf. 13x13½	
1571	A1050 1r blue & black	1.25	.65

Sister Alphonsa (1910-46).

A1051

1996, Aug. 2	Litho.	Perf. 14	
1572	A1051 5r multicolored	2.25	1.40

VSNL, 125th anniv.

A1052

1r, Chembai Vaidyanatha Bhagavathar. 2r, Ahilyabai Holkar.

1996	Photo.	Perf. 13x13½	
1573	A1052 1r dk bl grn & brn	.80	.55
1574	A1052 2r rose brn & lt brn	.80	.65

Issued: 1r, 8/28; 2r, 8/25.

Sir Pherozeshah Mehta — A1053

1996, Aug. 4	Photo.	Perf. 13	
1575	A1053 1r gray blue	.80	.80

Poultry Production A1054

1996, Sept. 2			
1576	A1054 5r Gallus gallus	5.75	2.25

Rani Gaidinliu — A1055

1996, Sept. 12			
1577	A1055 1r dark blue green	.80	.80

Barrister Nath Pai — A1056

1996, Sept. 25			
1578	A1056 1r blue	.80	.80

Indepex '97 World Philatelic Exhibition — A1057

1996, Oct. 5	Litho.	Perf. 13x13½	
1579	A1057 2r lake & bister	1.00	.50

Children's Day — A1058

1996, Nov. 14	Photo.	Perf. 13½x13	
1580	A1058 8r multicolored	2.00	1.25

South Asian Assoc. for Regional Cooperation (SAARC), 10th Anniv. — A1059

1996, Dec. 8		Perf. 13	
1581	A1059 11r multicolored	2.40	1.60

Abai Konunbaev (1845-1904), Poet — A1060

1996, Dec. 9		Perf. 13x13½	
1582	A1060 5r red brown & lake	3.00	.80

Dated 1995.

2nd Intl. Crop Science Congress — A1061

1996, Nov. 17		Perf. 13	
1583	A1061 2r multicolored	1.10	.70

Sikh Regiment, 150th Anniv. — A1062

1996, Oct. 19			
1584	A1062 5r multicolored	3.00	1.00

Natl. Rail Museum, 25th Anniv. A1063

1996, Oct. 7	Litho.	Perf. 13½	
1585	A1063 5r multicolored	4.00	1.75

Jananayak Debeswar Sarmah (1896-1993), Politician — A1064

1996, Oct. 10			
1586	A1064 2r lt brn & red brn	1.25	.60

Dr. Salim Ali, Birth Cent. A1065

1996, Nov. 12	Photo.	Perf. 13	
1587	8r Dr. Salim Ali	3.00	2.50
1588	11r Water fowl	3.00	2.50
a.	A1065 Pair, #1587-1588	6.50	6.50

Second Battalion, The Grenadiers, Bicent. — A1066

1996, Dec. 4		Perf. 14	
1589	A1066 5r multicolored	2.25	1.25

Vijay Divas — A1067

1996, Dec. 16			
1590	A1067 2r multicolored	.90	.30

Vivekananda Rock Memorial, Kanyakumari — A1068

1996, Dec. 26	Litho.	Perf. 13	
1591	A1068 5r multicolored	3.25	1.90

Use of Anesthesia, 150th Anniv. — A1069

1996, Dec. 27		Perf. 13	
1592	A1069 5r multicolored	2.40	1.40

University of Roorkee, 150th Anniv. — A1070

1997, Jan. 1	Photo.	Perf. 13	
1593	A1070 8r multicolored	1.50	1.10

Vrindavan Lal Verma, Writer — A1071

1997, Jan. 9	Photo.	Perf. 13x13½	
1594	A1071 2r red	.80	.50

Army Postal Service Corps. (APS), 25th Anniv. — A1072

1997, Jan. 22		Perf. 13½x13	
1595	A1072 5r multicolored	2.00	1.50

INDIA

Jose Marti (1853-95), Cuban Revolutionary — A1073

1997, Jan. 28   Perf. 13x13½
1596 A1073 11r multicolored   3.00   1.00

Inter-Parliamentary Specialized Conference, New Dehli — A1074

1997, Feb. 15   Photo.   Perf. 13
1597 A1074 5r multicolored   1.50   .40

A1075

1997, Mar. 4   Photo.   Perf. 13
1598 A1075 1r lake, dk brn, flesh   .80   .50
Shyam Lal Gupt (b. 1896), composer of song on natl. flag.

A1076

1997, Mar. 8   Perf. 13x13½
1599   5r Parijat Tree   2.50   1.50
1600   6r Branch, flower   2.50   1.50
   a. A1076 Pair, #1599-1600   5.00   5.00

Rashtriya Indian Military College, Dehra Dun, 75th Anniv. — A1077

1997, Mar. 13   Perf. 13½
1601 A1077 2r multicolored   1.25   .60

Netaji Subhas Chandra Bose (1897-1945), Nationalist Leader — A1078

1997, Jan. 23   Perf. 13
1602 A1078 1r dk brn & lt brn   .80   .45

St. Andrews Church — A1079

1997, Feb. 25   Photo.   Perf. 13x13½
1603 A1079 8r multicolored   2.00   .80

Morarji Desai, Prime Minister, 1977-79 — A1080

1997, Feb. 28   Photo.   Perf. 13
1604 A1080 1r brown & buff   .80   .45

Saint Dnyaneshwar (1274-95), Poet — A1081

1997, Mar. 5   Photo.   Perf. 13
1605 A1081 5r multicolored   1.75   .80

Ram Manohar Lohia (1910-67), Politician — A1082

1997, Mar. 23   Litho.   Perf. 13x13½
1606 A1082 1r multicolored   .75   .40

CENTIPEX '97 — A1083

Philatelic Society of India, Cent.: No. 1608, #1, Front cover of "The Philatelic Journal of India," 1897.

1997, Mar. 27
1607   2r multicolored   2.25   1.75
1608   2r multicolored   2.25   1.75
   a. Pair, #1607-1608   4.50   4.50

Jnanpith Award Winners — A1084

K.V. Puttappa, D.R. Bendre, Prof. V.K. Gokak, Dr. Masti V. Iyengar, writers.

1997, Mar. 28   Photo.   Perf. 13
1609 A1084 2r multi   1.00   .50

Madhu Limaye (1922-95), Politician — A1085

1997, May 1
1610 A1085 2r green   .80   .50

Pandit Omkarnath Thakur — A1086

1997, June 24   Photo.   Perf. 13x13½
1611 A1086 2r black & blue   .80   .50

A1087

1997, Aug. 6   Photo.   Perf. 13
1612 A1087 2r brown   1.25   1.00
Thirumathi Rukmini Lakshmipathi (1892-1951), reformer.

Independence, 50th Anniv. — A1088

Officers from Indian Natl. Army, Shah Nawaz Khan, G.S. Dhillon, P.K. Sahgal.

1997, Aug. 15
1613 A1088 2r multicolored   .70   .40

Newspaper Swantantra Bharat, 50th Anniv. — A1089

1997, Aug. 15   Perf. 13½x13
1614 A1089 2r multicolored   .80   .50

A1090

1997, Aug. 20   Perf. 13
1615 A1090 2r black & gray   1.50   .75
Sir Ronald Ross (1857-1932), physician, medical researcher.

A1091

1997, Sept. 6
1616 A1091 5r red brown   1.50   1.00
Swami Bhaktivedanta (b. 1896), humanitarian.

A1092

1997, Sept. 14
1617 A1092 2r black & gray   .60   .40
Swami Brahmanand (1894-1984), social reformer.

A1093

1997, Aug. 8
1618 A1093 2r Sri Basaveswara   .60   .40

Maratha Parachute Regiment, Bicent. — A1094

1997, Sept. 7   Perf. 13½x13
1619 A1094 2r multicolored   .90   .50

Hazari Prasad Dwivedi — A1095

1997, Dec. 13   Photo.   Perf. 13x13½
1620 A1095 2r gray brown   .60   .40

Firaq Gorakhpuri — A1096

1997, Aug. 28
1621 A1096 2r brown   .60   .40

Fossil Plants — A1097

No. 1622, Birbalsahnia divyadarshanii. No. 1623, Glossopteris. 6r, Pentoxylon. 10r, Williamsonia sewardiana.

1997, Sept. 11
1622 A1097   2r multicolored   1.50   1.00
1623 A1097   2r multicolored   1.50   1.00
1624 A1097   6r multicolored   4.50   2.75
1625 A1097   10r multicolored   6.75   4.50
   Nos. 1622-1625 (4)   14.25   9.25

Sir William Jones, 250th Birth Anniv. — A1098

1997, Sept. 28
1626 A1098 4r multicolored   1.50   .75

Lawrence School, Sanawar, 150th Anniv. — A1099

1997, Oct. 4   Perf. 13½x13
1627 A1099 2r multicolored   .90   .55

Indepex '97 — A1100

1997, June 6   Photo.   Perf. 13½x13
1628 A1100   2r Nalanda   .55   .45
1629 A1100   6r Bodhgaya   .90   .55
1630 A1100   10r Vaishali   1.40   .90
1631 A1100   11r Kushinagar   1.75   .90
   a. Block of 4, #1628-1631   5.00   5.00

INDIA

66th General Assembly Session of Interpol, 1997 — A1101

1997, Oct. 15 — Perf. 13½
1632 A1101 4r multicolored 1.25 .80

V.K. Krishna Menon — A1102

1997, Oct. 6 — Perf. 13
1633 A1102 2r brown carmine .75 .75

Indepex '97 World Philatelic Exhibition — A1103

Rural Indian women: 2r, Arunachal Pradesh. 6r, Gujarat. 10r, Ladakh. 11r, Kerala.

1997, Oct. 15 Photo. Perf. 13x13½
1634 A1103 2r multicolored .50 .30
1635 A1103 6r multicolored .95 .50
1636 A1103 10r multicolored 1.25 .70
1637 A1103 11r multicolored 1.50 .95
a. Block of 4, #1634-1637 4.50 4.50

Scindia School, Cent. A1104

Designs: No. 1638, Outdoor class. No. 1639, Founder, school building, aerial view.

1997, Oct. 20 — Perf. 14
1638 5r multicolored 10.00 5.00
1639 5r multicolored 10.00 5.00
a. A1104 Pair, #1638-1639 20.00 20.00

Medicinal Plants — A1105

2r, Ocimum sanctum. 5r, Curcuma longa. 10r, Rauvolfia serpentina. 11r, Aloe barbadensis.

1997, Oct. 28
1640 A1105 2r multicolored .60 .35
1641 A1105 5r multicolored 1.25 .60
1642 A1105 10r multicolored 1.60 1.10
1643 A1105 11r multicolored 1.90 1.10
a. Block of 4, #1640-1643 5.50 4.50

A1106

1997, July 2 Litho. Perf. 13x13½
1644 A1106 2r brown & sepia .60 .40
Ram Sewak Yadav (1926-74), politician, social reformer.

A1107

1997, July 11
1645 A1107 2r multicolored .60 .40
Sibnath Banerjee (1897-1982), politician, union leader.

Indepex '97 — A1110

Indian beaches: 2r, Gopalpur on Sea, Orissa. 6r, Kovalam Beach, Thiruvananthapuram. 10r, Anjuna Beach, Goa. 11r, Bogmalo Beach, Goa.

1997, Aug. 11 Perf. 13½x13
1648 A1110 2r multicolored .60 .30
1649 A1110 6r multicolored .90 .55
1650 A1110 10r multicolored 1.60 .80
1651 A1110 11r multicolored 2.25 1.00
Nos. 1648-1651 (4) 5.35 2.65

Sant Kavi Sunderdas (1596-1689) — A1111

1997, Nov. 8 Photo. Perf. 13x13½
1652 A1111 2r lt brn & dk brn 1.00 .50

Kotamraju Rama Rao — A1112

1997, Nov. 9
1653 A1112 2r dk brn & yel brn 1.25 .70

Children's Day — A1113

1997, Nov. 14 Perf. 13½x13
1654 A1113 2r Nehru with child .70 .40

A1114

1997, Nov. 23 Photo. Perf. 13
1655 A1114 4r multicolored 2.50 1.25
World Convention on Reverence for All Life.

A1115

1997, Dec. 15 Photo. Perf. 13½x13
1656 A1115 2r dk brn & lt brn .60 .40
Sardar Vallabhbhai Patel (1875-1950), politician.

Indepex '97 — A1116

Designs: 2r, Post Office Heritage Building. 6r, Indian River Mail. 10r, Cancellations, Jal Cooper. 11r, Mail ship, SS Hindosthan.

1997, Dec. 15 Photo. Perf. 13½x13
1657 A1116 2r multicolored .65 .55
1657A A1116 6r multicolored 1.40 .60
1657B A1116 10r multicolored 1.75 1.25
1657C A1116 11r multicolored 2.50 1.40
d. Block of 4, #1657-1657C 6.25 5.25

Souvenir Sheet

Mother Teresa (1910-97) — A1117

1997, Dec. 15 Litho. Perf. 13x13½
1658 A1117 45r multicolored 15.00 15.00

Indian Armed Forces, 50th Anniv. — A1118

1997, Dec. 16 Photo. Perf. 13½x13
1659 A1118 2r multicolored 1.10 .50

Dr. B. Pattabhi Sitaramayya (1880-1959), Author, Politician — A1119

1997, Dec. 17 Perf. 13x13½
1660 A1119 2r dk brn & lt brn 1.25 .65

Fr. Jerome D'Souza (1897-1977) A1120

1997, Dec. 18 Perf. 13½x13
1661 A1120 2r red brown 1.00 .50

Ashfaquallah Khan and Ram Prasad Bismil, Revolutionaries A1121

1997, Dec. 19 Perf. 13
1662 A1121 2r dk brn & brn 1.25 .50

Cellular Jail Natl. Memorial, Port Blair — A1122

1997, Dec. 30
1663 A1122 2r multicolored .70 .50

A1123

1998, Jan. 2
1664 A1123 2r red brown 1.00 .50
Nanak Singh (1897-1971), novelist.

A1124

1998, Jan. 9
1665 A1124 2r plum .75 .50
Nahar Singh, minor leader of Great Mutiny.

Rotary Intl., 1998 Council on Legislation, New Delhi — A1125

1998, Jan. 12 Perf. 13½x13
1666 A1125 8r multicolored 3.00 1.00

A1126   A1127

No. 1667, Maharana Pratap (1540-97), ruler, warrior. No. 1668, Vishnu S. Khandekar (b. 1898), writer.

1998, Jan. 19 Perf. 13x13½
1667 A1126 2r violet brown .80 .50
1668 A1127 2r rose red & dull red .80 .50

A1128

1998, Jan. 25
1669 A1128 10r multicolored 2.25 1.50
Bharat Paryatan Diwas (India Tourism Day).

A1129

1998, Jan. 2 Perf. 13½x13
1670 A1129 4r multicolored 2.25 1.00
11th Gurkha Rifles, 50th anniv.

INDIA

A1130

Mahatma Gandhi, 50th Anniv. of Death: 2r, Peasants' welfare. 6r, Social upliftment. 10r, Salt Satyagraha. 11r, Communal harmony.

1998, Jan. 30		Photo.		Perf. 14
1671		2r multicolored	.65	.50
1672		6r multicolored	1.00	.85
1673		10r multicolored	1.25	1.25
1674		11r multicolored	2.00	1.40
a.	A1130 Block of 4, #1671-1674		5.25	4.75

A1131

1998, Mar. 8   Photo.   Perf. 13x13½
1675   A1131   6r multicolored   2.00   .60
Universal Declaration of Human Rights, 50th anniv.

Savitribai Phule (1831-97), Educator, Women's Reformer — A1132

1998, Mar. 10   Perf. 13½x13
1676   A1132   2r dk brn & lt brn   .80   .50

Jagdish Chandra Jain — A1133

1998, Jan. 28   Photo.   Perf. 13x13½
1677   A1133   2r red brown   .80   .50

Syed Ahmad Khan (1817-98), Philosopher and Scholar — A1134

1998, Mar. 27
1678   A1134   2r brn & olive brn   .80   .50

Sardar A. Vedaratnam — A1135

1998, Feb. 25
1679   A1135   2r violet black   .80   .50

Global Environment Facility First Assembly Meeting — A1136

1998, Apr. 1   Perf. 13
1680   A1136   11r multicolored   2.00   1.10

A1137

1998, Apr. 16   Photo.   Perf. 14
1681   A1137   6r carmine   2.25   .70
Defense Services Staff College.

A1138

Design: Pres. Zakir Husain (1897-1969).

1998, May 3   Photo.   Perf. 13
1682   A1138   2r sepia   .70   .40

A1139

Jnanpith Literary Award winners, year: Shri Bishnu Dey (1909-82), 1971; Shri Tarashankar Bandopadhyay (1898-1971), 1966; Smt. Ashapurna Devi (1909-95), 1976.

1998, June 5
1683   A1139   2r olive brown   .70   .40

A1140

Designs: 5r, Parliament Clock Tower, London. 6r, Airplane, mascot, Gateway of India, Bombay.

1998, June 8		Photo.	Perf. 13
1684		5r multicolored	3.50 1.10
		Size: 56x35mm	
1685		6r multicolored	4.50 1.40
a.	A1140 Pair, #1684-1685		8.00 5.00

Air India's 1st intl. flight, 50th anniv.

A1141

Design: Salem C. Vijiaraghavachariar (1852-1944), freedom fighter.

1998, June 18
1686   A1141   2r red brown   .80   .40

A1142

1998, May 1
1687   A1142   2r N.G. Goray   .70   .50

Sri Ramana Maharshi — A1143

1998, Apr. 14
1688   A1143   2r violet black   .70   .50

Konkan Railway A1143a

1998, May 1   Photo.   Perf. 13
1689   A1143a   8r multicolored   2.25   1.00

A1144

Mohammed Abdurahiman Shahib.

1998, May 15
1690   A1144   2r red brown   .70   .50

A1145

1998, May 21   Photo.   Perf. 14
1691   A1145   2r brown & sepia   .70   .40
Lokanayak Omeo Kumar Das, freedom fighter.

Revolutionaries A1146

Design: Satyendra Chandra Bardhan, Vakkom Abdul Khader, Fouja Singh.

1998, May 25   Perf. 13
1692   A1146   2r brn & red brn   .70   .40

Natl. Savings Organization, 50th Anniv. — A1147

Design: 6r, Hand dropping coin into bank.

1998, June 30		
1693	5r multicolored	5.00 1.40
1694	6r multicolored	6.25 2.40
a.	A1147 Pair, #1693-1694	12.00 6.00

Bhagwan Gopinathji, Spiritual Leader, Birth Cent. — A1148

1998, July 3   Perf. 13½
1695   A1148   3r brown & sepia   .70   .40

Ardeshir (1868-1926) & Pirojsha (1882-1972) Godrej, Inventors and Manufacturers A1149

1998, July 11   Perf. 13
1696   A1149   3r green   1.10   .50

Aruna Asaf Ali, Revolutionay — A1150

1998, July 16
1697   A1150   3r brown   .70   .40

Vidyasagar College, 125th Anniv. — A1151

1998, July 29
1698   A1151   2r dark gray   .70   .40

Shivpujan Sahai (1893-1963), Writer — A1152

1998, Aug. 9   Photo.   Perf. 13
1699   A1152   2r brown   1.10   .50

Homage to Martyrs — A1153

Designs: 3r, Minaret, silhouettes of soldiers standing in fort, flag of India. 8r, Symbols of industrial, scientific and technological developments.

1998, Aug. 15		Perf. 14
1700	A1153 3r multicolored	2.75 .65
1701	A1153 8r multicolored	6.25 1.15
a.	Pair, #1700-1701	9.00 3.00

Gostha Behari Paul (1896-1976), Soccer Player — A1154

1998, Aug. 20   Perf. 13
1702   A1154   3r sepia   1.10   .40

Youth Hostels Assoc. of India, 50th Anniv. — A1155

1998, Aug. 23   Perf. 14
1703   A1155   5r multicolored   1.00   .50

Brigade of the Guards, Fourth Battalion, Bicent. — A1156

1998, Sept. 15   Photo.   Perf. 13½
1704   A1156   6r multicolored   1.75   .70

INDIA

Bhai Kanhaiyaji — A1157

1998, Sept. 18   *Perf. 13*
1705   A1157   2r red   1.00   .40

20th Intl. Congress of Radiology A1158

1998, Sept. 18   *Perf. 13½x13*
1706   A1158   8r multicolored   1.75   .80

28th IBBY Congress — A1159

1998, Sept. 20   *Perf. 13*
1707   A1159   11r multicolored   2.00   .75

Dr. Tristao Braganza Cunha — A1160

1998, Sept. 26
1708   A1160   3r dark brown   .80   .40

Jananeta Hijam Irawat Singh — A1161

1998, Sept. 30
1709   A1161   3r brown   .70   .40

Acharya Tulsi (1914-97) A1162

1998, Oct. 20   *Photo.*   *Perf. 13½x13*
1710   A1162   3r brown & orange   .70   .40

Indian Women in Aviation — A1163

1998, Oct. 15   *Perf. 13*
1711   A1163   8r blue   1.60   .85

Pulse Polio Immunization — A1164

1998, Sept. 21
1712   A1164   3r maroon   .50   .30

2nd Battalion of the Rajput Regiment (Kalichindi), Bicent. — A1165

1998, Nov. 30
1713   A1165   3r multicolored   1.00   .40

David Sassoon Library & Reading Room, Mumbai — A1166

1998, Nov. 30
1714   A1166   3r lt blue & dk blue   .80   .50

Army Postal Service Center, Kamptee, 50th Anniv. — A1167

1998, Dec. 2
1715   A1167   3r multicolored   1.00   .55

Connemara Public Library, Chennai — A1168

1998, Dec. 5   *Perf. 13½x13*
1716   A1168   3r bister & brown   1.00   .50

A1169

1998, Dec. 10   *Litho.*   *Perf. 13½*
1717   A1169   3r multicolored   1.50   .60
Indian Pharmaceutical Cong. Assoc., 50th anniv.

A1170

Design: Baba Raghav Das (1896-1958), reformer, freedom fighter.

1998, Dec. 12   *Photo.*   *Perf. 13*
1718   A1170   2r deep gray violet   .80   .40

Indra Lal Roy (1898-1918), World War I Pilot — A1171

1998, Dec. 19
1719   A1171   3r multicolored   1.50   .40

Sant Gadge Baba (1876-1956), Religious Philosopher A1172

1998, Dec. 20
1720   A1172   3r multicolored   .70   .40

Traditional Musical Instruments A1173

Designs: 2r, Rudra veena (stringed instrument). 6r, Flute (wind instrument). 8r, Pakhawaj (percussion instrument). 10r, Sarod (stringed instrument).

1998, Dec. 29
1721   A1173   2r multicolored   .55   .40
1722   A1173   6r multicolored   1.35   .65
1723   A1173   8r multicolored   1.75   .85
1724   A1173   10r multicolored   2.40   1.00
Nos. 1721-1724 (4)   6.05   2.90

Children's Day — A1174

1998, Nov. 14   *Photo.*   *Perf. 13½*
1725   A1174   3r multicolored   .90   .40

INS Delhi — A1175

1998, Nov. 15
1726   A1175   3r multicolored   1.25   .60

President's Bodyguard — A1176

1998, Nov. 16
1727   A1176   3r multicolored   1.50   .60

Shells — A1177

Designs: No. 1728, Cypraea staphylaea. No. 1729, Cassis cornuta. No. 1730, Chicoreus brunneus. 11r, Lambis lambis.

1998, Dec. 30
1728   A1177   3r multicolored   .65   .80
1729   A1177   3r multicolored   .90   .80
1730   A1177   3r multicolored   1.60   .80
1731   A1177   11r multicolored   2.25   1.60
Nos. 1728-1731 (4)   5.40   4.00

Indian Police Service, 50th Anniv. — A1178

1999, Jan. 13   *Litho.*   *Perf. 13½x13¼*
1732   A1178   3r multicolored   1.25   .50

Defense Research & Development Organization A1179

1999, Jan. 26   *Photo.*   *Perf. 13*
1733   A1179   10r multicolored   2.00   1.00

Newpapers in Assam, 150th Anniv. — A1180

1999, Jan. 29   *Perf. 13x13½*
1734   A1180   3r multicolored   1.00   .60

Sanskrit College, Calcutta, 175th Anniv. — A1181

1999, Feb. 25   *Perf. 13½x13*
1735   A1181   3r brown & yellow   .90   .50

National Defense Academy, 50th Anniv. — A1182

Perf. 13½x13¼
1999, Feb. 19   *Litho.*
1736   A1182   3r multicolored   1.75   .70

Hindu College, Delhi, Cent. — A1183

1999, Feb. 17   *Photo.*   *Perf. 13½x13*
1737   A1183   3r blue   .90   .40

Biju Patnaik (1916-97), Politician — A1184

1999, Mar. 5
1738   A1184   3r multicolored   1.00   .50

A1185

1999, Mar. 12   *Perf. 13*
1739   A1185   15r multicolored   2.25   1.00
Press Trust of India, 50th anniv.

A1186

1999, Mar. 6
1740   A1186   15r multicolored   2.25   1.00
Temple Complex of Khajuraho, 1000th anniv.

Dr. K.B. Hedgewar (1889-1940) — A1187

1999, Mar. 18
1741   A1187   3r multicolored   .70   .40

INDIA

Bethune Collegiate School, 150th Anniv. — A1188

1999   *Photo.*   *Perf. 13*
1742 A1188 3r green   .70   .50

Creation of the Khalsa, 300th Anniv. — A1189

1999, Apr. 14
1743 A1189 3r multicolored   1.25   .55

Maritime Heritage — A1190

No. 1744, Boat from 2200 B.C. No. 1745, Ship from 1700.

1999, Apr. 5   *Litho.*   *Perf. 13½x13¼*
1744 A1190 3r multicolored   .70   .50
1745 A1190 3r multicolored   .70   .50

Technology Day — A1191

1999, May 11   *Litho.*   *Perf. 13½x13¼*
1746 A1191 3r multicolored   1.00   .50

Mumbai Port Trust, 125th Anniv. — A1192

1999, June 26   *Photo.*   *Perf. 12¾x13*
1747 A1192 3r blue gray   .80   .50

A1193

1999, June 30   *Photo.*   *Perf. 13x12¾*
1748 A1193 3r multicolored   .80   .40
Mizoram Accord.

A1194

1999, July 4   *Photo.*   *Perf. 13¼*
1749 A1194 3r multicolored   .70   .40
Gulzari Lal Nanda (b. 1899), interim Prime Minister.

Jijabai, Mother of Shivaji — A1195

1999, July 7   *Photo.*   *Perf. 14x13½*
1750 A1195 3r claret   .75   .40

P. S. Kumaraswamy Raja — A1196

1999, July 8   *Photo.*   *Perf. 13¼*
1751 A1196 3r sky blue & brown   .70   .40

Balai Chand Mukhopadhyay (1879-1979), Writer — A1197

1999, July 19   *Photo.*   *Perf. 13¼*
1752 A1197 3r slate blue   .70   .40

Sindh River Festival — A1198

Perf. 13½x13¼
1999, July 28   *Photo.*
1753 A1198 3r multicolored   .80   .40

Geneva Conventions, 50th Anniv. — A1199

1999, Aug. 12   *Photo.*   *Perf. 13¾*
1754 A1199 15r black & red   3.50   1.60

Freedom Fighters — A1200

No. 1755, Swami Ramanand Teerth. No. 1756, Vishwambhar Dayalu Tripathi. No. 1757, Swami Keshawanand. No. 1758, Sardar Ajit Singh.

Perf. 13½x13¼
1999, Aug. 15   *Photo.*
1755 A1200 3r multicolored   .60   .40
1756 A1200 3r multicolored   .60   .40
1757 A1200 3r multicolored   .60   .40
1758 A1200 3r multicolored   .60   .40
Nos. 1755-1758 (4)   2.40   1.60

Kalki Krishnamurthy (1899-1954), Novelist — A1201

1999, Sept. 9   *Photo.*   *Perf. 13¾*
1759 A1201 3r black   1.00   .50

Qazi Nazrul Islam (1899-1976), Poet — A1202

Rambriksh Benipuri, Writer — A1203

Ramdhari Sinha "Dinkar," Poet — A1204

Jhaverchand Kalidas Meghani (b. 1896), Poet — A1205

1999, Sept. 14   *Photo.*   *Perf. 13x13¼*
1760 A1202 3r multicolored   .60   .50
Perf. 13¼
1761 A1203 3r multicolored   .60   .50
Perf. 13¼x13
1762 A1204 3r multicolored   .60   .50
1763 A1205 3r multicolored   .60   .50
Nos. 1760-1763 (4)   2.40   2.00

Arati Gupta, First Asian Woman to Swim Across English Channel — A1206

1999, Sept. 29   *Photo.*   *Perf. 13x13¼*
1764 A1206 3r multi   .90   .50

Worldwide Fund for Nature — A1207

Asiatic lion: No. 1765, Male atop female. No. 1766, Two lions. No. 1767, Three lions. 15r, Two lions, diff.

1999, Oct. 4   *Perf. 13¼x13*
1765 A1207 3r multi   1.75   .60
1766 A1207 3r multi   1.75   .60
1767 A1207 3r multi   1.75   .60
1768 A1207 15r multi   3.25   1.75
Nos. 1765-1768 (4)   8.50   3.55

UPU, 125th Anniv. — A1208

No. 1769, Muria ritual object. No. 1770, Mask for Chhau dance. No. 1771, Rathva wall painting. 15r, Angami ornament.

1999, Oct. 9   *Perf. 13¼x13, 13x13¼*
1769 A1208 3r multi   .70   .35
1770 A1208 3r multi   .70   .35
1771 A1208 3r multi, vert.   .70   .35
1772 A1208 15r multi, vert.   2.25   1.40
Nos. 1769-1772 (4)   4.35   2.45

Dr. T. M. A. Pai (1898-1979) A1209

Chhaganlal K. Parekh (1894-1968) A1209a

A. B. Walawalkar, Draftsman for Konkar Railway A1209b

A. D. Shroff — A1209c

1999, Oct. 9   *Perf. 13x13¼*
1773 A1209 3r yel & brn   .60   .60
Perf. 12¾x13¼
1774 A1209a 3r org brn & ind   .60   .60

Perf. 13¼
1775 A1209b 3r lilac & maroon   .60   .60
1776 A1209c 3r bister & olive   .60   .60
Nos. 1773-1776 (4)   2.40   2.40

Veerapandia Kattabomman (1760-99), Freedom Fighter — A1210

1999, Oct. 16   *Photo.*   *Perf. 13x13¼*
1777 A1210 3r olive green   1.00   .50

Musicians — A1211

No. 1778, Ustad Allauddin Khan Saheb (1870-1972), sarod player. No. 1779, Musiri Subramania Iyer (1899-1975), music teacher.

1999, Oct. 19   *Photo.*   *Perf. 13¾*
1778 A1211 3r multicolored   .75   .60
1779 A1211 3r multicolored   .75   .60

A1212

Perf. 13¼x13½
1999, Oct. 27   *Photo.*
1780 A1212 3r violet brown   1.00   .50
Brigadier Rajinder Singh (1899-1947).

Children's Day — A1213

1999, Nov. 14   *Photo.*   *Perf. 14*
1781 A1213 3r multi   .70   .40

Sri Sathya Sai Water Supply Project — A1214

Perf. 12¾x13¼
1999, Nov. 23   *Photo.*
1782 A1214 3r multi   1.00   .50

Supreme Court, 50th Anniv. — A1215

Perf. 12¾x13¼
1999, Nov. 26   *Photo.*
1783 A1215 3r multi   .80   .50

Dr. Punjabrao Deshmukh, Agriculture Minister — A1215a

A. Vaidyanatha Iyer (d. 1955), Advocate of Untouchables A1216

INDIA

P. Kakkan, Politician — A1217

Indulal Kanaiyalal Yagnik, Politician — A1218

1999, Dec. 9   *Perf. 13¼*
1784	A1215a	3r brown & grn	.70 .40
1785	A1216	3r orange brown	.70 .40
1786	A1217	3r green & brn	.70 .40
1787	A1218	3r tan & black	.70 .40
	Nos. 1784-1787 (4)		2.80 1.60

Thermal Power, Cent. — A1219

1999, Dec. 14   *Photo.*   *Perf. 13¼x13*
1788   A1219   3r bister & brn   .75 .50

Hindustan Times Newspaper, 75th Anniv. — A1220

1999, Dec. 16   *Photo.*   *Perf. 13¼*
1789   A1220   15r multi   2.25 1.60

Family Planning Assoc. of India, 50th Anniv. — A1221

1999, Dec. 18   *Perf. 14x13¾*
1790   A1221   3r multi   .80 .50

Birth of Jesus Christ, 2000th Anniv. — A1222

1999, Dec. 25
1791   A1222   3r multi   1.00 .70

Tabo Monastery — A1223

1999, Dec. 31   *Perf. 12¾x13¼*
1792		5r shown	6.25 2.75
1793		10r People	7.00 3.00
a.	A1223 Pair, #1792-1793		14.00 6.00

First Sunrise of the Millennium A1224

2000, Jan. 1   *Perf. 13¼x13*
1794   A1224   3r multi   1.25 1.25

Agni II Missile — A1225

2000, Jan. 1   *Litho.*   *Perf. 13x13¼*
1795   A1225   3r multi   .95 .95

Mahatma Gandhi — A1226

2000, Jan. 27   *Perf. 14x13¾*
1796   A1226   3r red & black   1.00 1.00
Republic of India, 50th anniv.

Gallantry Award Winners — A1227

Designs: No. 1797, Karam Singh, regimental crest. No. 1798, Abdul Hamid, jeep-mounted artillery gun. No. 1799, Albert Ekka, grenades, knife. No. 1800, N. J. S. Sekhon, airplane. No. 1801, M. N. Mulla, ship.

2000, Jan. 27   *Perf. 13¼x13*
1797	A1227	3r multi	1.60 1.60
1798	A1227	3r multi	1.60 1.60
1799	A1227	3r multi	1.60 1.60
1800	A1227	3r multi	1.60 1.60
1801	A1227	3r multi	1.60 1.60
a.	Strip of 5, #1797-1801		8.00 8.00

Republic of India, 50th anniv.

Millepex 2000 — A1228

Endangered reptiles: No. 1802, Batagur terrapin. No. 1803, Olive ridley turtle.

2000, Jan. 29   *Perf. 13¼*
1802		3r multi	1.10 1.10
1803		3r multi	1.10 1.10
a.	A1228 Pair, #1802-1803		4.50 4.50

Famous Men — A1229

Designs: No. 1804, Balwantrai Mehta. No. 1805, Arun Kumar Chanda. No. 1806, Dr. Harekrushna Mahatab, politician.

2000, Feb. 17   *Litho.*   *Perf. 13x13¼*
1804	A1229	3r multi	.50 .50
1805	A1229	3r multi	.50 .50
1806	A1229	3r multi	.50 .50
	Nos. 1804-1806 (3)		1.50 1.50

Patna Medical College, 75th Anniv. — A1230

2000, Feb. 26   *Perf. 13¼x13*
1807   A1230   3r multi   .70 .70

Dr. Burgula Ramakrishna Rao, Politician — A1231

2000, Mar. 13   *Perf. 13x13¾*
1808   A1231   3r brn & ocher   .70 .70

Potti Sriramulu (1901-52), Advocate of Untouchables A1232

2000, Mar. 16   *Perf. 13¼x13*
1809   A1232   3r red   .70 .70

Basawon Sinha (1909-89), Socialist Party Leader — A1233

2000, Mar. 23   *Perf. 13x13¼*
1810   A1233   3r multi   .60 .60

Indepex Asiana 2000 — A1234

2000, Mar. 31   *Perf. 13x13¼*
1811	A1234	3r Siroi lily	.55 .55
1812	A1234	3r Wild guava	.55 .55
1813	A1234	3r Sangai deer	.55 .55
1814	A1234	15r Slow loris	2.00 2.00
a.	Souvenir sheet, #1811-1814		4.50 4.50
	Nos. 1811-1814 (4)		3.65 3.65

See Nos. 1831-1834.

Arya Samaj, 125th Anniv. — A1235

2000, Apr. 5   *Litho.*   *Perf. 13x13¼*   *Unwmk.*
1815   A1235   3r multi   1.10 1.10

Indigenous Cattle Breeds — A1236

2000, Apr. 25   *Litho.*   *Perf. 13¼x13*   *Unwmk.*
1816	A1236	3r Gir	.70 .60
1817	A1236	3r Kangayam	.70 .60
1818	A1236	3r Kankrej	.70 .60
1819	A1236	15r Hallikar	2.50 1.75
	Nos. 1816-1819 (4)		4.60 3.55

Blackbuck A1237

Patel A1237a

Smooth Indian Otter A1238

Leopard Cat A1239

Tiger A1240

Amaltaas A1241

50p, Nilgiri tahr. 1r, Sarus crane. 2r, Sardar Vallabhbhai Patel (1875-1950), Politician. 15r, Butterfly. 50r, Paradise flycatcher.

Perf. 12¾x13, 13x12¾
2000   *Photo.*   *Wmk. 324*
1820	A1237	25p olive brn	.30 .30
1821	A1237	50p yel brn	.30 .30
1822	A1237	1r blue	.30 .30
1823	A1237a	2r black	.30 .30
1824	A1238	3r gray vio	.30 .30
1825	A1239	5r multi	.30 .30
1826	A1240	10r multi	.70 .70
1827	A1240	15r multi	1.00 1.00
1828	A1241	20r multi	1.50 1.50
1829	A1241	50r multi	4.00 4.00
	Nos. 1820-1829 (10)		9.00 9.00

Issued: 25p, 50p, 1r, 3r, 7/20; 2r, 10/31; 5r, 10r, 4/30; 15r, 20r, 11/20; 50r, 10/30.

Railways in Doon Valley, Cent. A1244

Perf. 13¼
2000, May 6   *Litho.*   *Unwmk.*
1830   A1244   15r multi   2.50 2.50

Indepex Asiana Type of 2000

Birds: No. 1831, Rosy pastor. No. 1832, Garganey teal. No. 1833, Forest wagtail. No. 1834, White stork.

2000, May 24   *Perf. 13¼x13*
1831	A1234	3r multi, horiz.	1.10 1.10
1832	A1234	3r multi, horiz.	1.10 1.10
1833	A1234	3r multi, horiz.	1.10 1.10
1834	A1234	3r multi, horiz.	1.10 1.10
a.	Block of strip of 4, #1831-1834		4.50 4.50
b.	Souvenir sheet, #1831-1834		6.00 6.00

Dr. Nandamuri Taraka Rama Rao (1923-96), Actor, Politician — A1245

2000, May 28
1835   A1245   3r multi   .75 .75

Swami Sahajanand Saraswati (1889-1950), Freedom Fighter — A1246

2000, June 26   *Perf. 13x13¼*
1836   A1246   3r multi   .80 .80

Christian Medical College and Hospital, Vellore, Cent. — A1247

2000, Aug. 12   *Perf. 13¼x13*
1837   A1247   3r multi   .80 .80

Social and Political Leaders — A1248

INDIA

Designs: No. 1838, Radha Gobinda Baruah (1900-75), newspaper publisher. No. 1839, Vijaya Lakshmi Pandit (1900-90), President of UN General Assembly. No. 1840, Jaglal Choudhary (1895-1975), politician. No. 1841, R. Srinivasan (1859-1945), advocate of untouchables, newspaper founder.

2000, Aug. 15		Perf. 13x13¼	
1838	A1248 3r multi	1.75	1.75
1839	A1248 3r multi	1.75	1.75
1840	A1248 3r multi	1.75	1.75
1841	A1248 3r multi	1.75	1.75
	Nos. 1838-1841 (4)	7.00	7.00

Kodaikanal Intl. School, Cent. — A1249

2000, Aug. 26	Litho.	Unwmk.	
	Perf. 13¼x13		
1842	A1249 15r multi	2.25	2.25

2000 Summer Olympics, Sydney — A1250

Designs: 3r, Discus. 6r, Tennis. 10r, Field hockey. 15r, Weight lifting.

2000, Sept. 17		Perf. 13x13¼	
1843-1846	A1250 Set of 4	5.50	5.50

India in Space — A1251

No. 1847, Oceansat 1. No. 1848, Insat 3B in orbit. No. 1849, vert.: a, Astronaut on planet, spacecraft. b, Earth, spacecraft.

2000, Sept. 29	Perf. 13¼x13, 13x13¼		
1847-1848	A1251 3r Set of 2	2.00	2.00
1849	Pair	2.00	2.00
a.-b.	A1251 3r Any single	1.00	1.00

Madhubani-Mithila Painting — A1252

No. 1850, 3 figures. No. 1851, 2 figures and bird. No. 1852, 2 figures and cow, vert. No. 1853, vert.: a, Red fish, palanquin. b, Yellow fish, elephant.

2000, Oct. 15		Perf. 13¼	
1850-1852	A1252 3r Set of 3	1.50	1.50
1853	Pair	2.50	2.50
a.	A1252 5r multi	.65	.65
b.	A1252 10r multi	1.60	1.60

Raj Kumar Shukla (b. 1875), Farmer — A1253

2000, Oct. 16	Litho.	Perf. 13x13¼	
1854	A1253 3r multi	22.50	22.50

Pres. Shanker Dayal Sharma (1918-99) — A1254

2000, Oct. 29		Litho.	
1855	A1254 3r multicolored	.80	.80

Children's Day — A1255

2000, Nov. 14			
1856	A1255 3r multicolored	.90	.90

Maharaja Bijli Pasi — A1256

2000, Nov. 16		Perf. 13¼x13	
1857	A1256 3r multicolored	1.00	1.00

Gems and Jewelry A1257

No. 1858, 3r, Ancient India. No. 1859, 3r, Sarpech. No. 1860, 3r. Taxila. No. 1861, 3r, Navratna. No. 1862, 3r, Temple. No. 1863, 3r, Bridal.

2000, Dec. 7		Perf. 13¼	
1858-1863	A1257 Set of 6	7.00	7.00
a.	Block of 6, #1858-1863	8.00	8.00
b.	Souvenir sheet, #1858, 1860-1861, 1863	8.50	8.50

Issued: No. 1863b, 12/11. No. 1863b sold fo 15r.

Warship of Adm. Mohammed Kunjali Marakkar A1258

2000, Dec. 17		Perf. 13¼x13	
1864	A1258 3r multi	1.50	1.50

Ustad Hafiz Ali Khan (1888-1972), Musician — A1259

2000, Dec. 28			
1865	A1259 3r multi	1.00	1.00

Famous Men — A1260

No. 1866, Gen. Zorawar Singh (1786-1841). No. 1867, Rajarshi Bhagyachandra (1740-98), King of Manipur, vert. No. 1868, Samrat Prithviraj Chauhan (1162-92), ruler of Delhi, vert. No. 1869, Raja Bhamashah (c. 1542-98), military leader, vert.

2000, Dec. 31	Perf. 13¼x13, 13x13¼		
1866-1869	A1260 3r Set of 4	2.40	2.40

St. Aloysius College Chapel Paintings, Cent. — A1261

	Perf. 13¼		
2001, Jan. 12	Litho.	Unwmk.	
1870	A1261 15r multi	2.40	2.40

Subhas Chandra Bose A1262

Dr. B. R. Ambedkar A1263

	Perf. 12¾x13		
2001	Photo.	Wmk. 324	
1871	A1262 1r brown	.40	.40
1872	A1263 3r blue green	.40	.40

Issued: 1r, 1/23; 3r, 4/14.

Famous Men — A1264

Designs: No. 1873, 3r, Sane Guruji (1899-1950), social reformer. No. 1874, 3r, N. G. Ranga (1900-95), politician. No. 1875, 3r, E. M. S. Namboodiripad (1909-98), Marxist leader. No. 1876, 3r, Giani Gurmukh Singh Musafir (1899-1976), politician.

	Perf. 13x13¼		
2001, Jan.	Litho.	Unwmk.	
1873-1876	A1264 Set of 4	2.40	2.40

Issued: No. 1873, 1/25; others, 1/27.

Famous Men — A1265

Designs: No. 1877, 3r, Sheel Bhadra Yajee (1906-96), freedom figher. No. 1878, 3r, Jubba Sahni (1906-44), revolt leader. No. 1879, 3r, Yogendra (1896-1966) and Baikunth (1907-34) Shukla, freedom fighters.

2001, Jan.			
1877-1879	A1265 Set of 3	1.75	1.75

Issued: No. 1877, 1/28; others, 1/29.

Western Railways Building, Mumbai, Cent. (in 1999) — A1266

2001, Feb. 6		Perf. 13¼x13	
1880	A1266 15r multi	3.75	3.75

Dated 1999.

2001 Census — A1267

2001, Feb. 10		Perf. 13x13¼	
1881	A1267 3r multi	1.00	1.00

President's International Fleet Review — A1268

Designs: No. 1882, 3r, Pal. No. 1883, 3r, Galbat. No. 1884, 3r, Tarangini. 15r, Emblem.

2001, Feb. 18		Perf. 13¼x13	
1882-1885	A1268 Set of 4	5.50	5.50

Geological Survey of India, 150th Anniv. — A1269

2001, Mar. 4			
1886	A1269 3r multi	1.25	1.25

4th Battalion of Maratha Light Infantry, Bicent. — A1270

2001, Mar. 6		Perf. 13x13¼	
1887	A1270 3r multi	1.25	1.25

Bhagwan Mahavira, 2600th Anniv. of Birth — A1271

2001, Apr. 6			
1888	A1271 3r multi	1.25	1.25

First Manned Space Flight, 40th Anniv. — A1272

2001, Apr. 12		Perf. 13¼x13	
1889	A1272 15r multi	3.25	3.25

Frederic Chopin (1810-49), Composer A1273

2001, May 4			
1890	A1273 15r multi	3.25	3.25

Suraj Narain Singh (1908-73), Politician — A1274

2001, May 31		Perf. 13x13¼	
1891	A1274 3r multi	.80	.80

B. P. Mandal (1918-82), Politician — A1275

2001, June 1			
1892	A1275 3r multi	.80	.80

INDIA

Samanta Chandra Sekhar (1835-1904), Astronomer — A1276

2001, June 11
1893 A1276 3r multi ... 1.00 1.00

Sant Ravidas, 15th Cent Religious Leader — A1277

2001, June 24
1894 A1277 3r multi ... .80 .80

Famous Men — A1278

Designs: No. 1895, 4r, Krishna Nath Sarmah (1887-1947), social reformer. No. 1896, 4r, C. Sankaran Nair (1857-1934), President of Indian National Congress. No. 1897, 4r, Syama Prasad Mookerjee (1901-53), politician. No. 1898, 4r, U Kiang Nongbah (d. 1862), soldier.

2001, July 6 Litho. *Perf. 13x13¼*
1895-1898 A1278 Set of 4 ... 2.40 2.40

Chandragupta Maurya, Emperor, 3rd Cent. B.C. — A1279

2001, July 21 Litho. *Perf. 13¼*
1899 A1279 4r multi ... 1.00 1.00

Jhalkari Bai — A1280

2001, July 22 Litho. *Perf. 13x13¼*
1900 A1280 4r multi ... 1.10 1.10

Corals A1281

Designs: No. 1901, 4r, Acropora digitifera. No. 1902, 4r, Fungia horrida. 15r, Montipora acquituberculata. 45r, Acropora formosa.

2001, Aug. 2 *Perf. 13¼*
1901-1904 A1281 Set of 4 ... 6.50 6.50

Dwarka Prasad Mishra (1901-88), Politician — A1282

2001, Aug. 5 *Perf. 13x13¼*
1905 A1282 4r multi ... .80 .80

Chaudhary Brahm Parkash (1918-93), Government Minister — A1283

2001, Aug. 11
1906 A1283 4r multi ... .80 .80

Ballia Revolution of August 1942 — A1284

2001, Aug. 19
1907 A1284 4r multi ... .80 .80

Jagdev Prasad (1922-74), Socialist Politician — A1285

2001, Sept. 5
1908 A1285 4r multi ... .80 .80

Rani Avantibai (d. 1858), Queen of Ramgarh — A1286

2001, Sept. 19
1909 A1286 4r multi ... .80 .80

Painted Stork — A1287

Perf. 12¾x13
2001, Sept. 20 Photo. Wmk. 324
1910 A1287 4r bister brown ... 1.00 1.00

Rao Tula Ram (1825-63), Chieftain — A1288

Perf. 13x13¼
2001, Sept. 23 Litho. Unwmk.
1911 A1288 4r multi ... .90 .90

Chaudhary Devi Lal (1914-2001), Deputy Prime Minister — A1289

2001, Sept. 25
1912 A1289 4r multi ... .80 .80

Satis Chandra Samanta (1900-83), Politician — A1290

2001, Sept. 29
1913 A1290 4r multi ... .80 .80

Sivaji Ganesan (1928-2001), Actor — A1291

2001, Oct. 1
1914 A1291 4r multi ... .90 .90

Mahatma Gandhi, Man of the Millennium — A1292

No. 1915: a, Gandhi and followers, birds. b, Gandhi.
Type A Syncopation (1st stamp No. 1915): On the two longer sides, an oval hole equal in width to 3 holes is located in the center, with an equal number of normal round holes to either side.

Perf. 13x13¼ Syncopated Type A
2001, Oct. 2
1915 A1292 4r Horiz. pair, #a-b ... 3.25 3.25

Literary and Performing Arts Personalities A1293

Designs: No. 1916, 4r, Lachhu Maharaj (1901-78), choreographer. No. 1917, 4r, Master Mitrasen (1895-1946), playwright, theater founder. No. 1918, 4r, Bharathidasan (1891-1964), Tamil poet.

2001, Oct. 9 *Perf. 13¼x13*
1916-1918 A1293 Set of 3 ... 2.00 2.00

Jayaprakash Narayan (1902-79), Socialist Politician — A1294

2001, Oct. 11
1919 A1294 4r multi ... .90 .90

Panchatantra Fables — A1295

No. 1920 — The Monkey and the Crocodile, 4r: a, Monkey in tree. b, Monkey on crocodile's back.
No. 1921 — The Lion and the Rabbit, 4r: a, Lion and rabbit. b, Lion and rabbit on bridge.
No. 1922 — The Crows and the Snake, 4r: a, Crows with necklace. b, Villagers pursuing snake.
No. 1923 — The Tortoise and the Geese, 4r: a, Tortoise in pond. b, Tortoise flying with geese.
Sizes: Nos. 1920a-1923a, 58x39mm; Nos. 1920b-1923b, 29x39mm.

2001, Oct. 17 *Perf. 13x13¼*
Horiz. Pairs, #a-b
1920-1923 A1295 Set of 4 ... 6.00 6.00

Global Iodine Deficiency Disorders Day — A1296

2001, Oct. 21
1924 A1296 4r multi ... 1.25 1.25

Thangal Kunju Musaliar (1897-1966), Industrialist — A1297

2001, Oct. 26
1925 A1297 4r multi ... .90 .90

Children's Day — A1298

2001, Nov. 14 Litho. *Perf. 13x13¼*
1926 A1298 4r multi ... 1.00 1.00

Dr. V. Shantaram (1901-90), Movie Producer — A1299

Perf. 13¼x13 Syncopated
2001, Nov. 17
1927 A1299 4r multi ... 1.25 1.25

Sobha Singh (1901-86), Artist — A1300

2001, Nov. 29 Litho. *Perf. 13x13¼*
1928 A1300 4r multi ... 1.10 1.10

Sun Temple, Konark A1301

No. 1929: a, 4r, Carved wheel. b, 15r, Sun Temple.

Perf. 13¼x13 Syncopated
2001, Dec. 1
1929 A1301 Horiz. pair, #a-b ... 2.75 2.75

Intl. Volunteers Year — A1302

2001, Dec. 5 Litho. *Perf. 13¼x13*
1930 A1302 4r multi ... .80 .80

INDIA

Raj Kapoor (1924-88), Film Actor, Director and Producer — A1303

Perf. 13¼x13 Syncopated
2001, Dec. 14 Litho.
1931 A1303 4r multi 1.25 1.25

Greetings — A1304

Flowers and: 3r, Fireworks. 4r, Butterflies.

Perf. 13x13¼ Syncopated
2001, Dec. 18 Litho.
1932-1933 A1304 Set of 2 2.00 2.00

Digboi Refinery, Cent. — A1305

2001, Dec. 18 **Perf. 13¼x13**
1934 A1305 4r multi 1.25 1.25

Vijaye Raje Scindia (1919-2001), Politician — A1306

Perf. 13x13¼ Syncopated
2001, Dec. 20
1935 A1306 4r multi .80 .80

Temples — A1307

Designs: No. 1936, 4r, Kedarnath. No. 1937, 4r, Tryambakeshwar. No. 1938, 4r, Aundha Nagnath. 15r, Rameswaram.

2001, Dec. 22 **Perf. 13¼x13**
1936-1939 A1307 Set of 4 3.50 3.50

Cancer Awareness Day — A1308

2001, Nov. 7 **Perf. 13x13¼**
1940 A1308 4r multi 1.00 1.00

Maharaja Ranjit Singh (1780-1839), Founder of Sikh Kingdom of the Punjab — A1309

2001, Nov. 9
1941 A1309 4r multi 1.00 1.00

Directorate General of Mine Safety, Cent. — A1310

Perf. 13x13¼ Syncopated
2002, Jan. 7 Litho.
1942 A1310 4r multi 1.00 1.00

May 2001 Ascent of Mt. Everest by Indian Army Mountaineers — A1311

2002, Jan. 15 **Perf. 13x13¼**
1943 A1311 4r multi 1.50 1.50

Bauddha Mahotsav Festival — A1312

Designs: No. 1944, 4r, Dhamek Stupa, Sarnath. No. 1945, 4r, Gridhakuta Hills, Rajgir. 8r, Mahaparinirvana Temple, Kushinagar. 15r, Mahabodhi Temple, Bodhgaya.

Perf. 13¼x13 Syncopated
2002, Jan. 21
1944-1947 A1312 Set of 4 4.50 4.50

Book Year — A1313

2002, Jan. 28 **Perf. 13¼x13**
1948 A1313 4r multi 1.10 1.10

Swami Ramanand — A1314

2002, Feb. 4 **Perf. 13x13¼**
1949 A1314 4r multi 1.10 1.10

Indian Munitions Factories, 50th Anniv. — A1315

Perf. 13¼ Syncopated
2002, Mar. 18 Litho.
1950 A1315 4r multi 1.10 1.10

Sido and Kanhu Murmu, 1855-57 Revolt Leaders — A1316

2002, Apr. 6 **Perf. 13¼**
1951 A1316 4r multi 1.50 1.50

Indian Railways, 150th Anniv. — A1317

2002, Apr. 16 **Perf. 13¼x13**
1952 A1317 15r multi 4.25 4.25
 a. Souvenir sheet of 1 4.25 4.25

India — Japan Diplomatic Relations, 50th Anniv. — A1318

No. 1953: a, Kathakali actor, India. b, Kabuki actor, Japan.

2002, Apr. 26 Litho. **Perf. 13x13¼**
1953 A1318 15r Horiz. pair, #a-b 5.50 5.50
 c. Souvenir sheet, #1953a-1953b 4.50 4.50

Parliament, 50th Anniv. — A1319

Litho. & Embossed
2002, May 13 **Perf. 13¼**
1954 A1319 4r gold 1.00 1.00

Prabodhankar Thackeray (1885-1973), Writer — A1320

Perf. 13x13¼ Syncopated
2002, May 19 Litho.
1955 A1320 4r black 1.00 1.00

Cotton College, Guwahati — A1321

2002, May 26 Photo. Perf. 13¼x13
1956 A1321 4r grn & claret .80 .80

P. L. Deshpande (1919-2000), Actor — A1322

2002, June 16 Litho. **Perf. 13¼**
1957 A1322 4r multi .90 .90

Brajlal Biyani (1896-1968), Politician and Writer — A1323

Perf. 13x13¼ Syncopated
2002, June 22
1958 A1323 4r multi .90 .90

Writers — A1324

Designs: No. 1959, 5r, Babu Gulabrai (1888-1963). No. 1960, 5r, Pandit Suryanarayan Vyas (1902-76).

2002, June 22
1959-1960 A1324 Set of 2 1.60 1.60

Sree Thakur Satyananda (1902-69), Writer — A1325

2002, July 23 Litho. **Perf. 13x13¼**
1961 A1325 5r multi .80 .80

Anna Bhau Sathe (1920-69), Writer — A1326

Perf. 13x13¼ Syncopated
2002, Aug. 1 Litho.
1962 A1326 4r gray & black .80 .80

Anand Rishiji Maharaj (1900-92), Humanitarian A1327

2002, Aug. 9 **Perf. 13¼**
1963 A1327 4r multi .80 .80

Vithalrao Vikhe Patil (1901-80), Initiator of Cooperatives — A1328

Perf. 13x13¼ Syncopated
2002, Aug. 10
1964 A1328 4r multi .80 .80

Sant Tukaram (1608-50), Poet — A1329

2002, Aug. 10
1965 A1329 4r multi 1.00 1.00

Bhaurao Krishnaroao Gaikwad (1902-71), Politician — A1330

2002, Aug. 26
1966 A1330 4r multi .80 .80

Social Reformers A1331

Designs: No. 1967, 5r, Ayyan Kali (1863-1941), advocate of rights for untouchables. No. 1968, 5r, Chandraprabha Saikiani (1901-72), women's rights advocate. No. 1969, 5r, Gora (1902-75), advocate of atheism.

Perf. 13¼x13 Syncopated
2002, Sept. 12
1967-1969 A1331 Set of 3 2.00 2.00

Ananda Nilayam Vimanam — A1332

2002, Oct. 11 **Perf. 13¼x13**
1970 A1332 15r multi 1.50 1.50

INDIA

Kanika Bandopadhyay (1924-2000), Singer — A1333

2002, Oct. 12	Photo.	Perf. 13x13¼
1971 A1333 5r multi		1.00 1.00

Arya Vaidya Sala Health Organization, Cent. — A1334

Perf. 13¼x13 Syncopated
2002, Oct. 12		Litho.
1972 A1334 5r multi		2.00 2.00

Bhagwan Baba (1896-1965), Religious Leader — A1335

Perf. 13x13¼ Syncopated
2002, Oct. 15
1973 A1335 5r multi .90 .90

Bihar Chamber of Commerce, 75th Anniv. (in 2001) — A1336

2002, Oct. 28
1974 A1336 4r multi 1.25 1.25

UN Climate Change Convention A1337

Mangroves: No. 1975, 5r, Rhizophora mucronata. No. 1976, 5r, Nypa fruticans. No. 1977, 5r, Bruguiera gymnorrhiza. 15r, Sonneratia alba.

Perf. 13¼x13 Syncopated
2002, Oct. 30
1975-1978 A1337 Set of 4 5.00 5.00
1978a Souvenir sheet, #1975-1978 6.00 6.00

Rose — A1338

Perf. 12¾x13
2002, Aug. 16	Photo.	Wmk. 324
1979 A1338 2r multi		.50 .50

Swami Pranavananda (1896-1941), Religious Leader — A1339

Perf. 12¾x13¼
2002, Nov. 3	Litho.	Unwmk.
1980 A1339 5r multi		1.50 1.50

Nagpur, 300th Anniv. A1340

2002, Nov. 11		Perf. 13x13¼
1981 A1340 5r multi		2.00 2.00

Children's Day — A1341

2002, Nov. 14		Perf. 12¾x13¼
1982 A1341 5r multi		2.00 2.00

Crafts A1342

No. 1983: a, Cane and bamboo containers. b, Thewa. c, Patan's Patola. d, Dhokra.

2002, Nov. 15		Perf. 13¼
1983 A1342 5r Block of 4, #a-d		3.00 3.00
e. Souvenir sheet of 1 #1983		5.50 5.50

Santidev Ghose (1910-99), Dancer and Musician — A1343

2002, Dec. 1
1984 A1343 5r multi 1.40 1.40

Formation of Tamralipta Jatiya Sarkar (National Government of Tamluk), 60th Anniv. — A1344

No. 1985: a, Ajoy Kumar Mukherjee (1901-86). b, Matangini Hazra (d. 1942).

2002, Dec. 17		Perf. 13¼x13
1985 A1344 5r Horiz. pair, #a-b		7.25 7.25

Anglo-Bengali Inter College, Allahabad A1345

Perf. 13¼x13 Syncopated
2002, Dec. 23
1986 A1345 5r multi .80 .80

Gurukula Kangri Vishwavidyalaya, Hardwar — A1346

Perf. 13x13¼ Syncopated
2002, Dec. 24
1987 A1346 5r multi 1.00 1.00

Dhirubhai H. Ambani (1932-2002), Industrialist — A1347

2002, Dec. 28		Perf. 13¼
1988 A1347 5r multi		1.25 1.25

T. T. Krishnamachari (1899-1974), Finance Minister — A1348

2002, Dec. 31
1989 A1348 5r multi 1.25 1.25

Forts in Andhra Pradesh A1349

Designs: No. 1990, 5r, Golocondra Fort. No. 1991, 5r, Palace, Chandragiri Fort.

2002, Dec. 31		Perf. 13¼x13
1990-1991 A1349 Set of 2		1.75 1.75

Aircraft — A1350

Designs: No. 1992, 5r, HT-2 airplane. No. 1993, 5r, Marut airplane. No. 1994, 5r, LCA airplane. 15r, Dhruv helicopter.

2003, Feb. 5		Perf. 13¼
1992-1995 A1350 Set of 4		5.00 5.00
1995a Souvenir sheet, #1992-1995		12.00 12.00

Ghantasala (1922-74), Singer — A1351

2003, Feb. 11
1996 A1351 5r multi .80 .80

S. L. Kirloskar (1903-94), Industrialist A1352

2003, Feb. 26
1997 A1352 5r multi .80 .80

Kusumagraj (V. V. Shirwadkar) (1912-99), Poet — A1353

2003, Mar. 14
1998 A1353 5r multi .80 .80

Sant Eknath (1533-99) — A1354

2003, Mar. 23
1999 A1354 5r multi .80 .80

Frank Anthony (b. 1908), Philantropist — A1355

2003, Mar. 28		Perf. 13x13¼
2000 A1355 5r multi		.80 .80

Kakaji Maharaj (1918-86), Yogi — A1356

2003, Mar. 30		Perf. 13¼
2001 A1356 5r multi		.80 .80

Medicinal Plants A1357

No. 2002: a, Commiphora wightii. b, Bacopa monnieri. c, Withania somnifera. d, Emblica officinalis.

2003, Apr. 7	Litho.	Perf. 13x13¼
2002 A1357 5r Block of 4, #a-d		7.50 7.50
e. Souvenir sheet, #2002a-2002d		8.50 8.50

Durga Das (1900-74), Journalist — A1358

2003, May 2	Photo.	Perf. 13x13¼
2003 A1358 5r multi		.80 .80

Singers — A1359

Designs: No. 2004, 5r, Kishore Kumar (1929-87). No. 2005, 5r, Mukesh (1923-76). No. 2006, 5r, Mohammed Rafi (1924-80). No. 2007, 5r, Hemant Kumar (1920-89).

Perf. 13x13¼ Syncopated
2003, May 15		Litho.
2004-2007 A1359 Set of 4		3.50 3.50
2007a Souvenir sheet, #2004-2007		5.50 5.50

Ascent of Mt. Everest, 50th Anniv. — A1360

2003, May 29		Perf. 13x13¼
2008 A1360 15r multi		2.50 2.50
a. Souvenir sheet of 1		5.50 5.50

Muktabai (1279-99), Poet Saint — A1361

2003, May 30		Perf. 13¼x12½
2009 A1361 5r multi		.80 .80

269

INDIA

Government Museum, Chennai — A1362

Designs: No. 2010, 5r, Sculpted medallion, Amravati, c. 150. No. 2011, 5r, Natesa, 12th cent. bronze sculpture. 15r, Museum Theater (58x28mm).

2003, June 19 — Perf. 13x13¼
2010-2012 A1362 Set of 3 4.00 4.00
2012a Souvenir sheet, #2010-2012 8.00 8.00

V. K. Rajwade (1863-1926), Historian — A1363

2003, June 23 — Photo.
2013 A1363 5r multi 1.25 1.25

Bade Ghulam Ali Khan (1902-68), Singer — A1364

2003, June 30 — Litho.
2014 A1364 5r multi 1.10 1.10

Temples — A1365

Designs: No.2015, Vishal Badri Temple, Badrinath. No.2016, Mallikarjunaswamy Temple, Srisailam. No.2017, Tripureswari Temple, Udaipur. No.2018, Jagannath Temple, Puri.

2003, Sept. 15 — Photo. Perf. 13¼x13
2015 A1365 5r multicolored 1.00 1.00
2016 A1365 5r multicolored 1.00 1.00
2017 A1365 5r multicolored 1.00 1.00
2018 A1365 5r multicolored 1.00 1.00
a. Horiz. strip of 4, #2015-2018 4.00 4.00

Janardan Swami — A1366

2003, Sept. 24 — Photo. Perf. 13x13¼
2019 A1366 5r brown .80 .80

Intl. Autism Conference, Delhi — A1367

2003, Sept. 30 — Litho. Perf. 13¼x13
2020 A1367 5r multi 3.00 3.00

Waterfalls — A1368

Designs: No. 2021, 5r, Kempty Falls, No. 2022, 5r, Athirapalli Falls. No. 2023, 5r, Kakolat Falls. 15r, Jog Falls.

2003, Oct. 3 — Litho. Perf. 13x13¼
2021-2024 A1368 Set of 4 4.50 4.50
2024a Souvenir sheet, #2021-2024 6.00 6.00

Jnanpith Award Winners for Literature A1369

No. 2025: a, G. Sankara Kurup (1901-78), poet. b, S. K. Pottekkatt (1913-82), novelist. c, Thakazhi Sivasankara Pillai (1912-99), novelist.

2003, Oct. 9 — Photo. Perf. 13¼x13
2025 A1369 Horiz. strip of 3 15.00 15.00
a.-c. 5r Any single 2.00 2.00

Kota Shivarama Karanth (1902-97), Writer and Educator — A1370

2003, Oct. 10 — Perf. 13x13¼
2026 A1370 5r multi .80 .80

Narendra Mohan (1934-2002), Journalist — A1371

2003, Oct. 14 — Litho. Perf. 13¼
2027 A1371 5r brown .80 .80

Govindrao Pansare (1913-46), Martyr — A1372

2003, Oct. 21 — Photo. Perf. 13¾x14
2028 A1372 5r multi .80 .80

Greetings — A1373

No. 2029: a, Birds. b, Fish and starfish. c, Squirrels. d, Butterflies and flowers.

2003, Oct. 30 — Litho. Perf. 13¼x13
2029 Horiz. strip of 4 4.50 4.50
a.-b. A1373 4r Either single .95 .95
c.-d. A1373 5r Either single 1.25 1.25

First Telegraph Line in India, 150th Anniv. — A1374

2003, Nov. 1 — Perf. 13¼
2030 A1374 5r multi 1.50 1.50

Bengal Sappers, Bicent. — A1375

2003, Nov. 7 — Photo. Perf. 13¼x13
2031 A1375 5r multi 1.10 1.10

Kalka-Shimla Railway, Cent. — A1376

2003, Nov. 9 — Litho.
2032 A1376 5r multi 1.50 1.50

Snakes — A1377

Designs: No. 2033, 5r, Python. No. 2034, 5r, Bamboo pit viper. No. 2035, 5r, King cobra. No. 2036, 5r, Gliding snake.

2003, Nov. 12
2033-2036 A1377 Set of 4 4.00 4.00
2036a Souvenir sheet, #2033-2036 8.00 8.00

Children's Day — A1378

2003, Nov. 14
2037 A1378 5r multi 1.75 1.75

2nd Guards Battalion (1st Grenadiers Battalion), 225th Anniv. A1379

2003, Nov. 22 — Photo. Perf. 13
2038 A1379 5r multi 1.00 1.00

Harivansh Rai Bachchan (1907-2003), Poet — A1380

2003, Nov. 27 — Litho. Perf. 13x13¼
2039 A1380 5r sepia & blk .80 .80

French and Indian Artisan's Work A1381

No. 2040: a, Illumination depicting rooster, France, 15th cent. b, Jewelry design, India, 19th cent.

2003, Nov. 29
2040 A1381 22r Horiz. pair, #a-b 4.75 4.75
c. Souvenir sheet, #2040 8.50 8.50
See France Nos. 2986-2987.

Yashpal (1903-76), Writer — A1382

2003, Dec. 3 — Photo. Perf. 13¼
2041 A1382 5r multi .80 .80

India — South Korea Diplomatic Relations, 30th Anniv. — A1383

No. 2042: a, Cheomsongdae Astronomical Observatory, Gyeongju, Korea. b, Jantar Mantar, Jaipur, India.

2003, Dec. 10 — Litho.
2042 A1383 15r Pair, #a-b 4.50 4.50
See South Korea No. 2136.

Rajya Sabha, 200th Session A1384

2003, Dec. 11
2043 A1384 5r multi .80 .80

Mukut Behari Lal Bhargava (b. 1903), Politician — A1385

2003, Dec. 18 — Photo.
2044 A1385 5r multi .80 .80

Swami Swaroopanandji (1903-74), Religious Leader — A1386

2003, Dec. 20 — Litho. Perf. 13¼x13
2045 A1386 5r multi .80 .80

Sangeet Natak Akademi, 50th Anniv. — A1387

No. 2046: a, Musicians. b, Actors. c, Dancers.

2003, Dec. 22
2046 A1387 Strip of 3, #a-c 4.75 4.75
a.-c. 5r Any single 1.10 1.10
d. Souvenir sheet, #2046 7.00 7.00
A privately-produced booklet containing two strips of No. 2046 exists.

Folk Musicians — A1388

Designs: No. 2047, 5r, Allah Jilai Bai (1902-92). No. 2048, 5r, Lalan Fakir (1774-1890).

2003, Dec. 29
2047-2048 A1388 Set of 2 2.00 2.00

Siddavanahalli Nijalingappa (1902-2000), Politician — A1389

2003, Dec. 31 — Perf. 13x13¼
2049 A1389 5r multi 1.00 1.00

INDIA

271

Major Somnath Sharma (1923-47), Military Hero — A1390

2003, Dec. 31   Photo.
2050 A1390 5r multi   .80   .80

Chintaman D. Deshmukh (1896-1982), Finance Minister — A1391

2004, Jan. 14   Litho.   *Perf. 13¼x13*
2051 A1391 5r multi   .80   .80

Nani A. Palkhivala (1920-2002), Jurist — A1392

2004, Jan. 16
2052 A1392 5r multi   .80   .80

A privately-produced booklet containing six examples of No. 2052 exists.

Dr. Bhalchandra D. Garware, Businessman — A1393

2004, Feb. 6
2053 A1393 5r multi   .80   .80

Annamacharya, Mystic Saint — A1394

2004, Mar. 18   Photo.   *Perf. 13¾*
2054 A1394 5r multi   .80   .80

9th Battalion of Madras Regiment (Travancore), 300th Anniv. — A1395

2004, Apr. 1   Litho.   *Perf. 13¼x13*
2055 A1395 5r multi   1.00 1.00

V. Lakshminarayana, Violinist — A1396

2004, Apr. 14   Photo.
2056 A1396 5r multi   .80   .80

Indian Institute of Social Welfare and Business Management, 51st Anniv. — A1397

2004, Apr. 25   Litho.   *Perf. 13x13¼*
2057 A1397 5r multi   1.00 1.00

Baji Rao Peshwa, General, Statesman — A1398

2004, Apr. 25   Photo.
2058 A1398 5r multi   1.00 1.00

Circumnavigation of I.N.S. Tarangini — A1399

2004, Apr. 25   Litho.   *Perf. 13¼x13*
2059 A1399 5r multi   1.40 1.40
   a.   Souvenir sheet of 1   10.00 10.00

Siddhar Swamigal (1904-64), Spiritual Leader — A1400

2004, May 15   *Perf. 13x13¼*
2060 A1400 5r multi   .80   .80

Indra Chandra Shastri (1912-86), Philosopher — A1401

2004, May 27   Photo.
2061 A1401 5r black & green   .80   .80

Woodstock School, Mussoorie, 150th Anniv. — A1402

2004, June 2   Litho.   *Perf. 12½x13¼*
2062 A1402 5r multi   .80   .80

Jyotiprasad Agarwalla (1903-51), Musician, Cinematographer A1403

2004, June 17   Photo.   *Perf. 13x13¼*
2063 A1403 5r multi   1.00 1.00

P. N. Panicker (1909-95), Educator — A1404

2004, June 19
2064 A1404 5r multi   .80   .80

Great Trigonometrical Survey — A1405

Designs: No. 2065, 5r, Nain Singh (c. 1826-1882), Himalayan explorer. No. 2066, 5r, Radhanath Sikdar (1813-70), Surveyor who calculated height of Mt. Everest. No. 2067, 5r, Stylized map of India, triangles (38x28mm).

2004, June 27   Litho.   *Perf. 13¼*
2065-2067 A1405   Set of 3   2.50 2.50
2067a   Souvenir sheet, #2065-2067   8.00 8.00

A privately-produced booklet containing six examples of No. 2067 exists.

Aacharya Bhikshu, Founder of Jain Swetamber Terapanth Sect — A1406

2004, June 30   Photo.
2068 A1406 5r multi   .70   .70

2004 Summer Olympics, Athens — A1407

No. 2069: a, 5r, Wrestling. b, 5r, Women's long jump. c, 15r, Shooting. d, 15r, Field hockey.

   Perf. 13¾x14¼
2004, Aug. 13   Photo.
2069 A1407   Block of 4, #a-d   2.50 2.50

Poets A1408

No. 2070: a, Kabir (1440-1518), Indian poet. b, Hafiz Shirazi (c. 1325-c. 1389), Persian poet.

2004, Aug. 16   *Perf. 13¼*
2070 A1408 15r Horiz. pair, #a-b   2.50 2.50
See Iran No. 2894.

Murasoli Maran (1934-2003), Politician, Film Maker, Journalist A1409

2004, Aug. 17   *Perf. 12½x13¼*
2071 A1409 5r multi   1.00 1.00

Prime Minister Rajiv Gandhi (1944-91) and Windmills A1410

2004, Aug. 20   Litho.   *Perf. 13¼*
2072 A1410 5r multi   1.00 1.00
Rajiv Gandhi Renewable Energy Day.

S. S. Vasan (1904-69), Film Producer, Magazine Publisher — A1411

2004, Aug. 28   Photo.   *Perf. 13x13¼*
2073 A1411 5r multi   1.00 1.00

Panini (c. 520 B.C.-c. 460 B.C.), Grammarian A1412

2004, Aug. 30   *Perf. 13¼x13*
2074 A1412 5r multi   .80   .80

K. Subrahmanyam (1904-71), Film Director and Producer — A1413

2004, Sept. 10
2075 A1413 5r multi   .90   .90

M. C. Chagla (1900-81), Judge, Diplomat — A1414

2004, Oct. 1
2076 A1414 5r multi   .75   .75

Tirupur Kumaran (1904-32), Martyred Protester — A1415

2004, Oct. 4   *Perf. 13x13¼*
2077 A1415 5r multi   .60   .60

India Post, 150th Anniv. A1416

No. 2078: a, Boat, #2, coach, train on bridge. b, Train on bridge, airplane, man with spear, frame of #C1. c, Mail box, building, #201. d, Computer, emblems for postal consumer services.

2004, Oct. 4   *Perf. 14¼x13¾*
2078   Horiz. strip of 4   2.00 2.00
  a.-d.   A1416 5r Any single   .30 .30
  e.   Souvenir sheet, #2078, perf. 13¼   8.00 8.00

Ashoka Chakra Winners A1417

No. 2079: a, Neerja Bhanot (1963-86), airline purser killed in hijacking. b, Randhir Prasad Verma (1952-91), slain policeman.

2004, Oct. 8   *Perf. 13¼x13*
2079 A1417 5r Horiz. pair, #a-b   4.50 4.50

INDIA

Guru Dutt (1925-64), Film Actor, Director — A1418

2004, Oct. 10
2080 A1418 5r multi ... 1.10 1.10

Indian Soldiers in UN Peacekeeping Forces — A1419

2004, Oct. 24   Perf. 13¼
2081 A1419 5r multi ... 1.25 1.25
     a. Souvenir sheet of 1 ... 10.00 10.00

Periya (1748-1801) and Chinna (1753-1801) Marudhu, Rulers of Sivaganga, Rebellion Leaders — A1420

2004, Oct. 24   Perf. 13¾x14
2082 A1420 5r multi ... .80 .80

A privately-produced booklet containing six examples of No. 2082 exists.

Greetings A1421

No. 2083: a, Kites. b, Dolls.

2004, Oct. 25   Perf. 13½x13
2083 A1421 4r Horiz. pair, #a-b ... 1.10 1.10

Dr. Svetoslav Roerich (1904-93), Painter — A1422

2004, Oct. 27   Perf. 13¼x13
2084 A1422 5r multi ... .80 .80

Tenneti Viswanatham (1895-1979), Politician — A1423

2004, Nov. 10   Photo.   Perf. 13x13¼
2085 A1423 5r multi ... .80 .80

Children's Day — A1424

2004, Nov. 14
2086 A1424 5r multi ... .75 .75

Walchand Hirachand (1882-1953), Industrialist — A1425

2004, Nov. 23   Perf. 13¾
2087 A1425 5r multi ... .75 .75

Dula Bhaya Kag (1903-77), Poet — A1426

2004, Nov. 25   Perf. 13x13¼
2088 A1426 5r multi ... .75 .75

Aga Khan Award for Architecture — A1427

No. 2089: a, Khas Mahal (blue panel). b, Agra Fort (orange panel).

2004, Nov. 28   Perf. 14x13¾
2089   Horiz. pair ... 2.50 2.50
   a.-b. A1427 15r Either single ... .95 .95
   c. Souvenir sheet, #2089a, 2089b, perf. 13¼ ... 10.00 10.00

Bhagat Puran Singh (1904-92), Founder of Home for Poor — A1428

2004, Dec. 10   Litho.   Perf. 13x13¼
2090 A1428 5r multi ... .75 .75

Women's Insurrections of 1904 and 1939 — A1429

2004, Dec. 12   Photo.   Perf. 13¼x13
2091 A1429 5r multi ... .80 .80

Energy Conservation Day — A1430

2004, Dec. 14
2092 A1430 5r multi ... .90 .90

Completion of Taj Mahal, 350th Anniv. A1431

2004, Dec. 16   Perf. 14x13¾
2093 A1431 15r multi ... 1.25 1.25
   a. Souvenir sheet of 1, perf. 13¼ ... 10.00 10.00

A privately produced booklet containing 3 No. 2093 exists.

Sahitya Academy, 50th Anniv. — A1432

2004, Dec. 21   Perf. 13¼x13
2094 A1432 5r multi ... .80 .80

Bhaskara Sethupathy (1868-1903), Ramanathapuram Ruler — A1433

2004, Dec. 27   Perf. 13x13¼
2095 A1433 5r multi ... .75 .75

Dogs — A1434

No. 2096: a, Himalayan sheepdog. b, Rampur hound. c, Mudhol hound. d, Rajapalayam.

2005, Jan. 9   Perf. 13¼
2096   Horiz. strip of 4 ... 4.00 4.00
   a.-c. A1434 5r Any single ... .40 .40
   d. A1434 15r multi ... .90 .90

Padampat Singhania (1905-79), Industrialist — A1435

2005, Feb. 3
2097 A1435 5r multi ... .75 .75

Rotary International, Cent. — A1436

2005, Feb. 23   Perf. 13¼x13
2098 A1436 5r multi ... .90 .90

Vice-President Krishan Kant (1927-2002) — A1437

2005, Feb. 27   Photo.   Perf. 13¼
2099 A1437 5r multi ... .75 .75

Madhavrao Scindia (1945-2001), Government Minister — A1438

2005, Mar. 10
2100 A1438 5r multi ... .75 .75

Flora and Fauna A1439

No. 2101: a, Clouded leopard. b, Dillenia indica. c, Mishmi takin. d, Pitcher plant.

2005, Mar. 24   Photo.   Perf. 13¼
2101 A1439 5r Block of 4, #a-d ... 2.00 2.00
   e. Souvenir sheet, #2101 ... 8.00 8.00

Intl. Year of Physics — A1440

             Perf. 12¾x13
2005, Mar. 31   Wmk. 324
2102 A1440 5r multi ... 1.40 1.40

Salt March to Dandi, 75th Anniv. A1441

Mohandas Gandhi and: a, Marchers. b, Newspaper. c, Map of march. d, Text by Gandhi.

             Perf. 13¼
2005, Apr. 5   Photo.   Unwmk.
2103 A1441 5r Block of 4, #a-d ... 2.00 2.00
   e. Souvenir sheet, #2103 ... 8.00 8.00

15th Punjab (Patiala) Battalion, 300th Anniv. — A1442

2005, Apr. 13
2104 A1442 5r multi ... .80 .80

Bandung Conference, 50th Anniv. A1443

2005, Apr. 18
2105 A1443 15r multi ... 1.25 1.25

Narayan Meghaji Lokhande (1848-1897), Labor Activist — A1444

2005, May 3   Perf. 13¾
2106 A1444 5r multi ... .75 .75

Cooperative Movement in India, Cent. — A1445

2005, May 8   Perf. 13¼
2107 A1445 5r multi ... .75 .75

World Environment Day — A1446

2005, June 5
2108 A1446 5r multi ... 1.25 1.25

Guru Granth Sahib — A1447

2005, June 16   Photo.   Perf. 14x13¾
2109 A1447 10r multi ... 60.00 —
   a. Souvenir sheet of 1 ... 175.00 —

Because of a lack of an agreement with Indian postal officials and Sikh religious representatives, local post offices were alerted that the issuance of Nos. 2109 and 2109a was to be postponed and the stamps were not to be placed on sale on June 16. Examples were

INDIA

sold at several locations that apparently did not receive the message.

Abdul Qaiyum Ansari (1905-73), Nationalist Leader — A1448

2005, July 1	Photo.	Perf. 13¼
2110	A1448 5r brown	.75 .75

Dheeran Chinnamalai (1765-1805), Freedom Fighter — A1449

2005, July 31		
2111	A1449 5r multi	.90 .90

State Bank of India, Bicent. A1450

2005, Aug. 31		
2112	A1450 15r multi	1.25 1.25

Intl. Day of Peace — A1451

2005, Sept. 21	Photo.	Perf. 13x13¼
2113	A1451 5r multi	1.00 1.00

A. M. M. Murugappa Chettiar (1902-65), Industrialist — A1452

2005, Oct. 1		
2114	A1452 5r multi	.90 .90

Pratap Singh Kairon (1901-65), Government Minister — A1453

2005, Oct. 1		Perf. 13¼x13
2115	A1453 5r multi	.75 .75

Dr. T. S. Soundram (1904-84), Founder of Gandhigram Development Program — A1454

2005, Oct. 2		
2116	A1454 5r multi	.90 .90

Mailboxes — A1455

No. 2117: a, Victorian era box, horse-drawn carriage. b, Man inserting letter into Penfold box. c, Two cylindrical boxes. d, Two square letter boxes.

2005, Oct. 18		Perf. 13x13¼
2117	Horiz. strip of 4	3.50 3.50
a.-d.	A1455 5r Any single	.75 .75
e.	Souvenir sheet, #2117a-2117d, perf. 13¾	13.00 13.00

V. Kalyanasundarnar (1883-1953), Union Leader — A1456

2005, Oct. 21		Perf. 13¼
2118	A1456 5r multi	.75 .75

Ayothidhasa Pandithar (1845-1914), Social Reformer — A1457

2005, Oct. 21		
2119	A1457 5r multi	.75 .75

Kavimani Desiga Vinayagam Pillai (1876-1954), Poet — A1458

2005, Oct. 21		Perf. 13¼x13
2120	A1458 5r multi	.75 .75

Prabodh Chandra (1911-86), Writer — A1459

2005, Oct. 24		Perf. 13x13¼
2121	A1459 5r multi	.75 .75

Children's Day — A1460

2005, Nov. 14		
2122	A1460 5r multi	.80 .80

Children's Film Society, 50th Anniv. — A1461

2005, Nov. 14		Perf. 13¾
2123	A1461 5r multi	1.25 1.25

Progress, Harmony and Development Chamber of Commerce and Industry, Cent. — A1462

2005, Nov. 16		
2124	A1462 5r multi	.80 .80

World Summit on the Information Society, Tunis — A1463

2005, Nov. 17	Photo.	Perf. 13¼x13
2125	A1463 5r multi	.80 .80

Calcutta Police Commissionerate, 150th Anniv. — A1464

2005, Nov. 19		Perf. 13¾
2126	A1464 5r multi	.90 .90

Newborn Health — A1465

2005, Nov. 24		Perf. 13¼
2127	A1465 5r blue	.50 .50

Jawaharlal Darda, Politician — A1466

2005, Dec. 2		
2128	A1466 5r multi	.70 .70

Navy Ships Delhi, Kora and Udaygiri A1467

2005, Dec. 4		Perf. 13
2129	A1467 5r multi	.90 .90

M. S. Subbulakshmi (1916-2004), Singer — A1468

2005, Dec. 18		Perf. 13¼x13
2130	A1468 5r multi	.70 .70

Integral Coach Factory, 50th Anniv. A1469

2005, Dec. 19		Perf. 13¾
2131	A1469 5r multi	1.00 1.00

Jadavpur University, 50th Anniv. A1470

2005, Dec. 21		
2132	A1470 5r multi	.70 .70

16th Air Force Squadron, 55th Anniv. A1471

2005, Dec. 27		Perf. 14x13¾
2133	A1471 5r multi	.70 .70

De Facto Transfer of Pondicherry, 50th Anniv. (in 2006) — A1472

2005, Dec. 30		Perf. 13¼x13
2134	A1472 5r multi	.70 .70

Pongal Festival A1473

2006, Jan. 12		Perf. 13¾
2135	A1473 5r multi	1.00 1.00

A. V. Meiyappan (1907-79), Film Producer and Director — A1474

2006, Jan. 22		Perf. 13¼
2136	A1474 5r multi	1.10 1.10

N. M. R. Subbaraman, Politician, Cent. of Birth — A1475

2006, Jan. 29		Photo.
2137	A1475 5r multi	.70 .70

Dated 2005.

Third Battalion of the Sikh Regiment, 150th Anniv. — A1476

2006, Feb. 1		Perf. 13¼x13
2138	A1476 5r multi	.75 .75

President's Fleet Review, Visakhapatnam — A1477

No. 2139: a, Aircraft carrier and jet. b, Helicopter and two ships. c, Airplane and two ships. d, Two submarines.

2006, Feb. 12		Perf. 13¾x13
2139	A1477 5r Block of 4, #a-d	2.50 2.50

Thirumuruga Kirupananda Variyar (1906-93), Tamil Magazine Publisher A1478

INDIA

Devaneya Pavanar (1902-81), Tamil Writer — A1479

Dr. U. V. Swaminatha Iyer (1855-1942), Tamil Literature Researcher — A1480

Tamilavel Umamaheswarar, Editor of Tamil Literary Magazine — A1481

2006, Feb. 18   *Perf. 13¼*
2140   A1478   5r chestnut   .50   .50
2141   A1479   5r blue   .50   .50
2142   A1480   5r red brown   .50   .50
2143   A1481   5r black   .50   .50
     Nos. 2140-2143 (4)   2.00   2.00

St. Bede's College, Shimla, 102nd Anniv. — A1482

2006, Feb. 24
2144   A1482   5r multi   .65   .65   *Perf. 13x13¼*

Gemini Ganesan (1920-2005), Actor — A1483

2006, Feb. 25   *Perf. 13¼x13*
2145   A1483   5r black   1.00   1.00

Salesians of Don Bosco in India, Cent. — A1484

2006, Feb. 27   *Perf. 13x13¼*
2146   A1484   5r brown   .70   .70

M. Singaravelar (1860-1946), Communist Politician — A1485

2006, Mar. 2
2147   A1485   5r multi   .75   .75

World Consumer Rights Day — A1486

2006, Mar. 15   *Perf. 13¼x13*
2148   A1486   5r multi   .70   .70

Indian Agricultural Research Institute, Delhi, Cent. — A1487

2006, Mar. 30
2149   A1487   5r multi   .70   .70

62nd Cavalry Armored Regiment, 50th Anniv. — A1488

2006, Apr. 1
2150   A1488   5r multi   .70   .70

Folk Dances A1489

No. 2151 — Folk dances from: a, India. b, Cyprus.

2006, Apr. 12   *Perf. 13x13¾*
2151   A1489   15r Horiz. pair, #a-b   2.75   2.75
  c.   Souvenir sheet, #2151, perf. 13¾x13¼   8.50   8.50
     See Cyprus No. 1052.

Calcutta Girls' High School, 150th Anniv. — A1490

2006, Apr. 21   *Perf. 13¾x13*
2152   A1490   5r multi   .70   .70

Pannalal Barupal (1913-83), Politician — A1491

2006, Apr. 28   *Perf. 13x13¼*
2153   A1491   5r multi   .70   .70

Kurinji Flower — A1492

2006, Apr. 29   *Perf. 13x13¾*
2154   A1492   15r multi   2.00   2.00
  a.   Souvenir sheet of 1   9.00   9.00

Rainwater Harvesting A1493

2006, June 5   *Perf. 13¼x13*
2155   A1493   5r multi   .80   .80

Sri Pratap College, Srinigar, Cent. A1494

2006, June 15   *Perf. 13*
2156   A1494   5r multi   .70   .70

Indraprastha Girls' School, New Delhi, 102nd Anniv. — A1495

2006, July 8   *Perf. 13¾x13*
2157   A1495   5r multi   .70   .70

Voorhees College, Vellore, 111th Anniv. — A1496

2006, July 10   *Perf. 13¼*
2158   A1496   5r multi   .70   .70

Vellore Mutiny, Bicent. A1497

2006, July 10   *Litho.*   *Perf. 13¼*
2159   A1497   5r multi   .70   .70

High Court of Jammu and Kashmir A1498

Perf. 13¾x13¼
2006, July 29   *Photo.*
2160   A1498   5r multi   .70   .70

Pankaj Kumar Mullick (1904-78), Composer A1499

2006, Aug. 4   *Perf. 13¼x13*
2161   A1499   5r multi   .70   .70

Oil and Natural Gas Corporation, Limited — A1500

2006, Aug. 14
2162   A1500   5r multi   .70   .70

M. P. Sivagnanam, Tamil Politician, Cent. of Birth — A1501

2006, Aug. 15   *Litho.*   *Perf. 13¼*
2163   A1501   5r multi   .70   .70

University of Madras — A1502

2006, Sept. 4   *Photo.*
2164   A1502   5r multi   .70   .70

L. V. Prasad (1908-94), Film Actor and Director — A1503

2006, Sept. 5
2165   A1503   5r multi   .70   .70

Indian Merchants Chamber — A1504

2006, Sept. 7   *Perf. 13x13¼*
2166   A1504   5r multi   .70   .70

Horse Sculptures — A1505

No. 2167: a, Horse and rider. b, Horse only.

2006, Sept. 11   *Perf. 13¼x13¾*
2167   A1505   15r Horiz. pair, #a-b   2.75   2.75
  c.   Souvenir sheet, #2167   8.50   8.50
     See Mongolia No. 2621.

Birds — A1506

No. 2168: a, Greater adjutant stork. b, Nilgiri laughing thrush. c, Manipur bush-quail. d, Lesser florican.

2006, Oct. 5   *Perf. 13*
2168   Vert. strip of 4   1.75   1.75
  a.-d.   A1506 5r Any single   .40   .40
  e.   Souvenir sheet, #2168a-2168d   7.00   7.00

Madhya Pradesh Chamber of Commerce and Industry, Cent. — A1507

2006, Oct. 12   *Photo.*   *Perf. 13¼*
2169   A1507   5r multi   .70   .70

Bishwanath Roy (1906-84), Politician — A1508

2007, Oct. 31   *Litho.*   *Perf. 13¼x13*
2170   A1508   5r multi   .70   .70

G. Varadaraj, Industrialist (1936-90) — A1509

2006, Nov. 1
2171   A1509   5r multi   .70   .70

Lakes A1510

INDIA

No. 2172: a, Roop Kund. b, Chandra Tal. vert. c, Tsomo Riri. d, Sela. e, Tsangu.

2006, Nov. 6   **Photo.**   **Perf. 13**
2172   A1510   5r Block of 5, #a-e   3.00   3.00

Lala Deen Dayal (1844-1905), Photographer — A1511

2006, Nov. 11
2173   A1511   5r multi   .70   .70

Children's Day — A1512

2006, Nov. 14   **Litho.**   **Perf. 13**
2174   A1512   5r Horiz. pair, #a-b   1.25   1.25
   c.   Souvenir sheet of 2, #2174a-2174b

No. 2174 — Various children's drawings: a, Denomination at LL. b, Denomination at UL.

The Tribune, 125th Anniv. — A1513

2006, Nov. 24   **Photo.**   **Perf. 14**
2175   A1513   5r multi   .70   .70

World AIDS Day — A1514

2006, Dec. 1   **Perf. 13x13¼**
2176   A1514   5r multi   .70   .70

Bartholomaeus Ziegenbalg (1682-1719), First Lutheran Missionary to India — A1515

2006, Dec. 8   **Perf. 13¼**
2177   A1515   5r multi   .80   .80

Army Field Post Offices, 150th Anniv. — A1516

No. 2178: a, Soldier, cancel, ship, map of Bushire-Bombay route. b, Soldier writing letter, camel. c, Soldier reading letter, sign. d, Soldier reading letter, helicopter.

2006, Dec. 10   **Litho.**   **Perf. 13x13¼**
2178   Horiz. strip of 4   2.75   2.75
   a.-d.   A1516 5r Any single   .65   .65

Sandalwood Carving — A1517

2006, Dec. 18   **Photo.**   **Perf. 13¼x13**
2179   A1517   15r multi   2.00   2.00
   a.   Souvenir sheet of 1, perf. 13   8.50   8.50

Stamps are impregnated with a sandalwood scent.

Stop Child Labor — A1518

No. 2180: a, Girl on tightrope. b, Boy with hoe. c, Boy pouring tea. d, Boy with large basket.

2006, Dec. 28   **Perf. 13¼x13**
2180   A1518   5r Block of 4, #a-d   2.50   2.50

Bimal Roy (1909-66), Film Director — A1519

2007, Jan. 8   **Litho.**   **Perf. 13**
2181   A1519   5r multi   .60   .60

Tamil Nadu Cricket Association, 70th Anniv. — A1520

2007, Jan. 26   **Perf. 13x13¼**
2182   A1520   5r multi   .70   .70

Rose Varieties A1521

No. 2183: a, 5r, Bhim. b, 5r, Neelam. c, 15r, Delhi Princess. d, 15r, Jawahar.

2007, Feb. 7   **Photo.**   **Perf. 13x13¼**
2183   A1521   Block or horiz. strip of 4, #a-d   2.00   2.00
   e.   Souvenir sheet, #2183   5.00   5.00

Stamps are impregnated with a rose scent.

Manoharbhai Patel (1906-70), Politician — A1522

2007, Feb. 9
2184   A1522   5r multi   .65   .65

Fairs A1523

Designs: No. 2185, 5r, Sonepur Fair. No. 2186, 5r, Pushkar Fair. No. 2187, 5r, Goa Carnival. No. 2188, 5r, Baul Mela.

2007, Feb. 27   **Litho.**
2185-2188   A1523   Set of 4   1.60   1.60
2188a   Souvenir sheet, #2185-2188   3.00   3.00

Women's Day — A1524

No. 2189: a, Two women. b, Woman, three birds. c, Two women and birds. d, Woman and birds.

2007, Mar. 8   **Photo.**   **Perf. 13x13¼**
2189   Horiz. strip of 4   3.00   3.00
   a.-b.   A1524 5r Either single   .40   .40
   c.-d.   A1524 15r Either single   1.10   1.10
   e.   Souvenir sheet, #2189   5.50   5.50

Raj Narain (1917-86), Politician — A1525

2007, Mar. 23   **Litho.**   **Perf. 13¼**
2190   A1525   5r multi   .60   .60

Mehboob Khan (1907-64), Film Producer and Director — A1526

2007, Mar. 30
2191   A1526   5r multi   .60   .60

Dr. R. M. Alagappa Chettiar (1909-57), Industrialist and Philanthropist — A1527

2007, Apr. 6   **Photo.**   **Perf. 13x13¼**
2192   A1527   5r multi   .60   .60

A1528
A1529
A1530
A1531
A1532

Mahaparinirvana of Buddha, 2550th Anniv. — A1533

2007, May 2   **Perf. 13¼**
2193   A1528   5r multi   .60   .60
2194   A1529   5r multi   .60   .60
2195   A1530   5r multi   .60   .60
2196   A1531   5r multi   .60   .60
2197   A1532   5r multi   .60   .60
2198   A1533   5r multi   .60   .60
   a.   Miniature sheet, #2193-2198   4.00   4.00
     Nos. 2193-2198 (6)   3.60   3.60

Natl. Parks A1534

No. 2199: a, Bandhavgarh Natl. Park. b, Bandipur Natl. Park. c, Kaziranga Natl. Park. d, Mudumalai Natl. Park. e, Periyar Natl. Park.

2007, May 31
2199   Vert. strip of 5   3.00   3.00
   a.-e.   A1534 5r Any single   .60   .60

Battle of Lucknow A1535

Battle of Kanpur — A1535a

2007, Aug. 9   **Photo.**   **Perf. 13¼x13**
2200   A1535   5r multi   .40   .40
2200A   A1535a   15r multi   1.10   1.10
   b.   Vert. pair, #2200-2200A   1.50   1.50
   c.   Souvenir sheet, #2200-2200A   2.50   2.50

First War of Independence, 150th anniv.

INDIA

Saint Vallalar (1823-74) — A1536

Maraimalai Adigal (1876-1950), Tamil Scholar — A1537

V. G. Suryanarayana Sastriar (1870-1903), Tamil Writer — A1538

2007, Aug. 18   Litho.   Perf. 13x13¼
2201	A1536	5r multi	.40	.40
2202	A1537	5r multi	.40	.40
2203	A1538	5r multi	.40	.40
	Nos. 2201-2203 (3)		1.20	1.20

Bridges — A1539

No. 2204: a, Howrah Bridge. b, Mahatma Gandhi Bridge. c, Pamban Bridge. d, Vidyasagar Bridge.

2007, Aug. 17   Photo.
2204	Vert. strip or block of 4		2.40	2.40
a.-d.	A1539 5r Any single		.60	.60
e.	Souvenir sheet, #2204a-2204d		3.00	3.00

J. P. Naik (1907-81), Education Reformer — A1540

2007, Sept. 5   Litho.   Perf. 13¼x13
2205	A1540	5r multi	.50	.50

53rd Commonwealth Parliamentary Conference, New Delhi — A1541

2007, Sept. 23   Litho.   Perf. 13¼
2206	A1541	15r multi	1.10	1.10

Sachin Deb Burman (1906-75), Composer — A1542

2007, Oct. 1   Perf. 13¼x13
2207	A1542	15r multi	1.75	1.75

Satyagraha (Non-Violent Resistance), Cent. — A1543

No. 2208 — Mohandas Gandhi and: a, Train. b, House, newspaper article. c, Crowd, building. d, People marching.

2007, Oct. 2   Photo.   Perf. 13¼x13
2208	Horiz. strip of 4		2.00	2.00
a.-d.	A1543 5r Any single		.50	.50
e.	Souvenir sheet, #2208a-2208d		3.75	3.75

Indian Air Force, 75th Anniv. — A1544

Designs: No. 2209, 5r, DHRUV helicopter. No. 2210, 5r, Westland Wapiti biplane. No. 2211, 5r, AWACS airplane (84x32mm). 15r, IL-78 (84x32mm).

2007, Oct. 8   Litho.   Perf. 13¼x13
2209-2212	A1544	Set of 4	2.00	2.00
2212a	Souvenir sheet, #2209-2212		4.00	4.00

Fourth Military World Games, Hyderabad — A1545

No. 2213: a, Parachutist. b, Soccer player. c, Swimmer.

2007, Oct. 14   Perf. 13¼x13
2213	Vert. strip of 3		1.50	1.50
a.-c.	A1545 5r Any single		.50	.50
d.	Souvenir sheet, #2213, perf. 13		3.50	3.50

Maharashtra Police Academy — A1546

2007, Nov. 3   Photo.   Perf. 13¼
2214	A1546	5r multi	.70	.70

Children's Day — A1547

Children's art: No. 2215, 5r, Children and stars. No. 2216, 5r, Fishermen and canoes at night.

2007, Nov. 14   Litho.   Perf. 13¼x13
2215-2216	A1547	Set of 2	1.25	1.25
2216a	Souvenir sheet, #2215-2216		2.00	2.00

Renewable Energy — A1548

Designs: No. 2217, 5r, Solar energy. No. 2218, 5r, Wind energy. No. 2219, 5r, Small hydroelectric power, vert. No. 2220, 5r, Biomass energy, vert.

2007, Nov. 22   Photo.   Perf. 13
2217-2220	A1548	Set of 4	2.50	2.50
2220a	Souvenir sheet, #2217-2220, perf. 13¾x13¼, 13¼x13¾		3.50	3.50
2220b	Miniature sheet, 6 each #2217-2218, 3 each #2219-2220		20.00	20.00

First Battalion of the Fourth Gorkha Rifles, 150th Anniv. — A1549

2007, Nov. 27   Litho.   Perf. 13¼
2221	A1549	5r multi	.70	.70

Intl. Day of Disabled Persons — A1550

Photo. & Embossed

2007, Dec. 3   Perf. 13
2222	A1550	5r multi	.70	.70

Daly College, Indore, 125th Anniv. — A1551

2007, Dec. 8   Litho.   Perf. 13¼
2223	A1551	5r multi	.70	.70

Wilson College, Bombay, 175th Anniv. — A1552

2007, Dec. 11   Photo.   Perf. 13
2224	A1552	5r multi	.70	.70

Greetings — A1553

No. 2225: a, Sun, wheat, path. b, Fish, lotus flower. c, Bird. d, Man, flower, butterfly, deer. e, Flowers, stars and text, "Happy New Year," (58x29mm).

2007, Dec. 15   Photo.   Perf. 13
2225	Horiz. strip of 5		2.50	2.50
a.-e.	A1553 5r Any single		.50	.50

S. B. Chavan (1920-2004), Politician — A1554

2007, Dec. 17   Litho.   Perf. 13¼x13
2226	A1554	5r multi	.60	.60

Snows Basilica, 425th Anniv. — A1555

2007, Dec. 25   Perf. 13
2227	A1555	5r multi	.60	.60

Water Year — A1556

2007, Dec. 28
2228	A1556	5r multi	.50	.50

Ritwik Ghatak (1925-76), Film Director — A1557

2007, Dec. 31   Photo.   Perf. 13¼x13
2229	A1557	5r brown & black	.50	.50

Butterflies Of Andaman and Nicobar Islands — A1558

No. 2230: a, Male Papilio mayo. b, Female Papilio mayo. c, Female Pachliopta rhodifer. d, Male Pachliopta rhodifer.

2008, Jan. 2   Perf. 13
2230	A1558	5r Block of 4, #a-d	2.00	2.00
e.	Souvenir sheet, #2230		3.75	3.75

Dr. Benjamin Peary Pal (1906-89), Rose Breeder and Plant Scientist — A1559

2008, Jan. 5   Litho.
2231	A1559	5r multi	.60	.60

Dr. Dhananjaya Ramachandra Gadgil (1901-71), Economist — A1560

2008, Feb. 8   Photo.
2232	A1560	5r multi	.50	.50

Damodaram Sanjeevaiah (1921-72), Politician — A1561

2008, Feb. 14   Litho.
2233	A1561	5r multi	.70	.70

Maharshi Bulusu Sambamurthy (1886-1958), Lawyer — A1562

2008, Mar. 4
2234	A1562	5r multi	.70	.70

Madhubala (1933-1969), Film Actress — A1563

2008, Mar. 18   Photo.   Perf. 13
2235	A1563	5r multi	.60	.60
a.	Souvenir sheet of 1, perf. 13x13¾		2.50	2.50

Asrar Ul Haq (Majaaz) (1909-55), Urdu Poet — A1564

2008, Mar. 28   Litho.   Perf. 13
2236	A1564	5r multi	.60	.60

INDIA

Civil Service — A1565

Photo. & Embossed
2008, Apr. 21
2237 A1565 5r multi .60 .60

Tata Steel, Cent. A1566

2008, Apr. 22 **Litho.**
2238 A1566 5r multi .70 .70

Jasmine Flowers — A1567

2008, Apr. 26 **Photo.**
2239 A1567 5r shown .60 .60
2240 A1567 15r Flowers, horiz. 1.40 1.40
  a. Souvenir sheet, #2239-2240 4.00 4.00

Nos. 2239-2240, 2240a are impregnated with a jasmine scent.

Aga Khan Foundation, 30th Anniv. — A1568

No. 2241: a, 5r, Heritage restoration (46x39mm). b, 15r, Social commitment (70x39mm).

2008, May 17 **Photo.** **Perf. 13**
2241 A1568 Horiz. pair, #a-b 1.25 1.25
  c. Souvenir sheet, #2241a-2241b 3.50 3.50

Shri Shirdi Sai Baba (1835-1918), Hindu Saint — A1569

2008, May 20
2242 A1569 5r multi 1.00 1.00

Rajesh Pilot (1945-2008), Politician — A1570

2008, June 12 **Litho.** **Perf. 13**
2243 A1570 5r multi .60 .60

Henning Holck-Larsen (1907-2003), Engineer and Industrialist — A1571

2008, June 12 **Litho.** **Perf. 13¼x13**
2244 A1571 5r multi .70 .70

Madhav Institute of Technology, Gwalior, 50th Anniv. — A1572

2008, June 30 **Litho.** **Perf. 13¼**
2245 A1572 5r multi .60 .60

Temples A1573

No. 2246: a, Maha Bodhi Temple, India. b, White Horse Temple, China.

2008, July 11 **Photo.** **Perf. 13**
2246 A1573 15r Horiz. pair, #a-b 1.75 1.75
  c. Souvenir sheet, #2246 4.00 4.00

See People's Republic of China Nos. 3678-3679.

Punjab Regiment 14th Battalion, 250th Anniv. — A1574

2008, July 21 **Litho.** **Perf. 13¼**
2247 A1574 5r multi .60 .60

Damodar Dharmananda Kosambi (1907-66), Mathematician A1575

2008, July 31
2248 A1575 5r multi .60 .60

Aldabra Giant Tortoise — A1576

Tortoise facing: 5r, Left. 15r, Forward.

2008, Aug. 2 **Photo.** **Perf. 13**
2249-2250 A1576 Set of 2 1.40 1.40

2008 Summer Olympics, Beijing — A1577

No. 2251 — 2008 Summer Olympics emblem and: a, 5r, Olympic torch and mascot. b, 5r, Boxing. c, 15r, Shooting. d, 15r, Archery.

2008, Aug. 8
2251 A1577 Block of 4, #a-d 2.50 2.50
  e. Souvenir sheet, #2251a-2251d 4.00 4.00

Indian Coast Guard, 30th Anniv. A1578

No. 2252: a, Airplane. b, Helicopter. c, Hovercraft (large wave at LL). d, Patrol boat (large wave at LR).

2008, Aug. 12 **Litho.** **Perf. 13¼**
2252 A1578 5r Block of 4, #a-d 2.00 2.00
  e. Souvenir sheet, #2252a-2252d 4.00 4.00

Ustad Bismillah Khan (1916-2006), Musician A1579

2008, Aug. 21
2253 A1579 5r multi .70 .70

Sir Pitti Theagarayar (1853-1925) A1580

Dr. Taravat Mahadevan Nair (1868-1919) A1581

Dr. C. Natesan (1869-1937) — A1582

2008, Sept. 17 **Perf. 13x13¼**
2254 A1580 5r multi .60 .60
Perf. 13¾ Syncopated
2255 A1581 5r multi .60 .60
2256 A1582 5r multi .60 .60
  Nos. 2254-2256 (3) 1.80 1.80

Founders of South Indian Welfare Association.

Festivals A1583

Designs: No. 2257, 5r, Dussehra Festival, Calcutta (Kolkata). No. 2258, 5r, Dussehra Festival, Mysore. No. 2259, 5r, Deepavali Festival, vert.

2008, Oct. 7 **Photo.** **Perf. 13**
2257-2259 A1583 Set of 3 1.50 1.50
2259a Souvenir sheet, #2257-2259 4.00 4.00

3rd Commonwealth Youth Games, Pune — A1584

No. 2260: a, Tiger mascot. b, Wrestling. c, Badminton. d, Hurdling.

2008, Oct. 12 **Perf. 13x13¼**
2260 Horiz. strip of 4 2.00 2.00
  a.-d. A1584 5r Any single .50 .50
  e. Souvenir sheet, #2260a-2260d 3.50 3.50

Indian Post Office — A1585

Perf. 13¾ Syncopated
2008, Oct. 13 **Litho.**
2261 A1585 5r multi .60 .60

Philately Day. A souvenir sheet of one sold for 15r.

Food Safety and Quality Year — A1586

2008, Oct. 16
2262 A1586 5r multi .60 .60

19th Commonwealth Games, Delhi — A1587

2008, Oct. 18 **Photo.** **Perf. 13¼x13**
2263 A1587 5r multi .60 .60

A souvenir sheet of one sold for 15r.

A1588

A1589

Children's Day — A1590

2008, Nov. 14 **Litho.** **Perf. 13¼**
2264 A1588 5r multi .40 .40
2265 A1589 5r multi .40 .40
2266 A1590 5r multi .40 .40
  a. Souvenir sheet of 3, #2264-2266 2.75 2.75
  Nos. 2264-2266 (3) 1.20 1.20

Bomireddi N. Reddi (1908-77), Film Director — A1591

2008, Nov. 16
2267 A1591 5r multi .60 .60

Canonization of Saint Alphonsa (1910-46) — A1592

2008, Nov. 16 **Photo.** **Perf. 13x13¼**
2268 A1592 5r multi .60 .60

A souvenir sheet of one sold for 15r.

INDIA

Standard Chartered Bank, 150th Anniv. — A1593

2008, Nov. 17   Litho.   *Perf. 13¼*
2269   A1593   5r multi   .60   .60

Gas Authority of India Limited, 25th Anniv. — A1594

2008, Nov. 19   *Perf. 13*
2270   A1594   5r multi   .60   .60

Joachim (1907-79) and Violet (1908-69) Alva, Politicians A1595

Perf. 13¾ Syncopated
2008, Nov. 20
2271   A1595   5r multi   .60   .60

Sardar Vallabhbhai Patel Natl. Police Academy, Hyderabad — A1596

Building and: 5r, Police cadets training and marching. 20r, Statue, policeman with sword.

2008, Nov. 27
2272-2273 A1596 Set of 2   1.50   1.50
2273a   Souvenir sheet, #2272-2273   3.50   3.50

St. Joseph's Boys' High School, Bangalore, 150th Anniv. — A1597

2008, Nov. 28
2274   A1597   5r multi   .60   .60

Buddhadeva Bose (1908-74), Writer — A1598

2008, Nov. 30   *Perf. 13*
2275   A1598   5r multi   .65   .65

Prime Minister Jawaharlal Nehru (1889-1964) A1599

E.V. Ramasami (1879-1973), Politician A1600

Mahatma Gandhi (1869-1948) A1601

Dr. Bhimrao R. Ambedkar (1891-1956), Politician A1602

Satyajit Ray (1921-92), Film Director A1603

Homi Jahangir Bhabha (1909-66), Nuclear Physicist A1604

Prime Minister Indira Gandhi (1917-84) A1605

Prime Minister Rajiv Gandhi (1944-91) A1606

C.V. Raman (1888-1970), 1930 Nobel Physics Laureate A1607

J. R. D. Tata (1904-93), Industrialist A1608

Mother Teresa (1910-97), 1979 Nobel Peace Laureate A1609

Rukmini Devi Arundale (1904-86), Dancer A1610

Perf. 12¾x13¼
2008-09   Photo.   Wmk. 324
2276 A1599 25p rose lil & blk   .30   .30
2277 A1600 50p blue   .30   .30
2278 A1601 1r olive brown   .30   .30
2279 A1602 2r rose lilac   .30   .30
2280 A1603 3r vio brown   .30   .30
2281 A1604 4r brt blue   .35   .35
2282 A1605 5r gray grn & blk   .40   .40
2283 A1606 5r brown   .40   .40
2284 A1607 10r multi   .55   .55
2285 A1608 15r purple   .70   .70
2286 A1609 20r multi   1.00   1.00
2287 A1610 50r multi   2.50   2.50
Nos. 2276-2287 (12)   7.40   7.40

Issued: 25p, Nos. 2282, 2283, 12/1; 1r, 2r, 3r, 4r, 15r, 20r, 3/1/09; 50p, 10r, 5/11/09. 50r, 5/11/09.

Discovery of Evershed Effect at Kodaikanal Solar Observatory, Cent. — A1611

Perf. 13¾ Syncopated
2008, Dec. 2   Litho.   Unwmk.
2288   A1611   5r multi   .60   .60

Map, Handshake, Indian Ship and Helicopter A1612

2008, Dec. 4
2289   A1612   5r multi   .60   .60
Navy Day.

Dr. Laxmi Mall Singhvi (1931-2007), Jurist — A1613

2008, Dec. 8
2290   A1613   5r multi   .60   .60

Christmas — A1614

No. 2291: a, 5r, Lambs. b, 20r, Madonna and Child.

2008, Dec. 8   Photo.   *Perf. 13*
2291 A1614 Horiz. pair, #a-b   1.40   1.40

Universal Declaration of Human Rights, 60th Anniv. — A1615

2008, Dec. 10
2292   A1615   5r multi   .70   .70

Indian Institute of Science, Bangalore, Cent. — A1616

No. 2293: a, 5r, Building. b, 20r, Building and scientists.

2008, Dec. 14
2293 A1616 Horiz. pair, #a-b   1.40   1.40
c.   Souvenir sheet, #2293a-2293b   3.50   3.50

Swami Ranganathananda (1908-2005), Hindu Monk — A1617

Perf. 13¾ Syncopated
2008, Dec. 15   Litho.
2294   A1617   5r multi   .60   .60

Field Marshal S. H. F. J. Manekshaw (1914-2008) — A1618

2008, Dec. 16   Photo.   *Perf. 13x13¼*
2295   A1618   5r multi   .60   .60

Thazhuvia V. Ramasubbaiyer (1908-84), Founder of Dinamalar Newspaper — A1619

Perf. 13¾ Syncopated
2008, Dec. 21   Litho.
2296   A1619   5r multi   .60   .60

Brahmos Cruise Missile, 10th Anniv. — A1620

Designs: 5r, Missile in flight, airplane. 20r, Missiles, airplane, ship, launch vehicle, horiz.

2008, Dec. 22   Photo.   *Perf. 13*
2297-2298 A1620 Set of 2   1.40   1.40
2298a   Souvenir sheet, #2297-2298   3.50   3.50

Udumalai Narayana Kavi (1899-1981), Lyricist — A1621

2008, Dec. 31   *Perf. 13x13¼*
2299   A1621   5r multi   .60   .60

Thillaiyadi Valliammai (1898-1914), Freedom Fighter — A1622

2008, Dec. 31   *Perf. 13*
2300   A1622   5r multi   .60   .60

Sheik Thambi Pavalar (1874-1950), Freedom Fighter — A1623

2008, Dec. 31
2301   A1623   5r multi   .60   .60

A. T. Paneerselvam, Politician — A1624

2008, Dec. 31   *Perf. 13x13¼*
2302   A1624   5r multi   .60   .60

M. Bhakthavatsalam (1897-1987), Politician — A1625

2008, Dec. 31   *Perf. 13*
2303   A1625   5r multi   .60   .60

Velu Nachchiyar, Tamil Queen — A1626

2008, Dec. 31   Litho.
2304   A1626   5r multi   .60   .60

INDIA

Louis Braille (1809-52), Educator of the Blind — A1627

Photo. & Embossed
2009, Jan. 4   Perf. 13¼x13
2305   A1627   5r multi   .75   .75

Vaikom Muhammad Basheer (1908-94), Writer — A1628

2009, Jan. 21   Litho.   Perf. 13
2306   A1628   5r multi   .60   .60

St. Paul's Church, Madras — A1629

2009, Jan. 25   Perf. 13¾ Syncopated
2307   A1629   5r multi   .60   .60

Preservation of Heritage Monuments — A1630

No. 2308: a, Jaisalmer Fort, Jaisalmer. b, Mongyu Monastery, Laddakh. c, St. Anne Church, Goa. d, Qila Mubarak, Patiala.

2009, Jan. 28   Photo.   Perf. 13
2308   A1630   5r Block of 4, #a-d   1.60   1.60
   e.   Souvenir sheet, #2308a-2308d   3.00   3.00

Bishnu Prasad Rabha (1909-69), Writer, Singer — A1631

Perf. 13¾ Syncopated
2009, Jan. 31   Litho.
2309   A1631   5r multi   .75   .75

Steel Authority of India, 50th Anniv. A1632

2009, Mar. 3   Photo.   Perf. 13
2310   A1632   5r multi   .60   .60

Natl. Girl Child Day — A1633

2009, Feb. 5
2311   A1633   5r multi   .65   .65

Santaji Jagnade Maharaj (1624-88), Marathi Saint — A1634

Perf. 13¾ Syncopated
2009, Feb. 9   Litho.
2312   A1634   5r multi   .60   .60

Mahi Kavi Magh, 8th Cent. Poet — A1635

2009, Feb. 9   Photo.   Perf. 13
2313   A1635   5r multi   .60   .60

Postal Life Insurance, 125th Anniv. — A1636

Perf. 13¾ Syncopated
2009, Feb. 11   Litho.
2314   A1636   5r multi   .60   .60

Vallabh Suri (1870-1954), Jain Religious Leader — A1637

2009, Feb. 21
2315   A1637   5r multi   .60   .60

Harakh Chand Nahata (1936-99), Film Financer — A1638

2009, Feb. 28
2316   A1638   5r multi   .70   .70

Medical Council of India, 75th Anniv. — A1639

2009, Mar. 1   Photo.   Perf. 13
2317   A1639   5r multi   .60   .60

Pterospermum Acerifolium Tree and Flower — A1640

2009, Mar. 6   Litho.
2318   A1640   5r multi   .60   .60

Baburao Puleshwar Shedmake, 19th Cent. Freedom Fighter — A1641

2009, Mar. 12
2319   A1641   5r multi   .60   .60

Dr. Krishna Kumar Birla (1918-2008), Industrialist A1642

2009, Mar. 13
2320   A1642   5r multi   .60   .60

Spices A1643

No. 2321: a, Black pepper. b, Cinnamon. c, Cardamom d, Cloves. e, Turmeric, coriander and chili peppers.

2009, Apr. 29   Photo.
2321   Strip of 5   3.50   3.50
  a.-d.   A1643 5r Any single   .50   .50
  e.   A1643 20r multi   1.50   1.50
  f.   Souvenir sheet of 5, #2321a-2321e   4.75   4.75

R. Sankar (1909-72), Politician — A1644

Perf. 13¾ Syncopated
2009, Apr. 30   Litho.
2322   A1644   5r multi   .60   .60

Lifeline Express Hospital Train A1645

2009, May 12   Perf. 13
2323   A1645   5r multi   .60   .60

Madras Regiment, 250th Anniv. — A1646

Perf. 13¾ Syncopated
2009, May 28   Litho.   Unwmk.
2324   A1646   5r multi   .60   .60

Rev. J.J.M. Nichols Roy (1883-1959), Politician — A1647

2009, June 12   Photo.   Perf. 13
2325   A1647   5r multi   .60   .60

Sacred Heart Church, Pudducherry, Cent. — A1648

Perf. 13¾ Syncopated
2009, June 19
2326   A1648   5r multi   .25   .25

Raza Library, Rampur A1649

Ram, Laxman and Jatayu From Valmiki Ramayana, by Sumer Chand A1650

Madonna Holding Book A1651

Illustrated Page from Diwan-i-Hafiz of Akbar's Collection A1652

2009, June 19   Litho.
2327   A1649   5r multi   .55   .55
2328   A1650   5r multi   .55   .55
2329   A1651   5r multi   .55   .55
2330   A1652   5r multi   .55   .55
  a.   Souvenir sheet, #2327-2330   3.00   3.00
Nos. 2327-2330 (4)   2.20   2.20

Indian Oil Corporation, 50th Anniv. — A1653

2009, June 30   Perf. 13
2331   A1653   5r multi   .60   .60

Lal Bahadur Shastri Natl. Academy of Administration, Mussoorie, 50th Anniv. — A1654

2009, July 4   Photo.
2332   A1654   5r multi   .60   .60

Ramcharan Agarwal (1919-77), Politician — A1655

Perf. 13¾ Syncopated
2009, July 25   Litho.
2333   A1655   5r multi   .60   .60

A1656

INDIA

A1657

A1658

A1659

A1660

A1661

A1662

A1663

A1664

A1665

Scenes from Geetagovinda, Poem by Jayadeva — A1666

2009, July 27		Photo.	Perf. 13	
2334	Horiz. strip of 11		4.00	4.00
a.	A1656 5r multi		.35	.35
b.	A1657 5r multi		.35	.35
c.	A1658 5r multi		.35	.35
d.	A1659 5r multi		.35	.35
e.	A1660 5r multi		.35	.35
f.	A1661 5r multi		.35	.35
g.	A1662 5r multi		.35	.35
h.	A1663 5r multi		.35	.35
i.	A1664 5r multi		.35	.35
j.	A1665 5r multi		.35	.35
k.	A1666 5r multi		.35	.35
l.	Souvenir sheet, #2334a-2334k		5.00	5.00

St. Joseph's College, Bangalore — A1667

Perf. 13¾ Syncopated
2009, Aug. 1 Litho.
2335 A1667 5r multi .60 .60

Maharishi Patanjali, Compiler of Yoga Sutras — A1668

2009, Aug. 4 Perf. 13
2336 A1668 5r multi .60 .60

Pingali Venkaiah (1876-1963), Designer of Indian Flag — A1669

2009, Aug. 12 Photo. Perf. 13¼x13
2337 A1669 5r multi .60 .60

Railway Stations A1670

Designs: No. 2338, 5r, Howrah Station, Calcutta. No. 2339, 5r, Chennai Central Station. No. 2340, 5r, Mumbai CST (Chhatrapati Shivaji Terminus). No. 2341, 5r, Old Delhi Station.

2009, Aug. 16 Litho. Perf. 13
2338-2341 A1670 Set of 4 2.00 2.00
2341a Souvenir sheet, #2338-2341 3.25 3.25

Uttam Kumar (1926-80), Actor — A1671

Perf. 13¾ Syncopated
2009, Sept. 3 Litho.
2342 A1671 5r multi .60 .60

Sacred Heart Matriculation Higher Secondary School, Chennai — A1672

2009, Sept. 9 Photo. Perf. 13
2343 A1672 5r multi .60 .60

Holy Cross Church, Mapranam A1673

Perf. 13¾ Syncopated
2009, Sept. 14 Litho.
2344 A1673 5r multi .60 .60

Dushyant Kumar (1933-75), Writer — A1674

2009, Sept. 27 Perf. 13¼x13
2345 A1674 5r multi .60 .60

Mammals A1675

Designs: No. 2346, 5r, Red panda. No. 2347, 5r, Marbled cat, vert. No. 2348, 5r, Barbe's leaf monkey, vert.

Perf. 13¾ Syncopated
2009, Oct. 1 Litho.
2346-2348 A1675 Set of 3 1.50 1.50
2348a Souvenir sheet, #2346-2348 3.00 3.00

Mahatma Gandhi — A1676

Wmk. 324
2009, Oct. 2 Photo. Perf. 13¼
2349 A1676 25r multi 1.40 1.40

Bishop Cotton School, Shimla A1677

Unwmk.
2009, Oct. 6 Litho. Perf. 13
2350 A1677 5r multi .60 .60

R.K. Narayan (1906-2001), Writer — A1678

Perf. 13¼
2009, Oct. 10 Litho. Unwmk.
2351 A1678 5r multi .60 .60

Dineshnandini Dalmia (1928-2007), Writer — A1679

Perf. 13¾ Syncopated
2009, Oct. 11 Litho.
2352 A1679 5r multi .60 .60

India Post Airplane — A1680

2009, Oct. 12 Litho. Perf. 13¼x13
2353 A1680 5r multi .70 .70

Temples A1681

Designs: No. 2354, 5r, Dilwara Temple. No. 2355, 5r, Ranakpur Temple.

2009, Oct. 14 Perf. 13
2354-2355 A1681 Set of 2 1.25 1.25

Gulab Singh (1792-1857), First Maharaja of Jammu and Kashmir — A1682

Perf. 13¾ Syncopated
2009, Oct. 21 Litho.
2356 A1682 5r multi .60 .60

Major General Dewan Misri Chand (1907-70), Pilot — A1683

2009, Oct. 22
2357 A1683 5r multi .60 .60

Canonization of Jeanne Jugan — A1684

No. 2358: a, 5r, Little Sisters of the Poor Home for the Aged, Bangalore (40x32mm). b, 20r, St. Jeanne Jugan (1792-1879), Founder of Little Sisters of the Poor (29x32mm).

2009, Oct. 29 Perf. 13
2358 A1684 Horiz. pair, #a-b 1.25 1.25

Dr. Rajkumar (1929-2006), Actor — A1685

2009, Nov. 1
2359 A1685 5r multi .60 .60

Dr. Mahendra Lal Sircar (1833-1904), Founder of Indian Association for the Cultivation of Science — A1686

2009, Nov. 2 Perf. 13¾
2360 A1686 5r multi .60 .60

Apollo Hospitals — A1687

2009, Nov. 2
2361 A1687 5r multi .60 .60

Danmal Mathur, Scouting Leader — A1688

2009, Nov. 7 Photo. Perf. 13x13¼
2362 A1688 5r multi .60 .60

INDIA

Virchand Raghavji Gandhi (1864-1901), Representative of Jains at 1893 World Parliament of Religions — A1689

2009, Nov. 8   Litho.   Perf. 13
2363   A1689   5r multi   .60   .60

Horse Breeds — A1690

Designs: No. 2364, 5r, Kathiawan. No. 2365, 5r, Marwari. No. 2366, 5r, Zanskari. No. 2367, 5r, Manipuri.

2009, Nov. 9   Perf. 13¾ Syncopated
2364-2367   A1690   Set of 4   1.75   1.75
2367a   Souvenir sheet, #2364-2367   3.00   3.00

Rajabhau Khobragade (1925-84), Politician A1691

2009, Nov. 11
2368   A1691   5r multi   .60   .60

Gaurishankar Dalmia (1910-88), Magazine Publisher — A1692

2009, Nov. 12   Perf. 13¼
2369   A1692   5r multi   .60   .60

British Commonwealth, 60th Anniv. — A1693

2009, Nov. 13   Perf. 13
2370   A1693   5r multi   .60   .60

Children's Day — A1694

Designs: No. 2371, 5r, Deer at pond. No. 2372, 5r, Tiger.

2009, Nov. 14   Perf. 13¼
2371-2372   A1694   Set of 2   1.25   1.25

Silent Valley National Park A1695

2009, Nov. 15   Perf. 13
2373   A1695   5r multi   .60   .60
   a. Souvenir sheet of 1   2.25   2.25

Marine Life A1696

No. 2374: a, 5r, Gangetic dolphin. b, 20r, Butanding.

2009, Nov. 16
2374   A1696   Horiz. pair, #a-b   1.25   1.25
   c. Souvenir sheet, #2374a-2374b   3.00   3.00
See Philippines Nos. 3246-3247.

Ganpatrao Govindrao Jadhav (1908-87), Newspaper Publisher A1697

2009, Nov. 18   Perf. 13¼
2375   A1697   5r multi   .60   .60

Tamil Nadu Police, 150th Anniv. A1698

2009, Nov. 30   Perf. 13
2376   A1698   5r multi   .50   .50

A1699   A1700

A1701

Greetings — A1702

2009, Dec. 1
2377   A1699   5r multi   .50   .50
2378   A1700   5r multi   .50   .50
2379   A1701   5r brown   .50   .50
2380   A1702   5r multi   .50   .50
   a. Souvenir sheet, #2377-2380   2.50   2.50
   Nos. 2377-2380 (4)   2.00   2.00

Convent of Jesus and Mary, Ambala Cantonment, Cent. — A1703

2009, Dec. 2
2381   A1703   5r multi   .70   .70

Second Lancers (Gardiner's Horse) Regiment A1704

2009, Dec. 2   Perf. 13¼
2382   A1704   5r multi   .70   .70

Traditional Textiles — A1705

Designs: No. 2383, 5r, Kalamkari. No. 2384, 5r, Apa Tani weaves. No. 2385, 5r, Kanchipuram silk. No. 2386, 5r, Banaras silk.

2009, Dec. 10   Perf. 13
2383-2386   A1705   Set of 4   2.25   2.25
2386a   Souvenir sheet, #2383-2386   3.00   3.00

Henry Louis Vivian Derozio (1809-31), Poet — A1706

2009, Dec. 15   Perf. 13x13¼
2387   A1706   5r multi   .60   .60

Lal Pratap Singh, Prince of Kalakankar — A1707

Perf. 13¾ Syncopated
2009, Dec. 17
2388   A1707   5r multi   .60   .60

Preservation of Polar Regions and Glaciers — A1708

Designs: No. 2389, 5r, Penguins. No. 2390, 5r, Polar bear.

2009, Dec. 19   Perf. 13
2389-2390   A1708   Set of 2   1.25   1.25
2390a   Souvenir sheet, #2389-2390   2.00   2.00

Indian Mathematical Society, Cent. — A1709

2009, Dec. 27   Perf. 13¼
2391   A1709   5r multi   .70   .70

Venkataramana Bhagavathar (1781-1874), Composer — A1710

2009, Dec. 27   Perf. 13¾
2392   A1710   5r multi   .60   .60

Maharaja Surajmal (1707-63), Ruler of Bharatpur — A1711

Perf. 13¾ Syncopated
2009, Dec. 29
2393   A1711   5r multi   .60   .60

20th Conference of Speakers and Presiding Officers of the Commonwealth, New Delhi — A1712

2010, Jan. 5   Perf. 13¼
2394   A1712   5r multi   .60   .60

Reserve Bank of India, 75th Anniv. A1713

2010, Jan. 16   Perf. 13
2395   A1713   5r multi   .60   .60

Election Commission of India, 60th Anniv. — A1714

2010, Jan. 25   Litho.
2396   A1714   5r multi   .60   .60

Bible Society of India, Bicent. — A1715

2010, Feb. 21   Photo.   Perf. 13x13¼
2397   A1715   5r multi   .60   .60

P. C. Sorcar (1913-71), Magician — A1716

2010, Feb. 23   Litho.
2398   A1716   5r multi   .70   .70

16th Punjab (2nd Patiala) Regiment A1717

2009, Mar. 19   Photo.   Perf. 13¼x13
2399   A1717   5r multi   .50   .50

Muthuramalinga Sethupathi (1760-1809), King of Ramanathapuram A1718

2010, Mar. 30   Perf. 13x13¼
2400   A1718   5r multi   .60   .60

Special Protection Group A1719

2010, Mar. 30   Litho.   Perf. 13
2401   A1719   5r multi   .60   .60

Vallal Pachaiyappa (1754-94), Philantropist A1720

2010, Mar. 31   Photo.   Perf. 13¼x13
2402   A1720   5r multi   .60   .60

INDIA

Signs of the Zodiac — A1721

Designs: No. 2403, 5r, Aries. No. 2404, 5r, Taurus. No. 2405, 5r, Gemini. No. 2406, 5r, Cancer, vert. No. 2407, 5r, Leo, vert. No. 2408, 5r, Virgo, vert. No. 2409, 5r, Libra. No. 2410, 5r, Scorpio. No. 2411, 5r, Sagittarius. No. 2412, 5r, Capricorn, vert. No. 2413, 5r, Aquarius. vert. No. 2414, 5r, Pisces, vert.

Perf. 13¼x13, 13x13¼

2010, Apr. 14		Litho.		
2403-2414	A1721	Set of 12	6.00	6.00
2414a		Souvenir sheet, #2403-2414, perf. 13	7.00	7.00

Chandra Shekhar (1927-2007), Prime Minister — A1722

2010, Apr. 17	Photo.		Perf. 13x13¼	
2415	A1722	5r multi	.60	.60

Kanwar Ram Sahib (1885-1939), Religious Leader — A1723

2010, Apr. 26		Litho.		
2416	A1723	5r multi	.60	.60

Velu Thampi (1765-1809), Prime Minister of Travancore — A1724

2010, May 6		Perf. 13x13¼		
2417	A1724	5r multi	.60	.60

Robert Caldwell (1814-91), Bishop and Linguist — A1725

2010, May 7		Photo.		
2418	A1725	5r multi	.60	.60

Dr. Guduru Venkata Chalam (1909-67), Agricultural Scientist — A1726

2010, May 8		Litho.		
2419	A1726	5r multi	.60	.60

Indian Post Offices A1727

Post offices in: No. 2420, 5r, Lucknow. No. 2421, 5r, Cooch Behar. No. 2422, 5r, Nagpur. No. 2423, 5r, Udagamandalam. No. 2424, 5r, Delhi. No. 2425, 5r, Shimla.

2010, May 13		Litho.	Perf. 13	
2420-2425	A1727	Set of 6	3.00	3.00
2425a		Souvenir sheet, #2420-2425	5.00	5.00

Indipex 2011 World Philatelic Exhibition, New Delhi.

C. V. Raman Pillai (1858-1922), Writer — A1728

2010, May 19	Photo.	Perf. 13x13¼		
2426	A1728	5r multi	.60	.60

Intl. Year of Biodiversity — A1729

Designs: 5r, Owl, sunflower, people in rice paddy. 20r, Birds, crab, water lilies.

Perf. 13¾ Syncopated

2010, June 5		Litho.		
2427-2428	A1729	Set of 2	1.50	1.50
2428a		Souvenir sheet, #2427-2428	4.00	4.00

Deshbandhu Gupta (1905-51), Politician and Journalist A1730

2010, June 14				
2429	A1730	5r multi	.60	.60

2010 Commonwealth Games, Delhi — A1731

Map and: 5r, Tiger mascot holding torch. 20r, Hand holding torch, mascot running with torch.

2010, June 25	Photo.	Perf. 13		
2430-2431	A1731	Set of 2	1.50	1.50
2431a		Souvenir sheet, #2430-2431	4.00	4.00

Kumaraguruparar Swamigal (1625-88), Poet — A1732

Perf. 13¾ Syncopated

2010, June 27		Litho.		
2432	A1732	5r multi	.60	.60

World Classical Tamil Conference, Kovai — A1733

2010, June 27	Photo.	Perf. 13x13¼		
2433	A1733	5r multi	.60	.60

Indian Naval Air Squadron 300, 50th Anniv. — A1734

Perf. 13¾ Syncopated

2010, July 7		Litho.		
2434	A1734	5r multi	.60	.60

Birds — A1735

Designs: No. 2435, 5r, Pigeons. No. 2436, 5r, Sparrows.

2010, July 9		Litho.	Perf. 13	
2435-2436	A1735	Set of 2	1.10	1.10
2436a		Souvenir sheet of 2, #2435-2436	3.00	3.00

Rath Yatra Festival, Puri — A1736

2010, July 12	Photo.	Perf. 13		
2437	A1736	5r multi	.60	.60
a.		Souvenir sheet of 1		

Stadia for 2010 Commonwealth Games, Delhi — A1737

Designs: No. 2438, 5r, Jawaharlal Nehru Stadium. No. 2439, 5r, Talkatora Stadium.

2010, Aug. 1		Litho.	Perf. 13	
2438-2439	A1737	Set of 2	1.25	1.25
2439a		Souvenir sheet, #2438-2439	3.25	3.25

Syed Mohammed Ali Shihab Thangal (1936-2009), Politician — A1738

Perf. 13¾ Syncopated

2010, Aug. 2		Litho.		
2440	A1738	5r multi	.60	.60

Vethathiri (1911-2006), Founder of World Community Service Center — A1739

2010, Aug. 14				
2441	A1739	5r multi	.60	.60

P. Jeevanandham (1907-63), Tamil Communist Leader — A1740

Perf. 13¾ Syncopated

2010, Aug. 21		Litho.		
2442	A1740	5r multi	.60	.60

Omanthur P. Ramaswamy Reddiar (1895-1970), Politician — A1741

2010, Aug. 25				
2443	A1741	5r multi	.60	.60

G. K. Moopanar (1931-2001), Politician and Philanthropist — A1742

2010, Aug. 30	Photo.	Perf. 13x13¼		
2444	A1742	5r multi	.60	.60

Dr. Y. S. Rajasekhara Reddy (1949-2009), Politician — A1743

2010, Sept. 2		Litho.	Perf. 13¾x14	
2445	A1743	5r multi	.60	.60

Brihadeeswarar Temple, Thanjavur A1744

Perf. 13¾ Syncopated

2010, Sept. 26				
2446	A1744	5r multi	.60	.60

Sports of 2010 Commonwealth Games, Delhi — A1745

Designs: No. 2447, 5r, Badminton. No. 2448, 5r, Archery. No. 2449, 5r, Field hockey. No. 2450, 5r, Track.

2010, Oct. 3		Perf. 13¾ Syncopated		
2447-2450	A1745	Set of 4	1.50	1.50
2450a		Souvenir sheet, #2447-2450	4.75	4.75

Feudatory States Stamps — A1746

Designs: No. 2451, 5r, Indore #2, type A6, vignette of #1. No. 2452, 5r, Sirmoor #22, 2, 13. No. 2453, 5r, Bamra type A2, revenue stamp. No. 2454, 5r, Cochin #15, type A4.

2010, Oct. 6		Perf. 13¼x13		
2451-2454	A1746	Set of 4	1.50	1.50
2454a		Souvenir sheet, #2451-2454, perf. 13	4.75	4.75

Indipex 2011 World Philatelic Exhibition, New Delhi (No. 2454a).

INDIA

Doon School, Dehradun, 75th Anniv. — A1747

2010, Oct. 22   *Perf. 13¾ Syncopated*
2455   A1747   5r multi   .60   .60

Sant Shadaram Sahib (1708-93), Religious Leader — A1748

2010, Oct. 25   *Perf. 13x13¼*
2456   A1748   5r multi   .60   .60

Cathedral and John Connon School, Mumbai, 150th Anniv. — A1749

2010, Oct. 27   *Perf. 13¼x13*
2457   A1749   5r multi   .60   .60

Kranti Trivedi (1930-2009), Writer — A1750

2010, Oct. 29   *Perf. 13x13¼*
2458   A1750   5r multi   .60   .60

K. A. P. Viswanatham (1899-1994), Medical Writer — A1751

2010, Nov. 10   *Perf. 13¼x13*
2459   A1751   5r multi   .60   .60

Children's Day — A1752

Designs: No. 2460, 5r, Dolls depicting women carrying baskets on heads. No. 2461, 5r, Kite. No. 2462, 5r, Tops. No. 2463, 5r, Dolls depicting women in native costumes (28x38mm).

Perf. 13¼, 13x13¼ (#2463)
2010, Nov. 14
2460-2463   A1752   Set of 4   1.50   1.50
2463a   Souvenir sheet, #2460-2463, perf. 13   4.00   4.00

Lakshmipat Singhania (1910-76), Industrialist A1753

Perf. 13¾ Syncopated
2010, Nov. 15
2464   A1753   5r multi   .60   .60

Comptroller and Auditor General of India, 150th Anniv. — A1754

2010, Nov. 16   *Photo.*   *Perf. 13x13¼*
2465   A1754   5r multi   .60   .60

Chidambaram Subramaniam (1910-2000), Statesman A1755

Perf. 13¾ Syncopated
2010, Nov. 28   *Litho.*
2466   A1755   5r multi   .60   .60

Kamlapat Singhania (1884-1937), Industrialist — A1756

2010, Dec. 1
2467   A1756   5r multi   .60   .60

Performing Artists — A1757

Designs: No. 2468, 5r, Thanjavur Balasaraswathi (1918-84), dancer. No. 2469, 5r, T. N. Rajarathinam Pillai (1898-1956), musician. No. 2470, 5r, Veenai Dhanammai (1867-1938), musician, horiz.

2010, Dec. 3
2468-2470   A1757   Set of 3   1.75   1.75

Sri Sri Borda (1911-94), Philosopher — A1758

2010, Dec. 6   *Photo.*   *Perf. 13x13¼*
2471   A1758   5r multi   .60   .60

Prafulla Chandra Chaki (1888-1908), Assassin of British Colonialists — A1759

2010, Dec. 11
2472   A1759   5r multi   .70   .70

Dances — A1760

Designs: 5r, Jarabe Tapatío (Mexican Hat dance), Mexico. 20r, Kalbelia dance, India.

2010, Dec. 15   *Litho.*   *Perf. 13*
2473-2474   A1760   Set of 2   2.00   2.00
2474a   Souvenir sheet of 2, #2473-2474, perf. 13¼ syncopated   4.00   4.00
See Mexico No. 2726.

Crafts Museum, New Delhi — A1761

Designs: No. 2475, 5r, Tiger. No. 2476, 5r, Figurines of two men and dog.

2010, Dec. 21   *Litho.*   *Perf. 13*
2475-2476   A1761   Set of 2   1.25   1.25
2476a   Souvenir sheet of 2, #2475-2476   3.00   3.00

Yashwantrao Balwantrao Chavan (1913-84), Politician — A1762

2010, Dec. 22   *Photo.*   *Perf. 13x13¼*
2477   A1762   5r multi   .60   .60

Bhausaheb Hiray (1905-61), Social Reformer A1763

2010, Dec. 22   *Litho.*   *Perf. 13¼x13*
2478   A1763   5r multi   .60   .60

Central Bank of India, Cent. — A1764

Perf. 13¾ Syncopated
2010, Dec. 23
2479   A1764   5r multi   .60   .60

Bhai Jeevan Singh (1649-1705), Sikh Warrior — A1765

2010, Dec. 23   *Perf. 13x13¼*
2480   A1765   5r multi   .60   .60

A1766

No. 2481: a, National Council of Education Building (39x29mm). b, Dr. Triguna Sen (1905-98), educator.

2010, Dec. 24   *Perf. 13¼*
2481   A1766   5r Horiz. pair, #a-b   1.00   1.00

Immanuel Sekaranar (1924-57), Social Reformer — A1767

2010, Dec. 31   *Perf. 13¾*
2482   A1767   5r multi   .60   .60

National Academy of Art, New Delhi — A1768

Perf. 13¼ Syncopated
2010, Dec. 31
2483   A1768   5r multi   .60   .60

Doot Magazine, Cent. — A1769

2011, Jan. 15   *Perf. 13¼x13*
2484   A1769   5r multi   .60   .60

Krishnadevaraya (d. 1529), Vijayanagara Emperor A1770

2011, Jan. 27   *Perf. 13¼ Syncopated*
2485   A1770   5r multi   .60   .60
   a.   Souvenir sheet of 1   3.00   3.00

Chaudhary Ranbir Singh (1914-2009), Politician A1771

2011, Feb. 1   *Perf. 13¾ Syncopated*
2486   A1771   5r multi   .60   .60

Mary Ward (1585-1645), Nun and Educational Buildings — A1772

2011, Feb. 2   *Perf. 13¼ Syncopated*
2487   A1772   5r multi   .60   .60
Loreto Institutions founded by Ward, 400th anniv.

Army Corps of Signals, Cent. — A1773

2011, Feb. 4   *Perf. 13*
2488   A1773   5r multi   .70   .70

V. Subbiah (1911-93), Communist Leader — A1774

2011, Feb. 7   *Perf. 13¾ Syncopated*
2489   A1774   5r multi   .60   .60

2011 Census — A1775

2011, Feb. 8   *Litho.*
2490   A1775   5r multi   .60   .60

INDIA

V. Venkatasubba Reddiar (d. 1981), Politician
A1776

Perf. 13¾ Syncopated
2011, Feb. 11
2491 A1776 5r multi .60 .60

The souvenir sheet above was issued in limited quantities and sold for well above the face value of the stamp. Value, $17.50.

First Airmail Flight, Cent. — A1777

Designs: No. 2492, 5r, Henri Pequet (1888-1974), pilot for first airmail flight, his airplane, newspaper clipping. No. 2493, 5r, Covers and cancels. No. 2494, 5r, Map of first flight, fort, vert. (32x58mm). No. 2495, 5r, Airplane, cancel, boat, vert. (32x58mm).

Perf. 13¼x13, 13 (#2494-2495)
2011, Feb. 12
2492-2495 A1777 Set of 4 2.00 2.00
2495a Souvenir sheet of 4, #2492-2495 3.50 3.50

Taj Mahal A1778

Aries A1779

Taurus A1780

Gemini A1781

Cancer A1782

Leo A1783

Virgo A1784

Libra A1785

Scorpio A1786

Sagittarius — A1787

Capricorn — A1788

Aquarius A1789

Pisces A1790

Trains A1791

Aircraft A1792

Fables A1793

Wildlife A1794

No. 2509: a, 1WP/1, 1963. b, 2 WDM 2, 1963. c, 1 GIP NO 1, 1853. d, 1 F/1, 1895.
No. 2510: a, LCA-Tejas airplane. b, Dhruv helicopter with red paint at top of fuselage. c, Dhruv helicopter with camouflage paint. d, HT-2 airplane.
No. 2511: a, The Lion and the Rabbit. b, The Monkey and the Crocodile. c, The Crows and the Snake. d, The Tortoise and the Geese.
No. 2512: a, Indian lion. b, Indian elephant. c, Tiger. d, Rhinoceros.

2011, Feb. 12 **Perf. 13**
2496 A1778 5r multi + label 3.00 3.00
2497 A1779 5r multi + label 3.00 3.00
2498 A1780 5r multi + label 3.00 3.00
2499 A1781 5r multi + label 3.00 3.00
2500 A1782 5r multi + label 3.00 3.00
2501 A1783 5r multi + label 3.00 3.00
2502 A1784 5r multi + label 3.00 3.00
2503 A1785 5r multi + label 3.00 3.00
2504 A1786 5r multi + label 3.00 3.00
2505 A1787 5r multi + label 3.00 3.00
2506 A1788 5r multi + label 3.00 3.00
2507 A1789 5r multi + label 3.00 3.00
2508 A1790 5r multi + label 3.00 3.00
2509 A1791 5r Block of 4, #a-d, + 4 labels 8.00 8.00
2510 A1792 5r Block of 4, #a-d, + 4 labels 8.00 8.00
2511 A1793 5r Block of 4, #a-d, + 4 labels 8.00 8.00
2512 A1794 5r Block of 4, #a-d, + 4 labels 8.00 8.00
Nos. 2496-2512 (17) 71.00 71.00

Indipex 2011, New Delhi. Nos. 2496-2508 were each printed in sheets of 12 + 12 labels. Nos. 2509-2512 were each printed in sheets containing 3 blocks of 4 + 12 labels. Each sheet sold for 150r and labels could be personalized. Compare types A1779-A1790 with type A1727, type A1791 with type A439, and type A1793 with type A1295.

Film Actresses A1795

Designs: No. 2513, 5r, Devika Rani (1908-94). No. 2514, 5r, Nutan (1936-91). No. 2515, 5r, Kanan Devi (1916-92). No. 2516, 5r, Savithri (1935-81). No. 2517, 5r, Meena Kumari (1932-72). No. 2518, 5r, Leela Naidu (1940-2009).

2011, Feb. 13 **Perf. 13¼x13**
2513-2518 A1795 Set of 6 2.50 2.50
2518a Souvenir sheet of 6, #2513-2518 3.50 3.50

La Martiniere Schools, 175th Anniv. — A1796

2011, Mar. 1 **Perf. 13¾ Syncopated**
2519 A1796 5r multi .60 .60

Subhadra Joshi (1919-2003), Politician A1797

2011, Mar. 23 **Perf. 13¼x13**
2520 A1797 5r multi .60 .60

Chitralekha Magazine, 61st Anniv. — A1798

2011, Apr. 20 **Perf. 13¾ Syncopated**
2521 A1798 5r multi .60 .60

Umrao Kunwar Ji Archana (1922-2009), Hospital Founder — A1799

2011, Apr. 30
2522 A1799 5r multi .60 .60

Rabindranath Tagore (1861-1941), Poet — A1800

Designs: No. 2523, 5r, Tagore writing. No. 2524, 5r, Tagore, flower.

2011, May 7 **Perf. 13**
2523-2524 A1800 Set of 2 1.10 1.10
2524a Souvenir sheet of 2, #2523-2524 2.00 2.00

Second Africa-India Forum Summit, Addis Ababa, Ethiopia A1801

Designs: 5r, Asian elephants. 25r, African elephants.

2011, May 25 **Perf. 13¼x13**
2525-2526 A1801 Set of 2 2.50 2.50
2526a Souvenir sheet of 2, #2525-2526 3.50 3.50

Dr. Daulat Singh Kothari (1906-93), Physicist A1802

2011, July 6 **Perf. 13¾ Syncopated**
2527 A1802 5r multi .65 .65

United Theological College, Bangalore, 101st Anniv. — A1803

Perf. 13¼x13 Syncopated
2011, July 8
2528 A1803 5r multi .60 .60

Vitthal Sakharam Page (1910-90), Politician A1804

2011, July 21 **Perf. 13¼x13**
2529 A1804 5r multi .60 .60

Kasu Brahmananda Reddy (1909-94), Politician — A1805

2011, July 28 **Perf. 13¾ Syncopated**
2530 A1805 5r multi .60 .60

K. M. Mathew (1917-2010), Journalist — A1806

2011, Aug. 1 **Litho.**
2531 A1806 5r multi .65 .65

Rashtrapati Bhavan (Presidential Palace), New Delhi — A1807

Designs: No. 2532, 5r, Elephant statues. No. 2533, 5r, Flag over central dome. No. 2534, 5r, Latticed stone screen. No. 2535, 5r, Rashtrapati Bhavan, horiz. (87x35mm).

INDIA

2011, Aug. 5   *Perf. 13x13¼*
2532-2535 A1807 Set of 4   1.60   1.60
2535a   Souvenir sheet of 4, #2532-2535, perf. 13   3.00   3.00

Pandit K. Santanam (1885-1949), Life Insurance Company Founder — A1808

2011, Aug. 25   *Photo.*   *Perf. 13¼x13*
2536 A1808 5r multi   .75   .75

Dr. Madhav Srihari Aney (1880-1968), Politician — A1809

2011, Aug. 29   *Litho.*   *Perf. 13x13¼*
2537 A1809 5r multi   .65   .65

Surendranath Jauhar (1903-86), Founder of Youth and National Integration Camps A1810

2011, Sept. 2   *Perf. 13*
2538 A1810 5r multi   .65   .65

Dev Narayan, Rajasthan Folk Deity A1811

Tejaji Maharaj, Rajasthan Folk Deity A1812

2011, Sept. 7   *Perf. 13¾ Syncopated*
2539 A1811 5r multi   .65   .65
2540 A1812 5r multi   .65   .65

Tripuraneni Gopichand (1910-62), Writer — A1813

2011, Sept. 8   *Litho.*
2541 A1813 5r multi   .65   .65

Jaimalji Maharaj (1708-96), Religious Leader — A1814

2011, Sept. 25   *Litho.*   *Perf. 13¼*
2542 A1814 5r multi   .65   .65

Trained Nurses Association of India, 103rd Anniv. — A1815

Perf. 13¾ Syncopated
2011, Sept. 30
2543 A1815 5r multi   .65   .65

Chitrapur Math (Community Temple) — A1816

2011, Oct. 9
2544 A1816 5r multi   .65   .65

Punjab Regiment — A1817

Perf. 13¼ & 13¾ Syncopated x13¼
2011, Oct. 12
2545 A1817 5r multi   .65   .65

Indian Council of Medical Research, Cent. — A1818

2011, Nov. 8   *Perf. 13¾ Syncopated*
2546 A1818 5r multi   .65   .65

Children's Day — A1819

Designs: 5r, Tiger. 20r, Tiger, diff.

2011, Nov. 14   *Photo.*   *Perf. 13x13¼*
2547-2548 A1819 Set of 2   1.25   1.25
2548a   Souvenir sheet of 2, #2547-2548   4.00   4.00

Grand Masonic Lodge of India, New Delhi, 50th Anniv. — A1820

2011, Nov. 25   *Litho.*   *Perf. 13x13¼*
2549 A1820 5r multi   1.00   1.00

Cleft Palate Surgery of Smile Train Charity — A1821

2011, Dec. 6   *Perf. 13¼x13*
2550 A1821 5r multi   .70   .70

Kavi Pradeep (1915-98), Songwriter — A1822

2011, Dec. 14   *Photo.*   *Perf. 13x13¼*
2551 A1822 5r multi   .65   .65

President's Fleet Review, Mumbai — A1823

Designs: No. 2552, 5r, Submarine. No. 2553, 5r, Warship. No. 2554, 5r, President's yacht. No. 2555, 5r, Airplane.

Perf. 13¼ & 13¾ Syncopated x13¼
2011, Dec. 19   *Litho.*
2552-2555 A1823 Set of 4   2.00   2.00

Liberation of Goa, 50th Anniv. — A1824

2011, Dec. 19   *Perf. 13¼x13*
2556 A1824 5r multi   .70   .70

Archaeological Survey of India, 150th Anniv. — A1825

Designs: 5r, Zoomorphic figurines. 20r, Archaeological artifacts.

Perf. 13¾ Syncopated
2011, Dec. 20
2557-2558 A1825 Set of 2   1.25   1.25
2558a   Souvenir sheet of 2, #2557-2558   3.50   3.50

Chhatrapati Shahuji Maharaj Medical University (King George's Medical College), Lucknow, Cent. — A1826

2011, Dec. 23   *Perf. 13*
2559 A1826 5r multi   .65   .65

Srinivasa Ramanujan (1887-1920), Mathematician — A1827

Perf. 13¾ Syncopated
2011, Dec. 26
2560 A1827 5r multi   .75   .75

Madan Mohan Malaviya (1861-1946), President of Indian National Congress — A1828

2011, Dec. 27   *Perf. 13x13¼*
2561 A1828 5r multi   .65   .65

Puran Chandra Gupta (1912-86), Newspaper Publisher A1829

2012, Jan. 2   *Photo.*   *Perf. 13¼x13*
2562 A1829 5r multi   .65   .65

Bhai Jagta Ji, 19th Century Sikh Saint — A1830

2012, Jan. 15   *Perf. 13x13¼*
2563 A1830 5r multi   .65   .65

Shyam Narayan Singh (1901-68), Politician — A1831

2012, Jan. 24
2564 A1831 5r multi   .65   .65

Dedication of India International Center, New Delhi, 50th Anniv. A1832

2012, Feb. 9   *Litho.*   *Perf. 13*
2565 A1832 5r multi   .65   .65

Employees' State Insurance Corporation A1833

Perf. 13¾ Syncopated
2012, Feb. 24
2566 A1833 5r multi   .65   .65

Vasantdada Patil (1917-89), Politician — A1834

2012, Mar. 1
2567 A1834 5r multi   .65   .65

Shyama Charan Shukla (1925-2007), Politician — A1835

2012, Mar. 9   *Photo.*   *Perf. 13x13¼*
2568 A1835 5r multi   .65   .65

Civil Aviation in India, Cent. — A1836

Designs: No. 2569, 5r, Helicopter in flight above terminal, airplane on ground. No. 2570, 5r, Terminal, airplanes on ground and in flight, air traffic controllers. No. 2571, 5r, Control tower, airplanes on ground and in flight, members of runway crew. 20r, Early airplane.

2012, Mar. 14   *Perf. 13*
2569-2572 A1836 Set of 4   2.25   2.25
2572a   Souvenir sheet of 4, #2569-2572   4.25   4.25

INDIA

Isabella Thoburn College, Lucknow, 125th Anniv. (in 2011) — A1837

		Perf. 13¾ Syncopated		
2012, Apr. 12		*Litho.*		
2573	A1837	5r multi	.65	.65

Godiji Temple, Mumbai, 200th Anniv. — A1838

2012, Apr. 17		*Photo.*	*Perf. 13x13¼*
2574	A1838	5r multi	.75 .75

Pres. Ramaswamy Venkataraman (1910-2009) — A1839

2012, Apr. 18			
2575	A1839	5r multi	.65 .65

Karpoor Chandra Kulish (1926-2006), Founder of Rajasthan Patrika Newspaper A1840

		Perf. 13¾ Syncopated		
2012, May 16		*Litho.*		
2576	A1840	5r multi	.65	.65

M. B. Kadadi (1909-92), Founder of Sangameshwar College, Solapur — A1841

2012, May 17			
2577	A1841	5r multi	.65 .65

800th Urs of Moinuddin Chishti, Dargah Sharif, Ajmer — A1842

Designs: 5r, Muslims seated. 20r, Dargah.

2012, May 27			
2578-2579	A1842	Set of 2	1.50 1.50
2579a		Souvenir sheet of 2, #2578-2579	3.50 3.50

Warli Painting A1843

Shekhawati Painting A1844

		Perf. 13¼ Syncopated		
2012, June 20				
2580	A1843	5r red brown	.50	.50
2581	A1844	20r multi	1.10	1.10
a.		Sheet of 16, 8 each #2580-2581	15.00	15.00

2012, Summer Olympics, London — A1845

Designs: No. 2582, 5r, Rowing. No. 2583, 5r, Sailboarding. No. 2584, 20r, Volleyball. No. 2585, 20r, Badminton.

2012, July 25			*Perf. 13¼x13*
2582-2585	A1845	Set of 4	2.00 2.00
2585a		Souvenir sheet of 4, #2582-2585, perf. 13	5.25 5.25

Customs Act, 50th Anniv. — A1846

2012, July 26	*Photo.*	*Perf. 13x13¼*
2586	A1846	5r multi	.65 .65

Durga Prasad Chaudhary, Newspaper Publisher — A1847

		Perf. 13¾ Syncopated		
2012, July 31		*Litho.*		
2587	A1847	5r multi	.65	.65

Armed Forces Medical College, Pune, 50th Anniv. A1848

2012, Aug. 4		*Perf. 13¼*
2588	A1848	5r multi	.70 .70

Husain Ahmad Madani (1879-1957), Islamic Scholar — A1849

2012, Aug. 29		*Perf. 13x13¼*
2589	A1849	5r multi	.65 .65

Motilal Nehru (1861-1931), President of Indian National Congress — A1850

2012, Sept. 25		*Photo.*
2590	A1850	5r multi	.65 .65

Indo-Tibetan Border Police Force, 50th Anniv. — A1851

2012, Oct. 1	*Litho.*	*Perf. 13¼x13*
2591	A1851	5r multi	.65 .65

AWACS (Airborne Warning and Control System) Airplane — A1852

2012, Oct. 8			
2592	A1852	5r multi	.65 .65

Souvenir Sheet

India Nos. 6c and 200 A1853

2012, Oct. 12		*Perf. 13*
2593	A1853	20r multi	2.50 2.50

Philately Day.

Fauna — A1854

Designs: No. 2594, 5r, Nicobar megapode. No. 2595, 5r, Hoolock gibbon. No. 2596, 5r, Venated gliding frog. 25r, Bugun liocichla.

2012, Oct. 16		*Perf. 13¾*
2594-2597	A1854	Set of 4	2.00 2.00
2597a		Souvenir sheet of 4, #2594-2597	4.75 4.75

Flowers A1855

Designs: No. 2598, 5r, Lilies. No. 2599, 5r, Pansies. No. 2600, 5r, Cinerarias. No. 2601, 5r, Dahlias.

2012, Oct. 19	*Litho.*	*Perf. 13*
		Stamps + Label
2598-2601	A1855	Set of 4	17.50 17.50

Nos. 2598-2601 each were printed in sheets of 12 + 12 labels. Labels could be personalized. Generic labels depict various flowers.

Deepavali, Hindu Festival of Lights — A1856

Hanukkah, Jewish Festival of Lights — A1857

		Perf. 13¾ Syncopated		
2012, Nov. 5		*Litho.*		
2602	A1856	5r multi	.65	.65
2603	A1857	5r multi	.65	.65

See Israel Nos. 1956-1957.

T.S. Narayanawami (1911-68), Industrialist — A1858

2012, Nov. 11		*Perf. 13x13¼*
2604	A1858	5r multi	.65 .65

Children's Day — A1859

		Perf. 13¾ Syncopated		
2012, Nov. 14				
2605	A1859	5r multi	.65	.65

Scinde Horse Cavalry Regiment A1860

2012, Nov. 16		*Perf. 13¼x13*
2606	A1860	5r multi	.65 .65

Ramgopal Maheshwari (1911-99), Newspaper Publisher — A1861

2012, Nov. 20		*Perf. 13¼*
2607	A1861	5r multi	.65 .65

Consumer Protection Act of 1986 — A1862

		Perf. 13¾ Syncopated		
2012, Nov. 29				
2608	A1862	5r multi	.65	.65

Sri Shivarathri Shivayogi, 10th Century Saint — A1863

2012, Dec. 21		*Perf. 13x13¼*
2609	A1863	5r multi	.65 .65

Srinivasa Ramanujan (1887-1920), Mathematician A1864

2012, Dec. 22		*Perf. 13¼x13*
2610	A1864	5r multi	.65 .65

National Mathematics Day.

Lighthouses — A1865

Designs: 5r, Mahabalipuram Lighthouse. 20r, Alleppey Lighthouse.

2012, Dec. 23		*Perf. 13¼x13*
2611-2612	A1865	Set of 2	2.00 2.00
2612a		Souvenir sheet of 2, #2611-2612, perf. 13 syncopated	3.25 3.25

Indian Science Congress, Cent. — A1866

		Perf. 13¾ Syncopated		
2013, Jan. 3				
2613	A1866	5r multi	.65	.65

INDIA

Postgraduate Institute of Medical Education and Research, Chandigarh, 50th Anniv. A1867

2013, Jan. 7			Perf. 13¾x14
2614	A1867	5r multi	.65 .65

Ghadar Movement for Indian Independence, Cent. — A1868

2013, Jan. 8			Perf. 13x13¼
2615	A1868	5r multi	.65 .65

Uttar Pradesh Legislature, 125th Anniv. — A1869

2013, Jan. 8			Perf. 13¼x13
2616	A1869	5r multi	.65 .65

Silk Letter Movement for Indian Independence, Cent. — A1870

2013, Jan. 11			Perf. 13x13¼
2617	A1870	5r multi	.65 .65

A1871

A1872

A1873

Swami Vivekananda (1863-1902), Hindu Monk — A1874

2013, Jan. 12	Litho.		Perf. 13
2618	A1871	5r multi	.35 .35
2619	A1872	5r multi	.35 .35
2620	A1873	5r multi	.35 .35
2621	A1874	20r multi	1.00 1.00
	Nos. 2618-2621 (4)		2.05 2.05

Chelat Achyutha Menon (1913-91), Politician — A1875

2013, Jan. 13			Perf. 13x13¼
2622	A1875	5r multi	.65 .65

Aditya Vikram Birla (1943-95), Industrialist A1876

2013, Jan. 14			Perf. 13¾ Syncopated
2623	A1876	5r multi	.65 .65

Basilica of Our Lady of Good Health, Vailankanni A1877

2013, Jan. 22			Perf. 13¾
2624	A1877	5r multi	.65 .65

Third Battalion of Special Forces Parachute Regiment, Bicent. — A1878

2013, Mar. 2			Perf. 13¾ Syncopated
2625	A1878	5r multi	.65 .65

Officers Training Academy, Chennai, 50th Anniv. — A1879

2013, Mar. 7			Perf. 13x13¼
2626	A1879	5r multi	.65 .65

Sahir Ludhianvi (1921-80), Poet and Lyricist — A1880

2013, Mar. 8			Perf. 13¾ Syncopated
2627	A1880	5r multi	.65 .65

Malayala Manorama Newspaper, 125th Anniv. — A1881

2013, Mar. 16		Litho.	
2628	A1881	5r multi	.65 .65

Jhulelal Sahib, Sindhi God — A1882

2013, Mar. 17			
2629	A1882	5r multi	.65 .65

Shiv Ram Hari Rajguru (1908-31), Revolutionist A1883

2013, Mar. 22			Perf. 13¼x13
2630	A1883	5r multi	.65 .65

Architectural Heritage of Srikakulam — A1884

Designs: 5r, Srikurmam Temple. 20r, Arasavalli Temple.

2013, Apr. 11			Perf. 13¾ Syncopated
2631-2632	A1884	Set of 2	1.25 1.25
2632a		Souvenir sheet of 2, #2631-2632	3.25 3.25

Post Office Centenaries A1885

Designs: No. 2633, 5r, Mumbai General Post Office. No. 2634, 5r, Agra Head Post Office.

2013, Apr. 12			Perf. 13¼x13
2633-2634	A1885	Set of 2	1.00 1.00
2634a		Souvenir sheet of 2, #2633-2634, perf. 13	2.25 2.25

Chaitya Bhoomi, Mumbai, and B. R. Ambedkar (1891-1956), Law Minister — A1886

2013, Apr. 14			Perf. 13¼x13
2635	A1886	5r multi	.70 .70

Hari Singh Nalwa (1791-1837), General, Governor of Kashmir, Peshawar and Nazara — A1887

2013, Apr. 30			Perf. 13¾ Syncopated
2636	A1887	5r multi	.65 .65

Indian Cinema, Cent. A1888

No. 2637, 5r: a, Allu Ramalingiah (1922-2004), actor. b, Ashok Mehta (1947-2012), cinematographer. c, Balraj Sahni (1913-73), actor. d, Bhanumathi (1925-2005), actress. e, C. V. Sridhar (1933-2008), director. f, Chetan Anand (1921-97), director. g, Kamaal Amrohi (1918-93), director. h, Geeta Dutt (1930-72), singer.
No. 2638, 5r: a, Kannadasan (1927-81), lyricist. b, Madan Mohan (1924-75), music director. c, Mehmood (1932-2004), actor. d, Motilal (1910-65), actor. e, Nagesh (1933-2009), actor. f, O. P. Nayyar (1926-2007), music director. g, Prem Nazir (1926-89), actor. h, R. D. Burman (1939-94), music director.
No. 2639, 5r: a, Raj Khosla (1925-91), director. b, Rajendra Kumar (1929-99), actor. c, Rajesh Khanna (1942-2012), actor. d, S. V. Ranga Rao (1918-74), actor. e, Salil Chowdhury (1922-95), music director. f, Sanjeev Kumar (1938-85), actor. g, Shailendra (1923-66), lyricist. h, Shakeel Badayuni (1916-70), lyricist.
No. 2640, 5r: a, Shammi Kapoor (1930-2011), actor. b, Shankar Singh Raghuvanshi (1922-87), and Jaikishan Dayabhai Panchal (1929-71), composers. c, Smita Patil (1955-86), actress. d, Suraiya (1929-2004), actress. e, Tarachand Barjatya (1914-92), producer. f, T. R. Sundaram (1907-63), actor. g, Utpal Dutt (1929-93), actor. h, Vishnu Vardhan (1950-2009), actor.
No. 2641, 5r: a, Ashok Kumar (1911-2001), actor. b, B. N. Sircar (1901-80), producer. c, B. R. Chopra (1914-2008), director. d, Bhalji Pendharkar (1897-1994), director. e, Bhupen Hazarika (1926-2011), lyricist. f, Dev Anand (1923-2011), actor. g, Dhirendranath Ganguly (1893-1978), director. h, Durga Khote (1905-91), actress. i, Hrishikesh Mukherjee (1922-2006), director.
No. 2642, 5r: a, Majrooh Sultanpuri (1919-2000), lyricist. b, Naushad (1919-2006), music director. c, Nitin Bose (1897-1986), director. d, Prithviraj Kapoor (1901-72), actor. e, Raichand Boral (1903-81), director. f, Ruby Myers (1907-83), actress. g, Sohrab Modi (1897-1984), actor. h, Tapan Sinha (1924-2009), director. i, Yash Chopra (1932-2012), director.

2013, May 3		Perf. 13¾ Syncopated	Litho.
		Sheets of 8, #a-h	
2637-2640	A1888	Set of 4	11.00 11.00
		Sheets of 9, #a-i	
2641-2642	A1888	Set of 2	6.50 6.50

Wild Asses — A1889

Designs: 5r, Kiang, Ladakh Region. 20r, Ghor Khar, Kutch Region.

2013, May 10		Perf. 13¾ Syncopated	Litho.
2643-2644	A1889	Set of 2	1.25 1.25
2644a		Souvenir sheet of 2, #2643-2644	3.50 3.50

Securities and Exchange Board of India — A1890

2013, May 24	Litho.		Perf. 13¼x13
2645	A1890	5r multi	.65 .65

Peerzada Ghulam Ahmad Mejhoor (1885-1952), Poet — A1891

2013, June 25	Litho.		Perf. 13¼x13
2646	A1891	5r multi	.65 .65

Delhi Gymkhana Club, Cent. — A1892

2013, July 3	Litho.		Perf. 13¼x13
2647	A1892	5r multi	.65 .65

Kerala Legislative Assembly A1893

2013, Aug. 7	Litho.		Perf. 13
2648	A1893	5r multi	.65 .65

Raj Bahadur (1912-90), Politician — A1894

2013, Aug. 21	Litho.		Perf. 13x13¼
2649	A1894	5r multi	.65 .65

INDIA

Miniature Sheet

Flowers — A1895

No. 2650: a, Dibang chirita. b, Kashmir mallow. c, Himalayan mini-sunflower. d, Himalayan lantern. e, Roundleaf asiabell. f, Blue poppy. g, Globe thistle. h, Himalayan iris. i, Himalayan bellflower. j, Cobra lily. k, Bladder campion. l, Rhododendron.

2013, Sept. 3	Litho.	Perf. 13	
2650 A1895 5r Sheet of 12, #a-l		2.25	2.25
m.	Souvenir sheet of 4, #2650c, 2650f, 2650g, 2650l, perf. 13x13¼	2.25	2.25
n.	Souvenir sheet of 4, #2650d, 2650e, 2650h, 2650i, perf. 13x13¼	2.25	2.25
o.	Souvenir sheet of 4, #2650a, 2650b, 2650j, 2650k, perf. 13x13¼	2.25	2.25

Asian-Pacific Postal Union Congress, New Delhi.

Lala Jagat Narain (1899-1981), Politician and Newspaper Publisher — A1896

2013, Sept. 9	Litho.	Perf. 13x13¼
2651 A1896 5r multi		.65 .65

Acharya Gyansagar (1891-1973), Poet — A1897

Perf. 13¾ Syncopated

2013, Sept. 10		Litho.
2652 A1897 5r multi		.65 .65

Gurajada Venkata Apparao (c. 1861-1915), Writer — A1898

2013, Sept. 21	Litho.	Perf. 13x13¼
2653 A1898 5r multi		.65 .65

Pratap Narayan Mishra (1856-94), Writer — A1899

2013, Sept. 24	Litho.	Perf. 13x13¼
2654 A1899 5r multi		.65 .65

Joomdev (1921-96), Founder of Social Welfare Organizations — A1900

2013, Sept. 30	Litho.	Perf. 13x13¼
2655 A1900 5r multi		.65 .65

Souvenir Sheet

Mahatma Gandhi (1869-1948), India Nos. 205 and 498 — A1901

2013, Oct. 12	Litho.	Perf. 13
2656 A1901 20r multi		2.25 2.25

Philately Day.

Bhakra Dam, 50th Anniv. — A1902

2013, Oct. 22	Litho.	Perf. 13¼x13
2657 A1902 5r multi		.65 .65

Ruchi Ram Sahni (1863-1948), Scientist and Politician — A1903

2013, Oct. 24	Litho.	Perf. 13x13¼
2658 A1903 5r multi		.65 .65

Boys' High School, Allahabad — A1904

2013, Nov. 5	Litho.	Perf. 13¼x13
2659 A1904 5r multi		.65 .65

K. M. Munshi (1887-1971), Founder of Bharatiya Vidya Bhavan (Indian Educational Trust) — A1905

2013, Nov. 7	Litho.	Perf. 13
2660 A1905 5r multi		.65 .65

Indian Academy of Pediatrics, 50th Anniv. — A1906

2013, Nov. 8	Litho.	Perf. 13¼x13
2661 A1906 5r multi		.65 .65

Central Bureau of Investigation, 50th Anniv. — A1907

2013, Nov. 11	Litho.	Perf. 13¼x13
2662 A1907 5r multi		.65 .65

The Times of India Newspaper, 175th Anniv. — A1908

2013, Nov. 13	Litho.	Perf. 13x13¼
2663 A1908 5r multi		.65 .65

Children's Day — A1909

2013, Nov. 14	Litho.	Perf. 13¼x13
2664 A1909 5r multi		.65 .65

A1910

Retirement of Sachin Tendulkar, Cricket Player — A1911

2013, Nov. 14	Litho.	Perf. 13x13¼
2665 A1910 20r multi		.85 .85
2666 A1911 20r multi		.85 .85
a.	Souvenir sheet of 2, #2665-2666	3.75 3.75

Satya Sai Baba (1926-2011), Guru — A1912

2013, Nov. 23	Litho.	Perf. 13x13¼
2667 A1912 5r multi		.65 .65

Intelligence Bureau, 125th Anniv. — A1913

2013, Nov. 23	Litho.	Perf. 13x13¼
2668 A1913 5r multi		.65 .65

Locomotives and Railway Workshops — A1914

2013, Nov. 26	Litho.	Perf. 13¼x13
2669-2670 A1914	Set of 2	1.50 1.50
2670a	Souvenir sheet of 2, #2669-2670	3.25 3.25

Locomotive and: 5r, Kanchrapara Workshop. 20r, Jamalpur Workshop.

Railway workshops, 150th anniv. (in 2012).

Sashastra Seema Bal (Armed Border Force), 50th Anniv. — A1915

2013, Nov. 29	Litho.	Perf. 13¼x13
2671 A1915 5r multi		.70 .70

Nagaland, 50th Anniv. — A1916

Perf. 13¾ Syncopated

2013, Dec. 1		Litho.
2672 A1916 5r multi		.65 .65

Commissioning of Aircraft Carrier INS Vikramaditya — A1917

Perf. 13¾ Syncopated

2013, Dec. 4		Litho.
2673 A1917 5r multi		.65 .65

Souvenir Sheet

Qutub Minar, Delhi, and Tokyo Tower, Tokyo — A1918

Perf. 13¼ Syncopated

2013, Dec. 5		Litho.
2674 A1918 20r multi		3.00 3.00

State visit of Japanese Emperor Akihito and Empress Michiko.

Indian Institute of Foreign Trade, 50th Anniv. — A1919

2013, Dec. 10	Litho.	Perf. 13¼x13
2675 A1919 5r multi		.65 .65

Beant Singh (1924-95), Politician — A1920

Perf. 13¾ Syncopated

2013, Dec. 17		Litho.
2676 A1920 5r multi		.65 .65

Gulab Singh Lodhi (?-1935), Freedom Fighter — A1921

2013, Dec. 23	Litho.	Perf. 13x13¼
2677 A1921 5r multi		.65 .65

INDIA

Eklavya, Prince in the Mahabharata — A1922

2013, Dec. 27	**Litho.**	**Perf. 13x13¼**
2678	A1922 5r multi	.65 .65

Babu Banarsi Das (1912-85), Politician — A1923

2013, Dec. 31	**Litho.**	**Perf. 13x13¼**
2679	A1923 5r multi	.65 .65

Food Corporation of India, 49th Anniv. — A1924

Perf. 13¾ Syncopated

2014, Jan. 14		**Litho.**
2680	A1924 5r multi	.70 .70

International Year of Crystallography A1925

Perf. 13¾ Syncopated

2014, Jan. 30		**Litho.**
2681	A1925 20r multi	1.10 1.10

Souvenir Sheet

Indian Museum, Kolkata, 200th Anniv. A1926

No. 2682: a, 5r, Peacock (29x29mm). b, 20r, Museum (39x29mm). c, 20r, Archer on bull (29x29mm).

Perf. 13¾, 13¾ Syncopated (#2682b)

2014, Feb. 2		**Litho.**
2682	A1926 Sheet of 3, #a-c	2.50 2.50

Jagjit Singh (1941-2011), Musician — A1927

No. 2683: a, 5r, Singh (29x29mm). b, 20r, Singh with instrument (52x29mm).

2014, Feb. 8	**Litho.**	**Perf. 13**
2683	A1927 Horiz. pair, #a-b	1.25 1.25

Central Vigilance Commission, 50th Anniv. — A1928

Perf. 13¾ Syncopated

2014, Feb. 11		**Litho.**
2684	A1928 5r multi	.70 .70

Hasrat Mohani (1875-1951), Writer — A1929

Perf. 13¾ Syncopated

2014, Feb. 25		**Litho.**
2685	A1929 5r multi	.65 .65

National Council of Churches, Cent. — A1930

Perf. 13¾ Syncopated

2014, Apr. 25		**Litho.**
2686	A1930 5r multi	.65 .65

Chattampiswamikal (1853-1924), Social Reformer — A1931

Perf. 13¾ Syncopated

2014, Apr. 30		**Litho.**
2687	A1931 5r multi	.70 .70

Govind Ballabh Pant Hospital, Delhi, 50th Anniv. — A1932

Perf. 13¾ Syncopated

2014, Apr. 30		**Litho.**
2688	A1932 5r multi	.60 .60

Drukpa Lineage of Buddhism A1933

Perf. 13¾ Syncopated

2014, May 14		**Litho.**
2689	A1933 5r multi	.70 .70

2014 World Cup Soccer Championships, Brazil — A1934

Designs: No. 2690, 5r, Player readying shot on goal. No. 2691, 5r, Goalie diving for ball. No. 2692, 25r, Player making bicycle kick. No. 2693, 25r, Mascot.

2014, June 12	**Litho.**	**Perf. 13¼**
2690-2693	A1934 Set of 4	2.00 2.00
2693a	Souvenir sheet of 4, #2690-2693	7.50 7.50

Fairy Queen Locomotive — A1934a

Taj Mahal, Agra — A1934b

Red Fort, Delhi — A1934c

St. Francis Church, Goa — A1934d

Hawa Mahal, Jaipur — A1934e

Ajanta Caves, Aurangabad District — A1934f

Qutub Minar, Delhi — A1934h

Butterfly and Flower — A1934i

Mysore Palace at Night — A1934j

Mysore Palace in Daylight — A1934k

2014	**Litho.**	**Perf. 13, 13¾ (#2693l)**	
2693B	A1934a	5r multi + label	3.00 3.00
2693C	A1934b	5r multi + label	3.00 3.00
2693D	A1934c	5r multi + label	3.00 3.00
2693E	A1934d	5r multi + label	3.00 3.00
2693F	A1934e	5r multi + label	3.00 3.00
2693G	A1934f	5r multi + label	3.00 3.00
2693I	A1934h	5r multi + label	3.00 3.00
2693J	A1934i	5r multi + label	3.00 3.00
2693K	Horiz. pair + 2 labels		6.00 6.00
l.	A1934j 5r multi + label		3.00 3.00
m.	A1934k 5r multi + label		3.00 3.00
	Nos. 2693B-2693K (9)		30.00 30.00

Issued: No. 2693B, 7/16; Nos. 2693C-2693G, 8/4; Nos. 2693I-2693K, 8/5.

Nos. 2693B-2693G, 2693I-2693J were each printed in sheets of 12 + 12 labels. No. 2693K was printed in sheets of 12 containing 6 each of Nos. 2693l and 2693m + 12 labels. Each sheet sold for 300r. Labels could be personalized.

An additional stamp was issued in this set. The editors would like to examine any example of it.

Gaiety Theater Complex, Shimla, 125th Anniv. A1935

2014, Aug. 20	**Litho.**	**Perf. 13**
2694	A1935 5r multi	.65 .65

Musicians A1936

Designs: No. 2695, 5r, Damal Krishnaswamy Pattammal (1919-2009), singer. No. 2696, 5r, Gangubai Hangal (1913-2009), singer. No. 2697, 5r, Kumar Gandharva (1924-92), singer. No. 2698, 5r, Vilayat Khan (1928-2004), sitar player. No. 2699, 5r, Mallikarjun Mansur (1910-92), singer. No. 2700, 5r, Ali Akbar Khan (1922-2009), sarod player. No. 2701, 5r, Ravi Shankar (1920-2012), sitar player. No. 2702, 25r, Bhimsen Joshi (1922-2011), singer.

Perf. 13¾ Syncopated

2014, Sept. 3		**Litho.**
2695-2702	A1936 Set of 8	3.25 3.25
2702a	Sheet of 8, #2695-2702	9.50 9.50

Anagarika Dharmapala (1864-1933), Founder of Mahabodhi Society — A1937

Perf. 13¾ Syncopated

2014, Oct. 25		**Litho.**
2703	A1937 5r multi	.70 .70

Liver Transplantation in India, 15th Anniv. — A1938

Perf. 13¾ Syncopated

2014, Nov. 4		**Litho.**
2704	A1938 5r multi	.80 .80

Unit Trust of India, 50th Anniv. — A1939

Perf. 13¾ Syncopated

2014, Nov. 12		**Litho.**
2705	A1939 5r multi	.70 .70

Children's Art — A1940

Designs: 5r, Dancers, by Sara Zivkovic, Slovenia. 25r, Indian family and house, by Roshan V. Anvekar, India.

Perf. 13¾ Syncopated

2014, Nov. 28		**Litho.**
2706-2707	A1940 Set of 2	2.00 2.00
2707a	Souvenir sheet of 2, #2706-2707	4.25 4.25

See Slovenia No. 1097.

Sagol Kangjei, 150th Anniv. — A1941

Perf. 13¾ Syncopated

2014, Nov. 29		**Litho.**
2708	A1941 5r multi	.70 .70

Swami Ekrasanand Saraswati (1866-1938), Founder of Daivia Sampad Mandal — A1942

Perf. 13¾ Syncopated

2014, Dec. 4		**Litho.**
2709	A1942 5r multi	.70 .70

INDIA

Kendriya Vidyalaya Sanghthan, 50th Anniv. (in 2013) — A1943

Perf. 13¾ Syncopated
2014, Dec. 15 Litho.
2710 A1943 5r multi .70 .70

Kuka Movement A1944

Perf. 13¾ Syncopated
2014, Dec. 24 Litho.
2711 A1944 5r multi .70 .70

Baba Amte (1914-2008), Founder of Ashrams for Lepers — A1945

Perf. 13¾ Syncopated
2014, Dec. 30 Litho.
2712 A1945 5r multi .70 .70

Return of Mohandas Gandhi to India, Cent. — A1946

Gandhi and: 5r, Cover page of *Souvenir of the Passive Resistance Movement in South Africa 1906-1914.* 25r, Wife, Kasturba and ship.

Perf. 13¼ Syncopated
2015, Jan. 8 Litho.
2713-2714 A1946 Set of 2 2.00 2.00
2714a Souvenir sheet of 2, #2713-2714 4.25 4.25

Campaign to Eliminate Female Feticide and Increase Education of Girls — A1947

Perf. 13¾ Syncopated
2015, Jan. 22 Litho.
2715 A1947 5r multi .70 .70

A1948   A1949

Campaign to Clean India — A1950

Perf. 13¾ Syncopated
2015, Jan. 30 Litho.
2716 A1948 5r multi .40 .40
2717 A1949 5r multi .40 .40
2718 A1950 5r multi .40 .40
a. Souvenir sheet of 3, #2716-2718 2.75 2.75

Statue of Mahatma Gandhi A1951

Kite Festival A1952

Dandiya Dance A1953

2015, Jan. 7 Litho. **Perf. 13**
2719 A1951 5r multi + label 3.00 3.00
2720 A1952 5r multi + label 3.00 3.00
2721 A1953 5r multi + label 3.00 3.00
Nos. 2719-2721 (3) 9.00 9.00

Nos. 2719-2721 were printed in sheets of 12, containing 4 of each stamp, + 12 labels that could be personalized. Sheets sold for 300r.

Project Rukmani Military Satellite Communications System — A1954

Perf. 13¾ Syncopated
2015, Feb. 14 Litho.
2722 A1954 5r multi .70 .70

11th Cent. Emperor Rajendra Chola I and Ship on Indian Ocean — A1955

Perf. 13¾ Syncopated
2015, Mar. 20 Litho.
2723 A1955 5r multi .70 .70

Engineers India Limited, 50th Anniv. — A1956

Perf. 13¾ Syncopated
2015, Mar. 27 Litho.
2724 A1956 5r multi .70 .70

French and Indian Cooperation in Space, 50th Anniv. — A1957

Designs: 5r, Megha-Tropiques satellite. 25r, Saral satellite.

Perf. 13¾ Syncopated
2015, Apr. 10 Litho.
2725-2726 A1957 Set of 2 1.25 1.25
2726a Souvenir sheet of 2, #2725-2726 4.25 4.25
See France Nos. 4798-4799.

Patna High Court, Cent. A1958

Perf. 13¼x13 Syncopated
2015, Apr. 18 Litho.
2727 A1958 5r multi .70 .70

Old Seminary Theological College, Kottayam, 50th Anniv. — A1959

Perf. 13¾ Syncopated
2015, Apr. 21 Litho.
2728 A1959 5r multi .70 .70

International Day of Yoga — A1960

Perf. 13¾ Syncopated
2015, June 21 Litho.
2729 A1960 5r multi .70 .70
a. Souvenir sheet of 1 1.60 1.60

Godavari Pushkaram — A1961

2015, July 14 Litho. **Perf. 13**
2730 A1961 5r multi + label 3.00 3.00

No. 2730 was printed in sheets of 12 + 12 labels that could be personalized. Sheets sold for 300r.

Nabakalebara Ritual — A1962

Perf. 13¾ Syncopated
2015, July 17 Litho.
2731 A1962 5r multi .70 .70

Asoka the Great (304 B.C.-232 B.C.), Maurya Emperor — A1963

2015, Aug. 24 Litho. **Perf. 14½**
2732 A1963 5r multi .70 .70

A1964   Empowerment of Women — A1965

Designs: No. 2733, Mother and child, women in military, legal and medical professions. No. 2734, Women and elephant. No. 2735, Two women using laptop computer. No. 2736, Woman on bicycle, woman astronaut.

Perf. 14x13¼, 13¾ Syncopated (A1965)
2015, Sept. 2 Litho.
2733 A1964 5r multi .25 .25
a. Perf. 14x13¾ .80 .80
2734 A1965 5r multi .25 .25
2735 A1964 5r multi .25 .25
a. Perf. 14x13¾ .80 .80
2736 A1965 5r multi .25 .25
a. Souvenir sheet of 4, #2733a, 2734, 2735a, 2736 3.25 3.25
Nos. 2733-2736 (4) 1.00 1.00

10th World Hindi Conference, Bhopal — A1966

Perf. 13¾ Syncopated
2015, Sept. 10 Litho.
2737 A1966 5r multi .70 .70

India-Pakistan War, 50th Anniv. — A1967

Designs: No. 2738, 5r, Soldiers. No. 2739, 5r, Indian Navy ship. No. 2740, 5r, Airplane battle.

Perf. 13¾ Syncopated
2015, Sept. 15 Litho.
2738-2740 A1967 Set of 3 1.25 1.25

Dr. Bhimrao R. Ambedkar (1891-1956), Architect of Indian Constitution A1968

Perf. 13¾ Syncopated
2015, Sept. 30 Litho.
2741 A1968 5r multi .70 .70

Mahant Avaidyanath (1919-2014), Politician — A1969

Perf. 13¾ Syncopated
2015, Oct. 1 Litho.
2742 A1969 5r multi .70 .70

Dr. Avul Pakir Jainulabdeen Abdul Kalam (1931-2015), President of India and Space Program Administrator — A1970

2015, Oct. 15 Litho. **Perf. 14x13¾**
2743 A1970 5r multi .70 .70

Spinning Wheels — A1971

Inscriptions: No. 2744, 5r, Bardoli Charkha. No. 2745, 5r, Peti Charkha.

Perf. 13¾ Syncopated
2015, Oct. 15 Litho.
2744-2745 A1971 Set of 2 .80 .80
2745a Souvenir sheet of 2, #2744-2745 2.75 2.75

Border Security Force, 50th Anniv. — A1972

Perf. 13¾ Syncopated
2015, Oct. 21 Litho.
2746 A1972 5r multi .70 .70

Third India-Africa Forum Summit — A1973

Designs: No. 2747, 5r, Indian rhinoceros. No. 2748, 5r, African rhinoceros. No. 2749, 5r, Black buck. No. 2750, 5r, Thomson's gazelle. No. 2751, 25r, Indian lion. No. 2752, 25r, African lion.

INDIA

Perf. 13¾ Syncopated
2015, Oct. 29   Litho.
2747-2752   A1973   Set of 6   2.50   2.50
2752a   Souvenir sheet of 6, #2747-2752   6.00   6.00

A souvenir sheet like No. 2752a with foil application and embossing sold for 200r.

Famous People — A1974

Designs: 25p, Mahatma Gandhi (1869-1948). 50p, Subramania Bharati (1882-1921), writer. No. 2755, Deendayal Upadhyaya (1916-68), politician. No. 2756, Rajendra Prasad (1884-1963), first President of India. No. 2757, Shyama Prasad Mukherjee (1901-53), politician. No. 2758, Bhagat Singh (1907-31), revolutionary socialist. No. 2759, Ram Manohar Lohia (1910-67), independence activist. No. 2760, Swami Vivekananda (1863-1902), Hindu monk. No. 2761, Moulana Abul Kalam Azad (1888-1958), Minister of Education. No. 2762, Lal Bahadur Shastri (1904-66), Prime minister. No. 2763, Jayaprakash Narayan (1902-79), political leader.

Perf. 12¾x13
2015-16   Photo.   Wmk. 324
2753   A1974   25p slate lilac   .25   .25
2754   A1974   50p slate vio   .25   .25
2755   A1974   5r reddish lil   .25   .25
2756   A1974   5r chestnut   .25   .25
2757   A1974   5r dull mauve   .25   .25
2758   A1974   5r lt brown   .25   .25
2759   A1974   5r reddish pur   .25   .25
2760   A1974   5r brown   .25   .25
2761   A1974   5r mauve   .25   .25
2762   A1974   5r blue   .25   .25
2763   A1974   5r brn lake   .25   .25
Nos. 2753-2763 (11)   2.75   2.75

Issued: 25p, Jan. 2016; 50p, Feb. 2016; Nos. 2755-2561, Oct. 2015; Nos. 2762, 2763, Feb. 2016. Additional stamps were issued in this set. The editors would like to examine any examples.
See Nos. 2792-2802, 2804-2807.

First Gorkha Rifles, 200th Anniv. — A1975

Third Gorkha Rifles, 200th Anniv. — A1976

Perf. 13¾ Syncopated
2015, Nov. 2   Litho.   Unwmk.
2764   A1975   5r multi   .45   .45
2765   A1976   5r multi   .45   .45

Children's Day — A1977

Designs: 5r, Children playing in water. 25r, Children's drawing of children playing under rainbow.

Perf. 13¾ Syncopated
2015, Nov. 14   Litho.
2766-2767   A1977   Set of 2   1.25   1.25
2767a   Souvenir sheet of 2, #2766-2767   4.50   4.50

Bharat Heavy Electricals Limited, 51st Anniv. — A1978

Perf. 13¾ Syncopated
2015, Nov. 16   Litho.
2768   A1978   5r multi   .70   .70

Diplomatic Relations Between India and Singapore, 50th Anniv. — A1979

Presidential residences: 5r, Istana, Singapore. 25r, Rashtrapati Bhavan, India.

Perf. 13¾ Syncopated
2015, Nov. 24   Litho.
2769-2770   A1979   Set of 2   1.75   1.75

See Singapore Nos. 1758-1759. A perf. 12¾ example of No. 2770 is found in a souvenir sheet only sold in Singapore.

Engineering Export Promotion Council, 60th Anniv. — A1980

Perf. 13¾x13¼
2015, Nov. 24   Litho.
2771   A1980   5r multi   .70   .70

Zoological Survey of India, 99th Anniv. A1981

Designs: 5r, Lion, birds, antelope, bull. 25r, Elephant, antelope, peacock, tiger, leopard.

2015, Dec. 3   Litho.   Perf. 14½
2772-2773   A1981   Set of 2   1.25   1.25
2773a   Souvenir sheet of 2, #2772-2773   4.25   4.25

Sumitranandan Pant (1900-77), Poet — A1982

Perf. 13¼x13¾
2015, Dec. 23   Litho.
2774   A1982   5r multi   .70   .70

Alagumuthu Kone (1710-59), Freedom Fighter — A1983

Perf. 13¾x13¼
2015, Dec. 26   Litho.
2775   A1983   5r multi   .70   .70

Institute for Defense Studies and Analysis, 50th Anniv. — A1984

Perf. 13¼x13¾
2015, Dec. 30   Litho.
2776   A1984   5r multi   .70   .70

Income Tax Appellate Tribunal, 75th Anniv. — A1985

2016, Jan. 24   Litho.   Perf. 13¾x13¼
2777   A1985   5r multi   .25   .25

Souvenir Sheet

Vibrant India A1986

Perf. 13¾ Syncopated
2016, Jan. 25   Litho.
2778   A1986   25r multi   .75   .75

International Fleet Review — A1987

2016, Feb. 6   Litho.   Perf. 13¼x13¾
2779   A1987   5r multi   .25   .25

Stamps with Attached Labels

Beginning in 2016, Indian postal officials allowed "sponsored" stamps to be created. Such stamps, with attached labels much like earlier personalized stamp issues, could be designed by the sponsor (often a corporation), who would pay a fee for the printing of a minimum of 5,000 sheets of stamps (60,000 stamps total). While the sponsor may not receive the entire printing of the stamps, and some of these stamps, if not all, may be available from post offices, the sheets were sold at prices well above the face value of the stamps. Because the labels on the sheets were already printed with designs of the sponsor's choosing, it is presumed that any purchaser of a sheet could not have the sponsor-designed labels personalized with another image. Unlike normal commemorative and definitive stamps, information about these sponsored stamps is not provided to the editors by the India postal authorities. Listings for stamps with attached labels will be limited to items the editors believe had labels that could be personalized by the public, such as the items below.

Ellora Caves A1989

Victoria Memorial A1990

Ghats of Varanasi A1991

Ghats of Varanasi A1992

Perf. 13¼
2016, Feb. 15   Litho.   Unwmk.
2781   A1989   5r multi + label   1.60   1.60
2782   A1990   5r multi + label   1.60   1.60

Perf. 13¾ Syncopated
2783   A1991   5r multi + label   1.60   1.60
2784   A1992   5r multi + label   1.60   1.60
a.   Horiz. pair, #2783-2784, + 2 labels   3.20   3.20
Nos. 2781-2784 (4)   6.40   6.40

Nos. 2781 and 2782 were each printed in sheets of 12 + 12 labels that could be personalized. Nos. 2783-2784 were printed together in sheets of 12 (6 of each design) + 12 labels that could be personalized. Sheets sold for 300r.

Gateway of India A1993

Sun Temple, Konark A1994

Mahabodhi Temple — A1995

Perf. 13¾ Syncopated
2016, Feb. 29   Litho.
2785   A1993   5r multi + label   1.60   1.60
2786   A1994   5r multi + label   1.60   1.60

Perf. 13¾x13½
2787   A1995   5r multi + label   1.60   1.60
Nos. 2785-2787 (3)   4.80   4.80

Nos. 2785-2787 were each printed in sheets of 12 + 12 labels that could be personalized. Sheets sold for 300r.

Vasantrao Srinivassa Sinai Dempo (1916-2000), Industrialist — A1996

Perf. 13¾ Syncopated
2016, Mar. 4   Litho.
2788   A1996   5r multi   .25   .25

HeForShe Gender Equality Movement — A1997

No. 2789: a, 5r, Face at right. b, 25r, Face at left.

Perf. 13¾ Syncopated
2016, Mar. 8   Litho.
2789   A1997   Horiz. pair, #a-b   .90   .90
c.   Souvenir sheet of 2, #2789a-2789b, perf. 13¾x13¼   3.75   3.75

Intl. Women's Day.

National Archives of India, 125th Anniv. — A1998

Perf. 13¾ Syncopated
2016, Mar. 11   Litho.
2790   A1998   5r multi   .25   .25

Famous People Type of 2015-16 and

Yoga — A1999

Designs: 1r, Bal Gangadhar Tilak (1856-1920), independence activist. No. 2793, Madurai S. Subbulakshmi (1916-2004), Carnatic vocalist. No. 2794, Ravi Shankar (1920-

INDIA

2012), composer. 4r, Srinivasa Ramanujan (1887-1920), mathematician. No. 2795, Bismillah Khan (1916-2006), musician. No. 2796, Bhimsen Joshi (1922-2011), singer. No. 2798, Subhas Chandra Bose (1897-1945), nationalist leader. No. 2799, Sardar Vallabhbhai Patel (1875-1950), deputy prime minister. No. 2800, Dr. Bhimrao R. Ambedkar (1891-1956), politician. No. 2801, Jawaharlal Nehru (1889-1964), prime minister. No. 2802, Gopinath Bardoloi (1890-1950), Assamese politician. No. 2804, Chhtarapati Shri Shivaji Maharaj (c.1627-80), king. No. 2805, Maharana Pratap (1540-97), King of Mewar. 15r, Dr. A. P. J. Abdul Karam (1931-2015), 11th President of India. 50r, Rabindranath Tagore (1861-1941), 1913 Nobel Literature laureate.

Perf. 12¾x13
2016-20 Photo. Wmk. 324

2791	A1999	25p multi	.25	.25
2792	A1974	1r grnish gray	.25	.25
2793	A1974	3r chocolate	.25	.25
2794	A1974	3r deep claret	.25	.25
2795	A1974	3r brn rose	.25	.25
2796	A1974	3r dull pur	.25	.25
2797	A1974	4r green	.25	.25
2798	A1974	5r brown	.25	.25
2799	A1974	5r olive brown	.25	.25
2800	A1974	5r gray blue	.25	.25
2801	A1974	5r slate lil	.25	.25
2802	A1974	5r multi	.25	.25
2804	A1974	10r red brown	.25	.25
2805	A1974	10r dp turq blue	.30	.30
2806	A1974	15r violet ('19)	.45	.45
2807	A1974	50r brn pur ('20)	1.40	1.40
	Nos. 2791-2807 (16)		5.40	5.40

Issued: 1r, Nos. 2794, 2797, 2804, March. No. 2793, February. No. 2795, March; No. 2796, 6/16; No. 2798, April; No. 2799, 5/19; No. 2800, 5/25; Nos. 2801, 2805, June.

Additional stamps were issued in this set. The editors would like to examine any examples.

High Court of Allahabad, 150th Anniv. — A2000

No. 2808: a, 5r, Court building, Lucknow. b, 15r, Court building, Allahabad.

Perf. 13¾ Syncopated
2016, Mar. 13 Litho. Unwmk.

2808	A2000	Horiz. pair, a-b	.60	.60
c.		As "a", perf. 13¼x13¾	.85	.85
d.		As "b", perf. 13¼x13¾	.85	.85
e.		Souvenir sheet of 2, #2808c-2808d	3.25	3.25

Fire Services Day — A2001

Perf. 13¾ Syncopated
2016, Apr. 14 Litho.

2809	A2001	5r multi	.25	.25

Govardhanram Tripathi (1855-1907), Writer — A2002

Perf. 13¾ Syncopated
2016, Apr. 27 Litho.

2810	A2002	5r multi	.25	.25

Swami Chidananda (1916-2008), Religious Leader — A2003

2016, May 21 Litho. Perf. 13¾x13½

2811	A2003	5r multi	.25	.25

Tata Power, Cent. — A2004

Perf. 13½x13¾
2016, June 10 Litho.

2812	A2004	5r multi	.25	.25

Surya Namaskar — A2005

Designs: Nos. 2813, 2824, Pranamasana. Nos. 2814, 2823, Hastauttanasana. Nos. 2815, 2822, Padahastasana. Nos. 2816, 2821, Asvasanchalanasana, horiz. Nos. 2817, 2820, Parvatasana, horiz. No. 2818, Ashtanga Namaskara, horiz. No. 2819, Bhujangasana.

Perf. 13¾x13½, 13½x13¾
2016, June 20 Litho.

2813	A2005	5r multi	.25	.25
2814	A2005	5r multi	.25	.25
2815	A2005	5r multi	.25	.25
2816	A2005	5r multi	.25	.25
a.		Perf. 13¾ syncopated	.55	.55
2817	A2005	5r multi	.25	.25
a.		Perf. 13¾ syncopated	.55	.55
2818	A2005	5r multi	.25	.25
a.		Perf. 13¾ syncopated	.55	.55
2819	A2005	25r multi	.75	.75
a.		Perf. 13¾ syncopated	2.60	2.60
2820	A2005	25r multi	.75	.75
a.		Perf. 13¾ syncopated	2.60	2.60
2821	A2005	25r multi	.75	.75
a.		Perf. 13¾ syncopated	2.60	2.60
2822	A2005	25r multi	.75	.75
2823	A2005	25r multi	.75	.75
2824	A2005	25r multi	.75	.75
a.		Souvenir sheet of 12, #2813-2815, 2316a-2321a, 2322-2324	12.50	12.50
	Nos. 2813-2324 (12)		6.00	6.00

Bombay Stock Exchange, 140th Anniv. — A2006

Perf. 13¾ Syncopated
2016, July 9 Litho.

2825	A2006	5r multi	.25	.25

Tigers From Tadoba Andhari National Park — A2007

Designs: 5r, Two adults. 25r, Adult and cub, horiz.

Perf. 13¾ Syncopated
2016, July 29 Litho.

2826	A2007	5r multi	.25	.25
a.		Perf. 13¾x13½	.75	.75
2827	A2007	25r multi	.65	.65
a.		Perf. 13½x13¾	3.50	3.50
b.		Souvenir sheet of 2, #2826a, 2827a	4.25	4.25

2016 Summer Olympics, Rio de Janeiro — A2008

Designs: No. 2828, 5r, Badminton. No. 2829, 5r, Boxing. No. 2830, 25r, Shooting. No. 2831, 25r, Wrestling.

Perf. 13 Syncopated
2016, Aug. 5 Litho.

2828-2831	A2008	Set of 4	1.90	1.90
2831a		Souvenir sheet of 4, #2828-2831	6.75	6.75

Orchids — A2009

Designs: No. 2832, 5r, Esmerelda cathcartii. No. 2833, 5r, Paphiopedilum villosum. No. 2834, 15r, Dendrobium gibsonii. No. 2835, 15r, Esmerelda clarkei. No. 2836, 25r, Cypripedium himalacium. No. 2837, 25r, Dendrobium falconeri.

Perf. 13¾ Syncopated
2016, Aug. 8 Litho.

2832-2837	A2009	Set of 6	2.75	2.75
2837a		Souvenir sheet of 4, #2832-2837	9.50	9.50

Souvenir Sheet

Tourist Sites in India — A2010

Perf. 13½x13¾
2016, Aug. 15 Litho.

2838	A2010	25r multi	.75	.75

Independence Day.

Metal Crafts — A2011

Designs: No. 2839, 5r, Iron surahi. No. 2840, 5r, Bronze Nataraja. No. 2841, 15r, Copper pandan. No. 2842, 15r, Brass incense burner. No. 2843, 25r, Silver spouted lota. No. 2844, 25r, Gold Gajalakshmi lamp.

Perf. 13 Syncopated
2016, Aug. 26 Litho.

2839-2844	A2011	Set of 6	2.75	2.75
2844a		Souvenir sheet of 6, #2839-2844	9.50	9.50

Jagadguru Sri Shivarathri Rajendra Swamy (1916-86), Religious Leader — A2012

Perf. 13¾ Syncopated
2016, Aug. 27 Litho.

2845	A2012	5r multi	.25	.25

Souvenir Sheet

Canonization of St. Teresa of Calcutta (Mother Teresa) — A2013

2016, Sept. 4 Litho. Perf. 13¾x13½

2846	A2013	50r multi	1.50	1.50

Lady Hardinge Medical College, New Delhi, Cent. — A2014

Perf. 13½x13¾
2016, Sept. 23 Litho.

2847	A2014	5r multi	.25	.25

Swachh Bharat (Campaign to Clean India) — A2015

Winning art in stamp design contest depicting: 5r, People cleaning street. 25r, Sun, flowers, waves, water, hills.

Perf. 13¾ Syncopated
2016, Oct. 2 Litho.

2848	A2015	5r multi	.25	.25
a.		Perf. 13¾x13½	.65	.65
2849	A2015	25r multi	.65	.65
a.		Perf. 13¾x13½	3.25	3.25
b.		Souvenir sheet of 2, #2848a, 2849a	4.00	4.00

Central Water and Power Research Station, Bombay, Cent. — A2016

Perf. 13¾ Syncopated
2016, Oct. 4 Litho.

2850	A2016	5r multi	.25	.25

Introduction of C-130J Super Hercules Aircraft, 5th Anniv. — A2017

Perf. 13¾ Syncopated
2016, Oct. 6 Litho.

2851	A2017	5r multi	.25	.25

Threatened Birds — A2018

Designs: 5r, Nicobar pigeon. 10r, Nilgiri flycatcher. 15r, Andaman woodpecker. 25r, Black and orange flycatcher.

2016, Oct. 17 Litho. Perf. 13¾x13½

2852	A2018	5r multi	.25	.25
2853	A2018	10r multi	.30	.30

Perf. 13¾ Syncopated

2854	A2018	15r multi	.45	.45
a.		Perf. 13¾x13½	2.10	2.10
2855	A2018	25r multi	.75	.75
a.		Perf. 13¾x13½	3.50	3.50
b.		Souvenir sheet of 4, #2852-2853, 2854a, 2855a	6.25	6.25
	Nos. 2852-2855 (4)		1.75	1.75

Renaming of Banaras to Varanasi, 60th Anniv. — A2019

Perf. 13¾ Syncopated
2016, Oct. 24 Litho.

2856	A2019	5r multi	.25	.25

Sardar Vallabhbhai Patel (1875-1950), Deputy Prime Minister — A2020

Perf. 13¾ Syncopated
2016, Oct. 31 Litho.

2857	A2020	10r multi	.25	.25

National Unity Day.

INDIA

Haryana State, 50th Anniv. — A2021

Perf. 13¾ Syncopated
2016, Nov. 1   Litho.
2858   A2021   5r multi   .25   .25

Children's Day — A2022

Picnic scenes with "Children's Day" in: No. 2859, Royal blue. No. 2860, Red, horiz.

Perf. 13¾x13½
2016, Nov. 14   Litho.   Unwmk.
2859   A2022   15r multi   .45   .45
Perf. 13½x13¾
2860   A2022   15r multi   .45   .45
   a.   Perf. 13¾ Syncopated   .70   .70
   b.   Souvenir sheet of 2, #2859, 2860a   1.50   1.50

Third Battalion of the Garhwal Rifles, Cent. — A2023

Perf. 13¾x13½
2016, Nov. 19   Litho.
2861   A2023   5r multi   .25   .25

All India Institute of Medical Sciences, 60th Anniv. — A2024

Perf. 13¾ Syncopated
2016, Dec. 3   Litho.
2862   A2024   5r multi   .25   .25

Birds — A2025

Designs: No. 2863, 5r, Cape parrot. No. 2864, 5r, Blue-throated macaw, vert. No. 2865, 10r, Hyacinth macaw. No. 2866, 10r, Sun conure, vert. No. 2867, 15r, Lesser sulphur-crested cockatoo. No. 2868, 15r, Magnum Amazon.

Perf. 13¾ Syncopated
2016, Dec. 5   Litho.
2863-2868   A2025   Set of 6   1.75   1.75
2867a   Souvenir sheet of 3, #2863, 2865, 2867   3.50   3.50
2868a   Souvenir sheet of 3, #2864, 2866, 2868   3.50   3.50

A2026

No. 2869: a, 5r, Pramukh Swami Maharaj (1921-2016), religious leader (39x39mm). b, 15r, Akshardham Temple, New Delhi (52x39mm).

2016, Dec. 7   Litho.   Perf. 14¼
2869   A2026   Horiz. pair, #a-b   .60   .60

Acharya Vimal Sagar (1916-94), Jain Monk — A2027

Perf. 13¾ Syncopated
2016, Dec. 14   Litho.
2870   A2027   5r multi   .25   .25

Samrat Vikramadittya, Legendary Emperor of India — A2028

Perf. 13¾x13½
2016, Dec. 22   Litho.
2871   A2028   5r multi   .25   .25

Christmas — A2029

Designs: 10r, Christmas tree and gifts. 20r, Santa Claus, reindeer and sleigh, horiz.

Perf. 13¾ Syncopated
2016, Dec. 23   Litho.
2872   A2029   10r multi   .30   .30
   a.   Perf. 13¾x13¼   1.50   1.50
2873   A2029   20r multi   .60   .60
   a.   Perf. 13¼x13¾   2.75   2.75
   b.   Souvenir sheet of 2, #2872a, 2873a   4.25   4.25

Hardayal Municipal Heritage Public Library — A2030

Perf. 13¾ Syncopated
2016, Dec. 26   Litho.
2874   A2030   5r multi   .25   .25

Sachchidananda Sinha (1871-1950), Politician A2031

Kunwar Singh (1777-1858), Leader of Rebellion of 1857 A2032

Dashrath Manjhi (1934-2007), Mountain Path Builder A2033

Kailashpati Mishra (1923-2012), Politician A2034

Karpoori Thakur (1920-88), Politician A2035

Vidyapati (1352-1448), Writer A2036

Phanishwar Nath Renu (1921-77), Writer A2037

Sri Krishna Sinha (1887-1961), Politician A2038

Perf. 13¾ Syncopated
2016, Dec. 26   Litho.
2875   A2031   5r multi   .25   .25
2876   A2032   5r multi   .25   .25
2877   A2033   5r multi   .25   .25
2878   A2034   5r multi   .25   .25
2879   A2035   5r multi   .25   .25
2880   A2036   5r multi   .25   .25
Perf. 13¾x13¼
2881   A2037   5r multi   .25   .25
2882   A2038   5r multi   .25   .25
Nos. 2875-2882 (8)   2.00   2.00

Famous men of Bihar.

Deendayal Upadhyaya (1916-68), Politician — A2039

Perf. 13¾x13½
2016, Dec. 29   Litho.
2883   A2039   10r multi   .30   .30

Singers — A2040

Designs: No. 2884, Talat Mahmood (1924-98). No. 2885, Manna Dey (1919-2013). No. 2886, Mohammed Rafi (1924-80). No. 2887, Kishore Kumar (1929-87). No. 2888, Mukesh (1923-76). No. 2889, Hemant Kumar (1920-89). No. 2890, Bhupen Hazarika (1926-2011). No. 2891, Geeta Dutt (1930-72). No. 2892, T. M. Soundararajan (1922-2013). No. 2893, Shamshad Begum (1919-2013).

Perf. 13¾ Syncopated
2016, Dec. 30   Litho.
2884   A2040   5r multi   .25   .25
   a.   Perf. 13¾x13½   .30   .30
2885   A2040   5r multi   .25   .25
   a.   Perf. 13¾x13½   .30   .30
2886   A2040   5r multi   .25   .25
   a.   Perf. 13¾x13½   .30   .30
2887   A2040   5r multi   .25   .25
   a.   Perf. 13¾x13½   .30   .30
2888   A2040   5r multi   .25   .25
   a.   Perf. 13¾x13½   .30   .30
2889   A2040   5r multi   .25   .25
   a.   Perf. 13¾x13½   .30   .30
2890   A2040   5r multi   .25   .25
   a.   Perf. 13¾x13½   .30   .30
2891   A2040   5r multi   .25   .25
   a.   Perf. 13¾x13½   .30   .30
2892   A2040   5r multi   .25   .25
   a.   Perf. 13¾x13½   .30   .30
2893   A2040   5r multi   .25   .25
   a.   Perf. 13¾x13½   .30   .30
   b.   Souvenir sheet of 10, #2884a-2893a   3.00   3.00
Nos. 2884-2893 (10)   2.50   2.50

Miniature Sheet

New Year 2017 A2041

No. 2894: a, Ganesh Pol. b, Pashmina wool shawl. c, Chhau mask. d, Worship of the Bodhi Tree sculpture, Sanchi Stupa Complex. e, Sarota. f, Peacock Gate decoration, Chandra Mahal. g, Chaitya Hall, Karle. h, Thanjavur painting. i, Blue pottery. j, Stained-glass window, Bagore-Ki-Haveli, Udaipur. k, Peitra Dura table top. l, Zardozi carpet.

Perf. 13 Syncopated
2017, Jan. 1   Litho.
2894   A2041   25r Sheet of 12, #a-l   12.00   12.00

A calendar with each page bearing one each of Nos. 2894a-2894l in a larger size sold for 1000r.

Sikh Temple — A2042

2017, Jan. 5   Litho.   Perf. 14½
2895   A2042   10r multi   .30   .30
   a.   Souvenir sheet of 1   .70   .70

Guru Gobind Singh (1666-1708), 10th Sikh guru.

Dancers — A2043

Designs: 5r, Dandiya dancers, India. 25r, Pauliteiros dancers, Portugal.

2017, Jan. 7   Litho.   Perf. 13½x13¾
2896   A2043   5r multi   .25   .25
   a.   Perf. 13¾ Syncopated   .30   .30
2897   A2043   25r multi   .75   .75
   a.   Perf. 13¾ Syncopated   1.25   1.25
   b.   Souvenir sheet of 2, #2896a, 2897a   1.60   1.60

Diplomatic Relations between India and Portugal.
See Portugal Nos.

Dr. M. G. Ramachandran (1917-87), Film Actor and Politician — A2044

Perf. 13¾ Syncopated
2017, Jan. 17   Litho.
2898   A2044   15r multi   .45   .45

Indian Fauna — A2045

Designs: No. 2899, Peacock. No. 2900, Elephants. No. 2901, Cranes. No. 2902, Tiger, horiz. No. 2903, Butterfly, horiz. No. 2904, Deer, horiz.

2017, Jan. 25   Litho.   Perf. 13¾x13½
2899   A2045   5r multi   .25   .25
   a.   Perf. 13¾ Syncopated   .30   .30
2900   A2045   5r multi   .25   .25
   a.   Perf. 13¾ Syncopated   .30   .30

INDIA

2901	A2045 5r multi	.25	.25
a.	Perf. 13¾ Syncopated	.30	.30

Perf. 13½x13¾

2902	A2045 5r multi	.25	.25
a.	Perf. 13¾ Syncopated	.30	.30
2903	A2045 5r multi	.25	.25
a.	Perf. 13¾ Syncopated	.30	.30
2904	A2045 5r multi	.25	.25
a.	Perf. 13¾ Syncopated	.30	.30
b.	Souvenir sheet of 6, #2899a-2904a	1.90	1.90
	Nos. 2899-2904 (6)	1.50	1.50

India Post Payments Bank — A2046

Perf. 13¾ Syncopated

2017, Jan. 30   Litho.

| 2905 | A2046 5r multi | .25 | .25 |

Miniature Sheet

Traditional Headcoverings — A2047

No. 2906: a, Haryanvi turban. b, Hornbill warrior cap. c, Gujarati turban. d, Bison horn Maria tribal cap. e, Rajasthani turban. f, Himachali cap. g, Angami tribal cap. h, Japi cap. i, Puneri turban. j, Naga hat. k, Mysore peta. l, Dastar. m, Karakul cap. n, Mithila turban. o, Brokpa tribe tepi. p, Gonda Ladakhi cap.

2017, Feb. 10   Litho.   **Perf. 14½**

| 2906 | A2047 10r Sheet of 16, #a-p | 6.50 | 6.50 |

Poona Horse Regiment, 200th Anniv. — A2048

Perf. 13¾x13½

2017, Feb. 11   Litho.

| 2907 | A2048 5r multi | .25 | .25 |

Ramjas College, Cent. — A2049

Perf. 13¾ Syncopated

2017, Feb. 13   Litho.

| 2908 | A2049 5r multi | .25 | .25 |

A2050

A2051

A2052

Ladybugs A2053

Perf. 13½x13¾

2017, Feb. 23   Litho.

2909	A2050 5r multi	.25	.25
a.	Perf. 13¾ Syncopated	.30	.30
2910	A2051 5r multi	.25	.25
a.	Perf. 13¾ Syncopated	.30	.30
2911	A2052 15r multi	.45	.45
a.	Perf. 13¾ Syncopated	.80	.80
2912	A2053 15r multi	.45	.45
a.	Perf. 13¾ Syncopated	.80	.80
b.	Souvenir sheet of 4, #2909a-2912a	2.25	2.25
	Nos. 2909-2912 (4)	1.40	1.40

Yogoda Satsanga Society of India, Cent. — A2054

Perf. 13¾x13 Syncopated

2017, Mar. 7   Litho.

| 2913 | A2054 5r multi | .25 | .25 |

Methods of Transportation A2055

No. 2914: a, Long palanquin. b, Meeana palanquin. c, Boutcha palanquin. d, Chowpaul palanquin.
No. 2915: a, Bullock cart. b, Rath bullock cart. c, Tonga. d, Horse carriage.
No. 2916: a, Cycle rickshaw. b, Motorcycle rickshaw. c, Hand rickshaw. d, School rickshaw.
No. 2917: a, Tram. b, Metro. c, Double-decker bus. d, Bus.
No. 2918: a, 1909 Rolls-Royce. b, 1926 Austin. c, 1932 Chevrolet. d, 1938 Ford.

2017, Mar. 25   Litho.   **Perf. 13**

2914	Horiz. strip of 4	3.00	3.00
a.	A2055 5r multi	.25	.25
b.	A2055 10r multi	.55	.55
c.	A2055 15r multi	.80	.80
d.	A2055 25r multi	1.40	1.40
2915	Horiz. strip of 4	3.00	3.00
a.	A2055 5r multi	.25	.25
b.	A2055 10r multi	.55	.55
c.	A2055 15r multi	.80	.80
d.	A2055 25r multi	1.40	1.40
2916	Horiz. strip of 4	3.00	3.00
a.	A2055 5r multi	.25	.25
b.	A2055 10r multi	.55	.55
c.	A2055 15r multi	.80	.80
d.	A2055 25r multi	1.40	1.40
2917	Horiz. strip of 4	3.00	3.00
a.	A2055 5r multi	.25	.25
b.	A2055 10r multi	.55	.55
c.	A2055 15r multi	.80	.80
d.	A2055 25r multi	1.40	1.40
2918	Horiz. strip of 4	3.00	3.00
a.	A2055 5r multi	.25	.25
b.	A2055 10r multi	.55	.55
c.	A2055 15r multi	.80	.80
d.	A2055 25r multi	1.40	1.40
	Nos. 2914-2918 (5)	15.00	15.00

Cub Scouts, Cent. (in 2016) — A2056

Perf. 13½x13¾

2017, Mar. 30   Litho.

| 2919 | A2056 5r multi | .25 | .25 |

Deekshabhoomi — A2057

No. 2920: a, Statue of Buddha, Dr. B. R. Ambedkar (1891-1956), governmental minister (39x39mm). b, Deekshabhoomi Stupa (52x39mm).

2017, Apr. 14   Litho.   **Perf. 14¼**

| 2920 | A2057 5r Horiz. pair, #a-b | .30 | .30 |

Bharat Ratna Bhimrao Ambedkar Institute of Telecom Training, Jabalpur — A2058

Perf. 13¾ Syncopated

2017, Apr. 22   Litho.

| 2921 | A2058 15r multi | .50 | .50 |
| a. | Souvenir sheet of 1, perf. 13¾x13½ | .90 | .90 |

Souvenir Sheet

Coffee A2059

Perf. 13¾ Syncopated

2017, Apr. 23   Litho.

| 2922 | A2059 100r multi | 3.25 | 3.25 |

No. 2922 is impregnated with a coffee scent.

Viswanatha Satyanarayana (1895-1976), Writer A2060

Tarigonda Vengamamba (1730-1817), Poet A2061

Aatukuri Molla (1440-1530), Poet — A2062

Perf. 13¾ Syncopated

2017, Apr. 26   Litho.

2923	A2060 5r multi	.25	.25
2924	A2061 5r multi	.25	.25
2925	A2062 5r multi	.25	.25
	Nos. 2923-2925 (3)	.75	.75

Ramanujacharya (c. 1017-1137), Philosopher — A2063

2017, May 1   Litho.   **Perf. 13¾x13½**

| 2926 | A2063 25r multi | .80 | .80 |

Telecom Regulatory Authority, 20th Anniv. — A2064

2017, May 5   Litho.   **Perf. 14¼**

| 2927 | A2064 5r multi | .25 | .25 |

Champaran Satyagraha (First Civil Resistance Inspired by Mahatma Gandhi), Cent. — A2065

Designs: 5r, Gandhi and quotation. 10r, Gandhi's wife, Kasturbai, statue of Gandhi in Champaran (39x39mm). 25r, Gandhi, workers in indigo field (68x39mm).

2017, May 13   Litho.   **Perf. 13¾x13½**

| 2928 | A2065 5r multi | .25 | .25 |
| a. | Perf. 13¾x13x13¾x14¼ | .30 | .30 |

Perf. 14¼

| 2929 | A2065 10r multi | .30 | .30 |
| a. | Perf. 13¾x14¼x13¾x13 | .40 | .40 |

Perf. 13x13¾

2930	A2065 25r multi	.30	.30
a.	Perf. 13¾x14¼	.90	.90
b.	Souvenir sheet of 3, #2928a-2930a	1.60	1.60
	Nos. 2928-2930 (3)	.85	.85

Birth of Shri Hanagal Kumaraswamiji, Religious Leader, 150th Anniv. — A2066

2017, May 19   Litho.   **Perf. 13¾x13½**

| 2931 | A2066 5r multi | .25 | .25 |

Balwant Gargi (1916-2003), Writer A2067

Shrilal Shukla (1925-2011), Writer A2068

K. V. Puttappa (1904-94), Writer A2069

Bhisham Sahni (1915-2003), Writer A2070

Krishan Chander (1914-77), Writer — A2071

2017, May 31   Litho.   **Perf. 13¾x13½**

| 2932 | A2067 10r multi | .35 | .35 |
| 2933 | A2068 10r multi | .35 | .35 |

Perf. 13¾ Syncopated

2934	A2069 10r multi	.35	.35
a.	Perf. 13¾x13½	.50	.50
2935	A2070 10r multi	.35	.35
a.	Perf. 13¾x13½	.50	.50
2936	A2071 10r multi	.35	.35
a.	Perf. 13¾x13½	.50	.50
b.	Souvenir sheet of 5, #2932-2933, 2934a-2936a	2.50	2.50
	Nos. 2932-2936 (5)	1.75	1.75

Jhala Manna, 16th Cent. Rajput Warrior — A2072

Perf. 13¾ Syncopated

2017, June 18   Litho.

| 2937 | A2072 5r multi | .25 | .25 |

INDIA

Survey of India, 250th Anniv. — A2073

Designs: 5r, Emblem. 15r, Theodolite.

Perf. 13¾ Syncopated

2017, June 22			Litho.	
2938	A2073	5r multi	.25	.25
a.		Perf. 13¾x13½	.30	.30
2939	A2073	15r multi	.50	.50
a.		Perf. 13¾x13½	.95	.95
b.		Souvenir sheet of 2, #2938a-2939a	1.25	1.25

Passports Act, 50th Anniv. — A2074

2017, June 23	Litho.	Perf. 13¾		
2940	A2074	25r multi	.80	.80

Banaras Hindu University, Cent. (in 2016) — A2075

No. 2941: a, 5r, Gate (39x32mm). b, 15r, Building (58x32mm).

2017, June 28	Litho.	Perf. 13		
2941	A2075	Horiz. pair, #a-b	.70	.70

Shrimad Rajchandraji (1867-1901), Poet — A2076

Perf. 13½x13¾

2017, June 29			Litho.	
2942	A2076	5r multi	.25	.25

1942 Freedom Movement, 75th Anniv. — A2084

2017, Aug. 9	Litho.	Perf. 13¼		
2943	A2077	5r multi	.25	.25
a.		Perf. 13	.30	.30
2944	A2078	5r multi	.25	.25
a.		Perf. 13	.30	.30
2945	A2079	5r multi	.25	.25
a.		Perf. 13	.30	.30
2946	A2080	5r multi	.25	.25
a.		Perf. 13	.30	.30
2947	A2081	5r multi	.25	.25
a.		Perf. 13	.30	.30
2948	A2082	5r multi	.25	.25
a.		Perf. 13	.30	.30
2949	A2083	5r multi	.25	.25
a.		Perf. 13	.30	.30
2950	A2084	5r multi	.25	.25
a.		Perf. 13	.30	.30
b.		Souvenir sheet of 8, #2943a-2950a	2.40	2.40
		Nos. 2943-2950 (8)	2.00	2.00

Winning Photographs in "Beautiful India" Photography Competition — A2086

Perf. 13¾ Syncopated

2017, Aug. 15			Litho.	
2951	A2085	15r multi	.50	.50
a.		Perf. 13½x13¾	.75	.75
2952	A2086	15r multi	.50	.50
a.		Perf. 13¾x13½	.75	.75
b.		Souvenir sheet of 2, #2951a-2952a	1.50	1.50

Caves of Meghalaya — A2087

Designs: No. 2953, Krem Blang. No. 2954, Krem Khung, horiz. No. 2955, Krem Syndai, horiz. No. 2956, Krem Lymput.

Perf. 13¾ Syncopated (#2953, 2956), 13½x13¾

2017, Aug. 15			Litho.	
2953	A2087	5r multi	.25	.25
a.		Perf. 13¾x13½	.30	.30
2954	A2087	5r multi	.25	.25
2955	A2087	5r multi	.25	.25
2956	A2087	5r multi	.25	.25
a.		Perf. 13¾x13½	.30	.30
b.		Souvenir sheet of 4, #2953a, 2954-2955, 2956a	1.25	1.25
		Nos. 2953-2956 (4)	1.00	1.00

Diplomatic Relations Between India and Belarus, 25th Anniv. — A2088

Perf. 13½x13¾

2017, Sept. 12			Litho.	
2957	A2088	25r multi	.80	.80
a.		Souvenir sheet of 1, perf. 13¾ syncopated	1.25	1.25

See Belarus No. 1058.

Vulnerable Birds — A2089

Designs: No. 2958, Nilgiri wood pigeon. No. 2959, Broad-tailed grass warbler. No. 2960, Nilgiri pipit.

Perf. 13½x13¾

2017, Sept. 18			Litho.	
2958	A2089	5r multi	.25	.25
a.		Perf. 13¾ Syncopated	.30	.30
2959	A2089	5r multi	.25	.25
a.		Perf. 13¾ Syncopated	.30	.30
2960	A2089	5r multi	.25	.25
a.		Perf. 13¾ Syncopated	.30	.30
b.		Souvenir sheet of 3, #2958a-2960a	.90	.90
		Nos. 2958-2960 (3)	.75	.75

Diwali — A2090

Designs: 5r, Diwali lamp. 25r, Diwali lamp, diff.

Perf. 13¾x13½

2017, Sept. 21			Litho.	
2961	A2090	5r multi	.25	.25
a.		Perf. 13¾ Syncopated	.30	.30
2962	A2090	25r multi	.80	.80
a.		Perf. 13¾ Syncopated	1.10	1.10
b.		Souvenir sheet of 2, #2961a-2962a	1.50	1.50

See Canada Nos. 3023-3025. A perf. 13¼ version of No. 2962 is found on Canada No. 3023, which was sold by Canada Post.

Rama and Sita Marrying A2091

Banishment of Rama — A2092

Bharata Meeting Rama — A2093

Crossing the Ganges A2094

Rama and Jatayu — A2095

Rama and Shabari A2096

Hanuman and Sita — A2097

Building Bridge Across Sea — A2098

Hanuman Flying and Holding Mountain A2099

Rama Killing Ravana A2100

Rama and His Court A2101

2017, Sept. 22	Litho.	Perf. 13x13¾		
2963		Sheet of 11	3.00	3.00
a.	A2091	5r multi	.25	.25
b.	A2092	5r multi	.25	.25
c.	A2093	5r multi	.25	.25
d.	A2094	5r multi	.25	.25
e.	A2095	5r multi	.25	.25
f.	A2096	5r multi	.25	.25
g.	A2097	5r multi	.25	.25
h.	A2098	5r multi	.25	.25
i.	A2099	5r multi	.25	.25
j.	A2100	5r multi	.25	.25
k.	A2101	15r multi	.50	.50
l.		Sheet of 11, #2963a-2963k, green sheet margin	3.00	3.00

Epic poem, Ramayana. Nos. 2963 and 2963l were printed by different printers. No. 2963 has a 187x240mm sheet margin with a brown purple background. No. 2963l has a 236x141mm green and light green sheet margin. The colors on the stamps on No. 2963 are darker than the stamps on No. 2963l, most noticeable with dark blue shades. On No. 2963l, the separation between Nos. 2963b and 2963c and 2963h and 2963i is perf. 13.

Rapid Action Force, 25th Anniv. — A2102

2017, Oct. 7	Litho.	Perf. 13½x13¾		
2964	A2102	5r multi	.25	.25

Nanaji Deshmukh (1916-2010), Politician — A2103

2017, Oct. 11	Litho.	Perf. 13¾x13½		
2965	A2103	5r multi	.25	.25

Chhatrapati Shivaji International Airport, Mumbai, 75th Anniv. — A2104

Designs: 5r, Interior of terminal. 15r, Airplane and exterior of terminal (58x29mm).

2017, Oct. 15	Litho.	Perf. 13½x13¾		
2966	A2104	5r multi	.25	.25
a.		Perf. 13¾	.30	.30
		Perf. 13¾		
2967	A2104	15r multi	.50	.50
a.		Souvenir sheet of 2, #2966a, 2967	1.00	1.00

3 Kumaon Rifles Battalion, Cent. — A2105

2017, Oct. 23	Litho.	Perf. 13¾x13½		
2968	A2105	5r multi	.25	.25

INDIA

Beryozka Dancers, Russia — A2106

Bhavai Dancers, India — A2107

Perf. 13¾ Syncopated

2017, Oct. 26			Litho.
2969	A2106 5r multi	.25	.25
a.	Perf. 13½x13¾	.30	.30
2970	A2107 25r multi	.80	.80
a.	Perf. 13½x13¾	1.10	1.10
b.	Souvenir sheet of 2, #2969a, 2970a	1.50	1.50

Diplomatic Relation between India and Russia.
See Russia No. 7869.

Draksharamam Bhimeswara Temple — A2108

Adikavi Nannaya, 11th Cent. Writer — A2109

Kavi Muddana (1870-1901), Poet — A2110

Perf. 13¾ Syncopated

2017, Nov. 1			Litho.
2971	A2108 5r multi	.25	.25
2972	A2109 5r multi	.25	.25
2973	A2110 5r multi	.25	.25
	Nos. 2971-2973 (3)	.75	.75

Indian Cuisine — A2111

No. 2974: a, Modak. b, Mahaprasad rice dal. c, Chhappan bhog. d, Peda. e, Sandesh. f, Tirupati laddoo. g, Malpua. h, Pongal. i, Motichur laddoo. j, Gujhiya. k, Seviyan. l, Thekua. m, Poha jalebi. n, Golgappa. o, Dhokla. p, Chhole bhature. q, Idli dosa. r, Vada pav. s, Baby appam. t, Baghare baingan. u, Dal bati. v, Litti chokha. w, Makke ki roti sarson ka saag. x, Biryani.

Perf. 13¾ Syncopated

2017, Nov. 3			Litho.
2974	Sheet of 24	3.75	3.75
a.-x.	A2111 5r Any single	.25	.25
y.	Sheet of 6, #2974a-2974f	3.25	3.25
z.	Sheet of 6, #2974g-2974l	3.25	3.25
aa.	Sheet of 6, #2974m-2974r	3.25	3.25
ab.	Sheet of 6, #2974s-2974x	3.25	3.25

Children's Day — A2112

Designs: No. 2975, 15r, Birds and nest. No. 2976, 15r, Birds and nest, vert.

Perf. 13½x13¾

2017, Nov. 14			Litho.
2975	A2112 15r multi	.50	.50
a.	Souvenir sheet of 1	2.25	2.25

Perf. 13¾x13½

2976	A2112 15r multi	.50	.50
a.	Souvenir sheet of 1, perf. 13¾ syncopated	2.25	2.25

A2113

A2114

A2115

A2116

A2117

A2118

A2119

A2120

A2121

A2122

A2123

A2124

A2125

A2126

A2127

A2128

A2129

Mahabharat A2130

Perf. 13¼x13 (15r, 25r), 13¾x13 (50r), 13 (100r)

2017, Nov. 27			Litho.
2977	Sheet of 18	14.50	14.50
a.	A2113 15r multi	.50	.50
b.	A2114 15r multi	.50	.50
c.	A2115 15r multi	.50	.50
d.	A2116 15r multi	.50	.50
e.	A2117 15r multi	.50	.50
f.	A2118 15r multi	.50	.50
g.	A2119 15r multi	.50	.50
h.	A2120 15r multi	.50	.50
i.	A2121 15r multi	.50	.50
j.	A2122 15r multi	.50	.50
k.	A2123 15r multi	.50	.50
l.	A2124 15r multi	.50	.50
m.	A2125 25r multi	.80	.80
n.	A2126 25r multi	.80	.80
o.	A2127 25r multi	.80	.80
p.	A2128 25r multi	.80	.80
q.	A2129 50r multi	1.60	1.60
r.	A2130 100r multi	3.25	3.25
s.	Souvenir sheet of 1 #2977q	2.00	2.00
t.	Souvenir sheet of 1 #2977r	4.00	4.00

INS Kalvari — A2131

2017, Dec. 7		Litho.	Perf. 13¾
2978	A2131 5r multi	.25	.25
a.	Souvenir sheet of 3	1.25	1.25

Cent. of Death of Shri Shirdi Sai Baba, Religious Leader (in 2018) — A2132

Perf. 13¾x13½

2017, Dec. 15			Litho.
2979	A2132 5r multi	.25	.25

Dr. Shambhunath Singh (1916-91), Poet — A2133

Perf. 13¾x13½

2017, Dec. 26			Litho.
2980	A2133 5r multi	.25	.25

Dr. Shivajirao Ganesh Patwardhan (1892-1986), Physician and Founder of Tapovan Leprosarium — A2134

Perf. 13¾x13½

2017, Dec. 28			Litho.
2981	A2134 5r multi	.25	.25

Dadabhai Naoroji (1825-1917), Member of British House of Commons — A2135

Perf. 13¼ Syncopated

2017, Dec. 29			Litho.
2982	A2135 5r multi	.25	.25

Miniature Sheet

Stepwells — A2136

No. 2983: a, 5r, Chand Baori, Abhaneri. b, 5r, Raniji Ki Baori, Bundi. c, 5r, Toor Ji Ka Jhalra, Jodhpur. d, 5r, Panna Mian Ki Baori, Jaipur. e, 5r, Rani Ki Vav, Patan. f, 5r, Dada Harir Stepwell, Ahmedabad. g, 5r, Shahi Baori, Lucknow. h, 5r, Ghaus Ali Shah Baori, Farrukh Nagar. i, 15r, Nagar Sagar Kund, Bundi. j, 15r, Neemrana Stepwell, Alwar. k, 15r, Pushkarini Stepwell, Hampi. l, 15r, Muskin Bhanvi Stepwell, Lakkundi. m, 15r, Adalaj Stepwell, Adalaj. n, 15r, Surya Kund, Modhera. o, 15r, Agrasen Ki Baori, Delhi. p, 15r, Rajon Ki Baori, Delhi.

Perf. 13½x13¾

2017, Dec. 29			Litho.
2983	A2136 Sheet of 16, #a-p	5.00	5.00

Birds — A2137

Designs: 5r, Bird of paradise. 25r, Peacock.

Perf. 13½x13¾

2017, Dec. 30			Litho.
2984	A2137 5r multi	.25	.25
a.	Perf. 13¾ syncopated	.75	.75
2985	A2137 25r multi	.80	.80
a.	Perf. 13¾ syncopated	3.75	3.75
b.	Souvenir sheet of 2, #2984a, 2985a	4.50	4.50

See Papua New Guinea Nos. 1914-1915.

Hand Fans A2138

No. 2986: a, Applique fan, Rajasthan. b, Zardozi embroidered fan, Rajasthan. c, Painted fan, Rajasthan. d, Mirror work fan, Gujarat. e, Phadh fan, Uttar Pradesh. f, Beaded fan, Gujarat. g, Satin ceiling fan, Rajasthan. h, Palm leaf fan, Odisha. i, Feather fan, Delhi. j, Sola pith fan, Bengal. k, Temple fan, Rajasthan. l, Leather fan, Kutch, Gujarat. m, Date palm fan, Sindh. n, Embroidered fan, Gujarat. o, Palm leaf fan, Bengal. p, Bamboo fan, Bihar.

No. 2987, Embroidered fan, Gujarat, vert.

2017, Dec. 30	Litho.	Perf. 13
2986 A2138 15r Sheet of 16, #a-p	7.75	7.75
q. Souvenir sheet of 1, #2986c, perf. 13¾	2.25	2.25

Souvenir Sheet
Perf. 13¾

2987	A2138 15r multi	2.25	2.25

Mehr Chand Mahajan (1889-1967), Chief Justice of Supreme Court — A2139

Perf. 13½x13¾

2017, Dec. 31			Litho.
2989	A2139 5r multi	.25	.25

Central Plantation Crops Research Institute, Cent. (in 2016) — A2140

Designs: 5r, Coconuts. 15r, Building (58x32mm).

2018, Jan. 8		Litho.	Perf. 13
2990	A2140 5r multi	.25	.25
a.	Perf. 13 syncopated	1.75	1.75

Perf. 13¾

2991	A2140 15r multi	.50	.50
a.	Perf. 13 syncopated	4.75	4.75
b.	Souvenir sheet of 2, #2990a, 2991a	6.50	6.50

INDIA

Houses of Worship — A2141

Designs: 5r, Pho Minh Pagoda, Tuc Mac, Viet Nam. 25r, Sanchi Stupa, Sanchi, India, horiz.

Perf. 13¾ Syncopated
2018, Jan. 25 — Litho.
2992	A2141	5r multi	.25	.25
a.		Perf. 13½x13½	.75	.75
2993	A2141	25r multi	.80	.80
a.		Perf. 13½x13¾	3.75	3.75
b.		Souvenir sheet of 2, #2992a, 2993a	4.50	4.50

See Viet Nam Nos. 3587-3588.

Association of South East Asian National Commemorative Summit, New Delhi — A2142

Designs: No. 2994, 5r, Torana Gate, Malaysia. No. 2995, 5r, Menyembah, Brunei. No. 2996, 5r, Pattam Katha, India. No. 2997, 5r, Ramayana-Darangen, Philippines. No. 2998, 5r, Phralak Phralam, Hamuman, Laos. No. 2999, 5r, Ramayana, Indonesia. No. 3000, 5r, Yama Zatdaw, Myanmar. No. 3001, 5r, Hanuman, Khon, Thailand, horiz. No. 3002, 5r, Sri Mariamman Temple and Singha, Singapore, horiz. No. 3003, 5r, Kate Festival, Viet Nam, horiz. No. 3004, 5r, Kumbhakaran, Angkor, Cambodia, horiz.

Perf. 13¼ Syncopated
2018, Jan. 25 — Litho.
2994-3004	A2142	Set of 11	1.75	1.75
3004a		Souvenir sheet of 11, #2994-3004	6.25	6.25

Potters at Their Wheels — A2143

Designs: 5r, Potter, dull brown panel. 15r, Potter, light orange panel, vert.

Perf. 13¾ Syncopated
2018, Jan. 26 — Litho.
3005	A2143	5r multi	.25	.25
a.		Perf. 13½x13¾	.90	.90

Perf. 13¾x13½
3006	A2143	15r multi	.50	.50
a.		Perf. 13¾ syncopated	2.60	2.60
b.		Souvenir sheet of 2, #3005a, 3006a	3.50	3.50

Talimeren Ao (1918-98), Soccer Player and Physician — A2144

2018, Jan. 28 Litho. *Perf. 13¾x13½*
3007	A2144	5r multi	.25	.25

Ports of Iran and India — A2145

Designs: 5r, Shahid Beheshti Port, Iran. 25r, Deendayal Port, India.

Perf. 13½x13¾
2018, Feb. 17
3008	A2145	5r multi	.25	.25
a.		Perf. 13¾ syncopated	.75	.75
3009	A2145	25r multi	.80	.80
a.		Perf. 13¾ syncopated	3.75	3.75
b.		Souvenir sheet of 2, #3008a, 3009a	4.50	4.50

See Iran No. 3186.

B. Nagi Reddi (1912-2004), Film Producer — A2146

Perf. 13¾x13½
2018, Feb. 23 — Litho.
3010	A2146	5r multi	.25	.25

Auroville International Township, 50th Anniv. — A2147

Perf. 13½x13¾
2018, Feb. 25 — Litho.
3011	A2147	5r multi	.25	.25

Biju Patnaik (1916-97), Chief Minister of Odisha — A2148

2018, Mar. 5 Litho. *Perf. 13½x13¾*
3012	A2148	5r multi	.25	.25

Central Industrial Security Force, 50th Anniv. A2149

No. 3013: a, Security Force members marching (39x29mm). b, Three Security Force members standing guard at nuclear plant (30x29mm).

2018, Mar. 9 Litho. *Perf. 14*
3013	A2149	5r Horiz. pair, #a-b	.30	.30

Planets — A2150

Designs: No. 3014, 5r, Mercury. No. 3015, 5r, Venus, horiz. No. 3016, 5r, Earth, horiz. No. 3017, 5r, Mars. No. 3018, 5r, Jupiter, horiz. (53x39mm). No. 3019, 5r, Saturn, horiz. (53x39mm). No. 3020, 5r, Uranus. No. 3021, 5r, Neptune, horiz.

Perf. 13¾x13½, 13½x13¾, 14¼ (#3018-3019)
2018, Mar. 20 — Litho.
3014-3021	A2150	Set of 8	1.25	1.25
3021a		Souvenir sheet of 8, #3014-3021	5.75	5.75

Defense Research and Development Organization, 60th Anniv. — A2151

2018, Apr. 11 Litho. *Perf. 14*
3022	A2151	10r multi	.30	.30

Goan Tiatr, 125th Anniv. — A2152

Designs: 5r, Stage lights, horn, theater masks. 25r, Stage lights, horn, theater masks and silhouettes of actors.

2018, Apr. 17 Litho. *Perf. 13¾x13½*
3023	A2152	5r multi	.25	.25
a.		Perf. 13¾ syncopated	.75	.75
3024	A2152	25r multi	.80	.80
a.		Perf. 13¾ syncopated	3.75	3.75
b.		Souvenir sheet of 2, #3023a, 3024a	4.50	4.50

Hemwati Nandan Bahuguna (1919-89), Chief Minister of Uttar Pradesh — A2153

Perf. 13¾ Syncopated
2018, Apr. 24 — Litho.
3025	A2153	5r multi	.25	.25

Safdarjung Hospital, Delhi — A2154

No. 3026: a, Building and doctors (30x29mm). b, Building and doctors (39x29mm).

2018, Apr. 27 Litho. *Perf. 14*
3026	A2154	5r Horiz. pair, #a-b	.30	.30

Miniature Sheet

Prithviraj Chauhan (c.1166-92), King of Ajmer and Delhi — A2155

No. 3027 — Background color: a, 5r, Red. b, 5r, Pink. c, 15r, Yellow brown. d, 15r, Blue.

2018, Apr. 28 Litho. *Perf. 13¼*
3027	A2155	Sheet of 4, #a-d	1.25	1.25

M. V. Arunachalam (1929-96), Industrialist — A2156

2018, May 15 Litho. *Perf. 13¾x13½*
3028	A2156	5r multi	.25	.25

C. Kesavan (1891-1969), Chief Minister of Travancore-Cochin A2157

2018, May 23 Litho. *Perf. 13¾x13½*
3029	A2157	5r multi	.25	.25

Lions Clubs International, 100th Anniv. (in 2017) — A2158

2018, May 25 Litho. *Perf. 13½x13¾*
3030	A2158	15r multi	.45	.45

World Environment Day — A2159

Silhouettes of: No. 3031, 5r, Man and woman running (bright yellow green frame). No. 3032, 5r, Hikers (pale blue frame). No. 3033, 5r, Man and woman exercising (pale yellow frame). No. 3034, 5r, Children running, man playing volleyball, dog (pale mauve frame).

2018, June 5 Litho. *Perf. 13½x13¾*
3031-3034	A2159	Set of 4	.60	.60
3034a		Souvenir sheet of 4, #3031-3034	3.50	3.50

Strategic Partnership Between India and South Africa, 20th Anniv. — A2160

Designs: 5r, Oliver Reginald Tambo (1917-93), South African politician. 25r, Deendayal Upadhyaya (1916-68), Indian politician.

2018, June 7 Litho. *Perf. 13¾x13½*
3035	A2160	5r multi	.25	.25
a.		Perf. 13¾ syncopated	.75	.75
3036	A2160	25r multi	.75	.75
a.		Perf. 13¾ syncopated	3.75	3.75
b.		Souvenir sheet of 2, #3035a, 3036a	4.50	4.50

See South Africa Nos.

Dakshina Bharat Hindi Prachar Sabha (Hindi Literacy Organization), Madras, Cent. — A2161

Perf. 13½x13¾
2018, June 17 — Litho.
3037	A2161	5r multi	.25	.25

Scott Christian College, Nagercoil — A2162

Perf. 13¾ Syncopated
2018, June 28 — Litho.
3038	A2162	5r multi	.25	.25

Institute of Chartered Accountants, 70th Anniv. — A2163

Perf. 13¾ Syncopated
2018, July 1 — Litho.
3039	A2163	22r multi	.65	.65

M. L. Vasanthakumari (1928-90), Musician — A2164

Perf. 13¾ Syncopated
2018, July 3 — Litho.
3040	A2164	5r multi	.25	.25

INDIA

Damodar Hari Chapekar (1870-98), Assassin of British Plague Commissioner W. C. Rand — A2165

2018, July 8 Litho. Perf. 13¾x13½
3041 A2165 5r multi .25 .25

Famous Men — A2166

Designs: 5r, Nelson Mandela (1918-2013), President of South Africa. 25r, Mahatma Gandhi (1869-1948), Indian nationalist leader.

2018, July 26 Litho. Perf. 14¼
3042-3043 A2166 Set of 2 .90 .90
3043a Souvenir sheet of 2, #3042-3043 4.50 4.50

See South Africa No. 1576.

National Viral Hepatitis Control Program — A2167

2018, July 28 Litho. Perf. 13½x13¾
3044 A2167 5r multi .25 .25

Products of Handlooms A2168

Designs: No. 3045, 5r, Baluchari saree. No. 3046, 5r, Pochampally ikat. No. 3047, 5r, Kashmir pashmina. No. 3048, 5r, Bhagalpur silk. No. 3049, 5r, Tangaliya shawl.

2018, Aug. 7 Litho. Perf. 14¼
3045-3049 A2168 Set of 5 .70 .70
3049a Souvenir sheet of 5, #3045-3049 4.00 4.00

City Palace, Udaipur — A2169

Stone Chariot, Hampi — A2170

Perf. 13¼x13¾
2018, Aug. 15 Litho.
3050 A2169 15r multi .45 .45
3051 A2170 15r multi .45 .45
a. Souvenir sheet of 2, #3050-3051 4.50 4.50

Holiday destinations.

Patna University, Bihar, Cent. (in 2017) — A2171

2018, Aug. 25 Litho. Perf. 14
3052 A2171 5r multi .25 .25

Dancers — A2172

Designs: 5r, Hov Arek dancers, Armenia. 25r, Manipuri dancers, India.

Perf. 13½x13¾
2018, Aug. 29 Litho.
3053-3054 A2172 Set of 2 .85 .85
3054a Souvenir sheet of 2, #3053-3054 4.50 4.50

India and Armenia Joint Issue. See Armenia No. 1148.

Mailar Mahadevappa (1911-43), Leader of Anti-British Guerrilla Fighters A2173

2018, Sept. 3 Litho. Perf. 13¼
3055 A2173 5r multi .25 .25

Diplomatic Relations Between India and Serbia, 70th Anniv. — A2174

Designs: 5r, Nikola Tesla (1856-1943), inventor. 25r, Swami Vivekananda (1863-1902), lecturer on Indian philosophies in Western world.

Perf. 13¾ Syncopated
2018, Sept. 15 Litho.
3056 A2174 5r multi .25 .25
a. Perf. 13¾x13½ .75 .75
3057 A2174 25r multi .70 .70
a. Perf. 13¾x13½ 3.75 3.75
b. Souvenir sheet of 2, #3056a, 3057a 4.50 4.50

See Serbia No. 830.

Stephen Hislop (1817-63), Educator, and Hislop College, Nagpur — A2175

Perf. 13¾ Syncopated
2018, Sept. 17 Litho.
3058 A2175 5r multi .25 .25

Sant Ganinath, 11th Century Maharaja — A2176

Perf. 13½x13¾
2018, Sept. 23 Litho.
3059 A2176 5r multi .25 .25

Mahatma Gandhi (1869-1948), Indian Nationalist Leader A2177

Gandhi: 5r, In suit and tie. 12r, And building foundation. 20r, Looking at man on bed. 22r, And spinning wheel. No. 3064, 25r, And group of Indians. No. 3065, 25r, At seashore. 41r, And map and dove.

2018, Oct. 2 Litho. Perf. 13¾
3060-3066 A2177 Set of 7 4.25 4.25
3066a Souvenir sheet of 7, #3060-3066 11.50 11.50

Values are for stamps with surrounding selvage.

Third Battalion of the Rajputana Rifles, 200th Anniv. — A2178

Perf. 13 Syncopated
2018, Nov. 3 Litho.
3067 A2178 5r multi .25 .25

A2179

Children's Day — A2180

Perf. 13¾ Syncopated
2018, Nov. 14 Litho.
3068 A2179 15r multi .45 .45
a. Perf. 13¼x13¾ Syncopated 2.25 2.25
3069 A2180 15r multi .45 .45
a. Perf. 13¼x13¾ Syncopated 2.25 2.25
b. Souvenir sheet of 2, #3068a, 3069a 4.50 4.50

Utkal University, Bhubaneswar, 75th Anniv. — A2181

Perf. 13¾ Syncopated
2018, Nov. 27 Litho.
3070 A2181 5r multi .25 .25

A2182

A2183

A2184

A2185

2018 Men's Field Hockey World Cup, Bhubansewar A2186

2018, Nov. 28 Litho. Perf. 14¼
3071 A2182 5r multi .25 .25
3072 A2183 5r multi .25 .25
3073 A2184 5r multi .25 .25
3074 A2185 5r multi .25 .25
3075 A2186 5r multi .25 .25
a. Souvenir sheet of 5, #3071-3075 4.00 4.00
Nos. 3071-3075 (5) 1.25 1.25

Ustad Sabri Khan (1927-2015), Musician — A2187

Perf. 13¾x13¼
2018, Dec. 13 Litho.
3076 A2187 5r multi .25 .25

Raj Kumar Shukla (1875-1929), Farmer — A2188

Perf. 13¼ Syncopated
2018, Dec. 18 Litho.
3077 A2188 5r multi .25 .25

Gulabrao Maharaj (1881-1915), Hindu Saint — A2189

Perf. 13¾ Syncopated
2018, Dec. 19 Litho.
3078 A2189 5r multi .25 .25

Dedication of National Police Memorial, New Delhi — A2190

Designs: 10r, Men on steps. 15r, Central Sculpture.

Perf. 13¾ Syncopated
2018, Dec. 22 Litho.
3079-3080 A2190 Set of 2 .70 .70
3080a Souvenir sheet of 2, #3079-3080 4.00 4.00

Paika Rebellion, 201st Anniv. — A2191

2018, Dec. 24 Litho. Perf. 13¼
3081 A2191 5r multi .25 .25

Kakaji Maharaj (1918-86) and His Brother Pappaji, Religious Leaders A2192

2018, Dec. 28 Litho. Perf. 13
3082 A2192 5r multi .25 .25

Maharaja Suheldev, Legendary 11th Century King — A2193

Perf. 13¾x13¼
2018, Dec. 29 Litho.
3083 A2193 5r multi .25 .25

INDIA

Hill Forts of Rajasthan UNESCO World Heritage Sites — A2194

Designs: No. 3084, Kumbhalgarh Fort. No. 3085, Gagron Fort. No. 3086, Ranthambore Fort. No. 3087, Amer Fort. No. 3088, Jaisalmer Fort. No. 3089, Chittorgarh Fort.

Perf. 13¾ Syncopated, 13¼x13¾ (#3087)

		2018, Dec. 29		Litho.
3084	A2194	5r multi	.25	.25
3085	A2194	5r multi	.25	.25
3086	A2194	5r multi	.25	.25
3087	A2194	12r multi	.35	.35
a.		Perf. 13¾ Syncopated (3089a)	1.60	1.60
3088	A2194	12r multi	.35	.35
3089	A2194	12r multi	.35	.35
a.		Souvenir sheet of 6, #3084-3086, 3087a, 3088-3089	6.75	6.75
		Nos. 3084-3089 (6)	1.80	1.80

First Flag Hoisting Ceremony at Port Blair, 75th Anniv. — A2195

Designs: 12r, Cellular Jail. 22r, Subhas Chandra Bose (1897-1945), saluting flag raised by soldiers. 41r, Subhas Chandra Bose and flag of India.

Perf. 13, 13½x13 (22r)

		2018, Dec. 30		Litho.
3090	A2195	12r multi	.35	.35
3091	A2195	22r multi	.65	.65
a.		Perf. 13 (3092a)	3.00	3.00
3092	A2195	41r multi	1.25	1.25
a.		Souvenir sheet of 3, #3090, 3091a, 3092	9.75	9.75
		Nos. 3090-3092 (3)	2.25	2.25

Fashions — A2196

Garments of: No. 3093, 5r, Mughal Empress Nur Jahan (1577-1645). No. 3094, 5r, Ghazi-ud-din Haider (c. 1769-1827), king of Awadh, with woman and man. No. 3095, 15r, People from Harappa and Mohenjo-Daro, Mauryan and Sunga periods (58x54mm). No. 3096, 15r, People of Indian Princely States (58x54mm).

		2018, Dec. 31	Litho.	Perf. 13
3093-3096	A2196	Set of 4	1.25	1.25
3096a		Souvenir sheet of 4, #3093-3096	5.75	5.75

Atal Bihari Vajpayee (1924-2018), Prime Minister — A2197

		2018, Dec. 25	Litho.	Perf. 13
3097	A2197	2r brown	.25	.25

Handicrafts A2198

Designs: No. 3098, 5r, Blue pottery of Jaipur. No. 3099, 5r, Maddalam of Palakkad. No. 3100, 5r, Karnataka bronzeware. No. 3101, 5r, Kutch embroidery. No. 3102, 5r, Sikki grass products of Bihar.

		2018, Dec. 31	Litho.	Perf. 14¼
3098-3102	A2198	Set of 5	.75	.75
3102a		Souvenir sheet of 5, #3098-3102	4.00	4.00

Central Institute of Plastics Engineering and Technology, 50th Anniv. (in 2018) A2199

		2019, Jan. 24	Litho.	Perf. 13¾
3103	A2199	41r multi	1.25	1.25
a.		Souvenir sheet of 1	5.75	5.75

Mahamati Prannath (1618-94), Societal Reformer — A2200

Perf. 13¾ Syncopated

		2019, Jan. 25		Litho.
3104	A2200	5r multi	.25	.25

Financial Inclusion — A2201

		2019, Jan. 30	Litho.	Perf. 14¼
3105	A2201	5r multi	.25	.25

Kumbh Mela Festival, Prayagraj — A2202

		2019, Feb. 2	Litho.	Perf. 13¾
3106	A2202	5r multi	.25	.25

Indian Institute of Technology of Banaras Hindu University, Cent. — A2203

		2019, Feb. 19	Litho.	Perf. 13¾
3107	A2203	5r multi	.25	.25

2019 Aero India Air Show — A2204

Designs: 5r, Helicopters, airplanes and crew members. 25r, Military jets and female pilots, vert.

		2019, Feb. 23	Litho.	Perf. 13¾
3108-3109	A2204	Set of 2	.85	.85
3109a		Souvenir sheet of 2, #3108-3109	4.50	4.50

Ram Chand Paul (1919-2002), Chemist — A2205

Perf. 13¾ Syncopated

		2019, Mar. 6		Litho.
3110	A2205	5r multi	.25	.25

Kubernath Ray (1933-96), Writer — A2206

		2019, Mar. 9	Litho.	Perf. 13¾x13¼
3111	A2206	5r multi	.25	.25

Punjab National Bank, 125th Anniv. (in 2020) — A2207

		2019, Apr. 12	Litho.	Perf. 13¾
3112	A2207	5r multi	.25	.25

Jallianwala Bagh Massacre, Cent. — A2208

Designs: 5r, Martyr's Well. 25r, Jallianwala Bagh Massacre Memorial.

		2019, Apr. 13	Litho.	Perf. 14¼
3113-3114	A2208	Set of 2	.90	.90
3114a		Souvenir sheet of 2, #3113-3114	4.50	4.50

Vedanta Desikan (1268-1369), Poet and Philosopher — A2209

		2019, May 2	Litho.	Perf. 13
3115	A2209	5r multi	.25	.25

Fashion — A2210

Designs: No. 3116, 5r, Pathare Prabhu women and their saris. No. 3117, 5r, Women wearing Brahmika saris. No. 3118, 12r, Traditional Parsi attire. No. 3119, 12r, Movie actress wearing sari.

		2019, June 12	Litho.	Perf. 13
3116-3119	A2210	Set of 4	1.00	1.00
3119a		Souvenir sheet of 4, #3116-3119	5.00	5.00

Mohandas K. Gandhi (1869-1948), Indian Nationalist Leader A2211

Dove, Blackboard and Gandhi Holding Walking Stick A2212

		2019, June 17	Litho.	Perf. 13
3120	A2211	15r multi	.45	.45
3121	A2212	15r multi	.45	.45
a.		Souvenir sheet of 2, #3120-3121	4.50	4.50

Winning art in stamp design contest on theme of Gandhi's philosophy, Ahimsa Parmo Dharma.

Fakir Mohan College, Balasore, 75th Anniv. — A2213

Litho. & Embossed

		2019, July 6		Perf. 13¼x13¾
3122	A2213	5r multi	.25	.25

Hwang-ok Heo, Lewgendary Queen of Korea — A2214

Princess Suriratna (Later Queen Heo) — A2215

		2019, July 30	Litho.	Perf. 13¼x13¾
3123	A2214	5r multi	.25	.25

Perf. 13¾ Syncopated

3124	A2215	25r multi	.75	.75
a.		Perf. 13¼x13¾ (3124b)	3.75	3.75
b.		Souvenir sheet of 2, #3123, 3124a	4.50	4.50

See South Korea No. 2555.

Containers of Sandalwood Perfume A2216

Sandalwood Flowers A2217

Jasmine Flowers and Vial of Jasmine Perfume A2218

Jasmine Flowers and Vial of Jasmine Perfume A2219

Perf. 13¾ Syncopated

		2019, Aug. 1		Litho.
3125	A2216	25r multi	.75	.75
a.		Perf. 13¾x13¼	2.75	2.75
3126	A2217	25r multi	.75	.75
a.		Perf. 13¾x13¼	2.75	2.75
b.		Souvenir sheet of 2, #3125a, 3126a	5.50	5.50

INDIA

3127	A2218 25r multi	.75	.75
a.	Perf. 13¾x13¼	2.75	2.75

Perf. 13¾x13¼

3128	A2219 25r multi	.75	.75
a.	Souvenir sheet of 2, #3127a, 3128	5.50	5.50
	Nos. 3125-3128 (4)	3.00	3.00

Nos. 3125-3126 are impregnated with a sandalwood scent and Nos. 3127-3128 are impregnated with a jasmine scent.

Statue of Mohandas K. Gandhi and Girl, Goa — A2220

Gyarah Murti Statues, Delhi — A2221

Perf. 13¾ Syncopated
2019, Aug. 15   Litho.

3129	A2220 15r multi	.45	.45

Perf. 13¼x13¾

3130	A2221 25r multi	.70	.70

Indian Soldiers in Major Battle Theaters of World War I — A2222

Indian soldiers: No. 3131, 5r, In Mesopotamia. No. 3132, 5r, In France and Belgium. No. 3133, 5r, In East Africa. No. 3134, 15r, At Battle of Gallipoli.

Perf. 13¼x13¾
2019, Aug. 20   Litho.

3131-3134	A2222 Set of 4	.85	.85
3134a	Souvenir sheet of 4, #3131-3134	3.25	3.25

Indian Pilots of World War I — A2223

Designs: No. 3135, 5r, Lieutenant Shrikrishna G. Wellingkar. No. 3136, 5r, Lieutenant Erroll Suvo Chunder Sen. No. 3137, 15r, Lieutenant Indra Lal Roy. No. 3138, 15r, Lieutenant Hardit Singh Malik.

2019, Aug. 20   Litho.   **Perf. 13¾**

3135-3138	A2223 Set of 4	1.10	1.10
3138a	Souvenir sheet of 4, #3135-3138	4.25	4.25

Memorials to Indians in World War I — A2224

Designs: No. 3139, 5r, Menin Gate Memorial, Belgium. No. 3140, 5r, Chattri Memorial, Brighton, United Kingdom. No. 3141, 5r, Neuve Chapelle Memorial, France. No. 3142, 10r, India Gate, Delhi. No. 3143, 10r, Teen Murti Haifa, Delhi. No. 3144, 10r, Indian Great War Military Memorial, France.

Perf. 13¾x13¼
2019, Aug. 20   Litho.

3139-3144	A2224 Set of 6	1.25	1.25
3144a	Souvenir sheet of 4, #3139-3144	4.75	4.75

Signing of the Treaty of Versailles, Cent. — A2225

2019, Aug. 20   Litho.   **Perf. 13¾**

3145	A2225 25r multi	.70	.70
a.	Souvenir sheet of 1	2.75	2.75

Calavala Cunnan Chetty (1869-1920), Businessman and Philanthropist — A2226

Perf. 13¼x13¾
2019, Aug. 24   Litho.

3146	A2226 5r multi	.25	.25

Ayurveda, Yoga and Naturopathy, Unani, Siddha, Sowa Rigpa and Homeopathic Healers — A2227

No. 3147: a, Dinshaw Mehta (1903-93). b, Bhaskar Vishwanath Gokhale (1903-62). c, Brihaspati Dev Triguna (1920-2013). d, Swami Kuvalayananda (1883-1966). e, Maharishi Mahesh Yogi (1918-2008). f, Shastri Shankar Daji Pade (1867-1909). g, K. G. Saxena (1912-2003). h, T. V. Sambasivam Pillai (1880-1953). i, Mohammad Abdul Aziz Lakhnawi (1854-1911). j, K. Raghavan Thirumulpad (1920-2010). k, Yadav Ji Trikam Ji Acharya (1881-1956). l, Mohammad Kabiruddin (1894-1976).

2019, Aug. 30   Litho.   **Perf. 13¼**

3147	A2227 5r Block of 12, #a-l	1.75	1.75

A2228

Fashion — A2229

Designs: No. 3148, 10r, Costume designing. No. 3149, 10r, Mass production. No. 3150, 15r, Fashion designer. No. 3151, 15r, Fashion show.

2019, Sept. 6   Litho.   **Perf. 13¾**

3148	A2228 10r multi	.30	.30
3149	A2228 10r multi	.30	.30
3150	A2229 15r multi	.45	.45
3151	A2229 15r multi	.45	.45
a.	Souvenir sheet of 4, #3148-3151	6.75	6.75

Mohandas K. Gandhi (1869-1948), Indian Nationalist Leader — A2230

Designs: No. 3152, 25r, Gandhi as child. No. 3153, 25r, Gandhi as young attorney. No. 3154, 25r, Gandhi and wife, Kasturba. No. 3155, 25r, Gandhi and spinning wheel. No. 3156, 25r, Gandhi in train car doorway. No. 3157, 25r, Three Wise Monkeys.

Litho. With Foil Application
2019, Oct. 2   **Perf. 13**

3152-3157	A2230 Set of 6	4.25	4.25
3157a	Souvenir sheet of 6, #3152-3157	11.50	11.50

Gopabandhu Das (1877-1928), Founder of *Samaja* Newspaper — A2231

Perf. 13¾ Syncopated
2019, Oct. 6   **Litho. & Embossed**

3158	A2231 5r multi	.25	.25

Samaja newspaper, cent.

Arjan Singh (1939-2017), Marshal of Indian Air Force — A2232

2019, Oct. 9   Litho.   **Perf. 13**

3159	A2232 5r multi	.25	.25

Containers of Agarwood Perfume A2233

Incense Burner A2234

Orange Blossoms A2235

Oranges and Vial of Orange Blossom Perfume A2236

Perf. 13¾ Syncopated
2019, Oct. 15

3160	A2233 25r multi	.70	.70
a.	Perf. 13¾x13¼	2.50	2.50
3161	A2234 25r multi	.70	.70
a.	Perf. 13¾x13¼	2.50	2.50
b.	Souvenir sheet of 2, #3160a, 3161a	5.00	5.00
3162	A2235 25r multi	.70	.70
a.	Perf. 13¾x13¼	2.50	2.50
3163	A2236 25r multi	.70	.70
a.	Perf. 13¾x13¼	2.50	2.50
b.	Souvenir sheet of 2, #3162a, 3163a	5.00	5.00
	Nos. 3160-3163 (4)	2.80	2.80

Nos. 3160-3161 are impregnated with a agarwood scent and Nos. 3162-3163 are impregnated with a orange blossom scent.

Gates of Forts and Monuments — A2237

Designs: No. 3164, Kote Gate, Bikaner. No. 3165, Jorawar Singh Gate, Jaipur. No. 3166, Sardar Market Gate, Jodhpur. No. 3167, Kashmere Gate, Delhi. No. 3168, Roomi Darwaza, Lucknow. No. 3169, Magazine Gate, Ajmer. No. 3170, Buland Darwaza, Fatehpur Sikri. No. 3171, Delhi Gate, Delhi.

Perf. 13¾ Syncopated, 13¼x13¾ (#3168)
2019, Oct. 19   Litho.

3164	A2237 5r multi	.25	.25
a.	Perf. 13¼x13¾	.70	.70
3165	A2237 5r multi	.25	.25
a.	Perf. 13¼x13¾	.70	.70
3166	A2237 5r multi	.25	.25
a.	Perf. 13¼x13¾	.70	.70
3167	A2237 5r multi	.25	.25
a.	Perf. 13¼x13¾	.70	.70
3168	A2237 5r multi	.25	.25
a.	Perf. 13¼x13¾	.70	.70
3169	A2237 5r multi	.25	.25
a.	Perf. 13¼x13¾	.70	.70
3170	A2237 10r multi	.30	.30
a.	Perf. 13¼x13¾	1.40	1.40
3171	A2237 10r multi	.30	.30
a.	Perf. 13¼x13¾	1.40	1.40
b.	Souvenir sheet of 8, #3164a, 3165a, 3166a, 3167a, 3168, 3169a, 3170a, 3171a	7.00	7.00
	Nos. 3164-3171 (8)	2.10	2.10

Siachen Glacier — A2238

2019, Oct. 25   Litho.   **Perf. 14¼**

3172	A2238 5r multi	.25	.25

A2239

Buildings Associated With Guru Nanak Dev Ji (1469-1539), Founder of Sikhism — A2240

Designs: No. 3173, Gurudwara Nanak Lama Sahib, Chungthang. No. 3174, Gurudwara Darbar Sahib, Dera Baba Nanak, Gurdaspur. No. 3175, Gurudwara Nanak Jhira Sahib, Bidar. No. 3176, Gurudwara Janamasthan, Nankana Sahib. No. 3177, Gurudwara Ber Sahib, Sultanpur Lodhi.

Perf. 14¼, 13¾ (#3176)
2019, Nov. 9   Litho.

3173	A2239 10r multi	.30	.30
3174	A2239 10r multi	.30	.30
3175	A2239 10r multi	.30	.30
3176	A2240 10r multi	.30	.30
3177	A2239 15r multi	.45	.45
a.	Souvenir sheet of 5, 3173-3177	7.50	7.50
	Nos. 3173-3177 (5)	1.65	1.65

A2241

Children's Day — A2242

Perf. 13¾x13¼
2019, Nov. 14   Litho.

3178	A2241 15r multi	.45	.45
a.	Perf. 13¾ Syncopated	2.25	2.25
3179	A2242 15r multi	.45	.45
a.	Perf. 13¾ Syncopated	2.25	2.25
b.	Souvenir sheet of 2, #3178a, 3179a	4.50	4.50

Mathew M. Kushiveli (1905-74), Writer — A2243

Perf. 13¼x13¾
2019, Nov. 22   Litho.

3180	A2243 5r multi	.25	.25

INDIA

250th Rajya Sabha Session — A2244

2019, Nov. 26 Litho. Perf. 14
3181 A2244 5r multi .25 .25
Values are for stamps with surrounding selvage.

Yamunotri A2245
Gangotri A2246
Kedarnath A2247
Badrinath A2248

2019, Nov. 29 Litho. Perf. 13
3182 A2245 10r multi .30 .30
3183 A2246 10r multi .30 .30
3184 A2247 15r multi .40 .40
3185 A2248 15r multi .40 .40
  a. Block of 4, #3182-3185 1.40 1.40
  Nos. 3182-3185 (4) 1.40 1.40

Char Dham Pilgrimage Sites, Uttarakhand.

Remount Veterinary Corps — A2249

2019, Dec. 14 Litho. Perf. 14¼
3186 A2249 5r multi .25 .25

Phulkari Embroidery A2250
Kutch Embroidery A2251
Kasuti Embroidery A2252
Chikankari Embroidery A2253
Toda Embroidery A2254
Kantha Embroidery A2255
Kamal Kadhai Embroidery A2256
Kashmiri Embroidery A2257
Chamba Rumal Embroidery A2258
Shamilami Embroidery A2259
Sujani Embroidery A2260
Appliqué Embroidery A2261

2019, Dec. 19 Litho. Perf. 13x13¼
3187 A2250 10r multi .30 .30
3188 A2251 10r multi .30 .30
3189 A2252 10r multi .30 .30
3190 A2253 10r multi .30 .30
3191 A2254 10r multi .30 .30
3192 A2255 15r multi .40 .40
3193 A2256 15r multi .40 .40
3194 A2257 15r multi .40 .40
3195 A2258 20r multi .55 .55
3196 A2259 20r multi .55 .55
3197 A2260 20r multi .55 .55

Perf. 14x14¼
3198 A2261 20r multi .55 .55
  a. Perf. 13x13¼ Syncopated 1.50 1.50
  b. Sheet of 12, #3187-3197, 3198a 13.00 13.00
  Nos. 3187-3198 (12) 4.90 4.90

Directorate of Revenue Intelligence — A2262

2019, Dec. 26 Litho. Perf. 13¾
3199 A2262 5r multi .25 .25

Fashion — A2263

Clothing by: No. 3200, 5r, Vastra. No. 3201, 5r, Indica Emporia. No. 3202, 5r, Flared Sherwani. No. 3203, 5r, Timeless. No. 3204, 5r, Mystical Indian. No. 3205, 5r, Embellishment. No. 3206, 5r, Varanasi Weaves. No. 3207, 5r, The Ambika Jacket. No. 3208, 5r, Classic Jalabiya.

2020, Jan. 14 Litho. Perf. 13¼x13¾
3200-3208 A2263 Set of 9 1.25 1.25
3208a Sheet of 9, #3200-3208, perf. 13¾ 7.50 7.50

International Labor Organization, Cent. (in 2019) A2264

2020, Jan. 22 Litho. Perf. 14½x14¼
3209 A2264 5r multi .25 .25

Constitution of India, 70th Anniv. — A2265

No. 3210: a, Asoka Pillar (32x39mm). b, Politicians at table (58x39mm).

Perf. 13¼x14¼x13¼x13 Syncopated (#3210a), 14½x14¼x14¼x14¼ (#3210b)

2020, Jan. 26 Litho.
3210 A2265 10r Horiz. pair, #a-b .60 .60
  c. Souvenir sheet of 2, #3210a-3210b 3.50 3.50

4th Battalion (Outram's), the Rajaputra Rifles, 200th Anniv. — A2266

Perf. 14½x14¼
2020, Feb. 12 Litho.
3211 A2266 5r multi .25 .25

Jamshedpur, Cent. — A2267

2020, Feb. 17 Litho. Perf. 13
3212 A2267 5r multi .25 .25

UNESCO World Heritage Sites in India — A2268

Designs: No. 3213, Animals, Manas Wildlife Sanctuary. No. 3214, Animals, Great Himalayan National Park. No. 3215, Flower and valley, Nanda Devi and Valley of the Flowers National Park (58x29mm). No. 3216, Animals, Nanda Devi and Valley of the Flowers National Park. No. 3217, Animals, Western Ghats.

Perf. 13½x14, 13½x13¼ (#3215)
2020, Mar. 16 Litho.
3213 A2268 5r multi .25 .25
  a. Perf. 13¼x13½ .30 .30
3214 A2268 5r multi .25 .25
  a. Perf. 13¼x13½ .30 .30
3215 A2268 12r multi .30 .30
  a. Perf. 13¼x13½ .80 .80
3216 A2268 12r multi .30 .30
  a. Perf. 13¼x13½ .80 .80
3217 A2268 12r multi .30 .30
  a. Perf. 13¼x13½ .80 .80
  b. Souvenir sheet of 5, #3213a-3217a 3.00 3.00

Musical Instruments and Wandering Minstrels — A2269

No. 3218, 5r — Stamps inscribed "Kamaicha": a, Instrument (29x39mm). b, Minstrel playing instrument (39x39mm).
No. 3219, 5r — Stamps inscribed "Ravanhatha": a, Instrument (29x39mm). b, Minstrel playing instrument (39x39mm).
No. 3220, 5r — Stamps inscribed "Surando": a, Instrument (29x39mm). b, Minstrel playing instrument (39x39mm).
No. 3221, 5r — Stamps inscribed "Algoza": a, Instrument (29x39mm). b, Minstrel playing instrument (39x39mm).
No. 3222, 5r — Stamps inscribed "Burrakatha Dakki": a, Instrument (29x39mm). b, Minstrel playing instrument (39x39mm).
No. 3223, 5r — Stamps inscribed "Ektara": a, Instrument (29x39mm). b, Minstrel playing instrument (39x39mm).

Perf. 13¾x14¼
2020, June 25 Litho.
Horiz. Pairs, #a-b
3218-3223 A2269 Set of 6 1.60 1.60

Terracotta Temples A2270

Designs: No. 3224, 5r, Indralath Temple, Ranipur Jharial. No. 3225, 5r, Madan Mohan Temple, Bishnupur. No. 3226, 5r, Jor Bangla Temple, Bishnupur. No. 3227, 5r, Lakshman Temple, Sirpur. No. 3228, 5r, Nebiya Khear Temple, Bhadwara. No. 3229, 12r, Shyam Rai Temple, Bishnupur. No. 3230, 12r, Lalji Temple, Kalna.

2020, Aug. 8 Litho. Perf. 14½
3224-3230 A2270 Set of 7 1.40 1.40
3230a Souvenir sheet of 7, #3224-3230 3.00 3.00

UNESCO World Heritage Sites in India — A2271

Designs: No. 3231, 5r, Sarkhej Roza, Historic City of Ahmadabad UNESCO World Heritage Site. No. 3232, 5r, Church of Bom Jesus, Churches and Convents of Goa UNESCO World Heritage Site. No. 3233, 5r, Monument, Group of Monuments at Pattadakal UNESCO World Heritage Site, vert. No. 3234, 5r, Javari Temple, Khajuraho Group of Monuments UNESCO World Heritage Site, vert. No. 3235, 5r, Qutb Minar, Qutb Minar and its Monuments UNESCO World Heritage Site, vert.

Perf. 13¾ Syncopated
2020, Aug. 15 Litho.
3231-3235 A2271 Set of 5 .70 .70
3235a Souvenir sheet of 5, #3231-3235 1.60 1.60

Mohandas K. Gandhi (1869-1948), Indian Nationalist Leader — A2272

Gandhi and inscription: No. 3236, 5r, Health and Nature Cure. No. 3237, 5r, Ecology and Environment. 15r, Self-reliance. 25r, Experiments in Education - Nai Talim.

2020, Oct. 2 Litho. Perf. 14¼
3236-3239 A2272 Set of 4 1.40 1.40
3239a Souvenir sheet of 4, #3236-3239 3.00 3.00

United Nations, 75th Anniv. — A2273

2020, Oct. 23 Litho. Perf. 13¼x13¾
3240 A2273 5r multi .25 .25

Inder K. Gurjal (1919-2012), 12th Prime Minister of India — A2274

2020, Dec. 4 Litho. Perf. 13¼x13¾
3241 A2274 5r multi .25 .25

Sheikh Mujibur Rahman (1920-75), First President of Bangladesh A2275

2020, Dec. 17 Litho. Perf. 14¼x14
3242 A2275 5r multi .25 .25

INDIA

Tribute to Workers in the COVID-19 Pandemic — A2276, A2277, A2278, A2279

2020, Dec. 24   Litho.   Perf. 14¼
3243	A2276	10r multi	.30	.30
3244	A2277	10r multi	.30	.30
3245	A2278	10r multi	.30	.30
3246	A2279	10r multi	.30	.30
a.	Souvenir sheet of 4, #3243-3246		1.25	1.25
	Nos. 3243-3246 (4)		1.20	1.20

Manikchandra Vajpayee (1919-2005), Journalist — A2280

Perf. 13¾x13¼
2020, Dec. 27   Litho.
3247   A2280   5r multi   .25   .25

Subhas Chandra Bose (1897-1945), Indian Nationalist — A2281

2021, Jan. 23   Litho.   Perf. 13
3248   A2281   25r multi   .70   .70

Himachal Pradesh Statehood, 50th Anniv. — A2282

2021, Jan. 25   Litho.   Perf. 13¼x13¾
3249   A2282   5r multi   .25   .25

High Court of Gujarat, 60th Anniv. (in 2020) — A2283

Perf. 13¼x13¾
2021, Feb. 16   Litho.
3250   A2283   5r multi   .25   .25
Dated 2020.

First Visit of Mohandas K. Gandhi to Odisha, Cent. — A2284

2021, Mar. 23   Litho.   Perf. 14¼
3251   A2284   5r multi   .25   .25

National War Memorial, New Delhi, and National Martyr's Memorial, Savar, Bangladesh A2285

2021, Mar. 27   Litho.   Perf. 14¼
3252   A2285   5r multi   .25   .25

Friendship between India and Bangladesh, 50th anniv. See Bangladesh No. 967.

Rayjogini Dadi Janki (1916-2020), Brahma Kumaris Spiritual Leader — A2286

Perf. 13¾ Syncopated
2021, Apr. 12   Litho.
3253   A2286   5r multi   .25   .25

Friendship between India and Bangladesh, 50th anniv.

Diplomatic Relations Between India and Germany, 70th Anniv. A2287

2021, June 10   Litho.   Perf. 14¼
3254   A2287   25r multi   .70   .70

See Germany No. 3221.

Gayatri Teerth Ashram, Shantikunj, 50th Anniv. — A2288

Perf. 13¼x13¾
2021, June 20   Litho.
3255   A2288   5r multi   .25   .25

Mananiya Chaman Lal (1920-2003), Social Worker — A2289

Perf. 13¾ Syncopated
2021, Aug. 7   Litho.
3256   A2289   5r multi   .25   .25

Rao Jaimal Rathore (1507-1583), Ruler of Merta — A2290

Perf. 13¾x13¼
2021, Sept. 17   Litho.
3257   A2290   5r multi   .25   .25

Solapur Martyrs — A2291

2021, Oct. 2   Litho.   Perf. 13¼x13¾
3258   A2291   5r multi   .25   .25

After a protest in Solapur against the arrest of Mohandas K. Gandhi, Maliappa Dhanshetti (1898-1931), Shrikisan Sarada (1893-1931), Jagannath Shinde (1906-31), and Abdul Rasul Kurban Hussain (1910-31) were arrested in 1930 by British authorities and hanged the following year.

Deccan College, Pune, 200th Anniv. — A2292

2021, Oct. 6   Litho.   Perf. 14¼
3259   A2292   5r multi   .25   .25

Dattopant Thengadi (1920-2004), Trade Union Leader — A2293

2021, Nov. 10   Litho.   Perf. 14¼
3260   A2293   5r multi   .30   .30

Srirama Chandra Bhanja Medical College and Hospital, Cuttack, 75th Anniv. A2294

Perf. 13¾x13¼
2021, Nov. 27   Litho.
3261   A2294   5r multi   .30   .30

Mahindra Group, 75th Anniv. A2295

2021, Dec. 1   Litho.   Perf. 13¾
3262   A2295   12r multi   .35   .35

Indo-Pakistani War, 50th Anniv. — A2296

Perf. 13¾x14¼
2021, Dec. 16   Litho.
3263   A2296   5r multi   .30   .30

AIR POST STAMPS

De Havilland Hercules over Lake — AP1

Wmk. 196 Sideways
1929-30   Typo.   Perf. 14
C1	AP1	2a dull green	1.00	.50
C2	AP1	3a deep blue	1.40	.90
C3	AP1	4a gray olive	4.00	1.90
a.		4a olive green ('30)	5.00	1.90
C4	AP1	6a bister	5.00	1.10
C5	AP1	8a red violet	5.75	5.75
C6	AP1	12a brown red	17.50	17.50
	Nos. C1-C6 (6)		34.65	27.65
	Set, never hinged		60.00	

Catalogue values for unused stamps in this section, from this point to the end of the section, are for Never Hinged items.

Dominion of India

Lockheed Constellation AP2

Perf. 13½x14
1948, May 29   Litho.   Wmk. 196
C7   AP2   12a ultra & slate blk   6.00   6.00

Bombay-London flight of June 8, 1948.

Republic of India

The Spirit of '76, by Archibald M. Willard — AP3

1976, May 29   Perf. 13x13½
C8   AP3   2.80r multicolored   2.00   2.00

American Bicentennial.

INDIA '80 Emblem, De Havilland Puss Moth — AP4

1979, Oct. 15   Photo.   Perf. 14½x14
C9	AP4	30p shown	.70	.30
C10	AP4	50p Chetak helicopter	.85	.50
C11	AP4	1r Boeing 737	1.10	.90
C12	AP4	2r Boeing 747	1.40	1.10
	Nos. C9-C12 (4)		4.05	2.80

INDIA '80 Intl. Stamp Exhib., New Delhi, Jan. 25-Feb. 3, 1980.

MILITARY STAMPS

China Expeditionary Force

Regular Issues of India, 1882-99, Overprinted   C. E. F.

1900   Wmk. 39   Perf. 14
M1	A31	3p carmine rose	.70	2.10
M2	A17	½a dark green	1.25	.45
M3	A19	1a maroon	7.00	2.50
M4	A21	2a ultra	5.25	15.00
M5	A28	2a6p green	4.75	21.00
M6	A22	3a orange	4.75	27.50
M7	A23	4a olive green	4.75	13.00
M8	A25	8a red violet	4.75	30.00
M9	A26	12a violet, *red*	30.00	30.00
M10	A29	1r car rose & grn	37.50	37.50
a.	Double overprint			
	Nos. M1-M10 (10)		100.70	179.05

The 1a6p of this set was overprinted, but not issued. Value $250.

Overprinted on 1900 Issue of India
1904, Feb. 27
M11   A19   1a carmine rose   55.00   15.00

Overprinted on 1902-09 Issue of India
1904
M12	A32	3p gray	8.00	10.00
M13	A34	1a carmine rose	12.00	1.10
M14	A35	2a violet	22.50	3.75
M15	A36	2a6p ultra	5.25	*8.00*
M16	A37	3a brown org	5.75	*6.50*
M17	A38	4a olive green	13.50	*19.00*
M18	A40	8a red violet	13.00	*12.00*
M19	A41	12a violet, *red*	18.00	*30.00*

INDIA

M20	A42	1r car rose & grn	20.00	45.00
		Nos. M12-M20 (9)	118.00	135.35

Overprinted on 1906 Issue of India
1909
M21	A44	½a green	1.50	1.00
M22	A45	1a carmine rose	1.50	.40

Overprinted on 1911-19 Issues of India
1913-21
M23	A46	3p gray	8.00	35.00
M24	A47	½a green	6.25	7.50
M25	A48	1a car rose	7.25	4.75
M26	A58	1½a chocolate	40.00	95.00
M27	A49	2a violet	27.50	80.00
M28	A57	2a6p ultra	20.00	30.00
M29	A51	3a brn org	40.00	240.00
M30	A52	4a ol grn	37.50	210.00
M31	A54	8a red violet	40.00	400.00
M32	A55	12a claret	37.50	140.00
M33	A56	1r grn & red brn	110.00	375.00
		Nos. M23-M33 (11)	374.00	1,617.

Issue dates: No. M23, 1913; others, 1921.

Indian Expeditionary Force
Regular Issues of India, 1911-13, Overprinted **I. E. F.**

1914 Wmk. 39 Perf. 14
M34	A46	3p gray	.30	.55
a.		Double overprint	70.00	55.00
M35	A47	½a green	.80	.55
a.		Double overprint	175.00	300.00
M36	A48	1a car rose	2.10	.55
M37	A49	2a violet	2.10	.55
M38	A57	2a6p ultra	2.50	4.00
M39	A51	3a brn org	1.75	2.75
M40	A52	4a olive grn	1.75	2.75
M41	A54	8a red violet	2.10	4.25
M42	A55	12a claret	3.75	10.50
M43	A56	1r grn & red brn	4.50	7.25
		Nos. M34-M43 (10)	21.65	33.70

Catalogue values for unused stamps in this section, from this point to the end of the section, are for Never Hinged items.

Korea Custodial Unit
Regular Issues of India Overprinted in Black

Perf. 13½x14, 14x13½
1953 Wmk. 196
M44	A91	3p gray violet	.45	5.50
M45	A92	6p red brown	.45	5.50
M46	A91	9p green	.45	4.50
M47	A101	1a turquoise	.65	4.50
M48	A93	2a carmine	1.00	4.50
M49	A94	2½a brown lake	1.90	4.75
M50	A94	3a red orange	2.25	5.50
M51	A94	4a ultra	2.60	4.75
M52	A95	6a purple	10.00	9.00
M53	A95	8a blue green	7.25	11.00
M54	A95	12a blue	9.75	17.00
M55	A96	1r dk grn & pur	15.50	17.00
		Nos. M44-M55 (12)	52.25	93.50

Hindi overprint reads "Indian Custodial Unit, Korea."

Indian UN Force in Congo
Nos. 302-303, 305, 307, 282 and 313 Overprinted: "U.N. FORCE (INDIA) CONGO"

Wmk. 324, 196 (13np)
1962, Jan. 15 Photo. Perf. 14x14½
M56	A117	1np blue green	.90	.90
M57	A117	2np light brown	.90	.90
M58	A117	5np emerald	.90	.90
M59	A117	8np bright green	.90	.90
M60	A117	13np brt carmine	1.50	1.50
M61	A117	50np orange	2.75	2.75
		Nos. M56-M61 (6)	7.85	7.85

Indian UN Force in Gaza
No. 393 Overprinted in Carmine

1965, Jan. 15 Unwmk. Perf. 13½
M62	A190	15p blue gray	4.00	8.00

Overprint letters stand for "United Nations Emergency Force."

INTERNATIONAL COMMISSION IN INDO-CHINA

Catalogue values for all unused stamps in this section are for Never Hinged items.

Cambodia
India Nos. 207, 231, 211, 216 and 217 Overprinted in Black

Perf. 13½x14
1954, Dec. 1 Wmk. 196
1	A91	3p gray violet	.50	.50
2	A101	1a turquoise	.60	.60
3	A93	2a carmine	1.00	1.00
4	A95	8a blue green	4.00	4.25
5	A95	12a blue	5.50	6.25
		Nos. 1-5 (5)	11.60	12.60

The overprint reads "International Commission Cambodia." Top line is 18mm on Nos. 4-5; 15½mm on Nos. 1-3, 6-12.

Same Overprint on India Nos. 276, 279, 282, 286 and 287
1957, Apr. 1 Perf. 14x14½
6	A117	2np light brown	.40	.40
7	A117	6np gray	.40	.40
8	A117	13np bright carmine	1.00	.70
9	A117	50np orange	4.75	2.50
10	A117	75np plum	5.25	4.75
		Nos. 6-10 (5)	11.80	8.75

Same Overprint on India No. 303
1962 Wmk. 324
12	A117	2np light brown	.65	.65

Laos
India Nos. 207, 231, 211, 216 and 217 Overprinted in Black

Perf. 13½x14
1954, Dec. 1 Wmk. 196
1	A91	3p gray violet	.50	.50
2	A101	1a turquoise	.60	.60
3	A93	2a carmine	1.00	1.00
4	A95	8a blue green	4.00	4.25
5	A95	12a blue	5.50	6.25
		Nos. 1-5 (5)	11.60	12.60

The overprint reads "International Commission Laos." Top line is 18mm on Nos. 4-5; 15½mm on Nos. 1-3, 6-16.

Same Overprint on India Nos. 276, 279, 282, 286 and 287
1957, Apr. 1 Perf. 14x14½
6	A117	2np light brown	.40	.40
7	A117	6np gray	.40	.40
8	A117	13np brt carmine	1.00	.70
9	A117	50np orange	4.75	2.50
10	A117	75np plum	5.25	4.75
		Nos. 6-10 (5)	11.80	8.75

Same Overprint on India Nos. 303-305, 313-314
1962-65 Wmk. 324
12	A117	2np light brown	2.50	3.00
13	A117	3np brown ('63)	.60	.60
14	A117	5np emerald ('63)	.60	.60
15	A117	50np orange ('65)	2.00	2.25
16	A117	75np plum ('65)	4.25	4.75
		Nos. 12-16 (5)	9.95	11.20

Laos and Viet Nam
No. 393 Overprinted in Carmine

1965, Jan. 15 Unwmk. Perf. 13½
1	A190	15p blue gray	4.00	4.00

Overprint letters stand for "International Control Commission."

Nos. 406-408, 411-412, 417 and 419-420 Overprinted in Carmine

Perf. 14½x14, 14x14½
1968, Oct. 2 Photo. Wmk. 324
2	A202	2p reddish brown	.50	.50
3	A202	3p olive bister	.50	.50
4	A202	5p cerise	.50	.50
5	A203	10p bright blue	2.50	2.50
6	A203	15p green	1.00	1.00
7	A202	60p dark gray	1.10	1.10
8	A204	1r dp cl & red brn	1.75	2.25
9	A205	2r violet & brt green	4.00	5.50
		Nos. 2-9 (8)	11.85	13.85

The arrangement of the lines of the overprint varies on each denomination.

Viet Nam
India Nos. 207, 231, 211, 216 and 217 Overprinted in Black

Perf. 13½x14
1954, Dec. 1 Wmk. 196
1	A91	3p gray violet	.50	.50
2	A101	1a turquoise	.60	.60
3	A93	2a carmine	1.00	1.00
4	A95	8a blue green	4.00	4.25
5	A95	12a blue	5.50	6.25
		Nos. 1-5 (5)	11.60	12.60

The overprint reads "International Commission Viet Nam." Top line of overprint is 18mm on Nos. 4-5; 15½mm on Nos. 1-3, 6-16.

Same Overprint on India Nos. 276, 279, 282, 286 and 287
1957, Apr. 1 Perf. 14x14½
6	A117	2np light brown	.40	.40
7	A117	6np gray	.40	.40
8	A117	13np bright carmine	1.00	.70
9	A117	50np orange	4.75	2.10
10	A117	75np plum	5.25	4.75
		Nos. 6-10 (5)	11.80	8.35

Same Overprint on India Nos. 302-305, 313-314
1961-65 Wmk. 324
11	A117	1np blue green	1.40	1.40
12	A117	2np light brown ('62)	2.75	2.75
13	A117	3np brown ('63)	1.00	1.00
14	A117	5np emerald ('63)	.65	.80
15	A117	50np orange ('65)	2.25	2.75
16	A117	75np plum ('65)	4.25	4.75
		Nos. 11-16 (6)	12.30	13.45

OFFICIAL STAMPS

Nos. O1-O26 are normally found with very heavy cancellations, and values are for stamps so canceled. Lightly canceled stamps are seldom seen.

Nos. 11-12, 18, 20-22, 23a, 24, 26 Overprinted in Black

1866, Aug. 1 Unwmk. Perf. 14
O1	A7	½a blue	1,100.	140.00
a.		Inverted overprint		
O3	A7	1a brown		140.00
O4	A7	8a rose	22.50	50.00

The 8p lilac unwatermarked (No. 19) with "Service" overprint was not officially issued.

Wmk. 38
O5	A7	½a blue	300.00	12.50
a.		Inverted overprint		
b.		Without period		210.00
O6	A8	8p lilac	20.00	52.50
O7	A7	1a brown	300.00	15.00
a.		Inverted overprint		
O8	A7	2a yellow	300.00	85.00
a.		Imperf.		
b.		Inverted overprint		
O9	A7	4a green	200.00	80.00
a.		Inverted overprint		
O10	A7	4a green (I)	1,000.	250.00

Reprints were made of Nos. O5, O7, O10 (type II).

Revenue Stamps Surcharged or Overprinted

Queen Victoria — O1

Blue Glazed Paper
Black Surcharge
1866 Wmk. 36 Perf. 14 Vertically
O11	O1	2a violet	350.00	250.00

The note after No. 30 will apply here also.

No. O11 is often found with cracked surface or scuffs. Such examples sell for somewhat less.

Reprints of No. O11 are surcharged in either black or green, and have the word "SERVICE" 16½x2½mm, instead of 16½x2¾mm and "TWO ANNAS" 18x3mm, instead of 20x3¼mm.

O2   O3

O4

Green Overprint
1866
O12	O2	2a violet	1,000.	325.
O13	O3	4a violet	4,500.	1,250.
O14	O4	8a violet	5,000.	5,000.

The note after No. 30 will apply here also.

These stamps are often found with cracked surface or scuffs. Such examples sell for somewhat less.

Reprints of No. O12 have the overprint in sans-serif letters 2¼mm high, instead of Roman letters 2½mm high. On the reprints of No. O13 "SERVICE" measures 16½x2½mm, instead of 20¼x3mm and "POSTAGE" 18x2¼mm, instead of 22x3mm.

On No. O14 "SERVICE" is 20½mm long, instead of 20mm and "POSTAGE" is 23mm long, instead of 22mm. All three overprints are in a darker green than on the original stamps.

O5

Green Overprint
1866 Wmk. 40 Perf. 15½x15
Lilac Paper
O15	O5	½a violet	425.00	85.00
a.		Double overprint		3,000.

INDIA

Nos. 20, 31, 22-23, 23a, 26, 28 Overprinted in Black

1866-73   Wmk. 38   Perf. 14

O16	A7	½a blue	30.00	.35
O17	A7	½a bl, re-engraved	140.00	67.50
a.		Double overprint		
O18	A7	1a brown	32.50	.40
O19	A7	2a orange	4.50	2.00
a.		2a yellow	20.00	2.25
O20	A9	4a green (I)	2.75	1.50
O21	A11	8a rose	3.00	1.50
		Nos. O16-O21 (6)	212.75	73.25

The 6a8p with this overprint was not issued. Value $25.

Nos. 31, 22-23, 26, 28 Overprinted in Black

1874-82

O22	A7	½a blue, re-engraved	8.00	.25
a.		Blue overprint	350.00	45.00
O23	A7	1a brown	12.50	.25
a.		Blue overprint	550.00	120.00
O24	A7	2a orange	40.00	17.50
O25	A9	4a green (I)	12.50	2.75
O26	A11	8a rose	4.25	4.00
		Nos. O22-O26 (5)	77.25	24.75

Same Overprint on Nos. 36, 38, 40, 42, 44, 49

1883-97   Wmk. 39

O27	A17	½a green	.40	.25
a.		Pair, one without overprint		
b.		Double overprint		1,150.
O28	A19	1a maroon	.75	.25
a.		Inverted overprint	350.00	475.00
b.		Double overprint		1,150.
c.		1a violet brown	2.25	.35
O29	A21	2a ultramarine	4.50	.50
O30	A23	4a olive green	15.00	.40
O31	A25	8a red violet	7.00	.40
O32	A29	1r car rose & grn	11.00	.40
		Nos. O27-O32 (6)	38.65	2.20

Same Overprint on No. 54

1899

O33	A31	3p carmine rose	.25	.25

Same Overprint on Nos. 56-58

1900

O34	A17	½a light green	1.25	.30
O35	A19	1a carmine rose	2.50	.25
a.		Double overprint		1,350.
b.		Inverted overprint		1,400.
O36	A21	2a violet	27.50	.50
		Nos. O34-O36 (3)	31.25	1.05

Same Overprint on Nos. 60-63, 66-68, 70

1902-09

O37	A32	3p gray	.85	.25
O38	A33	½a green	1.00	.25
O39	A34	1a carmine rose	.85	.25
O40	A35	2a violet	2.50	.25
O41	A38	4a olive green	4.25	.25
O42	A39	6a bister	2.25	.25
O43	A40	8a red lilac	5.25	.50
O44	A42	1r car rose & green ('05)	4.50	.25
		Nos. O37-O44 (8)	21.45	2.25

Same Overprint on Nos. 78-79

1906-07

O45	A44	½a green	1.00	.25
O46	A45	1a carmine rose	1.75	.25
a.		Pair, one without overprint		—
b.		Overprint on back		

Same Overprint on Nos. 71, 73-76

1909

O47	A43	2r brown & rose	6.50	.90
O48	A43	5r violet & ultra	11.00	1.00
O49	A43	10r car rose & grn	21.00	8.50
a.		10r red & green	52.50	6.00
O50	A43	15r ol gray & ultra	52.50	30.00
O51	A43	25r ultra & org brn	130.00	50.00
		Nos. O47-O51 (5)	221.00	90.40

No. O51 also was used to pay for radio licenses, telephone and telegraphs, and stamps so used include "WIRELESS" in the cancel. Used values so canceled are worth 10-15% of the values shown, which are for postally used examples.

For surcharges see Nos. O67-O69.

Nos. 80-84, 88, 90-91 Overprinted in Black

1912-22

O52	A46	3p gray	.25	.25
O53	A47	½a green	.25	.25
a.		Double overprint	110.00	
O54	A48	1a carmine rose	.75	.25
a.		Double overprint		950.00
O55	A48	1a dk brn ('22)	1.00	.25
a.		Imperf., pair	75.00	
O56	A49	2a violet	.50	.25
O57	A52	4a olive green	.75	.25
O58	A53	6a bister	1.25	1.75
O59	A54	8a red violet	1.75	.75

Nos. 93-98 Overprinted in Black

O60	A56	1r green & red brn	2.00	.80
O61	A56	2r yel brn & car rose	2.50	3.50
O62	A56	5r violet & ultra	10.50	13.50
O63	A56	10r car & grn	35.00	32.50
O64	A56	15r ol grn & ultra	80.00	95.00
O65	A56	25r ultra & brn org	180.00	150.00
		Nos. O52-O65 (14)	316.50	299.30

For surcharge see No. O69b.

1921   Black Surcharge

O66	O6	9p on 1a rose	.75	.60

For overprints see Chamba No. O35, Gwalior No. O28.

Nos. O49-O51 Surcharged

1925

O67	A43	1r on 15r ol gray & ultra	4.00	3.00
O68	A43	1r on 25r ultra & org brn	20.00	60.00
O69	A43	2r on 10r red & grn	3.50	3.50
a.		2r on 10r car rose & green	210.00	55.00
b.		Surcharge on #O63 (error)	4,500.	

Nos. O64-O65 Surcharged

O70	A56	1r on 15r ol grn & ultra	19.00	65.00
a.		Inverted surcharge		
O71	A56	1r on 25r ultra & brn org	5.00	9.00
a.		Inverted surcharge	4,000.	
		Nos. O67-O71 (5)	51.50	140.50

1926   Black Surcharge

O73	O7	1a on 6a bister	.40	.40

Nos. 83, 101, 102, 99 Surcharged

O74	A48	1a on 1a dk brn (error)	180.00	180.00
O75	A58	1a on 1½a choc	.25	.25
O76	A59	1a on 1½a choc	1.75	4.00
b.		Double surcharge	30.00	
O77	A57	1a on 2a6p ultra	.50	.50
		Nos. O73-O77 (5)	182.90	185.15

Nos. O74, O75 and O76 have short bars over the numerals in the upper corners.

Nos. 106-108, 111, 126-127, 112, 116, 128, 118-119 Overprinted — a

1926-35   Wmk. 196

O78	A46	3p slate ('29)	.25	.25
O79	A47	½a green ('31)	5.00	.40
O80	A48	1a dark brown	.25	.25
a.		Overprint as on No. O55	100.00	4.75
O81	A49	2a vermilion ('35)	1.00	1.00
a.		Small die	.85	.25
O82	A60	2a dull violet	.25	.25
O83	A60	2a vermilion ('32)	.90	2.00
O84	A57	2a6p buff ('32)	.25	.25
O85	A52	4a olive green ('35)	1.00	.25
O86	A61	4a olive green	.35	.25
O87	A53	6a bister ('35)	18.00	9.00
O88	A54	8a red violet	.50	.25
O89	A55	12a claret	.50	1.75

Nos. 120-121, 123 Overprinted - b

O90	A56	1r grn & brn ('30)	2.25	.90
O91	A56	2r brn org & car rose ('30)	6.00	6.00
O92	A56	10r car & grn ('31)	70.00	50.00
		Nos. O78-O92 (15)	106.50	72.80

Nos. 138, 135, 139, 136 Overprinted Type "a"

1932-35

O93	A71	½a green ('35)	.60	.25
O94	A68	9p dark green	.25	.25
O95	A72	1a dark brown ('35)	1.90	.25
O96	A69	1a3p violet	.25	.25
		Nos. O93-O96 (4)	3.00	1.00

Nos. 151-153, 162-165 Overprinted Type "a"

1937-39   Perf. 13½x14

O97	A80	½a brown ('38)	22.50	.45
O98	A80	9p green	25.00	.60
O99	A80	1a carmine	4.75	.35

Type "b" Overprint

O100	A82	1r brn & slate ('38)	.70	.55
O101	A82	2r dk brn & dk vio ('38)	1.90	3.25
O102	A82	5r dp ultra & dk grn ('38)	3.25	7.50
O103	A82	10r rose car & dk violet ('39)	19.00	6.75
		Nos. O97-O103 (7)	77.10	19.45

No. 136 Surcharged in Black

1939, May   Wmk. 196   Perf. 14

O104	A69	1a on 1a3p violet	17.00	3.00

King George VI — O8

1939-43   Typo.   Perf. 13½x14

O105	O8	3p slate	.40	.40
O106	O8	½a brown	8.00	.40
O106A	O8	½a dk rose vio ('43)	.40	.40
O107	O8	9p green	.40	.40
O108	O8	1a car rose	.40	.40
O108A	O8	1a3p bister ('41)	7.00	1.25
O108B	O8	1½a dull pur ('43)	.40	.40
O109	O8	2a scarlet	.40	.40
O110	O8	2½a purple	.40	.40
O111	O8	4a dark brown	.40	.40
O112	O8	8a blue violet	.60	.40
		Nos. O105-O112 (11)	18.80	5.25

For overprints see Chamba Nos. O55-O65, Gwalior Nos. O52-O61, Nabha Nos. O40-O48, Patiala Nos. O63-O73, and Oman O1-O10.

Stamps overprinted "Postal Service" or "I. P. N." were not used as postage stamps.

Catalogue values for unused stamps in this section, from this point to the end of the section, are for Never Hinged items.

Nos. 203-206 (Gandhi Issue) Overprinted Type "a"

Perf. 11½

1948, Aug.   Unwmk.   Photo.

O112A	A90	1½a brown	65.00	45.00
O112B	A90	3½a violet	7,500.	750.00
O112C	A90	12a dk gray green	8,000.	2,500.
O112D	A90	10r rose brn & brn	225,000.	

Overprint forgeries exist.

Capital of Asoka Pillar
O9   O10

Perf. 13½x14

1950   Wmk. 196   Typo.

O113	O9	3p violet blue	.40	.40
O114	O9	6p chocolate	.40	.40
O115	O9	9p green	.45	.40
O116	O9	1a turquoise	.65	.40
O117	O9	2a red	.40	.40
O118	O9	3a vermilion	3.50	2.75
O119	O9	4a brown car	5.00	.40
O120	O9	6a purple	4.00	.40
O121	O9	8a orange brn	2.00	.40

Litho.
Perf. 14x13½

O122	O10	1r dark purple	2.60	.40
O123	O10	2r brown red	1.10	.40
O124	O10	5r dark green	2.00	2.25
O125	O10	10r red brown	6.00	22.50
		Nos. O113-O125 (13)	28.50	31.50

Issue dates: 1r-10r, Jan. 2, others, July 1.

1951, Oct. 1   Typo.

O126	O9	4a violet blue	.25	.25

Type of 1950 Redrawn, Denomination in Naye Paise
Typo. or Litho.

1957-58   Perf. 13½x14

O127	O9	1np slate blue	.90	.55
O128	O9	2np blue violet	.90	.55
O129	O9	3np chocolate	.90	.55
O130	O9	5np yellow green	.90	.55
O131	O9	6np turquoise	.90	.55
O132	O9	13np red	.90	.55
O133	O9	15np dk purple ('58)	.90	.55
O134	O9	20np vermilion	.90	.55
O135	O9	25np violet blue	.90	.55
O136	O9	50np reddish brown	1.60	.55
		Nos. O127-O136 (10)	9.70	5.50

Issue dates: 15np, June; others, Apr. 1.

Redrawn Type of 1957-58
Typo. or Litho.

1958-71   Wmk. 324   Perf. 13½x14

O137	O9	1np slate blue ('59)	.30	.30
O138	O9	2np blue violet ('59)	.30	.30
O139	O9	3np chocolate	.30	.30
O140	O9	5np yel green	.30	.30
O141	O9	6np turquoise ('59)	.30	.30
O142	O9	10np dk green ('63)	.30	.30
O142A	O9	13np red ('63)	.30	.30
O143	O9	15np dk purple	.30	.30
O144	O9	20np ver ('59)	.30	.30
O145	O9	25np vio blue ('59)	.30	.30
O146	O9	50np redsh brown ('59)	.30	.30

Litho.
Perf. 14

O147	O10	1r rose vio ('59)	.30	.30
O148	O10	2r rose red ('60)	.50	.30
a.		Watermark sideways ('69)		
O149	O10	5r green ('59)	1.00	1.40
a.		Watermark sideways ('69)	.90	.30
O150	O10	10r rose lake ('59)	1.50	1.10
a.		Watermark sideways ('71)	3.75	3.75
		Nos. O137-O150 (15)	6.60	6.40

INDIA — INDIA - CONVENTION STATES — CHAMBA

Perf. 14½x14
1967-76 Photo. Wmk. 360
Without Gum
O151	O11	2p violet black	.85	.85
O152	O11	3p dk red brown	.85	.85
O153	O11	5p bright green	.85	.85
O154	O11	6p Prussian blue	3.25	3.25
O155	O11	10p slate green	.85	.85
O156	O11	15p purple	.85	.85
O157	O11	20p orange ver	.85	.85
O158	O11	25p deep car ('76)	26.00	11.00
O159	O11	30p violet blue	.85	.85
O160	O11	50p red brown	.85	.85

Nos. O151-O160 (10)   36.05   21.05

No. O153 Overprinted

1971, Nov. 15 Wmk. 360
Without Gum
O161	O11	5p green	.40	.40

No. O153 Overprinted "Refugee / Relief"
O162	O11	5p green	1.00	1.00

No. O162 was used in Maharashtra state.

Capital of Asoka Pillar — O12

1971, Dec. 1(?) Without Gum
O163	O12	5p green	.35	.35

Nos. O161-O163 were obligatory on all official mail as a postal tax to benefit refugees from East Pakistan. The tax was paid out of the various governmental departments' budgets.

Type of 1968
1967-74 Wmk. 324 Perf. 14½x14
O164	O11	2p violet	.80	1.00
O165	O11	5p brt green ('74)	.80	.25
O166	O11	10p slate green ('74)	1.25	.25
O167	O11	15p purple ('73)	1.60	.40
O168	O11	20p dp orange ('74)	5.25	5.00
O169	O11	30p ultramarine	3.50	1.00
O170	O11	50p red brown ('73)	2.75	2.00
O171	O11	1r dull purple	.55	.25

Nos. O164-O171 (8)   16.50   10.15

O13   O14

Without Currency Designation
1976-80 Litho. Wmk. 360
Perf. 14½x14
Without Gum
O172	O13	2p violet black	.35	.35
O173	O13	5p bright green	.35	.35
O174	O13	10p slate green	.35	.35
O175	O13	15p purple	.35	.35
O176	O13	20p brown orange	.35	.35
O177	O13	25p carmine rose	.80	.80
O178	O13	30p blue ('79)	2.50	2.50
O179	O13	35p violet ('80)	.75	.35
O180	O13	50p org brown	3.50	1.75
O181	O13	1r dull purple ('80)	4.00	.90

Wmk. 324
O182	O13	1r dull purple	.90	.90

Perf. 14x13½
O183	O14	2r salmon rose	3.50	3.50
O184	O14	5r deep green	3.50	3.50
O185	O14	10r red brown	1.25	1.25

Nos. O172-O185 (14)   22.45   17.20

O15

Perf. 15x14
1981, Feb. Litho. Wmk. 360
Without Gum
O186	O15	2r orange vermilion	1.00	.60
O187	O15	5r dark green	3.00	1.40
O188	O15	10r dark red brown	6.00	3.00

Nos. O186-O188 (3)   10.00   5.00

Unwmk.
1981, Dec. 10 Litho. Imperf.
Cream Paper
O189	O13	5p bright green	.90	1.25
O190	O13	10p slate green	1.00	1.25
O191	O13	15p purple	1.00	1.25
O192	O13	20p brown orange	1.00	1.25
O193	O13	25p carmine rose	2.25	2.75
O194	O13	35p violet	1.25	.90
O195	O13	50p brown	2.25	2.25
O196	O13	1r dull purple	2.50	2.25
O197	O15	2r salmon rose	2.50	5.25
O198	O15	5r deep green	2.75	7.25
O199	O15	10r red brown	3.75	9.75

Nos. O189-O199 (11)   21.15   35.40

Perf. 12½x13
1982, Nov. 22 Photo. Wmk. 360
Without Gum
O200	O13	5p bright green	.80	1.10
O201	O13	10p slate green	1.00	1.25
O202	O13	15p purple	1.10	1.25
O203	O13	20p fawn	1.25	1.25
O204	O13	25p car rose	1.60	2.50
O205	O13	30p dark blue	1.60	2.50
O206	O13	35p violet	1.60	.70
O207	O13	50p light brown	2.50	2.50
O208	O13	1r dull purple	2.50	2.50
O209	O13	2r salmon rose	2.75	3.75
O210	O15	5r deep green	3.25	6.50
O211	O15	10r red brown	4.00	9.00

Nos. O200-O211 (12)   23.95   34.80

Perf. 12½x13
1984-99 Photo. Wmk. 324
Without Gum
O212	O13	5p green	.25	.25
O213	O13	10p dark green	.25	.25
O214	O13	15p rose lake	.25	.25
O215	O13	20p fawn	.25	.25
O216	O13	25p deep carmine	.25	.25
O217	O13	30p blue	.25	.25
O218	O13	35p purple	.25	.25
O219	O13	40p violet	.25	.25
O220	O13	50p brown	.25	.25
O221	O13	60p brown	.25	.25
O222	O15	1r violet brown	.25	.25
O223	O15	2r orange ver	.40	.25
O223A	O15	3r orange	.35	
O224	O15	5r gray green	1.00	1.00
O225	O15	10r red brown	2.00	1.00

Nos. O213-O225 (14)   6.15   4.50

Issued: 25p, 1986. 60p, 4/15/88; 40p, 10/15/88; 3r, 3/22/99; others, 4/16/84.

POSTAL TAX STAMPS

Catalogue values for unused stamps in this section are for Never Hinged items.

No. 408 Overprinted

Perf. 14½x14
1971, Nov. 15 Photo. Wmk. 324
RA1	A202	5p cerise	.50	.30

No. 408 Overprinted "Refugee/Relief"
RA2	A202	5p cerise	.30	.30

No. RA2 was used in Maharashtra. In order to make the obligatory tax stamps available immediately throughout India postmasters were authorized to overprint locally No. 408. This resulted in a great variety of mostly hand-stamped overprints of various types and sizes.

Refugees — PT1

Perf. 14x14½
1971, Dec. 1 Photo. Wmk. 324
RA3	PT1	5p cerise	.30	.30

Nos. RA1-RA3 were obligatory on all mail. The tax was for refugees from East Pakistan. See Nos. O161-O163.

INDIA - CONVENTION STATES

CONVENTION STATES OF THE BRITISH EMPIRE IN INDIA
Stamps of British India overprinted for use in the States of Chamba, Faridkot, Gwalior, Jhind, Nabha and Patiala. These stamps had franking power throughout all British India.

Forgeries
Numerous forgeries exist of the high valued Convention States stamps, unused and used. Most cancelled examples of those stamps whose value used is far greater than unused bear favor or counterfeit cancels. Such stamps are worth far less than the values below, which are for postally used examples. More valuable Indian States stamps should be expertized.

CHAMBA
'chəm-bə

LOCATION — A State of India located in the north Punjab, south of Kashmir.
AREA — 3,127 sq. mi.
POP. — 168,908 (1941)
CAPITAL — Chamba

The varieties with small letters in the overprint are not listed as the letters are merely broken and not from another font of type.

Indian Stamps Overprinted in Black

1887-95 Wmk. 39 Perf. 14
1	A17	½a green	2.25	2.00
a.		"CHMABA"	950.00	1,450.
c.		Double overprint	750.00	
2	A19	1a vio brn	4.50	5.00
a.		"CHMABA"	950.00	1,250.
3	A20	1a6p bis brn ('95)	6.00	21.00
4	A21	2a ultra	3.50	4.00
a.		2a dull blue	4.50	5.00
b.		As "a," "CHMABA"	3,300.	4,500.
5	A28	2a6p grn ('95)	52.50	175.00
6	A22	3a brn org	4.50	9.00
a.		"CHMABA"	2,800.	4,250.
b.		Inverted overprint		
d.		3a orange	32.50	37.50
7	A23	4a ol grn	9.50	16.00
a.		"CHMABA"	2,750.	4,250.
b.		4a slate green	9.00	21.00
8	A25	8a red violet	13.50	27.00
a.		"CHMABA"	6,000.	6,250.
9	A26	12a vio, red ('90)	10.50	24.00
a.		"CHMABA"	16,500.	
b.		1st "T" of "STATE" invtd	16,500.	
10	A27	1r gray	85.00	225.00
a.		"CHMABA"	21,000.	
11	A29	1r car rose & grn ('95)	19.00	26.00
12	A30	2r brn & rose ('95)	210.00	650.00
13	A30	3r grn & brn ('95)	210.00	525.00
14	A30	5r vio & bl ('95)	240.00	1,250.

Wmk. 38
15	A14	6a bis ('90)	11.00	32.50
c.		6a bister brn	29.00	29.00

Nos. 1-15 (15)   881.75   2,992.

1900 Wmk. 39
15B	A31	3p carmine rose	1.40	1.90

1902-04
16	A31	3p gray ('04)	1.00	3.50
a.		Inverted overprint	120.00	
17	A17	½a yellow green ('03)	1.00	3.50
a.		½a pale yel green ('02)	4.50	7.00
18	A19	1a carmine rose	2.50	.60
19	A21	2a violet ('03)	21.00	52.50

Nos. 16-19 (4)   25.50   60.10

1903-05
20	A32	3p gray	.35	2.40
a.		3p slate gray ('05)	.85	2.40
21	A33	½a green	3.25	1.90
22	A34	1a carmine rose	3.00	2.40
23	A35	2a violet	3.25	6.50
24	A37	3a brown org ('05)	8.50	12.00
25	A38	4a olive green ('04)	14.00	50.00
26	A39	6a bister ('05)	8.00	50.00
27	A40	8a red violet ('04)	12.00	50.00
28	A41	12a violet, red	16.00	70.00
29	A42	1r car rose & grn ('05)	14.00	50.00

Nos. 20-29 (10)   82.35   295.20

1907
30	A44	½a green	3.25	5.00
31	A45	1a carmine rose	3.75	6.00

1913-24
32	A46	3p gray	.60	1.75
a.		3p pale gray	3.25	
b.		3p bluish gray	4.50	
33	A47	½a green	3.75	4.00
a.		½a deep green	5.50	6.50
b.		½a brt redsh vio	21.00	
34	A48	1a carmine rose	21.00	24.00
a.		1p aniline carmine	4.00	8.00
35	A48	1a dk brn ('22)	5.25	9.00
36	A49	2a violet	7.50	22.50
37	A51	3a brown orange	11.00	17.50
38	A51	3a ultra ('24)	6.25	40.00
39	A52	4a olive green	5.00	10.00
40	A53	6a bister	7.50	15.00
41	A54	8a red violet	12.50	32.50
42	A55	12a carmine lake	7.50	25.00
a.		12a claret	25.00	22.50
43	A56	1r dp blue grn & red brn	35.00	75.00
b.		1r grn & brn	45.00	65.00
d.		1r dp turq grn & org brn ('23)	50.00	

Nos. 32-43 (12)   122.85   276.25

India No. 104 Overprinted

1921
44	A48	9p on 1a rose	1.25	21.00

India Stamps of 1913-26 Overprinted

1922-27
45	A58	1½a chocolate	40.00	250.00
46	A59	1½a chocolate	5.00	10.00
47	A59	1½a rose	1.90	35.00
48	A57	2a6p ultramarine	1.10	7.50
49	A57	2a6p brown orange	6.00	45.00

Nos. 45-49 (5)   54.00   347.50

India Stamps of 1926 Overprinted

1927-28 Wmk. 196
50	A46	3p slate	.30	2.75
51	A47	½a green	.45	3.75
52	A48	1a dark brown	2.50	3.50
53	A60	2a dull violet	3.00	7.50
54	A51	3a ultramarine	2.10	32.50
55	A61	4a olive green	1.40	14.00
57	A54	8a red violet	1.75	17.50
58	A55	12a claret	2.00	19.00

Overprinted

59	A56	1r green & brown	22.50	57.50

Nos. 50-55,57-59 (9)   36.00   157.75

India Stamps of 1926-35 Overprinted

1932-37
60	A71	½a green	1.25	17.50
61	A68	9p dark green	11.00	40.00
62	A72	1a dark brown	4.25	2.75
63	A69	1a3p violet	5.00	10.00
64	A59	1½a carmine rose	16.00	16.00
65	A49	2a vermilion	1.60	37.50
a.		Small die	160.00	175.00

305

INDIA - CONVENTION STATES — CHAMBA — FARIDKOT

66	A57	2a6p buff	9.00	30.00
67	A51	3a carmine rose	4.50	25.00
68	A52	4a ol grn ('36)	12.00	32.50
69	A53	6a bister ('37)	35.00	250.00
		Nos. 60-69 (10)	99.60	461.25

Same Overprint on India Stamps of 1937

1938   Wmk. 196   Perf. 13½x14

70	A80	3p slate	8.00	40.00
71	A80	½a brown	3.00	27.50
72	A80	9p green	12.50	60.00
73	A80	1a carmine	6.50	12.00

74	A81	2a scarlet	10.00	40.00
75	A81	2a6p purple	11.00	65.00
76	A81	3a yellow green	11.50	55.00
77	A81	3a6p ultra	11.50	60.00
78	A81	4a dark brown	30.00	55.00
79	A81	6a peacock blue	32.50	160.00
80	A81	8a blue violet	30.00	110.00
81	A81	12a carmine lake	22.50	120.00

Overprinted

82	A82	1r brown & slate	45.00	150.00
83	A82	2r dk brn & dk vio	75.00	600.00
84	A82	5r dp ultra & dk green	120.00	1,000.
85	A82	10r rose car & dk brown	190.00	1,900.
86	A82	15r dk grn & dk brown	200.00	2,750.
a.		Double overprint, one inverted	1,250.	
87	A82	25r dk vio & bl vio	290.00	2,600.
		Nos. 70-87 (18)	1,109.	9,805.
		Set, never hinged	1,300.	

India Nos. 151 and 153 Overprinted

1942

87B	A80	½a brown	62.50	87.50
		Never hinged	75.00	
88	A80	1a carmine	95.00	90.00
		Never hinged	160.00	

Same Ovpt. on India Stamps of 1941-42

1942-44

89	A83	3p slate	.75	8.25
90	A83	½a rose vio ('43)	.75	9.50
91	A83	9p lt green	1.00	30.00
92	A83	1a car rose ('43)	1.75	7.50
93	A84	1½a dk purple ('44)	3.00	18.00
94	A84	2a scarlet ('43)	3.50	20.00
95	A84	3a violet ('43)	10.00	65.00
96	A84	3½a ultra ('43)	3.50	60.00
97	A85	4a chocolate ('43)	3.50	20.00
98	A85	6a pck blue ('43)	15.00	50.00
99	A85	8a blue vio ('43)	15.00	75.00
100	A85	12a car lake ('43)	20.00	85.00
		Nos. 89-100 (12)	77.75	448.25
		Set, never hinged	200.00	

India Nos. 162-167 Overprinted

1943   Wmk. 196   Perf. 13½x14

101	A82	1r brown & slate	17.00	90.00
102	A82	2r dk brn & dk vio	17.00	500.00
103	A82	5r dp ultra & dk grn	30.00	575.00
104	A82	10r rose car & dk vio	60.00	900.00
105	A82	15r dk grn & dk brn	120.00	2,000.
106	A82	25r dk vio & bl vio	100.00	2,000.
		Nos. 101-106 (6)	344.00	6,065.
		Set, never hinged	850.00	

India No. 161A Ovptd.

1947

107	A81	14a rose violet	12.00	5.50

OFFICIAL STAMPS

Indian Stamps Overprinted in Black

1887-98   Wmk. 39   Perf. 14

O1	A17	½a green	1.25	.25
a.		"CHMABA"	575.00	575.00
c.		"SERV CE"		
O2	A19	1a vio brn	5.00	2.25
a.		"CHMABA"	850.00	850.00
c.		"SERV CE"	5,750.	
d.		"SERVICE" double	4,250.	1,600.
O3	A21	2a ultra	4.50	4.00
a.		2a dull blue	4.50	4.00
b.		"CHMABA"	1,750.	3,750.
O4	A22	3a brn org	3.00	19.00
a.		"CHMABA"	4,500.	5,250.
O5	A23	4a ol grn	7.00	12.00
a.		"CHMABA"	1,750.	3,750.
c.		"SERV CE"	6,000.	
O6	A25	8a red violet	10.00	10.00
a.		"CHMABA"	14,000.	14,000.
O7	A26	12a vio, red ('90)	15.00	72.50
a.		"CHMABA"	13,000.	
b.		1st "T" of "STATE" invtd.	16,000.	
d.		"CHMABA STATE" double, one inverted	100.00	
O8	A27	1r gray ('90)	27.50	300.00
a.		"CHMABA"	7,500.	
O9	A29	1r car rose & grn ('98)	9.00	62.50

Wmk. 38

O10	A14	6a bister	9.00	25.00
		Nos. O1-O10 (10)	91.25	507.50

1902-04   Wmk. 39

O11	A31	3p gray ('04)	.75	2.40
O12	A17	½a light green	3.00	6.00
O13	A19	1a carmine rose	2.50	2.00
O14	A21	2a violet ('03)	17.50	52.50
		Nos. O11-O14 (4)	23.75	62.90

A 2a value, Scott No. O14, was overprinted in Calcutta but never issued. Value, $50.

1903-05

O15	A32	3p pale gray	.40	.25
b.		3p slate gray	.55	.70
O16	A33	½a green	.40	.25
O17	A34	1a carmine rose	2.75	3.00
O18	A35	2a violet	1.50	2.25
O19	A38	4a olive green ('05)	4.25	30.00
O20	A40	8a red violet ('05)	16.00	30.00
O21	A42	1r car rose & grn ('05)	4.50	25.00
		Nos. O15-O21 (7)	29.80	90.75

1907

O22	A44	½a green	1.10	1.10
a.		Inverted overprint	9,500.	11,000.
O23	A45	1a carmine rose	3.25	3.75

1913

O24	A49	2a violet	17.50	
O25	A52	4a olive green	15.00	

India No. 63 Overprinted

O26	A35	2a violet	60.00

No. O26 was never placed in use.

India Stamps of 1911-29 Overprinted

1913-25

O27	A46	(a) 3p gray	.25	.60
a.		3p pale gray	1.60	3.50
b.		3p bluish gray	3.50	5.00
c.		3p slate	1.60	3.50
O28	A47	(a) ½a green	.25	.75
a.		½a dp green	4.50	1.60
b.		½a brt green	2.90	.35
O29	A48	(a) 1a carmine rose	.30	.25
O30	A48	(a) 1a dk brn ('25)	8.50	2.50
O31	A49	(a) 2a violet ('14)	1.40	26.00
O32	A52	(a) 4a olive green	1.75	30.00
O33	A54	(a) 8a red violet	5.00	42.50
O34	A56	(b) 1r dp blue grn & red brn	16.00	62.50
b.		1r green & brown ('23)	22.50	150.00
		Nos. O27-O34 (8)	33.45	165.10

India No. O66 Overprinted

1921

O35	O6	9p on 1a rose	.55	12.50

India Stamps of 1926-35 Overprinted

1927-39   Wmk. 196

O36	A46	3p slate ('28)	.55	.45
O37	A47	½a lt green ('28)	1.10	.25
O38	A48	9p dk grn ('32)	5.00	16.00
O39	A48	1a dark brown	.35	.25
O40	A69	1a3p violet ('32)	11.00	1.25
O41	A60	2a dull violet ('28)	5.50	1.90
O42	A61	4a olive green ('28)	3.90	4.50
O43	A54	8a red violet ('30)	22.50	22.50
O44	A55	12a claret ('28)	7.50	42.50

Overprinted

O45	A56	1r grn & brn	19.00	72.50
O45A	A56	2r brn org & car rose ('39)	30.00	425.00
O45B	A56	5r dk vio & ultra ('39)	52.50	525.00
O45C	A56	10r car & grn ('39)	82.50	450.00
		Nos. O36-O45C (13)	241.40	1,562.

India Stamps of 1926-35 Overprinted

1935-36

O46	A71	½a green	7.00	.75
O47	A72	1a dark brown	4.50	.50
O48	A49	2a vermilion	7.00	1.75
O49	A52	4a olive grn ('36)	15.00	12.50
		Nos. O46-O49 (4)	33.50	15.50

Same Overprint on India Stamps of 1937

1938   Perf. 13½x14

O50	A80	9p green	35.00	100.00
		Never hinged	52.50	
O51	A80	1a carmine	37.50	12.50
		Never hinged	70.00	

India Stamps of 1937 Overprinted

1940-41

O51A	A82	1r brn & sl ('41)	80.00	900.00
O52	A82	2r dk brn & dk vio	30.00	950.00
O53	A82	5r dp ultra & dk grn	40.00	1,000.
O54	A82	10r rose car & dk vio	65.00	1,700.

India Official Stamps of 1939-43 Overprinted

1941-46   Wmk. 196

O55	O8	3p slate ('44)	.50	1.75
O56	O8	½a brown	60.00	6.50
O57	O8	½a dk rose vio ('44)	.50	5.50
O58	O8	9p green	2.50	17.50
O59	O8	1a carmine rose	1.50	4.50
O60	O8	1a3p bister ('46)	105.00	27.50
O61	O8	1½a dull pur ('46)	9.50	12.50
O62	O8	2a scarlet ('44)	3.50	12.50
O63	O8	2½a purple ('43)	3.50	35.00
O64	O8	4a dk brn ('44)	3.50	27.50
O65	O8	8a blue vio ('41)	7.50	100.00
		Nos. O55-O65 (11)	197.50	250.75

India Nos. 162-165 Overprinted

1944

O66	A82	1r brown & slate	15.00	375.00
O67	A82	2r dk brn & dk vio	25.00	650.00
O68	A82	5r dp ultra & dk grn	50.00	950.00
O69	A82	10r rose car & dk vio	60.00	1,600.
		Nos. O66-O69 (4)	150.00	3,575.

FARIDKOT

fe-'rēd-,kōt

LOCATION — A State of India lying northeast of Nabha in the central Punjab.
AREA — 638 sq. mi.
POP. — 164,364
CAPITAL — Faridkot

Previous stamp issues are listed under Feudatory States. Stamps of Faridkot were superseded by those of India in 1901.

The varieties with small letters in the overprint are not listed as the letters are merely broken and not from another font.

India Stamps Overprinted in Black

1887-93   Wmk. 39   Perf. 14

4	A17	½a green	3.00	3.00
a.		"ARIDKOT"	—	4,250.
b.		"FAR DKOT"	—	4,250.
5	A19	1a violet brown	3.00	5.50
6	A21	2a ultramarine	3.50	13.00
a.		2a deep blue	6.50	15.00
7	A22	3a orange	12.50	22.50
a.		3a brown orange ('93)	6.00	12.50
8	A23	4a olive green	15.00	27.50
a.		"ARIDKOT"	2,900.	
b.		4a slate grn	12.00	50.00
9	A25	8a red violet	37.50	67.50
a.		"ARIDKOT"	4,500.	
10	A27	1r gray	67.50	550.00
a.		"ARIDKOT"	6,750.	
11	A29	1r car rose & grn ('93)	60.00	175.00

Wmk. 38

12	A14	6a bister	5.00	32.50
a.		6a olive bister	57.50	110.00
b.		As "a," "ARIDKOT"	2,750.	
		Nos. 4-12 (9)	207.00	896.50

1900   Wmk. Star. (39)

13	A31	3p car rose	4.00	80.00
14	A26	12a violet, red	67.50	625.00

OFFICIAL STAMPS

India Stamps Overprinted in Black

1886   Wmk. 39   Perf. 14

O1	A17	½a green	.90	1.90
a.		"SERV CE"	4,500.	
b.		"FAR DKOT"	5,000.	
c.		"ESRVICE"	5,250.	
O2	A19	1a violet brown	1.50	4.50
b.		1a plum	3.50	3.75
c.		As "b," "SERV CE"	5,500.	

INDIA - CONVENTION STATES — FARIDKOT — GWALIOR

O3	A21	2a ultramarine	3.00	19.00
a.		"SERV CE"	6,250.	
		2a dp blue	9.50	21.00
O4	A22	3a orange	6.00	57.50
		3a brn orange ('98)	10.00	8.00
O5	A23	4a olive green	8.50	60.00
d.		"SERVI CE" double, one albino	5,250. 60.00	
O6	A25	8a red lilac	22.50	50.00
a.		"SERV CE"	4,500.	
O7	A27	1r gray	82.50	450.00

Wmk. 38

O8	A14	6a bister	50.00	55.00
a.		6p olive bister	75.00	200.00
b.		"ARIDKOT"	2,500.	
c.		"SERVIC"	4,750.	
		Nos. O1-O8 (8)	174.90	697.90

1896   **Wmk. 39**

O9	A29	1r car rose & grn	140.00	1,000.

Obsolete March 31, 1901.

GWALIOR

ˈgwäl-ē-ˌoər

LOCATION — One of the Central Provinces of India
AREA — 26,008 sq. mi.
POP. — 4,006,159 (1941)
CAPITAL — Lashkar

The varieties with small letters in the overprint are not listed as the letters are merely broken and not from another font.

India Stamps Overprinted in Black

Lines Spaced 16-17mm

1885   **Wmk. 39**   **Perf. 14**

1	A17	½a green	120.00
2	A19	1a violet brown	120.00
3	A20	1a6p bister brown	190.00
4	A21	2a ultramarine	125.00
5	A25	8a red lilac	160.00
6	A27	1r gray	160.00

Wmk. 38

7	A9	4a green	200.00
8	A14	6a bister	200.00
		Nos. 1-8 (8)	1,275.

The Hindi overprint measures 13½-14x2mm and 15-15½x2½mm.

The two sizes are found in the same sheet in the proportion of one of the smaller to three of the larger.

The ½a, 1a, 2a, also exist with lines 13mm apart and the short Hindi overprint.

Reprints of the ½a and 1a have the 13mm spacing, the short Hindi overprint and usually carry the overprint "Specimen."

India Stamps Overprinted

Red Overprint

1885   **Wmk. 39**

9	A17	½a green	2.60	.35
10	A21	2a ultramarine	50.00	20.00
11	A27	1r gray	27.50	60.00

Wmk. 38

12	A9	4a green	70.00	35.00
		Nos. 9-12 (4)	150.10	115.35

Nos. 9-12 have been reprinted. They bear the short Hindi overprint. Most stamps bear the word "Reprint." Those without it cannot be distinguished from the originals.

1885-91   **Black Overprint**   **Wmk. 39**

13	A17	½a green	1.40	.25
a.		"GWALICR"	125.00	175.00
b.		Double overprint	1,750.	1,400.
14	A18	9p rose	50.00	85.00
15	A19	1a violet brown	3.75	.30
16	A20	1a6p bister brown	3.25	3.75
17	A21	2a ultramarine	7.50	.25
a.		"R" omitted	750.00	700.00
b.		2a deep blue	27.50	9.00
c.		As "b," small "G"	240.00	260.00
18	A22	3a brown orange	9.50	.35
		3a orange	32.50	32.50
19	A23	4a olive green	22.50	4.50
c.		4a slate green	22.50	4.50
c.		Small "G"	400.00	475.00
d.		Small raised "R"	750.00	

20	A25	8a red violet	11.00	2.75
21	A26	12a violet, red	5.00	1.40
a.		Pair, one without overprint	6,500.	
22	A27	1r gray	8.50	6.50

Wmk. 38

23	A14	6a bister	9.00	18.00
a.		6a olive bister	20.00	45.00
		Nos. 13-23 (11)	131.40	123.05

The Hindi overprint measures 13½-14x2mm and 15-15½x2½mm as in the preceding issue.

1896   **Wmk. 39**

24	A28	2a6p green	16.00	30.00
a.		"GWALICR"	1,250.	
25	A29	1r car rose & grn	17.00	10.00
a.		"GWALICR"	1,750.	3,750.
26	A30	2r bis brn & rose	7.00	3.50
27	A30	3r grn & brn	9.50	4.50
28	A30	5r vio & blue	17.50	8.50
		Nos. 24-28 (5)	67.00	56.50

The Hindi inscription varies from 13 to 15½mm long.

1899

29	A31	3p carmine rose	.75	.30
a.		Inverted overprint	2,900.	950.00

1901-04

30	A31	3p gray ('04)	8.50	62.50
31	A17	½a pale yellow green	3.75	3.75
b.		½a yellow green ('03)	5.50	2.40
32	A19	1a carmine rose	1.90	.50
33	A21	2a violet ('03)	6.50	2.00
34	A28	2a6p ultra ('03)	4.50	15.00
		Nos. 30-34 (5)	25.15	90.25

1903-08

"GWALIO" 14mm long, 1¾mm between lines

35	A32	3p pale gray	1.75	.30
a.		3p slate gray ('05)	1.75	.40
36	A33	½a green	.30	.25
37	A34	1a carmine rose	.25	.25
38	A35	2a pale violet ('04)	3.75	1.40
39	A36	2a6p ultra ('04)	37.50	100.00
40	A37	3a brn org ('04)	4.00	.55
41	A38	4a olive green	6.50	.65
b.		4a pale olive	24.00	8.50
42	A39	6a bister ('04)	4.00	4.50
43	A40	8a red violet ('05)	10.00	2.75
44	A41	12a vio, red ('05)	11.00	24.00
45	A42	1r car rose & grn ('05)	16.00	2.50
46	A43	2r brown & rose	50.00	60.00
		Nos. 35-46 (12)	143.75	527.50

1908-11

"GWALIOR" 13mm long, 2¾mm between lines

35A	A32	3p pale gray	5.00	.25
c.		3p slate gray	6.00	.55
36A	A33	½a green	.25	.75
37A	A34	1a carmine	14.00	4.50
38A	A35	2a violet	7.00	.30
39A	A36	2½a ultramarine	3.50	17.00
40A	A37	3a brn orange	8.00	.30
41A	A38	4a pale olive	6.50	.65
42A	A39	6a olive bister	17.00	2.25
43A	A40	8a red violet	17.50	1.75
44A	A41	12a violet, red	8.50	3.50
45A	A42	1r carmine & grn	17.00	1.40
46A	A43	2r brown & rose	10.00	12.00
47	A43	3r grn & brn ('08)	42.50	75.00
48	A43	5r vio & bl ('08)	27.50	40.00
		Nos. 35A-48 (14)	184.25	159.65

1907

"GWALIOR" 14mm long, 1¾mm between lines

49	A44	½a green	.25	.75

"GWALIOR" 13mm long, 2¾mm between lines

49A	A44	½a green	3.00	.30
50	A45	1a carmine rose	1.00	.30

1912-23

51	A46	3p gray	.25	.25
52	A47	½a light green	1.10	.25
a.		Inverted overprint	600.00	
53	A48	1a car rose	.45	.25
a.		Double overprint	27.50	
54	A48	1a dk brown ('23)	1.25	.25
55	A49	2a violet	3.50	.35
56	A51	3a orange	2.00	.25
57	A52	4a olive grn ('13)	1.00	.60
58	A53	6a bister	4.00	1.90
59	A54	8a red vio ('13)	5.50	1.60
60	A55	12a claret ('14)	2.50	4.25
61	A56	1r dp blue grn & red brn ('13)	19.00	2.25
62	A56	2r brn & car rose ('13)	19.00	5.50
63	A56	5r violet & ultra	45.00	7.50
		Nos. 51-63 (13)	104.55	25.20

India No. 104 Overprinted

1921

64	A48	9p on 1a rose	.30	.50

India Stamps of 1911-26 Overprinted

Hindi Overprint 15mm Long

1923-27

66	A59	1½a choc ('25)	5.50	1.00
67	A59	1½a rose ('27)	.30	.25
68	A57	2a6p ultra ('25)	4.50	2.00
69	A57	2a6p brown org ('27)	.40	.55
70	A51	3a ultra ('24)	6.50	.85
		Nos. 66-70 (5)	17.20	4.65

Similar Ovpt. on India Stamps of 1926-35

Hindi Overprint 13½mm Long

1928-32   **Wmk. 196**

71	A46	3p slate ('32)	1.25	.25
72	A47	½a green ('30)	1.75	.25
73	A48	1a dark brown	1.00	.25
74	A60	2a dull violet	.80	.35
75	A51	3a ultramarine	1.90	.45
76	A61	4a olive green	4.00	1.25
77	A54	8a red violet	5.00	1.25
78	A55	12a claret	7.00	4.25

Overprinted

79	A56	1r green & brown	9.00	7.00
80	A56	2r brn org & car rose	9.00	5.00
81	A56	5r dk vio & ultra ('29)	45.00	35.00
82	A56	10r car & grn ('30)	120.00	62.50
83	A56	15r ol grn & ultra ('30)	225.00	100.00
84	A56	25r bl & ocher ('30)	550.00	300.00
		Nos. 71-84 (14)	980.70	517.80

India Stamps of 1932-35 Overprinted in Black

Hindi Overprint 13½mm Long

1933-36

85	A71	½a green ('36)	.80	.25
86	A68	9p dk green ('33)	4.00	.55
87	A72	1a dk brown ('36)	.25	.25
88	A69	1a3p violet ('36)	2.25	.25
89	A49	2a vermilion ('36)	5.00	3.50
		Nos. 85-89 (5)	12.30	4.80

Same Ovpt. on India Stamps of 1937

1938-40   **Perf. 13½x14**

90	A80	3p slate ('40)	10.00	.25
91	A80	½a brown	11.00	.25
92	A80	9p green ('40)	60.00	6.00
93	A81	1a carmine	10.00	.25
94	A81	3a yel green ('39)	35.00	6.50
95	A81	4a dark brown	55.00	5.25
96	A81	6a pck blue ('39)	12.00	16.50
		Nos. 90-96 (7)	193.00	35.00

Same Overprinted on India Stamps of 1941-43

1942-49

100	A83	3p slate ('44)	.30	.25
101	A83	½a rose vio ('46)	.65	.25
102	A83	9p light green	1.00	.25
103	A83	1a car rose ('44)	.60	.25
104	A84	1½a dk purple ('44)	4.50	.30
105	A84	2a scarlet ('44)	1.00	.25
a.		Double overprint		450.00
106	A84	3a violet ('44)	4.00	3.00
a.		Double overprint		425.00
108	A85	4a choc ('44)	3.00	.25
109	A85	6a pck blue ('48)	9.00	32.50
110	A85	8a blue violet	1.50	2.75
111	A85	12a carmine lake	5.50	27.50

India Nos. 162-167 Overprinted

112	A82	1r brn & sl ('45)	9.00	2.00
113	A82	2r dk brn & dk vio ('49)	15.00	14.00
114	A82	5r dp ultra & dk grn ('49)	20.00	50.00
115	A82	10r rose car & dk vio ('49)	20.00	52.50
116	A82	15r dk grn & dk brn ('48)	60.00	250.00
117	A82	25r dk vio & blue vio ('48)	55.00	22.50
		Nos. 100-106,108-117 (17)	210.05	458.55

India Stamps of 1941-43 Overprinted

1949

118	A83	3p slate	3.00	1.00
119	A83	½a rose violet	3.00	1.00
120	A83	1a carmine rose	3.00	1.00
121	A84	2a scarlet	27.50	2.75
122	A84	3a violet	65.00	37.50
123	A85	4a chocolate	11.00	4.25
124	A85	6a pck blue	50.00	90.00
125	A85	8a blue violet	100.00	82.50
126	A85	12a carmine lake	525.00	325.00
		Nos. 118-126 (9)	787.50	545.00

OFFICIAL STAMPS

India Stamps Overprinted in Black

1895   **Wmk. 39**   **Perf. 14**

O1	A17	½a green	1.75	.25
a.		Double overprint	1,500.	
O2	A19	1a maroon	20.00	1.60
a.		1a plum	6.50	.25
O3	A21	2a ultramarine	7.00	.60
a.		2a deep blue	5.25	.55
O4	A23	4a olive green	8.50	2.75
a.		4a slate green	7.00	2.75
O5	A25	8a red violet	9.00	5.25
O6	A29	1r car rose & grn	14.00	3.50
		Nos. O1-O6 (6)	60.25	13.95

Nos. O1 to O6 inclusive are known with the last two characters of the lower word transposed.

1901-04

O7	A31	3p gray ('04)	2.75	4.25
O8	A17	½a yel green	2.25	.25
a.		½a pale yel green	9.00	.25
O9	A19	1a carmine rose	11.00	.25
O10	A21	2a ultra ('03)	4.00	4.25
		Nos. O7-O10 (4)	20.00	9.00

1902

O11	A31	3p carmine rose	3.00	.55

1903-05

Overprint 10mm between lines

O12	A32	3p gray	.75	.25
O13	A33	½a green	2.25	.25
b.		½a slate gray ('05)	.75	.25
O14	A34	1a carmine rose	1.25	.25
O15	A35	2a violet ('05)	7.00	1.00
b.		2a pale violet	5.50	.40
O16	A38	4a olive grn ('05)	17.50	.75
O17	A40	8a red violet	8.00	4.00
		8a claret	37.50	8.50
O18	A42	1r car rose & grn ('05)	3.50	3.00
		Nos. O12-O18 (7)	40.25	9.50

1908

Overprint 10mm between lines

O19	A16	½a green	16.00	.25
O20	A45	1a carmine rose	14.00	.25

No. O13 with 10mm spacing is known with the two overprint lines transposed. This is due to a shift in the positioning of the overprint, rather than an actual transposition of the overprint.

1907-08

Overprint 8mm between lines

O12A	A32	3p gray	12.50	.25
b.		3p slate gray	22.50	2.50
c.		8¾mm between lines	100.00	2.75
O13A	A33	½a green	9.00	.25
b.		8¾mm between lines	80.00	2.50
O14A	A34	1a carmine rose	6.50	.25
b.		8¾mm between lines	52.50	2.50
O15A	A35	2a pale violet	22.50	.80
b.		8¾mm between lines	160.00	8.00
O16A	A38	4a olive green	4.50	1.00
b.		8¾mm between lines	52.50	11.00
O17A	A40	8a red violet	12.00	4.00
b.		8¾mm between lines	95.00	32.50

307

INDIA - CONVENTION STATES — GWALIOR — JIND

O18A	A42	1r car rose & brn ('08)	70.00	14.00	
b.		8¾mm between lines	450.00	100.00	
		Nos. O12A-O18A (7)	137.00	20.55	

1907
Overprint 8mm between lines

O19A	A44	½a green	1.75	.25	
b.		8¾mm between lines	22.50	2.50	
O20A	A45	1a carmine rose	87.50	2.25	
b.		8¾mm between lines	575.00	22.50	

1913-23

O21	A46	3p gray	1.75	.25	
a.		Pair, one without overprint	2,750.		
b.		3p pale gray	.80		
c.		3p bluish gray	—	1.00	
d.		3p slate	1.40	.30	
O22	A47	½a light green	.25	.25	
a.		½a emerald		.25	
O23	A48	1a carmine rose	.55	.25	
		Double overprint	80.00		
O24	A49	2a reddish violet	2.25	1.25	
O25	A52	4a olive green	1.10	1.90	
O26	A54	8a red violet	3.25	3.75	
O27	A56	1r dp blue grn & red brn	75.00	55.00	
b.		1r green & brown	65.00	32.50	
c.		1r dp turq-grn & org brn ('23)	75.00	50.00	
		Nos. O21-O27 (7)	84.15	62.65	

India No. O66 Overprinted

1921

O28	O6	9p on 1a rose	.25	.30	

India No. 83 Overprinted

1923

O29	A48	1a dark brown	8.00	.30	

Similar Ovpt. on India Stamps of 1926-35

1927-35   **Wmk. 196**

O30	A46	3p slate	.30	.25	
O31	A47	½a green	.25	.25	
O32	A48	1a dark brown	.25	.25	
O33	A60	2a dull violet	.25	.25	
O34	A61	4a olive green	2.25	.30	
O35	A54	8a red violet ('28)	1.10	1.90	

Overprinted

O36	A56	1r green & brown	1.40	2.25	
O37	A56	2r brn org & car rose ('35)	32.50	40.00	
O38	A56	5r dk vio & ultra ('32)	50.00	375.00	
O39	A56	10r car & grn ('32)	275.00	750.00	
		Nos. O30-O39 (10)	363.30	1,170.	

India Stamps of 1926-35 Overprinted

1933-37   **Perf. 13½x14, 14**

O40	A71	½a green ('36)	.25	.25	
O41	A68	9p dk green ('35)	.25	.25	
O42	A72	1a dk brown ('36)	.25	.25	
O43	A69	1a3p violet ('33)	.55	.25	
O44	A49	2a ver ('36)	.25	.45	
a.		Small die ('36)	7.00	1.40	
O45	A52	4a olive green ('37)	.65	.80	
		Nos. O40-O45 (6)	2.20	2.25	

For surcharge see No. O62.

Same Overprint on India Stamps

1938   **Perf. 13½x14**

O46	A80	½a brown	6.00	.50	
		Never hinged	9.50		
O47	A80	1a carmine	3.00	.50	
		Never hinged	4.50		

India Nos. 162-165 Overprinted

1945-48   **Wmk. 196**   **Perf. 13½x14**

O48	A82	1r brown & slate	10.00	30.00	
O49	A82	2r dk brn & dk vio	12.00	160.00	
O50	A82	5r dp ultra & dk grn ('46)	20.00	900.00	
O51	A82	10r rose car & dk vio ('48)	55.00	2,100.	
		Nos. O48-O51 (4)	97.00	3,190.	

India Official Stamps of 1939-43 Overprinted

1940-44   **Wmk. 196**   **Perf. 13½x14**

O52	O8	3p slate	.35	.25	
O53	O8	3p brown	10.00	.25	
O54	O8	½a dk rose vio ('43)	1.00	.25	
O55	O8	9p green ('43)	.85	.75	
O56	O8	1a car rose ('41)	1.50	.25	
O57	O8	1a3p bister ('42)	45.00	1.90	
O58	O8	1½a dl pur ('43)	.65	.30	
O59	O8	2a scarlet ('41)	.65	.30	
O60	O8	4a dk brn ('44)	.75	3.75	
O61	O8	8a blue vio ('44)	5.00	12.50	
		Nos. O52-O61 (10)	65.75	20.50	

Gwalior No. O43 with Additional Surcharge in Black

1942

O62	A69	1a on 1a3p violet	17.50	4.00	
		Never hinged	27.50		

JIND
'jind
(Jhind)

LOCATION — A State of India in the north Punjab.
AREA — 1,299 sq. mi.
POP. — 361,812 (1941)
CAPITAL — Sangrur

Previous stamp issues are listed under Feudatory States.

The varieties with small letters are not listed as the letters are merely broken and not from another font.

India Stamps Overprinted in Black

1885   **Wmk. 39**   **Perf. 14**

33	A17	½a green	12.50	11.00	
a.		Overprint reading down	190.00	210.00	
34	A19	1a violet brown	90.00	125.00	
a.		Overprint reading down	2,100.	2,300.	
35	A21	2a ultra	47.50	32.50	
a.		Overprint reading down	1,400.	1,500.	
36	A25	8a red lilac	800.00		
a.		Overprint reading down		18,000.	
37	A27	1r gray	800.00		
a.		Overprint reading down		21,000.	

Wmk. 38

38	A9	4a green	140.00	160.00	
		Nos. 33-38 (6)	1,890.	328.50	

On the reprints of Nos. 33 to 38 "Jhind" measures 8mm instead of 9mm and "State" 9mm instead of 9½mm.
Examples of "inverted overprints" exist of the ½a, 1a and 2a with the lines much less curved. These are thought to come from a trial printing.

India Stamps Overprinted in Red or Black

1885   **Wmk. 39**

39	A17	½a green (R)	210.00		
40	A19	1a violet brown	210.00		
41	A21	2a ultra (R)	240.00		
42	A25	8a red lilac	325.00		
43	A27	1r gray (R)	350.00		

Wmk. 38

44	A9	4a green (R)	325.00		
		Nos. 39-44 (6)	1,660.		

India Stamps Overprinted

1886   **Wmk. 39**   **Red Overprint**

45	A17	½a green	75.00		
a.		"JEIND"	24.00		
46	A21	2a ultramarine	75.00		
a.		"JEIND"	2,400.		
47	A27	1r gray	120.00		
a.		"JEIND"	42.50		

Wmk. 38

48	A9	4a green	100.00		
		Nos. 45-48 (4)	370.00		

Nos. 46, 47 and 48 were not placed in use.

1886-98   **Wmk. 39**   **Black Overprint**

49	A17	½a green ('88)	1.25	.25	
		Inverted overprint	290.00		
50	A19	1a vio brn	6.50	.40	
a.		"JEIND"	900.00		
c.		1a plum ('99)	12.00	1.00	
51	A20	1a6p bis brn ('97)	6.00	9.00	
52	A21	2a ultra	6.00	1.00	
53	A22	3a brown orange ('91)	8.00	1.90	
54	A23	4a olive green	9.00	5.00	
		4a slate green	16.00	1.00	
55	A25	8a dull mauve	21.00	47.50	
		"JEIND"	2,900.		
b.		8a magenta ('97)	27.50	65.00	
56	A26	12a vio, *red* ('97)	15.00	50.00	
57	A27	1r gray ('91)	21.00	95.00	
58	A29	1r car rose & grn ('98)	22.50	95.00	
59	A30	2r brn & rose ('97)	600.00	2,300.	
60	A30	3r grn & brn ('97)	900.00	1,900.	
61	A30	5r vio & bl ('97)	950.00	1,600.	

Wmk. 38

62	A14	6a bister	11.00	40.00	
a.		6a olive bister ('91)	17.50	50.00	
		Nos. 49-62 (14)	2,577.	6,145.	

1900   **Wmk. 39**

63	A31	3p carmine rose	1.25	4.00	

1902-04

64	A31	3p gray ('04)	.45	5.50	
65	A17	½a pale yellow	8.50	11.00	
a.		½a yellow green ('03)	12.50	12.50	
66	A19	1a carmine rose	3.50	15.00	
		Nos. 64-66 (3)	12.45	31.50	

1903-09

67	A32	3p pale gray	.65	.30	
		3p slate gray ('05)	.85	.85	
68	A33	½a green	4.50	3.25	
69	A34	1a car rose ('09)	3.50	2.75	
70	A35	2a mauve ('06)	6.50	1.90	
d.		2a pale violet	9.00	3.50	
70A	A36	2a6p ultra ('09)	3.25	12.50	
71	A37	3a brown orange	8.50	1.75	
		Double overprint	175.00	325.00	
72	A38	4a olive green	17.50	19.00	
		4a pale olive	12.50	22.50	
73	A39	6a bister ('05)	15.00	50.00	
74	A40	8a red violet	12.00	37.50	
75	A41	12a vio, *red* ('05)	8.50	27.50	
76	A42	1r car rose & grn ('05)	12.00	47.50	
		Nos. 67-76 (11)	91.90	203.95	

1907

77	A44	½a green	1.90	.50	
78	A45	1a carmine rose	4.25	.75	

1913

80	A46	3p gray	.25	2.50	
81	A47	½a green	.25	.75	
82	A48	1a carmine rose	.25	.65	
83	A49	2a violet	.25	5.00	
84	A51	3a brown orange	1.90	20.00	
85	A53	6a bister	15.00	57.50	
		Nos. 80-85 (6)	17.90	86.40	

90	A48	1a carmine rose	3.00	.25	
91	A49	2a violet	4.50	2.00	
92	A51	3a brown orange	1.00	8.50	
93	A52	4a olive green	3.50	15.00	
94	A53	6a yellow bister	10.00	35.00	
a.		6a brn bister	15.00	30.00	
95	A54	8a red magenta	8.25	37.50	
a.		8a bright mauve ('18)		60.00	
b.		8a deep mauve ('25)	27.50	42.50	
96	A55	12a claret	6.50	42.50	
97	A56	1r dp blue grn & red brn	22.50	52.50	
b.		1r green & brown	42.50		
		Nos. 88-97 (10)	67.25	193.75	

India No. 104 Overprinted

1921

98	A48	9p on 1a rose	1.25	12.50	

India Stamps of 1913-19 Overprinted

1922

99	A58	1½a chocolate	8.50	11.00	
100	A57	2a6p ultramarine	.80	8.00	

Same Overprint on India Stamps of 1911-26

1924

101	A48	1a dark brown	7.00	4.00	
102	A59	1½a chocolate	1.75	1.00	

Same Overprint on India No. 87

1925

103	A51	3a ultramarine	4.50	10.00	

Same Overprint on India Stamps of 1911-26

1927

104	A59	1½a rose	.40	3.25	
105	A57	2a6p brn org	2.50	14.00	
106	A56	2r yel brn & car rose	24.00	225.00	
107	A56	5r vio & ultra	85.00	625.00	
		Nos. 104-107 (4)	111.90	867.25	

India Stamps of 1926-35 Overprinted

1927-32   **Wmk. 196**

108	A46	3p slate	.25	.25	
109	A47	½a green ('29)	.65	.35	
110	A48	9p dk grn ('32)	2.50	.45	
111	A48	1a dark brown ('28)	.25	.25	
112	A69	1a3p violet ('32)	.25	.30	
113	A59	1½a carmine rose	1.50	6.25	
114	A60	2a dull violet	6.50	1.50	
115	A57	2a6p buff	4.50	22.50	
116	A51	3a ultramarine	10.00	32.50	
117	A61	4a olive green	13.00	4.50	
118	A54	8a red violet	15.00	5.00	
119	A55	12a claret	15.00	40.00	

Indian Stamps of 1911-23 Overprinted

120	A56	1r grn & brn ('30)	17.00	26.00	
121	A56	2r buff & car rose ('30)	45.00	250.00	
122	A56	5r dk vio & ultra ('28)	22.50	62.50	
123	A56	10r car rose & grn ('28)	27.50	20.00	
124	A56	15r ol grn & blue ('29)	225.00	1,750.	
125	A56	25r blue & ocher ('29)	400.00	2,250.	
		Nos. 108-125 (18)	806.40	4,472.	

India Stamps of 1926-35 Overprinted

1934-37

126	A71	½a green	.30	.25	
127	A72	1a dark brown	2.25	.30	
128	A49	2a vermilion	8.50	.75	
129	A51	3a carmine rose	4.50	.45	
130	A70	3a6p deep blue ('37)	6.00	30.00	

INDIA - CONVENTION STATES — JIND — NABHA

131	A52	4a olive green	4.50	2.00
132	A53	6a bister ('37)	1.00	32.50
		Nos. 126-132 (7)	27.05	66.25

Same Overprint on India Stamps of 1937

1937-38   Wmk. 196   Perf. 13½x14

133	A80	3p slate ('38)	6.50	3.75
134	A80	½a brown ('38)	.65	7.50
135	A80	9p green	.65	4.50
136	A80	1a carmine	.50	.75
137	A81	2a scarlet ('38)	2.50	32.50
138	A81	2a6p purple ('38)	1.40	42.50
139	A81	3a yel grn ('38)	5.00	40.00
140	A81	3a6p ultra ('38)	5.50	42.50
141	A81	4a dk brown ('38)	12.50	35.00
142	A81	6a pck blue ('38)	9.00	65.00
143	A81	8a blue vio ('38)	10.00	50.00
144	A81	12a car lake ('38)	4.00	60.00

Indian Stamps of 1937-40 Overprinted

1938

145	A82	1r brn & slate	8.00	70.00
146	A82	2r dk brn & dk vio	10.00	290.00
147	A82	5r dp ultra & dk grn	20.00	175.00
148	A82	10r rose car & dk violet	40.00	150.00
149	A82	15r dk grn & dk brown	60.00	1,900.
150	A82	25r dk vio & bl vio	650.00	2,600.
		Nos. 133-150 (18)	846.20	5,569.

India Stamps of 1937 Overprinted

1942-43   Wmk. 196   Perf. 13½x14

155	A80	3p slate	12.50	30.00
156	A80	½a brown	.80	3.75
157	A80	9p green	12.50	32.50
158	A80	1a carmine	.65	9.00
159	A82	1r brn & slate	7.50	40.00
160	A82	2r dk brn & dk violet	12.50	62.50
161	A82	5r dp ultra & dk grn	30.00	200.00
162	A82	10r rose car & dk vio ('43)	40.00	150.00
163	A82	15r dk grn & dk brn ('43)	125.00	525.00
164	A82	25r dk vio & bl vio	40.00	525.00
		Nos. 155-164 (10)	281.45	1,578.

Same Overprint on India Stamps of 1941-43

165	A83	3p slate	.35	2.10
166	A83	½a rose vio ('43)	.35	2.75
167	A83	9p light green	.50	5.00
168	A83	1a car rose ('43)	.65	1.60
169	A84	1a3p bister ('43)	.65	7.00
170	A84	1½a dark purple	6.50	8.00
171	A84	2a scarlet	.65	7.50
172	A84	3a violet ('43)	4.00	12.00
173	A84	3½a ultramarine	6.00	17.50
174	A85	4a chocolate	2.00	9.00
175	A85	6a pck blue	6.00	25.00
176	A85	8a blue violet	4.50	20.00
177	A85	12a carmine lake	10.00	27.50
		Nos. 165-177 (13)	42.15	147.45

OFFICIAL STAMPS

India Stamps Overprinted in Black

1885   Wmk. 39   Perf. 14

O1	A17	½a green	4.25	.60
a.		"JHIND STATE" reading down	175.00	80.00
O2	A19	1a violet brown	1.00	.25
a.		"JHIND STATE" reading down	22.50	8.50
O3	A21	2a ultra	60.00	60.00
a.		"JHIND STATE" reading down	1,700.	2,250.
		Nos. O1-O3 (3)	65.25	60.85

The reprints may be distinguished by the same measurements as the reprints of the corresponding regular issue.

India Stamps Overprinted in Red or Black

1885

O4	A17	½a green (R)		150.00
O5	A19	1a violet brown		175.00
O6	A21	2a ultra (R)		165.00
		Nos. O4-O6 (3)		490.00

India Stamps Overprinted

1886   Red Overprint

O7	A17	½a green		62.50
a.		"JEIND"		1,050.
b.		"ERVICE"		6,000.
O8	A21	2a ultramarine		75.00
a.		"JEIND"		2,250.
b.		"ERVICE"		3,750.

No. O8 was not placed in use.

1886-96   Black Overprint

O9	A17	½a green ('88)	7.00	.25
O10	A19	1a violet brown	70.00	
a.		"JEIND"	750.00	
b.		"ERVICE"		
d.		1a plum ('02)	27.50	1.90
O11	A21	2a ultramarine	6.50	1.50
b.		2a dull blue	8.50	1.90
O12	A23	4a olive green ('92)	9.00	5.25
b.		4a slate green	12.00	7.50
O13	A25	8a dull mauve ('92)	12.50	10.00
b.		8p magenta ('97)	14.00	16.00
O14	A29	1r car rose & grn ('96)	14.00	75.00
		Nos. O9-O14 (6)	119.00	92.00

1902

O15	A17	½a light green	5.00	.50

1903-06

O16	A32	3p pale gray	1.90	.25
a.		3p slate gray ('06)	1.50	.25
O17	A33	1a car rose	6.50	.25
a.		"HIND"	4,500.	450.00
b.		"SERV CE"		650.00
O18	A34	1a carmine rose	7.50	.25
a.		"HIND"	6,250.	450.00
O19	A35	2a pale violet	7.00	1.50
a.		2a mauve	4.00	.25
O20	A38	4a olive green	5.00	.50
O21	A40	8a red violet	15.00	1.50
O22	A42	1r car rose & grn ('06)	3.25	2.50
		Nos. O16-O22 (7)	46.15	6.75

1907

O23	A44	½a green	2.50	.25
O24	A45	1a carmine rose	3.50	.25

Indian Stamps of 1911-26 Overprinted

a   b

1914-27

O25	A46(a)	3p gray	.25	.25
b.		3p pale gray	.45	.25
c.		3p bluish gray	—	1.60
O26	A47(a)	½a light green	.25	.25
a.		½a emerald	6.00	.45
b.		½a brt green ('23)	2.50	.45
O27	A48(a)	1a car rose	.80	.25
O28	A49(a)	2a violet	.55	.45
O29	A52(a)	4a olive green	2.10	.35
O30	A54(a)	8a red violet	1.25	1.50
O31	A56(b)	1r dp blue grn & red brn	9.00	2.50
b.		1r green & brown ('23)	40.00	
O32	A56(b)	2r brn & car rose ('27)	22.50	85.00
O33	A56(b)	5r vio & ultra ('27)	50.00	525.00
		Nos. O25-O33 (9)	86.70	615.55

India Nos. 83 and 89 Overprinted Type "a"

1924-27

O34	A48	1a dark brown	.65	.25
O35	A53	6a bister ('27)	4.50	2.50

India Stamps of 1926-35 Overprinted — c

1927-32

O36	A46	3p slate ('28)	.25	.25
O37	A47	½a green ('29)	.25	1.25
O38	A68	9p dark green ('32)	1.10	.25
O39	A48	1a dark brown	.25	.25
O40	A69	1a3p violet ('32)	.45	.25
O41	A60	2a dull violet ('29)	.40	.25
O42	A61	4a olive green ('29)	.40	.25
O43	A54	8a red violet ('29)	.90	3.50
O44	A55	12a claret ('28)	3.25	30.00

India Stamps of 1911-23 Overprinted — d

O45	A56	1r green & brown ('28)	10.00	12.00
O46	A56	2r buff & car rose ('30)	95.00	67.50
O47	A56	5r dk vio & ultra ('29)	15.00	525.00
O48	A56	10r car rose & grn	62.50	225.00
		Nos. O36-O48 (13)	189.75	865.75

India Stamps of 1926-35 Overprinted Type "c"

1934-37

O49	A71	½a green	.25	.25
O50	A72	1a dark brown	.25	.25
O51	A49	2a vermilion	.35	.25
O52	A57	2a6p buff ('37)	2.50	27.50
O53	A52	4a olive green	12.00	.30
O54	A53	6a bister ('37)	7.50	35.00
		Nos. O49-O54 (6)	22.85	63.55

India Nos. 151-153 Overprinted Type "c"

1937-42   Perf. 13½x14

O55	A80	½a brown ('42)	67.50	.50
O56	A80	9p green	4.00	30.00
O57	A80	1a carmine	4.50	.45

India Nos. 162-165 Overprinted Type "d"

O58	A82	1r brn & sl ('40)	45.00	90.00
O59	A82	2r dk brn & dk vio ('40)	55.00	600.00
O60	A82	5r dk grn & dk grn ('40)	100.00	800.00
O61	A82	10r rose car & dk vio ('40)	450.00	2,250.
		Nos. O55-O61 (7)	726.00	3,771.

India Official Stamps of 1939-43 Overprinted

1940-43

O62	O8	3p slate	.40	2.25
O63	O8	½a brown	3.00	1.50
O64	O8	½a dk rose vio ('43)	.40	.30
O65	O8	9p green	2.00	17.50
O66	O8	1a car rose	2.50	.25
O67	O8	1½a dull pur ('43)	6.00	3.25
O68	O8	2a scarlet	5.50	.30
O69	O8	2½a purple	3.50	14.00
O70	O8	4a dark brown	5.50	9.50
O71	O8	8a blue violet	8.00	15.00

India Nos. 162-165 Overprinted

1942   Wmk. 196   Perf. 13½x14

O72	A82	1r brown & slate	12.00	82.50
O73	A82	2r dk brn & dk vio	12.00	350.00
O74	A82	5r dp ultra & dk green	27.50	900.00
O75	A82	10r rose car & dk violet	125.00	1,500.
		Nos. O62-O75 (14)	213.30	2,896.

NABHA

'näb-hə

LOCATION — A State of India in the eastern and southeastern Punjab
AREA — 966 sq. mi.
POP. — 340,044 (1941)
CAPITAL — Nabha

The varieties with small letters in the overprint are not listed as the letters are merely broken and not from another font.

Indian Stamps Overprinted in Black

1885   Wmk. 39   Perf. 14

1	A17	½a green	8.50	15.00
2	A19	1a violet brown	110.00	425.00
3	A21	2a ultramarine	50.00	110.00
4	A25	8a red lilac	650.00	
5	A27	1r gray	650.00	

Wmk. 38

6	A9	4a green	150.00	425.00

On the reprints "Nabha" and "State" each measure 9½mm. On the originals they measure 11 and 10mm respectively.

Indian Stamps Overprinted

1885   Wmk. 39   Red Overprint

7	A17	½a green	6.00	3.50
8	A21	2a ultramarine	7.00	6.00
9	A27	1r gray	210.00	625.00

Wmk. 38

10	A9	4a green	85.00	425.00

1885-97   Wmk. 39   Black Overprint

11	A17	½a green ('88)	1.50	.25
12	A18	9p rose ('92)	3.50	8.50
13	A19	1a violet brown	6.00	1.50
a.		1a plum	7.00	2.25
14	A20	1a6p bister brn ('91)	4.50	9.00
		"ABHA"	525.00	
15	A21	2a ultramarine	6.50	3.50
a.		2a dull blue ('88)	7.50	3.25
16	A22	3a brn org ('88)	11.00	4.00
a.		3a orange ('89)	35.00	55.00
17	A23	4a olive green ('88)	12.50	7.50
a.		slate green	12.50	6.50
18	A25	8a red lilac	7.00	8.00
19	A26	12a vio, red ('89)	7.00	10.00
20	A27	1r gray ('88)	25.00	95.00
21	A29	1r car rose & grn ('93)	27.50	25.00
a.		"N BHA"		
22	A30	2r brn & rose ('97)	275.00	450.00
23	A30	3r grn & brn ('97)	300.00	700.00
24	A30	5r vio & blk ('97)	300.00	1,100.

Wmk. 38

25	A14	6a olive bister ('89)	27.50	30.00
a.		6a bister brown	5.00	8.50
		Nos. 11-25 (15)	1,015.	2,452.

Nos. 7, 8, 9, 10, 13, and 18 have been reprinted. They usually bear the overprint "Specimen."

1900   Wmk. 39

26	A31	3p carmine rose	.45	.25

1903-09

27	A32	3p gray	.85	.25
a.		"NAB STA" for "NABHA STATE"	1,400.	
c.		3p slate gray (06)	.85	.25
28	A33	½a green	1.25	.80
a.		"NABH"	1,650.	
29	A34	1a car rose	3.50	2.25
30	A35	2a pale violet	9.00	5.25
c.		2a mauve	7.50	.45
30A	A36	2a6p ultra ('09)	22.50	130.00
31	A37	3a brn org	3.25	.50
32	A38	4a olive green	12.50	3.75
33	A39	6a bister	12.50	45.00
34	A40	8a red violet	13.00	60.00
35	A41	12a vio, red	13.00	60.00
36	A42	1r car rose & grn	15.00	37.50
		Nos. 27-36 (11)	106.35	345.30

1907

37	A44	½a green	1.60	1.90
38	A45	1a carmine rose	2.25	.75

309

INDIA - CONVENTION STATES — NABHA — PATIALA

1913
40	A46	3p gray	2.40	1.75
a.		3p pale gray	2.25	.45
b.		3p bluish gray	4.50	3.50
c.		3p slate	5.00	
41	A47	½a light green	3.00	1.90
a.		½a emerald	6.50	1.40
b.		½a bright green	3.75	1.90
42	A48	1a carmine rose	1.25	.25
43	A49	2a violet	3.00	3.50
44	A51	3a orange	3.25	.85
a.		3a dull orange	6.00	3.50
45	A52	4a olive green	3.25	5.50
46	A53	6a bister	7.50	11.00
a.		6a brown ocher	8.00	15.00
47	A54	8a red violet	20.00	12.00
48	A55	12a claret	13.00	50.00
49	A56	1r dp blue green & red brn	25.00	27.50
b.		1r green & brown	60.00	32.50
c.		1r dp turq grn & org brown ('23)	65.00	
		Nos. 40-49 (10)	81.65	114.25

1924
50	A48	1a dark brown	12.50	10.00

India Stamps of 1926-35 Overprinted

1927-32   Wmk. 196
51	A46	3p slate ('32)	2.00	.25
52	A47	½a green	3.00	.35
53	A48	1a dark brn	2.75	.25
54	A60	2a dull vio ('32)	3.50	.50
55	A57	2a6p buff ('32)	5.00	20.00
56	A51	3a blue ('30)	8.00	4.00
57	A61	4a ol grn ('32)	12.50	5.50

Indian Stamps of 1937-40 Overprinted

58	A56	2r brn org & car rose ('32)	65.00	325.00
59	A56	5r dk vio & ultra ('32)	120.00	900.00
		Nos. 51-59 (9)	221.75	1,256.

India Stamps of 1926-35 Overprinted

1936-37
63	A71	½a green	.75	.60
64	A68	9p dark green ('37)	4.00	1.75
65	A72	1a dark brown	.75	.80
66	A69	1a3p violet ('37)	3.00	8.00
67	A51	3a car rose ('37)	6.50	25.00
68	A52	4a olive green ('37)	9.00	7.00
		Nos. 63-68 (6)	24.00	42.85

Same Overprint in Black on 1937 Stamps of India

1938-39   Perf. 13½x14
69	A80	3p slate	8.50	2.75
70	A80	½a brown	5.00	2.25
71	A80	9p green	12.50	6.00
72	A80	1a carmine	4.00	2.50
73	A81	2a scarlet	1.75	17.50
74	A81	2a6p purple	2.50	25.00
75	A81	3a yel green	1.75	11.00
76	A81	3a6p ultramarine	5.50	55.00
77	A81	4a dark brown	11.00	9.00
78	A81	6a peacock blue	6.00	60.00
79	A81	8a blue violet	3.00	55.00
80	A81	12a car lake	2.50	40.00

Overprinted
81	A82	1r brown & slate	11.00	55.00
82	A82	2r dk brn & dk vio	25.00	240.00
83	A82	5r dp ultra & dk green	30.00	500.00
84	A82	10r rose car & dk vio ('39)	40.00	1,000.
85	A82	15r dk grn & dk brn ('39)	250.00	2,100.
86	A82	25r dk vio & blue ('39)	125.00	2,100.
		Nos. 69-86 (18)	545.00	6,281.

India Stamps of 1937 Overprinted in Black

1942   Perf. 13½x14
87	A80	3p slate	30.00	10.00
88	A80	½a brown	100.00	50.00
89	A80	9p green	8.00	19.00
90	A80	1a carmine	9.00	6.50
		Nos. 87-90 (4)	147.00	85.50

Same on India Nos. 168-179

1942-46   Wmk. 196
100	A83	3p slate	.80	1.25
101	A83	½a rose vio ('43)	.65	2.50
102	A83	9p lt green ('43)	.65	2.75
103	A83	1a car rose ('46)	.65	5.50
104	A84	1a3p bister ('44)	.65	5.00
105	A84	1½a dark pur ('43)	1.50	3.50
106	A84	2a scarlet ('44)	1.20	5.00
107	A84	3a violet ('44)	1.20	8.00
108	A84	3½a ultramarine	6.00	110.00
109	A85	4a choc ('43)	.65	1.50
110	A85	6a pck blue ('44)	8.00	82.50
111	A85	8a blue vio ('44)	10.00	62.50
112	A85	12a car lake ('44)	12.00	100.00
		Nos. 100-112 (13)	43.95	390.00

OFFICIAL STAMPS

Indian Stamps Overprinted in Black

1885   Wmk. 39   Perf. 14
O1	A17	½a green	12.50	2.25
O2	A19	1a violet brown	.75	.30
a.		"SERVICE" double		3,500.
O3	A21	2a ultra	150.00	275.00
		Nos. O1-O3 (3)	163.25	277.55

The reprints have the same measurements as the reprints of the regular issue of the same date.

Indian Stamps Overprinted

1885   Red Overprint
O4	A17	½a green	15.00	8.25
O5	A21	2a ultramarine	3.25	.80

1885-97   Black Overprint
O6	A17	½a green	.45	.25
a.		Period after "SERVICE"	210.00	3.25
b.		"SERVICE" double, one albino		3,500.
O7	A19	1a violet brown	4.50	.65
a.		1a plum	5.25	.35
b.		As "a," period after "SERVICE"	16.00	.90
c.		As "b," "NABHA STATE" double	3,750.	375.00
O8	A21	2a ultra	9.00	4.25
a.		dull blue ('88)	8.50	3.75
O9	A22	3a orange	35.00	175.00
a.		3a brown orange	50.00	240.00
O10	A23	4a olive green ('88)	5.50	2.75
a.		4a slate green	7.00	1.75
O11	A25	8a red vio ('89)	8.50	3.25
O12	A26	12a vio, red ('89)	10.00	32.50
O13	A27	1r gray ('89)	90.00	625.00
O14	A29	1r car rose & grn ('97)	50.00	140.00

Wmk. 38
O15	A14	6a bister ('89)	35.00	60.00
b.		6a bister brown	900.00	
		Nos. O6-O15 (10)	247.95	1,044.

Nos. O4, O5, and O7 have been reprinted. They usually bear the overprint "Specimen."

1903-06   Wmk. 39
O16	A32	3p pale gray ('06)	12.50	47.50
a.		3p slate gray ('06)	8.00	32.50
O17	A33	½a green	1.00	1.00
O18	A34	1a carmine rose	.90	.90
O19	A35	2a pale violet	6.00	2.40
a.		2a mauve	7.00	.45
O20	A38	4a olive green	4.00	.55
O21	A40	8a red violet	4.50	1.60
		8a claret	40.00	15.00
O22	A42	1r car rose & grn	4.50	4.50
		Nos. O16-O22 (7)	33.40	58.45

1907
O23	A44	½a green	3.00	.55
O24	A45	1a carmine rose	1.60	.45

1913
O25	A52	4a olive green	12.00	85.00
O26	A56	1r grn & red brn	92.50	650.00

Indian Stamps of 1911-26 Overprinted

1913
O27	A46(a)	3p gray	3.50	15.00
a.		3p pale gray	2.75	12.50
b.		3p bluish gray	2.40	17.50
c.		3p slate	2.25	17.50
O28	A47(a)	½a light green	1.10	.50
a.		½a emerald	4.25	.25
b.		½a bright green	4.25	.25
O29	A48(a)	1a carmine rose	1.60	.25
O30	A49(a)	2a violet	1.60	.25
O31	A52(a)	4a olive green	2.25	1.10
O32	A54(a)	8a red violet	5.50	3.00
a.		8a deep mauve	13.00	
b.		8a bright mauve ('18)	22.50	
O33	A56(b)	1r dp blue grn & red brn	13.00	10.00
a.		1r green & brown	17.50	10.00
		Nos. O27-O33 (7)	28.55	30.10

India Stamps of 1926-35 Overprinted

Perf. 13½x14, 14
1932-45   Wmk. 196
O34	A46	3p slate	.25	.25
O35	A72	1a dk brn ('35)	.35	.25
O36	A52	4a ol grn ('45)	32.50	3.75
O37	A54	8a red violet ('37)	1.20	3.50
		Nos. O34-O37 (4)	34.30	7.75

Same Overprint in Black on India Stamps of 1937

1938
O38	A80	9p green	8.00	5.00
		Never hinged	15.00	
O39	A80	1a carmine	12.00	1.25
		Never hinged	22.50	

Official Stamps of India 1939-43 Overprinted in Black

1942-44   Perf. 13½x14
O40	O8	3p slate	.80	3.00
O41	O8	½a brown ('43)	.75	.30
O42	O8	½a dk rose vio ('44)	4.75	2.25
O43	O8	9p green ('43)	.80	.50
O44	O8	1a car rose ('43)	1.25	.25
O45	O8	1½a dull purple ('43)	.45	.40
O46	O8	2a scarlet ('43)	1.50	1.60
O47	O8	4a dark brown ('43)	2.00	4.50
O48	O8	8a blue violet ('43)	3.00	30.00

India Nos. 162-164 Overprinted in Black

O49	A82	1r brown & slate	5.50	62.50
O50	A82	2r dk brn & dk vio	32.50	500.00
O51	A82	5r dp ultra & dk green	175.00	1,100.
		Nos. O40-O51 (12)	228.30	1,706.

PATIALA
,pət-ē-'äl-ə,

LOCATION — A State of India in the central Punjab
AREA — 5,942 sq. mi.
POP. — 1,936,259 (1941)
CAPITAL — Patiala

The varieties with small letters in the overprint are not listed as the letters are merely broken and not from another font.

Indian Stamps Overprinted in Red

1884   Wmk. 39   Perf. 14
1	A17	½a green	9.00	5.00
a.		Double overprint, one horiz.	5,000.	1,200.
2	A19	1a violet brown	110.00	160.00
a.		Double overprint		1,050.
b.		Double ovpt., one in black	1,050.	
c.		Pair, one as "b," one without overprint		
3	A21	2a ultra	25.00	17.50
4	A25	8a red lilac	650.00	2,300.
a.		Double ovpt., one in black	250.00	1,000.
c.		Overprint reversed		
d.		Pair like "a," one with overprint reversed		
5	A27	1r gray	225.00	1,100.

Wmk. 38
6	A9	4a green	170.00	210.00
		Nos. 1-6 (6)	1,189.	3,793.

Indian Stamps Overprinted in Red (¾mm spacing between lines of overprint)

1885   Wmk. 39
7	A17	½a green	5.50	.45
a.		"AUTTIALLA"	32.50	85.00
b.		1¾mm spacing between lines of ovpt.	15.00	20.00
c.		"STATE" only		
8	A21	2a ultra	24.00	1.90
a.		"AUTTIALLA"	110.00	
9	A27	1r gray	70.00	175.00
a.		"AUTTIALLA"	800.00	
b.		1¾mm between lines of ovpt.	750.00	

Wmk. 38
10	A9	4a green	12.00	4.50
a.		Double overprint, one in black	450.00	
b.		Pair, one as "a," one with black overprint		

Same, Overprinted in Black
Wmk. 39
11	A19	1a violet brown	1.50	.65
a.		Double overprint, one in red	35.00	175.00
b.		Double overprint	350.00	400.00
c.		1¾mm between lines of ovpt.	600.00	
d.		"AUTTIALLA"	140.00	
e.		As "d," double ovpt., one in red	3,500.	
f.		Pair, one as "c," one without overprint		
12	A25	8a red lilac	70.00	160.00
a.		"AUTTIALLA"	675.00	
c.		1¾mm between lines of ovpt.	800.00	
		Nos. 7-12 (6)	183.00	342.50

Nos. 7-12 have been reprinted. Most of them bear the word "Reprint." The few stamps that escaped the overprint cannot be distinguished from the originals.
The error "AUTTIALLA" has been reprinted in entire sheets, in red on the ½, 2, 4a and 1r and in black on the ½, 1, 2, 4, 8a and 1r. "STATE" is 7¾mm long, instead of 8½mm. Most stamps are overprinted "Reprint."

Same, Overprinted in Black

1891-96
13	A17	½a green	3.25	.25
14	A18	9p rose	2.50	3.50
15	A19	1a violet brown	3.00	.45
a.		1a plum	4.25	2.25
b.		As "a," "STATE" only	425.00	650.00
16	A20	1a6p bister brown	3.50	3.75
17	A21	2a dull blue ('96)	5.00	.55
a.		2a ultramarine	6.00	1.90
18	A22	3a orange	4.25	1.90
19	A23	4a ol grn ('96)	8.50	1.60
a.		"STATE" only	850.00	400.00
b.		4a slate green	8.50	1.50
20	A25	8a red vio ('96)	15.00	19.00
21	A26	12a vio, red	6.50	20.00
22	A29	1r car rose & grn ('96)	9.50	70.00
23	A30	2r brn & rose ('95)	325.00	2,000.
24	A30	3r grn & brn ('95)	375.00	2,100.
25	A30	5r vio & bl ('95)	425.00	2,300.

INDIA - CONVENTION STATES — PATIALA

			Wmk. 38		
26	A14	6a bister		5.00	22.50
a.		6a olive bister		15.00	45.00
		Nos. 13-26 (14)		1,184.	6,544.

1899 Wmk. 39
27	A31	3p carmine rose	.35	.30
a.		Pair, one without overprint	6,500.	

1902
28	A17	½a light green	1.25	1.90
29	A19	1a carmine rose	2.50	3.00

1903-06
31	A32	3p pale gray	.45	.25
c.		3p slate gray ('06)	.90	.25
32	A33	½a green	1.60	.25
33	A34	1a carmine rose	4.00	.25
a.		Pair, one without overprint	1,600.	
34	A35	2a pale violet	4.25	.75
a.		2a mauve	21.00	1.40
35	A37	3a brown orange	3.50	.50
36	A38	4a olive green ('06)	7.50	2.25
37	A39	6a bister ('05)	7.50	22.50
38	A40	8a red violet ('06)	9.50	9.00
39	A41	12a vio, red ('06)	15.00	55.00
40	A42	1r car rose & grn ('05)	8.50	15.00
		Nos. 31-40 (10)	61.80	105.75

1908
41	A44	½a green	.60	.35
42	A45	1a carmine rose	2.00	1.50

1912-14
43	A46	3p gray	2.00	.25
a.		3p pale gray	3.00	.30
b.		3p bluish gray	3.00	
c.		3p slate	7.50	2.75
44	A47	½a light green	3.00	3.65
a.		½a emerald	7.50	1.60
b.		½a bright green	5.25	2.25
45	A48	1a carmine rose	2.50	.25
46	A49	2a violet	4.00	2.25
47	A51	3a brown orange	6.50	3.00
48	A52	4a olive green	6.50	4.00
49	A53	6a bister	5.00	6.50
		6p brown ocher ('21)	9.00	9.50
50	A54	8a red violet	8.50	6.00
51	A55	12a claret	8.50	15.00
52	A56	1r dp blue green & red brn	21.00	22.50
b.		1r green & brown ('24)	40.00	
		Nos. 43-52 (10)	67.50	63.40

1922-26
53	A48	1a dk brown ('23)	4.50	.60
54	A58	1½a chocolate	.55	.70
55	A51	3a ultra ('26)	8.50	21.00
56	A56	2r yel brn & car rose ('26)	25.00	175.00
57	A56	5r vio & ultra ('26)	65.00	450.00
		Nos. 53-57 (5)	103.55	647.30

India Stamps of 1926-35 Overprinted

1928-34 Wmk. 196
60	A46	3p slate	2.50	.25
61	A47	½a green	.50	.25
62	A68	9p dark green ('34)	2.50	1.25
63	A48	1a dark brown	2.25	.35
64	A69	1a3p violet ('32)	4.50	.25
65	A60	2a dull violet	2.50	.50
66	A57	2a6p buff ('34)	10.00	5.00
67	A51	3a blue ('29)	7.00	4.50
68	A61	4a olive green	12.50	3.00
69	A54	8a red violet ('33)	14.00	7.50

Indian Stamps of 1911-23 Overprinted
70	A56	1r green & brown ('29)	15.00	21.00
71	A56	2r buff & car rose	65.00	165.00
		Nos. 60-71 (12)	138.25	208.85

India Stamps of 1926-35 Overprinted Like Nos. 60-69

1935-37 Perf. 14
75	A71	½a green ('37)	2.00	.30
76	A72	1a dk brown ('36)	.70	.25
77	A49	2a ver ('36)	.30	1.75
78	A51	3a car rose ('37)	12.00	16.00
79	A52	4a olive green	2.75	5.00
		Nos. 75-79 (5)	17.75	23.30

Same Overprint in Black on Stamps of India, 1937

1937-38 Perf. 13½x14
80	A80	3p slate ('38)	9.00	.35
81	A80	½a brown ('38)	5.50	.60
82	A80	9p green	3.50	1.25
83	A80	1a carmine	2.00	.25
84	A81	2a scarlet ('38)	2.50	20.00
85	A81	2a6p purple ('38)	12.00	60.00
86	A81	3a yel green ('38)	12.00	21.00
87	A81	3a6p ultra ('38)	9.00	60.00
88	A81	4a dk brn ('38)	25.00	37.50
89	A81	6a pck blue ('38)	30.00	90.00
90	A81	8a blue violet ('38)	35.00	90.00
91	A81	12a car lake ('38)	20.00	130.00

Overprinted Like Nos. 70-71

1938
92	A82	1r brown & slate	25.00	62.50
93	A82	2r dk brn & dk vio	30.00	200.00
94	A82	5r dp ultra & dk green	30.00	525.00
95	A82	10r rose car & dk vio	40.00	950.00
96	A82	15r dk grn & dk brn	100.00	2,100.
97	A82	25r dk vio & bl vio	150.00	2,100.
		Nos. 80-97 (18)	540.50	6,448.

India Nos. 150-153 Overprinted in Black

1942-43 Perf. 13½x14
98	A80	3p slate	15.00	4.00
99	A80	½a brown ('43)	4.00	3.25
100	A80	9p green ('43)	350.00	17.00
101	A80	1a carmine	27.50	3.75
		Nos. 98-101 (4)	396.50	28.00

India Stamps of 1941-43 with same Overprint in Black

1942-47 Perf. 13½x14
102	A83	3p slate	.65	.25
103	A83	½a rose vio ('43)	.65	.25
104	A83	9p lt grn ('43)	1.20	.25
a.		Pair, one without overprint	4,750.	
105	A83	1a car rose ('46)	1.10	.25
106	A84	1a3p bister ('43)	1.25	4.50
107	A84	1½a dk pur ('43)	5.00	6.50
108	A84	2a scar ('46)	1.25	.50
109	A84	3a violet ('46)	1.25	3.75
110	A84	3½a ultra ('46)	14.00	52.50
111	A84	4a choc ('46)	2.00	5.00
112	A85	6a pck blue ('46)	1.25	45.00
113	A85	8a blue violet ('46)	1.25	17.50
114	A85	12a car lake ('45)	20.00	125.00

No. 102 India No. 162 Overprinted in Black

115	A82	1r brn & slate ('47)	8.00	90.00
		Nos. 102-115 (14)	58.85	351.25

OFFICIAL STAMPS

Indian Stamps Overprinted in Black and Red

1884 Wmk. 39 Perf. 14
O1	A17	½a green	35.00	.60
O2	A19	1a vio brown	1.50	.25
a.		"SERVICE" double	3,750.	950.00
b.		"SERVICE" inverted		2,500.
c.		"PUTTIALLA STATE" dbl.		175.00
d.		"PUTTIALLA STATE" invtd.	4,500.	450.00
O3	A21	2a ultra	14,000.	175.00

Overprinted in Red or Black

1885-90
O4	A17(a)	½a grn (R & Bk)	4.50	.35
a.		"SERVICE" double		1,050.
b.		"AUTTIALLA"	95.00	25.00
c.		"AUTTIALLA" and "SERVICE" double		8,000.
O5	A17(b)	½a green (Bk)	2.75	.25
O6	A19(a)	1a vio brn (Bk)	2.75	.25
a.		"AUTTILLA"	1,250.	72.50
b.		"SERVICE" dble., one invtd.		900.00
d.		"SERVICE" double	4,000.	
e.		"PUTTIAILLA STATE" double		2,500.
O7	A21(b)	2a ultra (R)	1.10	.60
a.		"SERVICE" dbl., one invtd.	35.00	225.00
		Nos. O4-O7 (4)	11.10	

There are reprints of Nos. O4, O6 and O7. That of No. O4 has "SERVICE" overprinted in red in large letters and that of No. O6 has the same overprint in black. The originals have the word in small black letters. The reprints of No. O7, except those overprinted "Reprint," cannot be distinguished from the originals. These three reprints also exist with the error "AUTTIALLA."

Same, Overprinted in Black

1891-1900
O8	A17	½a green ('95)	1.60	.25
a.		"SERVICE" inverted	75.00	
b.		"SERV CE"	3,000.	
c.		"STA E"	1,000.	850.00
d.		"S ATE"	1,000.	
O9	A19	1a vio brn ('00)	9.00	.25
a.		"SERVICE" inverted	75.00	
O10	A21	2a ultramarine ('98)	7.50	5.00
a.		2a deep blue	6.00	4.00
b.		As "a," "SERVICE" inverted	75.00	3.50
c.		"SERV CE" inverted	4,500.	
O11	A22	3a orange	5.00	4.75
a.		"SERV CE"	6,000.	
O12	A23	4a olive green	5.50	.75
a.		4a slate green ('95)	6.50	.50
O13	A25	8a red violet	6.50	2.00
a.		8a magenta ('98)	6.50	4.00
b.		"SERV CE"	7,000.	
O14	A26	12a violet, red	4.00	.80
a.		"SERV CE"	9,000.	
O15	A27	1r gray	4.50	.85

Wmk. 38
O16	A14	6a bister	4.00	.55
a.		6a olive bister	1,500.	
		Nos. O8-O16 (9)	47.60	15.20

1902 Wmk. 39
O17	A19	1a carmine rose	2.50	.25

1903
O18	A29	1r car rose & green	9.00	12.50

1903-09
O19	A32	3p gray	.60	.25
a.		3p slate gray ('09)	.60	.25
O20	A33	½a green	1.50	.25
O21	A34	1a carmine rose	.75	.25
O22	A35	2a pale violet ('05)	1.00	.35
a.		2a mauve	2.50	.25
O23	A37	3a brown orange	9.00	5.25
O24	A38	4a olive green ('05)	4.50	.30
O25	A40	8a red violet	3.50	.85
a.		8a claret ('10)	12.00	13.00
O26	A42	1r car rose & grn ('06)	3.25	1.00
		Nos. O19-O26 (8)	24.10	8.50

1907
O27	A44	½a green	.55	.25
O28	A45	1a carmine rose	1.40	.25

India Stamps of 1911-26 Overprinted

1913-26
O29	A46(a)	3p gray	.25	.25
a.		3p pale gray	1.40	.80
b.		3p slate ('26)	1.90	.80
O30	A47(a)	½a light green	.25	.25
a.		½a emerald	7.00	1.40
b.		½a bright green	3.75	.65
O31	A48(a)	1a car rose	.25	.25
O32	A49(a)	2a violet	1.90	1.40
O33	A52(a)	4a olive green	.55	.40
O34	A54(a)	8a red violet	.85	.80
O35	A56(b)	1r grn & red brn	3.25	1.60
O36	A56(b)	2r yel brn & car rose ('26)	27.50	65.00
O37	A56(b)	5r vio & ultra ('26)	25.00	47.50
		Nos. O29-O37 (9)	59.80	117.45

Same Overprint on India Nos. 83 and 89

1925-26
O38	A48(a)	1a dark brown	13.00	1.50
O39	A53(a)	6a bister ('26)	3.25	2.75

India Stamps of 1926-35 Overprinted

1927-36 Wmk. 196
O40	A46	3p slate	.25	.25
a.		Blue overprint	3.75	2.75
O41	A47	½a green ('32)	1.25	.80
O42	A48	1a dark brown	.25	.25
O43	A69	1a3p violet ('32)	.50	.25
O44	A60	2a dull violet	.30	.30
O45	A60	2a vermilion ('33)	1.40	.40
O46	A57	2a6p buff ('33)	5.50	.40
O47	A61	4a olive green ('35)	.55	.30
O48	A54	8a red violet ('29)	4.00	.75

Indian Stamps of 1911-23 Overprinted

O49	A56	1r green & brown ('29)	10.00	6.50
O50	A56	2r brn org & car rose ('36)	20.00	70.00
		Nos. O40-O50 (11)	44.00	80.25

India Stamps of 1926-34 Overprinted

1935-36
O51	A71	½a green ('36)	.80	.25
O52	A72	1a dark brown ('36)	.65	.35
O53	A49	2a vermilion	.25	.25
a.		Small die	30.00	7.50
O54	A52	4a olive green ('36)	6.50	1.90
		Nos. O51-O54 (4)	8.20	2.75

Same Overprint on India Nos. 151-153

1938-39 Perf. 13½x14
O55	A80	½a brown ('39)	.65	.25
O56	A80	9p green ('39)	10.00	95.00
O57	A80	1a carmine	.65	.50
		Nos. O55-O57 (3)	11.30	95.75

India No. 136 Surcharged in Black

1939 Perf. 14
O58	A69	1a on 1a3p violet	15.00	5.75
		Never hinged	24.00	

"SERVICE" measures 9¼mm.

No. 64 Surcharged in Black

1940
O59	A69	1a on 1a3p violet	12.50	6.50
		Never hinged	20.00	

"SERVICE" measures 8½mm.

India Nos. 162-164 Overprinted

Perf. 13½x14
O60	A82	1r brown & slate	.65	10.50
O61	A82	2r dk brn & dk vio	6.00	5.50
O62	A82	5r dp ultra & dk grn	15.00	95.00

INDIA - CONVENTION STATES — PATIALA

India Official Stamps of 1939-43 Overprinted

1940-45
O63	O8	3p slate ('41)	.65	.25
O64	O8	½a brown	1.00	.25
O65	O8	½a dk rose vio ('43)	.75	.25
O66	O8	9p green	1.00	.55
O67	O8	1a carmine rose	1.00	.25
O68	O8	1a3p bister ('41)	1.00	.25
O69	O8	1½a dull purple ('45)	3.00	1.75
O70	O8	2a scarlet ('41)	3.00	.40
O71	O8	2½a purple ('41)	2.50	1.10
O72	O8	4a dk brown ('45)	1.25	2.75
O73	O8	8a blue violet ('45)	3.50	7.50

India Nos. 162-164 Overprinted in Black

O74	A82	1r brn & slate ('43)	4.00	12.00
O75	A82	2r dk brn & dk vio ('45)	12.50	95.00
O76	A82	5r dp ultra & dk grn ('45)	22.50	125.00
		Nos. O63-O76 (14)	57.65	247.30
		Set, never hinged	145.00	

Scott Postage Stamp Checklist
$9.99-$19.99 *AA**

- Provides basic information about postage stamps listed with major numbers in the Scott *Standard Postage Stamp Catalogue*.
- Features the country name, issue date or year, the Scott number, a description and four checkboxes; unused and used. The other two boxes can be used to label other options such as never-hinged or on cover.

AmosAdvantage.com
1-800-572-6885

ORDERING INFORMATION: *AA prices apply to paid subscribers of Amos Media titles, or for orders placed online. Prices, terms and product availability subject to change. **SHIPPING & HANDLING:** U.S.: Orders total $0-$10.00 charged $4.99 shipping. U.S. Order total $10.01-$74.99 charged $9.99 shipping. Orders totaling $75+ will ship FREE! Taxes will apply in CA, OH, & IL. Canada: 20% of order total. Minimum charge $19.99 Maximum charge $200.00. Foreign orders are shipped via FedEx Intl. or USPS and billed actual freight.

INDIA - FEUDATORY STATES

FEUDATORY STATES

These stamps had franking power solely in the states in which they were issued, except for Cochin and Travancore which had a reciprocal postal agreement.

ALWAR

'ăl-wər

LOCATION — A Feudatory State of India, lying southwest of Delhi in the Jaipur Residency
AREA — 3,158 sq. mi.
POP. — 749,751.
CAPITAL — Alwar

Katar (Indian Dagger) — A1

1877	Unwmk.	Litho.		Rouletted
1	A1	¼a ultramarine	8.00	2.00
2	A1	1a brown	7.00	2.00

Redrawn

1899-1901			Pin-perf. 12	
3	A1	¼a sl blue, wide margins	15.00	5.00
a.		Horiz. pair, imperf. between	1,250.	750.00
b.		Vert. pair, imperf. between	3,000.	3,400.
4	A1	¼a yel grn, narrow margins ('01)	15.00	5.00
a.		Horiz. pair, imperf. between	775.00	1,000.
b.		Imperf. pair	1,750.	
c.		¼a emer, narrow margins	11.00	4.00
d.		As "d," imperf. pair	1,000.	
f.		As "d," vert. pair, imperf. horiz.	900.00	
g.		As "d," horiz. pair, imperf. vert.	900.00	900.00
h.		As "d," vert. pair, imperf. horiz.	450.00	900.00
5	A1	¼a emer, wide margins ('99)	1,750.	7,500.

Nos. 3 and 4b are printed farther apart in the sheet.
On Nos. 3 and 4, the shading of the left border line is missing.
Nos. 1 to 4 occasionally show portions of the papermaker's watermark, W. T. & Co.
Alwar stamps became obsolete in 1902.

BAMRA

'băm-rə

LOCATION — A Feudatory State in the Eastern States, Orissa States Agency, Bengal.
AREA — 1,988 sq. mi.
POP. — 151,259
CAPITAL — Deogarh

Stamps of Bamra were issued without gum.

A1

1888	Unwmk.	Typeset		Imperf.
1	A1	¼a black, yellow	4,000.	20,000.
2	A1	¼a black, rose	350.	
3	A1	1a black, blue	300.	
4	A1	2a black, green	500.	2,500.
5	A1	4a black, yellow	350.	2,500.
6	A1	8a black, rose	250.	

Used values for Nos. 7-13E are for CTO examples. Genuinely used examples are exceptionally rare.

1890-93				
7	A2	¼a blk, rose lil	13.00	25.00
7D	A2	¼a blk, rose	5.00	5.00
7F	A2	¼a blk, magenta	5.00	5.00
8	A2	½a black, green	15.00	15.00
a.		"Eeudatory"	200.00	300.00
8D	A2	½a black, bl green	15.00	15.00
9	A2	1a black, yellow	10.00	10.00
9C	A2	1a black, org yel	150.00	150.00
10	A2	2a blk, rose lil	50.00	125.00
10B	A2	2a blk, rose	15.00	15.00
11	A2	4a blk, brt rose	17.00	20.00
11B	A2	4a blk, rose lil	3,000.	4,500.
11D	A2	4a blk, dl rose	45.00	45.00
12	A2	8a blk, rose lil	75.00	200.00
12D	A2	8a blk, rose	30.00	50.00
12F	A2	8a blk, dl rose	100.00	50.00
13	A2	1r blk, rose lil	275.00	500.00
13E	A2	1r blk, rose	50.00	50.00

The central ornament varies in size and may be found in various positions.
Bamra stamps became obsolete Dec. 31, 1894.

BARWANI

bər-'wän-ē

LOCATION — A Feudatory State of Central India, in the Malwa Agency.
AREA — 1,178 sq. mi.
POP. — 255,157 (1931)
CAPITAL — Barwani

The stamps of Barwani were all typographed and normally issued in booklets containing panes of four. Exceptions are noted (Nos. 14-15, 20-25). The majority were completely perforated, but some of the earlier printings were perforated only between the stamps, leaving one or two sides imperf. Nos. 1-25 were issued without gum. Many shades exist.

Rana Ranjit Singh — A1

1921, April (?)	Unwmk.	Pin-Perf 7
Toned Medium Wove Paper		
Clear Impression		
1	A1	¼a dull Prus green	425.00	1,600.
2	A1	½a dull blue	950.00	2,400.

1921		Coarse Perf. 7 x Imperf.
White Thin Wove Paper		
Blurred Impression		
3	A1	¼a dull green	60.00	650.00
4	A1	½a pale blue	40.00	800.00

1921		Toned Laid Paper		Imperf.
5	A1	¼a light green	40.00	350.00
6	A1	½a light green	10.00	
a.		Perf. 11, top or bottom only	10.00	

1921		Coarse Perf. 7, 7 x Imperf.
Thick Wove Paper		
Very Blurred Impression		
7	A1	¼a dull blue	30.00	
8	A1	½a dull green	65.00	

Rana Ranjit Singh — A2

1922		Perf. 7 x Imperf.
Thick Glazed Paper		
9	A1	¼a dull ultra	325.00	

Rough Perf. 11 x Imperf.		
10	A2	1a vermilion	6.00	80.00
a.		Vert. pair, imperf. between	1,100.	
b.		Printed double	3,750.	
11	A2	2a violet	4.00	100.00
a.		Double impression	700.00	
b.		Horiz. pair, imperf. between	800.00	1,800.
c.		Vert. pair, imperf. between	275.00	

Shades of No. 11 include purple.

1921		Thick Toned Paper		Imperf.
11D	A2	2a violet	30.00	175.00

1923-26		Wove, Laid Paper
12	A1	¼a grayish ultra, perf. 8½	3.00	150.00
a.		imperf. pair	900.00	
b.		Vert. pair, imperf. between	400.00	
13	A1	¼a black, perf. 7 x imperf.	125.00	1,300.
a.		Horiz. pair, imperf. between	6,500.	
14	A1	¼a rose, perf. 12	3.75	21.00
a.		Vert. pair, imperf. between	1,250.	
b.		Horiz. pair, imperf. between	2,600.	
c.		Vert. pair, imperf. horiz.	3,500.	
d.		Perf. 6	425.00	250.00
e.		Perf. 7	2,500.	4,000.
f.		Perf. 7, wove paper	7,000.	
15	A1	¼a dk bl, perf. 11 ('26)	5.00	45.00
a.		Tete beche pair, horiz.	6,500.	
16	A1	½a grn, perf. 11 x imperf.	6.00	60.00
a.		Vert. pair, imperf. between	1,500.	

No. 12 was also printed on pale gray thin toned paper.
No. 14 was printed on horizontally laid paper in horizontal sheets of 12 containing three panes of 4.
No. 15 was printed on vertically laid paper in horizontal sheets of 8.

Rana Ranjit Singh — A3

1923		Perf. 11
Thin Smooth Unglazed Wove Paper		
17	A2	1a brown red	5,500.	11,000.

1927		Thin Wove Paper		Perf. 7
17A	A1	¼a milky blue	12.00	125.00
17B	A1	½a yellow green	13.00	200.00
a.		Horiz. pair, imperf. between	3,250.	
17C	A3	4a dull orange	225.00	1,500.
a.		Horiz. pair, imperf. between	4,500.	
17D	A3	4a orange brown	300.00	1,600.

1927		Thick Wove Paper		Perf. 6
17E	A3	4a yellow brown	250.00	
a.		Horiz. pair, imperf. between	8,500.	
17F	A3	4a orange brown	275.00	1,600.

1928		Coarse Perf. 7
Thick Glazed Paper		
18	A1	¼a bright blue	18.00	
19	A1	½a bright yel green	57.50	

1928, Nov.		Rough Perf. 10½
20	A1	¼a deep ultra	15.00	
a.		Tete beche pair	35.00	
21	A1	½a yellow green	9.00	
a.		Tete beche pair	25.00	

1929-31		Perf. 11
22	A1	¼a blue	5.00	50.00
a.		Horiz. pair, imperf. between	250.00	
b.		Horiz. strip of 4, imperf. between	1,000.	
c.		Vert. pair, imperf. between	800.00	
23	A1	½a emerald green	6.00	55.00
a.		Horiz. pair, imperf. between	700.00	
b.		Horiz. pair, imperf. between	1,300.	2,500.
24	A2	1a car pink ('31)	30.00	150.00
a.		Horiz. pair, imperf. between	10,000.	
25	A3	4a salmon	140.00	850.00
a.		Horiz. pair, imperf. between	6,500.	

Nos. 20-25 were printed in sheets of 8 (4x2).
No. 22 had five printings in various shades (bright to deep blue) in horizontal or vertical format.
No. 23 also printed in various shades including dark myrtle green.

Rana Devi Singh — A4

1932-47	Glazed Paper	Perf. 11, 12
Close Setting (Stamps printed 2½ mm-4½ mm apart)		
26	A4	¼a dark gray	6.00	60.00
27	A4	½a blue green	8.00	65.00
28	A4	1a brown	9.00	55.00
29	A4	2a purple	8.00	150.00
30	A4	4a olive green	9.00	100.00
Nos. 26-30 (5)			40.00	430.00

No. 29 exists in shades of purple.

1932-47	Glazed Paper	Perf. 11
Wide Setting (Stamps printed 6½ mm-7½ mm apart)		
26A	A4	¼a dark gray	10.00	100.00
27A	A4	½a blue green	13.00	70.00
28A	A4	1a brown	35.00	65.00
29A	A4	2a rose carmine	1,600.	4,000.
30A	A4	4a olive green	45.00	150.00

1933-41	Glazed Paper	Perf. 11
Close Setting (Stamps printed 3 mm-4½ mm apart)		
31	A1	¼a slate gray	12.00	250.00
32	A1	½a green	18.00	100.00
33	A2	1a brown	35.00	85.00
36	A3	4a olive green	100.00	375.00

Shades exist for Nos. 32 and 33.

1939-47	Glazed Paper	Perf. 11
Wide Setting (Stamps printed 7 mm-10 mm apart)		
31A	A1	¼a slate gray	10.00	110.00
32A	A1	½a green	10.00	120.00
33A	A2	1a brown	22.00	45.00
b.		Perf. 8½	16.00	160.00
34	A2	2a brt purple	225.00	1,200.
35	A2	2a rose car	60.00	400.00
36A	A3	4a olive green	60.00	175.00

Shades exist for Nos. 32A, 33A and 36A.

Rana Devi Singh — A5

1938				
37	A5	1a dark brown	50.00	110.00
a.		Booklet pane of 4		

Stamps of type A5 in red are revenues.
Barwani stamps became obsolete July 1, 1948.

BHOPAL

bō-'päl

LOCATION — A Feudatory State of Central India, in the Bhopal Agency.
AREA — 6,924 sq. mi.
POP. — 995,745
CAPITAL — Bhopal

Inscription in Urdu in an octagon embossed on Nos. 1-83, in a circle embossed on Nos. 84-90. On designs A1-A3, A7, A11-A12, A14-A15, A19-A21 the embossing makes up the central part of the design.
The embossing may be found inverted or sideways.

Expect irregular perfs on the perforated stamps, Nos. 19-77, due to a combination of imperfect perforating methods and the fragility of the papers.
Nos. 1-90 issued without gum.

A1

Double Lined Frame

1876	Unwmk.	Litho.		Imperf.
1	A1	¼a black	2,850.	2,000.
a.		"EGAM"	7,000.	4,750.
b.		"BFGAM"	7,000.	4,750.
c.		"BEGAN"	4,750.	3,250.
2	A1	½a red	30.00	100.00
a.		"EGAM"	130.00	425.00
b.		"BFGAM"	110.00	250.00
c.		"BEGAN"	85.00	260.00

A2

1877		Single Lined Frame
3	A2	¼a black		14,000.
4	A2	½a red	125.00	250.
a.		"NWAB"	600.00	1,200.

INDIA - FEUDATORY STATES — BHOPAL

A3
1878
5	A3	¼a black	12.00	37.50
a.	"J" diagonal, plate II		30.00	50.00

All stamps of type A3 are lettered "EEGAM" for "BEGAM."

A4
1878
6	A4	½a pale red	10.00	35.00
a.	"NWAB"		60.00	
b.	"JAHN"		100.00	
c.	"EEGAM"		100.00	

A5
1879-80
7	A5	¼a green	25.00	75.00
8	A5	½a red	25.00	45.00

Perf.
9	A5	¼a green	20.00	60.00
10	A5	½a red	30.00	
	Nos. 7-10 (4)		100.00	180.00

Nos. 7 and 9 have the value in parentheses; Nos. 8 and 10 are without parentheses.

A6
1881 — **Imperf.**
11	A6	¼a green	20.00	60.00
a.	"NAWA"		100.00	225.00
b.	"CHAH"		250.00	
c.	¼a red on laid paper		10.00	10.00

Perf.
12	A6	¼a green	30.00	
a.	"NAWA"		130.00	
b.	"CHAH"		350.00	
c.	¼a red on laid paper			1,800.

A7
1881-89 — **Imperf.**
13	A7	¼a black	10.00	65.00
a.	"NWAB"		30.00	175.00
14	A7	½a red	10.00	55.00
a.	"NWAB"		30.00	
15	A7	1a brown	10.00	55.00
a.	"NWAB"		25.00	
16	A7	2a blue	10.00	55.00
a.	"NWAB"		25.00	
17	A7	4a yellow	60.00	250.00
a.	"NWAB"		165.00	
	Nos. 13-17 (5)		100.00	480.00

A8 A9
1884 — **Perf.**
19	A8	¼a green	350.00	400.00
a.	"JAN"		350.00	400.00
b.	"BEGM"		900.00	1,000.
c.	"NWAB" and "JAN"		1,500.	
d.	"NWAB" and "JN"		1,500.	
e.	"SHAHAN"		1,500.	
f.	"JAHA"		700.00	
20	A9	¼a green	13.00	35.00

On type A9 there is a dash at the left of "JA" of "JAHAN" instead of a character like a comma as on types A5 and A6.

Imitations of No. 19 were printed about 1904 in black on wove paper and in red on laid paper, both imperf. and pin-perf.

A10
1884 **Laid Paper** **Imperf.**
21	A10	¼a blue green	450.00	450.00
a.	"NWAB"		1,100.	
b.	"NAWAJANAN"		1,100.	
c.	"SAH"		1,100.	
22	A10	½a black	3.25	3.25
a.	"NWAB"		21.00	25.00
b.	"NAWAJANAN"		21.00	25.00
c.	"SAH"		21.00	25.00

Perf.
23	A10	¼a blue green	1.50	10.00
a.	"NWAB"		7.50	
b.	"NAWAJANAN"		7.50	
c.	"SAH"		7.50	
d.	Vert. strip of 3, imperf. between		7,500.	
e.	Vert. strip of 4, imperf. between		7,500.	
24	A10	½a black	1.50	5.00
a.	"NWAB"		7.50	25.00
b.	"NAWAJANAN"		7.50	25.00
c.	"SAH"		7.50	25.00
	Nos. 21-24 (4)		456.25	468.25

Type Redrawn
1886 **Wove Paper** **Imperf.**
25	A10	¼a grayish green	.80	5.00
a.	¼a green		.80	5.00
b.	"NWAB"		4.50	13.50
c.	"NAWA"		3.00	10.50
d.	"NAWAA"		4.50	13.50
e.	"NAWABABEGAAM"		4.50	13.50
f.	"NWABA"		4.50	13.50
26	A10	½a red	1.00	2.50
a.	"SAH"		6.00	9.50
b.	"NAWABA"		4.50	7.50

Perf.
27	A10	¼a green	3.75	6.00
a.	"NWAB"		20.00	
b.	"NAWA"		12.00	
c.	"NAWAA"		20.00	
d.	"NAWABABEGAAM"		20.00	
e.	"NWABA"		20.00	
28	A10	½a red	1.20	3.00
a.	"SAH"		9.00	
b.	"NAWABA"		12.00	
	Nos. 25-28 (4)		6.75	16.50

On Nos. 25-28 the inscriptions are closer to the value than on Nos. 21-24.

A11 A12
1886 **Imperf.**
29	A11	½a red	5.00	22.00
a.	"BEGAM"		25.00	80.00
b.	"NWAB"		25.00	80.00

Laid Paper
c.	½a red, perf.		2,000.	
d.	As "c," "BEGAM"		6,000.	
e.	As "c," "NWAB"		6,000.	
30	A12	4a yellow	30.00	100.00
a.	"EEGAM"		40.00	150.00
b.	Wove paper		2,000.	
c.	As "b," "EEGAM"		2,600.	

Perf.
31	A12	4a yellow	10.00	50.00
a.	"EEGAM"		15.00	75.00
	Nos. 29-31 (3)		45.00	

A13 A14
1889 **Wove Paper** **Imperf.**
32	A13	¼a green	1.50	3.00
a.	"SAH"		6.50	10.50
b.	"NAWA"		6.50	10.50
33	A14	¼a black	3.25	8.25
a.	"EEGAN"		27.50	47.50

Perf.
34	A13	¼a green	3.00	4.00
a.	"SAH"		11.00	13.50
b.	"NAWA"		11.00	13.50
c.	Vert. pair, imperf between		325.00	
35	A14	¼a black	2.50	8.25
a.	"EEGAN"		22.50	47.50
b.	Horiz. pair, imperf. between		400.00	
	Nos. 32-35 (4)		10.25	23.50

Type A13 has smaller letters in the upper corners than Type A10.

A15
1890 **Imperf.**
36	A15	¼a black	3.00	5.00
37	A15	1a brown	5.00	10.00
a.	"EECAM"		35.00	60.00
b.	"BBGAM"		35.00	60.00
38	A7	2a greenish blue	4.00	7.00
a.	"BBEGAM"		25.00	35.00
b.	"NAWAH"		25.00	35.00
39	A7	4a yellow	5.00	6.00
40	A16	8a blue	130.00	260.00
a.	"HAH"		170.00	360.00
b.	"JABAN"		210.00	
	Nos. 36-40 (5)		147.00	288.00

An imperf. imitation of Nos. 36 and 41 was printed about 1904 in black on wove paper.

41	A15	¼a black	6.00	11.00
a.	Pair, imperf. between		1,000.	
42	A15	1a brown	7.00	19.00
a.	"EECAM"		55.00	110.00
b.	"BBGAM"		55.00	110.00
43	A7	2a greenish blue	4.00	8.00
a.	"BBEGAM"		25.00	40.00
b.	"NAWAH"		25.00	40.00
44	A7	4a yellow	5.00	14.00
45	A16	8a blue	130.00	260.00
a.	"HAH"		170.00	
b.	"JABAN"		210.00	
	Nos. 41-45 (5)		152.00	312.00

Nos. 40 and 45 have a frame line around each stamp.

Imperf
46	A12	½a red (BECAM)	3.00	5.50
47	A13	½a red (NWAB)	3.00	2.25
a.	Inverted "N"			
b.	"SAH"		9.00	

Perf.
48	A12	½a red (BECAM)	2.50	7.00
a.	Without embossing			
49	A13	½a red (NWAB)	1.20	3.00
a.	Inverted "N"			
b.	"SAH"		7.50	
	Nos. 46-49 (4)		9.70	17.75

1891-93 **Laid Paper** **Imperf.**
50	A16	8a deep green	155.00	400.00
a.	"HAH"		200.00	
b.	"JABAN"		225.00	

Perf.
51	A16	8a deep green	155.00	400.00
a.	"HAH"		200.00	475.00
b.	"JABAN"		225.00	

For overprint, see No. 83.

1894 **Redrawn** **Imperf.**
53	A10	¼a green	4.00	5.00
a.	"NAWAH"		22.00	25.00
54	A11	½a brick red	5.00	5.00
55	A16	8a blue black	32.50	32.50
a.	Laid paper		500.00	700.00

Perf.
56	A10	¼a green	5.00	5.00
a.	"NAWAH"		30.00	30.00
57	A11	½a brick red	2.00	4.00
58	A16	8a blue black	55.00	70.00
	Nos. 53-58 (6)		103.50	121.50

The ¼a redrawn has letters in corners larger; value in very small characters.
The 8a redrawn has no frame to each stamp but a frame to the sheet.

A17 A18 A19 A20 A21
1898 **Imperf.**
60	A16	8a black	90.00	120.00
b.	"E" of "BEGAM" inverted		200.00	225.00

A15 A16
1895 **Laid Paper**
61	A17	¼a green	8.00	40.00
62	A18	¼a red	10.00	7.00
63	A19	¼a black	6.50	6.50
a.	"A" inserted in "NAW B"		17.00	12.00
64	A20	½a black	4.00	3.00
65	A21	½a red	5.00	3.25
	Nos. 61-65 (5)		33.50	59.75

On No. 63a, the second "A" in "NAWAB" has been inserted by hand and varies somewhat in size.

Imperf. imitations of No. 65 were printed about 1904 in deep red on laid paper and in black on wove paper.

Stamps of types A16 and A19-A21 with a circular embossed seal and perforated, were prepared but not issued.

A22 A23
1898 **Imperf.**
72	A22	¼a black	.75	.75
a.	"SHAN"		5.00	5.00
73	A22	¼a green	1.10	1.20
a.	"SHAN"		5.25	5.25
74	A23	¼a black	2.10	2.10
	Nos. 72-74 (3)		3.95	4.05

1899 **Type of 1899**
75	A13	½a black ("NWAB")	11.00	20.00
a.	"BBGAM"		75.00	95.00
b.	"NWASBAHJAHNJ"		75.00	95.00
c.	"SHH"		75.00	95.00
d.	"SBAH"		22.00	45.00
e.	"SBAN"		75.00	95.00
f.	"NWIB"		75.00	95.00
g.	"BEIAM"		75.00	75.00
h.	"SBAH" and "BBGAM"		75.00	95.00

A24
1902
76	A24	¼a red	9.00	17.00
77	A24	½a black	8.00	13.00
a.	Printed on both sides		2,000.	2,000.
78	A24	1a brown	20.00	28.00
79	A24	2a blue	24.00	40.00
80	A24	4a orange	155.00	225.00
81	A24	8a violet	155.00	450.00
82	A24	1r rose	600.00	1,000.
	Nos. 76-82 (7)		971.00	1,773.

No. 50 Overprinted in Red

1903
83	A16	8a deep green, red ovpt 6 mm	485.00	525.00
a.	Inverted overprint		1,000.	1,150.
b.	Red ovpt 11 mm		1,000.	1,150.

There are two types of the overprint which is the Arabic S, initial of the Begum.

Inscription in Circle Embossed on Each Stamp

1903 **Wove Paper**
84	A24	¼a red	2.50	10.00
85	A24	½a black	2.50	7.00
86	A24	1a brown	11.50	20.00
87	A24	2a blue	20.00	50.00
88	A24	4a yellow	27.00	85.00
89	A24	8a violet	100.00	225.00
90	A24	1r rose	175.00	475.00
	Nos. 84-90 (7)		338.50	872.00

Laid Paper
84a	A24	¼a red	1.50	13.00
85a	A24	½a black	1.50	14.00
86a	A24	1a brown	175.00	20.00
87a	A24	2a blue	375.00	1,000.
88a	A24	4a orange	300.00	210.00
89a	A24	8a violet	4,000.	
90a	A24	1r rose	4,000.	4,000.
	Nos. 84a-90a (7)		8,853.	5,257.

The embossing in a circle, which was first used in 1903, has been applied to many early stamps and impressions from redrawn plates of early issues. So far as is now known, these should be classed as reprints.

INDIA - FEUDATORY STATES — BHOPAL — BHOR

Coat of Arms — A25

1908		Engr.		Perf. 13½
99	A25	1a yellow green	6.50	11.00
a.		Printed on both sides	240.00	
b.		imperf., pair	3,000.	

OFFICIAL STAMPS

O1

Overprinted

Size: 20½x25mm

1908		Unwmk. Engr.		Perf. 13½
O1	O1	½a yellow green	5.00	.30
a.		Pair, one without ovpt.	1,600.	
b.		Inverted overprint	400.00	260.00
c.		Double ovpt., one invtd.	275.00	
d.		As "c," imperf., pair	235.00	
e.		Horiz. pair (#O1, O1c)	1,750.	
f.		Horiz. pair, imperf. between	2,000.	
O2	O1	1a carmine	7.00	.50
a.		Inverted overprint	250.00	175.00
b.		Imperf. pair	260.00	
O3	O1	2a blue	40.00	.30
a.		imperf., pair	100.00	
O4	O1	4a red brown	20.00	1.00
		Nos. O1-O4 (4)	72.00	2.10

Nos. O1-O4 Overprinted

O5	O1	½a yellow green	17.00	3.00
O6	O1	1a carmine	21.00	1.50
O7	O1	2a blue	8.00	1.50
a.		Inverted overprint	33.00	
O8	O1	4a red brown	130.00	2.50
a.		Inverted overprint	25.00	90.00
b.		Double overprint	300.00	
c.		Imperf. pair	125.00	
d.		As "c," inverted overprint	125.00	
		Nos. O5-O8 (4)	176.00	8.50

The difference in the two overprints is in the shape of the letters, most noticeable in the "R."

Nos. O2-O3 and Types of 1908 Overprinted

Size: 25½x30½mm

1930-31		Litho.		Perf. 14
O9	O1	½a gray green ('31)	32.00	2.50
O10	O1	1a carmine	32.00	.30
O11	O1	2a blue	32.00	.65
O12	O1	4a brown	32.00	1.50
		Nos. O9-O12 (4)	128.00	4.95

½a, 2a, 4a are inscribed "POSTAGE" on the left side; 1a "POSTAGE AND REVENUE."

Similar to Type O1
Size: 21x25mm
"POSTAGE" at left
"BHOPAL STATE" at right

1932-33		Perf. 11½, 13, 13½, 14
O13	O1	¼a orange yellow	3.75	1.50
a.		Pair, one without overprint	350.00	
b.		Perf. 13½	16.00	.45
c.		Perf. 14	18.00	.45
d.		Perf. 11½	18.00	.45
e.		"S" of "SERVICE" omitted	750.00	

"BHOPAL GOVT." at right

Perf. 13½

O14	O1	½a yellow green	16.00	.30
		Perf 14 ('34)	26.00	1.00
O15	O1	1a brown red	16.00	.30
a.		Pair, one without ovpt.	375.00	
O16	O1	2a blue	25.00	1.50
O17	O1	4a brown	25.00	1.50
a.		Perf 14 ('34)	33.00	.40
		Nos. O13-O17 (5)	85.75	5.10

No. O14, O16-O17 Surcharged in Red, Violet, Black or Blue

a, b, c

1935-36		Perf. 13½
O18	O1(a)	¼a on ½a (R)	80.00	30.00
a.		Inverted surcharge	650.00	185.00
O19	O1(b)	3p on ½a (R)	8.50	6.50
a.		Inverted surcharge	225.00	60.00
b.		"THEEE"	220.00	100.00
c.		As "b," inverted surcharge	3,000.	3,000.
d.		"THRFE"	220.00	100.00
e.		As "d," inverted surcharge	3,000.	3,000.
f.		"THREF"	220.00	100.00
g.		"PIES" omitted	4,750.	
h.		"HREE" and "PIES" omitted	7,500.	
i.		Vertical pair (#O18, O19)	110.00	45.00
j.		As "i," inverted surcharge	1,500.	450.00
k.		"I." "I" of "PIES"	7,500.	
O20	O1(a)	¼a on 2a (R)	65.00	40.00
a.		Inverted surcharge	625.00	160.00
b.		As "a," "A" omitted	4,750.	
O21	O1(b)	3p on 2a (R)	6.00	8.00
a.		Inverted surcharge	225.00	60.00
b.		"THEEE"	220.00	100.00
c.		As "b," inverted surcharge	3,000.	3,000.
d.		"THRFE"	220.00	100.00
e.		As "d," inverted surcharge	3,000.	3,000.
g.		"PIES" omitted	4,750.	
h.		"THEE"	7,500.	
i.		Vertical pair (#O20, O21)	100.00	70.00
O22	O1(a)	¼a on 4a (R)	3,000.	900.00
O23	O1(a)	¼a on 4a (Bk) ('36)	200.00	55.00
O24	O1(b)	3p on 4a (R)	500.00	175.00
a.		"THEEE"	2,500.	1,700.
b.		"THRFE"	2,500.	1,700.
c.		Vertical pair (#O22, O24)	5,500.	1,700.
O25	O1(b)	3p on 4a (Bk) ('36)	5.00	5.00
a.		"THRER"	1,200.	650.00
b.		"FHREE"	1,325.	1,000.
c.		"PISE"	2,250.	1,700.
d.		"PIFS"	1,200.	650.00
e.		Vertical pair (#O22, O25)	275.00	100.00
f.		As "e," "FHREE"		12,500.
O26	O1(c)	1a on ½a (V)	7.50	2.50
a.		Inverted surcharge	185.00	70.00
O27	O1(c)	1a on 2a (V)	4.00	4.00
a.		Inverted surcharge	225.00	100.00
O28	O1(c)	1a on 2a (Bk) ('36)	1.50	4.00
a.		"ANNO"	3,750.	
b.		1a on 2a (V)	100.00	160.00
c.		Inverted surcharge	185.00	225.00
d.		First "N" of "ANNA" inverted	2,100.	2,100.
e.		As "d," inverted surcharge	3,000.	3,000.
O29	O1(c)	1a on 4a (Bl)	10.00	10.00
		Perf. 14	40.00	15.00

Nos. O18-O25 are arranged in composite sheets of 100. The 2 top horizontal rows of each value are surcharged "a" and the next 5 rows as "b." The next 3 rows as "b" but in a narrower setting.

Arms of Bhopal — O2

1935		Litho.
O30	O2	1a3p claret & blue	5.00	3.00

Inscribed: "Bhopal State Postage"
Ovptd. "SERVICE" 11mm long

1937		Perf. 12
O31	O2	1a6p dk clar & bl	3.50	2.50
a.		Overprint omitted	375.00	275.00
b.		Dbl. ovpt., one inverted	1,500.	1,500.
c.		Blue printing double		275.00
d.		Imperf, pair		375.00
e.		Pair, imperf between	475.00	475.00

See Nos. O42, O45.

Arms of Bhopal — O3

Brown or Black Overprint

1936-38				Typo.
O32	O3	¼a orange (Br)	1.50	1.00
a.		Inverted overprint	1,100.	1,100.
b.		Vert. pair, imperf between	400.00	
c.		Horiz. pair, imperf between		1,200.
d.		Black overprint	12.00	1.25
e.		As "d," inverted ovpt.		750.00
f.		As "d," double ovpt.		550.00
O32G	O3	¼a yel (Br) ('38)	17.00	4.00
O33	O3	1a carmine	2.00	.30
a.		Horiz. pair, imperf vert.		425.00
b.		Vert. pair, imperf. between		800.00
c.		Horiz. pair, imperf between	400.00	400.00
d.		Block of 4, imperf between	1,200.	1,200.
		Nos. O32-O33 (3)	20.50	5.30

Moti Mahal — O4

Overprinted in Black

1936		Perf. 11½
O34	O4	½a grn & choc	1.00	1.00
a.		Frame double	160.00	25.00
b.		Double overprint	450.00	250.00
c.		Vert. pair, imperf between		600.00
d.		Horiz. pair, imperf between		600.00

Moti Masjid — O5

4a, Taj Mahal and Be-Nazir Palaces.

Overprinted in Black

1937		Perf. 11½
O35	O5	2a dk blue & brown	6.00	1.00
a.		Inverted overprint	400.00	525.00
b.		Vert. pair, imperf between		800.00
c.		Horiz. pair, imperf between		600.00
d.		Overprint omitted	700.00	
e.		Double overprint		1,000.
f.		Pair, one without ovpt.	1,500.	
g.		As "e," inverted overprint	3,000.	
O36	O5	4a bister brn & blue	5.00	1.00
a.		Double overprint		350.00
b.		Center double		1,000.
c.		Horiz. pair, imperf between		2,100.
d.		Overprint omitted		800.00

Types of 1937
Overprinted "SERVICE" in Black or Brown

Designs: 4a, Taj Mahal. 8a, Ahmadabad Palace. 1r, Rait-Ghat.

1938-44				
O37	O4	½a dp grn & brn	1.00	1.00
O38	O5	2a vio & dp grn	25.00	.75
a.		Vert. pair, imperf. between		650.00
b.		Vert. strip of 3, imperf. between	400.00	525.00
c.		Frame double		900.00
d.		Center double		1,050.
e.		Double ovpt.		1,000.
O39	O5	4a red brn & brt bl	6.50	1.00
a.		Frame double		800.00
O40	O5	8a red vio & blue	15.00	4.00
a.		"SERVICE" in serifs	225.00	285.00
b.		Overprint omitted		425.00
c.		Double overprint		375.00
d.		Vert. pair, imperf between		1,100.
e.		Frame double		650.00
f.		As "b," horiz. pair, imperf. vertically		700.00
g.		As "a," "SERAICE" in serifs	1,400.	2,000.
h.		As "a," "1" for "I" in "SERVICE"	1,400.	2,000.
O41	O5	1r bl & red vio (Br)	45.00	15.00
a.		Black overprint ('44)	40.00	6.50
b.		"SERVICE" in serifs	110.00	225.00
c.		Overprint omitted	2,600.	
d.		Vert. pair, imperf horiz.		5,250.
e.		As "b," "SREVICE"	325.00	650.00
		Nos. O37-O41 (5)	92.50	21.75

No. O39 measures 36½x22½mm, No. O40 39x24mm, No. O41 45½x27¾mm.

Type of 1935

1939		Perf. 12
O42	O2	1a6p dark claret	10.00	4.00
a.		Overprint omitted		1,100.
b.		Double overprint		1,100.
c.		Double overprint, one inverted		1,250.
d.		Pair, imperf between	600.00	600.00

Tiger — O6

Design: 1a, Deer.

1940		Typo.		Perf. 11½
O43	O6	¼a ultramarine	12.00	3.00
O44	O6	1a red violet	80.00	6.50

Type of 1935
Inscribed: "Bhopal State Postage"

1941				
O45	O2	1a3p emerald	6.00	4.50
a.		Pair, imperf between	1,200.	1,200.

Moti Palace O7 **Coat of Arms O8**

2a, Moti Mosque. 4a, Be-Nazir Palaces.

Perf. 11½, 12

1944-46		Unwmk.		Typo.
O46	O8	3p ultramarine	1.50	1.50
a.		Vert. pair, imperf. between	275.00	275.00
b.		Horiz. pair, imperf. between		750.00
c.		Double impression	150.00	
O47	O7	½a light green	1.50	1.50
a.		imperf., pair		175.00
b.		Horiz. pair, imperf. between		500.00
c.		Double impression		325.00
O48	O8	9p org brn ('46)	15.00	6.00
a.		Imperf., pair		290.00
O49	O8	1a brt red vio ('45)	16.00	2.60
a.		Vert. pair, imperf. horizontally		1,100.
O50	O8	1½a deep plum	6.50	2.00
a.		Horiz. pair, imperf. between		900.00
b.		Horiz. pair, imperf. between		900.00
O51	O7	2a red violet ('45)	13.00	5.00
O52	O8	3a yellow ('46)	40.00	40.00
a.		Imperf., pair		400.00
b.		Vert. pair, imperf. horizontally		600.00
O53	O7	4a brown ('45)	20.00	3.00
a.		imperf., pair		225.00
b.		Horiz. pair, imperf. vertically		600.00
c.		Double impression		400.00
O54	O8	6a brt rose ('46)	50.00	100.00
a.		Imperf., pair		550.00
b.		Vert. pair, imperf. horizontally		700.00
c.		Horiz. pair, imperf. vertically		700.00
		Nos. O46-O54 (9)	163.50	161.60

An imperf. variety of No. O51 exists in chocolate. Values, $500 unused and used.
For surcharges see Nos. O58-O59.

1946-47		Unwmk.		Perf. 11½
O55	O8	1a violet	30.00	5.00
O56	O7	2a violet ('47)	20.00	20.00
O57	O8	3a deep orange	225.00	225.00
		Nos. O55-O57 (3)	275.00	250.00

No. O50 Surcharged "2 As." and Bars

1949		Perf. 12
O58	O8	2a on 1½a dp plum	6.00	15.00
a.		Imperf., pair	600.00	650.00

Same Surcharged "2 As." and Rosettes

1949		Imperf.
O59	O8	2a on 1½a dp plum	4,250.	4,250.
a.		Perf 12	4,250.	4,250.

Three or more types of "2" in surcharge.
Bhopal stamps became obsolete in 1950.

BHOR
¹bōə̱r

LOCATION — A Feudatory State in the Kolhapur Residency and Deccan States Agency.
AREA — 910 sq. mi.
POP. — 141,546
CAPITAL — Bhor

INDIA - FEUDATORY STATES — BHOR — BIJAWAR — BUNDI

A1

A2

Handstamped
1879   Unwmk.   *Imperf.*
     Without Gum

1	A1	½a carmine	7.00	10.00
a.		Double impression	500.00	
b.		Tete beche pair	4,500.	
2	A2	1a carmine	11.00	15.00
a.		Double impression	1,000.	

Pant Sachiv Shankarrao — A3

1901   **Without Gum**   **Typo.**

3	A3	½a red	30.00	150.00

BIJAWAR
bi-'jä-wər

LOCATION — A Feudatory State in the Bundelkhand Agency of Central India.
AREA — 973 sq. mi.
POP. — 115,852
CAPITAL — Bijawar

Maharaja Sir Sawant Singh — A1

1935-36   Typo.   Unwmk.   **Perf. 10½**

1	A1	3p brown	20.00	20.00
a.		Imperf., pair	40.00	
b.		Vert. pair, imperf. between	150.00	
c.		Vert. pair, imperf. horizontally	100.00	
d.		Rouletted 7 ('36)	15.00	20.00
e.		As "d," printed on gummed side	1,500.	
2	A1	6p carmine	20.00	20.00
a.		Imperf., pair	200.00	
b.		Vert. pair, imperf. between	150.00	
c.		Horiz. pair, imperf. between	150.00	250.00
d.		Vert. pair, imperf. horizontally	160.00	
e.		Rouletted 7 ('36)	15.00	50.00
3	A1	9p purple	20.00	20.00
a.		Imperf., pair	250.00	
b.		Vert. pair, imperf. between	150.00	
c.		Horiz. pair, imperf. between	150.00	
d.		Vert. pair, imperf. horizontally	160.00	
e.		Rouletted 7 ('36)	15.00	300.00
4	A1	1a dark blue	30.00	20.00
a.		Imperf., pair	200.00	
b.		Vert. pair, imperf. between	150.00	
c.		Horiz. pair, imperf. between	250.00	
d.		Vert. pair, imperf. horizontally	180.00	
e.		Horiz. strip of 3, imperf. vertically	300.00	
f.		Rouletted 7 ('36)	15.00	325.00
5	A1	2a slate green	20.00	20.00
a.		Imperf., pair	180.00	
b.		Vert. pair, imperf. horizontally	40.00	
c.		Vert. pair, imperf. between	65.00	
d.		Horiz. pair, imperf. between	100.00	175.00
e.		Rouletted 7 ('36)	30.00	350.00

Maharaja Sir Sawant Singh — A2

1937   **Perf. 9**

6	A2	4a red orange	40.00	300.00
a.		Imperf., pair	300.00	
b.		Vert. pair, imperf. between	250.00	
7	A2	6a yellow	40.00	325.00
a.		Imperf., pair	300.00	
b.		Vert. pair, imperf. between	250.00	
8	A2	8a emerald	55.00	400.00
a.		Imperf., pair	400.00	

9	A2	12a turquoise blue	55.00	450.00
a.		Imperf., pair	400.00	
10	A2	1r purple	90.00	600.00
a.		"1Rs" instead of "1R"	180.00	1,200.
		Nos. 1-10 (10)	390.00	2,175.

Bijawar stamps became obsolete in 1939.

BUNDI
'bün-dē

LOCATION — A Feudatory State in the Rajputana Agency of India.
AREA — 2,220 sq. mi.
POP. — 216,722
CAPITAL — Bundi

A1

Katar (Indian Dagger) — A1a

Laid Paper
Without Gum
Gutters between Stamps

1894   Unwmk.   Litho.   *Imperf.*

1	A1	½a slate	40,000.	6,000.
f.		Last two letters of value below the rest		24,000.

Redrawn; Blade Does Not Touch Oval
No Gutters between Stamps
Wove Paper

1A	A1a	½a slate	100.00	100.00
b.		Value above, name below	700.00	1,100.
c.		Top right ornament omitted	6,000.	7,500.
d.		Last two letters of value below the rest	3,500.	3,500.
e.		Bottom left ornament omitted	6,000.	7,500.

On No. 1A, the dagger is thinner and its point does not touch the oval inner frame.

A2

Without Gum

1896   **Laid Paper**

2	A2	½a slate	12.00	18.00
a.		Last two letters of value below the rest	700.00	1,000.

A3

1897-98   **Without Gum**

3	A3	1a red	35.00	60.00
4	A3	2a yellow green	40.00	65.00
5	A3	4a yellow green	165.00	240.00
6	A3	8a red	300.00	900.00
7	A3	1r yellow, *blue*	1,000.	1,500.
		Nos. 3-7 (5)	1,540.	2,765.

A4

A5

Redrawn; Blade Wider and Diamond-shaped

1898-1900   **Without Gum**

8	A3	½a slate	12.00	12.00
9	A4	1a red	12.00	12.00
10	A4	2a emerald	40.00	40.00
a.		1st 2 characters of value omitted	3,750.	3,750.
11	A3	4a yel grn	80.00	175.00
12	A4	8a red	55.00	55.00
13	A5	1r yellow, *blue*	75.00	150.00
		Wove paper	55.00	80.00
		Nos. 8-13 (6)	274.00	444.00

On Nos. 9-10, the blade is wider and nearly diamond-shaped.

Point of Dagger to Left

14	A4	4a green	150.00	175.00
a.		4a yellow green	60.00	75.00

Maharao Rajah with Symbols of Spiritual and Temporal Power — A6

Rouletted 11 to 13 in Color

1915   Typo.   **Without Gum**
"Bundi" in 3 Characters (word at top right)

15	A6	¼a ultramarine	3.00	10.00
16	A6	½a black	5.00	13.00
a.		Thick wove paper	250.00	250.00
17	A6	1a vermilion	10.00	30.00
a.		Laid paper	35.00	55.00
18	A6	2a emerald	11.00	65.00
19	A6	2½a yellow	35.00	55.00
20	A6	3a brown	26.00	65.00
21	A6	4a yel green	30.00	75.00
a.		On laid paper	30.00	75.00
23	A6	6a pale ultra	30.00	250.00
24	A6	8a orange	10.00	125.00
25	A6	10a brown olive	30.00	250.00
26	A6	12a dark green	35.00	250.00
27	A6	1r violet	55.00	250.00
28	A6	2r car brn & blk	175.00	500.00
29	A6	3r blue & brown	275.00	750.00
30	A6	4r pale grn & red brn	650.00	850.00
31	A6	5r ver & pale grn	650.00	850.00

Minor differences in lettering in top and bottom panels may be divided into 8 types, but not all values come in each type. In one subtype the top appears as one word. Nos. 30-31 have an ornamental frame around the design.
For overprints see Nos. O1-O39.

A6a

1935   **Rouletted 11 to 13 in Color**
"Bundi" in 4 Characters (word at top right)

32	A6a	½a black	10.00	55.00
a.		On laid paper	150.00	150.00
33	A6a	1a scarlet, laid paper	100.00	65.00
34	A6a	4a yellow green	3,750.	1,100.
a.		4a brt grn, laid paper	30.00	65.00
		Nos. 32-34 (3)	3,860.	1,220.

The 4-character spelling of "Bundi" is found also on stamps rouletted in color: on ½a and 4a in small characters, and on ¼a, ½a, 1a, 4a, 4r and 5r in large characters like those on Nos. 32-35.
For overprints see Nos. O41-O42.

A6b

1935-41   **Rouletted 11 to 13 in Color**
"Bundi" in 4 Characters (word at top right)

35	A6b	¼a ultramarine	35.00	55.00
36	A6b	½a black ('38)	100.00	100.00
37	A6b	1a dp red	12.00	60.00
38	A6b	4a emerald ('38)	40.00	55.00
39	A6b	4r red & pale grn ('41)	250.00	
40	A6b	5r pale grn & ver ('41)	350.00	

1939-41   **Perf. 11**
"Bundi" in 4 Characters (word at top right)

41	A6b	¼a light blue ('41)	3.00	65.00
42	A6b	½a black	55.00	60.00
43	A6b	1a carmine ('40)	300.00	90.00
44	A6b	2a yellow green ('41)	22.00	140.00

A6c

1940   **Perf. 11**
"Bundi" in 4 Characters (word at top right), bottom characters smaller

45	A6c	½a black	475.00	250.00
46	A6c	2a bright green	100.00	115.00

Arms of Bundi — A7

1941-45   Typo.   **Perf. 11**

47	A7	3p bright ultra	6.00	10.00
48	A7	6p indigo	10.00	15.00
49	A7	1a red orange	13.00	17.00
50	A7	2a fawn	15.00	35.00
51	A7	4a brt yel green	22.00	100.00
52	A7	8a dull green	30.00	525.00
53	A7	1r royal blue	65.00	650.00
		Nos. 36-42 (7)	161.00	1,352.

The 1st printing of Nos. 47-53 was gummed. All later printings were without gum. **Values are for stamps without gum.**
For overprints see Nos. O76-O82.

A8

Maj. Maharao Rajah Bahadur Singh — A9

View of Bundi — A10

1947   **Perf. 11**

54	A8	¼a deep green	3.00	65.00
55	A8	½a purple	3.00	65.00
56	A8	1a yellow green	3.00	65.00
57	A9	2a red	3.00	110.00
58	A9	4a deep orange	6.00	130.00
59	A10	8a violet blue	6.00	
60	A10	1r chocolate	30.00	
		Nos. 54-60 (6)	189.50	236.50

For overprints see Rajasthan Nos. 1-14.

OFFICIAL STAMPS
Nos. 15-31 Handstamped in Black

a

Rouletted 11 to 13 in Color

1918   Unwmk.   **Without Gum**

O1	A6	¼a ultramarine	3.00	
a.		Red overprint	2.00	
b.		Green overprint	15.00	
O2	A6	½a black	20.00	
a.		Red overprint	6.00	
b.		Green overprint	10.00	
c.		As "#O2," thick wove paper	425.00	
O3	A6	1a vermilion	13.00	
O4	A6	2a emerald	12.00	
O5	A6	2½a yellow	13.00	
a.		Red overprint	550.00	
O6	A6	3a brown	15.00	
a.		Red overprint	650.00	
b.		Green overprint	900.00	
O7	A6	4a yel green	16.00	
a.		Red overprint	800.00	
O8	A6	6a pale ultra	25.00	
a.		Red overprint	1,000.	
O9	A6	8a orange	30.00	
a.		Red overprint	850.00	

INDIA - FEUDATORY STATES — BUNDI

O10	A6	10a olive green	160.00
a.		Red overprint	1,200.
O11	A6	12a dark green	135.00
a.		Red overprint	1,000.
O12	A6	1r violet	125.00
a.		Red overprint	850.00
O13	A6	2r car brn & blk	900.00
a.		Green overprint	2,600.
b.		2r choc & blk	1,750.
O14	A6	3r blue & brown	650.00
a.		Red overprint	2,600.
O15	A6	4r pale grn & red brn	650.00
O16	A6	5r pale grn & ver	650.00

Nos. 15-31 Handstamped Type b in Black

1919 — Without Gum

O17	A6	¼a ultramarine	7.00
a.		Red overprint	7.00
b.		Green overprint	125.00
O18	A6	½a black	5.00
a.		Red overprint	10.00
b.		Green overprint	525.00
c.		As "#18," thick wove paper	400.00
O19	A6	1a vermilion	130.00
O20	A6	2a emerald	100.00
a.		Red overprint	400.00
O21	A6	2½a yellow	32.00
a.		Red overprint	600.00
O22	A6	3a brown	30.00
a.		Red overprint	925.00
O23	A6	4a yel green	200.00
a.		Red overprint	700.00
O24	A6	6a pale ultra	500.00
a.		Red overprint	1,000.
O25	A6	8a orange	185.00
a.		Red overprint	850.00
O26	A6	10a brown olive	250.00
a.		Red overprint	1,200.
O27	A6	12a dark green	260.00
O28	A6	1r violet	130.00
a.		Red overprint	1,100.
O29	A6	2r car brn & blk	300.00
a.		Red overprint	2,600.
O30	A6	3r blue & brown	325.00
O31	A6	4r pale grn & red brn	—
O32	A6	5r ver & pale grn	600.00

Nos. 15-31 Handstamped Type "c" in Black

1919

O33	A6	¼a ultramarine	10.00
a.		Red overprint	525.00
b.		¼a cobalt	850.00
O34	A6	½a black	65.00
a.		Red overprint	525.00
O35	A6	1a carmine	260.00
O36	A6	2a emerald	250.00
O36A	A6	2½a yellow	650.00
O36B	A6	6]a cobalt	650.00
e.		Red overprint	1,000.
O37	A6	8a orange	575.00
O38	A6	10a brown olive	1,050.
a.		Red overprint	1,550.
O39	A6	12a dark green	1,200.
a.		Red oveprint	1,400.

Nos. 32-34a Handstamped Type "a" in Black or Red

1941 — Perf. 11

O41	A6a	½a black	700.00
a.		Red overprint	600.00
b.		On laid paper	700.00
c.		As "b," red overprint	260.00
O42	A6a	2a bright green, laid paper	500.00
a.		Red overprint	525.00

Nos. 35-38 Handstamped Type "a" in Black

O43	A6b	¼a ultramarine	33.00
a.		Red overprint	325.00
O44	A6b	½a black	120.00
a.		Red overprint	100.00
O44B	A6b	1a deep red	700.00
O44C	A6b	4a emerald	525.00
e.		Red overprint	1,450.

Nos. 41-44 Handstamped Type "a" in Black

1941

O45	A6b	¼a light blue	100.00
a.		Red overprint	260.00
O46	A6b	½a black	70.00
a.		Red overprint	190.00
O47	A6b	1a carmine	700.00
O48	A6b	2a yellow green	1,200.

Nos. 45-46 Handstamped Type "a" in Black

1941

O49	A6c	½a black	500.
a.		Red overprint	1,550.
O50	A6c	2a bright green	1,300.

Nos. 32-34a Handstamped Type "b" in Black

1941

O51	A6a	½a black	950.00
a.		Red overprint	600.00
b.		On laid paper	950.00
c.		As "b," red overprint	400.00
O52	A6a	4a brt grn, laid paper	475.00
a.		Red overprint	625.00

Nos. 35-40 Handstamped Type "b" in Black

1941

O53	A6b	¼a ultramarine	120.00
a.		Red overprint	700.00
O54	A6b	½a black	190.00
O55	A6b	1a deep red	700.00
O56	A6b	4a emerald	550.00
O57	A6b	4r pale grn & red	7,500.
O58	A6b	5r ver & pale grn	7,500.

Nos. 41-44 Handstamped Type "b" in Black

1941

O59	A6b	¼a light blue	100.00
O60	A6b	¼a ultramarine	85.00
a.		Red overprint	200.00
O61	A6b	½a black	130.00
a.		Red overprint	900.00
O62	A6b	1a carmine	800.00
O63	A6b	2a yellow green	550.00

Nos. 45-46 Handstamped Type "b" in Black

1941

O64	A6c	½a black	700.00
a.		Red overprint	1,550.
O65	A6c	2a bright green	1,200.

Nos. 32a Handstamped Type "c" in Red

1941

O66	A6a	½a black, laid paper, red ovpt.	1,100.

Nos. 36-38 Handstamped Type "c" in Black

1941

O67	A6b	½a black, red ovpt.	1,250.
O68	A6b	1a rose	1,250.
O69	A6b	4a emerald	1,050.
a.		Red overprint	1,450.

Nos. 41-44 Handstamped Type "c" in Black or Red

1941

O70	A6b	¼a light blue	300.00
O71	A6b	½a black	650.00
a.		Red overprint	650.00
O72	A6b	1a carmine	1,450.
a.		1a rose	700.00
O73	A6b	2a yellow green	700.00

Nos. 45-46 Handstamped Type "c" in Black

1941

O74	A6c	½a black	1,050.
a.		Red overprint	—
O75	A6c	2a bright green	4,000.

Nos. 47 to 53 Overprinted in Black or Carmine

1941 — Perf. 11

O76	A7	3p brt ultra (C)	15.00	30.00
O77	A7	6p indigo (C)	33.00	30.00
O78	A7	1a red orange	28.00	30.00
O79	A7	2a fawn	45.00	30.00
O80	A7	4a brt yel green	150.00	350.00
O81	A7	8a dull green	525.00	1,600.
O82	A7	1r royal blue (C)	600.00	1,750.

317

INDIA - FEUDATORY STATES — BUSSAHIR — CHARKHARI

BUSSAHIR
ˈbus-ə-ˌhiˌər

(Bashahr)

LOCATION — A Feudatory State in the Punjab Hill States Agency
AREA — 3,439 sq. mi.
POP. — 100,192
CAPITAL — Bashahr

Tiger
A1 A2
A3 A4
A5 A6
A7 A8

Monogram "R S" Overprinted in Violet, Rose, Blue Green (BG) or Mauve

Laid Paper

			1895 Unwmk.	Litho.	Imperf.
1	A1	¼a pink (V)		12,500.	
a.		½a pink (R)		16,000.	
2	A2	½a slate (R)		1,850.	2,500.
a.		½a slate (M)			
3	A3	1a red (V)		650.00	
4	A4	2a yellow (V)		275.00	650.00
a.		2a yellow (R)		525.00	800.00
b.		2a yellow (BG)		1,000.	
5	A5	4a violet (V)		525.00	
a.		4a violet (R)		575.00	
b.		Without monogram		900.00	
6	A6	8a brown (V)		525.00	700.00
a.		Without monogram		700.00	
b.		8a brown (BG)		600.00	
c.		8a brown (R)		700.00	
7	A7	12a green (R)		800.00	
a.		Without monogram		1,500.	
b.		12a green (V)			
8	A8	1r ultra (R)		525.00	
a.		Without monogram		1,100.	
b.		1r ultra (V)		700.00	

Perf. 7 to 14

9	A1	¼a pink (BG)	250.00	325.00
a.		Without monogram	1,600.	525.00
b.		¼a pink (V)		525.00
10	A2	½a slate (R)	60.00	400.00
a.		Without monogram	3,250.	
11	A3	1a red (V)	60.00	300.00
a.		Without monogram		
12	A4	2a yel (BG)	70.00	300.00
a.		2a yel (R)		
b.		2a yel (V)	525.00	
c.		Without monogram		600.00
13	A5	4a vio (BG)	70.00	300.00
a.		4a vio (R)	100.00	375.00
b.		4a vio (V)	160.00	
c.		Without monogram	100.00	
14	A6	8a brown (V)	55.00	300.00
a.		8a brown (BG)	200.00	525.00
b.		8a brown (R)	400.00	
c.		Without monogram	300.00	800.00
15	A7	12a green (R)	200.00	400.00
a.		12a green (V)	500.00	
b.		Without monogram	600.00	
16	A8	1r ultra (R)	400.00	
a.		Without monogram	900.00	1,200.

Pin-perf.

11D	A3	1a red (V)	525.00	600.00
12D	A4	2a yel (BG)	600.00	
e.		2a yel (R)	325.00	
f.		2a yel (V)	425.00	
g.		Without monogram	1,100.	
13D	A5	4a vio (BG)	1,100.	
e.		4a vio (R)	1,050.	
f.		4a vio (V)	850.00	
15D	A7	12a green (R)	1,050.	1,300.
16D	A8	1r ultra (R)	1,050.	1,300.

"R. S." are the initials of Tika Raghunath Singh, son of the Raja.

Overprinted "R S" Like Nos. 1-16

A9 A10
A11 A12
A13 A14

Wove Paper

1896		Engr.		Pin-perf.
17	A9	¼a dk gray vio (R)	—	4,250.
18	A10	½a blue gray (R)	2,850.	1,000.

1900		Litho.		Imperf.
19	A9	¼a red (V)	12.00	20.00
a.		¼a red (BG)	15.00	35.00
b.		Without monogram		
20	A9	¼a violet (R)	30.00	
a.		¼a violet (V)	30.00	
b.		¼a violet (BG)	35.00	
21	A10	½a blue (R)	40.00	55.00
a.		½a blue (V)	30.00	55.00
b.		Without monogram	150.00	
c.		As "26," laid paper	850.00	
22	A11	1a olive (R)	45.00	125.00
a.		1a red (V)	145.00	
23	A11	1a red (V)	13.00	40.00
a.		1a red (BG)	20.00	33.00
b.		Without monogram		
24	A12	2a yellow (V)	175.00	
a.		2a yellow (BG)	175.00	300.00
b.		Without monogram	250.00	
26	A14	4a brn vio (R)	185.00	350.00
a.		4 brn vio (V)	200.00	400.00
b.		4 brn vio (BG)	300.00	425.00
c.		Without monogram	100.00	
		Nos. 19-26 (7)	500.00	

27	A9	¼a red (V)	15.00	33.00
a.		¼a red (BG)	15.00	
b.		Without monogram		
28	A9	¼a violet (V)	55.00	55.00
a.		¼a violet (V)	55.00	85.00
29	A10	½a blue (R)	45.00	85.00
a.		½a blue (V)	40.00	85.00
b.		½a blue (BG)	525.00	
c.		As "c," laid paper		
30	A11	1a olive (V)	70.00	
a.		1a olive (R)	225.00	225.00
31	A11	1a red (V)	30.00	45.00
a.		1a red (BG)	32.00	35.00
32	A12	2a yellow (BG)	4,000.	4,000.
33	A13	2a yellow (V)	185.00	225.00
a.		2a yellow (BG)	300.00	350.00
b.		2a yellow (R)	200.00	325.00
34	A13	2a ocher (V)	210.00	
a.		2a ocher (BG)		
34B	A13	2a orange (BG)	250.00	250.00
c.		2a orange (V)	200.00	210.00
d.		Without monogram		1,000.
35	A14	4a brn vio (R)	325.00	
a.		4a brn vio (V)	350.00	525.00
b.		4a brn vio (BG)	325.00	500.00

Obsolete March 31, 1901.

Stamps overprinted with the monogram above (RNS) or with the monogram "PS" were never issued for postal purposes. They are either reprints or remainders to which this overprint has been applied. Many other varieties have appeared since the stamps became obsolete. It is probable that all or nearly all of them are reprints.

CHARKHARI
chər-ˈkär-ē

LOCATION — A Feudatory State in the Bundelkhand Agency in Central India.
AREA — 880 sq. mi.
POP. — 120,351
CAPITAL — Maharajnagar

A1

Thin White or Blue Wove Paper
Value in the Plural "ANNAS"
Without Gum

1894		Unwmk.	Typo.	Imperf.
1	A1	¼a rose	20,000.	20,000.
2	A1	½a purple		20,000.
3	A1	1a green	8,000.	9,000.
a.		Pin-perf.	30,000.	
3B	A1	2a green	10,000.	
3C	A1	4a green	5,750.	

A1a

1897
Value in the Singular "ANNA"
Without Gum

3D	A1a	¼a rose	4,500.	1,750.
f.		Pin-perf.	30,000.	
3E	A1a	¼a magenta	350.00	350.00
4	A1a	¼a purple	5.50	6.00
a.		Pin-perf.	5,000.	
6	A1a	1a blue green	10.00	15.00
7	A1a	2a blue green	15.00	25.00
8	A1a	4a green	20.00	30.00
		Nos. 4-8 (5)	400.50	426.00

In a later printing, the numerals of Nos. 4-8 are smaller or of different shape.
Proofs are known on paper of various colors.

A2

Size: 19½x23mm

1909		Litho.		Perf. 11
9	A2	1p red brown	9.00	60.00
10	A2	1p turq blue	2.00	1.00
a.		Horiz. pair, imperf. between	325.00	
11	A2	½a scarlet	3.00	2.00
12	A2	1a sage green	8.00	5.00
13	A2	2a gray blue	5.00	5.00
14	A2	4a deep green	6.00	7.00
15	A2	8a brick red	11.00	33.00
16	A2	1r red brown	19.00	100.00
		Nos. 9-16 (8)	63.00	213.00

See Nos. 22-27, 39-43. For surcharges see Nos. 37-38A.

A3

1912-17 Handstamped Imperf.
Without Gum

21	A3	1p violet ('17)	12.00	7.00
e.		On laid paper		1,900.
f.		Double frameline	2,200.	1,225.00
g.		Tete beche pair	160.00	160.00

The 1p violet exists in a pair, with one stamp sideways. Value, $325 used.
The 1p black, type A3, is a proof.

A3a

Wove Paper
Handstamped
1922 Without Gum Imperf.

21A	A3a	1a violet	200.00	240.00
b.		on laid paper	400.00	450.00
c.		As "b," perf. 11	200.00	325.00

A3b

Size: 20x23½mm

1930-40		Without Gum		Typo.
22	A3b	1p dark blue	3.00	25.00
a.		Tete beche pair	2,600.	
b.		On laid paper		1,000.
c.		Pair, perf. 11 x imperf.	300.00	250.00
23	A3b	½a olive green	5.00	25.00
a.		cop brown ('40)	10.00	42.00
b.		Tete beche pair	2,100.	
23C	A3b	½a gray brown	200.00	200.00
24	A3b	1a light green	5.00	30.00
25	A3b	1a chocolate	23.00	45.00
c.		Tete beche pair	145.00	
25A	A3b	1a dull red ('40)	375.00	150.00
b.		On laid paper		1,000.
26	A3b	2a light blue	4.00	30.00
a.		Tete beche pair	22.00	
27	A3b	4a carmine	5.00	33.00
a.		Tete beche pair	22.00	
		Nos. 22-27 (7)	420.00	338.00

Guesthouse of Raja at Charkhari Reservoir — A4
Imlia Palace — A5
Industrial School — A6
View of City — A7
Maharajnagar Fort, Charkhari City — A8
Guesthouse A9
Palace Gate A10
Temples at Rampur — A11
Govordhan Temple — A12

1931 Perf. 11, 11½, 12

28	A4	½a dull green	3.50	.30
a.		Horiz. pair, imperf. between	90.00	15.00
b.		Vert. pair, imperf. between	90.00	50.00
c.		Vert. pair, imperf. horiz.	70.00	
29	A5	1a black brown	3.00	.30
a.		Horiz. pair, imperf. between	15.00	10.00
b.		Vert. pair, imperf. between	35.00	16.00
c.		Vert. pair, imperf. horiz.	25.00	
d.		Imperf. pair	40.00	
30	A6	2a purple	3.00	.30
a.		Horiz. pair, imperf. between	50.00	40.00
b.		Vert. pair, imperf. between	55.00	35.00
c.		Vert. pair, imperf. horiz.	30.00	30.00
d.		Double impression	15.00	
e.		Imperf. pair	40.00	
31	A7	4a olive green	3.50	.30
a.		Vert. pair, imperf. between	140.00	140.00
32	A8	8a magenta	6.00	.30
a.		Horiz. pair, imperf. between	130.00	45.00
b.		Vert. pair, imperf. between	110.00	70.00
c.		Vert. pair, imperf. horizontally	130.00	30.00
33	A9	1r rose & green	7.00	.30
a.		Vert. pair, imperf. between	200.00	175.00
b.		Green center omitted	500.00	
c.		Vert. pair, imperf. horiz.	200.00	
d.		Imperf. pair	100.00	
34	A10	2r brown & red	15.00	1.00
a.		Vert. pair, imperf. horiz.	425.00	45.00
35	A11	3r bl grn & choc	32.00	1.00
a.		Horiz. pair, imperf. between		525.00
b.		Tete beche pair	1,000.	30.00
c.		Chocolate center omitted	30.00	
36	A12	5r violet & blue	13.00	1.00
a.		Horiz. pair, imperf. between	525.00	
b.		Center inverted	225.00	65.00
c.		Center, double impression		450.00
		Nos. 28-36 (9)	86.00	4.80

Size range of A4-A12: 30-31x19½-24mm.
Many errors of perforation and printing exist.
Used values are for canceled to order stamps.

INDIA - FEUDATORY STATES — CHARKHARI — COCHIN

Nos. 15-16 Surcharged in Black

1940 Perf. 11
37	A2	½a on 8a brick red	80.00	260.00
a.		Surcharge inverted	650.00	900.00
b.		"1" of "½" inverted	625.00	
38	A2	1a on 1r red brown	300.00	900.00
b.		Surcharge inverted	800.00	
38A	A2	"1 ANNA" on 1r red brown	3,250.	2,000.

Type of 1930

1943 Unwmk. Typo. Imperf.
Size: 20x23½mm
39	A3b	1p violet	40.00	525.00
a.		Tete beche pair	120.00	
40	A3b	1p apple green	110.00	1,000.
41	A3b	½a orange red	40.00	80.00
a.		Tete beche pair	95.00	
b.		On laid paper		1,000.
42	A3b	½a black	110.00	800.00
43	A3b	2a grayish green	210.00	450.00
a.		2a greenish gray ('41)	125.00	250.00
b.		As "a," tete beche pair	250.00	
c.		As "a," laid paper ('44)		1,000.
44	A3b	2a yellow green ('45)	4,600.	2,750.
		Nos. 39-43 (5)	510.00	2,855.

COCHIN
kō-'chin

LOCATION — A Feudatory State in the Madras States Agency in Southern India.
AREA — 1,480 sq. mi.
POP. — 1,422,875 (1941)
CAPITAL — Ernakulam

See the United State of Travancore and Cochin.

6 Puttans = 5 Annas
12 Pies = 1 Anna
16 Annas = 1 Rupee

A1

State Seal
1892 Unwmk. Typo. Perf. 12
1	A1	½put yellow	5.00	5.00
a.		Imperf., pair		
b.		Laid paper	2,100.	375.00
2	A1	1put red violet	5.00	5.00
a.		Vert. pair, imperf. between		7,000.
b.		1p purple (error)	375.00	300.00
3	A1	2put purple	5.00	3.00
a.		Imperf.		
		Nos. 1-3 (3)	15.00	13.00

Nos. 1 to 3 sometimes have watermark large umbrella in the sheet.

A1a

Wmk. Coat of Arms and Inscription in Sheet
1896
4	A1a	1put violet	200.00	200.00

Wmk. 43
4A	A1a	1put violet	26.00	45.00

Originally intended for revenue use, Nos. 4-4A were later authorized for postal use. Beware of fraudulently removed fiscal markings.

1894 Wmk. 41 Thin Paper
5	A1	½put orange	9.00	2.00
a.		Imperf., pair		
6	A1	1put magenta	22.00	11.00
7	A1	2put purple	17.00	6.00
a.		Imperf., pair		
b.		Double impression		3,500.
c.		Printed on both sides	3,500.	
d.		Tete beche pair	10,000.	
		Nos. 5-7 (3)	48.00	19.00

A2 **A3** **A4** **A5**

1898 Thin Paper
8	A2	3put ultra	2.00	2.00
a.		Double impression	1,600.	7,500.
b.		Horiz. pair, imperf. between	1,600.	7,500.
c.		Vert. pair, imperf. between	4,500.	
9	A3	½p gray green	3.00	3.00
a.		Pair, one sideways		6,500.
b.		Horiz. pair, imperf. between	3,250.	3,250.
10	A4	1p rose	7.00	3.00
a.		Laid paper		3,500.
b.		Tete beche pair	12,000.	8,000.
c.		As "a," tete beche pair		20,000.
d.		Printed on both sides		12,500.
e.		Double impression		7,500.
11	A5	2p purple	6.00	3.00
a.		Vert. pair, imperf. between		1,500.
b.		Vert. strip of 3, imperf. between	2,000.	
c.		Imperf. pair		12,500.
		Nos. 8-11 (4)	18.00	11.00

One confirmed used example each of Nos. 8a, 8b, 10e and 11c are known to exist.

1903 Thick Paper
12	A2	3p ultra	2.00	.30
d.		Horiz. pair, imperf. between		3,000.
i.		Double impression		1,250.
m.		Vert. pair, imperf. between	—	5,500.
12A	A3	½put gray green	2.00	.50
e.		Double impression		600.00
f.		Pair, one sideways	3,000.	3,000.
j.		Horiz. pair, imperf. between		3,000.
12B	A4	1put rose	5.00	.30
e.		Tete beche pair		8,500.
k.		Printed on both sides		12,500.
o.		"." instead of "L" in "ANCHAL"	250.00	250.00
p.		Double impression		2,500.
12C	A5	2p purple	5.00	.75
h.		Double impression	3,250.	1,750.
		Nos. 12-12C (4)	14.00	1.85

Beware of fake overprint surcharge varieties, such as double, inverted, etc. This applies also to early Official varieties. Such varieties require expertization.

Type of 1898 Surcharged

1909
13	A2	2p on 3p red violet	1.00	1.00
a.		Inverted surcharge	275.00	275.00
b.		Pair, stamps tete beche	600.00	600.00
c.		Pair, stamps & surch. tete beche	650.00	700.00
d.		Double surcharge	4,500.	2,500.

The surcharge is also known in a thin "2" measuring 5½x7mm, with curving foot. Values: unused $3,500.; used $2,500. This variety also is known overprinted both sides. Value: $12,500 unused.

Sri Rama Varma I — A6

1911-13 Engr. Perf. 14
14	A6	2p brown	1.00	.30
15	A6	3p blue	4.00	.30
a.		Perf. 14x12½	45.00	1.50
16	A6	4p yel green	5.00	.30
16A	A6	4p apple green	5.00	.60
17	A6	9p car rose	5.00	.30
18	A6	1a orange buff	5.00	.30
19	A6	1½a lilac	16.00	.60
20	A6	2a gray	11.00	.60
21	A6	3a vermilion	100.00	65.00
		Nos. 14-21 (9)	152.00	68.20

For surcharge and overprints see Nos. 34, O2-O9, O23-O24, O27.

Sri Rama Varma II
A7 **A8**

1918-23 Engr. Perf. 14
23	A7	2p brown	11.00	.30
a.		Imperf., pair	1,200.	
24	A7	4p green	1.50	.30
25	A7	6p red brown ('22)	3.25	.30
26	A7	8p black brown ('23)	4.00	.30
27	A7	9p carmine rose	60.00	1.00
28	A7	10p blue	13.00	.30
29	A8	1a brown orange	30.00	6.50
30	A7	1½a red violet ('21)	11.00	.30
31	A7	2a gray	6.00	.30
32	A7	2¼a yel green ('22)	20.00	4.50
33	A7	3a vermilion	16.00	.50
		Nos. 23-33 (11)	175.75	14.60

The 2p and 1a are found in two types, the difference lying in the first of the three characters directly above the maharaja's head.

For surcharges and overprints see Nos. 36-40, 52-53, O10-O22, O25-O26, O28-O36, O71A.

No. 15 Surcharged

Type I — Numeral 8mm high. Curved foot. Top begins with a ball. (As illustrated.)
Type II — Numeral 9mm high. Curved foot. Top begins with a curved line.
Type III — Numeral 6mm high. Straight foot. "Two pies" 15mm wide.
Type IV — "2" as in type III. Capital "P" in "Pies." "Two Pies" 13mm wide.
Type V — Heavy gothic numeral. Capital "P" in "Pies."

1922-29
34	A6	2p on 3p blue (Type I)	2.00	1.00
a.		Type II	8.50	1.50
b.		Type III	18.00	.50
c.		Type IV	26.00	26.00
d.		Type V	225.00	325.00
e.		Double surcharge, I	600.00	600.00
f.		Double surcharge II	1,700.	
g.		As "b," perf. 14x12½	25.00	25.00
h.		As "a," double surcharge	100.00	28.00
i.		As "h," double surcharge		
j.		As "b," "Pies" for "pies"	150.00	20.00
k.		As "j," perf. 14x12½	850.00	850.00
m.		As "c", double surch.	850.00	
n.		As "d", double surch.		6,000.

Types II and III with a capital "P" in "Pies" occur once in each sheet of the second and third settings. There are four settings. Type V is the first stamp, fourth row, of the fourth setting.

No. 32 Surcharged

1928
36	A7	1a on 2¼a yel green	9.00	16.00
a.		Double surcharge	—	850.00
b.		"REVENUF" for "REVENUE"	130.00	210.00

Nos. 24, 26 and 28 Surcharged in Black

1932-33
38	A7	3p on 4p green	4.00	3.50
39	A7	3p on 8p black brown	4.00	4.00
40	A7	9p on 10p deep blue	4.00	4.00
		Nos. 38-40 (3)	12.00	11.50

Sri Rama Varma III
A9 **A10**

1933-38 Engr. Perf. 13x13½
41	A9	2p brown ('36)	2.25	1.00
42	A9	4p green	1.00	.30
43	A9	6p red brown	1.00	.30
44	A10	1a brown org ('34)	4.00	.50
45	A9	1a8p rose red	4.00	11.00
46	A9	2a gray black ('38)	18.00	3.00
47	A9	2¼a yellow green	3.50	.50
48	A9	3a red org ('38)	18.00	2.50
49	A9	3a4p violet	2.50	2.50
50	A9	6a8p black brown	2.50	26.00
51	A9	10a deep blue	4.00	26.00
		Nos. 41-51 (11)	60.75	73.60

See Nos. 55-58. For overprints and surcharges see Nos. 54, 59-62, 73A-74, 76-77, 89, O37-O57, O70-O71, O72-O77A, O89.

Nos. 26 and 28 Surcharged in Red

1934 Perf. 13½
52	A7	6p on 8p black brown	1.50	.75
53	A7	6p on 10p blue	2.50	2.50

No. 44 Overprinted in Black — a

1939 Engr.
54	A10(a)	1a brown orange	15.00	2.50

Types of 1933-38
1938-41 Litho. Perf. 11
55	A9	2p dull brown	2.00	.50
56	A9	4p dl grn ('41)	2.00	.50
57	A9	6p red brown	3.50	.30
57A	A10	1a brn org	165.00	185.00
58	A9	2¼a yellow green	8.50	.40
		Nos. 55-58 (5)	181.00	186.70

Perf. 13x13½
55B	A9	2p dull brown	16.00	1.00
56B	A9	4p dl grn ('41)	15.00	24.00
57C	A9	6p red brown	—	9,500.
57D	A10	1a brn org	250.00	350.00
58B	A9	2¼a yellow green	28.00	10.00

Type of 1934 Overprinted in Black Type "a" or — b

Perf. 11 (#58A, 59), 13x13½ (#60)
1941-42
59	A10(b)	1a brown org	1,000.	4.00
		Perf. 13		650.00
60	A10(b)	1a brn org (#57D) ('42)	25.00	1.00
a.		Perf. 11	2.50	2.50

No. 45 Surcharged in Black — c

1943-44 Engr. Perf. 13x13½
61	A9(c)	3p on 1a8p rose red ('44)	17.00	23.00
62	A9(c)	1a3p on 1a8p rose red	1.50	1.00

319

INDIA - FEUDATORY STATES — COCHIN

Maharaja Sri Kerala Varma
A11 A12

1943 Litho. Wmk. 294 Perf. 13
63	A11	2p dull gray brn, wmk. 41	12.00	12.00
c.		Perf. 11		10,000.
64	A11	4p gray green, wmk. 294	10.00	30.00
b.		Perf. 11	6.50	8.00
65	A11	6p red brown	13.00	.30
a.		Perf. 11	11.00	2.25
66	A11	9p ultra, perf. 11	120.00	2.00
a.		Horiz. pair, imperf. between		6,000.
67	A12	1a brn org, 13x13½	300.00	375.00
b.		Perf. 11		33.00 100.00
68	A11	2¼a lt ol green, perf. 13x13½	50.00	6.50
a.		2¼a lt ol green	50.00	12.00
		Nos. 63-68 (6)	505.00	425.80

For surcharges and overprints see Nos. 69-73, 75, 78, 78B, O58-O69.

1943 Litho. Wmk. 41 Perf. 13
63A	A11	2p dull gray brn	70.00	8.50
63B	A11	2p dull gray brn, perf. 11	—	5,000.
64A	A11	4p gray green	4,000.	1,200.
67A	A12	1a brn org	4,000.	1,500.

Nos. 64 and 64A Surcharged Type "c"
69	A11(c)	3p on 4p gray grn, wmk. 294	13.00	.30
69A	A11(c)	3p on 4p gray grn, wmk. 41	250.00	65.00

Nos. 45, 64, 64a and 65 Surcharged in Black — d

1943-48 Wmk. 294 Perf. 13
69B	A9(d)	3p on 1a8p rose red ('42)	700.00	285.00
70	A11(d)	2p on 6p red brown	1.75	6.50
70A	A11(d)	2p on 6p red brn, perf. 11	4.00	3.50
71	A11(d)	3p on 4p gray green	20.00	.30
72	A11(d)	3p on 6p red brown	5.00	.30
72A	A11(d)	3p on 6p red brn, perf. 11	2.00	1.00
73	A11(d)	4p on 6p red brown	13.00	22.00

Nos. 57A Surcharged in Black — e

1944 Litho. Wmk. 41 Perf. 11
73A	A10(e)	6p on 1a brn org	1,700.	525.00
b.		"SIX PIES" double		3,000.
74	A10(e)	9p on 1a brn org	400.00	250.00

No. 57A, 67A Surcharged in Black — f

1944 Litho. Wmk. 41 Perf. 13
74B	A10(f)	6p on 1a brn org, perf. 11	850.00	425.00
74C	A10(f)	6p on 1a brn org	425.00	150.00
74D	A10(f)	9p on 1a brn org	1,000.	55.00
75	A12(f)	9p on 1a brn org	20.00	8.50
76	A9(c)	3p on 4p dull grn, perf. 11	10.00	6.00
76A	A9(c)	3p on 4p dull grn, perf. 13	35.00	5.50

Nos. 57A, 67A Surcharged in Black — g

1944 Litho. Wmk. 41 Perf. 13
77	A10(g)	9p on 1a brown orange	70.00	17.00
78	A12(g)	9p on 1a brown orange	20.00	6.00

One mint example of No. 78B has been recorded.

No. 67a Surcharged Type "c"
1944 Wmk. 41
78B	A12(g)	1a3p on 1a brn org	—	17,500.

Maharaja Ravi Varma — A13

1944-46 Wmk. 294 Perf. 13
79	A13	9p ultra ('46)	55.00	11.00
a.		Perf. 11	45.00	11.00
b.		Perf. 13x13½	90.00	11.00
80	A13	1a3p magenta	15.00	13.00
a.		Perf. 13x13½	900.00	200.00
81	A13	1a9p ultra ('46)	15.00	22.00
		Nos. 79-81 (3)	85.00	46.00

For overprints and surcharges see Nos. O78-O80, Travancore-Cochin Nos. 12, 14, O10.

Maharaja Ravi Varma — A15

1946-50 Litho. Perf. 13
82	A15	2p dull brown	5.00	.30
a.		Perf. 11	16.00	1.00
b.		Perf. 11x13	800.00	250.00
c.		Vert. pair, imperf. horiz.	8,000.	8,000.
83	A15	3p carmine rose	1.50	.50
83A	A15	4p gray grn ('50)	5,250.	120.00
84	A15	6p red brn ('47)	35.00	15.00
a.		Perf. 11	400.00	12.00
85	A15	9p ultramarine	4.50	.30
a.		Horiz. pair, imperf. between		7,000.
b.		Printed on both sides		1,500.
86	A15	1a dp org ('47)	13.00	60.00
a.		Perf. 11		1,200.
86B	A15	1a3p magenta	250.00	—
87	A15	2a gray ('47)	250.00	16.00
a.		Perf. 11	300.00	13.00
88	A15	3a vermilion	160.00	5.50
		Nos. 82-83,84-88 (7)	469.00	97.60

For surcharges and overprints see Nos. 98-99, O81-O88, Travancore-Cochin Nos. 8, 13, 15-15A, O11.

No. 45 Surcharged Type "d"
Perf. 13x13½

1947-48 Wmk. 41 Engr.
89	A9	6p on 1a8p rose red	8.00	35.00

Maharaja Sri Kerala Varma II — A16

Die I Die II

Two dies on 2p:
Die I, back of headdress almost touches value tablet.
Die II, back of headdress farther away from value tablet.

Die I Die II

Two dies on 3a4p:
Die I, white frame line around head is continuous, and two white lines beneath value inscriptions at bottom.
Die II, white frame line around head broken by value tablets at the sides, and single white line beneath value inscriptions at bottom. Die II comes from the first two stamps of the bottom row of the sheet.

1948-49 Wmk. 294 Perf. 11
90	A16	2p olive brown	2.50	.30
a.		Die II	80.00	6.00
b.		#90, horiz. pair, imperf. vert.		7,000.
c.		As "#90," vert. pair, imperf. horiz.		7,000.
91	A16	3p car ('49)	4.50	.30
a.		As "#90," vert. pair, imperf. between		4,750.
92	A16	4p gray green	24.00	8.50
a.		Horiz. pair, imperf. vert.	450.00	650.00
93	A16	6p red brown	33.00	.35
a.		Horiz. pair, imperf. vert.		1,300.
94	A16	9p ultra ('49)	3.25	1.25
95	A16	2a black	160.00	4.25
96	A16	3a ver ('49)	185.00	1.50
a.		Horiz. pair, imperf. vert.		6,500.
97	A16	3a4p violet ('49)	95.00	625.00
a.		Die II	450.00	3,000.
		Nos. 90-97 (8)	507.25	641.45

For overprints see Nos. O90-O97, Travancore-Cochin Nos. 9-11, O8-O9, O24.

No. 86 Surcharged Type "d" in Black
1949
98	A15	6p on 1a dp org	200.00	400.00
99	A15	9p on 1a dp org	325.00	500.00

A17

Design: 2a, Chinese fishing net. 2¼a, Dutch Palace.

1949 Unwmk. Perf. 11
100	A17	2a gray black	13.00	23.00
a.		Imperf. vert., horiz. pair	1,000.	
101	A17	2¼a dull green	6.50	23.00
a.		Imperf. vert., horiz. pair	1,000.	

See Travancore-Cochin for succeeding issues.

OFFICIAL STAMPS

See note above No. 13.

Stamps and Type of 1911-14 Overprinted — h

1913-14 Wmk. 41 Engr. Perf. 14
O2	A6(h)	4p yel green	30.00	.30
a.		Inverted overprint		525.00
O3	A6(h)	9p car rose	50.00	.30
O4	A6(h)	1½a red violet	160.00	.30
a.		Double overprint		1,550.
O5	A6(h)	2a gray	32.00	.30
O6	A6(h)	3a vermilion	180.00	.60
O7	A6(h)	6a violet	220.00	3.00
O8	A6(h)	12a blue	100.00	10.00
O9	A6(h)	1½r deep green	70.00	110.00
		Nos. O2-O9 (8)	842.00	124.80

Values for Nos. O2 and O3 are for the cheaper varieties with watermark sideways.

Stamps and Type of 1918-23 Overprinted — i

1918-34
O10	A7(i)	4p green	24.00	.30
a.		Double overprint		1,175.
O11	A7(i)	6p red brn ('22)	45.00	.30
a.		Double overprint		1,175.
O12	A7(i)	8p blk brn ('26)	24.00	.30
O13	A7(i)	9p car rose	190.00	.30
O14	A7(i)	10p dp blue ('23)	55.00	.30
a.		Double ovpt.		1,450.
O16	A7(i)	1½a red vio ('21)	11.00	.30
a.		Double overprint		1,450.
O17	A7(i)	2a gray	110.00	.40
O18	A7(i)	2¼a yel grn ('22)	45.00	.30
b.		Double overprint		1,050.
O19	A7(i)	3a ver ('22)	35.00	.40
a.		Double overprint		1,050.
O20	A7(i)	6a violet ('22)	100.00	1.00
O21	A7(i)	12a blue ('29)	55.00	10.00
O22	A7(i)	1½r dk grn ('34)	60.00	250.00
		Nos. O10-O22 (12)	754.00	263.90

On Nos. O2-O22, width of overprint varies from 14¾mm to 16½mm.

No. 15 Overprinted in Red — j

1921
O23	A7(i)	3p blue	225.00	.30
a.		Overprint in black		2,500.
b.		Double overprint (R)		1,050.
c.		Inverted "S" in ovpt. (R)		100.00

Nos. O3 and O13 Surcharged with New Values

1923-29
O24	A6	8p on 9p car rose	700.00	2.50
a.		Double surcharge		600.00
O25	A7	8p on 9p car rose	90.00	.30
a.		Double surcharge	—	425.00
O26	A7	10p on 9p car rose ('25)	125.00	1.50
a.		Double surcharge		600.00
b.		Surcharge measures 25mm	600.00	3.00
c.		As "b," double surcharge		650.00
O27	A6	10p on 9p car rose ('29)	4,500.	30.00
a.		Double surcharge		1,100.

Surcharge measures 27½ mm.

Regular Issue of 1918-23 Overprinted — k

1929-31
O28	A7(k)	4p green ('31)	65.00	4.25
O29	A7(k)	6p red brn ('30)	45.00	.30
O30	A7(k)	8p blk brn ('30)	18.00	.30
O31	A7(k)	10p deep blue	14.00	.30
O32	A7(k)	2a gray ('30)	120.00	.40
O33	A7(k)	3a vermilion ('30)	30.00	.30
O34	A7(k)	6a dk violet ('30)	280.00	5.00
		Nos. O28-O34 (7)	572.00	10.85

Inverted "S" in Overprint
O28a	A7(k)	4p green ('31)	525.00	42.50
O29a	A7(k)	6p red brown ('30)	260.00	5.50
O30a	A7(k)	8p black brown	—	125.00
O31a	A7(k)	10p deep blue	125.00	7.00
O32a	A7(k)	2a gray ('30)	700.00	20.00
O33a	A7(k)	3a vermilion ('30)	250.00	20.00
O34a	A7(k)	6a dk violet ('30)	1,300.	160.00

Same with Additional Surcharge on Type of Regular Issue of 1918-23 in Red

1933
O35	A7(k)	6p on 8p black brown	5.25	.30
a.		Inverted "S"	60.00	8.00
O36	A7(k)	6p on 10p dk blue	5.25	.30
a.		Inverted "S"	65.00	5.25

Regular Issue of 1933 Overprinted Type "k" in Black as in 1933-34

1933-35 Perf. 13x13½
O37	A9(k)	4p green	13.00	.30
O38	A9(k)	6p red brown	13.00	.30
O39	A10(k)	1a brn org	55.00	.30
O40	A9(k)	1a8p rose red	2.00	.50
O41	A9(k)	2a gray	65.00	.30
O42	A9(k)	2¼a yel grn	20.00	.30
O43	A9(k)	3a vermilion	100.00	.30
O44	A9(k)	3a4p violet	2.00	.30
O45	A9(k)	6a8p blk brn	2.00	.30
O46	A9(k)	10a deep blue	2.00	2.50
		Nos. O37-O46 (10)	274.00	5.40

Regular Stamps of 1934-38 Overprinted in Black — m

INDIA - FEUDATORY STATES — COCHIN — DHAR — DUNGARPUR

1937-38   Perf. 11, 13x13½
O47	A10(m)	1a brn org	65.00	1.00
O48	A9(m)	2a gray black	50.00	4.00
O49	A9(m)	3a red orange	15.00	3.00
		Nos. O47-O49 (3)	130.00	8.00

Similar Overprint on Types of 1933-36
1938-44   Litho.   Wmk. 294
O50	A9(m)	4p dl grn, perf. 13x13½	3.50	1.00
a.		Perf. 11 ('42)	200.00	22.00

Wmk. 41
O51	A9(m)	6p red brn ('41)	26.00	9.00
a.		Wmk. 294	26.00	1.50
b.		As "a," perf. 11	400.00	15.00
c.		Overprinted on both sides		400.00
O52	A10(m)	1a brn org	1.50	.30
a.		Wmk. 294	7.00	5.25
b.		As "a," perf. 11	22.00	6.50
c.		Overprinted on both sides		700.00
O53	A9(m)	3a orange ('40)	5.50	4.25
a.		Wmk. 294	40.00	15.00
		Nos. O50-O53 (4)	36.50	14.55

Similar Overprint in Narrow Serifed Capitals on No. 57

Wmk. 41   Perf. 11
O53A	A9	6p red brown	2,100.	975.00

Type of 1933-36 Overprinted in Black — o

Perf. 10½, 11, 13x13½
O54	A9(o)	4p dl grn, perf. 13x13½ ('41)	40.00	5.00
a.		Perf. 11	65.00	4.00
b.		Inverted "S"	75.00	3.50
O55	A9(o)	6p red brown ('41)	65.00	.60
a.		Inverted "S"	75.00	.75
O56	A9(o)	2a gray black	26.00	1.50
a.		Inverted "S"	33.00	1.75
		Nos. O54-O56 (3)	131.00	7.10

Type of 1934 Overprinted in Black — p

1941   Perf. 11
O57	A10(p)	1a brn org	700.00	3.75

Stamps and Types of 1944 Overprinted in Black — q

Perf. 11, 13x13½
1944-48   Wmk. 294
O58	A11(q)	4p gray grn	140.00	15.00
a.		Perf. 11	425.00	10.00
b.		Perf. 13	975.00	95.00
O59	A11(q)	6p red brn, perf. 11	4.00	.30
a.		Perf. 13x13½	11.00	.30
b.		Perf. 13	11.00	5.00
c.		As "a," dbl. ovpt.		125.00
d.		As "b," dbl. ovpt.		125.00
O59E	A11(q)	1a brn org, perf. 13x13½	28,000.	100.00
O60	A11(q)	2a gray blk	9.00	1.50
O61	A11(q)	2¼a dl yel grn	8.00	1.50
a.		Additional ovpt. on reverse		550.00
O62	A11(q)	3a red org, 13x13½	20.00	5.50
a.		Perf. 11	22.00	.60
		Nos. O58-O62 (5)	181.00	23.80

Same Overprint with Additional Surcharge
O63	A11	3p on 4p gray grn, perf. 13x13½	8.00	.30
a.		Perf. 11	25.00	1.00
b.		As "a," additional overprint on reverse		600.00
O64	A12	3p on 1a brn org	65.00	17.00
O65	A11	9p on 6p red brn	25.00	1.00
a.		Printed on both sides		1,000.
O66	A12	1a3p on 1a brn org	30.00	6.50
		Nos. O63-O66 (4)	128.00	31.80

Same Overprint in Black on Types of 1944 Surcharged Type "c"
O67	A11	3p on 4p gray grn, perf. 13½x13	13.00	1.00
a.		Perf. 11	700.00	260.00
O68	A11	9p on 6p red brn	12.00	2.00
O69	A12	1a3p on 1a brn org	6.50	.30
		Nos. O67-O69 (3)	31.50	3.30

Nos. O52 and O16 Surcharged Type "d"
1944   Wmk. 41   Perf. 11, 13x13½, 14
O70	A10	3p on 1a brn org	10.00	6.50
O71	A10	9p on 1a brn org	700.00	100.00

Engr.
O71A	A7	9p on 1½a red vio	1,850.	55.00

No. O52 Surcharged Type "c"
O72	A10	1a3p on 1a brn org	700.00	185.00

No. 76 Overprinted in Black

Perf. 13x13½
O72A	A9	3p on 4p dl grn	525.00	125.00

No. 45 Overprinted Type "k" and Surcharged Type "d"
1944-48   Wmk. 41   Perf. 13x13½
O73	A9	9p on 1a8p rose red	325.00	55.00
O74	A9	1a9p on 1a8p rose red	7.00	5.25

No. 45 Overprinted Type "k" and Surcharged Type "c"
O75	A9	3p on 1a8p rose red	20.00	5.50
O76	A9	1a9p on 1a8p rose red	8.00	1.00

Type of 1939-41 Overprinted in Black
1946   Wmk. 294   Perf. 11
O77	A9	2a gray	175.00	2.00
b.		Overprint omitted		3,250.
O77A	A9	2¼a yellow green	7,500.	16.00

Same Overprint in Black on Nos. 79-81
1946   Litho.   Perf. 13
O78	A13	9p ultramarine	5.50	.30
a.		Perf. 13x13½	8.25	.30
b.		Printed on both sides		1,200.
O79	A13	1a3p magenta	2.50	.30
a.		Double overprint	40.00	16.00
b.		Printed on both sides	325.00	—
c.		As "b," overprint doubled and inverted	175.00	175.00
O80	A13	1a9p ultramarine	.50	2.00
a.		Double overprint		300.00
b.		Pair, one without overprint		4,500.
		Nos. O78-O80 (3)	8.50	2.60

Types and Stamps of 1946-48 Overprinted Type "h"
1946-48
O81	A15	3p car rose	3.50	.30
a.		Additional overprint on reverse		1,200.
O82	A15	4p gray green	50.00	10.00
O83	A15	6p red brown	40.00	6.00
O84	A15	9p ultra	2.00	.35
a.		Printed on both sides, one invtd.		1,200.
O85	A15	1a3p magenta	10.00	2.50
O86	A15	1a9p ultra	12.00	.60
O87	A15	2a gray black	22.00	4.00
O88	A15	2¼a olive green	50.00	15.00
		Nos. O81-O88 (8)	189.50	38.75

No. 56 Overprinted Type "q" and Surcharged Type "d"
1947   Wmk. 41   Engr.   Perf. 13x13½
O89	A9	3p on 4p dull green	100.00	25.00
a.		Double surcharge	870.00	465.00

Stamps and Type of 1948-49 Overprinted Type "o"
1948-49   Wmk. 294   Litho.   Perf. 11
O90	A16	3p car ('49)	2.00	.30
O91	A16	4p gray green	4.25	.60
b.		Additional overprint on reverse	200.00	200.00
c.		Horizontal pair, imperf. between		3,000.
d.		Vertical pair, imperf. between		3,250.
O92	A16	6p red brown	6.00	.50
b.		Vertical pair, imperf. between		5,250.
O93	A16	9p ultramarine	6.50	.30
O94	A16	2a black ('49)	5.00	.50
O95	A16	2¼a lt ol grn ('49)	7.00	12.00
O96	A16	3a ver ('49)	1.50	2.00
O97	A16	3a4p dp pur ('49)	110.00	100.00
a.		3a4p dp pur (II)		
		Nos. O90-O97 (8)	142.25	116.20

See Travancore-Cochin for succeeding issues.

DHAR
'där

LOCATION — A Feudatory State in the Malwa Agency in Central India.
AREA — 1,800 sq. mi.
POP. — 243,521
CAPITAL — Dhar

Used values are for canceled-to-order examples; postally used examples are extremely rare.

Arms of Dhar — A1

No. 1
अर्धा डबल.

No. 1a
अर्धा बलडे.

No. 1b
अर्धा ळबड.

No. 1f
आंधा डबल.

The stamps of type A1 have an oval control mark handstamped in black.

Unwmk.
1897-1900   Typeset   Imperf.
Without Gum
1	A1	½p black, *red*	6.00	7.50
a.		Characters for "pice" transposed	55.00	65.00
b.		Characters for "pice" transposed	200.00	1,500.
c.		Without control mark		1,500.
d.		Line below upper inscription	150.00	150.00
e.		Tete beche pair		15,000.
f.		Four characters in first word	6.00	10.00
g.		As "f," without control mark		1,500.
h.		½p black, *lil rose* (error)	7,500.	—
2	A1	¼a blk, *org red* ('00)	6.00	12.00
a.		Without control mark		1,500.
3	A1	½a black, *lil rose*	8.00	15.00
a.		Without control mark		1,500.
b.		Line below upper inscription	300.00	350.00
4	A1	1a black, *bl grn*	15.00	50.00
a.		Without control mark	3,000.	
b.		Stamp printed on both sides	7,500.	
5	A1	2a black, *yel* ('00)	75.00	200.00
a.		Top right corner ornament transposed	500.00	1,500.
		Nos. 1-5 (5)	110.00	284.50

One example of No. 1c is recorded on cover. No other used examples are known.

One used example of No. 2a has been recorded.

Arms of Dhar — A2

1898-1900   Typo.   Perf. 11½
6	A2	½a red	12.00	20.00
7	A2	½a rose ('00)	10.00	15.00
a.		Imperf., pair	120.00	
8	A2	1a maroon	15.00	20.00
9	A2	1a violet ('00)	15.00	40.00
a.		Horiz. pair, imperf. vert.	5,000.	
10	A2	1a claret ('00)	15.00	20.00
11	A2	2a dark green ('00)	20.00	80.00
		Nos. 6-11 (6)	87.00	195.00

Obsolete Mar. 31, 1901.

No. 9a comes from a unique sheet, with only five examples possible.

DUNGARPUR
ˈdəŋ-gə̇r-ˌpər

LOCATION — A princely state in Rajasthan, in northwestern India.
AREA — 1,447 sq. mi.
POP. — 100,103 (1901)
CAPITAL — Dungarpur

Arms of Dungarpur — A1

1933-47   Unwmk.   Litho.   Perf. 11
1	A1	¼a bister yellow	—	650.00
1A	A1	¼a lemon yellow ('34)	—	850.00
2A	A1	¼a salmon ('35)	—	3,000.
3	A1	1a turq bl	30,000.	500.00
a.		1a dk grn (error)		—
b.		1a rose (error)		—
4	A1	1a3p dp red vio ('35)		1,000.
5	A1	2a dp dl grn ('47)	20,000.	1,500.
6	A1	4a dull rose red		4,000.
a.		4a rose red ('34)	7,000.	1,400.

A2   A3   A4   A5

Maharawal Lakshman Singh

1934-38   Typo.   Perf. 12
7	A2	¼a org yel ('36)	400.00	
8	A3	½a vermilion, Die I	—	400.00
9	A4	1a blue	—	325.00
a.		Perf 11½ ('38)	750.00	125.00
9B	A6	2a brt green	40,000.	2,500.
10	A5	4a gray brown		1,000.

There are three dies of the ½ anna: Die I measures 21x25½mm, and width of turban is 7½mm; Die II measures 20x20½mm, Die III measures 21x25½mm, and width of turban is 6½mm. There are 4 distinct cliches of Die III, printed in a block of 4, differing in the space between the top of the turban and the frame: Pos. 1 = 2mm; Pos. 2 = 2.5mm; Pos. 3 = 1mm; Pos. 4 = 1.5mm.

INDIA - FEUDATORY STATES — DUNGARPUR — DUTTIA — FARIDKOT — HYDERABAD (DECCAN)

Maharawal Lakshman Singh — A6

1940-42			Perf. 11	
11	A2	¼a yel org ('41)	30,000.	400.00
12	A3	½a carmine, Die I	30,000.	350.00
13	A4	1a blue	26,000.	325.00

Maharawal Lakshman Singh

1941-44			Perf. 10½	
17	A2	¼a dull org('44)	—	325.00
18	A3	½a ver, Die I ('44)	6,000.	400.00
19	A7	½a ver, Die II ('44)	6,000.	400.00
a.		Horiz. pair, #18 + #19	15,000.	1,200.
20	A4	1a blue ('44)	7,500.	250.00
21	A8	1a3p mauve	30,000.	1,500.
22	A5	4a pale brown ('44)	—	1,500.

Maharawal Lakshman Singh

1945-46			Perf. 10	
23	A2	¼a orange	30,000.	400.00
24	A9	½a ver, Die III ('44)	15,000.	300.00
25	A4	1a blue	6,000.	300.00
26	A8	1a3p bright mauve	30,000.	1,500.
27	A10	1½a deep violet	32,500.	1,500.
28	A5	4a brown	32,500.	1,500.

The stamps of Dungarpur became obsolete in Sept. 1949.

DUTTIA

ˈdət-ē-ə,

(Datia)

LOCATION — A Feudatory State in the Bundelkhand Agency in Central India.
AREA — 912 sq. mi.
POP. — 158,834
CAPITAL — Datia

Ganesh, Elephant-headed God
A1   A2

All Duttia stamps have a circular control mark, about 23mm in diameter, handstamped in blue or black. All were issued without gum.

1893	Typeset	Unwmk.	Imperf.	
1	A1	¼a blk, org red		6,250.
2	A1	½a blk, grysh grn		24,000.
3	A2	1a black, red	4,750.	7,500.
4	A1	2a blk, yel		5,250.
5	A1	4a black, rose		1,900.

Type A2 with Frameline around God, Rosettes in Lower Corners

1896 (?)				
5A	A2	½ black, green		15,000.
5C	A2	2a dk blue, lemon		3,750.

A 1a in this revised type has been reported.

1897				
6	A2	½a black, green	100.00	675.00
7	A2	1a black	150.00	525.00
a.		Laid paper		32.50

8	A2	2a black, yellow	42.50	500.00
9	A2	4a black, rose	40.00	325.00
		Nos. 6-9 (4)	332.50	2,025.

10	A3	½a black, green	150.00	825.00
11	A3	1a black	290.00	
12	A3	2a black, yellow	175.00	825.00
13	A3	4a black, rose	175.00	825.00
		Nos. 10-13 (4)	790.00	2,475.

Rouletted in Colored Lines on 2 or 3 Sides

1899-1900				
14	A4	¼a red (shades)	5.00	32.50
b.		Tete beche pair	4,900.	
15	A4	½a black, green	4.00	30.00
16	A4	1a black	4.50	30.00
17	A4	2a black, yellow	5.25	35.00
18	A4	4a black, rose red	5.00	32.50
a.		Tete beche pair		
		Nos. 14-18 (5)	23.75	160.00

1904			Imperf.	
22	A4	¼a carmine	5.50	47.50
23	A4	½a black, green		27.50
24	A4	1a black	21.00	75.00
		Nos. 22-24 (3)	54.00	122.50

1911			Perf. 13½	
25	A4	¼a carmine	9.50	75.00

1916			Imperf.	
26	A4	¼a dull blue	8.25	40.00
27	A4	½a green	8.25	40.00
28	A4	1a violet	10.00	42.50
a.		Tete beche pair	35.00	
29	A4	2a brown	22.50	52.50
29A	A4	4a brick red	110.00	
		Nos. 26-29A (5)	159.00	175.00

1918				
31	A4	½a ultramarine	5.25	27.50
32	A4	1a rose	5.25	27.50
33	A4	2a violet	11.00	40.00
		Perf. 12		
34	A4	¼a black	7.50	37.50
		Nos. 31-34 (4)	29.00	132.50

1920			Rouletted	
35	A4	¼a blue	4.00	21.00
36	A4	½a rose	5.25	24.00
		Perf. 7		
37	A4	½a dull red	24.00	62.50
		Nos. 35-37 (3)	33.25	107.50

Duttia stamps became obsolete in 1921.

FARIDKOT

fe-ˈrēd-ˌkōt

LOCATION — A Feudatory State in the Punjab Agency of India.
AREA — 638 sq. mi.
POP. — 164,364
CAPITAL — Faridkot

4 Folus or Paisas = 1 Anna

Handstamped

1879-86	Unwmk.	Imperf.		
		Without Gum		
1	A1	1f ultramarine	4.00	6.00
a.		Laid paper	21.00	24.00
b.		Tete beche pair	400.00	
2	A2	1p ultramarine	7.50	16.00
a.		Laid paper	125.00	150.00
3	A3	1p ultramarine	2.25	
a.		Tete beche pair	340.00	
		Nos. 1-3 (3)	13.75	22.00

Several other varieties exist, but it is believed that only the stamps listed here were issued for postal use. They became obsolete Dec. 31, 1886. See Faridkot under Convention States for issues of 1887-1900.

HYDERABAD (DECCAN)

ˈhīd-ə-ˌrə-ˌbad

LOCATION — Central India
AREA — 82,313 sq. mi.
POP. — 16,338,534 (1941)
CAPITAL — Hyderabad

This independent princely state was occupied and annexed by India in 1948.

Catalogue values for unused stamps in this State are for Never Hinged items, beginning with Scott 51 in the regular postage section, and Scott O54 in the officials section.

Expect irregular perfs on the Nos. 1-14 and O1-O20 due to the nature of the paper.

A1   A2

1869-71	Engr.	Unwmk.	Perf. 11½	
1	A1	½a brown ('71)	6.00	6.50
2	A2	1a olive green	27.50	11.00
a.		Imperf. horiz., pair	900.00	175.00
3	A1	2a green ('71)	90.00	72.50
		Nos. 1-3 (3)	123.50	90.00

For overprints see Nos. O1-O3, O11-O13.
The reprints are perforated 12½.

A3

Wove Paper

1871-1909			Perf. 12½	
4	A3	½a org brn	4.00	.25
a.		½a red brown	4.00	.25
b.		½a magenta (error)	75.00	12.00
c.		Perf. 11½	27.50	30.00
d.		½a rose	4.00	.30
e.		½a bright vermilion	4.00	.25
5	A3	1a dark brown	1.90	.25
a.		Imperf., pair		550.00
b.		Horiz. pair, imperf. vert.		1,350.
c.		Vert. pair, imperf. horiz.		1,350.
d.		Perf. 11½	180.00	200.00
6	A3	1a black ('09)	3.50	.25
7	A3	2a green	5.50	.25
a.		2a olive green ('09)	5.50	.50
b.		Perf. 11½	1,900.	
8	A3	3a yellow brown	4.50	2.25
a.		Perf. 11½	60.00	82.50
9	A3	4a slate	11.00	5.25
a.		Imperf. horiz., pair	1,350.	1,350.
b.		Perf. 11½	225.00	225.00
10	A3	4a deep green	8.25	5.00
a.		4a olive green	9.00	3.75
11	A3	8a bister brown	5.25	6.50
a.		Perf. 11½		
12	A3	12a blue	7.00	12.00
a.		Perf. 11½	500.00	
b.		12a slate green	7.50	7.50
		Nos. 4-12 (9)	50.90	32.00

For overprints see Nos. 13, O4-O10, O14-O20, O25-O26.

Surcharged

1900				
13	A3	¼a on ½a brt ver	.75	1.25
a.		Inverted surcharge	57.50	35.00

A4

1900, Sept. 20				
14	A4	¼a blue	8.25	5.25

Seal of the Nizam — A5

Engraved by A. G. Wyon

1905			Wmk. 42	
17	A5	¼a blue	3.75	.90
18	A5	½a red	6.00	.35
19	A5	½a orange	9.00	.50
		Nos. 17-19 (3)	18.75	1.75

For overprints see Nos. O21-O23.

Perf. 11, 11½, 12½, 13½ and Compound

1908-11				
20	A5	¼a gray	1.50	.25
21	A5	½a green	7.00	.25
22	A5	1a carmine	5.25	.25
23	A5	2a lilac	2.40	.25
24	A5	3a brn orange ('09)	4.00	1.50
25	A5	4a olive green ('09)	4.50	1.90
26	A5	8a violet ('11)	1.90	1.20
27	A5	12a blue green ('11)	10.50	6.00
		Nos. 20-27 (8)	37.05	11.60

For overprints see Nos. O24, O27-O38.

Engr. by Bradbury, Wilkinson & Co.

1912				
28	A5	¼a brown violet	1.20	.25
29	A5	½a deep green	2.50	.25
a.		Imperf., pair		550.00

The frame of type A5 differs slightly in each denomination.
Nos. 20-21 measure 19½x20½mm.
Nos. 28-29 measure 20x21½mm.
For overprints see Nos 37, O39-O40, O44.

Seal of the Nizam — A6

1915-16				
30	A6	½a green	1.50	.25
31	A6	1a carmine rose	3.75	.25
32	A6	1a red	2.50	.25
		Nos. 30-32 (3)	7.75	.75

Unless used, imperf. stamps of types A5 and A6 are from plate proof sheets.
See No. 58. For overprints see Nos. 38, O41-O43, O45.

A7

1927		Wmk. 211	Perf. 13½	
36	A7	1r yellow	13.50	18.00

Stamps of 1912-16 Surcharged in Red

(4 pies)   (8 pies)

1930				
37	A5	4p on ¼a brn vio	.45	.25
a.		Perf. 11		675.00
b.		Double surcharge		350.00
38	A6	8p on ½a green	.60	.25
a.		Perf. 11	400.00	210.00

For overprints see Nos. O44-O45.

INDIA - FEUDATORY STATES — HYDERABAD (DECCAN) — IDAR — INDORE

Seal of Nizam — A8

Char Minar — A9

High Court of Justice — A10

Reservoir for City of Hyderabad — A11

Bidar College — A13

Entrance to Ajanta Caves — A12

Victory Tower at Daulatabad — A14

Wmk. 211

1931-48		Engr.		Perf. 13½
39	A8	4p black	.45	.25
a.		Laid paper ('47)	3.75	8.25
39B	A8	6p car lake ('48)	15.00	12.50
40	A8	8p green	.75	.25
a.		8p yel grn, laid paper ('47)	4.50	6.75
b.		Imperf., pair	90.00	180.00
41	A9	1a dark brown	.75	.25
42	A10	2a dark violet	4.50	.25
a.		Imperf., pair	195.00	400.00
43	A11	4a ultramarine	2.40	1.00
a.		Imperf., pair	210.00	500.00
44	A12	8a deep orange	10.50	6.00
45	A13	12a scarlet	11.00	18.00
46	A14	1r yellow	7.50	7.00
		Nos. 39-46 (9)	52.85	45.50

On No. 39B, "POSTAGE" has been moved to ribbon at bottom of design.

Nos. 39a and 40a are printed from worn plates. The background of the design is unshaded.

See No. 59. For overprints see Nos. O46-O53, O56.

Unani General Hospital — A15

Osmania General Hospital — A16

Osmania University — A17

Osmania Jubilee Hall — A18

Perf. 13½x14

1937, Feb. 13		Litho.		Unwmk.
47	A15	4p violet & black	.75	3.25
48	A16	8p brown & black	1.25	3.25
49	A17	1a dull orange & gray	1.75	2.10
50	A18	2a dull green & gray	2.25	6.75
		Nos. 47-50 (4)	6.00	15.35

The Nizam's Silver Jubilee.

Catalogue values for unused stamps in this section, from this point to the end of the section, are for Never Hinged items.

Returning Soldier — A19

1946		Typo.		Perf. 13½
51	A19	1a dark blue	.25	.25

Wmk. 211

| 52 | A19 | 1a blue | .25 | .25 |

Wmk. Nizam's Seal in Sheet Laid Paper

| 53 | A19 | 1a dark blue | 1.00 | 1.20 |
| | | Nos. 51-53 (3) | 1.50 | 1.70 |

Victory of the Allied Nations in WW II.

Town Hall, Hyderabad — A20

1947, Feb. 17		Litho.		Wove Paper
54	A20	1a black	2.00	2.90

Inauguration of the Reformed Legislature, Feb. 17th, 1947.

Power House, Hyderabad — A21

Designs: 3a, Kaktyai Arch, Warangal Fort. 6a, Golkunda Fort.

Perf. 13½x14

1947-49		Typo.		Wmk. 211
55	A21	1a4p dark green	1.50	3.25
56	A21	3a blue	2.50	6.50
57	A21	6a olive brown	5.50	27.50
a.		6a red brown ('49)	25.00	47.50
b.		Imperf., pair	190.00	
		Nos. 55-57 (3)	9.50	37.25

Seal Type of 1915

1947		Engr.		Perf. 13½
58	A6	½a rose lake	3.75	1.10

For overprint see No. O54.

Seal Type of 1931

1949				Litho.
59	A8	2p brown	3.00	3.50

For overprint see No. O55.

OFFICIAL STAMPS

Regular Issues of 1869-71 Overprinted

1873		Unwmk.	Perf. 11½, 12½
		Red Overprint	
O1	A1	½a brown	195.00	125.00
O2	A1	1a olive green	35.00	35.00
O3	A1	2a green	72.50	57.50
O4	A3	½a red brown	27.50	9.00
O5	A3	1a dark brown	195.00	125.00
O6	A3	2a green	72.50	57.50
O7	A3	3a yel brown	250.00	250.00
O8	A3	4a slate	120.00	72.50
O9	A3	8a bister	125.00	225.00
O10	A3	12a blue	195.00	240.00

Black Overprint

O11	A1	½a brown		52.50
O12	A2	1a olive green	4.50	3.75
O13	A1	2a green	7.50	9.00
O14	A3	½a red brown	16.00	5.25
O15	A3	1a dark brown	—	52.50
O16	A3	2a green	7.50	9.00
O17	A3	3a yel brown	62.50	52.50
O18	A3	4a slate	32.50	30.00
O19	A3	8a bister	75.00	62.50
O20	A3	12a blue	90.00	120.00

The above official stamps became obsolete in August, 1878. Since that date the "Official" overprint has been applied to the reprints and probably to original stamps. Two new varieties of the overprint have also appeared, both on the reprints and on the current stamps. These are overprinted in various colors, positions and combinations.

Same Ovpt. On Regular Issues of 1905-11

1908			Wmk. 42
O21	A5	½a green	30.00	.25
O22	A5	1a carmine	97.50	.25
O23	A5	2a lilac	97.50	.25
		Nos. O21-O23 (3)	225.00	.75

Perf. 11, 11½, 12½, 13½ and Compound

1909-11				
O24	A5	½a red	210.00	.25
O25	A3	1a black	140.00	.75
O26	A3	2a olive green	150.00	1.50
O27	A5	3a brown orange	11.00	5.00
O28	A5	4a olive green ('11)	45.00	1.90
O29	A5	8a violet ('11)	19.00	5.25
O30	A5	12a blue green ('11)	15.00	5.00
		Nos. O24-O30 (7)	590.00	19.65

Regular Issue of 1908-11 Overprinted

1911-12

O31	A5	¼a gray	6.75	1.10
O32	A5	½a green	5.25	.25
O33	A5	1a carmine	3.00	.25
O34	A5	2a lilac	2.50	1.90
O35	A5	3a brown orange	27.50	1.10
O36	A5	4a olive green	7.00	.25
O37	A5	8a violet	11.00	.30
O38	A5	12a blue green	36.00	3.75
		Nos. O31-O38 (8)	99.00	8.90

Same Overprint on Regular Issue of 1912

O39	A5	¼a brown violet	5.50	.25
a.		¼a gray violet	5.50	.25
O40	A5	½a deep green	5.25	.25

Same Ovpt. On Regular Issue of 1915-16

1917

O41	A6	½a green	5.25	.25
O42	A6	1a carmine rose	7.00	.25
O43	A6	1a red	4.00	.25
		Nos. O41-O43 (3)	16.25	.75

Same Overprint on Nos. 37 and 38

1930

| O44 | A5 | 4p on ¼a brown violet | 3.25 | .25 |
| O45 | A6 | 8p on ½a green | 2.25 | .25 |

Same Overprint on Regular Issue of 1931

1934-47			Wmk. 211	Perf. 13½
O46	A8	4p black	4.00	.25
a.		Laid paper ('47)		7.50
b.		Imperf., pair	120.00	
O47	A8	8p green	1.90	.25
a.		8p yel grn, laid paper ('47)	10.00	7.50
b.		Inverted overprint		240.00
O48	A9	1a dark brown	3.00	.25
O49	A10	2a dark violet	11.00	.25
O50	A11	4a ultramarine	6.00	.35
O51	A12	8a deep orange	21.00	.90
O52	A13	12a scarlet	19.00	2.50
O53	A14	1r yellow	30.00	3.75
		Nos. O46-O53 (8)	95.90	8.50

Catalogue values for unused stamps in this section, from this point to the end of the section, are for Never Hinged items.

Same Overprint on Nos. 58-59, 39B

1947-50				Perf. 13½
O54	A6	½a rose lake	9.00	10.50
O55	A8	2p brown ('49)	9.00	15.00
O56	A8	6p car lake ('50)	11.00	35.00
		Nos. O54-O56 (3)	29.00	60.50

IDAR

ˈē-dər

LOCATION — A Feudatory State in the Western India States Agency.
AREA — 1,669 sq. mi.
POP. — 262,660
CAPITAL — Himmatnagar

Stamps of Idar are in booklet panes of four. All stamps have one or two straight edges.

Maharaja Shri Himatsinhji — A1

1939		Unwmk.	Typo.	Perf. 11
1	A1	½a light green	21.00	37.50

1941			**Same Redrawn**
2	A1	½a green	17.50	40.00

The panels containing denomination and name of state are shaded.

Maharaja Shri Himatsinhji — A2

1944		Unwmk.		Perf. 12
3	A2	½a green	4.00	110.00
4	A2	1a purple	4.00	100.00
a.		Imperf., pair	250.00	
5	A2	2a blue	4.50	150.00
6	A2	4a red	4.75	160.00
		Nos. 3-6 (4)	17.25	

INDORE

in-ˈdō̱ə̱r

(Holkar)

LOCATION — A Feudatory State in the Indore Agency in Central India.
AREA — 9,902 sq. mi.
POP. — 1,513,966
CAPITAL — Indore

Maharaja Tukoji Rao II — A1   *A2*

1886		Unwmk.	Litho.	Perf. 15
1	A1	½a lilac	5.50	3.25

1889			**Handstamped**	*Imperf.*
3	A2	¼a black, rose	5.25	5.50

No. 3 exists in two types.
The originals of this stamp are printed in water color. The reprints are in oil color and on paper of a deeper shade of rose.

Maharaja Shivaji Rao — A3

1889-92		Engr.		Perf. 15
4	A3	¼a orange	2.25	1.20
5	A3	½a brown violet	3.75	.25
6	A3	1a green	4.50	1.90
7	A3	2a vermilion	10.50	3.00
		Nos. 4-7 (4)	21.00	6.35

For overprint see No. 14.

INDIA - FEUDATORY STATES — INDORE — JAIPUR

Maharaja Tukoji Rao III
A4   A5

1904-08   **Perf. 13½, 14**
8	A4	¼a orange	.90	.25
9	A5	½a lake ('08)	13.50	.25
a.		Imperf., pair	35.00	
10	A5	1a green ('07)	3.75	.25
a.		Imperf., pair	175.00	
11	A5	2a brown ('05)	22.50	1.50
a.		Imperf., pair	120.00	
12	A5	3a violet	35.00	10.50
13	A5	4a ultramarine	7.50	2.10
		Nos. 8-13 (6)	83.15	14.85

For overprints see Nos. O1-O7.

No. 5 Surcharged

1905   **Perf. 15**
14	A3	¼a on ½a brown violet	9.00	30.00

Maharaja Yeshwant Rao II
A6   A7

1928-38   **Engr.**   **Perf. 13½**
15	A6	¼a orange	.90	.30
16	A6	½a claret	3.25	.25
17	A6	1a green	4.00	.25
18	A6	1¼a green ('33)	6.00	1.25
19	A6	2a dark brown	19.00	3.25
20	A6	2a Prus blue ('36)	19.00	3.25
a.		Imperf., pair	37.50	275.00
21	A6	3a dull violet	3.00	14.00
22	A6	3½a dull violet ('34)	10.50	15.00
a.		Imperf., pair	100.00	650.00
23	A6	4a ultramarine	10.50	7.50
24	A6	4a bister ('38)	52.50	2.50
a.		Imperf., pair	45.00	500.00
25	A6	8a gray	9.50	6.50
26	A6	8a red orange ('38)	40.00	35.00
27	A6	12a rose red ('34)	7.50	15.00
		Perf. 14		
28	A7	1r lt blue & black	12.50	22.50
29	A7	2r car lake & black	82.50	90.00
30	A7	5r org brn & black	140.00	140.00
		Nos. 15-30 (16)	420.65	356.55

Imperforates of types A6 and A7 were used with official sanction at Indore City during a stamp shortage in 1938. They were from sheets placed by the printers (Perkins, Bacon) on top of packets of 100 perforated sheets as identification.

Stamps of 1929-33 Surcharged in Black

1940   **Perf. 13, 14**
31	A7	¼a on 5r org brn & blk	19.00	2.50
a.		Dbl. surch., black over green		700.00
32	A7	½a on 2r car lake & blk	32.50	5.00
33	A6	1a on 1¼a green	32.50	1.20
a.		Inverted surcharge	110.00	
		Nos. 31-33 (3)	84.00	8.70

Stamps with green surcharge only are proofs.

A8

1941-47   **Typo.**   **Perf. 11**
34	A8	¼a orange	2.50	.25
35	A8	½a rose lilac	4.75	.25
36	A8	1a dk olive green	12.50	.25
37	A8	1¼a yellow green	20.00	20.00
a.		Imperf., pair	275.00	
38	A8	2a turquoise blue	14.00	1.75
39	A8	4a bister ('47)	20.00	20.00
		Size: 23x28¼mm		
40	A8	2r car lake & blk ('47)	16.00	250.00
41	A8	5r brn org & blk	15.00	325.00
		Nos. 34-41 (8)	104.75	617.50

OFFICIAL STAMPS

Stamps and Type of 1904-08 Overprinted

SERVICE
HALF ANNA.

1904-06   **Perf. 13½, 14**
O1	A5	½a lake	1.10	1.90
a.		Inverted overprint	35.00	62.50
b.		Double overprint	35.00	
c.		Imperf., pair	110.00	
O2	A5	1a green	.25	.25
O3	A5	2a brown ('05)	.45	.45
O4	A5	3a violet ('06)	2.50	5.50
a.		Imperf., pair	425.00	
O5	A5	4a ultra	7.50	2.25
		Nos. O1-O5 (5)	11.80	10.35

No. O1-O5 has an "R" that has a curved foot that is wholly underneath the curve of the "R".

No. 8 Overprinted in Black

1907
O6	A4	¼a orange	1.10	1.90

No. 9 Overprinted

SERVICE
HALF ANNA.

O7	A5	½a lake	.25	1.75

No. O7 "SERVICE" in slightly thinner letters and the letter "R" has a straight foot which projects at a distinct angle beyond the curve of the "R" than No. O1.

JAIPUR
/ˈjī-ˌpu̇(ə)r/

LOCATION — A Feudatory State in the Jaipur Residency of India.
AREA — 15,610 sq. mi.
POP. — 3,040,876
CAPITAL — Jaipur

> Catalogue values for unused stamps in this State are for Never Hinged items, beginning with Scott 49 in the regular postage section, and Scott O30 in the officials section.

A1   A1a

Chariot of Surya, Sun God
Pin-perf. 14x14½

1904   **Typo.**   **Unwmk.**
1	A1	½a ultramarine	290.00	275.00
a.		½a pale blue	210.00	275.00
b.		½a gray blue	3,250.	300.00
c.		As "b," imperf.	525.00	900.00
1D	A1a	½a blue	5.00	10.00
e.		½a ultramarine	5.50	10.00
f.		Imperf.	5.50	10.00
2	A1	1a dull red	8.25	21.00
a.		1a chestnut	8.25	21.00
3	A1	2a pale green	8.25	21.00
a.		2a emerald	9.00	
		Nos. 1-3 (4)	311.50	327.00

No. 1 has 36 varieties (on 2 plates), differing in minor details. Nos. 1b and 1c are from plate II. No. 1D has 24 varieties (one plate).

Chariot of Surya — A2

Perf. 12½x12 and 13½

1904-06   **Engr.**
4	A2	¼a olive green ('06)	1.25	1.60
5	A2	½a deep blue	2.75	.75
6	A2	1a carmine	3.75	6.75
7	A2	2a dark green	5.25	2.25
8	A2	4a red brown	11.00	3.25
9	A2	8a violet	6.00	4.00
10	A2	1r yellow	35.00	24.00
		Nos. 4-10 (7)	65.00	42.60

For overprints see Nos. 21-22.

A3

Without Gum

1911   **Typo.**   **Imperf.**
11	A3	¼a yellow green	3.75	5.00
a.		¼a olive green	3.75	5.00
b.		"¼" inverted	9.00	
12	A3	¼a olive yellow	.45	1.50
a.		¼a blue (error)		
13	A3	½a ultramarine	.45	1.50
a.		½a dull blue	4.00	4.00
b.		"½" for "½"	7.00	
14	A3	1a carmine	.75	1.50
15	A3	2a deep green	3.00	9.50
a.		2a gray green	4.00	8.25
		Nos. 11-15 (5)	8.40	19.00

There are six types for each value and several settings of the ¼a and ½a in the 1911 issue.

A4

Wmk. "Dorling & Co., London" in Sheet

1913-18   **Perf. 11**
16	A4	¼a olive bister	1.00	2.25
a.		Vert. pair, imperf. between	300.00	300.00
b.		Horiz. pair, imperf. between	—	240.00
17	A4	½a ultramarine	2.25	1.90
18	A4	1a carmine ('18)	8.25	8.25
a.		1a scarlet	6.00	5.50
b.		Vert. pair, imperf. btwn.	1,250.	1,250.
c.		Vert. pair, imperf. horiz.		1,250.
19	A4	2a green ('18)	6.00	7.50
20	A4	4a red brown	10.50	15.00
		Nos. 16-20 (5)	28.00	34.90

For overprints see Nos. O1-O6, O9-O10.

Stamps of 1904-06 Surcharged

1926   **Unwmk.**   **Engr.**   **Perf. 13½**
21	A2	3a on 8a violet	3.00	5.25
a.		Inverted surcharge	275.00	210.00
22	A2	3a on 1r yellow	4.00	9.50
a.		Inverted surcharge	825.00	275.00

Wmk. "Overland Bank" in Sheet

1928   **Typo.**   **Perf. 12**
17a	A4	½a ultramarine	4.75	6.00
18d	A4	1a rose red	40.00	25.00
18e	A4	1a scarlet	62.50	17.50
19a	A4	2a green	140.00	45.00
20a	A4	4a pale brown		
23	A4	1r red orange	600.00	825.00

Durbar Commemorative Issue

Chariot of Surya, Sun God — A5

Maharaja Man Singh II — A6

Elephant with Standard A7

Sowar in Armor A8

Blue Peafowl — A9

Royal Bullock Carriage — A10

Royal Elephant Carriage — A11

Albert Museum — A12

Sireh-Deorhi Gate — A13

Chandra Palace — A14

Amber Palace — A15

Rajas Jai Singh II and Man Singh II — A16

Perf. 13½x14, 14, 14x13½

1931, Mar. 14   **Unwmk.**
24	A5	¼a red brn & blk	4.50	4.00
25	A6	½a dull vio & blk	.75	.30
26	A7	1a blue & black	13.50	14.00
27	A8	2a ocher & black	13.50	14.00
28	A9	2½a rose & black	47.50	90.00
29	A10	3a dk green & blk	27.50	67.50
30	A11	4a dull grn & blk	27.50	82.50
31	A12	6a dk blue & blk	9.00	82.50
32	A13	8a brown & black	30.00	140.00
33	A14	1r olive & black	60.00	500.00
34	A15	2r lt green & blk	62.50	550.00
35	A16	5r violet & black	82.50	600.00
		Nos. 24-35 (12)	378.75	2,145.

Investiture of the Maharaja Man Singh II with full ruling powers.

Eighteen sets of this issue were overprinted in red "INVESTITURE—MARCH 14, 1931" for presentation to distinguished personages.

For surcharges see Nos. 47, 48, 58. For overprints see Nos. O12-O16, O22-O32, Rajasthan 16.

Man Singh II Type of 1931 and

Raja Man Singh II — A18

1932-46   **Perf. 14**
36	A6	¼a red brn & blk	.75	.75
36A	A6	¾a brn org & blk ('43)	12.00	6.25
37	A18	1a blue & black	5.00	2.50

INDIA - FEUDATORY STATES — JAIPUR — JAMMU and KASHMIR

37A	A6	1a blue & black	14.00	6.75
38	A18	2a ocher & black	6.75	4.00
38A	A6	2a ocher & blk ('45)	19.00	7.50
39	A6	2½a dk car & blk	6.75	5.00
40	A6	3a green & black	6.00	1.00
41	A18	4a gray grn & blk	6.75	17.50
41A	A6	4a gray grn & blk ('45)	72.50	2.40
42	A6	6a blue & black	9.00	45.00
43	A18	8a choc & black	9.00	22.50
43A	A6	8a choc & blk	42.50	190.00
44	A18	1r bis & gray blk	40.00	175.00
44A	A6	1r bis & gray blk ('46)	30.00	240.00
45	A18	2r yel grn & blk	140.00	700.00
		Nos. 36-45 (16)	420.00	1,426.

For overprints see Nos. O17-O30, Rajasthan Nos. 15, 17-25.

Stamps of 1931-32 Surcharged in Red or Black

1936   Perf. 14x13½, 13½x14
46	A18	1r on 2r yel grn & blk (R)	15.00	160.00
47	A16	1r on 5r violet & blk	15.00	125.00

No. 25 Surcharged in Red

1938   Perf. 14x13½
48	A6	¼a on ½a dl vio & blk	17.50	25.00

Catalogue values for unused stamps in this section, from this point to the end of the section, are for Never Hinged items.

Amber Palace — A19

Designs: ¼a, Palace gate. ¾a, Map of Jaipur. 1a, Observatory. 2a, Palace of the Winds. 3a, Arms of the Raja. 4a, Gate of Amber Fort. 8a, Chariot of the Sun. 1r, Raja Man Singh II.

1947-48   Unwmk.   Engr.   Perf. 14
49	A19	¼a dk grn & red brn ('48)	2.25	7.50
50	A19	½a blue vio & dp grn	.75	6.75
51	A19	¾a dk car & blk ('48)	2.25	9.00
52	A19	1a dp ultra & choc	1.50	7.00
53	A19	2a car & blue vio	1.50	7.50
54	A19	3a dk gray & grn ('48)	2.50	9.50
55	A19	4a choc & dp ultra	1.50	7.50
56	A19	8a dk brown & red	1.50	9.00
57	A19	1r dk red vio & bl grn ('48)	4.00	67.50
		Nos. 49-57 (9)	17.75	131.25

25th anniv. of the enthronement of Raja Man Singh II.

No. 25 Surcharged in Carmine with New Value and Bars

1947
58	A6	3p on ½a	25.00	40.00
a.		"3 PIE"	75.00	160.00
b.		Inverted surcharge	72.50	62.50
c.		Double surch., one inverted	110.00	82.50
d.		As "a," inverted surcharge	375.00	325.00

For overprint see No. O31.

OFFICIAL STAMPS

Regular Issue of 1913-22 Overprinted in Black or Red

1929   Unwmk.   Perf. 12½x12, 11
O1	A4	¼a olive green	3.75	4.00
O2	A4	½a ultramarine	1.90	.30
a.		Inverted overprint	675.00	
O3	A4	½a ultra (R)	4.00	.45
O4	A4	1a red	2.25	.45
O5	A4	2a green	2.25	.60
O6	A4	4a red brown	3.00	2.50
O7	A4	8a purple (R)	25.00	82.50
O8	A4	1r red orange	57.50	550.00
		Nos. O1-O8 (8)	99.65	640.80

The 8a and 1r not issued without overprint. For overprint see No. O11.

Regular Issue of 1913-22 Overprinted in Black or Red — b

1931   Perf. 11, 12½x12
O9	A4	½a ultra	575.00	.25
O10	A4	½a ultra (R)	300.00	.25
O10A	A4	8a purple	800.00	300.00
O10B	A4	1r red orange	975.00	400.00
		Nos. O9-O10B (4)	2,650.	700.50

No. O5 Surcharged

1932
O11	A4	½a on 2a green	225.00	3.00

Regular Issue of 1931 Overprinted in Red

1931-37   Perf. 13½x14, 14
O12	A6	¼a red brn & blk ('36)	.60	.25
O13	A6	½a dull vio & blk	.45	.25
O14	A7	1a blue & black	400.00	4.50
O15	A8	2a ocher & blk ('36)	6.75	8.25
O16	A11	4a dl grn & blk ('37)	72.50	60.00

For overprint see No. O32.

Same on Regular Issue of 1932 in Red

1932-37   Perf. 14
O17	A18	1a blue & black	6.75	.30
O18	A18	2a ocher & black	8.25	.30
O19	A18	4a gray grn & blk ('37)	550.00	16.00
O20	A18	8a choc & black	17.50	1.60
O21	A18	1r bister & gray blk	45.00	40.00
		Nos. O17-O21 (5)	627.50	58.20

No. 36 Overprinted Type "b" in Black

1939   Perf. 14
O22	A6	¼a red brown & blk	140.00	110.00

Nos. 36A, 38A, 39, 41A, 43A, 44A and Type of 1931 Overprinted in Carmine

1941-46   Unwmk.   Perf. 13½, 14
O23	A6	¾a brn org & blk ('43)	2.25	.75
O24	A6	1a blue & blk ('41)	6.75	.45
O25	A6	2a ocher & black	6.00	5.00
O26	A6	2½a dk car & blk ('46)	16.00	160.00
O27	A6	4a gray grn & blk ('46)	9.00	11.00
O28	A6	8a choc & black	6.00	12.50
O29	A6	1r bis & gray blk	60.00	
		Nos. O23-O28 (6)	46.00	189.70

Catalogue values for unused stamps in this section, from this point to the end of the section, are for Never Hinged items.

No. O24 Surcharged with New Value and Bars in Carmine

1947   Perf. 13½
O30	A6	9p on 1a blue & blk	5.50	5.50

No. 58 Overprinted in Red "SERVICE"

   Perf. 14
O31	A6	3p on ½a	9.00	21.00
a.		Inverted surcharge	—	2,250.
b.		Double surch., one inverted	72.50	72.50
c.		"3 PIE"	400.00	450.00

No. O13 Surcharged "Three-quarter Anna" in Devanagari, similar to surcharge on No. 48, and Bars in Carmine

1949   Perf. 14x13½
O32	A6	¾a on ½a dl vio & blk	27.50	30.00

For later issues see Rajasthan.

JAMMU AND KASHMIR

ˈjəm-ˌü and ˈkash-ˌmiˌər

LOCATION — A Feudatory State in the Kashmir Residency in the extreme north of India.
AREA — 82,258 sq. mi.
POP. — 4,021,616 (1941)
CAPITAL — Srinagar

All stamps of Jammu and Kashmir were issued without gum.

½ Anna — A1   1 Anna — A2

4 Annas (¼ Rupee) — A3

Native Grayish Laid Paper
Handstamped
1866-67   Unwmk.   Imperf.
Printed in Water Colors
1	A1	½a gray black	375.00	150.00
		Cut to shape	75.00	30.00
2	A1	1a dull blue	900.00	180.00
a.		1a ultramarine	900.00	180.00
b.		1a royal blue	—	750.00
		Cut to shape		150.00
3	A2	1a gray black	2,400.	2,100.
		Cut to shape	475.00	425.00
4	A3	4a dull black	4,500.	4,500.
a.		4a ultramarine	4,500.	4,500.
b.		4a indigo	4,500.	4,500.
		Cut to shape	900.00	900.00
5	A3	4a gray black	3,000.	
		Cut to shape	1,600.	
		Nos. 1-5 (5)	11,175.	6,930.

It has now been proved by the leading authorities on Indian stamps that all stamps of ½ anna and 1 anna printed from the so-called Die A are forgeries and that no such die was ever in use.
See Nos. 24-59.

JAMMU

A part of the Feudatory State of Jammu & Kashmir, both being ruled by the same sovereign.

½ Anna   1 Anna
A4   A5

Printed in blocks of four, three types of the ½a and one of the 1a.

Native Grayish Laid Paper
Printed in Water Colors
1867-77   Unwmk.   Imperf.
6	A4	½a black	1,800.	625.00
7	A4	½a indigo	625.00	490.00
a.		½a deep ultramarine	490.00	290.00
b.		½a deep violet blue	325.00	160.00
8	A4	½a red	12.50	6.75
a.		½a orange red	375.00	120.00
b.		½a orange	195.00	225.00
9	A5	1a black	3,750.	2,600.
10	A5	1a indigo	1,350.	625.00
a.		1a deep ultramarine	1,200.	625.00
b.		1a deep violet blue	1,200.	625.00
11	A5	1a red	30.00	19.00
a.		1a orange red	1,250.	525.00
b.		1a orange	4,750.	2,750.

1876
12	A4	½a emerald	3,750.	1,900.
13	A4	½a bright blue	2,400.	550.00
14	A5	1a emerald	5,250.	3,000.
15	A5	1a bright blue	700.00	750.00

Native Grayish Laid Paper
Printed in Oil Colors
1877
16	A4	½a red	18.00	13.50
a.		½a brown red		67.50
17	A4	½a black		1,800.
18	A5	1a red	57.50	40.00
a.		1a brown red		225.00
19	A5	1a black	3,750.	2,750.

The formerly listed ½a dark blue, ½a dark green, 1a dark blue and 1a dark green are believed to be reprints.

European White Laid Paper
20	A4	½a red	—	1,600.
a.		Thin laid bâtonné paper		2,750.
21	A5	1a red		225.00
a.		Thin laid bâtonné paper	6,750.	

European White Wove Paper
22	A4	½a red		675.00
23	A5	1a red		

RE-ISSUES
For Jammu Only
Native Grayish Laid Paper
Printed in Water Colors
1869-76   Imperf.
24	A1	½a deep black	500.00	
25	A1	½a bright blue	550.00	675.00
26	A1	½a orange red	1,000.	1,100.
a.		½a orange to salmon	400.00	
b.		½a red	150.00	525.00
27	A1	½a emerald	175.00	450.00
28	A1	½a yellow	1,100.	1,400.
29	A2	1a deep black	500.00	
30	A2	1a bright blue	195.00	550.00
31	A2	1a orange red	1,000.	1,100.
b.		1a red	300.00	500.00
32	A2	1a emerald	195.00	450.00
33	A2	1a yellow	1,400.	
34	A3	4a deep black	450.00	—
35	A3	4a bright blue	325.00	
		4a indigo		
36	A3	4a orange red	325.00	425.00
a.		4a orange		
b.		4a red	325.00	425.00
37	A3	4a emerald	450.00	1,000.
38	A3	4a yellow	900.00	

Native Grayish Laid Paper
1877   **Printed in Oil Colors**
39	A1	½a red	52.50	90.00
40	A1	½a black	57.50	97.50
41	A1	½a slate blue	240.00	400.00
42	A1	½a sage green	210.00	
43	A2	1a red	72.50	290.00
45	A2	1a slate blue	57.50	450.00
46	A2	1a sage green		225.00
47	A3	4a red	475.00	825.00
50	A3	4a sage green		

European White Laid Paper
51	A1	½a red		1,800.
52	A1	½a black	47.50	97.50
53	A1	½a slate blue	82.50	450.00
54	A1	½a yellow	240.00	
56	A2	1a slate blue	90.00	600.00
57	A3	4a red	650.00	750.00
58	A3	4a sage green		2,250.

European Brownish Wove Paper
59	A1	½a red		1,400.

It is probable that the issues of 1876, 1877 and the re-issues of the circular stamps were made to supply the demands of philatelists more than for postal needs. They were, however, available for postage.

There exist also reprints, printed in a variety of colors, on native and European thin wove paper. Collectors are warned against official imitations, which are very numerous. They are printed on several kinds of paper and in a great variety of colors.

A5a

325

INDIA - FEUDATORY STATES — JAMMU and KASHMIR — JASDAN — JHALAWAR — JIND

Handstamped in Oil Color
1877, Nov.
60 A5a (½a) red — 1,900.

This provisional, made with a canceling device, was used only in Nov. 1877, at Jammu city.

KASHMIR

A part of the Feudatory State of Jammu & Kashmir, both being ruled by the same sovereign.

½ Anna — A6

Printed in Water Colors
Native Grayish Laid Paper
Printed from a Single Die

1866		Unwmk.		Imperf.
62	A6	½a black	5,250.	675.00

¼ Anna A7
½ Anna A8
1 Anna A9
2 Annas A10
4 Annas A11
8 Annas A12

The ¼a, 1a and 2a are printed in strips of five varieties, the ½a in sheets of twenty varieties and the 4a and 8a from single dies.

1866-70
63	A7	¼a black	6.75	7.00
64	A8	½a black	2,250.	300.00
65	A8	½a ultra	7.50	2.50
a.		½a blue	13.50	6.75
66	A9	1a black	4,000.	750.00
67	A9	1a red orange	22.50	17.50
68	A9	1a Venetian red	27.50	19.00
69	A9	1a orange brown	22.50	17.50
70	A9	1a ultra	6,500.	2,500.
71	A10	2a olive yellow	30.00	32.50
72	A11	4a emerald	75.00	72.50
73	A12	8a red	75.00	72.50

All the stamps printed in oil colors are reprints.

As in Jammu, official imitations are numerous and are found in many colors and on various papers.

JAMMU & KASHMIR

¼ Anna A13
½ Anna A14
1 Anna — A15

Laid Paper
Printed in Oil Colors
1878 — Rough Perf. 10-14
74	A13	¼a red	—	—
75	A14	½a red	21.00	25.00
a.		Wove paper		500.00
76	A14	½a slate blue	110.00	110.00
77	A15	1a red	1,900.	—
78	A15	1a bright violet	—	—

2 Annas A16
4 Annas A17

1878-80 — Imperf.
79	A13	¼a red	35.00	30.00
80	A14	½a red	15.00	16.00
81	A14	½a slate	27.50	24.00
82	A15	1a red	14.00	17.50
83	A15	1a violet	40.00	42.50
a.		1a dull purple	67.50	62.50
84	A16	2a red	140.00	140.00
85	A16	2a bright violet	60.00	57.50
86	A16	2a dull ultra	175.00	175.00
87	A17	4a red	340.00	290.00

Thick Wove Paper
88	A14	½a red	47.50	90.00
89	A14	1a red	75.00	37.50
90	A16	2a red	32.50	40.00

8 Annas — A18

1879-80 — **Thin Toned Wove Paper**
91	A13	¼a red	5.50	6.75
92	A14	½a red	1.50	1.50
93	A15	1a red	3.75	5.25
94	A16	2a red	5.00	7.00
95	A17	4a red	16.00	16.00
96	A18	8a red	17.50	20.00
	Nos. 91-96 (6)		49.25	56.50

Thin Laid Bâtonné Paper
1880 — **Printed in Water Color**
| 97 | A13 | ¼a ultramarine | 1,350. | 900.00 |

Thin Toned Wove Paper
1881 — **Printed in Oil Colors**
98	A13	¼a orange	17.50	24.00
99	A14	½a orange	35.00	25.00
100	A15	1a orange	37.50	21.00
101	A16	2a orange	27.50	21.00
102	A17	4a orange	67.50	82.50
103	A18	8a orange	110.00	120.00
	Nos. 98-103 (6)		295.00	293.50

⅛ Anna — A19

Thin White or Yellowish Wove Paper
1883-94
104	A19	⅛a yellow brown	2.25	3.00
a.		⅛a yellow	2.25	3.00
105	A14	½a brown	1.90	1.50
	Double impression		1,800.	
106	A14	½a red	1.90	1.25
a.		½a rose	2.40	
106B	A19	⅛a bright blue	82.50	
c.		⅛a dull blue	12.00	
107	A15	1a bronze green	1.50	1.50
108	A15	1a yel green	1.50	1.50
109	A15	1a blue green	3.00	
110	A15	1a bister	—	
111	A17	4a green	6.50	6.00
112	A17	4a olive green	6.00	7.00
113	A18	8a deep blue	19.00	22.50
114	A18	8a dark ultra	18.00	21.00
115	A18	8a gray violet	15.00	32.50

Printed in Water Color
| 116 | A18 | 8a gray blue | 225.00 | 225.00 |

Printed in Oil Colors
Yellow Pelure Paper
| 117 | A16 | 2a red | 4.00 | 1.90 |

Yellow Green Pelure Paper
| 118 | A16 | 2a red | 5.50 | 6.00 |

Deep Green Pelure Paper
| 119 | A16 | 2a red | 27.50 | 27.50 |

Coarse Green Pelure Paper
| 120 | A16 | 2a red | 4.00 | 1.90 |
| | Nos. 104-120 (18) | | 425.05 | 360.05 |

Thin Creamy Laid Paper
1886-94
121	A19	⅛a yellow	90.00	100.00
122	A13	¼a brown	13.50	10.00
123	A14	½a vermilion	15.00	9.50
124	A14	½a rose red	—	110.00
125	A15	1a green	150.00	150.00
126	A17	4a green	—	—

Printed in Water Color
| 127 | A18 | 8a gray blue | 160.00 | 150.00 |
| | Nos. 121-127 (7) | | 428.50 | 529.50 |

Impressions of types A13 to A19 in colors other than the issued stamps are proofs. Forgeries to defraud the post exist, and some are common.

A fugitive pigment in No. 104 often leaves the stamp a dull yellowish brown.

1/4 Anna

Stamps of the above type, printed in red or black, were never placed in use.

OFFICIAL STAMPS
Same Types as Regular Issues
White Laid Paper
1878 — Unwmk. — Rough Perf. 10-14
| O1 | A14 | ½a black | | 3,000. |

Imperf
O3	A14	½a black	150.00	140.00
O4	A15	1a black	100.00	100.00
O5	A16	2a black	82.50	90.00
	Nos. O3-O5 (3)		332.50	330.00

Thin White or Yellowish Wove Paper
1880
O6	A13	¼a black	2.50	3.00
O7	A14	½a black	.25	1.10
O8	A15	1a black	3.00	1.50
O9	A16	2a black	.45	.65
O10	A17	4a black	1.90	2.50
O11	A18	8a black	3.75	1.60
	Nos. O6-O11 (6)		11.85	10.35

Thin Creamy Laid Paper
1890-91
O12	A13	¼a black	12.50	13.50
O13	A14	½a black	7.00	7.00
O14	A15	1a black	4.00	5.25
O15	A16	2a black	22.50	
O16	A17	4a black	82.50	97.50
O17	A18	8a black	42.50	75.00
	Nos. O12-O17 (6)		171.00	

Obsolete October 31, 1894.

JASDAN
jas-dən

LOCATION — A Feudatory State in the Kathiawar Agency in Western India.
AREA — 296 sq. mi.
POP. — 34,056 (1931)
CAPITAL — Jasdan

In 1948 Jasdan was incorporated in the United State of Saurashtra (see Soruth).

Catalogue values for all unused stamps in this state are for Never Hinged items.

Sun — A1

Perf. 8½ to 10½
1942 — Unwmk. — Typo.
| 1 | A1 | 1a green | 30.00 | 240.00 |

Issued in booklet panes of 4 and 8. The 1a carmine is a revenue stamp. Jasdan's stamp became obsolete Feb. 15, 1948.

JHALAWAR
ˈjäl-ə-ˌwär

LOCATION — A Feudatory State in the Rajputana Agency of India.
AREA — 813 sq. mi.
POP. — 107,890
CAPITAL — Jhalrapatan

A1

Apsaras, Hindu Nymph — A2

Laid Paper
1887-90 — Unwmk. — Imperf.
Without Gum
| 1 | A1 | 1p yellow green | 7.00 | 22.50 |
| 2 | A2 | ¼a green | 1.90 | 3.75 |

Obsolete October 31, 1900.

JIND
ˈjind

(Jhind)

LOCATION — A State of India in the north Punjab.
AREA — 1,299 sq. mi.
POP. — 361,812 (1941)
CAPITAL — Sangrur

A1, A2, A3, A4, A5

1874 — Unwmk. — Litho. — Imperf.
Without Gum
Thin White Wove Paper
1	A1	½a blue	10.00	6.25
2	A2	1a lilac	10.00	9.50
3	A3	2a yellow	1.50	6.75
4	A4	4a green	37.50	9.00
5	A5	8a dark violet	340.00	140.00
	Nos. 1-5 (5)		399.00	171.50

Thick Blue Laid Paper
1875 — **Without Gum**
6	A1	½a blue	1.50	7.00
7	A2	1a red violet	4.00	16.00
8	A3	2a brown orange	6.50	22.50
9	A4	4a green	5.50	22.50
10	A5	8a purple	13.50	32.50
	Nos. 6-10 (5)		31.00	100.50

Nos. 3 and 6 were perforated 12 in 1885 for use as fiscal stamps.

A6, A7, A8, A9

INDIA - FEUDATORY STATES — JIND — KISHANGARH

A10, A11

1882-84 Without Gum Imperf.
Thin Yellowish Wove Paper

12	A6	¼a buff	.45	2.25
a.		Double impression	75.00	
13	A7	½a yellow	3.75	2.50
14	A8	1a brown	2.50	5.00
15	A9	2a blue	3.00	13.50
16	A10	4a green	2.25	1.50
17	A11	8a red	9.50	6.75
		Nos. 12-17 (6)	21.45	31.50

Perf. 12

18	A6	¼a buff	1.50	4.00
19	A7	½a yellow	240.00	240.00
20	A8	1a brown	3.75	8.25
21	A9	2a blue	5.50	15.00
22	A10	4a green	7.50	16.00
23	A11	8a red	18.00	
a.		Thick white paper	15.00	
		Nos. 18-23 (6)	276.25	283.25

Laid Paper Imperf

24	A6	¼a buff	1.90	
25	A7	½a yellow	1.90	
26	A8	1a brown	1.90	3.75
27	A9	2a blue	27.50	30.00
28	A11	8a red	3.75	16.00
		Nos. 24-28 (5)	36.95	49.75

Perf. 12

29	A6	¼a buff	12.50	
30	A7	½a yellow	190.00	40.00
31	A8	1a brown	2.25	
32	A11	8a red	3.75	15.00
		Nos. 29-32 (4)	208.50	55.00

As postage stamps these issues became obsolete in July, 1885, but some possibly remained in use as revenue stamps.
For later issues see Jind under Convention States.

KISHANGARH
ˈkish-ən-ˌgär

LOCATION — A Feudatory State in the Jaipur Residency of India.
AREA — 858 sq. mi.
POP. — 85,744
CAPITAL — Kishangarh

Kishangarh was incorporated in Rajasthan in 1947-49.
Stamps were issued without gum except Nos. 27-35.

Coat of Arms — A1

1899-1900 Unwmk. Typo. Imperf.
Soft Porous Paper

1	A1	1a green	32.50	90.00
2	A1	1a blue ('00)	600.00	

Pin-perf

3	A1	1a green	110.00	

A2, A3
Coat of Arms — A4
Maharaja Sardul Singh — A5

A6, A7
Coat of Arms — A8
A9

Thin Wove Paper
1899-1900 Handstamped Imperf.

4	A2	¼a rose pink	1.90	4.00
a.		¼a carmine	12.50	
5	A2	¼a green	825.00	1,200.
6	A3	½a light blue	1.90	2.50
7	A3	½a green	57.50	62.50
8	A3	½a carmine	3,750.	1,900.
9	A3	½a violet	240.00	490.00
10	A4	1a gray violet	1.60	1.50
a.		1a gray	7.50	7.50
11	A4	1a rose	110.00	300.00
11A	A5	2a orange	7.50	6.75
12	A6	4a chocolate	9.00	15.00
		Laid paper	125.00	125.00
13	A7	1r dull green	35.00	52.50
13A	A7	1r light brown	30.00	37.50
14	A8	2r brown red	125.00	190.00
		Laid paper	100.00	
15	A9	5r violet	120.00	150.00
a.		Laid paper	120.00	

Pin-perf

16	A2	¼a magenta	7.50	10.00
a.		¼a rose	.35	.60
17	A2	¼a green	400.00	700.00
		Imperf. vertically, pair	1,900.	
18	A3	½a blue	1.50	.75
		½a dark blue	3.75	5.00
19	A3	½a green	27.50	40.00
		Imperf. vert., pair	275.00	
20	A4	1a gray violet	1.10	1.50
a.		1a gray	8.25	5.25
b.		1a red lilac	2.25	3.00
d.		As "b," laid paper	62.50	19.00
20E	A4	1a rose	125.00	375.00
21	A5	2a orange	6.00	7.50
21B	A6	4a pale red brn	5.25	9.00
c.		4a chocolate	3.50	9.00
22	A7	1r dull green	16.00	22.50
b.		Laid paper	140.00	
23	A8	2r brown red	52.50	82.50
		Laid paper	67.50	
24	A9	5r red violet	52.50	82.50
d.		Laid paper	110.00	

Nos. 4-24 exist tête bêche and sell for a slight premium.
For overprints see Nos. O1-O11, Rajasthan Nos. 26-28, 30-32.

A9a, A9b

1901 Soft Porous Paper Typo.

24A	A9a	½a rose	12.00	9.00
24B	A9b	1a dull violet	72.50	40.00

For overprint see No. O12.

A10

1903 Stout Hard Paper Imperf.

25	A10	½a pink	20.00	5.25
a.		Printed on both sides	2,100.	

A11

1904 Thin Wove Paper Pin-perf.

25B	A11	8a gray	7.50	11.00
c.		Tete beche pair	40.00	

For overprints see Nos. O13, O33, Rajasthan No. 29.

A11a

25D	A11a	1r green	27.50	27.50

For overprint see No. O13A.

Maharaja Sardul Singh — A12

1903 Stout Hard Paper Imperf.

26	A12	2a yellow	4.50	9.00

For overprints see Nos. O14, O34.

Maharaja Madan Singh — A13

1904-05 Engr. Perf. 12½, 13½

27	A13	¼a carmine	.65	1.10
28	A13	½a chestnut	1.90	.45
29	A13	1a deep blue	3.75	4.00
30	A13	2a orange	22.50	10.00
31	A13	4a dark brown	22.50	25.00
32	A13	8a purple ('05)	19.00	37.50
33	A13	1r dark green	42.50	67.50
34	A13	2r lemon yellow	42.50	250.00
35	A13	5r purple brown	35.00	300.00
		Nos. 27-35 (9)	190.30	695.55

For overprints see Nos. O15-O22, O35-O38, Rajasthan Nos. 33-39.

Maharaja Madan Singh — A14

Thin Wove Paper
1913 Typo. Rouletted 9½

37	A14	2 "ANNA" violet	8.25	13.50
a.		Tete beche pair	18.00	60.00

See Nos. 40-50. For overprint see Rajasthan No. 43.

A15
Maharaja Madan Singh — A16

Thick, Chalk-surfaced Paper
1913 Rouletted 6½, 12

38	A15	¼a pale blue	.45	1.40
a.		"Kishangahr"	7.50	10.00
b.		Imperf., pair	11.00	
39	A16	2a purple	12.50	27.50
		"Kishangahr"	75.00	140.00

For overprint see No. O23.

1913-16 Rouletted 12, 14½

40	A14	¼a pale blue	.30	.65
41	A14	½a green ('15)	.30	1.50
a.		Printed on both sides	350.00	
42	A14	1a carmine	1.90	3.75
43	A14	2 "ANNAS" pur	9.00	12.00
44	A14	4a ultramarine	9.00	12.00
45	A14	8a brown	10.00	60.00
46	A14	1r rose lilac	24.00	190.00
47	A14	2r dark green	150.00	525.00
48	A14	5r brown	60.00	675.00
		Nos. 40-48 (9)	264.50	1,480.

On Nos. 40-48 the halftone screen covers the entire design.
Nos. 41-48 have ornaments on both sides of value in top panel.
For overprints see Nos. O24-O30, O39-O43, Rajasthan Nos. 40-42, 44-48.

Type of 1913-16 Redrawn
1918 Rouletted

50	A14	1a rose red	2.25	8.25

The redrawn stamp is 24¾mm wide instead of 26mm. There is a white oval around the portrait with only traces of the red line. There is less shading outside the wreath.
For overprint see No. O44.

Maharaja Jagjanarajan Singh
A17, A18

Thick Glazed Paper
1928-29 Pin-perf. 14½ to 16

52	A17	¼a light blue	1.90	3.00
53	A17	½a lt yellow green	6.00	3.50
a.		Imperf., pair	180.00	180.00
54	A18	1a carmine rose	1.10	2.25
55	A18	2a red violet	5.00	12.50
56	A17	4a yellow brown	2.50	2.50
57	A17	8a purple	8.25	42.50
58	A17	1r green	30.00	95.00
59	A17	2r lemon	42.50	340.00
60	A17	5r red brown	67.50	400.00
		Imperf., pair	190.00	
		Nos. 52-60 (9)	164.75	901.25

1945-47 Thick Soft Unglazed Paper

52a	A17	¼a gray blue	6.25	19.00
b.		¼a greenish blue ('47)	4.00	15.00
53b	A17	½a deep green	2.25	4.00
54a	A18	1a dull carmine	12.50	6.50
55a	A18	2a deep red violet	16.00	19.00
b.		2a violet brown, imperf.	125.00	30.00
56a	A17	4a brown	35.00	30.00
57a	A17	8a violet	60.00	240.00
58a	A17	1r deep green	75.00	250.00
59a	A17	2r lemon		
60b	A17	5r red brown	875.00	1,100.

For overprints see Rajasthan Nos. 49-58.
For later issues see Rajasthan.

OFFICIAL STAMPS

Used values are for CTO stamps.

Regular Issues of 1899-1916 Handstamped in Black

On Issue of 1899-1900
1918 Unwmk. Imperf.

O1	A2	¼a carmine		12.00
O2	A4	1a gray violet	82.50	8.25
O3	A6	4a chocolate	—	190.00

Pin-perf

O4	A2	¼a carmine	3.25	.90
O4A	A2	¼a green	—	175.00
O4B	A3	½a blue	640.00	67.50
O6	A4	1a gray violet	67.50	2.25
O7	A5	2a orange	—	225.00
O8	A6	4a chocolate	100.00	24.00
O9	A7	1r dull green	250.00	180.00
O10	A8	2r brown red	—	1,400.
O11	A9	5r red violet	—	3,000.

See tete beche note after No. 24.

On Issue of 1901

O12	A9b	1a dull violet	75.00	2.25

On Issue of 1904

O13	A11	8a gray	140.00	35.00
O13A	A11a	1r green		1,350.

Imperf.

O14	A12	2a yellow	125.00	7.50

On Issue of 1904-05
Perf. 12½, 13½

O15	A13	¼a carmine		450.00
O16	A13	½a chestnut	1.50	.50
O17	A13	1a deep blue	16.00	6.00
O18	A13	2a orange	—	1,500.
O19	A13	4a dk brn	90.00	27.50
O20	A13	8a purple	600.00	375.00

327

INDIA - FEUDATORY STATES — KISHANGARH — KOTAH — LAS BELA — MORVI — NANDGAON

O21	A13	1r dk grn	1,200.	1,100.
O22	A13	5r purple brn		

On Issue of 1913
Rouletted

O23	A15	¼a pale blue	11.00	

On Issue of 1913-16

O24	A14	¼a pale blue	.90	.75
O25	A14	½a green	1.50	1.10
O26	A14	1a carmine	24.00	13.50
O27	A14	2a purple	12.50	6.00
O28	A14	4a ultra	42.50	22.50
O29	A14	8a brown	190.00	67.50
O30	A14	1r rose lilac	525.00	500.00
O31	A14	2r dk grn		
O32	A14	5r brown	2,750.	

Red Handstamp
On Issue of 1904
Pin-perf

O33	A11	8a gray	—	450.00

Imperf

O34	A12	2a yellow	675.00	400.00

On Issue of 1904-05
Perf. 12½, 13½

O35	A13	1a deep blue	35.00	10.00
O36	A13	4a dk brn	140.00	62.50
O37	A13	8a purple	—	400.00
O38	A13	1r dk grn		1,000.

On Issue of 1913-16
Rouletted

O39	A14	¼a pale blue	3.00	2.50
O40	A14	½a green	6.50	2.40
O41	A14	2a purple	210.00	100.00
O42	A14	4a ultra	—	52.50
O43	A14	8a brown		140.00

On Issue of 1918
Redrawn

O44	A14	1a rose red		

The overprint on Nos. O1 to O44 is handstamped and, as usual with that style of overprint, is found inverted, double, etc. In this instance there is evidence that many of the varieties were deliberately made.

KOTAH
kō-tə

LOCATION — A Feudatory State in the Rajputana Agency of India.
AREA — 5714 sq. mi.
POP. — 526,827 (1880)
CAPITAL — Kotah City

All Kotah stamps are only known on cover, including the uncanceled stamps. Values are for covers bearing a single stamp.

A1

A2

A3

Wove Paper
Handstamped

1883 Unwmk. *Imperf.*

1	A1	2p green, *yellow*	20,000.	8,500.
a.		Double impression		
2	A2	2p black, *yellow*		20,000.
3	A3	2p indigo, *pink*		20,000.

A4

1886 Wove Paper

4	A4	1p green, *yellow*	—	

The stamps of Kotah became obsolete in 1886.

LAS BELA
ləs ˈbāl-ə

LOCATION — A Feudatory State in the Baluchistan District.
AREA — 7,132 sq. mi.
POP. — 63,008
CAPITAL — Bela

A1

1897-98 Unwmk. Typo. Perf. 12

1	A1	½a black, *white*	45.00	25.00
2	A1	½a black, *gray*	25.00	16.00
3	A1	½a black, *blue* ('98)	30.00	16.00
		Nos. 1-3 (3)	100.00	57.00

A2

1901

4	A2	1a black, *red orange*	40.00	75.00

1904 *Pin-perf*

5	A1	½a black, *lt blue*	24.00	13.50

Granite Paper

6	A1	½a black, *greenish gray*	24.00	13.50

Las Bela stamps became obsolete in Mar. 1907.

MORVI
ˈmor-vē

LOCATION — A Feudatory State in the Kathiawar Agency, Western India.
AREA — 822 sq. mi.
POP. — 113,023
CAPITAL — Morvi

In 1948 Morvi was incorporated in the United State of Saurashtra (see Soruth).

Sir Lakhdhirji Waghji
The Thakur Sahib of
Morvi — A1

Size: 21½x26½mm

1931 Unwmk. Typo. Perf. 12

1	A1	3p red	4.50	22.50
a.		3p deep blue (error)	6.50	35.00
2	A1	½a deep blue	40.00	67.50
3	A1	1a red brown	5.00	25.00
4	A1	2a yellow brown	6.00	60.00
		Nos. 1-4 (4)	55.50	175.00

Nos. 1-4 and 1a were printed in two blocks of four, with stamps 5½mm apart, and perforated on four sides. Nos. 1 and 2 were also printed in blocks of four, with stamps 10mm apart, and perforated on two or three sides.

A2

1932 Size: 21x25½mm Perf. 11

5	A2	3p rose	7.50	21.00
6	A2	6p gray green	12.00	25.00
7	A2	6p emerald	9.50	21.00
8	A2	1a ultramarine	6.50	21.00
9	A2	2a violet	16.00	60.00
		Nos. 5-9 (5)	51.50	148.00

A3

1934-48 Perf. 14, Rough Perf. 11

10	A3	3p carmine rose	3.75	5.25
a.		3p red	2.50	6.50
11	A3	6p emerald	2.50	10.00
a.		6p green	10.00	25.00
12	A3	1a red brown	2.75	21.00
a.		1a brown	15.00	25.00
13	A3	2a violet	3.75	30.00
		Nos. 10-13 (4)	12.75	66.25

The 1934 London printing of Nos. 10-13 is perf. 14; the later Morvi Press printing is rough perf. 11.

Morvi stamps became obsolete Feb. 15, 1948.

NANDGAON
ˈnän(d)-ˌgaun

LOCATION — A Feudatory State in the Chhattisgarh States Agency in Central India.
AREA — 871 sq. mi.
POP. — 182,380
CAPITAL — Rajnandgaon

A1

White Paper
1892, Feb. Unwmk. Typo. *Imperf.*
Without Gum

1	A1	½a blue	10.00	275.00
2	A1	2a rose	40.00	825.00

Some authorities claim that No. 2 was a revenue stamp.
For overprints see Nos. O1-O2.

A2

1893 Without Gum

4	A2	½a green	19.00	140.00
5	A2	2a rose	19.00	140.00

For overprint see No. O5.

Same Redrawn

1894 Without Gum

6	A2	½a yellow green	37.50	140.00
7	A2	1a rose	82.50	175.00
a.		Laid paper		375.00

The redrawn stamps have smaller value characters and wavy lines between the stamps.
For overprints see Nos. O3-O4.

OFFICIAL STAMPS

Regular Issues Handstamped in Violet

1893-94 Unwmk. *Imperf.*
Without Gum

O1	A1	½a blue	550.00	
O2	A1	2a red	1,350.	
O3	A2	½a yellow green	9.50	17.50
O4	A2	1a rose	16.00	37.50
a.		Laid paper	16.00	125.00
O5	A2	2a rose	3.00	3.00

Some authorities believe that this handstamp was used as a control mark, rather than to indicate a stamp for official mail.
The 1 anna has been reprinted in brown and in blue.
Nandgaon stamps became obsolete in July, 1895.

INDIA - FEUDATORY STATES — NOWANUGGUR — ORCHHA — POONCH — RAJASTHAN

NOWANUGGUR

ˌnau-ə-ˈnəg-ər

(Navanagar)

LOCATION — A Feudatory State in the Kathiawar Agency, Western India.
AREA — 3,791 sq. mi.
POP. — 402,192
CAPITAL — Navanagar

Stamps of Nowanuggur were superseded by those of India.

6 Dokra = 1 Anna
16 Annas = 1 Rupee

Kandjar (Indian Dagger) — A1

Without Gum
Laid Paper

		1877	Unwmk.	Typo.	Imperf.
1	A1	1d dull blue		1.00	37.50
a.		1d ultramarine		1.00	37.50
b.		Tete beche pair		1,900.	

Perf. 12½

2	A1	1d slate	120.00	175.00
a.		Tete beche pair	2,400.	

No. 2 on wove paper is of private origin.

A2

Wove Paper

		1877-88	Without Gum	Imperf.
3	A2	1d black, *red violet*	5.25	16.00
a.		1d black, *rose*		5.25
b.		Characters at beginning of 3rd line read "4102" instead of "418"		
4	A2	2d black, *green*	8.25	21.00
a.		2d black, *blue green*	12.50	
b.		"4102" instead of "418"		
5	A2	3d black, *yellow*	9.00	30.00
a.		3d black, *orange yellow*	19.00	
b.		"4102" instead of "418"		
c.		Laid paper	160.00	
d.		2d black, *yellow* (error in sheet of 3d)	600.00	
		Nos. 3-5 (3)	22.50	67.00

Nos. 3-5 range in width from 14 to 19mm.

Seal of the State — A3

Without Gum

1893		Thick Paper	Imperf.
6	A3	1d black	450.00

Perf. 12

7	A3	1d black	6.50
8	A3	3d orange	7.50

Imperf
Thin Paper

9	A3	1d black	350.00
10	A3	2d dark green	450.00
11	A3	3d orange	400.00
		Nos. 9-11 (3)	1,200.

Perf. 12

12	A3	1d black	2.50	9.00
13	A3	2d green	3.40	12.00
14	A3	3d orange	3.40	17.50
a.		Imperf. vert., pair		
		Nos. 12-14 (3)	9.30	38.50

Obsolete at end of 1895.

ORCHHA

ˈor-chə

(Orcha)

LOCATION — A Feudatory State in the Bundelkhand Agency in Central India.
AREA — 2,080 sq. mi.
POP. — 314,661
CAPITAL — Tikamgarh

Seal of Orchha — A1

Without Gum

		1913-17	Unwmk.	Litho.	Imperf.
1	A1	¼a ultra ('15)		3.00	7.50
2	A1	½a emerald ('14)		.85	9.50
a.		Background of arms unshaded		52.50	150.00
3	A1	1a carmine ('14)		3.75	10.00
a.		Background of arms unshaded		30.00	275.00
4	A1	2a brown ('17)		6.75	35.00
5	A1	4a orange ('14)		12.00	57.50
		Nos. 1-5 (5)		26.35	119.50

Essays similar to Nos. 2-5 are in different colors.

A2

Maharaja Singh Dev — A3

		1939-40		Perf. 13½, 13½x14
6	A2	¼a chocolate	5.00	12.00
7	A2	½a yellow green	4.50	100.00
8	A2	¾a ultramarine	7.00	150.00
9	A2	1a rose red	4.50	30.00
10	A2	1¼a deep blue	5.50	150.00
11	A2	1½a lilac	6.00	190.00
12	A2	2a vermilion	4.50	120.00
13	A2	2½a turq green	7.50	340.00
14	A2	3a dull violet	8.00	180.00
15	A2	4a blue gray	9.00	42.50
16	A2	8a rose lilac	15.00	340.00
17	A3	1r sage green	26.00	750.00
18	A3	2r lt violet ('40)	60.00	1,000.
19	A3	5r yel org ('40)	200.00	2,750.
20	A3	10r blue	700.00	4,500.
		Nos. 6-20 (15)	1,063.	10,655.

POONCH

ˈpünch

LOCATION — A Feudatory State in the Kashmir Residency in India.
AREA — 1,627 sq. mi.
POP. — 287,000 (estimated)
CAPITAL — Poonch

Poonch was feudatory to Jammu and Kashmir. Cancellations of Jammu and Kashmir are found on Poonch stamps, which became obsolete in 1894. The stamps are all printed in watercolor and handstamped from single dies. They may be found on various papers, including wove, laid, wove batonne, laid batonne and ribbed, in various colors and tones. Nearly all Poonch stamps exist tete beche and impressed sideways. Issued without gum.

A1

White Paper
Handstamped

1876		Unwmk.	Imperf.
		Size: 22x21mm	
1	A1	6p red	18,000. 240.

1877			**Size: 19x17mm**
1A	A1	½a red	22,500. 7,500.

1879			**Size: 21x19mm**
1B	A1	½a red	7,500.

A2

A3

A4

A5

A6

1880-88 White Paper

2	A2	1p red ('84)	40.00	40.00
3	A3	½a red	4.00	5.25
4	A4	1a red	6.75	
5	A5	2a red	16.00	19.00
6	A6	4a red	25.00	

Yellow Paper

7	A2	1p red	5.50	5.50
8	A3	½a red	9.50	9.50
9	A4	1a red	82.50	
10	A5	2a red	15.00	17.50
11	A6	4a red	7.50	7.50

Blue Paper

12	A2	1p red	4.00	3.75
13	A4	1a red	600.00	625.00

Orange Paper

14	A2	1p red	5.50	5.50
15	A3	½a red	42.50	
16	A5	2a red	150.00	
17	A6	4a red	37.50	

Green Paper

18	A3	½a red	67.50	
19	A4	1a red	5.00	7.50
20	A5	2a red	67.50	
21	A6	4a red	100.00	

Lavender Paper

22	A2	1p red	75.00	82.50
23	A4	1a red	125.00	160.00
24	A6	2a red	5.00	5.50

OFFICIAL STAMPS
White Paper
Handstamped

1888		Unwmk.	Imperf.
O1	A2	1p black	4.00	4.50
O2	A3	½a black	4.50	6.00
O3	A4	1a black	4.00	4.50
O4	A5	2a black	7.50	7.50
O5	A6	4a black	12.00	16.00
		Nos. O1-O5 (5)	32.00	38.50

1890			**Yellowish Paper**
O6	A2	1p black		3.75
O7	A3	½a black	4.50	5.25
O8	A4	1a black	22.50	21.00
O9	A5	2a black	9.50	9.50
O10	A6	4a black	15.00	
		Nos. O6-O10 (5)	55.25	35.75

Obsolete since 1894.

RAJASTHAN

ˈrä-jə-ˌstän

(Greater Rajasthan Union)

AREA — 128,424 sq. miles
POP. — 13,085,000

The Rajasthan Union was formed in 1947-49 by 14 Indian States, including the stamp-issuing States of Bundi, Dungarpur, Jaipur and Kishangarh.

> Catalogue values for all unused stamps in this state are for Never Hinged items.

Bundi Nos. 43 to 49
Overprinted — a

1948 Unwmk. Perf. 11
Handstamped in Black

1	A8	¼a dp grn	8.25	50.00
a.		Pair, one without overprint	550.00	
2	A8	½a purple	8.25	50.00
a.		Pair, one without overprint	600.00	
3	A8	1a yel green	7.00	42.50
4	A8	2a red	21.00	125.00
5	A9	4a dp orange	72.50	450.00
6	A10	8a vio blue	13.50	80.00
		Nos. 1-6 (6)	130.50	797.50

Handstamped in Violet

1b	A8	¼a dp grn	9.00	55.00
2b	A8	½a purple	9.00	55.00
c.		Pair, one without overprint	550.00	
3a	A8	1a yel green	24.00	140.00
b.		Pair, one without overprint	550.00	
4a	A9	2a red	47.50	275.00
5a	A9	4a dp orange	47.50	275.00
6a	A10	8a vio blue	14.00	80.00
7	A10	1r chocolate	400.00	2,400.
		Nos. 1b-7 (7)	551.00	3,280.

Handstamped in Blue

1c	A8	¼a dp grn	52.50	300.00
2d	A8	½a purple	72.50	450.00
3c	A8	1a yel green	67.50	400.00
5b	A9	4a dp orange	190.00	1,100.
6b	A10	8a vio blue	120.00	725.00
7a	A10	1r chocolate	140.00	825.00
		Nos. 1c-7a (6)	642.50	3,800.

Typo. in Black

11	A9	2a red	15.00	100.00
a.		Inverted overprint	450.00	
12	A9	4a deep orange	6.00	100.00
a.		Double overprint	400.00	
13	A10	8a violet blue	27.50	
a.		Inverted overprint	950.00	
b.		Double overprint	600.00	
14	A10	1r chocolate	11.00	
		Nos. 11-14 (4)	59.50	

Stamps of Jaipur, 1931-47, Overprinted in Blue or Carmine

1949 Center in Black Perf. 14

15	A6	¼a red brown (Bl)	12.00	32.50
16	A6	½a dull violet	9.50	35.00
17	A6	¾a brown org (Bl)	15.00	40.00
18	A6	1a blue	11.00	72.50
19	A6	2a ocher	12.50	100.00
20	A6	2½a rose (Bl)	13.50	45.00
21	A6	3a green	16.00	110.00
22	A6	4a gray green	14.00	125.00
23	A6	6a blue	14.00	180.00
24	A6	8a chocolate	24.00	250.00
25	A6	1r bister	35.00	375.00
		Nos. 15-25 (11)	176.50	1,365.

Kishangarh Stamps and Types of 1899-1904 Handstamped Type "a" in Rose

1949 Pin-perf., Rouletted

26	A3	½a blue (#18)	900.00	
27	A4	1a dull lilac (#20)	21.00	62.50
28	A6	4a pale red brn (#21B)	125.00	160.00
29	A11	8a gray (#25B)	160.00	275.00
30	A7	1r dull green (#22)	450.00	500.00
31	A8	2r brown red (#23)	550.00	
32	A9	5r red violet (#24)	525.00	525.00
		Nos. 26-32 (7)	2,731.	

Kishangarh Nos. 28, 31-36
Handstamped Type "a" in Rose or Green

1949 Engr. Perf. 13½, 12½

33	A13	½a chestnut (R)		300.00
34	A13	4a dark brown (G)	375.00	
35	A13	4a dark brown (R)	20.00	
36	A13	8a purple (R)	16.00	
37	A13	1r dark green (R)	21.00	

329

INDIA - FEUDATORY STATES — RAJASTHAN — RAJPEEPLA — SIRMOOR — SORUTH

38	A13	2r lemon yellow (R)	27.50	
39	A13	5r purple brown (R)	47.50	
		Nos. 33-39 (7)	507.00	

Kishangarh Nos. 40-42, 37, 43, 46-48 Handstamped Type "a" in Rose

1949		Typo.		Rouletted
40	A14	¼a pale blue	8.00	8.00
41	A14	½a green	675.00	375.00
42	A14	1a carmine	—	450.00
43	A14	2 "anna" violet	825.00	
44	A14	2 "annas" purple	4.50	12.50
45	A14	8a brown	7.50	
46	A14	1r rose lilac	15.00	
47	A14	2r dark green	15.00	
48	A14	5r brown	675.00	
		Nos. 40-48 (9)	2,225.	

Kishangarh Stamps and Types of 1928-29 Handstamped Type "a" in Rose

1949				Pin-perf
49	A17	¼a greenish blue	75.00	75.00
50	A17	½a yel green	60.00	60.00
51	A18	1a car rose	110.00	110.00
52	A18	2a red violet	325.00	325.00
53	A17	4a yel brown	4.00	12.50
54	A17	8a purple	21.00	90.00
55	A17	1r deep green	10.00	
56	A17	2r lemon	140.00	
57	A17	5r red brown	75.00	
		Nos. 49-57 (9)	820.00	

Type of Kishangarh 1928-29, Handstamped Type "a" in Rose

1949			Pin-perf
58	A18	1a dark violet blue	140.00

No. 58 exists imperf.
Rajasthan stamps became obsolete Apr. 1, 1950.

RAJPEEPLA

räj-'pē-plə

(Rajpipla)

LOCATION — A Feudatory State near Bombay in the Gujarat States Agency in India.
AREA — 1,517 sq. mi.
POP. — 206,086
CAPITAL — Nandod

4 Paisas = 1 Anna

Kandjar (Indian Daggers) — A1

				Without Gum	
1880		Unwmk.	Litho.	Perf. 11, 12½	
1	A1	1pa ultramarine		5.25	57.50
2	A2	2a green		45.00	160.00
	a.	Horiz. pair, imperf. btwn.		900.00	900.00
3	A3	4a red		24.00	100.00
		Nos. 1-3 (3)		74.25	317.50

The stamps of Rajpeepla have been obsolete since 1886.

SIRMOOR

sir-'mu͝e͡r

(Sirmur)

LOCATION — A Feudatory State in the Punjab District of India.
AREA — 1,046 sq. mi.
POP. — 148,568
CAPITAL — Nahan

A1

Wove Paper

1879		Unwmk.		Perf. 11½
1	A1	1p green	24.00	500.00
	a.	Imperf., pair		

Laid Paper

2	A1	1p blue	6.75	250.00
	a.	Imperf., pair		

Raja Sir Shamsher Prakash — A2

1885-88		Litho.	Perf. 14 and 14½	
3	A2	3p brown	1.00	.60
4	A2	3p orange	2.50	.45
5	A2	6p green	6.50	6.00
6	A2	1a blue	4.00	5.50
7	A2	2a carmine	6.25	21.00
		Nos. 3-7 (5)	20.25	33.55

There are several printings, dies and minor variations of this issue.
For overprints see Nos. O1-O16.

A3

1893			Perf. 11½	
9	A3	1p yellow green	1.60	1.60
	a.	1pa dark blue green	1.10	1.10
10	A3	1p ultramarine	1.90	1.20
	b.	Imperf., pair	110.00	

Nos. 9 and 10 are re-issues, which were available for postage.
The printed perforation, which is a part of the design, is in addition to the regular perforation.

Elephant — A4

1895-99		Engr.	Perf. 14	
11	A4	3p orange	5.45	.45
12	A4	6p green	1.10	.45
	a.	Vert. pair, imperf between.	15,000.	
13	A4	1a dull blue	6.50	5.25
14	A4	2a dull red	5.25	2.25
15	A4	3a yellow green	35.00	67.50
16	A4	4a dark green	24.00	35.00
17	A4	8a deep blue	27.50	42.50
18	A4	1r vermilion	57.50	110.00
		Nos. 11-18 (8)	162.30	263.40

No. 12a is unique.

Sir Surendar Bikram Prakash — A5

1899

19	A5	3a yellow green	6.25	32.50
20	A5	4a dark green	8.25	35.00
21	A5	8a blue	11.00	30.00
22	A5	1r vermilion	18.00	75.00
		Nos. 19-22 (4)	43.50	172.50

OFFICIAL STAMPS

Regular Stamps Overprinted in Black

On S. S. S.

1890-91		Unwmk.	Perf. 14, 14½	
O1	A2	3p orange	4.50	52.50
O2	A2	6p green	2.25	2.25
	a.	Double overprint	275.00	
	b.	Double ovpt., one in red	1,250.	
O3	A2	1a blue	600.00	700.00
O4	A2	2a carmine	27.50	100.00
		Nos. O1-O4 (4)	634.25	

1890-92			Red Overprint	
O5	A2	6p green	42.50	3.50
O6	A2	1a blue	37.50	47.50

O7	A2	6p green	8.25	.75
	b.	Inverted overprint	210.00	150.00
O8	A2	1a blue	27.50	6.25
	a.	Inverted overprint	500.00	300.00
	b.	Double overprint	500.00	

1892			Black Overprint	
O9	A2	3p orange	.90	.75
	a.	Inverted overprint	375.00	
O10	A2	6p green	12.00	3.25
O11	A2	1a blue	18.00	1.50
	a.	Double overprint	600.00	
O12	A2	2a carmine	10.00	10.00
	a.	Inverted overprint	1,350.	1,350.
		Nos. O9-O12 (4)	40.90	15.50

On S. S. S.

Black Overprint

O13	A2	3p orange	19.00	1.90
	a.	Inverted overprint		
	b.	Double overprint	1,000.	
O14	A2	6p green	8.25	.90
O15	A2	1a blue	11.00	1.90
O16	A2	2a carmine	25.00	21.00
		Nos. O13-O16 (4)	63.25	25.70

There are several settings of some of these overprints, differing in the sizes and shapes of the letters, the presence or absence of the periods, etc.
The overprints on Nos. O1-O16 are press printed. In addition, nine varieties of handstamped overprints were applied in 1894-96. Most of the handstamps are very similar to the press printed overprints.
Obsolete Mar. 31, 1901.

SORUTH

(Sorath)

(Junagarh)

(Saurashtra)

LOCATION — A Feudatory State near Bombay in the Western India States Agency in India.
AREA — 3,337 sq. mi.
POP. — 670,719
CAPITAL — Junagarh

The United State of Saurashtra (area 31,885 sq. mi.; population 2,900,000) was formed in 1948 by 217 States, including the stamp-issuing States of Jasdan, Morvi, Nowanuggur and Wadhwan.
Nos. 1-27 were issued without gum.

> Catalogue values for unused stamps in this State are for Never Hinged items, beginning with Scott 39 in the regular postage section, and Scott O19 in the officials section.

Junagarh

A1

Handstamped in Watercolor

1864		Unwmk.		Imperf.
		Laid Paper		
1	A1	(1a) black, bluish	950.00	125.00
	a.	Wove paper		275.00

1B	A1	(1a) black, gray	950.00	125.00
		Wove Paper		
2	A1	(1a) black, cream		1,500.

A2

1868		Typo.		Imperf.
		Wove Paper		
3	A2	1a black, yellowish		37,500.
4	A2	1a red, green		16,000.
5	A2	1a red, blue		12,500.
6	A2	1a black, pink	825.00	110.00
7	A2	2a black, yellow		16,000.
		Laid Paper		
8	A2	1a black, blue	140.00	13.50
	a.	Left character, 3rd line, omitted		
9	A2	1a red	32.50	37.50
	a.	Left character, 3rd line, omitted		
10	A2	4a black	400.00	675.00
	a.	Left character, 3rd line, omitted		

A 1a black on white laid paper exists in type A2. Value, used $9,500.
In 1890 official imitations of 1a and 4a stamps, type A2, were printed in sheets of 16 and 4. Original sheets have 20 stamps. Four of these imitations are perf. 12, six are imperf.

A3   A4

1877-86		Laid Paper		Imperf.
11	A3	1a green	1.50	.75
	a.	Printed on both sides	750.00	825.00
12	A4	4a vermilion	4.00	2.50
	a.	Printed on both sides	950.00	
13	A4	4a scarlet, bluish	5.50	5.00
		Nos. 11-13 (3)	11.00	8.25

Perf. 12

14	A3	1a green	.60	.25
	a.	1a blue (error)	900.00	900.00
	c.	Wove paper	5.25	2.25
	d.	Imperf., pair	120.00	160.00
	e.	As "a," wove paper	—	900.00
	f.	As "c," vert. pair, imperf horiz.	240.00	
15	A3	1a green, bluish	5.25	6.75
	a.	Vert. pair, imperf horiz.		525.00
	b.	Horiz. pair, imperf vert.	210.00	—
16	A4	4a red	4.00	1.90
	a.	4a carmine	6.50	5.25
	c.	Wove paper	7.50	18.00
	d.	As "c," imperf., pair	340.00	450.00
17	A4	4a scarlet, bluish	16.00	25.00
		Nos. 14-17 (4)	25.85	33.90

Nos. 14c and 16c Surcharged

1913-14		Wove Paper		Perf. 12
18	A3	3p on 1a green	.25	.45
	a.	Laid paper	110.00	45.00
	b.	Inverted surcharge	52.50	30.00
	c.	Imperf., pair	52.50	
19	A4	1a on 4a red	3.75	10.00
	a.	Laid paper	11.00	82.50
	b.	Imperf., pair	950.00	
	c.	Double surcharge	1,000.	

A5   A6

1914			Perf. 12	
20	A5	3p green	2.10	.50
	a.	Imperf., pair	12.50	40.00
21	A6	1a rose carmine	2.25	3.25
	a.	Imperf., pair	30.00	140.00
	b.	Laid paper	375.00	160.00

INDIA - FEUDATORY STATES — SORUTH — TONK — TRAVANCORE

SORUTH

Nawab Mahabat Khan III
A7   A8

1923-29   Wove Paper   Perf. 12
22	A7	3p violet	.50	.65
a.		Imperf, pair	450.00	
b.		Laid paper ('29)	7.50	6.50
c.		As "b," imperf, pair ('29)	5.25	52.50
d.		As "b," horiz. pair, imperf btwn.	4.50	37.50
23	A8	1a red	4.50	14.00
b.		Laid paper	4.50	14.00

Single examples of Nos. 23 and 23b cannot usually be distinguished.

Surcharged with New Value
27	A8	3p on 1a red	7.50	10.00

Two types of surcharge.

Junagarh City and The Girnar — A9

Gir Lion — A10

Nawab Mahabat Khan III — A11

Kathi Horse — A12

1929   Perf. 14
30	A9	3p dk green & blk	1.50	.25
31	A10	½a dk blue & blk	9.00	.25
32	A11	1a claret & blk	7.50	1.50
33	A12	2a org buff & blk	19.00	3.00
34	A9	3a car rose & blk	9.00	19.00
35	A10	4a dull vio & blk	19.00	42.50
36	A12	8a apple grn & blk	25.00	35.00
37	A11	1r dull blue & blk	21.00	45.00
		Nos. 30-37 (8)	111.00	146.50

For surcharges see Nos. 40-42, O20-O25.
For overprints see Nos. O1-O14.

Type of 1929
Inscribed "Postage and Revenue"

1937
38	A11	1a claret & black	15.00	1.50

For overprint see No. O15.

Catalogue values for unused stamps in this section, from this point to the end of the section, are for Never Hinged items.

United State of Saurashtra

A13

Bhavnagar Court Fee Stamp Overprinted in Black "U.S.S. Revenue & Postage Saurashtra"
1949   Unwmk.   Typo.   Perf. 11
39	A13	1a deep claret	16.00	15.00
a.		"POSTAGE" omitted	525.00	375.00
b.		Double overprint	525.00	600.00

Nos. 30, 31 Surcharged in Black or Carmine "POSTAGE & REVENUE ONE ANNA"
1949-50   Perf. 14
40	A9	1a on 3p dk grn & blk (bl) ('50)	60.00	82.50
a.		"OSTAGE"	750.00	900.00
41	A10	1a on ½a dk bl & blk (C)	14.00	7.50
a.		Double surcharge		825.00

For overprint see No. O19.

No. 33 Surcharged in Green "Postage & Revenue ONE ANNA"
1949
42	A12	1a on 2a org buff & blk	24.00	40.00
a.		"EVENUE" omitted		1,100.

For overprint see No. O26.

OFFICIAL STAMPS
Regular Issue of 1929 Overprinted in Red

a

1929   Unwmk.   Perf. 14
O1	A9	3p dk green & black	2.50	.25
O2	A10	½a dk blue & black	6.00	.25
O3	A11	1a claret & black	6.00	.25
O4	A12	2a org buff & black	3.75	.90
O5	A9	3a car rose & black	1.10	.75
O6	A10	4a dull violet & blk	6.25	.65
O7	A12	8a apple green & blk	5.50	4.50
O8	A11	1r dull blue & blk	5.50	35.00
		Nos. O1-O8 (8)	36.60	42.55

For surcharges see Nos. O20-O24.

Regular Issue of 1929 Overprinted in Red

b

1933-49
O9	A9	3p dk grn & blk ('49)	375.00	25.00
O10	A10	½a dk bl & blk ('49)	900.00	22.50
O11	A9	3a car rose & blk	32.50	27.50
O12	A10	4a dull vio & blk	42.50	24.00
O13	A12	8a apple grn & blk	47.50	27.50
O14	A11	1r dull blue & blk	52.50	140.00

The 3p is also known with ms. "SARKARI" overprint in carmine.
For surcharge see No. O25.

No. 38 Overprinted Type "a" in Red
1938
O15	A11	1a claret & black	21.00	2.25

Catalogue values for unused stamps in this section, from this point to the end of the section, are for Never Hinged items.

United State of Saurashtra No. 41 with Manuscript "Service" in Carmine
1949
O19	A10	1a on ½a dk bl & blk (C)		225.00

Used value for No. O19 is for an example used on piece, cancelled at Gadhda or Una between June and December, 1949.
No. 42 is also known with carmine ms. "Service" overprint in English or Gujarati.

Nos. O4-O8 and O14 Surcharged "ONE ANNA" in Blue or Black
1949   Surcharge 2¼mm high
O20	A12	1a on 2a (Bl)	21,000.	40.00
O21	A9	1a on 3a	5,250.	100.00
O22	A10	1a on 4a	600.00	100.00
O23	A12	1a on 8a	525.00	72.50

Surcharge 4mm High, Handstamped
O24	A11	1a on 1r (#O8)	3,250.	72.50
O25	A11	1a on 1r (#O14)	1,350.	75.00
		Nos. O20-O25 (6)	31,975.	460.00

No. 42 Overprinted Type "b" in Carmine
1949   Unwmk.   Perf. 14
O26	A12	1a on 2a	125.00	35.00

TONK
ˈtänk

LOCATION — A Feudatory State in the Rajputana Agency of India.
AREA — 2509 sq. mi.
POP. — 307,528 (1900)
CAPITAL — Nimbahera

Three examples of Tonk No. 1 are known. All are on covers dated 1906.

A1

Handstamped with black octagonal control seal
1906   Unwmk.   Litho.   Imperf. Wove Paper
1	A1	¼a yellow brown	—	

The stamps of Tonk became obsolete in 1907.

TRAVANCORE
ˈtrav-ən-ˌkō(ə)r

LOCATION — A Feudatory State in the Madras States Agency, on the extreme southwest coast of India.
AREA — 7,662 sq. mi.
POP. — 6,070,018 (1941)
CAPITAL — Trivandrum

16 Cash = 1 Chuckram
2 Chuckrams = 1 Anna

Conch Shell (State Seal) — A1

1888   Unwmk.   Typo.   Perf. 12   Laid Paper
1	A1	1ch ultramarine	5.00	5.00
2	A1	2ch orange red	8.00	12.00
3	A1	4ch green	20.00	14.50
		Nos. 1-3 (3)	33.00	31.50

The frame and details of the central medallion differ slightly on each denomination of type A1.
Nos. 1-3 are printed on horizontally laid paper. No. 1 exists on vertically laid paper and is worth more.
Nos. 1-3 were printed on paper with a sheet watermark in a design similar to Wmk. 294, with a conch in the middle, "GOVERNMENT" in the arch and "OF TRAVANCORE" underneath the conch. Due to the position and spacing of the watermark, many stamps are unwatermarked. Unwatermarked and watermarked stamps are worth the same.
Laid paper printings of Nos. 1-3, 5-7 in completely different colors are essays.

1889-99   Wmk. 43   Wove Paper
4	A1	½ch violet	.90	.35
a.		Vert. pair, imperf. between	450.00	450.00
b.		Double impression		450.00
5	A1	1ch ultramarine	2.25	.25
a.		Vert. pair, imperf. between		675.00
b.		Horiz. pair, imperf. between		675.00
c.		Double impression		600.00
d.		Tete beche pair	5,750.	5,000.
6	A1	2ch scarlet	5.00	1.25
a.		Horiz. pair, imperf. between	550.00	550.00
b.		Vert. pair, imperf. between	250.00	
c.		Double impression	300.00	
7	A1	4ch dark green	5.00	1.00
a.		Double impression		650.00
		Nos. 4-7 (4)	13.15	2.85

Shades exist for each denomination.
For Nos. 10-11. For type surcharged see No. 20. For overprints see Nos. O1-O2, O4, O6, O18, O24-O25, O27B, O32-O33, O42.

Conch Shell (State Seal) — A2

1901-32   Handmade Wove Paper
8	A2	¾ch black	3.00	1.50

Machine-made Paper   Wmk. 43A
8A	A2	¾ch black ('32)	11.50	.75
9	A2	¾ch brt violet ('32)	.50	.25
a.		Horizontal pair, imperf. between		275.00
d.		Perf. compound 12x12½ ('37)	25.00	10.00

For overprints see Nos. O26-O27, O44, O52.

No. 4 Surcharged

1906   Wmk. 43
10	A1	¼ch on ½ch violet	1.10	.25
a.		Inverted surcharge	100.00	55.00
11	A1	⅜ch on ½ch violet	.60	.50
a.		Pair, one without surcharge	—	
b.		Inverted surcharge		90.00
c.		Double surcharge		

A3   A4

1908-11
12	A3	4ca rose	.45	.25
a.		Vertical pair, imperf. between	450.00	425.00
13	A1	6ca red brown ('10)	.45	.25
a.		Printed on both sides	75.00	
b.		Horizontal pair, imperf. between		425.00
14	A4	3ch purple ('11)	4.00	.30
a.		Vertical pair, imperf. between	450.00	425.00
b.		Vertical strip of 3, imperf. between	500.00	
		Nos. 12-14 (3)	4.90	.80

For surcharge & overprints see Nos. 19, O3, O5, O8, O13, O15, O20, O22, O30-O31, O53.

A5   A6

1916
15	A5	7ch red violet	3.50	1.00
a.		7ch carmine-red		60.00
16	A6	14ch orange	4.00	3.75
a.		Horizontal strip of 3, imperf. vertically	625.00	

For overprints see Nos. O11-O12, O34-O35.

A7

1920-33
17	A7	1¼ch claret	.80	.80
a.		Horiz. pair, imperf. between	500.00	475.00

Wmk. 43A
18	A7	1½ch light red ('33)	4.00	.25
a.		Horizontal strip of 3, imperf. between	325.00	
b.		Perf. 12½	25.00	3.25
c.		Perf. compound 12x12½		60.00

For surcharges see Nos. 27-28. For overprints see Nos. O7, O17, O28-O29, O38, O56.

No. 12 and Type of 1888 Surcharged

INDIA - FEUDATORY STATES — TRAVANCORE

1921 — Wmk. 43
19	A3	1ca on 4ca rose	.25	.25
	a.	Inverted surcharge	37.50	25.00
20	A1	5ca on 1ch dull bl (R)	1.50	.25
	a.	Inverted surcharge	19.00	12.50
	b.	Double surcharge	100.00	75.00
	c.	Vertical pair, imperf. between		425.00

A8

1921-32
21	A8	5ca bister	1.20	.25
	a.	Horizontal pair, imperf. between	75.00	75.00

Wmk. 43A
22	A8	5ca brown ('32)	4.00	.35
	a.	Horizontal pair, imperf. between	55.00	
	b.	Vertical pair, imperf. between		300.00

Wmk. 43
23	A8	10ca rose	.60	.25
		Nos. 21-23 (3)	5.80	.85

For surcharges & overprints see Nos. 29-30, O9-O10, O14, O16, O19, O21, O23, O36-O37.

Sri Padmanabha Shrine at Trivandrum — A9

State Chariot — A10

Maharaja Sir Bala Rama Varma — A11

1931, Nov. 6 — Wmk. 43A
24	A9	6ca emer & blk	2.40	2.40
	a.	Horizontal pair, imperf. between	225.00	225.00
25	A10	10ca ultra & black	1.90	1.00
	a.	Vertical pair, imperf. between	750.00	
26	A11	3ch violet & black	4.00	4.50
		Nos. 24-26 (3)	8.30	7.90

Investiture of Sir Bala Rama Varma with full ruling powers.

No. 17 Surcharged

1932, Jan. 14 — Wmk. 43
27	A7	1ca on 1¼ch claret	.25	.75
	a.	Inverted surcharge	6.50	10.00
	b.	Double surcharge	50.00	47.50
	c.	Horizontal pair, imperf. between	190.00	
28	A7	2ca on 1¼ch claret	.25	.25
	a.	Inverted surcharge	6.50	10.00
	b.	Double surcharge	42.50	
	c.	Pair, one without surcharge	180.00	190.00
	d.	Double surcharge, one inverted	80.00	
	e.	Triple surcharge	100.00	
	f.	Triple surcharge, one inverted	85.00	85.00
	i.	Horizontal pair, imperf. between	180.00	
	j.	Vertical pair, imperf. between	190.00	

Type of 1932 and No. 23 Surcharged like Nos. 19-20

1932, Mar. 5 — Wmk. 43A
29	A8	1ca on 5ca chocolate	.25	.25
	a.	Double surcharge	11.00	15.00
	b.	Pair, one without surcharge	180.00	
	c.	Horizontal pair, imperf. between	190.00	
	e.	Surcharge inverted on reverse only	115.00	
30	A8	2ca on 10ca rose	.25	.25
	a.	Inverted surcharge	7.50	12.00
	b.	Double surcharge	32.50	35.00
	c.	Horizontal pair, imperf. between	200.00	
	d.	Double surcharge, one inverted	115.00	110.00
	e.	Double surcharge, both inverted	65.00	
31	A8	1ca on 5ca slate pur	2.25	.50
	a.	Inverted surcharge	450.00	

Untouchables Entering Temple and Maharaja — A12

Designs: Different temples and frames.

1937, Mar. 29 — Litho. — Perf. 11½
32	A12	6ca carmine	4.25	1.50
	b.	Horizontal strip of 3, imperf. between	750.00	
33	A12	12ca ultramarine	5.25	.90
	d.	Vertical pair, imperf. between	750.00	
34	A12	1½ch light green	2.25	3.50
	b.	Vertical pair, imperf. between	525.00	
35		3ch purple	6.50	3.50
		Nos. 32-35 (4)	18.25	9.40

Temple Entry Bill.

Perf. 12½
32A	A12	6ca carmine	3.75	3.00
	c.	Compound perf.	75.00	82.50
33A	A12	12ca ultramarine	7.00	1.25
	b.	Vertical pair, imperf. between	700.00	
	c.	Compound perf.	110.00	
34A	A12	1½ch light green	40.00	11.50
	c.	Compound perf.		175.00
35A	A12	3ch purple	6.50	5.50
		Nos. 32A-35A (4)	57.25	21.25

Lake Ashtamudi — A13

A14

A15

Sir Bala Rama Varma A16

Sri Padmanabha Shrine A17

View of Cape Comerin — A18

Pachipara Reservoir — A19

1939, May 9 — Litho. — Perf. 12½
36	A13	1ch yellow green	12.00	.25
37	A14	1½ch carmine	7.00	7.00
	d.	Perf. 13½	27.50	100.00
38	A15	2ch orange	12.00	4.00
39	A16	3ch chocolate	11.00	.25
40	A17	4ch henna brown	14.00	.60
41	A18	7ch light blue	17.50	30.00
42	A19	14ch turq green	10.00	100.00
		Nos. 36-42 (7)	83.50	142.10

Perf. 11
36A	A13	1ch yellow green	17.50	.25
	d.	Vert. pair, imperf. between	100.00	100.00
	e.	Vertical strip of 3, imperf. between	50.00	100.00
37A	A14	1½ch carmine	8.00	37.50
38A	A15	2ch orange	27.50	2.75
39A	A16	3ch chocolate	30.00	.50
40A	A17	4ch henna brown	62.50	.75
41A	A18	7ch light blue	150.00	62.50
42A	A19	14ch turq green	18.00	180.00

Perf. 12
36B	A13	1ch yellow green	37.50	3.50
	d.	Vert. pair, imperf. between	50.00	100.00
	e.	Vertical pair, imperf. between	50.00	100.00
37B	A14	1½ch carmine	62.50	9.00
38B	A15	2ch orange	175.00	10.00
39B	A16	3ch chocolate	65.00	7.50
40B	A17	4ch henna brown	55.00	14.00

Perf. Compound 11, 12, 12½
36C	A13	1ch yellow green	45.00	—
	d.	Vert. pair, imperf. between	—	5.00
37C	A14	1½ch carmine	85.00	15.00
38C	A15	2ch orange	175.00	10.00
39C	A16	3ch chocolate	75.00	1.50
40C	A17	4ch henna brown	275.00	200.00
41C	A17	7ch light blue	175.00	75.00

27th birthday of Maharaja Sir Bala Rama Varma.

For surcharges and overprints see Nos. 45, O45-O51, Travancore-Cochin 3-7, O3-O7.

Maharaja Sir Bala Rama Varma and Aruvikara Falls — A20

Maharaja and Marthanda Varma Bridge, Alwaye — A21

1941, Oct. 20 — Typo. — Perf. 12½
43	A20	6ca violet black	11.00	.25
	a.	Perf. 11	9.00	.25
	b.	As "a", vertical pair, imperf. between	35.00	
	c.	As "a", horiz. pair, imperf. horiz.	80.00	100.00
	d.	Perf. 12	40.00	5.00
	e.	As "d", horiz. pair, imperf. between	37.50	
	f.	As "d", vert. pair, imperf. between	90.00	
	h.	Compound perf.	14.50	3.00
44	A21	¾ch dull brown	12.50	.35
	a.	Vertical pair, imperf. between		750.00
	b.	Perf. 11	12.00	.25
	c.	As "b", horizontal pair, imperf. between	350.00	
	d.	As "b", vert. pair, imperf. between	37.50	85.00
	g.	Perf. 12	80.00	16.00
	h.	Compound perf.	22.50	1.25

29th birthday of the Maharaja, Oct. 20, 1941.
For overprints & surcharges see Nos. 46-47, 49, O54-O55, O58-O59, Travancore-Cochin Nos. 1, O1.

Stamps and Types of 1939-41 Surcharged in Black

Perf. 11, 12½

1943, Sept. 17 — Wmk. 43
45	A14	2ca on 1½ch car	2.25	1.90
	a.	Vertical pair, imperf. between	80.00	
	e.	Perf. 11	.50	.50
	h.	Compound perf.	1.15	2.40
	i.	As "h", vertical pair, imperf. between	240.00	
46	A21	4ca on ¾ch dl brn	6.00	.45
	a.	Perf. 11	8.00	1.00
	b.	Perf. 12		225.00
	c.	Compound perf.	10.00	2.00
47	A20	8ca on 6ca red	7.00	.25
	a.	Perf. 11	7.00	.25
	b.	As "a", horiz. pair, imperf. between	60.00	
	c.	Perf. 12		125.00
	d.	Compound perf.	25.00	13.50
		Nos. 45-47 (3)	15.25	2.60

For overprints see Nos. O57-O59.

Maharaja Sir Bala Rama Varma — A22

1946, Oct. 24 — Typo. — Perf. 11
48	A22	8ca rose red	3.50	3.00
	a.	Perf. 12½	50.00	7.00
	b.	Perf. 12	50.00	7.00
	c.	As "b," horizontal pair, imperf. between	100.00	100.00
	d.	As "b," horizontal strip of 3, imperf. between	100.00	

For overprint see No. O60. For surcharges see Travancore-Cochin Nos. 2, O2.

No. O54 Overprinted "SPECIAL" Vertically in Orange

1946 — Perf. 12½
49	A20	6ca violet black	9.50	5.00
	a.	Perf. 11	55.00	9.00
	b.	Compound perf.	9.00	

No. 49 was overprinted "SPECIAL" to validate previously overprinted "SERVICE" stamps for general use when supplies of the regular 6ca stamps became exhausted.

OFFICIAL STAMPS

Nos. O1-O60 were issued without gum.

Regular Issues of 1889-1911 Overprinted in Red or Black

Perf. 12, 12½

1911, Aug. 16 — Wmk. 43
O1	A1	1ch indigo (R)	1.65	.25
	a.	Inverted overprint	10.00	6.50
	b.	"nO" for "On"	120.00	120.00
	c.	Double overprint	100.00	75.00
	d.	Vertical pair, imperf. between		275.00
O2	A1	2ch scarlet	.50	.25
	a.	Inverted overprint	12.00	12.00
	b.	Blue overprint	180.00	
O3	A4	3ch purple	.50	.25
	a.	Inverted overprint	15.00	15.00
	b.	Double overprint	120.00	100.00
	c.	Vertical pair, imperf. between	325.00	300.00
	d.	Horizontal pair, imperf. vertically	225.00	
	e.	Blue overprint	225.00	110.00
O4	A1	4ch dark green	.80	.25
	a.	Inverted overprint	82.50	19.00
	b.	Double overprint	190.00	140.00
	c.	Horizontal pair, imperf. between	400.00	
		Nos. O1-O4 (4)	3.45	1.00

Same Ovpt. on Regular Issues of 1889-1920

1918-20
O5	A3	4ca rose	.25	.25
	a.	Imperf., pair	450.00	450.00
	b.	Inverted overprint		120.00
	c.	Double overprint	180.00	140.00
	d.	Double impression		425.00
O6	A1	½ch violet (R)	3.75	.50
	a.	Inverted overprint	19.00	6.00
	b.	"chuckram"	18.50	6.50
	c.	Double overprint, both inverted	240.00	
	d.	"On" omitted		210.00
	e.	Double impression	75.00	
	f.	Horizontal pair, imperf. between	240.00	210.00
	g.	Vertical pair, imperf. between	100.00	100.00
O7	A7	1¼ch claret	.60	.25
	a.	Inverted overprint	14.00	12.00
	b.	Double overprint	67.50	
	c.	Double impression		475.00
	e.	A7 1¼ch carmine (error of color)	60.00	
		Nos. O5-O7 (3)	4.60	1.00

Same Ovpt. on Regular Issues of 1909-21

1921
O8	A1	6ca red brown	.45	.25
	a.	Inverted overprint	200.00	18.00
	b.	Double overprint	200.00	180.00
	c.	Vertical pair, imperf. between		350.00
O9	A8	10ca rose	2.00	.25
	a.	Inverted overprint		27.50
	b.	Double overprint	100.00	100.00
	c.	Horizontal pair, imperf. between		225.00
	d.	10ca scarlet ('25)		18.00

Same Overprint on Regular Issue of 1921

1922
O10	A8	5ca bister	2.50	.25
	a.	Inverted overprint	21.00	13.50

For surcharge see No. O39B.

Same Overprint on Regular Issue of 1916

1925
O11	A5	7ch plum	2.50	.45
O12	A6	14ch orange	3.25	.60

Same Overprint in Blue on Regular Issues of 1889-1921
O13	A3	4ca rose	80.00	1.00
O14	A8	5ca bister	.90	.25
	a.	Horizontal pair, imperf. between	375.00	375.00
	b.	Inverted overprint	40.00	22.50
O15	A1	6ca red brown	22.00	2.50
O16	A8	10ca rose	120.00	32.50
O17	A7	1¼ch claret	—	120.00
O18	A1	4ch dark green	—	150.00

Some authorities question the authenticity of No. O14.

1930 — Black Overprint
O19	A8	5ca brown	.35	.90

INDIA - FEUDATORY STATES — TRAVANCORE — TRAVANCORE-COCHIN

Regular Issues of 1889-1932 Overprinted in Black or Red

1930-34
O20	A3	4ca rose	30.00	95.00
O21	A8	5ca brown	45.00	14.00
a.		Inverted overprint	100.00	110.00
O22	A1	6ca org brown	.25	.25
a.		Inverted overprint	30.00	
b.		Double overprint		100.00
d.			100.00	100.00
O23	A8	10ca rose	6.50	4.50
a.		Horizontal pair, imperf. between	20.00	35.00
b.		Vertical pair, imperf. between	15.00	32.50
O24	A1	½ch violet ('34)	.85	.25
O25	A1	½ch purple (R)	.25	.25
b.		Vertical pair, imperf. between	180.00	175.00
O26	A2	¾ch blk (R) ('32)	.60	.25
a.		Inverted overprint		375.00
O27	A2	¾ch brt vio ('33)	.45	.25
b.		Double overprint	200.00	
c.		Vertical pair, imperf. between	240.00	
d.		Compound perf. (12x12½)	50.00	32.50
O27B	A1	1ch gray blue (R) ('33)	1.50	.35
e.		Horizontal pair, imperf. between	200.00	200.00
f.		Vertical pair, imperf. between	32.50	47.50
g.		Perf. 12½	15.00	8.50
h.		Compound perf. (12x12½)	37.50	17.50
i.		As "h," vertical pair, imperf. between		325.00
O28	A7	1¼ch claret	2.10	2.00
O29	A7	1½ch dl red ('32)	.60	.25
a.		Double overprint	80.00	80.00
b.		Perf. 12½	70.00	18.00
c.		Compound perf. (12x12½)		45.00
d.		As "c," double impression		350.00
e.		Vertical pair, imperf. between		250.00
O30	A4	3ch purple ('33)	1.90	.90
				150.00
O31	A4	3ch purple (R)	1.20	.25
a.		Inverted overprint		80.00
b.		Horizontal pair, imperf. between	150.00	75.00
c.		Vertical pair, imperf. between	110.00	65.00
d.		Perf. 12½		5.00
e.		As "d," vertical pair, imperf. between		325.00
f.		Compound perf. (12x12½)		20.00
O32	A1	4ch dp grn (R)	3.00	.25
O33	A1	4ch deep green	2.75	7.50
O34	A5	7ch maroon	1.90	.45
a.		Vertical pair, imperf. between	65.00	65.00
b.		Perf. 12½		20.00
c.		Compound perf. (12x12½)	75.00	16.00
d.		As "c," vertical pair, imperf. between		190.00
O35	A6	14ch orange ('31)	2.50	.60
a.		Inverted overprint	500.00	425.00
b.		Horizontal pair, imperf. between	60.00	85.00
c.		Vertical pair, imperf. between	300.00	
		Nos. O20-O35 (17)	101.35	127.30

The overprint on Nos. O22, O26 and O28 is smaller than the illustration. There are three sizes of the overprint on No. O27.
For surcharges see Nos. O39, O40-O41.

Type of 1921-32 and No. 17 Surcharged and Overprinted

1932
O36	A8	6ca on 5ca dk brn	.50	.50
b.		Inverted surcharge	12.00	12.50
c.		Double surcharge	150.00	
d.		Double surcharge, one inverted	130.00	
e.		Pair, one without surcharge	500.00	
O36A	A8	6ca on 5ca bister	2.50	3.00
f.		Inverted surcharge	110.00	
O37	A8	12ca on 10a rose	.25	.25
a.		New value inverted	9.00	11.00
b.		Overprint and surcharge inverted	55.00	50.00
c.		Double surcharge		160.00
d.		Inverted overprint	11.00	11.00
k.		Surcharge on front and back	300.00	
O38	A7	1ch8ca on 1¼ch cl	.50	.30
a.		Inverted surcharge	200.00	
b.		Double surcharge	75.00	
c.		Vertical pair, imperf. between		500.00
e.		Wrong font "1c"	27.50	22.50
		Nos. O36-O38 (4)	3.75	4.05

Nos. O21, O10, O23 and O28 Surcharged in Black

1933
O39	A8	6ca on 5ca dk brown	.30	.45
a.		New value inverted	16.00	19.00
b.		Pair, one without surcharge	325.00	
O39B	A8	6ca on 5ca bis	50.00	20.00
O40	A8	12ca on 10ca rose	3.00	2.25
a.		New value inverted	10.00	10.00
b.		"On S S" inverted	24.00	27.50
c.		Ovpt. & surch. inverted	60.00	70.00
d.		Ovpt. & surch. inverted	60.00	62.50
O41	A7	1ch8ca on 1¼ch cl	4.50	1.90
a.		New value inverted		160.00
		Nos. O39-O41 (4)	57.80	24.60

No. O39B can be distinguished from O36A by the letters "S" in the overprint, which are closer together on No. O39B.

Regular Issue of 1889-94 Overprinted

1933
O42	A1	¾ch violet	5.50	.25
a.		Horizontal pair, imperf. between	130.00	100.00
b.		Horizontal strip of 3, imperf. between		250.00
c.		Vertical pair, imperf. between		200.00
d.		Double impression		325.00

Regular Issue of 1901 Overprinted in Red

1933
O44	A2	¾ch black	.50	.40

No. O44 can be distinguished from No. O26 by its overprint, which is significantly smaller than No. O26.

Regular Issue of 1939 Overprinted in Black

"SERVICE" 13mm wide, letter "R" with curved tail

1939   First Overprint   Perf. 12½
O45	A13	1ch yellow green	11.00	.50
O46	A14	1½ch carmine	20.00	2.50
a.		"SESVICE"	200.00	45.00
b.		Perf. 12	110.00	27.50
c.		As "b," "SESVICE"		325.00
d.		As "b," horizontal pair, imperf. between		450.00
e.		Compound perf. (12x12½)	37.50	5.50
O47	A15	2ch orange	11.00	11.00
a.		"SESVICE"	190.00	210.00
b.		Compound perf. (12x12½)	200.00	200.00
O48	A16	3ch chocolate	9.50	.30
a.		"SESVICE"	150.00	30.00
b.		Perf. 12	50.00	.75
c.		As "b," "SESVICE"	450.00	65.00
d.		Compound perf. (12x12½)	22.50	7.00
O49	A17	4ch henna brown	24.00	8.50
O50	A18	7ch light blue	25.00	6.50
O51	A19	14ch turq green	42.50	12.50
		Nos. O45-O51 (7)	143.00	41.80

27th birthday of Maharaja Sir Bala Rama Varma.

Overprinted "SERVICE" 13½mm wide, letter "R" with straight tail

1941-42   Second Overprint   Perf. 12½
O45F	A13	1ch yel grn	2.00	.25
a.		Inverted overprint		60.00
b.		Double overprint	30.00	
c.		Vertical pair, imperf. between	85.00	85.00
O46F	A14	1½ch scarlet	6.50	.25
a.		Horizontal pair, imperf. between		100.00
O47F	A15	2ch orange	5.50	.35
O48F	A16	3ch chocolate	4.00	.25
a.		Vertical pair, imperf. between		1,000.
O49F	A17	4ch hen brn	5.50	1.25
O50F	A18	7ch light blue	11.00	.45
O51F	A19	14ch turq green	19.00	.85

Perf. 11
O45G	A13	1ch yel grn	1.25	.25
a.		Double overprint	225.00	210.00
b.		Vertical pair, imperf. between	65.00	
O46G	A14	1½ch scarlet	5.00	.25
a.		Vertical pair, imperf. between	240.00	225.00
b.		Vertical strip of 3, imperf. between	175.00	
c.		Horizontal pair, imperf. between		225.00
O47G	A15	2ch orange	20.00	4.00
a.		Vertical pair, imperf. between		1,000.
O48G	A16	3ch chocolate	4.25	.25
O49G	A17	4ch hen brn	6.50	.65
O50G	A18	7ch light blue	11.00	.45
O51G	A19	14ch turq green	24.00	1.75

Perf. 12
O45H	A13	1ch yel grn	5.00	.60
a.		Inverted overprint		210.00
b.		Double overprint	27.50	42.50
c.		Double impression	180.00	
			140.00	135.00
O46H	A14	1½ch scarlet	11.00	1.25
a.		Vertical strip of 3, imperf. between	350.00	
O47H	A15	2ch orange	225.00	200.00
a.		Vertical pair, imperf. between	1,100.	1,000.
O48H	A16	3ch chocolate	10.00	4.00
a.		Vertical pair, imperf. between	1,000.	900.00
O49H	A17	4ch hen brn	32.50	9.00
O50H	A18	7ch light blue	37.50	15.00
O51H	A19	14ch turq green	17.50	3.00

Perf. Compound (12x12½)
O45I	A13	1ch yel grn	10.00	3.00
O46I	A14	1½ch scarlet	5.00	.50
O47I	A15	2ch orange	200.00	200.00
O48I	A16	3ch chocolate	32.50	1.00
O49I	A17	4ch hen brn	80.00	32.50
O50I	A18	7ch light blue	25.00	6.00
O51I	A19	14ch turq green	125.00	20.00

"SERVICE" Overprint 13mm

No. 9 Overprinted — b

1939   Wmk. 43   Perf. 12
O52	A2	¾ch violet	42.50	2.50
a.		Perf. 12½	260.00	125.00
b.		Compound perf. (12x12½)	240.00	120.00

"SERVICE" 13½mm

1941   Perf. 12½
O52F	A2	¾ch violet	25.00	.25
a.		Horizontal pair, imperf. between	220.00	220.00
b.		Perf. 11	100.00	1.25
c.		Perf. 12	30.00	.25
d.		Compound perf. (12x12½)	55.00	1.00

No. 13 Overprinted Type "b"

1941
O53	A1	6ca red brown	1.25	.50
a.		Perf. 11	2.00	.90
b.		Perf. 12	1.00	.40
c.		Compound perf. (12x12½)	1.00	1.25

Nos. 43-44 Overprinted Type "a"

1941   Perf. 12½
O54	A20	6ca violet black	.90	.75
a.		Perf. 11	1.00	.25
b.		Perf. 12	110.00	17.50
c.		Compound perf. (12x12½)	1.75	1.75
O55	A21	¾ch dull brown	9.50	.25
a.		Vertical pair, imperf. between		750.00
b.		Perf. 11	10.00	.25
c.		Perf. 12	110.00	5.00
d.		Compound perf. (12x12½)	12.50	1.00

29th birthday of the Maharaja, Oct. 20, 1941.
For overprint see No. 49.

No. 18 Overprinted Type "b"

1944   Perf. 12
O56	A7	1½ch light red	6.50	1.25
a.		Perf. 12½ ('44)	21.00	12.00
b.		Compound perf. (12x12½)	28.50	17.50

Nos. 45-48 Overprinted Type "a"

1945-49   Perf. 11, 12
O57	A14	2ca on 1½ch car	.90	1.50
a.		Pair, one without surcharge	500.00	
b.		Perf. 12½	.75	1.20
c.		Compound perf. (12x12½)	1.00	1.50
d.		As "c," "2" omitted in surcharge	750.00	750.00
e.				
O58	A21	4ca on ¾ch dl brn	6.00	.60
a.		Perf. 12½ ('45)	8.00	.75
b.		Compound perf. (12x12½)	4.50	1.75
O59	A20	8ca on 6ca red	2.00	.25
a.		Inverted surcharge		2,250.
b.		Perf. 12½	4.00	.40
c.		Compound perf. (12x12½)	10.00	1.50
O60	A22	8ca rose red ('49)	5.00	1.75
a.		Double impression of stamp	47.50	

b.		Horizontal pair, imperf. between	65.00	
c.		Vertical pair, imperf. between		375.00
d.		Perf. 12½	.75	1.20
e.		As "d," double impression	50.00	
f.		Perf. 12	4.50	1.75
g.		As "f," double impression	75.00	
		Nos. O57-O60 (4)	13.90	4.10

Travancore stamps became obsolete June 30, 1949.

TRAVANCORE-COCHIN

'trav-ən-ˌkō ə̣r kō-'chin

LOCATION — Southern India
AREA — 9,155 sq. mi.
POP. — 7,492,000

The United State of Travancore-Cochin was established July 1, 1949.

Catalogue values for all unused stamps in this state are for Never Hinged items.

Warning: Stamps of Travancore-Cochin are commonly forged, especially those with higher values. Stamps where used values are greater than unused values are commonly found with forged cancellations.

Travancore Stamps of 1939-47 Surcharged in Red or Black

a

1949, July 1   Wmk. 43A   Perf. 12
1	A20	2p on 6ca vio blk (R)	.95	.30
a.		Horiz. pair, imperf. between	110.00	
b.		Vert. pair, imperf. between	10.00	26.00
c.		Inverted surcharge	200.00	
d.		Vert. strip of 3, imperf. between	47.50	
e.		Horiz. strip of 3, imperf. between	110.00	
f.		Block of 4, imperf. between (horiz. & vert.)	100.00	
			60.00	30.00
w.		"O" inverted		
2	A22	4p on 8ca rose red	1.85	.40
a.		Vert. pair, imperf. between	30.00	
b.		Inverted surcharge	250.00	
c.		Pair, one without surcharge	325.00	
d.		"FOUP"	225.00	125.00
e.		"S" inverted	150.00	
3	A13	½a on 1ch yel grn	1.25	.50
a.		Horiz. pair, imperf. between	110.00	110.00
b.		Vert. pair, imperf. between	8.00	22.50
c.		Inverted surcharge	6.25	
d.		"NANA"	400.00	200.00
e.		Block of 4, imperf. between (horiz. & vert.)	80.00	
4	A15	1a on 2ch orange	6.25	.65
a.		Horiz. pair, imperf. between	17.50	
b.		Vert. pair, imperf. between	10.00	25.00
c.		Block of 4, imperf. between (horiz. & vert.)	80.00	
5	A17	2a on 4ch hen brn	6.25	.70
a.		"O" inverted	85.00	27.50
6	A18	3a on 7ch lt blue	16.00	5.00
7	A19	6a on 14ch turq grn	35.00	55.00
a.		Accent omitted from Malayalam surcharge	600.00	675.00
		Nos. 1-7 (7)	67.55	62.55

For overprints see Nos. O1-O7, O12-O17.
For types overprinted see Nos. O18-O23.

Perf. 11
1g	A20	2p on 6ca vio blk (R)	2.75	.50
h.		Vert. pair, imperf. between	375.00	375.00
i.		Pair, one without surcharge	190.00	
j.		"O" inverted	75.00	32.50
2g	A22	4p on 8ca rose red	3.50	.40
h.		Vert. pair, imperf. between	325.00	325.00
i.		Pair, one without surcharge	325.00	
j.		Inverted surcharge	200.00	
k.		"FOUP"	310.00	160.00
l.		"S" inverted	110.00	62.50
3g	A13	½a on 1ch yel grn	4.25	.25
h.		Vert. pair, imperf. between	55.00	
i.		Inverted surcharge	—	450.00
j.		"NANA"	400.00	185.00
k.		Inverted "H" in "HALF"	—	175.00
4g	A15	1a on 2ch orange	1.85	.40
h.		Double surcharge	67.50	
5g	A17	2a on 4ch hen brn	5.25	.75
i.		"O" inverted	—	27.50
6g	A18	3a on 2ch lt blue	8.00	5.50
h.		Blue	100.00	6.25
i.		"3" omitted		1,500.
7g	A19	6a on 14ch turq grn	30.00	50.00
h.		Accent omitted from Malayalam surcharge	550.00	650.00
		Nos. 1g-7g (7)	55.60	57.80

Perf. 12½
1m	A20	2p on 6ca vio blk (R)	4.25	2.25
n.		Inverted surcharge	62.50	
o.		"O" inverted	60.00	22.50

INDIA - FEUDATORY STATES — TRAVANCORE-COCHIN — WADHWAN

2m	A22	4p on 8ca rose red	2.25	.50
n.		Inverted surcharge	92.50	
o.		"S" inverted	150.00	62.50
3m	A13	½a on 1ch yel grn	5.25	.40
n.		Vert. pair, imperf. between	—	325.00
o.		"NANA"	350.00	135.00
p.		Inverted "H" in "HALF"	—	175.00
4m	A15	1a on 2ch orange	5.50	.40
5m	A17	2a on 4ch hen brn	6.25	.75
o.		Inverted surcharge	—	475.00
		"O" inverted	75.00	25.00
6m	A18	3a on 2ch lt blue	16.00	9.00
7m	A19	6a on 14ch turq grn	35.00	67.50
n.		Accent omitted from Malayalam surcharge	550.00	625.00
		Nos. 1m-7m (7)	74.50	80.80

Perf. 14

1q	A20	2p on 6ca vio blk (R)	—	800.00
3q	A13	½a on 1ch yel grn	—	775.00

Perf. 13½

2r	A22	4p on 8ca rose red	—	1,100.
4r	A15	1a on 2ch orange	275.00	2.50

Compound Perforation

1s	A20	2p on 6ca vio blk (R)	—	62.50
2s	A22	4p on 8ca rose red	—	67.50
3s	A13	½a on 1ch yel grn	—	67.50
4s	A15	1a on 2ch orange	75.00	30.00
5s	A17	2a on 4ch hen brn	85.00	52.50
6s	A18	3a on 7ch lt blue	—	125.00
t.		Blue	—	175.00
7s	A19	6a on 14ch turq grn	92.50	110.00
t.		Accent omitted from Malayalam surcharge	875.00	
		Nos. 1s-7s (7)	252.50	515.00

Imperforate Pairs

1u	A20	2p on 6ca vio blk (R)	12.00	—
2u	A22	4p on 8ca rose red	110.00	—
3u	A13	½a on 1ch yel grn	12.50	30.00
4u	A15	1a on 2ch orange	15.00	—
7u	A19	6a on 14ch turq grn	—	—
		Nos. 1u-7u (5)	149.50	30.00

Cochin Nos. 80, 91 and Types of 1944-46 Surcharged in Black or Carmine — b

1949-50   Wmk. 294   Perf. 11, 13

8	A15	3p on 9p ultra	15.00	32.50
9	A16	3p on 9p ultra	5.75	3.50
a.		Vert. pair, imperf. between	—	4,000.
b.		Double surcharge	975.00	
c.		Surcharged on both sides	725.00	
10	A16	3p on 9p ultra (C)	11.00	3.50
11	A16	6p on 9p ultra (C)	2.75	.60
12	A19	6p on 1a3p mag ('50)	11.50	8.50
13	A15	6p on 1a3p magenta	25.00	23.00
a.		Double surcharge	—	1,100.
14	A13	1a on 1a9p ultra (C)	3.00	1.90
15	A15	1a on 1a9p ultra (C)	7.25	3.25
b.		Black surcharge	—	5,500.
c.		Hindi characters 7.5mm long	—	7,500.
		Nos. 8-15 (8)	81.25	76.75

The surcharge exists with line of Hindi characters varying from 16½ to 23mm wide. For overprints see Nos. O10-O11, O24.

Cochin No. 86 Overprinted

1949

15A	A15	1a deep orange	11.00	125.00
d.		No period after "S"	110.00	—
e.		Raised period after "T"	110.00	—

1950, Apr. 1   Wmk. 294   Perf. 13, 11

18	A15	1a deep orange	11.00	110.00
a.		No period after "S"	80.00	450.00
b.		Inverted overprint	375.00	
c.		As No. 18b, raised period after "T"	2,450.	

No. 18 Surcharged in Black

20	A15	6p on 1a dp org	6.75	90.00
a.		Surcharge on No. 15A	18.00	
b.		As No. 20a, no period after "S"	275.00	
c.		As No. 20a, raised period after "T"	275.00	
21	A15	9p on 1a dp org	5.50	90.00
a.		Surcharge on No. 15A	275.00	
b.		As No. 21a, no period after "S"	1,150.	
c.		As No. 21a, raised period after "T"	1,150.	

OFFICIAL STAMPS

Travancore Stamps of 1939-46 Surcharged in Red or Black

c

1949   Wmk. 43A   Perf. 12

O1	A20	2p on 6ca vio blk (R)	1.80	.75
a.		Horiz. pair, imperf. between	15.00	35.00
b.		Vert. pair, imperf. between	8.00	
c.		Block of 4, imperf. between (horiz. & vert.)	35.00	
d.		"O" inverted	40.00	
O2	A22	4p on 8ca rose red	7.25	1.25
a.		"FOUB"	200.00	72.50
b.		Pair, one without 4p surcharge	1,350.	
O3	A13	½a on 1ch yel grn	24.50	3.50
a.		"NANA"	800.00	300.00
b.		Pair, one without surcharge	220.00	
c.		Inverted surcharge on back only	600.00	
O4	A15	1a on 2ch orange	—	—
O5	A17	2a on 4ch hen brn	12.00	6.75
a.		Pair, one without surcharge	1,050.	
O6	A18	3a on 7ch lt blue	6.00	9.75
a.		Horiz. pair, imperf. between	30.00	
b.		Vert. pair, imperf. between	11.00	
c.		Block of 4, imperf. between (hrz. & vert.)	60.00	
d.		blue	100.00	6.75
e.		As "d," horiz. pair, imperf. between	1,000.	
O7	A19	6a on 14ch turq grn	80.00	13.50
a.		Horiz. pair, imperf. between	40.00	
b.		Vert. pair, imperf. between	50.00	
c.		Block of 4, imperf. between (horiz. & vert.)	85.00	
		Nos. O1-O7 (7)	118.00	8.10

Perf. 11

O1f	A20	2p on 6ca vio blk (R)	1.50	.25
g.		Vert. pair, imperf. between	375.00	375.00
h.		"O" inverted	35.00	22.50
O2f	A22	4p on 8ca rose red	6.00	.35
g.		"FOUB"	160.00	40.00
O3f	A13	½a on 1ch yel grn	3.75	.30
g.		Inverted surcharge	110.00	
h.		"NANA"	500.00	160.00
i.		Pair, one without surcharge	300.00	
O4f	A15	1a on 2ch orange	19.50	9.00
g.		Pair, one without surcharge	1,150.	
O5f	A17	2a on 4ch hen brn	8.50	.75
g.		Inverted surcharge	1,700.	
O6f	A18	3a on 2ch lt blue	6.75	1.25
g.		blue	100.00	22.00
O7f	A19	6a on 14ch turq grn	19.50	14.50
		Nos. O1f-O7f (7)	65.50	26.40

Perf. 12½

O1j	A20	2p on 6ca vio blk (R)	2.50	1.00
k.		Vert. pair, imperf. between	375.00	375.00
l.		Pair, one without surcharge	325.00	
m.		"O" inverted	35.00	22.50
O2j	A22	4p on 8ca rose red	8.50	1.50
k.		"FOUB"	400.00	145.00
O3j	A13	½a on 1ch yel grn	2.75	.30
k.		"NANA"	500.00	135.00
l.		Pair, one without surcharge	175.00	
m.		Inverted surcharge	50.00	
O4j	A15	1a on 2ch orange	22.00	9.75
l.		Inverted surcharge	1,050.	
			125.00	
O5j	A17	2a on 4ch hen brn	4.50	1.25
O6j	A18	3a on 2ch lt blue	8.50	4.00
k.		Vert. pair, imperf. between	30.00	
O7j	A19	6a on 14ch turq grn	24.50	16.00
k.		Vert. pair, imperf. between	50.00	
		Nos. O1j-O7j (7)	73.25	33.80

Experts question the existence of No. O4. The editors are seeking additional information.

Compound Perforation

O1n	A20	2p on 6ca vio blk (R)	100.00	—
O2n	A22	4p on 8ca rose red	35.00	30.00
O3n	A13	½a on 1ch yel grn	—	50.00
O5n	A17	2a on 4ch hen brn	—	67.50
		Nos. O1n-O5n (4)	135.00	147.50

Imperforate Pairs

O1o	A20	2p on 6ca vio blk (R)	10.00	35.00
O5o	A17	2a on 4ch hen brn	17.00	
O6o	A18	3a on 7ch lt blue	16.00	
O7o	A19	6a on 14ch turq grn	20.00	
		Nos. O1o-O7o (4)	63.00	35.00

Cochin Nos. O90-O91 Surcharged Type "b" in Black

1950   Wmk. 294   Perf. 11

O8	A16	6p on 3p carmine	1.90	1.10
a.		Double surcharge	—	525.00
b.		Vert. pair, imperf. between	—	2,300.
c.		"C" in place of "G"	24.50	12.25
O9	A16	9p on 4p gray grn	1.60	4.00
a.		Horiz. pair, imperf. between	1,250.	1,350.
b.		Hindi characters 22mm long	1.35	1.55
c.		As "b," horiz. pair, imperf. between	1,175.	1,175.
d.		"C" in place of "G"	32.50	37.50

Hindi characters in surcharge on No. O9 are 18mm long.

Travancore-Cochin Nos. 14-15 Overprinted "ON C G S"

Perf. 13

O10	A13	1a on 1a9p ultra	.90	1.00
O11	A15	1a on 1a9p ultra	37.50	25.00

Nos. 2-7 Overprinted in Black — d

1949-51   Wmk. 43   Perf. 12

O12	A22	4p on 8ca rose red	.35	.25
a.		"FOUB" instead of "FOUR"	130.00	45.00
O13	A13	½a on 1ch yel green	1.50	.25
a.		"AANA"	170.00	80.00
O14	A15	1a on 2ch orange	.60	.25
O15	A17	2a on 4ch hen brn	18.00	1.35
O16	A18	3a on 7ch lt blue	6.00	2.50
O17	A19	6a on 14ch turq grn	60.00	8.00
		Nos. O12-O17 (6)	86.45	12.60

Perf. 11

O12b	A22	4p on 8ca rose red	.60	.25
c.		"FOUB" instead of "FOUR"	110.00	40.00
O13b	A13	½a on 1ch yel green	.60	.25
a.		"AANA"	110.00	50.00
O14b	A15	1a on 2ch orange	4.50	.60
O15b	A17	2a on 4ch hen brn	1.85	1.35
O16b	A18	3a on 7ch lt blue	1.85	1.35
O17b	A19	6a on 14ch turq grn	17.00	8.00
		Nos. O12b-O17b (6)	26.40	11.80

Perf. 12½

O12d	A22	4p on 8ca rose red	1.25	.25
e.		"FOUB" instead of "FOUR"	130.00	42.50
O13d	A13	½a on 1ch yel green	2.75	.25
e.		"AANA"	400.00	90.00
O14d	A15	1a on 2ch orange	.50	.35
O15d	A17	2a on 4ch hen brn	5.25	1.00
O16d	A18	3a on 7ch lt blue	10.50	1.35
O17d	A19	6a on 14ch turq grn	1.85	5.50
		Nos. O12d-O17d (6)	22.10	8.70

Compound Perforation

O12f	A22	4p on 8ca rose red	14.50	14.50
O13f	A13	½a on 1ch yel green	57.50	32.00
g.		"AANA"	—	425.00
O14f	A15	1a on 2ch orange	36.50	32.00
O15f	A17	2a on 4ch hen brn	36.50	24.50
O16f	A18	3a on 7ch lt blue	—	100.00
O17f	A19	6a on 14ch turq grn	170.00	170.00
		Nos. O12f-O17f (6)	315.00	373.00

Imperforate Pairs

O12h	A22	4p on 8ca rose red	10.00	
O13h	A13	½a on 1ch yel green	11.00	30.00
O14h	A15	1a on 2ch orange	29.00	—
O16h	A18	3a on 7ch lt blue	67.50	—
		Nos. O12h-O16h (4)	117.50	30.00

Types of 1949 Overprinted Type "d"

1951   Wmk. 294

O18	A13	½a on 1ch yel grn, perf. 12½	5.50	.80
a.		Perf. 11	.50	.50
b.		Perf. 12	28.00	19.50
c.		Compound perf.	21.00	3.75
O19	A15	1a on 2ch org, perf. 12½	2.75	1.25
a.		Perf. 11	.60	.50
b.		Perf. 12	16.00	5.00
c.		Perf. 13½	2.50	1.25
d.		Compound perf.	8.50	3.75

Type of 1949 Overprinted Type "c" Unwmk.

O20	A22	4p on 8ca rose red	1.40	1.10

No. O20 is not from an unwatermarked part of sheet with wmk. 294 but is printed on paper entirely without watermark.

Nos. 1, 3 and 5 Overprinted Type "c"

Wmk. 294

O21	A13	½a on 1ch yel grn	1.10	.50
O22	A20	2p on 6ca vio blk, perf. 12½	.50	2.75
a.		"SERVICE" double	22.00	—
b.		Perf. 11	.60	2.75
c.		Perf. 12	1.50	2.10
O23	A17	2a on 4ch hen brn, perf. 12½	4.00	3.25
a.		Perf. 11	1.85	1.35
b.		Vert. pair, imperf. between	525.00	525.00
c.		Perf. 12	—	115.00
d.		Compound perf.	90.00	55.00
		Nos. O21-O23 (3)	5.60	6.50

Experts question the existence of No. O21. The editors are seeking additional information.

No. 9 Overprinted in Black

1951

O24	A16	3p on 9p ultra	.90	1.20
a.		Horiz. pair, imperf. between	—	3,500.

WADHWAN

wə-'dwän

LOCATION — A Feudatory State in Kathiawar Agency, Western India.
AREA — 242 sq. mi.
POP. — 44,259
CAPITAL — Wadhwan

Coat of Arms — A1

1888   Litho.   Unwmk.   Pin-perf.

Thin Paper

1	A1	½p black		160.00

Perf. 12½

2	A1	½p black	30.00	100.00

1889   Perf. 12 and 12½

Thick Paper

3	A1	½p black	12.50	14.00
		Nos. 1-3 (3)	202.50	

INDO-CHINA

INDO-CHINA
ˌin-ˌdō-ˈchī-nə

LOCATION — French possessions on the Cambodian Peninsula in southeastern Asia, bordering on the South China Sea and the Gulf of Siam
GOVT. — French Colony and Protectorate
AREA — 280,849 sq. mi.
POP. — 27,030,000 (estimated 1949)
CAPITAL — Hanoi

In 1949, Indo-China was divided into Cambodia, Laos and Viet Nam each issuing its own stamps.

100 Centimes = 1 Franc
100 Cents = 1 Piaster (1918)

Stamps of French Colonies Surcharged in Black or Red

		a		b

1889 **Unwmk.** *Perf. 14x13½*
1	A9(a)	5c on 35c dp vio, *org*	14.00	12.00
a.		"89" omitted	275.00	250.00
b.		Pair, #1 and #1a	425.00	425.00
2	A9(b)	5c on 35c dp vio, *org* (R)	110.00	100.00
a.		Date in smaller type	275.00	260.00
b.		Inverted surcharge, #2	2,000.	2,000.
c.		Inverted surcharge, #2a	3,000.	3,000.
d.		Pair, #2 and #2a	575.00	575.00

Issue dates: No. 1, Jan. 8; No. 2, Jan. 10.
"R" is the Colonial Governor, P. Richaud,
"D" is the Saigon P.M. General P. Demars.

For other overprints on designs A3-A27a see various issues of French Offices in China.

Navigation & Commerce — A3

Name of Colony in Blue or Carmine

1892-1900 **Typo.** *Perf. 14x13½*
3	A3	1c blk, *lil bl*	1.25	1.25
a.		"INDO-CHINE" double	9,000.	
4	A3	2c brn, *buff*	1.75	1.75
5	A3	4c claret, *lav*	1.75	1.75
6	A3	5c grn, *grnsh*	2.50	2.50
7	A3	5c yel grn ('00)	2.10	1.25
8	A3	10c blk, *lavender*	8.00	2.00
9	A3	10c red ('00)	3.75	2.25
10	A3	15c blue, quadrille paper	42.50	2.25
11	A3	15c gray ('00)	9.00	2.40
12	A3	20c red, *grn*	12.00	7.25
13	A3	25c blk, *rose*	20.00	4.25
a.		"INDO-CHINE" omitted	7,500.	7,500.
14	A3	25c blue ('00)	24.00	5.00
15	A3	30c brn, *bis*	29.00	8.00
16	A3	40c red, *straw*	29.00	15.00
17	A3	50c car, *rose*	45.00	16.00
18	A3	50c brn, *az* ('00)	30.00	9.50
19	A3	75c dp vio, *org*	24.00	19.00
a.		"INDO-CHINE" inverted	7,750.	7,750.
b.		As "a", in pair with normal	10,000.	
20	A3	1fr brnz grn, *straw*	60.00	40.00
a.		"INDO-CHINE" double	1,200.	1,400.
21	A3	5fr red lil, *lav* ('96)	145.00	120.00
		Nos. 3-21 (19)	490.60	261.40

Perf. 13½x14 stamps are counterfeits.
For surcharges and overprints see Nos. 22-23, Q2-Q4.

Nos. 11 and 14 Surcharged in Black

1903
| 22 | A3 | 5c on 15c gray | 2.00 | 1.25 |
| 23 | A3 | 15c on 25c blue | 2.50 | 1.60 |

Issue dates: No. 22, Dec. 4; No. 23, Aug. 8.

France — A4

1904-06
24	A4	1c olive grn	.80	.80
25	A4	2c vio brn, *buff*	1.25	.80
26	A4	4c claret, *bluish*	.80	.80
27	A4	5c deep green	1.25	.50
a.		Double impression	450.00	450.00
28	A4	10c carmine	1.60	.75
29	A4	15c org brn, *bl*	1.60	1.00
30	A4	20c red, *grn*	3.50	1.60
31	A4	25c deep blue	15.00	1.60
32	A4	30c pale brn	6.00	3.00
33	A4	35c blk, *yel* ('06)	22.00	3.25
34	A4	40c blk, *bluish*	5.75	1.60
35	A4	50c bister brn	11.00	3.00
36	A4	75c red, *org*	45.00	30.00
37	A4	1fr pale grn	22.50	8.50
38	A4	2fr brn, *org*	55.00	42.50
39	A4	5fr dp vio, *lil*	150.00	120.00
40	A4	10fr org brn, *grn*	225.00	190.00
		Nos. 24-40 (17)	568.05	409.70

For surcharges see Nos. 59-64.

Annamite Girl — A5

Cambodian Girl — A6

Cambodian Woman A7

Annamite Women A8

Hmong Woman A9

Laotian Woman A10

Cambodian Woman — A11

1907 *Perf. 14x13½*
41	A5	1c ol brn & blk	.40	.40
42	A5	2c yel brn & blk	.40	.40
43	A5	4c blue & blk	1.25	1.25
44	A5	5c grn & blk	1.60	.80
45	A5	10c red & blk	1.60	.55
46	A5	15c vio & blk	1.40	1.25
47	A5	20c vio & blk	3.75	1.60
48	A6	25c bl & blk	8.50	1.25
49	A6	30c brn & blk	13.00	7.50
50	A6	35c ol grn & blk	2.75	2.25
51	A6	40c yel brn & blk	4.50	1.25
52	A6	45c org & blk	11.00	7.00
53	A6	50c car & blk	16.00	6.00

Perf. 13½x14
54	A7	75c ver & blk	14.00	9.00
55	A8	1fr car & blk	62.50	22.50
56	A9	2fr grn & blk	18.00	17.50
57	A10	5fr blue & blk	47.50	55.00
58	A11	10fr pur & blk	120.00	110.00
		Nos. 41-58 (18)	328.15	246.25

For surcharges see Nos. 65-93, B1-B7.
Nos. 41, 47-51, 54-55 exist imperf.

Stamps of 1904-06 Surcharged in Black or Carmine

1912, Nov. *Perf. 14x13½*
59	A4	5c on 4c cl, *bluish*	6.00	6.00
60	A4	5c on 15c org brn, *bl* (C)	1.25	1.25
61	A4	5c on 30c pale brn	1.60	1.60
62	A4	10c on 40c blk, *bluish* (C)	1.60	1.60
63	A4	10c on 50c bis brn (C)	2.00	2.00
64	A4	10c on 75c red, *org*	5.25	5.25
		Nos. 59-64 (6)	17.70	17.70

Two spacings between the surcharged numerals are found on Nos. 59-64.

Nos. 41-58 Surcharged in Cents or Piasters in Black, Red or Blue

1919, Jan.
65	A5	⅖c on 1c	.85	.55
66	A5	⅘c on 2c	1.40	.90
67	A5	1⅗c on 4c (R)	2.00	.80
68	A5	2c on 5c	1.75	.30
a.		Inverted surcharge	160.00	
69	A5	4c on 10c (Bl)	1.60	.55
a.		Closed "4"	32.50	3.25
b.		Double surcharge	160.00	
70	A5	6c on 15c	6.75	1.25
a.		Inverted surcharge	160.00	
71	A6	8c on 20c	5.50	1.90
72	A6	10c on 25c	5.25	1.00
a.		Pair, one without surcharge	675.00	
73	A6	12c on 30c	7.00	1.10
74	A6	14c on 35c	3.50	.75
a.		Closed "4"	12.00	5.75
75	A6	16c on 40c	6.75	2.00
76	A6	18c on 45c	8.50	2.75
77	A6	20c on 50c (Bl)	13.00	1.25
78	A7	30c on 75c (Bl)	16.00	2.75
79	A8	40c on 1fr (Bl)	25.00	2.75
80	A9	80c on 2fr (R)	29.00	8.50
a.		Double surcharge	400.00	300.00
81	A10	2pi on 5fr (R)	110.00	110.00
82	A11	4pi on 10fr (R)	150.00	150.00
		Nos. 65-82 (18)	393.85	289.10

Types of 1907 Issue Surcharged with New Values in Black or Red

Nos. 88-92

No. 93

1922
88	A5	1c on 5c ocher & blk	1.60	
89	A5	2c on 10c gray grn & blk	2.40	
90	A6	6c on 30c lt red & blk	2.75	
91	A6	10c on 50c lt bl & blk	2.75	
92	A6	11c on 55c vio & blk, *bluish*	3.00	
93	A6	12c on 60c lt bl & blk, *pnksh* (R)	3.00	
		Nos. 88-93 (6)	15.50	

Nos. 88-93 were sold officially in Paris but were never placed in use in the colony. Nos. 88-89 exist without surcharge but were not regularly issued in that condition. Value, Nos. 88-89, each $190; Nos. 90-91, each $140; Nos. 92-93, each $100.

A12

A13

Two types of "CENTS" for the 4c, 5c, 10c-12c values: Type 1, thin font (April 1922); type 2, thicker font (Oct. 1922 and later printings). All other denominations are type 2. For more detailed listings, see the Scott Classic Specialized Catalogue of Stamps and Covers.

"CENTS" below Numerals

1922-23 *Perf. 14x13½*
94	A12	⅒c blk & sal ('23)	.25	.25
a.		Double impression of frame		
95	A12	⅕c blue & blk	.25	.25
96	A12	⅖c ol brn & blk	.25	.25
a.		Head and value doubled	275.00	275.00
97	A12	⅘c rose & blk, *lav*	.40	.35
98	A12	1c yel brn & blk	.25	.25
99	A12	2c gray grn & blk	.75	.55
100	A12	3c vio & blk	.35	.35
101	A12	4c org & blk, type 2	.35	.35
b.		Head and value doubled	225.00	225.00
102	A12	5c car & blk, type 2	.35	.35
b.		Head and value doubled	300.00	300.00
103	A13	6c dl red & blk	.50	.30
104	A13	7c grn & blk	.75	.65
105	A13	8c blk, *lav*	2.00	1.25
106	A13	9c ocher & blk, *grnsh*	1.50	.90
107	A13	10c bl & blk, type 2	.80	.75
108	A13	11c vio & blk, type 2	.75	.75
109	A13	12c brn & blk, type 2	.55	.55
b.		Head and value double (11c+12c)	550.00	550.00
110	A13	15c org & blk	1.10	.80
111	A13	20c bl & blk, *straw*	1.75	.80
112	A13	40c ver & blk, *bluish*	2.75	1.40
113	A13	1pi bl grn & blk, *grnsh*	5.75	5.25
114	A13	2pi vio brn & blk, *pnksh*	13.00	13.00
		Nos. 94-114 (21)	34.40	29.35

For overprints see Nos. O17-O32.

Plowing near Tower of Confucius A14

Ha Long Bay A15

Angkor Wat, Cambodia — A16

Carving Wood — A17

That Luang Temple, Laos — A18

Founding of Saigon — A19

1927, Sept. 26
115	A14	⅒c lt olive grn	.25	.25
116	A14	⅕c yellow	.25	.25
117	A14	⅖c lt light blue	.25	.25
118	A14	⅘c dp brn	.55	.55
119	A14	1c orange	.65	.30
120	A14	2c blue grn	1.10	.50
121	A14	3c indigo	.70	.30
122	A14	4c lil rose	1.60	1.25
123	A14	5c dp vio	.80	.30
a.		Booklet pane of 10	200.00	
124	A14	6c deep red	2.25	.80
a.		Booklet pane of 10	200.00	
125	A15	7c lt brn	1.50	.80
126	A15	8c gray green	2.10	1.00
127	A15	9c red vio	1.50	1.00
128	A15	10c light blue	2.00	1.25
129	A15	11c orange	2.00	1.25
130	A15	12c myrtle grn	1.50	1.00
131	A16	15c dl rose & ol brn	8.00	7.50
132	A16	20c vio & slate	4.00	2.00
133	A17	25c org brn & lil rose	8.75	6.50
134	A17	30c dp bl & ol gray	4.25	4.00
135	A18	40c ver & lt bl	7.75	3.25
136	A18	50c lt grn & slate	9.50	4.00
137	A19	1pi dk bl, blk & yel	22.50	8.25
a.		Yellow omitted	300.00	
138	A19	2pi red, dp bl & org	30.00	16.00
		Nos. 115-138 (24)	113.75	62.20

Common Design Types pictured following the introduction.

INDO-CHINA

Colonial Exposition Issue
Common Design Types Surcharged

No. 140
No. 141
No. 142

1931, Apr. 13   **Engr.**   **Perf. 12½**
Name of Country in Black
140	CD71	4c on 50c violet	3.50	3.50
141	CD72	6c on 90c red org	3.75	3.50
142	CD73	10c on 1.50fr dl bl	4.75	4.50
	Nos. 140-142 (3)		12.00	11.50
	Set, never hinged		18.50	

Junk — A20

Tower at Ruins of Angkor Thom — A21

Planting Rice — A22

Apsaras, Celestial Dancer — A23

1931-41   **Photo.**   **Perf. 13½x13**
143	A20	1/10c Prus blue	.25	.25
144	A20	1/5c lake	.25	.25
145	A20	2/5c org red	.25	.25
146	A20	1/2c red brn	.25	.25
147	A20	4/5c dk vio	.25	.25
148	A20	1c blk brn	.25	.25
149	A20	2c dk grn	.25	.25
150	A20	3c dp brn	.25	.25
151	A21	3c dk grn ('34)	6.00	1.60
152	A21	4c dk bl	1.25	.50
153	A21	4c dk grn ('38)	.80	.55
153A	A21	4c yel org ('40)	.40	.40
154	A21	5c dp vio	.30	.30
154A	A21	5c dp grn ('41)	.40	.40
155	A21	6c org red	.25	
a.		Bklt. pane 5 + 1 label	100.00	
156	A21	7c blk ('38)	.30	.30
157	A21	8c rose lake ('38)	.40	.40
157A	A21	9c blk, yel ('41)	.75	.75
158	A22	10c dark blue	.65	.50
158A	A22	10c ultra, pink ('41)	.55	.55
159	A22	15c dk brn	5.75	1.40
160	A22	15c dk bl ('33)	.25	.25
161	A22	18c blue ('38)	.75	.50
162	A22	20c rose	.30	.25
163	A22	21c olive grn	.30	.30
164	A22	24c dk grn ('38)	.55	.55
165	A22	25c dp vio	3.50	1.60
165A	A22	25c dk bl ('41)	.55	.55
166	A22	30c org brn ('32)	.50	.30

Perf. 13½
167	A23	50c dk brn	.75	.25
168	A23	60c dl vio ('32)	.90	.65
168A	A23	70c lt bl ('41)	.55	.55
169	A23	1pi yel grn	.90	.65
170	A23	2pi red	3.00	.75
	Nos. 143-170 (34)		32.60	17.05

Nos. 166, 167, 169 and 170 were issued without the letters "RF" in 1943, by the Vichy Government.
For surcharge & overprints see Nos. 214A, O1-O16, Viet Nam, Democratic Republic No. 1L14.

Emperor Bao-Dai — A24

King Sisowath Monivong — A25

For Use in Annam
1936, Nov. 20   **Engr.**   **Perf. 13**
171	A24	1c brown	1.00	1.00
172	A24	2c green	1.00	1.00
173	A24	4c violet	1.00	1.00
174	A24	5c red brn	1.50	1.50
175	A24	10c lil rose	2.00	2.00
176	A24	15c ultra	2.75	2.75
177	A24	20c scarlet	2.75	2.75
178	A24	30c plum	3.50	3.50
179	A24	50c slate grn	3.50	3.50
180	A24	1pi rose vio	4.75	4.75
181	A24	2pi black	5.75	5.75
	Nos. 171-181 (11)		29.50	29.50

For Use in Cambodia
182	A25	1c brown	1.00	1.00
183	A25	2c green	1.00	1.00
184	A25	4c violet	1.10	1.10
185	A25	5c red brn	1.10	1.10
186	A25	10c lil rose	2.40	2.40
187	A25	15c ultra	3.25	3.25
188	A25	20c scarlet	2.75	2.75
189	A25	30c plum	3.25	3.25
190	A25	50c slate grn	3.25	3.25
191	A25	1pi rose vio	4.25	4.25
192	A25	2pi black	5.75	5.75
	Nos. 182-192 (11)		29.10	29.10

Paris International Exposition Issue
Common Design Types
1937, Apr. 15
193	CD74	2c dp vio	1.60	1.60
194	CD75	3c dk grn	1.10	1.10
195	CD76	4c car rose	1.10	1.10
196	CD77	6c dk brn	1.10	1.10
197	CD78	9c red	1.40	1.40
198	CD79	15c ultra	1.40	1.40
	Nos. 193-198 (6)		7.70	7.70
	Set, never hinged		14.00	

Colonial Arts Exhibition Issue
Souvenir Sheet
Common Design Type
1937, Apr. 15   **Imperf.**
199	CD79	30c dull violet	10.00	12.00
	Never hinged		16.50	

Governor-General Paul Doumer — A26

1938, June 8   **Photo.**   **Perf. 13½x13**
200	A26	5c rose car	1.00	.65
201	A26	6c brown	1.10	1.10
202	A26	18c brt bl	1.10	1.10
	Nos. 200-202, C18 (4)		3.95	3.10
	Set, never hinged		6.50	

Trans-Indo-Chinese Railway, 35th anniv.

New York World's Fair Issue
Common Design Type
1939, May 10   **Engr.**   **Perf. 12½x12**
203	CD82	13c car lake	.80	.80
	Never hinged		1.40	
204	CD82	23c ultra	1.25	1.25
	Never hinged		2.25	

Mot Cot Pagoda, Hanoi — A27

1939, June 12   **Perf. 13**
205	A27	6c blk brn	1.10	1.10
206	A27	9c vermilion	1.10	1.10
207	A27	23c ultra	1.10	1.10
208	A27	39c rose vio	1.50	1.50
	Nos. 205-208 (4)		4.80	4.80
	Set, never hinged		9.00	

Golden Gate International Exposition.

Angkor Wat and Marshal Pétain — A27a

1941   **Engr.**   **Perf. 12½x12**
209	A27a	10c dk car	.80	
209A	A27a	25c blue	.80	

Nos. 209-209A were issued by the Vichy government in France, but were not placed on sale in Indo-China.
For overprints, see Nos. 262-263. For surcharges, see B21A-B21B.

Gum
Nos. 210-261 issued without gum.

Imperfs
Many issues between Nos. 209-263, B19A-B26 and C1-C28, plus some postage dues and official stamps, exist imperf.

King Norodom Sihanouk of Cambodia — A28

Pin-perf. 12½
1941, Oct. 15   **Unwmk.**   **Litho.**
210	A28	1c red org	1.60	1.60
211	A28	6c violet	3.25	3.25
212	A28	25c dp ultra	21.00	21.00
	Nos. 210-212 (3)		25.85	25.85

Coronation of Norodom Sihanouk, King of Cambodia, October, 1941.
For surcharges see Viet Nam, Democratic Republic Nos. 1L27-1L29.

Harnessed Elephant on Parade — A29

1942, Mar. 29
213	A29	3c reddish brown	2.00	1.60
214	A29	6c crimson	2.00	1.60

Fête of Nam-Giao in Annam.
For surcharges see Viet Nam, Democratic Republic Nos. 1L32-1L33, 1L53-1L54.

No. 165 Surcharged in Black

1942   **Perf. 13**
214A	A22	10c on 25c dp vio, gum	.50	.30

View of Saigon Fair — A30

1942, Dec. 20   **Perf. 13½**
215	A30	6c carmine rose	.80	.80

Saigon Fair of 1942.
For surcharge see Viet Nam, Democratic Republic No. 1L51.

Nam-Phuong, Empress of Annam — A31

1942, Sept. 1   **Pin-perf. 11½**
216	A31	6c carmine rose	1.25	.80

For surcharge see Viet Nam, Democratic Republic No. 1L55.

Marshal Pétain — A32

Perf. 11½, 12, 13½ and Compound
1942-44
217	A32	1c blk brn	.35	.35
218	A32	3c olive brn ('43)	.35	.35
219	A32	6c rose red	.55	.55
220	A32	10c dull grn ('43)	1.20	1.20
221	A32	40c dk blue ('43)	1.60	1.60
222	A32	40c slate bl ('44)	.80	1.25
	Nos. 217-222 (6)		4.85	5.30

Values are for the lowest-valued perforation varieties.
For overprints see Viet Nam, Democratic Republic Nos. 1L6-1L10, 1L21.

Bao-Dai, Emperor of Annam — A33

1942   **Perf. 13½**
223	A33	½c brown	1.25	1.60
224	A33	6c carmine rose	1.25	1.25

Issue dates: ½c, Nov. 1; 6c, Sept. 1.
For surcharge see Viet Nam, Democratic Republic No. 1L56.

Norodom Sihanouk, King of Cambodia — A34

1943   **Perf. 12**
225	A34	1c brown	1.25	.80
a.		Perf. 13¾	8.00	8.00
226	A34	6c red	1.00	.55
a.		Perf. 13¾	8.00	8.00

Issue dates: 1c, Mar. 10; 6c, May 10.
For surcharge see Viet Nam, Democratic Republic No. 1L30.

Types of 1931-32 Without "RF"
1943   **Photo.**   **Perf. 13½x13**
226A	A22	30c orange brown	1.60	
226B	A23	50c dark brown	1.60	
226C	A23	1pi yellow green	2.75	
226D	A23	2pi red	3.50	
	Nos. 226A-226D (4)		9.45	

Nos. 226A-226D were issued by the Vichy government in France, but were not placed on sale in Indo-China. Nos. 226A-226D were issued with gum.

Sisavang-Vong, King of Laos — A35

1943   **Perf. 12**
227	A35	1c bister brown	.80	1.25
a.		Perf. 13¾	10.00	10.00

INDO-CHINA

228	A35	6c carmine rose	1.25	.65
a.		Perf. 11½x12	32.50	32.50
b.		Perf. 13¾	32.50	32.50

Issue dates: 1c, Mar. 10; 6c, June 1.
For surcharge see Viet Nam, Democratic Republic No. 1L31.

Family, Country and Labor — A36

1943, Nov. 5   *Perf. 12*

229	A36	6c carmine rose	.65	.50
a.		Perf. 11½	.80	.80

National revolution, 3rd anniversary.
For surcharge see Viet Nam, Democratic Republic No. 1L52.

Admiral Rigault de Genouilly A37

François Chasseloup-Laubat A38

Admiral André A. P. Courbet — A39

1943   *Perf. 11½, 12, 12x11½*

230	A37	6c carmine rose	.50	1.40
231	A38	6c carmine rose	.50	.35
232	A39	6c carmine rose	1.40	.25
		Nos. 230-232 (3)	2.40	2.00

Issued: Nos. 230, 232, 9/1; No. 231, 10/5.
A 5c dull brown, type A37, was not regularly issued without the Viet Nam overprint. Value, $10.
For overprints see Viet Nam, Democratic Republic Nos. 1L15-1L16, 1L25-1L26.
A 3c light brown, type A39, was prepared but not issued. Value, $10.

Pigneau de Behaine, Bishop of Adran — A40

1943, June 10   *Perf. 12*

233	A40	20c dull red	1.50	1.75

For surcharge see Viet Nam, Democratic Republic No. 1L50.

Alexandre Yersin — A41

1943-45   *Perf. 12x11½*

234	A41	6c carmine rose	1.50	1.50
235	A41	15c vio brn ('44)	.55	.55
236	A41	1pi yel grn ('45)	.75	.75
		Nos. 234-236 (3)	2.80	2.80

Issued to honor Dr. Alexandre Yersin (1863-1943), the Swiss bacteriologist who introduced rubber culture into Indo-China.
Issued: 6c, 10/5; 15c, 12/10; 1pi, 1/10.
For overprint and surcharges see Viet Nam, Democratic Republic Nos. 1L1, 1L49.

Lt. M. J. François Garnier — A42

1943, Sept.   *Perf. 12*

237	A42	1c olive brown	.90	1.25

A 15c brown violet was prepared but not issued. Value, $16.
For surcharges see Viet Nam, Democratic Republic Nos. 1L41-1L42.

Alexandre de Rhodes — A43

1943-45   *Pin-perf., Perf. 12*

238	A43	15c dk vio brn ('45)	.40	.40
239	A43	30c org brn	.80	.80
a.		30c yellow brown, perf. 13½	.80	.80

Nos. 239, 239a carry the monogram "EF."
Issue dates: 15c, Mar. 10; 30c, June 15.
For overprints see Viet Nam, Democratic Republic Nos. 1L2-1L3.

Athlete Giving Olympic Salute — A44

1944, July 10   *Perf. 12*

241	A44	10c dk vio brn & yel	2.40	2.40
242	A44	50c dl red	2.75	2.75

For overprints see Viet Nam, Democratic Republic Nos. 1L4-1L5.

Adm. Pierre de La Grandière — A45

1943-45

243	A45	1c dull brn	.25	1.25
244	A45	5c dark brn ('45)	.30	.30

The upper left corner of No. 244 contains the denomination "5c" instead of "EF" monogram.
Issue dates: 1c, Aug.; 5c, Jan. 10.
For surcharges see Viet Nam, Democratic Republic Nos. 1L39-1L40.

Auguste Pavie — A46

1944   *Perf. 12*

245	A46	4c org yel	.50	.30
246	A46	10c dl grn	.30	.65

Issue dates: 4c, Feb. 10; 10c, Jan. 5.
A 20c dark red, type A46, was not regularly issued without the Viet Nam overprint. Value without overprint, $10.
For overprints see Viet Nam, Democratic Republic Nos. 1L11-1L13.

Governor-General Pierre Pasquier — A47

1944

247	A47	5c brn vio	.65	.65
248	A47	10c dl grn	.30	1.25

Issue dates: 5c, Nov. 1; 10c, Sept.
For surcharges see Viet Nam, Democratic Republic Nos. 1L34-1L35.

Joost Van Vollenhoven A48

1944, Oct. 10

249	A48	1c olive brown	.35	.35
250	A48	10c green	.75	.90

For surcharges see Viet Nam, Democratic Republic Nos. 1L44-1L45.

Governor-General J. M. A. de Lanessan — A49

1944

251	A49	1c dl gray brn	.65	.50
252	A49	15c dl rose vio	1.90	1.60

Issued: 1c, 12/10; 15c, 10/16.
For surcharges see Viet Nam, Democratic Republic Nos. 1L43, 1L46.

Governor-General Paul Doumer — A50

1944

253	A50	2c red vio	.30	.30
254	A50	4c lt brn	.30	.30
255	A50	10c yel grn	.30	.30
		Nos. 253-255 (3)	.90	.90

Issue dates: 2c, 4/15; 4c, 6/15; 10c, 1/5.
For overprints see Viet Nam, Democratic Republic Nos. 1L18-1L20.

Admiral Charner — A51

1944

256	A51	10c green	.50	1.40
257	A51	20c brn red	.65	1.40
258	A51	1pi pale yel grn	1.00	1.00
		Nos. 256-258 (3)	2.15	3.80

Issue dates: 10c, 20c, 8/10; 1pi, July.
For overprints see Viet Nam, Democratic Republic Nos. 1L22-1L24.

Doudart de Lagrée — A52

1944-45

259	A52	1c dl gray brn ('45)	.25	.25
260	A52	15c dl rose vio	.50	.55
261	A52	40c brt bl	.65	1.00
		Nos. 259-261 (3)	1.40	1.80

Issue dates: 1c, 1/10; 15c, 40c, Nov.
For overprint and surcharges see Viet Nam, Democratic Republic Nos. 1L17, 1L37-1L38.

Nos. 209-209A Overprinted in Black

1946   *Unwmk.*   *Perf. 12½x12*

262	A27a	10c dk car	1.10	1.60
263	A27a	25c blue	2.75	3.25

SEMI-POSTAL STAMPS

No. 45 Surcharged

Perf. 14x13½

1914, Oct. 28   *Unwmk.*

B1	A5	10c +5c red & blk	1.60	1.60

Nos. 44-46 Surcharged

1915-17

B2	A5	5c + 5c grn & blk ('17)	1.60	1.60
a.		Double surcharge	220.00	210.00
B3	A5	10c + 5c red & blk	2.50	2.00
B4	A5	15c + 5c vio & blk ('17)	2.50	2.00
a.		Triple surcharge	200.00	
b.		Quadruple surcharge	200.00	
		Nos. B2-B4 (3)	6.60	5.60

Nos. B2-B4 Surcharged with New Values in Blue or Black

1918-19

B5	A5	4c on 5c + 5c (Bl)	4.25	4.25
a.		Closed "4"	220.00	
B6	A5	6c on 10c + 5c	3.75	4.00
B7	A5	8c on 15c + 5c ('19)	15.00	15.00
a.		Double surcharge	225.00	
		Nos. B5-B7 (3)	23.00	23.25

France Nos. B5-B10 Surcharged

1919 (?)

B8	SP5	10c on 15c + 10c	1.60	1.60
a.		"10 CENTS" double	525.00	525.00
B9	SP5	16c on 25c + 15c	4.00	4.00
B10	SP6	24c on 35c + 25c	7.25	7.25
a.		Double surcharge	800.00	800.00
b.		"CENTS" double	950.00	
B11	SP7	40c on 50c + 50c	12.50	12.50
B12	SP8	80c on 1fr + 1fr	27.50	27.50
B13	SP8	4pi on 5fr + 5fr	190.00	190.00
a.		"PIASTRES" double	6,250.	5,400.
		Nos. B8-B13 (6)	242.85	242.85

Curie Issue
Common Design Type
Inscription and Date in Upper Margin

1938, Oct. 24   *Engr.*   *Perf. 13*

B14	CD80	18c + 5c brt ultra	12.00	12.00
		Never hinged	20.00	

French Revolution Issue
Common Design Type
Name and Value Typo. in Black

1939, July 5   *Photo.*

B15	CD83	6c + 2c green	12.00	12.00
B16	CD83	7c + 3c brown	12.00	12.00
B17	CD83	9c + 4c red org	12.00	12.00
B18	CD83	13c + 10c rose pink	12.00	12.00
B19	CD83	23c + 20c blue	12.00	12.00
		Nos. B15-B19 (5)	60.00	60.00
		Set, never hinged	112.50	

Common Design Type and

Tonkinese Sharpshooter SP1

Legionary SP2

INDO-CHINA

1941   Photo.   Perf. 13½
- **B19A** SP1 10c + 10c red   3.00
- **B19B** CD86 15c + 30c maroon   3.00
- **B19C** SP2 25c + 10c blue   3.00
- Nos. B19A-B19C (3)   9.00

Nos. B19A-B19C were issued by the Vichy government in France, but were not placed on sale in Indo-China.

Gum
#B20-B31 issued without gum.

Portal and Flags, City University, Hanoi — SP3

Perf. 11½
1942, June 1   Unwmk.   Litho.
- **B20** SP3 6c + 2c car rose   1.25   1.25
-    a. Perf. 13¾   120.00
- **B21** SP3 15c + 5c brn vio   1.25   1.25

Nos. 209-209A Srchd. in Black or Red

1944   Engr.   Perf. 12½x12
- **B21A** 5c + 15c on 25c blue (R)   .95
- **B21B**   + 25c on 10c dk car   1.00

Colonial Development Fund.
Nos. B21A-B21B were issued by the Vichy government in France, but were not placed on sale in Indo-China.

No. B20 Surcharged in Black

1944, June 10
- **B22** SP3 10c + 2c on 6c + 2c   1.25   1.25

Coat of Arms and Sword — SP4

1942, Aug. 1   Perf. 12
- **B23** SP4 6c + 2c red & blue   .80   .80
- **B24** SP4 15c + 5c vio blk, red & bl   .80   .80

No. B23 Surcharged in Black Like No. B22

1944, Mar. 15
- **B25** SP4 10c + 2c on 6c + 2c   .80   .80

Aviator Do-Huu-Vi — SP5

1943, Aug. 1
- **B26** SP5 6c + 2c car rose   .65   1.60

No. B26 Surcharged in Black Like No. B22

1944, Feb. 10
- **B27** SP5 10c + 2c on 6c + 2c   .80   .80

Surcharge arranged to fit size of stamp.

Aviator Roland Garros — SP6

1943, Nov. 15
- **B28** SP6 6c + 2c rose car   .80   .80

No. B28 Surcharged in Black Like No. B22

1944, Feb. 10
- **B29** SP6 10c + 2c on 6c + 2c   .80   .80

Cathedral of Orléans — SP7

1944, Dec. 20
- **B30** SP7 15c + 60c brn vio   1.60   1.60
- **B31** SP7 40c + 1.10pi blue   1.60   2.75

For surcharges see Viet Nam, Democratic Republic Nos. 1L36, 1L47-1L48.

Type of France, 1945, Surcharged in Black

1945   Unwmk.   Engr.   Perf. 13
- **B32** A152 50c + 50c on 2fr green   1.00   1.00
- **B33** A152 1pi + 1pi on 2fr hn brn   1.00   1.00
- **B34** A152 2pi + 2pi on 2fr Prus grn   2.00   2.00
- Nos. B32-B34 (3)   4.00   4.00
- Set, never hinged   4.75

AIR POST STAMPS

Airplane — AP1

1933-41   Unwmk.   Photo.   Perf. 13½
- **C1** AP1 1c ol brn   .25   .25
- **C2** AP1 2c dk grn   .30   .25
- **C3** AP1 5c yel grn   .30   .25
- **C4** AP1 10c red brn   .65   .30
- **C5** AP1 11c rose car ('38)   .80   .30
- **C6** AP1 15c dp bl   .70   .25
- **C6A** AP1 16c brt pink ('41)   .35   .35
- **C7** AP1 20c grnsh gray   .50   .50
- **C8** AP1 30c org brn   .30   .25
- **C9** AP1 36c car rose   1.90   .35
- **C10** AP1 37c ol grn ('38)   .80   .30
- **C10A** AP1 39c dk ol grn ('41)   .35   .35
- **C11** AP1 60c dk vio   1.90   .35
- **C12** AP1 66c olive grn   .55   .25
- **C13** AP1 67c brt bl ('38)   1.20   1.00
- **C13A** AP1 69c brt ultra ('41)   .65   .65
- **C14** AP1 1pi black   .70   .25
- **C15** AP1 2pi yel org   1.00   .35
- **C16** AP1 5pi purple   1.90   .50
- **C17** AP1 10pi deep red   3.75   .90
- Nos. C1-C17 (20)   18.85   7.95

See Nos. C27-C28.
Issue dates: 11c, 37c, June 8; 67c, Oct. 5; 16c, 39c, 69c, Feb. 5; others, June 1, 1933.
See Nos. C18A-C18O, C27-C28.

Trans-Indo-Chinese Railway Type

1938, June 8
- **C18** A26 37c red orange   .75   .25

Type of 1933-38 Without "RF"

1942-44   Perf. 13½
- **C18A** AP1 5c yellow green   .25
- **C18B** AP1 10c red brown   .25
- **C18C** AP1 11c rose carmine   .30
- **C18D** AP1 15c deep blue   .40
- **C18E** AP1 20c greenish gray   .40
- **C18F** AP1 36c carmine rose   .40
- **C18G** AP1 37c olive green   .70
- **C18H** AP1 60c dark violet   .70
- **C18I** AP1 66c brown olive   .70
- **C18J** AP1 67c bright blue   .90
- **C18K** AP1 69c br ultramarine   .90
- **C18L** AP1 1pi black   1.30
- **C18M** AP1 2pi yellow orange   1.30
- **C18N** AP1 5pi purple   1.75
- **C18O** AP1 10pi deep red   3.50
- Nos. C18A-C18O (15)   13.65

Nos. C18A-C18O were issued by the Vichy government in France, but were not placed on sale in Indo-China.

Victory Issue
Common Design Type
Perf. 12½
1946, May 8   Unwmk.   Engr.
- **C19** CD92 80c red org   1.00   .55

Chad to Rhine Issue
Common Design Types
1946, June 6
- **C20** CD93 50c yel grn   .90   .90
- **C21** CD94 1pi violet   .90   .90
- **C22** CD95 1.50pi carmine   1.10   1.10
- **C23** CD96 2pi vio brn   1.10   1.10
- **C24** CD97 2.50pi dp bl   1.10   1.10
- **C25** CD98 5pi org red   1.30   1.30
- Nos. C20-C25 (6)   6.40   6.40
- Set, never hinged   10.00

UPU Issue
Common Design Type
1949, July 4   Perf. 13
- **C26** CD99 3pi dp bl, dk vio, grn & red   4.75   4.00
- Never hinged   8.50

Plane Type of 1933-41
1949, June 13   Photo.   Perf. 13½
- **C27** AP1 20pi dk bl grn   11.50   6.50
- **C28** AP1 30pi brown   13.00   6.50

AIR POST SEMI-POSTAL STAMP

French Revolution Issue
Common Design Type
Unwmk.
1939, July 5   Photo.   Perf. 13
Name and Value Typo. in Orange
- **CB1** CD83 39c + 40c brn blk   25.00   25.00
- Never hinged   45.00

Poor Family SPAP1

Orphans — SPAP2

Caring for Children SPAP3

Perf. 13½x12½, 13 (#CB4)
Photo, Engr. (#CB4)
1942, June 22
- **CB2** SPAP1 15c + 35c green   2.00
- **CB3** SPAP2 20c + 60c brown   2.00
- **CB4** SPAP3 30c + 90c car red   2.00
- Nos. CB2-CB4 (3)   6.00

Native children's welfare fund.
Nos. CB2-CB4 were issued by the Vichy government in France, but were not placed on sale in Indo-China.

Colonial Education Fund
Common Design Type
Perf. 12½x13½
1942, June 22   Engr.
- **CB5** CD86a 12c + 18c blue & red   2.00

No. CB5 was issued by the Vichy government in France, but was not placed on sale in Indo-China.

POSTAGE DUE STAMPS

French Colonies No. J21 Surcharged

1904, June 26   Unwmk.   Imperf.
- **J1** D1 5c on 60c brn, *buff*   14.50   14.50

French Colonies Nos. J10-J11 Surcharged in Carmine

1905, July 22
- **J2** D1 5c on 40c black   40.00   20.00
- **J3** D1 10c on 60c black   40.00   20.00
- **J4** D1 30c on 60c black   40.00   20.00
- Nos. J2-J4 (3)   120.00   60.00

Dragon from Steps of Angkor Wat — D1

1908   Typo.   Perf. 14x13½
- **J5** D1 2c black   1.40   1.00
- **J6** D1 4c dp bl   1.40   1.00
- **J7** D1 5c bl grn   1.75   1.10
- **J8** D1 10c carmine   3.00   1.10
- **J9** D1 15c redsh vio   3.75   2.75
- **J10** D1 20c chocolate   1.90   1.40
- **J11** D1 30c ol grn   1.90   1.40
- **J12** D1 40c claret   8.50   7.25
- **J13** D1 50c grnsh bl   7.25   1.60
- **J14** D1 60c orange   12.00   11.00
- **J15** D1 1fr gray   24.00   18.50
- **J16** D1 2fr brt brn   24.00   18.50
- **J17** D1 5fr red   40.00   37.50
- Nos. J5-J17 (13)   130.85   104.10

Surcharged in Cents or Piasters in Black, Blue or Red

1919
- **J18** D1 ⅖c on 2c blk   1.75   1.25
- **J19** D1 1⅘c on 4c dp bl   1.75   1.25
- **J20** D1 2c on 5c bl grn   3.00   1.60
- **J21** D1 4c on 10c car   4.25   1.25
- **J22** D1 6c on 15c redsh vio   9.50   3.00
- **J23** D1 8c on 20c choc   6.75   2.40
- **J24** D1 12c on 30c ol grn   9.50   2.40
- **J25** D1 16c on 40c cl   9.50   2.00
- **J26** D1 20c on 50c grnsh bl   12.50   6.50
- **J27** D1 24c on 60c org   3.25   2.00
-    a. Closed "4"   20.00   16.00
- **J28** D1 40c on 1fr gray   5.50   1.60
-    a. Closed "4"   20.00   16.00
- **J29** D1 80c on 2fr yel brn   42.50   20.00
- **J30** D1 2pi on 5fr red   62.50   42.50
-    a. Double surcharge   240.00   190.00
-    b. Triple surcharge   225.00   180.00
- Nos. J18-J30 (13)   172.25   87.75

Dragon from Steps of Angkor Wat — D2

"CENT" below Numerals

1922, Oct.
- **J31** D2 ⅖c black   .25   .25
- **J32** D2 ⅘c red   .30   .30
- **J33** D2 1c buff   .50   .40
- **J34** D2 2c gray grn   .65   .50
- **J35** D2 3c violet   .75   .75
- **J36** D2 4c orange   .75   .40
-    a. "4 CENTS" omitted   700.00
-    b. "4 CENTS" double   105.00   105.00
- **J37** D2 6c ol grn   1.60   .65
- **J38** D2 8c blk, *lav*   1.25   .65
- **J39** D2 10c dp bl   2.00   .65
- **J40** D2 12c ocher, *grnsh*   1.60   1.25
- **J41** D2 20c dp bl, *straw*   2.00   .90
- **J42** D2 40c red, *bluish*   3.00   1.10
- **J43** D2 1pi brn vio, *pnksh*   6.75   3.75
- Nos. J31-J43 (13)   20.40   11.55

Pagoda of Mot Cot, Hanoi D3

Dragon of Annam D4

INDO-CHINA — INDONESIA

Perf. 14x13½, 13½x14
1927, Sept. 26
J44	D3	⅖c vio brn & org	.25	.25
J45	D3	⅘c vio & blk	.25	.25
J46	D3	1c brn red & sl	.90	.90
J47	D3	2c grn & brn ol	1.00	1.00
J48	D3	3c red brn & rl	1.60	1.60
J49	D3	4c ind & brn	1.60	1.60
J50	D3	6c dp red & ver	2.00	1.60
J51	D3	8c ol brn & vio	1.60	1.25
J52	D4	10c dp bl	2.50	1.25
J53	D4	12c olive	5.75	4.75
J54	D4	20c rose	4.00	2.00
J55	D4	40c bl grn	4.00	3.50
J56	D4	1pi red org	20.00	20.00
		Nos. J44-J56 (13)	45.45	39.95

Surcharged in Black or Blue — D5

1931-41 Perf. 13
J57	D5	⅕c red, *org* ('38)	.25	.25
J58	D5	⅖c red, *org*	.25	.25
J59	D5	⅘c red, *org*	.25	.25
J60	D5	1c red, *org*	.25	.25
J61	D5	2c red, *org*	.25	.25
J62	D5	2.5c red, *org* ('40)	.25	.25
J63	D5	3c red, *org* ('38)	.40	.25
J64	D5	4c red, *org*	.30	.30
J65	D5	5c red, *org* ('38)	.40	.30
J66	D5	6c red, *org*	.30	.30
J67	D5	10c red, *org*	.30	.30
J68	D5	12c red, *org*	.50	.30
J69	D5	14c red, *org* ('38)	.50	.30
J70	D5	18c red, *org* ('41)	.50	.50
J71	D5	20c red, *org*	.50	.50
J72	D5	50c red, *org*	.75	.50
J72A	D5	1pi red, *org*	10.00	9.50
J73	D5	1pi red, *org* (Bl)	10.00	9.00
		Nos. J57-J73 (18)	25.95	23.55

Perf. 12, 13½ and Compound
1943-44 Litho. Unwmk.
J74	D6	1c red, *org*	.25	.25
J75	D6	2c red, *org*	.25	.25
J76	D6	3c red, *org*	.30	.30
J77	D6	4c red, *org*	.30	.30
J78	D6	6c red, *org*	.40	.40
J79	D6	10c red, *org*	.40	.40
J80	D7	12c blue, *pnksh*	.50	.50
J81	D7	20c blue, *pnksh*	.50	.50
J82	D7	30c blue, *pnksh*	.50	.50
		Nos. J74-J82 (9)	3.40	3.40

Issued: 2c, 3c, 7/15/43; 6c-30c, 8/43; 1c, 4c, 6/10/44. Issued without gum.

OFFICIAL STAMPS

Regular Issues of 1931-32 Overprinted in Blue or Red

Perf. 13, 13½
1933, Feb. 27 Unwmk.
O1	A20	1c black brown (Bl)	.80	.75
O2	A20	2c dark green (Bl)	.90	.50

Regular Issues of 1931-32 Overprinted in Blue or Red
O3	A21	3c deep brown (Bl)	1.25	.65
a.		Inverted overprint	160.00	
O4	A21	4c dark blue (R)	1.50	.90
a.		Inverted overprint	160.00	
O5	A21	5c deep violet (Bl)	2.40	.90
O6	A21	6c orange red (Bl)	2.40	1.25

Regular Issues of 1931-32 Overprinted in Blue or Red
O7	A22	10c dk blue (R)	1.25	1.00
O8	A22	15c dk brown (Bl)	3.00	1.75
O9	A22	20c rose (Bl)	3.25	.85
O10	A22	21c olive grn (Bl)	3.00	1.75
O11	A22	25c dp violet (Bl)	1.60	.50
O12	A22	30c orange brn (Bl)	3.25	.85

Regular Issues of 1931-32 Overprinted in Blue or Red
O13	A23	50c dark brown (Bl)	12.50	3.50
O14	A23	60c dull violet (Bl)	2.75	2.40
O15	A23	1pi yellow green (Bl)	30.00	11.00
O16	A23	2pi red (Bl)	11.50	9.50
		Nos. O1-O16 (16)	81.35	38.05

Type of 1922-23 Issue Overprinted diagonally in Black or Red

1934, Oct. 4 Perf. 14x13
O17	A13	1c olive green	1.25	.75
O18	A13	2c brown orange	1.25	.75
O19	A13	3c yellow green	1.40	.65
O20	A13	4c cerise	2.50	1.30
O21	A13	5c yellow	1.40	.75
O22	A13	6c orange red	6.00	5.25
O23	A13	10c gray grn (R)	3.50	2.25
O24	A13	15c ultra	2.10	1.50
O25	A13	20c gray black (R)	2.00	1.50
O26	A13	21c light violet	11.00	9.25
O27	A13	25c rose lake	13.00	11.00
O28	A13	30c lilac gray	1.75	1.30
O29	A13	50c brt violet	8.00	6.75
O30	A13	60c gray	15.00	11.00
O31	A13	1pi blue (R)	30.00	24.50
O32	A13	2pi deep red	47.50	37.50
		Nos. O17-O32 (16)	147.65	116.00

The value tablet has colorless numeral and letters on solid background.

PARCEL POST STAMPS

French Colonies No. 50 Overprinted

1891 Unwmk. Perf. 14x13½
Q1	A9	10c black, *lavender*	35.00	30.00

The overprint on No. Q1 was also hand-stamped in shiny ink. Value unused, $750.

Indo-China No. 8 Overprinted

1898
Q2	A3	10c black, *lavender*	35.00	35.00

Nos. 8 and 9 Overprinted

1902
Q3	A3	10c black, *lavender*	55.00	35.00
a.		Inverted overprint	115.00	50.00
Q4	A3	10c red	55.00	24.00
a.		Inverted overprint	85.00	50.00
b.		Double overprint	85.00	50.00

INDONESIA

ˌin-də-ˈnē-zhə

LOCATION — In the East Indies
GOVT. — Republic
AREA — 741,101 sq. mi.
POP. — 273,520,000 (2020 est.)
CAPITAL — Nusantara

Formerly Netherlands Indies, Indonesia achieved independence late in 1949 as the United States of Indonesia and became the Republic of Indonesia August 15, 1950. See Netherlands Indies for earlier issues.

100 Sen = 1 Rupiah

Catalogue values for all unused stamps in this country are for Never Hinged items.

Watermarks

Wmk. 404

Wmk. 228

REVOLUTIONARY ISSUES

Following the surrender of Japan to the Allies in 1945, Indonesian nationalists declared independence and formed the Republic of Indonesia. On Sept. 27, the Djawan PTT (now PT Pos Indonesia) was established and assumed reponsibility for the postal system. Within days, civil war had broken out between the nationalists and the returning Dutch, who sought to reestablish control over their East Indies colony. During the hostilities, which continued until Dec. 1949, a Dutch blockade of the rebel strongholds in Java and Sumatra made regular communications between the two islands impossible, and the Djawan PTT was forced to organize separate postal services, using locally produced stamps, on Java and Sumatra.

JAVA ISSUES

Netherlands Indies Nos. 168, 200, 201 Ovptd. in Black or Red (R)

1945, Nov. Perf. 11½
1L1	A17	1c lilac gray (R)	2.50	3.50
1L2	A17	2c plum	5.50	7.50
1L3	A17	3½c dark gray (R)	100.00	100.00
		Nos. 1L1-1L3 (3)	108.00	111.00

Forgeries of Nos. 1L1-1L3 exist.

Netherlands Indies Nos. 228-231 Ovptd. in Black or Red (R)

1945, Nov. Perf. 12½
1L4	A23	2½c rose violet	2.00	3.50
1L5	A24	3c green (R)	2.00	3.50
1L6	A25	4c olive green (R)	2.50	4.50
1L7	A26	5c blue (R)	150.00	175.00
		Nos. 1L4-1L7 (4)	156.50	186.50

Forgeries of Nos. 1L4-1L7 exist.

Netherlands Indies Nos. N2, N3 Ovptd. in Black or Red (R)

1945, Nov. Perf. 12½
1L8	OS2	3½s carmine	425.00	375.00
1L9	OS3	5s green (R)	25.00	22.50

Forgeries of Nos. 1L8-1L9 exist.

Netherlands Indies Nos. N5-N11 Ovptd. in Black or Red (R)

1945, Nov. Perf. 12½
1L10	OS5	3½s rose red	50.00	50.00
1L11	OS6	5s yel grn (R)	.80	1.50
1L12	OS7	10s dk blue (R)	.80	1.50
a.		Perf 12	2.50	2.50
1L13	OS8	20s gray ol (R)	.85	1.50
1L14	OS9	40s rose lilac (R)	.75	1.50
1L15	OS10	60s red orange	1.25	1.50
1L16	OS11	80s fawn	25.00	25.00
		Nos. 1L10-1L16 (7)	79.45	82.50

Forgeries of Nos. 1L10-1L16 exist.

Errors and Rare Stamps from Indonesia

Mint and Used Stamps from Asia

INDONESIA HALIM STAMP
JL. BANDENGAN SELATAN 58/NO. 9
JAKARTA UTARA — 14450 INDONESIA
TELP: 62-21-6690135 | FAX: 62-21-66691765
WA no: +62 815 5177 988 | EMAIL: lim_stamp@yahoo.co.id

INDONESIA

Netherlands Indies Nos. 200, 201, 228-230, N38 Overprinted in Red or Brown (Br)

Perf. 12½, 12x12½ (#A18, A19)

1945, Nov.
1L17	A17	1s lilac gray		2.25	3.50
1L18	A17	1s lilac gray (Br)		15.00	17.50
1L19	OS21	2s carmine		1.50	2.00
1L20	A23	2½s rose violet		25.00	25.00
1L21	A24	3s green		4.75	4.75
1L22	A25	4s olive green		4.50	4.50
		Nos. 1L17-1L22 (6)		53.00	57.25

Forgeries of Nos. 1L17-1L22 exist.

A large number of proofs, both perf and imperf, in original and in different colors, exist for Nos. 1L23-1L50. All are scarce.

Bull — A1

Bull & Flag — A2

Perf. 11½

1945, Dec. 1   Typo.   Unwmk.
With Gum
1L23	A1	10s chocolate		10.00	10.00
a.		Imperf		110.00	200.00
1L24	A2	20s choc & carmine red		8.25	9.50

Issued to celebrate the first half-year of Indonesian independence.

Nos. 1L25-1L49 were issued without gum.

Road & Mountains A3

Sentry A4

Boat in Storm A5

Wayang Puppet A6

Kris & Flag A7

Temple A8

1946-47   Various perfs
1L25	A3	5s pale gray blue		.75	1.25
1L26	A4	20s lt red brown		.75	1.25
1L27	A5	30s carmine red		.80	1.25
1L28	A6	50s deep blue		20.00	20.00
1L29	A7	60s deep rose		10.00	300.00
1L30	A8	80s dp red vio ('47)		75.00	600.00
		Nos. 1L25-1L30 (6)		107.30	923.75

Issued: 5s, 20s, 6/1/46. 30s, 50s, 7/1/46. 60s, 9/1/46. 80s, 7/1/47.

Buffalo Breaking Chains A9

Bandung, March 1946 A10

Bombing of Soerabaya, Nov. 1945 — A11

Anti-aircraft Crew — A12

Quai at Tandjong Priok — A13

Pilot — A14

Ambarawa A15

Wonokroma Dam, Soerabaya A16

Meeting, Jakarta A17

Mounted Soldier A18

1946-47   Various perfs
1L31	A9	3s dull carmine		.35	1.75
a.		Imperf		.25	.25
1L32	A10	5s gray blue		.60	.95
a.		Imperf		.35	.50
1L33	A11	10s blue black		11.50	6.25
a.		Imperf		11.50	11.50
1L34	A11	15s dark purple		.95	1.25
a.		Imperf		.95	.95
1L35	A12	30s green		2.40	5.75
a.		Imperf		1.75	2.90
1L36	A13	40s dk blue vio		.95	2.40
a.		Imperf		1.00	1.00
1L37	A9	50s violet black		1.75	2.90
a.		Imperf		1.20	1.20
1L38	A10	60s dp red vio		3.50	4.50
a.		Imperf		1.75	1.75
1L39	A14	80s br rose red		1.20	7.00
a.		Imperf			150.00
1L40	A15	100s dull brn red		1.75	3.50
a.		Imperf		1.20	1.20
1L41	A16	200s dull lilac		2.90	3.50
a.		Imperf		1.50	2.40
1L42	A17	500s car red		15.00	27.50
a.		Imperf		9.00	9.00
1L43	A18	1000s lt blue green		16.50	30.00
a.		Imperf		7.00	7.00
		Nos. 1L31-1L43 (13)		59.35	97.25

First anniv. of independence.
Issued: 3s, 10s-200s, 8/17/46. 5s, 500s, 1000s, 2/1/47.

Worker & Ship — A19

1948, Aug. 17   Imperf.
1L44	A19	50s dull blue		5.00	5.00
a.		Perf 11		14.50	
1L45	A19	100s dull scarlet		5.00	7.50
a.		Perf 11		14.50	

Nos. 1L44 and 1L45 were printed on paper with papermaker's watermark. Nos. 1L44a and 1L45a were printed on unwatermarked paper.

Flag Over Waves — A20

1949, July 20   Imperf.
1L46	A20	100s car rose		8.50	9.00
a.		Perf 11		200.00	350.00
1L47	A20	150s car rose		10.00	22.00
a.		Perf 11		62.50	225.00

Return of the Indonesian government to Jakarta.

Nos. 1L46-1L47 were printed on paper bearing papermaker's watermark "MADE IN U.S.A." once in each sheet, and a few stamps within each sheet bear portions of the watermark.

Nos. 1L46a, 1L47a overprinted in Black — No. A49

1949, Dec. 27   Perf. 11
1L48	A20	100s car rose		22.50	
1L49	A20	150s car rose		25.00	100.00

Return of the Indonesian government to Jakarta.

POSTAGE DUE STAMPS

Netherlands Indies Nos. J29, J32a Overprinted — No. AJ1

1948   Perf. 12½
1LJ1	D5	25s on 7½c salmon		50.00	50.00
1LJ2	D5	25s on 15c salmon		60.00	75.00

MILITARY STAMP

1949, Aug.   Without Gum   Imperf.
1LM1	M1	15r ultramarine		4,250.	5,250.

No. 1LM1 was issued for provisional use at Surakarta, a Dutch stronghold in central Java, occupied by Indonesian forces in August, 1949.

SUMATRA ISSUES

Netherlands Indies Nos. 231, 201 Overprinted in Black

1946
2L1	A26	15s on 5c blue		1.25	1.75
2L2	A17	40s on 2c plum		.80	2.00

Netherlands Indies Nos. 164//203 Overprinted

Overprint Bar is 5mm's thick.

1946
2L3	A17	20s on 3½c dk gray		32.50	40.00
2L4	A17	30s on 1c lilac gray		16.00	16.00
2L5	A17	40s on 2c plum		1.50	1.50
2L6	A17	60s on 2½c bister		200.00	250.00
2L7	A17	80s on 3c yel grn		16.50	20.00
		Nos. 2L3-2L7 (5)		266.50	327.50

Some examples of Nos. 2L3-2L7 bear handstamps previously applied by local authorities during and after the Japanese occupation. Such multiply-overprinted stamps command prices that may be more or less than the values shown, which are for examples without other overprints.

Netherlands Indies Nos. 234, 236 Overprinted

1946
2L8	A28	50s on 17½c orange		100.00	100.00
2L9	A28	1r on 10c red org		22.50	25.00

Nos. 2L10-2L84 were issued without gum.

Farmer & Oxen in Rice Paddy A23

Sentry & Flag A24

Airplane over City — A25

1946, May 17   Perf. 11½x10
2L10	A23	5s (+25s) yel grn		1.25	2.25
2L11	A24	15s (+35s) deep red		2.50	4.00
2L12	A25	40s (+60s) orange		1.25	2.50
		Nos. 2L10-2L12 (3)		5.00	8.75

Nos. 2L10-2L12 were sold at a premium over face value, not indicated on the stamps themselves, to benefit the Freedom Fund ("Fonds Kemerdekkan").

Pres. Soekarno — A26

1946, June 1   Perf. 10¾
2L13	A26	40s (+60s) red		1.25	2.00
2L14	A26	40s (+60s) deep red		15.00	15.00

Nos. 2L13-2L14 were sold at a premium over face value, not indicated on the stamps themselves, to benefit the Freedom Fund ("Fonds Kemerdekkan").

As Nos. 2L10-2L12, in different colors on thicker paper

1946, Aug. 17   Perf. 11½x10
2L15	A23	5s (+25s) turquoise		1.75	3.00
2L16	A24	15s (+35s) purple		1.75	3.00
2L17	A25	40s (+60s) deep red		9.00	9.00
2L18	A25	40s (+60s) bister		17.50	30.00
		Nos. 2L15-2L18 (4)		30.00	45.00

Nos. 2L15-2L18 were sold at a premium over face value, not indicated on the stamps themselves, to benefit the Freedom Fund ("Fonds Kemerdekkan").

Nos. 2L15-2L17, One- or two-bar Overprint

1946   Perf. 11½x10¾
2L19	A23	5s turquoise		80.00	125.00
2L20	A24	15s purple		80.00	125.00
2L21	A25	40s deep red		75.00	110.00
		Nos. 2L19-2L21 (3)		235.00	360.00

INDONESIA

Farmer & Oxen in Rice Paddy — A26a

Sentry & Flag — A26b

Airplane over City — A26c

First Issue
1946-47   Perf. 11¾x10½
2L22	A26a	2s red	1.50	4.00
2L23	A26a	3s green	2.25	10.00
2L24	A26a	5s turquoise	.65	8.00
2L25	A26b	15s purple	.75	3.50
2L26	A26c	40s brown	1.00	35.00
		Nos. 2L22-2L26 (5)	6.15	60.50

Second Issue
2L27	A26a	2s chocolate	5.00	7.50
2L28	A26a	3s orange	6.50	5.00
2L29	A26b	15s green	7.00	7.50
2L30	A26c	40s blue	30.00	50.00
		Nos. 2L27-2L30 (4)	48.50	70.00

Japanese Occupation of Sumatra Revenue Stamps Overprinted

1947, May 12   *Various Rough Perfs*
2L31	A27	50s light red	50.00	75.00
2L32	A27	1f light red	45.00	60.00
2L33	A27	2f light red	35.00	60.00
2L34	A27	2.50f light red	30.00	30.00
		Nos. 2L31-2L34 (4)	160.00	225.00

No. 2L13 Surcharged

1947, May 12
2L35	A26	50s on 40s red	10.00	10.00
2L36	A26	1f on 40s red	18.50	15.00
2L37	A26	1.50f on 40s red	12.00	10.00
2L38	A26	2.50f on 40s red	1.75	5.00
2L39	A26	3.50f on 40s red	2.50	6.00
2L40	A26	5f on 40s red	2.00	4.00
		Nos. 2L35-2L40 (6)	46.75	51.00

Nos. 2L24, 2L26 Srchd. With Small Ornament Covering Original Value

1947
2L41	A26a	50s on 5s turq	15.00	15.00
2L42	A26a	1f on 5s turq	15.00	15.00
2L43	A26a	1.50f on 5s turq	18.00	15.00
2L44	A26c	1r on 40s purple	1.50	3.00
2L45	A26a	2r on 5s turq	2.25	4.00
		Nos. 2L41-2L45 (5)	51.75	52.00

The tail of the surcharged "5" ends in a ball on No. 2L41. Compare with No. 2L65.

Types A26a-A26b Srchd., in Black or Red (R), with Large Ornament covering Original Value

1947
2L46	A26b	1s on 15s vio (R)	1.25	3.50
2L47	A26a	5s on 3s sl bl (R)	1.00	3.00
2L48	A26b	10s on 15s orange	1.25	2.50
2L49	A26a	50s on 3s br red	35.00	42.50
		Nos. 2L46-2L49 (4)	38.50	51.50

Nos. 2L48 and 2L49 were not issued without ovpt.

No. 2L15 Surcharged

1947
2L50	A25	30s on 40s dp red	1.50	2.00
2L51	A25	50s on 40s dp red	25.00	40.00
2L52	A25	1f on 40s dp red	5.00	4.00
2L53	A25	1.50f on 40s dp red	7.50	10.00
2L54	A25	2.50f on 40s dp red	1.50	2.50
		Nos. 2L50-2L54 (5)	40.50	58.50

Nos. 2L23-2L26, Srchd. in Black or Red, New Value 2.8mm High

1948
2L55	A26a	.50f on 5s turq	1,200.	1,000.
2L56	A26b	.50f on 15s pur	1,200.	1,000.
2L57	A26a	1f on 5s turq	200.00	175.00
2L58	A26b	1f on 15s pur	400.00	400.00
2L59	A26c	1f on 40s brn	750.00	1,250.
2L60	A26a	2.50f on 5s turq	1,250.	1,250.
2L61	A26b	2.50f on 15s pur	750.00	675.00
2L62	A26b	5f on 15s pur	1,350.	1,100.
2L63	A26c	5f on 40s brn	500.00	650.00
2L64	A26a	50s on 5s turq	1,650.	1,750.
2L65	A26b	50s on 15s pur	525.00	675.00
		Nos. 2L55-2L65 (11)	9,775.	9,925.

The tail of the surcharged "5" is plain on No. 2L64. Compare with No. 2L41.

New Currency
Values 3.2mm High

1949
2L66	A26a	2.50r on 3s grn	32.50	40.00
a.		Red overprint	35.00	50.00
2L67	A26b	5r on 15s pur	12.50	25.00
a.		Red overprint	15.00	45.00
2L68	A26a	10r on 3s grn	110.00	150.00
a.		Red overprint	125.00	160.00
		Nos. 2L66-2L68 (3)	155.00	215.00

Emergency provisional issue for Aceh Province.

Nos. 2L22, 2L23, 2L25, 2L26 Srchd. in Black or Red, New Value 4.5mm High

1949
2L69	A26a	2r on 3s grn	50.00	75.00
a.		Red overprint	55.00	80.00
2L70	A26a	2.50r on 3s grn	30.00	75.00
a.		Red overprint	32.50	80.00
2L71	A26b	5r on 15s pur	12.50	20.00
a.		Red overprint	14.00	20.00
2L72	A26a	10r on 3s grn	22.50	60.00
a.		Red overprint	25.00	70.00
2L73	A26a	20r on 2s red	400.00	500.00
a.		Red overprint	475.00	600.00
2L74	A26b	50r on 15s pur	525.00	700.00
a.		Red overprint	550.00	750.00
2L75	A26b	100r on 15s pur	225.00	225.00
a.		Red overprint	250.00	250.00
2L76	A26c	200r on 40s brn	250.00	250.00
a.		Red overprint	300.00	350.00
		Nos. 2L69-2L76 (8)	1,515.	1,905.

Nos. 2L22, 2L25, 2L26 Srchd. in Black, New Value 7.2mm High

1949
2L77	A26b	10s on 15s pur	25.00	25.00
2L78	A26b	20s on 15s pur	25.00	25.00
2L79	A26b	30s on 15s pur	22.50	20.00
2L80	A26a	1r on 2s red	100.00	200.00
2L81	A26b	1.50f on 15s pur		1,000.
2L82	A26b	2.50f on 15s pur	30.00	75.00
2L83	A26c	5r on 40s brn	375.00	250.00
		Nos. 2L77-2L83 (7)	577.50	1,595.

Nos. 1L46-1L47 Surcharged

1949
2L84	A20	15r on 100s car rose	40.00	100.00
2L85	A20	15r on 150s car rose	45.00	100.00

AIR POST STAMPS

Nos. 66, 75 Overprinted

1947
2LC1	A26	10r on 40s br red	5.00	12.50
2LC2	A26	20r on 5s turq	4.00	10.00

REPUBLIC OF INDONESIA

Nos. 1-119, C1-C61, CE1-CE4, CO1-CO16, E1-E1G, J1-J39 and O1-O24 were authorized by the Indonesia PTT and were produced in Vienna and Philadelphia. Because most were printed by the Austrian State Printing Office (Staatsdruckerei), they are usually described as the "Vienna" issues. The first issue was released in Dec. 1948, but supplies did not reach republican-held areas of Java and Sumatra until mid-Jan., 1949. Through 1949, small supplies of these issues were sent to some 20 post offices in Java and Sumatra, where they were used both for local mail and for mail to foreign destinations, which was carried through the Dutch blockade by overseas (largely Indian) air carriers.

Following independence, the Vienna issues continued to be valid for postage for several years. While most covers on the market are philatelic in nature, commercial covers dated 1949-53 exist.

The Vienna issues were produced and heavily marketed by a U.S. stamp dealer. Proofs, deluxe sheetlets of one, and various overprints exist for these issues, as well as several unissued sets.

Values for the Vienna Issues are for mint never hinged stamps. Hinged examples are generally offered at 50-75% of these values. Used stamps are scarce, though generally not rare, and pricing information on values for used stamps is not presently available.

Map, Indonesian Archipelago A28

Farmer A29

Red Cross Airplane — A30

Balinese Dancer — A31

Military Officer, Flag of Republic — A32

Designs: 1s, Map of Indonesian Archipelago. 2s, Republican sentry and Toba Lake, Sumatra. 2½, Military review, Gen. Soedirmari. 3s, Farmer working field with pitchfork. 3½s, Sultan Sjahrir and Thomas Jefferson. 4s, Buffalo Canyon, Sumatra. 5s, Policemen on motorcycles, Sastroamidjojo. 7½s, Red Cross nurse with wounded soldier. 10s, Dr. Maramis, Minister of Finance, and Alexander Hamilton. 15s, Construction of Great Postal Road, Java. 17½s, Hadji Agoes Salim, philosopher, and Benjamin Franklin. 20s, Red Cross Boeing aircraft. 30s, Djanger dancer, Bali. 35s, Planting rice. 40s, Vice Pres. Mohammed Hatta and Abraham Lincoln. 50s, Mountain, Sumatra. 60s, Rice fields, Java. 80s, Boy holding pineapple. 1r, Pres. Soekarno and George Washington. 2r, Mosque, Medan, Sumatra. 2½r, Fish ponds, Tjipanas. 5r, Officer presenting flag. 10r, Vice Pres. Hatta. 25r, Pres. Soekarno.

Perf. 14x13¾, 13¼x14 (#6), 13½x14¼ (#12, 14-16, 19, 20), 14¼x13½ (#13, 17, 17, 21), 12½ (#22-24)

Photo, Engr. (#22-24)

1948, Dec. 15   Unwmk.
1	A28	1s dk turq grn & brn	.50	—
2	A28	2s dp brn & dp blue	.25	—
3	A28	2½s dk brn & org red	.35	—
4	A29	3s dk lil & dp red brn	.25	—
5	A28	3½s dk bl vio & br grn	.25	—
6	A29	4s dk bl vio & dp ol grn	.40	—
7	A28	5s turq & dull blue	.25	—
8	A28	7½s dp brn & dk lil	.35	—
9	A28	10s dp blue & brn rose	.50	—
10	A28	15s brown & dk grn	.75	—
11	A28	17½s ultra & org brn	.30	—
12	A30	20s Prus grn & dp bis brn	.45	—
13	A31	30s dk brn & dull vio	.30	—
14	A30	35s dk lilac & brn	.30	—
15	A30	40s dk brn & blue	.30	—
16	A30	50s dk brn & turq	.30	—
17	A31	60s dk brn & lt red brn	.50	—
18	A31	80s dk lilac & slate	.45	—
19	A30	1r bl blue & pur brn	.35	—
20	A30	2r dk brn & dk grn	.55	—
21	A31	2½r dk lilac & blue	.65	—
22	A32	5r yel brn & black	5.00	—
23	A32	10r emerald & black	7.50	—
24	A32	25r rose red & blk	12.50	—
		Nos. 1-24 (24)	33.30	

See Nos. C1-C13.
For overprints, see Nos. 70-90, O1-O6.

A33

Designs: 10s, 25s, Map, ships. 15s, 60s, Dockworkers loading ship, vert. 1r, Ships.

1949, Aug. 17   Photo.   Perf. 12½
25	A33	10s gray & green	1.00	—
26	A33	15s gray & maroon	1.00	—
27	A33	25s gray & blue	1.00	—
28	A33	60s maroon & gray	5.00	—
29	A33	1r org & dull blue	14.00	—
		Nos. 25-29 (5)	22.00	

Failure of Dutch blockade.
See Nos. C14-C18.

Sentry A34

Soekarno Decorating Soldier A35

Planting Rice A36

Boy Holding Pineapple A37

INDONESIA

Military Officer, Flag of Republic — A38

Designs: 1s, Republican sentry and Toba Lake, Sumatra. 2s, Soekarno decorating soldier. 2½s, Woman weaving batik. 3s, Metalcraft worker. 3½s, Construction of Great Postal Road, Java. 4s, Farmer working field with pitchfork. 5s, Javanese Wajang Wong dancer. 7½s, Planting rice on the sawah. 10s, Red Cross nurse with wounded soldier. 15s, Buffalo Canyon, Sumatra. 17½s, Plowing with oxen. 20s, Planting rice. 30s, Mountain, Sumatra. 35s, Boy holding pineapple. 40s, Fish ponds, Tjipanas. 50s, Djanger dancer, Bali. 60s, Javanese Serimpi court dancer. 80s, Mosque, Medan, Sumatra. 1r, Overcoming illiteracy. 2r, Idol. 2½r, Map of Indonesian Archipelago. 5r, Officer presenting flag. 10r, Vice Pres. Mohammed Hatta. 25r, Pres. Soekarno.

Country name inscription has been changed from "Repoeblik" to "Republik," to make spelling more American and less Dutch. This spelling change also officially changed Pres. Soekarno's name to Sukarno.

Perf. 14x13¾, 13¾x14 (#31-33, 35, 36, 39), 13½x14¼ (#41, 42, 47, 50), 14¼x13½ (#43-46), 12½ (#51-53)

Photo, Engr. (#51-53)

1949, Aug. 17

30	A34	1s dp brn & dp blue	.30	—
31	A35	2s dk red vio & dp grn	.40	—
32	A35	2½s dk brn & br scarlet	.35	—
33	A35	3s dp turq & org ver	.45	—
34	A35	3½s dp brn & dp grn	.40	—
35	A35	4s turq & dull blue	.50	—
36	A35	5s dull vio & dk yel brn	.35	—
37	A34	7½s dp brn & dk lil	.40	—
38	A34	10s dk brn & dp vio	.50	—
39	A35	15s dk vio & dp dull grn	1.00	—
40	A34	17½s dk brn & red org	.75	—
41	A36	20s dull vio & dp brn	.25	—
42	A36	30s dp brn & dk blue vio	.60	—
43	A37	35s sl vio & blue	.25	—
44	A37	40s dull vio & dk yel brn	.45	—
45	A37	50s dk brn & Prus grn	.40	—
46	A37	60s br blue & dk yel brn	.75	—
47	A36	80s dull vio & dull bl	.75	—
48	A36	1r dp blue & dp choc	.50	—
49	A37	2r dp brn & org ver	.30	—
50	A36	2½r dp brn & br blue	1.50	—
51	A38	5r red vio & black	10.00	—
52	A38	10r green & black	6.00	—
53	A38	25r orange & black	10.00	—
		Nos. 30-53 (24)	37.15	

For overprints, see Nos. 91-111, O7-O12.

A39

A40

Designs: 10s, 25s, Map, ships. 15s, 60s, Dockworkers loading ship, vert. 1r, Ships.

1948, Dec. 15   Photo.   Perf. 14½

54	A39	10s gray & red	2.00	—
55	A39	15s gray & dp blue	2.00	—
56	A39	25s gray & red brn	1.45	—
57	A39	60s gray & maroon	2.50	—
58	A39	1r gray & maroon	7.50	—
		Nos. 54-58 (5)	15.45	

Souvenir Sheets

59	A40	10s, 15s, 25s, 60s	100.00	
a.		Imperf	450.00	
60	A40	30s, 50s, 1r, 2½r	45.00	—
a.		Imperf	250.00	
b.		A39 2½r gray & maroon	—	
c.		As "b," imperf	—	
61	A40	1r, 4½r	75.00	—
a.		Imperf	100.00	
b.		A39 4½r maroon	—	
c.		As "b," imperf	—	

Failure of Dutch blockade, second issue.

The stamps contained in No. 60 and the 4½r stamp contained in No. 61 are air post stamps and are inscribed "POS UDARA."

See Nos. C32-C36.

For overprints, see Nos. 112-119.

Map, UPU Emblem & *Banteng* (Nationalist Symbol) — A41

Wmk. 404

1949, Dec. 1   Photo.   Perf. 14

62	A41	10s multicolored	.55	—
a.		Imperf	.60	
63	A41	20s multicolored	.55	—
a.		Imperf	.60	
64	A41	50s multicolored	.60	—
a.		Imperf	.70	
65	A41	1r multicolored	.60	—
a.		Imperf	1.00	
b.		Souvenir Sheet of 4, #62-65	30.00	
c.		As "b," imperf	35.00	
		Nos. 62-65 (4)	2.30	

Unwatermarked

66	A41	10s multicolored	.45	—
a.		Imperf	.45	
67	A41	20s multicolored	.45	—
a.		Imperf	.45	
68	A41	50s multicolored	.45	—
a.		Imperf	.45	
69	A41	1r multicolored	.45	—
a.		Imperf	.45	
		Nos. 66-69 (4)	1.80	

Nos. 64, 65, 68 and 69 are air post stamps and are inscribed "POS UDARA."

Souvenir sheets of 4, as No. 65c, without watermark, are proofs.

Most varieties of Nos. 1-69 exist overprinted "RIS", "RIS Merdeka" and "RIS Djakarta." These were not issued in Indonesia.

Liberation of Jakarta

Nos. 1-21 Overprinted

1949, Dec. 7

70	A28	1s dk turq grn & brn	.25	—
71	A28	2s dp brn & dp blue	1.25	—
72	A28	2½s dk brn & org red	.25	—
73	A29	3s dk lil & dp red brn	.45	—
74	A28	3½s dk bl vio & br grn	.25	—
75	A29	4s dk bl vio & dp ol grn	.75	—
76	A28	5s turq & dull blue	.25	—
77	A28	7½s dp brn & dk lil	.45	—
78	A28	10s dp blue & brn rose	.25	—
79	A28	15s brown & dk grn	1.50	—
80	A28	17½s ultra & org brn	2.50	—
81	A30	20s Prus grn & dp bis brn	1.50	—
82	A31	30s dk brn & dull vio	5.00	—
83	A30	35s dk lilac & brn	7.00	—
84	A30	40s dk brn & blue	1.00	—
85	A30	50s dk brn & turq	7.00	—
86	A31	60s dk brn & lt red brn	8.00	—
87	A31	80s dk lilac & slate	2.50	—
88	A30	1r br blue & pur brn	5.00	—
89	A30	2r dk brn & dk grn	1.50	—
90	A31	2½r dk lilac & blue	12.50	—
		Nos. 70-90 (21)	59.15	

Nos. 30-50 overprinted

91	A34	1s dp brn & blue	.25	—
92	A35	2s dk red vio & dp grn	2.00	—
93	A35	2½s dk brn & br scarlet	.25	—
94	A35	3s dp turq & org ver	.25	—
95	A34	3½s dp brn & dp grn	.25	—
96	A35	4s turq & dull blue	.25	—
97	A35	5s dull vio & dk yel brn	.50	—
98	A34	7½s dp brn & dk lil	.75	—
99	A34	10s dk brn & dp vio	.75	—
100	A35	15s dk vio & dp dull grn	1.50	—
101	A34	17½s dk brn & red org	1.50	—
102	A36	20s dull vio & dp brn	4.00	—
103	A36	30s dp brn & dk blue vio	3.50	—
104	A37	35s sl vio & blue	3.50	—
105	A37	40s dull vio & dk yel brn	3.50	—
106	A37	50s dk brn & Prus grn	5.50	—
107	A37	60s br blue & dk yel brn	5.50	—
108	A36	80s dull vio & dull bl	6.00	—
109	A36	1r dp blue & dp choc	3.00	—
110	A37	2r dp brn & org ver	3.50	—
111	A36	2½r dp brn & br blue	7.50	—
		Nos. 91-111 (21)	53.75	

Nos. 54-61 overprinted

112	A39	10s gray & red	.40	—
113	A39	15s gray & dp blue	.40	—
114	A39	25s gray & red brn	1.40	—
115	A39	60s gray & blue	1.40	—
116	A39	1r gray & maroon	3.50	—
		Nos. 112-116 (5)	7.10	

Souvenir Sheets

117	A40	10s, 15s, 25s, 60s	1,000.	
a.		Imperf	2,500.	
118	A40	30s, 50s, 1r, 2½r	125.00	
a.		Imperf	250.00	
b.		A39 2½r gray & maroon	—	
c.		As "b," imperf	—	
119	A40	1r, 4½r	50.00	—
a.		Imperf	125.00	
b.		A39 4½r maroon	—	

The stamps contained in No. 118 and the 4½r stamp contained in No. 119 are air post stamps and are inscribed "POS UDARA."

United States of Indonesia

Mountain, Palms and Flag of Republic — A49

Perf. 12½x12

1950, Jan. 17   Photo.   Unwmk.
Size: 20½x26mm

| 333 | A49 | 15s red | 1.25 | .30 |

Exists imperf, without gum. Value $70.

1950, June   Perf. 11½
Size: 18x23mm

| 334 | A49 | 15s red | 6.25 | 1.25 |

Exists imperf, without gum. Value $50.

Netherlands Indies Nos. 307-315 Overprinted in Black

1950   Perf. 11½, 12½

335	A42	1s gray	1.00	.80
336	A42	2s claret	1.40	3.50
a.		Perf 11½	1.60	2.00
337	A42	2½s olive brown	1.00	.70
a.		Perf 12½	1.40	.70
338	A42	3s rose pink	1.00	.60
a.		Perf 12½	.90	.45
339	A42	4s green	1.00	.75
a.		Perf 12½	1.60	1.00
340	A42	5s blue	1.00	.75
341	A42	7½s dark green	1.00	.75
342	A42	10s violet	1.00	.75
a.		Perf 12½	1.60	1.60
343	A42	12½s bright red	1.10	.75

Netherlands Indies Nos. 317-330 Overprinted in Black

Perf. 11½, 12½

345	A43	20s gray black	25.00	32.50
346	A43	25s ultra	.85	.75
a.		Perf 12½	1.40	.75
347	A44	30s bright red	8.50	20.00
a.		Perf 12½	45.00	65.00
348	A44	40s gray green	1.00	.45
a.		Perf 12½	1.00	.45
349	A44	45s claret	1.80	1.10
350	A44	50s orange brown	1.50	1.00
351	A45	60s brown	7.25	12.50
a.		Perf 12½		35.00
352	A45	80s scarlet	3.50	1.20
a.		Perf 12½	2.90	1.00

Perf. 11½, 20s, 45s, 50s. Others, both perfs.

Overprint 12mm High

Perf. 12½

353	A46	1r purple	2.10	.50
354	A46	2r olive green	360.00	100.00
355	A46	3r red violet	130.00	65.00
356	A46	5r dark brown	55.00	19.00
357	A46	10r gray	95.00	45.00
358	A46	25r orange brown	22.50	16.00
		Nos. 335-358 (23)	723.50	324.40
		Set, hinged	325.00	

For overprints see Riau Archipelago Nos. 17-22.

Republic of Indonesia

Arms of the Republic — A50

Perf. 12½x12

1950, Aug. 17   Photo.   Unwmk.

359	A50	15s red	1.75	.30
360	A50	25s dull green	2.75	1.60
361	A50	1r sepia	9.00	2.25
		Nos. 359-361 (3)	13.50	4.15

5th anniv. of Indonesia's proclamation of independence.

Doves in Flight — A51

1951, Oct. 24   Engr.   Perf. 12

362	A51	7½s blue green	2.75	1.00
363	A51	10s violet	.85	.45
364	A51	20s red	1.75	1.00
365	A51	30s carmine rose	2.75	1.25
366	A51	35s ultra	2.75	1.25
367	A51	1r sepia	17.00	4.00
		Nos. 362-367 (6)	27.85	8.95

6th anniv. of the UN and the 1st anniv. of the Republic of Indonesia as a member.

A52

Post Office — A53

Mythological Hero — A54

Pres. Sukarno — A55

INDONESIA

1951-53 Photo. Perf. 12½

368	A52	1s gray	.45	.90
369	A52	2s plum	.45	.80
370	A52	2½s brown	6.50	.25
371	A52	5s car rose	.45	.25
372	A52	7½s green	.45	.25
373	A52	10s blue	.50	.25
a.		Perf 11½	8.75	8.75
374	A52	15s purple	.50	.25
375	A52	20s rose red	.50	.25
376	A52	25s deep green	.50	.25
377	A53	30s red orange	.25	.25
378	A53	35s purple	.40	.25
379	A53	40s dull green	.25	.25
380	A53	45s deep claret	2.50	.30
381	A53	50s brown	2.50	.25
382	A54	60s dark brown	.25	.25
383	A54	70s gray	.25	.25
384	A54	75s ultra	.25	.25
385	A54	80s claret	.25	.25
386	A54	90s gray green	.25	.25
		Nos. 368-386 (19)	15.20	6.00

Perf. 12½x12

387	A55	1r purple	.30	.25
388	A55	1.25r dp orange	1.25	.25
389	A55	1.50r brown	.30	.25
390	A55	2r green	.30	.25
391	A55	2.50r rose brown	.30	.25
392	A55	3r blue	.30	.25
392A	A55	4r apple green	.30	.25
393	A55	5r brown	.30	.25
394	A55	6r rose lilac	.30	.25
395	A55	10r slate	.30	.25
396	A55	15r yellow	.30	.25
397	A55	20r sepia	.30	.25
398	A55	25r scarlet	.80	.25
399	A55	40r yellow green	.80	2.75
400	A55	50r violet	1.20	.25
		Nos. 387-400 (15)	7.35	6.25

Nos. 368-376, 387, 390, 392, 393, 395, 398 were issued in 1951; Nos. 377-386, 388-389, 391, 392A, 394, 396-397, 399-400 in 1953.

Values are for the later Djakarta printings which have thicker numerals and a darker over-all impression. An earlier printing by Joh. Enschede and Sons, Haarlem, Netherlands, sell for more. The Enschede printing is on thicker paper and has more contrast between the portrait and the background.

For surcharge see No. B68. For overprints see Riau Archipelago Nos. 1-16, 32-40.

Melati Flowers — A56

1953, Dec. 22 Perf. 12½

401	A56	50s blue green	9.00	.70

25th anniv. of the formation of the Indonesian Women's Congress.

Crowd Releasing Doves — A57

1955, Apr. 18 Perf. 13x12½

402	A57	15s gray	.40	.75
403	A57	35s brown	.65	.75
404	A57	50s deep magenta	1.75	.75
405	A57	75s blue green	1.25	.75
		Nos. 402-405 (4)	4.05	3.00

Asian-African Conf., Bandung, April 18-24.

Proclamation of Independence — A58

1955, Aug. 17 Photo. Perf. 12½

406	A58	15s green	.75	.90
407	A58	35s ultra	.75	.90
408	A58	50s brown	4.50	.55
409	A58	75s magenta	.80	.80
		Nos. 406-409 (4)	6.80	3.15

Ten years of independence.

Voters — A59

1955, Sept. 29 Perf. 12

Without gum

410	A59	15s rose violet	.60	.75
411	A59	35s green	.60	.75
412	A59	50s carmine rose	2.10	.50
413	A59	75s lt ultra	.85	.65
		Nos. 410-413 (4)	4.15	2.65

First free elections in Indonesia.

Mas Soeharto Postmaster General — A60

1955, Sept. 27 Perf. 12½

414	A60	15s brown	.80	.75
415	A60	35s dark carmine	.80	.75
416	A60	50s ultra	5.00	2.00
417	A60	75s dull green	2.00	.75
		Nos. 414-417 (4)	8.60	4.25

Issued to mark 10 years of Indonesia's Postal, Telegraph and Telephone system.

Helmet, Wreath and Monument — A61

1955, Nov. 10

418	A61	25s bluish green	.40	.30
419	A61	50s ultra	1.25	.70
420	A61	1r dk car rose	8.00	.30
		Nos. 418-420 (3)	9.65	1.30

Issued in honor of the soldiers killed in the war of liberation from the Netherlands.

Torch, Book and Map — A62

1956, May 26 Photo.

421	A62	25s ultra	.90	.30
422	A62	50s carmine rose	4.50	1.25
423	A62	1r dark green	1.75	1.25
		Nos. 421-423 (3)	7.15	2.80

Asia-Africa Student Conf., Bandung, May, 1956.

Lesser Malay Chevrotain — A63

1956 Unwmk. Perf. 12½x13½

424	A63	5s deep ultra	.25	.25
425	A63	10s yellow brown	.25	.25
426	A63	15s rose violet	.25	.25
427	A63	20s dull green	.25	.25
428	A63	25s deep claret	.25	.25
429	A63	35s brt violet blue	.25	.25
430	A63	50s brown	.25	.25
431	A63	75s dark brown	.25	.25
		Nos. 424-431 (8)	2.00	2.00

See Nos. 450-456. For overprints see Riau Archipelago Nos. 23-31.

Dancing Girl and Gate — A64

1956, Oct. 7 Perf. 12½x12

432	A64	15s slate green	.50	.60
433	A64	35s brown violet	1.25	.60
434	A64	50s blue black	2.00	1.10
435	A64	75s deep claret	2.50	1.10
		Nos. 432-435 (4)	6.25	3.40

Founding of the city of Jogjakarta, 200th anniv.

Telegraph Key — A65

1957, May 10 Unwmk.

436	A65	10s lt crimson	2.00	.60
437	A65	15s brt blue	.50	.30
438	A65	25s gray	.40	.25
439	A65	50s brown red	.50	.30
440	A65	75s lt blue green	.50	.25
		Nos. 436-440 (5)	3.90	1.70

Indonesian telegraph system centenary.

Thrift Symbolism — A66

Design: 15s, 1r, People and hands holding wreath of rice and cotton.

1957, July 12 Photo. Perf. 12½

441	A66	10s blue	.45	.45
442	A66	15s rose carmine	.45	.45
443	A66	50s green	.90	.75
444	A66	1r brt violet	1.40	.25
		Nos. 441-444 (4)	3.20	1.90

Cooperation Day, July 12.

Douglas DC-3 — A67

Aircraft: 15s, Helicopter. 30s, Miles Magister. 50s, Two-motor plane of Indonesian Airways. 75s, De Havilland Vampire.

1958, Apr. 9 Perf. 12½x12

445	A67	10s reddish brown	.25	.25
446	A67	15s blue	.25	.25
447	A67	35s orange	.25	.25
448	A67	50s bright green	.45	.40
449	A67	75s gray	.80	.40
		Nos. 445-449 (5)	2.00	1.55

Issued for National Aviation Day, April 9.

Animal Type of 1956

Animals: 30s, Otter. 40s, 45s, Malayan pangolin. 60s, 70s, Banteng. 80s, 90s, Asiatic two-horned rhinoceros.

1958 Photo. Perf. 12½x13½

450	A63	30s orange	.25	.25
451	A63	40s brt yellow grn	.25	.25
452	A63	45s rose lilac	1.00	.25
453	A63	60s dark blue	.25	.25
454	A63	70s orange ver	1.75	.30
455	A63	80s red	.30	.25
456	A63	90s yellow green	.30	.25
		Nos. 450-456 (7)	4.10	1.80

Thomas Cup — A68

1958, Aug. 15 Perf. 13½x13

457	A68	25s rose carmine	.25	.25
458	A68	50s orange	.25	.25
459	A68	1r brown	.30	.25
		Nos. 457-459 (3)	.80	.75

Indonesia's victory in the 1958 Thomas Cup World Badminton Championship.

Satellite Circling Globe — A69

1958, Oct. 15 Litho. Perf. 12½x12

460	A69	10s dk grn, pink & lt bl	.85	.60
461	A69	15s vio, gray & pale bluish grn	.25	.25
462	A69	35s brown, blue & pink	.25	.25
463	A69	50s bl, redsh brn & gray	.25	.25
464	A69	75s black, vio & buff	.25	.25
		Nos. 460-464 (5)	1.85	1.60

International Geophysical Year, 1957-58.

Bicyclist and Map — A70

1958, Nov. 15 Photo. Perf. 13½x13

465	A70	25s bright blue	.45	.30
466	A70	50s brown carmine	.60	.30
467	A70	1r gray	.35	.30
		Nos. 465-467 (3)	1.40	.90

Bicycle Tour of Java, Aug. 15-30.

Man Looking into Light — A71

Designs: 15s, Hands and flame. 35s, Woman holding candle. 50s, Family hailing torch. 75s, Torch and "10."

1958, Dec. 10 Perf. 12½x12

468	A71	10s gray brown	.25	.25
469	A71	15s dull red brn	.25	.25
470	A71	35s ultra	.25	.25
471	A71	50s pale brown	.25	.25
472	A71	75s lt blue grn	.25	.25
		Nos. 468-472 (5)	1.25	1.25

10th anniv. of the signing of the Universal Declaration of Human Rights.

Wild Boar (Babirusa) — A72

Animals: 15s, Anoa (smallest buffalo). 20s, Orangutan. 50s, Javan rhinoceros. 75s, Komodo dragon (lizard). 1r, Malayan tapir.

1959, June 1 Photo. Perf. 12

473	A72	10s olive bis & sepia	.25	.25
474	A72	15s org brn & sepia	.25	.25
475	A72	20s lt ol grn & sepia	.30	.30
476	A72	50s bister brn & sepia	.45	.45
477	A72	75s dp rose & sepia	.45	.25
478	A72	1r blue grn & blk	.55	.25
		Nos. 473-478 (6)	2.25	1.75

Issued to publicize wildlife preservation.

A73

1959, Aug. 17 Litho. Perf. 12

479	A73	20s blue & red	.25	.25
480	A73	50s rose red & blk	.25	.25
481	A73	75s brown & red	.25	.25
482	A73	1.50r lt green & blk	.25	.25
		Nos. 479-482 (4)	1.00	1.00

Introduction of the constitution of 1945 embodying "guided democracy."

Factories — A74

Designs: 20s, 75s, Cogwheel and train. 1.15r, Means of transportation.

1959, Oct. 26 Photo. Perf. 12

483	A74	15s brt green & blk	.25	.25
484	A74	20s dull org & blk	.25	.25
485	A74	50s red & black	.25	.25
486	A74	75s brt grnsh bl & blk	.25	.25
487	A74	1.15r magenta & blk	.25	.25
		Nos. 483-487 (5)	1.25	1.25

11th Colombo Plan Conference, Jakarta.

INDONESIA

Mother & Child, WRY Emblem — A75

15s, 75s, Destroyed town & fleeing family. 20s, 1.15r, World Refugee Year emblem.

1960, Apr. 7		**Unwmk.**	**Perf. 12½x12**	
488	A75	10s claret & blk	.25	.25
489	A75	15s bister & blk	.25	.25
490	A75	20s org brn & blk	.25	.25
491	A75	50s green & blk	.25	.25
492	A75	75s dk blue & blk	.25	.25
493	A75	1.15r scarlet & blk	.25	1.10
		Nos. 488-493 (6)	1.50	2.35

World Refugee Year, 7/1/59-6/3/60.

Tea Plantation — A76

5s, Oil palms. 10s, Sugar cane and railroad. 15s, Coffee. 20s, Tobacco. 50s, Coconut palms. 75s, Rubber plantation. 1.15r, Rice.

1960			**Perf. 12x12½**	
494	A76	5s gray	.25	.25
495	A76	10s red brown	.25	.25
496	A76	15s plum	.25	.25
497	A76	20s ocher	.25	.25
498	A76	25s brt blue grn	.25	.25
499	A76	50s deep blue	.25	.25
500	A76	75s scarlet	.25	.25
501	A76	1.15r plum	.25	.25
		Nos. 494-501 (8)	2.00	2.00

For surcharges see Nos. B132-B134.

Anopheles Mosquito — A77

1960, Nov. 12		**Photo.**	**Perf. 12x12½**	
502	A77	25s carmine rose	.25	.25
503	A77	50s orange brown	.25	.25
504	A77	75s brt green	.25	.25
505	A77	3r orange	.30	.30
		Nos. 502-505 (4)	1.05	1.05

World Health Day, Nov. 12, 1960, and to promote malaria control.

Pres. Sukarno with Hoe — A78

1961, Feb. 15			**Perf. 12½x12**	
506	A78	75s gray	.70	.25

Planned National Development.

Dayak Dancer of Borneo — A79

Designs: 10s, Ambonese boat. 15s, Tangkubanperahu crater. 20s, Bull races. 50s, Toradja houses. 75s, Balinese temple. 1r, Lake Toba. 1.50r, Balinese dancer and musicians. 2r, Buffalo hole, view. 3r, Borobudur Temple, Java.

1961			**Perf. 13½x13**	
507	A79	10s rose lilac	.50	.55
508	A79	15s gray	.50	.55
509	A79	20s orange	.50	.55
510	A79	25s orange ver	.50	.55
511	A79	50s carmine rose	.50	.55
512	A79	75s red brown	.50	.55
513	A79	1r brt green	.90	.45
514	A79	1.50r bister brn	.90	.45
515	A79	2r grnsh blue	1.40	.45
516	A79	3r gray	1.40	.45
		Set of 4 souvenir sheets	24.00	22.50
		Nos. 507-516 (10)	7.60	5.10

Issued for tourist publicity.

The four souvenir sheets among them contain one each of Nos. 507-516 imperf., with two or three stamps to a sheet and English marginal inscriptions: "Visit Indonesia" and "Visit the Orient Year." Size: 139x105mm or 105x139mm.

Sports Hall and Thomas Cup — A80

1961, June 1		**Photo.**	**Perf. 13½x12½**	
517	A80	75s pale violet & blue	.25	.25
518	A80	1r citron & yel	.25	.25
519	A80	3r salmon pink & dk bl	.30	.25
		Nos. 517-519 (3)	.80	.75

1961 Thomas Cup World Badminton Championship.

New Buildings and Workers — A81

1961, July 6			**Unwmk.**	
520	A81	75s violet & grnsh bl	.25	.25
521	A81	1.50r emerald & buff	.25	.25
522	A81	3r dk red & salmon	.40	.25
		Nos. 520-522 (3)	.90	.75

16th anniversary of independence.

Sultan Hasanuddin A82

Portraits: 20s, Abdul Muis. 30s, Surjopranoto. 40s, Tengku Tjhik Di Tiro. 50s, Teuku Umar. 60s, K. H. Samanhudi. 75s, Captain Pattimura. 1r, Raden Adjeng Kartini. 1.25r, K. H. Achmad Dahlan. 1.50r, Tuanku Imam Bondjol. 2r, Si Singamangaradja XII. 2.50r, Mohammad Husni Thamrin. 3r, Ki Hadjar Dewantoro. 4r, Djenderal Sudirman. 4.50r, Dr. G. S. S. J. Ratulangie. 5r, Pangeran Diponegoro. 6r, Dr. Setyabudi. 7.50r, H. O. S. Tjokroaminoto. 10r, K. H. Agus Salim. 15r, Dr. Soetomo.

		Perf. 13½x12½		
1961-62		**Unwmk.**	**Photo.**	
		Black Inscriptions; Portraits in Sepia		
523	A82	20s olive	.25	.30
524	A82	25s gray olive	.25	.30
525	A82	30s brt lilac	.25	.30
526	A82	40s brown orange	.25	.30
527	A82	50s bluish green	.25	.30
528	A82	60s green ('62)	.25	.30
529	A82	75s lt red brown	.25	.30
530	A82	1r lt blue	.90	.30
531	A82	1.25r lt ol grn ('62)	.60	.30
532	A82	1.50r emerald	.90	.30
533	A82	2r org red ('62)	.60	.30
534	A82	2.50r rose claret	.90	.30
535	A82	3r gray blue	.75	.30
536	A82	4r olive green	.75	.30
537	A82	4.50r red lilac ('62)	.35	.30
538	A82	5r brick red	.85	.30
539	A82	6r bister ('62)	.75	.30
540	A82	7.50r violet bl ('62)	.85	.30
541	A82	10r green ('62)	1.25	.30
542	A82	15r dp org ('62)	.60	.30
		Nos. 523-542 (20)	11.80	6.00

National heroes. The 25s, 75s, 1.50r, 5r issued on 8/17, Independence Day; 40s, 50s, 4r on 10/5, Army Day; 20s, 30s, 1r, 2.50r, 3r on 11/10, Republic Day; 60s, 2r, 7.50r, 15r on 10/5/62; 1.25r, 4.50r, 6r, 10r on 11/10/62.

Symbols of Census — A83

1961, Sept. 15			**Perf. 13½x12½**	
543	A83	75s rose violet	.60	.25

First census in Indonesia.

Djataju — A84

Scenes from Ramayana Ballet: 40s, Hanuman. 1r, Dasamuka. 1.50r, Kidang Kentiana. 3r, Dewi Sinta. 5r, Rama.

			Perf. 12x12½	
1962, Jan. 15			**Unwmk.**	
544	A84	30s ocher & red brn	.35	.45
545	A84	40s rose lilac & vio	.35	.45
546	A84	1r green & claret	.45	.45
547	A84	1.50r sal pink & dk grn	.55	.45
548	A84	3r pale grn & dp bl	1.10	.45
549	A84	5r brn org & dk brn	1.40	.45
		Nos. 544-549 (6)	4.20	2.70

Asian Games Emblem — A85

Main Stadium A86

Designs: 10s, Basketball. 15s, Main Stadium, Jakarta. 20s, Weight lifter. 25s, Hotel Indonesia. 30s, Cloverleaf intersection. 40s, Discus thrower. 50s, Woman diver. 60s, Soccer. 70s, Press House. 75s, Boxers. 1r, Volleyball. 1.25r, 2r, 3r, 5r, Asian Games emblem. 1.50r, Badminton. 1.75r, Wrestlers. 2.50r, Woman rifle shooter. 4.50r, Hockey. 6r, Water polo. 7.50r, Tennis. 10r, Table tennis. 15r, Bicyclist. 20r, Welcome Monument.

1962		**Photo.**	**Perf. 12½**	
550	A85	10s green & yel	.25	.25
551	A86	15s grnsh blk & bis	.25	.25
552	A85	20s red lil & lt grn	.30	.25
553	A86	25s car & lt grn	.25	.25
554	A86	30s bl grn & yel	.35	.25
555	A85	40s ultra & pale bl	.35	.25
556	A85	50s choc & gray	.35	.30
557	A85	60s lil rose & vio gray	.35	.30
558	A85	70s dk brn & rose	.35	.30
559	A85	75s choc & org	.35	.25
560	A85	1r purple & lt bl	.35	.30
561	A85	1.25r dk bl & rose car	.35	.40
562	A85	1.50r red org & lil	1.25	.40
563	A85	1.75r dk car & rose	.80	.40
564	A85	2r brn & yel grn	.55	.40
565	A85	2.50r dp bl & lt grn	.70	.40
566	A85	3r black & dk red	.70	.40
567	A85	4.50r dk grn & red	.70	.40
568	A85	5r gray grn & lem	.70	.40
569	A85	6r brn red & dp yel	.75	.40
570	A85	7.50r red brn & sal	.75	.25
571	A85	10r dk blue & blue	1.00	.55
572	A85	15r dl vio & pale vio	1.25	1.10
573	A85	20r dk grn & ol bis	2.40	1.25
		Nos. 550-573 (24)	15.40	9.70

4th Asian Games, Jakarta.

Malaria Eradication Emblem — A87

1962, Apr. 7			**Perf. 12x12**	
574	A87	40s dull bl & vio bl	.25	.25
575	A87	1.50r yel org & brn	.25	.25
576	A87	3r green & indigo	.25	.25
577	A87	6r lilac & blk	.25	.25
		Nos. 574-577 (4)	1.00	1.00

WHO drive to eradicate malaria. The 1.50r and 6r have Indonesian inscription on top.

Atom Diagram — A88

1962, Sept. 24		**Photo.**	**Perf. 12x12½**	
578	A88	1.50r dk blue & yel	.25	.25
579	A88	4.50r brick red & yel	.25	.30
580	A88	6r green & yel	.30	.30
		Nos. 578-580 (3)	.80	.85

Development through science.

Pacific Travel Association Emblem — A89

1.50r, Prambanan Temple and Mount Merapi. 6r, Balinese Meru (Buildings), Pura Taman Ajun.

1963, Mar. 14			**Unwmk.**	
581	A89	1r grn & indigo	.25	.25
582	A89	1.50r olive & indigo	.25	.25
583	A89	3r ocher & indigo	.35	.25
584	A89	6r dp org & indigo	.35	.25
		Nos. 581-584 (4)	1.20	1.00

12th conf. of the Pacific Area Travel Assoc., Bandung.

Mechanized Plow — A90

1r, 3r, Hand holding rice stalks, vert.

1963, Mar. 21		**Perf. 12½x12, 12x12½**		
585	A90	1r blue & yel	.25	.25
586	A90	1.50r brt grn & indigo	.25	.25
587	A90	3r rose car & org	.25	.25
588	A90	6r orange & blk	.25	.25
		Nos. 585-588 (4)	1.00	1.00

FAO "Freedom from Hunger" campaign. English inscription on 3r and 6r.

Long-Armed Lobster A91

Fish: 1.50r, Little tuna. 3r, River roman. 6r, Chinese pompano.

1963, Apr. 6			**Perf. 12½x12**	
589	A91	1r ver, blk & yel	.25	.25
590	A91	1.50r ultra, blk & yel	.25	.25
591	A91	3r Prus bl, bis & car	.75	.40
592	A91	6r ol grn, blk & ocher	.75	.60
		Nos. 589-592 (4)	2.00	1.50

Pen and Conference Emblem A92

Designs: 1.50r, Pen, Emblem and map of Africa and Southeast Asia. 3r, Globe, pen and broken chain, vert. 6r, Globe, hand holding pen and broken chain, vert.

		Perf. 12½x12, 12x12½		
1963, Apr. 24		**Photo.**	**Unwmk.**	
593	A92	1r lt bl & dp org	.25	.25
594	A92	1.50r pale vio & mar	.25	.25
595	A92	3r bister, bl & brnsh blk	.30	.25
596	A92	6r dull ver & blk	.45	.25
		Nos. 593-596 (4)	1.25	1.00

Asian-African Journalists' Conference.

INDONESIA

"Indonesia's Flag from Sabang to Merauke" — A93

4.50r, Parachutist landing in New Guinea. 6r, Bird of paradise & map of New Guinea.

1963, May 1		Perf. 12½x12		
597	A93	1.50r org brn, blk & red	.25	.25
598	A93	4.50r multicolored	.25	.25
599	A93	6r multicolored	.65	.65
	Nos. 597-599 (3)		1.15	1.15

Issued to mark the acquisition of Netherlands New Guinea (West Irian).

Centenary Emblem — A94

Design: 1.50r, 6r, Red Cross.

1963, May 8		Perf. 12		
600	A94	1r brt grn & red	.25	.25
601	A94	1.50r lt bl & red	.25	.25
602	A94	3r gray & red	.25	.25
603	A94	6r yel bis & red	.25	.25
	Nos. 600-603 (4)		1.00	1.00

Centenary of the International Red Cross.

Bank of Indonesia, Djalan — A95

Daneswara, God of Prosperity — A96

1963, July 5		Photo.	Perf. 12	
604	A95	1.75r lt bl & pur	.25	.25
605	A96	4r citron & sl grn	.25	.25
606	A95	6r lt green & brn	.25	.25
607	A96	12r org & dk red brn	.25	.25
	Nos. 604-607 (4)		1.00	1.00

Issued for National Banking Day.

Standard Bearers — A97

Designs: 1.75r, "Pendet" dance. 4r, GANEFO building, Senajan, Jakarta. 6r, Archery. 10r, Badminton. 12r, Javelin. 25r, Sailing. 50r, Torch.

1963, Nov. 10		Unwmk.	Perf. 12½	
608	A97	1.25r gray vio & dk brn	.25	.25
609	A97	1.75r org & ol grn	.25	.25
610	A97	4r emer & dk grn	.25	.25
611	A97	6r rose brn & blk	.25	.25
612	A97	10r lt ol grn & dk brn	.25	.25
613	A97	12r rose car & grnsh blk	.30	.25
614	A97	25r blue & dk blue	.40	.40
615	A97	50r red & black	.45	.45
	Nos. 608-615 (8)		2.40	2.35

1st Games of the New Emerging Forces, GANEFO, Jakarta, Nov. 10-22.

Pres. Sukarno — A98

1964		Photo.	Perf. 12½x12	
616	A98	6r brown & dk bl	.25	.25
617	A98	12r bister & plum	.25	.25
618	A98	20r blue & org	.25	.25
619	A98	30r red org & bl	.25	.25
620	A98	40r green & brn	.25	.25
621	A98	50r red & dp grn	.25	.25
622	A98	75r vio & red org	.25	.25
623	A98	100r sil & red brn	.25	.25
624	A98	250r dk blue & sil	.25	.25
625	A98	500r red & gold	.30	.30
	Nos. 616-625 (10)		2.55	2.55

See Nos. B165-B179. For surcharges see Nos. 661, 663-667.

Trailer Truck — A99

Designs: 1r, Oxcart. 1.75r, Freighter. 2r, Lockheed Electra plane. 2.50r, Buginese sailboat, vert. 4r, Mailman with bicycle. 5r, Dakota plane. 7.50r, Teletype operator. 10r, Diesel train. 15r, Passenger ship. 25r, Convair Coronado Plane. 35r, Telephone switchboard operator.

1964		Perf. 12x12½, 12½x12		
626	A99	1r dull claret	.25	.25
627	A99	1.25r red brown	.25	.25
628	A99	1.75r Prus blue	.25	.25
629	A99	2r red orange	.25	.25
630	A99	2.50r brt blue	.25	.25
631	A99	4r bluish grn	.25	.25
632	A99	5r olive bister	.25	.25
633	A99	7.50r brt green	.25	.25
634	A99	10r orange	.25	.25
635	A99	15r dark blue	.25	.25
636	A99	25r violet blue	.25	.25
637	A99	35r red brown	.25	.25
	Nos. 626-637 (12)		3.00	3.00

For surcharges see Nos. 659-660, 662.

Ramses II — A100

Design: 6r, 18r, Kiosk of Trajan, Philae.

1964, Mar. 8		Perf. 12½x12		
638	A100	4r ol bis & ol grn	.25	.25
639	A100	6r grnsh bl & ol grn	.25	.25
640	A100	12r rose & ol grn	.30	.25
641	A100	18r emer & ol grn	.30	.25
	Nos. 638-641 (4)		1.10	1.00

UNESCO world campaign to save historic monuments in Nubia.

Stamps of Netherlands Indies and Indonesia A101

1964, Apr. 1		Perf. 12½		
642	A101	10r gold, dk bl & red org	1.00	.25

Centenary of postage stamps in Indonesia.

Indonesian Pavilion A102

1964, May 16		Perf. 12½x12		
643	A102	25r sil, blk, red & dk bl	.35	.45
644	A102	50r gold, Prus bl, red & grn	.75	.45

New York World's Fair, 1964-65.

Thomas Cup — A103

1964, Aug. 15		Perf. 12½x13½		
645	A103	25r brt grn, gold & red	.25	.25
646	A103	50r ultra, gold & red	.30	.30
647	A103	75r purple, gold & red	.45	.95
	Nos. 645-647 (3)		1.00	1.55

Thomas Cup Badminton World Championship, 1964.

Cruisers and Map of West Irian — A104

30r, Submarine. 40r, Torpedo boat.

1964, Oct. 5		Photo.	Unwmk.	
648	A104	20r yellow & brn	.30	.25
649	A104	30r rose & blk	.35	.25
650	A104	40r brt grn & ultra	.65	.95
	Nos. 648-650 (3)		1.30	1.45

Issued to honor the Indonesian Navy.

Map of Africa and Asia and Mosque — A105

15r, 50r, Mosque and clasped hands.

1965, Mar. 6		Photo.	Perf. 12½	
651	A105	10r lt blue & pur	.25	.25
652	A105	15r org & red brn	.25	.25
653	A105	25r brt grn & brn	.35	.25
654	A105	50r brn red & blk	.45	.70
	Nos. 651-654 (4)		1.30	1.45

Afro-Asian Islamic Conf., Bandung, Mar. 1965.

Hand Holding Scroll — A106

Design: 25r, 75r, Conference emblem (globe, cotton and grain).

1965, Apr. 18		Unwmk.	Perf. 12½	
655	A106	15r silver & dp car	.25	.25
656	A106	25r aqua, gold & red	.25	.25
657	A106	50r gold & dp ultra	.25	.25
658	A106	75r pale vio, gold & red	.45	.80
	Nos. 655-658 (4)		1.20	1.55

10th anniv. of the First Afro-Asian Conf.

Nos. 618-623 and Nos. 634-636 Surcharged in Orange or Black

1965, Dec.		Perf. 12x12½, 12½x12		
659	A99	10s on 10r (B)	.25	.25
660	A99	15s on 15r	.25	.25
661	A98	20s on 20r	.25	.25
662	A99	25s on 25r (B)	.25	.25
663	A98	30s on 30r	.25	.25
664	A98	40s on 40r	.25	.25
665	A98	50s on 50r	.25	.25
666	A98	75s on 75r	.25	2.00
667	A98	100s on 100r	.25	.25
	Nos. 659-667 (9)		2.25	4.00

The surcharge on Nos. 659-660 and No. 662 is in two lines and larger.

Pres. Sukarno — A107

1966-67		Photo.	Perf. 12½x12	
668	A107	1s sep & Prus grn	.25	.25
669	A107	3s sep & lt ol grn	.25	.25
670	A107	5s sep & dp car	.25	.25
671	A107	8s sep & Prus grn	.25	.25
672	A107	10s sep & vio bl	.25	.25
673	A107	15s sep & blk	.25	.25
674	A107	20s sep & dp grn	.25	.25
675	A107	25s sep & dk red brn	.25	.25
676	A107	30s sep & dp bl	.25	.25
677	A107	40s sep & red brn	.25	.25
678	A107	50s sep & brt vio	.25	.25
679	A107	80s sep & org	.25	.25
680	A107	1r sep & emer	.25	.25
681	A107	1.25r sep & dk gray ol	.25	.25
682	A107	1.50r sep & emer	.25	.25
683	A107	2r sep & mag	.25	.25
684	A107	2.50r sep & gray	.25	.25
685	A107	5r sep & ocher	.25	.30
686	A107	10r sep & ol grn	.25	.25
686A	A107	12r grn & org ('67)	.25	.25
686B	A107	25r grn & brt pur ('67)	.25	.30
	Nos. 668-686B (21)		5.25	5.35

The 12r is inscribed "1967" instead of "1966."

Dockyard Workers — A108

Designs: 40s, Lighthouse. 50s, Fishermen. 1r, Maritime emblem (wheel and eagle). 1.50r, Sailboat. 2r, Loading dock. 2.50r, Diver emerging from water. 3r, Ship in drydock.

1966		Photo.	Perf. 12x12½	
687	A108	20s lt ultra & grn	.25	.25
688	A108	40s pink & dk bl	.25	.25
689	A108	50s green & brn	.25	.25
690	A108	1r salmon, bl & yel	.25	.25
691	A108	1.50r dull lil & dl grn	.25	.25
692	A108	2r gray & dp org	.25	.25
693	A108	2.50r rose lil & dk red	.25	.25
694	A108	3r brt green & blk	.25	.25
a.		Souvenir sheet	10.50	13.50
	Nos. 687-694 (8)		2.00	2.00

Maritime Day. Issued: Nos. 687-690, 9/23; Nos. 691-694, 10/23.

No. 694a contains one imperf. stamp similar to No. 694.

Gen. Ahmad Yani — A109

Heroes of the Revolution: No. 696, Lt. Gen. R. Suprapto. No. 697, Lt. General Harjono. No. 698, Lt. Gen. S. Parman. No. 699, Maj. Gen. D. I. Pandjaitan. No. 700, Maj. Gen. Sutojo Siswomihardjo. No. 701, Brig. General Katamso. No. 702, Colonel Soegijono. No. 703, Capt. Pierre Andreas Tendean. No. 704, Adj. Insp. Karel Satsuit Tubun.

1966, Nov. 10		Deep Blue Frame		
695	A109	5r org brn	.25	.25
696	A109	5r brt grn	.25	.25
697	A109	5r gray brn	.25	.25
698	A109	5r olive	.25	.25
699	A109	5r gray	.25	.25
700	A109	5r brt purple	.25	.25
701	A109	5r red lilac	.25	.25
702	A109	5r slate green	.25	.25
703	A109	5r dull rose lil	.25	.25
704	A109	5r orange	.25	.25
	Nos. 695-704 (10)		2.50	2.50

Issued to honor military men killed during the Communist uprising, October, 1965.

Tjlempung, Java — A110

Musical Instruments and Maps: 1r, Sasando, Timor. 1.25r, Foi doa, Flores. 1.50r, Kultjapi, Sumatra. 2r, Arababu, Sangihe and Talaud Islands. 2.50r, Drums, West New Guinea. 3r, Katjapi, Celebes. 4r, Hape, Borneo. 5r, Gangsa, Bali. 6r, Serunai, Sumatra. 8r, Rebab, Java. 10r, Trompet, West New Guinea. 12r, Totobuang, Moluccas. 15r, Drums, Nias. 20r, Kulintang, Celebes. 25r, Keledi, Borneo.

INDONESIA

1967 Unwmk. Photo. Perf. 12½x12
705	A110	50s red & gray	.25	.40
706	A110	1r brn & dp org	.25	.40
707	A110	1.25r mar & ultra	.25	.40
708	A110	1.50r grn & lt vio	.25	.40
709	A110	2r vio bl & yel bis	.25	.40
710	A110	2.50r ol grn & dl red	.25	.40
711	A110	3r brt grn & dl cl	.25	.40
712	A110	4r vio bl & org	.35	.40
713	A110	5r dull red & bl	.35	.40
714	A110	6r blk & brt pink	.35	.45
715	A110	8r red brn & brt grn	.40	.45
716	A110	10r lilac & red	.45	.45
717	A110	12r ol grn & lil	.45	.65
718	A110	15r vio & lt ol grn	.45	.40
719	A110	20r gray & sepia	.45	.40
720	A110	25r black & green	.45	.40
		Nos. 705-720 (16)	5.45	6.75

Issued: 1.25r, 10r, 12r, 15r, 20r, 25r, Mar. 1; others Feb. 1.
For surcharges see Nos. J118-J137.

Aviator and MiG-21 — A111

Aviation Day: 4r, Traffic control tower and 990A Convair jetliner. 5r, Hercules transport plane.

1967, Apr. 9 Perf. 12½
721	A111	2.50r multicolored	.35	.30
722	A111	4r multicolored	.35	.30
723	A111	5r multicolored	.55	.30
		Nos. 721-723 (3)	1.25	.90

Thomas Cup with Victory Dates — A112

Design: 12r, Thomas Cup and globe.

1967, May 31 Perf. 12x12½
724	A112	5r multicolored	.25	.25
725	A112	12r multicolored	.50	.25

Issued to commemorate the Thomas Cup Badminton World Championship of 1967.

Balinese Girl in Front of Temple Gate — A113

1967, July 1 Photo. Perf. 12½
726	A113	12r multicolored	1.10	1.00
a.		Souv. sheet of 1, imperf.	4.00	5.00

Intl. Tourist Year, 1967. See No. 739.

Heroes of the Revolution Monument, Lubang Buaja — A114

Designs: 5r, Full view of monument, horiz. 7.50r, Shrine at monument.

Perf. 12x12½, 12½x12
727	A114	2.50r pale grn & dk brn	.25	.25
728	A114	5r brt rose lil & pale brn	.40	.30
729	A114	7.50r pink & Prus grn	.40	.30
		Nos. 727-729 (3)	1.05	.85

Issued to publicize the "Heroes of the Revolution" Monument in Lubang Buaja.

Forest Fire, by Raden Saleh — A115

50r, Fight to Death, by Raden Saleh.

1967, Oct. 30 Photo. Perf. 12½
730	A115	25r org & gray grn	.30	.50
a.		Souvenir sheet of 1	4.50	7.00
731	A115	50r vio brn & org	.50	.45

Indonesian painter Raden Saleh (1813-80).

Human Rights Flame — A116

1968, Jan. 1 Photo. Perf. 12½
732	A116	5r grn, lt vio bl & red	.30	.25
733	A116	12r grn, ol bis & red	.35	.25

International Human Rights Year 1968.

Armed Forces College Emblem — A117

1968, Jan. 29 Litho. Perf. 12½
| 734 | A117 | 10r lt blue, yel & brn | .60 | .30 |

Integration of the Armed Forces College.

WHO Emblem and "20" — A118

20th anniv. of WHO: 20r, WHO emblem.

1968, Apr. 7 Photo. Perf. 12½
735	A118	2r dp yel, pale yel & dk brn	.30	.30
736	A118	20r emerald & blk	.40	.30

Trains of 1867 and 1967 and Railroad's Emblem A119

1968, May 15 Photo. Perf. 12½x12
737	A119	20r multicolored	.30	.30
738	A119	30r multicolored	.50	1.00

Indonesian railroad centenary (in 1967).

Tourist Type of 1967

Tourist Publicity: 30r, Butterfly dancer from West Java.

1968, July 1 Perf. 12½
739	A113	30r gray & multi	1.20	1.60
a.		Souv. sheet of 1 + label	4.50	7.50

Bosscha Observatory and Andromeda Nebula A120

30r, Observatory, globe and sky, vert.

1968, Sept. 20 Photo. Perf. 12½x12
740	A120	15r ultra & yellow	.35	.30
741	A120	30r violet & orange	.55	.30

Bosscha Observatory, 40th anniversary.

Weight Lifting — A121

Designs: 7.50r+7.50r, Sailing, horiz. 12r, Basketball. 30r, Dove, Olympic flame and emblem, horiz.

1968, Oct. 12 Perf. 12½
742	A121	5r ocher, blk & grn	.25	.25
743	A121	Pair	.55	.55
a.		7.50r Left half	.25	.25
b.		7.50r Right half	.25	.25
c.		Souvenir sheet	5.00	8.00
744	A121	12r blue & multi	.30	.40
745	A121	30r blue grn & multi	.50	.20
		Nos. 742-745 (4)	1.60	1.45

19th Olympic Games, Mexico City, Oct. 12-27. No. 743 is perforated vertically in the center, dividing it into two separate stamps, each inscribed "Republic Indonesia" and "7.50r." There is no gutter along the center perforation; and the design is continous over the two stamps.
No. 743c contains one No. 743 with track design surrounding the stamps.

Eugenia Aquea Burm. f. — A122

Fruits: 15r, Papaya. 30r, Durian, vert.

Perf. 12½x12, 12x12½
1968, Dec. 20 Photo.
746	A122	7.50r multicolored	.25	.25
747	A122	15r multicolored	.45	.35
a.		Souvenir sheet of 1	4.00	6.00
748	A122	30r multicolored	.70	.50
a.		Souvenir sheet of 1	4.00	6.00
		Nos. 746-748 (3)	1.40	1.10

Issued for the 11th Social Day.

Globe, ILO and UN Emblems — A123

Designs: 7.50r, 25r, ILO and UN emblems.

1969, Feb. 1 Photo. Perf. 12½
749	A123	5r yel grn & scar	.25	.25
750	A123	7.50r org & dk grn	.25	.25
751	A123	15r lilac & org	.25	.25
752	A123	25r bl grn & dull red	.25	.25
		Nos. 749-752 (4)	1.00	1.00

50th anniv. of the ILO.

R. Dewi Sartika — A124

Heroes of Indonesian Independence: No. 754, Tjoet Nja Din. No. 755, Tjoet Nja Meuthia. No. 756, General Gatot Subroto. No. 757, Sutan Sjahrir. No. 758, Dr. F. L. Tobing. Nos. 753-755 show portraits of women.

1969, Mar. 1 Photo. Perf. 12½x12
753	A124	15r green & pur	.25	.25
754	A124	15r red lilac & grn	.25	.25
755	A124	15r dk blue & ver	.25	.25
756	A124	15r lilac & dk blue	.25	.25
757	A124	15r lemon & red	.25	.25
758	A124	15r pale brn & blue	.25	.25
		Nos. 753-758 (6)	1.50	1.50

Red Crosses — A125

20r, Red Cross surrounded by arms.

1969, May 5 Photo. Perf. 12
759	A125	15r green & dp red	.40	.25
760	A125	20r org yel & red	.45	.35

50th anniversary of the League of Red Cross Societies.

"Family Planning Leads to National Development and Prosperity" A126

Design: 10r, Family, birds and factories.

1969, June 2 Photo. Perf. 12½
761	A126	10r blue grn & org	.25	.25
762	A126	20r gray & magenta	.50	.30

Planned Parenthood Conference of Southeast Asia and Oceania, Bandung, June 1-7.

Map of Bali and Mask — A127

Designs: 15r, Map of Bali and woman carrying basket with offerings on head. 30r, Map of Bali and cremation ceremony.

1969, July 1 Litho. Perf. 12½x12
763	A127	12r gray & multi	.45	.35
764	A127	15r lilac & multi	.65	.40
765	A127	30r multicolored	.65	.40
a.		Souvenir sheet of 1	4.00	6.00
		Nos. 763-765 (3)	1.75	1.15

Issued for tourist publicity.

Agriculture — A128

Designs: 5r, Religious coexistence (roofs of mosques and churches). 10r, Social welfare (house and family). 12r, Import-export (cargo and ship). 15r, Clothing industry (cloth and spindles). 20r, Education (school children). 25r, Research (laboratory). 30r, Health care (people and syringe). 40r, Fishing (fish and net). 50r, Statistics (charts).

1969 Photo. Perf. 12x12½
766	A128	5r yel grn & bl	.25	.25
767	A128	7.50r rose brn & yel	.25	.25
768	A128	10r slate & red	.25	.25
769	A128	12r blue & dp org	1.40	.65
770	A128	15r slate & org	.25	.25
771	A128	20r purple & yel	.25	.25
772	A128	25r orange & blk	.25	.25
773	A128	30r car rose & gray	.40	.25
774	A128	40r green & org	.50	.25
775	A128	50r sepia & org	.50	.25
		Nos. 766-775 (10)	4.30	2.90

Five-year Development Plan.
See No. 968a.

Radar, Djatiluhur Station — A129

30r, Communications satellite and earth.

1969, Sept. 29 Perf. 12½
776	A129	15r multicolored	.40	.25
777	A129	30r multicolored	.60	.55

INDONESIA

Vickers Vimy and Borobudur Temple — A130

100r, Vickers Vimy and map of Indonesia.

1969, Nov. 1   *Perf. 13½x12½*
778 A130 75r dp org & dull pur   .40   .60
779 A130 100r yellow & green   .50   .60

50th anniv. of the 1st flight from England to Australia (via Java).

EXPO '70, Indonesian Pavilion — A131

Designs: 15r, Garuda, symbol of Indonesian EXPO '70 committee. 30r, like 5r.

1970, Feb. 15   *Photo.*   *Perf. 12x12½*
780 A131 5r brown, yel & grn   .40   .30
781 A131 15r dk bl, yel grn & red   .55   .40
782 A131 30r red, yel & dk bl   1.10   .65
    Nos. 780-782 (3)   2.05   1.35

Issued to publicize EXPO '70 International Exposition, Osaka, Japan, Mar. 15-Sept. 13.

Upraised Hands, Bars and Scales of Justice — A132

1970, Mar. 15   *Photo.*   *Perf. 12½*
783 A132 10r red orange & pur   .65   .40
784 A132 15r brt green & pur   .80   .40

Rule of law and justice in Indonesia.

UPU Monument, Bern — A133

Design: 30r, UPU Headquarters, Bern.

1970, May 20   *Photo.*   *Perf. 12x12½*
785 A133 15r emer & copper red   .40   .40
786 A133 30r ocher & blue   1.00   .95

Inauguration of the new UPU Headquarters in Bern, Switzerland.

Dancers — A134

1970, July 1   *Photo.*   *Perf. 12*
787 A134 20r Timor dancers   .80   .50
788 A134 45r Bali dancers   1.10   .85
   a.   Souvenir sheet of 1   7.00   9.00

Tourist publicity. No. 788a sold for 60r.

Asian Productivity Year — A135

1970, Aug. 1   *Photo.*   *Perf. 12*
789 A135 5r emerald, org & red   .40   .25
790 A135 30r violet, org & red   1.00   .65

Independence Proclamation Monument — A136

1970, Aug. 17
791 A136 40r lt ultra & magenta   10.00   4.50

The 25th anniversary of independence.

Post and Telecommunications Emblems — A137

Postal Worker and Telephone Dial — A138

Perf. 12x12½, 12½x12
1970, Sept. 27   *Photo.*
792 A137 10r green, ocher & yel   2.50   .30
793 A138 25r pink, blk & yel   6.00   .70

25th anniversary of the postal service.

UN Emblem — A139

1970, Oct. 10   *Photo.*   *Perf. 12½*
794 A139 40r pur, red & yel grn   10.00   6.00

25th anniversary of the United Nations.

Education Year and UNESCO Emblems — A140

Design: 50r, similar to 25r, but without oval background.

1970, Nov. 16   *Photo.*   *Perf. 12½*
795 A140 25r yel, dk red & brn   5.50   3.75
796 A140 50r lt blue, blk & red   12.00   5.00

International Education Year.

Batik Worker A141

50r, Woman with bamboo musical instrument (angklung). 75r, Menangkabau house & family in traditional costumes.

1971, May 26   *Litho.*   *Perf. 12½*
797 A141 20r multi   1.75   1.50
798 A141 50r multi, vert.   3.50   4.00
   a.   Souvenir sheet of 1   40.00   65.00
799 A141 75r multi   5.50   6.00
    Nos. 797-799 (3)   10.75   11.50

"Visit ASEAN lands." No. 798a sold for 70r.

Fatahillah Park, Djakarta A142

30f, City Hall. 65r, Lenong Theater performance. 80r, Ismail Marzuki Cultural Center.

1971, June 19   *Photo.*   *Perf. 12½*
800 A142 15r yel grn, brn & bl   2.00   1.10
801 A142 65r org brn, dk brn
     & lt grn   4.00   4.50
802 A142 80r olive, bl & mag   8.00   3.50
    Nos. 800-802 (3)   14.00   9.10

Souvenir Sheet
803 A142 30r bl, yel & lil rose   18.00   27.50

444th anniv. of Djakarta. No. 803 sold for 60r.

Rama and Sita — A143

Design: 100r, Rama with bow.

1971, Aug. 31
804 A143 30r yellow, grn & blk   1.50   .85
805 A143 100r blue, red & blk   3.50   2.00

International Ramayana Festival.

Carrier Pigeon and Conference Emblem — A144

1971, Sept. 20
806 A144 50r ocher & dp brown   1.60   1.10

5th Asian Regional Postal Conference.

Globes and UPU Monument, Berne — A145

1971, Oct. 4   *Photo.*   *Perf. 13½x13*
807 A145 40r blue & dull vio   1.60   1.10

Universal Postal Union Day.

Boy Writing, UNICEF Emblem — A146

40r, Boy with sheaf of rice, emblem.

1971, Dec. 11   *Perf. 12½*
808 A146 20r orange & multi   1.75   .60
809 A146 40r blue & multi   3.25   1.25

25th anniv. UNICEF.

Lined Tang — A147

Fish: 30r, Moorish goddess. 40r, Imperial angelfish.

1971, Dec. 27   *Litho.*   *Perf. 12½*
810 A147 15r lilac & multi   3.50   1.25
811 A147 30r dull grn & multi   7.25   3.50
812 A147 40r blue & multi   11.50   5.00
    Nos. 810-812 (3)   22.25   9.75

See Nos. 834-836, 859-861, 926-928, 959-961.

UN Emblem A148

Radio Tower A149

1972, Mar. 28   *Photo.*   *Perf. 12½*
813 A148 40r lt grnsh bl & bl   2.00   1.00
814 A149 75r dk car, yel &
     grnsh bl   3.25   1.00
815 A148 100r green, yel & blk   3.75   2.25
    Nos. 813-815 (3)   9.00   4.25

UN Economic Commission for Asia and the Far East (ECAFE), 25th anniv.

"Your Heart is your Health" — A150

1972, Apr. 7
816 A150 50r multicolored   1.60   .80

World Health Day.

Woman Weaver, Factories — A151

1972, Apr. 22
817 A151 35r orange, yel & pur   1.60   .80

Textile Technology Institute, 50th anniv.

Book Readers — A152

1972, May 15   *Perf. 13½x12½*
818 A152 75r blue & multi   2.50   1.25

International Book Year 1972.

Weather Satellite — A153

50r, Astronaut on moon. 60r, Indonesian rocket Kartika 1.

1972, July 20   *Photo.*   *Perf. 12½*
819 A153 35r shown   1.50   .65
820 A153 50r multicolored   3.00   3.50
821 A153 60r multicolored   4.50   1.25
    Nos. 819-821 (3)   9.00   5.40

Space achievements.

Hotel Indonesia A154

1972, Aug. 5
822 A154 50r grn, lt bl & car   2.00   1.10

Hotel Indonesia, 10th anniversary.

Silat (Self Defense) — A155

Olympic Emblems and: 35r, Running. 50r, Diving. 75r, Badminton. 100r, Olympic Stadium.

1972, Aug. 26   *Photo.*
823 A155 20r lt blue & multi   1.25   .25
824 A155 35r multicolored   1.25   .40
825 A155 50r yel grn & multi   2.10   .70
826 A155 75r multicolored   2.10   1.75
827 A155 100r multicolored   3.50   2.75
    Nos. 823-827 (5)   10.20   5.85

20th Olympic Games, Munich, 8/26-9/11.

INDONESIA

Family, Houses of Worship — A156

Family planning: 75r, Healthy family. 80r, Working family (national prosperity).

1972, Sept. 27			Perf. 12½x13½	
828	A156	30r lemon & multi	1.25	.70
829	A156	75r lilac & multi	2.50	2.50
830	A156	80r multicolored	4.25	3.25
		Nos. 828-830 (3)	8.00	6.45

Moluccas Dancer — A157

60r, Man, woman and Toradja house, Celebes. 100fr, West Irian house, horiz.

Perf. 12½x13½, 13½x12½

1972, Oct. 28			Photo.	
831	A157	30r olive pink & brn	1.75	.65
832	A157	60r multicolored	2.50	3.00
833	A157	100r lt bl, brn & dl yel	5.25	3.00
		Nos. 831-833 (3)	9.50	6.65

Fish Type of 1971

Fish: 30r, Butterflyfish. 50r, Regal angelfish. 100r, Spotted triggerfish.

1972, Dec. 4			Litho.	Perf. 12½
834	A147	30r blue & multi	5.50	2.00
835	A147	50r blue & multi	8.75	2.75
836	A147	100r blue & multi	11.50	5.00
		Nos. 834-836 (3)	25.75	9.75

Thomas Cup, Shuttlecock — A158

Thomas Cup, Shuttlecock and: 75r, National monument & Istora Sports Hall. 80r, Indonesian flag & badminton player.

1973, Jan. 2			Perf. 12½	
837	A158	30r emerald & brt bl	1.00	.30
838	A158	75r dull grn & dk car	1.50	.55
839	A158	80r gold & red	2.25	1.10
		Nos. 837-839 (3)	4.75	1.95

Thomas Cup Badminton World Championship 1973.

WMO Emblem, Anemometer, Wayang Figure — A159

Perf. 13½x12½

1973, Feb. 15				Litho.
840	A159	80r blue, grn & claret	1.60	.80

Cent. of intl. meteorological cooperation.

"Health Begins at Home" — A160

1973, Apr. 7			Photo.	Perf. 12½
841	A160	80r dk grn, org & ultra	1.40	.85

25th anniv. of WHO.

Ceremonial Mask, Java — A161

60r, Mask, Kalimantan. 100r, Mask, Bali.

1973, June 1			Photo.	Perf. 12½
842	A161	30r shown	2.75	.90
843	A161	60r multi	5.50	4.00
844	A161	100r multi	9.00	2.00
		Nos. 842-844 (3)	17.25	6.90

Tourist publicity.

Hand Putting Coin into Bank — A162

30r, Symbolic coin bank and hand, horiz.

1973, July 2			Photo.	Perf. 12½
845	A162	25r yellow, lt brn & blk	1.00	.55
846	A162	30r green, yel & gold	1.25	.55

National savings movement.

Chess — A163

8th National Sports Week: 60r, Karate. 75r, Hurdling, horiz.

1973, Aug. 4			Photo.	Perf. 12½
847	A163	30r red, yellow & blk	1.25	1.10
848	A163	60r black, ocher & lt grn	2.00	1.10
849	A163	75r black, lt bl & rose	3.25	.90
		Nos. 847-849 (3)	6.50	3.10

INTERPOL Emblem and Policemen — A164

Design: 50r, INTERPOL emblem and guard statue from Sewu Prambanan Temple, vert.

1973, Sept. 3				
850	A164	30r yellow, grn & blk	.90	.35
851	A164	50r yellow, brn & blk	1.60	.65

50th anniv. of Intl. Police Organization.

Batik Worker and Parang Rusak Pattern A165

Batik designs: 80r, Man and Pagi Sore pattern. 100r, Man and Merak Ngigel pattern.

1973, Oct. 9			Photo.	Perf. 12½
852	A165	60r multicolored	1.90	1.90
853	A165	80r multicolored	3.25	2.25
854	A165	100r multicolored	7.25	4.00
		Nos. 852-854 (3)	12.40	8.15

Farmer, Grain, UN and FAO Emblems A166

1973, Oct. 24			Photo.	Perf. 12½
855	A166	30r lilac & multi	1.75	.65

World Food Program, 10th anniversary.

Houses of Worship — A167

Family planning: 30r, Classroom. 60r, Family and home.

1973, Nov. 10				
856	A167	20r dk bl, lt bl & ver	.55	.45
857	A167	30r ocher, blk & yel	1.40	.70
858	A167	60r lt grn, yel & blk	2.75	.60
		Nos. 856-858 (3)	4.70	1.75

Fish Type of 1971

Fish: 40r, Acanthurus leucosternon. 65r, Chaetodon trifasciatus. 100r, Pomacanthus annularis.

1973, Dec. 10			Litho.	Perf. 12½
859	A147	40r multicolored	1.90	.95
860	A147	65r multicolored	7.50	2.00
861	A147	100r multicolored	9.50	3.25
		Nos. 859-861 (3)	18.90	6.20

Adm. Sudarso and Battle of Arafuru A168

1974, Jan. 15				
862	A168	40r brt blue & multi	2.00	.85

12th Navy Day.

Bengkulu Costume — A169

Designs: Regional Costumes: 7.50r, Kalimantan, Timor. 10r, Kalimantan, Tengah. 15r, Jambi. 20r, Sulawesi, Tenggara. 25r, Nusatenggara, Timor. 27.50r, Maluku. 30r, Lampung. 35r, Sumatra, Barat. 40r, Aceh. 45r, Nusatenggara, Barat. 50r, Riouw. 55r, Kalimantan, Barat. 60r, Sulawesi, Utara. 65r, Sulawesi, Tengah. 70r, Sumatra, Selatan. 75r, Java, Barat. 80r, Sumatra, Utara. 90r, Yogyakarta. 95r, Kalimantan, Selatan. 100r, Java, Timor. 120r, Irian, Jaya. 130r, Jawa Tengah. 135r, Sulawesi, Selatan. 150r, Bali. 160r, Djakarta.

1974, Mar. 28			Litho.	Perf. 12½
863	A169	5r shown	14.00	1.00
864	A169	7.50r multi	7.00	1.00
865	A169	10r multi	4.00	.80
866	A169	15r multi	1.25	.80
867	A169	20r multi	1.25	.80
868	A169	25r multi	1.40	.80
869	A169	27.50r multi	1.40	2.50
870	A169	30r multi	1.40	1.50
871	A169	35r multi	1.40	.80
872	A169	40r multi	1.40	.80
873	A169	45r multi	3.00	.80
874	A169	50r multi	1.75	2.00
875	A169	55r multi	2.60	.80
876	A169	60r multi	2.60	.80
877	A169	65r multi	2.60	.80
878	A169	70r multi	2.60	.80
879	A169	75r multi	2.60	.80
880	A169	80r multi	2.60	.80
881	A169	90r multi	3.00	4.00
882	A169	95r multi	2.60	.80
883	A169	100r multi	2.60	1.60
884	A169	120r multi	5.00	1.00
885	A169	130r multi	5.00	.80
886	A169	135r multi	6.00	.80
887	A169	150r multi	6.00	.80
888	A169	160r multi	6.00	1.60
		Nos. 863-888 (26)	91.05	29.80

Baladewa — A170

Designs (Figures from Shadow Plays): 80r, Kresna. 100r, Bima.

1974, June 1			Photo.	Perf. 12½
889	A170	40r lt violet & multi	1.75	1.25
890	A170	80r salmon & multi	4.50	2.75
891	A170	100r rose	5.50	2.75
		Nos. 889-891 (3)	11.75	6.75

Pres. Suharto — A171

1974-76 Photo. Perf. 12½
Portrait in Dark Brown

901	A171	40r lt green & blk	.70	.25
903	A171	50r ultra & blk	1.50	.25
906	A171	65r brt pink & blk	1.00	.65
908	A171	75r yellow & blk	1.60	.25
912	A171	100r buff & blk	1.60	.25
913	A171	150r citron & blk	1.60	.25
914	A171	200r green & blue	4.25	.25
915	A171	300r brn org & car	1.75	.25
916	A171	400r green & yellow	2.60	.30
917	A171	500r lilac & car	4.00	1.00
		Nos. 901-917 (10)	20.60	3.75

Nos. 914-917 have wavy lines in background.
Issued: Nos. 901-913, 8/17/74; Nos. 914-917, 8/17/76.

Family and WPY Emblem — A172

1974, Aug. 19				
918	A172	65r ultra, gray & ocher	1.25	.55

World Population Year 1974.

"Welfare" A173

"Development" A174

"Religion" A175

1974, Sept. 9				
919	A173	25r green & multi	.80	.45
920	A174	40r yellow grn & multi	1.25	.45
921	A175	65r dk vio brn & multi	2.00	.45
		Nos. 919-921 (3)	4.05	1.35

Family planning.

Mailmen with Bicycles, UPU Emblem A176

UPU cent.: 40r, Horse-drawn mail cart. 65r, Mailman on horseback. 100r, Sailing ship, 18th century.

1974, Oct. 9				
922	A176	20r dk green & multi	1.75	.45
923	A176	40r dull blue & multi	1.90	.70
924	A176	65r black brn & yel	2.10	.70
925	A176	100r maroon & multi	2.25	1.90
		Nos. 922-925 (4)	8.00	3.75

Fish Type of 1971

Fish: 40fr, Zebrasoma veliferum. 80r, Euxiphipops navarchus. 100r, Synchiropus splendidus.

1974, Oct. 30			Photo.	Perf. 12½
926	A147	40r blue & multi	2.75	.45
927	A147	80r blue & multi	4.00	1.90
928	A147	100r blue & multi	5.75	2.40
		Nos. 926-928 (3)	12.50	4.75

Drill Team Searching for Oil — A177

INDONESIA

Designs (Pertamina Emblem and): 75r, Oil refinery. 95r, Pertamina telecommunications and computer center. 100r, Gasoline truck and station. 120r, Plane over storage tanks. 130r, Pipes and tanker. 150r, Petro-chemical storage tanks. 200r, Off-shore drilling platform. 95r, 100r, 120r, 130r, vertical.

1974, Dec. 10			Perf. 13½	
929	A177	40r black & multi	.45	.30
930	A177	75r black & multi	.50	.30
931	A177	95r black & multi	.60	.30
932	A177	100r black & multi	.60	.30
933	A177	120r black & multi	.70	.30
934	A177	130r black & multi	.70	.30
935	A177	150r black & multi	.75	.30
936	A177	200r black & multi	.85	.30
		Nos. 929-936 (8)	5.15	2.40

Pertamina State Oil Enterprise, 17th anniv.

Spittoon, Sumatra — A178

Artistic Metalware: 75r, Condiment dish, Sumatra. 100r, Condiment dish, Kalimantan.

1975, Feb. 24		Photo.	Perf. 12½	
937	A178	50r red & black	1.40	1.40
938	A178	75r green & black	2.10	1.40
939	A178	100r brt blue & multi	3.00	1.40
		Nos. 937-939 (3)	6.50	4.20

Blood Donors' Emblem — A179

1975, Apr. 7				
940	A179	40r yellow, red & grn	1.20	.65

"Give blood, save lives."

Globe, Standard Meter and Kilogram — A180

1975, May 20				
941	A180	65r blue, red & yel	1.75	.65

Cent. of Intl. Meter Convention, Paris, 1875.

Farmer, Teacher, Mother, Policewoman and Nurse A181

IWY Emblem A182

1975, June 26		Photo.	Perf. 12½	
942	A181	40r multicolored	1.20	.65
943	A182	100r multicolored	2.00	.65

International Women's Year 1975.

Dendrobium Pakarena — A183

Orchids: 70r, Aeridachnis bogor. 85r, Vanda genta.

1975, July 21				
944	A183	40r multicolored	2.50	1.25
945	A183	70r multicolored	4.25	2.40
946	A183	85r multicolored	5.75	3.50
		Nos. 944-946 (3)	12.50	7.15

See Nos. 1010-1012, 1036-1038.

Stupas and Damaged Temple — A184

Designs (UNESCO Emblem and): 40r, Buddha statues, stupas and damaged wall. 65r, Stupas and damaged wall, horiz. 100r, Buddha statue and stupas, horiz.

1975, Aug. 10			Perf. 12½	
947	A184	25r yel, brn & org	2.10	.80
948	A184	40r black, grn & yel	2.60	1.00
949	A184	65r lemon, cl & grn	5.00	4.25
950	A184	100r bis, brn & sl bl	7.50	4.25
		Nos. 947-950 (4)	17.20	10.30

UNESCO campaign to save Borobudur Temple, Java.

Banjarmasin Battle — A185

Battle Scenes: 40r, Batua, 9/8/46. 75r, Margarana, 11/20/46. 100r, Palembang, 1/1/47.

1975, Aug. 17				
951	A185	25r yellow & blk	.65	.45
952	A185	40r org ver & red	.85	.45
953	A185	75r vermilion & blk	1.00	1.25
954	A185	100r orange & blk	1.40	.90
		Nos. 951-954 (4)	3.90	3.05

Indonesian independence, 30th anniversary.

"Education" — A186

Family plannings: 25r, "Religion." 40r, "Prosperity."

1975, Oct. 20		Photo.	Perf. 12½	
955	A186	20r blue, salmon & blk	.50	.25
956	A186	25r emerald, sal & blk	.80	.30
957	A186	40r dp org, blue & blk	1.25	.55
		Nos. 955-957 (3)	2.55	1.10

Heroes' Monument, Surabaya — A187

1975, Nov. 10				
958	A187	100r maroon & green	1.75	.55

War of independence, 30th anniversary.

Fish Type of 1971

Fish: 40r, Coris angulata. 75r, Chaetodon ephippium. 150r, Platax pinnatus, vert.

1975, Dec. 15		Litho.	Perf. 12½	
959	A147	40r multicolored	1.25	.45
960	A147	75r multicolored	3.75	1.40
961	A147	150r multicolored	5.00	2.75
		Nos. 959-961 (3)	10.00	4.60

Thomas Cup — A188

40r, Uber Cup. 100r, Thomas & Uber Cups.

1976, Jan. 31		Photo.	Perf. 12½	
962	A188	20r blue & multi	.80	.35
963	A188	40r multicolored	.80	.60
964	A188	100r green & multi	1.75	.60
		Nos. 962-964 (3)	3.35	1.55

Indonesia, Badminton World Champions.

Refugees on Truck and New Village A189

Designs: 50r, Neglected and restored village streets. 100r, Derelict and rebuilt houses.

1976, Feb. 28		Photo.	Perf. 12½	
965	A189	30r yellow & multi	.80	.25
966	A189	50r blue & multi	1.00	.45
967	A189	100r ocher & multi	1.60	.45
		Nos. 965-967 (3)	3.40	1.15

World Human Settlements Day.

Telephones, 1876 and 1976 — A190

1976, Mar. 10		Photo.	Perf. 12½	
968	A190	100r yel, org & brn	1.25	.55
a.		Bklt. pane of 8, 4 #968, 4 #775 + 2 labels ('78)	7.75	

Centenary of first telephone call by Alexander Graham Bell, Mar. 10, 1876. Stamps from No. 968a have straight edges.

Eye and WHO Emblem — A191

Design: 40r, Blind man, eye and World Health Organization emblem.

1976, Apr. 7		Photo.	Perf. 12½	
969	A191	20r yel, lt grn & blk	.40	.30
970	A191	40r yel, blue & blk	.85	.45

Foresight prevents blindness.

Montreal Stadium A192

1976, May 17				
971	A192	100r ultra	1.25	.65

21st Olympic Games, Montreal, Canada, July 17-Aug. 1.

Lake Tondano, Celebes — A193

Tourist publicity: 40r, Lake Kelimutu, Flores. 75r, Lake Maninjau, Sumatra.

1976, June 1				
972	A193	35r lt green & blk	.65	.45
973	A193	40r gray, rose & lt grn	.80	.45
974	A193	75r blue & sl grn	1.00	.55
a.		Bklt. pane of 8 (7 #974, #998, 2 labels) ('78)	8.50	
		Nos. 972-974 (3)	2.45	1.45

Stamps from No. 974a have straight edges.

Radar Station — A194

Designs: 50r, Master control radar station. 100r, Palapa satellite.

1976, July 8		Photo.	Perf. 12½	
975	A194	20r multicolored	.65	.40
976	A194	50r green & blk	.85	.40
977	A194	100r multicolored	1.40	.75
a.		Bklt. pane of 9 (4 #977, 5 #987, label) ('78)	12.00	
		Nos. 975-977 (3)	2.90	1.55

Inauguration of domestic satellite system. Stamps from No. 977a have straight edges.

Arachnis Flosaeris A195

Orchids: 40r, Vanda putri serang. 100r, Coelogyne pandurata.

1976, Sept. 7				
978	A195	25r multicolored	1.50	1.10
a.		Souvenir sheet of 1	50.00	72.50
979	A195	40r multicolored	2.00	1.10
980	A195	100r multicolored	3.50	2.40
		Nos. 978-980 (3)	7.00	4.60

Tree and Mountain — A196

1976, Oct. 4				
981	A196	20r green, blue & brn	.85	.40

16th National Reforestation Week.

Dagger and Sheath from Timor — A197

Historic Daggers and Sheaths: 40r, from Borneo. 100r, from Aceh.

1976, Nov. 1			Perf. 12½	
982	A197	25r multicolored	.80	.45
983	A197	40r multicolored	1.60	.85
a.		Souvenir sheet of 1, imperf	12.50	17.50
984	A197	100r green & multi	2.60	2.60
		Nos. 982-984 (3)	5.00	3.90

No. 983a exists perf. Value $15.

Open Book A198

Children Reading A199

1976, Dec. 8		Photo.	Perf. 12½	
985	A198	20r multicolored	.55	.30
986	A199	40r multicolored	1.10	.45

Better books for children.

UNICEF Emblem — A200

1976, Dec. 11				
987	A200	40r multicolored	1.25	.45

UNICEF, 30th anniv.
See No. 977a.

INDONESIA

Ballot Box — A201

1977 elections: 75r, Ballot box, grain and factory. 100r, Coat of arms.

1977, Jan. 5		Photo.		Perf. 12½	
988	A201	40r multicolored		1.40	.30
989	A201	75r multicolored		1.75	.45
990	A201	100r multicolored		3.00	1.40
	Nos. 988-990 (3)			6.15	2.15

Camp and Flags Scout Emblems, — A202

Designs: 30r, Tent, emblems and trees. 40r, Boy and Girl Scout flags and emblems.

1977, Feb. 28					
991	A202	25r multicolored		1.25	.55
992	A202	30r multicolored		1.25	.55
993	A202	40r multicolored		1.40	1.25
	Nos. 991-993 (3)			3.90	2.35

11th National Scout Jamboree.

Letter with "AOPU" — A203

Design: 100r, Stylized bird and letter.

1977, Apr. 1		Photo.		Perf. 12½	
994	A203	65r multicolored		.50	.40
995	A203	100r multicolored		1.25	.55

Asian-Oceanic Postal Union, 15th convention.

Anniversary Emblem, Djakarta Arms — A204

Designs: Anniversary emblem and arms of Djakarta in different arrangements.

1977, May 23		Photo.		Perf. 12½	
996	A204	20r orange & blue		.50	.45
997	A204	40r emerald & blue		.75	.45
998	A204	100r slate & blue		1.50	.85
a.	Souvenir sheet of 1			7.50	9.00
	Nos. 996-998 (3)			2.75	1.75

450th anniversary of Djakarta. No. 998a also issued imperf. Value $17.50.

Rose — A205

1977, May 26		Photo.		Perf. 12½	
999	A205	100r shown		1.25	.45
a.	Souvenir sheet of 4			7.00	12.00
1000	A205	100r Envelope		1.25	.45
a.	Souvenir sheet of 4			7.00	12.00
b.	Pair, Nos. 999-1000			2.75	1.50

Amphilex 77 Phil. Exhib., Amsterdam, May 26-June 5. No. 999a contains one stamp similar to No. 999 with blue background. No. 1000a contains 2 each of Nos. 999-1000.
Nos. 999a, 1000a exist imperf. Values: No. 999a, $6; No. 1000a, $20.
See No. 1013a.

Various Sports Emblems — A206

9th Natl. Sports Week: 50r, 100r, Different sports emblems.

1977, June 22					
1001	A206	40r silver & multi		2.25	1.75
1002	A206	50r silver & multi		2.75	1.75
1003	A206	100r gold & multi		5.75	4.00
	Nos. 1001-1003 (3)			10.75	7.50

Contest Trophy A207

Emblem A208

1977, July 20					
1004	A207	40r green & multi		1.75	.55
1005	A208	100r yellow & multi		2.75	1.00

10th Natl. Koran Reading Contest, 7/20-27.

Map of ASEAN Countries, Satellite — A209

35r, Map of ASEAN countries. 50r, Flags of founding members: Indonesia, Malaysia, Philippines, Singapore & Thailand; ship, plane & train.

1977, Aug. 8					
1006	A209	25r multicolored		.75	.25
1007	A209	35r multicolored		1.75	.70
1008	A209	50r multicolored		2.25	.85
	Nos. 1006-1008 (3)			4.75	1.80

Association of South East Asian Nations (ASEAN), 10th anniversary.

Uniform, Jakarta Regiment — A210

1977, Aug. 19					
1009	A210	25r green, gold & brn		.75	.30

Indonesia-Pakistan Economic and Cultural Organization, 1968-1977.

Orchid Type of 1975

Orchids: 25r, Taeniophyllum. 40r, Phalaenopsis violacea. 100r, Dendrobium spectabile.

1977, Oct. 28		Photo.		Perf. 12½	
1010	A183	25r orange & multi		1.25	.80
1011	A183	40r blue & multi		1.75	1.75
1012	A183	100r yel grn & multi		4.00	2.75
a.	Souvenir sheet of 1, imperf			9.00	12.00
	Nos. 1010-1012 (3)			7.00	5.30

No. 1012a contains one stamp similar to No. 1012 with blue background. No. 1012a exists perf. Value $7.

Child and Mosquito — A211

1977, Nov. 7				Perf. 12½	
1013	A211	40r brt grn, red & blk		.75	.35
	Bklt. pane of 9+label (4 #999, 5 #1013) ('78)			8.75	

Natl. health campaign to eradicate malaria. Stamps from No. 1013a have straight edges.
Issued: No. 1013a, 9/27/78.

Proboscis Monkey A212

Designs: 40r, Indian elephant. 100r, Tiger.

1977, Dec. 22					
1014	A212	20r multicolored		.90	.35
1015	A212	40r multicolored		1.75	.75
1016	A212	100r multicolored		5.50	1.50
a.	Souvenir sheet of 1			5.00	10.00
	Nos. 1014-1016 (3)			8.15	2.60

Wildlife protection. No. 1016a exists imperf. Value $6.

Conference Emblem — A213

1978, Mar. 27		Photo.		Perf. 12½	
1017	A213	100r lt blue & ultra		1.25	.60

United Nations Conference on Technical Cooperation among Developing Countries.

Mother and Child — A214

75r, Mother and child, symbolic design.

1978, Apr. 7		Photo.		Perf. 12½	
1018	A214	40r lt green & blue		.45	.30
1019	A214	75r orange red & brn		1.00	.45

Promotion of breast feeding.

Dome of The Rock, Jerusalem A215

1978, May 15		Photo.		Perf. 12½	
1020	A215	100r multicolored		1.40	.55

Palestinian fighters and their families.

Argentina '78 Emblem — A216

1978, June 1					
1021	A216	40r multicolored		.55	.30
1022	A216	100r multicolored		1.10	.70

11th World Cup Soccer Championships, Argentina, June 1-25.

Head and "Blood Circulation" — A217

1978, June 17		Photo.		Perf. 12½	
1023	A217	100r black, blue & red		1.00	.55

World Health Day and drive against hypertension.

Leather Puppets A218

Art from Wayang Museum, Djakarta: 75r, Wooden puppets. 100r, Actors with puppet masks.

1978, July 22		Litho.		Perf. 12½	
1024	A218	40r multicolored		1.75	.70
1025	A218	75r multicolored		2.25	1.40
1026	A218	100r multicolored		5.00	2.40
	Nos. 1024-1026 (3)			9.00	4.50

Congress Emblem — A219

1978, Aug. 1					
1027	A219	100r slate		1.00	.45

27th Congress of World Confederation of Organizations of Teachers (WCOTP), Djakarta, June 26-Aug. 2.

IAAY Emblem — A220

1978, Aug. 16		Photo.		Perf. 12½	
1028	A220	100r org & dk blue		1.20	.45

International Anti-Apartheid Year.

Congress Emblem — A221

Design: 100r, People and trees.

1978, Oct. 16		Photo.		Perf. 12½	
1029	A221	40r emerald & blue		.25	.25
1030	A221	100r emerald & blk		1.00	.55

8th World Forestry Congress, Djakarta.

Youth Pledge Emblem — A222

1978, Oct. 28					
1031	A222	40r dk brown & red		.55	.30
1032	A222	100r salmon, brn & red		.90	.45

50th anniv. of Youth Pledge. See No. 1044b.

Wildlife Protection A223

40r, Porcupine anteater. 75r, Deer. 100r, Clouded tiger.

1978, Nov. 1					
1033	A223	40r multi		1.20	.40
1034	A223	75r multi		2.00	.80
a.	Souv. sheet of 5, #1034, 4 #1035 + label			10.00	10.00
1035	A223	100r multi		3.25	1.10
a.	Souvenir sheet of 1			4.00	4.00
	Nos. 1033-1035 (3)			6.45	2.30

Stamps in No. 1034a are in changed colors. Souvenir sheets inscribed for Essen 2nd Intl. Stamp Fair.

Orchid Type of 1975

Orchids: 40r, Phalaenopsis sri rejeki. 75r, Dendrobium macrophilium. 100r, Cymbidium fynlaysonianum.

1978, Dec. 22		Photo.		Perf. 12½	
1036	A183	40r multicolored		1.20	.45
1037	A183	75r multicolored		1.60	.70
1038	A183	100r multicolored		2.75	1.00
a.	Souvenir sheet of 1			4.00	6.00
	Nos. 1036-1038 (3)			5.55	2.15

Douglas DC-3, 1949, over Volcano A224

INDONESIA

Designs: 75r, Douglas DC-9 over village. 100r, Douglas DC-10 over temple.

1979, Jan. 26		Photo.		Perf. 12½	
1039	A224	40r multicolored		.65	.40
1040	A224	75r multicolored		.80	.40
1041	A224	100r multicolored		1.60	1.10
		Nos. 1039-1041 (3)		3.05	1.90

Garuda Indonesian Airways, 30th anniv.

A225

40r, Thomas Cup and badminton player. No. 1043, Player hitting ball. No. 1044, Player facing left.

1979, Feb. 24		Photo.		Perf. 12½	
1042	A225	40r red & blue		.50	.50
1043	A225	100r red & brown		.85	.85
1044	A225	100r red & brown		.85	.85
a.	Pair, #1043-1044			1.90	
b.	Blkt. pane, 3 each #1032, 1043-1044 + label			7.75	
		Nos. 1042-1044 (3)		2.20	2.25

11th Thomas Cup, Djakarta, May 24-June 2. No. 1044a forms a continuous design. Stamps from No. 1044b have straight edges.

Paphiopedilum Lowii — A227

Orchids: 100r, 300r, Vanda limbata. 125r, Phalaenopsis gigantea. 250r, as 60r.

1979, Mar. 22		Photo.		Perf. 12½	
1045	A227	60r multi		.75	.40
1046	A227	100r multi		1.40	.55
1047	A227	125r multi		2.25	.85
a.	Souvenir sheet of 1			4.50	4.50
b.	Souv. sheet of 2 (250r, 300r)			7.00	7.00
		Nos. 1045-1047 (3)		4.40	1.80

No. 1047b, issued for Asian Phil. Exhib., Dortmund, West Germany, May 24-27. Sold for 650r.

Family and Houses — A228

Third Five-year Plan: 12.50r, Plane. 17.50r, Bridge. 60r, Pylon and fields. 100r, School and clinic. 125r, Factories and trucks. 150r, Motorized mail delivery.

1979-82					
1047C	A228	12.50r rose car, yel ol ('80)		.45	.25
1047D	A228	17.50r pur brn, grey ol ('82)		.50	.25
1048	A228	35r green & olive		.25	.25
1049	A228	60r blue & olive		.25	.25
1050	A228	100r blue & dk brn		.50	.25
1051	A228	125r red brn & ol		.75	.25
1052	A228	150r car & yel		.90	.45
		Nos. 1047C-1052 (7)		3.60	1.95

See No. 1058a.

R. A. Kartini and Girls' School A229

1979, Apr. 21		Photo.		Perf. 12½	
1053		100r Kartini		.65	.40
1054		100r School		.65	.40
a.	A229 Pair, #1053-1054			1.40	2.00

Mrs. R. A. Kartini, educator, birth centenary.

Bureau of Education, UNESCO Emblems — A231

1979, May 25		Photo.		Perf. 12½	
1055	A231	150r multicolored		1.25	.45

50th anniversary of the statutes of the International Bureau of Education.

Self Defense — A232

Designs: 125r, Games' emblem. 150r, Senayan Main Stadium.

1979, June 21		Photo.		Perf. 12½	
1056	A232	60r multicolored		.55	.30
1057	A232	125r multicolored		.90	.45
1058	A232	150r multicolored		1.10	.70
a.	Bklt. pane of 6+4 labels (#1052, 5 #1058)			6.50	
		Nos. 1056-1058 (3)		2.55	1.45

10th So. East Asia Games, Djakarta, Sept. 21-30. Stamps from No. 1058a have straight edges. Issue date: No. 1058a, 9/27.

Cooperation Emblem — A233

1979, July 12		Photo.		Perf. 12½	
1059	A233	150r multicolored		.90	.40

32nd Indonesian Cooperative Day.

A234

Designs: 60r, IYC and natl. IYC emblems. 150r, IYC emblem.

1979, Aug. 4		Photo.		Perf. 12½	
1060	A234	60r emerald & blk		.40	.25
1061	A234	150r blue & blk		.75	.45

International Year of the Child.

TELECOM 79 — A235

1979, Sept. 20		Photo.		Perf. 12½	
1062	A235	150r bl, red, grey		1.00	.55

3rd World Telecommunications Exhibition, Geneva, Sept. 20-26.

Fight Drug Abuse — A236

1979, Oct. 17		Photo.		Perf. 12½	
1063	A236	150r deep rose & blk		.90	.55

Dolphin A237

Wildlife Protection: 125r, Freshwater dolphin. 150r, Leatherback turtle.

1979, Nov. 24		Photo.		Perf. 12½	
1064	A237	60r multi		.90	.65
1065	A237	125r multi		2.75	.85
1066	A237	150r multi		4.50	1.25
		Nos. 1064-1066 (3)		8.15	2.75

Souvenir Sheet

| 1066A | A237 | 200r like #1066 | | 6.50 | 8.00 |

Ship Made of Cloves — A238

Spice Race, Jakarta-Amsterdam (Sailing Ships): 60r, Penisi, vert. 150r, Madurese boat, vert.

1980		Photo.		Perf. 12½	
1067	A238	60r bright blue		.40	.25
1068	A238	125r red brown		.75	.45
1069	A238	150r red lilac		1.25	.45
		Nos. 1067-1069 (3)		2.40	1.15

Souvenir Sheets

| 1069A | A238 | 300r like #1068 | | 4.00 | 5.00 |
| 1069B | A238 | 300r like #1067 | | 6.50 | 6.50 |

Issued: Nos. 1067-1069, 300r, 3/12. 500r, 5/6. No. 1069B for London 1980 Intl. Stamp Exhib.

Rubber Raft in Rapids — A239

125r, Mountain climbing, vert. 150r, Hang gliding, vert.

Perf. 13½x13, 13x13½

1980, Mar. 21				Photo.	
1070	A239	60r shown		.40	.25
1071	A239	125r multicolored		.75	.55
1072	A239	150r multicolored		1.40	.85
		Nos. 1070-1072 (3)		2.55	1.65

Souvenir Sheet

| 1072A | A239 | 300r like #1070 | | 4.00 | 5.00 |

Anti-Smoking Campaign — A240

1980, Apr. 15				Perf. 12½	
1073	A240	150r multicolored		1.00	.45

A241

1980, Apr. 21		Photo.		Perf. 12½	
1074	A241	125r Flowers in vase		.80	.45
1075	A241	150r Bouquet		1.00	.70

2nd Flower Festival, Jakarta, Apr. 19-21. See Nos. 1080a-1080b.

Conference Building — A242

1980, Apr. 24				Perf. 13x13½	
1076	A242	150r gold & lil rose		1.10	.45

Souvenir Sheet

| 1076A | A242 | 300r multicolored | | 4.00 | 5.25 |

1st Asian-African Conf., 25th anniv.

A243

Designs: 60r, Male figure. 125r, Elephant stone. 150r, Taman Bali Stone Sarcophagus, 2000 B.C.

1980, May 2				Perf. 12½	
1077	A243	60r multicolored		.55	.30
1078	A243	125r multicolored		.75	.55
1079	A243	150r multicolored		.90	.70
		Nos. 1077-1079 (3)		2.20	1.55

Flower and Sculpture Types of 1980
Souvenir Sheet

1980		Photo.		Perf. 12½	
1080		Sheet of 8		16.00	16.00
a.	A241 100r like #1074			1.10	1.10
b.	A241 100r like #1075			1.10	1.10
c.	A243 200r like #1077			2.00	2.00
d.	A243 200r like #1079			2.00	2.00

London 1980 Intl. Stamp Exhib., May 6-14. No. 1080 contains 2 stamps of each design (4x2).

Draftsman in Wheelchair — A244

1980, May 18		Photo.		Perf. 12½	
1081	A244	100r multicolored		.90	.30

Disabled Veterans Corp, 30th anniversary.

Discus Thrower — A245

1980, May 18					
1082	A245	75r dp orange & sep		.75	.30

Olympics for the Disabled, Arnhem, Netherlands, June 21-July 5.

Pres. Suharto — A246

A246a   A246b

Perf. 13½x12½, 12½

1980-83				Photo.	
1083	A246	12.50r lt grn & grn		.35	.25
1084	A246	50r lt grn & bl		.35	.30
1084A	A246	55r red rose & red lil		.50	.25
1085	A246	75r lem & gldn brn		.85	.25
1086	A246	100r brt pink & bl		2.25	.40
a.	Bklt pane of 8 + 2 labels (6 #1086, 2 #1088, Inscribed 1981)			26.00	
1087	A246a	110r dull org & dp red lil		.50	.25
1088	A246	200r dl org & brn		6.00	.85
1088A	A246a	250r dl org & brn		.90	.25
1089	A246a	275r lt ap grn & dk grn		1.25	.25
1090	A246	300r rose lil & gold		1.40	.25
1091	A246	400r multicolored		1.60	.25

Engr.
Perf. 12½x13

| 1092 | A246b | 500r dk red brown | | 3.75 | 1.00 |
| | | Nos. 1083-1092 (12) | | 19.70 | 4.55 |

Issued: 12.50r, 50r, 75r, 100r, 200r, 6/8; 300r, 400r, 8/8/81; 250r, 9/82; 500r, 3/11/83; 55r, 7/83; 110r, 275r, 9/27/83.
See Nos. 1257-1261, 1265, 1268. For surcharge see No. 1527.

Map of Indonesia, People — A247

351

INDONESIA

1980, July 17   *Perf. 12½*
1093 A247 75r blue & pink .45 .25
1094 A247 200r blue & dull yel .90 .40
1980 population census.

Ship Laying Cable — A248

1980, Aug. 8   Photo.   *Perf. 12½*
1095 A248 75r multicolored .55 .25
1096 A248 200r multicolored .90 .45
Singapore-Indonesia submarine cable opening.

50s Stamp of 1946 — A249

100r, 15s Battle of Surabaya stamp, 1946, horiz. 200r, 15s Independence Fund stamp, 1946.

1980, Aug. 17
1097 A249 75r dk brn & dp org .40 .40
1098 A249 100r gold & purple .90 .45
1099 A249 200r multicolored 1.10 .70
    Nos. 1097-1099 (3) 2.40 1.55
Independence, 35th anniversary.

Asian Oceanic Postal Training School — A250

1980, Sept. 10   Photo.   *Perf. 12½*
1100 A250 200r multicolored 1.40 .25

OPEC Anniv. Emblem — A251

1980, Sept. 14
1101 A251 200r multicolored 1.20 .30
Organization of Petroleum Exporting Countries, 20th anniversary.

Armed Forces, 35th Anniversary A252

200r, Service men and emblem.

1980, Oct. 5   Photo.   *Perf. 13½x13*
1102 A252 75r shown .65 .25
1103 A252 200r multicolored 1.00 .40

Vulturine Parrot — A253

Parrots: 100r, Yellow-backed lory. 200r, Red lory.

1980, Nov. 25   Photo.   *Perf. 13x12½*
1104 A253 75r shown 2.10 .70
1105 A253 100r multi 2.60 1.40
1106 A253 200r multi 3.50 2.00
    Nos. 1104-1106 (3) 8.20 4.10

Souvenir Sheet
Perf. 12½
1106A   Sheet of 3   21.00 21.00
   b.   A253 250r like #1105   7.00 7.00
   c.   A253 350r like #1104   7.00 7.00
   d.   A253 400r like #1106   7.00 7.00

One Day Beauty Orchid — A254

Orchids: 100r, Dendrobium discolor. 200r, Dendrobium lasianthera.

1980, Dec. 10   *Perf. 13x13½*
1107 A254 75r shown .75 .25
1108 A254 100r multicolored 1.10 1.00
1109 A254 200r multicolored 2.60 .70
    Nos. 1107-1109 (3) 4.45 1.95

Souvenir Sheet
1980   *Perf. 13x13½*
1110   Sheet of 2   13.00 15.00
   a.   A254 250r like #1109   6.50 6.50
   b.   A254 350r like #1108   6.50 6.50

Heinrich von Stephan (1831-1897), UPU Founder — A255

1981, Jan. 7   *Perf. 13½x12½*
1111 A255 200r brt bl & dk bl 1.25 .60

6th Asian Pacific Scout Jamboree A256

1981   *Perf. 13½x12½, 12½x13½*
1112 A256 75r Emblems .40 .40
1113 A256 100r Scouts, vert. 1.10 .40
1114 A256 200r Emblems, diff. 1.20 .85
    Nos. 1112-1114 (3) 2.70 1.65

Souvenir Sheet
1115 A256 150r like #1113 5.00 6.00
Issued: Nos. 1112-1114, 2/22; No. 1115, 8/14.

4th Asian-Oceanian Postal Union Congress — A257

1981, Mar. 18   *Perf. 12½*
1116 A257 200r multicolored 1.40 .30

Blood Donor Campaign — A258

75r, Girl holding blood drop. 100r, Hands holding blood drop. 200r, Hands, blood, diff.

1981, Apr. 22
1117 A258 75r multicolored .50 .25
1118 A258 100r multicolored .80 .40
1119 A258 200r multicolored 1.10 .70
    Nos. 1117-1119 (3) 2.40 1.35

Intl. Family Planning Conference — A259

1981, Apr. 26
1120 A259 200r multicolored 1.20 .40

Natl. Education Day — A260

Traditional Bali Paintings: Nos. 1121-1122, Song of Sritanjung. No. 1123, Birth of the Eagle.

1981, May 2
1121 100r multicolored .80 .30
1122 200r multicolored 1.20 .65
   a.   A260 Pair #1121-1122 2.50 1.10

Souvenir Sheet
1123   Sheet of 2 10.00 12.00
   a.   A260 400r multicolored 3.50 3.50
   b.   A260 600r multicolored 6.00 6.00
No. 1123 has margin showing WIPA '81 emblem. No. 1123 exists with marginal inscription "Indonesien grusst WIPA." Value, $17.50.

A262

1981, May 9
1124 A262 200r multicolored 1.40 .45
ASEAN Building Jakarta, opening.

A263

1981, May 22
1125 A263 200r multicolored 2.25 .45
Uber Cup '81 Badminton Championship, Tokyo.

World Environment Day — A264

Bas-reliefs, Candhi Merut Buddhist Temple, Central Java: 75r, Tree of Life. 200r, Reclining Buddha.

1981, June 5
1126 A264 75r multicolored .65 .25
1127 A264 200r multicolored .95 .30

12th Koran Reading Competition, June 7-14 — A265

1981, June 7   *Perf. 13½x12½*
1128 A265 200r multicolored 1.00 .45

Intl. Year of the Disabled — A266

75r, Blind man. 200r, Speech, hearing disabilities.

1981, July 31   *Perf. 12½*
1129 A266 75r multicolored .40 .25
1130 A266 200r multicolored .95 .45

Soekarno-Hatta Independence Monument, Jakarta — A267

1981, Aug. 17
1131 A267 200r multicolored 1.40 .40

Natl. Sports Week, Sept. 19-30 — A268

75r, Skydiving. 100r, Skin diving, horiz. 200r, Equestrian.

1981, Sept. 19
1132 A268 75r multicolored .40 .25
1133 A268 100r multicolored .65 .65
1134 A268 200r multicolored 1.20 .55
    Nos. 1132-1134 (3) 2.25 1.45
The horse on No. 1134 is brown black. See Nos. 1374-1375 for souvenir sheets containing No. 1134 in different colors.

World Food Day — A268a

1981, Oct. 16
1135 A268a 200r multicolored 2.10 .70

Provincial Arms — A269

Natl. Arms — A270

No. 1136, Aceh. No. 1137, Bali. No. 1138, Bengkulu. No. 1139, Jakarta. No. 1140, West Irian. No. 1141, West Java. No. 1142, Jambi. No. 1143, Central Java. No. 1144, East Java. No. 1145, South Kalimantan. No. 1146, East Kalimantan. No. 1147, West Kalimantan. No. 1148, Lampung. No. 1149, Central Kalimantan. No. 1150, Moluccas. No. 1151, West Nusa Tenggara. No. 1152, East Nusa Tenggara. No. 1153, Southeast Sulawesi. No. 1154, Central Sulawesi. No. 1155, West Sumatra. No. 1156, North Sulawesi. No. 1157, North Sumatra. No. 1158, South Sumatra. No. 1159, Riau. No. 1160, South Sulawesi. No. 1161, Yogyakarta. No. 1161A, Timor.

1981-83
1136 A269 100r multi 2.50 .75
1137 A269 100r multi 2.50 .75
1138 A269 100r multi 2.50 .75
1139 A269 100r multi 3.00 1.50
1140 A269 100r multi 10.00 .85
1141 A269 100r multi 1.00 .45
1142 A269 100r multi 1.00 .45
1143 A269 100r multi 1.00 .45
1144 A269 100r multi 1.00 .45
1145 A269 100r multi 1.00 .45
1146 A269 100r multi 1.00 .45
1147 A269 100r multi 1.00 .45
1148 A269 100r multi 1.10 .45
1149 A269 100r multi 1.00 .45
1150 A269 100r multi .80 .45
1151 A269 100r multi 1.10 .45
1152 A269 100r multi .80 .25
1153 A269 100r multi .80 .25
1154 A269 100r multi .80 .25
1155 A269 100r multi .90 .25
1156 A269 100r multi .90 .25
1157 A269 100r multi .80 .25
1158 A269 100r multi .80 .25
1159 A269 100r multi .80 .25
1160 A269 100r multi .80 .25
1161 A269 100r multi 2.00 .25
1161A A269 100r multi 1.00 .60
1162 A270 250r shown 4.50 1.00
    Nos. 1136-1162 (28) 46.40 13.65

Issued: Nos. 1136-1140, 1981; Nos. 1141-1161, 1162, 1982; No. 1161A, 1983.

INDONESIA

Barat = West; Timur = East; Utara = North; Selatan = South; Tenggara = Southeast; Tengah = Central.

Pink-crested Cockatoo — A271

100r, Sulphur-crested cockatoo. 200r, King cockatoo.

1981, Dec. 10
1163	A271	75r shown	2.50	.80
1164	A271	100r multi	2.75	.80
1165	A271	200r multi	4.50	2.75
		Nos. 1163-1165 (3)	9.75	4.35

Souvenir Sheet
1166		Sheet of 2	17.50	21.00
a.		A271 150r like #1164	4.00	4.00
b.		A271 350r like #1165	12.50	12.50

Bumiputra Mutual Life Insurance Co., 70th Anniv. A272

75r, Family. 100r, Family, diff. 200r, Hands holding symbols.

1982, Feb. 12
1167	A272	75r multi	.40	.25
1168	A272	100r multi	.65	.40
1169	A272	200r multi	1.00	.65
		Nos. 1167-1169 (3)	2.05	1.30

Search and Rescue Institute, 10th Anniv. — A273

1982, Feb. 28   Perf. 12½x13½
1170	A273	250r multicolored	1.40	.30

General Election — A274

1982, Mar. 1   Perf. 12½
1171	A274	75r Ballot, houses	.40	.25
1172	A274	100r Farm	.55	.30
1173	A274	200r Arms	1.10	.70
		Nos. 1171-1173 (3)	2.05	1.25

2nd UN Conference on Exploration and Peaceful Uses of Outer Space, Vienna, Aug. 9-21 — A275

1982, Apr. 19   Perf. 13½x13½
1174	A275	150r Couple	.65	.40
1175	A275	250r Emblem	1.10	.65

12th Thomas Badminton Cup, London, May — A276

1982, May 19
1176	A276	250r multicolored	1.50	.45
a.		Souvenir sheet of 2	6.50	

No. 1176a also exists overprinted "INDONESIE SALUE PHILEXFRANCE" in red or black. Value, each $45.

1982 World Cup — A277

1982, June 14
1177	A277	250r multi	1.75	.45
a.		Souvenir sheet of 2	10.00	
b.-c.		Souvenir sheets of 2, each	75.00	80.00

No. 1177b overprinted "ITALIA WORLD CHAMPION" in black; No. 1177c overprinted same in red. Fake overprints exist.

60th Anniv. of Taman Siswa Educational System — A278

1982, July 3
1178	A278	250r multicolored	1.25	.50

15th Anniv. of Assoc. of South East Asian Nations (ASEAN) — A279

1982, Aug. 8   Photo.   Perf. 12½
1179	A279	150r Members' flags	1.40	.45

Balinese Starling — A280

250r, King birds of paradise.

1982, Oct. 11   Photo.   Perf. 13x13½
1180	A280	100r shown	2.50	.40
1181	A280	250r multi	4.00	1.10

Souvenir Sheet
1181A	A280	500r like 100r	13.00	13.00

3rd World Natl. Park Cong., Denpasar Bali.

Red Birds of Paradise — A281

100r, Lawe's six-wired parotia. 150r, Twelve-wired birds of paradise.

1982, Dec. 20   Perf. 12½x13½
1182	A281	100r multi	1.75	.40
1183	A281	150r multi	2.50	.80
1184	A281	250r shown	4.25	1.25
		Nos. 1182-1184 (3)	8.50	2.45

Souvenir Sheet   Perf. 12½x13½
1184A		Sheet of 2	22.00	22.00
b.		A281 200r like 100r	7.75	7.75
c.		A281 300r like 250r	12.50	12.50

Scouting Year — A282

1983, Feb. 22   Photo.   Perf. 13½x13
1185	A282	250r multi	1.75	.30

Restoration of Borobudur Temple A283

100r, Scaffolding, crane, vert. 150r, Buddha statue, stupas, vert. 250r, Statue, temple.

500r, Temple.

1983, Feb. 23   Perf. 12½
1186	A283	100r multi	1.00	.45
1187	A283	150r multi	1.50	.45
1188	A283	250r multi	4.50	2.75
		Nos. 1186-1188 (3)	7.00	3.65

Souvenir Sheet
1189	A283	500r multi	15.00	19.00

Gas Plant — A284

1983, May 16   Photo.   Perf. 12½
1190	A284	275r multi	1.20	.40

7th Intl. Liquefied Natural Gas Conference and Exhibition, Jakarta, May 16-19.

World Communications Year — A285

75r, Dove, ships. 110r, Satellite. 175r, Dish antenna, jet. 275r, Airmail envelope, globe.

1983, May 17   Perf. 12½x13½
1191	A285	75r multi	.25	.25
1192	A285	110r multi	.45	.25
1193	A285	175r multi	.80	.40
1194	A285	275r multi	1.20	.65
		Nos. 1191-1194 (4)	2.70	1.55

See Nos. 1215-1216.

13th Natl. Koran Reading Competition, Padang, May 23-31 — A286

1983, May 23   Perf. 13½x13
1195	A286	275r multi	1.25	.55

Total Solar Eclipse, June 11 A287

1983, June 11   Perf. 12½
1196	A287	110r Map, eclipse	.65	.25
1197	A287	275r multi	2.10	.40

Souvenir Sheet
1198	A287	500r like 275r	14.00	17.00

Launch of Palapa B Satellite — A288

1983, June 18   Perf. 12½x13½
1199	A288	275r multi	1.40	.55

Agricultural Census — A289

1983, July 1   Photo.   Perf. 12½
1200	A289	110r Produce	.55	.25
1201	A289	275r Farmer	1.00	.25

15th Anniv. of Indonesia-Pakistan Economic and Cultural Cooperation Org. — A290

Weavings: No. 1202, Indonesian, Lombok. No. 1203, Pakistani, Baluchistan.

1983, Aug. 19
1202	A290	275r multicolored	1.25	.85
1203	A290	275r multicolored	1.25	.85

Krakatoa Eruption Centenary — A291

1983, Aug. 26
1204	A291	110r Volcano	.55	.30
1205	A291	275r Map	1.40	.45

CN-235, Light Air Transport A292

1983, Sept. 10   Photo.   Perf. 12½
1206	A292	275r multi	1.25	.55

Tropical Fish — A293

110r, Puntius tetrazona. 175r, Rasbora einthoveni. 275r, Toxotes jaculator.

1983, Oct. 17   Photo.   Perf. 12½
1207	A293	110r multi	1.75	.65
1208	A293	175r multi	1.75	.65
1209	A293	275r multi	5.50	2.00
		Nos. 1207-1209 (3)	9.00	3.30

Canderawasih Birds — A294

110r, Diphyllodes republica. 175r, Epimachus fastuosus. 275r, Drepanornis albertisi.

1983, Nov. 30   Photo.   Perf. 12½
1210	A294	110r multi	1.25	.25
1211	A294	175r multi	1.75	.25
1212	A294	275r multi	3.50	.25
1213	A294	500r as #1212	5.00	.40
a.		Souvenir sheet of 2	22.50	22.50
		Nos. 1210-1213 (4)	11.50	1.15

Inalienable Rights of the Palestinian People — A295

1983, Dec. 20   Perf. 13½x13
1214	A295	275r multi	1.25	.30

WCY Type of 1983
Souvenir Sheets

1983   Photo.   Perf. 12½x13½
1215	A285	400r like No. 1192	9.00	8.00
1216	A285	500r like No. 1194	11.00	7.00

Telecom '83 exhib., Geneva, Oct. 26-Nov. 1 (400r). Philatelic Museum opening, Jakarta (500r). Issued: 400r, Oct. 26; 500r, Sept. 29.

INDONESIA

Fight Against Polio — A296

1984, Feb. 17		**Photo.**	**Perf. 12½**	
1217	A296	110r Emblem	.40	.25
1218	A296	275r Stylized person	1.20	.30

4th Five-Year Development Plan — A297

1984, Apr. 1		**Photo.**	**Perf. 12½**	
1219	A297	55r Fertilizer industry	.25	.25
1220	A297	75r Aviation	.25	.25
1221	A297	110r Shipping	.45	.25
1222	A297	275r Communications	1.25	.60
		Nos. 1219-1222 (4)	2.20	1.35

Forestry Resources — A298

75r, Forest, paper mill. 110r, Seedling. 175r, Tree cutting. 275r, Logs.

1984, May 17		**Photo.**	**Perf. 12½**	
1223	A298	75r multi	1.10	.25
1224	A298	110r multi	1.10	.25
1225	A298	175r multi	1.10	.40
1226	A298	275r multi	1.10	.55
a.		Souv. sheet of 2, #1225-1226	17.00	12.00
		Nos. 1223-1226 (4)	4.40	1.45

17th Annual Meeting of ASEAN Foreign Ministers A299

1984, July 9		**Photo.**	**Perf. 12½**	
1227	A299	275r Flags	1.75	.55

1984 Summer Olympics — A300

1984, July 28		**Photo.**	**Perf. 12½**	
1228	A300	75r Pole vault	.35	.25
1229	A300	110r Archery	.40	.25
1230	A300	175r Boxing	.50	.25
1231	A300	250r Shooting	1.00	.45
1232	A300	275r Weight lifting	1.40	.45
1233	A300	325r Swimming	2.25	.25
		Nos. 1228-1233 (6)	5.90	1.90

Horse Dancers, Central Java — A301

Processions: 110r, Reyog Ponorogo, East Java. 275r, Lion Dance, West Java. 325r, Barong of Bali.

1984, Aug. 17			**Perf. 12½x13½**	
1234	A301	75r shown	.75	.25
1235	A301	110r multi	1.10	.25
1236	A301	275r multi	1.10	.60
1237	A301	325r multi	2.90	.60
a.		Souvenir sheet of 1 + label	—	—
		Nos. 1234-1237 (4)	5.85	1.70

Issued: No. 1237a, 9/9/84.
Filacento Philatelic Exhibition, The Hague, Netherlands (No. 1237a).

Natl. Sports Day — A302

110r, Thomas Cup victory. 275r, Gymnastics.

1984, Sept. 9		**Photo.**	**Perf. 13½x13**	
1238	A302	110r multi	.95	.30
1239	A302	275r multi	1.40	.45

Postcode System Inauguration — A303

1984, Sept. 27		**Photo.**	**Perf. 12½**	
1240	A303	110r multi	.40	.30
1241	A303	275r multi	.85	.70

Birds of Irian Jaya — A304

75r, Chlamydera lauterbachi. 110r, Sericulus aureus. 275r, Astrapia nigra. 325r, Lophorhina superba.

1984, Oct. 15			**Perf. 12½x13½**	
1242	A304	75r multi	2.10	.25
1243	A304	110r multi	3.50	.25
1244	A304	275r multi	3.75	.25
1245	A304	325r multi	4.25	.30
a.		Souv. sheet of 2, #1242, 1245	25.00	27.00
		Nos. 1242-1245 (4)	13.60	1.05

No. 1245a for PHILAKOREA '84.

Oath of the Youth — A305

1984, Oct. 28			**Perf. 12½**	
1246	A305	275r Emblem	1.20	.70

ICAO, 40th Anniversary A306

275r, Airplane, Emblem.

1984, Dec. 7		**Photo.**	**Perf. 13½x12½**	
1247	A306	275r multi	1.25	.70

Indonesia Netherlands Marine Exped., 1984-85 — A307

Survey ship Snellius II and: 50r, Marine geological and geophysical exploration. 100r, Mapping ocean currents. 275r, Studying marine flora and fauna.

1985, Feb. 27		**Photo.**	**Perf. 13x13½**	
1248	A307	50r multi	.65	.25
1249	A307	100r multi	1.10	.25
1250	A307	275r multi	1.25	.40
		Nos. 1248-1250 (3)	3.00	.90

75th Intl. Women's Day — A308

100r, Emblem. 275r, Silhouettes, emblem.

1985, Mar. 8				
1251	A308	100r dp mauve & red	2.00	.65
1252	A308	275r brown & red	3.00	2.50

Five Year Plan — A309

75r, Mecca pilgrimage program. 140r, Compulsory education. 350r, Cement industry, Padang works.

1985, Apr. 1			**Perf. 13½x13**	
1254	A309	75r brn & red	.35	.25
1255	A309	140r brn, grey grn	.50	.25
1256	A309	350r brn, turq grn	1.00	1.00
		Nos. 1254-1256 (3)	1.85	1.70

Suharto Type of 1980-83 and

A310 A310a A310b A310c

Perf. 13½x12½, 12½ (A310, A310a, A310b, A310c)

1983-93			**Photo.**	
1257	A246	10r pale grn & dk grn	1.00	.25
1258	A246	25r pale org & dk cop red	.45	.25
1259	A246	50r beige & dk brn	.25	.25
1260	A246	55r sal rose & rose	.25	.25
1261	A246	100r lt bl grn & ultra	.40	.25
1262	A310	140r rose & dp brn	.60	.25
1263	A310c	150r yel grn & multi	.25	.25
1264	A310b	200r pink, bl & red	.40	.25
1265	A246	300r lt dull grn, bl grn & gold	1.10	.25
1266	A310c	300r multicolored	.35	.25
1267	A310	350r red & brt lil	1.00	.35
1268	A246	400r bl grn, int bl & gold	1.00	.25
1268A	A310b	700r pale grn, rose lil & grn	.90	.25
1268B	A310c	700r red & multi	.65	.25
1269	A310a	1000r multi	.90	.25
		Nos. 1257-1269 (15)	9.50	3.85

Issued: 10r, 25r, 3/11; 140r, 350r, 4/10/85; 50r, 100r, No. 1265, 12/24/86; 55r, 400r, 12/87; 200r, 12/89; 700r, 3/90; 1000r, 8/17/88; 150r, Nos. 1266, 1268B, 8/17/93.
For surcharge see No. 1527.

Asia-Africa Conference, 30th Anniv. A311

350r, Emblem, inscription.

1985, Apr. 24			**Perf. 12½**	
1270	A311	350r multi	1.60	.45

Intl. Youth Year — A312

75r, Three youths, globe. 140r, Youths supporting globe.

1985, July 12			**Perf. 12½x13½**	
1271	A312	75r multi	.60	.25
1272	A312	140r multi	1.00	.25

UN Decade for Women — A313

55r, Profiles of women, emblem. 140r, Globe, emblem.

1985, July 26				
1273	A313	55r multi	.55	.25
1274	A313	140r multi	.90	.25

Indonesian Trade Fair — A314

140r, Hydro-electric plant. 350r, Farmer, industrial plant.

1985, Aug. 1				
1275	A314	140r multi	.65	.25
1276	A314	350r multi	1.40	.40

Republic of Indonesia, 40th anniv.

11th Natl. Sports Week, Jakarta, Sept. 9-20 — A315

55r, Sky diving. 100r, Combat sports. 140r, High jump. 350r, Wind surfing, vert.

		Perf. 13½x12½, 12½x13½		
1985, Sept. 9			**Photo.**	
1277	A315	55r multi	.35	.25
1278	A315	100r multi	.75	.25
1279	A315	140r multi	.80	.25
1280	A315	350r multi	1.40	.40
		Nos. 1277-1280 (4)	3.30	1.15

Org. of Petroleum Exporting Countries, OPEC, 25th Anniv. — A316

1985, Sept. 14			**Perf. 12½**	
1281	A316	140r multi	1.25	.30

Natl. Oil Industry, Cent. — A317

1985, Oct. 8			**Perf. 13½x13**	
1282	A317	140r Oil tankers	.55	.30
1283	A317	250r Refinery	1.00	.45
1284	A317	350r Offshore oil rig	1.40	.90
		Nos. 1282-1284 (3)	2.95	1.65

UN, 40th Anniv. — A318

Design: 140r, Doves, 40, emblem. 300r, Bombs transformed into plants.

1985, Oct. 24			**Perf. 12½**	
1285	A318	140r multicolored	.45	.25
1286	A318	300r multicolored	1.40	.45

INDONESIA

Wildlife — A318a

75r, Rhinoceros sondaicus. 150r, Anoa depressicornis. 300r, Varanus komodoensis.

1985, Dec. 27   Photo.   Perf. 14½x13
1286A	A318a	75r multi	1.10	.30
1286B	A318a	150r multi	1.60	.45
1286C	A318a	300r multi	2.75	.70
		Nos. 1286A-1286C (3)	5.45	1.45

1986 Industrial Census A319

1986, Feb. 8   Photo.   Perf. 12½
1287	A319	Pair	1.40	1.25
a.		175r Census emblem	.65	.25
b.		175r Symbols of industry	.65	.25

UN Child Survival Campaign — A320

1986, Mar. 15   Photo.   Perf. 12½
1288	A320	75r Breastfeeding	.65	.25
1289	A320	140r Immunization	.85	.30

UNICEF, 40th anniv.

4th 5-year Development Plan — A321

1986, Apr. 1   Photo.   Perf. 12½
1290	A321	140r Construction	.55	.30
1291	A321	500r Agriculture	.75	.40

14th Thomas Cup, 13th Uber Cup, Jakarta — A322

1986, Apr. 22
1292	A322	55r Cup, racket	.65	.25
1293	A322	110r Cups, horiz.	1.10	.25

EXPO '86, Vancouver — A323

75r, Pinisi junk. 150r, Kentongan, satellite. 300r, Pavilion emblem.

1986, May 2   Perf. 12½x14½
1294	A323	75r multi	.50	.25
1295	A323	150r multi	1.00	.30
1296	A323	300r multi	1.50	.40
		Nos. 1294-1296 (3)	3.00	.95

A324

Perf. 13½x12½, 12½x13½

1986, June 21   Photo.
1297	A324	100r Saluting flag	.35	.25
1298	A324	140r Cookout	1.40	.30
1299	A324	210r Map-reading, vert.	1.60	.40
		Nos. 1297-1299 (3)	3.35	.95

Natl. Scout Jamboree, JAMNAS '86, Cibubur Jakarta East.

Air Show '86, Jakarta, June 22-July 1   A325

1986, June 23   Perf. 13½x12½
| 1300 | A325 | 350r multi | 1.75 | .50 |

Folk Dances   A326

1986, July 30   Photo.   Perf. 12½
1301	A326	140r Legong Kraton	1.10	.25
1302	A326	350r Barong	1.75	.45
1303	A326	500r Kecak	2.60	.60
		Nos. 1301-1303 (3)	5.45	1.30

19th Congress of Intl. Society of Sugar Cane Technologists, Jakarta — A327

1986, Aug. 5   Perf. 12½x13½
1304	A327	150r Planting	.50	.25
1305	A327	300r Sugar	1.50	.25

Sea-Me-We Submarine Cable Inauguration A328

1986, Sept. 8   Perf. 12½
1306	A328	140r shown	.50	.25
1307	A328	350r Map, diff.	1.50	.45

Southeast Asia, Middle East, Western Europe Submarine Cable.

Intl. Peace Year — A329

500r, Dove circling Earth.

1986, Dec. 17   Photo.   Perf. 12½
1308	A329	350r shown	1.10	.30
1309	A329	500r multi	1.40	.25

1987 General Election — A330

75r, Tourism, party emblems, industry. 350r, Emblems, natl. eagle, ballot box.

1987, Jan. 19
1310	A330	75r multi	.45	.25
1311	A330	140r multi	.65	.25
1312	A330	350r multi	1.25	.40
		Nos. 1310-1312 (3)	2.35	.90

A331

350r, Satellite, horiz.

1987, Mar. 21   Photo.   Perf. 12½
1313	A331	350r multi	1.00	.40
1314	A331	500r multi	1.50	.25

Launch of Palapa B-2P, Cape Canaveral.

A332

140r, Boy carving figurines, horiz.

1987, Apr. 1
1315	A332	140r multi	.30	.25
1316	A332	350r shown	.80	.35

4th 5-Year Development Plan.

Folk Costumes — A333

140r, Kalimantan Timur. 350r, Daerah Aceh. 400r, Timor Timur.

1987, May 25   Perf. 13x13½
1317	A333	140r multi	1.75	.40
1318	A333	350r multi	7.50	4.75
1319	A333	400r multi	9.00	1.10
		Nos. 1317-1319 (3)	18.25	6.25

See Nos. 1358-1363, 1412-1417, 1448-1453, 1464-1469.

14th Southeast Asia Games, Jakarta, Sept. 9-20 — A334

1987, June 10   Perf. 12½
1320	A334	140r Weight lifting	.45	.25
1321	A334	250r Swimming	.85	.30
1322	A334	350r Running	1.25	.45
		Nos. 1320-1322 (3)	2.55	1.00

Anniv. Emblems — A335

1987, June 20
1323	A335	75r multi, horiz.	.75	.25
1324	A335	100r shown	1.25	.25

City of Jakarta, 460th anniv.; Jakarta Fair, 20th anniv.

Children's Day — A336

100r, Education, horiz. 250r, Universal immunization.

1987, July 23
1325	A336	100r multicolored	.60	.25
1326	A336	250r multicolored	1.00	.25

ASEAN Headquarters, Jakarta — A337

1987, Aug. 8
| 1327 | A337 | 350r multi | 1.40 | .45 |

ASEAN, 20th anniv.

Assoc. of Physicians Specializing in Internal Diseases, 30th Anniv. — A338

300r, Stylized man, caduceus.

1987, Aug. 23   Photo.
| 1328 | A338 | 300r multicolored | 1.25 | .25 |

Sand Craters, Mt. Bromo, Timur — A339

350r, Bratan (Bedugul) Lake, Bali. 500r, Sea gardens, Bunaken Island.

1987, Oct. 20   Perf. 13½x12½
1329	A339	140r shown	.40	.25
1330	A339	350r multi	1.60	.65
1331	A339	500r multi	2.00	.30
		Nos. 1329-1331 (3)	4.00	1.20

Tourism. See Nos. 1367-1370A, 1408-1410, 1420-1422.

Role of Women in the Fight for Independence A340

75r, Veteran. 100r, Soldiers, barbed wire (Laskar Wanita).

1987, Nov. 10   Perf. 12½
1332	A340	75r multicolored	.40	.25
1333	A340	100r multicolored	.85	.25

Fish — A341

150r, Osphronemus goramy. 200r, Cyprinus carpio. 500r, Clarias batrachus.

1987, Dec. 30
1334	A341	150r multicolored	1.10	.65
1335	A341	200r multicolored	1.75	.30
1336	A341	500r multicolored	3.75	.30
		Nos. 1334-1336 (3)	6.60	1.25

Natl. Veteran's League, 31st Anniv. — A342

1988, Jan. 2
| 1337 | A342 | 250r blue grn & org | 1.10 | .25 |

Occupational Health and Safety for Greater Efficiency and Productivity A343

350r, Worker using safety equipment.

1988, Jan. 12   Perf. 13½x12½
| 1338 | A343 | 350r multicolored | 1.25 | .45 |

See No. 1419.

Natl. Craft Council, 8th Anniv. — A344

Crafts: 120r, Carved wood snake and frog. 350r, Cane rocking chair. 500r, Ornate carved bamboo containers and fan.

1988, Mar. 3   Photo.   Perf. 12½
1339	A344	120r ultra & dark brn	.70	.25
1340	A344	350r lt bl & dk brn	1.00	.45
1341	A344	500r yel grn & dk brn	1.75	.25
		Nos. 1339-1341 (3)	3.45	.95

Pelita IV (Five-Year Development Plan) — A345

140r, Oil rig, refinery. 400r, Crayfish, trawler.

INDONESIA

1988, Apr. 1
1342	A345	140r multicolored	.30	.25
1343	A345	400r multicolored	.75	.30

World Expo '88, Brisbane, Australia — A346

Designs: 200r, Two children, Borobudur Temple in silhouette. 300r, Boy wearing armor and headdress. 350r, Girl, boy and a Tongkonan house, Toraja, South Sulawesi.

1988, Apr. 30 Photo. Perf. 12½
1344	A346	200r multi	.80	.25
1345	A346	300r multi	1.20	.25
1346	A346	350r multi	1.50	.30
a.		Souv. sheet of 3, #1344-1346	12.00	12.00
		Nos. 1344-1346 (3)	3.50	.80

No. 1346a exists imperf. Value: $30 unused or used.

Intl. Red Cross and Red Crescent Organizations, 125th Annivs. — A347

1988, May 8
1347	A347	350r black & red	1.10	.25

Orchids — A348

400r, Dendrobium none. 500r, Dendrobium abang.

1988, May 17 Perf. 13x13½
1348	A348	400r multi	1.60	.45
1349	A348	500r multi	1.60	.30

1988 Summer Olympics, Seoul — A349

1988, June 15 Photo. Perf. 12½
1350	A349	75r Running	.50	.25
1351	A349	100r Weight lifting	.75	.25
1352	A349	200r Archery	.90	.25
1353	A349	300r Table tennis	.50	.25
1354	A349	400r Swimming	.65	.30
a.		Souv. sheet of 3 + label, #1351-1352, 1354, imperf	13.00	15.00
1355	A349	500r Tennis	2.25	.35
a.		Souv. sheet of 3 + label, #1350, 1353, 1355, imperf	13.00	15.00
		Nos. 1350-1355 (6)	5.55	1.65

Sheets exist perf. Value, each $12.

Intl. Council of Women, Cent. — A350

1988, June 26
1356	A350	140r brt blue & blk	.85	.25

7th Natl. Farmers' Week — A351

1988, July 9
1357	A351	350r lake & bister	1.25	.55

Folk Costumes Type of 1987

Traditional wedding attire from: 55r, West Sumatra. 75p, Jambi. 100r, Bengkulu. 120r, Lampung. 200r, Moluccas. 250r, East Nusa.

1988, July 15 Perf. 12½x14½
1358	A333	55r multicolored	.25	.25

Perf. 12½x13½
1359	A333	75r multicolored	.25	.25
1360	A333	100r multicolored	.55	.25
1361	A333	120r multicolored	.80	.25

Perf. 12½x14½
1362	A333	200r multicolored	1.50	.25
1363	A333	250r multicolored	2.00	1.00
		Nos. 1358-1363 (6)	5.35	2.25

A352

1988, Sept. 29 Photo. Perf. 12½
1364	A352	500r multicolored	1.50	.30

13th Congress of the Non-Aligned News Agencies Pool, Jakarta, Sept. 29-Oct. 1.

A353

1988, Oct. 9
1365	A353	140r multicolored	.85	.25

Intl. Letter Writing Week.

Transportation and Communications Decade for Asia and the Pacific (1985-1995) — A354

1988, Oct. 24
1366	A354	350r blk & lt blue	1.40	.55

Tourism Type of 1987

Architecture: 250r, Al Mashun Mosque, Medan. 300r, Pagaruyung Palace, Batusangkar. 500r, 1000r, Keong Emas Taman Theater, Jakarta.

1988-89 Photo. Perf. 13½x13
1367	A339	250r multi	.50	.40
1368	A339	300r multi	1.00	.30
1369	A339	500r multi	2.25	.30
		Nos. 1367-1369 (3)	3.75	1.00

Souvenir Sheets
Imperf
1370	A339	1000r multi	7.50	7.50

Perf. 14½x13
1370A		Sheet of 2	20.00	15.00
b.		A339 1500r like No. 1367	8.75	1.60
c.		A339 2500r like No. 1368	11.50	2.75

No. 1370 exists perf 14½x12½. Value $10.
Issue dates: No. 1370A, Nov. 1989; others, Nov. 25, 1988. World Stamp Expo '89, Washington, DC.

Butterflies — A356

400r, Papilio gigon. 500r, Graphium androcles.

1988, Dec. 20 Perf. 12½x13½
1371	A356	400r multi	1.50	.45
1372	A356	500r multi	2.50	.65

Souvenir Sheet
Imperf
1373	A356	1000r like 500r	9.00	9.00

No. 1373 exists perf. 12½x14½. Value $26.

Equestrian Type of 1981
Souvenir Sheets
1988 Imperf.
1374		Sheet of 4	8.00	8.00
a.		A268 200r blk, dark red & grn	.50	.25
1375		Sheet of 1 + label, dk bl, dark red & deep org	9.00	9.00

FILACEPT '88, The Hague, Oct. 18-23, 1988. Nos. 1374-1375 exist perf. 12½. Value, as 1374, $8; as 1375, $18.

Flora — A357

200r, Rafflesia. 1000r, Amorphophallus titanum.

1989, Jan. 7 Photo. Perf. 13½x13
1376	A357	200r multi	1.00	.40
1377	A357	1000r multi	2.50	.40

Souvenir Sheet
Perf. 13½x14½
Value in Black
1378	A357	1000r like No. 1377	20.00	25.00

Garuda Indonesia Airlines, 40th Anniv. — A358

1989, Jan. 26 Perf. 12½
1379	A358	350r bl grn & brt bl	1.60	.65

World Wildlife Fund — A359

Orangutans, Pongo pygmaeus: 75r, Adult and young. 100r, Adult hanging in tree. 140r, Adult, young in tree. 500r, Adult's head.

1989, Mar. 6 Photo. Perf. 12½
1380	A359	75r multi	1.75	1.10
1381	A359	100r multi	2.25	.65
a.		Souv. sheet of 2, #1380-1381	60.00	60.00
1382	A359	140r multi	2.75	.65
1383	A359	500r multi	7.00	5.00
a.		Souv. sheet of 2, #1382-1383	60.00	60.00
		Nos. 1380-1383 (4)	13.75	7.40

Use of Postage Stamps in Indonesia, 125th Anniv. — A360

1989, Apr. 1
1384	A360	1000r grn, rose lil & dp blue	2.00	.25

5th Five-year Development Plan — A361

Industries: 55r, Fertilizer. 150r, Cilegon Iron and Steel Mill. 350r, Petroleum.

1989, Apr. 1
1385	A361	55r multi	.30	.25
1386	A361	150r multi	.30	.25
1387	A361	350r multi	.70	.25
		Nos. 1385-1387 (3)	1.30	.75

See Nos. 1427-1428, 1461-1462, 1488-1489, 1530-1532.

Natl. Education Day — A362

Ki Hadjar Dewantara (b. 1889), founder of Taman Siswa school and: 140r, Graduate. 300r, Pencil, globe and books.

1989, May 2
1388	A362	140r ver, lake & brt rose lil	.60	.25
1389	A362	300r vio & pale grn	.90	.30

Terbuka University (140r) and freedom from illiteracy (300r).

Asia-Pacific Telecommunity, 10th Anniv. — A363

1989, July 1 Photo. Perf. 12½
1390	A363	350r green & vio	1.25	.85

Sudirman Cup, Flag — A364

1989, July 3
1391	A364	100r scar, gold & dark red brn	1.50	.25

Sudirman Cup world badminton mixed team championships, Jakarta, May 24-28.

Natl. Children's Day — A365

1989, July 23
1392	A365	100r Literacy	.50	.25
1393	A365	250r Physical fitness	1.00	.30

CIRDAP, 10th Anniv. — A366

1989, July 29
1394	A366	140r bl & dk red brn	1.00	.25

Center on Integrated Rural Development for Asia and the Pacific.

A367

Paleoanthropological Discoveries in Indonesia: Fossils of *Homo erectus* and *Homo sapiens* men: 100r, Sangiran 17. 150r, Perning 1. 200r, Sangiran 10. 250r, Wajak 1. 300r, Sambungmacan. 350r, Ngandong 7.

1989, Aug. 31
1395	A367	100r multi	.50	.25
1396	A367	150r multi	.70	.25
1397	A367	200r multi	1.10	.40
1398	A367	250r multi	1.40	.30
1399	A367	300r multi	1.60	.45
1400	A367	350r multi	2.25	.30
		Nos. 1395-1400 (6)	7.55	1.95

Nos. 1398-1400 vert.

A368

1989, Sept. 4
1401	A368	350r dp bl & yel grn	1.25	.75

Interparliamentary Union, Cent.

INDONESIA

12th Natl. Sports Week — A369

1989, Sept. 18
1402	A369	75r Tae kwando	.30	.25
1403	A369	100r Tennis	.40	.25
1404	A369	140r Judo	.50	.25
1405	A369	350r Volleyball	1.25	.70
1406	A369	500r Boxing	2.25	.35
1407	A369	1000r Archery	3.25	.60
		Nos. 1402-1407 (6)	7.95	2.40

Tourism Type of 1987

Structures in Miniature Park: 120r, Taman Burung. 350r, Natl. Philatelic Museum. 500r, Istana Anak-Anak, vert.

Perf. 13½x12½, 12½x13½

1989, Oct. 9
1408	A339	120r multicolored	.65	.25
1409	A339	350r multicolored	1.00	.45
1410	A339	500r multicolored	1.75	.40
		Nos. 1408-1410 (3)	3.40	1.10

Film Festival — A370

1989, Nov. 11 *Photo.* *Perf. 12½*
1411	A370	150r yel bister & blk	1.20	.25

Folk Costumes Type of 1987

Traditional wedding attire from: 50r, North Sumatra. 75r, South Sumatra. 100r, Jakarta. 140r, North Sulawesi. 350r, Mid Sulawesi. 500r, South Sulawesi. 1500r, North Sulawesi.

1989, Dec. 11 *Perf. 13x13½*
1412	A333	50r multicolored	.35	.25
1413	A333	75r multicolored	.35	.25
1414	A333	100r multicolored	.35	.25
1415	A333	140r multicolored	.80	.25
1416	A333	350r multicolored	1.25	.90
1417	A333	500r multicolored	1.75	.50
		Nos. 1412-1417 (6)	4.85	2.40

Souvenir Sheet
Imperf
1418	A333	1500r multicolored	6.50	6.50

No. 1418 exists perf. 12½x13½. Value $11.

Health and Safety Type of 1988

200r, Lineman, power lines.

1990, Jan. 12 *Perf. 13x12½*
Size: 29x21mm
1419	A343	200r blue grn & org brn	1.10	.25

Tourism Type of 1987

Architecture: 200r, Fort Marlborough, Bengkulu. 400r, 1000r, National Museum, Jakarta. 500r, 1500r, Mosque of Baiturrahman, Banda Aceh.

1990, Feb. 1 *Perf. 13½x13*
1420	A339	200r multicolored	.75	.25
1421	A339	400r multicolored	1.25	.25
1422	A339	500r multicolored	1.50	.30
		Nos. 1420-1422 (3)	3.50	.80

Souvenir Sheet
1423		Sheet of 2	9.00	9.00
a.	A339	1000r multicolored	3.25	.50
b.	A339	1500r multicolored	5.75	.75

Flora — A371

75r, Mammilaria fragilis. 1000r, Gmelina ellipitca.

1990, Mar. 1
1424	A371	75r multi	.40	.25
1425	A371	1000r multi	2.10	.45

Souvenir Sheet
1426	A371	1500r like #1425	11.00	11.00

5th Five-year Development Plan Type of 1989

200r, Road construction. 1000r, Lighthouse, ship.

1990, Apr. 1 *Perf. 12½*
1427	A361	200r multi	.35	.25
1428	A361	1000r multi	1.25	1.10

Visit Indonesia Year, 1991 — A372

Perf. 13½x12½, 12½x13½
1990, May 1
1429	A372	100r shown	.40	.25
1430	A372	500r Steps, ruin	1.25	.40

Souvenir Sheet
Perf. 14½x12½
1430A	A372	5000r like #1429	16.00	11.00

No. 1430A, Stamp World London '90.

A373

1990, May 18 *Perf. 12½*
1431	A373	1000r gray grn & brn org	1.50	.90

Disabled Veterans Corps, 40th anniv.

A374

1990, June 8 *Perf. 12½*
1432	A374	75r shown	.60	.25
1433	A374	150r multi, diff.	.90	.25
1434	A374	400r multi, diff.	2.00	.40
		Nos. 1432-1434 (3)	3.50	.90

Souvenir Sheet
1435	A374	1500r multi	8.00	8.50

World Cup Soccer Championships, Italy.

Family Planning in Indonesia, 20th Anniv. — A375

1990, June 29
1436	A375	60r brown & red	.85	.25

Natl. Census — A376

1990, July 1
1437	A376	90r yel grn & dk grn	1.00	.25

Natl. Children's Day — A377

1990, July 23
1438	A377	500r multicolored	1.40	.40

Traditional Lampung Wedding Costumes — A378

Perf. 12½x14½
1990, June 10 *Photo.*
1439	A378	2000r multicolored	7.00	7.00

Natl. Philatelic Exhibition, Stamp World London '90 and New Zealand '90.

Independence, 45th Anniv. — A379

200r, Soldier raising flag. 500r, Skyscraper, highway.

1990, Aug. 17 *Perf. 12½x13½*
1440	A379	200r multicolored	.70	.25
1441	A379	500r multicolored	1.00	.45

Souvenir Sheet
1442	A379	1000r like #1441	7.50	7.50

Indonesia-Pakistan Economic & Cultural Cooperation Organization — A380

Designs: 400r, Woman dancing in traditional costume, vert.

Perf. 13½x12½, 12½x13½
1990, Aug. 19 *Litho.*
1443	A380	75r multicolored	.55	.25
1444	A380	400r multicolored	1.25	.45

Asian Pacific Postal Training Center, 20th Anniv. — A381

1990, Sept. 10 *Photo.* *Perf. 12½*
1445	A381	500r vio bl, bl & ultra	1.40	.25

A382

1990, Sept. 14
1446	A382	200r gray, blk & org	1.25	.25

Organization of Petroleum Exporting Countries (OPEC), 30th anniv.

A383

1990, Oct. 24
1447	A383	1000r multicolored	2.10	.30

Environmental Protection Laws, 40th anniv.

Folk Costumes Type of 1987

Traditional wedding attire from: 75r, West Java. 100r, Central Java. 150r, Yogyakarta. 200r, East Java. 400r, Bali. 500r, West Nusa Tenggara.

1990, Nov. 1 *Perf. 13x13½*
1448	A333	75r multicolored	.35	.25
1449	A333	100r multicolored	.45	.25
1450	A333	150r multicolored	.50	.25
1451	A333	200r multicolored	.70	.25
1452	A333	400r multicolored	1.00	.40
1453	A333	500r multicolored	1.10	.55
		Nos. 1448-1453 (6)	4.10	1.95

A385

Visit Indonesia Year 1991: Women in traditional costumes.

1991, Jan. 1 *Photo.* *Perf. 12½x13½*
1454	A385	200r multicolored	1.00	.25
1455	A385	500r multicolored	1.25	.60
1456	A385	1000r multicolored	2.60	.45
		Nos. 1454-1456 (3)	4.85	1.30

Souvenir Sheet
1456A	A385	1500r As No. 1454	13.00	12.00

A386

1991, Feb. 4 *Perf. 12½*
1457	A386	200r yel, grn & bl grn	1.25	.25

16th natl. Koran reading competition, Jogjakarta.

Palace of Sultan Ternate, the Moluccas A387

Design: 1000r, 2500r, Bari House, Palembang, South Sumatra.

1991, Mar. 1 *Perf. 13½x12½*
1458	A387	500r multicolored	1.10	.30
1459	A387	1000r multicolored	1.75	.35

Souvenir Sheet
1460	A387	2500r multicolored	6.50	6.00

5th Five Year Development Plan Type of 1989

1991, Apr. 1 *Perf. 12½*
1461	A361	75r Steel mill, vert.	.35	.25
1462	A361	200r Computers	.60	.25

Danger of Smoking — A388

1991, May 31 *Photo.* *Perf. 12½*
1463	A388	90r multicolored	1.20	.25

Folk Costumes Type of 1987

Traditional wedding attire from: 100r, West Kalimantan. 200r, Mid Kalimantan. 300r, South Kalimantan. 400r, Southeast Sulawesi. 500r, Riau. 1000r, Irian Jaya.

INDONESIA

1991, June 15   *Perf. 13x13½*
1464	A333	100r multicolored	.30	.25
1465	A333	200r multicolored	1.00	.25
1466	A333	300r multicolored	.60	.25
1467	A333	400r multicolored	.75	.25
1468	A333	500r multicolored	1.00	.30
1469	A333	1000r multicolored	1.25	.65
		Nos. 1464-1469 (6)	4.90	1.95

Natl. Scouting Jamboree, Cibubur — A389

1991, June 15   *Perf. 12½*
1470	A389	200r multicolored	1.25	.25

Monument — A390

1991, July 6
1471	A390	200r multicolored	1.25	.25

Natl. Farmers' Week — A391

1991, July 15
1472	A391	500r brt bl, yel & grn	1.50	.25

Indonesian Chemical Society, 4th Natl. Congress — A392

1991, July 28
1473	A392	400r grn, ver & dull grn	1.50	.25

Chemindo '91.

1991, Aug. 24   *Photo.*   *Perf. 12½*
1474	A393	300r blk, red & gray	1.50	.25

5th Junior Men's and 4th Women's Asian Weightlifting Championships.

A394

1991, Aug. 30
1475	A394	500r lilac & sky blue	1.50	.25

World Cup Parachuting Championships.

A395

1991, Sept. 17
1476	A395	200r multicolored	1.40	.25

Indonesian Red Cross, 46th aAnniv.

A396

1991, Oct. 6
1477	A396	300r yellow & blue	1.40	.25

Intl. Amateur Radio Union, 8th regional conf., Bandung.

Istiqlal (Independence) Festival, Jakarta — A397

1991, Oct. 15
1478	A397	200r gray, blk & ver	1.40	.25

Intl. Conference on the Great Apes — A398

Pongo pygmaeus: 200r, Sitting in tree. 500r, Walking. 1000r, 2500r, Sitting on ground.

1991, Dec. 18   *Perf. 12½x13½*
1479	A398	200r multicolored	1.00	.25
1480	A398	500r multicolored	1.25	.30
1481	A398	1000r multicolored	2.25	.60
		Nos. 1479-1481 (3)	4.50	1.15

Souvenir Sheet
1481A	A398	2500r multicolored	8.00	8.00

Intl. Convention on Quality Control Circles, Bali — A399

1991, Oct. 22   *Perf. 12½*
1482	A399	500r multicolored	1.75	.45

Automation of the Post Office — A400

200r, P.O. 500r, Mail sorting equipment.

1992, Jan. 9   *Photo.*   *Perf. 13½x13*
1483	A400	200r multicolored	.40	.25
1484	A400	500r multicolored	.95	.30

National Elections — A401

100r, Ballot boxes, globe. 500r, Hands dropping ballots in ballot boxes.

1992, Feb. 10   *Perf. 12½*
1485	A401	75r shown	.25	.25
1486	A401	100r multicolored	.45	.25
1487	A401	500r multicolored	1.00	.30
		Nos. 1485-1487 (3)	1.70	.80

5th Five-year Development Plan Type of 1989

150r, Construction worker. 300r, Aviation technology.

1992, Apr. 1   *Photo.*   *Perf. 12½*
1488	A361	150r multicolored	.30	.25
1489	A361	300r multicolored	.60	.25

Visit Asia Year, 1992 — A402

300r, Lembah Baliem, Irian Jaya. 500r, Tanah Lot, Bali. 1000r, Lombah Anai, Sumatra Barat.

1992, Mar. 1   *Perf. 13½x13*
1490	A402	300r multicolored	.45	.25
1491	A402	500r multicolored	.90	.40
1492	A402	1000r multicolored	2.25	.40
		Nos. 1490-1492 (3)	3.60	1.05

Souvenir Sheet
1493	A402	3000r like #1491	8.00	8.00

Birds — A403

100r, Garrulax leucolophus. 200r, Dinopium javanense. 400r, Buceros rhinoceros. 500r, Alisterus amboinensis.

1992, July 1   *Photo.*   *Perf. 12½x13½*
1494	A403	100r multi	.25	.25
1495	A403	200r multi	.50	.25
1496	A403	400r multi	.80	.45
1497	A403	500r multi	1.25	.55
		Nos. 1494-1497 (4)	2.80	1.50

Souvenir Sheet
1498	A403	3000r like #1494	8.00	8.00

Children's Day — A404

75r, Street scene. 100r, Children with balloons. 200r, Boating scene. 500r, Girl feeding bird.

1992, July 23   *Perf. 12½*
1499	A404	75r multicolored	.25	.25
1500	A404	100r multicolored	.30	.25
1501	A404	200r multicolored	.50	.25
1502	A404	500r multicolored	1.10	.75
		Nos. 1499-1502 (4)	2.15	1.50

1992 Summer Olympics, Barcelona — A405

75r, Weight lifting. 200r, Badminton. 300r, Symbols of events. 500r, Women's tennis. 1000r, Archery.
No. 1508a, 2000r, like #1504. b, 3000r, like #1507.

1992, June 1   *Perf. 12½x13½*
1503	A405	75r multi	.25	.25
1504	A405	200r multi	.35	.25
1505	A405	300r multi	.65	.25
1506	A405	500r multi	.85	.25
1507	A405	1000r multi	1.75	.40
		Nos. 1503-1507 (5)	3.85	1.40

Souvenir Sheet
1508	A405	Sheet of 2, #a.-b.	9.00	9.00

ASEAN, 25th Anniv. — A406

1992, Aug. 8   *Perf. 13½x12½*
1509	A406	200r shown	.40	.25
1510	A406	500r Flags, map	1.10	.40
1511	A406	1000r Flags on poles	2.10	.45
		Nos. 1509-1511 (3)	3.60	1.10

Flowers — A407

Designs: 200r, Phalaenopsis ambilis. 500r, Rafflesia arnoldii. 1000r, 2000r, Jasminum sambae.

1992, Jan. 20   *Perf. 13½x12½*   *Photo.*
1512	A407	200r multicolored	.40	.25
1513	A407	500r multicolored	1.10	.40
1514	A407	1000r multicolored	1.50	.65
		Nos. 1512-1514 (3)	3.00	1.30

Souvenir Sheet   *Perf. 13½x13*
1515	A407	2000r multicolored	8.00	8.00

A408

1992, Sept. 6   *Perf. 12½x13½*   *Photo.*
1516	A408	200r shown	.60	.25
1517	A408	500r Flags, emblem	.80	.45

10th Non-Aligned Summit, Jakarta.

A409

1992, Nov. 29   *Photo.*   *Perf. 12½*
1518	A409	200r green & blue	1.00	.25

Intl. Planned Parenthood Federation, 40th anniv.

A410

200r, Globe, satellite. 500r, Palapa satellite. 1000r, Old, new telephones.

1992, Aug. 16   *Perf. 12½x13½*   *Photo.*
1519	A410	200r multicolored	.70	.25
1520	A410	500r multicolored	.80	.40
1521	A410	1000r multicolored	2.00	.45
		Nos. 1519-1521 (3)	3.50	1.10

Satellite Communications in Indonesia, 16th anniv.

A411

Traditional Dances: 200r, 3000r, Tari Ngremo, Timor. 500r, Tari Gending Sriwijaya, Sumatra.

1992, Oct. 1   *Perf. 12½x13½*
1522	A411	200r multicolored	.35	.25
1523	A411	500r multicolored	1.20	1.20

Souvenir Sheet
1524	A411	3000r like #1522	6.00	6.00

No. 1523 was withdrawn from sale on 10/5.
See Nos. 1564-1567, 1596-1600, 1628-1632, 1688-1692, 1747-1751, 1815-1820.

Antara News Agency, 55th Anniv. — A412

1992, Dec. 13   *Photo.*   *Perf. 12½*
1525	A412	500r blue & black	1.25	.25

INDONESIA

Natl. Afforestation Campaign
A413

Perf. 13½x12½
1992, Dec. 24 Photo.
1526 A413 500r multicolored 1.25 .25

No. 1260 Surcharged

1993, Feb. 1 Photo. **Perf. 13½x12½**
1527 A246 50r on 55r #1260 .75 .25

1993 General Session of the People's Consultative Assembly A414

1993, Mar. 1 Photo. **Perf. 13½x12½**
1528 A414 300r Building exterior .50 .25
1529 A414 700r Building interior 1.10 .30

5th Five Year Development Plan Type of 1989

300r, Soldier's silhouettes over city. 700r, Immunizing children. 1000r, Runners.

1993, Apr. 1 **Perf. 12½**
1530 A361 300r multicolored .35 .30
1531 A361 700r multicolored .80 .75
1532 A361 1000r multicolored 1.10 1.00
Nos. 1530-1532 (3) 2.25 2.05

Ornithoptera Goliath A415

1993, Apr. 20 Photo. **Perf. 12½**
1533 A415 1000r multicolored 1.75 .30
For overprint see No. 1540.

Surabaya 700th Anniv. — A416

Designs: 300r, Siege of Yamato Hotel. 700r, World Habitat Award, Surabaya skyline. 1000r, Candi Bajang Ratu, natl. monument.

Perf. 13½x12½
1993, May 29 Photo.
1534 A416 300r multicolored .45 .40
1535 A416 700r multicolored .90 .80
1536 A416 1000r multicolored 1.25 1.25
Nos. 1534-1536 (3) 2.60 2.45
For overprints see Nos. 1538-1539, 1541.

Nos. 1533-1536 Ovptd. in Red

and

Indopex '93 A417

1993 **Perfs. as Before**
1538 A416 300r on #1534 .50 .25
1539 A416 700r on #1535 1.40 .40
1540 A415 1000r on #1533 2.00 .80
1541 A416 1000r on #1536 2.00 .60
Nos. 1538-1541 (4) 5.90 2.05

Souvenir Sheet
Perf. 13½x12½
1542 A417 3500r multicolored 4.50 4.50
Location of overprint varies. Issued: No. 1540, Apr. 20; others, May 29.

Environmental Protection — A418

Flowers: Nos. 1543a, 1545a, Jasminum sambac. No. 1543b, Phalaenopsis amabilis. No. 1543c, Rafflesia arnoldi.
Wildlife: Nos. 1544a, 1545b, Varanus komodoensis. No. 1544b, Scleropages formasus. No. 1544c, Spizaetus bartelsi.

Perf. 12½x13½
1993, June 5 Photo.
1543 A418 300r Tripytych, #a.-c. 1.40 1.40
1544 A418 700r Tripytych, #a.-c. 4.50 4.50

Souvenir Sheet of 2
1545 A418 1500r #a.-b. 5.00 5.00

1st World Community Development Camp — A419

Designs: 300r, Boy scouts working on road. 700r, Pres. Suharto shaking hands with scout.

Perf. 13½x12½
1993, July 27 Photo.
1546 A419 300r multicolored .35 .25
1547 A419 700r multicolored 1.10 .25

Papilio Blumei — A420

Perf. 12½x13½
1993, Aug. 24 Photo.
1548 A420 700r multicolored 1.40 .25

Souvenir Sheets
1549 A420 3000r multicolored 6.00 6.00
1550 A420 3000r multicolored 6.00 6.00

Inscription at top of No. 1549 is like that on No. 1548. No. 1550 contains a stamp inscribed "1993," a se-tenant label and Bangkok '93 Philatelic Exhibition inscription in sheet margin.

Armed Forces Day — A421

No. 1551, Soedirman. No. 1552, Oerip Soemohardjo.

1993, Oct. 5 **Perf. 12½**
1551 A421 300r brown & red .50 .25
1552 A421 300r brown & red .50 .25
a. Pair, #1551-1552 1.00 .75

Tourism — A422

300r, 3000r, Waterfall. 700r, Cave formations. 1000r, Dormant volcanic crater, horiz.

Perf. 12½x13½, 13½x12½
1993, Oct. 4
1553 A422 300r multicolored .45 .40
1554 A422 700r multicolored .85 .85
1555 A422 1000r multicolored 1.25 1.25
Nos. 1553-1555 (3) 2.55 2.50

Souvenir Sheet
1556 A422 3000r multicolored 4.00 4.00

13th Natl. Sports Week — A423

1993, Sept. 9 **Perf. 12½x13½**
1557 A423 150r Swimming .25 .25
1558 A423 300r Cycling .35 .30
1559 A423 700r Mascot .80 .70
1560 A423 1000r High jump 1.25 1.00
Nos. 1557-1560 (4) 2.65 2.25

Souvenir Sheet
1561 A423 3500r like No. 1560 5.00 5.00

Flora and Fauna — A424

Designs: a, Michelia champaca. b, Cananga odorata. c, Copsychus pyrropygus. d, Gracula religiosa robusta.

1993, Nov. 5 Photo. **Perf. 12½x13½**
1562 A424 300r Block of 4, #a.-d. 3.50 3.50

Migratory Farm Workers — A425

1993, Dec. 4 **Perf. 12½**
1563 A425 700r Field workers .90 .70

Traditional Dance Type of 1992
Dance and region: 300r, Gending Sriwijaya, South Sumatra. 700r, Tempayan, West Kalimantan. 1000r, 3500r, Tifa, Irian Jaya.

1993, Dec. 22 **Perf. 12½x13½**
1564 A411 300r multicolored .55 .25
1565 A411 700r multicolored .90 .25
1566 A411 1000r multicolored 1.25 .25
Nos. 1564-1566 (3) 2.70 .75

Souvenir Sheet
1567 A411 3500r multicolored 4.50 4.50

Intl. Year of the Family — A426

1994, Mar. 1 Photo. **Perf. 13½x12½**
1568 A426 300r multicolored .75 .25

Indonesian Postage Stamps, 130th Anniv. A427

Design: 700r, Netherlands Indies Nos. B7, N7, Indonesia No. B214.

1994, Apr. 1 **Perf. 12½**
1569 A427 700r multicolored 1.25 .55

Souvenir Sheet Imperf
1569A A427 3500r like #1569 5.50 5.50
PHILAKOREA '94 (No. 1569A).

6th Five Year Development Plan — A428

Buddhist dieties and: 100r, Professional women. 700r, Education. 2000r, Medical care for children.

1994, Apr. 1 **Perf. 12½**
1570 A428 100r multicolored .30 .25
1571 A428 700r multicolored 1.00 .70
1572 A428 2000r multicolored 2.75 2.00
Nos. 1570-1572 (3) 4.05 2.95

Tropical Fish — A429

Designs: 300r, Telmatherina ladigesi. 700r, 3500r, Melanotaenia boesemani.

1994, Apr. 20 Photo. **Perf. 13**
1573 A429 300r multicolored .60 .25
1574 A429 700r multicolored .80 .40

Souvenir Sheet
1575 A429 3500r multicolored 6.00 6.00
No. 1575 has continuous design.

Intl. Federation of Red Cross & Red Crescent Societies, 75th Anniv. — A429a

1994, May 5 **Perf. 12½x13**
1575A A429a 300r multicolored .80 .25

Second Asian and Pacific Ministerial Conference on Women, Jakarta — A430

1994, June 13 **Perf. 13½x12½**
1576 A430 700r multicolored 1.00 .25

A431

1994 World Cup Soccer Championships, US: 150r, Player dribbling ball, vert. 300r, Mascot chasing ball, vert. 700r, 1994 Tournament emblem. 1000r, Ball in net. 3500r, Soccer ball in net.

1994, June 17 **Perf. 12½x13½**
1577 A431 150r multicolored .30 .25
1578 A431 300r multicolored .50 .25

Perf. 13½x12½
1579 A431 700r multicolored .90 .40
1580 A431 1000r multicolored 1.50 .45
Nos. 1577-1580 (4) 3.20 1.35

Souvenir Sheet
1581 A431 3500r multicolored 5.00 5.00

Thomas & Uber Cups — A432

Designs: a, Uber Cup. b, Thomas Cup.

1994, June 22 **Perf. 12½**
1582 A432 300r Pair, #a.-b. 1.25 .55

Souvenir Sheet of 2
1583 A432 1750r #a.-b. 4.50 4.50

INDONESIA

Human Rights Day — A433

Perf. 12½x13½

1994, July 27   Photo.
1584   A433   700r multicolored   1.10   .25

A434

300r, Brown pottery vase. 700r, Blue & white vase.

Perf. 13]x13½

1994, Aug. 19   Photo.
1585   A434   300r multicolored   .55   .25
1586   A434   1000r multicolored   1.10   .60

Indonesia-Pakistan Econiomic & Cultural Cooperation Organization.
See Pakistan Nos. 822-823.

Bogoriense Zoological Museum, Cent. — A435

700r, Skeleton of Javan rhinoceros. 1000r, 3500r, Skeleton of blue whale.

1994, Aug. 20   *Perf. 13½x13*
1587   A435   700r multicolored   1.25   .55
    Size: 80x22mm
1588   A435   1000r multicolored   1.75   .60
   Souvenir Sheet
    Perf. 13x13½
1588A   A435   3500r multicolored   5.50   5.50

12th Asian Games, Hiroshima 1994 — A436

1994, Oct. 2   Litho.   *Perf. 13½x13*
1589   A436   300r Mascots   .50   .25
1590   A436   700r Hurdlers   1.00   .60

Bakosurtanal, 25th Anniv. — A437

1994, Oct. 17   Litho.   *Perf. 13½x13*
1591   A437   700r multicolored   1.25   .30

Flora & Fauna — A438

Designs: a, Morus macroura. b, Oncosperma tigillaria. c, Eucalyptus urophylla. d, Phalaenopsis amabilis. e, Pometia pinnata. f, Argusianus argus. g, Loriculus pusillus. h, Philemon buceroides. i, Alisterus amboinensis. j, Seleucidis melanoleuca.
3500r, Philemon buceroides, diff.

1994, Nov. 5   Photo.   *Perf. 12½x13½*
1592   A438   150r Block or strip
      of 10, #a.-j.   6.00   6.00
   Souvenir Sheet
1593   A438   3500r multicolored   5.50   5.50
   a.   With added inscription in blue   12.00

Inscription in sheet margin of No. 1593a contains emblem and "PRIMERA '95." Issued: No. 1593a, 8/21/95.
See Nos. 1622, 1680-1682, 1737-1738, 1812-1814.

Asian-Pacific Economic Cooperation Summit (APEC '94) — A439

Design: 700r, Presidential retreat, Bogor.

1994, Nov. 15   *Perf. 13½X13*
1594   A439   700r multicolored   1.20   .25

For overprint see No. 1616A.

ICAO, 50th Anniv. — A440

1994, Dec. 7
1595   A440   700r multicolored   1.40   .25

Traditional Dance Type of 1992

Dance, region: 150r, Mengaup, Jambi. 300r, Mask, West Java. 700r, Anging Mamiri, South Sulawesi. 1000r, Pisok, North Sulawesi. 2000r, Bidu, East Nusa Tenggara. 3500r, Mask dance, West Java.

1994, Dec. 27   *Perf. 12½x13½*
1596   A411   150r multicolored   .30   .25
1597   A411   300r multicolored   .50   .25
1598   A411   700r multicolored   1.00   .30
1599   A411   1000r multicolored   1.40   .25
1600   A411   2000r multicolored   2.75   1.00
   a.   Bklt. pane, 2 ea #1596-1600   12.00
      Complete booklet, #1600a   12.00
    Nos. 1596-1600 (5)   5.95   2.05
   Souvenir Sheet
1601   A411   multicolored   5.50   5.50

World Tourism Organization, 20th Anniv. — A441

Designs: 300r, Yogyakarta Palace. 700r, Floating market. 1000r, Pasola Sumba ritual.

1995, Jan. 2   *Perf. 13½x12½*
1602   A441   300r multicolored   .25   .25
1603   A441   700r multicolored   .75   .65
1604   A441   1000r multicolored   1.00   .85
    Nos. 1602-1604 (3)   2.00   1.75

Indonesian Children, First Lady & Pres. Suharto — A442

Perf. 13½x12½

1995, Mar. 11   Photo.
1605   A442   700r multicolored   1.25   .65

6th Five Year Development Plan — A443

Designs: 300r, Letter from King of Klungung, 18th-19th cent. 700r, Carrier pigeon mascot of natl. letter writing campaign.

1995, Apr. 1   Photo.   *Perf. 12½*
1606   A443   300r multicolored   .40   .25
1607   A443   700r multicolored   1.10   .70

4th Intl. Bamboo Conference — A444

Designs: 300r, Schizostachyum brachycladum. 700r, Dendrocalamus asper.

Perf. 12½x13½

1995, June 19   Photo.
1608   A444   300r multicolored   .40   .25
1609   A444   700r multicolored   1.10   .70

First Flight of N250 Turboprop Commuter Airplane — A445

1995, Aug. 10   *Perf. 13½x12½*
1610   A445   700r multicolored   1.20   .65

Independence, 50th Anniv. — A446

300r, Anniv. emblem. 700r, Boy, national flag.

1995, Aug. 17
1611   A446   300r multi   .40   .25
1612   A446   700r multi   1.10   .70
   Souvenir Sheet
1612A   A446   2500r like No. 1612   4.50   4.50

JAKARTA '95, 8th Asian Intl. Philatelic Exhibition A447

Scenes in Jakarta: 300r, Kota Intan Drawbridge. 700r, Fatahillah Historical Museum.

1995, Aug. 8
1613   A447   300r multicolored   .40   .25
1614   A447   700r multicolored   1.00   .70

No. 1613 exists in 7 souvenir sheets of 1, each with different color margins. Sold at the 2nd International Stamp Exhibition in Jakarta. Value, set of 7 sheets $75.

Sail Indonesia '95 — A448

1995, Aug. 19
1615   A448   700r multicolored   1.00   .60
   Souvenir Sheet
1616   A448   2500r multicolored   4.50   4.50

No. 1594 Overprinted "PRIMERA '95" in Blue

1995, Aug. 21   Photo.   *Perf. 13½x13*
1616A   A439   700r on #1594   2.75   2.75

Istiqlal (Independence) Festival II 1995, Jakarta — A449

1995, Sept. 23   *Perf. 12½x13½*
1617   A449   700r multicolored   1.00   .60

Takeover of Post, Telegraph, & Telephone Headquarters, 50th Anniv. — A450

1995, Sept. 27   *Perf. 13½x12½*
1618   A450   700r multicolored   1.00   .60

FAO, 50th Anniv. — A451

1995, Oct. 16   *Perf. 12½x13½*
1619   A451   700r multicolored   1.00   .60

UN, 50th Anniv. — A452

UN emblem, "50," and: 300r, Flags of nations. 700r, Rainbow over earth.

1995, Oct. 24   *Perf. 12½*
1620   A452   300r multicolored   .40   .25
1621   A452   700r multicolored   1.00   .70

Flora and Fauna Type of 1994

Designs: a, Cyrtostachys renda. b, Panthera tigris sumatrae. c, Bouea macrophylla. d, Rhinoceros sondaicus. e, Santalum album. f, Varanus komodoensis. g, Diospyros celebica. h, Macrocephalon maleo. i, Nephleium ramboutan-ake. j, Polyplectron schleiermacheri.
2500r, Panthera tigris sumatrae.

1995, Nov. 5   Photo.   *Perf. 12½x13½*
1622   A438   150r Block of 10,
       #a.-j.   5.00   4.00
   Souvenir Sheet
1623   A438   2500r multicolored   9.00   8.00

1995 Aga Khan Award for Architecture A453

Designs: 300r, Masjid Agung, Kraton Yogyakarta. 700r, Kraton Surakarta.

1995, Nov. 23   *Perf. 13½x13*
1624   A453   300r multicolored   .50   .25
1625   A453   700r multicolored   1.10   .70

Sir Rowland Hill (1795-1879) — A454

300r, Hill, letter carriers on motorcycles. 700r, Hill, Indonesian postal service logo.

1995, Dec. 3   *Perf. 13½x12½*
1626   A454   300r multicolored   .40   .25
1627   A454   700r multicolored   1.10   .70

Traditional Dance Type of 1992

Dance and region: 150r, Nguri, West Nusa Tenggara. 300r, Muli Betanggai, Lampung. 700r, Mutiara, Maluku. 1000r, Gantar, East Kalimantan. 2500r, Tari Nguri, Nusa Tenggara Barrat.

1995, Dec. 27   *Perf. 12½x13½*
1628   A411   150r multicolored   .40   .25
1629   A411   300r multicolored   .50   .25
1630   A411   700r multicolored   1.00   .60
1631   A411   1000r multicolored   1.25   .80
    Nos. 1628-1631 (4)   3.15   1.90
   Souvenir Sheet
1632   A411   2500r multicolored   4.00   3.00

1996 Economic Census — A455

Design: 300r, Economic sectors, vert.

1996, Jan. 2   *Perf. 12½*
1633   A455   300r multicolored   .40   .25
1634   A455   700r multicolored   1.00   .70

INDONESIA

Greetings Stamps — A456

Various flowers.

1996, Feb. 1   Photo.   Perf. 12½
1635	A456	150r multicolored	.30	.25
1636	A456	300r multicolored	.50	.25
1637	A456	700r multicolored	.80	.55
	Nos. 1635-1637 (3)		1.60	1.05

See Nos. 1657-1659.

PWI Journalists' Assoc., 50th Anniv. — A457

Designs: 300r, RM Soemanang Soeriowinoto. 700r, Djamaluddin Adinegoro.

1996, Feb. 9
1638	A457	300r multicolored	.40	.25
1639	A457	700r multicolored	1.10	.55

Australian Spotted Cuscus — A458

Design: Nos. 1640, 1642a, shown. Nos. 1641, 1642b, Indonesian bear cuscus.

1996, Mar. 21   Photo.   Perf. 13x13½
1640	A458	300r multicolored	.55	.40
1641	A458	300r multicolored	.55	.40
a.	Pair, Nos. 1640-1641		1.40	1.40
b.	Sheet of 5 #1641a		35.00	17.50

Souvenir Sheet
1642	A458	1250r Sheet of 2, #a.-b.	3.50	3.50
c.	#1642 with added inscription, ovpt.		7.00	7.00

Indonesia '96 (No. 1641b).

No. 1642c has black CHINA '96 exhibition emblem in upper right corner. The bottom sheet margin contains gold overprint: "CHINA '96 - 9th Asian International Philatelic Exhibition" in both Chinese and English.

No. 1641b exists folded and affixed to a booklet cover. Value, $10.

See Australia Nos. 1489-1490.

A459

Launching of Palapa C Satellite — A460

1996, Jan. 31   Perf. 13
1643	A459	300r multicolored	.65	.25

                  Perf. 12½
1644	A460	700r multicolored	1.60	.60

Indonesia '96, World Junior Philatelic Exhibition A461

Designs: 300r, No. 1647a, Building. 700r, No. 1647b, Decorated sun umbrellas.

1996, Mar. 21   Perf. 13½x13
1645	A461	300r multicolored	.45	.25
1646	A461	700r multicolored	1.25	.55

Souvenir Sheet of 2
1647	A461	1250r #a.-b.	6.50	3.25

No. 1647 exists imperf with different color margins. A souvenir sheet containing No. 1645-1646 and progressive color proofs of No. 1646 exists.

Education Day — A462

Children's drawings: 150r, Teachers, students with outstretched arms. 300r, Children carrying books to school. 700r, Classroom instruction.

1996, May 2   Photo.   Perf. 13½x13
1648	A462	150r multicolored	.35	.25
1649	A462	300r multicolored	.50	.25
1650	A462	700r multicolored	1.10	.55
	Nos. 1648-1650 (3)		1.95	1.05

Natl. Youth Kirab — A463

700r, Holding flag, emblem.

1996, June 8
1651	A463	300r shown	.40	.25
1652	A463	700r multicolored	1.00	.55

1996 Summer Olympics, Atlanta — A464

1996, May 15
1653	A464	300r Archery	.50	.30
1654	A464	700r Weight lifting	1.00	.60
1655	A464	1000r Badminton	1.40	1.00
	Nos. 1653-1655 (3)		2.90	1.90

Souvenir Sheet
1656	A464	2500r like #1653	3.50	3.00

No. 1656 is a continuous design.

Greetings Type of 1996

150r, Roses. 300r, Orchids. 700r, Chrysanthemums.

1996, Apr. 15   Photo.   Perf. 12½
1657	A456	150r multicolored	.35	.25
1658	A456	300r multicolored	.50	.25
1659	A456	700r multicolored	1.00	.55
	Nos. 1657-1659 (3)		1.85	1.05

Maritime and Aviation Year — A465

300r, N-2130 aircraft, control tower at Soekarno-Hatta Airport. 700r, Inter-island passenger ship.

1996, June 22
1660	A465	300r multicolored	.30	.25
1661	A465	700r multicolored	1.10	.55

1996 Natl. Scout Jamboree — A466

Designs: a, Climbing rope. b, Sliding down rope. c, Girls at bottom of ropes. d, Girls assembling wood and rope ladder. e, Riding unicycle, eagle emblem, boys building scaffolding. f, Girls building scaffolding, campground. g, Two boys with project. h, Woman seated at control center.

No. 1662l, like #1662a-1662d. No. 1662J, like #1662e-1662h.

1996, June 26
1662	A466	150r Block of 8, #a.-h.	2.50	1.75

Souvenir Sheets
1662I	A466	1250d multicolored	2.50	2.50
1662J	A466	1250d multicolored	2.50	2.50

Istanbul '96 (Nos. 1662I-1662J). Nos. 1662I-1662J each contain one 64x48mm stamp.

Nos. 1662a-1662d, 1663e-1662h are continuous designs.

Bank BNI, 50th Anniv. — A467

1996, July 5
1663	A467	300r shown	.40	.25
1664	A467	700r Sailing ship	1.10	.55

UNICEF, 50th Anniv. — A468

1996, July 23   Perf. 13½x13
1665	A468	300r Child reading	.40	.30
1666	A468	700r Two children	.80	.60
1667	A468	1000r Three children	1.25	.90
	Nos. 1665-1667 (3)		2.45	1.80

Ibu Tien Suharto (1923-96) First Lady — A469

1996, Aug. 5   Perf. 12½x13½
1668	A469	700r multicolored	1.00	.55

Souvenir Sheet
1669	A469	2500r like #1668	3.00	3.00

No. 1669 is a continuous design.

14th Natl. Sports Week, Jakarta — A470

    Perf. 13½x12½   Photo.

1996, Sept. 2
1670	A470	300r Softball	.40	.30
1671	A470	700r Field hockey	.85	.60
1672	A470	1000r Basketball	1.25	.90
	Nos. 1670-1672 (3)		2.50	1.80

World Wildlife Fund — A471

Rhinoceros sondaicus: a, Adult. b, Adult with young. Dicerorhinus sumatrensis: c, Up close. d, Adult.

No. 1674: a, Like No. 1673a; b, Like No. 1673d.

1996, Oct. 2   Photo.   Perf. 13½x13
1673	A471	300r Block of 4, #a.-d.	2.25	2.25
e.	Souvenir sheet, 2 #1673		4.50	4.50
f.	As "e," ovptd. in sheet margin		5.75	3.75

Souvenir Sheet
1674	A471	1500r Sheet of 2, #a.-b.	4.50	4.50

Overprint in margin of No. 1673f reads: "Bursa Filateli SEA Games XIX / Jakarta, 11-19 Oktober 1997" in gold. Value, $6.

Greetings Stamps — A472

Bouquets of various flowers.

1996, Oct. 15   Photo.   Perf. 12½

Background Colors
1675	A472	150r yellow & blue	.30	.25
1676	A472	300r yellow & green	.40	.25
1677	A472	700r pink & blue	.85	.55
	Nos. 1675-1677 (3)		1.55	1.05

Financial Day, 50th Anniv. — A473

1996, Oct. 30   Perf. 13½x12½
1678	A473	700r multicolored	1.40	.55

Flora & Fauna Type of 1994

Fauna: No. 1680: a, Aceros cassidix. b, Orcaella brevirostris. c, Oriolus chinensis. d, Helarctos malayanus. e, Leucopsar rothschildi.

Flora: f, Borassus flabellifer. g, Coelogyne pandurata. h, Michelia alba. i, Amorphophallus titanum. j, Dysoxylum densiflorium.

No. 1681, Like No. 1680e. No. 1682, Like No. 1680g.

1996, Nov. 5   Litho.   Perf. 12½x13½
1680	A438	300r Block or strip of 10, #a.-j.	4.50	4.50
a.-j.	Any single		.45	.30

Souvenir Sheets
1681	A438	1250r multicolored	3.50	3.50
1682	A438	1250r multicolored	3.50	3.50

Souvenir Sheet

Aceros Cassidix A474

  Perf. 12½x13½

1996, Dec. 14   Photo.
1683	A474	2000r multicolored	10.00	10.00

ASEANPEX '96.

Scenes from Timor — A475

Designs: 300r, Deep sea diving. 700r, Sailing ships entering harbor, 18th cent.

1996-97   Perf. 13½x12½
1684	A475	300r multicolored	.50	.30
1685	A475	700r multicolored	1.25	.60

Souvenir Sheet
1685A	A475	2000d like #1685	5.50	2.75

Hong Kong '97 (No. 1685A).

Issued: Nos. 1686-1687, 12/18/96; No. 1685A, 2/12/97.

Foster Parents — A476

150r, Children at playground, vert. 300r, Children, adult's hand holding picture of girl.

  Perf. 12½x13½, 13½x12½

1996, Dec. 20
1686	A476	150r multicolored	.30	.25
1687	A476	300r multicolored	.45	.25

Traditional Dance Type of 1992

Dance, region: 150r, Tari Baksa Kembang, Kalimantan Selatan. 300r, 2000r, Tari Ngarojeng, Jakarta. 700r, Tari Rampai, Aceh. 1000r, Tari Boituka, Timor.

INDONESIA

1996, Dec. 27 — Perf. 12½x13½
1688	A411	150r multicolored	.30	.25
1689	A411	300r multicolored	.40	.25
1690	A411	700r multicolored	.75	.55
1691	A411	1000r multicolored	1.25	.80
	Nos. 1688-1691 (4)		2.70	1.85

Souvenir Sheet
1692	A411	2000r multicolored	3.00	3.00

Telecommunications Year — A477

Designs: 300r, Satellite dish, men at computers, map. 700r, Telephone keypad, woman using telephone, satellite in earth orbit.

1997, Jan. 1 — Perf. 13½x12½
1693	A477	300r multicolored	.40	.25
1694	A477	700r multicolored	.80	.55

Greetings Stamps — A478

Designs: No. 1695, Heart, ribbon. No. 1696, Children, "Happy Birthday."

1997, Jan. 15 — Perf. 12½
1695	A478	600r multicolored	.70	.45
1696	A478	600r multicolored	.70	.45

1997 General Election — A479

Ballot box and: 300r, Means of transportation. 700r, Indonesian Archipelago, House of Representatives Building. 1000r, Map, symbols of development.

1997, Feb. 3 — Perf. 13½x13
1697	A479	300r multicolored	.45	.30
1698	A479	700r multicolored	.80	.60
1699	A479	1000r multicolored	1.40	.90
	Nos. 1697-1699 (3)		2.65	1.80

Birth of Indonesia's 200-millionth Citizen — A480

700r, Pres. Suharto, baby.

Perf. 13½x12½
1997, Mar. 24 — Litho.
1700	A480	700r multicolored	1.00	.55

A481

Indonesian Philatelists Assoc., 75th Anniv.: 300r, Youth examining stamps, #1672. 700r, Magnifying glass, #1660, #1592h, #1580.

1997, Mar. 29 — Perf. 12½x13½
1701	A481	300r multicolored	.50	.30
1702	A481	700r multicolored	.90	.60

A482

Indonesian Artists: 300r, Wage Rudolf Soepratman (1903-38), composer, violinist. 700r, Usmar Ismail (1921-71), film pioneer, director. 1000r, Affandi (1907-90), painter.

1997, Apr. 30 — Litho. Perf. 13x13½
1703	A482	300r multicolored	.40	.30
1704	A482	700r multicolored	.80	.60
1705	A482	1000r multicolored	1.40	.90
b.	Sheet, 3 each #1703-1705 + label		8.00	7.00
	Nos. 1703-1705 (3)		2.60	1.80

Souvenir Sheet
1705A	A482	2000r like #1705	2.50	2.50

Indonesia 2000 — A483

Gemstones: 300r, Picture jasper. 700r, Chrysocolla. 1000r, Geode. 2000r, Banded agate.

1997, May 20 — Litho. Perf. 13½x13
1706	A483	300r multicolored	.50	.30
1707	A483	700r multicolored	.75	.45
1708	A483	1000r multicolored	1.50	.90
a.	Sheet, 3 each, #1706-1708 + label		8.50	4.75
b.	As "a", control No. in margin		20.00	6.50
	Nos. 1706-1708 (3)		2.75	1.65

Souvenir Sheet
1709	A483	2000r multicolored	4.00	2.50
a.	Control No. in margin		4.75	2.50

Nos. 1708b, 1709a promote INDONESIA 2000, Jakarta, Aug. 15-21, 2000. Nos. 1708a-1709 and 1708b-1709a were issued in presentation packs with certificate of authenticity.

See Nos. 1764-1767A, 1848-1851, 1851A, 1888-1891.

A484

1997, May 31 — Photo. Perf. 12½
1710	A484	1000r multicolored	1.25	.80

World Day to Stop Smoking.

World Environment Day — A485

Various marine life of the coral reefs.

1997, June 5 — Litho. Perf. 13x13½
1711	A485	150r multicolored	.40	.25
1712	A485	300r multicolored	.45	.25
1713	A485	700r multicolored	.90	.55
	Nos. 1711-1713 (3)		1.75	1.05

Souvenir Sheet
1714	A485	2000r multicolored	4.00	4.00

ASEAN, 30th Anniv. — A486

300r, Hands reaching out to each other. 700r, Rice stalks arranged to form number 30, globe.

1997, Aug. 8 — Litho. Perf. 13½x13
1715	A486	300r multicolored	.40	.25
1716	A486	700r multicolored	.85	.55

19th Southeast Asia Games, Jakarta — A487

No. 1717, Logo, "Hanoman" mascot. No. 1718, Runner carrying torch, flags of participating nations, logo. No. 1719, Runner, track, discus thrower. No. 1720, Hurdler, runners.

1997, Sept. 9 — Litho. Perf. 12½
1717	A487	300r multicolored	.30	.25
1718	A487	300r multicolored	.30	.25
a.	Pair, #1717-1718		.75	.75
1719	A487	700r multicolored	.75	.50
1720	A487	700r multicolored	.75	.50
a.	Pair, #1719-1720		2.00	2.00
b.	Bklt. pane, 2 ea #1717-1720		5.50	
	Complete booklet, 1 #1720b		5.50	
	Nos. 1717-1720 (4)		2.10	1.50

Transportation A488

1997, Sept. 17
1721	A488	300r Buses, ox cart	.45	.25
1722	A488	300r Trains	.45	.25
a.	Pair, #1721-1722		.90	.50
1723	A488	700r Ships	1.25	.50
1724	A488	700r Airplanes	1.25	.50
a.	Pair, #1723-1724		2.50	1.00
	Nos. 1721-1724 (4)		3.40	1.50

Souvenir Sheet

Oriolus Chinensis A489

1997, May 25 — Perf. 12½x13½
1725	A489	2000r multicolored	6.50	3.25

PACIFIC 97.

Nusantara Royal Palace Festival — A490

Royal carriages: 300r, Singa Baraong wooden carriage, 1549, with carving of mythical animal. 700r, Paksi Naga Liman carriage, phoenix-like bird.

1997, July 1 — Litho. Perf. 13½x12½
1726	A490	300r multicolored	.45	.25
1727	A490	700r multicolored	.80	.50

18th Natl. Koran Reading Contest A491

Designs: 300r, Decorated roof peaks, windows. 700r, Al-Ikhsaniah Mosque.

1997, July 9 — Perf. 12½
1728	A491	300r multicolored	.45	.25
1729	A491	700r multicolored	.80	.50

Indonesian Membership in UPU, 50th Anniv. — A492

Emblem of UPU and: 300r, Mas Soeharto. 700r, Heinrich von Stephan.

1997, Sept. 27 — Litho. Perf. 13½x13
1730	A492	300r multicolored	.40	.25
1731	A492	700r multicolored	.80	.50

1997-98 General Session of People's Consultative Assembly A493

1997, Oct. 1 — Perf. 12½
1732	A493	700r multicolored	.75	.50

Indonesian Armed Forces Day — A494

Designs: a, ABRI Village Program. b, Jalesveva Jayamahe Monument. c, Blue Falcon Flight Demonstration Team. d, Police Fast Reaction Unit.

1997, Oct. 5 — Perf. 13½x12½
1733	A494	300r Block of 4, #a.-d.	1.50	1.00

Flora and Fauna Type of 1994

Fauna: No. 1737: a, Chitala lopis. b, Haliastur indus. c, Rhinoplax vigil. d, Cervus timorensis. e, Bubalus depressicornis.

Flora: f, Lansium domesticum. g, Salacca zalacca. h, Shorea stenoptera. i, Diospyros macrophylla. j, Diplocaulobium utile.

No. 1738: a, Shorea stenoptera. b, Haliastur indus.

1997, Nov. 5 — Perf. 12½x13½
1737	A438	300r Block of 10	3.50	2.50
a.-j.	Any single		.35	.25

Souvenir Sheet
1738	A438	1250r Sheet of 2, #a.-b.	2.50	2.00

A495

Indonesian Cooperatives Day — A496

Designs: No. 1739, Cooperatives Monument, Tasikmalaya. No. 1740, Cooperatives Monument, Jakarta. No. 1741, Adult taking child's hand. No. 1742, Globe, movement towards globalization. No. 1743, Dr. Mohammad Hatta, Pres. Suharto.

1997, July 12 — Litho. Perf. 12½x13½
1739	A495	150r multicolored	.30	.25
1740	A495	150r multicolored	.30	.25
a.	Pair, #1739-1740		.60	.40
1741	A495	300r multicolored	.40	.25
1742	A495	300r multicolored	.40	.25
a.	Pair, #1741-1742		.80	.50

Perf. 12½
1743	A496	700r multicolored	1.00	.55
	Nos. 1739-1743 (5)		2.40	1.50

ASCOPE '97 (Asian Council on Petroleum) A497

a, LNG tanker. b, Petroleum trucks. c, Drilling rig, pumping wells. d, Refinery.

1997, Nov. 24 — Perf. 13½x12½
1744	A497	300r Block of 4, #a.-d.	1.50	.90

Foster Parents Natl. Movement A498

1997, Dec. 20 — Photo.
1745	A498	700r multicolored	.80	.40

INDONESIA

Family Welfare Movement, 25th Anniv. — A499

1997, Dec. 27   Litho.
1746   A499   700r multicolored   .80   .45

Traditional Dance Type of 1992

Dance, region: 150r, Moputi Cengke (clove picking), Central Sulawesi. 300r, Mandau Talawang Nyai Balau, Central Kalimantan. 600r, 2000r, Gambyong, Central Java. 700r, Cawan (bowl,) North Sumatra. 1000r, Legong Keraton, Bali.

1997, Dec. 27
1747   A411   150r multicolored   .30   .25
1748   A411   300r multicolored   .40   .25
1749   A411   600r multicolored   .60   .40
1750   A411   700r multicolored   .75   .45
1751   A411   1000r multicolored   .90   .60
   Nos. 1747-1751 (5)   2.95   1.95

Souvenir Sheet
Perf. 12½x13½
1752   A411   2000r multicolored   2.50   1.60
   No. 1752 is a continuous design.

Sulawesi Selatan A500

1997, Oct. 11   Litho.   **Perf. 13½x12½**
1753   A500   2000r multicolored   2.50   1.50
Makasser '97 National Philatelic Exhibition.

Year of Art and Culture 1998 — A501

Designs: 300r, Erau Festival, East Kalimantan. 700r, Tabot Festival, Bengkulu.

1998, Jan. 1   Litho.   **Perf. 12½**
1754   A501   300r multicolored   .40   .30
1755   A501   700r multicolored   .60   .30

Indonesian Folktales — A502

Folktale, region — No. 1759; a-e, Malin Kundang, West Sumatra. f-j: Sangkuriang, West Java. k-o, Roro Jonggrang, Central Java. p-t: Tengger, East Java. Each horizontal strip of 5 has continuous design.
2500r, Kasodo Ceremony, Tenegger, East Java.

1998, Feb. 2   **Perf. 13½x12½**
1759   Sheet of 20   4.00   3.00
  a.-t.   A502 300r Any single   .30   .25

Souvenir Sheet
1760   A502   2500r like #1759e   1.75   1.00
See Nos. 1828-1829, 1886-1887, 1929-1930.

Presidential Palaces — A503

Designs: a, Jakarta. b, Bogor. c, Cipanas. d, Yogyakarta. e, Tampak Siring.

1998, Apr. 1
1761   A503   300r Strip of 5, #a.-e.   1.10   .60

World Health Organization, 50th Anniv. A504

Designs: 300r, Pregnant woman, man, vert. 700r, Woman holding baby.

1998, Apr. 7   Litho.   **Perf. 12½**
1762   A504   300r multicolored   .30   .25
1763   A504   700r multicolored   .60   .30

Indonesia 2000 Type of 1997

Gemstones: 300r, Chrysopal. 700r, Tektite. 1000r, Amethyst. No. 1767, Petrified wood. No. 1767A, opal.

1998, May 2   **Perf. 13½x12½**
1764   A483   300r multicolored   .40   .25
1765   A483   700r multicolored   .40   .25
1766   A483   1000r multicolored   .40   .35
  a.   Sheet, 3 each #1764-1766 + label   5.00   2.50
   Nos. 1764-1766 (3)   1.20   .85

Souvenir Sheets
1767   A483   2500r multicolored   1.75   1.00
Perf. 13½x14
1767A   A483   2500r multicolored   5.00   3.00
  b.   Sheet, 2 each, #1764-1766, 1 each #1767, 1767A   15.00   14.00

Nos. 1767A, 1767Ab were issued in presentation packs with control numbers printed in margin and certificate of authenticity.
No. 1767A sold for 10,000r. No. 1767Ab sold for 25,000r.

1998 World Cup Soccer Championships, France — A505

Young boys playing soccer in Indonesia: 300r, Outside school, boy on bicycle. 700r, In neighborhood lot. 1000r, 2500r, In rural area.

1998, June 1
1768   A505   300r multicolored   .30   .25
1769   A505   700r multicolored   .40   .25
1770   A505   1000r multicolored   .80   .35
   Nos. 1768-1770 (3)   1.50   .85

Souvenir Sheet
1771   A505   2500r multicolored   1.50   1.00

World Environment Day — A506

Trees along river bank, denomination at: No. 1772, lower right. No. 1773, lower left.

1998, June 5
1772   A506   700r multicolored   .60   .25
1773   A506   700r multicolored   .60   .25
  a.   Pair, #1772-1773   1.25   .70

Souvenir Sheet

Juvalux '98, World Philatelic Exhibition, Luxembourg A507

1998, June 18   **Perf. 12½x13½**
1774   A507   5000r Felis viverrina   4.00   2.50

World Day to Fight Drug Abuse and Illicit Drug Trafficking — A508

Cartoons depicting how to say no to drugs.

1998, June 26
1775   A508   700r red & multi   .50   .30
1776   A508   700r yellow & multi   .50   .30
  a.   Pair, #1775-1776   1.25   .70
  b.   Tete beche pair, #1775-1776   1.25   .70

Tourism — A509

Temples, shrines in Bali: Nos. 1777, 1779, Pura Besakih. No. 1778, Pura Taman Ayun.

1998, July 1   **Perf. 12½**
1777   A509   700r multicolored   .50   .25
1778   A509   700r shown   .50   .25
  a.   Pair, #1777-1778   1.00   .60

Souvenir Sheet
Perf. 13½x13
1779   A509   2500r multicolored   1.75   1.00
No. 1777 is 64x24mm. No. 1779 contains one 41x25mm stamp.

Souvenir Sheet

Panthera Tigris A510

1998, July 23   Litho.   **Perf. 13½x12½**
1780   A510   5000r multicolored   3.00   3.00
Singpex '98.

Trains — A511

Train going right: a, Cattle, freight cars. b, Freight, box cars. c, Passenger cars. d, Passenger car, tender. e, Locomotive 850.
Train going left: f, Locomotive D52. g, Coal tender. h, Car with 2 doors. i, Dining car with large windows. j, Car with two windows. 2500r, Locomotive.

1998, Aug. 10
1781   A511   300r Block of 10, #a.-j.   3.50   2.50

Souvenir Sheet
1782   A511   2500r multicolored   1.75   1.10
No. 1781 issued in sheets of 20 stamps consisting of two tete-beche blocks of 10. No. 1782 contains one 41x25mm stamp.

Pres. H.B.J. Habibie — A512

1998, Aug. 17   **Perf. 12½x13½**
1783   A512   300r pink & multi   .35   .25
1784   A512   700r blue & multi   .45   .25
1785   A512   4500r green & multi   1.60   .90
1786   A512   5000r yellow & multi   1.75   1.00
   Nos. 1783-1786 (4)   4.15   2.40

13th Asian Games — A513

1998, Sept. 9   **Perf. 13½x12½**
1787   A513   300r Fencing   .35   .25
1788   A513   700r Taekwondo   .45   .25
1789   A513   4000r Wushu   1.50   .85
  a.   Sovenir sheet, #1787-1789   2.40   1.50
   Nos. 1787-1789 (3)   2.30   1.35

Intl. Year of the Ocean — A514

Perf. 13½x12½
1998, Sept. 26   Litho.
1790   A514   700r multicolored   .75   .25

Souvenir Sheets

5th NVPH (Netherlands Philatelic Congress) Exhibition, The Hague — A514a

Birds: 5000r, Halcyon cyannoventris. 35,000r, Vannelus macropterus, vert.

1998, Oct. 8   Litho.   **Perf. 13½x12½**
1790A   A514a   5000r multi   2.00   2.00
1790B   A514a   35,000r multi   12.50   12.50

A515

1998, Oct. 9   **Perf. 12½x13½**
1791   A515   700r #922   .50   .25
1792   A515   700r #414   .50   .25
  a.   Pair, #1791-1792   1.25   .30
World Stamp Day.

A516

Ducks and Geese: 250r, No. 1805, Aythya australis. 500r, Anas superciliosa. 700r, Anas gibberifrons. 1000r, Nettapus coromandelianus. 1500r, Nettapus pulchelus. 2500r, Dendrocygna javanica. 3500r, Dendrocygna arcuata. 4000r, Anseranas semipalmata. No. 1801, Dendrocygna guttata. 10,000r, Anas waigiuensis. 15,000r, Tadorna radjah. 20,000r, Cairina scutulata.

Litho. (#1793-1799, 1805)

1998   **Perf. 12½**
1793   A516   250r multi   .25   .25
1794   A516   500r multi   .35   .25
1795   A516   700r multi   .40   .25
1796   A516   1000r multi   .50   .30
1797   A516   1500r multi   .65   .40
1798   A516   2500r multi   .80   .65
1799   A516   3500r multi   1.25   .85

Litho. With Hologram
Perf. 13½x12½
Size: 42x25mm
1800   A516   4000r horiz.   1.25   .90
1801   A516   5000r horiz.   1.50   1.25
1802   A516   10,000r horiz.   3.25   2.25
1803   A516   15,000r horiz.   4.00   3.25
1804   A516   20,000r horiz.   6.50   4.25
  a.   Sheet of 5, #1800-1804, + 4 labels   20.00   12.50
   Nos. 1793-1804 (12)   20.70   14.85

Souvenir Sheet
Perf. 12½
1805   A516   5000r lt blue sky   3.25   3.25

Soaking in water may affect the hologram on Nos. 1800-1804.
Issued: Nos. 1793-1799, 1805, 12/1; others 10/19.
See Nos. 1918-1919.

INDONESIA

Souvenir Sheet

Italia '98
A516a

5000r, Jakarta Cathedral.

1998, Oct. 23			Perf. 12½x13½	
1805A	A516a	5000r multi	2.25	2.25

National Flag — A517

Mountains and: No. 1806, Flagpole at right. No. 1807, Flagpole at left.

1998, Oct. 28	Litho.		Perf. 12½x13½	
1806	A517	700r multicolored	.50	.25
1807	A517	700r multicolored	.50	.25
a.		Pair, #1806-1807	1.10	.40

Reform Movement A518

No. 1809, Dove, national flag. No. 1810, Students, Parliament Building.

1998, Oct. 28			Perf. 13½x12½	
1808	A518	700r shown	.35	.25
1809	A518	700r multicolored	.35	.25
a.		Pair, #1808-1809	1.00	.40

Size: 83x25mm

1810	A518	1000r multicolored	.75	.30

Flora and Fauna Type of 1994

Flora — No. 1812: a, Stelechocarpus burahol. b, Polianthes tuberosa. c, Mirabilis jalapa. d, Mangifera casturi. e, Ficus minahassae.
Fauna — f, Geopelia striata. g, Gallus varius. h, Elephas maximus. i, Nasalis larvatus. j, Tarsius spectrum.
No. 1813, like #1812b. No. 1814, like #1812i.

1998, Nov. 5			Perf. 12½x13½	
1812	A438	500r Block of 10	4.00	2.00
a.-j.		Any single	.40	.25

Souvenir Sheets

1813	A438	2500r multicolored	1.50	1.50
1814	A438	2500r multicolored	1.50	1.50

Traditional Dance Type of 1992

Dance, region: 300r, Oreng-oreng Gae, Southeast Sulawesi. 500r, Tribute dance, Bengkulu. 700r, Fan dance, Riau. 1000r, Srimpi, Yogyakarta. 2000r, 5000r, Tribute dance, West Sumatra.

1998, Dec. 27				
1815	A411	300r multicolored	.35	.25
1816	A411	500r multicolored	.35	.25
1817	A411	700r multicolored	.45	.25
1818	A411	1000r multicolored	.55	.25
1819	A411	2000r multicolored	1.00	.40
		Nos. 1815-1819 (5)	2.70	1.40

Souvenir Sheet

1820	A411	5000r multicolored	3.00	1.40

Creation and Engineering Year — A519

Designs: 500r, Hydroelectric turbine, power lines. 700r, Plumbing fixture, water pipes.

1999, Jan. 1	Litho.		Perf. 12½	
1821	A519	500r multicolored	.40	.25
1822	A519	700r multicolored	.50	.25

7th Far East & South Pacific Games for Disabled — A520

No. 1823, Throwing shotput. No. 1824, Medals, wheelchair.

1999, Jan. 10			Perf. 12½x13½	
1823	A520	500r multi	.40	.25
1824	A520	500r multi	.40	.25
a.		Pair, #1823-1824	.80	.25

Garuda Indonesia Airways, 50th Anniv. — A521

500r, Logo. 700r, Aircraft maintenance. 2000r, Pilot, attendant.

1999, Jan. 26			Perf. 13x13½	
1825	A521	500r multi	.25	.25
1826	A521	700r multi	.35	.25
1827	A521	2000r multi	.70	.40
		Nos. 1825-1827 (3)	1.30	.90

Indonesian Folktales Type of 1998

Folktale, region — No. 1828: a-e, Danau Toba, North Sumatra. f-j, Banjarmasin, South Kalimantan. k-o, Buleleng, Bali. p-t, Woiram, Irian Jaya.
5000r, like #1828e.

1999, Feb. 15			Perf. 13½x12½	
1828		Sheet of 20	6.00	4.00
a.-e.	A502	500r Strip of 5	1.50	1.00
f.-j.	A502	500r Strip of 5	1.50	1.00
k.-o.	A502	500r Strip of 5	1.50	1.00
p.-t.	A502	500r Strip of 5	1.50	1.00

Souvenir Sheet

1829	A502	5000r multicolored	2.50	1.50

Nos. 1829 is a continuous design.

Surabaya '99, Natl. Philatelic Exhibition — A522

1999, Mar. 4	Litho.		Perf. 13½x12½	
1830	A522	5000r Apples	2.75	1.75
a.		Ovptd. in sheet margin	4.00	3.00

No. 1830a Overprinted in Gold in Sheet Margin with "APPI SHOW '99 / SURABAYA, 10-18 JULI 1999" and Emblem. Issued, 7/10.

Souvenir Sheet

Australia '99, World Stamp Expo A523

1999, Mar. 19			Perf. 12½x13½	
1831	A523	5000r Tarsius spectrum	2.50	2.50
a.		Ovptd. in sheet margin	4.00	4.00

No. 1831a Overprinted in Gold in Sheet Margin with "The 13th / Thaipex / China / Stamp Exhibition / Bangkok '99 / 4 -15. 8. 99" and Emblem. Issued, 8/15.

Mushrooms A524

No. 1832: a, Mutinus bambusinus. b, Ascoparassis heinricherii. c, Mycena sp.
No. 1833: a, Micropurus xanthopus. b, Gloeophyllum imponens. c, Termitomyces eurrhizus.
No. 1834: a, Aseroe rubra. b, Calostoma orirubra. c, Boedijnopeziza insititia.
5000r, Termitomyces eurrhizus.

1999, Apr. 1			Perf. 12½	
1832	A524	500r Triptych, #a.-c.	1.25	.70
1833	A524	700r Triptych, #a.-c.	1.50	.75
1834	A524	1000r Triptych, #a.-c.	2.25	1.00
d.		Souvenir sheet, #1832-1834	5.00	3.00

Souvenir Sheet

1835	A524	5000r multicolored	2.50	1.75

Booklet Stamps

Size: 32x24mm

1836	A524	500r Like #1832a	.80	.25
1837	A524	500r Like #1832b	.80	.25
1838	A524	500r Like #1832c	.80	.25
a.		Booklet pane, 3 each #1836-1838, + label	7.25	
		Complete booklet, #1838a	7.25	
		Nos. 1836-1838 (3)	2.40	.75

No. 1835 contains one 25x41mm stamp. Numbers have been reserved for additional values in this set.

Public Health Care Insurance A525

1999, Apr. 7			Perf. 13½x12½	
1845	A525	700r multicolored	.70	.25

Souvenir Sheet

IBRA '99, Intl. Philatelic Exhibition, Nuremberg — A526

5000r, Dendrobium abang betawi.

1999, Apr. 27			Perf. 12½x13½	
1846	A526	5000r multi	2.75	2.75

Y2K Millennium Bug — A527

Designs: a, "Bug." b, Circuit, android.

1999, May 2			Perf. 13½x12½	
1847	A527	500r Pair, #a.-b.	.90	.50

Indonesia 2000 Type of 1997

500r, Chrysoprase. 1000r, Smoky quartz. 2000r, Opal blue.
No. 1851, Silicified coral. No. 1851A, Javan jade.

1999, May 20	Litho.		Perf. 13½x12¾	
1848	A483	500r multi	.35	.25
1849	A483	1000r multi	.55	.30
1850	A483	2000r multi	1.00	.65
a.		Sheet, 3 ea #1848-1850 + label	6.00	6.00
		Nos. 1848-1850 (3)	1.90	1.20

Souvenir Sheet

1851	A483	4000r multi	3.50	3.50
1851A	A483	4000r multi	12.00	12.00
b.		Sheet, #1851-1851A, 2 ea # 1849-1850, 4 #1848	18.00	18.00

Nos. 1851A, 1851Ab were issued in presentation packs with certificate of authenticity. Control numbers and silver overprint "1 Tahun/ Lagi / 1 Year / to Go" printed in margin. No. 1851A sold for 10,000r; No. 1851Ab for 30,000r.

Environmental Care — A528

Winning designs of 1999 Ecophila Stamp Design Contest: 500r, Girl wrapped in blanket, people walking through water. 1000r, 3000r, Boy swimming with duck, plant, cherry. 2000r, Elderly woman drinking water from pitcher, outdoor scene.

1999, June 5				
1852	A528	500r multicolored	.30	.25
1853	A528	1000r multicolored	.60	.45
1854	A528	2000r multicolored	1.25	.80
		Nos. 1852-1854 (3)	2.15	1.50

Souvenir Sheet

1855	A528	3000r multicolored	2.00	1.10

1999 General Election A529

Designs: a, "48," Banner, people standing in line to vote. b, People waiting turn to enter election booth, map.

1999, June 4				
1856	A529	1000r Pair, #a.-b.	1.40	.75

Souvenir Sheet

PhilexFrance '99 — A530

1999, July 2	Litho.		Perf. 12¾x13½	
1858	A530	5000r multi		3.50 3.50

INDONESIA

Red Cross / Red Crescent Millennium Year Campaign — A531

Photo. & Litho.
1999, Aug. 12 — Perf. 12½
1859 A531 1000r multicolored ... .80 .40

National Heroes — A532

No. 1860: a, Dr. W. Z. Johannes (1895-1924). b, Martha Christina Tijahahu (1800-18), freedom fighter. c, Frans Kaisiepo (1921-79), politician. d, Maria Walanda Maramis (1872-1924), educator.

Litho. & Engr.
1999, Aug. 17 — Perf. 12½
1860 Strip of 4 ... 1.50 .80
  a.-d. A532 500r any single ... .40 .25
  e. Booklet pane of 4, #1860a ... 2.00
  f. Booklet pane of 4, #1860b ... 2.00
  g. Booklet pane of 4, #1860c ... 2.00
  h. Booklet pane of 4, #1860d ... 2.00
    Complete bklt., #1860e-1860h ... 8.00
Complete booklet sold for 10,000r.

Souvenir Sheet

China 1999 World Philatelic Exhibition — A533

Perf. 13½x12¾
1999, Aug. 21 — Litho.
1861 A533 5000r multi ... 2.50 2.00

Gadjah Mada University, 50th Anniv. A534

1999, Sept. 19 — Perf. 12½
1862 A534 500r shown ... .50 .25
1863 A534 1000r Building, diff. ... .60 .25

Intl. Year of Older Persons — A535

1999, Oct. 1 — Perf. 13½x12¾
1864 A535 500r multi ... .65 .25

UPU, 125th Anniv. A536

No. 1865, Postman on horse. No. 1866, Postman on motorcycle.

1999, Oct. 9 — Perf. 12½
1865 A536 500r multicolored ... .50 .25
1866 A536 500r multicolored ... .50 .25
  a. Pair, #1865-1866 + label ... 1.25 .50
1866B Pair + 2 labels ... 3.00 2.00
  c. A536 1000r Like #1865, 30x32mm ... 1.50 1.00
  d. A536 1000r Like #1866, 30x32mm ... 1.50 1.00

No. 1866B issued in sheets of 5 pairs. As the labels could be personalized, sheets were available only through special orders with Indonesia Post and sold for 20,000r.

Batik Designs — A537

1999, Oct. 1
1867 A537 500r Cirebon ... .40 .25
1868 A537 500r Madura ... .40 .25
1869 A537 500r Jambi ... .40 .25
1870 A537 500r Yogyakarta ... .40 .25
  Nos. 1867-1870 (4) ... 1.60 1.00

Domesticated Animals — A538

1999, Nov. 5 — Perf. 13½x12¾
1871 A538 500r Dogs ... .30 .25
1872 A538 500r Chickens ... .30 .25
  a. Pair, #1871-1872 ... .75 .50
1873 A538 500r Cat ... .30 .25
1874 A538 500r Rabbits ... .30 .25
  a. Pair, #1873-1874 ... .75 .50
1875 A538 1000r Pigeon ... .70 .40
1876 A538 1000r Geese ... .70 .40
  a. Pair, #1875-1876 ... 1.50 .80
  b. Sheet of 6, #1871-1876 ... 3.50 2.50
  Nos. 1871-1876 (6) ... 2.60 1.80

Souvenir Sheet
1877 A538 4000r Like #1874 ... 2.50 1.75

Millennium A539

Designs: No. 1878, 1000r, No. 1880, 20,000r, 1999 agenda book. No. 1879, 1000r, No. 1881, 20,000r, Clock, child.

Litho. & Photo.
1999-2000 — Perf. 13½x12¾
1878-1879 A539 Set of 2 ... 1.25 .75
  a. Sheet of 20 + 20 labels ... 25.00 25.00

Souvenir Sheets
1880-1881 A539 Set of 2 ... 20.00 20.00
Labels on No. 1879a could be personalized. The sheet sold for 38,000r.
Issued: Nos. 1878, 1880, 12/31/99; Nos. 1879, 1879a, 1881, 1/1/00.

Visit Indonesia Decade — A540

Designs: 500r, Satellite, fish. 1000r, Hydroponic agriculture.

2000, Jan. 1 — Perf. 12¾x13½
1882-1883 A540 Set of 2 ... 1.25 .65

University of Indonesia, 50th Anniv. A541

Designs: 500r, Salemba campus. 1000r, University building, Depok.

2000, Feb. 2 — Perf. 12½
1884-1885 A541 Set of 2 ... 1.25 .65

Indonesian Folktales Type of 1998

Folktale, region — No. 1886: a-e, Tapak Tuan, Aceh. f-j, Batu Ballah, West Kalimantan. k-o, Sawerigading, South Sulawesi. p-t, 7 Putri kahyangan, Moluccas.
5000r, Like #1886e

2000, Feb. 5 — Perf. 13½x12¾
1886 Sheet of 20 ... 10.00 10.00
  a.-e. 500r Strip of 5 ... 2.50 2.50
  f.-j. 500r Strip of 5 ... 2.00 2.00
  k.-o. 500r Strip of 5 ... 2.50 2.00
  p.-t. 500r Strip of 5 ... 2.50 2.00
1887 A502 5000r multi ... 3.00 2.50

Indonesia 2000 Type of 1997

Designs: 500r, Prehnite. 1000r, Chalcedony. 2000r, Volcanic obsidian.

2000, Mar. 1
1888-1890 A483 Set of 3 ... 2.50 1.50
1890a Souvenir sheet, 3 each #1888-1890 + label ... 7.50 3.50

Souvenir Sheet
1891 A483 5000r Jasperized limestone ... 3.50 3.50
  a. Sheet, #1891, 14 #1888, 2 #1889, 3 #1890 + 20 labels ... 20.00 —

No. 1891a sold for 41,000r with labels personalized.

Comic Strip Characters — A542

Designs: No. 1892, 500r, I Brewok, by Gungun. No. 1893, 500r, Pak Tuntung, by Basuki. No. 1894, Pak Bei, by Masdi Sunardi. No. 1895, 500r, Mang Ohle, by Didin D. Basuni. No. 1896, 500r, Panji Koming, by Dwi Koendoro.

Perf. 12¾x13½
2000, Mar. 13 — Photo.
1892-1896 A542 Set of 5 ... 1.75 1.10
1896a Souvenir sheet, 3 each #1892-1896 + label ... 6.50 3.50

World Meteorological Organization, 50th Anniv. — A543

Litho. & Photo.
2000, Mar. 23 — Perf. 12½
1897 A543 500r multi ... .80 .30

Souvenir Sheet

Bangkok 2000 Stamp Exhibition — A544

2000, Mar. 23 — Perf. 13½x12¾
1898 A544 5000r multi ... 4.00 2.50

15th Natl. Sports Week — A545

Designs: 500r, Cycling. 1000r, Canoeing. 2000r, High jump.

2000, Apr. 1
1899-1901 A545 Set of 3 ... 2.50 1.60

Souvenir Sheet

The Stamp Show 2000, London A546

2000, May 22
1902 A546 5000r multi ... 4.00 2.50

Environmental Care — A547

Designs; 500r, Birds in nest. 1000r, Monkeys. 2000r, Fish.

2000, June 5
1903-1905 A547 Set of 3 ... 2.75 1.75

Souvenir Sheet
1906 A547 4000r Like #1904 ... 4.00 2.00

2000 Summer Olympics, Sydney — A548

No. 1907, 500r: a, Boxing. b, Judo.
No. 1908, 1000r: a, Badminton. b, Weight lifting.
No. 1909, 2000r: a, Swimming. b, Running.

2000, July 1 — Pairs, #a-b
1907-1909 A548 Set of 3 ... 4.50 3.00

Souvenir Sheet
1910 A548 5000r Like #1908b ... 4.00 2.25

Worldwide Fund for Nature (WWF) — A549

Komodo dragon: No. 1911, 500r, No. 1915a, 2500r, With tongue extended. No. 1912, 500r, On log. No. 1913, 500r, Pair walking. No. 1914, 500r, No. 1915b, 2500r, Pair fighting.

2000, Aug. 13
1911-1914 A549 Set of 4 ... 2.50 2.00
  a. Souvenir sheet, 2 each #1911-1914 ... 9.00 7.50

Souvenir Sheet
1915 A549 2500r Sheet of 2, #a-b ... 5.50 4.00

Souvenir Sheet

Olymphilex 2000 Stamp Exhibition A550

2000, Sept. 15 — Perf. 12¾x13½
1916 A550 5000r multi ... 4.00 2.25

A551

No. 1917: a, Pres. Abdurrahman Wahid. b, Vice Pres. Megawati Soekarnoputri

Photo. & Engr.
2000, Sept. 27 — Perf. 12½
1917 A551 1000r Pair, #a-b ... 1.50 1.00

Ducks and Geese Type of 1998

2000, Sept. 27 — Photo. — Perf. 12½
1918 A516 800r Like #1798 ... 1.25 1.00
1919 A516 900r Like #1793 ... 1.25 1.00

365

INDONESIA

Traditional Costumes — A552

Provinces and regions: a, Aceh. b, Jambi. c, Banten. d, Yogyakarta. e, Central Kalimantan (Kalimantan Tengah). f, Southeast Sulawesi (Sulawesi Tenggara). g, East Nusa Tenggara (Nusa Tenggara Timur). h, North Sumatra (Sumatera Utara). i, Bengkulu. j, Jakarta. k, East Java (Jawa Timur). l, East Kalimantan (Kalimantan Timur). m, South Sulawesi (Sulawesi Selatan). n, Maluku. o, West Sumatra (Sumatera Barat). p, South Sumatra (Sumatera Selatan). q, West Java (Jawa Barat). r, West Kalimantan (Kalimantan Barat). s, North Sulawesi (Sulawesi Utara). t, Bali. u, North Maluku (Maluku Utara). v, Riau. w, Lampung. x, Central Java (Jawa Tengah). y, South Kalimantan (Kalimantan Selatan). z, Central Sulawesi (Sulawesi Tengah). aa, West Nusa Tenggara (Nusa Tenggara Barat). ab, Irian Jaya.

Litho. & Photo.
2000, Oct. 28   *Perf. 12½*
1920   A552   Sheet of 28 + 7 labels   25.00   15.00
   a.-ab.   900r Any single   .55   .50

Artists and Entertainers — A553

No. 1921, horiz.: a, Bing Slamet (1927-74), singer, comedian. b, S. Sudjojono (1913-86), painter. c, I Ketut Maria (1897-1968), dancer. d, Chairil Anwar (1922-49), poet. e, Ibu Sud (1908-93), musician.

2000, Nov. 1   *Perf. 13½x12¾*
1921   Horiz. strip of 5   3.50   2.00
   a.-e.   A553 900r Any single   .60   .40
   Souvenir Sheet
1922   A553   4000r Chairil Anwar   2.50   2.00

Indonesia Post in the 21st Century — A554

Designs: 800r, Philately, vert. 900r, Business communications. 1000r, Business financial services, vert. 4000r, Business logistics, vert.

Litho. & Photo.
2000, Dec. 20   *Perf. 12½*
1923   A554   800r multi   .60   .30
1924   A554   900r multi   .60   .40
1925   A554   1000r multi   1.00   .50
1926   A554   4000r multi   3.50   1.75
   Nos. 1923-1926 (4)   5.70   2.95

Solar System A555

No. 1927: a, Sun. b, Mercury. c, Venus. d, Earth. e, Mars. f, Jupiter. g, Saturn. h, Uranus. i, Neptune. j, Pluto.

2001, Jan. 1   Litho.   *Perf. 13½x12¾*
1927   Block of 10 + 5 labels   7.00   3.50
   a.-j.   A555 900r Any single   .60   .30
   k.   Sheet of 10 + 5 labels   8.00   4.00
   l.   Sheet of 20 + 20 labels   20.00   20.00
   Souvenir Sheet
1928   A555   5000r Sun   3.00   2.00

Labels on No. 1927l could be personalized. The sheet sold for 36,000r.

Indonesian Folktales Type of 1998

Folktale, region — No. 1929: a-e, Batang Tuaka, Riau. f-j, Si Pitung, Jakarta. k-o, Terusan Nusa, Central Kalimantan. p-t, Ile Mauraja, East Nusa Tenggara.

5000r, Like No. 1929h.

Litho. & Photo.
2001, Feb. 2   *Perf. 13½x12¾*
1929   Sheet of 20   10.00   6.00
   a.-e.   A502 900r Strip of 5   2.50   1.50
   f.-j.   A502 900r Strip of 5   2.50   1.50
   k.-o.   A502 900r Strip of 5   2.50   1.50
   p.-t.   A502 900r Strip of 5   2.50   1.50
   Souvenir Sheet
1930   A502   5000r multi   2.50   1.25

Topeng Masks A556

No. 1931, 500r — Arsa Wijaya, Bali: a, Denomination at L. b, Denomination at R.
No. 1932, 800r — Asmat, Irian Jaya: a, Denomination at L. b, Denomination at R.
No. 1933, 800r — Cirebon, West Java: a, Denomination at L. b, Denomination at R.
No. 1934, 900r — Hudoq, East Kalimantan: a, Denomination at L. b, Denomination at R.
No. 1935, 900r — Wayang Wong, Yogyakarta: a, Denomination at L. b, Denomination at R.

5000r, Like No. 1934b.

2001, Mar. 2   *Perf. 12¾x13½*
   Pairs, #a-b
1931-1935   A556   Set of 5   4.50   2.25
   c.   Sheet, #1931-1935 +2 labels   5.00
   Souvenir Sheet
1936   A556   5000r multi   3.00   2.00
   a.   Ovptd. in margin in silver   4.50   3.00

Issued: No. 1936a, 10/16/01. No. 1936 overprinted with "HAFNIA '01 / World Philatelic Exhibition / Copenhagen / 16-21 October 2001," show emblem and new price of 7500r.

Traditional Communication Instruments — A557

No. 1937: a, Beduk. b, Bendé. c, Kentongan. d, Nafiri.

2001, Mar. 10   *Perf. 12½*
1937   Vert. strip of 4   2.00   1.50
   a.-d.   A557 900r Any single   .50   .35
   e.   Sheet, 2 each #1937a-1937d   8.00   4.00

Greetings — A558

Various flowers. Denominations: 800, 900, 1000, 1500, 2000, 4000, 5000, 10000r.

Litho. & Typo.
2001, Apr. 21   *Perf. 12½*
1938-1945   A558   Set of 8   14.00   8.75

Greetings A558a

A558b

2001, Apr. 21   Litho. & Typo.
   Perf. 13½x12¾
1945A   A558a 900r multi + label   3.50   2.50
   Perf. 12½
1945B   A558b 900r multi + label   3.50   2.50

No. 1945A was issued in sheets of 20 + 20 labels that could be personalized. The sheet sold for 36,000r. No. 1945B was issued in sheets of 10 + 10 labels that could be personalized. The sheet sold for 20,000r.

Environmental Care — A559

Children and: 800r, Fish. 900r, 5000r, Deer. 1000r, Sea turtle.

Litho. & Photo.
2001, June 5   *Perf. 13½x12¾*
1946   A559   800r multi   .50   .30
   a.   Tete-beche pair   1.00   1.00
1947   A559   900r multi   .50   .30
   a.   Tete-beche pair   1.00   1.00
1948   A559   1000r multi   .75   .40
   a.   Tete-beche pair   1.50   1.50
   Nos. 1946-1948 (3)   1.75   1.00
   Souvenir Sheet
1949   A559   3000r multi   3.50   3.00

No. 1949 exists imperf. Value $3.50.

Pres. Sukarno (1901-70) A560

Various portraits: 500, 800, 900, 1000r. 5000r, Sukarno at microphone.

2001, June 6   *Perf. 12½*
1950-1953   A560   Set of 4   2.00   1.25
   a.   Sheet, 2 each #1950-1953   6.50   3.25
   Souvenir Sheet
   Perf. 13½x12¾
1954   A560   5000r multi   3.00   2.25

No. 1954 contains one 41x25mm stamp.

National Police A561

Police and: a, Children. b, Helicopter.

2001, July 1   Photo.   *Perf. 13½x12¾*
1955   A561   1000r Horiz. pair, #a-b   1.25   1.10

National Scouting Jamboree — A562

Scouts: a, Raising flag. b, Pitching tent.

2001, July 3
1956   A562   1000r Horiz. pair, #a-b   1.25   1.10

Children's Games — A563

Designs: 800r, Kaki Siapa. 900r, Egrang Bambu. 1000r, Dakon. 2000r, Kuda Pelepah Pisang.

Litho. & Photo.
2001, July 23   *Perf. 13½x12¾*
1957-1960   A563   Set of 4   2.50   1.25
   a.   Sheet, 2 each #1957-1960   6.00   4.50
   Souvenir Sheet

Phila Nippon '01, Japan A564

2001, Aug. 1   Photo.
1961   A564   10,000r multi   6.00   4.00

Dr. R. Soeharso Orthopedic Hospital, Surakarta, 50th Anniv. — A565

Litho. & Photo.
2001, Aug. 28   *Perf. 13½x12¾*
1962   A565   1000r multi   .85   .30

Traditional Transportation A566

Designs: No. 1963, 1000r, Rowboat. No. 1964, 1000r, Trishaw. No. 1965, Horse-drawn carriage.

2001, Sept. 17
1963-1965   A566   Set of 3   1.50   1.00
   a.   Sheet, 3 each #1963-1965 +label   6.00   6.00

Post Offices — A567

Buildings in: 800r, Makassar. 900r, Bandung. 1000r, Balikpapan. 2000r, Padang.

2001, Sept. 27
1966-1969   A567   Set of 4   2.50   1.60

Gemstones A568

Designs: 800r, Rose quartz. 900r, Brecciated jasper. 1000r, Malachite. 5000r, Diamond.

2001, Oct. 1
1970-1972   A568   Set of 3   1.75   1.10
   a.   Sheet, 3 each #1970-1972 + label   5.50   4.50
   Souvenir Sheet
1973   A568   5000r multi   3.00   2.25

Year of Dialogue Among Civilizations — A569

2001, Oct. 9   Litho.   *Perf. 12¾x13½*
1974   A569   1000r multi   1.25   .40

Beetles — A570

Designs: 800r, Agestrata dehaan. 900r, Mormolyce phyllodes. No. 1977, 1000r,

INDONESIA

Batocera rosenbergi. No. 1978, 1000r, Chrysochroa buqueti. 2000r, 5000r, Chalcosoma caucasus.

2001, Nov. 5   Litho. & Photo.
1975-1979	A570	Set of 5	3.50	2.25
a.	Booklet pane, #1975-1979 + label		6.00	—
	Booklet, 2 #1979a		12.00	

Souvenir Sheet
1980	A570	5000r multi	3.00	2.50

Folktales — A571

No. 1981, 1000r — Pulau Kembara, South Sumatra: a, Four people, lanterns. b, Two men, woman, boat. c, Man and woman standing in boat. d, Man and woman in water. e, Boat, snake, fish.

No. 1982, 1000r — Nyi Koro Kidul, Yogyakarta: a, Woman at tight pointing. b, Woman at foreground with hand at mouth. c, Two men with hats at right. d, Woman in sea. e, Sea and island.

No. 1983, 1000r — Aji Tatin, East Kalimantan: a, Bird in tree, woman, man with hand outstretched. b, Woman, bird boat. c, Sinking boat. d, Woman and tree. e, Bird in tree.

No. 1984, 1000r — Danau Tondano, North Sulawesi: a, Woman with long hair in foreground. b, Man holding spear. c, Man at left with arm to head. d, Man and woman embracing. e, Sea and island.

5000r, Like No. 1981e.
Illustration reduced.

2002, Feb. 2   Litho. & Photo.
Perf. 13½x12¾
Blocks of 5, #a-e
1981-1984	A571	Set of 4	8.00	4.00

Souvenir Sheet
1985	A571	5000r multi	3.00	2.00

Nos. 1981-1984 are printed in sheets of four blocks of five. Stamp "e" is always adjacent to the LL stamp in the block of the remaining four stamps, and is found tete beche to both stamps "a" and "e" from adjacent blocks of five.

2002 World Cup Soccer Championships, Japan and Korea — A572

Celebrations: 1000r, Player lifting shirt over face. 1500r, Four players with fists raised, horiz. 2000r, 5000r, Player with arms outstretched.

2002, Apr. 1   Perf. 12¾x13½, 13½x12¾
Litho. & Photo.
1986-1988	A572	Set of 3	2.50	2.00

Souvenir Sheet
1989	A572	5000r multi	3.00	2.00

Indonesian Cancer Foundation, 25th Anniv. — A573

2002, Apr. 17   Perf. 12¾x13½
1990	A573	1000r multi	.90	.45
a.	Tete-beche pair		1.80	1.25

Telecommunications — A574

No. 1991: a, Woman using telephone (2/4). b, Man using cellular phone (1/4). c, Satellite above Earth (4/4). d, Satellite, world map, computer, satellite dish (3/4).

2002, May 17
1991	A574	1000r Block of 4, #a-d	2.50	1.50
e.	Sheet, 2 each #1991a-1991d		5.00	4.00
f.	Booklet pane, 4 #1991a		2.50	
g.	Booklet pane, 4 #1991b		2.50	
h.	Booklet pane, 4 #1991c		2.50	
i.	Booklet pane, 4 #1991d		2.50	
	Booklet, #1991f-1991i		10.00	

Marine Life — A575

No. 1992, 1000r: a, Charonia tritonis. b, Symphyllia radians.
No. 1993, 1500r: a, Cromileptes altivelis. b, Acanthaster planci.
No. 1994, 2000r, horiz.: a, Paracanthurus hepatus. b, Tridacna gigas.
5000r, Acanthaster planci.

2002, June 5   Horiz. Pairs, #a-b
1992-1994	A575	Set of 3	5.00	3.50
1994c		Sheet, #1992, 1993, 1994a, 1994b	7.00	3.50

Souvenir Sheet
1995	A575	5000r multi	3.00	2.00

Aceh Province — A576

Designs: 1500r, Student, Aceh dance, map of Aceh. 3500r, Masjid Raya Banda Aceh, map of Indonesia.

2002, June 15   Perf. 12½
1996-1997	A576	Set of 2	2.75	.45

Natl. Family Day — A577

2002, June 29   Litho. & Typo.
Perf. 13½x12¾
1998	A577	1000r multi	.85	.45

33rd Intl. Physics Olympiad, Bali — A578

No. 1999: a, Eclipse (1/2). b, Spectrum colors and Balinese symbols (2/2).

2002, July 14   Perf. 12¾x13½
1999	A578	1000r Horiz. pair, #a-b	1.25	1.00

Kites — A579

No. 2000: a, Popotengan (bird-shaped) (1/5). b, Barong (dragon head) (2/5). c, Fighting (3/5). d, Bebean (4/5). e, Modern (box and wing) (5/5).
5000r, Popotengan.

2002, July 15   Litho. & Photo.
Perf. 13½x12¾
2000		Horiz. strip of 5	2.50	2.50
a.-e.	A579	1000r Any single	.50	.30

Souvenir Sheet
2001	A579	5000r multi	3.00	2.00

Fruit — A580

Designs: 300r, Morinda citrifolia. 500r, Mangifera indica. 1500r, Averrhoa carambola. 3000r, Durio zibethinus.

2002, Aug. 1   Photo.   Perf. 13½x12¾
2002	A580	300r multi	.35	.25
2003	A580	500r multi	.35	.25
2004	A580	1500r multi	.65	.65
2005	A580	3000r multi	1.40	1.10
		Nos. 2002-2005 (4)	2.75	2.25

Souvenir Sheet

Philakorea 2002 World Stamp Exhibition, Seoul — A581

2002, Aug. 2   Litho.   Perf. 12¾x13½
2006	A581	7000r multi	4.00	3.00

Mohammad Hatta (1902-80), Prime Minister A582

No. 2007, 1000r: a, Denomination at left. b, Denomination at right.
No. 2008, 1500r: a, Denomination at left. b, Denomination at right.
5000r, Hatta standing.

2002, Aug. 12   Litho. & Photo.
Perf. 12½
Pairs, #a-b
2007-2008	A582	Set of 2	2.50	2.00
2008c		Sheet, 2 each #2007-2008 + 2 labels	4.00	4.00

Souvenir Sheet
Perf. 12¾x13½
2009	A582	5000r multi	3.50	3.50

No. 2009 contains one 25x41mm stamp.

President and Vice-President — A583

No. 2010, 1500r: a, Pres. Megawati Soekarnoputri. b, Vice-president Hamzah Haz.

Photo. with Foil Application
2002, Aug. 17   Perf. 12½
2010	A583	Horiz. pair, #a-b, + central label	1.75	1.75

Souvenir Sheet

Amphilex 2002 Intl. Stamp Exhibition, Amsterdam — A584

2002, Aug. 30   Perf. 13½x12¾   Photo.
2011	A584	7000r multi	5.00	4.00

Souvenir Sheet

Panfila 2002 Philatelic Exhibition, Yogyakarta A585

2002, Sept. 19   Perf. 12¾x13½
2012	A585	6000r multi	3.00	3.00

Paintings A586

No. 2013, 1000r: a, Seko, Guerrilla Vanguard, by S. Sudjojono. b, Cat, by Popo Iskandar.
No. 2014, 1500r, vert.: a, Catching Lice, by Hendra Gunawan. b, Gatut Kaca with Prigiwa and Prigiwati, by R. Basuki Abdullah.

2002, Sept. 27   Litho. & Photo.
Perf. 12½
Pairs, #a-b
2013-2014	A586	Set of 2	2.50	2.50
2014c		Sheet, 2 each #2013-2014	6.50	6.50

Souvenir Sheet

España 2002 Youth Philatelic Exhibition, Salamanca — A587

2002, Oct. 4   Photo.   Perf. 13½x12¾
2015	A587	7000r multi	2.50	2.50

Flora and Fauna A588

No. 2016, 1000r: a, Trimeresurus hageni. b, Rafflesia micropylora.
No. 2017, 1500r: a, Panthera pardus. b, Terminalia catappa.

INDONESIA

No. 2018, 2000r: a, Papilionanthe hookeriana. b, Varanus salvator.
3500r, Panthera pardus.

Litho. & Photo.
2002, Nov. 5   *Perf. 12¾x13½*
Horiz. Pairs, #a-b
2016-2018   A588   Set of 3   4.50   3.50

Souvenir Sheet
2019   A588   3500r multi   2.00   2.00

No. 2019 exists imperf. Value $2.

Antara, Indonesian News Agency — A589

Litho. & Typo.
2002, Dec. 13   *Perf. 12½*
2020   A589   1500r multi   1.00   .45

Happy Birthday — A590

2003   *Photo.*   *Perf. 12½*
2021   Strip of 2 stamps and 2 alternating labels   2.00   1.75
a.-b.   A590 1500r Any single   .80   .50
c.   Sheet of 5 #2021   10.00   10.00

No. 2021 was printed in sheets containing 10 strips with labels that could be personalized. The sheet sold for 45,000r. The labels on No. 2021c could also be personalized, and that sheet sold for 30,000r.

Folklore A591

No. 2022 — Scenes from Danau Ranau, Lampung (Nos. a.-e.), Kongga Owose, Southeast Sulawesi (Nos. f.-j.), Putri Gading Cempaka, Bengkulu (Nos. k.-o.), Putri Mandalika Nyale, West Nusa Tenggara (Nos. p.-t.) and stamp numbers: a, 01/20. b, 02/20. c, 03/20. d, 04/20. e, 05/20. f, 06/20. g, 07/20. h, 08/20. i, 09/20. j, 10/20. k, 11/20. l, 12/20. m, 13/20. n, 14/20. o, 15/20. p, 16/20. q, 17/20. r, 18/20. s, 19/20. t, 20/20.
5000r, Like #2022e.

Litho. & Photo.
2003, Feb. 2   *Perf. 13½x12¾*
2022   A591   1500r Sheet of 20, #a-t   12.00   12.00

Souvenir Sheet
2023   A591   5000r multi   2.50   2.50

22nd South East Asia Games, Hanoi, Viet Nam — A592

Designs: 1000r, Billiards. 1500r, Rowing. 2500r, Rhythmic gymnastics.

Litho. & Photo.
2003, May 12   *Perf. 14*
2024-2026   A592   Set of 3   2.50   2.00

Values are for stamps with surrounding selvage.

Volcanoes — A593

Designs: 500r, Kerinci. No. 2028, 1000r, Krakatoa. No. 2029, 1000r, Merapi. No. 2030, 1000r, Tambora. 2000r, Ruang.

2003, June 5   *Perf. 12½*
2027-2031   A593   Set of 5   3.00   2.00
2031a   Sheet, 2 each #2027-2031 + 2 labels   6.00   4.50

Astronomy A594

No. 2032: a, Andromeda Galaxy (1/5). b, Earth and Mars (2/5). c, Moon (3/5).
No. 2033: a, External view of observatory (4/5). b, Zeiss telescope (5/5).
5000r, Like No. 2033a.

2003, June 7   *Perf. 12½*
2032   Strip of 3   1.40   1.40
a.-c.   A594 1000r Any single   .40   .30
2033   Pair   1.50   1.50
a.-b.   A594 1500r Either single   .60   .40
c.   Sheet, 2 each #2032a-2032c, 2033a-2033b   5.00   4.00

Souvenir Sheet
Perf. 13½x12¾
2034   A594   5000r multi   3.00   2.50

Stamps in No. 2033c are tete-beche. No. 2034 contains one 41x25mm stamp.

Bank Indonesia, 50th Anniv. — A595

Designs: 1000r, Tower and flowers. 1500r, People at graduation ceremony, books.

Perf. 13½x13¼ Syncopated
2003, July 1
2035-2036   A595   Set of 2   1.50   1.00

Sri Sultan Hamengku Buwono IX and Lord Robert Baden-Powell — A596

Perf. 13½x12¾
2003, Aug. 14   *Photo.*
2037   A596   1500r multi   1.00   .50

Independence Day Games A597

No. 2038, 1000r: a, Panjat Pinang (1/4). b, Pukul Bantal (2/4).
No. 2039, 1500r, horiz.: a, Balap Kelom (3/4). b, Balap Karung (4/4).

Perf. 12¾x13½, 13½x12¾
2003, Aug. 17   *Litho. & Photo.*
Pairs, #a-b
2038-2039   A597   Set of 2   2.50   1.75
2039c   Sheet, 2 each #2038a-2038b, 2039a-2039b   5.00   3.75

Souvenir Sheet

Paintings of Srihadi Soedarsono — A598

No. 2040: a, Pendet, Dinamika Remaja. b, Borobudur-Purnama dalam Keheningan.

2003   *Perf. 13½ Syncopated*
2040   A598   3000r Sheet of 2, #a-b   1.75   1.75
c.   Sheet with margin design in cyan only   1.75   1.75
d.   As "c," with magenta added to margin design   3.50   3.00
e.   As "d," with yellow added to margin design   3.50   3.00
f.   As "e," with black added to margin design, but lacking artist's face and signature   3.50   3.00
g.   Sheet, 2 each #2040a-2040b   6.50   6.00

Emmitan-Philex 2003, Surabaya (Nos. 2040, 2040c, 2040d, 2040e, 2040f), 10th ASEAN Postal Business Meeting (No. 2040g). Issued: No. 2040, 9/4; No. 2040c, 8/29; No. 2040d, 8/30; No. 2040e, 8/31; No. 2040f, 9/1; No. 2040g, 9/3. No. 2040 exists imperf, issued 9/2. Value, $6.

Tourism A599

No. 2041, 1000r: a, Jou Uci Sabea, North Maluku (1/4). b, Mome'ati, Gorontalo (2/4).
No. 2042, 1500r: a, Muang Jong, Bangka Belitung (3/4). b, Seba Baduy, Banten (4/4).
5000r, Like No. 2042a.

2003, Sept. 27   *Perf. 12½*
Vert. Pairs, #a-b
2041-2042   A599   Set of 2   3.00   1.50

Souvenir Sheet
2043   A599   5000r multi   3.00   2.50

Souvenir Sheet

Bangkok 2003 World Philatelic Exhibition — A600

2003, Oct. 4   *Perf. 13½x12¾*
2044   A600   8000r multi   3.00   1.75

Handshake — A601

Fish and Water Lily A602

Birds A603

Handshake and Flag — A604

Flower A605

2003, Oct. 27   *Litho.*   *Perf. 12½*
2045   A601   1000r multi + label   .85   .85
2046   A602   1500r multi + label   1.00   1.00
2047   A603   1500r multi + label   1.00   1.00
2048   A604   1500r multi + label   1.00   1.00
2049   A605   1500r multi + label   1.00   1.00
Nos. 2045-2049 (5)   4.85   4.85

Nos. 2045-2049 were each issued in sheets of 20 stamps + 20 labels that could be personalized. Sheets of No. 2045 sold for 35,000r, while sheets of Nos. 2046-2049 each sold for 45,000r.

Indonesian Youth Pledge, 75th Anniv. — A606

2003, Oct. 28   *Litho.*   *Perf. 12¾x13¼*
2050   A606   1500r Nos. 1031-1032, 1246   1.00   .50

Flowers and Insects A607

No. 2051: a, Paphiopedilum mastersianum (9/12). b, Platylomia flavida (8/12). c, Osmoxylon palmatum (7/12). d, Apis dorsata (12/12). e, Freycinetia pseudoinsignis (11/12). f, Sia ferox (10/12). g, Aularches miliaris (3/12). h, Butea monosperma (2/12). i, Orthetrum testaceum (1/12). j, Anaphalis javanica (6/12). k, Hierodula vitrea (5/12). l, Saraca declinata (4/12).
No. 2052: a, Like #2051j. b, Like #2051i.

Litho. & Photo.
2003, Nov. 5   *Perf. 12½*
2051   A607   1500r Block of 12, #a-l   8.00   8.00
m.   Booklet pane, #2051a, 2051c, 2051e, 2051h, 2051j, 2051l   7.50   —
n.   Booklet pane, #2051b, 2051d, 2051f, 2051g, 2051i, 2051k   7.50   —
   Complete booklet, #2051m, 2051n   15.00

Souvenir Sheet
2052   A607   3000r Sheet of 2, #a-b, + label   3.00   2.25

Famous Men — A608

No. 2053: a, Prof. Roosseno (1908-96) (3/4). b, Prof. Sutami (1928-80) (4/4). c, Nurtanio Pringgoadisuryo (1923-66) (1/4). d, Martinus Putuhena (1901-82) (2/4).

Litho. & Engr.
2003, Nov. 10   *Perf. 13¼x13*
2053   Strip of 4   3.50   2.25
a.-d.   A608 2000r Any single   .55   .55

Flowers A609

No. 2054: a, Styrax benzoin (1/30). b, Kopsia fruticosa (2/30). c, Impatiens tujuhensis (3/30). d, Hoya diversifolia (4/30). e, Etlingera elatior (5/30). f, Dillenia suffruticosa (6/30). g, Papilionanthe hookerianum (7/30). h, Medinilla speciosa (8/30). i, Costus speciosus (9/30). j, Melastoma sylvaticum (10/30). k, Nelumbo nucifera (11/30). l, Begonia robusta (12/30). m, Anaphalis longifolia (13/30). n, Pisonia grandis (14/30). o, Ixora javanica (15/30). p, Plumeria acuminata (16/30). q, Cassia fistula (17/30). r, Calotropis gigantea (18/30). s, Dimorphorchis lowii (19/30). t, Aeschynanthus radicans (20/30). u, Sonneratia caseolaris (21/30). v, Rhododendron orbiculatum (22/30). w, Passiflora edulis (23/30). x, Pterospermum celebicum (24/30). y, Quisqualis indica (25/30). z, Spathiphyllum commutatum (26/30). aa, Lilium longiflorum (27/30). ab, Clitoria ternatea (28/30). ac, Pecteilis susannae (29/30). ad, Grammatophyllum speciosum (30/30).

INDONESIA

Litho. & Photo.
2004, Jan. 5 — Perf. 12½
2054   Sheet of 30   17.00 17.00
a.-ad. A609 1500r Any single   .75 .30

Folktales A610

No. 2055 — Scenes from Putri Selaras Pinang Masak, Jambi (Nos. a.-e.), Tanjung Lesung, Banten (Nos. f.-j.), Patung Palindo, Central Sulawesi (Nos. k.-o.), Danau Tolire, North Maluku (Nos. p.-t.) and stamp number: a, 01/20. b, 02/20. c, 03/20. d, 04/20. e, 05/20. f, 06/20. g, 07/20. h, 08/20. i, 09/20. j, 10/20. k, 11/20. l, 12/20. m, 13/20. n, 14/20. o, 15/20. p, 16/20. q, 17/20. r, 18/20. s, 19/20. t, 20/20. 6000r, Like # 2055j.

Litho. & Photo.
2004, Feb. 20 — Perf. 13½x12¾
2055 A610 1500r Sheet of 20, #a-t   12.00 12.00

Souvenir Sheet
2056 A610 6000r multi   3.00 2.50

Museums A611

No. 2057: a, Sri Baduga Museum, Bandung (3/4). b, Bahari Museum, Jakarta (1/4). c, Telecommunications Museum, Jakarta (4/4). d, Geology Museum, Bandung (2/4).

2004, Feb. 29 — Perf. 13¼x12¾
2057   Vert. strip of 4   3.00 1.75
a.-d. A611 1500r Any single   .75 .40

General Elections A612

No. 2058: a, Man and woman pointing at people holding flags (1/2). b, Man and woman casting ballots (2/2).

2004, Apr. 5 — Litho. — Perf. 12¾x13¼
2058 A612 1500r Horiz. pair, #a-b   1.50 1.10

Famous Women — A613

No. 2059: a, Gedong Bagoes Oka (1921-2002), social worker, religious leader (2/4). b, Ani Idrus (1918-99), journalist (1/4). c, Nyonya Meneer (1895-1978), founder of herbal medicine factory (3/4). d, Sandiah (Ibu Kasur) (1926-2002), composer of children's songs, television personality (4/4).

Perf. 13¼x13½ Syncopated
2004, Apr. 21 — Litho. & Engr.
2059   Horiz. strip of 4   3.50 2.50
a.-d. A613 2500r Any single   .85 .60

2004 Summer Olympics, Athens — A614

No. 2060: a, Swimming (1/3). b, Women's high jump (2/3). c, Hurdling (3/3).

Litho. & Photo.
2004, May 5 — Perf. 14
2060   Horiz. strip of 3   3.00 2.25
a.-c. A614 2500r Any single   1.10 .65

Environmental Protection A615

Designs: Nos. 2061a, 2062a, Bird, killer whale (1/2). Nos. 2061b, 2062b, Shark, turtle (2/2).

2004, June 5 — Perf. 13¼x12¾
2061 A615 1500r Vert. pair, #a-b   1.50 1.00

Souvenir Sheet
2062 A615 2500r Sheet of 2, #a-b   2.50 2.25

Indonesian Cuisine — A616

No. 2063: a, Gajebo, West Sumatra (1/4). b, Sambal Udang Terung Pipit, West Kalimantan (3/4). c, Kare Rajungan, East Java (2/4). d, Tinotuan, North Sulawesi (4/4).

2004, July 6 — Litho. — Perf. 13¼x12¾
2063 A616 1500r Block of 4, #a-d 2.00 2.00

Presidential Limousines A617

No. 2064: a, 1939 Buick with REP-1 license plate (1/2). b, 1942 DeSoto with REP-2 license plate (2/2).

2004, Aug. 17
2064 A617 2500r Vert. pair, #a-b   2.00 2.00
c.   Souvenir sheet #2064a-2064b   2.00 2.00

16th National Games A618

No. 2065: a, Volleyball (1/2). b, Sepak takraw (2/2).

Litho. & Photo.
2004, Sept. 2 — Perf. 14
2065 A618 1500r Pair, #a-b   1.50 1.00

Flowers and Insects Type of 2003

No. 2066: a, Gryllotalpa hirsuta (4/6). b, Alstonia scholaris (5/6). c, Scolopendra subspinipes (6/6). d, Cinnamomun sintok (2/6). e, Heterometrus cyaneus (2/6). f, Parkia roxburghii (1/6).
No. 2067: a, Like #2066e. b, Like #2066f.

2004, Nov. 5 — Perf. 12½
2066 A607 1500r Block of 6, #a-f 3.50 3.00

Souvenir Sheet
2067 A607 3000r Sheet of 2, #a-b, + label   3.00 2.50

National Teacher's Day — A619

No. 2068: a, Teacher, students with microscope and book (1/2). b, Teacher students with pen and book (2/2).

2004, Nov. 25 — Perf. 12¾x13¼
2068 A619 1500r Horiz. pair, #a-b   1.25 1.00

Souvenir Sheet

National Philatelic Exhibition, Surabaya — A620

No. 2069 — Paintings by Sunaryo: a, Setagen Rhythm. b, Sebelum Pentas. c, Bercinta.

2004, Dec. 16 — Litho. — Perf. 12½
2069 A620 5000r Sheet of 3, #a-c   8.00 6.50
d.   Souvenir sheet of 1, #2069a 2.50 2.00
e.   Souvenir sheet of 1, #2069b 2.50 2.00
f.   Souvenir sheet of 1, #2069c 2.50 2.00
g.   Souvenir sheet of 1, #2069a, imperf. 2.50 2.00
h.   Souvenir sheet of 1, #2069b, imperf. 2.50 2.00
i.   Souvenir sheet of 1, #2069c, imperf. 2.50 2.00

Folktales A621

No. 2070 — Scenes from Lahilote, Gorontalo (Nos. a.-e.), Kolam Putri, Riau Islands (Nos. f.-j.), Batu Balai, Bangka Belitung (Nos. k.-o.), Bulan & Sagu di Ibuanari, Papua (Nos. p.-t.) and stamp number: a, 1/20. b, 2/20. c, 3/20. d, 4/20. e, 5/20. f, 6/20. g, 7/20. h, 8/20. i, 9/20. j, 10/20. k, 11/20. l, 12/20. m, 13/20. n, 14/20. o, 15/20. p, 16/20. q, 17/20. r, 18/20. s, 19/20. t, 20/20. 6000r, Like #2070j.

2005, Feb. 2 — Litho. — Perf. 13½x12¾
2070 A621 1500r Sheet of 20, #a-t   10.00 10.00

Souvenir Sheet
2071 A621 6000r multi   2.50 2.00

Asian-African Summit, 50th Anniv. — A622

No. 2072: a, Dove and "50." b, Dove, world map and people.

Perf. 13½x13¼ Syncopated
2005, Apr. 18 — Litho. & Photo.
2072   Horiz. pair + central label   1.75 1.50
a.-b. A622 2500r Either single   .85 .75
c.   Souvenir sheet, #2072b   1.50 .75

Mangrove Forest Protection A623

No. 2073 — Mangroves and: a, Bird. b, Fish.

2005, June 5 — Litho. — Perf. 12¾x13¼
2073 A623 1500r Horiz. pair, #a-b   1.25 1.00
c.   Souvenir sheet, #2073   1.50 1.00

Voyages of Admiral Zheng He, 600th Anniv. — A624

Litho. & Photo.
2005, June 28 — Perf. 13½x12¾
2074 A624 2500r multi   1.25 .45
a.   Souvenir sheet of 1   2.50 1.00

Traditional Food — A625

No. 2075: a, Sayur Tauco (North Sumatra) (1/4). b, Soto Banjar (South Kalimantan) (3/4). c, Nasi Timbel (West Java) (2/4). d, Langga Roko (South Sulawesi) (4/4).

2005, July 6 — Litho.
2075   Vert. strip of 4   2.00 1.40
a.-d. A625 1500r Any single   .50 .35

Energy Conservation — A626

Designs: 1500r, Bus, electric plug (1/3). 2000r, Electric plugs and outlet (2/3). 2500r, Automobile (3/3).

2005, Aug. 17 — Perf. 12½
2076-2078 A626 Set of 3   2.25 1.25

Indonesian Leaders — A627

Designs: Nos. 2079a, 2080a, Pres. Susilo Banbang Yudhoyono. Nos. 2079b, 2080b, Vice-president Muhammad Jusuf Kalla.

2005, Aug. 17 — Litho.
2079   Horiz. pair with central label   1.00 .75
a.-b. A627 1500r Either single   .50 .25

Litho. With Foil Application
2080   Horiz. pair with central label   1.50 1.50
a.-b. A627 2500r Either single   .75 .75
c.   Souvenir sheet, #2080a, 2080b   3.00 1.50

Borobudur Ship Expedition — A628

No. 2081: a, Ship, head of Buddha (2/2). b, Carving of ship (1/2).

2005, Sept. 17
2081 A628 1500r Pair, #a-b   1.50 1.25
c.   As "a," with "2/2" removed 2.00 1.00
d.   As "b," with "1/2" removed 2.00 1.00
e.   Souvenir sheet, #2081c, 2081d + central label   1.50 1.25

Souvenir Sheet

National Philatelic Exhibition, Cilegon — A629

INDONESIA

No. 2082 — Paintings by Sudjana Kerton: a, Nyawer. b, Makan Siang. c, Wayang Golek. d, Tanah Air Indonesia.

2005, Sept. 23			Perf. 12½	
2082	A629	Sheet of 4	7.00	6.00
a.-c.		5000r Any single	1.50	1.00
d.		8000r multi	2.50	1.50
e.		Souvenir sheet, #2082a, imperf.	1.60	.85
f.		Souvenir sheet, #2082b, imperf.	1.60	.85
g.		Souvenir sheet, #2082c, imperf.	1.60	.85
h.		Souvenir sheet, #2082d, imperf.	2.75	1.75

Sea Mammals and Plants — A630

No. 2083: a, Neophocaena phocaenoides (1/4). b, Dugong dugon (2/4). c, Gelidium latifolium (3/4). d, Halimeda opuntia (4/4).

2005, Nov. 5			Perf. 12½	
2083	A630	1500r Block of 4, #a-d	2.00	1.50
e.		As "a", with "1/4" removed	2.00	1.00
f.		As "b", with "3/4" removed	2.00	1.00
g.		Souvenir sheet, #2083e, 2083f + central label	1.50	1.00

Folktales — A631

No. 2084: a, Bawang Merah & Bawang Putih (1/4). b, Keong Emas (2/4). c, Si Kancil (3/4). d, Timun Emas (4/4).

2006, Feb. 6	Litho.		Perf. 12¾x13½	
2084	A631	Block or strip of 4	2.50	1.60
a.-d.		1500r Any single	.60	.30
e.		Souvenir sheet, #2084a-2084d, imperf.	3.00	2.50

Miniature Sheets

Philately Day A632

No. 2085, 1500r — Illustrations in brown: a, Family in coach (1/28). b, Horse pulling coach (2/28). c, Girl, standing, with three photographs (3/28). d, Boy with one photograph (4/28). e, Boy with three photographs (5/28). f, Girl, wearing sandals, holding photograph (6/28). g, Barefoot girl touching photograph (7/28). h, Boy drawing map (8/28). i, Boy and crate (9/28). j, Boy at potter's wheel, finished pottery (10/28). k, Boy at potter's wheel (11/28). l, Girl pointing (12/28). m, Boy touching pottery (13/28). n, Caparisoned pottery horses (14/28).

No. 2086, 1500r — Illustrations in color: a, Like #2085a (15/28). b, Like #2085b (16/28). c, Like #2085c (17/28). d, Like #2085d (18/28). e, Like #2085e (19/28). f, Like #2085f (20/28). g, Like #2085g (21/28). h, Like #2085h (22/28). i, Like #2085i (23/28). j, Like #2085j (24/28). k, Like #2085k (25/28). l, Like #2085l (26/28). m, Like #2085m (27/28). n, Like #2085n (28/28).

2006, Mar. 29	Litho.	Perf. 14		
		Sheets of 14, #a-n		
2085-2086	A632	Set of 2	16.00	12.00

2006 World Cup Soccer Championships, Germany — A633

No. 2087: a, World Cup emblem, goal, soccer ball (1/4). b, World Cup emblem, soccer ball (2/4). c, World Cup trophy at right, soccer ball at bottom (3/4). d, World Cup trophy at left, soccer ball at right (4/4).

Die Cut, With Perf. 14 Selvage Between Stamps

2006, May 6		Self-Adhesive		
2087	A633	2500r Block of 4, #a-d	4.00	2.75
e.		Booklet pane, #2087a-2087d, die cut, imperf. selvage between stamps	4.00	—
		Complete booklet, #2087e	4.50	

Individual stamps have various die cut soccer players in center. Values are for unused stamps with surrounding selvage. Used stamps may or may not have the die cut soccer players.

Environmental Care — A634

No. 2088: a, Village, flowers, butterfly (1/2). b, Girl (2/2).

2006, June 5	Litho.	Perf. 13¼x12¾		
2088	A634	1500r Pair, #a-b	1.25	.90
c.		Souvenir sheet, #2088a-2088b	1.50	.90

Local Foods — A635

No. 2089: a, Pempek (South Sumatra, 1/4). b, Gudeg (Yogyakarta, 2/4). c, Ayam Betutu (Bali, 3/4). d, Aunu Senebre (Papua, 4/4).

2006, July 6				
2089		Block or strip of 4	2.50	1.25
a.-d.		A635 1500r Any single	.60	.30

National Scout Jamboree — A636

No. 2090: a, Kak Mashudi and scouts around campfire (1/2). b, Jigsaw puzzle of scouts (2/2).

Litho. & Photo.

2006, July 16			Perf. 12½	
2090	A636	1500r Pair, #a-b	1.25	1.00

Sultans — A637

No. 2091: a, Sultan Ma'moen Al Rasyid Perkasa Alamsyah Sultan Deli IX (1873-1924) (1/4). b, Sultan Agung Sultan Mataram III (1613-45) (2/4). c, Sultan Adji Mohamad Parikesit Sultan Kutai Kertanegara XX (1920-60) (3/4). d, Sultan Hasanuddin Sultan Gowa XVI (1653-69) (4/4).

Litho., Litho. with Foil Application (#2091e)

Perf. 13½ Syncopated

2006, Aug. 17				
2091		Block or strip of 4	2.25	1.50
a.-d.		A637 1500r Any single	.50	.35
e.		As "d", overprinted in red foil	3.00	1.50
f.		Block or strip of 4, #2091a-2091c, 2091e	8.00	4.00

Puppets A638

No. 2092: a, Indonesian puppet (1/2). b, Slovakian marionette (2/2).

Litho. & Photo.

2006, Sept. 27		Perf. 13x13¼		
2092	A638	2500r Horiz. pair, #a-b	1.75	1.00
c.		Souvenir sheet, #2092	2.00	1.00

See Slovakia Nos. 506-507.

Miniature Sheet

Eid ul-Fitr A639

No. 2093: a, Man sitting with crossed legs in prayer (1/8). b, Drummer (5/8). c, Older woman hugging young woman (2/8). d, Woman and man with hands in prayer (6/8). e, Mosque (3/8). f, People getting on bus (7/8). g, Geometric design (4/8). h, People and horse cart (8/8).

Nos. 2093lj-2093lq: As Nos. 2039a-2093h, but with Prisma emblem in lower corner of stamp and persoanlized photo above arc.

2006, Oct. 3	Litho.		Perf. 12½	
2093	A639	1500r Sheet of 8, #a-h	4.50	3.50
2093l	A639	1500r Sheet of 8, #j-q	6.00	6.00

No. 2093l sold for 20,000r.

Flora and Fauna A640

No. 2094: a, Licuala arbuscula (3/4). b, Livistona mamberamoensis (4/4). c, Melipotes carolae (1/4). d, Amblyornis flavifrons (2/4).

2006, Nov. 5			Perf. 12½	
2094	A640	1500r Block of 4, #a-d	2.50	1.75
e.		As "a", with "3/4" removed	1.00	1.00
f.		As "d", with "2/4" removed	1.00	1.00
g.		Souvenir sheet, #2094e-2094f + label	3.00	2.00

Souvenir Sheet

Bandung '06 Natl. Philatelic Exhibition — A641

No. 2095: a, Panthera pardus (1/2). b, Bouea macrophylla (2/2).

2006, Nov. 30			Perf. 13½x12¾	Litho.
2095	A641	2500r Sheet of 2, #a-b	1.75	1.50
c.		Like #2095, with margin illustration in blue and black	1.75	1.50
d.		Like #2095, with margin illustration in red and black	1.75	1.50
e.		Like #2095, with margin illustration in yellow and black	1.75	1.50
f.		Like #2095, with margin illustration in black	1.75	1.50

On No. 2095, the code number at lower left of sheet ends with "5," that of Nos. 2095c-2095f end in "1" to "4" respectively. Margin illustrations show progressive color printing.

Containers — A642

No. 2096: a, Container from Bali (2/2). b, Lidded basket from East Kalimantan (1/2).

2006, Dec. 23			Perf. 13½x12¾	
2096	A642	1500r Horiz. pair, #a-b	1.50	.75

New Year 2007 (Year of the Pig) — A643

No. 2097: a, Chinese zodiac animals and lanterns (1/2). b, Chinese zodiac animals, people and temple (2/2).

No. 2098: a, Rat (1/13). b, Ox (2/13). c, Tiger (3/13). d, Rabbit (4/13). e, Dragon (5/13). f, Snake (6/13). g, Horse (7/13). h, Goat (8/13). i, Monkey (9/13). j, Rooster (10/13). k, Dog (11/13). l, Pig (12/13). m, Like #2097b (96x64mm, 13/13)

No. 2099, Like #2097b.

Litho., Litho. With Foil Application (#2098m, 2099)

2007, Feb. 1			Perf. 12½	
2097	A643	Pair	1.25	.70
a.-b.		1500r Either single	.60	.30
2098		Sheet of 13	10.00	10.00
a.-l.		A643 2000r Any single	.60	.30
m.		A643 6000r multi	2.00	1.00

Souvenir Sheet

2099	A643	6000r multi	2.00	1.00

Dances A644

No. 2100: a, Lion dance (1/2). b, Dragon dance (2/2).

Perf. 13¼x13½ Syncopated

2007, Apr. 13				Litho.
2100	A644	2500r Pair, #a-b	1.60	.80
c.		Souvenir sheet, #2100a-2100b	2.50	1.25

See People's Republic of China Nos. 3581-3582.

INDONESIA

Reading and Writing — A645

No. 2101: a, Boy writing in book, mother reading (2/2). b, Boy looking at girl writing in book (1/2).

2007, May 2   **Litho.**   *Perf. 13½x12¾*
| 2101 | A645 | 1500r Pair, #a-b | 1.10 | .55 |

A646

Environmental Care — A647

Nos. 2102, 2104: a, Iceberg, top of polar bear's head (1/4). b, Crying polar bear (2/4).
No. 2103: a, Forest fire (3/4). b, Burnt forest (4/4).

2007, June 5
| 2102 | A646 | 1500r Vert. pair, #a-b | 1.10 | .55 |
| 2103 | A647 | 1500r Vert. pair, #a-b | 1.10 | .55 |

Souvenir Sheet
| 2104 | A646 | 2500r Sheet of 2, #a-b | 2.00 | 1.50 |

Nos. 2102 and 2103 were each printed in sheets containing 10 pairs with the bottom stamp in the pair tete-beche with the same stamp.

Campaign Against Drug Abuse A648

No. 2105: a, Guitarist, Indonesian inscription (1/2). b, Basketball player, English inscription (2/2).

2007, June 26   *Perf. 12¾x13½*
| 2105 | A648 | 1500r Pair, #a-b | 1.75 | .85 |

Traditional Foods — A649

No. 2106: a, Roti Cane and Kari Kambing (Aceh, 1/4). b, Gecok (West Nusa Tenggara, 3/4). c, Soto Kudus (Central Java, 2/4). d, Ikan Air Garam (Maluku, 4/4).

2007, July 6   *Perf. 13½x12¾*
| 2106 | Strip of 4 | 2.00 | 1.50 |
| a.-d. | A649 1500r Any single | .50 | .30 |

A650

A651

A652

Greetings With Hands — A653

2007, June 3   **Litho.**   *Perf. 12½*
2107	A650	1500r multi + label	.60	.40
2108	A651	1500r multi + label	1.00	.75
a.	Pair, #2107-2108, + 2 labels	1.75	1.50
2109	A652	1500r multi + label	1.00	.75
2110	A653	1500r multi + label	1.00	.75
a.	Pair, #2109-2110, + 2 labels	3.00	3.00
	Nos. 2107-2110 (4)	3.60	2.65

Nos. 2107-2108 and 2109-2110 were each printed in sheets of 20 stamps + 20 labels, containing ten of each stamp. Sheets sold for 45,000r. Labels could be personalized. A sheet of 20 No. 2107 + 20 non-personalizable labels, issued in 2008, also sold for 45,000r.

Fireworks A654

Guitar and G Clef — A655

Paint Brushes A656

Film and Reel — A657

Perf. 12½x12½x12½x4

2007, July 21   **Litho.**
2111	A654	1500r multi + label	.75	.30
2112	A655	1500r multi + label	1.25	1.00
2113	A656	1500r multi + label	1.25	1.00
2114	A657	1500r multi + label	1.25	1.00
	Nos. 2111-2114 (4)	4.50	3.30

Nos. 2111-2114 were each printed in sheets of 8 stamps + 8 labels that sold for 15,000r face. No. 2111 also was printed in four different sheets of 12 stamps + 12 labels that each sold for 30,000r. Labels could not be personalized.

Scouting, Cent. A658

No. 2115, 2500r: a, Centenary emblem, full color background (1/4). b, Scout, full color (2/4).
No. 2116, 1500r: a, Centenary emblem, blue background (3/4). b, Scout in blue (4/4).

2007, Aug. 1   *Perf. 13½ Syncopated*
| 2115 | A658 | Horiz. pair, #a-b | 2.25 | 1.10 |

Booklet Stamps
2116	A658	Horiz. pair, #a-b	1.10	.55
c.	Booklet pane, 5 #2116	5.50	
	Complete booklet, #2116c	5.50	—

Nepenthes Mirabilis A659

Nepenthes Ampulliaria A660

2007, Aug. 3   *Perf. 13½x12¾*
| 2117 | A659 | 1500r multi | .60 | .30 |

Perf. 12¾x13½
| 2118 | A660 | 1500r multi | .60 | .30 |

Souvenir Sheet   *Perf. 13½x12¾*
2119	Sheet of 2	2.50	1.25
a.	A659 2500r multi	1.25	.60
b.	A660 2500r multi	1.25	.60

Bangkok 2007 Intl. Stamp Exhibition.

Association of South East Asian Nations (ASEAN), 40th Anniv. — A661

Designs: 1500r, Fatahillah Museum, Jakarta.
No. 2121: a, Secretariat Building, Bandar Seri Begawan, Brunei (1/10). b, National Museum of Cambodia (2/10). c, Fatahillah Museum, Jakarta (3/10). d, Typical house, Laos (4/10). e, Malayan Railway Headquarters Building, Kuala Lumpur, Malaysia (5/10). f, Yangon Post Office, Myanmar (6/10). g, Malacañang Palace, Philippines (7/10). h, National Museum of Singapore (8/10). i, Vimanmek Mansion, Bangkok, Thailand (9/10). j, Presidential Palace, Hanoi, Viet Nam (10/10).

2007, Aug. 8   *Perf. 13½ Syncopated*
2120	A661	1500r multi	.85	.30
2121		Sheet of 10	9.00	4.50
a.-j.	A661 2500r Any single	.90	.45

See Brunei No. 607, Burma No. 370, Cambodia No. 2339, Laos Nos. 1717-1718, Malaysia No. 1170, Philippines Nos. 3103-3105, Singapore No. 1265, Thailand No. 2315, and Viet Nam Nos. 3302-3311.

Lighthouses A662

No. 2122: a, Semarang Lighthouse (1/2). b, Cikoneng Lighthouse (2/2).

2007, Aug. 17   *Perf. 12¾x13½*
| 2122 | A662 | 1500r Horiz. pair, #a-b | 1.25 | .60 |

Padjadjaran University, 50th Anniv. — A663

No. 2123: a, Tiger and ram (1/4). b, Men and dancers (2/4). c, Building (3/4). d, Symbols and globe (4/4).

2007, Sept. 5   *Perf. 13½x12¾*
| 2123 | Horiz. strip of 4 + central label | 2.25 | 2.00 |
| a.-d. | A663 1500r Any single | .50 | .30 |

Butterflies — A664

No. 2124: a, Delias kristianiae (1/4). b, Ornithoptera aesacus (2/4). c, Ornithoptera croesus (3/4). d, Troides hypolitus (4/4).
No. 2125: a, Like #2124a. b, Like #2124c.

2007, Nov. 5   *Perf. 12½*
| 2124 | A664 | Block of 4 | 2.25 | 1.10 |
| a.-d. | 1500r Any single | .35 | .30 |

Souvenir Sheet
| 2125 | A664 | Sheet of 2 + central label | 2.00 | 1.00 |
| a.-b. | 2500r Either single | 1.00 | .50 |

No. 2125 Surcharged in Gold

2007, Nov. 21   **Litho.**   *Perf. 12½*
| 2126 | A664 | Sheet of 2 + central label | 4.00 | 3.00 |
| a.-b. | 5000r on 2500r Either single | 1.75 | 1.50 |

No. 2126 also is overprinted in gold in margin and label with emblem and text for Bandungfilex 2007 and Jakarta 2008 Intl. Stamp Exhibition.

24th South East Asian Games, Nakhon Ratchasima, Thailand — A665

No. 2127: a, Bowling (1/4). b, Indoor soccer (2/4). c, Kempo (3/4). d, Hammer throw (4/4).

2007, Dec. 6   *Perf. 14*
| 2127 | Horiz. strip of 4 | 4.00 | 2.00 |
| a.-d. | A665 2500r Any single | 1.00 | .50 |

Djuanda Declaration, 50th Anniv. — A666

No. 2128: a, Map of Indonesia, children (1/3). b, Prime Minister Djuanda Kartawidjaja, eagle, and procession (2/3). c, Djuanda Kartawidjaja and map of Indonesia (3/3).

2007, Dec. 13   *Perf. 13½x12¾*
| 2128 | Vert. strip of 3 | 1.50 | 1.25 |
| a.-c. | A666 1500r Any single | .80 | .40 |

Miniature Sheet

Jakarta 2008 Intl. Stamp Exhibition — A667

INDONESIA

No. 2129: a, Prasasti Tugu (2/7). b, Arca Dewa Visnu (statue of Vishnu) (3/7). c, Prasasti Padrao (4/7). d, Peta Nusantara Zaman Portugis (5/7). e, Naskah Perjanjian Sunda Kelapa (6/7). f, Kapal Bangsa Portugis (7/7). g, Bendera Singa Ali and Fatahillah (1/7). Nos. 2129a-2129f are 41x25mm; No. 2129g, 83x25mm.

2008, Jan. 20   Litho.   Perf. 13½x12¾
2129	A667	Sheet of 7	7.00	7.00
a.-f.		2500r Any single	.55	.35
g.		10,000r multi	2.75	2.25

A668

New Year 2008 (Year of the Rat) A669

No. 2130: a, Rat facing right (1/3). b, Rat facing left (2/3). c, Rat on hind legs (3/3).

2008, Jan. 26   Perf. 13½x12¾
| 2130 | | Vert. strip of 3 + label | 1.60 | .80 |
| a.-c. | | A668 2000r Any single | .50 | .25 |

Souvenir Sheet   Perf. 12½
| 2131 | A669 | 5000r black & gray | 2.25 | 1.10 |

Souvenir Sheet

Flora and Fauna A670

No. 2132: a, Casuarius casuarius (1/2). b, Crinum asiaticum (2/2).

2008, Mar. 7   Perf. 12¾x13½
| 2132 | A670 | 5000r Sheet of 2, #a-b | 3.00 | 2.00 |

Jakarta 2008 Intl. Stamp Exhibition, Taipei 2008 Intl. Stamp Exhibition, Stamp Passion '08 Stamp Exhibition, Netherlands.

2008 Summer Olympics, Beijing — A671

No. 2133: a, Sailboarding (1/4). b, Soccer (2/4). c, Badminton (3/4). d, Weight lifting (4/4).

2008, Mar. 18   Perf. 14
| 2133 | A671 | 2500r Block of 4, #a-d | 3.00 | 2.00 |

Miniature Sheet

Jakarta 2008 Intl. Stamp Exhibition — A672

No. 2134: a, Istana Pemerintahan Batavia (2/7). b, Gedung Keuangan (3/7). c, Penyerangan Batavia oleh Sultan Agung, denomination at LR (4/7). d, Penyerangan Batavia oleh Sultan Agung, denomination at LL (5/7). e, Perubahan Batavia Menjadi Jakarta (6/7). f, Penyerahan Kekuasaan Indonesia (7/7). g, Penangkapan Pangeran Jayawikarta oleh Pasukan Banten (1/7). Nos. 2134a-2134f are 41x25mm; No. 2134g, 83x25mm.

Perf. 13½x12¾
2008, Mar. 29   Litho.
2134	A672	Sheet of 7	6.50	6.50
a.-f.		2500r Any single	.65	.40
g.		10,000r multi	2.75	2.25

Diplomatic Relations Between Indonesia and Japan, 50th Anniv. — A673

No. 2135, 2500r: a, Kelimutu Volcano, Indonesia (1/10). b, Mt. Fuji, Japan (2/10). No. 2136, 2500r: a, Borobudur, Indonesia (3/10). b, Toji Temple, Japan (4/10). No. 2137, 2500r: a, Rafflesia arnoldi (5/10). b, Cherry blossoms (6/10). No. 2138, 2500r: a, Angklung (7/10). b, Gaku biwa (8/10). No. 2139, 2500r, horiz: a, Scleropages formosus (9/10). b, Nishiki-goi (10/10).

2008, Apr. 15   Perf. 12½
Horiz. Pairs, #a-b
| 2135-2139 | A673 | Set of 5 | 7.00 | 7.00 |
| 2139c | | Miniature sheet | 7.00 | 7.00 |

Nos. 2135-2139 were each printed in sheets of 4 pairs. See Japan No. 3018.

Special Needs Education A674

No. 2140: a, Boy in wheelchair waving flags (1/3). b, Man in racing wheelchair (2/3). c, Handicapped children playing anklungs (3/3).

Litho. & Embossed
2008, May 2   Perf. 13½x12¾
| 2140 | | Strip of 3 | 1.60 | 1.00 |
| a.-c. | | A674 1500r Any single | .50 | .25 |

National Awakening, Cent. A675

No. 2141: a, People with fists raised, flag. b, Flag, people, satellite.

2008, May 20   Litho.   Perf. 12¾x13½
| 2141 | A675 | 1500r Horiz. pair, #a-b | .80 | .40 |

Environmental Care — A676

Nos. 2142 and 2143: a, Cyclists, motor vehicles (1/2). b, Seedling, forest (2/2). Stamps from No. 2143 lack stamp numbers.

2008, June 5   Perf. 13½x12¾
| 2142 | A676 | 1500r Pair, #a-b | 1.00 | .75 |

Souvenir Sheet
| 2143 | A676 | 2500r Sheet of 2, #a-b | 1.40 | 1.40 |

Miniature Sheet

Jakarta 2008 Intl. Stamp Exhibition — A677

No. 2144: a, Jakarta Philatelic Center (Kantor Filateli Jakarta) (2/7). b, National Museum (3/7). c, Dunia Fantasi (4/7). d, Taman Mini Indonesia (5/7). e, Wisana Seni and Budaya (6/7). f, Wisata Bihari (7/7). g, Warna Warni Jakarta (1/7). Nos. 2144a-2144f are 41x25mm; No. 2144g, 83x25mm.

2008, June 22   Perf. 13½x12¾
2144	A677	Sheet of 7	7.00	7.00
a.-f.		2500r Any single	.55	.35
g.		10,000r multi	2.75	2.50

17th National Games A678

No. 2145: a, Mountain biking (1/4). b, Bodybuilding (2/4). c, Steeplechase (3/4). d, Palaran Main Stadium, Samarinda (4/4).

2008, July 5   Perf. 14
| 2145 | A678 | 1500r Block of 4, #a-d | 2.00 | 1.00 |

Traditional Foods Type of 2007

No. 2146: a, Nasi Lemak (Riau, 1/4). b, Sate Bandeng (Banten, 2/4). c, Ayem Cincane (East Kalimantan, 3/4). d, Kaledo (Central Sulawesi, 4/4).

2008, July 6   Perf. 13½x12¾
| 2146 | | Block of 4 | 1.60 | .80 |
| a.-d. | | A649 1500r Any single | .40 | .25 |

Printed in sheets containing four of each stamp + four labels.

Provincial Arms and Architecture A679

Arms of: Nos. 2147, 1500r, 2158a, 2500r, Bali (1/33). Nos. 2148, 1500r, 2158b, 2500r, Gorontalo (2/33). Nos. 2149, 1500r, 2158c, 2500r, Jawa Barat (West Java) (3/33). Nos. 2150, 1500r, 2158d, 2500r, Jawa Tengah (Central Java) (4/33). Nos. 2151, 1500r, 2158e, 2500r, Kalimantan Barat (West Kalimantan) (5/33). Nos. 2152, 1500r, 2158f, 2500r, Maluku (Moluccas) (6/33). Nos. 2153, 1500r, 2158g, 2500r, Aceh (7/33). Nos. 2154, 1500r, 2158h, 2500r, Papua (8/33). Nos. 2155, 1500r, 2158i, 2500r, Riau (9/33). Nos. 2156, 1500r, 2158j, 2500r, Sulawesi Barat (West Sulawesi) (10/33). Nos. 2157, 1500r, 2158k, 2500r, Sumatera Barat (West Sumatra) (11/33).

2008, Aug. 17   Perf. 12½
2147-2157	A679	Set of 11	5.50	2.75
2158		Sheet of 11 + label	7.50	4.00
a.-k.		A679 2500r Any single	.65	.30

Nos. 2147-2157 each were printed in sheets of 10.

See Nos. 2200-2211, 2253-2264.

Great Post Road of Java — A680

No. 2159: a, Lighthouse, map of western part of road (1/4). b, Building, map of central part of road (2/4). c, Lighthouse, map of eastern part of road (3/4). d, Letter from Governor General Herman Daendels (4/4). 10,000r, Map of entire road.

2008, Sept. 27   Perf. 13½x12¾
| 2159 | | Horiz. strip of 4 | 2.75 | 2.50 |
| a.-d. | | A680 2500r Any single | .65 | .35 |

Souvenir Sheet
| 2160 | A680 | 10,000r multi | 3.00 | 2.50 |

No. 2160 contains one 125x25mm stamp.

Souvenir Sheets

A681

A682

A683

A684

A685

INDONESIA

Jakarta 2008 Intl. Stamp
Exhibition — A686

2008   Perf. 13½x12¾
2161	A681	5000r multi	1.40	1.10
2162	A682	5000r multi	1.40	1.10
2163	A683	5000r multi	1.40	1.10
2164	A684	5000r multi	1.40	1.10
2165	A685	5000r multi	1.40	1.10
2166	A686	5000r multi	1.40	1.10
		Nos. 2161-2166 (6)	8.40	6.60

Issued: No. 2161, 10/23; No. 2162, 10/24; No. 2163, 10/25; No. 2164, 10/26; No. 2165, 10/27; No. 2166, 10/28.

Miniature Sheet

Friendship Between Indonesia and Turkey — A687

No. 2167: a, Blue Mosque, Turkey (1/10). b, Istiqlal Mosque, Indonesia (2/10). c, Bosporus Bridge, Turkey (3/10). d, Barelang Bridge, Indonesia (4/10). e, Whirling dervishes (5/10). f, Saman dance (6/10). g, Turkish tulip (7/10). h, Flame of Irian (8/10). i, Turkish Van cat (9/10). j, Flat-headed cat (10/10).

2008, Oct. 24   Perf. 13½ Syncopated
2167	A687	2500r Sheet of 10, #a-j	7.50	7.50

See Turkey No. 3142.

Miniature Sheet

Flora and Fauna of the Provinces — A688

No. 2168: a, Leucopsar rothschildi, Dysoxylum densiflorum, Bali (1/11). b, Liza dussumieri, Vitex cofassus, Gorontalo (2/11). c, Panthera pardus, Bouea macrophylla, Jawa Barat (West Java) (3/11). d, Oriolus chinensis, Michelia alba, Jawa Tengah (Central Java) (4/11). e, Rhinoplax vigil, Shorea stenoptera, Kalimantan Barat (West Kalimantan) (5/11). f, Alisterus amboinensis, Dendrobium phalaenopsis, Maluku (Moluccas) (6/11). g, Copsychus pyrropygus, Michelia champaca, Aceh (7/11). h, Seleucidis melanoleuca, Pometia pinnata, Papua (8/11). i, Loriculus galgulus, Oncosperma tigillarium, Riau (9/11). j, Aramidopsis plateni, Elmerrillia ovalis, Sulawesi Barat (West Sulawesi) (10/11). k, Argusianus argus, Morus macroura, Sumatera Barat (West Sumatra) (11/11).

2008, Nov. 5   Perf. 13½x12¾
2168	A688	2500r Sheet of 11, #a-k, + label	8.00	7.00

See Nos. 2217, 2249-2252.

Cut Nyak Dhien (1848-1908), Leader of Aceh Resistance to Dutch Rule — A689

No. 2169: a, House (1/2). b, Cut Nyak Dhien (2/2).

2008, Nov. 5
2169	A689	1500r Horiz. pair, #a-b	1.00	.75

Islands — A690

No. 2170: a, Damar Island (1/4). b, Sebatik Island (2/4). c, Batubawaikang Island (3/4). d, Bras Island (4/4).

2008, Dec. 3
2170		Block or strip of 4	2.00	1.00
a.-d.	A690	1500r multi	.50	.25
e.		Miniature sheet, 4 each #2170a-2170d	8.00	4.00

New Year 2009 (Year of the Ox) — A691

Designs: Nos. 2171, 2174a, 2000r, Head of ox (1/3). Nos. 2172, 2174b, 2000r, Ox looking left (2/3). Nos. 2173, 2174c, 2000r, Ox in water (3/3).
10,000r, Ox, diff.

2009, Jan. 10   Litho.
2171-2173	A691	Set of 3	1.75	.85

Litho. & Embossed With Foil Application (Chinese Character in Gold)
2174	A691	2000r Horiz. strip of 3, #a-c	2.00	1.00

Souvenir Sheet
2175	A691	10,000r multi	3.00	2.50

Nos. 2171-2173 were printed in a sheet of 24 stamps containing 8 of each stamp. No. 2174 was printed in a sheet containing 2 strips.

Bandung Institute of Technology, 50th Anniv. — A692

No. 2176: a, Building, colored triangles (1/4). b, Emblems, crowd of dignitaries (2/4). c, "89 Tahun," text (3/4). d, Emblem dated "1920" (4/4).

2009, Mar. 2   Litho.
2176		Horiz. strip of 4 + central label	2.00	2.00
a.-d.	A692	1500r Any single	.45	.30

A693

A694

A695

General Elections — A696

2009, Mar. 5   Perf. 13x13¼
2177		Strip of 4	1.60	.80
a.	A693	1500r multi	.40	.25
b.	A694	1500r multi	.40	.25
c.	A695	1500r multi	.40	.25
d.	A696	1500r multi	.40	.25

Souvenir Sheet

Preservation of Polar Regions and Glaciers — A697

No. 2178 — Snowflake emblem and: a, Iceberg, top of polar bear's head. b, Crying polar bear.

2009, Mar. 18   Perf. 13½x12¾
2178	A697	2500r Sheet of 2, #a-b	2.00	1.00

Compare with No. 2104.

Souvenir Sheet

China 2009 World Stamp Exhibition, Luoyang — A698

2009, Apr. 10
2179	A698	10,000r multi	2.75	1.40

Intl. Year of Astronomy — A699

Nos. 2180 and 2181: a, Galileo's telescope (1/3). b, Intl. Year of Astronomy emblem (2/3). c, Galileo Galilei (1564-1642) (3/3).

2009, May 2   Litho.   Perf. 13x13¼
2180	A699	Horiz. strip of 3	2.50	1.25
a.-c.		1500r Any single	.80	.40

Souvenir Sheet
Litho. With Hologram
2181	A699	Sheet of 3	5.00	2.50
a.-c.		5000r Any single	1.60	.80

World Ocean Conference, Manado — A700

No. 2182: a, Blue-ringed angelfish (1/4). b, Anemone shrimp and sea anemone (2/4). c, Goldback anthias (3/4). d, Coral reef (4/4).
5000r, Sea turtle.

2009, May 11   Perf. 13½x12¾
2182	A700	2500r Block or strip of 4, #a-d	3.00	1.50

Souvenir Sheet
2183	A700	5000r multi	1.75	.85

World Environment Day — A701

No. 2184: a, Boy holding plant, parched earth (3/3). b, Factories, people in bubble (2/3). c, Smokestacks, tree, boy near forest (1/3).
5000r, Like 2184c.

2009, June 5
2184		Strip of 3	1.50	1.00
a.-c.	A701	1500r Any single	.50	.30

Souvenir Sheet
2185	A701	5000r multi	1.50	1.00

Opening of Suramadu Bridge — A702

No. 2186: a, City, statue, end of bridge (1/3). b, Bridge towers (2/3). c, End of bridge, boat, farmer with oxen (3/3).
10,000r, Entire bridge, city, sculpture, boat, farmer with oxen.

2009, June 10
2186		Horiz. strip of 3	1.50	1.00
a.-c.	A702	1500r Any single	.50	.30

Souvenir Sheet
2187	A702	10,000r multi	3.00	2.50

No. 2187 contains one 126x25mm stamp.

Traditional Foods — A703

No. 2188: a, Ihutilinanga (Gorontalo, 1/6). b, Gulai Balak (Lampung, 2/6). c, Sate Tambulinas (Southeast Sulawesi, 3/6). d, Sambal Goreng Papai (Central Kalimantan, 4/6). e, Nasi Uduk (Jakarta, 5/6). f, Ikan Bobara Kuah Asam (West Papua, 6/6).

2009, July 6
2188		Block of 6	3.00	1.50
a.-f.	A703	1500r Any single	.50	.25

BirdLife International — A704

No. 2189, 2500r: a, Ciconia stormi, with first "0" in denomination below bird (6/6). b, Aceros corrugatus, with first "0" in denomination touching central line of leaf (1/6).
No. 2190, 2500r, horiz.: a, Harpactes kasumba, with "A" of "Indonesia" barely touching bird's tail (41x25mm, 2/6). b, Actenoides concretus, with entire center of "D" in "Indonesia" over tree branch (41x25mm, 3/6).
No. 2191, 2500r, horiz.: a, Cairina scutulata, with farthest extent of white water ripple line running through "5" in denomination (41x25mm, 4/6). b, Argusianus argus, with white water ripple line touching "2" and "5" in denomination (41x25mm, 5/6).
No. 2192, 2500r: a, Like #2189a, with first "0" in denomination touching bird. b, Like #2189b, with first "0" in denomination above central line of leaf. c, Like #2190a, with "A" of "Indonesia" half on bird's tail, and without "2/6." d, Like #2190b, with center of "D" of "Indonesia" partly on tree branch. e, Like #2191a, with farthest extent of white water ripple line to left of "5" in denomination. f, Like #2191b, with white water ripple line below "2" and "5" in denomination.

2009, July 15   Perf. 13½x12¾
Horiz. Pairs, #a-b
"Burung" in Blue
2189-2191	A704	Set of 3	5.00	2.50

Souvenir Sheet
"Burung" in Black
2192	A704	2500r Sheet of 6, #a-f	5.00	2.50

For overprint see No. 2212.

373

INDONESIA

Children's Day — A705

No. 2193 — Children: a, Jumping rope (1/4). b, Flying kites (2/4). c, Playing hide-and-seek (3/4). d, Riding bicycles (4/4).

2009, July 23
2193 A705 1500r Block of 4, #a-d 2.00 1.50

Souvenir Sheet

Philakorea 2009 Intl. Philatelic Exhibition, Seoul — A706

2009, July 30   Perf. 14
2194 A706 10,000r multi   3.00 2.50

A707
A708
A709
A710

Personalizable Stamps — A711

2009   Litho.   Perf. 12½x4x12½x12½
2195 A707 1500r multi + label 2.00 2.00
2196 A708 1500r multi + label 2.00 2.00
2197 A709 1500r multi + label 2.00 2.00
2198 A710 1500r multi + label 2.00 2.00
2199 A711 1500r multi + label 2.00 2.00
    Nos. 2195-2199 (5)   10.00 10.00

Nos. 2195-2199 each were printed in sheets of 8 stamps + 8 labels that could be personalized. Each sheet sold for 20,000r.

Provincial Arms Type of 2008

Arms of: Nos. 2200, 1500r, 2211a, 2500r, Banten (12/33). Nos. 2201, 1500r, 2211b, 2500r, Jawa Timur (East Java) (13/33). Nos. 2202, 1500r, 2211c, 2500r, Kalimantan Tengah (Central Kalimantan) (14/33). Nos. 2203, 1500r, 2211d, 2500r, Kalimantan Timur (East Kalimantan) (15/33). Nos. 2204, 1500r, 2211e, 2500r, Kepulauan Riau (Riau Archipelago) (16/33). Nos. 2205, 1500r, 2211f, 2500r, Lampung (17/33). Nos. 2206, 1500r, 2211g, 2500r, Nusa Tenggara Timur (East Nusa Tenggara) (18/33). Nos. 2207, 1500r, 2211h, 2500r, Papua Barat (West Papua) (19/33). Nos. 2208, 1500r, 2211i, 2500r, Sulawesi Tengah (Central Sulawesi) (20/33). Nos. 2209, 1500r, 2211j, 2500r, Sulawesi Tenggara (Southeast Sulawesi) (21/33). Nos. 2210, 1500r, 2211k, 2500r, Sumatera Selatan (South Sumatra) (22/33).

2009, Aug. 17   Litho.   Perf. 12½
2200-2210 A679 Set of 11 5.50 2.75
2211   Sheet of 11 + label 8.00 8.00
  a.-k. A679 2500r Any single .75 .35

No. 2192 Overprinted in Gold With JIPEX 2009 Emblem

Methods and Perfs As Before
2009, Oct. 28
2212 A704 2500r Sheet of 6, #a-f 5.50 4.00

Tourist Sites in Indonesia and Singapore A712

Designs: 1500r, Sentosa, Singapore (4/4). 2500r, Taman Mini Indonesia Indah (Beautiful Indonesia Miniature Park), Indonesia (3/4). 4000r, Merlion, Singapore (2/4). 7500r, Singaraja Statue, Indonesia (1/4).

2009, Oct. 28   Litho.   Perf. 13½x12¾
2213-2216 A712 Set of 4 4.50 2.75
2216a   Miniature sheet, 2 each
            #2213-2216   9.00 9.00

See Singapore Nos. 1402-1405.

Flora and Fauna of the Provinces Type of 2008
Miniature Sheet

No. 2217: a, Rhinoceros sondaicus, Vatica bantenensis, Banten (1/11). b, Gallus varius x Gallus gallus, Polyanthes tuberosa, Jawa Timur (East Java) (2/11). c, Polyplectron schleirmacheri, Nephelium rambutan-ake, Kalimantan Tengah (Central Kalimantan) (3/11). d, Orcaella brevirostris, Coelogyne pandurata, Kalimantan Timur (East Kalimantan) (4/11). e, Lutjanus sanguineus, Piper betle, Kepulauan Riau (Riau Archipelago) (5/11). f, Elephas maximus sumatranus, Magnolia candolili, Lampung (6/11). g, Varanus komodoensis, Santalum album, Nusa Tenggara Timur (East Nusa Tenggara) (7/11). h, Paradisaea rubra, Pandanus conoideus, Papua Barat (West Papua) (8/11). i, Macrocephalon maleo, Diospyros celebica, Sulawesi Tengah (Central Sulawesi) (9/11). j, Bubalus depressicornis, Diplocaulobium utile, Sulawesi Tenggara (Southeast Sulawesi) (10/11). k, Notopterus chitala, Lansium domesticum, Sumatera Selatan (South Sumatra) (11/11).

2009, Nov. 5
2217 A688 2500r Sheet of 11,
              #a-k, + label 9.00 9.00

Buildings in Indonesia and Iran — A713

Designs: 1500r, Soltanieh Dome, Iran (2/2). 3000r, Al-Markaz Mosque, Indonesia (1/2).

2009, Dec. 18   Perf. 13x13¼
2218 A713 1500r multi .50 .35
2219 A713 3000r multi 1.00 .70
  a. Miniature sheet of 12, 6 each
      #2218-2219   9.00 9.00

See Iran No. 3013.

New Year 2010 (Year of the Tiger) — A714

Tiger: No. 2220, 1500r, Head (1/3). No. 2221, 1500r, Walking (2/3). No. 2222, 1500r, Running (3/3).
5000r, Tiger, sky.

2010, Feb. 6   Litho.   Perf. 13½x12¾
2220-2222 A714 Set of 3 1.40 .75
2222a   Souvenir sheet of 6, 2
            each #2220-2222   2.25 2.00

Souvenir Sheet
2223 A714 5000r multi 2.25 2.25

UNESCO Intangible Cultural Heritage — A720

Designs: 1000r, Batik in Campuran design (4/6). 1500r, Hanoman puppet, vert. (3/6). 2000r, Arjuna puppet, vert. (1/6). 2500r, Kresna puppet, vert. (2/6). 3000r, Kris, vert. (6/6). No. 2234, 5000r, Batik in Kembangan design (5/6).
No. 2235, 5000r, Hanoman puppet, diff., vert. No. 2236, 5000r, Kris, diff., vert.

Perf. 13½x12¾, 12¾x13½
2010, Mar. 29   Litho.
2229-2234 A720 Set of 6 5.00 3.50

Souvenir Sheets
2235-2236 A720 Set of 2 4.50 4.00

Nos. 2235-2236 exist imperforate.

2010 World Cup Soccer Championships, South Africa — A721

No. 2237: a, Soccer player (1/4). b, Mascot (2/4). c, Emblem (3/4). d, Goalie making save (4/4).

2010, May 1   Perf. 12¾x13½
2237 A721 1500r Block or horiz.
            strip of 4, #a-d 2.00 2.00
  e. Booklet pane of 4, #2237a-
       2237d   2.00 —
      Complete booklet, #2237e 2.00

A722

Environmental Care — A723

Designs: No. 2238, Hands holding seedling (3/3).
No. 2239: a, Bird, sheep, palm tree, child (1/3). b, Earth and hands (2/3).
5000r, Like #2238.

Perf. 12¾x13½, 13½x12¾
2010, June 5
2238 A722 1500r multi   .70 .30
2239 A723 1500r Vert. pair, #a-b .70 .30

Souvenir Sheet
2240 A722 5000r multi 1.40 1.40

Muhammadiyah Islamic Organization, Cent. — A724

No. 2241: a, Building (1/3). b, Kyai Haji Ahmad Dahlan (1868-1923), founder (2/3). c, Student, graduate, building (3/3).

2010, July 3   Perf. 12½
2241   Strip of 3 1.25 1.25
  a.-c. A724 1500r Any single .35 .25
  d.   Souvenir sheet of 6, 2 each
        #2241a-2241c   2.50 2.50

Traditional Foods — A725

No. 2242: a, Sup Lobster Kelapa Muda, West Sulawesi (1/7). b, Gulai Iga Kemba'ang, Bengkulu (2/7). c, Ayam Cincane, East Kalimantan (3/7). d, Sate Udang Pentuk Asam Manis, Jambi (4/7). e, Lempah Kuning, Bangka Belitung (5/7). f, Asam Padeh Baung, Riau (6/7). g, Lapis Palaro, North Moluccas (7/7).

2010, July 6   Perf. 13½x12¾
2242   Block of 7 + label 4.00 4.00
  a.-g. A725 1500r Any single .50 .35

Elected Leaders — A726

No. 2243 — Flag and: a, Pres. Susilo Bambang Yudhoyono (1/2). b, Vice-president Boediono (2/2).

2010, Aug. 17   Perf. 14
2243   Pair 1.50 1.00
  a.-b. A726 2500r Either single .75 .35
  c.   Souvenir sheet of 2, #2243a-
        2243b   1.50 1.50

2010 Youth Olympic Games, Singapore — A727

No. 2244 — Badminton player with denomination at: a, LR. b, LL.

2010, July 15   Litho.   Perf. 13½x12¾
2244 A727 1500r Pair, #a-b 1.10 1.10

Bandung, 200th Anniv. A728

No. 2245: a, Soccer player. b, R. Dewi Sartika (1884-1947), advocate for women's education.
No. 2246: a, Pasupati Bridge. b, City street. 5000r, Pasupati Bridge.

2010, Sept. 25   Perf. 12¾x13½
2245 A728 1000r Pair, #a-b .75 .75
2246 A728 1500r Pair, #a-b 1.25 1.25

Souvenir Sheet
2247 A728 5000r multi 1.50 1.50

Worldwide Fund for Nature (WWF) — A729

No. 2248 — Sea turtles: a, Lepidochelys olivacea (1/4). b, Chelonia mydas (2/4). c,

INDONESIA

Dermochelys coriacea (3/4). d, Eretmochelys imbricata (4/4).

2010, Oct. 24   *Perf. 13½x12¾*
2248   Strip or block of 4   2.75   2.75
   a.-d.   A729 1500r Any single   .65   .25

Flora and Fauna of the Provinces Type of 2008

No. 2249: a, Haliastur indus, Salacca zalacca, Jakarta (5/11). b, Geopelia striata, Stelechocarpus burahol, Yogyakarta (6/11).
No. 2250: a, Gracula religiosa robusta, Cananga odorata, Sumatera Utara (North Sumatra) (1/11). b, Panthera tigris sumatrae, Cyrtostachys renda, Jambi (2/11). c, Helarctos malayanus, Amorphophallus titanum, Bengkulu (3/11). d, Tarsius bancanus saltator, Palaquium rostratum, Bangka Belitung (4/11). 2000r, Cervus timorensis, Diospyros macrophylla, Nusa Tenggara Barat (West Nusa Tenggara) (11/11).
No. 2252: a, Nasalis larvatus, Mangifera casturi, Kalimantan Selatan (South Kalimantan) (7/11). b, Aceros cassadix, Borassus flabellifer, Sulawesi Selatan (South Sulawesi) (8/11). c, Tarsius spectrum, Ficus minahassae, Sulawesi Utara (North Sulawesi) (9/11). d, Semioptera wallacii, Syzygium aromaticum, Maluku Utara (North Moluccas) (10/11).

2010, Nov. 5   *Litho.*
2249   A688   1000r Pair, #a-b   .75   .75
2250   A688   1500r Strip or block of 4, #a-d   2.00   2.00
2251   A688   2000r multi   .75   .35
2252   A688   2500r Strip or block of 4, #a-d   3.50   3.50
   e.   Souvenir sheet, #2249a-2249b, 2250a-2250d, 2251, 2252a-2252d, + labels   7.50   7.50
   Nos. 2249-2252 (4)   4.55   2.20

Provincial Arms Type of 2008

Arms of: No. 2253, 1500r, Sumatera Utara (North Sumatra) (23/33). No. 2254, 1500r, Jambi (24/33). No. 2255, 1500r, Bengkulu (25/35). No. 2256, 1500r, Kepulauan Bangka Belitung (26/33). No. 2257, 1500r, DKI Jakarta (27/33). No. 2258, 1500r, Yogyakarta (28/33). No. 2259, 1500r, Kalimantan Selatan (South Kalimantan) (29/33). No. 2260, 1500r, Sulawesi Selatan (South Sulawesi) (30/33). No. 2261, 1500r, Sulawesi Utara (North Sulawesi) (31/33). No. 2262, 1500r, Maluku Utara (North Maluku) (32/33). No. 2263, 1500r, Nusa Tenggara Barat (West Nusa Tenggara) (33/33).
No. 2264, Like #2257.

2010, Dec. 13   *Litho.*   *Perf. 12½*
2253-2263   A679   Set of 11   5.00   3.00
2263a   Sheet of 11, #2253-2263, + label   5.00   5.00

Souvenir Sheet
2264   A679   5000r multi   4.00   2.00

New Year 2011 (Year of the Rabbit) — A730

Indonesian flag and: 1500r, Brown rabbit (1/3). 3000r, Gray rabbit (2/3). 4000r, Gray and brown rabbits (3/3).
5000r, Head of brown rabbit.

2011, Jan. 25   *Litho.*   *Perf. 13½x12¾*
2265-2267   A730   Set of 3   3.00   .95
2267a   Sheet of 6, 2 each #2265-2267, + 2 labels   7.00   7.00

Souvenir Sheet
Litho. with Foil Application
2268   A730   5000r multi   2.00   2.00

Traditional Rituals — A731

No. 2269: a, Grebeg Syawal ritual, Yogyakarta (1/4). b, Ngaben ritual, Bali (2/4). c, Pasola ritual, Sumba, East Nusa Tenggara (3/4). d, Tiwah ritual, Dayak, Central Kalimantan (4/4).

Perf. 13½x12¾
2011, Feb. 24   *Litho.*
2269   A731   1500r Block or horiz. strip of 4, #a-d   2.25   2.25

Intl. Year of Chemistry A732

Designs: 1500r, Molecular model of Artoindonesianin C. 2500r, International Year of Chemistry emblem, vert.

Perf. 13½x12¾, 12¾x13½
2011, Mar. 1
2270-2271   A732   Set of 2   1.50   .75

Traditional Textiles — A733

No. 2272: a, Ulos Batak, Sulawesi Utara (North Sulawesi) (1/8). b, Tenun Tampan, Lampung (2/8). c, Batik Lasem, Jawa Tengah (Central Java) (3/8). d, Batik Parang Garuda, Yogyakarta (4/8). e, Sasirangan Banjar, Kalimantan Selatan (South Kalimantan) (5/8). f, Tenun Iban, Kalimantan Timur (East Kalimantan) (6/8). g, Tenun Toraja, Sulawesi Selatan (South Sulawesi) (7/8). h, Tenun Sumba, Nusa Tenggara Timur (East Nusa Tenggara) (8/8).
5000r, Woman weaving fabric.

2011, Mar. 30   *Perf. 13½x12¾*
2272   A733   2500r Sheet of 8, #a-h   8.00   8.00
   i.   As #2272, with Indonesia 2012 emblem overprinted in sheet margin in metallic red   8.00   8.00

Souvenir Sheet
2273   A733   5000r multi   2.00   2.00
   a.   As #2273, with Indonesia 2012 emblem overprinted in sheet margin in metallic red   2.00   2.00

See Nos. 2281-2282, 2292-2293, 2307-2308. Nos. 2272i and 2273a exist imperforate.

Spacecraft A734

No. 2274: a, Rocket on launch pad (1/2). b, TUBSAT (2/2).

2011, Apr. 12   *Perf. 12¾x13½*
2274   A734   2500r Pair, #a-b   1.75   1.50

Internet Safety A735

No. 2275 — Child in helmet and: a, Plug in outlet in globe (1/2). b, Children using laptop computer (2/2).

2011, Apr. 21   *Perf. 13½x12¾*
2275   A735   2500r Horiz. pair, #a-b   1.75   1.50

No. 2275 was printed in sheets containing eight pairs and four labels.

Environmental Care — A736

No. 2276: a, Pine cone on branch (1/2). b, Squirrel on pine tree (2/2).

2011, June 5   *Litho.*
2276   A736   2500r Vert. pair, #a-b   1.75   1.50
   c.   Souvenir sheet, #2276a-2276b   1.75   1.75

Fish and Seaweed Production — A737

Designs: 1500r, Fish and vegetables on plate (3/4). 2000r, Fish and vegetables (2/4). 3000r, Man processing seaweed (4/4). 5000r, Fisherman and fish (1/4).

2011, June 22   *Perf. 12½*
2277-2280   A737   Set of 4   3.50   2.00
2280a   Souvenir sheet of 4, #2277-2280   3.50   3.50

Traditional Textiles Type of 2011

No. 2281: a, Tenun Aceh Nanggroe, Aceh (1/8). b, Tenun Pandai Sikek, Sumatara Barat (West Sumatra) (2/8). c, Batik Basurek, Bengkulu (3/8). d, Songket Palembang, Sumatera Selatan (South Sumatra) (4/8). e, Batik Madura, Jawa Timur (East Java) (5/8). f, Tenun Sambas, Kalimantan Barat (West Kalimantan) (6/8). g, Tenun Bentenan, Sulawesi Utara (North Sulawesi) (7/8). h, Batik Masambo, Nusa Tenggara Barat (West Nusa Tenggara) (8/8).
5000r, Man behind team of oxen with Karapan Sabi, Jawa Timur (East Java).

2011, July 6   *Perf. 13½x12¾*
2281   A733   2500r Sheet of 8, #a-h   8.00   8.00
   i.   Like #2281, with gold design in sheet margin   8.00   8.00

Souvenir Sheet
2282   A733   5000r multi   2.00   2.00

Nos. 2281i, 2282 exist imperf.

Souvenir Sheet
PhilaNippon '11 World Stamp Exhibition, Yokohama, Japan — A738

2011, July 28
2283   A738   10,000r multi   3.25   3.25

Friendship Between Malaysia and Indonesia A739

No. 2284: a, Proclamation Monument, Indonesia (1/8). b, 1945 Indonesia 5-sen banknote (2/8). c, Indonesia #1LM1 (3/8). d, Gallus varius (4/8).
No. 2285: a, National Monument, Malaysia (5/8). b, 1959 Malaya and North Borneo $1 banknote (6/8). c, Malaya #84 (7/8). d, Gallus gallus (8/8).

2011, Aug. 8   *Perf. 13¼x13*
2284   A739   Vert strip of 4   4.00   4.00
   a.-d.   2500r Any single   1.00   .30
2285   A739   Vert strip of 4   4.00   4.00
   a.-d.   2500r Any single   1.00   .30
   e.   Sheet of 8, #2284a-2284d, 2285a-2285d   8.00   8.00

See Malaysia No. 1360.

Scouting In Indonesia, 50th Anniv. — A740

Designs: No. 2286, 2500r, Dove, Scout holding Scouting flag (1/3). No. 2287, 2500r, Four Scouts, Scouting and Indonesian flag (2/3). No. 2288, 2500r, Scout leaders teaching Scouts (3/3).
5000r, Like No. 2286.

2011, Apr. 14   *Perf. 13½x12¾*
2286-2288   A740   Set of 3   2.50   .90

Souvenir Sheet
2289   A740   5000r multi   1.75   1.75

Landmarks A741

No. 2290: a, Lawang Sewu Building, Semarang (2/5). b, Equator Monument, Pontianak (3/5). c, Garuda Wisnu Kencana Cultural Park, Denpasar (4/5). d, Fort Rotterdam, Makassar (5/5). e, Ampera Bridge, Palembang (1/5).

2011, Sept. 27   *Perf. 13½x12¾*
2290   Strip of 5   3.50   3.00
   a.-e.   A741 2500r Any single   .70   .30

Famous Men A742

No. 2291: a, Dr. Mohammed Natsir (1908-93), Prime minister. b, Sutomo (1920-81), politician.

2011, Aug. 17   *Perf. 13x13¼*
2291   A742   2500r Horiz. pair, #a-b   1.75   1.50

Traditional Textiles Type of 2011

No. 2292: a, Songket Malayu, Riau (1/8). b, Songket Mentok, Bangka Belitung (2/8). c, Batik Mega Mendung, Jawa Barat (West Java) (3/8). d, Tenun Sora Langi, Sulawesi Barat (West Sulawesi) (4/8). e, Tenun Tolaki,

INDONESIA

Sulawesi Tenggara (Southeast Sulawesi) (5/8). f, Tenun Tanimbar, Maluku (6/8). g, Batik Papua, Papua (7/8). h, Batik Papua Barat, Papua Barat (West Papua) (8/8).
5000r, Masked dancer, Tari Topeng, Jawa Barat (West Java).

2011, Oct. 2   Litho.   Perf. 13½x12¾
2292   A733   2500r Sheet of 8, #a-h   8.00   8.00

Souvenir Sheet
2293   A733   5000r multi   2.00   2.00

Operation Trikora, 50th Anniv. — A743

Designs: No. 2294, 2500r, Trikora Monument, ships, map of West Papua, helicopter (1/4). No. 2295, 2500r, Soldiers and armored personnel carrier (2/4). No. 2296, 2500r, Navy ships, soldiers in water (3/4). No. 2297, 2500r, Soldiers and jet fighter (4/4).

2011, Oct. 5   Perf. 13½x12¾
2294-2297   A743   Set of 4   3.50   1.50
2297a   Souvenir sheet of 8, 2 each #2294-2297 + 2 labels   7.00   6.00

Indonesian Historical Links With South Africa — A744

No. 2298: a, Sheikh Yusuf (1626-99), establisher of Islam in South Africa (1/10). b, Balla Lampoa Museum, Sulawesi Selantan (South Sulawesi) (2/10). c, Alat Musik Tifa, Papua (3/10). d, Topi Tilangga, Nusa Tenggara Timur, and Kelom Geulis, Jawa Barat (West Java) (4/10). e, Tari Pakarena, Sulawesi Selatan (South Sulawesi) (5/10).

2011, Oct. 15   Perf. 13¼x13
2298   A744   2500r Vert. strip of 5, #a-e   4.00   4.00
See South Africa No. 1469.

2011 South East Asian Games, Jakarta and Palembang A745

No. 2299: a, Mascot and tower in Jakarta (1/6). b, Mascot and towers in Palembang (2/6). c, Mascot playing soccer (5/6). d, Mascot in pencak silat outfit (6/6). e, Mascot playing table tennis (3/6). f, Mascot playing badminton (4/6).

2011, Oct. 18   Perf. 12¾x13½
2299   A745   2500r Block of 6, #a-f   5.00   5.00

Flora and Fauna A746

Nos. 2300 and 2301: a, Leptophryne cruentata. b, Nymphoides indica.

2011, Nov. 5   Perf. 13½x12¾
2300   A746   2500r Horiz. pair, #a-b   1.75   1.50
   c.   Vert. tete-beche pair   1.75   1.50

Souvenir Sheet
2301   A746   5000r Sheet of 2, #a-b   3.50   3.50
No. 2301 has a curved die-cut slit that encompasses the stamps and text in the sheet margin.

China 2011 International Stamp Exhibition, Wuxi, People's Republic of China — A747

2011   Litho.
2302   A747   10,000r multi   3.50   3.50

New Year 2012 (Year of the Dragon) — A748

No. 2303 — Various dragons: a, Green and multicolored (1/3). b, Red brown and multicolored (2/3). c, Indigo and multicolored (3/3). 5000r, Dragon, diff.

2012, Jan. 15   Perf. 13½x12¾
2303   Strip of 3   2.50   2.50
  a.-c.   A748 2500r Any single   .75   .30
   d.   Souvenir sheet of 6, 2 each #2303a-2303c, + 2 labels   5.00   5.00

Souvenir Sheet
2304   A748   5000r multi   2.25   2.25

National Sports Week A749

No. 2305 — Mascot: a, Parachuting (1/6). b, Shooting (2/6). c, On gymnastic rings (3/6). d, Playing sepak takraw (4/6). e, Sailboarding (5/6). f, Canoeing (6/6).

2012, Feb. 22
2305   A749   2500r Block of 6, #a-f   5.00   4.00

Asian-Pacific Postal Union, 50th Anniv. — A750

2012, Apr. 1
2306   A750   5000r multi   1.60   .80

Traditional Textiles Type of 2011

No. 2307: a, Batik Bongbong, Riau Kepulauan (25/33). b, Batik Angso Duo, Jambi (26/33). c, Tenun Baduy, Banten (27/33). d, Tenun Gringsing, Bali (28/33). e, Kain Benang Bintik, Kalimantan Tengah (Central Kalimantan) (29/33). f, Tenun Donggala, Sulawesi Tengah (Central Sulawesi) (30/33). g, Kain Kerawang, Gorontalo (31/33). h, Batik Ternate, Maluku Utara (North Moluccas) (32/33). i, As "a," numbered 1/8. j, As "b," numbered 2/8. k, As "c," numbered 3/8. l, As "d," numbered 4/8. m, As "e," numbered 5/8. n, As "f," numbered 6/8. o, As "g," numbered 7/8. p, As "h," numbered 8/8.
5000r, Tari Barong, Bali.

2012, Apr. 21
2307   A733   2500r Block of 8, #a-h   7.00   7.00
  i.-p.   Any single   .75   .30
   q.   Souvenir sheet of 8, #2307i-2307p   7.00   7.00

Souvenir Sheet
2308   A733   5000r multi   1.75   1.75
No. 2307 was printed in a sheet containing three blocks of eight stamps. No. 2308 is dated 2011.

Environmental Care — A751

No. 2309: a, Gasoline pump nozzle (1/2). b, Rhinoceros, Earth in drop of gasoline (2/2).
5000r, Gasoline pump nozzle, rhinoceros, Earth in drop of gasoline, vert.

2012, June 5   Perf. 13½x12¾
2309   A751   2000r Vert. pair, #a-b   1.40   1.20

Souvenir Sheet
2310   A751   5000r multi   1.60   1.20
No. 2310 contains one 42x51mm stamp.

Traditional Foods — A752

No. 2311: a, Daging Sei and Jagung Bose, Nusa Tenggara Timur (1/2). b, Gulai Asam Pedas, Kepulauan Riau (2/2).

2012, July 6   Litho.
2311   A752   2500r Pair, #a-b   1.75   1.40
No. 2311 was printed in sheets containing 10 pairs and a central label.

Endangered Birds — A753

No. 2312: a, Otus siaoensis (1/4). b, Nisaetus floris (2/4). c, Aethopyga duyvenbodei (3/4). d, Habroptila wallacii (4/4).

2012, July 15   Perf. 14
2312   A753   2500r Block of 4, #a-d   3.00   3.00
   e.   Souvenir sheet of 4, #2312a-2312d   3.00   3.00

Scouting in Indonesia, Cent. — A763

No. 2324 — Scouts at flag ceremony with denomination at: a, Left (1/2). b, Right (2/2).

2012, Aug. 14   Perf. 13½x12¾   Litho.
2324   A763   2500r Horiz. pair, #a-b   1.60   1.25
   c.   Souvenir sheet of 2, #2324a-2324b   1.60   1.60

Television Broadcasting in Indonesia, 50th Anniv. — A764

No. 2325: a, Black-and-white television (1/2). b, High-definition color television (2/2).

2012, Aug. 24
2325   A764   2500r Pair, #a-b   1.60   1.25

People at Building Site — A765

Various People — A766

People Holding Hands — A767

Perf. 12¾x13½, 13½x12¾ (A766)
2012, Oct. 1
2326   Strip of 3   2.50   2.00
  a.   A765 2500r multi (1/3)   .75   .30
  b.   A766 2500r multi (2/3)   .75   .30
  c.   A767 2500r multi (3/3)   .75   .30

Houses of Worship — A768

No. 2327: a, Masjid Agung, Palembang (3/5). b, Pura, Besakih (4/5). c, Wihara Dharma Bhakti, Jakarta (5/5). d, Gereja Blenduk, Semarang (1/5). e, Gereja Puhsarang, Kediri (2/5).

2012, Oct. 27   Perf. 13½x12¾
2327   Strip of 5   3.50   3.50
  a.-e.   A768 2500r Any single   .60   .30

INDONESIA

Flora and Fauna — A769

Nos. 2328 and 2329: a, Spilocuscus rufoniger (1/2). b, Kandelia candel (2/2). Stamps on No. 2329 lack "1/2" and "2/2."

2012, Nov. 5   Perf. 12¾x13½
2328   A769   2500r Pair, #a-b   1.75   1.25
Souvenir Sheet
2329   A769   5000r Sheet of 2, #a-b   3.50   3.50

New Year 2013 (Year of the Snake) — A770

Various depictions of snakes.

2013, Jan. 22
2330   Strip of 3   5.00   4.00
  a. A770 2500r multi (1/3)   .75   .30
  b. A770 5000r multi (2/3)   1.25   .65
  c. A770 7500r multi (3/3)   1.75   1.00
  d. Miniature sheet of 6, 2 each #2330a-2330c   6.50   3.25
Souvenir Sheet
2331   A770   10,000r multi   3.25   3.25

Ratu Boko Palace — A771

Sumunaring Abhayagiri Dancers — A772

2013, Feb. 20   Perf. 13½x12¾
2332   A771   2500r multi   .85   .30
2333   A772   2500r multi   .85   .30

Musical Instruments — A773

Designs: No. 2334, 2500r, Gambus, Riau (1/33). No. 2335, 2500r, Celempung, Jawa Barat (West Java) (4/33). No. 2336, 2500r, Kollatung, Kalimantan Barat (West Kalimantan) (6/33). No. 2337, 2500r, Calong, Sulawesi Barat (West Sulawesi) (7/33). No. 2338, 2500r, Tambua, Sumatera Barat (West Sumatra) (8/33). No. 2339, 2500r, Siter, Jawa Tengah (Central Java) (9/33). No. 2340, 3000r, Serune Kalee, NAD (Aceh) (2/33). No. 2341, 3000r, Fu, Maluku (Moluccas) (3/33). No. 2342, 3000r, Cengceng, Bali (5/33). No. 2343, 3000r, Tifa, Papua (10/33). No. 2344, 3000r, Polopalo, Gorontalo (11/33).

2013, Mar. 9   Litho.
2334-2344   A773   Set of 11   10.00   5.00
  2344a   Block of 11, #2334-2344, + label   10.00   10.00

Nos. 2334-2344 were printed in sheets containing two of each stamp and 2 labels in center of sheet. See Nos. 2371-2381, 2402-2412, 2423. For surcharges, see Nos. 2516-2521.

Diplomatic Relations Between Indonesia and Mexico, 60th Anniv. — A774

No. 2345: a, Clouded leopard, Indonesia (1/2). b, Mexican jaguar (2/2).

2013, Apr. 6   Perf. 13¼x13
2345   A774   8000r Horiz. pair, #a-b   5.00   4.00

See Mexico Nos. 2818-2819.

A775   A776

Transfer of Control of West Irian to Indonesia, 50th Anniv. — A777

2013, May 1   Perf. 13½x12¾
2346   Strip of 3   2.50   2.00
  a. A775 2500r multi (1/3)   .75   .30
  b. A776 2500r multi (2/3)   .75   .30
  c. A777 2500r multi (3/3)   .75   .30

Publication of Anti-Colonial Writings by Ki Hadjar Dewantara (1889-1959), Cent. — A778

2013, May 2   Perf. 13¼x13
2347   A778   2500r multi   .90   .30

Souvenir Sheets

Australia 2013 World Stamp Expo, Melbourne — A779

Designs: No. 2348, 10,000r, Orangutans. No. 2349, 10,000r, Kangaroos.

2013, May 10   Perf. 12¾x13½
2348-2349   A779   Set of 2   3.50   3.50

World Environment Day — A780

No. 2350: a, Fruit in top of hourglass (1/2). b, Garbage in bottom of hourglass (2/2). 5000r, Fruit and garbage in hourglass, vert.

2013, June 5   Perf. 13½x12¾
2350   A780   2500r Vert. pair, #a-b   1.75   1.40
Souvenir Sheet
2351   A780   5000r multi   1.75   1.75

No. 2351 contains one 42x51mm stamp.

Cave Painting, Uhallie — A781

Ramayana Epic, Prambanan Temple, Yogyakarta — A782

Buddha Attaining Enlightenment, Borobudur Temple — A783

2013, June 14
2352   A781   2500r multi   .85   .30
2353   A782   2500r multi   .85   .30
Souvenir Sheet
2354   A783   10,000r multi   3.25   3.25

Indonesian Archaeological Institute, Cent.

SOS Children's Villages — A784

No. 2355: a, Building, child on swing (1/2). b, Children and bicycle (2/2).

2013, July 23   Litho.   Perf. 13½x12¾
2355   A784   2500r Pair, #a-b   1.60   1.25

Souvenir Sheet

2013 Thailand World Stamp Expo, Bangkok — A785

2013, Aug. 2   Litho.   Perf. 12¾x13½
2356   A785   10,000r multi   3.00   3.00

Postal Services — A786   A787

Designs: 2500r, 4000r, PosPay (online bill paying) service. 3000r, 4500r, WeselPos (money order) service. 3500r, 5000r, PosExpress and Poskilat Khusus (express and document delivery) services.

Perf. 13½x12¾
2013, Aug. 26   Litho.
2357   A786   2500r multi   .70   .25
2358   A786   3000r multi   .85   .30
2359   A786   3500r multi   1.00   .50
Perf. 12¾ Syncopated
2360   A787   4000r multi   1.10   .60
2361   A787   4500r multi   1.10   .60
2362   A787   5000r multi   .90   .45
  Nos. 2357-2362 (6)   5.65   2.80

Diplomatic Relations Between Indonesia and South Korea, 40th Anniv. — A788

No. 2363: a, Large lion figure from Korean folk play, small bull figure from Indonesian folk play (1/2). b, Small lion figure, large bull figure (2/2).

2013, Sept. 17   Litho.   Perf. 13¼x13
2363   A788   7500r Horiz. pair, #a-b   4.50   3.50

See South Korea No. 2415

Souvenir Sheet

2013 National Philatelic Exhibition, Bandung — A789

Perf. 13½x12¾
2013, Sept. 25   Litho.
2364   A789   10,000r multi   3.00   3.00

Garuda Contingent (Indonesian Armed Forces in United Nations Peace-Keeping Missions) — A790

No. 2365: a, Boy and soldier wearing United Nations helmets saluting each other (1/4). b, Soldiers and United Nations vehicle (2/4). c, Ships at sea (3/4). d, Soldier and United Nations Peacekeepers flag (4/4).

2013, Oct. 5   Litho.   Perf. 13¼x13
2365   A790   2500r Block of 4, #a-d   3.00   2.50

Flora and Fish — A791

Nos. 2366 and 2367: a, Metroxylon sago (2/2). b, Pristis microdon (1/2).

2013, Nov. 5   Litho.   Perf. 13½x12¾
2366   A791   2500r Pair, #a-b   1.50   1.20
Souvenir Sheet
2367   A791   5000r Sheet of 2, #a-b   3.00   3.00

General Elections — A792

No. 2368: a, Voters at polls, woman showing finger mark (1/4). b, Map of Indonesia, hand with stylus, ballot boxes, vert. (2/4). c, Caricature of ballot box (4/4). d, Voters, hand placing Indonesian flag in ballot box, vert. (3/4).

2014, Jan. 9   Litho.   Perf. 13½x12¾
2368   A792   2500r Block of 4, #a-d   3.00   2.50

New Year 2014 (Year of the Horse) — A793

No. 2369 — Horse and rider with top panel color of: a, Dark gray (1/3). b, Greenish gray (2/3). c, Brown (3/3).
10,000r, Four horses.

2014, Jan. 15   Litho.   Perf. 12¾x13¼
2369   Strip of 3   2.50   2.00
  a.-c. A793 2500r Any single   .75   .30
  d. Souvenir sheet of 6, 2 each #2369a-2369c   5.00   5.00
Souvenir Sheet
2370   A793   10,000r multi   3.00   3.00

Musical Instruments Type of 2013

Designs: No. 2371, 3000r, Dogdog Lojor, Banten (12/33). No. 2372, 3000r, Terompet

INDONESIA

Reog, Jawa Timur (East Java) (13/33). No. 2373, 5000r, Japen, Kalimantan Tengah (Central Kalimantan) (14/33). No. 2374, 5000r, Sampek, Kalimantan Timur (East Kalimantan) (15/33). No. 2375, 5000r, Gendang Panjang, Kepulauan Riau (Riau Islands) (16/33). No. 2376, 5000r, Cetik, Lampung (17/33). No. 2377, 5000r, Lalove, Sulawesi Tengah (Central Sulawesi) (20/33). No. 2378, 5000r, Latatou, Sulawesi Tenggara (Southeast Sulawesi) (21/33). No. 2379, 5000r, Accordion, Sumatra Selatan (South Sumatra) (22/33). No. 2380, 8000r, Sasando, Nusa Tenggara Timur (East Nusa Tenggara) (18/33). No. 2381, 8000r, Tambur, Papua Barat (West Papua) (19/33).

2014, Mar. 9   Litho.   Perf. 13½x12¾
2371-2381 A773   Set of 11   10.00   5.00
2381a   Block of 11, #2371-2381, + label   10.00   5.00

Nos. 2371-2381 were printed in sheets containing two of each stamp and 2 labels in center of sheet. For surcharges, see Nos. 2522-2530.

Stamps of Netherlands Indies and Indonesia — A794

No. 2382: a, 5000r, Netherlands Indies #1. b, 8000r, Netherlands Indies #N1. c, 10,000r, Indonesia #1L23.
50,000r, Netherlands Indies #1.

Perf. 13¼x13½ Syncopated
2014, Apr. 1   Litho.
2382 A794 Horiz. strip of 3,
        #a-c   6.50   5.00

Litho. With Hologram Affixed
Souvenir Sheet
Perf. 14x14½
2383 A794 50,000r multi   15.00   10.00

First Netherlands Indies stamp, 150th anniv. No. 2383 contains one 48x66mm stamp.

Education A795

No. 2384: a, Children and teacher (1/3). b, Children making origami figures (2/3). c, Children and house, vert. (3/3).

2014, May 2   Litho.   Perf. 13½x12¾
2384   Strip of 3   2.50   2.00
a.-c.   A795 3000r Any single   .75   .30

Miniature Sheet

Worldwide Fund for Nature (WWF) — A796

No. 2385 — Panthera pardus melas: a, Head, denomination at UR (1/4). b, Head, denomination at UL (2/4). c, Entire animal, denomination at UR (3/4). d, Entire animal, denomination at UL (4/4).

2014, May 2   Litho.   Perf. 13½x12¾
2385 A796 5000r Sheet of 4, #a-
              d   5.00   5.00
2014 Four Nations Stamp Show, Bandung.

Environmental Care — A797

Nos. 2386 and 2387: a, Leptoptilos javanicus (1/2). b, Scylla serrata (2/2).

2014, June 5   Litho.   Perf. 13½x12¾
2386 A797 3000r Vert. pair, #a-b   1.75   1.40

Souvenir Sheet
2387 A797 5000r Sheet of 2, #a-
              b   2.75   2.75

Birds A798

No. 2388: a, Mycteria cinerea (1/4). b, Charadrius javanicus (2/4). c, Gymnocrex rosenbergii (3/4). d, Pseudibis davisoni (4/4).

2014, July 15   Litho.   Perf. 14
2388 A798 5000r Block of 4, #a-d 3.50 2.75
e.   Souvenir sheet of 4, #2388a-
     2388d   3.50   3.50

Indonesian First Ladies — A799

No. 2389: a, Fatmawati Soekarno (1923-80) (1/5). b, Tien Soeharto (1923-96) (2/5). c, Ainun Habibie (1937-2010) (3/5). d, Sinta Nuriyah Wahid (4/5). e, Ani Yudhoyono (5/5).

2014, July 23   Litho.   Perf. 12½
2389   Horiz. strip of 5   6.00   5.00
a.-e.   A799 5000r Any single   1.00   .40

Indonesian Paleoanthropology, 125th Anniv. — A800

No. 2390: a, Homo erectus family (1/2). b, Maps and Homo sapiens skull (2/2).

Perf. 13½x12¾
2014, Aug. 31   Litho.
2390 A800 3000r Horiz. pair, #a-
              b   1.50   1.20

Ancient Calendars and Inscriptions — A801

No. 2391: a, Batak calendar (4/4). b, Tanjung Tanah manuscript with post-Pallava inscriptions (1/4). c, Sundanese inscriptions on tablet (2/4). d, Balinese calendar (3/4).

2014, Sept. 8   Litho.   Perf. 12¾x13½
2391   Strip of 4   3.00   2.50
a.-d.   A801 3000r Any single   .75   .30

Postman With Bicycle A802

2014, Sept. 27   Litho.   Perf. 12½
2392 A802 10,000r shown   2.75   1.40
2393 A802 20,000r Post office   5.50   2.75

Armed Forces — A803

No. 2394: a, KRI Dewa Ruci and figurehead (1/3). b, Sukhoi jet and eagle (2/3) c, Leopard tank and leopard (3/3).

2014, Oct. 5   Litho.   Perf. 13¼x13
2394   Strip of 3   2.50   2.00
a.-c.   A803 3000r Any single   .75   .30

Flora and Fauna A804

No. 2395: a, Eretmochelys imbricata (1/2). b, Tacca leontopetaloides (2/2).
5000r, Like No. 2395a.

2014, Nov. 5   Litho.   Perf. 13½x12¾
2395 A804 3000r Pair, #a-b   1.75   1.25

Souvenir Sheet
2396 A804 5000r multi   1.50   1.50

Stamp on No. 2396 is surrounded by turtle-shaped rouletting in sheet margin. No. 2396 exists imperforate without the rouletting in the sheet margin.

National Health Day, 50th Anniv. — A805

No. 2397: a, 50th anniversary emblem (1/2). b, President Sukarno spraying insecticide (2/2).

Perf. 13½x12¾
2014, Nov. 12   Litho.
2397 A805 3000r Pair, #a-b   1.75   1.25

Souvenir Sheet

Malaysia 2014 World Youth Stamp Exhibition, Kuala Lumpur — A806

2014, Dec. 1   Litho.   Perf. 13½x12¾
2398 A806 10,000r multi   3.00   3.00
Discovery of Borobudur Temple, 200th anniv.

Bridges A807

No. 2399: a, Kelok Sembilan Bridge (2/2). b, Bali Mandara Bridge (1/2).

2014, Dec. 3   Litho.   Perf. 13½x12¾
2399 A807 5000r Pair, #a-b   3.00   2.00

New Year 2015 (Year of the Ram) — A808

No. 2400: a, Ram wearing decorations (1/3). b, Ram leaping to right (2/3). c, Ram leaping to left (3/3).
10,000r, Ram wearing decorations, vert.

2015, Feb. 4   Litho.   Perf. 13½x12¾
2400   Horiz. strip of 3   2.50   2.00
a.-c.   A808 3000r Any single   .75   .30
d.   Souvenir sheet of 6, 2 each
     #2400a-2400c   5.00   5.00

Souvenir Sheet
Perf. 12¾x13½
2401 A808 10,000r multi   3.00   3.00

Musical Instruments Type of 2013

Designs: No. 2402, 3000r, Dol, Bengkulu (23/33). No. 2403, 3000r, Tehyan, DKI Jakarta (24/33). No. 2404, 3000r, Cangor, Jambi (25/33). No. 2405, 3000r, Panting, Kalimantan Selatan (South Kalimantan) (26/33). No. 2406, 3000r, Kacapi, Sulawesi Selatan (South Sulawesi) (27/33). No. 2407, 3000r, Kendang, DI Yogyakarta (28/33). No. 2408, 3000r, Hasapi, Sumatera Utara (North Sumatra) (29/33). No. 2409, 3000r, Kolintang,Sulawesi Utara (North Sulawesi) (30/33). No. 2410, 3000r, Bambu Hitada, Maluku Utara (North Maluku) (31/33). No. 2411, 3000r, Dambus, Kepulauan Bangka Belitung (32/33). No. 2412, 3000r, Sarone, Nusa Tenggara Barat (West Nusa Tenggara) (33/33).

2015, Mar. 9   Litho.   Perf. 13½x12¾
2402-2412 A773 Set of 11   8.00   4.00
2412a   Block of 11, #2402-2412, + label   8.00   8.00

Nos. 2402-2412 were printed in sheets containing two of each stamp and 2 labels in center of sheet.

United Nations World Conference on Disaster Risk Reduction — A809

No. 2413: a, Erupting volcano, woman adjusting surgical mask over child's face (1/3). b, Rescuers saving flood victims (2/3). c, Rescue workers and victims, horiz. (3/3).
5000r, Eruption of Tambora Volcano, 200th anniv., horiz.

Perf. 12¾x13½, 13½x12¾
2015, Mar. 14   Litho.
2413   Vert. strip of 3   2.50   1.75
a.-c.   A809 3000r Any single   .75   .30

Souvenir Sheet
Perf. 13¼x13
2414 A809 5000r multi   2.00   2.00
No. 2414 contains one 40x30mm stamp.

Orchids and Past Leaders of Indonesia and North Korea — A810

No. 2415: a, Phalaenopsis amabila, Indonesian Pres. Sukarno (1901-70). b, Dendrobium kimilsung, North Korean Pres. Kim Il-sung (1912-94)

2015, Apr. 15   Litho.   Perf. 13x13¼
2415   Horiz. pair   5.00   3.00
a.-b.   A810 8000r Either single   2.50   1.25
Printed in sheets of 11 each Nos. 2415a-2415b + 2 central labels.

Musical Instruments Type of 2013 and

A811

A812

A813

A814

A815

INDONESIA

A816

Folklore, Arms, and Food of North Kalimantan Province — A817

Design: No. 2423, Babun (8/8).

2015, Apr. 22   Litho.   Perf. 13½x12¾
2416	A811	3000r multi	.80	.30
2417	A812	3000r multi	.80	.30
2418	A813	3000r multi	.80	.30
2419	A814	3000r multi	.80	.30
2420	A815	3000r multi	.80	.30
2421	A816	3000r multi	.80	.30
2422	A817	3000r multi	.80	.30
2423	A773	3000r multi	.80	.30
		Nos. 2416-2423 (8)	6.40	2.40

Nos. 2416-2423 were printed in sheets containing three of each stamp + label.

First Asian African Conference, Bandung, 60th Anniv — A818

2015, Apr. 24   Litho.   Perf. 13½x12¾
| 2424 | A818 | 3000r multi | .50 | .25 |

Environmental Care — A819

2015, June 5   Litho.   Perf. 14
| 2425 | A819 | 3000r multi | .90 | .30 |

Souvenir Sheet
Perf.
| 2426 | A819 | 5000r multi | 2.00 | 2.00 |

Value for No. 2425 is for stamp with surrounding selvage.

23rd World Scout Jamboree, Japan — A820

No. 2427: a, Neckerchief and knot slide (1/2). b, Hands and knots (2/2).

2015, July 28   Litho.   Perf. 13¼x13
| 2427 | A820 | 5000r Horiz. pair, #a-b | 2.50 | 1.75 |

Printed in sheets of 10 pairs + central label.

Flags and Emblem of Association of Southeast Asian Nations — A821

2015, Aug. 8   Litho.   Perf. 14
| 2428 | A821 | 7000r multi | 1.75 | 1.00 |

See Brunei No. 656, Burma Nos. 417-418, Cambodia No. 2428, Laos No. 1906, Malaysia No. 1562, Philippines No. 3619, Singapore No. 1742, Thailand No. 2875, Viet Nam No. 3529.

Souvenir Sheet

Singapore 2015 World Stamp Exhibition — A822

2015, Aug. 14   Litho.   Perf. 13x13¼
| 2429 | A822 | 5000r multi | 1.50 | 1.50 |

A823

New President and Vice-President — A824

No. 2430: a, Pres. Joko Widodo (1/2). b, Vice-President Muhammad Jusuf Kalla (2-2). No. 2431, 8000r, Pres. Widodo. No. 2432, 8000r, Vice-President Kalla.

2015, Aug. 17   Litho.   Perf. 13x13¼
| 2430 | A823 | 5000r Pair, #a-b | 2.50 | 1.75 |

Souvenir Sheets
| 2431-2432 | A824 | Set of 2 | 4.50 | 4.50 |

Indonesian House of Representatives, 70th Anniv. — A825

No. 2433 — House of Representatives Building and: a, Silhouettes of people and flagbearer (1/2). b, Map of Asia and Africa, computer keyboard (2/2).

2015, Aug. 29   Litho.   Perf. 13¼x13
| 2433 | A825 | 3000r Horiz. pair, #a-b | 1.60 | 1.20 |

Indonesian Red Cross Society, 70th Anniv. — A826

No. 2434: a, Mohammad Hatta, 1945-46 chairman, Red Cross workers raising Red Cross flag (1/2). b, Ambulances at Red Cross Headquarters, 1959 (2/2).

2015, Sept. 10   Litho.   Perf. 13¼x13
| 2434 | A826 | 3000r Horiz. pair, #a-b | 1.25 | .90 |

Pancasila Sanctity Day — A827

2015, Oct. 1   Litho.   Perf. 12¾x13½
| 2435 | A827 | 3000r multi | .90 | .30 |

Defense Industry Products — A828

No. 2436: a, KRI Banda Aceh. b, ANOA armored personnel carrier. c, CN 235 airplane.

2015, Oct. 5   Litho.   Perf. 13½x12¾
| 2436 | | Strip of 3 | 2.00 | 1.50 |
| a.-c. | A828 | 3000r Any single | .65 | .30 |

Miniature Sheet

Surabaya 2015 National Philatelic Exhibition — A829

No. 2437: a, Elephant facing right. b, Elephant facing left. c, Head of elephant. d, Adult and juvenile.

Sheet of 4, #a-d
2015, Nov. 2   Litho.   Perf. 13½x12¾
| 2437 | A829 | 5000r Sheet of 4, #a-d | 4.50 | 4.50 |

Flora and Fauna — A830

No. 2438: a, Gracula religiosa robusta. b, Amorphophallus paeoniifolius. 5000r, Like #2438a.

2015, Nov. 5   Litho.   Perf. 13½x12¾
| 2438 | A830 | 3000r Pair, #a-b | 1.40 | 1.10 |

Souvenir Sheet
| 2439 | A830 | 5000r multi | 1.10 | 1.10 |

Tourism A831

No. 2440: a, Scuba diving off Derawan Islands. b, Boat near Raja Ampat Islands. c, Scuba diving in Wakatobi National Marine Park. d, Rocks on Belitung Island. 5000r, Boat near Raja Ampat Islands, diff.

2016, Jan. 1   Litho.   Perf. 13¼x13
| 2440 | A831 | 3000r Block of 4, #a-d | 1.75 | .85 |

Souvenir Sheet
Perf. 13½x12¾
| 2441 | A831 | 5000r multi | .75 | .35 |

No. 2441 contains one 83x21mm stamp.

New Year 2016 (Year of the Monkey) A832

Various monkeys with background color of: a, Red. b, Bright yellow green. c, Pale blue. 10,000r, Monkey, diff.

2016, Jan. 24   Litho.   Perf. 12¾x13½
| 2442 | A832 | 3000r Horiz. strip of 3, #a-c | 2.00 | 1.50 |

Souvenir Sheet
Perf. 13x13¼
| 2443 | A832 | 10,000r multi | 3.00 | 3.00 |

March 9, 2016 Solar Eclipse A833

Nos. 2444 and 2445 — Map of Indonesia showing path of eclipse and: a, Moon at left. b, Total eclipse. c, Moon at right.

Perf. 12¾x12½
2016, Feb. 23   Litho.
| 2444 | A833 | 3000r Horiz. strip of 3, #a-c | 2.00 | 1.50 |

Souvenir Sheet
| 2445 | A833 | 5000r Sheet of 3, #a-c | 3.00 | 3.00 |

A834

Diplomatic Relations Between Indonesia and Thailand — A835

No. 2446 and 2447 — Scenes from the epic poem *Ramayana*: a, Four characters and tree. b, Characters kneeling.

Serpentine Die Cut 10¼
2016, May 5   Litho.
Self-Adhesive
| 2446 | A834 | 8000r Pair, #a-b | 3.00 | 2.00 |

Souvenir Sheet
Litho. With Hologram
| 2447 | A835 | 18,000r Sheet of 2, #a-b | 7.50 | 7.50 |

See Thailand No. 2914.

Souvenir Sheet

19th National Sports Week A837

Litho., Sheet Margin Litho. & Embossed With Foil Application
2016, Sept. 16   Perf.
| 2449 | A837 | 10,000r multi | 1.60 | .80 |

Spices — A838

No. 2450: a, Myristica fragrans. b, Cinnamomum burmanii. c, Piper nigrum. d, Syzygium aromaticum.

2016, Sept. 24   Litho.   Perf. 12½
| 2450 | | Vert. strip of 4 | 2.00 | 1.00 |
| a.-d. | A838 | 3000r Any single | .50 | .25 |

INDONESIA

Souvenir Sheet

Pavo Muticus — A840

2016, Oct. 21   Litho.   Perf. 13x13¼
2452 A840 10,000r multi   1.60   .80
2016 PhilaTaipei World Stamp Championship, Taipei, 2017 National Philatelic Exhibition, Bandung.

Miniature Sheet

Flowers and Butterflies — A841

No. 2453: a, Lantana camara and Troides haliphron. b, Archidendron sp. and Troides helena. c, Leea indica and Papilio peranthus. d, Lantana camara and Cethosia biblis. e, Lantana camara and Papilio ascalaphus. f, Leea indica and Junonia atlites.

2016, Nov. 5   Litho.   Perf. 12½
2453 A841 3000r Sheet of 6, #a-f   2.75   1.40
An additional sheet was issued in this set. The editors would like to examine it.

New Year 2017 (Year of the Rooster) — A843

No. 2456: a, Rooster facing right (1/3). b, Rooster, hen and chicks (2/3). c, Hen facing left (3/3).
10,000r, Rooster, vert.

2017, Jan. 21   Litho.   Perf. 12½x12¾
2456   Horiz. strip of 3   1.40   .75
a.-c. A843 3000r Any single   .45   .25
d.   Souvenir sheet of 6, 2 each
     #2456a-2456c   2.80   1.50

Souvenir Sheet
Perf. 12¾x13½
2457 A843 10,000r multi   1.50   .75

Tourism — A844

No. 2458: a, Danau Toba (1/4). b, Mount Bromo (2/4). c, Mandalika Island (3/4). d, Labuan Bajo (4/4).
8000r, Danau Toba, diff.

2017, Feb. 10   Litho.   Perf. 12½
2458   Block or horiz. strip of 4   3.00   1.40
a.-d. A844 5000r Any single   .75   .35

Souvenir Sheet
Perf. 12½
2459 A844 8000r multi   1.25   .60
No. 2459 contains one 96x32mm stamp.

World Press Freedom Day A845

No. 2460 — UNESCO and World Press Freedom Day emblems and: a, Building, reporters typing (1/2). b, Reporters with notebooks and cameras, doves, minarets, Eiffel Tower (2/2).

2017, May 3   Litho.   Perf. 13x13¼
2460 A845 4000r Horiz. pair, #a-b   1.25   .60
c.   Souvenir sheet of 8, 4 each
     #2460a-2460b   5.00   2.40

Kapitan Pattimura (1783-1817), Soldier and National Hero — A846

2017, May 15   Litho.   Perf. 12¾x13½
2461 A846 3000r multi   .45   .25

Orchids A847

No. 2462: a, Coelogyne mayeriana (1/34). b, Vanda sumatrana (2/34). c, Cymbidium ensifolium (3/34). d, Coelogyne rochussenii (4/34). e, Aerides odorata (5/34). f, Bulbophyllum flabellum veneris (6/34). g, Paphiopedilum tonsum (7/34). h, Papilionanthe hookeriana (8/34). i, Bulbophyllum medusae (9/34). j, Phalaenopsis cornu-cervi (10/34). k, Dendrobium crumenatum (11/34). l, Phalaenopsis javanica (12/34). m, Rhynchostylis retusa (13/34). n, Thrixspermum centipeda (14/34). o, Vanda tricolor (15/34). p, Acanthephippium javanicum (16/34). q, Dendrobium secundum (17/34). r, Vanda limbata (18/34). s, Vanda insignis (19/34). t, Bulbophyllum beccarii (20/34). u, Coelogyne pandurata (21/34). v, Paphiopedilum supardii (22/34). w, Phalaenopsis gigantea (23/34). x, Paraphalaenopsis labukensis (24/34). y, Aerides huttonii (25/34). z, Grammatophyllum scriptum (26/34). aa, Dendrobium anosmum (27/34). ab, Dendrobium smillieae (28/34). ac, Diplocaulobium utile (29/34). ad, Dendrobium bracteosum (30/34). ae, Bulbophyllum graveolens (31/34). af, Dendrobium macrophyllum (32/34). ag, Paphiopedilum glanduliferum (33/34). ah, Grammatophyllum speciosum (34/34).
20,000r, Coelogyne marthae.

2017, May 18   Litho.   Perf. 12½
2462   Sheet of 34 + central label   15.50   8.50
a.-ah. A847 3000r Any single   .45   .25

Souvenir Sheet
2463 A847 20,000r multi   3.00   1.50
Bogor Botanic Gardens, 200th anniv.

Lions Clubs International, Cent. — A848

No. 2464 — Centenary emblem and: a, Lion, lioness and cubs. b, Lion.

2017, June 1   Litho.   Perf. 12½x12¾
2464 A848 5000r Horiz. pair #a-b   1.50   .75
Printed in sheets containing 8 pairs + 4 central labels.

Environmental Care — A849

No. 2465: a, Hands and tree (2/2). b, Tree with "25" in leaves (1/2).
10,000d, Scouts planting tree.

2017, June 5   Litho.   Perf. 12½
2465 A849 4000r Vert. pair, #a-b   1.25   .60

Souvenir Sheet
2466 A849 10,000r multi   1.50   .75

Postcrossing — A850

No. 2467: a, Girl sitting on window sill. b, World landmarks, Indonesian man holding large airmail envelope above head. c, Temples, Indonesian woman wearing headdress.
10,000r, World landmarks, Indonesian man holding large airmail envelope above head, diff.

2017, July 14   Litho.   Perf. 13x13¼
2467 A850 3000r Horiz. strip of 3, #a-c   1.40   .70

Souvenir Sheet
2468 A850 10,000r multi   1.50   .75

Jasminum Sambac — A851

2017, Aug. 8   Litho.   Perf. 13¼x13
2469 A851 5000r multi   .75   .35
Association of Southeast Asian Nations, 50th anniv.

Corals and Fish A852

Nos. 2470 and 2471 — Various fish and corals with stamps numbered: a, 1/2. b, 2/2.

2017, Sept. 7   Litho.   Perf. 13x13¼
2470 A852 5000r Pair, #a-b   1.50   .75

Souvenir Sheet
2471 A852 10,000r Sheet of 2, #a-b   3.00   1.50
Indonesia and Singapore Joint Issue, 50 years.
See Singapore Nos. 1857-1858.

Goal to Make Indonesia a Maritime Axis by 2045 — A853

No. 2472: a, Factory, trucks, crane and ships (1/3). b, Ships (2/3). c, Ships, trucks, buildings and satellite dish (3/3).

2017, Sept. 27   Litho.   Perf. 13¼x13
2472   Horiz. strip of 3   1.40   .75
a.-c. A853 3000r Any single   .45   .25

Fruit — A854

Nos. 2473 and 2474: a, Nephelium lappaceum (1/4). b, Garcinia mangostana (2/4). c, Cocos nucifera (3/4). d, Durio graveolens (4/4).

Litho. & Embossed
2017, Oct. 16   Perf. 13¼x13
2473   Strip or block of 4   1.90   1.00
a.-d. A854 3000r Any single   .45   .25

Miniature Sheet
2474   Sheet of 4   3.00   1.50
a.-d. A854 5000r Any single   .75   .35

18th Asian Games, Jakarta A855

No. 2475: a, Swimming (1/9). b, Soccer (2/9). c, Badminton (3/9). d, Synchronized swimming (4/9). e, Basketball (5/9). f, Wushu (6/9). g, Judo (7/9). h, Equestrian jumping (8/9). i, Running (9/9).
No. 2476, 15,000r, Pencak silat. No. 2477, 15,000r, Volleyball.

2018, Jan. 18   Litho.   Perf. 13¼x13
2475 A855 3000r Block of 9, #a-i   4.00   2.00

Souvenir Sheets
Perf. 14
2476-2477 A855 Set of 2   4.50   2.25
Nos. 2476-2477 each contain one 40x40mm stamp.

New Year 2018 (Year of the Dog) — A856

No. 2478 — Dog and: a, Flower (2/3). b, Pagoda (3/3). c, Mountain (1/3).
10,000r, Dog, vert.

2018, Feb. 1   Litho.   Perf. 12½x12¾
2478   Strip of 3   1.40   .70
a.-c. A856 3000r Any single   .45   .25
d.   Souvenir sheet of 6, 2 each
     #2478a-2478c   2.80   1.50

Souvenir Sheet
Perf. 12¾x12½
2479 A856 10,000r multi   1.50   .75

Festival and Carnival Participants A857

No. 2480 — Scenes from: a, Banyuwangi Ethno Carnival (4/4). b, Batam International Culture Carnival (1/4). c, Gorontalo Karawo Carnival (2/4). d, Tomohon International Flower Festival (3/4).
10,000r, Jember Fashion Carnival.

Perf. 13½x13¼ Syncopated
2018, May 20   Litho.
2480   Strip of 4   2.40   1.25
a.-d. A857 4000r Any single   .60   .30

Souvenir Sheet
Perf. 13¼x13
2481 A857 10,000r multi   1.50   .75

Indonesian Amateur Radio Organization, 50th Anniv. — A858

No. 2482 — Emblem, globe, radio user and: a, Satellite, satellite dish (1/2). b, Automobile, antennas, palm trees (2/2).

2018, July 9   Litho.   Perf. 12½
2482 A858 5000r Horiz. pair, #a-b   1.40   .70

A859

A860

INDONESIA

Transportation — A861

2018, Aug. 17 Litho. Perf. 13¼x13
2483 A859 4000r multi .55 .25
2484 A860 4000r multi .55 .25

Litho. & Embossed With Foil Application
Perf. 13x13¼
2485 A861 4000r gold & multi .55 .25
Nos. 2483-2485 (3) 1.65 .75

18th Asian Games, Jakarta — A862

No. 2486 — Winning art in stamp design competition: a, Medalist on victory stand (3/3). b, Stylized athletes (1/3). Cyclist and stadium (2/3).

2018, Aug. 18 Litho. Perf. 13x13¼
2486 A862 3000r Strip of 3, #a-c 1.25 .60

Railroads — A863

No. 2487: a, RailClinic train. b, Light Rail Transit train.

2018, Sept. 28 Litho. Perf. 12½
Granite Paper
2487 A863 3000r Pair, #a-b .80 .40

In 2018, Indonesia began creating and selling stamps that could not be personalized by customers with its personalized stamp creating apparatus. The stamps, which were issued in sheets of four and in souvenir sheets, have the country name, denomination and "Prisma" emblem in a panel. An example of a souvenir sheet is shown here.

2018 Annual Meeting of the International Monetary Fund and World Bank Group, Nusa Dua — A864

2018, Oct. 8 Litho. Perf. 13x13¼
2488 A864 10,000r multi 1.40 .70

Airports — A865

No. 2489 — Airport in: a, Aceh. b, Kalimantan Timur (East Kalimantan).

2018, Oct. 27 Litho. Perf. 13½x12¾
Granite Paper
2489 A865 5000r Pair, #a-b 1.40 .70

Flora and Fauna A866

No. 2490: a, Rhyticeros cassidix (4/6). b, Dendrolagus ursinus (5/6). c, Macaca nigra (6/6). d, Koompassia excelsa (1/6). e, Eusideroxylon zwageri (2/6). f, Agathis borneensis (3/6).

10,000r, Rhyticeros cassidix, horiz.

2018, Nov. 5 Litho. Perf. 14
Granite Paper
2490 A866 3000r Block or horiz. strip of 6, #a-f 2.60 1.40

Souvenir Sheet
Perf. 13½x13
2491 A866 10,000r multi 1.40 .70

Famous Indonesians — A867

No. 2492: a, Radjiman Wediodiningrat (1879-1952), physician and politician (1/4). b, Mas Isman (1924-82), freedom fighter (2/4). c, Laksamana Malahayati, 16th cent admiral of Aceh Sultanate (3/4). d, Lambertus Nicodemus Palar (1900-81), diplomat (4/4).

2018, Nov. 10 Litho. Perf. 13x13¼
Granite Paper
2492 A867 5000r Block or horiz. strip of 4, #a-d 2.75 1.40

A868

Hats and Headdresses — A869

No. 2493: a, Kupiah Meukeutop, Aceh (1/34). b, Ampu, Sumatera Utara (North Sumatra) (2/34). c, Saluak Datuk, Sumatera Barat (West Sumatra) (3/34). d, Tanjak, Riau (4/34). e, Tanjak, Kepulauan Riau (Riau Island) (5/34). f, Lacak, Jambi (6/34). g, Tanjak Songket, Sumatera Selatan (South Sumatra) (7/34). h, Kopiah Resam, Bangka Belitung (8/34). i, Enggano, Bengkulu (9/34). j, Manuk Meghom, Bandar Lampung (10/34). k, Destar Alpie, DKI Jakarta (11/34). l, Totopong, Jawa Barat (West Java) (12/34). m, Lomar, Banten (13/34). n, Blangkon Solo, Jawa Tengah (Central Java) (14/34). o, Blangkon Jogja, Special Region of Yogyakarta (15/34). p, Udeng, Jawa Timur (East Java) (16/34). q, Laung Banjar, Kalimantan Selatan (South Kalimantan) (17/34). r, Paruh Burung Enggang, Kalimantan Barat (West Kalimantan) (18/34). s, Lawung, Kalimantan Tengah (Central Kalimantan) (19/34). t, Tapung Seraung, Kalimantan Timur (East Kalimantan) (20/34). u, Bluko, Kalimantan Utara (North Kalimantan) (21/34). v, Udeng, Bali (22/34). w, Sapuk, Nusa Tenggara Barat (West Nusa Tenggara) (23/34). x, Ti'i Langga, Nusa Tenggara Timur (East Nusa Tenggara) (24/34). y, Songkok Recca, Sulawesi Selatan (South Selatan) (25/34). z, Songkok Tobone, Sulawesi Barat (West Sulawesti) (26/34). aa, Siga, Sulawesi Tengah (Central Sulawesi) (27/34). ab, Paporong, Sulawesi Utara (North Sulawesi) (28/34). ac, Kampurui, Sulawesi Tenggara (Southeast Sulawesi) (29/34). ad, Tudung Makuta, Gorontalo (30/34). ae, Kain Berang Merah, Maluku (31/34). af, Toa Pulu, Maluku Utara (North Maluku) (32/34). ag, Witaupa, Papua (33/34). ah, Mankota, Papua Barat (West Papua) (34/34).

No. 2494: a, Peci. b, Map of Indonesia.

Litho., Label Litho. With Foil Application
2018, Dec. 13 Perf. 12½
Granite Paper
2493 Sheet of 34 + central label 14.50 7.25
a.-ah. A868 3000k Any single .40 .25

Souvenir Sheet
Litho.
Perf. 13½x12½
2494 A869 10,000r Sheet of 2, #a-b 2.75 1.40

New Year 2019 (Year of the Pig) — A870

No. 2495 — Various pig figurines facing left, numbered: a, 1/3. b, 2/3. c, 3/3.
No. 2496, Pig figurine facing right, building roof at UR.

Litho., Litho. & Embossed (#2495b)
2019, Jan. 28 Perf. 12½
Granite Paper
2495 Strip of 3 1.40 .75
a.-c. A870 3000r Any single .45 .25
d. Souvenir sheet of 6, 2 each #2495a-2495c 2.80 1.50

Souvenir Sheet
2496 A870 10,000r multi 1.00 .75

April 17, 2019 General Elections A871

No. 2498: a, Voters at ballot box. b, Women, election emblem.

2019, Jan. 31 Litho. Perf. 13
2498 A871 3000r Horiz. pair, #a-b .85 .45

Four Pillars of the People's Consultative Assembly — A872

No. 2499: a, Constitution Preamble (2/4). b, Five numbered principles (1/4). c, Coat of arms of Indonesia (4/4). d, Map of Indonesia (3/4).

2019, Mar. 29 Litho. Perf. 12½
Granite Paper
2499 A872 5000r Block of 4, #a-d 2.75 1.40

A873

Comic Book Heroes A874

No. 2500 — Gundala panels numbered: a, 1/15. b, 2/15. c, 3/15. d, 4/15. e, 5/15. Sri Asih panels numbered: f, 6/15. g, 7/15. h, 8/15. i, 9/15. j, 10/15. Si Buta Dari Gua Hantu panels numbered: k, 11/15. l, 12/15. m, 13/15. n, 14/15. o, 15/15.

No. 2501: a, Gundala. b, Sri Asih. c, Si Buta Dari Gua Hantu.

2019, Apr. 4 Litho. Perf. 13
Granite Paper
2500 A873 3000r Sheet of 15, #a-o 6.50 3.25

Souvenir Sheet
Perf. 12½
2501 A874 10,000r Sheet of 3, #a-c 4.25 2.10

Festivals — A875

No. 2502 — Inscription: a, Festival Danau, Sentani (4/4). b, Festival Pesona Selat Lembeh, Kota Bitung (1/4). c, Pawai Kemerdekaan, Jakarta (2/4). d, Wakatobi Wave Festival (3/4).

10,000r, Cap Go Meh, Singkawang, vert.

2019, May 24 Litho. Perf. 13¼x13
Granite Paper
2502 Strip of 4 1.90 1.00
a.-d. A875 3000r Any single .45 .25

Souvenir Sheet
Perf. 13x13¼
2503 A875 10,000r multi 1.40 .70

A876

INDONESIA

Tourism — A877

No. 2504: a, Batu Kodok (1/3). b, Puncak Darma (2/3). c, Leuit-Kasepuhan Ciptagelar (3/3).
10,000r, Curug Cimarinjung.

2019, June 7   Litho.   Perf. 12½
Granite Paper
| 2504 | A876 | 5000r Vert. strip of 3, #a-c | 2.10 | 1.10 |

Souvenir Sheet
Perf. 13½x13¼
| 2505 | A877 | 10,000r multi | 1.40 | .70 |

Souvenir Sheet

China 2019 World Stamp Exhibition, Wuhan, People's Republic of China — A878

No. 2506: a, Ailuropoda melanoleuca. b, Pongo pygmaeus.

2019, June 11   Litho.   Perf. 13x13¼
Granite Paper
| 2506 | A878 | 10,000r Sheet of 2, #a-b | 2.75 | 1.40 |

Campaign for Drug-free Villages — A879

No. 2507: a, Farmer (2/2). b, Field (1/2).

2019, June 26   Litho.   Perf. 13x13¼
Granite Paper
| 2507 | A879 | 3000r Pair, #a-b | .85 | .45 |

24th World Scout Jamboree, West Virginia — A880

No. 2508 — Emblem and: a, Knot and flagpoles (2/2). b, Scouts and world map (1/2).

2019, July 22   Litho.   Perf. 13
Granite Paper
| 2508 | A880 | 5000r Pair, #a-b | 1.40 | .70 |

Indonesian Man and Woman in Tradtional Clothing — A881

2019, Aug. 8   Litho.   Perf. 12¾
Granite Paper
| 2509 | A881 | 3000r multi | .45 | .25 |

Ancient Manuscripts — A882

No. 2510: a, La Galigo (3/4). b, Nagarakretagama (4/4). c, Babad Dipanegara (1/4). d, Panji (2/4).

2019, Sept. 5   Litho. With Foil Application   Perf. 13¼
Granite Paper
| 2510 | A882 | 4000r Block or horiz. strip of 4, #a-d | 2.25 | 1.10 |

Souvenir Sheet

2019 National Philatelic Exhibition, Makassar — A883

2019, Oct. 17   Litho.   Perf. 13¼x13
Granite Paper
| 2511 | A883 | 10,000r multi | 1.50 | .75 |

Poetry and Poets — A884

No. 2512 — Poetry by: a, Chairil Anwar (1922-49) (2/2). b, Raja Ali Haji (1808-73) (1/2).

2019, Oct. 19   Litho.   Perf. 13¼x13
Granite Paper
| 2512 | A884 | 3000r Pair, #a-b | .85 | .40 |

No. 2512 was printed in sheets of 14 containing seven each of Nos. 2512a-2512b + label.

A885

A886

Flora and Fauna — A887

No. 2513: a, Castanopsis argentea (3/6). b, Amorphophallus gigas (1/6). c, Rafflesia kemumu (2/6).
No. 2514: a, Stiphodon annieae (4/6). b, Myzomela irianawidodoae (6/6). c, Paucidentomys vermidax (5/6).
No. 2515: a, Begonia balgooyi. b, Caridina woltereckae.

2019, Nov. 5   Litho.   Perf. 12½
Granite Paper
2513		Strip of 3	1.40	.75
a.-c.	A885	3000r Any single		.45	.25
2514		Strip of 3	1.40	.75
a.-c.	A886	3000r Any single		.45	.25

Souvenir Sheet
| 2515 | A887 | 10,000r Sheet of 2, #a-b | 3.00 | 1.50 |

Nos. 2334-2339, 2373-2381 Surcharged in Metallic Red

Methods and Perfs. As Before
2020, Mar. 5
2516	A773	3000r on 2500r #2334 (1/33)	.40	.25
2517	A773	3000r on 2500r #2335 (4/33)	.40	.25
2518	A773	3000r on 2500r #2336 (6/33)	.40	.25
2519	A773	3000r on 2500r #2337 (7/33)	.40	.25
2520	A773	3000r on 2500r #2338 (8/33)	.40	.25
2521	A773	3000r on 2500r #2339 (9/33)	.40	.25
a.		Block of 11, #2340-2344, 2516-2521, + label	4.50	2.75
2522	A773	3000r on 5000r #2373 (14/33)	.40	.25
2523	A773	3000r on 5000r #2374 (15/33)	.40	.25
2524	A773	3000r on 5000r #2375 (16/33)	.40	.25
2525	A773	3000r on 5000r #2376 (17/33)	.40	.25
2526	A773	3000r on 5000r #2377 (20/33)	.40	.25
2527	A773	3000r on 5000r #2378 (21/33)	.40	.25
2528	A773	3000r on 5000r #2379 (22/33)	.40	.25
2529	A773	3000r on 8000r #2380 (18/33)	.40	.25
2530	A773	3000r on 8000r #2381 (19/33)	.40	.25
a.		Block of 11, #2371-2372, 2522-2530, + label	4.50	2.75
		Nos. 2516-2530 (15)	6.00	3.75

SEMI-POSTAL STAMPS

Symbols of Olympic Games — SP43

Perf. 12½x12
1951, Jan. 2   Photo.   Unwmk.
B58	SP43	5s + 3s gray grn	.25	.25
B59	SP43	10s + 5s dk vio bl	.25	.25
B60	SP43	20s + 5s org red	.25	.25
B61	SP43	30s + 10s dk brn	.25	.25
B62	SP43	35s + 10s ultra	2.50	2.10
		Nos. B58-B62 (5)	3.50	3.10

Issued to publicize the Asiatic Olympic Games of 1951 at New Delhi, India.

Wings and Flame — SP44

1951, Oct. 15
B63	SP44	5s + 3s olive green	.30	.30
B64	SP44	10s + 5s dull blue	.30	.30
B65	SP44	20s + 5s red	.30	.30
B66	SP44	30s + 10s brown	.30	.30
B67	SP44	35s + 10s ultra	.30	1.10
		Nos. B63-B67 (5)	1.50	2.30

2nd Natl. Games, Djakarta, 10/21-28/51.

No. 378 Surcharged in Black

1953, May 8   Perf. 12½
| B68 | A53 | 35s + 10s purple | .75 | .25 |

The surcharge reads "Natural Disaster." Surtax was for emergency relief following volcanic eruption and floods.

Merapi Erupting — SP45

1954, Apr. 15   Litho.   Perf. 12½x12
B69	SP45	15s + 10s bl grn	1.50	1.75
B70	SP45	35s + 15s pur	1.50	1.40
B71	SP45	50s + 25s red	1.50	1.40
B72	SP45	75s + 25s vio bl	1.50	1.40
B73	SP45	1r + 25s car	1.50	1.40
B74	SP45	2r + 50s blk brn	2.50	1.40
B75	SP45	3r + 1r gray grn	10.00	8.75
B76	SP45	5r + 2.50r org brn	12.00	12.00
		Nos. B69-B76 (8)	30.00	29.50

The surtax was for victims of the Merapi volcano eruption.

Young Musicians — SP46

15s+10s, Parasol dance. 35s+15s, Girls playing dakon. 50s+15s, Boy on stilts. 75s+25s, Bamboo flute players. 1r+25s, Javanese dancer.

1954, Dec. 22   Photo.   Perf. 12½
B77	SP46	10s + 10s dk pur	.30	.70
B78	SP46	15s + 10s dk grn	.30	.80
B79	SP46	35s + 15s car rose	.30	.80
B80	SP46	50s + 15s rose brn	.30	.80
B81	SP46	75s + 25s ultra	.30	3.00
B82	SP46	1r + 25s red org	.30	5.00
		Nos. B77-B82 (6)	1.80	11.10

The surtax was for child welfare.

Scout Emblem SP47   **Scout Signaling SP48**

Designs: 50s+25s, Campfire. 75s+25s, Scout feeding fawn. 1r+50s, Scout saluting.

1955, June 27   Unwmk.   Perf. 12½
B83	SP47	15s + 10s bl grn	.35	.50
B84	SP48	35s + 15s ultra	.35	.50
B85	SP48	50s + 25s scar	.35	.50
B86	SP48	75s + 25s brn	.35	.50
B87	SP48	1r + 50s vio	.35	.50
		Nos. B83-B87 (5)	1.75	2.50

First National Boy Scout Jamboree.

Blind Weaver — SP49

35s+15s, Basket weaver. 50s+25s, Boy studying map. 75s+50s, Woman reading Braille.

1956, Jan. 4
B88	SP49	15s + 10s dp grn	.25	.70
B89	SP49	35s + 15s yel brn	.30	.70
B90	SP49	50s + 25s rose car	2.25	1.50
B91	SP49	75s + 50s ultra	1.25	.70
		Nos. B88-B91 (4)	4.05	3.60

The surtax was for the benefit of the blind.

INDONESIA

Red Cross and Heart — SP50

Designs: 35s+15s, 50s+15s, Transfusion bottle. 75s+25s, 1r+25s, Outstretched hands.

1956, July 26   Cross in Red   Litho.
B92	SP50	10s + 10s ultra	.25	.25
B93	SP50	15s + 10s carmine	.25	.25
B94	SP50	35s + 15s lt brn	.25	.25
B95	SP50	50s + 15s bl grn	.25	.25
B96	SP50	75s + 25s orange	.40	.40
B97	SP50	1r + 25s brt pur	.60	.45
		Nos. B92-B97 (6)	2.00	1.75

Surtax for the Indonesian Red Cross.

Invalids Doing Batik Work — SP51

Designs: 15s+10s, Amputee painting. 35s+15s, Lathe operator. 50s+15s, Crippled child learning to walk. 75s+25s, Treating amputee. 1r+25s, Painting with artificial hand.

1957, Mar. 26   Photo.   Perf. 12½
B98	SP51	10s + 10s dp blue	.30	.25
B99	SP51	15s + 10s brown	.30	.25
B100	SP51	35s + 15s red	.30	.25
B101	SP51	50s + 15s dp vio	.30	.30
B102	SP51	75s + 25s green	.40	.40
B103	SP51	1r + 25s dk car rose	.45	.65
		Nos. B98-B103 (6)	2.05	2.10

The surtax was for rehabilitation of invalids.

Kembodja Flower — SP52

Designs: 15s+10s, Michelia. 35s+15s, Sunflower. 50s+15s, Jasmine. 75s+50s, Orchid.

1957, Dec. 23   Perf. 13½x12½
Flowers in Natural Colors
B104	SP52	10s + 10s blue	1.40	1.25
B105	SP52	15s + 10s dp yel grn	1.25	1.25
B106	SP52	35s + 15s dk red brn	.65	.95
B107	SP52	50s + 15s ol & dk brn	.40	.80
B108	SP52	75s + 50s rose brn	.50	.80
		Nos. B104-B108 (5)	4.20	5.05

Children — SP53

15s+10s, 50s+25s, 1r+50s, Girl and boy.

1958, July 1   Photo.   Perf. 12½x12
B109	SP53	10s + 10s blue	.25	.25
B110	SP53	15s + 10s rose brn	.25	.25
B111	SP53	35s + 15s gray green	.25	.25
B112	SP53	50s + 25s gray olive	.25	.25
B113	SP53	75s + 50s brn car	.25	.25
B114	SP53	1r + 50s brown	.25	.25
		Nos. B109-B114 (6)	1.50	1.50

The surtax was for orphans.

Indonesian Scout Emblem — SP54

Design: 15s + 10s, 50s + 25s, 1r + 50s, Scout emblem and compass.

Emblem in Red
1959, July 17   Photo.   Unwmk.
B115	SP54	10s + 5s bister	.25	.25
B116	SP54	15s + 10s bluish grn	.25	.25
B117	SP54	20s + 10s lilac gray	.25	.30
B118	SP54	50s + 25s olive	.30	.50
B119	SP54	75s + 35s yel brn	.30	.50
B120	SP54	1r + 50s dark gray	.30	.50
		Nos. B115-B120 (6)	1.65	2.30

10th World Scout Jamboree, Makiling National Park near Manila, July 17-26.

Palm-leaf Ribs, Gong and 5 Rings — SP55

Young Couple Holding Sharpened Bamboo Weapon — SP56

Design: 20s+10s, 75s+35s, Bamboo musical instrument and 5-ring emblem.

1960, Feb. 14   Perf. 12½x12
B121	SP55	15s + 5s bis & dk brn	.25	.30
B122	SP55	20s + 10s grn & blk	.25	.30
B123	SP55	50s + 25s bl & pur	.25	.30
B124	SP55	75s + 35s ol & dk grn	.25	.30
B125	SP55	1.15r + 50s car & blk	.35	.30
		Nos. B121-B125 (5)	1.35	1.50

All-Indonesian Youth Cong., Bandung, 2/14-21/60.

Social Emblem — SP57

Designs: 15s+15s, Rice, lotus and cotton. 20s+20s, Lotus blossom and tree. 50s+25s, Girl and boy. 75s+25s, Watering of plant in man's hand. 3r+50s, Woman nursing infant.

Perf. 12½x12
1960, Dec. 20   Photo.   Unwmk.
Inscribed: "Hari Sosial Ke III"
B126	SP57	10s + 10s ocher & blk	.25	.25
B127	SP57	15s + 15s dp cl & blk	.25	.25
B128	SP57	20s + 20s bl & blk	.25	.25
B129	SP57	50s + 25s bis brn & blk	.25	.30
B130	SP57	75s + 25s emer & blk	.25	.30
B131	SP57	3r + 50s red & blk	.30	.30
		Nos. B126-B131 (6)	1.55	1.65

3rd Social Day, Dec. 20.

Type of 1960 Surcharged:
"BENTJANA ALAM 1961"
1961, Feb. 17   Perf. 12x12½
B132	A76	15s + 10s plum	.25	.25
B133	A76	20s + 15s ocher	.25	.25
B134	A76	75s + 25s scarlet	.25	.25
		Nos. B132-B134 (3)	.75	.75

The surtax was for flood relief.

Pineapple — SP58

4th Social Day: 75s+25s, Mangosteen. 3r+1r, Rambutan.

1961, Dec. 20   Perf. 12½x13½
B135	SP58	20s + 10s bl, yel & red	.40	.50
B136	SP58	75s + 25s gray, grn & dp claret	.60	.50
B137	SP58	3r + 1r grn, yel & red	1.00	1.40
		Nos. B135-B137 (3)	2.00	2.40

Istiqlal Mosque, Djakarta SP59

40s+20s, 3r+1r, Different view of mosque.

1962, Feb. 22   Perf. 12½x12
B138	SP59	30s + 20s Prus grn & yel	.25	.30
B139	SP59	40s + 20s dk red & yel	.25	.30
B140	SP59	1.50r + 50s brn & yel	.35	.30
B141	SP59	3r + 1r grn & yel	.45	.30
		Nos. B138-B141 (4)	1.30	1.20

Issued for the benefit of the new Istiqlal Mosque.

National Monument, Djakarta — SP60

1.50r+50s, 6r+1.50r, Aerial view of monument.

1962, May 20   Photo.   Perf. 12x12½
B142	SP60	1r + 50s org brn & blk	.25	.25
B143	SP60	1.50r + 50s ol grn & ultra	.25	.25
B144	SP60	3r + 1r lil rose & dk brn	.30	.25
B145	SP60	6r + 1.50r vio bl & red	.30	.25
		Nos. B142-B145 (4)	1.10	1.00

Vanda Tricolor — SP61

Orchids: 1.50r+50s, Phalaenopsis amabilis, vert. 3r+1r, Dendrobium phalaenopsis, vert. 6r+1.50r, Paphiopedilum praestans.

Perf. 13½x12½, 12½x13½
1962, Dec. 20   Unwmk.
Orchids in Natural Colors
B146	SP61	1r + 50s ultra & yel	.35	.25
B147	SP61	1.50r + 50s grnsh bl & ver	.35	.25
B148	SP61	3r + 1r dp bl & ocher	.35	.25
B149	SP61	6r + 1.50r org & dl vio	.40	.25
		Nos. B146-B149 (4)	1.45	1.00

Issued for the 5th Social Day.

West Irian Monument, Djakarta — SP62

1963, Feb. 15   Perf. 12½x13½
B150	SP62	1r + 50s rose red & blk	.25	.25
B151	SP62	1.50r + 50s mag & dk brn	.25	.25
B152	SP62	3r + 1r bl & dk brn	.25	.25
B153	SP62	6r + 1.50r grn & brn	.25	.25
		Nos. B150-B153 (4)	1.00	1.00

The surtax was for the construction of the West Irian Monument in Djakarta.

Erupting Volcano — SP63

1963, June 29   Photo.   Perf. 13½x13
| B154 | SP63 | 4r + 2r rose red | .25 | .25 |
| B155 | SP63 | 6r + 3r grnsh bl | .25 | .25 |

The surtax was for victims of national natural disasters.

Papilio Blumei, Celebes — SP64

Butterflies: 4r+1r, Charaxes dehaani, Java. 6r+1.50r, Graphium, West Irian. 12r+3r, Troides amphrysus, Sumatra.

1963, Dec. 20   Perf. 12x12½
B156	SP64	1.75r + 50s multi	.30	.25
B157	SP64	4r + 1r multi	.30	.25
B158	SP64	6r + 1.50r multi	.30	.25
B159	SP64	12r + 3r multi	.50	.40
		Nos. B156-B159 (4)	1.40	1.15

Issued for the 6th Social Day.

Malaysian Fantails — SP65

Birds: 6r+1.50r, Zebra doves. 12r+3r, Black drongos. 20r+5r, Black-naped orioles. 30r+7.50r, Javanese sparrows.

Perf. 12½x13½
1965, Jan. 25   Photo.   Unwmk.
B160	SP65	4r + 1r dl yel, lil & blk	.25	.25
B161	SP65	6r + 1.50 grn, blk & pink	.25	.25
B162	SP65	12r + 3r ol & blk	.35	.30
B163	SP65	20r + 5r gray, yel & red	.40	.40
B164	SP65	30r + 7.50r car rose, sl bl & blk	.65	.40
		Nos. B160-B164 (5)	1.90	1.60

Issued for the 7th Social Day.

Type of Regular Issue, 1964, Inscribed Vertically "Confeo"

1965   Perf. 12½x12
B165	A98	1r + 1r org red & brn	.25	.25
B166	A98	1.25r + 1.25r org red & brn	.25	.25
B167	A98	1.75r + 1.75r org, red & brn blk	.25	.25
B168	A98	2r + 2r org red & sl grn	.25	.25
B169	A98	2.50r + 2.50r org red & red brn	.25	.25
B170	A98	4r + 3.50r org red & dp bl	.25	.25
B171	A98	6r + 4r org red & emer	.25	.25
B172	A98	10r + 5r org red & yel grn	.25	.25
B173	A98	12r + 5.50r org red & org	.25	.25
B174	A98	15r + 7.50r org red & bl grn	.25	.25
B175	A98	20r + 10r org red & dk gray	.25	.25
B176	A98	25r + 10r org red & pur	.25	.25
B177	A98	40r + 15r ver & plum	.25	.25
B178	A98	50r + 15r org red & dp vio	.25	.25
B179	A98	100r + 25r org red & dk ol gray	.25	.25
		Nos. B165-B179 (15)	3.75	3.75

Conference of New Emerging Forces.

Makara Mask and Magic Rays — SP66

1965, July 17   Perf. 12
| B180 | SP66 | 20r + 10r red & dk bl | .35 | .25 |
| B181 | SP66 | 30r + 15r bl & dk red | .35 | .25 |

Issued to publicize the fight against cancer.

Family and Produce — SP67

INDONESIA

State Principles: 20r+10r, Humanitarianism; clasped hands, globe, flags and chain. 25r+10r, Nationalism; map of Indonesia and tree. 40r+15r, Democracy; conference and bull's head. 50r+15r, Belief in God; houses of worship and star.

1965, Aug. 17 Photo. Perf. 12½
B182	SP67	10r + 5r fawn, yel & blk	.35	.25
B183	SP67	20r + 10r dp yel, red & blk	.25	.25
B184	SP67	25r + 10r rose red, red, grn & blk	.25	.25
B185	SP67	40r + 15r bl, red & blk	.40	.25
B186	SP67	50r + 15r lil, yel & blk	.40	.25
	Nos. B182-B186 (5)		1.65	1.25

Samudra Beach Hotel and Pres. Sukarno — SP68

Designs: 25r+10r, 80r+20r, Ambarrukmo Palace Hotel and Pres. Sukarno.

1965, Dec. 1 Photo. Perf. 12½
B187	SP68	10r + 5r dk bl & lt bl grn	.25	.25
B188	SP68	25r + 10r vio blk & yel grn	.25	.25
B189	SP68	40r + 15r dk brn & vio bl	.30	.30
B190	SP68	80r + 20r dk pur & org	.35	.30
	Nos. B187-B190 (4)		1.15	1.10

Issued for tourist publicity.

Gloriosa — SP69

40r+15r, Magaguabush. 80r+20r, Balsam. 100r+25r, Crape myrtle.

1965, Dec. 20 Photo. Perf. 12
Flowers in Natural Colors
B191	SP69	30r + 10r deep blue	.30	.95
B192	SP69	40r + 15r deep blue	.40	.95
B193	SP69	80r + 20r deep blue	.45	.95
B194	SP69	100r + 25r deep blue	.65	.95
	Nos. B191-B194 (4)		1.65	3.80

Dated "1966"

10s+5s, Senna. 20s+5s, Crested barleria. 30s+10s, Scarlet ixora. 40s+10s, Rose of China (hibiscus).

1966, Feb. 10
Flowers in Natural Colors
B195	SP69	10s + 5s Prus bl	.30	.95
B196	SP69	20s + 5s grn	.40	.95
B197	SP69	30s + 10s grn	.45	.95
B198	SP69	40s + 10s Prus bl	.55	.95
	Nos. B195-B198 (4)		1.70	3.80

Nos. B191-B198 issued for the 8th Social Day, Dec. 20, 1965. An imperf. souvenir sheet contains one No. B198. Size: 58x78mm. Value, $6.

Type of 1965 Inscribed: "BENTJANA ALAM / NASIONAL 1966"

15s+5s, Gloriosa. 25s+5s, Magaguabush. 30s+10s, Balsam. 80s+20s, Crape myrtle.

1966, May 2
Flowers in Natural Colors
B199	SP69	15s + 5s blue	.30	.65
B200	SP69	25s + 5s dk bl	.35	.65
B201	SP69	30s + 10s dk bl	.45	.65
B202	SP69	80s + 20s lt bl	.55	.65
	Nos. B199-B202 (4)		1.65	2.60

The surtax was for victims of national natural disasters.

Reticulated Python — SP70

Reptiles: 3r+50s, Bloodsucker. 4r+75s. Saltwater crocodile. 6r+1r, Hawksbill turtle (incorrectly inscribed *chelonia mydas,* "green turtle").

1966, Dec. 20 Photo. Perf. 12½x12
B203	SP70	2r + 25s multi	.30	.30
B204	SP70	3r + 50s multi	.30	.30
B205	SP70	4r + 75s multi	.35	.30
B206	SP70	6r + 1r multi	.55	.30
	Nos. B203-B206 (4)		1.50	1.20

Flooded Village — SP71

2.50r+25s, Landslide. 4r+40s, Fire destroying village. 5r+50s, Erupting volcano.

1967, Dec. 20 Photo. Perf. 12½
B207	SP71	1.25r + 10s dl vio bl & yel	.30	.40
B208	SP71	2.50r + 25s dl vio bl & yel	.30	.40
B209	SP71	4r + 40s dp org & blk	.30	.40
B210	SP71	5r + 50s dp org & blk	.30	.40
a.		Souv. sheet of 2, #B209-B210	30.00	45.00
	Nos. B207-B210 (4)		1.20	1.60

Surtax for victims of natl. natural disasters.

Buddha & Stupa, Borobudur Temple — SP72

Designs: No. B211, Musicians. No. B212, Sudhana and Princess Manohara. No. B213, Procession with elephant and horses.

1968, Mar. 1 Photo. Perf. 12½
B211	SP72	2.50r + 25s brt grn & gray ol	.35	.30
B212	SP72	2.50r + 25s brt grn & gray ol	.35	.30
B213	SP72	2.50r + 25s brt grn & gray ol	.35	.30
a.		Souv. sheet of 3, #B211-B213	30.00	40.00
b.		Strip of 3, #B211-B213	1.50	1.50
B214	SP72	7.50r + 75s org & gray ol	.55	.30
	Nos. B211-B214 (4)		1.60	1.20

The surtax was to help save Borobudur Temple in Central Java, c. 800 A.D. No. B213b has continuous design showing a frieze from Borobudur.

Scout with Pickax — SP73

Designs: 10r+1r, Bugler. 30r+3r, Scouts singing around campfire, horiz.

1968, June 1 Photo. Perf. 12½
Size: 28½x44½mm
B215	SP73	5r + 50 dp org & brn	.35	.30
B216	SP73	10r + 1r brn & gray ol	.50	.50

Size: 68x28½mm
B217	SP73	30r + 3r ol gray & grn	.65	.65
	Nos. B215-B217 (3)		1.50	1.45

Surtax for Wirakarya Scout Camp.

Woman with Flower — SP74

1969, Apr. 21 Perf. 13½x12½
B218	SP74	20r + 2r emer, red & yel	.75	.40

Emancipation of Indonesian women.

Noble Voluta — SP75

Sea shells: 7.50r+50s, Common hairy triton. 10r+1r, Spider conch. 15r+1.50r, Murex ternispina.

1969, Dec. 20 Photo. Perf. 12½
B219	SP75	5r + 50s multi	.40	.55
B220	SP75	7.50r + 50s multi	.45	.55
B221	SP75	10r + 1r multi	.75	.80
B222	SP75	15r + 1.50r multi	.65	.80
	Nos. B219-B222 (4)		2.25	2.70

Issued for the 12th Social Day, Dec. 20.

Chrysocoris Javanus — SP76

Insects: 15r+1.50r, Dragonfly. 20r+2r, Carpenter bee.

1970, Dec. 21 Photo. Perf. 12½
B223	SP76	7.50r + 50c multi	5.00	1.60
B224	SP76	15r + 1.50r multi	10.50	8.00
B225	SP76	20r + 2r multi	14.50	5.50
	Nos. B223-B225 (3)		30.00	15.10

The 13th Social Day, Dec. 20.

Fight Against Cancer — SP77

Patient receiving radiation treatment, Jakarta Hospital.

1983, July 1 Photo. Perf. 12½
B226	SP77	55r + 20r multi	.70	.50
B227	SP77	75r + 25r multi	1.00	.50

Children's Day — SP78

Children's Drawings. Surtax was for Children's Palace building fund.

1984, June 17 Photo. Perf. 13½x13
B228	SP78	75r + 25r multi	1.10	.25
B229	SP78	110r + 25r multi	.75	.25
B230	SP78	175r + 25r multi	1.75	.40
B231	SP78	275r + 25r multi	1.75	.40
a.		Souv. sheet of 2, #B230-B231	45.00	45.00
b.		Souv. sheet of 4 + 2 labels	20.00	20.00
	Nos. B228-B231 (4)		5.35	1.30

AUSIPEX '84. No. B231b for FILACENTO '84, Netherlands, Sept. 6-9.

SP79

1987, May 12 Photo. Perf. 12½
B232	SP79	350r +25r dark ultra & yel	1.50	.50

Yayasan Cancer Medical Assoc., 10th anniv.

SP80

1991, June 1 Photo. Perf. 12½
B233	SP80	200r +25r multi	1.25	.30

Natl. Fed. for Welfare of Mentally Handicapped, 24th anniv.

Yayasan Cancer Medical Assoc., 15th Anniv. — SP81

1992, May 12 Photo. Perf. 12½
B234	SP81	200r +25r brn & mag	.50	.25
B235	SP81	500r +50r bl & mag	1.00	.30

Natl. Kidney Foundation SP82

Perf. 13½x12½
1994, Apr. 30 Photo.
B236	SP82	300r +30r multi	.60	.30

Rehabilitation Intl., 10th Asia & Pacific Regional Conference SP83

Design: 700r+100r, Painting, Mother's Love, by disabled artist Patricia Saerang.

Perf. 13½x12½
1995, Sept. 12 Photo.
B238	SP83	700r +100r multi	1.25	.85

March 1, 1949, Day of Total Attack — SP84

Designs: No. B239, Natl. flag, tanks, map. No. B240, Soldiers fighting, soldiers standing at attention, natl. flag.

1996, Mar. 1 Photo. Perf. 13½x12½
B239	SP84	700r +100r multi	1.25	.65
B240	SP84	700r +100r multi	1.25	.65
a.		Pair, #B239-B240	2.75	1.60

World AIDS Day — SP85

1997, Dec. 1 Photo. Perf. 13½x12½
B241	SP85	700r +100r multi	1.00	.50

PETA (Pembela Tanah Air) Volunteer Army — SP86

Perf. 12½x13½
1998, Nov. 10 Litho.
B242	SP86	700r Statue, museum	.65	.25

National Disaster Fund — SP87

INDONESIA

2005, May 20   Litho.   *Perf. 12½*
B243 SP87 1500r +300r multi + label   1.00   .65

Surtax for victims of Dec. 26, 2004 tsunami.

International Red Cross, 150th Anniv. — SP88

No. B244: a, Jean Henri Dunant (1828-1910), founder of Red Cross, flags (1/2). b, Helicopter, boat, Red Cross worker carrying man (2/2).

2013, May 8   *Perf. 13½x12¾*
B244 SP88 2500r +500r Pair, #a-b   2.00   1.50

World Environment Day — SP89

No. B245: a, Bamboo and waterfall (1/2). b, Bamboo, waterfall and bird (2/2).

Perf. 13½x13¼ Syncopated
2018, June 5   Litho.
B245 SP89 3000r +500r Horiz. pair, #a-b   1.00   1.00

AIR POST STAMPS

Airplane, Marshal Surydarma — AP1

Airplane Over Buffalo Canyon — AP2

Designs: 10s, Airplane, Air Chief Marshal Suryadi Surydarma. 20s, Sentry and aircraft, Lake Toba, Sumatra. 30s, Pilots. 40c, Indian Red Cross plane, Sumatra. 50s, Red Cross plane. 75s, Airplane over Buffalo Canyon. 1r, Crew studying flight plan. 1½r, Aircraft over Tjipanas Fish Ponds, Java. 4½r, DC-3 over rice fields. 7½r, DC-4 over Indonesian Archipelago.
Nos. C10, C12 and C13 are overprinted ("POS UDARA" and Airplane) on Nos. 22-24.

Perf. 14½, 12½ (#C10, C12, C13)
1948, Dec. 15   Photo.
C1	AP1	10s dk lilac & brn	.35	—
C2	AP1	20s Pruss grn & org red	.40	—
C3	AP1	30s dp blue & dull lil	.45	—
C4	AP1	40s red brn & blue emerald	.25	—
C5	AP1	50s dp vio & dull bl	.25	—
C6	AP2	75s dp brn & org brn	.75	—
C7	AP1	1r dp choc & pur brn	.90	—
C8	AP2	1½r dk vio & dp yel brn	3.00	—
C9	AP2	4½r Pruss grn & dl pur	2.25	—
C10	A32	5r yel brn & black	10.00	—
C11	AP1	7½r brn & slate vio	5.00	—
C12	A32	10r emerald & black	12.50	—
C13	A32	25r rose red & black	15.00	—
		Nos. C1-C13 (13)	51.10	

AP3

Designs: 30s, 1r, Map, ships. 50s, Harbor scene, vert. 2½r, 4½r, Ships.

1949, Aug. 17   Photo.   *Perf. 12½*
C14	AP3	30s blue & orange	1.75	
C15	AP3	50s green & orange	3.00	
C16	AP3	1r brn & green	1.90	
C17	AP3	2½r blk & dull grn	7.50	
C18	AP3	4½r blue & rose red	22.50	
		Nos. C14-C18 (5)	36.65	

Failure of Dutch blockade.

Nos. 51-53 Ovptd. "POS UDARA" and airplaine and

Airplane, Indonesian Archipelago — AP4

DC-3 Over Rice Fields — AP5

Designs: 10s, DC-4 over Indonesian Archipelago. 20s, Aircraft mechanics working on plane. 30s, Servicing plane on runway. 40c, Pilots. 50s, Briefing pilots. 75s, Sentry and aircraft, Lake Toba, Sumatra. 1r, Plane, mountain in Sumatra. 4½r, Airplane over Buffalo Canyon. 7½r, Aircraft over Tjipanas Fish Ponds, Java.

Perf. 14½, 12½ (#C10, C12, C13)
1949, Aug. 17   Photo.
C19	AP4	10s pur & lt blue	.50	—
C20	AP5	20s brn & sl blue	1.00	
C21	AP4	30s red brn & bl grn	2.00	
C22	AP4	40s dk brn & pur	1.50	
C23	AP4	50s dp bl grn & red brn	3.50	
C24	AP4	75s bl grn & brn	.95	
C25	AP4	1r pur & dk grn	1.25	
C26	AP5	1½r blk bl & org	3.00	
C27	AP5	4½r pur & chestnut	3.50	
C28	A38	5r On No. 51	3.50	
C29	AP5	7½r dk grn & vio brn	3.50	
C30	A38	10r On No. 52	6.00	
C31	A38	25r On No. 53	17.50	
		Nos. C19-C31 (13)	47.70	

AP6

Designs: 50s, Map, airplanes, horiz. 30s, 1r, Harbor scene. 2½r, Airplane on runway, horiz. 4½r, Airplane landing, horiz.

1949   Photo.   *Perf. 14½*
C32	AP6	30s multicolored	1.75	
C33	AP6	50s multicolored	2.00	
C34	AP6	1r multicolored	1.25	
C35	A39	2½r multicolored	2.00	
C36	A39	4½r multicolored	3.50	
		Nos. C32-C36 (5)	10.50	

Liberation of Jakarta

Nos. C1-C9, C11 Overprinted

1949, Dec. 7
C37	AP1	10s dk lilac & brn	.35	
C38	AP1	20s Pruss grn & org red	.35	
C39	AP1	30s dp blue & dull lil	.35	
C40	AP1	40s red brn & blue emerald	15.00	
C41	AP1	50s dp vio & dull bl	.55	
C42	AP2	75s dp brn & org brn	.55	
C43	AP2	1r dp choc & pur brn	1.25	
C44	AP2	1½r dk vio & dp yel brn	1.40	
C45	AP2	4½r Pruss grn & dl pur	2.00	
C46	AP1	7½r brn & slate vio	15.00	
		Nos. C37-C46 (10)	36.80	

Nos. C19-C27, C29 Overprinted

C47	AP4	10s pur & lt blue	.25	
C48	AP5	20s brn & sl blue	1.25	
C49	AP4	30s red brn & bl grn	.30	
C50	AP4	40s dk brn & pur	1.10	
C51	AP4	50s dp bl grn & red brn	.30	
C52	AP4	75s bl grn & brn	.30	
C53	AP4	1r pur & dk grn	1.50	
C54	AP4	1½r blk bl & org	2.00	
C55	AP5	4½r pur & chestnut	2.50	
C56	AP5	7½r dk grn & vio brn	2.75	
		Nos. C47-C56 (10)	12.25	

Nos. C32-C36 Overprinted

C57	AP6	30s multicolored	5.00	
C58	AP6	50s multicolored	3.00	
C59	AP6	1r multicolored	3.00	
C60	A39	2½r multicolored	4.50	
C61	A39	4½r multicolored	6.50	
		Nos. C57-C61 (5)	22.00	

AIR POST SPECIAL DELIVERY STAMPS

Aircraft Over Beach — APSD1

Perf. 14½
1948, Dec. 15   Photo.   Unwmk.
| CE1 | APSD1 | 40s dk brn & blue emerald | .80 | — |

Type APSD1, inscribed "REPUBLIK"
1948, Dec. 15   *Perf. 13½x14*
| CE2 | APSD1 | 40s brn & blue emer | .75 | |

No. CE1, Overprinted "Merdeka Djojakarta 6 Djuli 1949"

1949, Dec. 7
| CE3 | APSD1 | 40s brn & blue emer | .75 | |

No. CE2 Overprinted

1949, Dec. 7
| CE4 | APSD1 | 40s brn & blue emer | 10.00 | |

AIR POST OFFICIAL STAMPS

Nos. C1, C3, C5, C7 Overprinted

1948, Dec. 15
CO1	AP1	10s dk lilac & brown	1.25	
CO2	AP1	30s dp blue & dull lil	2.00	
CO3	AP1	50s dp vio & dull blue	2.25	
CO4	AP1	1r dp choc & pur brn	5.00	
		Nos. CO1-CO4 (4)	10.50	

Nos. C19//C25 Overprinted

1949, Aug. 17
CO5	AP4	10s pur & lt blue	3.50	—
CO6	AP4	30s red brn & bl grn	2.00	—
CO7	AP4	50s dp bl grn & red brn	4.50	—
CO8	AP4	1r pur & dk grn	3.25	—
		Nos. CO5-CO8 (4)	13.25	

Nos. CO1-CO4 Overprinted

1949, Dec. 7
CO9	AP1	10s dk lilac & brown	3.00	—
CO10	AP1	30s dp blue & dull lil	6.50	—
CO11	AP1	50s dp vio & dull bl	3.50	—
CO12	AP1	1r dp choc & pur brn	3.00	—
		Nos. CO9-CO12 (4)	16.00	

Nos. CO5-CO8 Overprinted

1949, Dec. 7
CO13	AP4	10s pur & lt blue	2.00	—
CO14	AP4	30s red brn & bl grn	10.00	—
CO15	AP4	50s dp bl grn & red brn	1.25	—
CO16	AP4	1r pur & dk grn	3.50	—
		Nos. CO13-CO16 (4)	16.75	

SPECIAL DELIVERY STAMPS

Train & Minangkabau House — SD1

Perf. 13½x14¼
1948, Dec. 15   Unwmk.   Photo.
| E1 | SD1 | 10s dp bluish grn & chestnut | .35 | |
| E1A | SD1 | 15s ches & steel bl | .50 | |

Type SD1, Inscribed "REPUBLIK"
1949, Aug. 17
| E1B | SD1 | 10s red brn & dp blue | .50 | |
| E1C | SD1 | 15s turq & dk yel brn | .35 | |

Nos. E1-E1A Overprinted

1949, Dec. 7
| E1D | SD1 | 10s dp bluish grn & chestnut | .40 | |
| E1E | SD1 | 15s ches & steel bl | .90 | |

Nos. E1B-E1C Overprinted "Merdeka Djojakarta 6 Djuli 1949"

1949, Dec. 7
| E1F | SD1 | 10s red brn & dp blue | .40 | |
| E1G | SD1 | 15s urq & dk yel brn | .75 | |

INDONESIA

Garuda — SD2

Perf. 13½x12½
1967		Unwmk.	Photo.	
E1H	SD2	10r lt ultra & dl pur	.50	.25
E2	SD2	15r org & dl pur	.70	.50

1968			Inscribed "1968"	
E3	SD2	10r lt ultra & dl pur	.60	.25
E4	SD2	15r org & dl pur	.70	.25
E5	SD2	20r yel & dl pur	.70	.25
E6	SD2	30r brt grn & dl pur	1.10	.60
E7	SD2	40r lil & dl pur	.90	.25
		Nos. E3-E7 (5)	4.00	1.60

1969		Same Inscribed "1969"		
E8	SD2	20r yel & dl pur	.50	.25
E9	SD2	30r brt grn & dl pur	.50	.25
E10	SD2	40r lil & dl pur	.65	.25
		Nos. E8-E10 (3)	1.65	.75

POSTAGE DUE STAMPS

D1

Perf. 13¾x14, 14½ (#J8-J13)
1948			Unwmk.	
J1	D1	1s blue & brn	.30	—
J2	D1	2½s dk brn & dk pur	.45	—
J3	D1	3½s pur & lt grn	.25	—
J4	D1	5s dk grn & brn	.40	—
J5	D1	7½s dk brn & dk grn	.50	—
J6	D1	10s dk pur & brn	.45	—
J7	D1	20s brn & org yel	1.25	—
J8	D1	25s dk pur & dk brn	1.50	—
J9	D1	30s blue & car red	1.25	—
J10	D1	40s blue & org yel	1.50	—
J11	D1	50s lt brn & pur	2.00	—
J12	D1	75s dk bl & dk grn	3.50	—
J13	D1	1r brn & green	4.00	—
		Nos. J1-J13 (13)	17.35	

As Type D1, inscribed "REPUBLIK"
Perf. 13¾x14, 14½ (#J8-J13)
1949, Aug. 17			Unwmk.	
J14	D1	1s dk blue & brn	35.00	—
J15	D1	2½s brn & pur	35.00	—
J16	D1	3½s pur & grn	35.00	—
J17	D1	5s dk grn & brn	35.00	—
J18	D1	7½s dk brn & dk grn	35.00	—
J19	D1	10s pur & brn	35.00	—
J20	D1	20s dk brn & yel	35.00	—
J21	D1	25s vio & dk pur	35.00	—
J22	D1	30s blue & red	35.00	—
J23	D1	40s blue & yel	35.00	—
J24	D1	50s brn & pur	35.00	—
J25	D1	75s dk bl & dk grn	35.00	—
J26	D1	1r dk brn & green	35.00	—
		Nos. J14-J26 (13)	455.00	

Nos. J1-J13 Overprinted

1949, Dec. 7				
J27	D1	1s blue & brn	1.25	—
J28	D1	2½s dk brn & dk pur	.65	—
J29	D1	3½s pur & lt grn	.75	—
J30	D1	5s dk grn & brn	.75	—
J31	D1	7½s dk brn & dk grn	1.25	—
J32	D1	10s dk pur & brn	.35	—
J33	D1	20s brn & org yel	10.00	—
J34	D1	25s dk pur & dk brn	4.50	—
J35	D1	30s blue & car red	15.00	—
J36	D1	40s blue & org yel	20.00	—
J37	D1	50s lt brn & pur	9.00	—
J38	D1	75s dk bl & dk grn	25.00	—
J39	D1	1r brn & green	20.00	—
		Nos. J27-J39 (13)	108.50	

Netherlands Indies Nos. J57 to J59 Surcharged in Black

1950		Wmk. 228	Perf. 14½x14	
J60	D7	2½s on 50c yellow	1.10	.50
J61	D7	5s on 100c apple grn	2.60	.75
J62	D7	10s on 75c aqua	7.00	1.75
		Nos. J60-J62 (3)	10.70	3.00

D8

		Wmk. 228		
1951-52		Litho.	Perf. 12½	
J63	D8	2½s vermilion	.25	.50
J64	D8	5s vermilion	.25	.25
J65	D8	10s vermilion	.25	.25
J66	D8	20s blue ('52)	.25	.25
J67	D8	25s olive bister ('52)	.85	.75
J68	D8	50s vermilion	11.50	1.00
J69	D8	1r citron	1.90	1.75
		Nos. J63-J69 (7)	15.25	4.50

1953-55			Unwmk.	
J70	D8	15s lt magenta ('55)	.25	.25
J71	D8	30s red brown	.25	.25
J72	D8	40s green	.25	.25
		Nos. J70-J72 (3)	.75	.75

1958-61			Perf. 13½x12½	
J73	D8	10s orange	.30	.55
J74	D8	15s orange ('59)	.30	.55
J74A	D8	20s orange ('61)	.30	.55
J75	D8	25s orange	.30	.55
J76	D8	30s orange ('60)	.30	.55
J77	D8	50s orange	1.75	.55
J78	D8	100s orange ('60)	1.00	.55
		Nos. J73-J78 (7)	4.25	3.85

1962-65			Perf. 13½x12½	
J79	D8	50s light bluish green	.25	.25
J80	D8	100s bister	.25	.25
J81	D8	250s blue	.25	.25
J82	D8	500s dull yellow	.25	.25
J83	D8	750s pale lilac	.25	.25
J84	D8	1000s salmon	.25	.25
J85	D8	50r red ('65)	.25	.25
J86	D8	100r maroon ('65)	.25	.25
		Nos. J79-J86 (8)	2.00	2.00

"1966" — D9

1966-67			Unwmk.	Photo.
J91	D9	5s dl grn & dl yel	.30	.25
J92	D9	10s red & lt bl	.30	.25
J93	D9	20s dk bl & pink	.30	.25
J94	D9	30s brn & rose	.30	.25
J95	D9	40s plum & bis	.30	.25
J96	D9	50s ol grn & pale lil	.30	.25
J97	D9	100s dk red & yel grn	.30	.25
J98	D9	200s brt grn & pink ('67)	.30	.25
J99	D9	500s yel & lt bl ('67)	.30	.25
J100	D9	1000s rose lil & yel ('67)	.30	.25
		Nos. J91-J100 (10)	3.00	2.55

1967			Dated "1967"	
J101	D9	50s ol grn & pale lil	.30	.30
J102	D9	100s dk red & yel grn	.30	.30
J103	D9	200s brt grn & pink	.30	.30
J104	D9	500s yel & lt bl	.60	.40
J105	D9	1000s rose lil & yel	.60	.40
J106	D9	15r org & gray	1.25	.60
J107	D9	25r lil & citron	2.00	1.00
		Nos. J101-J107 (7)	5.35	3.30

Similar stamps inscribed "Bajar" or "Bayar", year date and "Sumbangan Ongkos Tjetak" or ". . . Cetak" are revenues.

Inscribed "BAYAR PORTO"
1973			Dated "1973"	
J108	D9	25r lilac & citron	1.40	.30

Inscribed "BAYAR PORTO"
1974			Dated "1974"	
J109	D9	65r olive grn & bister	1.90	.50
J110	D9	125r lil & pale pink	4.00	1.50

Dated "1975"
Inscribed "BAYAR PORTO"
1975		Photo.	Perf. 13½x12½	
J111	D9	25r lilac & citron	1.50	1.00

"1976" — D10

1976				
J112	D10	15r vermilion & dull gray	1.50	2.00
J112A	D10	25r violet & dl yel	.50	.70
J112B	D10	65r olive grn & bister	1.00	1.25
J112C	D10	125r red lil & pale pink	2.00	5.00

1977			Dated "1977"	
J113	D10	100r dp vio & pale pink	.75	.30
J114	D10	200r brt bl & lt lil	.80	.30
J115	D10	300r choc & lt sal	1.25	.50
J116	D10	400r brt grn & tan	1.50	.60
J117	D10	500r red & tan	1.75	.75
		Nos. J113-J117 (5)	6.05	2.45

See Nos. J138, J139, J142.

Nos. 706, 709, 712-713, 716, 718 Surcharged in Red

1978		Photo.	Perf. 12½x12	
J118	A110	25r on 1r	.40	.40
J119	A110	50r on 2r	.40	.40
J120	A110	100r on 4r	1.00	1.00
J121	A110	200r on 5r	1.50	1.50
J122	A110	300r on 10r	2.25	2.25
J123	A110	400r on 15r	2.50	2.50
		Nos. J118-J123 (6)	8.05	8.05

Surcharged in Black
J124	A110	25r on 1r	.50	.50
J125	A110	50r on 2r	.50	.50
J126	A110	100r on 4r	1.00	1.00
J127	A110	200r on 5r	1.50	1.50
J128	A110	300r on 10r	2.50	2.50
J129	A110	400r on 15r	3.50	3.50
		Nos. J124-J129 (6)	9.50	9.50

Nos. 710, 717 Surcharged

1978		Photo.	Perf. 12½x12	
J130	A110	40r on 2.50r	1.50	1.50
J131	A110	40r on 12r	1.00	1.00
J132	A110	65r on 2.50r	1.50	1.50
J133	A110	65r on 12r	2.50	2.50
J134	A110	125r on 2.50r	1.50	1.50
J135	A110	125r on 12r	3.50	3.50
J136	A110	150r on 2.50r	3.00	3.00
J137	A110	150r on 12r	1.00	1.00
		Nos. J130-J137 (8)	15.50	15.50

Type of 1976 Dated "1979"
1979			Perf. 13½x12½	
J138	D10	25r lilac & citron	1.00	.25

Type of 1976 and

D11

Perf. 13½x12½, 13½x13 (#J144-J148, J150-J153), 14½x13 (#J154-J156A)
1980-90		Photo.	Dated "1980"	
J139	D10	25r dk lil & beige	.25	.25
J140	D11	50r multi	.50	.50
J141	D11	75r rose lake & rose	.90	.80
J142	D10	125r rose lil & lt pink	1.25	1.00
		Nos. J139-J142 (4)	2.90	2.55

Dated "1981"
J144	D11	25r brt vio & pale yel grn	.30	.30
J145	D11	50r sl grn & lt vio	.45	.45
J146	D11	75r rose vio & pink	.75	.75
J147	D11	125r pur & yel grn	1.25	1.25
		Nos. J144-J147 (4)	2.75	2.75

Dated "1982"
| J148 | D11 | 125r dp rose lil & pink | 4.00 | .50 |

Dated "1983"
J149	D11	125r dp rose & lil pink	.30	.30
J150	D11	200r dp vio & lt bl	.60	.30
J151	D11	300r dk grn & cit	.75	.30
J152	D11	400r ol grn & brn ol	1.00	.50
J153	D11	500r sepia & beige	1.25	.75
		Nos. J149-J153 (5)	3.90	2.15

Dated "1984"
J154	D11	25r brt vio & pale yel grn	.75	.30
J155	D11	50r sl grn & lt vio	.90	.50
J156	D11	125r rose lil & lt pink	2.00	.30
J156A	D11	500r sepia & beige	7.50	1.25
		Nos. J154-J156A (4)	11.15	2.35

Dated "1988"
J157	D11	1000r dp vio & gray	1.00	.75
J158	D11	2000r red & dp rose lil	1.75	1.25
J159	D11	3000r brn & dl org	2.50	2.00
J160	D11	5000r grn & bl grn	5.00	2.50
		Nos. J157-J160 (4)	10.25	6.50

Dated "1990"
J161	D11	2000r emer & brt yel	3.50	2.50
J162	D11	3000r dk bl grn & rose lil	5.00	3.50
J163	D11	4000r brn vio & brt yel grn	9.00	6.50
		Nos. J161-J163 (3)	17.50	12.50

OFFICIAL STAMPS

Nos. 2//16 Overprinted

1948, Dec. 15				
O1	A28	2s dp brn & dp blue	.35	—
O2	A28	5s turq & dull blue	.50	—
O3	A28	10s dp blue & brn rose	.45	—
O4	A28	15s brown & dk grn	.35	—
O5	A31	30s dk brn & dull vio	3.00	—
O6	A30	50s dk brn & turq	.75	—
		Nos. O1-O6 (6)	5.40	

Nos. 31//45 Overprinted

1949, Aug. 17				
O7	A35	2s dk red vio & dp grn	.35	—
O8	A35	5s dk yel brn & dull vio	.35	—
O9	A34	10s dk brn & dp vio	1.00	—
O10	A35	15s dk vio & dp dull grn	1.50	—
O11	A36	30s dp brn & dk blue vio	.75	—
O12	A37	50s dk brn & Prus grn	2.50	—
		Nos. O7-O12 (6)	6.45	

Nos. O1-O6 Overprinted

1948, Dec. 15				
O13	A28	2s dp brn & dp blue	.75	—
O14	A28	5s turq & dull blue	1.60	—
O15	A28	10s dp blue & brn rose	1.60	—
O16	A28	15s brown & dk grn	1.60	—
O17	A31	30s dk brn & dull vio	4.00	—
O18	A30	50s dk brn & turq	4.00	—
		Nos. O13-O18 (6)	13.55	

Nos. O7-O12 Overprinted

1948, Dec. 15				
O19	A35	2s dk red vio & dp grn	1.00	—
O20	A35	5s dk yel brn & dull vio	.45	—

INDONESIA — INHAMBANE

O21	A34	10s dk brn & dp vio	.45	—
O22	A35	15s dk vio & dp dull grn	1.00	—
O23	A36	30s dp brn & dk blue vio	2.50	—
O24	A37	50s dk brn & Pruss grn	4.00	—
		Nos. O19-O24 (6)	9.40	

RIAU ARCHIPELAGO

(Riouw Archipelago)
100 Sen = 1 Rupiah
(1 rupiah = 1 Malayan dollar)

Indonesia Nos. 371-386 Overprinted in Black

a / b

Overprint "a"

1954   Unwmk.   Perf. 12½

1	A52	5s car rose	67.50	57.50
2	A52	7½s green	1.50	1.50
3	A52	10s blue	80.00	80.00
4	A52	15s purple	3.00	3.00
5	A52	20s rose red	3.00	3.00
6	A52	25s dp green	150.00	42.50

Overprint "b"

7	A53	30s red orange	6.00	6.00
8	A53	35s purple	1.50	1.50
9	A53	40s dull green	1.50	1.50
10	A53	45s dp claret	1.50	1.50
11	A53	50s brown	525.00	100.00
12	A54	60s dk brown	1.50	1.50
13	A54	70s gray	2.75	2.75
14	A54	75s ultra	12.00	3.25
15	A54	80s claret	2.40	3.50
16	A54	90s gray green	2.40	3.50

Netherlands Indies Nos. 325-330 Overprinted Type "a" in Black

17	A46	1r purple	15.00	5.25
18	A46	2r olive grn	3.25	6.00
19	A46	3r red violet	5.25	6.00
20	A46	5r dk brown	5.25	6.00
21	A46	10r gray	6.75	10.00
22	A46	25r orange brn	6.75	10.00
		Nos. 1-22 (22)	903.80	355.75

Mint values are for stamps with somewhat tropicalized gum (stained brown and cracked). Stamps with clean, clear gum sell for about twice as much.

Indonesia Nos. 424-428, 450 and 430 Overprinted Type "b" or

1957-64   Photo.   Perf. 12½x13½

23	A63(b)	5s dp ultra	.90	.90
24	A63	10s yellow brn	13.00	10.00
25	A63(b)	10s yellow brn	.90	.90
26	A63(b)	15s rose vio ('64)	.90	.90
27	A63(b)	20s dull grn ('60)	.90	.90
27A	A63	25s dp claret	40.00	40.00
28	A63(b)	25s dp claret	.90	.90
29	A63(b)	30s orange	.90	.90
30	A63(b)	50s brown	13.00	10.00
31	A63(b)	50s brown	.90	.90

The "b" overprint measures 12mm in this set.

Sukarno Type of Indonesia Overprinted Type "a"

1960   Perf. 12½x12

32	A55	1.25r dp orange	4.50	6.75
33	A55	1.50r brown	4.50	6.75
34	A55	2.50r rose brown	6.75	10.00
35	A55	4r apple green	1.25	.50
36	A55	6r rose lilac	1.25	.50
37	A55	15r yellow	1.25	.50
38	A55	20r sepia	1.25	.50
39	A55	40r yellow grn	1.25	.50
40	A55	50r violet	2.40	.50
		Nos. 23-40 (19)	96.70	92.80

Nos. 26, 35-37, 39-40 are valued CTO with Bandung cancels. Postally used sell for much more.

WEST IRIAN

'west ˌir-ē-'än

(Irian Barat)
(West New Guinea)
LOCATION — Western half of New Guinea, southwest Pacific Ocean
GOVT. — Province of Indonesia
AREA — 162,927 sq. mi.
POP. — 923,440 (1973)
CAPITAL — Djajapura (formerly Hollandia)

The former Netherlands New Guinea became a territory under the administration of the United Nations Temporary Executive Authority on Oct. 1, 1962.
The territory came under Indonesian administration on May 1, 1963.

100 Sen = 1 Rupiah
(1 rupiah = 1 former Netherlands New Guinea gulden)

Catalogue values for all unused stamps in this country are for Never Hinged items.

Netherlands New Guinea Stamps of 1950-60 Overprinted

Type 2 Overprint

Perf. 12½x12, 12½x13½

1962-63   Photo.   Unwmk.

1a	A4	1c vermilion & yel	.25	.25
2a	A4	2c deep orange	.25	.25
3a	A4	5c choc & yel	.25	.25
4a	A5	7c org red, bl & brn vio	.25	.25
5a	A4	10c aqua & red brn	.25	.25
6a	A5	12c grn, bl & brn vio	.25	.25
7a	A4	15c dp yel & red brn	.50	.25
8a	A5	17c brn vio & bl	.60	.35
9a	A4	20c lt bl grn & red brn	.60	.35
10a	A6	25c red	.35	.30
11a	A6	30c deep blue	.80	.35
12a	A6	40c deep orange	.80	.35
13a	A6	45c dark olive	1.40	.75
14a	A6	55c slate blue	1.25	.55
15a	A6	80c dl gray vio	8.00	10.00
16a	A6	85c dk vio brn	4.00	5.00
17a	A6	1g plum	3.50	1.90

Engr.

18a	A3	2g reddish brn	15.00	20.00
19a	A3	5g green	7.50	6.00
		Nos. 1a-19a (19)	45.80	47.65

The overprint exists in four types:
1) Size 17½mm. Applied locally and sold in 1962 in West New Guinea. Top of "N" is slightly lower than the "U", and the base of the "T" is straight, or nearly so. This set sells for about $20 more than Nos. 1a-19a.
2) Size 17½mm. Applied in the Netherlands and sold in 1963 by the UN in New York. Top of the "N" is slightly higher than the "U", and the base of the "T" is concave. This is the set listed above.
3) Size 14mm. Exists on eight values. Set value, $200.
4) Size 19mm. Exists on 1c and 10c. Set value, $160.
Types 3 and 4 were applied in West New Guinea and it is doubtful whether they were regularly issued.
See the Scott U.S. Specialized Catalogue for complete listings and values of the UNTEA overprints.

Indonesia Nos. 454, 456, 494-501, 387, 390, 392 and 393 Surcharged or Overprinted: "IRIAN BARAT"

Perf. 12½x13½

1963, May 1   Photo.   Unwmk.

20	A63	1s on 70s org ver	.25	.25
21	A63	2s on 90s yel grn	.25	.25

Perf. 12x12½

22	A76	5s gray	.25	.25
23	A76	6s on 20s ocher	.25	.25
24	A76	7s on 50s dp bl	.25	.25
25	A76	10s red brn	.25	.25
26	A76	15s plum	.25	.25
27	A76	25s brt bl grn	.25	.25
28	A76	30s on 75s scar	.25	.25
29	A76	40s on 1.15r plum	.25	.30

Perf. 12½x12

30	A55	1r purple	.45	.55
31	A55	2r green	.80	.90
32	A55	3r dk bl	1.40	1.50
33	A55	5r brown	2.25	3.00
		Nos. 20-33 (14)	7.40	8.50

"Indonesia's Flag from Sabang to Merauke" — A1

20s, 50s, Parachutist landing in New Guinea. 60s, 75s, Bird of paradise and map of New Guinea.

1963, May 1

34	A1	12s org brn, blk & red	.25	.30
35	A1	17s org brn, blk & red	.25	.40
36	A1	20s multi	.30	.60
37	A1	50s multi	.30	1.00
38	A1	60s multi	.70	1.10
39	A1	75s multi	.90	2.00
		Nos. 34-39 (6)	2.70	5.40

Liberation of West New Guinea.

Maniltoa Gemmipara — A2

15s, Dendrobium lancifolium (orchid). 30s, Gardenia gjellerupii. 40s, Maniltoa flower. 50s, Phalanger. 75s, Cassowary. 1r, Kangaroo. 3r, Crowned pigeons.

1968, Aug. 17   Photo.   Perf. 12½x12

40	A2	5s dl grn & vio blk	.60	.85
41	A2	15s emer & dk pur	.90	1.75
42	A2	30s org & dp grn	2.00	2.75
43	A2	40s lemon & brt pur	2.10	3.00
44	A2	50s rose car & blk	2.75	3.75
45	A2	75s dl bl & blk	3.00	5.25
46	A2	1r brn org & blk	5.00	8.00
47	A2	3r apple grn & blk	7.75	10.50
		Nos. 40-47 (8)	24.10	35.85

Man, Map of Indonesia and Torches — A3

1968, Aug. 17

48	A3	10s ultra & gold	4.00	2.75
49	A3	25s crimson & gold	6.25	3.50

Issued to publicize the pledge of the people of West Irian to remain unified and integrated with the Republic of Indonesia.

Carving, Mother and Child — A4

West Irian Wood Carvings: 6s, Shield with 3 human figures. 7s, Child atop filigree carving. 10s, Drum. 25s, Seated man. 30s, Drum (3-tiered base). 50s, Carved bamboo. 75s, Man-shaped ornament. 1r, Shield. 2r, Seated man (hands raised).

1970   Photo.   Perf. 12½x12

50	A4	5s multi	.40	.55
51	A4	6s multi	.40	.55
52	A4	7s multi	.55	1.50
53	A4	10s multi	.55	1.50
54	A4	25s multi	.55	.55
55	A4	30s multi	.65	.80
56	A4	50s multi	.70	.80
57	A4	75s multi	.80	.95
58	A4	1r multi	.90	1.25
59	A4	2r multi	1.25	1.40
		Nos. 50-59 (10)	6.75	9.85

Issued: Nos. 50-54, 4/30; Nos. 55-59, 4/15.

Black-capped Lory — A5

1970, Oct. 26   Photo.   Perf. 12x12½

60	A5	5r shown	2.50	6.00
61	A5	10r Bird of paradise	2.25	7.50

POSTAGE DUE STAMPS

Type of Indonesia Overprinted: "IRIAN BARAT"

Perf. 13½x12½

1963, May 1   Litho.   Unwmk.

J1	D8	1s light brown	.25	.50
J2	D8	5s light gray olive	.30	.55
J3	D8	10s light blue	.30	.55
J4	D8	25s gray	.30	1.00
J5	D8	40s salmon	.50	1.60
J6	D8	100s bister	1.10	3.75
		Nos. J1-J6 (6)	2.75	7.95

Type of Indonesia Dated "1968" and Overprinted: "IRIAN BARAT"

1968   Photo.   Perf. 13½x12½

J7	D9	1s blue & lt grn	.25	.60
J8	D9	5s grn & pink	.25	.70
J9	D9	10s red & gray	.30	.70
J10	D9	25s grn & yel	.30	1.10
J11	D9	40s vio brn & pale grn	.65	1.75
J12	D9	100s org & bister	1.25	4.75
		Nos. J7-J12 (6)	3.00	9.60

INHAMBANE

ˌin-yəm-'ban-ə

LOCATION — East Africa
GOVT. — A district of Mozambique, former Portuguese colony
AREA — 21,000 sq. mi. (approx.)
POP. — 248,000 (approx.)
CAPITAL — Inhambane

1000 Reis = 1 Milreis
100 Centavos = 1 Escudo (1913)

Stamps of Mozambique Overprinted

On 1886 Issue

1895, July 1   Unwmk.   Perf. 12½
Without Gum

1	A2	5r black	57.50	45.00
2	A2	10r green	62.50	40.00
a.		Perf. 13½	170.00	120.00
3	A2	20r rose	80.00	55.00
4	A2	25r lilac	400.00	275.00
5	A2	40r chocolate	80.00	55.00
6	A2	50r blue	80.00	45.00
a.		Perf. 13½	160.00	160.00
7	A2	100r yellow brown	550.00	425.00
8	A2	200r gray violet	100.00	80.00
9	A2	300r orange	100.00	80.00
		Nos. 1-9 (9)	1,510.	1,100.

On 1894 Issue

Perf. 11½, 12½

10	A3	50r lt blue	70.00	55.00
a.		Perf. 12½	140.00	110.00
11	A3	75r rose, perf. 12½	120.00	90.00
12	A3	80r yellow green	75.00	65.00
13	A3	100r brown, buff	290.00	290.00
14	A3	150r carmine, rose, 12½	120.00	90.00
		Nos. 10-14 (5)	675.00	590.00

700th anniv. of the birth of St. Anthony of Padua.
The status of Nos. 4 and 7 is questionable. No. 3 is always discolored.
Forged overprints exist. Genuine overprints are 21mm high.

King Carlos — A1

Name and Value in Black except 500r

1903, Jan. 1   Typo.   Perf. 11½

15	A1	2½r gray	.75	.70
16	A1	5r orange	.95	.70
17	A1	10r lt green	.95	.85
18	A1	15r gray green	2.50	1.75
19	A1	20r gray violet	2.50	1.75
20	A1	25r carmine	2.50	1.75

INHAMBANE — ININI

21	A1	50r brown		4.50	2.25
22	A1	65r dull blue		29.00	20.00
23	A1	75r lilac		3.50	2.40
24	A1	100r dk blue, *blue*		3.75	2.40
25	A1	115r org brn, *pink*		8.50	7.75
26	A1	130r brown, *straw*		8.50	7.75
27	A1	200r red vio, *pink*		8.50	7.75
28	A1	400r dull bl, *straw*		15.00	12.00
29	A1	500r blk & red, *bl*		27.50	20.00
30	A1	700r gray blk, *straw*		30.00	22.00
		Nos. 15-30 (16)		148.90	111.80

For surcharge & overprints see Nos. 31-47, 88-101.

No. 22 Surcharged in Black

1905

| 31 | A1 | 50r on 65r dull blue | 7.50 | 5.50 |

Nos. 15-21, 23-30 Overprinted in Carmine or Green

1911

32	A1	2½r gray	.75	.50
33	A1	5r orange	.75	.50
34	A1	10r lt green	.75	.50
35	A1	15r gray green	.75	.50
36	A1	20r gray violet	1.40	1.00
37	A1	25r carmine (G)	1.20	1.00
38	A1	50r brown	.70	.60
39	A1	75r lilac	.95	.70
40	A1	100r dk blue, *bl*	.95	.70
41	A1	115r org brn, *pink*	1.40	1.00
42	A1	130r brown, *straw*	2.75	1.90
43	A1	200r red vio, *pink*	1.60	1.30
44	A1	400r dull bl, *straw*	2.75	1.90
45	A1	500r blk & red, *bl*	2.90	1.90
46	A1	700r gray blk, *straw*	4.00	1.90
		Nos. 32-46 (15)	23.60	16.75

No. 31 Overprinted in Red

1914

| 47 | A1 | 50r on 65r dull blue | 3.75 | 2.10 |

Vasco da Gama Issue of Various Portuguese Colonies

Common Design Types CD20-CD27 Surcharged

1913 On Stamps of Macao

48	CD20	¼c on ½a bl grn	2.25	2.00
49	CD21	½c on 1a red	2.25	2.00
50	CD22	1c on 2a red vio	2.25	2.00
a.		Inverted surcharge	40.00	37.50
51	CD23	2½c on 4a yel grn	2.25	2.00
52	CD24	5c on 8a dk bl	2.25	2.00
53	CD25	7½c on 12a vio brn	3.75	3.50
54	CD26	10c on 16a bis brn	3.25	2.40
55	CD27	15c on 24a bis	3.25	2.40
		Nos. 48-55 (8)	21.50	18.30

On Stamps of Portuguese Africa

56	CD20	¼c on 2½r brn	2.00	1.75
57	CD21	½c on 5r red	2.00	1.75
58	CD22	1c on 10r red vio	2.00	1.75
59	CD23	2½c on 25r yel grn	2.00	1.75
60	CD24	5c on 50r dk bl	2.00	1.75
61	CD25	7½c on 75r vio brn	3.50	3.25
62	CD26	10c on 100r bis brn	3.00	2.75
63	CD27	15c on 150r bis	3.00	2.75
a.		Inverted surcharge	70.00	70.00
		Nos. 56-63 (8)	19.50	17.50

On Stamps of Timor

64	CD20	¼c on ½a bl grn	2.25	2.00
a.		Inverted surcharge	40.00	37.50
65	CD21	½c on 1a red	2.25	2.00
66	CD22	1c on 2a red vio	2.25	2.00
67	CD23	2½c on 4a yel grn	2.25	2.00
68	CD24	5c on 8a dk bl	2.25	2.00
69	CD25	7½c on 12a vio brn	3.50	3.25
70	CD26	10c on 16a bis brn	3.25	2.40
71	CD27	15c on 24a bis	3.25	2.40
		Nos. 64-71 (8)	21.25	18.05
		Nos. 48-71 (24)	62.25	53.85

Ceres — A2

Name and Value in Black Chalky Paper

1914 Typo. Perf. 15x14

72	A2	¼c olive brown	1.20	.85
73	A2	½c black	5.00	2.40
74	A2	1c blue green	1.10	.75
75	A2	1½c lilac brown	1.10	.75
76	A2	2c carmine	1.10	.75
77	A2	2½c lt violet	.70	.60
78	A2	5c deep blue	1.10	1.10
79	A2	7½c yellow brown	2.20	1.90
80	A2	8c slate	2.10	2.00
81	A2	10c orange brown	2.10	2.00
82	A2	15c plum	3.50	2.50
83	A2	20c yellow green	3.50	2.50
84	A2	30c brown, *grn*	4.75	3.00
85	A2	40c brown, *pink*	4.75	3.50
86	A2	50c orange, *sal*	8.00	6.00
87	A2	1e green, *blue*	8.50	6.25
		Nos. 72-87 (16)	50.70	36.85

No. 31 Overprinted in Carmine

1915 Perf. 11½

| 88 | A1 | 50c on 65r dull blue | 11.00 | 9.00 |

Nos. 15-21, 23-30 Overprinted Locally

1917

89	A1	2½r gray	16.00	12.00
90	A1	5r orange	16.00	12.00
91	A1	15r gray green	2.50	1.60
92	A1	20r gray violet	2.50	1.60
93	A1	50r brown	1.60	1.60
94	A1	75r lilac	2.40	1.60
95	A1	100r blue, *blue*	2.70	1.60
96	A1	115r org brn, *pink*	2.90	2.00
97	A1	130r brn, *straw*	2.90	1.75
98	A1	200r red vio, *pink*	2.90	1.75
99	A1	400r dull bl, *straw*	3.75	2.50
100	A1	500r blk & red, *bl*	3.75	2.75
101	A1	700r gray blk, *straw*	17.00	8.00
		Nos. 89-101 (13)	76.90	50.75

The stamps of Inhambane have been superseded by those of Mozambique.

ININI

ē-ni-'nē

LOCATION — In northeastern South America, adjoining French Guiana
GOVT. — Territory of French Guiana
AREA — 30,301 sq. mi.
POP. — 5,024 (1946)
CAPITAL — St. Elie

Inini was separated from French Guiana in 1930 and reunited with it when the colony became an integral part of the Republic, acquiring the same status as the departments of Metropolitan France, under a law effective Jan. 1, 1947.

100 Centimes = 1 Franc

Used values are for canceled-to-order stamps.

Stamps of French Guiana, 1929-40, Overprinted in Black, Red or Blue

Nos. 1-9

Nos. 10-26

Nos. 27-40

1932-40 Unwmk. Perf. 13½x14

1	A16	1c gray lil & grnsh bl	.40	.55
2	A16	2c dk red & bl grn	.40	.55
3	A16	3c dk red & grnsh bl ('40)	.55	.70
4	A16	4c ol brn & red vio ('38)	.55	.80
5	A16	5c Prus bl & red org	.55	.80
6	A16	10c magenta & brn	.40	.55
7	A16	15c vio brn & red org	.40	.55
8	A16	20c dk bl & ol grn	.40	.55
9	A16	25c dk red & dk brn	.90	1.25

Perf. 14x13½

10	A17	30c dl grn & lt grn	2.40	2.40
11	A17	30c grn & brn ('40)	.60	.90
12	A17	35c Prus grn & ol ('38)	1.20	1.40
13	A17	40c org brn & ol gray	.80	1.20
14	A17	45c ol grn & lt grn ('40)	1.40	1.50
15	A17	50c dk bl & ol gray	.70	1.05
16	A17	55c vio bl & car ('38)	5.50	6.50
17	A17	60c sal & grn ('40)	.70	1.05
18	A17	65c sal & grn ('38)	2.10	2.25
19	A17	70c ind & sl bl ('40)	1.00	1.10
20	A17	75c ind & sl bl (Bl)	4.25	3.50
21	A17	80c bl & vio bl (R) ('38)	1.25	1.25
22	A17	90c dk red & ver	3.50	2.25
23	A17	90c red vio & brn ('39)	1.75	1.40
24	A17	1fr lt vio & brn ('38)	21.00	23.00
25	A17	1fr car & lt red ('38)	2.75	1.75
26	A17	1fr blk & vio bl ('40)	1.00	1.40
27	A18	1.25fr blk brn & bl grn ('33)	2.25	1.60
28	A18	1.25fr rose & lt red ('39)	1.40	1.40
29	A18	1.40fr ol brn & red vio ('40)	1.25	1.40
30	A18	1.50fr dk bl & lt bl	1.05	1.50
31	A18	1.60fr ol brn & bl grn ('40)	1.00	1.40
32	A18	1.75fr brn, red & blk brn ('33)	25.00	24.00
33	A18	1.75fr vio bl ('38)	1.75	2.40
34	A18	2fr dk grn & rose red	1.25	1.75
35	A18	2.25fr vio bl ('39)	1.10	1.40
36	A18	2.50fr cop red & brn ('40)	1.00	1.40
37	A18	3fr brn red & red vio	1.50	1.75
38	A18	5fr dl vio & yel grn	1.25	1.75
39	A18	10fr ol gray & dp ultra (R)	1.75	2.10
40	A18	20fr indigo & ver	1.75	2.10
		Nos. 1-40 (40)	99.75	106.15

Without "RF," see Nos. 46-49.

Common Design Types pictured following the introduction.

Colonial Arts Exhibition Issue
Souvenir Sheet
Common Design Type

1937 Imperf.

| 41 | CD75 | 3fr red brown | 21.00 | 27.50 |
| | | Never hinged | 29.00 | |

New York World's Fair Issue
Common Design Type

1939, May 10 Engr. Perf. 12½x12

42	CD82	1.25fr car lake	3.75	4.50
43	CD82	2.25fr ultra	3.75	4.50
		Set, never hinged	11.50	

French Guiana Nos. 170A-170B Overprinted in Green or Red

1941 Engr. Perf. 12½x12

| 44 | A21a | 1fr deep lilac | 1.00 | |
| 45 | A21a | 2.50fr blue (R) | 1.00 | |

Nos. 44-45 were issued by the Vichy government in France, but were not placed on sale in Inini.
For surcharges, see Nos. B9-B10.

Types of 1932-40 Without "RF" Methods and Perfs as Before

1942

46	A16	20c dk bl & ol grn	2.25	
47	A17	1fr black & ultra	2.25	
48	A18	10fr ol gr & dp ultra (R)	2.75	
49	A18	20fr indigo & ver	5.00	
		Nos. 46-49 (4)	12.25	

Nos. 46-49 were issued by the Vichy government in France, but were not placed on sale in Inini.

SEMI-POSTAL STAMPS

French Revolution Issue
Common Design Type
Photo.; Name & Value Typo. in Black

1939, July 5 Unwmk. Perf. 13

B1	CD83	45c + 25c green	16.00	20.00
B2	CD83	70c + 30c brown	16.00	20.00
B3	CD83	90c + 35c red org	16.00	20.00
B4	CD83	1.25fr + 1fr rose pink	16.00	20.00
B5	CD83	2.25fr + 2fr blue	16.00	20.00
		Nos. B1-B5 (5)	80.00	100.00

"Defense" Common Design Type and French Guiana Nos. B9 and B11 Ovptd. in Blue or Red

1941 Photo. Perf. 13½

B6	SP1	1fr + 1fr red (B)	1.75	
B7	CD86	1.50fr + 3fr maroon	1.75	
B8	SP2	2.50fr + 1fr blue (B)	1.75	
		Nos. B6-B8 (3)	5.25	

Nos. B6-B8 were issued by the Vichy government in France, but were not placed on sale in Inini.

Nos. 44-45 Srchd. in Black or Red

1944 Engr. Perf. 12½x12

| B9 | A21a | 50c + 1.50fr on 2.50fr blue (R) | 1.10 | |
| B10 | A21a | + 2.50fr on 1fr dp lilac | 1.10 | |

Colonial Development Fund.
Nos. B9-B10 were issued by the Vichy government in France, but were not placed on sale in Inini.

ININI — IONIAN ISLANDS

AIR POST SEMI-POSTAL STAMPS

Nurse with Mother & Child — SPAP1

		1942, June 22	Unwmk.	Engr.	Perf. 13
CB1	SPAP1	1.50fr + 50c green			1.25
CB2	SPAP1	2fr + 6fr brn & red			1.25

Native children's welfare fund.
Nos. CB1-CB2 were issued by the Vichy government in France, but were not placed on sale in Inini.

Colonial Education Fund
Common Design Type

1942, June 22				
CB3	CD86a	1.20fr + 1.80fr blue & red		1.25

No. CB3 was issued by the Vichy government in France, but was not placed on sale in Inini.

POSTAGE DUE STAMPS

Postage Due Stamps of French Guiana, 1929, Overprinted in Black

1932, Apr. 7	Unwmk.		Perf. 13½x14
J1	D3	5c indigo & Prus bl	.25 .40
J2	D3	10c bis brn & Prus grn	.65 1.00
J3	D3	20c grn & rose red	.65 1.00
J4	D3	30c ol brn & rose red	.65 1.00
J5	D3	50c vio & ol brn	1.00 1.50
J6	D3	60c brn red & ol brn	1.10 1.50

Overprinted in Black or Red

J7	D4	1fr dp bl & org brn	1.75 1.75
J8	D4	2fr brn red & bluish grn	2.50 2.50
J9	D4	3fr vio & blk (R)	7.50 7.50
J10	D4	3fr vio & blk	4.25 5.00
		Nos. J1-J10 (10)	20.30 23.15

IONIAN ISLANDS

ī-ō-nē-ən ī-lənds

LOCATION — Seven Islands, of which six-Corfu, Paxos, Lefkas (Santa Maura), Cephalonia, Ithaca and Zante-are in the Ionian Sea west of Greece, and a seventh-Cerigo (Kithyra)-is in the Mediterranean south of Greece
GOVT. — Integral part of Kingdom of Greece
AREA — 752 sq. miles
POP. — 231,510 (1938)

These islands were acquired by Great Britain in 1815 but in 1864 were ceded to Greece on request of the inhabitants.

In 1941 the islands were occupied by Italian forces. The Italians withdrew in 1943 and German forces continued the occupation, using current Greek stamps without overprinting, except for Zante.

For stamps of the Italian occupation of Corfu, see Corfu.

10 Oboli = 1 Penny
12 Pence = 1 Shilling
100 Lepta = 1 Drachma
100 Centesimi = 1 Lira

Watermarks

Wmk. 138 — "2"
Wmk. 139 — "1"

ISSUES OF THE BRITISH PROTECTORATE

Queen Victoria — A1

1859	Unwmk.		Engr.	Imperf.
1	A1	(½p) orange	250.00	750.00
		Wmk. 138		
2	A1	(1p) blue	57.50	300.00
		Wmk. 139		
3	A1	(2p) lake	47.50	300.00
		Nos. 1-3 (3)	355.00	1,350.

Forged cancellations are plentiful.

ISSUED UNDER ITALIAN OCCUPATION

Values of stamps overprinted by letterpress in pairs are for unsevered pairs. Single stamps, unused, sell for one third the price of a pair; used, one half the price of a pair.
Handstamped overprints were also applied to pairs, with "isola" instead of "isole."

Issue for Cephalonia and Ithaca
Stamps of Greece, 1937-38, Overprinted in Pairs Vertically, Reading Down, or Horizontally (H) in Black

Perf. 12½x12, 13½x12, 12x13½

1941		Wmk. 252, Unwmk.		
N1	A69	5 l brn red & bl	55.00	55.00
N2	A70	10 l bl & red brn (#413) (H)	55.00	55.00
a.		On No. 397	400.00	400.00
N3	A71	20 l blk & grn (H)	55.00	55.00
a.		Overprint inverted	275.00	225.00
N4	A72	40 l grn & blk	55.00	55.00
N5	A73	50 l brn & blk	55.00	55.00
N6	A74	80 l ind & yel brn (H)	95.00	95.00
a.		Overprint inverted	350.00	275.00
N7	A67	1d green (H)	260.00	200.00
N8	A84	1.50d green (H)	200.00	130.00
a.		Overprint inverted	325.00	240.00
N9	A75	2d ultra	55.00	55.00
N10	A76	5d red	200.00	90.00
N11	A77	6d ol brn	200.00	90.00
N12	A78	7d dk brn	200.00	90.00
N13	A67	8d dp blue (H)	225.00	130.00
N14	A79	10d red brn	200.00	90.00
N15	A80	15d green	275.00	145.00
N16	A81	25d dk blue	300.00	200.00
a.		Overprint inverted	650.00	525.00
N17	A84	30d org brn (H)	1,400.	950.00
a.		Overprint inverted	2,100.	1,050.
		Nos. N1-N17 (17)	3,885.	2,540.

A variety with wrong font "C" in "Cephalonia" is found in several positions in each sheet of all denominations except those overprinted on single stamps. It sells for about three times the price of a normal pair.
Several other minor spelling errors in the overprint occur on several denominations in one of the printings.
Forgeries exist of many of the higher valued stamps and minor varieties of Nos. N1-N17, NC1-NC11 and NRA1-NRA5.

Overprint Reading Up

N1a	A69	5 l	55.00	55.00
N4a	A72	40 l	55.00	55.00
N5a	A73	50 l	55.00	55.00
N9a	A75	2d	72.50	65.00
N10a	A76	5d	200.00	87.50
N11a	A77	6d	200.00	87.50
N12a	A78	7d	200.00	87.50
N14a	A79	10d	200.00	95.00
N15a	A80	15d	275.00	145.00
		Nos. N1a-N15a (9)	1,313.	732.50

General Issue
Stamps of Italy, 1929, Overprinted in Red or Black

1941		Wmk. 140		Perf. 14
N18	A90	5c olive brn (R)	.80	2.75
N19	A92	10c dk brown (R)	.80	2.75
N20	A91	20c rose red	.80	2.75
N21	A94	25c deep green	.80	2.75
N22	A95	30c olive brn (R)	.80	2.75
a.		"SOLE" for "ISOLE"	72.50	
N23	A95	50c purple (R)	.80	2.75
N24	A94	75c rose red	.80	2.75
N25	A94	1.25 l dk blue (R)	.80	2.75
		Nos. N18-N25 (8)	6.40	22.00

The stamps overprinted "Isole Jonie" were issued for all the Ionian Islands except Cerigo which used regular postage stamps of Greece.

ISSUED UNDER GERMAN OCCUPATION

Zante Issue

Nos. N21 and N23 with Addtl. Handstamped Ovpt. in Black

1943		Wmk. 140		Perf. 14
N26	A94	25c deep green	25.00	45.00
a.		Carmine overprint	35.00	75.00
N27	A95	50c purple	25.00	45.00
a.		Carmine overprint	35.00	75.00

No. N19 with this overprint is a proof. Value, black $70; carmine $375.
Nos. N26-N27 were in use 8 days, then were succeeded by stamps of Greece.
Forgeries of Nos. N26-N27, NC13 and their cancellations are plentiful.

Greek stamps with Italian overprints for the islands of Cerigo (Kithyra), Paxos and Lefkas (Santa Maura) are fraudulent.

OCCUPATION AIR POST STAMPS

Issued under Italian Occupation

Issue for Cephalonia and Ithaca
Stamps of Greece Overprinted in Pairs Vertically, Reading Down, or Horizontally (H) in Black Like Nos. N1-N17

Perf. 13x12½, 12½x13

1941		Grayish Paper	Unwmk.	
On Greece Nos. C22, C23, C25 and C27 to C30				
NC1	AP16	1d dp red	145.00	130.00
NC1A	AP17	2d dl bl	80.00	65.00
NC2	AP19	7d bl vio (H)	160.00	190.00
a.		Overprint inverted	350.00	175.00
NC3	AP21	25d rose (H)	650.00	475.00
a.		Overprint inverted	1,050.	525.00
NC4	AP22	30d dk grn	800.00	550.00
a.		Overprint reading up	800.00	550.00
b.		Horizontal overprint on single stamp		
c.		As "b," inverted		
NC5	AP23	50d vio (H)	4,500.	3,500.
a.		Overprint inverted	6,500.	4,500.
NC6	AP24	100d brown	2,250.	1,900.
a.		Overprint reading up	2,250.	1,900.

No. NC1A is known only with overprint reading up.

On Greece Nos. C31-C34 Reengraved; White Paper

NC7	AP16	1d red	145.00	130.00
NC8	AP17	2d gray bl	120.00	110.00
a.		Overprint reading up	120.00	110.00
b.		Horiz. ovpt. on pair	2,400.	1,900.
c.		Horizontal overprint on single stamp		
NC9	AP18	5d vio (H)	130.00	105.00
a.		Overprint inverted	1,100.	500.00
b.		Vert. ovpt. on single stamp, up or down	1,100.	525.00
NC10	AP19	7d dp ultra (H)	325.00	250.00
a.		Overprint inverted	1,050.	450.00

Overprinted Horizontally on No. C36
Rouletted 13½

NC11	D3	50 l vio brn	2,400.	1,900.
a.		Pair, one without ovpt.		
b.		On No. C36a	—	—

See footnote following No. N17.

General Issue
Italy No. C13 Overprinted in Red Like Nos. N18-N25

1941		Wmk. 140		Perf. 14
NC12	AP3	50c olive brown	.80	3.25
a.		"SOLE" for "ISOLE"	65.00	

Used in all the Ionian Islands except Cerigo which used air post stamps of Greece.
No. NC12 with additional overprint "BOLLO" is a revenue stamp.

Issued under German Occupation
ZANTE ISSUE

No. NC12 with Additional Handstamped Overprint in Black Like Nos. N26-N27

1943		Wmk. 140		Perf. 14
NC13	AP3	50c olive brown	27.50	55.00
a.		"SOLE" for "ISOLE"	450.00	
b.		Carmine overprint	150.00	300.00

See note after N27.

OCCUPATION POSTAGE DUE STAMPS

General Issue
Postage Due Stamps of Italy, 1934, Overprinted in Black Like Nos. N18-N25

1941		Wmk. 140		Perf. 14
NJ1	D6	10c blue	3.25	6.50
NJ2	D6	20c rose red	3.25	6.50
NJ3	D6	30c red orange	3.25	6.50
NJ4	D7	1 l red orange	3.25	6.50
		Nos. NJ1-NJ4 (4)	13.00	26.00

See footnote after No. N25.

OCCUPATION POSTAL TAX STAMPS

Issued under Italian Occupation

Issue for Cephalonia and Ithaca
Greece No. RA56 with Additional Overprint on Horizontal Pair in Black Like Nos. N1-N17

Serrate Roulette 13½

1941			Unwmk.	
NRA1	D3	10 l car (Bl+Bk)	32.50	40.00
a.		Blue overprint double	105.00	105.00
b.		Inverted overprint	300.00	300.00

Same Overprint Reading Down on Vertical Pairs of Nos. RA61-RA63

Perf. 13½x12

NRA2	PT7	10 l brt rose, pale rose	35.00	35.00
a.		Overprint on horiz. pair	120.00	75.00
b.		Horizontal overprint on single stamp	1,100.	
c.		Overprint reading up	35.00	35.00
NRA3	PT7	50 l gray grn, pale grn	32.50	24.00
a.		Overprint reading up	32.50	24.00
b.		Ovpt. on horiz. pair		
c.		Horizontal overprint on single stamp	—	—
NRA4	PT7	1d dl bl, lt bl	90.00	72.50
a.		Overprint reading up	105.00	95.00

Same Overprint Reading Down on Vertical Pair of No. RA65

NRA5 PT7 50 l gray grn,
pale grn 875.00 875.00
a. Overprint reading up 875.00 875.00

Nos. NRA5 and NRA5a were not placed in use on any compulsory day.
See footnote following No. N17.

IRAN
i-'rän

(Persia)

LOCATION — Western Asia, bordering on the Persian Gulf and the Gulf of Oman
GOVT. — Islamic republic
AREA — 636,000 sq. mi.
POP. — 83,990,000 (2020 est.)
CAPITAL — Tehran

20 Shahis (or Chahis) = 1 Kran
10 Krans = 1 Toman
100 Centimes = 1 Franc = 1 Kran (1881)
100 Dinars = 1 Rial (1933)
100 Rials = 1 Pahlavi
100 Rials = 1 Toman

Catalogue values for unused stamps in this country are for Never Hinged items, beginning with Scott 1054 in the regular postage section, Scott B1 in the semi-postal section, Scott C83 in the airpost section, Scott O72 in the officials section, Scott Q36 in the parcel post section, and Scott RA4 in the postal tax section.

Values of early stamps vary according to condition. Quotations for Nos. 1-20, 33-40 are for fine copies. Very fine to superb specimens sell at much higher prices, and inferior or poor copies sell at reduced prices, depending on the condition of the individual specimen.
Cracked gum on unused stamps does not detract from the value.

Beware of forgeries and/or reprints of most Iran stamps between the years 1870-1925. Scott values are for genuine stamps. Collectors should be aware that forgeries of many issues outnumber genuine examples by factors of 10 or 20 to one. Failing specialized knowledge on the part of the collector, these stamps should be examined or authenticated by acknowledged experts before purchase.

Watermarks

Wmk. 306 — Arms of Iran

Wmk. 161 — Lion

Wmk. 316 — Persian Inscription

Wmk. 349 — Persian Inscription and Crown in Circle

Illustration of Wmk. 349 shown sideways. Circles in Wmk. 349 are 95mm apart.

Wmk. 353 — Persian Inscription and Coat of Arms in Circle

Wmk. 381 — "Islamic Republic of Iran" in Persian (Partial Illustration)

Wmk. 411

Many issues have handstamped surcharges. As usual with such surcharges there are numerous inverted, double and similar varieties.

Coat of Arms — A1

Design A2 has value numeral below lion.

1870		Unwmk.	Typo.	Imperf.
1	A1	1s dull violet		325.00
2	A1	2s green		275.00
3	A1	4s greenish blue		225.00
4	A1	8s red		275.00
		Nos. 1-4 (4)		1,100.

Values for used examples of Nos. 1-4 are omitted, since this issue was only pen canceled. After 1875, postmarked remainders were sold to collectors. Values same as unused.
Printed in blocks of 4. Many shades exist. Forgeries exist.

Coat of Arms — A2

Printed on Both Sides

1a	A1	1s	20,000.
2a	A1	2s	40,000.
3a	A1	4s	
4a	A1	8s	18,000.

Vertically Rouletted 10½ on 1 or 2 Sides

1875			Thick Wove Paper	
11	A2	1s black	225.00	75.00
a.		Imperf.	3,500.	5,000.
12	A2	2s blue	225.00	75.00
a.		Tête bêche pair	30,000.	
b.		Imperf.		
13	A2	4s vermilion	300.00	100.00
a.		4s bright red, thin paper, imperf.	750.00	750.00
14	A2	8s yellow green	200.00	175.00
b.		Tête bêche pair	15,000.	10,000.
c.		Imperf.	2,000.	1,250.
		Nos. 11-14 (4)	950.00	425.00

Four varieties of each.
Nos. 11-14 were printed in horizontal strips of 4 with 3-10mm spacing between stamps. The strips were then cut very close all around (generally touching or cutting the outer framelines). Then they were hand-rouletted between the stamps. Values are for stamps with rouletting on both sides and margins clear at top and bottom. Stamps showing the rouletting on only one side sell for considerably less.
Nos. 11 to 14 also exist pin-perforated and percé en scie.
No. 13b has spacing of 2-3mm.
See Nos. 15-20, 33-40.

Medium to Thin White or Grayish Paper

1876				Imperf.
14A	A2	1s black	400.00	600.00
15	A2	1s gray black	50.00	175.00
a.		Printed on both sides	1,500.	
b.		Laid paper	1,000.	1,500.
16	A2	2s gray blue	600.00	750.00
a.		Printed on both sides	7,000.	
17	A2	2s black	1,000.	
a.		Tête bêche pair	6,000.	
18	A2	4s vermilion	500.00	150.00
a.		Printed on both sides	5,000.	5,000.
19	A2	1k rose	1,500.	100.00
a.		Printed on both sides		4,000.
b.		Laid paper	6,000.	1,200.
c.		1k yellow (error)	35,000.	15,000.
d.		Tête bêche pair		120,000.
20	A2	4k yellow	3,000.	300.00
a.		Printed on both sides		5,000.
b.		Laid paper	5,000.	300.00
c.		Tête bêche pair		18,000.

Nos. 15-16, 18-20 were printed in blocks of 4, and Nos. 14A and 17 in vertical strips of 4, with spacing of 2mm or less.
Nos. 14A and 17 are on medium to thick grayish wove paper. Forgeries exist.
Official reprints of the 1s and 4s are on thick coarse white paper without gum. Value, each $350.

1875 and 1876 issues

Various forgeries exist including forgeries printed from the replica cliches of the genuine issues in Paris by the order of Fabius Boital, a French engineer who was a concession-hunter, living in Iran during the 1870s through 1890s. There also are modern forgeries made by laser printers.

Nasser-eddin Shah Qajar — A3

Perf. 10½, 11, 12, 13, and Compounds

1876				Litho.
27	A3	1s lilac & blk	30.00	6.00
28	A3	2s green & blk	35.00	7.50
29	A3	5s rose & blk	30.00	4.00
30	A3	10s blue & blk	45.00	8.00
		Nos. 27-30 (4)	140.00	25.50

Bisects of the 5s and 1s, the latter used with 2s stamps, were used to make up the 2½ shahis postcard rate. Bisects of the 10s were used in the absence of 5s stamps to make up the letter rate.
The 10s was bisected and surcharged "5 Shahi" or "5 Shahy" for local use in Azerbaijan province and Khoy in 1877.
"Imperfs" of the 5s are envelope cutouts.
Forgeries and official reprints exist.
Very fine examples will have perforations cutting the background net on one side. Genuine stamps withs perfs clear of net on all four sides are very scarce.

1878		Typo.		Imperf.
33	A2	1k car rose	950.00	175.00
34	A2	1k red, yellow	5,000.	175.00
a.		Tête bêche pair		10,000.
35	A2	4k ultramarine	450.00	175.00
a.		Printed on both sides		4,000.
36	A2	5k violet	1,500.	350.00
37	A2	5k gold	8,500.	750.00
38	A2	5k red bronze	35,000.	2,500.
39	A2	5k vio bronze	65,000.	4,000.
40	A2	1t bronze, bl	75,000.	8,000.

Four varieties of each except for 4k which has 3.
Nos. 33 and 34 are printed from redrawn cliches. They have wide colorless circles around the corner numerals.

Nasser-eddin Shah Qajar — A6

Perf. 10½, 12, 13, and Compounds

1879				Litho.
41	A6	1k brown & blk	450.00	7.00
a.		Pair, imperf between	—	
b.		Inverted center		5,000.
42	A6	5k blue & blk	400.00	5.00
a.		Imperf., pair	3,000.	600.00
b.		Inverted center		2,500.
c.		Inverted center, imperf		2,500.

1880				
43	A6	1s red & black	50.00	15.00
b.		Pair, imperf between	4,500.	
44	A6	2s yellow & blk	85.00	10.00
a.		Imperf., pair		2,500.
45	A6	5s green & blk	350.00	2.00
46	A6	10s violet & blk	700.00	30.00
		Nos. 43-46 (4)	1,185.	57.00

Forgeries and official reprints exist.
Imperf examples of No. 46 are proofs on thin yellow paper. Nos. 41-46 exist imperforate on thick white card paper with red cancellation line or overprint. These are proofs. Value, $100 each.
The 2, 5 and 10sh of this issue and the 1 and 5kr of the 1879 issue have been reprinted from a new die which resembles the 5 shahi envelope. The aigrette is shorter than on the original stamps and touches the circle above it.

Sun — A7

1881		Litho.	Perf. 12, 13, 12x13
47	A7	5c dull violet	50.00 25.00
48	A7	10c rose	50.00 25.00
49	A7	25c green	6,750. 100.00
		Nos. 47-49 (3)	6,850. 150.00

1882		Engr., Border Litho.	
50	A7	5c blue vio & vio	50.00 60.00
51	A7	10c dp pink & rose	50.00 60.00
52	A7	25c deep grn & grn	1,400. 40.00
		Nos. 50-52 (3)	1,500. 160.00

Very fine examples of Nos. 50-52 will have perforations cutting the outer colored border but clear of the inner framelines.

Counterfeits of Nos. 50-52, 53, 53a are plentiful and have been used to create forgeries of Nos. 66, 66a, 70 and 70a. They usually have a strong, complete inner frameline at right. On genuine stamps that line is weak or missing.

A8

Type I

Type II (error)

IRAN

Shah Nasr-ed-Din
A9 A10

A11

Type I: Three dots at right end of scroll.
Type II: Two dots at right end of scroll.

1882-84 Engr.
53	A8	5s green, type I	50.00	1.50
a.		5s green, type II	100.00	10.00
54	A9	10s buff, org & blk	85.00	10.00
55	A10	50c buff, org & blk	700.00	80.00
56	A10	50c gray & blk ('84)	150.00	70.00
57	A10	1fr blue & black	150.00	20.00
58	A10	5fr rose red & blk	140.00	20.00
59	A11	10fr buff, red & blk	150.00	30.00
		Nos. 53-59 (7)	1,425.	231.50

Crude forgeries of Nos. 58-59 exist. Halves of the 10s, 50c and 1fr surcharged with Farsi characters in red or black are frauds. The 50c and 1fr surcharged with a large "5" surrounded by rays are also frauds.

No. 59 used is valued for c-t-o.

For overprints and surcharges see Nos 66-72.

Very fine examples of Nos. 53-59 will have perforations cutting the outer colored border but clear of the inner framelines.

A12

1885, March-May Perf. 12-12½, 13 Litho.
59A	A12	5c blue	1,500.	50.00
a.		5c violet blue	1,500.	75.00
b.		5c ultramarine	1,500.	75.00
c.		5c dp reddish lilac	2,500.	300.00
d.		As "a," imperf	10,000.	

No. 59A was issued because of an urgent need for 5c stamps, pending the arrival of No. 62 in July. No. 59A has 88 sunrays instead of the 124 sunrays on the typographed stamp, No. 62.

A13

1885-86 Typo.
60	A12	1c green	25.00	2.00
61	A12	2c rose	25.00	2.00
62	A12	5c dull blue	200.00	1.00
63	A12	10c brown	40.00	2.00
64	A13	1k slate	100.00	3.00
65	A13	5k dull vio ('86)	800.00	40.00
		Nos. 60-65 (6)	1,190.	50.00

Nos. 53, 54, 56 and 58 Surcharged in Black

a b
c d

e f

1885
66	(a)	6c on 5s grn, type I	150.00	30.00
a.		6c on 5s green, type II	275.00	100.00
67	(b)	12c on 50c gray & blk	150.00	30.00
68	(c)	18c on 10s buff, org & black	150.00	30.00
69	(d)	1t on 5fr rose red & black	150.00	50.00
		Nos. 66-69 (4)	600.00	140.00

1887
70	(e)	3c on 5s grn, type I	150.00	30.00
a.		3c on 5s green, type II	275.00	100.00
71	(a)	6c on 10s buff, org & blk	150.00	30.00
72	(f)	8c on 50c gray & blk	150.00	30.00
		Nos. 70-72 (3)	450.00	90.00

The word "OFFICIEL" indicated that the surcharged stamps were officially authorized. Surcharges on the same basic stamps of values other than those listed are believed to be bogus.

Counterfeits of Nos. 66-72 abound.

Very fine examples of Nos. 66-72 will have perforations cutting the outer colored border but clear of the inner framelines.

Beware of forgeries and/or reprints of most Iran stamps between the years 1870-1925. Scott values are for genuine stamps. Collectors should be aware that forgeries of many issues outnumber genuine examples by factors of 10 or 20 to one. Failing specialized knowledge on the part of the collector, these stamps should be examined or authenticated by acknowledged experts before purchase.

A14 A15

1889 Typo. Perf. 11, 13½, 11x13½
73	A14	1c pale rose	2.50	.75
74	A14	2c pale blue	2.50	.75
75	A14	5c lilac	1.50	.50
76	A14	7c brown	7.50	1.50
77	A15	10c black	2.50	.75
78	A15	1k red orange	4.50	.75
79	A15	2k rose	40.00	6.00
80	A15	5k green	25.00	6.00
		Nos. 73-80 (8)	86.00	17.00

All values exist imperforate.
Canceled to order stamps of No. 76 abound.
For surcharges see Nos. 622-625.
Nos. 73-80 with average centering, faded colors and/or toned paper sell for much less.

A16 A17

1891 Perf. 10½, 11½
81	A16	1c black	2.50	1.00
82	A16	2c brown	2.50	1.00
83	A16	5c deep blue	2.50	.25
84	A16	7c gray	350.00	12.00
85	A16	10c rose	2.50	.50
86	A16	14c orange	2.50	1.50
87	A17	1k green	30.00	2.00
88	A17	2k orange	700.00	35.00
89	A17	5k ocher yellow	8.00	30.00
		Nos. 81-89 (9)	1,101.	73.25

For surcharges see Nos. 626-629.

A18

Nasser-eddin Shah Qajar — A19

1894 Perf. 12½
90	A18	1c lilac	1.00	.25
91	A18	2c blue green	1.00	.25
92	A18	5c ultramarine	1.00	.25
93	A18	8c brown	1.00	.25

Perf. 11½x11
94	A19	10c orange	1.25	.75
95	A19	16c rose	25.00	75.00
96	A19	1k red & yellow	3.00	.75
97	A19	2k brn org & pale bl	4.00	1.00
98	A19	5k violet & silver	10.00	1.50
99	A19	10k red & gold	20.00	10.00
100	A19	50k green & gold	50.00	15.00
		Nos. 90-100 (11)	117.25	105.00

Canceled to order stamps sell for one-third of listed values.
Reprints exist. They are hard to distinguish from the originals. Value, set $15.
See Nos. 104-112, 136-144. For overprints see Nos. 120-128, 152-167, 173-181. For surcharges see Nos. 101-103, 168, 206, 211.

Nos. 93, 98 With Violet or Magenta Surcharge

a b

1897 Perf. 12½, 11½x11
101	A18(a)	5c on 8c brn (V)	30.00	5.00
a.		Inverted surcharge	150.00	25.00
102	A19(b)	1k on 5k vio & sil (V)	40.00	10.00
103	A19(b)	2k on 5k vio & sil (M)	60.00	35.00
		Nos. 101-103 (3)	130.00	60.00

Forgeries exist.

Lion Type of 1894 and

Mozaffar-eddin Shah Qajar — A22

1898 Typo. Perf. 12½
104	A18	1c gray	5.00	.35
105	A18	2c pale brown	5.00	.35
106	A18	3c dull violet	10.00	3.00
107	A18	4c vermilion	10.00	3.00
108	A18	5c yellow	5.00	.25
109	A18	8c orange	20.00	7.00
110	A18	10c light blue	5.00	.50
111	A18	12c rose	15.00	1.00
112	A18	16c green	20.00	7.00
113	A22	1k ultramarine	10.00	1.00
114	A22	2k pink	10.00	2.00
115	A22	3k yellow	10.00	3.00
116	A22	4k gray	10.00	5.00
117	A22	5k emerald	10.00	6.00
118	A22	10k orange	40.00	15.00
119	A22	50k bright vio	60.00	25.00
		Nos. 104-119 (16)	245.00	79.45

Unauthorized reprints of Nos. 104-119 were made from original clichés. Paper shows a vertical mesh. These abound unused and canceled to order. Value set, unused, hinged, $20.
See Nos. 145-151. For overprints see Nos. 129-135, 182-188. For surcharges see Nos. 169, 171, 207, 209, 211.

Reprints have been used to make counterfeits of Nos. 120-135, 152-167.

Stamps of 1898 Handstamped in Violet

a b
c d
e f
g h

1899
120	(a)	1c gray	5.00	5.00
121	(b)	2c pale brown	5.00	8.00
122	(b)	3c dull violet	12.00	15.00
a.		Type "d" handstamp	150.00	150.00
123	(c)	4c vermilion	18.00	30.00
124	(c)	5c yellow	10.00	3.00
125	(d)	8c orange	15.00	40.00
126	(d)	10c light blue	10.00	15.00
a.		Type "b" handstamp	500.00	500.00
127	(d)	12c rose	15.00	8.00
128	(d)	16c green	25.00	30.00
129	(e)	1k ultramarine	25.00	10.00
130	(f)	2k pink	30.00	25.00
131	(f)	3k yellow	80.00	250.00
132	(g)	4k gray	100.00	250.00
133	(g)	5k emerald	30.00	40.00
134	(h)	10k orange	80.00	80.00
135	(h)	50k brt violet	120.00	150.00
		Nos. 120-135 (16)	580.00	959.00

The handstamped control marks on Nos. 120-135 exist inverted and double. Counterfeits are plentiful.

Persiphila
Buying, Selling, Expertizing

Publisher of
Persiphila Iran Specialized Catalogs

www.**Persi**.com

Persiphila, PO Box 1589, Glendora, CA 91740-1589

Email: **Persi@Persi.com**

IRAN

Types of 1894-98

1899   **Typo.**   **Perf. 12½**

136	A18	1c gray, *green*	7.50	.75
137	A18	2c brown, *green*	7.50	.75
138	A18	3c violet, *green*	20.00	5.00
139	A18	4c red, *green*	12.00	5.00
140	A18	5c yellow, *green*	5.00	.30
141	A18	8c orange, *green*	15.00	10.00
142	A18	10c pale blue, *grn*	5.00	.50
143	A18	12c lake, *green*	15.00	1.25
144	A18	16c green, *green*	25.00	5.00
145	A22	1k red	30.00	1.25
146	A22	2k deep green	35.00	8.50
147	A22	3k lilac brown	35.00	17.00
148	A22	4k orange red	35.00	17.00
149	A22	5k gray brown	40.00	17.00
150	A22	10k deep blue	400.00	150.00
151	A22	50k brown	100.00	45.00
		Nos. 136-151 (16)	787.00	279.30

Canceled to order stamps abound.

Unauthorized reprints of Nos. 136-151 were made from original clichés. Paper is chalky and has white gum. The design can be seen through the back of the reprints. Value unused, hinged, set, $30.

For surcharges and overprints see Nos. 171, 173-188, 206-207, 209, 211.

Nos. 104-111 Handstamped in Violet

(Struck once on every two stamps.)

1900

152	A18	1c gray	50.00	20.00
153	A18	2c pale brown	60.00	25.00
154	A18	3c dull violet	150.00	70.00
155	A18	4c vermilion	150.00	70.00
156	A18	5c yellow	25.00	10.00
158	A18	10c light blue	2,500.	2,500.
159	A18	12c rose	100.00	50.00
		Nos. 152-159 (7)	3,035.	2,745.

Values are for single authenticated stamps. Pairs sell for much more.

This control mark, in genuine state, was not applied to the 8c orange (Nos. 109, 125).

Same Overprint Handstamped on Nos. 120-127 in Violet

(Struck once on each block of 4.)

160	A18	1c gray	100.00	50.00
163	A18	4c vermilion	300.00	140.00
164	A18	5c yellow	50.00	20.00
166	A18	10c light blue	1,250.	600.00
a.		Type "b" handstamp	500.00	250.00
167	A18	12c rose	150.00	50.00
		Nos. 160-167 (5)	550.00	760.00

Values are for single authenticated stamps. Blocks are rare and worth much more.
Counterfeits exist of Nos. 152-167.

No. 93 Surcharged in Violet

1900

168	A18	5c on 8c brown	75.00	4.00
a.		Inverted surcharge	300.00	100.00

No. 145 Surcharged in Violet

1901

169	A22	12c on 1k red	150.00	125.00
a.		Blue surcharge	175.00	150.00

Counterfeits exist.
No. 169 with a black surcharge is a fake.

A23

1902   **Violet Surcharge**

171	A23	5k on 50k brown	250.00	100.00
a.		Blue surcharge	250.00	100.00

Counterfeits exist. See No. 207.

Nos. 136-151 Overprinted in Black

1902

173	A18	1c gray, *green*	50.00	20.00
174	A18	2c brown, *green*	50.00	20.00
175	A18	3c violet, *green*	300.00	300.00
176	A18	4c red, *green*	400.00	400.00
177	A18	5c yellow, *green*	20.00	5.00
178	A18	8c orange, *green*	400.00	400.00
179	A18	10c pale blue, *grn*	50.00	15.00
180	A18	12c lake, *green*	125.00	50.00
181	A18	16c green, *green*	500.00	400.00
182	A22	1k red	100.00	45.00
183	A22	2k deep green	250.00	100.00
188	A22	50k brown	650.00	300.00

Overprinted on No. 168

206	A18	5c on 8c brown	300.00	175.00

Overprinted on Nos. 171 and 171a

207	A23	5k on 50k brown	250.00	150.00
a.		On #171a	300.00	175.00

Overprinted on Nos. 169 and 169a

209	A22	12c on 1k red	125.00	75.00
a.		On #169a	125.00	

Counterfeits of the overprint of Nos. 173-183, 188, 206-207, 209 are plentiful. Practically all examples with overprint sideways, inverted, double and double with one inverted are frauds.

Nos. 142 Surcharged in Violet

1902

211	A18	5c on 10c pale bl, *grn*	100.00	40.00

Surcharges in different colors were made for collectors.

Initials of Victor Castaigne, Postmaster of Meshed — A24

1902   **Typo.**   **Imperf.**

222	A24	1c black	1,500.	450.00
a.		Inverted frame	—	3,000.
		Inverted center		
223	A24	2c black	1,250.	450.00
a.		Inverted frame		
b.		"2" in right upper corner	3,000.	1,750.
224	A24	3c black	3,250.	1,750.
225	A24	5c violet	750.00	300.00
a.		"5" in right upper corner		
b.		Frame printed on both sides	2,250.	1,000.
c.		Inverted center		
226	A24	5c black	900.00	400.00
a.		Persian "5" in lower left corner		—
b.		Inverted center		
227	A24	12c dull blue	4,000.	1,500.
a.		Inverted frame		—
b.		Inverted center		—
228	A24	1k rose	30,000.	3,500.

Used values for Nos. 222-228 canceled to order are about ⅓ to ½ the values shown, which are for postally used stamps.
The design of No. 228, shown, differs slightly from the design of Nos. 222-227.
Nos. 222-228 were printed in three operations. Inverted centers have frames and numerals upright. Inverted frames have centers and numerals upright.

Pin-perforated

234	A24	12c dull blue	4,000.	1,500.

Monsieur Victor Castaigne, the Belgian director of post and customs in the northwestern province of Khorassan, on his own initiative, prepared a set of provisional stamps to meet the shortage of low-denomination stamps. These stamps were printed individually from two clichés, one for the frame and one for the vignette, reading V.C. (Castaigne's initials taken from his ring). Printed stamps were initialed by the director in red in for the shahis (ch) denominations and in violet ink for the 1k. Remainders exist posthumously canceled with fake MECHED postmarks. Various forgeries exist, including examples printed by two clichés for the frame and vignette, as well as one cliche for both. Values quoted are for examples accompanied by certificates of authenticity.

A25

TWO TYPES:
Type I — "CHAHI" or "KRANS" are in capital letters.
Type II — Only "C" of "Chahi" or "K" of "Krans" is a capital. The handstamp appears only on type I stamps and comes in two varieties: black serpent's head and hollow serpent's head.
The 3c and 5c sometimes have a tall narrow figure in the upper left corner. The 5c is also found with the cross at the upper left broken or missing. These varieties are known with many of the overprints.
Stamps of Design A25 have a faint fancy background in the color of the stamp. All issued stamps have handstamped controls as listed.

Black Serpents Head   Hollow Serpents Head

Type I
Handstamp Overprinted in Black

1902   **Typeset**   **Imperf.**

235	A25	1c gray & buff	300.00	150.00
236	A25	2c brown & buff	400.00	150.00
237	A25	3c green & buff	400.00	150.00
238	A25	5c red & buff	300.00	100.00
239	A25	12c ultra & buff	500.00	150.00
		Nos. 235-239 (5)	1,900.	700.00

Counterfeits abound. Type II stamps with this overprint are forgeries.
The 3c with violet overprint is believed not to have been regularly issued.

Handstamp Overprinted in Bright Red

1902   **Type I**

247	A25	1c gray & buff	25.00	2.00
b.		"2" in 1c cliché	150.00	
248	A25	2c brown & buff	25.00	2.00
249	A25	3c dp grn & buff	25.00	2.00
250	A25	5c red & buff	25.00	.75
251	A25	10c ol yel & buff	50.00	3.00
252	A25	12c ultra & buff	75.00	5.00
253	A25	1k violet & bl	60.00	6.00
254	A25	2k ol grn & bl	100.00	12.50
256	A25	10k dk bl & bl	150.00	30.00
257	A25	50k red & blue	1,500.	800.00
		Nos. 247-257 (10)	2,035.	863.25

A 5k exists but its status is doubtful. Value $500.
Stamps with handstamps other than bright red are either fake or were not regularly issued.

Type II

280	A25	1c gray & yellow	250.00	200.00
281	A25	2c brown & yel	200.00	200.00
282	A25	3c dk grn & yel	2,000.	750.00
283	A25	5c red & yellow	50.00	15.00
284	A25	10c ol yel & yel	100.00	15.00
285	A25	12c blue & yel	150.00	25.00
290	A25	50k org red & bl	1,250.	600.00

Denominations with handstamps other than bright red are either fake or not regularly issued.
Remainders exist with fake control handstamps.
Type II stamps with high denominations of 10t (100k), 20t, 25t, 50t and 100t with blue rosette 1319 handstamps and black control numbers on the front were used on postal money orders. Denominations with control numbers in colors other than black are forgeries.

Beware of forgeries and/or reprints of most Iran stamps between the years 1870-1925. Scott values are for genuine stamps. Collectors should be aware that forgeries of many issues outnumber genuine examples by factors of 10 or 20 to one. Failing specialized knowledge on the part of the collector, these stamps should be examined or authenticated by acknowledged experts before purchase.

Handstamp Surcharged in Black

1902   **Type I**

308	A25	5k on 5k ocher & bl	200.00	75.00

Counterfeits of No. 308 abound.
This surcharge in rose, violet, blue or green is considered bogus.
This surcharge on 50k orange red and blue, and on 5k ocher and blue, type II, is considered bogus.

Handstamp Overprinted Diagonally in Black

1902   **Type I**

315	A25	2c brown & buff	250.00	150.00
a.		Rose overprint	500.00	500.00

Type II

316	A25	2c brown & yel	—	—
a.		Rose overprint		

"P. L." stands for "Poste Locale."
Counterfeits of Nos. 315-316 exist.
Some specialists believe that Type II stamps were not used officially for this overprint.

Handstamp Overprinted in Black or Rose

1902   **Type II**

317	A25	2c brn & yellow	250.00	125.00
318	A25	2c brown & yel (R)	500.00	500.00

Counterfeits of Nos. 317-318 exist.

Overprinted in Blue

1903   **Type I**

321	A25	1k violet & blue	125.00	125.00

Type II

336	A25	1c gray & yellow	60.00	60.00
337	A25	2c brown & yellow	60.00	60.00
338	A25	5c red & yellow	40.00	40.00
339	A25	10c olive yel & yel	75.00	75.00
340	A25	12c blue & yellow	90.00	90.00
		Nos. 321-340 (6)	450.00	450.00

A 3c Type I exists but was not regularly issued. Value $250.
The overprint also exists in violet and black, but it is doubtful whether such items were regularly issued.
Forgeries of Nos. 321, 336-340 abound. Genuine unused examples are seldom found.

Arms of Persia — A26

IRAN

Mozaffar-eddin Shah Qajar — A27

1902 (Dec.)-1904 Typo. Perf. 12½
351	A26	1c violet	2.00	.25
352	A26	2c gray	2.00	.25
353	A26	3c green	2.00	.25
354	A26	5c rose	2.00	.25
355	A26	10c yellow brn	3.00	1.50
356	A26	12c blue	4.00	.50

Engr. Perf. 11½x11
357	A27	1k violet	15.00	.50
358	A27	2k ultramarine	25.00	1.25
359	A27	5k orange brn	40.00	2.00
360	A27	10k rose red	50.00	4.00
361	A27	20k orange ('04)	45.00	5.00
362	A27	30k green ('04)	70.00	12.50
363	A27	50k green	550.00	100.00
		Nos. 351-363 (13)	810.00	128.25

No. 355 exists with blue diagonal surcharge "1 CHAHI"; its status is questioned.

A government decree in November, 1903, required that all picture postcards be censored by the Central Post Office, which would apply a control mark on each card to show that the 2c tax for this service had been paid. No. 352 was overprinted "Controle" in several styles, for this purpose. Value: unused $100; used, from $25.

See Nos. 428-433. For surcharges and overprints see #364-420, 446-447, 464-469, O8-O28, P1.

No. 353 Surcharged in Violet or Blue

1903
364	A26	1c on 3c green (V)	75.00	25.00
365	A26	2c on 3c green (Bl)	75.00	25.00

A 2c surcharge on No. 354 exists, but its status is dubious.

No. 360 Surcharged in Blue
366	A27	12c on 10k rose red	75.00	40.00
a.		Black surcharge	150.00	70.00
b.		Violet surcharge	150.00	70.00
		Nos. 364-366 (3)	225.00	90.00

Nos. 366, 366a and 366b used are valued canceled to order.

No. 363 Surcharged in Blue or Black

1903
368	A27	2t on 50k grn (Bl)	300.00	100.00
a.		Rose surcharge	325.00	125.00
		Black surcharge	325.00	125.00
370	A27	3t on 50k grn (Bk)	300.00	100.00
a.		Violet surcharge	350.00	150.00
b.		Rose surcharge	350.00	150.00

No. 363 Surcharged in Blue or Black

1904
372	A27	2t on 50k grn (Bl)	300.00	100.00
375	A27	3t on 50k grn (Bk)	300.00	100.00

The 2t on 50k also exists with surcharge in rose, violet, black and magenta; the 3t on 50k in rose, violet and blue. Values about the same unused; about 50 percent higher used.

No. 352 Overprinted in Violet

1904 Perf. 12½
393	A26	2c gray	100.00	25.00
a.		Black overprint	150.00	50.00
b.		Rose overprint	135.00	35.00

This overprint also exists in blue, violet blue, maroon and gray, but these were not regularly issued.

Stamps of 1903 Surcharged in Black

1904
400	A26(a)	3c on 5c rose	40.00	.75
401	A26(b)	6c on 10c brown	75.00	.75
402	A27(c)	9c on 1k violet	50.00	3.50
		Nos. 400-402 (3)	165.00	5.00

Stamps of 1903 Surcharged in Black, Magenta or Violet

1905-06
404	A26	1c on 3c green ('06)	80.00	40.00
405	A27	1c on 1k violet	75.00	45.00
406	A27	2c on 5k orange brn	75.00	45.00
407	A26	1c on 3c grn (M) ('06)	35.00	10.00
408	A27	1c on 1k violet (M)	55.00	25.00
409	A27	2c on 5k org brn (V)	55.00	35.00
		Nos. 404-409 (6)	375.00	200.00

Nos. 355 and 358 Surcharged in Violet

1906
419	A26	1c on 10c brown	150.00	—
420	A27	2c on 2k ultra	250.00	—

These stamps were prepared on the initiative of the Tabriz postmaster. Tabriz is the capital of the northeastern province of Azerbaijan.

Forgeries of Nos. 419-420 are common. Forgeries of No. 420, especially, are hard to distinguish since the original handstamp was used. Genuine used stamps may, in some cases, be identified by the cancellation.

Typeset; "Provisoire" Overprint Handstamped in Black

A28

1906 Imperf.
422	A28	1c violet	25.00	3.00
a.		Irregular pin perf. or perf. 10½	75.00	25.00
423	A28	2c gray	150.00	15.00
424	A28	3c green	25.00	2.00
425	A28	6c red	25.00	1.00
426	A28	10c brown	70.00	70.00
427	A28	13c blue	50.00	20.00
		Nos. 422-427 (6)	345.00	111.00

Stamps of type A28 have a faint background pattern of tiny squares within squares, an ornamental frame and open rectangles for the value corners.

The 3c and 6c also exist perforated.

Nos. 422-427 are known without overprint but were probably not issued in that condition. Nearly all values are known with overprint inverted and double.

Forgeries are plentiful.

Lion Type of 1903 and

Mohammed-Ali Shah Qajar
A29 A30

1907-09 Typo. Perf. 12½
428	A26	1c vio, blue	7.00	.30
429	A26	2c gray, blue	10.00	.30
430	A26	3c green, blue	7.00	.30
431	A26	6c rose, blue	7.00	.30
432	A26	9c org, blue	10.00	.40
433	A26	10c brown, blue	10.00	1.50

Engr. Perf. 11, 11½
434	A29	13c dark blue	17.50	2.00
435	A29	1k red	12.00	1.50
436	A29	26c red brown	12.00	2.00
437	A29	2k deep grn	35.00	1.50
438	A29	3k pale blue	35.00	1.00
439	A29	4k brt yellow	600.00	25.00
440	A29	4k bister	35.00	3.00
441	A29	5k dark brown	40.00	3.00
442	A29	10k pink	50.00	3.00
443	A29	20k gray black	50.00	10.00
444	A29	30k dark violet	60.00	15.00
445	A30	50k gold, ver & black ('09)	200.00	30.00
		Nos. 428-445 (18)	1,198.	100.10

Frame of No. 445 lithographed. Nos. 434-444 were issued in 1908.

Remainders canceled to order abound. Used values for Nos. 437-445 are for c-t-os.

Nos. 428-429 Overprinted in Black

1909 Perf. 12½
446	A26	1c violet, blue	90.00	50.00
447	A26	2c gray, blue	90.00	50.00

Counterfeits of Nos. 446-447 exist.

Coat of Arms — A31

1909 Typo. Perf. 12½x12
448	A31	1c org & maroon	.50	.35
449	A31	2c vio & maroon	.50	.35
450	A31	3c yel grn & mar	.50	.35
451	A31	6c red & maroon	.50	.25
452	A31	9c gray & maroon	.50	.35
453	A31	10c red vio & mar	.50	.35
454	A31	13c dk blue & mar	.50	2.00
455	A31	1k sil, vio & bis brn	1.00	2.00
456	A31	26c dk grn & mar	1.00	3.00
457	A31	2k sil, dk grn & bis brown	1.00	2.00
458	A31	3k sil, gray & bis brn	1.00	3.50
459	A31	4k sil, by & bis brn	1.00	3.50
460	A31	5k gold, brn & bis brn	2.50	3.50
461	A31	10k gold, org & bis brn	5.00	10.00
462	A31	20k gold, ol grn & bis brn	7.00	20.00
463	A31	30k gold, car & bis brn	12.00	20.00
		Nos. 448-463 (16)	35.00	71.50

Unauthorized reprints of Nos. 448-463 abound. Originals have clean, bright colors, centers stand out clearly, and paper is much thinner. Nos. 460-463 originals have gleaming gold margins; reprint margins appear as blackish yellow. Centers of reprints of Nos. 448-454, 456 are brown.

Values above are for unused reprints and for authenticated used stamps. Original unused stamps sell for much higher prices. Value, unused set, $2,500.

For surcharges & overprints see Nos. 516-519, 541-549, 582-585, 588-594, 597, 601-606, 707-722, C1-C16, O31-O40.

In 1909 two sets of 16 stamps were prepared for the coronation of Ahmad Shad Qajar. The first set with lion and sun high values and gold borders was for postal use, while the second set with city gate high values and silver borders was inscribed "SERVICE". While neither set was placed in use, both were sold to collectors at a later date.

Nos. 428-444, Imperf., Surcharged in Red or Black

1910 Blue Paper Imperf.
464	A26	1c on 1c violet	210.00	165.00
465	A26	1c on 2c gray	210.00	165.00
466	A26	1c on 3c green	210.00	165.00
467	A26	1c on 6c rose (Bk)	210.00	165.00
468	A26	1c on 9c orange	210.00	165.00
469	A26	1c on 10c brown	210.00	165.00

White Paper
470	A29	2c on 13c dp bl	210.00	165.00
471	A29	2c on 26c red brn (Bk)	210.00	165.00
472	A29	2c on 1k red (Bk)	210.00	165.00
473	A29	2c on 2k dp grn	210.00	165.00
474	A29	2c on 3k pale bl	210.00	165.00
475	A29	2c on 4k brt yel	210.00	165.00
476	A29	2c on 4k bister	210.00	165.00
477	A29	2c on 5k dk brn	210.00	165.00
478	A29	2c on 10k pink (Bk)	210.00	165.00
479	A29	2c on 20k gray blk	210.00	165.00
480	A29	2c on 30k dk vio	210.00	165.00
		Nos. 464-480 (17)	3,570.	2,805.

Nos. 464-480 were prepared for use on newspapers, but nearly the entire printing was sold to stamp dealers. The issue is generally considered speculative. Counterfeit surcharges exist on trimmed stamps.

Used values are for c-t-o.

Early printings of Nos. 481-500 were made by wet printing, while later issues were mostly produced by dry printing. As a result, there are two heights of the central (engraved) vignette, 23mm (dry printing) and 22½ (wet printing), caused by the shrinkage of the paper as it dried after printing.

Ahmad Shah Qajar — A32

Engr. center, Typo. frame

1911-21 Tall Portrait (23mm) Perf. 11½
481	A32	1c green & org	20.00	1.00
482	A32	2c red & sepia	.50	1.00
483	A32	3c gray brn & grn	.50	1.00
483B	A32	3c 3c bister brown & green	.50	1.00
484	A32	5c brn & car ('13)	.50	
485	A32	6c gray & car	.50	.30
486	A32	6c grn & red brn ('13)	.50	.40
487	A32	9c yel brn & vio	.75	2.00
488	A32	10c red & org brn	.75	35.00
489	A32	12c grn & ultra ('13)	.50	.50
490	A32	13c violet & ultra	1.00	2.00

IRAN

491	A32	1k ultra & car	1.00	4.00
492	A32	24c vio & grn ('13)	.50	.50
493	A32	26c ultra & green	—	125.00
494	A32	2k grn & red vio	—	50.00
495	A32	3k violet & blk	—	100.00
497	A32	5k red & ultra	3.00	4.00
498	A32	10k ol bis & cl	5.00	100.00
499	A32	20k vio brn & bis	5.00	100.00
500	A32	30k red & green	7.00	5.00
		Nos. 481-500 (20)	47.50	532.70

Values for Nos. 481-500 unused are for reprints, which cannot be distinguished from the late printings of the stamps.
The reprints include inverted centers for some denominations. Values, each $30-$50.
For surcharges and overprints see Nos. 501-515, 520-540, 586-587, 595, 596, 598, 600, 607-609, 630-634, 646-666.

Perf. 11½x11

481a	A32	1c green & org	—	1.00
482a	A32	2c red & sepia	20.00	1.00
483a	A32	3c gray brn & grn	35.00	1.00
483Ba	A32	3c bister brn & grn ('21)	60.00	2.00
484a	A32	5c brn & car ('13)	35.00	.40
485a	A32	6c gray & car	45.00	2.00
486a	A32	6c grn & red brown ('13)	35.00	.40
487a	A32	9c yel brn & violet	35.00	2.00
488a	A32	10c red & org brn	55.00	.25
489a	A32	12c ultra & ultra ('13)	45.00	.50
490a	A32	13c violet & ultra	75.00	2.00
492a	A32	24c vio & grn ('13)	60.00	.50
494a	A32	2k green & red vio	100.00	1.00
495a	A32	3k violet & black	140.00	4.00
497a	A32	5k red & ultra	150.00	4.00
498a	A32	10k ol bis & claret	435.00	45.00
499a	A32	20k vio brn & bister	600.00	5.00
500a	A32	30k red & green	550.00	5.00
		Nos. 481a-500a (18)	2,495.	76.15

Perf. 11½x12

488b	A32	10c red & org brn	70.00	60.00
490b	A32	13c violet & ultra	100.00	—
493b	A32	26c ultra & green	—	75.00
496	A32	4k ultra & gray ('13)	450.00	100.00
497b	A32	5k red & ultra	400.00	100.00
		Nos. 488b-497b (4)	570.00	245.00

No. 496 with inverted center is a reprint. Value, $50.

Short Portrait (22½mm)
Perf. 11½

481c	A32	1c green & org	75.00	20.00
482c	A32	2c red & sepia	75.00	25.00
483c	A32	3c gray brn & grn	70.00	10.00
484c	A32	5c brn & car ('13)	—	10.00
485c	A32	6c gray & car	35.00	5.00
487c	A32	9c yel brn & violet	10.00	10.00
491c	A32	1k ultra & carmine	—	—
493c	A32	26c ultra & green	165.00	20.00
494c	A32	2k green & red vio	—	—
495c	A32	3k violet & black	—	—
496c	A32	4k violet & black ('13)	—	—
500c	A32	30k red & green	800.00	100.00
		Nos. 481c-500c (12)	1,230.	190.00

No. 491c is known only with the "Controlle 1922" overprint. Nos. 494c and 495c were apparently never used.

Perf. 11½x11

481d	A32	1c green & org	75.00	10.00
482d	A32	2c red & sepia	85.00	10.00
483d	A32	3c gray brn & grn	75.00	10.00
485d	A32	6c gray & car	75.00	3.00
488d	A32	10c red & org brn	100.00	30.00
490d	A32	13c violet & ultra	100.00	10.00
491d	A32	1k ultra & carmine	200.00	10.00
493d	A32	26c ultra & green	80.00	20.00
494d	A32	2k green & red vio	150.00	5.00
495d	A32	3k violet & black	300.00	20.00
497d	A32	5k red & ultra	350.00	50.00
498d	A32	10k ol bis & claret	750.00	100.00
		Nos. 481d-498d (12)	2,340.	278.00

Perf. 11½x12

493e	A32	26c ultra & green	500.00	100.00
494e	A32	2k green & red vio	400.00	30.00
495e	A32	3k violet & black	400.00	35.00
496e	A32	4k violet & black ('13)	600.00	150.00
498e	A32	10k ol bis & claret	700.00	50.00

Stamps of 1911 Overprinted in Black

1911 "Officiel" Overprint On Nos. 481/500

1911 Tall Portrait Perf. 11½

503	A32	3c gray brn & grn	75.00	10.00
504	A32	6c gray & car	75.00	10.00
507	A32	13c vio & ultra	175.00	15.00
509	A32	26c ultra & green	200.00	20.00
513	A32	10k ol bis & claret	1,500.	200.00
		Nos. 503-513 (5)	2,025.	255.00

On Nos. 481a/500a
Perf. 11½x11

501	A32	1c green & org	75.00	10.00
502	A32	2c red & sepia	75.00	10.00
503a	A32	3c gray brn & grn	75.00	10.00
504a	A32	6c gray & carmine	—	25.00
506	A32	10c red & org brn	125.00	15.00
508	A32	1k ultra & car	—	150.00
510	A32	2k grn & red vio	250.00	75.00
511	A32	3k vio & black	—	100.00
512	A32	5k red & ultra	400.00	100.00
513a	A32	10k ol bis & claret	1,500.	250.00
514	A32	20k vio brn & bis	1,500.	250.00
515	A32	30k red & green	1,700.	300.00
		Nos. 501-515 (12)	5,700.	1,295.

Short Portrait On Nos. 481c/500c
Perf. 11½

501c	A32	1c green & org	—	75.00
502c	A32	2c red & sepia	—	25.00
503c	A32	3c gray brn & grn	200.00	30.00
504c	A32	6c gray & carmine	100.00	15.00
505	A32	9c yel brn & vio	100.00	15.00
515c	A32	30k red & green	1,950.	500.00
		Nos. 501c-515c (6)	2,350.	660.00

On Nos. 481d/514d
Perf. 11½x11

501d	A32	1c green & org	100.00	15.00
502d	A32	2c red & sepia	100.00	15.00
503d	A32	3c gray brn & grn	100.00	15.00
504d	A32	6c gray & carmine	100.00	15.00
506d	A32	10c red & org brn	125.00	25.00
507d	A32	13c violet & ultra	250.00	15.00
508d	A32	1k ultra & carmine	—	150.00
509d	A32	26c ultra & green	200.00	20.00
510d	A32	2k grn & red violet	250.00	75.00
511d	A32	3k violet & black	—	100.00
512d	A32	5k red & ultra	400.00	150.00
513d	A32	10k olive bister & claret	1,750.	300.00
514d	A32	20k vio brn & bis	1,750.	350.00
		Nos. 501d-514d (13)	5,125.	1,245.

The "Officiel" overprint does not signify that the stamps were intended for use on official correspondence but that they were issued by authority. It was applied to the stocks in Tabriz and all post offices in the Tabriz region after a large quantity of stamps had been stolen during the Russian occupation of Tabriz.
The "Officiel" overprint has been counterfeited.

Stamps of 1909-11 Overprinted in Black

1911, Oct.   On #449-451, 454

516	A31	2c vio & maroon	300.00	150.00
517	A31	3c yel grn & mar	300.00	150.00
518	A31	6c red & maroon	300.00	150.00
519	A31	13c dk blue & mar	300.00	150.00
		Nos. 516-519 (4)	1,200.	600.00

On Nos. 482a/490s

520	A32	2c red & sepia (on #482a)	300.00	150.00
b.		On #482c	—	—
c.		On #482d	—	—
521	A32	3c gray brn & grn (on #483d)	300.00	150.00
a.		On #483	—	—
b.		On 483c	—	—
522	A32	6c gray & car (on #485)	300.00	150.00
a.		On #485a	—	—
b.		On #485c	—	—
c.		On #485d	—	—
523	A32	13c violet & ultra (on #490)	300.00	150.00
a.		On #490a	—	—
b.		On #490d	—	—
		Nos. 520-523 (4)	900.00	450.00

Stamps were sold at a 10% discount to stagecoach station keepers on the Tehran-Recht route. To prevent speculation, these stamps were overprinted "Stagecoach Stations" in French and Farsi.
Forgeries exist, usually overprinted on reprints of the 1909 issue and used examples of the 1911 issue. Values are for authenticated stamps.

In 1912 this overprint, reading "Sultan Mohammad Ali Shah Qajar," was hand-stamped on outgoing mail in the Persian Kurdistan region occupied by the forces of the former Shah Mohammad Ali. It was applied after the stamps were on cover and is found on 8 of the Shah Ahmed stamps of 1911 (1c, 2c, 3c, 6c, 9c, 13c, 1k and 26c). Two covers are known with 10c stamp.

Nos. 490 and 493 Surcharged

a b

1914

535	A32(a)	1c on 13c (on #490)	30.00	2.00
a.		On #490a	30.00	2.00
b.		On #490b	30.00	2.00
c.		On #490d	30.00	2.00
536	A32(b)	3c on 26c (on #493)	30.00	4.00
a.		On #493b	30.00	2.00
b.		On #493c	30.00	2.00
c.		on 26c (on #493d)	30.00	2.00
d.		On #493e	30.00	2.00

In 1914 a set of 19 stamps was prepared as a coronation issue. The 10 lower values each carry a different portrait; the 9 higher values show buildings and scenes. Value $2,500 each set. The same set printed with black centers was overprinted in red "SERVICE."

Nos. 484 and 489 Surcharged in Black or Violet

c d

1915

537	A32(c)	1c on 5c (on #484a)	25.00	2.00
538	A32(c)	2c on 5c (on #484a)	200.00	40.00
539	A32(c)	2c on 5c (V) (on #484a)	25.00	2.00
540	A32(d)	6c on 12c (on #489a)	35.00	2.00
		Nos. 537-540 (4)	285.00	46.00

Nos. 455, 454 Surcharged

e f

1915   Perf. 12½x12

541	A31(e)	5c on 1k multi	100.00	10.00
542	A31(f)	12c on 13c multi	145.00	10.00

Counterfeit surcharges on reprints abound.

Nos. 448-453, 455 Overprinted

1915

543	A31	1c org & maroon	75.00	15.00
544	A31	2c vio & maroon	75.00	15.00
545	A31	3c grn & maroon	75.00	15.00
546	A31	6c red & maroon	75.00	15.00
547	A31	9c gray & maroon	100.00	20.00
548	A31	10c red vio & mar	225.00	40.00
549	A31	1k sil, vio & bis brn	275.00	50.00
		Nos. 543-549 (7)	920.00	170.00

This overprint ("1333") also exists on the 2k, but they were not issued.

Counterfeit overprints, usually on reprints, abound.

Beware of forgeries and/or reprints of most Iran stamps between the years 1870-1925. Scott values are for genuine stamps. Collectors should be aware that forgeries of many issues outnumber genuine examples by factors of 10 or 20 to one. Failing specialized knowledge on the part of the collector, these stamps should be examined or authenticated by acknowledged experts before purchase.

Imperial Crown
A33

King Darius, Farvahar overhead
A34

Ruins of Persepolis — A35

Perf. 11½ or Compound 11x11½
Engr., Typo.

1915, Mar.   Wmk. 161

560	A33	1c car & indigo	20.00	20.00
561	A33	2c bl & carmine	.25	15.00
562	A33	3c dark green	.25	15.00
a.		Inverted center		
564	A33	5c red	.25	5.00
565	A33	6c olive grn & car	.25	5.00
a.		Inverted center	20.00	20.00
566	A33	9c yel brn & vio	.25	20.00
567	A33	10c bl grn & yel brn	30.00	30.00
568	A33	12c ultramarine	40.00	40.00
569	A34	1k sil, yel brn & gray	40.00	40.00
570	A33	24c yel brn & dk brn	40.00	30.00
571	A34	2k silver, bl & rose	.65	30.00
572	A34	3k sil, vio & brn	.65	30.00
573	A34	5k sil, brn & green	.65	30.00
574	A35	1t gold, pur & blk	.65	60.00
575	A35	2t gold, grn & brn	1.00	60.00
576	A35	3t gold, cl & red brn	1.00	60.00
577	A35	5t gold, blue & ind	1.00	60.00
		Nos. 560-577 (17)	176.85	550.00

Coronation of Shah Ahmed.
Nos. 560-568, 570 are engraved. Nos. 569, 571-573 are engraved except for silver margins. Nos. 574-577 have centers engraved, frames typographed.
The 3c and 6c with inverted centers are considered genuine errors. Unauthorized reprints exist of these varieties and of other denominations with inverted centers. **Values unused for Nos. 560-577 are for reprints. Used values are for postally used examples.**
For surcharges and overprints see Nos. 610-616, 635-646, O41-O57, Q19-Q35.

Nos. 455, 461-463 Overprinted

1915 Unwmk. Typo. Perf. 12½x12

582	A31	1k sil, vio & bis brn	2.00	35.00
583	A31	10k multicolored	5.00	35.00
584	A31	20k multicolored	10.00	150.00
585	A31	30k multicolored	12.00	100.00
		Nos. 582-585 (4)	29.00	320.00

Genuine unused examples are rare. Most unused stamps offered in the marketplace are reprints, and the unused values above are for reprints. Used values for authenticated stamps.
Forgeries abound of Nos. 582-585.

IRAN

In May 1917, 17 contemporaneous Russian stamps overprinted "Occupation Azerbayedjan" appeared on the philatelic market. These were a bogus production, purportedly prepared by Anglo-Russian forces in occupation of the province of Azerbaijan in Iran. While British and Russian troops were indeed in the province at that time, they were there strictly to support Persian forces against the Turks, and were in no sense occupiers. Covers canceled with the consular handstamp of Tabriz were privately created to lend credence to the issue. Later, other covers were created using a forged October 1917 datestamp of Baku, causing subsequent catalogs to attribute them to the Russian province of Azerbaijan. The issue has been extensively forged.

No. 491 Surcharged

1917   Perf. 11½
586	A32	12c on 1k multi (on #491a)	2,500. 3,500.
587	A32	24c on 1k multi (on #491a)	1,500. 1,750.

Issued during the Turkish occupation of Kermanshah. Forgeries exist.

No. 448 Overprinted "1335" in Persian Numerals

1917   Perf. 12½x12
588	A31	1c org & maroon	350.00 250.00

Overprint on No. 588 is similar to date in "k" and "l" surcharges. Forgeries exist.

Nos. 449, 452-453, 456 Surcharged

k   l

1917
589	A31(k)	1c on 2c	45.00 5.00
590	A31(k)	1c on 9c	45.00 5.00
591	A31(k)	1c on 10c	45.00 5.00
592	A31(l)	3c on 9c	55.00 5.00
593	A31(l)	3c on 10c	55.00 5.00
594	A31(l)	3c on 26c	55.00 5.00

Same Surcharge on No. 488

595	A32(k)	1c on 10c (on #488)	100.00 4.00
a.		On #488a	100.00 4.00
b.		On #488d	100.00 4.00
596	A32(l)	3c on 10c (on #488)	100.00 4.00

Nos. 454 & 491 Surcharged Type "e"

597	A31	5c on 13c	100.00 10.00
598	A32	5c on 1k (on #489a)	100.00 5.00

Counterfeit surcharges on "canceled" reprints of Nos. 449, 452-454, 456 abound.

No. 489 Surcharged

600	A32	6c on 12c grn & ultra (on #489a)	125.00 20.00

No. 457 Overprinted

1918
601	A31	2k multi	250.00 30.00

No. 601 abound with counterfeit handstamps on reprints of No. 457.

Nos. 459-460 Surcharged

1918
602	A31	24c on 4k multi	250.00 35.00
603	A31	10k on 5k multi	250.00 45.00

Nos. 602-603 abound with counterfeit handstamps on reprints of Nos. 459-460.

Nos. 457-463 Overprinted

1918
603A	A31	2k multicolored	3.00 100.00
604	A31	3k multicolored	3.00 45.00
604A	A31	4k multicolored	5.00 250.00
604B	A31	5k multicolored	5.00 125.00
605	A31	10k multicolored	8.00 100.00
605A	A31	20k multicolored	20.00 450.00
606	A31	30k multicolored	15.00 200.00
		Nos. 603A-606 (7)	59.00 1,270.

Genuine unused examples are rare. Most unused stamps offered in the marketplace are reprints, and the unused values above are for reprints. Used values for authenticated stamps.

Forgeries abound of Nos. 603A-606.

Nos. 489, 488 and 491 Surcharged

m   n

607	A32(m)	3c on 12c (on #489a)	200.00 4.00
608	A32(n)	6c on 10c (on #488a)	200.00 4.00
609	A32(m)	6c on 1k (on #491)	125.00 4.00
a.		On #491a	125.00 4.00
		Nos. 607-609 (3)	525.00 12.00

Nos. 571-577 Overprinted in Black or Red

1918   Wmk. 161
610	A34	2k sil, blue & rose	50.00 25.00
611	A34	3k sil, vio & brn (R)	50.00 25.00
612	A34	5k sil, brn & grn (R)	50.00 25.00
613	A35	1t gold, pur & black (R)	75.00 35.00
614	A35	2t gold, grn & brn	75.00 35.00
615	A35	3t gold, cl & red brn	75.00 35.00
616	A35	5t gold, bl & ind (R)	75.00 35.00
		Nos. 610-616 (7)	450.00 215.00

The overprint commemorates the end of World War I. Counterfeits of this overprint are plentiful.

A36

Color Litho., Black Typo.

1919   Unwmk.   Perf. 11½
617	A36	1c yel & black	50.00 4.00
618	A36	3c green & black	50.00 4.00
619	A36	5c rose & black	150.00 15.00
620	A36	6c vio & black	100.00 4.00
621	A36	12c blue & black	250.00 30.00
		Nos. 617-621 (5)	600.00 57.00

Nos. 617-621 exist imperf.

This issue has been extensively counterfeited, and most examples in the marketplace are forgeries.

Counterfeits having double line over "POSTES" abound.

Nos. 75, 85-86 Surcharged in Various Colors

1919   Perf. 10½, 11, 11½, 13½
622	A14	2k on 5c lilac (Bk)	25.00 25.00
623	A14	3k on 5c lilac (Br)	25.00 25.00
624	A14	4k on 5c lilac (G)	25.00 25.00
625	A14	5k on 5c lilac (V)	25.00 25.00
626	A16	10k on 10c rose (Bl)	35.00 35.00
627	A16	20k on 10c rose (G)	40.00 40.00
628	A16	30k on 10c rose (Br)	50.00 50.00
629	A16	50k on 14c org (V)	75.00 75.00
		Nos. 622-629 (8)	300.00 300.00

Nos. 622-629 exist with inverted and double surcharge. Some specialists consider these fraudulent. Forgeries exist.

Nos. 486, 489 Handstamp Surcharged

1921   Perf. 11½, 11½x11
630	A32	10c on 6c (on #486)	125.00 35.00
631	A32	1k on 12c (on #489)	125.00 35.00
a.		On #489a	125.00 35.00

Counterfeits exist.

No. 489 Surcharged

632	A32	6c on 12c (on #489)	750.00 30.00
a.		On #489a	750.00 30.00

Surcharged in Black or Violet

1921
633	A32	10c on 6c (V) (on #486)	250.00 60.00
a.		Surcharge handstamped in black	450.00 400.00
634	A32	1k on 12c (V) (on #489)	350.00 75.00
a.		On #489a	350.00 75.00
b.		As "a," black surcharge	550.00 400.00

Counterfeits exist.

Coronation Issue of 1915 Overprinted

1921, May   Wmk. 161   Perf. 11, 11½
635	A33	3c dark grn	25.00 200.00
a.		Center and overprint inverted	1,000.
636	A33	5c red	25.00 200.00
637	A33	6c olive grn & car	25.00 200.00
638	A33	10c bl grn & yel brn	25.00 200.00
639	A33	12c ultramarine	25.00 200.00
640	A34	1k sil, yel brn & gray	40.00 300.00
641	A34	2k sil, blue & rose	40.00 300.00
642	A34	5k sil, brn & green	75.00 500.00
643	A35	2t gold, grn & brn	75.00 500.00
644	A35	3t gold, cl & red brn	75.00 500.00
645	A35	5t gold, blue & ind	75.00 500.00
		Nos. 635-645 (11)	505.00 3,600.

A limited number of sets exist with inverted overprints. Counterfeits of both regular and inverted overprints exist. A total of 413 sets were handstamped "SPECIMEN" to be sent to the Universal Postal Union.

Stamps of 1911-13 Overprinted

1922   Unwmk.   Perf. 11½, 11½x11
646	A32	1c grn & orange (on #481)	15.00 .50
a.		Inverted overprint	350.00
b.		On #481a	15.00 .50
c.		As "b," pair, one without	550.00 —
d.		On #481c	200.00 .50
647	A32	2c red & sepia (on #482)	15.00 .50
a.		On #482a	20.00 .50
648	A32	3c brn & green (on #483)	20.00 .50
a.		On #483a	20.00 .50
648C	A32	3c brn & green (on #483B)	20.00 2.00
a.		On #483Ba	20.00 2.00
649	A32	5c brown & car (on #484a)	150.00 65.00
a.		On #484c	200.00 65.00
650	A32	6c grn & red brn (on #486)	15.00 .50
a.		On #486a	15.00 .50
651	A32	9c yel brn & vio (on #487)	20.00 .75
a.		On #487a	20.00 .75
652	A32	10c red & org brn (on #488)	25.00 .75
a.		Double ovpt., one inverted	750.00
b.		On #488a	30.00 2.00
c.		On #488c	50.00 .50
653	A32	12c green & ultra (on #489)	40.00 1.00
a.		Double overprint	600.00
b.		On #489a	40.00 1.00
654	A32	1k ultra & car (on #491)	40.00 2.00
a.		On #491a	40.00 2.00
b.		On #491c	60.00 5.00
655	A32	24c vio & green (on #492)	40.00 2.00
a.		On #492a	40.00 2.00
656	A32	2k grn & red vio (on #494)	110.00 2.00
a.		On #494a	110.00 2.00
657	A32	3k vio & black (on #495)	120.00 3.00
a.		On #495a	120.00 3.00
658	A32	4k ultra & gray (on #496)	300.00 65.00
a.		On #496c	500.00 95.00
b.		On #496e	400.00 100.00
659	A32	5k red & ultra (on #497)	250.00 4.00
660	A32	10k ol bis & cl (on #498)	1,100. 10.00
a.		On #498a	1,100. 10.00
661	A32	20k vio brn & bis (on #499)	1,200. 12.00
a.		On #499a	1,200. 12.00
b.		On #499c	1,300. 30.00
662	A32	30k red & green (on #500)	1,200. 25.00
		Nos. 646-662 (18)	4,680. 196.50

The status of inverted overprints on 5c and 12c is dubious. Unlisted inverts on other denominations are generally considered fraudulent. Counterfeits of this overprint exist.

Nos. 653, 655 Surcharged

IRAN

1922

663	A32	3c on 12c (on #489)	125.00	3.00
a.		On #489a	125.00	3.00
664	A32	6c on 24c (on #492)	250.00	4.00
a.		On #492a	250.00	4.00

Nos. 661-662 Surcharged

Type I

Type II

1923

665	A32	10c on 20k (on #499)	200.00	20.00
666	A32	1k on 30k (on #500), Ty I	250.00	25.00
a.		1k on 30k, Ty 2	250.00	25.00

There are two types of 'K' in 'Kran' — Type I: No. 666, one with straight serifs. Type II: No. 666a with a curved serif on the top right bar. Values are the same for either type.

Forgeries exist, generally made by handstamps applied to mint reprints or postally used original stamps.

Ahmad Shah Qajar — A37

Perf. 11½, 11x11½, 11½x11

1924-25 — *Engr.*

667	A37	1c orange	3.00	.50
668	A37	2c magenta	3.00	.50
a.		Imperf. btwn., pair		6,000.
669	A37	3c org brn	3.00	.50
670	A37	6c blk brn	3.00	.50
671	A37	9c dark green	5.00	5.00
672	A37	10c dark violet	3.00	1.00
673	A37	12c red	3.00	1.00
674	A37	1k dark blue	3.00	1.00
675	A37	2k indigo & red	7.00	5.00
a.		Center inverted	50,000.	8,000.
676	A37	3k dk vio & red brn	20.00	5.00
677	A37	5k red & grn	30.00	35.00
678	A37	10k choc & lilac	35.00	35.00
679	A37	20k dk grn & brn	40.00	40.00
680	A37	30k org & blk brn	45.00	45.00
		Nos. 667-680 (14)	203.00	175.00

For overprints see Nos. 703-706.

A38

SIX CHAHIS

Type I

Type II

Dated 1924
Color Litho., Black Typo.

1924 — *Perf. 11*

681	A38	1c yel brn & blk	25.00	1.50
682	A38	2c gray & blk	25.00	1.50
683	A38	3c dp rose & blk	25.00	1.50
684	A38	6c orange & blk (I)	40.00	1.50
a.		6c orange & blk (II)		
		Nos. 681-684 (4)	115.00	6.00

The 1c was surcharged "Chahis" by error. Later the "s" was blocked out in black.

Counterfeits having double line over "POSTES" are plentiful.

1925 — Dated 1925

686	A38	2c yel grn & blk	15.00	2.00
687	A38	3c red & blk	15.00	2.00
689	A38	6c chalky bl & blk	15.00	2.00
690	A38	9c lt brn & blk	35.00	4.00
691	A38	10c gray & blk	80.00	10.00
694	A38	1k emer & blk	80.00	15.00
695	A38	2k lilac & blk	190.00	50.00
		Nos. 686-695 (7)	430.00	85.00

Values are for authenticated stamps. Like Nos. 617-621, the originals have one line over "POSTES," while there is a double line in the forgeries. Most stamps offered in the market are forgeries.

A39

Gold Overprint on Treasury Department Stamps

1925

697	A39	1c red	20.00	6.00
698	A39	2c yellow	20.00	6.00
699	A39	3c yellow green	20.00	6.00
700	A39	5c dark gray	75.00	30.00
701	A39	10c deep orange	45.00	10.00
702	A39	1k ultramarine	50.00	15.00
		Nos. 697-702 (6)	230.00	73.00

Deposition of Ahmad Shah Qajar and establishment of provisional government of Reza Shah Pahlavi.

Nos. 697-702 have same center (Persian lion in sunburst) with 6 different frames. Overprint reads: "Post / Provisional Government / of Pahlavi / 9th Abanmah / 1304 / 1925."

Nos. 667-670 Overprinted

1926 — *Perf. 11½, 11x11½, 11½x11*

703	A37	1c orange	5.00	3.00
704	A37	2c magenta	5.00	5.00
705	A37	3c orange brown	5.00	3.00
706	A37	6c black brown	125.00	85.00
		Nos. 703-706 (4)	140.00	96.00

Overprinted to commemorate the Pahlavi dynasty, dated 16 December 1925. Counterfeits exist.

Nos. 448-463 Overprinted

1926 — *Perf. 11½, 12½x12*

707	A31	1c org & maroon	20.00	.50
a.		Inverted overprint	2,000.	
708	A31	2c vio & maroon	20.00	.50
709	A31	3c yel grn & mar	20.00	.50
a.		Inverted overprint	2,000.	
710	A31	6c red & maroon	20.00	.50
711	A31	9c gray & mar	20.00	1.00
712	A31	10c red vio & mar	25.00	1.00
713	A31	13c dk bl & mar	30.00	1.00
714	A31	1k multi	65.00	1.00
715	A31	26c dk grn & mar	30.00	1.00
716	A31	2k multi	75.00	3.00
717	A31	3k multi	175.00	5.00
718	A31	4k sil, bl & bis brn	550.00	45.00
719	A31	5k multi	250.00	35.00
720	A31	10k multi	800.00	35.00
721	A31	20k multi	850.00	45.00
722	A31	30k multi	900.00	50.00
		Nos. 707-722 (16)	3,850.	225.00

Overprinted to commemorate the Pahlavi government in 1926.

Values for Nos. 707-722 are for stamps perf. 11½, on thick paper. Stamps perf. 12½x12 on thin paper are worth substantially more.

Forgeries exist perf. 12½x12, with either machine overprints or handstamps. Most of these fakes can be identified by the absence of the top serif of the "1" in "1926."

A40

Reza Shah Pahlavi — A41

1926-29 — *Typo.* — *Perf. 11*

723	A40	1c yellow green	6.00	.25
724	A40	2c gray violet	6.00	.25
725	A40	3c emerald	6.00	.25
727	A40	6c magenta	6.00	.25
728	A40	9c rose	12.00	.50
729	A40	10c bister brown	30.00	5.00
730	A40	12c deep orange	30.00	3.00
731	A40	15c pale ultra	35.00	2.00
733	A41	1k dull bl ('27)	60.00	15.00
734	A41	2k brt vio ('29)	180.00	75.00
		Nos. 723-734 (10)	371.00	101.50

1928 — *Redrawn*

740	A40	1c yellow green	30.00	1.00
741	A40	2c gray violet	30.00	1.00
742	A40	3c emerald	30.00	1.00
743	A40	6c rose	30.00	1.00
		Nos. 740-743 (4)	120.00	4.00

On the redrawn stamps much of the shading of the face, throat, collar, etc., has been removed.

The letters of "Postes Persanes" and those in the circle at upper right are smaller. The redrawn stamps measure 20¼x25¾mm instead of 19¾x25¼mm.

A42

Reza Shah Pahlavi — A43

Perf. 11½, 12, 12½, Compound

1929 — *Photo.*

744	A42	1c yel grn & cer	3.50	.50
745	A42	2c scar & brt blue	3.50	.50
a.		Center inverted	45,000.	7,500.
746	A42	3c mag & myr grn	3.50	.50
747	A42	6c yel brn & ol grn	3.50	.50
a.		Center inverted		7,500.
748	A42	9c Prus bl & ver	5.00	.50
749	A42	10c bl grn & choc	6.00	.50
750	A42	12c gray blk & pur	8.00	.75
751	A42	15c citron & ultra	10.00	.75
752	A42	1k dull bl & blk	15.00	1.00
753	A42	24c ol grn & red brn	12.00	1.00

Engr.
Perf. 11½

754	A42	2k brn org & dk vio	125.00	5.00
755	A42	3k dark grn & dp rose	150.00	7.00
756	A42	5k red brn & dp green	100.00	10.00
757	A42	1t ultra & dp rose	125.00	20.00
758	A42	2t carmine & blk	200.00	30.00

Engr. and Typo.

759	A43	3t gold & dp vio	175.00	60.00
		Nos. 744-759 (16)	945.00	138.50

For overprints see Nos. 810-817.

Reza Shah Pahlavi — A44

1931-32 — *Litho.* — *Perf. 11*

760	A44	1c ol brn & ultra	6.00	.50
761	A44	2c red brn & blk	6.00	.50
762	A44	3c lilac rose & ol	6.00	.50
763	A44	6c red org & vio	6.00	.50
764	A44	9c ultra & red org	12.00	.75
765	A44	10c ver & gray	40.00	2.00
766	A44	11c bl & dull red	37.50	40.00
767	A44	12c turq blue & lil rose	45.00	1.25
768	A44	16c black & red	50.00	2.50
769	A44	1k car & turq bl	85.00	2.50
770	A44	27c dk gray & dl bl	90.00	2.50
		Nos. 760-770 (11)	383.50	53.50

For overprints see Nos. 818-826.

A45

Reza Shah Pahlavi — A46

1933-34

771	A45	5d olive brown	3.00	.50
772	A45	10d blue	3.00	.50
773	A45	15d gray	3.00	.50
774	A45	30d emerald	3.00	.50
775	A45	45d turq blue	3.00	.75
776	A45	50d magenta	4.00	.75
777	A45	60d green	5.00	.75
778	A45	75d brown	8.00	2.00
779	A45	90d red	10.00	3.50
780	A46	1r dk rose & blk	25.00	3.00
781	A46	1.20r gray blk & rose	30.00	3.00
782	A46	1.50 citron & bl	35.00	3.00
783	A46	2r lt bl & choc	45.00	3.00
784	A46	3r mag & green	60.00	5.00
785	A46	5r dk brn & red org	225.00	55.00
		Nos. 771-785 (15)	462.00	81.75

For overprints see Nos. 795-809.

"Justice" A47

"Education" A49

Ruins of Persepolis — A48

Tehran Airport — A50

Sanatorium at Sakhtessar A51

Cement Factory, Chah-Abdul-Azim — A52

Gunboat "Palang" — A53

Railway Bridge over Karun River — A54

IRAN

Post Office and Customs Building, Tehran — A55

1935, Feb. 21		Photo.		Perf. 12½
786	A47	5d red brn & grn	1.00	.75
787	A48	10d red org & gray black	1.00	.75
788	A49	15d mag & Prus bl	1.50	.75
789	A50	30d black & green	1.50	.75
790	A51	45d ol grn & red brn	2.00	.75
791	A52	75d grn & dark brn	6.00	1.25
792	A53	90d blue & car rose	20.00	5.00
793	A54	1r red brn & pur	60.00	30.00
794	A55	1½r violet & ultra	25.00	10.00
		Nos. 786-794 (9)	118.00	50.00

Reign of Reza Shah Pahlavi, 10th anniv.

Stamps of 1933-34 Overprinted in Black

1935			Perf. 11	
795	A45	5d olive brown	4.00	1.00
796	A45	10d blue	4.00	1.00
797	A45	15d gray	4.00	1.00
798	A45	30d emerald	4.00	1.00
799	A45	45d turq blue	12.00	4.00
800	A45	50d magenta	7.00	1.00
801	A45	60d green	8.00	1.00
802	A45	75d brown	15.00	15.00
803	A45	90d red	45.00	45.00
804	A46	1r dk rose & blk	150.00	250.00
805	A46	1.20r gray blk & rose	20.00	3.00
806	A46	1.50r citron & bl	20.00	3.00
807	A46	2r lt bl & choc	50.00	4.00
808	A46	3r mag & green	100.00	15.00
809	A46	5r dk brn & red org	350.00	550.00
		Nos. 795-809 (15)	793.00	895.00

Same Overprint on Stamps of 1929

1935			Perf. 12, 12x12½	
810	A42	1c yel grn & cerise	500.00	600.00
811	A42	2c scar & brt blue	300.00	400.00
812	A42	3c mag & myr grn	200.00	200.00
813	A42	6c yel brn & ol grn	140.00	150.00
814	A42	9c Prus bl & ver	85.00	100.00
		Perf. 11½		
815	A42	1t ultra & dp rose	50.00	75.00
816	A42	2t carmine & blk	50.00	40.00
817	A43	3t gold & dp vio	70.00	50.00
		Nos. 810-817 (8)	1,395.	1,615.

No. 817 is overprinted vertically.
Forged overprints exist.

Same Ovpt. on Stamps of 1931-32

1935			Perf. 11	
818	A44	1c ol brn & ultra	400.00	400.00
819	A44	2c red brn & blk	150.00	150.00
820	A44	3c lil rose & ol	100.00	125.00
821	A44	6c red org & vio	200.00	200.00
822	A44	9c ultra & red org	200.00	225.00
823	A44	11c blue & dull red	12.50	3.50
824	A44	12c turq bl & lil rose	600.00	900.00
825	A44	16c black & red	15.00	5.00
826	A44	27c dk gray & dull bl	19.00	5.00
		Nos. 818-826 (9)	1,697.	2,014.

Forged overprints exist.

Reza Shah Pahlavi — A56

1935		Photo.		Perf. 11
		Size: 19x27mm		
827	A56	5d violet	3.00	.25
828	A56	10d lilac rose	3.00	.25
829	A56	15d turquoise bl	3.00	.25
830	A56	30d emerald	3.00	.25
831	A56	45d orange	3.00	.25
832	A56	50d dull lt brn	4.00	.30
833	A56	60d ultramarine	15.00	.65
834	A56	75d red orange	15.00	.75
835	A56	90d rose	15.00	.75
		Size: 21½x31mm		
836	A56	1r dull lilac	30.00	.50
837	A56	1.50r blue	45.00	2.00
838	A56	2r dk olive grn	45.00	1.25
839	A56	3r dark brown	50.00	4.00
840	A56	5r slate black	275.00	25.00
		Nos. 827-840 (14)	509.00	36.45

Reza Shah Pahlavi — A57

1936-37		Litho.		Perf. 11
		Size: 20x27mm		
841	A57	5d bright vio	4.00	.35
842	A57	10d magenta	4.00	.35
843	A57	15d bright ultra	6.00	.35
844	A57	30d yellow green	25.00	.35
845	A57	45d vermilion	25.00	.35
846	A57	50d blk brn ('37)	30.00	.35
847	A57	60d brown orange	25.00	.35
848	A57	75d rose lake	15.00	.35
849	A57	90d rose red	20.00	.65
		Size: 23x31mm		
850	A57	1r turq green	20.00	.35
851	A57	1.50r deep blue	20.00	.50
852	A57	2r bright blue	35.00	.50
853	A57	3r violet brown	45.00	1.00
854	A57	5r slate green	45.00	2.50
855	A57	10r dk brn & ultra ('37)	225.00	45.00
		Nos. 841-855 (15)	544.00	53.30

Reza Shah Pahlavi — A58

1938-39		Size: 20x27mm		Perf. 11
856	A58	5d light violet	2.50	.25
857	A58	10d magenta	2.50	.25
858	A58	15d violet blue	2.50	.25
859	A58	30d bright green	2.50	.25
860	A58	45d vermilion	4.00	.25
861	A58	50d black brown	4.00	.25
862	A58	60d brown orange	4.00	.25
863	A58	75d rose lake	4.00	.25
864	A58	90d rose red ('39)	7.50	.25
		Size: 22½x30mm		
865	A58	1r turq green	12.00	.25
866	A58	1.50r deep blue	17.00	.30
867	A58	2r lt blue ('39)	70.00	.30
868	A58	3r violet brown	35.00	.70
869	A58	5r gray grn ('39)	60.00	1.25
870	A58	10r dk brn & ultra ('39)	200.00	20.00
		Nos. 856-870 (15)	427.50	25.05

Reza Shah Pahlavi — A58a

1938, Mar. 15				Perf. 13
870A	A58a	5d gray blue	5.00	5.00
870B	A58a	10d brown	5.00	5.00
870C	A58a	30d green	5.00	5.00
870D	A58a	60d dk brn	5.00	5.00
870E	A58a	90d red	7.00	7.00
870F	A58a	1.50r blue	15.00	10.00
870G	A58a	5r lilac	45.00	45.00
870H	A58a	10r carmine	60.00	60.00
		Nos. 870A-870H (8)	147.00	142.00

60th birthday of Reza Shah Pahlavi. Printed in sheets of 4, perf. 13 and imperf. The 1r violet and 2r orange were not available to the public. Value, perf. 13 each, imperf, 35% more. Value of sheets (including 1r and 2r), perf. 13 $1,100, imperf. $1,500.

Crown Prince and Princess Fawziya — A59

1939, Apr. 25		Photo.		Perf. 11½
871	A59	5d red brown	1.00	.50
872	A59	10d bright violet	1.00	.50
873	A59	30d emerald	2.00	.50
874	A59	90d red	15.00	2.00
875	A59	1.50r bright blue	25.00	4.00
		Nos. 871-875 (5)	44.00	7.50

Wedding of Crown Prince Mohammad Reza Pahlavi to Princess Fawziya of Egypt.

Bridge over Karun River — A60

Veresk Bridge, North Iran — A61

Granary, Ahwaz — A62

Train and Bridge — A63

Museum, Side View A64 A67

Ministry of Justice — A65

School Building — A66

Mohammad Reza Shah Pahlavi A68 A69

1942-46		Unwmk.	Litho.	Perf. 11
876	A60	5d violet	5.00	.25
877	A60	5d red org ('44)	2.00	.25
878	A61	10d magenta	5.00	.25
879	A61	10d pck grn ('44)	2.00	.25
880	A62	20d lt red violet	7.50	.25
881	A62	20d mag ('44)	5.00	.25
882	A63	25d rose carmine	65.00	7.00
883	A63	25d violet ('44)	20.00	1.00
884	A64	35d emerald	5.00	.30
885	A65	50d ultramarine	7.50	.30
886	A65	50d emerald ('44)	5.00	.30
887	A66	70d dull vio brn	5.00	.35
888	A67	75d rose lake	25.00	.35
889	A67	75d rose car ('46)	25.00	.35
890	A68	1r carmine	25.00	.25
891	A68	1r maroon ('45)	25.00	.25
892	A68	1.50r red	25.00	.25
893	A68	2r light blue	75.00	.25
894	A68	2r sage grn ('44)	5.00	.30
895	A68	2.50r dark blue	30.00	.25
896	A68	3r peacock grn	150.00	5.00
897	A68	3r brt vio ('44)	75.00	.25
898	A68	5r sage green	400.00	10.00
899	A68	5r lt blue ('44)	50.00	.50
900	A69	10r brn org & blk	100.00	3.00
901	A69	10r dk org brn & black ('44)	75.00	1.00
902	A69	20r choc & vio	1,200.	150.00
903	A69	20r org & blk ('44)	200.00	
904	A69	30r gray blk & emer	1,750.	175.00
905	A69	30r emer & blk ('44)	175.00	7.50
906	A69	50r dl bl & brn red	450.00	40.00
907	A69	50r brt vio & blk ('45)	150.00	12.00
908	A69	100r rose red & blk ('45)	800.00	75.00
909	A69	200r bl & blk ('45)	800.00	75.00
		Nos. 876-909 (34)	6,789.	572.35

Sixteen denominations of this issue were handstamped at Tabriz in 1945-46 in Persian characters: "Azerbaijan National Government, Dec. 12, 1945." A rebel group did this overprinting while the Russian army held that area. Value, set: unused $900; used $140.

Flag of Iran — A70

Designs: 50d, Docks at Bandar Shapur. 1.50r, Motor convoy. 2.50r, Gorge and railway viaduct. 5r, Map and Mohammad Reza Shah Pahlavi.

Inscribed: "En souvenir des efforts de l'Iran pour la Victoire"

1949, Apr. 28		Engr. & Litho.		Perf. 12½
910	A70	25d multicolored	15.00	15.00
		Engr.		
911	A70	50d purple	5.00	3.00
	a.	Imperf.	650.00	
912	A70	1.50r carmine rose	15.00	3.00
913	A70	2.50r deep blue	20.00	5.00
	a.	Imperf.	700.00	
914	A70	5r green	50.00	5.00
	a.	Imperf.	850.00	
		Nos. 910-914 (5)	105.00	31.00

Iran's contribution toward the victory of the Allied Nations in World War II.

Bank Melli Building, Tehran — A71

Post and Customs House, Tehran — A72

Former Ministry of P.T.T. — A73

Mohammad Reza Shah Pahlavi — A74

Shah and: 5d, Ramsar Hotel, Caspian Sea. 10d, Bridge over Zaindeh River. 25d, Old Royal Palace, Isfahan. 50d, Chaharbagh Madrassa, Isfahan. 75d, Railway Station. 1r, Ministry of Justice, Tehran. 1.50r, Shah Mosque, Tehran. 2.50r, Parliament, Tehran. 3r, Great Gate, Isfahan. 5r, Building, Isfahan.

1949-50		Unwmk.	Litho.	Perf. 10½
915	A71	5d rose & dk grn	2.00	.25
916	A71	10d ultra & brown	2.00	.25
917	A71	20d vio & ultra	2.00	.25
918	A71	25d blk brn & dp blue	2.00	.25
919	A71	50d grn & ultra	3.00	.25
920	A71	75d dk brn & red	3.50	.25
921	A72	1r vio & green	3.50	.25
922	A72	1.50r dk grn & ver	4.50	.25
923	A72	2r dp car & blk brn	6.00	.25
924	A72	2.50r chlky bl & bl	7.00	.25

IRAN

Scott #	Type	Description	Unused	Used
925	A72	3r vio bl & red org	8.00	.25
926	A72	5r dp car & vio	15.00	.25
927	A73	10r car & bl grn ('50)	45.00	.50
a.		Inverted center	3,500.	
928	A73	20r brn blk & red ('50)	350.00	20.00
929	A74	30r choc & dp blue ('50)	120.00	20.00
930	A74	50r red & dp blue ('50)	125.00	20.00
		Nos. 915-930 (16)	697.50	63.50

Globes and Pigeons — A75

Symbols of UPU — A76

1950, Mar. 16 — Photo.

| 931 | A75 | 50d brn carmine | 25.00 | 20.00 |
| 932 | A76 | 2.50r deep blue | 30.00 | 27.50 |

UPU, 75th anniv. (in 1949).

Reza Shah Pahlavi and his Tomb A77

1950, May 8

| 933 | A77 | 50d brown | 20.00 | 12.50 |
| 934 | A77 | 2r sepia | 30.00 | 15.00 |

Re-burial of Reza Shah Pahlavi, May 12, 1950.

Mohammad Reza Shah Pahlavi, 31st Birthday — A78

Various portraits.

1950, Oct. 26 — Engr. — Perf. 12½
Center in Black

935	A78	25d carmine	10.00	2.00
936	A78	50d orange	10.00	2.00
937	A78	75d brown	30.00	12.00
938	A78	1r green	25.00	10.00
939	A78	2.50r deep blue	25.00	10.00
940	A78	5r brown lake	40.00	10.00
		Nos. 935-940 (6)	140.00	46.00

Shah and Queen Soraya — A79

A80

1951, Feb. 12 — Litho. — Perf. 10½

941	A79	5d rose violet	4.50	1.00
942	A79	25d orange red	4.50	1.00
943	A79	50d emerald	7.50	1.00
944	A80	1r brown	12.00	2.00
945	A80	1.50r carmine	17.00	2.00
946	A80	2.50r blue	35.00	4.50
		Nos. 941-946 (6)	80.50	11.50

Wedding of Mohammad Reza Shah Pahlavi to Soraya Esfandiari.

Farabi — A81

1951, Feb. 20

| 947 | A81 | 50d red | 15.00 | 2.00 |
| 948 | A81 | 2.50r blue | 20.00 | 3.00 |

Death millenary of Farabi, Persian philosopher.

Mohammad Reza Shah Pahlavi
A82   A83

1951-52 — Unwmk. — Photo. — Perf. 10½

950	A82	5d brown orange	1.00	.25
951	A82	10d violet	1.00	.25
952	A82	20d choc ('52)	2.00	.35
953	A82	25d blue ('52)	2.50	.25
954	A82	50d green	3.00	.25
955	A82	75d rose	4.00	.30
956	A83	1r gray green	4.00	.25
957	A83	1.50r cerise	4.00	.45
958	A83	2r chocolate	6.00	.25
959	A83	2.50r deep blue	7.00	.25
960	A83	3r red orange	8.00	.25
961	A83	5r dark green	15.00	.25
962	A83	10r olive ('52)	45.00	.50
963	A83	20r org brn ('52)	20.00	3.00
964	A83	30r vio bl ('52)	35.00	2.00
965	A83	50r blk brn ('52)	75.00	7.50
		Nos. 950-965 (16)	247.50	16.35

See Nos. 975-977.

Oil Well and Mosque A84

Oil Well, Mosque and Monument A85

1953, Feb. 20 — Litho.

966	A84	50d green & yel	4.00	1.00
967	A85	1r lil rose & yel	4.00	1.00
968	A84	2.50r blue & yellow	7.00	2.50
969	A85	5r blk brn & yel	10.00	5.00
		Nos. 966-969 (4)	25.00	9.50

Discovery of oil at Qum.

Abadan Oil Refinery A86

Super Fractionators A87

1953, Mar. 20 — Photo.

970	A86	50d blue green	5.00	2.50
971	A86	1r rose	6.00	2.50
972	A87	2.50r bright ultra	10.00	5.00
973	A86	5r red orange	15.00	7.00
974	A86	10r dark violet	20.00	8.00
		Nos. 970-974 (5)	56.00	25.00

Nationalization of oil industry, 2nd anniv.

Shah Types of 1951-52

1953-54 — Photo. — Perf. 10½

975	A82	50d dark gray grn	100.00	.50
976	A83	1r dk blue green	5.00	.50
977	A83	1.50r cerise ('54)	7.00	.50
		Nos. 975-977 (3)	112.00	1.50

The background has been highlighted on the 1r and 1.50r.

Gymnast A88

Archery A89

Designs: 3r, Climbing Mt. Demavend. 5r, Ancient polo. 10r, Lion hunting.

1953, Oct. 26

978	A88	1r deep green	12.00	7.00
979	A89	2.50fr brt grnsh bl	20.00	10.00
980	A89	3r gray	25.00	10.00
981	A88	5r bister	25.00	15.00
982	A88	10r rose lilac	75.00	30.00
		Nos. 978-982 (5)	157.00	72.00

Mother with Children and UN Emblem — A90

1953, Oct. 24

| 983 | A90 | 1r bl grn & dk grn | 2.00 | .75 |
| 984 | A90 | 2.50r lt bl & indigo | 3.00 | 1.25 |

United Nations Day, Oct. 24.

Herring A91

Refrigeration Compressor A92

Processing Equipment, National Fisheries — A93

Designs: 2.50r, Sardines. 10r, Sturgeon.

1954, Jan. 31

985	A91	1r multi	15.00	10.00
986	A91	2.50r multi	45.00	20.00
987	A92	3r vermilion	20.00	10.00
988	A93	5r deep bl grn	20.00	10.00
989	A91	10r multi	75.00	35.00
		Nos. 985-989 (5)	175.00	85.00

Nationalization of fishing industry.

Broken Shackles — A94

3r, Torch flag. 5r, Citizen holding flag of Iran.

1954, Aug. 19 — Litho.

990	A94	2r multicolored	15.00	5.00
991	A94	3r multicolored	20.00	10.00
992	A94	5r multicolored	30.00	15.00
		Nos. 990-992 (3)	65.00	30.00

Return of the royalist government, 1st anniv.

Mother Feeding Baby — A95

1954, Oct. 24 — Photo.

| 993 | A95 | 2r red lil & org | 2.50 | 1.00 |
| 994 | A95 | 3r vio bl & org | 3.50 | 1.50 |

Issued to honor the United Nations.

Woodsman Felling Tree — A96

Designs: 2.50r, Laborer carrying firewood. 5r, Worker operating saw. 10r, Wooden galley.

1954, Dec. 11

995	A96	1r brn & grnsh black	40.00	30.00
996	A96	2.50r grnsh blk & bl	50.00	35.00
997	A96	5r lil & dk brn	75.00	60.00
998	A96	10r bl & claret	100.00	80.00
		Nos. 995-998 (4)	265.00	205.00

4th World Forestry Congress, Dehra Dun, India, 1954.

Mohammad Reza Shah Pahlavi
A97   A98

1954-55 — Unwmk.

999	A97	5d yellow brn	2.00	.25
1000	A97	10d violet	2.00	.25
1001	A97	25d scarlet	2.00	.25
1002	A97	50d black brn	2.00	.25
1003	A98	1r blue green	2.00	.25
1004	A98	1.50r cerise	2.00	.25
1005	A98	2r ocher	3.50	.25
1006	A98	2.50r blue	4.00	.25
1007	A98	3r olive	10.00	.25
1008	A98	5r dk sl grn	10.00	1.50
1009	A98	10r lilac rose	30.00	1.50
1010	A98	20r indigo	60.00	12.00
1011	A98	30r dp yel brn	200.00	35.00
1012	A98	50r dp orange	75.00	25.00
1013	A98	100r light vio	500.00	125.00
1014	A98	200r yellow	175.00	50.00
		Nos. 999-1014 (16)	1,080.	252.25

See Nos. 1023-1036.

Regional Costume — A99

Regional Costumes: 1r, 2r, Men's costumes. 2.50r, 3r, 5r, Women's costumes.

1955, June 26 — Photo. — Perf. 11

1015	A99	1r bluish gray & multi	15.00	10.00
1016	A99	2r dl rose & multi	15.00	10.00
1017	A99	2.50r buff & multi	35.00	20.00
1018	A99	3r rose lil & multi	20.00	10.00
1019	A99	5r gray brn & multi	40.00	20.00
		Nos. 1015-1019 (5)	125.00	70.00

Parliament Gate — A100

Designs: 3r, Statue of Liberty, vert. 5r, Old Gate of Parliament.

1955, Aug. 6 — Wmk. 306 — Perf. 11

1020	A100	2r red vio & grn	5.00	3.00
1021	A100	3r dk bl & aqua	12.00	4.00
1022	A100	5r Prus grn & red org	15.00	8.00
		Nos. 1020-1022 (3)	32.00	15.00

50th anniversary of constitution.

Shah Types of 1954-55

1955-56 — Wmk. 306 — Perf. 11

1023	A97	5d violet ('56)	5.00	1.50
1024	A97	10d carmine ('56)	2.00	.25
1025	A97	25d brown	2.00	.25
1026	A97	50d dk carmine	2.00	.25
1027	A98	1r dark bl grn	2.00	.25
1028	A98	1.50r red brn ('56)	85.00	3.00

IRAN

1029	A98	2r ol grn ('56)	40.00	.25
1030	A98	2.50r blue ('56)	7.00	.30
1031	A98	3r bister	10.00	.25
1032	A98	5r red lilac	12.00	.25
1033	A98	10r brt grnsh bl	10.00	.35
1034	A98	20r slate green	50.00	5.00
1035	A98	30r red org ('56)	90.00	30.00
1036	A98	50r red brn ('56)	175.00	40.00
	Nos. 1023-1036 (14)		492.00	81.90

UN Emblem and Globes — A101

1955, Oct. 24 — Perf. 11x12½
1039	A101	1r dp car & org	1.25	.75
1040	A101	2.50r dk bl & grnsh blue	1.50	1.25

UN, 10th anniv., Oct. 24, 1955.

Wrestlers — A102

1955, Oct. 26 — Wmk. 306 — Perf. 11
1041	A102	2.50r multi	12.00	6.00

Victory in intl. wrestling competitions.

Garden, Namazi Hospital A103

Immortal Guardsman A105

Namazi Hospital, Shiraz — A104

5r, Gate of the Koran. 10r, Ha'fez of Shiraz.

1956, Mar. 21 — Perf. 11x12½
1042	A103	50d multi	5.00	2.00
1043	A104	1r multi	6.00	2.50
1044	A105	2.50r multi	9.00	7.00
1045	A104	5r multi	15.00	6.00
1046	A105	10r multi	25.00	10.00
	Nos. 1042-1046 (5)		60.00	27.50

Opening of Namazi Hospital, Shiraz.

Arms of Iran and Olympic Rings — A106

1956, May 15 — Wmk. 306
1047	A106	5r rose lilac	35.00	22.50

National Olympic Committee, 10th anniv.

Tomb at Maragheh — A107

2.50r, Astrolabe. 5r, Nasr-ud-Din of Tus.

1956, May 26 — Photo. — Perf. 11x12½
1048	A107	1r orange	6.50	2.00
1049	A107	2.50r deep ultra	8.50	2.50
1050	A107	5r sepia & pur	12.50	3.00
	Nos. 1048-1050 (3)		27.50	7.50

700th death anniv. of Nasr-up-Din of Tus, mathematician and astronomer.

WHO Emblem — A108

Perf. 11x12½
1956, Sept. 19 — Wmk. 306
1051	A108	6r cerise	4.00	1.50

6th Regional Congress of the WHO.

Scout Bugler and Camp — A109

1956, Aug. 5 — Perf. 12½x11
1052	A109	2.50r ultra & blue	20.00	7.50
1053	A109	5r lil & red lil	20.00	12.50

National Boy Scout Jamboree.

Catalogue values for unused stamps in this section, from this point to the end of the section, are for Never Hinged items.

Former Telegraph Office, Tehran — A110

6r, Telegraph lines & ancient monument.

1956, Oct. 26
1054	A110	2.50r brt bl & grn, bluish	15.00	6.00
1055	A110	6r rose car & lil	20.00	7.00

Centenary of Persian telegraph system.

UN Emblem and People of the World — A111

Design: 2.50r, UN Emblem and scales.

1956, Oct. 24
1056	A111	1r bluish green	1.25	.40
1057	A111	2.50r blue & green	2.75	.60

United Nations Day, Oct. 24.

Shah and Pres. Iskander Mirza of Pakistan — A112

1956, Oct. 31
1058	A112	1r multicolored	15.00	2.50

Visit of Pres. General Iskander Mirza of Pakistan to Tehran, Oct. 31-Nov. 10.

Mohammad Reza Shah Pahlavi
A113   A114

Perf. 13½x11
1956-57 — Wmk. 306 — Photo.
1058A	A113	5d brt car & red	.90	.90
1058B	A113	10d vio bl & dl vio	.90	.90
1059	A113	25d dk brn & brn	1.10	.35
1059A	A113	50d brn & ol brn	1.10	.25
1060	A113	1r brn & brt grn	1.25	.25
1061	A113	1.50r brt lil & brn	1.25	.25
1062	A113	2r red vio & red	1.75	.25
1063	A113	2.50r ultra & blue	1.75	.25
1064	A113	3r brn & dk ol bis	2.25	.25
1065	A113	5r ver & mar	2.75	.25
1066	A114	6r dk vio & brn lil	9.00	.25
1067	A114	10r lt blue & grn	15.00	.25
1068	A114	20r green & blue	30.00	3.00
1069	A114	30r rose red & org	55.00	7.50
1070	A114	50r dk grn & ol grn	60.00	17.50
1071	A114	100r lilac & cer	400.00	30.00
1072	A114	200r dp plum & vio bl	250.00	20.00
	Nos. 1058A-1072 (17)		834.00	82.40

b. Inverted center 3,750.

Issued: 1.50r, 2r, 3r, 5r, 6r, 1956; others, 1957.
See Nos. 1082-1098.

Lord Baden-Powell — A115

1957, Feb. 22 — Perf. 12½
1073	A115	10r dk grn & brn	12.00	7.50

Birth cent. of Robert Baden-Powell, founder of the Boy Scout movement.

Railroad Tracks A116   **Train and Map A117**

Design: 10r, Train and mosque.

1957, May 2 — Perf. 11x12½, 12½x11
1074	A116	2.50r grnsh blk, bl & ocher	30.00	7.00
1075	A117	5r multi	35.00	10.00
1076	A116	10r blk, yel & bl	45.00	20.00
	Nos. 1074-1076 (3)		110.00	37.00

Opening of the Tehran Meshed-Railway.

Pres. Giovanni Gronchi of Italy and Shah A118

Design: 6r, Ruins of Persepolis and Colosseum in Rome and flags.

1957, Sept. 7 — Wmk. 316 — Photo. — Perf. 11
1077	A118	2r slate bl, grn & red	10.00	3.00
1078	A118	6r slate bl, grn & red	15.00	4.00

Visit of Pres. Giovanni Gronchi of Italy to Iran, Sept. 7.

Queen Soraya and Hospital — A119

1957, Sept. 29 — Wmk. 316 — Perf. 11
1079	A119	2r lt bl & grn	10.00	3.00

Sixth Medical Congress, Ramsar.

Globes Showing Location of Iran A120

1957, Oct. 22 — Litho. — Perf. 12½x11
1080	A120	10r blk, lt bl, yel & red	10.00	3.00

Intl. Cartographic Conference, Tehran.

Shah and King Faisal II — A121

1957, Oct. 18 — Photo.
1081	A121	2r slate bl, grn & red	15.00	4.00

Visit of King Faisal of Iraq, Oct. 19.

Shah Types of 1956-57

1957-58 — Wmk. 316 — Perf. 11
1082	A114	5d violet & pur	1.00	2.00
1083	A114	10d claret & rose car	1.00	2.00
1084	A114	25d rose car & brick red	1.00	.35
1085	A114	50d grn & ol grn	1.25	.25
1086	A114	1r dark green	1.50	.25
1087	A114	1.50r claret & red lil	2.00	.25
1088	A114	2r bl & grnsh blue	3.00	.25
1089	A114	2.50r dk bl & blue	3.00	.25
1090	A114	3r rose car & ver	3.50	.25
1091	A114	5r violet blue	3.50	.25
1092	A113	6r bright blue	5.00	.25
1093	A113	10r deep green	7.50	.30
1094	A113	20r grn & olive grn	45.00	1.00
1095	A113	30r vio bl & dk brn	60.00	15.00
1096	A113	50r dk brn & lt brn	65.00	15.00
1097	A113	100r rose lil & car rose	200.00	35.00
1098	A113	200r vio & yel brn	175.00	40.00
	Nos. 1082-1098 (17)		578.25	112.65

Issued: 1.50r, 2r, 3r, 1957; others, 1958.

Weight Lifter — A122

1957, Nov. 8 — Perf. 11x14½
1099	A122	10r bl, grn & red	13.00	4.50

Iran's victories in weight lifting.

IRAN

Modern and Old Houses, Radio Transmitter — A123

1958, Feb. 22   Litho.
1100   A123   10r brn, ocher & bl   10.00   5.00
30th anniversary of radio in Iran.

Oil Derrick and Symbolic Flame — A124

Wmk. 316
1958, Mar. 10   Photo.   Perf. 11
1101   A124   2r gray & multi   7.50   1.50
1102   A124   10r multicolored   10.00   2.50
Drilling of Iran's 1st oil well, 50th anniv.

Train on Viaduct — A125

Design: 8r, Train and map.

1958, Apr. 24   Wmk. 306   Perf. 11
1103   A125   6r dull purple   20.00   6.00
1104   A125   8r green   30.00   7.50
Opening of Tehran-Tabriz railway line.

Exposition Emblem — A126

1958, Apr. 17   Perf. 12½x11
1105   A126   2.50r bl & light bl   1.25   .30
1106   A126   6r car & salmon   2.25   .50
World's Fair, Brussels, Apr. 17-Oct. 19.

Mohammad Reza Shah Pahlavi — A127

1958-59   Wmk. 316   Photo.   Perf. 11
1107   A127   5d blue violet   1.00   .25
1108   A127   10d lt vermilion   1.00   .25
1109   A127   25d crimson   1.00   .25
1110   A127   50d brt blue   1.00   .25
1111   A127   1r dark green   2.00   .25
1113   A127   2r dark brown   12.50   .25
1115   A127   3r dk red brown   20.00   .25
1117   A127   6r bright blue   10.00   .45
1118   A127   8r magenta   10.00   .35
1120   A127   14r blue violet   17.50   2.00
1121   A127   20r green   35.00   1.00
   a.   Wmk. 306   35.00   20.00
1122   A127   30r brt car rose   30.00   5.00
1123   A127   50r rose violet   65.00   15.00
1124   A127   100r red orange   35.00   10.00
1125   A127   200r slate green   125.00   15.00
   Nos. 1107-1125 (15)   366.00   50.55
See Nos. 1138-1151, 1173-1179.

UN Emblem and Map of Iran — A128

1958, Oct. 24
1126   A128   6r bright blue   1.50   1.00
1127   A128   10r dk violet & grn   2.50   1.25
Issued for United Nations Day, Oct. 24.

Globe and Hands — A129

1958, Dec. 10
1128   A129   6r dk red brn & brn   1.50   .50
1129   A129   8r dk grn & gray grn   2.50   .75
Universal Declaration of Human Rights, 10th anniv.

Rudaki — A130

Design: 5r, Rudaki, different pose. 10r, Same design as No. 1130.

1958, Dec. 24   Photo.   Wmk. 306
1130   A130   2.50r bluish black   10.00   3.50
1131   A130   5r violet   15.00   5.00
1132   A130   10r dark brown   27.50   8.00
   Nos. 1130-1132 (3)   52.50   16.50
1100th birth anniv. of Rudaki, blind Persian poet.

Flag — A130a

Design: 1r & 6r, Red Lion & Sun flag (Iranian Red Cross Organization).

1959, May 8   Perf. 14½x11   Wmk. 316
1132A   A130a   1r multicolored   5.00   2.00
1132B   A130a   6r multicolored   7.00   3.00
Centenary of the Red Cross.

Wrestlers, Flag and Globe — A131

1959   Litho.   Perf. 11x12½
1133   A131   6r multicolored   17.50   10.00
World Wrestling Championships, Tehran.

Globe, UN Building and Hand Holding Torch of Freedom — A132

1959, Oct. 24   Photo.   Perf. 11
1134   A132   6r gray brn, red & bister   2.00   .60
Issued for United Nations Day, Oct. 24.

Shah and Pres. Ayub Khan of Pakistan A133

1959, Nov. 9   Litho.   Perf. 11x16
1135   A133   6r multicolored   12.50   5.00
Visit of Pres. Khan to Iran.

ILO Emblem — A134

1959, Nov. 12   Perf. 16
1136   A134   1r blue   2.00   .50
1137   A134   5r brown   3.00   .75
ILO, 40th anniversary.

Shah Type of 1958-59

1959-63   Wmk. 316   Photo.   Perf. 11
1138   A127   5d red brn ('60)   1.00   .30
1139   A127   10d Prus grn ('60)   1.00   .30
   a.   10d Prussian blue ('63)   1.50   .50
1140   A127   25d orange   2.00   .25
   a.   Perf. 12x11½   100.00   30.00
1141   A127   50d scarlet   2.00   .25
1142   A127   1r deep violet   2.00   .25
1142A   A127   2r brown   12.50   .25
1143   A127   3r olive   5.00   .25
1143A   A127   6r cobalt blue   10.00   .25
1144   A127   8r brown olive   3.00   .25
1145   A127   10r ol blk ('60)   3.00   .25
1146   A127   14r yel green   4.00   .25
   a.   14r emerald green   6.50   .50
1147   A127   20r sl grn ('60)   10.00   .35
1148   A127   30r choc ('60)   20.00   4.00
1149   A127   50r dp blue ('60)   20.00   4.00
1150   A127   100r green ('60)   175.00   15.00
1151   A127   200r cer ('60)   275.00   20.00
   Nos. 1138-1151 (16)   545.50   46.20
See Pakistan 274-276, Turkey 1813-1815.

Pahlavi Foundation Bridge, Karun River — A135

Design: 5r, Bridge, different view.

1960, Feb. 29   Litho.   Perf. 16x11
1152   A135   1r dk brn & brt bl   2.50   1.00
   a.   Perf. 13½x11   150.00
1153   A135   5r blue & emerald   3.50   1.50
Opening of Pahlavi Foundation Bridge at Khorramshahr on the Karun River.

A136   Uprooted Oak Emblem — A136a

Design: 6r, Arched frame.

1960, Apr. 7   Perf. 11
1154   A136   1r brt ultra   2.25   .50
1155   A136a   6r gray & sage grn   1.00   .75
World Refugee Year, 7/1/59-6/30/60.

Mosquito A137   Man with Spray Gun A138

Design: 3r, Mosquito on water.

1960, Apr. 7   Wmk. 316
1156   A137   1r blk & red, yel   2.50   2.00
1157   A138   2r lt bl, ultra & blk   4.50   2.00
1158   A137   3r blk & red, yel grn   6.00   3.00
   Nos. 1156-1158 (3)   13.00   7.00
Issued to publicize malaria control.

Polo Player — A139

Design: 6r, Persian archer.

1960, June 9   Litho.   Wmk. 316
1159   A139   1r deep claret   2.50   .50
1160   A139   6r dk blue & lt blue   4.00   1.00
17th Olympic Games, Rome, 8/25-9/11.

Shah and King Hussein of Jordan A140

1960, July 6   Perf. 11
1161   A140   6r multicolored   10.00   4.00
Visit of King Hussein of Jordan to Tehran.

Iranian Scout Emblem in Flower A141   Tents and Pillars of Persepolis A142

1960, July 18
1162   A141   1r green   1.50   .50
1163   A142   6r brn, brt bl & buff   2.50   .75
3rd National Boy Scout Jamboree.

Shah and Queen Farah A143

1960, Sept. 9   Litho.   Perf. 11
1164   A143   1r green   5.00   1.50
1165   A143   5r blue   10.00   2.00
Marriage of Shah Mohammad Reza Shah Pahlavi and Farah Diba.

UN Emblem and Globe — A144

1960, Oct. 24   Wmk. 316
1166   A144   6r bl, blk & lt brn   2.50   .50
15th anniversary of the United Nations.

Shah and Queen Elizabeth II — A145

1961, Mar. 2   Litho.   Perf. 11
1167   A145   1r lt red brown   2.50   .45
1168   A145   6r bright ultra   4.00   .65
Visit of Queen Elizabeth II to Tehran, Feb. 1961.

IRAN

Girl Playing Arganoon — A146

Safiaddin Amavi — A147

1961, Apr. 10   **Wmk. 316**   *Perf. 11*
1169	A146	1r dk brown & buff	1.25	.50
1170	A147	6r greenish gray	2.00	.75

International Congress of Music, Tehran.

Shah Type of 1958-59 Redrawn

1961-62   *Litho.*   *Perf. 11*
1173	A127	25d orange	5.00	.50
1174	A127	50d scarlet	5.00	.40
1175	A127	1r deep violet	8.00	.25
1176	A127	2r chocolate	10.00	.25
1177	A127	3r olive brown	12.00	.50
1178	A127	6r brt blue ('62)	65.00	3.50
1179	A127	8r brown ol ('62)	35.00	2.25
		Nos. 1173-1179 (7)	140.00	7.65

On Nos. 1173-1179 (lithographed), a single white line separates the lower panel from the shah's portrait. On Nos. 1107-1125, 1138-1151 (photogravure), two lines, one in color and one in white, separate panel from portrait. Other minor differences exist.

Shah and Queen Farah Holding Crown Prince — A148

1961, June 2   *Litho.*
1186	A148	1r bright pink	4.50	1.25
1187	A148	6r light blue	7.50	4.00

Birth of Crown Prince Reza Kourosh Pahlavi, Oct. 31, 1960.

Swallows and UN Emblem — A149

1961, Oct. 24   *Perf. 11*
1188	A149	2r blue & car rose	1.00	.25
1189	A149	6r blue & violet	1.50	.35

Issued for United Nations Day, Oct. 24.

Planting Tree — A150

1962, Jan. 11
1190	A150	2r ol grn, citron & dk bl	1.50	.25
1191	A150	6r ultra, grn & pale bl	2.50	.35

Tree Planting Day.

Worker and Symbols of Labor and Agriculture — A151

1962, Mar. 15   *Litho.*
1192	A151	2r bl grn, brn & blk	1.75	.25
1193	A151	6r lt ultra, brn & blk	2.25	.35

Issued for Workers' Day.

Map, Family and Cogwheel — A152

1962, Mar. 20   *Perf. 11*
1194	A152	2r black, yel & lil	1.50	.30
1195	A152	6r black, bl & ultra	2.50	.65

Social Insurance Week.

Sugar Refinery, Khuzistan — A153

1962, Apr. 14   *Wmk. 316*
1196	A153	2r dk & lt blue & grn	1.50	.35
1197	A153	6r ultra, buff & blue	2.00	.65

Opening of sugar refinery in Khuzistan.

Karaj Dam — A154

1962, May 15
1198	A154	2r dk brn & gray grn	2.25	.25
1199	A154	6r vio bl & lt blue	1.75	.50

Inauguration of Karaj Dam, renamed Amir Kabir Dam.

Sefid Rud Dam — A155

1962, May 19   *Litho.*
1200	A155	2r dk grn, lt bl & buff	2.00	.35
1201	A155	6r red brn, sl grn & lt blue	3.00	.65

Inauguration of Sefid Rud Dam.

"UNESCO" and UN Emblem — A156

1962, June 2   *Wmk. 316*   *Perf. 11*
1202	A156	2r black, emer & red	1.50	.30
1203	A156	6r blue, emer & red	2.00	.50

15th anniv. of UNESCO.

Malaria Eradication Emblem and Sprayer — A157

2r, Emblem & arrow piercing mosquito, horiz. 10r, Emblem & globe, horiz. Sizes: 2r, 10r, 40x25mm; 6r, 29½x34½mm.

1962, June 20
1204	A157	2r black & bluish grn	1.50	.35
1205	A157	6r pink & vio blue	1.75	.50
1206	A157	10r lt blue & ultra	2.00	.75
		Nos. 1204-1206 (3)	5.25	1.60

WHO drive to eradicate malaria.

Oil Field and UN Emblem — A158

1962, Sept. 1   *Photo.*
1207	A158	6r grnsh blue & brn	2.50	.50
1208	A158	14r gray & sepia	3.00	1.00

2nd Petroleum Symposium of ECAFE (UN Economic Commission for Asia and the Far East).

Mohammad Reza Shah Pahlavi — A159

Palace of Darius, Persepolis — A160

1962   *Photo.*   *Wmk. 316*   *Perf. 11*
1209	A159	5d green	.90	.25
1210	A159	10d chestnut	.90	.50
1211	A159	25d dark blue	.90	.35
1212	A159	50d Prus green	.90	.25
a.		Perf. 10½x11	1.75	.25
b.		Perf. 11x10½	1.75	.25
1213	A159	1r orange	2.75	.25
a.		Perf. 10½x11	3.50	.25
b.		Perf. 11x10½	3.50	.25
1214	A159	2r violet blue	2.75	.25
a.		Perf. 10½x11	3.50	.25
b.		Perf. 11x10½	3.50	.25
1215	A159	5r dark brown	3.50	.25
a.		Perf. 10½x11	3.50	.25
1216	A160	6r blue	10.00	.25
a.		Perf. 10½x11	13.50	2.50
1217	A160	8r yellow grn	6.25	1.00
a.		Perf. 10½x11	9.50	1.00
1218	A160	10r grnsh blue	9.00	.50
a.		Perf. 10½x11	9.50	.50
b.		Perf. 11x10½	9.50	.50
1219	A160	11r slate green	5.50	.65
a.		Perf. 10½x11	9.50	.65
1220	A160	14r purple	11.00	.65
a.		Perf. 10½x11	13.50	.65
1221	A160	20r red brown	13.50	1.50
a.		Perf. 10½x11	18.00	1.50
1222	A160	50r vermilion	16.00	1.50
a.		Perf. 10½x11	22.50	1.50
		Nos. 1209-1222 (14)	83.85	10.40

See Nos. 1331-1344.

Hippocrates and Avicenna — A161

1962, Oct. 7   *Litho.*
1226	A161	2r brown, buff & ultra	2.75	.50
1227	A161	6r grn, pale grn & ultra	3.75	.75

Near and Middle East Medical Congress.

Hands Laying Bricks — A162

Design: 6r, Houses and UN emblem, vert.

1962, Oct. 24
1228	A162	6r dk blue & ultra	2.00	.35
1229	A162	14r dk blue & emer	2.50	.60

Issued for United Nations Day, Oct. 24.

Crown Prince Receiving Flowers — A163

1962, Oct. 31
1230	A163	6r blue gray	6.00	1.00
1231	A163	14r dull green	12.00	1.90

Children's Day, Oct. 31; 2nd birthday of Crown Prince Reza.

Map of Iran and Persian Gulf — A164

1962, Dec. 12   *Wmk. 316*   *Perf. 11*
1232	A164	6r dk & lt bl, vio bl & rose	2.00	.35
1233	A164	14r dk & lt bl, pink & rose	2.50	.60

The Persian Gulf Seminar.

Hilton Hotel, Tehran — A165

1963, Jan. 21   *Photo.*
1234	A165	6r deep blue	4.00	.45
1235	A165	14r dark red brown	6.00	.60

Opening of the Royal Tehran Hilton Hotel.

Mohammad Reza Shah Dam — A166

1963, Mar. 14   *Litho.*   *Center Multicolored*
1236	A166	6r violet blue	4.50	.70
1237	A166	14r dark brown	7.00	1.00

Mohammad Reza Shah Dam inauguration (later Dez Dam).

Worker with Pickax — A167

1963, Mar. 15
1238	A167	2r cream & black	1.25	.25
1239	A167	6r lt blue & blk	2.25	.30

Issued for Labor Day.

Stylized Bird over Globe — A168

Designs: 6r, Stylized globe and "FAO." 14r, Globe in space and wheat emblem.

1963, Mar. 21   *Perf. 11*
1240	A168	2r ultra, lt bl & bis	2.00	.25
1241	A168	6r lt ultra, ocher & blk	3.00	.30
1242	A168	14r slate bl & ocher	4.00	.85
		Nos. 1240-1242 (3)	9.00	1.40

FAO "Freedom from Hunger" campaign.

Shah and List of Bills — A169

IRAN

1963, Mar. 21   Wmk. 316
1243	A169	6r green & lt blue	5.00	3.00
1244	A169	14r green & dull yel	9.00	4.00

Signing of six socioeconomic bills by Shah, 1st anniv.

Shah and King of Denmark — A170

1963, May 3   Litho.   Perf. 11
1245	A170	6r indigo & dk ultra	4.50	1.00
1246	A170	14r dk brn & red brn	5.50	1.50

Visit of King Frederik IX of Denmark.

Flags, Shah Mosque, Isfahan, and Taj Mahal, Agra — A171

1963, May 19
1247	A171	6r blue, yel grn & red	5.00	1.00
1248	A171	14r multicolored	6.00	1.50

Visit of Dr. Sarvepalli Radhakrishnan, president of India.

Chahnaz Dam — A172

1963, June 8   Wmk. 316   Perf. 11
1249	A172	6r ultra, bl & grn	4.00	.75
1250	A172	14r dk grn, bl & buff	6.00	.90

Inauguration of Chahnaz Dam (later Hamadan Dam).

Cent. Emblem with Red Lion and Sun — A173

1963, June 10
1251	A173	6r blue, gray & red	4.50	.65
1252	A173	14r buff, gray & red	5.50	.90

Centenary of International Red Cross.

Shah and Queen Juliana — A174

Perf. 11x10½
1963, Oct. 3   Wmk. 349
1253	A174	6r ultra & blue	6.00	.50
1254	A174	14r sl grn & dull grn	7.00	.75

Visit of Queen Juliana of the Netherlands.

Literacy Corps Emblem and Soldier Teaching Village Class — A175

1963, Oct. 15   Litho.   Perf. 10½
1255	A175	6r multicolored	4.50	1.00
1256	A175	14r multicolored	5.50	1.00

Issued to publicize the Literacy Corps.

Gen. Charles de Gaulle and View of Persepolis — A176

1963, Oct. 16
1257	A176	6r ultra & blue	4.50	1.00
1258	A176	14r brn & pale brn	6.00	1.00

Visit of General de Gaulle of France.

Fertilizer Plant, Oil Company Emblem and Map — A177

Design: 14r, Factory and Iranian Oil Company emblem, horiz.

Perf. 10½x11, 11x10½
1963, Oct. 18   Wmk. 316
1259	A177	6r black, yel & red	7.00	2.00
1260	A177	14r black, bl & yel	8.00	3.00

Opening of Shiraz Chemical Factory.

A178

6r, 14r, Pres. Heinrich Lübke of Germany & Mosque in Isfahan

1963, Oct. 23   Wmk. 349   Perf. 10½
1261	A178	6r ultra & dk blue	5.00	.65
1262	A178	14r gray & brown	6.00	1.60

Visit of Pres. Lubke of Germany.

UN Emblem and Iranian Flag — A179

1963, Oct. 24
1263	A179	8r multicolored	3.50	.50

Issued for United Nations Day.

UN Emblem and Jets — A180

1963, Oct. 24
1264	A180	6r multicolored	3.50	1.00

Iranian jet fighters with UN Force in the Congo.

Crown Prince Reza — A181

1963, Oct. 31
1265	A181	2r brown	2.50	.25
1266	A181	6r blue	4.50	.50

Children's Day; Crown Prince Reza's 3rd birthday.

Pres. Brezhnev of USSR — A182

1963, Nov. 16   Wmk. 349   Perf. 10½
1267	A182	6r dk brn, yel & bl	4.50	.50
1268	A182	11r dk brn, yel & red	6.50	1.00

Visit of Pres. Leonid I. Brezhnev.

Atatürk's Mausoleum, Ankara — A183

1963, Nov. 28   Litho.
1269	A183	4r shown	3.50	.30
1270	A183	5r Kemal Ataturk	4.50	.30

25th death anniv. of Kemal Atatürk, president of Turkey.

Scales and Globe — A184

1963, Dec. 10
1271	A184	6r brt yel grn, blk & ultra	3.00	.35
1272	A184	14r org brn, blk & buff	4.00	.45

Universal Declaration of Human Rights, 15th anniv.

Mother and Child — A185

1963, Dec. 16
1273	A185	2r multicolored	3.00	.25
1274	A185	4r multicolored	4.00	.50

Issued for Mother's Day.

Map of Iran, Chamber of Industry and Mines Emblem — A186

1963, Dec. 17   Litho.
1275	A186	8r bl grn, buff & dk bl	5.00	.40

Chamber of Industry and Mines.

Factories and Hand Holding Bill — A187

Designs: 4r, Factories and bills on scale. 6r, Man on globe carrying torch of education. 8r, Tractor, map and yardstick. 10r, Forest. 12r, Gate of Parliament and heads of man and woman.

1964, Jan. 26   Wmk. 349   Perf. 10½
1276	A187	2r multicolored	3.50	1.00
1277	A187	4r brown & gray	4.25	1.00
1278	A187	6r multicolored	5.00	1.00
1279	A187	8r multicolored	5.50	1.50
1280	A187	10r multicolored	6.00	1.75
1281	A187	12r red org & brn	9.00	2.00
	Nos. 1276-1281 (6)		33.25	8.25

2nd anniv. of six socioeconomic bills: 2r, Shareholding for factory workers. 4r, Sale of shares in government factories. 6r, Creation of Army of Education. 8r, Land reforms. 10r,

Nationalization of forests. 12r, Reforms in parliamentary elections.

"ECAFE" and UN Emblem — A188

1964, Mar. 2   Wmk. 349
1282	A188	14r brt green & blk	3.00	.45

20th session of ECAFE (Economic Commission for Asia and the Far East), Mar. 2-17.

Flowering Branch — A189

1964, Mar. 5   Perf. 10½
1283	A189	50d emerald, blk & org	.50	.25
1284	A189	1r brt blue, blk & org	.60	.25

Novrooz, Iranian New Year, Mar. 21.

Anemometer — A190

1964, Mar. 23   Litho.
1285	A190	6r brt blue & vio bl	2.25	.50

4th World Meteorological Day.

Mosque and Arches, Isfahan — A191

11r, Griffon & winged bull, Persepolis.

1964, Apr. 7   Perf. 10½
1286	A191	6r lilac, grn & blk	2.50	.40
1287	A191	11r orange, brn & blk	3.50	.55

Issued for tourist publicity.

Rudaki and Harp — A192

1964, May 16   Photo.   Wmk. 349
1288	A192	6r blue	3.00	.45
1289	A192	8r red brown	4.50	.55

Opening of an institute for the blind. The inscription translates: "Wisdom is better than eye and sight."

Sculpture, Persepolis A193

Designs: 4r, Achaemenian horse-drawn mail cart, map of Iran, horiz. 6r, Vessel with sculptured animals. 10r, Head of King Shapur, sculpture.

IRAN

1964, June 5 — Wmk. 349 — Litho.

1290	A193	2r gray & blue	6.00	2.25
1291	A193	4r vio bl, lt bl & bl	9.00	3.00
1292	A193	6r brown & yellow	12.00	3.50
1293	A193	10r yel & ol grn	12.00	4.50
	Nos. 1290-1293 (4)		39.00	13.25

Opening of the "7000 Years of Persian Art" exhibition in Washington, D.C.

Shah and Emperor Haile Selassie — A194

1964, Sept. 14 — Wmk. 349 — Perf. 10½

1294	A194	6r ultra & lt blue	5.00	1.00

Visit of Emperor Haile Selassie of Ethiopia.

Tooth and Dentists' Assoc. Emblem — A195

"2 I.D.A." — A196

1964, Sept. 14 — Litho.

1295	A195	2r blue, red & dk blue	3.50	.30
1296	A196	4r ultra, bl & pale brn	4.50	.35

Iranian Dentists' Association, 2nd congress.

Research Institute, Microscope, Wheat and Locust — A197

Beetle under Magnifying Glass — A198

1964, Sept. 23 — Wmk. 349 — Perf. 10½

1297	A197	2r red, orange & brn	3.00	.40
1298	A198	6r blue, brn & indigo	4.50	.60

Fight against plant diseases and damages.

Mithras (Mehr) on Ancient Seal — A199

1964, Oct. 8 — Litho.
Size: 26x34mm

1299	A199	8r org & brn org	3.00	1.00

Mehragan celebration. See No. 1406.

Eleanor Roosevelt (1884-1962) — A200

1964, Oct. 11

1300	A200	10r vio bl & rose vio	5.00	1.00

Exists imperf pair, $75 mint, $50 used.

Clasped Hands and UN Emblem — A201

Symbolic Airplane and UN Emblem — A202

1964, Oct. 24 — Wmk. 349 — Perf. 10½

1301	A201	6r ultra, yel, red & blk	2.00	.40
1302	A202	14r org, ultra & red	2.75	.60

Issued for United Nations Day.

Persian Gymnast — A203

Polo Player — A204

1964, Oct. 26

1303	A203	4r tan, sep & Prus bl	2.25	.40
1304	A204	6r red & black	2.50	.60

18th Olympic Games, Tokyo, Oct. 10-25.

Crown Prince Reza — A205

1964, Oct. 31 — Litho.

1305	A205	1r dull green & brn	2.50	.30
1306	A205	2r deep rose & ultra	3.00	.50
1307	A205	6r ultra & red	4.50	.65
	Nos. 1305-1307 (3)		10.00	1.45

Children's Day; Crown Prince Reza's 4th birthday.

UN Emblem, Flame and Smokestack — A206

1964, Nov. 16 — Wmk. 349 — Perf. 10½

1308	A206	6r black, lt bl & car	2.25	.35
1309	A206	8r black, emer & car	3.00	.40

Petro-Chemical Conference and Gas Seminar, Nov.-Dec. 1964.

Shah and King Baudouin — A207

1964, Nov. 17

1310	A207	6r black, org & yel	2.50	.35
1311	A207	8r black, org & emer	3.50	.75

Visit of King Baudouin of Belgium.

Rhazes — A208

1964, Dec. 27 — Wmk. 349 — Perf. 10½

1312	A208	2r multicolored	2.50	.35
1313	A208	6r multicolored	3.50	.60

1100th birth anniv. of Rhazes (abu-Bakr Mohammad Zakariya Razi), Persian physician.

Shah and King Olav V — A209

1965, Jan. 7 — Litho.

1314	A209	2r dk brown & lilac	2.50	.35
1315	A209	4r brown & green	3.50	.75

Visit of King Olav V of Norway.

Map of Iran and Six-pointed Star — A210

1965, Jan. 26 — Wmk. 349 — Perf. 10½

1316	A210	2r black, brt bl & org	1.75	.25

Shah's six socioeconomic bills, 3rd anniv.

Woman and UN Emblem — A211

1965, Mar. 1 — Wmk. 349 — Perf. 10½

1317	A211	6r black & blue	.75	.25
1318	A211	8r ultra & red	2.00	.25

18th session of the UN commission on the status of women.

Green Wheat and Tulip — A212

1965, Mar. 6

1319	A212	50d multicolored	.45	.25
1320	A212	1r multicolored	.55	.25

Novrooz, Iranian New Year, Mar. 21.

Pres. Habib Bourguiba and Minarets of Tunis Mosque — A213

1965, Mar. 14 — Litho. — Perf. 10½

1321	A213	4r multicolored	1.75	.35

Visit of Pres. Habib Bourguiba of Tunisia.

Map of Iran and Trade Mark of Iranian Oil Co. — A214

1965, Mar. 20 — Litho.

1322	A214	6r multicolored	4.00	.25
1323	A214	14r multicolored	4.50	.55

Oil industry nationalization, 14th anniv.

ITU Emblem, Old and New Communication Equipment — A215

1965, May 17 — Wmk. 349 — Perf. 10½

1324	A215	14r dp car rose & gray	2.00	.60

ITU, centenary.

ICY Emblem — A216

1965, June 22 — Litho. — Perf. 10½

1325	A216	10r sl grn & gray bl	4.00	.60

International Cooperation Year, 1965.

Iran Airways Emblem — A217

1965, July 17 — Wmk. 349 — Perf. 10½

1326	A217	14r multicolored	3.00	.75

Tenth anniversary of Iran Airways.

Hands Holding Book — A218

Map and Flags of Turkey, Iran and Pakistan — A219

1965, July 21 — Litho.

1327	A218	2r dk brn, org brn & buff	1.00	.25
1328	A219	4r multicolored	1.25	.25

Signing of the Regional Cooperation for Development Pact by Turkey, Iran and Pakistan, 1st anniv.
See Pakistan 217-218, Turkey 1648-1649.

Iranian Scout Emblem and Ornament — A220

1965, July 23

1329	A220	2r multicolored	1.25	.25
a.	Vert. pair, imperf. horiz.		200.00	

Middle East Rover Moot (senior Boy Scout assembly).

Majlis Gate — A221

1965, Aug. 5 — Wmk. 349 — Perf. 10½

1330	A221	2r lilac rose & brn	.75	.25

60th anniversary of Iranian constitution.

Types of Regular Issue, 1962
Wmk. 349

1964-65 — Photo. — Perf. 10½

1331	A159	5d dk sl grn ('65)	.50	.30
a.	Wmk. 353		.50	.30
1332	A159	10d chestnut	.50	.30
1333	A159	25d dk blue ('65)	1.00	.25
1334	A159	50d Prus green	1.00	.25
1335	A159	1r orange	1.00	.25
1336	A159	2r violet blue	1.00	.25
1337	A159	5r dark brown	4.00	.50
1338	A160	6r blue ('65)	12.00	1.00

IRAN

1339	A160	8r yel grn ('65)	5.00	.25
1340	A160	10r grnsh bl ('65)	5.00	.25
1341	A160	11r sl grn ('65)	12.00	1.50
1342	A160	14r purple ('65)	10.00	1.40
1343	A160	20r red brn ('65)	10.00	2.00
1344	A160	50r org ver ('65)	12.00	2.00
	Nos. 1331-1344 (14)		75.00	10.50

Perf. 11x10½

1331b	A159	5d Wmk. 353	7.00	1.00
1332a	A159	10d	1.00	.50
1333a	A159	25d	1.00	
1334a	A159	50d	4.00	2.00
1335a	A159	1r	4.00	2.00
1337a	A159	5r	7.00	.50
	Nos. 1331b-1337a (6)		24.00	6.25

Dental Congress Emblem — A222

1965, Sept. 7   Litho.   Perf. 10½

1345	A222	6r gray, ultra, & car	1.00	.25

Iranian Dentists' Association, 3rd congress.

Classroom and Literacy Corps Emblem — A223

Alphabets on Globe — A224

Designs: 6r, UNESCO emblem and open book (diamond shape). 8r, UNESCO emblem and inscription, horiz. 14r, Mohammad Reza Shah Pahlavi and inscription in six languages.

1965, Sept. 8

1346	A223	2r multi	.50	.25
1347	A224	5r multi	.65	.30

Size: 30x30mm

1348	A223	6r multi	1.10	.40

Size: 35x23mm

1349	A223	8r dk bl, car emer & buff	1.25	.45

Size: 34x46mm

1350	A223	14r cit, dk bl & brn	2.75	.75
	Nos. 1346-1350 (5)		6.25	2.15

World Congress Against Illiteracy, Tehran, Sept. 8-19.

Mohammad Reza Pahlavi A225

1965, Sept. 16   Litho.   Perf. 10½

1351	A225	1r crim, rose red & gray	1.50	.50
1352	A225	2r dk red, rose red & yel	2.00	.75

Reign of Shah, 25th year. (in 1966).

Emblem of Persian Medical Society — A226

1965, Sept. 21   Wmk. 349

1353	A226	5r ultra, dp ultra & gold	.90	.25

14th Medical Congress, Ramsar.

Pres. Jonas of Austria — A227

1965, Sept. 30

1354	A227	6r bl, brt bl & gray	2.00	.25

Visit of President Franz Jonas of Austria.

Mithras (Mehr) on Ancient Seal A228

1965, Oct. 8   Litho.   Wmk. 353

1355	A228	4r brt grn, gold, brn & blk	1.00	.25

Mehragan celebration during month of Mehr, Sept. 23-Oct. 22. Persian inscription of watermark vertical on No. 1355.

UN Emblem — A229

1965, Oct. 24   Wmk. 353   Perf. 10½

1356	A229	5r bl, grn & rose car	.75	.25

20th anniversary of the United Nations.

Symbolic Arches — A230

1965, Oct. 26

1357	A230	3r vio bl, blk, yel & red	.80	.25

Exhibition of Iranian Commodities.

Crown Prince Reza — A231

1965, Oct. 31

1358	A231	2r brown & yellow	1.75	.45

Children's Day; Crown Prince Reza's 5th birthday.

Weight Lifters — A232

1965, Nov. 1

1359	A232	10r brt bl, vio & brt pink	.90	.25

World Weight Lifting Championships, Tehran.

Open Book — A233

1965, Dec. 1   Wmk. 353   Perf. 10½

1360	A233	8r bl, brt pink & blk	.80	.25

Issued for Book Week.

Shah and King Faisal — A234

1965, Dec. 8   Litho.

1361	A234	4r olive bister & brn	2.75	.50

Visit of King Faisal of Saudi Arabia.

Scales and Olive Branch — A235

1965, Dec. 12

1362	A235	14r multicolored	1.00	.25

Human Rights Day (Dec. 10).

Tractor, "Land Reform" — A236

Symbols of Reform Bills: 2r, Trees, nationalization of forests. 3r, Factory and gear wheel, sale of shares in government factories. 4r, Wheels, shareholding for factory workers. 5r, Parliament gate, women's suffrage. 6r, Children before blackboard, Army of Education. 7r, Caduceus, Army of Hygiene. 8r, Scales, creation of rural courts. 9r, Two girders, creation of Army of Progress.

1966, Jan. 26   Wmk. 353   Perf. 10½

1363	A236	1r orange & brown	.40	.25
1364	A236	2r dl grn & green	.50	.25
1365	A236	3r silver & gray	.55	.40
1366	A236	4r light & dk vio	.80	.50
1367	A236	5r rose & brown	1.20	.55
1368	A236	6r olive & brown	1.60	.65
1369	A236	7r bl & vio blue	2.00	.75
1370	A236	8r ultra & dp ultra	2.40	.85
1371	A236	9r brn org & dk brn	2.75	.90
	Nos. 1363-1371 (9)		12.20	5.10

Parliamentary approval of the Shah's reform plan.

Shah A237

Ruins of Persepolis A238

Wmk. 353

1966-71   Photo.   Perf. 10½

1372	A237	5d green	.50	.25
1373	A237	10d chestnut	.50	.25
1374	A237	25d dark blue	.50	.25
1375	A237	50d Prussian green	.60	
a.		50d blue green ('71)	.60	.30
b.		Printed on reverse	750.00	
1376	A237	1r orange	.60	.25
1377	A237	2r violet	.60	.25
1377A	A237	4r cl brn ('68)	7.50	1.00
1378	A237	5r dark brn	2.00	.25
1379	A238	6r deep blue	2.50	.25
1380	A238	8r yellow grn	2.50	.25
a.		8r dull green ('71)	2.50	.25
1381	A238	10r Prus bl	2.50	.25
1382	A238	11r slate grn	2.50	.25
1383	A238	14r purple	3.00	.25
1384	A238	20r brown	19.00	.50
1385	A238	50r cop red	10.00	1.50
1386	A238	100r brt blue	20.00	2.50
1387	A238	200r chnt brn	20.00	4.50
	Nos. 1372-1387 (17)		94.80	13.00

Set, except 4r, issued Feb. 22, 1966.

Student Nurse Taking Oath — A239

1966, Feb. 24   Litho.

1388	A239	5r brt pink & mag	1.00	.50
1389	A239	5r lt bl & brt bl	1.00	.50
a.		Se-tenant pair, #1388-1389	3.00	3.00

Nurses' Day. Nos. 1388-1389 printed in sheets of 50 arranged checkerwise.

Narcissus — A240

1966, Mar. 7

1390	A240	50d ultra, yel & emer	.30	.25
1391	A240	1r lilac, yel & emer	.50	.30

Novrooz, Iranian New Year, Mar. 21.

Oil Derricks in Persian Gulf A241

1966, Mar. 20   Perf. 10½

1392	A241	14r blk, brt bl & brt rose lil	2.75	.75

Formation of six offshore oil companies.

Radio Tower — A242

2r, Radar, horiz. 6r, Emblem & waves. 8r, Compass rose & waves. 10r, Tower & waves.

1966, Apr. 27   Litho.   Wmk. 349

1393	A242	2r dark grn	.25	.35
1394	A242	4r ultra & dp org	.40	.35
1395	A242	6r gray ol & plum	.50	.40
1396	A242	8r brt bl & dk bl	1.00	.50
1397	A242	10r brn & bister	1.25	.55
	Nos. 1393-1397 (5)		3.40	2.15

Inauguration of the radio telecommunication system of the Central Treaty Organization of the Middle East (CENTO).

WHO Headquarters, Geneva — A243

1966, May 3   Wmk. 353

1398	A243	10r brt bl, yel & blk	.80	.30

Opening of the WHO Headquarters, Geneva.

World Map — A244

1966, May 14   Litho.

1399	A244	6r bl & multi	.50	.30
1400	A244	8r multicolored	1.00	.30

Intl. Council of Women, 18th Conf., Tehran, May 1966.

IRAN

Globe, Map of Iran and Ruins of Persepolis — A245

1966, Sept. 5   Wmk. 353   *Perf. 10½*
1401   A245   14r multicolored   1.50   .50
International Iranology Congress, Tehran.

Emblem of Iranian Medical Society — A246

1966, Sept. 21
1402   A246   4r ultra, lt bl & bis   .75   .30
15th Medical Congress, held at Ramsar.

Gate of Parliament, Mt. Demavend and Congress Emblem A247

8r, Senate building, Mt. Demavend & emblem.

1966, Oct. 2   Wmk. 353   *Perf. 10½*
1403   A247   6r brick red, ultra & dk grn   .65   .30
1404   A247   8r lt lil, ultra & dk grn   .85   .30
55th Interparliamentary Union Conf., Tehran.

Visit of President Cevdet Sunay of Turkey A248

1966, Oct. 2   Litho.
1405   A248   6r vio & dk brn   .75   .25

Mithras Type of 1964
1966, Oct. 8   Size: 30x40mm
1406   A199   6r olive bister & brn   .75   .30
Mehragan celebration.

Farmers A249

1966, Oct. 13
1407   A249   5r olive bister & brn   3.50   .75
Establishment of rural courts of justice.

UN Emblem A250

1966, Oct. 24   Wmk. 353   *Perf. 10½*
1408   A250   6r brn org & blk   .75   .30
21st anniversary of United Nations.

Crown Prince Reza — A251

1966, Oct. 31   Litho.
1409   A251   1r ultramarine   .75   .75
1410   A251   2r violet   1.10   .75
   a.   Pair, #1409-1410   2.00   2.00
Children's Day; Crown Prince Reza's 6th birthday.

Symbolic Woman's Face — A252

1966, Nov. 6
1411   A252   5r gold, blk & ultra   .60   .25
Founding of the Iranian Women's Org.

Film Strip and Song Bird — A253

1966, Nov. 6
1412   A253   4r blk, red lil & vio   .75   .25
First Iranian children's film festival.

"Census Count" — A254

1966, Nov. 11
1413   A254   6r dk brn & gray   .60   .25
National census.

Book Cover — A255

1966, Nov. 15
1414   A255   8r tan, brn & ultra   .60   .25
Issued to publicize Book Week.

Reza Shah Pahlavi — A256

Design: 2r, Reza Shah Pahlavi without kepi.

1966, Nov. 16   Litho.
1415   A256   1r slate blue   2.00   .75
1416   A256   1r brown   2.00   .75
   a.   Pair, #1415-1416   4.50   2.50
1417   A256   2r gray green   2.50   .75
1418   A256   2r violet blue   2.50   .75
   a.   Pair, #1417-1418   6.00   2.50
     Nos. 1415-1418 (4)   9.00   3.00
Reza Shah Pahlavi (1877-1944), founder of modern Iran.

EROPA Emblem and Map of Persia — A257

1966, Dec. 4   Wmk. 353   *Perf. 10½*
1419   A257   8r dk brn & emerald   1.50   .25
4th General Assembly of the Org. of Public Administrators, EROPA.

Shah Giving Deeds to Farmers A258

1967, Jan. 9   Wmk. 353   *Perf. 10½*
1420   A258   6r ol bis, yel & brn   1.75   .25
Approval of land reform laws, 5th anniv.

Shah and 9-Star Crescent A259

Design: 2r, Torch and 9-star crescent.

1967, Jan. 26   Wmk. 353   Litho.
1421   A259   2r multicolored   1.25   .50
1422   A259   6r multicolored   1.75   .50
5th anniv. of Shah's reforms, the "White Revolution."

Ancient Sculpture of Bull — A260

Designs: 5r, Sculptured mythical animals. 8r, Pillar from Persepolis.

1967, Feb. 25   Wmk. 353   *Perf. 10½*
1423   A260   3r dk brn & ocher   1.25   .35
1424   A260   5r Prus grn, brn & ocher   1.50   .45
1425   A260   8r vio, blk & sil   2.00   .65
     Nos. 1423-1425 (3)   4.75   1.45
Issued to publicize Museum Week.

Planting Tree — A261

1967, Mar. 6
1426   A261   8r brn org & grn   .60   .25
Tree Planting Day.

Goldfish — A262

1967, Mar. 11   Size: 26x20mm
1427   A262   1r shown   .40   .25
   Size: 35x27mm
1428   A262   8r Swallows   1.25   .30
Issued for Novrooz, Iranian New Year.

Microscope, Animals and Emblem A263

1967, Mar. 11   *Perf. 10½*
1429   A263   5r blk, gray & mag   .65   .25
Second Iranian Veterinary Congress.

Pres. Arif of Iraq, Mosque A264

1967, Mar. 14   Litho.   Wmk. 353
1430   A264   6r brt bl & grn   .55   .30
Visit of Pres. Abdul Salam Mohammad Arif.

Fireworks — A265

1967, Mar. 17
1431   A265   5r vio bl & multi   2.50   .50
Issued for United Nations Stamp Day.

Map of Iran and Oil Company Emblem A266

1967, Mar. 20
1432   A266   6r multicolored   1.75   .45
Nationalization of Iranian Oil Industry.

Fencers — A267

1967, Mar. 23
1433   A267   5r vio & bister   .85   .60
Intl. Youth Fencing Championships, Tehran.

Shah and King of Thailand A268

1967, Apr. 23   Wmk. 353   *Perf. 10½*
1434   A268   6r brn org & dk brn   3.00   .45
Visit of King Bhumibol Adulyadej.

Old and Young Couples A269

1967, Apr. 24   Litho.
1435   A269   5r ol bis & vio bl   .75   .25
15th anniversary of Social Insurance.

IRAN

Skier and Iranian Olympic Emblem — A270

Designs: 6r, Assyrian soldiers, Olympic rings and tablet inscribed "I.O.C." 8r, Wrestlers and Iranian Olympic emblem.

1967, May 5
1436	A270	3r brown & black	.75	.25
1437	A270	6r multicolored	1.00	.50
1438	A270	8r ultra & brown	1.25	.75
		Nos. 1436-1438 (3)	3.00	1.45

65th Intl. Olympic Cong., Tehran, May 2-11.

Lions International A271

Emblem — A271a

1967, May 11   Size: 41½x30½mm
1439	A271	3r multicolored	1.00	.50

Size: 36x42mm
1440	A271a	7r multicolored	1.50	.75

50th anniversary of Lions International.

Visit of Pres. Chivu Stoica of Romania A272

1967, May 13
1441	A272	6r orange & dk bl	.50	.25

International Tourist Year Emblem — A273

1967, June 6   Wmk. 353   Perf. 10½
1442	A273	3r brick red & ultra	.50	.25

Iranian Pavilion and Ornament — A274

1967, June 7   Litho.
1443	A274	4r dk brn, red & gold	.50	.25
1444	A274	10r red, dk brn & gold	.75	.30

EXPO '67, Montreal, Apr. 28-Oct. 27.

Stamp of 1870, No. 1 — A275

1967, July 23   Wmk. 353   Perf. 10½
1445	A275	6r multi	.50	.30
1446	A275	8r multi	.75	.30

Centenary of first Persian postage stamp.

World Map and School Children — A276

1967, Sept. 8   Litho.   Wmk. 353
1447	A276	3r ultra & brt & brt bl	.25	.25
1448	A276	5r brown & yellow	.75	.25

World campaign against illiteracy.

Globe and Oriental Musician — A277

1967, Sept. 10   Perf. 10½
1449	A277	14r brn org & dk brn	1.00	.35

Intl. Conf. on Music Education in Oriental Countries, Sept. 1967.

Child's Hand Holding Adult's — A278

1967, Sept. 14   Litho.   Wmk. 353
1450	A278	8r dk brn & yel	4.00	2.00

Introduction of Children's Villages in Iran. (Modelled after Austrian SOS Villages for homeless children).

Winged Wild Goat — A279

1967, Sept. 19
1451	A279	8r dk brn & lemon	1.00	.25

Festival of Arts, Persepolis.

UN Emblem — A280

1967, Oct. 17
1452	A280	6r olive bister & vio bl	.75	.25

Issued for United Nations Day.

Shah and Empress Farah — A281

1967, Oct. 26   Wmk. 353   Perf. 10½
Various Frames
1453	A281	2r sil, bl & brn	1.25	.40
1454	A281	10r sil, bl & vio	2.00	.60
1455	A281	14r lt bl, bl, gold & vio	3.50	1.50
		Nos. 1453-1455 (3)	6.75	2.50

Coronation of Shah Mohammad Reza Pahlavi and Empress Farah, Oct. 26, 1967.
Nos. 1453-1455 exist in imperf between pairs, with top sheet margin, value set, $50, and in imperf between blocks of 4, ungummed, value set, $25. Fake imperf between pairs, lacking the top sheet margin, have been manufactured by fraudulently perforating imperf-between blocks.

1967, Oct. 31   Litho.
Design: Crown Prince Reza.
1456	A281	2r silver & violet	1.00	.35
1457	A281	8r sil & red brown	1.50	.45

Children's Day; Crown Prince Reza's 7th birthday.

Visit of Pres. Georgi Traikov of Bulgaria — A283

1967, Nov. 20
1458	A283	10r lilac & dk brn	.50	.25

Persian Boy Scout Emblem — A284

1967, Dec. 3   Wmk. 353   Perf. 10½
1459	A284	8r olive & red brn	1.40	.50

Cooperation Week of the Iranian Boy Scouts, Dec. 5-12.

Hands Holding Chain Link — A285

1967, Dec. 6   Litho.
1460	A285	6r multicolored	.50	.25

Issued to publicize Cooperation Year.

Visit of Sheik Sabah of Kuwait — A286

1968, Jan. 10   Wmk. 353   Perf. 10½
1461	A286	10r lt bl & slate grn	.75	.25

List of Shah's 12 Reform Laws 4 — A287

1968, Jan. 27   Litho.   Wmk. 353
1462	A287	2r sl grn, brn & sal	.85	.30
1463	A287	8r vio, dk grn & lt grn	1.75	.35
1464	A287	14r brn, pink & lt lil	3.00	.50
		Nos. 1462-1464 (3)	5.60	1.15

"White Revolution of King and People."

Almond Blossoms A288

Haji Firooz (New Year Singer) A289

Design: 2r, Tulips.

1968, Mar. 12   Wmk. 353   Perf. 10½
1465	A288	1r multi	.35	.25
1466	A288	2r bluish gray & multi	.35	.25
1467	A288	2r brt rose lil & multi	.35	.25
1468	A289	6r multi	1.00	.45
		Nos. 1465-1468 (4)	2.05	1.20

Issued for Novrooz, Iranian New Year.

Oil Worker and Derrick — A290

1968, Mar. 20   Litho.
1469	A290	14r grn, blk & org yel	1.25	.50

Oil industry nationalization, 17th anniv.

WHO Emblem — A291

1968, Apr. 7   Wmk. 353   Perf. 10½
1470	A291	14r brn, bl & org	.85	.25

WHO, 20th anniversary.

Marlik Chariot, Ancient Sculpture — A292

1968, Apr. 13
1471	A292	8r blue, brn & buff	.75	.25

Fifth World Congress of Persian Archaeology and Art, Tehran.

Shah and King Hassan II — A293

1968, Apr. 16
1472	A293	6r bright vio & buff	1.25	.25

Visit of King Hassan II of Morocco.

Human Rights Flame — A294

Design: 14r, Frameline inscription reads, "International Conference on Human Rights Tehran 1968"; "Iran" at left.

1968, May 5   Wmk. 353   Perf. 10½
1473	A294	8r red & dk grn	.50	.25
1474	A294	14r vio bl & bl	.75	.30

Intl. Human Rights Year. The 8r commemorates the Iranian Human Rights Committee; the 14r, the Intl. Conference on Human Rights, Tehran, 1968.

Soccer Player — A295

1968, May 10   Litho.
1475	A295	8r multicolored	.50	.30
1476	A295	10r multicolored	.75	.30

Asian Soccer Cup Finals, Tehran.

IRAN

Tehran Oil Refinery — A296

1968, May 21 Wmk. 353 Perf. 10½
1477 A296 14r brt bl & multi 1.50 .35
Opening of the Tehran Oil Refinery.

Queen Farah as Girl Guide — A297

1968, June 24 Litho. Perf. 10½
1478 A297 4r brt rose lil & green 2.50 .75
1479 A297 6r car & brn 3.00 1.00
Great Camp of Iranian Girl Guides.

A set of 2 stamps (8r, 14r) were prepared for the International Tennis Congress, Tehran. The stamps were not released when the congress was cancelled. Value, set $4,000.

Anopheles Mosquito, Congress Emblem — A298

1968, Sept. 7 Wmk. 353 Perf. 10½
1480 A298 6r brt pur & blk .50 .35
1481 A298 14r dk grn & mag .75 .40
8th Intl. Congress on Tropical Medicine and Malaria, Tehran, Sept. 7-15.

Winged Figure with Banner, and Globe — A299

1968, Sept. 8 Litho.
1482 A299 6r lt vio, bis & bl .50 .25
1483 A299 14r dl yel, sl grn & brn .75 .30
World campaign against illiteracy.

Oramental Horse and Flower — A300

1968, Sept. 11
1484 A300 14r sl grn, org & yel grn .85 .25
2nd Festival of Arts, Shiraz-Persepolis.

INTERPOL Emblem and Globe — A301

1968, Oct. 6 Wmk. 353 Perf. 10½
1485 A301 10r dk brn & bl .85 .25
37th General Assembly of the Intl. Police Org. (INTERPOL) in Tehran.

Police Emblem on Iran Map in Flag Colors — A302

1968, Oct. 7 Litho.
1486 A302 14r multicolored 1.00 .30
Issued for Police Day.

Peace Dove and UN Emblem — A303

1968, Oct. 24
1487 A303 14r bl & vio bl 1.00 .25
Issued for United Nations Day.

Empress Farah A304

Designs: 8r, Mohammad Reza Shah Pahlavi. 10r, Shah, Empress and Crown Prince.

1968, Oct. 26
1488 A304 6r multi 8.00 3.75
1489 A304 8r multi 10.00 5.50
1490 A304 10r multi 12.00 6.75
Nos. 1488-1490 (3) 30.00 16.00
Coronation of Mohammad Reza Shah Pahlavi and Empress Farah, 1st anniv.

Shah's Crown and Bull's Head Capital — A305

1968, Oct. 30
1491 A305 14r ultra, gold, sil & red 1.00 .25
Festival of Arts and Culture.

UNICEF Emblem and Child's Drawing — A306

Children's Drawings and UNICEF Emblem: 3r, Boat on lake, house and trees, horiz. 5r, Flowers, horiz.

1968, Oct. 31 Litho.
1492 A306 2r dk brn & multi .35 .25
1493 A306 3r dk grn & multi .50 .30
1494 A306 5r multicolored .70 .40
Nos. 1492-1494 (3) 1.55 .95
Issued for Children's Day.

Labor Union Emblem — A307

Factory and Insurance Company Emblem — A308

Designs: 8r, Members of Army of Hygiene, and Insurance Company emblem. 10r, Map of Persia, Insurance Company emblem, car, train, ship and plane.

1968, Nov. 6 Wmk. 353 Perf. 10½
1495 A307 4r sil & vio bl .30 .35
1496 A308 5r multicolored .40 .35
1497 A308 8r ultra, gray & yel .50 .35
1498 A308 10r multicolored .55 .40
Nos. 1495-1498 (4) 1.75 1.45
Issued to publicize Insurance Day.

Human Rights Flame, Man and Woman — A309

1968, Dec. 10 Litho. Perf. 10½
1499 A309 8r lt bl, vio bl & car .60 .25
International Human Rights Year.

Symbols of Shah's Reform Plan A310

Design: Each stamp shows symbols of 3 of the Shah's reforms. No. 1503a shows the 12 symbols in a circle with a medallion in the center picturing 3 heads and a torch.

1969, Jan. 26 Wmk. 353 Perf. 10½
1500 2r ocher, grn & lil 1.50 .50
1501 4r lil, ocher & grn 1.75 .60
1502 6r lil, ocher & grn 1.75 .75
1503 8r lil, ocher & grn 2.50 1.10
 a. A310 Block of 4, #1500-1503 9.00 4.50
Nos. 1500-1503 (4) 7.50 2.95
Declaration of the Shah's Reform Plan.

Shah and Crowd — A311

1969, Feb. 1 Litho.
1504 A311 6r red, bl & brn 2.50 .35
10,000th day of the reign of the Shah.

European Goldfinch — A312

2r, Ring-necked pheasant. 8r, Roses.

1969, Mar. 6 Wmk. 353 Perf. 10½
1505 A312 1r multicolored .35 .25
1506 A312 2r multicolored .50 .25
1507 A312 8r multicolored 1.25 .25
Nos. 1505-1507 (3) 2.10 .75
Issued for Novrooz, Iranian New Year.

"Woman Lawyer" Holding Scales of Justice — A313

1969, Apr. 8 Litho. Perf. 10½
1508 A313 6r blk & brt bl .75 .25
15th General Assembly of Women Lawyers, Tehran, Apr. 8-14.

Workers, ILO and UN Emblems — A314

1969, Apr. 30 Wmk. 353 Perf. 10½
1509 A314 10r bl & vio bl .75 .25
ILO, 50th anniversary.

Freestyle Wrestlers and Aryamehr Cup A315

1969, May 6 Litho.
1510 A315 10r lilac & multi 1.50 .75
Intl. Freestyle Wrestling Championships, 3rd round.

Birds and Flower — A316

1969, June 10 Wmk. 353 Perf. 10½
1511 A316 10r vio bl & multi 1.00 .25
Issued to publicize Handicrafts Day.

Boy Scout Symbols — A317

1969, July 9 Wmk. 353 Perf. 10½
1512 A317 6r lt bl & multi 1.50 .30
Philia 1969, an outdoor training course for Boy Scout patrol leaders.

IRAN

Lady Serving Wine, Safavi Miniature, Iran — A318

No. 1514, Lady on Balcony, Mogul miniature, Pakistan. No. 1515, Sultan Suleiman Receiving Sheik Abdul Latif, 16th cent. miniature, Turkey.

1969, July 21   *Litho.*
1513	A318	25r multi	3.50	1.00
1514	A318	25r multi	3.50	1.00
1515	A318	25r multi	3.50	1.00
		Nos. 1513-1515 (3)	10.50	3.00

Signing of the Regional Cooperation for Development Pact by Turkey, Iran and Pakistan, 5th anniv.

Neil A. Armstrong and Col. Edwin E. Aldrin on Moon — A319

1969, July 26
1516	A319	24r bister, bl & brn	10.00	5.00

See note after Algeria No. 427.

Quotation from Shah's Declaration on Education and Art — A320

1969, Aug. 6   *Wmk. 353*   *Perf. 10½*
1517	A320	10r car, cream & emer	.85	.25

Anniv. of educational and art reforms.

Offshore Oil Rig in Persian Gulf — A321

1969, Sept. 1   *Litho.*
1518	A321	8r multicolored	1.75	.35

Marine drillings by the Iran-Italia Oil Co., 10th anniv.

Dancers Forming Flower — A322

1969, Sept. 6   *Wmk. 353*   *Perf. 10½*
1519	A322	6r multicolored	.45	.25
1520	A322	8r multicolored	.55	.25

3rd Festival of Arts, Shiraz and Persepolis, Aug. 30-Sept. 9.

Crossed-out Fingerprint, Moon and Rocket — A323

1969, Sept. 8   *Litho.*
1521	A323	4r multicolored	.50	.25

World campaign against illiteracy.

Persepolis, Simulated Stamp with UPU Emblem, and Shah — A324

1969, Sept. 28
1522	A324	10r lt bl & multi	3.00	1.00
1523	A324	14r multicolored	5.00	1.50

16th Congress of the UPU, Tokyo.

Fair Emblem — A325

14r, like 8r, inscribed "ASIA 69." 20r, Fair emblem, world map and "ASIA 69," horiz.

1969, Oct. 5   *Wmk. 353*   *Perf. 10½*
1524	A325	8r rose & multi	.50	.30
1525	A325	14r blue & multi	.75	.30
1526	A325	20r tan & multi	1.25	.40
		Nos. 1524-1526 (3)	2.50	1.00

2nd Asian Trade Fair, Tehran.

Justice — A326

1969, Oct. 13   *Litho.*
1527	A326	8r bl grn & dk brn	1.00	.25

Rural Courts of Justice Day.

UN Emblem — A327

1969, Oct. 24
1528	A327	2r lt bl & dp bl	.75	.25

25th anniversary of the United Nations.

Emblem and Column Capital, Persepolis — A328

1969, Oct. 28
1529	A328	2r deep blue & multi	1.00	.25

2nd Festival of Arts and Culture. See Nos. 1577, 1681, 1735.

Child's Drawing and UNICEF Emblem — A329

Children's Drawings and UNICEF Emblem: 1r, Boy and birds, vert. 5r, Dinner.

1969, Oct. 31   *Wmk. 353*   *Perf. 10½*
Size: 28x40mm, 40x28mm
1530	A329	1r lt blue & multi	.40	.25
1531	A329	2r lt grn & multi	.50	.25
1532	A329	5r lt lil & multi	.85	.25
		Nos. 1530-1532 (3)	1.75	.75

Children's Week. See Nos. 1578-1580.

Globe Emblem — A330

1969, Nov. 6
1533	A330	8r dk brn & bl	.75	.25

Meeting of the Natl. Society of Parents and Educators, Tehran.

Satellite Communications Station — A331

1969, Nov. 19   *Litho.*
1534	A331	6r blk brn & bis	.75	.30

1st Iranian Satellite Communications Earth Station, Hamadan.

Mahatma Gandhi (1869-1948) — A332

1969, Dec. 29   *Wmk. 353*   *Perf. 10½*
1535	A332	14r gray & dk rose brn	8.00	3.50

Globe, Flags and Emblems — A333

Design: 6r, Globe and Red Cross, Red Lion and Sun, and Red Crescent Emblems.

1969, Dec. 31
1536	A333	2r red & multi	1.25	.35
1537	A333	6r red & multi	1.50	.45

League of Red Cross Societies, 50th anniv.

Symbols of Reform Laws and Shah — A334

1970, Jan. 26   *Litho.*   *Wmk. 353*
1538	A334	1r bister & multi	1.50	.40
1539	A334	2r multicolored	2.00	.60

Declaration of the Shah's Reform Plan.

Pansies — A335

New Year's Table — A336

1970, Mar. 6   *Wmk. 353*   *Perf. 10½*
1540	A335	1r multicolored	.40	.25
1541	A336	8r multicolored	2.10	.30

Issued for the Iranian New Year.

Chemical Plant, Kharg Island, and Iranian Oil Company Emblem — A337

Designs (Iranian Oil Company Emblem and): 2r, Shah's portrait and quotation. 4r, Laying of gas pipe line and tractor. 8r, Tankers at pier of Kharg Island, vert. 10r, Tehran refinery.

1970, Mar. 20   *Wmk. 353*   *Perf. 10½*
1542	A337	2r gray & multi	1.50	.45
1543	A337	4r multicolored	2.00	.65
1544	A337	6r lt bl & multi	2.50	.75
1545	A337	8r multicolored	2.75	.90
1546	A337	10r multicolored	4.00	1.00
		Nos. 1542-1546 (5)	12.75	3.75

Nationalization of the oil industry, 20th anniv.

EXPO '70 Emblem — A338

1970, Mar. 27   *Litho.*
1547	A338	4r brt rose lil & vio bl	.50	.25
1548	A338	10r lt bl & pur	1.00	.25

EXPO '70, Osaka, Japan, Mar. 15-Sept. 13.

Radar, Satellite and Congress Emblem — A339

1970, Apr. 20   *Wmk. 353*   *Perf. 10½*
1549	A339	14r multicolored	1.40	.35

Asia-Australia Telecommunications Congress, Tehran.

UPU Headquarters, Bern — A340

1970, May 10
1550	A340	2r gray, brn & lil rose	1.00	.25
1551	A340	4r lil, brn & lil rose	1.00	.25

Inauguration of the new UPU Headquarters, Bern.

Asia Productivity Year Emblem — A341

1970, May 19   *Wmk. 353*   *Perf. 10½*
1552	A341	8r gray & multi	.75	.25

Asian Productivity Year, 1970.

Bird Bringing Baby — A342

1970, June 15   *Litho.*
1553	A342	8r brn & dk blue	.75	.25

Iranian School for Midwives, 50th anniv.

IRAN

Tomb of Cyrus the Great, Meshed-Morghab in Fars — A343

Designs: 8r, Pillars of Apadana Palace, Persepolis, vert. 10r, Bas-relief from a Mede tomb, Iraq. 14r, Achaemenian officers, bas-relief, Persepolis.

1970, June 21   Photo.   Perf. 13
1554	A343	6r gray, red & vio	2.25	.25
1555	A343	8r pale rose, blk & bl grn	2.25	.50
1556	A343	10r yel, red & brn	2.50	.65
1557	A343	14r bl, blk & red brn	3.00	1.00
		Nos. 1554-1557 (4)	10.00	2.40

2500th anniversary of the founding of the Persian Empire by Cyrus the Great.
See Nos. 1561-1571, 1589-1596, 1605-1612.

Seeyo-Se-Pol Bridge, Isfahan — A344

Wmk. 353
1970, July 21   Litho.   Perf. 10½
1558	A344	2r multicolored	1.10	.30
1559	A344	2r multicolored	1.10	.30
1560	A344	2r multicolored	1.10	.30
		Nos. 1558-1560 (3)	3.30	.90

Signing of the Regional Cooperation for Development Pact by Iran, Turkey and Pakistan, 6th anniv.
See Pakistan 290-292, Turkey 1857-1859.
No. 1559, Saiful Malook Lake, Pakistan, vert. No. 1560, View of Fethiye, Turkey, vert.

Queen Buran, Dirhem Coin — A345

Wine Goblet with Lion's Head — A346

Designs: No. 1562, Achaemenian eagle amulet. No. 1563, Mithridates I, dirhem coin. No. 1564, Sassanidae art (arch, coin, jugs). No. 1565, Shapur I, dirhem coin. No. 1567, Achaemenian courier. No. 1568, Winged deer. No. 1569, Ardashir I, dirhem coin. No. 1570, Seal of Darius I (chariot, palms, lion). 14r, Achaemenian tapestry.

1970   Wmk. 353   Photo.   Perf. 13
1561	A345	1r gold & multi	2.25	.50
1562	A346	2r green & multi	1.50	.40
1563	A345	2r gold & multi	2.25	.50
1564	A346	2r lilac & multi	2.75	.50
1565	A346	6r green & multi	1.75	.40
1566	A345	6r gold & multi	2.75	.60
1567	A345	6r lilac & multi	3.00	.60
1568	A345	8r pink & multi	2.25	.50
1569	A345	8r gold & multi	2.75	.75
1570	A345	8r lilac & multi	3.50	.75
1571	A345	14r lt bl & multi	2.75	1.10
		Nos. 1561-1571 (11)	27.50	6.60

2500th anniversary of the founding of the Persian Empire by Cyrus the Great.
Issued: 1r, Nos. 1563, 1566, 1569, 8/22; #1562, 1565, 1568, 14r, 8/6; others, 9/22.

Candle and Globe — A347

1970, Sept. 8   Litho.   Perf. 10½
1572	A347	1r lt bl & multi	.30	.25
1573	A347	2r pale sal & multi	.40	.25

Issued to publicize World Literacy Day.

Persian Decoration — A348

1970, Sept. 14
1574	A348	6r multi	.75	.25

Isfahan Intl. Cong. of Architects, Sept. 1970.

Emblem — A349

1970, Sept. 28   Perf. 10½
1575	A349	2r lt bl & pur	.40	.25

Congress of Election Committees of Persian States and Tehran.

UN Emblem, Dove and Scales — A350

1970, Oct. 24   Litho.   Wmk. 353
1576	A350	2r lt bl, mag & dk bl	.50	.25

Issued for United Nations Day.

Festival Type of 1969
1970, Oct. 28   Perf. 10½
1577	A328	2r org & multi	1.20	.25

3rd Festival of Arts and Culture.

UNICEF Type of 1969

Children's Drawings and UNICEF Emblem: 50d, Herdsman and goats. 1r, Family picnic. 2r, Mosque.

1970, Oct. 31   Size: 43½x31mm
1578	A329	50d black & multi	.35	.25
1579	A329	1r black & multi	.45	.25
1580	A329	2r black & multi	.65	.25
		Nos. 1578-1580 (3)	1.45	.75

Issued for Children's Week.

Mohammad Reza Shah Pahlavi — A351

1971, Jan. 26   Wmk. 353   Perf. 10½
1581	A351	2r lt bl & multi	3.50	1.00

Publicizing the "White Revolution of King and People" and the 12 reform laws.

Sheldrake — A352

2r, Ruddy shelduck. 8r, Flamingo, vert.

1971, Jan. 30   Litho.
1582	A352	1r multicolored	1.50	.50
1583	A352	2r multicolored	1.25	.75
1584	A352	8r multicolored	3.00	1.00
		Nos. 1582-1584 (3)	5.75	2.25

Intl. Wetland and Waterfowl Conf., Ramsar.

Reza Shah Pahlavi — A353

1971, Feb. 22   Wmk. 353   Perf. 10½
1585	A353	6r multicolored	6.00	2.75

50th anniversary of the Pahlavi dynasty's accession to power.

Rooster — A354

1971, Mar. 6   Photo.   Perf. 13½x13
1586	A354	1r multicolored	1.25	.45
1587	A354	2r multicolored	1.75	.75
1588	A354	6r multicolored	3.00	1.00
		Nos. 1586-1588 (3)	6.00	2.20

Novrooz, Iranian New Year.

Shapur II Hunting A355

Bull's Head, Persepolis — A356

1r, Harpist, mosaic. No. 1591, Investiture of Ardashir I, bas-relief. 5r Winged lion ornament. 6r, Persian archer, bas-relief. 8r, Royal audience, bas-relief. 10r, Bronze head of Parthian prince.

1971   Litho.   Perf. 10½
1589	A356	1r multicolored	3.50	.45
1590	A355	2r blk & brn org	4.00	.45
1591	A355	2r lil, gldn brn & blk	4.00	.45
1592	A356	4r pur & multi	2.25	.45
1593	A356	5r multicolored	2.50	.55
1594	A356	6r multicolored	2.50	.55
1595	A356	8r lt bl & multi	3.00	.80
1596	A356	10r dp bis, blk & slate	4.00	.90
		Nos. 1589-1596 (8)	25.75	4.60

2500th anniversary of the founding of the Persian Empire by Cyrus the Great.
Issued: 4r, 5r, 6r, 8r, 5/15; others, 6/15.

Prisoners Leaving Jail — A357

1971, May 20   Litho.   Wmk. 353
1597	A357	6r multicolored	2.25	.25
1598	A357	8r multicolored	3.50	.25

Rehabilitation of Prisoners Week.

Religious School, Chaharbagh, Ispahan — A358

No. 1600, Mosque of Selim, Edirne, Turkey. No. 1601, Badshahi Mosque, Lahore, Pakistan, horiz.

1971, July 21   Litho.   Perf. 10½
1599	A358	2r multicolored	.75	.25
1600	A358	2r multicolored	.75	.25
1601	A358	2r multicolored	.75	.25
		Nos. 1599-1601 (3)	2.25	.75

7th anniversary of Regional Cooperation among Iran, Pakistan and Turkey.
See Pakistan 305-307, Turkey 1886-1888.

"Fifth Festival of Arts" — A359

1971, Aug. 26   Litho. & Typo.
1602	A359	2r lt & dk grn, red & gold	.90	.30

5th Festival of Arts, Shiraz-Persepolis.

"Fight Against Illiteracy" A360

1971, Sept. 8   Litho.
1603	A360	2r grn & multi	.65	.30

International Literacy Day, Sept. 8.

Kings Abdullah and Hussein II of Jordan — A361

1971, Sept. 11
1604	A361	2r yel grn, blk & red	.75	.35

Hashemite Kingdom of Jordan, 50th anniv.

Shahyad Aryamehr Monument A362

Designs: 1r, Aryamehr steel mill, near Isfahan. 3r, Senate Building, Tehran. 11r, Shah Abbas Kabir Dam, Zayandeh River.

IRAN

1971, Sept. 22
1605	A362	1r blue & multi	1.50	.50
1606	A362	2r multicolored	1.75	.50
1607	A362	3r brt pink & multi	2.25	.50
1608	A362	11r org & multi	3.00	1.00
		Nos. 1605-1608 (4)	8.50	2.50

2500th anniversary of the founding of the Persian empire by Cyrus the Great.

Mohammad Reza Shah Pahlavi — A363

Designs: 2r, Reza Shah Pahlavi. 5r, Stone tablet with proclamation of Cyrus the Great, horiz. 10r, Crown of present empire (erroneously inscribed *Le Couronne*).

1971, Oct. 12
1609	A363	1r gold & multi	5.00	2.50
1610	A363	2r gold & multi	5.50	2.50
1611	A363	5r gold & multi	6.50	3.00
1612	A363	10r gold & multi	8.00	3.00
		Nos. 1609-1612 (4)	25.00	11.00

2500th anniversary of the founding of the Persian empire by Cyrus the Great.

Ghatour Railroad Bridge A364

1971, Oct. 7
1613	A364	2r multicolored	3.00	.85

Iran-Turkey railroad.

Racial Equality Emblem — A365

1971, Oct. 24
1614	A365	2r lt blue & multi	.35	.25

Intl. Year Against Racial Discrimination.

Mohammad Reza Shah Pahlavi — A366

Perf. 13½x13

1971, Oct. 26   Photo.   Wmk. 353

Size: 20½x28mm
1615	A366	5d lilac	.25	.25
1616	A366	10d henna brown	.25	.25
1617	A366	50d brt bl grn	.25	.25
1618	A366	1r dp yel grn	.30	.25
1619	A366	2r brown	.30	.25

Size: 27x36½mm
1620	A366	6r slate green	1.10	.25
1621	A366	8r violet blue	2.00	1.10
1622	A366	10r red lilac	2.00	.30
1623	A366	11r blue green	6.00	1.10
1624	A366	14r brt blue	9.00	.50
1625	A366	20r car rose	9.50	.65
1626	A366	50r yellow bis	10.00	1.25
		Nos. 1615-1626 (12)	40.95	6.40

See Nos. 1650-1661B, 1768-1772.

Child's Drawing and Emblem A367

Designs: No. 1631, Ruins of Persepolis, vert. No. 1632, Warrior, mosaic, vert.

1971, Oct. 31   Litho.   Perf. 10½
1630	A367	2r multicolored	.45	.25
1631	A367	2r multicolored	.45	.25
1632	A367	2r multicolored	.45	.25
		Nos. 1630-1632 (3)	1.35	.75

Children's Week.

UNESCO Emblem and "25" — A368

1971, Nov. 4
1633	A368	6r ultra & rose claret	.60	.25

25th anniversary of UNESCO.

Domestic Animals and Emblem — A369

1971, Nov. 22
1634	A369	2r gray, blk & car	.60	.30

4th Iranian Veterinarians' Congress.

ILO Emblem, Cog Wheels and Globe — A370

1971, Dec. 4
1635	A370	2r black, org & bl	.60	.25

7th ILO Conference for the Asian Region.

UNICEF Emblem, Bird Feeding Young — A371

1971, Dec. 16   Perf. 13x13½
1636	A371	2r lt bl, mag & blk	.60	.30

25th anniversary of UNICEF.

Mohammad Reza Shah Pahlavi — A372

1972, Jan. 26   Wmk. 353   Perf. 10½
1637	A372	2r lt green & multi	4.50	2.00
a.		20r Souvenir sheet	17.50	11.50

"White Revolution of King and People" and the 12 reform laws. No. 1637a contains one stamp with simulated perforations.

Pintailed Sandgrouse A373

No. 1639, Rock ptarmigan. 2r, Yellow-billed waxbill and red-cheeked cordon-bleu.

1972, Mar. 6   Litho.   Perf. 13x13½
1638	A373	1r green & multi	1.00	.40
1639	A373	1r lt blue & multi	1.00	.40
1640	A373	2r yellow & multi	2.00	.50
		Nos. 1638-1640 (3)	4.00	1.30

Iranian New Year.

"Your Heart is your Health" — A374

1972, Apr. 4   Perf. 10½
1641	A374	10r lemon & multi	3.00	.30

World Health Day; Iranian Society of Cardiology.

Film Strip and Winged Antelope — A375

8r, Film strips and winged antelope.

1972, Apr. 16   Litho. & Engr.
1642	A375	6r ultra & gold	1.50	.30
1643	A375	8r yellow & multi	2.00	.35

Tehran International Film Festival.

Rose and Bud — A376

1972, May 5   Litho.
1644	A376	1r shown	.50	.30
1645	A376	2r Yellow roses	.80	.35
1646	A376	5r Red rose	.90	.40
		Nos. 1644-1646 (3)	2.20	1.05

See Nos. 1711-1713.

Persian Woman, by Behzad — A377

Paintings: No. 1648, Fisherman, by Cevat Dereli (Turkey). No. 1649, Young Man, by Abdur Rehman Chughtai (Pakistan).

1972, July 21   Wmk. 353
1647	A377	5r gray & multi	1.75	.30
1648	A377	5r gray & multi	1.75	.30
1649	A377	5r gray & multi	1.75	.30
		Nos. 1647-1649 (3)	5.25	.90

Regional Cooperation for Development Pact among Iran, Turkey and Pakistan, 8th anniv. See Pakistan 322-324, Turkey 1912-1914.

Shah Type of 1971

1972-73   Photo.   Perf. 13½x13

Bister Frame & Crown

Size: 20½x28mm
1650	A366	5d lilac	.25	.25
1651	A366	10d henna brown	.25	.25
1652	A366	50d brt blue grn	.25	.25
1653	A366	1r dp yel grn		
a.		Brn frame & crown ('73)	.50	.25
b.		As No. 1653, dp yel grn (Shah) omitted	500.00	
1654	A366	2r brown	.40	.25

Size: 27x36½mm
1655	A366	6r slate grn	.80	.25
1656	A366	8r violet blue	.80	.25
a.		Frame omitted	500.00	
b.		Violet blue (Shah) omitted	650.00	
1657	A366	10r red lilac	1.20	.25
a.		Red lilac (Shah) omitted	650.00	
1658	A366	11r blue green	1.60	.80
1659	A366	14r dull blue	4.75	.60
1660	A366	20r car rose	8.00	.50
1661	A366	50r grnsh blue	6.00	1.00
1661A	A366	100r violet ('73)	8.00	2.00
1661B	A366	200r slate ('73)	10.00	3.50
		Nos. 1650-1661B (14)	42.55	10.40

Festival Emblem A378

1972, Aug. 31   Litho.   Perf. 10½
1662	A378	6r emerald, red & blk	1.00	.25
1663	A378	8r brt mag, blk & grn	1.50	.25

6th Festival of Arts, Shiraz-Persepolis, Aug. 31-Sept. 8.

Pens and Emblem — A379

1972, Sept. 8
1664	A379	1r lt blue & multi	.40	.25
1665	A379	2r yellow & multi	.60	.25

World Literacy Day, Sept. 8.

"10" and Emblems — A380

1972, Sept. 18
1666	A380	1r lilac & multi	.40	.25
1667	A380	2r dull yel & multi	.60	.25

10th Congress of Iranian Dentists' Assoc., Sept. 18-22.

Asian Broadcasting Union Emblem — A381

1972, Oct. 1
1668	A381	6r lt green & multi	.50	.25
1669	A381	8r gray & multi	1.00	.25

9th General Assembly of Asian Broadcasting Union, Tehran, Oct. 1972.

No. 450 on Cover — A382

1972, Oct. 9
1670	A382	10r lt blue & multi	2.50	.25

International Stamp Day.

IRAN

Chess and Olympic Rings — A383

Olympic Rings and: 2r, Hunter. 3r, Archer. 5r, Equestrians. 6r, Polo. 8r, Wrestling.

1972, Oct. 17
1671	A383	1r brown & multi	2.50	1.25
1672	A383	2r blue & multi	2.50	.40
1673	A383	3r lilac & multi	2.50	.40
1674	A383	5r bl grn & multi	2.75	.60
1675	A383	6r red & multi	3.00	.60
1676	A383	8r yel grn & multi	5.00	.80
a.		Souv. sheet of 6, #1671-1676, imperf.	25.00	15.00
		Nos. 1671-1676 (6)	18.25	4.05

20th Olympic Games, Munich, 8/26-9/11.

Communications Symbol, UN Emblem — A384

1972, Oct. 24
1677	A384	10r multicolored	1.75	.25

United Nations Day.

Children and Flowers — A385

Children's Drawings and Emblem: No. 1679, Puppet show. 6r, Boys cutting wood, horiz.

1972, Oct. 31   Litho.   Wmk. 353
1678	A385	2r gray & multi	.60	.25
1679	A385	2r bister & multi	.60	.25
1680	A385	6r pink & multi	1.25	.25
		Nos. 1678-1680 (3)	2.45	.75

Children's Week.

Festival Type of 1969

Design: 10r, Crown, emblems and column capital, Persepolis.

1972, Nov. 11
1681	A328	10r dp blue & multi	6.00	1.75

10th anniv. of White Revolution; Festival of Culture and Art.

Family Planning Emblem — A386

1972, Dec. 5
1682	A386	1r blue & multi	.35	.25
1683	A386	2r brt pink & multi	.55	.25

To promote family planning.

Iranian Scout Organization, 20th anniv. — A387

1972, Dec. 9
1684	A387	2r multicolored	.80	.25

Ancient Seal — A388

Designs: Various ancient seals.

1973, Jan. 5   Perf. 10½
1685	A388	1r blue, red & brn	.70	.25
1686	A388	1r yellow & multi	.70	.25
1687	A388	1r pink & multi	.70	.25
1688	A388	2r lt brick red & multi	.80	.25
1689	A388	2r dull org & multi	.80	.25
1690	A388	2r olive & multi	.80	.25
		Nos. 1685-1690 (6)	4.50	1.50

Development of writing.

Books and Book Year Emblem — A389

Design: 6r, Illuminated page, 10th century, from Shahnameh, by Firdousi.

1973, Jan. 10
1691	A389	2r black & multi	.65	.25
1692	A389	6r yellow & multi	.85	.25

International Book Year.

"12 Improvements by the King" — A390

Designs: 2r, 10r, 12 circles symbolizing 12 improvements. 6r, like 1r.

1973, Jan. 26   Litho.
Size: 29x43mm
1693	A390	1r gold, ultra, red & yel	.30	.25
1694	A390	2r sil, plum, ol & yel	.35	.25

Size: 65x84mm
1695	A390	6r gold, ultra, red & yel	2.50	1.50
		Nos. 1693-1695 (3)	3.15	2.00

Souvenir Sheet
Imperf
1696	A390	10r sil, plum, ol & yel	4.25	2.50

Introduction of the King's socioeconomic reforms, 10th anniv.

Acenthurus (Blue Surgeonfish) — A391

Fish: No. 1698, Sparus spinifer (Gilthead). No. 1699, Abdulef (Banded sergeant major). No. 1700, Anisotremus (Porkfish). No. 1701, Lutyanus Fulniflamma (Black-spot snapper).

1973, Mar. 6   Wmk. 353   Perf. 10½
1697	A391	1r multicolored	.65	.30
1698	A391	1r multicolored	.65	.30
1699	A391	2r multicolored	.90	.45
1700	A391	2r multicolored	.90	.45
1701	A391	2r multicolored	.90	.45
		Nos. 1697-1701 (5)	4.00	1.95

Iranian New Year.

WHO Emblem — A392

1973, Apr. 7   Litho.   Wmk. 353
1702	A392	10r brn, grn & red	1.50	.25

25th anniversary of the WHO.

Soccer — A393

1973, Apr. 13
1703	A393	14r orange & multi	2.00	.25

15th Asian Youth Football (soccer) Tournament.

Tracks and Globe — A394

1973, May 10   Wmk. 353   Perf. 10½
1704	A394	10r dk grn, lil & vio bl	3.00	.60

13th International Railroad Conference.

Clay Tablet with Aryan Script — A395

Designs: Clay tablets with various scripts.

1973, June 5   Perf. 10½
1705	A395	1r shown	.50	.25
1706	A395	1r Kharoshthi	.50	.25
1707	A395	1r Achaemenian	.50	.25
1708	A395	2r Parthian (Mianeh)	.90	.25
1709	A395	2r Parthian (Arsacide)	.90	.25
1710	A395	2r Gachtak (Dabireh)	.90	.25
		Nos. 1705-1710 (6)	4.20	1.50

Development of writing.

Flower Type of 1972

1973, June 20
1711	A376	1r Orchid	.35	.25
1712	A376	2r Hyacinth	.65	.25
1713	A376	6r Columbine	1.75	.25
		Nos. 1711-1713 (3)	2.75	.75

Regional Cooperation for Development Pact Among Iran, Turkey and Pakistan, 9th Anniv. — A396

Designs: No. 1714, Head from mausoleum of King Antiochus I (69-34 B.C.), Turkey. No. 1715, Statue, Shahdad Kerman, Persia, 4000 B.C. No. 1716, Street, Mohenjo-Daro, Pakistan.

1973, July 21
1714	A396	2r brown & multi	.40	.25
1715	A396	2r green & multi	.40	.25
1716	A396	2r blue & multi	.40	.25
a.		Strip of 3, #1714-1716	1.50	.75

See Pakistan 343-345, Turkey 1941-1943.

Shah, Oil Pump, Refinery and Tanker — A397

1973, Aug. 4
1717	A397	5r blue & black	2.50	.75

Nationalization of oil industry.

Soldiers and Rising Sun — A398

1973, Aug. 19   Litho.   Wmk. 353
1718	A398	2r ultra & multi	.65	.25

20th anniversary of return of monarchy.

Gymnasts and Globe — A399

1973, Aug. 23   Perf. 10½
1719	A399	2r olive & multi	.40	.25
1720	A399	2r violet bl & multi	.40	.25

7th Intl. Congress of Physical Education and Sports for Girls and Women, Tehran, Aug. 19-25.

Shahyad Monument (later Azadi Monument), Rainbow and WMO Emblem A400

1973, Sept. 4
1721	A400	5r multicolored	1.00	.25

Intl. meteorological cooperation, centenary.

Festival Emblem — A401

1973, Aug. 31
1722	A401	1r silver & multi	.35	.25
1723	A401	5r gold & multi	.50	.25

7th Festival of Arts, Shiraz-Persepolis.

Wrestlers — A402

1973, Sept. 6   Litho.   Wmk. 353
1724	A402	6r lt green & multi	1.25	.40

World Wrestling Championships, Tehran, Sept. 6-14.

IRAN

"Literacy as Light" — A403

1973, Sept. 8
1725 A403 2r multicolored .45 .25
World Literacy Day, Sept. 8.

Audio-Visual Equipment — A404

1973, Sept. 11
1726 A404 10r yellow & multi 1.00 .35
Tehran Intl. Audio-Visual Exhib., Sept. 11-24.

Warrior Taming Winged Bull — A405

1973, Sept. 16
1727 A405 8r blue gray & multi 1.00 .25
Intl. Council of Military Sports, 25th anniv.

Abu Rayhan Biruni (973-1048), Philosopher and Mathematician — A406

1973, Sept. 16
1728 A406 10r brown & black 1.50 .50

Soccer Cup — A407

1973, Oct. 2 Wmk. 353 Perf. 10½
1729 A407 2r lilac, blk & buff .50 .25
Soccer Games for the Crown Prince's Cup.

INTERPOL Emblem — A408

1973, Oct. 7
1730 A408 2r multicolored .75 .25
50th anniversary of INTERPOL.

Symbolic Arches and Globe — A409

1973, Oct. 8
1731 A409 10r orange & multi 1.00 .25
World Federation for Mental Health, 25th anniv.

UPU Emblem, Letter, Post Horn — A410

1973, Oct. 9
1732 A410 6r blue & orange .75 .25
World Post Day, Oct. 9.

Honeycomb A411

1973, Oct. 24
1733 A411 2r lt brown & multi .35 .25
1734 A411 2r gray olive & multi .35 .25
UN Volunteer Program, 5th anniv.

Festival Type of 1969
2r, Crown & column capital, Persepolis.

1973, Oct. 26
1735 A328 2r yellow & multi .65 .25
Festival of Culture and Art.

Turkish Bosporus Bridge, Flag — A412
8r, Kemal Ataturk & Reza Shah Pahlavi.

1973, Oct. 29 Litho. Perf. 10½
1736 A412 2r multicolored 1.00 .25
1737 A412 8r multicolored 2.00 .25
50th anniversary of the Turkish Republic.

Mother and Child, Emblem — A413

Children's Drawings and Emblem: No. 1739, Wagon, horiz. No. 1740, House and garden with birds.

1973, Oct. 31
1738 A413 2r multicolored .45 .25
1739 A413 2r multicolored .45 .25
1740 A413 2r multicolored .45 .25
Nos. 1738-1740 (3) 1.35 .75
Children's Week.

Cow, Wheat and FAO Emblem A414

1973, Nov. 4
1741 A414 10r multicolored 1.50 .25
10th anniversary of World Food Program.

Proclamation of Cyrus the Great; Red Cross, Lion and Crescent Emblems — A415

1973, Nov. 8
1742 A415 6r lt blue & multi 1.00 .25
22nd Intl. Red Cross Conf., Tehran, 1972.

"Film Festival" — A416

1973, Nov. 26 Wmk. 353 Perf. 10½
1743 A416 2r black & multi .45 .25
2nd International Tehran Film Festival.

Globe and Travelers — A417

1973, Nov. 26 Litho.
1744 A417 10r orange & multi .75 .25
12th annual Congress of Intl. Assoc. of Tour Managers.

Human Rights Flame — A418

1973, Dec. 10
1745 A418 8r lt blue & multi .65 .25
Universal Declaration of Human Rights, 25th anniv.

Score and Emblem — A419

Design: No. 1747, Score and emblem, diff.

1973, Dec. 21
1746 A419 10r yel grn, red & blk 1.00 .25
1747 A419 10r lt bl, ultra & red 1.00 .25
Dedicated to the art of music.

Forestry, Printing, Education A420

Designs (Symbols of Reforms): No. 1749, Land reform, sales of shares, women's suffrage. No. 1750, Army of progress, irrigation, women's education. No. 1751, Hygiene, rural courts, housing.

1974, Jan. 26 Litho. Perf. 10½
1748 1r lt blue & multi .25 .25
1749 1r lt blue & multi .25 .25
1750 2r lt blue & multi .25 .25
1751 2r lt blue & multi .25 .25
a. A420 Block of 4, #1748-1751 2.00 1.50
Imperf
Size: 76½x102mm
1752 A420 20r multicolored 5.00 3.00
"White Revolution of King and People" and 12 reform laws.

Pir Amooz Ketabaty Script — A421

Various Scripts: No. 1754, Mo Eghely Ketabaty. No. 1755, Din Dabireh, Avesta script. No. 1756, Pir Amooz, Naskh style. No. 1757, Pir Amooz, decorative style. No. 1758, Decorative and architectural style.

1974, Feb. 14 Wmk. 353 Perf. 10½
1753 A421 1r silver, ocher & multi .75 .25
1754 A421 1r gold, gray & multi .75 .25
1755 A421 1r silver, yel & multi .75 .25
1756 A421 2r gold, gray & multi 1.00 .25
1757 A421 2r gold, slate & multi 1.00 .25
1758 A421 2r gold, claret & multi 1.00 .25
Nos. 1753-1758 (6) 5.25 1.50
Development of writing.

Fowl, Syringe and Emblem — A422

1974, Feb. 23
1759 A422 6r red brown & multi .85 .25
5th Iranian Veterinary Congress.

Monarch Butterfly — A423

Designs: Various butterflies.

1974, Mar. 6 Litho. Perf. 10½
1760 A423 1r rose lilac & multi 1.00 .30
1761 A423 1r brt rose & multi 1.00 .30
1762 A423 2r lt blue & multi 1.40 .40
1763 A423 2r green & multi 1.40 .40
1764 A423 2r bister & multi 1.75 .45
Nos. 1760-1764 (5) 6.55 1.85
Novrooz, Iranian New Year.

Jalaludin Mevlana (1207-1273), Poet — A424

1974, Mar. 12 Perf. 13
1765 A424 2r pale violet & multi 1.00 .25

Shah Type of 1971
1974 Photo. Perf. 13½x13
Size: 20½x28mm
1768 A366 50d orange & bl .55 .25
1769 A366 1r emerald & bl .55 .25
1770 A366 2r red & blue .55 .25
Size: 27x36½mm
1771 A366 10r lt green & bl 4.50 .25
1772 A366 20r lilac & bl 3.75 .25
Nos. 1768-1772 (5) 9.90 1.25

IRAN

Palace of the Forty Columns, Hippocrates, Avicenna — A425

1974, Apr. 11   **Litho.**   **Perf. 10½**
1773   A425   10r multicolored   1.00   .25

9th Medical Congress of the Near and Middle East, Isfahan.

Onager — A426

1974, Apr. 13
1774   A426   1r shown   1.00   .25
1775   A426   2r Great bustard   1.25   .25
1776   A426   6r Fawn and deer   2.00   .35
1777   A426   8r Caucasian black grouse   3.00   .40
   a.   Strip of 4, #1774-1777   9.00   .63
   Nos. 1774-1777 (4)   7.25   1.25

Intl. Council for Game and Wildlife Preservation.

Athlete and Games Emblem — A427

1974, Apr. 30
1778   A427   1r shown   .75   .25
1779   A427   1r Table tennis   .75   .25
1780   A427   2r Boxing   1.25   .25
1781   A427   2r Hurdles   1.25   .25
1782   A427   6r Weight lifting   2.00   .25
1783   A427   8r Basketball   3.00   .25
   Nos. 1778-1783 (6)   9.00   1.50

7th Asian Games, Tehran; first issue.

Lion of Venice A428

Painting: 8r, Audience with the Doge of Venice.

1974, May 5
1784   A428   6r multicolored   .75   .25
1785   A428   8r multicolored   1.25   .35

Safeguarding Venice.

Links and Grain — A429

1974, May 13   **Litho.**   **Perf. 10½**
1786   A429   2r multicolored   .45   .25

Cooperation Day.

Military Plane, 1924 — A430

1974, June 1
1787   A430   10r shown   3.25   .50
1788   A430   10r Jet, 1974   3.25   .50

50th anniversary of Iranian Air Force.

Swimmer and Games Emblem — A431

No. 1790, Tennis, men's doubles. No. 1791, Wrestling. No. 1792, Hockey. No. 1793, Volleyball. No. 1794, Tennis, women's singles.

1974, July 1   **Wmk. 353**   **Perf. 10½**
1789   A431   1r shown   .75   .25
1790   A431   1r multi   .75   .25
1791   A431   2r multi   1.00   .25
1792   A431   2r multi   1.00   .25
1793   A431   4r multi   1.50   .40
1794   A431   10r multi   3.00   .50
   Nos. 1789-1794 (6)   8.00   1.90

7th Asian Games, Tehran; second issue.

Bicyclists and Games Emblem — A432

1974, Aug. 1
1795   A432   2r shown   1.25   .25
1796   A432   2r Soccer   1.25   .25
1797   A432   2r Fencing   1.25   .25
1798   A432   2r Small-bore rifle shooting   1.25   .25
   Nos. 1795-1798 (4)   5.00   1.00

7th Asian Games, Tehran; third issue.

Ghaskai Costume — A433

Regional Costumes: No. 1800, Kurdistan, Kermanshah District. No. 1801, Kurdistan, Sanandaj District. No. 1802, Mazandaran. No. 1803, Bakhtiari. No. 1804, Torkaman.

1974, July 6
1799   A433   2r lt ultra & multi   2.00   .75
1800   A433   2r buff & multi   2.00   .75
1801   A433   2r green & multi   2.00   .75
1802   A433   2r lt blue & multi   2.00   .75
1803   A433   2r gray & multi   2.00   .75
1804   A433   2r dull grn & multi   2.00   .75
   a.   Block of 6, #1799-1804   12.00   7.00

Gold Winged Lion Cup — A434

1974, July 13
1805   A434   2r dull green & multi   .45   .25

Iranian Soccer Cup.

Tabriz Rug, Late 16th Century — A435

Designs: No. 1807, Anatolian rug, 15th century. No. 1808, Kashan rug, Lahore.

1974, July 21
1806   A435   2r brown & multi   .50   .25
1807   A435   2r blue & multi   .50   .25
1808   A435   2r red & multi   .50   .25
   a.   Strip of 3, #1806-1808   2.00   .30

Regional Cooperation for Development Pact among Iran, Turkey and Pakistan, 10th anniv. See Pakistan 365-367, Turkey 1979-1981

King Carrying Vases, Bas-relief — A436

1974, Aug. 15   **Litho.**   **Perf. 10½**
1809   A436   2r black & multi   .45   .25

8th Iranian Arts Festival, Shiraz-Persepolis.

Aryamehr Stadium, Tehran A437

No. 1811, Games' emblem and inscription. No. 1812, Aerial view of games' site.

1974
1810   A437   6r multicolored   1.25   .25

Souvenir Sheets
1811   A437   10r multicolored   3.50   1.50
1812   A437   10r multicolored   3.50   1.50

7th Asian Games, Tehran; fourth and fifth issues. Nos. 1811-1812 contain one imperf 51x38mm stamp each.
Issued: Nos. 1811-1812, 9/1; No. 1810, 9/16.

"Welfare" A438

"Education" A439

1974, Sept. 11
1813   A438   2r orange & multi   .35   .25
1814   A439   2r blue & multi   .35   .25

Welfare and free education.

Map of Hasanlu, 1000-800 B.C. — A440

1974, Sept. 24
1815   A440   8r multicolored   .70   .25

2nd Intl. Congress of Architecture, Shiraz-Persepolis, Sept. 1974.

Achaemenian Mail Cart and UPU Emblem A441

Design: 14r, UPU emblem and letters.

1974, Oct. 9   **Wmk. 353**   **Perf. 10½**
1816   A441   6r orange, grn & blk   1.00   .40
   a.   Unwatermarked   300.00
1817   A441   14r multicolored   1.50   .50
   a.   Unwatermarked   300.00

Centenary of Universal Postal Union.

Road Through Farahabad Park — A442

1974, Oct. 16
1818   A442   1r shown   .30   .25
1819   A442   2r Recreation Bldg.   .35   .25

Inauguration of Farahabad Park, Tehran.

Farahnaz Dam and Mohammad Reza Shah Pahlavi — A443

Designs: 5d, Kharg Island petro-chemical plant. 10d, Ghatour Railroad Bridge. 1r, Tehran oil refinery. 2r, Satellite communication station, Hamadan, and Mt. Alvand. 6r, Aryamehr steel mill, Isfahan. 8r, University of Tabriz. 10r, Shah Abbas Kabir Dam. 14r, Rudagi (later Vahdat) Music Hall. 20r, Shayad Monument. 50r, Aryamehr Stadium.

1974-75   **Photo.**   **Perf. 13x13½**
   Size: 28x21mm
   Frame & Shah in Brown
1820   A443   5d slate green   .25   .25
1821   A443   10d orange   .25   .25
1822   A443   50d blue green   .25   .25
1823   A443   1r ultra   .25   .25
1824   A443   2r deep lilac   .25   .25
   Size: 36x26½mm
   Frame & Shah in Dark Blue
1825   A443   6r brown   .55   .25
1826   A443   8r grnsh blue   1.10   .35
1827   A443   10r deep lilac   .75   .25
   a.   Value in Farsi omitted   40.00   30.00
1828   A443   14r deep green   12.50   .50
1829   A443   20r magenta   3.75   .40
1830   A443   50r violet   5.25   1.00
   Nos. 1820-1830 (11)   25.15   4.00

Issued: 50d, 1r, 2r, 10/16/74; 14r, 11/1974; others 3/6/75.
See Nos. 1831-1841. For overprints see Nos. 2008, 2010.

1975-77   **Size: 28x21mm**
   Frame & Shah in Green
1831   A443   5d orange ('77)   .30   .25
1832   A443   10d rose mag ('77)   .30   .25
1833   A443   50d lilac   .30   .25
1834   A443   1r dark blue   .30   .25
1835   A443   2r brown   .30   .25
   Size: 36x26½mm
   Frame & Shah in Brown
1836   A443   6r vio bl ('76)   .75   .35
1837   A443   8r deep org ('77)   2.00   .30
1838   A443   10r dp yel grn ('76)   2.25   .25
   a.   Brown (Shah and frame) omitted   400.00
1839   A443   14r lilac   10.00   .25
   a.   Brown (Shah and frame) omitted   300.00
1840   A443   20r brt green ('76)   5.00   .40
1841   A443   50r dp blue ('76)   7.00   .90
   Nos. 1831-1841 (11)   28.50   3.70

Festival Emblem, Crown and Column Capital, Persepolis — A444

1974, Oct. 26   **Litho.**   **Perf. 10½**
1842   A444   2r multicolored   .65   .25

Festival of Culture and Art.

IRAN

Destroyer "Palang" and Flag — A445

1974, Nov. 5
1843　A445　10r multicolored　2.00　.35
Navy Day.

Girl at Spinning Wheel — A446

1974, Nov. 7　　　　**Perf. 10½**
1844　A446　2r shown　.25　.25
1845　A446　2r Scarecrow, vert.　.25　.25
1846　A446　2r Picnic　.25　.25
　　　Nos. 1844-1846 (3)　.75　.75
Children's Week.

Winged Ibex — A447

1974, Nov. 25　Litho.　Wmk. 353
1847　A447　2r vio, org & blk　.60　.25
Third Tehran International Film Festival.

WPY Emblem — A448

1974, Dec. 1
1848　A448　8r orange & multi　.85　.25
World Population Year.

Gold Bee — A449

Design: 8r, Gold crown, gift of French people to Empress Farah. Bee pin was gift of the Italian people.

1974, Dec. 20
1849　A449　6r multicolored　.75　.30
1850　A449　8r multicolored　1.00　.35
15th wedding anniv. of Shah and Empress Farah.

Angel with Banner A450

1975, Jan. 7　Litho.　Perf. 10½
1851　A450　2r org & vio bl　.35　.25
International Women's Year.

Symbols of Agriculture, Industry and the Arts — A451

1975, Jan. 26　　　　Wmk. 353
1852　A451　2r multicolored　.35　.25
"White Revolution of King and People."

Tourism Year 75 Emblem — A452

1975, Feb. 17
1853　A452　6r multicolored　.35　.25
South Asia Tourism Year.

"Farabi" in Shape of Musical Instrument or Alembic — A453

1975, Mar. 1
1854　A453　2r brn red & multi　.45　.25
Abu-Nasr al-Farabi (870?-950), physician, musician and philosopher, 1100th birth anniversary.

Ornament, Rug Pattern — A454

No. 1856, Blossoms and cypress trees. No. 1857, Shah Abbasi flower.

1975, Mar. 6
1855　A454　1r shown　.25　.25
1856　A454　1r multicolored　.25　.25
1857　A454　1r multicolored　.25　.25
　　a.　Strip of 3, #1855-1857　1.00　.60
Novrooz, Iranian New Year. Nos. 1855-1857 printed in sheets of 45 stamps + 5 labels.

Nasser Khosrov, Poet, Birth Millenary — A455

1975, Mar. 11
1858　A455　2r blk, gold & red　.40　.25

Formula — A456

1975, May 5　Litho.　Perf. 10½
1859　A456　2r buff & multi　.50　.25
5th Biennial Symposium of Iranian Biochemical Society.

Charioteer, Bas-relief, Persepolis A457

Design: 2r, Heads of Persian warriors, bas-relief from Persepolis, vert.

1975, May 5
1860　A457　2r lt brn & multi　3.00　.75
1861　A457　10r blue & multi　5.00　1.25
Rotary International, 70th anniversary.

Signal Fire, Persian Castle — A458

Design: 8r, Communications satellite.

1975, May 17
1862　A458　6r multicolored　1.25　.45
1863　A458　8r lil & multi　1.75　.55
7th World Telecommunications Day.

Cooperation Day — A459

1975, May 13
1864　A459　2r multicolored　.35　.25

Jet, Shayad Monument, Statue of Liberty — A460

1975, May 29　Litho.　Wmk. 353
1865　A460　10r org & multi　1.00　.40
Iran Air's 1st flight to New York, May 1975.

Emblem — A461

1975, June 5
1866　A461　6r blue & multi　.45　.25
World Environment Day.

Dam — A462

1975, June 10
1867　A462　10r multicolored　.70　.25
9th Intl. Congress on Irrigation & Drainage.

Resurgence Party Emblem — A463

1975, July 1　Wmk. 353　Perf. 10½
1868　A463　2r multicolored　.35　.25
Organization of Resurgence Party.

Girl Scout Symbols — A464

1975, July 16
1869　A464　2r multicolored　.50　.25
2nd Natl Girl Scout Camp, Tehran, July 1976.

Festival of Tus — A465

1975, July 17
1870　A465　2r gray, lil & vio　.45　.25
Festival of Tus in honor of Firdausi (940-1020), Persian poet born near Tus in Khorasan.

Ceramic Plate, Iran — A466

No. 1872, Camel leather vase, Pakistan, vert. No. 1873, Porcelain vase, Turkey, vert.

1975, July 21
1871　A466　2r bister & multi　.35　.25
1872　A466　2r bister & multi　.35　.25
1873　A466　2r bister & multi　.35　.25
　　Nos. 1871-1873 (3)　1.05　.75
Regional Cooperation for Development Pact among Iran, Pakistan and Turkey.
See Pakistan 383-385, Turkey 2006-2008.

Majlis Gate — A467

1975, Aug. 5　Litho.　Perf. 10½
1874　A467　10r multi　.75　.25
Iranian Constitution, 70th anniversary.

Column with Stylized Branches — A468

1975, Aug. 21　Litho.　Wmk. 353
1875　A468　8r red & multi　.50　.25
9th Iranian Arts Festival, Shiraz-Persepolis.

IRAN

Flags over Globe — A469

1975, Sept. 8
1876 A469 2r vio bl & multi .40 .25
Intl. Literacy Symposium, Persepolis.

Stylized Globe — A470

1975, Sept. 13
1877 A470 2r vio & multi .40 .25
3rd Tehran International Trade Fair.

World Map and Envelope A471

1975, Oct. 9 Litho. *Perf. 10½*
1878 A471 14r ultra & multi 1.00 .25
World Post Day, Oct. 9.

Crown, Column Capital, Persepolis — A472

1975, Oct. 26 Litho. *Wmk. 353*
1879 A472 2r ultra & multi .40 .25
Festival of Culture and Art. See No. 1954.

Face and Film — A473

1975, Nov. 2
1880 A473 6r multicolored .50 .25
Tehran Intl. Festival of Children's Films.

"Mother's Face" — A474

Girl — A475

Design: No. 1882, 2r, "Our House," horiz. All designs after children's drawings.

1975, Nov. 5
1881 A474 2r multicolored .35 .25
1882 A474 2r multicolored .35 .25
1883 A475 2r multicolored .35 .25
Nos. 1881-1883 (3) 1.05 .75
Children's Week.

"Film" — A476

1975, Dec. 4 *Wmk. 353* *Perf. 10½*
1884 A476 8r multicolored .50 .25
4th Tehran International Film Festival.

Symbols of Reforms A477

People A478

No. 1887, Five reform symbols.

1976, Jan. 26 Litho. *Perf. 10½*
1885 A477 2r shown .35 .25
1886 A478 2r shown .35 .25
1887 A477 2r multi .35 .25
Nos. 1885-1887 (3) 1.05 .75
"White Revolution of King and People."

Motorcycle Policeman A479

Police Helicopter A480

1976, Feb. 16
1888 A479 2r multicolored 1.25 .75
1889 A480 6r multicolored 2.00 1.00
Highway Police Day.

Soccer Cup — A481

1976, Feb. 24 Litho. *Wmk. 353*
1890 A481 2r org & multi .40 .25
3rd Intl. Youth Soccer Cup, Shiraz and Ahvaz.

Candlestick — A482

Designs: No. 1892, Incense burner. No. 1893, Rose water container.

1976, Mar. 6
1891 A482 1r olive & multi .35 .25
1892 A482 1r claret & multi .35 .25
1893 A482 1r Prus bl & multi .35 .25
a. Strip of 3, #1891-1893 1.25 1.00
Novrooz, Iranian New Year.

Telephones, 1876 and 1976 — A483

1976, Mar. 10
1894 A483 10r multicolored .75 .25
Centenary of first telephone call by Alexander Graham Bell, Mar. 10, 1876.

Eye Within Square — A484

1976, Apr. 29 Litho. *Perf. 10½*
1895 A484 6r blk & multi 1.75 .25
a. Perf. 12½ 9.50 7.50
World Health Day: "Foresight prevents blindness."

Nurse with Infant — A485

Young Man Holding Old Man's Hand — A486

No. 1897, Engineering apprentices.

1976, May 10
1896 A485 2r shown .65 .25
1897 A485 2r multi .65 .25
1898 A486 2r shown .65 .25
Nos. 1896-1898 (3) 1.95 .75
Royal Org. of Social Services, 30th anniv.

Map of Iran, Men Linking Hands — A487

1976, May 13 *Wmk. 353*
1899 A487 2r yel & multi .40 .25
Iranian Cooperatives, 10th anniversary.

Waves and Ear Phones — A488

1976, May 17
1900 A488 14r gray & multi .75 .25
World Telecommunications Day.

Emblem, Woman with Flag, Man with Gun — A489

1976, June 6
1901 A489 2r bister & multi .60 .25
To publicize the power of stability.

Map of Iran, Columns of Persepolis, Nasser Khosrow — A490

1976, July 6 Litho. *Perf. 10½*
1902 A490 6r yel & multi .50 .25
Tourist publicity.

Reza Shah Pahlavi — A491

6r, Mohammad Ali Jinnah. 8r, Kemal Ataturk.

1976, July 21 Litho. *Wmk. 353*
1903 A491 2r gray & multi .65 .25
1904 A491 6r gray & multi .80 .25
1905 A491 8r gray & multi 1.00 .25
Nos. 1903-1905 (3) 2.45 .75
Regional Cooperation for Development Pact among Iran, Turkey and Pakistan, 12th anniversary.
See Pakistan 412-414, Turkey 2041-2043.

Torch, Montreal and Iranian Olympic Emblems — A492

1976, Aug. 1
1906 A492 14r multicolored 1.00 .25
21st Olympic Games, Montreal, Canada, July 17-Aug. 1.

Reza Shah Pahlavi in Coronation Robe — A493

Designs: 2r, Reza Shah and Mohammad Reza Shah Pahlavi, horiz. 14r, 20r, Mohammad Reza Shah Pahlavi in coronation robe and crown.

1976, Aug. 19 *Wmk. 353* *Perf. 10½*
1907 A493 2r lilac & multi 1.75 .75
1908 A493 6r blue & multi 2.75 1.00
1909 A493 14r grn & multi 4.00 1.50
Nos. 1907-1909 (3) 8.50 3.25

Souvenir Sheet

1976, Oct. 8 *Imperf.*
1910 A493 20r multi 8.50 7.50
50th anniv. of Pahlavi dynasty; 35th anniv. of reign of Mohammad Reza Shah Pahlavi. No. 1910 contains one stamp 43x62mm.

IRAN

Festival Emblem — A494

1976, Aug. 29   Litho.   Perf. 10½
1911 A494 10r multicolored   .65   .25
10th Iranian Arts Festival, Shiraz-Persepolis.

Iranian Scout Emblem — A495

1976, Oct. 2   Litho.   Perf. 10½
1912 A495 2r lt bl & multi   .50   .25
10th Asia Pacific Conference, Tehran 1976.

Cancer Radiation Treatment — A496

1976, Oct. 6
1913 A496 2r black & multi   .50   .25
Fight against cancer.

Target, Police Woman Receiving Decoration — A497

1976, Oct. 7
1914 A497 2r lt bl & multi   .50   .25
Police Day.

UPU Emblem, No. 1907 on Cover — A498

1976, Oct. 9
1915 A498 10r multicolored   1.50   .25
International Post Day.

Crown Prince Reza with Cup — A499

1976, Oct. 10
1916 A499 6r multicolored   .50   .25
Natl. Soc. of Village Culture Houses, anniv.

Reza Shah and Mohammad Reza Shah Pahlavi, Railroad — A500

1976, Oct. 15
1917 A500 8r black & multi   5.00   2.00
Railroad Day.

Emblem & Column Capital, Persepolis — A501

1976, Oct. 26
1918 A501 14r blue & multi   .80   .30
Festival of Culture and Art.

Census Emblem — A502

1976, Oct. 30
1919 A502 2r gray & multi   .40   .25
Natl. Population & Housing Census, 1976.

Flowers and Birds — A503

Designs: No. 1921, Flowers and bird. No. 1922, Flowers and butterfly. Designs are from covers of children's books.

1976, Oct. 31   Perf. 10½
1920 A503 2r multicolored   .35   .25
1921 A503 2r multicolored   .35   .25
1922 A503 2r multicolored   .35   .25
       Nos. 1920-1922 (3)   1.05   .75
Children's Week.

Mohammad Ali Jinnah — A504

1976, Dec. 25   Litho.   Wmk. 353
1923 A504 10r multicolored   .60   .25
Jinnah (1876-1948), 1st Governor General of Pakistan.

Development and Agriculture Corps — A505

17-Point Reform Law: 5d, Land reform. 10d, Nationalization of forests. 50d, Sale of shares of state-owned industries. 1r, Profit sharing for factory workers. 2r, Parliament Gate, Woman suffrage. 3r, Education Corps formation. 5r, Health Corps. 8r, Establishment of village courts. 10r, Nationalization of water resources. 12r, Reconstruction program, urban and rural. 14r, Administrative and educational reorganization. 20r, Sale of factory shares. 30r, Commodity pricing. 50r, Free education. 100r, Child care. 200r, Care of the aged (social security).

1977, Jan. 26   Photo.   Perf. 13x13½
Frame and Shah's Head in Gold
Size: 28x21mm
1924 A505 5d rose & green   .25   .25
1925 A505 10d lt grn & brn   .25   .25
1926 A505 50d yel & vio bl   .25   .25
1927 A505 1r lil & vio bl   .25   .25
1928 A505 2r org & green   .25   .25
1929 A505 3r lt bl & red   .30   .25
1930 A505 5r bl grn & mag   .30   .25

Size: 37x27mm
1931 A505 6r brn, mar & black   .50   .25
1932 A505 8r ultra, mar & blk   .50   .25
1933 A505 10r lt grn, bl & black   1.25   .25
1934 A505 12r vio, mar & black   1.25   .25
1935 A505 14r org, red & blk   1.25   .75
1936 A505 20r gray, ocher & black   2.75   .50
1937 A505 30r bl, grn & blk   2.75   .65
1938 A505 50r yel, brn & blk   4.00   .60
1939 A505 100r multi   5.00   1.25
1940 A505 200r multi   8.50   2.50
       Nos. 1924-1940 (17)   29.60   9.00
"White Revolution of King and People" reform laws.

Man in Guilan Costume — A506

2r, Woman in Guilan costume (Northern Iran).

1977, Mar. 6   Wmk. 353   Perf. 13
1941 A506 1r multicolored   .35   .25
1942 A506 2r multicolored   .40   .25
Novrooz, Iranian New Year.

Electronic Tree — A507

1977, May 17   Photo.   Perf. 13
1943 A507 20r multicolored   1.10   .35
World Telecommunications Day.

Reza Shah Dam — A508

1977, May 31   Perf. 13x13½
1944 A508 5r multicolored   .60   .25
Inauguration of Reza Shah Dam.

Olympic Rings — A509

1977, June 23   Litho.   Perf. 10½
1945 A509 14r multicolored   .90   .25
Olympic Day.

Terra-cotta Jug, Iran — A510

No. 1947, Terra-cotta bullock cart, Pakistan. No. 1948, Terra-cotta pot with human face, Turkey.

Perf. 13x13½
1977, July 21   Photo.   Wmk. 353
1946 A510 5r violet & multi   .50   .25
1947 A510 5r emer & multi   .50   .25
1948 A510 5r green & multi   .50   .25
       Nos. 1946-1948 (3)   1.50   .75
Regional Cooperation for Development Pact among Iran, Turkey and Pakistan, 13th anniv. See Pakistan 431-433, Turkey 2053-2055.

Flowers with Scout Emblems, Map of Asia — A511

1977, Aug. 5   Litho.   Perf. 13
1949 A511 10r multicolored   .80   .25
2nd Asia-Pacific Jamboree, Nishapur.

Map of Eastern Hemisphere with Iran — A512

1977, Sept. 20   Photo.   Wmk. 353
1950 A512 3r multicolored   .40   .25
9th Asian Electronics Conference, Tehran.

Tree of Learning, Symbolic Letters — A513

1977, Oct. 8   Wmk. 353   Perf. 13
1951 A513 10r multicolored   .60   .25
Honoring the teachers.

Globe, Envelope, UPU Emblem — A514

1977, Oct. 9   Photo.
1952 A514 14r multicolored   .65   .25
Iran's admission to the UPU, cent.

Folk Art — A515

1977, Oct. 16
1953 A515 5r multicolored   .60   .25
Festival of Folk Art.

Festival Type of 1975

Design: 20r, similar to 1975 issue, but with small crown within star.

1977, Oct. 26   Perf. 10½
1954 A472 20r bis, grn, car & blk   1.00   .25
Festival of Culture and Art.

Joust — A516

No. 1956, Rapunzel. No. 1957, Little princess with attendants.

1977, Oct. 31   Photo.
1955 A516 3r multicolored   .30   .25
1956 A516 3r multicolored   .30   .25
1957 A516 3r multicolored   .30   .25
  a. Strip of 3, #1955-1957   1.00   1.00
Children's Week.

IRAN

Emblem — A517

1977, Nov. 7   Wmk. 353   Perf. 13
1958   A517   5r multicolored   .40   .25
First Regional Seminar on the Education and Welfare of the Deaf.

Mohammad Iqbal — A518

1977, Nov. 9   Litho.   Perf. 10½
1959   A518   5r multicolored   .60   .25
Iqbal (1877-1938) of Pakistan, poet and philosopher.

African Sculpture — A519

1977, Dec. 14
1960   A519   20r multicolored   4.00   .55
African art.

Shah Mosque, Isfahan — A520

Designs: 1r, Ruins, Persepolis. 2r, Khajou Bridge, Isfahan. 5r, Imam Reza Shrine, Meshed. 9r, Warrior frieze, Persepolis. 10r, Djameh Mosque, Isfahan. 20r, King on throne, bas-relief. 25r, Sheik Lotfollah Mosque. 30r, Ruins, Persepolis, diff. view. 50r, Ali Ghapou Palace, Isfahan. 100r, Bas-relief, Tagh Bastan. 200r, Horseman and prisoners, bas-relief, Naqsh Rostam.

1977-78   Photo.   Perf. 13x13½
"Iran" and Head in Gold
Size: 28x21mm
1961   A520   1r deep brn   .25   .25
1962   A520   2r emerald   .25   .25
1963   A520   3r magenta   .40   .25
1964   A520   5r Prus blue   .50   .25
Size: 36x27mm
1965   A520   9r sepia ('78)   1.40   .75
1966   A520   10r brt bl ('78)   4.00   .85
1967   A520   20r rose   1.40   .55
1968   A520   25r ultra ('78)   17.00   9.75
1969   A520   30r magenta   2.00   .55
1970   A520   50r deep yel grn ('78)   4.00   3.50
1971   A520   100r dk bl ('78)   10.00   9.75
1972   A520   200r vio bl ('78)   14.00   19.00
Nos. 1961-1972 (12)   55.20   45.70
For overprints see Nos. 2009, 2011-2018.

Persian Rug — A521

Designs: Persian rugs.

1978, Feb. 11   Litho.   Perf. 10½
1973   A521   3r sil & multi   .35   .25
1974   A521   5r sil & multi   .45   .25
1975   A521   10r sil & multi   .75   .35
Nos. 1973-1975 (3)   1.55   .85
Opening of Carpet Museum.

Mazanderan Man — A522

Design: 5r, Mazanderan woman.

1978, Mar. 6   Perf. 13
1976   A522   3r yel & multi   .30   .25
1977   A522   5r lt bl & multi   .45   .25
Novrooz, Iranian New Year.

Mohammad Reza Shah Pahlavi — A523

1978, Jan. 26
1978   A523   20r multicolored   3.00   1.00
Shah's White Revolution, 15th anniv.

Reza Shah Pahlavi and Crown Prince Inspecting Girls' School — A524

Designs (Reza Shah Pahlavi and Crown Prince Mohammad Reza Shah Pahlavi): 5r, Inauguration of Trans-Iranian railroad. 10r, At stairs of Palace, Persepolis. 14r, Shah handing Crown Prince (later Shah) officer's diploma at Tehran Officers' Academy.

1978, Mar. 15
1979   A524   3r multicolored   .75   .25
1980   A524   5r multicolored   .75   .35
1981   A524   10r multicolored   1.10   .40
1982   A524   14r multicolored   1.50   .70
Nos. 1979-1982 (4)   4.10   1.70
Reza Shah Pahlavi (1877-1944), founder of Pahlavi dynasty.

Communications Satellite over Map of Iran — A525

1978, Apr. 19   Litho.   Perf. 10½
1983   A525   20r multicolored   .65   .25
ITU, 7th meeting, Tehran; 10th anniv. of Iran's membership.

Antenna, ITU Emblem — A526

1978, May 17   Litho.   Perf. 10½
1984   A526   15r multicolored   .65   .25
10th World Telecommunications Day.

Welfare Legion Emblem — A527

1978, June 13   Photo.   Perf. 13x13½
1985   A527   10r multicolored   .65   .25
Universal Welfare Legion, 10th anniversary.

Pink Roses, Iran — A528

Designs: 10r, Yellow rose, Turkey. 15r, Red roses, Pakistan.

Perf. 13½x13
1978, July 21   Wmk. 353
1986   A528   5r multicolored   .60   .25
1987   A528   10r multicolored   .90   .25
1988   A528   15r multicolored   1.00   .40
Nos. 1986-1988 (3)   2.50   .90
Regional Cooperation for Development Pact among Iran, Turkey and Pakistan, 14th anniversary.
See Pakistan 449-451, Turkey 2094-2096.

Rhazes, Pharmaceutical Tools — A529

1978, Aug. 26   Wmk. 353   Perf. 13
1989   A529   5r multicolored   .65   .25
Pharmacists' Day. Rhazes (850-923), chief physician of Great Hospital in Baghdad.

Girl Scouts, Aryamehr Arch — A530

1978, Sept. 2   Perf. 10½
1990   A530   5r multicolored   .65   .30
23rd World Girl Scouts Conference, Tehran, Sept. 1978.

Reza Shah Pahlavi — A531

Design: 5r, Mohammad Reza Shah Pahlavi.

1978, Sept. 11   Litho.   Perf. 10½
1991   A531   3r multicolored   1.40   .40
1992   A531   5r multicolored   1.50   .50
Bank Melli Iran, 50th anniversary.

Girl and Bird — A532

1978, Oct. 31   Photo.   Perf. 13
1993   A532   3r multicolored   .75   .30
Children's Week.

Envelope, Map of Iran, UPU Emblem — A533

1978, Nov. 22   Perf. 13x13½
1994   A533   14r gold & multi   1.25   .40
World Post Day, Oct. 22.

Communications Symbols and Classroom — A534

1978, Nov. 22   Perf. 10½
1995   A534   10r multicolored   1.25   .40
Faculty of Communications, 50th anniv.

Human Rights Flame — A535

1978, Dec. 17   Photo.   Perf. 13
1996   A535   20r bl, blk & gold   3.00   .50
Universal Declaration of Human Rights, 30th anniv.

Kurdistani Man — A536

Design: 5r, Kurdistani woman.

1979, Mar. 17
1997   A536   3r multicolored   .90   .25
1998   A536   5r multicolored   1.25   .25

Rose — A537

1979, Mar. 17
1999   A537   2r multicolored   .25   .25
Novrooz, Iranian New Year.
See No. 2310i.

Islamic Republic

A538

Islamic revolution: 3r, 10r, Demonstrators. 5r, Hands holding rose, gun and torch breaking through newspaper. 20r, Hands breaking prison bars, and dove, vert.

1979, Apr. 20   Perf. 10½
2000   A538   3r multicolored   2.00   .35
2001   A538   5r multicolored   1.40   .35
2002   A538   10r multicolored   1.40   .65
2003   A538   20r multicolored   3.00   .75
Nos. 2000-2003 (4)   7.80   2.10

IRAN

Nos. 1837-1838, 1966, 1970 and Type A520 Overprinted

Designs: 15r, Warriors on horseback, bas-relief, Naqsh-Rostam. 19r, Chehel Sotoon Palace, Isfahan.

1979   Wmk. 353   Perf. 13x13½
2008	A443	8r org & brown	3.00	1.50
2009	A520	9r gold & dp brn	1.50	1.50
2010	A443	10r dp yel grn	50.00	10.00
2011	A520	10r gold & brt bl	1.75	1.00
2012	A520	15r gold & red lil	1.75	1.00
2013	A520	19r gold & slate grn	1.75	1.00
2016	A520	50r gold & dp yel grn	5.00	2.00
2017	A520	100r gold & vio bl	10.00	4.00
2018	A520	200r gold & vio bl	12.50	8.50
	Nos. 2008-2018 (9)		87.25	30.00

Overprint means Islamic revolution. Forgeries of No. 2010 exist.

Symbolic Tulip — A539

1979, June 5   Photo.   Perf. 13
2019	A539	5r multicolored	1.50	.40

Potters, by Kamalel Molk — A540

No. 2021, at the Well, by Allah Baksh, Pakistan. No. 2022, Threshing, by Namik Ismail, Turkey.

1979, July 21   Litho.   Perf. 10½
2020	A540	5r multicolored	4.75	.35
2021	A540	5r multicolored	3.50	.35
2022	A540	5r multicolored	3.50	.35
	Nos. 2020-2022 (3)		11.75	1.05

Regional Cooperation for Development Pact among Iran, Turkey and Pakistan, 15th anniv. No. 2020 exists imperf. Value, pair $100. See Pakistan 486-488, Turkey 2112-2114.

"TELECOM 79" — A541

1979, Sept. 20   Perf. 10½
2023	A541	20r multicolored	15.00	.30

3rd World Telecommunications Exhibition, Geneva, Sept. 20-26.

Greeting the Sunrise — A542

Children's Drawings and IYC Emblem: 2r, Tulip over wounded man. 2r, Children with banners.

1979, Sept. 23
2024	A542	2r multicolored	1.25	.50
2025	A542	3r multicolored	1.25	.50
2026	A542	5r multicolored	1.50	.50
	Nos. 2024-2026 (3)		4.00	1.50

International Year of the Child.

Persian Rug Design — A543

1979-80   Photo.   Perf. 13½x13
2027	A543	50d brn & pale sal	.25	.25
2028	A543	1r dark & lt bl	.25	.25
2029	A543	2r red & yellow	.25	.25
2030	A543	3r dk bl & lt lil	.25	.25
2031	A543	5r slate grn & lt grn	.25	.25
2032	A543	10r blk & salmon pink ('80)	.30	.25
2033	A543	20r brn & gray ('80)	.40	.25

Size: 27x37½mm
2034	A543	50r dp violet & gray ('80)	1.00	.50
2035	A543	100r blk & slate grn ('80)	3.50	1.40
2036	A543	200r dk bl & cr ('80)	4.00	2.75
	Nos. 2027-2036 (10)		10.45	6.40

Globe in Envelope — A544

1979, Oct. 9   Litho.   Perf. 10½
2041	A544	10r multicolored	3.00	.40

World Post Day.

Ghyath-al-din Kashani, Astrolabe — A545

1979, Dec. 5   Litho.   Perf. 10½
2042	A545	5r ocher & blk	1.75	.40

Kashani, mathematician, 550th death anniv.

Ka'aba, Flame and Mosque A546

Hegira (Pilgrimage Year): 5r, Koran open over globe, vert. 10r, Salman Farsi (follower of Mohammad), map of Iran.

1980, Jan. 19
2043	A546	3r multicolored	.30	.25
2044	A546	5r multicolored	.30	.25
2045	A546	10r multicolored	.75	.25
	Nos. 2043-2045 (3)		1.35	.75

Reissued in May-June, 1980, with shiny gum and watermark position changed.

People, Map and Flag of Iran — A547

Islamic Revolution, 1st Anniversary: 3r, Blood dripping on broken sword. 5r, Window open on sun of Islam, people.

1980, Feb. 11
2046	A547	1r multicolored	.25	.25
2047	A547	3r multicolored	.35	.25
2048	A547	5r multicolored	.65	.30
	Nos. 2046-2048 (3)		1.25	.80

For similar stamps measuring 24x36mm see Nos. 2310a, 2310b, 2310d.

Dehkhoda, Dictionary Editor, Birth Cent. — A548

1980, Feb. 26
2049	A548	10r multicolored	.50	.25

East Azerbaijani Woman — A549

Novrooz (Iranian New Year): 5r, East Azerbaijani man.

1980, Mar. 5
2050	A549	3r multicolored	.35	.25
2051	A549	5r multicolored	.35	.25

Mohammad Mossadegh — A550

1980, Mar. 19   Photo.   Perf. 13x13½
2052	A550	20r multi	.70	.25

Oil industry nationalization, 29th anniv.; Mohammad Mossadegh, prime minister who initiated nationalization.

Professor Morteza Motahhari, 1st Death Anniversary — A551

1980, May 1   Litho.   Perf. 10½
2053	A551	10r black & red	.70	.25

World Telecommunications Day — A552

1980, May 17   Photo.   Perf. 13x13½
2054	A552	20r multicolored	.70	.25

Interior of Mosque — A553

1r, Demonstration. 3r, Avicenna, al-Biruni, Farabi. 5r, Hegira emblem.

1980, June 11   Litho.   Perf. 10½
2055	A553	50d shown	.25	.25
2056	A553	1r multicolored	.25	.25
2057	A553	3r multicolored	.40	.25
2058	A553	5r multicolored	.30	.25
	Nos. 2055-2058 (4)		1.20	1.00

Hegira, 1400th anniv.

Ali Sharyati, Educator — A554

1980, June 15   Photo.   Perf. 13x13½
2059	A554	5r multicolored	.50	.25

Holy Ka'aba and Hand Waving Banner — A555

1980, June 28
2060	A555	5r multicolored	.50	.25

Hazrat Mehdi, 12th Imam's birth anniv.

A556

1980, Sept. 10   Perf. 13½x13
2061	A556	5r multicolored	.60	.25

Ayatollah Seyed Mahmood Talegani, death anniv. Compare with design A829.

OPEC Emblem — A557

10r, Men holding OPEC emblem.

1980, Sept. 15
2062	A557	5r shown	.60	.25
2063	A557	10r multicolored	1.40	.25

20th anniversary of OPEC.

"Let Us Liberate Jerusalem" — A558

1980, Oct. 9   Perf. 13x13½
2064	A558	5r multicolored	.60	.25
2065	A558	20r multicolored	1.40	.25

Tulip and Fayziyye Seminary, Qum — A559

5r, Blood spilling on tulip. 20r, Tulip, Republic emblem.

1981, Feb. 11   Perf. 13
2066	A559	3r shown	.35	.25
2067	A559	5r multicolored	.35	.25
2068	A559	20r multicolored	.80	.25
	Nos. 2066-2068 (3)		1.50	.75

Islamic Revolution, 2nd anniversary. See Nos. 2310c, 2310e, 2310j, watermark 381 (3r, unserifed "R" in denomination. 5r, bright yellow background; 20r, light blue background behind flower.)

Lorestani Man — A560

Novrooz (Iranian New Year): 10r, Lorestani woman.

1981, Mar. 11
2069	A560	5r multicolored	.30	.25
2070	A560	10r multicolored	.45	.25

IRAN

Telecommunications Day — A561

Perf. 13½x13
1981, May 17   Photo.   Wmk. 353
2071 A561 5r dk grn & org   .50   .25

Ayatollah Kashani Birth Centenary — A562

Perf. 13x13½
1981, July 21   Wmk. 381
2072 A562 15r dk grn & dl pur   .50   .25

Adult Education — A563

50d, Citizens bearing arms. 2r, Irrigation. 3r, Friday prayer service. 5r, Paasdaar emblem and members. 10r, Koran text. 20r, Hejaab (women's veil). 50r, Industrial development. 100r, Religious ceremony, Mecca. 200r, Mosque interior. 5r, 10r, 200r vert.

Perf. 13x13½, 13½x13 (5r, 10r, 200r)
1981, Aug.
2073 A563 50d blk & dp bister   .25   .25
2074 A563 1r dl pur & grn   .25   .25
2075 A563 2r brn & grnsh bl   .25   .25
   Size: 38x28mm, 28x38mm
2076 A563 3r brt yel grn & black   .25   .25
2077 A563 5r dk bl & brn org   .25   .25
2078 A563 10r dk bl & grnsh blue   .25   .25
2079 A563 20r red & black   .55   .25
2080 A563 50r lilac & black   1.25 .30
2081 A563 100r org brn & blk   2.75 .60
2082 A563 200r blk & bl grn   5.25 1.25
   Nos. 2073-2082 (10)   11.30 3.90

Islamic Iranian Army — A564

1981, Sept. 21   Photo.   Perf. 13
2087 A564 5r multicolored   .65   .30

World Post Day and 12th UPU Day — A565

Perf. 13x13½
1981, Oct. 9   Wmk. 381
2088 A565 20r black & blue   .75   .45

Millennium of Nahjul Balaghah (Sacred Book) — A566

1981, Oct. 17   Perf. 13
2089 A566 25r multicolored   .75   .35

Martyrs' Memorial A567

3r, June 28, 1981 victims. 5r, Pres. Rajai, Prime Minister Bahonar. 10r, Gen. Chamran.

1981, Nov. 9   Photo.   Perf. 13
2090 A567 3r multicolored   .35   .25
2091 A567 5r multicolored   .35   .25
2092 A567 10r multicolored   .35   .25
   Nos. 2090-2092 (3)   1.05   .75

Ayatollah M. H. Tabatabaee, Scholar — A568

1981, Dec. 25   Photo.   Perf. 13
2093 A568 5r multicolored   .45   .25

Literacy Campaign — A569

1982, Jan. 20   Photo.   Perf. 13½x13
2094 A569 5r blue & gold   .45   .25

Islamic Revolution, 3rd Anniv. — A570

1982, Feb. 11   Wmk. 381   Perf. 13
2095 A570 5r Map   .25   .25
2096 A570 10r Tulip   .25   .25
2097 A570 20r Globe   .50   .25
   a. Strip of 3, #2095-2097   1.50 1.00

See Nos. 2310f, 2310g, 2310k (5r, orange background, Arabian "5" 6mm above black panel. 10r, dark green background, gray dove with thick black lines around it. 20r, pink background, bright blue globe, faint latitude and longitude lines.)

Unity Week — A571

1982, Feb. 20   Photo.   Perf. 13
2098 A571 25r multicolored   1.00   .25

Koran Verse Relative to Christ — A572

1982, Mar. 11   Photo.   Wmk. 381
2099 A572 20r multicolored   .80   .25

Khuzestan Man — A573

5r, Khuzestan woman.

1982, Mar. 13
2100 A573 3r shown   .25   .25
2101 A573 5r multicolored   .25   .25
   a. Pair, #2100-2101   .50   .50

Novrooz (New Year).

3rd Anniv. of Islamic Revolution A574

1982, Apr. 1
2102 A574 30r multicolored   1.00   .25

Seyed Mohammad Bagher Sadr — A575

1982, Apr. 8   Photo.   Perf. 13½x13
2103 A575 50r multicolored   1.10   .40

Martyrs of Altar (Ayatollahs Madani and Dastgeyb) A576

1982, Apr. 21   Perf. 13
2104 A576 50r multicolored   1.10   .40

A577

1982, May 1   Photo.   Perf. 13½x13
2105 A577 100r multi   2.25   .80

Intl. Workers' Solidarity Day.

A578

1982, May 17   Perf. 13½x13
2106 A578 100r multi   3.00   .80

14th World Telecommunications Day.

Mab'as Day (Mohammad's Appointment as Prophet) — A579

1982, May 21   Perf. 13½x13
2107 A579 32r multicolored   1.00   .30

1963 Islamic Rising, 19th Anniv. — A580

1982, June 5   Wmk. 381   Perf. 13
2108 A580 28r multicolored   .75   .30

Lt. Islambuli, Assassin of Anwar Sadat — A581

1982, June 17
2109 A581 2r multicolored   .50   .25

1st Death Anniv. of Ayatollah Beheshti — A582

1982, June 28
2110 A582 10r multicolored   .60   .25
   a. Missing dot in Arabic numeral 1.00 1.00

Iran-Iraq War — A583

1982, July 7   Perf. 13x13½
2111 A583 5r multicolored   .35   .25

Universal Jerusalem Day — A584

1982, July 15   Perf. 13
2112 A584 1r Dome of the Rock   .35   .25

Pilgrimage to Mecca — A585

1982, Sept. 28
2113 A585 10r multicolored   .45   .25

13th World UPU Day — A586

1982, Oct. 9   Perf. 13½x13
2114 A586 30r multicolored   .90   .25

4th Anniv. of Islamic Revolution — A587

1983, Feb. 11   Photo.   Perf. 13
2115 A587 30r multicolored   1.00   .25

See No. 2310n for stamp with orange or orange red crowd and thick sharp lettering in black panels.

4th Anniv. of Islamic Republic — A588

1983, Apr. 1   Photo.   Perf. 13
2116 A588 10r multicolored   .45   .25

Teachers' Day — A589

IRAN

	Perf. 13½x13		
1983, May 1		**Wmk. 381**	
2117 A589	5r multicolored	.50	.25

World Communications Year — A590

1983, May 17			
2118 A590	20r multicolored	.80	.25

First Session of Islamic Consultative Assembly — A591

1983, May 28		**Perf. 13**	
2119 A591	5r multicolored	.50	.25

20th Anniv. of Islamic Movement — A592

1983, June 5	**Photo.**	**Perf. 13**	
2120 A592	10r multicolored	.60	.25

Iraqi MiG Bombing Now Rooz Oil Well — A593

1983, June 11		**Perf. 13x13½**	
2121 A593	5r multicolored	.75	.35

Ecology week.

Ayatollah Mohammad Sadooghi — A594

1983, July 2	**Photo.**	**Perf. 13½**	
2122 A594	20r blk & dl red	.70	.25

Universal Day of Jerusalem — A595

1983, July 8			
2123 A595	5r Dome of the Rock	.50	.25

Government Week — A596

1983, Aug. 30		**Wmk. 381**	**Perf. 13**
2124 A596	3r multicolored	.50	.25

Death of Pres. Rajai and Prime Minister Bahonar, 2nd anniv.

Iran-Iraq War, 3rd Anniv. — A597

1983, Sept. 28	**Photo.**	**Perf. 13**	
2125 A597	5r rose red & blk	.50	.25

Ayatollah Ashrafi Esphahani, Martyr of Altar — A598

1983, Oct. 15	**Photo.**	**Perf. 13**	
2126 A598	5r multicolored	.50	.25

Mirza Kuchik Khan — A599

Religious and Political Figures: 1r, Sheikh Mohammad Khiabani. 3r, Seyd Majtaba Navab Safavi. 5r, Seyd Jamal-ed-Din Assadabadi. 10r, Seyd Hassan Modaress. 20r, Sheikh Fazel Assad Nouri. 30r, Mirza Mohammad Hossein Naiyni. 50r, Sheikh Mohammad Hossein Kashef. 100r, Seyd Hassan Shirazi. 200r, Mirza Reza Kermani.

1983-84		**Photo.**	**Perf. 13**	
2128 A599	1r black & pink		.25	.25
2129 A599	2r org & black		.25	.25
2130 A599	3r brt bl & blk		.25	.25
a.	Unwatermarked			
2131 A599	5r rose red & blk		.25	.25
2132 A599	10r yel grn & blk		.30	.25
2133 A599	20r lilac & blk		.50	.25
2134 A599	30r gldn brn & blk		.75	.30
a.	Unwatermarked			
2135 A599	50r blk & lt bl		1.25	.50
2136 A599	100r blk & org		2.50	1.00
a.	Unwatermarked			
2137 A599	200r blk & bluish grn		5.00	2.00
a.	Unwatermarked			
Nos. 2128-2137 (10)			11.30	5.30

Issue dates: 1r, 50r-200r, Feb. 1984. Others, Oct. 23, 1983.

UPU Day — A600

1983, Oct. 9	**Photo.**	**Wmk. 381**	
2138 A600	10r multi	.70	.25

Takeover of the US Embassy, 4th Anniv. — A601

1983, Nov. 4	**Photo.**	**Perf. 13**	
2139 A601	28r multicolored	1.00	.50

UN Day — A602

1983, Oct. 24		**Perf. 13½**	
2140 A602	32r multicolored	1.25	.25

Protest of veto by US, Russia, People's Rep. of China, France and Great Britain.

Intl. Medical Seminar, Tehran — A603

1983, Nov. 20			
2141 A603	3r Avicenna	.60	.25

People's Forces Preparation Day — A604

1983, Nov. 26		**Perf. 13**	
2142 A604	20r multicolored	.80	.25

Conference on Crimes of Iraqi Pres. Saddam Hussein — A605

1983, Nov. 28		**Perf. 13½x13**	
2143 A605	5r multicolored	.55	.25

Mohammad Mofatteh — A606

1983, Dec. 18	**Photo.**	**Perf. 13**	
2144 A606	10r multicolored	.50	.25

Birth Anniversary of the Prophet Mohammad — A607

1983, Dec. 22	**Photo.**	**Perf. 13**	
2145 A607	5r multicolored	1.00	.25

Approximately 700,000 examples of No. 2145 were issued before a spelling error was discovered, and the remainder of the issue was then withdrawn from sale.

5th Anniv. of Islamic Revolution — A608

1984, Feb. 11	**Photo.**	**Perf. 13x13½**	
2146 A608	10r multicolored	.75	.25

See No. 2310h for stamp with splotchy colors in blue background and denomination, flag colors and darker, thicker black lines around tulips. Background and denominations on No. 2146 have a screened appearance.

Nurses' Day — A609

20r, Attending wounded soldiers.

1984, Feb. 24		**Perf. 13**	
2147 A609	20r multicolored	.80	.25

Invalids' Day — A610

5r, Man in wheelchair.

1984, Feb. 29			
2148 A610	5r multicolored	.50	.25

Local Flowers — A611

3r, Lotus gebelia. 5r, Tulipa chrysantha. 10r, Glycyrhiza glabra. 20r, Matthiola alyssifolia.

1984, Mar. 10		**Perf. 13½x13**	
2149 A611	3r multicolored	.50	.25
2150 A611	5r multicolored	.50	.25
2151 A611	10r multicolored	.50	.25
2152 A611	20r multicolored	1.00	.25

Novrooz (New Year).

Islamic Republic, 5th Anniv. — A612

1984, Apr. 1	**Photo.**	**Perf. 13**	
2153 A612	5r Flag, globe, map	.50	.25

World Health Day — A613

1984, Apr. 7			
2154 A613	10r Children	.50	.25

Sheik Ragheb Harb, Lebanese Religious Leader — A614

1984, Apr. 18			
2155 A614	5r multicolored	.50	.25

World Red Cross Day — A615

1984, May 8	**Photo.**	**Perf. 13½x13**	
2156 A615	5r multicolored	.75	.25

16th World Telecommunications Day — A616

1984, May 17			
2157 A616	20r multicolored	.80	.25

Martyrdom of Seyyed Ghotb — A617

1984, May 28		**Perf. 13**	
2158 A617	10r multicolored	.70	.25

IRAN

Struggle Against Discrimination — A618

1984, Mar. 21   **Photo.**   *Perf. 13*
2159   A618   5r Malcolm X   .75   .25

Conquest of Mecca Anniv. — A619

1984, June 20
2160   A619   5r Holy Ka'aba, idol destruction   .55   .25

Universal Day of Jerusalem — A620
Id Al-fitr Feast — A621

5r, Map, Koran. 10r, Moon, praying crowd, mosque.

1984, June 29
2161   A620   5r multicolored   .25   .25
2162   A621   10r multicolored   .25   .25
   a.   Pair, #2161-2162   1.00   .50

Tchogha Zanbil Excavation, Susa — A622

Cultural Heritage Preservation: b, Emamzadeh Hossein Shrine, Kazvin. c, Emam Mosque, Isfahan. d, Ark Fortress, Tabriz. e, Mausoleum of Daniel Nabi, Susa.

1984, Aug. 20   *Perf. 13½*
2163   Strip of 5   1.50   .25
   a.-e.   A622 5r, any single   .25   .25

"Eid Ul-Adha" — A623

Perf. 13x13½
1984, Sept. 6   **Photo.**   *Wmk. 381*
2164   A623   10r Holy Ka'aba   .55   .25

Feast of Sacrifices (end of pilgrimage to Mecca).

10th Tehran Intl. Trade Fair — A624

1984, Sept. 11
2165   A624   10r multicolored   .55   .25

Iraq-Iran War, 4th Anniv. — A625

1984, Sept. 22   **Photo.**   *Perf. 13x13½*
2166   A625   5r Flower, bullets   .55   .25

UPU Day — A626

20r, Dove, UPU emblems.

1984, Oct. 9   *Perf. 13½*
2167   A626   20r multicolored   .80   .25

Haj Seyyed Mostafa Khomeini Memorial — A627

1984, Oct. 23
2168   A627   5r multicolored   .55   .25

Ghazi Tabatabaie Memorial — A628

1984, Nov. 1   *Perf. 13x13½*
2169   A628   5r Portrait   .55   .25

Intl. Saadi Congress — A629

10r, Portrait, mausoleum, emblem.

1984, Nov. 25   *Perf. 13½*
2170   A629   10r multicolored   .65   .25

Saadi (c. 1213-1292), Persian poet.

Mohammad's Birthday, Unity Week — A630

1984, Dec. 6   *Perf. 13x13½*
2171   A630   5r Koran, mosque   .55   .25

Islamic Revolution, 6th Anniv. — A631

1985, Feb. 11   *Perf. 13x13½*
2172   A631   40r multicolored   1.00   .40

See No. 2310o for stamp with bright pink denomination and dove tail.

Arbor Day — A632

3r, Sapling, deciduous trees. 5r, Maturing trees.

1985, Mar. 6   *Perf. 13*
2173   A632   3r multicolored   .30   .25
2174   A632   5r multicolored   .30   .25
   a.   Pair, #2173-2174   .65   .55

Local Flowers — A633

No. 2175, Fritillaria imperialis. No. 2176, Ranunculus ficarioides. No. 2177, Crocus sativus. No. 2178, Primula heterochroma stapf.

1985, Mar. 9   *Perf. 13½x13*
2175   A633   5r multicolored   .50   .25
2176   A633   5r multicolored   .50   .25
2177   A633   5r multicolored   .50   .25
2178   A633   5r multicolored   .50   .25
   a.   Block of 4, #2175-2178   2.50   2.00

Novrooz (New Year).

Women's Day — A634

10r, Procession of women.

1985, Mar. 13   *Perf. 13x13½*
2179   A634   10r multicolored   .55   .25

Birth anniv. of Mohammad's daughter, Fatima.

Republic of Iran, 6th Anniv. — A635

20r, Tulip, ballot box.

1985, Apr. 1
2180   A635   20r multicolored   .65   .25

Mab'as Festival — A636

1985, Apr. 18
2181   A636   10r Holy Koran   .65   .25

Religious festival celebrating the recognition of Mohammad as the true prophet.

Day of the Oppressed — A637

1985, May 6
2182   A637   5r Koran, flag, globe   .50   .25

Birthday of the 12th Imam.

World Telecommunications Day — A638

1985, May 17   *Perf. 13½x13*
2183   A638   20r ITU emblem   .70   .25

Liberation of Khorramshahr, 1st Anniv. — A639

1985, May 24
2184   A639   5r Soldier, bridge   .60   .25

Fist, Theological Seminary, Qum — A640

1985, June 5   *Perf. 13x13½*
2185   A640   10r multicolored   .60   .25

1963 Uprising, 22nd Anniv.

World Handicrafts Day — A641

1985, June 10   *Perf. 13½*
2186   A641   20r Plates, flasks   .80   .25

Day of Jerusalem — A642

1985, June 14
2187   A642   5r multicolored   .50   .25

Id Al-fitr Feast — A643

1985, June 20   *Perf. 13x13½*
2188   A643   5r multicolored   .55   .25

Founding of the Islamic Propagation Org. — A644

1985, June 22
2189   A644   5r tan & emerald   .55   .25

Ayatollah Sheikh Abdolhossein Amini — A645

1985, July 3   **Photo.**   *Perf. 13*
2190   A645   5r multicolored   .50   .25

IRAN

Pilgrimage to Mecca — A646

1985, July 20 Photo. Perf. 13½
2191 A646 10r multicolored   .65 .25

Cultural Heritage Preservation A647

Ceramic plates from Nishabur: a, Swords. b, Farsi script. c, Peacock. d, Four leaves.

1985, Aug. 20
2192 Block of 4   1.25 .75
a.-d. A647 5r, any single   .30 .25

Goharshad Mosque Uprising, 50th Anniv. — A648

1985, Aug. 21 Perf. 13x13½
2193 A648 10r multicolored   .60 .25

Week of Government — A649

Designs: a, Industry and communications. b, Industry and agriculture. c, Health care, red crescent. d, Education.

1985, Aug. 30 Photo. Perf. 13x13½
2194 Block of 4   1.25 .75
a.-d. A649 5r, any single   .25 .25

Bleeding Tulips — A650

1985, Sept. 8
2195 A650 10r multicolored   .60 .25

17th Shahrivar, Bloody Friday memorial.

OPEC, 25th Anniv. — A651

Design: No. 2196b, OPEC emblem and 25.

1985, Sept. 14 Perf. 13½
2196 Pair   .65 .35
a.-b. A651 5r, any single   .25 .25

Iran-Iraq War, 5th Anniv. — A652

Designs: a, Dead militiaman. b, Mosque and Ashura in Persian. c, Rockets descending on doves. d, Palm grove, rifle shot exploding rocket.

1985, Sept. 22
2197 Block of 4   1.50 1.00
a.-d. A652 5r any single   .35 .25

Ashura mourning.

Ash-Sharif Ar-Radi — A653

1985, Sept. 26 Photo. Perf. 13x13½
2198 A653 20r brt bl, lt bl & gold   .75 .25

Ash-Sharif Ar-Radi, writer, death millennium.

UPU Day — A654

1985, Oct. 9 Perf. 13½
2199 A654 20r multicolored   .85 .25

World Standards Day — A655

1985, Oct. 14
2200 A655 20r Natl. Standards Office emblem   .85 .25

Agricultural Training and Development Year — A656

1985, Oct. 19 Perf. 13x13½
2201 A656 5r Hand, wheat   .55 .25

Takeover of US Embassy, 6th Anniv. — A657

1985, Nov. 4 Perf. 13
2202 A657 40r multicolored   1.75 .40

Moslem Unity Week — A658

1985, Nov. 25 Perf. 13x13½
2203 A658 10r Holy Ka'aba   .70 .25

Birth of prophet Mohammad, 1015th anniv.

High Council of the Cultural Revolution — A659

1985, Dec. 10
2204 A659 5r Roses   .55 .25

Intl. Youth Year — A660

Designs: a, Education. b, Defense. c, Construction. d, Sports.

1985, Dec. 18 Photo. Perf. 13x13½
2205 Block of 4   1.25 .25
a.-d. A660 5r, any single   .25 .25

Ezzeddin al-Qassam, 50th Death Anniv. — A661

1985, Dec. 20 Perf. 13½
2206 A661 20r sil, sep & hn brn   .80 .25

Map, Fists, Bayonets — A662

1985, Dec. 25 Wmk. 381
2207 A662 40r multicolored   1.25 .40

Occupation of Afghanistan and Moslem resistance, 6th anniv.

Mirza Taqi Khan Amir Kabir (d. 1851) — A663

1986, Jan. 8 Litho. Perf. 13
2208 A663 5r multicolored   1.25 .25

Students Destroying Statue of the Shah, Tulips — A664

1986, Feb. 11 Photo. Perf. 13½
2209 A664 20r multicolored   .60 .25

Iranian Revolution, 7th anniv.
See No. 2310l for 24x36mm stamp with yellow Arabic script.

Sulayman Khater, 40th Death Anniv. — A665

1986, Feb. 15 Perf. 13
2210 A665 10r multicolored   .60 .25

Women's Day — A666

1986, Mar. 3 Perf. 13½
2211 A666 10r multicolored   .55 .25

Birth anniv. of Mohammad's daughter, Fatima.

Flowers — A667

a, Papaver orientale. b, Anemone coronaria. c, Papaver bracteatum. d, Anemone biflora.

1986, Mar. 11 Photo. Perf. 13½
2212 Block of 4   2.25 .25
a.-d. A667 5r any single   .40 .25

Novrooz (New Year).

2000th Day of Sacred Defense — A668

1986, Mar. 14 Photo. Perf. 13x13½
2213 A668 5r scarlet & grn   .50 .25

Intl. Day Against Racial Discrimination — A669

1986, Mar. 21
2214 A669 5r multicolored   .55 .25

Islamic Republic of Iran, 7th Anniv. — A670

1986, Apr. 1 Perf. 13
2215 A670 10r Flag, map   .55 .25

Mab'as Festival — A671

1986, Apr. 7
2216 A671 40r multicolored   1.10 .25

Army Day — A672

1986, Apr. 18 Perf. 13½
2217 A672 5r multicolored   .55 .25

Day of the Oppressed — A673

1986, Apr. 25 Perf. 13x13½
2218 A673 10r blk, gold & dk red   .50 .25

IRAN

Helicopter Crash — A674

1986, Apr. 25   **Wmk. 381**
2219   A674   40r multicolored   1.25   .40
US air landing at Tabass Air Base, 6th anniv.

Teacher's Day — A675

1986, May 2   **Photo.**   **Perf. 13x13½**
2220   A675   5r multicolored   .55   .25

World Telecommunications Day — A676

1986, May 17   **Perf. 13½x13**
2221   A676   20r blk, sil & ultra   .70   .25

Universal Day of the Child — A677

No. 2222, Child's war drawing. No. 2223, Hosein Fahmide, Iran-Iraq war hero.

1986, June 1   **Perf. 13**
2222   A677   15r multicolored   .45   .25
2223   A677   15r multicolored   .45   .25
   a. Pair, #2222-2223   1.00   .30

1963 Uprising, 23rd Anniv. — A678

1986, June 5   **Perf. 13x13½**
2224   A678   10r Qum Theological Seminary   .65   .25

Day of Jerusalem — A679

1986, June 6
2225   A679   10r multicolored   .70   .25

Id Al-Fitr Feast — A680

1986, June 9   **Perf. 13**
2226   A680   10r Moslems praying   .75   .25

World Handicrafts Day — A681

a, Baluchi cross-hatched rug. b, Craftsman. c, Qalamkar flower rug. d, Copper repousse vase.

1986, June 10   **Perf. 13½**
2227   Block of 4   2.00   .40
   a.-d. A681 10r, any single   .45   .25

Intl. Day for Solidarity with Black So. Africans — A682

1986, June 26
2228   A682   10r multicolored   .70   .25

Ayatollah Beheshti — A683

1986, June 28   **Perf. 13x13½**
2229   A683   10r multicolored   .60   .25
Death of Beheshti and Islamic Party workers, Tehran headquarters bombing, 5th anniv.

Ayatollah Mohammad Taqi Shirazi, Map of Iraq — A684

1986, June 30   **Photo.**   **Wmk. 381**
2230   A684   20r multicolored   .80   .25
Iraqi Moslem uprising against the British.

Shrine of Imam Reza — A685

1986, July 19   **Perf. 13½**
2231   A685   10r multicolored   .50   .25

Eid Ul-Adha, Feast of Sacrifice — A686

1986, Aug. 17   **Perf. 13x13½**
2232   A686   10r multicolored   .55   .25

Cultural Heritage Preservation A687

Designs: No. 2233, Bam Fortress. No. 2234, Kabud (Blue) Mosque, Tabriz. No. 2235, Mausoleum of Sohel Ben Ali at Astenah, Arak. No. 2236, Soltanieh Mosque, Zendjan Province.

1986, Aug. 20
2233   A687   5r Hilltop   .35   .25
2234   A687   5r shown   .35   .25
2235   A687   5r Intact roof   .35   .25
2236   A687   5r Damaged roof   .35   .25
   Nos. 2233-2236 (4)   1.40   1.00

Eid Ul-Ghadir Feast — A688

1986, Aug. 25
2237   A688   20r multicolored   .70   .25

Population and Housing Census — A689

1986, Sept. 9   **Perf. 13½x13**
2238   A689   20r multicolored   .80   .25

Iran-Iraq War, 6th Year — A690

1986, Sept. 22   **Perf. 13**
2239   A690   10r Battleship Paykan   .50   .25
2240   A690   10r Susangerd   .50   .25
2241   A690   10r Khorramshahr   .50   .25
2242   A690   10r Howeizeh   .50   .25
2243   A690   10r Siege of Abadan   .50   .25
   Nos. 2239-2243 (5)   2.50   1.25

10th Asian Games, Seoul — A691

1986, Oct. 2   **Photo.**   **Wmk. 381**
2244   A691   15r Wrestling   .65   .25
2245   A691   15r Rifle shooting   .65   .25

World Post Day — A692

1986, Oct. 9
2246   A692   20r multicolored   .70   .25

UNESCO, 40th Anniv. — A693

1986, Nov. 4   **Photo.**   **Perf. 13x13½**
2247   A693   45r blk, sky bl & brt rose   1.25   .45

Ayatollah Tabatabaie (d. 1981) — A694

1986, Nov. 15   **Photo.**   **Perf. 13½x13**
2248   A694   10r multicolored   .55   .25

Unity Week — A695

1986, Nov. 20
2249   A695   10r multicolored   .55   .25
Birth anniv. of Mohammad.

People's Militia — A696

1986, Nov. 26   **Perf. 13**
2250   A696   5r multicolored   .55   .25
Mobilization of the Oppressed Week.

Afghan Resistance Movement, 7th Anniv. — A697

1986, Dec. 27
2251   A697   40r multicolored   1.25   .40

Nurses' Day — A698

1987, Jan. 12   **Photo.**   **Perf. 13**
2252   A698   20r multicolored   .70   .25
Hazrat Zainab birth anniv.

Fifth Islamic Theology Conference, Tehran — A699

Wmk. 381
1987, Jan. 29   **Photo.**   **Perf. 13**
2253   A699   20r multicolored   .65   .25

Islamic Revolution, 8th Anniv. — A700

1987, Feb. 11
2254   A700   20r multicolored   .80   .25
See No. 2310m for 24x36mm stamp.

IRAN

Islamic Revolutionary Committees, 8th Anniv. — A701

1987, Feb. 12
2255 A701 10r brt bl, scar & yel .65 .25

Women's Day — A702

1987, Feb. 19
2256 A702 10r multicolored .60 .25
Birthday of Fatima, daughter of Mohammad.

Iran Air, 25th Anniv. — A703

1987, Feb. 24
2257 A703 30r multicolored 1.00 .30

Ayatollah Mirza Mohammad Hossein Naeini, 50th Death Anniv. — A704

1987, Mar. 6   Photo.   Perf. 13
2258 A704 10r multicolored .55 .25

New Year — A705

Flowers: a, Iris persica. b, Rosa damascena. c, Iris paradoxa. d, Tulipa clusiana.

1987, Mar. 11   Perf. 13½x13
2259   Block of 4   2.75 .50
a.-d. A705 5r, any single .60 .25
See Nos. 2313, 2361, 2411, 2443.

Mab'as Festival — A706

1987, Mar. 28   Perf. 13
2260 A706 45r gold, dk grn & grn 1.40 .45

Universal Day of the Oppressed — A707

1987, Apr. 14
2261 A707 20r multicolored .65 .25
Savior Mahdi's birthday.

Memorial to Lebanese Hizbollah Martyrs — A708

1987, Apr. 5
2262 A708 10r grn, gray & brt car .55 .25

Revolutionary Guards Day — A709

1987, Apr. 2
2263 A709 5r multi .60 .25
Imam Hossein's birthday.

8th Anniv. of Islamic Republic — A710

1987, Apr. 1
2264 A710 20r multicolored .70 .25

World Health Day — A711

Child survival through immunization: 3r, Intravenous. 5r, Oral.

1987, Apr. 7   Perf. 13x13½
2265 A711 3r multicolored .30 .25
2266 A711 5r multicolored .40 .25
a.   Pair, #2265-2266 .80 .25

Int'l. Labor Day — A712

1987, May 1   Photo.   Perf. 13
2267 A712 5r multicolored .55 .25

Teachers' Day — A713

1987, May 2   Wmk. 381
2268 A713 5r Ayatollah Mottahari .55 .25

A714

1987, May 17   Perf. 13½x13
2269 A714 20r multicolored .90 .25
World Telecommunications Day.

A715

No. 2270, Sassanian silver gilt vase. No. 2271, Bisque pot, Rey, 12th cent.

1987, May 18   Perf. 13
2270 A715 20r multicolored .90 .25
2271 A715 20r multicolored .90 .25
Intl. Museum Day.

Universal Day of Jerusalem — A716

1987, May 22   Perf. 13½x13
2272 A716 20r multicolored .60 .25

World Crafts Day — A717

a, Blown glass tea service. b, Stained glass window. c, Ceramic plate. d, Potter.

1987, June 10   Perf. 13x13½
2273   Block of 4   1.00 .25
a.-d. A717 5r any single .25 .25

1963 Uprising, 24th Anniv. — A718

1987, June 5   Photo.   Perf. 13½
2274 A718 20r multicolored .80 .25

Tax Reform Week — A719

1987, July 10   Perf. 13
2275 A719 10r black, sil & gold .55 .25

Welfare Week — A720

1987, July 17
2276 A720 15r multicolored .70 .25

Eid Ul-adha, Feast of Sacrifice A721

1987, Aug. 6
2277 A721 12r sil, blk & Prus grn .65 .25

Eid Ul-Ghadir Festival — A722

1987, Aug. 14
2278 A722 18r black, green & gold .60 .25

Banking Week — A723

1987, Aug. 17   Perf. 13½x13
2279 A723 15r red brn, gold & pale grnsh bl .65 .25

1st Cultural and Artistic Congress of Iranian Calligraphers — A724

1987, Aug. 21   Photo.   Perf. 13x13½
2280 A724 20r multicolored 1.00 .25

Memorial to Iranian Pilgrims Killed in Mecca — A725

1987, Aug. 26   Wmk. 381   Perf. 13
2281 A725 8r multicolored .65 .25

Assoc. of Iranian Dentists, 25th Anniv. — A726

1987, Aug. 27   Photo.   Perf. 13½x13
2282 A726 10r multicolored 1.00 .25

IRAN

Intl. Peace Day — A727

1987, Sept. 1   *Perf. 13*
2283 A727 20r gold & lt ultra   .80   .25

No. 2285, Soldier, battle scene.

Iran-Iraq War, 7th Anniv. — A728

1987, Sept. 22   *Perf. 13½x13*
2284 A728 25r shown   .75   .25
2285 A728 25r multicolored   .75   .25
   a. Pair, #2284-2285   1.75   1.25

Police Day — A729

1987, Sept. 28
2286 A729 10r multicolored   .75   .25

Intl. Social Security Week, Oct. 4-10 — A730

1987, Oct. 4   *Wmk. 381*
2287 A730 15r blk, gold & brt blue   .60   .25

World Post Day — A731

UPU emblem and: No. 2288, M. Ghandi, minister of the Post and Telecommunications Bureau. No. 2289, Globe, dove.

1987, Oct. 9   *Perf. 13x13½*
2288 A731 15r multicolored   .55   .25
2289 A731 15r multicolored   .55   .25

Importation Prohibited
Importation of stamps was prohibited effective Oct. 29, 1987.

A732

Wmk. 381

1987, Nov. 4   *Photo.*   *Perf. 13*
2290 A732 40r multicolored   1.25   .25

Takeover of US Embassy, 8th anniv.

A733

1987, Nov. 5
2291 A733 20r multicolored   .90   .25

1st Intl. Tehran Book Fair.

Mohammad's Birthday, Unity Week — A734

1987, Nov. 10
2292 A734 25r multicolored   .60   .25

Ayatollah Modarres Martyrdom, 50th Anniv. — A735

1987, Dec. 1
2293 A735 10r brn & bister   .50   .25

Agricultural Training and Extension Week — A736

1987, Dec. 6
2294 A736 10r multicolored   .50   .25

Afghan Resistance, 8th Anniv. — A737

1987, Dec. 27
2295 A737 40r multicolored   1.25   .40

Main Mosques — A738

1987-92   *Perf. 13x13½, 13½x13*
Silver Background
2295A A738 1r Shoushtar   .50   .25
2296 A738 2r Ouroumieh   .50   .25
2296A A738 3r Kerman   .50   .25
2297 A738 5r Kazvin   .50   .30
2298 A738 10r Varamin   .50   .30
   a. Unwatermarked ('91)   3.00   2.00
2299 A738 20r Saveh   .75   .75
   a. Unwatermarked ('91)   2.00   1.25
2300 A738 30r Natanz, vert.   1.50   1.40
2301 A738 40r Shiraz   2.00   1.75
   a. Unwatermarked ('92)   10.00   5.00
2302 A738 50r Isfahan, vert.   1.50   1.25
   a. Unwatermarked ('91)   3.00   2.00
2303 A738 100r Hamadan   2.00   2.00
   a. Unwatermarked ('91)   5.00   3.00
2304 A738 200r Dezfoul, vert.   4.00   3.50
   a. Unwatermarked ('91)   15.00   10.00
2305 A738 500r Yazd, vert.   13.00   10.00
   a. Unwatermarked ('91)   20.00   15.00
   Nos. 2295A-2305 (12)   27.25   22.00
   Nos. 2298a-2305a (7)   58.00   33.25

Issued: 10r, 12/1; 5r, 12/30; 500r, 1/10/88; 20r, 1/14/88; 2r, 1/24/88; 50r, 1/24/89; 100r, 10/21/89; 200r, 10/28/89; 30r, 40r, 3/17/90; 1r, 3r, 3/92.
For surcharges see Nos. 2750-2751.
Watermarks on this issue can be difficult to discern. The paper of the unwatermarked stamps show fluoresence under long wave ultraviolet light.

Qum Uprising, 10th Anniversary A739

1988, Jan. 9   *Perf. 13*
2306 A739 20r multicolored   .65   .25

Bombing of Schools by Iraq — A740

1988, Feb. 1   *Perf. 13x13½*
2307 A740 10r multicolored   .80   .25

Gholamreza Takhti, World Wrestling Champion A741

1988, Feb. 4   *Perf. 13½*
2308 A741 15r multicolored   .50   .50

Women's Day — A742

1988, Feb. 9   *Perf. 13*
2309 A742 20r multicolored   .65   .25

Birth anniv. of Mohammad's daughter, Fatima.

Types of 1979-88 and Souvenir Sheet

Islamic Revolution, 9th Anniv. — A743

1988, Feb. 11   *Wmk. 381*   *Perf. 13*
2310 Sheet of 16   13.00
   a. A547 1r like #2046
   b. A547 3r like #2047
   c. A559 3r like #2066
   d. A547 5r like #2048
   e. A559 5r like #2067
   f. A570 5r like #2095
   g. A570 10r like #2096
   h. A608 10r like #2146
   i. A537 18r like #1999
   j. A559 20r like #2068
   k. A570 20r like #2097
   l. A664 20r like #2209
   m. A700 20r like #2254
   n. A587 30r like #2115
   o. A631 40r like #2172
   p. A743 40r shown

Nos. 2310a, 2310b, 2310d, 2310l, 2310m are smaller than the original issues. See original issues for distinguishing features on other stamps.
Exists imperf. Value $16.

Tabriz Uprising, 10th Anniv. — A744

1988, Feb. 18   *Perf. 13*
2311 A744 25r multicolored   .80   .75

Arbor Day — A745

1988, Mar. 5
2312 A745 15r multicolored   .50   .25

New Year Festival Type of 1987

Flowers: a, Anthemis hyalina. b, Malva silvestria. c, Viola odorata. d, Echium amaenum.

1988, Mar. 10   *Perf. 13½x13*
2313 Block of 4   1.50   1.25
   a.-d. A705 10r any single   .35   .25

Islamic Republic, 9th Anniv. — A746

1988, Apr. 1   *Perf. 13*
2314 A746 20r multicolored   .65   .25

Universal Day of the Oppressed — A747

1988, Apr. 3
2314A A747 20r multicolored   .65   .25

Savior Mahdi's Birthday.

Cultural Heritage A748

1988, Apr. 18
2315 A748 10r Mosque   .35   .25
2316 A748 10r Courtyard   .35   .25
   a. Pair, #2315-2316   .75   .75
2317 A748 10r Minarets, vert.   .35   .25
2318 A748 10r Corridor, vert.   .35   .25
   a. Pair, #2317-2318   1.25   1.00

Chemical Bombardment of Halabja, Iraq — A749

1988, Apr. 26
2319 A749 20r multicolored   1.00   .40

426   IRAN

Palestinian Uprising — A750b

1988, May 13
2320   Strip of 5   2.75 1.75
     a.   A750 10r multi   .50   .25
     b.   A750a 10r multi   .50   .25
     c.   A750b 10r multi   .50   .25
     d.   A750b 10r multi, diff.   .50   .25
     e.   A750b 10r Rock in hand, rioters   .50   .25

World Telecommunications Day — A751

1988, May 17   Perf. 13x13½
2321   A751   20r green & blue   .65   .25

Intl. Museum Day — A752

Designs: a, Ceramic vase, 1982. b, Bastan Museum, entranceway. c, Tabriz silk rug, 14th cent. d, Gold ring, 7th cent. B.C.

1988, May 18   Perf. 13
2322   Block of 4   1.50 1.50
     a.-d. A752 10r any single   .30   .25

Mining Day — A753

1988, May 22   Photo.   Wmk. 381
2323   A753   20r multicolored   1.25   .50

Intl. Day of the Child — A754

1988, June 1
2324   A754   10r multicolored   .50   .30

June 5th Uprising, 25th Anniv. — A755

1988, June 5
2325   A755   10r multicolored   .65   .40

World Crafts Day — A756

1988, June 10   Perf. 13x13½
2326   A756   10r Straw basket   .30   .25
2327   A756   10r Weaver   .30   .25
     a.   Pair, #2326-2327   .65   .55
2328   A756   10r Tapestry, vert.   .30   .25
2329   A756   10r Miniature, vert.   .30   .25
     a.   Pair, #2328-2329   .65   .55

Child Health Campaign — A757

1988, July 6   Perf. 13
2330   A757   20r blk, blue & green   .45   .25

Tax Reform Week — A758

1988, July 10
2331   A758   20r multicolored   .45   .25

Allameh Balkhi — A759

1988, July 15   Perf. 13½x13
2332   A759   20r multicolored   .45   .25

A760

No. 2333, Holy Ka'aba, dove, stars.

1988, July 21   Perf. 13
2333   A760   10r multicolored   .40   .25
2334   A760   10r shown   .40   .25

Massacre of Muslim Pilgrims at Mecca. Nos. 2333-2334 were printed together in one sheet, with alternating placement.

Destruction of Iranian Airliner — A761

1988, Aug. 11
2335   A761   45r multicolored   1.75 1.00

Seyyed Ali Andarzgou — A762

1988, Aug. 13
2336   A762   20r multicolored   .50   .25

Islamic Banking Week — A763

1988, Sept. 1   Perf. 13½x13
2337   A763   20r multicolored   .50   .25

Divine Day of 17 Shahrivar, 10th Anniv. — A764

1988, Sept. 8
2338   A764   25r multicolored   .70   .25

1988 Summer Olympics, Seoul — A765

Designs: a, Weightlifting. b, Pommel horse. c, Judo. d, Soccer. e, Wrestling.

1988, Sept. 10
2339   Strip of 5   2.00 1.50
     a.-e. A765 10r any single   .35   .25

Agricultural Census — A766

1988, Sept. 17   Perf. 13½x13
2340   A766   30r blk, grn & yel   .60   .25

Iran-Iraq War, 8th Anniv. — A767

1988, Sept. 22   Perf. 13x13½
2341   A767   20r multicolored   .50   .25

World Post Day — A768

1988, Oct. 9   Perf. 13
2342   A768   20r blk, ultra & grn   .60   .30

Parents and Teachers Cooperation Week — A769

1988, Oct. 16
2343   A769   20r multicolored   .50   .25

Mohammad's Birthday, Unity Week — A770

1988, Oct. 29
2344   A770   10r multicolored   .50   .30

A771

1988, Nov. 4
2345   A771   45r multicolored   1.10   .50

Takeover of US embassy, 9th anniv.

Insurance Day — A772

1988, Nov. 6   Perf. 13½x13
2346   A772   10r multicolored   .45   .30

Intl. Congress on the Writings of Hafiz — A773

1988, Nov. 19   Perf. 13x13½
2347   A773   20r blue, gold & pink   .50   .30

Agricultural Training and Extension Week — A774

1988, Dec. 6   Perf. 13
2348   A774   15r multicolored   .60   .30

Scientists, Artists and Writers — A775

No. 2349, Parvin E'Tessami. No. 2350, Jalal Al-Ahmad. No. 2351, Muhammad Mo'in. No. 2352, Qaem Maqam Farahani. No. 2353, Kamal Al-Molk.

1988, Dec. 18   Perf. 13x13½
2349   A775   10r multi   .35   .35
2350   A775   10r multi   .35   .35
2351   A775   10r multi   .35   .35
     a.   Pair, #2350-2351   .80   .35

IRAN

2352	A775	10r multi	.35	.35
2353	A775	10r multi	.35	.35
a.		Pair, #2352-2353	.80	.75

See Nos. 2398-2402.

Afghan Resistance, 9th Anniv. — A776

1988, Dec. 27 — Perf. 13
2354 A776 40r multicolored 1.10 .40

Transportation and Communication Decade — A777

No. 2355, Satellite, envelopes, microwave dish. No. 2356, Cargo planes. No. 2357, Train, trucks. No. 2358, Ships.

Perf. 13x13½
1989, Jan. 16 — Wmk. 381
2355	A777	20r multicolored	.60	.35
2356	A777	20r multicolored	.60	.35
a.		Pair, #2355-2356	1.40	1.25
2357	A777	20r multicolored	.60	.35
2358	A777	20r multicolored	.60	.35
a.		Pair, #2357-2358	1.40	1.25

Prophethood of Mohammad — A778

1989, Mar. 6 — Perf. 13
2359 A778 20r multicolored .75 .40
Mab'as festival.

Arbor Day — A779

1989, Mar. 6
2360 A779 20r multicolored .70 .40

New Year Festival Type of 1987

Flowers: a, Cephalanthera kurdica. b, Dactylorhiza romana. c, Comperia comperiana. d, Orchis mascula.

1989, Mar. 11 — Perf. 13½x13
2361 Block of 4 1.25 1.25
a.-d. A705 10r any single .25 .25

A780

30r, Meteorological devices, ship.

1989, Mar. 23
2362 A780 20r shown .60 .60
2363 A780 30r multicolored .60 .60
a. Pair, #2362-2363 1.50 1.25
World Meteorology Day.

A781

1989, Apr. 1 — Perf. 13
2364 A781 20r multicolored .65 .40
Islamic Republic, 10th anniv.

Reconstruction of Abadan Refinery — A782

1989, Apr. 1
2365 A782 20r multicolored .70 .30

Ayatollah Morteza Motahhari, 10th Death Anniv. — A783

1989, May 2
2366 A783 20r multicolored .50 .30
Teachers' Day.

A784

1989, May 5
2367 A784 30r multicolored .90 .30
Universal Day of Jerusalem.

A785

1989, May 17 — Perf. 13½x13
2368 A785 20r multicolored .80 .30
World Telecommunications Day.

A786

Intl. Museum Day: Gurgan pottery, 6th cent.

1989, May 18 — Perf. 13x13½
2369	A786	20r Jar	.50	.50
2370	A786	20r Bottle	.50	.50
a.		Pair, #2369-2370	1.25	1.10

Nomads' Day — A787

1989, June 4 — Perf. 13
2371 A787 20r multicolored .50 .25

World Crafts Day — A788

No. 2372, Engraver. No. 2373, Copper vase. No. 2374, Copper plate, vert. No. 2375, Copper wall hanging, vert.

1989, July 5 — Perf. 13x13½
2372	A788	20r multicolored	.40	.40
2373	A788	20r multicolored	.40	.40
a.		Pair, #2372-2373	1.10	1.00
2374	A788	20r multicolored	.40	.40
2375	A788	20r multicolored	.40	.40
a.		Pair, #2374-2375	1.10	1.00

Ayatollah Khomeini (1900-89) — A789

1989, July 6 — Perf. 13
2376 A789 20r multicolored .60 .30

Pasteur and Avicenna — A790

1989, July 7
2377	A790	30r multicolored	.70	.40
2378	A790	50r multicolored	1.00	.60
a.		Pair, #2377-2378	2.00	2.00

PHILEXFRANCE.

Asia-Pacific Telecommunity, 10th Anniv. — A791

1989, July 25
2379 A791 30r blk, org brn & bl .80 .40

Mehdi Araghi, 10th Death Anniv. — A792

1989, Aug. 30
2380 A792 20r brn org & org brn .50 .25

M.H. Shahryar, Poet — A793

1989, Sept. 17
2381 A793 20r multicolored .50 .25

Iran-Iraq War, 9th Anniv. — A794

20r, UN Security Council res. 598.

1989, Sept. 22
2382 A794 20r multi .60 .60

Ayatollah Khomeini A795

Designs: 1r, Khomeini's birthplace, flower. 2r, Portrait as youth. 3r, Giving speech. 5r, Map, rifles, exile. 10r, Khomeini returns to Iran, Feb. 1, 1979. 20r, Khomeini seated before microphone. 30r, Khomeini with grandson. 40r, Other mullahs. 50r, Khomeini gesturing with hands. 70r, On balcony before crowd. 100r, Slogan. 200r, Empty lectern. 500r, Mausoleum. 1000r, Sun rays.

1989-92 Litho. Unwmk. Perf. 13½
2382A	A795	1r grn & multi	.25	.25
2382B	A795	2r grn & multi	.25	.25
2383	A795	3r grn & multi	.25	.25
2384	A795	5r brt vio & multi	.25	.25
2385	A795	10r brt bl & multi	.35	.25
2386	A795	20r blue & multi	.30	.25
2387	A795	30r pink & multi	.35	.25
2388	A795	40r red & multi	.35	.30
2389	A795	50r gray & multi	.40	.30
2390	A795	70r brt grn & multi	.55	.35
2391	A795	100r ultra & multi	.75	.45
2392	A795	200r red brn & multi	1.50	.75
2393	A795	500r blk & multi	3.50	1.75
2393A	A795	1000r multi	7.50	9.15
		Nos. 2382A-2393A (14)	16.55	9.15

Issued: 1r, 1/3/91; 3r, 3/16/90; 5r, 12/13; 10r, 10/22; 20r, 30r, 50r, 9/23/90; 40r, 2/9/90; 100, 200r, 9/26/90; 70r, 500r, 6/4/91; 2r, 1000r, 3/16/92.

World Post Day — A796

Wmk. 381
1989, Oct. 9 Photo. Perf. 13
2394 A796 20r multicolored .65 .40

Mohammad's Birthday, Unity Week — A797

1989, Oct. 18
2395 A797 10r multicolored .40 .30

427

IRAN

Takeover of US Embassy, 10th Anniv. — A798

1989, Nov. 4   Perf. 13½x13
2396   A798   40r multicolored   1.00   .30

Bassij of the Oppressed (Militia), 10th Anniv. — A799

1989, Nov. 27   Perf. 13
2397   A799   10r multicolored   .40   .30

Scientists, Artists and Writers Type of 1988

No. 2398, Mehdi Elahi Ghomshei. No. 2399, Dr. Abdulazim Gharib. No. 2400, Seyyed Hossein Mirkhani. No. 2401, Ayatollah Seyyed Hossein Boroujerdi. No. 2402, Ayatollah Sheikh Abdulkarim Haeri.

1989, Dec. 18   Perf. 13x13½
2398   A775   10r gold, red, blk   .30   .30
2399   A775   10r gold, grn, blk   .30   .30
2400   A775   10r gold, pink, blk   .30   .30
    a.   Pair, #2399-2400   .80   .75
2401   A775   10r gold, bl grn, blk   .30   .30
2402   A775   10r gold, buff, blk   .30   .30
    a.   Pair, #2401-2402   .80   .75

Intl. Literacy Year — A800

    Wmk. 381
1990, Jan. 1   Photo.   Perf. 13½
2403   A800   20r multicolored   .60   .35

Cultural Heritage — A801

Designs: No. 2404, Drinking vessel, 1980. No. 2405, Footed vase, 1979.

1990, Jan. 21   Perf. 13
2404   A801   20r blk & deep org   .50   .30
2405   A801   20r blk & yel grn   .50   .30
    a.   Pair, #2404-2405   1.25   1.00

New Identification Card System — A802

1990, Feb. 9
2406   A802   10r multicolored   .30   .25

Islamic Revolution, 11th Anniv. — A803

1990, Feb. 11
2407   A803   50r multicolored   1.25   .40

Intl. Koran Recitation Competition — A804

1990, Feb. 23
2408   A804   10r blk, bl & grn   .35   .25

Invalids of Islamic Revolution — A805

1990, Mar. 2   Perf. 13½x13
2409   A805   10r multicolored   .35   .25

Arbor Day — A806

1990, Mar. 6   Perf. 13
2410   A806   20r multicolored   .55   .30

New Year Festival Type of 1987

Flowers: a, Coronilla varia. b, Astragalus cornu-caprae. c, Astragalus obtusifolius. d, Astragalus straussii.

1990, Mar. 11   Perf. 13½x13
2411   Block of 4   1.00   .80
    a.-d.   A705 10r any single   .25   .25

Islamic Republic, 11th Anniv. — A807

1990, Apr. 1   Perf. 13
2412   A807   30r multicolored   .80   .60

World Health Day — A808

1990, Apr. 7
2413   A808   40r multicolored   1.00   .50

A809

1990, June 4   Unwmk.   Perf. 11x10½
2414   A809   50r multicolored   1.25   .50

Ayatollah Khomeini, 1st death anniv.

Jerusalem Day — A810

1990, Dec. 15   Litho.   Perf. 10½
2415   A810   100r multicolored   2.50   .60

World Crafts Day — A811

20r, Turkoman jewelry. 50r, Gilded steel bird.

1990, Oct. 20   Perf. 13
2416   A811   20r multicolored   .60   .40
2417   A811   50r multicolored   1.40   1.00
    a.   Pair, #2416-2417   2.50   2.00

Intl. Day of the Child — A812

1990, Nov. 17   Perf. 10½
2418   A812   20r multicolored   .60   .30

Aid to Earthquake Victims — A813

1990, Nov. 19   Perf. 13x13½
2419   A813   100r multicolored   2.50   .30

Return and Tribute to Former Prisoners of Iran-Iraq War — A814

1990, Nov. 21   Perf. 13
2420   A814   250r multicolored   7.50   1.50

Ferdowsi Intl. Congress — A815

No. 2421, Portrait. No. 2422, Statue. No. 2423, Monument. No. 2424, Slogan, diamond cartouche. No. 2425, Rectangular slogan. No. 2426, Slogan, diff. No. 2427, Two riders embracing. No. 2428, Archer, birds. No. 2429, Six men. No. 2430, White elephant. No. 2431, Warrior, genie, horse. No. 2432, Hunting scene. No. 2433, Riding through fire. No. 2434, Four slogan tablets. No. 2435, Man with feet shackled. No. 2436, Palace scene.

1990, Dec. 22   Litho.   Imperf.
    Size: 60x75mm
2421   A815   100r multi   3.00   4.00
2422   A815   100r multi   3.00   4.00
2423   A815   100r multi   3.00   4.00
2424   A815   100r multi   3.00   4.00
2425   A815   100r multi   3.00   4.00
2426   A815   100r multi   3.00   4.00
2427   A815   200r multi   4.00   6.00
2428   A815   200r multi   4.00   6.00
2429   A815   200r multi   4.00   6.00
2430   A815   200r multi   4.00   6.00
2431   A815   200r multi   4.00   6.00
2432   A815   200r multi   4.00   6.00
2433   A815   200r multi   4.00   6.00
2434   A815   200r multi   4.00   6.00
2435   A815   200r multi   4.00   6.00
2436   A815   200r multi   4.00   6.00
    Nos. 2421-2436 (16)   58.00   84.00

Conference on epic poem "Book of Kings" by Ferdowsi.
In 1991 some imperf between blocks of 4 were released. Value, set $250.

"Victory Over Iraq" — A816

1991, Feb. 25   Perf. 13
2437   A816   100r multicolored   1.25   .50

Intl. Museum Day — A817

Designs: No. 2438, Gold jug with Kufric inscription, 10th cent. A.D. No. 2439, Silver-inlaid brass basin, 14th cent. A.D.

1991, Feb. 25
2438   A817   50r multicolored   1.10   .50
2439   A817   50r multicolored   1.10   .50
    a.   Pair, #2438-2439   2.25   1.50

A818

1991, Mar. 12   Perf. 10½
2440   A818   50r multicolored   1.00   .50

World Telecommunications Day.
No. 2440 exists imperf. Value, pair $25.

Opening of Postal Museum — A819

1991, Feb. 25   Perf. 13
2441   A819   200r org brn & blk   5.00   2.00

IRAN

Islamic Revolution, 12th Anniv. — A820

1991, Feb. 11	**Photo.**		**Perf. 13**
2442	A820	100r multicolored	2.50 1.00

New Year Festival Type of 1987

Designs: No. 2443a, Iris spuria. b, Iris lycotis. c, Iris demawendica. d, Iris meda.

1991, Mar. 11			**Perf. 13½x13**
2443	A705	20r Block of 4, #a.-d.	2.50 1.50

Saleh Hosseini, 10th Death Anniv. — A821

1991, Mar. 19			**Perf. 13½x13**
2444	A821	30r red & black	.90 .50

Mab'as Festival — A822

1991, Mar. 19			**Perf. 13x13½**
2445	A822	100r multicolored	2.00 .50

Universal Day of the Oppressed — A823

1991, Mar. 25			**Perf. 13**
2446	A823	50r multicolored	1.00 .50

Savior Mahdi's Birthday.

Revolutionaries, 25th Death Anniv. — A824

1990, June 16			
2447	A824	50r maroon & red org	1.00 .50

Dated 1990.

Islamic Republic, 12th Anniv. — A825

1991, Apr. 1	**Photo.**	**Unwmk.**	**Perf. 13**
2448	A825	20r blk, slate, grn & red	.60 .50

World Health Day — A826

1991, Apr. 7			**Perf. 13½x13**
2449	A826	100r multicolored	1.50 .50

Day of Jerusalem — A827

1991, Apr. 12			**Perf. 13**
2450	A827	100r bl, blk & brn	1.75 .75

A828

1991, Apr. 12	**Litho.**		**Perf. 10½**
2451	A828	50r multicolored	.80 .50

Women's Day. Birth anniv. of Mohammad's daughter, Fatima.

A829

1991, Apr. 28	**Photo.**	**Unwmk.**	**Perf. 13½x13**
2452	A829	200r bl grn & blk	5.00 .50

Ayatollah Borujerdi, 30th death anniv.

Teachers' Day — A830

1991, May 2			**Perf. 13x13½**
2453	A830	50r multicolored	1.25 .50

Decade for Natural Disaster Reduction — A831

1991, May 11	**Litho.**		**Perf. 10½**
2454	A831	100r multicolored	1.75 .50

World Telecommunications Day — A832

			Perf. 13½x13
1991, May 17	**Photo.**	**Unwmk.**	
2455	A832	100r multicolored	1.50 .50

Intl. Museum Day — A833

Ewers, Kashan, 13th cent.: 20r, With spout. 40r, Baluster.

1991, May 18			**Perf. 13**
2456	A833	20r multicolored	.50 .50
2457	A833	40r multicolored	1.00 .50
a.		Pair, #2456-2457	2.00 1.10

Flags — A834

1991, May 24			**Perf. 13x13½**
2458	A834	30r multicolored	.85 .50

Liberation of Khorramshahr, 7th anniv.

Abol-Hassan Ali-ebne-Mosa Reza, Birth Anniv. — A835

Views of shrine, Meshed.

1991, May 26			**Perf. 13**
2459		10r Mausoleum	.25 .25
2460		30r Gravestone	.75 .50
a.	A835	Pair, #2459-2460	1.25 1.10

First Intl. Conf. on Seismology and Earthquake Engineering — A836

1991, May 27			**Perf. 13½x13**
2461	A836	100r multicolored	2.00 .50

World Child Day — A837

1991, June 1	**Photo.**		**Perf. 13½**
2462	A837	50r multicolored	1.00 .50

Holy Shrine at Karbola, Iraq Destroyed by Invasion A838

		Unwmk.	
1991, June 3	**Photo.**		**Perf. 13**
2463	A838	70r multicolored	1.50 .50

Ayatollah Khomeini, 2nd Death Anniv. — A839

1991, June 4			
2464	A839	100r multicolored	2.50 .75

World Handicrafts Day — A840

Designs: No. 2465, Engraved brass wares. No. 2466, Gilded samovar set.

1991, June 10			**Perf. 13½x13**
2465	A840	40r multicolored	.90 .45
2466	A840	40r multicolored	.90 .45
a.		Pair #2465-2466	2.10 1.25

Intl. Congress on Poet Nezami A841

1991, June 22			**Perf. 13**
2467	A841	50r multicolored	1.25 .50

A842

1991, July 15	**Photo.**		**Perf. 13**
2468	A842	50r multicolored	1.40 .50

Ali Ibn Abi Talib, 1330th death anniv.

Blood Transfusion Week — A843

		Unwmk.	
1991, July 29	**Photo.**		**Perf. 13**
2469	A843	50r multicolored	1.40 .50

Return of Prisoners of War, First Anniv. — A844

1991, Aug. 27			**Perf. 13x13½**
2470	A844	100r multicolored	1.75 .50

IRAN

Ayatollah Marashi, Death Anniv. — A845

1991, Aug. 29   Perf. 13½x13
2471   A845   30r multicolored   1.10   .50

Ayatollah-ol-Ozma Seyyed Abdol-Hossein Lary, Revolutionary — A846

Design includes 1909 stamp issued by Lary.

1991, Sept. 9   Perf. 13x13½
2472   A846   30r multicolored   .70   .50

Start of Iran-Iraq War, 11th Anniv. — A847

1991, Sept. 22   Perf. 13½x13
2473   A847   20r multicolored   .65   .50

Mosque, Kaaba, Unity Week — A848

1991, Sept. 22   Perf. 13
2474   A848   30r multicolored   .70   .50

World Tourism Day — A849

1991, Sept. 27   Photo.   Perf. 13½
2475   A849   200r multicolored   4.50   1.00

Dr. Mohammad Gharib, Pediatrician — A849a

1991, Sept. 29   Photo.   Perf. 13
2475A   A849a   100r bl & blk   1.50   .50

Official first day covers are dated 1/19/1991.

World Post Day — A850

  Unwmk.
1991, Oct. 9   Photo.   Perf. 13
2476   A850   70r #2071 on cover   1.00   .50

Khaju-ye Kermani Intl. Congress — A851

1991, Oct. 15
2477   A851   30r multicolored   1.00   .50

World Food Day — A852

1991, Oct. 16
2478   A852   80r multicolored   .90   .50

A853

1991, Oct. 19   Perf. 13½x13
2479   A853   40r bl vio & gold   .70   .50

Intl. Conference Supporting Palestinians.

Illustrators of Children's Books, 1st Asian Biennial — A854

1991, Oct. 25   Perf. 13
2480   A854   100r Hoopoe   2.50   .50

"Children" misspelled.

World Standards Day — A855

1991, Oct. 14   Perf. 13½
2481   A855   100r multicolored   2.00   .50

1st Seminar on Adolescent and Children's Literature — A856

1991, Nov. 3   Perf. 13
2482   A856   20r multicolored   .70   .50

Roshid Intl. Educational Film Festival — A857

1991, Nov. 6
2483   A857   50r multicolored   1.50   .75

7th Ministerial Meeting of the Group of 77 — A858

1991, Nov. 16
2484   A858   30r vio & bl grn   .70   .50

Bassij of the Oppressed (Militia), 12th Anniv. — A859

1991, Nov. 25
2485   A859   30r multicolored   .80   .50

Ayatollah Aref Hosseini — A860

1991, Dec. 18   Perf. 13½
2486   A860   50r multicolored   1.10   .50

Sadek Ghanji — A861

1991, Dec. 20
2487   A861   50r multicolored   1.10   .50

Agricultural Training and Extension Week — A862

1991, Dec. 22   Perf. 13
2488   A862   70r multicolored   1.75   .50

World Telecommunications Day — A863

No. 2489: a, 20r, Telegraph key. b, 20r, Phone lines. c, 20r, Early telephones. d, 40r, Satellite dishes. e, 40r, Telecommunications satellite.

1992, May 17   Photo.   Perf. 13
2489   A863   Strip of 5, #a.-e.   3.50   1.50

New Year — A863a

Flora of Iran: Nos. 2490a, 2490d, 20r. Nos. 2490b, 2490c, 40r.

1992, Apr. 18   Perf. 13½x13
2490   A863a   Block of 4, #a.-d.   4.00   1.50

Mosque of Jerusalem — A864

1992, Mar. 27   Perf. 13x13½
2491   A864   200r multicolored   2.50   1.25

Day of Jerusalem and honoring A. Mousavi, the Shiva leader of Lebanon, with Sheikh Ragheb Harb in background.

Reunification of Yemen — A865

1992, May 22   Perf. 13½x13
2492   A865   50r multicolored   .90   .50

World Child Day — A866

1992, June 1   Perf. 13x13½
2493   A866   50r multicolored   .90   .50

Intl. Conference of Surveying and Mapping — A867

1992, May 25   Perf. 13
2494   A867   40r multicolored   .70   .50

21st FAO Regional Conference — A868

1992, May 17   Perf. 13x13½
2495   A868   40r blk, bl & grn   .50   .35

South and West Asia Postal Union — A869

Mosques: No. 2496, Imam's Mosque, Isfahan. No. 2497, Lahore Mosque, Pakistan. No. 2498, St. Sophia Mosque, Turkey.

1992, Mar. 27   Perf. 13½x13
2496   A869   50r multicolored   .75   .40
2497   A869   50r multicolored   .75   .40
2498   A869   50r multicolored   .75   .40

Economic Cooperation Organization Summit — A870

Design: 20r, Flags, emblem, vert.

IRAN

1992   *Perf. 13½x13, 13x13½*
2499	A870	20r multicolored	.75	.50
2500	A870	200r multicolored	5.00	1.00

Issued: 20r, Apr. 25; 200r, Feb. 17.

Natural Resources — A871

1992, Apr. 15   *Litho.*   *Perf. 13½x13*
2501	A871	100r multicolored	2.00	1.00

Islamic Republic, 13th Anniv. — A872

1992, Apr. 1   *Perf. 13½x13*
2502	A872	50r multicolored	.70	.50

Establishment of Postal Airline — A873

1992, Apr. 1   *Perf. 13x13½*
2503	A873	60r multicolored	1.00	.50

Islamic Revolution, 13th Anniv. — A874

1992, Feb. 11   *Unwmk.*   *Photo.*   *Perf. 13*
2504		30r multicolored	1.00	.50
2505		50r multicolored	1.25	.50
a.	A874	Pair, #2504-2505	2.50	1.25

A875

1992, Mar. 23   *Photo.*   *Perf. 13½x13*
2506	A875	100r multicolored	1.10	.50

World Meteorological Day.

A876

Famous Men: No. 2507, Mohammad Bagher Madjlessi. No. 2508, Hadi Sabzevari, wearing turban. No. 2509, Omman Samani, wearing fez. No. 2510, Chapter of praise from Koran (Arabic script), by Ostad Mir Emad.

1991-92   *Perf. 13x13½*
2507	A876	50r shown	.70	.50
2508	A876	50r brown & multi	.70	.50
2509	A876	50r multicolored	.70	.50
2510	A876	50r multicolored	.70	.50

Issued: No. 2510, 12/18/91; others, 5/17/92. First day covers of Nos. 2507-2509 may be dated 12/18/91.

Intl. Museum Day — A877

No. 2511, Gray ceramic ware, 1st millennium B.C. No. 2512, Painted ceramic bowl.

1992, May 18
2511	A877	40r multicolored	.90	.50
2512	A877	40r multicolored	.90	.50

Ayatollah Khomeini, 3rd Anniv. of Death — A878

1992, June 4   *Perf. 13*
2513	A878	100r multicolored	1.40	.50

Intl. Conference on Engineering Applications of Mechanics — A879

1992, June 9   *Perf. 13½x13*
2514	A879	50r multicolored	.80	.50

A880

1992, June 13   *Perf. 13x13½*
2515	A880	20r multicolored	.60	.40

In memory of clergy-lady Amini.

Sixth Conference of Nonaligned News Agencies — A881

1992, June 15
2516	A881	100r multicolored	1.10	.50

A882

1992, June 23   *Perf. 13x13½*
2517	A882	100r grn, blk & gold	1.25	.50

Meeting of Ministers of Industry and Technology.

A883

1992, June 26   *Perf. 13½x13*
2518	A883	100r multicolored	1.75	.60

World Anti-narcotics Day.

Holy Ka'aba — A884   **Prayer Calligraphy — A885**

Designs: No. 2520, Ayatollah Khomeini in prayer. No. 2521, Khomeini holding prayer beads. No. 2522, Khomeini unwrapping turban. Nos. 2523-2524, Islamic prayers.

1992   *Photo.*   *Perf. 13½x13*
2519	A884	50r multicolored	.70	.50
2520	A884	50r multicolored	.70	.50
2521	A884	50r multicolored	.70	.50
2522	A884	50r multicolored	.70	.50

Perf. 13x13½
2523	A885	50r dk grn & lt grn	.70	.50
2524	A885	50r dk blue & lt blue	.70	.50

Issue dates: July 27, Aug. 24.

Iran Shipping Line, 25th Anniv. — A886

1992, Aug. 24   *Photo.*   *Perf. 13½x13*
2525	A886	200r multicolored	2.00	1.00

A887

1992, Sept. 15   *Perf. 13½x13*
2526	A887	40r multicolored	.60	.45

Mohammad's Birthday, Unity Week.

A888

Iranian Defense Forces: 20r, Soldiers on patrol. 40r, Soldier seated at water's edge, horiz.

Perf. 13½x13, 13x13½

1992, Sept. 22
2527	A888	20r multicolored	.50	.40
2528	A888	40r multicolored	.50	.40

Intl. Congress on the History of Islamic Medicine — A889

20r, Avicenna, child. 40r, Physician's instruments.

1992, Sept. 23   *Litho.*   *Perf. 13*
2529		20r multi	.60	.50
2530		40r multi	.90	.50
a.	A889	Pair, #2529-2530	1.75	1.10

Mobarake Steel Plant — A890

1992, Sept. 26   *Photo.*   *Perf. 13x13½*
2531		20r Inside plant	.40	.50
2532		70r Outside plant	.70	.50
a.	A890	Pair, #2531-2532	1.40	1.25

Intl. Tourism Day — A891

1992, Sept. 27   *Perf. 13x13½*
2533	A891	20r Mazandaran	.45	.35
2534	A891	20r Isfahan	.45	.35
2535	A891	30r Bushehr (Bushire)	.65	.50
2536	A891	30r Hormozgan	.65	.50

Intl. Trade Fair — A892

1992, Oct. 2   *Perf. 13½x13*
2537	A892	200r multicolored	2.25	1.00

World Post Day — A893

1992, Oct. 9   *Perf. 13x13½*
2538	A893	30r Early post office	.80	.50

World Food Day — A894

1992, Oct. 16   *Perf. 13*
2539	A894	100r blk, bl & yel	1.25	1.00

Intl. Youth Photo Festival — A895

1992, Nov. 1   *Photo.*   *Perf. 13½x13*
2540	A895	40r multicolored	1.00	.50

A896

a, Seizure of US embassy, 12th anniv. b, Student's day (Eagles flying over dead doves). c, Khomeini's exile (Eagles, dove).

1992, Nov. 4   *Perf. 13*
2541	A896	100r Strip of 3, #a.-c.	4.50	1.50

IRAN

Fighting in Bosnia and Herzegovina — A897

1992, Nov. 4   Perf. 13½x13
2542 A897 40r multicolored .90 .50

Islamic Development Bank — A898

1992, Nov. 10   Litho.   Perf. 13½x13
2543 A898 20r multicolored .50 .40

Iran-Azerbaijan Telecommunications — A899

1992, Nov. 21   Photo.   Perf. 13x13½
2544 A899 40r multicolored .90 .50

Azad (Open) University, 10th Anniv. — A900

1992, Nov. 23   Perf. 13½x13
2545 A900 200r dark grn & emer 2.10 .50

Week of the Basij (Militia) — A901

1992, Nov. 26   Perf. 13x13½
2546 A901 40r multicolored .65 .50

Seyed Mohammad Hosseyn Shahrian, Poet — A902

1992, Dec. 1
2547 A902 80r multicolored 1.00 .50

Women's Day — A903

1992, Dec. 15
2548 A903 70r multicolored 1.00 .50
Birth anniv. of Fatima.

Famous Iranians A904

Scientists and writers: No. 2551a, Ayatollah Mirza Abolhassan Shar'rani (in turban). b, Prof. Mahmoud Hessabi, U=o formula. c, Mohiyt Tabatabaiy, books on shelves. d, Mehrdad Avesta, calligraphy.

1992, Dec. 18
2549 A904 20r Block of 4, #a.-d. 2.50 1.25

Natl. Iranian Oil Drilling Co. — A905

No. 2551, Ocean drilling platform.

1992, Dec. 22
2550 A905 100r shown 1.50 .50
2551 A905 100r multi 1.50 .50

A906

1992, Dec. 28   Perf. 13½x13
2552 A906 80r multicolored 1.00 .50
Promotion of literacy.

A907

20r, Narcissus. 30r, Iris. 35r, Tulips. 40r, Tuberose. 50r, White jasmine. 60r, Guelder rose. 70r, Pansies. 75r, Snapdragons. 100r, Lily. 120r, Petunia. 150r, Hyacinth. 200r, Damascus rose. 500r, Morning glory. 1000r, Corn rose.

1993-95   Photo.   Perf. 13½x13
2553 A907 20r multi .25 .25
2554 A907 30r multi .30 .25
2555 A907 35r multi .30 .25
2556 A907 40r multi .50 .25
2557 A907 50r multi .40 .25
2558 A907 60r multi .60 .30
2559 A907 70r multi .75 .35
2560 A907 75r multi .75 .35
2561 A907 100r multi .75 .35
2562 A907 120r multi .90 .35
2563 A907 150r multi .90 .35
2564 A907 200r multi 1.50 .60
2565 A907 500r multi 3.00 1.00
2566 A907 1000r multi 5.00 2.50
   Nos. 2553-2566 (14) 15.90 7.40

The 60r exists with inverted flowers. Value $9.
Issued: 20r, 1/12/93; 40r, 2/22/93; 100r, 4/21/93; 200r, 4/29/93; 500r, 6/27/93; 1000r, 7/19/93; 30r, 60r, 10/93; 50r, 8/93; 120r, 5/94; 35r, 75r, 3/95; 70r, 150r, 5/95.
For surcharges see Nos. 2759-2760, 2792-2794.

Prophethood of Mohammad A908

1993, Jan. 21   Photo.   Perf. 13x13½
2567 A908 200r multicolored 2.25 .50
Mab'as Festival.

Day of the Disabled A909

Designs: 40r, Player wearing medal, team members with hands raised.

1993, Jan. 27
2568 20r multicolored .50 .50
2569 40r multicolored .50 .50
  a. A909 Pair, #2568-2569 1.25 1.10

Cultural Heritage Preservation — A910

1993, Jan. 31   Perf. 13½x13
2570 A910 40r Mosque, exterior .50 .35
2571 A910 40r Mosque, interior .50 .35
  a. Pair, #2570-2571 1.25 1.25

Planning Day — A911

1993, Jan. 31   Perf. 13
2572 A911 100r multicolored 2.00 .50

Universal Day of the Oppressed A912

1993, Feb. 8   Litho.   Perf. 13
2573 A912 60r multicolored .80 .50
Savior Mahdi's Birthday.

Islamic Revolution, 14th Anniv. — A913

a, Iranian flag. b, Flag, soldiers. c, Soldiers, shellbursts. d, Oil derricks, storage tanks, people harvesting. e, Crowd, car, Ayatollah Khomeini.

1993, Feb. 11   Photo.   Perf. 13x13½
2574 A913 20r Strip of 5, #a.-e. 4.00 4.00

A914

1st Islamic Women's Games: a, Volleyball. b, Basketball. c, Medal. d, Swimming. e, Running.

1993, Feb. 13   Perf. 13
2575 A914 40r Strip of 5, #a.-e. 6.00 6.00

Morteza Ansari — A915

1993, Feb. 16   Perf. 13½
2576 A915 40r multicolored .80 .50

Arbor Day — A916

1993, Mar. 6
2577 A916 70r multicolored 1.10 .50

New Year — A917

a, 20r, Butterfly, tulip. b, 20r, Butterfly, lily. c, 40r, Butterfly, flowers. d, 40r, Butterfly, 3 roses.

1993, Mar. 11   Perf. 13½x13
2578 A917 Block of 4, #a.-d. 2.50 2.00

World Jerusalem Day — A918

1993, Mar. 14   Perf. 13½x13
2579 A918 20r multicolored .65 .35

End of Ramadan — A919

1993, Mar. 26   Perf. 13½x13
2580 A919 100r multicolored 2.00 1.00

Islamic Republic, 14th Anniv. — A920

40r, National anthem.

1993, Apr. 1   Perf. 13x13½
2581 A920 40r multicolored .90 .50

Intl. Congress on the Millennium of Sheik Mofeed A921

1993, Apr. 17   Perf. 13
2582 A921 80r multicolored 1.10 .50

A922

1993, Apr. 21   Perf. 13½x13
2583 A922 100r multicolored 1.25 .50
13th Conference of Asian and Pacific Labor Ministers.

IRAN

A924

1993, May 17 Perf. 13½x13
2585 A924 50r multicolored 1.20 .50
Intl. Congress for Advancement of Science and Technology in Islamic World.

Intl. Museum Day — A925

1993, May 1
2586 A925 40r multicolored 1.00 .50

Intl. Child Day — A928

1993, June 1 Photo. Perf. 13½x13
2589 A928 50r multicolored 1.00 .50

Ayatollah Khomeini, 4th Death Anniv. — A929

1993, June 4 Perf. 13
2590 A929 20r multicolored .70 .50

World Crafts Day — A930

1993, June 10 Perf. 13½x13
2591 A930 70r multicolored 1.25 .60

World Population Day — A931

1993, July 11 Perf. 13
2592 A931 30r multicolored .90 .50

1st Cultural-Athletic Olympiad of Iran University Students — A932

Various sports.

1993, July 22 Perf. 13x13½
Background Colors
2593 A932 20r blue .50 .25
2594 A932 40r henna brown .75 .40
2595 A932 40r ocher .75 .40

Intl. Festival of Films for Children and Young Adults, Isfahan A935

1993, Sept. 11 Photo. Perf. 13
2598 A935 60r multicolored 1.00 .50

World Post Day — A937

1993, Oct. 9 Photo. Perf. 13
2600 A937 60r multicolored 1.00 .50

A939

World of water with fish and: a, Birds. b, Girl. c, Angel with trumpet. d, Trees.

1993, Nov. 5 Photo. Perf. 13½x13
2602 A939 30r Block of 4, #a.-d. 3.50 2.00
Illustrators of Children's Books, Intl. Biennial.

A940

1993, Nov. 16 Photo. Perf. 13
2603 A940 30r multicolored .80 .50
Khaje Nassireddin Tussy, scientist and astronomer.

Week of the Bassij (Militia) — A941

Designs: No. 2604, Woman tying bandana around militiman's head. No. 2605, Militiaman facing line of tanks.

1993, Dec. 1 Perf. 13x13½
2604 A941 50r multicolored 1.00 .50
2605 A941 50r multicolored 1.00 .50

Death of Grand Ayatollah Mohammad Reza Golpaigani — A942

1993, Dec. 20 Perf. 13
2606 A942 300r multicolored 4.00 2.00

Support for Bosnia and Herzegovina — A943

No. 2607, Children playing hopscotch. No. 2608, Soldier, minaret. No. 2609, Woman, mosque.

1993, Dec. 27
2607 A943 40r multicolored .85 .50
2608 A943 40r multicolored .85 .50
2609 A943 40r multicolored .85 .50
 a. Strip of 3, #2607-2609 3.00 2.00

Day of Invalids — A944

1994, Jan. 18
2610 A944 80r multicolored .90 .50

Agriculture Week — A945

1994, Jan. 23
2611 A945 60r multicolored .90 .50

Conf. on Islamic Law — A946

1994, Feb. 20
2612 A946 60r multicolored .90 .50

Islamic Revolution, 15th Anniv. — A947

Designs: a, Town, farm, telephone lines. b, Flag, Ayatollah Khomeini, revolutionaries. c, Fisherman, bridge. d, Women working.

1994, Feb. 11
2613 A947 40r Block of 4, #a.-d. 3.00 2.25

Youth Welfare — A948

1994, Mar. 1
2614 A948 30r multicolored .90 .50

A949

1994, Mar. 28 Photo. Perf. 13½x13
2615 A949 30r multicolored .90 .50
25th Iranian Mathematics Conference, Shareef Industrial University.

A950

1994, Mar. 11 Perf. 13
2616 A950 50r multicolored .90 .50
World Jerusalem Day.

New Year — A951

No. 2617, Partridges, horiz. No. 2618, Heron. No. 2619, Bustard. No. 2620, Pheasants, horiz.

1994, Mar. 16 Perf. 13x13½, 13½x13
2617 A951 40r multi 1.00 .75
2618 A951 40r multi 1.00 .75
2619 A951 40r multi 1.00 .75
2620 A951 40r multi 1.00 .75

Islamic Republic, 15th Anniv. — A952

1994, Apr. 1 Photo. Perf. 13
2621 A952 40r multicolored .90 .50

A953

1994, Apr. 7
2622 A953 100r multicolored 1.50 .50
Intl. congress of Dentist's Assoc. and World Health Day.

Re-els Ali Delvary, 80th Anniv. of Death — A954

1994, Apr. 9 Perf. 13x13½
2623 A954 50r multicolored 1.00 .50

Intl. Year of the Family — A955

1994, May 10 Photo. Perf. 13½x13
2624 A955 50r multicolored .75 .50

IRAN

World Telecommunications Day — A956

1994, May 17   Perf. 13x13½
2625 A956 50r multicolored   1.00   .50

World Museum Day — A957

1994, May 18   Perf. 13
2626 A957 40r Marlik gold cup   .65   .40

A958

Cultural Preservation: 40r, Enameled pot with Kufic inscription, 13th cent.

1994, May 21
2627 A958 40r multicolored   .65   .25

Ayatollah Khomeini, 5th Death Anniv. — A959

1994, June 4
2628 A959 30r multicolored   .65   .25

Ayatollah Motahari, 15th Anniv. of Death — A961

1994, June 10
2630 A961 30r multicolored   .65   .25

World Crafts Day — A962

1994, June 10   Photo.   Perf. 13
2631 A962 60r Weaver   .90   .50
2632 A962 60r Glass pitcher   .90   .50

Islamic University Students' Solidarity Games — A963

1994, July 18
2633 A963 60r multicolored   .80   .40

Mohammad's Birthday, Unity Week — A964

1994, Aug. 26
2634 A964 30r multicolored   .65   .40

Seyed Mortaza Avini, Sacred Defense Week — A965

1994, Sept. 22   Perf. 13x13½
2635 A965 70r multicolored   .90   .50

World Post Day — A966

1994, Oct. 9
2636 A966 50r multicolored   .65   .50

Women's Day — A967

1994, Nov. 24   Perf. 13
2637 A967 70r multicolored   1.00   .50

Birth anniv. of Fatima.

Week of the Bassij (Militia) — A968

1994, Nov. 26
2638 A968 30r multicolored   .65   .25

Book Week — A969

1994, Dec. 10
2639 A969 40r multicolored   .65   .50

Support for Moslems of Bosnia & Herzegovina — A970

No. 2640, Moslem family. No. 2641, Map, arms, homes.

1994, Dec. 27
2640 A970 80r multicolored   1.10   .50
2641 A970 80r multicolored   1.10   .50

Grand Ayatollah Araky — A971

1995, Jan. 5
2642 A971 100r multicolored   1.25   .50

Universal Day of the Oppressed — A972

1995, Jan. 17
2643 A972 50r multicolored   .65   .40

Savior Mahdi's birthday.

Major General Mehdi Zin-el-Din A973

Major General Mehdi Bakeri A974

Major General Hasan Bagheri — A975

Martyred commanders: No. 2647, Major General Hosein Kherazi.

1995, Feb. 2
2644 A973 50r multicolored   .55   .25
2645 A974 50r multicolored   .55   .25
2646 A975 50r multicolored   .55   .25
2647 A975 50r multi, diff.   .55   .25

A976

1995, Feb. 11
2648 A976 100r multicolored   1.50   .50

Islamic Revolution, 16th anniv.

World Jerusalem Day — A977

1995, Feb. 24
2649 A977 100r multicolored   1.25   .50

Arbor Day — A978

1995, Mar. 6
2650 A978 50r multicolored   .80   .40

New Year — A979

1995, Mar. 16   Perf. 13½x13
2651 A979 50r shown   .75   .40
2652 A979 50r Pansies   .75   .40
2653 A979 50r Hyacinths   .75   .40
2654 A979 50r Tulips, fish bowl   .75   .40

Opening of Bafq-Bandar Abbas Railway Line — A980

1995, Mar. 17
2655 A980 100r multicolored   1.75   1.00

Islamic Republic of Iran, 16th Anniv. — A981

1995, Apr. 1   Photo.   Perf. 13
2656 A981 100r multicolored   1.10   .50

Second Press Festival — A982

1995, Apr. 26
2657 A982 100r multicolored   1.10   .50

Ayatollah Ahmad Khomeini — A983

1995, Apr. 27
2658 A983 50r multicolored   .75   .50

Day of Invalids — A984

1995, June 1
2659 A984 80r Arabic script   1.00   .50

IRAN

Ayatollah Ali Vaziri — A985

1995, May 4
2660 A985 100r multicolored 1.10 .50

World Telecommunications Day — A986

1995, May 17
2661 A986 100r multicolored 1.10 .50

Ayatollah Khomeini, 6th Death Anniv. — A987

1995, June 4
2662 A987 100r multicolored 1.25 .50

UN, 50th Anniv. A988

a, Infant, hand holding vaccination (WHO). b, Child laughing (UNICEF). c, Shafts of grain, world map (FAO). d, Woman reading (UNESCO).

1995, June 10   Perf. 13x13½
2663 A988 100r Block of 4, #a.-d. 4.50 3.00

Iqbal Ashtiany, Writer — A989

1995, Aug. 14   Perf. 13
2664 A989 100r multicolored 1.10 .50

Government Week — A990

1995, Aug. 28   Perf. 13x13½
2665 A990 100r Workers, dam 1.10 .50
Construction of the Karun dam and hydo-electric power station.

Sacred Defense Week — A991

1995, Sept. 22   Perf. 13
2666 A991 100r Gun, Koran 1.25 .50

World Post Day — A992

100r, Globe, envelopes.

1995, Oct. 9   Perf. 13½x13
2667 A992 100r multicolored 1.25 .50

M.J. Tondgooyan, Oil Minister — A993

1995, Dec. 20   Perf. 13
2668 A993 100r multicolored 1.10 .50

Prophet Mohammad — A994

100r, Arabic calligraphy.

1995, Dec. 20
2669 A994 100r multicolored 1.25 .50

Fathi Shaghaghi, Islamic Jihad Secretary General — A995

1995, Dec. 31
2670 A995 100r multicolored 1.25 .50

Islamic Revolution, 17th Anniv. — A996

1996, Feb. 11
2671 A996 100r multicolored 1.40 .60

World Jerusalem Day — A997

100r, Dome of the Rock.

1996, Feb. 17
2672 A997 100r multicolored 1.25 .60

Birds — A998

1996, Mar. 15
2673 A998 100r shown 1.40 .60
2674 A998 100r Crested head 1.40 .60
2675 A998 100r blue & multi 1.40 .60
2676 A998 100r yel, grn & multi 1.40 .60
New year.

Air Force Maj. Gen. Abbas Babai A999

Major Ali Akbar Shiroody A1000

Maj. Gen. Mahammed Ebrahim Hemmat A1001

Maj. Gen. Mohammad Broujerdi A1002

1996, Mar. 18
2677 A999 100r multicolored 1.40 .60
2678 A1000 100r multicolored 1.40 .60
2679 A1001 100r multicolored 1.40 .60
2680 A1002 100r multicolored 1.40 .60
See Nos. 2700-2707 for similar stamps dated 1997.

Islamic Republic of Iran, 17th Anniv. — A1003

1996, Mar. 31   Photo.   Perf. 13
2681 A1003 200r multicolored 2.25 1.00

Intl. Book Fair, Tehran — A1004

1996, May 8
2682 A1004 85r multicolored 1.25 .50
For surcharge see No. 2759A.

Mashhad-Sarakhs-Tajan Intl. Railway — A1005

1996, May 13
2683 A1005 200r multicolored 2.00 1.00
Turkmenistan intl. railway link,

Prisoners of War — A1006

1996, May 29
2684 A1006 200r multicolored 2.25 1.00
Captives and Missing Day.

Ayatollah Khomeini, 7th Death Anniv. — A1007

1996, June 3
2685 A1007 200r multicolored 2.10 1.00

World Crafts Day — A1008

1996, June 24   Photo.   Perf. 13
2686 A1008 200r multicolored 2.10 1.00

Third PTT Ministerial Conference, Tehran — A1009

1996, July 8
2687 A1009 200f multicolored 2.00 .50

Prophet Mohammad's Birthday, Unity Week — A1010

Designs: a, Zouqeblateyne Mosque. b, Tomb of Imam Hossein (red flag on top of dome). c, Mohammad's Mosque (dome without flag). d, Tomb of Imam Reza (green flag on top of dome). e, Qaba Mosque (four minarets).

1996, Aug. 3
2688 A1010 200r Strip of 5, #a.-e. 10.50 5.00

Government Week — A1011

Flag colors and: a, Tehran Subway. b, Iron works, Isfahan. c, Merchant fleet. d, Oil refinery, Bandar-e-Imam (clouds in sky). e, Satellite dish, Boumehen.

1996, Aug. 23
2689 A1011 200r Strip of 5, #a.-e. 10.50 5.00

IRAN

Ayatollah Moqddas Ardebily — A1012

1996, Sept. 12   Photo.   Perf. 13
2690   A1012   200r multicolored   2.10   .75

Sacred Defense Week — A1013

1996, Sept. 21
2691   A1013   200r multicolored   2.10   .60

World Standards Day — A1014

1996, Oct. 13
2692   A1014   200r multicolored   2.00   .50

World Food Day — A1015

1996, Oct. 16
2693   A1015   200r multicolored   1.60   .60

Natl. Census — A1016

1996, Oct. 22
2694   A1016   200r multicolored   2.00   .65

2nd World University Wrestling Championships, Tehran — A1017

1996, Dec. 10
2695   A1017   500r multicolored   5.00   2.00

Islamic Revolution, 18th Anniv. — A1018

   a, Ayatollah Khomeini holding man to his chest. b, Martyrs. c, Khomeini waving. d, Khomeini, leaders, airplane. e, Soldiers wearing helmets.

1997, Feb. 10
2696   A1018   200r Strip of 5, #a.-
           e.   9.00   7.50

Arbor Day — A1019

1997, Mar. 5
2697   A1019   200r multicolored   2.00   .80

Islamic Republic, 18th Anniv. — A1020

1997, Apr. 1
2698   A1020   200r multicolored   1.60   .60

8th Intl. Conference on Rainwater Catchment Systems — A1021

1997, Apr. 21
2699   A1021   200r multicolored   1.50   .60

Sheikh Fazlollah Mahallati A1022

Brig. Gen. Abbas Karimi A1023

Brig. Gen. Alireza Movahed Danesh A1024

Sheikh Abdollah Mishmi A1025

Brig. Gen. Naser Kazemi A1026

Gen. Mohammad Reza Vasture A1027

Maj. Gen. Yousef Kolahdooz A1028

Brig. Gen. Yadollah Kalhor A1029

1997, May 4
2700   A1022   100r multicolored   .70   .40
2701   A1023   100r multicolored   .70   .40
2702   A1024   100r multicolored   .70   .40
2703   A1025   100r multicolored   .70   .40
2704   A1026   100r multicolored   .70   .40
2705   A1027   100r multicolored   .70   .40
2706   A1028   100r multicolored   .70   .40
2707   A1029   100r multicolored   .70   .40
    Nos. 2700-2707 (8)   5.60   3.20

   Martyred commanders. See Nos. 2677-2680 for similar stamps.

Post, Telecommunications A1030

1997, May 22
2708   A1030   200r multicolored   1.50   .50

Ayatollah Khomeini, 8th Death Anniv. — A1031

1997, June 4
2709   A1031   200r multicolored   1.50   .50

Montreal Protocol on Substances that Deplete Ozone Layer, 10th Anniv. — A1032

1997, Sept. 16   Photo.   Perf. 13
2710   A1032   200r multicolored   1.50   .50

Tehran Subway — A1033

   Designs: 50r, Grain elevator. 65r, Medals, Students' Science Olympiad. 70r, Mobarake Steel Plant. 100r, Telecommunications. 130r, Port facilities. 150r, Bandar Abbas Oil Refinery. 200r, Rajai Dam. 350r, Rajai power station. 400r, Front of Foreign Affairs office. 500r, Child receiving oral polio vaccine. 650r, Printing house for Koran. 1000r, Imam Khomeini Intl. Airport. 2000r, Prayer place and tomb of Ayatollah Khomeini, Teheran.

1997   Photo.   Perf. 13½x13
2711   A1033   40r multicolored
2712   A1033   50r multicolored
2713   A1033   65r multicolored
2714   A1033   70r multicolored
2715   A1033   100r multicolored
2716   A1033   130r multicolored
2717   A1033   150r multicolored
2718   A1033   200r multicolored
2719   A1033   350r multicolored
2720   A1033   400r multicolored
2721   A1033   500r multicolored
2722   A1033   650r multicolored
2723   A1033   1000r multicolored
2724   A1033   2000r multicolored
    Nos. 2711-2724 (14)   24.00   10.00
   Issued: 2000r, 10/22; others, Sept.

Sacred Defense Week — A1034

1997, Sept. 28   Photo.   Perf. 13
2725   A1034   200r multicolored   1.25   .50

Poets — A1035

   No. 2726, Maitre Eqbal Lahouri. No. 2727, Molana Djalaleddin Mohammad Molavi.

1997, Oct. 15
2726   A1035   200r green & multi   1.40   .50
2727   A1035   200r salmon & multi   1.40   .50
   Compare with Pakistan 870-871.

World Post Day — A1036

1997, Oct. 15
2728   A1036   200r multicolored   1.40   .50

Naim Frasheri (1846-1900), Albanian Moslem Poet — A1037

1997, Nov. 5
2729   A1037   200r multicolored   1.40   .50

Eighth Islamic Summit — A1038

   Various ornate designs, Islamic texts: a, Seven ornaments. b, Ornament at bottom. c, Ornament at right. d, Ornament at upper left. e, Ornament above crescent.

1997, Dec. 9
2730   A1038   300r Strip of 5, #a.-
           e.   9.00   7.50

2nd Islamic Countries Women's Sports Games, Tehran — A1039

1997, Dec. 12
2731   A1039   200r multicolored   1.40   .50

IRAN

Islamic Revolution, 19th Anniv. — A1040

a, Natl. flags. b, Harvesting grain, factory. c, Soldiers carrying flags. d, Crowd cheering, picture of Ayatollah Khomeini. e, Ayatollah Khomeini.

1998, Feb. 11
2732 A1040 200r Strip of 5, #a.-e.   7.50 5.00

World Jerusalem Day — A1041

1998, Feb. 17
2733 A1041 250r multicolored   1.60 .80

New Year — A1042

1998, Mar. 5
2734 A1042 200r Still life   1.40 .60

Arbor Day — A1043

1998, Mar. 11
2735 A1043 200r multicolored   1.40 .90

Islamic Republic, 19th Anniv. A1044

1998, Apr. 1   Photo.   Perf. 13
2736 A1044 250r multicolored   1.50 .75

A1045

1998, May 17   Perf. 13½x13
2737 A1045 200r multicolored   1.40 .60
World Telecommunications Day.

Election Day — A1046

1998, May 23   Photo.   Perf. 13
2738 A1046 200r multicolored   1.40 .60

War Martyrs

A1047   A1048

A1049   A1050

1998, May 24   Photo.   Perf. 13
2739 A1047 100r multicolored   .60 .30
2740 A1048 100r multicolored   .60 .30
2741 A1049 100r multicolored   .60 .30
2742 A1050 100r multicolored   .60 .30

Shahriyar, Poet — A1051

1998, May 27
2743 A1051 200r multicolored   1.25 .50

Ayatollah Khomeini, 9th Death Anniv. — A1052

1998, June 4   Perf. 13
2744 A1052 200r multicolored   1.25 .50

2nd Congress of the South West Asia Postal Union, Tehran — A1053

1998, June 8
2745 A1053 250r multicolored   1.40 .60

1998 World Cup Soccer Championships, France — A1054

1998, June 10
2746 A1054 500r multicolored   2.75 1.00

World Handicrafts Day — A1055

1998, June 10
2747 A1055 200r multicolored   1.25 .50

Union Day — A1056

1998, Sept. 4
2748 A1056 250r multicolored   1.25 .50

1000th Friday of Public Prayer — A1057

1998, Oct. 30   Litho.   Perf. 13
2749 A1057 250r multicolored   1.25 .50

Nos. 2295A & 2296A Surcharged in Black or Green

1998, Nov. 11   Perf. 13x13½
2750 A738 200r on 1r Shoustar   8.00 5.00
2751 A738 200r on 3r Kerman (G)   8.00 5.00

Intl. Year of the Ocean — A1058

1998, Nov. 14   Perf. 13
2752 A1058 250r multicolored   1.25 .65

Sacred Defense Week — A1059

1998, Nov. 23
2753 A1059 250r multicolored   1.25 .50

World Post Day — A1060

1998, Dec. 2
2754 A1060 200r multicolored   1.25 .50

1998 World Wrestling Championships, Tehran — A1061

1998, Dec. 8
2755 A1061 250r multicolored   1.25 .50

Children and Cancer — A1062

1998, Dec. 13
2756 A1062 250r multicolored   1.25 .50

Cultural Development A1063

1998, Dec. 16   Photo.   Perf. 13
2757 A1063 250r multicolored   1.25 .50

Islamic Revolution, 20th Anniv. — A1064

1999, Feb. 11   Photo.   Perf. 13
2758 A1064 250r multicolored   1.25 .50

Nos. 2554, 2682, 2555 Surcharged in Black or Red

Nos. 2759, 2760   No. 2759A

1999, Feb.   Photo.   Perf. 13, 13½x13
2759   A907   200r on 35r (#2555)   — —
2759A A1004 250r on 85r (R, #2682) — —
2760   A907   900r on 30r (#2554)   — —

Establishment of Islamic Republic, 20th Anniv. A1065

1999, Apr. 1   Photo.   Perf. 13
2761 A1065 250r multicolored   1.25 .50

Ghadir Khom Religious Feast — A1066

1999, Apr. 5   Photo.   Perf. 13
2762 A1066 250r multicolored   1.25 .50

Ayatollah Khomieni's Charity Account A1067

IRAN

No. 2763, Houses. No. 2764, Village, palm trees.

1999, Apr. 10   Photo.   Perf. 13
2763 A1067 250r multi   1.25   .50
2764 A1067 250r multi   1.25   .50

Army Day — A1068

1999, Apr. 18
2765 A1068 250r multicolored   1.25   .50

Mullah Sadra — A1069

1999, May 22
2766 A1069 250r multicolored   1.25   .60

Ayatollah Khomeini, 10th Anniv. of Death — A1070

1999, May 25
2767 A1070 250r multicolored   2.00 1.00

Islamic Parliament, 20th Anniv. A1071

1999, May 28   Photo.   Perf. 13
2768 A1071 250r multicolored   1.25   .60

Islamic Interparliamentary Conference — A1072

1999, June 15   Photo.   Perf. 13
2769 A1072 250r multicolored   1.25   .60

Unity Week — A1073

1999, July 1   Photo.   Perf. 13
2770 A1073 250r multicolored   1.25   .60

Handicrafts Day — A1074

1999, July 25   Photo.   Perf. 13
2771 A1074 250r multicolored   1.50   .75

Total Solar Eclipse, Aug. 11 — A1075

Designs: a, Moon over right portion of sun. b, Baily's beads at top. c, Totality. d, Baily's beads at right. e, Moon over left portion of sun.

1999, Feb. 11   Photo.   Perf. 13
2772 A1075 250r Strip of 5, #a.-e.   20.00 20.00

Birds — A1076

100r, Hoopoe. 150r, Kingfisher. 200r, Robin. 250r, Lark. 300r, Red-backed shrike. 350r, Eurasian roller. 400r, Blue tit. 500r, Eurasian bee-eater. 1000r, Redwing. 2000r, Twite. 3000r, White throat. 4500r, Turtle dove.

1999-2002   Photo.   Perf. 13x13½
2773 A1076 100r multi   .50
2774 A1076 150r multi   .50
2775 A1076 200r multi   .50
2776 A1076 250r multi   .50
2777 A1076 300r multi   .60
2778 A1076 350r multi   .70
2779 A1076 400r multi   .80
2780 A1076 500r multi   1.00
2781 A1076 1000r multi   2.00
2782 A1076 2000r multi   4.00
2783 A1076 3000r multi   6.00
2784 A1076 4500r multi   9.00
Nos. 2773-2784 (12)   26.10

Issued: 150r, 8/6; 250r, 8/4; 100r, 6/17/00; 300r, 5/31/00; 500r, 8/30/00; 1000r, 10/30/00; 2000r, 1/13/01; 3000r, 1/23/01. 200r, 4/24/02; 400r, 5/18/02; 4500r, 7/16/02; 350r, 4/17/01.

UPU, 125th Anniv. A1077

1999, Oct. 2   Photo.   Perf. 13
2787 A1077 250r multicolored   1.50 1.00

Children's Day — A1078

a, Iranian girl. b, Latin American boy. c, Eskimo boy. d, African girl. e, Russian boy. f, French girl. g, Chinese girl. h, Asian Indian girl. i, American Indian girl. j, Arabian boy.

1999, Oct. 8
2788 A1078 150r Strip of 10, #a.-j.   15.00 15.00
Order of stamps in strip varies.

Intl. Exhibition of Children's Book Illustrators — A1079

Background colors: a, Blue. b, Yellow. c, Red. d, Green.

1999, Nov. 15
2789 A1079 250r Block of 4, #a.-d.   15.00 10.00

Ayatollah Mohammad Taghi Jafari — A1080

1999, Nov. 16
2790 A1080 250r multicolored   1.50 1.00

Islamic Revolution, 21st Anniv. — A1081

2000, Feb. 11   Photo.   Perf. 13
2791 A1081 300r multi   1.50 1.00

Nos. 2558, 2560, 2562 Surcharged Like No. 2759
Methods and Perfs. as Before
2000, Feb.
2792 A907 250r on 60r   3.00 2.00
2793 A907 250r on 75r   3.00 2.00
2794 A907 250r on 120r   3.00 2.00

The 60r stamp with the inverted flowers footnoted after No. 2566 is known with the 250r surcharge. Value $30.

New Year — A1082

2000, Mar. 13   Photo.   Perf. 13
2795 A1082 300r multi   1.50   .75

Science & Technology University, 70th Anniv. A1083

2000, July 9   Photo.   Perf. 13
2796 A1083 300r multi   8.00 5.00
Dated 1999.

Dr. Mohammad Mofatteh (1928-79), Martyr A1084

2000, July 22
2797 A1084 300r multi   1.75 1.00

A1085   A1086

A1087   A1088

A1089   A1090

A1091

Martyrs — A1092

2000
2798 A1085 150r multi   1.00 .50
2799 A1086 150r multi   1.00 .50
2800 A1087 150r multi   1.00 .50
2801 A1088 150r multi   1.00 .50
2802 A1089 150r multi   1.00 .50
2803 A1090 150r multi   1.00 .50
2804 A1091 150r multi   1.00 .50
2805 A1092 150r multi   1.00 .50
Nos. 2798-2805 (8)   8.00 4.00

Issued: Nos. 2798-2801, 8/6/00; Nos. 2802-2805, 7/30.

National Archives Day — A1093

2000, May 5   Photo.   Perf. 13
2806 A1093 300r multi   1.50 1.00

University Jihad Movement — A1094

2000, Aug. 6
2807 A1094 300r multi   2.00 1.25

IRAN

439

8th Asia-Pacific Postal Union Congress, Tehran — A1095

2000, Sept. 12
2808 A1095 300r multi   2.25 1.25

World Space Week — A1096

Satellite and: No. 2809, 500r, Dish at R. No. 2810, 500r, Dish at L.

2000, Oct. 4
2809-2810 A1096 Set of 2   6.00 4.00

World Breastfeeding Week — A1097

2000, Oct.
2811 A1097 300r multi   1.50 1.00

Ghadir Khom Festival — A1098

2001, Mar. 14
2812 A1098 500r multi   2.25 1.25

Year of H. H. Ali — A1099

2001, Mar. 14
2813 A1099 500r multi   1.50 .75

New Year — A1100

Birds: No. 2814, 300r, shown. No. 2815, 300r, Bird, diff., vert.

2001, Mar. 18   Perf. 13½, 13½x13
2814-2815 A1100 Set of 2   5.00 2.50

Palestinian Intifada A1100a

2001, Apr. 24   Photo.   Perf. 13
2815A A1100a 350r multi   5.50 2.75

Belgica 2001 Intl Stamp Exhibition, Brussels A1101

Designs: No. 2816, 350r, Chaffinch (shown). No. 2817, 350r, Waxwing. No. 2818, 350r, National Garden, vert.

2001, June 9
2816-2818 A1101 Set of 3   5.00 3.00

Phila Nippon '01, Japan — A1102

Emblem and: No. 2819, 250r, Mount Fuji, Japan. No. 2820, 250r, Mount Damavand, Iran.

2001, Aug. 1   Photo.   Perf. 13
2819-2820 A1102 Set of 2   1.50 1.00

World Tourism Day — A1103

2001, Sept. 22
2821 A1103 500r multi   1.25 .50

Police Week A1104

No. 2822: a, Helicopters, parachutists, police cars, motorcycle police. b, Parachutists, officer saluting flag, motorcycle police, naval patrol.

2001, Sept. 29   Perf. 13x13½
2822 A1104 250r Horiz. pair,
          #a-b   2.00 1.50

Year of Dialogue Among Civilizations — A1105

Designs: No. 2823, 250r, Shown. No. 2824, 250r, Cubist and Oriental art, horiz.

2001, Oct. 9   Perf. 13
2823-2824 A1105 Set of 2   4.50 2.50

Third Moslem Women's Games, Tehran — A1106

2001, Oct. 24
2825 A1106 250r multi   1.00 .50

Spring of the Holy Koran — A1107

2001, Nov. 26
2826 A1107 500r multi   1.50 .75

Honeybee A1108

2001, Dec. 3
2827 A1108 500r multi   2.00 1.00

UN High Commissioner for Refugees, 50th Anniv. — A1109

2001, Dec. 10
2828 A1109 500r multi   1.25 .50

Transportation Day — A1110

No. 2829: a, Truck on road. b, Truck on bridge, truck on road, gate.

2001, Dec. 17   Perf. 13x13½
2829 A1110 350r Horiz. pair,
          #a-b   2.50 2.00

Navy Day — A1111

No. 2830, 500r: a, Ship heading right. b, Ship heading left.
No. 2831, 500r: a, Helicopter, hovercraft. b, Submarine.

2001, Nov. 28   Photo.   Perf. 13
                Vert. Pairs, #a-b
2830-2831 A1111 Set of 2   5.00 5.00

Tehran Subway A1112

No. 2832: a, Train headed right. b, Train headed left.

2001, Dec. 13
2832 A1112 500r Vert. pair, #a-b   2.50 2.00

Iranian-made Automobiles A1113

Designs: No. 2833, 500r, shown. No. 2834, 500r, Automobile, vert.

2002, Jan. 15
2833-2834 A1113 Set of 2   2.00 1.00

Arbor Day — A1114

2002, Mar. 6
2835 A1114 500r multi   1.25 .75

A1115

New Year's Day A1116

No. 2836: a, Bird with yellow breast. b, Parrot.
No. 2837: a, Stork facing left. b, Hoopoe facing right.

2002, Mar. 16
2836 A1115 500r Horiz. pair,
          #a-b   2.50 2.00
2837 A1116 500r Horiz. pair,
          #a-b   2.50 2.00

Imam Hossein A1117

2002, July 8   Photo.   Imperf.
2838 A1117 400r multi   1.00 1.00

Butterflies A1118

No. 2839: a, Danaus sita. b, Polygonia c-album. c, Precis orithya. d, Vanessa cardui. e, Papilio maacki.

2002, July 29   Perf. 13
2839   Horiz. strip of 5   5.00 5.00
a.-e.   A1118 400r Any single   .75 .45

A1119

IRAN

PhilaKorea 2002 World Stamp Exhibition, Seoul — A1120

No. 2840 — Flowers: a, Hyoscyamus muticus. b, Frittillaria. c, Calotropis procera. d, Ranuculus.
No. 2841 — Horse breeds: a, Caspian. b, Kurd. c, Turkoman. d, Arab.

2002, Aug. 2
2840 A1119 400r Block of 4, #a-d, + 2 labels   6.00 6.00
2841 A1120 400r Block of 4, #a-d, + 2 labels   6.00 6.00

Ayatollah Khomeini (1900-89) — A1121

2002, Aug. 20
2842 A1121 400r multi   1.00 .50
No. 2842 exists imperf. Value, pair $25.

Jerusalem Day — A1122

2002, Nov. 29
2843 A1122 400r multi   1.25 .50

Iran — Brazil Diplomatic Relations, Cent. — A1123

No. 2844: a, Iranian ceramics. b, Brazilian ceramics.

2002, Dec. 15
2844   Horiz. pair + label   3.00 3.00
a.-b. A1123 400r Either single   1.25 .75
See Brazil Nos. 2868-2869.

2nd Biennial of Contemporary Painting of the Islamic World — A1124

2002, Dec. 25
2845 A1124 400r multi   1.50 .75

Esco Production Line, 30th Anniv. — A1125

2003, Jan. 13   Perf. 13x13½
2846 A1125 400r multi   2.00 1.00

Air Force Day — A1126

Various aircraft: 300r, 400r, 500r, 600r, 700r.

2003, Feb. 8   Photo.   Perf. 13
2847-2851 A1126 Set of 5   5.00 2.50

New Year 2003 — A1127

Mammals: No. 2852, 1000r, Goitered gazelle without horns. No. 2853, 1000r, Goitered gazelle with horns. No. 2854, 1000r, Red deer. No. 2855, 1000r, Urial.

2003, Mar. 15
2852-2855 A1127   Set of 4   7.00 4.00

Iranian and Chinese Buildings A1128

No. 2856: a, Mosque, Isfahan. b, Bell Tower, Xian, People's Republic of China.

2003, Apr. 15   Perf. 13x13½
2856   Horiz. pair + label   4.50 4.50
a.-b. A1128 400r Either single   1.50 1.25
Joint issue between Iran and China, People's Republic. See China (People's Republic) Nos. 3271-3272.

Book, Children and Family — A1129

2003, May 4   Photo.   Perf. 13
2857 A1129 500r multi   1.50 .75

Butterflies — A1130

100r, Zygaena sp. 200r, Issoria lathonia. 250r, Utethesia pulchella. 300r, Argynnis paphia. 500r, Polygonia egea. 600r, Papilio machaon. 650r, Colias aurorina. 1000r, Inachis io. 2000r, Papilio demoleus. 2100r, Papilio domoleus. 3000r, Euphydryas aurinia. 4400r, Danaus melanippus. 5500r, Colias aurorina.

2003-05   Photo.   Perf. 13x13½
2858 A1130 100r multi   .25 —
2859 A1130 200r multi   .40 —
2859A A1130 250r multi   .50 —
2860 A1130 300r multi   .60 —
   a.   Longer "Rls." + label ('04)   1.50 —
2862 A1130 500r multi   1.00 —
2863 A1130 600r multi   1.25 —
   a.   Longer "Rls." + label ('04)   2.50 —
2864 A1130 650r multi ('04)   1.25 —
2866 A1130 1000r multi ('04)   1.40 —
2867 A1130 2000r multi ('04)   4.00 —
2867A A1130 2100r multi ('05)   2.25 —
2868 A1130 3000r multi ('04)   3.75 —
2868A A1130 4400r multi   4.25 —
2869 A1130 5500r multi   5.50 —

Issued: 100r, 7/14; 200r, 5/12; 300r, 5/14; 500r, 8/25; 600r, 6/10; 250r, 12/17; 1000r, 1/6/04; Nos. 2860a, 2863a, 1/21/04; 1000r, 2/22/04; 3000r, 3/10/04, 650r, 2004. 2100r, 4/18/05; 4400r, 3/15/05; 5500r, 4/13/05.
The period in "Rls." is under the second zero on Nos. 2860a and 2863a. It is under the first zero on Nos. 2860 and 2863. Examples of No. 2860a exist with and without perforations separating the stamp from the label.

Social Security Organization, 50th Anniv. — A1131

2003, Aug. 16   Photo.   Perf. 13
2870 A1131 600r multicolored   1.50 .75

Government Martyrs — A1132

2003, Aug. 24
2871 A1132 600r multi + label   2.00 2.00

Government Week — A1133

2003, Aug. 25
2872 A1133 600r multicolored   1.50 1.00

Caspian Sea Fauna — A1134

No. 2873: a, Caspian seal. b, Beluga.

2003, Sept. 9
2873   Horiz. pair + label   3.00 3.00
a.-b. A1134 600r Either single   1.25 1.25
c. Souvenir sheet, 2 each #2873a-2873b   5.00 5.00
See Russia No. 6795.

World Post Day — A1135

No. 2874: a, Computer, UPU emblem, satellite. b, Post office loading dock, mail box, airplanes. c, Postal clerk at desk, truck. d, Post rider, ruins and statues.

2003, Oct. 9
2874   Horiz. strip of 4   5.00 5.00
a.-d. A1135 600r Any single   1.00 .75

Shared Functions of the Police and Post Office — A1136

2003, Oct. 5   Photo.   Perf. 13
2875 A1136 500r multicolored   1.50 .75

Worldwide Fund for Nature (WWF) — A1137

No. 2876 — Cheetah: a, Cub. b, Two adults lying in grass. c, Two adults standing. d, Head of adult.

2003, Nov. 18
2876 A1137 500r Block of 4, #a-d   4.00 4.00

Eid ul-Fitr — A1138

2003, Nov. 26
2877 A1138 600r multicolored   1.50 .75

Miniature Sheet

Bam Earthquake, Dec. 26, 2003 — A1139

No. 2878: a, Landmarks in Bam before earthquake. b, Earthquake devastation. c, Doctors treating injured people. d, Rescue personnel, map of world.

2004, Feb. 4
2878 A1139 500r Sheet of 4, #a-d   3.25 3.25

Islamic Revolution, 25th Anniv. — A1140

2004, Feb. 11
2879 A1140 600r multicolored   .75 .40

Hossein Rezazadeh, Weightlifter — A1141

2004, Feb. 15
2880 A1141 1200r multicolored   1.50 1.00
Dated 2003.

IRAN

ISO 9001-2000 Certification — A1142

2004, Feb. 29
2881 A1142 600r multicolored 1.00 .75

Freshwater Fish — A1143

Designs: Nos. 2882, 2888a, 100r, Carassius auratus. Nos. 2883, 2888b, 200r, Carassius auratus, diff. Nos. 2884, 2888c, 300r, Poecilia reticlate. Nos. 2885, 2888d, 400r, Betta splendens. Nos. 2886, 2888e, 500r, Carassius auratus, diff. Nos. 2887, 2888f, 600r, Carassius auratus, diff.

2004, Mar. 6 Stamps With White Frames
2882-2887 A1143 Set of 6 4.00 4.00
Miniature Sheet Stamps Without White Frames
2888 A1143 Sheet of 6, #a-f 4.00 4.00

FIFA (Fédération Internationale de Football Association), Cent. — A1144

2004, May 21 Perf. 13
2889 A1144 600r multicolored 1.50 1.00

Miniature Sheet

Saltwater Fish A1145

No. 2890: a, 250r, Balistoides conspicillum. b, 350r, Acanthurus glaucopareius. c, 450r, Pterois volitans. d, 550r, Zebrasoma veliferum. e, 650r, Pygoplites diacanthus. f, 750r, Pseudobalistes fuscus.

2004, May 22 Perf. 13
2890 A1145 Sheet of 6, #a-f 3.25 3.25

España 2004 Intl. Philatelic Exhibition, Riccione Philatelic Exhibition.

Reporter's Day — A1147

2004, Aug. 7
2892 A1147 650r multicolored .80 .80

2004 Summer Olympics, Athens — A1148

No. 2893: a, Taekwondo. b, Weight lifting. c, Wrestling. d, Judo.

2004, Aug. 12
2893 A1148 650r Block of 4, #a-d 3.50 3.50

Poets A1149

No. 2894: a, Kabir (1440-1518), Indian poet. b, Hafiz Shirazi (c. 1325-c. 1389), Persian poet.

2004, Aug. 16 Perf. 13
2894 A1149 600r Horiz. pair, #a-b 2.00 2.00

See India No. 2070.

International Avicenna Congress — A1150

No. 2895: a, Memorial. b, Avicenna (980-1037), scientist, philosopher.

2004, Aug. 22
2895 A1150 650r Horiz. pair, #a-b 1.60 1.60

Miniature Sheet

Primates A1151

No. 2896: a, Chacma baboons. b, Chimpanzee. c, Chimpanzees. d, Mandrill.

2004, Aug. 28
2896 A1151 500r Sheet of 4, #a-d 5.00 5.00

World Stamp Championship 2004, Singapore.

Miniature Sheet

Cats A1152

No. 2897: a, Gray cat, no tail visible. b, Gray cat, tail at right. c, Brown and white cat. d, White cat. e, Gray cat on rock. f, Gray cat, tail at left.

2004, Aug. 31
2897 A1152 500r Sheet of 6, #a-f 6.00 6.00

12th Paralympic Games, Athens — A1153

2004, Sept. 17
2898 A1153 650r multicolored 1.25 .50

Iran - Iraq War, 24th Anniv. — A1154

2004, Sept. 21
2899 A1154 650r multicolored 1.25 .50

Tehran University, 70th Anniv. — A1155

2004, Oct. 22
2900 A1155 650r multicolored 1.25 .50

Poets A1156

No. 2901: a, Dr. Jalal-eddin Ashtiani (wearing turban). b, Mahmoud Farschian (with hand on chin). c, Dr. Jafar Shahidi (looking right). d, Dr. Hosain Mirshamsi (looking left).

2004, Nov. 9 Photo. Perf. 13
2901 A1156 500r Block of 4, #a-d 3.00 3.00

Mountains — A1157

No. 2902: a, Damavand Mountain, Iran. b, Bolivar Peak, Venezuela.

2004, Nov. 28 Photo. Perf. 13
2902 A1157 650r Horiz. pair, #a-b 2.00 2.00

First Intl. Biennale of Islamic Poster Art A1158

No. 2903: a, Hand. b, Dove in nest. c, Slingshot. d, Crescent.

2004, Nov. 29
2903 A1158 500r Block of 4, #a-d 2.50 2.00

Imam Reza's Birthday A1159

No. 2904: a, Corner of mosque. b, Dome. c, Facade. d, Archway.

2004, Dec. 24 Photo. Perf. 13x13¼
2904 A1159 500r Block of 4, #a-d 2.50 2.00

Ali Daei, Soccer Player — A1160

2005, Feb. 2 Photo. Perf. 13
2905 A1160 650r multicolored 1.25 .50

Iran Film Museum A1161

No. 2906: a, Scene from *Where is the Friend's Home?* b, Scene from *The Children of Heaven*. c, Museum building. d, Scene from *The Cow*.

2005, Feb. 10
2906 A1161 500r Block of 4, #a-d 2.00 1.00

Airplanes A1162

No. 2907: a, AN-140. b, IR-140.

2005, Mar. 6 Perf. 13x13½
2907 Horiz. pair with central label 2.00 1.00
a.-b. A1162 850r Either single

See Ukraine No. 568.

Souvenir Sheet

Expo 2005, Aichi, Japan A1163

IRAN

No. 2908: a, Persepolis. b, Yazd air ventilation towers. c, Iranian flag, typical Iranian desert architecture. d, Clay tablet with inscriptions.

2005, Mar. 24 — **Perf. 13**
2908 A1163 650r Sheet of 4, #a-d   2.50   2.00

Tehran University of Medical Sciences, 70th Anniv. — A1164

2005, May 2
2909 A1164 650r multicolored   1.25   .50

Police Week — A1165

2005, Oct. 29
2910 A1165 650r multicolored   1.00   .50

Mevlana Jalal ad-Din ar-Rumi (1207-73), Islamic Philosopher — A1166

2005, Dec. 3
2911 A1166 650r multicolored   2.00   1.00

See Afghanistan Nos. 1449-1451, Syria No. 1574, Turkey No. 2971.

Gardens — A1167

No. 2912: a, Gardens of Royal Palace of La Granja de San Ildefonso, Segovia, Spain. b, Bagh-e-Shahzadeh, Kerman, Iran.

2005, Dec. 17
2912 A1167 650r Horiz. pair, #a-b   2.00   2.00

See Spain No. 3374.

Self-Sufficiency in Wheat Production — A1168

2006, Jan. 4
2913 A1168 650r multicolored   1.00   .50

Souvenir Sheet

Maps of the Persian Gulf — A1169

No. 2914: a, German map, 16th cent. b, Egyptian Ministry of Culture map, 1966. c, Saudi Arabian map, 1952. d, Map by Scoteri Motthaei, 18th cent.

2006, June 7
2914 A1169 650r Sheet of 4, #a-d   5.00   2.50

2006 World Cup Soccer Championships, Germany — A1170

2006, June 10
2915 A1170 650r multicolored   1.25   .50

Abbas Shafi A1171

Alama Mohammed Reza Hakimi A1172

Mohamed Hossein Gandji — A1173

Alama Mohammed Hassan Amoli — A1174

2006, Sept. 18   **Litho.**   **Perf. 13**
2916   Block of 4   5.00   5.00
   a. A1171 650r multi   1.00   .75
   b. A1172 650r multi   1.00   .75
   c. A1173 650r multi   1.00   .75
   d. A1174 650r multi   1.00   .75

Dated 2005.

Third Meeting of Economic Cooperation Organization Postal Authorities, Tehran — A1175

2006, Sept. 20
2917 A1175 650r multicolored   2.00   1.00

See Kazakhstan No. 526, Pakistan No. 1101 and Turkey No. 3041.

Basij, 27th Anniv. — A1176

2006, Nov. 26
2918 A1176 650r multicolored   2.00   1.00

Souvenir Sheet

Isfahan, 2006 Islamic Cultural Capital A1177

No. 2919: a, Chehel Sotun Palace. b, Emam Mosque. c, Aliqapu Palace. d, Khajo Bridge.

2006, Dec. 30
2919 A1177 650r Sheet of 4, #a-d   5.00   2.50

A1177a   A1177b
Iran Post Emblem
Hologram on Foil
2006, Dec.   **Self-Adhesive**   **Die Cut**
2919E A1177a 4400r silver   3.50   3.50
2919F A1177b 5500r silver   4.50   4.50

Martyrs A1178

No. 2920: a, Man and flags. b, Ten men.

2007, Jan. 7
2920 A1178 650r Horiz. pair, #a-b   2.00   1.00

Dated 2006.

Souvenir Sheet

Iranian Constitution, Cent. — A1179

No. 2921: a, Man, gate. b, Parliament. c, Three men, gate. d, Two men, gate.

2006, May 8   **Litho.**   **Perf. 13**
2921 A1179 650r Sheet of 4, #a-d   4.00   3.00

Souvenir Sheet

Seventh General Assembly of Association of Asian Parliaments for Peace, Tehran — A1180

No. 2922: a, Emblem of Association of Asian Parliaments for Peace. b, Dove, colors of Iranian flag. c, Gate and flags. d, Emblem of Islamic Consultative Assembly.

2006, Nov. 14
2922 A1180 650r Sheet of 4, #a-d   4.00   3.00

Peaceful Nuclear Energy A1181

2007, Feb. 11
2923 A1181 650r multicolored   1.50   .75

Iranian-built Engine — A1182

2007, Feb. 26
2924 A1182 650r multicolored   1.50   .60

Shrine of Fatima, Qom — A1183

2007, Mar. 18
2925 A1183 650r multicolored   1.50   .50

New Year A1184

No. 2926: a, Flowers, man with drum. b, Trumpeters, fishbowl, Koran, apples, grass.

2007, Mar. 19
2926 A1184 650r Horiz. pair, #a-b   2.00   1.00

Map of Persian Gulf — A1185

2007   **Litho.**   **Perf. 13x13½**
   Side Panel Color
2927 A1185 200r brown   1.00   .50
2928 A1185 300r yellow   1.00   .50
   a. Taller Arabic "Rls." + label   3.00   3.00
2929 A1185 650r orange   1.00   .50
   a. Wider "650" + label   3.00   3.00
2930 A1185 2100r blue   4.00   2.00
2931 A1185 4400r blue   8.00   3.00

Issued: 200r, 9/9; 300r, 5/23; 4400r, 7/25. 650r, 10/30; 2100r, 11/24; No. 2929a, 1/27/09. See Nos. 2943-2945, 2956-2960.

Chemical Weapons Convention, 10th Anniv. A1186

2007, June 29   **Perf. 13**
2932 A1186 650r multicolored   1.50   .50

38th Intl. Physics Olympiad, Isfahan A1187

2007, July 3
2933 A1187 650r multicolored   1.50   .50

IRAN

K. K. Sarughy — A1188

2007, Aug. 22
2934 A1188 650r multicolored .... 1.50 .50

Imam Moussa Sadr, Shiite Leader Who Disappeared in 1978 — A1189

2007, Aug. 31
2935 A1189 650r multicolored .... 1.00 .50

Worldwide Fund for Nature (WWF) — A1190

No. 2936 — Grus leucogranus: a, Pair, one with head raised, other with head lowered. b, Pair, facing each other. c, Pair, both standing on one leg. d, Running with wings extended.

2007, Sept. 9
2936 A1190 650r Block of 4, #a-d 3.50 3.00

Miniature Sheet

Great Messenger Year — A1191

No. 2937 — Arabic text and: a, Arch. b, Arabic text in diamond. c, Roman Colosseum. d, Pyramids.

2007, Jan. 6   Litho.   **Perf. 13**
2937 A1191 650r Sheet of 4, #a-d 5.00 2.50

Communications and Public Relations Day — A1192

2007, May 17
2938 A1192 650r multicolored .... 1.50 .50

Miniature Sheet

Return of Prisoners of War — A1193

No. 2939 — Flowers and: a, Geese. b, Iranian man, hand symbol. c, Prisoners of war on bus. d, People on motorcycles greeting prisoners of war.

2007, Aug. 17
2939 A1193 650r Sheet of 4, #a-d 5.00 2.50

Jamkaran Mosque — A1194

2007, Aug. 29
2940 A1194 650r multicolored .... 1.00 .50

World Post Day — A1195

2007, Sept. 10
2941 A1195 650r multicolored 2.00 1.00

Mevlana Jalal ad-Din ar-Rumi (1207-73), Islamic Philosopher — A1196

2007, Oct. 28
2942 A1196 650r multicolored 1.50 1.00

Map of Persian Gulf Type of 2007

2008   **Perf. 13x13½**
Side Panel Color
2943 A1185 1000r green 2.00 1.00
2944 A1185 2000r lilac 4.00 2.00
2945 A1185 5500r red 10.00 4.00
Issued: 1000r, 1/16; 2000r, 2/5; 5500r, 1/5.

Information Technology Infrastructure Development A1197

2008, Jan. 16   **Perf. 13**
2946 A1197 650r multicolored .... 1.50 .75

Navvab Safavi (1924-55), Founder of Islamic Fedayeen — A1198

2008, Jan. 17
2947 A1198 650r multicolored .... 1.25 .60

Falsafi, Preacher, 100th Anniv. of Birth — A1199

2008, Feb. 27
2948 A1199 650r multicolored .... 1.25 .60

Death of Emad Moghnie, Hezbollah Leader — A1200

2008, Mar. 10
2949 A1200 650r multicolored .... 1.50 .75

New Year — A1201

2008, Mar. 15
2950 A1201 650r multicolored .... 1.25 .60

Abdulazim Shrine — A1202

2008, Apr. 11   **Perf. 13x13½**
2951 A1202 650r multicolored .... 1.25 .60

Children and Youth Water Festival — A1203

2008, Apr. 21   **Perf. 13**
2952 A1203 650r multicolored .... 1.25 .60

Islamic City Councils, 10th Anniv. — A1204

2008, Apr. 28
2953 A1204 650r multicolored .... 1.25 .60

Thiqat al-Islam Kulayni, Islamic Legal Scholar, 1100th Anniv. of Death — A1205

2008, May 8
2954 A1205 650r multicolored .... 1.25 .60

Buildings in Morocco and Iran A1206

No. 2955: a, Kasbah, Oudayas, Morocco. b, Falak-Ol-Aflak Castle, Iran.

2008, May 12   Litho.   **Perf. 13**
2955 A1206 650r Horiz. pair, #a-b, + label 2.50 1.50
See Morocco No. 1061.

Map of Persian Gulf Type of 2007

2008-09   Litho.   **Perf. 13x13½**
Side Panel Color
2956 A1185 100r blue .... .50 .50
2957 A1185 250r pale orange .... .50 .50
2958 A1185 400r red .... .50 .50
2959 A1185 500r dark green .... .50 .50
2960 A1185 3000r pink 3.00 3.00
Nos. 2956-2960 (5) 5.00 5.00

Issued: 100r, 9/8; 250r, 10/20; 400r, 9/13; 500r, 5/28; 3000r, 2/15/09.

Handicrafts Day — A1207

No. 2961: a, Engraved copper cup. b, Mina vase.

2008, June 10   Litho.   **Perf. 13**
2961 A1207 650r Horiz. pair, #a-b 2.50 1.50

Miniature Sheet

Trenchless Trench Makers — A1207a

No. 2962 — Men and: a, Construction equipment with extendable arm. b, Bulldozer under roof. c, Utility vehicle. d, Ship on truck's flat-bed trailer.

2008, June 16   Litho.   **Perf. 13**
2962 A1207a 650r Sheet of 4, #a-d 4.50 4.50

Javid-al-Asar Haj Ahmed Motevasselian, Diplomat — A1208

2008, July 3
2963 A1208 650r multicolored .... 1.50 .75

Mountains in Kyrgyzstan and Iran — A1209

No. 2964: a, Khan-Tengri, Kyrgyzstan. b, Sabalan Peak, Iran.

2008, Aug. 15
2964 A1209 650r Horiz. pair, #a-b, + central label 2.50 1.50
See Kyrgyzstan No. 313.

IRAN

Ancient Jewelry From Iran and Kazakhstan — A1210

No. 2965: a, Gold medal depicting lions, 7th cent. B.C., Iran. b, Buckle depicting snow leopard and mountains, 4th-5th cent. B.C., Kazakhstan.

2008, Sept. 7
2965 A1210 650r Horiz. pair, #a-b 2.50 1.50
See Kazakhstan No. 578.

Iran Post Corporation, 20th Anniv. — A1211

2008, Oct. 8   Perf. 13x13½
2966 A1211 1200r multicolored 1.25 .60

Consumer Rights Day — A1212

2008, Feb. 28   Perf. 13
2967 A1212 650r multicolored 1.25 .60

Ayatollah Sheikh Hashem Ghazvini — A1213

2008, May 5
2968 A1213 650r multicolored 1.25 .60

Bank Melli Iran, 80th Anniv. — A1214

2008, Sept. 10
2969 A1214 650r multicolored 1.25 .60

World Jerusalem Day — A1215

2008, Sept. 26
2970 A1215 650r multicolored 1.25 .60

Statue of Sheikh Abulhassan Kharaghani — A1216

2008, Nov. 6
2971 A1216 650r multicolored 1.50 .75

Commander M. R. Pourkian and Tank — A1217

2008, Nov. 13
2972 A1217 650r multicolored 1.25 .60

28-Year Achievements of Security Services — A1218

2008, Nov. 19
2973 A1218 650r multicolored 1.25 .60

Zabol Burnt City Archaeological Site — A1219

2008, Dec. 21
2974 A1219 650r multicolored 1.50 .75

National Day of Exports — A1220

2008, Oct. 21   Perf. 13
2975 A1220 650r multicolored 1.25 .60

Musical Instruments — A1221

No. 2976: a, Gijak of Badahshon. b, Khorasan local dotaar.

2008, Dec. 15
2976 A1221 650r Horiz. pair, #a-b 4.50 2.25
See Tajikistan No. 340.

Support for Gaza Palestinians A1222

2009, Jan. 27
2977 A1222 1200r multicolored 3.00 1.50

Ayatollah Khomeini (1900-89) A1223

2009, Feb. 10
2978 A1223 650r multicolored 2.00 1.00
Islamic Revolution, 30th anniv.

Abbas, Karimi, Reza Cheraghi, and Mohammad Hemat — A1224

2009, Mar. 3
2979 A1224 650r multicolored 1.25 .60

Safir Omid, First Iranian Satellite A1225

No. 2980: a, Iranian flag, rocket on launch pad, emblem. b, Satellite, Earth.

2009, Mar. 7
2980 A1225 1300r Horiz. pair, #a-b 2.50 2.50

10th Economic Cooperation Organization Summit, Tehran A1226

2009, Mar. 11
2981 A1226 1300r multicolored 2.50 1.25
See Azerbaijan 895, compare with Pakistan 1111.

New Year 2009 — A1227

2009, Mar. 25
2982 A1227 1300r multicolored 2.00 1.00

Nurse's Day — A1228

2009, Apr. 28
2983 A1228 1300r multicolored 1.50 .75

Fish — A1229

Designs: 100r, Chaetodon mesoleucos. 200r, Holacanthus ciliaris. 250r, Euxiphipops xanthomelapon. 300r, Pomacanthus maculosus. 350r, Pomacanthus annularis. 400r, Chaetodon rafflesi. 500r, Centropyge bicolor. 1000r, Chaetodontoplus septentrionalis. 2000r, Chaetodon larvatus. 3000r, Chaetodon auriga. 3100r, Chaetodon semilarvatus. 4000r, Pomacanthus chrysurus. 5000r, Pomacanthus navarchus. 6400r, Paracanthurus hepatus. 7500r, Premnas biaculeatus.

2009-11   Litho.   Perf. 13x13½
Size: 32x25mm
2984	A1229	100r multi	.25	.25
2985	A1229	200r multi	.25	.25
2986	A1229	250r multi	.25	.25
2987	A1229	300r multi	.25	.25
2988	A1229	350r multi	.25	.25
2989	A1229	400r multi	.25	.25
2990	A1229	500r multi	.25	.25
2993	A1229	1000r multi	1.00	.25
2994	A1229	2000r multi	2.00	.40
2994A	A1229	3000r multi	3.00	.60
2995	A1229	3100r multi	3.00	.65
2996	A1229	4000r multi	4.00	.80
2997	A1229	5000r multi	5.00	1.00
2998	A1229	6400r multi	5.50	1.40
2999	A1229	7500r multi	6.00	1.50

Nos. 2984-2999 (15) 31.25 8.35

Issued: 100r, 9/25/10; 200r, 10/26; 250r, 4/7/10; 300r, 4/12/10; 350r, 2/26/11. 400r, 12/27/10. 500r, 12/21; 1000r, 6/22; 2000r, 8/1/10; 3000r, 5/8/11; 3100r, 1/19/10; 4000r, 7/18/10; 5000r, 6/15/10; 6400r, 11/10; 7500r, 10/12.
See Nos. 3055A-3055I.

Epic of Presence — A1230

2009, June 12   Litho.   Perf. 13
3000 A1230 1300r multicolored 1.50 .75

Mother's Day — A1231

2009, June 14
3001 A1231 1100r multicolored 1.75 1.00

Birds A1232

No. 3002: a, White-tailed eagle. b, Osprey.

2009, June 24
3002 A1232 2000r Horiz. pair, #a-b 6.00 6.00
See Portugal Nos. 3155-3156.

IRAN

Left Part of Stamp

Center Part of Stamp

Birds (Right Part of Stamp) A1233

The illustration of No. 3003 is broken into the three sections shown on the stamp.

2009, July 11   Perf. 13x13½
3003   A1233   1500r multicolored   3.00   3.00
See Cuba No. 4835.

Marwa El-Sherbini (1977-2009), Woman Murdered in German Courtroom — A1234

2009, July 19   Perf. 13
3004   A1234   1300r multicolored   1.50   .75

Islamic Human Rights and Human Dignity Day — A1235

2009, Aug. 5
3005   A1235   1200r multicolored   2.00   1.00

Rural Information and Communication Technologies in Iran — A1236

2009, Aug. 11
3006   A1236   1000r multicolored   2.00   1.00

Miniature Sheet

Conservation of Marine Turtles — A1237

No. 3007: a, 650r, Eretmochelys imbricata. b, 1000r, Eretmochelys imbricata, diff. c, 1500r, Chelonia mydas. d, 1850r, Chelonia mydas, diff.

2009, Aug. 26
3007   A1237   Sheet of 4, #a-d   5.00   5.00

A1238

No. 3008: a, World Post Day. b, World Child Day.

2009, Oct. 9
3008   A1238   1200r Horiz. pair, #a-b   3.50   3.50

17th Book Week — A1239

2009, Nov. 14
3009   A1239   1200r multicolored   2.00   1.00

Rob'e Rashidi University Endowment Document A1240

2009, Dec. 1
3010   A1240   1200r multicolored   1.50   .75

Ghadir Khom Festival — A1240a

2009, Dec. 6   Litho.   Perf. 13¾x14¼
3010A   A1240a   1200r multicolored   2.00   1.00

Universal Declaration of Human Rights, 60th Anniv. A1241

2009, Dec. 13   Perf. 13
3011   A1241   1200r multicolored   2.00   1.00

Ayatollah Mohammad Mofatteh (1928-79) — A1242

2009, Dec. 18   Perf. 13¾x14¼
3012   A1242   1200r multicolored   2.00   1.00

Buildings in Indonesia and Iran — A1243

No. 3013: a, Soltanieh Dome, Iran. b, Al-Markaz Mosque, Indonesia.

2009, Dec. 23   Perf. 13
3013   A1243   2000r Horiz. pair, #a-b, + central label   4.50   4.50
See Indonesia Nos. 2218-2219.

Intl. Year of Astronomy — A1244

No. 3014: a, 1000r, Artificial plan of Maragheh Observatory. b, 1200r, Al-Tafhim, by Abu Ryehan Biruni. c, 1300r, Armillary sphere. d, 1500r, Taqi al-Din and astronomers, 16th cent.

2010, Feb. 24   Perf. 13¾x14¼
3014   A1244   Block of 4, #a-d   4.50   4.50

Mullah Sadra (c. 1571-1641) — A1245

2010, May 18
3015   A1245   1300r multicolored   2.50   1.25

Khaje Abdullah Ansari (1006-88), Religious Commentator A1246

2010, July 25   Perf. 13¾
3016   A1246   2000r multicolored   3.00   1.50
See Afghanistan No. 1465, Tajikistan No. 366.

Destroyer Jamaran A1247

2010, Sept. 1   Perf. 14¼x13¾
3017   A1247   2000r multicolored   2.50   1.25

Martyred Engineers of the Sacred Defense — A1248

2010, Oct. 20   Perf. 13¾x14¼
3018   A1248   2000r multicolored   2.50   1.25

Shah-e-Cheragh Holy Shrine, Shiraz — A1249

No. 3019: a, 1200r, Mosque dome and minaret. b, 1300r, Shrine.

2010, Nov. 14   Perf. 13¾
3019   A1249   Horiz. pair, #a-b   3.50   3.50

A1250

New Year A1251

No. 3021: a, Flowers and ribbon. b, Candle and Iranian inscription. c, Goldfish in bowl and apples. d, Koran on bookstand and oranges.

    Perf. 13¾x14¼
2010, Mar. 27   Litho.
3020   A1250   2000r multicolored   2.25   1.25
    Perf. 14¼x13¾
3021   A1251   1250r Sheet of 4, #a-d   6.00   6.00

Nature Day — A1252

No. 3022 — Trees in: a, Spring. b, Summer. c, Autumn. d, Winter.

2010, Apr. 2   Perf. 13¾x14¼
3022   Horiz. strip of 4   5.00   5.00
  a.   A1252   1100r pink & multi   .75   .40
  b.   A1252   1200r green & multi   .75   .40
  c.   A1252   1300r orange & multi   .75   .40
  d.   A1252   1400r blue & multi   .75   .40

Towers in Pakistan and Iran A1253

No. 3023: a, Minar-e-Pakistan, Lahore. b, Milad Tower, Tehran.

2010, July 28
3023   A1253   2000r Horiz. pair, #a-b, + flanking label   3.50   3.50
See Pakistan No. 1149.

Miniature Sheet

Products of Iranian Military Industries — A1254

No. 3024: a, 1000r, Sedjil missile. b, 1500r, Saegheh airplane. c, 2000r, Mersad radar system. d, 2500r, Ghadir submarine.

2010, Aug. 22   Perf. 14¼x13¾
3024   A1254   Sheet of 4, #a-d   3.50   3.50

IRAN

Martyrs of Holy Defense — A1255

2010, Sept. 27			Perf. 13¾x14¼	
3025	A1255	2000r multicolored	2.50	1.25

Miniature Sheet

World Post Day A1256

2010, Oct. 9			Perf. 14¼	
3026	A1256	Sheet of 7, #a-g	8.00	8.00

No. 3026: a, 1000r, Airplane and S.P.S. emblem. b, 1100r, Financial Post emblem. c, 1300r, Mail truck and EMS emblem. d, 1400r, Shopping cart and "@" symbol. e, 1500r, Iran Post e-mail emblem. f, 1700r, Mailman on motorcycle. g, 2000r, UPU emblem, map of Iran.

Embroidery — A1257

2010, Nov. 10			Perf. 14¼x13¾	
3027	A1257	2000r Horiz. pair, #a-b	3.00	3.00

See Hungary Nos. 4178-4179.

No. 3027: a, Jazygian embroidery designs, Hungary. b, Termeh embroidery designs, Yazd, Iran.

18th Book Week — A1258

2010, Nov. 14			Perf. 13¾x14¼	
3028	A1258	2000r multicolored	2.50	1.25

Sheikh Abbas Qummi (1877-1940), Historian — A1259

2010, Dec. 2				
3029	A1259	2000r multicolored	2.50	1.25

A1259a A1259b

Personalized Stamps — A1259c

No. 3029E: f, 300r, Rainbow, denomination on green and blue stripes. g, 700r, Rainbos, denomination on orange, yellow and green stripes. h, 900r, Rainbow and tree, denomination on tree and grass. i, 1200r, Clouds, butterfly and city, denomination on city.

2010-11	Litho.	Perf. 13¾x14¼	
Denomination on One Line Country Name at Center			
3029A	A1259a	300r multi + label	3.00 3.00
3029B	A1259a	650r multi + label	6.00 6.00
3029C	A1259a	1000r multi + label	9.50 9.50
Country Name at Left Above Denomination on Two Lines			
3029D	A1259b	650r multi + label	6.00 6.00

Souvenir Sheet
Country Name Not Shown in English
Perf. 14¼x13¾ on 3 Sides

3029E	A1259c	Sheet of 4, #f-i + 4 labels	6.00 6.00

Issued: No. 3029A, 2010, others, 2011. Labels on Nos. 3029A-3029E are separated from the stamps by a line of simulated perforations. Other labels exist for No. 3029A. Other labels may exist for Nos. 3029B-3029E.

Space — A1259d

No. 3029J — Inscriptions: k, Space Technology Day. l, Kavoshgar 2. m, Tolou National Satellite. n, Mesbah 2 National Satellite. o, Satellite Ground Stations.

2010, Dec. 6	Litho.	Perf. 13¾x14¼	
3029J		Horiz. strip of 5	4.00 4.00
k.-l.	A1259d	1200r Either single	.50 .25
m.	A1259d	1400r multi	.50 .25
n.	A1259d	1600r multi	.50 .30
o.	A1259d	1800r multi	.50 .35

Bank Maskan Mehr Housing Project, 73rd Anniv. — A1260

2011, Jan. 15				
3030	A1260	2000r multicolored	2.50	1.25

Electronic Communication Between People and Government A1261

2011, Jan. 17				
3031	A1261	2000r multicolored	2.50	1.75

Islamic Revolution, 32nd Anniv. — A1262

No. 3032 — Ayatollah Khomeini and: a, Red flowers at LR. b, Candle at UL. c, White flowers and three candles at top. d, Birds and white flowers.

2011, Feb. 11				
3032		Horiz. strip of 4	3.50	3.50
a.-d.	A1262	1000r Any single	.50	.25

Convergence of Monotheistic Religions A1263

2011, Feb. 15			Perf. 14¼x13¾	
3033	A1263	2000r multicolored	2.50	1.50

Ayatollah Mahmoud Taleghani (1911-79) — A1264

2011, Mar. 5			Perf. 13¾x14¼	
3034	A1264	2500r multicolored	3.00	1.50

Miniature Sheet

New Year A1265

No. 3035: a, 1000r, Bowl of coins. b, 1100r, Grass and painted eggs in bowl. c, 1300r, Bowl of sumac. d, 1400r, Apples in bowl. e, 1500r, Garlic bulbs in bowl. f, 1700r, Oleaster in bowl. g, 2000r, Hyacinth and Koran.

2011, Mar. 26			Perf. 14¼	
3035	A1265	Sheet of 7, #a-g	7.00	7.00

Bridges — A1266

Designs: 10,000r, Jahanara Bridge. 14,800r, Khajoo Bridge. 20,000r, Veresk Bridge. 20,700r, Javadieh Bridge.

2011	Litho.	Perf. 14	
3036	A1266	10,000r multi	6.00 1.90
3037	A1266	14,800r multi	7.00 2.75
3038	A1266	20,000r multi	8.00 3.50
3039	A1266	20,700r multi	12.00 4.00
Nos. 3036-3039 (4)			33.00 12.15

Issued: 10,000r, 6/15; 14,800r, 7/20; 20,000r, 5/22; 20,700r, 7/6.

World Crafts Day A1267

No. 3040: a, Vase. b, Lidded container.

2011, June 10			Perf. 13¾x14¼	
3040	A1267	2000r Horiz. pair, #a-b	4.50	2.00

Ayatollah Muhammad Fazel Lankarani (1931-2007) — A1268

2011, June 15				
3041	A1268	2000r multicolored	2.50	1.25

Souvenir Sheet

Green Pheasants — A1269

2011, July 26			Perf. 14¼x13¾	
3042	A1269	5000r multicolored	5.00	5.00

PhilaNippon '11 Intl. Philatelic Exhibition, Yokohama, Japan.

Souvenir Sheet

Iranian Men's Volleyball Team, Champions of 16th Asian Tournament — A1269a

2011, Sept. 29			Perf. 14	
3042A	A1269a	3400r multi	3.50	3.50

National Veterinary Day — A1270

2011, Oct. 6			Perf. 14¼x13¾	
3043	A1270	2200r multicolored	2.00	1.00

2011 Population and Housing Census — A1271

2011, Oct. 23			Perf. 13¾x14¼	
3044	A1271	2200r multi	2.00	1.00

Shams Tabrizi (1185-c.1248), Teacher of Poet Mevlana — A1272

2011, Oct. 30				
3045	A1272	2200r multi	2.00	1.00

IRAN

Souvenir Sheet
Buildings in Belarus and Iran — A1273

No. 3046: a, Mir Castle, Mir, Belarus. b, Karimkhani Citadel, Shiraz, Iran.

2011, Sept. 28 Litho. **Perf. 14¼x13¾**
3046 A1273 2200r Sheet of 2,
#a-b 3.50 3.50
See Belarus No. 783.

World Post Day — A1274

2011, Oct. 9 **Perf. 13¾**
3047 A1274 2000r multi 2.50 1.25

19th Book Week — A1275

2011, Nov. 13 **Perf. 13¾x14¼**
3048 A1275 2200r multi 2.00 1.00

Souvenir Sheet
Revival Week A1276

2011, Nov. 27 **Perf. 14¼x13¾**
3049 A1276 2200r multi 3.00 3.00

Personalized Stamp — A1276a

2011, Dec. 6 Litho. **Perf. 13¾**
3049A A1276a 2600r multi + label 2.00 2.00
Label on No. 3049A separated from the stamp by a line of simulated perforations. Another label exists for No. 3049A.

Worldwide Fund for Nature (WWF) A1277

Designs: Nos. 3050, 3054a, 600r, Long-eared owl. Nos. 3051, 3054b, 1100r, Spotted owlet. Nos. 3052, 3054c, 1600r, Pallid scops owl. Nos. 3053, 3054d, 2200r, Brown fish owl.

2011, Dec. 14 Litho.
Stamps With White Frames
3050-3053 A1277 Set of 4 3.00 3.00
Souvenir Sheet
Stamps Without White Frame
3054 A1277 Sheet of 4, #a-d 4.00 4.00
No. 3054 exists imperf. Value, $125.

Islamic Awakening — A1278

2011, Dec. 22 **Perf. 13¾x14¼**
3055 A1278 2200r multi 2.00 1.00

Fish Type of 2009-11
Designs as before.

2011 Litho. **Perf. 14**
Size: 30x23mm
3055A	A1229	300r multi	1.00	.50
3055B	A1229	400r multi	1.00	.50
3055C	A1229	500r multi	1.00	.50
3055D	A1229	1000r multi	1.00	.50
3055E	A1229	2000r multi	2.00	1.00
3055F	A1229	4000r multi	4.00	2.00
3055G	A1229	5000r multi	5.00	2.25
3055H	A1229	6400r multi	6.00	2.50
3055I	A1229	7500r multi	7.00	3.00

No. 3055G exists imperf. Value, pair $50.

Islamic and Iranian Culture and Civilization A1279

2012, Feb. 1 **Perf. 14¼x13¾**
3056 A1279 2200r multi 2.00 1.00

Souvenir Sheet
Islamic Revolution, 33rd Anniv. — A1280

No. 3057: a, Toppled statue of Shah of Iran, flames. b, Ayatollah Khomeini, tulips.

2012, Feb. 11 **Perf. 13¾x14¼**
3057 A1280 2200r Sheet of 2,
#a-b 3.00 3.00

New Year 2012 A1281

No. 3058 — Flowers and: a, Pen, goldfish in bowl. b, Apples, oil lamp.

2012, Mar. 26 **Perf. 14¼x13¾**
3058 A1281 2200r Horiz. pair,
#a-b 2.50 2.50
A souvenir sheet containing Nos. 3058a-3058b was printed in limited quantities. Value $25.

Grand Ayatollah Mohammed Taghi Bahjat (1913-2009) A1282

2012, May 17 **Perf. 13¾x14¼**
3059 A1282 2200r multi 2.00 .75

Bridges — A1284 / A1283

Designs: 200r, Broken Bridge. 1000r, Khosro Abad Bridge. 3000r, Khatoon Bridge. 5000r, Martyr Kalantari Bridge. 8000r, Qishlaq Bridge. 9000r, Mardogh Bridge. 20,000r, Veresk Bridge.

Perf. 14 (A1283), 13x13½ (A1284)
2012-13
3060	A1283	200r multi	.25	.25
3061	A1284	1000r multi	.25	.25
3062	A1284	3000r multi	.50	.50
3063	A1284	5000r multi	.85	.85
3064	A1283	8000r multi	2.00	1.40
3065	A1283	9000r multi	3.00	1.60
3066	A1283	20,000r multi	7.00	3.25
Nos. 3060-3066 (5)			6.20	6.20

Issued: 200r, Dec. 2012; 1000r, 5000r, Jan. 2013; 3000r, 1/13/13; 8000r, 10/30; 9000r, 2/9. 20,000r, 2012.
See Nos. 3075-3080, 3106-3108, 3110-3112.

Islamic Republic of Iran Day — A1285

2012, Mar. 30 Litho. **Perf. 13¾x14**
3067 A1285 2200r multi 2.00 1.50

25th Tehran Intl. Book Fair — A1286

2012, May 5
3068 A1286 2200r multi 2.00 1.00

Ramadan — A1287

2012, July 21
3069 A1287 2200r multi 2.00 1.00

Souvenir Sheet
Dedication and Sacrifice — A1288

No. 3070: a, Mohammad Hussein Fahmideh (1967-80), war hero. b, Riz Ali Khajavi, farmer who prevented 1962 train crash.

2012, Dec. 11 **Perf. 14 Syncopated**
3070 A1288 2200r Sheet of 2,
#a-b 3.50 3.50

Miniature Sheet
World Crafts Day A1289

No. 3071 — Various textile crafts with: a, Green panel, denomination at LL. b, Green panel, denomination at LR. c, Red panel, denomination at UL. d, Red panel, denomination at UR.

Perf. 14x13¾ Syncopated
2012, Dec. 11
3071 A1289 2000r Sheet of 4,
#a-d 4.00 4.00

A1290

Personalized Stamps A1291

2012 **Perf. 13¾x14**
3072 A1290 2200r multi + label 1.25 .50
Perf. 13¾
3073 A1291 2500r multi + label 1.50 .50

Labels on Nos. 3072-3073 are separated from the stamps by a line of simulated perforations. Another label exists for No. 3073. Other labels may exist for No. 3072.

Non-Aligned Movement, 16th Summit, Tehran — A1292

2012, Aug. 28
3074 A1292 2200r multicolored 2.25 .50

Bridge Types of 2012-13
Designs: 100r, Earthen Bridge. 500r, Zamankhan Bridge. 800r, Yaqubie Bridge. 2000r, Tinoj Bridge. 4000r, Ghotoor Bridge. 15,700r, Bahrami Bridge.

Perf. 14 (A1283), 13x13½ (A1284)
2012-13
3075	A1284	100r multi	.25	.25
3076	A1284	500r multi	.25	.25
3077	A1284	800r multi	.25	.25
3078	A1284	2000r multi	.35	.35
3079	A1284	4000r multi	.65	.65
3080	A1283	15,700r multi	4.50	2.60
Nos. 3075-3080 (6)			6.25	4.35

Issued: 100r, 2/19/13; 500r, 2/13/13; 800r, 3/6/13; 2000r, 3/27/13; 4000r, 3/13/13; 15,700r, 9/5.

IRAN

Souvenir Sheet
Sacred Defense Week and World Post Day — A1293

2012, Oct. 8			Perf. 14	
3081	A1293	3400r multi	2.50	2.50

20th Book Week — A1294

2012, Nov. 15			Perf. 13¾x14	
3082	A1294	2200r multi	1.75	.50

The Canon of Medicine, by Avicenna, 1000th Anniv. of Completion — A1295

2013, Mar. 5				
3083	A1295	3000r multi	2.50	.75

Arbor Day — A1297

2013, Mar. 5	Litho.		Perf. 13¾x14¼	
3084	A1297	3000r multi	2.50	.75

Miniature Sheet
Fish — A1298

No. 3085: a, 3000r, Cyprinus carpio. b, 3600r, Rutilus frisii kutum. c, 3900r, Stizostedion lucioperca. d, 4600r, Salmon trutta caspius.

			Perf. 14¼x13¾	
2013, Mar. 20			Litho.	
3085	A1298	Sheet of 4, #a-d	5.00	5.00

Souvenir Sheet
New Year — A1299

2013, Mar. 25	Litho.		Perf. 14x13¾	
3086	A1299	15,000r multi	4.50	4.50

Personalized Stamps — A1300, A1301

2013		Litho.	Perf. 13¾	
3087	A1300	650r multi + label	18.00	18.00
		Perf. 13¾x14¼		
3088	A1301	4500r multi + label	5.00	5.00

Labels on Nos. 3087-3088 are separated from the stamps by a line of simulate perforations. issued: No. 3087, 7/8; No. 3088, 4/7.

Souvenir Sheet
World Health Day — A1302

No. 3089 — Electrocardiogram waves and: a, Running skeleton. b, Heart and sphygmomanometer dial.

2013, Apr. 7	Litho.		Perf. 14¼x13¾	
3089	A1302	4500r Sheet of 2, #a-b	4.00	4.00

Souvenir Sheet
Ebrat Museum, Tehran — A1303

2013, May 6	Litho.		Perf. 14¼x13¾	
3090	A1303	6000r multi	3.50	3.50

Miniature Sheet
Martyrs — A1304

No. 3091: a, 3000r, Dr. Mostafa Chamran (1932-81), Minister of Defense. b, 3600r, Javad Fakori (1939-81), Minister of Defense. c, 3900r, Mousa Namjoo (1938-81), Minister of Defense. d, 4600r, Mohsen Safavi, combat engineer.

2013, May 9	Litho.		Perf. 14¼x13¾	
3091	A1304	Sheet of 4, #a-d	4.00	4.00

World Crafts Day — A1305

No. 3092 — Chalice with background color of: a, 4500r, Red. b, 5400r, Purple. c, 5800r, Red violet. d, 6900r, Brown orange.

		Perf. 13¾x14¼		
2013, June 10	Litho.	Wmk. 411		
3092	A1305	Block of 4, #a-d	6.00	6.00

Unknown Soldiers of Imam Zaman — A1306

		Perf. 13¾		
2013, June 23	Litho.	Unwmk.		
3093	A1306	3000r multi	2.50	1.00

World Children's Day — A1307

		Wmk. 411		
2013, Nov. 8	Litho.		Perf. 13¾	
3094	A1307	4500r multi	2.50	.75

Economic Cooperation Organization — A1308

		Perf. 13¾x14¼		
2013, Nov. 25	Litho.	Wmk. 411		
3095	A1308	4500r multi	2.50	.75

Persian Alphabet — A1309, A1310, A1311, A1312, A1313, A1314, A1315, A1316, A1317, A1318

2014		Litho.	Wmk. 411	Perf. 14	
3096	A1309	500r multi		.25	.25
3097	A1310	1000r multi		.25	.25
3098	A1311	2000r multi		.25	.25
3099	A1312	3000r multi		.25	.25
3100	A1313	4000r multi		1.50	1.50
3101	A1314	5000r multi		1.75	1.75
3102	A1315	8000r multi		2.50	2.50
3103	A1316	9000r multi		3.00	3.00
3104	A1317	10,000r multi		4.50	4.50
3105	A1318	30,000r multi		7.50	7.50
		Nos. 3096-3105 (10)		21.75	21.75

Issued; 500r, 5/7; 1000r, 5/5; 2000r, 5/29; 3000r, 3/1; 4000r, 9/6; 5000r, 3/12; 8000r, 3/10; 9000r, 7/5; 10,000r, 5/15; 30,000r, 2/16.

Persian Alphabet Type of 2014
2015	Litho.	Unwmk.	Perf. 13x13¼
		Size: 32x25mm	
		Wider Orange Frames	
3105A	A1311	2000r multi	.25 .25
3105B	A1314	5000r multi	.35 .35
3105C	A1317	10,000r multi	.70 .70
3105D	A1318	30,000r multi	2.00 2.00
		Nos. 3105A-3105D (4)	3.30 3.30

Bridges Type of 2012-13
Designs: 250r, Latidan Bridge. 300r, Doab Bridge. 400r, Mirbaha Bridge.

2014		Litho.	Wmk. 411	Perf. 14	
3106	A1283	250r multi		.90	.35
3107	A1283	300r multi		.90	.35
3108	A1283	400r multi		.90	.35
		Nos. 3106-3108 (3)		2.70	1.05

Issued: 250r, 2/19; 300r, 400r, 2/23.

World Telecommunications Day — A1319

		Wmk. 411		
2014, May 17	Litho.		Perf. 13¾	
3109	A1319	4500r multi	2.00	1.00

Bridges Type of 2012-13
Designs: 9000r, Mardogh Bridge. 10,000r, Martyr Jahanara Bridge. 20,000r, Veresk Bridge.

2014		Litho.	Unwmk.	Perf. 13x13½	
3110	A1284	9000r multi		3.00	.70
3111	A1284	10,000r multi		3.00	.75
3112	A1284	20,000r multi		6.00	1.50
		Nos. 3110-3112 (3)		12.00	2.95

"Customized Stamp" Inscription — A1320

IRAN

"Commercial Stamp" Inscription — A1320a

"Customized Stamp" Inscription, Larger Type Font — A1320b

"Customized Stamp" Inscription — A1320c

Perf. 13¾x14

		2014-18	Litho.		Unwmk.	
3113	A1320	10,000r multi + label			.75	.75
3113A	A1320a	10,000r multi + label			.55	.55
3113B	A1320b	10,000r multi + label			.45	.45
3113C	A1320c	20,000r multi + label			1.40	1.40
		Nos. 3113-3113C (4)			3.15	3.15

Issued: No. 3113, 2014; No. 3113A, 2017, No. 3113B, 2018; No. 3113C, 8/17/15. Labels on Nos. 3113-3113C, which could be personalized, are separated from the stamps by a line of simulated perforations. Other labels exist for Nos. 3113 and 3113C. Compare with No. 3180.

Persian Alphabet — A1330

2014		Litho.	Wmk. 411	Perf. 14	
3115	A1322	1000r multi		.25	.25
3116	A1323	3000r multi		.25	.25
3117	A1324	5000r multi		.40	.40
3118	A1325	6000r multi		.45	.45
3119	A1326	7000r multi		2.50	.55
3120	A1327	8000r multi		.60	.60
3121	A1328	10,000r multi		3.00	.75
3122	A1329	20,000r multi		5.50	1.50
3123	A1330	30,000r multi		8.00	2.25
		Nos. 3115-3123 (9)		20.95	7.00

Issued: 6000r, 10/18; 7000r, 9/16; 20,000r, 8/12; others, 2014. An additional stamp was issued in this set. The editors would like to examine any example of it.

World Post Day — A1331

Perf. 14x13¾
2014, July 9		Litho.		Wmk. 411	
3124	A1331	4500r multi		3.00	2.00

Dated 2013.

27th Tehran International Book Fair — A1332

2014, July 9		Litho.	Perf. 13¾x14		
3125	A1332	4500r multi		2.00	1.00

Martyr's Day — A1333

Perf. 14x13¾
2014, July 9		Litho.		Wmk. 411	
3126	A1333	10,000r multi		3.50	2.25

Souvenir Sheet

New Year A1334

Perf. 14¼x13¾
2014, Aug. 10		Litho.		Unwmk.	
3127	A1334	10,000r multi		2.75	2.00

Souvenir Sheet

Ayatollah Khomeini (1900-89) — A1335

Perf. 13¾ (Partial)
2014, Aug. 18		Litho.		Wmk. 411	
3128	A1335	5000r multi		2.75	2.25

Dated 2013.

Ayatollah Khomeini Movement, 50th Anniv. — A1336

		Unwmk.			
2014, Sept. 17		Litho.		Perf. 14	
3129	A1336	9000r multi		3.50	2.00

World Post Day — A1337

Perf. 14¼x13¾
2014, Nov. 16		Litho.		Wmk. 411	
3130	A1337	6000r multi		2.60	1.25

Diplomatic Relations Between Iran and Mexico, 50th Anniv. — A1338

		Wmk. 411		Perf. 14	
2014, Nov. 16		Litho.			
3131	A1338	8000r multi		4.00	1.25

See Mexico No. 2923.

Souvenir Sheet

Samarkand Observatory — A1339

Perf. 14x13¾
2014, July 1		Litho.		Wmk. 411	
3132	A1339	6000r Sheet of 2, #a-b		3.00	1.25

No. 3132: a, Observatory. b, Open almanac.

Miniature Sheet

Worldwide Fund for Nature (WWF) — A1340

No. 3133 — Lesser white-fronted goose: a, 5000r, Standing. b, 6000r, In flight. c, 7000r, On water. d, 8000r, Standing, flock flying in background.

Perf. 14x13¾
2014, Dec. 15		Litho.		Unwmk.	
3133	A1340	Sheet of 4, #a-d		5.00	4.00

Miniature Sheet

Schools and Their Emblems A1341

No. 3134: a, School of Charbagh, Isfahan. b, Emblem of University of Jondishapour. c, Emblem of University of Tehran. d, School of Darol Fonoun.

Perf. 14x13¾
2015, Feb. 3		Litho.		Wmk. 411	
3134	A1341	6000r Sheet of 4, #a-d		6.50	6.50

Mosques A1342

No. 3135: a, Green Mosque, Bursa, Turkey. b, Kabood Mosque, Tabriz, Iran.

Perf. 14x13¾
2015, Feb. 18		Litho.		Unwmk.	
3135		Horiz. pair + central label		3.50	3.50
a.-b.	A1342	5000r Either single		1.75	1.00

See Turkey No. 3425.

New Year A1343

Perf. 14x13¾
2015, Mar. 25		Litho.		Unwmk.	
3136	A1343	9000r multi		2.75	2.00

World Telecommunications Day — A1344

Perf. 14x13¾
2015, May 10		Litho.		Wmk. 411	
3137	A1344	9000r multi		2.75	1.50

Flowers — A1347

Designs: Nos. 3138, 3139, Origanum majorana. Nos. 3140, 3141, Viola tricolor. Nos. 3142, 3143, Orchis simia. 3000r, Rheum rhaponticum. Nos. 3145, 3146, Matricaria chamomilla. 7000r, Ricinus communis. 10,000r, Glycyrrhiza glabra. Nos. 3150, 3151, Echium amoenum. 30,000r, Crocus sativus.

2015-16		Litho.	Wmk. 411	Perf. 14	
3138	A1345	500r multi		.25	.25
3139	A1346	500r multi		.25	.25
3140	A1345	1000r multi		.25	.25
3141	A1346	1000r multi		.25	.25
3142	A1346	2000r multi		.25	.25
3143	A1346	2000r multi		.25	.25
3144	A1346	3000r multi		.30	.25

IRAN

3145	A1345	5000r multi	.50	.35
3146	A1346	5000r multi	.70	.35
3147	A1346	7000r multi	2.00	.50
3148	A1345	10,000r multi	2.00	.70
3149	A1346	10,000r multi	2.00	.70
3150	A1346	20,000r multi	4.00	1.40
3151	A1347	20,000r multi	6.50	2.00
3152	A1346	30,000r multi	6.50	2.00
		Nos. 3138-3152 (14)	19.50	7.75

Issued: No. 3138, 8/23; No. 3140, 7/5; No. 3142, 9/26; No. 3145, 10/5; No. 3148, 10/10. No. 3151, 2015. 30,000r, 1/5/16. See Nos. 3164-3165.

Return to Iran of Bodies of 175 Divers Killed in 1986 Operation Karbala-4 — A1348

2015, Aug. 11   Perf. 14x13¾   Litho.   Wmk. 411
3153 A1348 9000r multi   2.75 2.00

Miniature Sheet

Expo 2015, Milan A1349

No. 3154: a, Folio of Iran Miniature. b, Iran Pavilion. c, Saffron and crocus. d, Persian garden carpet.

2015, Aug. 23   Perf. 14x13¾   Litho.   Wmk. 411
3154 A1349 9000r Sheet of 4, #a-d   9.00 9.00

Antiquities From Sialk-Kashan — A1350

No. 3155 — Clay pots: a, Left pot with bull design. b, Left pot with diamond pattern.

2015, Sept. 15   Perf. 14x13¾   Litho.   Wmk. 411
3155 A1350 9000r Vert. pair, #a-b   3.00 1.50

Alam-al-Hoda (c. 965-1009), Islamic Scholar — A1351

2015   Perf. 13¾x14   Litho.   Wmk. 411
3156 A1351 9000r multi   3.00 1.50

World Children's Day — A1352

Perf. 13¾x14
2016   Litho.   Wmk. 411
3157 A1352 9000r multi   3.00 1.50
Dated 2015.

Birth Anniversary of Prophet Mohammad — A1353

Perf. 13¾x14
2016   Litho.   Wmk. 411
3158 A1353 9000r multi   3.00 1.50
Dated 2015.

Cinema Day — A1354

Perf. 14x13¾
2016   Litho.   Wmk. 411
3159 A1354 9000r multi   3.00 1.50

Navvab Safavi (c. 1924-56), Cleric — A1355

Perf. 13¾x14
2016, Jan. 17   Litho.   Wmk. 411
3160 A1355 9000r multi   3.00 1.50

Souvenir Sheet

New Year 2016 A1356

Perf. 14x13¾
2016   Litho.   Wmk. 411
3161 A1356 9000r multi   4.00 4.00

Eurasian Lynx A1357

No. 3162: a, Lynx facing right. b, Head of lynx.

Perf. 14x13¾
2016   Litho.   Wmk. 411
3162 A1357 9000r Horiz. pair, #a-b   3.50 3.00

Poets A1358

No. 3163: a, Awhadi Maraghei (1271-1338). b, Mir Sayyid Ali Hamadani (1314-84). c, Sheikh Ahmad Jami (1048-1141).

Perf. 13¾x14
2016, Aug. 5   Litho.   Wmk. 411
3163 A1358 9000r Horiz. strip of 3, #a-c   4.50 4.50

Flower Types of 2015-16

Designs: 8000r, Salix aegyptiaca. 9000r, Carum carvi.

2016   Litho.   Wmk. 411   Perf. 14
3164 A1346 8000r multi   3.50 .55
3165 A1346 9000r multi   4.00 .60

Naser Khosrow (1004-1088), Poet — A1359

Perf. 13¾x14
2016   Litho.   Wmk. 411
3167 A1359 9000r multi   3.00 1.50
Dated 2015.

International Tourism Day — A1360

Perf. 14x13¾
2016   Litho.   Wmk. 411
3168 A1360 15,000r multi   4.00 2.00

Nationalization of Postal Service A1361

Perf. 14x13¾
2016, Aug. 18   Litho.   Unwmk.
3169 A1361 9000r multi   4.00 2.00

World Children's Day — A1362

Perf. 13¾x14
2016, Sept. 7   Litho.   Wmk. 411
3170 A1362 9000r multi   4.00 2.00

2015 Pilgrimage Stampede at Mena, Saudi Arabia — A1363

Perf. 13¾x14
2016, Sept. 12   Litho.   Unwmk.
3171 A1363 15,000r multi   4.00 2.00

Islamic Revolution, 38th Anniv. — A1364

Perf. 13¾x14
2017, Feb. 10   Litho.   Unwmk.
3172 A1364 9000r multi   3.00 1.50

Souvenir Sheet

Pres. Akbar Hashemi Rafsanjani (1934-2017) — A1365

Perf. 14x13¾
2017, Feb. 16   Litho.   Unwmk.
3173 A1365 9000r multi   3.50 1.75

Fatimah (c. 616-33), Daughter of Mohammed A1366

2017   Litho.   Unwmk.   Perf. 13¾x14
3174 A1366 15,000r multi   3.50 1.75
International Woman's Day.

New Year 2017 — A1367

Perf. 13¾x14
2017, Mar. 25   Litho.   Unwmk.
3175 A1367 9000r multi   4.00 2.00

Firefighters A1368

2017   Litho.   Unwmk.   Perf. 13¾x14
3176 A1368 9000r multi   4.00 2.00

2017 Asia Pacific Postal Union Congress, Tehran — A1369

2017   Litho.   Unwmk.   Perf. 14x13¾
3177 A1369 9000r multi   4.00 2.00

Souvenir Sheet

Houses of Worship A1370

No. 3178: a, Blue Mosque, Yerevan, Armenia. b, Holy Savior Cathedral, Isfahan, Iran.

IRAN

Perf. 14x13¾ on 3 Sides
2017, Oct. 25 Litho. Unwmk.
3178 A1370 15,000r Sheet of 2, 6.50 6.50
#a-b
Diplomatic Relations between Iran & Armenia.
See Armenia No. 1116.

Martyrs of Terror — A1371

2017 Litho. Unwmk. Perf. 13¾x14
3179 A1371 9000r multi 3.00 1.50

Personalized Stamp — A1372

2017 Litho. Unwmk. Perf. 13¾x14
3180 A1372 10,000r multi 3.50 1.75
Label on No. 3180 separated from the stamp by a line of simulated perforations. No. 3180 exists with different labels. Compare with Nos. 3113-3113B.

Iran Bastan Museum and Malek National Library and Museum, 80th Anniv. — A1373

2017 Litho. Unwmk. Perf. 13¾x14
3181 A1373 12,000r multi 4.00 2.00

Historic City of Yazd UNESCO World Heritage Site — A1374

2017 Litho. Unwmk. Perf. 14x13¾
3182 A1374 12,000r multi 4.00 2.00

A1375

No. 3183: a, Persian Garden carpet. b, Persian Garden architecture.

2017 Litho. Unwmk. Perf. 13¾x14
3183 A1375 12,000r Horiz. pair, 6.50 3.25
#a-b

Melissa Officinalis — A1376

Litho. With Hologram Affixed
2017 Die Cut Perf. 12
Self-Adhesive
3184 A1376 50,000r multi 2.75 2.75

Mohsen Hojaji (1991-2017), Military Officer Executed by ISIS — A1377

Perf. 14x13¾
2017, Aug. 28 Litho. Unwmk.
3185 A1377 12,000r multi .75 .75

Souvenir Sheet

Ports of Iran and India A1378

No. 3186 — Ships at: a, Deendayal Port, India. b, Shahid Beheshti Port, Iran.

Perf. 14x13¾
2018, Feb. 17 Litho. Unwmk.
3186 A1378 12,000r Sheet of 2, 1.40 1.40
#a-b
See India Nos. 3008-3009.

Souvenir Sheet

Nowruz A1379

Perf. 14x13¾
2018, Mar. 25 Litho. Unwmk.
3187 A1379 12,000r multi .65 .65

Attar of Nishapur (c. 1145-c. 1221), Poet — A1380

2018 Litho. Unwmk. Perf. 13¾x14
3188 A1380 12,000r multi .65 .65

World Crafts Day A1381

2018, June 10 Litho. Unwmk. Perf. 14
3189 A1381 12,000r multi .60 .60

Souvenir Sheet

2018 World Cup Soccer Championships, Russia — A1382

Perf. 14x13¾
2018, June 14 Litho. Unwmk.
3190 A1382 12,000r multi .60 .60

Hakim Khayyam Neishabouri (Omar Khayyam, 1048-1131), Mathematician and Poet, and His Mausoleum, Nishapur A1383

2018 Litho. Perf. 14x13¾
3191 A1383 12,000r multi .60 .60

World Post Day — A1384

2018 Litho. Perf. 13¾x14
3192 A1384 12,000r multi .60 .60

Police Week — A1385

2018 Litho. Perf. 14x13¾
3193 A1385 12,000r multi .60 .60

Souvenir Sheet

Map of the Silk Road A1386

2018 Litho. Perf. 14x13¾
3194 A1386 12,000r multi .60 .60

Lions A1387

No. 3195: a, Korean incense burner cover, c. 8th-9th cent., and flag of South Korea. b, Persian gold rhyton, c. 5th cent. B.C. and flag of Iran.

2018 Litho. Perf. 14x13¾
3195 A1387 12,000r Horiz. pair, 1.25 1.25
#a-b
Iran and South Korea joint issue.

Islamic Revolution, 40th Anniv. — A1389

2019, Feb. 11 Litho. Perf. 14x13¾
3197 A1389 12,000r multi 4.00 4.00

Central Insurance Building A1390

Iran Zamin Bank Emblem A1391

Ala Mirmohammad Sadeghi, Vice-president of Tehran Chamber of Commerce A1392

Sarmad Insurance Emblem A1393

Bank Saderat and Sarmad Insurance Emblems A1394

Alim Marvasti Family Revolving Loan Fund Institution A1395

Abadan Petroleum Industry Apprentice Museum — A1396

IRAN

Water Preservation — A1397

Achievement of 8 Percent Profit Rate in Housing Payment Facilities — A1398

No. 3204: a, Oil refinery equipment. b, Statue holding picture.
No. 3205: a, Field of flowers in mirror with legs. b, Man in parched field.
No. 3206: a, Buildings, Arabian numeral "8" and percent sign. b, Building and Arabian numeral "8."

2019		Litho.		Perf. 14x13¾
3198	A1390	5000r multi		2.50 2.50
3199	A1391	5000r multi		2.50 2.50
3200	A1392	5000r multi		2.50 2.50
3201	A1393	5000r multi		1.50 1.50
3202	A1394	5000r multi		1.50 1.50
3203	A1395	5000r multi		2.00 2.00
3204	A1396	5000r Horiz. pair, #a-b		3.00 3.00
3205	A1397	5000r Horiz. pair, #a-b		2.00 2.00
3206	A1398	5000r Horiz. pair, #a-b		2.50 2.50
Nos. 3198-3206 (9)				20.00 20.00

Simulated perforations do not separate the labels on Nos. 3198-3206 from stamps at bottom.

Nowruz — A1399

2019		Litho.	Perf. 13¾x14
3207	A1399	12,000r multi	4.00 4.00

Ceremony for Making Rosewater — A1400

2019		Litho.	Perf. 14x13¾
3208	A1400	18,000r multi	2.50 2.50

Souvenir Sheet

Mohandas K. Gandhi (1869-1948), Indian Nationalist Leader — A1401

2019		Litho.	Perf. 14x13¾
3209	A1401	18,000r multi	2.50 2.50

Polo — A1402

2019		Litho.	Perf. 14x13¾
3210	A1402	18,000r multi	3.00 3.00

Souvenir Sheet

Tehran Day A1403

2019		Litho.	Perf. 14x13¾
3211	A1403	60,000r multi	6.00 6.00

World Crafts Day — A1404

2020		Litho.	Perf. 13¾x14
3212	A1404	18,000r multi	2.50 2.50

Dated 2019.

Miniature Sheet

Persian Cuisine A1405

No. 3213: a, Fish on platter. b, Stew with vegetables. c, Stew with lentils. d, Meat dish with orange half.

2020		Litho.	Perf. 14¼x13¾
3213	A1405	18,000r Sheet of 4, #a-d	4.25 4.25

Dated 2019.

COVID-19 and Medical Workers A1406

2020, Mar. 17		Litho.	Perf. 14x13¾
3214	A1406	18,000r multi	2.50 2.50

Monastery of St. Thaddeus, Chaldiran — A1407

2020		Litho.	Perf. 14x13¾
3215	A1407	18,000r multi	2.00 2.00

Nowruz A1408

No. 3216: a, Purple flowers. b, White flowers.

2020		Litho.	Perf. 14x13¾
3216	A1408	18,000r Horiz. pair, #a-b	3.25 3.25

Souvenir Sheet

White-headed Duck — A1409

2020		Litho.	Perf. 13¾x14
3217	A1409	18,000r multi	2.50 2.50

Souvenir Sheet

Persian Qanat UNESCO World Heritage Site — A1410

2020		Litho.	Perf. 14x13¾
3218	A1410	18,000r multi	2.25 2.25

Constitution of the Islamic Republic of Iran — A1411

2020		Litho.	Perf. 14x13¾
3219	A1411	18,000r multi	2.00 2.00

Mohsen Fakhrizadeh (1958-2020), Assassinated Nuclear Scientist — A1412

2020		Litho.	Perf. 14
3220	A1412	18,000r multi	2.00 2.00

Souvenir Sheet

Qasem Soleimani (1957-2020), General — A1413

2020		Litho.	Perf. 13¾
3221	A1413	40,000r multi	4.00 4.00

Souvenir Sheet

Musical Instruments — A1414

No. 3222: a, Tar. b, Setar.

2020		Litho.	Perf. 13¾x14
3222	A1414	18,000r Sheet of 2, #a-b	3.50 3.50

Landscapes — A1415

No. 3223: a, Hyrcanian Forest. b, Maranjab Desert.

2020		Litho.	Perf. 14¼x13¾
3223	A1415	18,000r Vert. pair, #a-b	1.75 1.75

Miniature Sheet

Fruits A1416

No. 3224: a, Grapes. b, Figs. c, Pomegranates. d, Dates. e, Olives.

2020		Litho.	Perf. 14¼
3224	A1416	18,000r Sheet of 5, #a-e	4.25 4.25

IRAN

Miniature Sheet

Waterfalls — A1417

No. 3225: a, Latun Waterfall. b, Gazou Waterfall. c, Piran Waterfall. d, Shevi Waterfall.

2020		Litho.	Perf. 13¾x14¼	
3225	A1417	18,000r Sheet of 4, #a-d	3.50	3.50

Seyyed Hassan Shodjaat (1853-1941), Wrestler — A1418

2020		Litho.	Perf. 14¼x14	
3226	A1418	18,000r multi	.85	.85

Karafarin Bank, 21st Anniv. A1419

Designs: Nos. 3227a, 3228b, Squares with rounded corners. Nos. 3227b, 3228a, Gear, factory, flame, broadcasting tower, cellphone, Earth.

2021		Litho.	Perf. 13¾x14	
3227	A1419	5000r Horiz. pair, #a-b	1.50	1.50

Souvenir Sheet

3228	A1419	25,000r Sheet of 2, #a-b	4.00	4.00

Miniature Sheet

Novruz A1420

No. 3229: a, Flowers in lined container, with yellow background. b, Flowers, in black container with lines at side, with brown orange background. c, Inscription in frame of flowers, horiz. d, Flowers in vase, with dark green background. e, Flowers in container, chocolate background. f, Flowers, no container, brown lake background.

2021		Litho.	Perf. 13¾x14	
3229	A1420	18,000r Sheet of 6, #a-f	4.50	4.50

Miniature Sheet

Contemporary Art — A1421

No. 3230 — Painting depicting: a, Man sleeping by open window, by Iraj Eskandari. b, Soldiers and man with raised fist, by Habibollah Sadeghi. c, Woman holding flowers, and open door, by Kazem Chalipa. d, Birds, flowers, and silhouette of man, by Abolfazl Aali. e, Flower in vase, pomegranate, and woman, by Naser Palangi. f, Woman and injured child, by Mostafa Goodarzi.

Serpentine Die Cut 5¾x6

2021				Litho.
		Self-Adhesive		
3230	A1421	18,000r Sheet of 6, #a-f	5.25	5.25

Souvenir Sheet

Writers A1422

No. 3231: a, Simin Daneshvar (woman at left), (1921-2012), and Jalal Al-e-Ahmad (1923-69). b, Al-e-Ahmad (at left), Daneshvar.

Litho. With Foil Application
2021 Serpentine Die Cut 6x5¾
Self-Adhesive

3231	A1422	36,000r Sheet of 2, #a-b	3.50	3.50

Diplomatic Relations Between Iran and People's Republic of China, 50th Anniv. — A1423

No. 3232: a, Khaju Bridge, Iran, and blue sky. b, Guangji Bridge, People's Republic of China, and orange sky.

2021		Litho.	Perf. 14x13¾	
3232	A1423	40,000r Horiz. pair, #a-b	3.75	3.75

See People's Republic of China Nos.

Tehran Nature Bridge A1425

2022		Litho.	Perf. 14x13¾	
3233		Horiz. pair	3.80	3.80
	a.	A1424 40,000r multi	1.90	1.90
	b.	A1425 40,000r multi	1.90	1.90

Martyred Commanders — A1426

No. 3234, 40,000r: a, M. Ebrahim Hemmat. b, Mahdi Bakeri. c, Mahdi Zeinoddin. d, Hossein Kharrazi.
No. 3235, 40,000r: a, Mohammad Jahanara. b, Ahmad Kazemi. c, Mohammad Boroujerdi. d, Hasan Bagheri.

2022		Litho.	Perf. 13¾	
		Blocks of 4, #a-d		
3234-3235	A1426	Set of 2	15.00	15.00

Souvenir Sheet

Diplomatic Relations Between Iran and Kenya, 50th Anniv. — A1427

No. 3236: a, Map of Kenya and coffee beans. b, Map of Iran, saffron threads and crocus.

2022, June 24		Litho.	Perf. 14¼x14	
3236	A1427	40,000r Sheet of 2, #a-b		

SEMI-POSTAL STAMPS

Catalogue values for unused stamps in this section, from this point to the end of the section, are for Never Hinged items.

Lion and Bull, Persepolis SP1
Persian Soldier, Persepolis SP2
Palace of Darius the Great SP3
Tomb of Cyrus the Great, Pasargadae SP4
King Darius on his Throne — SP5

Perf. 13x13½, 13½x13

1948, Jan. 30		Engr.	Unwmk.	
B1	SP1	50d + 25d emer	2.50	2.50
B2	SP2	1r + 50d red	2.50	2.50
B3	SP3	2½r + 1¼r blue	2.50	2.50
B4	SP4	5r + 2½r pur	3.50	3.50
B5	SP5	10r + 5r vio brn	4.50	4.50
		Nos. B1-B5 (5)	15.50	15.50

The surtax was for reconstruction of the tomb of Avicenna (980-1037), Persian physician and philosopher, at Hamadan.

Ardashir II — SP6
Shapur I and Valerian — SP7

Designs: 1r+50d, King Narses, Naqsh-i-Rustam. 5r+2½r, Taq-i-Kisra, Ctesiphon. 10r+5r, Ardashir I and Ahura Mazda.

1949, June 11				
B6	SP6	50d + 25d green	2.50	2.50
B7	SP6	1r + 50d ver	2.50	2.50
B8	SP7	2½r + 1½r blue	2.50	2.50
B9	SP7	5r + 2½r magenta	3.50	3.50
B10	SP7	10r + 5r grnsh gray	4.50	4.50
		Nos. B6-B10 (5)	15.50	15.50

The surtax was for reconstruction of Avicenna's tomb at Hamadan.

Gunbad-i-Ali SP8
Alaviyan, Hamadan SP9
Seldjukide Coin — SP10

Designs: 1r+½r, Masjid-i-Jami, Isfahan. 5r+2½r, Masjid-i-Jami, Ardistan.

1949, Dec. 22				
B11	SP8	50d + 25d bl grn	2.00	2.00
B12	SP8	1r + ½r dk brn	2.00	2.00
B13	SP9	2½r + 1¼r blue	2.00	2.00
B14	SP9	5r + 2½r red	3.00	3.00
B15	SP10	10r + 5r olive gray	3.50	3.50
		Nos. B11-B15 (5)	12.50	12.50

The surtax was for reconstruction of Avicenna's tomb at Hamadan.

Koran, Crescent and Flag — SP11

1950, Oct. 2		Litho.	Perf. 11	
B16	SP11	1.50r + 1r multi	40.00	25.00

Economic Conference of the Islamic States.

IRAN

Tomb of Baba Afzal at Kashan — SP12

Gorgan Vase — SP13

Designs: 2½r+1¼r, Tower of Ghazan. 5r+2½r, Masjid-i Gawhar. 10r+5r, Mihrab of the Mosque at Rezaieh.

Perf. 13x13½, 13½x13
1950, Aug. 23   Engr.
B17	SP12	50d + 25d dk grn	2.00	2.00
B18	SP13	1r + ½r blue	2.00	2.00
B19	SP13	2½r + 1¼r choc	2.00	2.00
B20	SP12	5r + 2½r red	3.00	3.00
B21	SP12	10r + 5r gray	3.50	3.50
		Nos. B17-B21 (5)	12.50	12.50

The surtax was for reconstruction of Avicenna's tomb at Hamadan.

Mohammad Reza Shah Pahlavi and Map — SP14

Monument to Fallen Liberators of Azerbaijan — SP15

Designs: 1r+50d, Marching troops. 1.50r+75d, Running advance with flag. 2.50r+1.25r, Mohammad Reza ShahPahlavi. 3r+1.50r, Parade of victors.

1950, Dec. 12   Litho.
B22	SP14	10d + 5d blk brn	17.50	10.00
B23	SP15	50d + 25d blk brn	17.50	10.00
B24	SP15	1r + 50d brn lake	25.00	12.00
B25	SP14	1.50r + 75d org ver	25.00	12.00
B26	SP14	2.50r + 1.25r blue	40.00	25.00
B27	SP15	3r + 1.50r ultra	45.00	25.00
		Nos. B22-B27 (6)	170.00	94.00

Liberation of Azerbaijan Province from communists, 4th anniv.
The surtax was for families of Persian soldiers who died in the struggle.

Koran Gate at Shiraz — SP16

Saadi — SP17

Design: 50d+50d, Tomb of Saadi, Shiraz.

Perf. 11x10½, 10½x11
1952, Apr. 30   Photo.   Unwmk.
B28	SP16	25d + 25d dl bl grn	5.00	3.00
B29	SP16	50d + 50d brn ol	5.00	3.00
B30	SP17	1.50r + 50d vio bl	30.00	9.00
		Nos. B28-B30 (3)	40.00	15.00

770th birthday of Saadi, Persian poet. The surtax was to help complete Saadi's tomb at Shiraz.
Three stamps of same denominations and colors, with values enclosed in tablets, were prepared but not officially issued.
Value, set, $4,000.

View of Hamadan — SP18

Avicenna — SP19

Designs: 2½r+1¼r, Gonbad Qabus (tower of tomb). 5r+2½r, Old tomb of Avicenna. 10r+5r, New tomb.

Perf. 13x13½, 13½x13
1954, Apr. 21   Engr.   Unwmk.
B31	SP18	50d + 25d dp grn	2.00	2.00
B32	SP19	1r + ½r gray vio	2.00	2.00
B33	SP19	2½r + 1¼r blue	2.00	2.00
B34	SP18	5r + 2½r ver	3.00	3.00
B35	SP18	10r + 5r ol gray	4.00	4.00
		Nos. B31-B35 (5)	13.00	13.00

The surtax was for reconstruction of Avicenna's tomb at Hamadan.

Mother with Children and Ruins — SP20

1963, Feb. 4   Wmk. 316   Litho.   Perf. 10½
B36	SP20	14r + 6r dk bl grn & lt brn	3.00	1.00

The surtax was for the benefit of survivors of the Kazvin earthquake.
For overprints see Nos. C86-C88.

AIR POST STAMPS

Type of 1909 Overprinted

1927   Unwmk.   Typo.   Perf. 11½
C1	A31	1c org & maroon	3.50	1.50
C2	A31	2c vio & maroon	3.50	1.50
C3	A31	3c grn & maroon	3.50	1.50
C4	A31	6c red & maroon	3.50	1.50
C5	A31	9c gray & maroon	5.00	2.00
C6	A31	10c red vio & mar	7.00	2.50
C7	A31	13c dk bl & mar	8.00	3.00
C8	A31	1k sil, vio & bis brn	8.00	3.00
C9	A31	26c dk grn & mar	8.00	4.00
C10	A31	2k sil, dk grn & bis brown	15.00	5.00
C11	A31	3k sil, gray & bis brn	25.00	7.50
C12	A31	4k sil, bl & bis brn	45.00	17.50
C13	A31	5k gold, brn & bis brown	45.00	15.00
C14	A31	10k gold, org & bis brown	275.00	300.00
C15	A31	20k gold, ol grn & bis brn	275.00	300.00
C16	A31	30k gold, car & bis brown	275.00	300.00
		Nos. C1-C16 (16)	1,005.	965.50

Counterfeit overprints are plentiful. They are found on Nos. 448-463, perf. 12½x12 instead of 11½.
Exist without overprint. Value, set $5,000.

Airplane, Value and "Poste aérièn" Surcharged on Revenue Stamps

1928   Perf. 11
C17	AP1	3k yellow brn	125.00	40.00
C18	AP2	5k dark brown	30.00	20.00
C19	AP3	1t gray vio	40.00	30.00
C20	AP4	2t olive bister	40.00	30.00
C21	AP5	3t deep green	55.00	40.00
		Nos. C17-C21 (5)	290.00	160.00

1928-29   "Poste aerienne"
C22	AP6	1c emerald	2.50	.50
a.		1c yellow green	2.50	.50
b.		Double overprint	35.00	
C23	AP6	2c light blue	2.50	.25
a.		Rosette in place of "2"	150.00	100.00
C24	AP6	3c bright rose	2.50	.25
C25	AP6	5c olive brn	1.25	.25
a.		"5" omitted	3,000.	2,250.
b.		Horiz. pair, imperf. btwn.	300.00	
C26	AP6	10c dark green	2.00	.25
a.		"10" omitted	40.00	
b.		"1" inverted	75.00	
C27	AP7	1k dull vio	3.00	1.00
a.		"1" inverted	100.00	
C28	AP7	2k orange	10.00	3.50
a.		"S" for "s" in "Krs"	300.00	175.00
		Nos. C22-C28 (7)	23.75	6.00

Counterfeits exist.

Revenue Stamps Similar to Nos. C17 to C21, Overprinted like Nos. C22 to C28: "Poste aerienne"

1929
C29	AP1	3k yellow brn	100.00	25.00
C30	AP2	5k dark brn	25.00	10.00
C31	AP3	10k violet	40.00	30.00
C32	AP4	20k olive grn	45.00	35.00
C33	AP5	30k deep grn	55.00	45.00
a.		"80" instead of "30"		5,000.
		Nos. C29-C33 (5)	265.00	145.00

Reza Shah Pahlavi and Eagle — AP8

1930, July 6   Photo.   Perf. 12½x11½
C34	AP8	1c ol bis & brt bl	1.00	1.50
C35	AP8	2c bl & gray blk	1.00	1.50
C36	AP8	3c ol grn & dk vio	1.00	1.50
C37	AP8	4c dk vio & pck bl	1.00	1.50
C38	AP8	5c lt grn & mag	1.00	1.50
C39	AP8	6c mag & bl grn	1.00	1.50
C40	AP8	8c dk gray & dp vio	1.00	1.50
C41	AP8	10c dp ultra & ver	1.00	1.50
C42	AP8	12c slate & org	1.00	1.50
C43	AP8	15c org brn & ol grn	1.00	1.50
C44	AP8	1k Prus bl & scar	8.00	7.00
		Engr.		
C45	AP8	2k black & ultra	10.00	7.00
C46	AP8	3k dk brn & gray grn	20.00	8.00
C47	AP8	5k dp red & gray black	15.00	10.00
C48	AP8	1t orange & vio	52.00	20.00
C49	AP8	2t dk grn & red brown	50.00	50.00
C50	AP8	3t brn vio & sl bl	250.00	100.00
		Nos. C34-C50 (17)	415.00	217.00

Nos. C34-C50 Overprinted in Black

1935   Photo.
C51	AP8	1c ol bis & brt bl	1.00	1.00
C52	AP8	2c blue & gray blk	1.00	1.00
C53	AP8	3c ol grn & dk vio	1.00	1.00
C54	AP8	4c dk vio & pck bl	1.00	1.00
C55	AP8	5c lt grn & mag	1.00	1.00
C56	AP8	6c mag & bl grn	1.00	1.00
C57	AP8	8c dk gray & dp violet	1.00	1.00
C58	AP8	10c dp ultra & ver	1.00	1.00
C59	AP8	12c slate & org	1.00	1.00
C60	AP8	15c org brn & ol green	1.00	1.00
C61	AP8	1k Prus bl & scar	100.00	150.00

		Engr.		
C62	AP8	2k blk & ultra	75.00	100.00
C63	AP8	3k dk brn & gray green	25.00	15.00
C64	AP8	5k dp red & gray black	10.00	10.00
C65	AP8	1t orange & vio	225.00	175.00
C66	AP8	2t dk grn & red brown	55.00	45.00
C67	AP8	3t brn vio & sl bl	85.00	55.00
		Nos. C51-C67 (17)	585.00	560.00

Plane Over Mt. Demavend — AP9

Plane above Mosque — AP10

1953, Jan. 21   Unwmk.   Photo.   Perf. 11
C68	AP9	50d bl green	1.50	.25
C69	AP10	1r car rose	1.50	.25
C70	AP10	2r dark blue	1.50	.25
C71	AP10	3r dark brn	2.50	.25
C72	AP10	5r purple	4.50	.25
C73	AP10	10r org ver	5.00	.30
C74	AP10	20r vio blue	8.00	.50
C75	AP10	30r olive	15.00	7.00
C76	AP10	50r brown	30.00	4.00
C77	AP10	100r black brn	85.00	15.00
C78	AP10	200r dk bl grn	75.00	20.00
		Nos. C68-C78 (11)	229.50	48.05

AP11

Golden Dome Mosque and Oil Well — AP12

1953, May 4   Litho.   Perf. 10½
Mosque in Deep Yellow
C79	AP11	3r violet	15.00	15.00
C80	AP12	5r chocolate	20.00	20.00
C81	AP11	10r bl green	55.00	40.00
C82	AP12	20r red vio	110.00	70.00
		Nos. C79-C82 (4)	200.00	145.00

Discovery of oil at Qum.

Catalogue values for unused stamps in this section, from this point to the end of the section, are for Never Hinged items.

Globe and UN Emblem — AP13

1957, Oct. 24   Photo.   Wmk. 316   Perf. 10½x12½
C83	AP13	10r brt red lil & rose	3.00	.90
C84	AP13	20r dl vio & rose vio	6.00	1.25

United Nations Day, Oct. 24, 1957.

UNESCO Emblem — AP14

1966, June 20   Wmk. 353   Litho.   Perf. 10½
C85	AP14	14r multicolored	2.00	.50

20th anniversary of UNESCO.

IRAN

No. B36 Surcharged in Maroon, Brown or Red

1969, Dec. 4   **Wmk. 316**   **Perf. 10½**
C86	SP20	4r on 14r + 6r (M)	3.00	2.00
C87	SP20	10r on 14r + 6r (B)	3.50	3.00
C88	SP20	14r on 14r + 6r (R)	4.00	4.00
		Nos. C86-C88 (3)	10.50	9.00

1st England-Australia flight, via Iran, made by Capt. Ross Smith and Lt. Keith Smith, 50th anniv.

IATA Emblem and Persepolis AP15

Perf. 13x13½
1970, Oct. 27   **Photo.**   **Wmk. 353**
C89	AP15	14r multicolored	7.50	3.00

26th meeting of the Intl. Air Transport Assoc. (IATA), Tehran.

"UIT" — AP16

1972, May 17   **Litho.**   **Perf. 10½**
C90	AP16	14r multicolored	3.25	.75

4th World Telecommunications Day.

Shah and Jet — AP17

1974, June 1   **Photo.**   **Perf. 13**
C91	AP17	4r org & black	1.00	.25
C92	AP17	10r blue & black	2.00	.25
C93	AP17	12r dull yel & blk	2.00	.40
C94	AP17	14r lt green & blk	2.50	.40
C95	AP17	20r red lilac & blk	3.00	.65
C96	AP17	50r dull bl & blk	7.50	1.60
		Nos. C91-C96 (6)	18.00	3.55

Crown Prince at Controls of Light Aircraft AP18

1974, Oct. 31   **Litho.**   **Perf. 10½**
C97	AP18	14r gold & multi	2.00	.65

Crown Prince Reza's 14th birthday.

Importation Prohibited
Importation of stamps was prohibited effective Oct. 29, 1987.

Islamic Revolution, 10th Anniv. — AP19

1989, Feb. 11   **Perf. 13x13½**
C98	AP19	40r red vio, blk & gold	.75	.50
C99	AP19	50r bl vio, blk & gold	.75	.50
a.		Pair, #C98-C99	1.75	1.50

Ayatollah Khomeini AP20

1989, July 11   **Perf. 13**
C100	AP20	70r multicolored	1.00	.50

OFFICIAL STAMPS

Four bicolored stamps of this design (1s, 2s, 5s, 10s), with centers embossed, exist, but were never issued or used in Iran. Value $40. They are known imperforate and in many trial colors.

Shah Muzaffar-ed-Din — O1

No. 145 Surcharged in Black

1902   **Perf. 12½**
O5	O1	5c on 1k red	30.00	30.00
O6	O1	10c on 1k red	30.00	30.00
O7	O1	12c on 1k red	40.00	40.00
		Nos. O5-O7 (3)	100.00	100.00

Nos. 351-363 Overprinted in Black

1903-06
O8	A26	1c violet	5.00	.75
O9	A26	2c gray	5.00	.75
O10	A26	3c green	5.00	.75
O11	A26	5c rose	5.00	.75
O12	A26	10c yel brown	8.00	.75
O13	A26	12c blue	12.00	.75

Perf. 11½x11
O14	A27	1k violet	14.00	7.50
O15	A27	2k ultra	25.00	12.50
a.		Violet overprint	75.00	
O16	A27	5k org brown	40.00	20.00
O17	A27	10k rose red	50.00	19.00
a.		Violet overprint		75.00
O18	A27	20k orange ('06)	200.00	40.00
O19	A27	30k green ('06)	250.00	90.00
O20	A27	50k green	250.00	125.00
		Nos. O8-O20 (13)	869.00	318.50

Overprinted on Nos. 368, 370a
O21	A27	2t on 50k grn (Bl)	175.00	75.00
O22	A27	3t on 50k grn (V)	175.00	75.00

Overprinted on Nos. 372, 375, New Value Surcharged in Blue or Black

1905
O23	A27	2t on 50k grn (Bl)	200.00	75.00
O28	A27	3t on 50k grn (Bk)	200.00	75.00

The 2t on 50k also exists with surcharge in black and magenta; the 3t on 50k in violet and magenta. Values about the same.

Regular Issue of 1909 Overprinted

There is a space between the word "Service" and the Persian characters.

1911   **Perf. 12½x12**
O31	A31	1c org & maroon	15.00	7.50
O32	A31	2c vio & maroon	15.00	7.50
O33	A31	3c yel grn & mar	15.00	7.50
O34	A31	6c red & maroon	15.00	7.50
O35	A31	9c gray & maroon	25.00	13.00
O36	A31	10c multicolored	30.00	13.00
O38	A31	1k multicolored	60.00	45.00
O40	A31	2k multicolored	150.00	90.00
		Nos. O31-O40 (8)	325.00	191.00

The 13c, 26c and 3k to 30k denominations were not regularly issued with this overprint. Dangerous counterfeits exist, usually on reprints.

Regular Issue of 1915 Overprinted

1915   **Wmk. 161**   **Perf. 11, 11½**
O41	A33	1c car & indigo	4.00	10.00
O42	A33	2c bl & carmine	4.00	10.00
O43	A33	3c dark green	4.00	10.00
O44	A33	5c red	4.00	10.00
O45	A33	6c ol grn & car	4.00	10.00
O46	A33	9c yel brn & vio	4.00	10.00
O47	A33	10c multicolored	4.00	10.00
O48	A33	12c ultramarine	5.00	10.00
O49	A34	1k multicolored	5.00	20.00
O50	A34	24c multicolored	9.00	15.00
O51	A34	2k sil, bl & rose	9.00	20.00
O52	A34	3k sil, vio & brn	9.00	25.00
O53	A34	5k multicolored	10.00	30.00
O54	A35	1t gold, pur & blk	15.00	45.00
O55	A35	2t gold, grn & brn	15.00	50.00
O56	A35	3t multicolored	17.50	65.00
O57	A35	5t gold, bl & ind	20.00	75.00
		Nos. O41-O57 (17)	142.50	425.00

Coronation of Shah Ahmed.
Reprints have dull rather than shiny overprint. Value, set, $17.50.

Coat of Arms — O2

1941   **Unwmk.**   **Litho.**   **Perf. 11**
For Internal Postage
O58	O2	5d violet	15.00	.25
O59	O2	10d magenta	15.00	.25
O60	O2	25d carmine	15.00	.25
a.		Printed on both sides	20,000.	
O61	O2	50d brown black	20.00	.25
O62	O2	75d claret	25.00	.45

Size: 22½x30mm
O63	O2	1r peacock grn	40.00	.45
O64	O2	1½r deep blue	40.00	1.50
O65	O2	2r light blue	60.00	1.50
O66	O2	3r vio brown	75.00	1.50
O67	O2	5r gray green	150.00	2.00
O68	O2	10r dk brn & bl	550.00	5.00
O69	O2	20r chlky bl & brt pink	700.00	65.00
O70	O2	30r vio & brt grn	900.00	150.00
O71	O2	50r turq grn & dk brown	1,900.	350.00
		Nos. O58-O71 (14)	4,505.	578.40

Catalogue values for unused stamps in this section, from this point to the end of the section, are for Never Hinged items.

Coat of Arms — O3

Perf. 13½x13
1974, Feb. 25   **Photo.**   **Wmk. 353**
Size: 20x28mm
O72	O3	5d vio & lilac	.35	.30
O73	O3	10d mag & grnsh bl	.35	.30
O74	O3	50d org & lt green	.35	.30
O75	O3	1r gold & yellow	.45	.30
O76	O3	2r emerald & org	.75	.30

Perf. 13
Size: 23x37mm
O77	O3	6r slate grn & org	1.00	.50
O78	O3	8r ultra & yellow	1.25	.50
O79	O3	10r dk bl & lilac	4.50	.19
O80	O3	11r pur & light bl	2.50	1.25
O81	O3	14r red & lt ultra	2.50	1.25
O82	O3	20r vio blue & org	4.00	2.00
O83	O3	50r dk brn & brt grn	10.00	4.00
		Nos. O72-O83 (12)	28.00	11.50

1977-79   **Wmk. 353**   **Perf. 13½x13**
Size: 20x28mm
O87	O3	1r black & lt grn	.40	.30
O88	O3	2r brown & gray	.45	.30
O89	O3	3r ultra & orange	.60	.30
O90	O3	5r green & rose	.75	.30

Perf. 13
Size: 23x37mm
O91	O3	6r dk bl & lt bl ('78)	1.00	.30
O92	O3	8r red & bl grn ('78)	1.25	.30
O93	O3	10r dk grn & yel grn	2.00	.50
O94	O3	11r dk blue & brt yellow ('79)	2.50	.50
O95	O3	14r dl grn & gray	2.50	1.25
O96	O3	15r bl & rose lil ('78)	4.00	1.25
O97	O3	20r purple & yel	5.75	2.00
O98	O3	30r brn & ocher ('78)	12.00	4.00
O99	O3	50r blk & gold ('78)	10.00	7.00
		Nos. O87-O99 (13)	43.20	18.30

NEWSPAPER STAMP

No. 429 Overprinted

1909   **Typo.**   **Unwmk.**   **Perf. 12½**
P1	A26	2c gray, *blue*	60.00	30.00

PARCEL POST STAMPS

Regular issues of 1907-08 (types A26, A29) with the handstamp above in blue, black or green are of questionable status as issued stamps. The handstamp probably is a cancellation.

No. 436 Overprinted in Black

1909   **Engr.**   **Perf. 11½**
Q18	A29	26c red brown	25.00	20.00

The overprint is printed.

Regular Issue of 1915 Overprinted in Black

1915   **Wmk. 161**   **Perf. 11, 11½**
Q19	A33	1c car & indigo	5.00	5.00
Q20	A33	2c bl & carmine	5.00	5.00
Q21	A33	3c dark green	5.00	5.00
Q22	A33	5c red	5.00	5.00
Q23	A33	6c ol green & car	5.00	5.00
Q24	A33	9c yel brn & vio	5.00	5.00
Q25	A33	10c bl grn & yel brn	5.00	5.00
Q26	A33	12c ultramarine	7.00	7.00
Q27	A34	1k multicolored	12.00	12.00
Q28	A33	24c multicolored	7.00	7.00
Q29	A34	2k multicolored	12.00	12.00
Q30	A34	3k multicolored	15.00	15.00
Q31	A34	5k multicolored	15.00	15.00
Q32	A35	1t multicolored	15.00	15.00
Q33	A35	2t gold, grn & brn	20.00	20.00
Q34	A35	3t multicolored	25.00	25.00
Q35	A35	5t multicolored	30.00	30.00
		Nos. Q19-Q35 (17)	193.00	193.00

Coronation of Shah Ahmed.

IRAN — IRAQ

Reprints have dull rather than shiny overprint. Value, set, $16.

> Catalogue values for unused stamps in this section, from this point to the end of the section, are for Never Hinged items.

Post Horn — PP1

Black frame and "IRAN" (reversed) are printed on back of Nos. Q36-Q65, to show through when stamp is attached to parcel.

1958	Wmk. 306	Typo.	Perf. 12½
Q36 PP1	50d olive bis	.75	.25
Q37 PP1	1r carmine	1.00	.25
Q38 PP1	2r blue	1.00	.25
a.	Imperf., pair	300.00	
Q39 PP1	3r green	1.00	.25
Q40 PP1	5r purple	1.00	.25
Q41 PP1	10r orange brn	3.75	.25
Q42 PP1	20r dp orange	10.00	.35
Q43 PP1	30r lilac	12.50	1.60
Q44 PP1	50r dk carmine	19.00	2.50
Q45 PP1	100r yellow	40.00	5.00
Q46 PP1	200r light grn	60.00	9.00
	Nos. Q36-Q46 (11)	150.00	19.95

1961-66		Wmk. 316	
Q51 PP1	5r purple ('66)	12.50	5.00
Q52 PP1	10r org brn ('62)	12.50	5.00
Q53 PP1	20r orange	17.50	7.00
Q54 PP1	30r red lil ('63)	17.50	8.00
Q55 PP1	50r dk car ('63)	25.00	10.00
Q56 PP1	100r yellow ('64)	65.00	30.00
Q57 PP1	200r emer ('64)	80.00	30.00
	Nos. Q51-Q57 (7)	230.00	95.00

1967-74		Wmk. 353	Shiny Gum
Q58 PP1	2r blue ('74)	5.00	—
Q59 PP1	5r dk pur ('69)	5.00	—
Q60 PP1	10r orange brn	5.00	—
Q61 PP1	20r orange ('69)	10.00	—
Q62 PP1	30r red lilac	12.00	—
Q63 PP1	50r red brn ('68)	15.00	—
Q64 PP1	100r yellow	50.00	—
Q65 PP1	200r emerald ('69)	80.00	—
	Nos. Q58-Q65 (8)	182.00	

1977	Wmk. 353	White Dry Gum	
Q58a PP1	2r blue	1.50	.25
Q59a PP1	5r dk pur	1.50	.25
Q60a PP1	10r orange brn	2.25	.25
Q61a PP1	20r orange	3.00	.25
Q62a PP1	30r pink	3.75	.25
Q63a PP1	50r red brn	5.25	.50
Q64a PP1	100r yellow	7.50	1.00
Q65a PP1	200r emerald	11.50	3.00
	Nos. Q58a-Q65a (8)	36.25	5.75

Without Black Frame and IRAN on Back

Perf. 13½x13, 10½ (#100r)

1981	Typo.	Wmk. 353	
Q67 PP1	50r orange brown	45.00	25.00
Q68 PP1	100r yellow	400.00	150.00
a.	100r dull orange	400.00	150.00
Q69 PP1	200r green	50.00	25.00

Nos. Q67, Q69 printed from new dies. Numerals are larger and higher in the value tablet on No. Q67. Numerals read down from upper left to lower right in value tablet on No. Q69.

POSTAL TAX STAMPS

Iranian Red Cross Lion and Sun Emblem — PT1

1950	Unwmk.	Litho.	Perf. 11
RA1 PT1	50d grn & car rose	20.00	.90
RA2 PT1	2r vio & lil rose	10.00	1.50

1955		Wmk. 306	
RA3 PT1	50d emer & car rose	300.00	5.00

> Catalogue values for unused stamps in this section, from this point to the end of the section, are for Never Hinged items.

1957-58		Wmk. 316	
RA4 PT1	50d emer & rose lil	7.50	.90
RA5 PT1	2r vio & car rose ('58)	3.00	1.00

1965	Wmk. 349	Perf. 10½	
RA6 PT1	50d emer & car rose	3.00	.50
RA7 PT1	2r vio & lil rose	8.00	.65

1965-66		Wmk. 353	
RA8 PT1	50d emer & car rose (I)	2.00	.25
a.	Type II	4.00	.25
RA9 PT1	2r vio & car rose ('66)	3.00	.50

No. RA8 was printed in two types: I. Without diagonal line before Persian "50." II. With line.

1976, Sept.-78	Photo.	Perf. 13x13½	
RA10 PT1	50d emerald & red	3.00	.30
RA11 PT1	2r slate & red ('78)	3.00	2.50

Nos. RA10-RA11 are redrawn and have vertical watermark.

Nos. RA1-RA11 were obligatory on all mail. 50d stamps were for registered mail, 2r stamps for parcel post. The tax was for hospitals.

The 2.25r and 2.50r of type PT1 were used only on telegrams.

IRAQ

i-räk

LOCATION — In western Asia, bounded on the north by Syria and Turkey, on the east by Iran, on the south by Saudi Arabia and Kuwait, and on the west by Jordan

GOVT. — Republic
AREA — 167,925 sq. mi.
POP. — 40,220,000 (2020 est.)
CAPITAL — Baghdad

Iraq, formerly Mesopotamia, a province of Turkey, was mandated to Great Britain in 1920. The mandate was terminated in 1932. For earlier issues, see Mesopotamia.

16 Annas = 1 Rupee
1000 Fils = 1 Dinar (1932)

> Catalogue values for unused stamps in this country are for Never Hinged items, beginning with Scott 79 in the regular postage section, Scott C1 in the air post section, Scott CO1 in the air post official section, Scott O90 in the officials section, Scott RA1 in the postal tax section, and Scott RAC1 in the air post postal tax section.

Issues under British Mandate

Sunni Mosque — A1
Gufas on the Tigris — A2
Assyrian Winged Bull — A4
Ctesiphon Arch — A5
Motif of Assyrian Origin — A3
Colors of the Dulaim Camel Corps — A6
Golden Shiah Mosque of Kadhimain — A7
Conventionalized Date Palm or "Tree of Life" — A8

1923-25	Engr.	Wmk. 4	Perf. 12	
1	A1	½a olive grn	1.30	.25
2	A2	1a brown	2.25	.25
3	A3	1½a car lake	1.30	.25
4	A4	2a brown org	1.30	.25
5	A5	3a dp blue	2.60	.25
6	A6	4a dull vio	5.75	.35
7	A7	6a blue grn	3.50	.35
8	A6	8a olive bis	5.25	.75
9	A8	1r grn & brn	8.50	.90
10	A1	2r black	29.00	8.50
11	A1	2r bister ('25)	80.00	4.00
12	A6	5r orange	72.50	17.50
13	A7	10r carmine	90.00	25.00
	Nos. 1-13 (13)		303.25	58.60

For overprints see Nos. O1-O24, O42, O47, O51-O53.

King Faisal I — A9

1927				
14	A9	1r red brown	15.00	2.00

See No. 27. For overprint and surcharges see Nos. 43, O25, O54.

King Faisal I — A10, A11

1931				
15	A10	½a green	1.60	.60
16	A10	1a chestnut	1.60	.60
17	A10	1½a carmine	2.50	.85
18	A10	2a orange	2.10	.50
19	A10	3a light blue	2.50	.50
20	A10	4a pur brown	3.50	3.50
21	A10	6a Prus blue	4.25	1.55
22	A10	8a dark green	5.00	4.00
23	A11	1r dark brown	9.25	3.50
24	A11	2r yel brown	13.00	9.50
25	A11	5r dp orange	50.00	67.50
26	A11	10r red	150.00	170.00
27	A9	25r violet	1,900.	2,100.
	Nos. 15-27 (13)		2,145.	2,363.

See Nos. 44-60. For overprints see Nos. O26-O41, O43-O46, O48-O50, O54-O71.

Issues of the Kingdom
Nos. 6, 15-27 Surcharged in "Fils" or "Dinars" in Red, Black or Green

1932, Apr. 1				
28	A10(a)	2f on ½a (R)	.50	.25
29	A10(a)	3f on ½a	.50	.25
a.	Double surcharge		170.00	
b.	Inverted surcharge		170.00	
c.	Pair, one without surcharge		1,400.	
30	A10(a)	4f on 1a (G)	1.75	.35
31	A10(a)	5f on 1a	.65	.25
a.	Double surcharge		290.00	
b.	Inverted Arabic "5"		35.00	40.00
c.	Inverted surcharge		240.00	
32	A10(a)	8f on 1½a	.75	.50
a.	Inverted surcharge		175.00	
33	A10(a)	10f on 2a	.80	.25
a.	Inverted surcharge		275.00	
34	A10(a)	15f on 3a	1.75	1.50
35	A10(a)	20f on 4a	2.75	1.50
36	A6(b)	25f on 4a	4.50	3.75
a.	"Fils" for "Fils"		475.00	850.00
b.	Inverted Arabic "5"		500.00	900.00
c.	Pair, #a.-b.		2,500.	
37	A10(a)	30f on 6a	5.00	.75
38	A10(a)	40f on 8a	4.25	2.75
39	A11(c)	75f on 1r	4.50	4.50
a.	Inverted Arabic "5"		125.00	150.00
40	A11(c)	100f on 2r	10.00	4.75
41	A11(c)	200f on 5r	42.50	42.50
42	A11(d)	½d on 10r	125.00	150.00
a.	Bar in "½" omitted		1,900.	1,550.
43	A9(d)	1d on 25r	275.00	275.00
	Nos. 28-43 (16)		480.20	488.85

King Faisal I — A12, A13
A14

Values in "Fils" and "Dinars"

1932, May 9			Engr.	
44	A12	2f ultra	.50	.25
45	A12	3f green	.50	.25
46	A12	4f vio brown	.50	.25
47	A12	5f gray green	.60	.25
48	A12	8f deep red	2.00	.25
49	A12	10f yellow	1.75	.25
50	A12	15f deep blue	1.90	.25
51	A12	20f orange	3.25	.75
52	A12	25f rose lilac	1.75	.25
53	A12	30f olive grn	5.25	.25
54	A12	40f dark violet	2.25	1.40
55	A13	50f deep brown	3.25	.40
56	A13	75f lt ultra	4.25	2.75
57	A13	100f deep green	10.00	1.75
58	A13	200f dark red	25.00	9.75
59	A14	½d gray blue	92.50	55.00
60	A14	1d claret	200.00	150.00
	Nos. 44-60 (17)		355.25	224.55

For overprints see Nos. O55-O71.

A15
A16
King Ghazi — A17

1934-38			Unwmk.	
61	A15	1f purple ('38)	.75	.25
62	A15	2f ultra	.45	.25
63	A15	3f green	.45	.25
64	A15	4f pur brown	.45	.25
65	A15	5f gray green	.45	.25
66	A15	8f deep red	.75	.25
67	A15	10f yellow	.95	.25
68	A15	15f deep blue	.95	.25
69	A15	20f orange	.95	.25
70	A15	25f brown vio	1.75	.35
71	A15	30f olive grn	1.50	.25
72	A15	40f dark vio	1.75	.25
73	A16	50f deep brown	3.50	.25
74	A16	75f ultra	4.00	.40
75	A16	100f deep green	5.00	.50
76	A16	200f dark red	7.50	3.00
77	A17	½d gray blue	27.50	20.00
78	A17	1d claret	85.00	32.50
	Nos. 61-78 (18)		143.65	59.75

For overprints see Nos. 226, O72-O89.

> Catalogue values for unused stamps in this section, from this point to the end of the section, are for Never Hinged items.

IRAQ

Sitt Zubaidah Mausoleum — A18

Mausoleum of King Faisal I — A19

Lion of Babylon A20

Malwiye of Samarra (Spiral Tower) A21

Oil Wells A22

Shrine of the Golden Dome, Samarra A23

Perf. 14, 13½, 12½, 12x13½, 13½x12, 14x13½

1941-42 Engr.

79	A18	1f dk vio ('42)	.45	.25
80	A18	2f chocolate ('42)	.45	.25
81	A19	3f brt green ('42)	.45	.25
82	A19	4f purple ('42)	.45	.25
83	A19	5f dk car rose ('42)	.45	.25
84	A20	8f carmine	.75	.25
85	A20	8f ocher ('42)	.60	.25
86	A20	10f ocher	16.00	3.25
87	A20	10f carmine ('42)	1.50	.25
88	A20	15f dull blue	2.10	.25
89	A20	15f black ('42)	2.75	.25
90	A20	20f black	4.50	.60
91	A20	20f dull blue ('42)	1.25	.25
92	A21	25f dark violet	.50	.30
93	A21	30f deep orange	.50	.30
94	A21	40f brn orange	2.00	.50
95	A21	40f chestnut ('42)	2.00	.45
96	A21	50f ultra	3.25	.60
97	A21	75f rose violet	2.75	.60
98	A22	100f ol grn ('42)	3.50	1.00
99	A22	200f dp org ('42)	11.00	1.00
100	A23	½d lt bl, perf. 12x13½ ('42)	35.00	6.50
a.		Perf. 14	40.00	9.00
101	A23	1d grnsh bl ('42)	55.00	15.00
		Nos. 79-101 (23)	147.20	32.85

Nos. 92-95 measure 17¾x21½mm, Nos. 96-97 measure 21x24mm.
For overprints see Nos. O90-O114, O165, RA5.

King Faisal II — A24

Photo.; Frame Litho.

1942 *Perf. 13 x 13½*

102	A24	1f violet & brown	.65	.50
103	A24	2f dk blue & brown	.65	.50
104	A24	3f lt green & brown	.65	.50
105	A24	4f dull brown & brn	.65	.50
106	A24	5f sage green & brn	.65	.50
107	A24	6f red orange & brn	.65	.50
108	A24	10f dl rose red & lt brn	.65	.50
109	A24	12f yel green & brown	.65	.50
		Nos. 102-109 (8)	5.20	4.00

For overprints see Nos. O115-O122.

King Faisal II — A25

Perf. 11½x12

1948, Jan. 15 Engr. Unwmk.
Size: 17¾x20½mm

110	A25	1f slate	.60	.25
111	A25	2f sepia	.35	.25
112	A25	3f emerald	.35	.25
113	A25	4f purple	.35	.25
114	A25	5f rose lake	.35	.25
115	A25	6f plum	2.00	.25
116	A25	8f ocher	4.50	.55
117	A25	10f rose red	.45	.25
118	A25	12f dark olive	.45	.25
119	A25	15f black	7.50	1.50
120	A25	20f blue	1.00	.25
121	A25	25f rose violet	1.10	.25
122	A25	30f red orange	1.10	.25
123	A25	40f orange brn	2.25	.55

Perf. 12x11½
Size: 22x27½mm

124	A25	60f deep blue	1.75	.50
125	A25	75f lilac rose	1.75	.50
126	A25	100f olive green	8.00	1.00
127	A25	200f deep orange	7.25	1.00
128	A25	½d blue	22.50	4.00
129	A25	1d green	70.00	14.00
		Nos. 110-129 (20)	133.60	26.35

Sheets of 6 exist, perforated and imperforate, containing Nos. 112, 117, 120 and 125-127, with arms and Arabic inscription in blue green in upper and lower margins. Value perf or imperf, unused $100 each, used $160 each.
See Nos. 133-138. For overprints see Nos. 188-194, O123-O142, O166-O177, O257, O258, O272-O282, RA1-RA4, RA6.

Post Rider and King Ghazi — A26

Designs: 40f, Equestrian statue & Faisal I. 50f, UPU symbols & Faisal II.

1949, Nov. 1 *Perf. 13x13½*

130	A26	20f blue	2.75	2.00
131	A26	40f red orange	3.75	3.00
132	A26	50f purple	10.00	7.00
		Nos. 130-132 (3)	16.50	11.00

75th anniv. of the UPU.

Type of 1948

1950-51 Unwmk. *Perf. 11½x12*
Size: 17¾x20½mm

133	A25	3f rose lake	8.00	2.00
134	A25	5f emerald	8.50	4.00
135	A25	14f dk olive ('50)	2.25	.75
136	A25	16f rose red	2.00	.75
137	A25	28f blue	2.25	.45

Perf. 12x11½
Size: 22x27½mm

138	A25	50f deep blue ('50)	6.50	1.50
		Nos. 133-138 (6)	29.50	9.45

For overprints see Nos. 160, O143-O148, O258, O273, O275-O276.

King Faisal II — A27

1953, May 2 Engr. *Perf. 12*

139	A27	3f deep rose car	1.25	1.25
140	A27	14f olive	2.50	1.25
141	A27	28f blue	7.00	1.75
b.		Souv. sheet of 3, #139-141	115.00	200.00
		Nos. 139-141 (3)	10.75	4.25

Coronation of King Faisal II, May 2, 1953.

King Faisal II — A28

1954-57 *Perf. 11½x12*
Size: 18x20½mm

141A	A28	1f blue ('56)	.65	.25
142	A28	2f chocolate	.30	.25
143	A28	3f rose lake	.30	.25
144	A28	4f violet	.25	.25
145	A28	5f emerald	.30	.25
146	A28	6f plum	.30	.25
147	A28	8f ocher	.30	.25
148	A28	10f blue	.30	.25
149	A28	15f black	1.75	1.25
149A	A28	16f brt rose ('57)	2.75	2.25
150	A28	20f olive	1.25	.30
151	A28	25f rose vio ('55)	1.25	.25
152	A28	30f ver ('55)	1.25	.25
153	A28	40f orange brn	1.50	.45

Size: 22x27½mm

154	A28	50f blue	2.00	.70
155	A28	75f pink	3.00	.75
156	A28	100f olive green	6.00	.80
157	A28	200f orange	10.00	1.75
		Nos. 141A-157 (18)	33.45	10.75

For overprints see Nos. 158-159, 195-209, 674, 676, 678, O148A-O161A, O178-O191, O259-O260, O263, O266, O268, O270, O283-O291.

No. 143, 148 and 137 Overprinted in Black

1955, Apr. 6 *Perf. 11½x12*

158	A28	3f rose lake	1.50	.45
159	A28	10f blue	1.25	.45
160	A25	28f blue	2.10	1.00
		Nos. 158-160 (3)	4.85	1.90

Abrogation of Anglo-Iraq treaty of 1930.

King Faisal II — A29

1955, Nov. 26 *Perf. 13½x13*

161	A29	3f rose lake	1.25	.40
162	A29	10f light ultra	1.90	.60
163	A29	28f blue	2.50	1.50
		Nos. 161-163 (3)	5.65	2.50

6th Arab Engineers' Conf., Baghdad, 1955.
For surcharge see No. 227.

Faisal II and Globe — A30

1956, Mar. 3 *Perf. 13x13½*

164	A30	3f rose lake	1.25	.60
165	A30	10f light ultra	1.60	.60
166	A30	28f blue	2.25	1.25
		Nos. 164-166 (3)	5.10	2.45

Arab Postal Conf., Baghdad, Mar. 3.
For overprint see No. 173. For surcharge see No. 251.

Mechanical Loom — A31

Designs: 3f, Dam. 5f, Modern city development. 10f, Pipeline. 40f, Tigris Bridge.

1957, Apr. 8 Photo. *Perf. 11½*
Granite Paper

167	A31	1f Prus bl & org yel	.50	.25
168	A31	3f multicolored	.50	.25
169	A31	5f multicolored	.60	.25
170	A31	10f lt bl, ocher & red	1.00	.25
171	A31	40f lt bl, blk & ocher	2.00	.70
		Nos. 167-171 (5)	4.60	1.70

Development Week, 1957. See Nos. 185-187.

Fair Emblem — A32

1957, June 1 Unwmk.
Granite Paper

| 172 | A32 | 10f brown & buff | 1.00 | 1.00 |

Agricultural and Industrial Exhibition, Baghdad, June 1.

No. 166 Overprinted in Red

1957, Nov. 14 *Perf. 13x13½*

173	A30	28f blue	3.75	1.50
a.		Double overprint	300.00	275.00

Iraqi Red Crescent Soc., 25th anniv.

King Faisal II — A33

Perf. 11½x12

1957-58 Unwmk. Engr.

174	A33	1f blue	.40	.40
175	A33	2f chocolate	.40	.40
176	A33	3f dark car ('57)	.40	.40
177	A33	4f dull violet	.40	.40
177A	A33	5f emerald	1.00	1.00
178	A33	6f plum	1.00	1.00
179	A33	8f ocher	2.00	1.25
180	A33	10f blue	2.00	1.25
		Nos. 174-180 (8)	7.60	6.10

Higher denominations exist without Republic overprint. They were probably not regularly issued.
See note below No. 225.
For overprints see Nos. 210-225, 675, O162-O164, O192-O199, O269, O292-O294. For types overprinted see Nos. 677, 679, O261, O264, O267, O271, O295.

Tanks — A34

King Faisal II — A35

Army Day, Jan. 6: 10f, Marching soldiers. 20f, Artillery and planes.

1958, Jan. 6 *Perf. 13x13½*

181	A34	8f green & black	1.25	.85
182	A34	10f brown & black	1.50	1.10
183	A34	20f blue & red brown	1.50	1.10
184	A35	30f car & purple	2.25	1.50
		Nos. 181-184 (4)	6.50	4.55

Type of 1957

3f, Sugar beet, bag & refining machinery, vert. 5f, Farm. 10f, Dervendi Khan dam.

1958, Apr. 26 Photo. *Perf. 11½*
Granite Paper

185	A31	3f gray vio, grn & lt gray	.60	.35
186	A31	5f multicolored	.90	.55
187	A31	10f multicolored	2.25	1.10
		Nos. 185-187 (3)	3.75	2.00

Development Week, 1958.

Republic

Stamps of 1948-51 Overprinted

Perf. 11½x12, 12x11½

1958 Engr. Unwmk.
Size: 17¾x20½mm

188	A25	12f dark olive	.80	.25
189	A25	14f olive	1.00	.25
190	A25	16f rose red	15.00	4.50
191	A25	28f blue	1.25	.65

Size: 22x27½mm

192	A25	60f deep blue	4.00	.75
193	A25	½d blue	27.50	6.00
194	A25	1d green	55.00	25.00
		Nos. 188-194 (7)	104.55	37.40

Nos. 110 and 133 exist with this overprint, but these were probably not regularly issued.

Stamps of 1954-57 Overprinted

Size: 18x20½mm

195	A28	1f dark blue	.70	.25
196	A28	2f chocolate	.70	.25
196A	A28	4f violet	.70	.25
196B	A28	5f emerald	.70	.25
197	A28	6f plum	.70	.25
198	A28	8f ocher	.70	.25
199	A28	10f blue	.80	.25

IRAQ

200	A28	15f black	1.00	.25
201	A28	16f bright rose	2.60	.50
202	A28	20f olive	1.20	.65
203	A28	25f rose violet	.80	.40
204	A28	30f vermilion	1.40	.35
205	A28	40f orange brn	1.40	.25

Size: 22½x27½mm

206	A28	50f blue	6.50	3.50
207	A28	75f pink	5.25	1.00
208	A28	100f olive green	6.25	3.50
209	A28	200f orange	17.50	7.50
		Nos. 195-209 (17)	48.90	19.65

The lines of this overprint are found transposed on Nos. 195, 196 and 199.

Type of 1957-58 Stamps Overprinted

Size: 18x20mm

210	A33	1f blue	3.25	.75
211	A33	2f chocolate	.70	.25
212	A33	3f dark carmine	.70	.25
213	A33	4f dull violet	.75	.25
214	A33	5f emerald	.70	.25
215	A33	6f plum	.70	.25
216	A33	8f ocher	.70	.50
217	A33	10f blue	.70	.25
218	A33	20f olive	.70	.25
219	A33	25f rose violet	1.45	.80
220	A33	30f vermilion	1.60	.25
221	A33	40f orange brn	4.25	1.60

Size: 22x27½mm

222	A33	50f rose violet	3.25	.75
223	A33	75f olive	3.25	1.50
224	A33	100f orange	4.75	1.50
225	A33	200f blue	12.50	2.50
		Nos. 210-225 (16)	39.95	11.40

Nos. 218-225 were not issued without overprint.
The lines of this overprint are found transposed on Nos. 210 and 214.
Many errors of overprint exist of Nos. 188-226.
For overprint see No. O198.

Same Overprint on No. 78

Perf. 12

226	A17	1d claret	30.00	30.00

No. 163 Surcharged in Red

1958, Nov. 26   *Perf. 13x13½*

227	A29	10f on 28f blue	1.50	.95

Arab Lawyers' Conf., Baghdad, Nov. 26.

Soldier and Flag — A36

1959, Jan. 6   *Photo.*   *Perf. 11½*

228	A36	3f bright blue	.40	.25
229	A36	10f olive green	.65	.35
230	A36	40f purple	1.10	.70
		Nos. 228-230 (3)	2.15	1.30

Issued for Army Day, Jan. 6.

Orange Tree — A37

1959, Mar. 21   *Unwmk.*   *Perf. 11½*

231	A37	10f green, dk grn & org	.90	.25

Issued for Arbor Day.

Emblem of Republic — A38

Emblem in Gold, Red and Blue; Blue Inscriptions

1959-60   *Litho. & Photo.*   *Perf. 11½*
Granite Paper

232	A38	1f gray	.25	.25
233	A38	2f salmon	.25	.25
234	A38	3f pale violet	.25	.25
235	A38	4f bright yel	.25	.25
236	A38	5f light blue	.25	.25
237	A38	10f bright pink	.25	.25
238	A38	15f light green	.75	.25
239	A38	20f bister brn	.75	.25
240	A38	30f light gray	.75	.25
241	A38	40f orange yel	1.40	.35
242	A38	50f yel green	5.50	.90
243	A38	75f pale grn ('60)	2.25	.50
244	A38	100f orange ('60)	4.00	1.00
245	A38	200f lilac ('60)	7.00	1.00
246	A38	500f bister ('60)	11.00	4.00
247	A38	1d brt grn ('60)	24.00	10.00
		Nos. 232-247 (16)	58.90	20.00

See Nos. 305A-305B. For overprints see Nos. 252, 293-295, O200-O221.

Worker and Buildings A39

Victorious Fighters A40

Perf. 12½x13, 13x12½

1959, July 14   *Photo.*

248	A39	10f ocher & blue	.60	.55
249	A40	30f ocher & emerald	1.10	.70

1st anniv. of the Revolution of July 14 (1958), which overthrew the kingdom.

Harvest — A41

1959, July 14   *Perf. 11½*

250	A41	10f lt grn & dk grn	.70	.25

No. 166 Surcharged in Dark Red

1959, June 1   *Engr.*   *Perf. 13x13½*

251	A30	10f on 28f blue	2.00	.75

Issued for Children's Day, 1959.

No. 237 Overprinted

Litho. and Photo.

1959, Oct. 23   *Perf. 11½*

252	A38	10f multicolored	1.25	.50

Health and Sanitation Week.

Abdul Karim Kassem and Army Band — A42

Abdul Karim Kassem and: 16f, Field maneuvers, horiz. 30f, Antiaircraft. 40f, Troops at attention, flag and bugler. 60f, Fighters and flag, horiz.

1960, Jan. 6   *Photo.*   *Perf. 11½*

253	A42	10f blue, grn & mar	.70	.55
254	A42	16f brt blue & red	1.00	.70
255	A42	30f ol grn, yel & brn	1.00	.70
256	A42	40f deep vio & buff	1.50	.90
257	A42	60f dk brown & buff	2.00	1.00
		Nos. 253-257 (5)	6.20	3.85

Issued for Army Day, Jan. 6.

Prime Minister Abdul Karim Kassem — A43

1960, Feb. 1   *Engr.*   *Perf. 12½*

258	A43	10f lilac	1.10	.45
259	A43	30f emerald	1.90	.65

Issued to honor Prime Minister Kassem on his recovery from an assassination attempt.

Maroof el Rasafi — A44

1960, May 10   *Photo.*   *Perf. 13½x13*

260	A44	10f maroon & blk	3.25	1.50
a.		Inverted overprint	150.00	150.00
b.		Without overprint ('66)	10.00	10.00

No. 260b was released for postal use in 1966.

Symbol of the Army — A45

Unknown Soldier's Tomb and Kassem with Freedom Torch — A46

1960, July 14   *Perf. 11½*

261	A45	6f ol grn, red & gold	.75	.55
262	A46	10f green, blue & red	.80	.55
263	A46	16f vio, blue & red	.90	.80
264	A45	18f ultra, red & gold	.90	.80
265	A45	30f brown, red & gold	1.25	1.00
266	A46	60f dk brn, bl & red	2.00	1.50
		Nos. 261-266 (6)	6.60	5.20

2nd anniv. of the July 14, 1958 revolution.

Gen. Kassem and Marching Troops A47

Gen. Kassem and Arch A48

1961, Jan. 6   **Granite Paper**

267	A47	3f gray ol, emer, yel & gold	.65	.25
268	A47	6f pur, emer, yel & gold	.75	.25
269	A47	10f sl, emer, yel & gold	.90	.25
270	A48	20f bl grn, blk & buff	1.10	.25
271	A48	30f bis brn, blk & buff	1.40	.35
272	A48	40f ultra, black & buff	1.60	.65
		Nos. 267-272 (6)	6.40	2.00

Issued for Army Day, Jan. 6.

Gen. Kassem and Children — A49

1961, June 1   *Photo.*   *Unwmk.*
Granite Paper

273	A49	3f yellow & brown	.80	.45
274	A49	6f blue & brown	1.00	.45
275	A49	10f pink & brown	1.40	.45
276	A49	30f yellow & brown	1.60	.45
277	A49	50f lt grn & brown	2.40	.70
		Nos. 273-277 (5)	7.20	2.50

Issued for World Children's Day.

Gen. Kassem and Flag — A50

Gen. Kassem Saluting and Flags — A50a

1961, July 14   *Perf. 11½*
Granite Paper

278	A50	1f multicolored	.65	.25
279	A50	3f multicolored	.65	.25
280	A50a	5f multicolored	.65	.25
281	A50	6f multicolored	.65	.25
282	A50	10f multicolored	.65	.25
283	A50a	30f multicolored	1.00	.55
284	A50a	40f multicolored	1.25	.55
285	A50	50f multicolored	2.00	1.00
286	A50	100f multicolored	5.00	1.00
		Nos. 278-286 (9)	12.50	5.10

3rd anniv. of the July 14, 1958 revolution.

Gen. Kassem and Flag — A51

Gen. Kassem and Symbol of the Army — A52

Perf. 11½

1962, Jan. 6   *Unwmk.*   *Photo.*
Granite Paper

287	A51	1f multicolored	.70	.25
288	A51	3f multicolored	.75	.25
289	A51	6f multicolored	.85	.25
290	A52	10f blk, lilac & gold	1.40	.45
291	A52	30f black, org & gold	1.60	.45
292	A52	50f blk, pale grn & gold	2.50	.50
		Nos. 287-292 (6)	7.80	1.80

Issued for Army Day, Jan. 6.

Nos. 234, 237 and 240 Overprinted

Litho. & Photo.

1962, May 29   *Perf. 11½*

293	A38	3f multicolored	.70	.25
294	A38	10f multicolored	.70	.25
295	A38	30f multicolored	1.35	.35
		Nos. 293-295 (3)	2.75	.85

Fifth Islamic Congress.

Hands Across Map of Arabia and North Africa — A53

1962, July 14   *Photo.*

296	A53	1f brn, org, grn & gold	.65	.25
297	A53	3f brn, yel grn, grn & gold	.70	.25
298	A53	6f blk, lt brn, grn & gold	.80	.25
299	A53	10f brn, lil, grn & gold	1.05	.25

IRAQ

300	A53	30f brn, rose, grn & gold	1.30	.30
301	A53	50f brn, gray, grn & gold	2.10	.45
		Nos. 296-301 (6)	6.60	1.75

Revolution of July 14, 1958, 4th anniv.

al-Kindi — A54

Designs: 3f, Horsemen with standards and trumpets. 10f, Old map of Baghdad and Tigris. 40f, Gen. Kassem, modern building and flag.

1962, Dec. 1   **Perf. 14x13½**   **Litho.**   **Unwmk.**

302	A54	3f multicolored	.90	.25
303	A54	6f multicolored	.95	.25
304	A54	10f multicolored	1.10	.35
305	A54	40f multicolored	3.00	1.00
		Nos. 302-305 (4)	5.95	1.85

9th century Arab philosopher al-Kindi; millenary of the Round City of Baghdad.

Emblem of Republic — A54a

1962, Dec. 20   **Perf. 13½x14**

305A	A54a	14f brt green & blk	2.25	.50
305B	A54a	35f ver & black	2.75	.75

Nos. 305A-305B were originally sold affixed to air letter sheets, obliterating the portrait of King Faisal II. They were issued in sheets for general use in 1966.

For overprints see Nos. RA15-RA16.

Tanks on Parade and Gen. Kassem — A55

1963, Jan. 6   **Photo.**   **Perf. 11½**

306	A55	3f black & yellow	.70	.25
307	A55	5f brown & plum	.75	.25
308	A55	6f blk & lt green	.80	.25
309	A55	10f blk & lt blue	.85	.25
310	A55	10f black & pink	.90	.25
311	A55	20f black & ultra	1.10	.25
312	A55	40f blk & rose lilac	1.40	.25
313	A55	50f brn & brt ultra	2.00	.40
		Nos. 306-313 (8)	8.50	2.15

Issued for Army Day, Jan. 6.

Malaria Eradication Emblem — A56

1962, Dec. 31   **Perf. 14**
Republic Emblem in Red, Blue & Gold

314	A56	3f yel grn, blk & dk grn	.75	.25
315	A56	10f org, blk & dark blue	1.25	.25
316	A56	40f lilac, black & blue	1.50	.30
		Nos. 314-316 (3)	3.50	.80

WHO drive to eradicate malaria.

Gufas on the Tigris — A57

Designs: 2f, 500f, Spiral tower, Samarra. 4f, 15f, Ram's head harp, Ur. 5f, 75f, Map and Republic emblem. 10f, 50f, Lion of Babylon. 20f, 40f, Baghdad University. 30f, 200f, Kadhimain mosque. 100f, 1d, Winged bull, Khorsabad.

Engr.; Engr. and Photo. (bicolored)
1963, Feb. 16   **Unwmk.**   **Perf. 12x11**

317	A57	1f green	.75	.25
318	A57	2f purple	.75	.25
319	A57	3f black	.75	.25
320	A57	4f black & yel	.75	.25
321	A57	5f lilac & lt grn	1.00	.25
322	A57	10f rose red	1.50	.25
323	A57	15f brn & buff	2.25	.25
324	A57	20f violet blue	2.40	.25
325	A57	30f orange	1.55	.35
326	A57	40f brt green	2.60	.25
327	A57	50f dark brown	11.50	.65
328	A57	75f blk & lt grn	5.75	.45
329	A57	100f brt lilac	6.25	.25
330	A57	200f brown	12.00	.55
331	A57	500f blue	16.00	2.25
332	A57	1d deep claret	22.50	4.50
		Nos. 317-332 (16)	88.30	11.25

For overprints see Nos. O314-O317, RA7-RA12.

Shepherd and Sheep — A58

10f, Man holding sheaf. 20f, Date palm grove.

1963, Mar. 21   **Litho.**   **Perf. 13½x14**

333	A58	3f emerald & gray	.50	.25
334	A58	10f dp brn & lil rose	.75	.25
335	A58	20f dk bl & red brn	1.25	.35
a.		Souv. sheet of 3, #333-335	8.00	8.00
		Nos. 333-335 (3)	2.50	.85

FAO "Freedom from Hunger" campaign. No. 335a sold for 50f.
No. 335a was overprinted in 1970 in black to commemorate the UN 25th anniv. Denominations on the 3 stamps were obliterated, leaving "Price 50 Fils" in the margin. Value $7.50.

Cent. Emblem — A59

A59a

Design: 30f, Iraqi Red Crescent Society Headquarters.

Perf. 11x11½, 11½x11
1963, Dec. 30   **Photo.**

336	A59	3f violet & red	.40	.30
337	A59	10f gray & red	.60	.30
338	A59a	30f lt blue & red	1.25	.65
		Nos. 336-338 (3)	2.25	1.25

Centenary of International Red Cross.

Rifle, Helmet and Flag — A60

1964, Jan. 6   **Unwmk.**   **Perf. 11½**
Granite Paper

339	A60	3f brn, blue & emer	.50	.30
340	A60	10f brn, pink & emer	.70	.30
341	A60	30f brown, yel & emer	1.40	.70
		Nos. 339-341 (3)	2.60	1.30

Issued for Army Day, Jan. 6.

Flag and Soldiers Storming Ministry of Defense — A61

1964, Feb. 8   **Perf. 11½**
Granite Paper

342	A61	10f pur, red, grn & blk	.65	.30
343	A61	30f red brn, red, grn & blk	1.10	.65
a.		Souv. sheet of 2, imperf	5.75	2.50
b.		Souv. sheet of 2 (4th anniv.) ('67)	8.00	2.75

Revolution of Ramadan 14, 1st anniv. No. 343a contains stamps similar to Nos. 342-343 in changed colors (10f olive, red, green & black; 30f ultra, red, green & black). Sold for 50f.
No. 343b consists of various block-outs and overprints on No. 343a. It commemorates the 4th anniv. of the Revolution of Ramadan 14. Sold for 70f. Issued 2/8/67.

Hammurabi and a God from Stele in Louvre — A62

UN Emblem and Scales — A62a

1964, June 10   **Litho.**   **Perf. 13½**

344	A62	6f reddsh pur & tan	.60	.50
345	A62	10f org & vio blue	1.10	.50
346	A62a	30f blue & pale grn	1.80	.75
		Nos. 344-346 (3)	3.50	1.75

15th anniv. (in 1963) of the Universal Declaration of Human Rights.

"Industrialization of Iraq" — A63

Soldier Planting New Flag — A64

1964, July 14   **Perf. 11**

347	A63	3f gray, org & black	.40	.30
348	A64	10f rose red, blk & emer	.40	.30
349	A64	20f rose red, blk & emer	.60	.30
350	A63	50f gray, org & black	1.25	.60
		Nos. 347-350 (4)	2.65	1.50

6th anniv. of the July 14, 1958 revolution.

Star and Fighters — A65

1964, Nov. 18   **Photo.**   **Perf. 11½**

351	A65	5f sepia & orange	.35	.25
352	A65	10f lt bl & orange	1.00	.25
353	A65	50f vio & red orange	1.00	.50
		Nos. 351-353 (3)	2.35	1.00

Revolution of Nov. 18, 1963, 1st anniv.

Musician with Lute — A66

Perf. 13x13½
1964, Nov. 28   **Litho.**   **Unwmk.**

354	A66	3f bister & multi	1.00	.30
355	A66	10f dl grn & multi	1.00	.30
356	A66	30f dl rose & multi	1.50	.90
		Nos. 354-356 (3)	3.50	1.50

International Arab Music Conference.

Map of Arab Countries and Emblem — A67

1964, Dec. 13   **Perf. 12½x14**

| 357 | A67 | 10f lt grn & rose lilac | .75 | .25 |

9th Arab Engineers' Conference, Baghdad.

Arab Postal Union Emblem — A67a

1964, Dec. 21   **Photo.**   **Perf. 11**

358	A67a	3f sal pink & blue	.40	.25
359	A67a	10f brt red lil & brn	.50	.25
360	A67a	30f orange & blue	1.40	.50
		Nos. 358-360 (3)	2.30	1.00

10th anniv. of Permanent Office of APU
For overprint see No. 707.

Soldier, Flag and Rising Sun — A68

Perf. 14x12½
1965, Jan. 6   **Litho.**   **Unwmk.**

361	A68	5f dull green & multi	.50	.25
362	A68	15f henna brn & multi	.50	.30
363	A68	30f black brn & multi	1.50	.65
		Nos. 361-363 (3)	2.50	1.20

Issued for Army Day, Jan. 6.
An imperf. souvenir sheet carries a revised No. 363 with "30 FILS" omitted, and a portrait of Pres. Abdul Salam Arif. Violet inscriptions including "PRICE 60 FILS." Value $8.

Symbols of Agriculture and Industry — A69

1965, Jan. 8   **Perf. 12½x14**

| 364 | A69 | 10f ultra, brn & blk | .60 | .25 |

Arab Labor Ministers' Conference.

Tanker — A70

1965, Jan. 30   **Perf. 14**

| 365 | A70 | 10f multicolored | 1.00 | .45 |

Inauguration (in 1962) of the deep sea terminal for oil tankers.

Soldier with Flag and Rifle — A71

1965, Feb. 8   **Litho.**   **Perf. 13½**

| 366 | A71 | 10f multicolored | .60 | .25 |

Revolution of Ramadan 14, 2nd anniv.

Tree Week — A72

IRAQ

1965, Mar. 6   Unwmk.   *Perf. 13*
367   A72   6f multicolored   .40   .30
368   A72   20f multicolored   1.25   .30

Federation Emblem — A73

1965, Mar. 24   Unwmk.   *Perf. 14*
369   A73   3f lt bl, vio bl & gold   .40   .30
370   A73   10f gray, black & gold   .40   .30
371   A73   30f rose, car & gold   1.00   .75
     Nos. 369-371 (3)   1.80   1.35

Arab Federation of Insurance.

Dagger in Map of Palestine — A74

1965, Apr. 9   Litho.   *Perf. 14x12½*
372   A74   10f gray & black   3.50   .35
373   A74   20f lt brn & dk blue   6.50   .55

Deir Yassin massacre, Apr. 9, 1948.
See Jordan No. 499 and Kuwait Nos. 281-282.

Smallpox Attacking People A75

1965, Apr. 30   Litho.   *Perf. 14*
374   A75   3f multicolored   .60   .30
375   A75   10f multicolored   .75   .30
376   A75   20f multicolored   1.60   .80
     Nos. 374-376 (3)   2.95   1.40

WHO's fight against smallpox. Exist imperf. Value $6.

ITU Emblem, Old and New Telecommunication Equipment — A76

1965, May 17   *Perf. 14, Imperf.*
377   A76   10f multicolored   .75   .25
378   A76   20f multicolored   1.90   .55
   a.   Souv. sheet of 2, #377-378   18.00   15.00

ITU, centenary. No. 378a sold for 40f and exists imperf. Value same.

Map of Arab Countries and Banner — A77

1965, May 26   Litho.   *Perf. 14x12½*
379   A77   10f multicolored   .50   .25

Anniversary of the treaty with the UAR.

Library Aflame and Lamp — A78

1965, June   Photo.   *Perf. 11*
380   A78   5f black, grn & red   .50   .30
381   A78   10f blk, green & red   .75   .30

Burning of the Library of Algiers, 6/7/62.

Revolutionist with Club, Cannon, Sun and Flames — A79

1965, June 30   Litho.   *Perf. 13*
382   A79   5f multicolored   .50   .25
383   A79   10f multicolored   .75   .25

45th anniversary, Revolution of 1920.

Mosque A80

1965, July 12   Photo.   *Perf. 12*
384   A80   10f multicolored   1.25   .60

Prophet Mohammed's birthday. A souvenir sheet contains one imperf. stamp similar to No. 384. Sold for 50f. Value $6.25.

Factories and Grain — A81

1965, July 14   Litho.   *Perf. 13*
385   A81   10f multicolored   .55   .55

7th anniv. of the July 14, 1958 Revolution.

Arab Fair Emblem — A82

1965, Oct. 22   Unwmk.   *Perf. 13*
386   A82   10f multicolored   .55   .25

Second Arab Fair, Baghdad.

Pres. Abdul Salam Mohammed Arif — A83

1965, Nov. 18   Photo.   *Perf. 11½*
     Granite Paper
387   A83   5f org, buff & dk blue   .65   .25
388   A83   10f lt ultra, gray & dk brn   .90   .25
389   A83   50f lil, pale pink & sl blk   2.50   .90
     Nos. 387-389 (3)   4.05   1.40

Revolution of Nov. 18, 1963, 2nd anniv.

Census Chart and Adding Machine A84

1965, Nov. 29   Litho.   *Perf. 13*
390   A84   3f gray & plum   .50   .25
391   A84   5f brown red & brn   .60   .25
392   A84   15f olive bis & dl bl   1.40   .50
     Nos. 390-392 (3)   2.50   1.00

Issued to publicize the 1965 census.

Date Palms — A85

1965, Dec. 27   Litho.   *Perf. 13½x14*
393   A85   3f olive bis & multi   .35   .25
394   A85   10f car rose & multi   .80   .25
395   A85   15f blue & multi   2.00   .90
     Nos. 393-395 (3)   3.15   1.40

2nd FAO Intl. Dates Conference, Baghdad, Dec. 1965.
For surcharges see Nos. 694-695.

Soldiers' Monument — A86

1966, Jan. 6   Photo.   *Perf. 12*
396   A86   2f car rose & multi   .45   .25
397   A86   5f multicolored   .45   .25
398   A86   40f yel grn & multi   1.60   .75
     Nos. 396-398 (3)   2.50   1.25

Issued for Army Day.

Eagle and Flag of Iraq — A87

     Perf. 12½
1966, Feb. 8   Photo.   Unwmk.
399   A87   5f dl bl & multi   .40   .25
400   A87   10f orange & multi   .75   .25

3rd anniv. of the Revolution of Ramadan 14, which overthrew the Kassem government.

Arab League Emblem — A88

1966, Mar. 22   *Perf. 11x11½*
401   A88   5f org, brn & brt grn   .50   .25
402   A88   15f ol, rose lil & ultra   .50   .25

Arab Publicity Week.

Soccer Players — A89

1966, Apr. 1   *Perf. 12*
403   A89   2f multicolored   .75   .25
404   A89   5f multicolored   .50   .25
405   A89   15f multicolored   1.50   .45
     Nos. 403-405 (3)   2.75   .95

Miniature Sheet
Imperf
406   A89   50f vio & multi   7.50   10.50

3rd Arab Soccer Cup, Baghdad, Apr. 1-10.
For overprint, see No. O296.

Steam Shovel Within Cogwheel — A90

1966, May 1   Litho.   *Perf. 13½*
407   A90   15f multicolored   .40   .25
408   A90   25f red, blk, & sil   .50   .25

Issued for Labor Day, May 1, 1966.

Queen Nefertari A91   Facade of Abu Simbel A92

     Perf. 12½x13, 13½
1966, May 20   Litho.
409   A91   5f olive, yel & blk   .40   .25
410   A91   15f blue, yel & brn   .40   .25
411   A92   40f bis brn, red & blk   2.00   1.50
     Nos. 409-411 (3)   2.80   2.00

UNESCO world campaign to save historic monuments in Nubia.

President Arif and Flag — A93

1966, July 14   Photo.   *Perf. 11½*
412   A93   5f multicolored   .40   .25
413   A93   15f multicolored   .50   .25
414   A93   50f multicolored   1.75   1.00
     Nos. 412-414 (3)   2.65   1.50

8th anniv. of the July 14, 1958 revolution.

A94

1966, July 22   Litho.   *Perf. 12*
     Multicolored Vignette
415   A94   5f lt olive green   .40   .25
416   A94   15f lt greenish blue   .40   .25
417   A94   30f lt yellow green   1.25   .75
     Nos. 415-417 (3)   2.05   1.25

Mohammed's 1,396th birthday.

Iraqi Museum, Baghdad — A95   Golden headdress, Ur — A95a

Carved Sumerian Head — A95b

IRAQ

1966, Nov. 9   Litho.   *Perf. 14*
418	A95	15f multicolored	1.00	.25
419	A95a	50f lt bl, blk, gold & pink	1.50	.80
420	A95b	80f crim, blk, bl & gold	3.50	1.00
		Nos. 418-420 (3)	6.00	2.05

Opening of New Iraqi Museum, Baghdad.

UNESCO Emblem — A96

1966, Dec.   *Perf. 13½*
421	A96	5f blue, black & tan	.40	.25
422	A96	15f brt org brn, blk & gray	.40	.30

20th anniv. of UNESCO.

Iraqi Citizens — A97

1966, Nov. 18   *Perf. 13½x13*
423	A97	15f multicolored	.60	.25
424	A97	25f multicolored	1.10	1.10

3rd anniv. of the Revolution of 11/18/63.

Rocket Launchers and Soldier — A98

1967, Jan. 6   Photo.   *Perf. 11½*
425	A98	15f citron, dk brn & dp bis	.50	.25
426	A98	20f brt lil, dk brn & dp bis	.70	.25

Issued for Army Day, Jan. 6.

Oil Derrick, Pipeline, Emblem — A99

15f, 50f, Refinery and emblem, horiz.

1967, Mar. 6   Litho.   *Perf. 14*
427	A99	5f ol grn, pale yel & blk	.65	.25
428	A99	15f multicolored	.65	.25
429	A99	40f vio, yel & blk	1.30	.70
430	A99	50f multicolored	3.00	1.00
		Nos. 427-430 (4)	5.60	2.20

6th Arab Petroleum Congress, Baghdad, Mar. 1967.

New Year's Emblem and Spider's Web — A100

1967, Apr. 11   Litho.   *Perf. 13½*
431	A100	5f multicolored	.50	.25
432	A100	15f multicolored	.50	.25

Issued for Hegira (Pilgrimage) Year.

Worker Holding Cogwheel and Map of Arab Countries — A101

1967, May 1   *Perf. 12½x13*
433	A101	10f gray & multi	.40	.25
434	A101	15f lt ultra & multi	.40	.25

Issued for Labor Day.

A102

1967, June 20   Litho.   *Perf. 14*
435	A102	5f multicolored	.50	.25
436	A102	15f blue & multi	.60	.25

Mohammed's 1,397th birthday.

Flag, Hands with Clubs — A103

1967, July 7   *Perf. 13x13½*
437	A103	5f multicolored	.40	.25
438	A103	15f multicolored	.50	.25

47th anniversary of Revolution of 1920.

Um Qasr Harbor — A104

10f, 15f, Freighter loading in Um Qasr harbor.

1967, July 14   Litho.   *Perf. 14x13½*
439	A104	5f multicolored	.40	.25
440	A104	10f multicolored	.60	.30
441	A104	15f multicolored	1.10	.30
442	A104	40f multicolored	2.00	1.00
		Nos. 439-442 (4)	4.10	1.85

9th anniv. of the July 14, 1958 revolution and the inauguration of the port of Um Qasr.

Iraqi Man — A105

Iraqi Costumes: 5f, 15f, 25f, Women's costumes. 10f, 20f, 30f, Men's costumes.

1967, Nov. 10   Litho.   *Perf. 13*
443	A105	2f pale brn & multi	.40	.25
444	A105	5f ver & multi	.40	.25
445	A105	10f multicolored	.70	.25
446	A105	15f ultra & multi	.95	.50
447	A105	20f lilac & multi	1.25	.50
448	A105	25f lemon & multi	1.25	.60
449	A105	30f fawn & multi	1.50	.60
		Nos. 443-449,C19-C21 (10)	17.95	6.85

For overprints see Nos. 597-599, O228-O231, RA17.

President Arif — A106

Pres. Arif and Map of Iraq — A106a

Perf. 11x11½, 11½x11
450	A106	5f bl, vio blk & yel	.40	.25
451	A106a	15f rose & multi	.75	.40

4th anniversary of Nov. 18th revolution.

Ziggurat of Ur — A107

Designs: 5f, Gate with Nimrod statues. 10f, Gate, Babylon. 15f, Minaret of Mosul, vert. 25f, Arch and ruins of Ctesiphon.

1967, Dec. 1   Litho.   *Perf. 13*
452	A107	2f orange & multi	.40	.25
453	A107	5f lilac & multi	.40	.25
454	A107	10f orange & multi	.40	.25
455	A107	15f rose red & multi	.60	.25
456	A107	25f vio bl & multi	.80	.25
		Nos. 452-456,C22-C26 (10)	45.10	22.35

International Tourist Year.

For overprints see Nos. 593, 680, O225-O227, O308, RA18.

Iraqi Girl Scout Emblem and Sign — A108

Girl Scouts at Campfire & Girl Scout Emblem — A108a

10f, Boy Scout emblem & Boy Scout sign. 15f, Boy Scouts pitching tent & Boy Scout sign.

1967, Dec. 15
457	A108	2f orange & multi	1.30	.40
458	A108a	5f blue & multi	1.50	.40
459	A108	10f green & multi	1.60	.65
460	A108	15f blue & multi	1.60	.80
a.		Souv. sheet of 4	9.00	6.00
		Nos. 457-460 (4)	6.00	2.25

Issued to honor the Scout movement.
No. 460a contains 4 stamps similar to Nos. 457-460 with simulated perforations. Sold for 50f.

For overprint see No. RA19.

Soldiers on Maneuvers — A109

1968, Jan. 6   Photo.   *Perf. 11½*
461	A109	5f lt bl, brn & brt grn	.50	.25
462	A109	15f lt bl, ind & olive	.70	.25

Issued for Army Day 1968.

White-cheeked Bulbul — A110

Birds: 10f, Hoopoe. 15f, Eurasian jay. 25f, Peregrine falcon. 30f, White stork. 40f, Black partridge. 50f, Marbled teal.

1968, Jan.   Litho.   *Perf. 14*
463	A110	5f org & black	.85	.25
464	A110	10f blue, blk & brn	.95	.25
465	A110	15f pink & multi	1.35	.25
466	A110	25f dl org & multi	2.10	.50
467	A110	30f emer, blk & brn	2.25	.50
468	A110	40f rose lil & multi	3.00	.75
469	A110	50f multicolored	4.75	1.25
		Nos. 463-469 (7)	15.25	3.75

For overprint, see No. O311.

Fighting Soldiers — A111

1968, Feb. 8   *Perf. 11½*
470	A111	15f blk, org & brt bl	3.50	.90

Revolution of Ramadan 14, 5th anniv.

Factories, Tractor and Grain — A112

1968, May 1   Litho.   *Perf. 13*
471	A112	15f lt bl & multi	.40	.25
472	A112	25f multicolored	.70	.25

Issued for Labor Day.

Soccer — A113

5f, 25f, Goalkeeper holding ball, vert.

1968, June 14   *Perf. 13½*
473	A113	2f multicolored	.45	.25
474	A113	15f multicolored	.45	.25
475	A113	15f multicolored	.55	.25
476	A113	25f multicolored	2.25	.75
a.		Souv. sheet, 70f, imperf.	8.75	9.00
		Nos. 473-476 (4)	3.70	1.50

23rd C.I.S.M. (Conseil Internationale du Sports Militaire) Soccer Championships.
No. 476a shows badge of Military Soccer League.

Soldier, Flag, Chain and Rising Sun — A114

1968, July 14   Photo.   *Perf. 13½x14*
478	A114	15f multicolored	.50	.25

10th anniv. of the July 14, 1958 revolution.

World Health Organization Emblem — A115

5f, 10f, Staff of Aesculapius over emblem, vert.

1968, Nov. 29   Litho.   *Perf. 13½*
479	A115	5f multicolored	.40	.25
480	A115	10f multicolored	.40	.25
481	A115	15f blue, red & black	.50	.25
482	A115	25f yel grn, red & blk	.75	.30
		Nos. 479-482 (4)	2.05	1.05

WHO, 20th anniv. Exist imperf. Value $5.75.
For overprints, see Nos. O222-O224.

Human Rights Flame — A116

1968, Dec. 22   Litho.   *Perf. 13½*
483	A116	10f lt bl, yel & car	.40	.25
484	A116	25f yel grn, yel & car	.50	.25
a.		Souv. sheet, 100f, imperf.	5.00	5.00

International Human Rights Year.
For overprint, see No. O232.

Mother and Children — A117

IRAQ

1968, Dec. 31   Litho.   Perf. 13½
485 A117 15f multi   .50   .25
486 A117 25f bl & multi   1.25   .35
  a. Souv. sheet, 100f, imperf.   7.50   5.00
  UNICEF. For overprints see Nos. 624-625,
O234-O235.

Tanks — A118

1969, Jan. 6   Photo.
487 A118 25f vio, car & brn   4.00   2.25
  Issued for Army Day, Jan. 6.
  For overprint, see No. O244.

Harvester A119

1969, Feb.   Photo.   Perf. 13½
488 A119 15f yel brn & multi   .75   .25
  6th anniv. of the Revolution of Ramadan 14.

Mosque A119a

1969, Mar. 19   Photo.   Perf. 13x13½
488A A119a 15f multicolored   2.10   .75
  Issued for Hegira (Pilgrimage) Year.

Emblem — A120

1969, Apr. 12   Litho.   Perf. 12½x12
489 A120 10f yel grn & multi   .60   .30
490 A120 15f orange & multi   1.00   .30
  1st conference of the Arab Veterinary Union,
Baghdad, Apr. 1969.

Barbus Grypus — A121

Fish: 3f, Barbus puntius sharpeyi. 10f, Pampus argenteus. 100f, Barbus esocinus.

1969, May 9   Perf. 14
491 A121 2f multicolored   1.75   .45
492 A121 3f multicolored   1.90   .45
493 A121 10f multicolored   2.00   .45
494 A121 100f multicolored   6.00   3.75
  Nos. 491-494 (4)   11.65   5.10
  For overprints, see Nos. O312-O313.

Holy Kaaba, Mecca — A122

1969, May 28   Photo.   Perf. 12
495 A122 15f blue & multi   .75   .40
  Mohammed's 1,399th birthday.

ILO Emblem — A123

1969, June 6   Litho.   Perf. 13x12½
496 A123 5f lt vio, yel & blk   .25   .25
497 A123 15f grnsh gray, yel &
         black   .25   .25
498 A123 50f rose, yel & blk   1.25   .80
  a. Souv. sheet, 100f, imperf.   5.75   6.50
  Nos. 496-498 (3)   1.75   1.30
  ILO, 50th anniv.
  For overprint, see No. O297.

Weight Lifting — A124   High Jump — A124a

1969, June 20   Perf. 13½x13
500 A124 3f org yel & multi   .55   .25
501 A124a 5f blue & multi   .55   .25
502 A124 10f rose pink &
         multi   .65   .30
503 A124a 35f yellow & multi   1.25   1.00
  a. Souv. sheet of 4, #500-503,
      imperf.   11.00 11.00
  Nos. 500-503 (4)   3.00   1.80
  19th Olympic Games, Mexico City, Oct. 12-
27, 1968. No. 503a sold for 100f.

Coat of Arms, Symbols of Industry — A125

1969, July 14   Photo.   Perf. 13
504 A125 10f brn org & multi   .40   .25
505 A125 15f multicolored   .60   .25
  11th anniv. of the July 14, 1958 revolution.

Street Paving — A126

Baghdad International Airport — A126a

Pres. Ahmed Hassan al-Bakr — A127

1969, July 17   Perf. 13½
506 A126   10f yel & multi   .50   .30
507 A126   15f blue & multi   .50   .30
508 A126a 20f blue & multi   1.60   .45
509 A127   200f gold & multi   20.00   9.00
  Nos. 506-509 (4)   22.60 10.05
  Coup of July 17, 1968, 1st anniv. No. 508
also for the inauguration of Baghdad Intl.
Airport.
  No. 509 exists imperf. Value $25.

Wheat and Fair Emblem — A128

1969, Oct. 1   Photo.   Perf. 13½
510 A128 10f brt grn, gold & dl
         red   .65   .25
511 A128 15f ultra, gold & red   .80   .35
  6th International Fair, Baghdad.
  For overprints see Nos. 567A-567B.

Motor Ship Al-Waleed — A129

Designs: 15f, Floating crane Antara. 30f, Pilot ship Al-Rasheed. 35f, Suction dredge Hillah. 50f, Survey ship Al-Fao.

1969, Oct. 8   Litho.   Perf. 12½
512 A129 15f black & multi   .50   .25
513 A129 20f black & multi   .65   .40
514 A129 30f black & multi   1.00   .50
515 A129 35f black & multi   1.60   .80
516 A129 50f black & multi   4.75   2.25
  Nos. 512-516 (5)   8.50   4.20
  50th anniversary of Basrah Harbor.

Radio Tower and Map of Palestine — A130

1969, Nov. 9   Litho.   Perf. 12½x13
517 A130 15f multicolored   2.50   .35
518 A130 50f multicolored   4.50   .80
  10th anniversary of Iraqi News Agency.
  For overprints see Nos. 698-699.

"Search for Knowledge" — A131

1969, Nov. 21   Photo.   Perf. 13
519 A131 15f blue & multi   .35   .25
520 A131 20f green & multi   .50   .30
  Campaign against illiteracy.

Front Page of First Baghdad Newspaper — A132

1969, Dec. 26   Litho.   Perf. 13½
521 A132 15f yel, org & black   .50   .30
  Centenary of the Iraqi press.
  For overprint see No. 552.

Soldier, Map of Iraq and Plane A133

1970, Jan. 6   Photo.   Perf. 13
522 A133 15f lt vio & multi   .70   .30
523 A133 20f yellow & multi   1.40   .65
  Issued for Army Day 1970.

Soldier, Farmer and Worker Shoring up Wall in Iraqi Colors — A134

1970, Feb. 8   Photo.   Perf. 13
524 A134 10f multicolored   .25   .25
525 A134 15f brick red & multi   .40   .25
  7th anniv. of the Revolution of Ramadan 14.

Poppies — A135

Flowers: 3f, Poet's narcissus. 5f, Tulip. 10f, 50f, Carnations. 15f, Rose.

1970, June 12   Litho.   Perf. 13
526 A135 2f emer & multi   .40   .25
527 A135 3f lt bl & multi   .40   .25
528 A135 5f multicolored   .40   .25
529 A135 10f lt grn & multi   .60   .35
530 A135 50f pale sal & multi   1.10   .55
531 A135 50f lt grn & multi   3.25   1.25
  Nos. 526-531 (6)   6.15   2.90
  The overprinted sets Nos. 532-543 were released before Nos. 526-531.
  For overprints see Nos. 621-623, RA20. For surcharge see No. 726.

Nos. 526-531 Overprinted in Ultramarine

1970, Mar. 21
532 A135 2f emer & multi   .45   .30
533 A135 3f lt bl & multi   .45   .30
534 A135 5f multicolored   .45   .30
535 A135 10f lt grn & multi   .80   .30
536 A135 50f pale sal & multi   1.10   .90
537 A135 50f lt grn & multi   3.25   1.25
  Nos. 532-537 (6)   6.50   2.75
  Issued for Novrooz (New Year).

Nos. 526-531 Overprinted in Black

1970, Apr. 18
538 A135 2f emer & multi   .50   .50
539 A135 3f lt bl & multi   .50   .50
540 A135 5f multicolored   .50   .50
541 A135 10f lt grn & multi   .50   .50
542 A135 15f pale sal & multi   1.40   .90
543 A135 50f lt grn & multi   3.00   1.10
  Nos. 538-543 (6)   6.40   4.00
  Issued for the Spring Festival, Mosul.

Map of Arab Countries, Slogans A136

People, Flag, Sun and Map of Palestine — A136a

1970, Apr. 7   Perf. 13x12½
544 A136   15f gold & multi   .45   .25
545 A136   35f sil & multi   .65   .55
546 A136a 50f red & multi   2.10   .70
  a. Souv. sheet, 150f, imperf.   10.00 11.00
  Nos. 544-546 (3)   3.20   1.50
  23rd anniversary of Al-Baath Party.

Workers and Cogwheel A137

IRAQ

1970, May 1
547	A137	10f silver & multi	.40	.25
548	A137	15f silver & multi	.50	.35
549	A137	35f silver & multi	1.50	.75
		Nos. 547-549 (3)	2.40	1.35

Issued for Labor Day.

Kaaba, Mecca, and Koran — A138

1970, May 17   *Photo.*   *Perf. 13*
| 550 | A138 | 15f brt bl & multi | .40 | .25 |
| 551 | A138 | 20f orange & multi | .40 | .25 |

Mohammed's 1,400th birthday.

No. 521 Ovptd. "1970" and Arabic Inscription in Prussian Blue

1970, June 15   *Litho.*   *Perf. 13½*
| 552 | A132 | 15f yel, org & black | .55 | .55 |

Day of Iraqi press.

Revolutionists and Guns — A139

Designs: 35f, Revolutionist and rising sun.

1970, June 30   *Litho.*   *Perf. 13*
553	A139	10f blk & apple grn	.25	.25
554	A139	15f black & gold	.40	.25
555	A139	35f blk & red org	.90	.45
	a.	Souv. sheet, 100f, imperf.	5.00	5.00
		Nos. 553-555 (3)	1.55	.95

50th anniversary, Revolution of 1920.

Broken Chain and New Dawn — A140

1970, July 14   *Perf. 13x13½*
| 557 | A140 | 15f multicolored | .35 | .25 |
| 558 | A140 | 20f multicolored | .50 | .25 |

12th anniv. of the July 14, 1958 revolution.

Map of Arab Countries and Hands — A141

1970, July 17   *Perf. 13*
| 559 | A141 | 15f gold & multi | .30 | .25 |
| 560 | A141 | 25f gold & multi | .55 | .25 |

2nd anniversary of coup of July 17, 1968.

Pomegranates A142

1970, Aug. 21   *Perf. 14*
561	A142	3f shown	.40	.25
562	A142	5f Grapefruit	.40	.25
563	A142	10f Grapes	.40	.25
564	A142	15f Oranges	1.10	.35
565	A142	35f Dates	3.50	1.90
		Nos. 561-565 (5)	5.80	3.00

The Latin inscriptions on the 5f and 10f have been erroneously transposed.
For overprints & surcharge see Nos. 613-615, 725, O240-O245.

Kaaba, Mecca, Moon over Mountain and Spider Web — A143

1970, Sept. 4   *Photo.*   *Perf. 13*
| 566 | A143 | 15f multicolored | .40 | .25 |
| 567 | A143 | 25f multicolored | .55 | .25 |

Issued for Hajeer (Pilgrimage) Year.

Nos. 510-511 Overprinted in Red

1970, Sept.   *Photo.*   *Perf. 13½*
| 567A | A128 | 10f multi | 3.50 | 2.00 |
| 567B | A128 | 15f multi | 3.50 | 2.00 |

7th International Fair, Baghdad.

Intl. Education Year Emblem — A144

1970, Nov. 13   *Photo.*   *Perf. 13*
| 568 | A144 | 5f yel green & multi | .35 | .25 |
| 569 | A144 | 15f brick red & multi | .50 | .25 |

Flag and Map of Arab League Countries A145

1970   *Perf. 11*
| 570 | A145 | 15f olive & multi | .40 | .25 |
| 571 | A145 | 35f gray & multi | .50 | .40 |

25th anniversary of the Arab League.

Baghdad Hospital and Emblem A146

1970, Dec. 7   *Litho.*   *Perf. 12*
| 572 | A146 | 15f yellow & multi | .40 | .25 |
| 573 | A146 | 40f lt green & multi | 1.25 | .60 |

Iraqi Medical Society, 50th anniv.

Sugar Beet — A147   **Sugar Factory — A147a**

30f, like 5f.

Perf. 13x13½, 13½x13

1970, Dec. 25   *Photo.*
574	A147	5f ocher, grn & blk	.30	.25
575	A147a	15f black & multi	.50	.25
576	A147	30f org ver, grn & blk	1.75	.75
		Nos. 574-576 (3)	2.55	1.25

Publicity for Mosul sugar factory.

OPEC Emblem — A148

1970, Dec. 30   *Litho.*   *Perf. 13x13½*
| 577 | A148 | 10f rose claret, bis & bl | .75 | .40 |
| 578 | A148 | 40f emer, bis & blue | 3.25 | 1.25 |

OPEC, 10th anniversary.

Soldiers A149   **Soldiers, Maps of Arab Countries and Israel A150**

Perf. 13½x14, 11½x12½

1971, Jan. 6
579	A149	15f multicolored	1.00	.40
580	A150	40f red org & multi	4.00	1.50
	a.	Souv. sheet of 2, #579-580, imperf.	10.00	10.00

Army Day, 50th anniversary.
No. 580a sold for 100f.

Marchers and Map of Arab Countries A151

1971, Feb. 8   *Litho.*   *Perf. 11½x12½*
| 581 | A151 | 15f yellow & multi | .45 | .25 |
| 582 | A151 | 40f pink & multi | 1.40 | .50 |

Revolution of Ramadan 14, 8th anniversary.

Spider Web, Pilgrims — A152

1971, Feb. 26   *Photo.*   *Perf. 13*
| 583 | A152 | 10f pink & multi | .25 | .25 |
| 584 | A152 | 15f buff & multi | .50 | .25 |

Hajeer (New) Year.

President al-Bakr — A153

1971, Mar. 11   *Litho.*   *Perf. 14*
| 585 | A153 | 15f orange & multi | .60 | .40 |
| 586 | A153 | 100f emer & multi | 2.75 | 1.50 |

First anniversary of Mar. 11th Manifesto.

Marshland — A154

Tourist Publicity: 10f, Stork flying over Baghdad. 15f, "Summer Resorts." 100f, Return of Sindbad the Sailor.

1971, Mar. 15   *Perf. 13*
587	A154	5f multicolored	.45	.25
588	A154	10f lt grn & multi	.75	.25
589	A154	15f pink & multi	.90	.45
590	A154	100f multicolored	4.75	2.40
		Nos. 587-590 (4)	6.85	3.35

Blacksmith Taming Serpent A155

1971, Mar. 21   *Perf. 11½x12*
| 591 | A155 | 15f multicolored | .85 | .35 |
| 592 | A155 | 25f yel & multi | 1.75 | .70 |

Novrooz Festival.

No. 455 Overprinted

1971, Mar. 23   *Litho.*   *Perf. 13*
| 593 | A107 | 15f rose red & multi | 3.25 | 1.25 |

World Meteorological Day. See No. C39.

Workers, Soldier, Map of Arab Countries A156

1971, Apr. 7
594	A156	15f yel & multi	.80	.45
595	A156	35f multicolored	1.60	.75
596	A156	250f multicolored	10.00	10.00
		Nos. 594-596 (3)	12.40	11.20

24th anniv. of the Al Baath Party. No. 596 has circular perforation around vignette set within a white square of paper, perforated on 4 sides. The design of No. 596 is similar to Nos. 594-595, but with denomination within the circle and no inscriptions in margin.

Nos. 443-444, 448 Overprinted

1971, Apr. 14
597	A105	2f pale brn & multi	.50	.25
598	A105	5f ver & multi	.70	.25
599	A105	25f lemon & multi	2.25	1.00
		Nos. 597-599 (3)	3.45	1.50

Mosul Festival.

Worker, Farm Woman with Torch — A157

1971, May 1   *Litho.*   *Perf. 13*
| 600 | A157 | 15f ocher & multi | .35 | .25 |
| 601 | A157 | 40f olive & multi | 1.25 | .30 |

Labor Day.

Muslim Praying in Mecca — A158

1971, May 7
| 602 | A158 | 15f yellow & multi | .55 | .25 |
| 603 | A158 | 100f pink & multi | 2.75 | 1.25 |

Mohammed's 1,401st birthday.

IRAQ

People, Fists, Map of Iraq — A159

1971, July 14   Photo.   Perf. 14
604 A159 25f green & multi   .55   .25
605 A159 50f lt bl & multi   1.60   .60
13th anniv. of the July 14, 1958 revolution.

Surveyor, Preacher, Rising Sun — A160

1971, July 17   Perf. 13
606 A160 25f multicolored   .55   .25
607 A160 70f orange & multi   1.75   .75
3rd anniversary of July 17, 1968, coup.

Rafidain Bank Emblem — A161

1971, Sept. 24   Photo.   Perf. 13½
Diameter: 27mm
608 A161 10f multicolored   .55   .55
609 A161 15f multicolored   .90   .90
610 A161 25f multicolored   1.75   1.75
Diameter: 32mm
611 A161 65f multicolored   8.00   6.50
612 A161 250f multicolored   21.00   21.00
Nos. 608-612 (5)   32.20   30.70
30th anniversary of Rafidain Bank. Nos. 608-612 have circular perforation around design within a white square of paper, perforated on 4 sides.

Nos. 561, 564-565 Overprinted

1971, Oct. 15   Litho.   Perf. 14
613 A142 3f bl grn & multi   2.25   2.25
614 A142 15f red & multi   2.25   2.25
615 A142 35f orange & multi   2.25   2.25
Nos. 613-615 (3)   6.75   6.75
Agricultural census, Oct. 15, 1971.

Soccer — A162

Designs: 25f, Track and field. 35f, Table tennis. 75f, Gymnastics. 95f, Volleyball and basketball.

1971, Nov. 17   Litho.   Perf. 13½
616 A162 15f green & multi   .30   .30
617 A162 25f pink & multi   .80   .40
618 A162 35f lt bl & multi   1.00   .90
619 A162 70f lt grn & multi   4.25   1.50
620 A162 95f yel grn & multi   7.50   2.50
   a. Souvenir sheet of 5   24.00   24.00
Nos. 616-620 (5)   13.85   5.60
4th Pan-Arab Schoolboys Sports Games, Baghdad. No. 620a contains 5 stamps similar to Nos. 616-620 with simulated perforations. Sold for 200f.

Nos. 527-528, 530 Overprinted and Surcharged

1971, Nov. 23   Litho.   Perf. 13
621 A135 15f multicolored   1.75   .40
622 A135 25f on 5f multi   2.50   1.25
623 A135 70f on 3f multi   9.50   3.00
Nos. 621-623 (3)   13.75   4.65
Students' Day. The 15f has only first 3 lines of Arabic overprint.

Nos. 485-486 Overprinted

1971, Dec. 11   Litho.   Perf. 13½
624 A117 15f multicolored   2.75   1.00
625 A117 25f blue & multi   7.25   3.25
25th anniv. of UNICEF.

Children Crossing Street — A162a

1971, Dec. 17   Litho.   Perf. 13x12½
625A A162a 15f yel & multi   2.50   .80
625B A162a 25f brt rose & multi   4.50   2.50
2nd Traffic Week. For overprints see Nos. 668-669.

Arab Postal Union Emblem — A163

1971, Dec. 24   Photo.   Perf. 11½
626 A163 25f emer, yel & brn   .45   .25
627 A163 70f vio bl, yel & red   1.75   .65
25th anniv. of the Conf. of Sofar, Lebanon, establishing Arab Postal Union.

Racial Equality Emblem — A164

1971, Dec. 31   Perf. 13½x14
628 A164 25f brt grn & multi   .25   .25
629 A164 70f orange & multi   1.00   .90
Intl. Year Against Racial Discrimination.

Soldiers with Flag and Torch — A165

1972, Jan. 6   Photo.   Perf. 14x13½
630 A165 25f blue & multi   1.20   .65
631 A165 70f brt grn & multi   4.00   2.50
Army Day, Jan. 6.

Workers — A166

1972, Feb. 8
632 A166 25f brt grn & multi   2.50   .60
633 A166 95f lilac & multi   4.50   2.50
Revolution of Ramadan 14, 9th anniv.

Mosque, Minaret, Crescent and Caravan — A167

1972, Feb. 26   Litho.   Perf. 12½x13
634 A167 25f bl grn & multi   .35   .25
635 A167 35f purple & multi   .70   .40
Hegira (Pilgrimage) Year.

Peace Symbols and "11" — A168

1972, Mar. 11   Photo.   Perf. 11x12½
636 A168 25f lt blue & blk   1.50   .30
637 A168 70f brt lilac & blk   4.25   1.25
2nd anniversary of Mar. 11 Manifesto.

Mountain Range and Flowers A169

1972, Mar. 21   Perf. 11½x11
638 A169 25f vio blue & multi   1.25   .25
639 A169 70f vio blue & multi   4.25   1.50
Novrooz, New Year Festival.

Party Emblem — A170

Symbolic Design A171

Perf. 14 (A170), 13 (A171)

1972   Litho.
640 A170 10f brn org & multi   .35   .25
641 A171 25f bister & multi   .80   .40
642 A170 35f brn org & multi   .90   .50
643 A171 70f red & multi   2.75   2.10
Nos. 640-643 (4)   4.80   3.25
Iraqi Arab Baath Socialist Party, 25th anniv. Issued: 25f, 70f, Mar. 23; 10f, 35f, Apr. 7.

Emblem, Map, Weather Balloons and Chart — A172

1972, Mar. 23   Photo.   Perf. 14x13½
644 A172 25f multicolored   2.00   .50
645 A172 35f yel & multi   3.50   1.50
12th World Meteorological Day.

Cogwheel and Ship — A173

1972, Mar. 25   Perf. 11x11½
646 A173 25f ocher & multi   .50   .25
647 A173 35f pink & multi   1.00   .40
Arab Chamber of Commerce.

Derrick and Flame — A174

1972, Apr. 7   Perf. 13x13½
648 A174 25f multicolored   1.50   .30
649 A174 35f multicolored   2.00   1.00
Opening of North Rumaila (INOC, North Iraq Oil Fields).

Quill Pens, Map of Arab Countries — A175

1972, Apr. 17   Photo.   Perf. 11x11½
650 A175 25f orange & multi   .55   .25
651 A175 35f blue & multi   1.75   1.00
3rd Congress of Arab Journalists.

Women's Federation Emblem — A176

1972, Apr. 22   Litho.   Perf. 13½
652 A176 25f green & multi   .55   .30
653 A176 35f lilac & multi   1.75   1.20
Iraqi Women's Federation, 4th anniversary.

Hand Holding Globe-shaped Wrench — A177

1972, May 1   Photo.   Perf. 11½
654 A177 25f yel grn & multi   .45   .25
655 A177 35f orange & multi   .80   .40
Labor Day.

Kaaba, Mecca, and Crescent A178

1972, May 26
656 A178 25f green & multi   .55   .25
657 A178 35f purple & multi   1.75   1.10
Mohammed's 1,402nd birthday.

Soldier, Civilian and Guns A179

IRAQ

1972, July 14   **Photo.**   *Perf. 13½x14*
658   A179   35f multicolored   .90   .40
659   A179   70f lilac & multi   3.00   1.20
14th anniv. of July 14, 1958, revolution.

Dome of the Rock, Arab Countries' Map, Fists — A180

1972, July 17   *Perf. 13*
660   A180   25f citron & multi   1.20   .70
661   A180   95f blue & multi   3.25   3.00
4th anniv. of July 17, 1968 coup.

Congress Emblem, Scout Saluting Iraqi Flag — A182

1972, Aug. 12   **Photo.**   *Perf. 13½x14*
664   A182   20f multicolored   2.25   1.00
665   A182   25f lilac & multi   3.25   1.10
10th Arab Boy Scouts Jamboree and Conference, Mosul, Aug. 10-19.

1972, Aug. 24
666   A182   10f yellow & multi   1.50   .65
667   A182   45f multicolored   4.75   1.40
4th Arab Guides Camp & Conf., Mosul, Aug. 24-30.

No. 625B Ovptd.

No. 625A Ovptd. and Srchd.

1972, Oct. 4   **Photo.**   *Perf. 13x12½*
668   A162a   25f brt rose & multi   6.75   3.00
669   A162a   70f on 15f multi   8.50   7.00
Third Traffic Week.

Central Bank of Iraq — A183

1972, Nov. 16   **Photo.**   *Perf. 13*
670   A183   25f lt blue & multi   .80   .40
671   A183   70f lt green & multi   2.25   .90
25th anniversary, Central Bank of Iraq.

UIC Emblem — A184

1972, Dec. 29
672   A184   25f dp rose & multi   1.75   .70
673   A184   45f brt vio & multi   5.00   3.00
50th anniv., Intl. Railroad Union (UIC).

Nos. 148-149, 151, 180 and Type of 1957-58 Overprinted with 3 Bars

1973, Jan. 29   **Engr.**   *Perf. 11½x12*
674   A28   10f blue   3.50   1.25
675   A33   10f blue   3.50   1.25
676   A28   15f black   3.50   1.25
677   A33   15f black   3.50   1.25
678   A28   25f rose violet   3.50   1.25
679   A33   25f rose violet   3.50   1.25
   Nos. 674-679 (6)   21.00   7.50
The size and position of the bottom bar of overprint differs; the bar can be same size as 2 top bars, short and centered or moved to the right.

No. 455 Overprinted

1973, Mar. 25   **Litho.**   *Perf. 13*
680   A107   15f rose red & multi   10.00   4.00
Intl. History Cong. See Nos. C52-C53.

Workers and Oil Wells — A185

1973, June 1   **Litho.**   *Perf. 13*
681   A185   25f yel & multi   2.00   .90
682   A185   70f rose & multi   9.50   4.00
1st anniv. of nationalization of oil industry. For overprint, see No. O298.

Ram's-head Harp — A186

Designs: 25f, 35f, 45f, Minaret, Mosul, 50f, 70f, 95f, Statue of goddess. 10f, 20f, like 5f.

1973, June   **Litho.**   *Perf. 13x12½*
683   A186   5f orange & blk   .25   .25
684   A186   10f bister & blk   .35   .25
685   A186   20f brt rose & blk   .35   .25
686   A186   25f ultra & blk   .35   .25
687   A186   35f emer & blk   .60   .30
688   A186   45f blue & black   .70   .30
689   A186   50f olive & yel   .95   .30
690   A186   70f violet & yel   1.25   .50
691   A186   95f brown & yel   2.25   .75
   Nos. 683-691 (9)   7.05   3.15
For overprints see Nos. O299-O307, RA21.

People with Flags, Grain — A187

1973, July 14
692   A187   25f multicolored   .70   .30
693   A187   35f multicolored   1.40   .40
July Festivals.

Nos. 393 and 395 Surcharged

1973   **Litho.**   *Perf. 13½x14*
694   A85   25f on 3f multi   3.25   2.25
695   A85   70f on 15f multi   8.25   5.00
Festival of Date Trees.

INTERPOL Headquarters — A188

1973, Sept. 20   **Litho.**   *Perf. 12*
696   A188   25f multicolored   1.00   .60
697   A188   70f brt bl & multi   5.50   3.75
50th anniv. of Intl. Criminal Police Org.

Nos. 517-518 Overprinted in Silver

1973, Sept. 29   **Litho.**   *Perf. 12½x13*
698   A130   15f multicolored   4.75   2.50
699   A130   50f multicolored   9.00   3.50
Meeting of Intl. Org. of Journalists' Executive Committee, Sept. 26-29.

Flags and Fair Emblem — A189

1973, Oct. 10   **Photo.**   *Perf. 11*
700   A189   10f brt grn & dk brn   .45   .25
701   A189   20f ocher & multi   .80   .30
702   A189   65f blue & multi   1.75   .90
   Nos. 700-702 (3)   3.00   1.45
10th International Baghdad Fair, Oct. 1-21.

WMO Emblem — A190

1973, Nov. 15   **Litho.**   *Perf. 12*
703   A190   25f org, blk & green   .70   .25
704   A190   35f brt rose, blk & grn   2.25   1.00
Intl. meteorological cooperation, cent.

Flags of Arab League and Iraq, Maghreb Emblem — A191

1973, Dec. 1   **Photo.**   *Perf. 14*
705   A191   20f dl org & multi   .40   .25
706   A191   35f blue & multi   1.40   .90
11th session of Civil Aviation Council of Arab States, Baghdad, Dec. 1973.

No. 360 Overprinted

1973, Dec. 12   **Photo.**   *Perf. 11*
707   A67a   30f orange & blue   5.00   2.75
6th Executive Council Meeting of APU, Baghdad.

Human Rights Flame — A192

1973, Dec. 25   *Perf. 11½*
708   A192   25f multicolored   .25   .25
709   A192   70f ultra & multi   .90   .50
Universal Declaration of Human Rights, 25th anniv.

Military College Crest and Cadets — A193

1974, Jan. 6   *Perf. 12x11½*
710   A193   25f ocher & multi   .45   .25
711   A193   35f ultra & multi   1.60   1.00
50th anniversary of the Military College.

UPU and Arab Postal Union Emblems — A194

1974, May 28   **Photo.**   *Perf. 11½x12*
712   A194   25f gold & multi   .90   .25
713   A194   35f gold & multi   .90   .40
714   A194   70f gold & multi   1.60   .90
   Nos. 712-714 (3)   3.40   1.55
Centenary of the Universal Postal Union.

Symbols of Ancient Mesopotamia and Oil Industry — A195

1974, June 1   **Litho.**   *Perf. 12½*
715   A195   10f blue & multi   .40   .25
716   A195   25f ocher & multi   .85   .25
717   A195   70f rose & multi   2.75   2.00
   Nos. 715-717 (3)   4.00   2.50
Nationalization of the oil industry, 2nd anniv.

Festival — A196

1974, July 17   *Perf. 11½x12*
718   A196   20f lilac & multi   .35   .25
719   A196   35f dull org & multi   1.00   .50
July Festivals.

National Front Emblem and People — A197

1974, July 17   *Perf. 12x11½*
720   A197   25f blue & multi   .65   .25
721   A197   70f brt grn & multi   1.50   .75
1st anniv. of Progressive National Front.

IRAQ

Cement Plant and Brick Wall — A198

1974, Oct. 19		Perf. 11½x12	
722	A198 20f gray bl & multi	.45	.25
723	A198 25f red & multi	.65	.30
724	A198 70f emerald & multi	1.40	1.00
	Nos. 722-724 (3)	2.50	1.55

25th anniversary of Iraqi Cement Plant.

Nos. 561 and 527 Surcharged

a b

1975, Jan. 9	Litho.	Perf. 13, 14	
725	A142 (a) 10f on 3f multi	3.50	2.50
726	A135 (b) 25f on 3f multi	11.00	7.25

Globe and WPY Emblem — A199

1975, Jan. 30		Perf. 11½x12	
727	A199 25f dull bl & blk	.60	.25
728	A199 35f brt pink & ind	1.25	.65
729	A199 70f yel grn & vio	3.50	1.40
	Nos. 727-729 (3)	5.35	2.30

World Population Year 1974.

Festival Symbols A200

1975, July 17	Litho.	Perf. 12x11½	
730	A200 5f lt brn & multi	.25	.25
731	A200 10f lt brn & multi	.25	.25
732	A200 35f lt brn & multi	1.75	.75
	Nos. 730-732 (3)	2.25	1.25

Festivals, July 1975.

Map of Arab Countries — A201

1975, Aug. 5	Photo.	Perf. 13	
733	A201 25f rose & multi	.50	.25
734	A201 35f multicolored	.90	.60
735	A201 45f multicolored	1.00	.65
	Nos. 733-735 (3)	2.40	1.50

Arab Working Org., 10th anniv.

Symbols of Women, Oil Industry and Agriculture — A202

1975, Aug. 15		Perf. 14	
736	A202 10f lilac & multi	.50	.30
737	A202 35f multicolored	1.00	.85
738	A202 70f bl & multi	4.25	1.50
a.	Souv. sheet, 100f, imperf.	9.75	9.75
	Nos. 736-738 (3)	5.75	2.65

International Women's Year.

Euphrates Dam and Causeway A203

1975, Sept. 5	Litho.	Perf. 12x11½	
739	A203 3f orange & multi	.25	.25
740	A203 25f purple & multi	.70	.25
741	A203 70f rose red & multi	2.75	1.25
	Nos. 739-741 (3)	3.70	1.75

Intl. Commission on Irrigation and Drainage, 25th anniv.

National Insurance Co. Seal — A204

1975, Oct. 11	Photo.	Perf. 13	
742	A204 20f brt bl & multi	.80	.25
743	A204 25f crim & multi	1.00	.40
a.	Souv. sheet, 100f, imperf.	7.00	8.50

Natl. Insurance Co., Baghdad, 25th anniv.

Musician Entertaining King — A205

1975, Nov. 21		Perf. 14	
744	A205 25f silver & multi	.65	.25
745	A205 45f gold & multi	1.50	.90

Baghdad Intl. Music Conf., Nov. 1975.

Telecommunications Center — A206

1975, Dec. 22	Litho.	Perf. 12½	
746	A206 5f lil rose & multi	.25	.25
747	A206 10f blue & multi	.30	.25
748	A206 60f green & multi	1.90	1.20
	Nos. 746-748 (3)	2.45	1.70

Inauguration of Telecommunications Center Building during July 1975 Festival.

Diesel Locomotive A207

Conference Emblem and: 30f, Diesel passenger locomotive #511. 35f, 0-3-0 steam tank locomotive with passenger train. 50f, 2-3-0 German steam locomotive, c. 1914.

1975, Dec. 22	Photo.	Perf. 14	
749	A207 25f tan & multi	5.50	1.00
750	A207 30f tan & multi	8.50	2.00
751	A207 35f yel grn & multi	11.00	3.50
752	A207 50f yel grn & multi	16.00	9.50
	Nos. 749-752 (4)	41.00	16.00

15th Taurus Railway Conference, Baghdad.

A208

Design: Soldier on guard.

1976, Jan. 6		Perf. 13	
753	A208 5f silver & multi	.25	.25
754	A208 25f silver & multi	.55	.25
755	A208 50f gold & multi	1.60	.60
	Nos. 753-755 (3)	2.40	1.10

55th Army Day.

Arab Day Eliminate Illiteracy — A209

Fingerprint crossed out, Arab world.

1976, Jan. 8	Photo.	Perf. 13½x13	
756	A209 5f violet & multi	.25	.25
757	A209 15f blue & multi	.45	.25
758	A209 35f green & multi	1.60	1.00
	Nos. 756-758 (3)	2.30	1.50

Statue of Goddess — A210

20f-30f, Two female figures forming column. 35f-75f, Head of bearded man.

1976, Jan. 1	Litho.	Perf. 13x12½	
759	A210 5f lilac & multi	.25	.25
760	A210 10f rose & multi	.25	.25
761	A210 15f yellow & multi	.35	.25
762	A210 20f bister & multi	.35	.25
763	A210 25f lt grn & multi	.60	.25
764	A210 30f blue & multi	.90	.25
765	A210 35f lil rose & multi	.90	.30
766	A210 50f citron & multi	1.50	.30
767	A210 75f violet & multi	2.10	.90
	Nos. 759-767 (9)	7.20	3.00

Iraq Earth Station — A211

1976, Feb. 8		Perf. 13x13½	
768	A211 10f silver & multi	.40	.25
769	A211 25f silver & multi	1.20	.45
770	A211 75f gold & multi	4.25	2.00
	Nos. 768-770 (3)	5.85	2.70

Revolution of Ramadan 14, 13th anniv.

Telephones 1876 and 1976 — A212

1976, Mar. 17	Litho.	Perf. 12x12½	
771	A212 35f multicolored	1.25	.45
772	A212 50f multicolored	2.50	.70
773	A212 75f multicolored	4.00	1.00
	Nos. 771-773 (3)	7.75	2.15

Centenary of first telephone call by Alexander Graham Bell, Mar. 10, 1876.

Map of Maghreb, ICATU Emblem — A213

1976, Mar. 24	Photo.	Perf. 13½	
774	A213 5f green & multi	.35	.25
775	A213 10f multicolored	.35	.25
	Nos. 774-775,C54 (3)	5.20	2.50

20th Intl. Conf. of Arab Workers Syndicates.

Map of Iraq, Family, Torch and Wreath — A214

1976, Apr. 1		Perf. 12½	
776	A214 5f multicolored	.25	.25
777	A214 15f lilac & multi	.45	.25
778	A214 35f multicolored	2.25	.90
	Nos. 776-778 (3)	2.95	1.40

Police Day.

Pipeline, Map of Iraq — A215

Pres. A. H. al-Bakr Embracing Vice Pres. Saddam Hussein — A216

1976, June 1	Photo.	Perf. 13	
779	A215 25f multicolored	1.50	.25
780	A215 75f multicolored	3.75	1.90

Souvenir Sheet
Imperf

781	A216 150f multicolored	30.00	30.00

4th anniversary of oil nationalization.

"Festival" — A217

1976, July 17		Perf. 14	
782	A217 15f orange & multi	.40	.25
783	A217 35f orange & multi	1.60	.80

Festivals, July 1976.

Archbishop Capucci, Map of Palestine — A218

1976, Aug. 18	Litho.	Perf. 12	
784	A218 25f multicolored	.75	.25
785	A218 35f multicolored	1.15	.45
786	A218 75f multicolored	3.25	1.50
	Nos. 784-786 (3)	5.15	2.20

Detention of Archbishop Hilarion Capucci in Israel, Aug. 18, 1974.

Common Kingfisher — A219

IRAQ

10f, Turtle dove. 15f, Pin-tailed sandgrouse. 25f, Blue rock thrush. 50f, Purple and gray herons.

1976, Sept. 15   Litho.   Perf. 13½x14
787	A219	5f multicolored	2.75	.85
788	A219	10f multicolored	2.75	.85
789	A219	15f multicolored	3.75	.85
790	A219	25f multicolored	7.25	1.10
791	A219	50f multicolored	11.00	1.50
		Nos. 787-791 (5)	27.50	5.15

For overprints see Nos. O327-O331.

"15" — A220

1976, Nov. 23   Photo.   Perf. 13½
792	A220	30f multicolored	.65	.25
793	A220	70f multicolored	2.00	.75

15th anniv. of National Students Union.

Oil Tanker and Emblems — A221

25f, 50f, Pier, refinery, pipeline.

1976, Dec. 25   Perf. 12½x12
794	A221	10f multicolored	.70	.25
795	A221	15f multicolored	.90	.40
796	A221	25f multicolored	2.10	.75
797	A221	50f multicolored	3.00	1.25
		Nos. 794-797 (4)	6.70	2.65

1st Iraqi oil tanker (10f, 15f) and Nationalization of Basrah Petroleum Co. Ltd., 1st anniv. (25f, 50f).

Happy Children — A222

UNESCO Emblem and: 25f, Children with flowers and butterflies. 75f, Children planting flowers around flagpole.

1976, Dec. 25   Perf. 12x12½
798	A222	10f multicolored	.25	.25
799	A222	25f multicolored	2.00	.40
800	A222	75f multicolored	3.50	1.10
		Nos. 798-800 (3)	5.75	1.75

30th anniv. of UNESCO, and Books for Children Campaign.

Ornament — A223

1977, Mar. 2   Photo.   Perf. 13½
801	A223	25f gold & multi	.80	.25
802	A223	35f gold & multi	1.25	.30

Birthday of Mohammed (570-632).

Peace Day — A224

25f, 30f, Peace Dove.

1977, Mar. 11   Perf. 14x13½
803	A224	25f lt bl & multi	.40	.25
804	A224	30f buff & multi	.75	.30

Dahlia — A225

Flowers: 10f, Sweet peas. 35f, Chrysanthemums. 50f, Verbena.

1977, Mar. 21   Litho.   Perf. 12½
805	A225	5f multicolored	.25	.25
806	A225	10f multicolored	.45	.25
807	A225	35f multicolored	1.10	.30
808	A225	50f multicolored	2.25	.65
		Nos. 805-808 (4)	4.05	1.45

Spring Festivals, Baghdad.

Emblem with Doves — A226

Designs: 75f, Emblematic Hindu "7" with flame. 100f, Dove with olive branch.

1977, Apr. 7   Photo.   Perf. 13
809	A226	25f yel & multi	.60	.25
810	A226	75f yel & multi	2.25	1.00

Souvenir Sheet
Imperf
811	A226	100f multicolored	6.00	6.00

Al Baath Party, 30th anniversary. No. 811 contains one 49x35mm stamp.

APU Emblem, Members' Flags — A227

1977, Apr. 12   Litho.   Perf. 14
812	A227	25f orange & multi	.35	.25
813	A227	35f gray & multi	.70	.40

25th anniversary of Arab Postal Union.

Cogwheel, Globe and "1" — A228

1977, May 1   Litho.   Perf. 14½x14
814	A228	10f multicolored	.25	.25
815	A228	30f multicolored	.60	.25
816	A228	90f multicolored	.90	.60
		Nos. 814-816 (3)	1.75	1.10

Labor Day.

Weight Lifting — A229

75f, Weight lifter, standing up. 100f, Symbolic weight lifter with Iraqi flag, laurel wreath.

1977, May 8   Photo.   Perf. 14
817	A229	25f multicolored	.90	.60
818	A229	75f multicolored	2.50	1.10

Souvenir Sheet
Imperf
819	A229	100f multicolored	7.50	7.50

8th Asian Weight Lifting Championship, Baghdad, May 1977. No. 819 contains one 42x52mm stamp.

Arabian Garden — A230

Arab Tourist Year: 10f, View of town with minarets, horiz. 30f, Landscape with bridge and waterfall. 50f, Hosts welcoming tourists, and drum, horiz.

Perf. 11½x12, 12x11½
1977, June 15   Litho.
820	A230	5f multicolored	.25	.25
821	A230	10f multicolored	.25	.25
822	A230	30f multicolored	.80	.25
823	A230	50f multicolored	2.25	1.60
		Nos. 820-823 (4)	3.55	2.35

Grain and Dove — A231

1977, July 17   Photo.   Perf. 14
824	A231	25f multicolored	.55	.25
825	A231	30f multicolored	.70	.30

Festivals, July 1977.

Map of Arab Countries — A232

1977, Sept. 9   Photo.   Perf. 13½x14
826	A232	30f multicolored	.75	.45
827	A232	70f multicolored	2.25	.90

UN Conference on Desertification, Nairobi, Kenya, Aug. 29-Sept. 9.

Census Emblem — A233

1977, Oct. 17   Litho.   Perf. 14x14½
828	A233	20f ultra & multi	.30	.25
829	A233	30f brown & multi	.70	.25
830	A233	70f gray & multi	1.40	.80
		Nos. 828-830 (3)	2.40	1.30

Population Census Day, Oct. 17.

Festival Emblem — A234

1977, Nov. 1   Photo.   Perf. 14
831	A234	25f silver & multi	.30	.25
832	A234	50f gold & multi	.65	.40

Al Mutanabby Festival, Nov. 1977.

A235

Jumblatt, caricatures of Britain, US, Israel.

1977, Nov. 16   Photo.   Perf. 14
833	A235	20f multicolored	.80	.25
834	A235	30f multicolored	1.00	.25
835	A235	70f multicolored	2.50	.60
		Nos. 833-835 (3)	4.30	1.10

Kemal Junblatt, Druse leader, killed in Lebanese war.

A236

1977, Dec. 12   Photo.   Perf. 14
836	A236	30f gold & multi	.40	.25
837	A236	35f silver & multi	.50	.25

Hegira (Pilgrimage) Year.

Young People and Flags — A237

1978, Apr. 7   Photo.   Perf. 11½x11
838	A237	10f multicolored	.25	.25
839	A237	25f multicolored	.25	.25
840	A237	35f multicolored	.55	.35
		Nos. 838-840 (3)	1.05	.85

Youth Day.

Coins and Coin Bank — A238

1978, Apr. 15
841	A238	15f multicolored	.25	.25
842	A238	25f multicolored	.45	.25
843	A238	35f multicolored	.90	.40
		Nos. 841-843 (3)	1.60	.90

6th anniversary of postal savings law.

Microwave Transmission and Receiving — A239

1978, May 17   Photo.   Perf. 14
844	A239	25f org & multi	.40	.25
845	A239	35f lilac & multi	.40	.25
846	A239	75f emer & multi	1.00	.60
		Nos. 844-846 (3)	1.80	1.10

10th World Telecommunications Day and 1st anniversary of commissioning of national microwave network.

Emblems and Flags of Participants — A240

Perf. 12½x11½
1978, June 19   Litho.
847	A240	25f multicolored	.55	.25
848	A240	35f multicolored	.85	.50

Conference of Postal Ministers of Arabian Gulf Countries, Baghdad (Saudi Arabia, United Arab Emirates, Qatar, Bahrain, Kuwait, Oman, People's Republic of Yemen).

Ancient Coin — A241

Designs: Ancient Iraqi coins. 75f vertical.

IRAQ

1978, June 25   *Perf. 11½x12½*   *Photo.*
849	A241	1f citron & multi	.25	.25
850	A241	2f lt blue & multi	.25	.25
851	A241	3f salmon & multi	.25	.25
852	A241	4f yel grn & multi	.50	.50
853	A241	75f bl grn & multi	3.00	3.00
		Nos. 849-853 (5)	4.25	4.25

Festival Emblem — A242

Festival Poster A243

1978, July 17   *Perf. 13½x13*
854	A242	25f multicolored	1.50	.30
855	A242	35f multicolored	1.75	.40

Souvenir Sheet   *Perf. 13x13½*
856	A243	100f multicolored	6.00	6.00

Festivals, July 1978.

WHO Emblem, Nurse, Hospital, Sick Child — A244

1978, Aug. 18   *Photo.*   *Perf. 14*
857	A244	25f multicolored	.50	.25
858	A244	35f multicolored	1.00	.50
859	A244	75f multicolored	2.50	1.25
		Nos. 857-859 (3)	4.00	2.00

Eradication of smallpox.

Maritime Union Emblem — A245

1978, Aug. 30   *Photo.*   *Perf. 11½x12*
860	A245	25f multicolored	.70	.30
861	A245	75f multicolored	1.75	.60

1st World Maritime Day.

Workers — A246

1978, Sept. 12   *Perf. 14*
862	A246	10f multicolored	.25	.25
863	A246	25f multicolored	.55	.25
864	A246	35f multicolored	1.00	.65
		Nos. 862-864 (3)	1.80	1.15

10th anniv. of People's Work Groups.

Fair Emblem with Atom Symbol — A247

1978, Oct. 1
865	A247	25f multicolored	.25	.25
866	A247	35f multicolored	.30	.25
867	A247	75f multicolored	1.40	.85
		Nos. 865-867 (3)	1.95	1.35

15th International Fair, Baghdad, Oct. 1-15.

Map of Iraq, Ruler and Globe — A248

1978, Oct. 14
868	A248	25f multicolored	.25	.25
869	A248	35f multicolored	.30	.25
870	A248	75f multicolored	1.40	.85
		Nos. 868-870 (3)	1.95	1.35

World Standards Day.

Altharthar-Euphrates Dam — A249

1978   *Photo.*   *Perf. 11½*
871	A249	5f multicolored	.25	.25
872	A249	10f multicolored	.25	.25
873	A249	15f multicolored	.25	.25
874	A249	25f multicolored	.30	.25
875	A249	35f multicolored	.40	.25
876	A249	50f multicolored	.65	.30
		Nos. 871-876 (6)	2.10	1.55

Arab Summit Conference — A250

1978, Nov. 2   *Photo.*   *Perf. 14*
890	A250	25f multicolored	.25	.25
891	A250	35f multicolored	.45	.25
892	A250	75f multicolored	1.10	.85
		Nos. 890-892 (3)	1.80	1.35

9th Arab Summit Conference, Baghdad, Nov. 2-5.

Surgeons' Conference Emblem — A251

1978, Nov. 8   *Litho.*   *Perf. 12x11½*
893	A251	25f multicolored	.35	.25
894	A251	75f multicolored	1.00	.65

4th Cong. of the Assoc. of Thoracic & Cardiovascular Surgeons of Asia, Baghdad, Nov. 6-10.

Pilgrims at Mt. Arafat and Holy Ka'aba — A252

1978, Nov. 9   *Photo.*   *Perf. 14*
895	A252	25f multicolored	.35	.25
896	A252	35f multicolored	.55	.25

Pilgrimage to Mecca.

Atom Symbol, Map of South America, Africa, Arabia — A253

1978, Nov. 11   *Perf. 13½*
897	A253	25f multicolored	.25	.25
898	A253	50f multicolored	.55	.25
899	A253	75f multicolored	.90	.55
		Nos. 897-899 (3)	1.70	1.05

Technical Cooperation Among Developing Countries Conf., Buenos Aires, Argentina, Sept. 1978.

Hands Holding Emblem — A254

1978, Nov. 30   *Litho.*   *Perf. 13½x13*
900	A254	25f multicolored	.40	.25
901	A254	50f multicolored	.70	.30
902	A254	75f multicolored	2.00	.65
		Nos. 900-902 (3)	3.10	1.20

Anti-Apartheid Year.

Globe and Flame Emblem — A255

1978, Dec. 20   *Perf. 14*
903	A255	25f multicolored	.50	.25
904	A255	75f multicolored	1.50	1.00

Declaration of Human Rights, 30th anniv.

Candle and Emblem — A256

1979, Jan. 9   *Photo.*   *Perf. 14*
905	A256	10f multicolored	.35	.25
906	A256	25f multicolored	.35	.25
907	A256	35f multicolored	.65	.25
		Nos. 905-907 (3)	1.35	.75

Police Day.

Book, Pencil and Flame — A257

1979, Feb. 15   *Photo.*   *Perf. 14*
908	A257	15f multicolored	.25	.25
909	A257	25f multicolored	.35	.25
910	A257	35f multicolored	.90	.25
		Nos. 908-910 (3)	1.50	.75

Application of Compulsory Education Law, anniversary.

Pupils, School and Teacher — A258

1979, Mar. 1   *Perf. 13*
911	A258	10f multicolored	.25	.25
912	A258	15f multicolored	.25	.25
913	A258	50f multicolored	.80	.50
		Nos. 911-913 (3)	1.30	1.00

Teacher's Day.

Pupils, Flag, Pencil — A259

1979, Mar. 10   *Perf. 13½x13*
914	A259	15f multicolored	.25	.25
915	A259	25f multicolored	.45	.25
916	A259	35f multicolored	.70	.25
		Nos. 914-916 (3)	1.40	.75

National Comprehensive Compulsory Literacy Campaign.

Book, World Map, Arab Achievements A260

1979, Mar. 22   *Perf. 13*
917	A260	35f multicolored	.50	.25
918	A260	75f multicolored	1.50	.65

Achievements of the Arabs.

Girl Playing Flute — A261

1979, Apr. 15   *Litho.*   *Perf. 13½*
919	A261	15f multicolored	.35	.25
920	A261	25f multicolored	.55	.25
921	A261	35f multicolored	1.00	.45
		Nos. 919-921 (3)	1.90	.95

Mosul Spring Festival.

Iraqi Flag, Globe, UPU Emblem — A262

1979, Apr. 22   *Photo.*   *Perf. 13x13½*
922	A262	25f multicolored	.60	.25
923	A262	35f multicolored	.60	.25
924	A262	75f multicolored	1.50	.65
		Nos. 922-924 (3)	2.70	1.15

50th anniv. of Iraq's admission to the UPU.

Soccer Tournament Emblem — A263

1979, May 4   *Photo.*   *Perf. 13*
925	A263	10f multicolored	.25	.25
926	A263	15f multicolored	.30	.25
927	A263	50f multicolored	1.00	.50
		Nos. 925-927 (3)	1.55	1.00

5th Arabian Gulf Soccer Championship.

Child With Globe and Candle — A264

Design: 100f, IYC emblem, boy and girl reaching for UN emblem, vert.

1979, June 1   *Photo.*   *Perf. 13x13½*
928	A264	25f multicolored	.70	.30
929	A264	75f multicolored	1.75	1.00

Souvenir Sheet
930	A264	100f multicolored	30.00	27.50

International Year of the Child.
No. 930 contains one 30x42mm stamp.

Leaf and Flower — A265

1979, July 17   *Litho.*   *Perf. 12½*
931	A265	15f multicolored	.25	.25
932	A265	25f multicolored	.35	.25
933	A265	35f multicolored	.35	.25
		Nos. 931-933 (3)	.95	.75

July festivals.

IRAQ

Students Holding Globe, UNESCO Emblem — A266

1979, July 25

934	A266	25f multicolored	.50	.25
935	A266	40f multicolored	.90	.45
936	A266	100f multicolored	2.00	.90
		Nos. 934-936 (3)	3.40	1.60

Intl. Bureau of Education, Geneva, 50th anniv.

S. al Hosari, Philosopher — A267

Designs: No. 938, Mustapha Jawad, historian. No. 939, Jawad Selim, sculptor.

1979, Oct. 15   Litho.   Perf. 12½

937	A267	25f multicolored	.45	.25
938	A267	25f multicolored	.45	.25
939	A267	25f multicolored	.45	.25
		Nos. 937-939 (3)	1.35	.75

Pilgrimage to Mecca — A268

1979, Oct. 25   Litho.   Perf. 12½

940	A268	25f multicolored	.60	.25
941	A268	50f multicolored	1.25	.40

Iraqi News Agency, 20th Anniversary — A269

1979, Nov. 9   Photo.   Perf. 11½

942	A269	25f multicolored	.45	.25
943	A269	50f multicolored	1.00	.25
944	A269	75f multicolored	1.25	.40
		Nos. 942-944 (3)	2.70	.90

Telecom 79 — A270

1979, Nov. 20   Litho.   Perf. 11½

945	A270	25f multicolored	.45	.25
946	A270	50f multicolored	.70	.30
947	A270	75f multicolored	1.25	.65
		Nos. 945-947 (3)	2.40	1.20

3rd World Telecommunications Exhibition, Geneva, Sept. 20-26.

International Palestinian Solidarity Day — A271

1979, Nov. 29   Photo.   Perf. 11½x12

948	A271	25f multicolored	1.25	.25
949	A271	50f multicolored	2.25	.45
950	A271	75f multicolored	3.50	.85
		Nos. 948-950 (3)	7.00	1.55

A272

Designs: 25f, 75f, Ahmad Hassan Al-Bakr. 35f, 100f, Pres. Saddam Hussein.

1979, Dec. 1   Photo.   Perf. 13x13½

951	A272	25f multicolored	.35	.25
952	A272	35f multicolored	.50	.25
953	A272	75f multicolored	1.00	.40
954	A272	100f multicolored	4.00	2.25
		Nos. 951-954 (4)	5.85	3.15

A273

Vanguard Emblem and: 10f, Boy and violin. 15f, Children, map of Iraq. 25f, Youths. 35f, Vanguard emblem alone.

1979, Dec. 10   Perf. 14

955	A273	10f multicolored	.25	.25
956	A273	15f multicolored	.25	.25
957	A273	25f multicolored	.40	.25
958	A273	35f multicolored	.50	.25
		Nos. 955-958 (4)	1.40	1.00

World Meteorological Day — A274

1980, Mar. 23   Photo.   Perf. 14

959	A274	15f multicolored	.25	.25
960	A274	25f multicolored	.30	.25
961	A274	35f multicolored	.70	.25
		Nos. 959-961 (3)	1.25	.75

World Health Day — A275

1980, Apr. 7   Photo.   Perf. 14

962	A275	25f multicolored	.35	.25
963	A275	35f multicolored	.50	.25
964	A275	75f multicolored	1.90	.50
		Nos. 962-964 (3)	2.75	1.00

Festivals Emblem — A276

Pres. Hussein A277

1980, July 17   Photo.   Perf. 13½x13

965	A276	25f multicolored	.50	.30
966	A276	35f multicolored	.75	.35

Souvenir Sheet
Perf. 13½

967	A277	100f multicolored	14.00	12.00

July Festivals.

Hurdles, Moscow '80 Emblem — A278

20f, Weight lifting, vert. 30f, Boxing. 35f, Soccer, vert. 100f, Wrestling.

1980, July 30   Photo.   Perf. 14

968	A278	15f shown	.25	.25
969	A278	20f multi	.45	.35
970	A278	30f multi	.85	.40
971	A278	35f multi	1.75	.75
		Nos. 968-971 (4)	3.30	1.75

Souvenir Sheet

972	A278	100f multi	10.50	10.50

22nd Summer Olympic Games, Moscow, July 19-Aug. 3.

Fruits — A279

1980, Aug. 15

973	A279	5f Blackberries	.25	.25
974	A279	15f Apricots	.50	.25
975	A279	20f Pears	.70	.25
976	A279	25f Apples	.85	.25
977	A279	35f Plums	1.10	.35
		Nos. 973-977 (5)	3.40	1.35

World Tourism Conference, Manila, Sept. 27 — A279a

1980, Aug. 30   Litho.   Perf. 12½

978	A279a	25f multicolored	.35	.25
979	A279a	50f multicolored	.85	.25
980	A279a	100f multicolored	1.75	.85
		Nos. 978-980 (3)	2.95	1.35

Postal Union Emblem, Posthorn, Map of Arab States — A280

1980, Sept. 8   Perf. 12

981	A280	10f multicolored	.25	.25
982	A280	30f multicolored	.35	.25
983	A280	35f multicolored	.70	.25
		Nos. 981-983 (3)	1.30	.75

Arab Postal Union, 11th Congress, Baghdad.

20th Anniversary of OPEC — A281

1980, Sept. 30

984	A281	30f multicolored	1.00	.25
985	A281	75f multicolored	1.60	.75

Papilio Machaon — A282

15f, Danaus chrysippus. 20f, Vanessa atalanta. 30f, Colias croceus.

1980, Oct. 20   Photo.   Perf. 13½x14

987	A282	10f shown	2.00	.35
988	A282	15f multicolored	2.25	.65
989	A282	20f multicolored	3.25	.80
990	A282	30f multicolored	5.25	1.25
		Nos. 987-990 (4)	12.75	3.05

Hegira, 1,500th Anniv. — A283

1980, Nov. 9   Litho.   Perf. 11½x12

991	A283	15f multicolored	.40	.25
992	A283	25f multicolored	.75	.25
993	A283	35f multicolored	1.00	.35
		Nos. 991-993 (3)	2.15	.85

International Palestinian Solidarity Day — A284

1980, Nov. 29

994	A284	25f multicolored	1.25	.50
995	A284	35f multicolored	1.75	.50
996	A284	75f multicolored	3.50	2.00
		Nos. 994-996 (3)	6.50	3.00

Army Day — A285

1981, Jan. 6   Photo.   Perf. 14x13½

997	A285	25f multicolored	.30	.25
998	A285	30f multicolored	.55	.25
999	A285	75f multicolored	1.60	.70
		Nos. 997-999 (3)	2.45	1.20

February Revolution, 18th Anniversary — A286

1981, Feb. 8   Perf. 12

1000	A286	15f multicolored	.25	.25
1001	A286	25f multicolored	.45	.25
1002	A286	35f multicolored	.70	.25
		Nos. 1000-1002 (3)	1.40	.75

Map of Arab Countries — A287

1981, Mar. 22   Litho.   Perf. 12½

1003	A287	5f multicolored	.25	.25
1004	A287	25f multicolored	.50	.25
1005	A287	35f multicolored	.70	.25
		Nos. 1003-1005 (3)	1.45	.75

Battle of Qadisiya — A288

1981, Apr. 7   Photo.   Perf. 13½x13

1006	A288	30f multicolored	.45	.25
1007	A288	35f multicolored	.60	.25
1008	A288	75f multicolored	1.10	.50
		Nos. 1006-1008 (3)	2.15	1.00

Souvenir Sheet

1009	A288	100f multicolored	6.50	6.50

No. 1009 contains one horiz. stamp.

IRAQ

Helicopters and Tank — A289

1981, June 1   *Photo.*
1010 A289 5f shown .25 .25
1011 A289 10f Plane .35 .25
1012 A289 15f Rocket .50 .25
    Nos. 1010-1012,C66 (4) 5.10 3.25
    Air Force, 50th anniv.

Natl. Assembly Election, First Anniv. — A290

1981, June 20   *Perf. 12½*
1013 A290 30f multicolored .45 .25
1014 A290 35f multicolored .60 .25
1015 A290 45f multicolored .95 .35
    Nos. 1013-1015 (3) 2.00 .85

July Festivals — A291

1981, July 17   *Photo.*
1016 A291 15f multicolored .25 .25
1017 A291 25f multicolored .40 .25
1018 A291 35f multicolored .70 .25
    Nos. 1016-1018 (3) 1.35 .75

Pottery Maker — A292

Designs: Popular industries.

1981, Aug. 15   *Perf. 14*
1019 A292 5f Straw weaver .25 .25
1020 A292 30f Metal worker .55 .25
1021 A292 35f shown .75 .25
1022 A292 50f Rug maker, horiz. 1.00 .35
    Nos. 1019-1022 (4) 2.55 1.10

Islamic Pilgrimage A293

1981, Oct. 7   *Photo.*   *Perf. 12x11½*
1023 A293 25f multicolored .55 .25
1024 A293 45f multicolored 1.00 .30
1025 A293 50f multicolored 1.00 .30
    Nos. 1023-1025 (3) 2.55 .85

World Food Day — A294

1981, Oct. 16   *Photo.*   *Perf. 14*
1026 A294 30f multicolored .55 .25
1027 A294 45f multicolored 1.00 .40
1028 A294 75f multicolored 1.50 .75
    Nos. 1026-1028 (3) 3.05 1.40

Intl. Year of the Disabled — A295

1981, Nov. 15
1029 A295 30f multicolored .45 .25
1030 A295 45f multicolored .75 .30
1031 A295 75f multicolored 1.10 .60
    Nos. 1029-1031 (3) 2.30 1.15

5th Anniv. of United Arab Shipping Co. — A296

1981, Dec. 2   *Perf. 13x13½*
1032 A296 50f multicolored 1.40 .60
1033 A296 120f multicolored 4.00 1.75

Saddam Hussein Gymnasium — A297

50f, Palace of Conferences.

1981, Sept. 26   *Litho.*   *Perf. 12x12½*
1034 A297 45f shown .70 .25
1035 A297 50f multicolored .70 .30
1036 A297 120f like #1035 2.10 1.25
1037 A297 150f like #1034 2.75 1.50
    Nos. 1034-1037 (4) 6.25 3.30
    For surcharges see Nos. 1097-1099.

35th Anniv. of Al Baath Party — A298

25f, 45f, Pres. Hussein, flowers. 30f, 50f, Iraq Flag as rainbow and "7 7 7". 150f, Pres. Hussein, globe, arabic "7".

1982, Apr. 7   *Photo.*   *Perf. 13½x13*
1038 A298 25f peach & multi .55 .25
1039 A298 30f cream & multi .55 .25
1040 A298 45f gray blue & multi .90 .40
1041 A298 50f white & multi .90 .40
    Nos. 1038-1041 (4) 2.90 1.30

Souvenir Sheet
Imperf
1042 A298 150f emer & multi 6.75 6.75

Mosul Spring Festival — A299

1982, Apr. 15   *Litho.*   *Perf. 11½x12*
1043 A299 25f Birds 1.10 .25
1044 A299 30f Girl .70 .25
1045 A299 45f like 25f 1.10 .50
1046 A299 50f like 30f 1.10 .40
    Nos. 1043-1046 (4) 4.00 1.40

Intl. Workers' Day — A300

1982, May 1   *Perf. 12½*
1047 A300 25f multicolored .45 .25
1048 A300 45f multicolored .70 .30
1049 A300 50f multicolored .75 .40
    Nos. 1047-1049 (3) 1.90 .95

14th World Telecommunications Day — A301

1982, May 17   *Photo.*   *Perf. 13x13½*
1050 A301 5f multicolored .25 .25
1051 A301 45f multicolored .70 .35
1052 A301 100f multicolored 1.60 .90
    Nos. 1050-1052 (3) 2.55 1.50

10th Anniv. of Oil Nationalization — A302

1982, June 1   *Litho.*   *Perf. 12½*
1053 A302 5f Oil gusher .25 .25
1054 A302 25f like 5f .60 .25
1055 A302 45f Statue 1.25 .25
1056 A302 50f like 45f 1.50 .35
    Nos. 1053-1056 (4) 3.60 1.10

Martyrs' Day — A303

1981, Dec. 1   *Photo.*   *Perf. 14*
1057 A303 45f multicolored .45 .35
1058 A303 50f multicolored .55 .45
1059 A303 120f multicolored 1.50 1.00
    Nos. 1057-1059,O339A-O339C (6) 9.50 3.80

Women's Day — A304

1982, Mar. 4   *Litho.*   *Perf. 12½x13*
1060 A304 25f multicolored .55 .25
1061 A304 45f multicolored .90 .40
1062 A304 50f multicolored .90 .50
    Nos. 1060-1062 (3) 2.35 1.15

A305

1982, Apr. 12   *Perf. 12½*
1063 A305 25f multicolored .55 .25
1064 A305 45f multicolored .90 .30
1065 A305 50f multicolored .90 .30
    Nos. 1063-1065 (3) 2.35 .85
    Arab Postal Union, 30th anniv.

A305a

30f, 50f, Nuclear power emblem, lion. 45f, 120f, Bomb aimed at egg.

1982, June 7   *Photo.*   *Perf. 14*
1065A A305a 30f ol grn & multi .60 .30
1065B A305a 45f rose & multi 1.00 .35
1065C A305a 50f yel & multi 1.10 .50
1065D A305a 120f pur & multi 2.40 1.50
    Nos. 1065A-1065D (4) 5.10 2.65
    First anniv. of attack on nuclear power reactor.

July Festivals — A306

1982, July 17   *Photo.*   *Perf. 14½x14*
1066 A306 25f multicolored .50 .25
1067 A306 45f multicolored .70 .25
1068 A306 50f multicolored .80 .30
    Nos. 1066-1068 (3) 2.00 .80

Lacerta Viridis — A307

30f, Vipera aspis. 45f, Lacerta viridis, diff. 50f, Natrix tessellata.

1982, Aug. 20   *Litho.*   *Perf. 12½*
1069 A307 25f shown 2.25 .75
1070 A307 30f multi 2.25 .75
1071 A307 45f multi 3.00 1.10
1072 A307 50f multi 3.50 1.50
    Nos. 1069-1072 (4) 11.00 4.10

7th Non-aligned Countries Conference, Baghdad, Sept. — A308

No. 1073, Tito. No. 1074, Nehru. No. 1075, Nasser. No. 1076, Kwame Nkrumah. No. 1077, Hussein.

1982, Sept. 6   *Photo.*   *Perf. 13x13½*
1073 A308 50f multicolored .85 .40
1074 A308 50f multicolored .85 .40
1075 A308 50f multicolored .85 .40
1076 A308 50f multicolored .85 .40
1077 A308 100f multicolored 1.90 .55
    Nos. 1073-1077 (5) 5.30 2.15

TB Bacillus Centenary A309

1982, Oct. 1   *Perf. 14x14½*
1078 A309 20f multicolored .65 .25
1079 A309 50f multicolored 1.10 .30
1080 A309 100f multicolored 2.10 .85
    Nos. 1078-1080 (3) 3.85 1.40

1982 World Cup — A310

Designs: Various soccer players. 150f horiz.

1982, July 1   *Litho.*   *Perf. 11½x12*
1081 A310 5f multicolored .50 .25
1082 A310 45f multicolored 1.00 .45
1083 A310 50f multicolored 1.10 .50
1084 A310 100f multicolored 2.00 1.00
    Nos. 1081-1084 (4) 4.60 2.20

Souvenir Sheet
Perf. 12½
1085 A310 150f multicolored 4.00 4.00

13th UPU Day — A311

IRAQ

1982, Oct. 9   *Perf. 12x11½*
1086	A311	5f multicolored	.25	.25
1087	A311	45f multicolored	.70	.30
1088	A311	100f multicolored	1.60	.85
		Nos. 1086-1088 (3)	2.55	1.40

Musical Instruments — A312

5f, Drums. 10f, Zither. 35f, Stringed instrument. 100f, Lute.

1982, Nov. 15   *Perf. 12½x13*
1089	A312	5f multicolored	.25	.25
1090	A312	10f multicolored	.25	.25
1091	A312	35f multicolored	.85	.35
1092	A312	100f multicolored	2.75	.95
		Nos. 1089-1092 (4)	4.10	1.80

Birth Anniv. of Mohammed — A313

Baghdad and Medina Mosque views.

1982, Dec. 27   *Litho.*   *Perf. 12x11½*
1093	A313	25f multicolored	.25	.25
1094	A313	30f multicolored	.40	.25
1095	A313	45f multicolored	.55	.25
1096	A313	50f multicolored	.70	.35
		Nos. 1093-1096 (4)	1.90	1.10

Nos. 1034-1036 Surcharged

1983, May 15   *Litho.*   *Perf. 12x12½*
1097	A297	60f on 50f multi	1.25	.50
1098	A297	70f on 45f multi	1.75	.60
1099	A297	160f on 120f multi	4.50	2.00
		Nos. 1097-1099 (3)	7.50	3.10

July Festivals — A314

1983, July 17   *Litho.*   *Perf. 14½x14*
1100	A314	30f multicolored	.45	.25
1101	A314	60f multicolored	1.00	.35
1102	A314	70f multicolored	1.40	.45
		Nos. 1100-1102 (3)	2.85	1.05

Local Flowers — A315

1983, June 15   *Photo.*   *Perf. 15x14*
         Border Color
1103	A315	10f shown, light blue	.25	.25
1104	A315	20f Flowers, diff., pale yellow	.45	.25
1105	A315	30f like 10f, yellow	.55	.25
1106	A315	40f like 20f, gray	.95	.40
1107	A315	50f like 10f, pale green	1.10	.50
1108	A315	100f like 20f, pink	2.25	1.00
a.		Bklt. pane of 6, #1103-1108	9.75	
		Nos. 1103-1108 (6)	5.55	2.65

Nos. 1103-1108 issued in booklets only.
For surcharges see Nos. 1501-1506.

Battle of Thi Qar — A317   A316

1983, Oct. 30   *Photo.*   *Perf. 12½x13*
1109	A316	20f silver & multi	.25	.25
1110	A317	50f silver & multi	.75	.30
1111	A316	60f gold & multi	1.00	.35
1112	A317	70f gold & multi	1.10	.40
		Nos. 1109-1112 (4)	3.10	1.30

World Communications Year — A318

25f, 70f show emblem and hexagons.

1983, Oct. 20   *Photo.*   *Perf. 11½x12*
1113	A318	5f brt yel grn & multi	.25	.25
1114	A318	25f rose lil & multi	.30	.25
1115	A318	60f brt org yel & multi	.90	.35
1116	A318	70f brt bl vio & multi	1.10	.40
		Nos. 1113-1116 (4)	2.55	1.25

Souvenir Sheet
| 1117 | A318 | 200f apple grn & multi | 4.25 | 4.25 |

Baghdad Intl. Fair — A319

1983, Nov. 1   *Photo.*   *Perf. 12½*
1118	A319	60f multicolored	.75	.40
1119	A319	70f multicolored	.95	.50
1120	A319	160f multicolored	2.10	1.25
		Nos. 1118-1120 (3)	3.80	2.15

Symbolic "9" — A320

9th Natl. Congress of Arab Baath Socialist Party: 30f, 70f, Symbols of development. 60f, 100f, Torch, eagle, globe, open book.

1983, Nov. 10   *Photo.*   *Perf. 14*
1121	A320	30f multicolored	.35	.25
1122	A320	60f multicolored	.75	.40
1123	A320	70f multicolored	.95	.50
1124	A320	100f multicolored	1.40	.70
		Nos. 1121-1124 (4)	3.45	1.85

Festival Crowd A321

Various Paintings: No. 1126, Men hauling boat, vert. No. 1127,

1983, Nov. 20   *Litho.*   *Perf. 12½*
1125	A321	60f shown	1.50	.60
1126	A321	60f multicolored	1.50	.60
1127	A321	60f Decorations	1.50	.60
1128	A321	70f Village	2.00	.85
1129	A321	70f Crowd	2.00	.85
		Nos. 1125-1129 (5)	8.50	3.50

Sabra and Shattela Palestinian Refugee Camp Massacre — A322

Various Victims.

1983, Nov. 29   *Perf. 11½x12*
1130	A322	10f multicolored	.25	.25
1131	A322	60f multicolored	1.00	.40
1132	A322	70f multicolored	1.25	.50
1133	A322	160f multicolored	2.75	1.25
		Nos. 1130-1133 (4)	5.25	2.40

Pres. Hussein, Map — A323

1983   *Photo.*   *Perf. 13½x13*
1134	A323	60f multicolored	.75	.30
1135	A323	70f multicolored	1.00	.50
1136	A323	250f multicolored	3.50	2.00
		Nos. 1134-1136 (3)	5.25	2.80

Hussein as head of Al Baath Party, 4th anniv.

Modern Building — A324

Various buildings.

1983, Dec. 31   *Litho.*   *Perf. 14*
1137	A324	60f multicolored	.70	.40
1138	A324	90f multicolored	.90	.50
1139	A324	160f multicolored	2.25	1.10
1140	A324	200f multicolored	2.75	1.40
		Nos. 1137-1140,O340-O341 (6)	8.60	4.55

Medical Congress Emblem — A325

1984, Mar. 10   *Perf. 13x12½*
1141	A325	60f multicolored	.80	.40
1142	A325	70f multicolored	1.00	.50
1143	A325	200f multicolored	3.00	1.40
		Nos. 1141-1143 (3)	4.80	2.30

25th Intl. Congress of Military Medicine and Pharmacy, Baghdad, Mar. 10-15.

Pres. Hussein's Birthday — A326

Various portraits of Hussein.

1984, Apr. 28   *Litho.*   *Perf. 12½x13*
1144	A326	60f multicolored	.65	.30
1145	A326	70f multicolored	.70	.40
1146	A326	160f multicolored	2.10	1.25
1147	A326	200f multicolored	2.50	1.60
		Nos. 1144-1147 (4)	5.95	3.55

Souvenir Sheet
Imperf
| 1148 | A326 | 250f multicolored | 6.50 | 6.50 |

Gold ink on Nos. 1144-1147 and dark green ink in "margin" of No. 1148 was applied by a thermographic process, producing a raised effect. No. 1148 has perf. 12½x13 label picturing Pres. Hussein.

1984 Summer Olympics, Los Angeles — A327

1984, Aug. 12   *Litho.*   *Perf. 12x11½*
1149	A327	50f Boxing	.70	.50
1150	A327	60f Weight lifting	.90	.50
1151	A327	70f like 50f	1.10	.60
1152	A327	100f like 60f	1.60	.90

Size: 80x60mm
Imperf
| 1153 | A327 | 200f Soccer | 5.00 | 5.00 |
| | | Nos. 1149-1153 (5) | 9.30 | 7.50 |

Nos. 1153 contains one 32x41mm perf. 12½ label within the stamp.

A328

50f, 70f, Pres. Hussein, flaming horses heads, map. 60f, 100f, Abstract of woman, sapling, rifle. 200f, Shield, heraldic eagle.

1984, Sept. 22   *Perf. 11½x12*
1154	A328	50f multicolored	.55	.30
1155	A328	60f multicolored	.70	.40
1156	A328	70f multicolored	.85	.50
1157	A328	100f multicolored	1.25	.65

Size: 80x60mm
Imperf
| 1158 | A328 | 200f multicolored | 3.50 | 3.50 |
| | | Nos. 1154-1158 (5) | 6.85 | 5.35 |

Battle of Qadisiya. No. 1158 contains one 32x41mm perf. 12½ label within the stamp.

A329

Martyrs' Day: 50f, 70f, Natl. flag as flame. 60f, 100f, Woman holding rifle, medal.

1984, Dec. 1   *Perf. 13½*
1159	A329	50f multicolored	.45	.35
1160	A329	60f multicolored	.65	.35
1161	A329	70f multicolored	.75	.40
1162	A329	100f multicolored	1.00	.65
		Nos. 1159-1162 (4)	2.85	1.75

For overprints see Nos. O342-O345.

Pres. Hussein's Visit to Al-Mustansiriyah University, 5th Anniv. — A330

1985, Apr. 2   *Photo.*   *Perf. 12x11½*
1163	A330	60f dk bl gray & dk pink	.55	.35
1164	A330	70f myr grn & dk pink	.65	.40
1165	A330	250f blk & dk pink	2.50	1.40
		Nos. 1163-1165 (3)	3.70	2.15

Iraqi Air Force, 54th Anniv. — A331

10f, 160f, Pres. Hussein, fighter planes, pilot's wings. 60f, 70f, 200f, Planes, flag, "54," horiz.

Perf. 13x12½, 13½ (60f, 70f)
1985, Apr. 22   *Litho.*
1166	A331	10f multicolored	.30	.25
1167	A331	60f multicolored	1.50	.75
1168	A331	70f multicolored	1.60	.75
1169	A331	160f multicolored	4.00	2.00
		Nos. 1166-1169 (4)	7.40	3.75

Souvenir Sheet
Perf. 12½
| 1170 | A331 | 200f multicolored | 6.75 | 6.75 |

Pres. Hussein, 48th Birthday — A332

30f, 70f, Pres. Hussein, sunflower. 60f, 100f, Pres., candle & flowers. 200f, Flowers & text.

IRAQ

1985, Apr. 28 — Perf. 13½
1171	A332	30f multicolored	.35	.25
1172	A332	60f multicolored	.65	.30
1173	A332	70f multicolored	.75	.40
1174	A332	100f multicolored	1.10	.60
		Nos. 1171-1174 (4)	2.85	1.55

Souvenir Sheet
Perf. 13x12½
1175	A332	200f multicolored	4.50	4.50

Posts and Telecommunications Development Program — A333

Designs: 20f, 60f, Graph, woman in modern office. 50f, 70f, Satellite dish and graphs.

1985, June 30 — Perf. 12½
1176	A333	20f multicolored	.35	.25
1177	A333	50f multicolored	.70	.30
1178	A333	60f multicolored	.70	.30
1179	A333	70f multicolored	.95	.50
		Nos. 1176-1179 (4)	2.70	1.35

Battle of Qadisiya — A334

Designs: 10f, 60f, Shown. 20f, 70f, Pres. Hussein, Al-Baath Party emblem. 200f, Dove, natl. flag as shield, soldier.

1985, Sept. 4 — Perf. 11½x12
1180	A334	10f multicolored	.25	.25
1181	A334	20f multicolored	.25	.25
1182	A334	60f multicolored	.90	.40
1183	A334	70f multicolored	1.10	.65
		Nos. 1180-1183 (4)	2.50	1.55

Souvenir Sheet
Perf. 12x12½
1184	A334	200f multicolored	3.25	3.25

No. 1184 contains one stamp 30x45mm.

Solar Energy Research Center — A335

1985, Sept. 19 — Perf. 13½
1185	A335	10f multicolored	.25	.25
1186	A335	50f multicolored	.95	.40
1187	A335	100f multicolored	1.90	.95
		Nos. 1185-1187 (3)	3.10	1.60

UN Child Survival Campaign — A336

Designs: 10f, 50f, Stop Polio Campaign. 15f, 100f, Girl, infant.

1985, Oct. 10
1188	A336	10f multicolored	.25	.25
1189	A336	15f multicolored	.25	.25
1190	A336	50f multicolored	.75	.30
1191	A336	100f multicolored	1.50	.85
		Nos. 1188-1191 (4)	2.75	1.65

Al Sharif, Poet, Death Millennium — A337

1985, Oct. 20
1192	A337	30f multicolored	.25	.25
1193	A337	50f multicolored	.55	.30
1194	A337	100f multicolored	1.25	.80
		Nos. 1192-1194 (3)	2.05	1.35

UN, 40th Anniv. — A338

1985, Oct. 24
1195	A338	10f multicolored	.25	.25
1196	A338	40f multicolored	.55	.25
1197	A338	100f multicolored	1.40	.75
		Nos. 1195-1197 (3)	2.20	1.25

Death of Iraqi Prisoners of War in Iran — A339

30f, 100f, Knife, Geneva Convention declaration, red crescent, red cross. 70f, 200f, POWs, gun shell, natl. flag, cherub & dove.

1985, Nov. 10 — Perf. 14
1198	A339	30f multicolored	.35	.25
1199	A339	70f multicolored	.75	.40
1200	A339	100f multicolored	1.10	.65
1201	A339	200f multicolored	2.50	1.25

Size: 110x80mm
Imperf
1202	A339	250f multicolored	5.00	5.00
		Nos. 1198-1202 (5)	9.70	7.55

No. 1202 contains 2 perf. 14 labels similar to 100f and 200f designs within the stamp.

Intl. Palestinian Solidarity Day — A341

1985, Nov. 29 — Litho. Perf. 13½
1207	A341	10f multicolored	.25	.25
1208	A341	50f multicolored	.95	.40
1209	A341	100f multicolored	2.10	.95
		Nos. 1207-1209 (3)	3.30	1.60

Martyrs' Day — A342

1985, Dec. 1 — Perf. 11½x12
1210	A342	10f multicolored	.25	.25
1211	A342	40f multicolored	.45	.25
1212	A342	100f multicolored	1.40	.75
		Nos. 1210-1212 (3)	2.10	1.25

Intl. Youth Year — A343

IYY emblem and: 40f, 100f, Soldier holding flag. 50f, 200f, Youths, flag. 250f, Flag, cogwheel, rifle muzzle, symbols of industry.

1985, Dec. 12 — Litho. Perf. 11½x12
1213	A343	40f multicolored	.45	.25
1214	A343	50f multicolored	.65	.30
1215	A343	100f multicolored	1.40	.75
1216	A343	200f multicolored	2.75	2.00
		Nos. 1213-1216 (4)	5.25	3.30

Souvenir Sheet
Perf. 12x12½
1217	A343	250f multicolored	5.00	5.00

No. 1217 contains one stamp 30x45mm. Exists imperf.

Army Day — A344

Pres. Hussein, "6" and: 10f, 50f, Soldier, flowers, vert. 40f, 100f, Flag, cogwheel, rockets. 200f, Al-Baath Party emblem, rifle, waves.

1986, Jan. 6 — Perf. 11½x12, 12x11½
1218	A344	10f multicolored	.25	.25
1219	A344	40f multicolored	.65	.25
1220	A344	50f multicolored	.85	.30
1221	A344	100f multicolored	1.75	.95
		Nos. 1218-1221 (4)	3.50	1.75

Miniature Sheet
Perf. 12½x11½
1222	A344	200f multicolored	6.25	6.25

No. 1222 contains one stamp 52x37mm.

Women's Day — A345

Designs: 30f, 100f, Women in traditional and modern occupations, vert. 50f, 150f, Emblem, green flag, battle scene, grapes.

Perf. 11½x12, 12x11½

1986, Mar. 8 — Litho.
1223	A345	30f multicolored	.45	.25
1224	A345	50f multicolored	.65	.25
1225	A345	100f multicolored	1.40	.75
1226	A345	150f multicolored	2.25	1.00
		Nos. 1223-1226 (4)	4.75	2.30

Pres. Hussein, 49th Birthday — A346

Designs: 30f, 100f, Children greeting Pres. 50f, 150f, Portrait. 250f, Portrait, flag.

1986, Apr. 28 — Litho. Perf. 11½x12
1227	A346	30f multicolored	.45	.25
1228	A346	50f multicolored	.75	.25
1229	A346	100f multicolored	1.50	.45
1230	A346	150f multicolored	2.10	.65

Size: 80x60mm
Imperf
1231	A346	250f multicolored	5.00	5.00
		Nos. 1227-1231 (5)	9.80	6.60

Oil Nationalization Day, June 1 — A347

Designs: 10f, 100f, Symbols of industry, horiz. 40f, 150f, Oil well, pipeline to refinery.

Perf. 12x11½, 11½x12

1986, July 25 — Litho.
1232	A347	30f multicolored	.25	.25
1233	A347	40f multicolored	.55	.25
1234	A347	100f multicolored	1.50	.75
1235	A347	150f multicolored	2.10	1.25
		Nos. 1232-1235 (4)	4.40	2.50

Labor Day — A348

Designs: 10f, 100f, Laborer, cog wheel. 40f, 150f, May Day emblem.

1986, July 28 — Perf. 11½x12
1236	A348	10f multicolored	.25	.25
1237	A348	40f multicolored	.75	.25
1238	A348	100f multicolored	1.40	.65
1239	A348	150f multicolored	2.10	.95
		Nos. 1236-1239 (4)	4.50	2.10

Iraqi Air Force, 55th Anniv. — A349

Designs: 30f, 100f, Fighter plane, pilot's wings, natl. flag. 50f, 150f, Fighter planes. 250f, Medal, aircraft in flight.

1986, July 28 — Perf. 12x11½
1240	A349	30f multicolored	.70	.25
1241	A349	50f multicolored	1.40	.30
1242	A349	100f multicolored	2.75	1.40
1243	A349	150f multicolored	4.25	1.90

Size: 81x61mm
Imperf
1244	A349	250f multicolored	5.00	5.00
		Nos. 1240-1244 (5)	14.10	8.85

No. 1244 also exists perf.

July Festivals — A350

Pres. Hussein and: 20f, 100f, Flag. 30f, 150f, "17." 250f, Inscription, portrait inside medal of honor.

1986, July 29 — Perf. 11½x12
1245	A350	20f multicolored	.30	.25
1246	A350	30f multicolored	.40	.25
1247	A350	100f multicolored	1.50	.75
1248	A350	150f multicolored	2.25	1.25

Size: 81x61mm
Imperf
1249	A350	250f multicolored	4.00	4.00
		Nos. 1245-1249 (5)	8.45	6.50

1st Qadisiya Battle — A351

Designs: 20f, 70f, Warrior, shield, vert. 60f, 100f, Pres. Hussein, star, battle scene.

Perf. 13x13½, 13½x13

1986, Sept. 4 — Litho.
1250	A351	20f multicolored	.35	.25
1251	A351	60f multicolored	.80	.40
1252	A351	70f multicolored	.95	.50
1253	A351	100f multicolored	1.60	.65
		Nos. 1250-1253 (4)	3.70	1.80

Battle between the Arabs and Persian Empire.

Hussein's Battle of Qadisiya A352

30f, 100f, Pres. Hussein, soldiers saluting peace, vert. 40f, 150f, Pres., armed forces. 250f, Pres., soldiers, flags, military scenes.

Perf. 11½x12½, 12½x11½

1986, Sept. 4
1254	A352	30f multicolored	.90	.25
1255	A352	40f multicolored	1.25	.25
1256	A352	100f multicolored	2.50	.50
1257	A352	150f multicolored	4.25	.70

Size: 80x60mm
Imperf
1258	A352	250f multicolored	4.75	4.75
		Nos. 1254-1258 (5)	13.65	6.45

IRAQ

Intl. Peace Year — A353

50f, 150f, Dove, flag, G clef. 100f, Globe, dove, rifle. 200f, Emblem, flag, map, fist.

1986, Nov. 15   Litho.   *Perf. 11½x12*
1259	A353	50f lt blue & multi	.65	.25
1260	A353	100f grn & multi	1.10	.60
1261	A353	150f yel & multi	1.75	1.00
1262	A353	250f org & multi	2.50	1.40

Size: 80x69mm
Imperf
1263	A353	200f multi	2.75	2.75
		Nos. 1259-1263 (5)	8.75	6.00

Pres. Hussein
A354   A355
1264	A354	30f multicolored	.70	.25
1265	A355	30f multicolored	.70	.25
1266	A354	50f multicolored	.90	.25
1267	A355	50f multicolored	.90	.25
1268	A354	100f multicolored	1.90	.65
1269	A355	100f multicolored	1.90	.65
1270	A355	150f multicolored	2.40	.85
1271	A355	150f multicolored	2.60	.85
1272	A354	250f multicolored	4.75	1.40
1273	A354	350f multicolored	6.25	1.90
		Nos. 1264-1273 (10)	23.00	7.85

For overprints & surcharges see Nos. 1347-1348, 1455, 1480-1481, 1484, 1499-1500, 1518-1519.

Army Day — A356

40f, Hussein, armed forces.

1987, Jan. 6   Litho.   *Perf. 12x12½*
1274	A356	20f shown	.25	.25
1275	A356	40f multicolored	.35	.30
1276	A356	90f like 20f	.95	.90
1277	A356	100f like 40f	1.00	1.00
		Nos. 1274-1277 (4)	2.55	2.45

United Arab Shipping Co., 10th Anniv. (in 1986) — A357

50f, Cargo ship. 100f, Container ship Chaleb Ibn Al Waleeb. 200f, Loading cargo aboard the Waleeb.

1987, Apr. 3   Litho.   *Perf. 12½*
1278	A357	50f multi	.55	.50
1279	A357	100f multi	1.10	.60
1280	A357	150f like 50f	1.75	.85
1281	A357	250f like 100f	3.00	1.40

Size: 102x91mm
Imperf
1282	A357	200f multi	4.50	4.50
		Nos. 1278-1282 (5)	10.90	7.60

Arab Baath Socialist Party, 40th Anniv. — A358

40f, Hussein, "7," map.

1987, Apr. 7   Litho.   *Perf. 12x12½*
1283	A358	20f shown	.25	.25
1284	A358	40f multicolored	.35	.30
1285	A358	90f like 20f	.95	.90
1286	A358	100f like 40f	1.00	1.00
		Nos. 1283-1286 (4)	2.55	2.45

Pres. Hussein's 50th Birthday — A359

1987, Apr. 28   *Perf. 12½x12*
1287	A359	20f shown	.25	.25
1288	A359	40f Portrait	.35	.30
1289	A359	90f like 20f	.95	.90
1290	A359	100f like 40f	1.10	1.00
		Nos. 1287-1290 (4)	2.65	2.45

July Festivals — A360

20f, Hussein, star, flag, horiz.

1987, July 17   *Perf. 12½x12, 12x12½*
1291	A360	20f multi	.25	.25
1292	A360	40f shown	.35	.30
1293	A360	90f like 20f, horiz.	.95	.90
1294	A360	100f like 40f	1.00	1.00
		Nos. 1291-1294 (4)	2.55	2.45

UNICEF, 40th Anniv. — A361

1987, Oct. 4   *Perf. 12x12½, 12x12½*
1295	A361	20f shown	.25	.25
1296	A361	40f "40," horiz.	.35	.30
1297	A361	90f like 20f	.95	.90
1298	A361	100f like 40f, horiz.	1.00	1.00
		Nos. 1295-1298 (4)	2.55	2.45

Census Day — A362

30f, Graph, Arabs, diff.

1987, Nov. 1   *Perf. 12x11½*
1299	A362	20f shown	.25	.25
1300	A362	30f multicolored	.35	.25
1301	A362	50f like 30f	.55	.35
1302	A362	500f like 20f	5.25	4.00
		Nos. 1299-1302 (4)	6.40	4.85

Army Day — A363

20f, "6," Hussein, troops, vert.

Perf. 11½x12, 12x11½

1988, Jan. 6   Litho.
1303	A363	20f multicolored	.25	.25
1304	A363	30f shown	.25	.25
1305	A363	50f like 20f, vert.	.55	.25
1306	A363	150f like 30f	1.60	.60
		Nos. 1303-1306 (4)	2.65	1.35

Art Day — A364

30f, Hussein, rainbow, gun barrel, music. 150f, Notes, instruments, floral ornament.

1988, Jan. 8   Litho.   *Perf. 11½x12*
1307	A364	20f shown	.35	.25
1308	A364	30f multicolored	.50	.30
1309	A364	50f like 20f	.70	.35
1310	A364	100f like 30f	1.25	.40

Size: 60x80mm
Imperf
1311	A364	150f multicolored	3.50	3.50
		Nos. 1307-1311 (5)	6.30	4.80

A365

20f, "8," troops, Hussein, horiz. 30f, "8," Hussein, eagle.

1988, Feb. 8   *Perf. 11½x12, 12x11½*
1312	A365	20f multicolored	.35	.25
1313	A365	30f multicolored	.45	.25
1314	A365	50f like 20f, horiz.	.65	.35
1315	A365	150f like 30f	2.10	.65
		Nos. 1312-1315 (4)	3.55	1.50

Popular Army, 18th anniv. (20f, 50f); Feb. 8th Revolution, 25th anniv. (30f, 150f).

Al-Baath Arab Socialist Party, 50th Anniv. — A366

20f, Flag, grain, convention, horiz.

1988, Apr. 7   *Perf. 12x12½, 12½x12*
1316	A366	20f multicolored	.35	.25
1317	A366	30f shown	.45	.30
1318	A366	50f like 20f, horiz.	.65	.30
1319	A366	150f like 30f	2.10	.60
		Nos. 1316-1319 (4)	3.55	1.45

President Hussein, 51st Birthday — A367

30f, Hussein, 3 hands, flowers. 150f, Sun, Hussein, heart, flowers.

1988, Apr. 28   *Perf. 12x12½*
1320	A367	20f shown	.40	.30
1321	A367	30f multicolored	.50	.40
1322	A367	50f like 20f	.75	.40
1323	A367	100f like 50f	1.50	.60

Size: 90x99mm
Imperf
1324	A367	150f multicolored	4.50	4.50
		Nos. 1320-1324 (5)	7.65	6.20

World Health Organization, 40th Anniv. — A368

20f, WHO anniv. emblem, horiz.

1988, June 1   *Perf. 12½x12, 12x12½*
1325	A368	20f multicolored	.35	.25
1326	A368	40f shown	.45	.30
1327	A368	90f like 20f, horiz.	1.25	.40
1328	A368	100f like 40f	1.40	.40
		Nos. 1325-1328 (4)	3.45	1.35

Regional Marine Environment Day, Apr. 4 — A369

40f, Flag in map, fish, horiz.

1988, Apr. 24   *Perf. 12x12½, 12x12*
1329	A369	20f shown	.45	.25
1330	A369	40f multicolored	.45	.30
1331	A369	90f like 20f	1.25	.40
1332	A369	100f like 40f, horiz.	1.25	.40
		Nos. 1329-1332 (4)	3.40	1.35

Shuhada School Victims Memorial — A370

A371

40f, Girl caught in explosion, horiz.

1988, June 1   *Perf. 11½x12, 12x11½*
1333	A370	20f shown	.35	.25
1334	A370	40f multicolored	.45	.30
1335	A370	90f like 20f	1.25	.40
1336	A370	100f like 40f, horiz.	1.40	.40
		Nos. 1333-1336 (4)	3.45	1.35

Souvenir Sheet
Perf. 12½
1337	A371	150f red, blk & brt grn	3.00	3.00

Pilgrimage to Mecca — A372

1988, July 24   Litho.   *Perf. 13½*
1338	A372	90f multicolored	1.25	.40
1339	A372	100f multicolored	1.50	.60
1340	A372	150f multicolored	2.25	.70
		Nos. 1338-1340 (3)	5.00	1.70

Basra, 1350th Anniv. — A373

1988, Oct. 22   *Perf. 12x11½*
1341	A373	100f multicolored	1.40	.60

Natl. Flag, Grip on Lightning — A374

Pres. Hussein, Natl. Flag — A375

IRAQ

90f, Map, Hussein, desert.

1988, July 17   *Perf. 12x12½*
1342	A374	50f shown	.75	.40
1343	A374	90f multicolored	1.40	.50
1344	A374	100f like 50f	1.50	.50
1345	A374	150f like 90f	2.00	.60

Size: 90x70mm
Imperf
| 1346 | A375 | 250f shown | 6.00 | 4.50 |
| | | Nos. 1342-1346 (5) | 11.65 | 6.50 |

July Festivals and 9th anniv. of Pres. Hussein's assumption of office.

Nos. 1272-1273 Overprinted

1988, Aug. 7   *Litho.*   *Perf. 12½x12*
| 1347 | A354 | 250f multicolored | 6.00 | 2.00 |
| 1348 | A354 | 350f multicolored | 8.50 | 4.00 |

Victory.

Navy Day — A376

90f, Map, boats. 250f, Emblem, Pres. Hussein decorating officers.

1988, Aug. 12   *Perf. 12x12½*
1349	A376	50f shown	1.10	.40
1350	A376	90f multi	2.00	.60
1351	A376	100f like 50f	2.25	.85
1352	A376	150f like 90f	3.50	1.00

Size: 91x70mm
Imperf
| 1353 | A376 | 250f multi | 9.00 | 9.00 |
| | | Nos. 1349-1353 (5) | 17.85 | 11.85 |

1988 Summer Olympics, Seoul — A377

100f, Boxing, character trademark. 150f, Flag, emblems. 500f, Emblem, trademark, Hussein, trophy.

1988, Sept. 19   *Perf. 12x12½*
| 1354 | A377 | 100f multi | 2.25 | .80 |
| 1355 | A377 | 150f multi | 3.50 | 1.10 |

Size: 101x91mm
Imperf
| 1356 | A377 | 500f multi | 17.00 | 17.00 |
| | | Nos. 1354-1356 (3) | 22.75 | 18.90 |

Liberation of Fao — A378

500f, Hussein, text.

1988, Sept. 1   *Perf. 12x11½*
| 1357 | A378 | 100f multicolored | 2.00 | .60 |
| 1358 | A378 | 150f multicolored | 3.00 | .95 |

Size: 60x80mm
Imperf
| 1359 | A378 | 500f multicolored | 16.50 | 16.50 |
| | | Nos. 1357-1359 (3) | 21.50 | 18.05 |

Mosul A379   Baghdad A380

Ancient cities: 50f, Fortress. 150f, Astrolabe, modern architecture.

1988, Oct. 22   *Perf. 12x11½, 11½x12*
| 1360 | A379 | 50f multicolored | .95 | .25 |
| 1361 | A380 | 150f multicolored | 3.00 | .95 |

Al-Hussein Missile — A381

500f, Hussein, map, missile.

1988, Sept. 10   *Perf. 11½x12*
| 1362 | A381 | 100f multicolored | 1.40 | .50 |
| 1363 | A381 | 150f multicolored | 2.25 | .70 |

Size: 80x60mm
Imperf
| 1364 | A381 | 500f multicolored | 10.00 | 10.00 |
| | | Nos. 1362-1364 (3) | 13.65 | 11.20 |

2nd Intl. Festival, Babylon — A382

1988, Sept. 30   *Perf. 11½x12*
| 1365 | A382 | 100f multicolored | 1.40 | .60 |
| 1366 | A382 | 150f multicolored | 2.00 | .70 |

Size: 60x80mm
Imperf
| 1367 | A382 | 500f Medallions | 8.50 | 8.50 |
| | | Nos. 1365-1367 (3) | 11.90 | 9.80 |

Victorious Iraq — A383

1988, Aug. 8   *Litho.*   *Perf. 12x11½*
1368	A383	50f multicolored	6.00	6.00
1369	A383	100f multicolored	10.00	10.00
1370	A383	150f multicolored	14.50	14.50
		Nos. 1368-1370 (3)	30.50	30.50

Birthday of Mohammed — A384

1988, Oct. 23   *Litho.*   *Perf. 11½x12*
1371	A384	100f multicolored	1.50	.60
1372	A384	150f multicolored	2.00	.90
1373	A384	1d multicolored	14.00	5.25
		Nos. 1371-1373 (3)	17.50	6.75

Martyrs' Day — A385

1988, Dec. 1   *Litho.*   *Perf. 13½*
1374	A385	100f multicolored	1.00	.40
1375	A385	150f multicolored	1.90	.75
1376	A385	500f multicolored	6.50	2.00
		Nos. 1374-1376 (3)	9.40	3.15

Police Day — A386

1989, Jan. 9   *Litho.*   *Perf. 12x11½*
1377	A386	50f multicolored	.60	.40
1378	A386	100f multicolored	1.40	.45
1379	A386	150f multicolored	2.00	.90
		Nos. 1377-1379 (3)	4.00	1.75

Postal Savings Bank — A387   a

1988   *Litho.*   *Perf. 11½x12*
| 1380 | A387 | 50f shown | 1.60 | .80 |

Size: 23½x25mm
Perf. 13½x13
1381	A387(a)	100f multi	6.25	3.00
1382	A387(a)	150f multi	6.75	3.25
		Nos. 1380-1382 (3)	14.60	7.05

Nos. 1381-1382 have a line of Arabic at the top.
Nos. 1381-1382 without overprint are postal savings stamps.
For surcharges see Nos. 1507-1510, 1512-1514.

Arab Cooperation Council — A388

1989, Feb. 12   *Litho.*   *Perf. 12x11½*
| 1383 | A388 | 100f shown | 1.40 | .40 |
| 1384 | A388 | 150f Statesmen, diff. | 2.00 | .70 |

52nd Birthday of Pres. Hussein — A392

1989, Apr. 28   *Litho.*   *Perf. 12x11½*
| 1392 | A392 | 100f multicolored | 1.25 | .50 |
| 1393 | A392 | 150f multicolored | 1.75 | .50 |

Size: 60x81mm
Imperf
| 1394 | A392 | 250f Hussein, diff. | 6.00 | 6.00 |
| | | Nos. 1392-1394 (3) | 9.00 | 7.00 |

Fao Liberation, 1st Anniv. — A393

1989, Apr. 18   *Perf. 12x11½*
| 1395 | A393 | 100f multi | 1.25 | .50 |
| 1396 | A393 | 150f multi | 2.00 | .50 |

Size: 60x81mm
Imperf
| 1397 | A393 | 250f Calendar | 3.75 | 3.75 |
| | | Nos. 1395-1397 (3) | 7.00 | 4.75 |

Gen. Adnan Khairalla — A394

1989, May 6   *Litho.*   *Perf. 13½*
1398	A394	50f gold & multi	.80	.30
1399	A394	100f copper & multi	1.60	.40
1400	A394	150f silver & multi	2.40	.75
		Nos. 1398-1400 (3)	4.80	1.45

Gen. Adnan Khairalla (1940-1989), deputy commander-in-chief of the armed forces and minister of defense.

Reconstruction of Basra — A395

1989, June 14
| 1401 | A395 | 100f multi | 1.60 | .40 |
| 1402 | A395 | 150f multi | 2.40 | .75 |

Reconstruction of Fao — A396

1989, June 25
| 1403 | A396 | 100f multi | 1.60 | .40 |
| 1404 | A396 | 150f multi | 2.40 | .75 |

Women — A397

1989, June 25   *Litho.*   *Perf. 11½x12*
1405	A397	100f yel & multi	1.25	.35
1406	A397	150f brt pink & multi	1.40	.55
1407	A397	1d brt blue & multi	12.00	3.75
1408	A397	5d white & multi	50.00	16.00
		Nos. 1405-1408 (4)	64.65	20.65

For surcharges see Nos. 1485-1486, 1511, 1522.

July Festivals — A398

1989, July 17   *Litho.*   *Perf. 12x12½*
1409	A398	50f multicolored	.65	.30
1410	A398	100f multicolored	1.25	.40
1411	A398	150f multicolored	2.10	.65
		Nos. 1409-1411 (3)	4.00	1.35

Election of Pres. Hussein, 10th anniv.

Family — A399

1989, July 19   *Perf. 13½*
1412	A399	50f multicolored	1.20	.45
1413	A399	100f multicolored	2.00	.75
1414	A399	150f multicolored	5.75	1.25
		Nos. 1412-1414 (3)	8.95	2.45

A400

IRAQ

Victory Day — A401

		1989, Aug. 8		**Perf. 12x12½**
1415	A400	100f multicolored	1.25	.40
1416	A400	150f multicolored	2.10	.65

Size: 71x91mm
Imperf

1417	A401	250f multicolored	4.25	4.25
		Nos. 1415-1417 (3)	7.60	5.30

Interparliamentary Union, Cent. — A402

		1989, Sept. 15		**Perf. 12½x12**
1418	A402	25f multicolored	.35	.25
1419	A402	100f multicolored	1.25	.40
1420	A402	150f multicolored	2.10	.65
		Nos. 1418-1420 (3)	3.70	1.30

Ancient Cities — A403

		1989, Oct. 15		**Perf. 11½x12**
1421	A403	100f Dhi Qar-ur	1.90	.60
1422	A403	100f Erbil	1.90	.60
1423	A403	100f An Najaf	1.90	.60
		Nos. 1421-1423 (3)	5.70	1.80

A404

Designs: 100f, Land, air and sea transport, diff. 150f, Modes of transport, flags, vert.

		1989, Oct. 21	**Perf. 12x11½, 11½x12**	
1424	A404	50f shown	1.25	.55
1425	A404	100f multicolored	2.60	.75
1426	A404	150f multicolored	4.00	1.10
		Nos. 1424-1426 (3)	7.85	2.40

5th Session of the Arab Ministers of transport council, Baghdad, Oct. 21.

Iraqi News Agency, 30th Anniv. — A405

		1989, Nov. 9		**Perf. 13½**
1427	A405	50f multicolored	.55	.30
1428	A405	100f multicolored	1.10	.40
1429	A405	150f multicolored	1.75	.65
		Nos. 1427-1429 (3)	3.40	1.35

Declaration of Palestinian State, 1st Anniv. — A406

50f, Palestinian uprising.

		1989, Nov. 15		**Perf. 12x12½**
1430	A406	25f shown	.25	.25
1431	A406	50f multicolored	.65	.30
1432	A406	100f like 25f	1.25	.40
1433	A406	150f like 50f	2.10	.60
		Nos. 1430-1433 (4)	4.25	1.55

Flowers — A407

25f, Viola sp. 50f, Antirrhinum majus. 100f, Hibiscus trionum. 150f, Mesembryanthemum sparkles.

		1989, Nov. 20		**Perf. 13½x13**
1434	A407	25f multi	.35	.35
1435	A407	50f multi	.75	.35
1436	A407	100f multi	1.50	.45
1437	A407	150f multi	2.40	.45
		Nos. 1434-1437 (4)	5.00	1.60

Miniature Sheet
Perf. 12½x11½

1438		Sheet of 4	9.50	9.50
a.	A407	25f like No. 1434	2.10	2.10
b.	A407	50f like No. 1435	2.10	2.10
c.	A407	100f like No. 1436	2.10	2.10
d.	A407	150f like No. 1437	2.10	2.10

No. 1438 has a continuous design. No. 1438 sold for 500f.
For overprints and surcharges see Nos. 1450-1451, 1456, 1516, 1524.

A408

		1989, Oct. 25	**Litho.**	**Perf. 13½**
1439	A408	100f multicolored	1.40	.40
1440	A408	150f multicolored	2.10	.65

Reconstruction of Fao.

A409

		1989, Dec. 4	**Litho.**	**Perf. 13½**
1441	A409	50f multicolored	.65	.30
1442	A409	100f multicolored	1.25	.40
1443	A409	150f multicolored	1.75	.65
		Nos. 1441-1443 (3)	3.65	1.35

Martyrs' Day.

Iraqi Red Crescent Soc. — A410

		1989, Dec. 10	**Litho.**	**Perf. 13½**
1444	A410	100f multicolored	.70	.35
1445	A410	150f multicolored	2.00	.80
1446	A410	500f multicolored	6.75	2.50
		Nos. 1444-1446 (3)	9.45	3.65

Arab Cooperation Council, 1st Anniv. — A411

		1990, Feb. 16	**Litho.**	**Perf. 13x13½**
1447	A411	50f yellow & multi	1.00	.50
1448	A411	100f orange & multi	2.75	.90

Size: 80x62mm
Imperf

1449	A411	250f blue & multi	7.50	7.50
		Nos. 1447-1449 (3)	11.25	8.90

For surcharge see No. 1523.

Nos. 1435, 1437 Ovptd.

		1990, May 28	**Litho.**	**Perf. 13½x13**
1450	A407	50f multicolored	1.40	.85
1451	A407	150f multicolored	4.25	2.50

Arab League Summit Conf., Baghdad.

End of Iran-Iraq War, 2nd Anniv. — A412

		1990, Aug. 30	**Litho.**	**Perf. 13½x13**
1452	A412	50f purple & multi		.80
1453	A412	100f blue & multi		1.60

Imperf
Size: 59x81mm

1454	A412	250f Saddam Hussein, dove		5.00

For surcharge see No. 1525.

The surcharged issues of 1992-97 have been extensively forged. Collectors are urged to purchase these stamps with certificates of authenticity or from expert sellers who can attest to their authenticity.

No. 1269 Surcharged

		1992(?)	**Litho.**	**Perf. 12½x12**
1455	A355	1d on 100f #1269		8.50

No. 1434 Surcharged

Type I

Type II

		1993, Aug. 1	**Litho.**	**Perf. 13½x13**
1456	A407	10d on 25f Type I		30.00
a.		Type II		40.00

No. RA23 Surcharged

		1992	**Photo.**	**Perf. 14**
1457	PT3	100f on 5f multi		3.00

Reconstruction of Iraq — A413

Designs: 250f, Satellite dish. 500f, Bridges. 750f, Power plant, horiz. 1d, Factory.

		1993, Sept.	**Photo.**	**Perf. 14**
1459	A413	250f red & multi		.85
1460	A413	500f blue & multi		1.50
1461	A413	750f yellow & multi		2.25
1462	A413	1d multicolored		3.00
		Nos. 1459-1462 (4)		7.60

Stamps of this issue may be poorly centered or have perforations running through the design.
For surcharge see No. 1526.

Peace Ship — A414

		1993	**Photo.**	**Perf. 14**
1463	A414	2d red & multi		2.50
1464	A414	5d green & multi		6.50

No. RA23 Surcharged

b c
d e
f g
h i
ia j

IRAQ

     k   l

     m   n

     o   p

     q   r

     s   t

1994-1996		Photo.	Perf. 14	
1465	PT3(b)	500f on 5f multi, ovpt. 17mm wide	40.00	
a.		Overprint 14½mm wide	3.00	
1466	PT3(c)	1d on 5f multi	1.25	
1467	PT3(d)	1d on 5f multi	6.50	
a.	PT3(e)	1d on 5f multi	12.50	
b.	PT3(f)	1d on 5f multi	2.00	
c.	PT3(g)	1d on 5f multi	2.00	
1468	PT3(h)	2d on 5f multi	17.50	
1469	PT3(i)	2d on 5f multi	2.10	
a.	PT3(ia)	2d on 5f multi	2.10	2.10
1470	PT3(j)	3d on 5f multi	2.00	
1471	PT3(k)	3d on 5f multi	2.00	
1472	PT3(l)	5d on 5f multi	2.00	
a.	PT3(m)	5d on 5f multi	1.50	
b.	PT3(n)	5d on 5f multi	12.50	
1473	PT3(o)	5d on 5f multi	6.50	
1474	PT3(p)	10d on 5f multi	2.00	
1475	PT3(q)	25d on 5f multi	8.50	
a.	PT3(r)	25d on 5f multi	12.50	
1476	PT3(s)	25d on 10d on 5f	5.00	
1477	PT3(t)	50d on 5f multi	10.00	

Issue dates: No. 1476, Feb. 1996; all others Feb. 5, 1994.

No. 1273 Surcharged

     u   v

1994, Apr. 28		Litho.	Perf. 12½x12
1480	A354(u)	5d on 350f #1273	7.00
1481	A354(v)	5d on 350f #1273	7.00
a.		Pair, #1480-1481	22.50

Alqa'id Two-Deck Bridge — A415

1994, July 17			Perf. 14
1482	A415	1d pink & multi	3.50
1483	A415	3d blue & multi	3.50
a.		Pair, #1482-1483	8.50

No. 1273 Surcharged

1994, Aug. 8			Perf. 12½x12
1484	A354	5d on 350f #1273	4.75

No. 1406 Surcharged

     w   x

1995, Jan. 2			Perf. 11½x12
1485	A397(w)	5d on 150f #1406	5.00
1486	A397(x)	5d on 150f #1406	5.00
a.		Pair	20.00

Baghdad Clock — A416

1995, Feb. 28			Perf. 11
1487	A416	7d blue & black	2.50

Size: 76x98mm

Imperf

| 1488 | A416 | 25d multicolored | 15.00 |

Saddam Tower — A417

1995, Mar. 12			Perf. 14
1489	A417	2d multicolored	1.00
1490	A417	5d multicolored	3.25
a.		Vert. pair, #1489-1490	4.50

Honoring Dead From Battle of Um Almariq (Mother of All Battles) A418

1995			Imperf.
1491	A418	100d multicolored	14.00

Saddam Hussein, 58th Birthday — A419

1995, Apr. 28			Imperf.
1492	A419	25d multicolored	16.00
1493	A419	25d multicolored	16.00

Design: No. 1492, Saddam seated, flowers & flag behind him, vert.

Saddam River Canal Project — A420

1995, July 17			Perf. 11
1494	A420	4d ol yel & blue	4.00
1495	A420	4d red & blue	4.00

Size: 97x57mm

Imperf

| 1496 | A420 | 25d multi, denom. in black | 13.50 |
| a. | | Denomination in red | 13.50 |

Embargo of Iraq — A421

1995, Aug. 6			Perf. 11
1497	A421	10d bl grn & rose lil	3.00

Size: 77x100mm

Imperf

| 1498 | A421 | 25d multicolored | 14.00 |

No. 1273 Surcharged

     y   z

1995, Oct. 15		Litho.	Perf. 12½x12
1499	A354(y)	25d on 350f #1273	3.00
1500	A354(z)	25d on 350f #1273	3.00
a.		Pair	20.00

Nos. 1103-1108 Surcharged

     aa   ab

1995(?)		Photo.	Perf. 15x14
1501	A315(aa)	25d on 10f #1103	2.00
1502	A315(ab)	100d on 20f #1104	8.00
1503	A315(aa)	25d on 30f #1105	2.00
1504	A315(ab)	100d on 40f #1106	8.00
1505	A315(aa)	25d on 50f #1107	2.00
1506	A315(ab)	100d on 100f #1108	8.00
a.		Bklt. pane of 6, #1501-1506	32.00

No. 1380, Postal Savings Stamps Similar to Type A387 Surcharged in Red or Black

     ac   ad

     ae

1995(?)		Litho.	Perf. 11½x12
		Size: 23½x25mm	
1507	A387(ac)	25d on 100f multi	2.00
1508	A387(ad)	25d on 150f blue & multi	2.00
1509	A387(ad)	50d on 250f yel & multi (R)	4.00
1510	A387(ae)	50d on 50f #1380	4.00

The 250f postal savings stamp was also overprinted in denominations of 500f, 2500f and 5000f. These were not issued and were demonitized Feb. 1, 1996. They were subsequently surcharged with new values and with a bar obliterating the original overprint. See Nos. 1512-1514.

No. 1406 Surcharged

1995(?)			
1511	A397	100d on 150f multi	5.00

Postal Savings Stamps Similar to Type A387 Surcharged in Red

     af   ag

     ah

1996		Litho.	Perf. 11½x12
		Size: 23½x25mm	
		On 250f Yellow & Multi	
1512	A387(af)	25d on 500d	6.00
1513	A387(ag)	25d on 5000d	5.00
1514	A387(ah)	50d on 2500d	10.00
		Nos. 1512-1514 (3)	21.00

A421a   A421b

Children, Bank — A421c

1996		Litho.	Perf. 13½
1514A	A421a	25d on 10f grn & multi	35.00
1514B	A421b	25d on 25f bl & multi	2.00
1514C	A421c	50d on 10f grn & multi	110.00

Children, Bank — A422

1996		Litho.	Perf. 13½
1515	A422	50d on 50f multi	3.00

No. 1515 without surcharge is a postal savings stamp.

No. 1435 Surcharged

1996			Perf. 13½x13
1516	A407	100d on 50f multi	6.50

No. O341 Surcharged

1996			Perf. 14
1517	A324	100d on 70f #O341	5.75

IRAQ

No. 1273 Surcharged

ak / al

	1996		Litho.	Perf. 12½x12
1517A	A354(ak)	25d on 350f		1.25
1519A	A354(al)	1000d on 350f		50.00

No. 1273 Surcharged in Blue or Black

ai / aj

	1996			Perf. 12½x12
1518	A354(ai)	250d on 350f (Bl)		7.50
1519	A354(aj)	350d on 350f		18.00

No. O345 Surcharged

	1996		Litho.	Perf. 13½
1519B	A329	100d on 60f		5.00

Battle of Um Al Maarik — A423

	1997, Feb. 13		Photo.	Perf. 11
1520	A423	25d blk, red & green		1.00
1521	A423	100d blue, red & grn		5.25
a.	Arabic word at right center reversed			20.00

No. 1406 Surcharged

	1997, Apr. 22		Litho.	Perf. 11½x12
1522	A397	25d on 150f #1406		4.25

Post Day.

No. 1448 Surcharged

	1997			Perf. 13x13½
1523	A411	25d on 100f #1448		2.00

Baath Party, 50th anniv.

No. 1450 Surcharged

	1997		Litho.	Perf. 13½
1524	A407	100d on 50f multi		45.00

No. 1452 Surcharged

	1997			Perf. 13½x13
1525	A412	100d on 50f multi		8.00

No. 1459 Surcharged

	1997			Perf. 14
1526	A413	25d on 250f multi		1.25

Science Day.

A424

Referendum Day: 250d, Saddam Hussein, map of Arab nations.

	1997			Perf. 14
1527	A424	25d shown		1.50
1527A	A424	100d multicolored		6.00

Imperf
Size: 91x77mm

| 1528 | A424 | 250d multicolored | 10.00 |

A425

Saddam Hussein and: 25d, 100d, No. 1531, Water irrigating trees, grain. No. 1532, Water pipeline, flowers, grain.

	1997, Dec. 19			Perf. 14
	Self-Adhesive (#1530)			
1529	A425	25d multicolored		1.00
1530	A425	100d multicolored		3.00

Imperf
Size: 68x81mm

| 1531 | A425 | 250d multicolored | 6.00 |

Size: 64x82mm

| 1532 | A425 | 250d multicolored | 6.00 |

Wafa'a Alqa'id project.

Saladin (1169-1250), Founder of Ayyubid Dynasty, Saddam Hussein — A426

	1998, Feb.		Litho.	Perf. 14
	Self-Adhesive			
1533	A426	25d multicolored		1.00
1534	A426	100d multicolored		3.00

Size: 79x67mm
Imperf

| 1535 | A426 | 250d multicolored | 18.00 |

Nos. 1533-1534 exist imperf. No. 1535 has water-activated gum.

New Year — A427

	1998, Mar. 21			Imperf.
1536	A427	250d Zinnias		9.00
1537	A427	250d Irises		9.00

1998 World Cup Soccer Championship, France — A428

	1998, June			Imperf.
1538	A428	250d shown		7.50

Size: 63x76mm

| 1539 | A428 | 250d Two players, vert. | 7.50 |

Souvenir Sheet

Arab Police & Security Leaders Conf., 25th Anniv. — A429

	1998, July 12		Litho.	Imperf.
1540	A429	250d multicolored		7.50

A430

"Zad" Day (Arabic Alphabet) — A431

	1998, Oct. 25			Perf. 14
1541	A430	25d multicolored		.50
1542	A431	100d multicolored		2.00

Flowers — A432

Designs: 25d, Chamomilla recutita. 50d, Helianthus annuus. 1000d, Carduus nutans.

	1998, Oct. 27			
1543	A432	25d multicolored		.40
1544	A432	50d brown leaves		.75
1545	A432	50d green leaves		—
1546	A432	1000d multicolored		8.50

Self-Adhesive

| 1547 | A432 | 25d like #1543 | 7.50 |

No. 1547 is printed on glossy paper.

A433 / Martyr's Day — A434

	1998, Dec. 1			
1548	A433	25d multicolored		.50
1549	A434	100d multicolored		1.75

Nos. 1548-1549 exist imperf.

Martyr's Day — A434a

	1998, Dec. 1		Litho.	Imperf.
1550	A434a	250d multicolored		5.00

Anthocharis Euphome — A435

	1998, Dec. 20			
1551	A435	100d Precis orithya		3.00
1552	A435	150d shown		4.50

Exist imperf. Value, set $15.

Intl. Conference on Tower of Babel and Ziggurat of Borsippa — A436

	1999, Jan. 23		Litho.	Perf. 14
1553	A436	25d multicolored		1.00
1554	A436	50d multicolored		2.00

Imperf
Size: 71x89mm

| 1555 | A436 | 250d multicolored | 9.00 |

Great Dam — A437

25d, Dam. 100d, Dam, Saddam Hussein.

	1999, Apr. 28			Perf. 14
1556	A437	25d multicolored		1.00

477

IRAQ

1557	A437 100d multicolored		2.50
Imperf			
Size: 70x92mm			
1558	A437 250d Like #1557		9.00

Saddamiya, Aththerthar City — A438

25d, Saddam Hussein, emblem. 100d, Al-Saddamiyah City. 250d, Clock tower.

1999, May 7 — **Perf. 14**
| 1559 | A438 | 25d multicolored | 1.00 |
| 1560 | A438 | 100d multicolored | 2.00 |

Imperf
Size: 92x70mm
| 1561 | A438 | 250d multicolored | 9.00 |

Saddam Hussein, 62nd Birthday — A439

1999, May 17 — **Perf. 14**
1562	A439	25d multicolored	.25
1563	A439	50d multicolored	.50
1564	A439	150d multicolored	1.75
1565	A439	500d multicolored	6.00
1566	A439	1000d multicolored	14.00
1567	A439	5000d multi, horiz.	55.00
	Nos. 1562-1567 (6)		77.50

1998 World Cup, France — A440

1999, July 17
| 1568 | A440 | 25d Two players | 1.75 |
| 1569 | A440 | 100d Goalie save, horiz. | 4.00 |

Honey Bees — A441

1999, Sept. 18
| 1570 | A441 | 25d brown & multi | 2.00 |
| 1571 | A441 | 50d black & multi | 3.00 |

Al Fat'h Day — A442

Saddam Hussein and: 25d, Eagle, flowers. 50d, People. 250d, Eagle, flag.

1999, Dec. 12 — **Litho.** — **Perf. 14**
| 1572-1573 | A442 | Set of 2 | 2.00 |

Imperf
Size: 93x71mm
| 1574 | A442 | 250d multi | 6.75 |

A443   A444

A445   **Jerusalem Day — A446**

2000, Feb. — **Perf. 14**
1575	A443	25d multi	1.00
1576	A444	50d multi	1.25
1577	A445	100d multi	2.50
1578	A446	150d multi	3.50
	Nos. 1575-1578 (4)		8.25

Imperf
Size: 93x71mm
| 1579 | A446 | 250d multi | 10.00 |

A447   **Saddam Hussein's Birthday — A448**

500d, Saddam Hussein, stars.

2000, May 17 — **Perf. 14**
| 1580 | A447 | 25d multi | .50 |
| 1581 | A448 | 50d multi | .75 |

Imperf
Size: 92x71mm
| 1582 | A448 | 500d multi | 9.00 |

Sculpture — A449

Text "July Festivals 2000": a, At right. b, At left. c, At bottom center on two lines. d, At lower left. e, At bottom center on 3 lines.

2000, July 12 — **Perf. 14**
| 1583 | | Horiz. strip of 5 | 2.00 |
| a.-e. | A449 25d Any single | | .35 |

Exists imperf. Value, strip $10.

Victory Day — A450

Designs: 25d, 250d, Saddam Hussein. 50d, Saddam Hussein, flag.

2000, Aug. 8 — **Perf. 14**
| 1584-1585 | A450 | Set of 2 | 2.50 |

Imperf
Size: 71x91mm
| 1586 | A450 | 250d multi | 4.50 |

Birds — A451

Designs: 25d, Anas platyrhynchos. 50d, Passer domesticus. 150d, Porphyrio poliocephalus. 500d, Carduelis carduelis.

2000, Aug. 28 — **Perf. 14**
| 1587-1589 | A451 | Set of 3 | 5.00 |

Imperf
Size: 93x71mm
| 1590 | A451 | 500d multi | 10.00 |

Prophet Mohammad's Birthday — A452

Designs: 25d, Green background. 50d, Tan background.

2000, Oct. 11 — **Perf. 14**
| 1591-1592 | A452 | Set of 2 | 2.00 |

A453   **Referendum Day — A454**

250d, Saddam Hussein, crowd.

2000, Oct. 15 — **Perf. 14**
| 1593 | A453 | 25d multi | .35 |
| 1594 | A454 | 50d multi | .75 |

Imperf
Size: 93x72mm
| 1595 | A453 | 250d multi | 4.50 |

Baytol Hikma, 1200th Anniv. — A455

2001, Jan. — **Perf. 14**
| 1596-1597 | A455 | Set of 2 | 1.50 |
| a. | Pair, #1596-1597 | | 4.50 |

A456   A457

Writing, 5th Millennium — A458

2001, Mar. — **Litho.** — **Perf. 14**
1598	A456	25d multi	.30
1599	A457	50d multi	.55
1600	A456	75d multi	.80
1601	A457	100d multi	1.10
1602	A458	150d multi	1.75
1603	A458	250d multi	2.75
	Nos. 1598-1603 (6)		7.25

Bombing of Al Amiriya Shelter, 10th Anniv. — A459

Designs: 25d, 150d, Mother, injured child, rescue workers. 50d, Doves, wreath, picture frames, vert.

2001, Mar. — **Perf. 14**
| 1604-1605 | A459 | Set of 2 | 1.50 |

Imperf
Size: 91x71mm
Without Gum
| 1606 | A459 | 150d multi | 4.00 |

Al Baath Party, 54th Anniv. — A460

Designs: 25d, People, torch. 50d, Al Baath Party founder Michel Aflaq, Saddam Hussein. 100d, Map of Middle East.

2001, Apr. 7 — **Perf. 14**
| 1607-1609 | A460 | Set of 3 | 2.00 |

Saddam Hussein's 64th Birthday — A461

Saddam Hussein: 25d, Seated, with flowers, vert. 50d, Seated. 100d, Seated, with people. 250d, Standing, with crowd.

2001, Apr. 28 — **Perf. 14**
| 1610-1612 | A461 | Set of 3 | 1.50 |

Imperf
Size: 89x69mm
Without Gum
| 1613 | A461 | 250d multi | 4.50 |

Fish — A462

Designs: 25d, Barbus sharpeyi. 50d, Barbus esocinus. 100d, Barbus xanthopterus. 150d, Pampus argenteus.

2001, Aug. 4 — **Perf. 14**
| 1614-1617 | A462 | Set of 4 | 5.00 |

Battle of Um Al Maarik, 10th Anniv. — A463

Frame color: 25d, Red. 100d, Black.

2001, Aug.
| 1618-1619 | A463 | Set of 2 | 1.25 |

Mammals — A464

Designs: 100d, Gazella subgutturosa. 250d, Lepus europaeus. 500d, Camelus dromedarius. 1000d, Various mammals.

2001, Aug. — **Perf. 14**
| 1620-1622 | A464 | Set of 3 | 7.50 |

Imperf
Size: 92x70mm
Without Gum
| 1623 | A464 | 1000d multi | 9.00 |

Nationalization of Oil Industries, 29th Anniv. — A465

Designs: 25d, Oil rig, workers, soldier, Iraqi flag. 50d, Oil rig, refinery, pipeline.

2001, Sept. 15 — **Litho.** — **Perf. 14**
| 1624-1625 | A465 | Set of 2 | 1.00 |

IRAQ

Support for Palestinians — A466

Designs: No. 1626, 25d, Saddam Hussein, map of Israel and Iraq. No. 1627, 25d, Dome of the Rock, Palestinian flag, gunman, vert. 50d, Dome of the Rock, Palestinian flag, gunman with arms raised, vert.

No. 1629, 250d, Dome of the Rock, Israeli tank and Palestinian rock-thrower. No. 1630, 250d, Dome of the Rock, doves, Palestinian flag and Mohammad J. Durra and father.

2001, Sept. 20
1626-1628 A466   Set of 3   1.25
Imperf
Size: 88x67mm
Without Gum
1629-1630 A466   Set of 2   5.00

2001 Youth Soccer World Cup — A467

Designs: 25d, Players, map of world. 50d, Map of Asia, player, trophy, vert.

2001, Oct. 7   *Perf. 14*
1631-1632 A467   Set of 2   1.00

Iraqi Claim of Depleted Uranium US Bombs Dropped on Iraqi Citizens — A468

Falling bombs and: No. 1633, 25d, Woman and children. No. 1634, 25d, No. 1636, 250d, Disfigured people. 50d, People, Iraqi flag, horiz.

2001, Nov.
1633-1635 A468   Set of 3   4.00
Imperf
Size: 70x91mm
Without Gum
1636 A468 250d multi   7.00

Army Day — A469

Designs: 25d, Iraqi flag, soldiers, airplanes, ship and tank. No. 1638, 50d, No. 1640, 250d, Monument, vert. 100d, Soldier, Iraqi flag, tank, vert.

2002, Jan. 6   *Perf. 14*
1637-1639 A469   Set of 3   3.50
Imperf
Size: 73x91mm
Without Gum
1640 A469 250d multi   3.50

Liberation of Fao — A470

Saddam Hussein and: 25d, Mosque. 100d, Soldier, map of Iraq, horiz.

2002, Apr. 17   *Perf. 14*
1641-1642 A470   Set of 2   1.50

February 8 Revolution, 39th Anniv. — A470a

February 8 Revolution, 39th Anniv. — A470b

2002, Feb. 8   Litho.   *Perf. 14*
1642A A470a 50d multi   8.00   —
1642B A470b 100d multi 12.00   —

Jerusalem Day — A471

Frame color: 25d, Blue. 50d, Yellow. 100d, Pink.

2002, Apr.
1643-1645 A471   Set of 3   2.00

Hegira, Year 1423 — A472

Designs: 25d, Mosques, Holy Kaaba. 50d, Minaret and mosque, vert. 75d, Bird, spider web.

2002, Apr.
1646-1648 A472   Set of 3   1.75

Bombardment of Al Amirya Shelter, 11th Anniv. — A473

Frame color: 25d, Black. 50d, Red.

2002, Apr.
1649-1650 A473   Set of 2   1.00

War Against Iraq, 11th Anniv. — A474

2002, Apr.
1651 A474 100d multi   1.75

Flowers — A475

Designs: 25d, Roses. 50d, Roses, diff. 150d, Poppies, carnations. 250d, Roses, diff.

2002, Apr.   *Perf. 14*
1652-1654 A475   Set of 3   3.50
Imperf
Size: 73x91mm
Without Gum
1655 A475 250d multi   5.00

Saddam Hussein's 65th Birthday — A476

Color of vignette frame and country name: 25d, Red. 50d, Purple. 75d, Green. 100d, Dark blue.

No. 1660, 250d, Saddam Huseein, hearts and flowers. No. 1661, 250d, Saddam Hussein with headdress.

2002, Apr. 28   *Perf. 14*
1656-1659 A476   Set of 4   2.75
Imperf
Size: 74x91mm
Without Gum
1660-1661 A476   Set of 2   6.00

Palestinian Unity — A477

2002   Litho.   *Perf. 14*
1662 A477 5000d multi   35.00

Mosques — A478

Designs: 25d, Sheikh Maroof Mosque. 50d, Al-Mouiz Mosque. 75d, Um Al Marik Mosque.

2002
1663-1665 A478   Set of 3   2.00

Post Day — A479

Air mail envelope and: 50d, Stamp with dove. 100d, Airplane, ship, train, map of world. 250d, Globe and dove.

2002
1666-1667 A479   Set of 2   2.00
Imperf
Size: 70x91mm
Without Gum
1668 A479 250d multi   4.50

2002 World Cup Soccer Championships, Japan and Korea — A480

World Cup, various players and background color of: 50d, Blue. 100d, Yellow. 150d, Red violet. 250d, Purple.

2002   *Perf. 14*
1669-1671 A480   Set of 3   3.00
Imperf
Size: 70x92mm
Without Gum
1672 A480 250d multi   4.00

Ancient Ships — A481

Various ships: 150d, 250d, 500d.

2002   *Perf. 14*
1673-1675 A481   Set of 3   9.00

Victory Day — A482

Frame color: 25d, Blue. 50d, Pink. 150d, Eagle, vert.

2002   *Perf. 14*
1676-1677 A482   Set of 2   1.75
Imperf
Size: 71x90mm
Without Gum
1678 A482 150d multi   4.00

A483   A484

A485   A486

Poets — A487

2002   Litho.   *Perf. 14*
1679 A483 25d multi   .35
1680 A484 50d multi   .50
1681 A485 75d multi   1.00
1682 A486 100d multi   1.25
    Nos. 1679-1682 (4)   3.10
Size: 70x92mm
Without Gum
1683 A487 150d multi   4.00

A488   A489

A490

IRAQ

Baghdad Day — A491

2002			Perf. 14
1684	A488	25d multi	.35
1685	A489	50d multi	.50
1686	A490	75d multi	1.00
	Nos. 1684-1686 (3)		1.85

Imperf
Size: 91x70mm
Without Gum

1687	A491	250d multi	5.00

Referendum Day — A492

Designs: 100d, 250d, Saddam Hussein, people, hands, heart and flowers. 150d, Fist, ballot box.

2002			Perf. 14
1688-1689	A492	Set of 2	2.50

Imperf
Size: 71x92mm
Without Gum

1690	A492	250d multi	2.75

Mammals — A493

Designs: 25d, Oryx leucoryx. 50d, Acionyx jubatus, vert. 75d, 250d, Panthera leo persica, vert. 100d, Castor fiber. 150d, Equus hemionus hemippus.

2002			Perf. 14
1691-1695	A493	Set of 5	7.00

Imperf
Size: 70x93mm
Without Gum

1696	A493	250d multi	8.00

Saddam University — A494

Background colors: 50d, Brown. 100d, Blue.

2002			Perf. 14
1697-1698	A494	Set of 2	2.00

Iraqi Coalition Provisional Authority postal officials have declared as illegal 13 Iraqi stamps of the Saddam Hussein regime with various overprints and surcharges that read "Iraq / In Coalition / Occupation."

Issues of the Coalition Provisional Authority

Transportation A495

Designs: 50d, Raft. 100d, Horse-drawn carriage. 250d, Horse-drawn rail car. 500d, Boat. 5000d, Camel caravan.

2004, Jan. 15		Litho.	Perf. 14
1699-1703	A495	Set of 5	9.75 9.75

Dated 2003.

New Year — A496

2006, Mar. 16		Litho.	Perf. 13
1704	A496	250d multi	1.00 1.00

A497

June 30, 2004 Installation of Iraqi Interim Government — A498

2006, Sept. 7		Litho.	Perf. 14½
1705	A497	100d multi	.35 .35
1706	A498	250d multi	.90 .90

Iraq Civilization — A499

Designs: 100d, Mannequin with headdress. 150d, Golden bull. 200d, Stone carving. 250d, Paintings of horses on walls.

2006, Sept. 11		Litho.	Perf. 14½
1707-1709	A499	Set of 3	1.75 1.75

Imperf
Size: 80x61mm

1710	A499	250d multi	2.00 2.00

2004 Summer Olympics, Athens — A500

Designs: 100d, Soccer players. 150d, Runners. 500d, Various athletes.

2006, Sept. 24			Perf. 14¼
1711-1712	A500	Set of 2	1.50 1.50

Imperf
Size: 100x70mm

1713	A500	500d multi	2.75 2.75

Paintings A501

Unnamed paintings by: 100d, Akram Shukri. 150d, Hafidh Al Duroubi. 200d, Faiq Hassan. 250d, Atheer M. G.

2006, Oct. 9			Perf. 14¼
1714-1716	A501	Set of 3	2.00 2.00

Imperf
Size: 88x70mm

1717	A501	250d multi	2.25 2.25

The items shown above were prepared in 2006 but not issued.

Flowers — A502

Designs: 250d, Anemone. 750d, Viola mammola. 1000d, Atropa belladonna.

2007		Litho.	Die Cut
		Self-Adhesive	
1718-1720	A502	Set of 3	3.50 3.50
1720a		Souvenir sheet, #1718-1720	3.75 3.75

Issued: Nos. 1718-1720, 4/11; No. 1720a, 5/7.

Street Vendor A502a   Two Women A502b

2007, Apr. 23		Litho.	Perf. 13½x13¼
1720B	A502a	100d multi	.30 .30
1720C	A502b	250d multi	.75 .75

Singers and Cat — A503

2007, Apr. 23			Perf. 13½x13¼
1721	A503	5000d multi	15.00 15.00

Dated 2006.

Butterflies A504

Designs: 100d, Papilio demodocus. 250d, Precis orithua. 500d, Coitas croceus. 1000d, Papilio demodocus, diff.

2007, Apr. 23			Perf. 13½x13¼
1722-1724	A504	Set of 3	2.50 2.50

Size: 80x61mm
Imperf

1725	A504	1000d multi	2.75 2.75

Artisans — A505

Designs: 250d, Rug maker. 350d, Blanket maker. 500d, Basket maker.

2007, May 22		Litho.	Die Cut
		Self-Adhesive	
1726-1728	A505	Set of 3	3.50 3.50
1728a		Miniature sheet, #1726-1728	4.00

Folklore A506

2007, June 7			Imperf.
1729	A506	1000d multi	2.75 2.75

Dated 2006.

Rafidain Bank, 65th Anniv. (in 2006) — A507

Background colors: 100d, Light blue. 150d, Orange red. 250d, Brown. 500d, Lilac.

2007, July 10			Perf. 14
1730-1733	A507	Set of 4	2.75 2.75

Dated 2006.

Birds — A508

Designs: 150d, Anser anser. 250d, Merops superciliosus. 500d, Pterocles alchata. 1500d, Ducks in flight.

2007, Sept.			Perf. 14
1734-1736	A508	Set of 3	2.25 2.25

Imperf
Size: 80x80mm

1737	A508	1500d multi	3.75 3.75

A509   Musicians and Actors — A510

Designs: 250d, Mohammad al-Qubanchi, singer. 500d, Haqi al-Shibly, actor, horiz. 750d, Nazem al-Ghazaly, singer, horiz. 1000d, Munir Bashir, musician.

2007, Oct. 1			Die Cut
		Self-Adhesive	
1738	A509	250d multi	1.25 1.25
1739	A509	500d multi	2.25 2.25
1740	A509	750d multi	3.25 3.25
1741	A510	1000d multi	4.50 4.50
a.		Miniature sheet, #1738-1741	12.00
	Nos. 1738-1741 (4)		11.25 11.25

IRAQ

481

A511

A512

National Reconciliation A513

2008, Oct. 27 Litho. Perf. 12¾x13¼
1742 A511 250d multi .75 .75
Perf. 13
1743 A512 500d multi 1.50 1.50
1744 A513 750d multi 2.25 2.25
Nos. 1742-1744 (3) 4.50 4.50

Diplomatic Relations Between Iraq and People's Republic of China, 50th Anniv. A514

2008, Oct. 28 Perf. 12
1745 A514 500d multi 1.75 1.75

A three-dimensional souvenir sheet of one 500d stamp without white borders was presented as a gift to Chinese and Iraqi officials.

Wasit Poetry Festival A515

2008, Nov. 24 Perf. 13¼x13
1746 A515 5000d multi 12.00 12.00

Collective Cemeteries A516

Rose and: 250d, Corpses and mourners. 500d, Skeletal remains.

2008, Dec. 14
1747-1748 A516 Set of 2 2.10 2.10

Campaign to Regain Stolen Antiquities A517

Buildings and various antiquities: 250d, 500d, 750d.

2009, Mar. 17 Perf. 13x13¼
1749-1751 A517 Set of 3 3.75 3.75

Environmental Protection A518

2009, Mar. 29
1752 A518 1000d multi 3.00 3.00

Campaign to Restore Marshes A519

2009, Apr. 22
1753 A519 10,000d multi 32.50 32.50

Intl. Children's Day A520

Children's art: No. 1754, 50d, Shown. No. 1755, 50d, Two women wearing traditional clothing. No. 1756, 50d, Three men, palm trees. No. 1757, 50d, Woman hugging daughter. No. 1758, 50d, Three women. 500d, Woman holding baby, horiz.

2009, June 1 Litho. Perf. 13¼x13
1754-1758 A520 Set of 5 2.50 2.50
Imperf
Size:80x60mm
1759 A520 500d multi 3.00 3.00

2009 FIFA Confederations Cup Soccer Tournament A521

Emblem and: 100d, Goalie. 250d, Player dribbling ball. 500d, Player kicking ball. 750d, Emblem only.

2009, June 13 Perf. 13x13¼
1760-1762 A521 Set of 3 2.50 2.50
Imperf
Size: 80x80mm
1763 A521 750d multi 2.00 2.00

Iraqi Tourism Week (in 2008) A522

No. 1764, 250d — "Iraqi Tourism Week" in white, with denomination at: a, Right (5-1). b, Left (5-2).
No. 1765, 250d — "Iraqi Tourism Week" in black, with denomination at: a, Right (5-3). b, Left (5-4).
500d, Horsemen (5-5).

2009, July 14 Perf. 13¼x13
Horiz. Pairs, #a-b
1764-1765 A522 Set of 2 3.00 3.00
Imperf
Size: 90x60mm
1766 A522 500d multi 1.50 1.50
Dated 2009.

Jerusalem, Capital of Arab Culture A523

2009, Aug. 2 Perf. 13¼x13
1767 A523 250d lt org & multi .80 .80

Imperf
Size: 60x80mm
1768 A523 750d ol grn & multi 2.10 2.10

Emmanuel Baba Dawud (1934-2009), Soccer Player and Coach A524

Dawud and: 250d, Pink frame. 500d, Green frame.

2009, Dec. 30 Litho. Perf. 13x13¼
1769-1770 A524 Set of 2 1.75 1.75

Iraqi Republic Railways A525

Designs: 250d, Steam locomotive. 500d, Diesel locomotive. 750d, Steam locomotive, diff. 1000d, Diesel locomotive, building.

2010, Jan. 25 Litho. Perf. 13¼x13
1772-1774 A525 Set of 3 3.75 3.75
Size: 80x80mm
Imperf
1775 A525 1000d multi 2.50 2.50

Elections A526

Color of stylized people: 250d, Purple. 500d, Green. 1000d, Red.

2010, Mar. 7 Perf. 13¼x13
1776-1778 A526 Set of 3 4.25 4.25

Arabian Brotherhood Scouts Day A527

Designs: No. 1779, 250d, Bugler. No. 1780, 250d, Girls in field. No. 1781, 250d, Boys saluting flag. No. 1782, 250d, Girls standing at attention. 1000d, Scouts carrying flags.

2010, Mar. 23 Perf. 13¼x13
1779-1782 A527 Set of 4 2.50 2.50
Size: 80x60mm
Imperf
1783 A527 1000d multi 2.50 2.50

Iraqi Post Day A528

Designs: 250d, Envelope in mail slot. 500d, Dove, envelope, clay tablet.

2010, Apr. 27 Perf. 13¼x13
1784-1785 A528 Set of 2 1.90 1.90

A529

Prehistoric Animals A530

No. 1786 — Various prehistoric animals with stamps numbered: a, 10-1. b, 10-2. c, 10-3. d, 10-4. e, 10-5. f, 10-6. g, 10-7. h, 10-8.
No. 1787, 500d, 10-9. No. 1788, 500d, 10-10.

2010, June 28 Perf. 13¼x13
1786 Block of 8 7.25 7.25
a.-h. A529 250d Any single .90 .90
Imperf
1787-1788 A530 Set of 2 2.50 2.50

2010 World Cup Soccer Championships, South Africa A531

Emblem and various soccer players with frame in: 250d, Maroon. 500d, Brown. 750d, Purple. No. 1792, 1000d, Red.
No. 1793, Emblem and two soccer players.

2010, July 13 Perf. 13¼x13
1789-1792 A531 Set of 4 6.25 6.25
Size: 125x70mm
Imperf
1793 A531 1000d multi 2.50 2.50

Koran A532

2010, Aug. 11 Litho. Perf. 13¼x13
1794 A532 250d multi .65 .65
Size:90x70mm
Imperf
1795 A532 500d multi 1.25 1.25

Intl. Youth Year A533

"2010," Arabic text and: No. 1796, 250d, Youths, candle, olive branch. No. 1797, 250d, Young woman and man, leaves.

2010, Sept. 8 Perf. 13¼x13
1796-1797 A533 Set of 2 1.25 1.25

Organization of Petroleum Exporting Countries, 50th Anniv. A534

Sites in Iraq, OPEC 50th anniversary emblem and: 250d, Map of Iraq. 500d, World map.

2010, Sept. 14 Perf. 13x13¼
1798-1799 A534 Set of 2 1.90 1.90

IRAQ

Kirkuk, City of Iraqi Culture — A535

2010, Oct. 4		Litho.	Perf. 13¼x13
1800	A535	1000d multi	2.50 2.50

Convention on the Rights of the Child, 20th Anniv. — A536

Stylized faces in oval and: 500d, Child holding adult's hand. 750d, Child solving math problem on blackboard. 1000d, Children on carousel.

2010, Nov.			
1801-1803	A536	Set of 3	5.50 5.50

Intl. Year of Biodiversity — A537

Designs: 250d, Coccinella septempunctata. 500d, Egretta alba. 750d, Persian gazelle, horiz. No. 1807, 1000d, Ophisops elegans, horiz.
No. 1808, 1000d, Butterfly, dragonfly, ladybug, frog, various birds, horiz.

Perf. 13x13¼, 13¼x13			
2011, Jan. 11			Litho.
1804-1807	A537	Set of 4	6.25 6.25
Size: 150x75mm			
Imperf			
1808	A537	1000d multi	2.60 2.60

2011 Asian Cup Soccer Tournament, Qatar A538

Designs: 250d, Goalie. 500d, Player. 750d, Player, diff. No. 1812, 1000d, Player scissor kicking ball.
No. 1813, 1000d, Silhouettes of players, vert.

2011, Jan. 27			Perf. 13¼x13
1809-1812	A538	Set of 4	6.25 6.25
Size: 60x60mm			
Imperf			
1813	A538	1000d multi	2.60 2.60

Biodiversity of Shatt al-Arab and Persian Gulf — A539

Designs: 250d, Metapenaeus affinis. 500d, Torpedo panthera. 750d, Hermit crab. No. 1817, 1000d, Carp.
No. 1818, 1000d, Lionfish.

2011, Feb. 13			Perf. 13¼x13
1814-1817	A539	Set of 4	6.25 6.25
Size: 80x61mm			
Imperf			
1818	A539	1000d multi	2.60 2.60

Desertification Control Day — A540

Desert and: 750d, Boy examining seedling. 1000d, Hands holding seedling.

2011, Apr. 19			Perf. 13x13¼
1819-1820	A540	Set of 2	4.25 4.25

Intl. Day Against Tuberculosis — A541

Frame color: 250d, Blue. 500d, Green.

2011, June 21			Perf. 13¼x13
1821-1822	A541	Set of 2	1.90 1.90

Archaeological Sites — A542

Designs: 250d, Babylon. 500d, Hatra. 750d, Ziggurat of Ur. No. 1826, 1000d, Nineveh.
No. 1827, 1000d, Spiral Minaret, vert.

2011, June 29			Perf. 13x13¼
1823-1826	A542	Set of 4	6.50 6.50
Size: 60x80mm			
Imperf			
1827	A542	1000d multi	2.60 2.60

Poets — A543

Designs: 250d, Abdul al-Wahhab al-Bayati (1926-99). 500d, Muhammad Mahdi al-Jawahiri (1899-1997). 750d, Nazek al-Malaeka (1923-2007).

2011, July 7			Perf. 13¼x13
1828-1830	A543	Set of 3	3.75 3.75

Musical Instruments — A544

Designs: 250d, Zarna. 500d, Rababa. 750d, Ud. 1000d, Qanun.

2011, July 31			
1831-1834	A544	Set of 4	6.50 6.50

Arabian Horses A545

Designs: 250d, Two black horses. 500d, Two white horses. 750d, Gray and brown horses. No. 1838, 1000d, Gray and white horses.
No. 1839, 100d, Five horses.

2011			
1835-1838	A545	Set of 4	8.00 8.00
Imperf			
Size: 105x85mm			
1839	A545	1000d multi	3.00 3.00

Halabja Chemical Attack, 23rd Anniv. — A546

2011, Oct. 24			Perf. 13x13¼
1840	A546	1000d multi	2.75 2.75

Iraqi Philatelic and Numismatic Society, 60th Anniv. — A547

Designs: 250d, Emblem, stamps and coins. 500d, Coins, emblem and stamps, horiz.

2011, Nov. 3			Perf. 13x13¼, 13¼x13
1841-1842	A547	Set of 2	2.00 2.00

Traditional Iraqi Costumes — A548

Various men and women in costumes with frame color of: No. 1843, 500d, Brown (6-1). No. 1844, 500d, Purple (6-2). No. 1845, 500d, Gray green (6-3). No. 1846, 500d, Bister (6-4). No. 1847, 500d, Pink (6-5).
No. 1848, 500d, Orange brown (6-6).

2011, Nov. 3			Perf. 13¼x13
1843-1847	A548	Set of 5	6.75 6.75
Size: 80x80mm			
Imperf			
1848	A548	500d multi	1.40 1.40

Ramsar Convention, 40th Anniv. — A549

Various birds: 500d, 750d, 1000d. 1000d is vert.

Perf. 13x13¼, 13¼x13			
2011, Nov. 3			Litho.
1849-1851	A549	Set of 3	6.00 6.00

Discovery of AIDS, 30th Anniv. — A550

2012, Jan. 3			Perf. 13x13¼
1852	A550	10,000d multi	26.00 26.00
Dated 2011.			

Battle of Al-Taaf (Karbala), 680 — A551

Revolution of Imam Hussain — A552

No. 1853: a, Camel caravan. b, Riderless horse. c, Battle scene. d, Birds over battle camp, rider heading to battle.

Litho. With Foil Application

2012, Jan. 11			Perf. 13¼x13
1853		Horiz. strip of 4	6.75 6.75
a.	A551	250d multi	.65 .65
b.	A551	500d multi	1.40 1.40
c.	A551	750d multi	2.00 2.00
d.	A551	1000d multi	2.60 2.60
Imperf			
1854	A552	1000d multi	2.60 2.60
No. 1854 is dated 2011.			

Martyr's Day — A553

Emblem, doves and: 750d, Protesters with flag, coffins, two mourning women. 1000d, Coffins, mourning man.

2012, Mar. 4		Litho.	Perf. 13¼x13
1855-1856	A553	Set of 2	4.75 4.75

Arab Summit Conference, Baghdad — A554

Emblem with background color of: 250d, Pink. 500d, Blue. 750d, Orange.

2012, May 3			Perf. 13¼x13
1857-1859	A554	Set of 3	5.75 5.75

Flowers — A555

Designs: No. 1860, 250d, Sunflowers. No. 1861, 500d, Gardenias. No. 1862, 750d, Weasel's snouts. No. 1863, 1000d, Carnations. No. 1864, 1000d, Various flowers
No. 1865, 250d, Zinnias. No. 1866, 500d, Anemones. No. 1867, 750d, Roses. No. 1868, 1000d, Chrysanthemums.

2012, May 6			Perf. 13¼x13
1860-1863	A555	Set of 4	6.75 6.75
Size: 80x80mm (#1864)			
Imperf			
1864	A555	1000d multi	2.75 2.75
Self-Adhesive			
Die Cut			
1865-1868	A555	Set of 4	6.75 6.75

Al-Kadhimiya Mosque, Baghdad A556

Various views of mosque numbered: No. 1869, 250d, 4-1. No. 1870, 250d, 4-2. No. 1871, 250d, 4-3.
500d, Mosque, doves, scroll, horiz (4-4).

IRAQ

2012, June 12   Perf. 13¼x13
1869-1871   A556   Set of 3   2.25   2.25
Size: 100x70mm
Imperf
1872   A556   500d multi   1.50   1.50

Genocide of Kurdish Faylees — A557

Map of Iraq and various Kurdish refugees: 750d, 1000d.

2012, June 19   Perf. 13¼x13
1873-1874   A557   Set of 2   4.75   4.75

National Commission on Education, Culture and Science — A558

2012, July 27
1875   A558   5000d multi   14.00   14.00

2012 Summer Olympics, London — A559

Designs: 250d, Archery. 500d, Gymnastics. 750d, Fencing. No. 1879, 1000d, Hurdles. No. 1880, 1000d, Olympic rings, torch bearer, runner, high jump, equestrian, kayaker, swimmer. No. 1881, 1000d, Olympic rings, torch, mascots, stadiums, flags, javelin.

2012, Sept. 9   Perf. 13x13¼
1876-1879   A559   Set of 4   7.00   7.00
Size: 120x70mm
Imperf
1880-1881   A559   Set of 2   5.50   5.50

Kings of Iraq — A560

Designs: 500d, King Faisal II (1935-1958). 750d, King Ghazi (1912-1939). No. 1884, 1000d, King Faisal I (1885-1933). No. 1885, Kings Faisal I, Ghazi and Faisal II, equestrian statue, arms.

2012, Oct. 2   Perf. 14¼
1882-1884   A560   Set of 3   6.25   6.25
Size: 90x70mm
On Thin Card Stock Without Gum
Imperf
1885   A560   1000d multi   2.75   2.75

Arab Post Day — A561

2012, Nov. 26   Perf. 13x13¼
1886   A561   250d multi   .70   .70

Kirkuk Castle A562

2012, Nov. 26   Perf. 13¼x13
1887   A562   500d multi   1.40   1.40

Water Wheel — A563

2012, Dec. 4   Perf. 13¼
1888   A563   10,000d multi   27.50   27.50

Evacuation of Coalition Troops, 1st Anniv. A564

Frame color: 250d, Silver. 1000d, Gold.

2012, Dec. 13   Perf. 13¼x13
1889-1890   A564   Set of 2   3.50   3.50

Falcons — A565

Designs: 250d, Gyrfalcons. 500d, Lanner falcons. 750d, Saker falcons (cherrug). No. 1894, 1000d, Peregrine falcons. No. 1895, 1000d, Falcon on perch.

2012, Dec. 20   Perf. 13¼x13
1891-1894   A565   Set of 4   7.00   7.00
Size: 90x70mm
Imperf
1895   A565   1000d multi   2.75   2.75

Landmarks A566

Map of Iraq and various landmarks, with stamps numbered: No. 1896, 250d, (8-1). No. 1897, 250d, (8-2). No. 1898, 250d, (8-3). No. 1899, 250d, (8-4). 500d, (8-5), horiz. 750d, (8-6), horiz. No. 1902, 1000d, (8-7), horiz. No. 1903, 1000d, Map of Iraq, frame, various landmarks (8-8), horiz.

2013, Jan. 28   Perf. 13x13¼, 13¼x13
1896-1902   A566   Set of 7   9.00   9.00
Size: 100x80mm
Imperf
1903   A566   1000d multi   2.75   2.75

Baghdad, Capital of Arab Culture A567

Emblem and: 250d, Man (5-1). 500d, Woman (5-2). 750d, Man, diff. (5-3). No. 1907, 1000d, Man, diff. (5-4). No. 1908, 1000d, Round City of Baghdad (5-5).

2013, Apr. 25   Perf. 13¼x13
1904-1907   A567   Set of 4   7.00   7.00
Size: 80x60mm
Imperf
1908   A567   1000d multi   2.75   2.75

World Telecommunications Day — A568

Telecommunications satellites, map of Iraq, flags and: 250d, Globe. 1000d, Binary code, horiz.

Perf. 13¼x13, 13x13¼
2013, Sept. 1   Litho.
1909-1910   A568   Set of 2   3.75   3.75

Butterflies — A569

Designs: 200d, Anthocharis cardamines. 250d, Precis orithya. 500d, White glider. 750d, Colias croceus. 1000d, Papilio machaon. 5000d, Vanessa atalanta. 10,000d, Danaus chrysippus.

2013, Sept. 4   Litho.   Perf. 13¼x13½
1911-1917   A569   Set of 7   52.50   52.50

Camels — A570

Designs: 250d, Two camels in foreground facing left, two camels in background (6-1). 500d, One camel facing right (6-2). 750d, Two camels facing right (6-3). No. 1921, 1000d, One camel standing, three camels resting on ground (6-4). No. 1922, 1000d, Four camels in foreground facing right, group of camels on sand dune in background, horiz. (6-5). No. 1923, 1000d, Two camels in foreground facing left, two camels on sand dune in background facing left, horiz. (6-6).

2013, Sept. 9   Litho.   Perf. 13½
1918-1921   A570   Set of 4   6.00   6.00
Size: 110x75mm
Imperf
1922-1923   A570   Set of 2   16.50   16.50

Clock Towers — A571

Various clock towers with background color of: 250d, Greenish gray (4-1). 500d, Blue gray (4-2). 750d, Tan (4-3). 1000d, Lilac (4-4).

2013, Sept. 13   Litho.   Perf. 13¼x13
1924-1927   A571   Set of 4   7.50   7.50

Iraqi Women's Day — A572

2013, Dec. 4   Litho.   Perf. 13¼x13
1928   A572   1500d multi   4.50   4.50

World Arab Language Day — A573

Background color: 500d, Light blue. 1000d, Yellow green.

2013, Dec. 18   Litho.   Perf. 13x13¼
1929-1930   A573   Set of 2   4.50   4.50

Intl. Civil Aviation Organization, 70th Anniv. — A574

ICAO emblem, jet and: 500d, Control tower. 1000d, Terminal building. 1500d, World map.

2014, Jan. 28   Litho.   Perf. 13x13¼
1931-1933   A574   Set of 3   8.75   8.75

Environmental Year — A575

Background color: 250d, Purple. 500d, Green. 750d, Red.

2014, Apr. 16   Litho.   Perf. 13¼x13
1934-1936   A575   Set of 3   4.50   4.50

Parliamentary Elections — A576

Stylized voters, map of Iraq, and: 500d, Iraqi tourist attractions. 1000d, Dove and flag. 1500d, Flag, horiz.

Perf. 13¼x13, 13x13¼
2014, Apr. 30   Litho.
1937-1939   A576   Set of 3   8.75   8.75

Army Day — A577

Designs: 250d, Ship. 500d, Tank. 750d, Soldiers. 1000d, Airplane.

2015, Jan. 14   Litho.   Perf. 13¼
1940-1943   A577   Set of 4   7.50   7.50

Diplomatic Relations Between Iraq and Japan, 75th Anniv. — A578

Background colors: 250d, Green. 500d, Yellow green. No. 1946, 1000d, Blue. No. 1947, 1000d, 75th anniversary emblem, vignettes of Nos. 1944-1946 decreased in size.

2015, Jan. 15   Litho.   Perf. 13½x13
1944   A578   250d multi   .90   .90
1945   A578   500d multi   1.75   1.75
   a.   With top line of Arabic text under flags extending to left and right frame lines   1.75   1.75
1946   A578   1000d multi   3.50   3.50
   Nos. 1944-1946 (3)   6.15   6.15

IRAQ

Size: 90x62mm
Imperf
1947 A578 1000d multi 3.50 3.50
Dated 2014. First day covers are dated 11/1/14, but stamps were not made available until 2015. On No. 1945a, the lines of Arabic text under the flags are nonsensical.

2014 World Cup Soccer Championships, Brazil — A579

Designs: 250d, World Cup, flags of participating nations, soccer field. 500d, World Cup, flags, soccer player and ball. 650d, Flags, mascot with ball. No. 1951, 1000d, World Cup, various players, soccer ball in net. No. 1952, 1000d, Flags, emblem of 2014 World Cup.

2015, Jan. 18   Litho.   Perf. 13¾
1948-1951 A579 Set of 4 7.50 7.50
Imperf
Size: 70x70mm
1952 A579 1000d multi 10.50 10.50
Dated 2014. First day cancels are dated 6/12/14 but stamps were not made available until 2015. Values for Nos. 1948-1951 are for stamps with surrounding selvage.

Birds — A580

Designs: 250d, Tree sparrow. 500d, Blue-cheeked bee-eater. 750d, Robin. No. 1956, 1000d, Goldfinch. No. 1957, 1000d, Common kingfisher.
1500d, Tree sparrow, blue-cheeked bee-eater, robin, goldfinch, common kingfisher, horiz.

2015, Jan. 21   Litho.   Perf. 13¼
1953-1957 A580 Set of 5 10.50 10.50
Imperf
Size: 136x102mm
1958 A580 1500d multi + 3 labels 11.50 11.50
Dated 2014.

Craftsmen — A581

Designs: 250d, Potter. 500d, Coppersmith. 750d, Weaver. 1000d, Knife sharpener.

2015, Jan. 25   Litho.   Perf. 14¼x14
1959-1962 A581 Set of 4 7.50 7.50

Fruit — A582

Designs: 250d, Apricots. 500d, Pomegranates. 750d, Figs. No. 1966, 1000d, Apples. No. 1967, 1000d, Grapes.

2015, Jan. 26   Litho.   Perf. 13¼x13
1963-1967 A582 Set of 5 10.50 10.50
Dated 2014. First day cancels are dated 1/26/14, but stamps were not made available until 2015.

Cars Owned by Royalty — A583

Car in: 250d, Black. 500d, Red. 750d, Silver. 1000d, Dark red.

2015, Jan. 26   Litho.   Perf. 13¼
1968-1971 A583 Set of 4 7.50 7.50
Dated 2014. First day cancels are dated 1/26/14 but stamps were not made available until 2015.

Scenes From Southern Iraq Marshes — A584

Designs: 250d, Man standing in small boat. 500d, Cattle.

2015, Feb. 8   Litho.   Perf. 13x13¼
1972-1973 A584 Set of 2 3.00 3.00

Mosques A585

Various mosques with side panel in: 250d, Brown ochre. 500d, Blue. 750d, Purple. 1000d, Yellow brown.

2015, Feb. 9   Litho.   Perf. 13½
1974-1977 A585 Set of 4 7.50 7.50
Dated 2014.

National Day of the Disabled A586

Designs: 250d, Hexagons showing disabilities. 500d, Stylized people helping person in wheelchair, rectangles showing disabilities. 1000d, Umbrella, rectangles and flower petals showing disabilities.

2015, Sept. 17   Litho.   Perf. 14¼x14
1978-1980 A586 Set of 3 5.00 5.00

A587

A588

War Campaign Against Islamic State of Iraq and the Levant — A589

2015, Oct. 26   Litho.   Perf. 14¼x14
1981 A587 500d multi 1.50 1.50
1982 A588 750d multi 2.25 2.25
1983 A589 1000d multi 3.00 3.00
Nos. 1981-1983 (3) 6.75 6.75

Destruction of Iraqi Antiquities by Islamic State of Iraq and the Levant — A590

Designs: 500d, Toppled statue. 1000d, Cracked statues, vert. 1500d, Toppled statue and sledgehammer.

2015, Nov. 23   Litho.   Perf. 14¼
1984-1985 A590 Set of 2 3.25 3.25
Imperf
Size: 64x64mm
1986 A590 1500d multi 3.25 3.25
No. 1986 have simulated perforations.

Farm Pets — A591

Designs: 250d, Rabbits. 500d, Pigeons. 750d, Cat and dog, vert. 1000d, Chickens, vert.
1500d, Ducks, cat, dog, rabbits, pigeons and chickens.

Perf. 14x14¼, 14¼x14
2016, Mar. 23   Litho.
1987-1990 A591 Set of 4 7.50 7.50
Size: 103x84mm
Imperf
1991 A591 1500d multi 4.50 4.50
No. 1991 has simulated perfs around details of Nos. 1987-1990.

International Year of Light (in 2015) — A592

2016, Apr. 3   Litho.   Perf. 14x14¼
1992 A592 10,000d multi 29.00 29.00
UNESCO, 70th anniv. (in 2015).

Children at Play — A593

Designs: 250d, Girls playing hop scotch. 500d, Boys playing marbles, horiz. 750d, Boys playing game, horiz. 1000d, Girls skipping rope.

2016, Apr. 14   Litho.   Perf. 14
1993-1996 A593 Set of 4 7.25 7.25

Zaha Hadid (1950-2016), Architect A594

Mohammad Makeyah (1914-2015), Architect A595

2016, June 16   Litho.   Perf. 14
1997 A594 750d multi 2.25 2.25
1998 A595 1000d multi 3.00 3.00

Flowers — A596

Various flower arrangements: 250d, 500d, 750d, 1000d, 1500d. 750d is horiz.

2016, July 13   Litho.   Perf. 14
1999-2003 A596 Set of 5 11.50 11.50

Arab Postal Day A597

No. 2004 — Background color: a, 500d, Green. b, 1000d, Blue and purple.

2016, Sept. 5   Litho.   Perf. 14x14¼
2004 A597 Horiz. pair, #a-b 4.50 4.50

Health Organizations — A598

No. 2005: a, 250d, Syndicate of Iraqi Pharmacists. b, 250d, Iraqi Medical Association. c, 500d, Iraqi Red Crescent Society. d, 500d, Anti-tuberculosis and Chest Diseases Society in Iraq.

2016, Sept. 21   Litho.   Perf. 14
2005 A598 Block of 4, #a-d 4.50 4.50

Liberation of Anbar Province — A599

2016, Oct. 5   Litho.   Perf. 14
2006 A599 1000d multi 3.00 3.00

2016 Summer Olympics, Rio de Janeiro — A600

No. 2007: a, 250d, Track. b, 250d, Soccer. c, 500d, High jump. d, 500d, Handball. e, 750d, Equestrian show jumping. f, 750d, Javelin. g, 1000d, Boxing. h, 1000d, Fencing.
No. 2008, 1000d, Pole vault, gymnastics, basketball, long jump.

2016, Oct. 23   Litho.   Perf. 14
2007 A600 Sheet of 8, #a-h 15.50 15.50
Size: 140x70mm
Imperf
2008 A600 1000d multi 3.00 3.00

Sheikh Ahmed Al-Waili (1928-2003), Islamic Cleric and Poet — A601

2016, Nov. 13   Litho.   Perf. 14
2009 A601 1000d multi 3.00 3.00

Addition of South Iraq Marshes to UNESCO World Heritage List — A602

UNESCO and World Heritage Site emblem and: 250d, Gilgamesh. 500d, Statue. 750d, Ziggurat of Ur, horiz. No. 2013, 1000d, Boat in marsh waterway, horiz.
No. 2014, 1000d, Scroll, Gilgamesh, statue, Ziggurat of Ur, boat in marsh waterway.

2016, Dec. 1   Litho.   Perf. 14
2010-2013 A602 Set of 4 7.25 7.25
Size: 99x92mm
Imperf
2014 A602 1000d multi 3.00 3.00

IRAQ

Diplomatic Relations Between Iraq and Spain, 70th Anniv. — A603

2017, Feb. 5	Litho.	Perf. 14
2015 A603 1000d multi		3.25 3.25

Brothers Meeting Festival for Hobbies and Miscellaneous Crafts — A604

Emblem and: 500d, Rugs, stringed instrument, books, lantern, cup and coffee pot. 1000d, Rugs, large stringed instrument, plate, musical notes, artist's palette.

2017, Mar. 1	Litho.	Perf. 14
2016 A604 500d multi		1.60 1.60

Size: 84x84mm
Imperf
| 2017 A604 1000d multi | | 3.25 3.25 |

Al Rasheed Street, Baghdad, Cent. (in 2016) — A605

2017, Mar. 30	Litho.	Perf. 14
2018 A605 1000d multi		3.25 3.25

Airplanes, Trains and Buses — A606

No. 2019: a, 250d, Gipsy Moth biplane, 1931. b, 250d, DHL136 train, 2004. c, 250d, Ikarus bus, 1971. d, 500d, De Havilland Dragon biplane, 1933. e, 500d, DEM2745 train, 2001. f, 500d, Leyland bus, 1976. g, 750d, Gloster Gladiator biplane, 1937. h, 750d, DEM2006 train, 1964. i, 750d, AC bus, 1956. j, 1000d, De Havilland Dove airplane, 1948. k, 1000d, DMU train, 2014. l, 1000d, Albs bus, 2013.
No. 2020, Steam train, airplane and bus.

2017, July 5	Litho.	Perf. 14x14¼
2019 A606 Sheet of 12, #a-l		24.00 24.00

Size: 120x90mm
Imperf
| 2020 A606 1000d multi | | 3.00 3.00 |

Liberation of Mosul — A607

Designs: 500d, Troops, tanks, airplanes, damaged mosque. 1000d, Woman holding Iraqi flag, soldiers, horiz.

2017, July 18	Litho.	Perf. 14
2021 A607 500d multi		1.60 1.60

Size: 100x68mm
Imperf
| 2022 A607 1000d multi | | 3.25 3.25 |

"Baghdad" Overprinted Stamps of Mesopotamia, Cent. — A608

Designs: 250d, Mesopotamia #N1. 500d, Mesopotamia #N5, horiz. 1000d, Mesopotamia #N7, horiz. 1500d, Magnifying glass, canceler, covers bearing various stamps of Mesopotamia, horiz.

2017, Oct. 21	Litho.	Perf. 14
2023-2025 A608 Set of 3		6.00 6.00

Size: 94x70mm
Imperf
| 2026 A608 1500d multi | | 5.25 5.25 |

Al-Abbas Holy Shrine, Karbala — A609

Designs: 250d, Sepulcher of Al-Abbas ibn Ali. 1000d, Worshiper. 1500d, Mosque dome and minarets.

2017, Dec. 3	Litho.	Perf. 14
2027-2028 A609 Set of 2		4.25 4.25

Size: 100x70mm
Imperf
| 2029 A609 1500d multi | | 5.00 5.00 |

Mohammed Redha Al-Shibibi (1889-1965), Minister of Education and Poet — A610

2018, Jan. 15	Litho.	Perf. 14
2030 A610 1000d multi		3.25 3.25

Baghdad, 2017-18 Arab Media Capital — A611

Background color: No. 2031, 1000d, Turquoise green. No. 2032, 1000d, Ochre.

2018, Feb. 13	Litho.	Perf. 14
2031-2032 A611 Set of 2		6.75 6.75

Minerals — A612

Map of Iraq and: 250d, Phosphate ore. 500d, Sulfur ore. 1000d, Silica sand.

2018, Feb. 25	Litho.	Perf. 14
2033-2035 A612 Set of 3		5.75 5.75

Miniature Sheets

Actors and Actresses in *The Eagle and the City Eyes* Television Series — A613

No. 2036, 250d: a, Rasim Al-Gumaili. b, Gafar Al-Sadi. c, Fawziya Arif. d, Toama Al-Timimi. e, Sammi Abdul-Hameed. f, Fatima Al-Rubaiai. g, Qasim Al-Melak. h, Sana'a Abdul-Rahman.
No. 2037, 250d: a, Kheleel Shaoqi. b, Bedri Hassan Fereed. c, Moqdad Abdul-Ridha. d, Ibtsam Fereed. e, Betool Aziz. f, Muhsin Al-Ali. g, Seleema Al-Basri. h, May Gemal.

2018, May 27	Litho.	Perf. 14
Sheets of 8, #a-h, + 4 labels
2036-2037 A613 Set of 2		13.50 13.50

International Music Day — A614

Designs: 500d, Conductor and orchestra. 1000d, Conductor and orchestra, diff.

2018, June 25	Litho.	Perf. 14
2038-2039 A614 Set of 2		5.00 5.00

2018 World Cup Soccer Championships, Russia — A615

Designs: 250d, Soccer player. 500d, Palyer in white and red shirt, other in yellow green shirt. 750d, Player in white shirt, othe in yellow green shirt. No. 2043, 1000d, Player in white and violet shirt, other in red and white shirt. No. 2044, 1000d, Mascot and flags of competing countries.

2018, July 3	Litho.	Perf. 14
2040-2043 A615 Set of 4		8.25 8.25

Size: 71x100mm
Imperf
| 2044 A615 1000d multi | | 3.50 3.50 |

Mudhafar Al-Nawab, Poet — A616

Design: 1500d, Side view of Al-Nawab at podium with poem in hand.

2018, Sept. 5	Litho.	Perf. 13¼
2045 A616 1000d multi		3.50 3.50

Litho. w/Holographic Film
Size: 80x59mm
Imperf
| 2046 A616 1500d multi | | 5.50 5.50 |

Paintings A617

Unnamed paintings by: 250d, Nezar Seleem (1925-82), light turquoise green frame. 500d, Layla Alattar (1944-93), gray frame. 750d, Noori Alrawi (1925-2014), tan frame. No. 2050, 1000d, Fayek Hassan (1919-94), beige frame.
No. 2051, 1000d, Four paintings shown on Nos. 2047-2050, paint on artist's palette and paint brushes.

2018, Oct. 3	Litho.	Perf. 14
Stamps + Labels
2047-2050 A617 Set of 4		8.75 8.75

Size: 109x90mm
Imperf
| 2051 A617 1000d multi | | 3.50 3.50 |

National Industry — A618

Designs: 250d, Stylized people, factory and chemical plant. 500d, Stylized people and factory.

2018, Nov. 8	Litho.	Perf. 14
2052-2053 A618 Set of 2		2.75 2.75

Miniature Sheet

Diplomatic Relations Between Iraq and People's Republic of China, 60th Anniv. — A619

No. 2054: a, Spiral Minaret of Samara, Iraq. b, Songyue Pagoda, People's Republic of China. c, Replica of Ishtar Gate, Babylon, Iraq. d, Jiayu Guan, People's Republic of China.

2019, Jan. 22	Litho.	Perf. 12
2054 A619 1000d Sheet of 4, #a-d		15.00 15.00

No. 2054 was printed with sheet margins in blue as well as brown. Values are for either color sheet margin.

Mustansiriyah University, Baghdad, 55th Anniv. — A620

2019, Feb. 3	Litho.	Perf. 14
2055 A620 1000d multi		3.75 3.75

School Savings Program — A621

Designs: 250d, Car, children, Iraq postal savings stamps. 500d, Boy examining Iraq postal savings stamps. 750d, Iraq postal savings stamps, flower, collection container, stylized children. 1000d, Airplane, bicycle, children at table, children with flowers and balloon.

2019, Mar. 12	Litho.	Perf. 14
2056-2059 A621 Set of 4		9.25 9.25

IRAQ

2019 International Flower Festival, Baghdad — A622

Flowers and butterflies with background color of: 250d, Pink. 1000d, Light orange. 1500d, Olive bister.

2019, May 21	Litho.		Perf. 14	
2060-2061	A622	Set of 2	4.75	4.75

Size: 70x89mm
Litho. With Holographic Foil Affixed
Imperf

| 2062 | A622 | 1500d multi | 26.00 | 26.00 |

Mohandas K. Gandhi (1869-1948), Indian Nationalist Leader — A623

2019, June 17	Litho.		Perf. 14	
2063	A623	1000d multi	7.50	7.50

Doves, Dome of the Rock, Jerusalem, and Flag of Palestinian Authority — A624

2019, July 2	Litho.		Perf. 14	
2064	A624	1000d multi	5.75	5.75

Birds — A625

Designs: 250d, Luscinia svecica. 500d, Coccothraustes coccothraustes. 750d, Fringilla coelebs. 1000d, Parus caeruleus.

2019, Aug. 25	Litho.		Perf. 14	
2065-2068	A625	Set of 4	9.25	9.25

Fish — A626

Designs: 250d, Lizea abu. 500d, Alosa sapidissima. 750d, Spondyliosoma cantharus. 1000d, Pilchard.

2019, Sept. 30	Litho.		Perf. 14
2070-2073	A626	Set of 4	

Universal Postal Union, 145th Anniv. — A627

2019, Oct. 21	Litho.		Perf. 14
2074	A627	1000d multi	

Babylon UNESCO World Heritage Site — A628

Designs: 250d, King Hammurabi standing before a god. 500d, Dragon on Ishtar Gate. 750d, Tablet of Shamash, vert. 1000d, Aerial view.
1500d, Ishtar gate and Lion of Babylon sculpture, vert.

2019, Dec. 22	Litho.		Perf. 14
2075-2078	A628	Set of 4	

Size: 69x89mm
Imperf

| 2079 | A628 | 1500d multi | |

Diplomatic Relations Between Iraq and Armenia, 20th Anniv. — A629

2020, Mar. 9	Litho.		Perf. 14
2080	A629	1000d multi	

Baghdad Churches — A630

Designs: No. 2081, 250d, St. Trazia Chaldean Church. No. 2082, 250d, Seventh Day Adventist Church. No. 2083, 500d, Virgin Mary Armenian Orthodox Church. No. 2084, 500d, Mar Gorgis Assyrian Church. No. 2085, 750d, Virgin Mary Latin Church. No. 2086, 750d, Saints Peter and Paul Syriac Orthodox Cathedral. No. 2087, 1000d, St. Gregory the Illuminator Armenian Orthodox Church. No. 2088, 1000d, Lady of Salvation Syriac Catholic Church.
1500d, Mother of Sorrows Chaldean Church.

2020, Sept. 28	Litho.		Perf. 14
2081-2088	A630	Set of 8	
2088a		Souvenir sheet of 8, #2081-2088	

Size: 112x78mm
Imperf

| 2089 | A630 | 1500d multi | |

No. 2089 was printed using hologram lenticular method.

Iraqi Ministry of Health, Cent. — A631

2020, Nov. 11	Litho.		Perf. 14
2090	A631	250d multi	

Baghdad Statues and Monuments — A632

Designs: 250d, Kahramana Statue. 500d, Abbas Ibn Firnas Statue. 750d, Al-Nisour Monument. No. 2094, 1000d, Al-Mutanabbi Statue. 1500d, Poet Abo Noas Statue.
No. 2096, 1000d, Statues of Scheherazade and Shahryar, horiz.

2020, Dec. 23	Litho.		Perf. 14
2091-2095	A632	Set of 5	

Size: 100x72mm
Imperf

| 2096 | A632 | 1000d multi | |

Abu Mahdi Al-Muhandis (1954-2020), Politician and Commmander of Popular Mobilization Committee — A633

2021, Jan. 3	Litho.		Perf. 14
2097	A633	1500d multi	

Christmas — A634

Nos. 2098 and 2099: a, 500d, Christmas tree and ornaments. b, 1000d, Bells, ornaments and stylized Holy Family.
No. 2100, 1000d, Holy Family, bells, ornaments and candle, horiz.

2021, Jan. 19	Litho.		Perf. 14
2098	A634	Horiz. pair, #a-b	

Self-Adhesive

| 2099 | A634 | Horiz. pair, #a-b | |

Litho. & Embossed
Size: 84x68mm
Without Gum
Imperf

| 2100 | A634 | 1000d multi | |

Used examples of Nos. 2099a-2099b are the same as used examples of Nos. 2098a-2098b.

Shiite Clerics — A635

Designs: No. 2101, 1500d, Sayyid Mohammed Baqir Al-Hakeem (1939-2003). No. 2102, 1500d, Sayyid Mohammed Sadiq Al-Sadr (1943-99). No. 2103, 1500d, Sayyid Mohammed Baqir Al-Sadr (1935-80).

2021, Feb. 11	Litho.		Perf. 14
2101-2103	A635	Set of 3	

Iraqi Army, Cent. — A636

Designs; 250d, Soldiers and jets. 500d, Soldiers and artillery gun. 750d, Troop of old soldiers, modern soldiers on parade. No. 2107, 1000d, Jet, helicopter, old soldiers on vehicle, modern soldiers with tanks.
No. 2108, 1000d, Troop of old soldiers and officer, horiz.

2021, Mar. 15	Litho.		Perf. 14
2104-2107	A636	Set of 4	

Size: 100x75mm
Imperf

| 2108 | A636 | 1000d multi | |

First Baghdad International Water Conference — A637

2021, Mar. 23	Litho.		Perf. 14
2109	A637	1000d multi	

Ahmed Radhi (1964-2020), Soccer Player — A638

Designs: 1000d, Radhi and his uniform number "8." 1500d, Radhi and Iraqi flag on soccer ball.

2021, June 21	Litho.		Perf. 14
2110	A638	1000d multi	

Size: 84x83mm
Imperf

| 2111 | A638 | 1500d multi | |

Dhiqar Industrial Zone — A639

2021, July 4	Litho.		Perf. 14
2112	A639	1000d multi	

Coins and Banknotes of Iraq — A640

Coins and banknotes of: No. 2113, 250d, 1931-32. No. 2114, 250d, 1934-41. No. 2115, 500d, 1955-57. No. 2116, 500d, 1959-68. No. 2117, 750d, 1968-71. No. 2118, 750d, 1973-75. No. 2119, 1000d, 1978-86. No. 2120, 1000d, 2003.

2021, Aug. 2	Litho.		Perf. 14
2113-2120	A640	Set of 8	

Visit of Pope Francis to Iraq — A641

Pope Francis and: 500d, Statue, Chaldean Catholic Church, Baghdad. 750d, Ziggurat of Ur. 1000d, Grand Ayatollah Ali al-Sistani.
1500d, Pope Francis, dove and map of Iraq.

2021, Sept. 10	Litho.		Perf. 14
2121-2123	A641	Set of 3	

Size: 118x89mm
Imperf

| 2124 | A641 | 1500d multi | |

An imperforate 5000d stamp was issued in limited quantities.

A642

A643

A644

Baghdad Conference for Cooperation and Partnership — A645

2021, Oct. 5	Litho.		Perf. 14
2125	A642	1000d multi	
2126	A643	1000d multi	
2127	A644	1000d multi	

Size: 139x87mm
Imperf

| 2128 | A645 | 1500d multi | |

IRAQ

Ayatollah Mohammed Saeed Al-Hakim (1936-2021) — A646

2021, Oct. 10   Litho.   *Perf. 14*
2129   A646   1500d multi   —   —

Ali Hadi (1967-2020), Soccer Player and Manager — A647

2021, Nov. 2   Litho.   *Perf. 14*
2130   A647   1000d multi   —   —

A648

State of Iraq, Cent. A649

2021, Dec. 20   Litho.   *Perf. 14*
2131   A648   1500d multi   —   —
Size: 141x190mm
Imperf
2132   A649   5000d multi   —   —

Iraqi Police, Cent. — A650

Designs: 500d, Policemen parading. 1000d, Police officers. No. 2135, 1500d, Policemen parading, diff. No. 2136, Centenary emblem.

2022, Jan. 6   Litho.   *Perf. 14*
2133-2135   A650   Set of 3   —   —
Size: 110x110mm
Imperf
2136   A650   1500d multi   —   —

Diplomatic Relations Between Iraq and India — A651

2022, Feb. 17   Litho.   *Perf. 14*
2137   A651   1000d multi   —   —

International Day for the Elimination of Violence Against Women — A652

2022, Mar. 13   Litho.   *Perf. 14*
2138   A652   1000d multi   —   —

Traditional Knowledge of Iraq — A653

Designs: 250d, Tailor. 500d, Woman spinning thread. 750d, Woman grinding grain. 1000d, Man pouring tea. 1500d, Musicians, horiz.

2022, Apr. 3   Litho.   *Perf. 14*
2139-2142   A653   Set of 4   —   —
Size: 120x89mm
Imperf
2143   A653   1500d multi   —   —

Nadia Murad, Human Rights Activist and 2018 Nobel Peace Laureate A654

Litho. With Hologram Affixed
2022, Apr. 3   *Imperf.*
Size: 90x64mm
2144   A654   1500d multi   —   —

Iraqi Post Day — A655

2022, May 8   Litho.   *Perf. 14*
2145   A655   1000d multi   2.75   2.75

Karim Al-Iraqi, Poet and Song Writer — A656

2022, July 25   Litho.   *Perf. 14*
2146   A656   1000d multi   —   —

Yazidi Prince Esmael A657

Baba Chawish, Yazidi Religious Leader A658

2022, Aug. 10   Litho.   *Perf. 14*
2147   A657   500d multi   —   —
2148   A658   1000d multi   —   —

Monasteries A659

Designs: 250d, Rabban Hormizd Monastery, Alqosh. 1000d, Monastery of Mar Matta, Mount Alfaf.

2022, Aug. 10   Litho.   *Perf. 14*
2149-2150   A659   Set of 2   —   —

Mandaeism A660

Designs: 250d, Sabean Mandaeans celebrating Golden Baptism Day. 500d, Sabean Mandaean Bible. 1000d, Baptism of Sabean Mandaean.

2022, Aug. 10   Litho.   *Perf. 14*
2151-2153   A660   Set of 3   —   —

Muhammad Mahdi al-Jawahiri (1899-1997), Poet — A661

Jawahiri with: 1000d, Hand touching his face. 1500d, Hand not visible.

2022, Aug. 10   Litho.   *Perf. 14*
2154   A661   1000d multi   —   —
Size: 114x85mm
Imperf
2155   A661   1500d multi   —   —

World Post Day — A662

2022, Nov. 1   Litho.   *Perf. 14*
2156   A662   1000d multi   —   —

Arab League Summit, Algiers — A663

2022, Nov. 1   Litho.   *Perf. 14*
2157   A663   1000d multi   —   —

AIR POST STAMPS

Catalogue values for unused stamps in this section are for Never Hinged items.

Basra Airport AP1

Diyala Railway Bridge AP2

Vickers Viking over: 4f, 20f, Kut Dam. 5f, 35f, Faisal II Bridge.

Perf. 11½, 11½x12

		Engr.	Unwmk.	
1949, Feb. 1				
C1	AP1	3f blue green	.90	.25
C2	AP1	4f red violet	.90	.25
C3	AP1	5f red brown	.90	.25
C4	AP1	10f carmine	5.00	1.50
C5	AP1	20f blue	3.50	.65
C6	AP1	35f red orange	3.50	.65
C7	AP2	50f olive	4.50	1.10
C8	AP2	100f violet	8.75	2.25
		Nos. C1-C8 (8)	27.95	6.90

Sheets exist, perf. and imperf., containing one each of Nos. C1-C8, with arms and Arabic inscription in blue green in upper and lower margin. Value (2 sheets), each $80.

Republic

ICY Emblem AP3

1965, Aug. 13   Litho.   *Perf. 13½*
C9   AP3   5f brn org & black   .75   .25
C10   AP3   10f citron & dk brn   1.25   .25
C11   AP3   30f ultra & black   2.75   1.10
Nos. C9-C11 (3)   4.75   1.60
International Cooperation Year.

Trident 1E Jet Plane — AP4

1965, Dec. 1   *Photo.*   *Perf. 11½*
Granite Paper
C12   AP4   5f multicolored   .90   .55
C13   AP4   10f multicolored   .90   .55
C14   AP4   40f multicolored   6.00   4.75
Nos. C12-C14 (3)   7.80   5.85
Introduction by Iraqi Airways of Trident 1E jet planes.

Arab International Tourist Union Emblem AP5

Travelers on Magic Carpet AP6

1966, Dec. 3   Litho.   *Perf. 13½, 14*
C15   AP5   2f multicolored   1.00   .30
C16   AP6   5f yellow & multi   1.50   .30
C17   AP5   15f blue & multi   1.75   .50
C18   AP6   50f multicolored   3.00   .80
Nos. C15-C18 (4)   7.25   1.90
Meeting of the Arab Intl. Tourist Union, Baghdad.
For overprint see No. RAC1.

Costume Type of Regular Issue

Iraqi Costumes: 40f, Woman's head. 50f, Woman's costume. 80f, Man's costume.

1967, Nov. 10   Litho.   *Perf. 13*
C19   A105   40f multicolored   2.50   .90
C20   A105   50f blue & multi   3.50   1.25
C21   A105   80f green & multi   5.50   1.75
Nos. C19-C21 (3)   11.50   3.90
For overprints, see CO1-CO3.

International Tourist Year Type of Regular Issue

Designs: 50f, Female statue, Temples of Hatra. 80f, Spiral Tower (Malwiye of Samarra). 100f, Adam's Tree. 200f, Aladdin's Cave. 500f, Golden Shiah Mosque of Kadhimain. 50f, 80f, 100f and 200f are vert.

1967, Dec. 1   Litho.
C22   A107   50f multicolored   2.75   .40
C23   A107   80f multicolored   3.00   .65
C24   A107   100f multicolored   2.75   .80
C25   A107   200f ver & multi   6.00   3.25
C26   A107   500f brn & multi   28.00   16.00
Nos. C22-C26 (5)   42.50   21.10
For overprints see Nos. C39, C52, C53, CO4.

Arabian — AP7

Animals: 2f, Striped hyena. 3f, Leopard. 5f, Mountain gazelle. 200f, Arabian stallion.

1969, Sept. 1   Litho.   *Perf. 14*
C27   AP7   2f multicolored   .85   .25
C28   AP7   3f multicolored   .85   .25
C29   AP7   5f multicolored   .85   .25

IRAQ

C30	AP7	10f multicolored	1.10	.30
C31	AP7	200f multicolored	12.00	6.00
		Nos. C27-C31 (5)	15.65	7.05

For overprints, see Nos. CO5-CO7.

Ross Smith's Vickers Vimy — AP8

1969, Dec. 4   Litho.   *Perf. 14*

C32	AP8	15f dk bl & multi	3.50	1.20
C33	AP8	35f multicolored	5.00	2.75
	a.	Souv. sheet of 2, #C32-C33, imperf.	15.00	13.00

50th anniv. of the first England to Australia flight of Capt. Ross Smith and Lt. Keith Smith. No. C33a sold for 100f.

View Across Euphrates AP9

Iraqi Banknotes and Pres. Hassan al-Bakr — AP10

1970, Oct. 30   Litho.   *Perf. 13*

C34	AP9	10f brt bl & multi	2.25	.50
C35	AP9	15f multicolored	3.50	1.10
C36	AP10	1d multicolored	65.00	24.00
		Nos. C34-C36 (3)	70.75	25.60

National Development Plan.
For overprints see Nos. C42-C43.

Telecommunications Emblem — AP11

1970, Dec. 15   Litho.   *Perf. 14x13½*

C37	AP11	15f gray & multi	.85	.25
C38	AP11	25f lt bl & multi	1.00	.50

10th Conf. of Arab Telecommunications Union.

No. C23 Overprinted

1971, Apr. 23   *Perf. 13*

C39	A107	80f multicolored	9.00	5.50

World Meteorological Day.

Iraqi Philatelic Society Emblem — AP12

1972, Feb. 25   Litho.   *Perf. 13*

C40	AP12	25f multicolored	1.10	.95
C41	AP12	70f pink & multi	3.75	2.40

Iraqi Philatelic Society, 20th anniversary.

Nos. C34-C35 Overprinted

1972, Feb. 25

C42	AP9	10f brt bl & multi	2.50	2.40
C43	AP9	15f multicolored	2.50	2.40
	a.	Overprint inverted	150.00	

9th Cong. of Natl. Union of Iraqi Students.

Soccer and C.I.S.M. Emblem AP13

20f, 35f, Players, soccer ball, C.I.S.M. emblem. 100f, Winged lion, Olympic & C.I.S.M. emblems.

1972, June 9   Litho.   *Perf. 13½*

C46	AP13	10f lt bl & multi	.75	.30
C47	AP13	20f dp bl & multi	1.75	.30
C48	AP13	25f green & multi	1.75	.30
C49	AP13	35f brt bl & multi	4.50	.80
	a.	Souv. sheet, 100f, imperf.	22.50	22.50
		Nos. C46-C49 (4)	8.75	1.70

25th Military Soccer Championships (C.I.S.M.), Baghdad, June 9-19.

Statue of Athlete — AP14

Design: 70f, Mesopotamian archer on horseback, ancient and modern athletes.

1972, Nov. 15   Photo.   *Perf. 14x13½*

C50	AP14	25f multicolored	2.00	.65
C51	AP14	70f multicolored	5.00	2.10

Cong. of Asian and World Body Building Championships, Baghdad, Nov. 15-23, 1972.

Nos. C23, C26 Overprinted

1973, Mar. 25   Litho.   *Perf. 13*

C52	A107	80f multi	21.00	7.25
C53	A107	500f multi	75.00	75.00

International History Congress.

ICATU Type of 1976

1976, Mar. 24   Photo.   *Perf. 13½*

C54	A213	75f blue & multi	4.50	2.00

Symbolic Eye — AP15

1976, June 20   Photo.   *Perf. 14*

C55	AP15	25f ultra & dk brn	.70	.25
C56	AP15	35f brt grn & dk brn	1.00	.25
C57	AP15	50f orange & multi	2.10	.60
		Nos. C55-C57 (3)	3.80	1.10

World Health Day: Foresight prevents blindness.

Basketball — AP16

Montreal Olympic Games Emblem and: 35f, Volleyball. 50f, Wrestling. 75f, Boxing. 100f, Target shooting, horiz.

1976, July 30   Litho.   *Perf. 12x12½*

C58	AP16	25f yel & multi	.75	.25
C59	AP16	35f blue & multi	1.00	.50
C60	AP16	50f ver & multi	1.25	.95
C61	AP16	75f yel grn & multi	2.25	1.25
		Nos. C58-C61 (4)	5.25	2.95

Souvenir Sheet
Imperf

C62	AP16	100f grn & multi	7.00	7.00

21st Olympic Games, Montreal, Canada, July 17-Aug. 1.

13th World Telecommunications Day — AP17

1981, May 17   Photo.   *Perf. 12½*

C63	AP17	25f multicolored	.65	.25
C64	AP17	50f multicolored	1.25	.40
C65	AP17	75f multicolored	2.10	.85
		Nos. C63-C65 (3)	4.00	1.50

Air Force Type of 1981

1981, June 1   Photo.   *Perf. 14x13½*

C66	A289	120f Planes, vert.	4.00	2.50

AIR POST OFFICIAL STAMPS

Catalogue values for all unused stamps in this section are for Never Hinged items.

Nos. C19-C22 Overprinted

1971   Litho.   *Perf. 13*

CO1	A105	40f multicolored	4.75	1.40
CO2	A105	50f multicolored	6.00	1.40
CO3	A105	80f multicolored	5.50	1.40

"Official" Reading Down

CO4	A107	50f multicolored	5.25	3.25
		Nos. CO1-CO4 (4)	21.50	7.45

Nos. C27-C28, C30 Overprinted or Surcharged

1971   *Perf. 14*

CO5	AP7	10f multicolored	7.50	5.00
CO6	AP7	15f on 3f multi	7.50	5.00
CO7	AP7	25f on 2f multi	7.50	5.00
		Nos. CO5-CO7 (3)	22.50	15.00

No bar and surcharge on No. CO5.

OFFICIAL STAMPS

British Mandate
Regular Issue of 1923 Overprinted

k   l

1923   *Wmk. 4*   *Perf. 12*

O1	A1(k)	½a olive grn	1.50	1.25
O2	A2(k)	1a brown	1.75	.25
O3	A3(l)	1½a car lake	3.75	1.75
O4	A4(k)	2a brown org	2.75	.30
O5	A5(k)	3a deep blue	4.50	1.00
O6	A6(l)	4a dull violet	4.75	2.00
O7	A7(k)	6a blue green	7.00	1.40
O8	A6(l)	8a olive bister	7.00	1.30
O9	A8(l)	1r grn & brn	17.50	4.00
O10	A1(k)	2r black (R)	30.00	12.50
O11	A6(l)	5r orange	75.00	40.00
O12	A7(k)	10r carmine	160.00	62.50
		Nos. O1-O12 (12)	315.50	128.25

Regular Issue of 1923-25 Overprinted

m

n

1924-25

O13	A1(m)	½a olive green	2.00	.30
O14	A2(m)	1a brown	1.75	.30
O15	A3(n)	1½a car lake	2.00	.30
O16	A4(m)	2a brown org	2.75	.30
O17	A5(m)	3a deep blue	3.25	.30
O18	A6(m)	4a dull violet	6.50	.30
O19	A7(m)	6a blue green	3.50	.30
O20	A6(m)	8a olive bister	6.50	.40
O21	A8(n)	1r grn & brn	18.00	1.00
O22	A1(m)	2r bister ('25)	42.50	4.50
O23	A6(n)	5r orange	85.00	55.00
O24	A7(m)	10r brown red	155.00	55.00
		Nos. O13-O24 (12)	328.75	118.00

For overprint see Nos. O42, O47, O51-O53.

No. 14 Overprinted Type "n"

1927

O25	A9	1r red brown	16.00	2.50

Regular Issue of 1931 Overprinted Vertically

o

1931

O26	A10	½a green	.75	3.00
O27	A10	1a chestnut	2.25	.25
O28	A10	1½a carmine	6.50	16.00
O29	A10	2a orange	1.00	.25
O30	A10	3a light blue	1.75	.70
O31	A10	4a purple brown	2.00	.90
O32	A10	6a Pruss blue	6.00	15.00
O33	A10	8a dark green	6.00	15.00

Overprinted Horizontally

p

O34	A11	1r dark brown	17.50	20.00
O35	A11	2r yellow brown	32.50	65.00
O36	A11	5r deep orange	52.50	125.00
O37	A11	10r red	175.00	250.00
		Nos. O26-O37 (12)	303.75	511.10

Overprinted Vertically Reading Up

O38	A9(p)	25r violet	1,600.	2,100.

For overprints see Nos. O39-O41, O43-O46, O48-O50, O54.

IRAQ

Kingdom

Nos. O15, O19, O22-O24, O26-O31, O33-O35, O38 Surcharged with New Values in Fils and Dinars, like Nos. 28-43

1932, Apr. 1

O39	A10	3f on ½a	9.50	4.00
a.	Pair, one without surcharge		1,500.	
O40	A10	4f on 1a (G)	6.75	.25
O41	A10	5f on 1a	6.75	.25
a.	Inverted Arabic "5"		60.00	40.00
O42	A3	8f on 1½a	15.00	.60
O43	A10	10f on 2a	9.00	.25
O44	A10	15f on 3a	12.00	2.75
O45	A10	20f on 4a	12.00	2.75
O46	A10	25f on 4a	12.50	2.25
O47	A7	30f on 6a	13.00	2.00
O48	A10	40f on 8a	11.50	4.00
a.	"Flis" for "Fils"		975.00	1,100.
O49	A11	50f on 1r	15.00	4.00
O50	A11	75f on 1r	17.00	7.00
O51	A1	100f on 2r	50.00	4.00
O52	A6	200f on 5r	65.00	26.00
O53	A7	½d on 10r	18.00	100.00
a.	Bar in "½" omitted		1,200.	1,350.
O54	A9	1d on 25r	330.00	210.00
	Nos. O39-O54 (16)		603.00	370.10

Regular Issue of 1932 Overprinted Vertically like Nos. O26-O33

1932, May 9

O55	A12	2f ultramarine	1.25	.30
O56	A12	3f green	1.25	.30
O57	A12	4f violet brn	1.50	.30
O58	A12	5f gray	1.50	.30
O59	A12	8f deep red	1.50	.30
O60	A12	10f yellow	2.75	.30
O61	A12	15f deep blue	3.25	.30
O62	A12	20f orange	3.25	.30
O63	A12	25f rose lilac	3.25	.45
O64	A12	30f olive grn	4.50	.45
O65	A12	40f dark violet	6.50	.45

Overprinted Horizontally Like Nos. O34 to O37

O66	A13	50f deep brown	4.00	.55
O67	A13	75f lt ultra	3.00	1.10
O68	A13	100f deep green	8.25	1.75
O69	A13	200f dark red	27.50	10.00

Overprinted Vertically like No. O38

O70	A14	½d gray blue	20.00	30.00
O71	A14	1d claret	100.00	125.00
	Nos. O55-O71 (17)		193.25	172.15

Regular Issue of 1934-38 Overprinted Type "o" Vertically Reading up in Black

1934-38 Unwmk.

O72	A15	1f purple ('38)	2.10	.75
O73	A15	2f ultramarine	2.10	.30
O74	A15	3f green	1.00	.30
O75	A15	4f purple brn	2.10	.30
O76	A15	5f gray green	1.75	.30
O77	A15	8f deep red	7.25	.30
O78	A15	10f yellow	.35	.30
O79	A15	15f deep blue	15.50	2.00
O80	A15	20f orange	1.40	.30
O81	A15	25f brown violet	28.00	7.00
O82	A15	30f olive green	7.25	.30
O83	A15	40f dark violet	8.75	.45

Overprinted Type "p"

O84	A16	50f deep brown	1.40	.75
O85	A16	75f ultramarine	10.00	1.10
O86	A16	100f deep green	2.75	1.25
O87	A16	200f dark red	7.25	3.50

Overprinted Type "p" Vertically Reading Up

O88	A17	½d gray blue	19.00	25.00
O89	A17	1d claret	75.00	75.00
	Nos. O72-O89 (18)		192.95	119.20

Catalogue values for unused stamps in this section, from this point to the end of the section, are for Never Hinged items.

Stamps of 1941-42 Overprinted in Black or Red

r   s

Perf. 11½x13½, 13 to 14 and Compound

1941-42

O90	A18(r)	1f dk vio ('42)	.60	.25
O91	A18(r)	2f choc ('42)	.60	.25
O92	A19(r)	3f brt grn ('42)	.60	.25
O93	A19(r)	4f pur (R) ('42)	.60	.25
O94	A19(r)	5f dk car rose ('42)	.60	.25
O95	A20(s)	8f carmine	1.60	.25
O96	A20(s)	8f ocher ('42)	.60	.25
O97	A20(s)	10f ocher	11.50	.75
O98	A20(s)	10f car ('42)	1.40	.25
O99	A20(s)	15f dull blue	11.50	1.40
O100	A20(s)	15f blk (R) ('42)	2.25	.60
O101	A20(s)	20f black (R)	3.50	.60
O102	A20(s)	20f dl bl ('42)	1.20	.25
O103	A21(r)	25f dark vio	1.75	.60
O104	A21(r)	25f dk vio ('42)	2.00	.60
O105	A21(s)	30f dp org	1.75	.60
O106	A21(r)	30f dk org ('42)	1.75	.60
O107	A21(r)	40f brn org	1.00	.60
O108	A21(r)	40f chnt ('42)	1.75	.60
O109	A21(r)	50f ultra	3.00	.25
O110	A21(r)	75f rose vio	2.00	.75
O111	A22(s)	100f ol grn ('42)	4.00	.60
O112	A22(s)	200f dp org ('42)	5.75	1.60
O113	A23(r)	½d blue ('42)	18.00	16.00
O114	A23(r)	1d grnsh bl ('42)	32.00	23.00
	Nos. O90-O114 (25)		111.30	51.05

The space between the English and Arabic on overprints "r" and "s" varies with the size of the stamps.

For overprints see Nos. O165, RA5.

Stamps of 1942 Overprinted in Black

1942 Unwmk. **Perf. 13x13½**

O115	A24	1f violet & brown	.75	.70
O116	A24	2f dark blue & brn	.75	.70
O117	A24	3f lt green & brn	.75	.70
O118	A24	4f dl brown & brn	.75	.70
O119	A24	5f sage grn & brn	1.00	.90
O120	A24	6f red org & brn	1.00	.90
O121	A24	10f dl rose red & brn	1.25	1.15
O122	A24	12f yel green & brn	1.75	1.60
	Nos. O115-O122 (8)		8.00	7.35

Stamps of 1948 Overprinted in Black

1948, Jan. 15   **Perf. 11½x12**
Size: 17¾x20½mm

O123	A25	1f slate	.40	.40
O124	A25	2f sepia	.40	.50
O125	A25	3f emerald	.40	.50
O126	A25	4f purple	.40	.40
O127	A25	5f rose lake	.40	.25
O128	A25	6f plum	.40	.45
O129	A25	8f ocher	.40	.45
O130	A25	10f rose red	.40	.40
O131	A25	12f dark olive	.40	.40
O132	A25	15f black	4.50	6.75
O133	A25	20f blue	.40	.25
O134	A25	25f rose violet	.40	.25
O135	A25	30f red org	.40	.25
O136	A25	40f org brn	.70	.45

Perf. 12x11½
Size: 22x27½mm

O137	A25	60f deep blue	.95	.25
O138	A25	75f lilac rose	1.75	.40
O139	A25	100f olive grn	1.75	1.00
O140	A25	200f dp orange	2.75	1.00
O141	A25	½d blue	22.50	16.00
O142	A25	1d green	32.50	35.00
	Nos. O123-O142 (20)		72.20	65.35

For overprints see Nos. O166-O177, O257, O272, O274, O277, O282, RA1, RA3, RA4.

Same Overprint on Nos. 133-138

1949-51 **Perf. 11½x12**
Size: 17¾x20½mm

O143	A25	3f rose lake ('51)	3.25	1.00
O144	A25	5f emerald ('51)	3.50	1.00
O145	A25	14f dk olive ('50)	1.75	.35
O146	A25	16f rose red ('51)	3.25	1.00
O147	A25	28f blue ('51)	1.00	.35

Perf. 12x11½
Size: 22x27½mm

O148	A25	50f deep blue	1.50	.50
	Nos. O143-O148 (6)		14.25	3.55

For overprints see #O258, O273, O275, O276.

Same Overprint in Black on Stamps and Type of 1954-57

1955-59   **Perf. 11½x12**

O148A	A28	1f blue ('56)	.25	.25
O149	A28	2f chocolate	.25	.25
O150	A28	3f rose lake	.25	.25
O151	A28	4f violet	.25	.25
O152	A28	5f emerald	.25	.25
O153	A28	6f plum ('56)	.25	.25
O154	A28	8f ocher ('56)	.25	.25
O155	A28	10f blue	.25	.25
O155A	A28	16f brt rose ('57)	22.50	22.50
O156	A28	20f olive	.50	.25
O157	A28	25f rose violet	2.25	1.00
O158	A28	30f vermilion	1.00	.25
O159	A28	40f orange brn	.50	.25

Size: 22½x27½mm

O160	A28	50f deep blue	2.25	.75
O161	A28	60f pale pur	14.00	5.75
O161A	A28	100f ol grn ('59)	32.50	16.00
	Nos. O148A-O161A (16)		77.50	48.75

Dates of issue for Nos. O155A and O161A are suppositional.

For overprints see Nos. O178-O191, O259-O260, O283-O291.

Same Ovpt. on Stamps of 1957-58

O162	A33	1f blue	4.25	1.75
O162A	A33	2f chocolate	5.00	3.75
O162B	A33	3f dk carmine	6.50	2.75
O162C	A33	4f dull violet	7.75	1.75
O162D	A33	5f emerald	4.25	1.75
O163	A33	6f plum	4.25	2.75
O164	A33	10f blue	4.25	1.40
	Nos. O162-O164 (7)		36.25	15.90

For overprints see #O192-O199, O292-O293.

Republic

Official Stamps of 1942-51 with Additional Overprint

Perf. 13½x14

1958-59 Engr. Unwmk.

O165	A22	200f dp orange	10.00	5.75

Perf. 11½x12, 12x11½

O166	A25	12f dk olive	1.00	.75
O167	A25	14f olive	1.10	.95
O168	A25	15f black	1.00	.50
O169	A25	16f rose red	3.75	2.10
O170	A25	25f rose vio	3.50	2.00
O171	A25	28f blue	2.00	1.60
O172	A25	40f orange brn	1.25	.95
O173	A25	60f deep blue	5.00	2.50
O174	A25	75f lilac rose	2.25	1.90
O175	A25	200f dp orange	2.75	2.40
O176	A25	½d blue	17.00	6.25
O177	A25	1d green	27.50	12.50
	Nos. O166-O177 (12)		68.10	34.40

Other denominations of types A22 and A25 exist with this overprint, but these were probably not regularly issued.

Same Ovpt. on Nos. O148A-O161A

O178	A28	1f blue	.60	.25
O179	A28	2f chocolate	.60	.25
O180	A28	3f rose lake	.60	.25
O181	A28	4f violet	.60	.25
O181A	A28	5f emerald	.65	.40
O182	A28	6f plum	.60	.25
O183	A28	8f ocher	.55	.25
O183A	A28	10f blue	.80	.25
O184	A28	16f bright rose	7.50	7.00
O185	A28	20f olive	.65	.25
O186	A28	25f rose violet	.65	.25
O187	A28	30f vermilion	.70	.25
O188	A28	40f orange brn	1.00	.40
O189	A28	50f blue	1.00	.50
O190	A28	60f pale purple	1.00	.60
O191	A28	100f olive grn	2.10	.60
	Nos. O178-O191 (16)		19.60	12.15

Same Ovpts. on #O162-O164, 216

O192	A33	1f blue	.25	.25
O193	A33	2f chocolate	.25	.25
O194	A33	3f dark carmine	.45	.25
O195	A33	4f dull violet	.25	.25
O196	A33	5f emerald	.25	.25
O197	A33	6f plum	.25	.25
O198	A33	8f ocher	.65	.25
O199	A33	10f blue	.70	.25
	Nos. O192-O199 (8)		3.05	2.00

Nos. 232-233, 235-237, 242 Overprinted

Litho. & Photo.

1961, Apr. 1 Unwmk. **Perf. 11½**

O200	A38	1f multi	.40	.30
O201	A38	2f multi	.40	.30
O202	A38	4f multi	.40	.30
O203	A38	5f multi	.50	.30
O204	A38	10f multi	.80	.60
O205	A38	50f multi	13.50	10.50
	Nos. O200-O205 (6)		16.00	12.30

Nos. 232-247 Overprinted

Emblem in Gold, Red and Blue; Blue Inscriptions

1961

O206	A38	1f gray	.40	.30
O207	A38	2f salmon	.40	.30
O208	A38	3f pale violet	.40	.30
O209	A38	4f bright yel	.40	.30
O210	A38	5f light blue	.40	.30
O211	A38	10f bright pink	.40	.30
O212	A38	15f lt green	.40	.30
O213	A38	20f bister brn	.40	.30
O214	A38	30f light gray	.50	.30
O215	A38	40f orange yel	.50	.30
O216	A38	50f yel green	.60	.30
O217	A38	75f pale green	.80	.40
O218	A38	100f orange	.90	.65
O219	A38	200f lilac	3.25	1.40
O220	A38	500f bister	11.50	5.50
O221	A38	1d brt green	22.50	11.50
	Nos. O206-O221 (16)		43.75	22.75

Nos. 480-482 Overprinted

1971 **Litho.** **Perf. 13½**

O222	A115	10f multicolored	.90	1.50
O223	A115	15f blue & multi	9.00	1.50
O224	A115	25f multicolored	9.00	3.00
	Nos. O222-O224 (3)		18.90	6.00

Overprint lines are spaced 16mm on No. O222, 32½mm on Nos. O223-O224.

Same Overprint on Nos. 453, 455-456

1971 **Perf. 13**

O225	A107	5f lilac & multi	7.00	.30
O226	A107	15f rose red & multi	7.00	.50
O227	A107	25f vio bl & multi	10.00	1.50
	Nos. O225-O227 (3)		24.00	2.30

Overprint horizontal on Nos. O225 and O227; vertical, reading down on No. O226. Distance between English and Arabic words: 8mm.

See No. O308 for 15f stamp with horizontal overprint.

Nos. 446, 448-449 Overprinted

1971 **Litho.** **Perf. 13**

O228	A105	15f multicolored	1.60	.65
O229	A105	15f multi, wide ovpt. setting	62.50	7.50
a.	Narrow setting		47.50	
O230	A105	15f multicolored	11.50	3.00
O231	A105	30f multicolored	11.50	3.00
	Nos. O228-O231 (4)		87.10	14.15

No. O229 overprinted "Official" horizontally. Two overprint settings on O229: wide, 6.5mm between English and Arab inscriptions; narrow, 2mm between inscriptions.

Same Overprint on Nos. 483-486

1972 **Perf. 13½**

O232	A116	10f multicolored	5.00	.50
O233	A116	25f multicolored	5.00	1.00

1972

O234	A117	15f multicolored	5.00	.50
O235	A117	25f multicolored	5.00	1.00

IRAQ

Same Overprint, "Official" Reading Down on Nos. 562-565
1972
O240	A142	5f multicolored	5.00	3.75
O241	A142	10f multicolored	5.00	3.75
O242	A142	15f multicolored	5.00	3.75
O243	A142	35f multicolored	5.00	3.75
Nos. O240-O243 (4)			20.00	15.00

Latin inscription on Nos. O240-O241 obliterated with heavy bar.

No. 487 Overprinted "Official" like No. CO5
1972 *Photo. Perf. 13½*
O244	A118	25f multicolored	10.50	3.00

Nos. O134, O148 Ovptd. with 3 Bars
Perf. 11½x12, 12x11½
1973, Jan. 29 *Engr.*
O257	A25	25f rose violet	6.00	1.50
O258	A25	50f deep blue	6.00	5.50

Same on Nos. O157 and O160
O259	A28	25f rose violet	6.00	1.50
O260	A28	50f blue	6.00	1.50

Type of 1957 Overprinted
Size: 22x27½mm
O261	A33	50f deep blue	6.00	1.50
Nos. O257-O261 (5)			30.00	11.50

See note after No. 679. No. O261 not issued without overprints.

King Faisal Issues Overprinted

Two sizes of overprint: Arabic 6½mm or 9mm.

1973
O263	A28	15f black (#149)	4.00	3.75
O264	A33	15f black	4.00	1.00
O265	A25	25f rose vio (#121)	15.00	6.00
O266	A28	25f rose vio (#151)	4.00	1.00
O267	A33	25f rose violet	4.00	1.00

Same Overprint on Nos. 674-677
O268	A28	10f blue	3.75	3.75
O269	A28	10f black	52.50	60.00
O270	A28	15f black	67.50	75.00
O271	A33	15f black	2.50	2.00
Nos. O263-O271 (9)			157.25	153.50

Official Stamps of 1948-51 Overprinted

Overprint design faces left or right.

1973
O272	A25	12f (#O131)	2.00	.30
O273	A25	14f (#O145)	2.00	.50
O274	A25	15f (#O132)	2.00	.50
O275	A25	16f (#O146)	3.25	.85
O276	A25	28f (#O147)	6.75	1.10
O277	A25	30f (#O135)	6.75	.95
O278	A25	40f (#O136)	6.75	1.40
O279	A25	60f (#O137)	6.75	5.25
O280	A25	100f (#O139)	22.50	8.50
O281	A25	½d (#O141)	57.50	22.50
O282	A25	1d (#O142)	110.00	110.00
Nos. O272-O282 (11)			226.25	151.85

Same Overprint on Official Stamps of 1955-59
O283	A28	3f (#O150)	1.75	.60
O284	A28	6f (#O153)	1.75	.60
O285	A28	8f (#O154)	1.75	.60
O286	A28	16f (#O155A)	17.50	17.50
O287	A28	20f (#O156)	1.75	.60
O288	A28	30f (#O158)	1.75	.95
O289	A28	40f (#O159)	1.75	1.60
O290	A28	60f (#O161)	8.75	2.00
O291	A28	100f (#O161A)	27.50	8.00
Nos. O283-O291 (9)			64.25	32.45

Same Overprint on 1957-58 Issues
O292	A33	3f dk car (#O162B)	5.50	1.25
O293	A33	6f plum (#O163)	5.50	1.25
O294	A33	8f ocher (#179)	5.50	1.25
O295	A33	30f red orange	5.50	1.25
Nos. O292-O295 (4)			22.00	5.00

The overprint on Nos. O294-O295 includes the "On State Service" overprint; No. O295 was not issued without overprints. The overprint leaf design faces left or right and varies in size.

Nos. 403, 497, 681 Overprinted
Perf. 12½, 13x12½, 13½
1974 (?) *Photo., Litho.*
O296	A89	2f multicolored	5.00	
O297	A123	15f multicolored	6.00	.50
O298	A185	25f multicolored	4.00	1.00
Nos. O296-O298 (3)			15.00	

Size of "Official" on Nos. O297-O298 9mm.

Nos. 683-691 Overprinted
1974 *Litho. Perf. 13x12½*
O299	A186	5f orange & blk	.30	.30
O300	A186	10f bister & blk	.30	.30
O301	A186	20f brt rose & blk	.65	.30
O302	A186	25f ultra & blk	1.25	1.25
O303	A186	35f emerald & blk	1.25	.50
O304	A186	45f blue & black	1.25	.60
O305	A186	50f olive & yel	1.75	.65
O306	A186	70f violet & yel	1.75	.95
O307	A186	95f brown & yel	2.75	1.10
Nos. O299-O307 (9)			11.25	5.95

Nos. 455 and 467 Overprinted
1975 *Litho. Perf. 13, 14*
O308	A107	15f multicolored	3.50	3.50
O311	A110	30f multicolored	6.75	4.25

Space between Arabic and English lines of overprint is 4mm on No. O308, 13mm on No. O311.

See No. O226 for 15d stamp with vertical overprint.

Nos. 491-493 Overprinted or Surcharged like Nos. CO5-CO7
1975 *Perf. 14*
O312	A121	10f multicolored	7.00	4.00
O312A	A121	15f on 3f multi	7.00	4.00
O313	A121	25f on 2f multi	7.00	4.00
Nos. O312-O313 (3)			21.00	12.00

Nos. 322-325 Overprinted

Engr.; Engr. & Photo.
1975 *Perf. 12x11*
O314	A57	10f rose red	8.50	8.50
O315	A57	15f brown & buff	8.50	8.50
O316	A57	20f violet blue	8.50	8.50
O317	A57	30f orange	16.00	16.00
Nos. O314-O317 (4)			41.50	41.50

Arms of Iraq — O1
1975 *Photo. Perf. 14*
O318	O1	5f multicolored	.35	.35
O319	O1	10f blue & multi	.35	.35
O320	O1	15f yel & multi	.45	.45
O321	O1	20f ultra & multi	.70	.70
O322	O1	25f org & multi	.95	.95
O323	O1	30f rose & multi	1.05	1.05
O324	O1	50f multicolored	2.00	2.00
O325	O1	100f multicolored	3.50	3.50
Nos. O318-O325 (8)			9.35	9.35

Nos. 787-791 Overprinted "OFFICIAL" in English and Arabic
1976, Sept. 15 *Litho. Perf. 13½x14*
O327	A219	5f multicolored	1.50	.75
O328	A219	10f multicolored	1.50	.95
O329	A219	15f multicolored	1.75	.95
O330	A219	25f multicolored	4.00	1.25
O331	A219	50f multicolored	6.50	2.25
Nos. O327-O331 (5)			15.25	6.15

Altharthar - Euphrates Canal — O2
1978 *Photo. Perf. 11½*
O332	O2	5f multicolored	.35	.30
O333	O2	10f multicolored	.35	.30
O334	O2	15f multicolored	.50	.30
O335	O2	25f multicolored	.95	.30
Nos. O332-O335 (4)			2.15	1.20

Baghdad University Entrance — O3
1981, Oct. 21 *Litho. Perf. 12x12½*
O336	O3	45f multicolored	.70	.40
O337	O3	50f multicolored	3.25	.50

Nos. O336-O337 Surcharged
1983, May 15 *Litho. Perf. 12x12½*
O338	O3	60f on 45f multi	2.75	.50
O339	O3	70f on 50f multi	3.25	.75

Martyrs Type of 1981 Inscribed "OFFICIAL" in English and Arabic
1981 *Photo. Perf. 14*
O339A	A303	45f silver border	1.50	.40
O339B	A303	50f gold border	1.50	.50
O339C	A303	120f metallic bl border	4.00	1.10
Nos. O339A-O339C (3)			7.00	2.00

Building Type of 1983 Inscribed "OFFICIAL" in English and Arabic
1982, Dec. 31 *Litho. Perf. 14*
O340	A324	60f multicolored	.95	.50
O341	A324	70f multicolored	1.05	.65

For surcharge see No. 1517.

Martyr Type of 1984 Inscribed "OFFICIAL" in English and Arabic
1984, Dec. 1 *Perf. 13½*
O342	A329	20f multicolored	.35	.30
O343	A329	30f multicolored	.35	.30
O344	A329	50f multicolored	.60	.40
O345	A329	60f multicolored	.75	.40
Nos. O342-O345 (4)			2.05	1.40

No. RA22 Overprinted
1985 (?) *Litho. Perf. 13x12½*
O346	PT2	5f bister, blk & yel	3.75	1.00

POSTAL TAX STAMPS

Catalogue values for unused stamps in this section are for Never Hinged items.

Nos. O125 and 115 Surcharged in Carmine or Black
1949 *Unwmk. Perf. 11½x12*
RA1	A25	2f on 3f emer (C)	25.00	15.00
RA2	A25	2f on 6f plum	32.50	14.00

Similar Overprint in Carmine or Black on Nos. O124, O127 and O94, Middle Arabic Line Omitted
Perf. 11½x12
RA3	A25	2f sepia (C)	20.00	9.00
RA4	A25	5f rose lake	40.00	20.00

Perf. 12x13½, 14
RA5	A19	5f dark car rose	20.00	10.50

Larger overprint on #RA5, 20½mm wide. Value $22.50.

No. 115 Surcharged in Black
Perf. 11½x12
RA6	A25	5f on 6f plum	45.00	17.00

The tax on Nos. RA1-RA6 was to aid the war in Palestine.

Nos. 317, 322-326 Surcharged

Engr.; Engr. & Photo.
1963 *Perf. 12x11*
RA7	A57	5f on 1f green	4.00	5.00
RA8	A57	5f on 10f rose red	4.00	5.00
RA9	A57	5f on 15f brn & buff	4.00	5.00
RA10	A57	5f on 20f vio blue	4.00	5.00
RA11	A57	5f on 30f orange	4.00	5.00
RA12	A57	5f on 40f brt green	4.00	5.00
Nos. RA7-RA12 (6)			24.00	30.00

Surtax was for the Defense Fund.

1967, Aug. *Photo. Perf. 13½*
RA13	PT1	5f brown	5.00	.40

Surtax was for flood victims.

No. RA13 Overprinted
1967, Nov.
RA14	PT1	5f brown	5.00	.45

Surtax was for Defense Fund.

Nos. 305A-305B with Surcharge Similar to Nos. RA7-RA12
1972 *Litho. Perf. 13½x14*
RA15	A54a	5f on 14f	6.75	6.75
RA16	A54a	5f on 35f	6.75	6.75

Surtax was for the Defense Fund. The 2 disks obliterating old denominations are on one line at the bottom. Size of Arabic inscription: 17x12mm.

No. 452 with Surcharge Similar to Nos. RA7-RA12, and Nos. 443, 457 and 526 Srchd.
1973 *Litho. Perf. 13*
RA17	A105	5f on 2f multi	8.50	8.50
RA18	A107	5f on 2f multi	8.50	8.50
RA19	A108	5f on 2f multi	8.50	8.50
RA20	A135	5f on 2f multi	8.50	8.50
Nos. RA17-RA20 (4)			34.00	34.00

Surtax was for the Defense Fund. Surcharges on Nos. RA17-RA20 are adjusted to fit shape of stamps and to obliterate old denominations.

IRAQ — IRELAND

No 683 Overprinted

1974	Litho.		Perf. 13x12½
RA21	A186	5f orange & blk	6.00 4.00

Soldier — PT2

1974			
RA22	PT2	5f bister, blk & yel	2.50 2.50

Surtax of Nos. RA21-RA22 was for the Defense Fund.
For overprint see No. O346.

Dome of the Rock, Jerusalem — PT3

1977	Photo.		Perf. 14
RA23	PT3	5f multicolored	2.75 .50

Surtax was for families of Palestinians.
For surcharges see Nos. 1457, 1465-1477.

AIR POST POSTAL TAX STAMPS

Catalogue values for unused stamps in this section are for Never Hinged items.

No. C15 Surcharged Like Nos. RA17-RA20

1973	Litho.		Perf. 13½
RAC1	AP5	5f on 2f multi	7.50 7.50

Surtax was for the Defense Fund.

IRELAND

'ir-lənd

(Eire)

LOCATION — Comprises the entire island of Ireland, except 5,237 square miles at the extreme north
GOVT. — Republic
AREA — 27,136 sq. mi.
POP. — 3,626,087 (1996)
CAPITAL — Dublin

12 Pence = 1 Shilling
100 Pence = 1 Pound (Punt) (1971)
100 Cents = 1 Euro (2002)

Catalogue values for unused stamps in this country are for Never Hinged items, beginning with Scott 99 in the regular postage section, Scott C1 in the air post section, and Scott J5 in the postage due section.

Watermarks

Wmk. 44 — SE in Monogram

The letters "SE" are the initials of "Saorstat Eireann" (Irish Free State).

Wmk. 262 — Multiple "e"

Overprinted by Dollard, Ltd.

Great Britain Nos. 159-167, 170-172, 179-181 Overprinted

Overprint means "Provisional Government of Ireland."

Overprint measures 15x17½mm
Black or Gray Black Overprint

1922, Feb. 17		Wmk. 33	Perf. 15x14	
1	A82	½p green	2.00	1.35
		Never hinged	3.40	
a.		Inverted overprint	450.00	625.00
		Never hinged	750.00	
b.		Date omitted	110.00	90.00
2	A83	1p scarlet	3.40	1.35
		Never hinged	5.00	
a.		Inverted overprint	300.00	500.00
		Never hinged	450.00	
b.		Double overprint		1,600.
3	A86	2½p ultra	3.40	14.50
		Never hinged	13.50	
4	A87	3p violet	9.00	12.00
		Never hinged	16.00	
5	A88	4p slate green	9.00	22.50
		Never hinged	15.00	
6	A89	5p yel brown	9.00	20.00
		Never hinged	16.00	
7	A90	9p black brown	26.00	40.00
		Never hinged	47.50	
8	A90	10p light blue	16.00	32.50
		Never hinged	27.00	
		Nos. 1-8 (8)	77.80	144.20

The ½p with red overprint is a proof. Value, $150.

Red or Carmine Overprint

1922, Apr.-July				
9	A86	2½p ultra (R)	2.75	8.50
		Never hinged	5.50	
10	A88	4p sl grn (R)	16.00	27.00
		Never hinged	32.50	
10A	A88	4p sl grn (C)	80.00	130.00
		Never hinged	135.00	
11	A90	9p blk brn (R)	32.50	35.00
		Never hinged	55.00	
11A	A90	9p blk brn (C)	135.00	160.00
		Never hinged	200.00	
		Nos. 9-11A (5)	266.25	360.50

Overprinted in Black

There is a variation that is 21x14mm. The "h" and "é" are 1mm apart. See Nos. 36-38.

Overprint measures 21½x14mm

1922, Feb. 17		Wmk. 34	Perf. 11x12	
12	A91	2sh6p brown	55.00	100.00
		Never hinged	145.00	
a.		Double overprint, one albino	1,200.	—
13	A91	5sh car rose	90.00	190.00
		Never hinged	210.00	
a.		Double overprint, one albino	1,200.	—
14	A91	10sh gray blue	225.00	400.00
		Never hinged	450.00	
		Nos. 12-14 (3)	370.00	690.00

Overprinted by Alex. Thom & Co.

Overprinted in Black

TWO PENCE
Die I — Four horizontal lines above the head. Heavy colored lines above and the bottom tablet. The inner frame line is closer to the central design than it is to the outer frame line.
Die II — Three lines above the head. Thinner lines above and below the bottom tablet. The inner frame line is midway between the central design and the outer frame line.

Overprint measures 14½x16mm

1922, Feb. 17		Wmk. 33	Perf. 15x14	
15	A84	1½p red brown	3.25	2.75
		Never hinged	4.50	
a.		"PENCF"	540.00	475.00
16	A85	2p orange (II)	5.50	2.00
		Never hinged	6.50	
a.		Inverted overprint (II)	375.00	450.00
b.		2p orange (I)	5.00	1.75
		As "b," never hinged	6.50	
c.		Inverted overprint (I)	200.00	300.00
17	A89	6p red violet	20.00	27.50
		Never hinged	27.50	
18	A90	1sh bister	22.50	20.00
		Never hinged	42.50	
		Nos. 15-18 (4)	51.25	52.25

Important: see Nos. 25-26, 31, 35.

Overprinted by Harrison & Sons

Overprinted in Black in Glossy Black Ink

Overprint measures 15¼x17mm

1922, June			Coil Stamps	
19	A82	½p green	5.50	22.50
		Never hinged	7.00	
20	A83	1p scarlet	4.50	18.00
		Never hinged	6.75	
21	A84	1½p red brown	7.25	52.50
		Never hinged	11.00	
22	A85	2p orange (I)	27.00	45.00
		Never hinged	42.50	
a.		2p orange (II)	27.00	42.50
		Never hinged	45.00	
		Nos. 19-22 (4)	44.25	138.00

In Harrison overprint, "i" of "Rialtas" extends below the base of the other letters.
The Harrison stamps were issued in coils, either horizontal or vertical. The paper is double where the ends of the strips were overlapped. Mint pairs with the overlap sell for about three times the price of a single. The perforations are often clipped.

Overprinted by Alex. Thom & Co.

Stamps of Great Britain, 1912-22 Overprinted as Nos. 15 to 18, in Shiny to Dull Blue Black, or Red

Note: The blue black overprints can best be distinguished from the black by use of 50-power magnification with a light source behind the stamp.

Overprint measures 14½x16mm

1922, July-Nov.			Perf. 15x14	
23	A82	½p green	3.50	1.80
		Never hinged	5.00	
24	A83	1p scarlet	3.00	2.00
		Never hinged	3.50	
25	A84	1½p red brown	6.00	9.00
		Never hinged	13.50	
26	A85	2p orange (II)	5.50	2.00
		Never hinged	6.50	
a.		Inverted overprint (II)	375.00	500.00
b.		2p orange (I)	32.50	3.75
		Never hinged	45.00	
27	A86	2½p ultra (R)	9.00	32.50
		Never hinged	18.00	
28	A87	3p violet	10.00	6.50
		Never hinged	12.50	
29	A88	4p sl grn (R)	4.50	11.00
		Never hinged	11.00	
30	A89	5p yellow brown	9.00	16.00
		Never hinged	18.00	
31	A89	6p red violet	15.00	6.75
		Never hinged	18.00	
32	A90	9p blk brn (R)	20.00	26.00
		Never hinged	35.00	
33	A90	9p ol grn (R)	11.00	45.00
		Never hinged	20.00	
34	A90	10p light blue	27.50	67.50
		Never hinged	60.00	
35	A90	1sh bister	15.00	15.00
		Never hinged	32.50	
		Nos. 23-35 (13)	139.00	241.05

Nos. 23, 24, 28, 34 overprinted in dull black, rather than the normal blue-black, are believed to be proofs, pressed into use when supplies of the issued values ran low.

Overprinted as Nos. 12 to 14 in Blue Black (Shiny to Dull)

The "h" and "é" are ½mm apart.

Overprint measures 21x13½mm

1922		Wmk. 34	Perf. 11x12	
36	A91	2sh6p gray brn	290.	400.
		Never hinged	500.	
37	A91	5sh car rose	300.	450.
		Never hinged	525.	
38	A91	10sh gray blue	1,700.	2,000.
		Never hinged	2,400.	
		Nos. 36-38 (3)	2,290.	2,850.

Overprinted in Blue Black

Overprint measures 15¾x16mm

1922, Dec.		Wmk. 33	Perf. 15x14	
39	A82	½p green	1.35	2.50
		Never hinged	2.50	
40	A83	1p scarlet	5.50	4.50
		Never hinged	8.00	
41	A84	1½p red brown	3.25	16.00
		Never hinged	7.25	
42	A85	2p orange (II)	13.50	13.50
		Never hinged	22.50	
43	A90	1sh bister	45.00	72.50
		Never hinged	60.00	
		Nos. 39-43 (5)	68.60	109.00

Stamps of Great Britain, 1912-22, Overprinted in Shiny to Dull Blue Black or Red

This overprint means "Irish Free State"

The inner loop of the "9" is an upright oval.
The measurement of "1922" is made across the bottom of the numerals and does not include the serif at the top of the "1."
There were 5 plates for printing the overprint on Nos. 44-55. In the impressions from plate I the 12th stamp in the 15th row has no accent on the 2nd "A" of "SAORSTAT." To correct this an accent was inserted by hand, sometimes this was in a reversed position.
On Nos. 56-58 the accent was omitted on the 2nd stamp in the 3rd and 8th rows. Damage to the plate makes the accent look reversed on the 4th stamp in the 7th row. The top of the "t" slants down in a line with the so-called accent.

Overprint measures 15x8½mm
"1922" is 6¼mm long

1922-23		Wmk. 33	Perf. 15x14	
44	A82	½p green	1.80	1.35
		Never hinged	2.50	
a.		Accent omitted	1,275.	900.00
b.		Accent added	115.00	135.00
45	A83	1p scarlet	2.25	1.35
		Never hinged	2.50	
a.		Accent omitted	15,250.	9,000.
b.		Accent added	145.00	165.00
c.		Accent and final "t" omitted	13,500.	7,250.
d.		Accent and final "t" added	225.00	270.00
46	A84	1½p red brn	3.25	16.00
		Never hinged	9.00	
47	A85	2p org (II)	2.75	4.50
		Never hinged	7.50	
48	A86	2½p ultra (R)	6.75	13.00
		Never hinged	9.00	
a.		Accent omitted	145.00	180.00
49	A87	3p violet	9.00	11.50
		Never hinged	20.00	
a.		Accent omitted	300.00	390.00
50	A88	4p sl grn (R)	5.50	12.50
		Never hinged	10.00	
a.		Accent omitted	200.00	270.00
51	A89	5p yel brn	5.25	5.25
		Never hinged	9.50	
52	A89	6p dull vio	3.50	2.75
		Never hinged	6.50	
a.		Accent added	825.00	825.00
53	A90	9p ol grn (R)	10.00	11.00
		Never hinged	12.50	
a.		Accent omitted	250.00	315.00
54	A90	10p lt blue	18.00	52.50
		Never hinged	45.00	
55	A90	1sh bister	13.50	13.50
		Never hinged	35.00	
a.		Accent omitted	11,000.	11,000.
b.		Accent added	750.00	825.00

Perf. 11x12
Wmk. 34

56	A91	2sh6p lt brown	57.50	90.00
		Never hinged	125.00	
a.		Accent omitted	410.00	540.00
57	A91	5sh car rose	90.00	180.00
		Never hinged	225.00	
a.		Accent omitted	550.00	825.00
58	A91	10sh gray blue	200.00	450.00
		Never hinged	500.00	
a.		Accent omitted	2,750.	3,600.
		Nos. 44-58 (15)	429.05	865.20

Overprinted by Harrison & Sons
Coil Stamps
Same Ovpt. in Black or Blue Black

1923		Wmk. 33	Perf. 15x14	
59	A82	½p green	3.00	13.50
		Never hinged	6.50	
a.		Tall "1"	18.00	50.00
		Never hinged	27.50	

IRELAND

60	A83	1p scarlet	7.75	21.00
		Never hinged	15.00	
a.		Tall "1"	72.50	145.00
		Never hinged	95.00	
61	A84	1½p red brown	7.75	50.00
		Never hinged	22.50	
a.		Tall "1"	90.00	225.00
		Never hinged	170.00	
62	A85	2p orange (II)	11.00	18.00
		Never hinged	17.00	
a.		Tall "1"	32.50	55.00
		Never hinged	40.00	
		Nos. 59-62 (4)	29.50	102.50

These stamps were issued in coils, made by joining horizontal or vertical strips of the stamps. See 2nd paragraph after No. 22. In some strips there were two stamps with the "1" of "1922" 2½mm high and with serif at foot.

In this setting the middle "e" of "eireann" is a trifle above the line of the other letters, making the word appear slightly curved. The lower end of the "1" of "1922" is rounded on Nos. 59-62 instead of flat as on Nos. 44-47.

The inner loop of the "9" is round.

See Nos. 77b, 78b and 79b.

Booklet Panes

For very fine, the perforation holes at top or bottom of the pane should be visible, though not necessarily perfect half circles.

"Sword of Light" A1

Map of Ireland A2

Coat of Arms A3

Celtic Cross A4

Perf. 15x14
1922-23 Typo. Wmk. 44
Size: 18x22mm

65	A1	½p emerald	2.75	1.50
		Never hinged	4.50	
a.		Booklet pane of 6	350.00	
66	A2	1p car rose	2.25	1.50
		Never hinged	4.50	
a.		Booklet pane of 6	350.00	
b.		Booklet pane of 3 + 3 labels	400.00	
67	A2	1½p claret	3.75	3.00
		Never hinged	8.50	
68	A2	2p deep green	2.25	.75
		Never hinged	3.50	
a.		Booklet pane of 6	350.00	
b.		Perf. 15 horiz. ('35)	12,500.	2,000.

No. 68b is valued in the grade of fine.

69	A3	2½p chocolate	5.50	8.50
		Never hinged	11.00	
70	A4	3p ultra	3.50	3.00
		Never hinged	7.25	
71	A3	4p slate	6.25	6.25
		Never hinged	12.50	
72	A1	5p deep violet	22.50	15.00
		Never hinged	57.50	
73	A1	6p red violet	7.25	5.75
		Never hinged	14.50	
74	A3	9p violet	35.00	25.00
		Never hinged	125.00	
75	A4	10p brown	17.00	35.00
		Never hinged	57.50	
76	A1	1sh light blue	35.00	17.00
		Never hinged	110.00	
		Nos. 65-76 (12)	143.00	122.25

The 2p was issued in 1922; other denominations in 1923.

No. 68b is a vertical coil stamp.

See Nos. 87, 91-92, 105-117, 137-138, 225-226, 326. For types overprinted see Nos. 118-119.

Overprinted by the Government Printing Office, Dublin Castle and British Board of Inland Revenue at Somerset House, London

Great Britain Nos. 179-181 Ovptd. in Black or Gray Black

The measurement of "1922" is made across the bottom of the numerals and does not include the serif at the top of the "1".

"1922" is 5½mm long
1925 Wmk. 34 Perf. 11x12

77	A91	2sh6p gray brown	70.00	175.00
		Never hinged	125.00	
78	A91	5sh rose red	95.00	275.00
		Never hinged	160.00	
79	A91	10sh gray blue	225.00	575.00
		Never hinged	425.00	
		Nos. 77-79 (3)	390.00	1,025.

In 1927 the 2sh6p, 5sh and 10sh stamps were overprinted from a plate in which the Thom and Castle clichés were combined, thus including wide and narrow "1922" in the same setting.

Overprinted by British Board of Inland Revenue at Somerset House, London

Pair with "1922" Wide and Narrow

1927

77a	A91	2sh6p		400.
		Never hinged		775.
78a	A91	5sh		700.
		Never hinged		1,350.
79a	A91	10sh		1,700.
		Never hinged		3,750.
		Nos. 77a-79a (3)		2,800.

Wide "1922"
"1922" is 6¼mm long

1927-28

77b	A91	2sh6p	60.00	60.00
		Never hinged	110.00	
78b	A91	5sh ('28)	90.00	140.00
		Never hinged	225.00	
79b	A91	10sh ('28)	250.00	425.00
		Never hinged	550.00	
		Nos. 77b-79b (3)	400.00	625.00

Daniel O'Connell — A5

Perf. 15x14
1929, June 22 Wmk. 44

80	A5	2p dark green	.75	.55
		Never hinged	1.25	
81	A5	3p dark blue	4.25	14.00
		Never hinged	15.00	
82	A5	9p dark violet	4.75	13.50
		Never hinged	16.00	
		Nos. 80-82 (3)	9.75	28.05

Catholic Emancipation in Ireland, centenary.

Shannon River Hydroelectric Station — A6

1930, Oct. 15

83	A6	2p black brown	1.25	2.75
		Never hinged	4.25	

Opening of the hydroelectric development of the River Shannon.

Farmer with Scythe — A7

1931, June 12

84	A7	2p pale blue	1.00	1.50
		Never hinged	2.50	

Bicentenary of Royal Dublin Society.

Cross of Cong and Chalice — A8

1932, May 12

85	A8	2p dark green	2.50	.85
		Never hinged	3.50	
86	A8	3p bright blue	4.50	8.00
		Never hinged	7.00	

International Eucharistic Congress.

Type of 1922-23 Issue
Coil Stamp

1933-34 Perf. 15 Horizontally

87	A2	1p rose ('34)	27.50	60.00
		Never hinged	45.00	
a.		1p carmine rose	125.00	300.00
		Never hinged	200.00	

No. 87a has a single perforation at each side near the top, while No. 87 is perforated top and bottom only.

See No. 68b.

Adoration of the Cross — A9

1933, Sept. 18 Perf. 15x14

88	A9	2p slate green	1.25	.55
		Never hinged	2.50	
89	A9	3p deep blue	3.00	6.00
		Never hinged	8.75	

Holy Year.

Hurling — A10

1934, July 27

90	A10	2p green	1.00	1.50
		Never hinged	2.50	

50th anniv. of the Gaelic Athletic Assoc.

Types of 1922-23
Coil Stamps
Wmk. 44 Sideways

1934 Perf. 14 Vertically

91	A1	½p green	30.00	75.00
		Never hinged	45.00	
92	A2	2p gray green	50.00	125.00
		Never hinged	85.00	

Overprinted by Harrison & Sons
Great Britain Nos. 222-224
Overprinted in Black

1935 Wmk. 34 Perf. 11x12

93	A91	2sh6p brown	52.50	70.00
		Never hinged	100.00	
94	A91	5sh carmine	200.00	225.00
		Never hinged	350.00	
95	A91	10sh dark blue	400.00	650.00
		Never hinged	1,100.	
		Nos. 93-95 (3)	652.50	945.00

Waterlow printing can be distinguished by the crossed lines in the background of portrait. Previous issues have horizontal lines only.

St. Patrick and Paschal Fire — A11

1937, Sept. 8 Wmk. 44 Perf. 14x15

96	A11	2sh6p bright green	90.00	90.00
		Never hinged	225.00	
97	A11	5sh brown violet	110.00	110.00
		Never hinged	250.00	
98	A11	10sh dark blue	90.00	90.00
		Never hinged	225.00	
		Nos. 96-98 (3)	290.00	290.00

See Nos. 121-123.

Catalogue values for unused stamps in this section, from this point to the end of the section, are for Never Hinged items.

Allegory of Ireland and Constitution A12

1937, Dec. 29 Perf. 15x14

99	A12	2p plum	2.00	.30
100	A12	3p deep blue	7.00	5.50

Constitution Day.
See Nos. 169-170.

Father Theobald Mathew — A13

1938, July 1

101	A13	2p black brown	2.50	.50
102	A13	3p ultramarine	9.00	8.50

Temperance Crusade by Father Mathew, centenary.

Washington, US Eagle and Harp — A14

1939, Mar. 1

103	A14	2p bright carmine	1.50	.50
104	A14	3p deep blue	10.00	9.00

US Constitution, 150th anniv.

Type of 1922-23
Coil Stamp

1940-46 Wmk. 262 Perf. 15 Horiz.

105	A2	1p car rose ('46)	40.00	32.50
a.		Perf. 14 horiz.	60.00	60.00

Types of 1922-23

1940-42 Perf. 15x14
Size: 18x22mm

106	A1	½p emerald ('41)	2.75	1.40
a.		Booklet pane of 6	500.00	
107	A2	1p car rose ('41)	2.00	1.40
a.		Booklet pane of 6	6.00	
b.		Bklt. pane of 3 + 3 labels	9,500.	
108	A2	1½p claret ('41)	17.00	1.40
a.		Booklet pane of 6	140.00	
109	A2	2p deep green	2.50	1.40
a.		Booklet pane of 6	12.50	
110	A3	2½p choc ('41)	17.00	3.50
a.		Booklet pane of 6	95.00	
111	A4	3p dull blue ('41)	2.75	1.40
a.		Booklet pane of 6	40.00	
112	A3	4p slate	2.75	1.40
a.		Booklet pane of 6	65.00	
113	A1	5p deep violet	2.75	1.40
114	A1	6p red violet ('42)	2.75	1.40
115	A3	9p violet	2.75	1.40
116	A4	10p olive brown	2.75	1.40
117	A1	1sh blue	175.00	42.50
		Nos. 106-117 (12)	232.75	60.00

Types of 1922-23
Overprinted in Green or Violet

Overprint reads: "In memory of the Rebellion of 1916."

1941, Apr. 12 Perf. 15x14

118	A2	2p yellow orange	3.00	1.10
119	A4	3p blue (V)	35.00	15.50

Volunteer Soldier and Dublin Post Office — A15

1941, Oct. 27

120	A15	2½p bluish black	2.00	.85

Nos. 118-120 commemorate the 25th anniv. of the Easter Rebellion.

St. Patrick Type of 1937

1943-45 Wmk. 262 Perf. 14x15

121	A11	2sh6p bright green	45.00	1.40
122	A11	5sh brown violet	45.00	1.90
123	A11	10sh dark blue ('45)	1.00	6.75
		Nos. 121-123 (3)	91.00	10.05

Nos. 121-123 exist on chalky paper. Value, set $40.

Dr. Douglas Hyde — A16

1943, July 31 Perf. 15x14

124	A16	½p green	1.20	.75
125	A16	2½p red lilac	1.90	.25

50th anniv. of the Gaelic League.

IRELAND

Sir Rowan Hamilton — A17

1943, Nov. 13 **Typo.** **Wmk. 262**
126 A17 ½p deep green .75 .75
127 A17 2½p dk red brown 1.60 1.00
Centenary of discovery of the mathematical formula of Quaternions by William Rowan Hamilton.

Brother Michael O'Clery — A18

1944, June 30 **Perf. 14x15**
128 A18 ½p emerald .30 .25
 a. Booklet pane of 6 25.00
129 A18 1sh reddish brown 1.10 1.00
300th anniv. of the death of Michael O'Clery, Irish historian.

Edmund Rice — A19

1944, Aug. 29 **Perf. 15x14**
130 A19 2½p slate 1.90 .50
Death centenary of Edmund Ignatius Rice, founder of the Christian Brothers of Ireland.

Sower — A20

1945, Sept. 15
131 A20 2½p ultramarine 1.00 .25
132 A20 6p red violet 9.00 6.75
Commemorates the work of the Young Irelanders and the death centenary of Thomas Davis, Sept. 16, 1845.

Plowman — A21

1946, Sept. 16 **Typo.**
133 A21 2½p red 1.50 .25
134 A21 3p dark blue 5.00 6.00
Birth centenary of Charles Stewart Parnell and Michael Davitt, leaders in the struggle for Irish political independence.

Theobald Wolfe Tone — A22

 Perf. 15x14
1948, Nov. 19 **Wmk. 262**
135 A22 2½p deep plum 1.40 .25
136 A22 3p deep violet 6.25 6.25
Insurrection of 1798, 150th anniversary.

Types of 1922-23

1949
137 A1 8p bright red 2.75 3.75
138 A4 11p carmine rose 3.25 4.95

Leinster House, Dublin — A23

1949, Nov. 21
139 A23 2½p red brown 1.50 .25
140 A23 3p violet blue 7.50 4.75
International recognition of the Republic, Easter Monday, 1949.

James Clarence Mangan — A24

1949, Dec. 5
141 A24 1p dark green 2.90 .45
Mangan (1803-1849), poet.

Statue of St. Peter — A25

 Wmk. 262
1950, Sept. 11 **Engr.** **Perf. 12½**
142 A25 2½p violet 1.00 1.40
143 A25 3p blue 6.00 9.00
144 A25 9p brown 8.50 10.00
 Nos. 142-144 (3) 15.50 20.40
Holy Year, 1950.

Thomas Moore — A26

1952, Nov. 10 **Perf. 13**
145 A26 2½p deep plum 1.10 .25
146 A26 3½p dk olive green 2.50 3.75
Death centenary of Thomas Moore (1779-1852), poet.

Irish Harp — A27

1953, Feb. 9 **Typo.** **Perf. 14x15**
147 A27 2½p bright green 2.25 .40
148 A27 1sh4p bright blue 20.00 22.00
Ireland's National festival "An Tostal."

Robert Emmet — A28

1953, Sept. 21 **Engr.** **Perf. 12½x13**
149 A28 3p deep green 3.25 .25
150 A28 1sh3p carmine rose 24.50 13.25
150th anniv. of the execution of Robert Emmet (1778-1803), Irish nationalist.

Madonna by della Robbia — A29

1954, May 24 **Perf. 15**
151 A29 3p blue 1.10 .25
152 A29 5p deep green 2.00 3.25
Marian Year, 1953-54.

John Henry Cardinal Newman — A30

1954, July 19 **Typo.** **Perf. 15x14**
153 A30 2p rose lilac 2.50 .25
154 A30 1sh3p blue 13.00 8.00
Opening of the Catholic University of Ireland, centenary.

Statue of John Barry — A31

1956, Sept. 16 **Engr.** **Perf. 15**
155 A31 3p dull purple .75 .25
156 A31 1sh3p blue 5.00 7.00
John Barry (1745-1803), "Father of the American Navy," on the occasion of the unveiling of a statue in Wexford, Ireland, his birthplace.

Redmond — A32

 Perf. 14x15
1957, June 11 **Wmk. 262**
157 A32 3p dark blue 1.25 .25
158 A32 1sh3p rose lake 9.00 9.75
Birth cent. of John Edward Redmond (1856-1918), Irish political leader.

O'Crohan — A33

1957, July 1
159 A33 2p dull purple 1.20 .25
160 A33 5p violet 4.75 4.95
Birth cent. of Thomas O'Crohan (Tomas O'Criomhthain) (1856-1937), fisherman and author.

Brown — A34

1957, Sept. 23 **Typo.** **Perf. 15x14**
161 A34 3p blue 1.80 .25
162 A34 1sh3p carmine rose 20.75 15.50
Adm. William (Guillermo) Brown (1777-1857), founder of the Argentine Navy.

Father Luke Wadding — A35

1957, Nov. 25 **Engr.** **Perf. 15**
163 A35 3p dark blue 1.00 .25
164 A35 1sh3p deep claret 11.50 9.00
Luke Wadding (1588-1657), Irish Franciscan friar and historian.

Clarke — A36

1958, July 28 **Wmk. 262**
165 A36 3p deep green .50 .25
166 A36 1sh3p red brown 8.50 6.50
Thomas J. Clarke (1858-1916), patriot.

Aikenhead — A37

1958, Oct. 20 **Perf. 15x14**
167 A37 3p blue .70 .25
168 A37 1sh3p carmine 10.50 7.50
Mother Mary Aikenhead (1787-1858), founder of the Irish Sisters of Charity.

Constitution Type of 1937

1958, Dec. 29 **Typo.** **Wmk. 262**
169 A12 3p brown 1.00 .25
170 A12 5p bright green 1.00 4.50
21st anniv. of the constitution.

Arthur Guinness — A38

1959, July 20 **Engr.** **Perf. 15**
171 A38 3p rose lake 1.60 .25
172 A38 1sh3p dark blue 10.00 6.50
Bicentenary of Guinness Brewery.

Flight of the Holy Family — A39

1960, June 20 **Perf. 15**
173 A39 3p rose violet .30 .25
174 A39 1sh3p sepia 1.15 2.50
World Refugee Year, 7/1/59-6/30/60.

Europa Issue

Symbolic Wheel — CD3

1960, Sept. 19 **Engr.** **Perf. 15**
175 CD3 6p orange brown 2.25 1.50
176 CD3 1sh3p violet 11.00 14.50
 Nos. 175-176 (2) 13.25 16.00
No. 176 has fugitive ink.

De Havilland Dragon, Boeing 707 Jet and Dublin Airport — A41

1961, June 26 **Perf. 15**
177 A41 6p dull blue 1.10 3.25
178 A41 1sh3p green 2.90 4.50
25th anniv. of the founding of Aer Lingus, Irish International Airlines.

St. Patrick — A42

1961, Sept. 25 **Perf. 14½**
179 A42 3p blue .75 .25
180 A42 8p pale purple 1.90 5.00
181 A42 1sh3p green 2.10 1.50
 Nos. 179-181 (3) 4.75 6.75
1,500th anniv. of St. Patrick's death.

John O'Donovan and Eugene O'Curry — A43

1962, Mar. 26 **Perf. 15**
182 A43 3p crimson .30 .25
183 A43 1sh3p purple 2.75 2.50
Death centenaries of John O'Donovan (1806-1861) and Eugene O'Curry (1794-1862), Gaelic scholars and translators.

IRELAND

Europa Issue

19 Leaves on Young Tree — CD5

1962, Sept. 17   Engr.   Wmk. 262
| 184 | CD5 | 6p pink & dark red | .35 | 1.10 |
| 185 | CD5 | 1sh3p bluish grn & dk blue grn | 1.10 | 1.65 |

Wheat Emblem and Globe — A45

1963, Mar. 21   Wmk. 262
| 186 | A45 | 4p violet | .50 | .25 |
| 187 | A45 | 1sh3p red | 3.00 | 3.00 |

FAO "Freedom from Hunger" campaign.

Europa Issue

Stylized Links, Symbolizing Unity — CD6

1963, Sept. 16   Perf. 15
| 188 | CD6 | 6p rose carmine | .75 | 1.25 |
| 189 | CD6 | 1sh3p dark blue | 2.00 | 2.00 |

Centenary Emblem — A47

1963, Dec. 2   Photo.   Perf. 14½x14
| 190 | A47 | 4p gray & red | .50 | .25 |
| 191 | A47 | 1sh3p brt green, gray & red | 1.30 | 2.25 |

Centenary of the International Red Cross.

Wolfe Tone — A48

1964, Apr. 13   Engr.   Perf. 15
| 192 | A48 | 4p black | .30 | .25 |
| 193 | A48 | 1sh3p dark blue | 2.50 | 2.00 |

Birth bicentenary of Theobald Wolfe Tone (1763-1798), Irish revolutionist.

Irish Pavilion — A49

1964, July 20   Photo.   Perf. 14½x14
194	A49	5p multicolored	.40	.25
a.		Brown omitted	6,500.	
195	A49	1sh5p multicolored	2.35	2.50

New York World's Fair, 1964-65.

Europa Issue

CEPT Daisy (22 Petals) — CD7

Perf. 14x14½
1964, Sept. 14   Litho.   Wmk. 262
| 196 | CD7 | 8p dull grn & ultra | 1.00 | 1.25 |
| 197 | CD7 | 1sh5p red brown & org | 3.50 | 3.00 |

ITU Emblem, Globe and Communication Waves — A51

1965, May 17   Photo.   Perf. 14½x14
| 198 | A51 | 3p dp blue & emerald | .30 | .25 |
| 199 | A51 | 8p black & emerald | 1.60 | 1.50 |

ITU, cent.

William Butler Yeats — A52

1965, June 14   Perf. 15
200	A52	5p orange brn & blk	.30	.25
201	A52	1sh3p gray grn, brn & blk	3.00	1.75
a.		brown omitted	7,500.	

Birth centenary of William Butler Yeats (1865-1939), poet and dramatist.

ICY Emblem — A53

1965, Aug. 16   Photo.   Perf. 15
| 202 | A53 | 3p brt blue & vio bl | .35 | .35 |
| 203 | A53 | 10p redsh brn & dk brn | 2.40 | 2.50 |

International Cooperation Year.

Europa Issue

Leaves and Fruit — CD8

1965, Sept. 27   Perf. 15
| 204 | CD8 | 8p brick red & blk | 1.25 | .85 |
| 205 | CD8 | 1sh5p lt blue & claret | 4.50 | 3.75 |

James Connolly — A55

Designs: No. 207, Thomas J. Clarke. No. 208, Patrick Henry Pearse. No. 209, Symbolic of lives lost in fight for independence, and of Ireland marching into freedom. No. 210, Eamonn Ceannt. No. 211, Sean MacDiarmada. No. 212, Thomas MacDonagh. No. 213, Joseph Plunkett.

1966, Apr. 12   Wmk. 262   Perf. 15
206	A55	3p blue & black	.85	.55
207	A55	3p olive green	.85	.55
a.		Pair, #206-207	2.15	2.25
208	A55	5p olive & black	1.05	.55
209	A55	5p brt grn, blk & orange	1.05	.55
a.		Pair, #208-209	2.65	2.50
210	A55	7p dull org & blk	1.05	4.00
211	A55	7p blue grn & blk	1.05	4.00
a.		Pair, #210-211	2.75	12.00
212	A55	1sh3p grnsh bl & blk	1.10	3.50
213	A55	1sh5p emerald & blk	1.10	3.50
a.		Pair, #212-213	3.75	17.50
		Nos. 206-213 (8)	8.10	17.20

50th anniv. of the Easter Week Rebellion, and to honor the signers of the Proclamation of the Irish Republic.

Roger Casement — A56

1966, Aug. 3   Perf. 15
| 214 | A56 | 5p black | .30 | .25 |
| 215 | A56 | 1sh dark red brown | .45 | .55 |

50th death anniv. of Roger Casement (1864-1916), British consular agent and Irish rebel who was executed for treason.

Europa Issue

Symbolic Sailboat — CD9

1966, Sept. 26   Photo.   Perf. 15
| 216 | CD9 | 7p orange & green | .60 | 1.00 |
| 217 | CD9 | 1sh5p gray & green | 1.75 | 2.75 |

Ballintubber Abbey — A58

1966, Nov. 8   Perf. 15
| 218 | A58 | 5p red brown | .30 | .25 |
| 219 | A58 | 1sh black | .35 | .35 |

750th anniversary of Ballintubber Abbey.

Cross and Sword Types of 1922

1966-67   Photo.   Perf. 15
Size: 17x20½mm
225	A4	3p blue ('67)	.35	.25
226	A1	5p brt vio, type II ('68)	.35	.25
a.		Booklet pane of 6, No. 226b	62.50	
b.		Type I ('66)	8.25	8.25

Type I has irregularly spaced lines in shading behind sword.

Europa Issue

Cogwheels — CD10

1967, May 2
| 232 | CD10 | 7p green & gold | .50 | .80 |
| 233 | CD10 | 1sh5p dk red & gold | 1.75 | 1.50 |

Maple Leaves — A60

1967, Aug. 28   Photo.
| 234 | A60 | 5p multicolored | .30 | .25 |
| 235 | A60 | 1sh5p multicolored | .40 | .55 |

Centenary of the Canadian Confederation.

Rock of Cashel — A61

1967, Sept. 25   Wmk. 262   Perf. 15
| 236 | A61 | 7p sepia | .30 | .25 |
| 237 | A61 | 10p Prussian blue | .40 | .55 |

International Tourist Year.

One Cent Fenian Fantasy — A62

Design: 1sh, 24c Fenian fantasy.

1967, Oct. 23   Photo.   Perf. 15
| 238 | A62 | 5p lt green & slate grn | .30 | .25 |
| 239 | A62 | 1sh pale pink & gray | .40 | .40 |

Fenian Rising, centenary. The Fenian fantasy was created by S. Allan Taylor.

Swift's Bust and St. Patrick's Cathedral, Dublin — A63

Design: 1sh5p, Gulliver, Lilliputian army.

1967, Nov. 30   Perf. 15
| 240 | A63 | 3p gray & sepia | .30 | .25 |
| 241 | A63 | 1sh5p lt blue & sepia | .40 | .55 |

Birth tercentenary of Jonathan Swift (1667-1745), author of Gulliver's Travels.

Europa Issue

Golden Key with CEPT Emblem — CD11

1968, Apr. 29   Photo.   Wmk. 262
| 242 | CD11 | 7p multicolored | .65 | .55 |
| 243 | CD11 | 1sh5p multicolored | 1.85 | 1.15 |

St. Mary's Cathedral, Limerick — A65

1968, Aug. 26   Engr.   Perf. 15
| 244 | A65 | 5p dull blue | .30 | .25 |
| 245 | A65 | 10p olive | .40 | .90 |

800th anniv. of the founding of St. Mary's Cathedral by Donal Mor O'Brien, last King of Munster.

Countess Markievicz — A66

1968, Sept. 23   Photo.   Wmk. 262
| 246 | A66 | 3p black | .30 | .25 |
| 247 | A66 | 1sh5p dark blue | .40 | .75 |

Birth centenary of Countess Constance Markievicz (1868-1927), champion of Irish Independence and first Minister of Labor.

James Connolly — A67

1968, Sept. 23   Perf. 15
| 248 | A67 | 6p brown, dk brn & blk | .30 | .50 |
| 249 | A67 | 1sh dull grn, grn & blk | .40 | .35 |

Birth centenary of James Connolly (1868-1916), founder of the Irish Socialist Party, editor of "Workers' Republic" and Commander of the Irish Citizen Army.

Dog from Ancient Brooch, County Kilkenny A68

Winged Ox from Lichfield Gospel Book A69

Designs: ½p, 1p, 2p, 3p, 4p, 5p, 6p, Dog. 7p, 8p, 9p, 10p, 1sh, 1sh9p, Stag from ancient bowl, Kent. 2sh6p, 5sh, Winged ox. 10sh, Eagle, from ancient manuscript.

1968-70   Photo.   Wmk. 262   Perf. 15
250	A68	½p orange	.30	.25
251	A68	1p yellow green	.30	.25
252	A68	2p ocher	.50	.25
253	A68	3p bright blue	.35	.25
254	A68	4p dark red	.30	.25
255	A68	5p deep green	1.25	.85

IRELAND

256	A68	6p brown	.30	.25
a.		Booklet pane of 6 ('70)	27.50	
257	A68	7p yel & brown	.45	3.25
258	A68	8p red org & blk	.45	2.75
259	A68	9p ol grn & dk bl	.50	.25
260	A68	10p violet & dk brn	1.50	2.75
261	A68	1sh dk red brn & brown	.40	.25
262	A68	1sh9p grnsh bl & dk brown	4.00	2.50
263	A69	2sh6p red org, bl, ol & dull yel	1.75	.25
264	A69	5sh ol, gray, bis & yel	3.00	3.50
265	A69	10sh dk red brn, yel & dp org	4.75	4.75
		Nos. 250-265 (16)	20.10	22.60

Issued: 2p, 8p, 2sh6p, 10sh, 10/14/68; 6p, 9p, 1sh9p, 5sh, 2/24/69; 4p, 5p, 10p, 1sh, 3/31/69; ½p, 1p, 3p, 7p, 6/9/69.

See Nos. 290-304, 343-359, 395-402, 466-475.

1970 Coil Stamps Perf. 14x15
251a	A68	1p yellow green	1.10	3.25
252a	A68	2p ocher	1.10	7.00
253a	A68	3p bright blue	1.10	4.00
		Nos. 251a-253a (3)	3.30	14.25

Human Rights Flame — A70

1968, Nov. 4 Wmk. 262 Perf. 15
266	A70	5p black, ocher & gold	.30	.25
267	A70	7p crim, ocher & gold	.40	.45

International Human Rights Year.

First Meeting of Irish Parliament — A71

1969, Jan. 21 Perf. 15x14½
268	A71	6p dark slate green	.30	.25
269	A71	9p dark blue gray	.40	.40

50th anniv. of the first meeting of the Dail Eireann at the Mansion House, Dublin, Jan. 21, 1919.

"EUROPA" and "CEPT" — CD12

1969, Apr. 28 Photo. Perf. 15
270	CD12	9p ultra, gray & ocher	.70	.75
271	CD12	1sh9p car, gray & gold	1.30	1.25

Europa and CEPT, 10th anniv.

ILO Emblem — A73

1969, July 14 Perf. 15
272	A73	6p gray & black	.30	.25
273	A73	9p yellow & black	.40	.40

ILO, 50th anniv.

Last Supper and Crucifixion, by Evie Hone — A74

Perf. 15x14½
1969, Sept. 1 Photo. Wmk. 262
274	A74	1sh multicolored	.30	1.50

The design is after a stained-glass window by Evie Hone (1894-1955) in the Eton College Chapel.

Mahatma Gandhi — A75

1969, Oct. 2 Perf. 15
275	A75	6p dk yel grn & blk	.40	.25
276	A75	1sh9p yel, grn & black	1.25	1.25

Mohandas K. Gandhi (1869-1948), leader in India's fight for independence.

Stylized Bird, Tree and Shamrock — A76

1970, Feb. 23 Perf. 15
277	A76	6p olive bister & black	.30	.25
278	A76	9p violet & black	.55	.55

Nature Conservation Year.

Europa Issue

Interwoven Threads — CD13

1970, May 4 Photo. Perf. 15
279	CD13	6p purple & silver	.55	.25
280	CD13	9p yel brn & silver	.80	1.00
281	CD13	1sh9p dk gray & sil	1.20	1.25
		Nos. 279-281 (3)	2.55	2.50

Sailing Boats, by Peter Monamy (1670-1749) A78

1970, July 13 Perf. 15
282	A78	4p gold & multi	.30	.30

250th anniv. of the Royal Cork Yacht Club.

Madonna of Eire, by Mainie Jellett (1896-1943) — A79

1970, Sept. 1 Photo. Perf. 15
283	A79	1sh violet blue & multi	.30	.30

Tomás MacCurtain — A80

1970, Oct. 26 Perf. 15
284	A80	9p violet & black	.45	.25
285	A80	9p violet & black	.45	.25
a.		Pair, #284-285	1.65	3.50
286	A80	2sh9p brt blue & blk	1.15	4.00
287	A80	2sh9p brt blue & blk	1.15	4.00
a.		Pair, #286-287	3.75	12.00

50th anniv. of the deaths of Tomás Mac-Curtain (1884-1920) and Terence MacSwiney (1879-1920), lord mayors of Cork, who died during the Irish war of independence.

Kevin Barry — A81

1970, Nov. 2
288	A81	6p olive green	.30	.25
289	A81	1sh2p violet blue	.40	.75

50th anniv. of the death of Kevin Barry (1902-1920), who was hanged during the Irish war of independence.

Decimal Currency Issue
Types of 1968-69 (Numerals only)

Designs: ½p, 1p, 1½p, 2p, 2½p, 3p, 3½p, 4p, No. 298A, Dog. No. 298, 6p, 7p, 7½p, 9p, Stag. 10p, 12p, 20p, Winged ox. 50p, Eagle.

Two types of 10p:
I — Ox outlined in lilac
II — Outlined in brown

1971-75 Wmk. 262 Photo. Perf. 15
290	A68	½p yellow green	.30	.25
a.		Booklet pane of 6	27.50	40.00
291	A68	1p bright blue	.45	.25
a.		Booklet pane of 6	1.65	7.00
c.		Bklt. pane of 5 + label ('74)	1.10	
292	A68	1½p brown red	.30	.55
293	A68	2p dark green	.30	.25
b.		Booklet pane of 5 + label ('75)	1.10	
294	A68	2½p sepia	.30	.25
a.		Booklet pane of 6	5.50	
295	A68	3p yel orange	.30	.25
296	A68	3½p deep orange	.30	.25
297	A68	4p violet	.30	.25
298	A68	5p ap grn & brn	1.10	.25
298A	A68	5p apple grn ('74)	1.65	.55
d.		Booklet pane of 6 ('74)	5.50	
d.		Bklt. pane of 5 + label ('74)	2.75	
299	A68	6p bl gray & dk brn	3.25	2.20
299A	A68	7p ol grn & ind ('74)	3.75	1.10
300	A68	7½p rose vio & dk brn	.85	1.55
301	A68	9p bl grn & blk	1.10	.55
302	A69	10p lil & multi (I)	20.00	4.50
b.		Type II	16.50	.75
302A	A69	12p multi ('74)	.65	1.10
303	A69	20p slate & multi	.80	.25
304	A69	50p rose brn & multi	2.75	1.10
		Nos. 290-304 (18)	38.45	15.45

Booklet panes have watermark sideways.
Issued: No. 298A, 7p, 12p, 1/29/74; others, 2/15/71.
See Nos. 343-359, 395-402, 466-475.

1971-74 Coil Stamps Perf. 14x15
291b	A68	1p bright blue	.70	1.10
292a	A68	1½p brown red	.30	.55
293a	A68	2p dark green ('72)	.30	.65
294b	A68	2½p sepia	.30	.95
c.		Strip of 3 (1p, 1½p, 2½p)	1.10	4.00
297a	A68	4p violet ('72)	.75	.65
b.		Strip of 4 (1½p, 2p, 2½p, 4p) ('72)	1.10	4.00
298b	A68	5p apple green ('74)	.85	1.20
e.		Strip of 4 (2x1½p, 2p, 5p) ('74)	1.10	4.00

Common Design Type

Europa Issue, 1971 — CD14

1971, May 3 Wmk. 262 Perf. 15
305	CD14	4p apple green & blk	.55	.25
306	CD14	6p blue & black	1.90	1.25

John M. Synge — A82

1971, July 19 Photo. Perf. 15
307	A82	4p gray, black & gold	.30	.25
308	A82	10p org, black & gold	.60	.60

Birth cent. of John Millington Synge (1871-1909), poet and dramatist.

An Island Man, by Jack B. Yeats — A83

1971, Aug. 30 Perf. 15
309	A83	6p multicolored	.75	.75

Jack Butler Yeats (1871-1957), painter.

Racial Equality Emblem — A84

Perf. 14x14½
1971, Oct. 18 Litho. Unwmk.
310	A84	4p red	.30	.25
311	A84	10p black	.50	.50

Intl. Year Against Racial Discrimination.

Madonna, by John Hughes, Loughrea Cathedral — A85

1971, Nov. 15 Photo. Perf. 15
312	A85	2½p dp bl grn, gold & slate	.30	.25
313	A85	6p ultra, gold & slate	.50	.50

Christmas.

"Your Heart is your Health" — A86

1972, Apr. 7 Photo. Wmk. 262
314	A86	2½p gold & brown	.35	.25
315	A86	12p silver & black	1.50	1.50

World Health Day.

Europa Issue

Sparkles, Symbolic of Communications CD15

1972, May 1 Perf. 15
316	CD15	4p red, black & sil	1.40	.30
317	CD15	6p blue, black & sil	3.85	2.75

Dove Soaring Past Rising Moon — A88

1972, June 1 Photo.
318	A88	4p gray blue, org & dk bl	.30	.25
319	A88	6p olive, yel & dk green	.70	.70

The patriot dead of 1922-23.

Black Lake, by Gerard Dillon — A89

1972, July 10 Perf. 15
320	A89	3p indigo & multi	.75	.45

Rider from Clonmacnoise Slab and Olympic Rings — A90

1972, Aug. 28 Photo. Wmk. 262
321	A90	3p yellow, black & gold	.30	.25
322	A90	6p salmon, black & gold	.50	.70

20th Olympic Games, Munich, Aug. 26-Sept. 11, and 50th anniversary of the Olympic Council of Ireland.

IRELAND

Madonna and Child — A91

1972, Oct. 16   Unwmk.   Perf. 15
323 A91 2½p dk green & multi   .30 .25
324 A91 4p tan & multi   .30 .25
325 A91 12p multicolored   1.00 1.00
       Nos. 323-325 (3)   1.60 1.50

Christmas. The design is after a miniature in the Book of Kells, 9th century.

Ireland No. 68 — A92

1972, Dec. 6   Photo.
326 A92 6p blue gray & dp grn   .55 .65
     a.   Souvenir sheet of 4   5.00 8.50

50th anniv. of 1st Irish postage stamp.

Recurrent Celtic Head Motif — A93

1973, Jan. 1   Unwmk.
327 A93 6p orange & multi   .50 .75
328 A93 12p green & multi   1.00 1.00

Ireland's entry into the European Community.

Europa Issue

Post Horn of Arrows — CD16

1973, Apr. 30
329 CD16 4p bright ultra   .95 .25
330 CD16 6p black   3.00 1.75

"Berlin Blues I," by William Scott — A95

Perf. 15x14½
1973, Aug. 9   Photo.   Unwmk.
331 A95 5p lt blue, blue & dk brn   .60 .60

Weather Map of Northwest Europe — A96

1973, Sept. 4   Perf. 14½x15
332 A96 3½p ultra & multi   .30 .25
333 A96 12p lilac & multi   1.30 1.60

Intl. meteorological cooperation, cent.

Tractor Plowing and Birds — A97

1973, Oct. 5   Perf. 15x14½
334 A97 5p emerald & multi   .30 .25
335 A97 7p emerald & multi   .85 .45

World Plowing Championships, Wellington Bridge, County Wexford, Oct. 1-7.

Flight into Egypt, by Jan de Cock — A98

1973, Nov. 1   Perf. 15
336 A98 3½p black & multi   .30 .25
337 A98 12p gold & multi   1.00 1.50

Christmas.

Rescue, by Bernard Gribble — A99

Design: Ballycotton lifeboat rescuing crew of Daunt Rock Lightship, 1936.

1974, Mar. 28   Photo.   Wmk. 262
338 A99 5p multicolored   .50 .40

Sesquicentennial of the founding of the Royal National Lifeboat Institution.

Europa Issue

Edmund Burke, by John Henry Foley — A100

Perf. 14½x15
1974, Apr. 29   Unwmk.
339 A100 5p lt ultra & black   1.75 .25
340 A100 7p lt green & black   3.75 2.75

Oliver Goldsmith, by John Henry Foley — A101

1974, June 24   Photo.
341 A101 3½p brt citron & blk   .40 .25
342 A101 12p emerald & black   1.25 1.25

Oliver Goldsmith (1728-1774), writer.

Types of 1968-69

Type I - Fine Screen

Type II - Coarse Screen

½p, 1p, 2p, 3p, 3½p, 5p, Nos. 350, 352, Dog. Nos. 349, 351, 8p, 9p, Stag. 10p, 15p, 20p, Winged ox. 50p, £1, Eagle.

1974-78   Unwmk.   Perf. 15
343 A68 ½p yel green ('78)   .30 .25
344 A68 1p brt blue ('75)   .30 .25
345 A68 2p dark green ('76)   .30 .25
346 A68 3p ocher ('75)   .30 .25
347 A68 3½p deep orange   2.75 4.50
348 A68 5p apple green   .65 .25
349 A68 6p bl gray & dk brn   .65 2.75
350 A68 6p blue gray ('75)   .30 .25
351 A68 7p lt ol grn & indigo   1.10 .40
352 A68 7p olive green ('75)   .55 .25
     a.   Bklt. pane of 5 + label ('77)   4.95 16.00
353 A68 8p brn & dk brn ('75)   .65 .55
354 A68 9p lt bl grn & blk ('75)   .75 .35
355 A69 10p lil & multi ('75)   1.05 .35
356 A69 15p multi ('75)   .90 1.10
357 A69 20p slate & multi   .65 .25
358 A69 50p rose brn & multi, type I ('74)   1.65 .35
     a.   Type II ('83)   4.95 3.25
359 A69 £1 multi ('75)   2.50 .35
       Nos. 343-359 (17)   15.35 12.70

Coil Stamps

1977, Mar. 21   Perf. 14x15
344b A68 1p bright blue   1.10 1.65
345b A68 2p dark green   .45 .55
348b A68 5p apple green   1.10 .95
    c.   Strip of 4 (1p, 2x2p, 5p)   2.50 2.75

Kitchen Table, by Norah McGuinness — A102

1974, Aug. 19   Photo.   Perf. 14x15
360 A102 5p multicolored   .70 .35

Rugby — A103

1974, Sept. 2   Engr.   Perf. 15x14
361 A103 3½p slate green   .45 .25
     a.   3½ deep slate green   7.25 4.95
362 A103 12p multicolored   2.25 2.25

Centenary of Irish Rugby Union.
No. 361a was printed from a reengraved plate with more deeply engraved lines. The original printing (No. 361) was considered to be of unsatisfactory quality.

UPU "Postmark" — A104

1974, Oct. 9   Photo.   Perf. 14½x15
363 A104 5p emerald & black   .30 .25
364 A104 7p ultra & black   .45 .45

Centenary of Universal Postal Union.

Virgin and Child, by Bellini — A105

1974, Nov. 14
365 A105 5p multicolored   .30 .30
366 A105 15p multicolored   .95 .95

Christmas.

"Peace" — A106

1975, Mar. 25   Photo.   Perf. 14½x15
367 A106 8p dp rose lil & ultra   .30 .25
368 A106 15p ultra & emerald   .95 .95

International Women's Year.

Europa Issue

Castletown Hunt (detail), by Robert Healy — A107

1975, Apr. 28   Photo.   Perf. 15x14½
369 A107 7p black   1.25 .25
370 A107 9p green   3.00 2.00

Chipping from the Fringe — A108

1975, June 26   Photo.   Perf. 15x14½
371 A108 6p shown   .45 .25
372 A108 9p Putting   2.40 1.40

9th European Amateur Golf Team Championships, Killarney.

Bird of Prey, by Oisín Kelly — A109

1975, July 28
373 A109 15p ocher   1.10 1.50

Nano Nagle and Pupils, Engraving by Charles Turner — A110

1975, Sept. 1   Photo.   Perf. 14½x15
374 A110 5p light blue & black   .30 .25
375 A110 7p buff & black   .55 .35

Presentation Order of Nuns, bicentenary.

IRELAND

Clock Tower, St. Ann's Church, Shandon — A111

Designs: 7p, 9p, Holycross Abbey.

1975, Oct. 6   Photo.   Perf. 12½
376	A111	5p sepia	.30	.25
377	A111	6p ultra & multi	.45	.90
378	A111	7p sapphire	.45	.25
379	A111	9p multicolored	.45	.85
		Nos. 376-379 (4)	1.65	2.25

European Architectural Heritage Year.

St. Oliver Plunkett, by Imogen Stuart — A112

1975, Oct. 13   Engr.   Perf. 14x14½
380	A112	7p black	.30	.25
381	A112	15p dull red	.85	.90

Canonization of Oliver Plunkett (1625-1681), Primate of Ireland.

Madonna and Child, by Fra Filippo Lippi — A113

1975, Nov. 13   Photo.   Perf. 15
382	A113	5p multicolored	.30	.25
383	A113	7p multicolored	.30	.25
384	A113	10p gold & multi	.65	.65
		Nos. 382-384 (3)	1.25	1.15

Christmas.

James Larkin — A114

1976, Jan. 21   Photo.   Perf. 14½x15
385	A114	7p gray & slate grn	.30	.25
386	A114	11p ocher & brown	.50	.60

James Larkin (1876-1947), trade union leader.

Bell Making First Call — A115

1976, Mar. 10   Photo.   Perf. 14½x15
387	A115	9p multicolored	.30	.25
388	A115	15p multicolored	.50	.55

Centenary of first telephone call by Alexander Graham Bell, March 10, 1876.

13 Stars and Stripes — A116

Designs: 8p, 50 stars, and stripes. 9p, 15p, Benjamin Franklin on Albany essay of 1847.

1976, May 17   Litho.   Perf. 15x14
389	A116	7p ultra, sil & red	.30	.25
a.		Silver (inscription) omitted	1,875.	
390	A116	8p ultra, sil & red	.30	1.20
391	A116	9p bl, sil & ocher	.35	.25
392	A116	15p red, sil & bl	.50	.80
a.		Silver (inscription) omitted	1,325.	1,100.
b.		Souvenir sheet of 4, #389-392	3.85	8.75
c.		As No. 392b, silver (inscription) omitted	12,500.	
		Nos. 389-392 (4)	1.45	2.50

American Bicentennial.

Irish Delft Spirit Barrel — A117

Europa: 11p, Bowl, Irish Delft. Designs show mark of Henry Delamain's Factory, Dublin, both pieces c. 1756.

1976, July 1   Photo.   Perf. 15x14½
393	A117	9p gray & magenta	1.00	.25
394	A117	11p gray & blue	1.75	1.00

Types of 1968

Designs: 8p, 9p, 9½p, No. 399, Dog. No. 398, 11p, 12p, Stag. 17p, Winged ox.

1976-79   Photo.   Unwmk.   Perf. 15
395	A68	8p brown	.30	.25
396	A68	9p blue green	.35	.25
397	A68	9½p red ('79)	.35	.25
398	A68	10p lilac & black	.75	.25
399	A68	10p purple ('77)	.75	.25
400	A68	11p carmine & black	.50	1.65
401	A68	12p emer & black ('77)	.80	.25
402	A69	17p ol, bl & ocher ('77)	.85	1.90
		Nos. 395-402 (8)	4.65	5.05

The Lobster Pots, by Paul Henry — A118

1976, Aug. 30   Photo.   Perf. 15
405	A118	15p gold & multi	.65	.65

Paul Henry (1876-1958), birth centenary.

Radio Waves — A119

Radio Tower and Waves, Globe — A120

Perf. 14½x14, 14x14½

1976, Oct. 5   Litho.
406	A119	9p brt blue & black	.30	.25
407	A120	11p black & multi	.80	.80

Irish broadcasting, 50th anniversary.

Nativity, by Lorenzo Monaco — A121

1976, Nov. 11   Perf. 15x14½
408	A121	7p multicolored	.30	.25
409	A121	9p multicolored	.30	.25
410	A121	15p multicolored	.60	.90
		Nos. 408-410 (3)	1.20	1.40

Christmas.

Irish Manuscript, 16th Century — A122

Stone from Newgrange Burial Mound — A123

1977, May 9   Photo.   Perf. 15x14½
411	A122	8p multicolored	.30	.25
412	A123	10p multicolored	.70	.65

Centenaries of National Library (8p) and National Museum (10p).

Europa Issue

View of Ballynahinch A124

Lugalla Lake A125

1977, June 27   Litho.   Perf. 14x14½
413	A124	10p multicolored	.90	.25
414	A125	12p multicolored	3.00	1.40

Head, by Louis le Brocquy, 1973 — A126

1977, Aug. 8   Perf. 14x14½
415	A126	17p multicolored	1.10	1.00

Girl Guide and Tents — A127

Design: 17p, Boy Scout and tents.

1977, Aug. 22   Photo.   Perf. 15x14½
416	A127	8p multicolored	.40	.25
417	A127	17p multicolored	1.10	1.25

European Scout and Guide Conference, Ireland, and 50th anniversary of Catholic Boy Scouts of Ireland.

The Shanachie, by Jack B. Yeats — A128

Eriugena — A129

Perf. 14x14½, 14½x14

1977, Sept. 12   Litho.
418	A128	10p black	.45	.25
419	A129	12p black	.85	1.35

Folklore of Ireland Society, 50th anniv. and 1100th death anniv. of Johannes Scottus Eriugena, philosher, poet and mystic.

"Electricity," Mural by Robert Ballagh — A130

Bulls, from Contemporary Coin — A131

Greyhound A132

Litho. (10p, 17p); Photo. (12p)
Perf. 14½x14; 15x14½ (12p)

1977, Oct. 10
420	A130	10p multicolored	.30	.25
421	A131	12p multicolored	.35	1.55
422	A132	17p multicolored	1.00	.90
		Nos. 420-422 (3)	1.65	2.70

50th anniversaries of: Electricity Supply Board (10p); Agricultural Credit Act (12p); introduction of greyhound racing (17p).

Holy Family, by Giorgione — A133

1977, Nov. 3   Photo.   Perf. 14½x15
423	A133	8p multicolored	.30	.25
424	A133	10p multicolored	.40	.40
425	A133	17p multicolored	.60	.55
		Nos. 423-425 (3)	1.30	1.20

Christmas.

Bremen, Junkers Monoplane — A134

1978, Apr. 13   Litho.   Perf. 14
426	A134	10p ultra & black	.35	.25
427	A134	17p lt brown & black	1.00	1.00

50th anniversary of first East-West transatlantic flight from Baldonnel, County Dublin, to Greenly Island, Gulf of St. Lawrence.

Spring Gentian — A135

Wild flowers: 10p, Strawberry tree. 11p, Large-flowered butterwort. 17p, St. Daboec's heath.

1978, June 12   Litho.   Perf. 14x14½
428	A135	8p multicolored	.30	.35
429	A135	10p multicolored	.30	.25
430	A135	11p multicolored	.30	.45
431	A135	17p multicolored	.50	1.80
		Nos. 428-431 (4)	1.40	2.85

Catherine McAuley A136

Vaccination, lithograph by Manigaud A137

William Orpen, Self-portrait — A138

IRELAND

1978, Sept. 18   Litho.   Perf. 14
432 A136 10p multicolored   .30   .25
433 A137 11p multicolored   .45   .70
434 A138 17p multicolored   .80   .95
     Nos. 432-434 (3)   1.55 1.90

Catherine McAuley (1778-1841), founder of Sisters of Mercy (10p); eradication of smallpox (11p); William Orpen (1878-1931), painter (17p).

Offshore Oil Well — A139

1978, Oct. 18   Litho.   Perf. 14
435 A139 10p multicolored   .55   .55

First natural gas coming in off the Irish Coast at Kinsale.

Woodcock on Farthing — A140

Coins: 10p, Salmon on florin. 11p, Hen and chicks on penny. 17p, Horse on half crown.

1978, Oct. 26   Photo.   Perf. 15x14½
436 A140   8p multicolored   .30   .25
437 A140 10p multicolored   .30   .25
438 A140 11p multicolored   .30   .45
439 A140 17p multicolored   .35   .85
     Nos. 436-439 (4)   1.25 1.80

Irish currency, 50th anniversary.

Virgin and Child, by Guercino — A141

1978, Nov. 16   Photo.   Perf. 14½x15
440 A141   8p multicolored   .30   .25
441 A141 10p multicolored   .30   .25
442 A141 17p multicolored   .90   1.00
     Nos. 440-442 (3)   1.50 1.50

Christmas.

Conolly Folly, Castletown A142

Europa: 11p, Belvedere on Tower Hill at Dromoland.

1978, Dec. 6   Perf. 15x14½
443 A142 10p brown   1.40   .25
444 A142 11p dull green   1.40 1.75

Cross-country Runners — A143

1979, Aug. 20   Litho.   Perf. 14½x14
445 A143   8p multicolored   .30   .30

7th World Cross-country Championships, Greenpark Racecourse, Limerick, March 25.

Rowland Hill, Bronze Statue — A144

1979, Aug. 20   Perf. 14x14½
446 A144 17p multicolored   .65   .75

Sir Rowland Hill (1795-1879), originator of penny postage.

"European Communities" (7 Languages) — A145

1979, Aug. 20   Photo.   Perf. 14½x15
447 A145 10p lt greenish gray .30   .25
448 A145 11p rose lilac   .30   .25

European Parliament, first direct elections, June 7-10.

Wren — A146

Birds: 10p, Great crested grebe. 11p, Greenland white-fronted geese. 17p, Peregrine falcon.

1979, Aug. 30   Litho.   Perf. 14½x14
449 A146   8p multicolored   .35   .75
450 A146 10p multicolored   .35   .25
451 A146 11p multicolored   .40   .75
452 A146 17p multicolored   .55   1.90
     Nos. 449-452 (4)   1.65 3.65

A Happy Flower — A147

Children's Drawings: 11p, "Me and my skipping rope," vert. 17p, "Swans on a lake."

Perf. 14½x14, 14x14½
1979, Sept. 13   Litho.
453 A147 10p multicolored   .30   .25
454 A147 11p multicolored   .30   .55
455 A147 17p multicolored   .40   .75
     Nos. 453-455 (3)   1.00 1.55

International Year of the Child.

Pope John Paul II — A148

1979, Sept. 29   Litho.   Perf. 14½x14
456 A148 12p multicolored   .35   .25

Visit of Pope John Paul II to Ireland.

Hospitaller Brother Teaching Child — A149

1979, Oct. 4
457 A149 9½p rose & black   .45   .25

Hospitaller Order of St. John of God, centenary in Ireland.

Windmill and Sun — A150

1979, Oct. 4   Photo.   Perf. 14½x15
458 A150 11p multicolored   .60   .70

Energy conservation.

"Seated Figure," by F.E. McWilliam A151

1979, Oct. 4   Litho.   Perf. 14½x14
459 A151 20p multicolored   .75   1.25

Patrick Pearse — A152

1979, Nov. 10   Photo.   Perf. 15x14½
460 A152 12p multicolored   .60   .60

Patrick Henry Pearse (1879-1916), Irish writer and leader of Easter Rebellion.

Mother and Child, Panel, Domnach Argid Shrine — A153

1979, Nov. 15   Photo.   Perf. 14½x15
461 A153 9½p multicolored   .30   .25
462 A153 20p multicolored   .40   .80

Christmas.

Europa Issue

Bianconi Long Car, 1836 — A154

Laying Transatlantic Cable, Steamer William Cory, 1866 — A155

1979, Dec. 6   Litho.   Perf. 15x14
463 A154 12p multicolored   1.10   .30
464 A155 13p multicolored   1.50   1.40

Type of 1968

Designs: 13p, 16p, Stag; others, Dog.

1980-82   Photo.   Perf. 15
466 A68 12p green   .50   .25
467 A68 13p red brn & dk brn   .55   2.20
468 A68 15p ultra   .40   .25
469 A68 16p olive green & blk .65   1.10

Litho.
Perf. 14x15
470 A68 18p dull red brn ('81) .50   .55
471 A68 19p dull blue ('81)   .60   2.75
472 A68 22p gray blue ('81)   .70   .25
473 A68 24p brown olive ('81) 1.10 2.20
474 A68 26p bluish green ('82) 1.65   .45
475 A68 29p dp rose lilac ('82) 1.65 3.50
     Nos. 466-475 (10)   8.30 13.50

Issued: 12p, 13p, 3/26/80; 15p, 16p, 7/10/80; 18p, 19p, 4/27/81; 22p, 9/1/81; 24p, 10/29/81; 26p, 29p, 4/1/82.

St. Jean Baptiste de la Salle — A156

1980, Mar. 19   Litho.   Perf. 14x15
477 A156 12p multicolored   .45   .35

The Brothers of the Christian School (founded by St. Jean Baptiste), centenary in Ireland.

Europa Issue

George Bernard Shaw, by Alick Ritchie A157

Oscar Wilde, by Toulouse-Lautrec A158

1980, May 7   Litho.   Perf. 14x15
478 A157 12p multicolored   1.00   .50
479 A158 13p multicolored   1.00   2.50

Irish Ermine — A159

1980, July 30   Litho.   Perf. 14x15
480 A159 12p shown   .35   .30
481 A159 15p Irish hare   .40   .35
482 A159 16p Fox   .40   .30
483 A159 25p Red deer   .85   .75
  a. Miniature sheet of 4, #480-483 2.50 3.00
     Nos. 480-483 (4)   2.00 1.70

Bodhran Drum and Whistle Players — A160

15p, Piper, Uilleann pipes. 25p, Irish jig.

1980, Sept. 25 Photo. Perf. 14x15
484 A160 12p shown   .30   .25
485 A160 15p multicolored   .30   .25
486 A160 25p multicolored   .40   .50
     Nos. 484-486 (3)   1.00 1.00

Sean O'Casey (1880-1964), Playwright — A161

1980, Oct. 23   Litho.   Perf. 14x14½
487 A161 12p multicolored   .45   .25

IRELAND

499

Gold Painting No. 57, by Patrick Scott — A162

1980, Oct. 23 **Perf. 14x15**
488 A162 25p multicolored   1.00 1.15

A163

1980, Dec. 4 **Photo.** **Perf. 15x14½**
489 A163 12p multicolored   .30 .25
490 A163 15p multicolored   .30 .25
491 A163 25p multicolored   .45 1.35
 Nos. 489-491 (3)   1.05 1.85
Christmas.

A164

Scientists and Inventions: 12p, Robert Boyle (1627-1691), and Air Pump, 1659. 15p, Harry Ferguson (1884-1960), hydraulic tractor, 1936. 16p, Charles Parsons (1854-1931), Parsons' turbine, 1884. 25p, John Holland (1841-1914), Holland submarine, 1878.

1981, Mar. 12 **Litho.** **Perf. 14x14½**
492 A164 12p multicolored   .30 .25
493 A164 15p multicolored   .30 .25
494 A164 16p multicolored   .35 1.00
495 A164 25p multicolored   .40 1.30
 Nos. 492-495 (4)   1.35 2.80

The Cock and the Pot, Rubbing, 1841 — A165

Europa: 19p, The Scales of Judgment, rubbing, 1827.

1981, May 4 **Litho.** **Perf. 14½x15**
496 A165 18p multicolored   1.10 .25
497 A165 19p multicolored   2.20 2.20

Hiking — A166

15p, Bicycling, vert. 19p, Mountain climbing. 30p, Rock climbing, vert.

Perf. 14x15, 15x14
1981, June 24 **Litho.**
498 A166 15p multicolored   .30 .35
499 A166 18p shown   .30 .25
500 A166 19p multicolored   .30 1.10
501 A166 30p multicolored   .90 .85
 Nos. 498-501 (4)   1.80 2.55
Youth Hostel Assn., 50th anniv.

Jeremiah O'Donovan Rossa (1831-1915), Journalist A167

Railway Embankment, by William John Leech (1881-1968) A168

Perf. 14½x15, 15x14½
1981, Aug. 31
502 A167 15p multicolored   .45 .45
503 A168 30p multicolored   .90 .75

James Hoban (1762-1831), White House Architect — A169

1981, Sept. 29 **Perf. 15x14**
504 A169 18p multicolored   .65 .65
See US Nos. 1935-1936.

Draft Horse King of Diamonds A170

Famous Horses: No. 505, Show-jumper Boomerang. No. 506, Steeplechaser Arkle. 24p, Flat racer Ballymoss. 36p, Connemara pony Coosheen Finn.

1981, Oct. 23 **Litho.** **Perf. 15x14**
505 A170 18p multicolored   .60 1.00
506 A170 18p multicolored   .60 1.00
 a. Pair, #505-506   1.40 1.25
507 A170 22p multicolored   .60 .25
508 A170 24p multicolored   .60 .65
509 A170 36p multicolored   .65 .85
 Nos. 505-509 (5)   3.05 3.75

Nativity, by Federico Barocci — A171

1981, Nov. 19 **Litho.** **Perf. 14x15**
510 A171 18p multicolored   .35 .25
511 A171 22p multicolored   .50 .40
512 A171 36p multicolored   .90 .80
 Nos. 510-512 (3)   1.75 1.45
Christmas 1981.

Land Law Act Cent. — A172

1981, Dec. 10 **Litho.** **Perf. 14x14½**
513 A172 18p multicolored   .55 .40
Land Law Act centenary.

250th Anniv. of Royal Dublin Society — A173

1981, Dec. 10 **Perf. 14½x14**
514 A173 22p multicolored   .55 .60

50th Anniv. of Killarney Natl. Park — A174

1982, Feb. 26 **Litho.** **Perf. 14½x14**
515 A174 18p Upper Lake   .40 .25
516 A174 36p Eagle's Nest   .70 1.10

The Stigmatization of St. Francis, by Sassetta A175

Francis Makemie, Old Presbyterian Church, Ramelton A176

1982, Apr. 2 **Perf. 14x15, 15x14**
517 A175 22p multicolored   .45 .25
518 A176 24p brown   .65 1.55
800th birth anniv. of St. Francis of Assisi; 300th anniv. of Francis Makemie's ordination (father of American Presbyterianism).

Europa Issue

Great Famine of 1845-50 A177

Conversion of Ireland to Christianity (St. Patrick and his Followers, by Vincenzo Valdre) A178

1982, May 4
519 A177 26p tan & brown   2.50 .50
520 A178 29p multicolored   4.50 6.50

Padraic O'Connaire (1882-1928), Writer — A179

Designs: 26p, James Joyce (1882-1941), writer and poet, by Brancusi. 29p, John Field (1782-1837), Composer and pianist, Nocturne score. 44p, Charles Joseph Kickham (1828-1882), journalist and writer. 29p, 44p by Colin Harrison.

1982, June 16 **Litho.** **Perf. 14x15**
521 A179 22p blue & black   .30 .30
522 A179 26p black & brown   .40 .30
523 A179 29p black & blue   .60 1.60
524 A179 44p gray green & black   .90 1.50
 Nos. 521-524 (4)   2.20 3.70

Porbeagle Shark — A180

No. 526, Oyster. No. 527, Salmon. No. 528, Dublin Bay prawn.

1982, July 29 **Perf. 15x14**
525 A180 22p shown   .55 1.10
526 A180 22p multicolored   .55 1.10
527 A180 26p multicolored   .65 .25
528 A180 29p multicolored   .90 1.60
 Nos. 525-528 (4)   2.65 4.05

Currach — A181

No. 530, Galway hooker, vert. No. 531, Asgard II training ship. No. 532, Howth 17-footer, vert.

1982, Sept. 21 **Perf. 15x14, 14x15**
529 A181 22p shown   .55 1.10
530 A181 22p multicolored   .55 1.10
531 A181 26p multicolored   .85 .25
532 A181 29p multicolored   .85 1.60
 Nos. 529-532 (4)   2.80 4.05

The Irish House of Commons, by Francis Wheatley — A182

1982, Oct. 14 **Litho.** **Perf. 14½x15**
533 A182 22p multicolored   .75 1.10
Bicentenary of Grattan's Parliament.

Portrait of Eamon de Valera (1882-1975), President, by Robert Ballagh — A183

1982, Oct. 14 **Perf. 14x14½**
534 A183 26p multicolored   .85 .45

A183a — 535

Madonna and Child, by Andrea della Robbia (1435-1525).

1982, Nov. 11 **Litho.** **Perf. 14½x15**
535 A183a 22p lt violet & multi   .65 .90
536 A183a 26p gray & multi   .65 .30
Christmas.

A184

A185

Killarney Cathedral, 1855 — A186

Designs: 1p-5p, Central Pavilion, Dublin Botanical Gardens. 6p, 7p, 10p, 12p, Dr. Steeven's Hospital, Dublin. 15p, 20p, 22p, Aughnanure Castle, Oughterard, 16th cent. 23p, 26p, Cormac's Chapel, 1134. 29p, 30p, St. Mac Dara's Church. 50p, Casino, Marino. £1, Cahir Castle, 15th century. £5 Central Bus Station, Dublin, 1953.
50p, £1, £5 horiz.

1982-90 **Litho.** **Perf. 14x15, 15x14**
537 A184 1p dull blue   .30 .25
538 A184 2p gray green   .30 .25
539 A184 3p black   .30 .25
540 A184 4p rose lake   .30 .25
 a. Perf. 13½ on 3 or 4 sides   .95 .25
541 A184 5p brown   .30 .30
542 A184 6p dull blue   .30 .30
543 A184 7p gray green   .30 1.50
544 A184 10p black   .30 .30
545 A184 12p rose lake   .30 2.00
546 A185 15p gray green   .50 .40
547 A185 20p rose lake   .55 .50

IRELAND

548	A185	22p dull blue	.55	.25
a.		Bklt. pane of 7+label (3 4p, 4 22p) ('83)	9.00	
549	A185	23p gray green	.95	1.35
550	A185	26p black	.85	.25
a.		Bklt. pane, 2 ea 2p, 22p, 26p	10.50	
b.		Bklt. pane, 4 ea 2p, 22p, 26p	21.00	
c.		Bklt. pane, 3 4p, 5 22p, 4 26p ('88)	32.50	
d.		Perf. 13½ on 3 sides	3.25	4.50
551	A184	29p gray green	.75	2.50
552	A184	30p black	.75	.35
a.		Perf. 13½ on 3 or 4 sides	4.10	7.25

Perf. 14x15, 15x14

553	A186	44p gray & black	1.10	1.10
554	A186	50p gray & dull blue	1.90	.70
555	A186	£1 gray & brown	5.50	1.40
556	A186	£5 gray & rose lake	10.00	6.75
		Nos. 537-556 (20)	26.10	20.90

Stamps from No. 550c imprinted "Booklet Stamp" in green on reverse side. No. 550c sold for £2.

Issued: 4p, 6p-7p, 20p, 23p, 30p, 50p, 3/16/83; 1p-3p, 5p, 10p-15p, 7/6/83; Nos. 540a, 550d, 552a, 5/3/90; others, 12/15/82. See Nos. 638-645, 803a, 804b.

Dublin Chamber of Commerce Bicentenary A187

Bank of Ireland Bicentenary A188

22p, Ouzel Galley goblet. 26p, Bank.

1983, Feb. 23   *Litho.*

557	A187	22p blue & black	.60	1.00
558	A188	26p multicolored	.60	.60

Padraig Siochfhradha (1883-1964), Writer A189

Boys' Brigade Centenary A190

1983, Apr. 7   *Litho.*   *Perf. 14x14½*

559	A189	26p multicolored	.60	.45
560	A190	29p multicolored	1.00	.75

Europa — A191

Design: 26p, Newgrange Winter Solstice, Neolithic Pattern Drawing by Louis le Brocquy. 29p, Quaternion formula, by William Rowan Hamilton (1805-1865).

1983, May 4   *Litho.*   *Perf. 14½x14*

561	A191	26p dk gray & gold	1.40	.45
562	A191	29p multicolored	3.75	4.00

Kerry Blue Terrier — A192

Drawings of dogs by Wendy Walsh: No. 564, Irish wolfhound. No. 565, Irish water spaniel. No. 566, Irish terrier. No. 567, Irish setters.

1983, June 23

563	A192	22p shown	.70	.70
564	A192	26p multicolored	.75	.85
565	A192	26p multicolored	.75	.85
566	A192	29p multicolored	.80	1.40
567	A192	44p multicolored	1.40	2.25
a.		Miniature sheet of 5, #563-567	5.00	5.75
		Nos. 563-567 (5)	4.40	6.05

Sean Mac Diarmada (1883-1916), Nationalist A193

Society for the Prevention of Cruelty to Animals A194

Society of St. Vincent de Paul Sesquicentennial A195

Industrial Credit Co., 50th Anniv. A196

US Pres. Andrew Jackson (1767-1845) — A197

Perf. 14x14½, 14½x14

1983, Aug. 11

568	A193	22p multicolored	.55	.70
569	A194	22p multicolored	.55	.55
570	A195	26p multicolored	.55	.55
571	A196	26p multicolored	.55	.90
572	A197	44p gray	1.35	2.00
		Nos. 568-572 (5)	3.55	4.70

WCY — A198

1983, Sept. 15   *Litho.*   *Perf. 14x15*

573	A198	22p Mailman	1.00	.90
574	A198	29p Dish antenna	1.25	1.80

Handicrafts — A199

1983, Oct. 13   *Litho.*   *Perf. 14x15*

575	A199	22p Weaving	.60	.45
576	A199	26p Basketweaving	.60	.30
577	A199	29p Irish crochet	.65	1.10
578	A199	44p Harpmaking	1.10	2.00
		Nos. 575-578 (4)	2.95	3.85

La Natividad by Rogier van der Weyden — A200

1983, Nov. 30   *Litho.*   *Perf. 14x14½*

579	A200	22p multicolored	.40	.25
580	A200	26p multicolored	.65	.25

Christmas.

Irish Railways Sesquicentenary A201

Locomotives: 23p, Princess, Dublin and Kingstown Railway. 26p, Macha, Great Southern Railways. 29p, Kestrel, Great Northern Railway. 44p, Link-Hoffman railcar, Coras Iompair Eireann.

1984, Jan. 30   *Perf. 14½x14*

581	A201	23p multicolored	.70	1.10
582	A201	26p multicolored	.70	.30
583	A201	29p multicolored	.80	1.35
584	A201	44p multicolored	1.25	1.80
a.		Souvenir sheet of 4, #581-584	3.25	5.00
		Nos. 581-584 (4)	3.45	4.55

Private Overprints

Nos. 584a, 684a, 708a, 708b, 803a, 804a, 811a, 826a, 847a, 855a, 876b, and others, exist with privately applied show overprints.

Local Trees — A202

1984, Mar. 1   *Litho.*   *Perf. 15x14*

585	A202	22p Irish whitebeam	.60	.60
586	A202	26p Irish yew	.65	.25
587	A202	29p Irish willow	.75	1.60
588	A202	44p Birch	1.10	2.25
		Nos. 585-588 (4)	3.10	4.70

St. Vincent's Hospital, Dublin, Sesquicentenary A203

Royal College of Surgeons in Ireland Bicentenary A204

1984, Apr. 12   *Litho.*

589	A203	26p multicolored	.55	.25
590	A204	44p multicolored	1.30	1.35

2nd European Parliament Election — A205

1984, May 10   *Litho.*   *Perf. 15x14*

591	A205	26p multicolored	.75	.75

Europa (1959-84) — A206

1984, May 10

592	A206	26p multicolored	1.90	.45
593	A206	29p multicolored	4.10	3.80

John McCormack (1884-1945), Singer — A207

1984, June 6   *Litho.*   *Perf. 14x14½*

594	A207	22p multicolored	.60	.65

See US No. 2090.

1984 Summer Olympics — A208

1984, June 21   *Litho.*   *Perf. 14½x14*

595	A208	22p Hammer throw	.45	.70
596	A208	26p Hurdles	.55	.60
597	A208	29p Running	.65	1.10
		Nos. 595-597 (3)	1.65	2.40

Gaelic Athletic Assoc. Centenary A209

1984, Aug. 23   *Litho.*   *Perf. 14x15*

598	A209	22p Hurlers	.55	.75
599	A209	26p Soccer, vert.	.65	.75

Mayoral City of Galway, 500th Anniv. A210

St. Brendan (484-577) A211

26p, Medal. 44p, Portrait, manuscript.

1984, Sept. 18   *Perf. 14x15, 15x14*

600	A210	26p multicolored	.60	.45
601	A211	44p multicolored	1.25	1.35

Post Office Bicentenary A212

26p, Handing sealed letter.

1984, Oct. 19   *Perf. 15x14*

602	A212	26p multicolored	.75	.75

Virgin And Child by Sassoferrato — A214

Perf. 14½x14, 14x14½

1984, Nov. 26   *Litho.*

603	A213	17p multicolored	.50	.75
604	A214	22p multicolored	.50	1.10
605	A214	26p multicolored	.70	.35
		Nos. 603-605 (3)	1.70	2.15

Christmas.

Love — A215

A216

22p, Heart-shaped balloon. 26p, Bouquet of hearts.

1985, Jan. 31   *Litho.*   *Perf. 15x14*

606	A215	22p multicolored	.55	.70
607	A216	26p multicolored	.65	.70

IRELAND

Dunsink Observatory, 200th Anniv. A217

Cork City Charter, 800th Anniv. A218

Irish UN Defense Forces in the Congo, 1960 A224

Thomas Ashe (1885-1917), Patriot and Educator A225

Candle, Holly A230

Virgin and Child in a Landscape, by Adrian van Ijsenbrandt A231

24p, Robertstown Grand Canal. 28p, Fishing, County Mayo, vert. 30p, Yachting, River Shannon.

1986, May 27   *Perf. 15x14, 14x15*
662	A236	24p multicolored	1.15	.90
663	A236	28p multicolored	1.25	.90
664	A236	30p multicolored	1.35	2.25
		Nos. 662-664 (3)	3.75	4.05

British & Irish Steam Packet Co., 150th Anniv. — A237

24p, Steamer Severn, 1836. 28p, M.V. Leinster, 1986.

1986, July 10   *Perf. 15x14*
| 665 | A237 | 24p multicolored | 1.10 | .90 |
| 666 | A237 | 28p multicolored | 1.20 | .55 |

Royal Irish Academy, 200th Anniv. A219

1st Manned Flight in Ireland, 200th Anniv. A220

Bishop George Berkeley (1685-1753), Philosopher and Educator — A226

1985, Mar. 14   *Litho.*
608	A217	22p black	.45	.45
609	A218	26p multicolored	.45	.25
610	A219	37p multicolored	1.00	1.60
611	A220	44p multicolored	1.00	1.60
		Nos. 608-611 (4)	2.90	3.90

1985, June 20   *Perf. 15x14, 14x15*   *Litho.*
621	A224	22p multicolored	.75	.70
622	A225	26p multicolored	.75	.45
623	A226	44p multicolored	1.10	2.70
		Nos. 621-623 (3)	2.60	3.95

Irish forces as part of the UN Defense Forces, 25th anniv. (22p).

Christmas: No. 651, The Holy Family, by Murillo. 26p, Adoration of the Shepherds, by Louis Le Nain, horiz.

1985, Nov. 26   *Perf. 14x15, 15x14*   *Litho.*
649	A230	22p shown	.55	.45
650	A231	22p shown	1.00	1.75
651	A231	22p multicolored	1.00	1.75
a.		Pair, #650-651	2.25	4.00
652	A231	26p multicolored	1.10	.25
		Nos. 649-652 (4)	3.65	4.20

No. 649 was issued in discount sheets of 16 that sold for £3. Value $7.50.

Lighthouses — A238

1986, July 10   *Perf. 14½x15*
| 667 | A238 | 24p Kish, helicopter | 1.10 | .70 |
| 668 | A238 | 30p Fastnet | 1.65 | 2.50 |

Butterflies — A221

1985, Apr. 4   *Litho.*   *Perf. 14x15*
612	A221	22p Common blue	1.05	.90
613	A221	26p Red admiral	1.05	.60
614	A221	28p Brimstone	1.05	2.25
615	A221	44p Marsh fritillary	1.60	2.75
		Nos. 612-615 (4)	4.75	6.50

Intl. Youth Year — A227

1985, Aug. 1   *Litho.*
| 624 | A227 | 22p multi, horiz. | .60 | .45 |
| 625 | A227 | 26p multicolored | .60 | .45 |

Architecture Type of 1982

Designs: 24p, 39p, Cormac's Chapel. 28p, 32p, 37p, St. Mac Dara's Church. 46p, Cahir Castle. £1, Killarney Cathedral. £2, Casino, Marino. 46p, £2, horiz.

Perf. 15x14, 14x15 (A184, No. 644)

1985-88   *Litho.*
638	A185	24p brown	1.35	.40
639	A184	28p rose lake	.85	.30
a.		Bklt. pane, 4 2p, 2 24p, 1 4p, 5 28p ('88)	8.00	
c.		Bklt. pane, 2 2p, 3 4p, 3 24p, 4 28p ('88)	8.50	
640	A184	32p brown	2.75	3.25
641	A184	37p dull blue	1.10	3.00
642	A184	39p rose lake	2.75	3.00
643	A186	46p gray & gray grn	7.25	2.20
644	A186	£1 gray & dull bl	7.75	4.50
645	A186	£2 gray & gray grn	10.00	6.00
		Nos. 638-645 (8)	33.80	22.65

Issued: 24p, 28p, 37p, £1, June 27, 1985; 32p, 39p, 46p, May 1, 1986; £2, July 26, 1988.

Love — A232

26p, Heart-shaped mailbox.

1986, Jan. 30   *Perf. 14x15*
| 653 | A232 | 22p shown | 1.10 | .80 |
| 654 | A232 | 26p multicolored | 1.10 | .80 |

Ferns — A233

1986, Mar. 20   *Litho.*   *Perf. 14½x15*
655	A233	24p Hart's tongue	.65	.60
656	A233	28p Rusty-back	.70	.60
657	A233	46p Killarney	1.10	1.90
		Nos. 655-657 (3)	2.45	3.10

Dublin Council of Trade Unions, Cent. A239

Arthur Griffith (1871-1922), Statesman A240

Europa — A222

26p, Charles Villiers Stanford (1852-1924), composer. 37p, Turlough O'Carolan (1670-1738), Composer.

1985, May 16   *Litho.*   *Perf. 15x14*
| 616 | A222 | 26p multicolored | 2.00 | .45 |
| 617 | A222 | 37p multicolored | 5.00 | 5.50 |

Women in Society, Construction Surveyor — A241

A242

European Music Year — A223

Composers: No. 618, Giuseppe Domenico Scarlatti (1685-1757). No. 619, George Frideric Handel (1685-1759). No. 620, Johann Sebastian Bach (1685-1750).

1985, May 16   *Litho.*   *Perf. 14x15*
618	A223	22p multicolored	1.00	2.25
619	A223	22p multicolored	1.00	2.25
a.		Pair, #618-619	2.00	4.50
620	A223	26p multicolored	1.25	.45
		Nos. 618-620 (3)	3.25	4.95

Industrial Innovations A228

Institution of Engineers, 150th Anniv. — A229

22p, Computer technology. 26p, Peat production. 44p, The Key Man, by Sean Keating.

1985, Oct. 3   *Litho.*   *Perf. 15x14*
646	A228	22p multicolored	.55	.70
647	A228	26p multicolored	.55	.50
648	A229	44p multicolored	1.10	2.25
		Nos. 646-648 (3)	2.20	3.45

Europa — A234

28p, Industry and nature. 39p, Hedgerows, horiz.

1986, May 1   *Perf. 14x15, 15x14*
| 658 | A234 | 28p multicolored | 3.25 | .70 |
| 659 | A234 | 39p multicolored | 10.00 | 5.50 |

Aer Lingus, 50th Anniv. — A235

28p, Jet, 1986. 46p, The Eagle, 1936.

1986, May 27   *Perf. 15x14*
| 660 | A235 | 28p multicolored | 1.30 | .70 |
| 661 | A235 | 46p multicolored | 1.90 | 3.25 |

Inland Waterways A236

Intl. Peace Year — A242a

Perf. 14½x15, 14x15 (#670, 672), 15x14½, 15x14

1986, Aug. 21
669	A239	24p multicolored	.60	.80
670	A240	28p multicolored	.70	.70
671	A241	28p multicolored	.70	.70
672	A242	30p multi, vert.	.75	.90
673	A242a	46p shown	1.00	1.60
		Nos. 669-673 (5)	3.75	4.70

See Nos. 699, 711, 749, 807, 836.

William Mulready (1786-1863), Letter Sheet Designer — A243

Carriages by Charles Bianconi (1786-1875) A244

IRELAND

Perf. 15x14, 14x15
1986, Oct. 2   Litho.
674 A243 24p multicolored   .80 .65
675 A244 28p multi, vert.   .95 .50
676 A244 39p shown   1.25 1.60
     Nos. 674-676 (3)   3.00 2.75

Adoration of the Shepherds, by Francesco Pascucci — A245

Adoration of the Magi, by Frans Francken III (1542-1616) — A246

1986, Nov. 20   Perf. 15x14, 14½x15
677 A245 21p multicolored   1.20 1.25
678 A246 28p multicolored   .70 .55

Christmas. No. 677 was issued in discount sheets of 12 that sold for £2.50. Value $13.50.

Love — A247

Perf. 15x14, 14x15
1987, Jan. 27   Litho.
679 A247 24p Flowers, butterfly   .85 1.10
680 A247 28p Postman, vert.   1.25 1.10

Trolleys — A248

1987, Mar. 4   Litho.   Perf. 15x14
681 A248 24p Cork Electric   .60 .50
682 A248 28p Dublin Standard   .65 .70
683 A248 30p Howth (G.N.R.)   .75 1.60
684 A248 46p Galway Horse   1.00 1.80
   a. Miniature sheet of 4, #681-684   3.75 4.00
     Nos. 681-684 (4)   3.00 4.60

See note following No. 584.

Waterford Chamber of Commerce, 200th Anniv. — A249

Muintir Na Tire, 50th Anniv. A250

Trinity College Botanical Gardens, Dublin, 300th Anniv. A251

Medical Missionaries of Mary, 50th Anniv. — A252

Anniversaries and events: 24p, Three ships, Chamber crest. 28p, Canon Hayes (1887-1957), founder, and symbols of Muintir Na Tire activities. 30p, College crest, Calceolaria burbidgei. 39p, Intl. Missionary Training Hospital, Drogheda, and Mother Mary Martin.

Perf. 15x14, 14x15
1987, Apr. 9   Litho.
685 A249 24p vio bl, blk & dk grn   .65 .40
686 A250 28p multicolored   .65 .40
687 A251 30p multicolored   .65 1.75
688 A252 39p multicolored   .70 1.60
     Nos. 685-688 (4)   2.65 4.15

Europa — A253

Modern architecture, art: 28p, Borda na Mona headquarters, Dublin, and The Turf Cutter, by sculptor John Behan. 39p, St. Mary's Church and ruins of Romanesque monastery at Cong.

1987, May 14   Perf. 15x14
689 A253 28p multicolored   2.75 .55
690 A253 39p multicolored   5.00 6.50

Cattle — A254

1987, July 2
691 A254 24p Kerry   .65 .60
692 A254 28p Friesian   .85 .45
693 A254 30p Hereford   .85 1.75
694 A254 39p Shorthorn   1.15 1.75
     Nos. 691-694 (4)   3.50 4.55

Festivals — A255

24p, Fleadh Nua, Ennis. 28p, Festival Queen, Tralee. 30p, Wexford opera festival. 46p, Ballinasloe horse fair.

1987, Aug. 27   Perf. 14x15
695 A255 24p multicolored   .60 .55
696 A255 28p multicolored   .70 .40
697 A255 30p multicolored   .90 1.75
698 A255 46p multicolored   1.10 1.75
     Nos. 695-698 (4)   3.30 4.45

Nos. 695-696 vert.

Statesmen Type of 1986 and

Ewer and Chalice, Company Crest — A256

Harp in Shield, Preamble Excerpt A257

Woman Leading Board Meeting A258

Design: No. 699, Cathal Brugha, vert.

Perf. 14x15, 15x14
1987, Oct. 1   Litho.
699 A240 24p black   .70 .70
700 A256 24p multicolored   .70 .70
   a. Yellow omitted   3,750.
701 A257 28p multicolored   .80 .55
702 A258 46p multicolored   1.20 1.00
     Nos. 699-702 (4)   3.40 2.95

Company of Goldsmiths of Dublin, 350th anniv. (No. 700); Irish Constitution, 50th anniv. (28p); Women in Society, (46p).

A259

Christmas — A260

21p, 12 Days of Christmas (1st 3 days). 24p, Embroidery (detail), Waterford Vestments, 15th cent. 28p, Neapolitan creche (detail), 1850.

Perf. 15x14, 14x15
1987, Nov. 17   Litho.
703 A259 21p multicolored   .55 .90
704 A260 24p multicolored   .70 .90
705 A260 28p multicolored   .70 .70
     Nos. 703-705 (3)   1.95 2.50

No. 703 issued in discount sheets of 14 + center label; sheet sold for £2.90. Value $17.50.

Love — A261

Perf. 15x14½, 14½x15
1988, Jan. 27   Litho.
706 A261 24p shown   .80 .55
707 A261 28p Pillar box, vert.   .80 .60

Dublin Millennium A262

1988, Mar. 1   Perf. 15x14
708 A262 28p multicolored   .75 .65
   a. Booklet pane of 4, Gaelic   2.00
   b. Booklet pane of 4, English   2.00

Nos. 708a, 708b consist of two vert. pairs separated by a history in Gaelic or English. See note following No. 584.

A263

Impact of the Irish Abroad — A264

Designs: No. 709, Robert O'Hara Burke (1820-1861), by Sir Sidney Nolan; 19th cent. map of Australia with Burke & Wills expedition route. 46p, Mural (detail) of the Eureka Stockade by Nolan.

1988, Mar. 1
709 A263 24p multicolored   1.10 1.25
710 A264 46p multicolored   1.10 1.25

Statesmen Type of 1986 and

1988 Summer Olympics, Seoul — A265

Order of Malta Ambulance Corps, 50th Anniv. — A266

Barry Fitzgerald (1888-1961), Actor — A267

Designs: 24p, William T. Cosgrave (1880-1965), president of the United Ireland and Fine Gael party. No. 713, Cycling.

Perf. 14x15, 15x14
1988, Apr. 7   Litho.
711 A240 24p black   .40 .40
712 A265 28p multicolored   .90 1.25
713 A265 28p multicolored   .90 1.25
   a. Pair, #712-713   3.60 6.25
714 A266 30p multicolored   .85 .90
715 A267 50p multicolored   1.05 1.70
     Nos. 711-715 (5)   4.10 5.50

Nos. 712-713 printed in sheets of 5 each plus two labels. Value, $10.

Sirius Sailing from Passage West, County Cork — A268

1988, May 12   Litho.   Perf. 15x14
716 A268 24p multicolored   1.30 .45

1st scheduled transatlantic crossing by steamship, sesquicentennial.

Europa — A269

28p, Air traffic controllers and A320 Airbus. 39p, Europe on globe, letters.

1988, May 12   Litho.   Perf. 15x14
717 A269 28p multicolored   1.75 .50
718 A269 39p multicolored   3.75 3.00

Maia and Mercury Flying Boats in Foynes Harbor — A269a

1988, May 12   Litho.   Perf. 15x14
719 A269a 46p multicolored   2.20 2.70

1st east-west transatlantic crossing by seaplane, 50th anniv.

Conservation of Flora — A270

24p, Otanthus maritimus. 28p, Saxifraga hartii. 46p, Astragalus danicus.

1988, June 21   Litho.   Perf. 14x15
720 A270 24p multicolored   .55 .35
721 A270 28p multicolored   .60 .35
722 A270 46p multicolored   1.00 2.25
     Nos. 720-722 (3)   2.15 2.95

Irish Security Forces — A271

No. 723, Garda Siochana (police). No. 724, Army. No. 725, Navy, air corps. No. 726, FCA, Slua Muiri.

IRELAND

1988, Aug. 23   Litho.   Perf. 15x14
723	A271	28p multicolored	.90	1.00
724	A271	28p multicolored	.90	1.00
725	A271	28p multicolored	.90	1.00
726	A271	28p multicolored	.90	1.00
a.		Strip of 4, #723-726	3.75	4.75
		Nos. (4)	3.60	4.00

Institute of Chartered Accountants, Cent. — A272

Defeat of the Spanish Armada, 400th Anniv. — A273

46p, Duquesa Santa Ana off Donegal Coast.

Perf. 14x15, 15x14
1988, Oct. 6   Litho.
| 727 | A272 | 24p multicolored | .45 | .35 |
| 728 | A273 | 46p multicolored | 1.75 | 1.35 |

John F. Kennedy, Portrait by James Wyeth — A274

1988, Nov. 24   Litho.   Perf. 15x14
| 729 | A274 | 28p multicolored | 1.10 | .70 |

A275

Christmas — A276

21p, St. Kevin's Church, Glendalough. 24p, Adoration of the Magi. 28p, Flight into Egypt. 46p, Holy Family.

1988, Nov. 24   Perf. 14x15
730	A275	21p multicolored	.75	.90
731	A276	24p multicolored	.45	.55
732	A276	28p multicolored	.55	.40
733	A276	46p multicolored	.85	2.75
		Nos. 730-733 (4)	2.60	4.60

No. 730 issued only in discount sheets of 14. Sheet sold for £2.90. Value $11.

Love A277

The Sonnet, by William Mulready (1786-1863) A278

Perf. 15x14, 14x15
1989, Jan. 24   Litho.
| 734 | A277 | 24p multicolored | .80 | .50 |
| 735 | A278 | 28p multicolored | .80 | .50 |

Mulready, designer of Rowland Hill's first stamped envelope.

Classic Automobiles A279

1989, Apr. 11   Litho.   Perf. 15x14
736	A279	24p Silver Stream	.45	.50
737	A279	28p Benz Comfortable	.45	.50
a.		Booklet pane, 2 each 24p, 28p	1.90	
738	A279	39p Thomond Car	1.10	1.35
739	A279	46p Chambers Car	1.35	1.35
a.		Booklet pane of 4, #736-739	3.25	
		Nos. 736-739 (4)	3.35	3.70

Parks and Gardens — A280

24p, Garinish Island. 28p, Glenveagh. 32p, Connemara Natl. Park. 50p, St. Stephen's Green.

1989, Apr. 11
740	A280	24p multicolored	.55	.50
741	A280	28p multicolored	.65	.50
742	A280	32p multicolored	.75	1.15
743	A280	50p multicolored	1.10	1.55
		Nos. 740-743 (4)	3.05	3.70

Europa — A281

28p, Ring-a-ring-a-rosie. 39p, Hopscotch.

1989, May 11
| 744 | A281 | 28p multicolored | .85 | .70 |
| 745 | A281 | 39p multicolored | 1.10 | 2.00 |

Irish Red Cross Soc., 50th Anniv. — A282

1989, May 11   Perf. 14x15
| 746 | A282 | 24p multicolored | .60 | .60 |

European Parliament 3rd Elections — A283

1989, May 11
| 747 | A283 | 28p Stars from flag | 1.00 | 1.00 |

Sts. Kilian, Colman and Totnan (d. 689), Martyred Missionaries, and Shamrock A284

1989, June 15   Litho.   Perf. 13½
748	A284	28p multicolored	.50	1.00
a.		Booklet pane of 4, English	2.75	
b.		Booklet pane of 4, Gaelic	2.75	
c.		Booklet pane of 4, German	2.75	
d.		Booklet pane of 4, Latin	2.75	

See Federal Republic of Germany No. 1580.

RIAI Emblem A285

Dublin-Cork Coach, 1789 A286

Singer, Scene from La Boheme A287

Nehru A288

Design: 24p, Sean Thomas O'Kelly (1883-1966), 2nd president.

Perf. 14x15, 15x14
1989, July 27   Litho.
749	A240	24p black	.60	.50
750	A285	28p multicolored	.60	.50
751	A286	28p multicolored	1.10	.60
752	A287	30p multicolored	1.90	2.00
753	A288	46p red brown	3.25	2.90
		Nos. 749-753 (5)	7.45	6.80

Royal Institute of Architects, 150th anniv.; Mail coach in Ireland, bicent.; Margaret Burke Sheridan (1889-1958), soprano; Jawaharlal Nehru, 1st prime minister of independent India.

Flags and Sail Ireland Yacht Rounding Cape Horn, by Des Fallon — A289

1989, Aug. 31   Litho.   Perf. 15x14
| 754 | A289 | 28p multicolored | 1.10 | 1.15 |

Whitbread round of the World Yacht Race 1989-90.

Wildlife: Game Birds — A290

24p, Lagopus lagopus. 28p, Vanellus vanellus. 39p, Scolopax rusticola. 46p, Phasianus colchicus.

1989, Oct. 5   Litho.   Perf. 13½
755	A290	24p multicolored	.95	.60
756	A290	28p multicolored	.95	.60
757	A290	39p multicolored	1.20	2.75
758	A290	46p multicolored	1.20	2.75
a.		Miniature sheet of 4, #755-758	4.50	6.25
		Nos. 755-758 (4)	4.30	6.70

Children and Creche A291

Miniatures from a Flemish Psalter, 13th Cent. A292

24p, Annunciation. 28p, Nativity. 46p, Adoration of the Magi.

Statesmen Type of 1986 and

1989, Nov. 14   Litho.   Perf. 14x15
759	A291	21p multicolored	.70	.70
760	A292	24p multicolored	.70	.55
761	A292	28p multicolored	.70	.70
762	A292	46p multicolored	1.00	2.25
		Nos. 759-762 (4)	3.10	4.00

No. 759 issued only in discount sheets of 14. Sheet sold for £2.90. Value $11.

Ireland's Presidency of the European Communities A293

European Tourism Year — A294

1990, Jan. 9   Litho.   Perf. 15x14
| 763 | A293 | 30p multicolored | .85 | .55 |
| 764 | A294 | 50p multicolored | 1.90 | 2.75 |

A295

Love Issue — A296

26p, Heart Hot Air Balloon with Love underneath. 30p, "Love!".

1990, Jan. 30   Litho.   Perf. 14x15
| 765 | A295 | 26p multicolored | 1.30 | 1.15 |
| 766 | A295 | 30p multicolored | 1.35 | 1.15 |

Enamel Latchet Brooch A297

Ardagh Chalice A298

Art treasures of Ireland: 1p, 2p, Silver Kite Brooch, vert. 4p, 5p, Dunamase Food Vessel, vert. 10p, Derrinboy Armlets. 20p, Gold Dress Fastener. 26p, 28p, Lismore Crosier, vert. 32p, Broighter Collar. 34p, 37p, 38p, 40p, Gleninsheen Collar, vert. 41p, 44p, 45p, Silver thistle brooch, vert. 50p, 52p, Broighter boat, vert. £2, Tara Brooch. £5, St. Patrick's Bell Shrine, vert.

1990-95   Litho.   Perf. 15x14, 14x15
767	A297	1p blue & blk	.30	.25
768	A297	2p orange & blk	.30	.25
770	A297	4p violet & blk	.30	.25
a.		Perf. 13x13½	1.60	.65
b.		Photo.	.75	1.35
771	A297	5p green & blk	.30	.25
774	A297	10p orange & blk	.30	.25
777	A297	20p yel & blk (I)	.55	.25
778	A297	26p violet & blk	1.60	.65
a.		Perf. 13½ on 3 or 4 sides	1.90	4.00
779	A297	28p org & blk (I)	.75	.45
a.		Bklt. pane, 3 #770, 4 #779 + label	5.50	
b.		Photo.	2.20	4.00
780	A297	30p brt blue & blk	1.35	1.40
a.		Perf. 13½	2.20	3.50
b.		Bklt. pane, 3 #540a, 1 #550d, 2 #778a, 2 #780a	6.50	
c.		Bklt. pane, #768, 3 #770, #778, 2 #780 + label	6.00	
781	A297	32p green & blk	1.60	.70
a.		Bklt. pane, 2 #770b, #779b, 2 #781d	4.50	
b.		Perf. 13½x13	2.20	2.50
c.		Bklt. pane, #770a, 3 #781b	6.50	
d.		Photo.	.75	1.10
e.		Booklet pane, 1 #770, 3 #781	6.50	
782	A297	34p yellow & blk	1.60	1.60
783	A297	37p green & blk	1.90	2.50
784	A297	38p purple & blk	1.90	2.50
785	A297	40p blue & black	2.20	1.35
786	A297	41p orange & blk	1.90	2.25
787	A297	44p yellow & blk	2.00	1.90
788	A297	45p violet & black	4.00	2.50
789	A297	50p yellow & blk	1.90	2.00
790	A297	52p blue & blk (I)	2.75	1.90
791	A298	£1 yellow & blk (III)	3.50	1.50
792	A298	£2 green & blk (III)	4.95	3.00

IRELAND

793	A298	£5 blue & blk (III)	11.00	9.00

Self-Adhesive
Die cut perf 11
Size: 27x21mm

794	A297	32p like #781	1.90	.90
a.		Die cut perf. 11½	3.50	3.50
b.		Die cut perf. 9½x9	1.90	1.35
		Nos. 767-794 (23)	48.85	37.60

Issued: 26p, 30p, 32p, 41p, 50p, £1, 3/8; No. 780b, 5/3; 1p, 2p, 4p, 10p, 34p, £2, 7/26; No. 780c, 11/15; 5p, 20p, £5, 1/26/91; No. 781a, 5/14/91; 28p, 37p, 38p, 44p, 52p, 4/3/91; No. 779a, 10/17/91; No. 794, 10/31/91; 40p, 45p, 5/14/92; Nos. 770a, 781b, 9/24/93; No. 781e, 11/16/95; No. 794b, 6/8/95.

No. 794 was printed on phosphored paper; No. 794a on normal paper.

52 #777, 779, 790, Type I - Coarse Dot Structure
52 #777a, 779c, 790a, Type II - Fine Dot Structure

£1 #791-793, Type III
£1 #791a-793a, Type IV

Perf. 14x15, 15x14
1995, Nov. 15 Litho.

777a	A297	20p Type II	1.90	1.15
779c	A297	28p Type II	1.90	1.80
790a	A297	52p Type II	2.75	2.75
791a	A298	£1 Type IV	4.50	3.00
792a	A298	£2 Type IV	7.00	6.50
793a	A298	£5 Type IV	26.50	26.50
		Nos. 777a-793a (6)	44.55	41.70

A299

1990, Mar. 22 Litho. Perf. 14x15
Booklet Stamps

795	A299	26p Gift boxes	1.25	2.00
796	A299	26p Nosegay	1.25	2.00
797	A299	30p Horseshoe	1.25	2.00
798	A299	30p Balloons	1.25	2.00
a.		Bklt. pane of 4, #795-798 English labels		4.75
b.		As "a," 4 English, 4 Gaelic labels		4.75

Greetings. Available only in discount booklets containing Nos. 798a, 798b. Bklts. sold for £1.98.

A300

1990, Apr. 5 Litho. Perf. 14x15

799	A300	30p Tackle	1.00	1.45
800	A300	30p Heading the ball	1.00	1.45
a.		Pair, #799-800	2.25	3.00

1990 World Cup Soccer Championships, Italy. Printed in sheets of 4 No. 800a plus label. Value, $7.50.

Williamite Wars, 300th Anniv. — A301

No. 801, Siege of Limerick. No. 802, Battle of the Boyne.

1990, Apr. 5 Litho. Perf. 13½

801	A301	30p multicolored	1.60	1.60
802	A301	30p multicolored	1.60	1.60
a.		Pair, #801-802	3.50	3.75

Penny Black, 150th Anniv. — A302

1990, May 3 Litho. Perf. 15x14

803	A302	30p #780	1.00	.90
a.		Bklt. pane, #803, 2 each #552a, 780a		.50
804	A302	50p #68, 255, 550, 780	1.35	2.25
a.		Bklt. pane, 2 ea #803-804	6.50	
b.		Bklt. pane of 4, #552a, 780a, 803-804	6.50	
		Complete bklt., #803a, 804a, 804b, 780b	15.00	

See note following No. 584.

Europa 1990 — A303

Post offices: 30p, GPO, Dublin. 41p, Westport P.O., County Mayo.

1990, May 3 Perf. 14x15

805	A303	30p multicolored	.60	.45
806	A303	41p multicolored	1.15	2.25

Printed in sheets of 10+2 labels. Value $27.50.

Statesman Type of 1986
1990, June 12 Litho. Perf. 14x15

807	A240	30p Michael Collins	1.10	1.60

Irish Missionaries A304

Design: 50p, Working at water pump.

1990, June 21 Perf. 15x14

808	A304	26p multicolored	.90	.35
809	A304	50p multicolored	1.10	1.60

Garden Flowers — A305

1990, Aug. 30 Litho. Perf. 14x15

810	A305	26p Narcissus	.55	.50
811	A305	30p Rosa x hibernica	.60	.70
a.		Bklt. pane, 2 each #810-811	3.75	
812	A305	41p Primula	1.10	2.25
813	A305	50p Erica erigena	1.35	2.50
a.		Booklet pane of 4, #810-813	3.75	
		Nos. 810-813 (4)	3.60	5.95

See note following No. 584.

Theater — A306

Designs: No. 814, Playboy of the Western World. No. 815, Juno and the Paycock. No. 816, The Field. No. 817, Waiting for Godot.

1990, Oct. 18 Litho. Perf. 13½

814	A306	30p multicolored	.95	1.25
815	A306	30p multicolored	.95	1.25
816	A306	30p multicolored	.95	1.25
817	A306	30p multicolored	.95	1.25
a.		Block or strip of 4, #814-817	4.00	5.50

Christmas — A308

No. 818, Child praying. No. 819, Nativity scene. No. 820, Madonna and Child. No. 821, Adoration of the Magi.

1990, Nov. 15 Litho. Perf. 14x15

818	A307	26p multicolored	.70	.70
819	A308	26p multicolored	.55	.55
820	A308	30p multicolored	.80	.80
821	A308	50p multicolored	1.60	3.00
		Nos. 818-821 (4)	3.65	5.05

No. 818 sold only in discount sheets of 12 for $2.86. Value $11.

Love — A309

1991, Jan. 29 Litho. Perf. 14x15

822	A309	26p shown	.90	.90
823	A309	30p Boy, girl kissing	1.10	.90

Irish Cycles — A310

26p, Starley rover. 30p, Child's horse tricycle. 50p, Penny farthing.

1991, Mar. 5

824	A310	26p multicolored	.80	.55
825	A310	30p multicolored	1.10	.90
826	A310	50p multicolored	1.65	2.25
a.		Souvenir sheet of 3, #824-826	3.50	3.50
		Nos. 824-826 (3)	3.55	3.70

See note following No. 584.

1916 Rising, 75th Anniv. — A311

Design: Statue of Cuchulainn by Oliver Sheppard, 1916 Proclamation.

1991, Apr. 3 Litho. Perf. 15x14

827	A311	32p multicolored	1.10	1.35

Dublin, European City of Culture — A312

Designs: 28p, La Traviata, performed by Dublin Grand Opera Society. 32p, Dublin City Hall. 44p, St. Patrick's Cathedral, 800th anniv. 52p, Custom House, 200th anniv.

1991, Apr. 11 Perf. 15x14

828	A312	28p multicolored	.90	.90
829	A312	32p multicolored	1.00	1.45
830	A312	44p multicolored	.80	1.45
a.		Booklet pane of 3, #828-830	4.00	4.00

Size: 41x25mm
Perf. 13½

831	A312	52p multicolored	.90	1.45
a.		Booklet pane of 4, #828-831	4.00	
		Complete booklet, #830a, 831a	7.50	
		Nos. 828-831 (4)	3.60	5.25

50th anniv. of Dublin Grand Opera Soc. (No. 828).

Europa — A313

1991, May 14 Litho. Perf. 15x14

832	A313	32p Giotto probe	1.10	.90
833	A313	44p Hubble telescope	1.40	2.75

Williamite Wars, 300th Anniv. — A314

1991, May 14

834	A314	28p Siege of Athlone	1.00	1.25
835	A314	28p Treaty of Limerick	1.00	1.25
a.		Pair, #834-835	2.00	2.50

Statesman Type of 1986 and

Charles Stewart Parnell (1846-1891), Politician A315

Society of United Irishmen, Bicent. A316

28p, John A. Costello (1891-1976), politician.

Perf. 14x15, 15x14
1991, July 2 Litho.

836	A240	28p black	.65	.55
837	A315	32p multicolored	.75	.70
838	A316	52p multicolored	.90	2.25
		Nos. 836-838 (3)	2.30	3.50

A317

28p, Golfer putting, horiz.

Perf. 15x14, 14x15
1991, Sept. 3 Litho.

839	A317	28p multicolored	1.10	.90
840	A317	32p shown	1.35	.90

Walker Cup Competition, Portmarnock Golf Club (No. 839).

Irish Sheep — A318

1991, Sept. 3 Perf. 14x15, 15x14

841	A318	32p Wicklow Cheviot	.95	.70
842	A318	38p Donegal Blackface	1.05	1.35
843	A318	52p Galway, horiz.	1.50	2.90
		Nos. 841-843 (3)	3.50	4.95

IRELAND

505

Fishing Fleet — A319

1991, Oct. 17   Litho.   Perf. 15x14
844	A319	28p Boatyard	.55	.45
845	A319	32p Inshore trawler	.65	.60
a.		Bklt. pane of 5, #845, 2 each #768, 783	5.00	
b.		Bklt. pane, 2 each #844, 845	5.00	
846	A319	44p Inshore potter	1.15	2.00
847	A319	50p Factory ship	1.50	2.25
a.		Booklet pane of 4, #844-847	8.00	
		Nos. 844-847 (4)	3.85	5.30

See note following No. 584.

Christmas — A321

1991, Nov. 14   Litho.   Perf. 14x15
848	A321	28p Wise men, star	.75	.90
849	A321	28p Annunciation	.75	.60
850	A321	32p Nativity	.80	.70
851	A321	52p Adoration of the Magi	1.40	2.90
		Nos. 848-851 (4)	3.70	5.10

No. 848 issued only in discount sheets of 13+2 labels which sold for £3.36. Value $11.

Love — A322

Design: 32p, Rainbow over meadow, love etched in stone, vert.

Perf. 15x14, 14x15

1992, Jan. 28   Litho.
852	A322	28p shown	.95	.85
853	A322	32p multicolored	1.00	1.00

1992 Summer Olympics, Barcelona A323

1992, Feb. 25   Litho.   Perf. 15x14
854	A323	32p Boxing	1.15	.80
855	A323	44p Sailing	1.40	2.10
a.		Sheet of 4, 2 each #854-855	4.25	6.25

See note following No. 584.

Healthy Lifestyle — A324

1992, Feb. 25   Perf. 14x15
| 856 | A324 | 28p multicolored | 1.35 | .90 |

Galway Chamber of Commerce and Industry, Bicent. — A325

1992, Apr. 2   Litho.   Perf. 15x14
| 857 | A325 | 28p multicolored | 1.00 | .90 |

Intl. Maritime Heritage Year — A326

Perf. 15x14, 14x15

1992, Apr. 2   Litho.
858	A326	32p Mari Cog	1.10	.80
859	A326	52p Ovoca, vert.	1.65	2.50

Greetings — A327

1992, Apr. 2   Perf. 14x15
860	A327	28p Coastline	1.00	1.00
861	A327	28p Mountain	1.00	1.00
862	A327	32p Flowers	1.00	1.00
863	A327	32p Pond	1.00	1.00
a.		Bklt. pane of 4, #860-863, 8 English labels	4.50	
b.		Bklt. pane of 4, #860-863, 4 English labels + 4 Gaelic labels	4.50	
		Nos. 860-863 (4)	4.00	4.00

No. 863a contains Nos. 860-863 in order.
No. 863b contains Nos. 862, 863, 860 and 861 in order.

Discovery of America, 500th Anniv. — A328

Europa: 44p, Landing in New World.

1992, May 14   Litho.   Perf. 15x14
864	A328	32p multicolored	1.35	.80
865	A328	44p multicolored	2.25	2.75

Irish in the Americas A329

Design: No. 867, The White House, bridge, railroad workers, musicians, workers.

1992, May 14   Perf. 13½
866	A329	52p multicolored	1.60	1.70
867	A329	52p multicolored	1.60	1.70
a.		Pair, #866-867	3.25	3.50

Pine Marten — A330

1992, July 9   Litho.   Perf. 15x14
868	A330	28p shown	.90	.60
869	A330	32p In tree	.90	.70
a.		Imperf. btwn (vert. pair)	950.00	
870	A330	44p With young	1.45	1.35
871	A330	52p Holding bird	1.80	2.25
		Nos. 868-871 (4)	5.05	4.90

World Wildlife Fund.

Trinity College, Dublin, 400th Anniv. — A331

1992, Sept. 2   Litho.   Perf. 13½
872	A331	32p Library	1.10	.90
873	A331	52p Main entrance	1.40	2.00

Views of Dublin by James Malton, Bicent. — A332

28p, Rotunda, Assembly rooms. 44p, Charlemont House.

1992, Sept. 2   Perf. 15x14
874	A332	28p multicolored	1.00	.60
875	A332	44p multicolored	1.25	1.75

Single European Market — A333

1992, Oct. 15   Litho.   Perf. 15x14
876	A333	32p multicolored	.50	.70
a.		Bklt. pane of 3	1.65	
b.		Bklt. pane of 4	2.10	

No. 876b comes with stamps in three formats: four singles, two pairs, and block of four. See note following No. 584.

Food and Farming — A334

No. 877, Fresh food. No. 878, Cattle. No. 879, Combine harvesting grain. No. 880, Growing vegetables.

1992, Oct. 15   Perf. 14x15
877	A334	32p multicolored	1.10	1.10
878	A334	32p multicolored	1.10	1.10
879	A334	32p multicolored	1.10	1.10
880	A334	32p multicolored	1.10	1.10
a.		Strip of 4, #877-880	4.50	4.50
		Nos. (4)	4.40	4.40

A335

Christmas — A336

Designs: No. 881, Rural churchyard. No. 882, The Annunciation, manuscript illustration, Chester Beatty Library, Dublin. 32p, Adoration of the Shepherds, by Jocopo da Empoli. 52p, Adoration of the Magi, by Johann Rottenhammer.

1992, Nov. 19
881	A335	28p multicolored	.70	.60
882	A336	28p multicolored	.70	.60
883	A336	32p multicolored	1.00	.90
884	A336	52p multicolored	1.25	1.35
		Nos. 881-884 (4)	3.65	3.45

No. 881 issued only in discount sheets of 13+2 labels which sold for £3.36. Value $11.

Love — A337

Design: 28p, Queen of Hearts, vert.

Perf. 14x15, 15x14

1993, Jan. 26   Litho.
885	A337	28p multicolored	1.00	.70
886	A337	32p multicolored	1.10	.80

Irish Impressionist Paintings — A338

Designs: 28p, Evening at Tangier, by Sir John Lavery. 32p, The Goose Girl, by William J. Leech. 44p, La Jeune Bretonne, by Roderic O'Conor, vert. 52p, Lustre Jug, by Walter Osborne, vert.

1993, Mar. 4   Perf. 13
887	A338	28p multicolored	.60	.60
888	A338	32p multicolored	.65	.65
a.		Booklet pane of 2, #887-888	2.75	
889	A338	44p multicolored	.70	1.75
890	A338	52p multicolored	.75	2.50
a.		Booklet pane of 2, #889-890	2.75	
b.		Booklet pane of 4, #887-890	2.75	
		Nos. 887-890 (4)	2.70	5.50

No. 890b exists in two formats with different margin inscriptions.

Orchids — A339

28p, Bee orchid. 32p, O'Kelly's orchid. 38p, Dark red helleborine. 52p, Irish lady's tresses.

1993, Apr. 20   Litho.   Perf. 14x15
891	A339	28p multi	.70	.40
892	A339	32p multi	.75	.65
893	A339	38p multi	1.00	1.75
894	A339	52p multi	1.50	2.25
a.		Souvenir sheet of 4, #891-894	4.00	5.50
b.		As "a," with blue inscription	8.00	11.00
		Nos. 891-894 (4)	3.95	5.05

No. 894b has a larger top margin than No. 894a. Added Inscription includes text and flags of Ireland and Thailand.

Contemporary Paintings — A340

Europa: 32p, Pears in a Copper Pan, by Hilda van Stockum. 44p, Arrieta Orzola, by Tony O'Malley.

1993, May 18   Litho.   Perf. 13x13½
895	A340	32p multicolored	.60	.70
896	A340	44p multicolored	1.05	1.00

Issued in sheets of 10 + 2 labels. Value for sheet $28.

Gaelic League, Cent. — A341

Design: 52p, Illuminated manuscript presented to founder Douglas Hyde, vert.

IRELAND

Perf. 15x14, 14x15   Litho.
1993, July 8
| 897 | A341 | 32p multicolored | .95 | .70 |
| 898 | A341 | 52p multicolored | 1.40 | 1.35 |

Irish Amateur Swimming Assoc., Cent. — A342

Designs: No. 899, Swimmer diving into water. No. 900, Woman swimming.

1993, July 8   *Perf. 15x14*
899	A342	32p multicolored	.85	1.35
900	A342	32p multicolored	.85	1.35
a.	Pair, #899-900		1.75	2.75

Royal Hospital Donnybrook, 250th Anniv. A343

Carlow College, Bicent. A344

Ceide Fields, County Mayo A345

Edward Bunting (1773-1843), Composer A346

Perf. 15x14, 14x15, 13½ (52p)   Litho.
1993, Sept. 2
901	A343	28p multicolored	.95	.55
902	A344	32p multicolored	.60	.55
903	A345	44p multicolored	.85	1.45
904	A346	52p multicolored	1.30	1.80
	Nos. 901-904 (4)		3.70	4.35

Irish Buses — A347

Designs: 28p, Great Northern Railways Gardner. 32p, CIE Leyland Titan. No. 907, Horse-drawn omnibus. No. 908, Char-a-banc.

1993, Oct. 12   Litho.   *Perf. 15x14*
905	A347	28p multicolored	.95	.65
906	A347	32p multicolored	1.10	.65
a.	Booklet pane, 2 each #905-906		2.25	
907	A347	38p multicolored	1.90	2.25
908	A347	52p multicolored	1.90	2.25
a.	Pair, #907-908		4.00	4.50
b.	Booklet pane of 4, #905-908		3.50	
	Nos. 905-908 (4)		5.85	5.80

A348

Christmas — A349

Designs: 32p, Mary placing infant Jesus in manger. 52p, Adoration of the shepherds.

Perf. 14x15, 15x14
1993, Nov. 16   Litho.
909	A348	28p multicolored	.65	.70
910	A349	28p multicolored	.65	.50
911	A349	32p multicolored	.70	.65
912	A349	52p multicolored	.90	2.25
	Nos. 909-912 (4)		2.90	4.10

No. 909 issued only in discount sheets of 13+2 labels which sold for £3.36. Value $8.50.

Love — A350

32p, Man, woman in shape of heart, vert.

Perf. 15x14, 14x15   Litho.
1994, Jan. 27
| 913 | A350 | 28p multicolored | .75 | .70 |
| 914 | A350 | 32p multicolored | .90 | .75 |

Greetings Stamps — A351

1994, Jan. 27   *Perf. 14x15*
915	A351	32p Face in sun	1.10	1.15
916	A351	32p Face in flower	1.10	1.15
917	A351	32p Face in heart	1.10	1.15
a.	Souv. sheet of 3, #915-917		7.00	8.50
918	A351	32p Face in rose	1.10	1.15
a.	Booklet pane of 4, #915-918, 4 English + 4 Gaelic labels		4.50	
b.	As "a," 8 English labels		4.50	
	Nos. 915-918 (4)		4.40	4.60

New Year 1994 (Year of the Dog), Hong Kong '94 (No. 917a).
No. 918a contains Nos. 915-918 in order. No. 918b contains Nos. 917, 918, 915, 916 in order.

Macra na Feirme, 50th Anniv. — A352

The Taking of Christ, by Caravaggio A353

Irish Co-operative Organization Society, Cent. — A354

Irish Congress of Trade Unions, Cent. — A355

1994, Mar. 2   Litho.   *Perf. 15x14*
919	A352	28p blue & gold	.55	.60
920	A353	32p multicolored	.70	.70
921	A354	38p multicolored	1.75	1.75
922	A355	52p blue, blk & lt blue	.90	1.75
	Nos. 919-922 (4)		3.90	4.80

Voyages of St. Brendan (484-577) A356

Europa: 32p, St. Brendan, Irish monks sailing past volcano. 44p, St. Brendan on island with sheep, monks in boat.

1994, Apr. 18   *Perf. 15x14*
923	A356	32p multicolored	.65	.70
924	A356	44p multicolored	1.40	1.75
a.	Miniature sheet of 2, #923-924		3.50	4.00

See Faroe Islands Nos. 264-265; Iceland Nos. 780-781.

Parliamentary Anniversaries A357

No. 925, 1st meeting of the Dail, 1919. No. 926, 4th direct elections to European Parliament.

1994, Apr. 27
925	A357	32p multicolored	.75	.90
926	A357	32p multicolored	.75	.90
a.	Booklet pane, 1 each #925-926		1.40	
b.	Booklet pane, 2 each #925-926		2.25	
	Complete booklet, #926a, 926b		5.00	

1994 World Cup Soccer Championships, US — A358

Players from: No. 927, Argentina in striped shirt, Ireland in green. No. 928, Ireland, Germany.

1994, May 31   *Perf. 14x15*
927	A358	32p multicolored	.85	1.10
928	A358	32p multicolored	.85	1.10
a.	Pair, #927-928		1.75	2.25

Printed in sheets of 4 No. 928a plus label. Value, $7.50.

Women's Hockey — A359

32p, 1994 Women's Hockey World Cup, Dublin. 52p, Irish Ladies' Hockey Union, cent.

1994, May 31   *Perf. 13x13½*
| 929 | A359 | 32p multicolored | 1.40 | 1.10 |
| 930 | A359 | 52p multicolored | 1.65 | 2.25 |

Moths — A360

28p, Garden tiger. 32p, Burren green. 38p, Emperor. 52p, Elephant hawkmoth.

1994, July 12   Litho.   *Perf. 14½x14*
931	A360	28p multi	.50	.35
932	A360	32p multi	.60	.50
933	A360	38p multi	.70	.80
934	A360	52p multi	.95	1.35
a.	Souvenir sheet of 4, #931-934		4.50	4.50
b.	As "a," overprinted		6.00	6.00
	Nos. 931-934 (4)		2.75	3.00

Size: 34x23mm
Self-Adhesive
Die Cut Perf. 11½
935	A360	32p like #932	1.75	1.60
936	A360	32p like #931	1.75	1.60
937	A360	32p like #934	1.75	1.60
938	A360	32p like #933	1.75	1.60
a.	Strip of 4, #935-938		10.00	10.00

Overprint on No. 934b shows PHILAKOREA '94 exhibition emblem and Korean inscription.

A361

A362

A363

Anniversaries and Events — A364

28p, Medieval view of Drogheda. No. 940, Edmund Ignatius Rice (1762-1844), philanthropist. No. 941, Edmund Burke (1729-97), political commentator. No. 942, Eamonn Andrews (1922-87), broadcaster. No. 943, Vickers Vimy aircraft.

1994, Sept. 6   Litho.   *Perf. 13½*
| 939 | A361 | 28p multicolored | .90 | 1.10 |

Perf. 14x14½
| 940 | A362 | 32p multicolored | .75 | 1.10 |

Perf. 14x13½
| 941 | A363 | 32p multicolored | .75 | 1.10 |
| 942 | A363 | 52p multicolored | 1.25 | 1.35 |

Perf. 15x14
| 943 | A364 | 52p multicolored | 1.45 | 1.35 |
| | Nos. 939-943 (5) | | 5.10 | 6.00 |

Drogheda, 800th anniv. (No. 939). First Newfoundland-Ireland transatlantic flight, 75th anniv. (No. 943).

Nobel Prize Winners — A365

No. 944, George Bernard Shaw (1856-1950), dramatist, essayist. No. 945, Samuel Beckett (1906-89), playwright. 32p, Sean McBride (1904-88), statesman. 52p, William Butler Yeats (1865-1939), poet.

1994, Oct. 18   Litho.   *Perf. 15x14*
944	A365	28p multicolored	.45	.65
945	A365	28p multicolored	.45	.65
a.	Pair, #944-945		1.75	2.25
946	A365	32p multicolored	.50	.70
a.	Booklet pane of 3, #944-946		2.25	
b.	Bklt. pane, #944-945, 2 #946		2.25	
947	A365	52p multicolored	.75	1.35
a.	Booklet pane, 1 #946, 2 #947		2.25	
b.	Booklet pane of 4, #944-947		2.25	
	Complete bklt., #946a-946b, 947a-947b		11.00	
	Nos. 944-947 (4)		2.15	3.35

A366

Christmas — A367

No. 948, Stained glass nativity scene. No. 949, Annunciation, detail, 11th cent. ivory plaque. 32p, Flight Into Egypt, 15th cent. wood carving. 52p, Nativity, detail, 11th cent. ivory plaque.

1994, Nov. 17   Litho.   *Perf. 14x15*
948	A366	28p multicolored	.55	.45
949	A367	28p multicolored	.55	.45
950	A367	32p multicolored	.70	.50
951	A367	52p multicolored	1.10	1.60
	Nos. 948-951 (4)		2.90	3.00

No. 948 issued only in discount sheets of 13 plus 2 labels which sold for £3.36. Value $6.75.

IRELAND

Greetings Stamps — A368

No. 952, Tree of hearts. No. 953, Teddy bear, balloon. No. 954, Clown juggling hearts. No. 955, Bouquet of flowers.

1995, Jan. 24   Litho.   Perf. 14x15

952	A368	32p multicolored	1.35	1.35

Booklet Stamps

953	A368	32p multicolored	1.35	1.35
954	A368	32p multicolored	1.35	1.35
955	A368	32p multicolored	1.35	1.35
a.		Booklet pane, #952-955 + 4 English, 4 Gaelic labels	3.75	
b.		As "a," 8 English labels	3.75	
		Complete booklet, #955a-955b	12.50	
c.		Souvenir sheet, #952, 954-955 + 3 English, 3 Gaelic labels	4.25	5.00

New Year 1995 (Year of the Boar) (No. 955c).

No. 955a contains Nos. 953-954, 952, 955 in order. No. 955b contains Nos. 952, 955, 953-954 in order.

The falling heart on No. 952 has a black outline. The falling heart without an outline comes from Nos. 955a-955c.

Narrow Gauge Railways — A369

28p, West Clare. 32p, Co. Donegal. 38p, Cork & Muskerry. 52p, Cavan & Leitrim.

1995, Feb. 28   Litho.   Perf. 15x14

956	A369	28p multi	.60	.35
957	A369	32p multi	.65	.55
958	A369	38p multi	.80	1.35
959	A369	52p multi	1.60	1.80
a.		Souvenir sheet of 4, #956-959	4.00	4.25
		Nos. 956-959 (4)	3.65	4.05

No. 959a exists with Singapore '95 overprint in sheet margin. Value $10.

Peace & Freedom — A370

Europa: Nos. 960, 962, Stylized dove, reconstructed city. 44p, No. 963, Stylized dove, map of Europe.

1995, Apr. 6   Litho.   Perf. 15x14

960	A370	32p multicolored	.65	.70
961	A370	44p multicolored	1.35	1.60

Size: 34½x23mm

Self-Adhesive Coil Stamps

Die Cut Perf. 11½

962	A370	32p multicolored	1.30	1.30
963	A370	32p multicolored	1.30	1.30

Nos. 962-963 are coil stamps, printed in horizontal rolls of 100, with 50 of each design alternating.

1995 Rugby World Cup — A371

52p, Player being tackled.

1995, Apr. 6   Perf. 14

964	A371	32p shown	.80	.70
965	A371	52p multicolored	1.40	1.60

Souvenir Sheet

966	A371	£1 like #964	2.75	3.00

No. 966 has a continuous design.

A372

32p, Irish soldiers, Cross of Fontenoy.

1995, May 15   Photo.   Perf. 11½

967	A372	32p multicolored	1.10	.80

Battle of Fontenoy, 250th Anniv. See Belgium No. 1583.

A373

Military uniforms: 28p, Irish Brigade, French Army, 1745. No. 969, Tercio Irlanda, Army of Flanders, 1605. No. 970, Royal Dublin Fusiliers, 1914. 38p, St. Patrick's Battalion, Papal Army, 1860. 52p, The Fighting 69th, Army of Potomac, 1861.

1995, May 15   Litho.   Perf. 14x15

968	A373	28p multicolored	.60	.55
969	A373	32p multicolored	.70	.70
a.		Bklt. pane, 2 ea #968-969	2.20	
970	A373	32p multicolored	.70	.70
971	A373	38p multicolored	.80	1.10
a.		Bklt. pane of 3, #968-969, #971	2.20	
972	A373	52p multicolored	.95	1.60
a.		Bklt. pane of 3, #968-969, 972	2.20	
b.		Bklt. pane of 4, #968-969, 971-972	2.20	
		Complete booklet, #969a, 971a, 972a, 972b	10.00	
		Nos. 968-972 (5)	3.75	4.65

Radio, Cent. — A374

Designs: No. 973, Guglielmo Marconi, transmitting equipment. No. 974, Radio channel dial.

1995, June 8   Litho.   Perf. 13½

973	A374	32p multicolored	6.00	6.50
974	A374	32p multicolored	6.00	6.50
a.		Pair, #973-974	12.50	14.50

See Germany No. 1900, Italy Nos. 2038-2039, San Marino No. 1336-1337, Vatican City No. 978-979.

Anniversaries & Events — A378

Designs: 28p, Dr. Bartholomew Mosse, Rotunda Hospital. No. 976, Piper, laurel wreath over map of Europe. No. 977, St. Patrick's College. 52p, Geological map of Ireland.

1995, July 27   Litho.   Perf. 14½x14

975	A375	28p multicolored	1.25	.65
976	A376	32p multicolored	.70	.70
		Perf. 14½		
977	A377	32p multicolored	.70	.70
		Perf. 13½		
978	A378	52p multicolored	1.15	1.35
		Nos. 975-978 (4)	3.80	3.40

Rotunda Hospital, 250th anniv. (No. 975). End of World War II, 50th anniv. (No. 976). St. Patrick's College, Maynooth, bicent. (No. 977). Geological survey of Ireland, 150th anniv. (No. 978).

Reptiles & Amphibians A379

No. 979, Natterjack toad. No. 980, Common lizard. No. 981, Smooth newt. No. 982, Common frog.

1995, Sept. 1   Litho.   Perf. 15x14

979	A379	32p multi	1.00	1.05
980	A379	32p multi	1.00	1.05
981	A379	32p multi	1.00	1.05
982	A379	32p multi	1.00	1.05
a.		Strip of 4, #979-982	5.00	5.75

Die Cut Perf. 9¼

Size: 34½x22½mm

Self-Adhesive

982B	A379	32p like No. 979	2.25	2.25
982C	A379	32p like No. 980	2.25	2.25
982D	A379	32p like No. 981	2.25	2.25
982E	A379	32p like No. 982	2.25	2.25
f.		Strip of 4, Nos. 982B-982E	9.00	9.00

Natl. Botanic Gardens, Bicent. — A380

Designs: 32p, Crinum moorei. 38p, Sarracenia x moorei. 44p, Solanum crispum "glasnevin".

1995, Oct. 9   Litho.   Perf. 14x15

983	A380	32p multicolored	.95	.65
984	A380	38p multicolored	.85	1.80
985	A380	44p multicolored	1.40	2.25
a.		Booklet pane of 3, #983-985	3.25	
b.		Bklt. pane of 4, #984-985, 2 #983	3.25	
		Complete booklet, #985a-985b	7.50	
		Nos. 983-985 (3)	3.20	4.70

UN, 50th Anniv. — A381

1995, Oct. 19   Perf. 13x13½

986	A381	32p shown	.60	.35
987	A381	52p UN, "50" emblem	.85	.90

Christmas A383

Designs: No. 988, Adoration of the Magi. No. 989, Adoration of the Shepherds. 32p, Adoration of the Magi. 52p, Nativity.

1995, Nov. 16   Litho.   Perf. 14½x14

988	A382	28p multicolored	.70	.40
989	A383	32p multicolored	.60	.40
990	A383	32p multicolored	.70	.45
991	A383	32p multicolored	.95	2.00
		Nos. 988-991 (4)	2.95	3.25

No. 988 issued only in discount sheets of 13+2 labels, which sold for £3.36. Value $9.

Greetings/Love Stamps — A384

Television cartoon characters from "Zog, Zig and Zag:" No. 992, With hearts. No. 993, Waving hands. No. 994, In car, wearing space helmets. No. 995, Holding out hands, wearing hats.

1996, Jan. 23   Litho.   Perf. 14x15

992	A384	32p multicolored	1.35	.70

Booklet Stamps

993	A384	32p multicolored	2.25	2.25
994	A384	32p multicolored	2.25	2.25
995	A384	32p multicolored	2.25	2.25
a.		Booklet pane, Nos. 992-995, 5 English, 3 Gaelic labels	7.50	
b.		As "a," 7 English, 1 Gaelic label	7.50	
		Complete booklet, #995a-995b	15.00	
c.		Souvenir sheet, Nos. 992, 994-995 + 4 English, 2 Gaelic labels, 1 large label with Chinese inscription	6.00	6.50

No. 995a contains Nos. 993-995, 992 in order. No. 995b contains Nos. 995, 992-994 in order.

New Year 1996 (Year of the Rat) (No. 995c).

A385

1996 Summer/Paralympic Games, Atlanta — A386

1996, Feb. 1

996	A385	28p shown	.65	.60
997	A386	32p Discus	.70	.75
998	A386	32p Canoeing	.70	.75
999	A386	32p Running	.70	.75
a.		Strip of 3, Nos. 997-999	3.00	3.00

No. 999a printed in sheets of 9 stamps. Value $14.

L'Imaginaire Irlandais — A387

1996, Mar. 12   Litho.   Perf. 15x14

1000	A387	32p multicolored	1.10	1.10

Irish Horse Racing — A388

1996, Mar. 12   Litho.   Perf. 15x14

1001	A388	28p Fairyhouse	.60	.65
1002	A388	32p Punchestown	.65	.70
1003	A388	32p The Curragh	.65	.70
a.		Pair, #1002-1003	1.50	1.60
b.		Booklet pane, 2 #1001, 1 each #1002-1003	3.00	3.00
c.		Souv. sheet, #1002-1003	11.00	12.50
1004	A388	38p Galway	.85	1.10
a.		Booklet pane, 2 #1002, 1 #1004	3.00	
1005	A388	52p Leopardstown	1.05	1.35
a.		Bklt. pane, #1005, 2 #1003	3.00	
b.		Bklt. pane, 1 ea #1004, 1 #1005	3.00	
		Complete bklt., Nos. 1003b, 1004a, 1005a, 1005b	11.50	
		Nos. 1001-1005 (5)	3.80	4.50

No. 1003c for China '96.

IRELAND

UNESCO World Heritage Site — A389

UNICEF, 50th Anniv. — A390

Designs: 28p, Passage tombs, Bru na Bóinne National Monument, Boyne Valley. 32p, Children.

1996, Apr. 2	Litho.		Perf. 14	
1006	A389	28p sepia & black	.75	.55
1007	A390	32p multicolored	.95	.80

Europa — A391

32p, Louie Bennett (1870-1956), Suffragette, trade unionist. 44p, Lady Augusta Gregory (1852-1932), playwright, co-founder of Abbey Theatre.

1996, Apr. 2			Perf. 15x14	
1008	A391	32p violet	.95	.95
1009	A391	44p green	1.25	1.25

Die Cut Perf. 9¼
Self-Adhesive Coil Stamps

| 1009A | A391 | 32p like #1008 | 1.60 | 1.60 |
| 1009B | A391 | 32p like #1009 | 1.60 | 1.60 |

Nos. 962-963 are coil stamps, printed in horizontal rolls with each value alternating.

Irish Winners of Tourist Trophy Motorcycle Races — A392

32p, Stanley Woods. 44p, Artie Bell. No. 1012, Alec Bennett. 52p, No. 1014, Robert & Joey Dunlop.

1996, May 30			Perf. 14	
1010	A392	28p multicolored	.60	.90
1011	A392	44p multicolored	.75	1.35
1012	A392	50p multicolored	.85	1.35
1013	A392	52p multicolored	.85	1.35
	Nos. 1010-1013 (4)		3.05	4.50

Souvenir Sheet

| 1014 | A392 | 50p multicolored | 2.00 | 2.50 |

See Isle of Man Nos. 701-705.

Michael Davitt (1846-1906), Nationalist Leader — A393

1996, July 4	Litho.		Perf. 13½x13	
1015	A393	28p multicolored	.60	.55

Ireland's Presidency of the European Union — A394

1996, July 4			Perf. 13x13½	
1016	A394	32p multicolored	.60	.65

Thomas A. McLaughlin (1896-1971), Designer of Ardnacrusha Hydroelectric Power Station — A395

1996, July 4				
1017	A395	38p multicolored	.95	1.00

Bord na Móna (Irish Peat Corp.), 50th Anniv. — A396

1996, July 4				
1018	A396	52p multicolored	1.20	1.65

Irish Naval Service, 50th Anniv. — A397

Designs: 32p, Coastal patrol vessel. 44p, Corvette. 52p, Motor torpedo boat, vert.

1996, July 18			Perf. 15x14	
1019	A397	32p multicolored	.60	.65
a.	Booklet pane, 3 #1019		2.65	
1020	A397	44p multicolored	1.20	1.35
1021	A397	52p multicolored	1.20	1.45
a.	Booklet pane of 3, #1019-1021		2.65	
	Complete booklet, #1019a, 1021a		7.25	
	Nos. 1019-1021 (3)		3.00	3.45

People with Disabilities — A398

No. 1022, Man in wheelchair. No. 1023, Blind woman, child.

1996, Sept. 3	Litho.		Perf. 14x15	
1022	A398	28p multicolored	1.25	1.25
1023	A398	28p multicolored	1.25	1.25
a.	Pair, #1022-1023		2.75	2.75

Freshwater Ducks — A399

Designs: 32p, Anas crecca. 38p, Anas clypeata. 44p, Anas penelope. 52p, Anas platyrhynchos.

1996, Sept. 24			Perf. 15x14	
1024	A399	32p multicolored	.75	.90
1025	A399	38p multicolored	.85	1.15
1026	A399	44p multicolored	.95	1.25
1027	A399	52p multicolored	1.20	1.60
a.	Souvenir sheet, #1024-1027		4.00	4.50
	Nos. 1024-1027 (4)		3.75	4.90

No. 1027a is a continuous design.

Motion Pictures, Cent. — A400

No. 1028, Man of Aran. No. 1029, My Left Foot. No. 1030, The Commitments. No. 1031, The Field.

1996, Oct. 17	Litho.		Perf. 13½	
1028	A400	32p multicolored	1.10	1.15
1029	A400	32p multicolored	1.10	1.15
1030	A400	32p multicolored	1.10	1.15
1031	A400	32p multicolored	1.10	1.15
a.	Strip of 4, #1028-1031		4.50	4.75

Christmas — A402

No. 1032, Stained glass scene of Holy Family. No. 1033, Adoration of the Magi. 32p, The Annunciation. 52p, Shepherds receive news of Christ's birth.

1996, Nov. 19			Perf. 14	
1032	A401	28p multicolored	.60	.55
1033	A402	28p multicolored	.45	.35
1034	A402	32p multicolored	.50	.45
1035	A402	52p multicolored	.85	1.45
	Nos. 1032-1035 (4)		2.40	2.80

No. 1032 sold only in discount sheets of 15 for £3.92. Value $11.

Spideog Robin A403

Greenland White-fronted Goose A404

28p, Blue tit. horiz. 44p, Puffin. 52p, Barn owl.

Perf. 15x14, 14x15

1997, Jan. 16			Litho.	
1036	A403	28p multi	2.60	.45
1037	A403	32p shown	1.60	.90
b.	Perf. 14		3.00	3.00
1038	A403	44p multi	4.00	3.50
1039	A403	52p multi	5.00	2.75
1040	A404	£1 shown	3.75	1.10

Booklet Stamp
Size: 18x21mm, 21x18mm

1040A	A403	32p Like #1037	1.60	2.75
b.	Booklet pane, 3 #1040A, 1 #770		6.50	
	Complete booklet, #1040b		6.50	

Size: 20x23mm
Perf. 14x15

1040C	A403	32p Like #1037, "Eire" 8½mm wide ('99)	1.60	2.75
d.	Bklt. pane of 5 + 5 labels		10.00	
	Complete booklet		10.00	
	Nos. 1036-1040C (7)		20.15	14.20

On Nos. 1037,1037b "Eire" is 9mm wide, and size of design is 21x24mm.
See Nos. 1053-1054C, 1067, 1076-1081A, 1094, 1105-1115C, 1314-1319B, 1340-1343. Compare with Nos. 1353-1373.
Issued: No. 1040C, 6/30/99

Greetings Stamps — A405

Designs: No. 1041, Doves on tree limb. No. 1042, Cow jumping over moon. No. 1043, Pig going to market. No. 1044, Rooster on fence.

1997, Jan. 28	Litho.		Perf. 14x15	
1041	A405	32p multicolored	.95	.45

Booklet Stamps

1042	A405	32p multicolored	1.40	1.35
1043	A405	32p multicolored	1.40	1.35
1044	A405	32p multicolored	1.40	1.35
a.	Booklet pane, #1041-1044, 5 English, 3 Gaelic labels		4.75	
b.	As "a," #1041-1044, 7 English, 1 Gaelic label		4.75	
	Complete booklet, #1044a, 1044b		10.00	
c.	Souvenir sheet, 1042-1044, 3 English, 3 Gaelic labels + 1 large label with "Year of the Ox," Hong Kong '97		5.50	5.50

No. 1044a contains Nos. 1042, 1041, 1043-1044 in order. No. 1044b contains Nos. 1043-1044, 1041-1042 in order.

Irish State, 75th Anniv. — A406

Designs: No. 1045, Dáil, national flag, constitution. No. 1046, Defense forces, badges, UN flag. No. 1047, Four Courts, scales of justice. No. 1048, Garda badge, Garda Siochána.

1997, Feb. 18			Perf. 15x14	
1045	A406	32p multicolored	.75	1.10
1046	A406	32p multicolored	.75	1.10
a.	Pair, #1045-1046		1.50	2.25
1047	A406	52p multicolored	1.30	1.75
1048	A406	52p multicolored	1.30	1.75
a.	Pair, #1047-1048		2.60	3.50

See Nos. 1055-1058, 1082-1084, 1095-1096.

Marine Mammals A407

Designs: 28p, Halichoerus grypus, vert. 32p, Tursiops truncatus, vert. 44p, Phocaena phocaena. 52p, Orcinus orca.

Perf. 14x15, 15x14

1997, Mar. 6			Litho.	
1049	A407	28p multicolored	.45	.35
1050	A407	32p multicolored	.55	.45
1051	A407	44p multicolored	.85	1.25
1052	A407	52p multicolored	.95	1.35
a.	Souvenir sheet, #1049-1052		4.50	4.50
	Nos. 1049-1052 (4)		2.80	3.40

Bird Type of 1997
Die Cut Perf. 9x9½

1997, Mar. 6			Litho.	

Self-Adhesive Coil Stamps

1053	A403	32p Peregrine falcon	3.25	4.25
1054	A403	32p like #1037	3.25	4.25
a.	Pair, #1053-1054		7.50	8.75

Die Cut Perf. 11x11¼

1054B	A403	32p Like #1053	4.50	8.00
1054C	A403	32p Like #1053	8.50	6.00
d.	Pair, #1054B-1054C		20.00	22.50
	Nos. 1053-1054C (4)		19.50	22.50

Issued: Nos. 1053-1054, 3/6/97; Nos. 1054B-1054C, 4/97.

Irish State, 75th Anniv. Type of 1997

No. 1055, Singer, violinist, bodhran player. No. 1056, Athlete, soccer and hurling players. No. 1057, Irish currency, blueprint, food processing plant. No. 1058, Abbey Theatre emblem, books, palette, paintbrushes, Séamus Heaney manuscript.

1997, Apr. 3			Perf. 15x14	
1055	A406	32p multicolored	.75	1.10
1056	A406	32p multicolored	.75	1.10
a.	Pair, #1055-1056		1.50	2.25
1057	A406	52p multicolored	1.30	1.80
1058	A406	52p multicolored	1.30	1.80
a.	Pair, #1057-1058		3.00	3.75

Irish Coinage, Millennium A408

1997, Apr. 3			Perf. 15x14	
1059	A408	32p First Irish coin	1.10	1.10

Stories and Legends — A409

IRELAND

Europa: 32p, "The Children of Lir" flying as swans. 44p, "Oisin & Niamh" on horse.

		1997, May 14	Litho.	Perf. 14
1060	A409	32p multicolored	.55	.45
1061	A409	44p multicolored	1.40	1.75

Die Cut Perf. 9x9½
Self-Adhesive Coil Stamps

1062	A409	32p like #1060	1.35	1.60
1063	A409	44p like #1061	1.35	1.60
a.		Pair, #1062-1063	2.75	3.25

The Great Famine, 150th Anniv. — A410

Designs: 28p, Passengers waiting to board emigrant ship. 32p, Family group attending dying child. 52p, Irish Society of Friends soup kitchen.

		1997, May 14	Litho.	Perf. 15x14
1064	A410	28p multicolored	.75	.65
1065	A410	32p multicolored	.95	.65
1066	A410	52p multicolored	1.40	1.75
		Nos. 1064-1066 (3)	3.10	3.05

Bird Type of 1997
Souvenir Sheet

		1997, May 29		Perf. 14
1067	A404	£2 Pintail, horiz.	8.00	7.75

PACIFIC 97.

No. 1067 shows the duck's head in brown. See No. 1111 for stamp with duck's head in black.

Kate O'Brien (1897-1974), Novelist — A411

		1997, July 1	Litho.	Perf. 14
1068	A411	28p multicolored	.70	.90

St. Columba (521-97), Irish Patron Saint — A412

		1997, July 1		Perf. 14x15
1069	A412	28p multicolored	.70	.90

Designs: 32p, Daniel O'Connell (1775-1847), politician. 52p, John Wesley (1703-91), founder of Methodism, first visit to Ireland, 250th anniv.

		1997, July 1		Perf. 14x14½
1070	A413	32p multicolored	.80	.65
				Perf. 14¼x13¾
1071	A414	52p multicolored	1.30	2.25

Lighthouses A415

Designs: No. 1072, Baily. No. 1073, Tarbert. 38p, Hook Head, vert. 50p, Fastnet, vert.

		1997, July 1	Perf. 15x14, 14x15
1072	A415	32p multicolored	1.15	1.45
1073	A415	32p multicolored	1.15	1.45
a.		Pair, #1072-1073	2.25	2.25
b.		Bklt. pane, #1073, 2 #1072	3.00	
c.		Bklt. pane, 2 ea #1072-1073	4.00	
1074	A415	38p multicolored	1.15	1.35
1075	A415	50p multicolored	1.50	1.80
a.		Booklet pane, #1074-1075	3.00	
b.		Bklt. pane of 4, #1073a, 1074-1075	5.00	
		Complete booklet, #1073b, 1073c, 1075a, 1075b	13.50	

Bird Type of 1997
Perf. 14x15, 15x14

		1997, Aug. 27		Litho.
1076	A403	1p Magpie	.30	.70
1077	A403	2p Gannet	.30	.70
1078	A403	4p Corncrake	.55	.65
1079	A403	10p Kingfisher	.75	1.35
1080	A403	20p Lapwing	.70	1.10
1081	A404	£5 Shelduck	13.25	13.25

Booklet Stamp
Size: 18x21mm

		1997, Dec. 6		
1081A	A403	4p Like #1078	8.75	13.25
		Nos. 1076-1081A (7)	24.60	31.00

Irish State, 75th Anniv. Type of 1997

28p, Quill, page from Annals of Four Masters, No. 128. 32p, Stained glass window, No. 82. 52p, Aer Lingus airplane, letter, No. C7.

		1997, Aug. 27		Perf. 15x14
1082	A406	28p multicolored	.80	.60
1083	A406	32p multicolored	.85	1.10
1084	A406	52p multicolored	1.90	1.65
		Nos. 1082-1084 (3)	3.55	3.35

St. Patrick's Battalion, 150th Anniv. — A416

		1997, Sept. 12	Litho.	Perf. 14x13½
1085	A416	32p multicolored	1.40	1.55

See Mexico No. 2049.

Bram Stoker's "Dracula" — A417

Scenes of Dracula: 28p, Being transformed into a bat, vert. 32p, With potential victim, vert. 38p, Emerging from coffin. 52p, With wolf.

		1997, Oct. 1	Perf. 14x15, 15x14
1086	A417	28p multicolored	.45	.35
1087	A417	32p multicolored	.50	.45
a.		Souvenir sheet of 1	3.50	3.50
1088	A417	38p multicolored	.60	.75
1089	A417	52p multicolored	.75	1.35
a.		Souv. sheet of 4, #1086-1089	5.00	5.00
		Nos. 1086-1089 (4)	2.30	2.90

Stamps from Nos. 1087a, 1089a have souvenir sheet background framing vignette.

Christmas — A419

Nos. 1090-1092: Different images of Holy Family in stained glass. No. 1093, Christmas tree.

		1997, Nov. 18	Litho.	Perf. 14x15
1090	A418	28p multicolored	.55	.30
1091	A418	32p multicolored	.65	.40
1092	A418	52p multicolored	1.20	2.00
		Nos. 1090-1092 (3)	2.40	2.70

Self-Adhesive
Serpentine Die Cut 9x9½

1093	A419	28p multicolored	.65	.65
a.		Booklet pane, 20 #1093	12.50	

By its nature, No. 1093a is a complete booklet. The peelable paper backing serves as a booklet cover.

No. 1093 sold only in discount booklets for £5.32.

Bird Type of 1997
Perf. 15x14 (on 3 Sides)

		1997, Dec. 6		Litho.
		Booklet Stamp		
1094	A403	32p like #1053	1.90	1.65
a.		Bklt. pane, #1081a, 3 #1094	8.75	
		Complete booklet, #1094a	9.50	

Irish State, 75th Anniv. Type of 1997

No. 1095, General Post Office, No. 68. No. 1096: a, like No. 1048. b, like No. 1047. c, like No. 1057. d, like No. 1058. e, like No. 1082. f, like No. 1084.

		1997, Dec. 6	Litho.	Perf. 15x14
1095	A406	32p multicolored	.90	1.10

Sheet of 12

1096	A406	32p #a.-f. + #1045-1046, 1055-1056, 1083, 1095	11.00	17.50

Greetings Stamps — A420

Love is: No. 1097, "...from my heart." No. 1098, "...a birthday wish." No. 1099, "...thinking of you." No. 1100, "...keeping in touch."

		1998, Jan. 26	Litho.	Perf. 14x15
1097	A420	32p multicolored	1.40	.45
1098	A420	32p multicolored	1.40	1.35
1099	A420	32p multicolored	1.40	1.35
1100	A420	32p multicolored	1.40	1.35
a.		Bklt. pane, #1097-1100 + 8 labels	6.00	
		Complete booklet, 2 #1100a	9.00	
b.		Souv. sheet, #1098-1100 + 7 labels	5.00	5.50

No. 1100a exists with stamps in two different orders. No. 1100b has 1 English, 4 Chinese, 1 Gaelic labels + 1 large label with "Year of the Tiger," in English and Chinese. Same value.

See Nos. 1120-1123.

Aviation Pioneers — A421

28p, Lady Mary Heath (Sophie Catherine Pierce), 1st solo flight, Capetown-Croydon via Cairo, 1928. 32p, Col. James Fitzmaurice, navigator on "Bremen," 1st east-west Atlantic flight, 1928. 44p, Capt. J.P. (Paddy) Saul, navigator aboard Southern Cross, Dublin-Newfoundland, 1930. 52p, Capt. Charles Blair, 1st non-stop commercial flight Foynes-NYC, 1942.

		1998, Feb. 24		Perf. 15x14
1101	A421	28p multicolored	.55	.50
1102	A421	32p multicolored	.60	.55
a.		Bklt. pane, 2 ea #1101-1102	3.00	
1103	A421	44p multicolored	1.15	1.15
a.		Bklt. pane, #1103, 2 #1102	3.00	
1104	A421	52p multicolored	1.40	1.40
a.		Bklt. pane, #1102, 2 #1104	3.00	
b.		Bklt. pane of 4, #1101-1104	3.50	
		Complete booklet, #1102a, 1103a, 1104a, 1104b	12.50	
		Nos. 1101-1104 (4)	3.70	3.60

Bird Types of 1997

No. 1105, Woodpigeon, horiz. No. 1106, Blackbird. No. 1106B, Goldcrest, bklt. stamp. No. 1107, Stonechat. No. 1108, Ringed plover, horiz. No. 1109, Song thrush. No. 1110, Sparrowhawk, horiz. No. 1111, Pintail. No. 1111A: b, Like No. 1107. c, Like No. 1080. d, Like No. 1077. e, Like No. 1078. f, Like No. 1076. g, Like No. 1106B, "Eire" 8½mm wide. h, Like No. 1079. i, Like No. 1053. j, Like No. 1039. k, Like No. 1037. l, Like No. 1109. m, Like No. 1106, "Eire" 8½mm wide. n, Wren. o, Pied wagtail. p, Like No. 1038.

		1998-99	Litho.	Perf. 15x14, 14x15
1105	A403	5p multi	2.20	1.10
1106	A403	30p multi	2.50	1.35
a.		Perf. 14	1.35	1.65
1106B	A403	30p multi	1.35	2.40
c.		Booklet pane, 5 each #1106, 1106B	12.75	
		Complete booklet, #1106Bc	12.75	
1107	A403	35p multi	2.75	2.25
a.		Perf. 14	2.75	2.25
1108	A403	40p multi	2.75	2.75
a.		Perf. 14	2.75	1.40
1109	A403	45p multi	2.50	3.75
a.		Perf. 14	2.25	2.25
1110	A403	50p multi	3.25	2.50
a.		Perf. 14	3.25	1.65
1111	A404	£2 multi	3.60	2.75

Sheet of 15

1111A	A403	30p #b.-p.	19.00	19.00

See note under No. 1067.

Booklet Stamps
Size: 18x21mm, 21x18mm

1112	A403	5p Like #1105	1.90	2.50
1113	A403	30p Like #1106	2.20	2.50
a.		Booklet pane, 2 #1112, 3 #1113	7.25	
		Complete booklet, #1113a	7.25	
1113B	A403	30p like #1106B	1.35	2.50
c.		Bklt. pane, 2 #1112, 3 #1113B + label	7.00	
		Complete booklet, #1113c	7.00	

Size: 20x23mm

1113D	A403	45p Like #1109, "Eire" 8½mm wide	2.50	3.75
e.		Booklet pane of 4 + 4 labels	10.00	
		Complete booklet	10.00	

Size: 21x24mm
Perf. 10¾x13 on 3 sides

1113F	A403	30p Like #1106, "Eire" 8½mm wide	2.00	2.00
i.		Like #1113F, perf. 14¼x14¾ on 3 sides ('99)	2.00	2.00
1113G	A403	30p Like #1106B, "Eire" 8½mm wide	2.00	2.00
h.		Booklet pane, 5 each #1113F-1113G	20.00	—
		Booklet, #1113Gh	20.00	
j.		Like #1113G, perf. 14¼x14¾ on 3 sides ('99)	2.00	2.00
k.		Pair, #1113F-1113G	4.00	4.00

Die Cut Perf. 9x9½
Self-Adhesive

1114	A403	30p like #1106	1.65	2.25
1115	A403	30p like #1106B	1.65	2.25
d.		Pair, #1114-1115	3.25	4.50

Litho.
Die Cut Perf. 11x11¼
Self-Adhesive Coil Stamps

1115B	A403	30p Like #1114	4.50	2.50
1115C	A403	30p Like #1115	2.25	2.50
d.		Pair, #1115B-1115C	9.00	13.50

Issued: No. 1115B-1115C, 5/98; No. 1106B, 1113B, 9/4/98; No. 1111A, 2/16/99; No. 1113D, 6/30/99; No. 1113F, 1113G, 5/3/01.

Equestrian Sports — A422

30p, Show jumping. 32p, Three-day event. 40p, Gymkhana. 45p, Dressage, vert.

		1998, Apr. 2		
1116	A422	30p multicolored	.85	.55
1117	A422	32p multicolored	.90	.60
1118	A422	40p multicolored	.95	1.60
1119	A422	45p multicolored	.95	1.60
a.		Souvenir sheet #1116-1119	4.25	4.00
		Nos. 1116-1119 (4)	3.65	4.35

Greetings Type of 1998
Booklet Stamps

		1998, May 6	Litho.	Perf. 14x15
1120	A420	30p like #1098	1.25	.85
1121	A420	30p like #1099	1.25	.85
1122	A420	30p like #1100	1.25	.85
1123	A420	30p like #1097	1.25	.85
a.		Bklt. pane, #1120-1123 + 8 labels	5.25	5.25
		Complete booklet, 2 #1123a	11.00	

No. 1123a exists with stamps in different order. Complete booklet contains two different panes.

509

IRELAND

Festivals — A423

Europa: 30p, Crinniú na mBáid, Kinvara (sailboats). 40p, Puck Fair, Killorglin.

1998, May 6   *Perf. 15x14*
1124 A423 30p multicolored   1.60   1.60
1125 A423 40p multicolored   1.60   1.60

Serpentine Die Cut Perf 9x9½
Self-Adhesive
1126 A423 30p like #1124   3.00   3.00
1127 A423 30p like #1125   3.00   3.00
   a. Pair, #1126-1127   6.00   6.00
   Nos. 1124-1127 (4)   9.20   9.20

1798 Rebellion, Bicent. — A424

Battle scene and: No. 1128, "Liberty." No. 1129, Pikeman. No. 1130, French soldier. No. 1131, Wolfe Tone. No. 1132, Henry Joy McCracken.

1998, May 6
1128 A424 30p multicolored   .85   .90
1129 A424 30p multicolored   .85   .90
1130 A424 30p multicolored   .85   .90
   a. Strip of 3, #1128-1130   2.50   2.95
1131 A424 45p multicolored   .85   1.15
1132 A424 45p multicolored   .85   1.15
   a. Pair, #1131-1132   1.90   2.75

Tour de France Bicycle Race — A425

No. 1133, 4 cyclists. No. 1134, 2 cyclists, 1 wearing dark glasses. No. 1135, 2 cyclists, 1 wearing hat. No. 1136, Leading rider in yellow jersey.

1998, June 2   *Litho.*   *Perf. 15x14*
1133 A425 30p multicolored   1.10   .85
1134 A425 30p multicolored   1.10   .85
1135 A425 30p multicolored   1.10   .85
1136 A425 30p multicolored   1.10   .85
   a. Strip of 4, #1133-1136   4.50   4.00

Democracy Stamps — A426

Designs: 30p, Local government (Ireland Act), cent. 32p, Entrance into European Union, 25th anniv. 35p, Women's vote in local elections, cent. 45c, Republic of Ireland Act, 50th anniv.

1998, June 2
1137 A426 30p multicolored   .65   .45
1138 A426 32p multicolored   .65   .50
1139 A426 35p multicolored   .75   1.15
1140 A426 45p multicolored   .95   1.25
   Nos. 1137-1140 (4)   3.00   3.35

1998 Tall Ships Race — A427

No. 1141, Asgard II. No. 1142, Eagle. No. 1143, Boa Esperanza, horiz. No. 1144, T.S. Royalist, horiz.

Perf. 14x15, 15x14
1998, July 20   *Litho.*
1141 A427 30p multi   .95   .95
   a. Perf. 15   1.00   1.15
1142 A427 30p multi   .95   .95
   a. Pair, #1141-1142   1.90   1.90
   b. Perf. 15   1.25   1.60
   c. Bklt. pane, #1142b, 2 #1141a   2.75
1143 A427 45p multi   1.15   .90
   a. Perf. 15   1.65   2.25

1144 A427 £1 multi   1.85   2.50
   a. Perf. 15   2.75   2.00
   b. Bklt. pane of 3, #1142b, 1143a, 1144a   7.50
   Complete booklet, #1142c, 1144b   14.50
   Nos. 1141-1144 (4)   4.90   5.30

Souvenir Sheet
1145 A427 £2 like #1143   7.50   9.25

Die Cut Perf. 9x9½, 9½x9
Self-Adhesive
1145A A427 30p like #1143   2.00   2.00
1145B A427 30p like #1141   2.00   2.00
1145C A427 30p like #1142   2.00   2.00
1145D A427 30p like #1144   2.00   2.00
   e. Strip of 4, #1145A-1145D   8.00   8.00
Portugal '98 (No. 1145).
Issued at £2, 9/4; others, 7/20.

Postboxes — A428

No. 1146, Ashworth, 1856. No. 1147, Wallbox, 1922. No. 1148, Double Pillarbox, 1899. No. 1149, Penfold, 1866.

1998, Sept. 3
1146 A428 30p multicolored   .75   .90
1147 A428 30p multicolored   .75   .90
1148 A428 30p multicolored   .75   .90
1149 A428 30p multicolored   .75   .90
   a. Strip of 4, #1146-1149   3.00   3.25

Mary Immaculate College, Limerick, Cent. A429
Newton School, Waterford, Bicent. A430

1998, Sept. 3   *Perf. 15x14, 14x15*
1150 A429 30p multicolored   .70   .55
1151 A430 40p multicolored   .95   1.10

Universal Declaration of Human Rights, 50th Anniv. — A431

1998, Sept. 3   *Perf. 15x14*
1152 A431 45p multicolored   1.15   1.35

Endangered Animals — A432

No. 1153, Cheetah. No. 1154, Scimitar-horned oryx. 40p, Golden lion tamarin. 45p, Tiger.

1998, Oct. 8   *Litho.*   *Perf. 14*
1153 A432 30p multi   1.00   .90
1154 A432 30p multi   1.00   .90
   a. Pair, #1153-1154   2.00   1.80
1155 A432 40p multi, vert.   .85   1.15
1156 A432 45p multi, vert.   1.15   1.35
   a. Souvenir sheet, #1153-1156, perf. 15   4.25   4.50
   b. As "a," inscription on extended margin   7.00   7.00
   Nos. 1153-1156 (4)   4.00   4.30

Stamps on Nos. 1156a, 1156b have a white border. No. 1156b contains exhibition logo and "National Stamp Exhibition RDS-Dublin-6-8 November 1998" in sheet margin.

Christmas — A434

No. 1157, Holy family. 32p, Adoration of the Shepherds. 45p, Adoration of the Magi. No. 1160, Choir singers.

1998, Nov. 17   *Litho.*   *Perf. 14x15*
1157 A433 30p multicolored   .65   .55
1158 A433 32p multicolored   .75   .60
1159 A433 45p multicolored   1.00   1.60
   Nos. 1157-1159 (3)   2.40   2.75

Booklet Stamp
Self-Adhesive
Serpentine Die Cut Perf. 11x11½
1160 A434 30p multicolored   .55   .55
   a. Booklet pane of 20   10.00

No. 1160a is a complete booklet. The Peelable paper backing serves as a booklet cover. No. 1160 sold only in discount booklets at £5.40.

A435
Pets greetings stamps.

1999, Jan. 26   *Litho.*   *Perf. 14x15*
1161 A435 30p Dog   .75   .45

Booklet Stamps
1162 A435 30p Cat   .95   1.30
1163 A435 30p Fish   .95   1.30
1164 A435 30p Rabbit   .95   1.30
   a. Booklet pane, #1161-1164 + 5 English, 3 Gaelic labels   4.95
   b. Booklet pane, #1161-1164 + 7 English, 1 Gaelic label   4.95
   Complete booklet, #1164a-1164b   10.00
   c. Souvenir sheet, #1162-1164 (see footnote)   5.50   5.50

No. 1164a contains Nos. 1161-1164 in order. No. 1164b contains stamps in reverse order. No. 1164c has 1 English, 2 Chinese, 3 Gaelic labels + 1 large label with "Year of the Rabbit" in English and Chinese. New Year 1999 (Year of the Rabbit) (No. 1164c).

A436
Irish Actors: 30p, Micheál Mac Liammóir (1899-1978). 45p, Siobhán McKenna (1923-86). 50p, Noel Purcell (1900-85).

1999, Feb. 16   *Litho.*   *Perf. 14x15*
1165 A436 30p brown   .70   .55
1166 A436 45p green   .95   1.00
1167 A436 50p blue   .95   1.10
   Nos. 1165-1167 (3)   2.60   2.65

Irish Emigration A437

1999, Feb. 26   *Litho.*   *Perf. 15x14*
1168 A437 45p multicolored   1.40   .90
See US No. 3286.

Maritime Heritage — A438

30p, Polly Woodside. 35p, Ilen. 45p, Royal Natl. Lifeboat Institution. £1, Titanic.

1999, Mar. 19   *Litho.*   *Perf. 14*
1169 A438 30p multi, vert.   .55   .55
1170 A438 35p multi, vert.   .65   .65
1171 A438 45p multi   .80   .80
1172 A438 £1 multi   1.95   2.25
   a. Souvenir sheet of 2   6.50   6.50
   b. As "a" ovptd. in sheet margin   10.00   10.00
   Nos. 1169-1172 (4)   3.95   4.25

Souvenir Sheet
Perf. 14x14½
1173 Sheet of 2, #1173a, Australia #1729   2.50   2.50
   a. A438 30p like #1169   1.25   .50

Australia '99, World Stamp Expo. (No. 1172b, No. 1173). See Australia No. 1729a. No. 1172b is overprinted in gold in sheet margin with Australia '99, World Stamp Expo exhibition emblem.

Sky is gray blue, country and denomination are 3mm high on No. 1169. Sky is blue, country and denomination are 4mm high on No. 1173a.

Natl. Parks — A438a

Europa: Nos. 1174, 1176, Whooping swans, Kilcolman Nature Reserve. 40p, No. 1177, Fallow deer, Wellington Memorial Obelisk, Phoenix Park.

1999, Apr. 29   *Litho.*   *Perf. 15x14*
1174 A438a 30p multicolored   .95   .55
1175 A438a 40p multicolored   1.10   1.90

Die Cut Perf. 9x9½
Self-adhesive
1176 A438a 30p Like #1174   2.25   2.75
1177 A438a 30p Like #1175   2.25   2.75
   a. Pair, #1176-1177   4.50   5.50

A439

1999, Apr. 29   *Litho.*   *Perf. 14x15*
1178 A439 30p green & black   1.55   1.10

Prime Minister Sean Lemass (1899-1971).

A440

1999, Apr. 29   *Perf. 15x14*
1179 A440 30p multicolored   .80   .70

Introduction of the Euro. No. 1179 is denominated in both pence and euros.

A441

1999, Apr. 29   *Perf. 14x15*
1180 A441 45p multicolored   1.10   1.10

Council of Europe, 50th anniv.

IRELAND

Intl. Year of Older Persons — A442

1999, June 15		Perf. 15x14
1181	A442 30p multicolored	.75 .70

UPU, 125th Anniv. — A443

No. 1182, Modern mail truck. No. 1183, Early mail truck.

1999, June 15		
1182	A443 30p multicolored	1.50 1.35
1183	A443 30p multicolored	1.50 1.35
a.	Pair, #1182-1183	3.00 2.75

Pioneer Total Abstinence Assoc., Cent. — A444

1999, June 15		Perf. 14x15
1184	A444 32p Fr. James Cullen	.85 .70

Gaelic Football Team of the Millennium — A445

No. 1185: a, Danno Keeffe. b, Enda Colleran. c, Joe Keohane. d, Seán Flanagan. e, Seán Murphy. f, John Joe Reilly. g, Martin O'Connell. h, Mick O'Connell. i, Tommy Murphy. j, Seán O'Neill. k, Seán Purcell. l, Pat Spillane. m, Mikey Sheehy. n, Tom Langan. o, Kevin Heffernan.

1999, Aug. 17		Perf. 14¾x14¼ Litho.
1185	Sheet of 15 + label	20.00 20.00
a.-o.	A445 30p any single	1.25 1.25

Booklet Stamps
Size: 33x22mm
Self-Adhesive
Serpentine Die Cut Perf. 11¼x11½

1186	A445 30p like #1185a	1.75 1.75
1187	A445 30p like #1185c	1.75 1.75
1188	A445 30p like #1185e	1.75 1.75
1189	A445 30p like #1185h	1.75 1.75
1190	A445 30p like #1185l	1.75 1.75
1191	A445 30p like #1185m	1.75 1.75
a.	Bklt. pane, #1186-1189, 2 each #1190-1191	16.50
1192	A445 30p like #1185d	1.75 1.75
1193	A445 30p like #1185b	1.75 1.75
1194	A445 30p like #1185n	1.75 1.75
1195	A445 30p like #1185k	1.75 1.75
a.	Bklt. pane, 2 ea #1192-1195	6.75
1196	A445 30p like #1185o	1.75 1.75
1197	A445 30p like #1185g	1.75 1.75
1198	A445 30p like #1185i	1.75 1.75
a.	Bklt. pane, 3 ea #1196-1197, 2 #1198	4.95
1199	A445 30p like #1185f	1.75 1.75
1200	A445 30p like #1185j	1.75 1.75
a.	Bklt. pane, 4 ea #1199-1200	3.60

Nos. 1191a, 1195a, 1198a, 1200a are each complete booklets. The peelable paper backing serves as a booklet cover. No. 1185 exists imperf.

See Nos. 1246-1261.

Airplanes — A446

Designs: 30p, Douglas DC-3. 32p, Britten Norman Islander. 40p, Boeing 707. 45p, Lockheed Constellation.

1999, Sept. 9	Litho.	Perf. 14¾x14¼
1201	A446 30p multicolored	.60 .45
a.	Booklet pane of 4	2.75
1202	A446 32p multicolored	.70 .50
a.	Bklt. pane, 2 ea #1201, 1202	3.00
1203	A446 40p multicolored	.75 1.25
a.	Bklt. pane, #1203, 2 #1201	2.75
1204	A446 45p multicolored	.85 1.35
a.	Booklet pane, #1201-1204	3.00
	Complete bkt., #1201a-1204a	12.50
	Nos. 1201-1204 (4)	2.90 3.55

Extinct Irish Animals — A447

| Perf. 14¼x14¾, 14¾x14¼ |
1999, Oct. 11	Litho.
1205	A447 30p Mammoth, vert.	.65 .65
1206	A447 30p Giant deer, vert.	.65 .65
a.	Pair, #1205-1206	1.30 1.30
1207	A447 45p Wolf	.85 1.10
1208	A447 45p Brown bear	.85 1.10
a.	Pair, #1207-1208	1.75 2.25
b.	Souvenir sheet, #1205-1208, perf. 13¾	3.95 4.50

Stamps from No. 1208b do not have white border.

Die Cut Perf. 9¼x9½, 9½x9¼
1999, Oct. 11	Self-Adhesive	Litho.
1209	A447 30p Like #1208	1.25 .90
1210	A447 30p Like #1205	1.25 .90
1211	A447 30p Like #1207	1.25 .90
1212	A447 30p Like #1206	1.25 .90
a.	Strip, #1209-1212	5.00 3.50

Christmas A448

1999, Nov. 4	Litho.	Perf. 14¾x14¼
1213	A448 30p Holy Family	.50 .45
1214	A448 32p Shepherds	.70 .50
1215	A448 45p Magi	1.10 1.35
	Nos. 1213-1215 (3)	2.30 2.30

Self-Adhesive Booklet Stamp
Size: 19x27mm
Die Cut 11x11¼

| 1216 | A448 30p Angel, vert. | .60 .60 |
| a. | Booklet pane of 20 | 12.50 12.50 |

No. 1216a sold for £5.40 and is a complete booklet.

Millennium — A449

People of the 20th Century — No. 1217: a, Grace Kelly. b, Jesse Owens. c, John F. Kennedy. d, Mother Teresa. e, John McCormack. f, Nelson Mandela.

Irish Historic Events — No. 1218: a, horiz.: Norman invasion, 1169. b, Flight of the Earls, 1607. c, Irish Parliament, 1782. d, Land league. e, Irish independence. f, UN peacekeeping.

Discoveries — No. 1219: a, Rev. Nicholas Callan, electrical scientist. b, Birr Telescope. c, Thomas Edison. d, Albert Einstein. e, Marie Curie. f, Galileo.

The Arts — No. 1220: a, Ludwig van Beethoven. b, Dame Ninette de Valois, ballet director. c, James Joyce. d, Mona Lisa, by Leonardo da Vinci. e, Painting by Sir John Lavery. f, William Shakespeare.

World Events — No. 1221, horiz.: a, French Revolution, 1789. b, Industrial Revolution. c, Peace, 1945. d, Women's liberation. e, Fall of the Berlin Wall, 1989. f, Modern communications.

Epic Journeys — No. 1222, horiz.: a, Marco Polo. b, Capt. James Cook. c, Australian explorers Robert O'Hara Burke and William Wills. d, Antarctic explorer Ernest Shackleton. e, Charles Lindbergh. f, Astronaut on moon.

| Perf. 14¼x14¾, 14¾x14¼ |
1999-2001	Litho.
1217	Sheet of 12, 2 ea #a.-f.	20.00 20.00
a.-f.	A449 30p Any single	1.60 1.60
1218	Sheet of 12, 2 ea #a.-f.	20.00 20.00
a.-f.	A449 30p Any single	1.60 1.60
1219	Sheet of 12, 2 each #a.-f.	20.00 20.00
a.-f.	A449 30p Any single	1.60 1.60
1220	Sheet of 12, 2 each #a.-f.	20.00 20.00
a.-f.	A449 30p Any single	1.60 1.60
1221	A449 Sheet of 12, each #a-f	16.50 16.50
	30p Any single	1.60 1.60
1222	A449 Sheet of 12, each #a-f	18.50 18.50
a.-f.	30p Any single	1.60 1.60

Issued: No. 1217, 12/31; No. 1218, 1/1/00; No. 1219, 2/29/00; No. 1220, 6/16/00; No. 1221, 12/31/00; No. 1222, 1/1/01.

Mythical Creatures — A450

2000, Jan. 26	Litho.	Perf. 14¼x14¾
1223	A450 30p Frog Prince	1.50 .65
1224	A450 30p Pegasus	1.50 1.35
1225	A450 30p Unicorn	1.50 1.35
1226	A450 30p Dragon	1.50 1.35
a.	Booklet pane, #1223-1226, + 3 Gaelic, 5 English labels	6.00
b.	Booklet pane, #1223-1226, + 2 Gaelic, 6 English labels	4.50
c.	Booklet pane, #1223, 1226, + 14 labels	2.00
	Complete booklet, #1226a-1226c	10.00
d.	Souvenir sheet, #1224-1226, + 7 labels	3.25 3.25
	Nos. 1223-1226 (4)	6.00 4.70

New Year 2000 (Year of the Dragon), No. 1226d.

Emigrant Ship Jeanie Johnston — A451

| 2000, Mar. 9 | Litho. | Perf. 14¾x14¼ |
| 1227 | A451 30p multi | 1.10 1.10 |

Common Design Type

Europa, 2000 — CD17

| 2000, May 9 | Litho. | Perf. 14¼x14¾ |
| 1230 | CD17 32p multi | 1.10 1.10 |

Die Cut Perf 9¼x9¼
Self-Adhesive
Size: 22x34mm

| 1231 | CD17 30p multi | 1.50 1.50 |

Oscar Wilde (1854-1900), Playwright — A453

No. 1232, Portrait. No. 1233, The Happy Prince. No. 1234, The Importance of Being Earnest. No. 1235, The Picture of Dorian Gray. No. 1236, £2, Like No. 1232, signature at left.

| Perf. 14¼x14¾, 14¼x14 (#1236) |
2000, May 22	Litho.
1232	A453 30p multi	.90 1.10
1233	A453 30p multi	.90 1.10
1234	A453 30p multi	.90 1.10
1235	A453 30p multi	.90 1.10
a.	Block, #1232-1235	5.00 5.00
	Size: 27x27mm
1236	A453 30p multi + label	10.00 10.00
	Sheet of 20	110.00
	Nos. 1232-1236 (5)	13.60 14.40

Souvenir Sheet

| 1237 | A453 £2 multi | 3.75 3.75 |
| a. | With Stamp Show 2000 emblem in margin | 4.50 4.50 |

No. 1237 contains one 30x40mm stamp. No. 1236 was printed in sheets of 20 stamps and 20 labels for £10. These sheets were not available at Irish post offices, but were sold at the Irish Post booths at The Stamp Show 2000 in London and World Stamp Expo in Ahaheim, California. Labels were blank, but purchasers could provide Irish Post with photographic images or other artwork that would be reproduced on the labels.

2000 Summer Olympics, Sydney — A454

2000, July 7	Litho.	Perf. 13¼
1238	A454 30p Running	.50 .65
1239	A454 30p Javelin	.50 .65
a.	Pair, #1238-1239	1.25 1.50
1240	A454 50p Long jump	.75 1.10
1241	A454 50p High jump	.75 1.10
a.	Pair, #1240-1241	1.75 2.25

Stampin' the Future — A455

Children's Stamp Design Contest Winners: 30p, Marguerite Nyhan (rocket and flowers), vert. 32p, Kyle Staunton (2000). No. 1244, Jennifer Branagan (Earth, sun and moon). No. 1245, Diarmuid O'Ceochain (rocket, building on moon).

| Perf. 14¼x14¾, 14¾x14¼ |
2000, July 7	
1242	A455 30p multi	.70 .45
1243	A455 32p multi	.70 .55
1244	A455 45p multi	.75 .75
1245	A455 45p multi	.75 .75
a.	Pair, #1244-1245	1.50 1.50
	Nos. 1242-1245 (4)	2.90 2.50

Team of the Millennium Type of 1999

Hurling — No. 1246: a, Tony Reddin. b, Bobby Rackard. c, Nick O'Donnell. d, John Doyle. e, Brian Whelahan. f, John Keane. g, Paddy Phelan. h, Lory Meagher. i, Jack Lynch. j, Jim Langton. k, Mick Mackey. l, Christy Ring. m, Jimmy Doyle. n, Ray Cummins. o, Eddie Keher.

2000, Aug. 2	Litho.	Perf. 14¾x14¼
1246	Sheet of 15 + label	13.50 13.50
a.-o.	A445 30p Any single	1.25 1.25

No. 1246 exists imperf. Value, $125.

Booklet Stamps
Self-Adhesive
Size: 33x22mm
Serpentine Die Cut 11¼x11½

1247	A445 30p Like #1246a	1.00 .90
1248	A445 30p Like #1246m	1.00 .90
1249	A445 30p Like #1246d	1.00 .90
a.	Booklet, 3 each #1247-1248, 4 #1249	7.00
1250	A445 30p Like #1246b	1.00 .90
1251	A445 30p Like #1246c	1.00 .90
a.	Booklet, 5 each #1250-1251	6.50
1252	A445 30p Like #1246k	1.00 .90
1253	A445 30p Like #1246e	1.00 .90
1254	A445 30p Like #1246f	1.00 .90
a.	Booklet, 4 #1252, 3 each #1253-1254	6.00
1255	A445 30p Like #1246g	1.00 .90
1256	A445 30p Like #1246j	1.00 .90
1257	A445 30p Like #1246n	1.00 .90
1258	A445 30p Like #1246o	1.00 .90
a.	Booklet, 2 each #1255-1256, 3 each #1257-1258	6.50
1259	A445 30p Like #1246i	1.00 .90
1260	A445 30p Like #1246h	1.00 .90
1261	A445 30p Like #1246l	1.00 .90
a.	Booklet, 3 each #1259-1260, 4 #1261	6.50
	Nos. 1247-1261 (15)	15.00 13.50

No. 1246 exists imperf.

IRELAND

Butterflies — A456

Designs: 30p, Peacock. 32p, Small tortoiseshell. 45p, Silver-washed fritillary. 50p, Orange-tip.

2000, Sept. 6			Perf. 13¼x12¾
1262	A456 30p multi	.75	.45
1263	A456 32p multi	.80	.50
1264	A456 45p multi	1.20	1.55
1265	A456 50p multi	1.30	2.25
a.	Souvenir sheet, #1262-1265	10.00	10.00

Stamps from No. 1265a lack year date.

Military Aircraft — A457

Designs: No. 1266, Bristol F.2b Mk II fighter. No. 1267, Hawker Hurricane Mk IIc. No. 1268, Alouette III helicopter. No. 1269, De Havilland DH.115 Vampire T.55.

2000, Oct. 9	Litho.	Perf. 14¾x14¼
1266	A457 30p multi	1.40 1.60
1267	A457 30p multi	1.40 1.60
a.	Pair, #1266-1267	2.75 1.75
b.	Booklet pane, 2 each #1266-1267	4.50
1268	A457 45p multi	1.75 2.00
a.	Booklet pane, #1266-1268	4.50
1269	A457 45p multi	1.75 2.00
a.	Pair, #1268-1269	3.50 3.50
b.	Booklet pane, 2 each #1268-1269	5.50
c.	Booklet pane, #1266-1269	5.50
	Booklet, #1267b, 1268a, 1269b, 1269c	16.00
	Nos. 1266-1269 (4)	6.30 7.20

Coil Stamps
Self-Adhesive
Die Cut Perf. 9¼x9½

1270	A457 30p Like #1266	1.40 1.40
1271	A457 30p Like #1267	1.40 1.40
1272	A457 30p Like #1269	1.40 1.40
1273	A457 30p Like #1268	1.40 1.40
a.	Strip, #1270-1273	6.00

Dept. of Agriculture, Cent. — A458

2000, Nov. 14	Litho.	Perf. 13½
1274	A458 50p multi	1.40 1.50

Christmas — A459

Designs: No. 1275, Nativity. 32p, Adoration of the Magi. 45p, Adoration of the Shepherds. No. 1278, Flight to Egypt.

2000, Nov. 14		Perf. 14¼x14¾
1275	A459 30p multi	.60 .25
1276	A459 32p multi	.70 .50
1277	A459 45p multi	.90 1.35

Booklet Stamp
Self-Adhesive
Size: 21x26mm
Serpentine Die Cut 11¼

1278	A459 30p multi	.80 .45
a.	Booklet of 24	22.50
	Nos. 1275-1278 (4)	3.00 2.55

No. 1278 sold for £6.60.

Pets — A460

Designs: Nos. 1279, 1283, Goldfish, hearts. Nos. 1280a, 1284, Snake. Nos. 1280b, 1282, Frog, four-leaf clover. Nos. 1280c, 1285, Turtle, stars. No. 1281, Lizard, daisy.

2001, Jan. 24	Litho.	Perf. 14¼x14¾
1279	A460 30p multi	1.35 1.10

Souvenir Sheet

1280	Sheet of 3	6.50 7.00
a.-c.	A460 30p Any single	1.75 1.75

Booklet Stamps
Size: 25x30mm
Self-Adhesive
Serpentine Die Cut 12

1281	A460 30p multi	.90 1.00
1282	A460 30p multi	.90 1.00
1283	A460 30p multi	.90 1.00
1284	A460 30p multi	.90 1.00
1285	A460 30p multi	.90 1.00
a.	Booklet, 2 each #1281-1285 + 10 labels	13.00
	Nos. 1281-1285 (5)	4.50 5.00

New Year 2001 (Year of the Snake), No. 1280.

Broadcasting in Ireland — A461

Designs: 30p, Camera, audience, man. 32p, Microphone, announcers. 45p, People listening to radio. 50p, Television.

2001, Feb. 27		Perf. 14¾x14¼
1286	A461 30p multi	.85 .45
1287	A461 32p multi	1.00 .50
1288	A461 45p multi	1.25 1.00
1289	A461 50p multi	1.40 1.15
	Nos. 1286-1289 (4)	4.50 3.10

Literary Anniversaries — A462

Designs: 30p, Marsh's Library, first public library in Ireland, 300th anniv. 32p, Book of Common Prayer, first book printed in Ireland, 450th anniv.

2001, Mar. 14		Perf. 14¼x14¾
1290	A462 30p multi	.85 .55
1291	A462 32p multi	.85 1.10

Comhaltas Ceoltóirí Eirann, 50th Anniv. — A463

Musician with: No. 1292, Bagpipes. No. 1293, Tambourine. No. 1294, Flute, horiz. No. 1295, Violin, horiz.

Perf. 14¼x14¾, 14¾x14¼

2001, Mar. 14		
1292	A463 30p multi	.60 .90
1293	A463 30p multi	.60 .90
a.	Pair, #1292-1293	1.35 1.80
1294	A463 45p multi	1.25 1.50
1295	A463 45p multi	1.25 1.50
a.	Pair, #1294-1295	2.90 3.25
	Nos. 1292-1295 (4)	3.70 4.80

Race Cars — A464

Designs: Nos. 1296, 1300, 1301, Jordan Grand Prix Formula 1. Nos. 1297, 1304, Hillman Imp, Tulip Rally. Nos. 1298, 1303, Mini Cooper S, Monte Carlo Rally. Nos. 1299, 1302, Mercedes SSK, Irish Grand Prix.

2001, Apr. 26		Perf. 13¾x14¼
1296	A464 30p multi	.70 .45
1297	A464 32p multi	.75 .50
1298	A464 45p multi	1.15 .75
1299	A464 £1 multi	1.90 2.25
	Nos. 1296-1299 (4)	4.50 3.95

Souvenir Sheet

1300	A464 £2 multi	4.75 4.50
a.	With Belgica show emblem in margin	5.75 5.50

Booklet Stamps
Size: 36x24mm
Self-Adhesive
Serpentine Die Cut 11¾

1301	A464 30p multi	3.50 .90
1302	A464 30p multi	3.50 1.60
1303	A464 30p multi	3.50 1.60
1304	A464 30p multi	3.50 1.60
a.	Booklet, 4 #1301, 2 each #1302-1304	16.00
	Nos. 1301-1304 (4)	14.00 5.70

Issued: No. 1300a, 6/9/01.

Irish Heritage in Australia — A465

2001, May 3		Perf. 14¾x14¼
1305	A465 30p Ned Kelly	.65 .55
1306	A465 30p Peter Lalor	.65 .55
a.	Pair, #1305-1306	1.40 1.25
1307	A465 45p Settlers	1.40 1.40
1308	A465 45p Emigrants	1.40 1.40
a.	Pair, #1307-1308	2.90 2.90
	Nos. 1305-1308 (4)	4.10 3.90

Souvenir Sheet

1309	A465 £1 Like #1305	3.00 3.25

Europa — A466

2001, May 16	Litho.	Perf. 14¾x14¼
1310	A466 30p Wading	1.35 .55
1311	A466 32p Fishing	1.65 .85

Coil Stamps
Self-Adhesive
Die Cut Perf. 9¼x9½

1312	A466 30p Wading	2.00 2.00
1313	A466 30p Fishing	2.00 2.00
a.	Strip, #1312-1313	4.00

Bird Types of 1997 With Added Euro Denominations

Designs: Nos. 1314, 1319A, Blackbird. 1319B, Goldcrest. 32p, Robin. 35p, Puffin. 40p, Wren. 45p, Song thrush. £1, Greenland white-fronted goose.

Perf. 14¼x14¾

2001, June 11		Litho.
1314	A403 30p multi	1.10 2.25
1315	A403 32p multi	1.10 2.75
1316	A403 35p multi	2.25 3.25
1317	A403 40p multi	2.25 3.25
1318	A403 45p multi	2.25 3.50

Perf. 14¾x14¼

1319	A404 £1 multi	4.15 7.00
	Nos. 1314-1319 (6)	13.10 22.00

Self-Adhesive
Coil Stamps
Die Cut Perf. 11¼
Size: 21x26mm

1319A	A403 30p multi	1.60 1.60
1319B	A403 30p multi	1.60 1.60
c.	Pair, #1319A-1319B	3.25 3.25

Battle of Kinsale, 400th Anniv. — A467

Designs: No. 1320, Soldiers on horseback. No. 1321, Soldiers in stream. 32p, Soldiers and ramparts. 45p, View of Kinsale.

2001, July 10		Perf. 13½
1320	A467 30p multi	.90 .90
1321	A467 30p multi	.90 .90
a.	Pair, #1320-1321	2.25 1.75
1322	A467 32p multi	.95 .75
1323	A467 45p multi	1.30 1.35
	Nos. 1320-1323 (4)	4.05 3.90

Hall of Fame Athletes — A468

Designs: Nos. 1324, 1328, Padraic Carney, soccer player. Nos. 1325, 1329, Frank Cummins, hurler. Nos. 1326, 1330, Jack O'Shea, soccer player. Nos. 1327, 1331, Nicky Rackard, hurler.

2001, Sept. 5	Litho.	Perf. 14¾x14
1324	A468 30p multi	1.30 1.10
1325	A468 30p multi	1.30 1.10
1326	A468 30p multi	1.30 1.10
1327	A468 30p multi	1.30 1.10
a.	Horiz. strip, #1324-1327	5.50 4.50

Booklet Stamps
Size: 33x22mm
Self-Adhesive
Serpentine Die Cut 11x11½

1328	A468 30p multi	1.65 1.65
1329	A468 30p multi	1.65 1.65
1330	A468 30p multi	1.65 1.65
1331	A468 30p multi	1.65 1.65
a.	Booklet, 2 each #1328, 1331, 3 each #1329-1330	9.00
	Nos. 1324-1331 (8)	11.80 11.00

See Nos. 1429-1432.

Sailboats — A469

Designs: No. 1332, Ruffian 23. No. 1333, Howth 17. No. 1334, 1720 Sportsboat. No. 1335, The Glen. No. 1336, Ruffian 23. No. 1337, Howth 17. No. 1338, The Glen. No. 1339, 1720 Sportsboat.

2001, Sept. 5		Perf. 14x14¾
1332	A469 30p multi	.80 .35
1333	A469 30p multi	.80 .40
1334	A469 45p multi	1.15 .90
1335	A469 45p multi	1.15 .90
a.	Horiz. pair, #1334-1335	2.40 2.50
	Nos. 1332-1335 (4)	3.90 2.55

Coil Stamps
Self-Adhesive
Serpentine Die Cut 9½x9¼

1336	A469 30p multi	1.20 .90
1337	A469 30p multi	1.20 .90
1338	A469 30p multi	1.20 .90
1339	A469 30p multi	1.20 .90
a.	Strip of 4, #1336-1339	5.25 3.75

Bird Type of 1997
Serpentine Die Cut 11¼

2001, Oct. 9		Litho.

Booklet Stamps
Self-Adhesive

1340	A403 N Blackbird	2.40 .90
1341	A403 N Goldcrest	2.20 .90
a.	Booklet, 5 each #1340-1341	17.50
1342	A403 E Robin	2.20 .90
a.	Booklet of 10 + 10 etiquettes	19.50
1343	A403 W Song thrush	2.40 1.75
a.	Booklet of 10 + 10 etiquettes	22.50
	Nos. 1340-1343 (4)	9.20 4.45

On the date of issue Nos. 1340-1341 sold for 30p each, no. 1342 sold for 32p and No. 1343 sold for 45p.

Fish — A470

IRELAND

Designs: 30p, Perch. No. 1345, Arctic char. No. 1346, Pike. 45p, Common bream.

2001, Oct. 9			Perf. 14¾x14	
1344	A470	30p multi	.55	.25
1345	A470	32p multi	.90	.75
1346	A470	32p multi	.90	.75
a.	Horiz. pair, #1345-1346		2.00	1.50
1347	A470	45p multi	.90	.90
a.	Booklet pane, #1344-1347		3.75	—
b.	Booklet pane, #1345, 1346, 2 #1347		3.75	—
c.	Booklet pane, 2 each #1344, 1347		6.00	—
	Booklet, #1347b, 1347c, 2 #1347a		13.50	

No. 1347a exists with stamps in different order. The booklet contains the two different panes.

Governmental Support of Arts, 50th Anniv. — A471

2001, Nov. 5			Perf. 14x14¾	
1348	A471	50p multi	1.65	1.90

Christmas — A472

Designs: No. 1349, Nativity. 32p, Annunciation. 45p, Presentation in the Temple. No. 1352, Madonna and Child.

2001, Nov. 5			Perf. 14x14¾	
1349	A472	30p multi	.95	.45
1350	A472	32p multi	.95	.50
1351	A472	45p multi	1.40	1.35

Booklet Stamp
Size: 21x27mm
Self-Adhesive
Serpentine Die Cut 11x11¼

1352	A472	30p multi	1.15	.50
a.	Booklet of 24		25.00	
	Nos. 1349-1352 (4)		4.45	2.80

No. 1352a sold for £6.60.

100 Cents = 1 Euro (€)

A473

Birds (With Euro Denominations Only) — A474

Designs: 1c, Magpie. 2c, Gannet. 3c, Blue tit, horiz. 4c, Corncrake. 5c, Wood pigeon, horiz. Nos. 1358, 1370, 10c, Kingfisher. 20c, Lapwing. Nos. 1360, 1371, 1372, 38c, Blackbird. No. 1373, 38c, Goldcrest. 41c, Chaffinch. 44c, Robin. 50c, Gray heron, horiz. 51c, Roseate tern, horiz. 57c, Curlew. €1, Barnacle goose. €2, Greenland white-fronted goose, vert. €5, Pintail. €10, Shelduck, vert.

Perf. 14x14¾, 14¾x14

2002, Jan. 1			Litho.	
1353	A473	1c multi	.30	.25
1354	A473	2c multi	.30	.25
1355	A473	3c multi	.30	.25
1356	A473	4c multi	.30	.25
1357	A473	5c multi	.30	.25
1358	A473	10c multi	.45	.30
1359	A473	20c multi	.50	.90
1360	A473	38c multi	1.40	.70
1361	A473	41c multi	1.60	.55
1362	A473	44c multi	1.50	.60
1363	A473	50c multi	1.65	.80
1364	A473	51c multi	1.65	.70
1365	A473	57c multi	1.65	.70
1366	A474	€1 multi	2.40	1.25
1367	A474	€2 multi	3.85	2.25
1368	A474	€5 multi	9.50	5.50
1369	A474	€10 multi	19.00	12.50

Booklet Stamps
Size: 18x20mm
Perf. 14¾x14¼ on 3 Sides

1370	A473	10c multi	7.25	5.00
1371	A473	38c multi	1.10	1.35
a.	Booklet pane, #1370, 5 #1371		7.50	—
	Booklet, #1371a		7.50	

Coil Stamps
Size: 21x26mm
Self-Adhesive
Serpentine Die Cut 11x11¼

1372	A473	38c multi	2.25	1.10
1373	A473	38c multi	2.25	1.10
a.	Pair, #1372-1373		4.50	5.50
	Nos. 1353-1373 (21)		59.50	36.55

See Nos. 1392-1398, 1421-1423, 1433-1434, 1447-1449, 1492-1495, 1511-1515, 1523-1526.

Introduction of the Euro — A475

Designs: 38c, 1 euro coin introduced in 2002. 41c, 50p coin used from 1971-2001. 57c, 1p coin used from 1928-71.

2002, Jan. 1			Litho.	Perf. 14¾x14¼
1374	A475	38c multi	.80	.45
1375	A475	41c multi	.90	.55
1376	A475	57c multi	1.25	1.15
	Nos. 1374-1376 (3)		2.95	2.15

Toys — A476

Designs: Nos. 1377, 1379, Teddy bear. Nos. 1378a, 1381, Rocking horse. Nos. 1378b, 1382, Wooden locomotive. Nos. 1378c, 1380, Doll. No. 1383, Blocks.

2002, Jan. 22			Perf. 14¼x14¾	
1377	A476	38c multi	1.40	1.40

Souvenir Sheet
Perf. 14¼x14¾ on 3 or 4 Sides

1378		Sheet of 3	5.50	6.50
a.-c.	A476 38c Any single		1.75	2.10

Booklet Stamps
Self-Adhesive
Size: 21x27mm
Serpentine Die Cut 11¼

1379	A476	38c multi	.95	.75
1380	A476	38c multi	.95	.75
1381	A476	38c multi	.95	.75
1382	A476	38c multi	.95	.75
1383	A476	38c multi	.95	.75
a.	Booklet of 10, 2 each #1379-1383, + 10 labels		10.00	
	Nos. 1379-1383 (5)		4.75	3.75

New Year 2002 (Year of the Horse), No. 1378.

Steeplechasing in Ireland, 250th Anniv. — A477

2002, Mar. 12			Perf. 14¾x14¼	
1384	A477	38c Arkle	.95	.95
1385	A477	38c L'Escargot	.95	.95
1386	A477	38c Dawn Run	.95	.95
1387	A477	38c Istabraq	.95	.95
a.	Horiz. strip of 4, #1384-1387		3.80	3.80

Scouting — A478

Designs: No. 1388, Scout with peg and mallet. No. 1389, Scouts and leader around camp fire. No. 1390, Scouts on hike. No. 1391, Scouts kayaking.

2002, Mar. 12				
1388	A478	41c multi	.90	.80
1389	A478	41c multi	.90	.80
a.	Horiz. pair, #1388-1389		1.80	1.65
1390	A478	57c multi	1.50	1.50
1391	A478	57c multi	1.50	1.50
a.	Horiz. pair, #1390-1391		3.25	3.25
	Nos. 1388-1391 (4)		4.80	4.60

Bird Type of 2002

Designs: No. 1395, Chaffinch. No. 1396, Goldcrest. 44c, Robin. 47c, Kestrel, horiz. 55c, Oystercatcher, horiz. 57c, Song thrush. 60c, Jay, horiz.

2002			Litho.	Perf. 14¾x14
1392	A473	47c multi	1.65	.75
1393	A473	55c multi	1.90	2.20
1394	A473	60c multi	2.75	1.35

Self-Adhesive
Serpentine Die Cut 11x11¼
Size: 21x26mm

1395	A473	41c multi	2.20	1.10
1396	A473	41c multi	2.20	1.10
a.	Coil pair, #1395-1396		4.25	5.25
b.	Booklet of 10, 5 each #1395-1396		15.00	

Booklet Stamps

1397	A473	44c multi	1.65	1.10
a.	Booklet of 10		15.00	
1398	A473	57c multi	2.20	1.65
a.	Booklet of 10		24.00	
	Nos. 1392-1398 (7)		14.55	9.25

Issued: Nos. 1395-1398, 4/2. Nos. 1392-1394, 6/17.
Compare Nos. 1395-1396 with Nos. 1433-1434.

Mammals A479

Designs: 41c, Meles meles. 50c, €5, Lutra lutra. 57c, Sciurus vulgaris, vert. €1, Erinaceus europaeus, vert.

Perf. 14¾x14¼, 14¼x14¾

2002, Apr. 23			Litho.	
1399	A479	41c multi	.75	.55
1400	A479	50c multi	.90	.65
1401	A479	57c multi	1.00	.70
1402	A479	€1 multi	1.80	2.25
	Nos. 1399-1402 (4)		4.45	4.15

Souvenir Sheet

| 1403 | A479 | €5 multi | 15.00 | 15.00 |

Europa — A480

Designs: Nos. 1404, 1406, Clown. Nos. 1405, 1407, Equestrian act.

2002, May 14			Litho.	Perf. 14¾x14
1404	A480	41c multi	.85	.75
1405	A480	44c multi	1.35	.95

Coil Stamps
Size: 34x23mm
Self-Adhesive
Die Cut Perf. 9¼x9½

1406	A480	41c multi	1.10	.75
1407	A480	41c multi	1.10	.75
a.	Horiz. pair, #1406-1407		2.25	1.50
	Nos. 1404-1407 (4)		4.40	3.00

Soccer Stars — A481

Designs: Nos. 1408, 1415, Packie Bonner. Nos. 1409, 1412, Roy Keane, vert. Nos. 1410, 1413, Paul McGrath, vert. Nos. 1411, 1414, David O'Leary, vert.

2002, May 14			Perf. 14¾x14, 14x14¾	
1408	A481	41c multi	.75	.55
1409	A481	41c multi	.75	.55
1410	A481	41c multi	.75	.55
1411	A481	41c multi	.75	.55
a.	Vert. strip of 3, #1409-1411		3.00	2.20

Booklet Stamps
Sizes: 23x34, 34x23mm
Self-Adhesive
Serpentine Die Cut 11½x11¾, 11¾x11½

1412	A481	41c multi	.95	.95
1413	A481	41c multi	.95	.95
1414	A481	41c multi	.95	.95
1415	A481	41c multi	.95	.95
a.	Booklet, 3 #1412-1413, 2 #1414-1415		8.25	

Canonization of St. Pio of Pietrelcina (1887-1968) — A482

2002, June 17			Litho.	Perf. 14x14¾
1416	A482	41c multi	1.10	1.00

BrianBorú, 1000th Anniv of High Kingship — A483

Designs: 41c, Leading troops into battle. 44c, Commanding ships. 57c, On throne. €1, Decreeing Armagh as the primacy of the Irish church.

2002, July 9			Perf. 14¾x14	
1417	A483	41c multi	.70	.55
1418	A483	44c multi	.95	.90
1419	A483	57c multi	1.40	.90
1420	A483	€1 multi	1.90	2.25
	Nos. 1417-1420 (4)		4.95	4.60

Bird Type of 2002

Designs: No. 1421, Goldcrest. No. 1422, 36c, Wren. No. 1423, Chaffinch.

Perf. 14x14¾ on 3 Sides

2002, Aug. 6			Litho.	
Booklet Stamps				
1421	A473	41c multi	1.65	.65
a.	Booklet pane of 10, 5 each #1361, 1421		16.50	—
	Booklet, #1421a		16.50	

Size: 18x21mm
Perf. 14¾x14¼ on 3 Sides

1422	A473	36c multi	7.75	6.00
1423	A473	41c multi	1.30	.90
a.	Booklet pane of 5, #1422, 4 #1423 + label		12.25	
	Booklet, #1423a		12.25	

Paintings in National Gallery — A484

Designs: No. 1424, Before the Start, by Jack B. Yeats. No. 1425, The Conjuror, by Nathaniel Hone. No. 1426, The Colosseum and Arch of Constantine, Rome, by Giovanni Paolo Panini. No. 1427, The Gleaners, by Jules Breton.

2002, Aug. 29			Perf. 14¾x14	
1424	A484	41c multi	.85	.85
a.	Booklet pane of 4		2.75	—
1425	A484	41c multi	.85	.85
a.	Booklet pane of 4		2.75	—
1426	A484	41c multi	.85	.85
a.	Booklet pane of 4		2.75	—
1427	A484	41c multi	.85	.85
a.	Horiz. strip, #1424-1427		2.75	2.75
b.	Booklet pane of 4		2.75	—
	Booklet, #1424a, 1425a, 1426a, 1427b		12.00	

See Nos. 1496-1499, 1572-1575.

Archbishop Thomas Croke (1823-1902) — A485

2002, Sept. 17			Perf. 14x14¾	
1428	A485	44c multi	1.30	1.00

IRELAND

Hall of Fame Athletes Type of 2001

Designs: No. 1429, Peter McDermott, soccer player. No. 1430, Jimmy Smyth, hurler. No. 1431, Matt Connor, soccer player. No. 1432, Seanie Duggan, hurler.

2002, Sept. 17   Perf. 14¾x14

1429	A468	41c multi	.85	.90
1430	A468	41c multi	.85	.90
1431	A468	41c multi	.85	.90
1432	A468	41c multi	.85	.90
a.	Horiz. strip, #1429-1432		3.40	3.60

Bird Type of 2002 Redrawn

Designs: No. 1433, Chaffinch. No. 1434, Goldcrest.

Serpentine Die Cut 11x11¼

2002, Oct. 17 Coil Stamps Photo. Self-Adhesive

1433	A473	41c multi	2.75	1.10
1434	A473	41c multi	2.75	1.10
a.	Coil pair, #1433-1434		7.00	

Text appears grayer on Nos. 1433-1434 than on Nos. 1395-1396. On No. 1433, the second "h" of "Chaffinch" touches the branch, while it does not touch on No. 1395. On No. 1434, the points of the pine needles at the bottom of the stamp are shown, while they are cut off on No. 1396.

Irish Rock Musicians — A486

Designs: Nos. 1435, 1439, U2. Nos. 1436, 1440, Phil Lynott. Nos. 1437, 1441, Van Morrison. Nos. 1438, 1442, Rory Gallagher.

2002, Oct. 17 Litho. Perf. 13¼x12¾

1435	A486	41c multi	1.15	1.15
1436	A486	41c multi	1.15	1.15
a.	Horiz. pair, #1435-1436		2.30	2.30
1437	A486	57c multi	1.25	1.75
1438	A486	57c multi	1.25	1.75
a.	Horiz. pair, #1437-1438		2.50	3.50
	Nos. 1435-1438 (4)		4.80	5.80

Souvenir Sheets
Perf. 12¾x13¼

1439	A486	€2 multi	4.00	6.50
1440	A486	€2 multi	4.00	6.50
1441	A486	€2 multi	4.00	6.50
1442	A486	€2 multi	4.00	6.50

Christmas — A487

Scenes from *Les Très Riches Heures du Duc de Berry*: No. 1443, Adoration of the Magi. 44c, The Annunciation. 57c, Angels Announcing Birth to Shepherds. No. 1446, Adoration of the Shepherds.

2002, Nov. 7 Litho. Perf. 14¼x14¾

1443	A487	41c multi	.75	.55
1444	A487	44c multi	.85	.55
1445	A487	57c multi	1.20	1.00

Booklet Stamp Self-Adhesive Size: 21x27mm
Serpentine Die Cut 11x11¼

1446	A487	41c multi	1.10	.65
a.	Booklet pane of 24		22.50	
	Nos. 1443-1446 (4)		3.90	2.75

No. 1446a sold for €9.43.

Bird Type of 2002

Designs: 50c, Puffin. 75c, Ringed plover, horiz.. 95c, Sparrowhawk, horiz.

2003, Jan. 6 Litho. Perf. 14¾x14

1447	A473	75c multi	3.75	1.20
1448	A473	95c multi	5.25	1.55

Booklet Stamp Self-Adhesive Size: 21x27mm
Serpentine Die Cut 11x11¼

1449	A473	50c multi	2.50	2.50
a.	Booklet pane of 10 + 10 etiquettes		22.00	

Baby Animals — A488

Designs: Nos. 1450, 1452, Puppies. Nos. 1451a, 1454, Goats. Nos. 1451b, 1453, Chicks. Nos. 1451c, 1455, Kittens. No. 1456, Rabbits.

2003, Jan. 28   Perf. 14x14¾

1450	A488	41c multi	.95	.60

Souvenir Sheet
Perf. 14x14¾ on 3 or 4 Sides

1451	Sheet of 3	5.50	6.00
a.-c.	A488 50c Any single	1.75	1.90

Booklet Stamps
Size: 22x28mm
Self-Adhesive
Serpentine Die Cut 11x11¼

1452	A488	41c multi	1.40	.75
1453	A488	41c multi	1.40	.75
1454	A488	41c multi	1.40	.75
1455	A488	41c multi	1.40	.75
1456	A488	41c multi	1.40	.75
a.	Booklet pane of 10, 2 each #1452-1456 + 10 labels		14.00	
	Nos. 1452-1456 (5)		7.00	3.75

New Year 2003 (Year of the Goat), No. 1451.

St. Patrick's Day — A489

Designs: Nos. 1457, 1460, St. Patrick. Nos. 1458, 1461, St. Patrick's Day Parade, Dublin. Nos. 1459, 1462, St. Patrick's Day Parade, New York.

2003, Feb. 28   Perf. 14x14¾

1457	A489	41c multi	1.00	.55
a.	Booklet pane of 4		4.00	
1458	A489	50c multi	1.25	1.15
a.	Booklet pane of 4		5.00	
1459	A489	57c multi	1.50	1.35
a.	Booklet pane of 4		6.00	
b.	Booklet pane of 3, #1457-1459		3.75	
	Complete booklet, #1457a, 1458a, 1459a, 1459b		19.00	
	Nos. 1457-1459 (3)		3.75	3.05

Booklet Stamps
Self-Adhesive
Size: 22x32mm
Serpentine Die Cut 11¼

1460	A489	41c multi	1.15	.80
a.	Booklet pane of 10		13.25	
1461	A489	50c multi	1.40	1.35
a.	Booklet pane of 10		20.00	
1462	A489	57c multi	1.40	1.35
a.	Booklet pane of 10		26.00	
	Nos. 1460-1462 (3)		3.95	3.50

Beetles — A490

Designs: 41c, €2, Seven-spotted ladybug. 50c, Great diving beetle. 57c, Leaf beetle. €1, Green tiger beetle.

2003, Apr. 1   Perf. 13¾x14

1463	A490	41c multi	.85	.55
1464	A490	50c multi	.95	.65
1465	A490	57c multi	1.15	.70
1466	A490	€1 multi	2.00	2.25
	Nos. 1463-1466 (4)		4.95	4.15

Souvenir Sheet

1467	A490	€2 multi	4.95	7.50

European Year of People With Disabilities — A491

2003, May 9   Perf. 14¾x14

1468	A491	41c multi	1.10	.80

Europa — A492

Posters by Paul Henry: 41c, Dingle Peninsula (Ireland for Holidays). 57c, Connemara (Ireland This Year).

2003, May 9   Perf. 14x14¾

1469	A492	41c multi	.85	.70
1470	A492	57c multi	1.35	1.35

11th Special Olympics World Summer Games — A493

Designs: 41c, Competitors waving. 50c, Swimmer. 57c, Sprinter. €1, Shot put.

2003, May 20   Perf. 13¾x14

1471	A493	41c multi	.80	.25
1472	A493	50c multi	1.00	.40
1473	A493	57c multi	1.15	.50
1474	A493	€1 multi	2.00	1.60
	Nos. 1471-1474 (4)		4.95	2.75

Ford Motor Company, Cent. — A494

2003, June 30 Litho. Perf. 14¼x14

1475	A494	41c multi	1.10	1.10

Gordon Bennett Race in Ireland, Cent. — A495

Race map and 1903 automobiles: Nos. 1476, 1483, Napier. Nos. 1477, 1482, Mercedes. Nos. 1478, 1481, Mors. Nos. 1479, 1480, Winton.

2003, June 30 Litho. Perf. 14¼x14

1476	A495	41c multi	1.10	1.10
1477	A495	41c multi	1.10	1.10
1478	A495	41c multi	1.10	1.10
1479	A495	41c multi	1.10	1.10
a.	Horiz. strip of 4, #1476-1479		4.40	4.50

Coil Stamps
Size: 33x22mm
Self-Adhesive
Serpentine Die Cut 11¼

1480	A495	41c multi	1.10	1.10
1481	A495	41c multi	1.10	1.10
1482	A495	41c multi	1.10	1.10
1483	A495	41c multi	1.10	1.10
a.	Strip of 4, #1480-1483		4.40	4.50

Rebellion of 1803, Bicent. — A496

Designs: 41c, Robert Emmet (1778-1803), rebellion leader. 50c, Thomas Russell (1767-1803), rebellion leader. 57c, Anne Devlin (1780-1851), assistant to Emmet.

2003, July 29 Litho. Perf. 14¾x14

1484	A496	41c multi	.75	.55
1485	A496	50c multi	1.00	1.00
1486	A496	57c multi	1.35	1.45
	Nos. 1484-1486 (3)		3.10	3.00

Powered Flight, Cent. — A497

Designs: 41c, First Irish-built monoplane, built by Harry Ferguson, 1909. 50c, John Alcock & Arthur Brown's non-stop transatlantic flight, 1919. No. 1489, Lillian Bland, first female aircraft designer, 1910. Nos. 1490, 1491, Wright Flyer.

2003, July 29

1487	A497	41c multi	.75	.55
1488	A497	50c multi	1.00	.70
1489	A497	57c multi	1.60	1.35
1490	A497	57c multi	1.60	1.35
a.	Horiz. strip, #1489-1490		3.25	2.75

Souvenir Sheet

1491	A497	€5 multi	11.00	13.00

Bird Type of 2002

Designs: 7c, Stonechat. 48c, No. 1494, Peregrine falcon. No. 1495, Pied wagtail.

2003, Aug. 25 Litho. Perf. 14¾x14

1492	A473	7c multi	1.65	.85
1493	A473	48c multi	6.50	3.75

Self-Adhesive
Serpentine Die Cut 11x11¼

1494	A473	N multi	2.75	1.90
1495	A473	N multi	2.25	1.90
a.	Coil pair, #1494-1495		5.50	5.50
b.	Booklet pane, 5 each #1494-1495		25.00	

Nos. 1494-1495 each sold for 48c on day of issue.

National Gallery Paintings Type of 2002, Vert.

Designs: No. 1496, Self-portrait as Timanthes, by James Barry. No. 1497, Man Writing a Letter, by Gabriel Metsu. No. 1498, Woman Reading a Letter, by Metsu. No. 1499, Woman Seen From the Back, by Antoine Watteau.

2003, Sept. 9   Perf. 14x14¾

1496	A484	48c multi	1.00	1.10
a.	Booklet pane of 4		3.35	
1497	A484	48c multi	1.00	1.10
1498	A484	48c multi	1.00	1.10
a.	Booklet pane, 2 each #1497-1498		3.35	
1499	A484	48c multi	1.00	1.10
a.	Horiz. strip, #1496-1499		3.35	5.00
b.	Booklet pane of 4		3.35	
	Complete booklet, #1496a, 1499b, 2 #1498a		14.00	

Frank O'Connor (1903-66), Writer — A498

2003, Sept. 16 Litho. Perf. 14x14¼

1500	A498	50c multi	1.60	1.35

Ernest Thomas Sinton Walton (1903-95), 1951 Nobel Laureate in Physics — A499

2003, Sept. 16

1501	A499	57c multi	1.90	2.25

Mariners — A500

Designs: Nos. 1502, 1507, Argentine Admiral William (Guillermo) Brown (1777-1857). Nos. 1503, 1506, 1510, American Commodore John Barry (1745-1803). Nos. 1504, 1508, Captain Robert Halpin (1836-94). Nos. 1505, 1509, Captain Richard Roberts (1803-41).

IRELAND

Perf. 14¼x14 (#1502-1505, 1510)
2003, Sept. 30
1502	A500	48c multi	1.10	1.10
1503	A500	48c multi	1.10	1.10
a.	Horiz. pair, #1502-1503		2.50	2.50
1504	A500	57c multi	1.25	1.25
1505	A500	57c multi	1.25	1.25
a.	Horiz. pair, #1504-1505		2.75	2.75

Coil Stamps
Self-Adhesive (#1506-1509)
Size: 33x22mm (#1506-1509)
Serpentine Die Cut 11x11¼ (#1506-1509)
1506	A500	48c multi	1.20	1.50
1507	A500	48c multi	1.20	1.50
1508	A500	48c multi	1.20	1.50
1509	A500	48c multi	1.20	1.50
a.	Horiz. strip, #1506-1509		5.00	5.00
Nos. 1502-1509 (8)			9.50	10.70

Souvenir Sheet
| 1510 | A500 | €5 multi | 13.00 | 13.00 |

Bird Type of 2002
Designs: 4c, Corncrake. Nos. 1511, 1515, Pied wagtail. Nos. 1513, 1514, Peregrine falcon.

Perf. 14x14¾ on 3 Sides
2003, Sept. 30   Litho.
Booklet Stamps (#1511-1513)
1511	A473	48c multi	2.20	1.65
a.	Booklet pane, 5 each #1493, 1511		15.50	—
	Complete booklet, #1511a		15.50	

Size: 18x20mm
Perf. 15x14 on 3 Sides
1512	A473	4c multi	3.75	1.90
1513	A473	48c multi	2.25	1.65
a.	Booklet pane, 2 #1512, 4 #1513		17.50	
	Complete booklet, #1513a		17.50	
Nos. 1511-1513 (3)			8.20	5.20

Self-Adhesive
Size: 20x25mm
Serpentine Die Cut 11x11¼
1514	A473	48c multi	2.75	1.40
1515	A473	48c multi	2.75	1.40
a.	Coil pair, #1514-1515		5.50	
b.	Booklet pane, 5 each #1514-1515		27.50	

Examples of Nos. 1514-1515 from booklets are on a heavy, opaque paper, while those from coils are on a thinner, semi-transparent paper.

Election of Pope John Paul II, 25th Anniv. — A501

Pope John Paul II: 48c, In Ireland, 1979. 50c, At Vatican. 57c, At United Nations.

2003, Oct. 16   Perf. 14x14¾
1516	A501	48c multi	1.25	.80
1517	A501	50c multi	1.25	.85
1518	A501	57c multi	1.40	1.25
Nos. 1516-1518 (3)			3.90	2.90

Christmas — A502

Designs: No. 1519, Flight into Egypt. 50c, Angel. 57c, Three Kings. No. 1522, Nativity.

2003, Nov. 10   Perf. 13¼
| 1519 | A502 | 48c multi | .85 | .75 |

Size: 37x27mm
Perf. 14¾x14
1520	A502	50c multi	.90	.75
1521	A502	57c multi	1.85	1.15
Nos. 1519-1521 (3)			3.60	2.65

Booklet Stamp
Self-Adhesive
Size: 26x21mm
Serpentine Die Cut 11¼
| 1522 | A502 | 48c multi | 1.10 | .75 |
| a. | Booklet pane of 24 | | 26.00 | |

No. 1522a sold for €11.04.

Bird Type of 2002
Designs: Nos. 1523, 1525, Puffin. Nos. 1524, 1526, Song thrush.

2004, Jan. 5   Litho.   Perf. 14x14¾
| 1523 | A473 | 60c multi | 2.20 | 1.10 |
| 1524 | A473 | 65c multi | 2.20 | 1.10 |

Booklet Stamps
Self-Adhesive
Size: 21x26mm
Serpentine Die Cut 11x11¼
1525	A473	60c multi	2.20	1.90
a.	Booklet pane of 10		22.00	
1526	A473	65c multi	2.20	1.90
a.	Booklet pane of 10		22.00	

Irish Presidency of the European Union — A503

2004, Jan. 15   Perf. 14x14¾
| 1527 | A503 | 48c multi | 1.60 | 1.10 |

Love — A504

Designs: Nos. 1528, 1529a, 1530, Chimpanzees. Nos. 1529b, 1531, Panda. Nos. 1529c, 1532, Koala. No. 1533, Hippopotamus.

2004, Jan. 30   Perf. 14x14¾
| 1528 | A504 | 48c multi | 1.65 | 1.40 |

Souvenir Sheet
Perf. 14x14¾ on 3 or 4 Sides
| 1529 | Sheet of 3 | | 4.95 | 6.00 |
| a.-c. | A504 60c Any single | | 1.65 | 2.00 |

Booklet Stamps
Self-Adhesive
Size: 21x26mm
Serpentine Die Cut 11x11¼
1530	A504	48c multi	.90	1.10
1531	A504	48c multi	.90	1.10
1532	A504	48c multi	.90	1.10
1533	A504	48c multi	.90	1.10
a.	Booklet pane, 3 each #1530-1531, 2 each #1532-1533 + 10 labels		15.00	
Nos. 1530-1533 (4)			3.60	4.40

New Year 2004 (Year of the Monkey), No. 1529.

Abbey Theater, Dublin, Cent. — A505

2004, Feb. 27   Perf. 14x14¾
| 1534 | A505 | 48c multi | 1.20 | 1.20 |

St. Patrick's Day — A506

2004, Feb. 27
| 1535 | A506 | 65c multi | 1.65 | 1.65 |

Antarctic Expedition of Ernest Shackleton, 90th Anniv. — A507

Designs: No. 1536, Ship's stern, expedition members, dogs. No. 1537, Ship's bow, expedition members, dogs. No. 1538, 1540a, Man emerging from tent. Nos. 1539, 1540b, Tents, expedition members.

2004, Mar. 19   Perf. 13½
1536	A507	48c multi	1.50	1.50
1537	A507	48c multi	1.50	1.50
a.	Horiz. pair, #1536-1537		3.00	3.00
b.	Booklet pane, 2 #1537a		6.00	
1538	A507	65c multi	2.00	2.00
1539	A507	65c multi	2.00	2.00
a.	Horiz. pair, #1538-1539		4.00	4.00
b.	Booklet pane, 2 #1539a		8.00	
c.	Booklet pane, 2 #1537a, 1539a		7.00	
	Complete booklet, #1537b, 1539b, 2 #1539c		25.00	
Nos. 1536-1539 (4)			7.00	7.00

Souvenir Sheet
Perf. 13½ on 2 or 3 Sides
| 1540 | Sheet of 2 | | 7.00 | 7.00 |
| a.-b | A507 €1 Either single | | 3.00 | 3.00 |

No. 1539c exists with two different margins, both of which are in complete booklet.

FIFA (Fédération Internationale de Football Association), Cent. — A508

2004, Mar. 31   Perf. 13½x13
| 1541 | A508 | 60c multi | 1.40 | 1.55 |

Expansion of the European Union — A509

2004, May 1   Litho.   Perf. 14¾x14
| 1542 | A509 | 65c multi | 1.65 | 1.65 |

Europa — A510

Designs: 48c, Ross Castle. 65c, Cliffs of Moher.

2004, May 11   Perf. 14x13¾
| 1543 | A510 | 48c multi | 1.20 | .75 |
| 1544 | A510 | 65c multi | 1.60 | 1.60 |

Ducks — A511

Designs: 48c, Tufted duck. 60c, Red-breasted merganser. 65c, Gadwall. €1, Garganey.

2004, May 11   Perf. 13x13¼
1545	A511	48c multi	.95	.65
1546	A511	60c multi	1.40	1.15
1547	A511	65c multi	1.40	1.15
1548	A511	€1 multi	2.25	1.80
a.	Souvenir sheet of #1545-1548		7.00	5.25
Nos. 1545-1548 (4)			6.00	4.75

Intl. Year of the Family, 10th Anniv. — A512

2004, May 15   Litho.   Perf. 13¼x13
| 1549 | A512 | 65c multi | 1.40 | 1.65 |

Winning Artwork in Texaco Children's Art Competition — A513

Designs: 48c, Untitled work (Frog), by Daire Lee. 60c, Marmalade Cat, by Cian Colman. 65c, Ralleshin Dipditch, by Daire O'Rourke. €1, Fish on a Dish, by Ailish Fitzpatrick, horiz.

2004, May 19   Perf. 14x14¾
1550	A513	48c multi	.90	.65
1551	A513	60c multi	1.20	1.15
1552	A513	65c multi	1.20	1.15

Perf. 14¾x14
| 1553 | A513 | €1 multi | 1.95 | 1.80 |
| Nos. 1550-1553 (4) | | | 5.25 | 4.75 |

Publication of *Ulysses*, by James Joyce, Cent. — A514

Designs: 48c, Caricature of Joyce, by Tullio Percoli. 65c, Photograph of Joyce.

2004, June 16   Litho.   Perf. 13¼
| 1554 | A514 | 48c multi | 1.15 | 1.15 |
| 1555 | A514 | 65c multi | 1.40 | 1.40 |

Irish College, Paris, France — A515

2004, June 26   Perf. 14x14¾
| 1556 | A515 | 65c multi | 1.40 | 1.40 |

Inauguration of LUAS Tram System, Dublin — A516

2004, June 30   Perf. 13¼
1557	A516	48c Environment	1.35	1.35
1558	A516	48c Accessibility	1.35	1.35
a.	Horiz. pair, #1557-1558		2.75	2.75

2004 Summer Olympics, Athens — A517

Olympic flame, rings and: 48c, Javelin thrower. 60c, Myron's Discobolus.

2004, July 22   Perf. 13¾x14
| 1559 | A517 | 48c multi | 1.20 | .75 |

Perf. 14¼x14
| 1560 | A517 | 60c multi | 1.65 | 1.90 |

Camogie, Cent. — A518

Camogie players and: No. 1561, Camogie Association emblem. No. 1562, Cup.

2004, July 22   Perf. 14¾x14
1561	A518	48c multi	1.25	1.25
1562	A518	48c multi	1.25	1.25
a.	Horiz. pair, #1561-1562		2.50	2.50

IRELAND

Flowers — A519

Designs: 4c, Common dog-violet. 5c, Dandelion. Nos. 1565, 1571, Primrose. Nos. 1569A, 1570, Daisy. 60c, Hawthorn. 65c, Bluebell. €2, Lords-and-ladies. €5, Dog-rose, horiz.

Perf. 14x14¾, 14¾x14

2004, Sept. 9   Litho.
1563	A519	4c multi	.30	.25
1564	A519	5c multi	1.35	.25
1565	A519	48c multi	1.35	.75
1566	A519	60c multi	1.35	.95
1567	A519	65c multi	1.65	1.05

Size: 23x44mm
1568	A519	€2 multi	3.00	2.75

Size: 44x23mm
1569	A519	€5 multi	9.50	6.75
	Nos. 1563-1569 (7)		18.50	12.75

Booklet Stamp
Perf. 14x14¾ on 3 Sides
1569A	A519	48c multi	1.75	1.75
b.	Booklet pane 5 each #1565, 1569A		18.00	—
	Complete booklet, #1569Ab		18.00	—

Self-Adhesive
Size: 20x25mm
Serpentine Die Cut 11x11¼
1570	A519	48c multi	1.90	2.20
1571	A519	48c multi	1.90	2.20
a.	Vert. coil pair, #1570-1571		3.85	4.40
b.	Booklet pane, 5 each #1570-1571		16.50	

No. 1571 is on the left side of No. 1571b.
See Nos. 1606-1610, 1650-1655, 1708-1713, 1723-1729, 1770-1773, 1814, 1852, 1865.

National Gallery Paintings Type of 2002

Designs: No. 1572, The House Builders, by Walter Osborne. No. 1573, Kitchen Maid with the Supper at Emmaus, by Diego Velázquez. No. 1574, The Lamentation Over the Dead Christ, by Nicolas Poussin. No. 1575, The Taking of Christ, by Caravaggio.

2004, Sept. 16   *Perf. 14¾x14*
1572	A484	48c multi	.90	.90
a.	Booklet pane of 4		3.85	
1573	A484	48c multi	.90	.90
a.	Booklet pane of 4		3.85	
1574	A484	48c multi	.90	.90
a.	Booklet pane of 4		3.85	
1575	A484	48c multi	.90	.90
a.	Horiz. strip of 4, #1572-1575		3.85	3.85
b.	Booklet pane of 4		3.85	
	Complete booklet, #1572a, 1573a, 1574a, 1575b		15.00	

Complete booklet sold for €8.

Nobel Prize Winners for Literature A520

Designs: No. 1576, William Butler Yeats (1865-1939), 1923 winner. No. 1577, George Bernard Shaw (1856-1950), 1925 winner. No. 1578, Samuel Beckett (1906-89), 1969 winner. No. 1579, Seamus Heaney (b. 1939), 1995 winner.

Perf. 12½x13½

2004, Oct. 1   Litho. & Engr.
1576	A520	N multi	1.50	1.50
1577	A520	N multi	1.50	1.50
1578	A520	N multi	1.50	1.50
1579	A520	N multi	1.50	1.50
a.	Block of 4, #1576-1579		6.00	6.00
b.	Booklet pane of 4, #1576-1579		6.00	
	Complete booklet, #1579b		6.00	

Nos. 1576-1579 each sold for 48c on day of issue. See Sweden No. 2492.

Patrick Kavanagh (1904-67), Poet — A521

2004, Oct. 21   Litho.   *Perf. 13x13¼*
1580	A521	48c green & black	1.10	1.10

Quakerism in Ireland, 350th Anniv. — A522

2004, Oct. 21
1581	A522	60c multi	1.40	1.40

Christmas — A523

Designs: 48c, Holy Family. 60c, Flight into Egypt. 65c, Adoration of the Magi.

2004, Nov. 10   Litho.   *Perf. 14x14¾*
1582	A523	48c multi	.80	.45
1583	A523	60c multi	1.35	1.15
1584	A523	65c multi	1.70	1.25
	Nos. 1582-1584 (3)		3.85	2.85

Booklet Stamp
Self-Adhesive
Serpentine Die Cut 11x11¼
Size: 21x27mm
1585	A523	48c multi	1.10	.75
a.	Booklet pane of 24		25.00	

No. 1585a sold for €11.04.

Love — A524

Birds: Nos. 1586, 1587b, 1590, Parrots. Nos. 1587a, 1588, Rooster. Nos. 1587c, 1591, Owl. No. 1589, Storks.

2005, Jan. 28   *Perf. 14¾x14*
1586	A524	48c multi	1.10	1.10
1587		Sheet of 3	7.00	7.00
a.-c.	A524 60c Any single		2.30	2.30

Booklet Stamps
Self-Adhesive
Serpentine Die Cut 11¼x11
Size: 27x21mm
1588	A524	48c multi	1.40	1.40
1589	A524	48c multi	1.40	1.40
1590	A524	48c multi	.90	.90
1591	A524	48c multi	1.15	1.15
a.	Booklet pane, 3 each #1588, 1590, 2 each #1589, 1591 + 10 labels		8.25	

New Year 2005 (Year of the Rooster).

St. Patrick's Day — A525

2005, Feb. 17   Litho.   *Perf. 14x14¾*
1592	A525	65c multi	1.40	1.40

Works of Women Artists — A526

Designs: No. 1593, Landscape, Co. Wicklow, by Evie Hone (1894-1955). No. 1594, Seabird and Landmarks, by Nano Reid (1905-81). No. 1595, Threshing, by Mildred Anne Butler (1858-1941), vert. No. 1596, Three Graces, by Gabriel Hayes (1909-78), vert.

2005, Feb. 24   *Perf. 14¾x14, 14¾x14*
1593	A526	48c multi	1.10	1.10
1594	A526	48c multi	1.10	1.10
a.	Horiz. pair, #1593-1594		2.25	2.25
1595	A526	65c multi	1.60	1.60
1596	A526	65c multi	1.60	1.60
a.	Horiz. pair, #1595-1596		3.25	3.25

Cork, 2005 European Cultural Capital — A527

2005, Mar. 7   Litho.   *Perf. 13¼*
1597	A527	48c shown	1.10	1.10
1598	A527	48c Buildings, bridge	1.10	1.10
a.	Horiz. pair, #1597-1598		2.20	2.20

Intl. Year of Physics A528

Designs: 48c, William Rowan Hamilton (1805-65), mathematician and astronomer. 60c, UNESCO Headquarters, Paris. 65c, Albert Einstein (1879-1955), physicist.

2005, Mar. 14
1599	A528	48c multi	1.10	1.10
1600	A528	60c multi	1.40	1.40
1601	A528	65c multi	1.50	1.50
	Nos. 1599-1601 (3)		4.00	4.00

Dublin-Belfast Railway, 150th Anniv. — A529

Designs: No. 1602, Modern train. No. 1603, Steam locomotive at Connolly Station, Dublin. 60c, Steam locomotive on Boyne Valley Viaduct. 65c, Modern train at station platform.

2005, Apr. 5   Litho.   *Perf. 14¾x14*
1602	A529	48c multi	1.20	1.20
a.	Booklet pane of 4		4.50	
1603	A529	48c multi	1.20	1.20
a.	Booklet pane of 4		4.50	
b.	Horiz. pair, #1602-1603		2.40	2.40
1604	A529	60c multi	1.50	1.50
a.	Booklet pane of 4		5.50	
1605	A529	65c multi	1.60	1.60
a.	Booklet pane of 4		6.00	
	Complete booklet, #1602a, 1603a, 1604a, 1605a		21.00	
b.	Souvenir sheet, #1602-1605		6.00	6.00
	Nos. 1602-1605 (4)		5.50	5.50

Complete booklet sold for €9.

Flowers Type of 2004

Designs: 1c, Bloody crane's-bill. 2c, Irish orchid. 7c, Fly orchid. 10c, Mountain avens. €10, Spring gentian, horiz.

2005, Apr. 12   *Perf. 14x14¾*
1606	A519	1c multi	.30	.25
1607	A519	2c multi	.30	.25
1608	A519	7c multi	.55	.40
1609	A519	10c multi	1.10	.40

Size: 44x23mm
1610	A519	€10 multi	17.50	15.50
	Nos. 1606-1610 (5)		19.75	16.80

Biosphere Reserves in Ireland and Canada A530

Designs: 48c, Deer, Killarney National Park, Ireland. 65c, Saskatoon berries, Waterton Lakes National Park, Canada.

2005, Apr. 22   *Perf. 13¼x13*
1611	A530	48c multi	.95	.65
1612	A530	65c multi	1.90	1.40
a.	Souvenir sheet, #1611-1612		2.75	2.75

See Canada Nos. 2105-2106.

Europa — A531

2005, May 9   Litho.   *Perf. 14¼x14*
1613	A531	48c Irish stew	1.10	1.10
1614	A531	65c Oysters	1.65	1.65

Worldwide Fund for Nature (WWF) — A532

Butterflies: 48c, Small copper. 60c, Green hairstreak. 65c, €5, Painted lady. €1, Pearl-bordered fritillary.

2005, May 24   *Perf. 13¼*
1615	A532	48c multi	.95	.65
1616	A532	60c multi	1.30	1.15
1617	A532	65c multi	1.30	1.15
1618	A532	€1 multi	2.15	2.15
	Nos. 1615-1618 (4)		5.70	5.20

Souvenir Sheet
1619	A532	€5 multi	13.25	13.25

Tall Ships — A533

2005, July 4   Litho.   *Perf. 13½*
1620	A533	48c Dunbrody	1.05	.90
1621	A533	60c Tenacious	1.20	1.15
1622	A533	65c Eagle	1.20	1.15
	Nos. 1620-1622 (3)		3.45	3.20

Round Towers — A534

2005, July 27   Litho.   *Perf. 13¼*
1623	A534	48c Glendalough	1.20	.80
1624	A534	48c Ardmore	1.20	.80
1625	A534	48c Clones	1.20	.80
1626	A534	48c Kilmacduagh	1.20	.80
a.	Horiz. strip of 4, #1623-1626		5.00	3.25

Apimondia 2005 Apriarists Congress, Dublin — A535

2005, Aug. 19   *Perf. 13½x13*
1627	A535	65c multi	1.65	1.35

2006 Ryder Cup Golf Tournament, K Club, Straffan — A536

Designs: No. 1628, Golfers Darren Clark, Paul McGinley, and Pádraig Harrington. No. 1629, Golfers Eamonn Darcy, Christy O'Connor, Jr., and Philip Walton. 60c, Golfers Harry Bradshaw, Ronan Rafferty, and Christy O'Connor, Sr. 65c, K Club.

2005, Sept. 27   Litho.   *Perf. 14¾x14*
1628	A536	48c multi	1.20	1.20
a.	Booklet pane of 4		4.25	
1629	A536	48c multi	1.20	1.20
a.	Pair, #1628-1629		2.50	2.50
b.	Booklet pane of 4		4.25	
1630	A536	60c multi	1.40	1.40
a.	Booklet pane of 4		5.75	
b.	Booklet pane, 2 each #1628-1630 ('06)		7.25	
1631	A536	65c multi	1.40	1.40
a.	Booklet pane of 4		5.75	
b.	Booklet pane, 2 #1631 ('06)		2.75	
	Complete booklet, #1628a, 1629b, 1630a, 1631a		20.00	
	Nos. 1628-1631 (4)		5.20	5.20

Nos. 1630b, 1631b issued 9/14/06.

IRELAND

Pres. Erskine Childers (1905-74) — A537

2005, Oct. 10 — Perf. 14x14¾
1632 A537 48c multi — 1.10 1.10

Ireland in the United Nations — A538

Designs: No. 1633, Irish Defense Force member assisting man in East Timor. No. 1634, Medical worker aiding child in East Timor. 60c, F. H. Boland, Ireland's signer of United Nations Charter. 65c, Irish Defense Force member in classroom in Lebanon.

2005, Oct. 14 — Perf. 14¾x14
1633 A538 48c multi — 1.10 .90
1634 A538 48c multi — 1.10 .90
   a. Horiz. pair, #1633-1634 — 2.25 2.25
1635 A538 60c multi — 1.35 1.15
1636 A538 65c multi — 1.45 1.15
   Nos. 1633-1636 (4) — 5.00 4.10

Arthur Griffith's Policy Establishing Sinn Féin, Cent. — A539

2005, Nov. 10 — Perf. 13½
1637 A539 48c multi — 1.10 1.10

Christmas — A540

Designs: 48c, Nativity. 60c, Choir of angels. 65c, Choir of angels, diff.

2005, Nov. 10 — Perf. 14x14¾
1638 A540 48c multi — 1.10 .45
1639 A540 60c multi — 1.30 1.15
1640 A540 65c multi — 1.40 1.35
   Nos. 1638-1640 (3) — 3.80 2.95

Booklet Stamp
Self-Adhesive
Size: 21x27mm
Serpentine Die Cut 11x11¼

1641 A540 48c multi — .95 .90
   a. Booklet pane of 26 — 23.00 23.00
No. 1641a sold for €12.

Patrick Gallagher and Templecrone Cooperative Store — A541

2006, Jan. 16 Litho. Perf. 14¾x14
1642 A541 48c sepia — 1.10 1.10
Templecrone Cooperative Agricultural Society, cent.

New Year 2006 (Year of the Dog) — A542

Designs: Nos. 1643, 1644b, 1647, Dog, man and woman. Nos. 1644a, 1645, Two dogs, man. Nos. 1644c, 1646, Dog on leash, woman. No. 1648, Dog biting sneaker.

2006, Jan. 16 — Perf. 14¾x14
1643 A542 48c multi — 1.10 .95

Souvenir Sheet
1644 Sheet of 3 — 5.50 5.50
   a.-c. A542 65c Any single — 1.80 1.80

Booklet Stamps
Self-Adhesive
Size: 26x21mm
Serpentine Die Cut 11¼x11

1645 A542 48c multi — 1.75 1.75
1646 A542 48c multi — 1.75 1.75
1647 A542 48c multi — 1.75 1.75
1648 A542 48c multi — 1.75 1.75
   a. Booklet pane, 3 each #1645-1646, 2 each #1647-1648, + 10 labels — 20.00
   Nos. 1645-1648 (4) — 7.00 7.00

St. Patrick Lights the Paschal Fire at Slane, by Sean Keating — A543

2006, Feb. 16 — Perf. 14¾x14
1649 A543 65c multi — 1.90 1.35
St. Patrick's Day.

Flowers Type of 2004

Designs: 12c, Autumn gorse. 25c, Common knapweed. 75c, Navelwort. 90c, Viper's bugloss. €1, Foxglove.

2006, Feb. 20 — Perf. 14x14¾
1650 A519 12c multi — .45 .45
1651 A519 25c multi — .55 .55
1652 A519 75c multi — 2.20 1.20
1653 A519 90c multi — 2.50 1.75

Size: 23x44mm
1654 A519 €1 multi — 2.75 1.65
   Nos. 1650-1654 (5) — 8.45 5.60

Booklet Stamp
Self-Adhesive
Size: 21x27mm
Serpentine Die Cut 11x11¼

1655 A519 75c multi — 2.25 2.25
   a. Booklet pane of 10 — 22.50

Trees — A544

2006, Mar. 7 — Perf. 13¼
1656 A544 48c Sessile oak — .55 .80
1657 A544 60c Yew — 1.05 1.00
1658 A544 75c Ash — 1.35 1.25
1659 A544 €1 Strawberry tree — 1.70 1.80
   a. Souvenir sheet, #1656-1659 — 5.50 6.50
   b. As "a," with Washington 2006 World Philatelic Exhibition emblem in margin — 8.00 8.00
   Nos. 1656-1659 (4) — 4.65 4.85
No. 1659b issued in June. No. 1659b sold for €3.

St. Hubert, Stained Glass Window by Harry Clarke (1889-1931) — A545

2006, Mar. 21 — Perf. 13¼
1660 A545 48c multi — 1.15 1.15

Easter Rebellion, 90th Anniv. — A546

2006, Apr. 12 — Perf. 13½
1661 A546 48c multi — 1.40 1.40

Adoption of European Union Flag, 20th Anniv. — A547

2006, May 9 — Perf. 14¼x14
1662 A547 48c multi — 1.10 .95

Europa — A548

Winning art in children's stamp design contest: 48c, People holding Irish and European Union flags, by Katie McMillan. 75c, Flowers with flags, by Sarah Naughter.

2006, May 9 — Perf. 14x14¼
1663 A548 48c multi — 1.10 .45
1664 A548 75c multi — 3.00 3.00

University Church, Dublin, 150th Anniv. — A549

2006, May 25 Litho. Perf. 14x14¾
1665 A549 48c multi — 1.10 1.10

Department of the Gaeltacht, 50th Anniv. — A550

2006, June 6 — Perf. 13¼
1666 A550 48c multi — 1.40 1.40

TG4 Television Channel, 10th Anniv. — A551

2006, June 6
1667 A551 48c multi — 1.40 1.40

Celtic Scholars — A552

Designs: No. 1668, Máirtín O Cadhain (1906-70), writer. No. 1669, Johann Caspar Zeuss (1806-56), philologist.

2006, June 6 — Perf. 14x14¾
1668 A552 48c multi — 1.10 1.10
1669 A552 48c multi — 1.10 1.10
   a. Pair, #1668-1669 — 2.20 2.20

Rosslare-Fishguard Ferry Service, Cent. — A553

Designs: No. 1670, Steam ferry. No. 1671, Modern ferry.

2006, June 20 — Perf. 14¾x14
1670 A553 48c multi — 1.30 1.30
1671 A553 48c multi — 1.30 1.30
   a. Pair, #1670-1671 — 2.60 2.60
   b. Souvenir sheet, #1670-1671 — 3.25 3.25

Battle of the Somme, 90th Anniv. — A554

2006, June 26 — Perf. 13½x13¾
1672 A554 75c multi — 2.50 2.50

Guide Dog — A555

Litho. & Embossed
2006, July 7 — Perf. 13¼x13
1673 A555 48c multi — 1.50 1.25

A556

2006 Ryder Cup Golf Tournament, K Club, Straffan — A557

Golf ball: Nos. 1674, 1678, On tee. Nos. 1675, 1679, In rough. Nos. 1676, 1680, In sand trap. Nos. 1677, 1681, Near green. No. 1682: a, Tee shot. b, Sand trap shot.

2006 Litho. Perf. 14x14¾
1674 A556 48c multi — 1.25 1.25
1675 A556 48c multi — 1.25 1.25
1676 A556 48c multi — 1.25 1.25
1677 A556 48c multi — 1.25 1.25
   a. Horiz. strip, #1674-1677 — 5.00 5.00
   b. Souvenir sheet #1674-1677 — 5.50 5.50
   c. Booklet pane, 2 each #1674-1677 — 10.00 —
   d. Booklet pane, #1674-1677 — 5.00

Coil Stamps
Self-Adhesive
Size: 21x27mm
Serpentine Die Cut 11x11¼

1678 A556 48c multi — 1.25 1.25
1679 A556 48c multi — 1.25 1.25
1680 A556 48c multi — 1.25 1.25
1681 A556 48c multi — 1.25 1.25
   a. Vert. strip, #1678-1681 — 5.00

Souvenir Sheet
Self-Adhesive
Litho. With Three-Dimensional
Plastic Affixed
Serpentine Die Cut 9¼

1682 A557 Sheet of 2 — 5.00
   a.-b. 75c Either single — 2.40 2.40
   Complete booklet, #1630b, 1631b, 1677c, 1677d, and unbound #1682 — 27.50 27.50

Issued: Nos. 1674-1678, 7/25; No. 1682, 9/14. Complete booklet sold for €12. No. 1677b has Ryder Cup emblem in margin while No. 1677d does not.

IRELAND

Winning of Olympic 1500-Meter Running Gold Medal by Ronnie Delany, 50th Anniv. — A558

		Perf. 13¾x13½		
2006, Aug. 16			Litho.	
1683	A558	48c multi	1.10	1.10

Michael Cusack (1847-1906), Sports Journalist — A559

2006, Aug. 23		Perf. 14x14¾		
1684	A559	48c multi	1.10	1.10

Michael Davitt (1846-1906), Founder of National Land League — A560

2006, Sept. 5				
1685	A560	48c multi	1.10	1.10

National Concert Hall, Dublin, 25th Anniv. — A561

2006, Sept. 8				
1686	A561	48c multi	1.10	1.10

Inland Waterways A562

Designs: No. 1687, Barrow River at Graiguenamanagh. No. 1688, Belturbet Marina, Erne River. No. 1689, Grand Canal at Cornalaur. No. 1690, Meelick Pier, Shannon River.

2006, Oct. 20	**Litho.**	**Perf. 13½x13¾**		
1687	A562	75c multi	1.60	2.10
a.	Booklet pane of 4		6.00	—
1688	A562	75c multi	1.60	2.10
a.	Booklet pane of 4		6.00	—
1689	A562	75c multi	1.60	2.10
a.	Booklet pane of 4		6.00	—
1690	A562	75c multi	1.60	2.10
a.	Booklet pane of 4		6.00	—
	Complete booklet, #1687a-1690a		24.00	

Traditional Irish Music Groups — A563

Designs: No. 1691, The Chieftains. No. 1692, The Dubliners. No. 1693, The Clancy Brothers and Tommy Makem. No. 1694, Altan.

2006, Nov. 7	**Litho.**	**Perf. 13½x13¾**		
1691	A563	48c multi	1.20	1.60
a.	Booklet pane of 4		3.75	—
1692	A563	48c multi	1.20	1.60
a.	Booklet pane of 4		3.75	—
1693	A563	75c multi	1.40	2.25
a.	Booklet pane of 4		5.00	—
1694	A563	75c multi	1.40	2.25
a.	Booklet pane of 4		5.00	—
	Complete booklet, #1691a, 1692a, 1693a, 1694a		17.50	
b.	Souvenir sheet, #1691-1694		6.00	6.00

c.	As "b," with Belgica '06 emblem added in margin	7.00	7.00
d.	As "b," with MonacoPhil 2006 emblem added in margin	7.00	7.00

Complete booklet sold for €10.
No. 1694c issued 11/16; No. 1694d, 12/1.

Christmas
A564   A565

Designs: No. 1695, Madonna and Child. 75c, Shepherd and lamb. No. 1697, Nativity.

2006, Nov. 9		**Perf. 14x14¾**		
1695	A564	48c multi	1.10	.55
1696	A564	75c multi	1.90	2.50

Booklet Stamp
Self-Adhesive
Serpentine Die Cut 11x11¼

1697	A565	48c multi	1.40	6.65
a.	Booklet pane of 26		28.00	
	Nos. 1695-1697 (3)		4.40	9.70

No. 1697a sold for €12.

Father Luke Wadding (1588-1657) A566

Irish Franciscan College, Louvain, 400th Anniv. A567

2007, Jan. 24	**Litho.**	**Perf. 14x14¾**		
1698	A566	75c multi	1.90	2.45
1699	A567	75c multi	1.90	2.45

Hands With Wedding Rings A568

Greetings A569

Designs: No. 1701, Stamp with hat, heart balloon. No. 1702, Birthday cake.

Serpentine Die Cut 11¼

2007, Jan. 26	**Booklet Stamps**			
	Self-Adhesive			
1700	A568	N multi	1.10	1.10
a.	Booklet pane of 10		8.00	
1701	A569	N multi	1.10	1.10
1702	A569	N multi	1.10	1.10
a.	Booklet pane of 10, 5 each #1701-1702		7.75	
	Nos. 1700-1702 (3)		3.30	3.30

Nos. 1700-1702 each sold for 48c on day of issue.

New Year 2007 (Year of the Pig) — A570

2007, Feb. 9	**Litho.**	**Perf. 14¾x14**		
1703	A570	75c grn & multi	1.90	2.50

Souvenir Sheet

1704	Sheet of 3, #1704a, 2 #1703		5.75	7.00
a.	A570 75c red & multi		2.00	2.50

St. Patrick's Day — A571

2007, Feb. 9		**Perf. 13½**		
1705	A571	75c multi	1.90	2.50

Flight of the Earls, 400th Anniv. — A572

Designs: No. 1706, Hugh O'Neill, Earl of Tyrone, and ship at right. No. 1707, Rory O'Donnell, Earl of Tyrconnell, and rowboat at left.

2007, Feb. 23		**Perf. 14x14¾**		
1706	A572	48c multi	1.10	1.35
1707	A572	48c multi	1.10	1.35
a.	Horiz. pair, #1706-1707		2.75	3.00
b.	Souvenir sheet, #1707a		3.25	3.75

Flowers Type of 2004

Designs: 3c, Yellow flag. 55c, No. 1712, Large-flowered butterwort. 78c, Black bog-rush. 95c, Purple loosestrife. No. 1713, Blue-eyed grass.

2007, Mar. 1	**Litho.**	**Perf. 14x14¾**		
1708	A519	3c multi	.30	.25
1709	A519	55c multi	1.50	1.50
1710	A519	78c multi	2.20	2.10
1711	A519	95c multi	2.50	2.50
	Nos. 1708-1711 (4)		6.50	6.35

Self-Adhesive
Size: 21x26mm
Serpentine Die Cut 11x11¼

1712	A519	N multi	3.85	1.90
1713	A519	N multi	3.85	1.90
a.	Booklet pane, 5 each #1712-1713		38.50	
b.	Vert. coil pair, #1712-1713		7.75	

Nos. 1712-1713 each sold for 55c on day of issue.

Castles — A573

Designs: No. 1714, Trim Castle. No. 1715, Dunluce Castle. No. 1716, Lismore Castle. No. 1717, Portumna Castle.

2007, Mar. 9		**Perf. 14¾x14**		
1714	A573	55c multi	1.40	1.40
1715	A573	55c multi	1.40	1.40
1716	A573	55c multi	1.40	1.40
1717	A573	55c multi	1.40	1.40
b.	Souvenir sheet, #1714-1717		5.75	5.75

Treaty of Rome, 50th Anniv. — A574

2007, Mar. 28		**Perf. 14x14¾**		
1718	A574	55c multi	1.60	1.60

Planets A575

Earth and: No. 1719, Jupiter. No. 1720, Neptune. No. 1721, Saturn. No. 1722, Uranus.

2007, May 25	**Litho.**	**Perf. 13¼**		
1719	A575	55c multi	1.35	1.60
1720	A575	55c multi	1.35	1.60
a.	Horiz. pair, #1719-1720		3.25	3.25

1721	A575	78c multi	1.60	2.40
1722	A575	78c multi	1.60	2.40
a.	Horiz. pair, #1721-1722		3.25	5.00
b.	Souvenir sheet, #1719-1722		7.00	7.00
c.	Booklet pane, #1719-1722		6.25	—
	Complete booklet, 4 #1722c		25.00	
	Nos. 1719-1722 (4)		5.90	8.00

No. 1722c has stamps with straight edges at right. Complete booklet contains four examples of No. 1722c with different margins.

Flower Type of 2004

Designs: 5c, Dandelion. 25c, Common knapweed. 55c, Large-flowered butterwort. 78c, Black bog-rush.

Die Cut Perf. 12¾

2007, Apr. 20	**Coil Stamp**	**Litho.**		
	Self-Adhesive (#1723, 1728-1729)			
	Size: 21x26mm			
1723	A519	55c multi	1.65	1.65

Booklet Stamps
Size: 17x20mm
Perf. 14¾x14 on 3 Sides

1724	A519	5c multi	1.10	1.65
1725	A519	25c multi	6.75	5.50
1726	A519	55c multi	1.55	1.55
a.	Booklet pane of 6, #1725, 2 #1724, 3 #1726		9.00	—
	Complete booklet, #1726a		9.00	

Size: 20x23mm
Perf. 14¾x14 on 3 Sides

1727	A519	55c multi	1.65	1.65
a.	Booklet pane of 10		16.50	—
	Complete booklet, #1727a		16.50	

Size: 21x26mm
Serpentine Die Cut 11x11¼

1728	A519	55c multi	2.50	2.75
a.	Booklet pane of 10		15.00	
1729	A519	78c multi	2.25	2.25
a.	Booklet pane of 10		22.50	
	Nos. 1723-1729 (7)		17.45	17.00

Europa — A576

2007, May 9		**Perf. 14¼x14**		
1730	A576	55c Female Scout	1.40	.55
1731	A576	78c Male Scout	2.00	2.75

Scouting, cent.

Canonization of St. Charles of Mount Argus (1821-93) — A577

2007, June 5		**Perf. 13¼**		
1732	A577	55c multi	1.40	1.40

Institute of Public Administration, 50th Anniv. — A578

2007, June 13				
1733	A578	55c multi	1.40	1.40

RTE Performing Groups — A579

Designs: Nos. 1734, 1742, National Symphony Orchestra (Ceolfhoireann Shiansach Náisiúnta). Nos. 1735, 1740, Concert Orchestra (Ceolfhoireann Cheolchoirme). Nos. 1736, 1743, Vanbrugh Quartet (Ceathairéad Vanbrugh). Nos. 1737, 1741, Philharmonic Choir (Cór Fiolarmónach). Nos. 1738, 1739, Children's Choir (Cór na nÓg).

IRELAND

2007, June 19		Perf. 13¼x13½	
1734 A579 55c multi		1.20	1.40
1735 A579 55c multi		1.20	1.40
1736 A579 55c multi		1.20	1.40
a. Booklet pane, 2 each #1734-1736		3.50	—
1737 A579 55c multi		1.20	1.40
1738 A579 55c multi		1.20	1.40
a. Horiz. strip of 5, #1734-1738		5.50	7.00
b. Booklet pane, 2 each #1736a, 1738b		2.50	—
Complete booklet, 2 each #1736a, 1738b		12.00	

Booklet Stamps
Self-Adhesive
Serpentine Die Cut 11¼x11½

1739 A579 55c multi	.80	1.15
1740 A579 55c multi	.80	1.15
1741 A579 55c multi	.80	1.15
1742 A579 55c multi	.80	1.15
1743 A579 55c multi	.80	1.15
a. Booklet pane of 10, 2 each #1739-1743	7.00	7.00
Nos. 1734-1743 (10)	10.00	12.75

Revival of Honorable Society of King's Inns, 400th Anniv. — A580

2007, July 10		Perf. 13¼
1744 A580 55c multi	1.40	1.40

Registry of Deeds Act, 300th Anniv. — A581

2007, July 10		Perf. 14¾x14
1745 A581 78c multi	2.10	2.10

National Anthem, Cent. — A582

2007, July 17	Litho.	Perf. 13½
1746 A582 55c multi	1.40	1.40

Weddings Type of 2007
Serpentine Die Cut 11¼
Booklet Stamp

2007, July 25	Self-Adhesive	
1747 A568 55c multi	1.65	1.40
a. Booklet pane of 10	8.75	

Viking Ship Skuldelev 2 — A583

Designs: 55c, Ship. €3, Ship on water.

2007, Aug. 7	Litho.	Perf. 14¾x14
1748 A583 55c multi	2.20	2.20

Souvenir Sheet

| 1749 A583 €3 multi | 7.50 | 7.50 |

2007 Rugby World Cup, France — A584

Designs: 55c, Player carrying ball. 78c, Player catching ball.

2007, Aug. 20		Perf. 13¼
1750 A584 55c multi	1.10	.85
a. Souvenir sheet of 1	2.25	1.70
1751 A584 78c multi	2.25	2.75
a. Souvenir sheet of 1	4.50	5.25

Cat Caricatures by Martyn Turner — A585

Designs: Nos. 1752, 1756a, Fat Cat. Nos. 1753, 1756b, Celtic Tigress. Nos. 1754, 1756c, Cool Cats. Nos. 1755, 1756d, Kilkenny Cat.

2007, Sept. 6		Perf. 14x14¾
1752 A585 55c multi	1.50	1.50
1753 A585 55c multi	1.50	1.50
a. Horiz. pair, #1752-1753	3.00	3.00
1754 A585 78c multi	2.25	2.25
1755 A585 78c multi	2.25	2.25
a. Horiz. pair, #1754-1755	4.50	4.50

Souvenir Sheet
Perf. 13¼

1756 Sheet of 4	6.75	7.50
a.-b. A585 55c Either single, 16x16mm	1.50	1.50
c.-d. A585 78c Either single, 16x16mm	2.25	2.25

Excavations of San Clemente Basilica, Rome, 150th Anniv. — A586

2007, Sept. 12		Perf. 14¾x14
1757 A586 55c multi	1.60	1.60

James Fintan Lalor (1807-49), Political Writer — A587

2007, Sept. 18		Perf. 14x14¾
1758 A587 55c multi	1.40	1.40

Natural History Museum, Dublin, 150th Anniv. — A588

2007, Oct. 25	Litho.	Perf. 13¼
1759 A588 55c multi	1.40	1.40

Christmas — A589

Designs: No. 1760, Presentation in the Temple. No. 1761, Three Magi. No. 1762, Adoration of the Shepherds.

2007, Nov. 8		Perf. 14¾x14
1760 A589 55c multi	1.40	.80
1761 A589 78c multi	2.20	3.75

Self-Adhesive
Booklet Stamp
Size: 21x27mm
Serpentine Die Cut 11x11¼

1762 A589 55c multi	1.40	1.40
a. Booklet pane of 26	27.50	

No. 1762a sold for €13.75.

Charles Wesley (1707-88), Hymn Writer — A590

2007, Nov. 15		Perf. 14x14¾
1763 A590 78c multi	2.10	2.40

Bride and Groom — A591
Serpentine Die Cut 11¼

2008, Jan. 16	Litho.	
Booklet Stamp		
Self-Adhesive		
1764 A591 55c multi	1.40	1.60
a. Booklet pane of 10	8.75	

Greetings — A592
Serpentine Die Cut 11¼

2008, Jan. 16	Self-Adhesive	
Booklet Stamps		
1765 A592 55c Frog	1.40	1.55
1766 A592 55c Elephant	1.40	1.55
a. Booklet pane of 10, 5 each #1765-1766	11.00	

New Year 2008 (Year of the Rat) — A593

2008, Jan. 23		Perf. 14¾x14
1767 A593 78c multi	2.40	2.40
a. Souvenir sheet of 3	7.25	7.25

Liam Whelan (1935-58), Soccer Player Killed in Airplane Crash — A594

2008, Feb. 4		Perf. 13½x13¾
1768 A594 55c multi	2.20	1.55

St. Patrick's Day — A595

2008, Feb. 11		Perf. 13¼x13
1769 A595 78c multi	2.20	2.40

Flower Type of 2004

Designs: 20c, Thrift. 50c, Biting stonecrop. 82c, Sea aster.

2008, Mar. 3	Litho.	Perf. 14x14¾
Size: 20x23mm		
1770 A519 20c multi	.45	.45
1771 A519 50c multi	1.40	.85
1772 A519 82c multi	1.90	1.55
a. Booklet pane of 10	18.50	
Complete booklet, #1772a	18.50	
Nos. 1770-1772 (3)	3.75	2.85

Booklet Stamp
Self-Adhesive
Size: 21x25mm
Serpentine Die Cut 11x11¼

1773 A519 82c multi	3.00	3.00
a. Booklet pane of 10	28.50	

European Year of Intercultural Dialogue — A596

2008, Mar. 7		Perf. 13¼
1774 A596 55c multi	1.55	1.55

Hugh Lane, by Antonio Mancini — A597

2008, Mar. 28	Litho.	Perf. 13½
1775 A597 55c multi	1.55	1.55

Dublin City Gallery, cent. (founded by Lane).

Paintings by Paul Henry (1876-1958) — A598

Designs: No. 1776, A Connemara Village (left half, "Paul Henry" in blue). No. 1777, A Connemara Village (right half, "Paul Henry" in white). No. 1778, West of Ireland Landscape (left half, "Paul Henry" in gray at left). No. 1779, West of Ireland Landscape (right half, "Paul Henry" in gray at right).

2008, Apr. 17		Perf. 13¼
1776 A598 55c multi	1.30	1.40
1777 A598 55c multi	1.30	1.40
1778 A598 55c multi	1.30	1.40
1779 A598 55c multi	1.30	1.40
a. Horiz. strip of 4, #1776-1779	5.25	5.75
b. Booklet pane of 4, #1776-1779	4.00	
Complete booklet, 4 #1779b	16.00	

No. 1779b has example of No. 1779 with straight edge at right. The four examples of No. 1779b in the complete booklet have different margins. The complete booklet sold for €9.

Credit Union Movement, 50th Anniv. — A599

2008, Apr. 23		Perf. 14¾x14
1780 A599 55c multi	1.65	1.65

Intl. Year of Planet Earth — A600

Plasticine sculptures of Earth created by children: No. 1781, Africa and Europe, by Mohammed Rahman. No. 1782, South and North America, by Conor Reid.

2008, Apr. 28		Die Cut Perf.
Self-Adhesive		
1781 A600 55c red & multi	1.40	1.65
1782 A600 55c blue & multi	1.40	1.65
a. Horiz. pair, #1781-1782, on backing paper without back printing	2.80	
b. Booklet pane of 10, 5 each #1781-1782	11.00	

Institute of Creative Advertising and Design, 50th Anniv. — A601

2008, May 23		Perf. 13¼
1783 A601 55c multi	1.65	1.65

IRELAND

R. M. S. Leinster, 90th Anniv. of Sinking — A602

2008, May 30   **Perf. 14¾x14**
1784   A602   55c multi   2.20   1.65

Europa — A603

Designs: 55c, Boy writing letter. 82c, Girl writing letter.

2008, June 9   **Perf. 14x14¾**
1785   A603   55c multi   1.65   1.65
1786   A603   82c multi   2.20   2.20

Nos. 1785-1786 come printed in sheets of 10.

Tidy Towns Competition, 50th Anniv. — A604

2008, June 19
1787   A604   55c multi   1.65   1.65

Participation of Irish Defense Forces in UN Missions, 50th Anniv. — A605

2008, June 26   **Perf. 14¾x14**
1788   A605   55c multi   2.20   1.65

Movies Filmed in Ireland — A606

Designs: No. 1789, Kings. No. 1790, Cré na Cille. No. 1791, The Wind that Shakes the Barley. No. 1792, Garage.

2008, July 8   **Litho.**   **Perf. 14¾x14**
1789   A606   55c multi   1.20   1.15
1790   A606   55c multi   1.20   1.15
1791   A606   82c multi   1.40   1.70
1792   A606   82c multi   1.40   1.70
  a.   Booklet pane of 4, #1789-1792   5.75   —
     Complete booklet, 4 #1792a   22.50
  b.   Souvenir sheet of 4, #1789-1792   5.50   6.00
     Nos. 1789-1792 (4)   5.20   5.70

No. 1792b has a printed margin. The complete booklet, which sold for €12, contains 4 examples of No. 1792a, each with a different order of stamps and without a printed margin.

2008 Summer Olympics, Beijing — A607

Designs: 52c, Rowing. 82c, Shot put.

2008, July 15
1793   A607   55c multi   1.20   1.20
1794   A607   82c multi   1.55   1.90

Souvenir Sheet
Stamps Inscribed "Olympex 2008"
1795   Sheet of 2   3.75   3.75
  a.   A607 55c multi   1.45   1.45
  b.   A607 82c multi   2.20   2.20

Mushrooms — A608

Designs: No. 1796, Parasol. No. 1797, Orange birch bolete. 82c, Pink waxcap. 95c, Scarlet elfcup.

2008, Aug. 1   **Litho.**   **Perf. 14x14¾**
1796   A608   55c multi   1.40   1.40
1797   A608   55c multi   1.40   1.40
  a.   Horiz. pair, #1796-1797   2.80   2.80
1798   A608   82c multi   1.90   1.90
     Nos. 1796-1798 (3)   4.70   4.70

Souvenir Sheet
1799   A608   95c multi   3.85   4.50

First Transatlantic Cable Message From Europe to US, 150th Anniv. A609

2008, Aug. 15   **Perf. 13¼**
1800   A609   82c multi   2.75   2.40

Old Age Pensions Act, Cent. A610

2008, Sept. 19   **Litho.**   **Perf. 13¼**
1801   A610   55c multi   1.65   1.65

National University of Ireland, Cent. — A611

2008, Sept. 19   **Perf. 13½**
1802   A611   55c multi   1.65   1.50

Patrick Pearse (1879-1916), Patriot, and Founder of St. Enda's School — A612

Pearse and school buildings: No. 1803, Cullenswood House. No. 1804, The Hermitage.

2008, Sept. 25   **Perf. 14¾x14¼**
1803   A612   55c multi   1.50   1.50
1804   A612   55c multi   1.50   1.50

Irish Bands — A613

2008, Oct. 10   **Litho.**   **Perf. 13½**
1805   A613   55c   Planxty   1.30   1.40
1806   A613   55c   De Danann   1.30   1.40
1807   A613   82c   Tulla Ceili Band   1.65   1.80
1808   A613   82c   Bothy Band   1.65   1.80
  a.   Souvenir sheet, #1805-1808   6.00   7.00
     Nos. 1805-1808 (4)   5.90   6.40

Dancers — A614

2008, Nov. 7   **Litho.**   **Perf. 13½**
1809   A614   55c Irish dancer   1.75   1.75

Souvenir Sheet
1810   Sheet of 2, #1809, 1810a   3.85   4.15
  a.   A614 82c Flamenco dancer   2.30   2.50

See Spain No. 3609.

Christmas — A616

Creche figures: No. 1811, Flight into Egypt. 82c, Annunciation. No. 1813, Infant Jesus.

2008, Nov. 7   **Perf. 14¾x14**
1811   A615   55c multi   1.65   1.10
1812   A615   82c multi   2.10   2.50

Booklet Stamp
Self-Adhesive
Serpentine Die Cut 11x11¼
1813   A616   55c multi   1.40   1.40
  a.   Booklet pane of 26   27.50

No. 1813a sold for €13.75.

Flowers Type of 2004
Design: N, Yellow horned poppy.

Booklet Stamp
Self-Adhesive
Size: 17x21mm
Serpentine Die Cut 14

2008, Dec. 5   **Litho.**
1814   A519   N multi   2.40   2.40
  a.   Booklet pane of 10   22.25

No. 1814 sold for 55c on day of issue.

Eye — A617

Litho. & Embossed
2009, Jan. 23   **Perf. 14¼**
1815   A617   55c black   1.50   1.50

Louis Braille (1809-52), educator of the blind.

Love — A618

Die Cut Perf. 13¼
2009, Jan. 23   **Litho.**
Self-Adhesive
1816   A618   55c multi   1.50   1.50
  a.   Vert. pair on backing paper without back printing   3.00
  b.   Booklet pane of 10   15.00

All pairs from booklet pane are on backing paper with printing.

New Year 2009 (Year of the Ox) — A619

2009, Jan. 23   **Perf. 14¾x14**
1817   A619   82c multi   1.90   2.25
  a.   Souvenir sheet of 3   6.00   6.75

St. Patrick Climbs Croagh Patrick, by Margaret Clarke — A620

2009, Feb. 19   **Perf. 14x14¾**
1818   A620   82c multi   2.10   2.10

St. Patrick's Day.

Greetings — A621

Designs: No. 1819, Man lifting girl with letter to mailbox slot. No. 1820, Woman with letter, dog.

2009, Mar. 6   **Die Cut Perf. 12¾x13¼**
Self-Adhesive
1819   A621   55c multi   1.40   1.40
1820   A621   55c multi   1.40   1.40
  a.   Horiz. pair, #1819-1820, on backing paper withour back printing   2.80
  b.   Booklet pane of 10, 5 each #1819-1820, + 10 stickers   12.00

All pairs from booklet pane are on backing paper with printing.

Charles Darwin (1809-82), Naturalist — A622

2009, Mar. 20   **Perf. 13½**
1821   A622   82c multi   2.25   2.25

Scene from "The Playboy of the Western World" — A623

2009, Mar. 24   **Perf. 14x14¾**
1822   A623   55c multi   1.50   1.50

John Millington Synge (1871-1909), writer.

Irish Times Newspaper, Cent. A624

2009, Mar. 27   **Perf. 13¼**
1823   A624   55c multi   1.50   1.50

IRELAND

A625, A626

A627, A628

A629, A630

A631, A632

A633, A634

An Post, 25th Anniv.
A633   A634

Serpentine Die Cut 11x11¼

2009, Apr. 3   Litho.
Coil Stamps
Self-Adhesive
Size: 25x30mm

1824	A625 55c multi	2.00	2.00
1825	A626 55c multi	2.00	2.00
1826	A627 55c multi	2.00	2.00
1827	A628 55c multi	2.00	2.00
1828	A629 55c multi	2.00	2.00
a.	Vert. strip of 5, #1824-1828	10.00	
1829	A630 55c multi	2.00	2.00
1830	A631 55c multi	2.00	2.00
1831	A632 55c multi	2.00	2.00
1832	A633 55c multi	2.00	2.00
1833	A634 55c multi	2.00	2.00
a.	Vert. strip of 5, #1829-1833	10.00	
b.	Vert. strip of 10, #1824-1833	20.00	
	Nos. 1824-1833 (10)	20.00	20.00

Serpentine Die Cut 14

1834	Booklet pane of 10	17.50	
a.	A625 55c multi, 20x24mm	1.75	2.00
b.	A626 55c multi, 20x24mm	1.75	2.00
c.	A627 55c multi, 20x24mm	1.75	2.00
d.	A628 55c multi, 20x24mm	1.75	2.00
e.	A629 55c multi, 20x24mm	1.75	2.00
f.	A630 55c multi, 20x24mm	1.75	2.00
g.	A631 55c multi, 20x24mm	1.75	2.00
h.	A632 55c multi, 20x24mm	1.75	2.00
i.	A633 55c multi, 20x24mm	1.75	2.00
j.	A634 55c multi, 20x24mm	1.75	2.00

No. 1833b was only available in a full roll of 100 stamps. The philatelic bureau sold Nos. 1828a and 1833a as a convenience to collectors rather than No. 1833b.

Paintings by Francis Bacon (1909-92) — A635

Designs: 55c, Self-portrait. 82c, Artist's Studio.

2009, Apr. 24   Perf. 13½
1835 A635 55c multi   2.50 1.50
Souvenir Sheet
1836 A635 82c multi   6.00 5.50

James Larkin (1875-1947), Union Organizer — A636

2009, Apr. 30   Perf. 13¼
1837 A636 55c multi   1.40 1.40

Irish Transport and General Workers' Union, cent.

Volvo Ocean Race Stopover in Galway — A637

Designs: 55c, Green Dragon yacht. €3, Green Dragon and another yacht, vert.

2009, May 8   Perf. 13¾x14
1838 A637 55c multi   1.60 1.60
Souvenir Sheet
1839 A637 €3 multi   8.50 10.00

No. 1839 contains one 27x48mm stamp.

European Conference of Postal and Telecommunications Administrations, 50th Anniv. — A638

2009, May 15   Perf. 13¼
1840 A638 82c multi   2.20 2.20

Europa — A639

Designs: 55c, Crab Nebula. 82c, Jets from a brown dwarf.

2009, May 15
1841 A639 55c multi   1.60 1.60
1842 A639 82c multi   1.90 2.20

Intl. Year of Astronomy.

European Dog Show, Dublin — A640

2009, May 21   Die Cut Perf. 13x13¼
Self-Adhesive
1843 A640 55c multi   1.60 1.60
a. Horiz. pair on backing paper without back printing   3.25
b. Booklet pane of 10 #1843   15.00

City Status of Kilkenny, 400th Anniv. — A641

2009, June 16   Perf. 13½
1844 A641 55c multi   1.90 1.60

Anthony Trollope (1815-82), Writer — A642

2009, June 26   Perf. 14x14¾
1845 A642 82c multi   2.20 2.40

Birrell Land Act, Cent. — A643

2009, July 15   Perf. 13¼
1846 A643 82c multi   2.20 2.40

Composers — A644

Designs: No. 1847, Wolfgang Amadeus Mozart (1756-91). No. 1848, George Frideric Handel (1685-1759). No. 1849, Joseph Haydn (1732-1809). No. 1850, Frédéric Chopin (1810-49).

2009, Aug. 14   Perf. 13¼x13
1847	A644 55c multi	1.60	1.60
1848	A644 55c multi	1.60	1.60
a.	Horiz. pair, #1847-1848	3.25	3.25
1849	A644 82c multi	2.20	2.20
1850	A644 82c multi	2.20	2.20
a.	Horiz. pair, #1849-1850	4.50	4.50
b.	Souvenir sheet of 4, #1847-1850	8.25	8.25
c.	Booklet pane of 4, #1847-1850	5.50	
	Complete booklet, 4 #1850c	22.00	
	Nos. 1847-1850 (4)	7.60	7.60

On No. 1850b, stamps are at upper left with No. 1847 having straight edges at top and left, No. 1848 having straight edge at top and No. 1849 having straight edge at left. On No. 1850c, stamps are at right with Nos. 1848 and 1850 having straight edges at right. Complete booklet sold for €12 and contains four examples of No. 1850c, each with different margins.

Arthur Guinness (1725-1803), Founder of Guinness Brewery — A645

2009, Aug. 28   Perf. 14x14¾
1851 A645 82c multi   2.75 2.65

Guinness Brewery, 250th anniv.

Flower Type of 2004
Design: 82c, Sea aster.

2009, Aug. 7   *Serpentine Die Cut 14*
Booklet Stamp
Self-Adhesive
Size: 17x20mm
1852 A519 82c multi   3.00 3.00
a. Booklet pane of 10   26.50

Compare No. 1852 with No. 1773.

Plantation of Ulster, 400th Anniv. — A646

Designs: No. 1853, English text. No. 1854, Gaelic text.

2009, Sept. 4   Perf. 14¾x14
1853 A646 55c multi   1.60 1.60
1854 A646 55c multi   1.60 1.60
a. Horiz. pair, #1853-1854   3.20 3.20

Playwrights A647

Designs: No. 1855, Brian Friel. No. 1856, Tom Murphy. No. 1857, Frank McGuinness.

2009, Sept. 18
1855 A647 55c multi   1.35 1.50
1856 A647 55c multi   1.35 1.50
1857 A647 55c multi   1.35 1.50
Nos. 1855-1857 (3)   4.05 4.50

Dragonflies — A648

Designs: No. 1858, Large red damselfly. No. 1859, Irish bluet. 82c, Four-spotted chaser, horiz. 95c, Banded demoiselle, horiz.

2009, Oct. 16   Litho.   Perf. 14x14¾
1858 A648 55c multi   1.40 1.60
1859 A648 55c multi   1.40 1.60
a. Horiz. pair, #1858-1859   2.80 3.20
Perf. 14¾x14
1860 A648 82c multi   2.10 2.50
Nos. 1858-1860 (3)   4.90 5.70

Souvenir Sheet
Perf. 13¼
1861 A648 95c multi   4.65 4.65

No. 1861 contains one 60x25mm stamp.

Illustrations From Gospel Book, Monastery of Gamaghiel, Armenia A649

Virgin and Child, by Simon Bening A650

Christmas: No. 1862, Nativity. 82c, Annunciation.

2009, Nov. 6   Perf. 14¾x14
1862 A649 55c multi   1.75 .75
1863 A649 82c multi   2.50 3.25

Booklet Stamp
Self-Adhesive
Serpentine Die Cut 11x11¼
1864 A650 55c multi   1.55 1.55
a. Booklet pane of 26   31.00

No. 1864a sold for €13.75.

Flowers Type of 2004
Design: Large-flowered butterwort.

Serpentine Die Cut 14
2009, Oct. 16   Litho.
Booklet Stamp
Self-Adhesive
Size: 17x21mm
1865 A519 55c multi   1.65 1.65
a. Booklet pane of 10   16.50

Compare with No. 1728.

IRELAND

Douglas Hyde (1860-1949), First President of Ireland — A651

2010, Jan. 21	Litho.	Perf. 14x14¾
1866	A651 55c multi	1.40 1.40

Lovebirds — A652

2010, Jan. 21		Die Cut Perf. 13¼
		Self-Adhesive
1867	A652 55c multi	1.50 1.50
a.	Vert. pair on backing paper without back printing	3.20
b.	Booklet pane of 10	13.25

Greetings — A653

Designs: No. 1868, Girl astronaut in spaceship, birthday cake. No. 1869, Boy astronaut, heart.

		Die Cut Perf. 13¼x12¾
2010, Jan. 28		Self-Adhesive
1868	A653 55c multi	1.90 1.90
1869	A653 55c multi	1.90 1.90
a.	Vert. pair, #1868-1869, on backing paper without back printing	3.75
b.	Booklet pane of 10, 5 each #1868-1869 + 10 stickers	17.50

New Year 2010 (Year of the Tiger) — A654

2010, Feb. 11		Perf. 13¼
1870	A654 82c multi	2.25 2.25
a.	Souvenir sheet of 3	6.75 6.75

St. Patrick's Day — A655

2010, Feb. 18		Perf. 14x14¾
1871	A655 82c multi	2.25 2.25

President's Award, 25th Anniv. — A656

2010, Mar. 11	Litho.	Perf. 13¼
1872	A656 55c multi	1.40 1.40

Irish Countrywoman's Association, Cent. — A657

2010, Mar. 25		
1873	A657 55c multi	1.40 1.40

Crosses — A658

Designs: No. 1874, Monasterboice Cross, County Louth. No. 1875, Carndonagh Cross, County Donegal. No. 1876, Drumcliffe Cross, County Sligo. No. 1877, Ahenny Cross, County Tipperary.

2010, Apr. 8		
1874	A658 55c black	1.50 1.50
1875	A658 55c black	1.50 1.50
1876	A658 55c black	1.50 1.50
1877	A658 55c black	1.50 1.50
a.	Horiz. strip of 4, #1874-1877	6.00 6.00
	Nos. 1874-1877 (4)	6.00 6.00

Europa — A659

Scenes from children's books: 55c, The Happy Prince, by Oscar Wilde. 82c, Gulliver's Travels, by Jonathan Swift.

2010, May 6		
1878	A659 55c multi	1.40 1.30
1879	A659 82c multi	2.10 2.20

Nos. 1878-1879 were printed in sheets of 10.

Máirtín O Direáin (1910-88), Poet — A660

2010, May 27		Perf. 14¾x14
1880	A660 55c multi	1.40 1.40

Paintings by Roderic O'Conor (1860-1940) — A661

Designs: No. 1881, The Breton Girl (shown). No. 1882, Self-portrait.

2010, May 27		Perf. 13¼
1881	A661 55c multi	1.60 1.60
1882	A661 55c multi	1.60 1.60

Humanitarians — A662

Designs: No. 1883, Mother Teresa (1910-97), 1979 Nobel Laureate for Peace. No. 1884, Henry Dunant (1828-1910), founder of the Red Cross, 1901 Nobel Laureate for Peace.

2010, June 17		
1883	A662 55c multi	1.90 1.90
1884	A662 55c multi	1.90 1.90
a.	Horiz. pair, #1883-1884	3.90 3.90

Fashion Designers — A663

Work of Irish designers: No. 1885, Paul Costelloe. No. 1886, Louise Kennedy. No. 1887, Lainey Keogh. No. 1888, John Rocha. No. 1889, Philip Treacy. No. 1890, Orla Kiely.

	Litho. & Embossed	
2010, July 15		Perf. 13¼
1885	A663 55c multi	2.25 2.40
a.	Booklet pane of 3	3.25
1886	A663 55c multi	2.25 2.40
a.	Booklet pane of 3	3.25
1887	A663 55c multi	2.25 2.40
a.	Horiz. strip of 3, #1885-1887	4.50 4.50
b.	Booklet pane of 3	3.25
1888	A663 82c multi	2.75 2.75
a.	Booklet pane of 3	4.75
1889	A663 82c multi	2.75 2.75
a.	Booklet pane of 3	4.75
1890	A663 82c multi	2.75 2.75
a.	Horiz. strip of 3, #1888-1890	5.50 5.50
b.	Booklet pane of 3	4.75
	Complete booklet, #1885a, 1886a, 1887b, 1888a, 1889a, 1890b	24.00
	Nos. 1885-1890 (6)	15.00 15.45

Complete booklet sold for €13.

Birds — A664

2010, July 29	Litho.	Perf. 13¼
1891	A664 55c Buzzard	1.50 1.50
1892	A664 55c Golden eagle	1.50 1.50
a.	Horiz. pair, #1891-1892	3.00 3.00
1893	A664 82c Peregrine falcon	2.25 2.25
1894	A664 95c Merlin	2.50 2.50
a.	Souvenir sheet, #1891-1894	7.75 7.75
	Nos. 1891-1894 (4)	7.75 7.75

Romeo and Juliet (Vignette of Sweden No. 1141) — A665

	Litho. & Engr.	
2010, Aug. 26		Perf. 12¾
1895	A665 55c multi	2.00 1.50

Stamp engraving work of Czeslaw Slania. Joint issue between Ireland and Sweden. See Sweden No. 2642.

Irish Wheelchair Association, 50th Anniv. — A666

2010, Sept. 8	Litho.	Perf. 14¾x14
1896	A666 55c multi	1.40 1.40

Showbands A667

Designs: No. 1897, The Miami Showband. No. 1898, The Drifters Showband. No. 1899, The Royal Showband. No. 1900, The Freshmen.

2010, Sept. 23		Perf. 13½
1897	A667 55c multi	1.20 1.20
1898	A667 55c multi	1.20 1.20
1899	A667 82c multi	1.70 1.70
1900	A667 82c multi	1.70 1.70
a.	Souvenir sheet of 4, #1897-1900	6.50 7.50
b.	Booklet pane of 4, #1897-1900	5.50 —
	Complete booklet, 4 #1900b	22.00
	Nos. 1897-1900 (4)	7.50 7.50

On No. 1900a, stamps are not near the edge of the sheet and stamps have perforations on all four sides. On No. 1900b, Nos. 1898 and 1900 are at the right side of the sheet and have a straight edge at right. The complete booklet sold for €12 and contains four examples of No. 1900b, each with different margins.

Ireland Automobile Association, Cent. — A668

2010, Oct. 14		Perf. 14¾x14
1901	A668 55c multi	1.60 1.40

Irishmen Involved With Chilean Independence — A669

Designs: No. 1902, Commander General John Mackenna (1771-1814). No. 1903, Supreme Director Bernardo O'Higgins (1778-1842).

2010, Oct. 28		Perf. 13¼
1902	A669 82c multi	3.00 2.75
1903	A669 82c multi	3.00 2.75
a.	Horiz. pair, #1902-1903	6.00 5.50

See Chile No. 1562.

Christmas — A670

A670

Stained-glass windows from churches in Roscommon: No. 1904, Holy Family. 82c, Joseph and Mary.

2010, Nov. 4		Perf. 13¼
1904	A670 55c multi	1.75 1.10
1905	A670 82c multi	2.25 2.20
	Self-Adhesive	
	Serpentine Die Cut 11¼x11	
1906	A671 55c multi	1.60 1.60
a.	Vert. pair on backing paper without printing on back	3.25
b.	Booklet pane of 26 #1906	31.00

No. 1906b sold for €13.75 and all stamps have printing on the back of the backing paper.

Bride and Groom — A672

2011, Jan. 20		Die Cut Perf. 13¼
		Self-Adhesive
1907	A672 55c multi	1.30 1.35
a.	Horiz. pair on backing paper without printing on back	3.00
b.	Booklet pane of 10	10.00

IRELAND

Tulips A673

Balloons A674

2011, Jan. 27   *Die Cut Perf. 13¼x13*
Self-Adhesive
1908	A673	55c multi	1.20	1.50
1909	A674	55c multi	1.20	1.50
a.	Vert. pair, #1908-1909 on backing paper without printing on back		3.00	
b.	Booklet pane of 10, 5 each #1908-1909, + 10 stickers		11.00	

American Chamber of Commerce, Ireland, 50th Anniv. — A675

2011, Feb. 3   *Perf. 14x14¾*
1910	A675	55c multi	1.50	1.50

Pres. Cearbhall O Dáleaigh (Carroll O'Daly) (1911-78) — A676

2011, Feb. 10   *Perf. 13¾*
1911	A676	55c multi	1.50	1.50

St. Patrick's Day — A677

2011, Feb. 17   *Perf. 14¼x14¾*
1912	A677	82c multi	2.20	2.40

A678

Women's Rights — A679

2011, Mar. 3   *Perf. 13¼*
1913	A678	55c multi	1.40	1.40
1914	A679	82c multi	1.75	1.90

Irish Amateur Boxing Association, Cent. — A680

2011, Apr. 14   *Litho.*   *Perf. 14¾x14*
1915	A680	55c multi	1.40	1.40

Europa — A681

Designs: 55c, Girl under tulip tree, Knockabbey Gardens. 82c, River Walk, Avondale Forest Park.

2011, May 5
1916	A681	55c multi	1.40	1.20
1917	A681	82c multi	1.90	2.40
	Intl. Year of Forests.			

Year of Craft — A682

Craft object made of: No. 1918, Ceramics, by Deirdre McLoughlin. No. 1919, Glass, by Róisín de Buitléar. No. 1920, Metal, by Inga Reed. No. 1921, Textiles, by Helen McAllister. No. 1922, Wood, by Liam Flynn.

2011, May 12   *Perf. 13¼*
Booklet Stamps
1918	A682	55c multi	1.15	1.35
a.	Booklet pane of 3		3.50	
1919	A682	55c multi	1.15	1.35
a.	Booklet pane of 3		3.50	
1920	A682	55c multi	1.15	1.35
a.	Booklet pane of 3		3.50	
1921	A682	55c multi	1.15	1.35
a.	Booklet pane of 3		3.50	
1922	A682	55c multi	1.15	1.35
a.	Booklet pane of 3		3.50	
	Complete booklet, #1918a, 1919a, 1920a, 1921a, 1922a		17.50	
b.	Booklet pane of 5, #1918-1922		6.75	—
	Complete booklet, #1922b		6.75	—
	Nos. 1918-1922 (5)		5.75	6.75

National Parks — A683

Designs: No. 1923, Ballycroy National Park. No. 1924, The Burren National Park. No. 1925, Connemara National Park. No. 1926, Glenveagh National Park. No. 1927, Killarney National Park. No. 1928, Wicklow Mountains National Park.

2011, June 6   *Perf. 14¾x14*
1923	A683	55c multi	1.40	1.40
a.	Booklet pane of 3		3.25	
1924	A683	55c multi	1.40	1.40
a.	Booklet pane of 3		3.25	
1925	A683	55c multi	1.40	1.40
a.	Booklet pane of 3		3.25	
b.	Horiz. strip of 3, #1923-1925		4.80	4.80
c.	Souvenir sheet of 3, #1923-1925		4.80	4.80
1926	A683	82c multi	1.90	2.25
a.	Booklet pane of 3		4.75	
1927	A683	82c multi	1.90	2.25
a.	Booklet pane of 3		4.75	
1928	A683	82c multi	1.90	2.25
a.	Booklet pane of 3		4.75	
	Complete booklet, #1923a, 1924a, 1925a, 1926a, 1927a, 1928a		24.00	
b.	Horiz. strip of 3, #1926-1928		7.25	7.25
c.	Souvenir sheet of 3, #1926-1928		7.25	7.25
	Nos. 1923-1928 (6)		9.90	10.95
	Complete booklet sold for €13.			

Amnesty International, 50th Anniv. — A684

2011, June 30   *Perf. 13½*
1929	A684	55c multi	1.40	1.40

Hermit Crab — A685

Serpentine Die Cut 14
2011, June 22   *Litho.*
Booklet Stamp
Self-Adhesive
1930	A685	55c multi	2.20	2.20
a.	Booklet pane of 10		20.00	
b.	Die cut perf. 14		2.20	
c.	Booklet pane of 10 #1930b		20.00	
	Issued: No. 1930b, 5/1/12.			

Renewable Energy — A686

Designs: No. 1931, House with solar panels. No. 1932, Ardnacrusha Hydroelectric Station. No. 1933, Wind turbines. No. 1934, Ocean Energy Development Unit. No. 1935, Field of rape flowers for biofuel.

Die Cut Perf. 13¼x13
2011, Aug. 5   *Litho.*
Self-Adhesive
1931	A686	55c multi	1.60	1.60
a.	Booklet pane of 3		5.25	
1932	A686	55c multi	1.60	1.60
a.	Booklet pane of 3		5.25	
1933	A686	55c multi	1.60	1.60
a.	Booklet pane of 3		5.25	
1934	A686	55c multi	1.60	1.60
a.	Booklet pane of 3		5.25	
1935	A686	55c multi	1.60	1.60
a.	Booklet pane of 3		5.25	
	Complete booklet, #1931a, 1932a, 1933a, 1934a, 1935a		17.50	
b.	Booklet pane of 10, 2 each #1931-1935		16.00	
c.	Horiz. strip of 5, #1931-1935, on backing paper without back printing		8.00	
	Nos. 1931-1935 (5)		8.00	8.00
	Complete booklet sold for €9.			

Horses — A687

Designs: No. 1936, Colored horse. No. 1937, Irish draft horse. No. 1938, Thoroughbred. No. 1939, Connemara pony.

2011, Sept. 1   *Litho.*   *Perf. 13¼*
1936	A687	55c multi	1.50	1.50
1937	A687	55c multi	1.50	1.50
1938	A687	55c multi	1.50	1.50
1939	A687	55c multi	1.50	1.50
a.	Block of 4, #1936-1939		6.00	6.00
b.	Souvenir sheet of 4, #1936-1939		6.00	6.00
	Nos. 1936-1939 (4)		6.00	6.00

2011 Solheim Cup Women's Golf Tournament, Killeen Castle Golf Course, Dunsany — A688

2011, Sept. 15   *Perf. 14¾x14¼*
1940	A688	55c multi	1.65	1.40

Wildlife — A689

Coil Stamps
Serpentine Die Cut 11x11¼
2011, Sept. 29   **Self-Adhesive**
1941	A689	55c Red squirrel	2.20	2.20
1942	A689	55c Bottlenose dolphin	2.20	2.20
a.	Vert. pair, #1941-1942		4.50	4.50

Brian O'Nolan (1911-66), Writer — A690

2011, Oct. 6   *Perf. 13¾*
1943	A690	55c multi	1.40	1.40

Christmas — A691

Serpentine Die Cut 11x11¼
2011, Nov. 10
Self-Adhesive
1944	A691	55c multi	1.65	.85
a.	Horiz. pair on backing paper without back printing		3.25	
b.	Booklet pane of 26		25.00	
	No. 1944b sold for €13.75.			

Television Broadcasting in Ireland, 50th Anniv. — A692

Designs: No. 1945, Gay Byrne hosting *The Late Late Show*. No. 1946, Emma O'Driscoll and puppet on children's show *Hubble*. No. 1947, Newscaster Anne Doyle.

2011, Nov. 24   *Perf. 14¾x14*
1945	A692	55c multi	1.10	1.10
1946	A692	55c multi	1.10	1.10
1947	A692	55c multi	1.10	1.10
a.	Horiz. strip of 3, #1945-1947		3.30	3.30
	Nos. 1945-1947 (3)		3.30	3.30

Bride, Groom and Limousine — A693

2012, Jan. 19   *Die Cut Perf. 13¼*
Self-Adhesive
1948	A693	55c multi	1.40	1.40
a.	Vert. pair on backing paper without printing on back		2.75	
b.	Booklet pane of 10		8.75	

Gift A694

Birthday Candles A695

Die Cut Perf. 12¾x13½
2012, Jan. 26   **Self-Adhesive**
1949	A694	55c multi	1.40	1.10
1950	A695	55c multi	1.40	1.10
a.	Horiz. pair, #1949-1950, on backing paper without printing on back		2.75	
b.	Booklet pane of 10, 5 each #1949-1950 + 10 stickers		8.75	

Ireland's Chairmanship of Organization for Security and Cooperation in Europe — A696

2012, Feb. 2   *Perf. 13½x13¼*
1951	A696	55c multi	1.40	1.40

St. Patrick's Day — A697

2012, Feb. 9   *Perf. 14x14¾*
1952	A697	82c multi	2.25	2.25

Dancer From Fabulous Beast Dance Theater A698

IRELAND

Dancers From Dance Theater of Ireland — A699

Dancer From Irish Modern Dance Theater — A700

Dancer from CoisCéim Dance Theater — A701

2012, Mar. 22 Die Cut Perf. 13¼ Litho.
Booklet Stamps
Self-Adhesive
1953 A698 55c multi 1.40 1.15
1954 A699 55c multi 1.40 1.15
1955 A700 55c multi 1.40 1.15
1956 A701 55c multi 1.40 1.15
  a. Block of 4, #1953-1956 5.60
  b. Booklet pane of 8, 2 each #1953-1956 11.50
Nos. 1953-1956 (4) 5.60 4.60

Sinking of the Titanic, Cent. — A702

Designs: No. 1957, Thomas Andrews, shipbuilder in charge of construction of the Titanic, and Titanic under construction. No. 1958, Father Frank Browne, amateur photographer and passenger on Titanic from Southampton to Cork, and Titanic off Cobh. No. 1959, Edward John Smith, ship's captain, and Titanic. No. 1960, Molly Brown, passenger, and Titanic's staircase.

2012, Apr. 12 Perf. 13¼
1957 A702 55c multi 1.75 1.75
1958 A702 55c multi 1.75 1.75
  a. Horiz. pair, #1957-1958 3.50 3.50
1959 A702 82c multi 2.75 2.75
1960 A702 82c multi 2.75 2.75
  a. Horiz. pair, #1959-1960 5.50 5.50
  b. Booklet pane of 4, #1957-1960 9.75 —
Complete booklet, 4 #1960b 26.50
Nos. 1957-1960 (4) 9.00 9.00

On No. 1960b, Nos. 1958 and 1960 are at the right side of the pane and have a straight edge at right. The complete booklet sold for €12 and contains four examples of No. 1960b, each with different pane margins.

Bram Stoker (1847-1912), Writer — A703

Designs: No. 1961, Stoker. No. 1962, Count Dracula biting woman's neck.

2012, Apr. 19 Perf. 14x14¾
1961 A703 55c multi 1.35 1.35
1962 A703 55c multi 1.35 1.35
  a. Horiz. pair, #1961-1962 2.75 2.75
  b. Souvenir sheet of 2, #1961-1962 2.75 2.75

Europa — A704

Designs: 55c, Little Skellig Island. 82c, Ha'penny Bridge, Dublin.

2012, May 3 Perf. 13½
1963 A704 55c multi 1.50 1.50
1964 A704 82c multi 2.25 2.25

50th Intl. Eucharistic Congress, Dublin — A705

Designs: 55c, Chalice and host. 82c, Monstrance and host.

2012, June 7 Perf. 14x14¾
1965 A705 55c multi 1.10 .85
1966 A705 82c multi 1.90 2.20

Volvo Ocean Race — A706

Designs: 55c, Sailboats. €3, Sailboats, diff., vert.

2012, June 14 Perf. 14¾x14¼
1967 A706 55c multi 1.65 1.65
Souvenir Sheet
1968 A706 €3 multi 8.75 8.75
No. 1968 contains one 28x48mm stamp.

Common Frog — A707

2012, May 1 Die Cut Perf. 14x14¼
Booklet Stamp
Self-Adhesive
1969 A707 82c multi 3.00 3.00
  a. Booklet pane of 10 27.50

Dublin Fire Brigade, 150th Anniv. — A708

Designs: No. 1970, Firefighter carrying baby. No. 1971, Firefighters in chemical suits. No. 1972, Firefighters at car accident. No. 1973, Firefighter rescuing drowning man.

2012, June 28 Perf. 13¼
1970 A708 55c multi 1.40 1.40
  a. Booklet pane of 4 6.25 6.25
1971 A708 55c multi 1.40 1.40
  a. Booklet pane of 4 6.25 6.25
1972 A708 55c multi 1.40 1.40
  a. Booklet pane of 4 6.25 6.25
1973 A708 55c multi 1.40 1.40
  a. Booklet pane of 4 6.25 6.25
    Complete booklet, #1970a, 1971a, 1972a, 1973a 25.00
  b. Horiz. strip of 4, #1970-1973 5.60 5.60
Nos. 1970-1973 (4) 5.60 5.60

Nos. 1970a-1973a each have straight edge at right. Complete booklet sold for €10.

Science — A709

Designs: No. 1974, Conference Center, Dublin, molecular structure of DNA. No. 1975, Robert Boyle (1627-91), chemist and physicist, formula and graph of Boyle's Law.

2012, July 5
1974 A709 55c multi 1.60 1.80
1975 A709 55c multi 1.60 1.80
  a. Horiz. pair, #1974-1975 3.25 3.75
  b. Souvenir sheet of 2, #1974-1975 4.25 4.75

2012 City of Science Festival, Dublin (No. 1974); Boyle's Law, 350th anniv. (No. 1975).

2012 Summer Olympics, London — A710

Emblem of 2012 Summer Olympics and: 55c, Stylized winner's platform. 82c, Vertical bars.

2012, July 19 Perf. 14x14¾
1976 A710 55c multi 1.00 1.00
1977 A710 82c multi 1.75 1.90

Myths and Legends — A711

Designs: No. 1978, The Children of Lir (swans in flight). No. 1979, Deirdre of the Sorrows (couple embracing). No. 1980, Fionn Mac Cumhaill (man in water, fish). No. 1981, Setanta (Setanta swinging hurling stick at dog).

2012, Sept. 13 Perf. 14¾x14¼ Litho.
1978 A711 55c multi 1.10 1.10
1979 A711 55c multi 1.10 1.10
  a. Horiz. pair, #1978-1979 2.25 2.25
1980 A711 82c multi 2.10 1.90
1981 A711 82c multi 2.10 1.90
  a. Horiz. pair, #1980-1981 4.20 4.00
Nos. 1978-1981 (4) 6.40 6.00

Barnardos Ireland Children's Charity, 50th Anniv. — A712

2012, Oct. 11 Perf. 13¼
1982 A712 55c multi 1.40 1.40

Christmas — A713

2012, Nov. 8 Serpentine Die Cut 11x11¼ Self-Adhesive
1983 A713 55c multi 1.40 .85
  a. Horiz. pair on backing paper without back printing 2.80
  b. Booklet pane of 26 25.00

No. 1983b sold for €13.75.

Irish Presidency of Council of the European Union — A714

2013, Jan. 17 Perf. 14x14¾
1984 A714 55c multi 1.50 1.50

The Gathering Ireland 2013 Tourism Initiative — A715

2013, Jan. 24 Perf. 13¼
1985 A715 82c multi 2.25 1.90

St. Patrick's Day — A716

2013, Feb. 7 Perf. 14¾x14
1986 A716 82c multi 2.25 1.90

Bride and Groom Lighting Candles — A717

2013, Feb. 14 Die Cut Perf. 13¼
Self-Adhesive
1987 A717 N multi 2.40 2.20
  a. Vert. pair on backing paper without back printing 4.75
  b. Booklet pane of 10 24.00

No. 1987 sold for 55c on day of issue.

Greetings A718 A719

2013, Mar. 7 Die Cut Perf. 12¾x13½
Booklet Stamps
Self-Adhesive
1988 A718 N multi 1.90 .85
1989 A719 N multi 1.90 .85
  a. Booklet pane of 10, 5 each #1988-1989, + 10 stickers 17.50

On day of issue, Nos. 1988-1989 each sold for 55c.

Daffodil — A720

2013, Mar. 21 Perf. 14¾x14
1990 A720 N multi 1.40 1.40

Irish Cancer Society, 50th anniv. No. 1990 sold for 55c on day of issue.

Wildlife A721 A722

Designs: No. 1991, Golden eagle. No. 1992, Red deer. No. 1993, Goldfinch. 90c, Beadlet anemone, horiz.

IRELAND

Serpentine Die Cut 11x11¼
2013, Apr. 2
Coil Stamps
Self-Adhesive
1991	A721 60c multi	2.20	2.20
1992	A721 60c multi	2.20	2.20
a.	Vert. pair, #1991-1992	4.40	4.95

Booklet Stamps
Serpentine Die Cut 14
1993	A722 60c multi	2.20	2.20
a.	Booklet pane of 10	20.00	
1994	A722 90c multi	3.00	3.00
a.	Booklet pane of 10	27.50	
	Nos. 1991-1994 (4)	9.60	9.60

Contemporary Arts — A723

No. 1995: a, Doors and Sunlight, painting by Stephen McKenna. b, Ghost Ship, painting by Dorothy Cross. c, The Fall, performance art by Amanda Coogan. d, Smoke Tree, virtual sculpture by John Gerrard.

2013, Apr. 25 — *Perf. 14¼*
1995	Booklet pane of 4	6.50	
a.-d.	A723 60c Any single	1.60	1.60
	Complete booklet, #1995	6.50	

See No. 2027.

Europa — A724

Designs: 60c, Postman pushing cart, postman on bicycle. 90c, Postman and van.

2013, May 2 — *Perf. 14¾x14*
| 1996 | A724 60c multi | 1.50 | 1.35 |
| 1997 | A724 90c multi | 2.20 | 2.10 |

Description of Dublin by Eoin Moore — A725

2013, May 16 — *Litho.*
| 1998 | A725 60c yel & blk | 1.60 | 1.60 |

Selection of Dublin in 2010 as UNESCO City of World Literature.

State Visit to Ireland of Pres. John F. Kennedy, 50th Anniv. — A726

Photographs of Pres. Kennedy: 60c, With distant relative at Kennedy ancestral home in Dunganstown. 90c, Placing wreath on graves of victims of Easter Rising.

2013, June 6 — *Perf. 13½x13¼*
| 1999 | A726 60c multi | 1.30 | 1.10 |
| 2000 | A726 90c multi | 2.75 | 1.90 |

Port of Cork — A727

Designs: No. 2001, Container ship and tugboat. No. 2002, Sailboats. 90c, Cruise liner.

2013, July 17 — *Perf. 14¾x14*
2001	A727 60c multi	1.50	1.50
2002	A727 60c multi	1.50	1.50
a.	Horiz. pair, #2001-2002	3.00	3.00
2003	A727 90c multi	2.30	2.30
a.	Souvenir sheet of 3, #2001-2003	5.50	6.50
	Nos. 2001-2003 (3)	5.30	5.30

General Lockout, Cent. A728

Photographs of lockout and: No. 2004, Jim Larkin (1876-1947), trade union leader. No. 2005, James Connolly (1868-1916), founder of Irish Socialist Party. No. 2006, Countess Constance Markievicz (1868-1927), socialist leader.

2013, Aug. 22 — *Perf. 13¼*
2004	A728 60c multi	1.60	1.60
a.	Booklet pane of 3	4.00	
2005	A728 60c multi	1.60	1.60
a.	Booklet pane of 3	4.00	
2006	A728 60c multi	1.60	1.60
a.	Horiz. strip of 3, #2004-2006	4.80	4.80
b.	Booklet pane of 3 #2006	4.00	
c.	Booklet pane of 3, #2004-2006	4.00	
	Complete booklet, #2004a, 2005a, 2006b, 2 #2006c	20.00	
	Nos. 2004-2006 (3)	4.80	4.80

Complete booklet sold for €10 and contains two examples of No. 2006c with different margins.

Irish Defense Forces A729

Designs: No. 2007, Helicopter. No. 2008, Troops and helicopter. No. 2009, Ships. No. 2010, Soldier and United Nations tank.

2013, Sept. 12
2007	A729 60c multi	1.60	1.60
a.	Booklet pane of 4	5.00	
2008	A729 60c multi	1.60	1.60
a.	Booklet pane of 4	5.00	
2009	A729 60c multi	1.60	1.60
a.	Booklet pane of 4	5.00	
2010	A729 60c multi	1.60	1.60
a.	Block of 4, #2007-2010	6.25	6.25
b.	Booklet pane of 4 #2010	5.00	
	Complete booklet, #2007a, 2008a, 2009a, 2010b	20.00	

Complete booklet sold for €10. The bottom two stamps in each booklet pane have straight edges at bottom.

Integrated Ireland — A730

Designs: No. 2011, Oriental woman in police uniform. No. 2012, Black transit employee and tram. No. 2013, Young black and white hurlers. No. 2014, White woman near window.

2013, Sept. 26 — *Perf. 14¾x14*
2011	A730 60c multi	1.35	1.45
2012	A730 60c multi	1.35	1.45
a.	Horiz. pair, #2011-2012	2.75	3.00
2013	A730 90c multi	1.65	2.00
2014	A730 90c multi	1.65	2.00
a.	Horiz. pair, #2013-2014	3.50	5.00
	Nos. 2011-2014 (4)	6.00	6.90

Irish Volunteer Force, Cent. A731

2013, Oct. 3 — *Perf. 13¼*
| 2015 | A731 60c black & green | 1.60 | 1.60 |

Contemporary Architecture — A732

Designs: No. 2016, Lewis Glucksman Gallery, Cork. No. 2017, Cork Institute of Technology. No. 2018, Fingal County Hall, Swords. No. 2019, Croke Park, Dublin.

2013, Oct. 17 — *Litho.* — *Perf. 13¼x13½*
2016	A732 60c multi	1.25	1.25
2017	A732 60c multi	1.25	1.25
a.	Horiz. pair, #2016-2017	2.50	2.50
2018	A732 90c multi	1.75	1.75
2019	A732 90c multi	1.75	1.75
a.	Horiz. pair, #2018-2019	3.50	3.50
b.	Souvenir sheet of 4, #2016-2019	6.00	6.00
	Nos. 2016-2019 (4)	6.00	6.00

Christmas — A733

Serpentine Die Cut 11x11¼
2013, Nov. 7 — *Litho.*
Self-Adhesive
2020	A733 60c multi	1.10	.85
a.	Horiz. pair on backing paper without back printing	2.25	
b.	Booklet pane of 26	25.00	

No. 2020b sold for €15.

Irish Citizen Army, Cent. A734

2014, Jan. 23 — *Litho.* — *Perf. 13¼*
| 2021 | A734 60c multi | 750.00 | 925.00 |

No. 2021 was quickly withdrawn from sale on day of issue after questions were raised as to whether the correct image of Captain Jack White was actually shown on the stamp.

Greetings — A735

Designs: No. 2022, Robot and alien creature shaking hands. No. 2033, Robots and birthday cake.

Die Cut Perf. 13¼x13
2014, Jan. 30 — *Litho.*
Booklet Stamps
Self-Adhesive
2022	A735 60c multi	1.10	1.10
2023	A735 60c multi	1.10	1.10
a.	Booklet pane of 10, 5 each #2022-2023, + 10 stickers	10.00	

Rose — A736

Die Cut Perf. 13¼x13
2014, Feb. 13 — *Litho.*
Booklet Stamp
Self-Adhesive
2024	A736 60c multi	1.60	.85
a.	Vert. pair on backing paper without back printing	3.20	
b.	Booklet pane of 10	16.00	

See No. 2039.

St. Patrick's Day — A737

2014, Feb. 20 — *Litho.* — *Perf. 14x14¾*
| 2025 | A737 90c multi | 1.90 | 1.65 |

Brendan Behan (1923-64), Writer — A738

Perf. 14¼x14¾
2014, Mar. 20 — *Litho.*
| 2026 | A738 60c multi | 1.65 | 1.65 |

Contemporary Arts Type of 2013

No. 2027: a, Maesta, painting by Sean Scully. b, Light Receiver, sculpture by Eilis O'Connell. c, Patterned Behavior, painting by Diana Copperwhite. d, Chaplet, photograph by Alice Maher.

2014, Mar. 27 — *Litho.* — *Perf. 14¼*
2027	Booklet pane of 4	5.25	5.25
a.-d.	A723 60c Any single	1.30	1.30
	Complete booklet, #2027	5.25	

Cumann na mBan (Auxiliary of Irish Volunteers), Cent. — A739

2014, Apr. 3 — *Litho.* — *Perf. 14¼*
| 2028 | A739 60c sepia | 1.35 | 1.35 |

Irish Citizen Army, Cent. A740

2014, Apr. 17 — *Litho.* — *Perf. 13¼*
| 2029 | A740 60c sepia | 1.35 | 1.35 |

See note under No. 2021.

Viking Heritage — A741

Designs: No. 2030, Waterford Kite brooch. No. 2031, Sword.

2014, Apr. 24 — *Litho.* — *Perf. 13¼*
2030	A741 60c multi	1.60	1.60
2031	A741 60c multi	1.60	1.60
a.	Horiz. pair, #2030-2031	3.25	3.25

Europa — A742

Musical instruments: 60c, Bodhrán (drum). 90c, Harp.

2014, May 8 — *Litho.* — *Perf. 13¼*
| 2032 | A742 60c multi | 1.35 | .90 |
| 2033 | A742 90c multi | 1.90 | 2.50 |

Home Rule Act, Cent. — A743

2014, May 22 — *Litho.* — *Perf. 13¼*
| 2034 | A743 60c multi | 1.65 | 1.40 |

Bloom Garden Festival, Dublin A744

Designs: No. 2035, Garden. No. 2036, Woman holding box of vegetables.

IRELAND

2014, May 22   Litho.   Perf. 13¼
2035	A744	60c multi	1.60	1.85
2036	A744	60c multi	1.60	1.85
a.	Horiz. pair, #2035-2036		3.25	3.75
b.	Souvenir sheet of 2, #2035-2036		3.75	4.50

World Flower Show, Dublin — A745

X-ray photograph of Phalaenopsis orchid with denomination at: No. 2037, LR. No. 2038, UR.

2014, June 12   Litho.   Perf. 13¼
2037	A745	60c multi	1.60	1.50
2038	A745	60c multi	1.60	1.50
a.	Horiz. pair, #2037-2038		3.25	3.75
b.	Souvenir sheet of 2, #2037-2038		4.50	4.75

Rose Type of 2014
Die Cut Perf. 13¼x13

2014, July 21   Litho.
Self-Adhesive
With White Frame
2039	A736	68c multi	1.65	1.35
a.	Vert. pair on backing paper without back printing		3.30	
b.	Booklet pane of 10		16.50	

Wildlife   A746   A747

Designs: No. 2040, Black-legged kittiwake. No. 2041, Green crab. No. 2042, Cushion star. €1, Fireworks anemone.

Serpentine Die Cut 11x11¼

2014, July 21   Litho.
Coil Stamps
Self-Adhesive
2040	A746	68c multi	2.20	2.20
2041	A746	68c multi	2.20	2.20
a.	Vert. pair, #2040-2041		4.95	

Booklet Stamps
Serpentine Die Cut 14
2042	A747	68c multi	2.20	2.20
a.	Booklet pane of 10		20.00	
2043	A747	€1 multi	3.25	3.25
a.	Booklet pane of 10		27.50	

World War I, Cent. — A748

Recruiting posters with slogan at bottom: 68c, "Join an Irish Regiment Today." €1, "The Real Irish Spirit."

2014, July 24   Litho.   Perf. 13¼
2044	A748	68c multi	1.50	1.40
2045	A748	€1 multi	2.75	2.75

Irish Prison Service A749

Designs: No. 2046, Prison guards on patrol. No. 2047, Prisoner polishing bowl. No. 2048, Prisoner cleaning graffiti. No. 2049, Teacher with prisoners.

2014, Aug. 7   Litho.   Perf. 13¼
2046	A749	68c multi	1.50	1.50
2047	A749	68c multi	1.50	1.50
2048	A749	68c multi	1.50	1.50
2049	A749	68c multi	1.50	1.50
a.	Block of 4, #2046-2049		6.00	6.00
	Nos. 2046-2049 (4)		6.00	6.00

Seamus Heaney (1939-2013), 1995 Nobel Laureate in Literature — A750

2014, Aug. 28   Litho.   Perf. 13¾
| 2050 | A750 | 68c multi | 1.65 | 1.30 |

Cats — A751

Designs: No. 2051, Maine Coon cat. No. 2052, Burmese cat. No. 2053, British Shorthair cat. No. 2054, Persian cat.

2014, Sept. 4   Litho.   Perf. 13¼
2051	A751	68c multi	1.55	1.55
a.	Booklet pane of 4		6.50	
2052	A751	68c multi	1.55	1.55
a.	Booklet pane of 4		6.50	
2053	A751	68c multi	1.55	1.55
a.	Booklet pane of 4		6.50	
2054	A751	68c multi	1.55	1.55
a.	Block of 4, #2051-2054		6.50	7.00
b.	Booklet pane of 4		6.50	
	Complete booklet, #2051a, 2052a, 2053a, 2054b		26.50	

Complete booklet sold for €12. The stamps on the right side of each booklet pane have a straight edge at the right.

Thomas Davis (1814-45), Poet and Newspaper Publisher — A752

2014, Oct. 9   Litho.   Perf. 14¼x14¾
| 2055 | A752 | 68c blk & bl grn | 1.50 | 1.50 |

Electronic Game Screens and Characters — A753

Designs: No. 2056, Pac-Man. b, Space Invaders. c, Sonic the Hedgehog. d, Mario.

2014, Oct. 16   Litho.   Perf. 13¾x13½
2056	A753	68c multi	1.60	1.60
2057	A753	68c multi	1.60	1.60
2058	A753	68c multi	1.60	1.60
2059	A753	68c multi	1.60	1.60
a.	Block of 4, #2056-2059		6.50	6.50
	Nos. 2056-2059 (4)		6.40	6.40

Christmas — A754

Serpentine Die Cut 11x11¼

2014, Nov. 6   Litho.
Self-Adhesive
2060	A754	68c multi	1.40	1.20
a.	Horiz. pair on backing paper without printing on back		3.00	
b.	Booklet pane of 26		33.00	

No. 2060b sold for €17.

Circles and Squares in Dots A755

Rocket A756

2015, Jan. 7   Litho.   Perf. 14¼x14¾
2061	A755	68c multi	1.60	1.35
2062	A756	68c multi	1.60	1.60
a.	Horiz. pair, #2061-2062		3.20	3.20

Trinity College Science Gallery, Dublin (No. 2061), BT Young Scientist Exhibition (No. 2062).

Northern Ireland Peace Talks Between Seán Lemass (1899-1971) and Terence O'Neill (1914-90), 50th Anniv. A757

2015, Jan. 22   Litho.   Perf. 13¼x13½
| 2063 | A757 | 68c black | 1.50 | 1.50 |

Love — A758

Serpentine Die Cut 9x10¾

2015, Feb. 12   Litho.
Self-Adhesive
2064	A758	N multi	2.20	2.20
a.	Vert. pair on backing paper without printing on back		4.50	
b.	Booklet pane of 10		16.50	

No. 2064 sold for 68c on day of issue.

St. Patrick's Day — A759

Perf. 13½x13¼

2015, Feb. 26
| 2065 | A759 | €1 org & grn | 2.25 | 2.25 |

Animation Production in Ireland — A760

No. 2066: a, Roy. b, Give Upu Yer Aul Sins. c, The Secret of Kells. d, Nelly and Nora.

2015, Mar. 20   Litho.   Perf. 13¼x13
2066	A760	Sheet of 4	6.00	6.00
a.-d.	68c Any single		1.25	1.25
e.	Booklet pane of 4, #2066a-2066d		6.00	—
	Complete booklet, 4 #2066e		20.00	

The complete booklet sold for €12 and contains four examples of No. 2066e with different margins.

Battle of Gallipoli, Cent. — A761

Designs: 68c, Irish soldiers in trench. €1, Troop ship SS River Clyde.

2015, Apr. 23   Litho.   Perf. 13¼
2067	A761	68c multi	1.60	1.20
2068	A761	€1 multi	2.25	2.25

Sinking of the RMS Lusitania, Cent. — A762

Designs: 68c, Torpedo approaching RMS Lusitania. €1, RMS Lusitania listing.

2015, May 7   Litho.   Perf. 14¼x14
2069	A762	68c multi	1.90	1.20
2070	A762	€1 multi	2.25	2.50
a.	Souvenir sheet of 2, #2069-2070		3.75	3.75

Europa — A763

2015, May 14   Litho.   Perf. 14x14¼
2071	A763	68c Toy truck	1.40	.85
2072	A763	€1 Teddy bear	2.40	2.75

Mountain Rescue Ireland, 50th Anniv. — A764

Designs: No. 2073, Resucers hanging on rock face with litter. No. 2074, Rescuers carrying litter.

2015, June 4   Litho.   Perf. 14x14¼
2073	A764	68c multi	1.65	1.35
2074	A764	68c multi	1.20	1.40
a.	Horiz. pair, #2073-2074		3.25	3.75

William Butler Yeats (1865-1939), Poet — A765

2015, June 11   Litho.   Perf. 14x14¼
| 2075 | A765 | 68c black | 1.50 | 1.50 |

Wildlife   A766   A767

Designs: No. 2076, Mute swan. No. 2077, Great spotted woodpecker. No. 2078, Red fox. €1.05, Otter.

Serpentine Die Cut 11x11¼

2015, July 1   Litho.
Coil Stamps
Self-Adhesive
2076	A766	70c multi	2.20	2.20
2077	A766	70c multi	2.20	2.20
a.	Vert. pair, #2076-2077		4.40	

Booklet Stamps
Serpentine Die Cut 14
2078	A767	70c multi	2.40	2.40
a.	Booklet pane of 10		20.00	

IRELAND

2079	A767	€1.05 multi	3.85	3.85
a.		Booklet pane of 10 + 10 etiquettes		33.00

Food Production — A768

Designs: No. 2080, Rancher and steaks. No. 2081, Cheese maker and cheese. No. 2082, Fisherman, lobsters and fish. No. 2083, Farmer, bowl of cereal and fruit.

2015, July 16   Litho.   Perf. 13¼x13½

2080	A768	70c multi	1.50	1.25
2081	A768	70c multi	1.50	1.25
a.		Horiz. pair, #2080-2081	3.00	2.50
2082	A768	€1.05 multi	1.75	1.85
2083	A768	€1.05 multi	1.75	1.85
a.		Horiz. pair, #2082-2083	3.50	3.75
b.		Souvenir sheet of 4, #2080-2083	6.50	6.50
		Nos. 2080-2083 (4)	6.50	6.20

Speech of Patrick Pearse at Gravesite of Jeremiah O'Donovan Rossa, Cent. — A769

2015, July 30   Litho.   Perf. 13¼x13½

2084	A769	70c black	1.60	1.60

Toiletry Cabinet and Screen — A770

Transat Chair — A771

Adjustable Table — A772

Cabinet With Pivoting Drawers — A773

2015, Aug. 13   Litho.   Perf. 13¼

2085	A770	70c multi	1.20	1.20
2086	A771	70c multi	1.20	1.20
2087	A772	70c multi	1.20	1.20
2088	A773	70c multi	1.20	1.20
a.		Block of 4, #2085-2088	4.80	4.80
b.		Booklet pane of 4, #2085-2088	5.00	—
		Complete booklet, 4 #2088b	20.00	
		Nos. 2085-2088 (4)	4.80	4.80

Furniture designed by Eileen Gray (1878-1976). The complete booklet sold for €12 and contains four examples of No. 2088b with different margins.

Five Senses — A774

Senses: 70c, Taste. €1.05, Touch. €1.25, Vision. €1.70, Hearing. €2.80, Smell.

Litho., Litho. & Thermography (€1.70)

2015, Sept. 10   Perf. 13½

2089	A774	70c pink & blk	1.00	1.00
2090	A774	€1.05 org & blk	1.90	1.90
2091	A774	€1.70 blue & blk	2.85	2.85
2092	A774	€2.80 bl grn & blk	4.75	4.75

Self-Adhesive
On Plastic Film
Serpentine Die Cut 11

2093	A774	€1.25 white & blk	1.90	1.90
		Nos. 2089-2093 (5)	12.40	12.40

No. 2089 has strawberry-flavored gum. Portions of the design on No. 2090 was printed with thermochromic ink, which changes color when warmed. Gritty crystals are embedded in the film covering the ear on No. 2091. No. 2092 is impregnated with a mint scent.

St. Columban (c. 543-615), Missionary A775

2015, Oct. 22   Litho.   Perf. 14¼x14

2094	A775	€1.05 multi	2.40	2.20

Madonna and Child, by Marco Palmezzano — A776

Serpentine Die Cut 11x11¼

2015, Nov. 5   Litho.
Self-Adhesive

2095	A776	70c multi	1.20	1.20
a.		Horiz. pair on backing paper without back printing	2.50	
b.		Booklet pane of 26	27.50	

Christmas. No. 2095b sold for €17.50.

Irish Republic Flag A777

Proclamation of the Irish Republic A778

Easter Rising at General Post Office, Sackville Street, Dublin A779

Roger Casement (1864-1916), Rebellion Leader A780

Serpentine Die Cut 11¼x11

2016, Jan. 21   Litho.
Coil Stamps
Self-Adhesive

2096	A777	70c multi	1.60	1.20
2097	A778	70c multi	1.60	1.20
a.		Horiz. pair, #2096-2097	3.20	

Booklet Stamps
Serpentine Die Cut 14

2098	A779	70c multi	1.60	1.20
a.		Booklet pane of 10	15.00	
2099	A780	€1.05 multi	2.20	1.75
a.		Booklet pane of 10 + 10 etiquettes	20.00	

Easter Rising, Cent.

Irish Heart Foundation, 50th Anniv. — A781

2016, Jan. 28   Litho.   Perf. 13¼x13½

2100	A781	70c multi	2.20	1.40

Love — A782

Serpentine Die Cut 9x10¾

2016, Feb. 11   Litho.
Self-Adhesive

2101	A782	N multi	2.20	1.40
a.		Vert. pair on paper without back printing	4.50	
b.		Booklet pane of 10	16.50	

No. 2101 sold for 70c on day of issue.

St. Patrick's Day — A783

2016, Feb. 25   Litho.   Perf. 14¼

2102	A783	€1.05 multi	2.25	2.25

Dogs — A784

Designs: No. 2103, Irish wolfhound. No. 2104, Irish red setter. No. 2105, Sheepdog. No. 2106, Kerry Blue terrier.

2016, Mar. 10   Litho.   Perf. 14x14¼

2103	A784	70c multi	1.40	1.40
2104	A784	70c multi	1.40	1.40
2105	A784	70c multi	1.40	1.40
2106	A784	70c multi	1.40	1.40
a.		Block of 4, #2103-2106	6.00	6.00
b.		Souvenir sheet of 4, #2103-2106	7.00	7.00
		Nos. 2103-2106 (4)	5.60	5.60

Miniature Sheet

Easter Rising, Cent. A785

No. 2107: a, Executed Republican revolutionaries Thomas James Clarke (facing forward, wearing glasses) (1858-1916), Seán MacDiarmada (1883-1916) and Eammon Ceannt (1881-1916). b, Executed Republican revolutionaries Patrick Henry Pearse (facing right, without glasses) (1879-1916), Joseph Mary Plunkett (1887-1916) and Thomas MacDonagh (1878-1916). c, James Connolly (1869-1916), executed Republican revolutionary, Starry Plow flag. d, Irish Republic flag. e, Police Constable James O'Brien (1868-1916) and Sean Connolly, (1883-1916) rebel, first casualties of Easter Rising. f, Michael Malone (1888-1916) participant in Battle of Mount Street Bridge and brother, William Malone, soldier killed at Battle of Ypres. g, Dr. Kathleen Lynn (1874-1955) and Elizabeth O'Farrell (1894-1957), nurse. h, Rebels Jack Doyle and Tom McGrath. i, Proclamation of the Irish Republic. j, Seán Foster (1914-16), youngest child killed in Eater Rising. k, Louisa Nolan, recipient of British Military Medal for tending to wounded. l, Sir Francis Fletcher-Vane (1861-1934), British officer who exposed murders of unarmed civilians, and Francis Sheehy-Skeffington (1878-1916), civilian summarily executed by British. m, Easter Rising at General Post Office, Sackville Street. n, Children gathering firewood. o, Two prisoners at Richmond Barracks and British soldier. p, Roger Casement (1864-1916), rebellion leader.

2016, Mar. 24   Litho.   Perf. 13½

2107	A785	Sheet of 16	16.00	26.00
a.-p.		70c Any single	1.60	1.60
q.		Souvenir sheet of 4, #2107a-2107d	5.25	8.50
r.		Souvenir sheet of 4, #2107e-2107h	5.25	8.50
s.		Souvenir sheet of 4, #2107i-2107l	5.25	8.50
t.		Souvenir sheet of 4, #2107m-2107p	5.25	8.50

Nos. 2107q-2107t were sold together as a set in a folder for €15.

Charles Gavan Duffy (1816-1903), Writer, Prime Minister of Victoria — A786

2016, Apr. 7   Litho.   Perf. 14x14¼

2108	A786	70c multi	1.90	1.90

Europa — A788
A787

2016, May 12   Litho.   Perf. 13½

2109	A787	70c multi	1.60	.85
2110	A788	€1.05 multi	3.25	3.25

Think Green Issue.

Battle of the Somme, Cent. — A789

2016, June 23   Litho.   Perf. 13½

2111	A789	W multi	3.25	3.25

No. 2111 sold for €1.05 on day of issue.

Police Constable James O'Brien (1868-1916) and Sean Connolly (1883-1916) A790

Michael and William Malone A791

Dr. Kathleen Lynn (1874-1955) and Elizabeth O'Farrell (1894-1957), Nurse A792

Rebels Jack Doyle and Tom McGrath A793

Serpentine Die Cut 11¼x11

2016, July 21   Litho.
Coil Stamps
Self-Adhesive

2112	A790	72c multi	1.60	1.20
2113	A791	72c multi	1.60	1.20
a.		Horiz. pair, #2112-2113	3.20	

Booklet Stamps
Serpentine Die Cut 14

2114	A792	72c multi	1.60	1.20
a.		Booklet pane of 10	15.00	
2115	A793	€1.10 multi	2.20	1.75
a.		Booklet pane of 10 + 10 etiquettes	20.00	

Easter Rising, cent.

Wild Atlantic Way — A794

IRELAND

Designs: No. 2116, Horse riding at Grange. No. 2117, Fly fishing at Glenbeg Lough. No. 2118, Cycling on the Aran Islands. No. 2119, Surfing at Inch.

2016, July 28   Litho.   Perf. 13¼
2116	A794	72c multi	1.35	1.35
a.		Booklet pane of 4	4.75	—
2117	A794	72c multi	1.35	1.35
a.		Horiz. pair, #2116-2117	3.20	3.20
b.		Booklet pane of 4	4.75	
2118	A794	€1.10 multi	1.55	1.55
a.		Booklet pane of 4	7.50	
2119	A794	€1.10 multi	1.55	1.55
a.		Horiz. pair, #2118-2119	4.00	4.00
b.		Booklet pane of 4	7.50	
		Complete booklet, #2116a, 2117b, 2118a, 2119b	25.00	
		Nos. 2116-2119 (4)	5.80	5.80

Complete booklet sold for €15. See Nos. 2228, 2232.

Store Fronts — A795

Designs: No. 2120, Vibes & Scribes Arts and Hobby Shop, Cork. No. 2121, The Winding Stair Bookstore, Dublin. No. 2122, Clerke Grocery Store, Skibbereen. No. 2123, Thomas Moran Souvenir Shop, Westport.

2016, Aug. 18   Litho.   Perf. 12x12¼
2120	A795	72c multi	1.35	1.35
2121	A795	72c multi	1.35	1.35
a.		Horiz. pair, #2120-2121	3.20	3.20
2122	A795	€1.10 multi	1.65	1.65
2123	A795	€1.10 multi	1.65	1.65
a.		Horiz. pair, #2122-2123	4.75	4.75
		Nos. 2120-2123 (4)	6.00	6.00

A796

A797

A798

Cycling — A799

2016, Sept. 15   Litho.   Perf. 13¼
2124	A796	72c multi	1.50	1.50
2125	A797	72c multi	1.50	1.50
2126	A798	72c multi	1.50	1.50
2127	A799	72c multi	1.50	1.50
a.		Block of 4, #2124-2127	6.40	6.40
b.		Souvenir sheet of 4, #2124-2127	6.40	6.40
		Nos. 2124-2127 (4)	6.00	6.00

Commissioners of Irish Lights — A800

Designs: No. 2128, Crane moving buoy. No. 2129, Helicopter and Fanad lighthouse. No. 2130, Computerized navigational technology. No. 2131, ILV Granuaile near lighthouse.

2016, Oct. 6   Litho.   Perf. 13¼x13½
2128	A800	72c multi	1.50	1.50
2129	A800	72c multi	1.50	1.50
2130	A800	72c multi	1.50	1.50
2131	A800	72c multi	1.50	1.50
a.		Block of 4, #2128-2131	6.40	6.40
b.		Booklet pane of 4, #2128-2131	5.75	—
		Complete booklet, 4 #2131b	22.50	
		Nos. 2128-2131 (4)	6.00	6.00

Complete booklet sold for €13, and contains four examples of No. 2131b, each with a different pane margin.

Christmas — A801

2016, Nov. 3   Serpentine Die Cut 11x11¼   Litho.
2132	A801	72c multi	1.40	1.20
a.		Horiz. pair on backing paper without back printing	2.80	
b.		Booklet pane of 26	28.50	

No. 2132b sold for €18.

Artifacts
A802   A803

Designs: No. 2133, Castlederg bronze cauldron, 700-600 B.C. No. 2134, Armlet, 362-175 B.C. No. 2135, Gold disc, 2200-2000 B.C. No. 2136, Gleninsheen gold gorget, c. 800-700 B.C.

2017, Jan. 12   Serpentine Die Cut 11¼   Litho.
Coil Stamps
Self-Adhesive
2133	A802	N multi	1.60	1.20
2134	A802	N multi	1.60	1.20
a.		Vert. pair, #2133-2134	3.20	3.20

Booklet Stamps
Serpentine Die Cut 14
2135	A803	N multi	1.40	1.20
a.		Horiz. pair on paper without back printing	2.80	
b.		Booklet pane of 10	18.50	
2136	A803	W multi	2.20	1.75
a.		Horiz. pair on paper without back printing	4.40	
b.		Booklet pane of 10 + 10 etiquettes	20.00	

On day of issue, Nos. 2133-2135 each sold for 72c, and No. 2136 sold for €1.10.

Love — A804

2017, Feb. 2   Serpentine Die Cut 9x10¾   Litho.
Self-Adhesive
2137	A804	N gold	1.60	1.20
a.		Horiz. pair on paper without back printing	3.20	
b.		Booklet pane of 10	10.00	

No. 2137 sold for 72c on day of issue.

Japanese Noh Mask and Signature of William Butler Yeats (1865-1939), Writer — A805

2017, Feb. 9   Litho.   Perf. 13¼
Stamp With White Frame
2138	A805	W blk, red, gold	2.20	1.75

Souvenir Sheet
Stamps Without White Frame
2138A	A805	W multi	3.25	3.25

No. 2138 sold for €1.10 on day of issue.

St. Patrick's Day — A806

2017, Feb. 23   Litho.   Perf. 13¼
2139	A806	W emerald	2.20	2.20

No. 2139 sold for €1.10 on day of issue.

Emojis and "Don't Worry" — A807

Emojis and "Be Happy" — A808

2017, Mar. 16   Litho.   Perf. 13¼
2140	A807	N multi	1.60	1.20
2141	A808	N multi	1.60	1.20
a.		Horiz. pair, #2140-2141	3.20	3.20

On day of issue Nos. 2140-2141 each sold for 72c.

Royal Sites in Ireland
A809

Designs: No. 2142, Hill of Tara, County Meath. No. 2143, Eamhain Mhacha (Navan Fort), County Armagh. No. 2144, Rathcroghan, County Roscommon. No. 2145, Rock of Cashel, County Tipperary.

2017, Apr. 20   Litho.   Perf. 13¼
2142	A809	N multi	2.00	2.00
2143	A809	N multi	2.00	2.00
2144	A809	N multi	2.00	2.00
2145	A809	N multi	2.00	2.00
a.		Block of 4, #2142-2145	8.25	8.25
		Nos. 2142-2145 (4)	8.00	8.00

On day of issue, Nos. 2142-2145 each sold for €1. See No. 2229.

Europa — A810

Castles: €1, Dublin Castle. €1.35, King John's Castle, Limerick.

2017, May 4   Litho.   Perf. 13¼x13½
2146	A810	€1 multi	2.25	2.25
2147	A810	€1.35 multi	2.75	2.75

Lions Clubs International, Cent. A811

2017, June 1   Litho.   Perf. 13¼
2148	A811	€1.35 multi	2.75	2.75

Battle of Messines Ridge, Cent. — A812

2017, June 8   Litho.   Perf. 13¼
2149	A812	€1.35 multi	2.75	2.75

Thomas Francis Meagher (1823-67), American Civil War Brigadier General and Acting Territorial Governor of Montana — A813

2017, June 29   Litho.   Perf. 14x14¼
2150	A813	€1 multi	2.25	2.25

2017 Women's Rugby World Cup, Dublin and Belfast, Northern Ireland — A814

2017, July 13   Litho.   Perf. 13¼
2151	A814	€1 multi	2.25	2.25

Railroad Stations A815

Designs: No. 2152, Heuston Station. No. 2153, Clarke Station. No. 2154, Kent Station. No. 2155, Bagenalstown Station.

2017, July 20   Litho.   Perf. 13¼
2152	A815	€1 multi	1.65	1.65
2153	A815	€1 multi	1.65	1.65
2154	A815	€1 multi	1.65	1.65
2155	A815	€1 multi	1.65	1.65
a.		Block of 4, #2152-2155	7.00	7.00
b.		Souvenir sheet of 4, #2152-2155	7.00	7.00
		Nos. 2152-2155 (4)	6.60	6.60

Francis Ledwidge (1887-1917), Poet — A816

2017, July 27   Litho.   Perf. 14x14¼
2156	A816	€1 multi	2.20	1.90

John Mary "Jack" Lynch (1917-99), Hurler and Taoiseach of Ireland — A817

2017, Aug. 10   Litho.   Perf. 14x14¼
2157	A817	€1 multi	2.20	2.20

Free Secondary School Education, 50th Anniv. — A818

2017, Sept. 7   Litho.   Perf. 13¼
2158	A818	€1 multi	2.20	2.20

National Plowing Championships — A819

Designs: No. 2159, Tractor plowing field. No. 2160, Horse-drawn plow.

2017, Sept. 14   Litho.   Perf. 13¼
2159	A819	€1 multi	1.75	1.75
2160	A819	€1 multi	1.75	1.75
a.		Horiz. pair, #2159-2160	3.50	3.50
b.		Souvenir sheet of 2, #2159-2160	3.50	3.50

IRELAND

Urban Street Art — A820

Art by: No. 2161, Conor Harrington. No. 2162, Fin DAC. No. 2163, James Earley. No. 2164, Maser.

2017, Sept. 21   Litho.   Perf. 14x14¼
2161	A820	€1 multi	1.75	1.75
2162	A820	€1 multi	1.75	1.75
2163	A820	€1 multi	1.75	1.75
2164	A820	€1 multi	1.75	1.75
a.		Horiz. strip of 4, #2161-2164	6.00	6.00
b.		Booklet pane of 4, #2161-2164	6.25	—
		Complete booklet 4 #2164b	25.00	
		Nos. 2161-2164 (4)	7.00	7.00

Complete booklet contains four examples of No. 2164b, each with a different pane margin. See No. 2230.

Ernesto "Che" Guevara (1928-67), Cuban Revolutionary and Government Minister — A821

2017, Oct. 5   Litho.   Perf. 14x14¼
| 2165 | A821 | €1 red & black | 2.75 | 2.75 |

Postcrossing A822

2017, Oct. 5   Litho.   Perf. 13¼
| 2166 | A822 | €1.35 multi | 2.10 | 2.10 |

Apparition of the Virgin Mary at Fatima, Portugal, Cent. — A823

2017, Oct. 12   Litho.   Perf. 13¼
| 2167 | A823 | €1.35 multi | 2.10 | 2.10 |

Christmas — A824

Serpentine Die Cut 11x11¼
2017, Nov. 2   Self-Adhesive   Litho.
2168	A824	€1 multi	1.65	1.40
a.		Horiz. pair on paper without back printing	3.30	
b.		Booklet pane of 26	35.00	

No. 2168b sold for €25.

General Post Office, Dublin, 200th Anniv. — A825

2018, Jan. 11   Litho.   Perf. 13¼x13½
| 2169 | A825 | €1 multi | 1.75 | 1.75 |

Sir Alfred Chester Beatty (1875-1968), Philanthropist and Art Collector A826

Birth of the Virgin, by Simon Bening A827

Shah Jahan, by Bichitr A828

Allusions to the Seven Lucky Gods, by Yashima Gakutei A829

2018, Jan. 18   Litho.   Perf. 13¼
2170	A826	€1 multi	1.75	1.75
2171	A827	€1 multi	1.75	1.75
2172	A828	€1 multi	1.75	1.75
2173	A829	€1 multi	1.75	1.75
a.		Horiz. strip of 4, #2170-2173	7.25	7.25
b.		Souvenir sheet of 4, #2170-2173	7.25	7.25
		Nos. 2170-2173 (4)	7.00	7.00

See No. 2234.

Artifacts A830   A831

Designs: N, Paten, 8th-9th cent. W, Donore handle, 700-720.

Serpentine Die Cut 14
2018, Jan. 25   Booklet Stamps   Self-Adhesive   Litho.
2174	A830	N multi	2.20	1.75
a.		Horiz. pair on paper without back printing	4.40	
b.		Booket pane of 10	20.00	
2175	A831	W multi	2.50	2.10
a.		Horiz. pair on paper without back printing	5.00	
b.		Booklet pane of 10 + 10 etiquettes	22.50	

On day of issue, No. 2174 sold for €1; No. 2175, for €1.35.

Artifacts A832   A833

Designs: No. 2176, Corleck head, 1st-2nd cent. No. 2177, Ballindery brooch, c. 600.

Serpentine Die Cut 11x11¼
2018, Jan. 25   Coil Stamps   Self-Adhesive   Litho.
2176	A832	N multi	2.50	1.75
2177	A833	N multi	2.50	1.75
a.		Vert. pair, #2176-2177	5.00	

On day of issue, Nos. 2176-2177 each sold for €1.

Love — A834

Serpentine Die Cut 13
2018, Feb. 8   Booklet Stamp   Self-Adhesive   Litho.
| 2178 | A834 | N red | 2.20 | 1.75 |
| a. | | Booklet pane of 10 | 13.50 | |

No. 2178 sold for €1 on day of issue.

St. Patrick's Day — A835

2018, Feb. 22   Litho.   Perf. 13¼
| 2179 | A835 | €1.35 gold & multi | 2.40 | 2.20 |

John Redmond (1856-1918), Politician — A836

2018, Mar. 1   Litho.   Perf. 14x14¼
| 2180 | A836 | €1 multi | 2.20 | 2.20 |

Irish National Teachers' Organization, 150th Anniv. — A837

Perf. 13½x13¼
2018, Mar. 22   Litho.
| 2181 | A837 | €1 multi | 1.75 | 1.75 |

Dr. Martin Luther King, Jr. (1929-68), Civil Rights Leader — A838

Nelson Mandela (1918-2013), President of South Africa — A839

2018, Apr. 5   Litho.   Perf. 13½
2182	A838	W black	3.25	3.25
2183	A839	W black	3.25	3.25
a.		Horiz. pair, #2182-2183	6.50	6.50

On day of issue Nos. 2182-2183 each sold for €1.50.

Europa — A840

Designs: €1, Mizen Head Footbridge. €1.50, Boyne Viaduct.

2018, May 3   Litho.   Perf. 13½
| 2184 | A840 | €1 multi | 1.90 | 1.40 |
| 2185 | A840 | €1.50 multi | 3.00 | 2.75 |

See No. 2233.

Society of Uilleann Pipers, 50th Anniv. — A841

2018, May 24   Litho.   Perf. 14x14¼
| 2186 | A841 | €1 multi | 2.20 | 2.20 |

St. Kevin (498 ?-618) A842

2018, May 31   Litho.   Perf. 13¼
| 2187 | A842 | €1 multi | 2.20 | 2.20 |

Bees — A843

Designs: No. 2188, Garden bumblebee. No. 2189, Tawny mining bee. No. 2190, Ashy mining bee. No. 2191, Heather bee.

2018, July 12   Litho.   Perf. 13
2188	A843	€1 gold & multi	2.25	2.25
2189	A843	€1 gold & multi	2.25	2.25
2190	A843	€1 gold & multi	2.25	2.25
2191	A843	€1 gold & multi	2.25	2.25
a.		Horiz. strip of 4, #2188-2191	9.00	9.00
b.		Souvenir sheet of 4, #2188-2191	9.00	9.00
		Nos. 2188-2191 (4)	9.00	9.00

See No. 2231.

2018 World Meeting of Families Congress, Dublin — A844

Designs: €1, Pope Francis. €1.50, Family and dog.

2018, July 26   Litho.   Perf. 13½
2192	A844	€1 multi	2.75	1.40
2193	A844	€1.50 multi	2.75	2.75
a.		Souvenir sheet of 2, #2192-2193	5.50	5.50

Royal Dublin Society — A845

Emblem of the Royal Dublin Society and: No. 2194, Entrance to Society Showgrounds. No. 2195, Show jumping. No. 2196, Hand holding bowl. No. 2197, Child looking at science display.

2018, Aug. 2   Litho.   Perf. 13¼
2194	A845	€1 multi	1.75	1.75
2195	A845	€1 multi	1.75	1.75
2196	A845	€1 multi	1.75	1.75
2197	A845	€1 multi	1.75	1.75
a.		Block of 4, #2194-2197	8.25	8.25
		Nos. 2194-2197 (4)	7.00	7.00

Scientific Discoveries — A846

Designs: No. 2198, New form of light wave, discovered by Center for Adaptive Nanostructures and Nanodevices Institute. No. 2199, Mackerel bacteria that kills superbugs, discovered by APC Microbiome Institute. No. 2200, Emission adsorption, discovered by University of Limerick. No. 2201, Neonatal seizures recognition, discovered by Irish Center for Fetal and Neonatal Translational Research.

IRELAND

2018, Sept. 6	Litho.	Perf. 13¼		
2198	A846	€1 multi	1.75	1.75
a.	Booklet pane of 3		5.50	—
2199	A846	€1 multi	1.75	1.75
a.	Booklet pane of 3		5.50	
2200	A846	€1 multi	1.75	1.75
a.	Booklet pane of 3		5.50	
2201	A846	€1 multi	1.75	1.75
a.	Booklet pane of 3		5.50	
	Complete booklet, #2198a, 2199a, 2200a, 2201a		22.50	
b.	Block of 4, #2198-2201		8.25	8.25
	Nos. 2198-2201 (4)		7.00	7.00

Complete booklet sold for €13.

Sinking of the RMS Leinster, Cent. — A847

2018, Oct. 10	Litho.	Perf. 13¼		
2202	A847	€1.50 multi	2.75	2.75

See No. 2235.

Popular Democracy — A848

Designs: No. 2203, Pres. Eamon de Valera (1882-1975). No. 2204, Hanna Sheehy-Skeffington (1877-1946), suffragette.

2018, Oct. 18	Litho.	Perf. 13¼		
2203	A848	€1 multi	2.25	1.75
2204	A848	€1 multi	2.25	1.75
a.	Horiz. pair, #2203-2204		4.50	4.50

Star of Bethlehem A849

Holiday Foods A850

Family, Christmas Tree and Television A851

People at Airport A852

Child Holding Christmas Stocking A853

People Near Church A854

Nativity Scene A855

Elf A856

Serpentine Die Cut 10¾x11¼
2018, Nov. 1		Litho.		
		Self-Adhesive		
2205	A849	50c multi	1.10	.90
2206	A850	€1 multi	2.20	1.75
2207	A851	€1 multi	2.20	1.75
2208	A852	€1 multi	2.20	1.75
2209	A853	€1 multi	2.20	1.75
a.	Horiz. pair, #2208-2209 on backing paper without back printing		4.50	
2210	A854	€1 multi	2.20	1.75
2211	A855	€1 multi	2.20	1.75
a.	Booklet pane of 22, 4 each #2205, 2210, 2211, 3 each #2206, 2207, 2 each #2208, 2209		35.00	
b.	Booklet pane of 6, #2206, 2207, 2210, 2211, 2 #2205		10.00	

Die Cut Perf. 13x13¼ Syncopated
2212	A856	€1 multi	3.75	3.75
	Nos. 2205-2212 (8)		18.05	15.15

Christmas. No. 2211a sold for €19. No. 2212 was printed in a sheet of six that was sold together with six picture postcards in a package that sold for €9.95.

End of World War I, Cent. A857

Lines from: No. 2213, "In Flanders Fields," poem by John McCrae. No. 2214, "To My Daughter Betty, the Gift of God," poem by Thomas Kettle.

2018, Nov. 8	Litho.	Perf. 13¼		
2213	A857	€1.50 red & black	3.00	3.00
2214	A857	€1.50 dk grn & bl grn	3.00	3.00
a.	Horiz. pair, #2213-2214		6.00	6.00

A858

First Public Meeting of Dáil Eireann (Assembly of Ireland), Cent. A859

2019, Jan. 17	Litho.	Perf. 13¼		
2215	A858	N multi	2.25	1.75
2216	A859	N multi	2.25	1.75
a.	Horiz. pair, #2215-2216		4.50	4.50

On day of issue, Nos. 2215-2216 each sold for €1.

Apples and Apple Blossoms — A860

Serpentine Die Cut 9x10¾
2019, Jan. 24		Litho.		
		Self-Adhesive		
2217	A860	N multi	2.25	2.25
a.	Vert. pair on backing paper without back printing		4.50	
b.	Booklet pane of 10		16.00	

No. 2217 sold for €1 on day of issue.

Artifacts A861 A862

Designs: N, Gaelic Athletic Association Medal, 1887. W, Rococo silver candlestick holder, c. 1745.

Serpentine Die Cut 14
2019, Jan. 31		Litho.		
		Booklet Stamps		
		Self-Adhesive		
2218	A861	N multi	2.25	1.75
a.	Booklet pane of 10		20.00	
2219	A862	W multi	3.00	3.00
a.	Horiz. pair on backing paper without back printing		6.00	
b.	Booklet pane of 10 + 10 etiquettes		26.50	

On day of issue, No. 2218 sold for €1 and No. 2219 sold for €1.50.

Artifacts A863 A864

Designs: No. 2220, Penrose glas decanter, late 18th cent. No. 2221, Wicker cradle, 19th-20th cent.

Serpentine Die Cut 11x11¼
2019, Jan. 31		Litho.		
		Coil Stamps		
		Self-Adhesive		
2220	A863	N multi	3.25	2.25
2221	A864	N multi	3.25	2.25
a.	Vert. pair, #2220-2221		6.50	

On day of issue, Nos. 2220-2221 each sold for €1.

Gaelic and English Words Describing Wet Weather A865

2019, Feb. 21	Litho.	Perf. 13¼		
2222	A865	W multi	3.75	3.75

On day of issue, No. 2222 sold for €1.50.

Irish Coast Guard Rescue Helicopter A866

Irish Coast Guard Rescue Boat — A867

2019, Mar. 7	Litho.	Perf. 14¼		
2223	A866	N multi	2.25	2.25
2224	A867	N multi	2.25	2.25
a.	Vert. pair, #2223-2224		4.50	4.50

On day of issue, Nos. 2223-2224 each sold for €1.

Organ Donation — A868

2019, Mar. 21	Litho.	Perf. 13½		
2225	A868	N multi	1.90	1.90

On day of issue, No. 2225 sold for €1.

Europa — A869

Designs: N, Roseate tern. W, Golden plover.

2019, Apr. 11	Litho.	Perf. 13¼		
2226	A869	N multi	2.25	2.25
2227	A869	W multi	4.00	4.00
	Souvenir sheet of 2, #2226-2227		6.25	6.25

On day of issue, No. 2226 sold for €1 and No. 2227 sold for €1.70.

Types of 2016-18 Redrawn

Designs: No. 2228, Surfing at Inch. No. 2229, Rock of Cashel, County Tipperary. No. 2230, Urban street art by Fin DAC. No. 2231, Tawny mining bee. No. 2232, Horse riding at Grange. No. 2233, Boyne Viaduct. No. 2234, Shah Jahan, by Bichitr. No. 2235, Sinking of the RMS Leinster.

Serpentine Die Cut 9x10¾, 10¾x9
2019, Apr. 15		Litho.		
		Booklet Stamps		
		Self-Adhesive		
		Size: 37½x26mm, 26x37½mm		
2228	A794	N multi	2.25	2.25
2229	A809	N multi	2.25	2.25
2230	A820	N multi	2.25	2.25
2231	A843	N multi	2.25	2.25
a.	Booklet pane of 4, #2228-2231		9.00	
2232	A794	W multi	2.25	2.25
2233	A840	W multi	2.25	2.25
2234	A828	W multi	2.25	2.25
2235	A847	W multi	2.25	2.25
a.	Booklet pane of 4, #2232-2235, + 4 etiquettes		9.00	
	Nos. 2228-2235 (8)		18.00	18.00

On day of issue, Nos. 2228-2231 each sold for €1, and Nos. 2232-2235 each sold for €1.70.

Dreams, by The Cranberries A870

On Raglan Road, by Luke Kelly (1940-84) A871

With or Without You, by U2 A872

Danny Boy, by John McCormack (1884-1945) A873

Litho. With Foil Application
2019, May 2			Perf. 13¼	
		Stamps With White Frames		
2236	A870	N multi	2.25	2.25
2237	A871	N multi	2.25	2.25
2238	A872	W multi	3.00	3.00
2239	A873	W multi	4.00	4.00
	Nos. 2236-2239 (4)		11.50	11.50

Lyrics from songs performed by Irish musicians. On day of issue, Nos. 2236-2237 each sold for €1, and Nos. 2238-2239 each sold for €1.70. A set of four souvenir sheets of 1 containing stamps similar to Nos. 2236-2239, but lacking white frames around the stamps were sold initially for €17, and later for €15. The souvenir sheets were packaged in plastic mounts that were affixed to cardboard circles that resembled phonograph records.

First Transatlantic Flight of John Alcock and Arthur Brown, Cent. A874

2019, June 13	Litho.	Perf. 13¼		
2240	A874	W multi	3.75	3.25

On day of issue, No. 2240 sold for €1.70.

IRELAND

Space Exploration
A875

Designs: No. 2241, Astronaut and Lunar Module on the Moon, 50th anniv. No. 2242, Eileen Collins, U.S. astronaut with Irish ancestry, and Space Shuttle. No. 2243, Cady Coleman, U.S. astronaut with Irish ancestry, and International Space Station. No. 2244, Apollo 11 Command Module and astronaut, 50th anniv.

2019, July 4	Litho.		Perf. 13¼	
2241	A875	€1 multi	1.75	1.75
2242	A875	€1 multi	1.75	1.75
2243	A875	€1 multi	1.75	1.75
2244	A875	€1 multi	1.75	1.75
a.	Block of 4, #2241-2244		7.25	7.25
b.	Souvenir sheet of 4, #2241-2244		8.25	8.25
	Nos. 2241-2244 (4)		7.00	7.00

Iris Murdoch (1919-99), Writer — A876

2019, July 11	Litho.		Perf. 14x14½	
2245	A876	N multi	2.25	2.25

On day of issue, No. 2245 sold for €1.

100th Liffey River Swimming Race A877

2019, Aug. 1	Litho.		Perf. 13¼	
2246	A877	N gold & multi	2.25	2.25

On day of issue, No. 2246 sold for €1.

Carnegie Libraries A878

Library in: No. 2247, Kilkenny. No. 2248, Clondalkin. No. 2249, Enniskerry. No. 2250, Athea.

2019, Aug. 8	Litho.		Perf. 13¼	
2247	A878	N multi	2.50	2.50
2248	A878	N multi	2.50	2.50
2249	A878	N multi	2.50	2.50
2250	A878	N multi	2.50	2.50
a.	Block of 4, #2247-2250		10.00	10.00
	Nos. 2247-2250 (4)		10.00	10.00

On day of issue, Nos. 2247-2250 each sold for €1.

2019 Rugby World Cup, Japan — A879

Designs: No. 2251, Joe Schmidt, 2018 World Rugby Manager of the Year. No. 2252, Johnny Sexton, 2018 World Rugby Player of the Year.

2019, Aug. 29	Litho.		Perf. 13	
2251	A879	N multi	2.50	2.50
a.	Perf. 13½		2.25	2.25
2252	A879	N multi	2.50	2.50
a.	Perf. 13½		2.25	2.25
b.	Souvenir sheet of 2, #2251a, 2252a		5.00	5.00

On day of issue, Nos. 2251-2252 each sold for €1.

A880

A881

A882

People Celebrating Culture Night A883

2019, Sept. 5	Litho.		Perf. 13¼x13	
2253	A880	N multi	2.50	2.50
2254	A881	N multi	2.50	2.50
2255	A882	N multi	2.50	2.50
2256	A883	N multi	2.50	2.50
a.	Block of 4, #2253-2256		10.00	10.00
	Nos. 2253-2256 (4)		10.00	10.00

On day of issue, Nos. 2253-2256 each sold for €1.

Cover of Thin Lizzy's Album, *Black Rose* — A884

Philip Lynott (1949-86), Lead Vocalist of Thin Lizzy — A885

2019, Oct. 3	Litho.		Perf. 13¼	
2257	A884	N multi	2.25	2.25
2258	A885	N multi	2.25	2.25
a.	Souvenir sheet of 2, #2257-2258		4.50	4.50

On day of issue, Nos. 2257-2258 each sold for €1.

Woman Placing Letters in Pillar Box — A886

Swimmers With Stocking Caps — A887

Carolers A888

Journey to Bethlehem A889

Star of Bethlehem A890

Holly Leaves and Berries, Trees and Field A891

Serpentine Die Cut 11¼x10½

2019, Oct. 17		Litho.		
	Booklet Stamps			
	Self-Adhesive			
2259	A886	€1 multi	1.90	1.90
2260	A887	€1 multi	1.90	1.90
2261	A888	€1 multi	1.90	1.90
2262	A889	€1 multi	1.90	1.90
a.	Booklet pane of 5, #2259-2261, 2 #2262		11.50	
b.	Booklet pane of 20, 5 each #2259-2262		38.50	

Serpentine Die Cut 11¼x10¾

2263	A890	€1.70 multi	3.00	3.00
2264	A891	€1.70 multi	3.00	3.00
a.	Vert. pair, #2263-2264, on backing paper without back printing		6.00	
b.	Booklet pane of 5, 2 #2263, 3 #2264 + 5 etiquettes		17.50	
	Nos. 2259-2264 (6)		13.60	13.60

Christmas. No. 2262b sold for €19.

Rijeka, Croatia, 2020 European Capital of Culture — A892

Galway, Ireland, 2020 European Capital of Culture — A893

2020, Jan. 23	Litho.		Perf. 13¼x13¾	
2265	A892	N multi	2.50	2.50
2266	A893	N multi	2.50	2.50
a.	Souvenir sheet of 1		2.50	2.50

Joint Issue between Ireland and Croatia. On day of issue, Nos. 2265-2266 each sold for €1. See Croatia Nos. 1155-1156.

Love — A894

Litho. With Hologram Affixed
Serpentine Die Cut 10¼x11

2020, Jan. 30		**Self-Adhesive**		
	Booklet Stamp			
2267	A894	N multi	2.75	2.75
a.	Booklet pane of 10		22.50	

No. 2267 sold for €1 on day of issue.

Men of the South, Painting by Sean Keating (1889-1977) A895

2020, Feb. 2	Litho.		Perf. 13¼x14	
2268	A895	N multi	4.50	4.50

Irish War of Independence, cent. No. 2268 sold for €1 on day of issue.

Irish Emigrants at Galtymore Dancehall, London A896

Dame Kathleen Lonsdale (1903-71), Crystallographer, Richard Harris (1930-2002), Actor, and Patrick Sarsfield Gilmore (1829-92), Composer — A897

Edna O'Brien, Writer, Father Michael Kelly, Aid Worker, and Mary Elmes (1908-2002), Rescuer of Jewish children in World War II — A898

People Leaving Dublin Airport, 1969 — A899

An Emigrant's Letter and Envelope, Painting by Geraldine O'Reilly A900

2020, Feb. 27	Litho.		Perf. 13¼x14	
2269	A896	N multi	2.25	2.25
2270	A897	N multi	2.25	2.25
2271	A898	N multi	2.25	2.25
a.	Vert. strip of 3, #2269-2271		6.75	6.75
2272	A899	W multi	3.75	3.75
2273	A900	W multi	3.75	3.75
a.	Vert. pair, #2272-2273		7.50	7.50
	Nos. 2269-2273 (5)		14.25	14.25

On day of issue, Nos. 2269-2271 each sold for €1, and Nos. 2272-2273 each sold for €1.70.

Carmel Snow (1887-1961), Editor of American Edition of *Harper's Bazaar* Magazine A901

Maureen O'Hara (1920-2015), Actress A902

Lilian Bland (1878-1971), Journalist and Aviatrix A903

Maeve Kyle, Olympic Sprinter A904

Sarah Purser (1848-1943), Stained Glass Artist — A905

2020, Mar. 5	Litho.		Perf. 14x13¼	
2274	A901	N multi	2.25	2.25
2275	A902	N multi	2.25	2.25
2276	A903	N multi	2.25	2.25
2277	A904	N multi	2.25	2.25
2278	A905	N multi	2.25	2.25
a.	Horiz. strip of 5, #2274-2278		11.50	11.50
	Nos. 2274-2278 (5)		11.25	11.25

On day of issue, Nos. 2274-2278 each sold for €1.

IRELAND

Portrait of Liam Cosgrave, by Edward McGuire (1932-86) — A906

2020, Apr. 9	Litho.		Perf. 14x13¼
2279	A906 N multi		2.25 2.25

Cosgrave (1920-2017), Taoiseach. On day of issue, No. 2279 sold for €1.

Europa — A907

Designs: N, Letter writer and letter carriers in boat. W, Courier on horseback and letter recipient.

2020, July 16	Litho.		Perf. 13¼x14
2280	A907 N multi		2.40 2.40
2281	A907 W multi		4.00 4.00

Ancient Postal Routes. On day of issue, No. 2280 sold for €1, and No. 2281 sold for €1.70.

Father Ted Television Series, 25th Anniv. — A908

Script lines: Nos. 2282a, 2283, "Will you have a cup of tea, Father?" Nos. 2282b, 2284, "That's mad, Ted." Nos. 2282c, 2285, "That would be an ecumenical matter." Nos. 2282d, 2286, 2287, "That money was just resting in my account."

2020, Aug. 27	Litho.		Perf. 13¼
2282	A908 Sheet of 4		8.75 8.75
a.-d.	N Any single		2.25 2.25

Booklet Stamps
Self-Adhesive
Serpentine Die Cut 11

2283	A908 N multi	2.40	2.40
2284	A908 N multi	2.40	2.40
2285	A908 N multi	2.40	2.40
2286	A908 N multi	2.40	2.40
2287	A908 W multi	4.25	4.25
a.	Booklet pane of 5, #2283-2287	14.00	
	Nos. 2283-2287 (5)	13.85	13.85

On day of issue, Nos. 2282a-2282d, 2283-2286 each sold for €1, and No. 2287 sold for €1.70.

Irish Republican Army Court, Westport Town Hall, 1920 — A909

Headline From May 21 1920 Freeman's Journal A910

2020, Sept. 24	Litho.		Perf. 13¼x14
2288	A909 N multi		2.40 2.40
2289	A910 N multi		2.40 2.40
a.	Horiz. pair, #2288-2289		4.80 4.80

Irish War of Independence, cent. Nos. 2288-2289 each sold for €1 on day of issue.

Members of U2 and Band's Stage Structure in Wembley Stadium, London A911

U2 Albums A912

No. 2291: a, Achtung Baby (39mm diameter). b, Songs of Experience (40x39mm heptagonal stamp). c, The Joshua Tree (36x36mm). c, All That You Can't Leave Behind (50x50mm diamond-shaped stamp).

2020, Oct. 15	Litho.		Perf. 13¼x13¾
2290	A911 €3.60 Souvenir sheet of 1		8.50 8.50

Miniature Sheet
Self-Adhesive
Litho. With Foil Application (#2291a, 2291c), Litho. (#2291b, 2291d)
Die Cut Perf. (#2291a), Die Cut Perf. 13¼ (#2291b-2291d)

2291	A912 Sheet of 4	11.00	9.00
a.-b.	N Either single	2.20	2.20
c.-d.	W Either single	4.00	4.00
e.	Booklet pane of 4, #2291a-2291d	11.00	

On day of issue, Nos. 2291a-2291b each sold for €1, and Nos. 2291c-2291d each sold for €1.70. No. 2291e was sold folded, has a different arrangement of stamps, and the booklet pane margin lacks inscriptions and dots found on sheet margin of No. 2291.

Postal Worker Delivering Mail — A913

Mother and Children Making Christmas Food — A914

Holy Family — A915

Santa Claus Flying Over Village — A916

Family Celebrating Christmas Via Computer Link — A917

Angel — A918

Serpentine Die Cut 11¼x10½

2020, Nov. 5			Litho.

Booklet Stamps
Self-Adhesive

2292	A913 N multi	2.20	2.20
2293	A914 N multi	2.20	2.20
2294	A915 N multi	2.20	2.20
a.	Booklet pane of 5, 3 #2292, 2 #2293	10.00	
2295	A916 N multi	2.20	2.20
a.	Booklet pane of 20, 8 #2294, 4 each #2292-2293, 2295	35.00	
2296	A917 W multi	4.00	4.00
2297	A918 W multi	4.00	4.00
a.	Horiz. pair, #2296-2297 on backing paper without back printing	8.00	
b.	Booklet pane of 5, 3 #2296, 2 #2297 + 5 etiquettes	14.00	
	Nos. 2292-2297 (6)	16.80	16.80

Christmas. On day of issue, Nos. 2292-2295 each sold for €1, and Nos. 2296-2297 each sold for €1.70. No. 2295a sold for €19.

Disestablishment of the Church of Ireland, 150th Anniv. — A919

Die Cut Perf. 13¼
2021, Jan. 7			Litho.

Self-Adhesive

| 2298 | A919 N multi | 2.20 | 2.20 |

No. 2298 sold for €1 on day of issue.

Meditation Painting 28, by Patrick Scott (1921-2014) — A920

Litho. With Foil Application
2021, Jan. 21			Perf. 13¼x13¾
2299	A920 €3 gold & multi		7.25 7.25

No. 2299 was printed in sheets of 2 + central label.

Love — A921

Litho. With Hologram Affixed
Serpentine Die Cut 10¼x11
| 2021, Jan. 28 | | | |

Booklet Stamp
Self-Adhesive

| 2300 | A921 N red | 2.20 | 2.20 |
| a. | Booklet pane of 10 + 6 stickers | 22.00 | |

No. 2300 sold for €1 on day of issue.

"Fáilte" (Welcome) A922

Die Cut Perf. 13½
2021, Feb. 18			Litho.

Self-Adhesive

| 2301 | A922 W gold & sil | 3.85 | 3.85 |

No. 2301 sold for €1.70 on day of issue.

Jane, Lady Wilde (Speranza) (1821-96), Poet — A923

Litho. With Foil Application
2021, Mar. 8	Die Cut Perf. 13¼

Self-Adhesive

| 2302 | A923 N multi | 1.75 | 1.75 |

No. 2302 sold for €1 on day of issue.

For People For Planet Campaign A924

Designs: N, Postwoman in ebike. W, Hand holding smiling globe.

Die Cut Perf. 13½
2021, Mar. 25			Litho.

Self-Adhesive

| 2303 | A924 N multi | 2.40 | 2.40 |
| 2304 | A924 W multi | 4.00 | 4.00 |

On day of issue, No. 2303 sold for €1, and No. 2304 sold for €1.70.

Ship of Antarctic Explorer Edward Bransfield (c. 1785-1852), Penguins and map of Bransfield Strait A925

HMS Terror, 1839-43 Ross Expedition Ship Commanded by Francis Crozier (1796-1848), HMS Erebus and Compass Rose — A926

Members of 1910-13 Terra Nova Expedition Pulling Sled, and Compass Rose A927

Tom Crean (1877-1938), Antarctic Explorer, Compass Rose and Pipe — A928

Die Cut Perf. 13¼
2021, Apr. 15			Litho.

Self-Adhesive

2305	A925 N multi	2.20	2.20
2306	A926 N multi	2.20	2.20
a.	Horiz. pair, #2305-2306	4.40	
2307	A927 W multi	3.85	3.85
2308	A928 W multi	3.85	3.85
a.	Horiz. pair, #2307-2308	7.75	
	Nos. 2305-2308 (4)	12.10	12.10

On day of issue Nos. 2305-2306 each sold for €1, and Nos. 2307-2308 each sold for €1.70.

Europa — A929

Endangered animals: N, White prominent moth. W, Freshwater pearl mussels.

Die Cut Perf. 13¼
2021, May 6			Litho.

Self-Adhesive

| 2309 | A929 N multi | 2.20 | 2.20 |
| 2310 | A929 W multi | 3.85 | 3.85 |

On day of issue, No. 2309 sold for €1, and No. 2310 sold for €1.70.

Rainbow Pride Flag — A930

Inscription on flag: Nos. 2311, 2313, "Pride." No. 2312, "Bród."

IRELAND

Serpentine Die Cut 11½x11
2021, June 10   Litho.
Booklet Stamps
Self-Adhesive

2311	A930	N multi	2.20	2.20
2312	A930	N multi	2.20	2.20
2313	A930	W multi	3.85	3.85
a.	Booklet pane of 5, #2313, 2 each #2311-2312		20.00	
	Nos. 2311-2313 (3)		8.25	8.25

On day of issue, Nos. 2311-2312 each sold for €1.10, and No. 2313 sold for €2.

Excerpt From Letter by Eamon de Valera to David Lloyd George — A931

Date of Anglo-Irish Truce — A932

Die Cut Perf. 13¼
2021, July 8   Litho.
Self-Adhesive

2314	A931	N multi	2.60	2.60
2315	A932	N multi	2.60	2.60
a.	Horiz. pair, #2314-2315		4.50	

On day of issue, Nos. 2314-2315 each sold fo €1.10.

A932a, A932b, A932c, Artifacts — A932d

Designs: No. 2315B, Emigrant's teapot, late 19th-mid 20th century. No. 2315C, Kavanagh charter horn, 12th and 15th centuries. No. 2315D, Silver coin, mid 10th century. W, Morion, late 16th century.

Serpentine Die Cut 11¼
2021, July 14   Litho.
Coil Stamps
Self-Adhesive

2315B	A932a	N multi	3.25	2.25
2315C	A932b	N multi	3.25	2.25
f.	Vert. pair, #2315B-2315C		6.75	

Booklet Stamps
Serpentine Die Cut 11½

2315D	A932c	N multi	2.60	2.60
g.	Vert. pair on backing paper without back printing		5.20	
h.	Booklet pane of 10		26.00	
2315E	A932d	W multi	3.25	3.25
i.	Vert. pair on backing paper without back printing		9.50	
j.	Booklet pane of 10 + 10 etiquettes		32.50	

On day of issue, Nos. 2315B-2315D each sold for €1.10, and No. 2315E sold for €2.

Singers Who Have Performed at the Glastonbury Music and Arts Festival — A933

Designs: No. 2316, Christy Moore. No. 2317, Sinéad O'Connor. No. 2318, Lisa Hannigan. No. 2319, Hozier.

Die Cut Perf. 13¼
2021, July 15   Litho.
Booklet Stamps
Self-Adhesive

2316	A933	N multi	2.60	2.60
2317	A933	N multi	2.60	2.60
2318	A933	N multi	2.60	2.60
2319	A933	N multi	2.60	2.60
a.	Booklet pane of 4, #2316-2319		10.50	
	Nos. 2316-2319 (4)		10.40	10.40

On day of issue, Nos. 2316-2319 each sold for €1.10.

1948 Production of *Abdication* — A934

Maureen Potter and Jimmy O'Dea Performing, 1957 — A935

Production of *Riverdance* — A936

2018 Production of *Sive* — A937

Die Cut Perf. 13¼
2021, Oct. 7   Litho.
Self-Adhesive

2320	A934	N multi	2.60	2.60
2321	A935	N multi	2.60	2.60
2322	A936	N multi	2.60	2.60
2323	A937	N multi	2.60	2.60
a.	Block of 4, #2320-2323		10.50	
	Nos. 2320-2323 (4)		10.40	10.40

Gaiety Theater, Dublin, 150th anniv. On day of issue, Nos. 2320-2323 each sold for €1.10.

Christmas — A938

Inscriptions: No. 2324, "Sending Hugs." No. 2325, "Ho ho ho." No. 2326, "Naughty or Nice?" No. 2327, "Peace & Joy." No. 2328, "Nollaig Shona." No. 2329, "Love."

Serpentine Die Cut 11¼x10½
2021, Nov. 4   Litho.
Booklet Stamps
Self-Adhesive

2324	A938	N multi	2.50	2.50
2325	A938	N multi	2.50	2.50
2326	A938	N multi	2.50	2.50
2327	A938	N multi	2.50	2.50
a.	Booklet pane of 20, 5 each #2324-2327		50.00	
b.	Booklet pane of 5, 2 #2325, 3 #2327		12.50	
2328	A938	W multi	4.50	4.50
2329	A938	W multi	4.50	4.50
a.	Horiz. pair, #2328-2329 on backing paper without back printing		9.00	
b.	Booklet pane of 5, 3 #2328, 2 #2329		22.50	
	Nos. 2324-2329 (6)		19.00	19.00

On day of issue, Nos. 2324-2327 each had a franking value of €1.10, and Nos. 2328-2329 each sold for €2. No. 2327a sold for €20.

1921 Anglo-Irish Treaty With Signatures of Irish Delegates — A939

Message Written by Arthur Griffith After Signing of Treaty — A940

Die Cut Perf. 13¼
2021, Dec. 2   Litho.
Self-Adhesive

2330	A939	N yel grn & multi	2.50	2.50
2331	A940	N bl grn & multi	2.50	2.50
a.	Horiz. pair, #2330-2331		5.00	

Anglo-Irish Treaty, cent. On day of issue, Nos. 2330-2331 each sold for €1.10.

Formation of Irish Army, Cent. — A941

Handover of Dublin Castle, Cent. — A942

Formation of the Civic Guard, Cent. — A943

2022, Jan. 13   Engr.   Perf. 13¼x14

2332	A941	N black & gold	2.50	2.50
2333	A942	N black & gold	2.50	2.50
2334	A943	N black & gold	2.50	2.50
	Nos. 2332-2334 (3)		7.50	7.50

On day of issue, Nos. 2332-2334 each sold for €1.10.

A944

Publication of *Ulysses*, by James Joyce, Cent. — A945

2022, Jan. 17   Litho.   Perf. 13½x14

2335	A944	N multi	2.50	2.50
2336	A945	W multi	4.50	4.50

On day of issue, No. 2335 sold for €1.10, and No. 2336 sold for €2.

Love — A946

Serpentine Die Cut
2022, Feb. 3   Litho.
Self-Adhesive

2337	A946	N multi	2.50	2.50
a.	Vert. pair on backing paper without back printing		5.00	
b.	Booklet pane of 10		25.00	

No. 2337 sold for €1.10 on day of issue.

Irish Women in Sports — A947

Designs: No. 2338, Sonia O'Sullivan, long-distance runner. No. 2339, Rachael Blackmore, jockey. No. 2340, Katie Taylor, boxer. No. 2341, Kellie Harrington, boxer. No. 2342, Irish women's field hockey team. No. 2343, Ellen Keane, paralympic swimmer.

Serpentine Die Cut 12x11
2022, Mar. 3   Litho.
Booklet Stamps
Self-Adhesive

2338	A947	N multi	2.75	2.75
2339	A947	N multi	2.75	2.75
2340	A947	N multi	2.75	2.75
2341	A947	N multi	2.75	2.75
2342	A947	N multi	2.75	2.75
2343	A947	N multi	2.75	2.75
a.	booklet pane of 6, #2338-2343		16.50	
	Nos. 2338-2343 (6)		16.50	16.50

On day of issue, Nos. 2338-2343 each sold for €1.25.

Academy Award Winners From Ireland — A948

Designs: No. 2344, Brenda Fricker and Daniel Day-Lewis, actors in *My Left Foot*. No. 2345, Neil Jordan, screenplay writer for *The Crying Game*. No. 2346, Martin McDonagh, director of short film *Six Shooter*. No. 2347, Glen Hansard and Markéta Irglová, actors and musicians in *Once*.

Die Cut Perf. 10¾x11x11x11
2022, Mar. 24   Litho.
Booklet Stamps
Self-Adhesive

2344	A948	N multi	2.75	2.75
2345	A948	N multi	2.75	2.75
2346	A948	N multi	2.75	2.75
2347	A948	N multi	2.75	2.75
a.	Booklet pane of 4, #2344-2347		11.00	
	Nos. 2344-2347 (4)		11.00	11.00

On day of issue, Nos. 2344-2347 each sold for €1.25.

AIR POST STAMPS

Catalogue values for unused stamps in this section are for Never Hinged items.

Angel over Rock of Cashel — AP1

Designs: 1p, 1sh3p, 1sh5p, Rock of Cashel. 3p, 8p, Lough Derg. 6p, Croagh Patrick. 1sh, Glendalough.

1948-65   Perf. 15x14   Wmk. 262   Engr.

C1	AP1	1p dk brown ('49)	6.50	6.50
C2	AP1	3p blue	11.00	9.50
C3	AP1	6p rose lilac	1.10	.90
C4	AP1	8p red brown ('54)	4.50	3.50
C5	AP1	1sh green ('49)	2.25	1.15
C6	AP1	1sh3p ver ('54)	5.50	1.15

Perf. 15

C7	AP1	1sh5p dark blue ('65)	4.50	.90
	Nos. C1-C7 (7)		35.35	23.60

POSTAGE DUE STAMPS

D1

1925   Typo.   Wmk. 44   Perf. 14x15

J1	D1	½p emerald	13.00	19.00
		Never hinged	65.00	
J2	D1	1p carmine	14.25	5.75
		Never hinged	50.00	
J3	D1	2p dark green	32.50	8.75
		Never hinged	125.00	

IRELAND — ISRAEL

J4	D1	6p plum	8.25	6.50
		Never hinged	35.00	
		Nos. J1-J4 (4)	68.00	40.00

Catalogue values for unused stamps in this section, from this point to the end of the section, are for Never Hinged items.

1940-70   **Wmk. 262**

J5	D1	½p emerald ('43)	12.75	19.50
J6	D1	1p brt carmine ('41)	.95	.60
J7	D1	1½p vermilion ('52)	3.50	12.75
J8	D1	2p dark green	2.35	.60
J9	D1	3p blue ('52)	2.50	4.75
J10	D1	5p royal purple ('43)	4.25	1.90
J11	D1	6p plum ('60)	5.00	4.00
J12	D1	8p orange ('62)	4.25	12.75
J13	D1	10p red lilac ('65)	6.50	7.25
J14	D1	1sh lt yel grn ('69)	8.50	10.25
		Nos. J5-J14 (10)	50.55	74.35

1971, Feb. 15   **Typo.**   **Wmk. 262**

J15	D1	1p sepia	.30	.55
J16	D1	1½p bright green	.30	1.40
J17	D1	3p gray green	.55	2.25
J18	D1	4p orange	.70	1.15
J19	D1	5p bright blue	.95	2.75
J20	D1	7p yellow	.45	3.25
J21	D1	8p scarlet	.35	2.10
		Nos. J15-J21 (7)	3.60	13.45

1978   **Unwmk.**

J25	D1	3p gray green	1.85	6.75
J26	D1	4p orange	4.75	9.50
J27	D1	5p bright blue	1.85	4.75
		Nos. J25-J27 (3)	8.45	21.00

Celtic Knot — D2

1980-85   **Photo.**   **Perf. 15**

J28	D2	1p brt yel green	.30	.65
J29	D2	2p ultramarine	.30	.65
J30	D2	4p dark green	.30	.65
J31	D2	6p yel orange	.30	.75
J32	D2	8p violet blue	.30	.80
J33	D2	18p green	.50	1.15
J33A	D2	20p org brown ('85)	2.15	6.00
J34	D2	24p emerald	.55	1.85
J35	D2	30p violet blue ('85)	2.50	7.00
J36	D2	50p rose pink ('85)	2.85	7.00
		Nos. J28-J36 (10)	10.05	26.50

Issue dates: 1p, 2p, 4p, 6p, 8p, 18p, 24p, June 11; 20p, 30p, 50p, Aug. 22.

D3

1988, Oct. 6   **Litho.**   **Perf. 14x15**

J37	D3	1p blk, dp yel & brt red	.30	.55
J38	D3	2p blk, vio brn & brt red	.30	.55
J39	D3	3p blk, dull vio & brt red	.30	.55
J40	D3	4p blk, vio & brt red	.30	.95
J41	D3	5p blk, vio bl & brt red	.30	.55
J42	D3	17p blk, brt ol grn & brt red	.45	.75
J43	D3	20p blk, bluish gray & brt red	.60	1.00
J44	D3	24p blk, bl grn & brt red	.70	.95
J45	D3	30p blk & brt red	.85	1.50
J46	D3	50p blk, gray & brt red	1.30	1.65
J47	D3	£1 blk, dk ol brn & brt red	1.85	2.40
		Nos. J37-J47 (11)	7.25	11.40

ISRAEL

ˈiz-rē-əl

LOCATION — Western Asia, bordering on the Mediterranean Sea
GOVT. — Republic
AREA — 8,017 sq. mi.
POP. — 8,660,000 (2020 est.)
CAPITAL — Jerusalem

When the British mandate of Palestine ended in May 1948, the Jewish state of Israel was proclaimed by the Jewish National Council in Palestine.

1000 Mils = 1 Pound
1000 Prutot = 1 Pound (1949)
100 Agorot = 1 Pound (1960)
100 Agorot = 1 Shekel (1980)

Catalogue values for all unused stamps in this country are for Never Hinged items.

Tabs

Stamps of Israel are printed in sheets with tabs (labels) usually attached below the bottom row, sometimes at the sides.

Tabs of the following numbers are in two parts, perforated between: 9, 15, 23-37, 44, 46-47, 50, 55, 62-65, 70-72, 74-77, 86-91, 94-99, 104-118, 123-126, 133-136B, 138-141, 143-151, 160-161, 165-167, 178-179, 182, 187-189, 203, 211-213, 222-223, 228-237, 243-244, 246-250, 256-258, 269-270, 272-273, 275, 294-295, 312, 337-339, 341-344, 346-347, 353-354, C1-C13, C22-C30. Both parts must be present to qualify for with tab value. Stamps with only one part sell for about one-quarter to one-third of full tab prices.

Watermarks

Wmk. 301 — ISRAEL in Hebrew

Wmk. 302 — Multiple Stag

Ancient Judean Coins
A1   A2

Designs: Nos. 1-6, Various coins.

Perf. 10, 11 and Compound

1948, May 16   **Typo.**   **Unwmk.**

1	A1	3m orange	.30	.25
2	A1	5m yellow grn	.30	.25
3	A1	10m red violet	.45	.25
4	A1	15m red	.70	.25
5	A1	20m bright ultra	2.00	.30
6	A1	50m orange brown	.80	.70
		Nos. 1-6 (6)	11.75	2.00
		Nos. 1-6 (6) with tabs	200.00	
		Set, with tabs, hinged	85.00	

Size: 34½x22mm

7	A2	250m dark sl grn	27.50	9.00
8	A2	500m red brn, cr	100.00	45.00

Size: 36½x24mm

9	A2	1000m blk bl, pale bl	175.00	90.00
		Nos. 7-9 (3)	302.50	144.00
		Nos. 7-9 with tabs	5,250.	
		Set, hinged	125.00	

Nos. 1-9 exist imperf. Value: singles set $3,000; tab set $13,000.
See design A6. For overprints see Nos. J1-J5.

Rouletted

1a	A1	3m	.45	.25
2b	A1	5m	.60	.25
3b	A1	10m	10.00	.90
		Nos. 1a-3b (3)	11.05	1.40
		Set, with tabs	225.00	
		Set with tabs, hinged	75.00	

Flying Scroll — A3

1948, Sept. 26   **Litho.**   **Perf. 11½**

10	A3	3m brn red & ultra	.35	.25
11	A3	5m dl grn & ultra	.35	.25
12	A3	10m dp car & ultra	.35	.25
13	A3	20m dp ultra & ultra	1.75	.70
14	A3	65m brown & red	8.00	3.00
		Nos. 10-14 (5)	10.80	4.45
		With tabs	225.00	
		With tabs, hinged	90.00	

Jewish New Year, 5709.

Flag of Israel — A4

1949, Mar. 31

15	A4	20m bright blue	.50	.25
		With tab	42.50	

Appointment of the government by the Knesset.

Souvenir Sheet

A5

1949, May 1   **Imperf.**

16	A5	Sheet of 4	55.00	22.50
a.		10m dark carmine rose	12.50	4.00

1st anniv. of Israeli postage stamps.
The sheet was sold at "TABUL," First National Stamp Exhibition, in Tel Aviv, May 1-6, 1949. Tickets, costing 100 mils, covered the entrance fee and one sheet.

Bronze Half-Shekel of 67 A.D. — A6

Approach to Jerusalem A8

Hebrew University, Jerusalem A7

"The Negev" by Reuven Rubin — A9

1949-50   **Unwmk.**   **Perf. 11½, 14**

17	A6	3p gray black	.25	.25
18	A6	5p purple	.25	.25
19	A6	10p green	.25	.25
20	A6	15p deep rose	.25	.25
21	A6	30p dark blue	.25	.25
22	A6	50p brown	.90	.25
23	A7	100p Prus grn	.25	.25
		With tab	17.50	
24	A8	250p org brn & gray	.80	.55
		With tab	32.50	
25	A9	500p dp org & brown	6.00	5.00
		With tab	200.00	
		Nos. 17-25 (9)	9.30	7.30
		Nos. 17-22 with tabs (6)	65.00	
		Tete beche pairs, Nos. 18-21	85.00	85.00

Each of Nos. 17-22 portrays a different coin. 25th anniv. of the Hebrew University in Jerusalem (No. 23).

Issued: 250p, 2/16; 3p-50p, 12/18; 100p, 5/9/50; 500p, 12/26/50.
See Nos. 38-43, 56-61, 80-83, and design A1. For overprints see Nos. O1-O4.

Well at Petah Tikva — A10

1949, Aug. 10   **Perf. 11**

27	A10	40p dk grn & brn	6.00	.30
		With tab	80.00	

70th anniv. of Petah Tikva.

Arms and Service Insignia — A11

1949, Sept. 20   **Perf. 11½**

28	A11	5p Air Force	.30	.25
29	A11	10p Navy	.85	.25
30	A11	35p Army	3.00	2.00
		Nos. 28-30 (3)	4.15	2.50
		With tabs	575.00	

Jewish New Year, 5710.

Running Stag — A12

1950, Mar. 26

31	A12	40p purple	.50	.30
a.		Booklet pane of 4	3.50	
32	A12	80p rose red	.60	.35
a.		Booklet pane of 4	7.00	
		Complete booklet, 1 ea. #31a, 32a	25.00	
b.		Nos. 31 and 32 tête bêche	42.50	22.50
		With tabs	55.00	

75th anniv. (in 1949) of the UPU.

Struggle for Free Immigration A13

Arrival of Immigrants A14

1950, Apr. 23

33	A13	20p dull brown	2.00	1.25
34	A14	40p dull green	4.00	3.00
		With tabs	500.00	

Independence Day, Apr. 22, 1950.

Fruit and Star of David — A15

1950, Aug. 31   **Litho.**   **Perf. 14**

35	A15	5p vio blue & org	.25	.25
36	A15	15p red brn & grn	.25	.25
		With tabs	42.50	

Jewish New Year, 5711.

Runner and Track — A16

1950, Oct. 1

37	A16	80p olive & sl blk	1.00	.55
		With tab	57.50	

3rd Maccabiah, Ramat Gan, Sept. 27, 1950.

Coin Type of 1949 Redrawn

Designs: Various coins.

ISREAL

1950
38	A6 3p gray black	.25	.25
39	A6 5p purple	.25	.25
a.	Tête bêche pair	3.00	3.00
40	A6 10p green	.25	.25
a.	Tête bêche pair	1.25	1.00
41	A6 15p deep rose	.25	.25
a.	Tête bêche pair	2.00	1.75
42	A6 30p dark blue	.25	.25
a.	Tête bêche pair	4.00	4.00
43	A6 50p brown	.25	.25
	Nos. 38-43 (6)	1.50	1.50
	With tabs	2.90	

Inscription at left measures 11mm on Nos. 38-43; 9mm on Nos. 17-22.

Detail from Tablet, "Founding of Tel Aviv" — A17

1951, Mar. 22
44	A17 40p dark brown	.25	.25
	With tab	17.50	

40th anniversary of Tel Aviv.

Young Man Holding Outline Map of Israel — A18

1951, Apr. 30 Litho.
45	A18 80p red brown	.25	.25
	With tab	3.25	

Issued to promote the sale of Independence Bonds.

Metsudat Yesha — A19

Hakastel — A20

1951, May 9 Unwmk.
46	A19 15p red brown	.25	.25
47	A20 40p deep blue	.40	.25
	With tabs	40.00	

Proclamation of State of Israel, 3rd anniv.

Tractor and Wheat A21

Tree A22

Plower and National Fund Stamp of 1902 — A23

1951, June 24 Perf. 14
48	A21 15p red brown	.25	.25
49	A22 25p Prussian green	.25	.25
50	A23 80p dull blue	.30	.25
	Nos. 48-50 (3)	.80	.75
	With tabs	80.00	

Jewish National Fund, 50th anniversary.

Theodor Zeev Herzl — A24

1951, Aug. 14
51	A24 80p gray green	.25	.25
	With tab	3.50	

23rd Zionist Congress, Jerusalem.

Carrier Pigeons — A25

Designs: 15p, Girl holding dove and fruit. 40p, Scrolls of the law.

1951, Sept. 16
52	A25 5p blue	.25	.25
53	A25 15p cerise	.25	.25
54	A25 40p rose violet	.25	.25
	Nos. 52-54 (3)	.75	.75
	With tabs	3.00	

Jewish New Year, 5712.

Menorah and Emblems of Twelve Tribes — A26

1952, Feb. 27
55	A26 1000p dk bl & gray	10.00	4.50
	With tab	225.00	

Redrawn Coin Type of 1950

Designs: Various coins.

1952, Mar. 30
56	A6 20p orange	.25	.25
a.	Tête bêche pair	2.25	2.25
57	A6 35p olive green	.25	.25
58	A6 40p orange brown	.25	.25
59	A6 45p red violet	.25	.25
a.	Tête bêche pair	4.00	4.00
60	A6 60p carmine	.25	.25
61	A6 85p aquamarine	.25	.25
	Nos. 56-61 (6)	1.50	1.50
	With tabs	11.00	

Thistle and Yad Mordecai Battlefield — A27

Battlefields: 60p, Cornflower and Deganya. 110p, Anemone and Safed.

1952, Apr. 29
62	A27 30p lil rose & vio brn	.25	.25
63	A27 60p ultra & gray blk	.25	.25
64	A27 110p crimson & gray	.35	.25
	Nos. 62-64 (3)	.85	.75
	With tabs	18.00	

Proclamation of State of Israel, 4th anniv.

Manhattan Skyline and American Zionists' House — A28

1952, May 13
65	A28 220p dark blue & gray	.30	.25
	With tab	10.00	

Opening of American Zionists' House, Tel Aviv.

Figs — A29

1952, Sept. 3 Unwmk. Litho. Perf. 14
66	A29 15p shown	.25	.25
67	A29 40p Lily	.25	.25
68	A29 110p Dove	.25	.25
69	A29 220p Nut cluster	.40	.25
	Nos. 66-69 (4)	1.15	1.00
	With tabs	20.00	

Jewish New Year, 5713.

Pres. Chaim Weizmann (1874-1952) and Presidential Standard — A30

1952, Dec. 9
70	A30 30p slate	.25	.25
71	A30 110p black	.25	.25
	With tabs	8.00	

Weizmann, president of Israel 1948-52.

Numeral Incorporating Agricultural Scenes — A31

1952, Dec. 31
72	A31 110p brown, buff & emer	.25	.25
	With tab	8.00	

70th anniversary of B.I.L.U. (Bet Yaakov Lechu Venelcha) immigration.

Five Anemones and State Emblem — A32

1953, Apr. 19
73	A32 110p grnsh bl, bl blk & red	.25	.25
	With tab	2.50	

5th anniversary of State of Israel.

Rabbi Moshe ben Maimon (Maimonides) — A33

1953, Aug. 3 Wmk. 301 Perf. 14x13
74	A33 110p brown	.30	.25
	With tab	6.00	

7th International Congress of History of Science, Jerusalem, Aug. 4-11.

Holy Ark, Jerusalem — A34

Holy Arks: 45p, Petah Tikva. 200p, Safed.

1953, Aug. 11
75	A34 20p sapphire	.25	.25
76	A34 45p brown red	.25	.25
77	A34 200p purple	.25	.25
	Nos. 75-77 (3)	.75	.75
	With tabs	6.50	

Jewish New Year, 5714.

Combined Ball-Globe — A35

1953, Sept. 20 Unwmk. Litho. Perf. 14
78	A35 110p blue & dark brn	.25	.25
	With tab	2.75	

4th Maccabiah, Sept. 20-29, 1953.

Desert Rose — A36

1953, Sept. 22
79	A36 200p multicolored	.25	.25
	With tab	3.00	

Conquest of the Desert Exhib., 9/22-10/14.

Redrawn Type of 1950

Designs: Various coins.

1954, Jan. 5
80	A6 80p olive bister	.25	.25
81	A6 95p blue green	.25	.25
82	A6 100p fawn	.25	.25
83	A6 125p violet blue	.25	.25
	Nos. 80-83 (4)	1.00	1.00
	With tabs	2.00	

Marigold and Ruins at Yehiam — A37

350p, Narcissus and bridge at Gesher.

1954, May 5 Litho.
84	A37 60p dk bl, mag & ol gray	.25	.25
85	A37 350p dk brn, grn & yel	.25	.25
	With tabs	1.75	

Memorial Day and 6th anniversary of proclamation of State of Israel.

ISRAEL

NEW ISRAEL PRICE LIST
Tabs, Singles, FDC's, Booklets, Year Sets 1958-2023, Scott Listed varieties

Separate Israel Price List
Specialized, gutters, Phosphorus, varieties, Errors, Doar Ivri
Palestine & Judaica Also Available!

1-800-94-STAMP
(1-800-947-8267)

WE BUY ISRAEL
Tabs & Singles, 1948 Interim, Palestine including Forerunners, Worldwide Judaica, JNF, Documents, Covers & Postal History

Henry Gitner Philatelists, Inc. HGP
P.O. Box 3077-S, Middletown, NY 10940
Tel: 845-343-5151 Fax: 845-343-0068
Toll Free: 1-800-947-8267
E-mail: hgitner@hgitner.com
PHILATELY - THE QUIET EXCITEMENT

ISRAEL

Theodor Zeev Herzl (1860-1904), Founder of Zionist Movement — A38

1954, July 21		Wmk. 302	
86	A38	160p dk bl, dk brn & cr	.25 .25
		With tab	.60

Bearers with Grape Cluster — A39

1954, Sept. 8		Perf. 13x14	
87	A39	25p dark brown	.25 .25
		With tab	.25

Jewish New Year, 5715.

19th Century Mail Coach and Jerusalem Post Office — A40

200p, Mail truck & present G.P.O., Jerusalem.

1954, Oct. 13		Perf. 14	
88	A40	60p blue, blk & yel	.25 .25
89	A40	200p dk grn, blk & red	.25 .25
		With tabs	1.75

TABIM, National Stamp Exhibition, Jerusalem, Oct. 13-18.

Baron Edmond de Rothschild (1845-1934) and Grape Cluster — A41

1954, Nov. 23		Perf. 13x14	
90	A41	300p dark blue green	.25 .25
		With tab	.50

Lighted Oil Lamp — A42

1955, Jan. 13		Perf. 13x14	
91	A42	250p dark blue	.25 .25
		With tab	.50

Teachers' Association, 50th anniversary.

Parachutist and Barbed Wire — A43

1955, Mar. 31	Litho.	Perf. 14	
92	A43	120p dk Prus green	.25 .25
		With tab	.35

Jewish volunteers from Palestine who served in British army in World War II.

Lighted Menorah — A44

1955, Apr. 26			
93	A44	150p dk grn, blk & org	.25 .25
		With tab	.30

Proclamation of State of Israel, 7th anniv.

Immigration by Ship — A45

Designs: 10p, Immigration by plane. 25p, Agricultural training. 30p, Gardening. 60p, Vocational training. 750p, Scientific education.

1955, May 10	Unwmk.	Perf. 14	
94	A45	5p brt blue & black	.25 .25
95	A45	10p red & black	.25 .25
96	A45	25p deep grn & black	.25 .25
97	A45	30p orange & black	.25 .25
98	A45	60p lilac rose & blk	.25 .25
99	A45	750p olive bis & blk	.25 .25
		Nos. 94-99 (6)	1.50 1.50
		With tabs	1.25

Israel's Youth Immigration Institution, 20th anniv.

Musicians with Tambourine and Cymbals — A46

Musician with: 60p, Ram's Horn. 120p, Loud Trumpet. 250p, Harp.

1955, Aug. 25	Photo.	Wmk. 302	
100	A46	25p dark green & org	.25 .25
		Unwmk.	
101	A46	60p dk gray & orange	.25 .25
102	A46	120p dark blue & yel	.25 .25
103	A46	250p red brn & org	.25 .25
		#100-103, with tabs	.45

Jewish New Year, 5716.
See Nos. 121-123.

Ambulance A47

1955, Nov. 1	Wmk. 301	Perf. 14	
104	A47	160p grn, red & blk	.25 .25
		With tab	.25

Magen David Adom (Israeli Red Cross), 25th anniv.

Mandrake, Reuben — A48

Twelve Tribes: 20p, Gates of Sechem, Simeon. 30p, Ephod, Levi. 40p, Lion, Judah. 50p, Scales, Dan. 60p, Stag, Naphtali. 80p, Tents, Gad. 100p, Tree, Asher. 120p, Sun and stars, Issachar. 180p, Ship, Zebulon. 200p, Sheaf of wheat, Joseph. 250p, Wolf, Benjamin.

1955-57	Wmk. 302	Perf. 13x14	
105	A48	10p bright green	.25 .25
106	A48	20p red lilac ('56)	.25 .25
107	A48	30p bright ultra	.25 .25
108	A48	40p brown ('56)	.25 .25
109	A48	50p grnsh bl ('56)	.25 .25
110	A48	60p lemon	.25 .25
111	A48	80p deep vio ('56)	.25 .25
112	A48	100p vermilion	.25 .25
113	A48	120p olive ('56)	.25 .25
114	A48	180p lil rose ('56)	.25 .25
115	A48	200p green ('56)	.25 .25
116	A48	250p gray ('56)	.25 .25
		#105-116, with tabs	2.00

See Nos. 133-136B.

Albert Einstein (1879-1955) and Equation of his Relativity Theory — A49

1956, Jan. 3		Perf. 13x14	
117	A49	350p brown	.25 .25
		With tab	.40

Technion, Haifa — A50

1956, Jan. 3		Wmk. 302	
118	A50	350p lt ol grn & blk	.25 .25
		With tab	.25

Israel Institute of Technology, 30th anniv.

"Eight Years of Israel" — A51

1956, Apr. 12	Litho.	Perf. 14	
119	A51	150p multicolored	.25 .25
		With tab	.25

Proclamation of State of Israel, 8th anniv.

Jaffa Oranges — A52

1956, May 20	Wmk. 302	Perf. 14	
120	A52	300p bl grn & orange	.25 .25
		With tab	.25

4th Intl. Congress of Mediterranean Citrus Growers.

New Year Type of 1955

Musician with: 30p, Lyre. 50p, Cymbals. 150p, Double oboe, horiz.

1956, Aug. 14	Photo.	Perf. 14x13	
121	A46	30p brown & brt blue	.25 .25
		Perf. 14	
122	A46	50p purple & orange	.25 .25
123	A46	150p dk bl grn & org	.25 .25
		#121-123, with tabs	.25

Jewish New Year, 5717.

Haganah Insignia — A54

1957, Jan. 1		Perf. 13x14	
124	A54	20p + 80p brt grn	.25 .25
125	A54	50p + 150p car rose	.25 .25
126	A54	50p + 350p ultra	.25 .25
		#124-126, with tabs	.25

Defense issue. Divided denomination used to show increased postal rate.

Bezalel Museum and Antique Lamp — A55

1957, Apr. 29	Litho.	Perf. 14	
127	A55	400p multicolored	.25 .25
		With tab	.25

Bezalel Natl. Museum, Jerusalem, 50th anniv.

Jet Plane and "9" — A56

1957, Apr. 29			
128	A56	250p deep bl & blk	.25 .25
		With tab	.25

Proclamation of State of Israel, 9th anniv.

Horse and Seal — A57

Ancient Seals: 160p, Lion. 300p, Gazelle.

1957, Sept. 4	Wmk. 302	Perf. 14	
129	A57	50p ocher & blk, lt bl	.25 .25
		Perf. 14x13	
		Photo. **Unwmk.**	
130	A57	160p grn & blk, bis brn	.25 .25
131	A57	300p dp car & blk, pink	.25 .25
		#130-131, with tabs	.25

Jewish New Year, 5718.

TABIL Souvenir Sheet

Bet Alpha Synagogue Mosaic — A58

1957, Sept. 17	Litho.	Roulette 13	
132	A58	Sheet of 4	.30 .30
	a.	100p multicolored	.25 .25
	b.	200p multicolored	.25 .25
	c.	300p multicolored	.25 .25
	d.	400p multicolored	.25 .25

1st Intl. stamp exhib. in Israel, Tel Aviv, 9/17-23.

Tribes Type of 1955-57

Perf. 13x14

1957-59		Unwmk.	Photo.
133	A48	10p brt grn ('58)	.25 .25
133A	A48	20p red lilac	.25 .25
133C	A48	40p brown ('59)	.55 .45
134	A48	50p greenish blue	.25 .25
135	A48	60p lemon	.25 .25
136	A48	100p vermilion	.25 .25
136B	A48	120p olive ('58)	.25 .25
		Nos. 133-136B (7)	2.05 1.95
		With tabs	25.00

Hammer Thrower — A59

1958, Jan. 20		Perf. 14x13	
137	A59	500p bister & car	.25 .25
		With tab	.25

Maccabiah Games, 25th anniversary.

Ancient Ship — A60

Ships: 20p, Three-master used for "illegal immigration." 30p, Cargo ship "Shomron." 1000p, Passenger ship "Zion."

	Wmk. 302		
1958, Jan. 27	Litho.	Perf. 14	

Size: 36½x22½mm

138	A60	10p ocher, red & blk	.25 .25

Perf. 13x14
Photo.

| 139 | A60 | 20p brt grn, blk & brn | .25 .25 |

ISRAEL

140 A60 30p red, blk & grnsh bl .25 .25
    Size: 56½x22½mm
141 A60 1000p brt bl, blk & grn .25 .25
    #138-141, with tabs .35

Issued to honor Israel's merchant fleet.

Menorah and Olive Branch — A61

1958, Apr. 21 Litho. Unwmk. Perf. 14
142 A61 400p gold, blk & grn .25 .25
  With tab .25

Memorial Day and 10th anniversary of proclamation of State of Israel.

Dancing Youths Forming "10" — A62

1958, July 2
143 A62 200p dk org & dk grn .25 .25
  With tab .25

First World Conference of Jewish Youth, Jerusalem, July 28-Aug. 1.

Convention Center, Jerusalem — A63

1958, July 2
144 A63 400p vio & org, *yellow* .25 .25
  With tab .25

10th Anniversary of Independence Exhibition, Jerusalem, June 5-Aug. 21.

Wheat — A64

1958, Aug. 27 Photo. Perf. 14x13
145 A64 50p shown .25 .25
146 A64 60p Barley .25 .25
147 A64 160p Grapes .25 .25
148 A64 300p Figs .25 .25
  #145-148, with tabs .30

Jewish New Year, 5719.

"Love Thy Neighbor..." A65

1958, Dec. 10 Litho. Perf. 14
149 A65 750p yel, gray & grn .25 .25
  With tab .60

Universal Declaration of Human Rights, 10th anniversary.

Designing and Printing Stamps A66

Radio and Telephone A67

120p, Mobile post office. 500p, Teletype.

1959, Feb. 25 Wmk. 302 Perf. 14
150 A66 60p olive, blk & red .25 .25
151 A66 120p olive, blk & red .25 .25
152 A67 250p olive, blk & red .25 .25
153 A67 500p olive, blk & red .25 .25
  #150-153, with tabs .45

Decade of postal activities in Israel.

Shalom Aleichem — A68

1959 Unwmk. Photo. Perf. 14x13
154 A68 250p yel grn & red brn .25 .25
155 A68 250p ocher & ol gray .25 .25
  #154-155, with tabs .35

Perf. 14
Litho.
156 A68 250p bl & vio bl .25 .25
  With tab .35

Portraits: No. 155, Chaim Nachman Bialik. No. 156, Eliezer Ben-Yehuda.

Birth cent. of Aleichem (Solomon Rabinowitz), Yiddish writer (No. 154); 25th death anniv. of Bialik, Hebrew poet (No. 155); birth cent. of Ben-Yehuda, father of modern Hebrew (No. 156).

Issued: No. 154, 3/30; No. 155, 7/22; No. 156, 11/25.

Cyclamen — A69

Flowers: 60p, Anemone. 300p, Narcissus.

1959, May 11 Wmk. 302 Perf. 14
Flowers in Natural Colors
157 A69 60p deep green .25 .25
158 A69 120p brt purple .25 .25
159 A69 300p blue .25 .25
  #157-159, with tabs .35

Memorial Day and 11th anniversary of proclamation of State of Israel.

Buildings, Tel Aviv — A70

1959, May 4
160 A70 120p multicolored .25 .25
  With tab .25

50th anniversary of Tel Aviv.

Bristol Britannia and Windsock — A71

1959, July 22
161 A71 500p multicolored .25 .25
  With tab .30

Civil Aviation in Israel, 10th anniversary.

Pomegranates — A72

Perf. 14x13
1959, Sept. 9 Photo. Unwmk.
162 A72 60p shown .25 .25
163 A72 200p Olives .25 .25
164 A72 350p Dates .25 .25
  Nos. 162-164 (3) .75 .75
  With tabs 1.00

Jewish New Year, 5720.

Merhavya — A73

Settlements: 120p, Yesud Ha-Maala. 180p, Deganya.

1959, Nov. 25 Photo. Perf. 13x14
165 A73 60p citron & dk grn .25 .25
166 A73 120p red brn & ocher .25 .25
167 A73 180p blue & dk grn .25 .25
  Nos. 165-167 (3) .75 .75
  With tabs 1.25

Settlements of Merhavya and Deganya, 50th anniv.; Yesud Ha-Maala, 75th anniv.

Judean Coin (66-70 A.D.) — A74

1960 Unwmk. Perf. 13x14
Denominations in Black
168 A74 1a brn, *pinkish* .25 .25
  a. On surface colored paper As "a", with tab .25 .25
  b. Black overprint omitted .75
169 A74 3a brt red, *pinkish* .25 .25
170 A74 5a gray, *pinkish* .25 .25
171 A74 6a brt grn, *lt bl* .25 .25
171A A74 7a gray, *bluish* .25 .25
172 A74 8a mag, *lt blue* .25 .25
173 A74 12a grnsh bl, *lt bl* .25 .25
  a. Black overprint omitted
174 A74 18a orange .25 .25
175 A74 25a blue .25 .25
176 A74 30a carmine .25 .25
177 A74 50a bright lilac .25 .25
  #168-177, with tabs 1.50

Issue dates: 7a, July 6; others, Jan. 6.

Operation "Magic Carpet" — A75

Design: 50a, Resettled family in front of house, grapes and figs.

1960, Apr. 7 Unwmk. Perf. 13x14
178 A75 25a red brown .25 .25
179 A75 50a green .25 .25
  #178-179, with tabs .30

World Refugee Year, July 1, 1959-June 30, 1960.

Sand Lily — A76

Design: 32a, Evening primrose.

1960, Apr. 27 Litho. Perf. 14
180 A76 12a multicolored .25 .25
181 A76 32a brn, yel & grn .25 .25
  #180-181, with tabs .45

Memorial Day; proclamation of State of Israel, 12th anniv. See Nos. 204-206, 238-240.

Atom Diagram and Atomic Reactor — A77

1960, July 6 Wmk. 302 Perf. 14
182 A77 50a blue, red & blk .25 .25
  With tab .45

Installation of Israel's first atomic reactor.

Theodor Herzl and Rhine at Basel — A78

1960, Aug. 31 Litho. Perf. 14
183 A78 25a gray brown .25 .25
  With tab .40

King Saul — A79

Designs: 25a, King David. 40a, King Solomon.

Kings in Multicolor
1960, Aug. 31 Wmk. 302
184 A79 7a emerald .25 .25

Unwmk.
185 A79 25a brown .25 .25
186 A79 40a blue .25 .25
  Nos. 184-186 (3) .75 .75
  With tabs 1.25

Jewish New Year, 5721. See Nos. 208-210.

Jewish Postal Courier, Prague, 18th Century — A80

1960, Oct. 9 Perf. 13x14
187 A80 25a olive blk, *gray* .25 .25
  With tab 1.50
  a. Souvenir sheet 9.00 7.00

TAVIV Natl. Stamp Exhib., Tel Aviv, Oct. 9-19.
No. 187a sold only at Exhibition for 50a.

Henrietta Szold and Hadassah Medical Center — A81

1960, Dec. 14 Perf. 13x14
188 A81 25a turq bl & vio gray .25 .25
  With tab .30

Birth cent. of Henrietta Szold, founder of Hadassah, American Jewish women's organization.

Shields of Jerusalem and First Zionist Congress — A82

1960, Dec. 14 Unwmk. Perf. 14
189 A82 50a vio bl & turq blue .25 .25
  With tab .60

25th Zionist Congress, Jerusalem, 1960.

Ram A83

Signs of Zodiac A84

1961, Feb. 27 Photo. Perf. 13x14
190 A83 1a Ram .25 .25
191 A83 2a Bull .25 .25
192 A83 6a Twins .25 .25
193 A83 7a Crab .25 .25
194 A83 8a Lion .25 .25
  a. Booklet pane of 6 ('65) .45

ISRAEL

195	A83	10a Virgin	.25	.25
196	A83	12a Scales	.25	.25
a.		Booklet pane of 6 ('65)		.45
197	A83	18a Scorpion	.25	.25
198	A83	20a Archer	.25	.25
199	A83	25a Goat	.25	.25
200	A83	32a Water bearer	.25	.25
201	A83	50a Fishes	.25	.25

Perf. 14
Litho.

202	A84	£1 dk bl, gold & lt bl	.25	.25
		Nos. 190-202 (13)	3.25	3.25
		With tabs		5.50

Booklet pane sheets (Nos. 194a, 196a) of 36 (9x4) contain 6 panes of 6, with gutters dividing the sheet in four sections. Each sheet yields 4 tete beche pairs and 4 tete beche gutter pairs, or strips.

For surcharges see Nos. 215-217.

Vertical strips of 6 of the 1a, 10a and No. 216 (5a) are from larger sheets from which coils were produced. Regular sheets of 50 are arranged 10x5.

Javelin Thrower and "7" — A85

1961, Apr. 18   Litho.   Perf. 14

203	A85	25a multicolored	.25	.25
		With tab		.40

7th Intl. Congress of the Hapoel Sports Org., Ramat Gan, May 1961.

Flower Type of 1960

7a, Myrtle. 12a, Sea onion. 32a, Oleander.

1961, Apr. 18   Unwmk.
Flowers in Natural Colors

204	A76	7a green	.25	.25
205	A76	12a rose carmine	.25	.25
206	A76	32a brt greenish bl	.25	.25
		Nos. 204-206 (3)	.75	.75
		With tabs		.80

Memorial Day; proclamation of State of Israel, 13th anniv.

Scaffold Around "10" and Sapling — A86

1961, June 14   Photo.   Perf. 14

207	A86	50a Prussian blue	.25	.25
		With tab		.40

Israel bond issue 10th anniv.

Type of 1960

Designs: 7a, Samson. 25a, Judas Maccabaeus. 40a, Bar Cocheba.

1961, Aug. 21   Litho.   Perf. 14
Multicolored Designs

208	A79	7a red orange	.25	.25
209	A79	25a gray	.25	.25
210	A79	40a lilac	.25	.25
		Nos. 208-210 (3)	.75	.75
		With tabs		1.60

Jewish New Year, 5722.

Bet Hamidrash Synagogue, Medzibozh — A87

1961, Aug. 21   Photo.   Perf. 13x14

211	A87	25a dk brn & yel	.25	.25
		With tab		.40

Bicentenary of death of Rabbi Israel Baal-Shem-Tov, founder of Hasidism.

Pine Cone — A88

Design: 30a, Symbolic trees.

1961, Dec. 26   Unwmk.   Perf. 13x14

212	A88	25a green, yel & blk	.25	.25
213	A88	30a org, green & ind	.25	.25
		#212-213, with tabs		1.50

Achievements of afforestation program.

Cello, Harp, French Horn and Kettle Drum — A89

1961, Dec. 26   Litho.   Perf. 14

214	A89	50a multicolored	.25	.25
		With tab		1.50

Israel Philharmonic Orchestra, 25th anniv.

Zodiac Type of 1961 Surcharged with New Value

1962, Mar. 18   Photo.   Perf. 13x14

215	A83	3a on 1a lt lilac	.25	.25
a.		Without overprint	60.00	
216	A83	5a on 7a gray	.25	.25
217	A83	30a on 32a emerald	.25	.25
a.		Without overprint	50.00	
		#215-217, with tabs		.40
		#215a and 217a, with tabs		400.00

See note after No. 202.

Anopheles Maculipennis and Chart Showing Decline of Malaria in Israel — A90

1962, Apr. 30   Perf. 14x13

218	A90	25a ocher, red & blk	.25	.25
		With tab		.40

WHO drive to eradicate malaria.

View of Rosh Pinna — A91

1962, Apr. 30   Unwmk.

219	A91	20a yel, green & brn	.25	.25
		With tab		.35

Rosh Pinna agricultural settlement, 80th anniv.

Flame ("Hear, O Israel . . .") A92

Yellow Star of David and Six Candles A93

1962, Apr. 30   Photo.

220	A92	12a black, org & red	.25	.25

Perf. 14

221	A93	55a multicolored	.25	.25
		#220-221, with tabs		1.25

Heroes and Martyrs Day, in memory of the 6,000,000 Jewish victims of Nazi persecution.

Vautour Fighter-Bomber A94

Design: 30a, Fighter-Bombers in formation.

1962, Apr. 30   Perf. 13x14

222	A94	12a blue	.25	.25
223	A94	30a olive green	.25	.25
		#222-223, with tabs		1.50

Memorial Day; proclamation of the state of Israel, 14th anniv.

Symbolic Flags — A95

1962, June 5   Perf. 14

224	A95	55a multicolored	.25	.25
		With tab		.75

Near East Intl. Fair, Tel Aviv, June 5-July 5.

Wolf and Lamb, Isaiah 11:6 — A96

Designs: 28a, Leopard and kid, Isaiah 11:6. 43a, Child and asp, Isaiah 11:8.

1962, Sept. 5

225	A96	8a buff, red & black	.25	.25
226	A96	28a buff, lilac & black	.25	.25
227	A96	43a buff, org & black	.25	.25
		Nos. 225-227 (3)	.75	.75
		With tabs		2.25

Jewish New Year, 5723.

Boeing 707 — A97

1962, Nov. 7   Perf. 13x14

228	A97	55a bl, dk bl & rose lil	.30	.25
		With tab		.95
a.		Souvenir sheet	2.00	1.75

El Al Airlines; El Al Philatelic Exhibition, Tel Aviv, Nov. 7-14. Issued in sheets of 15.

No. 228a contains one stamp in greenish blue, dark blue & rose lilac with greenish blue color continuing into margin design (No. 228 has white perforations). Sold for £1 for one day at philatelic counters in Jerusalem, Haifa and Tel Aviv and for one week at the El Al Exhibition.

Cogwheel Symbols of UJA Activities — A98

1962, Dec. 26   Unwmk.   Perf. 13x14

229	A98	20a org red, sil & bl	.25	.25
		With tab		.35

25th anniv. of the United Jewish Appeal (United States) and its support of immigration, settlement, agriculture and care of the aged and sick.

Janusz Korczak — A99

1962, Dec. 26   Photo.

230	A99	30a olive grn & blk	.25	.25
		With tab		.35

Dr. Janusz Korczak (Henryk Goldszmit, 1879-1942), physician, teacher and writer, killed in Treblinka concentration camp.

Orange butterflyfish A100

Red Sea fish: 3a, Pennant Coral Fish. 8a, Lionfish. 12a, Zebra-striped angelfish.

1962, Dec. 26   Litho.   Perf. 14
Fish in Natural Colors

231	A100	3a green	.25	.25
232	A100	6a purple	.25	.25
233	A100	8a brown	.25	.25
234	A100	12a dark blue	.25	.25
		#231-234, with tabs		.60

See Nos. 246-249.

Stockade at Dawn — A101

Design: 30a, Completed stockade at night.

1963, Mar. 21   Unwmk.   Perf. 14

235	A101	12a yel brn, blk & yel	.25	.25
236	A101	30a dp plum, blk & lt bl	.25	.25
		#235-236, with tabs		.75

25th anniv. of the "Stockade and Tower" villages.

Hand Offering Food to Bird — A102

1963, Mar. 21   Photo.   Perf. 13x14

237	A102	55a gray & black	.25	.25
		With tab		.70
a.		Booklet pane of 4		27.50

FAO "Freedom from Hunger" campaign.

Issued in sheets of 15 (5x3) with 5 tabs. The booklet pane sheet of 16 (4x4) is divided into 2 panes of 8 (4x2) by horizontal gutter. The 4 stamps at left in each pane are inverted in relation to the 4 at right, making 4 horizontal tete beche pairs down the center of the sheet.

Flower Type of 1960

8a, White lily. 30a, Hollyhock. 37a, Tulips.

1963, Apr. 25   Litho.   Perf. 14
Flowers in Natural Colors

238	A76	8a slate	.25	.25
239	A76	30a yellow green	.25	.25
240	A76	37a sepia	.25	.25
		Nos. 238-240 (3)	.75	.75
		With tabs		2.00

Memorial Day; proclamation of the State of Israel, 15th anniv.

Typesetter, 19th Century — A103

1963, June 19   Photo.   Perf. 14x13

241	A103	12a tan & vio brn	.35	.35
		With tab		1.10
a.		Sheet of 16	30.00	30.00

Hebrew press in Palestine, cent. The background of the sheet shows page of 1st issue of "Halbanon" newspaper, giving each stamp a different background.

"The Sun Beat upon the Head of Jonah" — A104

Designs: 30a, "There was a mighty tempest in the sea." 55a, "Jonah was in the belly of the fish." 30a, 55a horiz.

1963, Aug. 21   Perf. 14x13, 13x14

242	A104	8a org, lil & blk	.25	.25
243	A104	30a multicolored	.25	.25
244	A104	55a multicolored	.25	.25
		Nos. 242-244 (3)	.75	.75
		With tabs		1.40

Jewish New Year, 5724.

ISRAEL

Hoe Clearing Thistles — A105

1963, Aug. 21   **Perf. 14**
245 A105 37a multicolored   .25   .25
   With tab   .65

80 years of agricultural settlements in Israel; "Year of the Pioneers."

Fish Type of 1962
Red Sea Fish: 2a, Undulate triggerfish. 6a, Radiate turkeyfish. 8a, Bigeye. 12a, Imperial angelfish.

1963, Dec. 16   **Litho.**   **Perf. 14**
Fish in Natural Colors
246 A100 2a violet blue   .25   .25
247 A100 6a green   .25   .25
248 A100 8a orange   .25   .25
249 A100 12a olive green   .25   .25
   Nos. 246-249 (4)   1.00   1.00
   With tabs   1.25

S.S. Shalom, Sailing Vessel and Ancient Map of Coast Line — A106

1963, Dec. 16   **Photo.**   **Perf. 13x14**
250 A106 £1 ultra, brt grn & lil   .70   .40
   With tab   5.50

Maiden voyage of S.S. Shalom.

"Old Age and Survivors Insurance" — A107

Designs (Insurance): 25a, Maternity. 37a, Large family. 50a, Workers' compensation.

1964, Feb. 24   **Litho.**   **Perf. 14**
251 A107 12a multicolored   .25   .25
252 A107 25a multicolored   .25   .25
253 A107 37a multicolored   .25   .25
254 A107 50a multicolored   .25   .25
   Nos. 251-254 (4)   1.00   1.00
   With tabs   4.00

Natl. Insurance Institute 10th anniv.

Pres. Izhak Ben-Zvi (1884-1963) — A108

1964, Apr. 13   **Photo.**   **Perf. 14x13**
255 A108 12a dark brown   .25   .25
   With tab   .35

Terrestrial Spectroscopy A109

Designs: 35a, Macromolecules of the living cell. 70a, Electronic computer.

1964, Apr. 13   **Perf. 14**
256 A109 8a multicolored   .25   .25
257 A109 35a multicolored   .25   .25
258 A109 70a multicolored   .25   .25
   Nos. 256-258 (3)   .75   .75
   With tabs   2.50

Proclamation of the State of Israel, 16th anniv.; Israel's contribution to science.

Basketball Players — A110

8a, Runner. 12a, Discus thrower. 50a, Soccer.

1964, June 24   **Perf. 14x13**
259 A110 8a brt brick red & dk brown   .25   .25
260 A110 12a rose lil & dk brn   .25   .25
261 A110 30a bl, car & dk brn   .25   .25
262 A110 50a yel grn, org red & dk brown   .25   .25
   Nos. 259-262 (4)   1.00   1.00
   With tabs   .90

Israel's participation in the 18th Olympic Games, Tokyo, Oct. 10-25.

Serpent of Aesculapius and Menorah — A111

1964, Aug. 5   **Unwmk.**
263 A111 £1 ol bis & slate grn   .30   .25
   With tab   .65

6th World Congress of the Israel Medical Association, Haifa, Aug. 3-13.

Ancient Glass Vase — A112

Different glass vessels, 1st-3rd centuries.

1964, Aug. 5   **Litho.**
264 A112 8a vio, brn & org   .25   .25
265 A112 35a ol, grn & bl grn   .25   .25
266 A112 70a brt car rose, blue & violet blue   .25   .25
   Nos. 264-266 (3)   .75   .75
   With tabs   .60

Jewish New Year, 5725.

Steamer Bringing Immigrants — A113

1964, Nov. 2   **Litho.**   **Perf. 14**
267 A113 25a slate bl, bl grn & blk   .25   .25
   With tab   .30

30th anniv. of the blockade runners bringing immigrants to Israel.

Eleanor Roosevelt (1884-1962) — A114

1964, Nov. 2   **Photo.**   **Perf. 14x13**
268 A114 70a dull purple   .25   .25
   With tab   .40

Chess Board, Knight and Emblem of Chess Olympics A115

1964, Nov. 2   **Perf. 13x14**
269 A115 12a shown   .25   .25
270 A115 70a Rook   .35   .30
   With tabs   1.75

16th Chess Olympics, Tel Aviv, Nov. 1964.

"Africa-Israel Friendship" — A116

1964, Nov. 30   **Photo.**   **Perf. 14x13**
271 A116 57a ol, blk, gold & red brown   .35   .25
   With tab   1.75
   a. Souvenir sheet   1.50   1.50

TABAI, Natl. Stamp Exhibition, dedicated to African-Israel friendship, Haifa, Nov. 30-Dec. 6. No. 271a contains one imperf. stamp. Sold for £1.

View of Masada from West — A117

Designs: 36a, Northern Palace, lower terrace. £1, View of Northern Palace, vert.

1965, Feb. 3   **Photo.**   **Perf. 13x14**
272 A117 25a dull green   .25   .25
273 A117 36a bright blue   .25   .25
274 A117 £1 dark red brn   .25   .25
   Nos. 272-274 (3)   .75   .75
   With tabs   1.40

Ruins of Masada, the last stronghold in the war against the Romans, 66-73 A.D.

Book Fair Emblem — A118

1965, Mar. 24   **Photo.**   **Perf. 13x14**
275 A118 70a gray ol, brt bl & blk   .25   .25
   With tab   .25

2nd Intl. Book Fair, Jerusalem, April.

Arms of Ashdod — A119

Town Emblems: 1a, Lydda (Lod). 2a, Qiryat Shemona. 5a, Petah Tikva. 6a, Nazareth. 8a, Beersheba. 10a, Bet Shean. 12a, Tiberias. 20a, Elat. 25a, Acre (Akko). 35a, Dimona. 37a, Zefat. 50a, Rishon Leziyyon. 70a, Jerusalem. £1, Tel Aviv-Jaffa. £3, Haifa.

Size: 17x22½mm

1965-66   **Perf. 13x14**
276 A119 1a brown   .25   .25
277 A119 2a lilac rose   .25   .25
278 A119 5a gray   .25   .25
279 A119 6a violet   .25   .25
280 A119 8a orange   .25   .25
   a. Booklet pane of 6   .45
281 A119 10a emerald   .25   .25
282 A119 12a dark purple   .25   .25
   a. Booklet pane of 6   .50
283 A119 15a green   .25   .25
284 A119 20a rose red   .25   .25
285 A119 25a ultramarine   .25   .25
286 A119 35a magenta   .25   .25
287 A119 37a olive   .25   .25
288 A119 50a greenish bl   .25   .25

Perf. 14x13
Size: 22x27mm
289 A119 70a dark brown   .25   .25
290 A119 £1 dark green   .25   .25
291 A119 £3 dk carmine rose   .55   .25
   Nos. 276-291 (16)   4.30   4.00
   With tabs   8.00

Issued: Nos. 283-286, 3/24/65; No. 290, 11/24/65; No. 291, 3/14/66; others, 2/2/66.

The uncut booklet pane sheets of 36 are divided into 4 panes (2 of 6 stamps, 2 of 12) by horizontal and vertical gutters. alf of the stamps in the 2 panes of 12 are inverted, causing 4 horizontal tête bêche pairs and 4 horizontal tête bêche gutter pairs.

Vertical strips of 6 of the 1a, 5a and 10a are from larger sheets, released Jan. 10, 1967, from which coils were produced. Regular sheets of 50 are arranged 10x5.

No. 290 also comes tagged (1975). See Nos. 334-336, 386-393.

Hands Reaching for Hope, and Star of David — A120

1965, Apr. 27   **Unwmk.**   **Perf. 14x13**
292 A120 25a gray, black & yel   .25   .25
   With tab   .40

Liberation of Nazi concentration camps, 20th anniv.

"Irrigation of the Desert" — A121

1965, Apr. 27   **Photo.**
293 A121 37a olive bister & blue   .25   .25
   With tab   .25

Memorial Day; proclamation of the state of Israel, 17th anniv.

Telegraph Pole and Syncom Satellite — A122

1965, July 21   **Unwmk.**   **Perf. 13x14**
294 A122 70a vio, blk & grnsh bl   .25   .25
   With tab   .30

ITU, centenary.

Symbol of Cooperation and UN Emblem — A123

1965, July 21   **Litho.**   **Perf. 14**
295 A123 36a gray, dp claret, bl, red & bis   .25   .25
   With tab   .30

International Cooperation Year.

Dead Sea Extraction Plant — A124

1965, July 21
296 A124 12a Crane   .25   .25
297 A124 50a shown   .25   .25
   #296-297, with tabs   .60

Dead Sea chemical industry.

"Let There be Light . . ." — A125

Genesis 1, The Creation: 8a, Firmament and Waters. 12a, Dry land and vegetation. 25a, Heavenly lights. 35a, Fish and fowl. 70a, Man.

ISRAEL

1965, Sept. 7   Photo.   *Perf. 13x14*
298 A125 6a dk pur, lil & gold .25 .25
299 A125 8a brt grn, dk bl & gold .25 .25
300 A125 12a red brn, blk & gold .25 .25
301 A125 25a dk pur, pink & gold .25 .25
302 A125 35a lt & dk bl & gold .25 .25
303 A125 70a dp cl, car & gold .25 .25
  Nos. 298-303 (6) 1.50 1.50
  With tabs 1.10

Jewish New Year, 5726. Sheets of 20 (10x2).

Charaxes Jasius — A126

Butterflies & Moths: 6a, Papilio alexanor maccabaeus. 8a, Daphnis nerii. 12a, Zegris eupheme uarda.

1965, Dec. 15   Litho.   *Perf. 14*
Butterflies in Natural Colors
304 A126 2a lt olive green .25 .25
305 A126 6a lilac .25 .25
306 A126 8a ocher .25 .25
307 A126 12a blue .25 .25
  #304-307, with tabs .50

Flags over Rooftops — A127

Designs: 30a, Fireworks over Tel Aviv. 80a, Warships and Super Mirage jets, Haifa.

1966, Apr. 20   Litho.   *Perf. 14*
308 A127 12a multi .25 .25
309 A127 30a multi .25 .25
310 A127 80a multi .25 .25
  #308-310, with tabs .40

Proclamation of state of Israel, 18th anniv.

Memorial, Upper Galilee — A128

1966, Apr. 20   Photo.   *Perf. 14x13*
311 A128 40a olive gray .25 .25
  With tab .35

Issued for Memorial Day.

Knesset Building, Jerusalem — A129

1966, June 22   Photo.   *Perf. 13x14*
312 A129 £1 deep blue .25 .25
  With tab .35

Inauguration of the Knesset Building (Parliament). Sheets of 12.

Road Sign and Motorcyclist — A130

Road Signs and: 5a, Bicyclist. 10a, Pedestrian. 12a, Child playing ball. 15a, Automobile.

1966, June 22   *Perf. 14*
313 A130 2a sl, red brn & lil rose .25 .25
314 A130 5a ol bis, sl & lil rose .25 .25
315 A130 10a vio, lt bl & lil rose .25 .25
316 A130 12a bl, grn & lil rose .25 .25
317 A130 15a grn, red & lil rose .25 .25
  #313-317, with tabs .35

Issued to publicize traffic safety.

Spice Box — A131

Ritual Art Objects: 15a, Candlesticks. 35a, Kiddush cup. 40a, Torah pointer. 80a, Hanging lamp.

1966, Aug. 24   Photo.   *Perf. 13x14*
318 A131 12a sil, gold, blk & bl .25 .25
319 A131 15a sil, gold, blk & lil .25 .25
320 A131 35a sil, gold, blk & emer .25 .25
321 A131 40a sil, gold, blk & vio bl .25 .25
322 A131 80a sil, gold, blk & red .25 .25
  #318-322, with tabs .65

Jewish New Year, 5727.

Bronze Panther, Avdat, 1st Century, B.C. — A132

30a, Stone menorah, Tiberias, 2nd Cent. 40a, Phoenician ivory sphinx, 9th cent., B.C. 55a, Gold earring (calf's head), Ashdod, 6th-4th cents. B.C. 80a, Miniature gold capital, Persia, 5th cent., B.C. £1.15, Gold drinking horn (ram's head), Persia, 5th cent., B.C., vert.

1966, Oct. 26   Litho.   *Perf. 14*
323 A132 15a dp bl & yel brn .25 .25
324 A132 30a vio brn & bister .25 .25
325 A132 40a sepia & yel bis .30 .25
326 A132 55a Prus grn, dp yel & brown .30 .25
327 A132 80a lake, dp yel & brown .50 .25
  Perf. 13x14
328 A132 £1.15 vio, gold & brn 1.00 .60
  Nos. 323-328 (6) 2.60 1.85
  With tabs 5.50

Israel Museum, Jerusalem. Sheets of 12.

Coach and Mailman of Austrian Levant — A133

Designs: 15a, Turkish mailman and caravan. 40a, Palestinian mailman and locomotive. £1, Israeli mailman and jet liner.

1966, Dec. 14   Photo.   *Perf. 14*
329 A133 12a ocher & green .25 .25
330 A133 15a lt grn, brn & dp car .25 .25
331 A133 40a brt rose & dk blue .25 .25
332 A133 £1 grnsh bl & brown .25 .25
  Nos. 329-332 (4) 1.00 1.00
  With tabs .65

Issued for Stamp Day.

Microscope and Cells — A134

1966, Dec. 14   *Perf. 14x13*
333 A134 15a red & dark slate grn .25 .25
  With tab .25

Campaign against cancer.

Arms Type of 1965-66

Town Emblems: 40a, Mizpe Ramon. 55a, Ashkelon. 80a, Rosh Pinna.

1967, Feb. 8   Unwmk.   *Perf. 13x14*
334 A119 40a dark olive .25 .25
335 A119 55a dk carmine rose .25 .25
336 A119 80a red brown .25 .25
  Nos. 334-336 (3) .75 .75
  With tabs 1.25

Port of Acre — A135

Ancient Ports: 40a, Caesarea. 80a, Jaffa.

1967, Mar. 22   Photo.   *Perf. 13x14*
337 A135 15a purple brown .25 .25
338 A135 40a dark blue grn .25 .25
339 A135 80a deep blue .25 .25
  Nos. 337-339 (3) .75 .75
  With tabs .80

Page of Shulhan Aruk and Crowns — A136

1967, Mar. 22   *Perf. 13½x13*
340 A136 40a dk & lt bl, gray & gold .25 .25
  With tab .25

400th anniv. of the publication (in 1565) of the Shulhan Aruk, a compendium of Jewish religious and civil law, by Joseph Karo (1488-1575).

War of Independence Memorial — A137

1967, May 10   Unwmk.   *Perf. 13x14*
341 A137 55a lt bl, indigo & sil .25 .25
  With tab .30

Issued for Memorial Day, 1967.

Auster Plane over Convoy on Jerusalem Road — A138

Military Aircraft: 30a, Mystère IV jet fighter over Dead Sea area. 80a, Mirage jet fighters over Masada.

1967, May 10   Photo.
342 A138 15a lt ol grn & dk bl grn .25 .25
343 A138 30a ocher & dark brn .25 .25
344 A138 80a grnsh bl & vio bl .25 .25
  Nos. 342-344 (3) .75 .75
  With tabs .60

Issued for Independence Day, 1967.

Israeli Ships in Straits of Tiran — A139

15a, Star of David, sword & olive branch, vert. 80a, Wailing (Western) Wall, Jerusalem.

1967, Aug. 16   *Perf. 14x13, 13x14*
345 A139 15a dk red, blk & yel .25 .25
346 A139 40a Prussian green .25 .25
347 A139 80a deep violet .25 .25
  #345-347, with tabs .60

Victory of the Israeli forces, June, 1967.

Torah, Scroll of the Law — A140

Various ancient, decorated Scrolls of the Law.

1967, Sept. 13   *Perf. 13x14*
348 A140 12a gold & multi .25 .25
349 A140 15a silver & multi .25 .25
350 A140 35a gold & multi .25 .25
351 A140 40a silver & multi .25 .25
352 A140 80a gold & multi .25 .25
  #348-352, with tabs .70

Jewish New Year, 5728. Sheets of 20 (10x2).

Chaim Weizmann — A141

Design: 40a, Lord Balfour.

1967, Nov. 2   Photo.   *Perf. 13x14*
353 A141 15a dark green .25 .25
354 A141 40a brown .25 .25
  #353-354, with tabs .25

50th anniv. of the Balfour Declaration, which established the right to a Jewish natl. home in Palestine. Issued in sheets of 15.

Emblem and Doll — A142

Inscriptions: 30a, Hebrew. 40a, French.

1967, Nov. 2   Litho.   *Perf. 14*
355 A142 30a yellow & multi .25 .25
356 A142 40a brt bl & multi .25 .25
357 A142 80a brt grn & multi .25 .25
  #355-357, with tabs .40

Intl. Tourist Year. Issued in sheets of 15.

Nubian Ibex — A143

18a, Caracal lynx. 60a, Dorcas gazelles.

1967, Dec. 27   Litho.   *Perf. 13*
Animal in Ocher & Brown
358 A143 12a dull purple .25 .25
359 A143 18a bright green .25 .25
360 A143 60a bright blue .25 .25
  #358-360, with tabs .40

Flags Forming Soccer Ball — A144

1968, Mar. 11   Photo.   *Perf. 13*
361 A144 80a ocher & multi .25 .25
  With tab .25

Pre-Olympic soccer tournament.

Welcoming Immigrants — A145

Design: 80a, Happy farm family.

1968, Apr. 24   Litho.   *Perf. 14*
362 A145 15a lt green & multi .25 .25
363 A145 80a cream & multi .25 .25
  #362-363, with tabs .25

Issued for Independence Day, 1968.

ISRAEL

Resistance Fighter — A146

1968, Apr. 24   Photo.   Perf. 14x13
364 A146 60a brown olive   .25 .25
        With tab   .25

Warsaw Ghetto Uprising, 25th anniv. Design from Warsaw Ghetto Memorial.

Sword and Laurel A147

Rifles and Helmet A148

1968, Apr. 24   Litho.   Perf. 14
365 A147 40a gold & multi   .25 .25
366 A148 55a black & multi   .25 .25
        #365-366, with tabs   .25

Zahal defense army, Independence Day (No. 365); Memorial Day (No. 366).

Candle and Prison Window — A149

1968, June 5   Photo.   Perf. 14x13
367 A149 80a blk, gray & sepia .25 .25
        With tab   .25

Issued to honor those who died for freedom.

Prime Minister Moshe Sharett (1894-1965) — A150

1968, June 5   Unwmk.
368 A150 £1 deep brown   .25 .25
        With tab   .25

27th Zionist Congress.

Knot Forming Star of David — A151

1968, Aug. 21   Litho.   Perf. 13
369 A151 30a multi   .25 .25
        With tab   .25

50 years of Jewish Scouting. Sheets of 15.

Dome of the Rock and Absalom's Tomb — A152

Views of Jerusalem: 15a, Church of the Resurrection. 35a, Tower of David and City Wall. 40a, Yemin Moshe District and Mount of Olives. 60a, Israel Museum and "Shrine of the Book."

1968, Aug. 21   Photo.   Perf. 14x13
370 A152 12a gold & multi   .25 .25
371 A152 15a gold & multi   .25 .25
372 A152 35a gold & multi   .25 .25
373 A152 40a gold & multi   .25 .25
374 A152 60a gold & multi   .25 .25
        #370-374, with tabs   .40

Jewish New Year, 5729. Sheets of 15.

Detail from Lions' Gate, Jerusalem (St. Stephen's Gate) — A153

1968, Oct. 8   Unwmk.   Perf. 13x14
375 A153 £1 brown org   .25 .25
        With tab   .25
  a.   Souvenir sheet   .35 .30

TABIRA Natl. Philatelic Exhibition. No. 375a contains one imperf. stamp. Sold only at exhibition for £1.50. No. 375 Issued in sheets of 15.

Abraham Mapu — A154

1968, Oct. 8   Photo.   Perf. 14x13
376 A154 30a dark olive grn   .25 .25
        With tab   .25

Mapu (1808-1867), novelist and historian.

Wheelchair Basketball — A155

1968, Nov. 6   Photo.   Perf. 14x13
377 A155 40a green & yel grn   .25 .25
        With tab   .25

17th Stoke-Mandeville Games for the Paralyzed, Nov. 4-13. Sheets of 15.

Port of Elat A156

Ports of Israel: 60a, Ashdod. £1, Haifa.

1969, Feb. 19   Unwmk.   Perf. 13x14
378 A156 30a deep magenta   .25 .25
379 A156 60a brown   .25 .25
380 A156 £1 dull green   .25 .25
        Nos. 378-380 (3)   .75 .75
        With tabs   1.75

Tank — A157

1969, Apr. 16   Photo.   Perf. 13x14
381 A157 15a shown   .25 .25
382 A157 80a Destroyer   .25 .25
        #381-382, with tabs   .40

Issued for Independence Day 1969.

Israel's Flag at Half-mast — A158

1969, Apr. 16
383 A158 55a vio, gold & bl   .25 .25
        With tab   .25

Issued for Memorial Day.

Worker and ILO Emblem — A159

1969, Apr. 16
384 A159 80a dark blue grn   .25 .25
        With tab   .25

ILO, 50th anniversary.

Hand Holding Torch — A160

1969, July 9   Photo.   Perf. 14x13
385 A160 60a gold & multi   .25 .25
        With tab   .40

Issued to publicize the 8th Maccabiah.

Arms of Hadera — A161

Town Emblems: 3a, Hertseliya. 5a, Holon. 15a, Bat Yam. 18a, Ramla. 20a, Kefar Sava. 25a, Giv'atayim. 30a, Rehovot. 40a, Netanya. 50a, Bene Beraq. 60a, Nahariyya. 80a, Ramat Gan.

1969-73   Perf. 13x14
386   A161 2a green   .25 .25
387   A161 3a deep magenta   .25 .25
388   A161 5a orange   .25 .25
389   A161 15a bright rose   .25 .25
  c.   Bklt. pane of 6 (2 #389 + 4 #389A) ('71)   .65
389A A161 18a ultra ('70)   .25 .25
  d.   Bklt. pane of 6 ('71)   .70
  e.   Bklt. pane of 6 (1 #281 + 5 #389A) ('73)   .65
389B A161 20a brown ('70)   .25 .25
  f.   Bklt. pane of 5 + label ('73) .90
390   A161 25a dark blue   .25 .25
390A A161 30a brt pink ('70)   .25 .25
391   A161 40a purple   .25 .25
392   A161 50a greenish bl   .25 .25
392A A161 60a olive ('70)   .25 .25
393   A161 80a dark green   .25 .25
        Nos. 386-393 (12)   3.00 3.00
        With tabs   3.00

Nos. 389c and 389d were also sold in uncut sheets of 36, No. 389e in uncut sheet of 18. See note after No. 291 about similar sheets.

Noah Building the Ark — A162

The Story of the Flood: 15a, Animals boarding the Ark. 35a, The Ark during the flood. 40a, Noah sending out the dove. 60a, Noah and the rainbow.

1969, Aug. 13   Unwmk.   Perf. 14
394 A162 12a multicolored   .25 .25
395 A162 15a multicolored   .25 .25
396 A162 35a multicolored   .25 .25
397 A162 40a multicolored   .25 .25
398 A162 60a multicolored   .25 .25
        #394-398, with tabs   .70

Jewish New Year, 5730. Sheets of 15.

King David by Marc Chagall — A163

1969, Sept. 24   Photo.   Perf. 14
399 A163 £3 multicolored   .65 .55
        With tab   1.00

Atom Diagram and Test Tube — A164

1969, Nov. 3   Perf. 14x13
400 A164 £1.15 vio bl & multi   .55 .40
        With tab   1.25

Weizmann Institute of Science, 25th anniv.

Joseph Trumpeldor — A165

1970, Jan. 21   Photo.   Perf. 14x13
401 A165 £1 dark purple   .25 .25
        With tab   .60

50th anniv. of the defense of Tel Hay under the leadership of Joseph Trumpeldor.

Dum Palms, Emeq Ha-Arava — A166

Views: 3a, Tahana Waterfall. 5a, Nahal Baraq Canyon, Negev. 6a, Cedars in Judean Hills. 30a, Soreq Cave, Judean Hills.

1970, Jan. 21
402 A166 2a olive   .25 .25
403 A166 3a deep blue   .25 .25
404 A166 5a orange red   .25 .25
405 A166 6a slate green   .25 .25
406 A166 30a brt purple   .25 .25
        #402-406, with tabs   .35

Issued to publicize nature reserves.

Magic Carpet Shaped as Airplane — A167

1970, Jan. 21   Litho.   Perf. 13
407 A167 30a multicolored   .25 .25
        With tab   .25

20th anniv. of "Operation Magic Carpet" which airlifted the Yemeni Jews to Israel.

Prime Minister Levi Eshkol (1895-1969) — A168

1970, Mar. 11   Litho.   Perf. 14
408 A168 15a bl & multi   .25 .25
        With tab   .25

Mania Shochat — A169

Portrait: 80a, Ze'ev Jabotinsky (1880-1940), writer and Zionist leader.

ISRAEL

1970, Mar. 11   Photo.   *Perf. 14x13*
409	A169	40a dp plum & buff	.25 .25
410	A169	80a green & cream	.25 .25
		#409-410, with tabs	.90

Ha-Shomer (Watchmen defense organization), 60th anniv. (No. 409); defense of Jerusalem, 50th anniv. (No. 410)

Camel and Train — A170

1970, Mar. 11   Litho.   *Perf. 13*
411	A170	80a orange & multi	.40 .25
		With tab	.50

Opening of Dimona-Oron Railroad.

Scene from "The Dibbuk" A171

1970, Mar. 11   Photo.   *Perf. 14x13*
412	A171	£1 multicolored	.25 .25
		With tab	.50

Habimah Natl. Theater, 50th anniv.

Memorial Flame — A172

1970, May 6   Photo.   *Perf. 13x14*
413	A172	55a vio, pink & blk	.25 .25
		With tab	.25

Issued for Memorial Day, 1970.

Orchis Laxiflorus — A173

Flowers: 15a, Iris mariae. 80a, Lupinus pilosus.

1970, May 6   Litho.   *Perf. 14*
414	A173	12a pale gray, plum & grn	.25 .25
415	A173	15a multicolored	.25 .25
416	A173	80a pale bl & multi	.25 .25
		Nos. 414-416 (3)	.75 .75
		With tabs	.80

Issued for Independence Day, 1970.

Charles Netter — A174

80a, Agricultural College (Mikwe Israel) & garden.

1970, May 6   Photo.   *Perf. 14x13*
417	A174	40a lt grn, dk brn & gold	.25 .25
418	A174	80a gold & multi	.25 .25
		With tabs	.80

Centenary of first agricultural college in Israel; its founder, Charles Netter.

420 Class Yachts — A175

Designs: Various 420 Class yachts.

1970, July 8   Photo.   *Perf. 14x13*
419	A175	15a grnsh bl, blk & sil	.25 .25
420	A175	30a ol, red, blk & sil	.25 .25
421	A175	80a ultra, blk & silver	.25 .25
		Nos. 419-421 (3)	.75 .75
		With tabs	.90

World "420" Class Sailing Championships.

Hebrew Letters Shaped Like Ship and Buildings — A176

1970, July 8   *Perf. 13x14*
422	A176	40a gold & multi	.25 .25

Keren Hayesod, a Zionist Fund to maintain schools and hospitals in Palestine, 50th anniv.

Arava Plane — A177

1970, July 8
423	A177	£1 brt blue, blk & sil	.25 .25
			.30

First Israeli designed and built aircraft.

Bird (Exiles) and Sun (Israel) — A178

1970, Sept. 7   Litho.   *Perf. 14*
424	A178	80a yel & multi	.25 .25
		With tab	.25

"Operation Ezra and Nehemiah," the exodus of Iraqi Jews.

Old Synagogue, Cracow — A179

Historic Synagogues: 15a, Great Synagogue, Tunis. 35a, Portuguese Synagogue, Amsterdam. 40a, Great Synagogue, Moscow. 60a, Shearith Israel Synagogue, New York.

Perf. 14, 13 (15a)

1970, Sept. 7   Photo.
425	A179	12a gold & multi	.25 .25
426	A179	15a gold & multi	.25 .25
427	A179	35a gold & multi	.25 .25
428	A179	40a gold & multi	.25 .25
429	A179	60a gold & multi	.25 .25
		#425-429, with tabs	.40

Jewish New Year, 5731.

Tel Aviv Post Office, 1920 — A180

1970, Oct. 18   Photo.   *Perf. 14*
430	A180	£1 multicolored	.25 .25
		With tab	
a.		Souvenir sheet	1.50 1.50

TABIT Natl. Stamp Exhibition, Tel Aviv, Oct. 18-29. No. 430a contains an imperf. stamp similar to No. 430. Sold for £1.50.

Mother and Child — A181

1970, Oct. 18   *Perf. 13x14*
431	A181	80a dp grn, yel & gray	.25 .25
		With tab	.30

WIZO, Women's Intl. Zionist Org., 50th anniv.

Paris Quai, by Camille Pissarro — A182

Paintings from Tel Aviv Museum: 85a, The Jewish Wedding, by Josef Israels. £2, Flowers in a Vase, by Fernand Leger.

1970, Dec. 22   Litho.   *Perf. 14*
432	A182	85a black & multi	.25 .25
433	A182	£1 black & multi	.25 .25
434	A182	£2 black & multi	.25 .25
		Nos. 432-434 (3)	.75 .75
		With tabs	1.40

Hammer and Menorah Emblem — A183

1970, Dec. 22
435	A183	35a gold & multi	.25 .25
		With tab	

General Federation of Labor in Israel (Histadrut), 50th anniversary.

Persian Fallow Deer — A184

Animals of the Bible: 3a, Asiatic wild ass. 5a, White oryx. 78a, Cheetah.

1971, Feb. 16   Litho.   *Perf. 13*
436	A184	2a multicolored	.25 .25
437	A184	3a multicolored	.25 .25
438	A184	5a multicolored	.25 .25
439	A184	78a multicolored	.25 .25
		#436-439, with tabs	.45

"Samson and Dalila," Israel National Opera A185

Theater Art in Israel: No. 441, Inn of the Ghosts, Cameri Theater. No. 442, A Psalm of David, Inbal Dance Theater.

1971, Feb. 16   *Perf. 14x13*
440	A185	50a bister & multi	.25 .25
441	A185	50a lt grn & multi	.25 .25
442	A185	50a blue & multi	.25 .25
		Nos. 440-442 (3)	.75 .75
		With tabs	.50

Basketball — A186

No. 444, Runner. No. 445, Athlete on rings.

1971, Apr. 13   Litho.   *Perf. 14*
443	A186	50a green & multi	.25 .25
444	A186	50a ocher & multi	.25 .25
445	A186	50a lt vio & multi	.25 .25
		#443-445, with tabs	.45

9th Hapoel Games.

Defense Forces Emblem — A187

1971, Apr. 13   Photo.   *Perf. 14x13*
446	A187	78a multicolored	.25 .25
		With tab	.25

Memorial Day, 1971, and the war dead.

Jaffa Gate, Jerusalem A188

Gates of Jerusalem: 18c, New Gate. 35c, Damascus Gate. 85c, Herod's Gate.

1971, Apr. 13   *Perf. 14*
Size: 41x41mm
447	A188	15a gold & multi	.25 .25
448	A188	18a gold & multi	.25 .25
449	A188	35a gold & multi	.25 .25
450	A188	85a gold & multi	.60 .40
a.		Souvenir sheet of 4	2.75 2.75
		Nos. 447-450 (4)	1.35 1.15
		With tabs	1.75

Independence Day, 1971. No. 450a contains 4 stamps similar to Nos. 447-450, but smaller (27x27mm). Sold at the Jerusalem Exhibition for £2.
See Nos. 488-491.

"He Wrote ... Words of the Covenant" — A189

85a, "First Fruits ..." Exodus 23:19. £1.50, "... Feast of Weeks" Exodus 34:22. The quotation on 50a is from Exodus 34:28. The quotations are in English on the tabs.

1971, May 25   Photo.   *Perf. 14x13*
451	A189	50a yellow & multi	.25 .25
452	A189	85a yellow & multi	.25 .25
453	A189	£1.50 yellow & multi	.25 .25
		Nos. 451-453 (3)	.75 .75
		With tabs	1.35

For the Feast of Weeks (Shabuoth).

"You shall rejoice in your feast" — A190

Designs: 18a, "You shall dwell in booths for seven days ..." Leviticus 23:42. 20a, "That I made the people of Israel dwell in booths ..." Lev. 23:43. 40a, "... when you have gathered in the produce of the land" Lev. 23:39. 65a, "... then I will give you your rains in their season" Lev. 26:4. The quotation on 15a is from Deuteronomy 16:14. The quotations are in English on tabs.

1971, Aug. 24   Photo.   *Perf. 14x13*
454	A190	15a yellow & multi	.25 .25
455	A190	18a yellow & multi	.25 .25
456	A190	20a yellow & multi	.25 .25
457	A190	40a yellow & multi	.25 .25
458	A190	65a yellow & multi	.25 .25
		#454-458, with tabs	.60

For the Feast of Tabernacles (Sukkoth).

ISRAEL

Sun Shining on Fields — A191

1971, Aug. 24   **Perf. 14**
459 A191 40a gold & multi .25 .25
   With tab .25

1st cooperative settlement in Israel, at Emeq (Valley of Israel), 50th anniv.

Retort and Grain — A192

1971, Oct. 25   **Litho.**   **Perf. 14**
460 A192 £1 green & multi .25 .25

50th anniversary of Volcani Institute of Agricultural Research.

Tagging

Starting in 1975, vertical luminescent bands were overprinted on various regular and commemorative stamps. In the 1971-75 regular series, values issued both untagged and tagged are: 20a, 25a, 30a, 35a, 45a, 50a, 65a, £1.10, £1.30, £2 and £3. Also No. 290 was re-issued with tagging in 1975.

Regular issues from 1975 onward, including the £1.70, are tagged unless otherwise noted.

Tagged commemoratives include Nos. 562-563 and all from Nos. 567-569 onward unless otherwise noted.

Negev — A193

Landscapes: 3a, Judean desert. 5a, Gan Ha-Shelosha. 18a, Kinneret. 20a, Tel Dan. 22a, Fishermen, Yafo. 25a, Arava. 30a, En Avedat. 35a, Brekhat Ram, Golan Heights. 45a, Grazing sheep, Mt. Hermon. 50a, Rosh Pinna. 55a, Beach and park, Netanya. 65a, Plain of Zebulun. 70a, Shore, Engedi. 80a, Beach at Elat. 88a, Boats in Akko harbor. 95a, Hamifratz Hane'elam. £1.10, Aqueduct near Akko. £1.30, Zefat. £1.70, Upper Nazareth. £2, Coral Island. £3, Haifa.

1971-75   **Photo.**   **Perf. 13x14**
461 A193 3a deep blue .25 .25
462 A193 5a green .25 .25
463 A193 15a deep org .25 .25
464 A193 18a bright mag .65 .25
464A A193 20a dark green .25 .25
465 A193 22a brt blue 1.25 .25
465A A193 25a orange red .25 .25
466 A193 30a brt rose .25 .25
466A A193 35a plum .25 .25
467 A193 45a dull vio blue .25 .25
468 A193 50a green .25 .25
469 A193 55a olive .25 .25
469A A193 65a black .25 .25
470 A193 70a deep car .25 .25
470A A193 80a deep ultra .25 .25
471 A193 88a greenish blue 1.25 .25
472 A193 95a org ver .80 .25
472A A193 £1.10 olive .25 .25
472B A193 £1.30 deep blue .25 .25
472C A193 £1.70 dark brown .40 .25
473 A193 £2 brown .40 .25
474 A193 £3 deep violet .55 .25
   Nos. 461-474 (22) 9.05 5.50
   With tabs 15.00

Issued: 15a, 18a, 50a, 88a, 10/25; 22a, 55a, 70a, 1/4/72; 3a, 5a, 30a, £3, 11/7/72; 45a, 95a, £2, 1/16/73; 20a, 65a, 10/23/73; 35a, £1.10, 12/20/73; 25a, 80a, £1.30, 11/5/74; £1.70, 6/17/75.
See No. 592.

"Get Wisdom" Proverbs 4:7 — A194

Abstract Designs: 18a, Mathematical and scientific formula. 20a, Tools and engineering symbols. 40a, Abbreviations of various college degrees.

1972, Jan. 4   **Litho.**   **Perf. 14**
475 A194 15a brt grn & multi .25 .25
476 A194 18a multicolored .25 .25
477 A194 20a multicolored .25 .25
478 A194 40a red, blk & gold .25 .25
   #475-478, with tabs .30

The Scribe, Sculpture by Boris Schatz — A195

Works by Israeli Artists: 55a, Young Girl (Sarah), by Abel Pann. 70a, Zefat (landscape), by Menahem Shemi, horiz. 85a, Old Jerusalem, by Jacob Steinhardt. £1, Resurrection (abstract), by Aharon Kahana.

Perf. 13x14 (40a, 85a), 14
1972, Mar. 7
479 A195 40a black & tan .25 .25
480 A195 55a red brn & multi .25 .25
481 A195 70a lt grn & multi .25 .25
482 A195 85a blk & yellow .25 .25
483 A195 £1 blk & multi .25 .25
   Nos. 479-483 (5) 1.25 1.25
   With tabs 1.00

Exodus — A196

Passover: 45a, Baking unleavened bread. 95a, Seder.

1972, Mar. 7   **Litho.**   **Perf. 13**
484 A196 18a buff & multi .25 .25
485 A196 45a buff & multi .25 .25
486 A196 95a buff & multi .25 .25
   Nos. 484-486 (3) .75 .75
   With tabs 1.10

"Let My People Go" — A197

1972, Mar. 7   **Perf. 14**
487 A197 55a blk, bl & yel grn .40 .30
   With tab 2.00

No. 487 inscribed in Hebrew, Arabic, Russian and English.

Gate Type of 1971

Gates of Jerusalem: 15a, Lions' Gate. 18a, Golden Gate. 45a, Dung Gate. 55a, Zion Gate.

1972, Apr. 17   **Photo.**   **Perf. 14**
Size: 40x40mm
488 A188 15a gold & multi .25 .25
489 A188 18a gold & multi .25 .25
490 A188 45a gold & multi .25 .25
491 A188 55a gold & multi .25 .25
   a. Souvenir sheet of 4 2.50 2.50
   Nos. 488-491 (4) 1.00 1.00
   With tabs 1.75

Independence Day. No. 491a contains 4 27x27mm stamps similar to Nos. 488-491. Sold for £2.

Jethro's Tomb — A198

1972, Apr. 17   **Litho.**   **Perf. 13**
492 A198 55a multicolored .25 .25
   With tab .25

Memorial Day — A199

1972, Apr. 17   **Perf. 14**
493 A199 55a Flowers .25 .25
   With tab .25

Hebrew Words Emerging from Opened Ghetto — A200

1972, June 6   **Perf. 13**
494 A200 70a blue & multi .35 .30
   With tab 1.50

Rabbi Isaac ben Solomon Ashkenazi Luria ("Ari") (1534-72), Palestinian cabalist.

International Book Year — A201

1972, June 6   **Perf. 14x13**
495 A201 95a Printed page .25 .25
   With tab .30

Satellite Earth Station, Satellite and Rainbow — A202

1972, June 6   **Perf. 13**
496 A202 £1 tan & multi .25 .25
   With tab .30

Opening of satellite earth station in Israel.

17th Cent. Ark, Ancona — A203

Holy Arks from: 45a, Padua, 1729. 70a, Parma, 17th century. 95a, Reggio Emilia, 1756. Arks moved to Israel from Italian synagogues.

1972, Aug. 8   **Photo.**   **Perf. 14x13**
497 A203 15a deep brn & yel .25 .25
498 A203 45a dp grn, yel grn & gold .25 .25
499 A203 70a brn red, yel & bl .25 .25
500 A203 95a magenta & gold .25 .25
   Nos. 497-500 (4) 1.00 1.00
   With tab 1.00

Jewish New Year, 5733.

Menorah and "25" — A204

1972, Aug. 8
501 A204 £1 silver, bl & mag .25 .25
   With tab .25

25th anniversary of the State of Israel.

Brass Menorah, Morocco, 18th-19th Century — A205

Menorahs: 25a, Brass, Poland, 18th century. 70a, Silver, Germany, 17th century.

1972, Nov. 7   **Litho.**   **Perf. 14x13**
502 A205 12a emer, blk & bl grn .25 .25
503 A205 25a lil rose, blk & org .25 .25
504 A205 70a blue, blk & vio .25 .25
   #502-504, with tabs .50

Hanukkah (Festival of Lights), 1972.

Child's Drawing — A206

Designs: Children's drawings.

Sizes: 22½x37mm (2a, 55a); 17x48mm (3a)

1973, Jan. 16   **Litho.**   **Perf. 14**
505 A206 2a blk & multi .25 .25
506 A206 3a multicolored .25 .25
507 A206 55a multicolored .25 .25
   #505-507, with tabs .30

Youth Wing of Israel Museum, Jerusalem (2a, 3a) and Youth Workshops, Tel Aviv Museum (55a).

Pendant — A207

1973, Jan. 16   **Photo.**   **Perf. 14x13**
508 A207 18a silver & multi .25 .25
   With tab .25

Immigration of North African Jews.

Levi, by Marc Chagall — A208

Tribes of Israel: No. 510, Simeon. No. 511, Reuben. No. 512, Issachar. No. 513, Zebulun. No. 514, Judah. No. 515, Dan. No. 516, Gad. No. 517, Asher. No. 518, Naphtali. No. 519, Joseph. No. 520, Benjamin.

1973   **Litho.**   **Perf. 14**
509 A208 £1 multicolored .35 .35
510 A208 £1 gray grn & multi .35 .35
511 A208 £1 olive & multi .35 .35
512 A208 £1 gray bl & multi .35 .35
513 A208 £1 lemon & multi .35 .35
514 A208 £1 gray & multi .35 .35
515 A208 £1 bl grn & multi .35 .35
516 A208 £1 gray & multi .35 .35
517 A208 £1 yel grn & multi .35 .35
518 A208 £1 sepia & multi .35 .35
519 A208 £1 olive & multi .35 .35
520 A208 £1 tan & multi .35 .35
   Nos. 509-520 (12) 4.20 4.20
   With tabs 7.00

Designs from stained glass windows by Marc Chagall, Hadassah-Hebrew University Medical Center Synagogue, Jerusalem.

Issued: Nos. 509-514, 3/26; Nos. 515-520, 8/21.

ISRAEL

Israel's Declaration of Independence — A209

1973, May 3		Photo.		
521	A209	£1 ocher & multi	.25	.25
		With tab	.25	
a.		Souvenir sheet	.60	.60

25 years of Independence. No. 521a sold for £1.50.

Star of David and Runners — A210

1973, May 3		Litho.		
522	A210	£1.10 multicolored	.25	.25
		With tab	.25	

9th Maccabiah.

Prison-cloth Hand — A211

1973, May 3		Photo.		
523	A211	55a blue black	.25	.25
		With tab	.25	

Heroes and martyrs of the Holocaust, 1933-1945.

Flame — A212

1973, May 3		Litho.		
524	A212	65a multicolored	.25	.25
		With tab	.25	

Memorial Day.

Prophets — A213

1973, Aug. 21		Photo.	Perf. 13x14	
525	A213	18a Isaiah	.25	.25
526	A213	65a Jeremiah	.25	.25
527	A213	£1.10 Ezekiel	.25	.25
		#525-527, with tabs	.35	

Jewish New Year, 5734.

Torch of Learning, Cogwheel — A214

1973, Oct. 23			Perf. 14x13	
528	A214	£1.25 slate & multi	.25	.25
		With tab	.25	

50th anniversary of the Technion, Israel Institute of Technology.

Rescue Boat and Danish Flag — A215

1973, Oct. 23			Perf. 13x14	
529	A215	£5 bister, red & blk	.30	.25
		With tab	.50	

30th anniversary of the rescue by the Danes of the Jews in Denmark.

Spectators at Stamp Show — A216

Design: £1, Spectators, different design.

1973, Dec. 20		Litho.	Perf. 13	
530	A216	20a brown & multi	.25	.25
531	A216	£1 brown & multi	.25	.25
		#530-531, with tabs	.25	

JERUSALEM '73 Philatelic Exhibition, Mar. 25-Apr. 2, 1974.

Souvenir Sheets

Israel No. 7 — A217

Designs: £2, No. 8. £3, No. 9.

1974, Mar. 25		Photo.	Perf. 14x13	
532	A217	£1 silver & dk slate grn	.25	.25
533	A217	£2 silver & red brn	.25	.25
534	A217	£3 silver & blk blue	.25	.25
		Nos. 532-534 (3)	.75	.75

Jerusalem '73 Philatelic Exhibition, Mar. 25-Apr. 2, 1974 (postponed from Dec. 1973), 25th anniv. of State of Israel. Each sheet was sold with a 50 per cent surcharge.

Soldier with Prayer Shawl — A218

1974, Apr. 23			Perf. 13x14	
535	A218	£1 blk & light bl	.25	.25
		With tab	.25	

Memorial Day.

Quill and Inkwell with Hebrew Letters — A219

1974, Apr. 23			Perf. 14x13	
536	A219	£2 gold & black	.25	.25
		With tab	.25	

50th anniversary of Hebrew Writers Assn.

Lady in Blue, by Moshe Kisling — A220

Designs: £2, Mother and Child, Sculpture by Chana Orloff. £3, Girl in Blue, by Chaim Soutine.

1974, June 11		Litho.	Perf. 14	
537	A220	£1.25 multicolored	.25	.25
538	A220	£2 multicolored	.25	.25
539	A220	£3 multicolored	.25	.25
		#537-539, with tabs	.90	

Art works from Tel Aviv, En Harod and Jerusalem Museums.

Wrench — A221

1974, June 11				
540	A221	25a multicolored	.25	.25
		With tab	.25	

50th anniv. of Working Youth Movement.

Istanbuli Synagogue, Jerusalem — A222

Designs: Interiors of restored synagogues in Jerusalem's Old City: 70a, Emtzai Synagogue. £1, Rabbi Yohanan Synagogue.

1974, Aug. 6		Photo.	Perf. 13x14	
541	A222	25a shown	.25	.25
542	A222	70a multicolored	.25	.25
543	A222	£1 multicolored	.25	.25
		#541-543, with tabs	.25	

Jewish New Year, 5735.

Lady Davis Technical Center "AMAL," Tel Aviv A223

60a, Elias Sourasky Library, Tel Aviv University. £1.45, Mivtahim Rest Home, Zikhron Yaaqov.

1974, Aug. 6			Perf. 13½x14	
544	A223	25a violet black	.25	.25
545	A223	60a dark blue	.25	.25
546	A223	£1.45 maroon	.25	.25
		#544-546, with tabs	.25	

Modern Israeli architecture.

David Ben-Gurion A224

1974, Nov. 5			Perf. 14	
547	A224	25a brown	.25	.25
548	A224	£1.30 slate green	.25	.25
		#547-549, with tabs	.25	

David Ben-Gurion (1886-1973), first Prime Minister and Minister of Defense of Israel.

Arrows on Globe A225

Dove Delivering Letter A226

1974, Nov. 5		Litho.	Perf. 14	
549	A225	25a black & multi	.25	.25
		Photo.		
550	A226	£1.30 gold & multi	.25	.25
		#549-550, with tabs	.25	

Centenary of Universal Postal Union.

Hebrew University, Mount Scopus, Jerusalem — A227

1975, Jan. 14		Litho.	Perf. 13	
551	A227	£2.50 multicolored	.25	.25
		With tab	.25	

Hebrew University, 50th anniv.

Girl Carrying Plant — A228

Arbor Day: 35a, Bird singing in tree. £2, Boy carrying potted plant.

1975, Jan. 14			Perf. 14	
552	A228	1a multicolored	.25	.25
553	A228	35a multicolored	.25	.25
554	A228	£2 multicolored	.25	.25
		#552-554, with tabs	.25	

Welder — A229

80a, Tractor driver. £1.20, Electrical lineman.

1975, Jan. 14		Photo.	Perf. 14x13	
555	A229	30a multicolored	.25	.25
556	A229	80a multicolored	.25	.25
557	A229	£1.20 ultra & multi	.25	.25
		#555-557, with tabs	.25	

Occupational safety and publicity for the Institute for Safety and Hygiene.

Hebrew University Synagogue, Jerusalem A230

Modern Israeli architecture: £1.30, Yad Mordecai Museum. £1.70, Bat Yam City Hall.

Perf. 14, 13½x14 (#559)

1975, Mar. 4			Photo.	
558	A230	80a brown	.25	.25
559	A230	£1.30 slate green	.25	.25
560	A230	£1.70 brown olive	.25	.25
		#558-560, with tabs	.35	

US President Harry S Truman (1884-1972) — A231

ISRAEL

1975, Mar. 4	**Engr.**		**Perf. 14**
561 A231	£5 dark brown		.25 .25
	With tab		.30

Eternal Flame over Soldier's Grave — A232

1975, Apr. 10	**Photo.**		**Perf. 14x13**
562 A232	£1.45 black & multi		.25 .25
	With tab		.25

Memorial Day.

Memorial Tablet — A233

1975, Apr. 10			
563 A233	£1.45 blk, red & gray		.25 .25
	With tab		.25

In memory of soldiers missing in action.

Hurdling — A234

1975, Apr. 10			**Perf. 13x14**
564 A234	25a shown		.25 .25
565 A234	£1.70 Bicycling		.25 .25
566 A234	£3 Volleyball		.25 .25
	#564-566, with tabs		.35

10th Hapoel Games; 50th anniv. of Hapoel Org.

Yom Kippur, by Maurycy Gottlieb — A235

Paintings of religious holidays: £1.00 Hanukkah, by Mortiz D. Oppenheim. 1.40, The Purim Players, by Jankel Adler, horiz.

1975, June 17	**Litho.**		**Perf. 14**
567 A235	£1 multicolored		.25 .25
568 A235	£1.40 multicolored		.25 .25
569 A235	£4 multicolored		.25 .25
	#567-569, with tabs		.50

Old Couple — A236

1975, June 17	**Photo.**		**Perf. 13x14**
570 A236	£1.85 multicolored		.25 .25
	With tab		.25

International Gerontological Association, 10th triennial conference, Jerusalem.

Pres. Zalman Shazar (1889-1974) — A237

1975, Aug. 5	**Photo.**		**Perf. 14x13**
571 A237	35a silver & blk		.25 .25
	With tab		.25

Pioneer Women, 50th Anniv. — A238

1975, Aug. 5			**Perf. 14½**
572 A238	£5 Emblem		.30 .25
	With tab		.35

Judges of Israel — A239

1975, Aug. 5			**Perf. 13x14**
573 A239	35a Gideon		.25 .25
574 A239	£1 Deborah		.25 .25
575 A239	£1.40 Jephthah		.25 .25
	#573-575, with tabs		.35

Jewish New Year, 5736.

Hebrew University, Mt. Scopus A240

1975, Oct. 14	**Photo.**		**Perf. 14x13**
576 A240	£4 multicolored		.25 .25
	With tab		.25

Return of Hadassah to Mt. Scopus, Jerusalem.

Collared Pratincoles — A241

Protected Birds: £1.70, Spur-winged plover. £2, Black-winged stilts.

1975, Oct. 14	**Litho.**		**Perf. 13**
577 A241	£1.10 pink & multi		.25 .25
578 A241	£1.70 lemon & multi		.25 .25
579 A241	£2 multicolored		.25 .25
	#577-579, with tabs		.40

Butterfly and Factory (Air Pollution) — A242

Designs: 80a, Fish and tanker (water pollution). £1.70, Ear and jet (noise pollution).

1975, Dec. 9	**Photo.**		**Perf. 14**
580 A242	50a car & multi		.25 .25
581 A242	80a green & multi		.25 .25
582 A242	£1.70 orange & multi		.25 .25
	With tabs		.40

Environmental protection.

Star of David — A243

1975-80			**Perf. 13x14**
583 A243	75a vio bl & car		.25 .25
584 A243	£1.80 violet bl & gray		.25 .25
585 A243	£1.85 vio bl & lt brn		.25 .25
586 A243	£2.45 vio bl & brt green		.25 .25
587 A243	£2.70 vio bl & purple		.25 .25
588 A243	£4.30 ultra & red		.25 .25
589 A243	£5.40 vio bl & ol		.25 .25
590 A243	£8 vio bl & bl		.25 .25
	Nos. 583-590 (8)		2.00 2.00
	With tabs		2.50

Issued: £1.85, 12/9; £2.45, 6/22/76; 75a, 12/77; £5.40, 5/23/78; £1.80, £8, 5/22/79; £2.70, 12/25/79; £4.30, 5/26/80.

Landscape Type of 1971-75

Design: £10, View of Elat and harbor.

1976, Aug. 17	**Photo.**		**Perf. 14x14½**
592 A193	£10 Prussian blue		.50 .25
	With tab		1.00

No. 592 issued both tagged and untagged.

"In the days of Ahasuerus." — A247

Designs (from Book of Esther): 80a, "He set the royal crown on her head." £1.60, "Thus shall it be done to the man whom the king delights to honor."

1976, Feb. 17	**Photo.**		**Perf. 14**
593 A247	40a multicolored		.25 .25
594 A247	80a multicolored		.25 .25
595 A247	£1.60 multicolored		.25 .25
a.	Souv. sheet of 3, #593-595, perf 13x14		.35 .35
	#593-595, with tabs		.30

Purim Festival. No. 595a sold for £4.

Border Settlement, Barbed Wire — A248

1976, Feb. 17			
596 A248	£1.50 olive & multi		.25 .25
	With tab		.25

Border settlements, part of Jewish colonization of Holy Land.

Symbolic Key — A249

1976, Feb. 17			
597 A249	£1.85 multicolored		.25 .25
	With tab		.25

Bezalel Academy of Arts and Design, Jerusalem, 70th anniv.

"200" US Flag — A250

1976, Apr. 25	**Photo.**		**Perf. 13x14**
598 A250	£4 gold & multi		.25 .25
	With tab		.30

American Bicentennial.

Dancers of Meron, by Reuven Rubin — A251

1976, Apr. 25	**Litho.**		**Perf. 14**
599 A251	£1.30 multicolored		.25 .25
	With tab		.25

Lag Ba-Omer festival.

8th Brigade Monument, Ben-Gurion Airport — A252

1976, Apr. 25	**Photo.**		**Perf. 14x13**
600 A252	£1.85 multicolored		.25 .25
	With tab		.25

Memorial Day.

Souvenir Sheet

Tourism, Sport and Industry A253

1976, Apr. 25			
601 A253	Sheet of 3		.50 .50
a.	£1 multicolored		.25 .25
b.	£2 multicolored		.25 .25
c.	£4 multicolored		.25 .25

No. 601 sold for £10.

High Jump — A254

1976, June 22			**Perf. 13x14**
602 A254	£1.60 shown		.25 .25
603 A254	£2.40 Diving		.25 .25
604 A254	£4.40 Gymnastics		.25 .25
	#602-604, with tabs		.50

21st Olympic Games, Montreal, Canada, July 17-Aug. 1.

Tents and Suns — A255

1976, June 22			**Perf. 14**
605 A255	£1.50 green & multi		.25 .25
	With tab		.25

Israel Camping Union.

"Truth" — A256

Design: £1.50, "Judgment" (scales). £1.90, "Peace" (dove and olive branch).

1976, Aug. 17	**Photo.**		**Perf. 14x13 Tagged**
606 A256	45a gold & multi		.25 .25
607 A256	£1.50 gold & multi		.25 .25
608 A256	£1.90 gold & multi		.25 .25
	#606-608, with tabs		.30

Festivals 5737.

Pawn — A257

1976, Oct. 19	**Litho.**		**Perf. 14**
609 A257	£1.30 shown		.25 .25
610 A257	£1.60 Rook		.25 .25
	#609-610, with tabs		.35

22nd Men's and 7th Women's Chess Olympiad, Haifa, Oct. 24-Nov. 11.

ISRAEL

Byzantine Building, 6th Century — A258

70a, City wall, 7th cent. B.C. £2.40, Robinson's Arch. £2.80, Steps to Gate of Hulda. Both from area leading to 2nd Temple, 1st cent. B.C. £5, Wall, Omayyad Palace, 8th cent. A.D.

1976		Litho.		Perf. 14	
611	A258	70a multicolored		.25	.25
612	A258	£1.30 multicolored		.25	.25
613	A258	£2.40 multicolored		.25	.25
614	A258	£2.80 multicolored		.25	.25
615	A258	£5 multicolored		.25	.25
		Nos. 611-615 (5)		1.25	1.25
		With tabs		1.25	

Excavations in Old Jerusalem.
Issued: Nos. 612-614, 10/19; Nos. 611, 615, 12/23.

Clearing the Land, 1890 — A259

Designs: 10a, Building harbor wall. 60a, Road building, vert. £1.40, Plower and horse-drawn plow. £1.80, Planting trees.

1976, Dec. 23		Photo.		Perf. 13	
616	A259	5a brown & gold		.25	.25
617	A259	10a purple & gold		.25	.25
618	A259	60a gold & car		.25	.25
619	A259	£1.40 gold & blue		.25	.25
620	A259	£1.80 green & gold		.25	.25
		#616-620, with tabs			.40

Work of the pioneers.

"Let's Pull up Grandfather's Carrot" — A260

1977, Feb. 15		Litho.		Perf. 14	
621	A260	£2.60 multicolored		.25	.25
		With tab			.30

Voluntary service.

Doves, Jew and Arab Shaking Hands — A261

£1.40, Arab & Jew holding hands, and flowers. £2.70, Peace dove, Arab and Jew dancing. Illustrations for the book "My Shalom-My Peace."

1977, Feb. 15					
622	A261	50a multicolored		.25	.25
623	A261	£1.40 multicolored		.25	.25
624	A261	£2.70 multicolored		.25	.25
		622-#624, with tabs			.45

Children's drawings for peace.

"By the Rivers of Babylon..." A262

Drawings by Efraim Moshe Lilien: £1.80, Abraham, vert. £2.10, "May our eyes behold thee when thou returnest to Zion in compassion."

		Perf. 14x13, 13x14			
1977, Feb. 15				Photo.	
625	A262	£1.70 gray, brn & blk		.25	.25
626	A262	£1.80 yel, blk & brn		.25	.25
627	A262	£2.10 lt grn & dk grn		.25	.25
		Nos. 625-627 (3)		.75	.75
		With tabs			.60

Souvenirs for 5th Zionist Congress, 1902.

Trumpet — A263

1977, Apr. 19		Litho.		Perf. 14	
628	A263	£1.50 shown		.25	.25
629	A263	£2 Lyre		.25	.25
630	A263	£5 Cymbals		.25	.25
		#628-630, with tabs			.50

Ancient musical instruments, Haifa Music Museum and Amli Library.

Embroidered Sabbath Cloth — A264

1977, Apr. 19				Perf. 13x14	
631	A264	£3 buff & multi		.25	.25
		With tab			.30

Importance of Sabbath observation in Jewish life.

Parachutists' Memorial, Bilu-Gedera, Tel Aviv — A265

1977, Apr. 19				Perf. 13x14	
632	A265	£3.30 gray, blk & grn		.25	.25
		With tab			.40

Memorial Day.

10th Maccabiah — A266

1977, June 23		Photo.		Perf. 14x13	
633	A266	£1 Fencing		.25	.25
634	A266	£2.50 Shot put		.25	.25
635	A266	£3.50 Judo		.25	.25
		Nos. 633-635 (3)		.75	.75
		With tabs			.55

ZOA Convention Emblem — A267

1977, June 23				Perf. 14	
636	A267	£4 silver & multi		.25	.25
		With tab			.35

Convention of Zionist Organization of America (ZOA), Jerusalem, June 1977.

Petah Tikva Centenary A268

1977, June 23				Perf. 14x13	
637	A268	£1.50 multicolored		.25	.25
		With tab			.25

Matriarchs of the Bible — A269

1977, Aug. 16		Photo.		Perf. 14	
638	A269	70a Sarah		.25	.25
639	A269	£1.50 Rebekah		.25	.25
640	A269	£2 Rachel		.25	.25
641	A269	£3 Leah		.25	.25
		#638-641, with tabs			.65

Jewish New Year, 5738.

Frontier Guards — A270

1977, Aug. 16		Litho.		Perf. 14	
642	A270	£1 shown		.25	.25
643	A270	£1 Police		.25	.25
644	A270	£1 Civil Guard		.25	.25
		#642-644, with tabs			.35

Israel Police Force, established Mar. 26, 1948.

Illuminated Page — A271

1977, July 21		Photo.		Perf. 14x13	
645	A271	£4 blk, gold & red		.25	.25
		With tab			.25

4th cent. of Hebrew printing at Safad.

Farm Growing from Steel Helmet — A272

1977, Oct. 18		Litho.		Perf. 14	
646	A272	£3.50 multicolored		.25	.25
		With tab			.25

Fighting Pioneer Youth (NAHAL), established 1949.

Koffler Accelerator — A273

1977, Oct. 18		Photo.		Perf. 14x13	
647	A273	£8 black & blue		.35	.35
		With tab			.50

Inauguration of Koffler accelerator at Weizmann Institute of Science, Rehovot. Untagged.

Caesarea — A274

Scenes: £1, Arava on the Dead Sea. £20, Rosh Pinna.

1977-78				Perf. 13½x14	
		Size: 27x22mm			
649	A274	10a violet blue		.25	.25
664	A274	£1 olive bister		.25	.25

		Perf. 14½x14			
		Size: 27½x26½mm			
672	A274	£20 org & dk grn ('78)		.65	.25
		#649-672, with tabs		1.40	

The 10a is untagged. The £1, £20 issued tagged and untagged.
Issued: 10a, £1, 10/18/77; £20, 7/4/78.

First Holy Land Locomotive A276

Locomotives: £1.50, Jezreel Valley train. £2, British Mandate period. £2.50, Israel Railways.

1977, Dec. 13		Photo.		Perf. 13x14	
674	A276	65a multicolored		.25	.25
675	A276	£1.50 multicolored		.25	.25
676	A276	£2 multicolored		.25	.25
677	A276	£2.50 multicolored		.25	.25
a.		Souvenir sheet of 4, #674-677		1.25	1.10
		#674-677, with tabs			.90

Railways in the Holy Land. No. 677a sold for £10.

Cypraea Isabella — A277

Red Sea shells: No. 679, Lioconcha castrensis. No. 680, Gloripallium pallium. No. 681, Malea pomum.

1977, Dec. 13		Litho.		Perf. 14	
678	A277	£2 shown		.25	.25
679	A277	£2 multicolored		.25	.25
680	A277	£2 multicolored		.25	.25
681	A277	£2 multicolored		.25	.25
		#678-681, with tabs			.50

Street in Jerusalem, by Haim Glicksberg (1904-1970) A278

Paintings: £3.80, Thistles, by Leopold Krakauer (1890-1954). £4.40, An Alley in Zefat, by Mordekhai Levanon (1901-1968).

1978, Feb. 14					
682	A278	£3 multicolored		.25	.25
683	A278	£3.80 multicolored		.25	.25
684	A278	£4.40 multicolored		.25	.25
		Nos. 682-684 (3)		.75	.75
		With tabs			.65

Marriage Contract, Netherlands, 1648 — A279

Marriage Contracts (Ketubah): £3.90, Morocco, 1897. £6, Jerusalem, 1846.

1978, Feb. 14					
685	A279	75a multicolored		.25	.25
686	A279	£3.90 multicolored		.25	.25
687	A279	£6 multicolored		.25	.25
		#685-687, with tabs			.50

Eliyahu Golomb — A280

Designs: Portraits.

ISRAEL

1978, Apr. 23   Photo.   Perf. 14x13
688	A280	£2 shown	.25	.25
689	A280	£2 Dr. Moshe Sneh	.25	.25
690	A280	£2 David Raziel	.25	.25
691	A280	£2 Yitzhak Sadeh	.25	.25
692	A280	£2 Abraham Stern	.25	.25
		#688-692, with tabs		.60

Heroes of underground movement. Nos. 688-692 issued in sheets of 15.

See Nos. 695-696, 699-700, 705-706, 712-714, 740-742.

Souvenir Sheet

Jerusalem, Mosaic, from Madaba Map — A281

1978, Apr. 23   Litho.   Perf. 14
693	A281	Sheet of 4	1.25	1.25
a.		£1 multicolored	.25	.25
b.		£2 multicolored	.25	.25
c.		£3 multicolored	.30	.30
d.		£4 multicolored	.35	.35

Tabir '78 National Stamp Exhibition, Jerusalem, Apr. 23. No. 693 sold for £15.

Flowers — A282

Design: Flowers, after children's paintings on Memorial Wall in Yad-Lebanim Museum, Petah Tikva. Each stamp shows different flowers.

1978, Apr. 23   Perf. 14
694		Sheet of 15	1.25 1.25
a.-o.	A282	£1.50 single stamp	.25 .25

Memorial Day.

Heroes Type

Designs: No. 695, Theodor Herzl. No. 696, Chaim Weizmann.

1978, July 5   Photo.   Perf. 14x13
695	A280	£2 gray & gray ol	.25	.25
696	A280	£2 buff & vio bl	.25	.25
		#695-696, with tabs		.25

Herzl, founder of Zionism; Weizmann, 1st President of Israel.

Hatiqwa, 1st Verse — A285

1978, July 4   Perf. 13x14
697	A285	£8.40 multicolored	.30	.30
		With tab		.40

Centenary of Israeli National Anthem, Hatiqwa, by poet Naftali Herz Imber.

YMCA Building, Jerusalem — A286

1978, July 4   Litho.   Perf. 13
698	A286	£5.40 multicolored	.25	.25
		With tab		.30

Centenary of YMCA in Jerusalem.

Heroes Type

Designs: No. 699, Rabbi Kook (1865-1935). No. 700, Rabbi Ouziel (1880-1963).

1978, Aug. 22   Photo.   Perf. 14x13
699	A280	£2 pale gray & slate grn	.25	.25
700	A280	£2 pale gray & dk pur	.25	.25
		#699-700, with tabs		.25

Patriarchs — A288

1978, Aug. 22   Perf. 14
701	A288	£1.10 Abraham & Isaac	.25	.25
702	A288	£5.20 Isaac	.25	.25
703	A288	£6.60 Jacob	.25	.25
		#701-703, with tabs		.55

Festivals 5739.

Families and Houses — A289

1978, Aug. 22   Perf. 13x14
704	A289	£5.10 multicolored	.25	.25
		With tab		.30

Social welfare.

Heroes Type

Designs: No. 705, David Ben-Gurion. No. 706, Ze'ev Jabotinsky.

1978, Oct. 31   Photo.   Perf. 14x13
705	A280	£2 buff & vio brn	.25	.25
706	A280	£2 gray & indigo	.25	.25
		#705-706, with tabs		.25

30 years of independence. Ben-Gurion, first Prime Minister, and Ze'ev Vladimir Jabotinsky (1880-1940), leader of World Union of Zionist Revisionists.

Star of David and Growing Tree — A291

1978, Oct. 31   Litho.   Perf. 14
707	A291	£8.40 multicolored	.35	.30
		With tab		.45

United Jewish Appeal, established 1939 in US to help Israel.

Old and New Hospital Buildings — A292

1978, Oct. 31
708	A292	£5.40 multicolored	.25	.25
		With tab		.30

Opening of new Shaare Zedek Medical Center, Jerusalem.

Silver and Enamel Vase, India — A293

£3, Elephant with howdah, Persia, 13th cent. £4, Mosque lamp, glass and enamel, Syria, 14th cent.

1978, Oct. 31
709	A293	£2.40 multicolored	.25	.25
710	A293	£3 multicolored	.25	.25
711	A293	£4 multicolored	.25	.25
		Nos. 709-711 (3)		.75
		With tabs		.55

Leo Arie Mayer Memorial Museum for Islamic Art, Jerusalem.

Heroes Type

No. 712, Menachem Ussishkin (1863-1941). No. 713, Berl Katzenelson (1878-1944). No. 714, Max Nordau (1849-1923).

1978, Dec. 26   Photo.   Perf. 14x13
712	A280	£2 citron & sl grn	.25	.25
713	A280	£2 gray & vio blue	.25	.25
714	A280	£2 buff & black	.25	.25
		#712-714, with tabs		.40

30th anniversary of independence.

Iris Lortetii — A295

Protected Wild Flowers: £5.40, Iris haynei. £8.40, Iris nazarena.

1978, Dec. 26   Litho.   Perf. 14
715	A295	£1.10 multicolored	.25	.25
716	A295	£5.40 multicolored	.25	.25
717	A295	£8.40 multicolored	.25	.25
		Nos. 715-717 (3)		.75
		With tabs		.80

Agricultural Mechanization — A296

Symbolic Designs: £2.40, Seawater desalination. £4.30, Electronics. £5, Chemical fertilizers.

1979, Feb. 13   Litho.   Perf. 13
718	A296	£1.10 multicolored	.25	.25
719	A296	£2.40 multicolored	.25	.25
720	A296	£4.30 multicolored	.25	.25
721	A296	£5 multicolored	.25	.25
		#718-721, with tabs		.60

Technological Achievements.

"Hope from Darkness" — A297

1979, Feb. 13
722	A297	£5.40 multicolored	.30	.25
		With tab		.35

Salute to "the Righteous among Nations," an award to those who helped during Nazi period.

Jewish Brigade Flag — A298

1979, Feb. 13   Photo.   Perf. 14
723	A298	£5.10 blue, yel & blk	.25	.25
		With tab		.30

Jewish Brigade served with British Armed Forces during WWII.

Paper (Prayer for Peace) in Crevice of Western Wall — A299

1979, Mar. 26   Photo.   Perf. 14x13
724	A299	£10 multicolored	.25	.25
		With tab		.35
a.		Souv. sheet of 1, imperf.	.40	.40

Signing of peace treaty between Israel and Egypt, Mar. 26.

11th Hapoel Games — A300

1979, Apr. 23   Litho.   Perf. 13
725	A300	£1.50 Weightlifting	.25	.25
726	A300	£6 Tennis	.25	.25
727	A300	£11 Gymnastics	.30	.25
		Nos. 725-727 (3)	.80	.75
		With tabs		.90

"50" and Rotary Emblem — A301

1979, Apr. 23   Photo.   Perf. 14x13
728	A301	£7 multicolored	.25	.25
		With tab		.35

Rotary Intl. in Israel, 50th anniv.

Navy Memorial, Ashdod — A302

1979, Apr. 23
729	A302	£5.10 multicolored	.25	.25
		With tab		.30

Memorial Day.

Rabbi Yehoshua ben Hananya — A303

Craftsmen-Sages: £8.50, Rabbi Meir Baal Ha-Ness, scribe. £13, Rabbi Johanan, sandal maker.

1979, Sept. 4   Photo.   Perf. 14x13
730	A303	£1.80 multicolored	.25	.25
731	A303	£8.50 multicolored	.25	.25
732	A303	£13 multicolored	.25	.25
		Nos. 730-732 (3)	.75	.75
		With tabs		.70

Jewish New Year 5740.

Flag Colors as Search Light — A304

1979, Sept. 4
733	A304	£10 multicolored	.25	.25
		With tab		.30

Jewish Agency, 50th anniversary.

Hot Springs, Tiberias — A305

Design: £12, Dead Sea health resorts.

1979, Sept. 4   Litho.   Perf. 14
734	A305	£8 multicolored	.25	.25
735	A305	£12 multicolored	.25	.25
		#734-735, with tabs		.55

ISRAEL

Boy Riding Rainbow — A306

1979, Nov. 13   Photo.   Perf. 13x14
736	A306	£8.50 multicolored	.25	.25
		With tab		.25

International Year of the Child.

Jerusalem — A307

Children's Drawings of Jerusalem: £4, People of different nationalities, horiz. £5, Praying at the Western Wall, horiz.

1979, Nov. 13   Perf. 14
737	A307	£1.80 multicolored	.25	.25
738	A307	£4 multicolored	.25	.25
739	A307	£5 multicolored	.25	.25
		#737-739, with tabs		.30

Heroes Type

Designs: £7, Arthur Ruppin (1876-1943). £9, Joseph Trumpeldor (1880-1920). £13, Aaron Aaronsohn (1876-1919).

1979, Nov. 13   Photo.   Perf. 14x13
740	A280	£7 gray & magenta	.25	.25
741	A280	£9 pale grn & Prus bl	.25	.25
742	A280	£13 pale yel & dk ol	.25	.25
		Nos. 740-742 (3)	.75	.75
		With tabs		1.00

Sorek Cave — A308

1980, Jan. 15   Litho.   Perf. 13x14
743	A308	£50 multicolored	.75	.40
		With tab		1.10

Star of David in Cogwheel — A309

1980, Jan. 15   Perf. 14
744	A309	£13 multicolored	.30	.25
		With tab		.40

Organization for Rehabilitation through Training (ORT), centenary.

Scolymus Maculatus — A310

Thistles: £5.50, Echinops viscosus. £8.50, Cynara syriaca.

1980, Jan. 15
745	A310	50a multicolored	.25	.25
746	A310	£5.50 multicolored	.25	.25
747	A310	£8.50 multicolored	.25	.25
		#745-747, with tabs		.45

Men and Drop of Blood A311

Mobile Intensive Care Unit A312

1980, Apr. 15   Photo.   Perf. 14x13
748	A311	£2.70 multicolored	.25	.25
749	A312	£13 multicolored	.25	.25
	a.	Souv. sheet, 2 each #748-749	1.00	1.00
		#748-749, with tabs		.40

Magen David Adom (Red Star of David), 50th anniv.

Road of Courage Monument — A313

1980, Apr. 15   Litho.   Perf. 14
750	A313	£12 multicolored	.25	.25
		With tab		.35

Memorial Day.

Sabbath Lamp, Netherlands, 18th Century — A314

Sabbath Lamps: £20, Germany, 18th century. £30, Morocco, 19th century.

1980, Aug. 5   Photo.   Perf. 13x14
751	A314	£4.30 multicolored	.25	.25
752	A314	£20 multicolored	.25	.25
753	A314	£30 multicolored	.25	.25
		Nos. 751-753 (3)	.75	.75
		With tabs		.80

Yizhak Gruenbaum — A315

1980, Aug. 5   Perf. 14x13
754	A315	£32 sepia	.60	.60
		With tab		.85

Yizhak Gruenbaum (1879-1970), first minister of the interior.

Renewal of Jewish Settlement in Gush Etzion — A316

1980, Aug. 5
755	A316	£19 multicolored	.25	.25
		With tab		.35

View of Haifa and Mt. Carmel, 17th Century A317

1980, Sept. 28   Litho.   Perf. 14x13
756	A317	Sheet of 2	1.75	1.75
	a.	2s multicolored	.60	.50
	b.	3s multicolored	.80	.75

Haifa 80 National Stamp Exhibition, Haifa, Sept. 28-Oct. 7.

A318

1980-81   Photo.   Perf. 13x14
757	A318	5a brt yel grn & green	.25	.25
758	A318	10a red & brt mag	.25	.25
759	A318	20a grnsh bl & dk blue	.25	.25
760	A318	30a lil & dp vio	.25	.25
761	A318	50a red org & red brown	.25	.25
762	A318	60a brt yel grn & dk brown	.25	.25
762A	A318	70a Prus bl & black	.25	.25
763	A318	1s brt mag & dk green	.25	.25
764	A318	2s dk bl grn & brn red	.25	.25
765	A318	2.80s brown & grn	.25	.25
766	A318	3.20s gray & red	.25	.25
767	A318	4.20s ultra & dk pur	.30	.25
768	A318	5s green & blk	.35	.25
769	A318	10s brn org & brn	.50	.25
		#757-769, with tabs		6.00

Issued: 70a, 5/5/81; others, 12/16/80. See Nos. 784-786, 807-808

Prime Minister Golda Meir (1898-1978) — A319

1981, Feb. 10   Photo.   Perf. 14x13
770	A319	2.60s rose violet	.25	.25
		With tab		.40

View of Jerusalem, by Mordechai Ardon A320

Paintings of Jerusalem by: 50a, Anna Ticho. 1.50s, Joseph Zaritsky, vert.

1981, Feb. 10   Litho.   Perf. 14
771	A320	50a multicolored	.25	.25
772	A320	1.50s multicolored	.25	.25
773	A320	2.50s multicolored	.25	.25
		Nos. 771-773 (3)	.75	.75
		With tabs		.95

Hand Putting Coin in Light Bulb — A321

1981, Mar. 17   Photo.   Perf. 14
774	A321	2.60s shown	.25	.25
775	A321	4.20s Hand squeezing solar energy	.30	.25
		#774-775, with tabs		.70

Shmuel Yosef Agnon (1880-1970), Writer — A322

Designs: 2.80s, Moses Montefiore (1784-1885), first knighted English Jew. 3.20s, Abba Hillel Silver (1893-1963), statesman.

Perf. 14x13, 14 (3.20s)
1981, Mar. 17
776	A322	2s dk blue & blk	.25	.25
777	A322	2.80s dk bl grn & blk	.25	.25
778	A322	3.20s deep bis & blk	.30	.30
		Nos. 776-778 (3)	.80	.80
		With tabs		1.00

Wind Surfing — A323

1981, May 5   Perf. 14x13
779	A323	80a shown	.25	.25
780	A323	4s Basketball	.30	.30
781	A323	6s High jump	.40	.40
		Nos. 779-781 (3)	.95	.95
		With tabs		1.40

11th Maccabiah Games, July 8-16.

Biq'at Hayarden Memorial — A324

1981, May 5   Perf. 13x14
782	A324	1s red & black	.25	.25
		With tab		.25

Jewish Family Heritage — A325

1981, May 5   Litho.   Perf. 14
783	A325	3s multicolored	.30	.25
		With tab		.45

Type of 1980

1981, Aug. 25   Photo.   Perf. 13x14
784	A318	90a dp vio & brn org	.25	.25
785	A318	3s red & dk blue	.35	.25
786	A318	4s dk brn vio & dp lil rose	.40	.25
		Nos. 784-786 (3)	1.00	.75
		With tabs		1.40

The Burning Bush — A326

Festivals 5742 (Book of Exodus): 1s "Let my people go . . ." 3s, Crossing of the Red Sea. 4s, Moses with Tablets.

1981, Aug. 25
787	A326	70a multicolored	.25	.25
788	A326	1s multicolored	.25	.25
789	A326	3s multicolored	.30	.25
790	A326	4s multicolored	.35	.25
		Nos. 787-790 (4)	1.15	1.00
		With tabs		1.25

Roses — A327

90a, Rosa damascena. 3.50s, Rosa phoenicia. 4.50s, Rosa hybrida.

ISREAL

1981, Oct. 22 — Litho. — Perf. 14
- 791 A327 90a multicolored .25 .25
- 792 A327 3.50s multicolored .30 .30
- 793 A327 4.50s multicolored .35 .35
- Nos. 791-793 (3) .90 .75
- With tabs 1.25

Ha-Shiv'a Interchange, Morasha-Ashod Highway — A328

1981, Oct. 22 — Photo. — Perf. 14x13
- 794 A328 8s multicolored .50 .50
- With tab .75

Elat Stone — A329

1981, Dec. 29 — Litho. — Perf. 14
- 795 A329 2.50s shown .25 .25
- 796 A329 5.50s Star sapphire .40 .40
- 797 A329 7s Emerald .55 .55
- Nos. 795-797 (3) 1.20 1.20
- With tabs 1.75

Arbutus Andrachne — A330

No. 799, Cercis siliquastrum. No. 800, Quercus ithaburensis.

1981, Dec. 29
- 798 A330 3s shown .25 .25
- 799 A330 3s multicolored .25 .25
- 800 A330 3s multicolored .25 .25
- a. Vert. or horiz. strip of 3, #798-800 .80 .80
- #800a, horiz. strip of 3 with tabs 1.50

Nos. 798-800 issued in sheets of 9.

Road Safety — A331

1982, Mar. 2 — Photo. — Perf. 14x13
- 801 A331 7s multicolored .60 .60
- With tab .90
- a. Souvenir sheet 1.25 1.25

No. 801a sold for 10s.

Joseph Gedalyah Klausner (1874-1958), Historian and Philosopher — A331a

7s, Perez Bernstein (1890-1971), writer and editor. 8s, Rabbi Arys Levin (1885-1969).

1982, Mar. 2
- 802 A331a 7s multi .30 .25
- 803 A331a 8s multi .35 .25
- 804 A331a 9s cream & dk bl .40 .25
- Nos. 802-804 (3) 1.05 .75
- With tabs 1.75

Type of 1980 and Produce — A332

1982-83 — Photo. — Perf. 13 x 14
- 805 A332 40a Prus bl & grn .25 .25
- 806 A332 80a lt bl & pur .25 .25
- 807 A318 1.10s ol & red .25 .25
- 808 A318 1.20s bl & red .25 .25
- 809 A332 1.40s ol grn & red .25 .25
- 810 A332 6s red vio & brn org .25 .25
- 811 A332 7s brn org & ol .25 .25
- 812 A332 8s brt grn & red brn .25 .25
- 813 A332 9s ol & brn .25 .25
- 814 A332 15s ver & brt grn .25 .25
- Nos. 805-814 (10) 2.50 2.50
- With tabs 5.00

Issued: 1.10s, 2/11; 1.20s, 3/16; 1.40s, 6/22/82; 40a, 80a, 6s, 1/11/83; 7s-15s, 10/11/83.
See Nos. 876-879.

Tel Aviv Landscape, by Aryeh Lubin (d. 1980) — A333

Landscapes by: 8s, Sionah Tagger, vert. 15s, Israel Paldi (1892-1979).

1982, Apr. 22 — Litho. — Perf. 14
- 815 A333 7s multicolored .30 .25
- 816 A333 8s multicolored .30 .25
- 817 A333 15s multicolored .60 .45
- Nos. 815-817 (3) 1.20 .95
- With tabs 2.25

Gedudei Nouar Youth Corps — A334

1982, Apr. 22 — Photo. — Perf. 14x13
- 818 A334 5s multicolored .30 .25
- With tab .50

Armour Memorial, En Zetim — A335

1982, Apr. 22 — Litho. — Perf. 14
- 819 A335 1.50s multicolored .25 .25
- With tab .25

Memorial Day.

Joshua Addressing Crowd — A336

Festivals 5743 (Book of Joshua): 5.50s, Crossing River Jordan. 7.50s, Blowing down walls of Jericho. 9.50s, Battle with five kings of Amorites.

1982, Aug. 10 — Perf. 14
- 820 A336 1.50s multicolored .25 .25
- 821 A336 5.50s multicolored .25 .25
- 822 A336 7.50s multicolored .30 .25
- 823 A336 9.50s multicolored .30 .25
- Nos. 820-823 (4) 1.10 1.00
- With tabs 1.25

Hadassah, 70th Anniv. — A337

1982, Aug. 10 — Litho.
- 824 A337 12s multicolored .85 .70
- With tab 1.25

Rosh Pinna Settlement Centenary — A338

1982 — Photo. — Perf. 13x14
- 825 A338 2.50s shown .25 .25
- 826 A338 3.50s Rishon Leziyyon .25 .25
- 827 A338 6s Zikhron Yaaqov .25 .25
- 828 A338 9s Mazkeret Batya .25 .25
- Nos. 825-828 (4) 1.00 1.00
- With tabs 1.25

Issued: 2.50s, 3.50s, Aug. 10; others, Oct. 5.
See Nos. 849-850.

Olive Branch — A339

1982, Sept. 12
- 829 A339 multicolored .25 .25
- With tab .40
- a. Booklet pane of 8 + 8 ('84) 3.00

Sold at various values.

Emblem of Council for a Beautiful Israel — A340

1982, Oct. 5 — Litho. — Perf. 14
- 830 A340 17s multicolored .60 .30
- With tab .80
- a. Souv. sheet of 1, imperf. 2.00 2.00

No. 830a was for Beer Sheva '82 National Stamp Exhibition. Sold for 25s.

Independence Martyrs — A341

a, Eliahu Bet Tzuri. b, Hannah Szenes. c, Shlomo Ben Yosef. d, Yosef Lishanski. e, Naaman Belkind. f, Eliezer Kashani. g, Yechiel Dresner. h, Dov Gruner. i, Mordechai Alkachi. j, Eliahu Hakim. k, Meir Nakar. l, Avshalom Haviv. m, Yaakov Weiss. n, Meir Feinstein. o, Moshe Barazani. p, Eli Cohen. q, Samuel Azaar. r, Moshe Marzouk. s, Shalom Salih. t, Yosef Basri.

1982, Dec. — Perf. 14x13½
- 831 A341 Sheet of 20 5.50 5.50
- a.-t. 3s multicolored .25 .25

Anti-Smoking Campaign — A342

1983, Feb. 15 — Litho. — Perf. 13
- 832 A342 7s Candy in ash tray .30 .25
- With tab .50

Beekeeping A343

1983, Feb. 15 — Photo. — Perf. 13x14
- 833 A343 30s multi 1.00 .75
- With tab 1.50

A343a

8s, Golan. 15s, Galil. 20s, Yehuda and Shomeron.

1983, Feb. 15 — Litho. — Perf. 14
- 834 A343a 8s multicolored .25 .25
- 835 A343a 15s multicolored .50 .35
- 836 A343a 20s multicolored .75 .45
- Nos. 834-836 (3) 1.50 1.05
- With tabs 2.40

Memorial Day (Apr. 17) — A344

3s, Division of Steel Memorial, Besor Region.

1983, Apr. 12 — Perf. 13
- 837 A344 3s multicolored .25 .25
- With tab .25

Independence Day — A345

1983, Apr. 12 — Perf. 14
- 838 A345 25s multicolored .65 .50
- With tab .95
- a. Souvenir sheet, imperf. 2.25 2.25

No. 838a sold for 35s.

12th Hapoel Games A346

1983, Apr. 12 — Perf. 14x13
- 839 A346 6s multicolored .25 .25
- With tab .35

50th Anniv. of Israel Military Industries — A347

1983, Apr. 12
- 840 A347 12s multicolored .40 .35
- With tab .50

Souvenir Sheet

WWII Uprising Leaders A348

Designs: a, Yosef Glazman (1908-1943), Founder of United Partisans Org. b, Text.1 c, Mordechai Anilewicz (1919-1943), leader of Warsaw Ghetto revolt. No. 841 sold for 45s.

1983, June 7 — Perf. 14
- 841 A348 Sheet of 3 2.50 2.50
- a. 10s multicolored .60 .40
- b. 10s multicolored .60 .40
- c. 10s multicolored .60 .40

Raoul Wallenberg (1912-1945), Swedish Diplomat — A349

1983, June 7 — Perf. 14x13
- 842 A349 14s multicolored .55 .40
- With tab .90

ISRAEL

The Last Way, by Yosef Kuzkovski — A350

1983, June 7		Perf. 14	
843	A350 35s multicolored	.75	.60
	With tab	1.10	

Ohel Moed Synagogue, Tel Aviv — A351

12s, Yeshurun Society, Jerusalem. 16s, Ohel Aharon, Haifa. 20s, Eliyahu Khakascni, Beer Sheva.

1983, Aug. 23			
844	A351 3s shown	.25	.25
845	A351 12s multicolored	.25	.25
846	A351 16s multicolored	.30	.25
847	A351 20s multicolored	.30	.25
	Nos. 844-847 (4)	1.10	1.00
	With tabs	1.50	

View of Afula, Jezreel Valley — A352

1983, Aug. 23			
848	A352 15s multicolored	.35	.35
	With tab	.50	

Settlement Type of 1982

1983, Aug. 23			
849	A338 11s Yesud Ha-Maala	.25	.25
850	A338 13s Nes Ziyyona	.40	.30
	#849-850, with tabs	.90	

Souvenir Sheet

Tel Aviv Seashore Promenade — A353

1983, Sept. 25		Perf. 14x13	
851	A353 Sheet of 2	8.00	8.00
a.	30s multicolored	2.00	2.00
b.	50s multicolored	3.75	3.50

Tel Aviv '83, 13th Natl. Stamp Show, Sept. Sold for 120s.

KFIR-C2 Tactical Fighter — A354

18s, Reshef class missile boat. 30s, Merkava-MK1 battle tank.

1983, Dec. 13	Photo.	Perf. 14	
852	A354 8s shown	.25	.25
853	A354 18s multicolored	.25	.25
854	A354 30s multicolored	.25	.25
	Nos. 852-854 (3)	.75	.75
	With tabs	.85	

Rabbi Meir Bar-Ilan (1880-1949), Founder of Mizrachi Movement — A355

1983, Dec. 13	Photo.	Perf. 14x13	
855	A355 9s multicolored	.25	.25
	With tab	.25	

Jewish Immigration from Germany, 50th Anniv. — A356

1983, Dec. 13	Photo.	Perf. 13x14	
856	A356 14s multicolored	.35	.30
	With tab	.45	

Michael Halperin (1860-1919), Zionist — A357

Uri Zvi Grinberg (1896-1981), Poet — A358

15s, Yigal Allon (1918-1980), military commander, founder of Israel Labor Party.

1984, Mar. 15	Photo.	Perf. 14x13	
857	A357 7s multicolored	.25	.25
	Litho.		
	Perf. 14		
858	A357 15s multicolored	.30	.30
	Perf. 13		
859	A358 16s multicolored	.25	.25
	Nos. 857-859 (3)	.80	.80
	With tabs	1.00	

Hevel Ha-Besor Settlement — A359

1984, Mar. 15		Perf. 14	
860	A359 12s shown	.25	.25
861	A359 17s Arava	.30	.25
862	A359 40s Gaza Strip	.40	.40
	Nos. 860-862 (3)	.95	.90
	With tabs	1.40	

Monument of Alexander Zaid, by David Polus — A360

Monuments: No. 864, Tel Hay Defenders (seated lion), by Abraham Melnikov (1892-1960). No. 865, Dov Gruner, by Chana Orloff (1888-1968).

1984, Mar. 15		Perf. 13x14	
863	A360 15s multicolored	.30	.25
864	A360 15s multicolored	.30	.25
865	A360 15s multicolored	.30	.25
	Nos. 863-865 (3)	.90	.75
	With tabs	1.25	

Memorial Day — A361

Design: Oliphant House (Druse military memorial), Dalyat Al Karmil.

1984, Apr. 26	Photo.	Perf. 14x13	
866	A361 10s multicolored	.25	.25
	With tab	.25	

Natl. Labor Fed., 50th Anniv. — A362

1984, Apr. 26			
867	A362 35s multicolored	.25	.25
	With tab	.35	

Produce Type of 1982-83

1984	Photo.	Perf. 13x14	
876	A332 30s vio brn & red	.25	.25
877	A332 50s dp bis & rose mag	.30	.30
878	A332 100s gray & green	.80	.50
879	A332 500s dp org & bl blk	1.50	.75
	Nos. 876-879 (4)	2.85	1.80
	With tabs	4.50	

Issued: 500s, 11/27; others 4/26.

Leon Pinsker (1821-91), — A363

Gen. Charles O. Wingate (1903-44) — A364

No. 880, Hovevei Zion founder. No. 881, British soldier.

1984, July 3		Perf. 14x13	
880	A363 20s lilac and purple	.25	.25
881	A364 20s blk, grn & gray	.25	.25
	#880-881, with tabs	.45	

Hearts, Stars — A365

1984, July 3			
882	A365 30s multicolored	.25	.25
	With tab	.30	

70th anniv. of American Jewish Joint Distribution Committee (philanthropic org. created during World War I).

1984 Summer Olympics — A366

1984, July 3	Litho.	Perf. 14	
883	A366 80s Dove	.55	.55
	With tab	.80	

Souvenir Sheet
Perf. 14x13

884	A366 240s like 80s	5.00	4.50

No. 884 contains one 23x32mm stamp. Sold for 350s.

Biblical Women — A367

1984, Sept. 4	Photo.	Perf. 13x14	
885	A367 15s Hannah	.25	.25
886	A367 70s Ruth	.30	.25
887	A367 100s Huldah	.35	.25
	Nos. 885-887 (3)	.90	.75
	With tabs	1.20	

David Wolffsohn (1856-1914), Jewish Colonial Trust Founder — A368

1984, Sept. 4		Perf. 14x14½	
888	A368 150s multicolored	.90	.60
	With tab	1.25	

Nahalal Settlement (Founded 1921) — A369

1984, Sept. 4		Perf. 14	
889	A369 80s multicolored	.35	.25
	With tab	.45	

World Food Day, Oct. 16 — A370

1984, Nov. 27		Litho.	
891	A370 200s Bread, wheat	.55	.55
	With tab	.80	

Rabbi Isaac Herzog (1888-1959), Statesman, Scholar — A371

1984, Nov. 27	Photo.	Perf. 14½	
892	A371 400s multicolored	1.00	1.00
	With tab	1.60	

A372

Children's Book Illustrations (Authors and their books): 20s, Apartment to Let, by Leah Goldberg (1911-70). 30s, Why is the Zebra Wearing Pajamas, by Omer Hillel (b. 1926) (30x30mm). 50s, Across the Sea, by Haim Nahman Bialik (1873-1934).

Perf. 14, 13 (30s)

1984, Nov. 27		Litho.	
893	A372 20s multicolored	.25	.25
894	A372 30s multicolored	.25	.25
895	A372 50s multicolored	.25	.25
	Nos. 893-895 (3)	.75	.75
	With tabs	.75	

Birds of Prey — A373

100s, Lappet faced vulture. 200s, Bonelli's eagle. 300s, Sooty falcon. 500s, Griffon vulture.

ISRAEL

1985, Feb. 5	Litho.		Perf. 14	
896	A373	100s multi	.30	.30
897	A373	200s multi	.45	.40
898	A373	300s multi	.70	.65
899	A373	500s multi	1.00	.90
	Nos. 896-899 (4)		2.45	2.25
	With tabs		5.50	

Souvenir Sheet

899A		Sheet of 4	7.50	7.50
b.	A373	100s like #896	.35	.30
c.	A373	200s like #897	.45	.40
d.	A373	300s like #898	.75	.65
e.	A373	500s like #899	1.25	1.00

No. 899A sold for 1650s. Nos. 899Ab-899Ad do not have inscriptions below the design.

Aviation in the Holy Land — A374

50s, Bleriot XI, 1913. 150s, Scipio-Short S-17 Kent, 1931. 250s, Tiger Moth DH-82, 1934. 300s, Scion-Short S-16, 1937.

1985, Apr. 2	Litho.		Perf. 14	
900	A374	50s multi	.25	.25
901	A374	150s multi	.35	.25
902	A374	250s multi	.50	.25
903	A374	300s multi	.45	.40
	Nos. 900-903 (4)		1.55	1.15
	With tabs		2.25	

Natl. Assoc. of Nurses A375

1985, Apr. 2	Litho.		Perf. 14	
904	A375	400s multicolored	.85	.80
	With tab		1.25	

Golani Brigade Memorial and Museum A376

1985, Apr. 2	Photo.		Perf. 14x13	
905	A376	50s multicolored	.25	.25
	With tab		.40	

Zivia (1914-1978) and Yitzhak (1915-1981) Zuckerman, Resistance Heroes, Warsaw Ghetto — A377

1985, Apr. 2	Photo.		Perf. 13x14	
906	A377	200s multicolored	.50	.50
	With tab		.80	

Souvenir Sheets

A378

World Stamp Exhibition, Tel Aviv — A379

Adam, Eve and the Serpent (detail) — A380

No. 907: a, Dome of the Rock. b, The Western Wall. c, Church of the Holy Sepulchre.
No. 908: a, 16th Cent. Bas-relief, Ottoman period. b, Hand, 18th cent. bas-relief, Jewish Quarter. c, Rosette carving, 12th-13th cent. Crusader capital.
No. 909, Frontispiece and detail, Schocken Bible, South Germany, ca. 1290.

1985, May 14	Litho.		Perf. 13x14	
907	A378	Sheet of 3	2.75	2.75
a.-c.		200s any single	.60	.60
	Sold for 900s.			

Perf. 14x13

908	A379	Sheet of 3	3.50	3.50
a.-c.		350s any single	.90	.90
	Sold for 1500s.			

Perf. 14

909	A380	800s multi	3.25	3.25
	Nos. 907-909 (3)		9.50	9.50
	Sold for 1200s.			

The Israeli postal administration authorized the Intl. Philatelic Federation (FIP) to overprint a limited number of these souvenir sheets for sale exclusively at ISRAPHIL '85 to raise funds. The FIP overprints have control numbers and are inscribed "Under the Patronage of the Philatelic Federation" in the sheet margin. The sheets remained valid for postage but were not sold by the post office. Value for set of sheets $45.

12th Maccabiah Games — A381

1985, July 16	Litho.		Perf. 14	
910	A381	400s Basketball	.50	.35
911	A381	500s Tennis	.70	.45
912	A381	600s Windsurfing	.90	.55
	Nos. 910-912 (3)		2.10	1.35
	With tabs		3.00	

1985 Festivals — A382

Tabernacle utensils: 100sh, Ark of the Covenant. 150sh, Acacia showbread table. 200sh, Menora. 300sh, Incense altar.

1985, July 16	Litho.		Perf. 14	
913	A382	100s multi	.25	.25
914	A382	150s multi	.30	.30
915	A382	200s multi	.35	.35
916	A382	300s multi	.55	.55
	Nos. 913-916 (4)		1.45	1.45
	With tabs		2.25	

A383

1985, July 16	Litho.		Perf. 14	
917	A383	150s Emblem, badges	.30	.25
	With tab		.50	

Intl. Youth Year.

A384

1985, Nov. 5	Litho.		Perf. 14	
918	A384	200s multi	.70	.25
	With tab		.95	

Leon Yehuda Recanati (1890-1945), financier and philanthropist.

Meir Dizengoff (1861-1936), Founder and Mayor of Tel Aviv — A385

1985, Nov. 5				
919	A385	500s multi	1.00	.65
	With tab		2.00	

Gedera Settlement, Cent. — A386

1985, Nov. 5	Photo.		Perf. 13x14	
920	A386	600s multi	.85	.75
	With tab		1.40	

The Kibbutz A387

1985, Nov. 5	Litho.		Perf. 14	
921	A387	900s multi	1.00	.80
	With tab		1.50	

Theodor Herzl A388

Capital, Second Temple, Jerusalem A389

Designs: 1s, Corinthian, A.D. 1st cent. 3s, Ionic, 1st cent. B.C.

1986, Jan. 1	Photo.		Perf. 13x14	
922	A388	1a red & ultra	.25	.25
923	A388	2a green & ultra	.25	.25
924	A388	3a brown & ultra	.25	.25
925	A388	5a blue & ultra	.25	.25
926	A388	10a org & ultra	.25	.25
927	A388	20a pink & ultra	.25	.25
928	A388	30a lemon & ultra	.25	.25
929	A388	50a pur & ultra	.25	.25
930	A389	1s multi	.75	.50
931	A389	3s multi	1.50	1.00
	Nos. 922-931 (10)		4.25	3.50
	With tabs		5.75	

1s and 3s designs with 1000a and 1500a values were not issued.
See Nos. 1014-1020, 1699.

Red Sea Coral — A390

1986, Mar. 4	Litho.		Perf. 14	
932	A390	30a Balanophyllia	.30	.25
933	A390	40a Goniopora	.45	.25
934	A390	50a Dendronephthya	.60	.25
	Nos. 932-934 (3)		1.35	.75
	With tabs		2.00	

Arthur Rubinstein (1887-1982), Pianist — A391

1986, Mar. 4	Photo.		Perf. 13x14	
935	A391	60a Picasso portraits	.50	.30
	With tab		1.25	

Broadcasting from Jerusalem, 50th Anniv. — A392

70a, Map and microphone, 1936.

1986, Mar. 4	Litho.		Perf. 14	
936	A392	70a multicolored	.65	.50
	With tab		.85	

Negev Brigade Memorial, Beer Sheva — A393

1986, May 4	Litho.		Perf. 13	
937	A393	20a multicolored	.25	.25
	With tab		.30	

Memorial Day.

Al Jazzar Mosque, Akko — A394

1986, May 4	Photo.		Perf. 14x13	
938	A394	30a multicolored	.25	.25
	With tab		.35	

Id Al-Fitr Feast.

Institutes of Higher Learning in the US — A395

Designs: No. 939, 942a, Hebrew Union College, Jewish Institute of Religion, 1875, Cincinnati. No. 940, 942b, Yeshiva University, 1886, NYC. No. 941, 942c, Jewish Theological Seminary of America, 1886, NYC.

1986, May 4	Litho.		Perf. 14	
939	A395	50a multicolored	.45	.25
940	A395	50a multicolored	.45	.25
941	A395	50a multicolored	.45	.25
	Nos. 939-941 (3)		1.35	.75
	With tabs		2.00	

Souvenir Sheet

942		Sheet of 3 + label	3.00	2.50
a.-c.	A395	75a any single	.75	.60

AMERIPEX '86. Size of Nos. 942a-942c: 36x23mm. No. 942 sold for 3s.

Ben Gurion Airport, 50th Anniv. — A396

90a, Terminal from aircraft.

ISRAEL

1986, July 22   **Perf. 14x13**
943   A396   90a multicolored   1.00   .50
     With tab   1.25

"No to Racism" in Graffiti — A397

1986, July 22   **Perf. 14**
944   A397   60a multicolored   .65   .40
     With tab   .80

Druze Feast of Prophet Nabi Sabalan — A398

1986, July 22   **Photo.**   **Perf. 14**
945   A398   40a Tomb, Hurfeish   .30   .25
     With tab   .45

Joseph Sprinzak (1885-1959), 1st Speaker of Knesset — A399

1986, July 22   **Litho.**   **Perf. 13**
946   A399   80a multicolored   .65   .30
     With tab   .85

Worms Illuminated Mahzor, 13th Cent. — A400

20a, Gates of Heaven. 40a, Sheqalim, prayer. 90a, Rose flower prayer introduction.

1986, Sept. 23   **Litho.**   **Perf. 13x14**
947   A400   20a multicolored   .25   .25
948   A400   40a multicolored   .25   .25
949   A400   90a multicolored   .40   .40
     Nos. 947-949 (3)   .90   .90
     With tabs   1.75

David Ben-Gurion (1886-1973) — A401

1986, Oct. 19   **Litho.**   **Perf. 14x13**
950   A401   1s multicolored   .80   .80
     With tab   1.10

Souvenir Sheet

Map of the Holyland, by Gerard de Jode, 1578 — A402

1986, Oct. 19   **Perf. 14½**
951   A402   2s multicolored   4.00   3.50

NATANYA '86 Stamp Exhibition; Organized philately in Natanya, 50th anniv. Sold for 3s.

Israel Meteorological Service, 50th Anniv. — A403

1986, Dec. 18   **Litho.**   **Perf. 13**
952   A403   50a multicolored   .40   .30
     With tab   .60

Basilica of the Annunciation, Nazareth — A404

1986, Dec. 18   **Litho.**   **Perf. 14**
953   A404   70a multicolored   .55   .30
     With tab   .75

Israel Philharmonic Orchestra, 50th Anniv. — A405

No. 9.54, Bronislaw Huberman, violinist. No. 955, Arturo Toscanini, conductor.

1986, Dec. 18
954   A405   1.50s multicolored   1.50   .75
955   A405   1.50s multicolored   1.50   .75
     a.   Pair, #954-955   3.50   3.25
     With tabs   5.00

Owls — A406

Designs: 30a, Bubo bubo. 40a, Otus brucei. 50a, Tyto alba. 80a, Strix butleri.

1987, Feb. 24   **Litho.**   **Perf. 14x13**
956   A406   30a sil & multi   .50   .30
957   A406   40a sil & multi   .60   .40
958   A406   50a sil & multi   .75   .50
959   A406   80a sil & multi   1.10   .70
     Nos. 956-959 (4)   2.95   1.90
     With tabs   6.50

Souvenir Sheet

960   Sheet of 4   8.00   5.00
  a.   A406 30a like #956   .70   .50
  b.   A406 40a like #957   1.25   1.00
  c.   A406 50a like #958   1.75   1.25
  d.   A406 80a like #959   2.25   1.50

Sold for 3s. Nos. 960a-960d do not have inscriptions below the design.

Ammunition Hill Memorial, Jerusalem — A407

1987, Apr. 16   **Litho.**   **Perf. 14**
961   A407   30a multicolored   .30   .30
     With tab   .45

Memorial Day.

13th Hapoel Games — A408

1987, Apr. 16
962   A408   90a multicolored   .50   .50
     With tab   .80

Souvenir Sheet

HAIFA '87 Stamp Exhibition — A409

1987, Apr. 16   **Perf. 14x13**
963   A409   2.70s No. C8   6.00   6.00

Sold for 4s.

Amateur Radio Operators — A410

1987, June 14   **Litho.**   **Perf. 14**
964   A410   2.50s multi   2.25   2.25
     With tab   3.50

World Dog Show, June 23-27 — A411

1987, June 14
965   A411   40a Saluki   .40   .35
966   A411   50a Sloughi   .55   .45
967   A411   2s Canaan   2.25   2.00
     Nos. 965-967 (3)   3.20   2.80
     With tabs   8.00

Clean Environment — A412

1987, June 14   **Perf. 13**
968   A412   40a multicolored   .40   .40
     With tab   .60

Rabbi Moshe Avigdor Amiel (1883-1945), Founder of Yeshivas — A413

1987, Sept. 10   **Perf. 14**
969   A413   1.40s multi   1.00   1.00
     With tab   1.30

Synagogue Models, Nahum Goldmann Museum, Tel Aviv — A414

30a, Altneuschul, Prague, 13th cent. 50a, Aleppo, Syria, 9th cent. 60a, Florence, Italy, 19th cent.

1987, Sept. 10   **Perf. 13x14**
970   A414   30a multicolored   .30   .25
971   A414   50a multicolored   .35   .30
972   A414   60a multicolored   .40   .35
     Nos. 970-972 (3)   1.05   .90
     With tabs   1.40

See Nos. 996-998.

Kupat Holim Health Insurance Institute, 75th Anniv. — A415

1987, Sept. 10   **Perf. 14**
973   A415   1.50s multi   .90   .90
     With tab   1.25

Pinhas Rosen (1887-1978), First Minister of Justice — A416

1987, Nov. 24   **Litho.**   **Perf. 13**
974   A416   80a multicolored   .45   .45
     With tab   .70

A417

Exploration of the Holy Land, 19th cent.: 30a, Thomas Howard Molyneux (1847) and Christopher Costigan (1835). 50a, William Francis Lynch (1848). 60a, John MacGregor (1868-1869).

1987, Nov. 24   **Perf. 14**
975   A417   30a multi   .30   .30
976   A417   50a multi   .40   .40
977   A417   60a multi   .50   .50
     Nos. 975-977 (3)   1.20   1.20
     With tabs   2.00

Souvenir Sheet

978   Sheet of 3   3.50   3.50
  a.   A417 40a like #975   .50   .50
  b.   A417 50a like #976   1.00   1.00
  c.   A417 80a like #977   1.25   1.25

No. 978 sold for 2.50s.

A418

10a, Computer technology. 80a, Genetic engineering. 1.40s, Medical engineering.

1988, Jan. 26
979   A418   10a multicolored   .25   .25
980   A418   80a multicolored   .40   .35
981   A418   1.40s multicolored   .75   .50
     Nos. 979-981 (3)   1.40   1.10
     With tabs   2.00

Industrialization of Israel, cent.

Water Conservation — A419

1988, Jan. 26
982   A419   40a multicolored   .25   .25
     With tab   .40

Australia Bicentennial — A420

1988, Jan. 26   **Perf. 14**
983   A420   1s multi   1.25   1.25
     With tab   1.25

Sunflower — A421

1988, Mar. 9   **Photo.**   **Perf. 13x14**
984   A421   (30a) dk yel grn & yel   .25   .25
     With tab   .30

A422

Design: Anne Frank (1929-45), Amsterdam house where she hid.

1988, Apr. 19   **Litho.**
985   A422   60a multicolored   .50   .50
     With tab   .70

ISRELAEL

Independence 40 Stamp Exhibition, Jerusalem — A423

Design: Modern Jerusalem.

1988, Apr. 19
986	A423	1s shown	.50	.40
		With tab		.65

Souvenir Sheet
987	A423	2s detail from 1s	3.25	3.00

No. 987 sold for 3s.

Memorial Day — A424

1988, Apr. 19 *Perf. 14x13*
988	A424	40a multicolored	.25	.25
		With tab		.30
a.		Souvenir sheet of 1	1.00	1.00

Natl. independence, 40th anniv. No. 988a contains one stamp like No. 988 but without copyright inscription LR. Sold for 60a.

Souvenir Sheet

Israel's 40th Anniv. Exhibition, Tel Aviv — A425

Stamps on stamps: a, No. 245. b, No. 297. c, No. 120. d, No. 96. e, Like No. 794. f, No. 252. g, No. 333. h, No. 478.

1988, June 9 *Litho. Perf. 14*
989	A425	Sheet of 8 + label	3.00	3.00
a.-h.		20a any single	.30	.30

Sold for 2.40s. Center label pictures Israel 40 emblem.

B'nai B'rith in Jerusalem, Cent. — A426

1988, June 27 *Perf. 14*
990	A426	70a multicolored	.35	.35
		With tab		.45

Nature Reserves in the Negev — A427

1988, June 27
991	A427	40a Ein Zin	.25	.25
992	A427	60a She'Zaf	.40	.30
993	A427	70a Ramon	.50	.35
		Nos. 991-993 (3)	1.15	.90
		With tabs		1.60

See Nos. 1052-1054, 1154-1156.

Agents Executed During World War II — A428

Portraits: 40a, Havivah Reik (1914-1944). 1.65s, Enzo Hayyim Sereni (1905-1944).

1988, Sept. 1 *Litho.*
994	A428	40a multicolored	.35	.35
995	A428	1.65s multicolored	1.00	1.00
		#994-995, with tabs		1.75

Synagogue Models Type of 1987

Models in the Nahum Goldmann Museum, Tel Aviv: 35a, Kai-Feng Fu Synagogue, 12th cent., China. 60a, Zabludow Wooden Synagogue, 17th cent., Poland. 70a, Touro Synagogue, 1763, Newport, Rhode Island, designed by Peter Harrison.

1988, Sept. 1 *Perf. 13x14*
996	A414	35a multicolored	.25	.25
997	A414	60a multicolored	.30	.30
998	A414	70a multicolored	.50	.30
		Nos. 996-998 (3)	1.05	.85
		With tabs		1.50

A429

1988, Nov. 9 *Perf. 14*
999	A429	80a multicolored	.60	.60
		With tab		.80

Kristallnacht, Nazi pogrom in Germany, 50th anniv.

Moshe Dayan (1915-1981), Foreign Minister, Minister of Defense — A430

1988, Nov. 9 *Perf. 13*
1000	A430	40a multicolored	.25	.25
		With tab		.45

Jewish Legion, 70th Anniv. — A431

1988, Nov. 9 *Perf. 14*
1001	A431	2s yel brn, sepia & lem	1.00	.75
		With tab		1.30

Agricultural Achievements A433

50a, Avocado (fruit-growing). 60a, Lilium longiflorum (horticulture). 90a, Irrigation.

1988, Dec. 22 *Perf. 14*
1004	A433	50a multicolored	.30	.30
1005	A433	60a multicolored	.40	.40
1006	A433	90a multicolored	.50	.50
		Nos. 1004-1006 (3)	1.20	1.20
		With tabs		1.75

Natl. Tourism — A434

40a, Red Sea. 60a, Dead Sea. 70a, Mediterranean Sea. 1.70s, Sea of Galilee.

1989, Mar. 12 *Litho. Perf. 13*
1007	A434	40a multicolored	.25	.25
1008	A434	60a multicolored	.30	.30
1009	A434	70a multicolored	.40	.40
1010	A434	1.70s multicolored	.60	.60
		Nos. 1007-1010 (4)	1.55	1.55
		With tabs		2.75

Rabbi Judah Leib Maimon (1875-1962) — A435

1989, Mar. 12 *Perf. 14*
1011	A435	1.70s multi	1.00	1.00
		With tab		1.50

Rashi, Rabbi Solomon Ben Isaac (b. 1039), Talmudic Commentator A436

1989, Mar. 12
1012	A436	4s buff & black	2.50	1.50
		With tab		3.00

Memorial Day — A437

Fallen Airmen's Memorial at Har Tayassim.

1989, Apr. 30 *Litho. Perf. 14*
1013	A437	50a multi	.40	.40
		With tab		.50

Archaeology Type of 1986

Gates of Huldah, Temple Compound, Mt. Moriah: 40a, Rosettes and rhomboids, frieze and columns, facade of the eastern gate, 1st cent. B.C. 60a, Corinthian capital, 6th cent. 70a, Bas-relief from the Palace of Umayade Caliphs, 8th cent. 80a, Corinthian capital from the Church of Ascension on the Mount of Olives, 12-13th cent. 90a, Star of David, limestone relief, northern wall, near the new gate, Suleiman's Wall. 2s, Mamluk relief, 14th century. 10s, Carved frieze from a sepulcher entrance, end of the Second Temple Period.

1988-90 *Litho. Perf. 14*
1014	A389	40a multi	.25	.25
1015	A389	60a multi	.30	.25
1016	A389	70a multi	.40	.25
1017	A389	80a multi	.40	.25
1018	A389	90a multi	.90	.25
1019	A389	2s multi	1.00	.75
1020	A389	10s multi	4.50	3.00
		Nos. 1014-1020 (7)	7.75	5.00
		With tabs		12.00

Issued: 40a, 60a, 12/22/88; 70a, 80a, 6/11/89; 10s, 4/30/89; 90a, 10/17/89; 2s, 6/12/90.

UNICEF — A438

1989, Apr. 30
1022	A438	90a multicolored	.60	.50
		With tab		.75

Moshe Smoira (1888-1961), 1st Pres. of Israeli Supreme Court — A439

1989, June 11 *Litho. Perf. 13*
1023	A439	90a deep blue	.60	.60
		With tab		.75

13th Maccabiah Games, July 3-13 — A440

1989, June 11 *Perf. 13x14*
1024	A440	80a multi	.60	.60
		With tab		.70

Ducks — A441

Designs: a, Garganey. b, Mallard. c, Teal. d, Shelduck.

1989, July 18 *Litho. Perf. 14*
1025		Strip of 4	3.00	3.00
		With tabs		4.00
a.-d.	A441	80a any single	1.25	.85

Souvenir Sheet
1025E		Sheet of 4	6.00	5.50
f.	A441	80a like No. 1025d	1.00	1.00
g.	A441	80a like No. 1025b	1.00	1.00
h.	A441	80a like No. 1025a	1.00	1.00
i.	A441	80a like No. 1025c	1.00	1.00

World Stamp Expo '89. No. 1025E contains four 29x33mm stamps. Sold for 5s.

Graphic Design Industry — A442

1989, July 18
1026	A442	1s multi	.60	.35
		With tab		.80

Souvenir Sheet

French Revolution, Bicent. — A443

1989, July 7
1027	A443	3.50s multi	5.50	4.00

Sold for 5s.

Hebrew Language Council, Cent. — A444

1989, Sept. 3 *Litho. Perf. 13x14*
1028	A444	1s multi	.60	.35
		With tab		.75

Rabbi Yehuda Hai Alkalai (1798-1878), Zionist — A445

1989, Sept. 3 *Perf. 14*
1029	A445	2.50s multi	2.00	1.00
		With tab		4.50

Mizrah Festival — A446

Paper cutouts: 50a, Menorah and lions, by Gadoliahu Neminsky, Holbenisk, Ukraine, 1921. 70a, Menorah and hands, Morocco, 19th-20th cent. 80a, "Misrah," hunting scene and deer, Germany, 1818.

1989, Sept. 3 *Perf. 14x13*
1030	A446	50a multi	.30	.25
1031	A446	70a multi	.40	.30
1032	A446	80a multi	.60	.30
		Nos. 1030-1032 (3)	1.30	.85
		With tabs		1.75

Tevel '89 Youth Stamp Exhibition, Oct. 15-21 — A447

ISRAEL

1989, Oct. 12   Photo.   *Perf. 13x14*
1033 A447 50a multi .35 .30
         With tab .45

1st Israeli Stamp Day — A448

1989, Oct. 17   Litho.   *Perf. 14*
1034 A448 1s multi .50 .35
         With tab .70

Special Occasions — A449

1989, Nov. 17   Photo.   *Perf. 13½x14*
1035 A449 (50a) Good luck .45 .35
1036 A449 (50a) With love .45 .35
  a. Booklet pane of 10 5.00
1037 A449 (50a) See you again .45 .35
  a. Booklet pane of 10 + 2 labels 5.75
  b. Sheet of 20 + 5 labels 11.50
         Nos. 1035-1037 (3) 1.35 1.05
         With tab 1.75

Nos. 1036a, 1037a contain 5 tete-beche pairs. No. 1037b contains 10 tete-beche pairs. Nos. 1037a-1037b had value of 80a when released.
Issued: No. 1036a, 8/7/90. Nos. 1037a-1037b, 6/22/93.
See Nos. 1059-1061, 1073-1075.

A450

Design: Tapestry and Rebab, a Stringed Instrument, from the Museum of Bedouin Culture.

1990, Feb. 13   Litho.   *Perf. 13*
1038 A450 1.50s multicolored .80 .80
         With tab 1.10

The Circassians in Israel — A451

Designs: Circassian folk dancers.

1990, Feb. 13   Photo.   *Perf. 14x13*
1039 A451 1.50s multicolored .75 .75
         With tab 1.00

Rehovot City, Cent. — A452

1990, Feb. 13   *Perf. 14*
1040 A452 2s multicolored 1.20 1.00
         With tab 1.60

Souvenir Sheet

Isaiah's Vision of Eternal Peace, by Mordecai Ardon — A453

Series of 3 stained-glass windows, The Hall of Eternal Jewishness and Humanism, Hebrew University Library, Jerusalem: a, "Roads to Jerusalem" (inscription at L). b, Isaiah's prophecy of broken guns beaten into ploughshares (inscription at R).

1990, Apr. 17   Litho.   *Perf. 14*
1041 A453 Sheet of 2 5.50 5.50
  a.-b. 1.50s any single 1.50 1.00

Stamp World London '90. Sold for 4.50s. Also exists imperf. Value $47.50.

Architecture — A454

Design: 75a, School, Deganya Kibbutz, 1930. 1.10s, Dining hall, Kibbutz Tel Yosef by Leopold Krakauer, 1933. 1.20s, Engel House by Ze'ev Rechter, 1933. 1.40s, Home of Dr. Chaim Weizmann, Rehovot by Erich Mendelsohn, 1936. 1.60s, Jewish Agency for Palestine, Jerusalem, by Yohanan Ratner, 1932.

1990-92   Photo.   *Perf. 14x13½*
1044 A454 75a blk, pale grn & buff .50 .35
1045 A454 1.10s blk, yel & grn .60 .35
1046 A454 1.20s blk, bl & yel .60 .35
1047 A454 1.40s blk, lt lil & buff .70 .35
1048 A454 1.60s multicolored .75 .35
  a. Dotted rose lilac background .75 .35
         Nos. 1044-1048 (5) 3.15 1.75
         With tabs 5.25

No. 1048 has a solid bluish lilac background.
Issued: 75a, 4/17; 1.10s, 1.20s, 12/12; 1.40s, 4/9/91; 1.60s, 4/26/92; No. 1048a, 7/14/96.

Nature Reserves Type of 1988

60a, Gamla, Yehudiyya. 80a, Huleh. 90a, Mt. Meron.

1990, Apr. 17   Litho.   *Perf. 14*
1052 A427 60a multicolored .30 .25
1053 A427 80a multicolored .50 .25
1054 A427 90a multicolored .70 .25
         Nos. 1052-1054 (3) 1.50 .75
         With tabs 2.25

Memorial Day — A456

60a, Artillery Corps Memorial.

1990, Apr. 17   Photo.   *Perf. 13x14*
1055 A456 60a multi .45 .25
         With tab .60

Intl. Folklore Festival, Haifa A457

1990, June 12   Litho.   *Perf. 14*
1056   1.90s Denom at UL 1.75 1.75
1057   1.90s Denom at UR 1.75 1.75
  a. A457 Pair, #1056-1057 4.00 4.00
         With tabs 5.00

Hagana, 70th Anniv. — A459

1990, June 12
1058 A459 1.50s multicolored 1.40 1.40
         With tab 1.50

Special Occasions Type of 1989

1990, June 12   *Perf. 13½x14*
1059 A449 55a Good luck .30 .30
1060 A449 80a See you again .40 .30
1061 A449 1s With love .50 .30
         Nos. 1059-1061 (3) 1.20 .90
         With tab 2.00

Spice Boxes — A460

55a, Austro-Hungarian spice box, 19th cent. 80a, Italian, 19th cent. 1s, German, 18th cent.

1990, Sept. 4   Litho.   *Perf. 13x14*
1062 A460 55a sil, gray & blk .30 .25
1063 A460 80a sil, gray & blk .50 .30
1064 A460 1s multicolored .60 .35
  a. Bklt. pane of 6 (3 #1062, 2 #1063, #1064) 7.50 7.50
         Nos. 1062-1064 (3) 1.40 .90
         With tabs 1.50

A461

1990, Sept. 4   *Perf. 13*
1065 A461 1.10s Aliya absorption .75 .75
         With tab .90

Electronic Mail — A462

1990, Sept. 4   *Perf. 14x13*
1066 A462 1.20s black & grn .80 .80
         With tab 1.00

Souvenir Sheet

Beersheba '90 Stamp Exhibition — A463

1990, Sept. 4   *Perf. 13x14*
1067 A463 3s multicolored 4.25 4.00

Sold for 4s.

Computer Games — A464

1990, Dec. 12   Litho.   *Perf. 13x14*
1068 A464 60a Basketball .30 .30
1069 A464 60a Chess .30 .30
1070 A464 60a Auto racing .30 .30
         Nos. 1068-1070 (3) .90 .90
         With tabs 1.25

Ze'ev Jabotinsky (1880-1940), Zionist Leader — A465

1990, Dec. 12   Litho.   *Perf. 13x14*
1071 A465 1.90s multicolored 1.00 1.00
         With tab 1.30

Philately Day — A466

1990, Dec. 12   *Perf. 14*
1072 A466 1.20s P.O., Yafo, #5 .80 .80
         With tab 1.15

Special Occasions Type of 1989

1991, Feb. 19   Photo.   *Perf. 13½x14*
1073 A449 (60a) Happy birthday .40 .30
1074 A449 (60a) Keep in touch .40 .30
  a. Booklet pane of 10 + 2 labels 5.75
  b. Sheet of 20 + 5 labels 11.50
1075 A449 (60a) Greetings .40 .30
         Nos. 1073-1075 (3) 1.20 .90
         With tabs

No. 1074a contains 5 tete-beche pairs. No. 1074b contains 10 tete-beche pairs.
Nos. 1074a-1074b had value of 85a when released.
Issued: Nos. 1074a-1074b, 4/18/94.

Famous Women — A467

Designs: No. 1076, Sarah Aaronsohn (1890-1917), World War I heroine. No. 1077, Rahel Bluwstein (1890-1931), poet. No. 1078, Lea Goldberg (1911-1970), poet.

1991, Feb. 19   *Perf. 14*
1076 A467 1.30s multicolored .75 .75
1077 A467 1.30s multicolored .75 .75
1078 A467 1.30s multicolored .75 .75
         Nos. 1076-1078 (3) 2.25 2.25
         With tabs 2.75

See Nos. 1096-1097, 1102-1103.

Hadera, Cent. — A468

1991, Feb. 19   *Perf. 13*
1079 A468 2.50s multicolored 1.40 1.00
         With tab 2.00

Intelligence Services Memorial, G'lilot — A469

1991, Apr. 9   Litho.   *Perf. 14*
1080 A469 65a multicolored .50 .30
         With tab .60

14th Hapoel Games — A470

1991, Apr. 9
1081 A470 60a multicolored .40 .30
1082 A470 90a multicolored .50 .40
1083 A470 1.10s multicolored .60 .40
         Nos. 1081-1083 (3) 1.50 1.20
         With tabs 2.00

Electrification — A471

Designs: 70a, First power station, Tel Aviv, 1923. 90a, Yarden Power Station, Naharayim, 1932. 1.20s, Rutenberg Power Station, Ashqelon, 1991.

1991, June 11   Litho.   *Perf. 13*
1084 A471 70a multicolored .35 .35
1085 A471 90a multicolored .60 .45
1086 A471 1.20s multicolored .75 .55
         Nos. 1084-1086 (3) 1.70 1.35
         With tabs 2.25

ISRAEL

Rabbi Shimon Hakham (1843-1910) — A472

1991, June 11
1087	A472	2.10s multicolored	1.20	1.20
	With tab			1.80

Souvenir Sheet

Postal and Philatelic Museum, Tel Aviv — A473

Israel #5, Palestine #70, Turkey #133.

1991, June 11   *Perf. 14x13*
1088	A473	3.40s multicolored	5.50	5.50

No. 1088 sold for 5s. Exists imperf. Value $40.

A474

Jewish Festivals: 65a, Man blowing ram's horn, Rosh Hashanah. 1s, Father blessing children, Yom Kippur. 1.20s, Family seated at harvest table, Sukkoth.

1991, Aug. 27   *Litho.*   *Perf. 14*
1089	A474	65a multicolored	.35	.30
1090	A474	1s multicolored	.55	.30
1091	A474	1.20s multicolored	.75	.30
	Nos. 1089-1091 (3)		1.65	.90
	With tabs		2.00	

Jewish Chronicle, 150th Anniv. — A475

1991, Aug. 27
1092	A475	1.50s multicolored	.80	.80
	With tab			1.10

Baron Maurice De Hirsch (1831-1896), Founder of Jewish Colonization Assoc. — A476

1991, Aug. 27   *Perf. 14*
1093	A476	1.60s multicolored	.80	.80
	With tab			1.00

Souvenir Sheet

Haifa, by Gustav Bauernfeind — A477

1991, Aug. 27   *Perf. 14x13*
1094	A477	3s multicolored	5.00	4.00

Haifa '91, Israeli-Polish Philatelic Exhibition. Sold for 4s.

Philately Day — A478

1991, Dec. 2   *Litho.*   *Perf. 13*
1095	A478	70a #2 on piece	.40	.40
	With tab			.50

Famous Women Type of 1991

Designs: 1s, Rahel Yanait Ben-Zvi (1886-1979), politician. 1.10s, Dona Gracia (Nasi, 1510?-1569), philanthropist.

1991, Dec. 2   *Litho.*   *Perf. 14*
1096	A467	1s multicolored	.40	.40
1097	A467	1.10s multicolored	.50	.50
	#1096-1097, with tabs		1.30	

1992 Summer Olympics, Barcelona — A479

1991, Dec. 2
1098	A479	1.10s multicolored	.80	.50
	With tab			1.10

Lehi — A480

1991, Dec. 2   *Perf. 14*
1099	A480	1.50s multicolored	.60	.60
	With tab			1.00

Etzel — A481

1991, Dec. 2
1100	A481	1.50s blk & red	.60	.60
	With tab			1.00

Wolfgang Amadeus Mozart, Death Bicent. — A482

1991, Dec. 2   *Perf. 13*
1101	A482	2s multicolored	1.75	1.50
	With tab		3.25	
a.	Booklet pane of 4		13.00	

One pair in No. 1101a is tete beche.

Famous Women Type of 1991

80a, Hanna Rovina (1889-1980), actress. 1.30s, Rivka Guber (1902-81), educator.

1992, Feb. 18   *Litho.*   *Perf. 14*
1102	A467	80a multicolored	.40	.40
1103	A467	1.30s multicolored	.60	.60
	#1102-1103, with tabs		1.40	

Sea of Galilee — A483

1992, Feb. 18
1104	A483	85a Trees	1.00	.65
1105	A483	85a Sailboat	1.00	.65
1106	A483	85a Fish	1.00	.65
a.	Strip of 3, #1104-1106		3.25	2.00
	With tabs		5.00	

Anemone — A483a

1992, Feb. 18   *Photo.*   *Perf. 13x14*
1107	A483a	(75a) multi	.30	.25
	With tab			.40

PALMAH, 50th Anniv. — A484

1992, Feb. 18   *Litho.*   *Perf. 14*
1108	A484	1.50s multicolored	.60	.60
	With tab			1.00

The Samaritans — A485

1992, Feb. 18
1109	A485	2.60s multicolored	1.00	1.00
	With tab			1.40

Rabbi Hayyim Joseph David Azulai (1724-1806) — A486

Rabbi Joseph Hayyim Ben Elijah (1834-1909) — A487

1992, Apr. 26   *Perf. 13*
1110	A486	85a multicolored	.35	.35
	Perf. 14			
1111	A487	1.20s multicolored	.50	.50
	#1110-1111, with tabs		1.40	

Discovery of America, 500th Anniv. — A488

1992, Apr. 26   *Perf. 14*
1112	A488	1.60s multicolored	.75	.75
	With tab			1.00

Memorial Day — A488a

1992, Apr. 26   *Litho.*   *Perf. 13*
1113	A488a	85a multicolored	.40	.40
	With tab			.55

Souvenir Sheet

Expulsion of Jews from Spain, 500th Anniv. — A489

Designs: No. 1114a, 80a, Map of Palestine. b, 1.10s, Map of Italy, Sicily, Greece and central Mediterranean. c, 1.40s, Map of Spain and Portugal.

1992, Apr. 26   *Perf. 14*
1114	A489	Sheet of 3, #a.-c.	3.50	3.50

Jaffa-Jerusalem Railway, Cent. — A490

Different train and four scenes on each stamp showing railroad equipment and memorabilia.

1992
1115	A490	85a multicolored	.40	.30
1116	A490	1s multicolored	.50	.40
1117	A490	1.30s multicolored	.70	.50
1118	A490	1.60s multicolored	.90	.60
	#1115-1118, with tabs		3.25	
a.	Bklt. pane of 4, #1115-1118		3.50	

Souvenir Sheet

1118B	Sheet of 4 + 4 labels		4.50	4.50
c.	A490 50a like #1118		.85	.75
d.	A490 50a like #1117		.85	.75
e.	A490 50a like #1115		.85	.75
f.	A490 50a like #1116		.85	.75

Nos. 1115 and 1118, 1116 and 1117 are tete beche in No. 1118a. Nos. 1118c and 1118f, 1118d and 1118e are tete beche in No. 1118B.

Issued: No. 1118B, 9/17; others 6/16.

Rabbi Hayyim Benatar (1696-1743) A491

Rabbi Shalom Sharabi (1720-1777) A492

1992, June 16   *Perf. 13*
1119	A491	1.30s multicolored	.55	.55
1120	A492	3s multicolored	1.25	1.25
	#1119-1120, with tabs		2.25	

Jewish Natl. & University Library, Jerusalem, Cent. — A493

85a, Parables, 1491. 1s, Italian manuscript, 15th cent. 1.20s, Bible translation by Martin Buber.

1992, Sept. 17   *Litho.*   *Perf. 13x14*
1121	A493	85a multicolored	.30	.30
1122	A493	1s multicolored	.50	.50
1123	A493	1.20s multicolored	.70	.70
	Nos. 1121-1123 (3)		1.50	1.50
	With tabs		2.00	

Supreme Court — A494

1992, Sept. 17   *Perf. 14*
1124	A494	3.60s multicolored	1.60	.75
	With tab		2.00	

Wild Animals — A495

No. 1125, Panthera pardus saxicolor. No. 1126, Elephas maximus. No. 1127, Pan troglodytes. No.1128, Panthera leo persica.

1992, Sept. 17
1125	A495	50a multicolored	.40	.35
1126	A495	50a multicolored	.40	.35
1127	A495	50a multicolored	.40	.35
1128	A495	50a multicolored	.40	.35
a.	Strip of 4, #1125-1128		1.75	1.75
	With tabs		2.75	

European Unification — A496

ISREAL

1992, Dec. 8		**Litho.**		***Perf. 13***
1129	A496	1.50s multicolored	.55	.55
		With tab		.90

Stamp Day.

First Hebrew Film, 75th Anniv. — A497

Films: 80a, Liberation of the Jews, 1918. 2.70s, Oded, the Vagabond, 1932, first Hebrew feature film. 3.50s, The Promised Land, 1935, first Hebrew talkie.

1992, Dec. 8				
1130	A497	80a multicolored	.50	.30
1131	A497	2.70s multicolored	1.00	.45
1132	A497	3.50s multicolored	1.25	.70
		Nos. 1130-1132 (3)	2.75	1.45
		With tabs	4.75	

Birds — A498

10a, Wallcreeper. 20a, Tristram's grackle. 30a, White wagtail. 50a, Palestine sunbird. 85a, Sinai rosefinch. 90a, Swallow. 1s, Trumpeter finch. 1.30s, Graceful warbler. 1.50s, Black-eared wheatear. 1.70s, Common bulbul.

1992-98		**Photo.**		***Perf. 13x14***
1133	A498	10a multi	.25	.25
1134	A498	20a multi	.25	.25
1135	A498	30a multi	.25	.25
1137	A498	50a multi	.25	.25
1141	A498	85a multi	.30	.25
1142	A498	90a multi	.25	.25
1142A	A498	1s multi	.30	.25
b.		Violet background	.55	.55
1143	A498	1.30s multi	.60	.45
1144	A498	1.50s multi	.50	.40
1146	A498	1.70s multi	.65	.55
		Nos. 1133-1146 (10)	3.60	3.15
		With tabs	5.25	

No. 1142A has a gray background.

Souvenir Sheet

Designs: a, like #1133. b, like #1137. c, like #1135. d, like #1134. e, like #1141. f, like #1144. g, like #1146. h, like #1142A. i, like #1143. j, like #1142.

		Litho.		***Perf. 14***
1152		Sheet of 10	3.75	3.75
a.-j.		A498 30a Any single	.30	.25

Nos. 1152a-1152j, issued for China '96, 9th Asian Intl. Philatelic Exhibition, have color variations and a gray border.

Issued: 10a, 20a, 30a, 90a, 12/8; 1.30s, 1.70s, 12/9/93; 50a, 1.50s, 2/16/93; 85a, 2/8/94; 1s, 6/7/95; No. 1152, 4/17/96; No. 1142Ab, 11/22/98.

Menachem Begin (1913-92), Prime Minister 1977-83 — A499

1993, Feb. 16		**Litho.**		***Perf. 13***
1153	A499	80a multicolored	.30	.25
		With tab		.45

Nature Reserves Type of 1988

1993, Feb. 16				***Perf. 14***
1154	A427	1.20s Hof Dor	.45	.45
1155	A427	1.50s Nahal Ammud	.55	.55
1156	A427	1.70s Nahal Ayun	.65	.65
		Nos. 1154-1156 (3)	1.65	1.65
		With tabs	2.00	

Baha'i World Center, Haifa — A500

1993, Feb. 16				***Perf. 13***
1157	A500	3.50s multicolored	2.00	1.00
		With tab	3.25	

Medical Corps Memorial — A501

1993, Apr. 18		**Litho.**		***Perf. 13***
1158	A501	80a multicolored	.30	.30
		With tab		.50

Scientific Concepts — A502

1993, Apr. 18				***Perf. 14***
1159	A502	80a Principle of lift	.40	.35
1160	A502	80a Waves	.40	.35
1161	A502	80a Color mixing	.40	.35
1162	A502	80a Eye's memory	.40	.35
a.		Strip of 4, #1159-1162	1.75	1.75
		With tabs	2.75	

Warsaw Ghetto Uprising, 50th Anniv. — A503

1993, Apr. 18				***Perf. 14***
1163	A503	1.20s gray, black & yel	.50	.35
		With tab	.75	

See Poland No. 3151.

Independence, 45th Anniv. — A504

1993, Apr. 18				***Perf. 14***
1164	A504	3.60s multicolored	1.60	1.60
		With tab	2.00	

Giulio Racah (1909-1965), Physicist — A505

1.20s, Aharon Katchalsky-Katzir (1913-72), chemist.

1993, June 29		**Photo.**		***Perf. 13x14***
1165	A505	80a mag, bis & blue	.35	.35
1166	A505	1.20s mag, bis & blue	.45	.45
		#1165-1166, with tabs	1.10	

Traffic Safety — A506

Children's drawings: 80a, Family crossing street. 1.20s, Traffic signs. 1.50s, Traffic director with hand as face.

1993, June 29		**Litho.**		***Perf. 14***
1167	A506	80a multicolored	.40	.30
1168	A506	1.20s multicolored	.45	.30
1169	A506	1.50s multicolored	.60	.30
		Nos. 1167-1169 (3)	1.45	.90
		With tabs	2.00	

Fight Against Drugs — A507

1993, June 29				***Perf. 14***
1170	A507	2.80s multicolored	1.10	1.10
		With tab	1.50	

14th Maccabiah Games — A508

1993, June 29				***Perf. 14***
1171	A508	3.60s multicolored	1.60	1.10
		With tab	2.00	

Respect for the Elderly — A509

1993, Aug. 22		**Litho.**		***Perf. 14***
1172	A509	80a multicolored	.30	.25
		With tab	.50	

Festivals — A510

1993, Aug. 22				***Perf. 14***
1173	A510	80a Wheat	.35	.25
1174	A510	1.20s Grapes	.40	.25
1175	A510	1.50s Olives	.50	.25
		Nos. 1173-1175 (3)	1.25	.75
		With tabs	1.75	

Environmental Protection A511

1993, Aug. 22				
1176	A511	1.20s multicolored	.45	.45
		With tab	.60	

B'nai B'rith, 150th Anniv. — A512

1993, Aug. 22				***Perf. 13***
1177	A512	1.50s multicolored	.60	.60
		With tab	.75	

Souvenir Sheet

Telafila '93, Israel-Romania Philatelic Exhibition — A513

3.60s, Immigrant Ship, by Marcel Janco.

1993, Aug. 21		**Litho.**		***Perf. 14x13***
1178	A513	3.60s multicolored	2.75	2.75

Hebrew Magazines for Children, Cent. — A514

1993, Dec. 9		**Litho.**		***Perf. 14***
1179	A514	1.50s multicolored	.60	.40
		With tab	.75	

Philately Day.

Hanukkah A515

Hanukkah lamp with candles lit and: 90a, Oil lamp, Talmudic Period. 1.30s, Hanukkah Lamp, Eretz Israel carved stone, 20th cent. 2s, Lighting the Hanukkah Lamp, Rothschild Miscellany illuminated manuscript, c. 1470. No. 1183, Moroccan lamp, Mazagan. No. 1184: Folding Hanukkah Lamp, Lodz Ghetto, 1944. 2.10s, Coin of the Bar-Kokhba War. 1.80s, Cubic copper savivon (dreidel). 2.15s, Hanukkah lamp "Mattathias the Hasmonean," by Boris Schatz.

1993-99				
1180	A515	90a multicolored	.40	.40
1181	A515	1.30s multicolored	.50	.50
1182	A515	2s multicolored	.60	.60
1183	A515	1.50s multicolored	.40	.80
1184	A515	1.50s multicolored	.50	.50
1185	A515	2.10s multicolored	.65	.35
1186	A515	1.80s multicolored	.55	.35
1187	A515	2.15s multicolored	.60	.50
		Nos. 1180-1187 (8)	4.20	4.00
		With tabs	8.75	

The numbering of this set reflects the lighting of the candles on the Menorah.

Issued: 90a, 1.30s, 2s, 12/9/93; No. 1183, 11/27/94; No. 1184, 12/14/95; Nos. 1185-1186, 12/23/97; 2.15s, 1/5/99.

Beetles — A516

No. 1189, Graphopterus serrator. No. 1190, Potosia cuprea. No. 1191, Coccinella septempunctata. No. 1192, Chlorophorus varius.

1994, Feb. 8		**Litho.**		***Perf. 14***
1189	A516	85a multicolored	.35	.35
1190	A516	85a multicolored	.35	.35
1191	A516	85a multicolored	.35	.35
1192	A516	85a multicolored	.35	.35
a.		Bklt. pane, 2 each #1189-1192	5.50	
		Nos. 1189-1192 (4)	1.40	1.40
		With tabs	1.75	

Health — A517

1994, Feb. 8				***Perf. 13***
1193	A517	85a Exercise	.35	.35
1194	A517	1.30s Don't smoke	.45	.45
1195	A517	1.60s Eat sensibly	.55	.55
		Nos. 1193-1195 (3)	1.35	1.35
		With tabs	1.75	

Mordecai Haffkine (1860-1930), Developer of Cholera Vaccine — A518

1994, Feb. 8				***Perf. 14***
1196	A518	3.85s multicolored	1.50	1.50
		With tab	1.75	

Intl. Style Architecture in Tel Aviv, 1930-39 — A519

No. 1197, Citrus House, by Karl Rubin, 1936-38. No. 1198, Assuta Hospital, by Yosef Neufeld, 1934-35. No. 1199, Cooperative Workers' Housing, by Arieh Sharon, 1934-36.

ISRAEL

1994, Apr. 5 — Litho. — Perf. 14
1197	A519	85a multicolored	.40	.40
1198	A519	85a multicolored	.40	.40
1199	A519	85a multicolored	.40	.40
		Nos. 1197-1199 (3)	1.20	1.20
		With tabs	1.90	

Memorial Day — A520

85a, Monument to fallen soldiers of Communications, Electronics & Computer Corps, Yehud.

1994, Apr. 5 — Litho. — Perf. 14
| 1200 | A520 | 85a multicolored | .35 | .35 |
| | | With tab | .45 | |

Prevent Violence — A521

1994, Apr. 5 — Litho. — Perf. 13
| 1201 | A521 | 3.85s black & red | 1.60 | 1.60 |
| | | With tab | 2.00 | |

Saul Adler (1895-1966), Scientist — A522

1994, Apr. 5 — Litho. — Perf. 14
| 1202 | A522 | 4.50s multicolored | 1.75 | 1.75 |
| | | With tab | 2.25 | |

Hot Air Ballooning A523

No. 1203, Filling balloon. No. 1204, Balloons in flight. No. 1205, Marking target.

1994, June 21 — Litho. — Perf. 14
1203	A523	85a multicolored	.30	.30
1204	A523	85a multicolored	.30	.30
1205	A523	85a multicolored	.30	.30
		Nos. 1203-1205 (3)	.90	.90
		With tabs	1.25	

Tarbut Elementary Schools, 75th Anniv. — A524

1994, June 21
| 1206 | A524 | 1.30s multicolored | .50 | .50 |
| | | With tab | .70 | |

Antoine de St. Exupery (1900-44) — A525

1994, June 21
| 1207 | A525 | 5s multicolored | 2.75 | 2.75 |
| | | With tab | 4.00 | |

Intl. Olympic Committee, Cent. — A526

1994, June 21
| 1208 | A526 | 2.25s multicolored | .85 | .85 |
| | | With tab | 1.10 | |

Peace — A527

1994, Aug. 23 — Litho. — Perf. 14
| 1209 | A527 | 90a multicolored | .50 | .50 |
| | | With tab | .70 | |

Peace Between Arabs and Israelis.

Children's Drawings of Bible Stories — A528

Designs: 85a, Adam and Eve. 1.30s, Jacob's Dream. 1.60s, Moses in the Bulrushes. 4s, Parting of the Red Sea.

1994, Aug. 23
1210	A528	85a multicolored	.40	.25
1211	A528	1.30s multicolored	.50	.25
1212	A528	1.60s multicolored	.65	.25
		Nos. 1210-1212 (3)	1.55	.75
		With tabs	2.00	

Souvenir Sheet
Perf. 13x14
| 1213 | A528 | 4s multicolored | 3.00 | 3.00 |

No. 1213 contains one 40x51mm stamp.

Immigration to Israel — A529

1994, Aug. 23 — Perf. 13
1214	A529	1.40s Third Aliya	.50	.25
1215	A529	1.70s Fourth Aliya	.70	.25
		#1214-1215, with tabs	1.60	

Israel-Jordan Peace Treaty — A530

1994, Oct. 26 — Litho. — Perf. 14
| 1216 | A530 | 3.50s multicolored | 1.35 | .50 |
| | | With tab | 1.75 | |

Public Transportation A531

Designs: 90a, Ford Model T's, 1920's. 1.40s, White Super buses, 1940's. 1.70s, Leyland Royal Tiger buses, 1960's.

1994, Nov. 27
1217	A531	90a multicolored	.35	.25
1218	A531	1.40s multicolored	.50	.35
1219	A531	1.70s multicolored	.75	.55
		Nos. 1217-1219 (3)	1.60	1.15
		With tabs	2.00	

Computerization of Post Offices — A532

1994, Nov. 27
| 1220 | A532 | 3s multicolored | 1.25 | .90 |
| | | With tab | 1.60 | |

Dreyfus Affair, Cent. — A533

1994, Nov. 27
| 1221 | A533 | 4.10s multicolored | 1.75 | 1.75 |
| | | With tab | 2.75 | |

Outdoor Sculpture — A534

Designs: 90a, Serpentine, by Itzhak Danziger (1916-77), Yarkon Park, Tel Aviv. 1.40s, Stabile, by Alexander Calder (1898-1976), Mount Herzl, Jerusalem. 1.70s, Gate to the Hall of Remembrance, by David Palombo (1920-66), Yad Vashem, Jerusalem.

1995, Feb. 7 — Litho. — Perf. 14x13
1222	A534	90a multicolored	.50	.50
1223	A534	1.40s multicolored	.80	.80
1224	A534	1.70s multicolored	.90	.90
		Nos. 1222-1224 (3)	2.20	2.20
		With tabs	2.50	

Jewish Composers A535

Title of work, composer: No. 1225, Schelomo, by Ernest Bloch (1880-1959). No. 1226, Symphony No. 1 - Jeremiah, by Leonard Bernstein (1918-90).

1995, Feb. 7
1225	A535	4.10s multicolored	2.40	2.40
1226	A535	4.10s multicolored	2.40	2.40
		#1225-1226, with tabs	5.25	

See Nos. 1231-1232, 1274-1275.

Ordnance Corps Monument, Netanya — A536

1995, Apr. 25 — Litho. — Perf. 13
| 1227 | A536 | 1s multicolored | .60 | .60 |
| | | With tab | .65 | |

End of World War II, Liberation of Concentration Camps, 50th Anniv. — A537

1995, Apr. 25 — Perf. 14x13
| 1228 | A537 | 1s multicolored | 1.40 | 1.40 |
| | | With tab | 1.60 | |

Souvenir Sheet
| 1229 | A537 | 2.50s like #1228 | 3.50 | 3.50 |

No. 1229 contains one 51x40mm stamp.

UN, 50th Anniv. — A538

1995, Apr. 25 — Perf. 14
| 1230 | A538 | 1.50s multicolored | .80 | .80 |
| | | With tab | .90 | |

Composer Type of 1995

No. 1231, Arnold Schoenberg (1874-1951). No. 1232, Darius Milhaud (1892-1974).

1995, Apr. 25
1231	A535	2.40s multicolored	1.25	1.25
1232	A535	2.40s multicolored	1.25	1.25
		#1231-1232, with tabs	2.75	

Souvenir Sheet

Jewish Volunteers to British Army in World War II — A539

1995, Apr. 25
| 1233 | A539 | 2.50s multicolored | 3.25 | 3.25 |
| | | With tab | 3.50 | 3.50 |

15th Hapoel Games, Ramat Gan — A540

1995, June 7 — Litho. — Perf. 14
| 1234 | A540 | 1s Kayak | .65 | .65 |
| | | With tab | .70 | |

Kites A541

Designs: No. 1235, Hexagonal "Tiara" kite, bird-shaped kite, rhombic Eddy kite. No. 1236, Drawing of kite glider, "Cody War Kite," box kite. No. 1237, Rhombic aerobatic kites, aerobatic "Delta" kite, drawing by Otto Lilienthal.

1995, June 7
1235		1s multicolored	.50	.50
1236		1s multicolored	.50	.50
1237		1s multicolored	.50	.50
	a.	A541 Strip of 3, #1235-1237	1.50	1.50
		With tabs	1.75	

Children's Books — A542

Designs: 1s, Stars in a Bucket, by Anda Amir-Pinkerfeld. 1.50s, Hurry, Run, Dwarfs, by Miriam Yallan-Stekelis. 1.80s, Daddy's Big Umbrella, by Levin Kipnis.

1995, June 7
1238	A542	1s multicolored	.45	.45
1239	A542	1.50s multicolored	.70	.70
1240	A542	1.80s multicolored	.85	.85
		Nos. 1238-1240 (3)	2.00	2.00
		With tabs	2.25	

Zim Israel Navigation Co. Ltd., 50th Anniv. — A543

1995, June 7
| 1241 | A543 | 4.40s multicolored | 2.40 | 2.40 |
| | | With tab | 2.60 | |

Festivals — A544

Designs: 1s, Elijah's Chair for circumcision, linen cloth. 1.50s, Tallit bag, usually a Bar-Mitzvah gift. 1.80s, Marriage Stone for breaking glass at wedding, cloth.

1995, Sept. 4 — Litho. — Perf. 14
1242	A544	1s multicolored	.45	.45
1243	A544	1.50s multicolored	.70	.70
1244	A544	1.80s multicolored	.85	.85
		Nos. 1242-1244 (3)	2.00	2.00
		With tabs	2.25	

Jerusalem, 3000th Anniv. — A545

ISRAEL

Designs: 1s, 6th Cent. mosaic pavement, Gaza Synagogue. 1.50s, 19th Cent. illustration of city from map of Eretz Israel, by Rabbi Pinie of Safed. 1.80s, Aerial photograph of Knesset, Supreme Court.

1995, Sept. 4
1245	A545	1s multicolored	.45	.45
1246	A545	1.50s multicolored	.70	.70
1247	A545	1.80s multicolored	.85	.85
		Nos. 1245-1247 (3)	2.00	2.00
		With tabs	2.25	

See Nos. 1862-1863.

Veterinary Services, 75th Anniv. — A546

1995, Sept. 4
1248	A546	4.40s multicolored	2.50	2.50
		With tab	2.75	

Yitzhak Rabin (1922-95), Prime Minister — A547

1995, Dec. 5
1249	A547	5s multicolored	2.50	2.50
		With tab	2.75	

Fire Fighting and Rescue Service, 70th Anniv. — A548

Designs: No. 1250, Fighting fire. No. 1251, Rescue vehicle, fireman beside car.

1995, Dec. 14
1250	A548	1s multicolored	.60	.60
1251	A548	1s multicolored	.60	.60
		#1250-1251, with tabs	1.40	

Model Planes — A549

1995, Dec. 14
1252	A549	1.80s multicolored	.80	.80
		With tab	.90	

Philately Day.

Motion Pictures, Cent. — A550

Silhouettes of people in theater viewing: 4.40s, Marx Brothers, Simone Signoret, Peter Sellers, Danny Kaye, Al Jolson.

1995, Dec. 14
1253	A550	4.40s multicolored	2.25	2.25
		With tab	2.40	

Souvenir Sheet

Jerusalem, City of David, 3000th Anniv. — A551

Designs: a, Mosaic pavement of King David playing harp, Gaza Synagogue, 6th cent. CE. b, Map of Eretz Israel drawn by Rabbi Pinie, 19th cent. c, Present day aerial view of Knesset and Supreme Court.

1995, Dec. 16
1254	A551	Sheet of 3	3.00	3.00
a.		1s multicolored	.65	.65
b.		1.50s multicolored	.95	.95
c.		1.80s multicolored	1.40	1.40

Sports — A552

1.05s, Mountain cycling. 1.10s, Horseback riding. 1.80s, Water skiing. 1.90s, Paragliding. 2s, Women's volleyball. 2.20s, Whitewater rafting. 3s, Beach bat & ball. 5s, Archery. 10s, Rappelling.

1996-98   Photo.   Perf. 13x14
1256	A552	1.05s multi	.60	.60
1257	A552	1.10s multi	.80	.80
a.		Booklet pane of 20	16.00	
		Complete booklet, #1257a	16.00	
1258	A552	1.80s multi	.90	.90
1259	A552	1.90s multi	1.10	1.10
1260	A552	2s multi	1.10	1.10
1261	A552	2.20s multi	1.10	1.10
1262	A552	3s multi	1.60	1.60
1263	A552	5s multi	2.75	2.75
1264	A552	10s multi	5.25	5.25
		Nos. 1256-1264 (9)	15.20	15.20
		With tabs	17.00	

Issued: 1.05s, 1.90s, 2s, 2/20/96; 1.10s, 5s, 2/13/97; 10s, 7/8/97; 3s, 9/23/97; 1258, 1261, 2/17/98.

Souvenir Sheet

Synagogue, Dura-Europos, Syria, 3rd Century A.D. — A553

Murals from synagogue walls: a, Temple, walls of Jerusalem. b, Torah Ark niche. c, Anointing of David as king by Prophet Samuel.

1996, Feb. 20   Perf. 14x13
1266	A553	Sheet of 3	2.50	2.50
a.		1.05s multicolored	.55	.55
b.		1.60s multicolored	.85	.85
c.		1.90s multicolored	1.10	1.10

Jerusalem, 3000th anniv.

Israel Cattle Breeders' Assoc., 70th Anniv. — A554

1996, Feb. 20   Perf. 14
1267	A554	4.65s multicolored	3.00	3.00
		With tab	3.50	

Hebrew Writers' Assoc., 75th Anniv. — A555

No. 1269: a, M.J. Berdyczewski. b, Yehuda Burla. c, Devorah Baron. d, Haim Hazaz. e, J.L. Gordon. f, Joseph Hayyim Brenner. g, Abraham Shlonsky. h, Yaakov Shabtai. i, I.L. Peretz. j, Nathan Alterman. k, Saul Tchernichowsky. l, Amir Gilboa. m, Yokheved Bat-Miriam. n, Mendele Mokher Sefarim.

1996, Apr. 17   Litho.   Perf. 14
1269		Pane of 14	4.00	4.00
a.-n.		A555 40a Any single	.25	.25

Manufacturers Assoc. of Israel, 75th Anniv. — A556

1996, Apr. 17
1271	A556	1.05s multicolored	.65	.65
		With tab	.75	

Monument to the Fallen Israel Police — A557

1996, Apr. 17
1272	A557	1.05s multicolored	.65	.65
		With tab	.75	

Settlement of Metulla, Cent. — A558

1996, Apr. 17
1273	A558	1.90s multicolored	.95	.95
		With tab	1.10	

Composer Type of 1995

Designs: No. 1274, Felix Mendelssohn (1809-47). No. 1275, Gustav Mahler (1860-1911).

1996   Litho.   Perf. 14
1274	A535	4.65s multicolored	3.75	3.75
1275	A535	4.65s multicolored	3.75	3.75
		#1274-1275, with tabs	8.00	

Issued: No. 1275, 4/17/96; No. 1274, 6/25/96.

A559

1996, June 25
1276	A559	1.05s multicolored	.40	.40
		With tab	.50	

Eleven Jewish settlements in Negev Desert, 50th Anniv.

A560

1996, June 25
1277	A560	1.05s Fencing	.40	.40
1278	A560	1.60s Pole vault	.60	.60
1279	A560	1.90s Wrestling	.75	.75
a.		Booklet pane of 6, 1 #1277, 2 #1278, 3 #1279	12.00	
		Complete booklet, #1279a	12.00	
		Nos. 1277-1279 (3)	1.75	1.75
		With tabs	2.00	

1996 Summer Olympics, Atlanta.

Fruit — A561

1.05s, Orange, "sweety", kumquat, lemon. 1.60s, Avocado, persimmon, date, mango, grapes. 1.90s, Carambola, lychee, papaya.

1996, June 25
1280	A561	1.05s multicolored	.45	.45
1281	A561	1.60s multicolored	.70	.70
1282	A561	1.90s multicolored	.85	.85
		Nos. 1280-1282 (3)	2.00	2.00
		With tabs	2.25	

Public Works Department, 75th Anniv. — A562

1996, Sept. 3   Litho.   Perf. 14
1283	A562	1.05s multicolored	.65	.65
		With tab	.75	

Festivals — A563

Stylized designs: 1.05s, Bowl of honey, two lighted candles, Rosh Hashanah. 1.60s, Sukka booth, Sukkot. 1.90s, Inside of synagogue during Torah reading, Simchat Torah.

1996, Sept. 3
1284	A563	1.05s multicolored	.45	.45
1285	A563	1.60s multicolored	.70	.70
1286	A563	1.90s multicolored	.85	.85
		Nos. 1284-1286 (3)	2.00	2.00
		With tabs	2.25	

1st Zionist Congress, Cent. — A564

Designs: 4.65s, Tapestry of Theodore Herzl, David's Tower, shining sun. 5s, Casino building, Basel, site of first congress.

1996, Sept. 3
1287	A564	4.65s multicolored	2.25	2.25
		With tab	2.50	

Souvenir Sheet
1288	A564	5s multicolored	3.00	3.00

No. 1288 contains one 40x51mm stamp. See No. 1867.

Hanukkah A565

Serpentine Die Cut 11

1996, Oct. 22   Photo.
1289	A565	2.50s multicolored	1.15	1.15
		With tab	1.25	

See US No. 3118.

Ha-Shilo'ah, Cent., edited by Ahad Ha'am (1856-1927) — A566

1996, Dec. 5   Litho.   Perf. 14
1290	A566	1.15s multicolored	.60	.60
		With tab	.70	

Coexistence: Man and Animals — A567

1996, Dec. 5
1291	A567	1.10s Birds, aircraft	.50	.50
1292	A567	1.75s Pets	.90	.90
1293	A567	2s Dolphins	1.00	1.00
		Nos. 1291-1293 (3)	2.40	2.40
		With tabs	2.60	

Space Research in Israel — A568

1996, Dec. 5
1294	A568	2.05s multicolored	1.05	1.05
		With tab	1.20	

Philately Day.

UOAD (Umbrella Organization of Associations for the Disabled) — A569

1996, Dec. 5
1295	A569	5s multicolored	2.50	2.50
		With tab	2.75	

ISRAEL

Souvenir Sheet

Inventors — A570

Designs: a, 1.50s, Alexander Graham Bell (1847-1922). b, 2s, Thomas Alva Edison (1847-1931).

1997, Feb. 13	Litho.	Perf. 13
1296	A570 Sheet of 2, #a.-b.	3.50 3.50

Hong Kong '97.

Ethnic Costumes — A571

1.10s, Ethiopia. 1.70s, Kurdistan. 2s, Salonica.

1997, Feb. 13		Perf. 14
1297	A571 1.10s multicolored	.55 .55
1298	A571 1.70s multicolored	.85 .85
1299	A571 2s multicolored	1.05 1.05
	Nos. 1297-1299 (3)	2.45 2.45
	With tabs	2.75

Miguel de Cervantes (1547-1616), Writer — A572

1997, Feb. 13		
1300	A572 3s multicolored	1.75 1.75
	With tab	2.00

Monument to the Fallen Soldiers of the Logistics Corps — A573

1997, Apr. 30	Litho.	Perf. 14
1301	A573 1.10s multicolored	.45 .45
	With tab	.65

A574

Jewish monuments in Prague: No. 1302, Tombstone of Rabbi Judah Loew MaHaRal. No. 1303, Altneuschul Synagogue.

1997, Apr. 30		
1302	A574 1.70s blue & multi	1.00 1.00
1303	A574 1.70s red & multi	1.00 1.00
a.	Sheet, 4 each, #1302-1303	17.00 17.00
	#1302-1303, with tabs	2.25

Stamps in No. 1303a do not have tabs. See Czech Republic Nos. 3009-3010.

A575

Design: "The Vilna Gaon," Rabbi Elijah Ben Solomon Zalman (1720-97).

1997, Apr. 30		
1304	A575 2s multicolored	.90 .90
	With tab	1.00

Organized Clandestine Immigration (1934-48) — A576

1997, Apr. 30		
1305	A576 5s multicolored	2.25 2.25
	With tab	2.50

Souvenir Sheet

Discovery of the Cairo Geniza, Cent., Discovery of Dead Sea Scrolls, 50th Anniv. — A577

Designs: a, 2s, Ben Ezra Synagogue, Cairo. b, 3s, Cliffs, Dead Sea, Prof. Sukenik examining scrolls.

1997, May 29	Litho.	Perf. 13
1306	A577 Sheet of 2, #a.-b.	4.25 4.25

Pacific '97.

Hello First Grade — A578

1997, July 8	Litho.	Perf. 14
1307	A578 1.10s multicolored	.50 .50
	With tab	.60

Road Safety — A579

No. 1308, "Keep in Lane," car sinking into lake, fish. No. 1309, "Keep Your Distance," car with bird on front grille. No. 1310, "Don't Drink and Drive," man holding drink, car balanced on edge of cliff.

1997, July 8		Perf. 13
1308	A579 1.10s multicolored	.45 .45
1309	A579 1.10s multicolored	.45 .45
1310	A579 1.10s multicolored	.45 .45
	Nos. 1308-1310 (3)	1.35 1.35
	With tabs	1.60

15th Maccabiah Games — A580

1997, July 8		Perf. 14
1311	A580 5s Ice skating	2.25 2.25
	With tab	2.50

Festival Stamps — A581

The Visiting Patriarchs, Sukkot: 1.10s, Abraham. 1.70s, Isaac. 2s, Jacob.

1997, Sept. 23	Litho.	Perf. 14
1312	A581 1.10s multicolored	.55 .55
1313	A581 1.70s multicolored	.90 .90
1314	A581 2s multicolored	1.00 1.00
a.	Booklet pane, 1 #1312, 2 #1313, 3 #1314	9.00
	Complete booklet, #1314a	9.00
	Nos. 1312-1314 (3)	2.45 2.45
	With tabs	2.75

Compare with Nos. 1375-1378.

Music and Dance in Israel — A582

Designs: 1.10s, Zimriya, World assembly of choirs. 2s, Karmiel Dance Festival. 3s, Festival of Klezmers (musical instruments).

1997, Sept. 23		Perf. 13
1315	A582 1.10s multicolored	.50 .50
1316	A582 2s multicolored	.90 .90
1317	A582 3s multicolored	1.40 1.40
	Nos. 1315-1317 (3)	2.80 2.80
	With tabs	3.00

UN Resolution on Creation of Jewish State, 50th Anniv. — A583

1997, Sept. 23		Perf. 13x14
1318	A583 5s multicolored	2.25 2.25
	With tab	2.60

Souvenir Sheet

Pushkin's "Eugene Onegin," Translated by Abraham Shlonsky — A584

1997, Nov. 19		Perf. 14x13
1319	A584 5s multicolored	3.00 3.00

See Russia No. 6418.

State of Israel, 50th Anniv. in 1998 — A585

1997, Dec. 23		Perf. 14
1320	A585 (1.10s) multicolored	.60 .60
	With tab	1.00
a.	Size: 17x22mm	.60 .60
	With tab	1.00
b.	Booklet pane, 20 #1320a	20.00
	Complete booklet, #1320b	18.00
c.	As "a", perf. 13x14, photo.	— —
	With tab	

No. 1320b consists of two blocks of 10 stamps, tete-beche in relationship to each other. No. 1320 is 18x23mm. No. 1320a has brighter blue stripes in flag.
Issued: No. 1320a, 2/17/98; No. 1320c, 5/3/98.

"MACHAL," Overseas Volunteers — A586

Designs: 1.80s, "GACHAL," recruitment in the Diaspora.

1997, Dec. 23		
1321	A586 1.15s multicolored	.50 .50
1322	A586 1.80s multicolored	.75 .75
	#1321-1322, with tabs	1.50

Chabad's Children of Chernobyl — A587

1997, Dec. 23		
1323	A587 2.10s multicolored	.85 .85
	With tab	1.00

A588

1997, Dec. 23		
1324	A588 2.50s Julia Set Fractal	1.10 1.10
	With tab	1.25

Philately Day.

A589

Three battle fronts during war: Nos. 1325, 1328a (1.50s), Northern Front, photograph of people, Zefat, 1948. Nos. 1326, 1328b (2.50s), Central Front, drawing over photograph of vehicles coming down mountain, outskirts of Jerusalem, 1948. Nos. 1327, 1328c (3s), Southern Front, raising Israeli flag, Elat, 1949.

1998, Feb. 17	Litho.	Perf. 14x13
1325	A589 1.15s multicolored	.65 .65
1326	A589 1.15s multicolored	.65 .65
1327	A589 1.15s multicolored	.65 .65
	Nos. 1325-1327 (3)	1.95 1.95
	With tabs	2.25

Souvenir Sheet

| 1328 | A589 Sheet of 3, #a.-c. | 4.25 4.25 |

War of Independence, 1947-49. No. 1328b is 51x40mm.
See No. 1861.

Chaim Herzog (1918-97), President of Israel — A590

1998, Feb. 17		Perf. 14
1329	A590 5.35s multicolored	2.25 2.25
	With tab	2.50

A591

Jewish Contributions to Modern World Culture: a, Franz Kafka (1883-1924), writer. b, George Gershwin. c, Lev Davidovich Landau (1908-68), physicist. d, Albert Einstein. e, Leon Blum (1872-1950), statesman. f, Elizabeth Rachel Felix (1821-58), actress.

1998, Apr. 27	Litho.	Perf. 14
1330	Sheet of 6 + 6 labels	4.50 4.50
a.-f.	A591 90a Any single	.75 .75

See No. 1362.

A592

1998, Apr. 27		
1331	A592 1.15s multicolored	.50 .50
	With tab	.60

Memorial Day.

A593

ISRAEL

1998, Apr. 27
1332 A593 1.15s multicolored .50 .50
With tab .75

Declaration of the Establishment of the State of Israel, 50th anniv.

A594

1998, Apr. 27
1333 A594 5.35s multicolored 2.10 2.10
With tab 2.50

Israel Defense Forces, 50th anniv.

Holocaust Memorial Day — A595

Non-Jews who risked their lives to save Jews during Holocaust: Giorgio Perlasca, Aristides de Sousa Mendes, Carl Lutz, Sempo Sugihara, Selahattin Ulkumen.

1998, Apr. 27 Perf. 13
1334 A595 6s multicolored 2.50 2.50
With tab 3.00

Children's Pets — A596

Israel '98: a, Cat. b, Dog. c, Bird. d, Goldfish. e, Hamster. f, Rabbit.

1998, May 13
1335 Sheet of 6 4.00 4.00
a.-f. A596 60a Any single .35 .35

No. 1335 contains diagonal perforations so that lower left corner of each stamp can be removed leaving denominated portion in shape of a pentagon.

Postal and Philatelic Museum — A597

Illustrations by Kariel Gardosh featuring cartoon character, "Srulik:" a, At post office counter. b, Looking at stamp with magnifying glass. c, Putting mail into post box.

1998, May 13 Perf. 14
1336 Sheet of 3 4.25 4.25
a. A597 1.50s multicolored .90 .90
b. A597 2.50s multicolored 1.40 1.40
c. A597 3s multicolored 1.75 1.75

Aircraft Used in War of Independence, 1948 — A598

No. 1337, Dragon Rapide. No. 1338, Spitfire. No. 1339, B-17 Flying Fortress.

1998, May 3 Litho. Perf. 14
1337 A598 2.20s multi 1.25 1.25
1338 A598 2.20s multi 1.25 1.25
1339 A598 2.20s multi 1.25 1.25
a. Strip of 3, #1337-1339 3.75 3.75
With tabs 4.00 4.00

Israel '98.

No. 1339a was issued in sheets containing 2 strips printed tete beche separated by strip of three labels.

A limited-edition booklet exists. It contains the following panes: 1 each Nos. 1305, 1318, 1320, 1320b, 1321-1322, 1325-1327, 1332, 1333, 1339a. Value, $77.50.

Souvenir Sheet

Mosaic of a Young Woman, Zippori A599

1998, May 13
1340 A599 5s multicolored 3.25 3.25

Israel '98. Sold for 6s.

Souvenir Sheet

King Solomon's Temple — A600

a, Drawing of the temple. b, Inscribed ivory pomegranate.

1998, May 13
1341 A600 Sheet of 2 3.75 3.75
a. 2s multicolored 1.50 1.50
b. 3s multicolored 2.25 2.25

Israel '98. Sold for 7s.

Israel Jubilee Exhibition — A601

1998, Aug. 3 Litho. Perf. 14x13
1342 A601 5.35s multicolored 2.00 2.00
With tab 2.25 2.25

Child's Drawing "Living in a World of Mutual Respect" — A602

1998, Sept. 8 Perf. 14
1343 A602 1.15s multicolored .45 .45
With tab .50

Holy Cities — A603

1998, Sept. 8
1344 A603 1.80s Hebron .80 .80
1345 A603 2.20s Jerusalem .95 .95
#1344-1345, with tabs 2.00
1346 A603 1.15s Zefat .60 .60
1347 A603 5.35s Tiberias 2.75 2.75
#1346-1347, with tabs 3.75

See No. 1864.

Festival Stamps — A604

Holy ark curtains: 1.15s, Peacocks on both sides of menorah, text, Star of David. 1.80s, Menorah, text, two lions. 2.20s, Text surrounded by ornate floral pattern.

1998, Sept. 8
1348 A604 1.15s multicolored .55 .55
1349 A604 1.80s multicolored .80 .80
1350 A604 2.20s multicolored .90 .80
Nos. 1348-1350 (3) 2.25 2.15
With tabs 2.75

Natl. Flag — A605

1998, Dec. 17 Litho. Die Cut Self-Adhesive
1351 A605 1.15s dk bl & bl .95 .95
1352 A605 2.15s dk bl & grn 1.75 1.75
1353 A605 3.25s dk bl & rose red 2.75 2.75
1354 A605 5.35s dk bl & yel org 4.75 4.75
Nos. 1351-1354 (4) 10.20 10.20

Hyacinth — A606

1999, Feb. 1 Photo. Perf. 15
1355 A606 (1.15s) multicolored .60 .60
With tab .65

See Nos. 1492A, 1539D-1540.

Knesset, 50th Anniv. — A607

1999, Feb. 1 Litho. Perf. 14
1356 A607 1.80s multicolored .60 .60
With tab .75

Manuscript of Rabbi Shalem Shabazi (1619-80), Poet — A608

1999, Feb. 1
1357 A608 2.20s multicolored 1.10 1.10
With tab 1.25

Jewish Colonial Trust, Cent. — A609

Drawings from one pound sterling share.

1999, Feb. 16
1358 A609 1.80s multicolored .60 .60
With tab .75

Ethnic Costumes A610

Designs: 2.15s, Yemenite Jewry, Yemen. 3.25s, Bene Israel Community, India.

1999, Feb. 16
1359 A610 2.15s multicolored .80 .80
1360 A610 3.25s multicolored 1.20 1.20
#1359-1360, with tabs 2.25

See Nos. 1373-1374.

Souvenir Sheet

Ancient Boat from Sea of Galilee A611

a, 3s, Reconstructed boat. b, 5s, Ancient boat.

1999, Mar. 19 Litho. Perf. 13
1361 A611 Sheet of 2, #a.-b. 4.50 4.50

Australia '99, World Stamp Expo.

Jewish Contributions to Modern World Culture Type of 1998

Designs: a, Emile Durkheim (1858-1917), social scientist. b, Paul Ehrlich (1854-1915), medical researcher. c, Rosa Luxemburg (1870-1919), politician. d, Norbert Wiener (1894-1964), mathematician, developer of computer science. e, Sigmund Freud (1856-1939), psychologist, founder of psychoanalysis. f, Martin Buber (1878-1965), religious philosopher.

1999, Apr. 18 Litho. Perf. 14
1362 Sheet of 6 + 6 labels 3.75 3.75
a.-f. A591 90a Any single .60 .60

Monument for Fallen Bedouin Soldiers — A612

1999, Apr. 18
1363 A612 1.20s multicolored .45 .45
With tab .50

Israel's Admission to UN, 50th Anniv. — A613

1999, Apr. 18
1364 A613 2.30s multicolored .85 .85
With tab 1.00

A614

Design: Simcha Holtzberg (1924-94), Holocaust survivor, "Father of Wounded Soldiers."

1999, Apr. 18
1365 A614 2.50s multicolored .85 .85
With tab 1.00

Painting, "My Favorite Room," by James Ensor (1860-1949) A614a

1999, May 16 Photo. Perf. 11½
1365A A614a 2.30s multi 1.30 1.30
With tab 1.50 1.50

See Belgium No. 1738.

"Lovely Butterfly," Children's Television Show — A615

Puppets: No. 1366, Ouza, the goose. No. 1367, Nooly, the chick & Shabi, the snail. No. 1368, Batz, the tortoise, and Pingi, the penguin.

1999, June 22 Litho. Perf. 14
1366 A615 1.20s multicolored .65 .65
1367 A615 1.20s multicolored .65 .65
1368 A615 1.20s multicolored .65 .65
a. Strip of 3, #1366-1368 2.00 2.00
With tabs 2.25

Pilgrimage to the Holy Land — A616

1999, June 22 Perf. 14x13
1369 A616 3s Nazareth 1.50 1.50
1370 A616 3s River Jordan 1.50 1.50
1371 A616 3s Jerusalem 1.50 1.50
Nos. 1369-1371 (3) 4.50 4.50
With tabs 5.00

Rabbi Or Sharga (?-1794) — A617

ISRAEL

Illustration from Musa-Nameh manuscript, by Shahin, depicting battle of Isreal over Amalek.

1999, June 22   *Perf. 14*
1372   A617   5.60s multicolored   2.00   2.00
     With tab   2.25   2.25

Ethnic Costumes Type of 1999

Designs: 2.30s, Jewish woman in traditional Moroccan costume. 3.40s, Jewish man in traditional costume of Bukhara.

1999, Sept. 1   *Litho.*   *Perf. 14*
1373   A610   2.30s multicolored   .70   .70
1374   A610   3.40s multicolored   1.00   1.00
     #1373-1374, with tab   2.00

"Ushpizin," Guests in the Sukkah, Festival of Sukkoth — A619

1999, Sept. 1
1375   A619   1.20s Joseph   .60   .60
1376   A619   1.90s Moses   .90   .90
1377   A619   2.30s Aaron   1.00   1.00
1378   A619   5.60s David   2.50   2.50
   a.   Bklt. pane, #1376-1378, 3
        #1375   11.00   11.00
     Complete booklet, #1378a   11.00
     Nos. 1375-1378 (4)   5.00   5.00
     With tabs   5.50

Stamp Day — A620

1999, Sept. 1
1379   A620   5.35s multicolored   2.10   2.10
     With tab   2.40

Ceramic Urns, Museum of Jewish Culture, Bratislava, Slovakia — A621

Designs: No. 1380, Urn from 1776 showing man on sick bed, denomination at UL. No. 1381, Urn from 1734 showing funeral procession, denomination at UR.

1999, Nov. 23   *Litho.*   *Perf. 14*
1380   A621   1.90s multi   .80   .80
1381   A621   1.90s multi   .80   .80
     #1380-1381, with tabs   1.90

See Slovakia Nos. 344-345.

Kiryat Shemona, 50th Anniv. — A622

1999, Dec. 7
1382   A622   1.20s multicolored   .45   .45
     With tab   .55

Proclamation of Jerusalem as Israel's Capital, 50th Anniv. — A623

1999, Dec. 7   *Perf. 13x14*
1383   A623   3.40s multicolored   1.25   1.25
     With tab   1.40

Sidna "Baba Sali" The Admor, Israel Abihssira (1890-1984) — A624

1999, Dec. 7   *Perf. 13*
1384   A624   4.40s multi   1.50   1.50
     With tab   1.75

Millennium — A625

Designs: 1.40s, Joggers in park. 1.90s, Researcher with flask. 2.30s, Man at computer. 2.80s, Astronaut in space.

2000, Jan. 1
1385   A625   1.40s multi   .70   .70
1386   A625   1.90s multi   .95   .95
1387   A625   2.30s multi   1.10   1.10
1388   A625   2.80s multi   1.40   1.40
     Nos. 1385-1388 (4)   4.15   4.15
     With tabs   4.75

Stampin' the Future Children's Stamp Design Contest Winners — A626

Various children's drawings.

2000, Jan. 1   *Perf. 13x13½*
Background Colors
1389   A626   1.20s blue   .60   .60
1390   A626   1.90s yel org   .95   .95
1391   A626   2.30s red   1.10   1.10
1392   A626   3.40s green   1.60   1.60
     Nos. 1389-1392 (4)   4.25   4.25
     With tabs   4.75

Fairy Tales of Hans Christian Andersen (1805-75) — A627

1.20s, The Little Mermaid. 1.90s, The Emperor's New Clothes. 2.30s, The Ugly Duckling.

2000, Feb. 15   *Litho.*   *Perf. 13x14*
1393   A627   1.20s multi   .60   .60
1394   A627   1.90s multi   .95   .95
1395   A627   2.30s multi   1.10   1.10
     Nos. 1393-1395 (3)   2.65   2.65
     With tabs   3.00

Pilgrimage to the Holy Land — A628

Churches: 1.40s, All Apostles, Capernaum. 1.90s, St. Andrew's, Jerusalem. 2.30s, Church of the Visitation, Ein Kerem.

2000, Feb. 15   *Perf. 14x13*
1396   A628   1.40s multi   .70   .70
1397   A628   1.90s multi   .95   .95
1398   A628   2.30s multi   1.10   1.10
     Nos. 1396-1398 (3)   2.75   2.75
     With tabs   3.00

King Hussein of Jordan (1935-99) — A629

2000, Feb. 15   *Litho.*   *Perf. 14*
1399   A629   4.40s multi   2.25   2.25
     With tab   2.50

Shuni Historic Site — A630

Perf. 14 Syncopated
2000, Feb. 15   *Photo.*
1400   A630   2.30s multi   1.10   1.10
     With tab   1.25

See Nos. 1409, 1427-1428, 1442, 1478, 1492, 1601.

A631

Worldwide Fund for Nature: Various depictions of Blanford's fox.

2000, May 3   *Litho.*   *Perf. 14*
Denomination Color
1401   A631   1.20s red violet   .65   .65
1402   A631   1.20s green   .65   .65
1403   A631   1.20s blue   .65   .65
1404   A631   1.20s yellow   .65   .65
   a.   Strip, #1401-1404 + central label   3.00   3.00
     With tabs   3.75

See Nos. 1435-1438.

Memorial Day — A632

2000, May 3
1405   A632   1.20s multi   .50   .50
     With tab   .60

Intl. Communications Day — A633

2000, May 3   *Perf. 13*
1406   A633   2.30s multi   .90   .90
     With tab   1.10

Land of Three Religions — A634

2000, May 3
1407   A634   3.40s multi   1.30   1.30
     With tab   1.50

See No. 1866.

Johann Sebastian Bach (1685-1750) — A635

2000, May 3
1408   A635   5.60s multi   2.25   2.25
     With tab   2.60

Historic Site Type of 2000
Perf. 14 Syncopated
2000, July 25   *Photo.*
1409   A630   1.20s Juara   .50   .50
     With tab   .75
   a.   Perf. 14¾x15 Syncopated   6.00   6.00
     With tab   7.00

The line containing the country name in English and Arabic is 10mm long on No. 1409, 11 mm long on No. 1409a. Issued: No. 1409a, 2001.

2000 Summer Olympics, Sydney — A636

2000, July 25   *Litho.*   *Perf. 13*
1410   A636   2.80s multi   1.00   1.00
     With tab   1.10

A637

2000, July 25   *Perf. 14*
1411   A637   4.40s multi   1.50   1.50
     With tab   1.75

King Hassan II of Morocco (1929-99).

Israeli Food — A638

2000, June 25   *Perf. 13½x13*
1412   A638   1.40s Couscous   .65   .65
1413   A638   1.90s Gefilte fish   .85   .85
1414   A638   2.30s Falafel   1.00   1.00
   a.   Booklet pane, #1412, 2 #1413, 3 #1414   8.75
     Booklet, #1414a   8.75
     Nos. 1412-1414 (3)   2.50   2.50
     With tabs   2.75

Dental Health — A639

2000, Sept. 19   *Litho.*   *Perf. 14*
1415   A639   2.20s multi   .90   .90
     With tab   1.10

Dohany Synagogue, Budapest — A640

2000, Sept. 19   *Perf. 13x14*
1416   A640   5.60s multi   2.75   2.75
     With tab   3.00

See Hungary No. 3710.

Jewish New Year Cards — A641

Designs: 1.20s, Boy giving girl a gift. 1.90s, Girl holding Zionist flag. 2.30s, Man giving flowers and greetings to woman.

2000, Sept. 19   *Perf. 14*
1417   A641   1.20s multi   .45   .45
1418   A641   1.90s multi   .70   .70
1419   A641   2.30s multi   .85   .85
     Nos. 1417-1419 (3)   2.00   2.00
     With tabs   2.25

See Nos. 1455-1457.

Aleppo Codex — A642

2000, Dec. 5   *Perf. 13*
1420   A642   4.40s multi   1.75   1.75
     With tab   2.00

ISRAEL

Dinosaurs — A643

Designs: No. 1421, Struthiomimuses on beach. No. 1422, Struthiomimuses in forest. No. 1423, Struthiomimus on hill.

2000, Dec. 5		Litho.	Perf. 13	
1421	A643	2.20s multi	.85	.85
1422	A643	2.20s multi	.85	.85
1423	A643	2.20s multi	.85	.85
a.	Strip of 3, #1421-1423		2.60	2.60
	With tabs		2.75	

Science Fiction — A644

Designs: 2.80s, Robot. 3.40s, Time travel. 5.60s, Space flight.

2000, Dec. 5			Perf. 14	
1424	A644	2.80s multi	1.10	1.10
1425	A644	3.40s multi	1.35	1.35
1426	A644	5.60s multi	2.10	2.10
	Nos. 1424-1426 (3)		4.55	4.55
	With tabs		5.00	

Historic Sites Type of 2000
Perf. 14 Syncopated

2000-2001			Photo.	
1427	A630	2.20s Mitzpe Revivim	1.10	1.10
	With tab		1.25	
1428	A630	3.40s Ilaniyya	1.60	1.60
	With tab		1.75	1.75

Issued: 2.20s, 12/5; 3.40s, 2/13/01.

Settlements, Cent. — A645

2001, Feb. 13		Litho.	Perf. 14	
1429	A645	2.50s Yavne'el	1.10	1.10
1430	A645	4.70s Menahamia	2.00	2.00
1431	A645	5.90s Kefar Tavor	2.60	2.60
	Nos. 1429-1431 (3)		5.70	5.70
	With tabs		6.25	

Hebrew Letters Aleph and Beth — A646

No. 1432: a, Aleph. b, Beth. c, Gimel. d, Daleth. e, He. f, Waw. g, Zayin. h, Heth. i, Teth. j, Yod. k, Kaph. l, Lamed. m, Mem. n, Nun. o, Samekh. p, Ayin. q, Pe. r, Sadhe. s, Qoph. t, Resh. u, Sin. v, Taw.
No. 1433 — End-of-word letters: a, Kaph. b, Mem. c, Nun. d, Pe. e, Sadhe.

2001, Feb. 13		Photo.	Perf. 15	
1432		Sheet of 22	2.00	2.00
a.-v.	A646 10a Any single		.25	.25
		Litho.		
		Perf. 14		
1433		Horiz. strip of 5	1.10	1.10
a.-e.	A646 10a Any single		.25	.25
1434	A646	1s shown	.45	.45
	With tab		.55	

No. 1433 issued in sheets of two tete-beche strips. The horizontal strips of stamps in No. 1432 are printed tete-beche.

Worldwide Fund for Nature Type of 2000 Without WWF Emblem

Designs: 1.20s, Lesser kestrel. 1.70s, Kuhl's pipistrelle. 2.10s, Roe deer. 2.50s, Greek tortoise.

2001, Mar. 18		Litho.	Perf. 14	
1435	A631	1.20s multi	.55	.55
1436	A631	1.70s multi	.70	.70
1437	A631	2.10s multi	.90	.90
1438	A631	2.50s multi	1.15	1.15
a.	Booklet pane, 2 each #1435-1438		8.00	
	Nos. 1435-1438 (4)		3.30	3.30
	With tabs		3.50	

Flowers — A647

No. 1439: a, Prairie gentian (purple). b, Barberton daisy (yellow) c, Star of Bethlehem (orange). d, Calla lily (white).

2001, Mar. 18				
1439		Horiz. strip of 4 + 6 labels	3.00	3.00
a.-d.	A647 1.20s Any single		.60	.60

No. 1439 was printed in sheets of four strips. The second and fourth strips in the sheet have the stamps in reverse order. Sheets sold at the Jerusalem 2001 Stamp Exhibition could have their labels personalized by the purchaser.
See No. 1463.

Souvenir Sheet

Jerusalem 2001 Stamp Exhibition — A648

2001, Mar. 18				
1440	A648	10s multi	4.25	4.25

Monument to Fallen Nahal Soldiers — A649

2001, Apr. 18		Litho.	Perf. 13	
1441	A649	1.20s multi	.50	.50
	With tab		.60	

Memorial Day.

Historic Sites Type of 2000
Perf. 14 Syncopated

2001, May 23			Photo.	
1442	A630	2s Sha'ar HaGay Inn	.95	.95
	With tab		1.10	

Shrine of the Báb Terraces, Haifa — A650

2001, May 23			Perf. 13x13¼	
1443	A650	3s multi	1.75	1.75
	With tab		2.00	

Karaite Jews — A651

2001, May 23		Litho.	Perf. 14	
1444	A651	5.60s multi	2.50	2.50
	With tab		2.75	

Souvenir Sheet

Belgica 2001 Intl. Stamp Exhibition, Brussels — A652

Cut diamonds: a, 1.40s, Marquise. b, 1.70s, Round. c, 4.70s, Square.

2001, May 23			Perf. 14¾x14½	
1445	A652	Sheet of 3	4.25	4.25
a.	1.40s multi		.75	.75
b.	1.70s multi		.90	.90
c.	4.70s multi		2.50	2.50

No. 1445 sold for 10s.

Youth Movements A653

2001, July 17			Perf. 14	
1446	A653	5.60s multi	2.50	2.50
	With tab		2.75	

Bezalel School of Art Ceramic Facade Tiles — A654

Landscapes of: 1.20s, Hebron. 1.40s, Jaffa. 1.90s, Haifa. 2.30s, Tiberias.

2001, July 17			Perf. 13x14	
1447	A654	1.20s multi	.55	.55
1448	A654	1.40s multi	.65	.65
1449	A654	1.90s multi	.90	.90
1450	A654	2.30s multi	1.10	1.10
	Nos. 1447-1450 (4)		3.20	3.20
	With tabs		3.50	

Souvenir Sheet

Phila Nippon '01, Japan A655

Children's stamp design contest winners: a, 1.20s, Balloons. b, 1.40s, Cat. c, 2.50s, Veterinarian with dog. d, 4.70s, Dolphins.

2001, July 17			Perf. 14¾	
1451	A655	Sheet of 4	4.25	4.25
a.	1.20s multi		.50	.50
b.	1.40s multi		.60	.60
c.	2.50s multi		1.10	1.10
d.	4.70s multi		2.00	2.00

No. 1451 sold for 10s.

Shota Rustaveli (c. 1172-c. 1216), Georgian Poet — A656

2001, Sept. 3		Litho.	Perf. 13x14	
1452	A656	3.40s multi	1.45	1.45
	With tab		1.60	

Yehuda Amichai (1924-2000), Poet — A657

2001, Sept. 3				
1453	A657	5.60s multi	2.25	2.25
	With tab		2.50	

Jewish National Fund, Cent — A658

2001, Sept. 3			Perf. 14	
1454	A658	5.60s multi	2.50	2.50
	With tab		2.75	

Jewish New Year Cards Type of 2000

Designs: 1.20s, Soldier, dove with olive branch. 1.90s, Two women. 2.30s, Boy with flowers.

2001, Sept. 3				
1455	A641	1.20s multi	.50	.50
1456	A641	1.90s multi	.80	.80
1457	A641	2.30s multi	1.00	1.00
	Nos. 1455-1457 (3)		2.30	2.30
	With tabs		2.50	

Selection of Col. Ilan Ramon as Israel's First Astronaut — A659

2001, Dec. 11		Litho.	Perf. 13	
1458	A659	1.20s multi	.65	.65
	With tab		.80	

Akim Association for the Rehabilitation of the Mentally Handicapped, 50th Anniv. — A660

2001, Dec. 11			Perf. 13x14	
1459	A660	2.20s multi	1.00	1.00
	With tab		1.10	

Heinrich Heine (1797-1856), Poet — A661

2001, Dec. 11				
1460	A661	4.40s multi	2.00	2.00
	With tab		2.25	

Institute for the Blind, Jerusalem, Cent. — A662

Litho. & Embossed

2001, Dec. 11			Perf. 14¾	
1461	A662	5.60s multi	2.10	2.10
	With tab		2.50	

Coastal Conservation — A663

2001, Dec. 11		Litho.	Perf. 13	
1462	A663	10s multi	4.50	4.50
	With tab		5.00	

Flower Type of 2001

2002, Feb. 24		Litho.	Perf. 14	
1463	A647	1.20s Yellow lily	.60	.60
	With tab		.70	

No. 1463 has small picture of flower at left, while No. 1439b has small picture of flower at right.

ISRAEL

Languages — A664

2002, Feb. 24   *Perf. 13x14*
1464	A664	2.10s Yiddish	.90	.90
1465	A664	2.10s Ladino	.90	.90
		With tabs	2.00	

Mushrooms — A665

Designs: 1.90s, Agaricus campester. 2.20s, Amanita muscaria. 2.80s, Suillus granulatus.

2002, Feb. 24
1466	A665	1.90s multi	.80	.80
1467	A665	2.20s multi	.95	.95
1468	A665	2.80s multi	1.25	1.25
		Nos. 1466-1468 (3)	3.00	3.00
		With tabs	3.50	

Months of the Year A666

Designs: a, Tishrei (shofar, pomegranates). b, Heshvan (dried leaves). c, Kislev (dreidel, Hanukkah candles). d, Tevet (orange, flowers). e, Shevat (seedling, flowers, seeds). f, Adar (party hat, noisemaker, hamentashen). g, Nisan (cup, matzoh, flowers). h, Iyyar (bow and arrows, seeds). i, Sivan (wheat, sickle). j, Tammuz (flower, shells). k, Av (bride, groom, grapes). l, Elul, (cotton, dates, prayer book).

2002, Feb. 24   *Photo.*   *Perf. 14x14¼*
| 1469 | A666 | Sheet of 12 | 6.75 | 6.75 |
| a.-l. | | 1.20s Any single | .55 | .55 |

Self-Adhesive
Serpentine Die Cut 16
| 1470 | A666 | Booklet of 12 | 11.50 | |
| a.-l. | | 1.20s Any single | .95 | .95 |

Monument to Fallen Military Police — A667

2002, Apr. 10   *Litho.*   *Perf. 14*
| 1471 | A667 | 1.20s multi | .50 | .50 |
| | | With tab | .60 | |

Hakhel Le Yisrael — A668

2002, Apr. 10   *Perf. 13x14*
1472	A668	4.70s multi	2.00	2.00
		With tab	2.25	
a.		Perf. 13¼x13 (1830a)	—	—

Issued: No. 1472a, 11/21/10.

Israel Foundation for Handicapped Children, 50th Anniv. — A669

2002, Apr. 10
| 1473 | A669 | 5.90s multi | 2.25 | 2.25 |
| | | With tab | 2.50 | |

Historians — A670

Designs: No. 1474, Heinrich Graetz (1817-91). No. 1475, Simon Dubnow (1860-1941). No. 1476, Benzion Dinur (1884-1973). No. 1477, Yitzhak Baer (1888-1980).

2002, Apr. 10   *Perf. 14*
1474	A670	2.20s multi	.90	.90
1475	A670	2.20s multi	.90	.90
1476	A670	2.20s multi	.90	.90
1477	A670	2.20s multi	.90	.90
		Nos. 1474-1477 (4)	3.60	3.60
		With tabs	4.00	

See Nos. 1553-1555.

Historic Sites Type of 2000
Perf. 14 Syncopated
2002, June 18   *Photo.*
| 1478 | A630 | 3.30s Hatsar Kinneret | 1.40 | 1.40 |
| | | With tab | 1.60 | |

Cable Cars — A671

2002, June 18   *Litho.*   *Perf. 14*
1479	A671	2.20s Haifa	.95	.95
1480	A671	2.20s Massada	.95	.95
1481	A671	2.20s Menara	.95	.95
1482	A671	2.20s Rosh Haniqra	.95	.95
		Nos. 1479-1482 (4)	3.80	3.80
		With tabs	4.25	

Souvenir Sheet

Geology A672

2002, June 18
1483	A672	Sheet of 3	5.00	5.00
a.		2.20s Fish fossil	1.10	1.10
b.		3.40s Copper minerals	1.75	1.75
c.		4.40s Ammonite	2.10	2.10

No. 1483 sold for 12s.

Rechavam Ze'evy (1926-2001), Assassinated Tourism Minister — A673

2002, Aug. 27   *Litho.*   *Perf. 14*
| 1484 | A673 | 1.20s multi | .50 | .50 |
| | | With tab | .60 | |

Baruch Spinoza (1632-77), Philosopher — A674

2002, Aug. 27   *Perf. 13x14*
| 1485 | A674 | 5.90s multi | 2.25 | 2.25 |
| | | With tab | 2.50 | 2.50 |

Wine — A675

Designs: 1.20s, Clippers, bunch of grapes. 1.90s, Corkscrew, cork. 2.30s, Wine glass, bottle.

2002, Aug. 27   *Perf. 14*
1486	A675	1.20s multi	.45	.45
1487	A675	1.90s multi	.75	.75
1488	A675	2.30s multi	.90	.90
		Nos. 1486-1488 (3)	2.10	2.10
		With tabs	2.40	

Birds of the Jordan Valley — A676

2002, Aug. 27   *Perf. 14½x14*
1489	A676	2.20s Golden eagle	.90	.90
1490	A676	2.20s Black stork	.90	.90
1491	A676	2.20s Common crane	.90	.90
		Nos. 1489-1491 (3)	2.70	2.70
		With tabs	3.00	

Historic Sites Type of 2000
Perf. 14 Syncopated
2002, Aug. 27   *Photo.*
| 1492 | A630 | 4.60s Kadoorie School | 2.00 | 2.00 |
| | | With tab | 2.25 | |

Hyacinth Type of 1999
Perf. 14 Syncopated
2002, Oct. 21   *Photo.*
| 1492A | A606 | (1.20s) multi | 7.50 | 7.50 |
| | | With tab | 8.00 | |

Political Journalists A677

Designs: 1.20s, Abba Ahimeir (1897-1962). 3.30s, Israel Eldad (1910-96). 4.70s, Moshe Beilinson (1890-1936). 5.90s, Rabbi Binyamin (1880-1957).

2002, Nov. 26   *Litho.*   *Perf. 14*
1493	A677	1.20s multi	.45	.45
1494	A677	3.30s multi	1.30	1.30
1495	A677	4.70s multi	1.90	1.90
1496	A677	5.90s multi	2.25	2.25
		Nos. 1493-1496 (4)	5.90	5.90
		With tabs	6.75	

Toys — A678

2002, Nov. 26
1497	A678	2.20s Five Stones	.95	.95
1498	A678	2.20s Marbles	.95	.95
1499	A678	2.20s Spinning top	.95	.95
1500	A678	2.20s Yo-yo	.95	.95
		Nos. 1497-1500 (4)	3.80	3.80
		With tabs	4.25	

Menorah — A679

2002-03   *Photo.*   *Perf. 15x14¾*
1501	A679	20a red	.25	.25
1502	A679	30a gray olive	.25	.25
1503	A679	40a gray green	.25	.25
1504	A679	50a gray brown	.25	.25
1505	A679	1s purple	.40	.40
1506	A679	1.30s blue	.50	.50
		Nos. 1501-1506 (6)	1.90	1.90
		With tabs	2.75	

Issued: 30a, 1s, 11/26/02; 20a, 40a, 50a, 1.30s, 2/11/03. See Nos. 1758-1760.

Yeshivot Hahesder, 50th Anniv. (in 2004) — A680

2003, Feb. 11   *Litho.*   *Perf. 14*
| 1507 | A680 | 1.20s multi | .50 | .50 |
| | | With tab | .60 | |

11 September 2001, by Michael Gross — A681

2003, Feb. 11   *Perf. 13x14*
| 1508 | A681 | 2.30s multi | 1.10 | 1.10 |
| | | With tab | 1.25 | 1.25 |

Monument for the Victims of Hostile Acts, Jerusalem A682

2003, Feb. 11   *Perf. 14x13*
| 1509 | A682 | 4.70s multi | 1.75 | 1.75 |
| | | With tab | 2.00 | |

Powered Flight, Cent. — A683

Designs: 2.30s, Wright Flyer in flight. 3.30s, Engine, propellor, Wright brothers. 5.90s, Orville Wright piloting Wright Flyer.

2003, Feb. 11   *Perf. 14*
1510	A683	2.30s multi	.95	.95
1511	A683	3.30s multi	.90	.90
1512	A683	5.90s multi	1.35	1.35
		Nos. 1510-1512 (3)	3.20	3.20
		With tabs	5.00	

Memorial Day — A684

2003, Apr. 27   *Litho.*   *Perf. 14*
| 1513 | A684 | 1.20s multi | .50 | .50 |
| | | With tab | .60 | |

Holocaust Memorial Day — A685

2003, Apr. 27   *Perf. 13*
| 1514 | A685 | 2.20s multi | 1.00 | 1.00 |
| | | With tab | 1.10 | |

Yemeni Jewish Immigration A686

2003, Apr. 27   *Perf. 14*
| 1515 | A686 | 3.30s multi | 1.25 | 1.25 |
| | | With tab | 1.40 | |

Israeli Aircraft Industries, 50th Anniv. — A687

2003, Apr. 27
| 1516 | A687 | 3.30s multi | 1.40 | 1.40 |
| | | With tab | 1.50 | |

Independence, 55th Anniv. — A688

ISRAEL

2002, Apr. 27
1517 A688 5.90s multi ... 2.25 2.25
     With tab ... 2.50 2.50

Famous Men — A689

Designs: 1.90s, Ya'akov Meridor (1913-95), government minister. 2.20s, Ya'akov Dori (1899-1973), first chief of staff of the Israel Defense Forces. 2.80s, Sheikh Ameen Tarif (1898-1993), President of Druse Religious Court.

2003, Apr. 27 *Perf. 13*
1518 A689 1.90s multi ... .85 .85
1519 A689 2.20s multi ... 1.00 1.00
1520 A689 2.80s multi ... 1.25 1.25
     Nos. 1518-1520 (3) ... 3.10 3.10
     With tabs ... 3.50

Greetings — A690

Designs: No. 1521, Open box, Hebrew letters. No. 1522, Bride and groom. No. 1523, Heart as flower. No. 1524, Hot air balloon, flowers. No. 1525, Flowers and ladybug. No. 1526, Boy and teddy bear.

2003 *Perf. 14*
1521 A690 (1.20s) multi ... .70 .70
  a. Sheet of 12 + 12 labels ... 13.50 13.50
1522 A690 (1.20s) multi ... .70 .70
  a. Sheet of 12 + 12 labels ... 13.50 13.50
1523 A690 (1.20s) multi ... .70 .70
  a. Sheet of 12 + 12 labels ... 13.50 13.50
     Nos. 1521-1523 (3) ... 2.10 2.10
     With tabs ... 2.50
1524 A690 (1.20s) multi ... .70 .70
  a. Sheet of 12 + 12 labels ... 13.50 13.50
1525 A690 (1.20s) multi ... .70 .70
  a. Sheet of 12 + 12 labels ... 13.50 13.50
1526 A690 (1.20s) multi ... .70 .70
  a. Sheet of 12 + 12 labels ... 13.50 13.50
     Nos. 1524-1526 (3) ... 2.10 2.10
     With tabs ... 2.50

Issued: Nos. 1521-1523, 4/27; Nos. 1524-1526, 6/24; Nos. 1521a-1523a, 1524a-1526a, 10/19. Nos. 1521a-1526a each sold for 21.20s. Labels could be personalized.

A sheet containing three No. 1524 + three labels that could not be personalized was issued in 2011 and sold for 15s.

Self-adhesive examples of Nos. 1521, 1523, 1524-1526 come from sheets issued in 1999 that sold for much more than face value.

Village Centenaries A691

2003, June 24 *Litho.* *Perf. 14*
1527 A691 3.30s Atlit ... 1.50 1.50
1528 A691 3.30s Givat-Ada ... 1.50 1.50
1529 A691 3.30s Kfar-Saba ... 1.50 1.50
     Nos. 1527-1529 (3) ... 4.50 4.50
     With tabs ... 5.00

Evolution of the Israeli Flag — A692

Designs: 1.90s, Flag of the Prague Jewish community, 15th cent. 2.30s, Ness Ziona flag, 1891. 4.70s, Theodor Herzl's "Der Judenstaat" flag design, 1896. 5.90s, Israeli flag, 1948.

2003, June 24
1530 A692 1.90s multi ... .85 .85
1531 A692 2.30s multi ... 1.00 1.00
1532 A692 4.70s multi ... 1.90 1.90
1533 A692 5.90s multi ... 2.50 2.50
     Nos. 1530-1533 (4) ... 6.25 6.25
     With tabs ... 7.00

Yad Vashem, 50th Anniv. — A693

Stars of David and: No. 1534, List of Jewish forced laborers. No. 1535, Teddy bear, page of testimony.

2003, Sept. 9 *Litho.* *Perf. 14*
1534 A693 2.20s multi ... 1.00 1.00
1535 A693 2.20s multi ... 1.00 1.00
  a. Pair, #1534-1535 ... 2.00 2.00
     Pair with tabs ... 2.25
  b. Miniature sheet, 3 #1535a ... 6.00 6.00

No. 1535b issued 2004.

Olive Oil — A694

Designs: 1.30s, Olives. 1.90s, Olive press. 2.30s, Jars of oil.

2003, Sept. 9
1536 A694 1.30s multi ... .60 .60
1537 A694 1.90s multi ... .90 .90
1538 A694 2.30s multi ... 1.10 1.10
  a. Booklet pane, #1536, 2 #1537, 3 #1538 ... 5.75 —
     Complete booklet, #1538a ... 5.75
     Nos. 1536-1538 (3) ... 2.60 2.60
     With tabs ... 3.00

Souvenir Sheet

Armenian Ceramics in Jerusalem — A695

No. 1539: a, Deer, by Karakashian-Balian Studio, 1930s-1940s. b, Bird, by Stepan Karakashian, 1980s. c, Tree of Life, by Marie Balian, 1990s.

2003, Sept. 9 *Perf.*
1539 A695 Sheet of 3 ... 6.75 6.75
  a. 2.30s multi ... 1.50 1.50
  b. 3.30s multi ... 2.25 2.25
  c. 4.70s multi ... 3.00 3.00

No. 1539 contains three 31mm diameter stamps and sold for 15s.

Hyacinth Type of 1999
2003 *Photo.* *Perf. 15 Syncopated*
1539D A606 (1.20s) multi ... 8.00 8.00

Booklet Stamp
Self-Adhesive
Serpentine Die Cut 13½x14
1540 A606 (1.30s) multi ... 1.50 1.50
  a. Booklet pane of 20 ... 30.00

Issued: 1.20s, 10/8; 1.30s, 12/4.

Immigrants to Israel — A696

Designs: 2.10s, Leibowitch family, clerical house, Zikhron Ya'acov. 6.20s, Second Aliya immigrants, Rothschild Ave., Tel Aviv.

2003, Dec. 9 *Litho.* *Perf. 13*
1541 A696 2.10s multi ... .75 .75
1542 A696 6.20s multi ... 2.25 2.25
     With tabs ... 3.50

Famous Men — A697

Designs: 3.30s, Aharon David Gordon (1856-1922), laborer. 4.90s, Emile Habiby (1921-96), journalist, politician. 6.20s, Yehoshua Hankin (1865-1945), land developer.

2003, Dec. 9 *Perf. 14*
1543 A697 3.30s multi ... 1.00 1.00
1544 A697 4.90s multi ... 1.50 1.50
1545 A697 6.20s multi ... 2.00 2.00
     Nos. 1543-1545 (3) ... 4.50 4.50
     With tabs ... 5.00

Children on Wheels — A698

No. 1546: a, Boy on bicycle. b, Girl on roller blades. c, Girl on scooter. d, Boy on skateboard.

2003, Dec. 9 *Perf. 13¾*
1546 Horiz. strip of 4 ... 2.10 2.10
  a.-d. A698 1.30s Any single ... .50 .50
     Strip with tabs ... 2.25

Philately Day.

Red Sea Fish — A699

Designs: No. 1547, Amphiprion bicinctus. No. 1548, Pseudanthias squamipinnis. No. 1549, Pseudochromis fridmani. No. 1550, Chaetodon paucifasciatus.

2004, Jan. 30 *Litho.* *Perf. 14*
1547 A699 1.30s multi ... .50 .50
1548 A699 1.30s multi ... .50 .50
1549 A699 1.30s multi ... .50 .50
1550 A699 1.30s multi ... .50 .50
  a. Souvenir sheet, #1547-1550 ... 3.00 3.00
     Nos. 1547-1550 (4) ... 2.00 2.00
     With tabs ... 2.25

2004 Hong Kong Stamp Expo (No. 1550a). No. 1550a sold for 7.50s.

Menachem Begin Heritage Center, Jerusalem — A700

2004, Feb. 24 *Perf. 13*
1551 A700 2.50s multi ... 1.10 1.10
     With tab ... 1.25

Col. Ilan Ramon (1954-2003), First Israeli Astronaut — A701

2004, Feb. 24
1552 A701 2.60s multi ... 1.25 1.25
     With tab ... 1.40

Historians Type of 2002

Designs: 2.40s, Emanuel Ringelblum (1900-44). 3.70s, Jacob Talmon (1916-80). 6.20s, Jacob Herzog (1921-72).

2004, Feb. 24 *Perf. 14*
1553 A670 2.40s multi ... 1.00 1.00
1554 A670 3.70s multi ... 1.45 1.45
1555 A670 6.20s multi, Type I ... 2.50 2.50
  a. Type II ... —
     Nos. 1553-1555 (3) ... 4.95 4.95
     With tabs ... 5.50

Type II has thicker shadows behind the Hebrew characters and numerals, with the shadow at the top of the "6" with a projection, the shadow is visible below, to the right, and above the horizontal line of the "2," and a shadow all around the "0." The background and face are greener, and the width of the color band at the bottom is wider.

Type I has thin shadows behind the Hebrew characters and numerals, with the shadow at the top of the "6" without a projection, the shadow visible below and to the right only of the horizontal line of the "2," and a partial shadow around the "0." The background and face have a lighter shade. The width of the color band at the bottom is narrower.

Memorial Day — A702

2004, Apr. 20 *Litho.* *Perf. 14*
1556 A702 1.30s multi ... .60 .60
     With tab ... .65

FIFA (Fédération Internationale de Football Association), Cent. — A703

2004, May 3 *Perf. 13*
1557 A703 2.10s multi ... .85 .85
     With tab ... 1.00

Printed in sheets of 12 + 4 central labels.

UEFA (European Football Union), 50th Anniv. — A704

2004, May 3 *Perf. 14*
1558 A704 6.20s multi ... 2.50 2.50
     With tab ... 2.75

Ottoman Clock Towers — A705

2004, May 3 *Perf. 13x14*
1559 A705 1.30s Acre ... .65 .65
1560 A705 1.30s Safed ... .65 .65
1561 A705 1.30s Jaffa ... .65 .65
1562 A705 1.30s Jerusalem ... .65 .65
1563 A705 1.30s Haifa ... .65 .65
     Nos. 1559-1563 (5) ... 3.25 3.25
     With tabs ... 3.50

Booklet Stamps
1563A A705 3.10s Safed ... 2.75 2.75
  f. Booklet pane of 1 ... 2.75
1563B A705 3.70s Acre ... 3.25 3.25
  g. Booklet pane of 1 ... 3.25
1563C A705 5.20s Haifa ... 4.50 4.50
  h. Booklet pane of 1 ... 4.50
1563D A705 5.50s Jerusalem ... 4.75 4.75
  i. Booklet pane of 1 ... 4.75
1563E A705 7s Jaffa ... 6.00 6.00
  j. Booklet pane of 1 ... 6.50
  k. Booklet pane of #1563A-1563E ... 21.50 —
     Complete booklet, #1563Af, 1563Bg, 1563Ch, 1563Di, 1563Ej, 1563Ek ... 45.00
     Nos. 1563A-1563E (5) ... 21.25 21.25

A706 — **Great Synagogue of Rome — A707**

2004, May 20 *Litho.* *Perf. 13x14*
1564 A706 2.10s multi ... .85 .85
1565 A707 2.10s multi ... .85 .85
     With tab ... 2.00

See Italy Nos. 2607-2608.

Theodor Herzl (1860-1904), Zionist Leader — A708

2004, July 6 *Perf. 13*
1566 A708 2.50s multi ... 1.10 1.10
     With tab ... 1.25

See Austria No. 1960, Hungary No. 3903.

ISRAEL

National Insurance Institute, 50th Anniv. — A709

2004, July 6
1567 A709 7s multi ... 2.75 2.75
    With tab ... 3.25 3.25

2004 Summer Olympics, Athens — A710

Medals won by Israeli athletes in previous Olympics: 1.50s, 1992 Silver medal, Judo. 2.40s, 1996 Bronze medal, Men's Mistral (windsurfing). 6.90s, 2000 Bronze medal, Kayaking.

2004, July 6 — *Perf. 14*
1568 A710 1.50s multi ... .55 .55
1569 A710 2.40s multi ... .95 .95
1570 A710 6.90s multi ... 3.00 3.00
    Nos. 1568-1570 (3) ... 4.50 4.50
    With tabs ... 5.00

Founding of Herzliya Hebrew High School, Tel Aviv, Cent. (in 2005) — A711

2004, Aug. 31 *Litho.* *Perf. 13x14*
1571 A711 2.20s multi ... 1.00 1.00
    With tab ... 1.10

Ben-Gurion Heritage Institute — A712

2004, Aug. 31 *Perf. 13*
1572 A712 2.50s multi ... 1.10 1.10
    With tab ... 1.25

Adventure Stories — A713

Designs: 2.20s, Eight on the Trail of One, by Yemima Avidar-Tchernovitz (parachutist). 2.50s, The "Hasamba" Series, by Igal Mossinsohn (children, donkey). 2.60s, Our Gang, by Pucho (four people).

2004, Aug. 31
1573 A713 2.20s multi ... .80 .80
1574 A713 2.50s multi ... .90 .90
1575 A713 2.60s multi ... 1.00 1.00
    Nos. 1573-1575 (3) ... 2.70 2.70
    With tabs ... 3.00

Festivals — A714

Bread making: 1.50s, Wheat ears, sickle. 2.40s, Mill, wooden fork. 2.70s, Oven, bread shovel.

2004, Aug. 31 *Perf. 14x13*
1576 A714 1.50s multi ... .60 .60
1577 A714 2.40s multi ... 1.00 1.00
1578 A714 2.70s multi ... 1.15 1.15
    Nos. 1576-1578 (3) ... 2.75 2.75
    With tabs ... 3.00

Opening of Third Terminal at Ben-Gurion Airport — A715

2004, Nov. 2 *Litho.* *Perf. 14x13*
1579 A715 2.70s multi ... 1.10 1.10
    With tab ... 1.25

Winning Design of Telabul 2004 Stamp Designing Contest — A716

2004, Dec. 14
1580 A716 1.30s multi ... .65 .65
    With tab ... .75

Bank of Israel, 50th Anniv. — A717

2004, Dec. 14
1581 A717 6.20s multi ... 2.75 2.75
    With tab ... 3.00

Philately Day — A718

Designs: 2.10s, Mailbox of Austrian Postal Services, Jerusalem Post Office. 2.20s, Mailbox of British Mandate era, Lilienblum St. Post Office, Tel Aviv. 3.30s, Modern mailbox, Main Post Office, Tel Aviv.

2004, Dec. 14
1582 A718 2.10s multi ... .85 .85
1583 A718 2.20s multi ... .90 .90
1584 A718 3.30s multi ... 1.40 1.40
    Nos. 1582-1584 (3) ... 3.15 3.15
    With tabs ... 3.50

Ancient Water Systems — A719

Designs: 2.10s, Hazor water tunnel and ivory cosmetics spoon. 2.20s, Megiddo water system and seal. 3.30s, Caesarea Aqueduct, coin from Caesarea. 6.20s, Hezekiah's tunnel, pool of Siloam, Jerusalem, and imprinted piece of clay.

2005, Feb. 22 *Litho.* *Perf. 14x13*
1585 A719 2.10s multi ... .80 .80
1586 A719 2.20s multi ... .85 .85
1587 A719 3.30s multi ... 1.30 1.30
1588 A719 6.20s multi ... 2.60 2.60
    Nos. 1585-1588 (4) ... 5.55 5.55
    With tabs ... 6.25

Animals in the Bible — A720

Designs: Nos. 1589, 1593a, Ostrich. Nos. 1590, 1593b, Brown bear. Nos. 1591, 1593c, Wolf. Nos. 1592, 1592d, Nile crocodile.

2005, Feb. 22 *Perf. 14x13*
1589 A720 1.30s yel & multi ... .60 .60
1590 A720 1.30s blue & multi ... .60 .60
1591 A720 2.20s org & multi ... 1.00 1.00
1592 A720 2.20s pink & multi ... 1.00 1.00
    Nos. 1589-1592 (4) ... 3.20 3.20
    With tabs ... 3.50

Souvenir Sheet
Perf. 14
1593   Sheet of 4 ... 5.00 5.00
  a. A720 1.30s yel & multi ... .75 .75
  b. A720 2.10s blue & multi ... 1.25 1.25
  c. A720 2.30s org & multi ... 1.35 1.35
  d. A720 2.80s pink & multi ... 1.60 1.60

No. 1593 sold for 12s and contains four 40x25mm stamps.

Memorial Day — A721

2005, May 3 *Litho.* *Perf. 14x13½*
1594 A721 1.50s multi ... .60 .60
    With tab ... .70

Reserve Force — A722

2005, May 3
1595 A722 2.20s multi ... .90 .90
    With tab ... 1.00

Bar-Ilan University, 50th Anniv. — A723

2005, May 3
1596 A723 2.20s multi ... .90 .90
    With tab ... 1.00

End of World War II, 60th Anniv. A724

No. 1597: a, Jewish partisan and underground fighters. b, Jewish soldiers in Allied forces.

2005, May 3
1597 A724 Horiz. pair ... 3.00 3.00
  a.-b. 3.30s Either single ... 1.50 1.50
    With tab ... 3.25

Schools — A725

Designs: 2.10s, Hebrew kindergarden, Rishon Le-Zion. 6.20s, Lemel Elementary School, Jerusalem.

2005, May 3 *Perf. 13½x14*
1598 A725 2.10s multi ... .85 .85
1599 A725 6.20s multi ... 2.50 2.50
    With tabs ... 3.75

Pope John Paul II (1920-2005) — A726

2005, May 18 *Litho.* *Perf. 13¾x14*
1600 A726 3.30s multi ... 1.50 1.50
    With tab ... 1.75

See No. 1865.

Historic Sites Type of 2000
Serpentine Die Cut 11¼x11
2005, June 7 *Litho.*
Booklet Stamp
Self-Adhesive
1601 A630 2.20s Mitzpe Revivim ... 1.15 1.15
  a. Booklet pane of 12 ... 14.00

2005 Maccabiah Games — A727

2005, July 11 *Perf. 13¾x14*
1602 A727 3.30s multi ... 1.25 1.25
    With tab ... 1.50

Gagea Commutate — A728

Perf. 14 Syncopated
2005, July 26 *Photo.*
1603 A728 (1.30s) multi ... .60 .60
    .70

See Nos. 1618, 1656D.

Maimonides (1138-1204), Rabbi, Philosopher — A729

2005, July 26 *Litho.* *Perf. 13¾x14*
1604 A729 8.20s multi ... 3.25 3.25
    With tab ... 3.75

Paintings — A730

Designs: 2.20s, Agrippas Street, by Arie Aroch. 4.90s, Tablets of the Covenant, by Moshe Castel. 6.20s, The Rift in Time, No. 7, by Moshe Kupferman.

2005, July 26 *Perf. 13¾x14*
1605 A730 2.20s multi ... .90 .90
1606 A730 4.90s multi ... 2.00 2.00
1607 A730 6.20s multi ... 2.40 2.40
    Nos. 1605-1607 (3) ... 5.30 5.30
    With tabs ... 6.00

Prime Minister Yitzhak Rabin (1922-95) and Yitzhak Rabin Center, Tel Aviv — A731

2005, Sept. 27 *Litho.* *Perf. 13*
1608 A731 2.20s multi ... .85 .85
    With tab ... 1.00

Albert Einstein (1879-1955), Physicist — A732

2005, Sept. 27
1609 A732 3.30s multi ... 1.50 1.50
    With tab ... 1.60

Intl. Year of Physics.
See No. 1620.

Priestly Blessing at Western Wall — A733

565

ISRAEL

2005, Sept. 27 — **Perf. 13½x14**
1610 A733 6.20s multi 2.50 2.50
    With tab 2.75
  a. Perf. 13½ (1866a) — —
    Issued: No. 1610a, 11/21/10.

Medicine in Israel — A734

2005, Sept. 27 — **Perf. 14x13½**
1611 A734 1.40s Geriatrics .55 .55
1612 A734 2.20s Pediatrics .80 .80
1613 A734 2.20s Rehabilitation .80 .80
1614 A734 6.20s Mental Health 2.40 2.40
    Nos. 1611-1614 (4) 4.55 4.55
    With tabs 5.25

Orders of the Mishnah — A735

2005, Sept. 27
1615 A735 1.30s Zeraim .55 .55
1616 A735 2.10s Moed .80 .80
1617 A735 2.30s Nashim .90 .90
    Nos. 1615-1617 (3) 2.25 2.25
    With tabs 2.50

See Nos. 1653-1655.

Gagea Commutate Type of 2005
Serpentine Die Cut 13½x14

2005, Nov. 3 — **Photo.**
1618 A728 (1.30s) multi .85 .85
  a. Booklet pane of 20 17.00

Diplomatic Relations With Germany, 40th Anniv. — A736

2005, Nov. 3 — **Litho.** — **Perf. 13**
1619 A736 2.10s multi .90 .90
    With tab 1.00

See Germany No. 2359.

Einstein Type of 2005
Souvenir Sheet

2005, Dec. 27
1620 A732 8.20s multi 5.00 5.00
    Philately Day, Jerusalem 2006 National Stamp Exhibition. No. 1620 sold for 12s.

Children's Rights — A737

Inscriptions: No. 1621, Childhood is happiness. No. 1622, Indifference hurts. No. 1623, A warm home.

2005, Dec. 27 — **Perf. 13½x14**
1621 A737 1.30s multi .50 .50
1622 A737 1.30s multi .50 .50
1623 A737 1.30s multi .50 .50
    Nos. 1621-1623 (3) 1.50 1.50
    With tabs 1.75

Theater Personalities — A738

Designs: No. 1624, Joseph Millo (1916-97), director. No. 1625, Moshe Halevy (1895-1974), director. No. 1626, Shai K. Ophir (1928-87), actor. No. 1627, Nissim Aloni (1926-98), playwright.

2005, Dec. 27
1624 A738 2.20s multi .80 .80
1625 A738 2.20s multi .80 .80
1626 A738 6.20s multi 2.40 2.40
1627 A738 6.20s multi 2.40 2.40
    Nos. 1624-1627 (4) 6.40 6.40
    With tabs 7.25

Manufacturers Association of Israel, 85th Anniv. — A739

2005, Dec. 29 — **Litho.** — **Perf. 13¾x14**
1628 A739 1.50s multi .55 .55
    With tab .65

Emblem of Israel Post — A740

2006 — **Perf. 14x13¾**
1629 A740 1.50s multi .55 .55
    With tab .65

Souvenir Sheet
Imperf

2006
1630 A740 5.90s multi 3.25 3.25
    Issued: 1.50s, 2/28; 5.90s, 5/8. Jerusalem 2006 National Stamp Exhibition (No. 1630). No. 1630 sold for 7.50s.
    Embossed and numbered examples of No. 1630 were given as gifts and were not available for sale. Value, $40.

Headquarters of Chabad Lubavitch Hasidism, Brooklyn, NY — A741

2006, Feb. 28 — **Perf. 14x13¾**
1631 A741 2.50s multi .95 .95
    With tab 1.10

Pres. Ezer Weizman (1924-2005) — A742

2005, Feb. 28 — **Perf. 13¾x14**
1632 A742 7.40s multi 3.00 3.00
    With tab 3.25

Children's Art — A743

Contest-winning art by Jewish children in US: Nos. 1633, 1637a, Desert Bloom, by Yael Bildner. Nos. 1634, 1637c, Harmony, by Michela T. Janower. Nos. 1635, 1637d, Together in Israel, by Jessica Deutsch. Nos. 1636, 1637b, Colors of Israel, by Marissa Galin.

2006 — **Perf. 14x13¾**
1633 A743 1.50s multi .60 .60
1634 A743 2.40s multi .90 .90
1635 A743 3.60s multi 1.50 1.50
1636 A743 7.40s multi 3.00 3.00
    Nos. 1633-1636 (4) 6.00 6.00
    With tabs 6.75

Souvenir Sheet
Perf. 14

1637 Sheet of 4 5.75 5.75
  a. A743 2.20s multi .95 .95
  b. A743 2.40s multi 1.05 1.05
  c. A743 3.60s multi 1.50 1.50
  d. A743 5.10s multi 2.25 2.25

Issued: Nos. 1633-1636, 2/28; No. 1637, 5/28. Washington 2006 World Philatelic Exhibition (No. 1637). No. 1637 sold for 15s and contains four 40x35mm stamps.

Yad Lashiron Armored Corps Memorial, Latrun — A744

2006, Apr. 11 — **Perf. 14x13¾**
1638 A744 1.50s multi .70 .70
    With tab .80

Memorial Day.

Tel Aviv University, 50th Anniv. — A745

2006, May 8
1639 A745 3.60s multi 1.35 1.35
    With tab 1.50

Tulips — A746

2006, May 8 — **Perf. 14x14¼**
1640 A746 1.50s shown .70 .70
  a. Sheet of 12 + 12 labels 30.00 30.00
1641 A746 1.50s Columbines .70 .70
    With tab 1.60
  a. Sheet of 12 + 12 labels 30.00 30.00

Nos. 1640a and 1641a each sold for 27s. Labels could be personalized. Compare with type A647.

Souvenir Sheet

Jerusalem 2006 National Stamp Exhibition — A747

2006, May 8 — **Perf. 14**
1642 A747 10s multi 6.25 6.25

The Solar System — A748

Designs: Nos. 1643a, 1644d, Sun, Mercury and Venus. Nos. 1643b, 1644c, Earth, Moon and Mars. Nos. 1643c, 1644e, Neptune, Pluto, and moons. Nos. 1643d, 1644b, Jupiter, moons and asteroids. Nos. 1643e, 1644f, Saturn, moon, Sun and asteroids. Nos. 1643f, 1644a, Uranus, moons, asteroids, part of Saturn.

2006, May 8 — **Perf. 13**
1643 A748 Sheet of 6 7.75 7.75
  a.-f. 2.50s Any single 1.25 1.25

Self-Adhesive
Serpentine Die Cut 11

1644 A748 Booklet pane of 6 10.00
  a.-f. 2.50s Any single 1.60 1.60

Jerusalem 2006 National Stamp Exhibition. The six individual stamps, when separated, could be rearranged to produce a Star of David over the planets.

Religious Zionist Education, Cent. — A749

2006, July 25 — **Perf. 13¾x14**
1645 A749 3.60s multi 1.35 1.35
    With tab 1.50

Rabbis of Jerusalem — A750

Rabbis: 1.50s, Jacob Saul Eliachar (1817-1906). 2.20s, Samuel Salant (1816-1909). 2.40s, Jacob Meir (1856-1939).

2006, July 25
1646 A750 1.50s multi .65 .65
1647 A750 2.20s multi .90 .90
1648 A750 2.40s multi 1.00 1.00
    Nos. 1646-1648 (3) 2.55 2.55
    With tabs 2.75

Silver Khamsas — A751

Khamsa from: 1.50s, Morocco, 1920. 2.50s, Tunisia, 1930. 7.40s, Iran, 1925.

2006, July 26
1649 A751 1.50s multi .60 .60
1650 A751 2.50s multi .95 .95
1651 A751 7.40s multi 3.00 3.00
    Nos. 1649-1651 (3) 4.55 4.55
    With tabs 5.00

Abba Eban (1915-2002), Foreign Minister — A752

2006, Sept. 12 — **Perf. 14x13¾**
1652 A752 7.30s multi 2.60 2.60
    With tab 3.00

Orders of the Mishnah Type of 2005

2006, Sept. 12
1653 A735 1.50s Nezikin .70 .70
1654 A735 2.20s Kodashim 1.00 1.00
1655 A735 2.40s Tohorot 1.10 1.10
    Nos. 1653-1655 (3) 2.80 2.80
    With tabs 3.00

Bezalel Academy of Arts and Design, Cent. — A753

2006, Sept. 12 — **Perf. 13**
1656 Horiz. strip of 3 2.75 2.75
  a. A753 2.50s green .85 .85
  b. A753 2.50s blue .85 .85
  c. A753 2.50s orange .85 .85
    Strip with tabs 3.25

ISRAEL

Gagea Commutate Type of 2005
Redrawn With Two Leaves at Right
2006, Sept. 20   Litho.   Perf. 14
1656D A728 (1.50s) multi — —

Medicinal Herbs and Spices — A754

Designs: 1.50s, Coriandrum sativum. 2.50s, Micromeria fruticosa. 3.30s, Mentha piperita.

2006, Dec. 17   Litho.   Perf. 14¼x14
1657 A754 1.50s multi .60 .60
1658 A754 2.50s multi 1.10 1.10
1659 A754 3.30s multi 1.40 1.40
    Nos. 1657-1659 (3) 3.10 3.10
    With tabs 3.50

See Nos. 1700-1701, 1747.

Creation of Esperanto Language, 120th Anniv. — A755

2006, Dec. 17   Perf. 14x13¾
1660 A755 3.30s multi 1.60 1.60
    With tab 1.75

Israeli Fashions — A756

Women's fashions from: 1.50s, 1882-1948. 2.50s, 1948-73. 3.30s, 1973-90. 7.30s, 1990-2005.

2006, Dec. 17   Perf. 13
1661 A756 1.50s multi .60 .60
1662 A756 2.50s multi 1.10 1.10
1663 A756 3.30s multi 1.40 1.40
1664 A756 7.30s multi 3.00 3.00
    Nos. 1661-1664 (4) 6.10 6.10
    With tabs 6.75

Crusader Sites in Israel — A757

2006, Dec. 17   Litho.   Perf. 14x13¾
1665 A757 2.50s Atlit 1.10 1.10
1666 A757 2.50s Caesarea 1.10 1.10
1667 A757 2.50s Montfort 1.10 1.10
1668 A757 2.50s Belvoir 1.10 1.10
    Nos. 1665-1668 (4) 4.40 4.40
    With tabs 4.75

Development A758

Development of the: 2.50s, Negev. 3.30s, Galilee.

2007, Feb. 20   Litho.   Perf. 14x13¾
1669 A758 2.50s multi 1.15 1.15
1670 A758 3.30s multi 1.45 1.45
    With tabs 3.00

Sports and Physical Education A759

Inscriptions: 2.90s, Physical education in schools. 3s, Wingate Institute. 7.30s, Sport for all.

2007, Feb. 20
1671 A759 2.90s multi 1.15 1.15
1672 A759 3s multi 1.25 1.25
1673 A759 7.30s multi 3.00 3.00
    Nos. 1671-1673 (3) 5.40 5.40
    With tabs 6.00

Educational Television — A760

Designs: Nos. 1674a, 1675, Ma Pit'om (green panel). Nos. 1674b, 1676, Krovim Krovim (blue panel). Nos. 1674c, 1677, No Secrets (orange panel).

2007, Feb. 20   Perf. 13¾x14
1674   Strip of 3 3.25 3.25
  a.-c. A760 2.50s Any single 1.05 1.05
    Strip with tabs 3.75

Booklet Stamps
Self-Adhesive
Serpentine Die Cut 10¾x11
1675 A760 2.50s multi 1.75 1.75
1676 A760 2.50s multi 1.75 1.75
1677 A760 2.50s multi 1.75 1.75
  a.   Booklet pane, 2 each #1675-1677 10.50

Memorial Day — A761

2007, Apr. 17   Litho.   Perf. 14x13¾
1678 A761 1.50s multi .60 .60
    With tab .70

Scouting, Cent. — A762

2007, Apr. 17
1679 A762 2.50s multi 1.10 1.10
    With tab 1.25

Regional Development Towns — A763

Towns in: 2.50s, Northern region. 3.30s, Central region. 7.30s, Southern region.

2007, Apr. 17
1680 A763 2.50s multi 1.00 1.00
1681 A763 3.30s multi 1.40 1.40
1682 A763 7.30s multi 3.00 3.00
    Nos. 1680-1682 (3) 5.40 5.40
    With tabs 6.00

Souvenir Sheet

Neve-Tzedek Neighborhood of Tel Aviv, 120th Anniv. — A764

2007, Apr. 17   Perf. 13¾x14
1683 A764   Sheet of 3 6.50 6.50
  a.   2.20s Founders 1.30 1.30
  b.   3.30s Neve-Tzedek 1.90 1.90
  c.   5.80s Intellectuals 3.25 3.25
    No. 1683 sold for 15s.

Reunification of Jerusalem, 40th Anniv. — A765

2007, May 16
1684 A765 1.50s multi .75 .75
    With tab .85

Volunteer Organizations A766

2007, June 20   Perf. 13
1685 A766 1.50s multi .75 .75
    With tab .85

Israel Prison Service — A767

2007, June 20   Perf. 13¾x14
1686 A767 2.50s multi 1.10 1.10
    With tab 1.25

Dance — A768

No. 1687: a, Ballet. b, Ethnic dance. c, Israeli folk dance. d, Modern dance.

2007, June 20
1687   Horiz. strip of 4 3.75 3.75
  a.-d. A768 2.20s Any single .90 .90
    Strip with tabs 4.25

UNESCO World Heritage Sites — A769

Designs: 3.30s, Akko (Acre). 5s, †0s, Tel Aviv. 5.80s, Masada.

2007   Perf. 14x13¾
1688 A769 3.30s multi 1.40 1.40
1689 A769 5s multi 2.00 2.00
1690 A769 5.80s multi 2.25 2.25
    Nos. 1688-1690 (3) 5.65 5.65
    With tabs 6.50

Souvenir Sheet
1691 A769 10s multi 6.50 6.50
    Issued: 3.30s, 5s, 5.80s, 6/20; 10s, 8/27. Tel Aviv, cent. (No. 1691). No. 1691 sold for 15s.

Beach — A770

2007, Aug. 27   Perf. 14
1692 A770 (1.50s) multi .75 .75
    With tab .85
  a.   Miniature sheet of 12 + 12 labels 20.00 20.00

No. 1692a sold for 27s. Labels could be personalized. Self-adhesive examples of No. 1692 come from sheets issued in 1999 that sold for much more than face value.

Hashomer A771

2007, Aug. 27   Perf. 14x13¾
1693 A771 3.30s multi 1.35 1.35
    With tab 1.50

Israel Reserve Forces — A772

2007, Aug. 27   Perf. 13¾x14
1694 A772 7.30s multi 3.00 3.00
    With tab 3.50

Chalom Messas (1909-2003), Chief Rabbi of Morocco and Jerusalem — A773

2007, Aug. 27
1695 A773 7.30s multi 3.00 3.00
    With tab 3.50

Women of the Bible — A774

2007, Aug. 27
1696 A774 1.50s Jael .65 .65
1697 A774 2.20s Esther .95 .95
1698 A774 2.40s Miriam 1.05 1.05
    Nos. 1696-1698 (3) 2.65 2.65
    With tabs 3.00

Theodor Herzl Type of 1986
Serpentine Die Cut 13½x13¾
2007, Nov. 1   Litho.
Self-Adhesive
1699 A388 5a blue & ultra .60 .60

Medicinal Herbs and Spices Type of 2006

Designs: 1.55s, Laurus nobilis. 2.25s, Coridothymus capitatus.

2007, Nov. 5   Perf. 14
1700 A754 1.55s multi .70 .70
1701 A754 2.25s multi 1.10 1.10
    With tabs 2.00

Rabbi Itzhak Kaduri (1902-2006) — A775

2007, Dec. 5   Perf. 13½x14
1702 A775 8.15s multi 3.25 3.25
    With tab 3.75

Tel Aviv Movie Theaters — A776

Designs: 4.50s, Eden Cinema. 4.60s, Mograbi Cinema.

2007, Dec. 5   Perf. 14x13½
1703 A776 4.50s multi 2.10 2.10
1704 A776 4.60s multi 2.10 2.10
    With tabs 4.75

ISRAEL

Family Love — A777

Designs: 1.55s, Boy giving flower to mother. 2.25s, Girl with baby brother. 3.55s, Father and son.

2007, Dec. 5			Perf. 13½x14	
1705	A777	1.55s multi	.70	.70
1706	A777	2.25s multi	1.05	1.05
1707	A777	3.55s multi	1.60	1.60
	Nos. 1705-1707 (3)		3.35	3.35
	With tabs		3.75	

Hula Nature Reserve — A778

Designs: Nos. 1708a, 1710, Pelicans, Caspian terrapins, iris (denomination in yellow). Nos. 1708b, 1709, Water buffalos, marbled duck, reed warbler, wildcat, wild raspberry (denomination in red violet). Nos. 1708c, 1711, Otter, catfish, cranes, willow herb (denomination in orange).

2007, Dec. 5			Perf. 14x13½	
1708		Strip of 3	3.00	3.00
a.-c.	A778 2.25s Any single		.95	.95
	Strip with tabs		3.50	

Booklet Stamps
Self-Adhesive
Serpentine Die Cut 11x10¼

1709	A778	2.25s multi	1.25	1.25
1710	A778	2.25s multi	1.25	1.25
1711	A778	2.25s multi	1.25	1.25
a.	Booklet pane, 2 each #1709-1711		7.50	
	Nos. 1709-1711 (3)		3.75	3.75

Miniature Sheet

Noah's Ark A779

No. 1712: a, Dove and olive branch. b, Noah and family, animals, leaving ark. c, Camels, giraffes, zebra, elephants, whale. d, Peafowl, bears, tiger. e, Lions, wolf. f, Wolf, leopards, goats, kangaroos.

2007, Dec. 5			Perf. 14	
1712	A779	Sheet of 6	8.50	8.50
a.-f.	2.25s Any single		1.40	1.40

World Stamp Championship Israel 2008. No. 1712 sold for 16s.
A limited edition booklet containing two self-adhesive examples of Nos. 1712a-1712f sold at the Israel 2008 World Stamp Championship Philatelic Exhibtion, Tel Aviv. Value, $25.

Israel Rokach (1896-1959), Mayor of Tel Aviv — A780

2008, Jan. 27	Litho.		Perf. 14x13¾	
1713	A780	2.25s multi	1.10	1.10
	With tab		1.25	

Tel Aviv Land Lottery, Cent. (in 2009) A781

2008, Jan. 27			Perf. 13	
1714	A781	4.50s multi	2.00	2.00
	With tab		2.25	

No. 1714 has an imperf. tab on the bottom margin. Examples with a perforated bottom margin come from a limited edition of the prestige booklet noted under No. 1733.

Intl. Holocaust Remembrance Day — A782

2008, Jan. 27			Perf. 14	
1715	A782	4.60s multi	2.10	2.10
	With tab		2.50	

See United Nations No.948, United Nations Offices in Geneva No.479, United Nations Offices in Vienna No. 412.

Mekorot, National Water System, 70th Anniv. — A783

2008, Jan. 27			Perf. 13¾x14	
1716	A783	5.80s multi	2.75	2.75
	With tab		3.25	

Akiva Aryeh Weiss (1868-1947), Tel Aviv Builder and Developer — A784

2008, Jan. 27			Perf. 14x13¾	
1717	A784	8.15s multi	3.50	3.50
	With tab		4.00	

UNESCO World Heritage Sites — A785

Designs: 2.25s, Biblical Tels. 3.40s, Incense Route.

2008, Jan. 27				
1718	A785	2.25s multi	1.05	1.05
1719	A785	3.40s multi	1.60	1.60
	With tabs		3.00	

A booklet inscribed "World Heritage Sites in Israel" sold for 55s. It contained 1 pane of 3 each for Nos. 1688, 1690 and 1718-1719, and a pane of 2 of No. 1689. Value, $35.

Israeli Boy and Flag — A786

2008, Apr. 28	Litho.		Perf. 14	
1720	A786	(1.55s) multi	.70	.70
	With tab		.80	

Booklet Stamp
Self-Adhesive
Serpentine Die Cut 13½x14

1721	A786	(1.55s) multi	.90	.90
a.	Booklet pane of 20		18.00	

Flowers — A787

No. 1722, White roses. No. 1723, Cyclamen persicum.

2008, Apr. 28			Perf. 14	
1722	A787	(1.55s) multi	.90	.90
1723	A787	(1.55s) multi	.90	.90
	With tabs		1.05	

Self-adhesive examples of Nos. 1722-1723 come from sheets issued in 1999 that sold for much more than face value.

Independence, 60th Anniv. — A788

2008, Apr. 28			Perf. 14x13¾	
1724	A788	1.55s multi	.80	.80
	With tab		.90	

Memorial Day — A789

2008, Apr. 28			Perf. 13¾x14	
1725	A789	1.55s multi	.80	.80
	With tab		.90	

Israel Export Institute, 50th Anniv. — A790

2008, Apr. 28			Perf. 14x13¾	
1726	A790	2.80s multi	1.25	1.25
	With tab		1.40	

Souvenir Sheet

Hatikva (National Anthem), 120th Anniv. A791

2008, Apr. 28			Perf. 13¾	
1727	A791	10s multi	7.50	7.50

No. 1727 sold for 15s.

Miniature Sheet

Independence Day Posters — A792

No. 1728 — Poster from: a, 1981 (green panel). b, 1991 (brown panel). c, 2006 (blue panel). d, 1971 (purple panel). e, 1965 (dark red panel). f, 1952 (orange panel).

2008, Apr. 28			Perf. 13¾x14	
1728	A792	Sheet of 6	6.75	6.75
a.-f.	2.25s Any single		1.05	1.05

Children's Art — A793

Designs: No. 1729, I Love Israel (numbers, symbols, Hebrew and Roman letters), by Etai Epstein. No. 1730, Israel is My Home (Hebrew letters, house and map of Israel), by Yuval Sulema and Eden Vilker. No. 1731, Israel's 60th, (girl, telescope, cat, butterflies, flowers and "60"), by Daniel Hazan.

2008, May 14	Litho.		Perf. 13½x14	
1729	A793	2.25s multi	1.20	1.20
1730	A793	2.25s multi	1.20	1.20
1731	A793	2.25s multi	1.20	1.20
	Nos. 1729-1731 (3)		3.60	3.60
	With tabs		4.00	

Souvenir Sheet

Jerusalem of Gold — A794

Litho. & Embossed With Foil Application

2008, May 14			Perf. 14½x14¼	
1732	A794	18s multi	12.00	12.00

No. 1732 sold for 22.50s.
No. 1732 exists imperf. Value, $80.

Souvenir Sheet

Tel Aviv, Cent. (in 2009) A795

No. 1733 — Sketches of Tel Aviv life by Nahum Gutman: a, The First Concert. b, The First Lamp Post. c, Dr. Hisin.

2008, May 14	Litho.		Perf. 14x13¾	
1733	A795	Sheet of 3	9.00	9.00
a.	3.50s multi		2.25	2.25
b.	4.50s multi		3.00	3.00
c.	5.50s multi		3.75	3.75

2008 World Stamp Championships, Israel. No. 1733 sold for 18s.
A booklet containing Nos. 1713 and 1717 in panes of 2, Nos. 1691, 1714 and 1733 with an additional border in panes of 1, and a pane of 1 each for Nos. 1703-1704, was sold at the 2008 World Stamp Chamionships, Tel Aviv. Value, $40. A limited number contained No. 1714 perforated on four sides. Value, $125.

Gush Katif, 1970-2005 Gaza Strip Settlement A796

2008, July 14	Litho.		Perf. 14x13	
1734	A796	1.55s multi	.80	.80
	With tab		.90	

Promenades A797

Designs: 4.50s, Tabgha Promenade (on Sea of Galilee), Capernaum. 4.60s, Armon Hanatziv Promenade, Jerusalem. 8.15s, Rishonim Promenade, Netanya.

2008, July 14				
1735	A797	4.50s multi	2.10	2.10
1736	A797	4.60s multi	2.25	2.25
1737	A797	8.15s multi	3.75	3.75
	Nos. 1735-1737 (3)		8.10	8.10
	With tabs		8.75	

2008 Summer Olympics, Beijing — A798

2008, July 14				
1738	A798	1.55s Swimming	.80	.80
1739	A798	1.55s Gymnastics	.80	.80
1740	A798	2.25s Sailing	1.25	1.25
1741	A798	2.25s Tennis	1.25	1.25
	Nos. 1738-1741 (4)		4.10	4.10
	With tabs		4.50	

ISRAEL

Rabbis — A799

Designs: 2.30s, Rabbi Samuel Mohilewer (1824-98). 8.50s, Rabbi Zvi Hirsch Kalischer (1795-1874).

2008, Sept. 17   Perf. 12½x13
1742	A799	2.30s multi	1.20	1.20
1743	A799	8.50s multi	4.25	4.25
	With tabs		6.00	

Torah Crowns — A800

Torah crown from: 1.60s, Aden, late 19th cent. No. 1745, Turkey, 19th cent. No. 1746, Poland, 1729.

2008, Sept. 17   Perf. 14x13
1744	A800	1.60s multi	.80	.80
1745	A800	3.80s multi	1.90	1.90
1746	A800	3.80s multi	1.90	1.90
	Nos. 1744-1746 (3)		4.60	4.60
	With tabs		5.00	

Herbs and Spices Type of 2006 and

Salvia Fruticosa — A801

Design: 1.60s, Artemisia arborescens.

2008-09   Perf. 13
1747	A754	1.60s multi	.80	.80
1748	A801	(2.90s) multi	1.45	1.45
	With tabs		2.50	

Self-Adhesive Booklet Stamps
Serpentine Die Cut 11x10¾
1749	A801	(2.90s) multi	2.00	2.00
a.	Booklet pane of 10 + 10 etiquettes		20.00	

With Different Arabic Inscription and Dash Before "24"
1749B	A801	(2.90s) multi	2.00	2.00
c.	Booklet pane of 10 + 10 etiquettes		20.00	

Issued: Nos. 1747-1749, 9/17/08. No. 1749B, 1/25/09.

Landmarks of France and Israel A802

Airplane, stamped first flight cover and: 1.60s, Haifa waterfront, Israel. 3.80s, Eiffel Tower, Paris.

2008, Nov. 6   Litho.   Perf. 14
1750	A802	1.60s multi	.80	.80
1751	A802	3.80s multi	1.90	1.90
	With tab		3.00	

First flight between France and Israel, 60th anniv. See France Nos. 3533-3534.

2008 Census — A803

2008, Dec. 17   Perf. 14x13
1752	A803	1.60s multi	.75	.75
	With tab		.85	

Israeli Defense Forces Radio — A804

2008, Dec. 17   Perf. 14x13¾
1753	A804	2.30s multi	1.10	1.10
	With tab		1.25	1.25

Taglit-Birthright Israel — A805

2008, Dec. 17   Perf. 14x13
1754	A805	5.60s multi	3.00	3.00
	With tab		3.25	

Ancient Letters — A806

Designs: 1.60s, Bar Kokhba letters, A.D. 134. 2.30s, Lachish letters, 589 B.C. 8.50s, Letter from Ugarit, 1230 B.C.

2008, Dec. 17
1755	A806	1.60s multi	.70	.70
1756	A806	2.30s multi	1.05	1.05
1757	A806	8.50s multi	4.00	4.00
	Nos. 1755-1757 (3)		5.75	5.75
	With tabs		6.25	

Menorah Type of 2002-03
2009   Serpentine Die Cut 13½x13¾
Self-Adhesive
1758	A679	30a gray olive	.30	.30
1758A	A679	40a gray green	.40	.40
1759	A679	50a gray brown	.40	.40
1760	A679	1s purple	.50	.50
	Nos. 1758-1760 (4)		1.60	1.60

Issued: 30a, 50a, 1s, 2/17; 40a, 9/8.

Tel Aviv, Cent. — A807

People and: 1.60s, Boardwalk and beaches. 2.30s, Buildings with different architectural styles. 3.80s, Parks.

2009   Perf. 14x13¾
1761	A807	1.60s multi	.70	.70
1762	A807	2.30s multi	.95	.95
1763	A807	3.80s multi	1.60	1.60
	Nos. 1761-1763 (3)		3.25	3.25
	With tabs		3.75	

Extreme Sports — A808

2009, Feb. 17
1764	A808	4.40s Mountain biking	1.90	1.90
1765	A808	5.40s Skydiving	2.40	2.40
1766	A808	5.60s Surfing	2.50	2.50
	Nos. 1764-1766 (3)		6.80	6.80
	With tabs		7.50	

Fruit — A809

No. 1767: a, Grapes. b, Lemons. c, Avocados. d, Oranges. e, Pomegranates.

2009, Feb. 17   Perf. 14
1767	Vert. strip of 5		4.00	4.00
a.-e.	A809 (1.60s) Any single		.80	.80
	Strip with tabs		4.50	

See Nos. 1792-1796.

Memorial Day — A810

2009, Apr. 22   Perf. 14x13¾
1768	A810	1.60s multi	.70	.70
	With tab		.80	

Intl. Year of Astronomy A811

Designs: 2.30s, Gersonides using Jacob's staff. 3.80s, Gravitational lensing. 8.50s, Laser Interferometer Space Antenna.

2009, Apr. 22
1769	A811	2.30s multi	1.00	1.00
1770	A811	3.80s multi	1.75	1.75
1771	A811	8.50s multi	3.50	3.50
	Nos. 1769-1771 (3)		6.25	6.25
	With tabs		7.00	

Souvenir Sheet

Berek Joselewicz, A Jewish Fighter for Polish Freedom's Last Battle, Kock, by Juliusz Kossak — A812

2009, Apr. 22   Perf. 14
1772	A812	6.10s multi	3.00	3.00

See Poland No. 3935.

Miniature Sheet

Israeli Musicians — A813

No. 1773: a, Zohar Argov (1955-87). b, Sasha Argov (1914-95). c, Meir Ariel (1942-99). d, Yossi Banai (1932-2006). e, Naomi Shemer (1930-2004). f, Shoshana Damari (1923-2006). g, Yair Rosenblum (1944-96). h, Moshe Wilensky (1910-97). i, Ehud Manor (1941-2005). j, Arik Lavie (1927-2004). k, Uzi Hitman (1952-2004). l, Ofra Haza (1957-2000).

2009, Apr. 22   Perf. 13
1773	A813	Sheet of 12 + 4 labels	15.00	15.00
a.-l.	1.60s Any single		1.25	1.25

Love — A814

2009, June 30   Perf. 14
1774	A814	(1.60s) multi	.85	.85
	With tab		.95	

Dead Sea A815

2009, June 30   Perf. 13¾x14
1775	A815	2.30s multi	1.10	1.10
	With tab		1.25	

18th Maccabiah Games — A816

2009, June 30
1776	A816	5.60s multi	2.50	2.50
	With tab		2.75	

Intl. Harp Contest, 50th Anniv. — A817

2009, June 30
1777	A817	8.50s multi	3.75	3.75
	With tab		4.25	

Environmental Quality — A818

No. 1778: a, Geothermal energy (Earth as teakettle, 31x31mm). b, Global warming (Earth melting in frying pan, 62x31mm). c, Solar energy (house with solar panels on Earth, 31x31mm).

2009, June 30   Perf. 13
1778		Horiz. strip of 3	3.25	3.25
a.-c.	A818	2.30s Any single	1.05	1.05
	Strip with tabs		3.75	

Leumit Health Fund, 75th Anniv. — A819

2009, Sept. 8   Perf. 14x13¾
1779	A819	8.80s multi	4.00	4.00
	With tab		4.50	

Honey — A820

Honeycomb and: 1.60s, Bee on flower. 4.60s, Honeycomb on plate. 6.70s, Honey dripping on apple slice.

2009, Sept. 8
1780	A820	1.60s multi	.70	.70
1781	A820	4.60s multi	2.10	2.10
1782	A820	6.70s multi	3.25	3.25
	Nos. 1780-1782 (3)		6.05	6.05
	With tabs		6.75	

Virtual Communications A821

Designs: 2.40s, Instant messaging software. 5.30s, USB flash drive. 6.50s, Voice over Internet protocol.

2009, Sept. 8
1783	A821	2.40s multi	1.05	1.05
1784	A821	5.30s multi	2.50	2.50
1785	A821	6.50s multi	3.00	3.00
	Nos. 1783-1785 (3)		6.55	6.55
	With tabs		7.25	

Animal Assisted Therapy — A822

ISRAEL

Designs: Nos. 1786, 1789, Woman and dog. Nos. 1787, 1790, Girl and horse. Nos. 1788, 1791, Girl and dolphin.

2009, Sept. 8 — *Perf. 14x13¾*
1786	A822	2.40s multi	1.10	1.10
1787	A822	2.40s multi	1.10	1.10
1788	A822	2.40s multi	1.10	1.10
	Nos. 1786-1788 (3)		3.30	3.30
	With tabs		3.75	

Booklet Stamps
Self-Adhesive
Serpentine Die Cut 11x10¼
1789	A822	2.40s multi	1.50	1.50
1790	A822	2.40s multi	1.50	1.50
1791	A822	2.40s multi	1.50	1.50
a.	Booklet pane of 6, 2 each #1789-1791		9.00	
	Nos. 1789-1791 (3)		4.50	4.50

Fruit Type of 2009
Serpentine Die Cut 14¼x13

2009, Nov. 26 — Litho.

Booklet Stamps
Self-Adhesive
1792	A809	(1.60s) Lemons	1.00	1.00
1793	A809	(1.60s) Grapes	1.00	1.00
1794	A809	(1.60s) Pomegranates	1.00	1.00
1795	A809	(1.60s) Oranges	1.00	1.00
1796	A809	(1.60s) Avocados	1.00	1.00
a.	Booklet pane of 20, 4 each #1792-1796		20.00	
	Nos. 1792-1796 (5)		5.00	5.00

Yiddish Theater, Iasi, Romania — A823

2009, Nov. 26 Litho. *Perf. 14*
| 1797 | A823 | 4.60s multi | 2.25 | 2.25 |
| | With tab | | 2.50 | |

See Romania No. 5142.

Lighthouses A824

Lighthouses at: 4.60s, Jaffa. 6.70s, Tel Aviv. 8.80s, Ashdod.

2009, Nov. 26 — *Perf. 14x13¾*
1798	A824	4.60s multi	2.10	2.10
1799	A824	6.70s multi	3.00	3.00
1800	A824	8.80s multi	4.00	4.00
	Nos. 1798-1800 (3)		9.10	9.10
	With tabs		10.00	

Maritime Archaeology A825

Diver and: No. 1801, Earthenware jugs. No. 1802, Figurines. 3.60s, Weapons. 5s, Anchors.

2009, Nov. 26
1801	A825	2.40s multi	1.05	1.05
1802	A825	2.40s multi	1.05	1.05
1803	A825	3.60s multi	1.60	1.60
1804	A825	5s multi	2.40	2.40
	Nos. 1801-1804 (4)		6.10	6.10
	With tabs		6.75	

Arava Valley Settlements, 50th Anniv. — A826

2010, Jan. 27 Litho. *Perf. 14x13¾*
| 1805 | A826 | 1.60s multi | .75 | .75 |
| | With tab | | .85 | |

Lions Club of Israel, 50th Anniv. — A827

2010, Jan. 27
| 1806 | A827 | 4.60s multi | 2.00 | 2.00 |
| | With tab | | 2.25 | |

Intl. Holocaust Remembrance Day — A828

2010, Jan. 27 *Perf. 14*
| 1807 | A828 | 6.70s multi | 3.50 | 3.50 |
| | With tab | | 4.00 | |

Alliance Israelite Universelle, 150th Anniv. — A829

2010, Jan. 27 *Perf. 14x13¾*
| 1808 | A829 | 8.80s multi | 4.00 | 4.00 |
| | With tab | | 4.50 | |

Birds — A830

No. 1809: a, Carduelis carduelis. b, Upupa epops. c, Prinia gracilis.

2010, Jan. 27 *Perf. 13¾x14*
1809	Strip of 3, #a-c	4.00	4.00
a.-c.	A830 2.40s Any single	1.25	1.25
	Strip with tabs	4.50	

A booklet was issued in 2012 with Nos. 1489-1491, and 1809a-c, each stamp in a pane of 3. It sold for 49s. Value, $30.

Memorial Day — A831

2010, Apr. 14 Litho. *Perf. 13¾x14*
| 1810 | A831 | 1.60s multi | .80 | .80 |
| | With tab | | .90 | |

Tribute to World Trade Center Victims, by Eliezer Weishoff, Jerusalem — A832

2010, Apr. 14
| 1811 | A832 | 2.40s multi | 1.20 | 1.20 |
| | With tab | | 1.40 | 1.40 |

Friendship Between Israel and Canada, 60th Anniv. — A833

2010, Apr. 14 *Perf. 14x13¾*
| 1812 | A833 | 4.60s multi | 2.00 | 2.00 |
| | With tab | | 2.25 | |

See Canada No. 2379.

Israeli Innovations A834

Designs: No. 1813, Drip irrigation dripper and farm field. No. 1814, Computer chip and computer. No. 1815, Gastrointestinal camera and intestines.

2010, Apr. 14 *Perf. 14x13¾*
1813	A834	2.40s multi	1.10	1.10
1814	A834	2.40s multi	1.10	1.10
1815	A834	2.40s multi	1.10	1.10
	Nos. 1813-1815 (3)		3.30	3.30
	With tabs		3.75	

Expo 2010, Shanghai.

Souvenir Sheet

Children's Books — A835

No. 1816: a, Alice's Adventures in Wonderland, by Lewis Carroll. b, Peter Pan, by Sir James M. Barrie. c, Gulliver's Travels, by Jonathan Swift.

2010, Apr. 14 *Perf. 14¾x14*
| 1816 | A835 | Sheet of 3 | 6.50 | 6.50 |
| a.-c. | 4.60s Any single | | 2.10 | 2.10 |

London 2010 International Stamp Exhibition.

Souvenir Sheet

Theodor Herzl (1860-1904), Zionist Leader — A836

No. 1817: a, Herzl leaning on railing, settlers. b, Settlers at settlement. c, Boy waving Israeli flag, adults, city skyline.

2010, Apr. 14
1817	A836	Sheet of 3	7.00	7.00
a.	3.70s multi		1.75	1.75
b.	4.60s multi		2.00	2.00
c.	6.70s multi		3.25	3.25

Kibbutzim, Cent. — A837

2010, June 14 Litho. *Perf. 14x13½*
| 1818 | A837 | 2.50s multi | 1.15 | 1.15 |
| | With tab | | 1.30 | |

Rabbi Nachman of Breslev (1772-1810), Philosopher — A838

2010, June 14 *Perf. 13½x14*
| 1819 | A838 | 3.70s multi | 1.75 | 1.75 |
| | With tab | | 1.90 | |

Simon Wiesenthal (1908-2005), Hunter of Nazi War Criminals A839

2010, June 14 *Perf. 12½*
| 1820 | A839 | 5s multi | 2.10 | 2.10 |
| | With tab | | 2.50 | |

The Star of David is made up of tiny holes made by a laser. See Austria No. 2264.

World 420 Sailing Championships, Haifa — A840

2010, June 14 *Perf. 14x15*
| 1821 | A840 | 9s multi | 3.75 | 3.75 |
| | With tab | | 4.25 | |

Story Gardens, Holon — A841

Sculptures based on children's stories: No. 1822, Where is Pluto? (Dog). No. 1823, Shmuel the Hedgehog. No. 1824, Soul Bird.

2010, June 14 *Perf. 14x13½*
1822	A841	2.50s multi	1.20	1.20
1823	A841	2.50s multi	1.20	1.20
1824	A841	2.50s multi	1.20	1.20
	Nos. 1822-1824 (3)		3.60	3.60
	With tabs		4.00	

Musical Instruments — A842

No. 1825: a, Zoma and oboe. b, Rebab and violin. c, Darbouka and drum. d, Qanun and piano. e, Oud and guitar.

2010, June 14 *Perf. 13½x14*
1825	Horiz. strip of 5	3.75	3.75
a.-e.	A842 1.70s Any single	.75	.75
	Strip with tabs	4.25	

Tzevet (Israel Defense Forces Veterans Association), 50th Anniv. — A843

2010, Aug. 25 Litho. *Perf. 13¼x13*
| 1826 | A843 | 2.50s multi | 1.15 | 1.15 |
| | With tab | | 1.35 | |

Settlements Outside of Jerusalem's Old City Walls, 150th Anniv. — A844

2010, Aug. 25 *Perf. 13¼*
1827	A844	3.70s multi	1.60	1.60
	With tab		1.90	
a.	Booklet pane of 2		5.00	

Issued: No. 1827a, 11/21/10.

Urban Renaissance A845

2010, Aug. 25 *Perf. 13x13¼*
| 1828 | A845 | 8.90s multi | 4.00 | 4.00 |
| | With tab | | 4.50 | |

Shofars — A846

ISRAEL

Shofar blower and shofar made of: 1.70s, Ram's horn. 4.20s, Kudu horn. 6.10s, Ram's horn, diff.

2010, Aug. 25   **Perf. 13¼x13**
1829	A846	1.70s multi	.75	.75
1830	A846	4.20s multi	1.90	1.90
a.		Booklet pane of 2, #1472a, 1830	—	—
1831	A846	6.10s multi	2.75	2.75
		Nos. 1829-1831 (3)	5.40	5.40
		With tabs	6.00	

Issued: No. 1830a, 11/21/10.

Greetings
A847   A848

2010, Aug. 25   **Perf. 13¾x14**
1832	A847	(1.70s) multi	.90	.90
		With tab	1.00	
a.		Sheet of 12 + 12 labels	15.00	15.00
1833	A848	(1.70s) multi	.90	.90
		With tab	1.00	
a.		Sheet of 12 + 12 labels	15.00	15.00

Booklet Stamps
Self-Adhesive
Serpentine Die Cut 12½x12¾
1834	A847	(1.70s) multi	.90	.90
1835	A848	(1.70s) multi	.90	.90
a.		Booklet pane of 12, 6 each #1834-1835	11.00	

Nos. 1832a and 1833a each sold for 28s. Labels could be personalized.

Miniature Sheet
Animals and Their Young — A849

No. 1836: a, Chicks. b, Hen. c, Kitten with ball of yarn. d, Cat. e, Rabbit kit, flower, carrot. f, Rabbit.

2010, Aug. 25   **Perf. 13x13¼**
1836	A849	Sheet of 6 + 3 labels	4.75	4.75
a.-f.		1.70s Any single	.75	.75

Garden of Gethsemane, Jerusalem A850

2010, Nov. 15   **Litho.**   **Perf. 13x13¼**
1837	A850	4.20s multi	2.00	2.00
		With tab	2.40	

Printed in sheets of 4. See Vatican City No. 1456.

Flag of Israel — A851

2010, Nov. 21   **Perf. 13¾x14**
1838	A851	(1.70s) multi	.95	.95
		With tab	1.10	
a.		Sheet of 12 + 12 labels	15.50	15.50

No. 1838a sold for 28s. Labels could be personalized. See No. 1877.

Movie Theaters — A852

Designs: 4.20s, Armon Cinema, Haifa. 9s, Zion Cinema, Jerusalem.

2010, Nov. 21   **Perf. 13x13¼**
1839	A852	4.20s multi	1.90	1.90
1840	A852	9s multi	4.00	4.00
		With tabs	6.75	

Bible Stories A853

Designs: No. 1841, Adam and Eve. No. 1842, Samson and the Lion. No. 1843, Jonah and the Fish. 6s, Moses parting the Red Sea, vert.

2010, Nov. 21   **Perf. 14½x14¼**
1841	A853	1.70s multi	.95	.95
a.		Miniature sheet of 6	8.00	8.00
1842	A853	1.70s multi	.95	.95
a.		Miniature sheet of 6	8.00	8.00
1843	A853	1.70s multi	.95	.95
a.		Miniature sheet of 6	8.00	8.00
		Nos. 1841-1843 (3)	2.85	2.85
		With tabs	3.25	

Souvenir Sheet
Perf. 13½x13
1844	A853	6s multi	4.00	4.00

Jerusalem 2010 Intl. Philatelic Exhibition (No. 1844). No. 1844 contains one 30x40mm stamp.

A854, A855, A856, A857, A858, A859, A860, A861, A862, A863, A864, A865, A866, A867

Animation A868

2010, Nov. 21   **Litho.**   **Perf. 13x13¼**
1845		Sheet of 15	12.00	12.00
a.	A854	1.70s multi	.80	.80
b.	A855	1.70s multi	.80	.80
c.	A856	1.70s multi	.80	.80
d.	A857	1.70s multi	.80	.80
e.	A858	1.70s multi	.80	.80
f.	A859	1.70s multi	.80	.80
g.	A860	1.70s multi	.80	.80
h.	A861	1.70s multi	.80	.80
i.	A862	1.70s multi	.80	.80
j.	A863	1.70s multi	.80	.80
k.	A864	1.70s multi	.80	.80
l.	A865	1.70s multi	.80	.80
m.	A866	1.70s multi	.80	.80
n.	A867	1.70s multi	.80	.80
o.	A868	1.70s multi	.80	.80

Booklet Panes of 1
Self-Adhesive
Serpentine Die Cut 6¼
1846	A854	1.70s multi	.80	.80
1847	A855	1.70s multi	.80	.80
1848	A856	1.70s multi	.80	.80
1849	A857	1.70s multi	.80	.80
1850	A858	1.70s multi	.80	.80
1851	A859	1.70s multi	.80	.80
1852	A860	1.70s multi	.80	.80
1853	A861	1.70s multi	.80	.80
1854	A862	1.70s multi	.80	.80
1855	A863	1.70s multi	.80	.80
1856	A864	1.70s multi	.80	.80
1857	A865	1.70s multi	.80	.80
1858	A866	1.70s multi	.80	.80
1859	A867	1.70s multi	.80	.80
1860	A868	1.70s multi	.80	.80
		Complete booklet, #1846-1860	12.00	
		Nos. 1846-1860 (15)	12.00	12.00

Types of 1995-2010 Redrawn or In Different Sizes
2010, Nov. 21   **Litho.**   **Perf. 13½x13**
Booklet Stamps
1861	A589	1.15s Like #1326, 30x40mm (1863a)	.75	.75

Perf. 13x13½
1862	A545	1.50s Like #1246, 40x30mm (1866a)	1.00	1.00
1863	A545	1.80s Like #1247, 40x30mm (1863a)	1.25	1.25
a.		Booklet pane of 2, #1861, 1863	2.00	—
1864	A603	2.20s Like #1345, 40x30mm (1867a)	1.50	1.50

Perf. 13½
1865	A726	3.30s Like #1600, redrawn, 30x40mm (1866a)	2.25	2.25

Perf. 13½x13¼
1866	A634	3.40s Like #1407, redrawn, 30x30mm (1866a)	2.25	2.25
a.		Booklet pane of 4, #1610a, 1862, 1865, 1866	9.75	—

Perf. 13½
1867	A564	4.65s Like #1287, 30x40mm (1867a)	3.25	3.25
a.		Booklet pane of 2, #1864, 1867	4.75	
		Complete booklet, #1827a, 1830a, 1863a, 1866a, 1867a	30.00	
		Nos. 1861-1867 (7)	12.25	12.25

Complete booklet sold for 49s.

Intl. Year of Chemistry A869

Chemical models of: 4.20s, Ubiquitin, protein destroyer. 6.10s, Ribosome, protein constructor.

2011, Jan. 4   **Litho.**   **Perf. 14x13½**
1868	A869	4.20s multi	2.00	2.00
1869	A869	6.10s multi	3.00	3.00
		With tabs	5.50	

Roots of the Hebrew Language — A870

2011, Feb. 7   **Perf. 13½x14**
1870	A870	3.70s multi	1.75	1.75
		With tab	2.00	

Clalit Health Services, Cent. — A871

2011, Feb. 7   **Perf. 14x13½**
1871	A871	9s multi	4.25	4.25
		With tab	4.75	

Building Projects of King Herod — A872

2011, Feb. 7   **Perf. 13½x14**
1872	A872	1.70s Masada	.80	.80
1873	A872	1.70s Caesarea	.80	.80
1874	A872	2.50s Jerusalem	1.20	1.20
1875	A872	2.50s Herodian	1.20	1.20
		Nos. 1872-1875 (4)	4.00	4.00
		With tabs	4.50	

ISRAEL

Worldwide Fund for Nature (WWF) — A873

No. 1876 — Panthera pardus saxicolor: a, Leaping. b, Standing on hill with rams. c, Drinking. d, With cub.

2011, Feb. 7		Perf. 14x13½
1876	A873 Block of 4	3.25 3.25
a.-d.	1.70s Any single	.80 .80
	Nos. 1876a-1876d, with tabs	3.75

Flag of Israel Type of 2010
Serpentine Die Cut 13x14¼

2011, Apr. 12	Booklet Stamp Self-Adhesive	
1877	A851 (1.70s) multi	1.10 1.10
a.	Booklet pane of 20	22.00

Memorial Day — A874

2011, Apr. 12		Perf. 13½x13
1878	A874 1.70s multi	1.00 1.00
	With tab	1.10

Aliyah of Ethiopian Jews — A875

2011, Apr. 12		Perf. 14¼
1879	A875 2.50s multi	1.50 1.50
	With tab	1.75

Mount Carmel Training Center, 50th Anniv. — A876

2011, Apr. 12		Perf. 13x13½
1880	A876 5s multi	2.50 2.50
	With tab	3.00

Pres. Ephraim Katzir (1916-2009) A877

2011, Apr. 12		Perf. 13x13½
1881	A877 9s multi	4.75 4.75
	With tab	5.25

Tourism — A878

Designs: 4.20s, Sea of Galilee. 6s, Tower of David and Old City Wall, Jerusalem. 6.10s, Red Sea clownfish near Eilat.

2011, Apr. 12		Perf. 14x13½
1882	A878 4.20s multi	2.25 2.25
1883	A878 6s multi	3.25 3.25
1884	A878 6.10s multi	3.50 3.50
	Nos. 1882-1884 (3)	9.00 9.00
	With tabs	10.00

Miniature Sheet

Butterflies — A879

Designs: Nos. 1885a, 1888, Anaphaeis aurota. Nos. 1885b, 1887, Vanessa atalanta. Nos. 1885c, 1886, Papilio machaon syracus. Nos. 1885d, 1889, Apharitis acamas. Nos. 1885e, 1890, Danaus chrysippus. Nos. 1885f, 1891, Polyommatus icarus zelleri.

2011		Perf. 13¾x14
1885	A879 Sheet of 6	5.50 5.50
a.-f.	(1.70s) Any single	.90 .90

Booklet Stamps Self-Adhesive
Serpentine Die Cut 13x14¼

1886	A879 (1.70s) multi	1.00 1.00
1887	A879 (1.70s) multi	1.00 1.00
1888	A879 (1.70s) multi	1.00 1.00
1889	A879 (1.70s) multi	1.00 1.00
1890	A879 (1.70s) multi	1.00 1.00
1891	A879 (1.70s) multi	1.00 1.00
a.	Booklet pane of 20, 4 each #1886-1889, 2 each #1890-1891	20.00
	Nos. 1886-1891 (6)	6.00 6.00

Issued: No. 1885, 4/12; Nos. 1886-1891, 6/27.

Rabbi Shlomo Goren (1917-94), Chief Rabbi of Israel — A880

2011, June 27		Perf. 13x13½
1892	A880 1.70s multi	.90 .90
	With tab	1.00

Doctor in Clown Costume Treating Child — A881

2011, June 27		Litho.
1893	A881 9s multi	4.75 4.75
	With tab	5.25

Israeli Agricultural Achievements A882

Designs: No. 1894, Medjool date trees nourished by saline water in pots. No. 1895, Tomatoes growing in hothouse. No. 1896, Water purification pool, Dan Region Wastewater Treatment Facility.

2011, June 27		
1894	A882 2.50s multi	1.35 1.35
1895	A882 2.50s multi	1.35 1.35
1896	A882 2.50s multi	1.35 1.35
	Nos. 1894-1896 (3)	4.05 4.05
	With tabs	4.25

Miniature Sheet

Beaches A883

No. 1897: a, Sea of Galilee Beach, hot air balloons. b, Sea of Galilee Beach, no balloons. c, Caesarea Beach, no kites. d, Caesarea Beach, kites. e, Tel Aviv Beach, sailboats. f, Tel Aviv Beach, jetty. g, Dead Sea Beach, no airplane. h, Dead Sea Beach, airplane. i, Eilat Beach, speedboats. j, Eilat Beach, no speedboats.

2011, June 27		Perf. 14x13½
1897	A883 Sheet of 10	10.00 10.00
a.-j.	1.70s Any single	1.00 1.00

Admission of Israel to Organization for Economic Cooperation and Development A884

2011, Sept. 13		
1898	A884 9.30s multi	5.00 5.00
	With tab	5.50

Items at Rosh Hashanah Feast — A885

Designs: 1.70s, Apples and honey. 4s, Fish head. 5.90s, Pomegranates.

2011, Sept. 13		
1899	A885 1.70s multi	.80 .80
1900	A885 4s multi	1.90 1.90
1901	A885 5.90s multi	2.75 2.75
	Nos. 1899-1901 (3)	5.45 5.45
	With tabs	6.25

Children's Games — A886

Designs: Nos. 1902, 1905, Hopscotch. Nos. 1903, 1906, Hide and seek. Nos. 1904, 1907, Tag.

2011, Sept. 13		Perf. 14x13½
1902	A886 2.60s multi	1.40 1.40
1903	A886 2.60s multi	1.40 1.40
1904	A886 2.60s multi	1.40 1.40
	Nos. 1902-1904 (3)	4.20 4.20
	With tabs	4.75

Booklet Stamps Self-Adhesive
Serpentine Die Cut 12½

1905	A886 2.60s multi	1.40 1.40
1906	A886 2.60s multi	1.40 1.40
1907	A886 2.60s multi	1.40 1.40
a.	Booklet pane of 6, 2 each #1905-1907	8.50
	Nos. 1905-1907 (3)	4.20 4.20

Miniature Sheet

Israeli Record Albums A887

No. 1908: a, *Why Should I Take it to Heart*, by Arik Einstein and Shalom Hanoch, 1979. b, *Ways*, by Shlomo Artzi, 1979. c, *Barcelona*, by Israel Andalusian Orchestra and Jo Amar, 2000. d, *Poogy Tales*, by Kaveret, 1973. e, *To the Candle and the Spices*, by Lehakat Tsliley Ha'Ud, 1975. f, *HaKeves HaShisha Asar*, by HaKeves Ha Shisha Asar (tree in field with white calf), 1978. g, *Antarctica*, by Corinne Allal, 1989. h, *Ashes and Dust*, by Yehuda Poliker (boy watching train pass), 1988. i, *Continuing to Ride*, by Ehud Banai and the Refugees (abstract head), 1987. j, *The Middle of the Road*, by Yehoram Gaon, 1984. k, *The Flute*, by the Doodaim, 1959. l, *Out of the Depths*, by The Idan Raichel Project (woman sitting by door), 2005.

2011, Sept. 13		Perf. 13¼x14
1908	A887 Sheet of 12 + 4 central labels	11.50 11.50
a.-l.	1.70s Any single	.95 .95

Valley Railroad — A888

2011, Dec. 6		Perf. 14x13¼
1909	A888 2.60s multi	1.10 1.10
	With tab	1.30

Tribute to Rescue Forces — A889

2011, Dec. 6		Perf. 13¼x14
1910	A889 3.80s red & yel grn	1.75 1.75
	With tab	2.00

Israel Philharmonic Orchestra, 75th Anniv. — A890

2011, Dec. 6		
1911	A890 4s multi	1.75 1.75
	With tab	2.10

Miniature Sheet

Israeli Soccer Legends A891

No. 1912: a, Avi Cohen (1956-2010). b, Menachem Ashkenazi (1934-2000). c, Nahum Stelmach (1936-99). d, Jerry Beit Halevi (1912-97). e, Eli Fuchs (1924-92). f, Shmuel Ben-Dror (1924-2009). g, Natan Panz (1917-48). h, Ya'akov Grundman (1939-2004). i, Avi Ran (1963-87). j, Ya'akov Hodorov (1927-2006). English translations of names are on tabs adjacent to stamps.

ISRAEL

2011, Dec. 6   Perf. 14x13¼
1912 A891 Sheet of 10   8.50 8.50
a.-j. 1.70s Any single   .85 .85

Memorial Candle — A892

2012, Feb. 7   Perf. 13¾
1913 A892 (1.70s) multi   .90 .90
     With tab   1.00
a.   Sheet of 12 + 12 labels   15.00 15.00

No. 1913a sold for 28s. Labels could be personalized.

Rabbi Shneur Zalman of Lidai (1745-1812), Founder of Chabad Hasidism — A893

2012, Feb. 7   Perf. 13x13¼
1914 A893 1.70s multi   .90 .90
     With tab   1.00

Technion (Israel Institute of Technology), Cent. — A894

2012, Feb. 7
1915 A894 2.60s multi   1.40 1.40
     With tab   1.60

Trial, Sentencing and Execution of Nazi War Criminal Adolf Eichmann, 50th Anniv. — A895

2012, Feb. 7   Perf. 13¼x13
1916 A895 9.30s multi   5.00 5.00
     With tab   5.50

Famous Women — A896

Designs: 4s, Bracha Zefira (1910-90), singer. 5.90s, Batia Makov (1841-1912), business entrepreneur.

2012, Feb. 7   Perf. 13x13¼
1917 A896 4s multi   1.90 1.90
1918 A896 5.90s multi   3.00 3.00
     With tab   5.50

Gemstones From High Priest's Breastplate A897

Gemstones and inscribed tribe: No. 1919, Carnelian, Reuven. No. 1920, Topaz, Shimon. No. 1921, Emerald, Levi. No. 1922, Turquoise, Yehuda.

2012, Feb. 7   Litho.   Perf. 13x13¼
1919 A897 2.60s multi   1.30 1.30
1920 A897 2.60s multi   1.30 1.30
1921 A897 2.60s multi   1.30 1.30
1922 A897 2.60s multi   1.30 1.30
     Nos. 1919-1922 (4)   5.20 5.20
     With tabs   5.75

See Nos. 1925-1928, 1935-1938.

Diplomatic Relations Between Israel and People's Republic of China, 20th Anniv. — A898

Designs: 2s, Waxwing, five-pointed star. 3s, White dove, Star of David.

2012, Mar. 20   Litho.   Perf. 13¼x14
1923 A898 2s multi   1.10 1.10
1924 A898 3s multi   1.60 1.60
     With tabs   3.00

See People's Republic of China Nos. 3986-3987.

Gemstones From High Priest's Breastplate Type of 2012

Gemstones and inscribed tribe: No. 1925, Lazurite, Issachar. No. 1926, Quartz, Zevulun. No. 1927, Zircon, Dan. No. 1928, Amethyst, Naftali.

2012, Apr. 17   Perf. 14x13¼
1925 A897 3s multi   1.40 1.40
1926 A897 3s multi   1.40 1.40
1927 A897 3s multi   1.40 1.40
1928 A897 3s multi   1.40 1.40
     Nos. 1925-1928 (4)   5.60 5.60
     With tabs   6.25

Memorial Day — A899

2012, Apr. 17
1929 A899 1.70s multi   .95 .95
     With tab   1.10

Chain of Generations Center, Western Wall Plaza, Jerusalem — A900

2012, Apr. 17   Perf. 13¼x14
1930 A900 9.30s multi   5.00 5.00
     With tab   5.50

Jewish Seamanship A901

Designs: No. 1931, Hehalutz in Jaffa Harbor, 1919. No. 1932, Sara A in Haifa Harbor, 1935, and Jeremiah Helpern. No. 1933, Har Zion in Tel-Aviv Harbor, 1935, and Captain Erich Hirschfeld.

2012, Apr. 17   Perf. 14x13¼
1931 A901 3s multi   1.60 1.60
1932 A901 3s multi   1.60 1.60
1933 A901 3s multi   1.60 1.60
     Nos. 1931-1933 (3)   4.80 4.80
     With tabs   5.25

Nos. 1931-1933 exist imperf. Value, set with tabs, $50.

Miniature Sheet

Children's Books — A902

No. 1934 — Books and illustrations: a, A Tale of Five Balloons, by Miriam Roth (girl holding blue balloon). b, Raspberry Juice, by Haya Shenhav (lion and giraffe). c, Caspion the Little Fish, by Paul Kor (fish). d, The Absent-minded Guy from Kefar Azar, by Leah Goldberg (man with glasses holding umbrellas). e, Itamar Walks on Walls, by David Grossman (Itamar walking on wall). f, Hot Sweet Corn, by Miriam Roth (five children eating corn on the cob). g, The Lion that Loved Strawberries, by Tirtza Atar (lion and strawberries). h, Come to Me, Nice Butterfly, by Fania Bergstein (child reaching for butterfly in fenced garden).

2012, Apr. 17
1934 A902 Sheet of 8   9.00 9.00
a.-h. 2s Any single   1.10 1.10

Gemstones From High Preist's Breasplate Type of 2012

Gemstone and inscribed tribe: No. 1935, Agate, Gad. No. 1936, Aquamarine, Asher. No. 1937, Onyx, Yosef. No. 1938, Jasper, Binyamin.

2012, June 26   Perf. 13x13¼
1935 A897 3s multi   1.60 1.60
1936 A897 3s multi   1.60 1.60
1937 A897 3s multi   1.60 1.60
1938 A897 3s multi   1.60 1.60
     Nos. 1935-1938 (4)   6.40 6.40
     With tabs   7.25

Teddy Kollek (1911-2007), Mayor of Jerusalem — A903

2012, June 26   Perf. 13¼x13
1939 A903 9.40s multi   5.25 5.25
     With tab   5.75

2012 Summer Olympics, London — A904

London landmarks, 2012 Olympic Games emblem and: No. 1940, High jump. No. 1941, Artistic gymnastics. 4.50s, Taekwondo.

2012, June 26   Perf. 13¼x13
1940 A904 2s multi   1.05 1.05
1941 A904 2s multi   1.05 1.05
1942 A904 4.50s multi   2.50 2.50
     Nos. 1940-1942 (3)   4.60 4.60
     With tabs   5.25

Israeli Membership in Intl. Police Association, 50th Anniv. — A905

2012, Sept. 4
1943 A905 4.20s multi   2.00 2.00
     With tab   2.25

Dead Sea, Mt. Everest, Flags of Israel and Nepal — A906

2012, Sept. 4   Perf. 13¼x13
1944 A906 5s multi   2.60 2.60
     With tab   3.00

See Nepal Nos. 874-875.

Hadassah (Women's Zionist Organization of America), Cent. — A907

2012, Sept. 4
1945 A907 6.20s multi   3.00 3.00
     With tab   3.50

Contribution of Senior Citizens — A908

2012, Sept. 4   Perf. 13x13¼
1946 A908 9.40s multi   4.25 4.25
     With tab   4.75

Worshipers Casting Away Sins at Water's Edge on Rosh Hashanah A909

Synagogue Members Reciting Kol Nidrei Prayer on Yom Kippur — A910

Worshipers Holding Palm Fronds on Succoth — A911

2012, Sept. 4
1947 A909 2s multi   .90 .90
1948 A910 4.20s multi   2.00 2.00
1949 A911 6.20s multi   3.00 3.00
     Nos. 1947-1949 (3)   5.90 5.90
     With tabs   6.50

Tourist Attractions A912

Designs: Nos. 1950, 1953, Grotto, Rosh Hanikra. Nos. 1951, 1954, Jaffa. Nos. 1952, 1955, Solomon's Pillars, Timna Park.

2012, Sept. 4   Perf. 13x13¼
1950 A912 3s multi   1.50 1.50
1951 A912 3s multi   1.50 1.50
1952 A912 3s multi   1.50 1.50
     Nos. 1950-1952 (3)   4.50 4.50
     With tabs   5.00

Nos. 1950-1953 exist imperf. Value, set with tabs $32.50.

A booklet with a pane of 3, Nos. 1837, 1736 and 1883, a pane of 3, Nos. 1735, 1950 and 1882, a pane of 3, Nos. 1951, 1737 and 1897e, and a pane of 3, Nos. 1884, 1897h and 1952. Value, $30.

Booklet Stamps
Self-Adhesive
Serpentine Die Cut 12½

1953 A912 3s multi   1.75 1.75
1954 A912 3s multi   1.75 1.75
1955 A912 3s multi   1.75 1.75
a.   Booklet pane of 6, 2 each #1953-1955   10.50
     Nos. 1953-1955 (3)   5.25 5.25

Deepavali, Hindu Festival of Lights — A913

Hanukkah, Jewish Festival of Lights — A914

2012, Nov. 5   Perf. 13x13¼
1956 A913 2s multi   1.10 1.10
1957 A914 2s multi   1.10 1.10
     With tabs   2.50

See India Nos. 2602-2603.

ISRAEL

Offshore Gas Drilling Platform — A915

2012, Dec. 12
| 1958 | A915 | 4.20s multi | | 2.25 | 2.25 |
| | | With tab | | | 2.50 |

Philately Day.

Koren Jerusalem Bible, 50th Anniv. — A916

2012, Dec. 12 — Perf. 13¼x13
| 1959 | A916 | 9.50s multi | 4.25 | 4.25 |
| | | With tab | | 4.75 |

Wildlife Conservation A917

No. 1960 — Hands, bandage and: a, Mediterranean spur-thighed tortoise. b, Mountain gazelle fawn. c, Imperial eagle.

2012, Dec. 12 — Perf. 13x13¼
1960		Horiz. strip of 3	4.50	4.50
a.-c.	A917	3s Any single	1.45	1.45
		Strip with tabs		5.00

No. 1960 was printed in sheets containing two strips of three stamps.

Souvenir Sheet

High Priest Wearing Breastplate — A918

2012, Dec. 12 — Perf. 13¼x13
| 1961 | A918 | 5s multi | 3.50 | 3.50 |

Tel Aviv 2013 Intl. Stamp Exhibition. No. 1961 sold for 7s.

Arad, 50th Anniv. — A919

2013, Feb. 5 — Perf. 13x13¼
| 1962 | A919 | 2s multi | 1.30 | 1.30 |
| | | With tab | | 1.50 |

Water, The Source of Life — A920

2013, Feb. 5 — Perf. 14½
| 1963 | A920 | 3s multi | 1.90 | 1.90 |
| | | With tab | | 2.10 |

Hebrew Reali School, Haifa, Cent. — A921

2013, Feb. 5 — Perf. 13x13¼
| 1964 | A921 | 4.20s multi | 2.40 | 2.40 |
| | | With tab | | 2.60 |

Israel Customs Directorate — A922

2013, Feb. 5 — Perf. 13¼x13
| 1965 | A922 | 9.50s multi | 5.25 | 5.25 |
| | | With tab | | 5.75 |

Gerbera Daisy — A923

No. 1966 — Color of flower: a, Pink. b, Orange and yellow. c, White. d, Yellow. e, Red and white.

2013, Feb. 5 — Perf. 13¾
1966		Horiz. strip of 5	1.60	1.60
a.	A923	20a multi	.25	.25
b.	A923	30a multi	.25	.25
c.	A923	40a multi	.25	.25
d.	A923	50a multi	.30	.30
e.	A923	1s multi	.55	.55
		Strip with tabs		1.75

No. 1966 was printed in sheets containing two tete-beche strips of 5 stamps. See Nos. 2001-2001 A.

Gerbera Daisy Type of 2013
Serpentine Die Cut 13¼x13¾

2013-14 — Self-Adhesive — Typo.
1966F	A923	20a Like #1966a	.30	.30
1966G	A923	30a Like #1966b	.30	.30
1966H	A923	40a Like #1966c	.30	.30
1966I	A923	50a Like #1966d	.30	.30
1966J	A923	1s Like #1966e	.55	.55
		Nos. 1966F-1966J (5)	1.75	1.75

Issued: No. 1966F, 3/11; No. 1966G, 1/5/14; No. 1966H, 10/13; No. 1966I, 5/1; No. 1966J, 3/3.

Memorial Day — A924

2013, Apr. 2 — Litho. — Perf. 13¼x13
| 1967 | A924 | 2s multi | 1.10 | 1.10 |
| | | With tab | | 1.25 |

Pawel Frenkel (1920-43), Commander of Jewish Military Organization in Warsaw Ghetto — A925

2013, Apr. 2 — Perf. 13x13¼
| 1968 | A925 | 9.50s multi | 5.25 | 5.25 |
| | | With tab | | 5.75 |

Warsaw Ghetto Uprising, 70th anniv.

Vultures — A926

Designs: No. 1969, Torgos tracheliotus negevensis, Neophron percnopterus. No. 1970, Gypaetus barbatus. No. 1971, Gyps fulvus.

2013, Apr. 2 — Litho.
1969	A926	3s multi	1.75	1.75
1970	A926	3s multi	1.75	1.75
1971	A926	3s multi	1.75	1.75
		Nos. 1969-1971 (3)	5.25	5.25
		With tab		5.75

Nos. 1969-1971 exist imperf. Value, set with tabs $40.

Israeli Cardiological Achievements A927

Designs: 3s, Percutaneous heart valve. 4.20s, Stent. 5s, Implantable defibrillator.

2013, Apr. 2
1972	A927	3s multi	1.75	1.75
1973	A927	4.20s multi	2.40	2.40
1974	A927	5s multi	2.75	2.75
		Nos. 1972-1974 (3)	6.90	6.90
		With tabs		7.75

Battle of Beersheba, 96th Anniv. — A928

Designs: 2s, Statue of Australian Light Horseman, by Peter Corlett, Beersheva, Israel. 6.10s, Australian Light Horsemen, photograph of battle re-enactment.

2013, May 10 — Perf. 13x13¼
1975	A928	2s multi	1.00	1.00
1976	A928	6.10s multi	3.00	3.00
		With tabs		4.50

See Australia Nos. 3914-3915.

19th Maccabiah Games — A929

2013, May 26 — Perf. 14x13¼
| 1977 | A929 | 3s multi | 1.60 | 1.60 |
| | | With tab | | 1.75 |

Hashomer Hatzair Movement, Cent. — A930

2013, May 26 — Perf. 13¼x14
| 1978 | A930 | 3s multi | 1.60 | 1.60 |
| | | With tab | | 1.75 |

Yitzhak Shamir (1915-2012), Prime Minister — A931

2013, May 26
| 1979 | A931 | 9.50s multi | 5.25 | 5.25 |
| | | With tab | | 5.75 |

Souvenir Sheet

Postal Vehicles A932

No. 1980: a, Austrian Post horse-drawn mail carriage, Jaffa Gate, Jerusalem. b, Mail train, clerk sorting mail in train car. c, Mail van, airplane.

2013, May 26 — Perf. 14x13¼
1980	A932	Sheet of 3	8.50	8.50
a.		2s multi	1.75	1.75
b.		3s multi	2.50	2.50
c.		5s multi	4.25	4.25

Tel Aviv 2013 Intl. Stamp Exhibition. No. 1980 sold for 15s.
No. 1980 exists imperf. Value, $37.50.

Miniature Sheet

National Trail A933

No. 1981: a, Sun, hang glider, bird, hiker with backpack. b, Hiker looking at antelope, arch, hiker and statue, mountains, swimmer with pool toy. c, Kite flyer, windsurfer, guide, children, Antipatris Fortress. d, Picnickers, hiker and child, John F. Kennedy Memorial, people on ski lift, man under umbrella. e, Hikers at archaeological site, man in dune buggy. f, Woman climbing rocks, hiker at Beit Guvrin Cave, woman reading newspaper in Dead Sea, campers at campfire. g, Hiker near Solomon's Pillars and Mushroom rock formation, woman in small boat. h, Ostrich, ladder, hiker in tree looking at gazelle. i, Bicycle, dolphin, Underwater Observatory, Eilat, hiker looking at picture of mushroom. j, Tourists in automobile, hiker resting under palm tree.

2013, May 26
| 1981 | A933 | Sheet of 10 | 11.00 | 11.00 |
| a.-j. | | 2s Any single | 1.10 | 1.10 |

Betar (Zionist Youth Movement), 90th Anniv. — A934

2013, Aug. 26 — Litho. — Perf. 14x13½
| 1982 | A934 | 3.10s multi | 1.75 | 1.75 |
| | | With tab | | 1.90 |

Israel Military Industries, 80th Anniv. — A935

2013, Aug. 26 — Litho. — Perf. 14x13½
| 1983 | A935 | 9.60s multi | 5.50 | 5.50 |
| | | With tab | | 6.00 |

Etrog Boxes — A936

Etrog box made in: 2s, Jerusalem, 20th cent. 3.90s, Austria, 19th cent. 5.70s, Iraq, 19th cent.

2013, Aug. 26 — Litho. — Perf. 14x13½
1984	A936	2s multi	1.15	1.15
1985	A936	3.90s multi	2.40	2.40
1986	A936	5.70s multi	3.50	3.50
		Nos. 1984-1986 (3)	7.05	7.05
		With tabs		7.75

ISRAEL

Souvenir Sheet

Dorcas Gazelles — A937

2013, Aug. 26   Litho.   *Perf. 14x13½*
1987   A937   7s multi   4.50   4.50
See Greenland No. 646.

Miniature Sheet

Children's Songs — A938

No. 1988: a, A Brave Clock (Clock with eyes and mouth, child with clock's head). b, What Do the Does Do? (doe, elephants and balls). c, I Wanted You to Know (angel, girl in pajamas holding pillow). d, Buba Zehava (doll and teddy bear). e, I Am Always Me (boys with beach balls). f, Why Does the Zebra Wear Pajamas? (zebra wearing cap, pajamas on clothesline). g, Merry Choir (singing birds). h, The Prettiest Girl in Kindergarten (girl and block towers). i, Brave Danny (crying boy, boy and girl holding hands). j, Horse Rider (horse). k, My Dad (boy on father's shoulders, ladder and house). l, The Post Van (Post van with canceled cover).

Perf. 13¼x14, 14x13¼
2013, Aug. 26   Litho.
1988   A938   Sheet of 12 + 4 central labels   14.50   14.50
a.-l.   2s Any single   1.20   1.20

The Annunciation of Sarah, Painting by José Gurvich — A939

2013, Oct. 28   Litho.   *Perf. 13x13¼*
1989   A939   2s multi   1.25   1.25
With tab   1.40
Diplomatic relations between Israel and Uruguay, 65th anniv. See Uruguay No. 2445.

Rachel's Tomb, Gilo — A940

2013, Oct. 28   Litho.   *Perf. 13¼x13*
1990   A940   5s multi   3.00   3.00
With tab   3.25

Haifa Holiday of Holidays Festival, 20th Anniv. — A941

2013, Dec. 3   Litho.   *Perf. 13¼x13*
1991   A941   3.10s multi   1.90   1.90
With tab   2.10

Israeli Opera Production at Masada Opera Festival, and Giuseppe Verdi (1813-1901), Composer — A942

2013, Dec. 3   Litho.   *Perf. 13x13¼*
1992   A942   3.90s multi   2.50   2.50
With tab   2.75

Quasi-periodic Crystals of Aluminum-Managanese Alloy — A943

2013, Dec. 3   Litho.   *Perf. 13x13¼*
1993   A943   10s multi   5.75   5.75
With tab   6.50
Intl. Year of Crystallography, Philately Day.

Aviation in Israel, Cent. — A944

Designs: Nos. 1994, 1997, Bleriot XI, 1913 (first plane in Israel). Nos. 1995, 1998, Fouga Magister Air Force training plane, 1960. Nos. 1996, 1999, Heron I drone, 1994.

2013, Dec. 3   Litho.   *Perf. 13x13¼*
1994   A944   3.10s multi   1.90   1.90
1995   A944   3.10s multi   1.90   1.90
1996   A944   3.10s multi   1.90   1.90
  Nos. 1994-1996 (3)   5.70   5.70
  With tabs   6.25
Nos. 1994-1996 exist imperf. Value, set with tabs $42.50.

Booklet Stamps
Self-Adhesive
Die Cut Perf. 12½
1997   A944   3.10s multi   1.90   1.90
1998   A944   3.10s multi   1.90   1.90
1999   A944   3.10s multi   1.90   1.90
a.   Booklet pane of 6. 2 each #1997-1999   11.50   11.50
  Nos. 1997-1999 (3)   5.70   5.70

Halls of the Knights Hospitallers, Acre, Israel and Valletta, Malta — A945

2014, Jan. 28   Litho.   *Perf. 13x13½*
2000   A945   3.90s multi   2.50   2.50
With tab   2.75
See Malta No. 1506.

Gerbera Daisy Type of 2013

10a, Red Gerbera daisy.

2014   Litho.   *Perf. 13¾*
2001   A923   10a multicolored   .50   .50
With tab   .75

Typo.
Serpentine Die Cut 13¼x13¾
Self-Adhesive
2001A   A923   10a Like #2001   .30   .30
Issued: No. 2001, 2/11; No. 2001A, Aug.

Resistance Radio Broadcasts, 75th Anniv. — A946

2014, Feb. 11   Litho.   *Perf. 13½x13*
2002   A946   9.60s multi   5.50   5.50
With tab   6.00

Ancient Erosion Craters — A947

Designs: No. 2003, Makhtesh Gadol, vehicle caravan. No. 2004, Makhtesh Katan, bicyclists. No. 2005, Makhtesh Ramon, rock climber.

2014, Feb. 11   Litho.   *Perf. 13x13½*
2003   A947   3.10s multi   1.75   1.75
2004   A947   3.10s multi   1.75   1.75
2005   A947   3.10s multi   1.75   1.75
  Nos. 2003-2005 (3)   5.25   5.25
  With tabs   5.75
Nos. 2003-2005 exist imperf. Value, set with tabs $37.50.

Landmarks — A948

No. 2006: a, Independence Hall, Tel Aviv. b, Detention Camp, Atlit. c, Synagogue, Peki'in. d, Ein Keshatot, Golan. e, City of David, Jerusalem.

2014, Feb. 11   Litho.   *Perf. 13x13½*
2006   Horiz. strip of 5   6.25   6.25
a.-e.   A948 2s Any single   1.25   1.25
  Strip with tabs   7.00

Wedding Rings — A949

2014, Apr. 8   Litho.   *Perf. 14*
2007   A949   (2s) multi   1.35   1.35
With tab   1.50

Memorial Day — A950

2014, Apr. 8   Litho.   *Perf. 14x13½*
2008   A950   2s multi   1.35   1.35
With tab   1.50

Mateh Yehuda Regional Council, 50th Anniv. — A951

2014, Apr. 8   Litho.   *Perf. 14x13½*
2009   A951   3.10s multi   1.90   1.90
With tab   2.10

Violin and Auschwitz Concentration Camp — A952

2014, Apr. 8   Litho.   *Perf. 13½x14*
2010   A952   9.60s multi   5.25   5.25
With tab   5.75
Violins that survived the Holocaust.

Non-Olympic Sports — A953

Designs: 3.90s, Water skiing. 5s, Wushu. 5.70s, Paragliding.

2014, Apr. 8   Litho.   *Perf. 13½x14*
2011   A953   3.90s multi   1.75   1.75
2012   A953   5s multi   2.75   2.75
2013   A953   5.70s multi   3.00   3.00
  Nos. 2011-2013 (3)   7.50   7.50
  With tabs   8.00

Israeli Sign Language — A954

Signs for: Nos. 2014a, 2015, Thanks. Nos. 2014b, 2016, Kiss. Nos. 2014c, 2017, Friendship. Nos. 2014d, 2018, Love. Nos. 2014e, 2019, Goodbye.

2014, Apr. 8   Litho.   *Perf. 14*
2014   Horiz. strip of 5   5.75   5.75
a.-e.   A954 (2s) Any single   1.15   1.15
  Strip with tabs   6.50

Booklet Stamps
Self-Adhesive
Serpentine Die Cut 13½x14¼
2015   A954   (2s) multi   1.25   1.25
2016   A954   (2s) multi   1.25   1.25
2017   A954   (2s) multi   1.25   1.25
2018   A954   (2s) multi   1.25   1.25
2019   A954   (2s) multi   1.25   1.25
a.   Booklet pane of 20, 4 each #2015-2019   25.00
  Nos. 2015-2019 (5)   6.25   6.25
No. 2014 was printed in sheets containing two tete-beche strips.

Pomegranates, Mangosteens, Flags of Israel and Thailand — A955

2014, June 5   Litho.   *Perf. 14x13½*
2020   A955   3.10s multi   1.90   1.90
With tab   2.10
Diplomatic relations between Israel and Thailand, 60th anniv. See Thailand No. 2811.

Palmer Gate Street, Haifa — A956

2014, June 23   Litho.   *Perf. 14x13½*
2021   A956   9.60s multi   5.50   5.50
With tab   6.00

Famous Women — A957

Designs: 6s, Sara Levi-Tanai (1910-2005), choreographer. 10s, Esther Raab (1894-1981), poet.

2014, June 23   Litho.   *Perf. 14x13½*
2022   A957   6s multi   3.50   3.50
2023   A957   10s multi   6.00   6.00
  With tabs   10.50

Amphibians — A958

No. 2024: a, Pelobates syriacus. b, Salamandra infraimmaculata. c, Ommatotriton vittatus. d, Latonia nigriventer.

2014, June 23   Litho.   *Perf. 14xx13½*
2024   A958   Block of 4   5.00   5.00
a.-d.   2s Any single   1.25   1.25
  Nos. 2024a-2024b pair with tabs   2.75
  Nos. 2024c-2024d pair with tabs   2.75

ISRAEL

Global City of Tel Aviv — A959

2014, Sept. 9   Litho.   *Perf. 13x13½*
2025   A959   4.50s   multi   2.50   2.50
    With tab   2.75

Wolfgang von Weisl (1896-1974), Journalist and Zionist Leader — A960

2014, Sept. 9   Litho.   *Perf. 13x13½*
2026   A960   9.70s   multi   5.50   5.50
    With tab   6.00

Simchat Torah Flags — A961

Flag from: 2s, 1930s. 3.80s, 1950s. 5.60s, 1960s.

2014, Sept. 9   Litho.   *Perf. 13x13½*
2027   A961   2s   multi   1.05   1.05
2028   A961   3.80s   multi   1.90   1.90
2029   A961   5.60s   multi   3.00   3.00
    Nos. 2027-2029 (3)   5.95   5.95
    With tabs   6.75

Broadway Premiere of *Fiddler on the Roof*, 50th Anniv. — A962

Inscriptions: Nos. 2030, 2033, Fiddler on the Roof. Nos. 2031, 2034, Tevye the Dairyman. Nos. 2032, 2035, Do you love me?

2014, Sept. 9   Litho.   *Perf. 13x13½*
2030   A962   3.10s   multi   1.75   1.75
2031   A962   3.10s   multi   1.75   1.75
2032   A962   3.10s   multi   1.75   1.75
    Nos. 2030-2032 (3)   5.25   5.25
    With tabs   5.75

Nos. 2030-2032 exist imperf. Value, set with tabs $40.

Booklet Stamps
Self-Adhesive
Serpentine Die Cut 12½x12¼
2033   A962   3.10s   multi   1.90   1.90
2034   A962   3.10s   multi   1.90   1.90
2035   A962   3.10s   multi   1.90   1.90
    a.   Booklet pane of 6, 2 each #2033-2035   11.50
    Nos. 2033-2035 (3)   5.70   5.70

Ovadia Yosef (1920-2013), Chief Rabbi of Tel Aviv-Jaffa — A963

2014, Sept. 28   Litho.   *Perf. 13¼*
2036   A963   2s   multi   1.10   1.10
    With tab   1.25

Arik Einstein (1939-2013), Singer — A964

2014, Dec. 16   Litho.   *Perf. 13¼*
2037   A964   1.80s   multi   .95   .95
    With tab   1.10

Ophrys Fuciflora, Dracula Simia, Flags of Israel and Ecuador — A965

2014, Dec. 16   Litho.   *Perf. 13½x13*
2038   A965   5s   multi   2.75   2.75
    With tab   3.25

Friendship between Israel and Ecuador.

Hanukkah A966

2014, Dec. 16   Litho.   *Perf. 13x13½*
2039   A966   9.70s   multi   5.00   5.00
    With tab   5.50

Sundials — A967

Sundial from: 2.70s, Jewish Quarter, Jerusalem. 3.80s, Jezzar Pasha Mosque, Acre. 5.60s, Zoharei Chama Synagogue, Jerusalem.

2014, Dec. 16   Litho.   *Perf. 13x13½*
2040   A967   2.70s   multi   1.40   1.40
2041   A967   3.80s   multi   2.00   2.00
2042   A967   5.60s   multi   3.00   3.00
    Nos. 2040-2042 (3)   6.40   6.40
    With tabs   7.00

Automobiles Made in Israel — A968

Designs: 3.80s, 1936 Standard Carmel. 4s, 1961, Sabra Sport. 4.10s, 1951 Kaiser Manhattan. 8.30s, 1992 Sufa Jeep.

2014, Dec. 16   Litho.   *Perf. 13x13½*
2043   A968   3.80s   multi   2.00   2.00
2044   A968   4s   multi   2.10   2.10
2045   A968   4.10s   multi   2.10   2.10
2046   A968   8.30s   multi   4.25   4.25
    Nos. 2043-2046 (4)   10.45   10.45
    With tabs   11.50

Ariel Sharon (1928-2014), Prime Minister — A969

2015, Jan. 27   Litho.   *Perf. 13¼*
2047   A969   2.10s   multi   1.10   1.10
    With tab   1.25

Open Doors Monument, Rishon LeZion, Flags of Israel and the Philippines — A970

2015, Jan. 27   Litho.   *Perf. 13½x13*
2048   A970   4.50s   multi   2.25   2.25
    With tab   2.50

See Philippines No. 3567.

2015 European Individual Chess Championships, Jerusalem A971

2015, Feb. 10   Litho.   *Perf. 13x13½*
2049   A971   4.10s   multi   2.10   2.10
    With tab   2.40

International Year of Light — A972

2015, Feb. 10   Litho.   *Perf. 13x13½*
2050   A972   11.80s   multi   6.00   6.00
    With tab   6.75

Awarding of 2013 Nobel Prize in Chemistry to Martin Karplus, Michael Levitt and Arieh Warshel.

Flowers — A973

Designs: 1.80s, Anthemis leucanthemifolia. 2.10s, Alkanna tinctoria. 2.70s, Anemone coronaria.

2015, Feb. 10   Litho.   *Perf. 13½x13*
2051   A973   1.80s   multi   .95   .95
2052   A973   2.10s   multi   1.10   1.10
2053   A973   2.70s   multi   1.40   1.40
    Nos. 2051-2053 (3)   3.45   3.45
    With tabs   3.75

Memorial Day — A974

2015, Apr. 14   Litho.   *Perf. 13½x13*
2054   A974   2.20s   multi   1.10   1.10
    With tab   1.25

Port of Ashdod, 50th Anniv. — A975

2015, Apr. 14   Litho.   *Perf. 13½x13*
2055   A975   4.30s   multi   2.25   2.25
    With tab   2.50

Expo 2015, Milan — A976

2015, Apr. 14   Litho.   *Perf. 13x13*
2056   A976   6.50s   multi   3.50   3.50
    With tab   3.50

Cyrus Declaration A977

2015, Apr. 14   Litho.   *Perf. 13x13½*
2057   A977   8.30s   multi   4.25   4.25
    With tab   4.75

Zion Mule Corps, Cent. — A978

2015, Apr. 14   Litho.   *Perf. 13x13½*
2058   A978   11.80s   multi   6.25   6.25
    With tab   7.00

Eastern European Synagogue Hanukkah Lamp, 18th Cent. — A979

Dome of Shrine of the Book — A980

Turning the World Upside Down, Sculpture by Anish Kapoor — A981

2015, Apr. 14   Litho.   *Perf. 13x13½*
2059   A979   4.10s   multi   2.10   2.10
2060   A980   4.10s   multi   2.10   2.10
2061   A981   4.10s   multi   2.10   2.10
    Nos. 2059-2061 (3)   6.30   6.30
    With tabs   7.25

Israel Museum, Jerusalem, 50th anniv.

Diplomatic Relations Between Israel and Germany, 50th Anniv. — A982

2015, May 7   Litho.   *Perf. 13x13½*
2062   A982   7.40s   multi   4.00   4.00
    With tab   4.50

See Germany No. 2846.

Bell AH-1 Cobra Attack Helicopter A983

2015, June 16   Litho.   *Perf. 13x13½*
2063   A983   2.20s   multi   1.25   1.25
    With tab   1.40

Moshe Sharett and Turkish Military Railway — A984

2015, June 16   Litho.   *Perf. 13x13½*
2064   A984   11.80s   multi   6.25   6.25
    With tab   7.00

World War I, cent.

Jewish Bridal Jewelry — A985

Designs: No. 2065, Bridal Necklace, Yemen, 1930s. No. 2066, Wedding ring, Italy, 17th cent. No. 2067, Bridal Head ornament, Bukhara, 19th cent.

2015, June 16   Litho.   *Perf. 13½x13*
2065   A985   4.10s   multi   2.25   2.25
2066   A985   4.10s   multi   2.25   2.25
2067   A985   4.10s   multi   2.25   2.25
    Nos. 2065-2067 (3)   6.75   6.75
    With tabs   7.50

Vegetables — A986

Designs: Nos. 2068a, 2069, Carrots. Nos. 2068b, 2070, Purple cabbage. Nos. 2068c, 2071, Lettuce. Nos. 2068d, 2072, Onions. Nos. 2068e, 2073, Tomatoes.

2015, June 16   Litho.   *Perf. 14*
2068   Horiz. strip of 5   6.25   6.25
    a.-e.   A986 (2.20s) Any single   1.25   1.25
    Strip with tabs   7.00

ISRAEL

Booklet Stamps
Self-Adhesive
Serpentine Die Cut 13¼x14¼
2069	A986	(2.20s) multi	1.25	1.25
2070	A986	(2.20s) multi	1.25	1.25
2071	A986	(2.20s) multi	1.25	1.25
2072	A986	(2.20s) multi	1.25	1.25
2073	A986	(2.20s) multi	1.25	1.25
a.	Booklet pane of 20, 4 each #2069-2073		25.00	
	Nos. 2069-2073 (5)		6.25	6.25

Jewish Resistance Monument, Ramat Gan — A987

2015, Sept. 2 Litho. Perf. 14x13½
2074	A987	11.80s multi	6.00	6.00
	With tab		6.75	

Jewish Resistance Movement, 70th Anniv.

Souvenir Sheet
Church of the Holy Sepulchre, Jerusalem — A988

2015, Sept. 2 Litho. Perf. 14x13½
2075	A988	7s multi	3.75	3.75

Visit of Pope Francis to Israel. See Vatican City No. 1602.

Children Celebrating Jewish Holidays — A989

Children celebrating: 2.20s, Rosh Hashanah. 7.40s, Yom Kippur. 8.30s, Sukkot.

2015, Sept. 2 Litho. Perf. 14x13½
2076	A989	2.20s multi	1.10	1.10
2077	A989	7.40s multi	3.75	3.75
2078	A989	8.30s multi	4.25	4.25
	Nos. 2076-2078 (3)		9.10	9.10
	With tabs		10.00	

Rivers — A990

Designs: Nos. 2079, 2082, Kziv River. Nos. 2080, 2083, Taninim River. Nos. 2081, 2084, Zin River.

2015, Sept. 2 Litho. Perf. 14x13½
2079	A990	4.10s multi	2.10	2.10
2080	A990	4.10s multi	2.10	2.10
2081	A990	4.10s multi	2.10	2.10
	Nos. 2079-2081 (3)		6.30	6.30
	With tabs		7.00	

Booklet Stamps
Self-Adhesive
Serpentine Die Cut 12½
2082	A990	4.10s multi	2.10	2.10
2083	A990	4.10s multi	2.10	2.10
2084	A990	4.10s multi	2.10	2.10
a.	Booklet pane of 6, 2 each #2082-2084		13.00	
	Nos. 2082-2084 (3)		6.30	6.30

Nili Resistance Movement, Cent. — A991

2015, Dec. 8 Litho. Perf. 13x13¼
2085	A991	5s multi	2.60	2.60
	With tab		3.00	

Mamluk Postal Road — A992

2015, Dec. 8 Litho. Perf. 13x13¼
2086	A992	10s multi	5.25	5.25
	With tab		5.75	

Philately Day.

Pension Savings — A993

2015, Dec. 8 Litho. Perf. 13x13¼
2087	A993	11.70s multi	6.00	6.00
	With tab		6.75	

Entertainers — A994

Designs: 2.30s, Sefi Rivlin (1947-2013), comedian. 4.10s, Channa Marron (1923-2014), actress.

2015, Dec. 8 Litho. Perf. 13¼x13
2088	A994	2.30s multi	1.25	1.25
2089	A994	4.10s multi	2.10	2.10
	With tabs		3.75	

Nostalgia — A995

No. 2090: a, Soda siphon. b, Tembel hat. c, Sussita automobile.

2015, Dec. 8 Litho. Perf. 13x13¼
2090		Horiz. strip of 3	3.75	3.75
a.-c.	A995	2.30s Any single	1.25	1.25
	Strip with tabs		4.25	

Full Diplomatic Relations Between Israel and Greece, 25th Anniv. — A996

2016, Feb. 9 Litho. Perf. 14x13½
2091	A996	4.10s multi	2.10	2.10
	With tab		2.40	

See Greece No. 2719.

Winter — A997

2016, Feb. 9 Litho. Perf. 14x13½
2092	A997	4.10s multi	2.10	2.10
	With tab		2.40	

Ephraim Kishon (1924-2005), Writer — A998

2016, Feb. 9 Litho. Perf. 13½x14
2093	A998	11.70s multi	6.00	6.00
	With tab		6.75	

Famous Women — A999

Designs: 2.30s, Nehama Pohatchevsky (1869-1934), writer. 5s, Zelda Schneerson-Mishkovsky (1914-84), poet.

2016, Feb. 9 Litho. Perf. 14x13½
2094	A999	2.30s multi	1.25	1.25
2095	A999	5s multi	2.60	2.60
	With tabs		4.25	

Turtles A1000

No. 2096: a, Chelonia mydas. b, Caretta caretta. c, Eretmochelys imbricata. d, Dermochelys coriacea.

2016, Feb. 9 Litho. Perf. 14x13½
2096	A1000	Block of 4	5.00	5.00
a.-d.		2.30s Any single	1.25	1.25
	Nos. 2096a-2096d with tabs		5.50	

Memorial Day — A1001

2016, Apr. 19 Litho. Perf. 13x13¼
2097	A1001	2.30s multi	1.25	1.25
	With tab		1.40	

Knesset Building, Jerusalem, 50th Anniv. — A1002

2016, Apr. 19 Litho. Perf. 13x13¼
2098	A1002	2.30s multi	1.25	1.25
	With tab		1.40	

Spring — A1003

2016 Litho. Perf. 13x13¼
2099	A1003	4.10s multi	2.25	2.25
	With tab		2.50	
a.	Perf. 14x13½ (#2114a)		2.40	2.40

Issued: No. 2099, 4/19; No. 2099a, 9/13.

Chords Bridge, Jerusalem A1004

2016, Apr. 19 Litho. Perf. 13x13¼
2100	A1004	7.40s multi	4.00	4.00
	With tab		4.50	

Diplomatic relations between Israel and Spain, 30th anniv. See Spain No. 4120.

Israeli Achievements in Printing — A1005

Designs: 2.30s, Digital prepress. 8.30s, Digital printing.

2016, Apr. 19 Litho. Perf. 13x13¼
2101	A1005	2.30s multi	1.25	1.25
2102	A1005	8.30s multi	4.50	4.50
	With tabs		6.50	

Markets — A1006

Designs: No. 2103, Mahana Yehuda Market, Jerusalem. No. 2104, Old Acre Market. No. 2105, Flea Market, Jaffa.

2016, Apr. 19 Litho. Perf. 13x13¼
2103	A1006	4.10s multi	2.25	2.25
2104	A1006	4.10s multi	2.25	2.25
2105	A1006	4.10s multi	2.25	2.25
	Nos. 2103-2105 (3)		6.75	6.75
	With tabs		7.50	

Summer — A1007

2016 Litho. Perf. 13x13¼
2106	A1007	4.10s multi	2.25	2.25
	With tab		2.50	
a.	Perf. 14x13½ (#2114a)		2.40	2.40

Issued: No. 2106, 6/21; No. 2106a, 9/13.

German World War I Pilot and Airplane — A1008

2016, June 21 Litho. Perf. 13x13¼
2107	A1008	11.70s multi	6.25	6.25
	With tab		7.00	

Service Dogs — A1009

Designs: 2.30s, Guide dogs. 10s, Search and rescue dogs.

2016, June 21 Litho. Perf. 13x13¼
2108	A1009	2.30s multi	1.25	1.25
2109	A1009	10s multi	5.25	5.25
	With tabs		7.25	

2016 Summer Olympics, Rio de Janeiro — A1010

Designs: No. 2110, Triple jump. No. 2111, Judo. No. 2112, Windsurfing.

2016, June 21 Litho. Perf. 13¼x13
2110	A1010	4.10s multi	2.25	2.25
2111	A1010	4.10s multi	2.25	2.25
2112	A1010	4.10s multi	2.25	2.25
	Nos. 2110-2112 (3)		6.75	6.75
	With tabs		7.50	

Casualties of War and Terror Appreciation Day — A1011

2016, Sept. 13 Litho. Perf. 14x13½
2113	A1011	2.30s multi	1.25	1.25
	With tab		1.40	

Autumn — A1012

ISRAEL

2016, Sept. 13   Litho.   Perf. 14x13½
2114 A1012 4.10s multi   2.25 2.25
    With tab   2.50
a. Souvenir sheet of 4, #2092,
2099a, 2106a, 2114   9.75 9.75

Jerusalem 2016 Stamp Exhibition (No. 2114a). No. 2114a sold for 18s.

White Storks, Flags of Israel and Bulgaria — A1013

2016, Sept. 13   Litho.   Perf. 14x13½
2115 A1013 5s multi   2.75 2.75
    With tab   3.00

Israel-Bulgaria Joint Issue, Bird Migration. See Bulgaria No. 4772.

Hands of Artisans in Yom Kippur Poem, "As the Clay in the Hand of the Potter" — A1014

Designs: 2.40s, Potter. 7.40s, Glazier. 8.30s, Silversmith.

2016, Sept. 13   Litho.   Perf. 14x13½
2116 A1014 2.30s multi   1.25 1.25
2117 A1014 7.40s multi   4.00 4.00
2118 A1014 8.30s multi   4.50 4.50
    Nos. 2116-2118 (3)   9.75 9.75
    With tabs   10.50

Parables of the Sages — A1015

Designs: Nos. 2119, 2122, The Lion and the Heron. Nos. 2120, 2123, The Reed and the Cedar. Nos. 2121, 2124, The Fox in the Vineyard.

2016, Sept. 13   Litho.   Perf. 14x13½
2119 A1015 4.10s multi   2.25 2.25
2120 A1015 4.10s multi   2.25 2.25
2121 A1015 4.10s multi   2.25 2.25
    Nos. 2119-2121 (3)   6.75 6.75
    With tabs   7.50

Booklet Stamps Self-Adhesive
Die Cut Perf. 12½
2122 A1015 4.10s multi   2.25 2.25
2123 A1015 4.10s multi   2.25 2.25
2124 A1015 4.10s multi   2.25 2.25
  a. Booklet pane of 6, 2 each
    #2122-2124   13.50
    Nos. 2122-2124 (3)   6.75 6.75

Yitzhak Navon (1921-2015), President of Israel — A1016

2016, Nov. 13   Litho.   Perf. 13¼x13
2125 A1016 11.70s multi   6.25 6.25
    With tab   7.00

Mosaics — A1017

No. 2126 — Mosaic depicting: a, Leaping tiger, from 6th cent. synagogue, Gaza. b, Fish, from 3rd cent. villa, Lod. c, Peacock, from 6th cent. synagogue, Maon.

2016, Nov. 13   Litho.   Perf. 13x13¼
2126   Horiz. strip of 3   6.75 6.75
a.-c. A1017 4.10s Any single   2.25 2.25
    Strip with tabs   7.50

Tourist Attractions in Jerusalem A1018

No. 2127: a, Biblical Zoo. b, First train station. c, Via Dolorosa. d, Jaffa Road. e, Ramparts Promenade.

2016, Nov. 13   Litho.   Perf. 13x13¼
2127   Horiz. strip of 5   6.25 6.25
a.-e. A1018 2.40s Any single   1.25 1.25
  f. Booklet pane of 10, 2 each
    #2127a-2127e, + 2 central
    labels   12.50   —
    Complete booklet, #2127f   12.50
    Strip with tabs   7.00

Souvenir Sheet

King Solomon's Ships — A1019

2016, Nov. 13   Litho.   Perf. 13¼x13
2128 A1019 5s multi   2.60 2.60

Jerusalem 2016 Stamp Exhibition.

Etsel Combat Soldiers and Emblem of Brit Hayyale Ha'Etsel — A1020

2017, Feb. 7   Litho.   Perf. 13¼x13
2129 A1020 2.40s multi   1.40 1.40
    With tab   1.60

Zionist Organization of America, 120th Anniv. — A1021

2017, Feb. 7   Litho.   Perf. 13¼x13
2130 A1021 8.30s multi   4.75 4.75
    With tab   5.25

Krav Maga — A1022

2017, Feb. 7   Litho.   Perf. 13x13¼
2131 A1022 11.70s multi   6.50 6.50
    With tab   7.25

Aromatic Plants — A1023

Designs: No. 2132, Frankincense. No. 2133, Myrrh. No. 2134, Balsam.

2017, Feb. 7   Litho.   Perf. 13¼x13
2132 A1023 4.10s multi   2.25 2.25
2133 A1023 4.10s multi   2.25 2.25
2134 A1023 4.10s multi   2.25 2.25
    Nos. 2132-2134 (3)   6.75 6.75
    With tabs   7.50

See Nos. 2151-2153.

UNESCO World Heritage Sites — A1024

Designs: 2.40s, Nahal Me'arot Caves. 5s, Bet She'arim Necropolis. 10s, Maresha and Bet-Guvrin Caves.

2017, Feb. 7   Litho.   Perf. 13x13¼
2135 A1024 2.40s multi   1.40 1.40
2136 A1024 5s multi   2.75 2.75
2137 A1024 10s multi   5.50 5.50
    Nos. 2135-2137 (3)   9.65 9.65
    With tabs   11.00

National Memorial Hall, Jerusalem A1025

2017, Apr. 4   Litho.   Perf. 14½x14¼
2138 A1025 2.40s multi   1.40 1.40
    With tab   1.60

Memorial Day.

Dolphin Research A1026

2017, Apr. 4   Litho.   Perf. 13x13¼
2139 A1026 7.40s multi   4.25 4.25
    With tab   4.75

See Portugal No. 3894.

Illustrations From Modern Passover Haggadahs A1027

Designs: No. 2140, Jews returning to Israel on boat. No. 2141, Haganah soldiers. No. 2142, Kibbutz members on hill.

2017, Apr. 4   Litho.   Perf. 13x13¼
2140 A1027 4s multi   2.25 2.25
2141 A1027 4s multi   2.25 2.25
2142 A1027 4s multi   2.25 2.25
    Nos. 2140-2142 (3)   6.75 6.75
    With tabs   7.50

Settlements, 50th Anniv. — A1028

Settlement in: No. 2143, Golan (apples and Sa'ar River Waterfall). No. 2144, Jordan Valley (dates, date grove near Samaria Mountains). No. 2145, Judea and Samaria (olive branch, youths at Sebastia train station).

2017, Apr. 4   Litho.   Perf. 13¼x13
2143 A1028 2.40s multi   1.40 1.40
2144 A1028 2.40s multi   1.40 1.40
2145 A1028 2.40s multi   1.40 1.40
    Nos. 2143-2145 (3)   4.20 4.20
    With tabs   4.75

Souvenir Sheet

Reunification of Jerusalem, 50th Anniv. — A1029

No. 2146: a, Water tower of Hebrew University of Jerusalem. b, Jews at Western Wall.

2017, Apr. 4   Litho.   Perf. 13¼x13
2146   Sheet of 2   5.50 5.50
a.-b. 4.10s Either single   2.75 2.75

No. 2146 sold for 10s.

20th Maccabiah Games — A1030

2017, June 13   Litho.   Perf. 13¼x13
2147 A1030 2.40s multi   1.40 1.40
    With tab   1.60

Entry of Field Marshal Edmund Allenby into Jerusalem, Cent. — A1031

2017, June 13   Litho.   Perf. 13¼x13
2148 A1031 11.60s multi   6.75 6.75
    With tab   7.50

World War I, end of Turkish rule in Jerusalem, cent.

Love Songs — A1043

Litho., Labels Litho. With Foil Application
2017, June 13   Perf. 13¼
2149   Sheet of 12 + 4 central labels   17.00 17.00
  a. A1032 2.40s red & multi   1.40 1.40
  b. A1033 2.40s beige & multi   1.40 1.40
  c. A1034 2.40s blue gray & multi 1.40 1.40
  d. A1035 2.40s black, pink & multi 1.40 1.40
  e. A1036 2.40s sage grn, red & multi 1.40 1.40
  f. A1037 2.40s gray & multi   1.40 1.40
  g. A1038 2.40s azure & multi   1.40 1.40
  h. A1039 2.40s blk, yel ochre & multi 1.40 1.40
  i. A1040 2.40s lt brown & multi   1.40 1.40
  j. A1041 2.40s gray grn, pink & multi 1.40 1.40

ISRAEL

k. A1042 2.40s blk, pale blue & multi ... 1.40 1.40
l. A1043 2.40s orange & multi ... 1.40 1.40

Anemone Coronaria and Iris Croatica Prodán — A1044

2017, Sept. 4 Litho. Perf. 13x13¼
2150 A1044 6.50s multi ... 3.75 3.75
 With tab ... 4.25

Diplomatic relations between Israel and Croatia, 20th anniv. See Croatia No. 1045.

Aromatic Plants Type of 2017

Designs: No. 2151, Frankincense. No. 2152, Myrrh. No. 2153, Balsam.

Die Cut Perf. 12½x12¼

2017, Sept. 12 Photo.
Booklet Stamps
Self-Adhesive
2151 A1023 4.10s multi ... 2.40 2.40
2152 A1023 4.10s multi ... 2.40 2.40
2153 A1023 4.10s multi ... 2.40 2.40
 a. Booklet pane of 6, 2 each #2151-2153 ... 14.50
 Nos. 2151-2153 (3) ... 7.20 7.20

Shimon Peres (1923-2016), Prime Minister and Ninth President of Israel — A1045

2017, Sept. 12 Litho. Perf. 13¼
2154 A1045 2.40s multi ... 1.40 1.40
 With tab ... 1.60

Habimah National Theater, Cent. — A1046

2017, Sept. 12 Litho. Perf. 13x13¼
2155 A1046 2.40s multi ... 1.40 1.40
 With tab ... 1.60

Balfour Declaration, Cent. A1047

Perf. 14½x14¼

2017, Sept. 12 Litho.
2156 A1047 5s multi ... 3.00 3.00
 With tab ... 3.50

Activities of Jewish Festivals of the Month of Tishrei — A1048

Designs: 2.40s, Selichot prayers. 7.40s, Building a sukkah. 8.30s, Second Hakafot.

2017, Sept. 12 Litho. Perf. 13x13¼
2157 A1048 2.40s multi ... 1.40 1.40
2158 A1048 7.40s multi ... 4.25 4.25
2159 A1048 8.30s multi ... 4.75 4.75
 Nos. 2157-2159 (3) ... 10.40 10.40
 With tabs ... 11.50

Gorny Convent, Ein Karem — A1049

2017, Nov. 14 Litho. Perf. 14x13½
2160 A1049 6s multi ... 3.50 3.50
 With tab ... 4.00

Diplomatic Relations between Israel and Russia.
See Russia No. 7873.

Integration of the Handicapped into Society — A1050

2017, Dec. 19 Litho. Perf. 14x13½
2161 A1050 11.60s multi ... 6.75 6.75
 With tab ... 7.50

Submarines A1051

Designs: No. 2162, S Class submarine, 1959. No. 2163, T Class submarine, 1967. No. 2164, Gal Class submarine, 1976.

2017, Dec. 19 Litho. Perf. 14x13½
2162 A1051 2.50s multi ... 1.50 1.50
2163 A1051 2.50s multi ... 1.50 1.50
2164 A1051 2.50s multi ... 1.50 1.50
 Nos. 2162-2164 (3) ... 4.50 4.50
 With tabs ... 5.00

Ancient Roman Arenas — A1052

Designs: No. 2165, Amphitheater, Beit Guvrin. No. 2166, Theater, Beit She'an. No. 2167, Hippodrome, Caesarea.

2017, Dec. 19 Litho. Perf. 14x13½
2165 A1052 4.10s multi ... 2.40 2.40
2166 A1052 4.10s multi ... 2.40 2.40
2167 A1052 4.10s multi ... 2.40 2.40
 Nos. 2165-2167 (3) ... 7.20 7.20
 With tabs ... 8.00

Snakes — A1053

No. 2168: a, Dolichophis jugularis. b, Psammophis schokari. c, Daboia palaestinae.

2017, Dec. 19 Litho. Perf. 13½x14
2168 Horiz. strip of 3 ... 7.20 7.20
 a.-c. A1053 4.10s Any single ... 2.40 2.40
 Strip with tabs ... 8.00

Indian Cavalry in Haifa, 1918 — A1054

2018, Feb. 6 Litho. Perf. 13x13¼
2169 A1054 2.50s multi ... 1.50 1.50
 With tab ... 1.75

Israel Television, 50th Anniv. — A1055

2018, Feb. 6 Litho. Perf. 13x13¼
2170 A1055 4.20s multi ... 2.40 2.40
 With tab ... 2.60

Ha'Chizbatron Musical Troupe, 70th Anniv. — A1056

2018, Feb. 6 Litho. Perf. 13x13¼
2171 A1056 7.40s multi ... 4.25 4.25
 With tab ... 4.75

Gevatron Chorus, 70th Anniv. — A1057

2018, Feb. 6 Litho. Perf. 13¼x13
2172 A1057 10s multi ... 5.75 5.75
 With tab ... 6.50

Wildlife Repopulated by Yotvata Hai-Bar — A1058

No. 2173: a, Equus hemionus. b, Oryx leucoryx. c, Gazella gazella acacia.

2018, Feb. 6 Litho. Perf. 13x13¼
2173 Horiz. strip of 3 ... 4.50 4.50
 a.-c. A1058 2.50s Any single ... 1.50 1.50
 Strip with tabs ... 5.00

Yotvata Hai-Bar, 50th anniv.

Memorial Day — A1059

2018, Apr. 9 Litho. Perf. 13¼x13
2174 A1059 2.50s multi ... 1.40 1.40
 With tab ... 1.60

Independence, 70th Anniv. — A1060

2018, Apr. 9 Litho. Perf. 14½x14¼
2175 A1060 5s multi ... 2.75 2.75
 With tab ... 3.00

Civil Aviation in Israel, 70th Anniv. — A1061

2018, Apr. 9 Litho. Perf. 13x13¼
2176 A1061 11.60s multi ... 6.50 6.50
 With tab ... 7.25

Flowers — A1062

Designs: Nos. 2177, 2181, Chrysanthemum coronarium. Nos. 2178, 2182, Trifolium purpureum. Nos. 2179, 2183, Centaurea cyanoides. Nos. 2180, 2184, Tulipa agenensis.

2018, Apr. 9 Litho. Perf. 14x14¼
2177 A1062 4.10s multi ... 2.25 2.25
 a. Perf. 13½x13 ... 2.75 2.75
2178 A1062 4.10s multi ... 2.25 2.25
 a. Perf. 13½x13 ... 2.75 2.75
2179 A1062 4.10s multi ... 2.25 2.25
 a. Perf. 13½x13 ... 2.75 2.75
2180 A1062 4.10s multi ... 2.25 2.25
 a. Perf. 13½x13 ... 2.75 2.75
 b. Souvenir sheet of 4, #2177a-2180a ... 11.00 11.00
 Nos. 2177-2180 (4) ... 9.00 9.00
 With tabs ... 10.00

Booklet Stamps
Serpentine Die Cut 11¼x12¼

2181 A1062 4.10s multi ... 2.25 2.25
2182 A1062 4.10s multi ... 2.25 2.25
2183 A1062 4.10s multi ... 2.25 2.25
2184 A1062 4.10s multi ... 2.25 2.25
 a. Booklet pane of 8, 2 each #2181-2184 ... 18.00
 Nos. 2181-2184 (4) ... 9.00 9.00

No. 2180b sold for 20s.

Miniature Sheet

Hats of the Israeli Defense Forces A1063

No. 2185 — Hat of: a, Artillery Corps. b, Armor Corps. c, Combat Intelligence Collection Corps. d, Engineering Corps. e, General Service Corps. f, Paratroopers Brigade. g, Intelligence Corps. h, Nahal Brigade. i, Israel Air Force. j, Home Front Command. k, Givati Brigade. l, Golani Brigade. m, C4I and Cyber Defense. n, Kfir Brigade. o, Military Police Corps. p, Israeli Navy.

Litho., Labels Litho. With Foil Application

2018, Apr. 9 Perf. 13¼
2185 A1063 Sheet of 16 + 9 central labels ... 22.50 22.50
 a.-p. 2.50s Any single ... 1.40 1.40

Innovations of the Israeli Defense Force — A1064

Designs: 2.50s, Iron Dome missile defense system. 4.10s, Cyber defense.

2018, May 27 Litho. Perf. 13¼x13
2186 A1064 2.50s multi ... 1.40 1.40
2187 A1064 4.10s multi ... 2.40 2.40
 With tabs ... 4.25

"Jerusalem of Gold," Song by Naomi Shemer (1930-2004), 50th Anniv. — A1065

2018, May 27 Litho. Perf. 14¼x14½
2188 A1065 5s multi ... 3.00 3.00
 With tab ... 3.25

Souvenir Sheet
Litho. With Foil Application
2189 A1065 10s gold & multi ... 5.75 5.75

Comic Strip Characters Drawn by Michel Kichka — A1066

No. 2190 — Man: a, Pushing shopping cart. b, Driving military vehicle. c, Driving tractor.

2018, May 27 Litho. Perf. 13x13¼
2190 Horiz. strip of 3 ... 4.25 4.25
 a.-c. A1066 2.50s Any single ... 1.40 1.40
 Strip with tabs ... 4.75

Souvenir Sheet

Menorahs — A1067

ISRAEL

No. 2191 — Menorah: a, On Israel coat of arms. b, From Arch of Titus, Rome. c, From ruins of synagogue, Magdala.

2018, May 27 Litho. *Perf. 13*
2191 A1067 Sheet of 3 .... 9.00 9.00
a.-c. 5s Any single 3.00 3.00

2018 World Stamp Championship, Jerusalem.

Litwinsky House, Tel Aviv — A1068

2018, Aug. 28 Litho. *Perf. 13x13¼*
2192 A1068 6.50s multi 3.75 3.75
With tab 4.25

Joint Issue between Israel and Estonia. See Estonia No. 874.

Famous Women — A1069

Designs: No. 2193, Ada Sereni (1905-97), leader of Aliyah Bet clandestine immigration movement in Italy. No. 2194, Recha Freier (1892-1984), Youth Aliyah leader.

2018, Aug. 28 Litho. *Perf. 13x13¼*
2193 A1069 2.50s multi 1.40 1.40
2194 A1069 2.50s multi 1.40 1.40
With tabs 3.25

Archeozoology in Israel — A1070

Designs: No. 2195, Elephant, tusk found in Holon. No. 2196, Lioness, skull found in Jaffa.

2018, Aug. 28 Litho. *Perf. 13¼x13*
2195 A1070 2.50s multi 1.40 1.40
2196 A1070 2.50s multi 1.40 1.40
With tabs 3.25

Date Palms — A1071

Designs: 2.50s, Lulav and dates. 7.40s, Palm fronds and fibers. 8.30s, Roof made with palm tree trunks and fronds.

2018, Aug. 28 Litho. *Perf. 13¼x13*
2197 A1071 2.50s multi 1.40 1.40
2198 A1071 7.40s multi 4.25 4.25
2199 A1071 8.30s multi 4.75 4.75
Nos. 2197-2199 (3) 10.40 10.40
With tabs 11.50

Sukkot Festival.

Menorah — A1072

2018, Oct. 16 Litho. *Perf. 13¼x13*
2200 A1072 8.30s multi 4.50 4.50
With tab 5.00

Hanukkah. Israel and United States Joint Issue. See United States No. 5338.

Fireworks and Flags of Israel and Poland — A1073

2018, Nov. 5 Litho. *Perf. 13x13¼*
2201 A1073 6.50s multi 3.50 3.50
With tab 4.00

Independence of Israel, 70th anniv., and of Poland, cent. See Poland No. 4376.

Israel Securities Authority, 50th Anniv. — A1074

2018, Dec. 4 Litho. *Perf. 13x13¼*
2202 A1074 4.10s multi 2.25 2.25
With tab 2.50

Israeli Technological Innovations A1075

Designs: No. 2203, Robotic guidance of spine surgery. No. 2204, Collision avoidance system.

2018, Dec. 4 Litho. *Perf. 13x13¼*
2203 A1075 2.50s multi 1.40 1.40
2204 A1075 2.50s multi 1.40 1.40
With tabs 3.25

Trees — A1076

Designs: No. 2205, Cercis siliquastrum. No. 2206, Quercus ithaburensis. No. 2207, Arbutus andrachne.

2018, Dec. 4 Litho. *Perf. 13x13¼*
2205 A1076 2.50s multi 1.40 1.40
2206 A1076 2.50s multi 1.40 1.40
2207 A1076 2.50s multi 1.40 1.40
Nos. 2205-2207 (3) 4.20 4.20
With tabs 4.75

Balloon, Gift and Birthday Greetings — A1077

2019, Mar. 5 Litho. *Perf. 13¾*
2208 A1077 (2.50s) multi 1.40 1.40
With tab 1.60
a. Sheet of 12 + 12 labels .... 22.50 —

No. 2208a sold for 39s. Labels could be personalized.

Science Oriented Youth Educational Program — A1078

2019, Mar. 5 Litho. *Perf. 13¼x13*
2209 A1078 11.80s multi 6.50 6.50
With tab 7.25

Mountains A1079

Designs: 4.10s, Mount Maron. 7.40s, Mount Karkom.

2019, Mar. 5 Litho. *Perf. 13x13¼*
2210 A1079 4.10s multi 2.25 2.25
2211 A1079 7.40s multi 4.25 4.25
With tabs 7.25

Purim Mitzvahs — A1080

No. 2212: a, Gifts for the needy. b, Mishlo'ach manot. c, Festive Purim banquet. d, Reading the Book of Esther.

2019, Mar. 5 Litho. *Perf. 13x13¼*
2212 Horiz. strip of 4 .... 5.60 5.60
a.-d. A1080 2.50s Any single 1.40 1.40
Strip with tab 6.25

No. 2212 was printed in sheets containing two tete-beche strips.

Birds — A1081

No. 2213: a, Merops apiaster. b, Merops persicus. c, Merops orientalis. d, Alcedo atthis. e, Coracias garrulus.

2019, Mar. 5 Litho. *Perf. 13¾*
2213 Horiz. strip of 5 .... 7.00 7.00
a.-e. A1081 (2.50s) Any single 1.40 1.40
Strip with tabs 7.75
f. Tete-beche pair of #2213c 2.80 2.80

No. 2213 was printed in sheets containing two tete-beche strips, with only No. 2213c being the only pair containing the same stamp.

Memorial Day — A1082

2019, May 1 Litho. *Perf. 13¼x13*
2214 A1082 2.50s multi 1.40 1.40
With tab 1.60

Mimouna Festival — A1083

2019, May 1 Litho. *Perf. 13x13¼*
2215 A1083 4.10s multi 2.25 2.25
With tab 2.50

Lyrics of "Hava Nagila" and Dancers — A1084

2019, May 1 Litho. *Perf. 14¼x14½*
2216 A1084 11.80s multi 6.75 6.75
With tab 7.50

Israeli Newspapers A1085

Designs: No. 2217, Moshe Yosef Glikson (1878-1938), editor, and Isaac Leib Goldberg (1860-1935), founder of *Haaretz* newspaper. No. 2218, Ze'ev Jabotinsky (1880-1940) and Itamar Ben-Avi (1882-1943), editors of *Doar Hayom* newspaper. No. 2219, Shneur Zalman Rubashov (1889-1974), editor and President of Israel, and Berl Katznelson (1887-1944), founder of *Davar* newspaper.

2019, May 1 Litho. *Perf. 13x13¼*
2217 A1085 4.10s multi 2.25 2.25
2218 A1085 4.10s multi 2.25 2.25
2219 A1085 4.10s multi 2.25 2.25
Nos. 2217-2219 (3) 6.75 6.75
With tabs 7.50

Foundation of *Haaretz* and *Doar Hayom*, cent.

Endangered Animals — A1086

No. 2220: a, Hemiechinus auritus. b, Dryomys nitedula. c, Vulpes rueppellii.

2019, May 1 Litho. *Perf. 13x13¼*
2220 Horiz. strip of 3 .... 4.20 4.20
a.-c. A1086 2.50s Any single 1.40 1.40
Strip with tabs 4.75

Conversion of Hiriya Garbage Dump Into Ariel Sharon Park — A1087

2019, July 16 Litho. *Perf. 13x13¼*
2221 A1087 7.40s multi 4.25 4.25
With tab 4.75

Diplomatic Relations Between Israel and Singapore, 50th Anniv. — A1088

National bird of Israel (hoopoe) and Singapore (crimson sunbird) and: 2.50s, Flowers of Singapore (Bougainvillea glabra, Dendrobium lucian, Dendrobium crumenatum, and Ixora congesta). 7.40s, Flowers of Israel (Anemone, Cyclamen, Senecio and Narcissus).

2019, July 16 Litho. *Perf. 13¼x13*
2222 A1088 2.50s multi 1.50 1.50
2223 A1088 7.40s multi 4.25 4.25
With tabs 6.50

See Singapore Nos. 1967-1968.

Tourism — A1089

Designs: No. 2224, Camels carrying tourists at Makhtesh Ramon. No. 2225, Baptism in Jordan River. No. 2226, Birdwatcher in Hula Valley.

2019, July 16 Litho. *Perf. 13x13¼*
2224 A1089 2.50s multi 1.50 1.50
2225 A1089 2.50s multi 1.50 1.50
2226 A1089 2.50s multi 1.50 1.50
Nos. 2224-2226 (3) 4.50 4.50
With tabs 5.00

Cycling — A1090

Designs: 4.10s, Mountain biking. 4.30s, Road cycling. 4.50s, Urban cycling.

2019, July 16 Litho. *Perf. 13¼x13*
2227 A1090 4.10s multi 2.40 2.40
2228 A1090 4.30s multi 2.50 2.50
2229 A1090 4.50s multi 2.60 2.60
Nos. 2227-2229 (3) 7.50 7.50
With tabs 8.25

ISREAL 581

Souvenir Sheet

Ketubah (Marriage Agreement) — A1091

Litho., Sheet Margin Litho. With Foil Application

2019, July 16 — Perf. 14 Syncopated
2230 A1091 10s gold & multi 5.75 5.75

Souvenir Sheet

Church of St. Peter, Capernaum, Israel — A1092

2019, Sept. 10 — Litho. — Perf.
2231 A1092 10s multi 8.75 8.75

Diplomatic relations between Israel and Vatican City, 25th anniv. No. 2231 sold for 15s. See Vatican City No. 1725.

Campaign Against Breast Cancer — A1093

2019, Sept. 18 — Litho. — Perf. 13x13¼
2232 A1093 2.50s multi 1.50 1.50
   With tab 1.75

Sehrane Festival — A1094

2019, Sept. 18 — Litho. — Perf. 13x13¼
2233 A1094 4.10s multi 2.40 2.40
   With tab 2.60

Flowers — A1095

Designs: Nos. 2234, 2237, Sternbergia clusiana. Nos. 2235, 2238, Muscari parviflorum. Nos. 2236, 2239, Pancratium sickenbergeri.

2019 — Litho. — Perf. 13¼x13
2234 A1095 4.10s multi 2.40 2.40
2235 A1095 4.10s multi 2.40 2.40
2236 A1095 4.10s multi 2.40 2.40
   Nos. 2234-2236 (3) 7.20 7.20
   With tabs 8.00

Booklet Stamps
Self-Adhesive
Serpentine Die Cut 11¼x12¼

2237 A1095 4.10s multi 2.40 2.40
2238 A1095 4.10s multi 2.40 2.40
2239 A1095 4.10s multi 2.40 2.40
   a. Booklet pane of 6, 2 each #2237-2239 14.50
   Nos. 2237-2239 (3) 7.20 7.20

Issued: Nos. 2234-2236, 9/18; Nos. 2237-2239, 11/26.

Souvenir Sheet

Honeybees and Flowers — A1096

No. 2240 — Bee, honey drop and: a, Wildflowers. b, Citrus blossoms. c, Eucalyptus blossoms.

2019, Sept. 18 — Litho. — Perf. 13¼
2240 A1096 Sheet of 3 10.50 10.50
   a. 2.50s multi 1.50 1.50
   b. 7.40s multi 4.25 4.25
   c. 8.30s multi 4.75 4.75

Sigd Festival — A1097

2019, Nov. 26 — Litho. — Perf. 14x13½
2241 A1097 7.40s multi 4.25 4.25
   With tab 4.75

Dr. Chaim Weizmann (1874-1952), Biochemist and First President of Israel, and Symbols of Science — A1098

2019, Nov. 26 — Litho. — Perf. 13½x14
2242 A1098 8.30s multi 4.75 4.75
   With tab 5.25

Weizmann Institute of Science, 70th anniv.

Family Games — A1099

Designs: No. 2243, Rummikub. No. 2244, Taki.

2019, Nov. 26 — Litho. — Perf. 13½x14
2243 A1099 2.50s multi 1.50 1.50
2244 A1099 2.50s multi 1.50 1.50
   With tabs 3.50

Monsters — A1100

No. 2245 — Color of monster: a, Green. b, Purple. c, Red orange.

2019, Nov. 26 — Litho. — Perf. 14x13½
2245 Horiz. strip of 3 7.25 7.25
   a.-c. A1100 4.10s Any single 2.40 2.40
   Strip with tabs 8.00

Monsters exhibit at Eretz Israel Museum.

Histadrut (General Federation of Labor in Israel), Cent. — A1101

2020, Feb. 4 — Litho. — Perf. 13x13¼
2246 A1101 2.50s multi 1.50 1.50
   With tab 1.75

Keren Hayesod (United Israel Appeal), Cent. — A1102

2020, Feb. 4 — Litho. — Perf. 13x13¼
2247 A1102 4.10s multi 2.40 2.40
   With tab 2.60

Ben Gurion University of the Negev, 50th Anniv. — A1103

2020, Feb. 4 — Litho. — Perf. 13¼x13
2248 A1103 5s multi 3.00 3.00
   With tab 3.25

Rabbi Azriel Hildesheimer (1820-99) — A1104

2020, Feb. 4 — Litho. — Perf. 13¼x13
2249 A1104 11.80s multi 7.00 7.00
   With tab 7.75

Chlorusus and Other Marine Life — A1105

2020, Feb. 4 — Litho. — Perf. 14½
2250 A1105 16s multi 7.00 7.00
   With tab 7.75

Cyan, Magenta, Yellow and Black (CMYK) printing. No. 2250 was printed in sheets of 12 with four progressive proofs in the four ink colors that are not valid for postage.

Rose — A1106

2020, Feb. 4 — Litho. — Perf. 14
2251 A1106 (4.30s) multi 2.50 2.50
   With tab 2.75

Booklet Stamp
Self-Adhesive
Serpentine Die Cut 11x10½

2252 A1106 (4.30s) multi 2.50 2.50
   a. Booklet pane of 12 + 12 etiquettes 30.00

"Good Luck" — A1107

2020, Apr. 21 — Litho. — Perf. 13¾
2253 A1107 (2.50s) multi 1.50 1.50
   With tab 1.75
   a. Sheet of 12 + 12 labels 21.50 —

No. 2253a sold for 37.50s. Labels could be personalized.

Mikve Israel, 150th Anniv. — A1108

2020, Apr. 21 — Litho. — Perf. 13x13¼
2254 A1108 4.10s multi 2.40 2.40
   With tab 2.60

Liberation of World War II Concentration Camps, 75th Anniv. — A1109

2020, Apr. 21 — Litho. — Perf. 13¼x13
2255 A1109 8.30s multi 4.75 4.75
   With tab 5.25

Bees — A1110

No. 2256 — Flower and: a, Bombus terrestri. b, Anthophora. c, Apis mellifera.

2020, Apr. 21 — Litho. — Perf. 13x13¼
2256 Strip of 3 7.25 7.25
   a.-c. A1110 4.10s Any single 2.40 2.40
   Strip with tabs 8.00

Souvenir Sheet

Memorial Day — A1111

No. 2257: a, Ship carrying illegal immigrants arriving at Nahariya, 1948. b, Settlers building a guard tower at Kibbutz Masada, 1937. c, Haganah fighters in the Jezreel Valley, 1948.

2020, Apr. 21 — Litho. — Perf. 13x13¼
2257 A1111 Sheet of 3 8.50 8.50
   a.-c. 4.10s Any single 2.75 2.75

No. 2257 sold for 15s.

Writers — A1112

Designs: No. 2258, Haim Gouri (1923-2018). No. 2259, Ronit Matalon (1959-2017). No. 2260, Amos Oz (1939-2018).

2020, June 9 — Litho. — Perf. 13x13¼
2258 A1112 2.50s multi 1.50 1.50
2259 A1112 2.50s multi 1.50 1.50
2260 A1112 2.50s multi 1.50 1.50
   Nos. 2258-2260 (3) 4.50 4.50
   With tabs 5.00

ISREAL

Flowers — A1113

Designs: 7.40s, Dittricia viscosa. 8.30s, Epilobium hirsutum. 11.80s, Capparis zoharyi.

2020, June 9	Litho.	Perf. 13¼x13
2261	A1113 7.40s multi	4.25 4.25
2262	A1113 8.30s multi	5.00 5.00
2263	A1113 11.80s multi	6.75 6.75
	Nos. 2261-2263 (3)	16.00 16.00
	With tabs	17.50

Tel Aviv and Jaffa, Israel and Recife and Olinda, Brazil — A1114

2020, Sept. 8	Litho.	Perf. 13¼x13½
2264	A1114 11.80s multi	7.00 7.00
	With tab	7.75

Friendship between Israel and Brazil. See Brazil No. 3445.

Murals — A1115

Designs: 4.10s, Ades Synagogue Mural, by Yaakov Stark (1881-1915), Jerusalem. 5s, The Circle of Life Mural, by Avraham Ofek (1935-90), Kfar Uriah. 6.50s, The Painted House Mural, by Afia Zecharia (c. 1905-2002), Shlomi.

2020, Sept. 8	Litho.	Perf. 13x13¼
2265	A1115 4.10s multi	2.40 2.40
2266	A1115 5s multi	3.00 3.00
2267	A1115 6.50s multi	3.75 3.75
	Nos. 2265-2267 (3)	9.15 9.15
	With tabs	10.00

Mandalas A1116

Designs: 2.50s, Kingship. 7.40s, Remembrance. 8.30s, Shofars.

2020, Sept. 8	Litho.	Perf. 13½
2268	A1116 2.50s multi	1.50 1.50
a.	Tete-beche pair	3.00 3.00
2269	A1116 7.40s multi	4.50 4.50
a.	Tete-beche pair	9.00 9.00
2270	A1116 8.30s multi	5.00 5.00
a.	Tete-beche pair	10.00 10.00
	Nos. 2268-2270 (3)	11.00 11.00
	With tabs	12.00

Values are for stamps with surrounding selvage.

Ludwig van Beethoven (1770-1827), Composer A1117

2020, Dec. 15	Litho.	Perf. 13x13½
2271	A1117 11.80s multi	7.50 7.50
	With tab	8.25

Exhibits of Steinhardt Museum of Natural History, Tel Aviv — A1118

Inscription: No. 2272, The Web of Life. No. 2273, Beetles. No. 2274, Caracal and francolin.

2020, Dec. 15	Litho.	Perf. 13x13½
2272	A1118 4.10s multi	2.60 2.60
2273	A1118 4.10s multi	2.60 2.60
2274	A1118 4.10s multi	2.60 2.60
	Nos. 2272-2274 (3)	7.80 7.80
	With tabs	8.75

Biblical Meetings of Peace A1119

Inscriptions: 2.50s, "And they made a pact in Beer-sheba." (Abraham and Abimelech, King of Gerar). No. 2276, "And they built a palace for David." (King David and King Hiram of Tyre). No. 2277, "They came from a distant country, from Babylon." (King Hezekiah and the envoys of the King of Babylon). 10s, "And she came to test him with hard questions." (King Solomon and the Queen of Sheba), vert.

	Perf. 14½x14¼
2020, Dec. 15	Litho.
2275 A1119 2.50s multi	1.60 1.60
2276 A1119 4.10s multi	2.60 2.60
2277 A1119 4.10s multi	2.60 2.60
Nos. 2275-2277 (3)	6.80 6.80
With tabs	7.50

Souvenir Sheet
Perf. 14x13¾ Syncopated

| 2278 | A1119 10s multi | 6.25 6.25 |

No. 2278 contains one 40x55mm stamp.

Orri Mandarin Orange — A1120

2021, Feb. 9	Litho.	Perf. 13x13½
2279	A1120 5s multi	3.00 3.00
	With tab	3.50

Agricultural Research Organization's Volcani Center, cent.

Jewish National Fund, 120th Anniv. — A1121

2021, Feb. 9	Litho.	Perf. 13x13½
2280	A1121 11.70s multi	7.25 7.25
	With tab	8.00

Remote-Sensing Satellites — A1122

No. 2281: a, Venus Research Satellite. b, Opt-Sat 3000 Observation Satellite. c, TechSAR Radar Satellite.

2021, Feb. 9	Litho.	Perf. 13½x13⅔
2281	A1122 Horiz. strip of 3	7.50 7.50
a.-c.	4.10s Any single	2.50 2.50
	Strip with tabs	8.25

Memorial Day — A1123

2021, Apr. 6	Litho.	Perf. 13¼x13
2282	A1123 2.50s multi	1.60 1.60
	With tab	1.75

Jews Saving Other Jews During the Holocaust — A1124

2021, Apr. 6	Litho.	Perf. 13¼x13
2283	A1124 10s multi	6.25 6.25
	With tab	7.00

Bank Hapoalim, Cent. — A1125

2021, Apr. 6	Litho.	Perf. 13x13¼
2284	A1125 11.70s multi	7.25 7.25
	With tab	8.00

Occupations of the Past — A1126

No. 2285: a, Photographer. b, Ice seller. c, Milkman.

2021, Apr. 6	Litho.	Perf. 13x13¼
2285	Horiz. strip of 3	7.50 7.50
a.-c.	A1126 4.10s Any single	2.50 2.50
	Strip with tabs	8.25

Souvenir Sheet

House Blessing A1127

2021, Apr. 6	Litho.	Perf.
2286	A1127 10s multi	6.25 6.25

Manufacturers' Association of Israel, Cent. — A1128

2021, June 29	Litho.	Perf. 13x13¼
2287	A1128 5s multi	3.25 3.25
	With tab	3.50

Israel Police Orchestra, Cent. — A1129

2021, June 29	Litho.	Perf. 13x13¼
2288	A1129 11.70s multi	7.25 7.25
	With tab	8.00

2020 Summer Olympics, Tokyo — A1130

Designs: 2.50s, Rhythmic gymnastics. 4s, Equestrian show jumping. 6.50s, Swimming.

2021, June 29	Litho.	Perf. 13¼x13
2289	A1130 2.50s multi	1.60 1.60
2290	A1130 4s multi	2.50 2.50
2291	A1130 6.50s multi	4.00 4.00
	Nos. 2289-2291 (3)	8.10 8.10
	With tabs	9.00

The 2020 Summer Olympics were postponed until 2021 because of the COVID-19 pandemic.

Tu B'Av A1131

No. 2292: a, Man on bicycle. b, Woman holding bowl of grapes and tambourine.

2021, June 29	Litho.	Perf. 13¾
2292	A1131 Horiz. pair	6.25 6.25
a.	3s multi	1.90 1.90
b.	7s multi	4.25 4.25
	With tabs at left and right sides of horiz. pair	7.00

Shmuel Yosef Agnon (1888-1970), 1966 Nobel Literature Laureate — A1132

2021, Aug. 17	Litho.	Perf. 13
2293	A1132 6.50s multi	4.00 4.00
	With tab	4.50

See Ukraine No. 1310.

Yitzhak Nissim (1895-1973), Sephardic Chief Rabbi of Israel — A1133

2021, Aug. 24	Litho.	Perf. 13¼x13
2294	A1133 11.70s multi	7.25 7.25
	With tab	8.00

Festivals A1134

Themes on the circles of existence from the Book of Ecclesiastes: 2.50s, Sun, moon and tree (The sun rises, and the sun sets, and glides back to where it rises). 7.40s, Sun, rain clouds, mountain and stream (All streams flow into the sea, yet the sea is never full; to the place from which they flow the streams flow back again). 8.30s, Child and old man (The earlier ones are not remembered, so too those that will occur later).

2021, Aug. 24	Litho.	Perf. 13½
2295	A1134 2.50s multi	1.60 1.60
a.	Tete-beche pair	3.20 3.20
2296	A1134 7.40s multi	4.75 4.75
a.	Tete-beche pair	9.50 9.50
2297	A1134 8.30s multi	5.25 5.25
a.	Tete-beche pair	10.50 10.50
	Nos. 2295-2297 (3)	11.60 11.60
	With tabs	13.00

Values are for stamps with surrounding selvage.

Observatories A1135

No. 2298 — Telescope and user at: a, Wise Observatory, Mitzpe Ramon. b, Givatayim Observatory, Givatayim. c, Ramon Crater International Dark Sky Park.

2021, Aug. 24	Litho.	Perf. 13x13¼
2298	Horiz. strip of 3	8.00 8.00
a.-c.	A1135 4.10s Any single	2.60 2.60
	Strip of 3 with tabs	8.75

ISRAEL

Tomas G. Masaryk (1850-1937), President of Czechoslovakia, and Mosaic at Kfrar Masaryk Kibbutz — A1136

2021, Nov. 30	Litho.	Perf. 13x13¼
2299	A1136 6.50s multi	4.25 4.25
	With tab	4.75

See Czech Republic No. 3890.

Tribute to Workers During the COVID-19 Pandemic — A1137

2021, Nov. 30	Litho.	Perf. 13¼x13
2300	A1137 11.70s multi	7.50 7.50
	With tab	8.25

Waterfalls A1138

Designs: 5s, Banyas Waterfall and flower. 7.30s, David Waterfall and ibex. 8.40s, En Avdat Waterfall and hiker.

2021, Nov. 30	Litho.	Perf. 13x13¼
2301	A1138 5s multi	3.25 3.25
2302	A1138 7.30s multi	4.75 4.75
2303	A1138 8.40s multi	5.50 5.50
	Nos. 2301-2303 (3)	13.50 13.50
	With tabs	15.00

Painting by Disabled Artists A1139

No. 2304: a, Mouth painter. b, Foot painter.

2021, Nov. 30	Litho.	Perf. 13x13¼
2304	A1139 Pair	3.25 3.25
a.-b.	2.50s Either single	1.60 1.60
	Pair with tabs	3.75

Givatayim, Cent. — A1140

2022, Feb. 15	Litho.	Perf. 13x13¼
2305	A1140 5s multi	3.25 3.25
	With tab	3.75

Torah Arks and Bimahs From Synagogues in Gibraltar and Israel A1141

	Perf. 14½x14¼	
2022, Feb. 15		Litho.
2306	A1141 7.40s multi	4.75 4.75
	With tab	5.25

Joint issue between Israel and Gibraltar. See Gibraltar No. 1819.

Shaare Zedek Medical Center, Jerusalem, 120th Anniv. — A1142

2022, Feb. 15	Litho.	Perf. 13x13¼
2307	A1142 8.30s multi	5.25 5.25
	With tab	5.75

Farmers Federation of Israel, Cent. — A1143

2022, Feb. 15	Litho.	Perf. 13x13¼
2308	A1143 11.70s multi	7.25 7.25
	With tab	8.00

Cacti — A1144

No. 2309: a, Mammillaria. b, Ferocactus. c, Opuntia. d, Thelocactus. e, Echinopsis.

2022, Feb. 15	Litho.	Perf. 13¼x13
2309	Horiz. strip of 5	8.00 8.00
a.-e.	A1144 2.50s Any single	1.60 1.60
f.	Tete-beche pair, #2309c	3.20 3.20
	Strip with tabs	8.75

No. 2309 was printed in sheets containing two strips that are tete-beche in relation to each other.

Home Front Command Fallen Soldiers Memorial A1145

2022, Apr. 26	Litho.	Perf. 13x13¼
2310	A1145 2.60s multi	1.50 1.50
	With tab	1.75

Memorial Day.

Raanana, Cent. — A1146

2022, Apr. 26	Litho.	Perf. 13x13¼
2311	A1146 12s multi	7.25 7.25
	With tab	8.00

Art from the Holocaust A1147

Designs: 2.60s, The Refugee, painting by Felix Nussbaum (1904-44). No. 2313, To the Man Who Restored My Belief in Humanity, drawing by Yehuda Bacon (light green background). No. 2314, The Evacuation, watercolor by Ben Zion (Nolik) Schmidt (1926-44) (light gray blue background).

2022, Apr. 26	Litho.	Perf. 13x13¼
2312	A1147 2.60s multi	1.60 1.60
2313	A1147 4.20s multi	2.50 2.50
2314	A1147 4.20s multi	2.50 2.50
	Nos. 2312-2314 (3)	6.60 6.60
	With tabs	7.50

Souvenir Sheet

The Revelation at Mount Sinai — A1148

2022, Apr. 26	Litho.	Perf. 13¾x14
2315	A1148 10s multi	6.00 6.00

Christians for Israel — A1149

2022, June 28	Litho.	Perf. 13¼x13
2316	A1149 7.40s multi	4.25 4.25
	With tab	4.75

LGBTQ Community in Israel — A1150

2022, June 28	Litho.	Perf. 13¼x13
2317	A1150 8.30s multi	4.75 4.75
	With tab	5.25

21st Maccabiah Games — A1151

2022, June 28	Litho.	Perf. 13¼x13
2318	A1151 12s multi	7.00 7.00
	With tab	7.75

Scuba Diving Sites A1152

No. 2319: a, Canyon, Achziv. b, Marine archaeology site, Caesarea.
No. 2320: a, Moses Rock Reef, Eilat. b, Missile boat, Eilat.

2022, June 28	Litho.	Perf. 13x13¼
2319	A1152 Pair	3.00 3.00
a.-b.	2.60s Either single	1.50 1.50
2320	A1152 Pair	3.00 3.00
a.-b.	2.60s Either single	1.50 1.50
	With tab	3.75

Diplomatic Relations Between Israel and Mexico, 70th Anniv. — A1153

2022, Sept. 13	Litho.	Perf. 13x13¼
2321	A1153 8.30s multi	4.75 4.75
	With tab	5.25

See Mexico No. 3264.

Festivals A1154

Designs: 2.60s, Bull (Sukkoth). 7.40s, Goat (Yom Kippur). 12s, Ram (Rosh Hashana).

2022, Sept. 13	Litho.	Perf. 13½
2322	A1154 2.60s multi	1.50 1.50
a.	Tete-beche pair	3.00 3.00
2323	A1154 7.40s multi	4.25 4.25
a.	Tete-beche pair	8.50 8.50
2324	A1154 12s multi	6.75 6.75
a.	Tete-beche pair	13.50 13.50
	Nos. 2322-2324 (3)	12.50 12.50
	With tabs	14.00

Values are for stamps with surrounding selvage.

Shells — A1155

No. 2325: a, Bolinus brandaris. b, Charonia variegata. c, Columbella rustica.

2022, Sept. 13	Litho.	Perf. 13x13¼
2325	Horiz. strip of 3	7.25 7.25
a.-c.	A1155 4.20s Any single	2.40 2.40
	Strip with tabs	8.00

House of David Inscription Discovered at Tel Dan in 1993 — A1156

2022, Dec. 20	Litho.	Perf. 13¼x13
2326	A1156 4.40s multi	2.50 2.50
	With tab	2.75

ISRAEL

Year	Mint	Tab	Year	Mint	Tab	Year	Mint	Tab	Year	Mint	Tab
1948	370.00	POR	1965	5.95	13.95	1978	7.95	11.95	1993	27.95	28.95	2008	75.95	81.95
1949	62.50	599.00	1966	5.95	8.95	1979	6.95	8.95	1994	26.50	27.50	2009	75.95	81.95
1950	17.95	645.00	1967	5.95	8.95	1980	8.95	9.95	1995	22.95	25.95	2010	83.95	88.95
1951	3.50	145.00	1968	5.95	9.95	1981	10.95	11.95	1996	29.95	30.95	2011	83.95	88.95
1952	20.75	215.00	1969	6.95	8.95	1982	13.00	14.95	1997	32.95	35.95	2012	75.95	78.95
1953	5.95	59.95	1970	9.50	9.95	1983	11.95	12.95	1998	36.95	39.95	2013	75.95	76.95
1954	3.50	12.95	1971	9.95	13.50	1984	11.95	12.95	1999	39.95	41.95	2014	84.00	87.95
1955	4.00	14.95	1972	8.95	10.95	1985	15.95	20.95	2000	46.95	47.95	2015	80.95	86.95
1956	3.25	6.95	1973	7.95	9.50	1986	17.95	18.95	2001	53.95	54.95	2016	91.95	94.95
1957	4.00	6.95	1974	7.95	8.95	1987	15.95	17.95	2002	49.95	52.95	2017	88.95	95.95
1958	4.00	7.50	1975	7.95	10.95	1988	15.95	16.95	2003	56.95	61.95	2018	93.95	97.95
1959	5.00	7.50	1976	6.95	8.95	1989	24.95	26.95	2004	45.95	49.95	2019	119.95	124.95
1960	11.50	16.00	1977	19.95	25.95	1990	19.95	21.95	2005	65.95	71.95	2020	102.95	104.95
1961	6.95	13.50				1991	19.95	20.95	2006	69.95	75.95	2021	99.95	100.95
1962	7.95	13.50				1992	25.95	27.95	2007	75.95	81.95	2022	99.95	101.95
1963	9.50	22.00										2023	99.95	102.95
1964	6.50	14.00												

Terms: Check with order or payment via Paypal to sales@israelstamps.net. For payment with a credit card, please visit our website, ISRAELSTAMPS.NET.
Mint and tab year sets consist of mint singles and souvenir sheets only. All orders add 8.25 for shipping and handling. Orders outside the U.S. must be registered - insurance or registration extra. Also available: Sheets, sheetlets, booklets, postal stationery and specialty items. Prices subject to change without notice.

Send orders to: ISRAELSTAMPS.NET
P.O. Box 90784, Raleigh, NC 27675
FOR ORDERS ONLY, PLEASE CALL (919) 937-1577

Email us at: sales@israelstamps.net
OR: VISIT OUR WEBSITE WWW.ISRAELSTAMPS.NET FOR THE LATEST NEW ISSUES AS THEY BECOME AVAILABLE AND EASY ORDERING WITH YOUR CREDIT CARD! WE ALSO BUY ISRAEL AND UNITED NATIONS STAMPS!

ISRAEL

Tombstone Inscription in Georgian Script Discovered in Umm Leisun, Israel in 2002 — A1157

2022, Dec. 20		Litho.		Perf. 14½
2327	A1157	6.50s multi	3.75	3.75
		With tab		4.25

Diplomatic relations between Israel and Georgia, 30th anniv. See Georgia No.

Mount Hermon Resort, 50th Anniv. A1158

Resort in: 2.60s, Summer. 4.20s, Winter.

2022, Dec. 20		Litho.		Perf. 13¼
2328	A1158	2.60s multi	1.50	1.50
2329	A1158	4.20s multi	2.40	2.40
		With tabs		4.25

Food Processing Companies A1159

Designs: 7.40s, Osem, maker of noodles and ptitim. 8.30s, Elite, maker of chocolate bars. 12s, Strauss, maker of dairy products.

2022, Dec. 20		Litho.		Perf. 13x13¼
2330	A1159	7.40s multi	4.25	4.25
2331	A1159	8.30s multi	4.75	4.75
2332	A1159	12s multi	6.75	6.75
		Nos. 2330-2332 (3)	15.75	15.75
		With tabs		17.50

Israel Electric Corporation, Cent. — A1160

2023, Feb. 7		Litho.		Perf. 13¼x13
2333	A1160	7.40s multi	4.25	4.25
		With tab		4.75

Standards Institution of Israel, Cent. — A1161

2023, Feb. 7		Litho.		Perf. 13¼x13
2334	A1161	12s multi	6.75	6.75
		With tab		7.50

Women — A1162

Designs: 4.20s, Shoshana Shababo (1910-92), writer. 4.40s, Ada Fishman Maimon (1893-1973), politician.

2023, Feb. 7		Litho.		Perf. 13x13¼
2335	A1162	4.20s multi	2.40	2.40
2336	A1162	4.40s multi	2.50	2.50
		With tabs		5.50

Mammals — A1163

No. 2337: a, Vormela peregusna. b, Felis silvestris. c, Canis aureus. d, Herpestes ichneumon. e, Hyaena hyaena.

2023, Feb. 7		Litho.		Perf. 13¼x13
2337		Horiz. strip of 5	7.50	7.50
a.-e.		A1163 2.60s Any single	1.50	1.50
f.		Tete-beche pair, #2337c	3.00	3.00
		Strip with tabs		8.25

Souvenir Sheet

Traveler's Prayer Written by Rabbi Hisda A1164

2023, Feb. 7		Litho.		Perf.
2338	A1164	15s multi	8.25	8.25

Memorial Day — A1165

2023, Mar. 28		Litho.		Perf. 13x13¼
2339	A1165	3.30s multi	1.90	1.90
		With tab		2.10

Yom Kippur War, 50th anniv.

Meir Har-Zion (1934-2014), Commando A1166

2023, Mar. 28		Litho.		Perf. 13x13¼
2340	A1166	5.50s multi	3.25	3.25
		With tab		3.50

City of Nesher, Cent. — A1167

2023, Mar. 28		Litho.		Perf. 13x13¼
2341	A1167	12.50s multi	7.00	7.00
		With tab		7.75

Modes of Transport of International Mail Leaving Israel — A1168

Designs: 5.50s, Russian mail ship Chihachov, Jaffa skyline, envelope sent from French Post Office in Jaffa. 7.60s, Mail transport truck, Haifa railroad station, envelope sent from Baghdad to Haifa. 8.50s, Seaplane, aerial view of Tiberius, envelope sent from Cyprus to Tiberius.

2023, Mar. 28		Litho.		Perf. 13x13¼
2342	A1168	5.50s multi	3.25	3.25
2343	A1168	7.60s multi	4.25	4.25
2344	A1168	8.50s multi	4.75	4.75
		Nos. 2342-2344 (3)	12.25	12.25
		With tabs		13.50

State of Israel, 75th Anniv. — A1169

"75" and: No. 2345, Ashaim thermo-solar power plant, wind turbines, power lines, Leviathan gas field equipment, highway overpass, crane, building, electric train, electric car at charging station, recycling machine, water works. No. 2346, F-35 Adir fighter jet, Heron MKII drone, Oleq-16 satellite, Arrow 3 missile, Light Shield laser system, Merkava M4 tank, security wall, Dolphin submarine, Sa'ar 6 missile ship, SH-60 Seahawk marine helicopter. No. 2347, Robotic arm, computer processor, computer, gold bars in bank vault, microscope, molecular models, agricultural drone watering crops, computerized shopping cart, synthetic meat printer, diamond, airplane, container ship.

2023, Mar. 28		Litho.		Perf. 13¼
		Denomination	**Color**	
2345	A1169	3.30s	purple	1.90 1.90
2346	A1169	3.30s	green	1.90 1.90
2347	A1169	3.30s	brown	1.90 1.90
		Nos. 2345-2347 (3)		5.70 5.70
		With tabs		6.25

Air Tanker Fighting Fire — A1170

2023, Apr. 4		Litho.		Perf. 13½
2348	A1170	10.90s multi	6.00	6.00
		With tab		6.75

See Cyprus No.

AIR POST STAMPS

Doves Pecking at Grapes AP1

Marisa Eagle AP2

Designs: 30p, Beth Shearim eagle. 40p, Mosaic bird. 50p, Stylized dove. 250p, Mosaic dove and olive branch.

1950, June 25		Unwmk.	Litho.	
C1	AP1	5p brt grnsh bl	.65	.25
C2	AP1	30p gray	.35	.25
C3	AP1	40p dark green	.35	.25
C4	AP1	50p henna brown	.35	.25
C5	AP2	100p rose car	13.00	12.00
C6	AP2	250p dk gray bl	1.75	.60
		Nos. C1-C6 (6)	16.45	13.60
		With tabs		250.00

Haifa Bay and City Seal — AP3

120p, Haifa, Mt. Carmel and city seal.

1952, Apr. 13			Perf. 14
		Seal in Gray	
C7	AP3	100p ultramarine	.30 .25
C8	AP3	120p purple	.30 .25
		#C7-C8, with tabs	20.00

Stamps were available only on purchase of a ticket to the National Stamp Exhibition, Haifa. Price, including ticket, 340p.

Olive Tree AP4

Tanur Cascade AP5

Coast at Tel Aviv-Jaffa — AP6

70p, En Gev, Sea of Galilee. 100p, Road to Jerusalem. 150p, Lion Rock. 350p, Bay of Elat, Red Sea. 750p, Lake Hule. 3000p, Tomb of Rabbi Meir Baal Haness, Tiberias.

1953-56			Litho.	
C9	AP4	10p olive grn	.25	.25
C10	AP4	70p violet	.25	.25
C11	AP4	100p green	.25	.25
C12	AP4	150p orange brn	.25	.25
C13	AP4	350p car rose	.25	.25
C14	AP5	500p dull & dk bl	.25	.25
C15	AP6	750p brown	.30	.25
C16	AP6	1000p deep bl grn	4.50	1.00
		With tab		85.00
C17	AP6	3000p claret	.25	.25
		Nos. C9-C17 (9)	6.55	3.00
		Nos. C9-C15, C17 with tabs		7.50

Issued: 1000p, 3/16/53; 10p, 100p, 500p, 3/2/54; 70p, 150p, 350p, 4/6/54; 750p, 8/21/56; 3000p, 11/13/56.

Old Town, Zefat — AP7

Designs: 20a, Ashkelon, Afridar Center. 25a, Acre, tower and boats. 30a, Haifa, view from Mt. Carmel. 35a, Capernaum, ancient synagogue, horiz. 40a, Jethro's tomb, horiz. 50a, Jerusalem, horiz. 65a, Tiberias, tower and lake, horiz. £1, Jaffa, horiz.

1960-61		Photo.	Perf. 13x14, 14x13	
C18	AP7	15a light lil & blk	.25	.25
C19	AP7	20a brt yel grn & blk	.25	.25
C20	AP7	25a orange & blk ('61)	.25	.25
C21	AP7	30a grnsh bl & blk ('61)	.25	.25
C22	AP7	35a yel grn & blk ('61)	.25	.25
C23	AP7	40a lt vio & blk ('61)	.25	.25
C24	AP7	50a olive & blk ('61)	.25	.25
C25	AP7	65a lt ultra & black	.25	.25
C26	AP7	£1 pink & blk ('61)	.40	.30
		Nos. C18-C26 (9)	2.40	2.30
		With tabs		12.00

Issued: Nos. C18, C19, C25, 2/24/60; Nos. C20-C22, 6/14/61; Nos. C23, C24, C26, 10/26/61.

Port of Elat ('Aqaba) — AP8

Wmk. 302

1962, Feb. 21		Litho.	Perf. 14	
C27	AP8	£3 multicolored	1.60	1.00
		With tab		10.00

Houbara Bustard — AP9

ISRAEL — ITALIAN COLONIES

Birds: 5a, Sinai rose finch, horiz. 20a, White-breasted kingfisher, horiz. 28a, Mourning wheatear, horiz. 30a, Blue-cheeked bee eater. 40a, Graceful prinia. 45a, Palestine sunbird. 70a, Scops owl. £1, Purple heron. £3, White-tailed Sea eagle.

Perf. 13x14, 14x13

1963 Unwmk. Photo.

C28	AP9	5a dp vio & multi	.25	.25
C29	AP9	20a red & multi	.25	.25
C30	AP9	28a emerald & multi	.25	.25
C31	AP9	30a orange & multi	.25	.25
C32	AP9	40a multicolored	.25	.25
C33	AP9	45a yellow & multi	.25	.25
C34	AP9	55a multicolored	.25	.25
C35	AP9	70a black & multi	.25	.25
C36	AP9	£1 multicolored	.30	.30
C37	AP9	£3 ultra & multi	.75	.60
		Nos. C28-C37 (10)	3.05	2.90
		With tabs	7.50	

Issue dates: Nos. C28-C30, 4/15; Nos. C31-C33, 6/19; Nos. C34-C36, 2/13; No. C37, 10/23.

Diamond and Boeing 707 — AP10

Boeing 707 and: 10a, Textiles. 30a, Symbolic stamps. 40a, Vase, jewelry. 50a, Chick, egg. 55a, Melon, avocado, strawberries. 60a, Gladioli. 80a, Electronic equipment, chart. £1, Heavy oxygen isotopes (chemical apparatus). £1.50, Women's fashions.

1968 Photo. Perf. 13x14

C38	AP10	10a ultra & multi	.25	.25
C39	AP10	30a gray & multi	.25	.25
C40	AP10	40a multicolored	.25	.25
C41	AP10	50a multicolored	.25	.25
C42	AP10	55a multicolored	.25	.25
C43	AP10	60a sl grn, lt grn & red	.25	.25
C44	AP10	80a yel, brn & lt blu	.25	.25
C45	AP10	£1 dark bl & org	.25	.25
C46	AP10	£1.50 multicolored	.25	.25
C47	AP10	£3 pur & lt bl	.30	.25
		Nos. C38-C47 (10)	2.55	2.50
		With tabs	4.25	

Israeli exports. Sheets of 15 (5x3).
Issued: Nos. C38-C41, 3/11; No. C47, 2/7; Nos. C42-C43, C45, 11/6; Nos. C44, C46, 12/23.

POSTAGE DUE STAMPS

Types of Regular Issue Overprinted in Black

Various coins, as on postage denominations.

1948, May 28 Typo. Perf. 11
Unwmk. Yellow Paper

J1	A1	3m orange	3.00	1.25
J2	A1	5m yellow green	4.00	1.75
J3	A1	10m red violet	7.00	4.00
J4	A1	20m ultramarine	13.00	8.00
J5	A1	50m orange brown	55.00	55.00
		Nos. J1-J5 (5)	82.00	70.00
		With tabs (blank)	2,750.	

The 3m, 20m and 50m are known with overprint omitted.
Nos. J1-J5 exist imperf.

1949, Dec. 18 Litho. Perf. 11½

J6	D1	2p orange	.25	.25
J7	D1	5p purple	.40	.25
J8	D1	10p yellow green	.40	.25
J9	D1	20p vermilion	.50	.25
J10	D1	30p violet blue	.65	.30
J11	D1	50p orange brown	1.10	.95
		Nos. J6-J11 (6)	3.30	2.25
		With tabs (blank)	150.00	

Running Stag — D2

1952, Nov. 30 Unwmk. Perf. 14

J12	D2	5p orange brown	.25	.25
J13	D2	10p Prussian blue	.25	.25
J14	D2	20p magenta	.25	.25
J15	D2	30p gray black	.25	.25
J16	D2	40p green	.25	.25
J17	D2	50p brown	.25	.25
J18	D2	60p purple	.25	.25
J19	D2	100p red	.25	.25
J20	D2	250p blue	.25	.25
		Nos. J12-J20 (9)	2.25	2.25
		With tabs (blank)	10.00	

OFFICIAL STAMPS

Redrawn Type of 1950 Overprinted in Black

1951, Feb. 1 Unwmk. Perf. 14

O1	A6	5p bright red violet	.25	.25
O2	A6	15p vermilion	.25	.25
O3	A6	30p ultramarine	.25	.25
O4	A6	40p orange brown	.25	.25
		Nos. O1-O4 (4)	1.00	1.00
		With tabs	18.00	

ITALIAN COLONIES

ə-ˈtal-yən ˈkä-lə-nēz

General Issues for all Colonies

100 Centesimi = 1 Lira

Used values in italics are for postally used stamps. Cancelled-to-order examples sell for about the same as unused, hinged stamps.

Watermark

Wmk. 140

Type of Italy, Dante Alighieri Society Issue, in New Colors

Overprinted in Red or Black

1932, July 11 Wmk. 140 Perf. 14

1	A126	10c gray blk	1.00	3.50
2	A126	15c olive brn	1.00	3.50
3	A126	20c slate grn	1.00	2.00
4	A126	25c dk grn	1.00	2.00
5	A126	30c red brn (Bk)	1.00	2.00
6	A126	50c bl blk	1.00	1.35
7	A126	75c car rose (Bk)	1.75	5.75
8	A126	1.25 l dk bl	1.75	8.00
9	A126	1.75 l violet	1.75	13.00
10	A126	2.75 l org (Bk)	1.75	22.00
11	A126	5 l + 2 l ol grn	2.25	25.00
12	A126	10 l + 2.50 l dp bl	22.50	40.00
		Nos. 1-12, C1-C6 (18)	32.50	234.10

Types of Italy, Garibaldi Issue, in New Colors and Inscribed: "POSTE COLONIALI ITALIANE"

1932, July 1 Photo.

13	A138	10c green	3.25	15.00
14	A138	20c car rose	3.25	10.00
15	A138	25c green	3.25	10.00
16	A138	30c green	3.25	16.00
17	A138	50c car rose	3.25	10.00
18	A141	75c car rose	4.00	17.00
19	A141	1.25 l deep blue	4.00	17.00
20	A141	1.75 l + 25c dp bl	9.00	22.50
21	A144	2.55 l + 50c ol brn	9.00	40.00
22	A145	5 l + 1 l dp bl	9.00	50.00
		Nos. 13-22, C8-C12 (15)	85.25	306.50

See Nos. CE1-CE2.

Plowing with Oxen A1

Pack Camel A2

Lioness — A3

1933, Mar. 27 Wmk. 140

23	A1	10c ol brn	11.00	20.00
24	A2	20c dl vio	11.00	20.00
25	A3	25c green	11.00	20.00
26	A1	50c purple	11.00	20.00
27	A2	75c carmine	11.00	24.00
28	A3	1.25 l blue	11.00	24.00
29	A1	2.75 l red orange	22.50	42.50
30	A2	5 l + 2 l gray grn	45.00	85.00
31	A3	10 l + 2.50 l org brn	45.00	130.00
		Nos. 23-31, C13-C19 (16)	379.00	775.50

Annexation of Eritrea by Italy, 50th anniv.

Agricultural Implements A4

Arab and Camel A5

"Eager with New Life" — A7

Steam Roller — A6

1933 Photo. Perf. 14

32	A4	5c orange	6.00	12.50
33	A5	25c green	6.00	12.50
34	A6	50c purple	6.00	11.00
35	A4	75c carmine	6.00	22.00
36	A5	1.25 l deep blue	6.00	22.00
37	A6	1.75 l rose red	6.00	22.00
38	A4	2.75 l dark blue	6.00	32.00
39	A5	5 l brnsh blk	15.00	42.50
40	A6	10 l bluish blk	15.00	55.00
41	A7	25 l gray black	18.00	85.00
		Nos. 32-41, C20-C27 (18)	191.50	631.00

10th anniversary of Fascism. Each denomination bears a different inscription.
Issue dates: 25 l, Dec. 26; others, Oct. 5.

Mercury and Fasces — A8

1934, Apr. 18

42	A8	20c red orange	1.25	7.25
43	A8	30c slate green	1.25	7.25
44	A8	50c indigo	1.25	7.25
45	A8	1.25 l blue	1.25	14.50
		Nos. 42-45 (4)	5.00	36.25

15th annual Trade Fair, Milan.

Scoring a Goal A9

Soccer Kickoff A10

1934, June 5

46	A9	10c olive green	35.00	47.50
47	A9	50c purple	52.50	32.00
48	A9	1.25 l blue	52.50	110.00
49	A10	5 l brown	70.00	360.00
50	A10	10 l gray blue	70.00	360.00
		Nos. 46-50, C29-C35 (12)	586.50	1,835.

2nd World Soccer Championship.

SEMI-POSTAL STAMPS

Many issues of Italy and Italian Colonies include one or more semi-postal denominations. To avoid splitting sets, these issues are generally listed as regular postage, airmail, etc., unless all values carry a surtax.

AIR POST STAMPS

Italian Air Post Stamps for Dante Alighieri Society Issue in New Colors and Overprinted in Red or Black Like #1-12

1932, July 11 Wmk. 140 Perf. 14

C1	AP10	50c gray blk (R)	1.50	7.25
C2	AP11	1 l indigo (R)	1.50	7.25
C3	AP11	3 l gray (R)	3.00	11.00
C4	AP11	5 l ol brn (R)	3.00	16.00
C5	AP10	7.70 l + 2 l car rose	3.00	22.00
C6	AP11	10 l + 2.50 l org	3.00	42.50
		Nos. C1-C6 (6)	15.00	106.00

Leonardo da Vinci — AP1

1932, Sept. 7 Photo. Perf. 14½

C7	AP1	100 l dp grn & brn	14.50	125.00

Types of Italian Air Post Stamps, Garibaldi Issue, in New Colors and Inscribed: "POSTE AEREA COLONIALE ITALIANA"

1932, July 1

C8	AP13	50c car rose	4.25	11.00
C9	AP14	80c green	4.25	11.00
C10	AP13	1 l + 25c ol brn	8.50	21.00
C11	AP13	2 l + 50c ol brn	8.50	21.00
C12	AP14	5 l + 1 l ol brn	8.50	35.00
		Nos. C8-C12 (5)	34.00	99.00

Eagle — AP2

Savoia Marchetti 55 — AP3

Savoia Marchetti 55 Over Map of Eritrea — AP4

1933 Perf. 14

C13	AP2	50c org brn	16.00	20.00
C14	AP2	1 l blk vio	16.00	20.00
C15	AP3	3 l carmine	23.00	40.00
C16	AP3	5 l olive brn	23.00	40.00
C17	AP2	7.70 l + 2 l slate	40.00	90.00

ITALIAN COLONIES — ITALIAN EAST AFRICA

C18	AP3	10 l + 2.50 l dp bl	40.00	90.00
C19	AP4	50 l dk vio	42.50	90.00
		Nos. C13-C19 (7)	200.50	390.00

50th anniv. of Italian Government of Eritrea.
Issue dates: 50 l, June 1; others, Mar. 27.

Macchi-Costoldi Seaplane — AP5

Savoia S73 AP6

Winding Propeller AP7

"More Efficient Machinery" — AP8

1933-34

C20	AP5	50c org brn	8.00	19.00
C21	AP6	75c red vio	8.00	19.00
C22	AP5	1 l bis brn	8.00	19.00
C23	AP6	3 l olive gray	8.00	37.50
C24	AP5	10 l dp vio	8.00	37.50
C25	AP6	12 l bl grn	8.00	57.50
C26	AP7	20 l gray blk	21.00	65.00
C27	AP8	50 l blue ('34)	32.50	60.00
		Nos. C20-C27 (8)	101.50	314.50

Tenth anniversary of Fascism.
Issue dates: 50 l, Dec. 26; others, Oct. 5.

Natives Hailing Dornier Wal — AP9

1934, Apr. 24

C28	AP9	25 l brown olive	35.00	215.00

Issued in honor of Luigi Amadeo, Duke of the Abruzzi (1873-1933).

Airplane over Stadium AP10

Goalkeeper Leaping AP11

Seaplane and Soccer Ball — AP12

1934, June

C29	AP10	50c yel brn	9.50	47.50
C30	AP10	75c dp vio	9.50	47.50
C31	AP11	5 l brn blk	57.50	110.00
C32	AP11	10 l red org	57.50	110.00
C33	AP10	15 l car rose	57.50	110.00
C34	AP11	25 l green	57.50	250.00
C35	AP12	50 l bl grn	57.50	250.00
		Nos. C29-C35 (7)	306.50	925.00

World Soccer Championship Games, Rome.
Issued: 50 l, June 21; others, June 5.

AIR POST SPECIAL DELIVERY STAMPS

Garibaldi Type of Italy
Wmk. 140

1932, Oct. 6 Photo. Perf. 14

CE1	APSD1	2.25 l + 1 l dk vio & sl	10.00	21.00
CE2	APSD1	4.50 l + 1.50 l dk brn & grn	10.00	35.00

ITALIAN EAST AFRICA

ə-'tal-yən 'ēst 'a-fri-kə

LOCATION — In eastern Africa, bordering on the Red Sea and Indian Ocean
GOVT. — Italian Colony
AREA — 665,977 sq. mi. (estimated)
POP. — 12,100,000 (estimated)
CAPITAL — Asmara

This colony was formed in 1936 and included Ethiopia and the former colonies of Eritrea and Italian Somaliland. For previous issues see listings under these headings.

100 Centesimi = 1 Lira

Used values in italics are for postally used stamps. Cancelled-to-order examples sell for about the same as unused, hinged stamps.

Grant's Gazelle A1

Eagle and Lion A2

Victor Emmanuel III — A3

Fascist Legionary A5

Statue of the Nile A4

Desert Road — A6

Wmk. 140

1938, Feb. 7 Photo. Perf. 14

1	A1	2c red orange	2.25	1.00
2	A2	5c brown	2.25	.25
3	A3	7½c dk violet	3.00	4.25
4	A4	10c olive brown	3.00	.25
5	A5	15c slate green	2.25	.35
6	A3	20c crimson	2.25	.25
7	A6	25c green	3.00	.25
8	A1	30c olive brown	2.25	.70
9	A2	35c sapphire	3.00	11.00
10	A3	50c purple	2.25	.25

Engr.

11	A5	75c carmine lake	3.00	.35
12	A6	1 l olive green	1.90	.25
13	A3	1.25 l deep blue	3.00	.35
14	A4	1.75 l orange	15.50	.25
15	A2	2 l cerise	3.00	.35
16	A6	2.55 l dark brown	18.00	29.00
17	A1	3.70 l purple	57.50	85.00
18	A5	5 l blue	18.00	4.25
19	A2	10 l henna brown	25.00	18.00
20	A4	20 l dull green	36.00	42.50
		Nos. 1-20,C1-C11,CE1-CE2 (33)	381.30	343.30

Augustus Caesar (Octavianus) A7

Goddess Abundantia A8

1938, Apr. 25 Photo. Perf. 14

21	A7	5c bister brn	.75	1.80
22	A8	10c copper red	.75	1.20
23	A7	25c deep green	1.45	1.10
24	A8	50c purple	1.45	.75
25	A7	75c crimson	1.45	2.75
26	A8	1.25 l deep blue	1.45	7.75
		Nos. 21-26,C12-C13 (8)	9.10	22.85

Bimillenary of the birth of Augustus Caesar (Octavianus), first Roman emperor.

Rome-Berlin Axis.
Four stamps of type AP8, without "Posta Aerea," were prepared in 1941, but not issued. Value, each $2,400.

Native Boat A9

Native Soldier A10

Statue Suggesting Italy's Conquest of Ethiopia — A11

1940, May 11 Wmk. 140

27	A9	5c olive brown	.75	1.10
28	A10	10c red orange	.75	1.10
29	A11	25c green	2.25	1.80
30	A9	50c purple	2.25	1.10
31	A10	75c rose red	2.25	7.00
32	A11	1.25 l dark blue	2.25	5.50
33	A10	2 l + 75c carmine	2.25	20.00
		Nos. 27-33,C14-C17 (11)	23.25	52.10

Issued in connection with the first Triennial Overseas Exposition held at Naples.

Hitler and Mussolini ("Two Peoples, One War") — A12

1941, June 19

34	A12	5c ocher	2.25	
35	A12	10c chestnut	2.25	
36	A12	20c black	4.25	
37	A12	25c turquoise grn	4.25	
38	A12	50c rose lilac	4.25	
39	A12	75c rose car	4.25	
40	A12	1.25 l brt ultra	4.25	
		Nos. 34-40,C18-C19 (9)	174.75	

SEMI-POSTAL STAMPS

Many issues of Italy and Italian Colonies include one or more semi-postal denominations. To avoid splitting sets, these issues are generally listed as regular postage, airmail, etc., unless all values carry a surtax.

AIR POST STAMPS

Plane Flying over Mountains — AP1

Mussolini Carved in Stone Cliff — AP2

Airplane over Lake Tsana AP3

Bataleur Eagle AP4

Wmk. Crowns (140)

1938, Feb. 7 Photo. Perf. 14

C1	AP1	25c slate green	3.50	4.25
C2	AP2	50c olive brown	57.50	.25
C3	AP3	60c red orange	2.25	13.00
C4	AP1	75c orange brn	3.50	2.25
C5	AP4	1 l slate blue	1.40	.25

Engr.

C6	AP2	1.50 l violet	1.75	.35
C7	AP3	2 l slate blue	1.75	1.60
C8	AP1	3 l carmine lake	2.75	6.00
C9	AP1	5 l red brown	52.50	42.50
C10	AP2	10 l violet brn	10.50	13.00
C11	AP1	25 l slate blue	25.00	32.00
		Nos. C1-C11 (11)	162.40	115.45

Eagle Attacking Serpent — AP5

1938, Apr. 25 Photo.

C12	AP5	50c bister brown	.90	2.75
C13	AP5	1 l purple	.90	4.75

Bimillenary of the birth of Augustus Caesar (Octavianus), first Roman emperor.

Triennial Overseas Exposition Type

#C14, C16, Tractor. #C15, C17, Plane over city.

1940, May 11

C14	A10	50c olive gray	2.25	7.25
C15	A9	1 l purple	2.25	7.25
C16	A10	2 l + 75c gray blue	3.00	—
C17	A9	5 l + 2.50 l red brn	3.00	—
		Nos. C14-C17 (4)	10.50	14.50

Hitler and Mussolini ("Two Peoples, One War") — AP8

AP9

1941, Apr. 24

C18	AP8	1 l slate blue	140.00	
C19	AP9	1 l slate blue	9.00	

Rome-Berlin Axis.

ITALIAN EAST AFRICA — ITALIAN STATES — MODENA

AIR POST SPECIAL DELIVERY STAMPS

Plow and Airplane — APSD1

1938, Feb. 7   Engr.   **Wmk. 140**   Perf. 14
CE1	APSD1	2 l slate blue	7.00	11.00
CE2	APSD1	2.50 l dk brn	5.50	18.00

SPECIAL DELIVERY STAMPS

Victor Emmanuel III — SD1

1938, Apr. 16   Engr.   **Wmk. 140**   Perf. 14
E1	SD1	1.25 l dark green	11.00	11.00
E2	SD1	2.50 l dark carmine	11.00	32.00

POSTAGE DUE STAMPS

Italy, Nos. J28 to J40, Overprinted in Black

1941   **Wmk. 140**   Perf. 14
J1	D6	5c brown	1.60
J2	D6	10c blue	1.60
J3	D6	20c rose red	3.25
J4	D6	25c green	3.25
J5	D6	30c red orange	8.00
J6	D6	40c black brown	8.00
J7	D6	50c violet	8.00
J8	D6	60c slate black	11.00
J9	D7	1 l red orange	22.50
J10	D7	2 l green	22.50
J11	D7	5 l violet	35.00
J12	D7	10 l blue	22.50
J13	D7	20 l carmine rose	22.50
		Nos. J1-J13 (13)	169.70

In 1943 a set of 11 "Segnatasse" stamps, picturing a horse and rider and inscribed "A. O. I.," was prepared but not issued. Value, $17.50.

ITALIAN STATES

ə-ˈtal-yən ˈstāts

Watermarks

Wmk. 157 — Large Letter "A"

Wmk. 184 — Interlaced Wavy Lines

Wmk. 184 has double lined letters diagonally across the sheet reading: "II R R POSTE TOSCANE."

Wmk. 185 — Crowns in the sheet

The watermark consists of twelve crowns, arranged in four rows of three, with horizontal and vertical lines between them. Only parts of the watermark appear on each stamp.

Wmk. 186 — Fleurs-de-Lis in Sheet

MODENA

LOCATION — In northern Italy
GOVT. — Duchy
AREA — 1,003 sq. mi.
POP. — 448,000 (approx.)
CAPITAL — Modena

In 1852, when the first postage stamps were issued, Modena was under the rule of Duke Francis V of the House of Este-Lorraine. In June, 1859, he was overthrown and the Duchy was annexed to the Kingdom of Sardinia which on March 17, 1861, became the Kingdom of Italy.

100 Centesimi = 1 Lira

Values of Modena stamps vary tremendously according to condition. Values are for very fine examples, and values for unused stamps are for examples with original gum as defined in the catalogue introduction. Extremely fine or superb examples sell at much higher prices, and fine or poor examples sell at greatly reduced prices.

Coat of Arms — A1

1852-57   Unwmk.   Typo.   Imperf.
Without Period After Figures of Value

1	A1	5c blk, green	4,000.	127.50
2	A1	10c blk, rose	690.00	72.50
a.		"EENT. 10"	9,500.	2,875.
b.		"1" of "10" inverted	9,500.	2,875.
c.		"CNET"	1,575.	1,600.
d.		No period after "CENT"	2,150.	800.00
3	A1	15c blk, yellow	85.00	29.00
a.		"CETN 15."	9,500.	1,000.
b.		No period after "CENT"	345.00	500.00
4	A1	25c blk, buff	250.00	42.50
a.		No period after "CENT"	850.00	950.00
b.		"ENT.25" omitted	1,000.	—
c.		25c black, green (error)	5,000.	2,875.
d.		"N" of "CENT" omitted	750.00	1,750.
5	A1	40c blk, blue	460.00	100.00
a.		40c black, pale blue	20,000.	2,250.
b.		No period after "CENT"	2,000.	1,600.
c.		As "a," no period after "CENT"	—	—

Unused examples of No. 5a lack gum.
Used examples of No. 4c have a green administrative cancellation.

See Nos. PR3-PR4.
With Period After Figures of Value

6	A1	5c blk, green	45.00	45.00
a.		5c black, olive green ('55)	625.00	145.00
b.		"ENT"	—	3,100.
c.		"CNET"	4,500.	3,750.
d.		As "a," "CNET"	2,850.	2,000.
e.		"E" of "CENT" sideways	—	5,700.
f.		As "a," "CEN1"	3,425.	2,275.
g.		As "a," no period after "5"	850.00	525.00
h.		Double impression, no gum	1,600.	—
i.		As "a," double impression	1,600.	—
j.		Pair, #6a, 6g	1,140.	2,500.
7	A1	10c blk, rose ('57)	475.00	340.00
a.		"CENE"	1,600.	1,725.
b.		"CNET"	700.00	800.00
c.		"CE6T"	1,600.	1,700.
d.		"N" of "CENT" sideways	12,750.	4,500.
e.		Double impression	1,600.	5,500.
f.		Raised period after "10"	1,600.	1,650.
8	A1	40c blk, blue ('54)	57.50	100.00
a.		"CNET"	290.00	800.00
b.		"CENE"	700.00	1,700.
c.		"CE6T"	700.00	1,700.
d.		"49"	290.00	800.00
e.		"4C"	700.00	1,700.
f.		"CEN.T"	42,500.	—
g.		Space between "T" and period	290.00	800.00
h.		Pair, one with no period after value, on cover	—	2,300.

Wmk. 157

9	A1	1 l black ('53)	57.50	2,500.
a.		With period after "LIRA"	150.00	5,100.
b.		No period after "1"	135.00	4,800.

Provisional Government

Coat of Arms — A2

1859   Unwmk.

10	A2	5c green	1,375.	630.00
a.		5c emerald	1,425.	690.00
b.		5c dark green	1,425.	690.00
11	A2	15c brown	2,150.	3,725.
11A	A2	15c gray	350.00	
e.		Double impression	1,825.	
12	A2	20c lilac	87.50	1,700.
a.		20c violet	4,000.	260.00
b.		20c blue violet	2,850.	260.00
c.		As #12, no period after "20"	100.00	1,575.
d.		As #12, "ECNT"	230.00	3,400.
e.		As #12, "N" inverted	190.00	2,275.
f.		Double impression (#12b)	—	8,000.
13	A2	40c carmine	170.00	1,450.
a.		40c brown rose	175.00	1,450.
b.		No period after "40"	350.00	2,300.
c.		Period before "CENT"	345.00	2,300.
d.		Inverted "5" before the "C", no gum	50,000.	60,000.
e.		Large period after "40"	345.00	2,300.
14	A2	80c buff	175.00	20,000.
a.		80c brown orange	175.00	20,000.
b.		"CENT 8"	345.00	—
c.		"CENT 0"	1,250.	—
d.		No period after "80"	345.00	—
e.		"N" inverted	575.00	—

NEWSPAPER TAX STAMPS

NT1

Type I

Type II

1853   Unwmk.   Typo.   Imperf.
PR1	NT1	9c blk, violet (I)	—	3,100.
PR2	NT1	9c blk, violet (II)	850.00	70.00
a.		No period after "9"	1,350.	215.00

All known unused examples of #PR1 lack gum.

1855-57
PR3	A1	9c blk, violet	3.00	
a.		No period after "9"	5.75	
b.		No period after "CENT"	8.75	
PR4	A1	10c blk, gray vio ('57)	70.00	230.00
a.		"CEN1"	315.00	1,150.

No. PR3 was never placed in use.

NT2

1859
PR5	NT2	10c black	1,025.	1,875.
a.		Double impression	15,000.	18,750.
b.		Vert. guidelines between stamps	1,025.	

Values for unused pairs
PR5	NT2	10c black	2,150.

PARMA

LOCATION — Comprising the present provinces of Parma and Piacenza in northern Italy.
GOVT. — Independent Duchy
AREA — 2,750 sq. mi. (1860)
POP. — 500,000 (1860)
CAPITAL — Parma

Parma was annexed to Sardinia in 1860.

100 Centesimi = 1 Lira

Values of Parma stamps vary tremendously according to condition. Values are for very fine examples, and values for unused stamps are for examples with original gum as defined in the catalogue introduction except for No. 8 which is known only without gum. Extremely fine or superb copies sell at much higher prices, and fine or poor stamps sell at greatly reduced prices. In addition, very fine unused stamps without gum sell for about 20% of the values shown.

Crown and Fleur-de-lis — A1

1852		Unwmk.	Typo.	Imperf.
1	A1	5c blk, *yellow*	145.00	135.00
2	A1	10c blk, *white*	145.00	135.00
3	A1	15c blk, *pink*	6,750.	90.00
a.		Tête bêche pair, horiz.		90,000.
b.		Double impression		5,400.
4	A1	25c blk, *violet*	25,000.	225.00
5	A1	40c blk, *blue*	5,400.	550.00
a.		40c black, *pale blue*	11,400.	825.00

1853-55				
6	A1	5c org yel	14,500.	640.00
a.		5c lemon yellow	17,250.	825.00
b.		Double impression		18,000.
7	A1	15c red	17,250.	325.00
8	A1	25c red brn ('55)	64,000.	450.00
a.		Double impression		36,000.

No. 8 unused is without gum.

Crown and Fleur-de-lis — A2

1857-59				
9	A2	15c red ('59)	365.00	325.00
10	A2	25c red brown	675.00	225.00
11	A2	40c bl, wide "0" ('58)	70.00	550.00
a.		Narrow "0" in "40"	75.00	690.00

Provisional Government

A3

1859				
12	A3	5c yel grn	500.00	29,000.
a.		5c blue green	3,200.	4,250.
13	A3	10c brown	1,000.	525.00
a.		10c deep brown	1,000.	525.00
b.		"1" of "10" inverted	2,050.	4,250.
c.		Thick "0" in "10"	1,500.	675.00
14	A3	20c pale blue	1,000.	215.00
a.		20c deep blue	1,000.	240.00
b.		Thick "0" in "20"	1,500.	240.00
15	A3	40c red	550.00	8,000.
a.		40c brown red	30,000.	12,500.
b.		Thick "0" in "40" (#15)	825.00	10,000.
c.		Thick "0" in "40," (#15a)	32,000.	13,750.
16	A3	80c ol yel	8,200.	200,000.
a.		80c orange yellow	12,000.	
b.		80c bister	9,100.	
c.		80c orange bister	10,000.	

Nos. 12-16 exist in two other varieties: with spelling "CFNTESIMI" and with small "A" in "STATI." These are valued about 50 per cent more than normal stamps.
See Nos. PR1-PR2.

NEWSPAPER TAX STAMPS

Type of 1859
Normal Paper ('53)

1853-57		Unwmk.	Typo.	Imperf.
PR1	A3	6c blk, *dp rose*	2,750.	375.00
PR2	A3	9c black, *blue*	825.00	4,750.

Thin, Semitransparent Paper ('57)

| PR1a | A3 | 6c black, rose ('57) | 145.00 |
| PR2a | A3 | 9c black, *blue* | 90.00 |

These stamps belong to the same class as the Newspaper Tax Stamps of Modena, Austria, etc.
Note following #16 also applies to #PR1-PR2.
Nos. PR1a-PR2a were not issued.
The stamps of Parma were superseded by those of Sardinia in 1860.

ROMAGNA

LOCATION — Comprised the present Italian provinces of Forli, Ravenna, Ferrara and Bologna.
GOVT. — One of the Roman States
AREA — 5,626 sq. mi.
POP. — 1,341,091 (1853)
CAPITAL — Ravenna

Postage stamps were issued when a provisional government was formed pending the unification of Italy. In 1860 Romagna was annexed to Sardinia and since 1862 the postage stamps of Italy have been used.

100 Bajocchi = 1 Scudo

Values of Romagna stamps vary tremendously according to condition. Values are for very fine examples, and values for unused stamps are for examples with original gum as defined in the catalogue introduction. Extremely fine or superb stamps sell at much higher prices, and fine or poor stamps sell at greatly reduced prices. In addition, very fine unused stamps without gum sell for about 20% of the values shown.

A1

1859		Unwmk.	Typo.	Imperf.
1	A1	½b blk, *straw*	42.50	360.00
a.		Half used as ¼b on cover		16,250.
2	A1	1b blk, *drab*	42.50	180.00
3	A1	2b blk, *buff*	55.00	210.00
a.		Half used as 1b on cover		6,250.
4	A1	3b blk, *dk grn*	60.00	360.00
5	A1	4b blk, *fawn*	650.00	165.00
a.		Half used as 2b on cover		30,000.
6	A1	5b blk, *gray vio*	72.50	400.00
7	A1	6b blk, *yel grn*	500.00	9,000.
a.		Half used as 3b on cover		150,000.
8	A1	8b blk, *rose*	210.00	1,800.
a.		Half used as 4b on cover		150,000.
9	A1	20b blk, *gray grn*	200.00	2,400.

Forged cancellations are plentiful.
Bisects used Oct. 12, 1859 to Mar. 1, 1860.

These stamps have been reprinted several times. The reprints usually resemble the originals in the color of the paper but there are impressions on incorrect colors and also in colors on white paper. They often show broken letters and other injuries. The Y shaped ornaments between the small circles in the corners are broken and blurred and the dots outside the circles are often missing or joined to the circles.
The stamps of Romagna were superseded by those of Sardinia in February, 1860.

ROMAN STATES

LOCATION — Comprised most of the central Italian Peninsula, bounded by the former Kingdom of Lombardy-Venetia and Modena on the north, Tuscany on the west, and the Kingdom of Naples on the southeast.

GOVT. — Under the direct government of the See of Rome.
AREA — 16,000 sq. mi.
POP. — 3,124,758 (1853)
CAPITAL — Rome

Upon the formation of the Kingdom of Italy, the area of the Roman States was greatly reduced and in 1870 they disappeared from the political map of Europe. Postage stamps of Italy have been used since that time.

100 Bajocchi = 1 Scudo
100 Centesimi = 1 Lira (1867)

Values of Roman States stamps vary tremendously according to condition. Values are for very fine examples, and values for unused stamps are for examples with original gum as defined in the catalogue introduction. Extremely fine or superb stamps sell at much higher prices, and fine or poor stamps sell at greatly reduced prices. In addition, very fine unused stamps without gum sell for about 20% of the values shown.

Papal Arms
A1 A2
A3 A4
A5 A6
A7 A8
No. 10a A11
A9 A10
A12 A13
A14 A15
A16 A17
A18

1852		Unwmk.	Typo.	Imperf.
1	A1	½b blk, *dl vio*	55.00	135.00
a.		½b black, *gray blue*	675.00	90.00
b.		½b black, *gray lilac*	675.00	360.00
c.		½b black, *gray*	675.00	90.00
d.		½b black, *reddish vio*	3,500.	2,700.
e.		½b black, *dark violet*	295.00	315.00
f.		Vertical pair, tête bêche	—	30,000.
h.		As "a," half used as ¼b on wrapper		54,000.
		As "h," pen canceled		9,000.
i.		As #1, double impression		6,000.
j.		Impression on both sides	—	13,000.
2	A2	1b blk, *gray grn*	390.00	9.00
a.		1b black, *blue green*	800.00	50.00
b.		As "a," half used as ½b on cover		425.00
c.		Grayish oily ink	1,100.	27.50
d.		Double impression		5,750.
e.		Impression on both sides	—	12,750.
3	A3	2b blk, *grnsh white*	16.00	65.00
a.		2b black, *yel grn*	240.00	16.00
b.		As #3, half used as 1b on cover		5,400.
c.		As "a," half used as 1b on cover		360.00
d.		Grayish oily ink	1,275.	32.50
e.		No period after "BAJ"	145.00	32.50
f.		As "a" and "e"	500.00	32.50
g.		Double impression		5,750.
4	A4	3b blk, *brn*	275.00	55.00
a.		3b black, *light brown*	5,250.	160.00
b.		3b black, *yel brn*	2,500.	40.00
c.		3b black, *yellow buff*	2,500.	40.00
d.		3b black, *chrome yel*	42.50	160.00
e.		One-third used as 1b on circular		3,250.
f.		Two-thirds used as 2b on circular		10,500.
g.		Grayish oily ink	7,000.	210.00
h.		Impression on both sides	—	11,000.
i.		Double impression	—	6,000.
j.		Half used as 1½b on cover		11,500.
5	A5	4b blk, *lem*	240.00	70.00
a.		4b black, *yellow*	240.00	72.50
b.		4b black, *rose brown*	13,500.	120.00
c.		4b black, *gray brown*	11,500.	72.50
d.		Half used as 2b on cover		2,250.
e.		One-quarter used as 1b on cover		20,000.
f.		Impression on both sides	—	11,000.
g.		Ribbed paper	325.00	90.00
h.		Grayish oily ink	23,500.	325.00
i.		As "a," half used as 2b on cover		3,750.
j.		As "a," one-quarter used as 1b on cover		21,500.
6	A6	5b black, *rose*	225.00	14.00
a.		5b black, *pale rose*	225.00	16.00
c.		Impression on both sides	—	11,000.
d.		Double impression		5,500.
e.		Grayish oily ink	1,400.	32.50
f.		Half used as 2½b on cover		54,000.
7	A7	6b blk, *grnsh gray*	975.00	67.50
a.		6b black, *gray*	1,500.	72.50
b.		6b black, *grayish lil*	1,700.	210.00
c.		Grayish oily ink	3,750.	250.00
d.		Double impression	—	6,000.
e.		Half used as 3b on cover		4,250.
f.		One-third used as 2b on cover		16,000.
8	A8	7b black, *blue*	1,425.	72.50
a.		Half used as 3¼b on cover		30,000.
b.		Double impression	—	5,750.
c.		Grayish oily ink	5,000.	135.00
9	A9	8b used black	550.00	40.00
a.		Half used as 4b on cover		8,000.
b.		Quarter used as 2b on cover		80,000.
c.		Double impression	—	
d.		Grayish oily ink	2,250.	210.00
10	A10	50b dull blue	15,000.	1,650.
a.		50b deep blue (worn impression)	21,500.	2,950.
11	A11	1sc rose	4,000.	3,250.

Counterfeits exist of Nos. 10-11. Fraudulent cancellations are found on No. 11.

1867		**Glazed Paper**		Imperf.
12	A12	2c blk, *grn*	90.00	315.00
a.		No period after "Cent"	110.00	350.00
13	A13	3c blk, *gray*	1,300.	8,000.
a.		3c black, *lilac gray*	3,250.	2,150.
14	A14	5c blk, *lt bl*	190.00	215.00
a.		No period after "5"	375.00	450.00
15	A15	10c blk, *ver*	1,900.	95.00
a.		Double impression		5,750.
16	A16	20c blk, *cop red* (unglazed)	190.00	120.00
a.		No period after "20"	540.00	360.00
b.		No period after "CENT"	540.00	360.00
17	A17	40c blk, *yel*	200.00	160.00
a.		No period after "40"	260.00	200.00
18	A18	80c blk, *lil rose*	180.00	450.00
a.		No period after "80"	250.00	675.00

Imperforate stamps on unglazed paper, or in colors other than listed, are unfinished remainders of the 1868 issue.
Fraudulent cancellations are found on Nos. 13, 14, 17, 18.

1868		**Glazed Paper**		Perf. 13
19	A12	2c blk, *grn*	9.00	90.00
a.		No period after "CENT"	11.00	110.00

ITALIAN STATES — ROMAN STATES — SARDINIA — TUSCANY

20	A13	3c blk, gray	55.00	3,250.
		3c black, lilac gray	10,000.	18,000.
21	A14	5c blk, lt blue	60.00	60.00
a.		No period after "5"	75.00	72.50
b.		No period after "Cent"	150.00	350.00
c.		5c black, lt bl (unglazed, imperf., without gum)	120.00	—
22	A15	10c blk, org ver	3.00	15.00
a.		10c black, vermilion	60.00	15.00
b.		10c black, ver (unglazed)	1.25	—
c.		10c black, ver (unglazed, imperf., without gum)	1.25	—
23	A16	20c blk, dp crim	4.75	30.00
a.		20c black, magenta	6.00	42.50
b.		20c blk, mag (unglazed)	300.00	35.00
c.		20c blk, mag (imperf., without gum)	2.50	—
d.		20c blk, cop red (unglazed)	1,950.	42.50
e.		20c blk, dp crim (imperf., without gum)	2.50	—
f.		No period after "20" (copper red)	2,800.	350.00
g.		No period after "20" (mag)	24.00	180.00
h.		No period after "20" (deep crimson)	25.00	180.00
i.		No period after "CENT" (cop red)	2,800.	375.00
j.		No period after "CENT" (mag)	24.00	180.00
k.		No period after "CENT" (dp crim)	24.00	180.00
24	A17	40c blk, grnsh yel	11.00	125.00
a.		40c black, yellow	210.00	75.00
b.		40c black, org yel	90.00	750.00
c.		No period after "40"	15.00	95.00
25	A18	80c blk, rose lil	210.00	415.00
a.		80c blk, brt rose	6,250.	60,000.
b.		80c black, rose (unglazed)	65.00	—
c.		No period after "80" (rose lilac)	110.00	—
d.		80c black, pale rose lilac (unglazed)	77.50	—
e.		80c black, pale rose	55.00	425.00
f.		As "e", no period after "80"	65.00	650.00
g.		As "a", no period after "80"	7,000.	—
h.		As "e", double impression	—	—
		Nos. 19-25 (7)	352.75	3,985.

All values except the 3c are known imperforate vertically or horizontally, and in vertical and horizontal pairs, imperf between. See the *Scott Specialized Catalogue of Stamps and Covers* for detailed listings.

Double impressions are known of the 5c, 10c, 20c (all three colors), 40c and 80c.

Fraudulent cancellations are found on Nos. 20, 24 and 25.

The stamps of the 1867 and 1868 issues have been privately reprinted; many of these reprints are well executed and it is difficult to distinguish them from the originals. Most reprints show more or less pronounced defects of the design. On the originals the horizontal lines between stamps are unbroken, while on most of the reprints these lines are broken. Most of the perforated reprints gauge 11½.

Roman States stamps were replaced by those of Italy in 1870.

SARDINIA

LOCATION — An island in the Mediterranean Sea off the west coast of Italy and a large area in northwestern Italy, including the cities of Genoa, Turin and Nice.

GOVT. — Kingdom

As a result of war and revolution, most of the former independent Italian States were joined to the Kingdom of Sardinia in 1859 and 1860. On March 17, 1861, the name was changed to the Kingdom of Italy.

100 Centesimi = 1 Lira

Values of Sardinia stamps vary tremendously according to condition. Values are for very fine examples, and values for unused stamps are for examples with original gum as defined in the catalogue introduction. Extremely fine or superb stamps sell at much higher prices, and fine or poor stamps sell at greatly reduced prices.

King Victor Emmanuel II — A1

1851   Unwmk.   Litho.   Imperf.

1	A1	5c gray black	13,000.	2,000.
a.		5c black	13,000.	2,000.
2	A1	20c blue	9,500.	235.00
		20c deep blue	9,500.	235.00
a.		20c pale blue	9,500.	235.00
3	A1	40c rose	17,750.	4,000.
a.		40c violet rose	17,750.	5,250.

King Victor Emmanuel II — A2

Vignette & Inscriptions Embossed
1853

4	A2	5c blue green	17,500.	1,100.
a.		Double embossing		3,000.
5	A2	20c dull blue	18,500.	200.00
a.		Double embossing		1,250.
6	A2	40c pale rose	11,250.	800.00
b.		Double embossing		2,250.

King Victor Emmanuel II — A3

Lithographed Frame in Color, Colorless Embossed Vignette
1854

7	A3	5c yellow green	30,000.	575.00
a.		Double embossing		1,250.
		5c grayish green	3,600.	
8	A3	20c blue	16,000.	175.00
a.		Double embossing		525.00
		20c indigo	700.00	
9	A3	40c rose	82,500.	2,750.
a.		Double embossing		5,500.
		40c brown rose	180.00	

Nos. 7b, 8b and 9b, differing in shade from the original stamps, were prepared but not issued.

King Victor Emmanuel II — A4

Stamps of this issue vary greatly in color, paper and sharpness of embossing as between the early (1855-59) printings and the later (1860-63) ones. Year dates after each color name indicate whether the stamp falls into the Early or Late printing group.

As a rule, early printings are on smooth thick paper with sharp embossing, while later printings are usually on paper varying from thick to thin and of inferior quality with embossing less distinct and printing blurred. The outer frame shows a distinct design on the early printings, while this design is more or less blurred or even a solid line on the later printings.

Typographed Frame in Color, Colorless Embossed Vignette
1855-63   Unwmk.   Imperf.

10	A4	5c grn ('62-63)	4.50	11.00
a.		5c yel grn ('62-63)	95.00	17.00
b.		5c olive green ('60-61)	435.00	67.50
c.		5c yel grn ('55-59)	900.00	160.00
d.		5c myrtle green ('57)	7,500.	475.00
e.		5c emerald ('55-57)	3,900.	375.00
f.		Head inverted		3,700.
g.		Double head, one inverted		3,500.
11	A4	10c bister ('63)	4.50	24.00
a.		10c ocher ('62)	90.00	22.00
b.		10c olive bister ('62)	190.00	22.00
c.		10c olive brown ('61)	190.00	29.00
d.		10c reddish brn ('61)	1,800.	160.00
e.		10c gray brown ('61)	150.00	40.00
f.		10c olive gray ('60-61)	370.00	55.00
g.		10c gray ('60)	1,350.	180.00
h.		10c grayish brown ('59)	130.00	210.00
i.		10c violet brown ('59)	525.00	300.00
j.		10c dark brown ('58)	775.00	360.00
k.		Head inverted		4,000.
l.		Double head, one inverted		4,000.
m.		Pair, one without embossing	2,000.	
n.		Half used as 5c on cover (15c rate)		125,000.
12	A4	20c indigo ('62)	85.00	40.00
a.		20c blue ('61)	165.00	16.00
b.		20c light blue ('60-61)	165.00	16.00
c.		20c Prus bl ('59-60)	775.00	27.50
d.		20c indigo ('57-58)	460.00	40.00
e.		20c sky blue ('55-56)	7,100.	170.00
f.		20c cobalt ('55)	3,600.	100.00
g.		Head inverted	3,100.	1,600.
h.		Double head, one inverted		
i.		Pair, one without embossing	1,100.	
j.		Half used as 10c on cover		160,000.
k.		As "c", one without embossing	1,250.	
13	A4	40c red ('63)	17.00	40.00
a.		40c rose ('61-62)	135.00	60.00
b.		40c carmine ('60)	775.00	350.00
c.		40c light red ('57)	3,800.	110.00
d.		40c vermilion ('55-57)	7,250.	325.00
e.		Head inverted		6,250.
f.		Double head, one inverted		6,250.
g.		Pair, one without embossing	1,625.	
h.		Half used as 20c on cover		67,500.
14	A4	80c org yel ('62)	22.00	390.00
a.		80c yellow ('60-61)	25.00	360.00
b.		80c yellow ocher ('59)	900.00	690.00
c.		80c ocher ('58)	200.00	540.00
d.		80c brown orange ('58)	220.00	600.00
e.		Head inverted		22,500.
f.		Half used as 40c on cover		85,000.
15	A4	3 l bronze, thin paper ('61)	400.00	3,650.
		Nos. 10-15 (6)	533.00	4,155.

Forgeries of the inverted and double head varieties have been made by applying a faked head embossing to printer's waste without head. These forgeries are plentiful.

Fraudulent cancellations are found on #13-15.

The 5c, 20c and 40c have been reprinted; the embossing of the reprints is not as sharp as that of the originals, the colors are dull and blurred.

NEWSPAPER STAMPS

N1

Typographed and Embossed
1861   Unwmk.   Imperf.

P1	N1	1c black	6.75	15.00
a.		Numeral "2"	600.00	2,500.
b.		Figure of value inverted	2,400.	34,000.
c.		Double impression	2,750.	
P2	N1	2c black	175.00	105.00
a.		Numeral "1"	13,000.	32,500.
b.		Figure of value inverted	2,400.	34,000.

Forgeries of the varieties of the embossed numerals have been made from printer's waste without numerals.

See Italy No. P1 for 2c buff.

The stamps of Sardinia were superseded in 1862 by those of Italy, which were identical with the 1855 issue of Sardinia, but perforated. Until 1863, imperforate and perforated stamps were issued simultaneously.

TUSCANY

LOCATION — In the north central part of the Apennine Peninsula.
GOVT. — Grand Duchy
AREA — 8,890 sq. mi.
POP. — 2,892,000 (approx.)
CAPITAL — Florence

Tuscany was annexed to Sardinia in 1860.

60 Quattrini = 20 Soldi = 12 Crazie = 1 Lira

100 Centesimi = 1 Lira (1860)

Values of Tuscany stamps vary tremendously according to condition. Values are for very fine examples, and values for unused stamps are for examples with original gum as defined in the catalogue introduction. Extremely fine or superb stamps sell at much higher prices, and fine or poor stamps sell at greatly reduced prices.

Dangerous counterfeits exist of #1-PR1c.

Lion of Tuscany — A1

1851-52   Typo.   Wmk. 185   Imperf.
Blue, Grayish Blue or Gray Paper

1	A1	1q black, grayish ('52)	15,000.	2,250.
2	A1	1s ocher, grayish	17,250.	2,100.
a.		1s orange, grayish	19,250.	2,100.
b.		1s yellow, bluish	20,750.	2,350.
3	A1	2s scarlet	57,500.	9,600.
4	A1	1cr carmine	8,800.	145.00
a.		1cr brown carmine	11,600.	145.00
5	A1	2cr blue	5,250.	160.00
a.		2cr greenish blue	5,600.	160.00
6	A1	4cr green	8,800.	125.00
a.		4cr bluish green	9,600.	325.00
7	A1	6cr slate blue	9,600.	275.00
a.		6cr blue	8,800.	275.00
b.		6cr indigo	9,600.	300.00
8	A1	9cr gray lilac	21,000.	300.00
a.		9cr deep violet	21,000.	300.00
9	A1	60cr red ('52)	95,000.	27,500.

The first paper was blue, later paper more and more grayish. Stamps on distinctly blue paper sell about 20 percent higher, except Nos. 3 and 9 which were issued on blue paper only. Examples without watermark are proofs.
Reprints of Nos. 3 and 9 have re-engraved value labels, color is too brown and impressions blurred and heavy. Paper same as originals.

No. 14a

1857-59   White Paper   Wmk. 184

10	A1	1q black	1,750.	920.00
11	A1	1s yellow	52,500.	6,250.
12	A1	1cr carmine	11,600.	900.00
13	A1	2cr blue	3,850.	160.00
14	A1	4cr deep green	8,800.	175.00
a.		Inverted value tablet		1,100,000.
15	A1	6cr deep blue	12,500.	300.00
16	A1	9cr gray lil ('59)	52,500.	6,250.

Provisional Government

Coat of Arms — A2

1860

17	A2	1c brn lilac	3,800.	960.00
a.		1c red lilac	4,400.	1,075.
b.		1c gray lilac	3,800.	960.00
18	A2	5c green	14,000.	260.00
a.		5c olive green	15,200.	275.00
b.		5c yellow green	17,500.	360.00
19	A2	10c dp brn	4,800.	62.50
a.		10c gray brown	4,800.	62.50
b.		10c purple brown	4,125.	62.50
20	A2	20c blue	12,400.	180.00
a.		20c deep blue	12,400.	220.00
b.		20c gray blue	14,000.	220.00
21	A2	40c rose	18,000.	350.00
a.		40c carmine	18,000.	350.00
b.		Half used as 20c on cover		175,000.
22	A2	80c pale red brn	32,000.	1,500.
a.		80c brown orange	32,000.	1,525.
23	A2	3 l ocher	260,000.	125,000.

NEWSPAPER TAX STAMPS

NT1

1854   Unwmk.   Typo.   Imperf.
Yellowish Pelure Paper

PR1	NT1	2s black		80.00
a.		Tête bêche pair		750.00
b.		As "a," one stamp on back		750.00
c.		Double impression		560.00
d.		Gummed on the front side		225.00

This stamp represented a fiscal tax on newspapers coming from foreign countries. It was not canceled when used.

The stamps of Tuscany were superseded by those of Sardinia in 1861.

ITALIAN STATES — TWO SICILIES — ITALY

TWO SICILIES

LOCATION — Formerly comprised the island of Sicily and the lower half of the Apennine Peninsula.
GOVT. — Independent Kingdom
CAPITAL — Naples

The Kingdom was annexed to Sardinia in 1860.

200 Tornesi = 100 Grana = 1 Ducat

Values of Two Sicilies stamps vary tremendously according to condition. Values are for very fine examples, and values for unused stamps are for examples with original gum as defined in the catalogue introduction. Extremely fine or superb copies sell at much higher prices, and fine or poor copies sell at greatly reduced prices. In addition, very fine unused stamps without gum sell for about 20%-30% of the values shown.

Naples

Coat of Arms
A1   A2
A3   A4
A5   A6
A7

1858 Engr. Wmk. 186 Imperf.

1	A1	½g pale lake	2,200.	325.00
a.		½g rose lake	2,200.	325.00
b.		½g lake	2,740.	550.00
c.		½g carmine lake	3,300.	700.00
d.		Half used as ¼g on newspaper		225,000.
2	A2	1g pale lake	950.00	37.50
a.		1g rose lake	660.00	37.50
b.		1g brown lake	1,600.	82.50
c.		1g carmine lake	1,000.	65.00
d.		Printed on both sides		1,750.
e.		Printed on both sides, one inverted		900.00
3	A3	2g pale lake	660.00	14.00
a.		2g rose lake	660.00	14.00
b.		2g lake	900.00	22.50
c.		2g carmine lake	1,100.	22.50
d.		Impression of 1g on reverse		1,650.
e.		Double impression		9,000.
f.		Printed on both sides		1,775.
4	A4	5g brown lake	3,300.	67.50
a.		5g rose lake	2,750.	67.50
b.		5g carmine lake	4,000.	67.50
c.		Printed on both sides		5,000.
e.		5g rose carmine	6,000.	165.00
f.		5g bright carmine	6,600.	275.00
g.		5g dark carmine	7,600.	300.00
5	A5	10g rose lake	6,600.	190.00
a.		10g lake	7,400.	350.00
b.		10g carmine lake	7,250.	350.00
c.		Printed on both sides		15,000.
d.		Double impression		15,000.
6	A6	20g rose lake	6,000.	675.00
a.		20g lake	6,000.	800.00
b.		Double impression	55,000.	
c.		20g pale rose	9,000.	1,350.
d.		20g pale car rose	9,500.	1,600.
7	A7	50g rose lake	11,000.	2,400.
a.		50g lake	11,000.	2,400.

Nos. 1-2, 4-7 have been reprinted in bright rose and Nos. 1, 7 in dull brown. The reprints are on thick unwatermarked paper. Value $8 each.

Provisional Government

A8   A9

1860

8	A8	½t deep blue	250,000.	11,000.
9	A9	½t deep blue	50,000.	3,250.
a.		½t deep blue	50,000.	3,500.

100 varieties of each.

No. 8 was made from the plate of No. 1, which was altered by changing the "G" to "T."
No. 9 was made from the same plate after a second alteration erasing the coat of arms and inserting the Cross of Savoy. Dangerous counterfeits exist of Nos. 8-9.

Sicily

Ferdinand II — A10

1859 Unwmk. Engr. Imperf.
Soft Porous Paper, Brownish Gum
(Naples consignment)

10g	A10	½g orange	700.00	5,000.
c.		Printed on both sides		44,000.
11	A10	1g dk brn	20,000.	875.00
12h	A10	1g pale ol grn (III)	275.00	240.00
c.		Double impression	5,250.	4,750.
13g	A10	2g rose	200.00	120.00
b.		Printed on both sides		26,000.
14	A10	5g dark rose	950.00	700.00
15	A10	5g vermilion	875.00	2,350.
16	A10	10g dark blue	975.00	440.00
17	A10	20g dk gray vio	975.00	775.00
18	A10	50g dk brn red	975.00	5,850.

There were three plates each for the 1g and 2g, two each for the ½g and 5g and one plate each for the other values.

Nos. 10a, 10b, 11, 11a, 14, 14a, 14b and 15 are printed from Plate I on which the stamps are 2 to 2½mm apart. On almost all stamps from Plate I, the S and T of POSTA touch.

Nos. 12a, and 15a are from Plate II and No. 12 is from Plate III. On both Plates II and III stamps are spaced 1½mm apart. Most stamps from Plate II have a white line about 1mm long below the beard.

Nos. 10-18 are on soft, porous paper with brownish gum, while Nos. 10, 12 and 13 exist also on hard white paper, with white gum. Color shades exist, some on both types of paper. For detailed listings, see the *Scott Classic Specialized Catalogue of Stamps and Covers.*

The ½g blue is stated to be a proof of which two examples are known. Both originated on the same cover. One stamp is sound and still on its original partial cover. This item was sold at auction in 2011, where it realized $2.6 million. The second stamp is a faulty, loose single.

Fraudulent cancellations are known on Nos. 10, 15, 15a and 18.

Neapolitan Provinces

King Victor Emmanuel II — A11

Lithographed, Center Embossed
1861 Unwmk. Imperf.

19	A11	½t green	14.00	250.00
a.		½t yellow green	425.00	340.00
b.		½t emerald	7,850.	1,350.
c.		½t black (error)	135,000.	160,000.
d.		Head inverted (green)	200.00	
e.		Head inverted (yel grn)		11,250.
f.		Printed on both sides		32,250.
20	A11	½g bister	200.00	225.00
a.		½g brown	200.00	310.00
b.		½g gray brown	225.00	225.00
c.		Head inverted	1,950.	
21	A11	1g black	310.00	32.50
a.		Head inverted		1,675.
22	A11	2g blue	125.00	14.00
a.		2g deep blue	125.00	14.00
b.		Head inverted	400.00	1,000.
c.		2g black (error)		160,000.
23	A11	5g car rose	225.00	125.00
a.		5g vermilion	225.00	160.00
b.		5g lilac rose	250.00	250.00
c.		Head inverted	1,250.	8,400.
e.		Printed on both sides		21,000.
25	A11	10g orange	100.00	275.00
a.		10g ocher	1,250.	625.00
b.		10g bister	110.00	275.00
26	A11	20g yellow	425.00	3,350.
a.		Head inverted		42,000.
27	A11	50g gray	32.50	8,500.
a.		50g slate	40.00	8,500.
b.		50g slate blue	45.00	11,250.
	Nos. 19-27 (8)		1,432.	12,772.

Counterfeits of the inverted head varieties of this issue are plentiful. See note on forgeries after Sardinia No. 15.

Fraudulent cancellations are found on Nos. 19-20, 23-27.

Stamps similar to those of Sardinia 1855-61, type A4 but with inscriptions in larger, clearer lettering, were prepared in 1861 for the Neapolitan Provinces. They were not officially issued although a few are known postally used. Denominations: 5c, 10c, 20c, 40c and 80c.

Stamps of Two Sicilies were replaced by those of Italy in 1862.

ITALY

ˈi-t*ə*l-ē

LOCATION — Southern Europe
GOVT. — Republic
AREA — 119,764 sq. mi.
POP. — 60,460,000 (2020 est.)
CAPITAL — Rome

Formerly a kingdom, Italy became a republic in June 1946

100 Centesimi = 1 Lira
100 Cents = 1 Euro (2002)

Catalogue values for unused stamps in this country are for Never Hinged items, beginning with Scott 691 in the regular postage section, Scott B47 in the semi-postal section, Scott C129 in the airpost section, Scott D21 in the pneumatic post section, Scott E32 in the special delivery section, Scott EY11 in the authorized delivery section, Scott J83 in the postage due section, Scott Q77 in the parcel post section, Scott QY5 in the parcel post authorized delivery section, Scott 1N1 in the A.M.G. section, Scott 1LN1 in the Venezia Giulia section, 1LNC1 in the occupation air post section, 1LNE1 in the occupation special delivery section, and all of the items in the Italian Social Republic area with the exception of "G.N.R" overprints, which are valued Unused.

Watermarks

Wmk. 87 — Honeycomb

Wmk. 140 — Crown

Wmk. 277 — Winged Wheel

Wmk. 303 — Multiple Stars

Values of Italy stamps vary tremendously according to condition. Quotations are for very fine examples, and values for unused stamps are for examples with original gum as defined in the catalogue introduction. Extremely fine or superb copies sell at much higher prices, and fine or poor examples sell at greatly reduced prices. In addition, unused examples without gum are discounted severely.

Very fine examples of Nos. 17-21, 24-75, J2-J27, O1-O8 and Q1-Q6 will have perforations barely clear of the frameline or design due to the narrow spacing of the stamps on the plates.

King Victor Emmanuel II — A4

Typographed; Head Embossed
1862 Unwmk. Perf. 11½x12

17	A4	10c bister	8,000.	325.00
g.		Vert. half used as 5c on cover		125,000.
19	A4	20c dark blue	20.00	32.50
f.		Vert. half used as 10c on cover		170,000.
20	A4	40c red	250.00	175.00
21	A4	80c orange	50.00	1,900.

The outer frame shows a distinct design on the early printings, while this design is more or less blurred, or even a solid line, on the later printings.

Numerous shades of Nos. 17-21 exist. Some are very expensive. For listings, see the *Scott Classic Catalogue.*

The 20c and 40c exist perf. 11½. These are remainders of Sardinia with forged perforations.

Counterfeit cancellations are often found on No. 21.

Lithographed; Head Embossed
1863 Imperf.

22	A4	15c blue	57.50	45.00
a.		Head inverted		70,000.
b.		Double head	115.00	70.00
c.		Head omitted	575.00	40,000.
j.		Triple head	265.00	475.00

See note after Sardinia No. 15.
No. 22c is valued with original gum only.

King Victor Emmanuel II — A5

Type I — First "C" in bottom line nearly closed.
Type II — "C" open. Line broken below "Q."

1863 Litho.

23	A5	15c blue, Type II	7.00	11.50
a.		Type I	300.00	24.00
b.		No gum	35.00	
c.		As "a," double impression		3,800.
f.		As "a," printed on both sides		17,500.

One example of No. 23f is known used, cancelled "Milano, 25-VII-1863." Unused examples always lack gum and are from printer's waste. They are of little value.

A6   A7
A8   A13

1863-77 Typo. Wmk. 140 Perf. 14

24	A6	1c gray grn	6.00	3.00
25	A7	2c org brn ('65)	24.00	2.00
a.		Imperf., pair	210.00	300.00
26	A8	5c slate grn	1,825.	3.25
27	A8	10c buff	3,100.	4.25
28	A8	10c blue ('77)	5,850.	4.75
29	A8	15c blue	2,350.	3.00
30	A8	30c brown	9.00	9.00
a.		Imperf., single		

ITALY

31	A8	40c carmine	6,500.	5.75
a.		40c rose	8,750.	8.00
32	A8	60c lilac	9.00	14.00
33	A13	2 l vermilion	24.00	90.00

Nos. 26 to 32 have the head of type A8 but with different corner designs for each value.
Early printings of Nos. 24-27, 29-33 were made in London by De La Rue, later printings in Turin. Used examples can be determined by cancellation date. Unused singles cannot be distinguished.
For overprints see Italian Offices Abroad Nos. 1-5, 8-11.

No. 29 Surcharged in Brown

Type I — Dots flanking stars in oval, and dot in eight check-mark ornaments in corners.
Type II — Dots in oval, none in corners.
Type III — No dots.

1865

34	A8	20c on 15c bl (I)	645.00	4.00
a.		Type II	8,750.	15.00
b.		Type III	1,750.	6.00
c.		Inverted surcharge (I)		65,000.
d.		Double surcharge, on cover (I)		60,000.
e.		Double surcharge (III)		25,000.

A15

1867-77 Typo.

35	A15	20c sky blue (London)	1,600.	3.00
36	A15	20c orange ('77)	4,400.	3.00

For overprints see Italian Offices Abroad Nos. 9-10.

Official Stamps Surcharged in Blue

1878

37	O1	2c on 2c lake	180.00	25.00
38	O1	2c on 5c lake	225.00	30.00
39	O1	2c on 20c lake	800.00	3.50
40	O1	2c on 30c lake	700.00	12.50
41	O1	2c on 1 l lake	550.00	4.00
42	O1	2c on 2 l lake	550.00	10.00
43	O1	2c on 5 l lake	800.00	13.00
44	O1	2c on 10 l lake	550.00	16.50
		Nos. 37-44 (8)	4,355.	114.50

Inverted Surcharge

37a	O1	2c on 2c		1,625.
38a	O1	2c on 5c		1,300.
39a	O1	2c on 20c	38,000.	875.
40a	O1	2c on 30c		1,300.
41a	O1	2c on 1 l	44,000.	1,200.
42a	O1	2c on 2 l	44,000.	1,300.
43a	O1	2c on 5 l		1,300.
44a	O1	2c on 10 l		1,300.

King Humbert I — A17

1879 Typo. Perf. 14

45	A17	5c blue green	8.00	1.45
46	A17	10c claret	450.00	1.50
47	A17	20c orange	425.00	1.45
48	A17	25c blue	800.00	7.25
49	A17	30c brown	150.00	2,650.
50	A17	50c violet	20.00	22.00
51	A17	2 l vermilion	52.50	350.00

Nos. 45-51 have the head of type A17 with different corner designs for each value.
Beware of forged cancellations on No. 49, on or off cover.
For surcharges and overprints see Nos. 64-66, Italian Offices Abroad 12-17.

Arms of Savoy — A24

Humbert I — A25

A26

A27

A28

A29

1889

52	A24	5c dark green	775.00	3.00
53	A25	40c brown	13.00	17.50
a.		Horiz. pair, imperf. between		17,500.
54	A26	45c gray green	2,350.	8.50
55	A27	60c violet	17.00	42.50
56	A28	1 l brown & yel	17.00	22.00
a.		1 l brown & orange	19.00	27.00
57	A29	5 l grn & claret	35.00	1,075.

Forged cancellations exist on Nos. 51, 57.

Parcel Post Stamps of 1884-86 Surcharged in Black

1890

58	PP1	2c on 10c ol gray	5.40	7.00
a.		Inverted surcharge	500.00	3,250.
59	PP1	2c on 20c blue	5.40	7.00
60	PP1	2c on 50c claret	57.50	42.50
a.		Inverted surcharge		45,000.
61	PP1	2c on 75c bl grn	5.40	7.00
62	PP1	2c on 1.25 l org	50.00	37.50
a.		Inverted surcharge	85,000.	42,500.
63	PP1	2c on 1.75 l brn	22.00	55.00
		Nos. 58-63 (6)	145.70	156.00

Stamps of 1879 Surcharged

1890-91

64	A17	2c on 5c bl grn ('91)	20.00	50.00
a.		"2" with thin tail	125.00	290.00
65	A17	20c on 30c brn	425.00	11.00
66	A17	20c on 30c violet	500.00	42.50
		Nos. 64-66 (3)	945.00	103.50

Arms of Savoy — A33

Humbert I — A34

A35

A36

A37

A38

1891-96 Typo.

67	A33	5c green	500.00	2.25
68	A34	10c claret ('96)	8.50	2.25
69	A35	20c orange ('95)	8.50	2.25
70	A36	25c blue	8.50	9.00
71	A37	45c ol grn ('95)	8.50	9.00
72	A38	5 l blue & rose	85.00	230.00

Arms of Savoy — A39

A40

A41

1896-97

73	A39	1c brown	9.00	7.00
a.		Half used as ½c on cover		1,450.
74	A40	2c orange brown	10.00	1.80
75	A41	5c green ('97)	36.00	1.80
		Nos. 73-75 (3)	55.00	10.60

Coat of Arms
A43   A44

Victor Emmanuel III
A45   A46

1901-26

76	A42	1c brown	1.45	.35
a.		Imperf, single	400.00	650.00
b.		Vert. pair, lower stamp imperf.		3,000.
77	A43	2c org brn	1.45	.35
a.		Double impression	110.00	200.00
b.		Imperf, single	115.00	160.00
78	A44	5c blue grn	80.00	.55
a.		Imperf, single	1,800.	
79	A45	10c claret	110.00	1.10
a.		Imperf, single		10,000.
80	A45	20c orange	22.00	1.10
81	A45	25c ultra	250.00	3.75
82	A46	25c grn & pale grn ('26)	1.45	.30
a.		Frame & vignette double	75.00	3.60
b.		Floral design double	42.50	50.00
c.		Floral design omitted	12.00	6.00
d.		"POSTE ITALIANE" omitted	1,150.	
e.		Imperf., single	75.00	75.00
f.		Vert. pair, lower stamp imperf.	1,900.	
83	A45	40c brown	720.00	8.75
84	A45	45c olive grn	11.00	.35
a.		Imperf, single	145.00	190.00
85	A45	50c violet	850.00	16.00
86	A46	75c dk red & rose ('26)	4.25	.30
a.		Floral design omitted	115.00	
b.		Imperf., single	100.00	100.00
87	A46	1 l brn & grn	4.25	.35
a.		Imperf, single	72.50	110.00
b.		Floral design (green) omitted	145.00	
c.		Double impression of vignette (brown)	72.50	100.00
d.		"POSTE ITALIANE" omitted	550.00	
88	A46	1.25 l bl & ultra ('26)	11.00	.30
89	A46	2 l dk grn & org ('23)	22.00	7.25
90	A46	2.50 l dk grn & org ('26)	57.50	7.25
91	A46	5 l blue & rose	30.00	5.75
		Nos. 76-91 (16)	2,176.	53.80

Nos. 83, 85, unused, are valued in fine condition.
The borders of Nos. 79-81, 83-85, 87, 89 and 91 differ slightly for each denomination.
On Nos. 82, 86, 88 and 90 the value is expressed as "Cent. 25," etc.
See No. 87d in set following No. 174G.
For surcharges and overprints see Nos. 148-149, 152, 158, 174F-174G, B16; Austria N20-N21, N27, N30, N52-N53, N58, N60, N64-N65, N71, N74; Dalmatia 1, 6-7.

Overprints & Surcharges
See Castellorizo, Italian Offices in China, Crete, Africa, Turkish Empire (Albania to Valona) and Aegean Islands for types A36-A58 overprinted or surcharged.

No. 80 Surcharged in Black

1905

92	A45	15c on 20c org	70.00	1.80
a.		Double surcharge		5,000.

ITALY

No. 93

No. 111

No. 123

A47

	1906	Unwmk.	Engr.	Perf. 12	
93	A47	15c slate		70.00	.90
a.		Vert. pair, imperf horiz.		180.00	180.00
b.		Horiz. pair, imperf vert.		180.00	180.00
c.		Booklet pane of 6		3,300.	
d.		Complete bklt., 4 #93c		14,500.	
		On thin paper		92.50	3.00

A48

	1906-19	Wmk. 140	Typo.	Perf. 14	
94	A48	5c green		1.45	.35
a.		Imperf., single		36.00	36.00
b.		Printed on both sides		225.00	
95	A48	10c claret		3.00	.30
a.		Imperf., single		32.50	37.50
b.		Printed on both sides		225.00	
96	A48	15c slate ('19)		2.90	.30
a.		Imperf., single		125.00	200.00
		Nos. 94-96 (3)		7.35	.95

The frame of No. 95 differs in several details. See Nos. 96b-96d following No. 174G.
For overprints and surcharge see Nos. 142A-142B, 150, 174A, B5, B9-B10; Austria N22-N23, N31, N54-N55, N61-N62, N66-N67; Dalmatia 2-5.

A49

	1908-27				
97	A49	20c brn org ('25)		1.45	.90
98	A49	20c green ('25)		.35	.75
99	A49	20c lil brn ('26)		2.75	.30
100	A49	25c blue		2.25	.30
a.		Imperf., pair		105.00	105.00
b.		Printed on both sides		200.00	325.00
101	A49	25c lt grn ('27)		7.25	18.00
102	A49	30c org brn ('22)		3.00	.70
a.		Imperf., single		240.00	
103	A49	30c gray ('25)		4.25	.25
a.		Imperf., single		115.00	145.00
104	A49	40c brown		3.75	.30
a.		Imperf., pair		160.00	175.00
105	A49	50c violet		1.45	.30
a.		Imperf., pair		150.00	150.00
106	A49	55c dl vio ('20)		17.00	37.50
107	A49	60c car ('17)		2.25	.35
108	A49	60c blue ('23)		8.50	80.00
109	A49	60c brn org ('26)		11.50	.55
110	A49	85c red brn ('20)		22.00	30.00
		Nos. 97-110 (14)		87.75	170.20

A50

Redrawn
Perf. 13x13½, 13½x14

	1909-17	Typo.	Unwmk.		
111	A50	15c slate black		270.00	2.25
112	A50	20c brn org ('16)		57.50	4.25

No. 111 is similar to No. 93, but the design has been redrawn and the stamp is 23mm high instead of 25mm. There is a star at each side of the coat collar, but one is not distinct. See illustrations next to A47.
For overprints and surcharges see Nos. B6, B11; Austria N24, N32, N56, N63, N68.

		Wmk. 140		Perf. 14	
113	A50	20c brn org ('17)		7.25	.35
a.		Imperf., pair		50.00	

Stamps overprinted "Prestito Nazionale, 1917," or later dates, are Thrift or Postal Savings Stamps.

A51

1910, Nov. 1

114	A51	10 l gray grn & red	72.50	32.00
a.		Red inverted		6,600.

For surcharge see Dalmatia No. 8.

A52

Perf. 14x13½

	1910, Apr. 15		Unwmk.	
115	A52	5c green	29.00	25.00
116	A52	15c claret	50.00	50.00

50th anniversary of freedom of Sicily.

Giuseppe Garibaldi — A53

1910, Dec. 1

117	A53	5c claret	125.00	125.00
118	A53	15c green	225.00	180.00

50th anniversary of the plebiscite of the southern Italian provinces in 1860.
Nos. 115-118 sold for 5c above face value to benefit the anniversary committee. The stamps were valid only on mail to addresses within the Kingdom of Italy. Nos. 115-116 were valid to June 30, 1910; Nos. 117-118 were valid to Jan. 31, 1911.

Used values in italics are for postally used stamps. CTO's sell for about the same as unused, hinged stamps.

Symbols of Rome and Turin A54

Symbol of Valor A55

Genius of Italy A56

Glory of Rome A57

1911, May 1   Engr.   Perf. 14x13½

119	A54	2c brown	2.90	5.75
a.		Vert. pair, imperf horiz.	85.00	87.50
b.		Horiz. pair, imperf vert.	85.00	87.50
120	A55	5c deep green	40.00	36.00
121	A56	10c carmine	29.00	55.00
a.		Vert. pair, imperf horiz.	—	—
b.		Horiz. pair, imperf vert.	180.00	180.00
122	A57	15c slate	37.50	72.50
		Nos. 119-122 (4)	109.40	169.25

50th anniv. of the union of Italian States to form the Kingdom of Italy.
Nos. 119 to 122 were sold at a premium over their face value to benefit the anniversary committee. They were valid to Dec. 31, 1911. The stamps were valid only for mail to addresses within the Kingdom of Italy. They were used by military post offices in Libya. After 1913, No. 119 was sold without the premium.
For surcharges see Nos. 126-128.

Victor Emmanuel III — A58

1911, Oct.   Re-engraved   Perf. 13½

123	A58	15c slate	29.00	1.10
a.		Imperf., single	87.50	110.00
b.		Printed on both sides	360.00	475.00
c.		Bklt. pane of 6	1,500.	
		Cplt. bklt., 4 #123c	3,250.	

The re-engraved stamp is 24mm high. The stars at each side of the coat collar show plainly and the "C" of "Cent" is nearer the frame than in No. 93. See illustrations next to A47.
For surcharge see No. 129.

Campanile, Venice — A59

1912, Apr. 25   Perf. 14x13½

124	A59	5c indigo	8.50	13.00
125	A59	15c dk brn	47.50	60.00

Re-erection of the Campanile at Venice. Nos. 124-125 were sold only in Venice and were valid to Dec. 31, 1912. The stamps were valid only for mail within Italy.

Nos. 120-121 Surcharged in Black

1913, Mar. 1

126	A55	2c on 5c dp grn	2.25	6.00
127	A56	2c on 10c car	2.25	6.00

No. 122 Surcharged in Violet

128	A57	2c on 15c slate	2.25	6.00
		Nos. 126-128 (3)	6.75	18.00
		Set, never hinged	16.50	

No. 123 Surcharged

1916, Jan. 8

129	A58	20c on 15c slate	16.00	1.10
		Never hinged	40.00	
a.		Bklt. pane of 6	675.00	
		Cplt. bklt., 4 #129a	2,700.	
b.		Inverted surcharge	315.00	315.00
c.		Double surcharge	200.00	200.00
e.		Vert. pair, one without surcharge	1,600.	
g.		Imperf, single	145.00	180.00

Old Seal of Republic of Trieste — A60

Wmk. 140

1921, June 5   Litho.   Perf. 14

130	A60	15c blk & rose	6.50	50.00
a.		Horiz. pair, imperf btwn.	850.00	
131	A60	25c bl & rose	6.50	50.00
132	A60	40c brn & rose	6.50	50.00
		Nos. 130-132 (3)	19.50	150.00
		Set, never hinged	50.00	

Reunion of Venezia Giulia with Italy.

Allegory of Dante's Divine Comedy A61

Italy Holding Laurels for Dante A62

Dante Alighieri — A63

1921, Sept. 28   Typo.

133	A61	15c vio brn	6.50	32.00
a.		Imperf., single	36.00	36.00
134	A62	25c gray grn	6.50	32.00
a.		Imperf., single	36.00	36.00
135	A63	40c brown	6.50	32.00
a.		Imperf., single	36.00	36.00
		Nos. 133-135 (3)	19.50	96.00
		Set, never hinged	48.00	

600th anniversary of the death of Dante. A 15c gray was not issued. Value: hinged $145, never hinged $360, canceled $425; block of 4, hinged $600, never hinged $1,275; imperf., single, hinged $400, canceled $6,100. A 15c gray violet, never issued: hinged $700, never hinged $1,400.
Nos. 133-135 exist in part perforate pairs.

"Victory" — A64

1921, Nov. 1   Engr.   Perf. 14

136	A64	5c olive green	1.45	1.80
b.		Imperf., single	225.00	250.00
137	A64	10c red	2.10	2.25
c.		Imperf., single	225.00	475.00
138	A64	15c slate green	3.75	8.50
139	A64	25c ultra	2.10	5.75
c.		Imperf., single	145.00	145.00
d.		As "c," double impression	500.00	
		Nos. 136-139 (4)	9.40	18.30
		Set, never hinged	23.50	

3rd anniv. of the victory on the Piave.
For surcharges see Nos. 171-174.

ITALY

Flame of Patriotism Tempering Sword of Justice — A65

Giuseppe Mazzini — A66

Mazzini's Tomb — A67

1922, Sept. 20   Typo.   Perf. 14

140	A65	25c maroon	11.50	32.00
141	A66	40c vio brn	22.50	40.00
142	A67	80c dk bl	11.50	50.00
		Nos. 140-142 (3)	45.50	122.00
		Set, never hinged	145.00	

Mazzini (1805-1872), patriot and writer.

Nos. 95, 96, 100 and 104 Overprinted in Black

1922, June 4   Wmk. 140   Perf. 14

142A	A48	10c claret	425.00	425.00
142B	A48	15c slate	225.00	225.00
142C	A48	25c blue	225.00	225.00
142D	A49	40c brown	360.00	360.00
		Nos. 142A-142D (4)	1,235.	1,235.
		Set, never hinged	3,125.	

9th Italian Philatelic Congress, Trieste. Nos. 142A-142D were on sale to Sept. 30, 1922. Counterfeits exist.

Christ Preaching The Gospel — A68

Portrait at upper right and badge at lower right differ on each value. Portrait at upper left is of Pope Gregory XV. Others: 20c, St. Theresa. 30c, St. Dominic. 50c, St. Francis of Assisi. 1 l, St. Francis Xavier.

1923, June 11

143	A68	20c ol grn & brn org	5.75	175.00
a.		Imperf., single	500.00	650.00
b.		Vert. pair, imperf btwn.	1,100.	1,500.
144	A68	30c clar & brn org	5.75	175.00
a.		Imperf., single	500.00	650.00
c.		Horiz. pair, imperf btwn.	1,100.	1,500.
145	A68	50c vio & brn org	5.75	175.00
a.		Imperf., single	500.00	650.00
c.		Horiz. pair, imperf btwn.	1,750.	2,150.
d.		Vert. pair, imperf btwn.	1,100.	1,500.
146	A68	1 l bl & brn org	5.75	175.00
a.		Imperf., single	500.00	650.00
c.		Horiz. pair, imperf btwn.	1,100.	1,500.
d.		Vert. pair, imperf btwn.	1,100.	1,500.
		Nos. 143-146 (4)	23.00	700.00
		Set, never hinged	58.00	

300th anniv. of the Propagation of the Faith. Practically the entire issue was delivered to speculators.

Forged cancellations exist on Nos. 143-146.

Stamps of Previous Issues, Surcharged

a

b

1923-25

147	A49(a)	7½c on 85c	.35	1.20
a.		Double surcharge		1,450.
148	A42(b)	10c on 1c	.35	.35
a.		Inverted surcharge	22.00	36.00
149	A43(b)	10c on 2c	.35	.30
a.		Inverted surcharge	55.00	85.00
150	A48(c)	10c on 15c	.35	.30
a.		Vert. pair, one without surcharge	1,000.	—
b.		Surcharge on reverse only	200.00	
151	A49(a)	20c on 25c	.35	.30
152	A45(d)	20c on 45c	1.45	14.50
a.		Vert. pair, one without surcharge	1,000.	—
153	A49(a)	25c on 60c	3.00	.90
a.		Vert. pair, one without surcharge	1,000.	—
154	A49(a)	30c on 50c	.35	.30
155	A49(a)	30c on 55c	1.45	.30
156	A49(a)	50c on 40c	.40	.35
a.		Inverted surcharge	215.00	325.00
b.		Double surcharge	115.00	135.00
157	A49(a)	50c on 55c	20.00	14.50
a.		Inverted surcharge	1,100.	2,000.
158	A51(e)	1.75 l on 10 l	14.50	32.00
a.		Vert. pair, one without surcharge	1,600.	
		Nos. 147-158 (12)	46.50	65.30
		Set, never hinged	120.00	

Years of issue: Nos. 148-149, 156-157, 1923; Nos. 147, 152-153, 1924; others, 1925.

Emblem of the New Government — A69

Wreath of Victory, Eagle and Fasces — A70

Symbolical of Fascism and Italy — A71

Unwmk.

1923, Oct. 24   Engr.   Perf. 14

159	A69	10c dark green	4.25	10.00
a.		Imperf., single	725.00	850.00
160	A69	30c dark violet	4.25	10.00
161	A69	50c brn car	8.50	18.00

Wmk. 140   Typo.

162	A70	1 l blue	14.50	18.00
163	A70	2 l brown	17.00	22.00
164	A71	5 l blk & bl	29.00	57.50
a.		Imperf., single	290.00	
		Nos. 159-164 (6)	77.50	135.50
		Set, never hinged	195.00	

Anniv. of the March of the Fascisti on Rome.

Fishing Scene — A72

Designs: 15c, Mt. Resegone. 30c, Fugitives bidding farewell to native mountains. 50c, Part of Lake Como. 1 l, Manzoni's home, Milan. 5 l, Alessandro Manzoni. The first four designs show scenes from Manzoni's work "I Promessi Sposi."

1923, Dec. 29   Perf. 14

165	A72	10c brn red & blk	22.00	180.00
166	A72	15c bl grn & blk	22.00	180.00
167	A72	30c blk & slate	22.00	180.00
a.		Imperf., single	2,700.	
		Imperf., pair		
168	A72	50c org brn & blk	22.00	180.00
169	A72	1 l blue & blk	145.00	700.00
a.		Imperf., single, no gum	290.00	
170	A72	5 l vio & blk	725.00	3,950.
a.		Imperf., single	850.00	
		Imperf., pair		
		Nos. 165-170 (6)	958.00	5,370.
		Set, never hinged	2,375.	

50th anniv. of the death of Alessandro Manzoni.

Nos. 136-139 Surcharged

1924, Feb.

171	A64	1 l on 5c ol grn	22.50	225.00
172	A64	1 l on 10c red	14.50	225.00
173	A64	1 l on 15c slate grn	22.50	225.00
174	A64	1 l on 25c ultra	14.50	225.00
		Nos. 171-174 (4)	74.00	900.00
		Set, never hinged	180.00	

Surcharge forgeries exist.

Perf. 14x13½

171a	A64	1 l on 5c	32.00	300.00
172a	A64	1 l on 10c	18.00	300.00
173a	A64	1 l on 15c	32.00	300.00
174h	A64	1 l on 25c	18.00	300.00
		Nos. 171a-174h (4)	100.00	1,200.
		Set, never hinged	195.00	

Nos. 95, 102, 105, 108, 110, 87 and 89 Overprinted in Black or Red

1924, Feb. 16

174A	A48	10c claret	2.25	42.50
174B	A49	30c org brn	2.25	42.50
174C	A49	50c violet	2.25	42.50
174D	A49	60c bl (R)	14.50	125.00
174E	A49	85c choc (R)	7.25	125.00
174F	A46	1 l brn & grn	42.50	425.00
174G	A46	2 l dk grn & org	32.00	425.00
		Nos. 174A-174G (7)	103.00	1,228.
		Set, never hinged	260.00	

These stamps were sold on an Italian merchant ship which made a cruise to South American ports in 1924.

Overprint forgeries exist of Nos. 174D-174G.

Stamps of 1901-22 with Advertising Labels Attached

Perf. 14 all around, Imperf. between

1924-25

96b	A48	15c + Bitter Campari	3.75	25.00
96c	A48	15c + Cordial Campari	3.75	22.00
96d	A48	15c + Columbia	57.50	50.00
100c	A49	25c + Abrador	100.00	125.00
100d	A49	25c + Coen	215.00	65.00
100e	A49	25c + Piperno	1,450.	1,100.
100f	A49	25c + Reinach	100.00	85.00
100g	A49	25c + Tagliacozzo	850.00	1,150.
102	A49	30c + Columbia	29.00	40.00
105b	A49	50c + Coen	1,450.	85.00
105c	A49	50c + Columbia	22.00	16.00
105d	A49	50c + De Montel	3.75	16.00
105e	A49	50c + Piperno	2,000.	315.00
105f	A49	50c + Reinach	215.00	65.00
105g	A49	50c + Siero Casali	22.00	47.50
105h	A49	50c + Singer	3.75	11.00
105i	A49	50c + Tagliacozzo	2,175.	600.00
105j	A49	50c + Tantal	360.00	200.00
87d	A46	1 l + Columbia	850.00	950.00
		Nos. 96b-87d (19)	9,911.	4,968.
		Set, never hinged	20,000.	

No. 97 with Columbia label and No. E3 with Cioccolato Perugina label were prepared but not issued. Values: Columbia, unused $50, never hinged $125; Cioccolato, unused $18, never hinged $42.50.

King Victor Emmanuel III — A78

1925-26   Engr.   Unwmk.   Perf. 11

175	A78	60c brn car	1.45	.70
a.		Perf. 13½	7.25	2.25
b.		Imperf., pair	235.00	260.00
176	A78	1 l dk bl	1.45	.70
a.		Perf. 13½	14.50	14.50

b.		Imperf., pair	235.00	—

Perf. 13½

177	A78	1.25 l dk bl ('26)	4.25	2.25
a.		Perf. 11	100.00	125.00
b.		Imperf., pair	550.00	
		Nos. 175-177 (3)	7.15	3.65
		Set, never hinged	18.00	

25th year of the reign of Victor Emmanuel III.

Nos. 175 to 177 exist with sideways watermark of fragments of letters or a crown, which are normally on the sheet margin.

St. Francis and His Vision — A79

Monastery of St. Damien — A80

Assisi Monastery — A81

St. Francis' Death A82

St. Francis A83

1926, Jan. 30   Wmk. 140   Perf. 14

178	A79	20c gray grn	.70	.90
a.		Imperf single	1,100.	1,100.
179	A80	40c dk vio	.70	.90
180	A81	60c red brn	.90	.90
a.		Imperf single	500.00	500.00

Unwmk.   Perf. 11

181	A83	30c slate blk	.75	.90
a.		Perf. 13½	11.00	20.00
		Never hinged	27.00	
182	A82	1.25 l dark blue	3.75	.90
a.		Perf. 13½	425.00	40.00
		Never hinged	1,100.	

Perf. 13½

183	A83	5 l + 2.50 l dk brn	10.00	125.00
		Nos. 178-183 (6)	16.80	129.50
		Set, never hinged	40.00	

700th anniv. of the death of St. Francis of Assisi.

Alessandro Volta — A84

1927   Wmk. 140   Typo.   Perf. 14

188	A84	20c dk car	3.00	1.10
189	A84	50c grnsh blk	3.00	.75
a.		Vert. pair, imperf. between		2,750.
190	A84	60c chocolate	4.25	4.50
191	A84	1.25 l ultra	14.50	7.25
		Nos. 188-191 (4)	24.75	13.60
		Set, never hinged	50.00	

Cent. of the death of Alessandro Volta. The 20c in purple is Cyrenaica No. 25 with overprint omitted. Values: $4,000 unused; $6,000 never hinged.

A85

1927-29   Size: 17½x22mm   Perf. 14

192	A85	50c brn & slate	3.00	.35
a.		Imperf., pair		
b.		Double frame	400.00	325.00

Unwmk.   Engr.   Perf. 11   Size: 19x23mm

193	A85	1.75 l dp brn	3.75	.30
a.		Perf. 13½ ('29)	37,500.	3,150.
		Never hinged	57,500.	
b.		Perf. 11x13½ ('29)	—	3,150.
c.		Perf. 13½x11 ('29)	—	3,150.
d.		Imperf., single	4,750.	

ITALY

194	A85	1.85 l black	3.00	.65
195	A85	2.55 l brn car	3.75	8.50
196	A85	2.65 l dp vio	5.75	72.50
a.		Imperf., single	3,150.	
		Nos. 192-196 (5)	19.25	82.30
		Set, never hinged	45.00	

A86

1928-29 Wmk. 140 Typo. Perf. 14

197	A86	7½c lt brown	3.00	11.00
198	A86	15c brn org ('29)	3.00	.30
199	A86	35c gray blk ('29)	8.00	14.50
200	A86	50c dull violet	17.00	.30
a.		Imperf single	225.00	
		Nos. 197-200 (4)	31.00	26.10
		Set, never hinged	75.00	

Emmanuel Philibert, Duke of Savoy — A87

Statue of Philibert, Turin — A88

Philibert and Italian Soldier of 1918 — A89

1928 Perf. 11

201	A87	20c red brn & ultra	9.50	16.00
a.		Perf. 13½	240.00	240.00
202	A87	25c dp red & bl grn	9.50	16.00
a.		Perf. 13½	47.50	52.50
203	A87	30c bl grn & red brn	16.00	32.00
a.		Center inverted	67,500.	9,200.
b.		Perf. 13½	35.00	35.00

Perf. 14

204	A89	50c org brn & bl	4.00	1.25
205	A89	75c dp red	4.75	4.00
206	A88	1.25 l bl & blk	4.75	4.00
207	A89	1.75 l bl grn	32.50	40.00
208	A87	5 l vio & bl grn (Perf. 11)	29.00	110.00
209	A89	10 l blk & pink	35.00	225.00
210	A88	20 l vio & blk	70.00	725.00
		Nos. 201-210 (10)	215.00	1,173.
		Set, never hinged	535.00	

400th anniv. of the birth of Emmanuel Philibert, Duke of Savoy; 10th anniv. of the victory of 1918; Turin Exhibition.

She-wolf Suckling Romulus and Remus — A90

Julius Caesar A91

Augustus Caesar A92

"Italia" — A93

A94

A95

1929-42 Wmk. 140 Photo. Perf. 14

213	A90	5c olive brn	.25	.25
214	A91	7½c deep vio	1.60	.25
215	A92	10c dk brn	.25	.25
216	A93	15c slate grn	.25	.25
217	A91	20c rose red	.25	.25
218	A94	25c dp green	.25	.25
219	A95	30c olive brn	.25	.25
a.		Imperf., pair	1,100.	
220	A93	35c dp blue	.25	.25
221	A95	50c violet	.25	.25
a.		Imperf., pair	725.00	875.00
222	A94	75c rose red	.25	.25
222A	A91	1 l dk pur ('42)	.25	.25
223	A94	1.25 l dp blue	.25	.25
224	A92	1.75 l red org	.25	.25
225	A93	2 l car lake	.25	.25
226	A95a	2.55 l slate grn	.25	.80
226A	A95a	3.70 l pur ('30)	.25	.80
227	A95a	5 l rose red	.25	.25
228	A93	10 l purple	4.00	4.00
229	A91	20 l lt green	4.75	12.00
230	A92	25 l bluish sl	11.00	35.00
231	A94	50 l dp violet	13.00	40.00
		Nos. 213-231 (21)	38.35	96.35
		Set, never hinged	94.00	

Stamps of the 1929-42 issue overprinted "G.N.R." are 1943 local issues of the Guardia Nazionale Republicana. See Nos. 427-438, 441-459.

For surcharge and overprints see Nos. 460, M1-M13, 1N10-1N13, 1LN1-1LN1A, 1LN10; Italian Social Republic 1-5A; Yugoslavia-Ljubljana N36-N54.

Courtyard of Monte Cassino — A96

Monks Laying Cornerstone A98

St. Benedict of Nursia A100

Designs: 25c, Fresco, "Death of St. Benedict." 75c+15c, 5 l+1 l, Monte Cassino Abbey.

1929, Aug. 1 Photo. Wmk. 140

232	A96	2c red orange	1.60	1.60
233	A96	25c dk green	1.60	1.60
234	A98	50c + 10c ol brn	4.00	30.00
235	A98	75c + 15c crim	4.75	40.00
236	A96	1.25 l + 25c saph	6.50	45.00
237	A98	5 l + 1 l dk vio	9.50	175.00

Unwmk. Engr.

238	A100	10 l + 2 l slate grn	14.50	325.00
		Nos. 232-238 (7)	42.45	618.20
		Set, never hinged	105.00	

14th cent. of the founding of the Abbey of Monte Cassino by St. Benedict in 529 A.D. The premium on some of the stamps was given to the committee for the celebration of the centenary.

Prince Humbert and Princess Marie José — A101

1930, Jan. 8 Photo. Wmk. 140

239	A101	20c orange red	.80	.60
240	A101	50c + 10c ol brn	2.40	4.00
241	A101	1.25 l + 25c dp bl	5.50	13.00
		Nos. 239-241 (3)	8.70	17.60
		Set, never hinged	22.00	

Marriage of Prince Humbert of Savoy with Princess Marie José of Belgium.

The surtax on Nos. 240 and 241 was for the benefit of the Italian Red Cross Society.

The 20c in green is Cyrenaica No. 35 with overprint omitted. Values: $35,000 unused; $52,500 never hinged.

Ferrucci Leading His Army — A102

Fabrizio Maramaldo Killing Ferrucci A103

Francesco Ferrucci A104

1930, July 10

242	A102	20c rose red	.80	.80
243	A103	25c deep green	1.40	.80
244	A103	50c purple	.80	.40
245	A103	1.25 l deep blue	11.00	4.75
246	A104	5 l + 2 l org red	22.50	140.00
		Nos. 242-246 (5)	36.50	146.75
		Set, never hinged	90.00	
		Nos. 242-246,C20-C22 (8)	60.50	314.75
		Set, never hinged	150.00	

4th cent. of the death of Francesco Ferrucci, Tuscan warrior.

Overprints
See Castellorizo and Aegean Islands for types A103-A145 Overprinted.

Helenus and Aeneas — A106

Designs: 20c, Anchises and Aeneas watch passing of Roman Legions. 25c, Aeneas feasting in shade of Albunea. 30c, Ceres and her children with fruits of Earth. 50c, Harvesters at work. 75c, Woman at loom, children and calf. 1.25 l, Anchises and his sailors in sight of Italy. 5 l+1.50 l, Shepherd piping by fireside. 10 l+2.50 l, Aeneas leading his army.

1930, Oct. 21 Photo. Perf. 14

248	A106	15c olive brn	2.40	2.40
249	A106	20c orange	2.40	1.60
250	A106	25c green	3.20	1.60
251	A106	30c dull vio	9.50	4.00
252	A106	50c violet	16.00	.80
253	A106	75c rose red	4.00	12.00
254	A106	1.25 l blue	4.00	12.00

Unwmk. Engr.

255	A106	5 l +1.50 l red brn	60.00	525.00
256	A106	10 l +2.50 l gray grn	60.00	725.00
		Set, never hinged	405.00	
		Nos. 248-256 (9)	161.50	1,284.
		Nos. 248-256,C23-C26 (13)	332.00	2,019.
		Set, never hinged	835.00	

Bimillenary of the birth of Virgil. Surtax on Nos. 255-256 was for the National Institute Figli del Littorio.

Arms of Italy (Fascist Emblems Support House of Savoy Arms) — A115

1930, Dec. 16 Photo. Wmk. 140

257	A115	2c deep orange	1.60	.25
		Never hinged	4.00	

Olivares Hermitage, Portugal — A118

St. Anthony being Installed as a Franciscan A116

St. Anthony Freeing Prisoners — A120

St. Anthony's Death A121

St. Anthony Succoring the Poor A122

Designs: 25c, St. Anthony preaching to the fishes. 50c, Basilica of St. Anthony, Padua.

Wmk. 140
1931, Mar. 9 Photo. Perf. 14

258	A116	20c dull violet	4.00	1.25
259	A116	25c gray green	2.40	1.25
260	A118	30c brown	6.50	2.40
261	A118	50c violet	2.00	.80
262	A120	1.25 l blue	20.00	9.50

Unwmk. Engr.

263	A121	75c brown red	9.50	16.00
a.		Perf. 12	100.00	375.00
		Never hinged	240.00	
264	A122	5 l + 2.50 l ol grn	40.00	325.00
		Nos. 258-264 (7)	84.40	356.20
		Set, never hinged	210.00	

7th centenary of the death of Saint Anthony of Padua.

Tower of Meloria A123

Training Ship "Amerigo Vespucci" A124

Cruiser "Trento" — A125

1931, Nov. 29 Photo. Wmk. 140

265	A123	20c rose red	8.75	2.00
266	A124	50c purple	8.75	1.60
267	A125	1.25 l dk bl	24.00	4.75
		Nos. 265-267 (3)	41.50	8.35
		Set, never hinged	165.00	

Royal Naval Academy at Leghorn (Livorno), 50th anniv.

Giovanni Boccaccio A126

Designs: 15c, Niccolo Machiavelli. 20c, Paolo Sarpi. 25c, Count Vittorio Alfieri. 30c, Ugo Foscolo. 50c, Count Giacomo Leopardi. 75c, Giosue Carducci. 1.25 l, Carlo Giuseppe Botta. 1.75 l, Torquato Tasso. 2.75 l, Francesco Petrarca. 5 l+2 l, Ludovico Ariosto. 10 l+2.50 l, Dante Alighieri.

1932, Mar. 14 Perf. 14

268	A126	10c olive brn	3.25	1.60
269	A126	15c slate grn	3.25	2.00
270	A126	20c rose red	3.25	1.60
271	A126	25c dp green	3.25	1.25
272	A126	30c olive brn	4.00	1.60
273	A126	50c violet	2.40	.80
274	A126	75c car rose	16.00	8.00
275	A126	1.25 l dp blue	4.75	4.00
276	A126	1.75 l orange	12.00	8.00
277	A126	2.75 l gray	24.00	40.00
278	A126	5 l + 2 l car rose	29.00	300.00
279	A126	10 l + 2.50 l ol grn	35.00	450.00
		Nos. 268-279 (12)	140.15	818.85
		Set, never hinged	350.00	
		Nos. 268-279,C28-C33,C34 (19)	237.90	2,427.
		Set, never hinged	600.00	

Dante Alighieri Society, a natl. literary association founded to promote development of the

ITALY

Italian language and culture. The surtax was added to the Society funds to help in its work.

View of Caprera — A138

Garibaldi Carrying His Dying Wife A141

Garibaldi Memorial A144

Giuseppe Garibaldi — A145

Designs: 20c, 30c, Garibaldi meeting Victor Emmanuel II. 25c, 50c, Garibaldi at Battle of Calatafimi. 1.25 l, Garibaldi's tomb. 1.75 l+25c, Rock of Quarto.

1932, Apr. 6

280	A138	10c gray blk	2.40	1.60
281	A138	20c olive brn	2.40	1.25
282	A138	25c dull grn	3.25	1.60
283	A138	30c orange	3.25	2.40
284	A138	50c violet	1.60	.40
285	A141	75c rose red	16.00	9.50
286	A141	1.25 l dp blue	32.50	4.00
287	A141	1.75 l + 25c bl gray	40.00	87.50
288	A144	2.55 l + 50c red brn	32.50	125.00
289	A145	5 l + 1 l cop red	32.50	130.00
	Nos. 280-289 (10)		166.40	363.25
	Set, never hinged	410.00	
	Nos. 280-289,C35-C39,CE1-CE2 (17)		242.40	619.25
	Set, never hinged	600.00	

50th anniv. of the death of Giuseppe Garibaldi, patriot.

Plowing with Oxen and Tractor — A146

10c, Soldier guarding mountain pass. 15c, Marine, battleship & seaplane. 20c, Head of Fascist youth. 25c, Hands of workers & tools. 30c, Flags, Bible & altar. 35c, "New roads for the new Legions." 50c, Mussolini statue, Bologna. 60c, Hands with spades. 75c, Excavating ruins. 1 l, Steamers & galleons. 1.25 l, Italian flag, map & points of compass. 1.75 l, Flag, athlete & stadium. 2.55 l, Mother & child. 2.75 l, Emblems of drama, music, art & sport. 5 l+2.50 l, Roman emperor.

1932, Oct. 27 *Photo.*

290	A146	5c dk brown	2.40	1.25
291	A146	10c dk brown	2.40	.80
292	A146	15c dk gray grn	2.40	1.25
293	A146	20c car rose	2.40	.60
294	A146	25c dp green	2.40	.40
295	A146	30c dk brown	3.25	2.40
296	A146	35c dk blue	8.00	9.50
297	A146	50c purple	1.60	.40
298	A146	60c orange brn	12.00	8.00
299	A146	75c car rose	4.00	4.00
300	A146	1 l black vio	16.00	6.50
301	A146	1.25 l dp blue	4.00	1.60
302	A146	1.75 l orange	24.00	2.00
303	A146	2.55 l dk gray	29.00	40.00
304	A146	2.75 l slate grn	29.00	40.00
305	A146	5 l + 2.50 l car rose	40.00	450.00
	Nos. 290-305 (16)		182.85	568.70
	Set, never hinged	455.00	
	Nos. 290-305,C40-C41,E16-E17 (20)		201.75	758.30
	Set, never hinged	520.00	

10th anniv. of the Fascist government and the March on Rome.

Statue of Athlete — A162

1933, Aug. 16 *Perf. 14*

306	A162	10c dk brown	.80	.80
307	A162	20c rose red	.80	.80
308	A162	50c purple	.80	.40
309	A162	1.25 l blue	4.75	6.50
	Nos. 306-309 (4)		7.15	8.50
	Set, never hinged	18.00	

Intl. University Games at Turin, Sept., 1933.

Cross in Halo, St. Peter's Dome — A163

Designs: 25c, 50c, Angel with cross. 1.25 l, as 20c. 2.55 l, + 2.50 l, Cross with doves.

1933, Oct. 23

310	A163	20c rose red	4.75	1.25
311	A163	25c green	12.00	1.60
312	A163	50c purple	4.75	.40
313	A163	1.25 l dp blue	12.00	4.75
314	A163	2.55 l + l blk	8.00	240.00
	Nos. 310-314 (5)		41.50	248.00
	Set, never hinged	105.00	
	Nos. 310-314,CB1-CB2 (7)		47.90	435.50
	Set, never hinged	121.00	

Issued at the solicitation of the Order of the Holy Sepulchre of Jerusalem to mark the Holy Year.

Anchor of the "Emanuele Filiberto" — A166

Designs: 20c, Anchor. 50c, Gabriele d'Annunzio. 1.25 l, St. Vito's Tower. 1.75 l, Symbolizing Fiume's annexation. 2.55 l+2 l, Victor Emmanuel III arriving aboard "Brindisi." 2.75 l+2.50 l, Galley, gondola and battleship.

1934, Mar. 12

315	A166	10c dk brown	8.00	4.00
316	A166	20c rose red	1.60	1.60
317	A166	50c purple	1.60	1.60
318	A166	1.25 l blue	1.60	6.50
319	A166	1.75 l + 1 l indigo	1.60	35.00
320	A166	2.55 l + 2 l dull vio	1.60	55.00
321	A166	2.75 l + 2.50 l ol grn	1.60	55.00
	Nos. 315-321 (7)		17.60	158.70
	Set, never hinged	44.00	
	Nos. 315-321,C56-C61,CE5-CE7 (16)		29.95	308.60
	Set, never hinged	66.50	

10th anniversary of annexation of Fiume.

Antonio Pacinotti — A172

1934, May 23

322	A172	50c purple	.80	.40
323	A172	1.25 l sapphire	1.25	2.75
	Set, never hinged	5.00	

75th anniv. of invention of the dynamo by Antonio Pacinotti (1841-1912), scientist.

Guarding the Goal A173

Players A175

Soccer Players — A174

1934, May 23

324	A173	20c red orange	6.50	8.00
325	A174	25c green	6.50	2.40
326	A174	50c purple	6.50	1.25
327	A174	1.25 l blue	16.00	16.00
328	A175	5 l + 2.50 l brn	95.00	700.00
	Nos. 324-328 (5)		130.50	727.65
	Set, never hinged	330.00	
	Nos. 324-328,C62-C65 (9)		264.00	1,465.
	Set, never hinged	625.00	

2nd World Soccer Championship. For overprints see Aegean Islands Nos. 31-35.

Luigi Galvani — A176

1934, Aug. 16

329	A176	30c brown, *buff*	1.00	.80
330	A176	75c carmine, *rose*	1.40	3.25
	Set, never hinged	6.00	

Intl. Congress of Electro-Radio-Biology.

Carabinieri Emblem A177

Cutting Barbed Wire A178

Designs: 20c, Sardinian Grenadier and soldier throwing grenade. 25c, Alpine Infantry. 30c, Military courage. 75c, Artillery. 1.25 l, Acclaiming the Service. 1.75 l+1 l, Cavalry. 2.55 l+2 l, Sapping Detail. 2.75 l+2 l, First aid.

1934, Sept. 6 *Photo.* *Wmk. 140*

331	A177	10c dk brown	2.40	2.40
332	A178	15c olive grn	2.40	4.00
333	A178	20c rose red	2.40	1.60
334	A177	25c green	4.00	1.60
335	A178	30c dk brown	4.00	8.00
336	A178	50c purple	2.40	.80
337	A178	75c car rose	40.00	12.00
338	A178	1.25 l dk blue	40.00	8.00
339	A177	1.75 l + 1 l red org	17.50	60.00
340	A178	2.55 l + 2 l dp cl	17.50	80.00
341	A178	2.75 l + 2 l vio	21.00	80.00
	Nos. 331-341 (11)		153.60	258.40
	Set, never hinged	385.00	
	Nos. 331-341,C66-C72 (18)		202.10	421.40
	Set, never hinged	505.00	

Centenary of Military Medal of Valor. For overprints see Aegean Islands Nos. 36-46.

Man Holding Fasces — A187

Standard Bearer, Bayonet Attack — A188

Design: 30c, Eagle and soldier.

1935, Apr. 23 *Perf. 14*

342	A187	20c rose red	.80	.80
343	A187	30c dk brown	6.50	16.00
344	A188	50c purple	.80	.40
	Nos. 342-344 (3)		8.10	17.20
	Set, never hinged	20.00	

Issued in honor of the University Contests.

Fascist Flight Symbolism A190

Leonardo da Vinci A191

1935, Oct. 1

345	A190	20c rose red	20.00	2.00
346	A190	30c brown	35.00	6.50
347	A191	50c purple	72.50	4.75
348	A191	1.25 l dk blue	80.00	7.25
	Nos. 345-348 (4)		207.50	17.00
	Set, never hinged	830.00	

International Aeronautical Salon, Milan.

Vincenzo Bellini A192

Bellini's Villa A194

Bellini's Piano — A193

1935, Oct. 15

349	A192	20c rose red	16.00	4.00
350	A192	30c brown	24.00	14.50
351	A192	50c violet	24.00	1.60
352	A192	1.25 l dk blue	40.00	20.00
353	A193	1.75 l + 1 l red org	35.00	325.00
354	A194	2.75 l + 2 l ol blk	65.00	340.00
	Nos. 349-354 (6)		204.00	705.10
	Set, never hinged	510.00	
	Nos. 349-354,C79-C83 (11)		287.00	1,022.
	Set, never hinged	710.00	

Bellini (1801-35), operatic composer.

Map of Italian Industries — A195

Designs: 20c, 1.25 l, Map of Italian Industries. 30c, 50c, Cogwheel and plow.

1936, Mar. 23

355	A195	20c red	.80	.40
356	A195	30c brown	.80	1.25
357	A195	50c purple	.80	.35
358	A195	1.25 l blue	4.75	3.25
	Nos. 355-358 (4)		7.15	5.25
	Set, never hinged	18.00	

The 17th Milan Trade Fair.

Flock of Sheep A197

Ajax Defying the Lightning A199

ITALY

Bust of Horace — A200

Designs: 20c, 1.25 l+1 l, Countryside in Spring. 75c, Capitol. 1.75 l+1 l, Pan piping. 2.55 l+1 l, Dying warrior.

Wmk. Crowns (140)

1936, July 1   Photo.   Perf. 14

359	A197	10c dp green	6.50	1.25
360	A197	20c rose red	4.75	.80
361	A199	30c olive brn	6.50	2.40
362	A200	50c purple	6.50	.40
363	A197	75c rose red	16.00	12.00
364	A197	1.25 l + 1 l dk bl	27.50	160.00
365	A199	1.75 l + 1 l car rose	32.50	300.00
366	A197	2.55 l + 1 l sl blk	40.00	350.00
		Nos. 359-366 (8)	140.25	826.85
		Set, never hinged	350.00	
		Nos. 359-366,C84-C88 (13)	202.00	1,153.
		Set, never hinged	500.00	

2000th anniv. of the birth of Quintus Horatius Flaccus (Horace), Roman poet.

Child Holding Wheat — A204

Child Giving Salute — A205

Child and Fasces — A206

"Il Bambino" by della Robbia — A207

1937, June 28

367	A204	10c yellow brn	3.25	1.60
368	A205	20c car rose	3.25	1.25
369	A204	25c green	3.25	2.00
370	A206	30c dk brown	4.75	4.00
371	A205	50c purple	3.25	.40
372	A207	75c rose red	16.00	17.50
373	A205	1.25 l dk blue	20.00	17.50
374	A206	1.75 l + 75c org	40.00	250.00
375	A207	2.75 l + 1.25 l dk bl grn	32.50	275.00
376	A205	5 l + 3 l bl gray	40.00	375.00
		Nos. 367-376 (10)	166.25	944.25
		Set, never hinged	415.00	
		Nos. 367-376,C89-C94 (16)	262.25	1,378.
		Set, never hinged	655.00	

Summer Exhibition for Child Welfare. The surtax on Nos. 374-376 was used to support summer camps for children.

Rostral Column — A208

15c, Army Trophies. 20c, Augustus Caesar (Octavianus) offering sacrifice. 25c, Cross Roman Standards. 30c, Julius Caesar and Julian Star. 50c, Augustus receiving acclaim. 75c, Augustus Caesar. 1.25 l, Symbolizing maritime glory of Rome. 1.75 l+1 l, Sacrificial Altar. 2.55 l+2 l, Capitol.

1937, Sept. 23

377	A208	10c myrtle grn	3.25	.80
378	A208	15c olive grn	3.25	1.25
379	A208	20c red	3.25	.60
380	A208	25c green	3.25	.60
381	A208	30c olive bis	4.00	.80
382	A208	50c purple	3.25	.35
383	A208	75c scarlet	3.25	4.75
384	A208	1.25 l dk blue	8.00	5.50
385	A208	1.75 l + 1 l plum	40.00	225.00
386	A208	2.55 l + 2 l sl blk	52.50	300.00
		Nos. 377-386 (10)	124.00	539.65
		Set, never hinged	300.00	
		Nos. 377-386,C95-C99 (15)	259.00	812.65
		Set, never hinged	625.00	

Bimillenary of the birth of Emperor Augustus Caesar (Octavianus) on the occasion of the exhibition opened in Rome by Mussolini, Sept. 22, 1937.

No. 378 exists in violet (error).

For overprints see Aegean Islands Nos. 47-56.

Gasparo Luigi Pacifico Spontini A218

Antonius Stradivarius A219

Count Giacomo Leopardi A220

Giovanni Battista Pergolesi A221

Giotto di Bondone — A222

1937, Oct. 25

387	A218	10c dk brown	1.60	.80
388	A219	20c rose red	1.60	.80
389	A220	25c dk green	1.60	.80
390	A221	30c dk brown	1.60	1.60
391	A220	50c purple	1.60	.80
392	A221	75c crimson	2.25	4.75
393	A222	1.25 l dp blue	3.25	4.75
394	A218	1.75 l dp orange	3.25	4.75
395	A219	2.55 l + 2 l gray grn	16.00	260.00
396	A222	2.75 l + 2 l red brn	16.00	300.00
		Nos. 387-396 (10)	48.75	579.05
		Set, never hinged	125.00	

Centennials of Spontini, Stradivarius, Leopardi, Pergolesi and Giotto.

For overprints see Aegean Islands Nos. 57-58.

Guglielmo Marconi — A223

1938, Jan. 24

397	A223	20c rose pink	3.25	.80
398	A223	50c purple	.80	.40
399	A223	1.25 l blue	3.25	6.75
		Nos. 397-399 (3)	7.30	7.95
		Set, never hinged	18.00	

Guglielmo Marconi (1874-1937), electrical engineer, inventor of wireless telegraphy.

Augustus Caesar (Octavianus) — A224

10c, Romulus Plowing. 25c, Dante. 30c, Columbus. 50c, Leonardo da Vinci. 75c, Victor Emmanuel II and Garibaldi. 1.25 l, Tomb of Unknown Soldier, Rome. 1.75 l, Blackshirts' March on Rome, 1922. 2.75 l, Map of Italian East Africa and Iron Crown of Monza. 5 l, Victor Emmanuel III.

1938, Oct. 28

400	A224	10c brown	2.40	.80
401	A224	20c car rose	2.40	.80
402	A224	25c dk green	2.40	.80
403	A224	30c olive brn	2.40	2.00
404	A224	50c lt violet	2.40	.80
405	A224	75c rose red	3.25	3.25
406	A224	1.25 l dp blue	6.50	3.25
407	A224	1.75 l vio blk	8.00	4.00
408	A224	2.75 l slate grn	27.50	47.50
409	A224	5 l lt red brn	32.50	52.50
		Nos. 400-409 (10)	89.75	115.70
		Set, never hinged	220.00	
		Nos. 400-409,C100-C105 (16)	143.25	284.20
		Set, never hinged	350.00	

Proclamation of the Empire.

Wood-burning Engine and Streamlined Electric Engine — A234

1939, Dec. 15   Photo.   Perf. 14

410	A234	20c rose red	.80	.60
411	A234	50c brt violet	1.60	.80
412	A234	1.25 l dp blue	4.00	4.00
		Nos. 410-412 (3)	6.40	5.40
		Set, never hinged	16.00	

Centenary of Italian railroads.

Adolf Hitler and Benito Mussolini — A235

Hitler and Mussolini — A236

1941   Wmk. 140

413	A235	10c dp brown	2.00	2.10
414	A235	20c red orange	2.00	2.10
415	A235	25c dp green	6.50	2.10
416	A236	50c violet	5.00	2.10
417	A236	75c rose red	6.50	5.50
418	A236	1.25 l deep blue	8.00	7.00
		Nos. 413-418 (6)	30.00	20.90
		Set, never hinged	65.00	

Rome-Berlin Axis.

Stamps of type A236 in the denominations and colors of Nos. 413-415 were prepared but not issued. They were sold for charitable purposes in 1948. Value $35 each.

Galileo Teaching Mathematics at Padua — A237

Designs: 25c, Galileo presenting telescope to Doge of Venice. 50c, Galileo Galilei (1564-1642). 1.25 l, Galileo studying at Arcetri.

1942, Sept. 28

419	A237	10c dk org & lake	.65	.90
420	A237	25c gray grn & grn	.65	.90
421	A237	50c brn vio & vio	.65	.90
	a.	Frame missing	1,750.	
422	A237	1.25 l Prus bl & ultra	.65	2.50
		Nos. 419-422 (4)	2.60	5.20
		Set, never hinged	5.00	

Statue of Rossini A241

Gioacchino Rossini A242

1942, Nov. 23   Photo.

423	A241	25c deep green	.70	.45
424	A241	30c brown	.70	.45
425	A242	50c violet	.70	.45
426	A242	1 l blue	1.00	1.40
		Nos. 423-426 (4)	3.10	2.75
		Set, never hinged	5.00	

Gioacchino Antonio Rossini (1792-1868), operatic composer.

"Victory for the Axis" — A243

"Discipline is the Weapon of Victory" — A244

"Everything and Everyone for Victory" — A245

"Arms and Hearts Must Be Stretched Out Towards the Goal" — A246

Perf. 14 all around, Imperf. between

1942   Photo.   Wmk. 140

427	A243	25c deep green	.35	.85
428	A244	25c deep green	.35	.85
429	A245	25c deep green	.35	.85
430	A246	25c deep green	.35	.85
431	A243	30c olive brown	.35	3.50
432	A244	30c olive brown	.35	3.50
433	A245	30c olive brown	.35	3.50
434	A246	30c olive brown	.35	3.50
435	A243	50c purple	.35	.90
436	A244	50c purple	.35	.90
437	A245	50c purple	.35	.90
438	A246	50c purple	.35	.90
		Nos. 427-438 (12)	4.20	21.00
		Set, never hinged	10.00	

Issued in honor of the Italian Army.

The left halves of Nos. 431-438 are type A95.

For overprints see Italian Social Republic Nos. 6-17.

She-Wolf Suckling Romulus and Remus — A247

Perf. 10½x11½, 11x11½, 11½, 14

1944, Jan.   Litho.   Wmk. 87

Without Gum

439	A247	50c rose vio & bis rose	2.00	3.25

Unwmk.

440	A247	50c rose vio & pale rose	.30	1.40

Nos. 439-440 exist imperf., part perf.

No. 440 exists with triple impression. Value, $500.

Types of 1929

1945, May   Unwmk.   Perf. 14

441	A93	15c slate green	.25	.25
442	A93	35c deep blue	.25	.25
443	A91	1 l deep violet	.35	.25
		Nos. 441-443 (3)	.85	.75
		Set, never hinged	2.00	

Types of 1929 Redrawn Fasces Removed

Victor Emmanuel III A248

Julius Caesar A249

ITALY

Augustus Caesar — A250

"Italia" — A251

A252

1944-45　Wmk. 140　Photo.　Perf. 14
444	A248	30c dk brown	.35	.25
445	A248	50c purple	2.50	2.10
446	A248	60c slate grn ('45)	.35	.70
447	A249	1 l dp violet ('45)	.35	.25
		Nos. 444-447 (4)	3.55	3.30
		Set, never hinged	6.50	

1945　Unwmk.　Perf. 14
448	A250	10c dk brown	.50	.70
448A	A249	20c rose red	.25	.35
449	A251	50c dk violet	.25	.25
450	A248	60c slate grn	.25	.25
451	A251	60c red org	.25	.35
452	A249	1 l dp violet	.25	.25
452A	A249	1 l dp vio, redrawn	.25	.25
452B	A249	2 l dp car	1.25	.75
452C	A251	10 l purple	4.00	7.50
		Nos. 448-452C (9)	7.25	10.65
		Set, never hinged	15.00	

1945　　Wmk. 277
453	A249	20c rose red	.25	.60
454	A248	60c slate grn	.25	.60
455	A249	1 l dp violet	.25	.25
456	A251	1.20 l dk brown	.25	.60
457	A249	2 l dk red	.25	.25
458	A252	5 l dk red	.70	.60
459	A251	10 l purple	4.50	7.50
		Nos. 453-459 (7)	6.45	10.40
		Set, never hinged	16.00	

Nos. 452A and 457 are redrawings of types A249 and A251. In the redrawn 1 l, the "L" of "LIRE" extends under the "IRE" and the letters of "POSTE ITALIANE" are larger. In the original the "L" extends only under the "I."
In the redrawn 2 l, the "2" is smaller and thinner, and the design is less distinct.
For overprints see Nos. 1LN2-1LN8.

No. 224 Surcharged in Black

1945, Mar.　Wmk. 140
460	A92	2.50 l on 1.75 l red org	.25	.50
		Never hinged	.30	
a.		Six bars at left	2.50	3.75

Italian Social Republic Nos. 18-19 Surcharged in Black

No. 18

No. 19

1945, May 2　Photo.　Perf. 14
461	A1	1.20 l on 20c crim	.25	.25
462	A2	2 l on 25c green	.25	.25
a.		2½ mm between "2" and "LIRE"	2.75	5.50
		Set, never hinged	.75	

Breaking Chain — A255

Planting Tree — A257

Torch — A259

"Italia" and Sprouting Oak Stump — A260

1945-47　Wmk. 277　Photo.　Perf. 14
463	A255	10c rose brown	.25	.25
464	A255	20c dk brown	.25	.25
464A	A259	25c brt bl grn ('46)	.25	.25
465	A257	40c slate	.25	.25
465A	A255	50c dp vio ('46)	.25	.25
466	A258	60c dk green	.25	.40
467	A255	80c car rose	.25	.25
468	A257	1 l dk green	.25	.25
469	A259	1.20 l chestnut	.25	.90
470	A258	2 l dk claret brn	.25	.30
471	A259	3 l red	.25	.25
471A	A256	4 l red org ('46)	.25	.25
472	A256	5 l deep blue	.35	.25
472A	A257	6 l dp vio ('47)	7.50	.25
473	A257	10 l slate	1.20	.25
473A	A257	15 l dp bl ('46)	8.00	.25
474	A259	20 l dk red vio	3.00	.25
475	A260	25 l dk grn	20.00	.25
476	A260	50 l dk vio brn	8.50	.25
		Nos. 463-476 (19)	51.55	5.60
		Set, never hinged	175.00	

See Nos. 486-488.
For overprints see Nos. 1LN11-1LN12, 1LN14-1N19, Trieste 1-13, 15-17, 30-32, 58-68, 82-83.

United Family and Scales — A261

1946, July 29　Engr.　Perf. 14
477	A261	100 l car lake	160.00	1.75
		Never hinged	400.00	
a.		Perf. 14x13½	350.00	2.50
		Never hinged	500.00	

For overprints see No. 1LN13, Trieste Nos. 14, 69.
Forgeries exist perf. 11¼ and perf. 11½ on unwatermarked paper.

Cathedral of St. Andrea, Amalfi — A262

Church of St. Michael, Lucca — A263

"Peace" from Fresco at Siena — A264

Signoria Palace, Florence — A265

View of Cathedral Domes, Pisa — A266

Republic of Genoa — A267

"Venice Crowned by Glory," by Paolo Veronese — A268

Oath of Pontida — A269

1946, Oct. 30
478	A262	1 l brown	.25	.25
479	A263	2 l dk blue	.25	.25
480	A264	3 l dk bl grn	.25	.25
481	A265	4 l dp org	.25	.25
482	A266	5 l dp violet	.25	.25
483	A267	10 l car rose	.25	.25
484	A268	15 l dp ultra	1.25	1.00
485	A269	20 l red brown	.25	.25
		Nos. 478-485 (8)	3.00	2.75
		Set, never hinged	5.75	

Proclamation of the Republic.

Types of 1945

1947-48　Wmk. 277　Photo.　Perf. 14
486	A255	8 l dk green ('48)	4.00	.25
487	A256	10 l red orange	24.00	.25
488	A259	30 l dk blue ('48)	150.00	.25
		Nos. 486-488 (3)	178.00	.75
		Set, never hinged	450.00	

St. Catherine Giving Mantle to Beggar — A270

5 l, St. Catherine carrying cross. 10 l, St. Catherine, arms outstretched. 30 l, St. Catherine & scribe.

1948, Mar. 1　　Photo.
489	A270	3 l yel grn & gray grn	.25	.35
490	A270	5 l vio & bl	.25	.35
491	A270	10 l red brn & vio	1.25	3.25
492	A270	30 l bis & gray brn	9.00	22.50
		Nos. 489-492 (4)	10.75	26.45
		Set, never hinged	25.00	
		Nos. 489-492,C127-C128 (6)	83.25	90.45
		Set, never hinged	140.00	

600th anniv. of the birth of St. Catherine of Siena, Patroness of Italy.

"Constitutional Government" — A271

1948, Apr. 12
493	A271	10 l rose vio	.70	.85
494	A271	30 l blue	1.50	2.50
		Set, never hinged	6.00	

Proclamation of the constitution of 1/1/48.

Uprising at Palermo, Jan. 12, 1848 — A272

Designs (Revolutionary scenes): 4 l, Rebellion at Padua. 5 l, Proclamation of statute, Turin. 6 l, "Five Days of Milan." 8 l, Daniele Manin proclaming the Republic of Venice. 10 l, Defense of Vicenza. 12 l, Battle of Curtatone. 15 l, Battle of Gioto. 20 l, Insurrection at Bologna. 30 l, "Ten Days of Brescia." 50 l, Garibaldi in Rome fighting. 100 l, Death of Goffredo Mameli.

1948, May 3
495	A272	3 l dk brown	.65	1.00
496	A272	4 l red violet	.65	1.00
497	A272	5 l dp blue	3.25	1.00
498	A272	6 l dp yel grn	1.00	1.00
499	A272	8 l brown	1.00	1.15
500	A272	10 l orange red	1.25	1.00
501	A272	12 l dk gray grn	3.75	3.00
502	A272	15 l gray blk	9.00	2.00
503	A272	20 l car rose	20.00	10.00
504	A272	30 l brt ultra	6.25	2.50
505	A272	50 l violet	45.00	6.00
506	A272	100 l blue blk	55.00	22.50
		Nos. 495-506 (12)	146.80	52.15
		Set, never hinged	405.00	
		Nos. 495-506,E26 (13)	191.80	74.65
		Set, never hinged	540.00	

Centenary of the Risorgimento, uprisings of 1848-49 which led to Italian unification.
For overprints see Trieste Nos. 18-29, E5.

Alpine Soldier and Bassano Bridge — A273

1948, Oct. 1　Wmk. 277　Perf. 14
507	A273	15 l dark green	1.50	1.75
		Never hinged	3.00	

Bridge of Bassano, re-opening, Oct. 3, 1948.
For overprint see Trieste No. 33.

Gaetano Donizetti — A274

1948, Oct. 23　　Photo.
508	A274	15 l dark brown	1.15	2.10
		Never hinged	2.25	

Death cent. of Gaetano Donizetti, composer.
For overprint see Trieste No. 34.

Fair Buildings — A275

1949, Apr. 12
509	A275	20 l dark brown	3.00	3.75
		Never hinged	8.00	

27th Milan Trade Fair, April 1949.
For overprint see Trieste No. 35.

Standard of Doges of Venice — A276

15 l, Clock strikers, Lion Tower and Campanile of St. Mark's. 20 l, Lion standard and Venetian galley. 50 l, Lion tower and gulls.

1949, Apr. 12　Buff Background
510	A276	5 l red brown	.55	.25
511	A276	15 l dk green	2.00	2.25
512	A276	20 l dp red brn	4.25	.25
513	A276	50 l dk blue	20.00	2.50
		Nos. 510-513 (4)	26.80	5.25
		Set, never hinged	65.00	

Biennial Art Exhibition of Venice, 50th anniv.
For overprints see Trieste Nos. 36-39.

"Transportation" and Globes — A277

1949, May 2　Wmk. 277　Perf. 14
514	A277	50 l brt ultra	20.00	7.50
		Never hinged	45.00	

75th anniv. of the UPU.
For overprint see Trieste No. 40.

Workman and Ship — A278

ITALY

1949, May 30   Photo.
515 A278 5 l dk green   6.00   6.50
516 A278 15 l violet   11.50   17.50
517 A278 20 l brown   21.00   17.50
    Nos. 515-517 (3)   38.50   41.50
    Set, never hinged   80.00
European Recovery Program.
For overprints see Trieste Nos. 42-44.

The Vascello, Rome — A279

1949, May 18
518 A279 100 l brown   110.00   100.00
    Never hinged   225.00
Centenary of Roman Republic.
For overprint see Trieste No. 41.

Giuseppe Mazzini — A280

1949, June 1
519 A280 20 l gray   3.75   4.50
    Never hinged   11.50
Erection of a monument to Giuseppe Mazzini (1805-72), Italian patriot and revolutionary.
For overprint see Trieste No. 45.

Vittorio Alfieri — A281

1949, June 4   Photo.
520 A281 20 l brown   3.00   3.50
    Never hinged   8.00
200th anniv. of the birth of Vittorio Alfieri, tragic dramatist.
For overprint see Trieste No. 46.

Basilica of St. Just, Trieste — A282

1949, June 8
521 A282 20 l brown red   8.00   17.00
    Never hinged   12.00
Trieste election, June 12, 1949.
For overprint see Trieste No. 47.

Staff of Aesculapius, Globe — A283

1949, June 13   Wmk. 277   Perf. 14
522 A283 20 l violet   12.50   12.50
    Never hinged   32.50
2nd World Health Cong., Rome, 1949.
For overprint see Trieste No. 49.

Lorenzo de Medici — A284

1949, Aug. 4
523 A284 20 l violet blue   3.25   3.75
    Never hinged   10.00
Birth of Lorenzo de Medici, 500th anniv.
For overprint see Trieste No. 50.

Andrea Palladio — A285

1949, Aug. 4
524 A285 20 l violet   5.00   8.00
    Never hinged   12.50
Andrea Palladio (1518-1580), architect.
For overprint see Trieste No. 51.

Tartan and Fair Buildings — A286

1949, Aug. 16
525 A286 20 l red   2.60   3.00
    Never hinged   7.00
133th Levant Fair, Bari, September, 1949.
For overprint see Trieste No. 52.

Voltaic Pile A287

Alessandro Volta A288

1949, Sept. 14   Engr.   Perf. 14
526 A287 20 l rose car   3.00   2.00
  a. Perf. 13x14   12.00   9.50
527 A288 50 l deep blue   30.00   27.50
  a. Perf. 13x14   300.00   75.00
    Set, never hinged   97.50
Invention of the Voltaic Pile, 150th anniv.
For overprints see Trieste Nos. 53-54.

Holy Trinity Bridge — A289

1949, Sept. 19   Photo.
528 A289 20 l deep green   3.25   3.25
    Never hinged   7.50
Issued to publicize plans to reconstruct Holy Trinity Bridge, Florence.
For overprint see Trieste No. 55.

Gaius Valerius Catullus — A290

1949, Sept. 19   Wmk. 277   Perf. 14
529 A290 20 l brt blue   4.00   3.50
    Never hinged   10.00
2000th anniversary of the death of Gaius Valerius Catullus, Lyric poet.
For overprint see Trieste No. 56.

Domenico Cimarosa — A291

1949, Dec. 28
530 A291 20 l violet blk   3.25   2.75
    Never hinged   9.00
Bicentenary of the birth of Domenico Cimarosa, composer.
For overprint see Trieste No. 57.

Milan Fair Scene — A292

1950, Apr. 12   Photo.
531 A292 20 l brown   2.00   3.00
    Never hinged   3.50
The 28th Milan Trade Fair.
For overprint see Trieste No. 70.

Flags and Italian Automobile A293

1950, Apr. 29
532 A293 20 l vio gray   3.50   2.50
    Never hinged   10.00
32nd Intl. Auto Show, Turin, May 4-14, 1950.
For overprint see Trieste No. 71.

Pitti Palace, Florence A294

"Perseus" by Cellini A295

1950, May 22
533 A294 20 l olive grn   3.00   3.00
534 A295 55 l blue   25.00   16.50
    Set, never hinged   70.00
5th General Conf. of UNESCO.
For overprints see Trieste Nos. 72-73.

Composite of Italian Cathedrals and Churches — A296

1950, May 29
535 A296 20 l violet   5.00   .75
536 A296 55 l blue   27.50   3.00
    Set, never hinged   85.00
Holy Year, 1950.
For overprints see Trieste Nos. 74-75.

Gaudenzio Ferrari — A297

1950, July 1   Wmk. 277   Perf. 14
537 A297 20 l gray grn   6.50   3.25
    Never hinged   17.50
Issued to honor Gaudenzio Ferrari.
For overprint see Trieste No. 76.

Radio Mast and Tower of Florence — A298

1950, July 15   Photo.
538 A298 20 l purple   9.00   5.00
539 A298 55 l blue   70.00   80.00
    Set, never hinged   175.00
Intl. Shortwave Radio Conf., Florence, 1950.
For overprints Trieste see Nos. 77-78.

Ludovico A. Muratori — A299

1950, July 22
540 A299 20 l brown   2.25   2.60
    Never hinged   6.75
200th anniv. of the death of Ludovico A. Muratori, writer.
For overprint see Trieste No. 79.

Guido d'Arezzo — A300

1950, July 29
541 A300 20 l dark green   6.50   3.00
    Never hinged   20.00
900th anniv. of the death of Guido d'Arezzo, music teacher and composer.
For overprint see Trieste No. 80.

Tartan and Fair Buildings — A301

1950, Aug. 21
542 A301 20 l chestnut brown   3.75   2.60
    Never hinged   12.50
Levant Fair, Bari, September, 1950.
For overprint see Trieste No. 81.

G. Marzotto and A. Rossi — A302

1950, Sept. 11
543 A302 20 l indigo   2.00   2.00
    Never hinged   3.50
Pioneers of the Italian wool industry.
For overprint see Trieste No. 84.

Tobacco Plant — A303

Designs: 20 l, Mature plant, different background. 55 l, Girl holding tobacco plant.
1950, Sept. 11
544 A303 5 l dp claret & grn   2.00   3.00
545 A303 20 l brown & grn   2.75   1.00
546 A303 55 l dp ultra & brn   32.50   25.00
    Nos. 544-546 (3)   37.25   29.00
    Set, never hinged   80.00
Issued to publicize the European Tobacco Conference, Rome, 1950.
For overprints see Trieste Nos. 85-87.

Arms of the Academy of Fine Arts — A304

1950, Sept. 16
547 A304 20 l ol brn & red brn   2.00   2.60
    Never hinged   5.00
200th anniv. of the founding of the Academy of Fine Arts, Venice.
For overprint see Trieste No. 88.

ITALY

Augusto Righi — A305

1950, Sept. 16
548 A305 20 l cream & gray blk 2.00 2.75
  Never hinged 5.00
Centenary of the birth of Augusto Righi, physicist.
For overprint see Trieste No. 89.

Blacksmith, Aosta Valley — A306

Designs: 1 l, Auto mechanic. 2 l, Mason. 5 l, Potter. 6 l, Lace-making. 10 l, Weaving. 12 l, Sailor steering boat. 15 l, Shipbuilding. 20 l, Fisherman. 25 l, Sorting oranges. 30 l, Woman carrying grapes. 35 l, Olive picking. 40 l, Wine cart. 50 l, Shepherd and flock. 55 l, Plowing. 60 l, Grain cart. 65 l, Girl worker in hemp field. 100 l, Husking corn. 200 l, Woodcutter.

1950, Oct. 20 Wmk. 277 Perf. 14
549 A306 50c vio blue .25 .25
550 A306 1 l dk bl vio .25 .25
551 A306 2 l sepia .25 .25
552 A306 5 l dk gray .25 .25
553 A306 6 l chocolate .25 .25
554 A306 10 l dp green 3.25 .25
555 A306 12 l dp blue grn 1.75 .25
556 A306 15 l dk gray bl 1.50 .25
557 A306 20 l blue vio 9.00 .25
558 A306 25 l brn org 1.25 .25
559 A306 30 l magenta 1.25 .25
560 A306 35 l crimson 6.50 1.00
561 A306 40 l brown .50 .25
562 A306 50 l violet 12.00 .25
563 A306 55 l dp blue .75 .25
564 A306 60 l red 2.10 .25
565 A306 65 l dk grn 1.00 .25

Perf. 13x14, 14x13 Engr.
566 A306 100 l brn org 27.50 .35
  a. Perf. 13 27.50 .25
  b. Perf. 14 30.00 .25
567 A306 200 l ol brn 8.00 3.00
  a. Perf. 14 8.00 3.00
  Nos. 549-567 (19) 77.60 8.35
  Set, never hinged 190.00

See Nos. 668-673A. For overprints see Trieste Nos. 90-108, 122-124, 178-180.

1851 Stamp of Tuscany — A307

Design: 55 l, Tuscany 6cr.

1951, Mar. 27 Photo. Perf. 14
568 A307 20 l red vio & red 1.50 .95
569 A307 55 l ultra & blue 18.00 37.50
  Set, never hinged 45.00
Centenary of Tuscany's first stamps.
For overprints see Trieste Nos. 109-110.

Italian Automobile A308

1951, Apr. 2
570 A308 20 l dk green 4.50 3.50
  Never hinged 12.50
33rd Intl. Automobile Exhib., Turin, Apr. 4-15, 1951.
For overprint see Trieste No. 111.

Altar of Peace, Medea — A309

1951, Apr. 11
571 A309 20 l blue vio 2.50 3.00
  Never hinged 8.00
Consecration of the Altar of Peace at Redipuglia Cemetery, Medea.
For overprint see Trieste No. 112.

Helicopter over Leonardo da Vinci Heliport A310

P. T. T. Building, Milan Fair A311

1951, Apr. 12 Photo.
572 A310 20 l brown 8.00 1.90
573 A311 55 l dp blue 27.50 55.00
  Set, never hinged 85.00
29th Milan Trade Fair.
For overprints see Trieste Nos. 113-114.

Symbols of the International Gymnastic Festival — A312

Wmk. 277
1951, May 18 Photo. Perf. 14
Fleur-de-lis in Red
574 A312 5 l dk brown 20.00 500.00
575 A312 10 l Prus green 20.00 500.00
576 A312 15 l vio blue 20.00 500.00
  Nos. 574-576 (3) 60.00 1,500.
  Set, never hinged 80.00
International Gymnastic Festival and Meet, Florence, 1951.
Fake cancellations exist on Nos. 574-576.
For overprints see Trieste Nos. 115-117.

Statue of Diana, Spindle and Turin Tower — A313

1951, Apr. 26
577 A313 20 l purple 9.50 4.25
  Never hinged 24.00
Tenth International Exhibition of Textile Art and Fashion, Turin, May 2-16.
For overprint see Trieste No. 118.

Landing of Columbus A314

1951, May 5
578 A314 20 l Prus green 5.00 4.00
  Never hinged 15.00
500th anniversary of birth of Columbus.
For overprint see Trieste No. 119.

Reconstructed Abbey of Montecassino A315

Design: 55 l, Montecassino Ruins.

1951, June 18
579 A315 20 l violet 3.00 1.90
580 A315 55 l brt blue 30.00 50.00
  Set, never hinged 82.50
Issued to commemorate the reconstruction of the Abbey of Montecassino.
For overprints see Trieste Nos. 120-121.

Pietro Vannucci (Il Perugino) — A316

1951, July 23
581 A316 20 l brn & red brn 3.00 2.50
  Never hinged 4.00
500th anniversary (in 1950) of the birth of Pietro Vannucci, painter.
For overprint see Trieste No. 125.

Stylized Vase A317

Cartouche of Amenhotep III and Pitcher A318

1951, July 23
582 A317 20 l grnsh gray & blk 7.00 3.75
583 A318 55 l vio bl & pale sal 24.00 40.00
  Set, never hinged 40.00
Triennial Art Exhibition, Milan, 1951.
For overprints see Trieste Nos. 126-127.

Cyclist — A319

1951, Aug. 23
584 A319 25 l gray black 4.50 4.50
  Never hinged 9.00
World Bicycle Championship Races, Milan, Aug.-Sept. 1951.
For overprint see Trieste No. 128.

Tartan and Globes — A320

1951, Sept. 8 Photo.
585 A320 25 l deep blue 2.50 3.00
  Never hinged 6.50
15th Levant Fair, Bari, September 1951.
For overprint see Trieste No. 129.

"La Figlia di Jorio" by Michetti — A321

1951, Sept. 15 Wmk. 277 Perf. 14
586 A321 25 l dk brown 3.00 3.00
  Never hinged 7.50
Centenary of the birth of Francesco Paolo Michetti, painter.
For overprint see Trieste No. 130.

Sardinia Stamps of 1851 — A322

1951, Oct. 5
587 A322 10 l shown 2.00 3.00
588 A322 25 l 20c stamp 1.60 1.50
589 A322 60 l 40c stamp 8.50 10.00
  Nos. 587-589 (3) 12.10 14.50
  Set, never hinged 16.00
Centenary of Sardinia's 1st postage stamp.
For overprints see Trieste Nos. 131-133.

Mercury A323

Roman Census A324

1951, Oct. 31
590 A323 10 l green 1.00 1.50
591 A324 25 l vio gray 1.00 1.50
  Set, never hinged 6.00
3rd Industrial and the 9th General Italian Census.
For overprints see Trieste Nos. 134-135.

Winter Scene A325

Trees A326

1951, Nov. 21
592 A325 10 l ol & dl grn 2.00 3.00
593 A326 25 l dull grn 4.50 2.00
  Set, never hinged 8.00
Issued to publicize the Festival of Trees.
For overprints see Trieste Nos. 136-137.

Giuseppe Verdi — A327

Portraits of Verdi, various backgrounds.

1951, Nov. 19 Engr.
594 A327 10 l vio brn & dk grn 2.00 3.75
595 A327 25 l red brn & dk brn 5.00 1.50
596 A327 60 l dp grn & indigo 20.00 19.00
  Nos. 594-596 (3) 27.00 24.25
  Set, never hinged 50.00
50th anniversary of the death of Giuseppe Verdi, composer.
For overprints see Trieste Nos. 138-140.

Vincenzo Bellini — A328

Wmk. 277
1952, Jan. 28 Photo. Perf. 14
597 A328 25 l gray & gray blk 1.60 1.50
  Never hinged 5.00
150th anniversary of the birth of Vincenzo Bellini, composer.
For overprint see Trieste No. 141.

Palace of Caserta and Statuary — A329

1952, Feb. 1
598 A329 25 l dl grn & ol bis 1.25 1.15
  Never hinged 4.00
Issued to honor Luigi Vanvitelli, architect.
For overprint see Trieste No. 142.

ITALY

Statues of Athlete and River God Tiber — A330

1952, Mar. 22
599 A330 25 l brn & sl blk .75 1.05
  Never hinged 1.75
Issued on the occasion of the first International Exhibition of Sports Stamps.
For overprint see Trieste No. 143.

Milan Fair Buildings — A331

1952, Apr. 12 Engr.
600 A331 60 l blue 22.50 20.00
  Never hinged 45.00
30th Milan Trade Fair.
For overprint see Trieste No. 144.

Leonardo da Vinci — A332

Virgin of the Rocks — A332a

1952 Wmk. 277 Photo. Perf. 14
601 A332 25 l deep orange .25 .25

Unwmk.
Engr. Perf. 13
601A A332a 60 l ultra 2.25 8.75
Wmk. 277
601B A332 80 l brn car 11.50 .40
  c. Perf. 14x13 25.00 .40
Set, never hinged 35.00
Leonardo da Vinci, 500th birth anniv.
For overprints see Trieste Nos. 145, 163-164.

First Stamps and Cathedral Bell Towers of Modena and Parma — A333

1952, May 29 Perf. 14
602 A333 25 l blk & red brn 1.00 1.00
603 A333 60 l blk & ultra 4.00 12.00
Set, never hinged 8.50
Cent. of the 1st postage stamps of Modena and Parma.
For overprints see Trieste Nos. 146-147.

Globe and Torch — A334

1952, June 7
604 A334 25 l bright blue .85 1.00
  Never hinged 2.00
Issued to honor the Overseas Fair at Naples and Italian labor throughout the world.
For overprint see Trieste No. 148.

Lion of St. Mark — A335

1952, June 14
605 A335 25 l black & yellow 1.00 .90
  Never hinged 2.50
26th Biennial Art Exhibition, Venice.
For overprint see Trieste No. 149.

"P" and Basilica of St. Anthony — A336

1952, June 19
606 A336 25 l bl gray, red & dk bl 1.75 1.00
  Never hinged 5.00
30th International Sample Fair of Padua.
For overprint see Trieste No. 150.

Flag and Basilica of St. Just — A337

1952, June 28
607 A337 25 l dp grn, dk brn & red 1.20 1.20
  Never hinged 2.75
4th International Sample Fair of Trieste.
For overprint see Trieste No. 151.

Fair Entrance and Tartan — A338

1952, Sept. 6 Wmk. 277 Perf. 14
608 A338 25 l dark green .75 .70
  Never hinged 1.75
16th Levant Fair, Bari, Sept. 1952.
For overprint see Trieste No. 152.

Girolamo Savonarola — A339

1952, Sept. 20
609 A339 25 l purple 1.50 .95
  Never hinged 3.25
500th anniversary of the birth of Girolamo Savonarola.
For overprint see Trieste No. 153.

Mountain Peak and Climbing Equipment — A340

1952, Oct. 4
610 A340 25 l gray .55 .55
  Never hinged 1.00
Issued to publicize the National Exhibition of the Alpine troops, Oct. 4, 1952.
For overprint see Trieste No. 154.

Colosseum and Plane — A341

1952, Sept. 29
611 A341 60 l dp bl & blue 3.00 10.00
  Never hinged 5.50
Issued to publicize the first International Civil Aviation Conference, Rome, Sept. 1952.
For overprint see Trieste No. 155.

Guglielmo Cardinal Massaia and Map — A342

1952, Nov. 21 Engr. Perf. 13
612 A342 25 l brn & dk brn .80 .80
  Never hinged 1.75
Centenary of the establishment of the first Catholic mission in Ethiopia.
For overprint see Trieste No. 156.

Symbols of Army, Navy and Air Force A343

Sailor, Soldier and Aviator A344

Design: 60 l, Boat, plane and tank.

1952, Nov. 3 Photo. Perf. 14
613 A343 10 l dk green .25 .25
614 A344 25 l blk & dk brn .40 .25
615 A344 60 l black & lt blue 3.50 5.50
  Nos. 613-615 (3) 4.15 6.00
Set, never hinged 8.00
Armed Forces Day, Nov. 4, 1952.
For overprints see Trieste Nos. 157-159.

Antonio Mancini A345

Vincenzo Gemito A346

1952, Dec. 6
616 A345 25 l dark green .45 .75
617 A346 25 l brown .45 .75
Set, never hinged 1.75
Birth centenaries of Antonio Mancini, painter, and Vincenzo Gemito, sculptor.
For overprints see Trieste Nos. 160-161.

Martyrs, Jailer and Artist Boldini — A347

1952, Dec. 31
618 A347 25 l gray blk & dk blue .75 .75
  Never hinged 2.25
Centenary of the deaths of the five Martyrs of Belfiore.
For overprint see Trieste No. 162.

Antonello da Messina — A349

1953, Feb. 21 Photo. Perf. 14
621 A349 25 l car lake .75 .75
  Never hinged 2.00
Messina Exhibition of the paintings of Antonello and his 15th cent. contemporaries.
For overprint see Trieste No. 165.

Racing Cars — A350

1953, Apr. 24
622 A350 25 l violet .50 .50
  Never hinged 1.00
20th 1,000-mile auto race.
For overprint see Trieste No. 166.

Decoration "Knights of Labor" Bee and Honeycomb — A351

1953, Apr. 30
623 A351 25 l violet .50 .50
  Never hinged .90
For overprint see Trieste No. 167.

Arcangelo Corelli — A352

1953, May 30
624 A352 25 l dark brown .50 .50
  Never hinged 1.00
300th anniv. of the birth of Arcangelo Corelli, composer.
For overprint see Trieste No. 168.

St. Clare of Assisi and Convent of St. Damien — A353

1953, June 27
625 A353 25 l brown & dull red .35 .45
  Never hinged .65
St. Clare of Assisi, 700th death anniv.
For overprint see Trieste No. 169.

"Italia" after Syracusean Coin — A354

Size: 17x21mm

1953-54 Wmk. 277 Perf. 14
626 A354 5 l gray .25 .25
627 A354 10 l org ver .25 .25
628 A354 12 l dull green .25 .25
628A A354 13 l brt lil rose ('54) .25 .25
629 A354 20 l lt brown 2.00 .25
630 A354 25 l redsh lilac 2.00 .25
631 A354 35 l rose car .60 .25
632 A354 60 l blue 15.00 5.00
633 A354 80 l orange brn 32.50 .25
  Nos. 626-633 (9) 53.10 7.00
Set, never hinged 100.00
See Nos. 661-662, 673B-689, 785-788, 998A-998W, 1288-1290. For overprints see Trieste Nos. 170-177.

Mountain Peaks — A355

1953, July 11
634 A355 25 l grnsh blue .45 .45
  Never hinged 1.25
Festival of the Mountain.
For overprint see Trieste No. 181.

ITALY

Tyche, Goddess of Fortune — A356

1953, July 16
635	A356	25 l dark brown	.45	.25
636	A356	60 l deep blue	2.25	3.25
		Set, never hinged	6.00	

Intl. Exposition of Agriculture, Rome, 1953.
For overprints see Trieste Nos. 182-183.

Continents Joined by Rainbow — A357

1953, Aug. 6
637	A357	25 l org & Prus bl	1.25	.25
638	A357	60 l lil rose & dk vio bl	3.50	3.50
		Set, never hinged	12.00	

Signing of the North Atlantic Treaty, 4th anniv.
For overprints see Trieste Nos. 184-185.

Luca Signorelli — A358

1953, Aug. 13
639	A358	25 l dk brn & dull grn	.40	.40
		Never hinged	.90	

Issued to publicize the opening of an exhibition of the works of Luca Signorelli, painter.
For overprint see Trieste No. 186.

Agostino Bassi — A359

1953, Sept. 5
640	A359	25 l dk gray & brown	.35	.35
		Never hinged	.60	—

6th International Microbiology Congress, Rome, Sept. 6-12, 1953.
For overprint see Trieste No. 187.

Siena A360

Rapallo A361

Views: 20 l, Seaside at Gardone. 25 l, Mountain, Cortina d'Ampezzo. 35 l, Roman ruins, Taormina. 60 l, Rocks and sea, Capri.

1953, Dec. 31 — Perf. 14
641	A360	10 l dk brn & red brn	.25	.25
642	A361	12 l lt blue & gray	.25	.25
643	A361	20 l brn org & dk brn	.25	.25
644	A360	25 l dk grn & pale bl	.40	.25
645	A361	35 l cream & brn	.60	.40
646	A361	60 l bl grn & ind	1.15	1.75
		Nos. 641-646 (6)	2.90	3.15
		Set, never hinged	6.50	

For overprints see Trieste Nos. 188-193, 204-205.

Lateran Palace, Rome — A362

1954, Feb. 11
647	A362	25 l dk brown & choc	.35	.25
648	A362	60 l blue & ultra	1.75	2.50
		Set, never hinged	4.00	

Signing of the Lateran Pacts, 25th anniv.
For overprints see Trieste Nos. 194-195.

Television Screen and Aerial — A363

1954, Feb. 25
649	A363	25 l purple	.75	.25
650	A363	60 l dp blue grn	3.25	4.50
		Set, never hinged	7.50	

Introduction of regular natl. television service.
For overprints see Trieste Nos. 196-197.

"Italia" and Quotation from Constitution A364

1954, Mar. 20
651	A364	25 l purple	.45	.25
		Never hinged	1.75	

Propaganda for the payment of taxes.
For overprint see Trieste No. 198.

Vertical Flight Trophy — A365

1954, Apr. 24
652	A365	25 l gray black	.45	.70
		Never hinged	.80	

Issued to publicize the experimental transportation of mail by helicopter, April 1954.
For overprint see Trieste No. 199.

Eagle Perched on Ruins — A366

1954, June 1
653	A366	25 l gray, org brn & blk	.35	.35
		Never hinged		.45

10th anniv. of Italy's resistance movement.
For overprint see Trieste No. 200.

Alfredo Catalani, Composer, Birth Centenary — A367

1954, June 19 — Perf. 14
654	A367	25 l dk grnsh gray	.35	.30
		Never hinged		.45

For overprint see Trieste No. 201.

Marco Polo, Lion of St. Mark and Dragon — A368

1954, July 8 — Engr. — Perf. 14
655	A368	25 l red brown	.35	.25

Perf. 13
656	A368	60 l gray green	2.60	5.25
a.		Perf. 13x12	5.75	5.75
		Set, never hinged	5.25	

700th anniv. of the birth of Marco Polo.
For overprints see Trieste Nos. 202-203.

Automobile and Cyclist — A369

1954, Sept. 6 — Photo. — Perf. 14
657	A369	25 l dp green & red	.30	.30
		Never hinged	.60	

Italian Touring Club, 60th anniv.
For overprint see Trieste No. 206.

St. Michael Overpowering the Devil — A370

1954, Oct. 9
658	A370	25 l rose red	.25	.25
659	A370	60 l blue	.90	.90
		Set, never hinged	1.50	

23rd general assembly of the International Criminal Police, Rome 1954.
For overprints see Trieste Nos. 207-208.

Pinocchio and Group of Children — A371

1954, Oct. 26
660	A371	25 l rose red	.40	.30
		Never hinged	1.00	

Carlo Lorenzini, creator of Pinocchio.

Italia Type of 1953-54

1954, Dec. 28 — Engr. — Perf. 13
Size: 22½x27½mm
661	A354	100 l brown	55.00	.30
662	A354	200 l dp blue	3.00	.50
		Set, never hinged	125.00	

Madonna, Perugino — A372

1954, Dec. 31 — Photo. — Perf. 14
663	A372	25 l brown & bister	.25	.25
664	A372	60 l black & cream	.75	.50
		Set, never hinged	2.00	

Issued to mark the end of the Marian Year.

Amerigo Vespucci and Map — A373

1954, Dec. 31 — Engr. — Perf. 13
665	A373	25 l dp plum	.25	.25
a.		Perf. 13x14	6.00	.75
666	A373	60 l blue blk	1.00	1.00
a.		Perf. 13x14	3.00	2.75
		Set, never hinged	2.75	

500th anniv. of the birth of Amerigo Vespucci, explorer, 1454-1512.

60 l, Madonna of the Pieta, Michelangelo.

Silvio Pellico (1789-1854), Dramatist — A374

Wmk. 277
1955, Jan. 24 — Photo. — Perf. 14
667	A374	25 l brt blue & vio	.30	.25
		Never hinged	.60	

Italy at Work Type of 1950

1955-57 — Wmk. 303
668	A306	50c vio bl	.25	.25
669	A306	1 l dk bl vio	.25	.25
670	A306	2 l sepia	.25	.25
671	A306	15 l dk gray bl	.30	.25
672	A306	30 l magenta	25.00	.25
673	A306	50 l violet	10.00	.25
673A	A306	65 l dk grn ('57)	14.00	35.00
		Nos. 668-673A (7)	50.05	36.50
		Set, never hinged	125.00	

St. George, by Donatello — A374a

Italia Type of 1953-54 and

1955-58 — Wmk. 303 — Photo. — Perf. 14
Size: 17x21mm
673B	A354	1 l gray ('58)	.25	.25
674	A354	5 l slate	.25	.25
675	A354	6 l ocher ('57)	.25	.25
676	A354	10 l org ver	.25	.25
677	A354	12 l dull green	.25	.25
678	A354	13 l brt lil rose	.25	.25
679	A354	15 l gray vio ('56)	.25	.25
680	A354	20 l brown	.25	.25
681	A354	25 l purple	.25	.25
682	A354	35 l rose car	.25	.25
683	A354	50 l olive ('58)	.25	.25
685	A354	60 l blue	.25	.25
686	A354	80 l brown org	.25	.25
687	A354	90 l lt red brn ('58)	.25	.25

Size: 22½x28mm
Engr. — Perf. 13½
688	A354	100 l brn ('56)	4.25	.25
a.		Perf. 13½x12	7.50	.25
b.		Perf. 13½x14	1,225.	22.50
689	A354	200 l gray bl ('57)	3.00	.25
690	A374a	500 l grn ('57)	1.00	.25
b.		Perf. 14x13½	75.00	2.50
690A	A374a	1000 l rose car ('57)	1.50	.60
c.		Perf. 14x13½	5.00	.50
		Nos. 673B-690A (18)	13.25	4.85
		Set, never hinged	30.00	

Nos. 690-690A were printed on ordinary and fluorescent paper.
See Nos. 785-788. See Nos. 998A-998W for small-size set.

Catalogue values for unused stamps in this section, from this point to the end of the section, are for Never Hinged items.

"Italia" — A375

1955, Mar. 15 — Photo. — Perf. 14
691	A375	25 l rose vio	1.75	.25

Issued as propaganda for the payment of taxes.

Oil Derrick and Old Roman Aqueduct — A376

60 l, Marble columns and oil field on globe.

1955, June 6
692	A376	25 l olive green	.35	.25
693	A376	60 l henna brown	1.10	1.10

4th World Petroleum Cong., Rome, June 6-15, 1955.

ITALY

Antonio Rosmini, Philosopher, Death Centenary — A377

1955, July 1   **Wmk. 303**   *Perf. 14*
694 A377 25 l sepia   .65   .25

Girolamo Fracastoro and Stadium at Verona — A378

1955, Sept. 1
695 A378 25 l gray blk & brn   .50   .25
Intl. Medical Congress, Verona, Sept. 1-4.

Basilica of St. Francis, Assisi — A379

1955, Oct. 4
696 A379 25 l black & cream   .40   .25
Issued in honor of St. Francis and for the 7th centenary (in 1953) of the Basilica in Assisi.

Young Man at Drawing Board — A380

1955, Oct. 15
697 A380 25 l Prus green   .40   .25
Centenary of technical education in Italy.

Harvester A381

FAO Headquarters, Rome A382

1955, Nov. 3
698 A381 25 l rose red & brn   .40   .25
699 A382 60 l blk & brt pur   1.25   1.00
Intl. Institute of Agriculture, 50th anniv. and FAO, successor to the Institute, 10th anniv.

A383

1955, Nov. 10
700 A383 25 l rose brown   .65   .25
70th anniversary of the birth of Giacomo Matteotti, Italian socialist leader.

A384

1955, Nov. 19
701 A384 25 l dark green   .35   .25
Death of Battista Grassi, zoologist, 30th anniv.

"St. Stephen Giving Alms" — A385

"St. Lorenzo Giving Alms" — A386

1955, Nov. 26
702 A385 10 l black & cream   .25   .25
703 A386 25 l ultra & cream   .40   .25
Death of Fra Angelico, painter, 500th anniv.

Giovanni Pascoli — A387

1955, Dec. 31
704 A387 25 l gray black   .30   .25
Centenary of the birth of Giovanni Pascoli, poet.

Ski Jump "Italia" — A388

Stadiums at Cortina: 12 l, Skiing. 25 l, Ice skating. 60 l, Ice racing, Lake Misurina.

1956, Jan. 26   *Photo.*
705 A388 10 l blue grn & org   .25   .25
706 A388 12 l yellow & blk   .25   .25
707 A388 25 l vio blk & org brn   .35   .25
708 A388 60 l sapphire & org   1.60   2.25
Nos. 705-708 (4)   2.45   3.00
VII Winter Olympic Games at Cortina d'Ampezzo, Jan. 26-Feb. 5, 1956.

Mail Coach and Tunnel Exit — A389

1956, May 19   **Wmk. 303**   *Perf. 14*
709 A389 25 l dk blue grn   4.00   .65
50th anniv. of the Simplon Tunnel.

Arms of Republic and Symbols of Industry — A390

1956, June 2
710 A390 10 l gray & slate bl   .40   .25
711 A390 25 l pink & rose red   .40   .25
712 A390 60 l lt bl & brt bl   4.50   5.25
713 A390 80 l orange & brn   7.00   .25
Nos. 710-713 (4)   12.30   6.00
Tenth anniversary of the Republic.

Amedeo Avogadro — A391

1956, Sept. 8
714 A391 25 l black vio   .25   .25
Centenary of the death of Amedeo Avogadro, physicist.

Europa Issue

"Rebuilding Europe" — A392

1956, Sept. 15
715 A392 25 l dark green   1.25   .25
716 A392 60 l blue   8.00   1.00
Issued to symbolize the cooperation among the six countries comprising the Coal and Steel Community.

Globe and Satellites — A393

1956, Sept. 22
717 A393 25 l intense blue   .25   .25
7th Intl. Astronautical Cong., Rome, Sept. 17-22.

Globe — A394

1956, Dec. 29   *Litho.*   *Unwmk.*
718 A394 25 l red & bl grn, *pink*   .30   .25
719 A394 60 l bl grn & red, *pale bl grn*   .40   .25
Italy's admission to the United Nations. The design, viewed through red and green glasses, becomes three-dimensional.

Postal Savings Bank and Notes — A395

1956, Dec. 31   *Photo.*   **Wmk. 303**
720 A395 25 l sl bl & dp ultra   .25   .25
80th anniversary of Postal Savings.

Ovid — A396

1957, June 10   *Perf. 14*
721 A396 25 l ol grn & blk   .30   .25
2000th anniversary of the birth of the poet Ovid (Publius Ovidius Naso).

Antonio Canova A397

Paulina Borghese as Venus A398

60 l, Sculpture: Hercules and Lichas.

1957, July 15   *Engr.*
722 A397 25 l brown   .25   .25
723 A397 60 l gray   .25   .55
724 A398 80 l vio blue   .25   .25
Nos. 722-724 (3)   .75   1.05
Birth of Antonio Canova, sculptor, 200th anniv.

Traffic Light — A399

1957, Aug. 7   **Wmk. 303**   *Photo.*   *Perf. 14*
725 A399 25 l green, blk & red   .35   .25
Campaign for careful driving.

"United Europe" — A400

1957, Sept. 16   *Litho.*   *Perf. 14*
Flags in Original Colors
726 A400 25 l light blue   .75   .25
Perf. 13
727 A400 60 l violet blue   3.50   .60
United Europe for peace and prosperity.

Giosue Carducci — A401

1957, Oct. 14   *Engr.*   *Perf. 14*
728 A401 25 l brown   .30   .25
Death of the poet Giosue Carducci, 50th anniv.

Filippino Lippi — A402

1957, Nov. 25   **Wmk. 303**   *Perf. 14*
729 A402 25 l reddish brown   .30   .25
Birth of Filippino Lippi, painter, 500th anniv.

2000th Anniv. of the Death of Marcus Tullius Cicero, Roman Statesman and Writer — A403

1957, Nov. 30   *Photo.*
730 A403 25 l brown red   .25   .25

St. Domenico Savio and Students of Various Races — A404

1957, Dec. 14
731 A404 15 l brt redsh vio & gray   .25   .25
Cent. of the death of St. Domenico Savio.

St. Francis of Paola — A405

1957, Dec. 21   *Engr.*
732 A405 25 l black   .25   .25
450th anniv. of the death of St. Francis of Paola, patron saint of seafaring men.

ITALY

Giuseppe Garibaldi — A406

Design: 110 l, Garibaldi monument, horiz.

1957, Dec. 14   Perf. 14x13, 13x14
733 A406 15 l slate green   .25 .25
734 A406 110 l dull purple   .35 .25

150th anniv. of the birth of Giuseppe Garibaldi.

Peasant, Dams and Map of Sardinia — A407

1958, Feb. 1   Engr.   Perf. 14
738 A407 25 l bluish grn   .25 .25

Completion of the Flumendosa-Mulargia irrigation system.

Immaculate Conception Statue, Rome, and Lourdes Basilica — A408

1958, Apr. 16   Wmk. 303   Perf. 14
739 A408 15 l rose claret   .25 .25
740 A408 60 l blue   .25 .25

Apparition of the Virgin Mary at Lourdes, cent.

Book and Symbols of Labor Industry and Agriculture — A409

Designs: 60 l, "Tree of Freedom," vert. 110 l, Montecitorio Palace.

1958, May 9   Photo.   Perf. 14
741 A409 25 l bl grn & ocher   .25 .25
742 A409 60 l blk brn & bl   .25 .25
743 A409 110 l ol bis & blk brn .25 .25
    Nos. 741-743 (3)   .75 .75

10th anniversary of the constitution.

Brussels Fair Emblem — A410

1958, June 12
744 A410 60 l blue & yellow   .25 .25

Intl. and Universal Exposition at Brussels.

Prologue from Pagliacci — A411

1958, July 10
745 A411 25 l dk bl & dk red   .25 .25

Birth of Ruggiero Leoncavallo, composer, cent.

Scene from La Bohème — A412

1958, July 10   Engr.   Unwmk.
746 A412 25 l dark blue   .25 .25

Birth of Giacomo Puccini, composer, cent.

Giovanni Fattori, Self-portrait — A413

1958, Aug. 7 Wmk. 303 Perf. 13x14
747 A413 110 l redsh brown   .60 .30

Death of Giovanni Fattori, painter, 50th anniv.

"Ave Maria on the Lake" by Giovanni Segantini — A414

1958, Aug. 7   Perf. 14
748 A414 110 l slate, buff   .60 .25

Birth of Giovanni Segantini, painter, cent.

Map of Brazil, Plane and Arch of Titus — A415

1958, Aug. 23   Photo.   Perf. 14
749 A415 175 l Prus green   .75 .75

Italo-Brazilian friendship on the occasion of Pres. Giovanni Gronchi's visit to Brazil.

Common Design Types pictured following the introduction.

Europa Issue, 1958
Common Design Type

1958, Sept. 13   Size: 20½x35½mm
750 CD1 25 l red & blue   .25 .25
751 CD1 60 l blue & red   .80 .35

Issued to show the European Postal Union at the service of European integration.

½g Stamp of Naples — A416

Design: 60 l, 1g Stamp of Naples.

Perf. 14x13½, 13½
1958, Oct. 4   Engr.   Unwmk.
752 A416 25 l brown red   .25 .25
753 A416 60 l blk & red brn   .25 .25

Centenary of the stamps of Naples.

Evangelista Torricelli — A417

1958, Oct. 20   Wmk. 303   Perf. 14
754 A417 25 l rose claret   .55 .35

350th anniv. of the birth of Evangelista Torricelli, mathematician and physicist.

"The Triumph of Caesar," Montegna — A418

25 l, Coats of Arms of Trieste, Rome & Trento, horiz. 60 l, War memorial bell of Rovereto.

1958, Nov. 3   Engr.   Perf. 14x13½
755 A418 15 l green   .25 .25
756 A418 25 l gray   .25 .25
757 A418 60 l rose claret   .25 .25
    Nos. 755-757 (3)   .75 .75

40th anniv. of Italy's victory in World War I.

Persian Style Bas-relief, Sorrento — A419

1958, Nov. 27   sepia, bluish   Photo.
758 A419 25 l sepia, bluish   .25 .25
759 A419 60 l vio bl, bluish   .45 .45

Visit of the Shah of Iran to Italy.

Eleonora Duse — A420

Unwmk.
1958, Dec. 11   Engr.   Perf. 14
760 A420 25 l brt ultra   .25 .25

Cent. of the birth of Eleonora Duse, actress.

Dancers and Antenna — A421

Design: 60 l, Piano, dove and antenna.

1958, Dec. 29   Photo.   Wmk. 303
761 A421 25 l red, bl & blk   .25 .25
762 A421 60 l ultra & blk   .25 .25

10th anniv. of the Prix Italia (International Radio and Television Competitions).

Stamp of Sicily — A422

Design: 60 l, Stamp of Sicily, 5g.

Perf. 14x13½
1959, Jan. 2   Engr.   Unwmk.
763 A422 25 l Prus green   .25 .25
764 A422 60 l dp orange   .25 .25

Centenary of the stamps of Sicily.

Dome of St. Peter's and Tower of Lateran Palace — A423

Wmk. 303
1959, Feb. 11   Photo.   Perf. 14
765 A423 25 l ultra   .25 .25

30th anniversary of the Lateran Pacts.

Map of North Atlantic and NATO Emblem — A424

1959, Apr. 4
766 A424 25 l dk bl & ocher   .25 .25
767 A424 60 l dk bl & green   .25 .25

10th anniv. of NATO.

Arms of Paris and Rome — A425

1959, Apr. 9
768 A425 15 l blue & red   .25 .25
769 A425 25 l blue & red   .25 .25

Cultural ties between Rome and Paris.

"A Gentle Peace Has Come" — A426

1959, Apr. 13   Engr.   Unwmk.
770 A426 25 l olive green   .25 .25

International War Veterans Association convention, Rome.

Statue of Lord Byron — A427

1959, Apr. 21
771 A427 15 l black   .25 .25

Unveiling in Rome of a statue of Lord Byron by Bertel Thorvaldson, Danish sculptor.

Camillo Prampolini — A428

1959, Apr. 27   Unwmk.   Perf. 14
772 A428 15 l car rose   8.00 .40

Camillo Prampolini, socialist leader and reformer, birth centenary.

Fountain of Dioscuri and Olympic Rings A429

Baths of Carcalla A430

Designs: 25 l, Capitoline tower. 60 l, Arch of Constantine. 110 l, Ruins of Basilica of Massentius.

1959, June 23   Photo.   Wmk. 303
Designs in Dark Sepia
773 A429 15 l red orange   .25 .25
774 A429 25 l blue   .25 .25
775 A430 35 l bister   .25 .25
776 A430 60 l rose lilac   .25 .30
777 A430 110 l yellow   .30 .25
    Nos. 773-777 (5)   1.30 1.30

1960 Olympic Games in Rome.

603

ITALY

Victor Emanuel II, Garibaldi, Cavour, Mazzini — A431

Battle of San Fermo — A432

25 l, "After the Battle of Magenta" by Fattori and Red Cross, vert. 60 l, Battle of Palestro. 110 l, "Battle of Magenta" by Induno, vert.

Engr., Cross Photo. on 25 l
1959, June 27			Unwmk.	
778	A431	15 l gray	.25	.25
779	A431	25 l brn & red	.25	.25
780	A432	35 l dk violet	.25	.25
781	A432	60 l ultra	.25	.25
782	A432	110 l magenta	.25	.25
		Nos. 778-782 (5)	1.25	1.25

Cent. of the war of independence. No. 779 for the centenary of the Red Cross idea.

Labor Monument, Geneva — A433

1959, July 20			Perf. 14x13, 14	
783	A433	25 l violet	.25	.25
784	A433	60 l brown	.30	.25

40th anniv. of the ILO.

Italia Type of 1953-54
Photo.; Engr. (100 l, 200 l)
1959-66		Wmk. 303	Perf. 14	
		Size: 17x21mm		
785	A354	30 l bis brn ('60)	.25	.25
786	A354	40 l lil rose ('60)	1.25	.25
786A	A354	70 l Prus grn ('60)	.35	.25
787	A354	100 l brown	.65	.25
787A	A354	130 l gray & dl red ('66)	.25	.25
788	A354	200 l dp blue	.65	.25
		Nos. 785-788 (6)	3.40	1.50

Stamp of Romagna — A434

1959, Sept. 1			Photo.	
789	A434	25 l pale brn & blk	.25	.25
790	A434	60 l gray grn & blk	.25	.25

Centenary of the stamps of Romagna.

Europa Issue, 1959
Common Design Type
1959, Sept. 19		Size: 22x27½mm		
791	CD2	25 l olive green	.40	.25
792	CD2	60 l blue	.40	.25

Stamp of 1953 with Facsimile Cancellation — A435

1959, Dec. 20		Wmk. 303	Perf. 14	
793	A435	15 l gray, rose car & blk	.25	.25

Italy's first Stamp Day, Dec. 20, 1959.

Aeneas Fleeing with Father and Son, by Raphael — A436

1960, Apr. 7		Engr.	Unwmk.	
794	A436	25 l lake	.25	.25
795	A436	60 l gray violet	.25	.25

World Refugee Year, 7/1/59-6/30/60. Design is detail from "The Fire in the Borgo."

Garibaldi's Proclamation to the Sicilians — A437

King Victor Emmanuel and Garibaldi Meeting at Teano — A438

60 l, Volunteers embarking, Quarto, Genoa.

Wmk. 303
1960, May 5		Photo.	Perf. 14	
796	A437	15 l brown	.25	.25

Perf. 13x14, 14x13
		Engr.	Unwmk.	
797	A438	25 l rose claret	.25	.25
798	A437	60 l ultramarine	.25	.25

Cent. of the liberation of Southern Italy (Kingdom of the Two Sicilies) by Garibaldi.

Emblem of 17th Olympic Games A439

Olympic Stadium A440

Statues: 15 l, Roman Consul on way to the games. 35 l, Myron's Discobolus. 110 l, Seated boxer. 200 l, Apoxyomenos by Lysippus.
Stadia: 25 l, Velodrome. 60 l, Sports palace. 150 l, Small sports palace.

Photogravure, Engraved
Perf. 14x13½, 13½x14
1960		Wmk. 303, Unwmk.		
799	A439	5 l yellow brn	.25	.25
800	A440	10 l dp org & dk bl	.25	.25
801	A439	15 l ultra	.25	.25
802	A440	25 l lt vio & brn	.25	.25
803	A439	35 l rose cl	.25	.25
804	A440	60 l bluish grn & brn	.25	.25
805	A439	110 l plum	.25	.25
806	A440	150 l blue & brn	1.50	1.50
807	A439	200 l green	.75	.25
		Nos. 799-807 (9)	4.00	3.50

17th Olympic Games, Rome, 8/25-9/11. The photo. denominations (5-10, 25, 60, 150 l) are wmkd.; the engraved (15, 35, 110, 200 l) are unwmkd.

Bottego Statue, Parma — A441

1960		Unwmk.	Perf. 14	
808	A441	30 l brown	.25	.25

Birth cent. of Vittorio Bottego, explorer.

Europa Issue, 1960
Common Design Type
1960		Photo.	Wmk. 303	
		Size: 37x27mm		
809	CD3	30 l dk grn & bis brn	.25	.25
810	CD3	70 l dk bl & salmon	.25	.25

Michelangelo da Caravaggio — A442

1960		Unwmk. Engr.	Perf. 13x13½	
811	A442	25 l orange brn	.25	.25

350th anniv. of the death of Michelangelo da Caravaggio (Merisi), painter.

Mail Coach and Post Horn — A443

1960		Wmk. 303 Photo.	Perf. 14	
812	A443	15 l blk brn & org brn	.25	.25

Issued for Stamp Day, Dec. 20.

Slave, by Michelangelo — A444

Designs from Sistine Chapel by Michelangelo: 5 l, 10 l, 115 l, 150 l, Heads of various "slaves." 15 l, Joel. 20 l, Libyan Sybil. 25 l, Isaiah. 30 l, Eritrean Sybil. 40 l, Daniel. 50 l, Delphic Sybil. 55 l, Cumaean Sybil. 70 l, Zachariah. 85 l, Jonah. 90 l, Jeremiah. 100 l, Ezekiel. 200 l, Self-portrait. 500 l, Adam. 1000 l, Eve.

Wmk. 303
1961, Mar. 6		Photo.	Perf. 14	
		Size: 17x21mm		
813	A444	1 l gray	.25	.25
814	A444	5 l brown org	.25	.25
815	A444	10 l red org	.25	.25
816	A444	15 l brt lil	.25	.25
817	A444	20 l Prus grn	.25	.25
818	A444	25 l brown	.30	.25
819	A444	30 l purple	.25	.25
820	A444	40 l rose red	.25	.25
821	A444	50 l olive	.25	.25
822	A444	55 l red brn	.25	.25
823	A444	70 l blue	.25	.25
824	A444	85 l slate grn	.25	.25
825	A444	90 l lil rose	.40	.25
826	A444	100 l vio gray	.40	.25
827	A444	115 l ultra	.40	.25

Engr.
828	A444	150 l chocolate	.75	.25
829	A444	200 l dark blue	1.25	.35
a.		Perf. 13½	1.50	.25

Perf. 13½
Size: 22x27mm
830	A444	500 l blue grn	3.75	.35
831	A444	1000 l brown red	3.50	6.00
		Nos. 813-831 (19)	13.50	10.70

Map Showing Flight from Italy to Argentina — A445

185 l, Italy to Uruguay. 205 l, Italy to Peru.

1961, Apr.		Photo.	Perf. 14	
832	A445	170 l ultra	4.50	4.50
833	A445	185 l dull green	4.50	4.50
834	A445	205 l violet blk	15.00	14.00
a.		205 l rose lilac	1,250.	2,000.
		Nos. 832-834 (3)	24.00	23.00

Visit of Pres. Gronchi to South America, 4/61.
Nos. 832-833 and 834a were issued Apr. 4, to become valid on Apr. 6. The map of Peru on No. 834a was drawn incorrectly and the stamp was therefore withdrawn on Apr. 4. A corrected design in new color (No. 834) was issued Apr. 6. Forgeries of No. 834a exist.

Statue of Pliny, Como Cathedral — A446

1961, May 27				
835	A446	30 l brown	.25	.25

1900th anniversary of the birth of Pliny the Younger, Roman consul and writer.

Ippolito Nievo (1831-61), Writer — A447

1961, June 8		Wmk. 303	Perf. 14	
836	A447	30 l multi	.25	.25

St. Paul Aboard Ship — A448

1961, June 28				
837	A448	30 l multi	.25	.25
838	A448	70 l multi	.30	.30

1,900th anniversary of St. Paul's arrival in Rome. The design is after a miniature from the Bible of Borso D'Este.

Cavalli Gun and Gaeta Fortress — A449

Cent. of Italian unity: 30 l, Carignano palace, Turin. 40 l, Montecitorio palace, Rome. 70 l, Palazzo Vecchio, Florence. 115 l, Villa Madama, Rome. 300 l, Steel construction, Italia '61 Exhibition, Turin.

1961, Aug. 12			Photo.	
839	A449	15 l dk bl & redsh brn	.25	.25
840	A449	30 l dk bl & red brn	.25	.25
841	A449	40 l bl & brn	.35	.25
842	A449	70 l brn & pink	.35	.25
843	A449	115 l org brn & dk bl	1.75	.25
844	A449	300 l brt grn & red	6.00	8.25
		Nos. 839-844 (6)	8.95	9.50

Europa Issue, 1961
Common Design Type
1961, Sept. 18		Wmk. 303	Perf. 14	
		Size: 36½x21mm		
845	CD4	30 l carmine	.25	.25
846	CD4	70 l yel grn	.25	.25

Giandomenico Romagnosi — A450

Perf. 13½
1961, Nov. 28		Unwmk.	Engr.	
847	A450	30 l green	.25	.25

Bicentenary of the birth of Giandomenico Romagnosi, jurist and philosopher.

Design from 1820 Sardinia Letter Sheet — A451

Wmk. 303
1961, Dec. 3		Photo.	Perf. 14	
848	A451	15 l lil rose & blk	.25	.25

Issued for Stamp Day 1961.

ITALY

Family Scene "I am the Lamp that Glows so Gently..." A452

1962, Apr. 6   Wmk. 303   Perf. 14
849 A452 30 l red   .25 .25
850 A452 70 l blue   .25 .30
Death of Giovanni Pascoli, poet, 50th anniv.

Pacinotti's Dynamo — A453

1962, June 12
851 A453 30 l rose & blk   .25 .25
852 A453 70 l ultra & blk   .25 .25
Antonio Pacinotti (1841-1912), physicist and inventor of the ring winding dynamo.

St. Catherine of Siena, by Andrea Vanni — A454

70 l, St. Catherine, 15th century woodcut.

1962, June 26   Photo.
853 A454 30 l black vio   .25 .25

Engraved and Photogravure
854 A454 70 l red & blk   .25 .40
500th anniversary of the canonization of St. Catherine of Siena, Patroness of Italy.

Lion of St. Mark — A455

Design: 30 l, Stylized camera eye.

1962, Aug. 25   Photo.
855 A455 30 l bl & blk   .25 .25
856 A455 70 l red org & blk   .25 .25
Intl. Film Festival in Venice, 30th anniv.

Motorcyclist and Bicyclist — A456

70 l, Group of cyclists. 300 l, Bicyclist.

1962, Aug. 30
857 A456 30 l grn & blk   .25 .25
858 A456 70 l bl & blk   .25 .25
859 A456 300 l dp org & blk   3.50 3.50
    Nos. 857-859 (3)   4.00 4.00
World Bicycle Championship Races.

Europa Issue, 1962
Common Design Type

1962, Sept. 17   Size: 37x21mm
860 CD5 30 l carmine   .25 .25
861 CD5 70 l blue   .75 .30

A457

Design: Swiss and Italian Flags, Eugenio and Angela Lina Balzan Medal.

1962, Oct. 25   Wmk. 303   Perf. 14
862 A457 70 l rose red, grn & brn   .55 .35
1st distribution of the Balzan Prize by the Intl. Balzan Foundation for Italian-Swiss Cooperation.

Malaria Eradication Emblem — A458

1962, Oct. 31   Photo.
863 A458 30 l light violet   .25 .25
864 A458 70 l light blue   .25 .25
WHO drive to eradicate malaria.

Stamps of 1862 and 1961 — A459

1962, Dec. 2
865 A459 15 l pur, buff & bister   .25 .25
Stamp Day and cent. of Italian postage stamps.

A460

30 l, 70 l, Descent of the Holy Spirit on the twelve apostles.

1962, Dec. 8
866 A460 30 l org & dk bl grn, buff   .25 .25
867 A460 70 l dk bl grn & org, buff   .25 .30
21st Ecumenical Council of the Roman Catholic Church, Vatican II. The design is an illumination from the Codex Syriacus.

A461

Statue of Count Camillo Bensi di Cavour.

1962, Dec. 10   Engr.   Unwmk.
868 A461 30 l dk grn   .25 .25
Centenary of Court of Accounts.

Count Giovanni Pico della Mirandola — A462

Wmk. 303
1963, Feb. 25   Photo.   Perf. 14
869 A462 30 l gray blk   .25 .25
Mirandola (1463-94), Renaissance scholar.

Gabriele D'Annunzio — A463

1963, Mar. 12   Engr.   Unwmk.
870 A463 30 l dk grn   .25 .25
Issued to commemorate the centenary of the birth of Gabriele d'Annunzio, author and soldier.

Sower — A464

Design: 70 l, Harvester tying sheaf, sculpture from Maggiore Fountain, Perugia.

1963, Mar. 21   Photo.   Wmk. 303
871 A464 30 l rose car & brn   .25 .25
872 A464 70 l bl & brn   .25 .25
FAO "Freedom from Hunger" campaign.

Mt. Viso, Alpine Club Emblem, Ax and Rope — A465

1963, Mar. 30   Wmk. 303   Perf. 14
873 A465 115 l dk brn & brt bl   .25 .25
Italian Alpine Club founding, cent.

Map of Italy and "INA" Initials — A466

1963, Apr. 4
874 A466 30 l grn & blk   .25 .25
50th anniv. of the Natl. Insurance Institute.

Globe and Stamp — A467

1963, May 7   Photo.   Perf. 14
875 A467 70 l bl & grn   .25 .25
1st Intl. Postal Conf., Paris, 1863.

Crosses and Centenary Emblem on Globe — A468

1963, June 8   Wmk. 303   Perf. 14
876 A468 30 l dk gray & red   .25 .25
877 A468 70 l dl bl & red   .25 .25
International Red Cross founding, cent.

Roman Column, Globe and Highways — A469

1963, Aug. 21   Wmk. 303   Perf. 14
878 A469 15 l gray ol & dk bl   .25 .25
879 A469 70 l dl bl & brn   .25 .25
UN Tourist Conf., Rome, Aug. 21-Sept. 5.

Europa Issue, 1963
Common Design Type

1963, Sept. 16   Size: 27½x23mm
880 CD6 30 l rose & brn   .25 .25
881 CD6 70 l brn & grn   .25 .25

Bay of Naples, Vesuvius and Sailboats A470

Athlete on Greek Vase A471

1963, Sept. 21   Wmk. 303   Perf. 14
882 A470 15 l bl & org   .25 .25
883 A471 70 l dk grn & org brn   .25 .30
4th Mediterranean Games, Naples, Sept. 21-29.

Giuseppe Gioachino Belli (1791-1863), Poet — A472

1963, Nov. 14   Wmk. 303   Perf. 14
884 A472 30 l red brn   .25 .25

Stamps Forming Flower — A473

1963, Dec. 1
885 A473 15 l bl & car   .25 .25
Issued for Stamp Day.

Pietro Mascagni and Old Costanzi Theater, Rome — A474

No. 886, Giuseppe Verdi & La Scala, Milan.

1963   Photo.
886 A474 30 l gray grn & yel brn   .25 .25
887 A474 30 l yel brn & gray grn   .25 .25
Verdi (1813-1901), and Mascagni (1863-1945), composers. Issued: No. 886, 10/10; No. 887, 12/7.

Galileo Galilei — A475

1964, Feb. 15   Wmk. 303   Perf. 14
888 A475 30 l org brn   .25 .25
889 A475 70 l black   .25 .25
Galilei (1564-1642), astronomer & physicist.

Nicodemus by Michelangelo — A476

1964, Feb. 18   Photo.
890 A476 30 l brown   .25 .25
Michelangelo Buonarroti (1475-1564), artist. Head of Nicodemus (self-portrait?) from the Pieta, Florence Cathedral. See No. C137.

ITALY

Carabinieri
A477

70 l, Charge of Pastrengo, 1848, by De Albertis.

1964, June 5	Wmk. 303		Perf. 14
891	A477	30 l vio bl & red	.25 .25
892	A477	70 l brown	.25 .25

150th anniv. of the Carabinieri (police corps).

Giambattista Bodoni — A478

Perf. 14x13
1964, July 30	Engr.		Unwmk.
893	A478	30 l carmine	.25 .25
a.		Perf. 13	.25 .25

Death of Giambattista Bodoni (1740-1813), printer & type designer (Bodoni type), 150th anniv.

Europa Issue, 1964
Common Design Type
Wmk. 303

1964, Sept. 14	Photo.		Perf. 14
		Size: 21x37mm	
894	CD7	30 l brt rose lilac	.25 .25
895	CD7	70 l blue green	.25 .25

Walled City — A479

1964, Oct. 15	Photo.		Perf. 14
896	A479	30 l emer & dk brn	.25 .25
897	A479	70 l bl & dk brn	.25 .25
		Unwmk.	Engr.
898	A479	500 l red	1.50 1.75
	Nos. 896-898 (3)		2.00 2.25

7th Congress of European Towns. The buildings in design are: Big Ben, London; Campodoglio, Rome; Town Hall, Bruges; Römer, Frankfurt; Town Hall, Paris; Belfry, Zurich; Gate, Kampen (Holland).

Left Arch of Victor Emmanuel Monument, Rome — A480

1964, Nov. 4	Photo.		Wmk. 303
899	A480	30 l dk red brn	.25 .25
900	A480	70 l blue	.25 .25

Pilgrimage to Rome of veterans living abroad.

Giovanni da Verrazano and Verrazano-Narrows Bridge, New York Bay — A481

1964, Nov. 21	Wmk. 303		Perf. 14
901	A481	30 l blk & brn	.25 .25

Opening of the Verrazano-Narrows Bridge connecting Staten Island and Brooklyn, NY, and to honor Giovanni da Verrazano (1485-1528), discoverer of New York Bay. See No. C138.

Italian Sports Stamps, 1934-63 — A482

1964, Dec. 6	Photo.		Perf. 14
902	A482	15 l gldn brn & dk brn	.25 .25

Issued for Stamp Day.

Italian Soldiers in Concentration Camp A483

Victims Trapped by Swastika A484

15 l, Italian soldier, sailor and airman fighting for the Allies. 70 l, Guerrilla fighters in the mountains. 115 l, Marchers with Italian flag. 130 l, Ruins of city and torn Italian flag.

1965, Apr. 24	Photo.		Wmk. 303
903	A483	10 l black	.25 .25
904	A483	15 l grn & rose car	.25 .25
905	A484	30 l plum	.25 .25
906	A483	70 l deep blue	.25 .25
907	A484	115 l rose car	.25 .25
908	A484	130 l grn, sepia & red	.25 .25
	Nos. 903-908 (6)		1.50 1.50

Italian resistance movement during World War II, 20th anniv.

Antonio Meucci, Guglielmo Marconi and ITU Emblem — A485

1965, May 17			Perf. 14
909	A485	70 l red & dk grn	.25 .25

Cent. of the ITU.

Sailboats of Flying Dutchman Class — A486

Designs: 70 l, Sailboats of 5.5-meter class, vert. 500 l, Sailboats, Lightning class.

1965, May 31	Photo.		Wmk. 303
910	A486	30 l blk & dl rose	.25 .25
911	A486	70 l blk & ultra	.25 .25
912	A486	500 l blk & gray bl	.55 .35
	Nos. 910-912 (3)		1.05 .85

Issued to publicize the World Yachting Championships, Naples and Alassio.

Mont Blanc and Tunnel — A487

1965, June 16	Wmk. 303		Perf. 14
913	A487	30 l black	.25 .25

Opening of the Mont Blanc Tunnel connecting Entrayes, Italy, and Le Polerins, France.

Alessandro Tassoni and Scene from "Seccia Rapita" — A488

	Unwmk.		
1965, Sept. 20	Photo.		Perf. 14
914	A488	40 l blk & multi	.25 .25

Tassoni (1565-1635), poet. Design is from 1744 engraving by Bartolomeo Soliani.

Europa Issue, 1965
Common Design Type

1965, Sept. 27			Wmk. 303
		Size: 36½x27mm	
915	CD8	40 l ocher & ol grn	.25 .25
916	CD8	90 l ultra & ol grn	.25 .25

Dante, 15th Century Bust — A489

Designs (from old Manuscripts): 40 l, Dante in Hell. 90 l, Dante in Purgatory led by Angel of Chastity. 130 l, Dante in Paradise interrogated by St. Peter on faith, horiz.

Perf. 13½x14, 14x13½
1965, Oct. 21	Photo.		Unwmk.
917	A489	40 l multi	.25 .25
918	A489	90 l multi	.25 .25
919	A489	130 l multi	.25 .25
	Wmk. 303		Perf. 14
920	A489	500 l slate grn	.55 .35
	Nos. 917-920 (4)		1.30 1.10

Dante Alighieri (1265-1321), poet.

House under Construction — A490

1965, Oct. 31	Wmk. 303		Perf. 14
921	A490	40 l buff, blk & org brn	.25 .25

Issued for Savings Day.

Jet Plane, Moon and Airletter Border — A491

Design: 40 l, Control tower and plane.

1965, Nov. 3			
922	A491	40 l dk Prus bl & red	.25 .25
	Unwmk.		
923	A491	90 l red, grn, dp bl & buff	.25 .25

Night air postal network.

Map of Italy with Milan-Rome Highway — A492

1965, Dec. 5	Photo.		Perf. 13x14
924	A492	20 l bl, blk, ocher & gray	.25 .25

Issued for Stamp Day.

Two-Man Bobsled — A493

Design: 90 l, Four-man bobsled.

1966, Jan. 24	Wmk. 303		Perf. 14
925	A493	40 l dl bl, gray & red	.25 .25
926	A493	90 l vio & bl	.25 .25

Intl. Bobsled Championships, Cortina d'Ampezzo.

Woman Skater — A494

Winter University Games: 40 l, Skier holding torch, horiz. 500 l, Ice hockey.

1966, Feb. 5			Photo.
927	A494	40 l blk & red	.25 .25
928	A494	90 l vio & red	.25 .25
929	A494	500 l brn & red	.55 .35
	Nos. 927-929 (3)		1.05 .85

Benedetto Croce — A495

1966, Feb. 25	Wmk. 303		Perf. 14
930	A495	40 l brown	.25 .25

Benedetto Croce (1866-1952), philosopher, statesman and historian.

Arms of Venice and Other Cities in Venezia A496

1966, Mar. 22	Photo.		Unwmk.
932	A496	40 l gray & multi	.25 .25

Centenary of Venezia's union with Italy.

Battle of Bezzecca — A497

1966, July 21	Wmk. 303		Perf. 14
933	A497	90 l ol grn	.25 .25

Centenary of the unification of Italy and of the Battle of Bezzecca.

Umbrella Pine A498

Carnations62 A499

25 l, Apples. 50 l, Florentine iris. 55 l, Cypresses. 90 l, Daisies. 170 l, Olive tree. 180 l, Juniper.

1966-68	Unwmk.		Perf. 13½x14
934	A498	20 l multi	.25 .25
934A	A498	25 l multi ('67)	.25 .25
935	A499	40 l multi	.25 .25
935A	A498	50 l multi ('67)	.25 .25
935B	A498	55 l multi ('68)	.25 .25
936	A499	90 l multi	.25 .25
937	A498	170 l multi	.25 .25
937A	A498	180 l multi ('68)	.25 .25
	Nos. 934-937A (8)		2.00 2.00

ITALY

Tourist Attractions — A500

1966, May 28   Wmk. 303   Perf. 14
938 A500 20 l yel, org & blk   .25 .25

Issued for tourist publicity and in connection with the National Conference on Tourism, Rome.

"I" in Flag Colors — A501

Perf. 13½x14
1966, June 2   Photo.   Unwmk.
939 A501 40 l multi   .25 .25
940 A501 90 l multi   .25 .25

20th anniversary of the Republic of Italy.

Singing Angels, by Donatello — A502

Perf. 13½x14
1966, Sept. 24   Photo.   Unwmk.
941 A502 40 l multi   .25 .25

Donatello (1386-1466), sculptor.

Europa Issue, 1966
Common Design Type
1966, Sept. 26   Wmk. 303   Perf. 14
Size: 22x38mm
942 CD9 40 l brt pur   .25 .25
943 CD9 90 l brt bl   .25 .25

Madonna, by Giotto — A503

Perf. 13½x14
1966, Oct. 20   Photo.   Unwmk.
944 A503 40 l multi   .25 .25

700th anniversary of the birth of Giotto di Bondone (1266?-1337), Florentine painter.

Italian Patriots — A504

1966, Nov. 3   Wmk. 303   Perf. 14
945 A504 40 l gray & dl grn   .25 .25

50th anniv. of the execution by Austrians of 4 Italian patriots: Fabio Filzi, Cesare Battisti, Damiano Chiesa and Nazario Sauro.

Postrider — A505

Perf. 14x13½
1966, Dec. 4   Photo.   Unwmk.
946 A505 20 l multi   .25 .25

Issued for Stamp Day.

Globe and Compass Rose — A506

1967, Mar. 20   Photo.   Wmk. 303
947 A506 40 l dull blue   .25 .25

Centenary of Italian Geographical Society.

Arturo Toscanini (1867-1957), Conductor A507

1967, Mar. 25   Perf. 14
948 A507 40 l dp vio & cream   .25 .25

Seat of Parliament on Capitoline Hill, Rome — A508

1967, Mar. 25   Perf. 14
949 A508 40 l sepia   .25 .25
950 A508 90 l rose lil & blk   .25 .25

10th anniv. of the Treaty of Rome, establishing the European Common Market.

Europa Issue, 1967
Common Design Type
1967, Apr. 10   Wmk. 303   Perf. 14
Size: 22x28mm
951 CD10 40 l plum & pink   .25 .25
952 CD10 90 l ultra & pale gray   .35 .25

Alpine Ibex, Grand Paradiso Park — A509

National Parks: 40 l, Brown bear, Abruzzi Apennines, horiz. 90 l, Red deer, Stelvio Pass, Ortler Mountains, horiz. 170 l, Oak and deer, Circeo.

Perf. 13½x14, 14x13½
1967, Apr. 22   Photo.
953 A509 20 l multi   .25 .25
954 A509 40 l multi   .25 .25
955 A509 90 l multi   .25 .25
956 A509 170 l multi   .25 .25
Nos. 953-956 (4)   1.00 1.00

Claudio Monteverdi and Characters from "Orfeo" — A510

1967, May 15   Perf. 14
957 A510 40 l bis brn & brn   .25 .25

Monteverdi (1567-1643), composer.

Bicyclists and Mountains A511

50th Bicycle Tour of Italy: 90 l, Three bicyclists on the road. 500 l, Group of bicyclists.

Perf. 14x13½
1967, May 15   Photo.   Unwmk.
958 A511 40 l multi   .25 .25
959 A511 90 l brt bl & multi   .25 .25
960 A511 500 l yel grn & multi   1.50 .85
Nos. 958-960 (3)   2.00 1.35

Luigi Pirandello and Stage — A512

1967, June 28   Perf. 14x13
961 A512 40 l blk & multi   .25 .25

Pirandello (1867-1936), novelist & dramatist.

Stylized Mask — A513

1967, June 30   Wmk. 303   Perf. 14
962 A513 20 l grn & blk   .25 .25
963 A513 40 l car rose & blk   .25 .25

10th "Festival of Two Worlds," Spoleto.

Postal Card with Postal Zone Number — A514

Design: 40 l, 50 l, Letter addressed with postal zone number.

Wmk. 303, Unwmkd, (20 l, 40 l)
1967-68
964 A514 20 l multi   .25 .25
965 A514 25 l multi ('68)   .25 .25
966 A514 40 l multi   .25 .25
967 A514 50 l multi ('68)   .25 .25
Nos. 964-967 (4)   1.00 1.00

Introduction of postal zone numbers, 7/1/67.

Pomilio PC-1 Biplane and 1917 Airmail Postmark — A515

1967, July 18   Photo.   Wmk. 303
968 A515 40 l blk & lt bl   .25 .25

1st airmail stamp, Italy No. C1, 50th anniv.

St. Ivo Church, Rome — A516

1967, Aug. 2   Unwmk.   Perf. 14
969 A516 90 l multi   .25 .25

Francesco Borromini (1599-1667), architect.

Umberto Giordano and "Improvisation" from Opera Andrea Chenier — A517

1967, Aug. 28   Wmk. 303
970 A517 20 l blk & org brn   .25 .25

Umberto Giordano (1867-1948), composer.

Oath of Pontida, by Adolfo Cao — A518

1967, Sept. 2
971 A518 20 l dk brn   .25 .25

800th anniv. of the Oath of Pontida, which united the Lombard League against Emperor Frederick I.

ITY Emblem — A519

Perf. 13½x14
1967, Oct. 23   Photo.   Unwmk.
972 A519 20 l blk, cit & brt bl   .25 .25
973 A519 50 l blk, org & brt bl   .25 .25

Issued for International Tourist Year, 1967.

Lions Emblem — A520

1967, Oct. 30   Perf. 14x13½
974 A520 50 l multi   .25 .25

50th anniversary of Lions International.

Soldier at the Piave — A521

1967, Nov. 9   Perf. 13x14
975 A521 50 l multi   .25 .25

50th anniversary of Battle of the Piave.

Enrico Fermi at Los Alamos and Model of 1st Atomic Reactor — A522

Wmk. 303
1967, Dec. 2   Photo.   Perf. 14
976 A522 50 l org brn & blk   .25 .25

25th anniv. of the 1st atomic chain reaction under Enrico Fermi (1901-54), Chicago, IL.

"Day and Night" and Pigeon Carrying Italy No. 924 — A523

1967, Dec. 3   Unwmk.   Perf. 13½x14
977 A523 25 l multi   .25 .25

Issued for Stamp Day, 1967.

Scouts at Campfire — A524

1968, Apr. 23   Perf. 13x14
978 A524 50 l multi   .25 .25

Issued to honor the Boy Scouts.

Europa Issue, 1968
Common Design Type
Perf. 14x13
1968, Apr. 29   Wmk. 303
Size: 36½x26mm
979 CD11 50 l blk, rose & sl grn   .25 .25
980 CD11 90 l blk, bl & brn   .25 .25

ITALY

St. Aloysius Gonzaga, by Pierre Legros — A525

Perf. 13½x14
1968, May 28   Photo.   Wmk. 303
981 A525 25 l red brn & vio   .25   .25

Aloysius Gonzaga (1568-1591), Jesuit priest who ministered to victims of the plague.

Arrigo Boito and Mephistopheles A526

1968, June 10   Unwmk.   Perf. 14
982 A526 50 l multi   .25   .25

Boito (1842-1918), composer and librettist.

A527

Francesco Baracca and "Planes," by Giacomo Balla.

1968, June 19
983 A527 25 l multi   .25   .25

Major Francesco Baracca (1888-1918), World War I aviator.

Giambattista Vico — A528

Designs: No. 985, Tommaso Campanella. No. 986, Gioacchino Rossini.

Perf. 14x13½
1968   Engr.   Wmk. 303
984 A528 50 l ultra   .25   .25
985 A528 50 l black   .25   .25
  a.   Perf. 13½   .80   .25
986 A528 50 l car rose   .25   .25
  Nos. 984-986 (3)   .75   .75

Vico (1668-1744), philosopher; Campanella (1568-1639), Dominican monk, philosopher poet and teacher; Rossini (1792-1868), composer.
Issued: No. 984, 6/24; No. 985, 9/5; No. 986, 10/25.

Bicycle Wheel and Velodrome, Rome — A529

90 l, Bicycle and Sforza Castle, Imola.

Perf. 13x14
1968, Aug. 26   Photo.   Unwmk.
987 A529 25 l slate, rose & brown   .25   .25
988 A529 90 l slate, blue & ver   .25   .25

Bicycling World Championships: 25 l for the track championships at the Velodrome in Rome; 90 l, the road championships at Imola.

"The Small St. Mark's Place," by Canaletto A531

1968, Sept. 30   Unwmk.   Perf. 14
989 A531 50 l pink & multi   .25   .25

Canaletto (Antonio Canale, 1697-1768), Venetian painter.

"Mobilization" A533

Symbolic Designs: 25 l, Trench war. 40 l, The Navy. 50 l, The Air Force. 90 l, The Battle of Vittorio Veneto. 180 l, The Unknown Soldier.

1968, Nov. 2   Photo.   Unwmk.
990 A533 20 l brn & multi   .25   .25
991 A533 25 l bl & multi   .25   .25
992 A533 40 l multi   .25   .25
993 A533 50 l multi   .25   .25
994 A533 90 l grn & multi   .25   .25
995 A533 180 l bl & multi   .25   .25
  Nos. 990-995 (6)   1.50 1.50

50th anniv. of the Allies' Victory in WW I.

Emblem — A534

1968, Nov. 20   Perf. 14x13½
996 A534 50 l blk, bl grn & red   .25   .25

50th anniv. of the Postal Checking Service.

Parabolic Antenna, Fucino — A535

1968, Nov. 25   Photo.   Perf. 14
997 A535 50 l multi   .25   .25

Issued to publicize the expansion of the space communications center at Fucino.

Development of Postal Service — A536

1968, Dec. 1   Wmk. 303
998 A536 25 l car & yel   .25   .25

Issued for the 10th Stamp Day.

Fluorescent Paper

was introduced in 1968 for regular and special delivery issues. These stamps are about 1mm. smaller each way than the non-fluorescent ones they replaced, except Nos. 690-690A which remained the same size.
Commemorative or nonregular stamps issued only on fluorescent paper are Nos. 935B, 937A, 965, 967 and from 981 onward unless otherwise noted.

Italia Type of 1953-54
Small Size: 16x19½-20mm
Photo.; Engr. (100, 150, 200-400 l)
1968-76   Wmk. 303   Perf. 14
998A A354 1 l dk gray   .25   .25
998B A354 5 l slate   .25   .25
998C A354 6 l ocher   .25   .25
998D A354 10 l org ver   .25   .25
998E A354 15 l gray vio   .25   .25
998F A354 20 l brown   .25   .25
998G A354 25 l purple   .25   .25
998H A354 30 l bis brn   .25   .25
998I A354 40 l lil rose   .25   .25
998J A354 50 l olive   .25   .25
998K A354 55 l vio ('69)   .25   .25
998L A354 60 l blue   .25   .25
998M A354 70 l Prus grn   .25   .25
998N A354 80 l brn org   .25   .25
998O A354 90 l lt red brn   .25   .25
998P A354 100 l redsh brn   .25   .25
998Q A354 125 l ocher & lil red ('74)   .25   .25
998R A354 130 l gray & dl red   .25   .25
998S A354 150 l vio ('76)   .25   .25
998T A354 180 l gray & vio brn ('71)   .30   .25
998U A354 200 l slate blue .30   .25
998V A354 300 l Prus grn ('72)   .30   .25
998W A354 400 l dull red ('76)   .50   .25
  Nos. 998A-998W (23)   6.15 5.75

Memorial Medal — A537

Unwmk.
1969, Apr. 22   Photo.   Perf. 14
999 A537 50 l pink & blk   .25   .25

Centenary of the State Audit Bureau.

Europa Issue, 1969
Common Design Type
1969, Apr. 28   Perf. 14x13
Size: 35½x25½mm
1000 CD12 50 l mag & multi   .25   .25
1001 CD12 90 l bl & multi   .25   .25

Niccolo Machiavelli — A538

1969, May 3   Perf. 14x13½
1002 A538 50 l blue & multi   .25   .25

Niccolo Machiavelli (1469-1527), statesman and political philosopher.

ILO Emblem — A539

Wmk. 303
1969, June 7   Photo.   Perf. 14
1003 A539 50 l grn & blk   .25   .25
1004 A539 90 l car & blk   .25   .25

50th anniv. of the ILO.

A540

Design: Federation Emblem, Tower of Superga Basilica and Matterhorn.

1969, June 26   Unwmk.   Perf. 14
1005 A540 50 l gold, bl & car   .25   .25

Federation of Italian Philatelic Societies, 50th anniv.

Sondrio-Tirano Stagecoach, 1903 — A541

1969, Dec. 7   Engr.   Wmk. 303
1006 A541 25 l violet blue   .25   .25

Issued for the 11th Stamp Day.

Downhill Skier — A542

90 l, Sassolungo & Sella Group, Dolomite Alps.

Perf. 13x14
1970, Feb. 6   Unwmk.   Photo.
1007 A542 50 l blue & multi   .25   .25
1008 A542 90 l blue & multi   .25   .25

World Alpine Ski Championships, Val Gardena, Bolzano Province, Feb. 6-15.

Galatea, by Raphael — A543

Painting: 50 l, Madonna with the Goldfinch (detail), by Raphael, 1483-1520.

1970, Apr. 6   Photo.   Perf. 14x13
1009 A543 20 l multi   .25   .25
1010 A543 50 l multi   .25   .25

Symbol of Flight, Colors of Italy and Japan — A544

1970, May 2   Unwmk.   Perf. 14
1011 A544 50 l multi   .25   .25
1012 A544 90 l multi   .25   .25

50th anniv. of Arturo Ferrarin's flight from Rome to Tokyo, Feb. 14-May 31, 1920.

Europa Issue, 1970
Common Design Type
1970, May 4   Wmk. 303
Size: 36x20mm
1013 CD13 50 l red & org   .25   .25
1014 CD13 90 l bl grn & org   .25   .25

Gattamelata, Bust by Donatello — A545

1970, May 30   Engr.   Perf. 14x13
1015 A545 50 l slate green   .25   .25

Erasmo de' Narni, called Il Gattamelata (1370-1443), condottiere.

Runner — A546

Unwmk.
1970, Aug. 26   Photo.   Perf. 14
1016 A546 20 l shown   .25   .25
1017 A546 180 l Swimmer   .30   .25

1970 World University Games, Turin, 8/26-9/6.

Dr. Maria Montessori and Children — A547

1970, Aug. 31   Perf. 14x13
1018 A547 50 l multi   .25   .25

Montessori (1870-1952), educator & physician.

ITALY

Map of Italy and Quotation of Count Camillo Cavour — A548

1970, Sept. 19   Unwmk.   Perf. 14
1019   A548   50 l multi   .25   .25
Union of the Roman States with Italy, cent.

Loggia of St. Mark's Campanile, Venice — A549

Perf. 14x13½
1970, Sept. 26   Engr.   Wmk. 303
1020   A549   50 l red brown   .25   .25
Iacopo Tatti "Il Sansovino" (1486-1570), architect.

Garibaldi at Battle of Dijon — A550

1970, Oct. 15   Photo.   Perf. 14
1021   A550   20 l gray & dk bl   .25   .25
1022   A550   50 l brt rose lil & dk bl   .25   .25
Cent. of Garibaldi's participation in the Franco-Prussian War during Battle of Dijon.

Tree and UN Emblem — A551

1970, Oct. 24   Unwmk.   Perf. 13x14
1023   A551   25 l blk, sep & grn   .25   .25
1024   A551   90 l blk, brt bl & yel grn   .25   .25
25th anniversary of the United Nations.

Rotary Emblem — A552

1970, Nov. 12   Wmk. 303   Perf. 14
1025   A552   25 l bluish vio & org   .25   .25
1026   A552   90 l bluish vio & org   .25   .25
Rotary International, 65th anniversary.

Telephone Dial and Trunk Lines — A553

1970, Nov. 24
1027   A553   25 l yel grn & dk red   .25   .25
1028   A553   90 l ultra & dk red   .25   .25
Issued to publicize the completion of the automatic trunk telephone dialing system.

"Man Damaging Nature" — A554

1970, Nov. 28   Wmk. 303   Perf. 14
1029   A554   20 l car lake & grn   .25   .25
1030   A554   25 l dk bl & emer   .25   .25
For European Nature Conservation Year.

Mail Train — A555

1970, Dec. 6   Engr.
1031   A555   25 l black   .25   .25
For the 12th Stamp Day.

Virgin and Child, by Fra Filippo Lippi — A556

1970, Dec. 12   Photo.   Unwmk.
1032   A556   25 l multi   .25   .25
Christmas 1970. See No. C139.

Saverio Mercadante (1795-1870), Composer A557

1970, Dec. 17   Wmk. 303
1033   A557   25 l vio & gray   .25   .25

Mercury, by Benvenuto Cellini — A558

1971, Mar. 20   Photo.   Perf. 14
1034   A558   50 l Prussian blue   .25   .25
Benvenuto Cellini (1500-1571), sculptor.

Bramante's Temple, St. Peter in Montorio — A559

Photogravure and Engraved
1971, Apr. 8   Perf. 13x14
1035   A559   50 l ocher & blk   .25   .25
Honoring Bramante (Donato di Angelo di Antonio, 1444-1514), architect.

Adenauer, Schuman, De Gasperi — A560

Perf. 14x13½
1971, Apr. 28   Photo.   Wmk. 303
1036   A560   50 l blk & lt grnsh bl   .25   .25
1037   A560   90 l blk & lil rose   .25   .25
European Coal & Steel Community, 20th anniv.

Europa Issue, 1971
Common Design Type
1971, May 3   Perf. 14
1038   CD14   50 l ver & dk red   .25   .25
1039   CD14   90 l brt rose lil & dk lil   .40   .25

Giuseppe Mazzini, Italian Flag — A561

Perf. 14x13½
1971, June 12   Unwmk.
1040   A561   50 l multi   .25   .25
1041   A561   90 l multi   .25   .25
25th anniversary of the Italian Republic.

Kayak Passing Between Poles — A562

Design: 90 l, Kayak in free descent.

1971, June 16   Photo.   Perf. 14
1042   A562   50 l multi   .25   .25
1043   A562   90 l multi   .25   .25
Canoe Slalom World Championships, Merano.

Skiing, Basketball, Volleyball — A563

50 l, Gymnastics, cycling, track and swimming.

Perf. 13½x14
1971, June 26   Photo.   Unwmk.
1044   A563   20 l emer, ocher & blk   .25   .25
1045   A563   50 l dl bl, org & blk   .25   .25
Youth Games.

Plane Circling Globe and "A" — A564

Designs: 50 l, Ornamental "A." 150 l, Tail of B747 in shape of "A."

1971, Sept. 16   Perf. 14x13½
1046   A564   50 l multi   .25   .25
1047   A564   90 l multi   .25   .25
1048   A564   150 l multi   .25   .25
Nos. 1046-1048 (3)   .75   .75
ALITALIA, Italian airlines founding, 25th anniv.

Grazia Deledda (1871-1936), Novelist — A565

Photogravure and Engraved
Perf. 13½x14
1971, Sept. 28   Wmk. 303
1049   A565   50 l blk & salmon   .25   .25

Child in Barrel Made of Banknote — A566

Perf. 13x14
1971, Oct. 27   Photo.   Unwmk.
1050   A566   25 l blk & multi   .25   .25
1051   A566   50 l multi   .25   .25
Publicity for postal savings bank.

UNICEF Emblem and Children — A567

90 l, Children hailing UNICEF emblem.

1971, Nov. 26   Perf. 14x13
1052   A567   25 l pink & multi   .25   .25
1053   A567   90 l multi   .25   .25
25th anniv. of UNICEF.

Packet Tirrenia and Postal Ensign — A568

1971, Dec. 5   Wmk. 303   Perf. 14
1054   A568   25 l slate green   .25   .25
Stamp Day.

Nativity — A569

Christmas: 90 l, Adoration of the Kings. Both designs are from miniatures in Evangelistary of Matilda in Nonantola Abbey, 12th-13th centuries.

Perf. 14x13
1971, Dec. 10   Photo.   Unwmk.
1055   A569   25 l gray & multi   .25   .25
1056   A569   90 l gray & multi   .25   .25

Giovanni Verga and Sicilian Cart — A570

1972, Jan. 27
1057   A570   25 l org & multi   .25   .25
1058   A570   50 l multi   .25   .25
Verga (1840-1922), writer & playwright.

Giuseppe Mazzini (1805-1872), Patriot and Writer — A571

Wmk. 303
1972, Mar. 10   Engr.   Perf. 13
1059   A571   25 l blk & Prus grn   .25   .25
1060   A571   90 l black   .25   .25
1061   A571   150 l blk & rose red   .25   .25
Nos. 1059-1061 (3)   .75   .75

Flags, Milan Fair — A572

Designs: 50 l, 90 l, Different abstract views.

Perf. 14x13½
1972, Apr. 14   Photo.   Unwmk.
1062   A572   25 l emer & blk   .25   .25
1063   A572   50 l dp org & blk   .25   .25
1064   A572   90 l bl & blk   .25   .25
Nos. 1062-1064 (3)   .75   .75
50th anniversary of the Milan Sample Fair.

Europa Issue 1972
Common Design Type
1972, May 2   Perf. 13x14
Size: 26x36mm
1065   CD15   50 l multi   .25   .25
1066   CD15   90 l multi   .30   .25

ITALY

Alpine Soldier and Pack Mule — A573

50 l, Mountains, Alpinist's hat, pick & laurel.
90 l, Alpine soldier & mountains.

1972, May 10   *Perf. 14x13*
1067 A573 25 l ol & multi .25 .25
1068 A573 50 l bl & multi .25 .25
1069 A573 90 l grn & multi .25 .25
    Nos. 1067-1069 (3) .75 .75

Centenary of the Alpine Corps.

Brenta Mountains, Society Emblem — A574

Emblem and: 50 l, Mountain climber & Brenta Mountains. 180 l, Sunset over Mt. Crozzon.

Perf. 14x13
1972, Sept. 2   Photo.   Unwmk.
1070 A574 25 l multi .25 .25
1071 A574 50 l multi .25 .25
1072 A574 180 l multi .30 .25
    Nos. 1070-1072 (3) .80 .75

Tridentine Alpinist Society centenary.

Conference Emblem, Seating Diagram — A575

1972, Sept. 21
1073 A575 50 l multi .25 .25
1074 A575 90 l multi .25 .25

60th Conference of the Inter-Parliamentary Union, Montecitorio Hall, Rome.

St. Peter Damian, by Giovanni di Paoli, c. 1445 — A576

1972, Sept. 21   Photo.
1075 A576 50 l multi .25 .25

St. Peter Damian (1007-72), church reformer, cardinal, papal legate.

The Three Graces, by Antonio Canova (1757-1822), Sculptor — A577

1972, Oct. 13   Engr.   Wmk. 303
1076 A577 50 l black .25 .25

Page from Divine Comedy, Foligno Edition — A578

Designs (Illuminated First Pages): 90 l, Mantua edition, vert. 180 l, Jesina edition.

Perf. 14x13½, 13½x14
1972, Nov. 23   Photo.   Unwmk.
1077 A578 50 l ocher & multi .25 .25
1078 A578 90 l multi .25 .25
1079 A578 180 l multi .25 .25
    Nos. 1077-1079 (3) .75 .75

500th anniversary of three illuminated editions of Dante's Divine Comedy.

Angel — A579

Christmas: 25 l, Christ Child in cradle, horiz. 150 l, Angel. All designs from 18th century Neapolitan crèche.

Perf. 13x14, 14x13
1972, Dec. 6   Photo.
1080 A579 20 l multi .25 .25
1081 A579 25 l multi .25 .25
1082 A579 150 l multi .25 .25
    Nos. 1080-1082 (3) .75 .75

Passenger and Mail Autobus — A580

1972, Dec. 16   Engr.   Wmk. 303
1083 A580 25 l magenta .25 .25

Stamp Day.

Leòn Battista Alberti — A581

1972, Dec. 16   *Perf. 14*
1084 A581 50 l ultra & ocher .25 .25

Leòn Battista Alberti (1404-1472), architect, painter, organist and writer.

Lorenzo Perosi — A582

1972, Dec. 20   Photo.   Unwmk.
1085 A582 50 l dk vio brn & org .25 .25
1086 A582 90 l blk & yel grn .25 .25

Lorenzo Perosi (1872-1956), priest & composer.

Luigi Orione and Boys — A583

1972, Dec. 30
1087 A583 50 l lt bl & dk bl .25 .25
1088 A583 90 l ocher & slate grn .25 .25

Orione (1872-1940), founder of CARITAS; Catholic Welfare Organization.

Ship Exploring Ocean Floor — A584

1973, Feb. 15   Photo.   *Perf. 13x14*
1089 A584 50 l multi .25 .25

Cent. of the Naval Hydrographic Institute.

Palace Staircase, Caserta — A585

1973, Mar. 1   Engr.   *Perf. 14x13½*
1090 A585 25 l gray olive .25 .25

Luigi Vanvitelli (1700-1773), architect.

Schiavoni Shore A586

The Tetrarchs, 4th Century Sculpture A587

50 l, "Triumph of Venice," by Vittore Carpaccio. 90 l, Bronze horses from St. Mark's. 300 l, St. Mark's Square covered by flood.

1973   Photo.   *Perf. 14*
1091 A586 20 l ultra & multi .25 .25
1092 A587 25 l ultra & multi .25 .25
1093 A586 50 l ultra & multi .25 .25
1094 A587 90 l ultra & multi .25 .25
1095 A587 300 l ultra & multi .70 .45
    Nos. 1091-1095 (5) 1.70 1.45

Save Venice campaign. Issued: No. 1091, 3/5; others 4/10.

Verona Fair Emblem — A588

1973, Mar. 10   *Perf. 13x14*
1096 A588 50 l multi .25 .25

75th International Fair, Verona.

Title Page for Book about Rosa — A589

1973, Mar. 15   *Perf. 14*
1097 A589 25 l org & blk .25 .25

Salvator Rosa (1615-1673), painter & poet.

G-91 Jet Fighters — A590

Designs: 25 l, Formation of S-55 seaplanes. 50 l, G-91Y fighters. 90 l, Fiat CR-32's flying figure 8. 180 l, Camprini-Caproni jet, 1940.

1973, Mar. 28   *Perf. 14x13½*
1098 A590 20 l multi .25 .25
1099 A590 25 l multi .25 .25
1100 A590 50 l multi .25 .25
1101 A590 90 l multi .25 .25
1102 A590 180 l multi .25 .25
    Nos. 1098-1102, C140 (6) 1.55 1.50

50th anniversary of military aviation.

Soccer Field and Ball — A591

Design: 90 l, Soccer players and goal.

1973, May 19   Photo.   *Perf. 14x13½*
1103 A591 25 l ol, blk & lt grn .25 .25
1104 A591 90 l grn & multi .40 .40

75th anniv. of Italian Soccer Federation.

Alessandro Manzoni, by Francisco Hayez — A592

1973, May 22   Engr.
1105 A592 25 l blk & brn .25 .25

Manzoni (1785-1873), novelist and poet.

Villa Rotunda, by Andrea Palladio (1508-80), Architect. — A593

1973, May 30   Photo.   Unwmk.
Perf. 13x14
1106 A593 90 l blk, yel & lem .25 .25

Spiral and Cogwheels A594

1973, June 20   *Perf. 14x13*
1107 A594 50 l gold & multi .25 .25

50th anniversary of the State Supply Office.

Europa Issue 1973
Common Design Type

1973, June 30   Litho.   *Perf. 14*
Size: 36x20mm
1108 CD16 50 l lil, gold & yel .25 .25
1109 CD16 90 l lt bl grn, gold & yel .25 .25
    Nos. 1108-1109 (2) .50 .50

Catcher and Diamond — A595

Design: 90 l, Diamond and batter.

1973, July 21   Photo.   *Perf. 14x13½*
1110 A595 25 l multi .25 .25
1111 A595 90 l multi .25 .25

International Baseball Cup.

Viareggio by Night — A596

1973, Aug. 10   Photo.   *Perf. 13x14*
1112 A596 25 l blk & multi .25 .25

Viareggio Carnival.

Assassination of Giovanni Minzoni — A597

1973, Aug. 23   *Perf. 14x13*
1113 A597 50 l multi .25 .25

Minzoni (1885-1923), priest & social worker.

ITALY

Gaetano Salvemini (1873-1957), Historian, Anti-Fascist — A598

1973, Sept. 8   **Perf. 14x13½**
1114   A598   50 l   pink & multi   .25   .25

Palazzo Farnese, Caprarola, by Vignola — A599

1973, Sept. 21   **Engr.**   **Perf. 14x13½**
1115   A599   90 l   choc & yel   .25   .25

Giacomo da Vignola (real name, Giacomo Barocchio), 1507-1573, architect.

St. John the Baptist, by Caravaggio A600

Lithographed & Engraved
1973, Sept. 28   **Perf. 14**
1116   A600   25 l   blk & dl yel   .25   .25

400th anniversary of the birth of Michelangelo da Caravaggio (1573-1610?), painter.

Tower of Pisa — A601

1973, Oct. 8   **Photo.**
1117   A601   50 l   multi   .25   .25

8th century of Leaning Tower of Pisa.

Famous Men — A602

Designs: No. 1118, Sandro Botticelli. No. 1119, Giambattista Piranesi. No. 1120, Paolo Veronese. No. 1121, Andrea del Verrocchio. No. 1122, Giovanni Battista Tiepolo. No. 1123, Francesco Borromini. No. 1124, Rosalba Carriera. No. 1125, Giovanni Bellini (Giambellino). No. 1126, Andrea Mantegna. No. 1127, Raphael (Raffaello).

1973-74   **Photo.**   **Perf. 14x13½**
1118   A602   50 l   multi   .25   .25
1119   A602   50 l   multi   .25   .25
1120   A602   50 l   multi   .25   .25
1121   A602   50 l   multi   .25   .25
1122   A602   50 l   multi   .25   .25
1123   A602   50 l   multi   .25   .25
1124   A602   50 l   multi   .25   .25
1125   A602   50 l   multi   .25   .25
1126   A602   50 l   multi   .25   .25
1127   A602   50 l   multi   .25   .25
   Nos. 1118-1127 (10)   2.50   2.50

Famous artists.

Issued: Nos. 1118-1122, 11/5; Nos. 1123-1127, 5/25/74.

See Nos. 1204-1209, 1243-1247, 1266-1270.

Trevi Fountain, Rome — A603

Designs: No. 1129, Immacolatella Fountain, Naples. No. 1130, Pretoria Fountain, Palermo.

Photogravure and Engraved
1973, Nov. 10   **Perf. 13½x14**
1128   A603   25 l   blk & multi   .25   .25
1129   A603   25 l   blk & multi   .25   .25
1130   A603   25 l   blk & multi   .25   .25
   Nos. 1128-1130 (3)   .75   .75

See Nos. 1166-1168, 1201-1203, 1251-1253, 1277-1279, 1341-1343, 1379-1381.

Angels, by Agostino di Duccio — A604

Sculptures by Agostino di Duccio: 25 l, Virgin and Child. 150 l, Angels with flute and trumpet.

1973, Nov. 26
1131   A604   20 l   yel grn & blk   .25   .25
1132   A604   25 l   lt bl & blk   .25   .25
1133   A604   150 l   yel & blk   .25   .25
   Nos. 1131-1133 (3)   .75   .75

Christmas 1973.

Map of Italy, Rotary Emblems — A605

1973, Nov. 28   **Photo.**
1134   A605   50 l   red, grn & dk bl   .25   .25

50th anniv. of Rotary International of Italy.

Caravelle — A606

Wmk. 303
1973, Dec. 2   **Engr.**   **Perf. 14**
1135   A606   25 l   Prussian blue   .25   .25

15th Stamp Day.

Gold Medal of Valor, 50th Anniv. — A607

   Perf. 13½x14
1973, Dec. 10   **Photo.**   **Unwmk.**
1136   A607   50 l   gold & multi   .25   .25

Enrico Caruso (1873-1921), Operatic Tenor — A608

Design: 50 l, Caruso as Duke in Rigoletto.

1973, Dec. 15   **Engr.**
1137   A608   50 l   magenta   .25   .25

Christ Crowning King Roger — A609

Norman art in Sicily: 50 l, King William II offering model of church to the Virgin, mosaic from Monreale Cathedral. The design of 20 l, is from a mosaic in Martorana Church, Palermo.

Lithographed and Engraved
1974, Mar. 4   **Perf. 13½x14**
1138   A609   20 l   ind & buff   .25   .25
1139   A609   50 l   red & lt grn   .25   .25

Luigi Einaudi (1874-1961), Pres. of Italy — A610

1974, Mar. 23   **Engr.**   **Perf. 14x13½**
1140   A610   50 l   green   .25   .25

Guglielmo Marconi (1874-1937), Italian Inventor and Physicist — A611

Design: 90 l, Marconi and world map.

1974, Apr. 24   **Photo.**   **Perf. 14x13½**
1141   A611   50 l   bl grn & gray   .25   .25
1142   A611   90 l   vio & multi   .25   .25

David, by Giovanni L. Bernini — A612

Europa: 90 l, David, by Michelangelo.

1974, Apr. 29   **Photo.**   **Perf. 13½x14**
1143   A612   50 l   sal, ultra & gray   .25   .25
1144   A612   90 l   grn, ultra & buff   .25   .25

Customs Frontier Guards, 1774, 1795, 1817 — A613

Uniforms of Customs Service: 50 l, Lombardy Venetia, 1848, Sardinia, 1815, Tebro Battalion, 1849. 90 l, Customs Guards, 1866, 1880 and Naval Marshal, 1892. 180 l, Helicopter pilot, Naval and Alpine Guards, 1974. All bordered with Italian flag colors.

1974, June 21   **Photo.**   **Perf. 14**
1145   A613   40 l   multi   .25   .25
1146   A613   50 l   multi   .25   .25
1147   A613   90 l   multi   .25   .25
1148   A613   180 l   multi   .40   .25
   Nos. 1145-1148 (4)   1.15   1.00

Customs Frontier Guards bicentenary.

Sprinter — A614

1974, June 28   **Photo.**   **Perf. 14x13**
1149   A614   40 l   shown   .25   .25
1150   A614   50 l   Pole vault   .25   .25

European Athletic Championships, Rome.

Sharpshooter A615

Design: 50 l, Bersaglieri emblem.

1974, June 27
1151   A615   40 l   multi   .25   .25
1152   A615   50 l   grn & multi   .25   .25

Bersaglieri Veterans Association, 50th anniv.

View of Portofino A616

1974, July 10   **Perf. 14**
1153   A616   40 l   shown   .25   .25
1154   A616   40 l   View of Gradara   .25   .25

Tourist publicity.

See Nos. 1190-1192, 1221-1223, 1261-1265, 1314-1316, 1357-1360, 1402-1405, 1466-1469, 1520-1523, 1563A-1563D, 1599-1602, 1630-1633, 1708-1711, 1737-1740, 1776-1779, 1803-1806, 1830-1833, 1901-1904.

Petrarch (1304-74), Poet — A617

50 l, Petrarch at his desk (from medieval manuscript).

Lithographed and Engraved
1974, July 19   **Perf. 13½x14**
1155   A617   40 l   ocher & multi   .25   .25
1156   A617   50 l   ocher, yel & bl   .25   .25

Niccolo Tommaseo (1802-1874), Writer, Venetian Education Minister — A618

Tommaseo Statue, by Ettore Ximenes, Shibenik.

1974, July 19
1157   A618   50 l   grn & pink   .25   .25

Giacomo Puccini (1858-1924), Composer — A619

1974, Aug. 16   **Photo.**
1158   A619   40 l   multi   .25   .25

Lodovico Ariosto (1474-1533), Poet — A620

50 l, King Roland, woodcut.

1974, Sept. 9   **Engr.**   **Perf. 14x13½**
1159   A620   50 l   blue & red   .25   .25

The design is from a contemporary illustration of Ariosto's poem "Orlando Furioso."

Quotation from Menippean Satire by Varro — A621

1974, Sept. 21
1160   A621   50 l   ocher & dk red   .25   .25

Marcus Terentius Varro (116-27 BC), Roman scholar and writer.

ITALY

"October," 15th Century Mural — A622

1974, Sept. 28　Photo.　Perf. 14
1161　A622　50 l　multi　.25　.25

14th International Wine Congress, Trento.

"UPU" and Emblem — A623

Design: 90 l, Letters, "UPU" and emblem.

1974, Oct. 19　Photo.　Perf. 14
1162　A623　50 l　multi　.25　.25
1163　A623　90 l　multi　.25　.25

Centenary of Universal Postal Union.

St. Thomas Aquinas, by Francesco Traini — A624

1974, Oct. 25　　　　Perf. 13x14
1164　A624　50 l　multi　.25　.25

St. Thomas Aquinas (1225-1274), scholastic philosopher, 700th death anniversary.

Bas-relief from Ara Pacis — A625

1974, Oct. 26
1165　A625　50 l　multi　.25　.25

Centenary of the Ordini Forensi (Bar Association).

Fountain Type of 1973

Designs: No. 1166, Oceanus Fountain, Florence. No. 1167, Neptune Fountain, Bologna. No. 1168, Fontana Maggiore, Perugia.

Photogravure and Engraved
1974, Nov. 9　　　　Perf. 13x14
1166　A603　40 l　blk & multi　.25　.25
1167　A603　40 l　blk & multi　.25　.25
1168　A603　40 l　blk & multi　.25　.25
　　Nos. 1166-1168 (3)　.75　.75

St. Francis Adoring Christ Child, Anonymous A626

Photogravure and Engraved
1974, Nov. 26　　　Perf. 14x13½
1169　A626　40 l　multi　.25　.25

Christmas 1974.

Masked Dancers — A627

1974, Dec. 1　Photo.　Perf. 13½x14
1170　A627　40 l　Pulcinella　.25　.25
1171　A627　50 l　shown　.25　.25
1172　A627　90 l　Pantaloon　.25　.25
　　Nos. 1170-1172 (3)　.75　.75

16th Stamp Day 1974.

God Admonishing Adam, by Jacopo della Quercia — A628

Courtyard, Uffizi Gallery, Florence, by Giorgio Vasari — A629

1974, Dec. 20　Engr.　Perf. 14
1173　A628　90 l　dk vio bl　.25　.25
Lithographed and Engraved
1174　A629　90 l　multi　.25　.25

Italian artists: Jacopo della Quercia (1374-c. 1438), sculptor, and Giorgio Vasari (1511-1574), architect, painter and writer.

Angel with Tablet A630

Angel with Cross A632

Angels' Bridge, Rome — A631

Holy Year 1975: 50 l, Angel holding column. 150 l, Angel holding Crown of Thorns. The angels are statues by Giovanni Bernini on the Angels' Bridge (San Angelo).

1975, Mar. 25　Photo.　Perf. 14
1175　A630　40 l　multi　.25　.25
1176　A630　50 l　bl & multi　.25　.25
1177　A630　90 l　bl & multi　.25　.25
1178　A630　150 l　vio & multi　.25　.25
1179　A632　180 l　multi　.25　.25
　　Nos. 1175-1179 (5)　1.25　1.25

Pitti Madonna, by Michelangelo — A633

Works of Michelangelo: 50 l, Niche in Vatican Palace. 90 l, The Flood, detail from Sistine Chapel.

1975, Apr. 18　Engr.　Perf. 13½x14
1180　A633　40 l　dl grn　.25　.25
1181　A633　50 l　sepia　.25　.25
1182　A633　90 l　red brn　.25　.25
　　Nos. 1180-1182 (3)　.75　.75

Michelangelo Buonarroti (1475-1564), sculptor, painter and architect.

Flagellation of Jesus, by Caravaggio — A634

Europa: 150 l, Apparition of Angel to Hagar and Ishmael, by Tiepolo (detail).

1975, Apr. 29　Photo.　Perf. 13x14
1183　A634　100 l　multi　.25　.25
1184　A634　150 l　multi　.30　.25

Four Days of Naples, by Marino Mazzacurati A635

Resistance Fighters of Cuneo, by Umberto Mastroianni A636

Design: 100 l, Martyrs of Ardeatine Caves, by Francesco Coccia.

1975, Apr. 23
1185　A635　70 l　multi　.25　.25
1186　A636　100 l　ol & multi　.25　.25
1187　A636　150 l　multi　.25　.25
　　Nos. 1185-1187 (3)　.75　.75

Resistance movement victory, 30th anniv.

Globe and IWY Emblem — A637

1975, May　　　Perf. 14x13½
1188　A637　70 l　multi　.25　.25

International Women's Year 1975.

Satellite, San Rita Launching Platform — A638

1975, May 28　　　Perf. 13½x14
1189　A638　70 l　multi　.25　.25

San Marco satellite project.

Tourist Type of 1974

Paintings: No. 1190, View of Isola Bella. No. 1191, Baths of Montecatini. No. 1192, View of Cefalù.

1975, June 16　Photo.　Perf. 14
1190　A616　150 l　grn & multi　.25　.25
1191　A616　150 l　bl grn & multi　.25　.25
1192　A616　150 l　red brn & multi　.25　.25
　　Nos. 1190-1192 (3)　.75　.75

Artist and Model, Armando Spadini — A640

Painting: No. 1194, Flora, by Guido Reni.

1975, June 20　Engr.　Perf. 14
1193　A640　90 l　blk & multi　.25　.25
1194　A640　90 l　multi　.25　.25

50th death anniv. of Armando Spadini and 400th birth anniv. of Guido Reni.

Giovanni Pierluigi da Palestrina (1525-94), Composer of Sacred Music — A641

1975, June 27　Engr.　Perf. 13½x14
1195　A641　100 l　magenta & tan　.25　.25

Emmigrants and Ship — A642

1975, June 30　Photo.　Perf. 14x13½
1196　A642　70 l　multi　.25　.25

Italian emigration centenary.

Emblem of United Legal Groups — A643

1975, July 25　Photo.　Perf. 14x13½
1197　A643　100 l　yel, grn & red　.25　.25

Unification of Italian legal organizations, cent.

Locomotive Wheels — A644

1975, Sept. 15　Photo.　Perf. 14x13½
1198　A644　70 l　multi　.25　.25

Intl. Railroad Union, 21st cong., Bologna.

Salvo D'Acquisto, by Vittorio Pisano — A645

1975, Sept. 23
1199　A645　100 l　multi　.25　.25

D'Acquisto died in 1943 saving 22 people.

Stylized Syracusean Italia — A646

1975, Sept. 26　Photo.　Perf. 13½x14
1200　A646　100 l　org & multi　.25　.25

Cent. of unification of the State Archives.

Fountain Type of 1973

Designs: No. 1201, Rosello Fountain, Sassari. No. 1202, Fountain of the 99 Faucets, Aquila. No. 1203, Piazza Fontana, Milan.

Photogravure and Engraved
1975, Oct. 30　　　Perf. 13x14
1201　A603　70 l　blk & multi　.25　.25
1202　A603　70 l　blk & multi　.25　.25
1203　A603　70 l　blk & multi　.25　.25
　　Nos. 1201-1203 (3)　.75　.75

Famous Men Type of 1973-74

Designs: No. 1204, Alessandro Scarlatti. No. 1205, Antonio Vivaldi. No. 1206, Gaspare Spontini. No. 1207, Ferruccio Busoni. No. 1208, Francesco Cilea. No. 1209, Franco Alfano.

1975, Nov. 14　Photo.　Perf. 14x13½
1204　A602　100 l　multi　.25　.25
1205　A602　100 l　multi　.25　.25
1206　A602　100 l　multi　.25　.25
1207　A602　100 l　multi　.25　.25

ITALY

1208	A602	100 l multi	.25	.25
1209	A602	100 l multi	.25	.25
		Nos. 1204-1209 (6)	1.50	1.50

Famous musicians.

Annunciation to the Shepherds — A648

Christmas: 100 l, Nativity. 150 l, Annunciation to the Kings. Designs from painted wood panels, portal of Alatri Cathedral, 14th century.

Lithographed and Engraved
1975, Nov. 25 Perf. 13½x14
1210	A648	70 l grn & multi	.25	.25
1211	A648	100 l ultra & multi	.25	.25
1212	A648	150 l brn & multi	.25	.25
		Nos. 1210-1212 (3)	.75	.75

"The Magic Orchard" — A649

Children's Drawings: 70 l, Children on Horseback, horiz. 150 l, Village and procession, horiz.

Perf. 14x13½, 13½x14
1975, Dec. 7 Photo.
1213	A649	70 l multi	.25	.25
1214	A649	100 l multi	.25	.25
1215	A649	150 l multi	.25	.25
		Nos. 1213-1215 (3)	.75	.75

17th Stamp Day.

Boccaccio, by Andrea del Castagno — A650

Design: 150 l, Frontispiece for "Fiammetta," 15th century woodcut.

Engraved and Lithographed
1975, Dec. 22 Perf. 13½x14
| 1216 | A650 | 100 l yel grn & blk | .25 | .25 |
| 1217 | A650 | 150 l buff & multi | .25 | .25 |

Giovanni Boccaccio (1313-1375), writer.

State Advocate's Office, Rome — A651

1976, Jan. 30 Photo. Perf. 13½x14
| 1218 | A651 | 150 l multi | .25 | .25 |

State Advocate's Office, centenary.

ITALIA 76 Emblem — A652

Design: 180 l, Milan Fair pavilion.

1976, Mar. 27 Photo. Perf. 13½x14
| 1219 | A652 | 150 l blk, red & grn | .25 | .25 |
| 1220 | A652 | 180 l blk, red, grn & bl | | |

ITALIA 76 International Philatelic Exhibition, Milan, Oct. 14-24.

Tourist Type of 1974

Tourist publicity: No. 1221, Fenis Castle. No. 1222, View of Ischia. No. 1223, Itria Valley.

1976, May 21 Photo. Perf. 14
1221	A616	150 l grn & multi	.25	.25
1222	A616	100 l plum & multi	.25	.25
1223	A616	150 l yel & multi	.25	.25
		Nos. 1221-1223 (3)	.75	.75

Majolica Plate, Deruta — A653

Europa: 180 l, Ceramic vase in shape of woman's head, Caltagirone.

1976, May 22 Perf. 13½x14
| 1224 | A653 | 150 l multi | .25 | .25 |
| 1225 | A653 | 180 l brn & multi | .30 | .25 |

Italian Flags A654

Italian Presidents A655

1976, June 1
| 1226 | A654 | 100 l multi | .25 | .25 |
| 1227 | A655 | 150 l multi | .25 | .25 |

30th anniversary of Italian Republic.

Fortitude, by Giacomo Serpotta, 1656-1732 A656

Paintings: No. 1229, Woman at Table, by Umberto Boccioni, 1882-1916. No. 1230, The Gunner's Letter, by F. T. Marinetti, 1876-1944.

1976, July 26 Engr. Perf. 14
| 1228 | A656 | 150 l blue | .25 | .25 |

Lithographed and Engraved
1229	A656	150 l multi	.25	.25
1230	A656	150 l blk & red	.25	.25
		Nos. 1228-1230 (3)	.75	.75

Italian art.

Paintings by Vittore Carpaccio (1460-1526), Venetian Painter — A657

Designs: No. 1231, St. George. No. 1232, Dragon, after painting in Church of St. George Schiavoni, Venice.

1976, July 30 Engr. Perf. 14x13½
1231	A657	150 l rose lake	.25	.25
1232	A657	150 l rose lake	.25	.25
	a.	Pair, #1231-1232 + label	.50	.25

Flora, by Titian — A658

1976, Sept. 15 Engr. Perf. 14
| 1233 | A658 | 150 l carmine | .25 | .25 |

Titian (1477-1576), Venetian painter.

St. Francis, 13th Century Fresco — A659

1976, Oct. 2 Engr. Perf. 14
| 1234 | A659 | 150 l brown | .25 | .25 |

St. Francis of Assisi, 750th death anniv.

Cart, from Trajan's Column — A660

100 l, Emblem of Kingdom of Sardinia. 150 l, Marble mask, 19th cent. mail box. 200 l, Hand canceler, 19th cent. 400 l, Automatic letter sorting machine.

1976, Oct. 14 Photo. Perf. 14x13½
1235	A660	70 l multi	.25	.25
1236	A660	100 l multi	.25	.25
1237	A660	150 l multi	.25	.25
1238	A660	200 l multi	.25	.25
1239	A660	400 l multi	.45	.25
		Nos. 1235-1239 (5)	1.45	1.25

ITALIA 76 International Philatelic Exhibition, Milan, Oct. 14-24.

Girl and Animals — A661

Designs (Children' Drawings): 100 l, Trees, rabbit and flowers. 150 l, Boy healing tree.

1976, Oct. 17 Perf. 13½x14
1240	A661	40 l multi	.25	.25
1241	A661	100 l multi	.25	.25
1242	A661	150 l multi	.25	.25
		Nos. 1240-1242 (3)	.75	.75

18th Stamp Day and nature protection.

Famous Men Type of 1973-74

Designs: No. 1243, Lorenzo Ghiberti. No. 1244, Domenico Ghirlandaio. No. 1245, Sassoferrato. No. 1246, Carlo Dolci. No. 1247, Giovanni Piazzetta.

1976, Nov. 22 Photo. Perf. 14x13½
1243	A602	170 l multi	.25	.25
1244	A602	170 l multi	.25	.25
1245	A602	170 l multi	.25	.25
1246	A602	170 l multi	.25	.25
1247	A602	170 l multi	.25	.25
		Nos. 1243-1247 (5)	1.25	1.25

Famous painters.

The Visit, by Silvestro Lega — A662

1976, Dec. 7 Photo. Perf. 14x13½
| 1248 | A662 | 170 l multi | .25 | .25 |

Silvestro Lega (1826-1895), painter.

Adoration of the Kings, by Bartolo di Fredi — A663

Christmas: 120 l, Nativity, by Taddeo Gaddi.

1976, Dec. 11 Perf. 13½x14
| 1249 | A663 | 70 l multi | .25 | .25 |
| 1250 | A663 | 120 l multi | .25 | .25 |

Fountain Type of 1973

Designs: No. 1251, Antique Fountain, Gallipoli. No. 1252, Madonna Fountain, Verona. No. 1253, Silvio Cosini Fountain, Palazzo Doria, Genoa.

Lithographed and Engraved
1976, Dec. 21 Perf. 13½x14
1251	A603	170 l blk & multi	.25	.25
1252	A603	170 l blk & multi	.25	.25
1253	A603	170 l blk & multi	.25	.25
		Nos. 1251-1253 (3)	.75	.75

Snakes Forming Net — A664

Design: 170 l, Drug addict and poppy.

1977, Feb. 28 Photo. Perf. 14x13½
| 1254 | A664 | 120 l multi | .25 | .25 |
| 1255 | A664 | 170 l multi | .25 | .25 |

Fight against drug abuse.

Micca Setting Fire — A665

1977, Mar. 5
| 1256 | A665 | 170 l multi | .25 | .25 |

Pietro Micca (1677-1706), patriot who set fire to the powder magazine of Turin Citadel.

Globe with Cross in Center — A666

Design: 120 l, People of the World united as brothers by St. John Bosco.

1977, Mar. 29 Photo. Perf. 13x13½
| 1257 | A666 | 70 l multi | .25 | .25 |
| 1258 | A666 | 120 l multi | .25 | .25 |

Honoring the Salesian missionaries.

Italian Constitution, Article 53 — A667

1977, Apr. 14 Photo. Perf. 14
| 1259 | A667 | 120 l bis, brn & blk | .25 | .25 |
| 1260 | A667 | 170 l lt grn, grn & blk | .25 | .25 |

"Pay your taxes."

Tourist Type of 1974

Europa (Europa Emblem and): 170 l, Taormina. 200 l, Castle del Monte.

1977, May 2
| 1261 | A616 | 170 l multi | .65 | .25 |
| 1262 | A616 | 200 l multi | .85 | .25 |

Tourist Type of 1974

Paintings: No. 1263, Canossa Castle. No. 1264, Fermo. No. 1265, Castellana Caves.

1977, May 30 Photo. Perf. 14
1263	A616	170 l brn & multi	.25	.25
1264	A616	170 l vio & multi	.25	.25
1265	A616	170 l gray & multi	.25	.25
		Nos. 1263-1265 (3)	.75	.75

Famous Men Type of 1973-74

Designs: No. 1266, Filippo Brunelleschi. No. 1267, Pietro Aretino. No. 1268, Carlo Goldoni. No. 1269, Luigi Cherubini. No. 1270, Eduardo Bassini.

1977, June 27 Perf. 14x13½
1266	A602	70 l multi	.25	.25
1267	A602	70 l multi	.25	.25
1268	A602	70 l multi	.25	.25

ITALY

| 1269 | A602 | 70 l | multi | .25 | .25 |
| 1270 | A602 | 70 l | multi | .25 | .25 |

Nos. 1266-1270 (5)   1.25   1.25

Famous artists, writers and scientists.

Justice, by Andrea Delitio — A669

Painting: No. 1272, Winter, by Giuseppe Arcimboldi, 1527-c.1593.

Engraved and Lithographed
1977, Sept. 5   *Perf. 14*

| 1271 | A669 | 170 l | multi | .25 | .25 |
| 1272 | A669 | 170 l | multi | .25 | .25 |

Italian Ships — A670

No. 1273, Corvette Caracciolo. No. 1274, Hydrofoil gunboat Sparviero. No. 1275, Paddle steamer Ferdinando Primo. No. 1276, Passenger liner Saturnia.

Photogravure and Engraved
1977, Sept. 23   *Perf. 14x13½*

1273	170 l	multi	.25	.25
1274	170 l	multi	.25	.25
1275	170 l	multi	.25	.25
1276	170 l	multi	.25	.25

a. A670 Block or strip of 4, #1273-1276 + 2 labels   1.00   .50

See Nos. 1323-1326, 1382-1385, 1435-1438.

Fountain Type of 1973

Designs: No. 1277, Pacassi Fountain, Gorizia. No. 1278, Fraterna Fountain, Isernia. No. 1279, Palm Fountain, Palmi.

Lithographed and Engraved
1977, Oct. 18   *Perf. 13x14*

1277	A603	120 l	blk & multi	.25	.25
1278	A603	120 l	blk & multi	.25	.25
1279	A603	120 l	blk & multi	.25	.25

Nos. 1277-1279 (3)   .75   .75

Volleyball — A671

Designs (Children's Drawings): No. 1281, Butterflies and net. No. 1282, Flying kites.

1977, Oct. 23   *Photo.*   *Perf. 13x14*

1280	A671	120 l	multi	.25	.25
1281	A671	120 l	multi	.25	.25
1282	A671	120 l	multi	.25	.25

a. Block of 3, #1280-1282 + label   .50   .30

19th Stamp Day.

Symbolic Blood Donation — A672

Design: 70 l, Blood donation symbolized.

1977, Oct. 26   *Perf. 14x13½*

| 1283 | A672 | 70 l | multi | .30 | .25 |
| 1284 | A672 | 120 l | multi | .40 | .25 |

Blood donors.

Quintino Sella and Italy No. 24 — A673

1977, Oct. 23   *Perf. 13½x14*

| 1285 | A673 | 170 l | olive & blk brn | .30 | .25 |

Quintino Sella (1827-1884), statesman, engineer, mineralogist, birth sesquicentenary.

Italia Type of 1953-54 and

Italia — A674

1977-87   *Wmk. 303*   *Perf. 14*
Size: 16x20mm
Photo.

| 1288 | A354 | 120 l | dk bl & emer | .25 | .25 |

Photo. & Engr.

| 1289 | A354 | 170 l | grn & ocher | .25 | .25 |

Litho. & Engr.

| 1290 | A354 | 350 l | red, ocher & pur | .30 | .25 |

Perf. 14x13½
   Engr.   Unwmk.

1291	A674	1500 l	multi	2.25	.25
1292	A674	2000 l	multi	3.00	.25
1293	A674	3000 l	multi	4.00	.25
1294	A674	4000 l	multi	8.00	.25
1295	A674	5000 l	multi	.60	.35
1296	A674	10,000 l	multi	12.50	.50
1297	A674	20,000 l	multi	25.00	4.00

Nos. 1288-1297 (10)   56.15   6.60

Issued: 120 l, 170 l, 350l, 11/22/77; 5,000 l, 12/4/78; 4,000 l, 2/12/79; 3,000 l, 3/12/79; 2,000 l, 4/12/79; 1,500 l, 5/14/79; 10,000 l, 6/27/83; 20,000 l, 1/5/87.

Dina Galli (1877-1951), Actress — A675

1977, Dec. 2   *Photo.*   *Unwmk.*

| 1309 | A675 | 170 l | multi | .25 | .25 |

Adoration of the Shepherds, by Pietro Testa — A676

Christmas: 120 l, Adoration of the Shepherds, by Gian Jacopo Caraglio.

Lithographed and Engraved
1977, Dec. 13   *Perf. 14*

| 1310 | A676 | 70 l | blk & ol | .25 | .25 |
| 1311 | A676 | 120 l | blk & bl grn | .25 | .25 |

La Scala Opera House, Milan, Bicent. — A677

Designs: 170 l, Facade. 200 l, Auditorium.

1978, Mar. 15   *Litho.*   *Perf. 13½x14*

| 1312 | A677 | 170 l | multi | .25 | .25 |
| 1313 | A677 | 200 l | multi | .40 | .25 |

Tourist Type of 1974

Paintings: 70 l, Gubbio. 200 l, Udine. 600 l, Paestum.

1978, Mar. 30   *Photo.*   *Perf. 14*

1314	A616	70 l	multi	.25	.25
1315	A616	200 l	multi	.30	.25
1316	A616	600 l	multi	.75	.45

Nos. 1314-1316 (3)   1.30   .95

Giant Grouper — A678

Designs (outline of "Amerigo Vespucci" in background): No. 1318, Leatherback turtle. No. 1319, Mediterranean monk seal. No. 1320, Audouin's gull.

1978, Apr. 3   *Perf. 14x13*

1317	A678	170 l	multi	.40	.25
1318	A678	170 l	multi	.40	.25
1319	A678	170 l	multi	.40	.25
1320	A678	170 l	multi	.40	.25

a. Strip of 4, #1317-1320 + label   1.60   1.00

Endangered species in Mediterranean.

Castel Nuovo, Angevin Fortifications, Naples — A679

Europa: 200 l, Pantheon, Rome.

1978, Apr. 29   *Litho.*   *Perf. 14x13½*

| 1321 | A679 | 170 l | multi | .30 | .25 |
| 1322 | A679 | 200 l | multi | .40 | .25 |

Ship Type of 1977

Designs: No. 1323, Cruiser Benedetto Brin. No. 1324, Frigate Lupo. No. 1325, Ligurian brigantine Fortuna. No. 1326, Container ship Africa.

1978, May 8   *Litho. & Engr.*

1323	170 l	multi	.35	.25
1324	170 l	multi	.35	.25
1325	170 l	multi	.35	.25
1326	170 l	multi	.35	.25

a. A670 Block of 4, #1323-1326 + 2 labels   1.50   1.40

Matilde Serao — A680

Portraits of famous Italians: No. 1328, Vittorino da Feltre. No. 1329, Victor Emmanuel II. No. 1330, Pope Pius IX. No. 1331, Marcello Malpighi. No. 1332, Antonio Meucci.

1978, May 10   *Engr.*   *Perf. 14x13½*

1327	A680	170 l	pink & black	.25	.25
1328	A680	170 l	blue & black	.25	.25
1329	A680	170 l	blue & dk blue	.25	.25
1330	A680	170 l	green & black	.25	.25
1331	A680	170 l	green & brown	.25	.25
1332	A680	170 l	pink & blue	.25	.25

a. Block of 6, #1327-1332   1.50   .75

Constitution, 30th Anniv. — A681

1978, June 2   *Litho.*   *Perf. 13½x14*

| 1333 | A681 | 170 l | multi | .25 | .25 |

Telegraph Wires and Lens — A682

1978, June 30   *Photo.*

| 1334 | A682 | 120 l | lt bl & gray | .25 | .25 |

Photographic information.

The Lovers, by Tranquillo Cremona (1837-1878) — A683

Design: 520 l, The Cook (woman with goose), by Bernardo Strozzi (1581-1644).

Engraved and Lithographed
1978, July 12   *Perf. 14*

| 1335 | A683 | 170 l | multi | .50 | .25 |
| 1336 | A683 | 520 l | multi | 1.75 | .70 |

Holy Shroud of Turin, by Giovanni Testa, 1578 — A684

1978, Sept. 8   *Photo.*   *Perf. 14*

| 1337 | A684 | 220 l | yel, red & blk | .45 | .25 |

400th anniversary of the transfer of the Holy Shroud from Savoy to Turin.

Volleyball — A685

Design: 120 l, Volleyball, diff.

1978, Sept. 20

| 1338 | A685 | 80 l | multi | .25 | .25 |
| 1339 | A685 | 120 l | multi | .30 | .25 |

Men's Volleyball World Championship.

Mother and Child, by Masaccio — A686

1978, Oct. 18   *Engr.*   *Perf. 13½x14*

| 1340 | A686 | 170 l | indigo | .25 | .25 |

Masaccio (real name Tommaso Guidi; 1401-28), painter.

Fountain Type of 1973

Designs: No 1341, Neptune Fountain, Trent. No. 1342, Fortuna Fountain, Fano. No. 1343, Cavallina Fountain, Genzano di Lucania.

1978, Oct. 25   *Litho. & Engr.*

1341	A603	120 l	blk & multi	.25	.25
1342	A603	120 l	blk & multi	.25	.25
1343	A603	120 l	blk & multi	.25	.25

Nos. 1341-1343 (3)   .75   .75

ITALY

Virgin and Child, by Giorgione — A687

Adoration of the Kings, by Giorgione — A688

1978, Nov. 8   Engr.   *Perf. 13x14*
1344   A687   80 l   dark red   .25   .25

    Photo.   *Perf. 14x13½*
1345   A688   120 l   multi   .25   .25
Christmas 1978.

Flags as Flowers — A689

Designs: No. 1347, European flags. No. 1348, "People hailing Europe."

1978, Nov. 26   Photo.   *Perf. 13x14*
1346   A689   120 l   multi   .25   .25
1347   A689   120 l   multi   .25   .25
1348   A689   120 l   multi   .25   .25
    Nos. 1346-1348 (3)   .75   .75
20th Stamp Day on theme "United Europe."

State Printing Office, Stamps — A690

Design: 220 l, Printing press and stamps.

1979, Jan. 6   Photo.   *Perf. 14x13½*
1349   A690   170 l   multi   .25   .25
1350   A690   220 l   multi   .35   .25
1st stamps printed by State Printing Office, 50 anniv.

St. Francis Washing Lepers, 13th Century Painting — A691

1979, Jan. 22
1351   A691   80 l   multi   .25   .25
Leprosy relief.

Bicyclist Carrying Bike — A692

1979, Jan. 27   *Perf. 13½x14*
1352   A692   170 l   multi   .25   .25
1353   A692   220 l   multi   .35   .25
World Crosscountry Bicycle Championships.

Virgin Mary, by Antonello da Messina — A693

Painting: 520 l, Haystack, by Ardengo Soffici (1879-1964).

1979, Feb. 15   Engr.   *Perf. 14*
1354   A693   170 l   multi   .30   .25
1355   A693   520 l   multi   .70   .50

Albert Einstein (1879-1955), Theoretical Physicist and His Equation. — A694

Lithographed and Engraved
1979, Mar. 14   *Perf. 13x14*
1356   A694   120 l   multi   .25   .25

Tourist Type of 1974
Paintings: 70 l, Asiago. 90 l, Castelsardo. 170 l, Orvieto. 220 l, Scilla.

1979, Mar. 30   Photo.   *Perf. 14*
1357   A616   70 l   grn & multi   .25   .25
1358   A616   90 l   car & multi   .25   .25
1359   A616   170 l   ultra & multi   .25   .25
1360   A616   220 l   gray & multi   .35   .25
    Nos. 1357-1360 (4)   1.10   1.00

Famous Italians — A695

No. 1361, Carlo Maderno (1556-1629), architect. No. 1362, Lazzaro Spallanzani (1729-1799), physiologist. No. 1363, Ugo Foscolo (1778-1827), writer. No. 1364 Massimo Bontempelli (1878-1960), journalist. No. 1365, Francesco Severi (1879-1961), mathematician.

1979, Apr. 23   Engr.   *Perf. 14x13½*
1361   A695   170 l   multi   .25   .25
1362   A695   170 l   multi   .25   .25
1363   A695   170 l   multi   .25   .25
1364   A695   170 l   multi   .25   .25
1365   A695   170 l   multi   .25   .25
    Nos. 1361-1365 (5)   1.25   1.25

Telegraph — A696

Europa: 220 l, Carrier pigeons.

1979, Apr. 30   Photo.   *Perf. 14*
1366   A696   170 l   multi   .65   .25
1367   A696   220 l   multi   .65   .30

Flags and "E" — A697

1979, May 5   *Perf. 14x13½*
1368   A697   170 l   multi   .25   .25
1369   A697   220 l   multi   .30   .25
European Parliament, first direct elections, June 7-10.

Exhibition Emblem, Dome of Milan — A698

1979, June 22   Photo.   *Perf. 14*
1370   A698   170 l   multi   .25   .25
1371   A698   220 l   multi   .30   .25
3rd World Machine Tool Exhib., Milan, Oct. 10-18.

Aeneas and Rotary Emblem — A699

1979, June 9   *Perf. 13½x14*
1372   A699   220 l   multi   .30   .25
70th World Rotary Cong., Rome, June 1979.

Basket — A700

120 l, Basketball players.

1979, June 13   *Perf. 14*
1373   A700   80 l   shown   .25   .25
1374   A700   120 l   multicolored   .25   .25
21st European Basketball Championship, June 9-20.

A701

Patient & Physician, 16th cent. woodcut.

1979, June 16   Photo. & Engr.
1375   A701   120 l   multi   .25   .25
Digestive Ailments Study Week.

A702

Design: Ottorino Respighi (1879-1936), composer, Roman landscape.

Lithographed and Engraved
1979, July 9   *Perf. 13x14*
1376   A702   120 l   multi   .25   .25

Woman Making Phone Call — A703

200 l, Woman with old-fashioned phone.

1979, Sept. 20   Photo.   *Perf. 14*
1377   A703   170 l   red & gray   .25   .25
1378   A703   220 l   grn & slate   .30   .25
3rd World Telecommunications Exhibition, Geneva, Sept. 20-26.

Fountain Type of 1973
Designs: No. 1379, Great Fountain, Viterbo. No. 1380, Hot Springs, Acqui Terme. No. 1381, Pomegranate Fountain, Issogne Castle.

Lithographed and Engraved
1979, Sept. 22   *Perf. 13x14*
1379   A603   120 l   multi   .35   .25
1380   A603   120 l   multi   .35   .25
1381   A603   120 l   multi   .35   .25
    Nos. 1379-1381 (3)   1.05   .75

Ship Type of 1977
Designs: No. 1382, Cruiser Enrico Dandolo. No. 1383, Submarine Carlo Fecia. No. 1384, Freighter Cosmos. No. 1385, Ferry Deledda.

1979, Oct. 12   *Perf. 14x13½*
1382   170 l   multi   .35   .25
1383   170 l   multi   .35   .25
1384   170 l   multi   .35   .25
1385   170 l   multi   .35   .25
  a.   A670 Block of 4, #1382-1385 + 2 labels   1.60   1.40

Penny Black, Rowland Hill — A704

1979, Oct. 25   Photo.
1386   A704   220 l   multi   .30   .25

Minstrels and Church — A705

1979, Nov. 7   Photo.   *Perf. 14x13½*
1387   A705   120 l   multi   .25   .25
Christmas 1979.

Black and White Boys Holding Hands — A706

Children's Drawings: 120 l, Children of various races under umbrella map, vert. 150 l, Children and red balloons.

Perf. 14x13½, 13½x14
1979, Nov. 25   Photo.
1388   A706   70 l   multi   .25   .25
1389   A706   120 l   multi   .25   .25
1390   A706   150 l   multi   .25   .25
    Nos. 1388-1390 (3)   .75   .75
21st Stamp Day.

Solar Energy Panels — A707

Energy Conservation: 170 l, Sun & pylon.

1980, Feb. 25   Photo.   *Perf. 14x13½*
1391   A707   120 l   multi   .25   .25
1392   A707   170 l   multi   .25   .25

St. Benedict of Nursia, 1500th Birth Anniv. — A708

1980, Mar. 21   Engr.   *Perf. 13½x14*
1393   A708   220 l   dark blue   .30   .25

Royal Palace, Naples — A709

Lithographed and Engraved
1980, Apr. 16   *Perf. 13½x14*
1394   A709   220 l   multi   .30   .25
20th International Philatelic Exhibition, Europa '80, Naples, Apr. 26-May 4.

ITALY

Antonio Pigafetta, Caravel — A710

Europa: 220 l, Antonio Lo Surdo (1880-1949) geophysicist.

1980, Apr. 28   Litho.   Perf. 14x13½
| 1395 | A710 | 170 l multi | .40 | .25 |
| 1396 | A710 | 220 l multi | .70 | .30 |

St. Catherine, Reliquary Bust — A711

1980, Apr. 29   Photo.
| 1397 | A711 | 170 l multi | .25 | .25 |

St. Catherine of Siena (1347-1380).

Italian Red Cross — A712

1980, May 15   Photo.   Perf. 14x13½
| 1398 | A712 | 70 l multi | .25 | .25 |
| 1399 | A712 | 80 l multi | .25 | .25 |

Temples of Philae, Egypt A713

1980, May 20
1400	Pair + label		.70	.25
a.	A713 220 l shown		.35	.25
b.	A713 220 l Temple of Philae, diff.		.35	.25

Italian civil engineering achievements (Temples of Philae saved from ruin by Italian engineers).

Soccer Player — A714

1980, June 11
| 1401 | A714 | 80 l multi | 1.50 | 1.10 |

European Soccer Championships, Milan, Turin, Rome, Naples, June 9-22.

Tourist Type of 1974

Paintings: 80 l, Erice. 150 l, Villa Rufolo, Ravello. 200 l, Roseto degli Abruzzi. 670 l, Public Baths, Salsomaggiore Terme.

1980, June 28   Perf. 14
1402	A616	80 l multi	.25	.25
1403	A616	150 l multi	.25	.25
1404	A616	200 l multi	.30	.25
1405	A616	670 l multi	.90	.75
	Nos. 1402-1405 (4)		1.70	1.50

Cosimo I with his Artists, by Giorgio Vasari, and Armillary sphere A715

1980, July 2   Perf. 13½x14
1406	A715	Pair + label	.50	.50
a.		170 l Cosimo I	.25	.25
b.		170 l Armillary sphere	.25	.25

The Medici in Europe of the 16th Century Exhibition, Florence.

Fonte Avellana Monastery Millennium A716

1980, Sept. 3   Engr.   Perf. 14x13½
| 1407 | A716 | 200 l grn & brn | .30 | .25 |

Castles — A717

Designs: No. 1408, St. Angelo Castle, Rome. No. 1409, Sforzesco, Milan. No. 1410, Del Monte, Andria. No. 1411, Ursino, Catania. No. 1412, Rocca di Calascio. No. 1413, Norman Tower, St. Mauro Fort. No. 1414, Isola Capo Rizzuto. No. 1415, Aragonese, Ischia. No. 1416, Estense, Ferrarra. No. 1417, Miramare, Trieste. No. 1418, Ostia, Rome. No. 1419, Gavarone, Savona. No. 1420, Cerro al Volturno, Isernia. No. 1421, Rocca di Mondavio. No. 1422, Svevo, Bari. No. 1423, Mussomelli, Caltanissetta. No. 1424, Imperatore-Prato, Florence. No. 1425, Bosa, Nuoro. No. 1426, Rovereto, Trento. No. 1427, Scaligero, Sirmione. No. 1428, Ivrea, Turin. No. 1429, Rocca Maggiore, Assisi. No. 1430, St. Pierre, Aosta. No. 1431 Montagnana, Padua. No. 1432, St. Severna, Rome. No. 1433, Lombardia, Enna. No. 1434, Serralunga d'Alba, Cuneo.

Photo. (#1408-1417), Litho. and Engr. (#1418-1422, 1425, 1427-1428), Engr. (#1423-1424, 1426, 1429-1434)

Perf. 14x13½

1980, Sept. 22   Wmk. 303
1408	A717	5 l multi	.25	.25
1409	A717	10 l multi	.25	.25
1410	A717	20 l multi	.25	.25
1411	A717	40 l multi	.25	.25
1412	A717	50 l multi	.25	.25
1413	A717	60 l multi	.25	.25
1414	A717	90 l multi	.25	.25
1415	A717	100 l multi	.25	.25
1416	A717	120 l multi	.25	.25
1417	A717	150 l multi	.25	.25
1418	A717	170 l multi	.70	.25
1419	A717	180 l multi	1.20	1.00
1420	A717	200 l multi	.75	.25
1421	A717	250 l multi	.70	.25
1422	A717	300 l multi	.80	.25
1423	A717	350 l multi	.80	.25
1424	A717	400 l multi	.80	.25
1425	A717	450 l multi	1.00	.25
1426	A717	500 l multi	.80	.25
1427	A717	600 l multi	.90	.25
1428	A717	700 l multi	1.00	.25
1429	A717	800 l multi	1.10	.25
1430	A717	900 l multi	1.25	.25
1431	A717	1000 l multi	1.25	.25
	Nos. 1408-1431 (24)		15.55	6.75

Coil Stamps
Perf. 14 Vert.
Size: 16x21mm

1432	A717	30 l multi	.25	.25
1433	A717	120 l multi	.25	.25
a.	Pair, Nos. 1432-1433		.40	.25
1434	A717	170 l multi	.30	.25
a.	Pair, Nos. 1432, 1434		.75	.75
	Nos. 1432-1434 (3)		.75	.75

No. 1412 exists dated "1980."
See Nos. 1475-1484, 1657-1666, 1862-1866.

Ship Type of 1977

No. 1435, Corvette Gabbiano. No. 1436, Torpedo boat Audace. No. 1437, Sailing ship Italia. No. 1438, Floating dock Castoro Sei.

Lithographed and Engraved
1980, Oct. 11   Perf. 14x13½
1435		200 l multi	.60	.40
1436		200 l multi	.60	.40
1437		200 l multi	.60	.40
1438		200 l multi	.60	.40
a.	A670 Block of 4, #1435-1438 + 2 labels		6.00	6.00

Philip Mazzei (1730-1816), Political Writer in US — A718

1980, Oct. 18   Photo.   Perf. 13½x14
| 1439 | A718 | 320 l multi | .50 | .30 |

Villa Foscari Malcontenta, Venezia — A719

Villas: 150 l, Barbaro Maser, Treviso. 170 l, Godi Valmarana, Vicenza.

Lithographed and Engraved
1980, Oct. 31   Perf. 14x13½
1440	A719	80 l multi	.30	.30
1441	A719	150 l multi	.50	.25
1442	A719	170 l multi	.60	.25
	Nos. 1440-1442 (3)		1.40	.80

See Nos. 1493-1495, 1528-1530, 1565-1568, 1606-1609, 1646-1649, 1691-1695.

St. Barbara, by Palma the Elder (1480-1528) A720

Design: No. 1444, Apollo and Daphne, by Gian Lorenzo Bernini (1598-1680).

1980, Nov. 20   Perf. 14
| 1443 | A720 | 520 l multi | .75 | .55 |
| 1444 | A720 | 520 l multi | .75 | .55 |

Nativity Sculpture by Federico Brandini, 16th Cent. — A721

1980, Nov. 22   Engr.
| 1445 | A721 | 120 l brn org & blk | .25 | .25 |

Christmas 1980.

View of Verona — A722

22nd Stamp Day: Views of Verona drawings by school children.

1980, Nov. 30   Photo.   Perf. 14x13½
1446	A722	70 l multi	.25	.25
1447	A722	120 l multi	.25	.25
1448	A722	170 l multi	.25	.25
	Nos. 1446-1448 (3)		.75	.75

Daniele Comboni (1831-1881), Savior of the Africans — A723

1981, Mar. 14   Engr.
| 1449 | A723 | 80 l multi | .25 | .25 |

Alcide de Gasperi (1881-1954), Statesman — A724

1981, Apr. 3   Perf. 13½x14
| 1450 | A724 | 200 l olive green | .30 | .25 |

International Year of the Disabled — A725

1981, Apr. 11   Photo.
| 1451 | A725 | 300 l multi | .40 | .35 |

A726

1981, Apr. 27   Photo.   Perf. 13½x14
1452	A726	200 l Roses	.30	.25
1453	A726	200 l Anemones	.30	.25
1454	A726	200 l Oleanders	.30	.25
	Nos. 1452-1454 (3)		.90	.75

See Nos. 1510-1512, 1555-1557.

Europa — A727

Designs: No. 1455, Chess game with human pieces, Marostica. No. 1456, Horse race, Siena.

1981, May 4
| 1455 | A727 | 300 l shown | 1.00 | .25 |
| 1456 | A727 | 300 l multicolored | 1.00 | .25 |

St. Rita Offering Thorn — A728

1981, May 22
| 1457 | A728 | 600 l multi | .80 | .40 |

St. Rita of Cascia, 600th birth anniversary.

Ciro Menotti (1798-1831), Patriot — A729

1981, May 26   Engr.   Perf. 14x13½
| 1458 | A729 | 80 l brn & blk | .25 | .25 |

Italian Aircraft A730

No. 1459, G-222 Aeritalia transport. No. 1460, MB-339 Aermacchi jet. No. 1461, A-109 Agusta helicopter. No. 1462, P-68 Partenavia transport.

ITALY

1981, June 1 — Photo.
1459 200 l multicolored .30 .25
1460 200 l multicolored .30 .25
1461 200 l multicolored .30 .25
1462 200 l multicolored .30 .25
  a. A730 Block of 4, #1459-1462 + 2 labels   1.40 1.40
See Nos. 1505-1508, 1550-1553.

Hydro-geological Research — A731

1981, June 8   Perf. 13½x14
1463 A731 80 l multi   .25 .25

Sao Simao Dam and Power Station, Brazil — A732

Civil Engineering Works Abroad: No. 1465, High Island Reservoir, Hong Kong.

1981, June 26   Engr.   Perf. 14x13½
1464 A732 300 l dark blue   .45 .25
1465 A732 300 l red   .45 .25
  a. Pair, #1464-1465 + label   1.00 .80
See Nos. 1516-1517, 1538-1539.

Tourist Type of 1974
80 l, View of Matera. 150 l, Lake Garda. 300 l, St. Teresa di Gallura beach. 900 l, Tarquinia.

1981, July 4   Photo.   Perf. 14
1466 A616 80 l multi   .25 .25
1467 A616 150 l multi   .35 1.10
1468 A616 300 l multi   .50 .45
1469 A616 900 l multi   1.40 .55
  Nos. 1466-1469 (4)   2.50 2.35

Naval Academy, Livorno and Navy Emblem — A735

Naval Academy of Livorno Centenary: 150 l, View. 200 l, Cadet with sextant, training ship Amerigo Vespucci.

1981, July 24   Perf. 14x13½
1472 A735 80 l multi   .25 .25
1473 A735 150 l multi   .25 .25
1474 A735 200 l multi   .35 .25
  Nos. 1472-1474 (3)   .85 .75

Castle Type of 1980
30 l, Aquila. 70 l, Aragonese, Reggio Calabria. 80 l, Sabbionara, Avio. 550 l, Rocca Sinibalda. 1400 l, Caldoresco, Vasto.

   Perf. 14x13½
1981-84   Photo.   Wmk. 303
1475 A717 30 l multicolored   .25 .25
1476 A717 70 l multicolored   .25 .25
1477 A717 80 l multicolored   .25 .25
   Perf. 13½
1478 A717 550 l multicolored   .70 .25
   Engr.
1479 A717 1400 l multicolored   1.60 .50
  Nos. 1475-1479 (5)   3.05 1.50
Issue dates: Nos. 1475-1477, Aug. 20, 1981; Nos. 1478-1479, Feb. 14, 1984.

Coil Stamps
50 l, Scilla. 200 l, Angioina, Lucera. 300 l, Norman Castle, Melfi. 400 l, Venafro. 450 l, Piobbico Pesaro.

1981-88   Engr.   Perf. 14 Vert.
   Size: 16x21mm
1480 A717 50 l blue   .25 .25
1481 A717 200 l blue & pur   1.00 1.00
1482 A717 300 l bl grn & grn   .30 .25
1483 A717 400 l ol grn & red brn   .60 .25
1484 A717 450 l green   .50 .25
  a. Pair, #1480, 1484   1.00 .75
  Nos. 1480-1484 (5)   2.65 2.00
Issued: Nos. 1481-1482, 9/30; No. 1483, 6/25/83; Nos. 1480, 1484, 7/25/85; No. 1484a, 3/1/88.

Palazzo Spada, Rome (Council Seat) — A736

1981, Aug. 31   Engr.   Unwmk.
1485 A736 200 l multi   .30 .25
State Council sesquicentennial.

World Cup Races — A737

1981, Sept. 4   Photo.   Perf. 13½x14
1486 A737 300 l multi   .40 .25

Harbor View, by Carlo Carra (1881-1966) — A738

Lithographed and Engraved
1981, Sept. 7   Perf. 14
1487 A738 200 l multi   .30 .25
1488 A738 200 l multi   .30 .25
See Nos. 1532-1533, 1638-1639, 1697-1698, 1732.

No. 1488, Castle, by Guiseppe Ugonia (1881-1944).

Riace Bronze, 4th Cent. B.C. — A739

1981, Sept. 9   Photo.   Perf. 13½x14
1489 200 l Statue   .30 .25
1490 200 l Statue, diff.   .30 .25
  a. A739 Pair, #1489-1490   .70 .60
Greek statues found in 1972 in sea near Reggio di Calabria.

Virgil, Mosaic, Treviri — A740

1981, Sept. 19   Perf. 14
1491 A740 600 l multi   .75 .40
Virgil's death bimillennium.

Food and Wine, by Gregorio Sciltian — A741

1981, Oct. 16   Litho.   Perf. 14
1492 A741 150 l multi   .40 .25
World Food Day.

Villa Type of 1980
100 l, Villa Campolieto, Ercolano. 200 l, Cimbrone, Ravello. 300 l, Pignatelli, Naples.

Lithographed and Engraved
1981, Oct. 17   Perf. 14x13½
1493 A719 100 l multicolored   .25 .25
1494 A719 200 l multicolored   .30 .25
1495 A719 300 l multicolored   .50 .50
  Nos. 1493-1495 (3)   1.05 1.00

Adoration of the Magi, by Giovanni de Campione d'Italia (Christmas 1981) — A743

1981, Nov. 21   Engr.   Perf. 14
1496 A743 200 l multi   .30 .25

Pope John XXIII (1881-1963) — A744

1981, Nov. 25   Photo.   Perf. 13½x14
1497 A744 200 l multi   .65 .25

Stamp Day — A745

120 l, Letters, horiz. 200 l, Angel, letter chest. 300 l, Letter seal.

Photogravure, Photogravure and Engraved (200 l)
   Perf. 14x13½, 13½x14
1981, Nov. 29
1498 A745 120 l multicolored   .25 .25
1499 A745 200 l multicolored   .40 .55
1500 A745 300 l multicolored   .60 .25
  Nos. 1498-1500 (3)   1.25 1.05

St. Francis of Assisi, 800th Birth Anniv. — A746

Design: St. Francis Receiving the Stigmata, by Pietro Cavaro.

1982, Jan. 6   Perf. 13½x14
1501 A746 300 l dk bl & brn   .40 .25

Niccolo Paganini (1782-1840), Composer, Violinist — A748

1982, Feb. 19   Photo.   Perf. 13½x14
1503 A748 900 l multi   1.25 1.00

Anti-smoking Campaign — A749

1982, Mar. 2   Photo.   Perf. 14x13½
1504 A749 300 l multi   .40 .25

Aircraft Type of 1981
No. 1505, Aeritalia MRCA. No. 1506, SIAI 260 Turbo. No. 1507, Piaggio 166-dl3 Turbo. No. 1508, Nardi NH-500.

1982, Mar. 27   Litho.   Perf. 14x13½
1505 300 l multicolored   .55 .55
1506 300 l multicolored   .55 .55
1507 300 l multicolored   .55 .55
1508 300 l multicolored   .55 .55
  a. A730 Block of 4, #1505-1508 + 2 labels   3.50 3.00

Sicilian Vespers, 700th Anniv. — A750

1982, Mar. 31   Engr.   Perf. 13½x14
1509 A750 120 l multi   .25 .25

Flower Type of 1981
1982, Apr. 10   Photo.
1510 A726 300 l Cyclamens   .50 .50
1511 A726 300 l Camellias   .50 .50
1512 A726 300 l Carnations   .50 .50
  Nos. 1510-1512 (3)   1.50 1.50

Europa — A751

200 l, Coronation of Charlemagne, 799. 450 l, Treaty of Rome signatures, 1957.

Photogravure and Engraved
1982, May 3   Perf. 13½x14
1513 A751 200 l multicolored   .70 .70
1514 A751 450 l multicolored   1.10 .55

Engineering Type of 1981
No. 1516, Microwaves across Red Sea. No. 1517, Automatic letter sorting.

1982, May 29   Photo.   Perf. 14x13½
1516 A732 450 l multicolored   .60 .25
1517 A732 450 l multicolored   .60 .25
  a. Pair, #1516-1517 + label   1.50 1.50

Giuseppe Garibaldi (1807-82) — A753

1982, June 2   Perf. 13½x14
1518 A753 200 l multicolored   .60 .60

Game of the Bridge, Pisa — A754

1982, June 5
1519 A754 200 l multi   .35 .35
See Nos. 1562, 1603, 1628-1629, 1655, 1717, 1749, 1775, 1807.

Tourist Type of 1974
No. 1520, Frasassi Caves. No. 1521, Paganella Valley. No. 1522, Temple of Agrigento. No. 1523, Rodi Garganico Beach.

1982, June 28   Perf. 14
1520 A616 200 l multicolored   .50 .60
1521 A616 200 l multicolored   .50 .60
1522 A616 450 l multicolored   .75 .40
1523 A616 450 l multicolored   .75 .40
  Nos. 1520-1523 (4)   2.50 2.00

ITALY

World Junior Canoeing Championship A755

1982, Aug. 4   Photo.   *Perf. 14*
1524 A755 200 l multi   .40 .35

Duke Federico da Montefeltro (1422-1482) A756

200 l, Urbino Palace, Gubbio Council House.

Photogravure and Engraved
1982, Sept. 10   *Perf. 14x13½*
1525 A756 200 l multicolored   .30 .30

Italy's Victory in 1982 World Cup — A757

1982, Sept. 12   Photo.   *Perf. 14*
1526 A757 1000 l World Cup   1.75 1.50

69th Inter-Parliamentary Conference, Rome — A758

1982, Sept. 14   *Perf. 14x13½*
1527 A758 450 l multi   .55 .25

Villa Type of 1980
Designs: 150 l, Temple of Aesculapius, Villa Borghese, Rome. 250 l, Villa D'Este, Tivoli, Rome. 350 l, Villa Lante, Bagnaia, Viterbo.

Photogravure and Engraved
1982, Oct. 1   *Perf. 14x13½*
1528 A719 150 l multi   .45 .45
1529 A719 250 l multi   .65 .25
1530 A719 350 l multi   1.00 1.10
   Nos. 1528-1530 (3)   2.10 1.80

Thurn and Taxis Family Postal Service — A759

300 l, Franz von Taxis (1450-1517).

1982, Oct. 23   Engr.   *Perf. 13½x14*
1531 A759 300 l multicolored   .40 .25

Art Type of 1981
Paintings: No. 1532, The Fortune Teller by G.B. Piazzetta (1682-1754). No. 1533, Antonietta Negroni Prati Morosini as a Little Girl by Francesco Hayez (1791-1882).

Lithographed and Engraved
1982, Nov. 3   *Perf. 14*
1532 A738 300 l multi   .55 .50
1533 A738 300 l multi   .55 .50

24th Stamp Day — A761

Children's Drawings.

1982, Nov. 28   Photo.   *Perf. 14x13½*
1534 A761 150 l multi   .25 .25
1535 A761 250 l multi   .50 .30
1536 A761 350 l multi   .65 .55
   Nos. 1534-1536 (3)   1.40 1.10

Cancer Research — A762

1983, Jan. 14   Photo.   *Perf. 13½x14*
1537 A762 400 l multi   .55 .35

Engineering Type of 1981
No. 1538, Globe, factories. No. 1539, Automated assembly line.

1983, Jan. 20   *Perf. 13½*
1538 A732 400 l multicolored   .55 .35
1539 A732 400 l multicolored   .55 .35
  a.   Pair, #1538-1539   1.30 1.30

Crusca Academy, 400th Anniv. — A763

1983, Jan. 25   Engr.   *Perf. 14x13½*
1540 A763 400 l Emblem   .50 .35

World Biathlon Championship A764

1983, Feb. 5   Photo.   *Perf. 14*
1541 A764 200 l multi   .40 .40

Gabriele Rossetti (1783-1854), Writer — A765

1983, Feb. 28   Engr.   *Perf. 14x13½*
1542 A765 300 l dk brn & dk bl   .40 .30

Francesco Guicciardini (1483-1540), Historian — A766

1983, Mar. 5   Engr.   *Perf. 13½x14*
1543 A766 450 l sepia   .60 .35

Umberto Saba (1883-1957), Poet — A767

1983, Mar. 9   Photo.   *Perf. 14x13½*
1544 A767 600 l multi   .75 .45

Pope Pius XII (1876-1958) — A768

1983, Mar. 21   Engr.   *Perf. 13½x14*
1545 A768 1400 l dark blue   2.00 .95

Holy Year — A769

250 l, St. Paul's Basilica. 300 l, St. Maria Maggiore Church. 400 l, San Giovanni Church. 500 l, St. Peter's Church.

1983, Mar. 25   Photo.   *Perf. 14*
1546 A769 250 l multicolored   .35 .35
1547 A769 300 l multicolored   .50 .25
1548 A769 400 l multicolored   .55 .25
1549 A769 500 l multicolored   .70 .25
   Nos. 1546-1549 (4)   2.10 1.10

Aircraft Type of 1981
No. 1550, Caproni C22J glider. No. 1551, Aeritalia Macchi jet fighter. No. 1552, SIAI-211 jet trainer. No. 1553, A-129 Agusta helicopter.

1983, Mar. 28   Litho.   *Perf. 14x13½*
1550   400 l multicolored   .50 .50
1551   400 l multicolored   .50 .50
1552   400 l multicolored   .50 .50
1553   400 l multicolored   .50 .50
  a.   A730 Block or strip of 4, #1550-1553 + 2 labels   2.50 2.50

Intl. Workers' Day (May 1) — A770

1983, Apr. 29   Engr.   *Perf. 14x13½*
1554 A770 1200 l blue   1.40 .90

Flower Type of 1981
1983, Apr. 30   Photo.   *Perf. 13½x14*
1555 A726 200 l Mimosa   .50 .50
1556 A726 200 l Rhododendron   .50 .50
1557 A726 200 l Gladiolus   .50 .50
   Nos. 1555-1557 (3)   1.50 1.50

Europa 1983 — A771

400 l, Galileo, telescope, 160l. 500 l, Archimedes and his screw.

Litho. & Engr.
1983, May 2   *Perf. 14x13½*
1558 A771 400 l multicolored   1.50 1.00
1559 A771 500 l multicolored   2.00 .90

Ernesto T. Moneta (1833-1918), Nobel Peace Prize Winner, 1907 — A772

1983, May 5   Engr.   *Perf. 14x13½*
1560 A772 500 l multi   .65 .30

Monument, Globe, Computer Screen — A773

1983, May 9   Photo.   *Perf. 13½x14*
1561 A773 500 l multi   .65 .30

3rd Intl. Congress of Jurisdicial Information.

Folk Celebration Type of 1982
No. 1562, La Corsa Dei Ceri Procession, Gubbio.

1983, May 13   *Perf. 13½*
1562 A754 300 l multi   .55 .30

20th Natl. Eucharistic Congress — A775

1983, May 14   *Perf. 14*
1563 A775 300 l multi   .40 .30

Tourist Type of 1974
1983, July 30   Photo.   *Perf. 14*
1563A A616 250 l Alghero   .75 1.40
1563B A616 300 l Bardonecchia   .75 .75
1563C A616 400 l Riccione   .60 .65
1563D A616 500 l Taranto   .70 .40
   Nos. 1563A-1563D (4)   2.80 3.20

Girolamo Frescobaldi (1583-1643), Composer — A776

1983, Sept. 15   Engr.   *Perf. 13½x14*
1564 A776 400 l brn & grn   .50 .30

Villa Type of 1980
Designs: 250 l, Fidelia, Spello. 300 l, Imperiale, Pesaro. 400 l, Michetti Convent, Francavilla al Mare. 500 l, Riccia.

Photogravure and Engraved
1983, Oct. 10   *Perf. 14x13½*
1565 A719 250 l multi   .70 1.75
1566 A719 300 l multi   .70 .25
1567 A719 400 l multi   .80 .25
1568 A719 500 l multi   .80 .25
   Nos. 1565-1568 (4)   3.00 2.50

Francesco de Sanctis (1817-1883), Writer — A777

1983, Oct. 28   Photo.
1569 A777 300 l multi   .45 .30

Christmas 1983 — A778

Raphael Paintings: 250 l, Madonna of the Chair. 400 l, Sistine Madonna. 500 l, Madonna of the Candelabra.

1983, Nov. 10   *Perf. 13½x14*
1570 A778 250 l multi   .50 .30
1571 A778 400 l multi   .65 .25
1572 A778 500 l multi   .75 .25
   Nos. 1570-1572 (3)   1.90 .80

25th Stamp Day, World Communications Year — A779

Children's Drawings. 200 l, Letters holding hands, horiz. 300 l, Spaceman. 400 l, Flag train, globe, horiz.

Perf. 14x13½, 13½x14
1983, Nov. 27
1573 A779 200 l multicolored   .35 .35
1574 A779 300 l multicolored   .50 .25
1575 A779 400 l multicolored   .75 .30
   Nos. 1573-1575 (3)   1.60 .90

ITALY

Road Safety — A780

300 l, Bent road sign, vert. 400 l, Accident.

1984, Jan. 20   *Perf. 13½x14, 14x13½*   Photo.
1576	A780	300 l multicolored	.50	.50
1577	A780	400 l multicolored	.60	.50

Promenade in Bois de Boulogne, by Giuseppe de Nittis (1846-1884) A781

Design: 400 l, Portrait of Paul Guillaume, 1916, by Amedeo Modigliani (1884-1920).

Lithographed and Engraved
1984, Jan. 25   *Perf. 14*
1578	A781	300 l multicolored	.55	.45
1579	A781	400 l multicolored	.75	.65

Galaxy-Same Tractor — A782

Italian-made vehicles: No. 1581, Alfa-33 car. No. 1582, Maserati Biturbo car. No. 1583, Iveco 190-38 truck.

1984, Mar. 10   Photo.   *Perf. 14x13½*
1580	A782	450 l shown	.65	.55
1581	A782	450 l multicolored	.65	.55
1582	A782	450 l multicolored	.65	.55
1583	A782	450 l multicolored	.65	.55
a.		Block of 4, #1580-1583 + 2 labels	5.00	5.00

See Nos. 1620-1623, 1681-1684.

A783

1984, Apr. 10
1584	A783	300 l Mosaic, furnace	.40	.25
1585	A783	300 l Glass Blower	.40	.25
a.		Pair, #1584-1585 + label	1.10	1.10

2nd European Parliament Elections A784

400 l, Parliament Strasbourg.

1984, Apr. 16
1586	A784	400 l multicolored	.65	.65

Forest Preservation A785

No. 1587, Helicopter fire patrol. No. 1588, Hedgehog, squirrel, badger. No. 1589, Riverside waste dump. No. 1590, Plant life, animals.

1984, Apr. 24   Photo.   *Perf. 14x13½*
1587	A785	450 l multi	.55	.55
1588	A785	450 l multi	.55	.55
1589	A785	450 l multi	.55	.55
1590	A785	450 l multi	.55	.55
a.		Block of 4, #1587-1590	7.00	7.00

Italia '85 — A786

450 l, Ministry of Posts, Rome. 550 l, Via Appia Antiqua, Rome.

1984, Apr. 26   *Perf. 14*
1591	A786	450 l multi	.75	.25
1592	A786	550 l multi	.90	.25

Rome Pacts, 40th Anniv. — A787

Trade Unionists: Giuseppe di Vittorio, Bruno Buozzi, Achille Grandi.

1984, Apr. 30   *Perf. 14x13½*
1593	A787	450 l multi	.75	.70

Europa (1959-84) — A788

1984, May 5
1594	A788	450 l multi	2.50	.90
1595	A788	550 l multi	7.00	2.50

Intl. Telecommunications Symposium, Florence, May — A789

1984, May 7   *Perf. 14*
1596	A789	550 l multi	1.00	.65

Italian Derby Centenary A790

Lithographed and Engraved
1984, May 12   *Perf. 14x13½*
1597	A790	250 l Racing	.75	1.50
1598	A790	400 l Racing, diff.	1.25	.65

Tourist Type of 1974

350 l, Campione d'Italia. 400 l, Chianciano Terme baths. 450 l, Padula. 550 l, Greek ampitheater, Syracuse.

1984, May 19   Photo.   *Perf. 14*
1599	A616	350 l multi	1.75	1.60
1600	A616	400 l multi	.90	.80
1601	A616	450 l multi	.90	.80
1602	A616	550 l multi	1.00	.90
		Nos. 1599-1602 (4)	4.55	4.10

Folk Celebration Type of 1982

Design: La Macchina Di Santa Rosa.

1984, Sept. 3   Photo.   *Perf. 13½x14*
1603	A754	400 l multi	.60	.35

Peasant Farming — A792

250 l, Grain harvester, thresher. 350 l, Cart, hand press.

1984, Oct. 1   Photo.   *Perf. 14x13½*
1604	A792	250 l multicolored	.45	.40
1605	A792	350 l multicolored	.55	.40

Villa Type of 1980

Designs: 250 l, Villa Caristo, Stignano. 350 l, Villa Doria Pamphili, Genoa. 400 l, Villa Reale, Stupinigi. 450 l, Villa Mellone, Lecce.

Lithographed and Engraved
1984, Oct. 6   *Perf. 14x13½*
1606	A719	250 l multi	1.05	1.25
1607	A719	350 l multi	.90	.90
1608	A719	400 l multi	.90	.90
1609	A719	450 l multi	1.00	.50
		Nos. 1606-1609 (4)	3.85	3.15

Italia '85 — A793

No. 1610, Etruscan bronze statue. No. 1611, Italia '85 emblem. No. 1612, Etruscan silver mirror.

1984, Nov. 9   *Perf. 13½x14*
1610	A793	550 l multicolored	.55	.30
1611	A793	550 l multicolored	.55	.30
1612	A793	550 l multicolored	.55	.30
a.		Strip of 3, #1610-1612	3.25	3.00

Journalistic Information — A794

350 l, Globe, paper tape, microwave dish.

1985, Jan. 15   Photo.   *Perf. 13½x14*
1613	A794	350 l multicolored	.60	.35

Modern Problems — A795

1985, Jan. 23   Photo.   *Perf. 13½x14*
1614	A795	250 l Aging	.45	.45

A796

Italia '85. No. 1615, The Hunt, by Raphael (1483-1520). No. 1616, Emblem. No. 1617, Detail from fresco by Baldassare Peruzzi (1481-1536) in Bishop's Palace, Ostia Antica.

Photo. and Engr., Photo. (#1616)
1985, Feb. 13   *Perf. 13½x14*
1615	A796	600 l multi	.80	.30
1616	A796	600 l multi	.80	.30
1617	A796	600 l multi	.80	.30
a.		Strip of 3, #1615-1617	3.25	3.00

Faience Tiles, Plate, Flask and Covered Bowl A797

Italian ceramics: No. 1619, Tile mural, gladiators in combat.

1985, Mar. 2   Photo.   *Perf. 14x13½*
1618	A797	600 l multi	.60	.30
1619	A797	600 l multi	.60	.30
a.		Pair, #1618-1619 + label	2.25	1.75

Italian Vehicle Type of 1984
1985, Mar. 21
1620	A782	450 l Lancia Thema	.70	.55
1621	A782	450 l Fiat Abarth	.70	.55
1622	A782	450 l Fiat Uno	.70	.55
1623	A782	450 l Lamborghini	.70	.55
a.		Block of 4, #1620-1623 + 2 labels	9.00	9.00

A799

Italia '85: No. 1624, Church of St. Mary of Peace, Rome, by Pietro di Cortona (1596-1669). No. 1625, Exhibition emblem. No. 1626, Church of St. Agnes, Rome, fountain and obelisk.

Photo. and Engr., Photo. (#1625)
1985, Mar. 30   *Perf. 13½x14*
1624	A799	250 l multi	.30	.30
1625	A799	250 l multi	.30	.30
1626	A799	250 l multi	.30	.30
a.		Strip of 3, #1624-1626	2.00	1.50

Pope Sixtus V, (1520-1590), 400th Anniv. of Papacy — A800

Sixtus V, dome of St. Peter's Basilica, Rome.

1985, Apr. 24   *Litho. and Engr.*
1627	A800	1500 l multi	2.25	1.10

Folk Celebration Type of 1982

Folktales: No. 1628, The March of the Turks, Potenza. No. 1629, San Marino Republican Regatta, Amalfi.

1985, May 29   Photo.
1628	A754	250 l multi	.70	.60
1629	A754	350 l multi	1.00	.60

Tourist Type of 1974

Scenic views: 350 l, Bormio town center. 400 l, Mt. Vesuvius from Castellamare di Stabia. 450 l, Stromboli Volcano from the sea. 600 l, Beach, old town at Termoli.

1985, June 1   *Perf. 14*
1630	A616	350 l multi	.85	1.50
1631	A616	400 l multi	.80	.35
1632	A616	450 l multi	.90	.35
1633	A616	600 l multi	1.25	.70
		Nos. 1630-1633 (4)	3.80	2.90

Nature Conservation — A803

No. 1634, European beaver. No. 1635, Primula. No. 1636, Nebrodi pine. No. 1637, Italian sandpiper.

1985, June 5   *Perf. 13½x14*
1634	A803	500 l multicolored	.60	.45
1635	A803	500 l multicolored	.60	.45
1636	A803	500 l multicolored	.60	.45
1637	A803	500 l multicolored	.60	.45
a.		Block of 4, #1634-1637	10.00	10.00

Art Type of 1981

Designs: No. 1638, Madonna bu Il Sassoferrato, G.B. Salvi, 1609-1685. No. 1639, Pride of the Work by Mario Sironi, 1885-1961.

Lithographed and Engraved
1985, June 15   *Perf. 14*
1638	A738	350 l multi	1.00	1.00
1639	A738	400 l multi	1.20	.95

Europa — A805

ITALY

Tenors and Composers: 500 l, Aureliano Pertile (1885-1969) and Giovanni Martinelli (1885-1962). 600 l, Johann Sebastian Bach (1685-1750) and Vincenzo Bellini (1801-1835).

1985, June 20	Photo.	Perf. 13½x14
1640 A805 500 l multi		3.50 .80
1641 A805 600 l multi		5.00 1.10

San Salvatore Abbey, Monte Amiata, 950th Anniv. — A806

Lithographed and Engraved		
1985, Aug. 1		Perf. 14x13½
1642 A806 450 l multi		.60 .30

World Cycling Championships A807

1985, Aug. 21		Photo.
1643 A807 400 l multi		1.00 .35

7th Intl. Congress for Crime Prevention, Milan, Aug. 26-Sept. 6 — A808

1985, Aug. 26		
1644 A808 600 l multi		1.25 .45

Intl. Youth Year — A809

1985, Sept. 3		
1645 A809 600 l multi		1.25 .45

Villa Type of 1980

Designs: 300 l, Nitti, Maratea. 400 l, Aldrovandi Mazzacorati, Bologna. 500 l, Santa Maria, Pula. 600 l, De Mersi, Villazzano.

Lithographed and Engraved		
1985, Oct. 1		Perf. 14x13½
1646 A719 300 l multi		1.00 .35
1647 A719 400 l multi		1.50 .35
1648 A719 500 l multi		1.50 .30
1649 A719 600 l multi		2.25 .35
Nos. 1646-1649 (4)		6.25 1.35

Natl. and Papal Arms, Treaty Document A810

1985, Oct. 15		Photo.
1650 A810 400 l multi		.75 .35

Ratification of new Concordat with the Vatican.

Souvenir Sheets

Parma #10, View of Parma — A812

A813

Sardinia #1, Great Britain #1 — A814

No. 1651: b, Two Sicilies #3, Naples. c, Two Sicilies #10, Palermo. d, Modena #3, Modena. e, Roman States #8, Rome. f, Tuscany #5, Florence. g, Sardinia #15, Turin. h, Romagna #7, Bologna. i, Lombardy-Venetia #4, Milan.
No. 1652a, Switzerland #3L1. b, Japan #1. c, US #2. d, Western Australia #1. e, Mauritius #4.

Lithographed and Engraved		
1985, Oct. 25		Perf. 14
1651 A812 Sheet of 9		5.00 5.00
a.-i. 300 l, any single		.40 .40
		Perf. 14x13½
1652 A813 Sheet of 5 + label		5.00 5.00
a.-e. 500 l, any single		.85 .45
		Imperf.
1653 A814 4000 l multi		5.50 4.00

Italia '85, Rome, Oct. 25-Nov. 3.

Long-distance Skiing — A815

1986, Jan. 25	Photo.	Perf. 14x13½
1654 A815 450 l multi		.80 .45

Folk Celebration Type of 1982

Design: Procession of St. Agnes, Le Candelore Folk Festival, Catania.

1986, Feb. 3		Perf. 13½x14
1655 A754 450 l multi		.75 .25

Amilcare Ponchielli (1834-1886), Composer A816

2000 l, Scene from La Giaconda.

Photogravure and Engraved		
1986, Mar. 8		Perf. 14x13½
1656 A816 2000 l multicolored		3.00 .55

Castle Type of 1980

Designs: 380 l, Vignola, Modena. 650 l, Montecchio Castle, Castiglion Fiorentino. 750 l, Rocca di Urbisaglia.

		Perf. 14x13½
1986-90	Photo.	Wmk. 303
1657 A717 380 l multi ('87)		.55 .25
1658 A717 650 l multi		.90 .25
		Engr.
1659 A717 750 l multi ('90)		1.10 .25
Nos. 1657-1659 (3)		2.55 .75

Issue date: 750 l, Sept. 20.

Coil Stamps

100 l, St. Severa. 500 l, Norman Castle, Melfi. 600 l, Scaligero, Sirmione. 650 l, Serralunga D'Alba. 750 l, Venafro. 800 l, Rocca Maggiore, Assisi.

	Perf. 14 Vert.	
1988-91	Engr.	Wmk. 303
	Size: 16x21mm	
1661 A717 100 l brown		.25 .25
1662 A717 500 l blue		.80 .40
1663 A717 600 l green		.95 .55
1664 A717 650 l bright mauve		.90 .60
1665 A717 750 l violet		1.10 .65
1666 A717 800 l red		1.25 .65
Nos. 1661-1666 (6)		5.25 3.10

Issued: 600 l, 800 l, 2/20/91; others, 3/1/88.

Giovanni Battista Pergolesi (1710-1736), Musician — A817

		Perf. 13½x14
1986, Mar. 15	Photo.	Unwmk.
1667 A817 2000 l multi		3.25 1.00

The Bay, Acitrezza A818

450 l, Piazzetta, Capri. 550 l, Kursaal, Merano. 650 l, Lighthouse, San Benedetto del Tronto.

1986, Mar. 24		Perf. 14
1668 A818 350 l shown		.65 .50
1669 A818 450 l multicolored		.85 .50
1670 A818 550 l multicolored		1.00 .35
1671 A818 650 l multicolored		1.25 .50
Nos. 1668-1671 (4)		3.75 1.85

Europa 1986 — A819

Trees in special shapes: a, Heart (life). b, Star (poetry). c, Butterfly (color). d, Sun (energy).

1986, Apr. 28	Photo.	Perf. 13x14
1672 Block of 4		10.00 10.00
a.-d. A819 650 l, any single		1.10 .45

25th Intl. Opthalmological Congress, Rome, May 4-10 — A820

1986, May 3	Photo.	Perf. 14
1673 A820 550 l multi		.80 .25

Police in Uniform A821

1986, May 10		
1674 A821 550 l multi		1.25 .55
1675 A821 650 l multi		1.50 .90

European Police Conference, Chianciano Terme, May 10-12. Nos. 1674-1675 printed se-tenant with labels picturing male or female police.

Battle of Bezzecca, 120th Anniv. — A822

1986, May 31		Perf. 14x13½
1676 A822 550 l multi		.85 .35

Memorial Day for Independence Martyrs — A823

1986, May 31		Perf. 14
1677 A823 2000 l multi		3.25 .90

Bersaglieri Corps of Mountain Troops, 150th Anniv. — A824

1986, June 1		Perf. 13½x14
1678 A824 450 l multi		1.10 .35

Telecommunications — A825

1986, June 16		Perf. 14x13½
1679 A825 350 l multi		.55 .35

Sacro Monte di Varallo Monastery A826

1986, June 28	Engr.	Perf. 14
1680 A826 2000 l Prus bl & sage grn		3.25 1.00

Italian Vehicle Type of 1984

No. 1681, Alfa Romeo AR8 Turbo. No. 1682, Innocenti 650 SE. No. 1683, Ferrari Testarossa. No. 1684, Fiatallis FR 10B.

1986, July 4	Photo.	Perf. 14x13½
1681 A782 450 l multi		.65 .50
1682 A782 450 l multi		.65 .50
1683 A782 450 l multi		.65 .50
1684 A782 450 l multi		.65 .50
a. Block of 4, #1681-1684 + 2 labels		9.00 9.00

Ladies' Fashions A827

Breda Heavy Industry A828

Olivetti Computer Technology A829

1986, July 14		
1685 A827 450 l shown		1.20 .45
1686 A827 450 l Men's fashions		1.20 .45
a. Pair, #1685-1686 + label		7.50 7.50
1687 A828 650 l shown		2.00 .45
1688 A829 650 l shown		2.00 .45
Nos. 1685-1688 (4)		6.40 1.80

Alitalia, Italian Airlines, 40th Anniv. — A830

550 l, Anniv. emblem. 650 l, Jet, runway lights.

ITALY

1986, Sept. 16 **Photo.** *Perf. 14x13½*
1689 A830 550 l multi .... 1.00 .40
1690 A830 650 l multi .... 1.25 .40

Villa Type of 1980
No. 1691, Necker, Trieste. No. 1692, Borromeo, Cassano D'Adda. No. 1693, Palagonia, Bagheria. No. 1694, Medicea, Poggio a Caiano. No. 1695, Castello d'Issogne, Issogne.

1986, Oct. 1 **Photo. & Engr.**
1691 A719 350 l multi .... .60 .45
1692 A719 350 l multi .... .60 .45
1693 A719 450 l multi .... .85 .30
1694 A719 550 l multi .... .85 .30
1695 A719 650 l multi .... 1.15 .50
Nos. 1691-1695 (5) 4.05 2.00

Christmas — A831
Madonna and Child, bronze sculpture by Donatello, Basilica del Santo, Padua.

1986, Oct. 10 *Engr.* *Perf. 14*
1696 A831 450 l brown olive .... .70 .25

Art Type of 1981
Designs: 450 l, Seated Woman Holding a Book, drawing by Andrea del Sarto, Uffizi, Florence, vert. 550 l, Daphne at Pavarola, painting by Felice Casorati, Museum of Modern Art, Turin, vert.

1986, Oct. 11 **Litho. & Engr.**
1697 A738 450 l blk & pale org .... 1.50 .35
1698 A738 550 l multi .... 1.75 .40

Memorial, Globe, Plane — A832

Plane, Cross, Men — A833

1986, Nov. 11 **Photo.** *Perf. 13½x14*
1699 A832 550 l multi .... .95 .40
1700 A833 650 l multi .... 1.10 .40

Intl. Peace Year, memorial to Italian airmen who died at Kindu, Zaire, while on a peace mission.

Stamp Day — A834

1986, Nov. 29 *Perf. 14x13½*
1701 A834 550 l Die of Sardinia No. 2 .... 1.10 .25

Francesco Matraire, printer of first Sardinian stamps.

Industries A836

A835

No. 1702, Marzotto Textile, 1836. No. 1703, Italgas Energy Corp., 1837.

Perf. 14½x13½

1987, Feb. 27 **Photo.**
1702 A835 700 l multi .... 1.00 .55
1703 A836 700 l multicolored .... 1.00 .55

Environmental Protection — A837

Designs: a, Volturno River. b, Garda Lake. c, Trasimeno Lake. d, Tirso River.

1987, Mar. 6 **Litho.** *Perf. 14x13½*
1704 A837 Block of 4 .... 7.50 7.50
  a.-d. 500 l, any single .... .85 .40

Antonio Gramsci (1891-1937), Author and Artist — A838

1987, Apr. 27 **Litho.** *Perf. 14x13½*
1705 A838 600 l scar & gray black .... 1.00 .40

Europa 1987 — A839

Modern architecture: 600 l, Church of Sun Motorway, Florence, designed by Michelucci. 700 l, Railway station, Rome, designed by Nervi.

1987, May 4 **Photo.**
1706 A839 600 l multi .... 2.00 .60
1707 A839 700 l multi .... 2.75 .60

Tourist Type of 1974
380 l, Verbania Pallanza. 400 l, Palmi. 500 l, Vasto. 600 l, Villacidro.

1987, May 9 *Perf. 14*
1708 A616 380 l multi .... .75 .60
1709 A616 400 l multi .... .85 .60
1710 A616 500 l multi .... 1.00 .50
1711 A616 600 l multi .... 1.25 .50
Nos. 1708-1711 (4) 3.85 2.20

Naples Soccer Club, Nat'l. Champions — A840

1987, May 18 **Litho.** *Perf. 13½x14*
1712 A840 500 l multi 2.00 1.60

The Absinthe Drinkers, by Degas — A841

1987, May 29
1713 A841 380 l multi .... .90 .45
Fight against alcoholism.

St. Alfonso M. de Liguori (1696-1787) and Gulf of Naples — A842

1987, Aug. 1 *Perf. 14x13½*
1714 A842 400 l multi .... .70 .40

Events — A843

Emblems and natl. landmarks: No. 1715, OLYMPHILEX '87, Intl. Olympic Committee Building, Foro Italico, Rome. No. 1716, World Athletics Championships, Olympic Stadium, Rome.

1987, Aug. 29 **Photo.** *Perf. 14x14½*
1715 A843 700 l multi .... 1.10 .30
1716 A843 700 l multi .... 1.10 .30

Folk Celebration Type of 1982
Design: Quintana Joust, Foligno.

Perf. 13½x14½

1987, Sept. 12 **Photo.**
1717 A754 380 l multi .... .75 .35

Piazzas — A844

380 l, Piazza del Popolo, Ascoli Piceno. 500 l, Piazza Giuseppe Verdi, Palermo. 600 l, Piazza San Carlo, Turin. 700 l, Piazza dei Signori, Verona.

Litho. & Engr.
1987, Oct. 10 *Perf. 14x13½*
1718 A844 380 l multi .... .75 .45
1719 A844 500 l multi .... 1.00 .30
1720 A844 600 l multi .... 1.00 .30
1721 A844 700 l multi .... 1.00 .50
Nos. 1718-1721 (4) 3.75 1.55
See Nos. 1747-1748, 1765-1766.

Christmas — A845

Paintings by Giotto: 500 l, Adoration in the Manger, Basilica of St. Francis, Assisi. 600 l, The Epiphany, Scrovegni Chapel, Padua.

1987, Oct. 15 **Photo.** *Perf. 13½x14*
1722 A845 500 l multi .... 1.00 .30
1723 A845 600 l multi .... 1.25 .30

Battle of Mentana, 120th Anniv. — A846

Litho. & Engr.
1987, Nov. 3 *Perf. 14x13½*
1724 A846 380 l multi .... .90 .35

Il Pantocrator (Christ), Mosaic, Monreale Cathedral A847

Coat of Arms and San Carlo Theater, Naples, from an 18th Cent. Engraving A848

1987, Nov. 4 *Perf. 14*
1725 A847 500 l multi .... 1.25 .50
1726 A848 500 l multi .... 1.25 .50
Artistic heritage. See Nos. 1768-1769.

Nunziatella Military School, 200th Anniv. — A849

1987, Nov. 14 *Perf. 14x13½*
1727 A849 600 l multi .... 1.05 .40

Stamp Day — A850

Philatelist Marco DeMarchi (d. 1936) holding magnifying glass and stamp album, Milan Cathedral.

1987, Nov. 20 **Photo.** *Perf. 13½x14*
1728 A850 500 l multi .... 1.40 .45

Homo Aeserniensis (Flint Knapper) — A851

Photo. & Engr.
1988, Feb. 6 *Perf. 13½x14*
1729 A851 500 l multi .... .90 .55
Remains of Isernia Man, c. 736,000 years-old, discovered near Isernia.

E. Quirino Visconti School, Rome — A852

Litho. & Engr.
1988, Mar. 1 *Unwmk.* *Perf. 14x13½*
1730 A852 500 l multi .... .75 .40
See Nos. 1764, 1824, 1842.

St. John Bosco (1815-1888), Educator — A853

1988, Apr. 2 **Photo.** *Perf. 13½x14*
1731 A853 500 l multi .... .75 .55

Art Type of 1981
Painting: The Archaeologists, by Giorgio de Chirico (1888-1978).

1988, Apr. 7 *Engr.* *Perf. 14*
1732 A738 650 l multi, vert. .... 1.75 .65

1st Printed Hebrew Bible, 500th Anniv. — A854

Soncino Bible excerpt, 15th cent.

1988, Apr. 22 **Photo.** *Perf. 14x13½*
1733 A854 550 l multi .... .80 .45

Epilepsy Foundation A855

ITALY

Design: St. Valentine, electroencephalograph readout, epileptic in seizure and medieval crest.

1988, Apr. 23
1734 A855 500 l multi .85 .50

Transport and communication: 650 l, ETR 450 locomotive. 750 l, Electronic mail, map of Italy.

1988, May 2
1735 A856 650 l multi 1.75 .60
1736 A856 750 l multi 2.25 .85

Tourist Type of 1974
Scenic views: 400 l, Castiglione della Pescaia. 500 l, Lignano Sabbiadoro. 650 l, Noto. 750 l, Vieste.

1988, May 7 Photo. *Perf. 14*
1737 A616 400 l multi .60 .85
1738 A616 500 l multi .80 .65
1739 A616 650 l multi 1.00 .75
1740 A616 750 l multi 1.25 1.10
  Nos. 1737-1740 (4) 3.65 3.35

1988, May 16
1741 A858 500 l Golf .80 .45

1990 World Cup Soccer Championships A859

1988, May 16 Litho. *Perf. 14x13½*
1742 A859 3150 l blk, grn & dark red 3.75 2.75

1988 Natl. Soccer Championships, Milan — A860

1988, May 23 *Perf. 13½x14*
1743 A860. 650 l multi .75 .55

Bronze Sculpture, Pergola A861

1988, June 4 Engr. *Perf. 14*
1744 A861 500 l Horse .85 .75
1745 A861 650 l Woman .95 .75

Bologna University, 900th Anniv. — A862

1988, June 10 Engr. *Perf. 13½x14*
1746 A862 500 l violet .75 .50

Piazza Type of 1987
Designs: 400 l, Piazza del Duomo, Pistoia. 550 l, Piazza del Unita d'Italia, Trieste.

1988, July 2 Litho. & Engr. *Perf. 14x13½*
1747 A844 400 l multi .70 .55
1748 A844 550 l multi .95 .50

Folk Celebration Type of 1982
Discesa Dei Candelieri, Sassari: Man wearing period costume, column and bearers.

1988, Aug. 13 Photo. *Perf. 13½x14*
1749 A754 550 l multi 1.30 .40

Intl. Gastroenterology and Digestive Endoscopy Congress, Rome — A863

1988, Sept. 5
1750 A863 750 l multi 1.10 .55

Neorealistic Films — A864

Italian films amd directors: 500 l, *Ossessione*, 1942, by Luchino Visconti. 650 l, *Ladri di Biciclette*, 1948, by Vittorio DeSica. 2400 l, *Roma Citta Aperta*, 1945, by Roberto Rossellini. 3050 l, *Riso Amaro*, 1949, by Giuseppe DeSantis.

1988, Oct. 13 Litho. *Perf. 14x13½*
1751 A864 500 l multi .85 1.10
1752 A864 650 l multi 1.00 1.30
1753 A864 2400 l multi 4.00 1.50
1754 A864 3050 l multi 5.50 2.25
  Nos. 1751-1754 (4) 11.35 6.15

Elsag A865

Aluminia A866

State Mint and Polygraphic Insitute A867

Italian Industries.

1988, Oct. 19 Photo.
1755 A865 750 l multi 1.00 .60
1756 A866 750 l multi 1.00 .60

Photo. & Engr.
1757 A867 750 l multi 1.00 .60
  Nos. 1755-1757 (3) 3.00 1.80

Christmas: *Nativity*, by Pasquale Celommi, Church of the Virgin's Assumption — A868

1988, Oct. 29 Photo. *Perf. 13½x14*
1758 A868 650 l multi 1.40 .25

Christmas A869

Photo. & Engr.
1988, Nov. 12 *Perf. 14x13½*
1759 A869 500 l dark blue grn & chest brn 1.25 .45

St. Charles Borromeo (1538-1584), Ecclesiastical Reformer — A870

1988, Nov. 4 Litho. & Engr.
1760 A870 2400 l multi 3.50 1.25

Stamp Day — A871

Japan #69 & stamp designer Edoardo Chiossone.

1988, Dec. 9 Photo. *Perf. 13½x14*
1761 A871 500 l multi .80 .40

Campaign Against AIDS — A872

1989, Jan. 13
1762 A872 650 l multi 1.00 .35

Paris-Peking Rally A873

3150 l, Map, Itala race car.

1989, Jan. 21 *Perf. 14½x13½*
1763 A873 3150 l multicolored 4.25 4.25

School Type of 1988
1989 Photo. & Engr. *Perf. 14x13½*
1764 A852 650 l multi .85 .40

Piazza Type of 1987
No. 1765, Piazza Del Duomo, Catanzaro.
No. 1766, Piazza Di Spagna, Rome.

Litho. & Engr.
1989, Apr. 10 *Perf. 14x13½*
1765 A844 400 l multi .65 .65
1766 A844 400 l multi .65 .65

Velo World Yachting Championships — A875

1989, Apr. 8 Photo. *Perf. 14*
1767 A875 3050 l multi 4.25 1.00

Artistic Heritage Type of 1987
Art and architecture: 500 l, King with scepter and orb, Palazzo Della Ragione, Padova, vert. 650 l, Crypt of St. Nicolas, St. Nicolas Basilica, Bari, vert.

1989, Apr. 8 Litho. & Engr., Engr.
1768 A847 500 l multi .85 .75
1769 A847 650 l indigo 1.10 .75

Europa 1989 — A876

Children's games: 500 l, Leapfrog, horiz. 650 l, Playing dress-up. 750 l, Sack race, horiz.

  Perf. 14x13½, 13½x14
1989, May 8 Photo.
1770 A876 500 l multicolored 1.10 .50
1771 A876 650 l shown 1.40 .50
1772 A876 750 l multicolored 1.60 .50
  Nos. 1770-1772 (3) 4.10 1.50

European Parliament 3rd Elections — A877

1989, June 3 *Perf. 13½x14*
1773 A877 500 l multi 1.00 .55

No. 1773 also inscribed in European Currency Units "ECU 0,31."

Pisa University A878

1989, May 29 Engr. *Perf. 14x13½*
1774 A878 500 l violet .80 .40

Folk Celebration Type of 1982
Priest and Flower Feast street scene.

1989, May 27 Photo. *Perf. 13½x14*
1775 A754 400 l multi .65 .55

Tourist Type of 1974
1989, June 10 Photo. *Perf. 14*
1776 A616 500 l Naxos Gardens 1.00 .65
1777 A616 500 l Spotorno 1.00 .65
1778 A616 500 l Pompei 1.00 .65
1779 A616 500 l Grottammare 1.00 .65
  Nos. 1776-1779 (4) 4.00 2.60

Ministry of Posts, Cent. — A879

500 l, Posthorn, No. 52. 2400 l, Posthorn, Earth.

1989, June 24 *Perf. 14x13½*
1780 A879 500 l multicolored .80 1.25
1781 A879 2400 l multicolored 3.25 1.00

INTER Soccer Championships A880

1989, June 26
1782 A880 650 l multi .85 .55

Interparliamentary Union, Cent. — A881

1989, June 28
1783 A881 750 l multi .90 .65

ITALY

French Revolution, Bicent. — A882

1989, July 7	Photo.	Perf. 14
1784	A882 3150 l multi	4.25 4.25

Fortified Walls of Corinaldo, by Francesco di Giorgio Martini (1439-1502) — A883

1989, Sept. 2	Litho. & Engr.	Perf. 14
1785	A883 500 l multi	.90 .45

Charlie Chaplin (1889-1977) — A884

1989, Sept. 23	Engr.	Perf. 14x13½
1786	A884 750 l black & sepia	1.10 .50

Naples-Portici Railway, 150th Anniv. — A885

1989, Oct. 3		Litho. & Engr.
1787	550 l Denom at UL	.55 .25
1788	550 l Denom at UR	.55 .25
a.	A885 Pair, #1787-1788	1.60 1.60

Adoration of the Kings, by Correggio — A887

1989, Oct. 21	Photo.	Perf. 13½x14
1789	500 l multicolored	.65 .45
1790	500 l multicolored	.65 .45
a.	A887 Pair, #1789-1790	1.50 1.25

Christmas.

Fidardo Castle, the Stradella, Accordion — A889

Industries: No. 1791, Music. No. 1792, Arnoldo World Publishing.

1989, Oct. 14	Photo.	Perf. 14x13½
1791	A889 450 l multicolored	.65 .50
1792	A889 450 l multicolored	.65 .50

Stamp Day — A890

1989, Nov. 24		Perf. 13½x14
1793	A890 500 l Emilio Diena	.90 .45

1990 World Soccer Championships, Italy — A891

1989, Dec. 9	Engr.	Perf. 13½x14
1794	A891 450 l multicolored	.65 .40

Columbus's First Voyage, 1474-1484 — A892

1990, Feb. 24		Photo.
1795	700 l Denom at UL	.90 .30
1796	700 l Denom at UR	.90 .30
a.	A892 Pair, #1795-1796	2.00 1.75

Souvenir Sheets

1990 World Cup Soccer Championships, Italy — A894

Soccer club emblems and stadiums in Italy. No. 1797: a, Italy. b, US. c, Olympic Stadium, Rome. d, Municipal Stadium, Florence. e, Austria. f, Czechoslovakia.
No. 1798: a, Argentina. b, Russia. c, St. Paul Stadium, Naples. d, New Stadium, Bari. e, Cameroun. f, Romania.
No. 1799: a, Brazil. b, Costa Rica. c, Alps Stadium, Turin. d, Ferraris Stadium, Genoa. e, Sweden. f, Scotland.
No. 1800: a, UAE. b, West Germany. c, Dall'ara Stadium, Bologna. d, Meazza Stadium, Milan. e, Colombia. f, Yugoslavia.
No. 1801: a, Belgium. b, Uruguay. c, Bentegodi Stadium, Verona. d, Friuli Stadium, Udine. e, South Korea. f, Spain.
No. 1802: a, England. b, Netherlands. c, Sant'elia Stadium, Cagliari. d, La Favorita Stadium, Palermo. e, Ireland. f, Egypt.

1990, Mar. 24		Perf. 14x13½
1797	A894 Sheet of 6	3.00 3.00
a.-f.	450 l any single	.45 .85
1798	A894 Sheet of 6	4.00 4.00
a.-f.	600 l any single	.65 .85
1799	A894 Sheet of 6	4.50 4.50
a.-f.	650 l any single	.80 .65
1800	A894 Sheet of 6	5.00 5.00
a.-f.	700 l any single	.85 .65
1801	A894 Sheet of 6	5.50 5.50
a.-f.	800 l any single	1.00 .65
1802	A894 Sheet of 6	8.00 8.00
a.-f.	1200 l any single	1.40 1.25
	Nos. 1797-1802 (6)	30.00 30.00

See No. 1819.

Tourist Type of 1974

No. 1803, Sabbioneta. No. 1804, Montepulciano. No. 1805, Castellammare del Golfo. No. 1806, San Felice Circeo.

1990, Mar. 30	Photo.	Perf. 14
1803	A616 600 l multicolored	.75 .45
1804	A616 600 l multicolored	.75 .45
1805	A616 600 l multicolored	.75 .45
1806	A616 600 l multicolored	.75 .45
	Nos. 1803-1806 (4)	3.00 1.80

Folk Celebration Type of 1982

Design: Horse race, Merano.

1990, Apr. 9		Perf. 13½x14
1807	A754 600 l multicolored	.80 .45

Aurelio Saffi, Death Cent. — A895

1990, Apr. 10		Perf. 14
1808	A895 700 l multicolored	.85 .45

Giovanni Giorgi (1871-1950) — A896

1990, Apr. 23		Perf. 14x13½
1809	A896 600 l multicolored	.75 .45

Metric System in Italy, 55th. anniv.

Labor Day, Cent. — A897

1990, Apr. 28	Photo.	Perf. 13½x14
1810	A897 600 l multicolored	.75 .40

Naples Soccer Club, Italian Champions — A898

1990, Apr. 30		Perf. 13½x14
1811	A898 700 l multicolored	1.25 .75

Europa — A899

Post Offices: 700 l, San Silvestro Piazza, Rome. 800 l, Fondaco Tedeschi, Venice.

1990, May 7		Perf. 14x13½
1812	A899 700 l multicolored	1.25 .45
1813	A899 800 l multicolored	2.25 .45

Giovanni Paisiello (1740-1816), Composer — A900

1990, May 9		Perf. 14x13½
1814	A900 450 l multicolored	.65 .65

Dante Alighieri (1265-1321), Poet — A901

1990, May 12		Perf. 14x13½
1815	A901 700 l multicolored	.85 .45

Dante Alighieri Soc., cent.

Mosaic (Detail) — A902

Sculpture — A903

Photo. (#1816), Litho. & Engr. (#1817)

1990, May 19		Perf. 13½x14
1816	A902 450 l multicolored	.55 .85
1817	A903 700 l multicolored	.85 .55

Malatestiana Music Festival, Rimini, 40th Anniv. — A904

1990, June 15	Photo.	Perf. 14
1818	A904 600 l multicolored	.75 .45

World Cup Soccer Type of 1990 Inscribed "Campione Del Mondo"

1990, July 9	Litho.	Perf. 14x13½
1819	A894 600 l like No. 1800b	.90 .90

Still Life, by Giorgio Morandi (1890-1964) — A905

1990, July 20	Engr.	Perf. 14
1820	A905 750 l black	1.00 .65

Greco-Roman Wrestling, World Championships — A906

1990, Oct. 11	Litho.	Perf. 14x13½
1821	A906 3200 l multicolored	4.00 1.10

Christmas — A907

Paintings of the Nativity by: 600 l, Emidio Vangelli. 750 l, Pellegrino.

1990, Oct. 26		Perf. 14
1822	A907 600 l multicolored	.70 .35
1823	A907 750 l multicolored	1.00 .45

School Type of 1988 and

Italian Schools — A908

Designs: 600 l, Bernardino Telesio gymnasium, Cosenza. 750 l, University of Catania.

1990, Nov. 5	Litho. & Engr.	Perf. 14x13½
1824	A852 600 l multicolored	.70 .35
	Engr.	
1825	A908 750 l multicolored	.90 .45

ITALY

Stamp Day — A909

Self-portrait, Corrado Mezzana (1890-1952).

1990, Nov. 16   Litho.   Perf. 13½x14
1826 A909 600 l multicolored   .80 .45

The Nativity — A910

1991, Jan. 5   Litho.   Perf. 13½x14
1827 A910 600 l multicolored   .75 .45

Genoa Flower Show — A911

1991, Jan. 10   Perf. 14
1828 A911 750 l multicolored   .95 .45

Seal of the Univ. of Siena — A912

1991, Jan. 15   Photo.   Perf. 13½x14
1829 A912 750 l multicolored   .90 .45

Tourist Type of 1974

1991   Photo.
1830 A616 600 l San Remo   .80 .45
1831 A616 600 l Roccaraso   .80 .45
1832 A616 600 l La Maddalena   .80 .45
1833 A616 600 l Calgi   .80 .45
  Nos. 1830-1833 (4)   3.20 1.80

United Europe — A913

    Perf. 14x13½
1991, Mar. 12   Photo.   Unwmk.
1834 A913 750 l multi   .95 .25

No. 1834 also carries .48 ECU denomination.

Discovery of America, 500th Anniv. (in 1992) — A914

1991, Mar. 22   Litho.
1835   750 l Ships leaving port   1.00 .45
1836   750 l Columbus, Queen's court   1.00 .45
  a. A914 Pair, #1835-1836   2.00 2.00

Giuseppe Gioachino Belli (1791-1863), Poet — A916

1991, Apr. 15   Litho.   Perf. 14x13½
1837 A916 600 l bl & gray blk   .70 .45

Church of St. Gregory, Rome A917

1991, Apr. 20   Photo.   Perf. 14x13½
1838 A917 3200 l multicolored   3.75 1.40

Europa — A918

750 l, DRS satellite. 800 l, Hermes space shuttle.

1991, Apr. 29   Photo.   Perf. 14x13½
1839 A918 750 l multi   1.60 .70
1840 A918 800 l multi   1.60 .70

Santa Maria Maggiore Church, Lanciano — A919

1991, May 2   Engr.   Perf. 13½x14
1841 A919 600 l brown   .70 .45

Schools Type of 1988

Design: D. A. Azuni school, Sassari.

    Litho. & Engr.
1991, May 3   Perf. 14x13½
1842 A852 600 l multicolored   .70 .45

Team Genoa, Italian Soccer Champions, 1990-91 — A920

1991, May 27   Photo.   Perf. 13½x14
1843 A920 3000 l multicolored   3.00 2.25

Basketball, Cent. — A921

1991, June 5
1844 A921 500 l multicolored   .75 .50

No. 1844 exists with blue in place of purple at the bottom of the design. Value, $15,000.

Children's Rights — A922

750 l, Man, child with balloon.

1991, June 14
1845 A922 600 l shown   .70 .25
1846 A922 750 l multicolored   .90 .45

Art and Culture — A923

Designs: 600 l, Sculpture by Pericle Fazzini (b. 1913). 3200 l, Exhibition Hall, Turin, designed by Pier Luigi Nervi (1891-1979).

    Litho. & Engr.
1991, June 21   Perf. 14
1847 A923 600 l multicolored   .70 .70
1848 A923 3200 l multicolored   3.75 .90

Egyptian Museum, Turin — A924

1991, Aug. 31   Litho.   Perf. 13½x14
1849 A924 750 l grn, yel & gold   .95 .45

Luigi Galvani (1737-1798), Electrophysicist A925

1991, Sept. 24   Perf. 14x13½
1850 A925 750 l multicolored   .95 .30
  Radio, cent. (in 1995). See Nos. 1873, 1928, 1964.

Nature Protection A926

No. 1851, Marevivo posidonia. No. 1852, Falco pellegrino. No. 1853, Cervo sardo. No. 1854, Orso marsicano.

1991, Oct. 10   Photo.   Perf. 14x13½
1851 A926 500 l multicolored   .65 .60
1852 A926 500 l multicolored   .65 .60
1853 A926 500 l multicolored   .95 .60
1854 A926 500 l multicolored   .65 .60
  Nos. 1851-1854 (4)   2.90 2.40

World Wildlife Fund.

Wolfgang Amadeus Mozart, Death Bicent. — A927

1991, Oct. 7   Perf. 13½x14
1855 A927 800 l multicolored   1.00 .50

Christmas — A928

1991, Oct. 18
1856 A928 600 l multicolored   .75 .40

Giulio and Alberto Bolaffi, Philatelists A929

1991, Oct. 25   Perf. 14
1857 A929 750 l multicolored   .95 .50

Stamp Day.

Pietro Nenni (1891-1980), Politician A930

1991, Oct. 30
1858 A930 750 l multicolored   .95 .40

Fountain of Neptune, Florence, by Bartolomeo Ammannati (1511-1592) — A931

1992, Feb. 6   Photo.   Perf. 13½x14
1859 A931 750 l multicolored   .95 .50

22nd European Indoor Track Championships A932

1992, Jan. 30   Perf. 14x13½
1860 A932 600 l multicolored   .85 .40

University of Ferrara, 600th Anniv. — A933

1992, Mar. 4   Photo.   Perf. 13½x14
1861 A933 750 l multicolored   .90 .50

Castle Type of 1980

200 l, Cerro al Volturno. 250 l, Mondavio. 300 l, Bari. 450 l, Bosa. 850 l, Arechi, Salerno.

    Perf. 14x13½
1992-94   Photo.   Wmk. 303
1862 A717 200 l multicolored   .25 .25
1863 A717 250 l multicolored   .40 .25
1864 A717 300 l multicolored   .40 .25
1865 A717 450 l multicolored   .60 .25
1866 A717 850 l multicolored   .95 .40
  Nos. 1862-1866 (5)   2.60 1.40

Issued: 200 l, 250 l, 300 l, 450 l, 2/24/94; 850 l, 3/7/92.

University of Naples A934

1992, Mar. 9   Unwmk.   Perf. 14x13½
1872 A934 750 l multicolored   .95 .50

Radio Cent. Type of 1991

Alessandro Volta (1745-1827), Italian physicist.

1992, Mar. 26
1873 A925 750 l multicolored   1.10 .40
  Radio, cent. (in 1995).

ITALY

Genoa '92 Intl. Philatelic Exhibition — A935

1992, Mar. 27			Perf. 13½x14	
1874	A935	750 l multicolored	.90	.25

Lorenzo de Medici (1449-1492) A936

1992, Apr. 8			Perf. 14	
1875	A936	750 l bl & org brn	.90	.50

Filippini Institute, 300th Anniv. — A937

1992, May 2		Photo.	Perf. 13½x14	
1876	A937	750 l multicolored	.90	.45

Discovery of America, 500th Anniv. — A938

No. 1877, Columbus seeking Queen Isabella's support. No. 1878, Columbus' fleet. No. 1879, Sighting land. No. 1880, Landing in New World.

1992, Apr. 24		Photo.	Perf. 14x13½	
1877	A938	500 l multicolored	.75	.60
1878	A938	500 l multicolored	.75	.60
1879	A938	500 l multicolored	.75	.60
1880	A938	500 l multicolored	.75	.60
a.		Block of 4, #1877-1880	3.25	3.00

See US Nos. 2620-2623.

Discovery of America, 500th Anniv. — A939

Designs: 750 l, Monument to Columbus, Genoa. 850 l, Globe, Genoa '92 Exhibition emblem.

1992, May 2			Perf. 13½x14	
1881	A939	750 l multicolored	1.40	.65
1882	A939	850 l multicolored	1.75	.75

Europa.

Miniature Sheets

Voyages of Columbus — A940

Columbus: No. 1883: a, Presenting natives. b, Announcing his discovery. c, In chains. No. 1884: a, Welcomed at Barcelona. b, Restored to favor. c, Describing his 3rd voyage.
No. 1885: a, In sight of land. b, Fleet. c, Queen Isabella pledging her jewels.
No. 1886: a, Soliciting aid from Isabella. b, At La Rabida. c, Recall.
No. 1887: a, Landing. b, Santa Maria. c, Queen Isabella and Columbus. No. 1888, Columbus.
Nos. 1883-1888 are similar in design to US Nos. 230-245.

1992, May 22		Engr.	Perf. 10½	
1883	A940	Sheet of 3	6.50	5.50
a.		50 l olive black	.25	.25
b.		300 l dark blue green	.35	.25
c.		4000 l red violet	5.00	3.25
1884	A940	Sheet of 3	5.00	5.00
a.		100 l brown violet	.25	.25
b.		800 l magenta	.80	.60
c.		3000 l green	3.50	3.25
1885	A940	Sheet of 3	3.50	3.50
a.		200 l dark blue	.25	.25
b.		900 l ultra	1.10	.70
c.		1500 l orange	1.75	1.60
1886	A940	Sheet of 3	2.75	2.75
a.		400 l chocolate	.50	.50
b.		700 l vermillion	.90	.60
c.		1000 l slate blue	2.40	1.30
1887	A940	Sheet of 3	4.00	4.00
a.		500 l brown violet	.60	.50
b.		600 l dark green	.70	.60
c.		2000 l crimson lake	2.40	2.25
1888	A940	5000 l Sheet of 1	6.50	6.50
		Nos. 1883-1888 (6)	28.25	27.25

See US Nos. 2624-2629, Portugal Nos. 1918-1923 and Spain Nos. 2677-2682.

Tour of Italy Bicycle Race — A941

1992, May 23		Photo.	Perf. 14x13½	
1889	A941	750 l Ocean	.90	.35
1890	A941	750 l Mountains	.90	.35
a.		Pair, #1889-1890	2.00	1.75

No. 1890a printed in continuous design.

Milan, Italian Soccer Champions — A942

1992, May 25			Perf. 13½x14	
1891	A942	750 l black, red & grn	1.00	.50

Beach Resorts — A943

1992			Perf. 14x13½	
1892	A943	750 l Viareggio	.80	.45
1893	A943	750 l Rimini	.80	.45

Issued: No. 1892, 5/30; No. 1893, 6/13.

Tazio Nuvolari (1892-1953), Race Car Driver — A944

1992, June 5			Perf. 14x13½	
1900	A944	3200 l multicolored	4.00	1.40

Tourism Type of 1974

1992, June 30			Perf. 14	
1901	A616	600 l Arcevia	.70	.55
1902	A616	600 l Maratea	.70	.55
1903	A616	600 l Braies	.70	.55
1904	A616	600 l Pantelleria	.70	.55
		Nos. 1901-1904 (4)	2.80	2.20

The Shepherds, by Jacopo da Ponte — A945

Litho. & Engr.

1992, Sept. 5			Perf. 14	
1905	A945	750 l multicolored	.85	.45

Discovery of America, 500th Anniv. — A946

500 l, Columbus' house, Genoa. 600 l, Columbus' fleet. 750 l, Map. 850 l, Columbus pointing to land. 1200 l, Coming ashore. 3200 l, Columbus, art by Michelangelo.

1992, Sept. 18		Photo.	Perf. 13½x14	
1906	A946	500 l multicolored	.55	.50
1907	A946	600 l multicolored	.70	.30
1908	A946	750 l multicolored	.85	.40
1909	A946	850 l multicolored	.95	.60
1910	A946	1200 l multicolored	1.40	.90
1911	A946	3200 l multicolored	3.75	1.25
		Nos. 1906-1911 (6)	8.20	3.95

Genoa '92.

Stamp Day — A947

1992, Sept. 22			Perf. 14	
1912	A947	750 l multicolored	.95	.30

Self-Adhesive
Perf. 13½

| 1913 | A947 | 750 l multicolored | 2.00 | 1.50 |

Lions Intl., 75th Anniv. — A948

1992, Sept. 24			Perf. 14x13½	
1914	A948	3000 l multicolored	3.25	1.50

Single European Market — A949

1992, Oct. 5		Photo.	Perf. 14x13½	
1915	A949	600 l multicolored	.70	.50

Intl. Conference on Nutrition, Rome — A950

1992, Oct. 16		Photo.	Perf. 14x13½	
1916	A950	500 l multicolored	.65	.40

Christmas A951

1992, Oct. 31				
1917	A951	600 l multicolored	.80	.40

Miniature Sheet

United Europe A952

Buildings on natl. flags, inscriptions in native language: a, Italy (Benvenuta). b, Belgium (Bienvenue, Welkom). c, Denmark (Velkommen). d, France (Bienvenue L'Europe). e, Germany (Willkommen). f, Greece. g, Ireland (Failte). h, Luxembourg (Bienvenue Europe). i, Netherlands (Welkom). j, Portugal (Bem-Vinda). k, United Kingdom (Welcome). l, Spain (Bienvenida).

1993, Jan. 20		Photo.	Perf. 13½x14	
		Sheet of 12		
1918	A952	750 l #a.-l.	13.00	9.00

Meeting of Veterans of 1943 Battle of Nikolajewka, Russia — A953

1993, Jan. 23		Litho.	Perf. 14x13½	
1919	A953	600 l multicolored	1.25	.50

Carlo Goldoni (1707-93), Playwright — A954

Paintings depicting scenes from plays: No. 1920, Man in harlequin costume leaning on picture. No. 1921, Woman seated in front of harlequins.

1993, Feb. 6		Photo.	Perf. 13½x14	
1920	A954	500 l multicolored	.70	.55
1921	A954	500 l multicolored	.70	.55

Mosaic from the Piazza Armerina — A955

Photo. & Engr.

1993, Feb. 20			Perf. 14	
1922	A955	750 l multicolored	.95	.50

Natl. Health Day Promoting a Healthy Heart — A956

1993, Mar. 5		Photo.	Perf. 14x13½	
1923	A956	750 l multicolored	.95	.50

Cats — A957

No. 1924, European. No. 1925, Maine coon, vert. No. 1926, Devon Rex, vert. No. 1927, White Persian.

ITALY

1993, Mar. 6   *Perf. 14x13½, 13½x14*
1924	A957	600 l	multicolored	.75	.50
1925	A957	600 l	multicolored	.75	.50
1926	A957	600 l	multicolored	.75	.50
1927	A957	600 l	multicolored	.75	.50
Nos. 1924-1927 (4)   3.00   2.00

Radio Cent. Type of 1991
Design: 750 l, Temistocle Calzecchi Onesti.

1993, Mar. 26   Litho.   *Perf. 14x13½*
1928   A925   750 l   multicolored   .95   .30
Radio cent. (in 1995).

City Scene, by Francesco Guardi (1712-1793) — A958

1993, Apr. 6   Photo. & Engr.   *Perf. 14*
1929   A958   3200 l   multicolored   4.00   2.00

Horace (Quintus Horatius Flaccus), Poet and Satirist, 2000th Anniv. of Death — A959

1993, Apr. 19   Photo.   *Perf. 13½x14*
1930   A959   600 l   multicolored   .75   .40

Contemporary Paintings — A960

Europa: 750 l, Carousel Animals, by Lino Bianchi Barriviera. 850 l, Abstract, by Gino Severini.

1993, May 3
1931   A960   750 l   multicolored   .90   .60
1932   A960   850 l   multicolored   1.10   .50

Natl. Soccer Champions, Milan — A961

1993, May 24
1933   A961   750 l   multicolored   .95   .40

Natl. Academy of St. Luke, 400th Anniv. — A962

1993, May 31   Photo.
1934   A962   750 l   multicolored   .95   .40

St. Giuseppe Benedetto Cottolengo (1786-1842) — A963

1993, May   Photo. & Engr.
1935   A963   750 l   multicolored   .95   .30

Family Fest '93 — A964

1993, June 5   Photo.   *Perf. 14x13½*
1936   A964   750 l   multicolored   1.00   .50

Tourism — A965

No. 1937, Palmanova. No. 1938, Senigallia. No. 1939, Carloforte. No. 1940, Sorrento.

1993, June 28   Photo.   *Perf. 14x13½*
1937	A965	600 l	multicolored	.75	.45
1938	A965	600 l	multicolored	.75	.45
1939	A965	600 l	multicolored	.75	.45
1940	A965	600 l	multicolored	.75	.45
Nos. 1937-1940 (4)   3.00   1.80
See Nos. 1972-1975, 2032-2035.

1993 World Kayaking Championships, Trentino — A966

1993, July 1   *Perf. 13½x14*
1941   A966   750 l   multicolored   .95   .40

Regina Margherita Observatory, Cent. — A967

1993, Sept. 4   Photo.   *Perf. 14x13½*
1942   A967   500 l   multicolored   .75   .40

Museum Treasures — A968

Designs: No. 1943, Concert, by Bartolomeo Manfredi. No. 1944, Ancient map of Foggia. 750 l, Illuminated page with "S," vert. 850 l, The Death of Adonis, by Sebastiano Del Piombo.

Perf. 14x13½, 13½x14
1993, Nov. 27   Litho.
1943	A968	600 l	multicolored	.75	.40
1944	A968	600 l	multicolored	.75	.45
1945	A968	750 l	multicolored	1.00	.25
1946	A968	850 l	multicolored	1.00	.45
Nos. 1943-1946 (4)   3.50   1.55

Holy Stairway, Veroli — A969

1993, Sept. 25   Photo.   *Perf. 13½x14*
1947   A969   750 l   multicolored   .95   .30

World War II — A970

Events of 1943: No. 1948, Deportation of Jews from Italy, Oct. 16, 1943. No. 1949, Soldiers, helmet (Battle of Naples). No. 1950, Execution of the Cervi Brothers.

1993, Sept. 25
1948	A970	750 l	multicolored	1.00	.30
1949	A970	750 l	multicolored	1.00	.30
1950	A970	750 l	multicolored	1.00	.30
Nos. 1948-1950 (3)   3.00   .90
See Nos. 1984-1986.

Thurn and Taxis Postal History — A971

No. 1951, Coach. No. 1952, Coat of arms. No. 1953, Cart. No. 1954, Post rider on galloping horse. No. 1955, Post rider on walking horse.

1993, Oct. 2   *Perf. 14x13½*
1951	A971	750 l	multicolored	.90	.25
1952	A971	750 l	multicolored	.90	.25
1953	A971	750 l	multicolored	.90	.25
1954	A971	750 l	multicolored	.90	.25
1955	A971	750 l	multicolored	.90	.25
Nos. 1951-1955 (5)   4.50   1.25

Perf. 14 Horiz.
1951a	A971	750 l		.85	.65
1952a	A971	750 l		.85	.65
1953a	A971	750 l		.85	.65
1954a	A971	750 l		.85	.65
1955a	A971	750 l		.85	.65
   b.   Booklet pane of 5, #1951a-1955a   5.00   4.00

Bank Exterior — A972

1000 Lire Note — A972a

1993, Oct. 15   *Perf. 14x13½*
1956   A972   750 l   multi   1.00   .30
1957   A972a   1000 l   multi   2.00   .75
Bank of Italy, Cent. Nos. 1956-1957 were printed with se-tenant labels. Values, set of two with labels: $5.50 unused, $2.75 used.

Christmas — A973

Designs: 600 l, Living Creche in the town of Corchiano. 750 l, Detail of The Annunciation, by Piero Della Francesca.

1993, Oct. 26   Litho.   *Perf. 13½x14*
1958   A973   600 l   multicolored   .70   .40
1959   A973   750 l   multicolored   .95   .50

Stamp Day — A974

1993, Nov. 12   Photo.   *Perf. 14*
1960   A974   600 l   blue & red   .70   .40
First Italian colonial postage stamps, cent.

Circus — A975

600 l, Acrobat, horses. 750 l, Clown performing.

1994, Jan. 8   Litho.   *Perf. 13½x14*
1961   A975   600 l   multi   .75   .40
1962   A975   750 l   multi   .90   .50

Presence of Women in the Home — A976

1994, Feb. 14   Photo.   *Perf. 14*
1963   A976   750 l   multicolored   .95   .25

Radio Cent. Type of 1991
750 l, Augusto Righi (1850-1920), physicist.

Perf. 14x13½
1994, Mar. 11   Photo.   Unwmk.
1964   A925   750 l   multicolored   .95   .30
Radio cent. (in 1995).

Dogs — A977

No. 1965, German shepherd. No. 1966, Abruzzi sheepdog. No. 1967, Boxer. No. 1968, Dalmatian.

1994, Mar. 12   *Perf. 14x13*
1965	A977	600 l	multi	.75	.45
1966	A977	600 l	multi	.75	.45
1967	A977	600 l	multi	.75	.45
1968	A977	600 l	multi	.75	.45
Nos. 1965-1968 (4)   3.00   1.80

Italian Cuisine — A978

1994, Mar. 24   *Perf. 13x14*
1969   A978   500 l   Breads   .65   .45
1970   A978   600 l   Pasta   .90   .40

Procession Honoring Apparition of Christ, Tarquinia — A979

1994, Apr. 2   *Perf. 13½*
1971   A979   750 l   multicolored   1.00   .30

Tourism Type of 1993
No. 1972, Orta San Giulio. No. 1973, Santa Marinella. No. 1974, Messina. No. 1975, Monticchio, Potenza.

1994, Apr. 23   Photo.   *Perf. 14x13½*
1972	A965	600 l	multi	.75	.30
1973	A965	600 l	multi	.75	.30
1974	A965	600 l	multi	.75	.30
1975	A965	600 l	multi	.75	.30
Nos. 1972-1975 (4)   3.00   1.20

A981

Nobel Prize Winners: 750 l, Camillo Golgi (1844-1926), Physician, Medicine, 1906. 850 l, Guilio Natta (1903-), Chemistry, 1963.

1994, May 2   Photo.   *Perf. 13½x14*
1976   A981   750 l   multicolored   1.00   .40
1977   A981   850 l   multicolored   1.40   .50

ITALY

Publication of "Summa de Arithemtica, Geometria, Proportioni et Proportionalita," 500th Anniv. — A982

Fra Luca Pacioli (c. 1445-1514), mathematician.

1994, May 2   Photo.   Perf. 14x13
1978   A982   750 l   multicolored   1.00   .30

Lajos Kossuth (1802-94) — A983

1994, Apr. 30   Photo.   Perf. 13½x14
1979   A983   3750 l   multicolored   4.75   1.75

Milan, Winners of 1993-94 Italian Soccer Championships A984

1994, May 2   Perf. 14x13½
1980   A984   750 l   multicolored   1.25   .50

World Swimming Championships A985

1994, May 2   Photo.   Perf. 13½x14
1981   A985   600 l   Diving   .75   .45
1982   A985   750 l   Water polo   1.00   .30

Archaeology Exhibition, Rimini — A986

1994, May 6
1983   A986   750 l   multicolored   .95   .30

World War II Type of 1993

Events of 1944: No. 1984, Destruction of Monte Cassino. No. 1985, Massacre of the Ardeatine Caves. No. 1986, Massacre at Marzabotto.

1994, May 18
1984   A970   750 l   multicolored   .95   .25
1985   A970   750 l   multicolored   .95   .25
1986   A970   750 l   multicolored   .95   .25
  Nos. 1984-1986 (3)   2.85   .75

22nd Natl. Eucharistic Congress, Siena — A987

1994, May 28   Photo.   Perf. 13½x14
1987   A987   600 l   multicolored   .70   .40

Ariadne, Venus and Bacchus, by Tintoretto (1518-94) A988

1994, May 31   Perf. 14
1988   A988   750 l   multicolored   1.00   .40

Brotherhood of Mercy, Florence, 700th Anniv. — A989

1994, June 4   Perf. 14x13½
1989   A989   750 l   multicolored   .95   .25

European Parliamentary Elections — A990

1994, June 11   Photo.   Perf. 13½x14
1990   A990   600 l   multicolored   .95   .30

Natl. Museums — A991

No. 1991, Attic Krater, Natl. Archaeological Museum. No. 1992, Ancient drawing, Natl. Archives. 750 l, Statue, Natl. Roman Museum. 850 l, Medallion, Natl. Archives.

1994, June 16
1991   A991   600 l   multicolored   .75   .40
1992   A991   600 l   multicolored   .75   .40
1993   A991   750 l   multicolored   .90   .40
1994   A991   850 l   multicolored   .90   .40
  Nos. 1991-1994 (4)   3.30   1.60

Intl. Olympic Committee, Cent. — A992

1994, June 23
1995   A992   850 l   multicolored   1.25   .40

G-7 Summit, Naples — A993

1994, July 8
1996   A993   600 l   multicolored   .85   .40
A 750 l in this design was printed in error but not issued. Value, $17,000.

A995

1994, Sept. 8   Photo.   Perf. 14
1998   A995   500 l   multicolored   .95   .40
Basilica of Loreto, 500th anniv.

A996

1994, Sept. 19
1999   A996   750 l   multicolored   1.00   .25
Frederick II (1194-1250), Holy Roman Emperor.

Stamp Day — A998

Designs: 600 l, Pietro Miliani (1744-1817), paper manufacturer. 750 l, Convent of San Domenico.

1994, Sept. 16   Photo.   Perf. 13½x14
2001   A998   600 l   multicolored   .70   .45
2002   A998   750 l   multicolored   .90   .30

Basilica of St. Mark, 900th Anniv. — A999

1994, Oct. 8   Photo.   Perf. 13½x13
2003   A999   750 l   multicolored   1.00   .75
  a.   Souvenir sheet of 2, tete beche   2.25   2.25

No. 2003 printed with se-tenant label. No. 2003a contains one each No. 2003 and San Marino No. 1314. Only No. 2003 was valid for postage in Italy. See San Marino No. 1314.

Christmas — A1000

600 l, The Annunciation, by Melozzo da Forli. 750 l, Madonna and Child, by Lattanzio da Rimini.

1994, Nov. 5   Photo.   Perf. 13½x14
2004   A1000   600 l   multicolored   .80   .40
2005   A1000   750 l   multicolored   1.10   .30

Italian Touring Club, Cent. — A1001

1994, Nov. 8
2006   A1001   600 l   multicolored   .85   .40

CREDIOP, 75th Anniv. — A1002

1994, Nov. 11
2007   A1002   750 l   multicolored   .85   .30
No. 2007 was printed with a se-tenant label. Value with label attached: $2.

Giovanni Gentile (1875-1944), Philosopher — A1003

1994, Nov. 21
2008   A1003   750 l   multicolored   1.15   .40

Querini Dubois Palace, Venice — A1004

1994   Perf. 13½x14
2009   A1004   600 l   red & silver   .90   .40

New Italian Postal Emblem — A1005

1994   Perf. 14x13½
2010   A1005   750 l   red, blk & grn   1.40   .25
2011   A1005   750 l   red brown   1.40   .25
  a.   Pair, #2010-2011   3.50   2.00
See Nos. 2059-2060.

World Speed Skating Championships A1006

1995, Feb. 6   Photo.   Perf. 14x13½
2012   A1006   750 l   multicolored   1.10   .30

Achille Beltrame (1871-1945) — A1007

Design: 500 l, Cover of first issue of LA DOMENICA DEL CORRIERE.

1995, Feb. 18   Photo.   Perf. 13½x14
2013   A1007   500 l   multicolored   1.10   .40

Italian Food — A1008

1995, Mar. 4
2014   A1008   500 l   Rice   1.00   .55
2015   A1008   750 l   Olives, olive oil   1.25   .40
See Nos. 2068-2069.

Birds — A1009

1995, Mar. 11   Photo.   Perf. 14x13½
2016   A1009   600 l   Heron   .75   .45
2017   A1009   600 l   Vulture   .75   .45
2018   A1009   600 l   Royal eagle   .75   .45
2019   A1009   600 l   Alpine chaffinch   .75   .45
  Nos. 2016-2019 (4)   3.00   1.80

ITALY

UN, 50th Anniv. — A1010

1995, Mar. 24   Photo.   Perf. 14x13½
2020 A1010 850 l multicolored   1.00 .40

Fifth Day of Milan War Memorial, by Giuseppe Grandi, Cent. — A1011

1995, Mar. 25   Photo.   Perf. 14x13½
2021 A1011 750 l gold, black & blue   1.00 .30

Miniature Sheet

End of World War II, 50th Anniv. A1012

Designs: a, Mafalda de Savoy, concentration camp, barbed wire. b, Allied DUKW, Battles of Anzio and Nettuno. c, Women in World War II, Teresa Gullace. d, Gold Medal of Valor, Palazzo Vecchio, Florence. e, Gold Medal of Valor, building, Vittorio Veneto. f, Gold Medal of Valor, Cathedral, Cagliari. g. Mountain Battalion. h, Air dropping supplies, Balkans. i, Atlantic fleet.

1995, Mar. 31   Photo.   Perf. 14x13½
2022 A1012 750 l Sheet of 9, #a.-i.   9.50 9.50

Natl. Treasures — A1013

Designs: No. 2023, Illuminated manuscript with "P," State Archives, Rome. No. 2024, Painting of Port of Naples, by Tavola Strozzi, Natl. Museum of San Martino, horiz. No. 2025, Illuminated manuscript with "I," Christ, State Archives, Mantua. No. 2026, Painting, Sacred and Profane Love, by Titian, Borghese Gallery and Museum, Rome, horiz.

Perf. 13½x14, 14x13½

1995, Apr. 28   Photo.
2023 A1013 500 l multicolored   .65 .50
2024 A1013 500 l multicolored   .65 .45
2025 A1013 750 l multicolored   .90 .30
2026 A1013 850 l multicolored   1.00 .45
    Nos. 2023-2026 (4)   3.20 1.70

Venice Biennial, Cent. — A1014

1995, Apr. 29   Perf. 13½x14
2027 A1014 750 l multicolored   1.00 .30

Basilica of Santa Croce, Florence — A1015

1995, May 3   Engr.
2028 A1015 750 l vio black   1.00 .30

Peace & Freedom — A1016

Europa: 750 l, Family, liberating soldiers, Italian flag. 850 l, Stars of European flag, church, mosque.

1995, May 5   Photo.   Perf. 13½x14
2029 A1016 750 l multicolored   1.10 .30
2030 A1016 850 l multicolored   1.40 .45

Volleyball, Cent. — A1017

1995, May 8
2031 A1017 750 l multicolored   1.00 .30

Tourism Type of 1993

1995, May 12   Photo.   Perf. 14x13½
2032 A965 750 l Nuoro   1.00 .30
2033 A965 750 l Susa   1.00 .30
2034 A965 750 l Alatri   1.00 .30
2035 A965 750 l Venosa   1.00 .30
    Nos. 2032-2035 (4)   4.00 1.20

Discovery of the X-Ray, Cent. — A1018

1995, June 2
2036 A1018 750 l multicolored   1.00 .30

1994-95 Natl. Soccer Championship Team, Juventus — A1019

1995, June 5   Perf. 13½x14
2037 A1019 750 l multicolored   1.25 .40

Radio, Cent. — A1020

Designs: 750 l, Griffone House. 850 l, Guglielmo Marconi, transmitting equipment.

1995, June 8   Perf. 14x13½
2038 A1020 750 l multicolored   1.00 .30

Perf. 14
2039 A1020 850 l multicolored   1.25 .40

No. 2039 is 36x21mm. See Germany No. 1900, Ireland No. 974a, San Marino Nos. 1336-1337, Vatican City Nos. 978-979.

St. Anthony of Padua (1195-1231) A1022

Perf. 13½x14, 14x13½
1995, June 13
2040 A1021 750 l multicolored   1.10 .30
2041 A1022 850 l multicolored   1.25 .45

See Brazil No. 2539 and Portugal Nos. 2054-2057.

Historical Public Gardens A1023

Designs: No. 2042, Durazzo Pallavicini, Pegli. No. 2043, Boboli, Firenze. No. 2044, Ninfa, Cisterna di Latina. No. 2045, Royal Park, Caserta.

Litho. & Engr.
1995, June 24   Perf. 14x13½
2042 A1023 750 l multicolored   1.00 .25
2043 A1023 750 l multicolored   1.00 .25
2044 A1023 750 l multicolored   1.00 .25
2045 A1023 750 l multicolored   1.00 .25
    Nos. 2042-2045 (4)   4.00 1.00

Congress of European Society of Ophthalmology A1024

1995, June 24   Litho.   Perf. 13½x14
2046 A1024 750 l multicolored   1.00 .30

The Sailors' Wives, by Massimo Campigli (1895-1971) A1025

1995, July 4   Photo.   Perf. 14
2047 A1025 750 l multicolored   1.40 .30

14th World Conference on Relativity, Florence A1026

750 l, Galileo, Einstein.

1995, Aug. 7   Litho.   Perf. 14x13
2048 A1026 750 l dk blue & org brn   1.00 .30

Motion Pictures, Cent. — A1027

No. 2049, Son of the Shiek, Rudolph Valentino. No. 2050, L'oro Di Napoli, Toto. No. 2051, Le Notti Di Cabiria, F. Fellini. No. 2052, Cinecitta '95.

Litho. & Engr.
1995, Aug. 29   Perf. 13½x14
2049 A1027 750 l multicolored   1.00 .45
2050 A1027 750 l multicolored   1.00 .45
2051 A1027 750 l multicolored   1.00 .45
2052 A1027 750 l multicolored   1.00 .45
    Nos. 2049-2052 (4)   4.00 1.80

See Nos. 2099-2101, 2170-2172, 2269-2271.

FAO, 50th Anniv. — A1028

1995, Sept. 1   Photo.   Perf. 14x13½
2053 A1028 850 l multicolored   1.25 .40

Basilica of Pontida & Death of St. Albert of Prezzate, 900th Anniv. — A1029

1995, Sept. 2   Engr.
2054 A1029 1000 l blue & brown   1.40 .50

ROMA '95, First World Military Games — A1030

1995, Sept. 6   Photo.   Perf. 13½x14
2055 A1030 850 l multicolored   1.10 .40

Italian News Agency (ANSA), 50th Anniv. — A1031

1995, Oct. 27   Photo.   Perf. 14x13½
2056 A1031 750 l multicolored   1.25 .30

Christmas A1032

Designs: 750 l, Nativity figurines, Cathedral of Polignano a Mare, by Stefano da Putignano. 850 l, Adoration of the Magi, by Fra Angelico.

1995, Nov. 18
2057 A1032 750 l multicolored   1.75 .30
2058 A1032 850 l multicolored   2.25 .40

New Italian Postal Emblem Type of 1994

1995, Dec. 9   Photo.   Perf. 13½x14
Size: 26x18mm
2059 A1005 750 l like No. 2011   1.00 .25
  a.   Booklet pane of 8   8.50
        Complete booklet, #2059a   10.00
2060 A1005 850 l like No. 2010   1.25 .25
  a.   Booklet pane of 8   10.00
        Complete booklet, #2060a   11.50

Renato Mondolfo A1033

1995, Dec. 9   Photo.   Perf. 14x13½
2061 A1033 750 l multicolored   1.00 .30

Philately Day.

F.T. Marinetti (1876-1944), Poet and Ideologue A1034

1996, Jan. 19   Photo.   Perf. 14
2062 A1034 750 l multicolored   1.25 .30

Collections from Natl. Museum and Archives — A1035

No. 2063, Arms of the Academy of Georgofili, Florence. No. 2064, Illuminated manuscript from Lucca (1372), vert. No. 2065, Manuscript of Gabriele D'Annunzio (1863-

ITALY

1938), author, soldier, political leader. No. 2066, French miniature, c. 1486.

1996, Feb. 26 *Perf. 14x13½, 13½x14*
2063 A1035 750 l multicolored 1.00 .30
2064 A1035 750 l multicolored 1.00 .30
2065 A1035 850 l multicolored 1.40 .45
2066 A1035 850 l multicolored 1.40 .45
Nos. 2063-2066 (4) 4.80 1.50

Sarah and the Angel, by Tiepolo (1696-1770) A1036

1996, Mar. 5 *Perf. 14*
2067 A1036 1000 l multicolored 2.00 .50

Italian Food Type of 1995
500 l, White wine, grapes. 750 l, Red wine, grapes.

1996, Mar. 20 *Perf. 13½x14*
2068 A1008 500 l multi 1.20 .40
2069 A1008 750 l multi 1.75 .40

CHINA '96, 9th Asian Intl. Philatelic Exhibition A1037

1996, Mar. 22 *Perf. 14x13½*
2070 A1037 1250 l multicolored 2.25 1.00
Marco Polo's return from China, 700th anniv. (in 1995).
See San Marino No. 1350.

Cathedral of Milan — A1038

No. 2071, Front entrance. No. 2072, Corner, side view.

1996, Mar. 23 *Perf. 13½x14*
2071 A1038 750 l multicolored .75 .30
2072 A1038 750 l multicolored .75 .30
 a. Pair, #2071-2072 2.00 1.50
 b. Booklet pane, 4 #2072a 10.00
    Complete booklet, #2072b 10.00
No. 2072a is a continuous design.
ITALIA '98, Intl. Philatelic Exhibition, Milan.

A1039

1996, Apr. 3 *Perf. 13½x14, 14x13½*
2073 A1039 750 l shown 1.25 .40
2074 A1039 750 l Globe, "100" 1.40 .40
Natl. Press Federation, 50th anniv. (No. 2073). "La Gazzetta dello Sport," cent. (No. 2074), horiz.

Intl. Museum of Postal Images, Belvedere Ostrense — A1040

1996, Apr. 13 *Photo. Perf. 13½x14*
2075 A1040 500 l multicolored 1.25 .30

Academy of Finance Police, Cent. — A1040a

1996, Apr. 13
2076 A1040a 750 l multicolored 1.00 .60

RAMOGE Agreement Between France, Italy, Monaco, 20th Anniv. — A1041

Photo. & Engr.
1996, May 14 *Perf. 14x13½*
2077 A1041 750 l multicolored 1.25 .40
See France No. 2524, Monaco No. 1998.

Rome-New York Trans-Continental Drive — A1042

1996, Apr. 13 *Photo. Perf. 13½x14*
2078 A1042 4650 l multicolored 8.00 4.00

Europa (Famous Women) — A1043

750 l, Carina Negrone, pilot. 850 l, Adelaide Ristori, actress.

1996, Apr. 29 *Photo. Perf. 13½x14*
2079 A1043 750 l multicolored 1.10 .50
2080 A1043 850 l multicolored 1.40 .50

St. Celestine V (1215-96) A1044

Litho. & Engr.
1996, May 18 *Perf. 14x13½*
2081 A1044 750 l multicolored 1.25 .40

Tourism — A1045

No. 2082, Pienza Cathedral. No. 2083, St. Anthony's Church, Diano Marina. No. 2084, Belltower of Church of St. Michael the Archangel, Monte Sant'Angelo. No. 2085, Prehistoric stone dwelling, Lampedusa.

1996, May 18 *Photo. Perf. 14x13½*
2082 A1045 750 l multicolored 1.25 .40
2083 A1045 750 l multicolored 1.25 .40
2084 A1045 750 l multicolored 1.25 .40
2085 A1045 750 l multicolored 1.25 .40
Nos. 2082-2085 (4) 5.00 1.60

Consecration of Reconstructed Farfa Abbey, 500th Anniv. — A1046

1996, May 18 *Photo. Perf. 13½x14*
2086 A1046 1000 l multicolored 1.50 .60

Mediterranean Fair, Palermo — A1047

1996, May 25 *Perf. 14x13½*
2087 A1047 750 l multicolored 1.10 .30

Italian Republic, 50th Anniv. — A1048

1996, June 1 *Perf. 13½x14*
2088 A1048 750 l multicolored 1.10 .30

Production of Vespa Motor Scooters, 50th Anniv. — A1049

1996, June 20
2089 A1049 750 l multicolored 1.75 .40

First Meeting of European Economic Community, Messina and Venice, 40th Anniv. A1050

1996, June 21 *Perf. 14*
2090 A1050 750 l multicolored 1.25 .40

Modern Olympic Games, Cent. — A1051

Designs: 500 l, Runners, 1896. 750 l, Discus, Atlanta skyline, vert. 850 l, Gymnast on rings, basketball, Atlanta stadium. 1250 l, 1896 stadium, Athens, 1996 stadium, Atlanta, vert.

Perf. 14x13½, 13½x14
1996, July 1 *Photo.*
2091 A1051 500 l multicolored .60 .35
2092 A1051 750 l multicolored 1.00 .50
2093 A1051 850 l multicolored 1.00 .45
2094 A1051 1250 l multicolored 1.75 .80
Nos. 2091-2094 (4) 4.35 2.10

Butterflies A1052

No. 2095, Melanargia arge. No. 2096, Papilio hospiton. No. 2097, Zygaena rubicundus. No. 2098, Acanthobrahmaea europaea.

1996, Aug. 26 *Perf. 14x13½*
2095 A1052 750 l multicolored 1.10 .30
2096 A1052 750 l multicolored 1.10 .30
2097 A1052 750 l multicolored 1.10 .30
2098 A1052 750 l multicolored 1.10 .30
Nos. 2095-2098 (4) 4.40 1.20

Motion Picture Type of 1995
No. 2099, Massimo Troisi in "Scusate Il Ritardo." No. 2100, Aldo Fabrizi in "Prima Comunione." No. 2101, Bartolomeo Pagano as Maciste in "Cabiria."

Photo. & Engr.
1996, Aug. 30 *Perf. 13½x14*
2099 A1027 750 l multicolored 1.25 .45
2100 A1027 750 l multicolored 1.25 .45
2101 A1027 750 l multicolored 1.25 .45
Nos. 2099-2101 (3) 3.75 1.35

A1054

1996, Sept. 7 *Photo. Perf. 13½x14*
2102 A1054 750 l multicolored 2.00 .30
Milan, 1995-96 national soccer champions.

A1055

1996, Sept. 7 *Engr. Perf. 14x13½*
2103 A1055 750 l dark blue 1.25 .30
The Duomo, cathedral of Santa Maria del Fiore, Florence, 700th anniv.

13th Intl. Congress of Prehistoric Science — A1056

1996, Sept. 9 *Photo. Perf. 13½x14*
2104 A1056 850 l multicolored 1.25 .35

Levant Fair, Bari — A1057

1996, Sept. 13 *Photo. Perf. 14x13½*
2105 A1057 750 l multicolored 1.25 .30

1997 Mediterranean Games, Bari — A1058

1996, Sept. 13 *Perf. 13½x14*
2106 A1058 750 l multicolored 1.25 .30

Juventus, 1995-96 European Soccer Champions — A1059

1996, Sept. 14
2107 A1059 750 l multicolored 2.00 .40

Alessandro Pertini (1896-1990), Former President — A1060

1996, Sept. 25 *Photo. Perf. 13½x14*
2108 A1060 750 l multicolored 1.25 .30

ITALY

Eugenio Montale (1896-1981), Poet — A1061

1996, Oct. 12			Litho. & Engr.		
2109	A1061	750 l blue & brown		1.25	.30

Annunciation, by Pietro da Cortona (1596-1669) — A1062

1996, Oct. 31					Photo.
2110	A1062	500 l multicolored		.95	.35

Invitation to Philately — A1063

Designs: 750 l, Tex Willer, western scene. 850 l, Seagulls, gondola, city, Corto Maltese.

1996, Oct. 31		Litho. & Engr.	Perf. 14x13½		
2111	A1063	750 l multicolored		1.75	.30
2112	A1063	850 l multicolored		1.75	.45

Stamp Day — A1064

1996, Nov. 8		Photo.	Perf. 13½x14		
2113	A1064	750 l multicolored		1.25	.30

Universities of Italy — A1065

Designs: No. 2114, Agrarian School, cent., University of Perugia. No. 2115, University of Sassari (1562-1996), horiz. No. 2116, University of Salerno.

Perf. 13½x14, 14x13½

1996, Nov. 9			Engr.		
2114	A1065	750 l brown		1.25	.30
2115	A1065	750 l green		1.25	.30
2116	A1065	750 l blue		1.25	.30
		Nos. 2114-2116 (3)		3.75	.90

World Food Summit, Rome — A1066

1996, Nov. 13		Photo.	Perf. 14x13½		
2117	A1066	850 l green & black		1.40	.40

Christmas — A1067

Designs: 750 l, Madonna and Child, by Pisanello. 850 l, Santa, toys, horiz.

Perf. 13½x14, 14x13½

1996, Nov. 15					
2118	A1067	750 l multicolored		1.50	.30
2119	A1067	850 l multicolored		1.60	.45

UNESCO, 50th Anniv. — A1068

850 l, UNICEF 50th Anniv., baby, globe, emblem.

1996, Nov. 20			Perf. 13½x14		
2120	A1068	750 l multicolored		1.25	.30
2121	A1068	850 l multicolored		1.25	.45

Natl. Institute of Statistics, 70th Anniv. — A1069

1996, Nov. 26					
2122	A1069	750 l multicolored		1.00	.30

"Strega" Literary Award 50th Anniv. — A1070

1996, Nov. 29					
2123	A1070	3400 l multicolored		4.75	2.50

First Natl. Flag, Bicent. — A1071

1997, Jan. 7		Photo.	Perf. 13½x14		
2124	A1071	750 l multicolored		1.00	.25

Sestrieres '97, World Alpine Skiing Championships A1072

1997, Feb. 1		Photo.	Perf. 13½x14		
2125	A1072	750 l shown		1.00	.35
2126	A1072	850 l Ski of colors		1.25	.45

Galileo Ferraris (1847-97), Physicist, Electrical Engineer A1073

1997, Feb. 7			Perf. 14x13½		
2127	A1073	750 l multicolored		1.00	.35

Emanuela Loi (1967-92), Police Woman Killed by Mafia — A1074

1997, Mar. 8					
2128	A1074	750 l multicolored		1.00	.40

Italia '98, World Philatelic Exhibition, Milan — A1075

Designs: a, Airmail philately. b, Topical philately. c, Postal history. d, Philatelic literature.

1997, Mar. 21		Litho.	Perf. 13½x14		
2129		Sheet of 4		4.00	3.00
a.-d.	A1075	750 l any single		.90	.65

Statue of Marcus Aurelius (121-180), Roman Emperor — A1076

1997, Mar. 25					Photo.
2130	A1076	750 l multicolored		1.00	.40

Treaty of Rome, 40th anniv.

St. Ambrose (339-397), Bishop of Milan — A1077

1997, Apr. 4		Litho. & Engr.	Perf. 14		
2131	A1077	1000 l multicolored		1.50	.45

St. Geminian, 1600th Death Anniv. — A1078

1997, Apr. 4		Photo.	Perf. 13½x14		
2132	A1078	750 l multicolored		1.00	.40

University of Rome — A1079

Design: No. 2134, University of Padua.

1997, Apr. 14		Engr.	Perf. 14x13½		
2133	A1079	750 l claret		1.00	.30
2134	A1079	750 l blue		1.00	.30

Founding of Rome, 2750th Anniv. — A1080

1997, Apr. 21		Photo.	Perf. 14x13½		
2135	A1080	850 l multicolored		1.25	.40

Timoleontee Wall, Gela — A1081

1997, Apr. 24					
2136	A1081	750 l multicolored		1.00	.30

Antonio Gramsci (1891-1937), Politician — A1082

1997, Apr. 26		Photo.	Perf. 14		
2137	A1082	850 l multicolored		1.25	.40

Monastery Church, Pavia, 500th Anniv. — A1083

1997, May 3			Perf. 13½x14		
2138	A1083	1000 l multicolored		1.50	.45

Stories and Legends A1084

Europa: 800 l, Cobbler's workshop. 900 l, Street singer, vert.

Perf. 14x13, 13x14

1997, May 5					Photo.
2139	A1084	800 l multicolored		1.00	.30
2140	A1084	900 l multicolored		1.50	.30

Massimo Theatre, Palermo, Cent. — A1085

1997, May 16		Photo.	Perf. 13½x14		
2141	A1085	800 l multicolored		1.25	.25

Tourism — A1086

Designs: No. 2142, St. Vitalian Basilica, Ravenna. No. 2143, Tomb of Marcus Tullius Cicero (106-43BC), Formia. No. 2144, College of Assumption of the Holy Mary, Positano. No. 2145, St. Sebastian Church, Acireale.

1997, May 17		Photo.	Perf. 14x13		
2142	A1086	800 l multicolored		1.00	.25
2143	A1086	800 l multicolored		1.00	.25
2144	A1086	800 l multicolored		1.00	.25
2145	A1086	800 l multicolored		1.00	.25
		Nos. 2142-2145 (4)		4.00	1.00

Book Fair, Turin — A1087

1997, May 22			Perf. 13½x14		
2146	A1087	800 l multicolored		1.40	.40

Queen Paola of Belgium, 60th Birthday — A1088

750 l, San Angelo Castle.

1997, May 23		Photo.	Perf. 14x13½		
2147	A1088	750 l multi		1.25	.30

See Belgium No. 1652.

ITALY

Rome Fair — A1089

1997, May 24 Photo. Perf. 14x13½
2148 A1089 800 l multicolored 1.25 .30

Cathedral of Orvieto — A1090

1997, May 31 Engr. Perf. 13x14
2149 A1090 450 l deep violet .75 .40

Fr. Giuseppe Morosini (1913-44) — A1091

1997, June 4 Photo.
2150 A1091 800 l multicolored 1.25 .30

Bologna Fair — A1092

1997, June 7 Perf. 14x13
2151 A1092 800 l multicolored 1.25 .30

Juventus, 1996-97 Italian Soccer Champions — A1093

1997, June 7 Perf. 13½x14
2152 A1093 800 l multicolored 1.50 .35

Abruzzo Natl. Park, 75th Anniv. — A1094

1997, June 7 Photo. Perf. 13½x14
2153 A1094 800 l multicolored 1.25 .30

Italian Naval League, Cent. — A1095

1997, June 10 Photo. Perf. 13½x14
2154 A1095 800 l multicolored 1.25 .30

13th Mediterranean Games, Bari — A1096

1997, June 13 Perf. 14x13½
2155 A1096 900 l multicolored 1.25 .40

Public Gardens A1097

Designs: No. 2156, Miramare-Trieste Park. No. 2157, Cavour-Santena. No. 2158, Villa Sciarra, Rome. No. 2159, Orto Botanical Gardens, Palermo.

Photo. & Engr.
1997, June 14 Perf. 14x13½
2156 A1097 800 l multicolored 1.00 .30
2157 A1097 800 l multicolored 1.00 .30
2158 A1097 800 l multicolored 1.00 .30
2159 A1097 800 l multicolored 1.00 .30
   Nos. 2156-2159 (4) 4.00 1.20

Italian Labor Force — A1098

800 l, Industry. 900 l, Agriculture, horiz.

Perf. 13½x14, 14x13½
1997, June 20
2160 A1098 800 l multi 1.00 .30
2161 A1098 900 l multi 1.25 .40

John Cabot's Voyage to Canada, 500th Anniv. — A1099

1997, June 24 Litho. Perf. 14
2162 A1099 1300 l multicolored 2.00 2.00

Joint issue between Italy and Canada. See Canada No. 1649.

Pietro Verri (1728-97), Economist, Journalist — A1100

1997, June 28 Perf. 13½x14
2163 A1100 3600 l multicolored 4.75 2.50

Madonna of the Rosary by Pomarancio il Vecchio (Niccolo Cercignani)(d. 1597) — A1101

650 l, The Miracle of Ostia, by Paolo de Dono Uccello (1397-1475).

1997, July 19 Photo. Perf. 13½x14
2164 A1101 450 l multicolored .75 .30
   Size: 26x37mm
2165 A1101 650 l multicolored 1.25 .60

Varia di Palmi Festival — A1102

1997, Aug. 2 Perf. 13½x14
2166 A1102 800 l multicolored 1.25 .40

Universiade 97, Sicily — A1103

1997, Aug. 19 Photo. Perf. 14x13½
2167 A1103 450 l Basketball .75 .35
2168 A1103 800 l High jump 1.25 .30

Antonio Rosmini (1797-1855), Priest, Philosopher A1104

1997, Aug. 26
2169 A1104 800 l multicolored 1.25 .25

Motion Picture Type of 1995

No. 2170, Pietro Germi in "The Railway Man." No. 2171, Anna Magnani in "Mamma Roma." No. 2172, Ugo Tognazzi in "My Dear Friends."

Photo. & Engr.
1997, Aug. 27 Perf. 13½x14
2170 A1027 800 l multicolored 1.25 .40
2171 A1027 800 l multicolored 1.25 .40
2172 A1027 800 l multicolored 1.25 .40
   Nos. 2170-2172 (3) 3.75 1.20

Viareggio Literary Prize — A1106

1997, Aug. 30 Photo. Perf. 14x13½
2173 A1106 4000 l multicolored 4.75 2.00

Intl. Fair, Bolzano — A1107

1997, Sept. 1
2174 A1107 800 l multicolored 1.25 .30

A1108

Artifacts and Paintings from Natl. Museums and Galleries: 450 l, Bronze head, 500BC, National Museum, Reggio Calabria. 650 l, Madonna and Child with Two Vases of Roses, by Ercole di Roberti, Natl. Picture Gallery, Ferrara. 800 l, Miniature of troubadour, Sordello da Goito, Arco Palace Museum, Manta. 900 l, St. George and the Dragon, Vitale da Bologna, Natl. Picture Gallery, Bologna.

1997, Sept. 13 Photo. Perf. 13½x14
2175 A1108 450 l multicolored .75 .30
2176 A1108 650 l multicolored 1.00 .50
2177 A1108 800 l multicolored 1.25 .30
2178 A1108 900 l multicolored 1.25 .40
   Nos. 2175-2178 (4) 4.25 1.50

Pope Paul VI (1897-1978) — A1109

1997, Sept. 26 Engr. Perf. 13x14
2179 A1109 4000 l dark blue 5.75 2.50

Milan Fair — A1110

1997, Sept. 30 Photo. Perf. 14x13
2180 A1110 800 l multicolored 1.25 .40

Marshall Plan, 50th Anniv. — A1111

1997, Oct. 17
2181 A1111 800 l multicolored 1.25 .25

Christmas A1112

Nativity scenes: 800 l, Molded polychrome, from Church of St. Francis, Leonessa. 900 l, Fresco, from Baglioni Chapel, St. Mother Mary Church, Spello.

1997, Oct. 18
2183 A1112 800 l multicolored 1.50 .30
2184 A1112 900 l multicolored 1.50 .40

Aristide Merloni (1897-1970) — A1113

1997, Oct. 24 Perf. 13x14
2185 A1113 800 l multicolored 1.25 .30

Giovanni Battista Cavalcaselle (1819-97), Art Historian — A1114

Litho. & Engr.
1997, Oct. 31 Perf. 13½x14
2186 A1114 800 l multicolored 1.25 .30

Philately Day — A1115

1997, Dec. 5 Photo.
2187 A1115 800 l multicolored 1.25 .30

Emigration of Italian Population of Dalmatia, Istria & Fiume, 50th Anniv. — A1116

1997, Dec. 6 Perf. 14x13½
2188 A1116 800 l multicolored 1.25 .30

State Highway Police, 50th Anniv. — A1117

1997, Dec. 12
2189 A1117 800 l multicolored 1.25 .30

ITALY

Constitution, 50th Anniv. — A1118

1998, Jan. 2   Photo.   Perf. 13½x14
2190 A1118 800 l multicolored   1.25   .30

Hercules and the Hydra, by Antonio Del Pollaiolo (1429-98) A1119

1998, Jan. 3   Perf. 14
2191 A1119 800 l multicolored   1.25   .30
See Nos. 2278, 2319.

Famous Writers — A1120

450 l, Bertolt Brecht (1898-1956), playwright. 650 l, Federico Garcia Lorca (1898-1936), poet, dramatist. 800 l, Curzio Malaparte (Kurt Suckert) (1898-1957), journalist, writer. 900 l, Leonida Repaci (1898-1985), writer.

1998, Feb. 2   Perf. 14x13½
2192 A1120 450 l multi   .75   .40
2193 A1120 650 l multi   1.00   .40
2194 A1120 800 l multi   1.25   .25
2195 A1120 900 l multi, vert.   1.50   .25
   Nos. 2192-2195 (4)   4.50 1.30

Verona Fair, Cent. — A1121

1998, Feb. 11   Photo.   Perf. 14x13½
2196 A1121 800 l multicolored   1.40   .40

Jewish Emancipation, 150th Anniv. — A1122

1998, Mar. 28   Perf. 14
2197 A1122 800 l multicolored   1.25   .40

National Festivals — A1123

1998, Apr. 3   Litho.   Perf. 13½x14
2198 A1123 800 l Umbria Jazz   1.00   .30
2199 A1123 900 l Giffoni Film   1.50   .40
   Europa.

**Completion of "The Last Supper," by Leonardo da Vinci (1452-1519), 500th Anniv.
A1124**

1998, Apr. 4   Engr.   Perf. 14x13½
2200 A1124 800 l red brown   1.50   .40

Gaetano Donizetti (1797-1848), Composer A1125

1998, Apr. 8   Photo.
2201 A1125 800 l multicolored   1.10   .30

Italian Opera, 400th Anniv. — A1126

1998, Apr. 8   Perf. 13½x14
2202 A1126 800 l multicolored   1.10   .30

Cathedral of Turin, 500th anniv., and Shroud of Turin — A1127

1998, Apr. 18   Photo.   Perf. 13½x14
2203 A1127 800 l multicolored   1.25   .30

Tourism — A1128

No. 2204, Castle, Otranto. No. 2205, Mori Fountain and Castle, Marino. No. 2206, Village and chapel, Livigno. No. 2207, Marciana Marina, Elba Island.

1998, Apr. 18   Litho.   Perf. 14x13½
2204 A1128 800 l multicolored   1.00   .30
2205 A1128 800 l multicolored   1.00   .30
2206 A1128 800 l multicolored   1.00   .30
2207 A1128 800 l multicolored   1.00   .30
   Nos. 2204-2207 (4)   4.00 1.20
See Nos. 2283-2286.

Sardinia Intl. Fair — A1129

1998, Apr. 23   Photo.   Perf. 14x13½
2208 A1129 800 l multicolored   1.25   .30

The Charge of Carabinieri at Pastrengo, by Sebastiano de Albertis (1828-97) — A1130

1998, Apr. 30   Perf. 13½x14
2209 A1130 800 l multicolored   1.25   .30

A1131

1998, May 11   Photo.   Perf. 13½x14
2210 A1131 800 l Padua Fair   1.25   .30

Juventus, 1997-98 Italian Soccer Champions — A1132

1998, May 18
2211 A1132 800 l multicolored   1.25   .40

Polytechnical School, Turin — A1133

1998, May 18   Engr.   Perf. 14x13½
2212 A1133 800 l dark blue   1.25   .30

World Food Program — A1134

1998, May 22   Photo.
2213 A1134 900 l multicolored   1.50   .40

4th Intl. Convention on Fossils, Evolution, and Environment, Pergola — A1135

1998, May 30   Photo.   Perf. 14x13½
2214 A1135 800 l multicolored   1.25   .30

Carthusian Monastery of Santa Maria di Pesio, 825th Anniv. — A1136

1998, May 30
2215 A1136 800 l multicolored   1.25   .30

A1137

1998, June 2   Perf. 13½x14
2216 A1137 800 l multicolored   1.25   .30
Honoring the fallen of the Italian police corps.

6th World Congress of Endoscopic Surgery — A1138

1998, June 3
2217 A1138 900 l multicolored   1.25   .30

Italian Museums — A1139

No. 2218, Regional Archeological Museum, Agrigento. No. 2219, Natl. Museum of the Risorgimento, Turin. No. 2220, Peggy Guggenheim Collection, Venier Dei Leoni Palace, Venice.

1998, June 6   Perf. 13½x14, 14x13½
2218 A1139 800 l multi   1.00   .30
2219 A1139 800 l multi, horiz.   1.00   .30
2220 A1139 800 l multi, horiz.   1.00   .30
   Nos. 2218-2220 (3)   3.00   .90

Vicenza Fair — A1140

1998, June 13   Perf. 13½x14
2221 A1140 800 l multi   1.25   .30

Giacomo Leopardi (1798-1837), Poet — A1141

1998, June 29   Photo.   Perf. 14x13½
2222 A1141 800 l dark brn & sep   1.25   .30

Women in Art — A1142

Paintings: 100 l, "Young Velca," Etruscan tomb. 450 l, Detail from, "Herod's Feast," by Filippo Lippi. 650 l, Woman in profile, by Fra Benci. 800 l, "Lady with the Unicorn," by Raphael. 1000 l, sculpture of Constanza Buonarelli, by Gian Lorenzo Bernini.

1998, July 8   Photo.   Perf. 14x13½
2223 A1142   100 l blk & multi   .30   .25
2224 A1142   450 l vio & multi   .75   .25
2225 A1142   650 l gray grn &
                     multi   1.50   .25
**Engr.
Wmk. 303**
2226 A1142   800 l red brn &
                     multi   2.50   .25
2227 A1142 1000 l grn bl & multi   2.75   .25
   Nos. 2223-2227 (5)   7.80 1.25

Denominated in Lira and Euros
1999, Jan. 28   Photo.   Perf. 14x13½
2228 A1142   100 l blk & multi   .40   .25
2229 A1142   450 l vio & multi   1.00   .25
2230 A1142   650 l gray grn &
                     multi   1.40   .25
**Engr.
Wmk. 303**
2231 A1142   800 l red brn &
                     multi   1.75   .25
2232 A1142 1000 l grn bl & multi   2.00   .25
   Nos. 2228-2232 (5)   6.55 1.25
See Nos. 2436-2453.

33rd World Baseball Cup — A1143

Perf. 14x13½
1998, July 21   Photo.   Unwmk.
2251 A1143 900 l multicolored   1.25   .40

ITALY

A1144

1998, Aug. 12
2252 A1144 1300 l multicolored   2.00 1.00
Columbus' landing in Venezuela and exploration of Amerigo Vespucci, 500th anniv. Joint issue between Italy and Venezuela. See Venezuela No. 1595.

Riccione Intl. Stamp Fair, 50th Anniv. — A1145

1998, Aug. 28   *Perf. 13½x14*
2253 A1145 800 l multicolored   1.25 .40

Mother Teresa (1910-97) A1146

1998, Sept. 5   *Perf. 14x13½, 13½x14*
2254 A1146 800 l shown   1.25 .30
2255 A1146 900 l Portrait, vert.   1.75 .40
See Albania Nos. 2578-2579.

Father Pio da Pietrelcina (1887-1968) A1147

1998, Sept. 23   *Engr.*   *Perf. 14x13½*
2256 A1147 800 l deep blue   1.25 .30

1998 World Equestrian Championships, Rome — A1148

1998, Oct. 2   *Photo.*   *Perf. 14x13½*
2257 A1148 4000 l multicolored   5.00 1.75

School of Higher Education in Telecommunications, Rome — A1149

1998, Oct. 9   *Engr.*   *Perf. 14x13½*
2258 A1149 800 l deep blue   1.25 .30

Italia '98, Intl. Philatelic Exhibition A1150

800 l, Pope John Paul II.

1998, Oct. 23   *Photo.*   *Perf. 14*
2259 A1150 800 l multi   2.50 .30
See San Marino No. 1430 and Vatican City No. 1085.

Armed Forces Day — A1151

Emblem from branch of the military and: No. 2260, Aircraft carrier "Giuseppe Garibaldi," Navy. No. 2261, Eurofighter 2000, Air Force. No. 2262, Officer, Carabinieri (police force), vert. No. 2263, Italian monument, El Alamein battlefield, vert.

Perf. 14x13½, 13½x14
1998, Oct. 24   *Photo.*
2260 A1151 800 l multicolored   1.00 .35
2261 A1151 800 l multicolored   1.00 .35
2262 A1151 800 l multicolored   1.00 .35
2263 A1151 800 l multicolored   1.00 .35
Nos. 2260-2263 (4)   4.00 1.40
Air Force, 75th anniv. (No. 2261). Nos. 2260-2263 were printed se-tenant with Italia '98 label. Values, set with labels: $5 unused, $3 used.

Art Day — A1152

1998, Oct. 25   *Perf. 13½x14*
2264 A1152 800 l Dionysus   1.25 .35
Italia '98.

Enzo Ferrari (1898-1988) Automobile Manufacturer — A1153

a, 1931 Bobbio-Passo del Penice. b, 1952 Ferrari F1. c, 1963 Ferrari GTO. d, 1998 Ferrari F1.

1998, Oct. 26   *Litho.*   *Perf. 13½*
2265 A1153   800 l Sheet of 4, #a.-d.   7.00 6.00
Italia '98.

Universal Declaration of Human Rights, 50th Anniv. — A1154

1998, Oct. 27   *Photo.*   *Perf. 14x13½*
2266 A1154 1400 l multicolored   2.50 .80
Italia '98. Printed se-tenant with a label. Value with label, $2.

Europe Day — A1155

1998, Oct. 28   *Perf. 13½x14*
2267 A1155 800 l multicolored   1.25 .25

Die Cut Perf. 11
Self-Adhesive Booklet Stamp
2268 A1155 800 l multicolored   1.25 .40
  a.   Booklet pane of 6   8.00 7.00
       Complete booklet, #2268a   8.25

Motion Picture Type of 1995
Motion pictures, stars: 450 l, "Ti Conosco Mascherina," Eduardo de Filippo. 800 l, "Fantasmi a Roma," Antonio Pietrangeli. 900 l, "Il Signor Max," Mario Camerini.

1998, Oct. 29   *Litho. & Engr.*
2269 A1027 450 l multicolored   .45 .30
2270 A1027 800 l multicolored   .80 .35
2271 A1027 900 l multicolored   .90 .35
Nos. 2269-2271 (3)   2.15 1.00
Italia '98. Nos. 2269-2271 each printed se-tenant with label. Value, set with labels $3.25.

Communications Day — A1156

1998, Oct. 31   *Photo.*
2272 A1156 800 l multicolored   1.25 .30

Souvenir Sheet

Stamp Day A1157

1998, Nov. 1   *Litho.*
2273 A1157 4000 l multicolored   6.00 5.00
Italia '98.

Christmas A1158

800 l, Sculpture, "The Epiphany," Church of St. Mark, Seminara, vert. 900 l, Adoration of the shepherds, drawing by Giulio Romano.

Perf. 13½x14, 14x13½
1998, Nov. 28   *Engr.*
2274 A1158 800 l deep blue   1.25 .30
2275 A1158 900 l brown   1.25 .40

The Ecstasy of St. Teresa, Sculpture by Gian Lorenzo Bernini — A1159

1998, Dec. 1   *Photo.*   *Perf. 13½x14*
2276 A1159 900 l multicolored   1.40 .30

Emancipation of Valdesi, 150th Anniv. — A1160

1998, Dec. 4   *Perf. 14*
2277 A1160 800 l multicolored   1.25 .30

Art Type of 1998
Conception of Space, by Lucio Fontana (1899-1968).

1999, Feb. 19   *Photo.*   *Perf. 14*
2278 A1119 450 l multicolored   1.00 .40

National Parks — A1162

Europa: 800 l, Wolf, Calabria, vert. 900 l, Birds, Tuscan Archipelago.

Perf. 13¼x14, 14x13¼
1999, Mar. 12   *Photo.*
2279 A1162 800 l multicolored   1.10 .35
2280 A1162 900 l multicolored   1.50 .40

Holy Year 2000 — A1163

1999, Mar. 13   *Perf. 13¼x13¾*
2281 A1163 1400 l Holy Door   2.00 .45

St. Egidio Church, Cellere — A1164

1999, Apr. 10   *Engr.*   *Perf. 13¾x13½*
2282 A1164 800 l brown lake   1.25 .35

Tourism Type of 1998
No. 2283, Earthen pyramids, Segonzano. No. 2284, Waterfalls, river, Terni. No. 2285, Buildings, Lecce. No. 2286, Walls around Lipari.

1999, Apr. 17   *Photo.*   *Perf. 14x13¼*
2283 A1128 800 l multicolored   1.10 .40
2284 A1128 800 l multicolored   1.10 .40
2285 A1128 800 l multicolored   1.10 .40
2286 A1128 800 l multicolored   1.10 .40
Nos. 2283-2286 (4)   4.40 1.60

Museums A1165

No. 2287, Swan on Lake, Casina della Civette, Rome. No. 2288, "Iulia Bela," International Ceramics Museuam, Faenza, vert. No. 2289, Bells, Marinelli Historic Bell Museum, Agnone.

Perf. 14x13¼, 13¼x14
1999, Apr. 17   *Photo.*
2287 A1165 800 l multicolored   1.10 .40
2288 A1165 800 l multicolored   1.10 .40
2289 A1165 800 l multicolored   1.10 .40
Nos. 2287-2289 (3)   3.30 1.20

Constitutional Court — A1166

Perf. 13¾x13¼
1999, Apr. 23   *Photo.*
2290 A1166 800 l multicolored   1.25 .30

Natl. Firefighting Service — A1167

1999, Apr. 29
2291 A1167 800 l multicolored   1.40 .40

Military Academy of Modena — A1168

1999, May 3   *Photo.*   *Perf. 13¼x14*
2292 A1168 800 l multicolored   1.25 .40

ITALY

50th Anniv. of Death of Grande Torino Soccer Team in Airplane Crash — A1169

800 l, Plane, team members. 900 l, Superga Basilica, names.

1999, May 4   Photo.   Perf. 14x13¼
2293 A1169 800 l multi   1.50 .30
2294 A1169 900 l multi   1.90 .40

Council of Europe, 50th Anniv. — A1170

1999, May 5   Photo.   Perf. 14x13¼
2295 A1170 800 l multicolored   1.25 .30

Milan, 1998-99 Italian Soccer Champions — A1171

1999, June 7   Photo.   Perf. 13¼x14
2296 A1171 800 l multicolored   1.50 .35

Elections for European Parliament, 20th Anniv. — A1172

1999, June 10   Photo.   Perf. 14x13¼
2297 A1172 800 l multicolored   1.25 .30

Priority Mail — A1173

Typo. & Silk-screened
1999, June 14   Die Cut 11¼
Self-Adhesive
2298 A1173 1200 l multicolored   1.25 .30
   Se-tenant with etiquette   2.00 1.50
 a. Bklt. pane of 4 + 4 etiquettes   9.00
    Complete booklet, #2298a   9.50
 b. Bklt. pane of 8, no etiquettes   18.00
    Complete booklet, #2298b   18.00

No. 2298 was intended for Priority Mail service. Self-adhesive blue etiquettes to be used with each stamp on mail were provided on the sheets and in booklets of 4 stamps.
The backing paper from the sheet stamps is rouletted, while the backing paper in the booklets is not.
See No. 2324.

Fausto Coppi (1919-60), Cyclist — A1174

1999, June 12   Photo.   Perf. 14x13¼
2299 A1174 800 l multi   1.25 .35

Fiat Automobile Co., Cent. — A1175

1999, July 10   Photo.   Perf. 13¼x14
2300 A1175 4800 l multi   6.00 2.50

Statue of Our Lady of the Snows, Mt. Rocciamelone, Cent. — A1176

1999, July 19
2301 A1176 800 l multi   1.25 .35

Eleonora de Fonseca Pimentel (1752-1799), Writer — A1177

1999, Aug. 20   Perf. 14x13¼
2302 A1177 800 l multi   1.25 .30

30th World Canoe Championships A1178

1999, Aug. 26
2303 A1178 900 l multi   1.25 .30

Johann Wolfgang von Goethe (1749-1832), German Poet — A1179

1999, Aug. 28
2304 A1179 4000 l multi   5.00 2.00

World Cycling Championships A1180

1999, Sept. 15   Photo.   Perf. 13¼x14
2305 A1180 1400 l multi   2.00 .70

Stamp Day — A1181

1999, Sept. 25   Photo.   Perf. 13¼x14
2306 A1181 800 l multi   1.25 .35

Basilica of St. Francis, Assisi A1182

Litho. & Engr.
1999, Sept. 25   Perf. 14x13¼
2307 A1182 800 l multi   1.25 .35

Giuseppe Parini (1729-99), Poet — A1183

1999, Oct. 2   Engr.   Perf. 13¼x14
2308 A1183 800 l blue gray   1.25 .30

Alessandro Volta's Pile, Bicent. — A1184

1999, Oct. 11   Photo.
2309 A1184 3000 l multi   4.00 1.75

UPU, 125th Anniv. — A1185

1999, Oct. 18   Perf. 14x13¼
2310 A1185 900 l multi   1.25 .30

Goffredo Mameli (1827-49), Lyricist of Natl. Anthem, Nos. 506, 518 — A1186

1999, Oct. 22   Perf. 14
2311 A1186 1500 l multi   2.00 1.50

"Stamps, Our Friends" A1187

Various abstract designs: a, 450 l. b, 650 l. c, 800 l. d, 1000 l.

1999, Oct. 23   Perf. 13¼x14
2312 A1187 Sheet of 4, #a.-d.   4.50 4.00

First World War Soldiers — A1188

1999, Nov. 4
2313 A1188 900 l multi   1.25 .35

Christmas — A1189

Designs: 800 l, Santa Claus, reindeer and sleigh. 1000 l, Nativity, By Dosso Dossi.

1999, Nov. 5   Photo.
2314 A1189 800 l multi   1.25 .30
2315 A1189 1000 l multi   1.75 .40
   See Finland Nos. 1117-1119.

Holy Year 2000 — A1190

No. 2316, Map by Conrad Peutinger, 1507. No. 2317, 18th cent. print of pilgrims in Rome. No. 2318, Bas-relief, facade of Fidenza Duomo.

1999, Nov. 24   Photo.   Perf. 14x13¼
2316 A1190 1000 l multi   1.50 .50
2317 A1190 1000 l multi   1.50 .50
2318 A1190 1000 l multi   1.50 .50
    Nos. 2316-2318 (3)   4.50 1.50

Art Type of 1998

Design: Restless Leopard, by Antonio Ligabue (1899-1965), horiz.

1999, Nov. 27   Photo.   Perf. 14
2319 A1119 1000 l multi   1.50 .50

Schools — A1191

Designs: 450 l, State Institute of Art, Urbino. 650 l, Normal Superior School, Pisa.

1999, Nov. 27   Engr.   Perf. 14x13¼
2320 A1191 450 l black   .50 .30
2321 A1191 650 l brown   1.00 .40

Year 2000 — A1192

1999, Nov. 27   Photo.
2322 A1192 4800 l multi   6.00 2.50

Souvenir Sheet

Millennium — A1193

Designs: a, The past. b, The future.

2000, Jan. 1   Litho.   Perf. 14x13¼
2323 A1193 Sheet of 2   5.50 5.00
 a.-b. 2000 l Any single   2.40 .70
    See Nos. 2330-2332, 2365-2366.

Priority Mail Type of 1999 Redrawn With Yellow Rectangle at Center
Typo. & Silk-Screened
2000, Jan. 10   Die Cut 11¼
Self-Adhesive
2324 A1173 1200 l multi   5.00 .40

No. 2324 was intended for Priority Mail service. A self-adhesive blue etiquette is adjacent to the stamp. No. 2324 is valued with etiquette adjacent. See No. 2393 for similar stamp with Posta Prioritaria in lower case letters.

First Performance of Opera "Tosca," Cent. — A1194

2000, Jan. 14   Litho. & Engr.
**   Perf. 14x13¼**
2325 A1194 800 l multi   1.25 .35

Basilica of St. Paul — A1195

2000, Jan. 18   Photo.   Perf. 13¼x14
2326 A1195 1000 l multi   1.50 .40
    Holy Year 2000.

ITALY

Six Nation Rugby Tournament — A1196

2000, Feb. 5   *Perf. 14x13¼*
2327 A1196 800 l multi   1.25   .35

5th Symposium on Breast Diseases — A1197

1000 l, Woman holding rose.

2000, Feb. 12   *Perf. 13¼x14*
2328 A1197 800 l shown   1.25   .40
2329 A1197 1000 l multi   1.60   .50

Millennium Type of 2000
Souvenir Sheet

No. 2330: a, Art. b, Science.
No. 2331: a, Nature. b, The city.
No. 2332: a, Generations. b, Space.

2000   *Litho.*   *Perf. 14x13¼*
2330 A1193 Sheet of 2   2.75   2.75
   a.-b.   800 l Any single   1.25   .40
2331 A1193 Sheet of 2   2.75   2.75
   a.-b.   800 l Any single   1.25   .40
2332 A1193 Sheet of 2   2.75   2.75
   a.-b.   800 l Any single   1.25   .40

Issued: No. 2330, 3/4; No. 2331, 5/4; No. 2332, 7/4.

Skiing World Cup — A1198

2000, Mar. 7   *Photo.*   *Perf. 13¼x14*
2333 A1198 4800 l multi   6.50   2.50

Souvenir Sheet

Italian Design — A1199

Household furnishings designed by:
a, Achille & Pier Giacomo Castiglioni, Ettore Sottsass, Jr. Carlo Bartoli, Aldo Rossi. b, Mario Bellini, Alessandro Mendini, Vico Magistretti, Alberto Meda & Paolo Rizzatto. c, Gio Ponti, Gatti Paolini Teodoro, Massimo Morozzi, Tobia Scarpa. d, Pietro Chiesa, Joe Colombo, Cini Boeri & Tomu Katayanagi, Lodovico Acerbis & Giotto Stoppino. e, Gaetano Pesce, Antonio Citterio & Oliver Loew, Enzo Mari, De Pas D'Urbino Lomazzi. f, Marco Zanuso, Anna Castelli Ferrieri, Michele de Lucchi & Giancarlo Fassina, Bruno Munari.

2000, Mar. 9   *Litho.*   *Perf. 13¼*
2334 A1199 Sheet of 6   7.50   7.50
   a.-f.   800 l Any single   1.25   .60

Holy Year 2000 — A1200

Paintings depicting the life of Jesus:
450 l, The Adoration of the Shepherds, by Ghirlandaio. 650 l, The Baptism and Temptation of Christ, by Veronese, vert. 800 l, The Last Supper, by Ghirlandaio, vert. 1000 l, Fresco from Episodes of the Life of the Virgin Mary and Christ, by Giotto. 1200 l, The Resurrection of Christ, by Piero della Francesca, vert.

   Perf. 14x13¼, 13¼x14
2000, Mar. 10   *Litho.*
2335 A1200 450 l multi   .50   .30
2336 A1200 650 l multi   .75   .30
2337 A1200 800 l multi   1.00   .35
2338 A1200 1000 l multi   1.75   .50
2339 A1200 1200 l multi   2.25   .55
   Nos. 2335-2339 (5)   6.25   2.00

La Civiltá Cattolica, 150th Anniv. — A1201

2000, Apr. 6   *Photo.*   *Perf. 14x13¼*
2340 A1201 800 l multi   1.25   .40

San Giuseppe de Merode College, Rome, 150th Anniv. — A1202

2000, Apr. 8
2341 A1202 800 l multi   1.25   .40

Intl. Cycling Union, Cent. — A1203

2000, Apr. 14   *Photo.*   *Perf. 13¼x14*
2342 A1203 1500 l multi   2.00   .60

Tourism A1204

Designs: No. 2343, Terre di Franciacorta, Brescia. No. 2344, Dunarobba Petrified Forest, Avigliano Umbro. No. 2345, Ercolano. No. 2346, Bella di Taormina Island.

2000, Apr. 14   *Perf. 14x13¼*
2343 A1204 800 l multi   1.00   .40
2344 A1204 800 l multi   1.00   .40
2345 A1204 800 l multi   1.00   .40
2346 A1204 800 l multi   1.00   .40
   Nos. 2343-2346 (4)   4.00   1.60

Little Holy Society, Caltanissetta A1205

2000, Apr. 19
2347 A1205 800 l multi   1.25   .40

Niccolò Piccinni (1728-1800), Opera Composer — A1206

2000, May 6   *Perf. 13¼x14*
2348 A1206 4000 l multi   5.75   2.50

Europa, 2000
Common Design Type

2000, May 9
2349 CD17 800 l multi   1.50   .40

Post and Telecommunications Historical Museum — A1207

No. 2350, Ship, telecommunications equipment. No. 2351, #19, 20.

2000, May 9   *Litho.*   *Perf. 14x13¼*
2350 A1207 800 l multi   1.25   .40
2351 A1207 800 l multi   1.25   .40

Lazio, 1999-2000 Soccer Champions — A1208

2000, May 20   *Photo.*   *Perf. 13¼x14*
2352 A1208 800 l multi   1.25   .40

Monza Cathedral — A1209

2000, May 31
2353 A1209 800 l multi   1.25   .40

Rome, Headquarters of UN Food and Agriculture Agencies — A1210

2000, June 17   *Photo.*   *Perf. 13¼x14*
2354 A1210 1000 l multi   1.50   .50

Jesus the Redeemer Monument, Nuoro, Cent. — A1211

2000, June 24
2355 A1211 800 l multi   1.25   .40

Società Italiana per Condotte d'Acqua, Construction Company, 120th Anniv. — A1212

2000, June 28   *Perf. 14x13¼*
2356 A1212 800 l multi   1.25   .40

Stampin' the Future Children's Stamp Design Contest Winner — A1213

2000, July 7   *Perf. 13¼x14*
2357 A1213 1000 l multi   1.50   .55

Archery World Championships, Campagna — A1214

2000, July 8
2358 A1214 1500 l multi   2.25   .75

World Cycling Championships A1215

2000, July 31   *Photo.*   *Perf. 13¼x14*
2359 A1215 800 l multi   1.40   .40

Madonna and Child, by Carlo Crivelli — A1216

2000, Aug. 8   *Litho. & Engr.*   *Perf. 14*
2360 A1216 800 l multi   1.25   .40

Sant'Orso Fair, 1000th Anniv. — A1217

2000, Aug. 8   *Photo.*   *Perf. 14x13¼*
2361 A1217 1000 l multi   1.50   .45

18th World Congress of Transplantation Society — A1218

2000, Aug. 26   *Photo.*   *Perf. 13¼x14*
2362 A1218 1000 l multi   1.50   .50

2000 Summer Olympics, Sydney — A1219

Designs: 800 l, Celebrating athlete, Olympic stadium, Sydney. 1000 l, Myron's Discobolus, Sydney skyline.

2000, Sept. 1
2363 A1219 800 l multi   1.25   .30
2364 A1219 1000 l multi   1.50   .30

Millennium Type of 2000
Souvenir Sheets

No. 2365, vert.: a, War. b, Peace.
No. 2366: a, Meditation. b, Expression.

2000   *Litho.*   *Perf. 13¼x14, 14x13¼*
2365 A1193 Sheet of 2   2.75   2.00
   a.-b.   800 l Any single   1.25   .40
2366 A1193 Sheet of 2   2.75   2.00
   a.-b.   800 l Any single   1.25   .40

Issued: No. 2365, 9/4. No. 2366, 11/4.

ITALY

Battle of Marengo, Bicent. — A1220

2000, Sept. 8 Photo. Perf. 13¼x14
2367 A1220 800 l multi 1.25 .40

Fellini Film Year — A1221

2000, Sept. 20 Photo. Perf. 13¼x14
2368 A1221 800 l multi 1.25 .40

Philately Day — A1222

2000, Sept. 23 Photo. Perf. 14x13¼
2369 A1222 800 l multi 1.25 .40

Father Luigi Maria Monti (1825-1900) A1223

2000, Sept. 30 Photo. Perf. 14x13¼
2370 A1223 800 l multi 1.25 .40

Antonio Salieri (1750-1825), Composer — A1224

2000, Sept. 30 Perf. 13¼x14
2371 A1224 4800 l multi 6.50 3.00

2000 Paralympics, Sydney — A1225

2000, Oct. 2 Photo. Perf. 13¼x14
2372 A1225 1500 l multi 2.25 .75

World Mathematics Year — A1226

2000, Oct. 14 Photo. Perf. 14x13¼
2373 A1226 800 l multi 1.25 .40

Voluntarism — A1227

2000, Oct. 18 Perf. 13¼x14
2374 A1227 800 l multi 1.25 .40

Giordano Bruno (1548-1600), Philosopher A1228

2000, Oct. 20 Perf. 14x13¼
2375 A1228 800 l multi 1.25 .40

Madonna and Child, by Luca Della Robbia — A1229

Litho. & Engr.
2000, Oct. 25 Perf. 14
2376 A1229 800 l multi 1.25 .40

Accademia Roveretana Degli Agiati, 250th Anniv. — A1230

2000, Oct. 26 Photo. Perf. 13¼x14
2377 A1230 800 l multi 1.25 .40

Gaetano Martino (1900-67), Statesman A1231

2000, Nov. 3 Photo. Perf. 14
2378 A1231 800 l multi 1.25 .40

Perseus, by Benvenuto Cellini (1500-71), Sculptor A1232

Litho. & Engr.
2000, Nov. 3 Perf. 14
2379 A1232 1200 l multi 2.00 1.40

Schools — A1233

Designs: 800 l, Camerino University. 1000 l, Calabria University, Cosenza.

2000, Nov. 6 Engr. Perf. 14x13¼
2380 A1233 800 l blue 1.25 .40
2381 A1233 1000 l blue 1.75 .50

Christmas — A1234

Designs: 800 l, Snowflakes. 1000 l, Creche, Matera Cathedral, horiz.

Perf. 13¼x14, 14x13¼
2000, Nov. 6 Photo.
2382 A1234 800 l multi 1.40 .30
2383 A1234 1000 l multi 1.75 .50

World Snowboarding Championships A1235

2001, Jan. 15 Photo. Perf. 13¼x14
2384 A1235 1000 l multi 1.50 .50

The Annunciation, by Botticelli A1236

2001, Jan. 18 Perf. 14
2385 A1236 1000 l multi 1.50 .50

Exhibit of Italian art at Natl. Museum of Western Art, Tokyo.

Souvenir Sheet

Opera Composers — A1237

No. 2386: a, Vincenzo Bellini (1801-35). b, Domenico Cimarosa (1749-1801). c, Gaspare Luigi Pacifico Spontini (1774-1851). d, Giuseppe Verdi (1813-1901).

2001, Jan. 27 Litho. Perf. 13¼x14
2386 A1237 Sheet of 4 5.00 4.50
a.-d. 800 l Any single 1.25 .40

St. Rose of Viterbo (1235-1252) — A1238

2001, Mar. 6 Photo. Perf. 13¼x14
2387 A1238 800 l multi 1.25 1.25

Souvenir Sheet

Ferrari, 2000 Formula 1 World Champions — A1239

2001, Mar. 9 Litho. Perf. 14x13¼
2388 A1239 5000 l multi 7.50 7.00

Santa Maria Abbey, Sylvis A1240

2001, Mar. 10 Engr. Perf. 14
2389 A1240 800 l blue 1.25 .40

Postage Stamp Sesquicentennials A1241

Designs: No. 2390, Tuscany #1. No. 2391, Sardinia #1. No. 2392, Lombardy-Venetia #1.

2001, Mar. 31 Photo. Perf. 13¼x14
2390 A1241 800 l multi 1.50 .40
2391 A1241 800 l multi 1.50 .40
2392 A1241 800 l multi 1.50 .40
Nos. 2390-2392 (3) 4.50 1.20

Priority Mail — A1242

Serpentine Die Cut 11
Typo & Silk Screened
2001, Apr. 10 Self-Adhesive
2393 A1242 1200 l multi 2.50 1.00
a. Booklet pane of 4 + 4 etiquettes 12.00
Booklet. #2393a 12.00

Compare with No. 2324. No. 2393 was intended for Priority Mail service. A self-adhesive blue etiquette is adjacent to the stamp. No. 2393 is valued with etiquette adjacent.
See Nos. 2466-2471, 2582-2585B, 2613A-2615, 2691A-2691B.

Tourism — A1243

2001, Apr. 14 Photo. Perf. 14x13¼
2394 A1243 800 l Stintino 1.00 .40
2395 A1243 800 l Comacchio 1.00 .40
2396 A1243 800 l Diamante 1.00 .40
2397 A1243 800 l Pioraco 1.00 .40
Nos. 2394-2397 (4) 4.00 1.60

Nature and the Environment — A1244

Designs: 450 l, Campanula. 650 l, Marmots. 800 l, Storks. 1000 l, World Day Against Desertification.

2001, Apr. 21 Perf. 13¼x14
2398 A1244 450 l multi .50 .40
2399 A1244 650 l multi .75 .50
2400 A1244 800 l multi 1.25 .40
2401 A1244 1000 l multi 1.50 .60
Nos. 2398-2401 (4) 4.00 1.90

General Agricultural Confederation A1245

2001, Apr. 24 Photo. Perf. 13¼x14
2402 A1245 800 l multi 1.10 .40

ITALY

Gorizia, 1000th Anniv. — A1246

			Perf. 14x13¼	
2001, Apr. 28				
2403	A1246	800 l multi	1.10	.40

Europa — A1247

2001, May 4		Photo.	Perf. 14x13¼	
2404	A1247	800 l multi	1.50	.40

European Union's Charter of Fundamental Rights — A1248

2001, May 9		Photo.	Perf. 14x13¼	
2405	A1248	800 l multi	1.25	.40

Order of the Knights of Labor, Cent. — A1249

2001, May 9		Photo.	Perf. 13¼x14	
2406	A1249	800 l multi	1.10	.40

Workplace Injury Memorial Day — A1250

2001, May 19				
2407	A1250	800 l multi	1.10	.40

Art and Student Creativity Day — A1251

Children's art by: No. 2408, People staning on rainbow, by Lucia Catena. No. 2409, Painting with eye, by Luigi Di Cristo. No. 2410, Colors and Persons Profile, by Barbara Grilli. No. 2411, Child looking thru magnifying glass at stamp, by Rita Vergari, vert.

2001, May 26		Perf. 13¼x14, 14x13¼	
2408	A1251	800 l multi	1.10	.40
2409	A1251	800 l multi	1.10	.40
2410	A1251	800 l multi	1.10	.40
2411	A1251	800 l multi	1.10	.40
	Nos. 2408-2411 (4)		4.40	1.60

Masaccio (1401-28), Painter — A1252

2001, June 1			Perf. 13¼x14	
2412	A1252	800 l multi	1.10	.40

Madonna of Senigallia, by Piero della Francesca A1253

		Litho. & Engr.		
2001, June 9			Perf. 14	
2413	A1253	800 l multi	1.10	.40

Panathlon International, 50th Anniv. — A1254

2001, June 12		Photo.	Perf. 13¼x14	
2414	A1254	800 l multi	1.10	.40

Republic of San Marino, 1700th Anniv. — A1255

2001, June 23				
2415	A1255	800 l multi	1.25	.40

Rome, 2000-2001 Soccer Champions — A1256

2001, June 23		Photo.	Perf. 13¼x14	
2416	A1256	800 l multi	1.40	.40

Harbormaster's Corps and Coast Guard — A1257

2001, July 20		Photo.	Perf. 14x13¼	
2417	A1257	800 l multi	1.25	.40

Salvatore Quasimodo (1901-68), Writer — A1258

2001, Aug. 20			Perf. 13¼x14	
2418	A1258	1500 l multi	2.25	.60

Octagonal Room, Domus Aurea (Golden House of Nero), Rome A1259

2001, Aug. 31		Engr.	Perf. 14	
2419	A1259	1000 l multi	1.50	.50

Italian Design A1260

Household furnishings designed by: a, Piero Lissoni, Patricia Urquiola and Anna Bartoli. b, Monica Graffeo and Rodolfo Dordoni. c, Ferruccio Laviani and Massimo Iosa Ghini. d, Anna Gili and Miki Astori. e, Marco Ferreri, M. Cananzi and R. Semprini. f, Stefano Giovannoni and Massimiliano Datti.

2001, Sept. 1		Litho.	Perf. 13¼	
2420		Sheet of 6	8.00	8.00
a.-f.	A1260	800 l Any single	1.25	.40

Cent. of Il Quarto Stato, Painting by Giuseppe Pellizza da Volpedo A1261

2001, Sept. 15		Engr.	Perf. 14x13¼	
2421	A1261	1000 l brown	1.60	.50

Discovery of Mummified Man "Otzi" in Melting Glacier, 10th Anniv. — A1262

2001, Sept. 19		Photo.	Perf. 13¼x14	
2422	A1262	800 l multi	1.25	.40

Stamp Day — A1263

2001, Sept. 22			Perf. 14x13¼	
2423	A1263	800 l multi	1.10	.40

Enrico Fermi (1901-54), Physicist — A1264

2001, Sept. 29			Perf. 13¼x14	
2424	A1264	800 l multi	1.10	.40

Schools — A1265

Designs: No. 2425, Pavia University. No. 2426, Bari University, vert. No. 2427, Camilo Cavour State Science High School, Rome.

		Perf. 14x13¼, 13¼x14		
2001, Sept. 29			Engr.	
2425	A1265	800 l blue	1.10	.40
2426	A1265	800 l red brown	1.10	.40
2427	A1265	800 l Prus blue	1.10	.40
	Nos. 2425-2427 (3)		3.30	1.20

Latin Union — A1266

2001, Oct. 12		Photo.	Perf. 14x13¼	
2428	A1266	800 l multi	1.50	.45

Natl. Archaeological Museum, Taranto — A1267

2001, Oct. 12		Photo.	Perf. 14x13¼	
2429	A1267	1000 l multi	1.25	.40

Intl. Food and Agriculture Organizations — A1268

Wheat and emblem of: a, Intl. Fund for Agricultural Development. b, Food and Agriculture Organization and farmer (49x27mm). c, World Food Program.

2001, Oct. 16		Photo.	Perf. 14x13¼	
2430		Horiz. strip of 3	3.50	2.75
a.-c.	A1268	800 l Any single	1.00	.40

Enthroned Christ and Angels, Sancta Sanctorum, St. John Lateran Basilica — A1269

		Litho. & Engr.		
2001, Oct. 19			Perf. 14	
2431	A1269	800 l multi	1.10	.40

Madonna and Child, by Macrino d'Alba — A1270

2001, Oct. 20				
2432	A1270	800 l multi	1.20	.40

A1271

Christmas A1272

2001, Oct. 30		Photo.	Perf. 14x13¼	
2433	A1271	800 l multi	1.00	.40
2434	A1272	1000 l multi	1.25	.50

Souvenir Sheet

Italian Silk Industry A1273

		Silk-screened on Silk		
2001, Nov. 29			Imperf.	
2435	A1273	5000 l multi	6.50	4.50

100 Cents = 1 Euro (€)

Women in Art Type of 1998 With Denominations in Euros Only

Designs: 1c, Hebe, sculpture by Antonio Canova. 2c, Profile of woman from Syracuse tetradrachm. 3c, Queen of Sheba from "The Meeting of King Solomon and the Queen of Sheba," painting by Piero della Francesca. 5c,

ITALY

"Young Velca," Etruscan tomb. 10c, Head of terra cotta statue, 3rd cent. BC. 20c, Danae, painting by Correggio. 23c, Detail from "Herod's Feast," by Fra Filippo Lippi. 41c, "Lady with the Unicorn," by Raphael. 45c, "Venus of Urbina," by Titian. 50c, "Antea," by Parmigianino. 65c, "Princess of Trebizonde," by Antonio Pisano. 70c, "Neptune Gives to Venice," by Giovanni Battista Tiepolo. 77c, "Primavera," by Botticelli. 85c, "Courtesan," by Vittore Carpaccio. 90c, "Venus and Mars bound by Love", the detail of the face of Venus, by Antonio Ciaburro.

Perf. 14x13¼, 13¼x13½ (#2447, 2449, 2450, 2452, 2453)

2002-04			Photo.	
2436	A1142	1c multi	.25	.25
a.	Perf. 13¼x13½		.25	.25
2437	A1142	2c multi	.25	.25
a.	Perf. 13¼x13½		.25	.25
2438	A1142	3c multi	.25	.25
a.	Perf. 13¼x13½		.25	.25
2440	A1142	5c multi	.25	.25
a.	Perf. 13¼x13½		.25	.25
2441	A1142	10c multi	.25	.25
a.	Perf. 13¼x13½ ('04)		.30	.25
2443	A1142	20c multi	.50	.25
a.	Perf. 13¼x13½		.50	.25
2444	A1142	23c multi	.60	.25

Engr.
Wmk. 303

2446	A1142	41c multi	1.00	.45
a.	Perf. 13¼x13½		1.00	.35
2447	A1142	45c multi	1.10	.50
2448	A1142	50c multi	1.25	.55
a.	Perf. 13¼x13½		1.25	.55
2449	A1142	65c multi	1.75	.70
2450	A1142	70c multi	2.00	.75
2451	A1142	77c multi	2.10	.80
a.	Perf. 13¼x13½		2.10	.80
2452	A1142	85c multi	2.25	.90
2453	A1142	90c multi	2.50	1.00
	Nos. 2436-2453 (15)		16.30	7.40

Issued: 2c, 5c, 10c, 23c, 41c, 50c, No. 2451, 1/1. 1c, 3c, 20c, 3/1; Nos. 2437a, 2438a, 2004; No. 2446a, 2003. No. 2451a, 2004 (?); Nos. 2436a, 2440a, 2448a, 2004; 45c, 1/27/04; 65c, 3/20/04; 85c, 2/17/04; No. 2443a, 2004; 70c, 7/31/04; 90c, 6/26/04; No. 2441a, 2004.

No. 2446 was reprinted in 2003 with imprint "I.P.Z.S. S.p.A.-Roma."

Italia — A1274

Perf. 14x13¼, 13¼x13½ (#2460, 2461A, 2462)

2002-04		Engr.	Unwmk.	
2454	A1274	€1 multi	3.00	.60
2455	A1274	€1.24 multi	4.00	1.00
2457	A1274	€1.55 multi	4.50	1.00
2459	A1274	€2.17 multi	6.00	1.40
2460	A1274	€2.35 multi	6.50	1.40
2461	A1274	€2.58 multi	7.00	1.40
2461A	A1274	€2.80 multi	7.50	1.75
2462	A1274	€3 multi	8.00	1.75
2463	A1274	€3.62 multi	10.00	2.50
2465	A1274	€6.20 multi	17.00	5.50
	Nos. 2454-2465 (10)		73.50	17.90

Issued: €1, €1.24, €1.55, €2.17, €2.58, €3.62, 1/2. €6.20, 3/1. €2.35, 5/7/04; €2.80, 2/3/04; €3, 5/22/04.

Compare Type A1274 with Type A1407.

Priority Mail Type of 2001 with Euro Denominations Only
Typo. & Silk Screened

2002, Jan. 2 *Serpentine Die Cut 11*
Self-Adhesive
Background Color

2466	A1242	62c yellow	2.00	.30
	Booklet, 4 #2466		9.00	
2467	A1242	77c blue green	2.75	.75
2468	A1242	€1 blue	4.50	.50
2469	A1242	€1.24 yel green	5.00	1.50
2470	A1242	€1.86 rose	8.00	2.00
2471	A1242	€4.13 lilac	15.00	4.50
	Nos. 2466-2471 (6)		37.25	9.55

A self-adhesive etiquette is adjacent to each stamp. Nos. 2466-2471 are valued with etiquette adjacent.
No. 2466-2471 were reprinted in 2003 with imprint "I.P.Z.S. S.p.A.-Roma-2003." Values, same. No. 2468 was reprinted in 2004 with imprint "I.P.Z.S. S.p.A. - Roma - 2004."

Introduction of the Euro — A1275

No. 2472: a, 1285 Venetian ducat. b, 1252 Genoan genovino and Florentine florin.
No. 2473: a, Euro symbol and flags. b, 1946 Italian 1-lira coin and new 1-euro coin.

2002, Jan. 2 *Photo.* *Perf. 14x13¼*
2472	A1275	Horiz. pair	2.50	1.25
a.-b.	41c Either single		1.00	.40
2473	A1275	Horiz. pair	2.50	1.25
a.-b.	41c Either single		1.00	.40

Blessed Josemaría Escrivá (1902-75), Founder of Opus Dei — A1276

2002, Jan. 9
2474	A1276	41c multi	1.10	.40

Luigi Bocconi and Luigi Bocconi Commercial University, Milan — A1277

2002, Jan. 24
2475	A1277	41c multi	1.10	.40

Parma Stamps, 150th Anniv. — A1278

2002, Jan. 26 *Perf. 13¼x14*
2476	A1278	41c No. 1	1.10	.40

Intl. Year of Mountains — A1279

2002, Feb. 1
2477	A1279	41c multi	1.10	.40

2006 Winter Olympics, Turin — A1280

2002, Feb. 23
2478	A1280	41c multi	1.10	.40

Malato Alla Fonte, Sculpture by Arnolfo de Cambio A1281

2002, Mar. 8 *Engr.* *Perf. 14*
2479	A1281	41c red lilac	1.25	.40

Tourism — A1282

Designs: No. 2480, Venaria Reale. No. 2481, San Gimignano. No. 2482, Sannicandro di Bari. No. 2483, Capo d'Orlando.

2002, Mar. 23 *Photo.* *Perf. 14x13¼*
2480	A1282	41c multi	1.10	.40
2481	A1282	41c multi	1.10	.40
2482	A1282	41c multi	1.10	.40
2483	A1282	41c multi	1.10	.40
	Nos. 2480-2483 (4)		4.40	1.60

See Nos. 2542-2544, 2598-2600.

Santa Maria Della Grazie Sanctuary, Spezzano Albanese A1283

2002, Apr. 3 *Engr.* *Perf. 14*
2484	A1283	41c red brown	1.10	.40

State Police, 150th Anniv. — A1284

2002, Apr. 12 *Photo.* *Perf. 14x13¼*
2485	A1284	41c multi	1.40	.45

Fr. Matteo Ricci (1552-1610), Missionary in China, Geographer A1285

2002, Apr. 20
2486	A1285	41c multi	1.10	.40

Europa — A1286

2002, May 4 *Photo.* *Perf. 14x13¼*
2487	A1286	41c multi	1.25	.45

Francesco Morosini Naval School, Venice — A1287

2002, May 4
2488	A1287	41c multi	1.40	.40

Italian Cinema — A1288

Designs: No. 2489, Umberto D., directed by Vittorio De Sica. No. 2490, Miracle in Milan, written by Cesare Zavattini.

Litho. & Engr.
2002, May 10 *Perf. 13¼x14*
2489	A1288	41c multi	1.10	.40
2490	A1288	41c multi	1.10	.40

Juventus, 2001-02 Italian Soccer Champions — A1289

2002, May 18 *Photo.*
2491	A1289	41c multi	1.10	.40

Giovanni Falcone (1939-92) and Paolo Borsellino (1940-92), Judges Assassinated by Mafia — A1290

2002, May 23 *Perf. 14x13¼*
2492	A1290	62c multi	1.50	.60

NATO-Russia Summit Meeting, Rome — A1291

2002, May 28 *Photo.* *Perf. 14x13¼*
2493	A1291	41c multi	1.00	.40

World Kayak Championships, Valsesia — A1292

2002, May 30 *Perf. 13¼x14*
2494	A1292	52c multi	1.50	.50

Italian Military Forces in Peace Missions — A1293

2002, June 1
2495	A1293	41c multi	1.00	.40

Modena Stamps, 150th Anniv. — A1294

2002, June 1 *Photo.* *Perf. 13¼x14*
2496	A1294	41c multi	1.10	.40

Alfredo Binda (1902-86), Cyclist — A1295

2002, June 14 *Photo.* *Perf. 13¼x14*
2497	A1295	41c multi	1.25	.40

St. Pio of Pietrelcina (1887-1968) A1296

2002, June 16 *Perf. 14*
2498	A1296	41c multi	1.10	.40

Monument to the Massacre of the Acqui Division — A1297

2002, June 21 *Perf. 13¼x14*
2499	A1297	41c multi	1.10	.40

ITALY

The Crucifixion, by Cimabue — A1298

Litho. & Engr.
2002, June 22   Perf. 14
2500   A1298   €2.58 multi   7.00   2.50

Prefectural Institute, Bicent. — A1299

2002, June 24   Photo.   Perf. 14x13¼
2501   A1299   41c multi   1.10   .40

St. Maria Goretti (1890-1902) — A1300

2002, July 6   Perf. 13¼x14
2502   A1300   41c multi   1.10   .40

Jules Cardinal Mazarin (1602-61), and Birthplace A1301

2002, July 13   Photo.   Perf. 14x13¼
2503   A1301   41c multi   1.10   .40

Italians Around the World — A1302

2002, Aug. 8   Perf. 13¼x14
2504   A1302   52c multi   1.50   .50

Monument to Sant'Anna di Stazzema Massacre — A1303

2002, Aug. 17
2505   A1303   41c multi   1.10   .40

UNESCO World Heritage Sites — A1304

Designs: 41c, Pisa. 52c, Aeolian Islands.

2002, Aug. 30   Perf. 14
2506   A1304   41c multi + label   1.25   .40
2507   A1304   52c multi + label   1.50   .50

Italian Design — A1305

Apparel by: a, Krizia. b, Dolce e Gabbana. c, Gianfranco Ferre. d, Giorgio Armani. e, Laura Biagiotti. f, Prada.

2002, Aug. 30   Litho.
2508   Sheet of 6   7.50   6.50
   a.-f.   A1305 41c Any single   1.25   .40

Carlo Alberto Dalla Chiesa (1920-82), Prefect of Palermo Assassinated by Mafia — A1306

2002, Sept. 3   Photo.   Perf. 13¼x14
2509   A1306   41c multi   1.25   .40

Concordia Theater, Monte Castello de Vibio A1307

Litho. & Engr.
2002, Sept. 7   Perf. 14
2510   A1307   41c multi   1.25   .40

Sailboat Gathering, Imperia — A1308

2002, Sept. 11   Photo.   Perf. 14x13¼
2511   A1308   41c multi   1.25   .45

Santa Giulia Museum, Brescia A1309

Palazzo Altemps, Roman Natl. Museum A1310

Perf. 13¼x14, 14x13¼
2002, Oct. 4   Photo.
2512   A1309   41c multi   1.25   .40
2513   A1310   41c multi   1.25   .40

Roman States Postage Stamps, 150th Anniv. — A1311

2002, Oct. 4   Photo.   Perf. 13¼x14
2514   A1311   41c Roman States #6   1.10   .40

Flora and Fauna — A1312

2002, Oct. 11
2515   A1312   23c Orchid   .70   .40
2516   A1312   52c Lynx   1.50   .50
2517   A1312   77c Stag beetle   2.25   .75
   Nos. 2515-2517 (3)   4.45   1.65

World Food Day — A1313

2002, Oct. 16   Photo.   Perf. 13¼x14
2518   A1313   41c multi   1.10   .40

Forestry Corps — A1314

2002, Oct. 22
2519   A1314   41c multi   1.10   .40

Father Carlo Gnocchi (1902-56), Founder of Fondazione Pro Juventute — A1315

2002, Oct. 25
2520   A1315   41c multi   1.10   .40

2002 Muscular Dystrophy Telethon — A1316

2002, Oct. 31   Perf. 14x13¼
2521   A1316   41c multi   1.00   .40

Christmas A1317

Designs: 41c, Nativity. 62c, Child with candle, Christmas tree, vert.

Perf. 14x13¼, 13¼x14
2002, Oct. 31   Photo.
2522   A1317   41c multi   1.25   .40
2523   A1317   62c multi   1.75   .55

Women's Sports — A1318

2002, Nov. 20   Photo.   Perf. 13¼x14
2524   A1318   41c multi   1.10   .40

Stamp Day — A1319

2002, Nov. 29   Perf. 14x13¼
2525   A1319   62c multi   1.75   .50

2002 World Cup Soccer Championships, Japan and Korea — A1320

No. 2526: a, Flags, soccer ball and field (33mm diameter). b, Soccer player, years of Italian championships.

2002, Nov. 29   Litho.   Perf. 14
2526   A1320   Horiz. pair   3.50   2.50
   a.-b.   52c Either single   1.25   .50

See Argentina No. 2184, Brazil No. 2840, France No. 2891, Germany No. 2163 and Uruguay No. 1946.

Vittorio Emanuele Orlando (1860-1952), Politician — A1321

2002, Dec. 4   Photo.   Perf. 13¼x14
2527   A1321   41c multi   1.10   .40

2003 Winter Universiade Games, Tarvisio — A1322

2003, Jan. 16   Photo.   Perf. 13½x14
2528   A1322   52c multi   1.25   .45

"La Repubblica Italiana" Philatelic Exhibition, Rome — A1323

2003, Jan. 16   Perf. 14
2529   A1323   62c multi   2.00   .55
   a.   Booklet pane of 5   100.00   100.00
     Complete booklet, #2529a,   100.00

World Cyclocross Championships, Monopoli — A1324

2003, Feb. 1   Photo.   Perf. 13¼x14
2530   A1324   41c multi   1.25   .50

Alinari Brothers Photographic Studio, 150th Anniv. — A1325

2003, Feb. 1   Perf. 14x13¼
2531   A1325   77c multi + label   2.50   1.00

European Year of the Disabled A1326

2003, Feb. 14
2532   A1326   41c multi   1.10   .40

ITALY

World Nordic Skiing Championships, Val di Fiemme — A1327

2003, Feb. 18   *Photo.*   *Perf. 14x13¼*
2533   A1327   41c multi   1.10   .40

National Civil Service A1328

2003, Feb. 25   *Photo.*   *Perf. 14x13¼*
2534   A1328   62c multi + label   2.00   .65

Duel of Barletta, 500th Anniv. — A1329

2003, Mar. 6
2535   A1329   41c multi   1.25   .40

Torquato Tasso High School, Rome A1330

2003, Mar. 11   *Photo.*   *Perf. 14*
2536   A1330   41c multi   1.10   .40

Encounter at the Golden Door, by Giotto — A1331

2003, Mar. 20   *Litho. & Engr.*
2537   A1331   41c multi   1.10   .40

Gian Rinaldo Carli High School, Pisino d'Istria A1332

2003, Mar. 24   *Photo.*
2538   A1332   41c multi   1.10   .40

Lincei Academy, 400th Anniv. — A1333

2003, Mar. 26   *Litho. & Engr.*   *Perf. 13¼x14*
2539   A1333   41c multi   1.00   .40

World Junior Fencing Championships, Trapani — A1334

2003, Apr. 4   *Photo.*   *Perf. 14x13¼*
2540   A1334   41c multi   1.25   .40

Acquasanta Golf Club, Rome, Cent. — A1335

2003, Apr. 5
2541   A1335   77c multi   2.25   .75

Tourism Type of 2002

2003, Apr. 5
2542   A1282   41c Sestri Levante   1.25   .40
2543   A1282   41c Lanciano   1.25   .40
2544   A1282   41c Procida   1.25   .40
    Nos. 2542-2544 (3)   3.75   1.20

La Sapienza University, Rome, 700th Anniv. A1336

2003, Apr. 10   *Photo.*   *Perf. 14*
2545   A1336   41c multi   1.10   .40

Natl. Pasta Museum, Rome — A1337

2003, Apr. 17   *Perf. 13¼x14*
2546   A1337   41c multi   1.10   .40

Guido Carli Free Intl. University for Social Studies A1338

2003, Apr. 23   *Photo.*   *Perf. 14*
2547   A1338   €2.58 multi   6.50   2.50

Europa — A1339

Poster art by Marcello Dudovich: 41c, Woman in blue dress. 52c, Women in white dresses.

2003, May 5   *Photo.*   *Perf. 13¼x14*
2548   A1339   41c multi   1.25   .30
2549   A1339   52c multi   1.50   .40

Central State Archives, 50th Anniv. — A1340

2003, May 8   *Perf. 14x13¼*
2550   A1340   41c multi   1.00   .40

Veronafil Philatelic Exhibition, Verona — A1341

2003, May 9
2551   A1341   41c multi   1.10   .40

Aldo Moro (1916-78), Premier — A1342

2003, May 9   *Perf. 13¼x14*
2552   A1342   62c multi   1.60   .40

Souvenir Sheet

Antonio Meucci (1808-96), Telephone Pioneer — A1343

2003, May 28   *Litho.*
2553   A1343   52c multi   1.75   1.75

Father Eugenio Barsanti and Felice Matteucci, Internal Combustion Engine Pioneers A1344

2003, May 31   *Photo.*   *Perf. 14x13¼*
2554   A1344   52c multi   1.50   .50

Post Office, Latina A1345

2003, June 30   *Engr.*   *Perf. 14*
2555   A1345   41c blue   1.25   .40
    City of Latina, 70th anniv.

Italian Presidency of the Council of the European Union — A1346

2003, July 1   *Photo.*   *Perf. 14x13¼*
2556   A1346   41c multi   1.10   .40

Ezio Vanoni (1903-56), Economist — A1347

2003, July 1   *Perf. 13¼x14*
2557   A1347   €2.58 multi   7.00   3.00

The Assumption, by Corrado Giaquinto (c. 1694-1765) A1348

2003, July 2   *Perf. 14*
2558   A1348   77c multi   2.50   .70

Eugenio Balzan (1874-1953), Journalist A1349

2003, July 15   *Photo.*   *Perf. 14x13¼*
2559   A1349   41c multi   1.10   .40

Francesco Mazzola "Il Parmigianino," (1503-40), Painter — A1350

2003, Aug. 23   *Photo.*   *Perf. 14x14¼*
2560   A1350   41c multi   1.25   .50

Juventus, 2002-03 Italian Soccer Champions — A1351

2003, Aug. 30   *Perf. 13¼x14*
2561   A1351   41c multi   1.50   .40

Abbey of St. Sylvester I, Nonantola A1352

2003, Sept. 6   *Litho. & Engr.*   *Perf. 14*
2562   A1352   41c multi   1.25   .40

Italian Aviation Pioneers A1353

2003, Sept. 12   *Photo.*   *Perf. 13x13¼*
2563   A1353   52c Mario Calderara   1.40   .50
2564   A1353   52c Mario Cobianchi   1.40   .50
2565   A1353   52c Gianni Caproni   1.40   .50
2566   A1353   52c Alessandro Marchetti   1.40   .50
   a.   Souvenir sheet, #2563-2566   6.50   6.50
    Nos. 2563-2566 (4)   5.60   2.00

Giovanni Giolitti (1842-1928), Premier — A1354

2003, Sept. 13   *Photo.*   *Perf. 14x13¼*
2567   A1354   41c multi   1.10   .40

Europalia Italia Festival, Belgium — A1355

Designs: 41c, Still Life, by Giorgio Morandi. 52c, 1947 Cisitalia 202, designed by Battista Pininfarina.

2003, Sept. 13
2568   A1355   41c multi   1.10   .45
2569   A1355   52c multi   1.50   .55
    See Belgium Nos. 1980-1981.

ITALY

Cent. of First Publication of Leonardo Magazine, by Attilio Vallecchi (1880-1946) — A1356

2003, Sept. 27   *Photo.*   *Perf. 13x13¼*
2570   A1356   41c multi   1.10   .40

The Family — A1357

2003, Oct. 3   *Perf. 13¼x13*
2571   A1357   77c multi   2.25   .75

Maestà, by Duccio di Buoninsegna — A1358

2003, Oct. 4
2572   A1358   41c multi   1.10   .40
Exhibition of paintings by Duccio di Buoninsegna, Siena.

Vittorio Alfieri (1749-1803), Poet — A1359

2003, Oct. 8   *Perf. 13x13¼*
2573   A1359   41c multi   1.10   .40

Ugo La Malfa (1903-79), Government Minister — A1360

2003, Oct. 13   *Perf. 13¼x13*
2574   A1360   62c multi   1.75   .60

Bernardino Ramazzini (1633-1714), Physician A1361

2003, Oct. 15   *Perf. 13x13¼*
2575   A1361   41c multi   1.25   .40

Confedilizia Property Owner's Organization, 120th Anniv. — A1362

2003, Oct. 15   *Perf. 13¼x13*
2576   A1362   €2.58 multi   7.00   3.00

Nativity, by Gian Paolo Cavagna A1363

Poinsettia A1364

2003, Oct. 24
2577   A1363   41c multi   1.25   .35
2578   A1364   62c multi   1.75   .55
Christmas.

Futurist Art by Giacomo Balla — A1365

Designs: 41c, Forme Grido Viva L'Italia. 52c, Linee-Forza del Pugno di Boccioni.

2003, Nov. 26   *Photo.*   *Perf. 13x13¼*
2579   A1365   41c multi   1.25   .35
2580   A1365   52c multi   1.50   .45

Philately Day — A1366

2003, Nov. 28   *Photo.*   *Perf. 13x13¼*
2581   A1366   41c multi   1.10   .40

Priority Mail Type of 2001 With Euro Denominations Only
Self-Adhesive
Typo. & Silk Screened

2004   *Serpentine Die Cut 11*
Background Color
2582   A1242   60c org (gold frame)   2.00   .65
2583   A1242   80c yel brn   2.60   .80
2584   A1242   €1.40 green   5.50   1.00
2585   A1242   €1.50 gray   4.50   1.00
   Photo.
2585A   A1242   60c dl org (bronze frame)   1.75   .85
2585B   A1242   80c dl brn (bronze frame)   2.40   1.25
   Nos. 2582-2585B (6)   18.75   5.55

Issued: 60c, 1/2; €1.40, 1/10; 80c, €1.50, No. 2585A, 3/19/04. A self-adhesive etiquette is adjacent to each stamp. Values are for stamps with adjacent etiquette.
The frame has a splotchy appearance on Nos. 2585A and 2585B.
No. 2585A exists dated 2005. Undated examples of No. 2585B were issued in 2008. See No. 2613A.

A1367

Television Transmissions in Italy, 50th Anniv. — A1368

2004, Jan. 3   *Photo.*   *Perf. 13x13¼*
2586   A1367   41c multi   1.10   .40
2587   A1368   62c multi   1.50   .50

Giorgio La Pira (1904-77), Judge — A1369

2004, Jan. 9   *Photo.*   *Perf. 13x13¼*
2588   A1369   41c multi   1.00   .40

Genoa, 2004 European Cultural Capital — A1370

2004, Feb. 12   *Photo.*   *Perf. 13¼x13*
2589   A1370   45c multi   1.25   .40

2006 Winter Olympics, Turin — A1371

Designs: 23c, Santa Maria Assunta Church, Pragelato. 45c, San Pietro Apostolo Church, Bardonecchia. 62c, Mole Antonelliana, Turin. 65c, Fountain, Sauze d'Oulx.

2004, Mar. 9
2590   A1371   23c multi   .60   .25
2591   A1371   45c multi   1.25   .35
2592   A1371   62c multi   1.60   .45
2593   A1371   65c multi   1.75   .45
   Nos. 2590-2593 (4)   5.20   1.50

Petrarch (1304-74), Poet — A1372

2004, Mar. 18
2594   A1372   45c multi   1.25   .40

Giorgio Amarelli Licorice Museum, Rossano A1373

2004, Apr. 3   *Perf. 14*
2595   A1373   45c multi   1.25   .40

Road Safety — A1374

Designs: 60c, Car dashboard, traffic signs. 62c, Seat belt, map of Italy, vert.

2004, Apr. 7   *Perf. 13x13¼, 13¼x13*
2596   A1374   60c multi   1.50   .45
2597   A1374   62c multi   1.60   .45

Tourism Type of 2002

2004, Apr. 10   *Photo.*   *Perf. 13x13¼*
2598   A1282   45c Vignola   1.25   .35
2599   A1282   45c Viterbo   1.25   .35
2600   A1282   45c Isole Egadi   1.25   .35
   Nos. 2598-2600 (3)   3.75   1.05

Casa del Fascio, Como, Designed by Giuseppe Terragni (1904-43), Architect A1375

2004, Apr. 17   *Perf. 13x13¼*
2601   A1375   85c multi   2.50   .50

Souvenir Sheet

Rome-Bangkok Foundation — A1376

No. 2602: a, Wat Saket, Bangkok. b, Colosseum, Rome.

2004, Apr. 21   *Litho.*   *Perf. 14x13¼*
2602   A1376   Sheet of 2   3.75   3.75
   a.-b.   65c Either single   1.50   .95
See Thailand No. 2125.

Martyrdom of St. George, 1700th Anniv. A1377

2004, Apr. 23   *Photo.*   *Perf. 14*
2603   A1377   €2.80 multi   7.00   3.00

Europa — A1378

Map of Europe and: 45c, Closed suitcase. 62c, Open suitcase.

2004, May 7   *Perf. 13x13¼*
2604   A1378   45c multi   1.25   .45
2605   A1378   62c multi   1.50   .55

Souvenir Sheet

L'Aquila - Foggia Livestock Trail A1379

2004, May 8   *Litho.*   *Perf. 14x13¼*
2606   A1379   45c multi   1.50   1.50

Great Synagogue, Rome — A1380

2004, May 20   *Photo.*   *Perf. 13¼x14*
2607   A1380   60c shown   1.60   .40
2608   A1380   62c Synagogue, diff.   1.75   .40
See Israel Nos. 1564-1565.

Milan, 2003-04 Italian Soccer Champions A1381

2004, May 22   *Perf. 13x13¼*
2609   A1381   45c multi   1.50   .40

ITALY

50th Puccini Festival — A1382

2004, May 28   Photo.   *Perf. 13¼x13*
2610   A1382   60c multi   1.75   .40

University of Turin, 600th Anniv. — A1383

2004, June 3   Engr.   *Perf. 14*
2611   A1383   45c brown   1.25   .40

Achille Varzi (1904-48), Automobile and Motorcycle Racer — A1384

2004, June 5   Photo.   *Perf. 13x13¼*
2612   A1384   45c multi   1.25   .40

Penitentiary Police Corps — A1385

2004, June 16   Photo.   *Perf. 13x13¼*
2613   A1385   45c multi   1.25   .40

Priority Mail Type of 2001 With Euro Denominations Only
Self-Adhesive
Serpentine Die Cut 11

2004, June 16   Photo.
Background Color
2613A   A1242   €1.40 bl grn   5.00   1.00
2614   A1242   €2 sl grn (brnz frame)
2615   A1242   €2.20 rose   5.50   1.50
                                 6.00   2.25
Nos. 2613A-2615 (3)   16.50   4.75

Issued: €2, 6/16; €1.40, July; €2.20, 6/26.
A self-adhesive etiquette is adjacent to each stamp. Values are for stamps with adjacent etiquette.
No. 2613A has a less obvious coating over the circled "P" that shines most when viewed from an oblique angle. No. 2613A exists dated 2006. Undated examples of No. 2613A were issued in 2007. Undated examples of Nos. 2614 and 2615 were issued in 2008.

Ascent of K2 By Italian Mountaineers, 50th Anniv. — A1386

2004, July 31   Photo.   *Perf. 13¼x13*
2616   A1386   65c multi   1.75   .40

Italian Regions — A1387

2004, Aug. 27   *Perf. 14x13¼*
2617   A1387   45c Liguria   1.50   .40
2618   A1387   45c Emilia Romagna   1.50   .40
2619   A1387   45c Abruzzo   1.50   .40
2620   A1387   45c Basilicata   1.50   .40
     Nos. 2617-2620 (4)   6.00   1.60

See Nos. 2654-2657, 2746-2749, 2796-2799, 2876-2879.

Apparition of Madonna of Tirano, 500th Anniv. — A1388

2004, Sept. 4   *Perf. 13¼x13*
2621   A1388   45c multi   1.25   .40

St. Nilus of Rossano (c. 905-1005), Abbot A1389

2004, Sept. 25   Photo.   *Perf. 14¼x14*
2622   A1389   45c multi   1.25   .40

State Archives, Florence A1390

2004, Sept. 30   Photo.   *Perf. 14¼x14*
2623   A1390   45c multi   1.25   .40

Lacemaking A1391

2004, Oct. 8   Embroidered   *Imperf.*
              Self-Adhesive
2624   A1391   €2.80 blue & gray   8.25   4.00

Filo d'Oro Society — A1392

2004, Oct. 9   Photo.   *Perf. 13¼x13*
2625   A1392   45c multi   1.25   .40

Victor Emmanuel III State Technical Institute, Lucera — A1393

2004, Oct. 16   *Perf. 14x14¼*
2626   A1393   45c multi   1.25   .40

Father Luigi Guanella (1842-1915) — A1394

2004, Oct. 19   Photo.   *Perf. 13¼x13*
2627   A1394   45c multi   1.25   .40

Return of Trieste to Italy, 50th Anniv. — A1395

2004, Oct. 26   *Perf. 13x13¼*
2628   A1395   45c multi   1.50   .60
   a.   Booklet pane of 4   6.00   —
         Complete booklet, #2628a   6.00

Military Information and Security Service — A1396

2004, Oct. 27   Photo.   *Perf. 13x13¼*
2629   A1396   60c multi   1.50   .40

European Constitution A1397

2004, Oct. 29
2630   A1397   62c multi   1.75   .40

Venice Dockyards, 900th Anniv. — A1398

2004, Oct. 30   Photo.   *Perf. 13x13¼*
2631   A1398   €2.80 multi   7.00   2.00

Live Nativity Scene, Tricase — A1399

Christmas Tree — A1400

2004, Oct. 30   Photo.   *Perf. 13x13¼*
2632   A1399   45c multi   1.25   .40

Photo. & Embossed
Perf. 13¼x13
2633   A1400   62c multi   1.75   .40

Hands and Braille Book A1401

Photo. & Embossed
2004, Nov. 6   *Perf. 14*
2634   A1401   45c multi   1.25   .40

Martyrdom of St. Lucy, 1700th Anniv. — A1402

2004, Nov. 6   Photo.   *Perf. 13¼x13*
2635   A1402   45c multi   1.25   .40

Philately Day — A1403

2004, Nov. 12   Photo.   *Perf. 13¼x14*
2636   A1403   45c multi   1.25   .45

Tenth "Sport For All" World Congress — A1404

2004, Nov. 12   Photo.   *Perf. 13¼x13*
2637   A1404   65c multi   1.75   .50

Maria Santissima Assunta Free University, Rome A1405

2004, Nov. 15   *Perf. 14*
2638   A1405   45c multi   1.25   .40

Souvenir Sheet

Italian-made Footwear — A1406

No. 2639: a, Woman's shoe by Casadei. b, Men's shoes by Moreschi. c, Men's shoe by Fratelli Rosetti. d, Athletic shoe by Superga.

2004, Nov. 27   Photo.   *Perf. 13¼x13*
2639   A1406   Sheet of 4   5.75   5.00
  a.-d.   45c Any single   1.25   .40

Italia With Large Numerals — A1407

Perf. 13¼x13½
2005, Jan. 21   Engr.   *Unwmk.*
2640   A1407   €1 multi   2.75   .50

Compare type A1407 with type A1274.

Italian Auto Club, Cent. — A1408

2005, Jan. 21   Photo.   *Perf. 13¼x13*
2648   A1408   45c multi   1.25   .40

ITALY

Luigi Calabresi (1937-72), Assassinated Police Commissioner — A1409

2005, Jan. 26
2649 A1409 45c multi   1.25 .40

Exodus of Italians From Istria, Fiume and Dalmatia, 60th Anniv. — A1410

2005, Feb. 10 Photo. *Perf. 14x13¼*
2650 A1410 45c multi   1.25 .40

Rotary International, Cent. — A1411

2005, Feb. 23 *Perf. 13¼x14*
2651 A1411 65c multi   1.75 .45

Sassari Brigade — A1412

2005, Mar. 1 *Perf. 14x13¼*
2652 A1412 45c multi   1.25 .40

14th Art Quadrennial, Rome — A1413

2005, Mar. 4
2653 A1413 45c multi   1.25 .40

Italian Regions Type of 2004
No. 2654, Lombardy. No. 2655, Friuli-Venezia Giulia. No. 2656, Campania. No. 2657, Calabria.

2005, Mar. 18 *Perf. 13x13¼*
2654 A1387 45c multi   1.50 .35
2655 A1387 45c multi   1.50 .35
2656 A1387 45c multi   1.50 .35
2657 A1387 45c multi   1.50 .35
     Nos. 2654-2657 (4)   6.00 1.40

2006 Winter Olympics, Turin — A1414

Turin Olympics emblem and: 23c, Pinerolo. 45c, Cesana Torinese. 60c, Mascots Neve and Gliz. 62c, Sestriere.

2005, Mar. 21 *Perf. 13¼x13*
2658 A1414 23c multi   .75 .25
2659 A1414 45c multi   1.40 .35
2660 A1414 60c multi   1.75 .40
2661 A1414 62c multi   1.75 .40
     Nos. 2658-2661 (4)   5.65 1.40

Intl. Year of Physics — A1415

2005, Mar. 29 *Perf. 14x13¼*
2662 A1415 85c multi   2.50 .75

Opening of New Milan Fair Complex A1416

2005, Mar. 31
2663 A1416 45c multi   1.25 .40

State Railways, Cent. — A1417

2005, Apr. 22 Photo. *Perf. 13x13¼*
2664 A1417 45c multi   1.25 .40

Italian Army — A1418

2005, Apr. 29 *Perf. 13¼x13*
2665 A1418 45c multi   1.25 .40

Europa — A1419

2005, May 9 Photo. *Perf. 13¼x13*
2666 A1419 45c Wheat   1.00 .40
2667 A1419 62c Grapes   1.50 .40

St. Ignatius of Làconi (1701-81) — A1420

2005, May 11 Photo. *Perf. 13¼x13*
2668 A1420 45c multi   1.25 .40

Commercial Confederation, 60th Anniv. — A1421

2005, May 18
2669 A1421 60c multi   1.75 .50

Tommaso Campanella High School, Reggio Calabria — A1422

2005, May 20 Photo. *Perf. 13¼x13¼*
2670 A1422 45c multi   1.25 .40

San Giuseppe da Copertino Basilica — A1423

2005, May 21 Engr. *Perf. 14*
2671 A1423 45c blue gray   1.25 .40

Tourism A1424

No. 2672, Asolo. No. 2673, Rocchetta a Volturno. No. 2674, Amalfi.

2005, May 26   Photo.
2672 A1424 45c multicolored   1.25 .40
2673 A1424 45c multicolored   1.25 .40
2674 A1424 45c multicolored   1.25 .40
     Nos. 2672-2674 (3)   3.75 1.20

See Nos. 2734-2736, 2803-2806, 2887-2890, 2948-2951, 3080-3083, 3126-3129.

St. Gerardo Maiella (1726-55) A1425

2005, May 28 *Perf. 13¼x13¼*
2675 A1425 45c multi   1.25 .40

Juventus, 2004-05 Italian Soccer Champions — A1426

2005, June 6 *Perf. 13¼x13*
2676 A1426 45c multi   1.25 .40

Ratification of Modifications to Italy-Vatican Concordat, 20th Anniv. — A1427

Arms of Vatican City and Italy and: 45c, Map. €2.80, Pen.

2005, June 9 *Perf. 13¼x13¼*
2677 A1427   45c multi   1.25 .40
2678 A1427 €2.80 multi   7.75 2.25

See Vatican City Nos. 1301-1302.

First Italian Dirigible Flight by Almerico da Schio, Cent. — A1428

2005, June 17 Photo. *Perf. 13¼x13¼*
2679 A1428 €3 multi   7.50 2.75

European Youth Olympic Festival, Lignano Sabbiadoro A1429

2005, June 20 Photo. *Perf. 13¼x13*
2680 A1429 62c multi   1.75 .50

Intl. Day Against Illegal Drugs — A1430

2005, June 25 Photo. *Perf. 13x13¼*
2681 A1430 45c multi   1.25 .40

Institute for Maritime Trades Social Insurance A1431

2005, June 28
2682 A1431 45c multi   1.25 .40

Leo Longanesi (1905-57), Writer — A1432

2005, Aug. 26 Engr. *Perf. 13¼x14*
2683 A1432 45c dark blue   1.25 .40

Alberto Ascari (1918-55), Race Car Driver — A1433

2005, Sept. 2 Photo. *Perf. 13x13¼*
2684 A1433 €2.80 multi   7.50 3.00

A1434

National Military Aerobatic Team — A1435

2005, Sept. 3 Photo. *Perf. 13x13¼*
2685 A1434 45c multi   1.25 .40
2686 A1435 60c multi   1.75 .55

Pietro Savorgnan di Brazzà (1852-1905), Explorer of Africa — A1436

2005, Sept. 14 Photo. *Perf. 13¼x13*
2687 A1436 45c multi   1.25 .40

Guido Gonella (1905-82), Politician, Journalist — A1437

2005, Sept. 17
2688 A1437 45c multi   1.25 .40

Italian Participation in Exploration of Mars A1438

644   ITALY

Photo. With Hologram Applied
2005, Sept. 21   *Die Cut*
Self-Adhesive
2689   A1438   80c multi   2.25   1.25
Printed in sheets of 4.

Intercultura, 50th Anniv. — A1439

2005, Sept. 23   **Photo.**   *Perf. 13x13¼*
2690   A1439   60c multi   1.75   .50

Souvenir Sheet

Louis Vuitton Cup Acts 8 & 9 (Races to Determine America's Cup Challenger), Trapani — A1440

2005, Sept. 28   **Photo.**   *Perf. 13¼x13*
2691   A1440   €2.80 multi   7.00   7.00

Priority Mail Type of 2001 With Euro Denominations Only
Inscribed "I. P. Z. S. S. p. A. - ROMA 2005" at Bottom
2005   **Photo.**   *Serpentine Die Cut 11*
Self-Adhesive
Background Color
2691A   A1242   62c yellow   4.00   .55
2691B   A1242   €1.50 gray   9.00   1.00
Issued: 62c, Oct.; €1.50, Dec.
Nos. 2466 and 2585 have different printer's inscriptions and have a more easily seen coating over the circled "P" than on Nos. 2691A and 2691B. The coating over the circled "P" on Nos. 2691A and 2691B shines most when viewed from an oblique angle. A self-adhesive etiquette is adjacent to each stamp. Values are for stamps with adjacent etiquette.
Nos. 2691A and 2691B have self-adhesive selvage surrounding the stamp and etiquette. This selvage is not found on Nos. 2466 and 2585.
No. 2691B exists without year date and without etiquette, issued in 2007.

Stamp Day — A1441

2005, Oct. 7   **Photo.**   *Perf. 13¼x13*
2692   A1441   45c multi   1.25   .40

Italian Organ Donation Association — A1442

2005, Oct. 7   **Photo.**   *Perf. 13¼x13*
2693   A1442   60c multi   1.75   .50

National Association of Communities — A1443

2005, Oct. 19
2694   A1443   45c multi   1.25   .40

Story of Sts. Stephan and John The Baptist, by Fra Filippo Lippi — A1444

2005, Oct. 25   *Perf. 13x13¼*
2695   A1444   45c shown   1.25   .40
2696   A1444   €1.50 Four men   4.25   1.25

A1445

Christmas — A1446

2005, Oct. 31   **Photo.**   *Perf. 13¼x13¼*
2697   A1445   45c multi   1.25   .40
     Perf. 13¼x13
2698   A1446   62c multi   1.75   .50

Alcide De Gasperi (1881-1954), Prime Minister — A1447

2005, Nov. 9   **Photo.**   *Perf. 13¼x13*
2699   A1447   62c multi   1.75   .50

Giuseppe Mazzini (1805-72), Revolution Leader — A1448

2005, Nov. 10   **Photo.**   *Perf. 13¼x13¼*
2700   A1448   45c multi   1.25   .40

National Civil Protection — A1449

2005, Nov. 16   **Photo.**   *Perf. 13¼x13*
2701   A1449   45c multi   1.25   .40

Italian Red Cross — A1450

2005, Nov. 16
2702   A1450   45c multi   1.25   .40

Admission to United Nations, 50th Anniv. — A1451

2005, Nov. 23   *Perf. 13¼x13¼*
2703   A1451   70c multi   2.00   .50

Popes Reigning in 2005 — A1452

Designs: 45c, Pope John Paul II (1920-2005). 65c, Pope Benedict XVI.
2005, Nov. 26   **Photo.**   *Perf. 13x13¼*
2704   A1452   45c multi   1.40   .45
2705   A1452   65c multi   1.75   .60

Reconstitution of Caserta Province, 60th Anniv. — A1453

2005, Dec. 5   **Photo.**   *Perf. 13x13¼*
2706   A1453   45c multi   1.25   .40

A1454

Design: Opening of Enrico Toti Submarine Exhibit at Natl. Museum of Science and Technology, Milan.
2005, Dec. 7
2707   A1454   82c multi   1.75   .60

Eighteenth Birthday Greetings — A1455

2006, Jan. 1   **Photo.**   *Perf. 13½x13*
2708   A1455   45c blue & multi   1.50   .40
2709   A1455   45c pink & multi   1.50   .40
Souvenir sheets of 1 of redrawn stamps similar to Nos. 2708-2709 exist from a limited printing. Value, set of two sheets $1,300.

Panini, Soccer Card and Sticker Creators A1456

2006, Jan. 30   **Photo.**   *Perf. 13¼x13¼*
2710   A1456   €2.80 multi   8.00   3.00

Quattroruote Magazine, 50th Anniv. — A1457

2006, Feb. 1   *Perf. 13¼x13*
2711   A1457   62c multi   1.75   .50

Carlo Bo University, Urbino, 500th Anniv. — A1458

Ernesto Cairoli State High School, Varese A1459

Alessandron Tassoni State Science High School, Modena A1460

Agostino Nifo State High School, Sessa Aurunca A1461

2006, Feb. 6
2712   A1458   45c multi   1.25   .40
2713   A1459   45c multi   1.25   .40
2714   A1460   45c multi   1.25   .40
2715   A1461   45c multi   1.25   .40
Nos. 2712-2715 (4)   5.00   1.60

2006 Winter Olympics, Turin — A1462

2006, Feb. 8   *Perf. 13x13¼*
2716   A1462   23c Biathlon   .60   .25
2717   A1462   45c Figure skating   1.25   .40
2718   A1462   65c Ice hockey   1.60   .50
2719   A1462   70c Curling   1.75   .60
2720   A1462   85c Bobsled   2.10   .65
2721   A1462   90c Alpine skiing   2.25   .75
2722   A1462   €1 Torch   2.50   .80
2723   A1462   €1.30 Luge   3.25   .90
2724   A1462   €1.70 Medals   4.50   1.25
   a.   Souvenir sheet, #2716-2724   20.00   20.00
Nos. 2716-2724 (9)   19.80   6.10

Nos. 23, 45, 79 and 239 — A1463

2006, Feb. 9   **Photo.**   *Perf. 13¼x13*
2725   A1463   60c multi   1.75   .85
   a.   Booklet pane of 4   7.00   —
     Complete booklet, #2725a   7.50
Kingdom of Italy Stamp Show, Rome.

Dalmatian Historical Society, 80th Anniv. — A1464

2006, Feb. 10   **Engr.**   *Perf. 13x13¼*
2726   A1464   45c red vio & dk bl   1.25   .40

ITALY

Detail of Fresco From Mantua Castle Bridal Chamber, by Andrea Mantegna (1431-1506) — A1465

2006, Feb. 25		Photo.	Perf. 13x13¼
2727	A1465	45c multi	1.25 .40

2006 Winter Paralympics, Turin — A1466

2006, Mar. 9			Perf. 13¼x13
2728	A1466	60c multi	1.75 .40

Items Made in Italy — A1467

60c, Gelato. €2.80, Carrara marble.

2006, Mar. 11			Perf. 13¼x13
2729	A1467	60c multi	1.50 .50
2730	A1467	€2.80 multi	7.50 3.00

National Singers Association, 25th Anniv. — A1468

2006, Mar. 17			
2731	A1468	45c multi	1.25 .40

Aircraft Carrier "Cavour" A1469

2006, Mar. 17			
2732	A1469	60c multi	1.50 .50

Centenary of Sempione Tunnel — A1470

2006, Mar. 18			Perf. 13¼x13
2733	A1470	62c multi	1.50 .45

Tourism Type of 2005

No. 2734, Lago di Como. No. 2735, Marina di Pietrasanta. No. 2736, Pozzuoli.

2006, Mar. 24			
2734	A1424	45c multi	1.25 .40
2735	A1424	45c multi	1.25 .40
2736	A1424	45c multi	1.25 .40
	Nos. 2734-2736 (3)		3.75 1.20

Intl. Day of Mountains A1471

2006, Mar. 30			Perf. 13¼x13
2737	A1471	60c multi	1.60 .40

Madonna and Child Icon, Mondragone Basilica — A1472

2006, Apr. 1			
2738	A1472	45c multi	1.25 .40

First Vote for Italian Citizens Abroad — A1473

2006, Apr. 3			Perf. 13¼x13
2739	A1473	62c multi	1.60 .40

"Two Republics" Philatelic Exhibition A1474

2006, Apr. 5		Photo.	Perf. 13x13¼
2740	A1474	62c multi	1.60 .50
a.	Souvenir sheet, #2740, San Marino #1676a		3.50 3.50

See San Marino No. 1676. On No. 2740a, the Italian stamp is on the left. On San Marino No. 1676, the Italian stamp is on the right. Both stamps in No. 2740a have text printed on reverse.

Matterhorn Ski School, 70th Anniv. — A1475

2006, Apr. 13		Photo.	Perf. 13¼x13
2741	A1475	45c multi	1.25 .40

Madonna of Humility, by Gentile da Fabriano A1476

2006, Apr. 20		Photo.	Perf. 13x13¼
2742	A1476	€2.80 multi	7.00 2.50

Il Giorno Newspaper, 50th Anniv. — A1477

2006, Apr. 21			Perf. 13¼x13
2743	A1477	45c multi	1.25 .40

Constitutional Court, 50th Anniv. A1478

2006, Apr. 22			Engr.
2744	A1478	45c blue	1.25 .40

Enrico Mattei (1906-62), Public Administrator — A1479

2006, Apr. 29		Photo.	Perf. 13¼x13
2745	A1479	45c multi	1.25 .40

Italian Regions Type of 2004

2006, Apr. 29			Perf. 13¼x13
2746	A1387	45c Piedmont	1.25 .40
2747	A1387	45c Tuscany	1.25 .40
2748	A1387	45c Lazio	1.25 .40
2749	A1387	45c Puglia	1.25 .40
	Nos. 2746-2749 (4)		5.00 1.60

Targa Floria Automobile Race Track, Cent. A1480

2006, May 6		Photo.	Perf. 13¼x13
2750	A1480	60c multi	1.75 .50

Christopher Columbus (1451-1506), Explorer — A1481

2006, May 6		Photo.	Perf. 13¼x13
2751	A1481	62c multi	1.75 .50

Europa — A1482

People sitting on wall: 45c, View of faces. 62c, View of backs.

2006, May 8			
2752	A1482	45c multi	1.10 .40
2753	A1482	62c multi	1.50 .50

General Assembly of Intl. Military Sport Council, Rome — A1483

2006, May 9			
2754	A1483	45c multi	1.25 .40

2006 World Team Chess Championships, Turin — A1484

2006, May 20		Photo.	Perf. 13¼x13
2755	A1484	62c multi	1.60 .45

Constituent Assembly, 60th Anniv. — A1485

2006, June 1			Perf. 13¼x13
2756	A1485	60c multi	1.60 .40

Woman Suffrage, 60th Anniv. — A1486

2006, June 1			Perf. 13¼x13
2757	A1486	60c multi	1.60 .40

2006 World Bridge Championships, Verona — A1487

2006, June 9			Perf. 13¼x13
2758	A1487	65c multi	1.75 .45

Salto di Quirra Proving Grounds, 50th Anniv. — A1488

2006, June 13			Perf. 13¼x13
2759	A1488	60c multi	1.75 .40

Customs Department General Headquarters, Cent. A1489

Customs Cadet Legion, Cent. A1490

2006, June 21			Perf. 13¼x13
2760	A1489	60c multi	1.60 .40
			Perf. 13¼x13
2761	A1490	60c multi	1.60 .40

Reopening of Greek Theater, Tindari, 50th Anniv. — A1491

2006, July 6			Perf. 13¼x13
2762	A1491	€1.50 multi	4.25 1.25

Autostrada del Sole, 50th Anniv. — A1492

2006, July 10			Perf. 13¼x13
2763	A1492	60c multi	1.75 .40

Terrorist Bombing in Bologna, 26th Anniv. — A1493

2006, Aug. 2			Perf. 13¼x13
2764	A1493	60c multi	1.75 .40

ITALY

Italian Philatelic Union, 40th Anniv. A1494

2006, Sept. 1 Perf. 13x13¼
2765 A1494 60c multi + label   1.60   1.25

St. Gregory the Great (540-604) — A1495

2006, Sept. 2 Perf. 13¼x13
2766 A1495 60c multi   1.75   .40

Victory of Italian 2006 World Cup Soccer Team — A1496

2006, Sept. 9 Photo. Perf. 13x13¼
2767 A1496 €1 multi   2.75   .70

Victims of Terrorism A1497

2006, Sept. 16
2768 A1497 60c multi   1.60   .40

Ettore Majorana (1906-38?), Physicist — A1498

2006, Sept. 18 Perf. 13¼x13
2769 A1498 60c multi   1.75   .40

Saints — A1499

Designs: No. 2770, St. Ignatius of Loyola (1491-1556). No. 2771, St. Francis Xavier (1506-52).

2006, Sept. 27 Perf. 13x13¼
2770 A1499 60c multi   1.60   .40
2771 A1499 60c multi   1.60   .40

World Fencing Championships, Turin — A1500

2006, Sept. 29
2772 A1500 65c org, blk, white   1.75   .50

Lottery, 500th Anniv. — A1501

2006, Oct. 6 Photo. Perf. 13x13¼
2773 A1501 60c multi   1.60   .40

Philately Day — A1502

2006, Oct. 6
2774 A1502 60c multi   1.60   .40

Land and Marine Area Protection System — A1503

2006, Oct. 6
2775 A1503 65c multi   1.75   .40

Luchino Visconti (1906-76), Film Director — A1504

2006, Oct. 13 Perf. 13¼x13
2776 A1504 60c multi   1.60   .40

Dino Buzzati (1906-72), Writer — A1505

2006, Oct. 16
2777 A1505 60c multi   1.60   .40

Adoration of the Magi, by Jacopo Bassano — A1506

Christmas Tree — A1507

2006, Oct. 28 Engr. Perf. 13x13¼
2778 A1506 60c rose   1.60   .40
 Photo.
 Perf. 13¼x13
2779 A1507 65c multi   1.75   .50

Vittoriano Building, Tomb of the Unknown Soldier, Rome — A1508

2006, Nov. 11 Photo. Perf. 13x13¼
2780 A1508 60c multi   1.75   .40

Cathedral of St. Evasius, Casale Monteferrato A1509

2007, Jan. 4 Engr. Perf. 13x13¼
2781 A1509 60c rose   1.60   .40

First Montessori School, Cent. A1510

2007, Jan. 5 Photo. Perf. 13¼x13
2782 A1510 60c multi   1.60   .40

School for Public Administration, 50th Anniv. — A1511

2007, Jan. 10 Photo. Perf. 13x13¼
2783 A1511 65c multi   1.75   .45

Parma Cathedral A1512

2007, Jan. 13 Engr. Perf. 13¼x13
2784 A1512 60c green   1.60   .40

Arturo Toscanini (1867-1957), Conductor — A1513

2007, Jan. 16 Photo.
2785 A1513 60c multi   1.60   .40

St. Francis of Paola (1416-1507) A1514

2007, Jan. 27 Perf. 13x13¼
2786 A1514 60c multi   1.60   .40

Ferrante Gonzaga (1507-57), Soldier — A1515

2007, Jan. 27
2787 A1515 €1 multi   2.75   .65

Antonio Genovesi Salerno Foundation, 20th Anniv. — A1516

2007, Jan. 29 Photo. Perf. 13x13¼
2788 A1516 60c multi   1.60   .40

Relocation of Istrian Area Refugees to Giuliana di Fertilia District, Sardinia, 60th Anniv. — A1517

2007, Feb. 10 Photo. Perf. 13x13¼
2789 A1517 60c multi   1.60   .40

Father Lodovico Acernese (1835-1916) — A1518

2007, Feb. 16 Photo. Perf. 13¼x13
2790 A1518 23c multi   .70   .25

Giosuè Carducci (1835-1907), 1906 Nobel Laureate in Literature A1519

2007, Feb. 16 Photo. Perf. 13¼x13
2791 A1519 60c multi   1.60   .40

University of Brescia A1520

2007, Feb. 26 Perf. 13¼x13
2792 A1520 60c multi   1.60   .40

European Equal Opportunity Year — A1521

2007, Mar. 1 Photo. Perf. 13¼x13
2793 A1521 60c multi   1.60   .40

Scipione Maffei State High School, Verona A1522

2007, Mar. 14 Photo. Perf. 13¼x13
2794 A1522 60c multi   1.60   .40

Nicolò Carosio (1907-84), Radio Sportscaster A1523

2007, Mar. 15 Perf. 13¼x13
2795 A1523 65c multi   2.00   .50

Italian Regions Type of 2004

No. 2796, Trentino-Alto Adige. No. 2797, Marche. No. 2798, Umbria. No. 2799, Sardinia.

2007, Mar. 16 Photo. Perf. 13¼x13
2796 A1387 60c multi   1.75   .40
2797 A1387 60c multi   1.75   .40
2798 A1387 60c multi   1.75   .40
2799 A1387 60c multi   1.75   .40
 Nos. 2796-2799 (4)   7.00   1.60

Venice, UNESCO World Heritage Site — A1524

2007, Mar. 16 Engr. Perf. 13¼x13
2800 A1524 60c black   1.60   .40

ITALY

647

Intl. Electrotechnical Commission A1525

2007, Mar. 16 Photo. Perf. 13x13¼
2801 A1525 €1.50 multi   3.75   1.00

Souvenir Sheet

Treaty of Rome, 50th Anniv. A1526

2007, Mar. 25 Photo. Perf. 13x13¼
2802 A1526 Sheet of 2   3.50   3.50
  a. 60c Stars and "50"   1.50   .50
  b. 65c "Insieme dal 1957"   1.60   .50

Tourism Type of 2005

No. 2803, Brunico-Bruneck. No. 2804, Gaeta. No. 2805, Massafra. No. 2806, Cattolica Eraclea.

2005, Apr. 13 Perf. 13¼x13
2803 A1424 60c multi   1.60   .40
2804 A1424 60c multi   1.60   .40
2805 A1424 60c multi   1.60   .40
2806 A1424 60c multi   1.60   .40
  Nos. 2803-2806 (4)   6.40   1.60

Giuseppe Tomasi di Lampedusa (1896-1957), Writer — A1527

2007, Apr. 14 Photo. Perf. 13¼x13
2807 A1527 60c multi   1.60   .40

Forum, Rome — A1528

2007, Apr. 21 Perf. 13x13¼
2808 A1528 60c multi   1.60   .40

Europa A1529

Scouts: 60c, In canoe. 65c, At campfire.

2007, Apr. 23 Perf. 13¼x13
2809 A1529 60c multi   1.75   .45
2810 A1529 65c multi   2.00   .55
  a. Souvenir sheet, #2809-2810   5.00   5.00

Duccio Galamberti (1906-44), World War II Resistance Leader — A1530

2007, Apr. 24
2811 A1530 60c multi   1.60   .40

School of Economics and Finance, Rome, 50th Anniv. — A1531

2007, Apr. 27 Perf. 13x13¼
2812 A1531 €2.80 multi   7.00   2.25

Cinecittà Film Studios, Rome, 70th Anniv. — A1532

2007, Apr. 28
2813 A1532 65c multi   1.75   .50

Polirone Monastery, San Benedetto Po, 1000th Anniv. A1533

2007, May 5 Engr. Perf. 13¼x13
2814 A1533 60c blue & dark blue   1.60   .40

Malatesta Castle, Montefiore Conca A1534

2007, May 12
2815 A1534 60c brown   1.60   .40

Bancarella Musica Folk Music Project — A1535

2007, May 23 Photo.
2816 A1535 60c multi   1.60   .40

Emblem of Lamborghini Automobiles — A1536

2007, May 23
2817 A1536 85c multi   2.50   .75

F. C. Internazionale, 2006-07 Italian Soccer Champions — A1537

2007, June 4 Photo. Perf. 13¼
2818 A1537 60c multi   1.75   .40

Chianca Dolmen A1538

2007, June 9 Engr. Perf. 13¼x13
2819 A1538 60c brown   1.60   .40

Luigi Ganna, (1883-1957), Cyclist — A1539

2007, June 9 Photo. Perf. 13¼x13
2820 A1539 60c multi   1.60   .40

Altiero Spinelli (1907-86), Writer and Politician A1540

2007, June 21 Perf. 13x13¼
2821 A1540 60c multi   1.60   .40

Two Worlds Festival, 50th Anniv. — A1541

2007, June 29 Photo. Perf. 13x13¼
2822 A1541 60c multi   1.60   .40

San Vincenzo Basilica, Galliano A1542

On Wood Veneer Self-Adhesive

2007, July 2 Litho. Rouleted 7
2823 A1542 €2.80 black   7.50   2.75

Fiat 500 Automobile A1543

2007, July 4 Photo. Perf. 13x13¼
2824 A1543 60c multi   1.75   .40

Giuseppe Garibaldi (1807-82), Patriot — A1544

2007, July 4
2825 A1544 65c multi   1.75   .50

Capt. Maurizio Poggiali (1965-97), Pilot — A1545

2007, July 6
2826 A1545 60c multi   1.60   .40

Roman Speleology Club — A1546

2007, July 9
2827 A1546 €1.40 multi   3.75   1.25

Primo Carnera (1906-67), Boxer — A1547

2007, July 13
2828 A1547 60c multi   1.60   .40

Marco Foscarini School, Venice A1548

St. Pius V Institute for Political Studies, Rome A1549

Salerno Medical College A1550

2007, Sept. 17 Photo. Perf. 13¼x13
2829 A1548 60c multi   1.60   .40
2830 A1549 60c multi   1.60   .40
2831 A1550 60c multi   1.60   .40
  Nos. 2829-2831 (3)   4.80   1.20

Protected Donkey Breeds — A1551

2007, Sept. 22 Perf. 13x13¼
2832 A1551 60c multi   1.60   .40

31st European Women's Basketball Championships A1552

2007, Sept. 22 Perf. 13¼x13
2833 A1552 65c multi   1.75   .45

Sacra di San Michele Abbey, Sant'Ambroglio di Torino — A1553

2007, Sept. 29 Engr.
2834 A1553 60c red brown   1.60   .40

ITALY

Concetto Marchesi (1878-1957), Historian — A1554

2007, Oct. 1		Photo.
2835	A1554 60c multi	1.60 .40

Jacopo Barozzi (Il Vignola) (1507-73), Architect A1555

2007, Oct. 1		Perf. 13x13¼
2836	A1555 €2.80 multi	7.50 2.00

Grandparent's Day — A1556

2007, Oct. 2		
2837	A1556 60c multi	1.60 .40

Philately Day — A1557

2007, Oct. 12		Perf. 13¼x13
2838	A1557 60c multi	1.60 .40

Cupid and Psyche, Sculpture by Antonio Canova (1757-1822) A1558

2007, Oct. 12	Engr.	Perf. 13x13¼
2839	A1558 €1.50 black	4.00 1.40

Miniature Sheet

Entertainers — A1559

2007, Oct. 18	Photo.	Perf. 13¼x13
2840	A1559 Sheet of 3	5.00 4.50
a.-c.	60c Any single	1.60 .40

No. 2840: a, Beniamino Gigli (1890-1957), opera singer. b, Maria Callas (1923-77), opera singer. c, Amedeo Nazzari (1907-79), actor.

Giuseppe Di Vittorio (1892-1957), Union Leader — A1560

2007, Nov. 3		Perf. 13x13¼
2841	A1560 60c multi	1.60 .40

Mondadori Publishing House, Cent. — A1561

2007, Nov. 12		
2842	A1561 60c multi	1.60 .40

Madonna and Child, by Giovan Battista Cima da Conegliano A1562

Snow-covered House and Trees A1563

2007, Nov. 20	Engr.	Perf. 13¼x13
2843	A1562 60c green	1.50 .40
		Photo.
2844	A1563 65c multi	1.60 .45

Christmas.

Italian 2007-08 Term on UN Security Council — A1564

2007, Dec. 1	Photo.	Perf. 13x13¼
2845	A1564 85c multi	2.25 .80

Governor's Palace, Fiume (Rijeka, Croatia) — A1565

2007, Dec. 10		
2846	A1565 65c multi	1.75 .50

Italian Constitution, 60th Anniv. — A1566

2008, Jan. 2		Perf. 13¼x13
2847	A1566 60c multi	1.60 .40

Italian Red Cross Volunteer Nursing Corps, Cent. — A1567

2008, Jan. 29		
2848	A1567 60c multi	1.60 .40

Amintore Fanfani (1908-99), Politician A1568

2008, Feb. 6		Perf. 13x13¼
2849	A1568 €1 multi	2.50 .75

Italian Stock Exchange, Bicent. — A1569

2008, Feb. 8		Perf. 13¼x13
2850	A1569 65c multi	1.75 .50

Olivetti Typewriter and First Olivetti Factory — A1570

2008, Feb. 12		Perf. 13x13¼
2851	A1570 60c multi	1.60 .40

Olivetti Corporation, Cent.

Villa Reale, Monza, Designed by Giuseppe Piermarini A1571

2008, Feb. 18	Engr.	Perf. 13x13¼
2852	A1571 €1.40 black & blue	3.50 1.00

Natl. Council of Economics and Labor, 50th Anniv. — A1572

2008, Feb. 20		Photo.
2853	A1572 €1.50 multi	4.00 1.00

Dorando Pietri (1885-1942), Marathon Runner — A1573

2008, Feb. 23		
2854	A1573 60c multi	1.60 .40

Souvenir Sheet

Song, "Nel Blu, Dipinto di Blu," 50th Anniv. A1574

2008, Feb. 25		Perf. 13¼x13
2855	A1574 60c multi	2.00 2.00

Anna Magnani (1908-73), Actress — A1575

2008, Mar. 7		
2856	A1575 60c multi	1.60 .40

Emblem of Ricordi Publishing House and La Scala Theater, Milan — A1576

2008, Mar. 7	Photo.	Perf. 13¼x13
2857	A1576 60c indigo & gray	1.60 .40

Ricordi Music Publishing House, bicent.

Italia 2009 Intl. Philatelic Exhibition, Rome A1577

Exhibition emblem and: 60c, Congress Center. 65c, Colosseum.

2008, Mar. 7	Photo.	Perf. 13¼x13
2858	A1577 60c multi	1.75 .40
2859	A1577 65c multi	2.00 .50

Carlo Combi High School, Capodistria A1578

2008, Mar. 8		
2860	A1578 60c multi	1.60 .40

Edmondo de Amicis (1846-1908), Writer — A1579

2008, Mar. 11	Photo.	Perf. 13¼x13
2861	A1579 60c multi	1.60 .40

Self-portrait, by Bernardino di Betto (Pintoricchio, c. 1454-1513) A1580

2008, Mar. 14		Perf. 13x13¼
2862	A1580 60c multi	1.75 .40

Running of the Madonna, Sulmona — A1581

2008, Mar. 15		Perf. 13¼x13
2863	A1581 60c multi	1.60 .40

Italian Rowing Federation, 120th Anniv. — A1582

2008, Mar. 31	Photo.	Perf. 13x13¼
2864	A1582 65c multi	1.75 .50

Confirmation of the Rule, by Giotto — A1583

2008, Apr. 16	Photo.	Perf. 13¼x13
2865	A1583 60c multi	1.60 .40

Rule of life of St. Francis of Assisi, 700th anniv.

ITALY

Imperial Forum, Rome — A1584

2008, Apr. 21
2866 A1584 60c multi   1.60 .40

Italian National Press Federation, Cent. — A1585

2008, Apr. 23   Perf. 13¼x13
2867 A1585 60c multi   1.60 .40

Flight, Sculpture by Pasquale Basile — A1586

2008, Apr. 23   Perf. 13x13¼
2868 A1586 €1.40 multi   3.50 1.00
Intl. Decade of Education for Sustainable Development.

Giovannino Guareschi (1908-68), Journalist — A1587

2008, May 1   Photo.   Perf. 13¼x13
2869 A1587 60c multi   1.60 .40

Ludovico Geymonat (1908-91), Philosopher A1588

2008, May 8   Perf. 13x13¼
2870 A1588 60c multi   1.60 .40

Europa — A1589

Designs: 60c, Red mailbox. 65c, Brown mailbox.

2008, May 9   Photo.   Perf. 13¼x13
2871 A1589 60c multi   1.40 .45
2872 A1589 65c multi   1.60 .55

Works of Andrea Palladio (1508-80), Architect A1590

Designs: 60c, Alpini Bridge, Bassano. 65c, Palladian Basilica, Vicenza.

2008, May 10   Engr.   Perf. 13x13¼
2873 A1590 60c multi   1.50 .40
2874 A1590 65c multi   1.75 .50

St. Francis Caracciolo (1563-1608) A1591

2008, May 23   Photo.   Perf. 13x13¼
2875 A1591 60c multi   1.60 .40

Italian Regions Type of 2004

2008, May 23   Photo.   Perf. 13x13¼
2876 A1387 60c Valle d'Aosta   1.60 .40
2877 A1387 60c Veneto   1.60 .40
2878 A1387 60c Molise   1.60 .40
2879 A1387 60c Sicily   1.60 .40
Nos. 2876-2879 (4)   6.40 1.60

Guastalla School, Monza A1592

2008, May 24   Photo.   Perf. 13¼x13
2880 A1592 60c dk & lt blue   1.60 .40

Ducati Desmosedici GP7 Motorcycle A1593

2008, May 31   Perf. 13x13¼
2881 A1593 60c multi   2.00 .40

Giacomo Puccini (1858-1924), Composer — A1594

2008, June 21   Photo.   Perf. 13¼x13
2882 A1594 €1.50 multi   4.00 1.25

F. C. Internazionale, 2007-08 Italian Soccer Champions A1595

2008, July 4   Photo.   Perf. 13¼x13
2883 A1595 60c multi   1.75 .40

2008 Summer Olympics, Beijing — A1596

Olympic rings and: 60c, Torch bearer and map. 85c, Greek and Chinese athletes.

2008, July 7   Photo.   Perf. 13¼x13
2884 A1596 60c multi   1.60 .40
2885 A1596 85c multi   2.25 .75

Tommaso Landolfi (1908-79), Writer — A1597

2008, July 19   Photo.   Perf. 13¼x13
2886 A1597 60c multi   1.60 .40

Tourism Type of 2005

No. 2887, Tre Cime di Lavaredo. No. 2888, Introdacqua. No. 2889, Casamicciola Terme. No. 2890, Mamoiada.

2008, July 24   Photo.   Perf. 13¼x13
2887 A1424 60c multi   1.50 .40
2888 A1424 60c multi   1.50 .40
2889 A1424 60c multi   1.50 .40
2890 A1424 60c multi   1.50 .40
Nos. 2887-2890 (4)   6.00 1.60

Bowl of Saffron and Crocuses A1598

Ingredients for Spaghetti all'Amatriciana A1599

2008   Photo.   Perf. 13¼x13
2891 A1598 60c multi   1.60 .40
Perf. 13x13¼
2892 A1599 60c multi   1.60 .40
Issued: No. 2891, 7/26; No. 2892, 8/29.

Bell Tower, Treviglio — A1600

2008, Aug. 30   Engr.   Perf. 13x13¼
2893 A1600 60c multi   1.60 .40

Dante Alighieri High School, Gorizia A1601

Seal of the University of Perugia A1602

2008, Sept. 8   Photo.   Perf. 13¼x13
2894 A1601 60c multi   1.50 .40
2895 A1602 60c multi   1.50 .40

Cesare Pavese (1908-50), Writer — A1603

2008, Sept. 9
2896 A1603 65c multi   1.75 .50

Alberico Gentili (1552-1608), Jurist — A1604

2008, Sept. 13   Perf. 13x13¼
2897 A1604 65c multi   1.75 .50

Malatestiana Library, Cesena A1605

2008, Sept. 19   Engr.   Perf. 13¼x13
2898 A1605 60c black   1.60 .40

World Road Cycling Championships, Varese — A1606

2008, Sept. 22   Photo.   Perf. 13x13¼
2899 A1606 60c multi   1.60 .40

Philately Day — A1607

2008, Oct. 10   Perf. 13¼x13
2900 A1607 60c multi   1.60 .40

Italia 2009 Intl. Philatelic Exhibition, Rome — A1608

2008, Oct. 10   Photo.   Perf. 13¼x13
2901 A1608 85c multi   2.25 .60

Litho. on Gold Foil
Self-Adhesive
Rouletted 8
2902 A1608 €2.80 multi   8.00 5.00

Local Police — A1609

2008, Oct. 23   Photo.   Perf. 13¼x13
2903 A1609 60c multi   1.60 .40

Oath of the Plebian Tribune, 2500th Anniv. — A1610

2008, Oct. 24   Perf. 13x13¼
2904 A1610 60c multi   1.60 .40

ITALY

Madonna and Child Enthroned with Two Angels, by Lorenzo di Credi — A1611

2008, Oct. 30   **Photo.**   *Perf. 13¼x13*
2905   A1611   60c multi   1.60   .40

Litho. on Gold Foil Self-Adhesive
Rouletted 8
2906   A1612   €2.80 multi   8.00   5.00

Wreath — A1612

Christmas.

UNESCO World Heritage Sites — A1613

2008, Oct. 31   **Engr.**   *Perf. 13¼x13*
2907   A1613   60c multi   1.50   .40
2908   A1613   €2.80 blue & black   7.00   2.00

Designs: 60c, Val d'Orcia. €2.80, Historic Center of Urbino.

Messina Earthquake, Cent. — A1614

2008, Nov. 3   **Photo.**   *Perf. 13x13¼*
2909   A1614   60c multi   1.60   .40

Corriere dei Piccoli Comic Strips, Cent. — A1615

2008, Nov. 8
2910   A1615   60c multi   1.60   .40

Charles Darwin (1809-82), Naturalist — A1616

2009, Feb. 12
2911   A1616   65c multi   1.75   .50

Souvenir Sheet

Song, "Tintarella di Luna," 50th Anniv. — A1617

2009, Feb. 17   *Perf. 13¼x13*
2912   A1617   60c multi   1.75   1.75

5th Natl. Conference on Drugs, Trieste — A1618

2009, Mar. 12
2913   A1618   60c multi   1.60   .40

Valle Camonica Rock Drawing UNESCO World Heritage Site — A1619

2009, Mar. 27   **Engr.**
2914   A1619   €2.80 brown   7.00   2.00

Italia 2009 Intl. Philatelic Exhibition, Rome — A1620

People and: 60c, Italian stamps. €1, Map of Europe.

2009, Mar. 27   **Photo.**
2915   A1620   60c multi   1.75   .50
2916   A1620   €1 multi   2.75   .80

Father Primo Mazzolari (1890-1959), Writer on Social and Religious Issues — A1621

2009, Apr. 14   *Perf. 13x13¼*
2917   A1621   60c multi   1.60   .40

Sardinia Grenadier Corps, 350th Anniv. — A1622

2009, Apr. 16
2918   A1622   60c multi   1.60   .40

Piazza di Spagna, Spanish Steps, Fontana della Barcaccia, Rome — A1623

2009, Apr. 21
2919   A1623   60c multi   1.60   .40

Indro Montanelli (1909-2001), Journalist — A1624

2009, Apr. 22   *Perf. 13¼x13*
2920   A1624   60c multi   1.60   .40

Bulgari Jewelers, 125th Anniv. — A1625

2009, Apr. 24
2921   A1625   60c multi   1.60   .50

Italy-Switzerland Chamber of Commerce, Cent. — A1626

2009, May 2   *Perf. 13x13¼*
2922   A1626   60c multi   1.60   .40

Carabinieri Command for Cultural Heritage Protection — A1627

2009, May 4
2923   A1627   60c multi   1.60   .40

16th Mediterranean Games, Pescara — A1628

2009, May 5
2924   A1628   60c multi   1.60   .40

European Parliament Elections — A1629

2009, May 7
2925   A1629   60c multi   1.60   .40

Europa — A1630

Designs: 60c, Galileo National Telescope, La Palma, Canary Islands. 65c, AGILE astronomical satellite.

2009, May 7
2926   A1630   60c multi   1.60   .45
2927   A1630   65c multi   1.75   .55

Intl. Year of Astronomy.

Giro d'Italia Bicycle Race, Cent. — A1631

2009, May 9   *Perf. 13¼x13*
2928   A1631   60c multi   1.60   .55

Academy of Italian-German Studies, Merano, 50th Anniv. — A1632

2009, May 9   *Perf. 13x13¼*
2929   A1632   60c multi   1.60   .40

Mille Miglia Auto Race — A1633

2009, May 14   *Perf. 13x13¼*
2930   A1633   60c multi   1.60   .55

Festival of Mysteries, Campobasso — A1634

2009, May 22   *Perf. 13¼*
2931   A1634   60c multi   1.60   .55

See Nos. 3041, 3160, 3162-3163, 3262, 3283-3284, 3324.

Cathedral of Santa Maria Madre di Dio, Rieti — A1635

2009, May 27   **Engr.**   *Perf. 13¼x13*
2932   A1635   60c black   1.60   .55

Giovanni Palatucci (1909-45), Police Official Who Saved Jews From Deportation — A1636

2009, May 29   **Photo.**
2933   A1636   60c multi   1.60   .55

Gilera Motorbikes, Cent. — A1637

2009, June 6   *Perf. 13x13¼*
2934   A1637   60c multi   1.60   .55

Postage Stamps of Sicily, 150th Anniv. — A1638

2009, June 18   **Photo.**   *Perf. 13x13¼*
2935   A1638   60c multi   1.60   .55

Souvenir Sheet

2009 Baseball World Cup Tournament — A1639

2009, June 20   **Photo.**   *Perf. 13x13¼*
2936   A1639   60c multi   1.75   1.75

ITALY

St. Giovanni Leonardi
(1541-1609) — A1640

2009, June 23   *Perf. 13¼x13*
2937   A1640   60c multi   1.60   .55

F. C. Internazionale,
2008-09 Italian Soccer
Champions — A1641

2009, June 25
2938   A1641   60c multi   1.60   .55

San Daniele
Prosciutto, 500th
Anniv. of
Historical
Documentation of
Production
A1642

2009, June 26   *Perf. 13x13¼*
2939   A1642   60c multi   1.60   .55

St. Mark's
Square,
Venice — A1643

2009, July 2
2940   A1643   60c multi   1.60   .55

Envelope
A1644

2009   *Engr.*   *Serpentine Die Cut 11*
Self-Adhesive
          Denomination   Color
2941   A1644   60c   blue   1.60   .40
2942   A1644   €1.40   red   4.00   1.00
2943   A1644   €1.50   green   4.00   1.00
2944   A1644   €2   brown   5.25   1.50
2945   A1644   €3.30   black   8.50   1.50
     Nos. 2941-2945 (5)   23.35   6.40

Issued: Nos. 2941-2944, 7/7. No. 2945, 10/31. See Nos. 3074, 3166-3168A, 3273-3274, 3331.

Insurrection of
the Women of
Carrara, 65th
Anniv. — A1645

2009, July 7   *Photo.*   *Perf. 13x13¼*
2946   A1645   €1.50 multi   4.00   1.25

G8 Summit,
L'Aquila — A1646

2009, July 8   *Photo.*   *Perf. 13¼x13*
2947   A1646   65c multi   1.75   .80

Tourism Type of 2005
No. 2948, Verezzi. No. 2949, Isola del Giglio. No. 2950, Costa degli Dei, Capo Vaticano. No. 2951, Gole dell'Alcantara.

2009, July 10   *Photo.*   *Perf. 13¼x13*
2948   A1424   60c multi   1.60   .40
2949   A1424   60c multi   1.60   .40
2950   A1424   60c multi   1.60   .40
2951   A1424   60c multi   1.60   .40
     Nos. 2948-2951 (4)   6.40   1.60

La Nazione
Newspaper, Florence,
150th Anniv. — A1647

2009, July 14
2952   A1647   60c multi   1.60   .55

13th World Aquatics Championships,
Rome — A1648

2009, July 18   *Engr. & Embossed*
2953   A1648   €1.50 blue   4.00   1.25

Forest Fire
Prevention — A1649

2009, Aug. 1   *Photo.*
2954   A1649   60c multi   1.60   .50

30th Rimini
Meeting — A1650

2009, Aug. 25
2955   A1650   60c green & black   1.60   .50

Montebello Lancers
Cavalry Regiment,
150th Anniv. — A1651

2009, Sept. 4
2956   A1651   60c multi   1.60   .50

Painting by
Francesco
Solimena
A1652

2009, Sept. 17   *Photo.*   *Perf. 13¼x13*
2957   A1652   60c multi   1.60   .50

Portrait of a Woman, by Giovanni
Ambrogio de Predis, and Ambrosian
Academy Library and Gallery, Milan
A1653

2009, Sept. 21   *Engr.*   *Perf. 13¼x13*
2958   A1653   €1.40 black   3.75   1.25

Emilio Alessandrini
(1942-79), Magistrate
Killed by
Terrorists — A1654

2009, Sept. 26   *Photo.*   *Perf. 13¼x13*
2959   A1654   60c multi   1.60   .40

Souvenir Sheet

Christian
Roots of
Europe
A1655

No. 2960: a, Green cross, yellow brown map. b, Yellow brown cross, green map.

2009, Oct. 7   *Perf. 13x13¼*
2960   A1655   Sheet of 2   3.50   3.50
   a.   60c multi   1.60   .40
   b.   65c multi   1.75   .45

L'Unione Sarda
Newspaper, 120th
Anniv. — A1656

2009, Oct. 13   *Perf. 13¼x13*
2961   A1656   60c multi   1.60   .40

Father Luigi Sturzo
(1871-1959),
Politician — A1657

2009, Oct. 14
2962   A1657   €1.50 multi   4.00   1.00

Norberto Bobbio
(1909-2004),
Historian — A1658

2009, Oct. 16
2963   A1658   65c multi   1.75   .50

Fathers Giovanni Minozzi (1884-1959)
and Giovanni Semeria (1867-1931),
Founders of Natl. Institute of Southern
Italy — A1659

2009, Oct. 19
2964   A1659   60c multi   1.60   .50

Philately
Day — A1660

2009, Oct. 21   *Perf. 13x13¼*
2965   A1660   60c multi   1.60   .50

Italian Language Day — A1661

2009, Oct. 21   *Photo.*   *Perf. 13¼x13*
2966   A1661   60c multi + label   1.60   .40

Printed in sheets of 5 + 5 labels. Value, sheet $12.
See San Marino No. 1801; Vatican City No. 1426.

Sports Day at Italia
2009 Intl. Philatelic
Exhibition,
Rome — A1662

Sports figures: 60c, Gino Bartali (1914-2000), cyclist. 65c, Valentino Mazzola (1919-49), soccer player. €1.40, Michele Alboreto (1956-2001), race car driver.

2009, Oct. 22   *Photo.*   *Perf. 13¼x13*
2967   A1662   60c multi   1.60   .50
2968   A1662   65c multi   1.75   .55
2969   A1662   €1.40 multi   4.00   1.10
     Nos. 2967-2969 (3)   7.35   2.15

Souvenir Sheet

Diplomatic Relations Between Italy
and Bulgaria, 130th Anniv. — A1663

2009, Oct. 22   *Perf. 13¼*
2970   A1663   65c multi   2.00   2.00
   See Bulgaria No. 4525.

Adoration of the
Shepherds, by
Domenico Piola (1627-1703)
A1664

Ornaments
A1665

652　ITALY

2009, Oct. 23   Perf. 13¼x13
2971　A1664　60c multi　　1.60　.40

Self-Adhesive
Serpentine Die Cut 11
2972　A1665　60c multi　　2.50　.55

Christmas.

Souvenir Sheet

Comic Strips A1666

No. 2973: a, Cocco Bill, by Benito Jacovitti. b, Diabolik, by Angela and Luciana Giussani. c, Lupo Alberto, by Silver.

2009, Oct. 23   Perf. 13x13¼
2973　A1666　Sheet of 3　7.50　7.50
　a.-c.　€1 Any single　2.25　.90

Collector's Day at Italia 2009 Intl. Philatelic Exhibition, Rome.

Music Day at Italia 2009 Intl. Philatelic Exhibition, Rome — A1667

Designs: 65c, Luciano Pavarotti (1935-2007), singer. €1, Mino Reitano (1944-2009), singer. €1.50, Nino Rota (1911-79), composer.

2009, Oct. 24   Perf. 13¼
2974　A1667　65c multi　1.75　.55
2975　A1667　€1 multi　2.50　.75
2976　A1667　€1.50 multi　4.00　1.25
　Nos. 2974-2976 (3)　8.25　2.55

Europe Day at Italia 2009 Intl. Philatelic Exhibition, Rome — A1668

No. 2977 — Roman architectural works: a, Pont du Gard, France. b, Hadrian's Wall, Great Britain. c, Odeon of Patras, Greece. d, Porta Nigra, Trier, Germany. e, Segovia Aqueduct, Spain.

2009, Oct. 25　*Serpentine Die Cut 11*
Self-Adhesive
2977　Booklet pane of 5 + label　9.50　9.50
　a.-e.　A1668 65c Any single　1.75　.50
　Complete booklet, #2977　10.00

Art of the 20th Century — A1669

Designs: 60c, Guantanamera, sculpture by Giacomo Manzù (1908-91). 65c, Danza dell'Orzo (The Bear Dance), by Gino Severini (1883-1966). 85c, Donna e Ambiente, by Federico de Pistoris (1898-1975).

2009, Oct. 30   Perf. 13¼x13
2978　A1669　60c multi　1.75　.55
2979　A1669　65c multi　1.75　.60
2980　A1669　85c multi　2.50　.80
　Nos. 2978-2980 (3)　6.00　1.95

Giorgio Perlasca (1910-92), Rescuer of Jews in World War II — A1670

2010, Jan. 31　Photo.　Perf. 13x13¼
2981　A1670　60c multi　1.60　.50

Souvenir Sheet

Santa Maria de Collemaggio Basilica, L'Aquila — A1671

2010, Feb. 10　Photo.　Perf. 13¼x13
2982　A1671　60c multi　1.60　1.60

Folk Festivals Type of 2009

Designs: No. 2983, Acireale Carnival. No. 2984, Jousting tournament, Sa Sartiglia, Oristano.

2010, Feb. 12　Photo.　Perf. 13½
2983　A1634　60c multi　1.60　.50
2984　A1634　60c multi　1.60　.50

2010 Winter Olympics, Vancouver A1672

Serpentine Die Cut 11
2010, Feb. 12　**Self-Adhesive**
2985　A1672　85c multi　2.25　.75

2010 Youth Olympics, Singapore — A1673

2010, Feb. 12　　Photo.
Self-Adhesive
2986　A1673　85c multi　2.25　.75

Mario Pannunzio (1910-68), Journalist A1674

2010, Mar. 5　　Perf. 13x13¼
2987　A1674　60c multi　1.60　.50

Ennio Flaiano (1910-72), Screenwriter — A1675

2010, Mar. 5　Photo.　Perf. 13¼x13
2988　A1675　60c multi　1.60　.50

Madonna dei Miracoli Basilica, Motta di Livenza A1676

2010, Mar. 9
2989　A1676　60c black　1.60　.50

Massimo D'Azeglio, First President of Province of Milan, and Isimbardi Palace — A1677

2010, Mar. 19　　Perf. 13x13¼
2990　A1677　60c multi　1.60　.50

Province of Milan, 150th anniv.

Alfa Romeo Automobiles, Cent. — A1678

No. 2991: a, 1910 24HP. b, 2010 Giulietta.

2010, Mar. 20
2991　Horiz. pair + central label　3.50　3.00
　a.-b.　A1678 60c Either single　1.60　.50

Burial of Christ with Three Angels Holding the Shroud, by Gerolamo della Rovere — A1679

2010, Mar. 22　　Perf. 13¼x13
2992　A1679　60c multi　1.60　.50

Confindustria (Federation of Employers), Cent. — A1680

2010, May 5　　Perf. 13¼x13
2993　A1680　€1.40 multi　3.75　1.40

Miniature Sheet

Expedition of the Thousand, 150th Anniv. — A1681

No. 2994 — Paintings: a, Garibaldi Sets Sail From Quarto, by V. Azzola. b, Landing at Marsala, by unknown artist. c, Battle of Calatafimi, by Remigio Legat. d, Encounter in Teano of Garibaldi and Victor Emmanuel II, by Pietro Aldi.

2010, May 5
2994　A1681　Sheet of 4　8.00　7.00
　a.　60c multi　1.60　.50
　b.　65c multi　1.75　.55
　c.　85c multi　2.25　.80
　d.　€1 multi　2.50　.80

Rhaetian Railway in the Albula - Bernina Landscapes UNESCO World Heritage Site — A1682

2010, May 6　　Perf. 13¼x13
2995　A1682　65c multi　1.75　.60

Pinocchio, by Carlo Collodi A1683

Geronimo Stilton, by Elisabetta Dami A1684

2010, May 7
2996　A1683　60c multi　1.40　.60
2997　A1684　65c multi　1.60　.75

Europa.

Sister Maria Domenica Brun Barbentini (1789-1868), Founder of the Congregation of the Sister Servants of the Sick of St. Camillus A1685

2010, May 22　　Perf. 13x13¼
2998　A1685　60c multi　1.60　.50

Hanbury Botanic Gardens, Ventimiglia A1686

2010, May 29
2999　A1686　60c multi　1.60　.50

Tourism Type of 2005 and

1955 Tourism Poster — A1687

2010, June 4　　Perf. 13¼x13
3000　A1424　60c Courmayeur　1.60　.50
3001　A1424　60c Todi　1.60　.50
3002　A1424　60c Viggiano　1.60　.50
3003　A1424　60c Isole Tremiti　1.60　.50
　Nos. 3000-3003 (4)　6.40　2.00

Self-Adhesive
Serpentine Die Cut 11
3004　A1687　60c multi　1.60　.50

Camilo Benso, Count of Cavour (1810-61), Statesman — A1688

2010, June 6　　Perf. 13¼x13
3005　A1688　60c multi　1.60　.50

Association of Italian Joint Stock Companies, Cent. — A1689

2010, June 17　Photo.　Perf. 13x13¼
3006　A1689　60c multi　1.60　.50

ITALY

F.C. Internazionale, 2009-10 Italian Soccer Champions — A1690

2010, June 24			**Perf. 13¼x13**	
3007	A1690	60c multi	1.60	.50

Federacciai Iron and Steel Plant, Bagnoli, Cent. — A1691

Litho. & Silk-Screened

2010, June 28			**Perf. 13¼x14**	
3008	A1691	€3.30 black	8.50	3.00

No. 3008 is coated with a varnish producing a rough surface, and is printed with a special ink that allows the stamp to be lifted by a magnet.

Envelope — A1692

Serpentine Die Cut 11x11¼

2010, July 1   Self-Adhesive   **Photo.**
Color of Denomination

3009	A1692	5c dark blue	.25	.25
3010	A1692	10c black	.30	.25
3011	A1692	20c blue green	.60	.25
		Nos. 3009-3011 (3)	1.15	.75

See Nos. 3165, 3330.

Giovanni Virginio Schiaparelli (1835-1910), Astronomer A1693

2010, July 2			**Perf. 13x13¼**	
3012	A1693	65c multi	1.75	.50

Pope Benedict XVI, Statue of Pope Celestine V — A1694

2010, July 4			**Perf. 13¼x13**	
3013	A1694	60c multi	1.60	.50

Celestinian Jubliee Year.

David with the Head of Goliath, by Caravaggio (1571-1610) A1695

2010, July 16			**Perf. 13x13¼**	
3014	A1695	60c multi	1.75	.50

Ettore Paratore (1907-2000), Latin Scholar, Mosaic and Theater Mask A1696

2010, July 17			**Perf. 13¼x13**	
3015	A1696	65c multi	1.75	.55

50th Plautus Festival, Sarsina.

Samnite Theater, Pietrabbondante — A1697

2010, July 31			**Engr.**	
3016	A1697	60c brown	1.60	.50

Joe Petrosino (1860-1909), New York City Policeman, Statue of Liberty, Brooklyn Bridge — A1698

2010, Aug. 30		**Photo.**	**Perf. 13x13¼**	
3017	A1698	85c multi	2.25	.75

1960 Summer Olympics, Rome, 50th Anniv. — A1699

2010, Sept. 7				
3018	A1699	60c multi	1.60	.50

First National Gathering of Fire Brigades, Cortina d'Ampezzo A1700

2010, Sept. 10			**Perf. 13x13¼**	
3019	A1700	60c multi	1.60	.50

National Aerobatic Team, 50th Anniv. — A1701

2010, Sept. 11				
3020	A1701	60c multi	1.60	.50

Piazzale di Porta Pia, Rome — A1702

2010, Sept. 20				
3021	A1702	60c multi	1.60	.50

Men's Volleyball World Championships, Italy — A1703

Engr. & Embossed

2010, Sept. 24			**Perf. 13x13¼**	
3022	A1703	85c blue	2.25	.75

Torre Del Greco Coral A1704

2010, Sept. 30		**Photo.**	**Perf. 13¼x13**	
3023	A1704	60c multi	1.60	.55

Souvenir Sheet

Turin-Salerno High Speed Rail Line — A1705

2010, Oct. 2			**Perf. 13x13¼**	
3024	A1705	60c multi	1.60	1.60

Corriere Adriatico Newspaper, Ancona, 150th Anniv. — A1706

2010, Oct. 5			**Perf. 13¼x13**	
3025	A1706	60c multi	1.60	.50

National Anti-trust Authority, 20th Anniv. — A1707

2010, Oct. 10			**Perf. 13x13¼**	
3026	A1707	€1.40 multi	3.75	1.20

School of Oenology, Conegliano A1708

2010, Oct. 21			**Perf. 13x13¼**	
3027	A1708	60c multi	1.60	.50

Leonardo Sciascia (1921-89), Writer — A1709

2010, Oct. 23			**Engr.**	
3028	A1709	60c black	1.60	.50

Italian Tennis Federation, Cent. — A1710

2010, Oct. 25			**Photo.**	
3029	A1710	60c multi	1.60	.50

Self-Portrait of Pietro Annigoni (1910-88) A1711

2010, Oct. 27			**Perf. 13¼x13**	
3030	A1711	60c multi	1.75	.50

Souvenir Sheet

Italian Film Personalities — A1712

No. 3031: a, Federico Fellini (1920-93), director. b, Vittorio Gassman (1922-2000), actor, director. c, Alberto Sordi (1920-2003), actor, director.

2010, Oct. 28				
3031	A1712	Sheet of 3	5.00	5.00
a.-c.		60c Any single	1.60	.50

Philately Day — A1713

2010, Oct. 29				
3032	A1713	60c multi	1.60	.50

Frette Textiles, 150th Anniv. A1714

2010, Oct. 29				
3033	A1714	60c multi	1.60	.50

Adoration of the Magi, by Sandro Botticelli A1715

Toy Train — A1716

2010, Oct. 29			**Perf. 13¼x13**	
3034	A1715	60c multi	1.60	.50
			Perf. 13x13¼	
3035	A1716	65c multi	1.75	.60

Christmas.

Mario Mazzuca (1910-83), Rugby Player — A1717

2010, Oct. 30			**Perf. 13x13¼**	
3036	A1717	60c multi	1.60	.50

ITALY

Gentilini Cookies, 120th Anniv. A1718

2010, Oct. 31 Perf. 13¼x13
3037 A1718 60c multi 1.60 .50

Berlucchi Wines, 50th Anniv. (in 2011) A1719

2010, Nov. 5
3038 A1719 60c multi 1.60 .50

A1720

Italian Flag, 150th Anniv. — A1721

2011, Jan. 7 Photo. Perf. 13x13¼
Souvenir Sheet
3039 A1720 60c multi 1.60 .50
Self-Adhesive
Serpentine Die Cut 11
3040 A1721 60c multi 2.25 .60
Unification of Italy, 150th anniv.

Folk Festivals Type of 2009
Design: No. 3041, Battle of the Oranges, Carnival of Ivrea.

2011, Feb. 20 Photo. Perf. 13½
3041 A1634 60c multi 1.60 .50

Antonio Fogazzaro (1842-1911), Writer — A1722

2011, Mar. 7 Perf. 13x13¼
3042 A1722 60c multi 1.60 .50

Intl. Women's Day — A1723

2011, Mar. 8
3043 A1723 75c multi 1.75 .60

Miniature Sheet

Taxation Agencies, 10th Anniv. — A1724

No. 3044: a, Territorio (Land Registry). b, Dogane (Customs). c, Demanio (State Property). d, Entrate (Revenue).

2011, Mar. 10
3044 A1724 Sheet of 4 6.00 6.00
a.-d. 60c Any single 1.60 .50

Souvenir Sheet

Proclamation of the Kingdom of Italy, 150th Anniv. — A1725

2011, Mar. 17 Photo. Perf. 13x13¼
3045 A1725 60c multi 1.75 1.75

Souvenir Sheet

Piazza del Popolo, Rome A1726

2011, Mar. 21 Perf. 13¼x13
3046 A1726 €1.50 multi 4.50 4.50
Unification of Italy, 150th anniv. See Vatican City No. 1470.

Cheeses Made in Italy — A1727

Designs: No. 3047, Gorgonzola. No. 3048, Parmigiano Reggiano. No. 3049, Mozzarella di Bufala Campana (buffalo milk mozzarella). No. 3050, Ragusano.

2011, Mar. 25
3047 A1727 60c multi 1.60 .50
3048 A1727 60c multi 1.60 .50
3049 A1727 60c multi 1.60 .50
3050 A1727 60c multi 1.60 .50
Nos. 3047-3050 (4) 6.40 2.00

World Theater Day — A1728

Serpentine Die Cut 11
2011, Mar. 27 Self-Adhesive
3051 A1728 60c multi 1.60 .50

Italy No. 22 — A1729

Serpentine Die Cut 11¼
2011, Mar. 29 Photo.
Self-Adhesive
3052 A1729 60c aqua &dk blue 1.60 .50
a. Booklet pane of 10 16.00
Complete booklet, #3052a 17.50

First Man in Space, 50th Anniv. — A1730

Serpentine Die Cut 11
2011, Apr. 12 Photo.
Self-Adhesive
3054 A1730 75c multi 2.10 .75

Quadriga on King Victor Emmanuel II Monument, Rome — A1731

2011, Apr. 21 Perf. 13¼x13
3055 A1731 60c multi 1.60 .50

Emilion Salgari (1862-1911), Writer — A1732

2011, Apr. 23 Perf. 13x13¼
3056 A1732 60c multi 1.60 .50

Beatification of Pope John Paul II — A1733

Serpentine Die Cut 11
2011, Apr. 29 Self-Adhesive
3057 A1733 60c multi 1.60 .50

Europa — A1734

Forest and: 60c, Mushrooms, squirrel. 75c, Bird, flowers.

2011, May 9 Perf. 13¼x13
3058 A1734 60c multi 1.60 .50
3059 A1734 75c multi 2.00 1.00
Intl. Year of Forests.

Amnesty International, 50th Anniv. — A1735

Serpentine Die Cut 11¼
2011, May 28 Photo.
Self-Adhesive
3060 A1735 60c multi 1.60 .50

National Emigration Museum, Rome — A1736

2011, June 1 Perf. 13x13¼
3061 A1736 60c multi 1.60 .55

Souvenir Sheets

Unification of Italy, 150th Anniv. — A1737

Famous people and artwork: No. 3062, Camillo Benso, Conte di Cavour (1810-61), statesman, scene from 1856 Congress of Paris. No. 3063, Carlo Cattaneo (1801-69), writer, scene from 1848 Milan Revolt. No. 3064, Giuseppe Garibaldi (1807-82), military leader, scene of Garibaldi entering Naples, Sept. 7, 1860. No. 3065, Vincenzo Gioberti (1801-52), politician, scene of people celebrating in Naples. No. 3066, Clara Maffei (1814-86), Cristina Trivulzio Belgiojoso (1808-71), advocates of independence, scene of soldiers carrying injured Luciano Manara at Villa Spada, 1850. No. 3067, Giuseppe Mazzini (1805-72), politician, cover page of Giovine Italia, and Unione, Forza e Liberta flag. No. 3068, Carlo Pisacane (1818-57), patriot, and depiction of his murder. No. 3069, King Victor Emmanuel II (1820-78), and depiction of him on horseback

2011, June 2
3062 A1737 60c multi 1.75 1.75
3063 A1737 60c multi 1.75 1.75
3064 A1737 60c multi 1.75 1.75
3065 A1737 60c multi 1.75 1.75
3066 A1737 60c multi 1.75 1.75
3067 A1737 60c multi 1.75 1.75
3068 A1737 60c multi 1.75 1.75
3069 A1737 60c multi 1.75 1.75
Nos. 3062-3069 (8) 14.00 14.00

Souvenir Sheet

Anita and Giuseppe Garibaldi, First Tower of San Marino — A1738

2011, June 4
3070 A1738 €1.50 multi 4.00 4.00
Granting of San Marino citizenship to Garibaldis. See San Marino No. 1851.

Miniature Sheet

Italian Navy, 150th Anniv. A1739

No. 3071: a, Arms of the Savoia family, Navy arms and pennant. b, Naval Academy, Livorno. c, Training ship Amerigo Vespucci. d, Emblems of Italian Sailor's Union and National Association of Italian Sailors

2011, June 10
3071 A1739 Sheet of 4 6.00 6.00
a.-d. 60c Any single 1.60 .55

Italian Referees Association, Cent. — A1740

2011, June 18
3072 A1740 60c multi 1.60 .55

ITALY

655

Carlo Dapporto (1911-89), Actor — A1741

2011, June 25		Perf. 13¼x13
3073	A1741 60c multi	1.60 .55

Envelope Type of 2009
Self-Adhesive
Serpentine Die Cut 11

2011, June 28		Engr.
	Denomination	Color
3074	A1644 75c	lilac 2.00 .75

Parks and Gardens A1742

Designs: No. 3075, Flower Garden, Appenninica di Capracotta. No. 3076, Padua Botanical Gardens.

2011, July 4	Photo.	Perf. 13¼x13
3075	A1742 60c multi	1.60 .55
3076	A1742 60c multi	1.60 .55

Holy Trinity Benedictine Abbey, Cava de'Tirreni, 1000th Anniv. A1743

2011, July 7		Engr. Perf. 13¼x13
3077	A1743 60c black	1.60 .55

Compasso d'Oro Award for Industrial Design A1744

2011, July 12	Photo.	Perf. 13½
3078	A1744 60c multi	1.60 .55

Hadrian's Villa, Tivoli A1745

2011, July 14		Perf. 13¼x13
3079	A1745 60c multi	1.60 .55

Tourism Type of 2005 and

1955 Tourism Poster — A1746

No. 3080, Tarvisio. No. 3081, Riviera del Conero, Sirolo. No. 3082, Sepino. No. 3083, Bosa.

2011, July 23	Photo.	Perf. 13¼x13
3080	A1424 60c multi	1.60 .55
3081	A1424 60c multi	1.60 .55
3082	A1424 60c multi	1.60 .55
3083	A1424 60c multi	1.60 .55
	Nos. 3080-3083 (4)	6.40 2.20

Self-Adhesive
Serpentine Die Cut 11

| 3084 | A1746 60c multi | 1.60 .55 |

Souvenir Sheet

St. Luke Painting the Virgin, by Giorgio Vasari (1511-74) — A1747

2011, July 30		Perf. 13x13¼
3085	A1747 €1.40 multi	3.50 3.50

Folk Festivals Type of 2009
Design: Mastrogiurato Festival, Lanciano.

2011, Aug. 26		Perf. 13½
3086	A1634 60c multi	1.60 .75

Milan, 2010-11 Italian Soccer Champions A1748

F. C. Internazionale, 2010-11 Italy Cup Soccer Champions A1749

2011, Aug. 27		Perf. 13¼x13
3087	A1748 60c multi	1.60 .55
		Perf. 13x13¼
3088	A1749 60c multi	1.60 .55

World Sports Fishing Championships, Italy — A1750

Serpentine Die Cut 11

2011, Aug. 27		Self-Adhesive
3089	A1750 60c multi	1.60 .55

2011 European Field Archery Championships, Montevarchi A1751

Serpentine Die Cut 11

2011, Aug. 27		Self-Adhesive
3090	A1751 75c multi	2.00 .75

25th National Eucharistic Congress A1752

2011, Sept. 3		Photo. Self-Adhesive
3091	A1752 60c multi	1.60 .55

Arch of Trajan, Benevento A1753

2011, Sept. 9	Engr.	Perf. 13x13¼
3092	A1753 60c black	1.60 .55

Intl. Year of Chemistry A1754

Serpentine Die Cut 11

2011, Sept. 11		Photo. Self-Adhesive
3093	A1754 €1.40 multi	3.50 1.25

Council of State, 180th Anniv. — A1755

Serpentine Die Cut 11

2011, Sept. 13		Engr. Self-Adhesive
3094	A1755 60c black	1.60 .55

Organization for Economic Cooperation and Development, 50th Anniv. — A1756

2011, Sept. 30		Photo.
3095	A1756 60c multi	1.60 .55

European Year of Volunteers — A1757

Self-Adhesive

2011, Oct. 4	Serpentine Die Cut 11
3096	A1757 75c multi 2.00 .75

Marzotto Textiles, 175th Anniv. — A1758

2011, Oct. 14		Photo. Self-Adhesive
3097	A1758 60c multi	1.60 .55

Italo Svevo (1861-1928), Writer — A1759

Self-Adhesive

2011, Oct. 28	Serpentine Die Cut 11
3098	A1759 60c multi 1.60 .55

Equestrian Order of the Holy Sepulchre of Jerusalem A1760

2011, Nov. 3		Photo. Self-Adhesive
3099	A1760 60c multi	1.60 .55

Souvenir Sheets

Battles A1761

No. 3100: a, Battle of Pastrengo, 1848. b, Battle of Solferino, 1859. c, Battle of Volturno, 1860.
No. 3101: a, Battle of Bezzecca, 1866. b, Breach of Porta Pia, 1870. c, Battles of the Isonzo, 1915-17.

2011, Nov. 4		Perf. 13x13¼
3100	A1761 Sheet of 3	4.50 4.50
a.-c.	60c Any single	1.60 .75
3101	A1761 Sheet of 3	4.50 4.50
a.-c.	60c Any single	1.60 .75

Italian Military Missions in Foreign Countries A1762

Serpentine Die Cut 11

2011, Nov. 12		Self-Adhesive
3102	A1762 75c multi	2.00 .75

Philately Day — A1763

Self-Adhesive

2011, Nov. 18		Photo.
3103	A1763 60c multi	1.60 .80

Italian Mint, Cent. A1764

Self-Adhesive

2011, Nov. 18		
3104	A1764 60c multi	1.60 .55

ITALY

Postal Savings Booklets A1765

Designs: 60c, Old postal savings booklets. 75c, Modern postal savings booklets.

2011, Nov. 18   Self-Adhesive
3105 A1765 60c multi   1.60   .55
3106 A1765 75c multi   2.00   .75

Fratelli Carli Olive Oil, Cent. A1766

2011, Nov. 19   Self-Adhesive
3107 A1766 60c multi   1.60   .55

Madonna and Child with Pomegranate, by Unknown Artist A1767

Flying Reindeer A1768

2011, Nov. 19   Self-Adhesive
3108 A1767 60c multi   1.60   .55
3109 A1768 60c multi   1.60   .55
Christmas.

Russian-Italian Year of Culture — A1769

2011, Dec. 10   Self-Adhesive
3110 A1769 75c multi   2.00   .75
See Russia No. 7326.

Italian Olympic Committee Library and Stylized Athletes — A1770

2012, Jan. 4   *Serpentine Die Cut 11*
3111 A1770 60c multi   1.60   1.60
Giulio Onesti (1912-81), Member of Italian Olympic Committee and collector of books on sports.

Souvenir Sheet

Introduction of the Italian Lira, 150th Anniv. — A1771

No. 3112: a, Italia holding lira coin. b, "150" with coin as zero. c, Coin.

2012, Mar. 23   *Perf. 13x13¼*
3112 A1771 Sheet of 3   4.50 4.50
a.-c.   60c Any single   1.60   .55

Italian Regional Wine Grapes and Vineyards A1772

No. 3113 — Grapes and vineyards for wines guaranteed to be from specific regions: a, Aglianico del Vulture Superiore. b, Cannellino di Frascati. c, Barolo. d, Greco di Tufo. e, Brunello di Montalcino. f, Montepulciano d'Abruzzo Colline Teramane. g, Colli Orientali del Friuli Picolit. h, Montefalco Sagrantino. i, Prosecco Conegliano Valdobbiadene Superiore. j, Vernaccia di Serrapetrona. k, Cerasuolo di Vittoria. l, Vermentino di Gallura. m, Moscato di Scanzo. n, Romagna Albana. o, Primitivo di Manduria Dolce Naturale.

2012, Mar. 24   *Serpentine Die Cut 11*
     Self-Adhesive
3113   Sheet of 15   30.00 30.00
a.-o.   A1772 60c Any single   1.60   .55
Milanofil 2012 Intl. Philatelic Exhibition, Milan. See Nos. 3196, 3270, 3337, 3373.

Le Fracchie di San Marco — A1773

2012, Mar. 31   *Perf. 13¼*
3114 A1773 60c multi   1.60   .55

Giovanni Pascoli (1855-1912), Poet — A1774

2012, Apr. 6   *Serpentine Die Cut 11*
     Self-Adhesive
3115 A1774 60c multi   1.60   .80

Savings Banks Association (ACRI), Cent. — A1775

2012, Apr. 11   Self-Adhesive
3116 A1775 60c multi   1.60   .80

Publication of Lunario Barbanera (Almanac), 250th Anniv. — A1776

2012, Apr. 11   Self-Adhesive
3117 A1776 60c multi   1.60   .80

Balsamic Vinegar From Modena — A1777

2012, Apr. 17   Self-Adhesive
3118 A1777 60c multi   1.60   .80

Miniature Sheet

Italian Post Office, 150th Anniv. — A1778

No. 3119: a, Men and women in office with pillars and machinery. b, Postman on camel. c, Airplane ground crew handling mail sacks. d, Mail vehicles in arc. e, Man handling mail sack on streetcar. f, Woman and computer. g, Postman on scooter. h, Customers at postal bank. i, Postal workers in office with computers.

2012, May 5   Self-Adhesive
3119 A1778 Sheet of 9   17.50 17.50
a.-i.   60c Any single   1.50   .75

Europa — A1779

Woman and: 60c, Field of sunflowers, building, building pillars. 75c, Dancer, coastal village.

2012, May 9   Self-Adhesive
3120 A1779 60c multi   1.50   .75
3121 A1779 75c multi   2.00   .95

Santa Maria Novella Perfumes and Pharmaceuticals Shop, Florence, 400th Anniv. — A1780

2012, May 10   *Serpentine Die Cut 11*
3122 A1780 75c multi   2.00   1.25

Trani Cathedral A1781

2012, June 1   *Engr.*   *Perf. 13x13¼*
3123 A1781 60c black   1.50   .75

Pres. Luigi Einaudi (1874-1961) A1782

2012, July 2   *Photo.*
     Serpentine Die Cut 11
     Self-Adhesive
3124 A1782 60c multi   1.50   .75

Horse Battle, by Aligi Sassu (1912-2000) A1783

2012, July 17   *Perf. 13¼x13*
3125 A1783 60c multi   1.50   .75

Tourism Type of 2005 and

Travel Poster — A1784

2012, July 19   *Serpentine Die Cut 11*
     Self-Adhesive
3126 A1424 60c Baveno   1.50   .75
3127 A1424 60c Maiori   1.50   .75
3128 A1424 60c Monte Cassino   1.50   .75
3129 A1424 60c Ustica   1.50   .75
3130 A1784 60c multi   1.50   .75
Nos. 3126-3130 (5)   7.50   3.75

Juventus, 2011-12 Italian Soccer Champions A1785

2012, July 21   *Photo.*
     Self-Adhesive
3131 A1785 60c multi   1.50   .75

Expo 2015, Milan — A1786

2012, Aug. 1   *Serpentine Die Cut 11*
     Self-Adhesive
3132 A1786 60c multi   1.50   .75

Boniface VIII Baths, Fiuggi A1787

2012, Aug. 4   *Engr.*
     Self-Adhesive
3133 A1787 €1.50 black   4.00   4.00

Fermo Cathedral A1788

2012, Aug. 14   *Perf. 13x13¼*
3134 A1788 60c black   1.50   .55

Roma Newspaper, 150th Anniv. — A1789

2012, Sept. 10   *Serpentine Die Cut 11*
     Photo.
     Self-Adhesive
3135 A1789 60c multi   1.50   .75

ITALY

Souvenir Sheet

Battle of the Milvian Bridge, 1700th Anniv. — A1790

2012, Sept. 13		Perf. 13x13¼
3136	A1790 €1.40 multi	3.75 3.75

See Vatican City No. 1507.

Anti-Mafia Investigation Department — A1791

Serpentine Die Cut 11
2012, Sept. 21		Self-Adhesive
3137	A1791 60c multi	1.50 .80

Italian Surgery Congress, Rome — A1792

2012, Sept. 23		Photo.
	Self-Adhesive	
3138	A1792 60c red & green	1.50 .80

Botanical Gardens A1793

Botanical Gardens in: No. 3139, Rome. No. 3140, Catania.

Serpentine Die Cut 11
2012, Sept. 28		Self-Adhesive
3139	A1793 75c multi	2.00 1.00
3140	A1793 75c multi	2.00 1.00

See Nos. 3175-3177, 3235-3237.

Court of Auditors, 150th Anniv. — A1794

2012, Oct. 1		Engr.
	Self-Adhesive	
3141	A1794 60c green & black	1.50 .80

Cusano Milanino, Cent. — A1795

2012, Oct. 6		Photo.
	Self-Adhesive	
3142	A1795 60c multi	1.50 .80

Second Vatican Council (Vatican II), 50th Anniv. A1796

2012, Oct. 11	*Serpentine Die Cut 11*
	Self-Adhesive
3143	A1796 60c multi	1.75 .80

National Corps of Scouts and Guides, Cent. — A1797

2012, Oct. 12		Photo.
	Self-Adhesive	
3144	A1797 60c multi	1.50 .80

Philately Day — A1798

No. 3145 — Steps in the creation of an Italian stamp: a, Philatelic consultation group (Consulta filatelica). b, Signing of decree (Decretazione). c, Graphic design (Ideazione grafica). d, Philatelic commission inspecting designs (Commissione filatelica). e, Printing of stamps (Produzione carte valori).

2012, Oct. 12		Perf. 13¼x13
3145	Horiz. strip of 5	8.00 7.00
a.-e.	A1798 60c Any single	1.60 .55

See Nos. 3197, 3277.

Manger with Saints John the Baptist and Bartholomew, by Antonio del Massaro — A1799

Christmas Tree — A1800

2012, Oct. 12	*Serpentine Die Cut 11*
	Self-Adhesive
3146	A1799 60c multi	1.50 .80
3147	A1800 60c multi	1.50 .80

Christmas.

Guzzini Housewares A1801

2012, Oct. 13		Photo.
	Self-Adhesive	
3148	A1801 60c multi	1.50 .80

Ceramics A1802

No. 3149: a, Castelli ceramic plate. b, Caltagirone ceramic tiles. c, Ceramic tiles with inscription "Arte della ceramica" in square. d, Castellamonte ceramic stoves. e, Squillace ceramic plate.

2012, Oct. 14		Perf. 13¼x13
3149	Horiz. strip of 5	7.50 7.50
a.-e.	A1802 60c Any single	1.60 .55

Pope John Paul I (1912-78) A1803

2012, Oct. 17	*Serpentine Die Cut 11*
	Self-Adhesive
3150	A1803 60c multi	1.50 1.50

Astronomical Observatories A1804

Galaxy and: No. 3151, Brera Observatory, Milan. No. 3152, Capodimonte Observatory, Naples.

2012, Oct. 22		Self-Adhesive
3151	A1804 60c multi	1.50 .80
3152	A1804 60c multi	1.50 .80

Luigi Carlo Farini (1812-66), Prime Minister — A1805

2012, Oct. 22		Self-Adhesive
3153	A1805 60c multi	1.50 .80

Italian El Alamein War Memorial, Italian Base Q33, Emblem of Folgore Parachute Brigade — A1806

2012, Oct. 23	*Serpentine Die Cut 11*
	Self-Adhesive
3154	A1806 €1.40 multi	3.75 3.75

Battle of El Alamein, 70th anniv.

81st General Assembly of Interpol, Rome — A1807

2012, Nov. 3		Photo.
	Self-Adhesive	
3155	A1807 60c multi	1.50 .80

Italian National Electricity Company, 50th Anniv. — A1808

2012, Nov. 5	*Serpentine Die Cut 11*
	Self-Adhesive
3156	A1808 60c multi	1.50 .80

Elimination of Architectural Barriers to the Handicapped A1809

2012, Nov. 9		Photo.
	Self-Adhesive	
3157	A1809 60c multi	1.50 .80

Primo Levi (1919-87), Writer — A1810

Serpentine Die Cut 11
2012, Nov. 10		Self-Adhesive
3158	A1810 75c multi	2.00 1.00

Emblem of Health and Anti-Adulteration Center, 50th Anniv. — A1811

2012, Nov. 29		Photo.
	Self-Adhesive	
3159	A1811 60c multi	1.50 .80

Folk Festival Type of 2009

Design: Ndocciata Christmas Festival, Agnone.

2012, Dec. 7		Perf. 13¼
3160	A1634 60c multi	1.50 .80

Awarding of 2012 Nobel Peace Prize to the European Union A1812

2012, Dec. 10		Perf. 13¼x13
3161	A1812 75c multi	2.00 .75

Folk Festival Type of 2009

Designs: 60c, Carnival, Fano. 70c, Canival, Termini Imerese.

2013		Photo.	Perf. 13¼
3162	A1634 60c multi	1.50	.55
3163	A1634 70c multi	1.75	.65

Issued: 60c, 1/12; 70c, 2/4.

Nordic Skiing World Championships, Val di Fiemme — A1813

2013, Feb. 1	*Serpentine Die Cut 11*
	Self-Adhesive
3164	A1813 85c multi	2.25 1.25

Envelope Types of 2009-10

Serpentine Die Cut 11x11¼
2013			Photo.
	Self-Adhesive		
	Denomination Color		
3165	A1692	25c pale org	.65 .30
	Engr.		
	Serpentine Die Cut 11		
3166	A1644	70c black	1.75 .90
3167	A1644	85c orange	2.25 1.10
3168	A1644	€1.90 green	4.75 2.50
3168A	A1644	€3.60 brown	9.00 5.00
	Nos. 3165-3168A (5)		18.40 9.80

Issued: 25c, 2/13; 70c, 3/1. 85c, €1.90, 8/10; €3.60, 9/21.

Portrait of Anna Maria Luisa de'Medici (1667-1743), Patron of the Arts, by Antonio Franchi — A1814

Serpentine Die Cut 11
2013, Feb. 18		Photo.
	Self-Adhesive	
3169	A1814 €3.60 multi	9.50 6.50

657

ITALY

St. John the Baptist Preaching with a Self-Portrait of the Artist, by Mattia Preti (1613-99) A1815

Serpentine Die Cut 11
2013, Feb. 23   Self-Adhesive
3170   A1815   70c multi   1.75   .95

Sketches for Italian State Emblem and Stamp Designs, by Paolo Paschetto (1885-1963) A1816

2013, Mar. 9   Photo.
             Self-Adhesive
3171   A1816   70c multi   1.75   .95

Gabriele d'Annunzio (1863-1938), Writer — A1817

Serpentine Die Cut 11
2013, Mar. 12   Self-Adhesive
3172   A1817   70c multi   1.75   .95

Souvenir Sheet

Verona Opera Festival, Cent. A1818

2013, Mar. 15   Perf. 13¼x13
3173   A1818   €1.90 multi   5.00   5.00

Italian Air Force, 90th Anniv. — A1819

Serpentine Die Cut 11x11¼
2013, Mar. 28   Self-Adhesive
3174   A1819   70c multi   1.75   .95

Botanical Gardens Type of 2012

Designs: No. 3175, Gardens of Castel Trauttmansdorff, Merano. No. 3176, Cinque Terre National Park. No. 3177, Botanical Garden Museum, Bari.

2013, Apr. 5   *Serpentine Die Cut 11*
             Self-Adhesive
3175   A1793   70c multi   1.75   .95
3176   A1793   70c multi   1.75   .95
3177   A1793   70c multi   1.75   .95
      Nos. 3175-3177 (3)   5.25   2.85

Souvenir Sheet

Edict of Milan, 1700th Anniv. A1820

2013, Apr. 5   Perf. 13x13¼
3178   A1820   €1.90 multi   5.00   5.00
See Vatican City Nos. 1532-1535.

Election of Pope Francis — A1821

2013, May 2   *Serpentine Die Cut 11*
             Self-Adhesive
3179   A1821   70c multi   2.00   .95
See Argentina No. 2682, Vatican City Nos. 1523-1526.

Polytechnic University of Milan, 150th Anniv. — A1822

2013, May 7   Self-Adhesive
3180   A1822   70c multi   1.75   .95

Europa — A1823

Postal vehicles: 70c, Motorcycles. 85c, Vans.

2013, May 9   Photo.
             Self-Adhesive
3181   A1823   70c multi   1.75   .95
3182   A1823   85c multi   2.10   1.10

Municipal Theater of Bologna, 250th Anniv. A1824

2013, May 14   Engr.   Perf. 13¼x13
3183   A1824   70c black   1.75   .95

State Police Headquarters A1825

Serpentine Die Cut 11
2013, May 16   Photo.
             Self-Adhesive
3184   A1825   70c multi   1.75   .95

Gold Items Made in Italy — A1826

No. 3185: a, Etruscan earrings with amphora pendants, 3rd-2nd cent. B.C. (black background). b, Salt cellars depicting Neptune and Earth, by Benvenuto Cellini, 16th cent. (red background). c, Star-shaped buckle, 14th cent. (green background). d, Golden Sphere monstrance, by Leonardo Montalbano, 1640 (red background). e, Brooch depicting Venus, engraved by Antonio Bernini, 19th cent. (blue background).

2013, May 18   Photo.   Perf. 13x13¾
3185   Horiz. strip of 5   9.50   6.50
  a.-e.   A1826   70c Any single   1.90   .95

Twelve-Foot Dinghy, Cent. — A1827

Serpentine Die Cut 11
2013, May 22   Photo.
             Self-Adhesive
3186   A1827   70c multi   1.75   .95

50th Intl. Submariner Association Congress, Catania A1828

Serpentine Die Cut 11
2013, May 23   Photo.
             Self-Adhesive
3187   A1828   70c multi   1.75   .95

Italian Alpine Club, 150th Anniv. — A1829

2013, May 25   Photo.
             Self-Adhesive
3188   A1829   70c multi   1.75   .95

Italian Medicines Agency — A1830

2013, June 3   *Serpentine Die Cut 11*
             Self-Adhesive
3189   A1830   70c multi   1.75   .95

Giovanni Boccaccio (1313-75), Poet — A1831

2013, June 5   Engr.
             Self-Adhesive
3190   A1831   70c blue   1.75   .95

Miniature Sheet

Determination of San Marino Borders, 550th Anniv. — A1832

No. 3191 — Map of various border areas of San Marino and: a, Bird and flower (Monte Lupo and Serravalle area). b, Insect. c, Bird and flower (Penna Rossa, Fiorentino, Torricella and Valle Sant'Anastasio area). d, Bird.

2013, June 7   Photo.   Perf. 13x13¼
3191   A1832   Sheet of 4   7.50   7.50
  a.-d.   70c Any single   1.90   .95
See San Marino No. 1891.

Sacred Hermitage, Camaldoli A1833

2013, July 11   Photo.   Perf. 13¼x13
3192   A1833   70c multi   1.75   .95

2013 Road Cycling World Championships, Tuscany — A1834

Serpentine Die Cut 11
2013, Sept. 21   Photo.
             Self-Adhesive
3193   A1834   70c multi   1.75   .95

Giuseppe Verdi (1813-1901), Composer — A1835

Serpentine Die Cut 11
2013, Oct. 10   Photo.
             Self-Adhesive
3194   A1835   70c multi   1.75   .95

Olympic Victory, Sculpture by Emilio Greco (1913-95) A1836

2013, Oct. 11   Engr.   Perf. 13¼x13
3195   A1836   70c black   1.75   .95

Italian Regional Wine Grapes and Vineyards Type of 2012

No. 3196 — Grapes and vineyards for wines guaranteed to be from specific regions: a, Aglianico del Taburno. b, Alta Langa. c, Amarone della Valpolicella. d, Barbera d'Asti. e, Bardolino Superiore. f, Castel del Monte Bombino Nero. g, Cesanese del Piglio. h, Colli Bolognesi Classico Pignoletto. i, Morellino di Scansano. j, Oltrepò Pavese Metodo Classico. k, Ramandolo. l, Sfursat di Valtellina. m, Torgiano Rosso Riserva. n, Castelli di Jesi Verdicchio Riserva. o, Vino Nobile di Montepulciano.

ITALY

Serpentine Die Cut 11
2013, Oct. 18   Photo.   Self-Adhesive
3196   Sheet of 15   28.50   28.50
a.-o.   A1772 70c Any single   1.90   .95

Philately Day Type of 2013

No. 3197: a, Two Sicilies #9, Tuscany #23 on cover to Paris (blue background). b, First Italian postal card (pink background). c, Italy #116, 118 (green background). d, Italy #C49 on cover to Chicago, Italy #C48 (yellow brown background). e, Italian stamp catalog (dull rose background).

2013, Oct. 18   Photo.   Perf. 13¼x13
3197   Horiz. strip of 5   9.50   7.50
a.-e.   A1798 70c Any single   1.90   .95

Juventus, 2012-13 Italian Soccer Champions — A1837

Serpentine Die Cut 11
2013, Oct. 19   Photo.   Self-Adhesive
3198   A1837 70c multi   1.75   .95

Archimedean Year — A1838

Serpentine Die Cut 11
2013, Oct. 19   Photo.   Self-Adhesive
3199   A1838 70c multi   1.75   .95

St. Joseph with the Child, by Guido Reni — A1839

Envelope, Card, Pen, Ribbon and Ornaments — A1840

Serpentine Die Cut 11
2013, Oct. 20   Photo.   Self-Adhesive
3200   A1839 70c multi   1.75   .95
3201   A1840 85c multi   2.10   1.10
Christmas.

Social Theater of Como, 200th Anniv. A1841

2013, Oct. 28   Engr.   Perf. 13¼x13
3202   A1841 70c black   1.75   .95

La Fenice Theater, Venice A1842

Serpentine Die Cut 11
2013, Nov. 9   Photo.   Self-Adhesive
3203   A1842 70c multi   1.90   .95

Civita Association, 25th Anniv. — A1843

2013, Nov. 15   Photo.   Perf. 13¼
3204   A1843 70c multi   1.75   .75

Tourism A1844

1935 Italian Tourism Poster A1845

Designs: No. 3205, San Leo. No. 3206, Scanno. No. 3207, Ponza. No. 3208, Tropea.

Serpentine Die Cut 11
2013, Nov. 16   Photo.   Self-Adhesive
3205   A1844 70c multi   1.75   .95
3206   A1844 70c multi   1.75   .95
3207   A1844 70c multi   1.75   .95
3208   A1844 70c multi   1.75   .95
3209   A1845 70c multi   1.75   .95
    Nos. 3205-3209 (5)   8.75   4.75
See Nos. 3251-3254, 3291-3294, 3401-3404, 3467-3471.

Rita Levi-Montalcini (1909-2012), 1986 Nobel Laureate in Physiology or Medicine — A1846

Serpentine Die Cut 11
2013, Nov. 16   Photo.   Self-Adhesive
3210   A1846 70c multi   1.75   .95

Cola di Rienzo (1313-54), Roman Tribune — A1847

Serpentine Die Cut 11
2013, Nov. 23   Photo.   Self-Adhesive
3211   A1847 70c Prus grn & blk   1.75   .95

Giuseppe Gioachino Belli (1791-1863), Poet — A1848

Serpentine Die Cut 11
2013, Nov. 23   Photo.   Self-Adhesive
3212   A1848 85c multi   2.10   1.10

Mole Antonelliana, Turin — A1849

Nardo Cathedral A1850

Alba Fucens Archaeological Site — A1851

Santa Sofia Monument Complex, Benevento A1852

Renaissance Era City Walls of Lucca A1853

Serpentine Die Cut 11
2013, Nov. 13   Engr.   Self-Adhesive
3213   A1849 70c black   1.75   .95
3214   A1850 70c black   1.75   .95

    Photo.
3215   A1851 70c multi   1.75   .95
3216   A1852 70c multi   1.75   .95
3217   A1853 70c black   1.75   .95
    Nos. 3213-3217 (5)   8.75   4.75

Adnkronos News Agency, 50th Anniv. — A1854

2013, Dec. 4   Photo.   Perf. 13¼
3218   A1854 70c multi   1.75   .75

Birds of the Alps — A1855

No. 3219: a, Rock ptarmigan (Pernice bianca). b, Gray-headed woodpecker (Picchio cenerino). c, Bearded vulture (Gipeto). d, Boreal owl (Civetta capogrosso). e, Western capercaillie (Gallo cedrone).

2013, Dec. 4   Photo.   Perf. 13x13¼
3219   Horiz. strip of 5   10.00   7.50
a.-e.   A1855 70c Any single   2.00   1.00

Ordinary Public Consistory for the Creation of New Cardinals A1856

Serpentine Die Cut 11
2014, Feb. 22   Photo.   Self-Adhesive
3220   A1856 70c multi   1.75   .95

Father Martino Martini (1614-61), Missionary to China and Cartographer — A1857

Serpentine Die Cut 11
2014, Mar. 8   Photo.   Self-Adhesive
3221   A1857 85c multi   2.10   1.10

Miniature Sheet

Renewable Energy — A1858

No. 3222: a, Solar energy, b, Hydroelectric energy. c, Geothermal energy. d, Wind energy. e, Wave energy. f, Biomass energy.

Serpentine Die Cut 11
2014, Mar. 21   Photo.   Self-Adhesive
3222   A1858 Sheet of 6   12.00   12.00
a.-f.   70c Any single   2.00   1.00

Christ Bound at the Column, by Donato Bramante (1444-1514) A1859

Serpentine Die Cut 11
2014, Mar. 22   Photo.   Self-Adhesive
3223   A1859 70c multi   1.75   .95

David, by Michelangelo (1475-1564) A1860

2014, Mar. 23   Engr.   Perf. 13x13¼
3224   A1860 70c black   1.75   .75

Institute for International Political Studies, 80th Anniv. — A1861

Serpentine Die Cut 11
2014, Mar. 27   Photo.   Self-Adhesive
3225   A1861 70c multi   1.75   .95

ITALY

Galileo Galilei (1564-1642), Astronomer — A1862

2014, Apr. 5   Engr.   Perf. 13¼
3226 A1862 70c black   1.75 .75

New Town of Bari — A1863

Serpentine Die Cut 11
2014, Apr. 23   Photo.
Self-Adhesive
3227 A1863 70c multi   1.75 .95

Canonization of Popes A1864

Designs: No. 3228, Pope John XXIII. No. 3229, Pope John Paul II.

Serpentine Die Cut 11
2014, Apr. 24   Photo.
Self-Adhesive
3228 A1864 70c multi   1.75 .95
3229 A1864 70c multi   1.75 .95
See Vatican City No. 1557.

Bridge on Ancient Roman Road, Via Claudia Augusta A1865

Serpentine Die Cut 11
2014, May 2   Photo.
Self-Adhesive
3230 A1865 70c multi   1.75 .95

Tiberio Bridge, Rimini A1866

2014, May 2   Engr.   Perf. 13¼x13
3231 A1866 €1.90 black   4.75 2.50

Europa — A1867

Musicians: 70c, Zampogna player. 85c, Launeddas player.

Serpentine Die Cut 11
2014, May 9   Photo.
Self-Adhesive
3232 A1867 70c multi   1.75 .95
3233 A1867 85c multi   2.10 1.10

Nutella Chocolate-Hazelnut Spread, 50th Anniv. — A1868

Serpentine Die Cut 11
2014, May 14   Photo.
Self-Adhesive
3234 A1868 70c multi   1.75 .95

Botanical Gardens Type of 2012
Designs: No. 3235, Minerva Garden, Salerno. No. 3236, Etna Park. No. 3237, Gola del Furlo State Nature Reserve.

Serpentine Die Cut 11
2014, May 23   Photo.
Self-Adhesive
3235 A1793 70c multi   1.75 .95
3236 A1793 70c multi   1.75 .95
3237 A1793 70c multi   1.75 .95
Nos. 3235-3237 (3)   5.25 2.85

Bombing of Piazza della Loggia, Brescia, 40th Anniv. — A1869

Serpentine Die Cut 11
2014, May 28   Photo.
Self-Adhesive
3238 A1869 70c brn red & blk   1.75 .95

Libraries and Colleges — A1870

Designs: No. 3239, Oliveriana Library, Pesaro. No. 3240, Braidense National Library, Milan. No. 3241, Tulliano College, Arpino.

Serpentine Die Cut 11
2014, May 31   Photo.
Self-Adhesive
3239 A1870 70c multi   1.75 .95
3240 A1870 70c multi   1.75 .95
3241 A1870 70c multi   1.75 .95
Nos. 3239-3241 (3)   5.25 2.85
See Nos. 3288-3290, 3345-3347, 3420.

Italian Red Cross, 150th Anniv. — A1871

Serpentine Die Cut 11
2014, June 4   Photo.
Self-Adhesive
3242 A1871 70c multi   1.75 .95

Convention of Friendship With San Marino, 75th Anniv. — A1872

Serpentine Die Cut 11
2014, June 5   Photo.
Self-Adhesive
3243 A1872 70c multi   1.75 .95
See San Marino No. 1910.

Italian Olympic Committee, Cent. — A1873

Serpentine Die Cut 11
2014, June 7   Photo.
Self-Adhesive
3244 A1873 70c multi   1.75 .95

Enrico Berlinguer (1922-84), Communist Politician — A1874

Serpentine Die Cut 11
2014, June 11   Photo.
Self-Adhesive
3245 A1874 70c red & black   1.75 .95

Silvano Arieti (1914-81), Psychiatrist — A1875

Serpentine Die Cut 11
2014, June 28   Photo.
Self-Adhesive
3246 A1875 70c multi   1.75 .95

Italian Presidency of the Council of the European Union — A1876

Serpentine Die Cut 11
2014, July 1   Photo.
Self-Adhesive
3247 A1876 70c multi   1.75 .95

Agostino Gemelli Teaching Hospital, Rome, 50th Anniv. — A1877

Serpentine Die Cut 11
2014, July 7   Photo.
Self-Adhesive
3248 A1877 70c multi   1.75 .95

St. Camillus de Lellis (1550-1614) — A1878

Serpentine Die Cut 11
2014, July 14   Photo.
Self-Adhesive
3249 A1878 70c multi   1.75 .95

Miniature Sheet

Carabinieri Force, 200th Anniv. — A1879

No. 3250: a, Statue of Carabinier, by Edoardo Rubino. b, Bergia Carabinieri Barracks, Turin. c, Emblem of Carabinieri Force. d, Sculpture depicting two Carabinieri, by Antonio Berti.

2014, July 16   Photo.   Perf. 13x13¼
3250 A1879 Sheet of 4   7.00 7.00
a.-d. 70c Any single   1.75 .65

Tourism Type of 2013 and

1963 Italian Tourism Poster — A1880

Designs: No. 3251, Margherita di Savoia. No. 3252, Monsummano Terme. No. 3253, Lovere. No. 3254, Olbia.

Serpentine Die Cut 11
2014, July 19   Photo.
Self-Adhesive
3251 A1844 70c multi   1.75 .95
3252 A1844 70c multi   1.75 .95
3253 A1844 70c multi   1.75 .95
3254 A1844 70c multi   1.75 .95
3255 A1880 70c multi   1.75 .95
Nos. 3251-3255 (5)   8.75 4.75

Election of Pope Hormisdas, 1500th Anniv. — A1881

2014, July 20   Engr.   Perf. 13¼x13
3256 A1881 70c black   1.75 .95

Juventus, 2013-14 Italian Soccer Champions — A1882

Serpentine Die Cut 11
2014, Aug. 1   Photo.
Self-Adhesive
3257 A1882 70c multi   1.75 .95

Italian Catholic Guides and Scouts Association, 40th Anniv. — A1883

Serpentine Die Cut 11
2014, Aug. 7   Photo.
Self-Adhesive
3258 A1883 70c multi   1.75 .95

ITALY

Emperor Augustus (63 B.C.-14 A.D.) A1884

Serpentine Die Cut 11
2014, Aug. 19   Photo. & Engr.
Self-Adhesive
3259 A1884 70c pale yel & blk   1.75   .95

St. Pius X (1835-1914) — A1885

Serpentine Die Cut 11
2014, Aug. 20   Photo.
Self-Adhesive
3260 A1885 70c multi   1.75   .95

Gazzetta di Mantova Newspaper, 350th Anniv, — A1886

Serpentine Die Cut 11
2014, Sept. 1   Photo.
Self-Adhesive
3261 A1886 70c multi   1.75   .95

Folk Festivals Type of 2009
Design: 70c, Giro della Rua, Vicenza.
2014, Sept. 6   Photo.   Perf. 13¼
3262 A1634 70c multi   1.75   .90

National Nuclear Physics Laboratories A1887

No. 3263: a, KLOE kaon experiment equipment, Frascati National Laboratory. b, Borexino neutrino detection equipment, Gran Sasso National Laboratory. c, AGATA gamma ray detector, Legnaro National Laboratory. d, K800 Cyclotron, National Laboratory of the South.

Serpentine Die Cut 11
2014, Sept. 16   Photo.
Self-Adhesive
3263   Horiz. strip of 4   7.00   7.00
a.-d. A1887 70c Any single   1.75   .90

2015 Women's World Volleyball Championships, Italy — A1888

Serpentine Die Cut 11
2014, Sept. 23   Photo.
Self-Adhesive
3264 A1888 70c multi   1.75   .90

Vajont Dam and Basin and Church, Pirago A1889

Serpentine Die Cut 11
2014, Oct. 9   Photo.
Self-Adhesive
3265 A1889 70c multi   1.75   .85
Vajont Foundation, and 51st anniv. of Vajont Dam disaster.

Real Ferdinando Bridge A1890

Celtic Huts, Fiumalbo A1891

Trabocchi Coast A1892

Villa Nobel, Sanremo A1893

2014, Oct. 25   Engr.   Perf. 13¼x13
3266 A1890 70c black   1.75   .85
3267 A1891 70c blue & black   1.75   .85
   Photo.
Serpentine Die Cut 11
Self-Adhesive
3268 A1892 70c multi   1.75   .85
3269 A1893 70c multi   1.75   .85
   Nos. 3266-3269 (4)   7.00   3.40

Italian Regional Wine Grapes and Vineyards Type of 2012
No. 3270 — Grapes and vineyards for wines guaranteed to be from specific regions: a, Barbaresco. b, Castel del Monte Nero di Troia Riserva. c, Chianti. d, Fior d'Arancio Colli Euganei. e, Franciacorta. f, Frascati Superiore. g, Gattinara. h, Malanotte del Piave. i, Offida. j, Recioto di Soave. k, Rosazzo. l, Ruche di Castagnole Monferrato. m, Taurasi. n, Val di Cornia Rosso. o, Vernaccia di San Gimignano.

Serpentine Die Cut 11
2014, Nov. 22   Photo.
Self-Adhesive
3270   Sheet of 15   30.00   30.00
a.-o. A1772 80c Any single   2.00   1.00

Callipo Canned Fish, 101st Anniv. A1894

Serpentine Die Cut 11
2014, Nov. 29   Photo.
Self-Adhesive
3271 A1894 80c multi   2.00   1.00

Straw Hat Industry of Florence A1895

Serpentine Die Cut 11
2014, Nov. 29   Photo.
Self-Adhesive
3272 A1895 80c multi   2.00   1.00

Envelopes Type of 2009
Serpentine Die Cut 11
2014, Dec. 1   Engr.
Self-Adhesive
Denomination Color
3273 A1644 80c red   2.00   1.00
3274 A1644 95c dark blue   2.40   1.25

Madonna With Child and Saints, by Agostino Carracci A1896

Child Looking at Christmas Presents A1897

Serpentine Die Cut 11
2014, Dec. 1   Photo.
Self-Adhesive
3275 A1896 80c multi   2.00   1.00
3276 A1897 95c multi   2.40   1.25
   Christmas.

Philately Day Type of 2012
No. 3277 — Journey of a letter: a, Person writing letter. b, Person placing letter in mailbox. c, Letter sorting. d, Delivery of letter. e, Opening of letter.

2014, Dec. 15   Photo.   Perf. 13¼x13
3277   Horiz. strip of 5   10.00   10.00
a.-e. A1798 80c Any single   2.00   1.00

Giuseppe Mercalli (1850-1914), Vulcanologist — A1898

Serpentine Die Cut 11
2014, Dec. 15   Photo.
Self-Adhesive
3278 A1898 80c multi   1.75   1.00

Launch of San Marco 1 Satellite, 50th Anniv. — A1899

Serpentine Die Cut 11
2014, Dec. 15   Photo.
Self-Adhesive
3279 A1899 80c multi   2.00   1.00

Marsica Earthquake, Cent. — A1900

Serpentine Die Cut 11
2015, Jan. 13   Photo.
Self-Adhesive
3280 A1900 80c multi   1.90   .95

International Year of Light — A1901

Serpentine Die Cut 11
2015, Jan. 26   Photo.
Self-Adhesive
3281 A1901 80c multi   1.90   .95

Turin, 2015 European Capital of Sports — A1902

Serpentine Die Cut 11
2015, Jan. 30   Photo.
Self-Adhesive
3282 A1902 80c multi   1.90   .95

Folk Festivals Type of 2009
Designs: No. 3283, Sciacca Carnival. No. 3284, Putignano Carnival.
2015, Feb. 5   Photo.   Perf. 13¼
3283 A1634 80c multi   1.90   .75
3284 A1634 80c multi   1.90   .75

Aldo Manuzio (1449-1515), Printer — A1903

Serpentine Die Cut 11
2015, Feb. 6   Engr.
Self-Adhesive
3285 A1903 80c black   1.90   .90

Floranga 2015 Flower Competition A1904

Serpentine Die Cut 11
2015, Feb. 19   Photo.
Self-Adhesive
3286 A1904 80c multi   1.90   .90

SZ 1, by Alberto Burri A1905

Serpentine Die Cut 11
2015, Mar. 12   Photo.
Self-Adhesive
3287 A1905 80c multi   1.90   .90

Libraries and Colleges Type of 2014
Designs: No. 3288, Lucchesiana Library, Agrigento. No. 3289, Guglielmo Tagliacarne Institute, Rome. No. 3290, Victor Emmanuel III National Library, Naples.

Serpentine Die Cut 11
2015, Mar. 21   Photo.
Self-Adhesive
3288 A1870 80c multi   1.90   .90
3289 A1870 80c multi   1.90   .90
3290 A1870 80c multi   1.90   .90
   Nos. 3288-3290 (3)   5.70   2.70

ITALY

Tourism Type of 2013 and

1963 Travel Poster — A1906

Designs: No. 3291, Bressanone. No. 3292, Valnerina. No 3293, Tricarico. No. 3294, Isola di Burano.

Serpentine Die Cut 11
2015, Apr. 10   Photo.
Self-Adhesive

3291	A1844	80c multi	1.90	.95
3292	A1844	80c multi	1.90	.95
3293	A1844	80c multi	1.90	.95
3294	A1844	80c multi	1.90	.95
3295	A1906	80c multi	1.90	.95
	Nos. 3291-3295 (5)		9.50	4.75

Banco Popolare, Milan, 150th Anniv. — A1907

Serpentine Die Cut 11
2015, Apr. 11   Photo.
Self-Adhesive

| 3296 | A1907 | 80c multi | 1.90 | .95 |

Fernet Branca Liqueur, 170th Anniv. A1908

Gianduiotto Chocolates, 150th Anniv. A1909

Lavazza Coffee, 120th Anniv. — A1910

Serpentine Die Cut 11
2015, Apr. 24   Photo.
Self-Adhesive

3297	A1908	80c multi	1.90	.95
3298	A1909	80c multi	1.90	.95
3299	A1910	80c multi	1.90	.95
	Nos. 3297-3299 (3)		5.70	2.85

World War II Liberation, 70th Anniv. A1911

Serpentine Die Cut 11
2015, Apr. 25   Photo.
Self-Adhesive

| 3300 | A1911 | 80c multi | 1.90 | .95 |

Giorgio Armani Fashions, 40th Anniv. — A1912

Serpentine Die Cut 11
2015, Apr. 30   Photo.
Self-Adhesive

| 3301 | A1912 | 80c multi | 1.90 | .95 |

Europa — A1913

Old toys: 80c, Pinocchio on tricycle, 1940. 95c, Biplane W, 1938, horiz.

Serpentine Die Cut 11
2015, May 9   Photo.
Self-Adhesive

| 3302 | A1913 | 80c multi | 1.90 | .90 |
| 3303 | A1913 | 95c multi | 2.25 | 1.10 |

St. John Bosco (1815-88) A1914

Serpentine Die Cut 11
2015, May 19   Photo.
Self-Adhesive

| 3304 | A1914 | 80c multi | 1.90 | .90 |

See Vatican City No. 1589.

Miniature Sheet

World War I, Cent. A1915

No. 3305: a, Pilot Francesco Barraca and airplane. b, Machine gun emplacement on mountain. c, Anti-submarine boat. d, Soldiers in trench with machine guns.

2015, May 24   Photo.   Perf. 13x13½

| 3305 | A1915 | Sheet of 4 | 8.00 | 8.00 |
| a.-d. | | 80c Any single | 1.90 | .90 |

Teatro Stabile, Turin A1916

Teatro Petrarca, Arezzo A1917

Malatesta Castle, Longiano A1918

Colombaia Castle, Trapani A1919

National Archaeological Museum of Sybaris — A1920

Fenestrelle Fort — A1921

Santa Maria della Consolazione Church, Todi — A1922

Serpentine Die Cut 11
2015, May 27   Engr.
Self-Adhesive

3306	A1916	80c black	1.90	.90
3307	A1917	80c black	1.90	.90
3308	A1918	80c black	1.90	.90
3309	A1919	80c black	1.90	.90

Photo.

3310	A1920	80c multi	1.90	.90
3311	A1921	80c multi	1.90	.90
3312	A1922	80c multi	1.90	.90
	Nos. 3306-3312 (7)		13.30	6.30

Vignola and Local Cherries — A1923

Serpentine Die Cut 11
2015, June 6   Photo.
Self-Adhesive

| 3313 | A1923 | 80c multi | 1.90 | .90 |

Juventus, 2015 Italian Soccer Champions — A1924

Serpentine Die Cut 11
2015, June 11   Photo.
Self-Adhesive

| 3314 | A1924 | 80c multi | 1.90 | .90 |

Souvenir Sheet

Blood Donation A1925

2015, June 14   Photo.   Perf. 13x13½

| 3315 | A1925 | 80c multi | 1.90 | .90 |

Daughters of St. Paul, Cent. — A1926

Serpentine Die Cut 11
2015, June 15   Photo.
Self-Adhesive

| 3316 | A1926 | 80c multi | 1.90 | .90 |

Souvenir Sheet

Selection of Florence as Capital of Italy, 150th Anniv. A1927

2015, June 19   Photo.   Perf. 13½x13

| 3317 | A1927 | 80c multi | 1.90 | .90 |

Pesaro Film Festival, 50th Anniv. — A1928

Serpentine Die Cut 11
2015, June 22   Photo.
Self-Adhesive

| 3318 | A1928 | 80c multi | 1.90 | .90 |

Mascot of Expo 2015, Milan — A1929

Serpentine Die Cut 11
2015, July 3   Photo.
Self-Adhesive

| 3319 | A1929 | 80c multi | 1.90 | .90 |

Miniature Sheet

Expo 2015, Milan A1930

No. 3320: a, Beet. b, Fish. c, Cabbage. d, Plums. e, Wheat. f, Artichoke. g, Bees. h, Carrots. i, Peppers. j, Acorn. k, Parsley. l, Peach. m, Oranges. n, Beans. o, Deer.

Serpentine Die Cut 11
2015, July 3   Photo.
Self-Adhesive

| 3320 | A1930 | Sheet of 15 | 30.00 | 30.00 |
| a.-o. | | 80c Any single | 1.90 | .90 |

Italian Coast Guard, 150th Anniv. — A1931

Serpentine Die Cut 11
2015, July 20   Photo.
Self-Adhesive

| 3321 | A1931 | 80c multi | 1.90 | .90 |

St. Philip Neri (1515-95) — A1932

ITALY

Serpentine Die Cut 11
2015, July 22 — Photo. — Self-Adhesive
3322 A1932 80c multi 1.90 .90

Dolomites — A1933

Serpentine Die Cut 11
2015, July 25 — Photo. — Self-Adhesive
3323 A1933 95c multi 2.25 1.10

Folk Festivals Type of 2009
Design: Gulf of La Spezia boat race.

2015, Aug. 1 — Photo. — Perf. 13¼
3324 A1634 95c multi 2.25 1.10

Botanical Gardens Type of 2012
Designs: No. 3325, Municipal Botanical Garden of Trieste. No. 3326, Asinara National Park. No. 3327, Vulci Archaeological Park. No. 3328, Alpine Botanical Garden of Campo Imperatore.

Serpentine Die Cut 11
2015, Aug. 12 — Photo. — Self-Adhesive
3325 A1793 95c multi 2.25 1.10
3326 A1793 95c multi 2.25 1.10
3327 A1793 95c multi 2.25 1.10
3328 A1793 95c multi 2.25 1.10
Nos. 3325-3328 (4) 9.00 4.40

2015 Canoe Sprint World Championships, Milan — A1934

Serpentine Die Cut 11
2015, Aug. 19 — Photo. — Self-Adhesive
3329 A1934 95c multi 2.25 1.10

Envelope Types of 2009-10
Serpentine Die Cut 11x11¼
2015, Sept. 19 — Photo. — Self-Adhesive
Denomination Color
3330 A1692 15c cerise .35 .25
Engr.
Serpentine Die Cut 11
3331 A1644 €1 black 2.25 1.10

Vitruvian Man, by Leonardo da Vinci — A1935
Aerial Screw, by Leonardo da Vinci — A1936
Mechanical Wing, by Leonardo da Vinci — A1937
Giant Crossbow, by Leonardo da Vinci — A1938

Serpentine Die Cut 11
2015, Oct. 1 — Engr. — Self-Adhesive
3332 A1935 (€2.80) multi 6.50 3.25
3333 A1936 (€3.50) multi 8.25 4.00
3334 A1937 (€4.50) multi 10.50 5.00
3335 A1938 (€5.50) multi 13.00 6.25
Nos. 3332-3335 (4) 38.25 18.50
150th anniv. of the Unification of Italy.

Italian Banking Association, 70th Anniv. — A1939

Serpentine Die Cut 11
2015, Oct. 7 — Photo. — Self-Adhesive
3336 A1939 95c multi 2.25 1.10

Italian Regional Wine Grapes and Vineyards Type of 2012
No. 3337 — Grapes and vineyards for wines guaranteed to be from specific regions: a, Elba Aleatico Passito. b, Asti. c, Friularo di Bagnoli. d, Castel del Monte Rosso Riserva. e, Chianti Classico. f, Asolo Prosecco superiore. g, Dolcetto di Diano d'Alba. h, Fiano di Avellino. i, Gavi. j, Ghemme. k, Lison. l, Ovada. m, Recioto della Valpolicella. n, Valtellina Superiore. o, Verdicchio di Matelica Riserva.

Serpentine Die Cut 11
2015, Oct. 10 — Photo. — Self-Adhesive
3337   Sheet of 15 32.50 32.50
a.-o. A1772 95c Any single 2.25 1.10

End of World War I Postcard Illustration by Antonio Marchisio — A1940

Serpentine Die Cut 11
2015, Oct. 15 — Photo. — Self-Adhesive
3338 A1940 95c multi 2.25 1.10

10th Mediterranean and Black Sea Regional Sea Power Symposium, Venice — A1941

Serpentine Die Cut 11
2015, Oct. 21 — Photo. — Self-Adhesive
3339 A1941 95c multi 2.25 1.10

San Marino-Italy Techno Science Park — A1942

Designs: No. 3340, Balloon, flags of Italy and San Marino, stylized lightbulb, drone. No. 3341, Lightbulb in head.

2015, Oct. 23 — Photo. — Perf. 13x13¼
3340 A1942 95c multi 2.25 1.10
3341 A1942 95c multi 2.25 1.10
See San Marino Nos. 1946-1947.

Stamp Day — A1943

Designs: No. 3342, Bird on wall (stamp collecting in prison). No. 3343, Hot air balloon (stamp collecting in schools). No. 3344, Penny Black, 175th anniv.

Serpentine Die Cut 11
2015, Oct. 24 — Photo. — Self-Adhesive
3342 A1943 95c multi 2.25 1.10
3343 A1943 95c multi 2.25 1.10
3344 A1943 95c multi 2.25 1.10
Nos. 3342-3344 (3) 6.75 3.30

Libraries and Colleges Type of 2014
Designs: No. 3345, Library of the Italian Encyclopedia Institute, Rome. No. 3346, National Library, Rome. No. 3347, Polytechnic University, Bari.

2015, Oct. 31 — Photo. — Perf. 13x13¼
Souvenir Sheet — Self-Adhesive
3345 A1870 95c multi 2.25 1.10

Serpentine Die Cut 11
3346 A1870 95c multi 2.25 1.10
3347 A1870 95c multi 2.25 1.10

Truffles and Forest — A1944

Serpentine Die Cut 11
2015, Oct. 31 — Photo. — Self-Adhesive
3348 A1944 95c multi 2.25 1.10

Pier Paolo Pasolini (1922-75), Writer — A1945

Serpentine Die Cut 11
2015, Nov. 2 — Engr. — Self-Adhesive
3349 A1945 95c black 2.25 1.10

International Affairs Institute, 50th Anniv. — A1946

Serpentine Die Cut 11
2015, Nov. 13 — Photo. — Self-Adhesive
3350 A1946 95c multi 2.25 1.00

A1947

Christmas — A1948

Designs: No. 3351, Madonna and Child with Saints Joseph and Catherine of Alexandria, by Polidoro da Lanciano (1515-65). No. 3352, Stylized Christmas Tree.

Serpentine Die Cut 11
2015, Nov. 21 — Photo. — Self-Adhesive
3351 A1947 95c multi 2.25 1.10
3352 A1948 95c gold & multi 2.25 1.10

Souvenir Sheet — San Giovanni Battista Hospital, Rome — A1949

No. 3353: a, Exterior of old hospital entrance, tree. b, Exterior of modern hospital, bushes.

2015, Nov. 27 — Photo. — Perf. 13x13¼
3353   A1949 Sheet of 2 4.50 4.50
a.-b. 95c Either single 2.25 1.10

Women's Shoes by Salvatore Ferragamo, S.p.A. — A1950

Serpentine Die Cut 11
2015, Nov. 30 — Photo. — Self-Adhesive
3354 A1950 95c multi 2.25 1.10

Gaetano Perusini (1879-1915), Physician — A1951

Serpentine Die Cut 11
2015, Dec. 7 — Engr. — Self-Adhesive
3355 A1951 95c black 2.25 1.10

Extraordinary Jubilee of Mercy — A1952

Pope Francis and holy door of: 95c, St. Peter's Basilica. €1, Basilica of St. Mary Major. €2.20, Basilica of St. John Lateran. €2.90, Basilica of St. Paul Outside the Walls.

Serpentine Die Cut 11
2015, Dec. 7 — Engr. — Self-Adhesive
3356 A1952 95c black 2.25 1.10
Photo.
3357 A1952 €1 multi 2.25 1.10
3358 A1952 €2.20 multi 5.00 2.40
3359 A1952 €2.90 multi 7.00 3.25
Nos. 3356-3359 (4) 16.50 7.85

School of Barbiana and Students — A1953

Serpentine Die Cut 11
2015, Dec. 9 — Photo. — Self-Adhesive
3360 A1953 95c multi 2.25 1.10

La Repubblica Newspaper, 40th Anniv. — A1954

Serpentine Die Cut 11
2016, Jan. 14 — Photo. — Self-Adhesive
3361 A1954 95c lav gray & blk 2.25 1.10

ITALY

Nuova Antologia Magazine, 150th Anniv. — A1955

Serpentine Die Cut 11
2016, Jan. 31   **Self-Adhesive**   Photo.
3362   A1955   95c multi   2.25   1.10

Elio Vittorini (1908-66), Writer — A1956

Serpentine Die Cut 11
2016, Feb. 12   **Self-Adhesive**   Photo.
3363   A1956   95c multi   2.25   1.10

Carnival of Viareggio — A1957

Serpentine Die Cut 11
2016, Feb. 13   **Self-Adhesive**   Photo.
3364   A1957   95c multi   2.25   1.10

Terni Basilica Stained-Glass Window Depicting St. Valentine — A1958

2016, Feb. 14   Photo.   Perf. 13¼
3365   A1958   95c multi   2.25   1.10

Meyer Pediatric Hospital, Florence, 125th Anniv. — A1959

Serpentine Die Cut 11
2016, Feb. 19   **Self-Adhesive**   Photo.
3366   A1959   95c multi   2.25   1.10

Benedetto Croce (1866-1952), Philosopher and Politician A1960

Serpentine Die Cut 11
2016, Feb. 25   **Self-Adhesive**   Photo.
3367   A1960   95c multi   2.25   1.10

Father Carlo Gnocchi (1902-56), Educator — A1961

Serpentine Die Cut 11
2016, Feb. 27   **Self-Adhesive**   Photo.
3368   A1961   95c multi   2.25   1.10

Italian Boxing Federation, Cent. — A1962

Serpentine Die Cut 11
2016, Mar. 2   **Self-Adhesive**   Photo.
3369   A1962   95c multi   2.25   1.10

Corriere Della Sera Newspaper, 140th Anniv. A1963

Serpentine Die Cut 11
2016, Mar. 5   **Self-Adhesive**   Photo.
3370   A1963   95c multi   2.25   1.10

Church of the Holy Family, Cesano Boscone, Statue of Monsignor Domenico Pogliani (1838-1921) A1964

Serpentine Die Cut 11
2016, Mar. 18   **Self-Adhesive**   Photo.
3371   A1964   95c multi   2.25   1.10
Holy Family Institute Foundation, 120th anniv.

Holy Thorn of Andria A1965

Serpentine Die Cut 11
2016, Mar. 25   **Self-Adhesive**   Photo.
3372   A1965   95c multi   2.25   1.10

Italian Regional Wine Grapes and Vineyards Type of 2012

No. 3373 — Grapes and vineyards for wines guaranteed to be from specific regions: a, Barbera del Monferrate Superiore. b, Brachetto d'Acqui. c, Carmignano. d, Colli di Conegliano. e, Conero Riserva. f, Dogliani. g, Erbaluce di Caluso. h, Montecucco Sangiovese. i, Montello. j, Recioto di Gambellara. k, Roero. l, Soave Superiore. m, Suvereto.

Serpentine Die Cut 11
2016, Apr. 11   **Self-Adhesive**   Photo.
3373   Sheet of 13   29.50   29.50
   a.-m.   A1772 95c Any single   2.25   1.10

Vinitaly Wine Competition Emblem A1966

Vinitaly Wine Competition 50th Anniv. Emblem A1967

Serpentine Die Cut 11
2016, Apr. 11   **Self-Adhesive**   Photo.
3374   A1966   95c multi   2.25   1.10
3375   A1967   95c multi   2.25   1.10

Women's Health Day — A1968

Serpentine Die Cut 11
2016, Apr. 22   **Self-Adhesive**   Photo.
3376   A1968   95c multi   2.25   1.10

Italian Worldwide Fund for Nature (WWF), 50th Anniv. — A1969

Serpentine Die Cut 11
2016, Apr. 22   **Self-Adhesive**   Photo.
3377   A1969   95c multi   2.25   1.10

Totocalcio Soccer Pool, 70th Anniv. — A1970

Serpentine Die Cut 11
2016, May 5   **Self-Adhesive**   Photo.
3378   A1970   95c multi   2.25   1.10

Italian Sports Center, Rome, 110th Anniv. — A1971

Serpentine Die Cut 11
2016, May 6   **Self-Adhesive**   Photo.
3379   A1971   95c multi   2.25   1.10

100th Targa Florio Road Race — A1972

Serpentine Die Cut 11
2016, May 7   **Self-Adhesive**   Photo.
3380   A1972   95c multi   2.25   1.10

Judge Francesco Coco (1908-76) and Magistrate Vittorio Occorsio (1929-76), Victims of Terrorism A1973

Serpentine Die Cut 11
2016, May 9   **Self-Adhesive**   Photo.
3381   A1973   95c multi   2.25   1.10

A1974   Europa — A1975

Serpentine Die Cut 11
2016, May 9   **Self-Adhesive**   Photo.
3382   A1974   95c multi   2.25   1.10
3383   A1975   €1 multi   2.25   1.10
Think Green Issue.

Red Coral of Alghero and Alghero Buildings A1976

Serpentine Die Cut 11
2016, May 14   **Self-Adhesive**   Photo.
3384   A1976   95c multi   2.25   1.10

Military Corps of Italian Red Cross, 150th Anniv. — A1977

Serpentine Die Cut 11
2016, June 1   **Self-Adhesive**   Photo.
3385   A1977   95c multi   2.25   1.10

Italian Republic, 70th Anniv. — A1978

Serpentine Die Cut 11
2016, June 2   **Self-Adhesive**   Photo.
3386   A1978   95c multi   2.25   1.10

Woman Suffrage in Italy, 70th Anniv. A1979

Serpentine Die Cut 11
2016, June 2   **Self-Adhesive**   Photo.
3387   A1979   95c multi   2.25   1.10

ITALY

Appointment of First Female Government Minister, 40th Anniv. — A1980

Serpentine Die Cut 11
2016, June 2 Photo.
Self-Adhesive
3388 A1980 95c multi 2.25 1.10

Juventus, 2012-16 Italian Soccer Champions A1981

Serpentine Die Cut 11
2016, June 27 Photo.
Self-Adhesive
3389 A1981 95c multi 2.25 1.10
No. 3389 was printed in sheets of 5.

Piazza della Republica, Rome — A1982
Piazza del Plebiscito, Naples — A1983
Piazza Ruggiero Settimo, Palermo — A1984
Piazza del Duomo, Milan — A1985
Piazza San Carlo, Turin — A1986
Piazza Maggiore, Bologna — A1987
Piazza de Ferrari, Genoa — A1988
Piazza della Signoria, Florence A1989

Serpentine Die Cut 11
2016, July 2 Engr.
Self-Adhesive
3390 A1982 (95c) multi 2.25 1.10
3391 A1983 (€1) multi 2.40 1.10
3392 A1984 (€2.20) multi 5.25 2.50
3393 A1985 (€2.55) multi 6.00 2.75
3394 A1986 (€2.70) multi 6.50 3.00
3395 A1987 (€2.90) multi 7.00 3.25
3396 A1988 (€3.70) multi 8.75 4.00
3397 A1989 (€4.60) multi 11.00 5.25
Nos. 3390-3397 (8) 49.15 22.95

Italian Shooting Federation, 90th Anniv. — A1990

Serpentine Die Cut 11
2016, July 5 Photo.
Self-Adhesive
3398 A1990 95c multi 2.25 1.10

Canonization of St. Frances Xavier Cabrini (1850-1917), 70th Anniv. A1991

Serpentine Die Cut 11
2016, July 7 Photo.
Self-Adhesive
3399 A1991 95c multi 2.25 1.10

Slow Food Organization, 30th Anniv. — A1992

Serpentine Die Cut 11
2016, July 26 Photo.
Self-Adhesive
3400 A1992 95c multi 2.25 1.10

Tourism Type of 2013
Designs: No. 3401, Albenga. No. 3402, Camerino. No. 3403, Carovilli. No. 3404, Sperlinga.

Serpentine Die Cut 11
2016, Aug. 6 Photo.
Self-Adhesive
3401 A1844 95c multi 2.25 1.10
3402 A1844 95c multi 2.25 1.10
3403 A1844 95c multi 2.25 1.10
3404 A1844 95c multi 2.25 1.10
Nos. 3401-3404 (4) 9.00 4.40

Dynamism of a Man's Head, by Umberto Boccioni (1882-1916) A1993

Serpentine Die Cut 11
2016, Aug. 17 Photo.
Self-Adhesive
3405 A1993 95c multi 2.25 1.10

Anna Magnani (1908-73), Actress — A1994

Serpentine Die Cut 11
2016, Aug. 31 Photo.
Self-Adhesive
3406 A1994 95c multi 2.25 1.10

Luchino Visconti (1906-76), Theater and Film Director — A1995

Serpentine Die Cut 11
2016, Aug. 31 Photo.
Self-Adhesive
3407 A1995 95c multi 2.25 1.10

Aldo Moro (1916-78), Prime Minister — A1996

Serpentine Die Cut 11
2016, Sept. 23 Photo.
Self-Adhesive
3408 A1996 95c multi 2.25 1.10

Grand Duke Cosimo III of Tuscany (1642-1723) and Map of Tuscany A1997

Serpentine Die Cut 11
2016, Sept. 24 Photo.
Self-Adhesive
3409 A1997 95c multi 2.25 1.10
Declaration of boundaries of Chianti, Pomino Carmignano and Vald'Arno di Sopra, 300th anniv.

Salini Impreglio Group, 110th Anniv. — A1998

Serpentine Die Cut 11
2016, Sept. 27 Photo.
Self-Adhesive
3410 A1998 95c multi 2.25 1.10

Piero Calamandrei (1889-1956), Politician and Writer — A1999

Serpentine Die Cut 11
2016, Sept. 27 Photo.
Self-Adhesive
3411 A1999 95c multi 2.25 1.10

Antonio Mattei Biscotti A2000

Serpentine Die Cut 11
2016, Sept. 29 Photo.
Self-Adhesive
3412 A2000 95c multi 2.25 1.10

Il Secolo XIX Newspaper, 130th Anniv. — A2001

Serpentine Die Cut 11
2016, Sept. 30 Photo.
Self-Adhesive
3413 A2001 95c multi 2.25 1.10

Alto Adige Speck A2002

Serpentine Die Cut 11
2016, Oct. 1 Photo.
Self-Adhesive
3414 A2002 95c multi 2.25 1.10

Gallo Rice — A2003

Serpentine Die Cut 11
2016, Oct. 3 Photo.
Self-Adhesive
3415 A2003 95c multi 2.25 1.10

Statue of Virgil, Mantua — A2004

Serpentine Die Cut 11
2016, Oct. 15 Photo.
Self-Adhesive
3416 A2004 95c red 2.25 1.10
Mantua, 2016 Italian Capital of Culture.

Teresio Olivelli (1916-45), Beatified Soldier of World War II Resistance Movement — A2005

Serpentine Die Cut 11
2016, Oct. 15 Photo.
Self-Adhesive
3417 A2005 95c multi 2.25 1.10

La Leche League International, 60th Anniv. — A2006

Serpentine Die Cut 11
2016, Oct. 17 Photo.
Self-Adhesive
3418 A2006 95c multi 2.25 1.10

Santa Cecilia National Academy — A2007

Serpentine Die Cut 11
2016, Oct. 20 Photo.
Self-Adhesive
3419 A2007 95c black & red 2.25 1.10

Libraries and Colleges Type of 2014
Design: 95c, Bibliotecha Nazionale Marciana (St. Mark's National Library), Venice.

ITALY

Serpentine Die Cut 11
2016, Oct. 20 Photo.
Self-Adhesive
3420 A1870 95c multi 2.25 1.10

Philately Day — A2008

Serpentine Die Cut 11
2016, Oct. 21 Photo.
Self-Adhesive
3421 A2008 95c multi 2.25 1.10

50th Comics and Games Convention, Lucca — A2009

Serpentine Die Cut 11
2016, Oct. 28 Photo.
Self-Adhesive
3422 A2009 95c multi 2.25 1.10

A2010
Design: 95c, Children's Drawing Depicting Rescue of Art Treasures in 1967 Flood in Florence.

Serpentine Die Cut 11
2016, Nov. 4 Photo.
Self-Adhesive
3423 A2010 95c multi 2.25 1.10

International Bicycle and Motorcycle Exhibition, Milan — A2011

Serpentine Die Cut 11
2016, Nov. 8 Photo.
Self-Adhesive
3424 A2011 95c multi 2.25 1.10

DeCecco Pasta, 130th Anniv. — A2012

Serpentine Die Cut 11
2016, Nov. 18 Photo.
Self-Adhesive
3425 A2012 95c multi 2.25 1.10

UNICEF, 70th Anniv. — A2013

Serpentine Die Cut 11
2016, Nov. 20 Photo.
Self-Adhesive
3426 A2013 €1 blue 2.25 1.10

Victorious Youth Sculpture A2014

Villa Grock, Imperia A2015

Fort Bard — A2016

Santa Maria della Croce Church, Casarano A2017

Alessandro Bonci Theater, Cesena A2018

Santa Maria della Quercia Sanctuary and Bell Tower, Viterbo A2019

Serpentine Die Cut 11
2016, Nov. 25 Photo.
Self-Adhesive
3427 A2014 95c multi 2.25 1.10
3428 A2015 95c multi 2.25 1.10
3429 A2016 95c multi 2.25 1.10
3430 A2017 95c multi 2.25 1.10
3431 A2018 95c multi 2.25 1.10
3432 A2019 95c multi 2.25 1.10
Nos. 3427-3432 (6) 13.50 6.60

French Academy in Rome, 350th Anniv. — A2020

Serpentine Die Cut 11
2016, Nov. 30 Photo.
Self-Adhesive
3433 A2020 95c multi 2.25 1.10
See France No. 5149.

Sister Cities Agreement Between Rome and Paris, France, 60th Anniv. — A2021

Serpentine Die Cut 11
2016, Nov. 30 Photo.
Self-Adhesive
3434 A2021 95c multi 2.25 1.10

Tommaso Maestrelli (1922-76), Soccer Player and Coach — A2022

Serpentine Die Cut 11
2016, Dec. 2 Photo.
Self-Adhesive
3435 A2022 95c multi 2.25 1.10

Leonardo Ximenes (1716-86), Astronomer and Hydraulic Engineer A2023

Serpentine Die Cut 11
2016, Dec. 5 Photo.
Self-Adhesive
3436 A2023 95c multi 2.25 1.00

Italian Victory in Davis Cup Tennis Tournament, 40th Anniv. — A2024

Serpentine Die Cut 11
2016, Dec. 6 Photo.
Self-Adhesive
3437 A2024 95c multi 2.25 1.00

Madonna and Child, by Niccolò di Segna A2025

Reindeer A2026

Serpentine Die Cut 11
2016, Dec. 7 Photo.
Self-Adhesive
3438 A2025 95c multi 2.25 1.00
3439 A2026 €1 multi 2.40 1.10
Christmas.

Luigi Tenco (1938-67), Singer — A2027

Serpentine Die Cut 11
2017, Jan. 27 Photo.
Self-Adhesive
3440 A2027 95c multi 2.25 1.10

La Stampa Newspaper, 150th Anniv. — A2028

Serpentine Die Cut 11
2017, Feb. 9 Photo.
Self-Adhesive
3441 A2028 95c multi 2.25 1.00

Baccalà alla Vicentina A2029

Serpentine Die Cut 11
2017, Mar. 1 Photo.
Self-Adhesive
3442 A2029 95c multi 2.25 1.00

Penitentiary Police Corps, 200th Anniv. — A2030

Serpentine Die Cut 11
2017, Mar. 18 Photo.
Self-Adhesive
3443 A2030 95c multi 2.25 1.10

Padua Astronomical Observatory, 250th Anniv. — A2031

Serpentine Die Cut 11
2017, Mar. 21 Photo.
Self-Adhesive
3444 A2031 95c multi 2.25 1.10

Auricchio Cheese Company, 140th Anniv. — A2032

Serpentine Die Cut 11
2017, Mar. 22 Photo.
Self-Adhesive
3445 A2032 95c multi 2.25 1.10

Treaty of Rome, 60th Anniv. — A2033

Serpentine Die Cut 11
2017, Mar. 25 Photo.
Self-Adhesive
3446 A2033 95c multi 2.10 1.10

Borsalino Hats, 160th Anniv. — A2034

Serpentine Die Cut 11
2017, Apr. 4 Photo.
Self-Adhesive
3447 A2034 95c multi 2.10 1.10

ITALY

Christ as Savior with Martin Luther, by Lucas Cranach, the Elder (1472-1553) A2035

Serpentine Die Cut 11
2017, Apr. 24   Photo.
Self-Adhesive
3448   A2035   95c multi   2.10   1.10
Protestant Reformation and Lutheran Church, 500th anniv.

Pio La Torre (1927-82), and Rosario di Salvo (1946-82), Politicians Killed by the Mafia A2036

Serpentine Die Cut 11
2017, Apr. 28   Photo.
Self-Adhesive
3449   A2036   95c multi   2.10   1.10

Livy (59 B.C.- 17 A.D.), Historian A2037

Serpentine Die Cut 11
2017, May 2   Photo.
Self-Adhesive
3450   A2037   95c multi   2.10   1.10

Europa A2038
Designs: 95c, Doria Castle, Dolceacqua. €1, Scaligero Castle, Malcesine.

Serpentine Die Cut 11
2017, May 9   Photo.
Self-Adhesive
3451   A2038   95c multi   2.10   1.10
3452   A2038   €1 multi   2.25   1.10

Piccolo Theater, Milan A2039

People's Theater, Castelfiorentino — A2040

Serpentine Die Cut 11
2017, May 19   Photo.
Self-Adhesive
3453   A2039   95c multi   2.10   1.10
3454   A2040   95c multi   2.10   1.10

G7 Summit, Taormina A2041

Serpentine Die Cut 11
2017, May 26   Photo.
Self-Adhesive
3455   A2041   95c multi   2.10   1.10

Pistoia, 2017 Italian Capital of Culture A2042

Serpentine Die Cut 11
2017, May 19   Photo.
Self-Adhesive
3456   A2042   95c multi   2.10   1.10

Lambretta Motor Scooters, 70th Anniv. — A2043

Serpentine Die Cut 11
2017, June 3   Photo.
Self-Adhesive
3457   A2043   95c multi   2.25   1.10

15th World Paragliding Championships, Monte Avena — A2044

Serpentine Die Cut 11
2017, June 1   Photo.
Self-Adhesive
3458   A2044   95c multi   2.10   1.10

Historical Museum of the Carabinieri, 80th Anniv. A2045

Serpentine Die Cut 11
2017, June 6   Photo.
Self-Adhesive
3459   A2045   95c multi   2.25   1.10

Banca Popolare dell'Emilia Romagna, 150th Anniv. — A2046

Serpentine Die Cut 11
2017, June 12   Photo.
Self-Adhesive
3460   A2046   95c multi   2.25   1.10

Montelupo Fiorentino Ceramics A2047

Serpentine Die Cut 11
2017, June 17   Photo.
Self-Adhesive
3461   A2047   95c multi   2.25   1.10

Sixth Consecutive Championship of Juventus Soccer Team — A2048

Serpentine Die Cut 11
2017, July 1   Photo.
Self-Adhesive
3462   A2048   95c multi   2.25   1.10

Fiat Nuova 500, 60th Anniv. A2049

Serpentine Die Cut 11
2017, July 4   Photo.
Self-Adhesive
3463   A2049   95c multi   2.25   1.10

Vittorio Valletta (1883-1967), President of Fiat Automobiles A2050

Giuseppe di Vittorio (1892-1957), Politician A2051

Serpentine Die Cut 11
2017, July 4   Photo.
Self-Adhesive
3464   A2050   95c multi   2.25   1.10
3465   A2051   95c multi   2.25   1.10

British Institute of Florence, Cent. — A2052

Serpentine Die Cut 11
2017, July 22   Photo.
Self-Adhesive
3466   A2052   95c multi   2.25   1.10

Tourism Type of 2014
Designs: No. 3467, Introd. No. 3468, Isola del Liri. No. 3469, Pontelandolfo. No. 3470, Arbatax. No. 3471, Val Gardena Railway.

2017   Photo.   *Serpentine Die Cut 11*
Self-Adhesive
3467   A1844   95c multi   2.25   1.10
3468   A1844   95c multi   2.25   1.10
3469   A1844   95c multi   2.25   1.10
3470   A1844   95c multi   2.25   1.10
3471   A1844   95c multi   2.25   1.10
   Nos. 3467-3471 (5)   11.25   5.50
Issued: Nos. 3467-3470, 7/31; No. 3471, 9/9.

Abbey of San Gervasio di Bulgaria, Mondolfo A2053

San Nicola Basilica, Bari — A2054

Casamari Abbey A2055

Serpentine Die Cut 11
2017, Sept. 15   Photo.
Self-Adhesive
3472   A2053   95c multi   2.25   1.10
   Engr.
3473   A2054   95c sil & blk   2.25   1.10
3474   A2055   95c black   2.25   1.10
   Nos. 3472-3474 (3)   6.75   3.30

Piero Portaluppi (1888-1967), Architect — A2056

Serpentine Die Cut 11
2017, Sept. 29   Photo.
Self-Adhesive
3475   A2056   95c multi   2.25   1.10

Italian Association of Women Engineers and Architects, 60th Anniv. — A2057

Serpentine Die Cut 11
2017, Oct. 6   Photo.
Self-Adhesive
3476   A2057   95c multi   2.25   1.10

Stamp Day — A2058

Serpentine Die Cut 11
2017, Oct. 7   Photo.
Self-Adhesive
3477   A2058   95c multi   2.25   1.10

Italian Catholic Social Work, 110th Anniv. — A2059

Serpentine Die Cut 11
2017, Oct. 26   Photo.
Self-Adhesive
3478   A2059   95c multi   2.25   1.10

ITALY

Lions Clubs International, Cent. — A2060

Serpentine Die Cut 11
2017, Oct. 30 Photo.
Self-Adhesive
3479 A2060 95c multi 2.25 1.10

Mickey Mouse and Goofy A2061

Steamboat Willie A2062

Mickey and Minnie Mouse A2063

Mickey Mouse and Goofy A2064

Mickey Mouse and Pluto A2065

Mickey Mouse and Atomo Bleep-Bleep A2066

Mickey Mouse and Goofy Holding Sword A2067

Mickey and Minnie Mouse A2068

Serpentine Die Cut 11
2017, Nov. 3 Photo.
Self-Adhesive
3480 A2061 95c multi 2.25 1.10
Miniature Sheet
3481 Sheet of 8, #3480, 3481a-3481g 18.00
a. A2062 95c multi 2.25 1.10
b. A2063 95c multi 2.25 1.10
c. A2064 95c multi 2.25 1.10
d. A2065 95c multi 2.25 1.10
e. A2066 95c multi 2.25 1.10
f. A2067 95c multi 2.25 1.10
g. A2068 95c multi 2.25 1.10
Mickey Mouse, 90th anniv.

Franz von Taxis (1459-1517), Founder of Thurn and Taxis Postal System — A2069

Serpentine Die Cut 11
2017, Nov. 11 Photo.
Self-Adhesive
3482 A2069 95c multi 2.25 1.10

Italian Geographic Society, 150th Anniv. A2070

Serpentine Die Cut 11
2017, Nov. 14 Photo.
Self-Adhesive
3483 A2070 95c multi 2.25 1.10

Totò (1888-1967), Comedian A2071

Serpentine Die Cut 11
2017, Nov. 16 Engr.
Self-Adhesive
3484 A2071 95c black 2.25 1.10

Guardia di Finanza Historical Museum, 80th Anniv. A2072

Serpentine Die Cut 11
2017, Nov. 21 Photo.
Self-Adhesive
3485 A2072 95c multi 2.25 1.10

Granarolo Food Company, 60th Anniv. — A2073

Serpentine Die Cut 11
2017, Nov. 21 Photo.
Self-Adhesive
3486 A2073 95c multi 2.25 1.10

Museum of Liberation of Rome, 60th Anniv. — A2074

Serpentine Die Cut 11
2017, Nov. 23 Photo.
Self-Adhesive
3487 A2074 95c multi 2.25 1.10

Premiere of *Carosello* Television Show, 60th Anniv. — A2075

Serpentine Die Cut 11
2017, Nov. 27 Photo.
Self-Adhesive
3488 A2075 95c black 2.25 1.10

Italian Highway Patrol, 70th Anniv. — A2076

Serpentine Die Cut 11
2017, Nov. 28 Photo.
Self-Adhesive
3489 A2076 95c multi 2.25 1.10

Madonna and Child with Angels, by Filippino Lippi (1457-1504) A2077

Children and Santa Claus Made of Boxes A2078

Serpentine Die Cut 11
2017, Dec. 1 Photo.
Self-Adhesive
3490 A2077 95c multi 2.25 1.10
3491 A2078 €1 multi 2.40 1.25

Security Intelligence System, 10th Anniv. — A2079

Serpentine Die Cut 11
2017, Dec. 4 Photo.
Self-Adhesive
3492 A2079 95c multi 2.40 1.25

Souvenir Sheet

Alcide De Gasperi (1881-1954), Enrico De Nicola (1877-1959), and Umberto Terracini (1895-1983) at Signing of Italian Constitution, 70th Anniv. — A2080

Serpentine Die Cut 11
2017, Dec. 27 Photo.
Self-Adhesive
3493 A2080 95c multi 2.40 1.25

Singers — A2081

Designs: No. 3494, Domenico Modugno (1928-94). No. 3495, Mia Martini (1947-95).

Serpentine Die Cut 11
2018, Feb. 10 Photo.
3494 A2081 95c multi 2.40 1.25
3495 A2081 95c multi 2.40 1.25

Italian Presidency of International Holocaust Remembrance Alliance — A2082

Serpentine Die Cut 11
2018, Mar. 5 Photo.
Self-Adhesive
3496 A2082 95c multi 2.40 1.25

Famous Women — A2083

Designs: No. 3497, Maria Gaetana Agnesi (1718-99), mathematician. No. 3498, Eva Mameli Calvino (1886-1978), botanist. No. 3499, Ada Negri (1870-1945), poet. No. 3500, Elena Lucrezia Cornaro Piscopia (1646-84), philosopher.

Serpentine Die Cut 11
2018, Mar. 8 Photo.
Self-Adhesive
3497 A2083 95c multi 2.40 1.25
3498 A2083 95c multi 2.40 1.25
3499 A2083 95c multi 2.40 1.25
3500 A2083 95c multi 2.40 1.25
Nos. 3497-3500 (4) 9.60 5.00

Murdered Campaigners Against the Mafia — A2084

Designs: No. 3501, Peppino Impastato (1948-78). No. 3502, Father Pino Puglisi (1937-93).

Serpentine Die Cut 11
2018, Mar. 21 Photo.
Self-Adhesive
3501 A2084 95c multi 2.40 1.25
3502 A2084 95c multi 2.40 1.25

Polar Exploration by Crew of Airship Italia, 90th Anniv. A2085

Serpentine Die Cut 11
2018, Mar. 23 Photo.
Self-Adhesive
3503 A2085 95c multi 2.40 1.25

San Miniato al Monte Abbey, Florence A2086

Serpentine Die Cut 11
2018, Apr. 27 Engr.
Self-Adhesive
3504 A2086 95c black 2.40 1.25

ITALY

Europa — A2087

Designs: 95c, Metauro River Bridge, Fermignano. €1, Stone Bridge, Verona.

Serpentine Die Cut 11
2018, May 9 — Photo. Self-Adhesive
3505	A2087	95c	multi	2.25	1.10
3506	A2087	€1	multi	2.40	1.25

Marrucino Theater, Chieti, 200th Anniv. A2088

Serpentine Die Cut 11
2018, May 11 — Photo. Self-Adhesive
3507	A2088	95c	multi	2.25	1.10

Belìce Valley Earthquake, 50th Anniv. — A2089

Serpentine Die Cut 11
2018, May 16 — Photo. Self-Adhesive
3508	A2089	95c	multi	2.25	1.10

Cuirassiers' Regiment (Presidential Honor Guard), 150th Anniv. — A2090

Serpentine Die Cut 11
2018, May 19 — Photo. Self-Adhesive
3509	A2090	95c	multi	2.25	1.10

Eliseo Theater, Rome, Cent. A2091

Serpentine Die Cut 11
2018, May 24 — Engr. Self-Adhesive
3510	A2091	95c	black	2.25	1.10

National Autonomous Road Company, 90th Anniv. — A2092

Serpentine Die Cut 11
2018, May 25 — Photo. Self-Adhesive
3511	A2092	95c	multi	2.25	1.10

Maruzzella Canned Tuna, Cent. — A2093

Serpentine Die Cut 11
2018, May 26 — Photo. Self-Adhesive
3512	A2093	95c	multi	2.25	1.10

Salvatore Quasimodo (1901-68), 1959 Nobel Literature Laureate — A2094

Serpentine Die Cut 11
2018, June 14 — Photo. Self-Adhesive
3513	A2094	(95c)	multi	2.25	1.10

Carpenè Malvolti Wines, 150th Anniv. — A2095

Serpentine Die Cut 11
2018, June 15 — Photo. Self-Adhesive
3514	A2095	(95c)	multi	2.25	1.10

Presidents of Italy — A2096

Designs: No. 3515, Giovanni Gronchi (1887-1978). No. 3516, Giuseppe Saragat (1898-1988). No. 3517, Oscar Luigi Scalfaro (1918-2012).

Serpentine Die Cut 11
2018, June 22 — Photo. Self-Adhesive
3515	A2096	(95c)	multi	2.25	1.10
3516	A2096	(95c)	multi	2.25	1.10
3517	A2096	(95c)	multi	2.25	1.10
Nos. 3515-3517 (3)				6.75	3.30

Father Angelo Secchi (1818-78), Astronomer A2097

Serpentine Die Cut 11
2018, June 28 — Photo. Self-Adhesive
3518	A2097	(95c)	multi	2.25	1.10

Tourism A2098

Designs: No. 3519, Pineto. No. 3520, Grado. No. 3521, Soverato. No. 3522, Grammichele.

Serpentine Die Cut 11
2018, July 6 — Photo. Self-Adhesive
3519	A2098	(€1.10)	multi	2.60	1.40
3520	A2098	(€1.10)	multi	2.60	1.40
3521	A2098	(€1.10)	multi	2.60	1.40
3522	A2098	(€1.10)	multi	2.60	1.40
Nos. 3519-3522 (4)				10.40	5.60

See Nos. 3605-3608, 3764-3767, 3885-3888.

Italian Soccer Federation, 120th Anniv. — A2099

Serpentine Die Cut 11
2018, July 19 — Photo. Self-Adhesive
3523	A2099	(€1.10)	multi	2.60	1.40

Ca'Foscari University, Venice, 150th Anniv. A2100

Serpentine Die Cut 11
2018, July 20 — Photo. Self-Adhesive
3524	A2100	(€2.40)	multi	5.75	3.00

Giovannino Guareschi (1908-68), Cartoonist A2101

Serpentine Die Cut 11
2018, July 21 — Photo. Self-Adhesive
3525	A2101	(€1.10)	multi	2.60	1.40

Juventus, 2017-18 Italian Soccer Champions — A2102

Serpentine Die Cut 11
2018, July 28 — Photo. Self-Adhesive
3526	A2102	(€1.10)	multi	2.60	1.40

Community of Sant'Egidio Lay Catholic Organization, 50th Anniv. — A2103

Serpentine Die Cut 11
2018, Sept. 1 — Photo. Self-Adhesive
3527	A2103	(€1.10)	multi	2.60	1.40

Italian Movies — A2104

Designs: No. 3528, I Soliti Ignoti (Big Deal on Madonna Street), 1958. No. 3529, Il Giorno della Civetta (Mafia), 1968. No. 3530, C'era una Volta il West (Once Upon a Time in the West), 1968.

Serpentine Die Cut 11
2018, Sept. 6 — Photo. Self-Adhesive
3528	A2104	(€1.10)	multi	2.60	1.40
3529	A2104	(€1.10)	multi	2.60	1.40
3530	A2104	(€1.10)	multi	2.60	1.40
Nos. 3528-3530 (3)				7.80	4.20

Genoa Cricket and Soccer Club, 125th Anniv. — A2105

Serpentine Die Cut 11
2018, Sept. 7 — Photo. Self-Adhesive
3531	A2105	(€1.10)	multi	2.60	1.40

St. Pio of Pietrelcina (1878-1968) — A2106

Serpentine Die Cut 11
2018, Sept. 20 — Engr. Self-Adhesive
3532	A2106	(€1.10)	brown	2.60	1.40

Bandierai Degli Uffizi (Flag Wavers of Florence), 45th Anniv. — A2107

Serpentine Die Cut 11
2018, Sept. 26 — Photo. Self-Adhesive
3533	A2107	(€3.50)	multi	8.25	4.25

50th Barcolana Regatta — A2108

Serpentine Die Cut 11
2018, Sept. 27 — Photo. Self-Adhesive
3534	A2108	(€1.10)	multi	2.60	1.40

Palermo, 2018 Italian Capital of Culture A2109

Serpentine Die Cut 11
2018, Oct. 6 — Photo. Self-Adhesive
3535	A2109	(€1.10)	multi	2.50	1.25

Avvenire Newspaper, Milan, 50th Anniv. — A2110

Serpentine Die Cut 11
2018, Oct. 11 — Photo. Self-Adhesive
3536	A2110	(€1.10)	multi	2.50	1.25

ITALY

Serpentine Die Cut 11
2018, Oct. 12 Photo.
Self-Adhesive
3537 A2111 (€1.10) multi 2.50 1.25

Internazionale Milan Soccer Team, 110th Anniv. — A2111

Serpentine Die Cut 11
2018, Oct. 26 Photo.
Self-Adhesive
3538 A2112 (€1.10) multi 2.50 1.25

Special Intervention Group of the Carabinieri, 40th Anniv. — A2112

Il Ponte Center, Civitavecchia, 40th Anniv. — A2113

Serpentine Die Cut 11
2018, Oct. 31 Photo.
Self-Adhesive
3539 A2113 (€1.10) multi 2.50 1.25

Fresco to the Memory of the Fallen of Cortona, by Osvaldo Bignami (1856-1936) A2114

Serpentine Die Cut 11
2018, Nov. 3 Photo.
Self-Adhesive
3540 A2114 (€1.10) multi 2.50 1.25
End of World War I, cent.

National Cancer Association, 40th Anniv. — A2115

Serpentine Die Cut 11
2018, Nov. 9 Photo.
Self-Adhesive
3541 A2115 (€1.10) multi 2.50 1.25

Italian Multiple Sclerosis Association, 50th Anniv. — A2116

Serpentine Die Cut 11
2018, Nov. 9 Photo.
Self-Adhesive
3542 A2116 (€1.10) multi 2.50 1.25

Italian Soccer Association, 50th Anniv. — A2117

Serpentine Die Cut 11
2018, Nov. 12 Photo.
Self-Adhesive
3543 A2117 (€1.10) multi 2.50 1.25

Italian Soccer Technical Center and Training Grounds, Coverciano, 60th Anniv. — A2118

Serpentine Die Cut 11
2018, Nov. 12 Photo.
Self-Adhesive
3544 A2118 (€1.10) multi 2.50 1.25

Gioachino Rossini (1792-1868), Composer A2119

Serpentine Die Cut 11
2018, Nov. 13 Engr.
Self-Adhesive
3545 A2119 (€1.10) black 2.50 1.25

Souvenir Sheet

Chamber of Deputies in Palazzo Montecitorio, Rome, 100th Anniv. — A2120

Serpentine Die Cut 11
2018, Nov. 20 Photo.
Self-Adhesive
3546 A2120 (€1.10) multi 2.50 1.25

Italian Rowing Federation, 130th Anniv. A2121

Serpentine Die Cut 11
2018, Dec. 1 Photo.
Self-Adhesive
3547 A2121 (€1.10) multi 2.50 1.25

Fresco of Madonna and Child Attributed to Benvenuto di Giovanni (1436-c. 1518) in Church of Santa Maria Maddalena, Saturnia — A2122

Family and Christmas Tree — A2123

Serpentine Die Cut 11
2018, Dec. 1 Photo.
Self-Adhesive
3548 A2122 (€1.10) gold & multi 2.50 1.25
3549 A2123 (€1.15) multi 2.60 1.40
Christmas.

Door to Europe Monument, Lampedusa — A2124

Serpentine Die Cut 11
2018, Dec. 7 Photo.
Self-Adhesive
3550 A2124 (€1.10) multi 2.50 1.25

Carlo Besta Neurological Institute, Milan, Cent. — A2125

Serpentine Die Cut 11
2018, Dec. 20 Photo.
Self-Adhesive
3551 A2125 (€1.10) multi 2.50 1.25

Vittorio Pozzo (1886-1968), Soccer Player and Manager A2126

2018, Dec. 21 Photo. Perf. 13x13½
3552 A2126 (€1.10) multi 2.50 1.25

Pitti Immagine Fashion Exhibitions, 30th Anniv. — A2127

Serpentine Die Cut 11
2019, Jan. 8 Photo.
Self-Adhesive
3553 A2127 (€1.10) multi 2.60 1.40

Kingdom of Sardinia Stamped Postal Card, 200th Anniv. — A2128

Serpentine Die Cut 11
2019, Jan. 25 Photo.
Self-Adhesive
3554 A2128 (€1.10) multi 2.60 1.40

Valentino Mazzolla (1919-49), Soccer Player — A2129

Serpentine Die Cut 11
2019, Jan. 26 Photo.
Self-Adhesive
3555 A2129 (€1.10) multi 2.60 1.40

Conciliation Hall, Lateran Palace, Site of Signing of the Lateran Treaty A2130

Serpentine Die Cut 11
2019, Feb. 11 Photo.
Self-Adhesive
3556 A2130 (€1.10) multi 2.50 1.25
See Vatican City No. 1710.

Sant'Andrea Abbey, Vercelli A2131

Serpentine Die Cut 11
2019, Feb. 19 Engr.
Self-Adhesive
3557 A2131 (€2.40) black 5.50 2.75

Francesco Morosini (1619-94), Doge of Venice — A2132

Serpentine Die Cut 11
2019, Feb. 26 Photo.
Self-Adhesive
3558 A2132 (€1.10) multi 2.50 1.25

The Trial by Fire, St. Francis Offers to Walk Through Fire to Convert the Sultan of Egypt, by Giotto di Bondone (c. 1267-1337) — A2133

Serpentine Die Cut 11
2019, Mar. 1 Photo.
Self-Adhesive
3559 A2133 (€1.10) multi 2.50 1.25
Encounter of St. Francis and the Sultan of Egypt, 800th anniv.

Matera, 2019 European Cultural Capital — A2134

Serpentine Die Cut 11
2019, Mar. 4 Photo.
Self-Adhesive
3560 A2134 (€1.15) multi 2.60 1.40

Royal Gymnastics Society, Turin, 175th Anniv. — A2135

Serpentine Die Cut 11
2019, Mar. 15 Photo.
Self-Adhesive
3561 A2135 (€2.60) multi 6.00 3.00

Scouts and Giuseppe Diana (1958-94), Priest Killed by the Camorra A2136

Serpentine Die Cut 11
2019, Mar. 19 Photo.
Self-Adhesive
3562 A2136 (€1.10) multi 2.50 1.25

ITALY

Bambino Gesù Pediatric Hospital, Rome, 150th Anniv. — A2137

2019, Mar. 19　Photo.　Perf. 13½x13
3563　A2137　(€1.10) multi　　2.50　1.25
See Vatican City No. 1711.

Miniature Sheet

Philately Day — A2138

No. 3564 — Details of stamp vignettes from 1945-47: a, "Italia." b, United family. c, Torch. d, Breaking chain. e, Planting tree. f, Tying tree.

Serpentine Die Cut 11
2019, Mar. 22　　　　Photo.
Self-Adhesive
3564　A2138　Sheet of 6　　15.00
a.-f.　(€1.10) Any single　2.50　1.25

Nilla Pizzi (1919-2011), Singer — A2139

Serpentine Die Cut 11
2019, Apr. 16　　　　Photo.
Self-Adhesive
3565　A2139　(€1.10) multi　　2.50　1.25

St. Peter's Circle, 150th Anniv. — A2140

Serpentine Die Cut 11
2019, Apr. 28　　　　Photo.
Self-Adhesive
3566　A2140　(€1.10) multi　　2.50　1.25

Crucifixion, by Jacopo Tintoretto (1518-94) — A2141

Serpentine Die Cut 11
2019, Apr. 29　　　　Photo.
Self-Adhesive
3567　A2141　(€1.10) multi　　2.50　1.25

Miniature Sheet

Carabinieri Unit for Protection of Cultural Heritage, 50th Anniv. — A2142

No. 3568: a, Portrait of a Young Woman, by Raphael (1483-1520). b, Illuminated 15th century codex. c, Portrait of a Young Peasant (The Gardener), by Vincent van Gogh (1853-90). d, Roman ivory mask. e, The Holy Family, by Andrea Mantegna (c. 1431-1506). f, Headquarters of Carabinieri Unit for Protection of Cultural Heritage.

Serpentine Die Cut 11
2019, Apr. 29　　　　Photo.
Self-Adhesive
3568　A2142　Sheet of 6　　15.00
a.-f.　(€1.10) Any single　2.50　1.25
Joint Issue between Italy and Vatican City. See Vatican City No. 1717.

Sergio Leone (1929-89), Film Director — A2143

Serpentine Die Cut 11
2019, Apr. 30　　　　Photo.
Self-Adhesive
3569　A2143　(€2.40) multi　　5.50　2.75

Miniature Sheet

Art by Leonardo da Vinci (1452-1519) — A2144

No. 3570: a, Study of Proportions of the Eye. b, Adoration of the Magi. c, Portrait of a Musician. d, Head of a Woman (La Scapiliata).

Serpentine Die Cut 11
2019, May 2　　　　Photo.
Self-Adhesive
3570　A2144　Sheet of 4　　10.00
a.-d.　(€1.10) Any single　2.50　1.25

National Alpine Soldiers Association, Cent. — A2145

Serpentine Die Cut 11
2019, May 10　　　　Photo.
Self-Adhesive
3571　A2145　(€1.10) multi　　2.50　1.25

Blessed Virgin of Ghiara and Basilica of the Blessed Virgin of Ghiara, Reggio Emilia, 400th Anniv. — A2146

Serpentine Die Cut 11
2019, May 11　　　　Photo.
Self-Adhesive
3572　A2146　(€1.10) gold & multi　2.50　1.25

Italian Banking Association, Cent. — A2147

Serpentine Die Cut 11
2019, May 14　　　　Photo.
Self-Adhesive
3573　A2147　(€1.10) gold & multi　2.50　1.25

Confederation of Italian Cooperatives, Cent. — A2148

Serpentine Die Cut 11
2019, May 14　　　　Photo.
Self-Adhesive
3574　A2148　(€1.10) multi　　2.50　1.25

Santa Croce and Carle Hospital, Cuneo, 700th Anniv. — A2149

Serpentine Die Cut 11
2019, May 18　　　　Photo.
Self-Adhesive
3575　A2149　(€1.10) multi　　2.50　1.25

Italian Ophthalmological Society, 150th Anniv. — A2150

Serpentine Die Cut 11
2019, May 23　　　　Photo.
Self-Adhesive
3576　A2150　(€1.10) multi　　2.50　1.25

Aurora Pen Company, Cent. — A2151

Serpentine Die Cut 11
2019, May 24　　　　Photo.
Self-Adhesive
3577　A2151　(€1.10) multi　　2.50　1.25

International Labor Organization, Cent. — A2152

Serpentine Die Cut 11
2019, May 31　　　　Photo.
Self-Adhesive
3578　A2152　(€1.10) multi　　2.50　1.25

24th World Congress of Dermatology, Milan — A2153

Serpentine Die Cut 11
2019, June 10　　　　Photo.
Self-Adhesive
3579　A2153　(€1.10) multi　　2.50　1.25

Brera Art Gallery, Milan, 210th Anniv. — A2154

Serpentine Die Cut 11
2019, June 10　　　　Engr.
Self-Adhesive
3580　A2154　(€1.10) brown　　2.50　1.25

Cosimo I de' Medici (1519-74), Grand Duke of Tuscany — A2155

Serpentine Die Cut 11
2019, June 12　　　　Photo.
Self-Adhesive
3581　A2155　(€1.10) multi　　2.50　1.25

Springs, Cassano Irpino — A2156

Serpentine Die Cut 11
2019, June 15　　　　Photo.
Self-Adhesive
3582　A2156　(€1.10) multi　　2.50　1.25

Italian Celiac Association, 40th Anniv. — A2157

Serpentine Die Cut 11
2019, June 21　　　　Photo.
Self-Adhesive
3583　A2157　(€1.10) multi　　2.50　1.25

A2158

Serpentine Die Cut 11
2019, June 21　　　　Photo.
Self-Adhesive
3584　A2158　(€1.10) multi　　2.50　1.25
Italian Association against Leukemia, Lymphoma and Myeloma, 50th anniv.

Allied Landing at Anzio, 75th Anniv. — A2159

Serpentine Die Cut 11
2019, June 22　　　　Photo.
Self-Adhesive
3585　A2159　(€2.40) multi　　5.50　2.75

671

ITALY

Admission of General Public to Uffizi Gallery, Florence, 250th Anniv. A2160

Serpentine Die Cut 11
2019, June 24 Engr.
3586 A2160 (€1.10) black 2.50 1.25

2019 Summer Universiade, Naples — A2161

Serpentine Die Cut 11
2019, July 3 Photo.
Self-Adhesive
3587 A2161 (€3.90) multi 9.00 4.50

1899 Fiat Automobile A2162

Serpentine Die Cut 11
2019, July 4 Photo.
Self-Adhesive
3588 A2162 (€3.50) multi 7.75 4.00
Fiat Automobiles, 120th anniv.

Juventus, 2018-19 Italian Soccer Champions — A2163

Serpentine Die Cut 11
2019, July 5 Photo.
Self-Adhesive
3589 A2163 (€1.10) multi 2.50 1.25

National Association of Insurance Companies, 75th Anniv. — A2164

Serpentine Die Cut 11
2019, July 10 Photo.
Self-Adhesive
3590 A2164 (€1.10) multi 2.50 1.25

Roman Carratelli Codex A2165

Serpentine Die Cut 11
2019, Aug. 2 Photo.
Self-Adhesive
3591 A2165 (€1.10) multi 2.40 1.25

Ruggiero Leoncavallo (1857-1919), Opera Composer A2166

Serpentine Die Cut 11
2019, Aug. 9 Photo.
Self-Adhesive
3592 A2166 (€1.10) multi 2.40 1.25

Gianni Brera (1919-92), Sports Journalist A2167

Serpentine Die Cut 11
2019, Sept. 8 Photo.
Self-Adhesive
3593 A2167 (€1.10) gray & blk 2.40 1.25

Italian Publishers' Association, 150th Anniv. — A2168

Serpentine Die Cut 11
2019, Sept. 11 Photo.
Self-Adhesive
3594 A2168 (€1.10) gold & multi 2.40 1.25

Fausto Coppi (1919-60), Professional Cyclist — A2169

Serpentine Die Cut 11
2019, Sept. 15 Photo.
Self-Adhesive
3595 A2169 (€1.10) multi 2.40 1.25

Superior Court of Public Waters, Cent. — A2170

Serpentine Die Cut 11
2019, Sept. 19 Photo.
Self-Adhesive
3596 A2170 (€1.10) multi 2.40 1.25

A2171

Design: Selection of Sannio Falanghina wine growing region as 2019 European wine city.

Serpentine Die Cut 11
2019, Sept. 28 Photo.
Self-Adhesive
3597 A2171 (€1.10) multi 2.40 1.25

Enrico De Nicola (1877-1959), First President of Italy — A2172

Serpentine Die Cut 11
2019, Oct. 1 Photo.
Self-Adhesive
3598 A2172 (€1.10) multi 2.40 1.25

Singers — A2173

Designs: No. 3599, Lucio Dalla (1943-2012). No. 3600, Pino Daniele (1955-2015). No. 3601, Giorgio Gaber (1939-2003).

Serpentine Die Cut 11
2019, Oct. 2 Photo.
Self-Adhesive
3599 A2173 (€1.10) multi 2.50 1.25
3600 A2173 (€1.10) multi 2.50 1.25
3601 A2173 (€1.10) multi 2.50 1.25
Nos. 3599-3601 (3) 7.50 3.75

Bonelli's Eagle — A2174

Goldfinches A2175

Serpentine Die Cut 11
2019, Oct. 4 Photo.
Self-Adhesive
3602 A2174 (€1.10) multi 2.50 1.25
3603 A2175 (€2.60) multi 5.75 3.00
Europa.

Naval Arsenal, La Spezia, 150th Anniv. — A2176

Serpentine Die Cut 11
2019, Oct. 9 Photo.
Self-Adhesive
3604 A2176 (€1.10) multi 2.50 1.25

Tourism Type of 2018
Designs: No. 3605, Troia. No. 3606, Portoferraio. No. 3607, Orbetello. No. 3608, Saluzzo.

Serpentine Die Cut 11
2019, Oct. 10 Photo.
Self-Adhesive
3605 A2098 (€1.10) multi 2.50 1.25
3606 A2098 (€1.10) multi 2.50 1.25
3607 A2098 (€1.10) multi 2.50 1.25
3608 A2098 (€1.10) multi 2.50 1.25
Nos. 3605-3608 (4) 10.00 5.00

National Association of Small Italian Municipalities, 20th Anniv. — A2177

Serpentine Die Cut 11
2019, Oct. 11 Photo.
Self-Adhesive
3609 A2177 (€1.10) multi 2.50 1.25

Institute of the Innocents, Florence, 600th Anniv. — A2178

Serpentine Die Cut 11
2019, Oct. 22 Photo.
Self-Adhesive
3610 A2178 (€1.10) multi 2.50 1.25

Giovanni Goria (1943-94), Prime Minister — A2179

Serpentine Die Cut 11
2019, Oct. 26 Photo.
Self-Adhesive
3611 A2179 (€1.10) multi 2.50 1.25

A2180

A2181

A2182

A2183

A2184

A2185

A2186

Donald Duck, 85th Anniv. A2187

ITALY

Serpentine Die Cut 11
2019, Oct. 30   Photo.
Self-Adhesive

3612	A2180	(€1.10) multi	2.50	1.25
3613		Sheet of 8, #3612, 3613a-3613g	20.00	
a.	A2181	(€1.10) multi	2.50	1.25
b.	A2182	(€1.10) multi	2.50	1.25
c.	A2183	(€1.10) multi	2.50	1.25
d.	A2184	(€1.10) multi	2.50	1.25
e.	A2185	(€1.10) multi	2.50	1.25
f.	A2186	(€1.10) multi	2.50	1.25
g.	A2187	(€1.10) multi	2.50	1.25

Veterinary School of Turin, 250th Anniv. — A2188

Serpentine Die Cut 11
2019, Oct. 31   Photo.
Self-Adhesive

| 3614 | A2188 | (€1.10) multi | 2.50 | 1.25 |

Italian Handball Federation, 50th Anniv. — A2189

Serpentine Die Cut 11
2019, Nov. 5   Photo.
Self-Adhesive

| 3615 | A2189 | (€1.10) multi | 2.50 | 1.25 |

Italian Gymnastics Federation, 150th Anniv. — A2190

Serpentine Die Cut 11
2019, Nov. 5   Photo.
Self-Adhesive

| 3616 | A2190 | (€1.10) multi | 2.50 | 1.25 |

National Notarial Fund, Cent. — A2191

Serpentine Die Cut 11
2019, Nov. 9   Photo.
Self-Adhesive

| 3617 | A2191 | (€1.10) multi | 2.50 | 1.25 |

Campaign Against Violence Towards Women — A2192

Serpentine Die Cut 11
2019, Nov. 11   Photo.
Self-Adhesive

| 3618 | A2192 | (€1.10) multi | 2.50 | 1.25 |

Cicero Denounces Catilina, Fresco by Cesare Maccari (1840-1919) — A2193

2019, Nov. 15   Photo.   Perf. 13¼x13

3619	A2193	(€1.10) multi	2.50	1.25
a.		Booklet pane of 2 #3619 + label	5.00	—
		Complete booklet, #3619a	5.00	

Cassa Depositi e Prestiti Investment Bank, 170th Anniv. — A2194

Serpentine Die Cut 11
2019, Nov. 18   Photo.
Self-Adhesive

| 3620 | A2194 | (€1.10) multi | 2.50 | 1.25 |

Prosecco Producers' Consortium, 10th Anniv. — A2195

Serpentine Die Cut 11
2019, Nov. 19   Photo.
Self-Adhesive

| 3621 | A2195 | (€1.10) multi | 2.50 | 1.25 |

National Fire Brigade, 80th Anniv. — A2196

Serpentine Die Cut 11
2019, Nov. 21   Photo.
Self-Adhesive

| 3622 | A2196 | (€1.10) multi | 2.50 | 1.25 |

Souvenir Sheet

Naming of Virgin Mary as Patron Saint of the Carabinieri, 70th Anniv. — A2197

Serpentine Die Cut 11
2019, Nov. 21   Photo.
Self-Adhesive

| 3623 | A2197 | (€1.10) multi | 2.50 | 1.25 |

Federation of Italian Philatelic Societies, Cent. — A2198

Serpentine Die Cut 11
2019, Nov. 22   Photo.
Self-Adhesive

| 3624 | A2198 | (€1.10) multi | 2.50 | 1.25 |

St. Rocco and St. Erasmus (Detail), by Giovanni Antonio de'Sacchis (Il Pordenone) (c. 1484-1539) A2199

Serpentine Die Cut 11
2019, Nov. 23   Photo.
Self-Adhesive

| 3625 | A2199 | (€3.10) gold & multi | 7.00 | 3.50 |

Bibenda Wine Guide, 20th Anniv. — A2200

Serpentine Die Cut 11
2019, Nov. 30   Photo.
Self-Adhesive

| 3626 | A2200 | (€1.10) gold & multi | 2.50 | 1.25 |

Madonna and Child with St. John and St. Jerome, by Francesco Raibolini (1447-1517) A2201

Santa Claus and Christmas Tree A2202

Serpentine Die Cut 11
2019, Dec. 2   Photo.
Self-Adhesive

| 3627 | A2201 | (€1.10) gold & multi | 2.50 | 1.25 |
| 3628 | A2202 | (€1.15) multi | 2.60 | 1.40 |

Christmas.

National Amateur Soccer League, 60th Anniv. A2203

Serpentine Die Cut 11
2019, Dec. 12   Photo.
Self-Adhesive

| 3629 | A2203 | (€1.10) multi | 2.50 | 1.25 |

Free Port of Trieste, 300th Anniv. — A2204

Serpentine Die Cut 11
2019, Dec. 13   Photo.
Self-Adhesive

| 3630 | A2204 | (€1.10) multi | 2.50 | 1.25 |

Lazio Soccer Team, 120th Anniv. — A2205

Serpentine Die Cut 11
2020, Jan. 9   Photo.
Self-Adhesive

| 3631 | A2205 | (€1.10) multi | 2.50 | 1.25 |

Self-portrait of Federico Fellini (1920-93), Film Director — A2206

Serpentine Die Cut 11
2020, Jan. 20   Photo.
Self-Adhesive

| 3632 | A2206 | (€1.10) multi | 2.50 | 1.25 |

Reclining Nude on a White Cushion, by Amadeo Modigliani (1884-1920) — A2207

2020, Jan. 24   Photo.   Perf. 13¼x13

| 3633 | A2207 | (€2.80) multi | 6.25 | 3.25 |

70th Sanremo Music Festival — A2208

Serpentine Die Cut 11
2020, Feb. 7   Photo.
Self-Adhesive

| 3634 | A2208 | (€1.10) multi | 2.50 | 1.25 |

2020 World Biathlon Championships, Rasun-Anterselva A2209

Serpentine Die Cut 11
2020, Feb. 12   Photo.
Self-Adhesive

| 3635 | A2209 | (€1.10) multi | 2.50 | 1.25 |

110th Pont-Saint-Martin Carnival — A2210

Serpentine Die Cut 11
2020, Feb. 20   Photo.
Self-Adhesive

| 3636 | A2210 | (€1.10) multi | 2.50 | 1.25 |

Telethon Foundation, 30th Anniv. — A2211

Serpentine Die Cut 11
2020, Feb. 28   Photo.
Self-Adhesive

| 3637 | A2211 | (€1.10) multi | 2.50 | 1.25 |

Proclamation of Our Lady of Loreto as Patron Saint of Aviators, Cent. — A2212

Serpentine Die Cut 11
2020, May 8   Photo.
Self-Adhesive

| 3638 | A2212 | (€1.10) gold & multi | 2.50 | 1.25 |

FILA Group (Art Supply Company), Cent. — A2213

Serpentine Die Cut 11
2020, May 21   Photo.
Self-Adhesive

| 3639 | A2213 | (€1.10) multi | 2.50 | 1.25 |

ITALY

Eduardo De Filippo (1900-84), Actor — A2214

Serpentine Die Cut 11
2020, May 24 Photo.
Self-Adhesive
3640 A2214 (€1.10) multi 2.50 1.25

Bruno Ielo (1951-2017), Tobacconist Murdered by Mafia — A2215

Serpentine Die Cut 11
2020, May 25 Photo.
Self-Adhesive
3641 A2215 (€1.10) multi 2.50 1.25

Cagliari Soccer Team, Cent. — A2216

Serpentine Die Cut 11
2020, May 30 Photo.
Self-Adhesive
3642 A2216 (€1.10) multi 2.50 1.25

Giuseppe Ungaretti (1888-1970), Writer — A2217

Serpentine Die Cut 11
2020, June 1 Photo.
Self-Adhesive
3643 A2217 (€1.10) multi 2.50 1.25

Sanpaoloni (Papier-Mâché Statues of Apostles) of San Cataldo — A2218

Serpentine Die Cut 11
2020, June 5 Photo.
Self-Adhesive
3644 A2218 (€1.10) multi 2.50 1.25

Alberto Sordi (1920-2003), Actor — A2219

Serpentine Die Cut 11
2020, June 15 Photo.
Self-Adhesive
3645 A2219 (€1.10) multi 2.50 1.25

Divella Pasta Company, 130th Anniv. — A2220

Serpentine Die Cut 11
2020, June 19 Photo.
Self-Adhesive
3646 A2220 (€1.10) multi 2.50 1.25

1930 Map of Postal Routes — A2221

1695 Map of Postal Routes — A2222

Serpentine Die Cut 11
2020, June 29 Photo.
Self-Adhesive
3647 A2221 (€1.10) multi 2.50 1.25
3648 A2222 (€1.15) multi 2.60 1.30
Europa.

Zeno Colò (1920-93), Downhill Skiing Gold Medalist in 1952 Winter Olympics A2223

Serpentine Die Cut 11
2020, June 30 Photo.
Self-Adhesive
3649 A2223 (€1.10) multi 2.50 1.25

Mario Amato (1937-80), Magistrate Assassinated by Neo-Fascist Terrorists — A2224

Serpentine Die Cut 11
2020, July 2 Photo.
Self-Adhesive
3650 A2224 (€1.10) multi 2.60 1.30

Miniature Sheet

Paintings by Raphael (1483-1520) — A2225

No. 3651: a, Self-portrait. b, Triumph of Galatea. c, Madonna and Child. d, Marriage of the Virgin.

Serpentine Die Cut 8x9¼
2020, July 20 Photo.
Self-Adhesive
3651 A2225 Sheet of 4 37.00
a.-d. (€3.90) Any single 9.25 4.50

Terrorist Bombing of Bologna Centrale Railroad Station, 40th Anniv. — A2226

Serpentine Die Cut 11
2020, Aug. 2 Photo.
Self-Adhesive
3652 A2226 (€1.10) multi 2.60 1.30

Opening of Genoa-San Giorgio Viaduct Over Polcevera River A2227

Serpentine Die Cut 9¼x8
2020, Aug. 3 Photo.
Self-Adhesive
3653 A2227 (€1.10) multi 2.60 1.30

Pellegrino Artusi (1820-1911), Writer of Cookbooks — A2228

Serpentine Die Cut 11
2020, Aug. 4 Photo.
Self-Adhesive
3654 A2228 (€1.10) multi 2.60 1.30

Enzo Biagi (1920-2007), Journalist A2229

Serpentine Die Cut 11
2020, Aug. 9 Photo.
Self-Adhesive
3655 A2229 (€1.10) multi 2.60 1.30

2020 Euroscience Open Forum, Trieste — A2230

Serpentine Die Cut 11
2020, Sept. 2 Photo.
Self-Adhesive
3656 A2230 (€1.15) multi 2.75 1.40

Vecchia Romagna Brandy, 200th Anniv. — A2231

Serpentine Die Cut 11
2020, Sept. 3 Photo.
Self-Adhesive
3657 A2231 (€1.10) multi 2.60 1.30

Drawing of Angels and Cathedral of San Lorenzo, Scala, by Dario Fo A2232

Poster for Blessed Gerardo Sasso Celebrations, by Mimmo Paladino A2233

Serpentine Die Cut 11
2020, Sept. 3 Photo.
Self-Adhesive
3658 A2232 (€1.10) multi 2.60 1.30
3659 A2233 (€1.15) multi 2.75 1.40
Blessed Gerardo Sasso (c. 1040-1120), founder of the Order of Knights Hospitaller.

Tetradramma of Gela, 5th Cent. B. C. — A2234

Serpentine Die Cut 11
2020, Sept. 8 Photo.
Self-Adhesive
3660 A2234 (€1.10) multi 2.60 1.30

Tino Island — A2235

Serpentine Die Cut 11
2020, Sept. 11 Photo.
Self-Adhesive
3661 A2235 (€1.10) multi 2.60 1.30

Campari Liqueurs, 160th Anniv. — A2236

Serpentine Die Cut 11
2020, Sept. 14 Photo.
Self-Adhesive
3662 A2236 (€1.10) multi 2.60 1.30

Italian Dairy Association 75th Anniv. — A2237

Serpentine Die Cut 11
2020, Sept. 15 Photo.
Self-Adhesive
3663 A2237 (€1.10) multi 2.60 1.30

Miniature Sheet

Breach of the Porta Pia, 150th Anniv. A2238

No. 3664: a, Italian flag and Monument to the Bersaglieri, Rome. b, Internal façade of the Porte Pia. c, Emblem of the 2020 Rally of the Bersaglieri, Rome. d, The Bersaglieri, painting by Michele Cammarano (1835-1920).

Serpentine Die Cut 11
2020, July 20 Photo.
Self-Adhesive
3664 A2238 Sheet of 4 27.00
a.-d. (€2.80) Any single 6.75 3.50

Sandra Mondaini (1931-2010), and Her Husband, Raimando Vianello (1922-2010), Television Variety Show Hosts — A2239

Serpentine Die Cut 11
2020, Sept. 21 Photo.
Self-Adhesive
3665 A2239 (€1.10) multi 2.60 1.30

ITALY

Padua, 2020 European Capital of Voluntarism — A2240

Serpentine Die Cut 11
2020, Sept. 21   Photo.
Self-Adhesive
3666   A2240   (€1.15) multi   2.75   1.40

Parma, 2020-21 Capital of Italian Culture — A2241

Serpentine Die Cut 11
2020, Sept. 22   Photo.
Self-Adhesive
3667   A2241   (€1.10) multi   2.60   1.30

Gancia Sparkling Wines, 170th Anniv. — A2242

Serpentine Die Cut 11
2020, Sept. 24   Photo.
Self-Adhesive
3668   A2242   (€1.10) multi   2.60   1.30

Zingaro Nature Reserve — A2243

Serpentine Die Cut 11
2020, Sept. 25   Photo.
Self-Adhesive
3669   A2243   (€1.10) multi   2.60   1.30

Etruscan Coast — A2244

Serpentine Die Cut 11
2020, Sept. 25   Photo.
Self-Adhesive
3670   A2244   (€1.10) multi   2.60   1.30

Carlo Alberto Dalla Chiesa (1920-82), General Murdered by Mafia — A2245

Serpentine Die Cut 8¼x9¼
2020, Sept. 27   Photo.
Self-Adhesive
3671   A2245   (€1.10) multi   2.60   1.30

Artisan's Confederation of Genoa, 75th Anniv. — A2246

Serpentine Die Cut 11
2020, Sept. 28   Photo.
Self-Adhesive
3672   A2246   (€1.10) multi   2.60   1.30

Vatican Public Security Inspectorate, 75th Anniv. — A2247

Serpentine Die Cut 11
2020, Sept. 28   Photo.
Self-Adhesive
3673   A2247   (€1.10) multi   2.60   1.30
See Vatican City No. 1748.

Toscanini Clothes Hangers, Cent. — A2248

Serpentine Die Cut 11
2020, Oct. 1   Photo.
Self-Adhesive
3674   A2248   (€1.10) multi   2.60   1.30

Gino Bartali (1914-2000), Cyclist — A2249

Serpentine Die Cut 11
2020, Oct. 3   Photo.
Self-Adhesive
3675   A2249   (€1.10) multi   2.60   1.30

Italian Federation of Winter Sports, Cent. — A2250

Serpentine Die Cut 11
2020, Oct. 6   Photo.
Self-Adhesive
3676   A2250   (€1.10) multi   2.60   1.30

1970 Pininfarina Modulo, 50th Anniv. — A2251

Serpentine Die Cut 11
2020, Oct. 8   Photo.
Self-Adhesive
3677   A2251   (€1.10) multi   2.60   1.30

Italian Competition Authority, 30th Anniv. A2252

Serpentine Die Cut 9¼x8
2020, Oct. 10   Photo.
Self-Adhesive
3678   A2252   (€1.10) multi   2.60   1.30

Modica Chocolate — A2253

Serpentine Die Cut 11
2020, Oct. 15   Photo.
Self-Adhesive
3679   A2253   (€1.10) multi   2.60   1.30

Souvenir Sheet

Carabinieri Marshals and Brigadiers School, Florence, Cent. — A2254

2020, Oct. 15   Photo.   *Perf. 13¼x13*
3680   A2254   (€1.10) multi + 4 labels   2.60   1.30

G. P. Vieusseux Scientific Literary Library, Florence, 200th Anniv. — A2255

Serpentine Die Cut 11
2020, Oct. 17   Photo.
Self-Adhesive
3681   A2255   (€1.10) multi   2.60   1.30

Souvenir Sheet

Philately Day A2256

2020, Oct. 20   Photo.   *Perf. 13x13¼*
3682   A2256   (€1.10) multi + label   2.60   1.30

Grondona Biscuits, 200th Anniv. — A2257

Serpentine Die Cut 11
2020, Oct. 22   Photo.
Self-Adhesive
3683   A2257   (€1.10) multi   2.60   1.30

Marietti Publishing House, 200th Anniv. — A2258

Serpentine Die Cut 11
2020, Oct. 23   Photo.
Self-Adhesive
3684   A2258   (€1.10) multi   2.60   1.30

Ulrico Hoepli Publishing House, 150th Anniv. — A2259

Serpentine Die Cut 11
2020, Oct. 23   Photo.
Self-Adhesive
3685   A2259   (€1.10) multi   2.60   1.30

Gianni Rodari (1920-80), Writer of Children's Literature — A2260

Serpentine Die Cut 11
2020, Oct. 23   Photo.
Self-Adhesive
3686   A2260   (€1.10) blk & org   2.60   1.30

United Nations, 75th Anniv. — A2261

Serpentine Die Cut 11
2020, Oct. 24   Photo.
Self-Adhesive
3687   A2261   (€3.10) lt blue   7.25   3.75

Italian Union of the Blind and Visually Impaired, Cent. A2262

2020, Oct. 26   Photo.   *Perf. 13¼*
3688   A2262   (€1.10) multi   2.60   1.30

Napoli Soccer Team, Winner of the 2020 Coppa Italia — A2263

Serpentine Die Cut 11
2020, Oct. 27   Photo.
Self-Adhesive
3689   A2263   (€1.10) multi   2.60   1.30

Alpine School of the Guardia di Finanza, Predazzo, Cent. — A2264

Serpentine Die Cut 11
2020, Oct. 28   Photo.
Self-Adhesive
3690   A2264   (€1.10) gold & multi   2.60   1.30

Florence Nightingale (1820-1910), Nurse, and Ponte Vecchio, Florence — A2265

ITALY

Serpentine Die Cut 11
2020, Oct. 29 — Photo.
Self-Adhesive
3691 A2265 (€1.10) multi   2.60 1.30

Palermo Soccer Team, 120th Anniv. — A2266

Serpentine Die Cut 11
2020, Nov. 1 — Photo.
Self-Adhesive
3692 A2266 (€1.10) multi   2.60 1.30

Fedora Barbieri (1920-2003), Opera Singer — A2267

Serpentine Die Cut 11
2020, Nov. 4 — Photo.
Self-Adhesive
3693 A2267 (€1.10) multi   2.60 1.30

1980 Olympic Gold Medal and Pietro Mennea (1952-2013), Sprinter and Politician — A2268

Serpentine Die Cut 11
2020, Nov. 9 — Photo.
Self-Adhesive
3694 A2268 (€1.10) multi   2.60 1.30

Consecration of Volterra Cathedral, 900th Anniv. — A2269

Serpentine Die Cut 9¼x8
2020, Nov. 10 — Engr.
Self-Adhesive
3695 A2269 (€1.10) black   2.75 1.40
See Vatican City No. 1750.

Basilica of Aquileia — A2270

2020, Nov. 10   Photo.   Perf. 13x13¼
3696 A2270 (€1.10) multi   2.75 1.40
See Vatican City No. 1751.

International Year of Plant Health — A2271

Serpentine Die Cut 11
2020, Nov. 12 — Photo.
Self-Adhesive
3697 A2271 (€1.15) multi   2.75 1.40

Juventus, 2019-20 Italian Soccer Champions A2272

Serpentine Die Cut 11
2020, Nov. 17 — Photo.
Self-Adhesive
3698 A2272 (€1.10) multi   2.75 1.40

Assassinated Magistrates — A2273

Designs: No. 3699, Nicola Giacumbi (1928-80). No. 3700, Girolamo Minervini (1919-80). No. 3701, Gaetano Costa (1916-80). No. 3702, Guido Galli (1932-80).

Serpentine Die Cut 11
2020, Nov. 19 — Photo.
Self-Adhesive
3699 A2273 (€1.10) multi   2.75 1.40
3700 A2273 (€1.10) multi   2.75 1.40
3701 A2273 (€1.10) multi   2.75 1.40
3702 A2273 (€1.10) multi   2.75 1.40
  Nos. 3699-3702 (4)   11.00 5.60

Italian Regions With Ordinary Statutes, 50th Anniv. — A2274

Serpentine Die Cut 11
2020, Nov. 19 — Photo.
Self-Adhesive
3703 A2274 (€2.60) multi   6.25 3.25

University Concerts Institution, 75th Anniv. — A2275

Serpentine Die Cut 11
2020, Nov. 20 — Photo.
Self-Adhesive
3704 A2275 (€1.10) multi   2.75 1.40

Restoration of Winged Victory Statue, Brescia — A2276

Serpentine Die Cut 8x9¼
2020, Nov. 21 — Photo.
Self-Adhesive
3705 A2276 (€1.10) multi   2.75 1.40

Leonardo Fibonacci (c. 1170-c. 1242), Mathematician, Fibonacci Sequence and Spiral — A2277

Serpentine Die Cut 9¼x8
2020, Nov. 23 — Engr.
Self-Adhesive
3706 A2277 (€1.10) black   2.75 1.40

National Museum of 21st Century Arts, Rome, 10th Anniv. — A2278

Serpentine Die Cut 11
2020, Nov. 24 — Photo.
Self-Adhesive
3707 A2278 (€1.10) multi   2.75 1.40

Amadeo Peter Giannini (1870-1949), Founder of Bank of America — A2279

Serpentine Die Cut 11
2020, Nov. 25 — Photo.
Self-Adhesive
3708 A2279 (€1.15) multi   2.75 1.40

World AIDS Day — A2280

Serpentine Die Cut 11
2020, Dec. 1 — Photo.
Self-Adhesive
3709 A2280 (€1.10) multi   2.75 1.40

Chigi Palace, Rome — A2281

Serpentine Die Cut 11
2020, Dec. 1 — Photo.
Self-Adhesive
3710 A2281 (€3.50) multi   9.00 4.50
Start of Italian presidency of the G20 Nations.

Madonna and Child, by Perin del Vaga (1501-47) A2282

Comet Star, by Natino Chirico — A2283

Serpentine Die Cut 8x9¼
2020, Dec. 1 — Photo.
Self-Adhesive
3711 A2282 (€1.10) multi   2.75 1.40
Serpentine Die Cut 11
3712 A2283 (€1.15) multi   2.75 1.40
Christmas.

Caffé Florian Coffeehouse, Venice, 300th Anniv. — A2284

Serpentine Die Cut 8x9¼
2020, Dec. 3 — Engr.
Self-Adhesive
3713 A2284 (€1.10) car lake   2.75 1.40

A2285

Design: Onofrio Zappalà, railway worker killed in 1980 Bologna train station bombing, and station clock.

Serpentine Die Cut 11
2020, Dec. 4 — Photo.
Self-Adhesive
3714 A2285 (€1.10) multi   2.75 1.40
Friends of Onofrio Zappalà Association, 15th anniv.

A2286

Serpentine Die Cut 11
2020, Dec. 4 — Photo.
Self-Adhesive
3715 A2286 (€1.10) multi   2.75 1.40
Tommasino Bacciotti Foundation for childhood brain tumor research, 20th anniv.

Carlo Azeglio Ciampi (1920-2016), Prime Minister and President of Italy — A2287

Serpentine Die Cut 11
2020, Dec. 9 — Photo.
Self-Adhesive
3716 A2287 (€1.10) multi   2.75 1.40

Tonino Guerra (1920-2012), Screenwriter — A2288

Serpentine Die Cut 11
2020, Dec. 12 — Photo.
Self-Adhesive
3717 A2288 (€1.10) multi   2.75 1.40

Adriano Olivetti (1901-60), Typewriter Manufacturer and Politician A2289

Olivetti Lettera 22 Portable Typewriter, 70th Anniv. A2290

ITALY

Serpentine Die Cut 11
2020, Dec. 15   Photo.
Self-Adhesive
3718 A2289 (€1.10) multi   2.75 1.40
3719 A2290 (€1.10) multi   2.75 1.40

Conference of Regions and Autonomous Provinces, 40th Anniv. — A2291

Serpentine Die Cut 11
2021, Jan. 15   Photo.
Self-Adhesive
3720 A2291 (€1.10) multi   2.75 1.40

17th Congress of the Italian Socialist Party, Livorno, Cent. — A2292

Serpentine Die Cut 11
2021, Jan. 21   Photo.
Self-Adhesive
3721 A2292 (€1.10) multi   2.75 1.40

Rome as Capital of Italy, 150th Anniv. — A2293

Serpentine Die Cut 11
2021, Feb. 3   Photo.
Self-Adhesive
3722 A2293 (€1.10) multi   2.75 1.40

2021 Alpine Skiing World Championships, Cortina d'Ampezzo — A2294

Serpentine Die Cut 11
2021, Feb. 7   Photo.
Self-Adhesive
3723 A2294 (€1.15) multi   2.75 1.40

Camillo d'Errico (1821-97), Mayor of Palazzo San Gervasio — A2295

Serpentine Die Cut 11
2021, Feb. 13   Photo.
Self-Adhesive
3724 A2295 (€1.10) multi   2.75 1.40

Giovanni Agnelli (1866-1945), Founder of Fiat Automobiles — A2296

Serpentine Die Cut 11
2021, Mar. 12   Photo.
Self-Adhesive
3725 A2296 (€1.10) multi   2.60 1.30

Girolamo Luxardo Liqueurs, 200th Anniv. — A2297

Serpentine Die Cut 11
2021, Mar. 23   Photo.
Self-Adhesive
3726 A2297 (€1.10) multi   2.60 1.30

Venice, 1500th Anniv. — A2298

Serpentine Die Cut 11
2021, Mar. 25   Photo.
Self-Adhesive
3727 A2298 (€1.15) multi   2.75 1.40

Foundation of Leontinoi (Lentini) by Greeks, 2750th Anniv. — A2299

Serpentine Die Cut 11
2021, Mar. 26   Photo.
Self-Adhesive
3728 A2299 (€1.10) multi   2.60 1.30

Ernesto Nathan (1845-1921), Mayor of Rome — A2300

Serpentine Die Cut 11
2021, Apr. 9   Photo.
Self-Adhesive
3729 A2300 (€1.10) multi   2.75 1.40

Settimia Spizzichino (1921-2000), Only Woman to Survive Holocaust After Deportation From Rome's Jewish Ghetto — A2301

Serpentine Die Cut 11
2021, Apr. 15   Photo.
Self-Adhesive
3730 A2301 (€1.10) multi   2.75 1.40

Souvenir Sheet

Environmental Sustainability — A2302

2021, Apr. 22   Litho.   Perf. 13¼
3731 A2302 (€1.10) multi + 9 labels   2.75 1.40
See Slovakia No. 843.

Health Care Workers — A2303

Serpentine Die Cut 11
2021, Apr. 28   Photo.
Self-Adhesive
3732 A2303 (€1.10) multi   2.75 1.40

Movie Stars — A2304

Designs: No. 3733, Giulietta Masina (1921-94). No. 3734, Nino Manfredi (1921-2004). No. 3735, Alida Valli (1921-2006).

Serpentine Die Cut 11
2021, Apr. 30   Photo.
Self-Adhesive
3733 A2304 (€1.10) multi   2.75 1.40
3734 A2304 (€1.10) multi   2.75 1.40
3735 A2304 (€1.10) multi   2.75 1.40
     Nos. 3733-3735 (3)   8.25 4.20

Napoleon Bonaparte (1769-1821), Emperor of France and King of Italy — A2305

Serpentine Die Cut 11
2021, May 5   Photo.
Self-Adhesive
3736 A2305 (€1.15) multi   3.00 1.50

Animals and Giuseppe Garibaldi (1807-82), General and Founder of National Animal Protection Organization A2306

Serpentine Die Cut 11
2021, May 19   Photo.
Self-Adhesive
3737 A2306 (€1.10) multi   2.75 1.40
National Animal Protection Organization, 150th anniv.

Musicians — A2307

Designs: No. 3738, Rino Gaetano (1950-81). No. 3739, Ezio Bosso (1971-2020).

Serpentine Die Cut 11
2021, May 21   Photo.
Self-Adhesive
3738 A2307 (€1.10) multi   2.75 1.40
3739 A2307 (€1.10) multi   2.75 1.40

Miniature Sheet

Alta Murgia National Park A2308

No. 3740: a, Dinosaur footprint, Cava Pontrelli. b, Fossil of man, Lamalunga Cave. c, Spinazzola Bauxite Mines. d, Pulo di Altamua Sinkhole. e, Pulicchio di Gravina Sinkhole.

Serpentine Die Cut 11
2021, May 24   Photo.
Self-Adhesive
3740 A2308 Sheet of 5   14.00
   a.-e.   (€1.10) Any single   2.75 1.40

Guardia di Finanza Yellow Flames Athletic Team, Cent. — A2309

Serpentine Die Cut 11
2021, May 29   Photo.
Self-Adhesive
3741 A2309 (€1.10) multi   2.75 1.40

Souvenir Sheet

Detachment of Italian Carabinieri in San Marino, Cent. — A2310

2021, June 1   Photo.   Perf. 13x13¼
3742 A2310 (€1.10) multi   2.75 1.40
See San Marino No. 2109.

Arnoldo Mondadori (1889-1971), Publisher — A2311

Serpentine Die Cut 11
2021, June 8   Photo.
Self-Adhesive
3743 A2311 (€1.10) multi   2.75 1.40

San Francesco Patron Saint of Italy Magazine, Cent. — A2312

Serpentine Die Cut 11
2021, June 8   Photo.
Self-Adhesive
3744 A2312 (€1.10) multi   2.60 1.30

Rummo S.p.A. Pasta Makers, 175th Anniv. — A2313

Serpentine Die Cut 11
2021, June 9   Photo.
Self-Adhesive
3745 A2313 (€2.80) multi   6.75 3.50

2020 European Soccer Championships A2314

Serpentine Die Cut 11
2021, June 11   Photo.
Self-Adhesive
3746 A2314 (€1.15) multi   2.75 1.40

The 2020 European Soccer Championships were postponed until 2021 because of the COVID-19 pandemic.

ITALY

Cosimo II de'Medici Receiving His Knights, Fresco by Il Volterrano (1611-89) A2315

Battle of Lepanto, 450th Anniv. — A2316

Serpentine Die Cut 11
2021, June 18
Self-Adhesive   Photo.

| 3747 | A2315 | (€1.10) multi | 2.60 | 1.30 |
| 3748 | A2316 | (€3.50) multi | 8.25 | 4.25 |

Order of Saint Stephen, 460th anniv. (No. 3747).

Laudamo Philharmonic Orchestra, Messina, Cent. — A2317

Serpentine Die Cut 11
2021, June 21
Self-Adhesive   Photo.

| 3749 | A2317 | (€1.10) multi | 2.60 | 1.30 |

Gigi Proietta (1940-2020), Actor — A2318

Serpentine Die Cut 11
2021, June 29
Self-Adhesive   Photo.

| 3750 | A2318 | (€1.10) multi | 2.60 | 1.30 |

Ennio Morricone (1928-2020), Composer of Motion Picture Music — A2319

Serpentine Die Cut 11
2021, June 29
Self-Adhesive   Photo.

| 3751 | A2319 | (€1.10) multi | 2.60 | 1.30 |

Andrea Camilleri (1925-2019), Writer — A2320

Serpentine Die Cut 11
2021, June 29
Self-Adhesive   Photo.

| 3752 | A2320 | (€1.10) multi | 2.60 | 1.30 |

Tourism A2321

Designs: No. 3753, Basilica of Santa Croce, Florence (Firenze). No. 3754, Duomo and Galleria Vittorio Emanuele II, Milan (Milano). No. 3755, Piazza del Plebescito, Naples (Napoli). No. 3756, Piazza Vigliena, Palermo. No. 3757, Spanish Steps, Fontana della Barcaccia and Trinità dei Monti Church, Rome (Roma). No. 3758, Doge's Palace, Marciana National Library, Venice (Venezia).

Serpentine Die Cut 9¼x8
2021, June 30
Self-Adhesive   Photo.

3753	A2321	(€1.10) multi	2.60	1.30
3754	A2321	(€1.10) multi	2.60	1.30
3755	A2321	(€1.10) multi	2.60	1.30
3756	A2321	(€1.10) multi	2.60	1.30
3757	A2321	(€1.10) multi	2.60	1.30
3758	A2321	(€1.10) multi	2.60	1.30
Nos. 3753-3758 (6)			15.60	7.80

Italian Caritas, 50th Anniv. — A2322

Serpentine Die Cut 11
2021, July 2
Self-Adhesive   Photo.

| 3759 | A2322 | (€1.10) multi | 2.60 | 1.30 |

ITAS Mutua Insurance Company, 200th Anniv. — A2323

Serpentine Die Cut 8x9¼
2021, July 3
Self-Adhesive   Photo.

| 3760 | A2323 | (€1.10) multi | 2.60 | 1.30 |

Lagostina Cookware Company Factory, Omegna, 120th Anniv. — A2324

Serpentine Die Cut 11
2021, July 7
Self-Adhesive   Photo.

| 3761 | A2324 | (€1.10) multi | 2.60 | 1.30 |

Remo Gaspari (1921-2011), Politician — A2325

Serpentine Die Cut 11
2021, July 10
Self-Adhesive   Photo.

| 3762 | A2325 | (€1.10) multi | 2.60 | 1.30 |

Modugno, 1000th Anniv. — A2326

Serpentine Die Cut 11
2021, July 22
Self-Adhesive   Photo.

| 3763 | A2326 | (€1.10) multi | 2.60 | 1.30 |

Tourism Type of 2018

Designs: No. 3764, Piazza Maggiore, Bologna. No. 3765, Norcia. No. 3766, Christ the Redeemer Statue, Maratea. No. 3767, La Maddalena.

Serpentine Die Cut 9¼x8
2021, July 23
Self-Adhesive   Photo.

3764	A2098	(€1.10) multi	2.60	1.30
3765	A2098	(€1.10) multi	2.60	1.30
3766	A2098	(€1.10) multi	2.60	1.30
3767	A2098	(€1.10) multi	2.60	1.30
Nos. 3764-3767 (4)			10.40	5.20

Inter Milan, 2020-21 Italian Soccer Champions — A2327

Serpentine Die Cut 11
2021, July 30
Self-Adhesive   Photo.

| 3768 | A2327 | (€1.10) gold & multi | 2.60 | 1.30 |

Italy, Winners of 2020 European Soccer Championships A2328

Serpentine Die Cut 11
2021, Aug. 6
Self-Adhesive   Photo.

| 3769 | A2328 | (€1.15) multi | 2.75 | 1.40 |

The 2020 European Soccer Championships were postponed until 2021 because of the COVID-19 pandemic.

Giorgio Strehler (1921-97), Actor and Theater Director — A2329

Serpentine Die Cut 11
2021, Aug. 14
Self-Adhesive   Photo.

| 3770 | A2329 | (€1.10) multi | 2.60 | 1.30 |

Motion Picture Celebrities — A2330

Designs: No. 3771, Gino Cervi (1901-74), actor. No. 3772, Vittorio De Sica (1901-74), actor and director.

Serpentine Die Cut 11
2021, Aug. 27
Self-Adhesive   Photo.

| 3771 | A2330 | (€1.10) multi | 2.60 | 1.30 |
| 3772 | A2330 | (€1.10) multi | 2.60 | 1.30 |

Madonna and Sanctuary of Oropa — A2331

Serpentine Die Cut 8x9¼
2021, Aug. 29
Self-Adhesive   Photo.

| 3773 | A2331 | (€1.10) multi | 2.60 | 1.30 |

Fifth coronation of the Madonna of Oropa.

Ventotene Manifesto, 80th Anniv. — A2332

Serpentine Die Cut 11
2021, Aug. 31
Self-Adhesive   Photo.

| 3774 | A2332 | (€1.15) multi | 2.75 | 1.40 |

International Fair Play Award, 25th Anniv. — A2333

Serpentine Die Cut 11
2021, Sept. 1
Self-Adhesive   Photo.

| 3775 | A2333 | (€1.10) multi | 2.60 | 1.30 |

Tobacco Factory Complex, Battipaglia, Cent. — A2334

Serpentine Die Cut 11
2021, Sept. 2
Self-Adhesive   Photo.

| 3776 | A2334 | (€2.60) multi | 6.00 | 3.00 |

University of Ferrara Botanical Garden, 250th Anniv. — A2335

Serpentine Die Cut 11
2021, Sept. 6
Self-Adhesive   Photo.

| 3777 | A2335 | (€1.10) gold & multi | 2.60 | 1.30 |

Gucci Fashions, Cent. — A2336

Serpentine Die Cut
2021, Sept. 10
Self-Adhesive   Photo.

| 3778 | A2336 | (€1.10) multi | 2.60 | 1.30 |

Guzzi Motorcycles, Cent. A2337

Serpentine Die Cut 9¼x8
2021, Sept. 11
Self-Adhesive   Photo.

| 3779 | A2337 | (€1.15) multi | 2.75 | 1.40 |

ITALY

A2338

A2339

Dante Alighieri (c. 1265-1321), Writer — A2340

Serpentine Die Cut 9¼x8
2021, Sept. 14   **Photo.**
Self-Adhesive
3780   A2338   (€1.10) multi   2.60   1.30
3781   A2339   (€1.10) multi   2.60   1.30
Serpentine Die Cut 8x9¼
3782   A2340   (€1.10) multi   2.60   1.30
    Nos. 3780-3782 (3)   7.80   3.90

Frejus Railway Tunnel, 150th Anniv. — A2341

Serpentine Die Cut 11
2021, Sept. 17   **Photo.**
Self-Adhesive
3783   A2341   (€1.10) multi   2.60   1.30

Grazia Deledda (1871-1936), 1926 Nobel Laureate in Literature — A2342

Serpentine Die Cut 11
2021, Sept. 27   **Photo.**
Self-Adhesive
3784   A2342   (€1.10) multi   2.60   1.30

Sicilian Direct Cultivators Regional Federation, 70th Anniv. — A2343

Serpentine Die Cut 9¼x8
2021, Sept. 28   **Photo.**
Self-Adhesive
3785   A2343   (€1.10) multi   2.60   1.30

Mafalda, Comic Strip by Quino (1932-2020) — A2344

Serpentine Die Cut 11
2021, Sept. 29   **Photo.**
Self-Adhesive
3786   A2344   (€1.10) multi   2.60   1.30

A2345

Serpentine Die Cut 11
2021, Sept. 30   **Photo.**
Self-Adhesive
3787   A2345   (€1.15) multi   2.75   1.40
   Organization for Economic Cooperation and Development, 60th anniv.

Venini, Manufacturer of Murano Glass, Cent. — A2346

Serpentine Die Cut 11
2021, Oct. 2   **Photo.**
Self-Adhesive
3788   A2346   (€1.10) multi   2.60   1.30

Academy of Sciences, Letters and Fine Arts of the Zealots and Daphnics, Acireale, 350th Anniv. — A2347

Serpentine Die Cut 11
2021, Oct. 3   **Photo.**
Self-Adhesive
3789   A2347   (€1.10) multi   2.60   1.30

Revenue Agency, 20th Anniv. A2348

Serpentine Die Cut 9¼x8
2021, Oct. 6   **Photo.**
Self-Adhesive
3790   A2348   (€1.10) multi   2.60   1.30

Italo Tibaldi (1927-2010), Concentration Camp Survivor and Writer — A2349

Serpentine Die Cut 11
2021, Oct. 13   **Photo.**
Self-Adhesive
3791   A2349   (€1.15) multi   2.75   1.40

Jole Santelli (1968-2020), President of Calabria — A2350

Serpentine Die Cut 11
2021, Oct. 15   **Photo.**
Self-Adhesive
3792   A2350   (€1.10) multi   2.60   1.30

Souvenir Sheet

Tomb of the Unknown Soldier, Rome A2351

2021, Oct. 19   **Photo.**   *Perf. 13x13¼*
3793   A2351   (€1.10) multi   2.60   1.30

Opera Singers — A2352

Designs: No. 3794, Enrico Caruso (1873-1921). No. 3795, Giuseppe Di Stefano (1921-2008). No. 3796, Franco Corelli (1921-2003).

Serpentine Die Cut 11
2021, Oct. 25   **Photo.**
Self-Adhesive
3794   A2352   (€1.10) multi   2.60   1.30
3795   A2352   (€1.10) multi   2.60   1.30
3796   A2352   (€1.10) multi   2.60   1.30
   Nos. 3794-3796 (3)   7.80   3.90

Enchanted Curtains, Painting by Emanuele Luzzati (1921-2007), Film Director and Painter — A2353

Serpentine Die Cut 11
2021, Oct. 26   **Photo.**
Self-Adhesive
3797   A2353   (€1.10) multi   2.60   1.30

Turin as Host of 2021-25 Nitto Association of Tennis Professionals Finals — A2354

Serpentine Die Cut 8x9¼
2021, Oct. 29   **Photo.**
Self-Adhesive
3798   A2354   (€1.10) multi   2.60   1.30

Luigi Einaudi (1874-1961), President of Italy — A2355

Serpentine Die Cut 11
2021, Oct. 30   **Photo.**
Self-Adhesive
3799   A2355   (€1.10) multi   2.60   1.30

Bud Spencer (1929-2016), Film Actor — A2356

Serpentine Die Cut 11
2021, Oct. 31   **Photo.**
Self-Adhesive
3800   A2356   (€1.10) multi   2.60   1.30

Mario Rigoni Stern (1921-2008), Writer — A2357

Serpentine Die Cut 11
2021, Nov. 1   **Photo.**
Self-Adhesive
3801   A2357   (€1.10) multi   2.60   1.30

Italian Basketball Federation, Cent. — A2358

Serpentine Die Cut 11
2021, Nov. 2   **Photo.**
Self-Adhesive
3802   A2358   (€1.10) multi   2.50   1.25

Aeolian Wall Lizard — A2359

Marsican Brown Bear — A2360

Serpentine Die Cut 11
2021, Nov. 15   **Photo.**
Self-Adhesive
3803   A2359   (€1.10) multi   2.50   1.25
3804   A2360   (€2.60) multi   6.00   3.00
   Europa.

Italian Presidency of the Committee of Ministers of the Council of Europe — A2361

Serpentine Die Cut 11
2021, Nov. 17   **Photo.**
Self-Adhesive
3805   A2361   (€3.50) multi   8.00   4.00

Italian Protected Designation of Origin Food Crops — A2362

No. 3806: a, Tomato (pomidoro). b, Beans (fagiolo). c, Artichoke (carciofo). d, Orange (arancia). e, Pepper (peperone). f, Apple (mela). g, Eggplant (melanzana). h, Potatoes (patata). i, Chestnuts (castagna). j, Onions (cipolla). k, Hazelnuts (nocciola). l, Figs (fico). m, Basil (basilico). n, Garlic (aglio). o, Pistachios (pistacchio).

Serpentine Die Cut 8x9¼
2021, Nov. 20   **Photo.**
Self-Adhesive
3806   Sheet of 15   9.00
a.-o.   A2362 25c Any single   .60   .30

Sirti Telecommunications Company, Cent. — A2363

ITALY

Serpentine Die Cut 11
2021, Nov. 21   **Photo.**
Self-Adhesive
3807   A2363   (€1.10) multi   2.50   1.25

Doctors Without Borders, 50th Anniv. — A2364

Serpentine Die Cut 11
2021, Nov. 22   **Photo.**
Self-Adhesive
3808   A2364   (€3.10) multi   7.00   3.50

Leonardo Sciascia (1921-89), Writer — A2365

Serpentine Die Cut 11
2021, Nov. 27   **Photo.**
Self-Adhesive
3809   A2365   (€1.10) multi   2.50   1.25

Madonna Enthroned with Child Between St. Bernardino of Siena and St. Francis, by Bernardino Lanino (c. 1512-c. 1582) — A2366

Person Writing Christmas Greeting — A2367

Serpentine Die Cut 8x9¼
2021, Dec. 1   **Photo.**
Self-Adhesive
3810   A2366   (€1.10) multi   2.50   1.25

Serpentine Die Cut 9¼x8
3811   A2367   (€1.15) multi   2.60   1.30

Italian Association of Female Doctors, Cent. — A2368

Serpentine Die Cut 11
2021, Dec. 3   **Photo.**
Self-Adhesive
3812   A2368   (€1.10) multi   2.50   1.25

Roman Philharmonic Academy, 200th Anniv. — A2369

Serpentine Die Cut 11
2021, Dec. 4   **Photo.**
Self-Adhesive
3813   A2369   (€1.10) multi   2.50   1.25

Canons Regular of the Immaculate Conception, 150th Anniv. — A2370

Serpentine Die Cut 11
2021, Dec. 8   **Photo.**
Self-Adhesive
3814   A2370   (€1.10) multi   2.50   1.25

Il Piccolo Newspaper, Trieste, 140th Anniv. — A2371

Serpentine Die Cut 11
2021, Dec. 10   **Photo.**
Self-Adhesive
3815   A2371   (€1.10) multi   2.50   1.25

Association of Executive Classes of Public Administrations, 20th Anniv. — A2372

Serpentine Die Cut 9¼x8
2021, Dec. 14   **Photo.**
Self-Adhesive
3816   A2372   (€1.10) multi   2.50   1.25

Elmo Palazzi (1871-1915), Sculptor — A2373

Serpentine Die Cut 11
2021, Dec. 23   **Photo.**
Self-Adhesive
3817   A2373   (€1.10) multi   2.50   1.25

Procida, 2022 Italian Capital of Culture — A2374

Serpentine Die Cut 11
2022, Jan. 22   **Photo.**
Self-Adhesive
3818   A2374   (€1.10) multi   2.50   1.25

Giovanni Verga (1840-1922), Writer — A2375

Serpentine Die Cut 11
2022, Jan. 27   **Photo.**
Self-Adhesive
3819   A2375   (€1.10) multi   2.50   1.25

Pirelli Tires, 150th Anniv. — A2376

Serpentine Die Cut 11
2022, Jan. 28   **Photo.**
Self-Adhesive
3820   A2376   (€1.10) multi   2.50   1.25

Consecration of Cosenza Cathedral, 800th Anniv. — A2377

Serpentine Die Cut 8x9¼
2022, Jan. 30   **Photo.**
Self-Adhesive
3821   A2377   (€1.10) black & gray   2.50   1.25

Anatomical Theater, University of Padua — A2378

Serpentine Die Cut 11
2022, Feb. 2   **Photo.**
Self-Adhesive
3822   A2378   (€1.10) multi   2.50   1.25
University of Padua, 800th anniv.

Tina Modotti (1896-1942), Photographer and Actress — A2379

Serpentine Die Cut 11
2022, Feb. 18   **Photo.**
Self-Adhesive
3823   A2379   (€1.10) multi   2.50   1.25

Italian League for the Fight Against Cancer, Cent. — A2380

Serpentine Die Cut 11
2022, Feb. 25   **Photo.**
Self-Adhesive
3824   A2380   (€1.10) multi   2.50   1.25

St. Gabriel of Our Lady of Sorrows, (1838-62), and Shrine of St. Gabriel, Isola del Gran Sasso — A2381

Serpentine Die Cut 9¼x8
2022, Feb. 27   **Photo.**
Self-Adhesive
3825   A2381   (€1.10) multi   2.50   1.25

Beppe Fenoglio (1922-63), Writer — A2382

Serpentine Die Cut 11
2022, Mar. 1   **Photo.**
Self-Adhesive
3826   A2382   (€1.10) multi   2.50   1.25

Giuseppe Mazzini (1805-72), Italian Nationalist Leader, and Episode of the Five Days of Milan in Piazza Sant' Alessandro, Painting by Carlo Stragliati — A2383

Serpentine Die Cut 8x9¼
2022, Mar. 1   **Photo.**
Self-Adhesive
3827   A2383   (€2.60) multi   5.75   3.00

Ugo Tognazzi (1922-90), Film Actor and Director — A2384

Serpentine Die Cut 11
2022, Mar. 23   **Photo.**
Self-Adhesive
3828   A2384   (€1.10) multi   2.50   1.25

Santa Maria in Vado Church, Ferrara — A2385

Serpentine Die Cut 8x9¼
2022, Mar. 28   **Photo.**
Self-Adhesive
3829   A2385   (€1.10) multi   2.50   1.25

State Police, 170th Anniv. — A2386

Serpentine Die Cut 11
2022, Apr. 10   **Photo.**
Self-Adhesive
3830   A2386   (€1.10) multi   2.40   1.25

Spilimbergo Mosaic School, Friuli, Cent. — A2387

Serpentine Die Cut
2022, Apr. 22   **Photo.**
Self-Adhesive
3831   A2387   (€1.10) multi   2.40   1.25

Madonna and Child, San Martino Church, Vallecorsa — A2388

Serpentine Die Cut 11
2022, Apr. 23   **Photo.**
Self-Adhesive
3832   A2388   (€1.10) multi   2.40   1.25

ITALY

Souvenir Sheet

Poste Italiane, 160th Anniv. — A2389

2022, May 5   Photo.   Perf. 13x13¼
3833   A2389   (€1.10) multi + 6 labels   2.40   1.25

Young Philatelists and Gastone Rizzo (1922-2019), Founder of Franco Bollino Stamp Club — A2390

2022, May 7   Photo.   Perf. 13x13¼
3834   A2390   (€1.10) multi   2.40   1.25

Paolo Ruffini (1765-1822), Mathematician — A2391

Serpentine Die Cut 11
2022, May 10   Photo.   Self-Adhesive
3835   A2391   (€1.10) multi   2.40   1.25

Managed Savings Industry — A2392

Serpentine Die Cut 11
2022, May 12   Photo.   Self-Adhesive
3836   A2392   (€1.10) multi   2.40   1.25

St. Luigi Orione (1872-1940) — A2393

2022, May 16   Photo.   Perf. 13x13¼
3837   A2393   (€2.40) multi   5.25   2.60

No. 3837 was printed in sheets of 4. See Argentina No. 2959, Vatican City No. 1794.

Roncioniana Library, Prato, 300th Anniv. — A2394

Serpentine Die Cut 11
2022, May 21   Photo.   Self-Adhesive
3838   A2394   (€1.10) multi   2.40   1.25

Margherita Hack (1922-2013), Astrophysicist and Writer — A2395

Serpentine Die Cut 11
2022, June 12   Photo.   Self-Adhesive
3839   A2395   (€1.25) multi   2.60   1.30

Italian Federation of Judo, Fighting, Karate and Martial Arts, 120th Anniv. — A2396

Serpentine Die Cut 11
2022, June 21   Photo.   Self-Adhesive
3840   A2396   (€1.10) multi   2.40   1.25

Galup Baked Goods, Cent. — A2397

Serpentine Die Cut 11
2022, June 21   Photo.   Self-Adhesive
3841   A2397   (€1.10) multi   2.40   1.25

FS Class Three-Phase Electric Locomotive E.431, Cent. — A2398

2022, June 23   Photo.   Perf. 13¼x13
3842   A2398   (€1.10) multi   2.40   1.25

AC Milan, 2021-22 Italian Soccer Champions — A2399

Serpentine Die Cut
2022, June 30   Photo.   Self-Adhesive
3843   A2399   (€1.20) multi   2.50   1.25

No. 3843 was printed in sheets of 6.

Ferrari Trento Winery, 120th Anniv. — A2400

Serpentine Die Cut 11
2022, July 6   Photo.   Self-Adhesive
3844   A2400   (€1.25) multi   2.60   1.30

Souvenir Sheet

Carabinieri and Cernaia Barracks, Turin — A2401

Serpentine Die Cut 9¼x8
2022, July 23   Photo.   Self-Adhesive
3845   A2401   (€1.20) multi   2.50   1.25

Recruitment Station, Turin, 200th anniv.

52nd Giffoni Film Festival, Giffoni Valle Piana — A2402

Serpentine Die Cut 8x9¼
2022, July 25   Photo.   Self-Adhesive
3846   A2402   (€3.05) multi   6.25   3.25

European Youth Year.

Mexican Embassy, Rome, Cent. — A2403

Serpentine Die Cut 11
2022, July 28   Photo.   Self-Adhesive
3847   A2403   (€3.90) multi   8.00   4.00

Domenico Fioritto (1872-1952), Politician, and His Birthplace, San Nicandro Garganico — A2404

Serpentine Die Cut 11
2022, Aug. 3   Photo.   Self-Adhesive
3848   A2404   (€1.20) multi   2.40   1.25

Passion Play of Sordevolo — A2405

Serpentine Die Cut 9¼x8
2022, Aug. 6   Photo.   Self-Adhesive
3849   A2405   (€1.20) multi   2.40   1.25

2022 European Aquatics Championships, Rome — A2406

Serpentine Die Cut 9¼x8
2022, Aug. 11   Photo.   Self-Adhesive
3850   A2406   (€1.25) multi   2.50   1.25

Procession of the Vara and the Giants, Messina — A2407

Serpentine Die Cut 9¼x8
2022, Aug. 12   Photo.   Self-Adhesive
3851   A2407   (€1.20) multi   2.40   1.25

Renon Narrow-Gauge Cog Railway — A2408

Serpentine Die Cut 11
2022, Aug. 13   Photo.   Self-Adhesive
3852   A2408   (€1.20) multi   2.40   1.25

National Automobile Racetrack, Monza, Cent. — A2409

Serpentine Die Cut 11
2022, Sept. 3   Photo.   Self-Adhesive
3853   A2409   (€1.20) multi   2.40   1.25

The Rio dei Mendicanti and Scuola Grande di San Marco, Painting by Bernardo Bellotto (c.1721-80) — A2410

Serpentine Die Cut 9¼x8
2022, Sept. 7   Photo.   Self-Adhesive
3854   A2410   (€1.20) multi   2.40   1.25

Guarantor for the Protection of Personal Data, 25th Anniv. — A2411

Serpentine Die Cut 11
2022, Sept. 14   Photo.   Self-Adhesive
3855   A2411   (€1.20) multi   2.40   1.25

Ettore Bastianini (1922-67), Opera Singer — A2412

Serpentine Die Cut 11
2022, Sept. 24   Photo.   Self-Adhesive
3856   A2412   (€1.20) multi   2.40   1.25

ITALY

Santa Maria di Campagna Basilica, Piacenza, 500th Anniv. — A2413

Serpentine Die Cut 9¼x8
2022, Sept. 26   **Photo.**
Self-Adhesive
3857   A2413   (€1.20) multi   2.40   1.25

Piacenza Cathedral, 900th Anniv. — A2414

Serpentine Die Cut 9¼x8
2022, Sept. 26   **Photo.**
Self-Adhesive
3858   A2414   (€1.20) multi   2.40   1.25

Metamorphosis of the Phoenix, Sculpture by Antonio De Paoli — A2415

Serpentine Die Cut 11
2022, Sept. 28   **Photo.**
Self-Adhesive
3859   A2415   (€1.20) multi   2.40   1.25
Falconara powder magazine explosion, cent.

Roche Italia Pharmaceutical Company, 125th Anniv. — A2416

Serpentine Die Cut 9¼x8
2022, Oct. 4   **Photo.**
Self-Adhesive
3860   A2416   (€1.20) multi   2.40   1.25

Cosenza Chamber of Commerce, 210th Anniv. — A2417

Serpentine Die Cut 11
2022, Oct. 5   **Photo.**
Self-Adhesive
3861   A2417   (€1.20) multi   2.40   1.25

Items in Historic Museum of Communication, Rome — A2418

2022, Oct. 6   **Photo.**   **Perf. 13¼x13**
3862   A2418   (€1.20) multi   2.40   1.25

The Peace of Kyiv, Sculpture by Antonio Canova (1757-1822) — A2419

Serpentine Die Cut 11
2022, Oct. 13   **Photo.**
Self-Adhesive
3863   A2419   (€2.80) multi   5.75   3.00

1922 Lancia Lambda — A2420

Serpentine Die Cut 11
2022, Oct. 22   **Photo.**
Self-Adhesive
3864   A2420   (€1.20) multi   2.40   1.25
No. 3864 was printed in sheets of 27 + 18 labels.

Extra Virgin Olive Oil — A2421

Serpentine Die Cut 9¼x8
2022, Oct. 24   **Photo.**
Self-Adhesive
3865   A2421   (€1.20) multi   2.40   1.25

La Molisana Pasta, 110th Anniv. — A2422

Serpentine Die Cut 11
2022, Oct. 25   **Photo.**
Self-Adhesive
3866   A2422   (€1.20) multi   2.40   1.25

Legend of the Colapesce A2423

Legend of Romeo and Juliet — A2424

Serpentine Die Cut 11
2022, Oct. 25   **Photo.**
Self-Adhesive
3867   A2423   (€2.70) multi   5.50   2.75
3868   A2424   (€3.10) multi   6.25   3.25
Europa.

Franco Franchi (1928-92) and Ciccio Ingrassia (1922-2003), Comedians — A2425

Serpentine Die Cut 11
2022, Oct. 26   **Photo.**
Self-Adhesive
3869   A2425   (€1.20) multi   2.40   1.25

Erminio Macario (1902-80), Comedian A2426

Serpentine Die Cut 9¼x8
2022, Oct. 26   **Photo.**
Self-Adhesive
3870   A2426   (€1.20) multi   2.40   1.25

Bauli Baked Goods, Cent. — A2427

Serpentine Die Cut 11
2022, Oct. 27   **Photo.**
Self-Adhesive
3871   A2427   (€1.20) multi   2.40   1.25

Military Geographic Institute, 150th Anniv. — A2428

Serpentine Die Cut 11
2022, Oct. 27   **Photo.**
Self-Adhesive
3872   A2428   (€1.20) multi   2.40   1.25

Niccolò Paganini (1782-1840), Violinist and Composer A2429

Serpentine Die Cut 11
2022, Oct. 27   **Photo.**
Self-Adhesive
3873   A2429   (€4.80) multi   9.50   4.75

A2430

A2431

Philately Day — A2432

Serpentine Die Cut 8x9¼
2022, Oct. 28   **Photo.**
Self-Adhesive
3874   A2430   (€1.20) multi   2.40   1.25
3875   A2431   (€1.20) multi   2.40   1.25
3876   A2432   (€1.20) multi   2.40   1.25
  a.   Souvenir sheet of 3, #3874-3876   7.25
Nos. 3874-3876 (3)   7.20   3.75

Pierangelo Bertoli (1942-2002), Singer and Songwriter A2433

Serpentine Die Cut 11
2022, Oct. 29   **Photo.**
Self-Adhesive
3877   A2433   (€1.20) multi   2.40   1.25

Paulo Emilio Taviani (1912-2001), Governmental Minister and Historian — A2434

Serpentine Die Cut 11
2022, Nov. 6   **Photo.**
Self-Adhesive
3878   A2434   (€1.20) multi   2.50   1.25

Ukrainian Refugees — A2435

Serpentine Die Cut 11
2022, Nov. 7   **Photo.**
Self-Adhesive
3879   A2435   (€1.25) multi   2.60   1.30

Italian War Memorial, El Alamein, Egypt — A2436

Serpentine Die Cut 11
2022, Nov. 8   **Photo.**
Self-Adhesive
3880   A2436   (€1.20) multi   2.50   1.25
Second Battle of El Alamein, 80th anniv.

Angela Giussani (1922-87), Creator of *Diabolik* Comic Book Series — A2437

Serpentine Die Cut 11
2022, Nov. 10   **Photo.**
Self-Adhesive
3881   A2437   (€1.20) multi   2.50   1.25

Giuseppe Antonio Borgese (1882-1952), Writer — A2438

Serpentine Die Cut 11
2022, Nov. 12   **Photo.**
Self-Adhesive
3882   A2438   (€1.20) multi   2.50   1.25

Sapio Group, Supplier of Medical and Industrial Gases, Cent. — A2439

Serpentine Die Cut 11
2022, Nov. 17   **Photo.**
Self-Adhesive
3883   A2439   (€1.20) multi   2.50   1.25

ITALY

Piazza Ducale, Vigevano — A2440

Serpentine Die Cut 9¼x8
2022, Nov. 19 Photo.
Self-Adhesive
3884 A2440 (€1.20) multi 2.50 1.25

Tourism Type of 2018
Designs: No. 3885, Riccione. No. 3886, Candelo. No. 3887, Venafro. No. 3888, Siracusa.

Serpentine Die Cut 9¼x8
2022, Nov. 22 Photo.
Self-Adhesive
3885 A2098 (€1.20) multi 2.50 1.25
3886 A2098 (€1.20) multi 2.50 1.25
3887 A2098 (€1.20) multi 2.50 1.25
3888 A2098 (€1.20) multi 2.50 1.25
Nos. 3885-3888 (4) 10.00 5.00

Raffaella Carrà (1943-2021), Singer and Actress — A2441

Serpentine Die Cut 11
2022, Nov. 25 Photo.
Self-Adhesive
3889 A2441 (€1.20) multi 2.50 1.25

Carla Fracci (1936-2021), Ballet Dancer and Actress — A2442

Serpentine Die Cut 11
2022, Nov. 25 Photo.
Self-Adhesive
3890 A2442 (€1.20) multi 2.50 1.25

Monica Vitti (1931-2022), Actress — A2443

Serpentine Die Cut 11
2022, Nov. 25 Photo.
Self-Adhesive
3891 A2443 (€1.20) multi 2.50 1.25

Lina Wertmüller (1928-2021), Film Director — A2444

Serpentine Die Cut 11
2022, Nov. 25 Photo.
Self-Adhesive
3892 A2444 (€1.20) black 2.50 1.25

Singers — A2445

Designs: No. 3893, Milva (1939-2021). No. 3894, Franco Battiato (1945-2021).

Serpentine Die Cut 11
2022, Nov. 25 Photo.
Self-Adhesive
3893 A2445 (€1.20) multi 2.50 1.25
3894 A2445 (€1.20) multi 2.50 1.25

Souvenir Sheet

Tribute to Magistrates Killed Fighting the Mafia and Terrorism — A2446

Serpentine Die Cut 9¼x8
2022, Nov. 25 Photo.
3895 A2446 (€1.20) multi 2.50 1.25

Italian Confederation of Small and Medium-Size Private Industries, 75th Anniv. — A2447

Serpentine Die Cut 11
2022, Nov. 28 Photo.
Self-Adhesive
3896 A2447 (€1.20) multi 2.50 1.25

Gender Medicine A2448

Serpentine Die Cut 11
2022, Nov. 29 Photo.
Self-Adhesive
3897 A2448 (€4.50) multi 9.50 4.75

Palazzo Piacentini (Economic Development Ministry Building), Rome, 90th Anniv. — A2449

Serpentine Die Cut 11
2022, Nov. 30 Photo.
Self-Adhesive
3898 A2449 (€1.20) multi 2.50 1.25

Ennio Doris (1940-2021), Founder of Mediolanum (Insurance, Finance and Banking Company) — A2450

Serpentine Die Cut 11
2022, Dec. 1 Photo.
Self-Adhesive
3899 A2450 (€1.20) multi 2.50 1.25

Italian Society of Authors and Publishers, 140th Anniv. — A2451

Serpentine Die Cut 11
2022, Dec. 3 Photo.
Self-Adhesive
3900 A2451 (€1.20) multi 2.60 1.30

Italian Federation of Roller Sports, Cent. — A2452

Serpentine Die Cut
2022, Dec. 5 Photo.
Self-Adhesive
3901 A2452 (€1.20) multi 2.60 1.30

Italian Men's Soccer Team's 1982 World Cup Championship, 40th Anniv. — A2453

Serpentine Die Cut 11
2022, Dec. 5 Photo.
Self-Adhesive
3902 A2453 (€5.50) multi 11.50 5.75

Pres. Antonio Segni (1891-1972) — A2454

Serpentine Die Cut 11
2022, Dec. 6 Photo.
Self-Adhesive
3903 A2454 (€1.20) multi 2.60 1.30

E. Marinella, Necktie Manufacturer — A2455

Serpentine Die Cut 11
2022, Dec. 6 Photo.
Self-Adhesive
3904 A2455 (€1.20) multi 2.60 1.30

Barilla Foods, 145th Anniv. — A2456

Serpentine Die Cut 11
2022, Dec. 6 Photo.
Self-Adhesive
3905 A2456 (€1.20) multi 2.60 1.30

Bichvinta Cathedral, Pitsunda, Abkhazia, Georgia, and Flags of Italy and Georgia — A2457

Serpentine Die Cut 11
2022, Dec. 7 Photo.
Self-Adhesive
3906 A2457 (€2.40) multi 5.25 2.60
Diplomatic relations between Italy and Georgia, 30th anniv.

Self-Portrait of Ilario Fioravanti (1922-2012), Painter and Sculptor — A2458

Serpentine Die Cut 11
2022, Dec. 7 Photo.
Self-Adhesive
3907 A2458 (€1.20) multi 2.60 1.30

Detail from St. Francis Altarpiece, Santa Croce Basilica, Florence, by Coppo di Marcovaldo (c. 1225-c. 1276) — A2459

Ribbon Christmas Tree, Snowmen and Dog — A2460

Serpentine Die Cut 11
2022, Dec. 7 Photo.
Self-Adhesive
3908 A2459 (€1.20) multi 2.60 1.30
Die Cut Perf. 10¾x10¾x10½
3909 A2460 (€1.20) multi 2.60 1.30
Christmas.

David Sassoli (1956-2022), President of the European Parliament A2461

Serpentine Die Cut 11
2022, Dec. 19 Photo.
Self-Adhesive
3910 A2461 (€1.25) multi 2.75 1.40

Marcialonga Ski Race, 50th Anniv. — A2462

Serpentine Die Cut 11
2023, Jan. 29 Photo.
Self-Adhesive
3911 A2462 (€1.20) multi 2.60 1.30

Silvano Campeggi (1923-2018), Designer of Movie Posters — A2463

Serpentine Die Cut 11
2023, Jan. 31 Photo.
Self-Adhesive
3912 A2463 (€1.20) multi 2.60 1.30

Franco Zeffirelli (1923-2019). Film Director — A2464

Serpentine Die Cut 11
2023, Feb. 12 Photo.
Self-Adhesive
3913 A2464 (€1.20) multi 2.60 1.30

ITALY

Italian Carnivals — A2465

Carnival in: No. 3914, Venice (Venezia). No. 3915, Fano. No. 3916, Putignano. No. 3917, Acireale. No. 3918, Cento. No. 3919, Viareggio.

Serpentine Die Cut 9¼x8
2023, Feb. 16   Photo.
Self-Adhesive
3914	A2465	(€1.20) multi	2.60	1.30
3915	A2465	(€1.20) multi	2.60	1.30
3916	A2465	(€1.20) multi	2.60	1.30
3917	A2465	(€1.20) multi	2.60	1.30
3918	A2465	(€1.20) multi	2.60	1.30
3919	A2465	(€1.20) multi	2.60	1.30
a.	Souvenir sheet of 6, #3914-3919		16.00	
	Nos. 3914-3919 (6)		15.40	7.80

National Order of Journalists, 60th Anniv. — A2466

Serpentine Die Cut 11
2023, Feb. 24   Photo.
Self-Adhesive
| 3920 | A2466 | (€1.20) multi | 2.60 | 1.30 |

Promotion of Female Entrepreneurs — A2467

Serpentine Die Cut 11
2023, Mar. 8   Photo.
Self-Adhesive
| 3921 | A2467 | (€1.20) multi | 2.60 | 1.30 |

Cartoon Characters of Benito Jacovitti (1923-97), Cartoonist — A2468

2023, Mar. 11   Photo.   *Perf. 13¼x13*
| 3922 | A2468 | (€1.20) multi | 2.60 | 1.30 |

Italian Air Force, Cent. — A2470

Serpentine Die Cut 11
2023, Mar. 23   Photo.
Self-Adhesive
| 3924 | A2470 | (€1.20) multi | 2.60 | 1.30 |

Bergamo and Brescia, 2023 Capitals of Italian Culture — A2472

No. 3926: a, Porta San Giacomo and Baptistery, Bergamo ("2023" at UL). b, Palazzo della Loggia and Brescia Castle, Brescia ("2023" at UR).

2023, Mar. 23   Photo.   *Perf. 13x13¼*
| 3926 | A2472 | Horiz. pair | 5.25 | 2.60 |
| a.-b. | | (€1.20) Either single | 2.60 | 1.30 |

Franco Frattini (1957-2022), President of the Council of State — A2473

Serpentine Die Cut 11
2023, Mar. 27   Photo.
Self-Adhesive
| 3927 | A2473 | (€1.25) multi | 2.75 | 1.40 |

Training Ship Italia — A2474

Serpentine Die Cut 11
2023, Mar. 30   Photo.
Self-Adhesive
| 3928 | A2474 | (€1.20) multi | 2.60 | 1.30 |

Tender to Nave Italia Foundation, 16th anniv.

Hellas Verona Soccer Team, 120th Anniv. — A2475

Serpentine Die Cut 11
2023, Apr. 1   Photo.
Self-Adhesive
| 3929 | A2475 | (€1.20) multi | 2.60 | 1.30 |

Pliny the Elder (c. 23-79), Roman Military Commander, Author and Naturalist — A2476

Serpentine Die Cut 11
2023, Apr. 3   Photo.
Self-Adhesive
| 3930 | A2476 | (€1.20) multi | 2.60 | 1.30 |

Virgilio and Stefano Mattei, Brothers Killed in 1973 Terrorist Arson Attack on Their Home — A2477

Serpentine Die Cut 9¼x8
2023, Apr. 16   Photo.
Self-Adhesive
| 3931 | A2477 | (€1.20) multi | 2.75 | 1.40 |

Mattei Brothers Association, 50th anniv.

National Association of Civilian Casualties of War, 80th Anniv. — A2478

Serpentine Die Cut 11
2023, Apr. 18   Photo.
Self-Adhesive
| 3932 | A2478 | (€1.20) multi | 2.75 | 1.40 |

Abruzzo, Lazio and Molise National Park, Cent. — A2479

Serpentine Die Cut 9¼x8
2023, Apr. 22   Photo.
Self-Adhesive
| 3933 | A2479 | (€1.20) multi | 2.75 | 1.40 |

Lelio Luttazzi (1923-2010), Composer and Actor — A2480

Serpentine Die Cut 11
2023, Apr. 27   Photo.
Self-Adhesive
| 3934 | A2480 | (€1.20) multi | 2.75 | 1.40 |

Felce Azzurra Perfume and Bath Products, Cent. — A2481

Serpentine Die Cut 11
2023, May 3   Photo.
Self-Adhesive
| 3935 | A2481 | (€1.20) multi | 2.60 | 1.30 |

Ambrosoli Honey, Cent. — A2482

Serpentine Die Cut 8x9¼
2023, May 4   Photo.
Self-Adhesive
| 3936 | A2482 | (€1.20) multi | 2.60 | 1.30 |

Awarding of Columbian Exhibition Gold Medal to DeCecco Pasta, 130th Anniv. — A2483

Serpentine Die Cut 8x9¼
2023, May 4   Photo.
Self-Adhesive
| 3937 | A2483 | (€1.20) multi | 2.60 | 1.30 |

1920s Advertising Poster for Cirio Foods — A2484

Serpentine Die Cut 8x9¼
2023, May 4   Photo.
Self-Adhesive
| 3938 | A2484 | (€1.20) multi | 2.60 | 1.30 |

Vismara Cured Meats, 125th Anniv. — A2485

Serpentine Die Cut 8x9¼
2023, May 4   Photo.
Self-Adhesive
| 3939 | A2485 | (€1.20) multi | 2.60 | 1.30 |

First Session of the Senate of the Italian Republic, 75th Anniv. — A2487

Serpentine Die Cut
2023, May 8   Photo.
Self-Adhesive
| 3941 | A2487 | (€1.20) multi | 2.60 | 1.30 |

Europa — A2488

Serpentine Die Cut 11
2023, May 9   Photo.
Self-Adhesive
| 3942 | A2488 | (€1.25) multi | 2.75 | 1.40 |

Maimeri Art Supplies, Cent. — A2489

Serpentine Die Cut 11
2023, May 10   Photo.
Self-Adhesive
| 3943 | A2489 | (€1.20) multi | 2.60 | 1.30 |

Pope Benedict XVI (1927-2022) — A2490

Serpentine Die Cut 8x9¼
2023, May 16   Photo.
Self-Adhesive
| 3944 | A2490 | (€3.05) multi | 6.50 | 3.25 |

Alessandro Manzoni (1785-1873), Writer — A2491

Serpentine Die Cut
2023, May 22   Photo.
Self-Adhesive
| 3945 | A2491 | (€1.20) multi | 2.60 | 1.30 |

ITALY

Rigoni di Asiago Foods, Cent. — A2492

Serpentine Die Cut 11
2023, May 24   Photo.
Self-Adhesive
3946   A2492   (€1.20) multi   2.60   1.30

State General Accounting Law, Cent. — A2493

Serpentine Die Cut 11
2023, May 25   Photo.
Self-Adhesive
3947   A2493   (€1.20) multi   2.60   1.30

Father Lorenzo Milani (1923-67), Educator — A2494

Serpentine Die Cut 11
2023, May 27   Photo.
Self-Adhesive
3948   A2494   (€1.20) multi   2.60   1.30

Codogno, 2023 European Town of Sports — A2495

Serpentine Die Cut 11
2023, June 5   Photo.
Self-Adhesive
3949   A2495   (€1.20) multi   2.60   1.30

Francesco Bagnaia on Ducati Motorcycle A2496

Serpentine Die Cut 9¼x8
2023, June 9   Photo.
Self-Adhesive
3950   A2496   (€5.50) multi   12.00   6.00
Bagnaia and Ducati Motorcycles, 2022 Moto GP World Champions.

Cedral Tassoni Soft Drinks, 230th Anniv. — A2497

Serpentine Die Cut 11
2023, June 12   Photo.
Self-Adhesive
3951   A2497   (€1.20) multi   2.60   1.30

Pasquale Saraceno (1903-91), Economist, and Emblem of Association for the Development of Industry in Southern Italy — A2498

Serpentine Die Cut 11
2023, June 14   Photo.
Self-Adhesive
3952   A2498   (€1.20) multi   2.60   1.30

100th Arena di Verona Opera Festival — A2499

Serpentine Die Cut 11
2023, June 16   Photo.
Self-Adhesive
3953   A2499   (€2.40) multi   5.25   2.60

Triumphal Arch of the Artillery Corps, Turin — A2500

Serpentine Die Cut 11
2023, June 17   Photo.
Self-Adhesive
3954   A2500   (€1.20) multi   2.60   1.30
National Association of Artillerymen of Italy, cent.

End of 2022-23 Ocean Race in Genoa — A2501

Serpentine Die Cut 11
2023, June 22   Photo.
Self-Adhesive
3955   A2501   (€3.10) multi   6.75   3.50
Originally planned for 2021-22, the Ocean Race was postponed until 2022-23 because of the COVID-19 pandemic.

Madonna and Child, Fresco by Pietro Perugino (c. 1446-1523) A2502

Serpentine Die Cut 8x9¼
2023, June 23   Photo.
Self-Adhesive
3956   A2502   (€1.20) multi   2.60   1.30

Martini & Rossi Alcoholic Beverages, 160th Anniv. — A2503

Serpentine Die Cut 11
2023, July 5   Photo.
Self-Adhesive
3957   A2503   (€1.20) multi   2.60   1.30

Umbria Jazz Summer Festival, 50th Anniv. — A2504

30th Umbria Jazz Winter Festival A2505

Serpentine Die Cut 8x9¼
2023, July 7   Photo.
Self-Adhesive
3958   A2504   (€1.20) multi   2.60   1.30
Serpentine Die Cut 9¼x8
3959   A2505   (€1.20) multi   2.60   1.30

The Canonical Congregations of Europe, Painting by Unknown Artist — A2506

Serpentine Die Cut 8x9¼
2023, July 10   Photo.
Self-Adhesive
3960   A2506   (€1.20) multi   2.60   1.30
Lateran Union, 200th anniv.

Napoli, 2022-23 Italian Soccer Champions — A2509

Serpentine Die Cut 11
2023, July 13   Photo.
Self-Adhesive
3966   A2509   (€1.20) multi   2.75   1.40

Italian Academy of Cuisine, Milan, 70th Anniv. — A2510

Serpentine Die Cut 11
2023, July 29   Photo.
Self-Adhesive
3967   A2510   (€1.25) multi   2.75   1.40

2023 European Men's and Women's Volleyball Championships A2511

Serpentine Die Cut 11
2023, Aug. 5   Photo.
Self-Adhesive
3968   A2511   (€1.30) multi   2.75   1.40

Royal Spanish Academy, Rome, 150th Anniv. — A2512

Serpentine Die Cut 11
2023, Aug. 8   Photo.
Self-Adhesive
3969   A2512   (€1.30) multi   2.75   1.40

Vilfredo F. D. Pareto (1848-1923), Sociologist and Economist, and His Book *Treatise on General Sociology* A2513

Serpentine Die Cut 11
2023, Sept. 1   Photo.
Self-Adhesive
3970   A2513   (€2.75) multi   6.00   3.00

Higher School of Specialization in Telecommunications, Rome, Cent. — A2514

Serpentine Die Cut 11
2023, Sept. 4   Photo.
Self-Adhesive
3971   A2514   (€1.25) multi   2.75   1.40

Gina Lollobrigida (1927-2023), Actress — A2515

Serpentine Die Cut 11
2023, Sept. 6   Photo.
Self-Adhesive
3972   A2515   (€1.25) multi   2.75   1.40

Giovanni Minzoni (1885-1923), Anti-Fascist Priest Murdered by Fascists — A2516

Serpentine Die Cut 11
2023, Sept. 6   Photo.
Self-Adhesive
3973   A2516   (€1.25) multi   2.75   1.40

Queen Elizabeth II (1926-2022) A2517

Serpentine Die Cut 11
2023, Sept. 12   Photo.
Self-Adhesive
3974   A2517   (€1.30) multi   2.75   1.40

Miniature Sheet

Artwork in the Uffizi Gallery, Florence A2518

No. 3975: a, Baptism of Christ, by the workshop of Andrea de Verrochio. b, Adoration of the Magi, by Domenico Ghirlandaio (1448-94). c, Portrait of a Man with a Medal of Cosimo the Elder, by Sandro Botticelli (1445-1510). d, Tobias and the Three Archangels, by Francesco Botticini (1446-98). e, Study for the Head of Mary Magdalene, by Leonardo da Vinci (1452-1519). f, Allegory of Fertility and Abundance, by Luca Signorelli (c. 1441-1523).

ITALY

Serpentine Die Cut 8x9¼
2023, Sept. 15 — Photo. — Self-Adhesive
3975	A2518	Sheet of 6	16.50	
a.-f.		(€1.25) Any single	2.75	1.40

Saverio Tutino (1923-2011), Journalist — A2519

Serpentine Die Cut 11
2023, Sept. 16 — Photo. — Self-Adhesive
3976	A2519	(€1.25) multi	2.75	1.40

Andrea Bafile (1878-1918), World War I Hero — A2520

Serpentine Die Cut 11
2023, Sept. 20 — Photo. — Self-Adhesive
3977	A2520	(€1.25) multi	2.75	1.40

Salvo d'Acquisto (1920-43), World War II Hero Executed by Germans — A2521

Serpentine Die Cut 8x9¼
2023, Sept. 23 — Photo. — Self-Adhesive
3978	A2521	(€1.25) multi	2.75	1.40

Portrait of Franca Florio, by Giovanni Boldini (1842-1931) — A2522

Serpentine Die Cut 11
2023, Sept. 28 — Photo. — Self-Adhesive
3979	A2522	(€1.25) multi	2.75	1.40

Florio (1873-1950), socialite and patron of the arts.

2023 Ryder Cup Golf Matches, Guidonia Montecelio — A2523

Serpentine Die Cut
2023, Sept. 29 — Photo. — Self-Adhesive
3980	A2523	(€2.90) multi	6.25	3.25

Tex Willer, Comic Book Character by Gian Luigi Bonelli (1908-2001), 75th Anniv. — A2524

Serpentine Die Cut 11
2023, Sept. 30 — Photo. — Self-Adhesive
3981	A2524	(€1.25) multi	2.75	1.40

Italian Association for Organ, Tissue and Cell Donation, 50th Anniv. — A2525

Serpentine Die Cut 11
2023, Oct. 1 — Photo. — Self-Adhesive
3982	A2525	(€1.25) multi	2.75	1.40

SEMI-POSTAL STAMPS

Many issues of Italy and Italian Colonies include one or more semi-postal denominations. To avoid splitting sets, these issues are generally listed as regular postage, airmail, etc., unless all values carry a surtax.

Italian Flag — SP1

Italian Eagle Bearing Arms of Savoy — SP2

1915-16 — Typo. — Perf. 14
B1	SP1	10c + 5c rose	8.50	12.00
B2	SP2	15c + 5c slate	6.75	9.50
B3	SP2	20c + 5c orange	32.50	65.00
		Nos. B1-B3 (3)	47.75	86.50
		Set, never hinged	125.00	

No. B2 Surcharged

1916
B4	SP2	20c on 15c + 5c	20.00	55.00
		Never hinged	50.00	
a.		Double overprint	800.00	—
		Never hinged		
b.		Inverted overprint	800.00	1,400.
		Never hinged		
c.		Pair, one without surcharge	1,800.	
		Never hinged	2,600.	

Regular Issues of 1906-16 Overprinted in Blue or Red

1921
B5	A48	10c claret (Bl)	900.00	1,450.
a.		Double overprint	1,300.	
B6	A50	20c brn org (Bl)	1,250.	425.00
B7	A49	25c blue (R)	220.00	180.00
a.		Double overprint	360.00	
B8	A49	40c brn (Bl)	85.00	18.00
a.		Inverted overprint	425.00	700.00
		Nos. B5-B8 (4)	2,455.	2,073.
		Set, never hinged	5,000.	

Regular Issues of 1901-22 Overprinted in Black, Blue, Brown or Red

1922-23
B9	A48	10c cl ('23) (Bk)	110.00	100.00
a.		Blue ovpt.	85.00	80.00
		Never hinged	215.00	
b.		Brown ovpt.	85.00	80.00
		Never hinged	215.00	
d.		Blk ovpt. double	160.00	
e.		As "b," ovpt. double	160.00	
B10	A48	15c slate (Org)	290.00	475.00
a.		Blue ovpt.	900.00	725.00
		Never hinged	1,900.	
b.		Red overprint	360.00	575.00
		Never hinged	900.00	
B11	A50	20c brn org (Bk)	360.00	475.00
a.		Blue ovpt.	800.00	325.00
		Never hinged	1,575.	
B12	A49	25c blue (BK; '23)	100.00	87.50
b.		Red cverprint	200.00	475.00
		Never hinged	725.00	
c.		Orange overprint	325.00	540.00
		Never hinged	800.00	
B12A	A49	30c org brn (Bk)	220.00	200.00
		Never hinged	540.00	
B13	A49	40c brn (Bl)	170.00	87.50
a.		Black overpt.	190.00	87.50
		Never hinged	425.00	
b.		As "a," invtd. ovpt.	210.00	—
B14	A49	50c vio ('23) (Bk)	725.00	500.00
a.		Blue cverprint		
B15	A49	60c car (Bk)	2,200.	1,900.
		Never hinged	4,000.	
B15A	A49	85c choc (Bk)	290.00	475.00
		Never hinged	725.00	
B16	A46	1 l brn & grn ('23) (Bk)	3,250.	2,200.
a.		Inverted overprint	5,000.	
		Never hinged	6,250.	
		Set, never hinged	21,060.	

The stamps overprinted "B.L.P." were sold by the Government below face value to the National Federation for Assisting War Invalids. Most of them were affixed to special envelopes (Buste Lettere Postali) which bore advertisements. The Federation was permitted to sell these envelopes at a reduction of 5c from the face value of each stamp. The profits for the war invalids were derived from the advertisements.

Values of Nos. B5-B16 unused are for stamps with original gum. Most copies without gum or with part gum sell for about a quarter of values quoted. Uncanceled stamps affixed to the special envelopes usually sell for about half value.

The overprint on Nos. B9-B16 is wider (13½mm) than that on Nos. B5-B8 (11mm). The 1922-23 overprint exists both typo. and litho. on 10c, 15c, 20c and 25c; only litho. on 40c, 50c, 60c and 1 l; and only typo. on 30c and 85c.

Counterfeits of the B.L.P. overprints exist.

Administering Fascist Oath — SP3

1923, Oct. 29 — Perf. 14x14½
B17	SP3	30c + 30c brown	32.50	160.00
B18	SP3	50c + 50c violet	32.50	160.00
a.		Horiz. pair, imperf between	1,900.	
B19	SP3	1 l + 1 l gray	32.50	160.00
		Nos. B17-B19 (3)	97.50	480.00
		Set, never hinged	250.00	

The surtax was given to the Benevolent Fund of the Black Shirts (the Italian National Militia).

Anniv. of the March of the Fascisti on Rome.

St. Maria Maggiore — SP4

Pope Opening Holy Door — SP8

Designs: 30c+15c, St. John Lateran. 50c+25c, St. Paul's Church. 60c+30c, St. Peter's Basilica. 5 l+2.50 l, Pope closing Holy Door.

1924, Dec. 24 — Perf. 12
B20	SP4	20c + 10c dk grn & brn	4.50	12.50
B21	SP4	30c – 15c dk brn & brn	4.50	12.50
B22	SP4	50c – 25c vio & brn	4.50	12.50
B23	SP4	60c – 30c dp rose & brn	4.50	40.00
B24	SP8	1 l – 50c dp bl & vio	7.50	40.00
B25	SP8	5 l + 2.50 l org brn & vio	9.50	80.00
		Nos. B20-B25 (6)	35.00	197.50
		Set, never hinged	82.00	

The surtax was contributed toward the Holy Year expenses.

Castle of St. Angelo — SP10

Designs: 50c+20c, 60c+30c, Aqueduct of Claudius. 1.25 l+50c, 1.25 l+60c, Capitol, Roman Forum. 5 l+2 l, 5 l+2.50 l, People's Gate.

Unwmk.
1926, Oct. 26 — Engr. — Perf. 11
B26	SP10	40c + 20c dk brn & blk	3.25	24.00
B27	SP10	60c + 30c brn red & ol brn	3.25	24.00
B28	SP10	1.25 l + 60c bl grn & blk	3.25	72.50
B29	SP10	5 l + 2.50 l dk bl & blk	6.50	225.00
		Nos. B26-B29 (4)	16.25	345.50
		Set, never hinged	40.00	

Stamps inscribed "Poste Italiane" and "Fiere Campionaria di Tripoli" are listed in Libya.

1928, Mar. 1
B30	SP10	30c + 10c dl vio & blk	12.50	65.00
B31	SP10	50c + 20c ol grn & sl	21.00	65.00
B32	SP10	1.25 l + 50c dp bl & blk	25.00	140.00
B33	SP10	5 l + 2 l brn red & blk	55.00	450.00
		Nos. B30-B33 (4)	113.50	720.00
		Set, never hinged	275.00	

The tax on Nos. B26 to B33 was devoted to the charitable work of the Voluntary Militia for National Defense.
See Nos. B35-B38.

Victor Emmanuel II — SP14

1929, Jan. 4 — Photo. — Perf. 14
B34	SP14	50c + 10c ol grn	4.75	12.00
		Never hinged	12.00	

50th anniv. of the death of King Victor Emmanuel II. The surtax was for veterans.

Type of 1926 Issue
Designs in same order.

1930, July 1 — Engr.
B35	SP10	30c + 10c dk grn & vio	2.40	40.00
B36	SP10	50c + 10c dk grn & bl grn	3.25	30.00
B37	SP10	1.25 l + 30c ind & grn	8.00	95.00
B38	SP10	5 l + 1.50 l blk brn & ol brn	16.00	450.00
		Nos. B35-B38 (4)	29.65	615.00
		Set, never hinged	74.00	

The surtax was for the charitable work of the Voluntary Militia for National Defense.

Militiamen at Ceremonial Fire with Quotation from Leonardo da Vinci — SP15

Symbolical of Pride for Militia — SP16

ITALY

Symbolical of Militia Guarding Immortality of Italy SP17
Militia Passing Through Arch of Constantine SP18

1935, July 1   Photo.   Wmk. 140
B39	SP15	20c + 10c rose red	9.50	12.50
B40	SP16	25c + 15c grn	9.50	20.00
B41	SP17	50c + 30c pur	9.50	28.00
B42	SP18	1.25 l + 75c blue	9.50	42.50
		Nos. B39-B42 (4)	38.00	103.00
		Set, never hinged	96.00	
		Nos. B39-B42,CB3 (5)	47.50	143.00
		Set, never hinged	117.50	

The surtax was for the Militia.

Roman Battle SP19
Roman Warriors SP20

1941, Dec. 13
B43	SP19	20c + 10c rose red	.75	1.50
B44	SP19	30c + 15c brown	.75	1.90
B45	SP20	50c + 25c violet	.75	1.90
B46	SP20	1.25 l + 1 l blue	1.50	3.00
		Nos. B43-B46 (4)	3.75	8.30
		Set, never hinged	7.50	

2,000th anniv. of the birth of Livy (59 B.C.-17 A.D.), Roman historian.

Catalogue values for unused stamps in this section, from this point to the end of the section, are for Never Hinged items.

Aid for Flood Victims — SP21

1995, Jan. 2   Photo.   Perf. 13½x14
B47	SP21	750 l +2250 l multi	5.00	5.00

Queen Helen (1873-1952) — SP22

2002, Mar. 2   Photo.   Perf. 13¼x14
B48	SP22	41c + 21c multi	2.00	.85

Surtax for breast cancer research and prevention.

Intl. Commission on Occupational Health, 28th Congress SP23

2006, Mar. 8   Photo.   Perf. 13x13¼
B49	SP23	60c +30c multi	2.50	1.75

Surtax for breast cancer research.

Nursing — SP24

2010, May 16   Photo.
Serpentine Die Cut 11
Self-Adhesive
B50	SP24	60c +30c multi	2.25	2.25

Surtax for breast cancer research.

AIR POST STAMPS

Used values for Nos. C1-C105 are for postally used stamps with legible cancellations. Forged cancels on these issues abound, and expertization is strongly recommended.

Special Delivery No. E1 Ovptd.

1917, May   Wmk. 140   Perf. 14
C1	SD1	25c rose red	24.00	40.00
		Never hinged	60.00	

Type of SD3 Surcharged in Black

1917, June 27
C2	SD3	25c on 40c violet	24.00	47.50
		Never hinged	60.00	

Type SD3 was not issued without surcharge.

AP2

1926-28   Typo.
C3	AP2	50c rose red ('28)	19.00	12.00
C4	AP2	60c gray	4.75	12.00
C5	AP2	80c brn vio & brn ('28)	35.00	120.00
C6	AP2	1 l blue	12.00	12.00
C7	AP2	1.20 l brn ('27)	24.00	120.00
C8	AP2	1.50 l buff	19.00	32.50
C9	AP2	5 l gray grn	40.00	105.00
		Nos. C3-C9 (7)	153.75	413.50
		Set, never hinged	385.00	

Nos. C4 and C6 Surcharged

1927, Sept. 16
C10	AP2	50c on 60c gray	24.00	95.00
a.		Pair, one without surcharge	2,250.	
C11	AP2	80c on 1 l blue	60.00	450.00
		Set, never hinged	200.00	

Pegasus AP3
Wings AP4
Spirit of Flight AP5
Arrows AP6

1930-32   Photo.   Wmk. 140
C12	AP4	25c dk grn ('32)	.25	.25
C13	AP3	50c olive brn	.25	.25
C14	AP4	75c org brn ('32)	.40	.25
C15	AP4	80c org red	.25	.70
C16	AP5	1 l purple	.25	.25
C17	AP6	2 l deep blue	.40	.25
C18	AP3	5 l dk green	.80	1.60
C19	AP3	10 l org red	1.60	6.50
		Nos. C12-C19 (8)	4.20	10.05
		Set, never hinged	10.00	

The 50c, 1 l and 2 l were reprinted in 1942 with labels similar to those of Nos. 427-438, but were not issued. Value, set of 3: unused $550; never hinged $1,400.

For overprints see Nos. MC1-MC5. For overprints and surcharges on design AP6 see Nos. C52-C55; Yugoslavia-Ljubljana NB9-NB20, NC11-NC17.

Ferrucci Type of Postage
Statue of Ferrucci.

1930, July 10
C20	A104	50c purple	4.00	17.50
C21	A104	1 l orange brn	4.00	20.00
C22	A104	5 l + 2 l brn vio	16.00	130.00
		Nos. C20-C22 (3)	24.00	167.50
		Set, never hinged	60.00	

For overprinted types see Aegean Islands Nos. C1-C3.

Virgil Type of Postage
Jupiter sending forth his eagle.

1930, Oct. 21   Photo.   Wmk. 140
C23	A106	50c lt brown	24.00	40.00
C24	A106	1 l orange	24.00	45.00

Engr.
Unwmk.
C25	A106	7.70 l + 1.30 l vio brn	55.00	520.00
C26	A106	9 l + 2 l indigo	65.00	600.00
		Nos. C23-C26 (4)	168.00	1,205.
		Set, never hinged	430.00	

The surtax on Nos. C25-C26 was for the National Institute Figli del Littorio.

For overprinted types see Aegean Islands Nos. C4-C7.

Trans-Atlantic Squadron — AP9

1930, Dec. 15   Photo.   Wmk. 140
C27	AP9	7.70 l Prus bl & gray	450.00	1,600.
		Never hinged	900.00	
a.		Seven stars instead of six	2,000.	—
		Never hinged	4,000.	

Flight by Italian aviators from Rome to Rio de Janeiro, Dec. 1930-Jan. 12, 1931.

Leonardo da Vinci's Flying Machine — AP10
Leonardo da Vinci AP11
Leonardo da Vinci AP12

1932
C28	AP10	50c olive brn	4.75	14.50
C29	AP11	1 l violet	6.50	16.00
C30	AP11	3 l brown red	8.00	40.00
C31	AP11	5 l dp green	13.00	47.50
C32	AP10	7.70 l + 2 l dk bl	9.50	200.00
C33	AP11	10 l + 2.50 l blk brn	11.00	340.00
		Nos. C28-C33 (6)	52.75	658.00
		Set, never hinged	132.00	

Engr.
Unwmk.
C34	AP12	100 l brt bl & brn ol	45.00	950.00
		Never hinged	110.00	
a.		Thin paper	260.00	1,800.

Dante Alighieri Soc. and especially Leonardo da Vinci, to whom the invention of a flying machine has been attributed. Surtax was for the benefit of the Society.

Inscription on No. C34: "Man with his large wings by beating against the air will be able to dominate it and lift himself above it."

Issued: Nos. C28-C33, 3/14; No. C34, 8/6.

For overprinted types see Aegean Islands Nos. C8-C13.

Garibaldi's Home at Caprera AP13
Farmhouse where Anita Garibaldi Died AP14

50c, 1 l+25c, Garibaldi's home, Caprera. 2 l+50c, Anita Garibaldi. 5 l+1 l, Giuseppe Garibaldi.

1932, Apr. 6   Photo.   Wmk. 140
C35	AP13	50c copper red	4.75	8.00
C36	AP14	80c deep green	5.00	13.00
C37	AP13	1 l + 25c red brn	8.00	32.50
C38	AP13	2 l + 50c dp bl	13.00	45.00
C39	AP14	5 l + 1 l dp grn	13.00	52.50
		Nos. C35-C39 (5)	43.75	151.00
		Set, never hinged	110.00	

50th anniv. of the death of Giuseppe Garibaldi, patriot. The surtax was for the benefit of the Garibaldi Volunteers.

For overprinted types see Aegean Islands Nos. C15-C19.

ITALY & AREA 1863-DATE

Great Stock of Italy, Colonies & Offices. Want Lists Welcomed.

WANTED:
We urgently need better Mint NH & LH singles, sets, S/S, collections & stocks of all Italy, San Marino, Vatican, Trieste, Colonies, Venezia Guilia, Trentino, etc.

For buying or selling Italy and all other U.S. & Worldwide, call

1-800-94-STAMP
(1-800-947-8267)

WE BUY COVERS & POSTAL HISTORY TOO!

Visit our "Store" on our website - new items added weekly

Henry Gitner Philatelists, Inc.

P.O. Box 3077-S, Middletown, NY 10940
Tel: 845-343-5151 Fax: 845-343-0068
Toll Free: 1-800-947-8267
E-mail: hgitner@hgitner.com

PHILATELY - THE QUIET EXCITEMENT!

ITALY

March on Rome Type of Postage

50c, Eagle sculpture and airplane. 75c, Italian buildings from the air.

1932, Oct. 27   Perf. 14
C40	A146	50c dark brown	3.25	9.50
C41	A146	75c orange brn	9.50	32.50
	Set, never hinged		32.00	

Graf Zeppelin Issue

Zeppelin over Pyramid of Caius Cestius — AP19

5 l, Tomb of Cecilia Metella. 10 l, Stadium of Mussolini. 12 l, St. Angelo Castle and Bridge. 15 l, Roman Forum. 20 l, Imperial Avenue.

1933, Apr. 24
C42	AP19	3 l blk & grn	22.50	125.00
C43	AP19	5 l grn & brn	22.50	140.00
C44	AP19	10 l car & dl bl	22.50	325.00
C45	AP19	12 l dk bl & red org	22.50	575.00
C46	AP19	15 l dk brn & gray	22.50	725.00
C47	AP19	20 l org brn & bl	22.50	800.00
a.	Vertical pair, imperf. between		10,000.	
	Never hinged		15,000.	
	Nos. C42-C47 (6)		135.00	2,690.
	Set, never hinged		330.00	

Balbo's Trans-Atlantic Flight Issue

Italian Flag

King Victor Emmanuel III

Allegory "Flight" — AP25

No. C49, Colosseum at Rome, Chicago skyline. Nos. C48-C49 consist of 3 parts; Italian flag, Victor Emmanuel III, & scene arranged horizontally.

1933, May 20
C48	AP25	5.25 l + 19.75 l red, grn & ultra	125.00	2,000.
	Never hinged		250.00	
a.	Left stamp without ovpt.		37,500.	
	Never hinged		57,500.	
C49	AP25	5.25 l + 44.75 l grn, red & ultra	160.00	2,000.
	Never hinged		325.00	

Transatlantic Flight, Rome-Chicago, of 24-seaplane squadron led by Gen. Italo Balbo. Center and right sections paid postage. At left is registered air express label overprinted "APPARECCHIO" and abbreviated pilot's name. Twenty triptychs of each value differ in name overprint.

No. C49 overprinted "VOLO DI RITORNO/NEW YORK-ROMA" was not issued; flight canceled. Value: unused $36,000; never hinged $54,000.

Nos. C48-C49 exist imperf. at bottom. Value, set $112,000.

For overprints see Nos. CO1, Aegean Islands C26-C27.

Type of Air Post Stamp of 1930 Surcharged in Black

1934, Jan. 18
C52	AP6	2 l on 2 l yel	10.50	95.00
C53	AP6	3 l on 2 l yel grn	10.50	140.00
C54	AP6	5 l on 2 l rose	10.50	275.00
C55	AP6	10 l on 2 l vio	10.50	400.00
	Nos. C52-C55 (4)		42.00	910.00
	Set, never hinged		104.00	

For use on mail carried on a special flight from Rome to Buenos Aires.

Annexation of Fiume Type

25c, 75c, View of Fiume Harbor. 50c, 1 l+50c, Monument to the Dead. 2 l+1.50 l, Venetian Lions. 3 l+2 l, Julian wall.

1934, Mar. 12
C56	A166	25c green	.95	4.00
C57	A166	50c brown	.95	2.40
C58	A166	75c org brn	.95	9.50
C59	A166	1 l + 50c dl vio	.95	16.00
C60	A166	2 l + 1.50 l dl bl	.95	21.00
C61	A166	3 l + 2 l blk brn	.95	23.00
	Nos. C56-C61 (6)		4.80	76.40
	Set, never hinged		14.40	

Airplane and View of Stadium AP32

Soccer Player and Plane AP33

Airplane and Stadium Entrance AP35

Airplane over Stadium AP34

1934, May 24
C62	AP32	50c car rose	11.00	52.50
C63	AP33	75c gray blue	17.50	65.00
C64	AP34	5 l + 2.50 l ol grn	52.50	425.00
C65	AP35	10 l + 5 l brn blk	52.50	650.00
	Nos. C62-C65 (4)		133.50	1,193.
	Set, never hinged		332.50	

2nd World Soccer Championships.
For overprinted types see Aegean Islands Nos. C28-C31.

Zeppelin under Fire AP36

Air Force Memorial AP40

Designs: 25c, 80c, Zeppelin under fire. 50c, 75c, Motorboat patrol. 1 l+50c, Desert infantry. 2 l+1 l, Plane attacking troops.

1934, Apr. 24
C66	AP36	25c dk green	3.25	8.00
C67	AP36	50c gray	3.25	9.50
C68	AP36	75c dk brown	3.25	11.00
C69	AP36	80c slate blue	3.25	14.50
C70	AP36	1 l + 50c red brn	8.00	32.50
C71	AP36	2 l + 1 l brt bl	11.50	40.00
C72	AP40	3 l + 2 l brn blk	16.00	47.50
	Nos. C66-C72 (7)		48.50	149.00
	Set, never hinged		120.00	

Cent. of the institution of the Military Medal of Valor.

For overprinted types see Aegean Islands Nos. C32-C38.

King Victor Emmanuel III — AP41

1934, Nov. 5
C73	AP41	1 l purple	3.25	95.00
C74	AP41	2 l brt blue	3.25	105.00
C75	AP41	4 l red brown	7.50	325.00
C76	AP41	5 l dull green	7.50	425.00
C77	AP41	8 l rose red	23.00	525.00
C78	AP41	10 l brown	25.00	800.00
	Nos. C73-C78 (6)		69.50	2,275.
	Set, never hinged		160.00	

65th birthday of King Victor Emmanuel III and the nonstop flight from Rome to Mogadiscio.

For overprint see No. CO2.

Muse Playing Harp — AP42

Angelic Dirge for Bellini — AP43

Scene from Bellini Opera, La Sonnambula AP44

1935, Sept. 24
C79	AP42	25c dull yellow	4.75	13.00
C80	AP42	50c brown	4.75	11.00
C81	AP42	60c rose carmine	16.00	32.50
C82	AP43	1 l + 1 l purple	24.00	240.00
C83	AP44	5 l + 2 l green	32.50	325.00
	Nos. C79-C83 (5)		82.00	621.50
	Set, never hinged		204.00	

Vincenzo Bellini, (1801-35), operatic composer.

Quintus Horatius Flaccus Type

25c, Seaplane in Flight. 50c, 1 l+1 l, Monoplane over valley. 60c, Oak and eagle. 5 l+2 l, Ruins of ancient Rome.

1936, July 1
C84	A197	25c dp green	3.25	12.00
C85	A197	50c dk brown	5.00	12.00
C86	A197	60c scarlet	8.50	20.00
C87	A197	1 l + 1 l vio	19.00	240.00
C88	A197	5 l + 2 l slate bl	24.00	350.00
	Nos. C84-C88 (5)		59.75	634.00
	Set, never hinged		150.00	

Child of the Balilla AP49

Heads of Children AP50

1937, June 28
C89	AP49	25c dk bl grn	8.00	27.50
C90	AP50	50c brown	16.00	17.50
C91	AP49	1 l purple	12.00	35.00
C92	AP50	2 l + 1 l dk bl	16.00	200.00
C93	AP49	3 l + 2 l org	20.00	275.00
C94	AP50	5 l + 3 l rose lake	24.00	340.00
	Nos. C89-C94 (6)		96.00	895.00
	Set, never hinged		240.00	

Summer Exhibition for Child Welfare. The surtax on Nos. C92-C94 was used to support summer camps for poor children.

Prosperous Italy — AP51

50c, Prolific Italy. 80c, Apollo's steeds. 1 l+1 l, Map & Roman Standard. 5 l+1 l, Augustus Caesar.

1937, Sept. 23
C95	AP51	25c red vio	8.00	16.00
C96	AP51	50c olive brn	8.00	12.00
C97	AP51	80c orange brn	24.00	22.50
C98	AP51	1 l + 1 l dk bl	30.00	175.00
C99	AP51	5 l + 1 l dl vio	65.00	340.00
	Nos. C95-C99 (5)		135.00	565.50
	Set, never hinged		335.00	

Bimillenary of the birth of Augustus Caesar (Octavianus) on the occasion of the exhibition opened in Rome by Mussolini on Sept. 22nd, 1937.

For overprinted types see Aegean Islands Nos. C39-C43.

King Victor Emmanuel III — AP56

25c, 3 l, King Victor Emmanuel III. 50c, 1 l, Dante Alighieri. 2 l, 5 l, Leonardo da Vinci.

1938, Oct. 28
C100	AP56	25c dull green	4.75	6.50
C101	AP56	50c dk yel brn	4.75	6.50
C102	AP56	1 l violet	8.00	9.50
C103	AP56	2 l royal blue	8.00	36.00
C104	AP56	3 l brown car	13.00	45.00
C105	AP56	5 l dp green	15.00	65.00
	Nos. C100-C105 (6)		54.00	170.50
	Set, never hinged		134.00	

Proclamation of the Empire.

Plane and Clasped Hands — AP59

Swallows in Flight — AP60

1945-47   Wmk. 277   Photo.   Perf. 14
C106	AP59	1 l slate bl	.25	.25
C107	AP60	2 l dk blue	.25	.25
C108	AP59	3.20 l red org	.30	.25
C109	AP60	5 l dk green	.25	.25
C110	AP60	10 l car rose	.25	.25
C111	AP60	25 l dk bl ('46)	6.50	13.00
C112	AP60	25 l brown ('47)	.25	.25
C113	AP59	50 l dk grn ('46)	12.00	20.00
C114	AP59	50 l violet ('47)	20.30	34.75
	Nos. C106-C114 (9)		40.00	
	Set, never hinged			

Issued: Nos. C111, C113, 7/13/46; NOs. C112, C114, 4/21/47.

See Nos. C130-C131. For surcharges and overprints see Nos. C115, C136, 1LNC1-1LNC7, Trieste C1-C6, C17-C22.

No. C108 Surcharged in Black

1947, July 1
C115	AP59	6 l on 3.20 l	.25	.25
	Never hinged		.30	
a.	Horiz. pair, one without surcharge	2,000.		
b.	Inverted surcharge			26,000.

Radio on Land — AP61

Designs: 6 l, 25 l, Radio on land. 10 l, 35 l, Radio at sea. 20 l, 50 l, Radio in the skies.

1947, Aug. 1   Photo.   Perf. 14
C116	AP61	6 l dp violet	.25	.25
C117	AP61	10 l dk car rose	.25	.25
C118	AP61	20 l dp orange	.40	1.00
C119	AP61	25 l aqua	.90	1.50
C120	AP61	35 l brt blue	1.50	2.40
C121	AP61	50 l lilac rose	2.00	3.00
	Nos. C116-C121 (6)		5.30	8.40
	Set, never hinged		6.50	

50th anniv. of radio.
For overprints see Trieste Nos. C7-C12.

ITALY

Plane over Capitol Bell Tower — AP65

1948
C123	AP65	100 l green	.90	.25
C124	AP65	300 l lilac rose	.25	.60
C125	AP65	500 l ultra	.65	.75

Engr.
C126	AP65	1000 l dk brown	.65	2.50
a.		Vert. pair, imperf. btwn.	275.00	275.00
b.		Perf. 14x13	2.00	2.40
		Nos. C123-C126 (4)	2.45	4.10
		Set, never hinged	6.50	

See No. C132-C135. For overprints see Trieste Nos. C13-C16, C23-C26.

St. Catherine Carrying Cross — AP66

200 l, St. Catherine with outstretched arms.

1948, Mar. 1   Photo.
C127	AP66	100 l bl vio & brn org	45.00	40.00
C128	AP66	200 l dp blue & bis	27.50	24.00
		Set, never hinged	130.00	

600th anniversary of the birth of St. Catherine of Siena, patroness of Italy.

Catalogue values for unused stamps in this section, from this point to the end of the section, are for Never Hinged items.

Giuseppe Mazzini (1805-1872), Patriot — AP67

1955, Dec. 31   Wmk. 303   Perf. 14
C129	AP67	100 l Prus green	1.50	1.00

Types of 1945-46, 1948
1955-62   Wmk. 303   Perf. 14
C130	AP60	5 l green ('62)	.25	.25
C131	AP59	50 l vio ('57)	.25	.25
C132	AP65	100 l green	.60	.25
C133	AP65	300 l lil rose	.70	.55
C134	AP65	500 l ultra ('56)	1.00	.90

Engr.
Perf. 13½
C135	AP65	1000 l maroon ('59)	1.75	2.00
		Nos. C130-C135 (6)	4.55	4.20

Fluorescent Paper
See note below No. 998.
No. C132 was issued on both ordinary and fluorescent paper. The design of the fluorescent stamp is smaller. Airmail stamps issued only on fluorescent paper are Nos. C139-C140.

Type of 1945-46 Surcharged in Ultramarine

1956, Feb. 24
C136	AP59	120 l on 50 l mag	1.00	1.25

Visit of Pres. Giovanni Gronchi to the US and Canada.

Madonna of Bruges, by Michelangelo — AP68

1964, Feb. 18   Wmk. 303   Photo.   Perf. 14
C137	AP68	185 l black	.30	.25

Michelangelo Buonarroti (1475-1564), artist.

Verrazano Type of Regular Issue
1964, Nov. 21   Wmk. 303   Perf. 14
C138	A481	130 l blk & dull grn	.30	.25

See note after No. 901.

Adoration of the Kings, by Gentile da Fabriano — AP69

1970, Dec. 12   Photo.   Unwmk.
C139	AP69	150 l multicolored	.25	.25

Christmas 1970.

Aviation Type of Regular Issue
Design: F-104S Starfighter over Aeronautical Academy, Pozzuoli.

1973, Mar. 28   Photo.   Perf. 14x13½
C140	A590	150 l multicolored	.30	.25

AIR POST SEMI-POSTAL STAMPS

Holy Year Type of Postage
Dome of St. Peter's, dove with olive branch, Church of the Holy Sepulcher.

Wmk. 140
1933, Oct. 23   Photo.   Perf. 14
CB1	A163	50c + 25c org brn	2.40	27.50
CB2	A163	75c + 50c brn vio	4.00	160.00
		Set, never hinged	16.00	

Symbolical of Military Air Force — SPAP2

1935, July 1
CB3	SPAP2	50c + 50c brown	9.50	40.00

The surtax was for the Militia.

AIR POST SPECIAL DELIVERY STAMPS

Garibaldi, Anita Garibaldi, Plane — APSD1

Wmk. 140
1932, June 2   Photo.   Perf. 14
CE1	APSD1	2.25 l + 1 l	16.00	52.50
CE2	APSD1	4.50 l + 1.50 l	16.00	52.50
		Set, never hinged	80.00	

Death of Giuseppe Garibaldi, 50th anniv.
For overprinted types see Aegean Islands Nos. CE1-CE2.

Airplane and Sunburst APSD2

1933-34
CE3	APSD2	2 l gray blk ('34)	.25	3.25
CE4	APSD2	2.25 l slate	4.75	200.00
		Set, never hinged	12.50	

For overprint and surcharge see Nos. MCE1, Yugoslavia-Ljubljana NCE1.

Annexation of Fiume Type
Flag raising before Fascist headquarters.

1934, Mar. 12
CE5	A166	2 l + 1.25 l	4.75	27.50
CE6	A166	2.25 l + 1.25 l	.95	22.50
CE7	A166	4.50 l + 2 l	.95	24.00
		Nos. CE5-CE7 (3)	5.60	77.00
		Set, never hinged	17.00	

Triumphal Arch in Rome — APSD4

1934, Aug. 31
CE8	APSD4	2 l + 1.25 l brown	16.00	45.00
CE9	APSD4	4.50 l + 2 l cop red	20.00	45.00
		Set, never hinged	90.00	

Centenary of the institution of the Military Medal of Valor.
For overprinted types see Aegean Islands Nos. CE3-CE4.

AIR POST OFFICIAL STAMPS

Balbo Flight Type of Air Post Stamp of 1933 Overprinted

1933   Wmk. 140   Perf. 14
CO1	AP25	5.25 l + 44.75 l red, grn & red vio	3,300.	14,000.
		Never hinged	5,000.	

Air Post Stamp of 1934 Overprinted in Gold

1934
CO2	AP41	10 l blue blk	875.00	14,000.
		Never hinged	1,750.	

65th birthday of King Victor Emmanuel III and the non-stop flight from Rome to Mogadiscio.

PNEUMATIC POST STAMPS

PN1

1913-28   Wmk. 140   Typo.   Perf. 14
D1	PN1	10c brown	2.40	32.50
D2	PN1	15c brn vio ('28)	3.25	16.00
a.		15c dull violet ('21)	3.25	45.00
D3	PN1	15c rose red ('28)	16.00	40.00
D4	PN1	15c claret ('28)	4.75	16.00
D5	PN1	20c brn vio ('25)	24.00	65.00
D6	PN1	30c blue ('23)	8.00	225.00
D7	PN1	35c rose red ('27)	25.00	475.00
D8	PN1	40c dp red ('26)	27.50	450.00
		Nos. D1-D8 (8)	110.90	1,320.

Nos. D1, D2a, D5-D6, D8 Surcharged Like Nos. C10-C11

1924-27
D9	PN1	15c on 10c	4.75	40.00
D10	PN1	15c on 20c ('27)	9.50	72.50
D11	PN1	20c on 10c ('25)	9.50	80.00
D12	PN1	20c on 15c ('25)	12.50	47.50
D13	PN1	35c on 40c ('27)	21.00	400.00
D14	PN1	40c on 30c ('25)	12.50	425.00
		Nos. D9-D14 (6)	69.75	1,065.

Dante Alighieri — PN2

Galileo Galilei — PN3

1933, Mar. 29   Photo.
D15	PN2	15c dark violet	.45	1.60
D16	PN3	35c rose red	.45	7.25

Similar to Types of 1933, Without "REGNO"
1945, Oct. 22   Wmk. 277
D17	PN2	60c dull brown	.25	3.25
D18	PN3	1.40 l dull blue	.25	3.25

Minerva — PN6

1947, Nov. 15
D19	PN6	3 l rose lilac	4.50	9.50
D20	PN6	5 l aqua	.25	.25
		Set, never hinged	7.00	

Catalogue values for unused stamps in this section, from this point to the end of the section, are for Never Hinged items.

1958-66   Wmk. 303
D21	PN6	10 l rose red	.25	.25
D22	PN6	20 l sapphire ('66)	.25	.25

SPECIAL DELIVERY STAMPS

Victor Emmanuel III — SD1

1903-26   Typo.   Wmk. 140   Perf. 14
E1	SD1	25c rose red	47.50	1.20
a.		Imperf., pair	475.00	600.00
E2	SD1	50c dl red ('20)	4.75	1.60
E3	SD1	60c dl red ('22)	9.50	1.20
E4	SD1	70c dl red ('25)	1.60	.35
E5	SD1	1.25 l dp bl ('26)	.80	.25
		Nos. E1-E5 (5)	64.15	4.60

No. E1 is almost always found poorly centered, and it is valued thus.
For overprints and surcharges see Nos. C1, E11, E13, Austria NE1-NE2, Dalmatia E1, Offices in Crete, Offices in Africa, Offices in Turkish Empire.

Victor Emmanuel III — SD2

1908-26
E6	SD2	30c blue & rose	2.25	4.00
E7	SD2	2 l bl & red ('25)	8.00	160.00
E8	SD2	2.50 l bl & red ('26)	3.25	10.50
		Nos. E6-E8 (3)	13.50	174.50

The 1.20 lire blue and red (see No. E12) was prepared in 1922, but not issued. Value: unused $200; never hinged $400.
For surcharges and overprints see Nos. E10, E12, Austria NE3, Dalmatia E2, Offices in China, Offices in Africa, Offices in Turkish Empire.

ITALY

1917, Nov.
E9 SD3 25c on 40c violet ... 40.00 ... 125.00

Type SD3 not issued without surcharge. For surcharge see No. C2.

No. E6 Surcharged

1921, Oct.
E10 SD2 1.20 l on 30c ... 2.40 ... 27.50
  a. Comma in value omitted ... 12.50 ... 55.00
  b. Double surcharge ... 350.00

No. E2 Surcharged

1922, Jan. 9
E11 SD1 60c on 50c dull red ... 47.50 ... 1.60
  a. Inverted surcharge ... 275.00 ... 275.00
  b. Double surcharge ... 2,000.
  c. Imperf., pair ... 475.00 ... 600.00

Type of 1908 Surcharged

1924, May
E12 SD2 1.60 l on 1.20 l bl & red ... 3.25 ... 135.00
  a. Double surch., one inverted ... 350.00

No. E3 Surcharged like No. E11

1925, Apr. 11
E13 SD1 70c on 60c dull red ... 1.60 ... 1.20
  a. Inverted surcharge ... 340.00 ... 400.00

Victor Emmanuel III — SD4

1932-33   Photo.
E14 SD4 1.25 l green ... .30 ... .25
E15 SD4 2.50 l dp org ('33) ... .30 ... 6.50

For overprints and surcharges see Italian Social Republic Nos. E1-E2; Yugoslavia-Ljubljana NB5-NB8, NE1.

March on Rome Type of Postage
1.25 l, Ancient Pillars and Entrenchments.
2.50 l, Head of Mussolini, trophies of flags, etc.

1932, Oct. 27
E16 A146 1.25 l deep green ... 2.40 ... 1.60
E17 A146 2.50 l deep orange ... 8.00 ... 160.00
  Set, never hinged ... 26.00

"Italia" — SD7

1945, Aug.   Wmk. 277   Perf. 14
E18 SD7 5 l rose carmine ... .25 ... 1.00

Winged Foot — SD8

Rearing Horse and Torch-Bearer SD9

1945-51
E19 SD8 5 l henna brn ... .25 ... .25
E20 SD9 10 l deep blue ... .25 ... .25
E21 SD9 15 l dk car rose ('47) ... 1.60 ... .25
E22 SD9 25 l brt red org ('47) ... 15.00 ... .25
E23 SD8 30 l dp vio ('46) ... 3.00 ... 3.25
E24 SD8 50 l lil rose ('51) ... 17.50 ... .25
E25 SD9 60 l car rose ('48) ... 25.00 ... .25
  Nos. E19-E25 (7) ... 62.60 ... 4.75
  Set, never hinged ... 140.00

See No. E32. For overprints see Nos. 1LNE1-1LNE2, Trieste E1-E4, E6-E7.

Type of Regular Issue of 1948
Inscribed: "Espresso"

1948, Sept. 18   Photo.   Perf. 14
E26 A272 35 l violet (Naples) ... 45.00 ... 22.50
  Never hinged ... 120.00

Catalogue values for unused stamps in this section, from this point to the end of the section, are for Never Hinged items.

Type of 1945-51
1955, July 7   Wmk. 303   Perf. 14
E32 SD8 50 l lilac rose ... 4.50 ... .25

Etruscan Winged Horses — SD10

1958-76   Photo.
Size: 36½x20¼mm
E33 SD10 75 l magenta ... .25 ... .25
Size: 36x20mm
E34 SD10 150 l dl bl grn ('68) ... .25 ... .25
  a. Size: 36½x20¼mm ('66) ... .50 ... .25
E35 SD10 250 l blue ('74) ... .30 ... .25
E36 SD10 300 l brown ('76) ... .40 ... .25
  Nos. E33-E36 (4) ... 1.20 ... 1.00

Nos. E34-E36 are fluorescent.

AUTHORIZED DELIVERY STAMPS

For the payment of a special tax for the authorized delivery of correspondence privately instead of through the post office.

AD1

1928   Wmk. 140   Typo.   Perf. 14
EY1 AD1 10c dull blue ... 9.50 ... .60
  a. Perf. 11 ... 37.50 ... 4.75

Coat of Arms — AD2

1930   Photo.   Perf. 14
EY2 AD2 10c dark brown ... .25 ... .25

For surcharge and overprint see Nos. EY3, Italian Social Republic EY1.

No. EY2 Surcharged in Black

1945
EY3 AD2 40c on 10c dark brown ... .50 ... 1.50

Coat of Arms — AD3

1945-46   Photo.   Wmk. 277
EY4 AD3 40c dark brown ... .25 ... 1.00
EY5 AD3 1 l dk brown ('46) ... 3.25 ... 5.00

For overprint see Trieste No. EY1.

"Italia" — AD4

1947-52   Size: 27½x22½mm
EY6 AD4 1 l brt grnsh bl ... .25 ... .35
EY7 AD4 8 l brt red ('48) ... 12.00 ... .35
Size: 20½x16½mm
EY8 AD4 15 l violet ('49) ... 31.00 ... .30
EY9 AD4 20 l rose vio ('52) ... 2.00 ... .25
  Nos. EY6-EY9 (4) ... 45.25 ... 1.25
  Set, never hinged ... 125.00

For overprints see Trieste Nos. EY2-EY5.

Catalogue values for unused stamps in this section, from this point to the end of the section, are for Never Hinged items.

Italia Type of 1947
1955-90   Wmk. 303   Photo.   Perf. 14
Size: 20½x16½mm
EY11 AD4 20 l rose vio ... .25 ... .25
EY12 AD4 30 l Prus grn ('65) ... .25 ... .25
EY13 AD4 35 l ocher ('74) ... .25 ... .25
EY14 AD4 110 l lt ultra ('77) ... .25 ... .25
EY15 AD4 270 l brt pink ('84) ... .75 ... .25
Size: 19½x16½mm
EY16 AD4 300 l rose & grn ('87) ... .60 ... .40
EY17 AD4 370 l tan & brn vio ... .65 ... .40
  Nos. EY11-EY17 (7) ... 3.00 ... 2.05

Issue date: 370 l, Sept. 24, 1990.

POSTAGE DUE STAMPS

Unused values for Postage Due stamps are for examples with full original gum. Stamps with part gum or privately gummed sell for much less.

D1

1863   Unwmk.   Litho.   Imperf.
J1 D1 10c yellow ... 2,000. ... 240.00
  No gum ... 80.00
  a. 10c yellow orange ... 2,250. ... 260.00
  No gum ... 90.00

D2

1869   Wmk. 140   Typo.   Perf. 14
J2 D2 10c buff ... 9,000. ... 80.00

D3

1870-1925
J3 D3 1c dull org & car ... 4.00 ... 12.00
J4 D3 2c dull org & car ... 8.00 ... 24.00
J5 D3 5c dull org & car ... .80 ... .80
J6 D3 10c dull org & car ('71) ... .80 ... .80
  b. Imperf, single ... 2,200.
J7 D3 20c dull org & car ('94) ... 8.00 ... .80
  a. Imperf., pair ... 240.00 ... 240.00
J8 D3 30c dull org & car ... 2.40 ... 1.20
  b. Imperf, pair ... 6,000. ... 3,600.
J9 D3 40c dull org & car ... 2.40 ... 2.40
J10 D3 50c dull org & car ... 2.40 ... 1.20
  b. Imperf, single ... 2,000.
J11 D3 60c dull org & car ... 120.00 ... 4.75
J12 D3 60c buff & brn ('25) ... 40.00 ... 16.00
J13 D3 1 l lt bl & brn ... 8,000. ... 20.00
J14 D3 1 l bl & mag ('94) ... 45.00 ... 1.25
  a. Imperf., pair ... 400.00 ... 350.00
J15 D3 2 l lt bl & brn ... 7,250. ... 32.50
J16 D3 2 l bl & mag ('03) ... 65.00 ... 9.50
J17 D3 5 l lt bl & brn ('74) ... 500.00 ... 35.00
J18 D3 5 l bl & mag ('03) ... 250.00 ... 55.00
J19 D3 10 l lt bl & brn ('74) ... 9,500. ... 35.00
J20 D3 10 l bl & mag ('94) ... 225.00 ... 8.00

Early printings of 5c, 10c, 30c, 40c, 50c and 60c were in buff and magenta, later ones (1890-94) in stronger shades. The earlier, paler shades and their inverted-numeral varieties sell for considerably more than those of the later shades. Values are for the later shades.

For surcharges and overprints see Nos. J25-J27, Offices in China, Offices in Turkish Empire; Austria Nos. NJ1-NJ16; Somalia Nos. J1-J22, J31-J41.

Numeral Inverted
J3a D3 1c ... 4,750. ... 3,000.
J4a D3 2c ... 12,000. ... 4,500.
J5a D3 5c ... 6.50 ... 12.00
J6a D3 10c ... 8.00 ... 16.00
J7b D3 20c ... 65.00 ... 60.00
J8a D3 30c ... 12.00 ... 24.00
J9a D3 40c ... 550.00 ... 650.00
J10a D3 50c ... 60.00 ... 80.00
J11a D3 60c ... 550.00 ... 400.00
J13a D3 1 l
J14b D3 1 l ... 5,200. ... 4,500.
J15a D3 2 l ... 3,000.
J16a D3 2 l ... 4,500. ... 4,500.
J17a D3 5 l ... 1,400.
J19a D3 10 l ... 2,700. ... 450.00

D4

1884-1903
J21 D4 50 l green ... 87.50 ... 95.00
J22 D4 50 l yellow ('03) ... 95.00 ... 47.50
J23 D4 100 l claret ... 87.50 ... 47.50
J24 D4 100 l blue ('03) ... 72.50 ... 20.00
  Nos. J21-J24 (4) ... 342.50 ... 210.00

Nos. J3 & J4 Surcharged in Black

1890-91
J25 D3 10c on 2c ... 130.00 ... 35.00
J26 D3 20c on 1c ... 525.00 ... 27.50
  a. Inverted surcharge ... 10,000.
J27 D3 30c on 2c ... 2,000. ... 12.00
  a. Inverted surcharge ... 2,750.
  Nos. J25-J27 (3) ... 2,655. ... 74.50

Coat of Arms
D6   D7

1934   Photo.
J28 D6 5c brown ... .80 ... .40
J29 D6 10c blue ... .80 ... .40
J30 D6 20c rose red ... .80 ... .40
J31 D6 25c green ... .80 ... .40
J32 D6 30c red org ... .80 ... .40
J33 D6 40c blk brn ... .80 ... 4.75
J34 D6 50c violet ... .80 ... .40
J35 D6 60c slate blk ... .80 ... 14.00
J36 D7 1 l red org ... .80 ... .40
J37 D7 2 l green ... .80 ... .40
J38 D7 5 l violet ... 1.60 ... .80
J39 D7 10 l rose ... 6.50 ... 12.00
J40 D7 20 l car rose ... 12.50 ... 40.00
  Nos. J28-J40 (13) ... 28.60 ... 74.75

For overprints and surcharges see Italian Social Republic #J1-J13, Yugoslavia-Ljubljana NJ14-NJ22.

ITALY

D8 D9

1945-46 Unwmk. Perf. 14
J41	D8	5c brn, grayish ('46)		2.00	6.00
J42	D8	10c blue		.40	1.25
J43	D8	20c rose red, grayish ('46)		2.00	1.25
J44	D8	25c dk grn		.40	1.25
J45	D8	30c red org		.40	1.25
J46	D8	40c blk brn		.40	1.25
J47	D8	50c violet		.40	1.25
J48	D8	60c black		.40	6.00
J49	D9	1 l red org		.40	1.25
J50	D9	2 l green		.40	1.25
J51	D9	5 l violet		.40	1.25
J52	D9	10 l blue		.40	1.25
J53	D9	20 l car rose		.45	5.00
Nos. J41-J53 (13)				8.45	29.50

Nos. J41 and J43 have yellow gum.

Wmk. 277
J54	D8	10c dark blue	.40	4.50
J55	D8	25c dk grn	1.00	5.00
J56	D8	30c red org	1.00	9.00
J57	D8	40c blk brn	.40	.45
J58	D8	50c vio ('46)	5.75	7.00
J59	D8	60c bl blk ('46)	7.50	20.00
J60	D9	1 l red org	.40	.45
J61	D9	2 l dk grn	.40	.45
J62	D9	5 l violet	12.00	9.00
J63	D9	10 l dark blue	18.00	9.00
J64	D9	20 l car rose	29.00	25.00
Nos. J54-J64 (11)			75.85	89.85
Set, never hinged			175.00	

For overprints see Trieste Nos. J1, J3-J5.

D10

1947-54 Photo. Perf. 14
J65	D10	1 l red orange	.25	.25
J66	D10	2 l dk green	.40	.25
J67	D10	3 l carmine	1.10	2.00
J68	D10	4 l brown	.50	1.25
J69	D10	5 l violet	.80	.25
J70	D10	6 l vio blue	2.00	3.00
J71	D10	8 l rose vio	10.00	3.00
J72	D10	10 l deep blue	.75	.25
J73	D10	12 l golden brn	3.00	2.00
J74	D10	20 l lil rose	30.00	.25
J75	D10	25 l dk red ('54)	30.00	.80
J76	D10	50 l aqua	25.00	.25
J77	D10	100 l org yel ('52)	8.00	.25

Engr. Perf. 13½x14
J78	D10	500 l dp bl & dk car ('52)	10.00	.45
a.		Perf. 11x13	10.00	.45
b.		Perf. 13	10.00	.45
Nos. J65-J78 (14)			121.80	14.25
Set, never hinged			290.00	

For overprints see Trieste Nos. J2, J6-J29.

Catalogue values for unused stamps in this section, from this point to the end of the section, are for Never Hinged items.

1955-91 Wmk. 303 Photo. Perf. 14
J83	D10	5 l violet	.25	.25
J85	D10	8 l rose vio	175.00	175.00
J86	D10	10 l deep blue	.25	.25
J87	D10	20 l lil rose	.25	.25
J88	D10	25 l dk red	.25	.25
J89	D10	30 l gray brn ('61)	.25	.25
J90	D10	40 l dl brn ('66)	.25	.25
J91	D10	50 l aqua	.25	.25
a.		Type II	.30	.25
J92	D10	100 l org yel ('58)	.25	.25

Engr.
J93	D10	500 l dp bl & dk car ('61)	2.90	.25
J94	D10	900 l dp car & gray grn ('84)	1.20	.25
J95	D10	1500 l brn & org	2.50	.50
Nos. J83,J86-J95 (11)			8.60	3.00

Type I imprint on No. J91 reads: "1ST POL. STATO OFF. CARET VALORI". Type II reads: "I.P.Z.S. OFF. CARTE VALORI" (1992). No. J91 has lighter background with more distinguishable lettering and design.

No. J92 exists with both Type I & Type II imprints.

Nos. J92 and J93 exist with "I. P. Z. S. ROMA" imprint.

Issue date: 1500 l, Feb. 20, 1991.

MILITARY STAMPS

Regular Stamps, 1929-42, Overprinted

P.M.

1943 Wmk. 140 Perf. 14
M1	A90	5c ol brn	.40	2.50
M2	A92	10c dk brn	.40	2.50
M3	A93	15c slate grn	.40	2.50
M4	A91	20c rose red	.40	2.50
M5	A94	25c dp grn	.40	2.50
M6	A95	30c ol brn	.40	2.50
M7	A95	50c purple	.40	2.50
M8	A91	1 l dk pur	3.75	20.00
M9	A94	1.25 l deep blue	.40	4.00
M10	A92	1.75 l red org	.40	4.00
M11	A93	2 l car lake	.40	4.00
M12	A95a	5 l rose red	.40	4.00
M13	A93	10 l purple	3.00	29.00
Nos. M1-M13 (13)			11.15	82.50
Set, never hinged			27.50	

Due to a shortage of regular postage stamps during 1944-45, this issue was used for ordinary mail. "P. M." stands for "Posta Militare."

MILITARY AIR POST STAMPS

Air Post Stamps, 1930 Overprinted Like Nos. M1-M13 in Black

1943 Wmk. 140 Perf. 14
MC1	AP3	50c olive brown	.45	3.00
MC2	AP5	1 l purple	.45	3.00
MC3	AP6	2 l deep blue	.45	15.00
MC4	AP3	5 l dark green	3.75	25.00
MC5	AP3	10 l org red	3.75	32.50
Nos. MC1-MC5 (5)			8.85	78.50
Set, never hinged			25.00	

MILITARY AIR POST SPECIAL DELIVERY STAMPS

No. CE3 Overprinted Like Nos. M1-M13

1943 Wmk. 140 Perf. 14
MCE1	APSD2	2 l gray black	3.50	29.00

MILITARY SPECIAL DELIVERY STAMPS

No. E14 Overprinted Like Nos. M1-M13

1943 Wmk. 140 Perf. 14
ME1	SD4	1.25 l green	.45	10.00

OFFICIAL STAMPS

O1

1875 Wmk. 140 Typo. Perf. 14
O1	O1	2c lake	3.25	4.75
O2	O1	5c lake	3.25	4.75
O3	O1	20c lake	1.60	1.60
O4	O1	30c lake	1.60	3.25
O5	O1	1 l lake	4.75	20.00
O6	O1	2 l lake	12.50	60.00
O7	O1	5 l lake	55.00	225.00
O8	O1	10 l lake	95.00	160.00
Nos. O1-O8 (8)			176.95	479.35

For surcharges see Nos. 37-44.
Stamps inscribed "Servizio Commissioni" were used in connection with the postal service but not for the payment of postage.

NEWSPAPER STAMP

N1

Typographed, Numeral Embossed
1862 Unwmk. Imperf.
P1	N1	2c buff	52.50	110.00
a.		Numeral double	475.00	1,650.
b.		Printed on gummed side	500.00	

Black 1c and 2c stamps of similar type are listed under Sardinia.

PARCEL POST STAMPS

King Humbert I — PP1

1884-86 Wmk. 140 Typo. Perf. 14
Various Frames
Q1	PP1	10c olive gray	125.00	120.00
Q2	PP1	20c blue	260.00	175.00
Q3	PP1	50c claret	9.50	14.50
Q4	PP1	75c blue grn	9.50	14.50
Q5	PP1	1.25 l orange	20.00	32.50
Q6	PP1	1.75 l brown	24.00	120.00
Nos. Q1-Q6 (6)			448.00	476.50

For surcharges see Nos. 58-63.

Parcel Post stamps from No. Q7 onward were used by affixing them to the waybill so that one half remained on it following the parcel, the other half staying on the receipt given the sender. Most used halves are right halves. Complete stamps were and are obtainable canceled, probably to order.

Both unused and used values are for complete stamps.

PP2

1914-22 Wmk. 140 Perf. 13
Q7	PP2	5c brown	4.75	20.00
Q8	PP2	10c deep blue	4.75	20.00
Q9	PP2	20c black ('17)	17.50	20.00
Q10	PP2	25c red	24.00	20.00
Q11	PP2	50c orange	35.00	40.00
Q12	PP2	1 l violet	40.00	16.00
Q13	PP2	2 l green	40.00	20.00
Q14	PP2	3 l bister	47.50	55.00
Q15	PP2	4 l slate	60.00	72.50
Q16	PP2	10 l lilac ('22)	49.50	72.50
Q17	PP2	12 l red brn ('22)	160.00	450.00
Q18	PP2	15 l ol grn ('22)	140.00	450.00
Q19	PP2	20 l brn vio ('22)	120.00	450.00
Nos. Q7-Q19 (13)			788.50	1,706.

Halves Used
Q7-Q14, each	.40
Q15	.80
Q16	1.60
Q17	4.00
Q18	4.00
Q19	6.50

Imperfs exist. Value per pair: 20c, 25c, 50c, 2 l, 3l, 4 l: $50 each; 10l $225.

No. Q7 Surcharged
Q20	PP2	30c on 5c brown	1.60	24.00
		Half stamp		3.25
Q21	PP2	60c on 5c brown	1.60	24.00
		Half stamp		3.25
Q22	PP2	1.50 l on 5c brown	6.50	190.00
		Half stamp		6.50
a.		Double surcharge	250.00	

No. Q16 Surcharged
Q23	PP2	3 l on 10 l rose lil	6.50	80.00
		Half stamp		3.25
Nos. Q20-Q23 (4)			16.20	318.00

PP3

1927-39 Wmk. 140
Q24	PP3	5c brn ('38)	.80	3.25
Q25	PP3	10c dp bl ('39)	.80	3.25
Q26	PP3	25c red ('32)	.80	3.25
Q27	PP3	30c ultra	.80	4.00
Q28	PP3	50c org ('32)	.80	3.25
Q29	PP3	60c red	.80	4.00
Q30	PP3	1 l lilac ('31)	.80	3.25
Q31	PP3	1 l brn vio ('36)	24.00	87.50
Q32	PP3	2 l grn ('32)	.80	4.00
Q33	PP3	3 l yel bister	.80	9.50
a.		Printed on both sides	65.00	
Q34	PP3	4 l gray	.80	9.50
Q35	PP3	10 l rose lil ('34)	2.40	55.00
Q36	PP3	20 l lil brn ('33)	3.25	80.00
Nos. Q24-Q36 (13)			37.65	269.75

Value of used halves: Nos. Q24-Q34, each 40c; Q35 80c; Q36 $4.

For overprints see Italian Social Republic Nos. Q1-Q12.

Nos. Q24-Q30, Q32-Q36 Overprinted Between Halves in Black

1945 Wmk. 140 Perf. 13
Q37	PP3	5c brown	1.50	8.00
Q38	PP3	10c dp blue	1.50	8.00
Q39	PP3	25c red	1.50	8.00
Q40	PP3	30c ultra	15.00	20.00
Q41	PP3	50c orange	1.50	6.50
Q42	PP3	60c red	1.50	6.50
Q43	PP3	1 l lilac	1.50	6.50
Q44	PP3	2 l green	1.50	6.50
Q45	PP3	3 l yel bister	1.50	6.50
Q46	PP3	4 l gray	1.50	6.50
Q47	PP3	10 l rose lilac	17.50	65.00
Q48	PP3	20 l lilac brn	35.00	125.00
Nos. Q37-Q48 (12)			81.00	273.00
Set, never hinged			150.00	

Halves Used
Q37-48, each .25

Type of 1927 With Fasces Removed
1946 Typo.
Q55	PP3	1 l lilac	2.25	5.00
Q56	PP3	2 l green	1.50	5.00
Q57	PP3	3 l yellow org	2.25	8.50
Q58	PP3	4 l gray	4.50	8.50
Q59	PP3	10 l rose lilac	40.00	75.00
Q60	PP3	20 l lilac brn	50.00	250.00
Nos. Q55-Q60 (6)			100.50	352.00
Set, never hinged			200.00	

Halves Used
Q55-Q58, each	.25
Q59	.80
Q60	1.25

PP4

PP5

1946-54 Photo. Wmk. 277
Perf. 13¼, 13¼x14, 12¼x13x13¼
Q61	PP4	25c dl vio bl ('48)	.25	.25
Q62	PP4	50c brn ('47)	.40	.25
Q63	PP4	1 l gldn brn ('47)	.50	.25
Q64	PP4	2 l lt bl grn ('47)	.80	.75
Q65	PP4	3 l red org ('47)	.40	.25
Q66	PP4	4 l gray blk ('47)	6.00	9.00
Q67	PP4	5 l lil rose ('47)	.40	.25
a.		Perf. 13¼	.60	.25
Q68	PP4	10 l violet	6.00	.55
a.		Perf. 13¼	6.00	.55
Q69	PP4	20 l lilac brn	2.75	.60
a.		Perf. 13¼	6.50	.80
Q70	PP4	30 l plum ('52)	3.00	5.00
a.		Perf. 13¼	3.00	5.00
Q71	PP4	50 l rose red	12.00	2.00
a.		Perf. 13¼	12.00	2.00
Q72	PP4	100 l sapphire	30.00	30.00
a.		Perf. 13¼	30.00	30.00
Q73	PP4	200 l grn ('48)	45.00	75.00
a.		Perf. 13¼	45.00	80.00
Q74	PP4	300 l brn car ('48), perf 13¼	550.00	900.00
Q75	PP4	500 l brn ('48)	50.00	100.00
a.		Perf. 12¼x13¼	50.00	100.00

ITALY — A.M.G.

Engr. Perf. 13
Q76	PP5	1000 l ultra ('54)		2,000.	2,750.
	Nos. Q61-Q76 (16)			2,708.	3,874.
	Set, never hinged			5,000.	

Halves Used
Q61-Q73, each		.25
Q74		8.00
Q75		3.25
Q76		22.50

For overprints see Trieste Nos. Q1-Q26.

Catalogue values for unused stamps in this section, from this point to the end of the section, are for Never Hinged items.

Perf. 12½x13
1955-59 Wmk. 303 Photo.
Without Imprint
Q77	PP4	25c vio bl	.25	.25
Q77A	PP4	50c brn ('56)	3.50	4.00
Q78	PP4	5 l lil rose ('59)	.25	.25
Q79	PP4	10 l violet	.25	.25
Q80	PP4	20 l lil brn	.25	.25
Q81	PP4	30 l plum ('56)	.25	.25
Q82	PP4	40 l dl vio ('57)	.25	.25
Q83	PP4	50 l rose red	.25	.25
Q84	PP4	100 l sapphire	.25	.25
Q85	PP4	150 l org brn ('57)	.25	.25
Q86	PP4	200 l grn ('56)	.30	.25
Q87	PP4	300 l brn car ('58)	.60	.25
Q88	PP4	400 l gray blk ('57)	.55	.45
Q89	PP4	500 l brn ('57)	1.25	.50

Engr. Perf. 13
Q90	PP5	1000 l ultra ('57)	1.25	.75
Q91	PP5	2000 l red brn & car ('53)	4.50	4.00
	Nos. Q77-Q91 (16)		14.20	12.45

Halves Used
Q77-Q89, each	.25
Q90-Q91, each	.40

1960-66 Photo. Perf. 12½x13
Q92	PP4	60 l bright lilac	.25	.25
Q93	PP4	140 l dull red	.30	.25
Q94	PP4	280 l yellow	.60	.45
Q95	PP4	600 l olive bister	1.00	.50
Q96	PP4	700 l blue ('66)	2.00	.95
Q97	PP4	800 l dp org ('66)	2.40	.95
	Nos. Q92-Q97 (6)		6.55	3.35

Halves Used
Q92-Q93, each	.25
Q94	.25
Q95	.40
Q96-Q97, each	.25

Imprint: "I.P.S.-Off. Carte Valori- Roma"

1973, Mar. Photo. Wmk. 303
Q98	PP4	20 l lilac brown	.25	.25
Q99	PP4	30 l plum	.25	.25

PARCEL POST AUTHORIZED DELIVERY STAMPS

For the payment of a special tax for the authorized delivery of parcels privately instead of through the post office.

PAD1

1953 Wmk. 277 Photo. Perf. 13
QY1	PAD1	40 l org red	12.00	13.00
QY2	PAD1	50 l ultra	140.00	140.00
QY3	PAD1	75 l brown	80.00	80.00
QY4	PAD1	110 l lil rose	90.00	100.00
	Nos. QY1-QY4 (4)		322.00	333.00
	Set, never hinged		400.00	

Halves Used
QY1	.35
QY2	1.25
QY3	3.25
QY4	3.25

For overprints see Trieste Nos. QY1-QY4.

Catalogue values for unused stamps in this section, from this point to the end of the section, are for Never Hinged items.

1956-58 Wmk. 303 Perf. 12½x13
QY5	PAD1	40 l org red	2.25	2.25
QY6	PAD1	50 l ultra	2.50	2.50
QY7	PAD1	60 l brt vio bl ('58)	7.00	4.00
QY8	PAD1	75 l brown	325.00	140.00
QY9	PAD1	90 l lil ('58)	.35	.40
QY10	PAD1	110 l lil rose	325.00	200.00
QY11	PAD1	120 l grnsh bl ('58)	.35	.40
	Nos. QY5-QY11 (7)		662.45	349.55

Halves Used
QY5-QY6, each	.25
QY7	.90
QY8, QY10	8.00
QY9	.30
QY11	.25

1960-81
QY12	PAD1	70 l green ('66)	9.00	9.00
QY13	PAD1	80 l brown	.30	.30
QY14	PAD1	110 l org yel	.30	.30
QY15	PAD1	140 l black	.30	.30
QY16	PAD1	150 l car rose ('68)	.30	.30
QY17	PAD1	180 l red ('66)	.50	.50
QY18	PAD1	240 l dk bl ('66)	1.00	.70

Engr. Perf. 13½
QY19	PAD1	500 l ocher ('76)	1.40	1.40
QY20	PAD1	600 l bl grn ('79)	1.50	1.50
QY21	PAD1	900 l ultra ('81)	1.60	1.60
	Nos. QY12-QY21 (10)		16.20	15.90

Halves Used
QY12	4.00
QY13-QY15, QY18, QY21, each	.25
QY16, QY17, QY19, each	.25
QY20	.35

PAD2

Perf. 14x13½
1984 Photo. Wmk. 303
QY22	PAD2	3000 l multi	3.50	3.50

OCCUPATION STAMPS

Issued under Austrian Occupation

Austria Nos. M49-M64 Surcharged in Black

Austria Nos. M65-M67 Surcharged in Black

1918 Unwmk. Perf. 12½
N1	M3	2c on 1h grnsh bl	.25	.45
N2	M3	3c on 2h red org	.25	.40
N3	M3	4c on 3h ol gray	.25	.45
N4	M3	6c on 5h ol grn	.25	.40
N5	M3	7c on 6h vio	.25	.45
a.		Perf. 12.12½x11½	16.00	95.00
N6	M3	11c on 10h org brn	.25	.45
N7	M3	13c on 12h blue	.25	.45
N8	M3	16c on 15h brt rose	.25	.45
N9	M3	22c on 20h red brn	.25	.45
a.		Perf. 11½	24.00	80.00
N10	M3	27c on 25h ultra	.65	1.60
N11	M3	32c on 30h slate	.65	1.60
N12	M3	43c on 40h ol bis	.65	1.60
a.		Perf. 11½	16.00	72.50
N13	M3	53c on 50h dp grn	.65	1.60
N14	M3	64c on 60h rose	.65	1.60
N15	M3	85c on 80h dl bl	.65	1.20
N16	M3	95c on 90h dk vio	.65	1.20
N17	M4	2 l 11c on 2k rose, straw	.65	2.40
N18	M4	3 l 16c on 3k grn, bl	1.20	3.25
N19	M4	4 l 22c on 4k rose, grn	2.40	5.50
	Nos. N1-N19 (19)		11.05	25.45

Exist imperf. Values: unused, $160; never hinged, $325. See No. N33.

Austria Nos. M69-M82 Surcharged in Black

1918
N20	M5	2c on 1h grnsh bl	6.00	
N21	M5	3c on 2h orange	6.00	
N22	M5	4c on 3h ol gray	6.00	
N23	M5	6c on 5h yel grn	6.00	
N24	M5	11c on 10h dk brn	6.00	
N25	M5	22c on 20h red	6.00	
N26	M5	27c on 25h blue	6.00	
N27	M5	32c on 30h bister	6.00	
N28	M5	48c on 45h dk sl	6.00	
N29	M5	53c on 50h dp grn	6.00	
N30	M5	64c on 60h violet	6.00	
N31	M5	85c on 80h rose	6.00	
N32	M5	95c on 90h brn vio	6.00	
N33	M4	1 l 6c on 1k ol bister, blue	6.00	
	Nos. N20-N33 (14)		84.00	

Nos. N20 to N33 inclusive were never placed in use in the occupied territory. They were, however, on sale at the Post Office in Vienna for a few days before the Armistice. Exist imperf. Values unused, $325; never hinged, $800.

OCCUPATION SPECIAL DELIVERY STAMPS

Bosnia and Herzegovina Nos. QE1-QE2 Surcharged

1918 Unwmk. Perf. 12½
NE1	SH1	3c on 2h ver	12.00	24.00
NE2	SH1	6c on 5h dp grn	12.00	24.00

Nos. NE1-NE2 are on yellowish paper. Reprints on white paper sell for about $1.25 a set.

OCCUPATION POSTAGE DUE STAMPS

Bosnia Nos. J16, J18-J19, J21-J24 Surcharged Like Nos. NE1-NE2

1918 Unwmk. Perf. 12½
NJ1	D2	6c on 5h red	3.25	6.50
a.		Perf. 11½	8.00	12.00
NJ2	D2	11c on 10h red	2.40	8.00
a.		Perf. 11½	8.00	12.00
NJ3	D2	16c on 15h red	.80	3.25
NJ4	D2	27c on 25h red	.80	3.25
NJ5	D2	32c on 30h red	.80	4.00
NJ6	D2	43c on 40h red	.80	4.00
NJ7	D2	53c on 50h red	.80	4.00
	Nos. NJ1-NJ7 (7)		9.65	33.00

OCCUPATION NEWSPAPER STAMPS

Austrian Nos. MP1-MP4 Surcharged

1918 Unwmk. Perf. 12½
NP1	MN1	3c on 2h blue	.80	1.20
a.		Perf. 11½	12.00	40.00
NP2	MN1	7c on 6h org	1.10	2.40
NP3	MN1	11c on 10h car	1.10	2.40
NP4	MN1	22c on 20h brn	1.10	2.75
a.		Perf. 11½	125.00	250.00
	Nos. NP1-NP4 (4)		4.10	8.75

A.M.G.

Issued jointly by the Allied Military Government of the United States and Great Britain, for civilian use in areas under Allied occupation.

Catalogue values for unused stamps in this section are for Never Hinged items.

CS4

Offset Printing
"Italy Centesimi" (or "Lira") in Black
1943 Unwmk. Perf. 11
1N1	OS4	15c pale orange	1.00	1.50
1N2	OS4	25c pale citron	1.00	1.50
1N3	OS4	30c light gray	1.50	1.50
1N4	OS4	50c light violet	1.50	1.50
1N5	OS4	60c orange yellow	1.50	1.50
1N6	OS4	1 l lt yel green	1.50	1.50
1N7	OS4	2 l deep rose	1.50	4.00
1N8	OS4	5 l light blue	3.00	7.50
1N9	OS4	10 l buff	3.00	7.50
	Nos. 1N1-1N9 (9)		15.50	28.00

Italy Nos. 217, 220 and 221 Overprinted in Blue, Vermilion, Carmine or Orange

1943, Dec. 10 Wmk. 140 Perf. 14
1N10	A91	20c rose red (Bl)	2.00	4.00
1N11	A93	35c dp blue (C)	17.50	25.00
a.		35c deep blue (V)	35.00	35.00
1N13	A95	50c purple (C)	1.00	2.00
a.		50c purple (O)	1.00	2.00
	Nos. 1N10-1N13 (3)		20.50	31.00

Nos. 1N1-1N9 were for use in Sicily, Nos. 1N10-1N13 for use in Naples.

VENEZIA GIULIA

Catalogue values for unused stamps in this section are for Never Hinged items.

Stamps of Italy, 1929 to 1945 Overprinted in Black

a

On Stamps of 1929
1945-47 Wmk. 140 Perf. 14
1LN1	A92	(a) 10c dk brown	.30	.35
1LN1A	A91	(a) 20c rose red ('47)	.40	.50

b

On Stamps of 1945
1945 Wmk. 277 Perf. 14
1LN2	A249	(a) 20c rose red	.35	.50
1LN3	A248	(a) 60c sl grn	.45	.35
1LN4	A249	(a) 1 l dp vio	.30	.35
1LN5	A251	(a) 2 l dk red	.35	.35
1LN6	A252	(a) 5 l dk red	.65	.50
1LN7	A251	(a) 10 l purple	.90	1.25
	Nos. 1LN2-1LN7 (6)		3.00	3.30

On Stamps of 1945
1945-46 Unwmk.
1LN7A	A250	(a) 10c dk brn ('46)	.30	.25
1LN7B	A249	(a) 20c rose red ('46)	.25	.25
1LN8	A251	(a) 60c red org	.25	.25
	Nos. 1LN7A-1LN8 (3)		.80	1.00

On Air Post Stamp of 1930
1945 Wmk. 140 Perf. 14
1LN9	AP3	(a) 50c olive brn	.25	.50

1946 On Stamp of 1929
1LN10	A91	(a) 20 l lt green	2.25	6.50

On Stamps of 1945
Wmk. 277
1LN11	A260	(a) 25 l dk green	8.00	9.00
1LN12	A260	(a) 50 l dk vio brn	8.00	15.00

Italy No. 477 Overprinted in Black

1LN13	A261	100 l car lake	29.00	90.00
	Nos. 1LN10-1LN13 (4)		47.25	120.50

ITALY — A.M.G. — ITALIAN SOCIAL REPUBLIC

Stamps of Italy, 1945-47 Overprinted Type "a" in Black

1947

1LN14	A259	25c brt bl grn	.25	1.00
1LN15	A258	2 l dk claret brn	.60	.35
1LN16	A259	3 l red	.45	.25
1LN17	A259	4 l red org	.70	.25
1LN18	A257	6 l deep violet	2.00	1.90
1LN19	A259	20 l dk red vio	55.00	7.50
Nos. 1LN14-1LN19 (6)			59.00	11.25

Some denominations of the Venezia Giulia A.M.G. issues exist with inverted overprint; several values exist in horizontal and vertical pairs, one stamp without overprint.

OCCUPATION AIR POST STAMPS

Catalogue values for unused stamps in this section are for Never Hinged items.

Italy Nos. C106-C107 and C109-C113 Overprinted in Black

1946-47   Wmk. 277   Perf. 14

1LNC1	AP59	1 l sl blue ('47)	.40	5.00
1LNC2	AP60	2 l dk blue ('47)	.40	2.50
1LNC3	AP60	5 l dk grn ('47)	3.00	1.50
1LNC4	AP59	10 l car rose ('47)	3.00	1.50
1LNC5	AP60	25 l dk blue	3.00	1.50
1LNC6	AP60	25 l brown ('47)	35.00	47.50
1LNC7	AP59	50 l dk green	6.50	11.00
Nos. 1LNC1-1LNC7 (7)			51.30	70.50

Nos. 1LNC5 and 1LNC7 exist with inverted overprint; No. 1LNC5 with double overprint, one inverted.

OCCUPATION SPECIAL DELIVERY STAMPS

Catalogue values for unused stamps in this section are for Never Hinged items.

Italy Nos. E20 and E23 Overprinted in Black

1946   Wmk. 277   Perf. 14

1LNE1	SD9	10 l deep blue	4.00	1.60
1LNE2	SD8	30 l deep violet	8.75	19.00

ITALIAN SOCIAL REPUBLIC

On Sept. 15, 1943, Mussolini proclaimed the establishment of a Republican fascist party and a new fascist government. This government's authority covered only the Northern Italy area occupied by the Germans.

Catalogue values for unused stamps in this section are for hinged stamps. Never hinged examples are valued at 2-2.5 times the values shown.

"G.N.R." Overprints

Stamps of Italy were overprinted "G.N.R." for use in the territories in northern Italy that remained under Mussolini's regime after summer 1943. This included most of Italy north of Rome. "G.N.R." stands for "Guardia Nazionale Repubblicana".

Two printings exist, with different printers: Brescia printing (December 1943), Verona printing (May 1944). Differences between the two printings may be determined by examining sheets or multiples, such as horizontal strips. Otherwise, it is difficult to distinguish between the two printings. Scott catalog listings and values refer to the Verona printings. Values for used Brescia-printed stamps with readable dates between Dec. 12 1943, and April1944, are two to three times higher than stamps overprinted in Verona.

Italy Nos. 213, 215-231 Overprinted "G.N.R." in Black or Red

Italy No. 226A Overprinted

Italy No. 229 Overprinted

Italy No. 230 Overprinted

Italy No. 231 Overprinted

1944, May   Wmk. 140   Perf. 14

GN1	A90	5c ol brown	2.50	6.00
GN2	A92	10c brown	2.50	6.00
GN3	A93	15c sl grn (R)	2.50	6.00
GN4	A91	20c carmine	2.50	6.00
GN5	A94	25c green (R)	2.50	50.00
GN6	A95	30c ol brown	2.50	6.00
GN7	A93	35c dp bl (R)	105.00	325.00
GN8	A95	50c purple	2.50	6.00
GN9	A94	75c rose red	2.50	9.25
GN10	A91	1 l dk purple	2.50	6.00
GN11	A94	1.25 l dp bl (R)	2.50	6.00
GN12	A92	1.75 l red org	5.00	55.00
GN13	A93	2 l car lake	17.00	55.00
GN14	A95a	2.55 l sl grn (R)	110.00	390.00
GN15	A95a	3.70 l purple	37.50	300.00
GN16	A95a	5 l rose red	18.50	75.00
GN17	A93	10 l purple	150.00	75.00
GN18	A91	20 l lt grn (R)	190.00	775.00
GN19	A92	25 l bl slate (R)	550.00	2,800.
GN20	A94	50 l dp violet	500.00	3,250.
Nos. GN1-GN20 (20)			1,708.	8,207.

Nos. GN1-GN18 and GN20 exist with overprint inverted. Values for inverted overprints are substantially higher than the normal overprinted stamps.

Nos. GN1, GN2, GN4, GN10 and GN18 exist with double overprint.

Errors of overprint color exist on Nos. GN1-GN3, GN5-GN8, GN10, GN11, GN14 and GN15.

Italy Nos. 427-438 Overprinted "G.N.R." in Black or Red

1944

GN50	A243	25c dp grn (R)	10.00	65.00
GN51	A244	25c dp grn (R)	10.00	65.00
GN52	A245	25c dp grn (R)	10.00	65.00
GN53	A246	25c dp grn (R)	10.00	65.00
GN54	A243	30c ol brown	18.00	135.00
GN55	A244	30c ol brown	18.00	135.00
GN56	A245	30c ol brown	18.00	135.00
GN57	A246	30c ol brown	18.00	135.00
GN58	A243	50c purple	10.00	65.00
GN59	A244	50c purple	10.00	65.00
GN60	A245	50c purple	10.00	65.00
GN61	A246	50c purple	10.00	65.00
Nos. GN50-GN61 (12)			152.00	1,060.

Nos. GN50-GN61 exist with overprint inverted. Values for inverted overprints are substantially higher than the normal overprinted stamps.

No. GN51 exists with double overprint.

Italy Nos. 218, 219, 221 to 223 and 231 Overprinted in Black or Red

a   b

c

1944   Wmk. 140   Perf. 14

1	A94(a)	25c deep grn	.35	2.00
2	A95(b)	30c ol brn (R)	.35	2.00
3	A95(c)	50c vio (R)	.35	2.00
4	A94(a)	75c rose red	.35	2.40
5	A94(b)	1.25 l dp bl (R)	.35	2.40
5A	A94(b)	50 l dp vio (R)	200.00	4,000.
Nos. 1-5 (5)			1.75	10.80

Nos. 1 to 5 exist with overprint inverted. Value, each: unused $30; used $37.50.

No. 1 exists with overprint "b." Value: unused, $60; used $800.

Counterfeits of No. 5A exist.

Italy Nos. 427 to 438 Overprinted Same in Black or Red

6	A243(a)	25c deep green	.45	3.50
7	A244(a)	25c deep green	.45	3.50
8	A245(a)	25c deep green	.45	3.50
9	A246(a)	25c deep green	.45	3.50
10	A243(b)	30c ol brn (R)	.45	30.00
11	A244(b)	30c ol brn (R)	.45	30.00
12	A245(b)	30c ol brn (R)	.45	30.00
13	A246(b)	30c ol brn (R)	.45	30.00
14	A243(c)	50c purple (R)	.45	3.50
15	A244(c)	50c purple (R)	.45	3.50
16	A245(c)	50c purple (R)	.45	3.50
17	A246(c)	50c purple (R)	.45	3.50
Nos. 6-17 (12)			5.40	148.00

Loggia dei Mercanti, Bologna — A1

Drummer Boy A3

Basilica of San Lorenzo, Rome A2

1944   Photo.   Perf. 14

18	A1	20c crimson	.25	.75
19	A2	25c green	.25	.75
20	A3	30c brown	.25	.75
21	A3	75c dark red	.25	1.75
Nos. 18-21 (4)			1.00	4.00

For surcharges see Italy Nos. 461-462.

Church of St. Ciriaco, Ancona A4

Monte Cassino Abbey A5

Loggia dei Mercanti, Bologna A6

Basilica of San Lorenzo, Rome A7

Statue of "Rome" A8

Basilica of St. Maria delle Grazie, Milan A9

1944   Unwmk.

22	A4	5c brown	.25	.30
23	A5	10c brown	.25	.25
24	A6	20c rose red	.25	.25
25	A7	25c deep green	.25	.25
26	A3	30c brown	.25	.25
27	A8	50c purple	.25	.25
28	A3	75c dark red	1.00	21.00
29	A1	1 l purple	.25	.25
30	A9	1.25 l blue	.65	15.00
31	A9	3 l deep green	.65	50.00
Nos. 22-31 (10)			4.05	87.80

Bandiera Brothers — A10

1944, Dec. 6

32	A10	25c deep green	.25	1.00
33	A10	1 l purple	.25	1.00
34	A10	2.50 l rose red	.25	7.50
Nos. 32-34 (3)			.75	9.50

Cent. of the execution of Attilio (1811-44) and Emilio Bandiera (1819-44), revolutionary patriots who were shot at Cosenza, July 23, 1844, by Neapolitan authorities after an unsuccessful raid.

This set was overprinted in 1945 by the committee of the National Philatelic Convention to publicize that gathering at Venice.

AIR POST STAMPS

Italy Nos. C12-C19 Overprinted "G.N.R."

Italy No. C19 Overprinted

1944   Wmk. 140   Perf. 14

GNC1	AP4	25c dk grn (R)	21.00	175.00
GNC2	AP3	50c olive brown	2.50	6.00
GNC3	AP5	75c org brown	18.00	175.00
GNC4	AP4	80c red org	60.00	400.00
GNC5	AP5	1 l purple	2.40	6.00
GNC6	AP6	2 l dp bl (R)	90.00	350.00
GNC7	AP3	5 l dk grn (R)	60.00	425.00
GNC8	AP3	10 l org red	600.00	3,500.
Nos. GNC1-GNC8 (8)			853.90	5,037.

Nos. GNC1-GNC8 exist with overprint inverted. Values for inverted overprints are substantially higher than the normal overprinted stamps.

No. GNC2 exists with double overprint. Nos. GNC9, GNC14 and GNC18 exist with bold overprint.

ITALY — ITALIAN SOCIAL REPUBLIC — ITALY OFFICES ABROAD

AIR POST SPECIAL DELIVERY STAMPS

Italy No. CE3 Overprinted

1944		Wmk. 140		Perf. 14
GNCE1	APSD2	2 l slate (R)	275.00	2,100.

No. GNCE1 exists with bold overprint. Value, $500 unused, $4,250 used.
Exists with overprint inverted. Value, $1,900 unused.

SPECIAL DELIVERY STAMPS

Italy Nos. E14-E15 Overprinted "G.N.R." in Red or Black

1943-44		Photo. Wmk. 140		Perf. 14
GNE1	SD4	1.25 l green (R)	12.00	40.00
GNE2	SD4	2.50 l dp orange	170.00	575.00

No. GNE1-GNE2 exist with overprint inverted. Value unused, $500.
No. GNE1-GNE2 exist with bold overprint. Value GNE1, $10 unused, $40 used. Value GNE2, $145 unused, $600 used.

Italy Nos. E14 and E15 Overprinted in Red or Black

1944		Wmk. 140		Perf. 14
E1	SD4	1.25 l green (R)	.35	.80
E2	SD4	2.50 l deep orange	.35	20.00

Cathedral, Palermo — SD1

1944		Photo.		
E3	SD1	1.25 l green	.25	1.00

AUTHORIZED DELIVERY STAMP

Catalogue values for unused stamps in this section are for Never Hinged items.

Italy No. EY2 Overprinted

1944		Wmk. 140		Perf. 14
EY1	AD2	10c dark brown	.25	.80

Italy No. EY2 with overprint type a and type b were prepared but not issued. Values: type a, unused $135, never hinged $425; type b, unused $250, never hinged $800.

POSTAGE DUE STAMPS

Italy Nos. J28-J40 Overprinted

1944		Wmk. 140		Perf. 14
GNJ1	D6	5c brown	30.00	75.00
GNJ2	D6	10c blue (R)	30.00	75.00
GNJ3	D6	20c rose red	25.00	42.50
GNJ4	D6	20c green (R)	22.00	42.50
GNJ5	D6	30c red orange	30.00	75.00
GNJ6	D6	40c blk brn (R)	30.00	75.00
GNJ7	D6	50c violet	65.00	300.00
GNJ8	D6	60c sl black (R)	300.00	1,350.
GNJ9	D7	1 l red orange	25.00	50.00
GNJ10	D7	2 l green (R)	50.00	100.00
GNJ11	D7	5 l violet	220.00	550.00
GNJ12	D7	10 l blue (R)	90.00	350.00
GNJ13	D7	20 l car rose	90.00	350.00
		Nos. GNJ1-GNJ13 (13)	1,007.	3,435.

Nos. GNJ1-GNJ5 and GNJ10-GNJ13 exist with overprint inverted. Values for inverted overprints are substantially higher than the normal overprinted stamps.

Italy Nos. J28-J40 Overprinted Like No. EY1

1944				
J1	D6	5c brown	4.00	5.00
J2	D6	10c blue	4.00	5.00
J3	D6	20c rose red	4.00	5.00
J4	D6	25c green	4.00	5.00
J5	D6	30c red org	4.00	10.00
J6	D6	40c blk brn	4.00	15.00
J7	D6	50c violet	4.00	5.00
J8	D6	60c slate blk	20.00	50.00
J9	D7	1 l red org	7.00	5.00
J10	D7	2 l green	14.00	32.50
J11	D7	5 l violet	40.00	225.00
J12	D7	10 l blue	65.00	550.00
J13	D7	20 l car rose	65.00	850.00
		Nos. J1-J13 (13)	239.00	1,763.

PARCEL POST STAMPS

Both unused and used values are for complete stamps.

Italian Parcel Post Stamps and Types of 1927-39 Overprinted

1944		Wmk. 140		Perf. 13
Q1	PP3	5c brown	5.00	65.00
Q2	PP3	10c deep blue	5.00	65.00
Q3	PP3	25c carmine	5.00	65.00
Q4	PP3	30c ultra	5.00	65.00
Q5	PP3	50c orange	5.00	65.00
Q6	PP3	60c red	5.00	450.00
Q7	PP3	1 l lilac	5.00	65.00
Q8	PP3	2 l green	300.00	2,000.
Q9	PP3	3 l yel bister	45.00	750.00
Q10	PP3	4 l gray	75.00	850.00
Q11	PP3	10 l rose lilac	160.00	3,000.
Q12	PP3	20 l lilac brn	450.00	4,250.
		Nos. Q1-Q12 (12)	1,065.	11,690.

No parcel post service existed in 1944. Nos. Q1-Q12 were used undivided, for regular postage.

ITALY OFFICES ABROAD

Stamps listed under this heading were issued for use in the Italian Post Offices which, for various reasons, were maintained from time to time in foreign countries.

100 Centesimi = 1 Lira

GENERAL ISSUE

Values of Italian Offices Abroad stamps vary tremendously according to condition. Quotations are for very fine examples, and values for unused stamps are for examples with original gum as defined in the catalogue introduction. Extremely fine or superb examples sell at much higher prices, and fine or poor examples sell at greatly reduced prices. In addition, unused examples without gum are discounted severely.

Very fine examples of Nos. 1-17 will have perforations barely clear of the frameline or design due to the narrow spacing of the stamps on the plates.

Italian Stamps with Corner Designs Slightly Altered and Overprinted

1874-78		Wmk. 140		Perf. 14
1	A6	1c ol grn	47.50	47.50
a.		Inverted overprint	40,000.	
c.		2 dots in lower right corner	87.50	275.00
d.		Three dots in upper right corner	400.00	1,750.
e.		Without overprint	75,000.	
2	A7	2c org brn	52.50	55.00
a.		Without overprint	75,000.	
3	A8	5c slate grn	1,200.	55.00
a.		Lower right corner not altered	24,000.	2,600.
4	A8	10c buff	3,600.	120.00
a.		Upper left corner not altered	30,000.	1,800.
b.		None of the corners altered	—	75,000.
c.		Lower corners not altered	—	12,000.
5	A8	10c blue ('78)	725.00	35.00
6	A15	20c blue	2,800.	55.00
7	A15	20c org ('78)	13,000.	32.50
8	A8	30c brown	8.00	32.50
a.		None of the corners altered	—	55,000.
b.		Right lower corner not altered	—	—
c.		Double overprint	—	—
9	A8	40c rose	8.00	32.50
10	A8	60c lilac	27.50	350.00
11	A13	2 l vermilion	350.00	1,100.

1881				
12	A17	5c green	47.50	20.00
13	A17	10c claret	9.50	16.00
14	A17	20c orange	9.50	9.50
a.		Double overprint, on piece		
15	A17	25c blue	9.50	24.00
16	A17	50c violet	24.00	80.00
17	A17	2 l vermilion	47.50	
		Nos. 12-17 (6)	147.50	
		Nos. 12-16 (5)		149.50

The "Estero" stamps were used in various parts of the world, South America, Africa, Turkey, etc.
Forged cancellations exist on Nos. 1-2, 9-11, 16.

OFFICES IN CHINA

100 Cents = 1 Dollar

PEKING

Italian Stamps of 1901-16 Handstamped

1917		Wmk. 140, Unwmk.	Perf. 12, 13½, 14	
1	A48	2c on 5c green	450.00	300.00
a.		Inverted surcharge	400.00	275.00
b.		Double surcharge, one inverted	1,100.	875.00
c.		4c on 5c green	9,500.	
3	A48	4c on 10c claret (No. 95)	800.00	475.00
a.		Inverted surcharge	725.00	450.00
b.		Double surcharge, one inverted	1,750.	1,200.
c.		4c on 10c claret (No. 79)	—	
5	A58	6c on 15c slate	1,600.	1,100.
b.		8c on 15c slate	5,500.	5,200.
c.		Pair, one without surcharge	—	
7	A58	8c on 20c on 15c slate	6,000.	4,500.
a.		Inverted surcharge	5,500.	4,000.
8	A50	8c on 20c brn org (No. 112)	12,000.	4,500.
a.		Inverted surcharge	10,500.	4,200.
9	A49	20c on 50c vio	30,000.	25,000.
a.		Inverted surcharge	40,000.	27,000.
b.		40c on 50c violet	24,000.	24,000.
c.		As "b," inverted surcharge	22,000.	22,000.
11	A46	40c on 1 l brn & grn	350,000.	60,000.
a.		Inverted surcharge	300,000.	52,000.

Excellent forgeries exist of the higher valued stamps of Offices in China.

Italian Stamps of 1901-16 Overprinted

1917-18				
12	A42	1c brown	40.00	80.00
13	A43	2c orange brown	40.00	80.00
a.		Double overprint	450.00	
14	A48	5c green	12.00	27.50
a.		Double overprint	275.00	
15	A48	10c claret	12.00	27.50
16	A50	20c brn org (No. 112)	300.00	350.00
17	A49	25c blue	12.00	35.00
18	A49	50c violet	12.00	35.00
19	A46	1 l brown & grn	27.50	72.50
20	A46	5 l blue & rose	55.00	120.00
21	A51	10 l gray grn & red	400.00	675.00
		Nos. 12-21 (10)	910.50	1,503.

Italy No. 113, the watermarked 20c brown orange, was also overprinted "Pechino," but not issued. Value: hinged $32.50; never hinged $80.

Italian Stamps of 1901-16 Surcharged

Type I   Type II

TWO DOLLARS:
Type I — Surcharged "2 dollari Pechino"
Type II — Surcharged "2 DOLLARI."
Type III — Surcharged "2 dollari." "Pechino" measures 11½mm wide, instead of 13mm.

1918-19				Perf. 14
22	A42	½c on 1c brown	350.00	350.00
a.		Surcharged "1 cents"	1,100.	1,200.
23	A43	1c on 2c org brn	12.00	24.00
a.		Surcharged "1 cents"	550.00	650.00
24	A48	2c on 5c green	12.00	24.00
25	A48	4c on 10c clar	12.00	24.00
26	A50	8c on 20c brn org (No. 112)	65.00	47.50
a.		"8 CENTS" doubled	525.00	525.00
27	A49	10c on 25c blue	24.00	47.50
a.		"10 CENTS" doubled	525.00	525.00
28	A49	20c on 50c vio	32.50	47.50
29	A46	40c on 1 l brn & grn	350.00	450.00
30	A46	$2 on 5 l bl & rose (type I)	650.00	1,050.
a.		Type II	70,000.	60,000.
b.		Type III	20,000.	16,000.
		Nos. 22-30 (9)	1,508.	2,065.

Italy No. 100 Surcharged

1919				
32	A49	10c on 25c blue	11.00	27.50

Imperf. examples of No. 32 are proofs.

PEKING SPECIAL DELIVERY STAMPS

Italian Special Delivery Stamp 1908 Ovptd.

1917		Wmk. 140		Perf. 14
E1	SD2	30c blue & rose	16.00	60.00

No. E1 Surcharged

1918				
E2	SD2	12c on 30c bl & rose	125.00	450.00

PEKING POSTAGE DUE STAMPS

Italian Postage Due Stamps Overprinted Like Nos. 12-21

1917		Wmk. 140		Perf. 14
J1	D3	10c buff & magenta	5.50	14.00
a.		Double overprint	400.00	

ITALY — ITALY OFFICES ABROAD

J2	D3	20c buff & magenta	5.50	14.00
J3	D3	30c buff & magenta	5.50	14.00
J4	D3	40c buff & magenta	11.00	14.00
		Nos. J1-J4 (4)	27.50	56.00

Nos. J1-J4 Surcharged Like No. E2

1918
J5	D3	4c on 10c	125,000.	100,000.
J6	D3	8c on 20c	55.00	110.00
a.		Pair, one without surcharge	2,000.	
J7	D3	12c on 30c	125.00	275.00
J8	D3	16c on 40c	550.00	950.00

In 1919, the same new values were surcharged on Italy Nos. J6-J9 in a different style: four lines to cancel the denomination, and "-PECHINO- 4 CENTS." These were not issued. Value $17.50 each, never hinged $42.50 each.

TIENTSIN

Italian Stamps of 1906 Handstamped

Wmk. 140, Unwmk.
1917 — **Perf. 12, 13½, 14**
1	A48	2c on 5c green	575.00	575.00
a.		Surcharge inverted	575.00	475.00
b.		Double surcharge	1,200.	875.00
c.		4c on 5c green	16,000.	
d.		Double surcharge, one inverted	1,250.	950.00
2	A48	4c on 10c claret	875.00	475.00
a.		Surcharge inverted	875.00	425.00
b.		Double surcharge	1,900.	1,100.
c.		Double surcharge, one inverted	2,000.	1,200.
4	A58	6c on 15c slate	1,750.	1,500.
a.		Surcharge inverted	1,750.	1,100.
b.		4c on 15c slate	8,750.	8,000.
		Nos. 1-4 (3)	3,200.	2,550.

Italian Stamps of 1901-16 Overprinted

1917-18
5	A42	1c brown	30.00	45.00
a.		Inverted overprint	400.00	400.00
6	A43	2c orange brn	30.00	45.00
7	A48	5c green	10.00	18.00
8	A48	10c claret	10.00	18.00
a.		Double overprint	425.00	
9	A50	20c brn org (#112)	200.00	180.00
10	A49	25c blue	10.00	18.00
11	A49	50c violet	10.00	18.00
12	A46	1 l brown & grn	24.00	65.00
13	A46	5 l blue & rose	36.00	55.00
14	A51	10 l gray grn & red	240.00	550.00
		Nos. 5-14 (10)	600.00	1,012.

Italy No. 113, the watermarked 20c brown orange was also overprinted "Tientsin," but not issued. Value: hinged $32.50; never hinged $80.

Italian Stamps of 1901-16 Surcharged

Type I

TWO DOLLARS:
Type I — Surcharged "2 Dollari Tientsin."
Type II — Surcharged "2 dollari."
Type III — Surcharged "2 Dollari." "Tientsin" measures 10mm wide instead of 13mm.

1918-21 — **Perf. 14**
15	A42	½c on 1c brn	350.00	350.00
a.		Inverted surcharge	650.00	650.00
b.		Surcharged "1 cents"	1,100.	1,200.
16	A43	1c on 2c org brn	12.00	24.00
a.		Surcharged "1 cents"	550.00	650.00
b.		Inverted surcharge	650.00	650.00
17	A48	2c on 5c grn	12.00	24.00
18	A48	4c on 10c clar	12.00	24.00
19	A50	8c on 20c brn org (#112)	65.00	55.00
20	A49	10c on 25c blue	24.00	47.50
21	A49	20c on 50c vio	32.50	47.50
22	A46	40c on 1 l brn & grn	350.00	450.00
23	A46	$2 on 5 l bl & rose (type I)	650.00	1,050.
a.		Type II	20,000.	20,000.
b.		Type III ('21)	17,500.	16,000.
		Nos. 15-23 (9)	1,508.	2,072.

SPECIAL DELIVERY STAMPS

Italian Special Delivery Stamp of 1908 Overprinted

1917 — **Wmk. 140** — **Perf. 14**
E1	SD2	30c blue & rose	16.00	60.00

No. E1 Surcharged

1918
E2	SD2	12c on 30c bl & rose	125.00	450.00

POSTAGE DUE STAMPS

Italian Postage Due Stamps Overprinted

1917 — **Wmk. 140** — **Perf. 14**
J1	D3	10c buff & magenta	5.50	14.00
a.		Double overprint	400.00	
J2	D3	20c buff & magenta	5.50	14.00
J3	D3	30c buff & magenta	5.50	14.00
a.		Double overprint	400.00	
J4	D3	40c buff & magenta	11.00	14.00
		Nos. J1-J4 (4)	27.50	56.00

Nos. J1-J4 Surcharged

1918
J5	D3	4c on 10c	9,500.	9,500.
J6	D3	8c on 20c	55.00	110.00
a.		"8 CENTS" double	2,750.	
J7	D3	12c on 30c	120.00	275.00
J8	D3	16c on 40c	550.00	950.00

In 1919, the same new values were surcharged on Italy Nos. J6-J9 in a different style: four lines to cancel the denomination, and "-TIENTSIN- 4 CENTS." These were not issued. Value $17 each, never hinged $42.50 each.

OFFICES IN CRETE

40 Paras = 1 Piaster
100 Centesimi = 1 Lira (1906)

Italy Nos. 70 and 81 Surcharged in Red or Black

a   b

1900-01 — **Wmk. 140** — **Perf. 14**
1	A36(a)	1pi on 25c blue	8.00	80.00
2	A45(b)	1pi on 25c dp bl (Bk) ('01)	4.50	10.00

Italian Stamps Overprinted

1906
On Nos. 76-79, 92, 81, 83-85, 87, 91
3	A42	1c brown	2.75	6.00
a.		Pair, one without ovpt.	1,325.	
b.		Double overprint	375.00	
4	A43	2c org brn	2.75	6.00
a.		Imperf., pair	2,400.	
b.		Double overprint	375.00	
5	A44	5c bl grn	5.00	7.00
6	A45	10c claret	300.00	250.00
7	A45	15c on 20c org	5.00	7.00
8	A45	25c blue	11.50	23.00
9	A45	40c brown	11.50	23.00
10	A45	45c ol grn	11.50	23.00
11	A45	50c violet	11.50	23.00
12	A46	1 l brn & grn	45.00	85.00
13	A46	5 l bl & rose	375.00	500.00
		Nos. 3-13 (11)	781.50	953.00

On Nos. 94-95, 100, 104-105

1907-10
14	A48	5c green	1.90	2.00
a.		Inverted overprint	300.00	
15	A48	10c claret	1.90	2.00
a.		Double overprint	—	
16	A49	25c blue	2.75	14.50
17	A49	40c brown	30.00	45.00
18	A49	50c violet	2.75	14.50
		Nos. 14-18 (5)	39.30	78.00

On No. 111 in Violet

1912 — **Unwmk.** — **Perf. 13x13½**
19	A50	15c slate black	3.00	4.00

SPECIAL DELIVERY STAMPS

Special Delivery Stamp of Italy Overprinted

1906 — **Wmk. 140** — **Perf. 14**
E1	SD1	25c rose red	12.00	24.00

OFFICES IN AFRICA

40 Paras = 1 Piaster
100 Centesimi = 1 Lira (1910)

BENGASI

Italy No. 81 Surcharged in Black

1901 — **Wmk. 140** — **Perf. 14**
1	A45	1pi on 25c dp bl	65.00	160.00

Same Surcharge on Italy No. 100

1911
1A	A49	1pi on 25c blue	65.00	160.00

TRIPOLI

Italian Stamps of 1901-09 Overprinted in Black or Violet

1909 — **Wmk. 140**
2	A42	1c brown	4.75	3.25
a.		Inverted overprint	275.00	
3	A43	2c orange brn	2.40	3.25
4	A48	5c green	175.00	9.50
a.		Double overprint	325.00	
5	A48	10c claret	3.25	3.25
a.		Double overprint	225.00	225.00
6	A49	25c blue	2.40	3.25
7	A49	40c brown	8.00	8.00
8	A49	50c violet	9.50	9.50

Perf. 13½x14
Unwmk.
9	A50	15c slate blk (V)	4.75	4.75
		Nos. 2-9 (8)	210.05	44.75

Italian Stamps of 1901 Overprinted

1909 — **Wmk. 140** — **Perf. 14**
10	A46	1 l brown & grn	140.00	100.00
11	A46	5 l blue & rose	47.50	300.00

Same Overprint on Italy Nos. 76-77

1915
12	A42	1c brown		3.50
13	A43	2c orange brown		3.50

Nos. 12-13 were prepared but not issued. No. 12 exists as a pair, one without overprint, value $2,400 hinged, $3,600 never hinged. No. 12 also exists with inverted overprint. Value, $1,600.

SPECIAL DELIVERY STAMPS

Italy Nos. E1, E6 Ovptd. Like Nos. 10-11

1909 — **Wmk. 140** — **Perf. 14**
E1	SD1	25c rose red	19.00	12.00
E2	SD2	30c blue & rose	6.50	16.00

Tripoli was ceded by Turkey to Italy in Oct., 1912, and became known as the Colony of Libia. Later issues will be found under Libya.

OFFICES IN TURKISH EMPIRE

40 Paras = 1 Piaster

Various powers maintained post offices in the Turkish Empire before World War I by authority of treaties which ended with the signing of the Treaty of Lausanne in 1923. The foreign post offices were closed Oct. 27, 1923.

GENERAL ISSUE

Italian Stamps of 1906-08 Surcharged

Printed at Turin

1908 — **Wmk. 140**
1	A48	10pa on 5c green	8.00	4.75
2	A48	20pa on 10c claret	8.00	4.75
3	A49	40pa on 25c blue	3.25	3.25
4	A49	80pa on 50c violet	6.50	4.75

See Janina Nos. 1-4.

Surcharged in Violet

Unwmk.
5	A47	30pa on 15c slate	2.40	2.40
		Nos. 1-5 (5)	28.15	19.90

Nos. 1, 2, 3 and 5 were first issued in Janina, Albania, and subsequently for general use. They can only be distinguished by the cancellations.

Italian Stamps of 1901-08 Surcharged

Nos. 6-8   No. 9

Nos. 10-12

ITALY — ITALY OFFICES ABROAD

Printed at Constantinople

1908   **First Printing**

6	A48	10pa on 5c grn	400.00 500.00
a.		Vert. pair, one without surcharge	4,000.
7	A48	20pa on 10c claret	400.00 500.00
8	A47	30pa on 15c slate	1,200. 1,400.
9	A49	1pi on 25c blue	1,200. 1,400.
a.		"PIASTRE"	2,000. 2,000.
10	A49	2pi on 50c vio	3,250. 4,000.
11	A46	4pi on 1 l brn & grn	17,500. 12,000.
12	A46	20pi on 5 l bl & rose	40,000. 35,000.

On Nos. 8, 9 and 10 the surcharge is at the top of the stamp. No. 11 has the "4" closed at the top. No. 12 has the "20" wide.

Second Printing
Italian Stamps of 1901-08 Surcharged

Nos. 13-15   No. 16

Nos. 17-19

13	A48	10pa on 5c green	40.00 52.50
14	A48	20pa on 10c claret	40.00 52.50
15	A47	30pa on 15c slate	160.00 120.00
a.		Double surcharge	350.00 350.00
b.		Triple surcharge	800.00 800.00
16	A49	1pi on 25c blue	40.00 52.50
a.		"PIPSTRA"	250.00 250.00
b.		"1" omitted	250.00 250.00
17	A49	2pi on 50c violet	240.00 240.00
a.		Surcharged "20 PIASTRE"	2,400. 2,400.
b.		"20" with "0" scratched out	800.00 800.00
c.		"2" 5mm from "PIASTRE"	650.00 650.00
18	A46	4pi on 1 l brn & grn	1,600. 1,600.
19	A46	20pi on 5 l bl & rose	9,500. 5,200.
		Nos. 13-19 (7)	11,620. 7,318.

On No. 18 the "4" is open at the top.

Third Printing
Surcharged in Red

20	A47	30pa on 15c slate	9.50 9.50
a.		Double surcharge	240.00 240.00

Fourth Printing

20B	A46	4pi on 1 l brn & grn	65.00 95.00
c.		Inverted "S"	200.00 200.00
20D	A46	20pi on 5 l bl & rose	210.00 240.00
i.		Inverted "S"	550.00 550.00

Fifth Printing

20E	A46	4pi on 1 l brn & grn	55.00 72.50
f.		Surch. "20 PIASTRE"	2,750.
20G	A46	20pi on 5 l bl & rose	55.00 72.50
h.		Double surcharge	1,600. 1,600.

Italian Stamps of 1906-19 Surcharged

1921

21	A48	1pi on 5c green	350.00 475.00
22	A48	2pi on 15c slate	8.00 12.00
23	A50	4pi on 20c brn org (No. 113)	80.00 95.00
24	A49	5pi on 25c blue	80.00 95.00
a.		Double surcharge	350.00
25	A49	10pi on 60c carmine	4.75 8.00
		Nos. 21-25 (5)	522.75 685.00

No. 21 is almost always found poorly centered, and it is valued thus.
On No. 25 the "10" is placed above "PIASTRE."

Italian Stamps of 1901-19 Surcharged

n   o

1922

26	A42(n)	10pa on 1c brn	2.40 2.75
27	A43(n)	20pa on 2c org brn	2.40 2.75
28	A48(n)	30pa on 5c grn	6.50 6.50
29	A48(o)	1pi20pa on 15c slate	7.25 2.75
30	A50(n)	3pi on 20c brn org (#113)	9.50 17.50
31	A49(o)	3pi30pa on 25c blue	4.75 2.75
32	A49(o)	7pi20pa on 60c carmine	9.50 6.50
33	A46(n)	15pi on 1 l brn & grn	27.50 47.50
		Nos. 26-33 (8)	69.80 89.00

On No. 32, the distance between the two lines is 2mm. See note after No. 58A.

Italy No. 100 Surcharged

34	A49	3.75pi on 25c blue	2.40 2.75

Italian Stamps of 1901-20 Surcharged

q   r

1922

35	A48	30pi on 5c grn	4.00 17.50
36	A49	1.50pi on 25c blue	2.40 9.50
37	A49	3.75pi on 40c brn	3.25 11.00
a.		Double surcharge	325.00
38	A49	4.50pi on 50c vio	8.00 24.00
39	A49	7.50pi on 60c car	6.50 17.50
a.		Double surcharge	400.00
b.		Pair, one without surcharge	1,750.
40	A49	15pi on 85c red brn	12.00 40.00
41	A46	18.75pi on 1 l brn & grn	5.50 32.50

On No. 40 the numerals of the surcharge are above "PIASTRE."

Italian Stamps of 1901-20 Surcharged

42	A46	45pi on 5 l bl & rose	450.00 725.00
43	A51	90pi on 10 l gray grn & red	475.00 875.00

On No. 42 the figure "4" is open at top. See note after No. 61.
On No. 43 the figure "9" has a curved or arched bottom. See note after No. 62.

Italian Stamps of 1901-17 Surcharged Type "q" or:

44	A43	30pa on 2c org brn	2.40 6.50
45	A50	1.50pi on 20c brn org (#113)	2.40 6.50
		Nos. 35-45 (11)	971.45 1,765.

Italian Stamps of 1901-20 Surcharged in Black or Red

46	A48	30pa on 5c green	2.40 4.00
47	A48	1½pi on 10c claret	2.40 4.00
48	A49	3pi on 25c blue	20.00 8.00
49	A49	3¾pi on 40c brown	4.00 4.00
50	A49	4½pi on 50c violet	47.50 45.00
51	A49	7½pi on 85c red brn	9.50 12.00
a.		"PIASTRE"	47.50 47.50
52	A49	7½p on 1 l brn & grn (R)	12.00 14.00
a.		Double surcharge	175.00
b.		"PIASIRE"	55.00 55.00
53	A46	15p on 1 l brn & grn	72.50 175.00
54	A46	45p on 5 l blue & rose	110.00 110.00
55	A51	90p on 10 l gray grn & red	87.50 200.00
		Nos. 46-55 (10)	367.80 576.00

Italian Stamps of 1901-20 Surcharged Type "o" or

No. 58   No. 59

Nos. 61-62

1923

56	A49	1pi20pa on 25c blue	14.00
57	A49	3pi30pa on 40c brn	14.00
58	A49	4pi20pa on 50c vio	14.00
58A	A49	7pi20pa on 60c car	40.00
59	A49	15pi on 85c red brn	14.00
60	A46	18pi30pa on 1 l brn & grn	14.00
a.		Double surcharge	325.00
61	A46	45pi on 5 l bl & rose	40.00
62	A51	90pi on 10 l gray grn & red	35.00
		Nos. 56-62 (8)	185.00

On No. 58A the distance between the lines is 1.5mm. On No. 61 the figure "4" is closed at top. On No. 62 the figure "9" is nearly rectilinear at bottom.
Nos. 56-62 were not issued.

SPECIAL DELIVERY STAMPS

Italian Special Delivery Stamps Surcharged

1908   **Wmk. 140**   **Perf. 14**

E1	SD1	1pi on 25c rose red	3.25 4.75

Surcharged

1910

E2	SD2	60pa on 30c blue & rose	6.50 8.00

Surcharged

1922

E3	SD2	15pi on 1.20 l on 30c bl & rose	35.00 87.50

On No. E3, lines obliterate the first two denominations.

Surcharged

1922

E4	SD2	15pi on 30c bl & rose	525.00 1,050.

Surcharged

1923

E5	SD2	15pi on 1.20 l blue & red	16.00

No. E5 was not regularly issued.

ALBANIA

Stamps of Italy Surcharged in Black

1902   **Wmk. 140**   **Perf. 14**

1	A44	10pa on 5c green	4.75 2.40
2	A45	35pa on 20c orange	7.25 8.00
3	A45	40pa on 25c blue	14.00 8.00
		Nos. 1-3 (3)	26.00 18.40

Nos. 1-3 with red surcharges are proofs.

1907

4	A48	10pa on 5c green	55.00 65.00
5	A48	20pa on 10c claret	35.00 27.50
6	A45	80pa on 50c violet	35.00 27.50
		Nos. 4-6 (3)	125.00 120.00

No. 5 is almost always found poorly centered, and it is valued thus.

CONSTANTINOPLE

Stamps of Italy Surcharged in Black or Violet

Wmk. 140, Unwmk. (#3)

1909-11   **Perf. 14, 12**

1	A48	10pa on 5c green	2.40 2.40
2	A48	20pa on 10c claret	2.40 2.40
3	A47	30pa on 15c slate (V)	2.40 2.40
4	A49	1pi on 25c blue	2.40 2.40
a.		Double surcharge	210.00 210.00
5	A49	2pi on 50c violet	4.75 3.25

Surcharged

6	A46	4pi on 1 l brn & grn	4.75 4.00
7	A46	20pi on 5 l bl & rose	72.50 72.50
8	A51	40pi on 10 l gray grn & red	8.00 32.50
		Nos. 1-8 (8)	99.60 121.85

Italian Stamps of 1901-19 Surcharged

Nos. 10, 12-13   Nos. 9, 11

1922

9	A48	20pa on 5c green	20.00 32.50
10	A48	1pi20pa on 15c slate	2.40 2.40
11	A49	3pi on 30c org brn	2.40 2.40
12	A49	3pi30pa on 40c brown	2.40 2.40
13	A46	7pi20pa on 1 l brn & grn	2.40 2.40
		Nos. 9-13 (5)	29.60 42.10

ITALY — ITALY OFFICES ABROAD — AEGEAN ISLANDS

Italian Stamps of 1901-20 Surcharged

1923
14	A48	30pa on 5c grn	3.25	2.40
15	A49	1pi20pa on 25c blue	3.25	2.40
16	A49	3pi30pa on 40c brn	3.25	2.00
17	A49	4pi20pa on 50c vio	3.25	2.00
18	A49	7pi20pa on 60c car	3.25	2.00
19	A49	15pi on 85c red brn	3.25	3.25
20	A46	18pi30pa on 1 l brn & grn	3.25	3.25
21	A46	45pi on 5 l bl & rose	3.25	7.25
22	A51	90pi on 10 l gray grn & red	3.25	8.00
	Nos. 14-22 (9)		29.25	32.55

CONSTANTINOPLE SPECIAL DELIVERY STAMP

Unissued Italian Special Delivery Stamp of 1922 Surcharged in Black

1923   Wmk. 140   Perf. 14
E1	SD2	15pi on 1.20 bl & red	8.00	45.00

CONSTANTINOPLE POSTAGE DUE STAMPS

Italian Postage Due Stamps of 1870-1903 Overprinted

1922   Wmk. 140   Perf. 14
J1	D3	10c buff & mag	80.00	110.00
J2	D3	30c buff & mag	80.00	110.00
J3	D3	60c buff & mag	80.00	110.00
J4	D3	1 l blue & mag	80.00	110.00
J5	D3	2 l blue & mag	1,900.	3,400.
J6	D3	5 l blue & mag	875.00	1,200.
	Nos. J1-J6 (6)		3,095.	5,040.

A circular control mark with the inscription "Poste Italiane Constantinopoli" and with the arms of the Kingdom of Italy (Savoy Cross) in the center was applied to each block of four of these stamps in black. Value, set of 6 blocks of four with control marks: unused $20,000; used $28,000.

DURAZZO

Stamps of Italy Surcharged in Black or Violet

Wmk. 140, Unwmk. (#3)
1909-11   Perf. 14, 12
1	A48	10pa on 5c green	1.60	3.25
2	A48	20pa on 10c claret	1.60	3.25
3	A47	30pa on 15c slate (V)	80.00	4.00
4	A49	1pi on 25c blue	2.40	4.00
5	A49	2pi on 50c violet	2.40	4.00

Surcharged

6	A46	4pi on 1 l brn & grn	4.00	4.75
7	A46	20pi on 5 l bl & rose	325.00	275.00
8	A51	40pi on 10 l gray grn & red	20.00	140.00
	Nos. 1-8 (8)		437.00	438.25

No. 3 Surcharged

1916   Unwmk.   Perf. 12
9	A47	20c on 30pa on 15c slate	4.75	20.00

JANINA

Stamps of Italy Surcharged

1902-07   Wmk. 140   Perf. 14
1	A44	10pa on 5c green	9.50	3.75
2	A45	35pa on 20c orange	7.00	4.00
3	A45	40pa on 25c blue	35.00	11.50
4	A45	80pa on 50c vio ('07)	62.50	47.50
	Nos. 1-4 (4)		114.00	66.75

Surcharged in Black or Violet

Wmk. 140, Unwmk. (#7)
1909-11   Perf. 14, 12
5	A48	10pa on 5c green	1.25	2.50
6	A48	20pa on 10c claret	1.25	2.50
7	A47	30pa on 15c slate (V)	1.25	2.50
8	A49	1pi on 25c blue	1.25	2.50
9	A49	2pi on 50c violet	1.25	3.25

Surcharged

10	A46	4pi on 1 l brn & grn	4.00	4.75
11	A46	20pi on 5 l bl & rose	275.00	350.00
12	A51	40pi on 10 l gray grn & red	17.50	100.00
	Nos. 5-12 (8)		302.75	468.00

JERUSALEM

Stamps of Italy Surcharged in Black or Violet

Wmk. 140, Unwmk. (#3)
1909-11   Perf. 14, 12
1	A48	10pa on 5c green	8.00	20.00
2	A48	20pa on 10c claret	8.00	20.00
3	A47	30pa on 15c slate (V)	8.00	27.50
4	A49	1pi on 25c blue	8.00	20.00
5	A49	2pi on 50c violet	27.50	65.00

Surcharged

6	A46	4pi on 1 l brn & grn	35.00	87.50
7	A46	20pi on 5 l bl & rose	1,250.	1,400.
8	A51	40pi on 10 l gray grn & red	47.50	600.00
	Nos. 1-8 (8)		1,392.	2,240.

Forged cancellations exist on Nos. 1-8.

SALONIKA

Stamps of Italy Surcharged in Black or Violet

Wmk. 140, Unwmk. (#3)
1909-11   Perf. 14, 12
1	A48	10pa on 5c green	1.50	3.25
2	A48	20pa on 10c claret	1.50	3.25
3	A47	30pa on 15c slate (V)	1.75	3.50
4	A49	1pi on 25c blue	1.75	3.50
5	A49	2pi on 50c violet	2.40	4.25

Surcharged

6	A46	4pi on 1 l brn & grn	3.50	4.75
7	A46	20pi on 5 l bl & rose	475.00	600.00
8	A51	40pi on 10 l gray grn & red	16.50	95.00
	Nos. 1-8 (8)		503.90	717.50

SCUTARI

Stamps of Italy Surcharged in Black or Violet

Wmk. 140, Unwmk. (#3)
1909-11   Perf. 14, 12
1	A48	10pa on 5c green	1.60	3.25
2	A48	20pa on 10c claret	1.60	3.25
3	A47	30pa on 15c slate (V)	27.50	6.50
4	A49	1pi on 25c blue	1.60	3.25
5	A49	2pi on 50c violet	1.60	4.75

Surcharged

6	A46	4pi on 1 l brn & grn	3.25	4.75
7	A46	20pi on 5 l bl & rose	35.00	55.00
8	A51	40pi on 10 l gray grn & red	75.00	175.00
	Nos. 1-8 (8)		147.15	255.75

Surcharged like Nos. 1-5

1915
9	A43	4pa on 2c org brn	2.40	5.50

No. 3 Surcharged

1916   Unwmk.   Perf. 12
10	A47	20c on 30pa on 15c slate	6.50	27.50

SMYRNA

Stamps of Italy Surcharged in Black or Violet

Wmk. 140, Unwmk. (#3)
1909-11   Perf. 14, 12
1	A48	10pa on 5c green	1.60	1.60
2	A48	20pa on 10c claret	1.60	1.60
3	A47	30pa on 15c slate (V)	3.25	4.75
4	A49	1pi on 25c blue	3.25	4.75
5	A49	2pi on 50c violet	4.00	6.50

Surcharged

6	A46	4pi on 1 l brn & grn	4.75	8.00
7	A46	20pi on 5 l bl & rose	190.00	240.00
8	A51	40pi on 10 l gray grn & red	20.00	120.00
	Nos. 1-8 (8)		228.45	387.20

Italian Stamps of 1901-22 Surcharged

Nos. 10, 12-13

Nos. 9, 11

1922
9	A48	20pa on 5c green		32.50
10	A48	1pi20pa on 15c slate		1.60
11	A49	3pi on 30c org brn		1.60
12	A49	3pi30pa on 40c brn		4.00
13	A46	7pi20pa on 1 l brn & grn		4.00
	Nos. 9-13 (5)			43.70

Nos. 9-13 were not issued.

VALONA

Stamps of Italy Surcharged in Black or Violet

Wmk. 140, Unwmk. (#3)
1909-11   Perf. 14, 12
1	A48	10pa on 5c green	1.60	3.25
2	A48	20pa on 10c claret	1.60	3.25
3	A47	30pa on 15c slate (V)	20.00	6.50
4	A49	1pi on 25c blue	2.40	3.25
5	A49	2pi on 50c violet	2.40	4.00

Surcharged

6	A46	4pi on 1 l brn & grn	2.40	4.00
7	A46	20pi on 5 l bl & rose	55.00	65.00
8	A51	40pi on 10 l gray grn & red	65.00	175.00
	Nos. 1-8 (8)		150.40	264.25

Italy No. 123 Surcharged in Violet or Red Violet

1916
9	A58	30pa on 15c slate (V)	4.75	14.00
a.	Red violet surcharge		11.00	32.50

No. 9 Surcharged

10	A58	20c on 30pa on 15c slate	2.40	20.00

AEGEAN ISLANDS
(Dodecanese)

A group of islands in the Aegean Sea off the coast of Turkey. They were

ITALY — AEGEAN ISLANDS

occupied by Italy during the Tripoli War and were ceded to Italy by Turkey in 1924 by the Treaty of Lausanne. Stamps of Italy overprinted with the name of the island were in use at the post offices maintained in the various islands.

Rhodes, on the island of the same name, was capital of the entire group.

100 Centesimi = 1 Lira

GENERAL ISSUE

Italian Stamps of 1907-08 Overprinted

1912   Wmk. 140   Perf. 14

1	A49	25c blue	50.00	32.50
a.		Inverted overprint	270.00	270.00
2	A49	50c violet	50.00	32.50
a.		Inverted overprint	270.00	270.00

Virgil Issue

Italian Stamps of 1930 Ovptd. in Red or Blue

1930   Photo.   Wmk. 140   Perf. 14

3	A106	15c vio blk	1.45	19.00
4	A106	20c org brn	1.45	19.00
5	A106	25c dk green	1.35	8.50
6	A106	30c lt brown	1.45	8.50
7	A106	50c dull vio	1.45	8.50
8	A106	75c rose red	1.45	19.00
9	A106	1.25 l gray bl	1.45	25.00

Engr. Unwmk.

10	A106	5 l + 1.50 l dk vio	4.25	47.50
11	A106	10 l + 2.50 l ol brn	4.25	47.50

Nos. 3-11,C4-C7 (13)   31.45   384.50

St. Anthony of Padua Issue

Italian Stamps of 1931 Ovptd. in Blue or Red

1932   Photo.   Wmk. 140   Perf. 14

12	A116	20c black brn	30.00	25.00
13	A116	25c dull grn	30.00	25.00
14	A118	30c brown org	30.00	30.00
15	A118	50c dull vio	30.00	22.00
16	A120	1.25 l gray bl	32.50	42.50

Engr. Unwmk.

17	A121	75c lt red	30.00	35.00
18	A122	5 l + 2.50 l dp org	30.00	160.00

Nos. 12-18 (7)   212.50   339.50

Dante Alighieri Society Issue

Italian Stamps of 1932 Overprinted

1932   Photo.   Wmk. 140

19	A126	10c grnsh gray	1.45	7.25
20	A126	15c black vio	1.45	7.25
21	A126	20c brown org	1.45	7.25
22	A126	25c dp green	1.45	7.25
23	A126	30c dp org	1.45	7.25
24	A126	50c dull vio	1.45	8.50
25	A126	75c rose red	1.45	10.00
26	A126	1.25 l blue	1.45	8.50
27	A126	1.75 l ol brn	2.90	10.00
28	A126	2.75 l car rose	2.90	10.00
29	A126	5 l + 2 l dp vio	2.90	22.50
30	A126	10 l + 2.50 l dk brn	2.90	40.00

Nos. 19-30 (12)   23.20   140.75

See Nos. C8-C14.

Soccer Issue

Types of Italy, "Soccer" Issue, Overprinted in Black or Red

1934

31	A173	20c brn rose (Bk)	70.00	85.00
32	A174	25c green (R)	70.00	85.00
33	A174	50c violet (R)	250.00	55.00
34	A174	1.25 l gray bl (R)	70.00	155.00
35	A175	5 l +2.50 l bl (R)	70.00	400.00

Nos. 31-35 (5)   530.00   780.00

See Nos. C28-C31.

Same Overprint on Types of Medal of Valor Issue of Italy, in Red or Black

1935

36	A177	10c sl gray (R)	37.50	75.00
37	A178	15c brn (Bk)	37.50	75.00
38	A178	20c red org (Bk)	37.50	75.00
39	A177	25c dp grn (R)	37.50	75.00
40	A178	30c lake (Bk)	37.50	75.00
41	A178	50c ol grn (Bk)	37.50	75.00
42	A178	75c rose red (Bk)	37.50	75.00
43	A178	1.25 l dp bl (R)	37.50	75.00
44	A177	1.75 l + 1 l pur (R)	37.50	75.00
45	A178	2.55 l + 2 l dk car (Bk)	37.50	75.00
46	A178	2.75 l + 2 l org brn (Bk)	37.50	75.00

Nos. 36-46 (11)   412.50   825.00

See Nos. C32-C38, CE3-CE4.

Types of Italy, 1937, Overprinted in Blue or Red

1938   Wmk. 140   Perf. 14

47	A208	10c dk brn (Bl)	5.00	8.50
48	A208	15c pur (R)	5.00	8.50
49	A208	20c chestnut (Bl)	5.00	8.50
50	A208	25c myr grn (R)	5.00	8.50
51	A208	30c gr cl (Bl)	5.00	8.50
52	A208	50c sl grn (R)	5.00	13.00
53	A208	75c rose red (Bl)	5.00	13.00
54	A208	1.25 l dk bl (R)	5.00	13.00
55	A208	1.75 l + 1 l dp org (Bl)	7.25	27.50
56	A208	2.55 l + 2 l ol brn	7.25	27.50

Nos. 47-56 (10)   54.50   136.50

Bimillenary of birth of Augustus Caesar (Octavianus), first Roman emperor.
See Nos. C39-C43.

Same Overprint of Type of Italy, 1937, in Red

1938

57	A222	1.25 l deep blue	1.40	2.10
58	A222	2.75 l + 2 l brown	1.60	8.50

600th anniversary of the death of Giotto di Bondone, Italian painter.

Statue of Roman Wolf — A1

Arms of Rhodes — A2

Dante's House, Rhodes — A3

1940   Photo.

59	A1	5c lt brown	.70	1.10
60	A2	10c pale org	1.10	1.10
61	A3	25c blue grn	1.50	1.75
62	A1	50c rose vio	1.50	1.80
63	A2	75c dull ver	1.50	3.50
64	A3	1.25 l dull blue	1.50	3.50
65	A2	2 l + 75c rose	1.50	25.00

Nos. 59-65,C44-C47 (11)   17.50   75.85

Triennial Overseas Exposition, Naples.

AIR POST STAMPS

Ferrucci Issue

Types of Italian Air Post Stamps of 1930 Overprinted in Blue or Red Like Nos. 12-18

1930   Wmk. 140   Perf. 14

C1	A104	50c brn vio (Bl)	10.00	22.00
C2	A104	1 l dk bl (R)	10.00	22.50
C3	A104	5 l + 2 l dp car (Bl)	19.00	60.00

Nos. C1-C3 (3)   39.00   104.50

Nos. C1-C3 were sold at Rhodes only.

Virgil Issue

Types of Italian Air Post Stamps of 1930 Overprinted in Red or Blue Like Nos. 3-11

1930   Photo.

C4	A106	50c dp grn (R)	2.20	35.00
C5	A106	1 l rose red (Bl)	2.20	27.00

Engr. Unwmk.

C6	A106	7.70 l + 1.30 l dk brn	4.25	47.50
C7	A106	9 l + 2 l gray (R)	4.25	72.50

Nos. C4-C7 (4)   12.90   182.00

Dante Alighieri Society Issue

Types of Italian Air Post Stamps of 1932 Overprinted Like Nos. 19-30

1932   Wmk. 140

C8	AP10	50c car rose	1.40	5.50
C9	AP11	1 l dp grn	1.40	5.75
C10	AP11	3 l dl vio	1.40	8.50
C11	AP11	5 l dp org	1.40	8.50
C12	AP10	7.70 l + 2 l ol brn	4.25	20.00
C13	AP11	10 l + 2.50 l dk bl	4.25	26.00

Nos. C8-C13 (6)   14.10   74.25

Leonardo da Vinci — AP12

1932   Photo.   Perf. 14½

C14	AP12	100 l bl & grnsh gray	20.00	125.00

Garibaldi Types of Italian Air Post Stamps of 1932 Overprinted in Red or Blue

1932

C15	AP13	50c deep green	55.00	125.00
C16	AP14	80c copper red	55.00	125.00
C17	AP13	1 l + 25c dl bl	55.00	125.00
C18	AP13	2 l + 50c red brn	55.00	125.00
C19	AP14	5 l + 1 l bluish sl	55.00	125.00

Nos. C15-C19 (5)   275.00   625.00

See Nos. CE1-CE2.

Graf Zeppelin over Rhodes — AP17

1933   Perf. 14

C20	AP17	3 l olive brn	85.00	215.00
C21	AP17	5 l dp vio	85.00	250.00
C22	AP17	10 l dk green	85.00	400.00
C23	AP17	12 l dk blue	85.00	450.00
C24	AP17	15 l car rose	85.00	450.00
C25	AP17	20 l gray blk	85.00	450.00

Nos. C20-C25 (6)   510.00   2,215.

Balbo Flight Issue

Italian Air Post Stamps of 1933 Ovptd.

1933

C26	AP25	5.25 l + 19.75 l grn, red & bl gray	55.00	150.00
C27	AP25	5.25 l + 44.75 l red, grn & bl gray	55.00	150.00

Soccer Issue

Types of Italian Air Post Stamps of 1934 Overprinted in Black or Red Like #31-35

1934

C28	AP32	50c brown (R)	18.00	72.50
C29	AP33	75c rose red (R)	18.00	72.50
C30	AP34	5 l + 2.50 l red org	29.00	145.00
C31	AP35	10 l + 5 l grn (R)	29.00	170.00

Nos. C28-C31 (4)   94.00   460.00

Types of Medal of Valor Issue of Italy Overprinted in Red or Black Like Nos. 31-35

1935

C32	AP36	25c dp grn	60.00	100.00
C33	AP36	50c blk brn (R)	60.00	100.00
C34	AP36	75c rose	60.00	100.00
C35	AP36	80c dk brn	60.00	100.00
C36	AP36	1 l + 50c ol grn	42.50	100.00
C37	AP36	2 l + 1 l dp bl (R)	42.50	100.00
C38	AP40	3 l + 2 l vio (R)	42.50	100.00

Nos. C32-C38 (7)   367.50   700.00

Types of Italy Air Post Stamps, 1937, Overprinted in Blue or Red Like Nos. 47-56

1938   Wmk. 140   Perf. 14

C39	AP51	25c dl gray vio (R)	4.25	7.00
C40	AP51	50c grn (R)	4.25	7.00
C41	AP51	80c brt bl (R)	4.25	21.00
C42	AP51	1 l + 1 l rose lake	8.50	25.00
C43	AP51	5 l + 1 l rose red	11.00	50.00

Nos. C39-C43 (5)   32.25   110.00

Bimillenary of the birth of Augustus Caesar (Octavianus).

Statues of Stag and Roman Wolf — AP18

Plane over Government Palace, Rhodes — AP19

1940   Photo.

C44	AP18	50c olive blk	2.15	3.50
C45	AP19	1 l dk vio	2.15	3.60
C46	AP18	2 l + 75c dk bl	2.15	11.00
C47	AP19	5 l + 2.50 l cop brn	2.15	20.00

Nos. C44-C47 (4)   8.60   38.10

Triennial Overseas Exposition, Naples.

AIR POST SPECIAL DELIVERY STAMPS

Type of Italian Garibaldi Air Post Special Delivery Stamps Overprinted in Blue or Ocher Like Nos. 12-18

1932   Wmk. 140   Perf. 14

CE1	APSD1	2.25 l + 1 l bl & rose & (Bl)	85.00	230.00
CE2	APSD1	4.50 l + 1.50 l ocher & gray (O)	85.00	230.00

Type of Medal of Valor Issue of Italy, Ovptd. in Black

ITALY — AEGEAN ISLANDS

1935
CE3	APSD4	2 l + 1.25 l dp bl	42.50	100.00
CE4	APSD4	4.50 l + 2 l grn	42.50	100.00

ISSUES FOR THE INDIVIDUAL ISLANDS

Italian Stamps of 1901-20 Overprinted with Names of Various Islands as

a   b

c

The 1912-22 issues of each island have type "a" overprint in black on all values except 15c (type A58) and 20c on 15c, which have type "b" overprint in violet.
The 1930-32 Ferrucci and Garibaldi issues are types of the Italian issues overprinted type "c". Stamps with type "c" overprints are also listed in Castellorizo.

CALCHI

(Halki)

Overprinted "Karki" in Black or Violet

1912-22   Wmk. 140   Perf. 13½, 14
1	A43	2c orange brn	7.25	8.50
a.		Double overprint	360.00	540.00
2	A48	5c green	4.25	8.50
3	A48	10c claret	1.40	8.50
4	A48	15c slate ('22)	4.25	42.50
a.		Double overprint	360.00	
5	A50	20c brn org ('21)	4.25	40.00
6	A49	25c blue	1.40	8.50
7	A49	40c brown	1.40	8.50
8	A49	50c violet	1.40	17.00

Unwmk.
9	A58	15c slate (V)	42.50	17.00
10	A50	20c brn org ('17)	215.00	155.00
		Nos. 1-10 (10)	283.10	314.00

No. 9 Surcharged

1916   Perf. 13½
11	A58	20c on 15c slate	2.15	25.00

Ferrucci Issue
Types of Italy
Overprinted in Red or Blue

1930   Wmk. 140   Perf. 14
12	A102	20c vio (R)	3.50	8.50
13	A103	25c dk grn (R)	3.50	8.50
14	A103	50c blk (R)	3.50	14.00
15	A103	1.25 l dp bl (R)	3.50	14.00
16	A104	5 l + 2 l dp car (Bl)	10.00	25.00
		Nos. 12-16 (5)	24.00	70.00

Garibaldi Issue
Types of Italy
Overprinted "CARCHI" in Red or Blue

1932
17	A138	10c brown	17.00	30.00
18	A138	20c red brn (Bl)	17.00	30.00
19	A138	25c dp grn	17.00	30.00
20	A138	30c bluish sl	17.00	30.00
21	A138	50c red vio (Bl)	17.00	30.00
22	A141	75c cop red (Bl)	17.00	30.00
23	A141	1.25 l dl bl	17.00	30.00
24	A141	1.75 l + 25c brn	17.00	30.00
25	A144	2.55 l + 50c org (Bl)	17.00	32.50
26	A145	5 l + 1 l dl vio	17.00	32.50
		Nos. 17-26 (10)	170.00	305.00

CALINO

(Kalymnos, Kalimnos)

Overprinted "Calimno" in Black or Violet

1912-21   Wmk. 140   Perf. 13½, 14
1	A43	2c orange brn	8.50	8.50
2	A48	5c green	2.75	8.50
3	A48	10c claret	1.45	8.50
4	A48	15c slate ('21)	4.25	50.00
5	A50	20c brn org ('21)	4.25	50.00
6	A49	25c blue	8.50	8.50
7	A49	40c brown	1.10	8.50
8	A49	50c violet	1.10	17.00

Unwmk.
9	A58	15c slate (V)	35.00	17.00
10	A50	20c brn org ('17)	85.00	210.00
		Nos. 1-10 (10)	151.90	386.50

No. 9 Surcharged Like Calchi No. 11

1916   Perf. 13½
11	A58	20c on 15c slate	16.00	35.00

Ferrucci Issue
Types of Italy
Overprinted in Red or Blue

1930   Wmk. 140   Perf. 14
12	A102	20c violet (R)	3.50	8.50
13	A103	25c dk grn (R)	3.50	8.50
14	A103	50c black (R)	3.50	14.50
15	A103	1.25 l dp bl (R)	3.50	14.50
16	A104	5 l + 2 l dp car (Bl)	3.50	25.00
		Nos. 12-16 (5)	17.50	71.00

Garibaldi Issue
Types of Italy
Overprinted in Red or Blue

1932
17	A138	10c brown	17.00	30.00
18	A138	20c red brn (Bl)	17.00	30.00
19	A138	25c dp grn	17.00	30.00
20	A138	30c bluish sl	17.00	30.00
21	A138	50c red vio (Bl)	17.00	30.00
22	A141	75c cop red (Bl)	17.00	30.00
23	A141	1.25 l dull blue	17.00	30.00
24	A141	1.75 l + 25c brn	17.00	30.00
25	A144	2.55 l + 50c org (Bl)	17.00	30.00
26	A145	5 l + 1 l dl vio	17.00	30.00
		Nos. 17-26 (10)	170.00	300.00

CASO

(Kasos, Kassos)

Overprinted "Caso" in Black or Violet

1912-21   Wmk. 140   Perf. 13½, 14
1	A43	2c orange brn	7.25	8.50
2	A48	5c green	4.25	8.50
3	A48	10c claret	1.40	8.50
4	A48	15c slate ('21)	4.25	42.50
5	A50	20c brn org ('20)	3.50	30.00
6	A49	25c blue	1.45	8.50
7	A49	40c brown	1.45	8.50
8	A49	50c violet	1.45	17.00

Unwmk.
9	A58	15c slate (V)	42.50	17.00
10	A50	20c brn org ('17)	125.00	200.00
		Nos. 1-10 (10)	192.50	349.00

No. 9 Surcharged Like Calchi No. 11

1916   Perf. 13½
11	A58	20c on 15c slate	1.45	35.00

Ferrucci Issue
Types of Italy
Overprinted in Red or Blue

1930   Wmk. 140   Perf. 14
12	A102	20c violet (R)	3.50	7.00
13	A103	25c dk green (R)	3.50	7.00
14	A103	50c black (R)	3.50	12.50
15	A103	1.25 l dp bl (R)	3.50	12.50
16	A104	5 l + 2 l dp car (Bl)	10.00	22.50
		Nos. 12-16 (5)	24.00	61.50

Garibaldi Issue
Types of Italy
Overprinted in Red or Blue

1932
17	A138	10c brown	17.00	30.00
18	A138	20c red brn (Bl)	17.00	30.00
19	A138	25c dp grn	17.00	30.00
20	A138	30c bluish sl	17.00	30.00
21	A138	50c red vio (Bl)	17.00	30.00
22	A141	75c cop red (Bl)	17.00	30.00
23	A141	1.25 l dull blue	17.00	30.00
24	A141	1.75 l + 25c brn	17.00	30.00
25	A144	2.55 l + 50c org (Bl)	17.00	30.00
26	A145	5 l + 1 l dl vio	17.00	30.00
		Nos. 17-26 (10)	170.00	300.00

COO

(Cos, Kos)

Overprinted "Cos" in Black or Violet

1912-22   Wmk. 140   Perf. 13½, 14
1	A43	2c orange brn	8.00	9.50
2	A48	5c green	100.00	9.50
3	A48	10c claret	4.75	9.50
4	A48	15c slate ('22)	4.75	55.00
5	A50	20c brn org ('21)	4.00	35.00
6	A49	25c blue	40.00	9.50
7	A49	40c brown	1.60	9.50
8	A49	50c violet	1.60	19.00

Unwmk.
9	A58	15c slate (V)	60.00	19.00
10	A50	20c brn org ('17)	65.00	225.00
		Nos. 1-10 (10)	289.70	400.50

No. 9 Surcharged Like Calchi No. 11

1916   Perf. 13½
11	A58	20c on 15c slate	19.00	40.00

Ferrucci Issue
Types of Italy
Overprinted in Red or Blue

1930   Wmk. 140   Perf. 14
12	A102	20c violet (R)	4.00	9.50
13	A103	25c dk green (R)	4.00	9.50
14	A103	50c black (R)	4.00	16.00
15	A103	1.25 l dp bl (R)	4.00	16.00
16	A104	5 l + 2 l dp car (Bl)	11.00	27.50
		Nos. 12-16 (5)	27.00	78.50

Garibaldi Issue
Types of Italy
Overprinted in Red or Blue

1932
17	A138	10c brown	19.00	35.00
18	A138	20c red brn (Bl)	19.00	35.00
19	A138	25c dp grn	19.00	35.00
20	A138	30c bluish sl	19.00	35.00
21	A138	50c red vio (Bl)	19.00	35.00
22	A141	75c cop red (Bl)	19.00	35.00
23	A141	1.25 l dull blue	19.00	35.00
24	A141	1.75 l + 25c brn	19.00	35.00
25	A144	2.55 l + 50c org (Bl)	19.00	35.00
26	A145	5 l + 1 l dl vio	19.00	35.00
		Nos. 17-26 (10)	190.00	350.00

LERO

(Leros)

Overprinted "Leros" in Black or Violet

1912-22   Wmk. 140   Perf. 13½, 14
1	A43	2c orange brn	9.50	9.50
2	A48	5c green	8.00	9.50
3	A48	10c claret	3.25	9.50
4	A48	15c slate ('22)	4.75	40.00
5	A50	20c brn org ('21)	175.00	125.00
6	A49	25c blue	72.50	9.50
7	A49	40c brown	4.75	9.50
8	A49	50c violet	1.60	19.00

Unwmk.
9	A58	15c slate (V)	87.50	19.00
10	A50	20c brn org ('17)	65.00	225.00
		Nos. 1-10 (10)	431.85	475.50

No. 9 Surcharged Like Calchi No. 11

1916   Perf. 13½
11	A58	20c on 15c slate	19.00	40.00

Ferrucci Issue
Types of Italy
Overprinted in Red or Blue

1930   Perf. 14
12	A102	20c violet (R)	4.00	9.50
13	A103	25c dk green (R)	4.00	9.50
14	A103	50c black (R)	4.00	16.00
15	A103	1.25 l dp bl (R)	4.00	16.00
16	A104	5 l + 2 l dp car (Bl)	11.00	27.50
		Nos. 12-16 (5)	27.00	78.50

Garibaldi Issue
Types of Italy
Overprinted in Red or Blue

1932
17	A138	10c brown	19.00	35.00
18	A138	20c red brn (Bl)	19.00	35.00
19	A138	25c dp grn	19.00	35.00
20	A138	30c bluish sl	19.00	35.00
21	A138	50c red vio (Bl)	19.00	35.00
22	A141	75c cop red (Bl)	19.00	35.00
23	A141	1.25 l dull blue	19.00	35.00
24	A141	1.75 l + 25c brn	19.00	35.00
25	A144	2.55 l + 50c org (Bl)	19.00	35.00
26	A145	5 l + 1 l dl vio	19.00	35.00
		Nos. 17-26 (10)	190.00	350.00

LISSO

(Lipsi, Loipsoi)

Overprinted "Lipso" in Black or Violet

1912-22   Wmk. 140   Perf. 13½, 14
1	A43	2c orange brn	8.00	9.50
2	A48	5c green	4.75	9.50
3	A48	10c claret	3.25	9.50
4	A48	15c slate ('22)	4.75	40.00
5	A50	20c brn org ('21)	4.75	47.50
6	A49	25c blue	1.60	9.50
7	A49	40c brown	3.25	9.50
8	A49	50c violet	1.60	19.00

Unwmk.
9	A58	15c slate (V)	47.50	19.00
10	A50	20c brn org ('17)	95.00	225.00
		Nos. 1-10 (10)	174.45	398.00

No. 9 Surcharged Like Calchi No. 11

1916   Perf. 13½
11	A58	20c on 15c slate	1.60	40.00

Ferrucci Issue
Types of Italy
Overprinted in Red or Blue

1930   Wmk. 140   Perf. 14
12	A102	20c violet (R)	4.00	9.50
13	A103	25c dk green (R)	4.00	9.50
14	A103	50c black (R)	4.00	16.00
15	A103	1.25 l dp bl (R)	4.00	16.00
16	A104	5 l + 2 l dp car (Bl)	11.00	29.00
		Nos. 12-16 (5)	27.00	80.00

Garibaldi Issue
Types of Italy
Overprinted "LIPSO" in Red or Blue

1932
17	A138	10c brown	19.00	35.00
18	A138	20c red brn (Bl)	19.00	35.00
19	A138	25c dp grn	19.00	35.00
20	A138	30c bluish sl	19.00	35.00
21	A138	50c red vio (Bl)	19.00	35.00
22	A141	75c cop red (Bl)	19.00	35.00
23	A141	1.25 l dull blue	19.00	35.00
24	A141	1.75 l + 25c brn	19.00	35.00
25	A144	2.55 l + 50c org (Bl)	19.00	35.00
26	A145	5 l + 1 l dl vio	19.00	35.00
		Nos. 17-26 (10)	190.00	350.00

NISIRO

(Nissiros, Nisyros)

Overprinted "Nisiros" in Black or Violet

1912-22   Wmk. 140   Perf. 13½, 14
1	A43	2c orange brn	8.00	9.50
2	A48	5c green	4.75	9.50
3	A48	10c claret	1.60	9.50
4	A48	15c slate ('22)	32.50	55.00
5	A50	20c brn org ('21)	110.00	125.00
6	A49	25c blue	3.25	9.50
7	A49	40c brown	1.60	9.50
8	A49	50c violet	4.00	19.00

Unwmk.
9	A58	15c slate (V)	47.50	19.00
10	A50	20c brn org ('17)	140.00	225.00
		Nos. 1-10 (10)	353.20	490.50

No. 9 Surcharged Like Calchi No. 11

1916   Perf. 13½
11	A58	20c on 15c slate	1.60	40.00

Ferrucci Issue
Types of Italy
Overprinted in Red or Blue

1930   Wmk. 140   Perf. 14
12	A102	20c violet (R)	4.00	9.50
13	A103	25c dk grn (R)	4.00	9.50
14	A103	50c black (R)	4.00	16.00
15	A103	1.25 l dp bl (R)	4.00	16.00
16	A104	5 l + 2 l dp car (Bl)	11.00	27.50
		Nos. 12-16 (5)	27.00	78.50

ITALY — AEGEAN ISLANDS

Garibaldi Issue
Types of Italy
Overprinted in Red or Blue

1932
17	A138	10c brown	19.00	35.00
18	A138	20c red brn (Bl)	19.00	35.00
19	A138	25c dp grn	19.00	35.00
20	A138	30c bluish sl	19.00	35.00
21	A138	50c red vio (Bl)	19.00	35.00
22	A141	75c cop red (Bl)	19.00	35.00
23	A141	1.25 l dull blue	19.00	35.00
24	A141	1.75 l + 25c brn	19.00	35.00
25	A144	2.55 l + 50c org (Bl)	19.00	35.00
26	A145	5 l + 1 l dl vio	19.00	35.00
	Nos. 17-26 (10)		190.00	350.00

PATMO

(Patmos)
Overprinted "Patmos" in Black or Violet

1912-22   Wmk. 140   Perf. 13½, 14
1	A43	2c orange brn	8.00	9.50
2	A48	5c green	4.75	9.50
3	A48	10c claret	3.25	9.50
4	A48	15c slate ('22)	4.75	52.50
5	A50	20c brn org ('21)	175.00	225.00
6	A49	25c blue	1.60	9.50
7	A49	40c brown	4.00	9.50
8	A49	50c violet	1.60	19.00
		Unwmk.		
9	A58	15c slate (V)	47.50	19.00
10	A50	20c brn org ('17)	95.00	225.00
	Nos. 1-10 (10)		345.45	588.00

No. 9 Surcharged Like Calchi No. 11

1916   Perf. 13½
11	A58	20c on 15c slate	19.00	40.00

Ferrucci Issue
Types of Italy
Overprinted in Red or Blue

1930   Wmk. 140   Perf. 14
12	A102	20c violet (R)	4.00	9.50
13	A103	25c dk green (R)	4.00	9.50
14	A103	50c black (R)	4.00	16.00
15	A103	1.25 l dp bl (R)	4.00	16.00
16	A104	5 l + 2 l dp car (Bl)	11.00	29.00
	Nos. 12-16 (5)		27.00	80.00

Garibaldi Issue
Types of Italy
Overprinted in Red or Blue

1932
17	A138	10c brown	19.00	35.00
18	A138	20c red brn (Bl)	19.00	35.00
19	A138	25c dp grn	19.00	35.00
20	A138	30c bluish sl	19.00	35.00
21	A138	50c red vio (Bl)	19.00	35.00
22	A141	75c cop red (Bl)	19.00	35.00
23	A141	1.25 l dull blue	19.00	35.00
24	A141	1.75 l + 25c brn	19.00	35.00
25	A144	2.55 l + 50c org (Bl)	19.00	35.00
26	A145	5 l + 1 l dl vio	19.00	35.00
	Nos. 17-26 (10)		190.00	350.00

PISCOPI

(Episkopi, Tilos)
Overprinted "Piscopi" in Black or Violet

1912-21   Wmk. 140   Perf. 13½, 14
1	A43	2c orange brn	8.00	9.50
2	A48	5c green	4.75	9.50
3	A48	10c claret	1.60	9.50
4	A48	15c slate ('21)	19.00	52.50
5	A50	20c brn org ('21)	65.00	72.50
6	A49	25c blue	1.60	9.50
7	A49	40c brown	1.60	9.50
8	A49	50c violet	1.60	19.00
		Unwmk.		
9	A58	15c slate (V)	47.50	19.00
10	A50	20c brn org ('17)	95.00	225.00
	Nos. 1-10 (10)		245.65	435.50

No. 9 Surcharged Like Calchi No. 11

1916   Perf. 13½
11	A58	20c on 15c slate	1.60	40.00

Ferrucci Issue
Types of Italy
Overprinted in Red or Blue

1930   Wmk. 140   Perf. 14
12	A102	20c violet (R)	4.00	9.50
13	A103	25c dk green (R)	4.00	9.50
14	A103	50c black (R)	4.00	16.00
15	A103	1.25 l dp bl (R)	4.00	16.00
16	A104	5 l + 2 l dp car (Bl)	11.00	29.00
	Nos. 12-16 (5)		27.00	80.00

Garibaldi Issue
Types of Italy
Overprinted in Red or Blue

1932
17	A138	10c brown	19.00	35.00
18	A138	20c red brn (Bl)	19.00	35.00
19	A138	25c dp grn	19.00	35.00
20	A138	30c bluish sl	19.00	35.00
21	A138	50c red vio (Bl)	19.00	35.00
22	A141	75c cop red (Bl)	19.00	35.00
23	A141	1.25 l dull blue	19.00	35.00
24	A141	1.75 l + 25c brn	19.00	35.00
25	A144	2.55 l + 50c org (Bl)	19.00	35.00
26	A145	5 l + 1 l dl vio	19.00	35.00
	Nos. 17-26 (10)		190.00	350.00

RHODES

(Rodi)
Overprinted "Rodi" in Black or Violet

1912-24   Wmk. 140   Perf. 13½, 14
1	A43	2c org brn	1.60	9.50
2	A48	5c green	4.75	9.50
	a.	Double overprint	400.00	600.00
3	A48	10c claret	1.60	9.50
4	A48	15c slate ('21)	175.00	72.50
5	A45	20c org ('16)	3.25	8.00
6	A50	20c brn org ('19)	6.50	20.00
	a.	Double overprint	87.50	
7	A49	25c blue	4.75	9.50
8	A49	40c brown	6.50	9.50
9	A49	50c violet	1.60	19.00
10	A49	85c red brn ('22)	87.50	125.00
11	A46	1 l brn & grn ('24)	3.25	

No. 11 was not regularly issued.

Unwmk.
12	A58	15c slate (V)	47.50	19.00
13	A50	20c brn org ('17)	240.00	225.00
	Nos. 1-13 (13)		583.80	536.00

No. 12 Surcharged Like Calchi No. 11

1916   Perf. 13½
14	A58	20c on 15c slate	140.00	175.00

Windmill, Rhodes — A1
Medieval Galley — A2
Christian Knight — A3
Crusader Kneeling in Prayer — A4
Crusader's Tomb — A5

No Imprint

1929   Unwmk.   Litho.   Perf. 11
15	A1	5c magenta	11.00	2.40
16	A2	10c olive brn	11.00	1.60
17	A3	20c rose red	11.00	.80
18	A3	25c green	11.00	.80
19	A4	30c dk blue	72.50	2.40
20	A4	50c dk brown	11.00	.80
21	A5	1.25 l dk blue	11.00	2.40
22	A4	5 l magenta	80.00	140.00
23	A4	10 l olive brn	240.00	340.00
	Nos. 15-23 (9)		458.50	491.20

Visit of the King and Queen of Italy to the Aegean Islands. The stamps are inscribed "Rodi" but were available for use in all the Aegean Islands.

Nos. 15-23 and C1-C4 were used in eastern Crete in 1941-42 with Greek postmarks.

See Nos. 55-63. For surcharges and overprints see Nos. 29-44, B1-B18, E3-E4.

Ferrucci Issue
Types of Italy
Overprinted in Red or Blue

1930   Wmk. 140   Perf. 14
24	A102	20c violet (R)	4.00	9.50
25	A103	25c dk green (R)	4.00	9.50
26	A103	50c black (R)	4.00	16.00
27	A103	1.25 l dp blue (R)	4.00	16.00
28	A104	5 l + 2 l dp car (Bl)	11.00	29.00
	Nos. 24-28 (5)		27.00	80.00

Hydrological Congress Issue

Rhodes Issue of 1929 Overprinted

1930   Unwmk.   Perf. 11
29	A1	5c magenta	65.00	55.00
30	A2	10c olive brn	65.00	55.00
31	A3	20c rose red	72.50	55.00
32	A3	25c green	80.00	55.00
33	A4	30c dk blue	65.00	55.00
34	A4	50c dk brown	600.00	95.00
35	A5	1.25 l dk blue	450.00	140.00
36	A4	5 l magenta	400.00	600.00
37	A4	10 l olive grn	400.00	650.00
	Nos. 29-37 (9)		2,198.	1,760.

Rhodes Issue of 1929 Overprinted in Blue or Red

1931
38	A1	5c mag (Bl)	9.50	22.50
39	A2	10c ol brn (R)	9.50	22.50
40	A3	20c rose red (Bl)	9.50	37.50
41	A3	25c green (R)	9.50	37.50
42	A4	30c dk blue (R)	9.50	37.50
43	A5	50c dk brown (R)	65.00	87.50
44	A5	1.25 l dk bl (R)	55.00	125.00
	Nos. 39-44 (7)		167.50	370.00

Italian Eucharistic Congress, 1931.

Garibaldi Issue
Types of Italy
Overprinted in Red or Blue

1932   Wmk. 140   Perf. 14
45	A138	10c brown	19.00	35.00
46	A138	20c red brn (Bl)	19.00	35.00
47	A138	25c dp grn	19.00	35.00
48	A138	30c bluish sl	19.00	35.00
49	A138	50c red vio (Bl)	19.00	35.00
50	A141	75c cop red (Bl)	19.00	35.00
51	A141	1.25 l dl bl	19.00	35.00
52	A141	1.75 l + 25c brn	19.00	35.00
53	A144	2.55 l + 50c org (Bl)	19.00	35.00
54	A145	5 l + 1 l dl vio	19.00	35.00
	Nos. 45-54 (10)		190.00	350.00

Types of Rhodes Issue of 1929
Imprint: "Officina Carte-Valori Roma"

1932
55	A1	5c rose lake	1.60	.25
56	A2	10c dk brn	1.60	.25
57	A3	20c red	1.60	.25
58	A3	25c dl grn	1.60	.25
59	A4	30c dl bl	1.60	.25
60	A5	50c blk brn	1.60	.25
61	A5	1.25 l dp bl	1.60	.25
62	A4	5 l rose lake	1.60	2.25
63	A4	10 l ol brn	4.00	4.75
	Nos. 55-63 (9)		16.80	8.75

Aerial View of Rhodes — A6
Map of Rhodes — A7

1932   Wmk. 140   Litho.   Perf. 11

Shield in Red
64	A6	5c blk & grn	9.50	24.00
65	A6	10c blk & vio bl	9.50	20.00
66	A6	20c blk & dl yel	9.50	20.00
67	A6	25c lil & blk	9.50	20.00
68	A6	30c blk & pink	9.50	20.00

Shield and Map Dots in Red
69	A7	50c blk & gray	9.50	20.00
70	A7	1.25 l red brn & gray	9.50	40.00
71	A7	5 l dk bl & gray	24.00	100.00
72	A7	10 l dk grn & gray	65.00	180.00
73	A7	25 l choc & gray	250.00	1,200.
	Nos. 64-73 (10)		405.50	1,644.

20th anniv. of the Italian occupation and 10th anniv. of Fascist rule.

Deer and Palm — A8

1935, Apr.   Photo.   Wmk. 140
74	A8	5c orange	27.50	35.00
75	A8	10c brown	27.50	35.00
76	A8	20c car rose	27.50	45.00
77	A8	25c green	27.50	45.00
78	A8	30c purple	27.50	52.50
79	A8	50c red brn	27.50	52.50
80	A8	1.25 l blue	27.50	120.00
81	A8	5 l yellow	240.00	450.00
	Nos. 74-81 (8)		432.50	835.00

Holy Year.

The above overprints on No. 55 are stated to have been prepared locally for use on German military correspondence, but banned by postal authorities in Berlin.

RHODES SEMI-POSTAL STAMPS

Rhodes Nos. 55-62 Surcharged in Black or Red

1943   Wmk. 140   Perf. 14
B1	A1	5c + 5c rose lake	3.75	4.50
B2	A2	10c + 10c dk brn	3.75	4.50
B3	A3	20c + 20c red	3.75	4.50
B4	A3	25c + 25c dl grn	3.75	4.50
B5	A4	30c + 30c dl bl (R)	6.00	7.50
B6	A5	50c + 50c blk brn	6.00	7.50
B7	A5	1.25 l + 1.25 l dp bl (R)	7.50	11.00
B8	A4	5 l + 5 l rose lake	150.00	250.00
	Nos. B1-B8 (8)		184.50	294.00

The surtax was for general relief.

Rhodes Nos. 55-58, 60 and 61 Surcharged in Black or Red

1944
B9	A1	5c + 3 l rose lake	4.50	10.50
B10	A2	10c + 3 l dk brn (R)	4.50	10.50
B11	A3	20c + 3 l red	4.50	10.50
B12	A3	25c + 3 l dl grn (R)	4.50	10.50
B13	A5	50c + 3 l blk brn (R)	4.50	10.50
B14	A5	1.25 l + 5 l dp bl (R)	37.50	70.00
	Nos. B9-B14 (6)		60.00	122.50

The surtax was for war victims.

Rhodes Nos. 62 and 63 Surcharged in Red

1945
B17	A4	5 l + 10 l rose lake	15.00	34.00
B18	A4	10 l + 10 l ol brn	15.00	34.00

The surtax was for the Red Cross.

ITALY — AEGEAN ISLANDS — TRIESTE

RHODES AIR POST STAMPS

Symbolical of Flight — AP18

Wmk. 140 Upright (No. C1), Sideways (No. C2a-C4a)

1937-38		Typo.		Perf. 14	
C1	AP18	50c blk & yel		.80	.40
C2a	AP18	80c blk & mag		.80	2.40
C3a	AP18	1 l blk & grn		.80	.40
C4a	AP18	5 l blk & red vio		1.60	4.75
		Nos. C1-C4a (4)		4.25	8.30

Nos. C2a-C4a were issued in 1937-38, on paper with sideways watermark. The 1935 first printing, which includes C1, is on paper within which the watermark is upright. For detailed listings, see the *Scott Classic Specialized Catalogue*.

RHODES AIR POST SEMI-POSTAL STAMPS

Rhodes Nos. C1-C4 Surcharged in Silver

1944		Wmk. 140		Perf. 14	
CB1	AP18	50c + 2 l		12.00	3.75
CB2	AP18	80c + 2 l		12.00	7.50
CB3	AP18	1 l + 2 l		16.00	9.00
CB4	AP18	5 l + 2 l		100.00	110.00
		Nos. CB1-CB4 (4)		140.00	130.25

The surtax was for war victims.

RHODES SPECIAL DELIVERY STAMPS

Stag — SD1

1936		Photo.		Wmk. 140		Perf. 14	
E1	SD1	1.25 l green				4.75	4.75
E2	SD1	2.50 l vermilion				8.00	8.00

Nos. 58 and 57 Surcharged in Black

1943				
E3	A3	1.25 l on 25c dl grn	1.50	3.75
E4	A3	2.50 l on 20c red	1.50	3.75

RHODES SEMI-POSTAL SPECIAL DELIVERY STAMPS

Rhodes Nos. E1 and E2 Srchd. in Red or Black

1943		Wmk. 140		Perf. 14	
EB1	SD1	1.25 l + 1.25 l (R)		82.50	92.50
EB2	SD1	2.50 l + 2.50 l		97.50	150.00

The surtax was for general relief.

RHODES POSTAGE DUE STAMPS

Maltese Cross PD1

Immortelle PD2

1934		Photo.		Wmk. 140		Perf. 13	
J1	PD1	5c vermilion				4.75	8.00
J2	PD1	10c carmine				4.75	8.00
J3	PD1	20c dk grn				4.75	6.50
J4	PD1	30c purple				4.75	6.50
J5	PD1	40c dk bl				4.75	12.50
J6	PD2	50c vermilion				4.75	6.50
J7	PD2	60c carmine				4.75	24.00
J8	PD2	1 l dk grn				4.75	24.00
J9	PD2	2 l purple				4.75	12.50
		Nos. J1-J9 (9)				42.75	108.50

RHODES PARCEL POST STAMPS

Both unused and used values are for complete stamps.

PP1

PP2

1934		Photo.		Wmk. 140		Perf. 13	
Q1	PP1	5c vermilion				6.50	12.00
Q2	PP1	10c carmine				6.50	12.00
Q3	PP1	20c dk green				6.50	12.00
Q4	PP1	25c purple				6.50	12.00
Q5	PP1	50c dk blue				6.50	12.00
Q6	PP1	60c black				6.50	12.00
Q7	PP2	1 l vermilion				6.50	12.00
Q8	PP2	2 l carmine				6.50	12.00
Q9	PP2	3 l dk green				6.50	12.00
Q10	PP2	4 l purple				6.50	12.00
Q11	PP2	10 l dk blue				6.50	12.00
		Nos. Q1-Q11 (11)				71.50	132.00

Value of used halves, Nos. Q1-Q11, each 80 cents.

See note preceding No. Q7 of Italy.

SCARPANTO

(Karpathos)

Overprinted "Scarpanto" in Black or Violet

1912-22		Wmk. 140		Perf. 13½, 14	
1	A43	2c org brn		9.50	9.50
2	A48	5c green		3.25	9.50
3	A48	10c claret		1.60	9.50
4	A48	15c slate ('22)		19.00	40.00
5	A50	20c brn org ('21)		65.00	65.00
6	A49	25c blue		9.50	9.50
7	A49	40c brown		1.60	9.50
8	A49	50c violet		3.25	19.00

Unwmk.

9	A58	15c slate (V)		40.00	19.00
10	A50	20c brn org ('17)		140.00	225.00
		Nos. 1-10 (10)		292.70	415.50

No 9 Surcharged Like Calchi No. 11

1916				Perf. 13½	
11	A58	20c on 15c slate		1.60	40.00

Ferrucci Issue
Types of Italy
Overprinted in Red or Blue

1930		Wmk. 140		Perf. 14	
12	A102	20c violet (R)		4.00	9.50
13	A103	25c dk green (R)		4.00	9.50
14	A103	50c black (R)		4.00	16.00
15	A103	1.25 l dp bl (R)		4.00	16.00
16	A104	5 l + 2 l dp car (Bl)		11.00	27.50
		Nos. 12-16 (5)		27.00	78.50

Garibaldi Issue
Types of Italy
Overprinted in Red or Blue

1932					
17	A138	10c brown		19.00	35.00
18	A138	20c red brn (Bl)		19.00	35.00
19	A138	25c dp grn		19.00	35.00
20	A138	30c bluish sl		19.00	35.00
21	A138	50c red vio (Bl)		19.00	35.00
22	A141	75c cop red (Bl)		19.00	35.00
23	A141	1.25 l dull blue		19.00	35.00
24	A141	1.75 l + 25c brn		19.00	35.00
25	A144	2.55 l + 50c org (Bl)		19.00	35.00
26	A145	5 l + 1 l dl vio		19.00	35.00
		Nos. 17-26 (10)		190.00	350.00

SIMI

(Symi)

Overprinted "Simi" in Black or Violet

1912-21		Wmk. 140		Perf. 13½, 14	
1	A43	2c org brn		16.00	9.50
2	A48	5c green		40.00	9.50
3	A48	10c claret		1.60	9.50
4	A48	15c slate ('21)		140.00	72.50
5	A50	20c brn org ('21)		72.50	40.00
6	A49	25c blue		9.50	9.50
7	A49	40c brown		1.60	9.50
8	A49	50c violet		1.60	19.00

Unwmk.

9	A58	15c slate (V)		72.00	19.00
10	A50	20c brn org ('17)		72.50	125.00
		Nos. 1-10 (10)		427.30	323.00

No. 9 Surcharged Like Calchi No. 11

1916				Perf. 13½	
11	A58	20c on 15c slate		9.50	40.00

Ferrucci Issue
Types of Italy
Overprinted in Red or Blue

1930		Wmk. 140		Perf. 14	
12	A102	20c violet (R)		4.75	9.50
13	A103	25c dk green (R)		4.75	9.50
14	A103	50c black (R)		4.75	16.00
15	A103	1.25 l dp bl (R)		4.75	16.00
16	A104	5 l + 2 l dp car (Bl)		11.00	27.50
		Nos. 12-16 (5)		30.00	78.50

Garibaldi Issue
Types of Italy
Overprinted in Red or Blue

1932					
17	A138	10c brown		19.00	35.00
18	A138	20c red brn (Bl)		19.00	35.00
19	A138	25c dp grn		19.00	35.00
20	A138	30c bluish sl		19.00	35.00
21	A138	50c red vio (Bl)		19.00	35.00
22	A141	75c cop red (Bl)		19.00	35.00
23	A141	1.25 l dull blue		19.00	35.00
24	A141	1.75 l + 25c brn		19.00	35.00
25	A144	2.55 l + 50c org (Bl)		19.00	35.00
26	A145	5 l + 1 l dl vio		19.00	35.00
		Nos. 17-26 (10)		190.00	350.00

STAMPALIA

(Astipalea, Astypalaia)

Overprinted "Stampalia" in Black or Violet

1912-21		Wmk. 140		Perf. 13½, 14	
1	A43	2c org brn		9.50	9.50
2	A48	5c green		1.60	9.50
3	A48	10c claret		1.60	9.50
4	A48	15c slate ('21)		11.00	40.00
5	A50	20c brn org ('21)		55.00	72.50
6	A49	25c blue		1.60	9.50
7	A49	40c brown		4.75	9.50
8	A49	50c violet		1.60	19.00

Unwmk.

9	A58	15c slate (V)		47.50	19.00
10	A50	20c brn org ('17)		95.00	125.00
		Nos. 1-10 (10)		229.15	323.00

No. 9 Surcharged Like Calchi No. 11

1916				Perf. 13½	
11	A58	20c on 15c slate		1.60	40.00

Ferrucci Issue
Types of Italy
Overprinted in Red or Blue

1930		Wmk. 140		Perf. 14	
12	A102	20c violet (R)		4.00	9.50
13	A103	25c dk green (R)		4.00	9.50
14	A103	50c black (R)		4.00	16.00
15	A103	1.25 l dp bl (R)		4.00	16.00
16	A104	5 l + 2 l dp car (Bl)		11.00	27.50
		Nos. 12-16 (5)		27.00	78.50

Garibaldi Issue
Types of Italy
Overprinted in Red or Blue

1932					
17	A138	10c brown		19.00	35.00
18	A138	20c red brn (Bl)		19.00	35.00
19	A138	25c dp grn		19.00	35.00
20	A138	30c bluish sl		19.00	35.00
21	A138	50c red vio (Bl)		19.00	35.00
22	A141	75c cop red (Bl)		19.00	35.00
23	A141	1.25 l dull blue		19.00	35.00
24	A141	1.75 l + 25c brn		19.00	35.00
25	A144	2.55 l + 50c org (Bl)		19.00	35.00
26	A145	5 l + 1 l dl vio		19.00	35.00
		Nos. 17-26 (10)		190.00	350.00

TRIESTE

A free territory (1947-1954) on the Adriatic Sea between Italy and Yugoslavia. In 1954 the territory was divided, Italy acquiring the northern section and seaport, Yugoslavia the southern section (Zone B).

Catalogue values for all unused stamps in this country are for Never Hinged items.

ZONE A

Issued jointly by the Allied Military Government of the United States and Great Britain

Stamps of Italy 1945-47 Overprinted

a

b

c

The letters "F. T. T." are the initials of "Free Territory of Trieste."

1947, Oct. 1		Wmk. 277		Perf. 14	
1	A259(a)	25c brt bl grn		.30	1.60
2	A255(a)	50c dp vio		.30	1.60
3	A257(a)	1 l dk grn		.30	.25
4	A258(a)	2 l dk cl brn		.30	.25
5	A259(a)	3 l red		.30	.25
6	A259(a)	4 l red org		.30	.25
7	A256(a)	5 l deep blue		.30	.25
8	A257(a)	6 l dp vio		.30	.25
9	A255(a)	10 l slate		.30	.25
10	A257(a)	15 l deep blue		2.75	.25
11	A259(a)	20 l dk red vio		4.50	.25
12	A260(b)	25 l dk grn		6.50	13.00
13	A260(b)	50 l dk vio brn		7.00	8.00

Perf. 14x13½

| 14 | A261(c) | 100 l car lake | | 55.00 | 45.00 |
| | | Nos. 1-14 (14) | | 78.45 | 71.45 |

Italy Nos. 486-488 Ovptd. Type "a"

1948, Mar. 1				Perf. 14	
15	A255	8 l dk green		6.50	11.00
16	A256	1 l red org		20.00	.30
17	A259	30 l dk blue		275.00	19.00
		Nos. 15-17 (3)		301.50	30.30

Italy Nos. 495 to 506 Overprinted — d

1948, July 1					
18	A272	3 l dk brn		.45	.45
19	A272	4 l red vio		.45	.45
20	A272	5 l deep blue		.45	.45
21	A272	6 l dp yel grn		.90	.45
22	A272	8 l brown		.45	.45
23	A272	10 l org red		.90	.45
24	A272	12 l dk gray grn		.90	1.40
25	A272	15 l gray blk		20.00	17.50
26	A272	20 l car rose		35.00	17.50
27	A272	30 l brt ultra		2.75	2.75

ITALY — TRIESTE

28	A272	50 l violet		24.00	32.50
29	A272	100 l bl blk		52.50	80.00
	Nos. 18-29 (12)			138.75	154.35

Italy Nos. 486-488 Overprinted in Carmine

1948, Sept. 8

30	A255	8 l dk green		.30	.25
31	A256	10 l red org		.30	.25
32	A259	30 l dk blue		2.75	2.75
	Nos. 30-32,C17-C19 (6)			6.55	6.45

The overprint is embossed.

Italy No. 507 Overprinted in Carmine

1948, Oct. 15

33	A273	15 l dk green	6.00	6.00

Italy No. 508 Overprinted in Green — e

1948, Nov. 15

34	A274	15 l dk brown	20.00	4.00

Italy No. 509 Overprinted in Red

1949, May 2   Wmk. 277   Perf. 14

35	A275	20 l dk brown	16.00	8.00

Italy Nos. 510-513 Overprinted — f

1949, May 2   Buff Background

36	A276	5 l red brown		.80	1.60
37	A276	15 l dk green		13.00	24.00
38	A276	20 l dp red brn		7.25	1.60
39	A276	50 l dk blue		16.00	12.00
	Nos. 36-39 (4)			37.05	39.20

Italy No. 514 Overprinted in Red

1949, May 2

40	A277	50 l brt ultra	5.50	5.50

Italy No. 518 Overprinted in Red

1949, May 30

41	A279	100 l brown	72.50	120.00

Italy Nos. 515-517 Overprinted in Black

1949, June 15

42	A278	5 l dk green		14.50	9.50
43	A278	15 l violet		14.50	17.50
44	A278	20 l brown		14.50	14.50
	Nos. 42-44 (3)			43.50	41.50

Italy Nos. 519 and 520 Overprinted in Carmine

1949, July 16

45	A280	20 l gray	14.50	8.00
46	A281	20 l brown	14.50	8.00

Italy, No. 521 Ovptd. in Green — g

1949, June 8

47	A282	20 l brown red	8.00	8.00

Italy No. 522 Overprinted in Carmine

1949, July 8

49	A283	20 l violet	22.50	16.00

Italy No. 523 Overprinted in Black, Without Periods

1949, Aug. 27

50	A284	20 l violet blue	16.00	8.00

Italy No. 524 Overprinted

1949, Aug. 27

51	A285	20 l violet	24.00	24.00

Italy No. 525 Overprinted in Green

1949, Sept. 10

52	A286	20 l red	14.50	8.00

Italy Nos. 526 and 527 Overprinted — h

Wmk. 277

1949, Nov. 7   Photo.   Perf. 14

53	A287	20 l rose car	6.50	6.50
54	A288	50 l deep blue	24.00	26.00

No. 528 Overprinted

1949, Nov. 7

55	A289	20 l dp grn	8.75	6.50

No. 529 Overprinted

1949, Nov. 7

56	A290	20 l brt blue	5.50	4.75

No. 530 Overprint in Red

1949, Dec. 28

57	A291	20 l violet blk	7.25	4.00

Italian Stamps of 1945-48 Overprinted in Black

1949-50   Photo.

58	A257	1	dk green	.25	1.00
59	A258	2	dk cl brn	.25	.25
60	A259	3	red	.25	.25
61	A256	5	deep blue	.25	.25
62	A257	6	dp violet	.25	.25
63	A255	8	dk green	55.00	47.50
64	A256	10	red org	.25	.25
65	A257	15	deep blue	4.00	.80
66	A259	20	dk red vio	2.40	.25
67	A260	25	dk grn ('50)	40.00	4.75
68	A260	50	dk vio brn ('50)	60.00	4.00

Engr.

69	A261	100 l car lake	120.00	32.50
	Nos. 58-69 (12)		282.90	92.05

Issued: 3 l, 20 l, 10/21; 5 l, 11/5; 10 l, 11/7; 100 l, 11/23; 15 l, 11/28; 1 l, 2 l, 6 l, 8 l, 12/28; 50 l, 1/19; 25 l, 2/25.

Italy No. 531 Overprinted in Carmine

1950, Apr. 12

70	A292	20 l brown	7.25	4.00

Italy No. 532 Overprinted in Carmine

1950, Apr. 29

71	A293	20 l vio gray	5.50	5.50

Italy Nos. 533-534 Overprinted in Carmine

1950, May 22

72	A294	20 l olive green	5.50	5.50
73	A295	55 l blue	20.00	20.00

Italy Nos. 535-536 Overprinted in Black

1950, May 29

74	A296	20 l violet	9.00	4.75
75	A296	55 l blue	35.00	27.50

Italy No. 537 Overprinted in Carmine

1950, July 10

76	A297	20 l gray grn	5.50	5.50

Italy Nos. 538-539 Overprint in Carmine

1950, July 15

77	A298	20 l purple	9.50	5.50
78	A298	55 l blue	35.00	40.00

Italy No. 540 Overprinted

1950, July 22

79	A299	20 l brown	9.50	8.00

Italy, No. 541 Overprinted in Carmine — i

1950, July 29

80	A300	20 l dk grn	9.00	7.25

Italy No. 542 Overprinted

1950, Aug. 21

81	A301	20 l chnt brn	4.75	4.75

Italy Nos. 473A-474 Overprinted

1950, Aug. 27

82	A257	15 l blue	8.00	4.75
83	A259	20 l dk red vio	8.00	7.25

Trieste Fair.

ITALY — TRIESTE

Italy No. 543 Overprinted in Carmine

1950, Sept. 11
84 A302 20 l indigo 4.75 4.00

Italy Nos. 544-546 Overprinted

1950, Sept. 16   Wmk. 277   Perf. 14
85 A303   5 l dp cl & grn   2.00   4.75
86 A303 20 l brn & grn   4.75   4.75
87 A303 55 l dp ultra & brn 40.00 40.00
Nos. 85-87 (3)   46.75 49.50

Italy No. 547 Overprinted in Black

1950, Sept. 16
88 A304 20 l ol brn & red brn 5.50 4.75

Italy No. 548 Overprinted in Black

1950, Sept. 16
89 A305 20 l cream & gray blk 9.00 7.25

Italy Nos. 549 to 565 Overprinted in Black

1950, Oct. 20
90   A306 50c violet blue   .25   .25
91   A306   1 l dk blue vio   .25   .25
92   A306   2 l sepia   .25   .25
93   A306   5 l dk gray   .25   .25
94   A306   6 l chocolate   .25   .25
95   A306 10 l deep green   .80   .25
96   A306 12 l dp blue grn 2.40   .80
97   A306 15 l dk gray bl   2.40   .25
98   A306 20 l blue vio   2.40   .25
99   A306 25 l brown org   4.00   .25
100 A306 30 l magenta   1.60   .80
101 A306 35 l crimson   4.00   1.60
102 A306 40 l brown   1.75   1.60
103 A306 50 l violet   .80   .80
104 A306 55 l deep blue   .80   .80
105 A306 60 l red   12.00 14.50
106 A306 65 l dk green   .80   .80

Italy Nos. 566 and 567 Overprinted — k

Perf. 14, 14x13½
Engr.
107 A306 100 l brown org   9.00   .25
108 A306 200 l olive brn   8.00 9.00
Nos. 90-108 (19)   52.00 33.20

Italy Nos. 568-569 Overprinted in Black

1951, Mar. 27   Photo.   Perf. 14
109 A307 20 l red vio & red   8.00   8.00
110 A307 55 l ultra & bl   65.00 65.00

Italy No. 570 Overprinted

1951, Apr. 2
111 A308 20 l dk grn 4.00 4.00

Italy No. 571 Overprinted

1951, Apr. 11
112 A309 20 l bl vio 4.75 4.75

Italy Nos. 572-573 Overprinted

1951, Apr. 12
113 A310(h) 20 l brown   4.75 4.75
114 A311(g) 55 l deep blue 7.25 7.25

Italy Nos. 574-576 Overprinted in Black

1951, May 18   Fleur-de-Lis in Red
115 A312   5 l dk brown   11.00   75.00
116 A312 10 l Prus grn   11.00   75.00
117 A312 15 l vio bl   11.00   75.00
Nos. 115-117 (3)   33.00 225.00

Italy No. 577 Overprinted — m

1951, Apr. 26
118 A313 20 l violet 4.75 4.75

Italy No. 578 Overprinted

1951, May 5
119 A314 20 l Prus green 4.25 4.75

Italy Nos. 579-580 Ovptd. Type "g"

1951, June 18
120 A315 20 l violet   2.00 2.00
121 A315 55 l brt blue 4.75 4.75

Nos. 94, 98 and 104 Overprinted

1951, June 24
122 A306   6 l chocolate   .80 2.00
123 A306 20 l blue violet 2.00   .80
124 A306 55 l deep blue   2.00 2.00
Nos. 122-124 (3)   4.80 4.80

Issued to publicize the Trieste Fair, 1951.

Italy No. 581 Overprinted — n

1951, July 23
125 A316 20 l brn & red brn 4.00 4.00

Italy Nos. 582 and 583 Overprinted in Red

1951, July 23
126 A317(n) 20 l grnsh gray & blk   2.75 2.75
127 A318(h) 55 l vio bl & pale sal   5.25 5.25

Italy No. 584 Overprinted in Carmine

1951, Aug. 23
128 A319 25 l gray blk 17.50 8.00

Italy No. 585 Overprinted in Black

1951, Sept. 8
129 A320 25 l deep blue 4.00 4.00

Italy No. 586 Ovptd. in Red

1951, Sept. 15
130 A321 25 l dk brn 4.00 4.00

Italy Nos. 587-589 Ovptd. in Blue — o

1951, Oct. 11
131 A322 10 l dk brn & gray   2.00 2.00
132 A322 25 l rose red & grnsh bl 2.00 2.00
133 A322 60 l vio bl & red org   4.00 4.00
Nos. 131-133 (3)   8.00 8.00

Italy Nos. 590-591 Overprinted — p

Overprint Spaced to Fit Design

1951, Oct. 31   Photo.
134 A323 10 l blue green 2.50 2.50
135 A324 25 l vio gray   2.50 2.50

Italy Nos. 592-593 Ovprinted in Black

1951, Nov. 21
136 A325 10 l ol & dull grn 2.50 2.50
137 A326 25 l dull green   2.50 2.50

Italy Nos. 594-596 Overprinted in Black

No. 138

No. 139

Overprint "p" Spaced to Fit Design

1951, Nov. 23
138 A327(p) 10 l vio brn & dk grn   2.00 2.50
139 A327(k) 25 l red brn & dk brn   2.00 1.60
140 A327(p) 60 l dp grn & ind   4.00 4.00
Nos. 138-140 (3)   8.00 8.10

Italy No. 597 Overprinted

Overprint Spaced to Fit Design

1952, Jan. 28   Wmk. 277   Perf. 14
141 A328 25 l gray & gray blk 4.00 3.25

Italy No. 598 Ovptd. in Black

1952, Feb. 2
142 A329 25 l dl grn & ol bis 4.00 3.25

Italy No. 599 Overprinted in Black

1952, Mar. 26
143 A330 25 l brn & sl blk 4.00 3.25

Italy No. 600 Overprinted in Blue

1952, Apr. 12
144 A331 60 l ultra 4.00 4.75

ITALY — TRIESTE

Italy No. 601 Overprinted in Black

1952, Apr. 16
145	A332	25 l dp orange	.80	.40

Stamps of Italy Overprinted in Various Sizes and Arrangements

No. 146

On Nos. 602-603

1952, June 14 Wmk. 277 Perf. 14
146	A333	25 l blk & red brn	2.00	2.00
147	A333	60 l blk & ultra	2.75	2.75

1952, June 7 On No. 604
148	A334	25 l bright blue	4.00	4.00

Italy No. 605 Overprinted in Black

1952, June 14
149	A335	25 l black & yellow	4.00	4.00

1952, June 19 On No. 606
150	A336	25 l bl gray, red & dk bl (R)	4.00	4.00

1952, June 28 On No. 607
151	A337	25 l dp grn, dk brn & red	4.00	4.00

1952, Sept. 6 On No. 608
152	A338	25 l dark green	4.00	4.00

On No. 609 in Gold

1952, Sept. 20
153	A339	25 l purple	4.00	4.00

1952, Oct. 4 On No. 610
154	A340	25 l gray	4.00	4.00

1952, Oct. 1 On No. 611
155	A341	60 l dk bl & Prus bl	4.75	4.75

Italy No. 612 Overprinted in Black

1952, Nov. 21 Perf. 13
156	A342	25 l brn & dk brn	3.25	2.40

Italy Nos. 613-615 Overprinted in Black

1952, Nov. 3 Perf. 14
157	A343	10 l dk green	.80	.80
158	A344	25 l blk & dk brn	1.60	.80
159	A344	60 l blk & blue	2.25	2.25
		Nos. 157-159 (3)	4.65	3.85

1952, Dec. 6 On Nos. 616-617
160	A345	25 l dk green	4.00	4.00
161	A346	25 l brown	4.00	4.00

1953, Jan. 5 On No. 618
162	A347	25 l gray blk & bl gray (Bl)	4.00	4.00

On Nos. 601A-601B

1952, Dec. 31
163	A332a	60 l ultra (G)	3.25	3.25
164	A332	80 l brown car	4.00	4.50

1953, Feb. 21 On No. 621
165	A349	25 l car lake	4.00	4.00

1953, Apr. 24 On No. 622
166	A350	25 l violet	4.00	4.00

1953, Apr. 30 On No. 623
167	A351	25 l violet	4.00	4.00

1953, May 30 On No. 624
168	A352	25 l dark brown	4.00	4.00

1953, June 27 On No. 625
169	A353	25 l brn & dull red	4.00	4.00

1953-54 On Nos. 626-633
170	A354	5 l gray	.25	.35
171	A354	10 l org ver	.25	.25
172	A354	12 l dull grn	.25	.25
172A	A354	13 l brt lil rose ('54)	.25	.25
173	A354	20 l brown	.80	.80
174	A354	25 l purple	.80	.90
175	A354	35 l rose car	4.00	4.00
176	A354	60 l blue	6.50	6.50
177	A354	80 l org brn	20.00	20.00
		Nos. 170-177 (9)	33.10	33.70

Issue dates: 13 l, Feb. 1. Others, June 16.

Italy, Nos. 554, 558 and 564 Overprinted in Red or Green

1953, June 27
178	A306	10 l dp green (R)	.80	1.25
179	A306	25 l brown org	.80	.80
180	A306	60 l red	3.25	2.75
		Nos. 178-180 (3)	4.85	4.80

5th International Sample Fair of Trieste.

Italy No. 634 Overprinted in Black

1953, July 11
181	A355	25 l grnsh blue	4.00	4.00

1953, July 16 On Nos. 635-636
182	A356	25 l dark brown	2.00	.80
183	A356	60 l deep blue	2.75	4.00

1953, Aug. 6 On Nos. 637-638
184	A357	25 l org & Prus bl	2.50	2.50
185	A357	60 l lil rose & dk vio bl	4.00	4.00

1953, Aug. 13 On No. 639
186	A358	25 l dk brn & dl grn	4.00	4.00

1953, Sept. 5 On No. 640
187	A359	25 l dk gray & brn	4.00	4.00

1954, Jan. 26 On Nos. 641-646
188	A360	10 l dk brn & red brn	.40	.40
189	A361	12 l lt bl & gray	.40	.40
190	A361	20 l brn org & dk brn	.40	.40
191	A360	25 l dk grn & pale bl	.40	.40
192	A361	35 l cream & brn	3.25	3.25
193	A361	60 l bl grn & ind	3.25	3.25
		Nos. 188-193 (6)	8.10	8.10

1954, Feb. 11 On Nos. 647-648
194	A362	25 l dk brn & choc	1.60	.80
195	A362	60 l dp bl & ultra	3.25	4.00

1954, Feb. 25 On Nos. 649-650
196	A363	25 l redsh vio & lil	1.60	.80
197	A363	60 l dp bl grn & turq bl	3.25	4.00

1954, Mar. 20 On No. 651
198	A364	25 l purple	4.00	4.00

1954, Apr. 24 On No. 652
199	A365	25 l gray blk	4.00	4.00

1954, June 1 On No. 653
200	A366	25 l gray, org brn & blk	4.00	4.00

1954, June 19 On No. 654
201	A367	25 l dk grnsh gray	4.00	4.00

1954, July 8 On Nos. 655-656
202	A368	25 l red brown	1.60	1.60
203	A368	60 l gray green	3.25	3.25

Nos. 644, 646 With Additional Overprint

1954, June 17
204	A360	25 l dk grn & pale bl	1.60	1.60
205	A361	60 l bl grn & indigo	3.25	3.25

International Sample Fair of Trieste.

Italy No. 657 Overprinted in Black

1954, Sept. 6
206	A369	25 l dp grn & red	4.00	4.00

1954, Oct. 30 On Nos. 658-659
207	A370	25 l rose red	1.60	1.60
208	A370	60 l blue	3.25	3.25

OCCUPATION AIR POST STAMPS

Air Post Stamps of Italy 1945-47 Overprinted in Black

1947, Oct. 1 Wmk. 277 Perf. 14
C1	AP59	1 l slate bl	.25	.25
C2	AP60	2 l dk blue	.25	.25
C3	AP60	5 l dk green	9.00	8.75
C4	AP59	10 l car rose	9.00	8.75
C5	AP60	25 l brown	27.50	17.50
C6	AP59	50 l violet	120.00	25.00
		Nos. C1-C6 (6)	166.00	60.50

Italy Nos. C116-C121 Overprinted in Black

1947, Nov. 19
C7	AP61	6 l dp violet	2.40	4.00
C8	AP61	10 l dk car rose	2.40	4.00
C9	AP61	20 l dp org	21.00	16.00
C10	AP61	25 l aqua	3.25	4.75
C11	AP61	35 l brt blue	3.25	6.50
C12	AP61	50 l lilac rose	21.00	12.50
		Nos. C7-C12 (6)	53.30	47.75

Italy Nos. C123-C126 Overprinted in Black

1948
C13	AP65	100 l green	127.50	9.00
C14	AP65	300 l lil rose	27.50	40.00
C15	AP65	500 l ultra	50.00	55.00
C16	AP65	1000 l dk brown	275.00	360.00
		Nos. C13-C16 (4)	480.00	464.00

Issue date: Nos. C13-C15, Mar. 1.

Italy, No. C110, C113 and C114, Ovptd. in Black

1948, Sept. 8
C17	AP59	10 l carmine rose	.40	.40
C18	AP60	25 l brown	.80	.80
C19	AP59	50 l violet	2.00	2.00
		Nos. C17-C19 (3)	3.20	3.20

The overprint is embossed.

Italy Air Post Stamps of 1945-48 Overprinted in Black

1949-52
C20	AP59	10 l car rose	.25	.25
C21	AP60	25 l brown ('50)	.25	.25
C22	AP59	50 l violet	.25	.25
C23	AP65	100 l green	1.60	.25
C24	AP65	300 l lil rose ('50)	22.50	40.00
C25	AP65	500 l ultra ('50)	47.50	47.50
C26	AP65	1000 l dk brn ('52)	75.00	110.00
		Nos. C20-C26 (7)	147.35	198.50

No. C26 is found in two perforations: 14 and 14x13.

Issued: 100 l, 11/7; 50 l, 12/5; 10 l, 12/28; 25 l, 1/23; 300 l, 500 l, 11/25; 1000 l, 2/18.

OCCUPATION SPECIAL DELIVERY STAMPS

Special Delivery Stamps of Italy 1946-48 Overprinted in Black

1947-48 Wmk. 277 Perf. 14
E1	SD9	15 l dk car rose	.25	.30
E2	SD8	25 l brt red org ('48)	95.00	32.50
E3	SD8	30 l dp vio	.60	.60
E4	SD9	60 l car rose ('48)	95.00	45.00
		Nos. E1-E4 (4)	190.85	78.40

Issue dates: Oct. 1, 1947. Mar. 1, 1948.

Italy No. E26 Overprinted in Black

1948, Sept. 24
E5	A272	35 l violet	4.00	4.00

Italy No. E25 Overprinted in Black

1950, Sept. 27
E6	SD9	60 l car rose	9.00	3.25

ITALY — TRIESTE — IVORY COAST

Italy No. E32 Overprinted in Black

1952, Feb. 4
E7	SD8	50 l lilac rose	9.00	3.25

OCCUPATION AUTHORIZED DELIVERY STAMPS

Italy No. EY5 Overprinted in Black

1947, Oct. 1   Wmk. 277   Perf. 14
EY1	AD3	1 l dark brown	.80	1.60

Italy, No. EY7 Overprinted in Black

1947, Oct. 29
EY2	AD4	8 l bright red	14.50	4.75

Italy No. EY8 Overprinted in Black

1949, July 30
EY3	AD4	15 l violet	80.00	40.00

Italy No. EY8 Overprinted in Black

1949, Nov. 7
EY4	AD4	15 l violet	1.60	2.00

Italy No. EY9 Overprinted in Black

1952, Feb. 4
EY5	AD4	20 l rose violet	14.50	2.40

OCCUPATION POSTAGE DUE STAMPS

Postage Due Stamps of Italy, 1945-47, Overprinted Type "a"

1947, Oct. 1   Wmk. 277   Perf. 14
J1	D9	1 l red orange	.80	.80
J2	D10	2 l dk green	.40	.80
J3	D9	5 l violet	8.00	2.50
J4	D9	10 l dk blue	16.00	9.00
J5	D10	20 l car rose	32.50	12.00
J6	D10	50 l aqua	2.40	1.60
	Nos. J1-J6 (6)		60.10	26.70

Italy Nos. J65, J67-J74 Overprinted in Black

1949
J7	D10	1 l red orange	.40	.80
J8	D10	3 l carmine	.80	3.25
J9	D10	4 l brown	22.50	40.00
J10	D10	5 l violet	175.00	52.50
J11	D10	6 l vio blue	65.00	80.00
J12	D10	8 l rose vio	110.00	190.00
J13	D10	10 l deep blue	250.00	52.50
J14	D10	12 l bister brn	40.00	55.00
J15	D10	20 l lilac rose	40.00	17.50
	Nos. J7-J15 (9)		703.70	491.55

Issued: 3 l, 4 l, 6 l, 8 l, 12 l, 1/24; others, 4/15.

Italy Nos. J65-J78 Overprinted in Black

1949-54
J16	D10	1 l red orange	.25	.25
J17	D10	2 l dk green	.25	.25
J18	D10	3 l car ('54)	.25	.50
J20	D10	5 l violet	1.25	.25
J21	D10	6 l vio bl ('50)	.25	.25
J22	D10	8 l rose vio ('50)	.25	1.00
J23	D10	10 l deep blue	.35	1.00
J24	D10	12 l gldn brn ('50)	1.60	1.00
J25	D10	20 l lilac rose	4.00	1.00
J26	D10	25 l dk red ('54)	5.50	3.25
J27	D10	50 l aqua ('50)	6.50	1.00
J28	D10	100 l org yel ('52)	10.00	1.75
J29	D10	500 l dp bl & dk car ('52)	120.00	110.00
	Nos. J16-J29 (13)		150.45	120.00

Issued: 5 l, 10 l, 11/7; 1 l, 11/22; 2 l, 20 l, 12/28; 6 l, 8 l, 12 l, 5/16; 50 l, 11/25; 100 l, 11/11; 500 l, 6/19; 3 l, 1/24; 25 l, 2/1.

OCCUPATION PARCEL POST STAMPS

See note preceding Italy No. Q7.

Parcel Post Stamps of Italy, 1946-48, Overprinted

1947-48   Wmk. 277   Perf. 13½
Q1	PP4	1 l golden brn	.80	2.40
Q2	PP4	2 l lt bl grn	1.00	4.00
Q3	PP4	3 l red org	.80	4.00
Q4	PP4	4 l gray blk	1.25	4.75
Q5	PP4	5 l lil rose ('48)	27.50	35.00
Q6	PP4	10 l violet	8.00	20.00
Q7	PP4	20 l lilac brn	8.00	20.00
Q8	PP4	50 l rose red	12.00	37.50
Q9	PP4	100 l sapphire	17.50	47.50
Q10	PP4	200 l grn ('48)	575.00	1,000.
Q11	PP4	300 l brn car ('48)	350.00	525.00
Q12	PP4	500 l brn ('48)	200.00	300.00
	Nos. Q1-Q12 (12)		1,202.	2,000.

Halves Used
Q1-Q4	.40
Q5	.40
Q6-Q7	.40
Q8	.40
Q9	.40
Q10	.80
Q11	.60
Q12	.60

Issued: Nos. Q1-Q4, Q6-Q9, Oct. 1; others, Mar. 1.

Parcel Post Stamps of Italy, 1946-54, Overprinted

1949-54
Q13	PP4	1 l gldn brn ('50)	1.75	1.60
Q14	PP4	2 l lt bl grn ('51)	.85	1.00
Q15	PP4	3 l red org ('51)	.85	1.00
Q16	PP4	4 l gray blk ('51)	.85	1.00
Q17	PP4	5 l lilac rose	.85	1.00
Q18	PP4	10 l violet	2.25	2.25
Q19	PP4	20 l lil brn	2.25	2.25
Q20	PP4	30 l plum ('52)	.85	1.00
Q21	PP4	50 l rose red ('50)	1.75	2.00
Q22	PP4	100 l saph ('50)	4.00	7.00
Q23	PP4	200 l green	27.50	72.50
Q24	PP4	300 l brn car ('50)	140.00	225.00
Q25	PP4	500 l brn ('51)	77.50	135.00
	Perf. 13x13½			
Q26	PP5	1000 l ultra ('54)	200.00	600.00
	Nos. Q13-Q26 (14)		461.25	1,053.

Halves Used
Q13-Q18, Q20	.40
Q19, Q22	.40
Q21	.80
Q23	.80
Q24	.80
Q25	.80
Q26	.60
Nos. 1-17 (17)	580.75 436.00

Pairs of Q18 exist with 5mm between overprints instead of 11mm. Value $1,000.
Issued: 20 l, 200 l, 11/22; 5 l, 10 l, 11/28; 300 l, 1/19; 50 l, 3/10; 1 l, 10/7; 100 l, 11/9; 500 l, 11/25; 2 l, 3 l, 4 l, 8/1; 30 l, 3/6; 1000 l, 8/12.

PARCEL POST AUTHORIZED DELIVERY STAMPS

For the payment of a special tax for the authorized delivery of parcels privately instead of through the post office. Both unused and used values are for complete stamps.

Italy Nos. QY1-QY4 Overprinted in Black

1953, July 8   Wmk. 277
QY1	PAD1	40 l org red	21.00	7.00
QY2	PAD1	50 l ultra	21.00	7.00
QY3	PAD1	75 l brown	21.00	13.00
QY4	PAD1	110 l lilac rose	21.00	13.00
	Nos. QY1-QY4 (4)		84.00	40.00

Halves Used
QY1	.25
QY2	.25
QY3-QY4, each	.35

IVORY COAST

'iv-rē 'kōst

LOCATION — West coast of Africa, bordering on Gulf of Guinea
GOVT. — Republic
AREA — 127,520 sq. mi.
POP. — 26,380,000 (2020 est.)
CAPITAL — Yamoussoukro

The former French colony of Ivory Coast became part of French West Africa and used its stamps, starting in 1945. On December 4, 1958, Ivory Coast became a republic, with full independence on August 7, 1960.

100 Centimes = 1 Franc

> Catalogue values for unused stamps in this country are for Never Hinged items, beginning with Scott 165 in the regular postage section, Scott B8 in the semi-postal section, Scott C6 in the air-post section, Scott J19 in the postage due section, Scott M1 in the military section, and Scott O1 in the official section.

Navigation and Commerce — A1

Perf. 14x13½
1892-1900   Typo.   Unwmk.
Colony Name in Blue or Carmine
1	A1	1c black, lil bl	2.25	2.25
2	A1	2c brown, buff	3.75	3.00
3	A1	4c claret, lav	5.25	4.50
4	A1	5c green, grnsh	15.00	11.00
5	A1	10c black, lavender	20.00	15.00
6	A1	10c red ('00)	130.00	110.00
7	A1	15c blue, quadrille paper	32.50	13.50
8	A1	15c gray ('00)	22.00	4.75
9	A1	20c red, green	21.00	16.00
10	A1	25c black, rose	24.00	7.50
11	A1	25c blue ('00)	40.00	37.50
12	A1	30c brown, bister	35.00	27.50
13	A1	40c red, straw	30.00	16.00
14	A1	50c car, rose	75.00	65.00
15	A1	50c brn, azure ('00)	40.00	25.00
16	A1	75c deep vio, org	32.50	32.50
17	A1	1fr brnz grn, straw	52.50	45.00
	Nos. 1-17 (17)		580.75	436.00

Perf. 13½x14 stamps are counterfeits.
For surcharges see Nos. 18-20, 37-41.

Nos. 12, 16-17 Surcharged in Black

1904
18	A1	0,05c on 30c brn, bis	87.50	87.50
19	A1	0,10c on 75c vio, org	18.00	18.00
20	A1	0,15c on 1fr brnz grn, straw	26.00	26.00
	Nos. 18-20 (3)		131.50	131.50

Gen. Louis Faidherbe — A2

Oil Palm — A3

Dr. N. Eugène Ballay — A4

1906-07
Name of Colony in Red or Blue
21	A2	1c slate	2.00	2.00
a.	"CÔTE D'IVOIRE" omitted		225.00	225.00
22	A2	2c chocolate	2.00	2.00
23	A2	4c choc, gray bl	2.40	2.40
a.	"CÔTE D'IVOIRE" double		250.00	
b.	"CÔTE D'IVOIRE" omitted		275.00	
24	A2	5c green	4.00	2.75
a.	"CÔTE D'IVOIRE" omitted		175.00	140.00
25	A2	10c carmine (B)	9.50	6.50
a.	"CÔTE D'IVOIRE" double		210.00	400.00
b.	"CÔTE D'IVOIRE" omitted			400.00
26	A3	20c black, azure	11.00	9.50
27	A3	25c bl, pinkish	9.50	6.00
28	A3	30c choc, pnksh	15.00	8.75
30	A3	35c black, yel	15.00	5.75
a.	"CÔTE D'IVOIRE" omitted		300.00	
31	A3	45c choc, grnsh	18.00	12.50
32	A3	50c deep violet	16.00	12.50
33	A3	75c blue, org	16.00	12.50
34	A4	1fr black, azure	40.00	35.00
35	A4	2fr blue, pink	52.50	50.00
36	A4	5fr car, straw (B)	100.00	95.00
	Nos. 21-36 (15)		312.90	263.15

Stamps of 1892-1900 Surcharged in Carmine or Black

1912
37	A1	5c on 15c gray (C)	1.60	1.60
38	A1	5c on 30c brn, bis (C)	2.40	2.75
39	A1	10c on 40c red, straw	2.40	2.75
a.	Pair, one without surcharge		75.00	75.00
40	A1	10c on 50c brn, az	4.00	4.75
41	A1	10c on 75c dp vio, org	9.00	10.00
	Nos. 37-41 (5)		19.40	21.85

Two spacings between the surcharged numerals are found on Nos. 37 to 41. For detailed listings, see the *Scott Classic Specialized Catalogue of Stamps and Covers*.

River Scene — A5

1913-35
42	A5	1c vio brn & vio	.25	.25
43	A5	2c brown & blk	.30	.25
44	A5	4c vio & vio brn	.35	.30
45	A5	5c yel grn & bl grn	1.10	.50
46	A5	5c choc & ol brn ('22)	.35	.35
47	A5	10c red org & rose	2.00	.95
48	A5	10c yel grn & bl grn ('22)	.70	.70
49	A5	10c car rose, bluish ('26)	.35	.35
50	A5	15c org & rose ('17)	1.10	.75

IVORY COAST

51	A5	20c black & gray	.80	.55
52	A5	25c ultra & bl	11.00	6.50
53	A5	25c blk & vio ('22)	.75	.75
54	A5	30c choc & brn	2.40	2.00
55	A5	30c red org & rose ('22)	2.75	2.75
56	A5	30c lt bl & rose red ('26)	.40	.40
57	A5	30c dl grn & grn ('27)	.80	.80
58	A5	35c vio & org	1.10	.80
59	A5	40c gray & bl grn	1.60	.80
60	A5	45c red org & choc	1.10	.80
61	A5	45c dp rose & mar ('34)	5.25	4.50
62	A5	50c black & vio	5.00	3.50
63	A5	50c ultra & bl ('22)	2.25	2.25
64	A5	50c ol grn & bl ('25)	.80	.80
65	A5	60c vio, pnksh ('25)	.80	.80
66	A5	65c car rose & ol grn ('26)	1.60	1.60
67	A5	75c brn & rose	1.10	.80
68	A5	75c ind & ultra ('34)	3.75	3.75
69	A5	85c red vio & blk ('26)	1.60	1.60
70	A5	90c brn red & rose ('30)	11.00	11.00
71	A5	1fr org & black	1.10	1.00
72	A5	1.10fr dl grn & dk brn ('28)	7.50	7.50
73	A5	1.50fr lt bl & dp bl ('30)	7.50	7.50
74	A5	1.75fr lt ultra & mag ('35)	15.00	9.00
75	A5	2fr brn & blue	5.25	2.60
76	A5	3fr red vio ('30)	7.50	7.50
77	A5	5fr dk bl & choc	7.50	5.25
		Nos. 42-77 (36)	113.70	91.50

Nos. 45, 47, 50, 52, 56 and 58 exist on both ordinary and chalky paper. See the *Scott Classic Specialized Catalogue of Stamps & Covers 1840-1940* for listings.

For surcharges see Nos. 78-91, B1.

Nos. 45, 47 and 52, pasted on cardboard and overprinted "Valeur d'echange" and value of basic stamp, were used as emergency currency in 1920.

Stamps and Type of 1913-34 Srchd.

1922-34

78	A5	50c on 45c dp rose & mar ('34)	4.00	2.75
79	A5	50c on 75c indigo & ultra ('34)	3.00	2.00
80	A5	50c on 90c brn red & rose ('34)	3.00	2.25
81	A5	60c on 75c vio, pnksh	.75	.75
a.		Surcharge omitted	160.00	175.00
82	A5	65c on 15c org & rose ('25)	1.25	1.25
83	A5	85c on 75c brn & rose ('25)	1.40	1.10
		Nos. 78-83 (6)	13.40	10.10

Stamps and Type of 1913 Surcharged with New Value and Bars

1924-27

84	A5	25c on 2fr (R)	.35	1.00
85	A5	25c on 5fr	.35	1.00
86	A5	90c on 75c brn red & cer ('27)	2.00	1.60
a.		Surcharge omitted	240.00	
87	A5	1.25fr on 1fr dk bl & ultra (R) ('26)	1.25	1.25
88	A5	1.50fr on 1fr lt bl & dk blue ('27)	1.90	1.90
89	A5	3fr on 5fr brn red & bl grn ('27)	6.00	6.00
a.		Double surcharge	160.00	
90	A5	10fr on 5fr dl red & rose lil ('27)	19.00	16.00
91	A5	20fr on 5fr bl grn & ver ('27)	19.00	18.00
		Nos. 84-91 (8)	49.85	46.75

Common Design Types pictured following the introduction.

Colonial Exposition Issue
Common Design Types
Name of Country in Black

1931   Engr.   Perf. 12½

92	CD70	40c deep green	4.50	4.50
93	CD71	50c violet	6.00	6.00
94	CD72	90c red orange	6.00	6.00
95	CD73	1.50fr dull blue	6.00	6.00
		Nos. 92-95 (4)	22.50	22.50

Stamps of Upper Volta 1928, Overprinted

1933   Perf. 13½x14

96	A5	2c brown & lilac	.25	.25
a.		Inverted overprint	27.50	
b.		Double overprint	40.00	47.50
97	A5	4c blk & yellow	.25	.30
a.		Inverted overprint	100.00	
b.		Double overprint	65.00	72.50
98	A5	5c ind & gray bl	.35	.45
a.		Inverted overprint	47.50	
b.		Double overprint	65.00	
99	A5	10c indigo & pink	.35	.45
100	A5	15c brown & blue	1.10	.90
101	A5	20c brown & green	1.10	.90
102	A6	25c brn & yellow	2.25	1.90
103	A6	30c dp grn & grn	2.75	1.75
a.		Double overprint	75.00	
104	A6	45c brown & blue	8.25	6.00
a.		Inverted overprint	80.00	
b.		Double overprint	120.00	
105	A6	65c indigo & bl	3.00	2.60
a.		Double overprint	95.00	
106	A6	75c black & lilac	3.75	2.25
a.		Double overprint	95.00	
107	A6	90c brn red & lil	3.00	2.60

Burkina Faso Nos. 58 & 60 Ovptd.

108	A7	1fr brn & grn	3.75	3.00
a.		Inverted overprint	150.00	160.00
109	A7	1.50fr ultra & grysh	3.75	3.00
a.		Inverted overprint	150.00	
b.		Double overprint	95.00	

Burkina Faso Nos. 52 & 54 Surcharged

110	A6	1.25fr on 40c blk & pink	2.25	2.25
a.		Double overprint	100.00	
111	A6	1.75fr on 50c blk & green	3.75	3.00
a.		Double overprint	100.00	
		Nos. 96-111 (16)	39.90	31.60

Baoulé Woman — A6

Mosque at Bobo-Dioulasso — A7

Coastal Scene — A8

1936-44   Perf. 13

112	A6	1c carmine rose	.25	.25
113	A6	2c ultramarine	.25	.25
114	A6	3c dp grn ('40)	.25	.25
115	A6	4c chocolate	.25	.25
116	A6	5c violet	.25	.25
117	A6	10c Prussian bl	.25	.25
118	A6	15c copper red	.25	.25
119	A6	20c ultramarine	.25	.25
120	A7	25c copper red	.25	.25
121	A7	30c blue green	.25	.25
122	A6	30c brown ('40)	.25	.25
123	A7	35c dp grn ('38)	.75	.75
124	A7	40c carmine rose	.25	.25
125	A7	45c brown	.35	.35
126	A7	45c blue grn ('40)	.25	.25
127	A7	50c plum	.25	.25
128	A7	55c dark vio ('38)	.40	.75
129	A8	60c car rose ('40)	.25	.25
130	A8	65c red brown	.40	.40
131	A8	70c red brn ('40)	.40	.25
132	A8	75c dark violet	1.10	.75
133	A8	80c blk brn ('38)	1.20	.75
134	A8	90c carmine rose	8.25	5.25
135	A8	90c dk grn ('39)	.75	.75
136	A8	1fr dark green	3.75	2.75
137	A8	1fr car rose ('38)	1.50	.75
138	A8	1fr dk vio ('40)	.35	.35
139	A8	1.25fr copper red	.35	.35
140	A8	1.40fr ultra ('40)	.35	.35
141	A8	1.50fr ultramarine	.35	.35
141A	A8	1.50fr grnsh blk ('42)	1.90	1.50
142	A8	1.60fr blk brn ('40)	.75	.75
143	A9	1.75fr carmine rose	.35	.35
144	A9	1.75fr dull bl ('38)	1.50	.75
145	A9	2fr ultramarine	.75	.75
146	A9	2.25fr dark bl ('39)	1.10	1.10
147	A9	2.50fr rose red ('40)	1.10	1.10
148	A9	3fr green	.75	.75
149	A9	5fr chocolate	.75	.75
150	A9	10fr violet	1.10	1.10
151	A9	20fr copper red	1.50	1.50
		Nos. 112-151 (41)	35.65	29.15

For types A7, A8 and A9 without "RF," see Nos. 166A-166D.

For surcharges see Nos. B8-B11.

Paris International Exposition Issue
Common Design Types

1937   Perf. 13

152	CD74	20c deep violet	2.00	2.00
153	CD75	30c dark green	2.00	2.00
154	CD76	40c car rose	2.00	2.00
155	CD77	50c dk brn & bl	1.60	1.60
156	CD78	90c red	1.60	1.60
157	CD79	1.50fr ultra	2.00	2.00
		Nos. 152-157 (6)	11.20	11.20

Colonial Arts Exhibition Issue
Souvenir Sheet
Common Design Type

1937   Imperf.

158	CD76	3fr sepia	11.00	15.00

Louis Gustave Binger — A10

1937   Perf. 13

159	A10	65c red brown	.35	.35

Death of Governor General Binger; 50th anniv. of his exploration of the Niger.

Caillie Issue
Common Design Type

1939   Engr.   Perf. 12½x12

160	CD81	90c org brn & org	.35	.75
161	CD81	2fr bright violet	.35	.90
162	CD81	2.25fr ultra & dk bl	.35	.90
		Nos. 160-162 (3)	1.05	2.55

New York World's Fair Issue
Common Design Type

1939

163	CD82	1.25fr carmine lake	.75	1.50
164	CD82	2.25fr ultramarine	.75	1.50

Catalogue values for unused stamps in this section, from this point to the end of the section, are for Never Hinged items.

Ebrié Lagoon and Marshal Pétain — A11

1941

165	A11	1fr green	.80	—
166	A11	2.50fr deep blue	.85	—

For surcharges, see Nos. B14A-B14B.

Types of 1936-40 Without "RF"

1944   Perf. 13

166A	A7	30c brown	2.25	
166B	A8	60c car rose	2.25	
166C	A8	1fr dark violet	2.25	
166D	A9	20fr copper red	4.50	
		Nos. 166A-166D (4)	11.25	

Nos. 166A-166D were issued by the Vichy government in France, but were not placed on sale in Ivory Coast.

For other stamps inscribed Cote d'Ivoire and Afrique Occidentale Francaise see French West Africa Nos. 58, 72, 77.

Republic

Elephant — A12

1959, Oct. 1   Engr.   Perf. 13

167	A12	10fr black & emerald	.85	.35
168	A12	25fr vio brn & olive	1.25	.50
169	A12	30fr ol blk & grnsh bl	1.50	1.00
		Nos. 167-169 (3)	3.60	1.85

Imperforates

Most Ivory Coast stamps from 1959 onward exist imperforate in issued and trial colors, and also in small presentation sheets in issued colors.

President Felix Houphouet-Boigny — A13

1959, Dec. 4   Unwmk.

170	A13	25fr violet brown	1.00	.60

Proclamation of the Republic, 1st anniv.

Bété Mask — A14

Designs: Masks of 5 tribes: Bété, Guéré, Baoulé, Senufo and Guro. Nos. 174-176 horiz.

1960   Perf. 13

171	A14	50c pale brn & vio brn	.25	.25
172	A14	1fr violet & mag	.25	.25
173	A14	2fr ultra & bl grn	.25	.25
174	A14	4fr dk grn & org	.25	.25
175	A14	5fr ver & brown	.40	.25
176	A14	6fr dark brn & vio	.50	.40
177	A14	45fr dk grn & brn vio	1.80	1.00
178	A14	50fr dk brn & grnsh bl	2.75	1.20
179	A14	85fr car & slate grn	5.00	2.25
		Nos. 171-179 (9)	11.45	6.15

C.C.T.A. Issue
Common Design Type

1960, May 16   Engr.   Perf. 13

180	CD106	25fr grnsh bl & vio	1.10	.50

Emblem of the Entente — A14a

1960, May 29   Photo.   Perf. 13x13½

181	A14a	25fr multicolored	1.10	1.00

1st anniv. of the Entente (Dahomey, Ivory Coast, Niger and Upper Volta).

IVORY COAST

Young Couple with Olive Branch and Globe — A15

1961, Aug. 7   Engr.   Perf. 13
182 A15 25fr emer, bister & blk   1.00   .50
First anniversary of Independence.

Blood Lilies — A16

Designs: Various Local Plants & Orchids.
1961-62
183 A16   5fr dk grn, red & org ('62)   1.00   .35
184 A16 10fr ultra, claret & yel   .60   .35
185 A16 15fr org, rose lil & green ('62)   1.80   .50
186 A16 20fr brn, dk red & yel   1.00   .50
187 A16 25fr grn, red brn & yel   1.00   .50
188 A16 30fr blk, car & green   1.25   .75
189 A16 70fr green, ver & yel   3.25   1.60
190 A16 85fr brn, lil, yel & grn   5.25   2.00
    Nos. 183-190 (8)   15.15   6.55

Early Letter Carrier and Modern Mailman — A17

1961, Oct. 14   Unwmk.   Perf. 13
191 A17 25fr choc, emer & bl   1.00   .70
Issued for Stamp Day.

Ayamé Dam — A18

1961, Nov. 18   Engr.
192 A18 25fr grnsh bl, blk & grn   1.10   .50

Swimming Race — A19

1961, Dec. 23   Unwmk.   Perf. 13
193 A19   5fr shown   .45   .25
194 A19 20fr Basketball   .65   .30
195 A19 25fr Soccer   1.10   .45
    Nos. 193-195 (3)   2.20   1.00
Abidjan Games, Dec. 24-31. See No. C17.

Palms — A20

1962, Feb. 5   Photo.   Perf. 12x12½
196 A20 25fr brn, blue & org   1.10   .45
Commission for Technical Co-operation in Africa South of the Sahara, 17th session, Abidjan, 2/5-16.

Fort Assinie and Assinie River — A21

1962, May 26   Engr.   Perf. 13
197 A21 85fr Prus grn, grn & dl red brn   3.25   1.50
Centenary of the Ivory Coast post.

African and Malagasy Union Issue
Common Design Type

1962, Sept. 8   Photo.   Perf. 12½x12
198 CD110 30fr multicolored   2.10   .75
African and Malagasy Union, 1st anniv.

Fair Emblem, Cotton and Spindles A22

1963, Jan. 26   Engr.   Perf. 13
199 A22 50fr grn, brn org & sepia   2.75   1.25
Bouake Fair, Jan. 26-Feb. 4.

Stylized Map of Africa — A23

1963, May 25   Photo.   Perf. 12½x12
200 A23 30fr ultra & emerald   1.10   .90
Conference of African heads of state for African unity, Addis Ababa.

Hartebeest — A24

Designs: 1fr, Yellow-backed duiker, horiz. 2fr, Potto. 4fr, Beecroft's hyrax, horiz. 5fr, Water chevrotain. 15fr, Forest hog, horiz. 20fr, Wart hog, horiz. 25fr, Bongo (antelope). 45fr, Cape hunting dogs, or hyenas, horiz. 50fr, Black-and-white colobus (monkey).

1963-64   Engr.   Perf. 13
201 A24   1fr choc, grn & yel ('64)   .75   .25
202 A24   2fr blk, dk bl, gray ol & brown ('64)   .75   .25
203 A24   4fr red brn, dk bl, brn & black ('64)   .65   .30
204 A24   5fr sl grn, brn & citron ('64)   .65   .30
205 A24 10fr ol grn & ocher   .85   .30
206 A24 15fr red brn, grn & black ('64)   1.40   .45
207 A24 20fr red org grn & blk   1.75   .45
208 A24 25fr red brn & green   2.40   .60
209 A24 45fr choc, bl grn & yel green   5.00   1.50
210 A24 50fr red brn, grn & blk   7.00   2.00
    a. Min. sheet of 4, #205, 207, 209-210   25.00   25.00
    Nos. 201-210 (10)   21.20   6.40
See Nos. 218-220.

UNESCO Emblem, Scales and Globe — A25

1963, Dec. 10   Unwmk.
211 A25 85fr dk bl, blk & org   2.00   .80
Universal Declaration of Human Rights, 15th anniv.

Sun Radiating from Ivory Coast over Africa — A26

1964, Mar. 17   Photo.   Perf. 12x12½
212 A26 30fr dl vio & red   1.10   .45
Inter-African Conference of Natl. Education Ministers.

Weather Station and Balloon — A27

1964, Mar. 23   Perf. 13x12½
213 A27 25fr multicolored   1.25   .60
World Meteorological Day, Mar. 23.

Physician Vaccinating Child — A28

1964, May 8   Engr.   Perf. 13
214 A28 50fr dk brn, bl & red   1.90   .70
Issued to honor the National Red Cross.

Wrestlers, Globe and Torch — A29

35fr, Globe, torch, athletes, vert.

1964, June 27   Unwmk.   Perf. 13
215 A29 35fr multicolored   1.50   .55
216 A29 65fr shown   2.75   1.10
18th Olympic Games, Tokyo, Oct. 10-25.

Europafrica Issue, 1964
Common Design Type

Design: 30fr, White man and black man beneath tree of industrial symbols.

1964, July 20   Photo.   Perf. 12x13
217 CD116 30fr multicolored   1.10   .35

Animal Type of 1963-64

Designs: 5fr, Manatee, horiz. 10fr, Pygmy hippopotamus, horiz. 15fr, Royal antelope.

1964, Oct. 17   Engr.   Perf. 13
218 A24   5fr yel grn, sl grn & brn   .75   .30
219 A24 10fr sep, Prus grn & dp cl   1.75   .45
220 A24 15fr lil rose, grn & org brn   2.75   .45
    Nos. 218-220 (3)   5.25   1.20

Co-operation Issue
Common Design Type

1964, Nov. 7   Unwmk.   Perf. 13
221 CD119 25fr grn, dk brn & red   1.10   .35

Korhogo Mail Carriers with Guard, 1914 — A30

1964, Nov. 28   Engr.
222 A30 85fr blk, brn, bl & brn red   2.75   1.40
Issued for Stamp Day.

Potter — A31

Artisans: 10fr, Wood carvers. 20fr, Ivory carver. 25fr, Weaver.

1965, Mar. 27   Engr.   Perf. 13
223 A31   5fr mag, green & blk   .40   .25
224 A31 10fr red lil, grn & blk   .50   .25
225 A31 20fr bis, dp bl & dk brn   .90   .30
226 A31 25fr brn, olive & car   1.10   .45
    Nos. 223-226 (4)   2.90   1.25

Unloading Mail, 1900 — A32

1965, Apr. 24   Unwmk.   Perf. 13
227 A32 30fr multicolored   1.25   .70
Issued for Stamp Day.

A32a

ITU emblem, old and new telecommunication equipment.

1965, May 17
228 A32a 85fr mar, brt grn & dk bl   2.25   .70
ITU, centenary.

Abidjan Railroad Station — A33

1965, June 12   Engr.   Perf. 13
229 A33 30fr mag, bl & brn ol   1.25   .80

Pres. Felix Houphouet-Boigny and Map of Ivory Coast — A34

1965, Aug. 7   Photo.   Perf. 12½x13
230 A34 30fr multicolored   .90   .45
Fifth anniversary of Independence.

Hammerhead Stork — A35

Birds: 1fr, Bruce's green pigeon, horiz. 2fr, Spur-winged goose, horiz. 5fr, Stone partridge. 15fr, White-breasted guinea fowl. 30fr, Namaqua dove, horiz. 50fr, Lizard buzzard, horiz. 75fr, Yellow-billed stork. 90fr, Forest (or Latham's) francolin.

1965-66   Engr.   Perf. 13
231 A35   1fr yel grn, pur & yel ('66)   1.00   .30
232 A35   2fr slate grn, blk & red ('66)   1.00   .40
233 A35   5fr dk ol, dk brn & red ('66)   1.25   .45
234 A35 10fr red lil, blk & red brn   1.40   .30
235 A35 15fr sl grn, gray & ver   1.50   .40
236 A35 30fr sl grn, mar & red brown   2.00   .65
237 A35 50fr brn, blk & chlky bl   3.50   1.00
238 A35 75fr org, mar & sl grn   6.25   1.25

IVORY COAST

239 A35 90fr emer, blk & brn
('66) 7.25 3.00
Nos. 231-239 (9) 25.15 8.00

Mail Train, 1906 — A36

1966, Mar. 26   Engr.   Perf. 13
240 A36 30fr grn, blk & mar 2.90 1.00
Issued for Stamp Day.

Baoulé Mother and Child, Carved in Wood — A37

Designs: 10fr, Unguent vessel, Wamougo mask lid. 20fr, Atié carved drums. 30fr, Bété female ancestral figure.

1966, Apr. 9   Unwmk.
241 A37 5fr blk & emerald .45 .25
242 A37 10fr purple & blk .75 .30
243 A37 20fr orange & blk 2.00 .75
244 A37 30fr red & black 2.50 1.00
Nos. 241-244 (4) 5.70 2.30
Intl. Negro Arts Festival, Dakar, Senegal, 4/1-24.

Hotel Ivoire — A38

1966, Apr. 30   Engr.   Perf. 13
245 A38 15fr bl, grn, red & olive .90 .40

Farm Tractor — A39

1966, Aug. 7   Photo.   Perf. 12½x13
246 A39 30fr multicolored 1.00 .55
6th anniversary of independence.

Uniformed Teacher and Villagers — A40

1966, Sept. 1   Engr.   Perf. 13
247 A40 30fr dk red, indigo & dk brn 1.00 .50
National School of Administration.

Veterinarian Treating Cattle — A41

1966, Oct. 22   Engr.   Perf. 13
248 A41 30fr ol, bl & dp brn 1.10 .50
Campaign against cattle plague.

Man, Waves, UNESCO Emblem — A42

1966, Nov. 14   Engr.   Perf. 13
249 A42 30fr dp bl & vio brn 1.00 .55
UNESCO, 20th anniv.

Delivery of Gift Parcels — A43

1966, Dec. 11   Engr.   Perf. 13
250 A43 30fr dk bl, brn & blk 1.00 .55
UNICEF, 20th anniv.

Bouaké Hospital and Red Cross — A44

1966, Dec. 20
251 A44 30fr red brn, red & lilac 1.00 .55

Sikorsky S-43 Seaplane and Boats A45

1967, Mar. 25   Engr.   Perf. 13
252 A45 30fr indigo, bl grn & brn 3.00 1.20
Stamp Day. 30th anniv. of the Sikorsky S-43 flying boat route.

Pineapple Harvest — A46

1967   Engr.   Perf. 13
253 A46 20fr shown .60 .40
254 A46 30fr Palm nuts .85 .45
255 A46 100fr Bananas 3.50 1.10
Nos. 253-255 (3) 4.95 1.95
Issue dates: 30fr, June 24; others, Mar. 25.

Genie, Protector of Assamlangangan — A47

1967, July 31   Engr.   Perf. 13
256 A47 30fr grn, blk & maroon 1.00 .55
Intl. PEN Club (writers' organization), 25th Congress, Abidjan, July 31-Aug. 5.

Old and New Houses — A48

1967, Aug. 7   Photo.   Perf. 12½x12
257 A48 30fr multicolored 1.00 .55
7th anniversary of independence.

Lions Emblem and Elephant's Head — A49

1967, Sept. 2   Photo.   Perf. 12½x13
258 A49 30fr lt bl & multi 1.50 .60
50th anniversary of Lions International.

Monetary Union Issue
Common Design Type

1967, Nov. 4   Engr.   Perf. 13
259 CD125 30fr car, slate grn & blk .85 .40

Allegory of French Recognition of Ivory Coast — A50

1967, Nov. 17   Photo.   Perf. 13x12½
260 A50 90fr multicolored 2.50 .95
Days of Recognition, 20th anniv. See No. 298.

Tabou Radio Station — A51

1968, Mar. 9   Engr.   Perf. 13
261 A51 30fr dk grn, brn & brt grn 1.10 .55
Issued for Stamp Day.

Cotton Mill — A52

Designs: 5fr, Palm oil extraction plant. 15fr, Abidjan oil refinery. 20fr, Unloading raw cotton and spinning machine, vert. 30fr, Flour mill. 50fr, Cacao butter extractor. 70fr, Instant coffee factory, vert. 90fr, Saw mill and timber.

1968   Engr.   Perf. 13
262 A52 5fr ver, slate grn & blk .40 .25
263 A52 10fr dk grn, gray & ol bis .70 .25
264 A52 15fr ver, lt ultra & blk 1.50 .65
265 A52 20fr Prus blue & choc 1.10 .55
266 A52 30fr dk grn, brt bl & brown 1.10 .65
267 A52 50fr red, brt grn & blk 1.90 .90
268 A52 70fr dk brn, bl & brn 2.50 1.00
269 A52 90fr dp bl, blk & brn 3.25 1.60
Nos. 262-269 (8) 12.45 5.85
Issued: 5fr, 15fr, June 8; 10fr, 20fr, 90fr, Mar. 23; others, Oct. 5.

Canoe Race — A53

1968, Apr. 6   Engr.   Perf. 13
270 A53 30fr shown 1.00 .50
271 A53 100fr Runners 3.00 .90
19th Olympic Games, Mexico City, 10/12-27.

Queen Pokou Sacrificing her Son — A54

1968, Aug. 7   Photo.   Perf. 12½x12
272 A54 30fr multicolored 1.10 .50
8th anniversary of independence.

Vaccination, WHO Emblem and Elephant's Head — A55

1968, Sept. 28   Engr.   Perf. 13
273 A55 30fr choc, brt bl & mar 1.00 .50
WHO, 20th anniversary.

Antelope in Forest — A56

1968, Oct. 26   Engr.   Perf. 13
274 A56 30fr ultra, brn & olive 5.75 1.25
Protection of fauna and flora.

Abidjan Anthropological Museum and Carved Screen — A57

1968, Nov. 2
275 A57 30fr vio bl, ol & rose mag 1.00 .50

Human Rights Flame and Statues of "Justitia" — A58

1968, Nov. 9   Engr.   Perf. 13
276 A58 30fr slate, org & dk brn 1.00 .50
International Human Rights Year.

"Ville de Maranhao" at Grand Bassam — A59

1969, Mar. 8   Engr.   Perf. 13
277 A59 30fr brn, brt bl & grn 1.75 .55
Issued for Stamp Day.

Opening of Hotel Ivoire, Abidjan A60

1969, Mar. 29
278 A60 30fr ver, bl & grn 1.25 .50

Carved Figure — A61

1969, July 5   Engr.   Perf. 13
279 A61 30fr red lil, blk & red org 1.10 .60
Ivory Coast art exhibition, Fine Arts Museum, Vevey, Switzerland, 7/12-9/22.

Mountains and Radio Tower, Man — A62

1969, Aug. 7   Engr.   Perf. 13
280 A62 30fr dl brn, sl & grn 1.25 .50
9th anniversary of independence.

IVORY COAST

Development Bank Issue
Common Design Type
Design: Development Bank emblem and Ivory Coast coat of arms.

1969, Sept. 6
281 CD130 30fr ocher, grn & mar .70 .40

Arms of Bouake — A63

Coats of Arms: 15fr, Abidjan. 30fr, Ivory Coast.

1969 *Photo.* *Perf. 13*
282 A63 10fr multicolored .40 .25
283 A63 15fr multicolored .50 .25
284 A63 30fr multicolored .85 .25
 Nos. 282-284 (3) 1.75 .75

Issued: 10fr, 10/25; 15fr, 12/27; 30fr, 12/20. See Nos. 335-336, 378-382, design A297.

Sport Fishing and SKAL Emblem — A64

100fr, Vacation village, SKAL emblem.

1969, Nov. 22 *Engr.* *Perf. 13*
285 A64 30fr shown 3.75 .55
286 A64 100fr multi 4.75 1.40

1st Intl. Congress in Africa of the SKAL Tourist Assoc., Abidjan, Nov. 23-28.

ASECNA Issue
Common Design Type

1969, Dec. 13 *Engr.* *Perf. 13*
287 CD132 30fr vermilion .90 .40

University Center, Abidjan A65

1970, Feb. 26 *Engr.* *Perf. 13*
288 A65 30fr indigo & yel grn .90 .50

Higher education in Ivory Coast, 10th anniv.

Gabriel Dadié and Telegraph Operator — A66

1970, Mar. 7 *Engr.* *Perf. 13*
289 A66 30fr dk red, sl grn & blk .70 .35

Stamp Day; Gabriel Dadié (1891-1953) 1st native-born postal administrator.

University of Abidjan A67

1970, Mar. 21 *Photo.*
290 A67 30fr Prus bl, dk pur & dk yel grn .90 .50

3rd General Assembly of the Assoc. of French-language Universities (A.U.P.E.L.F.).

Safety Match Production — A68

20fr, Textile industry. 50fr, Shipbuilding.

1970, May 9 *Engr.* *Perf. 13*
291 A68 5fr shown .40 .45
292 A68 20fr multi .60 .40
293 A68 15fr multi 1.60 .50
 Nos. 291-293 (3) 2.60 1.35

Radar, Classroom with Television A69

1970, May 17
294 A69 40fr red, grn & gray ol 1.10 .55

Issued for World Telecommunications Day.

UPU Headquarters Issue
Common Design Type

1970, May 20
295 CD133 30fr lil, brt grn & olive 1.10 .50

UN Emblem, Lion, Antelopes and Plane — A70

1970, June 27 *Engr.* *Perf. 13*
296 A70 30fr dk red brn, ultra & dk green 3.25 1.25

25th anniversary of the United Nations.

Coffee Branch and Bags Showing Increased Production — A71

1970, Aug. 7 *Engr.* *Perf. 13*
297 A71 30fr org, bluish grn & gray 1.50 .50

Tenth anniversary of independence.

Type of 1967
1970, Oct. 29 *Photo.* *Perf. 12x12½*
298 A50 40fr multicolored 1.00 .50

Ivory Coast Democratic Party, 5th Congress.

Power Plant at Uridi — A73

1970, Nov. 21 *Engr.* *Perf. 13*
299 A73 40fr multicolored 2.00 .40

Independence, 10th Anniv. — A73a

Designs: Nos. 299A, 299D, Pres. Houphouet-Boigny, Gen. Charles DeGaulle. Nos. 299B, 299F, Pres. Houphouet-Boigny, elephants. Nos. 299C, 299E, Coat of arms.

1970, Nov. 27 *Embossed* *Perf. 10½*
 Die Cut
299A A73a 300fr Silver 15.00 15.00
299B A73a 300fr Silver 15.00 15.00
299C A73a 300fr Silver 15.00 15.00
 g. Pair, #299B-299C 35.00 35.00
299D A73a 1000fr Gold 45.00 45.00
299E A73a 1000fr Gold 45.00 45.00

Litho. & Embossed
299F A73a 1200fr Gold & multi 45.00 45.00
 h. Pair, #299E-299F 100.00 100.00

Nos. 299B, 299F are airmail.

Postal Service Autobus, 1925 — A74

1971, Mar. 6 *Engr.* *Perf. 13*
300 A74 40fr dp grn, dk brn & gldn brn 2.75 .50

Stamp Day.

Marginella Desjardini — A75

Marine Life: 1fr, Aporrhaispes gallinae. 5fr, Neptunus validus. 10fr, Hermodice carunculata, vert. No. 305, Natica fanel, vert. No. 306, Goniaster cuspidatus, vert. No. 307, Xenorhora digitata. 25fr, Conus prometheus. 35fr, Polycheles typhlops, vert. No. 310, Conus genuanus. No. 311, Chlamys flabellum. 45fr, Strombus bubonius. 50fr, Enoplometopus callistus, vert. 65fr, Cypraea stercoraria.

1971-72 *Engr.* *Perf. 13*
301 A75 1fr olive & multi .50 .25
302 A75 5fr red & multi .50 .30
303 A75 10fr emer & multi 1.00 .30
304 A75 15fr brt bl & multi 1.00 .35
305 A75 15fr dp car & multi 1.50 .40
306 A75 20fr ocher & car 1.90 .50
307 A75 20fr ver & multi 2.25 .65
308 A75 25fr dk car, rose brn & black 1.25 .35
309 A75 35fr yel & multi 2.50 .75
310 A75 40fr emer & multi 4.00 1.25
311 A75 40fr brown & multi 3.25 1.10
312 A75 45fr multi 4.50 1.50
313 A75 50fr green & multi 5.00 1.60
314 A75 65fr bl, rose brn & sl grn 3.50 1.50
 Nos. 301-314 (14) 32.65 10.80

Issued: Nos. 304, 306, 310, 4/24/71; 5fr, 35fr, 50fr, 6/5/71; 1fr, 10fr, No. 311, 10/23/71; 25fr, 65fr, 1/29/72; Nos. 305, 307, 45fr, 4/3/72.

Submarine Cable Station, 1891 — A76

1971, May 17
315 A76 100fr bl, ocher & olive 2.25 .85

3rd World Telecommunications Day.

Apprentice and Lathe — A77

1971, June 19 *Engr.* *Perf. 13*
316 A77 35fr grn, slate & org brn .90 .40

Technical instruction and professional training.

Map of Africa and Telecommunications System — A78

1971, June 26 *Perf. 13x12½*
317 A78 45fr magenta & multi .85 .40

Pan-African Telecommunications system.

Bondoukou Market A79

1971, Aug. 7 *Engr.* *Perf. 13*
 Size: 48x27mm
318 A79 35fr ultra, brn & slate 1.00 .45

11th anniv. of independence. See No. C46.

White, Black and Yellow Girls — A80

1971, Oct. 10 *Photo.* *Perf. 13*
319 A80 40fr shown .80 .25
320 A80 45fr Boys around globe .80 .25

Intl. Year Against Racial Discrimination.

Gaming Table and Lottery Tickets — A81

1971, Nov. 13 *Perf. 12½*
321 A81 35fr green & multi 1.00 .50

National lottery.

Electric Power Installations — A82

1971, Dec. 18 *Perf. 13*
322 A82 35fr red brn & multi 2.00 .50

Cogwheel and Workers — A83

1972, Mar. 18 *Engr.* *Perf. 13*
323 A83 35fr org, bl & dk brn .70 .40

Technical Cooperation Week.

"Your Heart is Your Health" — A84

1972, Apr. 7 *Photo.* *Perf. 12½x13*
324 A84 40fr blue, olive & red .85 .50

World Health Day.

Girls Reading, Book Year Emblem — A85

35fr, Boys reading, horiz.

 Perf. 12½x13, 13x12½
1972, Apr. 22 *Engr.*
325 A85 35fr multi .70 .25
326 A85 40fr shown .90 .40

International Book Year.

Postal Sorting Center, Abidjan — A86

1972, May 13 *Perf. 13*
327 A86 40fr dk grn, rose lil & bis 1.10 .40

Stamp Day.

709

IVORY COAST

Radio Tower, Abobo, and ITU Emblem — A87

1972, May 17   Engr.   Perf. 13
328   A87   40fr blue, red & grn   2.00   .65
4th World Telecommunications Day.

Computer Operator, Punch Card — A88

1972, June 24
329   A88   40fr brt grn, bl & red   2.00   .60
Development of computerized information.

View of Odienné A89

1972, Aug. 7   Engr.   Perf. 13
330   A89   35fr bl, grn & brn   1.00   .60
12th anniversary of independence.

West African Monetary Union Issue
Common Design Type

1972, Nov. 2   Engr.   Perf. 13
331   CD136   40fr brn, gray & red lilac   1.00   .50

Diamond and Diamond Mine — A90

1972, Nov. 4
332   A90   40fr Prus bl, slate & org brn   3.25   1.60

Pasteur Institute, Louis Pasteur — A91

1972, Nov. 21
333   A91   35fr vio bl, grn & brn   1.10   .50
Pasteur (1822-1895), chemist and bacteriologist.

Children at Village Pump — A92

1972, Dec. 9   Engr.   Perf. 13
334   A92   35fr dk red, grn & blk   1.25   .40
Water campaign. See No. 360.

Arms Type of 1969

1973   Photo.   Perf. 12
335   A63   5fr Daloa   .45   .25
336   A63   10fr Gagnoa   .45   .25
Nos. 335-336 are 16½-17x22mm and have "DELRIEU" below design at right. Nos. 282-284 are 17x23mm and have no name at lower right.

Dr. Armauer G. Hansen — A93

1973, Feb. 3   Engr.   Perf. 13
342   A93   35fr lil, dp bl & brn   1.10   .40
Centenary of the discovery of the Hansen bacillus, the cause of leprosy.

Lake Village Bletankoro A94

1973, Mar. 10   Engr.   Perf. 13
343   A94   200fr choc, bl & grn   4.75   2.00

Balistes Capriscus — A95

Fish: 20fr, Pseudupeneus prayensis. 25fr, Cephalopholis taeniops. 35fr, Priacanthus arenatus. 50fr, Xyrichthys novacula.

1973-74   Engr.   Perf. 13
344   A95   15fr ind & slate grn   1.50   .60
345   A95   20fr lilac & multi   2.50   .75
346   A95   25fr slate grn & rose ('74)   3.75   .80
347   A95   35fr rose red & slate grn   2.75   1.10
348   A95   50fr blk, ultra & rose red   4.00   1.20
Nos. 344-348 (5)   14.50   4.45
Issued: 50fr, 3/24; 15fr, 20fr, 7/7; 35fr, 12/1; 25fr, 3/2.

Children — A96

1973, Apr. 7   Engr.   Perf. 13
354   A96   40fr grn, blk & dl red   1.10   .45
Establishment of first children's village in Africa (SOS villages for homeless children).

Parliament, Abidjan A97

1973, Apr. 24   Photo.   Perf. 13x12½
355   A97   100fr multicolored   1.25   .45
112th session of the Inter-parliamentary Council.

Teacher and PAC Store — A98

1973, May 12   Photo.   Perf. 13x12½
356   A98   40fr multicolored   .70   .25
Commercial Action Program (PAC).

Mother, Typist, Dress Form and Pot — A99

1973, May 26
357   A99   35fr multicolored   .90   .40
Technical instruction for women.

Farmers, African Scout Emblem — A100

1973, July 16   Photo.   Perf. 13x12½
358   A100   40fr multicolored   1.00   .60
24th Boy Scout World Conference, Nairobi, Kenya, July 16-21.

Party Headquarters, Yamoussokro — A101

1973, Aug. 7   Photo.   Perf. 13
359   A101   35fr multicolored   .70   .50

Children at Dry Pump — A102

1973, Aug. 16   Engr.
360   A102   40fr multicolored   1.25   .45
African solidarity in drought emergency.

African Postal Union Issue
Common Design Type

1973, Sept. 12   Engr.   Perf. 13
361   CD137   100fr pur, blk & red   2.50   1.00

Decorated Arrow Heads, Abidjan Museum — A103

1973, Sept. 15   Photo.   Perf. 12½x13
362   A103   5fr blk, brn red & brn   .55   .25

Ivory Coast No. 1 — A104

1973, Oct. 9   Engr.   Perf. 13
363   A104   40fr emer, blk & org   1.25   .60
Stamp Day.

Highway Intersection A105

1973, Oct. 13
364   A105   35fr blue, blk & grn   .90   .45
Indenie-Abidjan intersection.

Map of Africa, Federation Emblem — A106

1973, Oct. 26   Photo.   Perf. 13
365   A106   40fr ultra, red brn & vio bl   .65   .30
Intl. Social Security Federation, 18th General Assembly, Abidjan, Oct. 26-Nov. 3.

Elephant Emblem — A107

1973, Nov. 19
366   A107   40fr blk & bister   .75   .30
7th World Congress of the Universal Federation of World Travel Agents' Associations, Abidjan.

Kong Mosque A108

1974, Mar. 9
367   A108   35fr bl, grn & brn   1.10   .60

People and Sun — A109

1974, Apr. 20   Photo.   Perf. 13
368   A109   35fr multicolored   .65   .35
Permanent Mission to UN.

Grand Lahou Post Office A110

1974, May 17   Engr.   Perf. 13
369   A110   35fr multicolored   1.00   .60
Stamp Day.

Map and Flags of Members A110a

1974, May 29   Photo.   Perf. 13x12½
370   A110a   40fr blue & multi   .70   .25
15th anniversary of the Council of Accord.

Pres. Houphouet-Boigny
A111   **A112**

1974-76   Engr.   Perf. 13
371   A111   25fr grn, org & brn   .65   .25
   a.   Booklet pane of 10   6.50
   b.   Booklet pane of 20   13.00
373   A112   35fr org, grn & brn   1.00   .25
   a.   Booklet pane of 10   10.00
   b.   Booklet pane of 20   20.00

IVORY COAST

374	A112	40fr grn, org & brn	1.00	.25
a.		Booklet pane of 10	10.00	
375	A112	60fr bl, car & brn ('76)	.90	.40
376	A112	65fr car, bl & brn ('76)	.90	.40
		Nos. 371-376 (5)	4.45	1.55

See Nos. 783-792.

Ivory Coast Arms Type of 1969 with smaller "P" and "s" in "Postes"

1974, June 29   Photo.   *Perf. 12*

378	A63	35fr brn, emer & gold	.70	.25
a.		Booklet pane of 10	7.50	
b.		Booklet pane of 20	15.00	
379	A63	40fr vio, bl, emer & gold	.90	.25
a.		Booklet pane of 10	10.00	
b.		Booklet pane of 20	20.00	

Inscribed: "COTE D'IVOIRE"

1976, Jan.

380	A63	60fr car, gold & emer	.90	.25
381	A63	65fr grn, gold & emer	.90	.30
382	A63	70fr bl, gold & emer	1.00	.40
		Nos. 378-382 (5)	4.40	1.45

See design A297.

WPY Emblem — A114

1974, Aug. 19   Engr.   *Perf. 13*

383   A114   40fr emerald & blue   .80   .30
World Population Year.

Cotton Harvest — A115

1974, Sept. 21   Litho.   *Perf. 12½x13*

384   A115   50fr multicolored   1.10   .50

UPU Centenary A116

1974, Oct. 9   Engr.   *Perf. 13*

385   A116   40fr multicolored   .80   .30
See Nos. C59-C60.

Plowing Farmer, Service Emblem — A117

1974, Dec. 7   Photo.   *Perf. 13*

386   A117   35fr multicolored   .75   .30
14th anniversary of independence.

National Library, First Anniv. A118

1975, Jan. 9   Photo.   *Perf. 13*

387   A118   40fr multicolored   .70   .30

Raoul Follereau and Blind Students — A119

1975, Jan. 26   Engr.   *Perf. 13*

388   A119   35fr multicolored   1.75   .80
Follereau, educator of the blind and lepers.

Congress Emblem — A120

1975, Mar. 4   Photo.   *Perf. 12½x13*

389   A120   40fr blk & emerald   .75   .30
52nd Congress of the Intl. Assoc. of Seed Crushers, Abidjan, Mar. 2-7.

Coffee Cultivation — A121

1975, Mar. 15   *Perf. 13½x13*

390	A121	5fr multicolored	.35	.25
391	A121	10fr multicolored	.65	.25

Sassandra Wharf A122

1975, Apr. 19   Engr.   *Perf. 13*

392   A122   100fr multicolored   2.25   1.25

Letter Sorting — A123

1975, Apr. 26   Photo.   *Perf. 13*

393   A123   40fr multicolored   1.10   .60
Stamp Day.

Cotton Flower A124   **Cotton Bolls A125**

1975, May 3   Photo.   *Perf. 13*

394	A124	5fr multicolored	.45	.35
395	A125	10fr multicolored	.70	.35

Cotton cultivation.

Marie Kore, Women's Year Emblem A126

1975, May 19   Engr.   *Perf. 13*

396   A126   45fr lt bl, yel grn & brn   .75   .50
International Women's Year.

Fort Dabou A127

1975, June 7   Engr.   *Perf. 13*

397   A127   50fr multicolored   .90   .60

Abidjan Harbor A128

40fr, Grand Bassam wharf, 1906. 100fr, Planned harbor expansion on Locodjro.

1975, July 1   Photo.   *Perf. 13*

398	A128	35fr multicolored	1.10	.60

Miniature Sheet

399		Sheet of 3	9.50	9.50
a.	A128	40fr multi, vert.	3.75	3.75
b.	A128	100fr multi	4.00	4.00

25th anniversary of Abidjan Harbor. No. 399 contains Nos. 398, 399a, 399b.

Cacao Pods on Tree — A129

1975, Aug. 2

400   A129   35fr multicolored   2.25   .65

Farm Workers — A130

1975, Oct. 4   Photo.   *Perf. 13x12½*

401   A130   50fr multicolored   .85   .60
Natl. Org. for Rural Development.

Railroad Bridge, N'zi River — A131

1975, Dec. 7   Photo.   *Perf. 13*

402   A131   60fr multicolored   4.75   1.25
15th anniversary of independence.

Baoulé Mother and Child, Carved in Wood — A132

1976, Jan. 24   Litho.   *Perf. 13*

403   A132   65fr black & multi   2.00   .65

Baoulé Mask — A133   **Chief Abron's Chair — A133a**

1976, Feb. 7   Photo.   *Perf. 12½*

404	A133	20fr multicolored	.60	.30
405	A133a	150fr multicolored	3.00	1.00

Senufo Statuette — A134

1976, Feb. 21   *Perf. 13x13½*

406   A134   25fr ocher & multi   .75   .45

Telephones 1876 and 1976 — A135

1976, Mar. 10   Litho.   *Perf. 12*

407   A135   70fr multicolored   1.10   .65
Centenary of first telephone call by Alexander Graham Bell, Mar. 10, 1876.

Ivory Coast Map, Pigeon, Carving — A136

1976, Apr. 10   Photo.   *Perf. 12½*

408   A136   65fr multicolored   1.25   .60
20th Stamp Day.

Smiling Trees and Cat — A137

1976, June 5   Litho.   *Perf. 12½*

409   A137   65fr multicolored   1.25   .60
Nature protection.

Children with Books — A138

1976, July 3   Photo.   *Perf. 12½x13*

410   A138   65fr multicolored   1.10   .60

IVORY COAST

Runner, Maple Leaf, Olympic Rings — A139

1976, July 17	Litho.		Perf. 12
411	A139 60fr Javelin, vert.	1.00	.55
412	A139 65fr shown	1.00	.55

21st Olympic Games, Montreal, Canada, July 17-Aug. 1.

Mohammad Ali Jinnah — A139a

1976, Aug. 14	Litho.		Perf. 13
412A	A139a 50fr multicolored	65.00	15.00

1st Governor-General of Pakistan.

Cashew — A140

1976, Sept. 18			Perf. 12½
413	A140 65fr blue & multi	1.90	.70

Highway and Conference Emblem A141

1976, Oct. 25	Litho.		Perf. 12½x12
414	A141 60fr multicolored	.90	.50

3rd African Highway Conference, Abidjan, July 25-30.

Pres. Houphouet-Boigny — A142

1976-77	Photo.		Perf. 13½x12½
415	A142 35fr brn, red lil & blk ('77)	125.00	—
416	A142 40fr brt grn, ocher & brn blk	4.50	.75
a.	Bklt. pane of 12 (8#416, 4#417)	55.00	
417	A142 45fr ocher, brt grn & brn blk	4.50	1.00
418	A142 60fr brn, mag & brn blk	6.00	1.00
419	A142 65fr grn, org & brn blk	7.00	1.50
	Nos. 416-419 (4)	22.00	4.25

The 40fr and 45fr issued in booklet and coil; 35fr, 60fr and 65fr in coil only. No. 416 coil sells for about the same as No. 415.
Stamps from booklets are imperf. on one side or two adjoining sides. Coils have control number on back of every 10th stamp.

John Paul Jones, American Marine and Ship — A143

American Bicentennial: 125fr, Count de Rochambeau and grenadier of Touraine Regiment. 150fr, Admiral Count Jean Baptiste d'Estaing and French marine. 175fr, Lafayette and grenadier of Soissons Regiment. 200fr, Jefferson, American soldier, Declaration of Independence. 500fr, Washington, US flag, Continental officer.

1976, Nov. 27	Litho.		Perf. 11
421	A143 100fr multicolored	1.50	.30
422	A143 125fr multicolored	1.75	.45
423	A143 150fr multicolored	2.00	.55
424	A143 175fr multicolored	2.00	.70
425	A143 200fr multicolored	2.50	.75
	Nos. 421-425 (5)	9.75	2.75

Souvenir Sheet
| 426 | A143 500fr multicolored | 7.00 | 2.50 |

"Development and Solidarity" A144

1976, Dec. 7	Photo.		Perf. 13
427	A144 60fr multicolored	.90	.60

16th anniversary of independence.

Benin Head, Ivory Coast Arms — A145

1977, Jan. 15	Photo.		Perf. 13
428	A145 65fr gold, dk brn & grn	1.10	.75

2nd World Black and African Festival, Lagos, Nigeria, Jan. 15-Feb. 12.

Musical Instruments A146

5fr, Baoule bells. 10fr, Senufo balafon. 20fr, Dida drum.

1977, Mar. 5	Engr.		Perf. 13
429	A146 5fr multi	.35	.25
430	A146 10fr multi	.35	.25
431	A146 20fr multi	.55	.25
	Nos. 429-431 (3)	1.25	.75

Air Afrique Plane Unloading Mail — A147

1977, Apr. 9	Litho.		Perf. 13
432	A147 60fr multicolored	1.25	.60

Stamp Day.

Sassenage Castle, Grenoble — A148

1977, May 21	Litho.		Perf. 12½
433	A148 100fr multicolored	2.00	.75

Intl. French Language Council, 10th anniv.

Orville and Wilbur Wright, "Wright Flyer," 1903 — A149

History of Aviation: 75fr, Louis Bleriot crossing English Channel, 1909. 100fr, Ross Smith and Vickers-Vimy (flew England-Australia, 1919). 200fr, Charles A. Lindbergh and "Spirit of St. Louis" (flew New York-Paris, 1927). 300fr, Supersonic jet Concorde, 1976. 500fr, Lindbergh in flying suit and "Spirit of St. Louis."

1977, June 27	Litho.		Perf. 14
434	A149 60fr multi	1.00	.30
435	A149 75fr multi	1.10	.30
436	A149 100fr multi	1.25	.30
437	A149 200fr multi	3.00	.75
438	A149 300fr multi	4.00	1.25
	Nos. 434-438 (5)	10.35	2.90

Souvenir Sheet
| 439 | A149 500fr multi | 6.50 | 2.00 |

Santos Dumont's "Ville de Paris," 1907 — A150

65fr, LZ1 at takeoff. 150fr, "Schwaben" LZ10 over Germany. 200fr, "Bodensee" LZ120, 1919. 300fr, LZ127 over Sphinx & pyramids.

1977, Sept. 3	Litho.		Perf. 11
440	A150 60fr multi	1.00	.25
441	A150 65fr multi	1.00	.35
442	A150 150fr multi	2.00	.55
443	A150 200fr multi	3.00	1.00
444	A150 300fr multi	4.00	1.25
	Nos. 440-444 (5)	11.00	3.40

History of the Zeppelin. Exist imperf. See No. C63.

Congress Emblem — A151

1977, Sept. 12	Photo.		Perf. 12½
445	A151 60fr lt & dk grn	.80	.50

17th Intl. Congress of Administrative Sciences in Africa, Abidjan, Sept. 12-16.

A152

1977, Nov. 12	Photo.		Perf. 13½x14
446	A152 65fr multicolored	3.25	.75

Yamoussoukro, 1st Ivory Coast container ship.

Butterflies — A152a

Designs: 30fr, Epiphora rectifascia boolana. 60fr, Charaxes jasius epijasius. 65fr, Imbrasia arata. 100fr, Palla decius.

1977, Nov.	Photo.		Perf. 14x13
446A	A152a 30fr multi	—	2.25
446B	A152a 60fr multi	—	17.50
446C	A152a 65fr multi	—	4.00
446D	A152a 100fr multi	—	6.00
	Nos. 446A-446D (4)		29.75
	Set, unused	280.00	

A153

1977, Dec. 7	Photo.		Perf. 13½
447	A153 60fr multicolored	.90	.65

17th anniversary of independence.

Flowers — A153a

5fr, Strophanthus hispidus. 20fr, Anthurium cultorum. 60fr, Arachnis flos-aeris. 65fr, Renanthera storiei.

1977	Photo.		Perf. 13x14
447A	A153a 5fr multi	125.00	62.50
447B	A153a 20fr multi	125.00	62.50
447C	A153a 60fr multi	125.00	62.50
447D	A153a 65fr multi	125.00	62.50
	Nos. 447A-447D (4)	500.00	250.00

Presidents Giscard d'Estaing and Houphouet-Boigny — A154

1978, Jan. 11			Perf. 13
448	A154 60fr multicolored	1.00	.35
449	A154 65fr multicolored	1.25	.35
450	A154 100fr multicolored	1.60	.75
a.	Souvenir sheet, 500fr	9.25	9.25
	Nos. 448-450 (3)	3.85	1.45

Visit of Pres. Valery Giscard d'Estaing. No. 450a contains one stamp.

St. George and the Dragon, by Rubens — A155

Paintings by Peter Paul Rubens (1577-1640): 150fr, Child's head. 250fr, Annunciation. 300fr, The Birth of Louis XIII. 500fr, Virgin & Child.

1978, Mar. 4	Litho.		Perf. 13½
451	A155 65fr gold & multi	.90	.35
452	A155 150fr gold & multi	2.00	.60
453	A155 250fr gold & multi	3.00	1.00
454	A155 300fr gold & multi	4.25	1.50
	Nos. 451-454 (4)	10.15	3.45

Souvenir Sheet
| 455 | A155 500fr gold & multi | 7.00 | 3.25 |

Royal Guards A156

65fr, Cosmological figures.

1978, Apr. 1	Litho.		Perf. 12½
456	A156 60fr shown	1.25	.40
457	A156 65fr multicolored	1.25	.40

IVORY COAST

Rural Postal Center — A157

1978, Apr. 8
458 A157 60fr multicolored 1.00 .60
Stamp Day.

Antenna, ITU Emblem — A158

1978, May 17 *Perf. 13*
459 A158 60fr multicolored .90 .50
10th World Telecommunications Day.

Svante August Arrhenius, Electrolytic Apparatus A159

Nobel Prize Winners: 75fr, Jules Bordet, child, mountains, eagle and Petri dish. 100fr, André Gide, and St. Peter's, Rome. 200fr, John Steinbeck and horse farm. 300fr, Children with flowers and UNICEF emblem. 500fr, Max Planck, rockets and earth.

1978, May 27 *Litho.* *Perf. 13½*
460 A159 60fr multi .75 .25
461 A159 75fr multi 1.00 .30
462 A159 100fr multi 1.00 .35
463 A159 200fr multi 2.00 .70
464 A159 300fr multi 4.00 1.00
  Nos. 460-464 (5) 8.75 2.60

Souvenir Sheet
465 A159 500fr multi 5.50 2.00

Soccer Ball, Player and Argentina '78 Emblem A160

Soccer Ball, Argentina '78 Emblem and: 65fr, Player, vert. 100fr, Player, diff. 150fr, Goalkeeper. 300fr, Ball as sun, and player, vert. 500fr, Ball as globe with Argentina on map of South America.

1978, June 17
466 A160 60fr multi .70 .25
467 A160 65fr multi .85 .30
468 A160 100fr multi 1.00 .55
469 A160 150fr multi 1.50 .60
470 A160 300fr multi 3.00 .95
  Nos. 466-470 (5) 7.05 2.65

Souvenir Sheet
471 A160 500fr multi 5.00 2.00
11th World Cup Soccer Championship, Argentina, June 1-25.

Miniodes Discolor — A161

Butterflies: 65fr, Charaxes lactetinctus. 100fr, Papilio zalmoxis. 200fr, Papilio antimachus.

1978, July 8 *Photo.* *Perf. 14x13*
472 A161 60fr multicolored 3.75 1.00
473 A161 65fr multicolored 3.75 1.00
474 A161 100fr multicolored 5.50 1.75
475 A161 200fr multicolored 10.00 4.00
  Nos. 472-475 (4) 23.00 7.75

Cricket — A162

Insects: 20fr, 60fr, Various hemiptera. 65fr, Goliath beetle.

1978, Aug. 26 *Litho.* *Perf. 12½*
476 A162 10fr multicolored 1.10 .40
477 A162 20fr multicolored 1.75 .40
478 A162 60fr multicolored 3.50 1.00
479 A162 65fr multicolored 5.00 1.25
  Nos. 476-479 (4) 11.35 3.05

Stylized Figures Emerging from TV Screen — A163

65fr, Passengers on train made up of TV sets.

1978, Sept. 18 *Perf. 13*
480 A163 60fr multicolored .90 .30
481 A163 65fr multicolored 1.10 .35
Educational television programs.

Map of Ivory Coast, Mobile Drill Platform Ship — A164

Map of Ivory Coast, Ram at Discovery Site and: 65fr, Gold goblets. 500fr, Pres. Houphouet-Boigny holding gold goblets.

1978, Oct. 18 *Litho.* *Perf. 12½x12*
482 A164 60fr multicolored 1.40 .50
483 A164 65fr multicolored 1.40 .50

Souvenir Sheet
484 A164 500fr multicolored 12.00 12.00
Announcement of oil discovery off the coast of Ivory Coast, 1st anniv.

National Assembly, Paris, UPU Emblem — A165

1978, Dec. 2 *Litho.* *Perf. 13½*
485 A165 200fr multicolored 2.00 .90
Congress of Paris, centenary.

Drummer — A166

1978, Dec. 7 *Photo.* *Perf. 12½x13*
486 A166 60fr multicolored 1.10 .60
18th anniversary of independence.

Poster — A167

Design: 65fr, Arrows made of flags, and television screen.

1978, Dec. 12
487 A167 60fr multicolored .90 .40
488 A167 65fr multicolored .90 .40
Technical cooperation among developing countries with the help of educational television.

Plowing A168

1979, Jan. 27 *Photo.* *Perf. 13*
489 A168 100fr multicolored 2.00 .60

King Hassan II, Pres. Houphouet-Boigny, Flags and Map of Morocco and Ivory Coast — A169

1979, Jan. 27 *Photo.* *Perf. 13*
490 A169 60fr multicolored 2.50 1.00
491 A169 65fr multicolored 3.50 1.25
492 A169 500fr multicolored 17.50 7.50
  Nos. 490-492 (3) 23.50 9.75
Visit of King Hassan of Morocco to Ivory Coast. The visit never took place and the stamps were not issued. To recover the printing costs the stamps were sold in Paris for one day.

Horus A170

500fr, Vulture with ankh, cartouches.

1979, Feb. 17 *Litho.* *Perf. 12½*
493 A170 200fr silver, turq & grn 3.00 1.25
494 A170 500fr gold, org & brn 6.50 3.25
UNESCO drive to save Temples of Philae.

Flowers — A171

30fr, Locranthus. 60fr, Vanda Josephine. 65fr, Renanthera storiei.

1979, Feb. 24
495 A171 30fr multicolored 1.00 .50
496 A171 60fr multicolored 1.50 .60
497 A171 65fr multicolored 1.75 .80
  Nos. 495-497 (3) 4.25 1.90

Wildlife Protection A172

1979, Mar. 24 *Photo.* *Perf. 13x13½*
498 A172 50fr Hippopotamus 2.25 .70

Globe and Emblem A173

Child Riding Dove A174

1979, Apr. 1 *Litho.* *Perf. 12x12½*
499 A173 60fr multicolored .60 .45
500 A174 65fr multicolored .70 .50
501 A173 100fr multicolored 1.50 .90
502 A174 500fr multicolored 5.50 3.00
  Nos. 499-502 (4) 8.30 4.85
International Year of the Child.

Rural Mail Delivery A175

1979, Apr. 7 *Perf. 12½*
503 A175 60fr multicolored 1.10 .35
Stamp Day.

Korhogo Cathedral A176

1979, Apr. 9 *Perf. 13*
504 A176 60fr multicolored .90 .45
Arrival of Catholic missionaries, 75th anniv.

Crying Child — A177

1979, May 17 *Litho.* *Perf. 12½*
505 A177 65fr multicolored .90 .50
10th anniv. of SOS Village (for homeless children).

Euphaedra Xypete — A178

Butterflies: 65fr, Pseudacraea bois duvali. 70fr, Auchenisa schausi.

1979, May 26 *Perf. 13x13½*
506 A178 60fr multicolored 2.50 1.00
507 A178 65fr multicolored 3.00 1.00
508 A178 70fr multicolored 4.50 1.50
  Nos. 506-508 (3) 10.00 3.50

Endangered Animals — A179

5fr, Antelopes. 20fr, Duikerbok. 60fr, Aardvark.

IVORY COAST

1979, June 2

509	A179	5fr multicolored	.75	.35
510	A179	20fr multicolored	1.25	.45
511	A179	60fr multicolored	4.00	1.40
		Nos. 509-511 (3)	6.00	2.20

UPU Emblem, Radar, Truck and Ship — A180

No. 513, Ancestral figure & antelope, vert.

1979, June 8   *Engr.*   *Perf. 13*

| 512 | A180 | 70fr multicolored | 3.00 | 2.00 |

Photo.

| 513 | A180 | 70fr multicolored | 3.00 | 2.00 |

Philexafrique II, Libreville, Gabon, June 8-17. Nos. 512, 513 each printed in sheets of 10 with 5 labels showing exhibition emblem.

Rowland Hill, Steam Locomotive, Great Britain No. 75 — A181

Rowland Hill, Locomotives and: 75fr, Ivory Coast #125. 100fr, Hawaii #4. 150fr, Japan #30, syll. 3. 300fr, France #2. 500fr, Ivory Coast #123.

1979, July 7   *Litho.*   *Perf. 13½*

514	A181	60fr multi	.70	.25
515	A181	75fr multi	.80	.30
516	A181	100fr multi	1.25	.40
517	A181	150fr multi	1.50	.65
518	A181	300fr multi	3.25	1.25
		Nos. 514-518 (5)	7.50	2.45

Souvenir Sheet

| 519 | A181 | 500fr multi | 6.75 | 3.00 |

Sir Rowland Hill (1795-1879), originator of penny postage.

Insects — A181a

30fr, Wasp. 60fr, Praying mantis, vert. 65fr, Cricket.

1979   *Photo.*   *Perf. 14x13, 13x14*

519A	A181a	30fr multi	15.00	2.50
519B	A181a	60fr multi	30.00	4.00
519C	A181a	65fr multi	40.00	4.00
		Nos. 519A-519C (3)	85.00	10.50

A181b

Musical instruments: 100fr, Harp. 150fr, Whistles.

1979   *Photo.*   *Perf. 13x14*

| 519D | A181b | 100fr multi | 35.00 | 14.00 |
| 519E | A181b | 150fr multi | 50.00 | 20.00 |

"TELECOM 79" — A182

1979, Sept. 20   *Litho.*   *Perf. 13x12½*

| 520 | A182 | 60fr multicolored | .90 | .40 |

3rd World Telecommunications Exhibition, Geneva, Sept. 20-26.

Culture Day — A183

1979, Oct. 13   *Perf. 12½*

| 521 | A183 | 65fr multicolored | .90 | .40 |

Fish — A183a

60fr, Pterois volitans. 65fr, Coelacanth.

1979   *Photo.*   *Perf. 14x13*

| 521A | A183a | 60fr multi | 150.00 | — |
| 521B | A183a | 65fr multi | 150.00 | — |

Boxing A184

65fr, Running. 100fr, Soccer. 150fr, Bicycling. 300fr, Wrestling. 500fr, Gymnastics.

1979, Oct. 27   *Litho.*   *Perf. 14x13½*

522	A184	60fr shown	.60	.25
523	A184	65fr multicolored	.65	.25
524	A184	100fr multicolored	1.00	.35
525	A184	150fr multicolored	1.50	.45
526	A184	300fr multicolored	3.25	1.25
		Nos. 522-526 (5)	7.00	2.55

Souvenir Sheet

| 527 | A184 | 500fr multicolored | 6.00 | 2.00 |

Pre-Olympic Year.

Wildlife Fund Emblem and Jentink's Duiker — A185

Wildlife Protection: 60fr, Colobus Monkey. 75fr, Manatees. 100fr, Epixerus ebii. 150fr, Hippopotamus. 300fr, Chimpanzee.

1979, Nov. 3   *Litho.*   *Perf. 14½*

528	A185	40fr multi	3.00	.30
529	A185	60fr multi	3.25	.50
530	A185	75fr multi	4.00	.60
531	A185	100fr multi	4.75	.85
532	A185	150fr multi	6.50	1.25
533	A185	300fr multi	15.00	2.50
		Nos. 528-533 (6)	36.50	6.00

Raoul Follereau Institute, Adzope — A186

1979, Dec. 6   *Litho.*   *Perf. 12½*

| 534 | A186 | 60fr multicolored | 1.40 | .70 |

Independence, 19th Anniversary — A187

1979, Dec. 7   *Litho.*   *Perf. 14x13½*

| 535 | A187 | 60fr multicolored | 1.10 | .35 |

Fireball — A188

Local Flora: 5fr, Clerodendron thomsonae, vert. 50fr, Costus incanusiamus, vert. 60fr, Ficus elastica abidjan, vert.

1980   *Litho.*   *Perf. 12½*

536	A188	5fr multicolored	.30	.25
537	A188	10fr multicolored	.40	.25
538	A188	50fr multicolored	1.10	.30
539	A188	60fr multicolored	1.25	.30
		Nos. 536-539 (4)	3.05	1.10

Issued: 5fr, 10fr, Jan. 26; 50fr, 60fr, Feb. 16.

Rotary Intl., 75th Anniv. — A189

1980, Feb. 23   *Photo.*   *Perf. 13½*

| 540 | A189 | 65fr multicolored | .90 | .50 |

International Archives Day — A190

1980, Feb. 26   *Litho.*

| 541 | A190 | 65fr multicolored | .90 | .50 |

Astronaut Shaking Hands with Boy — A191

Path of Apollo 11 — A192

1980, July 6   *Photo.*

542	A191	60fr multicolored	.90	.50
543	A192	65fr multicolored	.90	.50
544	A191	70fr multicolored	1.75	.75
545	A192	150fr multicolored	3.00	1.75
		Nos. 542-545 (4)	6.55	3.50

Apollo 11 moon landing, 10th anniv. (1979).

Jet and Map of Africa — A193

1980, Mar. 22   *Perf. 12½*

| 546 | A193 | 60fr multicolored | .90 | .45 |

ASECNA (Air Safety Board), 20th anniv.

Boys and Stamp Album, Globe A194

1980, Apr. 12   *Litho.*   *Perf. 12½*

| 547 | A194 | 65fr bl grn & red brn | 1.10 | .50 |

Stamp Day; Youth philately.

Missionary and Church, Aboisso — A195

1980, Apr. 26   *Photo.*   *Perf. 13x13½*

| 548 | A195 | 60fr multicolored | 1.10 | .50 |

Settlement of the Holy Fathers at Aboisso, 75th anniversary.

Fight Against Cigarette Smoking — A196

1980, May 3   *Perf. 12½*

| 549 | A196 | 60fr multicolored | 1.10 | .50 |

Pope John Paul II, Pres. Houphouet-Boigny — A197

1980, May 10   *Photo.*   *Perf. 13*

| 550 | A197 | 65fr multicolored | 2.50 | 1.00 |

Visit of Pope John Paul II to Ivory Coast.

Le Belier Locomotive A198

65fr, Abidjan Railroad Station, 1904. 100fr, Passenger car, 1908. 150fr, Steam locomotive, 1940.

1980, May 17   *Litho.*   *Perf. 13*

551	A198	60fr shown	.70	.35
552	A198	65fr multicolored	.80	.35
553	A198	100fr multicolored	1.60	.60
554	A198	150fr multicolored	2.00	1.00
		Nos. 551-554 (4)	5.10	2.30

Central Bank of West African States, 1st Anniversary — A199

1980, May 26   *Litho.*   *Perf. 12x12½*

| 555 | A199 | 60fr multicolored | .90 | .50 |

Lujtanus Sebae — A200

65fr, Monodactylus sebae, vert. 100fr, Colisa fasciata.

1980, Apr. 19   *Photo.*   *Perf. 14*

556	A200	60fr shown	3.25	.65
557	A200	65fr multicolored	3.50	1.00
558	A200	100fr multicolored	3.75	1.40
		Nos. 556-558 (3)	10.50	3.05

Snake A201

IVORY COAST

1980, July 12 Litho. *Perf. 12½*
559 A201 60fr shown 2.00 .75
560 A201 150fr Toad 4.75 1.75

Tourists in Village, by K. Ehouman Pierre — A202

Conference Emblem — A203

1980, Aug. 9
561 A202 60fr multicolored .75 .30
562 A203 65fr multicolored .75 .30
National Tourist Office, Abidjan; World Tourism Conference, Manila.

Insects — A204

60fr, Forticula auricularia (Common Earwig). 65fr, Mantis religiosa (Praying mantis), vert.

Perf. 14x13, 13x14
1980, Sept. 6 Photo.
563 A204 60fr shown 5.00 2.00
564 A204 65fr multicolored 5.00 2.00

Cicadas — A204a

60fr, Cicada (Cicadidae sp.). 200fr, Cicada (Cicadidae sp.), with wings.

Perf. 13½x13, 13x13½
1980, Oct. 11 Photo.
565 A204a 60fr multi, vert. 2.50 1.25
566 A204a 200fr multi 7.50 3.50

Hands Free from Chain, Map of Ivory Coast, Pres. Houphouet-Boigny — A205

Pres. Houphouet-Boigny, Symbols of Development — A206

Perf. 12½x13, 14x14½ (A206)
1980, Oct. 18
567 A205 60fr shown 1.25 .75
568 A206 65fr shown 1.25 .75
569 A205 70fr Map, colors, document 1.75 1.00
570 A205 150fr like #567 4.25 2.75
571 A206 300fr like #568 7.50 4.25
Nos. 567-571 (5) 16.00 9.50
Pres. Houphouet-Boigny, 75th birthday.

7th PDCI and RDA Congress — A207

1980, Oct. 25 *Perf. 12½*
572 A207 60fr multicolored .90 .40
573 A207 65fr multicolored .90 .40

River Cruise Boat Sotra — A208

1980, Dec. 6 Litho. *Perf. 13x13½*
574 A208 60fr multicolored 1.10 .60

View of Abidjan A209

1980, Dec. 7 *Perf. 13x12½*
575 A209 60fr multicolored .90 .30
20th anniversary of independence.

Universities Association Emblem — A210

1980, Dec. 16 *Perf. 12½*
576 A210 60fr multicolored .90 .50
African Universities Assoc., 5th General Conf.

African Postal Union, 5th Anniversary — A211

1980, Dec. 24 Photo. *Perf. 13½*
577 A211 150fr multi 1.50 .60

Herichtys Cyanoguttatum A212

65fr, Labeo bicolor. 200fr, Tetraodon fluviatilis.

1981, Mar. 14 Litho. *Perf. 12½*
578 A212 60fr shown 1.10 .65
579 A212 65fr multicolored 1.25 .75
580 A212 200fr multicolored 3.25 1.75
Nos. 578-580 (3) 5.60 3.15

Birds — A212a

No. 580A, Spreo superbus. No. 580B, Tockus camurus. No. 580C, Balearica pavonina. No. 580D, Ephippiorhyn-chus.

1980, Dec. 30 Photo. *Perf. 14½x14*
580A A212a 60fr multi 300.00 60.00
580B A212a 65fr multi 300.00 60.00
580C A212a 65fr multi 300.00 60.00
580D A212a 100fr multi 300.00 60.00
Nos. 580A-580D (4) 1,200. 240.00

Post Office, Grand Lahou — A213

25th Anniv. of Ivory Coast Philatelic Club — A214

1981, May 2 Litho. *Perf. 12½*
581 A213 60fr multicolored .90 .30
582 A214 65fr multicolored .90 .30
Stamp Day.

13th World Telecommunications Day — A215

1981, May 17
583 A215 30fr multicolored .45 .25
584 A215 60fr multicolored .90 .35

Viking Satellite Landing, 1976 A216

Space Conquest: Columbia space shuttle.

1981, June 13 Litho. *Perf. 13½*
585 A216 60fr multi .65 .25
586 A216 75fr multi .85 .30
587 A216 125fr multi 1.25 .55
588 A216 300fr multi 2.75 1.25
Nos. 585-588 (4) 5.50 2.35
Souvenir Sheet
589 A216 500fr multi 5.25 1.25

Local Flowers — A217

50fr, Amorphophallus. 60fr, Sugar Cane. 100fr, Heliconia ivoirea.

1981, July 4 Photo. *Perf. 14½x14*
590 A217 50fr multicolored 1.60 .55
591 A217 60fr multicolored 1.90 1.00
592 A217 100fr multicolored 3.75 1.50
Nos. 590-592 (3) 7.25 3.05

Prince Charles and Lady Diana, Coach — A218

Royal Wedding: Couple and coaches.

1981, Aug. 8 Litho. *Perf. 12½*
593 A218 80fr multi .80 .25
594 A218 100fr multi 1.00 .50
595 A218 125fr multi 1.50 .85
Nos. 593-595 (3) 3.30 1.60
Souvenir Sheet
596 A218 500fr multi 5.50 2.00
For overprints see Nos. 642-645.

Elephant on Flag and Map — A219

1981, Sept. Litho. *Perf. 12½*
597 A219 80fr multicolored .75 .25
598 A219 100fr multicolored 1.00 .50
599 A219 125fr multicolored 1.25 .60
Nos. 597-599 (3) 3.00 1.35
See Nos. 662-666, 833.

Soccer Players — A220

Soccer players.

1981, Sept. 19 *Perf. 14*
600 A220 70fr multi, horiz. .65 .35
601 A220 80fr multi, horiz. .75 .45
602 A220 100fr multi .90 .55
603 A220 150fr multi 1.25 .85
604 A220 350fr multi 3.25 1.60
Nos. 600-604 (5) 6.80 3.80
Souvenir Sheet
605 A220 500fr multi, horz. 4.75 2.00
ESPANA '82 World Cup Soccer Championship.
For overprints see Nos. 651-656.

West African Rice Development Assoc., 10th Anniv. — A221

1981, Oct. 3 *Perf. 12½*
606 A221 80fr multicolored 1.10 .50

World Food Day — A222

1981, Oct. 18
607 A222 100fr multicolored 1.10 .60

Post Day — A223

1981, Oct. 9 Litho. *Perf. 12½*
608 A223 70fr multicolored .65 .30
609 A223 80fr multicolored .75 .45
610 A223 100fr multicolored .95 .55
Nos. 608-610 (3) 2.35 1.30

75th Anniv. of Grand Prix — A224

Winners and their cars: 15fr, Felice Nazarro, 1907. 40fr, Jim Clark, 1962. 80fr, Fiat, 1907. 100fr, Auto Union, 1936. 125fr, Ferrari, 1961. 500fr, 1933 car.

IVORY COAST

1981, Nov. 21 — Perf. 14
611	A224	15fr multi	.25	.25
612	A224	40fr multi	.50	.25
613	A224	80fr multi	1.00	.45
614	A224	100fr multi	1.25	.50
615	A224	125fr multi	1.50	.60
	Nos. 611-615 (5)		4.50	2.05

Souvenir Sheet
616	A224	500fr multi	5.75	2.75

21st Anniv. of Independence — A225

1981, Dec. 7 — Perf. 13x12½
617	A225	50fr multicolored	.60	.30
618	A225	80fr multicolored	1.10	.50

Traditional Hairstyle — A226

Designs: Various hairstyles.

1981, Dec. 19 — Photo. — Perf. 14½x14
619	A226	80fr multicolored	1.50	.75
620	A226	100fr multicolored	2.50	1.10
621	A226	125fr multicolored	3.25	1.50
	Nos. 619-621 (3)		7.25	3.35

Stamp Day Africa A227

100fr, Bingerville P.O., 1902.

1982, Apr. 3 — Litho. — Perf. 12½x12
622	A227	100fr multicolored	1.10	.60

Rotary Emblem on Map of — A228

1982, Apr. 13 — Perf. 12½
623	A228	100fr ultra & gold	1.10	.60

Pres. Houphouet-Boigny's Rotary Goodwill Conference, Abidjan, Apr. 13-15.

250th Birth Anniv. of George Washington A229

Anniversaries: 100fr, Auguste Piccard (1884-1962), Swiss physicist. 350fr, Goethe (1749-1832). 450fr, 500fr, Princess Diana, 21st birthday (portraits).

1982, May 15 — Litho. — Perf. 13
624	A229	80fr multi	.75	.35
625	A229	100fr multi	1.00	.50
626	A229	350fr multi	3.75	1.25
627	A229	450fr multi	4.50	1.50
	Nos. 624-627 (4)		10.00	3.60

Souvenir Sheet
628	A229	500fr multi	4.50	2.00

Visit of French Pres. Mitterand, May 21-24 A230

1982, May 21 — Photo. — Perf. 13½
629	A230	100fr multicolored	1.40	.55

14th World Telecommunications Day — A231

1982, May 29 — Litho. — Perf. 13
630	A231	80fr multicolored	.85	.30

Scouting Year — A232

Scouts sailing, diff. 80fr, 150fr, 350fr, 500fr vert.

1982, May 29 — Perf. 12½
631	A232	80fr multi	.85	.30
632	A232	100fr multi	1.25	.35
633	A232	150fr multi	1.50	.60
634	A232	350fr multi	3.50	1.25
	Nos. 631-634 (4)		7.10	2.50

Souvenir Sheet
635	A232	500fr multi	6.00	2.50

TB Bacillus Centenary A233

1982, June 5 — Photo. — Perf. 13x13½
636	A233	30fr brown & multi	.70	.30
637	A233	80fr lt grn & multi	1.10	.50

UN Conference on Human Environment, 10th Anniv. — A234

1982, July — Photo. — Perf. 13½x13
638	A234	40fr multicolored	.70	.30
639	A234	80fr multicolored	1.25	.45

League of Ivory Coast Secretaries, First Congress — A235

1982, Aug. 9 — Litho. — Perf. 12½x13
640	A235	80fr tan & multi	1.00	.40
641	A235	100fr silver & multi	1.25	.50

593-596 Overprinted in Blue "NAISSANCE / ROYALE 1982"

1982, Aug. 21 — Perf. 12½
642	A218	80fr multi	.85	.45
643	A218	100fr multi	1.00	.55
644	A218	125fr multi	1.25	.65
	Nos. 642-644 (3)		3.10	1.65

Souvenir Sheet
645	A218	500fr multi	4.50	4.50

Birth of Prince William of Wales, June 21.

La Colombe de l'Avenir, 1962, by Pablo Picasso (1881-1973) A236

Picasso Paintings: 80fr, Child with Dove, 1901. 100fr, Self-portrait, 1901. 185fr, Les Demoiselles d'Avignon, 1907. 350fr, The Dream, 1932. Nos. 646-649 vert.

1982, Sept. 4 — Litho. — Perf. 13
646	A236	80fr multi	.85	.35
647	A236	100fr multi	1.00	.40
648	A236	185fr multi	2.50	.65
649	A236	350fr multi	4.00	1.25
650	A236	500fr multi	6.00	1.75
	Nos. 646-650 (5)		14.35	4.40

Nos. 600-605 Overprinted with World Cup Winners 1966-1982 in Black on Silver

1982, Oct. 9 — Litho. — Perf. 14
651	A220	70fr multi	.65	.30
652	A220	80fr multi	.80	.50
653	A220	100fr multi	1.00	.55
654	A220	150fr multi	1.50	.90
655	A220	350fr multi	3.50	1.50
	Nos. 651-655 (5)		7.45	3.75

Souvenir Sheet
656	A220	500fr multi	5.50	5.50

Italy's victory in 1982 World Cup.

13th World UPU Day — A237

Designs: 80fr, P.O. counter. 100fr, Postel-2001 building, Abidjan, vert. 350fr, Postal workers. 500fr, Postel-2001 interior.

1982, Oct. 23 — Perf. 12½
657	A237	80fr multi	.75	.45
658	A237	100fr multi	1.25	.50
659	A237	350fr multi	3.25	1.50

Size: 48x37mm — Perf. 13
660	A237	500fr multi	4.50	2.25
	Nos. 657-660 (4)		9.75	4.70

22nd Anniv. of Independence A238

1982, Dec. 7 — Perf. 13
661	A238	100fr multicolored	1.10	.60

Elephant Type of 1981

1982-84
662	A219	5fr multicolored	.25	.25
662A	A219	10fr multi ('84)	.45	.25
662B	A219	20fr multicolored	.45	.25
663	A219	25fr multicolored	.35	.25
664	A219	30fr multicolored	.35	.25
665	A219	40fr multicolored	.55	.25
666	A219	50fr multicolored	.55	.25
	Nos. 662-666 (7)		2.95	1.75

Man Waterfall A238a

No. 666B, Boisee Savanna.

1982 — Photo. — Perf. 15x14
666A	A238a	80fr shown	20.00	2.00
666B	A238a	80fr multi	30.00	1.75
666C	A238a	500fr like #666A	65.00	7.00
	Nos. 666A-666C (3)		115.00	10.75

Issued: No. 666B, 12/18; others, 11/27.

20th Anniv. of West African Monetary Union — A239

1982, Dec. 21 — Litho. — Perf. 12½
667	A239	100fr Emblem	1.10	.55

Abouissa Children's Village — A240

1983, Mar. 5 — Photo. — Perf. 13½x13
668	A240	125fr multicolored	1.50	.60

Fauna — A241

35fr, Pangolin manis (Scaly Anteater), vert. 90fr, Potamochoerus porcus (Red River Hog). 100fr, Colobus guereza (Colobus monkey), vert. 125fr, Syncerus caffer (African Buffalo).

1983, Mar. 12 — Litho. — Perf. 12½x13
669	A241	35fr multi	.55	.40
670	A241	90fr shown	1.00	.50
671	A241	100fr multi	1.25	.60
672	A241	125fr multi	1.50	.75
	Nos. 669-672 (4)		4.30	2.25

Stamp Day — A242

100fr, Grand Bassam P.O., 1903.

1983, Mar. 19 — Litho. — Perf. 12½
673	A242	100fr multi	1.10	.60

Easter 1983 — A243

Paintings by Rubens (1577-1640) 100fr, Descent from the Cross, vert. 125fr, Resurrection. 350fr, Crucifixion. 400fr, Piercing of the Sword, vert. 500fr, Descent, diff., vert.

1983, Apr. 9 — Perf. 13
674	A243	100fr multi	1.00	.30
675	A243	125fr multi	1.25	.50
676	A243	350fr multi	3.25	1.00
677	A243	400fr multi	4.00	1.25
678	A243	500fr multi	4.75	1.50
	Nos. 674-678 (5)		14.25	4.50

25th Anniv. of UN Economic Commission for Africa — A244

1983, Apr. 29 — Litho. — Perf. 13x12½
679	A244	100fr multicolored	1.10	.55

Gray Parakeet — A245

100fr, Fish eagle, vert. 150fr, Touracoes.

IVORY COAST

1983, June 11
680	A245	100fr multi	2.00	1.00
681	A245	125fr shown	2.75	.75
682	A245	150fr multi	4.25	1.00
	Nos. 680-682 (3)		9.00	2.75

World Communications Year — A245a

Designs: 100fr, Tower, telephone, operators. 125fr, Buildings, satellite dish.

1983, July 16 *Perf. 12½x13*
682A	A245a	100fr multi	125.00	—
682B	A245a	125fr multi	125.00	—

A246

50fr, Flali, Gouro. 100fr, Masked dancer, Guere. 125fr, Stilt dancer, Yacouba.

1983, Sept. 3 *Litho.* *Perf. 12½*
683	A246	50fr multi	.50	.30
684	A246	100fr multi	1.10	.45
685	A246	125fr multi	1.50	.55
	Nos. 683-685 (3)		3.10	1.30

20th Anniv. of the Ivory Hotel, Abidjan A249

1983, Sept. 7 *Perf. 13*
693	A249	100fr multicolored	1.10	.60

Ecology in Action — A250

25fr, Forest after fire. 100fr, Animals fleeing. 125fr, Animals grazing.

1983, Oct. 24 *Litho.*
694	A250	25fr multi	.65	.35
695	A250	100fr multi	1.75	.75
696	A250	125fr multi	2.25	1.10
	Nos. 694-696 (3)		4.65	2.20

Raphael (1483-1520), 500th Birth Anniv. — A252

Paintings: 100fr, Christ and St. Peter. 125fr, Study for St. Joseph, vert. 350fr, Virgin of the House of Orleans, vert. 500fr, Virgin with the Blue Diadem, vert.

1983, Nov. 5 *Litho.* *Perf. 13*
698	A252	100fr multi	1.00	.35
699	A252	125fr multi	1.25	.50
700	A252	350fr multi	3.00	1.50
701	A252	500fr multi	4.50	2.00
	Nos. 698-701 (4)		9.75	4.35

Auto Race — A253

1983, Oct. 24 *Litho.* *Perf. 12½*
702	A253	100fr Car, map	1.25	.60

Flowers — A254

100fr, Fleurs d'Ananas (Pineapple flower). 125fr, Heliconia Rostrata (Hanging lobster claw). 150fr, Rose de Porcelaine (Porcelain rose).

1983, Nov. 26 *Photo.* *Perf. 14x15*
703	A254	100fr multi	150.00	
704	A254	125fr multi	10.00	3.00
705	A254	150fr multi	10.00	3.00
	Nos. 703-705 (3)		170.00	

23rd Anniv. of Independence A255

1983, Dec. 7
706	A255	100fr multicolored	1.10	.50

First Audio-visual Forum, Abidjan — A256

1984, Jan. 25 *Litho.* *Perf. 13x12½*
707	A256	100fr Screen, arrow	1.10	.50

14th African Soccer Cup — A257

100fr, Emblem. 200fr, Maps shaking hands.

1984, Mar. 4 *Photo.* *Perf. 12½*
708	A257	100fr multi	1.00	.40
709	A257	200fr multi	2.00	.85

Local Insects — A258

100fr, Argiope, vert. 125fr, Polistes gallicus.

1984, Mar. 24 *Litho.* *Perf. 13*
710	A258	100fr multi	2.00	.70
711	A258	125fr multi	2.25	.90

Stamp Day — A259

100fr, Abidjan P.O., 1934.

1984, Apr. 7 *Litho.* *Perf. 12½*
712	A259	100fr multi	1.10	.55

Lions Emblem — A260

1984, Apr. 27 *Perf. 13½x13*
713	A260	100fr multicolored	1.00	.50
714	A260	125fr multicolored	1.50	.65

3rd Convention of Multi-district 403, Abidjan, Apr. 27-29.

16th World Telecommunications Day — A261

1984, May 17 *Perf. 12½*
715	A261	100fr multi	1.10	.55

Council of Unity, 25th Anniv. — A262

1984, May 29
716	A262	100fr multicolored	1.00	.35
717	A262	125fr multicolored	1.25	.45

First Governmental Palace, Grand-Bassam — A263

125fr, Palace of Justice, Grand-Bassam.

1984, July 14 *Litho.* *Perf. 12½*
718	A263	100fr shown	1.00	.35
719	A263	125fr multi	1.25	.50

Men Playing Eklan A264

1984, Aug. 11 *Perf. 13*
720	A264	100fr Board	1.40	.35
721	A264	125fr shown	1.50	.55

Locomotive "Gazelle" A265

No. 723, Cargo ship. No. 724, Superpacific. No. 725, Cargo ship, diff. No. 726, Pacific type 10. No. 727, Ocean liner. No. 728, Mallet class GT2. No. 729, Ocean liner, diff.

1984 *Perf. 12½*
722	A265	100fr shown	1.00	.40
723	A265	100fr multicolored	1.00	.40
724	A265	125fr multicolored	1.75	.50
725	A265	125fr multicolored	1.25	.50
726	A265	350fr multicolored	4.00	1.25
727	A265	350fr multicolored	3.50	1.25
728	A265	500fr multicolored	5.50	1.75
729	A265	500fr multicolored	5.50	1.75
	Nos. 722-729 (8)		23.50	7.80

Issue dates: trains, Aug. 25; ships, Sept. 1.

Stamp Day — A266

100fr, Map, post offices.

1984, Oct. 20 *Litho.* *Perf. 12½*
730	A266	100fr multicolored	1.50	.60

10th Anniv., West African Union — A267

100fr, Map, member nations.

1984, Oct. 27 *Litho.* *Perf. 13½*
731	A267	100fr multicolored	1.00	.50

Wildlife — A267a

100fr, Tragelaphus scriptus. 150fr, Felis serval.

1984, Nov. 3 *Photo.* *Perf. 14½x15*
731A	A267a	100fr multi	75.00	12.00
731B	A267a	150fr multi	75.00	12.00

Tourism — A267b

50fr, Le Club Valtur. 100fr, Grand Lahou.

1984, Nov. 10 *Photo.* *Perf. 15x14½*
731C	A267b	50fr multi	65.00	11.00
731D	A267b	100fr multi	65.00	11.00

Flowers — A267c

100fr, Allamanda carthartica. 125fr, Baobob.

1984, Nov. 17 *Photo.* *Perf. 14½x15*
731E	A267c	100fr multi	75.00	12.00
731F	A267c	125fr multi	75.00	12.00

90th Anniv., Ivory Coast Postage Stamps — A268

1984, Nov. 23 *Litho.* *Perf. 12½*
732	A268	125fr Book cover	1.40	.75

24th Anniv. of Independence A269

IVORY COAST

100fr, Citizens, outline map.

1984, Dec. 7	Litho.	Perf. 12½
733 A269 100fr multicolored	1.00	.60

Rotary Intl. Conf. — A270

1985, Jan. 16	Litho.	Perf. 12½x13
734 A270 100fr multicolored	.90	.50
735 A270 125fr multicolored	1.10	.55

Traditional Costumes — A271

90fr, Dan le Babou. 100fr, Post-natal gown.

1985, Feb. 16	Litho.	Perf. 13½
736 A271 90fr multicolored	1.50	.45
737 A271 100fr multicolored	1.50	.55

Birds — A271a

25fr, Marabout. 100fr, Jacana. 350fr, Ibis.

1985	Photo.	Perf. 14½x15
737A A271a 25fr multi	150.00	17.50
737B A271a 100fr multi	150.00	17.50
737C A271a 350fr multi	150.00	17.50
Nos. 737A-737C (3)	450.00	52.50

Issued: Nos. 737A, 737B, Mar. No. 737C, 8/17.

Stamp Day — A272

100fr, Riverboat Adjame.

1985, Apr. 13	Litho.	Perf. 12½
738 A272 100fr multicolored	2.25	.80

18th District of Zonta Intl., 7th Conference, Abidjan, Apr. 25-27 — A273

125fr, Zonta Intl. emblem.

1985, Apr. 25	Litho.	Perf. 13½
739 A273 125fr multicolored	1.25	.60

Bondoukou — A273a

100fr, Marche de Bondoukou. 125fr, Mosque, Samatiguila.

1985	Litho.	Perf. 14½x13½
739A A273a 100fr multi	140.00	9.00
739B A273a 125fr multi	140.00	9.00
739C A273a 140fr multi	140.00	9.00
Nos. 739A-739C (3)	420.00	27.00

PHILEXAFRICA '85, Lome — A274

No. 740, Factory, jet, van. No. 741, Youth sports, farming.

1985, May 15		Perf. 13
740 A274 200fr multicolored	2.00	1.10
741 A274 200fr multicolored	2.00	1.10
a. Pair, Nos. 740-741 + label	6.00	6.00

African Development Bank, 20th Anniv. — A275

100fr, Senegal chemical industry. 125fr, Gambian tree nursery.

1985, June 18		
742 A275 100fr multicolored	.95	.45
743 A275 125fr multicolored	1.10	.65

Intl. Youth Year A276

125fr, Map, profiles, dove.

1985, July 20		Perf. 12½
744 A276 125fr multicolored	1.20	.65

Natl. Armed Forces, 25th Anniv. — A277

Emblems: No. 745, Presidential Guard. No. 746, F.A.N.C.I. 125fr, Air Transport & Liaison Group, G.A.T.L. 200fr, National Marines. 350fr, National Gendarmerie.

1985, July 27		Perf. 12½x13
745 A277 100fr dp rose lil & gold	.85	.45
746 A277 100fr dark bl & gold	.90	.50
747 A277 125fr blk brn & gold	1.10	.55
748 A277 200fr blk brn & gold	1.75	1.00
749 A277 350fr brt ultra & sil	2.75	1.75
Nos. 745-749 (5)	7.35	4.25

1986 World Cup Soccer Preliminaries, Mexico — A279

100fr, Heading the ball. 150fr, Tackle. 200fr, Dribbling. 350fr, Passing. 500fr, Power shot.

1985, Aug.		Perf. 13
751 A279 100fr multicolored	.80	.45
752 A279 150fr multicolored	1.25	.75
753 A279 200fr multicolored	1.50	1.00
754 A279 350fr multicolored	3.00	1.75
Nos. 751-754 (4)	6.55	3.95

Souvenir Sheet

| 755 A279 500fr multicolored | 4.25 | 2.00 |

Ivory Coast Sovereign Military Order of Malta Postal Convention, Dec. 19, 1984 — A280

125fr, National arms. 350fr, S.M.O.M. arms.

1985, Aug. 31		Perf. 13x12½
756 A280 125fr multi	1.00	.65
757 A280 350fr multi	3.00	1.75

Visit of Pope John Paul II — A281

100fr, Portrait, St. Paul's Cathedral, Abidjan.

Overprint in Black

1985, Sept. 24		Perf. 13
758 A281 100fr multicolored	2.00	1.00

The overprint, "Consecration de la Cathedrale Saint Paul d'Abidjon," was added to explain the reason for the visit of the Pope. Stamps without overprint exist but were not issued.

UN Child Survival Campaign A282

No. 759, Breast-feeding. No. 760, Oral rehydration therapy. No. 761, Mother and child. No. 762, Vaccination.

1985, Oct. 5	Litho.	Perf. 13½x14
759 A282 100fr multi	.90	.50
760 A282 100fr multi	.90	.50
761 A282 100fr multi	.90	.50
762 A282 100fr multi	.90	.50
Nos. 759-762 (4)	3.60	2.00

UN 40th Anniv. A283

1985, Oct. 31		Perf. 13
763 A283 100fr multicolored	1.00	.60

Admission to UN, 25th anniv.

World Wildlife Fund A284

Striped antelopes.

1985, Nov. 30		
764 A284 50fr multicolored	7.00	1.00
765 A284 60fr multicolored	9.00	2.00
766 A284 75fr multicolored	18.00	3.00
767 A284 100fr multicolored	27.50	5.00
Nos. 764-767 (4)	61.50	11.00

City Skyline A285

1985, Nov. 21	Litho.	Perf. 13
768 A285 125fr multicolored	1.25	.65

Expo '85 national industrial exhibition.

Return to the Land Campaign — A286

1985, Dec. 7		Perf. 12½
769 A286 125fr multicolored	1.25	.65

Natl. independence, 25th anniv.

Flowers — A286a

100fr, L'Amorphophallus staudtii. 125fr, Crinum scillifolium. 200fr, Triphyophyllum peltatum.

1985, Dec. 28	Litho.	Perf. 14x15
769A A286a 100fr multi	140.00	10.00
769B A286a 125fr multi	140.00	10.00
769C A286a 200fr multi	140.00	10.00
Nos. 769A-769C (3)	420.00	30.00

Handicrafts — A287

125fr, Spinning thread. 155fr, Painting.

1986, Jan.		Perf. 13½
770 A287 125fr multicolored	1.25	.55
771 A287 155fr multicolored	1.50	.75

Flora — A288

40fr, Omphalocarpum elatum. 50fr, Momordica charantia. 125fr, Millettia takou. 200fr, Costus afer.

1986, Feb. 22	Litho.	Perf. 13½
772 A288 40fr multicolored	.45	.25
773 A288 50fr multicolored	.55	.30
774 A288 125fr multicolored	1.25	.75
775 A288 200fr multicolored	2.00	1.00
Nos. 772-775 (4)	4.25	2.30

Cooking Utensils, Natl. Museum, Abidjan — A289

20fr, We bowl. 30fr, Baoule bowl. 90fr, Baoule platter. 125fr, Dan scoop. 440fr, Baoule lidded pot.

1986, Mar. 6	Perf. 13x12½, 12½x13
776 A289 20fr multi	.25 .25
777 A289 30fr multi	.30 .25
778 A289 90fr multi	1.00 .45
779 A289 125fr multi	1.25 .65
780 A289 440fr multi	4.00 2.25
Nos. 776-780 (5)	6.80 3.85

Nos. 776-778 horiz.

IVORY COAST

Natl. Pedagogic and Vocational School, 10th Anniv. — A290

1986, Mar. 20			Perf. 13½	
781	A290	125fr multicolored	1.40	.60

Cable Ship Stephan, 1910 — A291

1986, Apr. 12		Litho.	Perf. 12½	
782	A291	125fr multicolored	2.25	.60

Stamp Day.

Houphouet-Boigny Type of 1974-76

1986, Apr.		Engr.	Perf. 13	
783	A112	5fr dk red, dp rose lil & brn	.25	.25
784	A112	10fr gray grn, brt bl & brn	.25	.25
785	A112	20fr brt ver, blk brn & brn	.25	.25
786	A112	25fr bl, dp rose lil & brn	.30	.25
787	A112	30fr brt ver, blk brn & brn	.30	.25
789	A112	50fr lake, dk vio & brn	.50	.25
790	A112	90fr dk brn vio, rose lake & brn	.90	.40
791	A112	125fr brt lil rose, brt ver & brn	1.25	.50
792	A112	155fr dk brn vio, Prus bl & brn	1.25	.60
		Nos. 783-792 (9)	5.25	3.00

The 1986 printing of the 40fr is in slightly darker colors than No. 374.

Natl. Youth and Sports Institute, 25th Anniv. — A293

1986, May 9		Litho.	Perf. 12½	
793	A293	125fr brt org & dk yel grn	1.10	.60

Fish — A294

5fr, Polypterus endlicheri. 125fr, Synodontis punctifer. 150fr, Protopterus annectens. 155fr, Synodontis koensis. 440fr, Malapterurus electricus.

1986, July 5		Litho.	Perf. 14½x13½	
794	A294	5fr multi	.25	.25
795	A294	125fr multi	1.25	.55
796	A294	150fr multi	1.75	.75
797	A294	155fr multi	2.00	.75
798	A294	440fr multi	5.00	2.00
		Nos. 794-798 (5)	10.25	4.30

Enthronement of a Chief, Agni District — A295

50fr, Drummer, vert. 350fr, Chief in litter. 440fr, Royal entourage.

1986, July 19			Perf. 13½x14½	
799	A295	50fr multi	.45	.40
800	A295	350fr multi	3.50	2.00
801	A295	440fr multi	4.50	3.00
		Nos. 799-801 (3)	8.45	5.40

Rural Houses — A296

125fr, Baoule aoulo. 155fr, Upper Antiam eva. 350fr, Lobi soukala.

1986, Aug. 2		Litho.	Perf. 14x15	
802	A296	125fr multi	1.25	.60
803	A296	155fr multi	1.50	.80
804	A296	350fr multi	3.00	1.75
		Nos. 802-804 (3)	5.75	3.15

Coat of Arms — A297

1986-87		Engr.	Perf. 13	
807	A297	50fr bright org	.40	.25
808	A297	125fr dark green	1.25	.35
809	A297	155fr crimson	1.50	.35
810	A297	195fr blue ('87)	1.75	.35
		Nos. 807-810 (4)	4.90	1.30

Issue dates: 50fr, 125fr, 155fr, Aug. 23.

Coastal Landscapes — A298

125fr, Grand Bereby. 155fr, Sableux Boubele, horiz.

		Perf. 14x15, 15x14		
1986, Aug. 30			Litho.	
820	A298	125fr multi	1.50	.75
821	A298	155fr multi	2.00	1.00

Oceanographic Research Center — A299

125fr, Fishing grounds. 155fr, Net fishing.

		Perf. 14½x13½		
1986, Sept. 13				
822	A299	125fr multicolored	1.10	.60
823	A299	155fr multicolored	1.50	.80

Intl. Peace Year — A300

1986, Oct. 16		Litho.	Perf. 14x13½	
824	A300	155fr multicolored	1.40	.75

Research and Development — A301

1986, Nov. 15			Perf. 13½x14	
825	A301	125fr Bull	1.50	.90
826	A301	155fr Wheat	1.50	.90

Natl. Independence, 26th Anniv. — A302

1986, Dec. 6		Litho.	Perf. 13½x14	
827	A302	155fr multicolored	1.50	.75

Rural Housing — A303

190fr, Guesseple Dan. 550fr, M'Bagui Senoufo.

1987, Mar. 14		Litho.	Perf. 13½x14	
828	A303	190fr multi	2.00	1.10
829	A303	550fr multi	5.50	3.00

Stamp Day — A304

155fr, Mailman, 1918.

1987, Apr. 4			Perf. 13x13½	
830	A304	155fr multicolored	1.40	.80

Jean Mermoz College, 25th Anniv. — A305

40fr, Cock, elephant. 155fr, Dove, children.

1987, Apr. 9			Perf. 13	
831	A305	40fr multicolored	.40	.30
832	A305	155fr multicolored	1.50	.70

Elephant Type of 1981

1987, Apr. 9				
833	A219	35fr multicolored	.50	.25

Fouilles, by Krah N'Guessan — A306

Paintings by local artists: 500fr, Cortege Ceremonial, by Santoni Gerard.

1987, Aug. 14		Litho.	Perf. 14½x15	
841	A306	195fr multi	1.75	1.00
842	A306	500fr multi	4.50	2.75

World Post Day, Express Mail Service — A307

1987, Oct. 9			Perf. 13½	
843	A307	155fr multi	1.50	.95
844	A307	195fr multi	1.75	1.00

Intl. Trade Cent. — A308

1987, Oct. 24				
845	A308	155fr multi	2.10	1.00

A309

1987, Dec. 5		Litho.	Perf. 14x13½	
846	A309	155fr multicolored	1.40	.90

Natl. Independence, 27th anniv.

A310

1988, Feb. 20		Litho.	Perf. 14x13½	
847	A310	155fr multicolored	1.40	.85

Lions Club for child survival.

The Modest Canary, by Monne Bou — A311

Paintings by local artists: 20fr, The Couple, by K.J. Houra, vert. 150fr, The Eternal Dance, by Bou, vert. 155fr, La Termitiere, by Mathilde Moro, vert. 195fr, The Sun of Independence, by Michel Kodjo, vert.

1988, Jan. 30		Perf. 12½x13, 13x12½		
848	A311	20fr multi	.30	.25
849	A311	30fr shown	.30	.25
850	A311	150fr multi	1.50	.75
851	A311	155fr multi	1.60	.85
852	A311	195fr multi	2.00	1.00
		Nos. 848-852 (5)	5.70	3.10

Stamp Day — A312

155fr, Bereby P.O., c. 1900.

1988, Apr. 4		Litho.	Perf. 13	
853	A312	155fr multicolored	1.40	.90

A313

1988, Apr. 18		Litho.	Perf. 15x14	
854	A313	195fr blk & dark red	2.25	1.40

15th French-Language Nations Cardiology Congress, Abidjan, Apr. 18-20.

A314

1988, May 21		Litho.	Perf. 12x13	
855	A314	195fr multicolored	2.00	1.00

Intl. Fund for Agricultural Development (IFAD), 10th anniv.

IVORY COAST

1st Intl. Day for the Campaign Against Drug Abuse and Drug Trafficking — A315

1988, Aug. 27	Litho.		Perf. 13½
856	A315	155fr multi	1.75 1.00

Stone Heads — A316

Various stone heads from the Niangoran-Bouah Archaeological Collection.

1988, July 9	Litho. & Engr.		Perf. 13x14½
857	A316	5fr beige & sep	.25 .25
858	A316	10fr buff & sep	.25 .25
859	A316	30fr pale grn & sep	.30 .25
860	A316	155fr pale yel & sep	1.50 .85
861	A316	195fr pale yel grn & sep	2.00 .95
		Nos. 857-861 (5)	4.30 2.55

World Post Day — A317

1988, Oct. 15	Litho.		Perf. 14
862	A317	155fr multi	1.50 .90

Natl. Independence 28th Anniv. — A318

Year of the Forest: 40fr, Healthy trees. No. 864, Stop forest fires. No. 865, Planting trees.

1988, Dec. 6			Perf. 11½x12
863	A318	40fr multi	.50 .25
864	A318	155fr multi	2.00 .90
865	A318	200fr multi	2.00 .90
		Nos. 863-865 (3)	4.50 2.05

History of Money — A319

195fr, Senegal bank notes, 1854, 1901.

1989, Feb. 25	Litho.		Perf. 12x11½
		Granite Paper	
866	A319	50fr shown	1.00 .25
867	A319	195fr multicolored	2.50 1.25

See Nos. 885-886, 896-898, 915. For surcharges see Nos. 904-905.

"Valeur d'echange 0fr.25" on 25c Type A5, 1920 — A320

1989, Apr.			Perf. 12½
868	A320	155fr multicolored	1.75 .95

Stamp Day.

Jewelry from the National Museum Collection A321

90fr, Voltaic bracelets. 155fr, Anklets.

1989, Mar. 25	Litho.		Perf. 14
869	A321	90fr multicolored	1.00 .60
870	A321	155fr multicolored	2.00 1.25

Sculptures by Christian Lattier — A322

40fr, The Old Man and the Infant, vert. 155fr, The Saxophone Player, vert. 550fr, The Panther.

1989, May 13	Perf. 11½x12, 12x11½		Granite Paper
871	A322	40fr multicolored	.50 .25
872	A322	155fr multicolored	1.75 1.00
873	A322	550fr multicolored	4.25 2.75
		Nos. 871-873 (3)	6.50 4.00

For surcharge see No. 903.

Council for Rural Development, 30th Anniv. — A323

75fr, Flags, well, tractor, field.

1989, May 29			Perf. 15x14
874	A323	75fr multicolored	1.40 .50

See Togo No. 1526.

Intl. Peace Congress A324

1989, June	Litho.		Perf. 13
875	A324	195fr multicolored	1.75 1.00

Rural Habitat — A325

155fr, Hut, Sirikukube Dida.

1989, June 10	Litho.		Perf. 14
876	A325	155fr multicolored	1.75 1.00

For surcharge see No. 902.

Sekou Watara, King of Kong (1710-1745) A326

Designs: No. 878, Bastille, Declaration of Human Rights and Citizenship.

1989, July 7	Litho.		Perf. 13
877	A326	200fr shown	2.75 1.50
878	A326	200fr multicolored	2.75 1.50
a.		Pair, Nos. 877-878 + label	8.50 7.50

PHILEXFRANCE '89, French revolution bicent.

Endangered Species — A327

25fr, Varanus niloticus. 100fr, Crocodylus niloticus.

1989, Sept. 16			Perf. 12x11½
		Granite Paper	
879	A327	25fr multicolored	.50 .30
880	A327	100fr multicolored	2.00 .90

World Post Day — A328

1989, Oct. 9	Litho.		Perf. 12½x13
881	A328	195fr multicolored	1.75 .90

CAPTEAO, 30th Anniv. — A329

1989, Oct. 28	Litho.		Perf. 12½
882	A329	155fr multicolored	1.50 .90

Conference of Postal and Telecommunication Administrations of West African Nations.

A330

1989, Dec. 7			Perf. 13
883	A330	155fr multicolored	1.50 .85

Natl. independence, 29th anniv.

A331

1990, Jan. 18	Litho.		Perf. 13
884	A331	155fr multicolored	1.25 .85

Pan-African Union, 10th anniv.

History of Money Type of 1989

155fr, 1923 25fr note. 195fr, 1, 2, 5fr notes.

1990, Mar. 17	Litho.		Perf. 12x11½
		Granite Paper	
885	A319	155fr grn & black	1.50 .85
886	A319	195fr org & black	2.50 1.25

Stamp Day — A332

1990, Apr. 21	Litho.		Perf. 13x12½
887	A332	155fr Packet Africa	1.75 .90

Multinational Postal School, 20th Anniv. — A333

1990, May 31			Perf. 12½
888	A333	155fr multicolored	1.50 .80

Rural Village — A334

1990, June 30			Perf. 14
889	A334	155fr multicolored	1.50 .60

Intl. Literacy Year — A335

1990, July 28			Perf. 15x14
890	A335	195fr multicolored	1.75 .90

Dedication of Basilica of Notre Dame of Peace, Yamoussoukro A336

1990, Sept. 8			Perf. 14½x13½
891	A336	155fr shown	1.50 .80
892	A336	195fr Basilica, diff.	2.50 1.25

Visit of Pope John Paul II — A337

1990, Sept. 9			Perf. 13
893	A337	500fr multicolored	5.00 2.75

World Post Day — A338

1990, Oct. 9	Litho.		Perf. 14x15
894	A338	195fr multicolored	3.25 1.50

Independence, 30th Anniv. — A339

1990, Dec. 6	Litho.		Perf. 13½x14½
895	A339	155fr multicolored	1.75 .90

History of Money Type of 1989

40fr, French West Africa 1942 5fr, 100fr notes. 195fr, French West Africa & Togo 50fr, 500fr notes.

1991, Mar. 1	Litho.		Perf. 11½
		Granite Paper	
896	A319	40fr yel & black	.45 .25
897	A319	155fr like #896	1.60 .85
898	A319	195fr mag & black	2.00 1.25
		Nos. 896-898 (3)	4.05 2.35

For surcharges see Nos. 904-905.

Stamp Day — A340

1991, May 18	Litho.		Perf. 13½
899	A340	150fr multicolored	1.50 .55

IVORY COAST

Miniature Sheets

French Open Tennis Championships, Cent. — A341

Tennis Players: No. 900a, Henri Cochet. b, Rene Lacoste. c, Jean Borotra. d, Don Budge. e, Marcel Bernard. f, Ken Rosewall. g, Rod Laver. h, Bjorn Borg. i, Yannick Noah.

No. 901a, Suzanne Lenglen. b, Helen Wills Moody. c, Simone Mathieu. d, Maureen Connolly. e, Francoise Durr. f, Margaret Court. g, Chris Evert. h, Martina Navratilova. i, Steffi Graf.

1991, May 24   Litho.   Perf. 13½
| 900 | A341 | 200fr #a.-i. | 22.50 | 22.50 |
| 901 | A341 | 200fr #a.-i. | 22.50 | 22.50 |

Nos. 872, 876, 897-898 Surcharged

Perfs. as Before
1991, July 15   Litho.
| 902 | A325 | 150fr on 155fr #876 | 1.75 | .55 |

Granite Paper
903	A322	150fr on 155fr #872	1.75	.55
904	A319	150fr on 155fr #897	1.75	.65
905	A319	200fr on 195fr #898	2.25	.80
		Nos. 902-905 (4)	7.50	2.55

Location of obliterator and surcharge varies.

Packet Boats — A342

1991, June 28   Litho.   Perf. 12x11½
Granite Paper
| 906 | A342 | 50fr Europe | .55 | .25 |
| 907 | A342 | 550fr Asia | 5.25 | 2.75 |

World Post Day — A343

1991, Oct. 9   Perf. 13
| 908 | A343 | 50fr shown | .55 | .25 |
| 909 | A343 | 100fr SIPE, globe | .95 | .50 |

Tribal Drums — A344

5fr, We. 25fr, Krou, Soubre region. 150fr, Sinematiali. 200fr, Akye, Alepe region.

1991   Litho.   Perf. 14x15
910	A344	5fr plum & dull mauve	.25	.25
911	A344	25fr red & rose	.25	.25
912	A344	150fr bl grn & turq grn	1.75	1.10
913	A344	200fr grey ol & sage grn	2.00	1.25
		Nos. 910-913 (4)	4.25	2.85

Independence, 31st Anniv. — A345

1991, Dec. 7   Litho.   Perf. 13½x14½
| 914 | A345 | 150fr multicolored | 1.75 | .80 |

History of Money Type of 1989
1991, Dec. 8   Perf. 12x11½
Granite Paper
| 915 | A319 | 100fr like #898 | 1.00 | .70 |

Flowers — A346

Various flowers.

1991, Dec. 20   Engr.   Perf. 13
| 916 | A346 | 150fr grn, blk & mag, vert. | 1.50 | .50 |
| 917 | A346 | 200fr grn, olive & rose car | 1.90 | .85 |

African Soccer Championships — A347

Designs: 150fr, Elephants holding trophy, map, soccer ball, vert.

1992, Apr. 22   Litho.   Perf. 13
| 918 | A347 | 20fr multicolored | .35 | .25 |
| 919 | A347 | 150fr multicolored | 1.75 | 1.25 |

Animals — A348

5fr, Viverra civetta. 40fr, Nandinia binotata. 150fr, Tragelaphus euryceros. 500fr, Panthera pardus.

1992, May 5   Engr.   Perf. 13x12½
920	A348	5fr multi	.25	.25
921	A348	40fr multi	.55	.25
922	A348	150fr multi	2.00	.80
923	A348	500fr multi	5.00	3.25
		Nos. 920-923 (4)	7.80	4.55

World Post Day — A349

1992, Oct. 7   Litho.   Perf. 13
| 924 | A349 | 150fr black & blue | 1.50 | .80 |

First Ivory Coast Postage Stamp, Cent. A350

Designs: a, #3. b, #197. b, #182, #909 with mail trucks, post office boxes.

1992, Oct. 7
| 925 | A350 | 150fr Pair, #a.-b. + label | 5.00 | 3.50 |

Funeral Monuments A351

Various grave site monuments.

1992, Dec. 30   Engr.   Perf. 13
926	A351	5fr multicolored	.25	.25
927	A351	50fr multicolored	.65	.25
928	A351	150fr multicolored	1.60	.80
929	A351	400fr multicolored	3.75	1.75
		Nos. 926-929 (4)	6.25	3.05

Intl. Abidjan Marathon A351a

150fr, Flags, runners. 200fr, Runners.

1992, Nov. 20   Litho.   Perf. 11½
Granite Paper
| 929A | A351a | 150fr multi | 1.10 | .50 |
| 929B | A351a | 200fr multi | 2.25 | .75 |

Nos. 929A-929B were not available in the philatelic market until Apr. 1994.

Gold Mine of Ity, 1st Anniv. — A351b

1992, Nov. 8   Litho.   Perf. 14x15
| 929C | A351b | 200fr multicolored | 2.00 | .75 |

No. 929C was not available in the philatelic market until Apr. 1994.

32nd Anniv. of Independence A351c

150fr, People, flag, Statue of Liberty, map.

1992, Dec. 4
| 929D | A351c | 30fr shown | .35 | .35 |
| 929E | A351c | 150fr multicolored | 1.75 | .75 |

Nos. 929D-929E were not available in the philatelic market until Apr. 1994.

Tourist Attractions — A351d

10fr, Modern hotel, horiz. 25fr, Dent de Man. 100fr, Resort, horiz. 200fr, Map of tourist sites.

Perf. 14x15, 15x14
1992, Sept. 4   Litho.
929F	A351d	10fr multi	—	—
929G	A351d	25fr multi	35.00	—
929H	A351d	100fr multi	45.00	10.00
929I	A351d	200fr multi	65.00	10.00

Environmental Summit — A351e

200fr, Prevent water pollution, horiz.

Perf. 11½x12, 12x11½
1992, June 5   Litho.
Granite Paper
| 929J | A351e | 150fr multicolored | 70.00 | 2.00 |
| 929K | A351e | 200fr multicolored | 70.00 | 5.00 |

Stamp Day — A352

Designs showing children interested in philately: No. 930, Girl, stamp collection, #169. No. 931, Girl, #431, #446B, #186, and #920. 150fr, Boy sitting under tree, stamp exhibition.

1993, Apr. 17   Litho.   Perf. 13½
930	A352	50fr multicolored	.45	.25
931	A352	50fr multicolored	.45	.25
932	A352	150fr multicolored	1.75	.75
		Nos. 930-932 (3)	2.65	1.25

A353

Medicinal plants: 5fr, Argemone mexicana. 20fr, Hibiscus esculentus. 200fr, Cassia alata.

1993, May 14   Litho.   Perf. 11½x12
Granite Paper
933	A353	5fr multi	.35	.25
934	A353	20fr multi	.45	.25
935	A353	200fr multi	2.00	1.25
		Complete booklet, 10 #935		
		Nos. 933-935 (3)	2.80	1.75

A354

Orchids: 10fr, Calyptrochilum emarginatum. 50fr, Plectrelminthus caudathus. 150fr, Eulophia guineensis.

1993, Aug. 27   Photo.   Perf. 12x11½
Granite Paper
936	A354	10fr multicolored	.25	.25
937	A354	50fr multicolored	.40	.30
938	A354	150fr multicolored	1.50	.90
		Nos. 936-938 (3)	2.15	1.45

Ivory Coast Colony, Cent. — A355

25fr, Organization charter. 100fr, Colonial Governor Louis Gustave Binger, Pres. F. Houphouet-Boigny. 500fr, Natives selecting goods for trade.

1993, Sept. 17   Perf. 13x12½
939	A355	25fr green & black	.35	.25
940	A355	100fr blue & black	1.10	.75
941	A355	500fr brown & black	5.00	3.50
		Nos. 939-941 (3)	6.45	4.50

Elimination Round of 1994 World Cup Soccer Championships, US — A356

Designs: 150fr, Cartoon soccer players. 200fr, Three players. 300fr, Two players. 400fr, Cartoon players, diff.

721

IVORY COAST

1993, Sept. 24 Litho. Perf. 14x15
942 A356 150fr multicolored 1.10 .45
943 A356 200fr multicolored 2.25 .85
944 A356 300fr multicolored 3.00 1.75
945 A356 400fr multicolored 4.00 2.25
Nos. 942-945 (4) 10.35 5.30

World Post Day — A357

Designs: 30fr, Map of Ivory Coast. 200fr, Post office, Bouake.

1993, Oct. 9 Perf. 13x13½
946 A357 30fr multicolored .35 .25
947 A357 200fr multicolored 2.00 1.25

African Biennial of Plastic Arts, Abidjan — A358

Perf. 14½x13½
1993, Nov. 24 Litho.
948 A358 200fr multicolored 1.75 .90

Independence, 33rd Anniv. — A359

1993, Dec. 7 Litho. Perf. 13½x13
950 A359 200fr multicolored 2.00 .95

Pres. Felix Houphouet-Boigny (1905-93) — A360

Pres. Houphouet-Boigny and: Nos. 951a, 952a, 953a, Modern buildings, technology. Nos. 951b, 952b, 953b, Agriculture, shipping. Nos. 951c, 952c, 953c, Dove, rainbow, Presidential palace.

1994, Feb. 5 Litho. Perf. 13
951 A360 150fr Strip of 3, #a.-c. 3.00 2.00
952 A360 200fr Strip of 3, #a.-c. 4.00 3.00

Souvenir Sheet
Perf. 12
953 A360 500fr Sheet of 3, #a.-c. 10.00 10.00

Raoul Follereau, Campaign Against Leprosy — A361

1994, Feb. 20 Litho. Perf. 13
954 A361 150fr multicolored 1.10 .85

RASCOM (Regional African Satellite Communications Organization), 1st Meeting, Abidjan — A362

1994, Jan. 19 Litho. Perf. 14x13
955 A362 150fr multicolored .85 .50

Woman Carrying Basket — A363

Litho. & Engr.
1994-95 Perf. 13½x13
Color of Border
956 A363 5fr orange .25 .25
956A A363 10fr green .25 .25
956B A363 20fr red .25 .25
957 A363 25fr blue .25 .25
957A A363 30fr olive bister .25 .25
958 A363 40fr yellow green .25 .25
959 A363 50fr brown .25 .25
960 A363 75fr lilac rose .30 .25
961 A363 150fr bright green .70 .35
961A A363 180fr pale lake .95 .50
961B A363 280fr gray 1.40 .70
962 A363 300fr violet 1.40 .70
Nos. 956-962 (12) 6.50 4.25

Issued: 30fr, 180fr, 280fr, 5/16/95, dated 1994; others, 11/4/94.

Stained Glass Windows, Basilica of Notre Dame of Peace, Yamoussoukro — A364

Designs: 25fr, Christ, world map. 150fr, Christ, fishermen. 200fr, Madonna and Child. 600fr, Aerial view of Cathedral, Yamoussoukro.

1994, Nov. 18 Litho. Perf. 14
963 A364 25fr lilac rose & multi .35 .25
964 A364 150fr pale org & multi 1.00 .60
965 A364 200fr yellow & multi 1.25 .80
a. Booklet pane of 10 —
Complete booklet #965a —
Nos. 963-965 (3) 2.60 1.65

Souvenir Sheet
966 A364 600fr multicolored 5.00 5.00

Natl. Independence, 34th Anniv. — A365

1994, Dec. 6 Litho. Perf. 12
967 A365 150fr multicolored 1.00 .40

Snakes — A366

Designs: 10fr, Python regius. 20fr, Philothamnus semivariegatus. 100fr, Dendroaspis veridis. 180fr, Bitis arietans. 500fr, Bitis nasicornis.

1995, June 23 Litho. Perf. 13
968 A366 10fr multicolored .25 .25
969 A366 20fr multicolored .25 .25
970 A366 100fr multicolored .65 .25
971 A366 180fr multicolored 1.40 .75
972 A366 500fr multicolored 3.00 1.50
Nos. 968-972 (5) 5.55 3.00

FAO, 50th Anniv. A367

UN, 50th Anniv. A368

1995, Aug. 4 Litho. Perf. 11½
973 A367 100fr multicolored .75 .35
974 A368 280fr multicolored 2.50 .75

Mushrooms — A369

Designs: 30fr, Lentinus tuber-regium. 50fr, Volvariella volvacea. 180fr, Dictyophora indusiata. 250fr, Termitomyces schimperi.

1995, Sept. 8 Perf. 14x13½
975 A369 30fr multicolored .45 .35
976 A369 50fr multicolored .85 .70
977 A369 180fr multicolored 2.50 1.00
978 A369 250fr multicolored 2.75 2.00
a. Block of 4, #975-978 8.50 6.00
b. Dated "1997" —

No. 978a was issued in sheets of 16 stamps.

Louis Pasteur (1822-95) — A370

1995, Sept. 28 Perf. 11½
979 A370 280fr multicolored 1.50 .80

School Philatelic Clubs — A371

1995, Oct. 6 Perf. 13½
980 A371 50fr GSR .50 .25
981 A371 180fr LBP 1.75 .80

Butterflies

Designs: 180fr, Pala decius. 280fr, Papilio dardanus. 550fr, Papilio menestheus.

1995 Litho. Perf. 15x14
981A A371a 180fr multi 13.50 2.00
981B A371a 280fr multi 19.00 3.00
981C A371a 550fr multi 24.00 4.00
Nos. 981A-981C (3) 56.50 9.00

Transportation in Abidjan — A372

Designs: 180fr, People pushing, pulling cart of grain, automobiles, bus on street. 280fr, People getting into bus in middle of traffic.

1996, May 24 Perf. 13½
982 A372 180fr multicolored 1.10 .60
983 A372 280fr multicolored 1.75 1.00

Fish — A373

Designs: 50fr, Heterotis niloticus. 180fr, Auchenoglanis occidentalis. 700fr, Schilbe mandibularis.

1996, June
984 A373 50fr multicolored .35 .30
985 A373 180fr multicolored 1.25 .65
986 A373 700fr multicolored 4.50 2.50
Nos. 984-986 (3) 6.10 3.45

A374

Orchids: 40fr, Cyrtorchis arcuata. 100fr, Eulophia horsfalii. 180fr, Eulophidium maculatum. 200fr, Anselia africana.

1996, July 12 Litho. Perf. 13½x13
987 A374 40fr multicolored .35 .30
988 A374 100fr multicolored .75 .45
989 A374 180fr multicolored 1.50 1.00
990 A374 200fr multicolored 1.60 1.10
Nos. 987-990 (4) 4.20 2.85

A375

200fr, Boxing. 280fr, Running. 400fr, Long jump. 500fr, Natl. Olympic Committee emblem.

1996, Nov. 19
991 A375 200fr multicolored 1.10 .60
992 A375 280fr multicolored 1.75 1.00
993 A375 400fr multicolored 2.25 1.25
994 A375 500fr multicolored 2.75 1.75
Nos. 991-994 (4) 7.85 4.60

1996 Summer Olympic Games, Atlanta.

Carved Canes — A376

180fr, Cane of Birifor hunter. 200fr, Cane of Chief Lobi. 280fr, Cane of Chief Lobi (Gboberi).

1996, Sept. 20 Litho. Perf. 11½
995 A376 180fr black & green 1.20 .60
996 A376 200fr black & org yel 1.20 .70
997 A376 280fr black & lilac 1.75 1.00
Nos. 995-997 (3) 4.15 2.30

Water Flowers — A377

Designs: 50fr, Nelumbo nucifera. 180fr, Nymphea lotus. 280fr, Nymphea capensis. 700fr, Nymphea alba.

1997, June 20 Litho. Perf. 13½x14
998 A377 50fr multicolored .30 .25
999 A377 180fr multicolored 1.10 .60
1000 A377 280fr multicolored 1.75 1.00
1001 A377 700fr multicolored 4.00 2.50
Nos. 998-1001 (4) 7.15 4.35

Basilica of Our Lady of Peace, Yamoussoukro — A378

a, 180fr, Pres. Felix Houphouet-Boigny, exterior view of basilica. b, 200fr, Interior view. c, 280fr, Aerial view, Pope John Paul II.

1997, July 8 Litho. Perf. 13
1002 A378 Strip of 3, #a.-c. 5.00 4.00

IVORY COAST

Traditional Jewelry — A379

Various beaded necklaces.

1997, Aug. 22			Perf. 11½	
1003	A379	50fr plum & black	.35	.25
1004	A379	100fr plum & black	.55	.50
1005	A379	180fr plum & black	1.10	.75
		Nos. 1003-1005 (3)	2.00	1.50

A379a

Various stone heads of Gohitafla.

1997, Oct. 10	Litho.		Perf. 11½	
		Granite Paper		
1006	A379a	100fr red & multi	.55	.25
1007	A379a	180fr blue & multi	1.10	.75
1008	A379a	500fr green & multi	2.75	1.50
		Nos. 1006-1008 (3)	4.40	2.50

A380

Work tools: 180fr, Pulley. 280fr, Comb. 300fr, Navette, horiz.

1997, Nov. 28			Perf. 13½	
1009	A380	180fr orange & multi	1.10	.50
1010	A380	280fr green & multi	1.50	.75
1011	A380	300fr blue & multi	1.60	.75
		Nos. 1009-1011 (3)	4.20	2.00

Endangered Species — A381

Designs: 180fr, African manatee. 280fr, Jentink's duiker. 400fr, Kob antelope.

1997, Dec. 19	Photo.		Perf. 11½	
1012	A381	180fr multicolored	1.60	1.00
1013	A381	280fr multicolored	1.75	1.00
1014	A381	400fr multicolored	2.25	1.25
		Nos. 1012-1014 (3)	5.60	3.25

1998 World Cup Soccer Championships, France — A382

Paris landmarks in background and: 180fr, Player, ball depicted with angry face. 280fr, Flags of nations inside outline of player. 400fr, Player taking shot on goal. 500fr, Two players, mascot, vert.

Perf. 13x13½, 13½x13

1998, June 5			Litho.	
1015	A382	180fr multicolored	1.10	.55
1016	A382	280fr multicolored	1.60	1.00
1017	A382	400fr multicolored	2.25	1.25
1018	A382	500fr multicolored	2.75	1.40
		Nos. 1015-1018 (4)	7.70	4.20

Mushrooms — A383

50fr, Agaricus bingensis. 180fr, Lactarius gymnocarpus. 280fr, Termitomyces le testui.

1998, June 26	Litho.		Perf. 13½x13	
1019	A383	50fr multicolored	.60	.40
1020	A383	180fr multicolored	1.25	1.00
1021	A383	280fr multicolored	2.10	1.25
		Nos. 1019-1021 (3)	3.95	2.65
		See No. B20A.		

Endemic Plants — A384

Designs: 40fr, Hutchinsonia barbata. 100fr, Synsepalum aubrevillei. 180fr, Cola lorougnonis.

1998, July 10			Perf. 12	
		Granite Paper		
1022	A384	40fr multicolored	.45	.25
1023	A384	100fr multicolored	.75	.50
1024	A384	180fr multicolored	1.10	.75
		Nos. 1022-1024 (3)	2.30	1.50
		See No. B20A.		

Traditional Costumes from Grand-Bassam Museum — A385

1998, Nov. 13	Litho.		Perf. 13½x13	
1025	A385	180fr Tapa	1.10	.75
1026	A385	280fr Raffia	1.60	1.10
		See No. B20C.		

Trains of Africa — A386

180fr, South African Railway, 1918. 280fr, Garret 2-8-2+2-8-2 Beyer Peacock, 1925. 500fr, Cecil Rhodes.

1999, Feb. 26	Litho.		Perf. 13½	
1027	A386	180fr multicolored	1.10	.75
1028	A386	280fr multicolored	1.75	1.10

Souvenir Sheet

1029	A386	500fr multicolored	2.50	2.50
		See No. B20B.		

PhilexFrance '99, World Philatelic Exhibition — A387

Animals: 180fr+20fr, Loxodonta africana. 250fr, Syncerus caffer. 280fr, Pan troglodytes. 400fr, Cercopithecus aethiops.

1999, July 2	Litho.		Perf. 13x13¼	
1030	A387	180fr +20fr multi	1.50	1.10
1031	A387	250fr multicolored	1.60	1.25
1032	A387	280fr multicolored	1.75	1.25
1033	A387	400fr multicolored	2.25	1.75
		Nos. 1030-1033 (4)	7.10	5.35

UPU, 125th Anniv. — A388

UPU emblem and: 180fr+20fr, Carved heads. 280fr, Methods of delivering mail.

1999, June 25			Perf. 11¾x11½	
1034	A388	180fr +20fr multi	1.10	.75
1035	A388	280fr multicolored	1.50	1.10

Flowers — A389

Designs: 100fr, Ancistrochilus rothschilianus. 180fr+20fr, Brachycorythis pubescens. 200fr, Bulbophyllum barbigerum. 280fr, Habenaria macrandra.

1999, July 27	Litho.		Perf. 13¼x13	
1036	A389	100fr multicolored	.55	.35
1037	A389	180fr +20fr multi	1.40	1.00
1038	A389	200fr multicolored	1.50	1.10
1039	A389	280fr multicolored	1.75	1.25
		Nos. 1036-1039 (4)	5.20	3.70

Ahouakro Rock Formations — A390

Various rock formations.

Perf. 13¼x14, 14x13¼

1999, Aug. 6			Litho.	
1040	A390	180fr +20fr multi, horiz.	1.60	.75
1041	A390	280fr multi, horiz.	1.60	1.00
1042	A390	400fr multicolored	2.40	1.50
		Nos. 1040-1042 (3)	5.60	3.25

PhilexFrance 99 — A391

1999, July 2	Litho.		Perf. 13	
1043	A391	280fr multicolored	2.75	2.75

No. 1043 has a holographic image. Soaking in water may affect hologram.

Birds — A392

Designs: 50fr, Oriolus auratus. 180fr + 20fr, Nectarinia cinnyris venusta. 280fr, Trenon vinago australis. 300fr, Psittacus eithacus.

1999, Oct. 29	Litho.		Perf. 13¼x13	
1044	A392	50fr multi	.45	.25
1045	A392	180fr + 20fr multi	1.50	1.00
1046	A392	280fr multi	2.25	1.25
1047	A392	300fr multi	2.25	1.25
		Nos. 1044-1047 (4)	6.45	3.75

Fish — A393

Designs: 100fr, Synodontis schall. 180fr + 20fr, Chromidotilapia guntheri. 280fr, Distichodus rostratus.

1999, Nov. 19			Perf. 13½x13¼	
1048	A393	100fr multi	.75	.35
1049	A393	180fr +20fr multi	1.50	1.00
1050	A393	280fr multi	2.25	1.50
		Nos. 1048-1050 (3)	4.50	2.85

Challenges for Ivory Coast in Third Millennium — A394

Designs: 100fr, Education. 180fr +20fr, Agriculture. 200fr, Industry. 250fr, Information. 280fr, Peace. 400fr, Culture.

1999, Dec. 10			Perf. 13½x13¾	
1051	A394	100fr multi	.55	.35
1052	A394	180fr +20fr multi	1.10	.75
1053	A394	200fr multi	1.10	.75
1054	A394	250fr multi	1.40	1.00
1055	A394	280fr multi	1.50	1.00
1056	A394	400fr multi	1.75	1.50
		Nos. 1051-1056 (6)	7.40	5.35

Native Masks — A395

50fr, Wambélé. 180fr+20fr, Djè. 400fr, Korobla, vert.

Perf. 13½x13¼, 13¼x13½

2000, June 30			Litho.	
1057	A395	50fr multi	.35	.25
1058	A395	180fr +20fr multi	1.25	.80
1059	A395	400fr multi	2.25	1.75
		Nos. 1057-1059 (3)	3.85	2.80

Edible Plants — A396

Designs: 30fr, Blighia sapida. 180fr+20fr, Ricinodendron heudelotii. 300fr, Telfaira occidentalis. 400fr, Napoleonaea vogelii.

2000, July 14			Perf. 13¼x13½	
1060	A396	30fr multi	.35	.25
1061	A396	180fr +20fr multi	1.40	.80
1062	A396	300fr multi	1.75	1.25
1063	A396	400fr multi	2.25	2.00
		Nos. 1060-1063 (4)	5.75	4.30

Pres. Robert Guei, Elephant, Map and Dove — A397

2000, Aug. 4			Perf. 13¾x13¼	
1064	A397	180fr +20fr red & multi	1.50	.80
1065	A397	400fr yel & multi	2.75	1.75

Independence, 40th anniv., coup d'etat of Robert Guei.

Cacao — A398

Frame colors: 5fr, Dark blue green. 10fr, Light brown. 20fr, Claret. 25fr, Blue. 30fr, Greenish black. 40fr, Cerise. 50fr, Golden brown. 100fr, Brown. 180fr+20fr, Orange. 300fr, Blue violet. 350fr, Prussian blue. 400fr, Emerald. 600fr, Olive green.

Perf. 11½x11¾

2000, Aug. 25			Photo.	
		Granite Paper		
1066-1078	A398	Set of 13	11.50	8.00

IVORY COAST

National Lottery, 30th Anniv. — A399

Denominations: 180fr+20fr, 400fr.

2000, Aug. 30		Litho.	Perf. 13¼x13
1079-1080	A399	Set of 2	4.25 2.75

2000 Summer Olympics, Sydney — A400

Designs: 180fr+20fr, Soccer. 400fr, Kangaroo. 600fr, Runners. 750fr, Bird over stadium.

2000, Sept. 8			Perf. 13½x13¼
1081-1084	A400	Set of 4	12.00 9.00

Hairstyles — A401

Various hairstyles: 180fr+20fr, 300fr, 400fr, 500fr.

2000, Sept. 22			Perf. 13¾x13¼
1085-1088	A401	Set of 4	8.50 6.50

Compare with design A424.

Release of Nelson Mandela, 10th Anniv. — A402

2000, Oct. 6	Photo.	Perf. 12x11¾
1089	A402 300fr multi	2.10 1.25

Historic Monuments — A403

Designs: 180fr+20fr, Queen Pokou. 400fr, Akwaba. 600fr, Invocation of the Spirits.

2000, Nov. 10		Litho.	Perf. 13½x13
1090-1092	A403	Set of 3	7.00 6.00

UN High Commisioner for Refugees, 50th Anniv. — A404

2000, Dec. 8	Photo.	Perf. 11¾x12
1093	A404 400fr multi	2.50 1.75

Abokouamekro Animal Park — A405

Designs: 50fr, Cattle. 100fr, Rhinoceroses. 180fr+20fr, Rhinoceros. 400fr, Cattle.

2001, May 14	Litho.	Perf. 13½x13¼
1094-1097	A405	Set of 4	6.50 3.25

Sculpted Columns in National Museum — A406

Designs: 100fr, Alingué, Wouo Anouman. 180fr+20fr, Blolo Bian, Blolo B1a. 300fr+20fr, Botoumo. 400fr+20fr, Odi Oka.

2001, June 18		Perf. 13¼x13
1098-1101	A406	Set of 4	5.00 5.00

Elimination Rounds for World Cup Soccer Championships A407

Various soccer plays: 180fr + 20fr, 400fr + 20fr, 600fr + 20fr, 700fr.

2001, Aug. 21	Litho.	Perf. 13x13¼
1102-1105	A407	Set of 4	10.00 10.00

The following items inscribed "Republique de Cote d'Ivoire" have been declared "illegal" by Ivory Coast postal authorities:

Sheets of nine 100fr stamps: Marilyn Monroe (2 different).

Sheets of six 100fr stamps: Shells and Rotary emblem (2 different), Dogs and Scouting emblem (2 different), Butterflies and Scouting emblem (2 different), Orchids (2 different), Motorbike races and Rotary emblem (2 different), Table tennis players (2 different), Old fire engines (2 different), Elvis Presley (2 different), Marilyn Monroe, Pope John Paul II.

Sheets of six stamps: Trains (4 different).

Souvenir sheets of one stamp: Trains (4 different).

Sheet of ten 200fr Stamps: Birds.

Sheets of nine stamps of various denominations: Japanese Women, Earle K. Bergey, Julie Bell, Michael Möbius, Nudes.

Sheet of eight stamps of various denominations: Nature Conservancy.

Sheets of eight 300fr stamps: Owls and Mushrooms, Lighthouses and Penguins.

Sheets of eight 100fr stamps: Anthony Hopkins, Ben Affleck, Eminem.

Sheets of six stamps of various denominations: Spirited Away, Nature Conservancy, Nudes

Sheets of six 500fr stamps: History of World Aircraft (5 different), Red Cross and Rotary emblem, Japanese Women, Actresses, Women Tennis Players, Marilyn Monroe.

Sheet of six 450fr stamps: The Lord of the Rings.

Sheets of six 400fr stamps: Beatles (2 different).

Sheets of six 350fr stamps: Uniforms of World War II (5 different).

Sheets of Six 300fr stamps: Harry Potter (3 different), Fire Engines (2 different), Owls and Mushrooms.

Sheets of six 200fr stamps: Dogs and Scouting emblem, Lighthouses and Rotary emblem.

Sheets of six 100fr stamps: Pope John Paul II, Celine Dion, Pierce Brosnan, Classic Automobiles.

Sheets of four 100fr stamps: AC/DC, Backstreet Boys, Bee Gees, Beatles, Doors, Freddie Mercury, KISS, Madonna, Metallica, Queen, Rolling Stones.

Sheets of three stamps of various denominations: Nature Conservancy (2 different), Fairy Tales, Fantasy Tales, Dinosaurs, Steam Railways.

Sheet of two 1000fr stamps: Pope John Paul II.

Sheets of Two 500fr stamps: Nature Conservancy, Mother Teresa and Pope John Paul II.

Sheets of two 250fr stamps: Pope John Paul II (3 different).

Souvenir sheets of one 1000fr stamp: Dinosaurs, Fish, Owl and Scouting emblem.

Souvenir sheets of one 500fr stamp: Snow White, Nature Conservancy, Pope John Paul II.

Souvenir sheets of one 300fr stamp: Harry Potter (2 different).

Souvenir sheets of one 250fr stamp: Disney Cartoons and Scouting emblem (10 different).

Souvenir sheets of one 150fr stamp: Fire Engines and Scouting emblem (5 different).

Souvenir sheets of one 100fr stamp: Sorayama (5 different), Locomotives (2 different).

Korhogo Art — A408

Designs: 100fr, Shown. 180fr+20fr, Hunters and wildlife. 400fr+20fr, Painter, vert.

2001, Nov. 27		Litho.	Perf. 14
1106-1108	A408	Set of 3	4.00 4.00

2002 World Cup Soccer Championships, Japan and Korea — A410

Design: 300fr+20fr, Caricatures of soccer players in action, horiz.

Perf. 13¾, 13x13¼ (#1110), 13¼x13 (#1112)

2002, June 6			Litho.	
1109	A409	180fr +20fr grn & multi	1.25	1.25
1110	A410	300fr +20fr multi	2.25	2.25
1111	A409	400fr +20fr red & multi	2.75	2.75
	Complete booklet, 10 #1111		30.00	30.00
1112	A410	600fr +20fr shown	4.00	4.00

Souvenir Sheet

| 1113 | A409 | 500fr red & multi | 3.50 | 3.50 |

Ivory Coast — People's Republic of China Diplomatic Relations, 20th Anniv. — A411

2003, July 9			Litho.	Perf. 12
1114	A411	180fr grn & multi	1.25	1.25
1115	A411	400fr org & multi	2.25	2.25
1116	A411	650fr red & multi	3.75	3.75
	Nos. 1114-1116 (3)		7.25	7.25

Sculpted Columns in Museum of Civilizations — A412

Designs: 20fr, Alinguè Bia column. 100fr, Laliè column. 180fr+20fr, Tre Ni Tre column. 300fr+20fr, Golikplé-Kplé column.

2003, Nov. 27		Litho.	Perf. 13½x13
1117	A412	20fr multi	.25 .25
1118	A412	100fr multi	.50 .50
1119	A412	180fr +20fr shown	1.00 1.00
1120	A412	300fr +20fr multi	1.50 1.50
	Nos. 1117-1120 (4)		3.25 3.25

Paintings by Unknown Artists — A413

Designs: 50fr, Au Revoir. 100fr, Ballet. 250fr, Le Chef, horiz. 500fr, Ligne de Main, horiz. 825fr, Appel, horiz.

Perf. 13¼x13, 13x13¼

2004, June 15			Litho.
1121-1125	A413	Set of 5	20.00 —

IVORY COAST

Independence, 44th Anniv. — A414

Denominations: 100fr, 250fr.

2004, Aug. 7		Perf. 13¼x13		
1126-1127	A414	Set of 2		

2004 Summer Olympics, Athens — A415

Designs: 50fr, Sprint race. 100fr, Greco-Roman wrestling, vert. 250fr, Torch bearer, vert. 825fr, Discus throw, vert. 1000fr, Sprint race.

2004, Aug. 13		Perf. 13x13¼, 13¼x13		
1128-1131	A415	Set of 4	—	—

Souvenir Sheet

| 1131A | A415 | 1000fr multi | 8.25 | 8.25 |

National Reconciliation — A416

2004, Sept. 28	Litho.	Perf. 13¼x13		
1132	A416	50fr shown	3.50	—
1133	A416	250fr multi	9.00	—

Promotion of Women — A417

2004, Nov. 26	Litho.	Perf. 14x13½		
1134	A417	250fr multi	—	—

Molothrus Bonariensis A418

Perf. 14¼x13½

2004, Dec. 22		Litho.		
1135	A418	50fr multi	—	—

Trichosurus Vulpecula — A419

2004, Dec. 22		Perf. 14x13¼		
1136	A419	100fr multi	2.25	2.25

Flora — A420

Design: 250fr, Cassia tuhovaliana. 500fr, Schumanniophyton problematicum.

2004, Dec. 22		Perf. 13½x14¼		
1137	A420	250fr multi		
1138	A420	500fr multi		

Tenth General Assembly of African Organization of Supreme Audit Institutions — A421

Frame color: 250fr, Blue. 350fr, Purple.

2005, July 18	Litho.	Perf. 13¼		
1139-1140	A421	Set of 2	10.00	—

"Culture and Excellence" A422

Designs: 100fr, Dan spoon. 250fr, Sénoufo cane, vert.

2005, July 25		Perf. 13x13½, 13½x13		
1141-1142	A422	Set of 2		

World Summit on the Information Society, Tunis — A423

Frame color: 30fr, Red. 220fr, Green.

2005, Sept. 28		Perf. 13¼		
1143-1144	A423	Set of 2	—	2.50

Women's Hairstyles — A424

Various hairstyles: 70fr, 100fr, 250fr, 350fr.

2005, Nov. 3				
1145-1148	A424	Set of 4	—	—

Compare with design A401.

Kings and Chiefs — A425

Designs: 30fr, Tchaman chief standing. 70fr, Tchaman chief, diff. 80fr, Yacouba, Baoulé and Abron chiefs, horiz. 250fr, Akan king and staff-bearer, horiz. 1000fr, Yacouba, Baoulé, and Abron chiefs, horiz.

2005, Nov. 22				
1149-1152	A425	Set of 4	—	—

Souvenir Sheet

| 1152A | A425 | 1000fr multi | 8.25 | 8.25 |

Masks — A426

Designs: 70fr, Dan. 220fr, Gu. 250fr, Zamblé.

2005, Dec. 22				
1153-1155	A426	Set of 3	15.00	—

Europa Stamps, 50th Anniv. (in 2006) — A427

Map of Ivory Coast and: 30fr, Corn and map of Ireland. 70fr, Rubber tree and map of Germany. 80fr, Cotton plant and map of Poland. 220fr, Bananas and map of Netherlands. 250fr, Pineapple and map of Czech Republic. 350fr, Cacao and map of Belgium. 400fr, Sweet potatoes and map of Great Britain. 650fr, Coffee beans and map of Italy. 1000fr, Peanuts and map of Portugal. 2775fr, Palm nut and map of Spain.

2005, Dec. 23	Litho.	Perf. 13¼		
1156-1165	A427	Set of 10	22.00	22.00
1160a		Miniature sheet, #1156-1160	2.40	2.40
1165a		Miniature sheet, #1161-1165	19.50	19.50
1165b		Miniature sheet, #1156-1165	22.00	22.00

Coffee Branches, Flowers and Cherries — A428

Designs: 220fr, Coffea arabusta. 250fr, Coffea liberica.

2005, Dec. 28	Litho.	Perf. 13¼		
1166-1167	A428	Set of 2	—	—

Mushrooms — A429

Designs: 220fr, Marasmius zenkeri. 250fr, Cantharellus rufopunctatus.

2005, Dec. 28				
1168-1169	A429	Set of 2		

Endangered Plants — A430

Designs: 30fr, Dorstenia astyanactis. 70fr, Monosalpinx guillaumetii. 80fr, Monanthotaxis capea. 100fr, Okoubaka aubrevillei.

2005, Dec. 28	Litho.	Perf. 13¼		
1170	A430	30fr multi	—	—
1171	A430	70fr multi	—	—
1172	A430	80fr multi	—	—
1173	A430	100fr multi	—	—

Urban Transportation A431

Designs: 30fr, Buses, automobiles, ferry. 80fr, Buses, automobiles, ferry, diff.

2005, Dec. 29	Litho.	Perf. 13¼		
1174-1175	A431	Set of 2		

Léopold Sédar Senghor (1906-2001), First President of Senegal — A432

Denominations: 50fr, 250fr.

2006, Mar. 20	Litho.	Perf. 13½		
1176-1177	A432	Set of 2	2.40	2.40

A433

2006 World Cup Soccer Championships, Germany — A434

Designs: 50fr, Emblem. 100fr, Goalie making save. 200fr, World Cup. 250fr, Mascot. 1000fr, Mascot.

2006, June 9	Litho.	Perf. 13x13¼		
1178	A433	50fr multi	—	—
1179	A434	100fr multi	—	2.00
1180	A433	200fr multi	—	2.00
1181	A433	250fr multi	—	—

Souvenir Sheet

Perf. 13¾

| 1182 | A433 | 1000fr multi | | |

China-Africa Forum, Beijing — A435

Designs: 250fr, Map of Africa and China. 650fr, Forum venue.

2006, Nov. 28		Perf. 12x12¼		
1183-1184	A435	Set of 2	7.50	7.50

Pardon — A436

2008, June 25		Perf. 13x13¼		
1185-1186	A436	Set of 2		

Diplomatic Relations Between Ivory Coast and People's Republic of China, 30th Anniv.
A437

No. 1187 — Flags of Ivory Coast and People's Republic of China and: a and c, Temple of Heaven, Beijing, Basilica of Our Lady of Peace, Yamoussoukro. b and d, Giant pandas and elephants.
500fr, Pres. Laurent Gbagbo and Chinese Prime Minister Wen Jiabao shaking hands.

2013, Mar. 2	Litho.	Perf. 12		
1187		Horiz. strip of 4	5.25	5.25
a.	A437	50fr multi	.35	.35
b.	A437	100fr multi	.70	.70
c.	A437	250fr multi	1.75	1.75
d.	A437	350fr multi	2.40	2.40

Souvenir Sheet On Plastic Without Gum

| 1188 | A437 | 500fr multi | — | — |
| a. | | As No. 1188, on plain paper, imperf. | — | — |

Nos. 1188 and 1188a contain one 76x50mm stamp.

IVORY COAST

Historic Structures — A438

Designs: 100fr, Great Mosque, Kong. 400fr, Old Governor's Palace, Bingerville, horiz. 825fr, Bandama-Tissalé Bridge, horiz.

Perf. 13½x13, 13x13½
2013, Aug. 1   Litho.
1189-1191 A438 Set of 3   6.25 6.25

Turtle and Waterfall — A439

2013, Aug. 12   Litho.   *Perf. 13x13½*
1192 A439 700fr multi   3.50 3.50

Flora — A440

Designs: 50fr, Tapinanthus belvisii. 250fr, Thonningia sanguinea. 650fr, Ottelia ulvifolia.

2013, Aug. 12   Litho.   *Perf. 13½x13*
1193-1195 A440 Set of 3   4.75 4.75

Animals A441

No. 1196 — Crocuta crocuta: a, 250fr, Hyena. b, 350fr, Hyena, diff. c, 500fr, Hyena, diff. d, 750fr, Hyena, diff.
No. 1197 — Syncerus caffer: a, 250fr, Facing left. b, 350fr, Hind leg raised. c, 500fr, Facing forward. d, 750fr, Two birds on back.
No. 1198 — Hippopotamus amphibius: a, 250fr, Adult and juvenile, juvenile at left. b, 350fr, Adult with mouth closed. c, 500fr, Adult with mouth open. d, 750fr, Adult and juvenile, juvenile at right.
No. 1199 — Primates: a, 250fr, Colobus polykomos. b, 350fr, Cercocebus torquatus. c, 500fr, Procolobus badius. d, 750fr, Cercopithecus diana.
No. 1200 — Bats: a, 250fr, Lavia frons. b, 350fr, Pipistrellus tenuipinnis. c, 500fr, Nycticeinops schlieffeni. d, 750fr, Micropteropus pusillus.
No. 1201 — Panthera leo: a, 250fr, Lion facing forward. b, 350fr, Lion climbing rock. c, 500fr, Lion looking left. d, 750fr, Lion looking right.
No. 1202 — Panthera pardus pardus: a, 250fr, Leopard on branch. b, 350fr, Leopard sitting with tail up. c, 500fr, Leopard sitting tail down. d, 750fr, Leopard walking left.
No. 1203 — Loxodonta africana: a, 250fr, Elephant front leg bent. b, 350fr, Elephant facing forward. c, 500fr, Elephant looking left trunk bent. d, 750fr, Elephant looking left trunk straight.
No. 1204 — Dolphins: a, 250fr, Sousa teuszii. b, 350fr, Steno bredanensis. c, 500fr, Stenella clymene. d, 750fr, Stenella frontalis.
No. 1205 — Whales: a, 250fr, Megaptera novaeangliae. b, 350fr, Feresa attenuata. c, 500fr, Globicephala macrorhynchus. d, 750fr, Pseudorca crassidens.
No. 1206 — Pigeons and doves: a, 250fr, Streptopelia senegalensis. b, 350fr, Treron calvus. c, 500fr, Columba guinea. d, 750fr, Turtur tympanistria.
No. 1207 — Water birds: a, 250fr, Phoenicopterus minor. b, 350fr, Scopus umbretta. c, 500fr, Plegadis falcinellus. d, 750fr, Phoenicopterus roseus.
No. 1208 — Owls: a, 250fr, Scotopelia peli. b, 350fr, Bubo shelleyi. c, 500fr, Glaucidium capense. d, 750fr, Otus icterorhynchus.
No. 1209 — Birds of prey: a, 250fr, Polyboroides typus. b, 350fr, Gyps rueppellii. c, 500fr, Aquila pennata. d, 750fr, Haliaeetus vocifer.
No. 1210 — Cuckoos: a, 250fr, Clamator levaillantii. b, 350fr, Clamator glandarius. c, 500fr, Chrysococcyx klaas. d, 750fr, Clamator jacobinus.
No. 1211 — Bee-eaters: a, 250fr, Merops albicollis. b, 350fr, Merops malimbicus. c, 500fr, Merops bulocki. d, 750fr, Merops orientalis.
No. 1212 — Wood hoopoes: a, 250fr, Phoeniculus purpureus. b, 350fr, Phoeniculus castaneiceps. c, 500fr, Rhinopomastus aterrimus. d, 750fr, Phoeniculus purpureus, diff.
No. 1213 — Butterflies: a, 250fr, Charaxes zingha. b, 350fr, Charaxes cyparissa. c, 500fr, Charaxes imperialis. d, 750fr, Papilio menestheus.
No. 1214 — Fish: a, 250fr, Abudefduf saxatilis. b, 350fr, Anthias nicholsi. c, 500fr, Astronotus ocellatus. d, 750fr, Antigonia capros.
No. 1215 — Turtles: a, 250fr, Eretmochelys imbricata. b, 350fr, Lepidochelys olivacea. c, 500fr, Lepidochelys olivacea, diff. d, 750fr, Chelonoidis carbonaria.
No. 1216 — Snakes and lizards: a, 250fr, Hapsidophrys smaragdina. b, 350fr, Trachylepis affinis. c, 500fr, Squamata amphisbaena. d, 750fr, Leptotyphlops albiventer.
No. 1217 — Frogs: a, 250fr, Hylarana occidentalis. b, 350fr, Hildebrandtia ornata. c, 500fr, Hyperolius fusciventris. d, 750fr, Phrynomantis microps.
No. 1218 — Dinosaurs: a, 250fr, Carcharodontosaurus. b, 350fr, Ceratosaurus. c, 500fr, Allosaurus. d, 750fr, Suchomimus.
No. 1219 — Endangered animals: a, 250fr, Cephalophus jentinki. b, 350fr, Pan troglodytes. c, 500fr, Gyps africanus. d, 750fr, Choeropsis liberiensis.
No. 1220, 2500fr, Crocuta crocuta, diff. No. 1221, 2500fr, Syncerus caffer, diff. No. 1222, 2500fr, Hippopotamus amphibius adult and juvenile, diff. No. 1223, 2500fr, Pan troglodytes, diff. No. 1224, 2500fr, Rousettus aegyptiacus. No. 1225, 2500fr, Panthera leo, diff. No. 1226, 2500fr, Panthera pardus pardus, diff. No. 1227, 2500fr, Loxodonta africana, diff. No. 1228, 2500fr, Delphinus delphis. No. 1229, 2500fr, Physeter macrocephalus. No. 1230, 2500fr, Oena capensis. No. 1231, 2500fr, Phalacrocorax carbo. No. 1232, 2500fr, Tyto alba. No. 1233, 2500fr, Elanus axillaris. No. 1234, 2500fr, Chrysococcyx cupreus. No. 1235, 2500fr, Merops muelleri. No. 1236, 2500fr, Phoeniculus bollei. No. 1237, 2500fr, Charaxes hansali. No. 1238, 2500fr, Balistes punctatus. No. 1239, 2500fr, Dermochelys coriacea. No. 1240, 2500fr, Trachylepis quinquetaeniata. No. 1241, 2500fr, Kassina arboricola. No. 1242, 2500fr, Afrovenator. No. 1243, 2500fr, Loxodonta cyclotis.

Litho. & Embossed
2014, Mar. 10   *Perf. 13¼*
Sheets of 4, #a-d
1196-1219 A441 Set of 24 185.00 185.00
Souvenir Sheets
1220-1243 A441 Set of 24 250.00 250.00

New Year 2014 (Year of the Horse) — A442

2014, Mar. 10   Litho.   *Perf. 13x13¼*
1243A A442 250fr multi   1.10 1.10
Souvenir Sheet
Perf. 13¼
1243B A442 2500fr multi 10.50 10.50
No. 1243B contains one 47x36mm stamp.

First Post Office, Grand-Bassam A443

Denominations: 250fr, 500fr.

2015, Aug. 27   Litho.   *Perf. 13x13¼*
1244-1245 A443 Set of 2   4.00 4.00
UPU Strategy Conference, Geneva.

Economic Community of West African States, 40th Anniv. — A444

2015, Dec. 17   Litho.   *Perf. 13x13¼*
1246 A444 250fr multi   1.50 1.50

8th Francophone Games, Abidjan — A445

Designs: 25fr, Francophone (ring and lines) emblem. 50fr, Games (elephant) emblem. 250fr, Games mascot. 400fr, Games emblem and Ivorian dancers. 500fr, Games emblem and Ivorian dancers, horiz. 650fr, Games emblem and athletes, horiz.

Perf. 13¼x13, 13x13¼
2017, July 22   Litho.
1247-1252 A445 Set of 6

Start of Operations of Soubré Dam — A446

Designs: 10cfr, Aerial view of dam. 250fr, Dam and construction equipment.

2017, Nov. 2   Litho.   *Perf. 13¼x13*
1253-1254 A446 Set of 2

Diplomatic Relations Between Ivory Coast and People's Republic of China, 35th Anniv. — A447

Designs: 200fr, Kong Mosque. 250fr, Forbidden City, Beijing. 400fr, Soubré Dam. 500fr, Ivorian Pres. Alassane Ouattara and People's Republic of China Pres. Xi Jinping shaking hands. 650fr, Comac C919 airplane.

2018, Mar. 2   Litho.   *Perf. 12*
1255-1259 A447 Set of 5

27th Universal Postal Congress, Abidjan (in 2020) — A448

2018, Sept. 6   Litho.   *Perf. 13¼*
Color of Denomination
1260 A448 250fr red
1261 A448 500fr green
Booklet Stamp
Self-Adhesive
Serpentine Die Cut 11
1262 A448 500fr green
  a. Booklet pane of 10

Mohandas K. Gandhi (1869-1948), Indian Nationalist Leader — A449

Gandhi, dove and: 250fr, Map of Ivory Coast. 500fr, Circle.

2019, Oct. 2   Litho.   *Perf. 13¼*
1263-1264 A449 Set of 2

Express Mail Service, 20th Anniv. — A450

Denominations: 50fr, 200fr, 500fr.

2019, Oct. 9   Litho.   *Perf. 13¼*
1265-1267 A450 Set of 3   —   —

27th Universal Postal Union Congress, Abidjan — A453

Designs: 25fr, 50fr, 750fr, Congress emblem and Abidjan buildings. 250fr, Congress emblem.

2021, Aug. 9   Litho.   *Perf. 13x13¼*
1276 A453 25fr org & multi   —   —
1277 A453 50fr green & multi   —   —
1278 A453 250fr multi   —   —
1280 A453 750fr multi   —   —

The 27th Universal Postal Union Congress was scheduled for 2020 but was postponed until 2021 because of the COVID-19 pandemic. An additional stamp was issued in this set. The editors would like to examine any example of it.

SEMI-POSTAL STAMPS

No. 47 Surcharged in Red

1915   Unwmk.   *Perf. 14x13½*
B1 A5 10c + 5c   1.60 1.60
  a. Double surcharge   80.00 80.00

Curie Issue
Common Design Type
1938   *Perf. 13*
B2 CD80 1.75fr + 50c brt ultra   11.00 7.50

French Revolution Issue
Common Design Type
1939   Photo.
Name and Value Typo. in Black
B3 CD83 45c + 25c grn   8.75 8.75
B4 CD83 70c + 30c brn   8.75 8.75
B5 CD83 90c + 35c red org   8.75 8.75
B6 CD83 1.25fr + 1fr rose pink 8.75 8.75
B7 CD83 2.25fr + 2fr blue 8.75 8.75
   Nos. B3-B7 (5)   43.75 43.75

Catalogue values for unused stamps in this section, from this point to the end of the section, are for Never Hinged items.

Stamps of 1936-38 Surcharged in Red or Black

1941
B8   A7 50c + 1fr plum (Bk)   3.75 3.75
B9   A8 80c + 2fr blk brn (R) 11.00 11.00
B10 A8 1.50fr + 2fr ultra (R) 11.00 11.00
B11 A9 2fr + 3fr ultra (Bk)   11.00 11.00
   Nos. B8-B11 (4)   36.75 36.75

Common Design Type and Native Engineer — SP1

IVORY COAST

Senegalese Light Artillery — SP2

	1941	Photo.	Perf. 13½
B12	SP1	1fr + 1fr red	1.50
B13	CD86	1.50fr + 3fr claret	1.50
B14	SP2	2.50fr + 1fr blue	1.50
		Nos. B12-B14 (3)	4.50

Nos. B12-B14 were issued by the Vichy government in France, but were not placed on sale in Ivory Coast.

Nos. 165-166 Surcharged in Black or Red

	1944	Engr.	Perf. 12½x12
B14A	50c + 1.50fr on 2.50fr deep blue (R)		.80
B14B	+ 2.50fr on 1fr green		.80

Colonial Development Fund.

Nos. B14A-B14B were issued by the Vichy government in France, but were not placed on sale in Ivory Coast.

Republic
Anti-Malaria Issue
Common Design Type

	1962, Apr. 7	Engr.	Perf. 12½x12
B15	CD108	25fr + 5fr ol grn	1.25 1.25

Freedom from Hunger Issue
Common Design Type

	1963, Mar. 21		Perf. 13
B16	CD112	25fr + 5fr red lil, dk vio & brn	1.50 1.50

Red Cross - Red Crescent Soc., Child Survival Campaign — SP3

	1987, May 8	Litho.	Perf. 13½
B17	SP3	195fr +5fr multi	2.50 2.50

No. B17 surcharged "+5fr" in red. Not issued without surcharge. Surtax for the Red Cross - Red Crescent Soc.

Organization of African Unity, 25th Anniv. — SP4

	1988, Nov. 19	Litho.	Perf. 12½x13
B18	SP4	195fr +5fr multi	2.25 2.25

Marie Therese Houphouet-Boigny and N'Daya Intl. Emblem — SP5

	1988, Dec. 9	Litho.	Perf. 13
B19	SP5	195fr +5fr multi	2.25 2.25

N'Daya Intl., 1st anniv.

See postage issues, beginning with No. 1030, for semi-postal stamps that are part of sets with regular postage stamps.

Council of Understanding, Solidarity & Rural Development, 40th Anniv. — SP6

	1999, May 29	Litho.	Perf. 13x13½
B20	SP6	180fr +20fr multi	1.20 1.20

Postage Types of 1998-99 With Added Surtax

	1999 ?	Litho.	Perf. 12
	Granite Paper (#B20A)		
B20A	A384	180fr +20fr Like #1024	—
		Perf. 13½	
B20B	A386	180fr +20fr Like #1027	—

Nos. B20A-B20B apparently were not issued with Nos. 1022-1024 and 1027-1029.

Postage Type of 1998 With Added Surtax

	1999 ?	Litho.	Perf. 13½x13
B20C	A385	180fr +20fr Like #1025	—

Independence, 41st Anniv. — SP7

	2001, Aug. 7	Litho.	Perf. 13¼x13½
B21	SP7	180fr +20fr multi	1.10 1.10

Year of Dialogue Among Civilizations SP8

	2001, Oct. 9	Litho.	Perf. 13x13¼
B22	SP8	400fr +20fr multi	2.25 2.25

Second Republic, 1st Anniv. — SP9

	2001, Oct. 26		
B23	SP9	180fr +20fr multi	1.10 1.10

Planned 2004 Universal Postal Union Congress, Abidjan — SP10

Vignette size: 180fr+20fr, 23x37mm. 400fr+20fr, 26x37mm. 600fr+20fr, 36x49mm.

Perf. 13, 13¼x13 (#B25)

	2001, Dec. 21		Litho.
B24	SP10	180fr +20fr multi	1.00 1.00
a.	Souvenir sheet of 1		5.00 5.00
B25	SP10	400fr +20fr multi	2.25 2.25
B26	SP10	600fr +20fr multi	3.25 3.25

On Nos. B24-B26 and B24a portions of the design were applied by a thermographic process producing a shiny raised effect. No. B24a sold for 1000fr and contains imperforate examples of Nos. B25 and B26 in the margin, which are surmised to be invalid for postage as the face value of these two stamps exceeds the selling price of the sheet. The 2004 UPU Congress was moved from Abidjan to Bucharest, Romania due to political unrest in the Ivory Coast.

St. Valentine's Day — SP11

Serpentine Die Cut

	2002, Feb. 14		Litho.
	Booklet Stamp		
	Self-Adhesive		
B27	SP11	180fr +20fr multi	1.10 1.10
a.	Booklet pane of 8		9.00

Jean Mermoz Intl. College, Abidjan, 40th Anniv. — SP12

Panel color: 180fr+20fr, Tan. 400fr+20fr, Red.

	2002, Apr. 19		Perf. 13½x13¼
B28-B29	SP12	Set of 2	3.00 3.00

Decentralization SP14

Denomination color: 180fr+20fr, Green. 400fr+20fr, Blue.

	2002, Dec. 4	Litho.	Perf. 13¼x13
B34-B35	SP14	Set of 2	3.00 3.00

Campaign Against AIDS — SP16

	2003, Dec. 22	Litho.	Perf. 13¼
B36	SP15	180fr +20fr multi	1.00 1.00
			Perf. 13¾
B37	SP16	400fr +20fr multi	2.00 2.00

Values for No. B37 are for stamps with surrounding selvage.

AIR POST STAMPS

Common Design Type

	1940	Unwmk.	Engr.	Perf. 12½x12
C1	CD85	1.90fr ultramarine	.40	.40
C2	CD85	2.90fr dark red	.40	.40
C3	CD85	4.50fr dk gray grn	.75	.75
C4	CD85	4.90fr yel bister	.75	.75
C5	CD85	6.90fr deep orange	1.50	1.50
		Nos. C1-C5 (5)	3.80	3.80

Catalogue values for unused stamps in this section, from this point to the end of the section, are for Never Hinged items.

Common Design Types

1942

C6	CD88	50c car & blue	.35
C7	CD88	1fr brn & black	.75
C8	CD88	2fr dk grn & red brn	1.10
C9	CD88	3fr dk blue & scar	1.10
C10	CD88	5fr vio & dk red	1.10

Frame Engraved, Center Typographed

C11	CD89	10fr multicolored	1.50
C12	CD89	20fr multicolored	2.25
C13	CD89	50fr multicolored	3.00
		Nos. C6-C13 (8)	11.15

There is doubt whether Nos. C6-C12 were officially placed in use.

Republic

Lapalud Place and Post Office, Abidjan AP1

Designs: 200fr, Houphouet-Boigny Bridge. 500fr, Ayamé dam.

	1959, Oct. 1	Engr.	Perf. 13
C14	AP1	100fr multicolored	3.00 .75
C15	AP1	200fr multicolored	5.00 2.25
C16	AP1	500fr multicolored	11.00 4.50
		Nos. C14-C16 (3)	19.00 7.50

Sports Type of 1961

	1961, Dec. 23		
C17	A19	100fr High jump	4.50 2.25

Air Afrique Issue
Common Design Type

	1962, Feb. 17	Unwmk.	Perf. 13
C18	CD107	50fr Prus bl, choc & org brn	2.00 1.25

Village in Man Region AP2

200fr, Street in Odienne, vert.

	1962, June 23	Engr.	Perf. 13
C19	AP2	200fr multi	5.50 2.75
C20	AP2	500fr shown	11.00 5.00

UN Headquarters, New York — AP3

	1962, Sept. 20		Perf. 13
C21	AP3	100fr multi	2.75 1.25

Admission to the UN, 2nd anniv.

Sassandra Bay — AP4

50fr, Moossou bridge. 200fr, Comoe River.

	1963	Unwmk.	Perf. 13
C22	AP4	50fr multi	2.25 .75
C23	AP4	100fr shown	3.25 1.75
C24	AP4	200fr multi	6.00 2.75
		Nos. C22-C24 (3)	11.50 5.25

African Postal Union Issue
Common Design Type

	1963, Sept. 8	Photo.	Perf. 12½
C25	CD114	85fr org brn, ocher & red	2.50 1.50

1963 Air Afrique Issue
Common Design Type

	1963, Nov. 19	Unwmk.	Perf. 13x12
C26	CD115	25fr crim, gray, blk & grn	1.00 .50

IVORY COAST

Ramses II and Queen Nefertari — AP5

1964, Mar. 7   Engr.   Perf. 13
C27   AP5   60fr car, blk & red brn   2.50   1.50

UNESCO campaign to save historic monuments in Nubia.

Arms of Republic — AP6

1964, June 13   Photo.
C28   AP6   200fr ultra, yel grn & gold   5.00   2.25

President John F. Kennedy (1917-63) — AP7

1964, Nov. 14   Unwmk.   Perf. 12½
C29   AP7   100fr gray, cl brn & blk   2.75   1.50
   a.   Souvenir sheet of 4   13.00   13.00

Liana Bridge, Lieupleu AP8

1965, Dec. 4   Engr.   Perf. 13
C30   AP8   100fr ol grn, dk grn & dk red brn   3.50   1.75

Street in Kong — AP9

1966, Mar. 5   Engr.   Perf. 13
C31   AP9   300fr brt bl, bis brn & vio brn   8.00   4.50

Air Afrique Issue, 1966
Common Design Type

1966, Aug. 20   Photo.   Perf. 13
C32   CD123   30fr dk grn, blk & gray   1.00   .60

Air Afrique Headquarters — AP10

1967, Feb. 4   Engr.   Perf. 13
C33   AP10   500fr emer, ind & ocher   11.50   5.50

Opening of Air Afrique headquarters in Abidjan.

African Postal Union Issue, 1967
Common Design Type

1967, Sept. 9   Engr.   Perf. 13
C34   CD124   100fr blk, vio & car lake   3.50   1.50

Senufo Village AP11

1968   Engr.   Perf. 13
C35   AP11   100fr shown   3.25   1.25
C36   AP11   500fr Tiegba village   11.50   4.50

Issue dates: 100fr, Feb. 17; 500fr, Apr. 27.

PHILEXAFRIQUE Issue
Common Design Type

Street in Grand Bassam, by Achalme AP12

1969, Jan. 11   Photo.   Perf. 12x12½
C37   AP12   100fr grn & multi   4.25   4.25

PHILEXAFRIQUE Phil. Exhib., Abidjan, Feb. 14-23. Printed with alternating green label. Value, single with attached label, $6.

2nd PHILEXAFRIQUE Issue
Common Design Type

50fr, Ivory Coast #130 & view of San Pedro. 100fr, Ivory Coast #149 & man wearing chief's garments, vert. 200fr, Ivory Coast #77 # Exhibition Hall, Abidjan.

1969, Feb. 14   Engr.   Perf. 13
C38   CD128   50fr grn, brn red & deep bl   3.00   3.00
C39   CD128   100fr brn, org & dp blue   4.50   4.50
C40   CD128   200fr brn, gray & dp blue   7.00   7.00
   a.   Min. sheet of 3, #C38-C40   18.50   18.50
Nos. C38-C40 (3)   14.50   14.50

Opening of PHILEXAFRIQUE.

Man Waterfall AP13

Mount Niangbo AP14

1970   Engr.   Perf. 13
C41   AP13   100fr multicolored   3.25   1.50
C42   AP14   200fr multicolored   4.25   2.00

Issue dates: 100fr, Jan. 6; 200fr, July 18.

San Pedro Harbor AP15

1971, Mar. 21   Engr.   Perf. 13
C43   AP15   100fr multicolored   2.25   1.00

Treichville Swimming Pool — AP16

1971, May 29   Photo.   Perf. 12½
C44   AP16   100fr multicolored   3.00   1.25

Aerial View of Coast Line AP17

1971, July 3   Engr.   Perf. 13
C45   AP17   500fr multi   12.00   6.00

Tourist publicity for the African Riviera.

Bondoukou Market Type of Regular Issue

Design: 200fr, Similar to No. 318, but without people at left and in center.

Embossed on Gold Paper

1971, Aug. 7   Perf. 12½
Size: 36x26mm
C46   A79   200fr gold, ultra & blk   4.75   2.50

African Postal Union Issue, 1971
Common Design Type

Design: 100fr, Ivory Coast coat of arms and UAMPT building, Brazzaville, Congo.

1971, Nov. 13   Photo.   Perf. 13x13½
C47   CD135   100fr bl & multi   2.00   1.00

Lion of St. Mark — AP18

1972, Feb. 5   Photo.   Perf. 12½
C48   AP18   100fr shown   3.50   1.75
C49   AP18   200fr multi   6.00   3.25

200fr, Waves, St. Mark's Basilica, Venice.
UNESCO campaign to save Venice.

Kawara Mosque AP19

1972, Apr. 29   Engr.   Perf. 13
C50   AP19   500fr bl, brn & ocher   12.00   6.00

View of Gouessesso AP20

200fr, Jacqueville Lake. 500fr, Kossou Dam.

1972   Engr.   Perf. 13
C51   AP20   100fr shown   3.25   1.25
C52   AP20   200fr multi   4.75   1.75
C53   AP20   500fr multi   10.00   6.00
Nos. C51-C53 (3)   18.00   9.00

Issued: 100fr, 6/10; 200fr, 1/8; 500fr, 11/17.

Akakro Radar Earth Station AP21

1972, Nov. 27   Engr.   Perf. 13
C54   AP21   200fr brt bl, sl grn & choc   4.50   1.75

The Judgment of Solomon, by Nandjui Legue — AP22

1973, Aug. 26   Photo.   Perf. 13
C55   AP22   500fr multi   12.00   5.75

6th World Peace Conference for Justice.

Sassandra River Bridge AP23

1974, May 4   Engr.   Perf. 13
C56   AP23   100fr blk & yel grn   2.25   .75
C57   AP23   500fr slate grn & brn   12.00   4.25

Vridi Soap Factory, Abidjan AP24

1974, July 6   Photo.   Perf. 13
C58   AP24   200fr multi   3.50   1.75

UPU Emblem, Ivory Coast Flag, Post Runner and Jet — AP25

1974, Oct. 9   Photo.   Perf. 13
C59   AP25   200fr multi   5.00   3.00
C60   AP25   300fr multi   6.00   4.00

Centenary of Universal Postal Union.

Fly Whisk and Panga Knife, Symbols of Akans Royal Family — AP26

1976, Apr. 3   Photo.   Perf. 12½x13
C61   AP26   200fr brt bl & multi   4.75   2.00

Tingrela Mosque AP27

1977, May 7   Engr.   Perf. 13
C62   AP27   500fr multi   7.50   4.50

Zeppelin Type of 1977
Souvenir Sheet

"Graf Zeppelin" LZ 127 over New York.

1977, Sept. 3   Litho.   Perf. 11
C63   A150   500fr multi   6.25   1.90

Exists imperf.

Philexafrique II - Essen Issue
Common Design Types

#C64, Elephant and Ivory Coast No. 239. #C65, Pheasant and Bavaria No. 1.

1978, Nov. 1   Litho.   Perf. 13x12½
C64   CD138   100fr multi   3.50   2.50
C65   CD139   100fr multi   3.50   2.50
   a.   Pair, #C64-C65 + label   9.00   9.00

Gymnast, Olympic Rings — AP28

Various gymnasts. 75fr, 150fr, 350fr, vert.

IVORY COAST

1980, July 24 Litho. *Perf. 14½*
C66 AP28 75fr multi .90 .25
C67 AP28 150fr multi 1.25 .45
C68 AP28 250fr multi 3.00 1.00
C69 AP28 350fr multi 3.50 1.25
  Nos. C66-C69 (4) 8.65 2.95

C70 AP28 500fr multi 5.50 2.00

22nd Summer Olympic Games, Moscow, July 19-Aug. 3.

President Houphouet-Boigny, 75th Birthday AP28a

Embossed Die Cut *Perf. 10½*
1980, Oct. 18
C70A AP28a 2000fr Silver 20.00 20.00
C70B AP28a 3000fr Gold 35.00 35.00

Manned Flight Bicentenary AP29

Various balloons: 100fr, Montgolfier, 1783, vert. 125fr, Hydrogen, 1783, vert. 150fr, Mail transport, 1870. 350fr, Double Eagle II, 1978, vert. 500fr, Dirigible.

1983, Apr. 2 Litho. *Perf. 13*
C71 AP29 100fr multi 1.00 .35
C72 AP29 125fr multi 1.50 .45
C73 AP29 150fr multi 1.75 .50
C74 AP29 350fr multi 4.50 1.00
C75 AP29 500fr multi 6.50 1.75
  Nos. C71-C75 (5) 15.25 4.05

Pre-Olympic Year — AP30

Various swimming events: 100fr, Crawl. 125fr, Diving. 350fr, Backstroke. 400fr, Butterfly. 500fr, Water polo.

1983, July 9 Litho. *Perf. 14*
C76 AP30 100fr multi .95 .35
C77 AP30 125fr multi 1.25 .45
C78 AP30 350fr multi 2.00 .75
C79 AP30 400fr multi 4.00 1.40
  Nos. C76-C79 (4) 8.20 2.95

Souvenir Sheet
C80 AP30 500fr multi 5.50 2.00

1984 Summer Olympics AP31

Pentathlon: 100fr, Swimming. 125fr, Running. 185fr, Shooting. 350fr, Fencing. 500fr, Equestrian.

1984, Mar. *Perf. 12½*
C81 AP31 100fr multi 1.00 .30
C82 AP31 125fr multi 1.25 .40
C83 AP31 185fr multi 1.75 .60
C84 AP31 350fr multi 3.75 1.25
  Nos. C81-C84 (4) 7.75 2.55

Souvenir Sheet
C85 AP31 500fr multi 5.50 2.00

Los Angeles Olympics Winners — AP32

100fr, Tiacoh, silver. 150fr, Lewis, gold. 200fr, Babers, gold. 500fr, Cruz, gold.

1984, Dec. 15 Litho. *Perf. 13*
C86 AP32 100fr multi 1.00 .25
C87 AP32 150fr multi 1.50 .40
C88 AP32 200fr multi 2.00 .75
C89 AP32 500fr multi 4.25 1.50
  Nos. C86-C89 (4) 8.75 2.90

Christmas AP33

Paintings: 100fr, Virgin and Child, by Correggio. 200fr, Holy Family with Angels, by Andrea del Sarto. 400fr, Virgin and Child, by Bellini.

1985, Jan. 12 *Perf. 13*
C90 AP33 100fr multi 1.00 .35
C91 AP33 200fr multi 1.75 .85
C92 AP33 400fr multi 3.75 1.75
  Nos. C90-C92 (3) 6.50 2.95
Nos. C91-C92 have incorrect frame inscriptions.

Audubon Birth Bicentenary AP34

Birds: 100fr, Mergus serrator. 150fr, Pelecanus erythrorhynchos. 200fr, Mycteria americana. 350fr, Melanitta deglandi.

1985, June 8 Litho. *Perf. 13*
C93 AP34 100fr multi 1.00 .45
C94 AP34 150fr multi, vert. 1.50 .70
C95 AP34 200fr multi, vert. 2.50 1.00
C96 AP34 350fr multi 3.50 1.75
  Nos. C93-C96 (4) 8.50 3.90

PHILEXAFRICA '85, Lome, Togo — AP35

No. C98, Soccer, boys and deer.

1985, Nov. 16 Litho. *Perf. 13*
C97 AP35 250fr shown 3.00 2.00
C98 AP35 250fr multi 3.00 2.00
  a. Pair, #C97-C98 + label 9.00 6.00

Edmond Halley, Computer Drawing of Comet AP36

Return of Halley's Comet: 155fr, Sir William Herschel, Uranus. 190fr, Space probe, comet. 350fr, MS T-5 probe, comet. 440fr, Skylab, Kohoutek comet.

1986, Jan. Litho. *Perf. 13*
C99 AP36 125fr shown 1.00 .50
C100 AP36 155fr multi 1.25 .75
C101 AP36 190fr multi 1.75 .90
C102 AP36 350fr multi 3.00 1.60
C103 AP36 440fr multi 3.75 2.10
  Nos. C99-C103 (5) 10.75 5.85

1986 World Cup Soccer Championships, Mexico — AP37

Various soccer plays.

1986, Apr. 26 Litho. *Perf. 13*
C104 AP37 90fr multi .80 .40
C105 AP37 125fr multi 1.25 .60
C106 AP37 155fr multi 1.50 .70
C107 AP37 440fr multi 4.00 2.10
C108 AP37 500fr multi 4.50 2.50
  Nos. C104-C108 (5) 12.05 6.30

Souvenir Sheet *Perf. 13½x13*
C109 AP37 600fr multi 6.25 2.50

AP38

1988 Summer Olympics, Seoul — AP39

Sailing sports: 155fr, Soling Class. 195fr, Windsurfing. 250fr, 470 Class. 550fr, Windsurfing, diff. 650fr, 470 Class, diff.

1987, May 23 Litho. *Perf. 12½*
C110 AP38 155fr multi 1.50 .60
C111 AP38 195fr multi 2.25 .75
C112 AP38 250fr multi 3.00 1.00
C113 AP38 550fr multi 6.00 2.50
  Nos. C110-C113 (4) 12.75 4.85

Souvenir Sheet
C114 AP39 650fr multi 7.00 2.25

1988 Summer Olympics, Seoul AP40

100fr, Gymnastic rings. 155fr, Women's handball. 195fr, Boxing. No. C118, 500fr, Parallel bars. No. C119, 500fr, Horizontal bar.

1988, June 18 Litho. *Perf. 13*
C115 AP40 100fr multi .90 .40
C116 AP40 155fr multi 1.25 .60
C117 AP40 195fr multi 2.00 .75
C118 AP40 500fr multi 5.00 2.00
  Nos. C115-C118 (4) 9.15 3.75

Souvenir Sheet
C119 AP40 500fr multi 14.00 2.00

1990 World Cup Soccer Championships, Italy — AP41

Italian monuments and various athletes: 195fr, Milan Cathedral. 300fr, Columbus Monument, Genoa. 450fr, Turin. 550fr, Bologna.

1989, Nov. 25 Litho. *Perf. 13*
C120 AP41 195fr multi 1.75 .75
C121 AP41 300fr multi 2.50 1.25
C122 AP41 450fr multi 3.50 1.75
C123 AP41 550fr multi 5.00 2.00
  Nos. C120-C123 (4) 12.75 5.75

World Cup Soccer Championships, Italy — AP42

Various plays.

1990, May 31 Litho. *Perf. 13*
C124 AP42 155fr multicolored 1.50 .60
C125 AP42 195fr multicolored 1.75 .85
C126 AP42 500fr multicolored 4.25 2.00
C127 AP42 600fr multicolored 5.75 2.50
  Nos. C124-C127 (4) 13.25 5.95

AIR POST SEMI-POSTAL STAMPS

Types of Dahomey Air Post Semi-Postal Issue
Perf. 13½x12½, 13 (#CB3)
Photo, Engr. (#CB3)

1942, June 22
CB1 SPAP1 1.50fr + 3.50fr green 1.00 5.50
CB2 SPAP2 2fr + 6fr brown 1.00 5.50
CB3 SPAP2 3fr + 9fr car red 1.00 5.50
  Nos. CB1-CB3 (3) 3.00 16.50
Native children's welfare fund.

Colonial Education Fund
Common Design Type
Perf. 12½x13½

1942, June 22 Engr.
CB4 CD86a 1.20fr + 1.80fr blue & red 1.00 5.50

POSTAGE DUE STAMPS

Natives — D1

Perf. 14x13½
1906-07 Unwmk. Typo.
J1 D1 5c grn, *greenish* 4.00 4.00
J2 D1 10c red brown 4.00 4.00
J3 D1 15c dark blue 6.50 6.50
J4 D1 20c blk, *yellow* 9.50 9.50
J5 D1 30c red, *straw* 9.50 9.50
J6 D1 50c violet 7.25 7.25
J7 D1 60c black, *buff* 32.50 32.50
J8 D1 1fr blk, *pinkish* 35.00 35.00
  Nos. J1-J8 (8) 108.25 108.25

D2

1914
J9 D2 5c green .25 .25
J10 D2 10c rose .30 .30
J11 D2 15c gray .30 .30
J12 D2 20c brown .55 .55
J13 D2 30c blue .55 .55
J14 D2 50c black .90 .90

IVORY COAST

J15	D2	60c orange	1.25	1.25
J16	D2	1fr violet	1.50	1.50
		Nos. J9-J16 (8)	5.60	5.60

Type of 1914 Issue Surcharged

1927

J17	D2	2fr on 1fr lilac rose	2.75	2.75
J18	D2	3fr on 1fr org brown	2.75	2.75

Catalogue values for unused stamps in this section, from this point to the end of the section, are for Never Hinged items.

Republic

Guéré Mask — D3

1960   Engr.   Perf. 14x13
Denomination Typographed in Black

J19	D3	1fr purple	.25	.25
J20	D3	2fr bright green	.25	.25
J21	D3	5fr orange yellow	.50	.50
J22	D3	10fr ultramarine	.90	.90
J23	D3	20fr lilac rose	1.60	1.60
		Nos. J19-J23 (5)	3.50	3.50

Mask — D4

Various masks and heads, Bingerville school of art.

1962, Nov. 3   Typo.   Perf. 13½x14

J24	D4	1fr org & brt blue	.25	.25
J25	D4	2fr black & red	.30	.30
J26	D4	5fr red & dark grn	.40	.40
J27	D4	10fr green & lilac	.90	.90
J28	D4	20fr dark pur & blk	1.60	1.60
		Nos. J24-J28 (5)	3.45	3.45

Baoulé Weight — D5

Various Baoulé weights.

1968, May 18   Photo.   Perf. 13

J29	D5	5fr cit, brn & bl grn	.25	.25
J30	D5	10fr lt bl, brn & bl grn	.30	.30
J31	D5	15fr sal, brn & bl grn	.80	.80
J32	D5	20fr gray, car & bl grn	1.10	1.10
J33	D5	30fr bis, brn & bl grn	1.50	1.50
		Nos. J29-J33 (5)	3.95	3.95

Gold Weight — D6

Various gold weights.

1972, May 27   Engr.

J34	D6	20fr vio bl & org red	.90	.90
J35	D6	40fr ver & ocher	1.50	1.50
J36	D6	50fr orange & chocolate	2.00	2.00
J37	D6	100fr slate grn & ocher	4.00	4.00
		Nos. J34-J37 (4)	8.40	8.40

It has been reported that Nos. J34-J37 were used briefly as regular postage for domestic use. Examples of use as postage to foreign addresses exists.

MILITARY STAMP

The catalogue value for the unused stamp in this section is for Never Hinged.

Coat of Arms — M1

Perf. 13x14
1967, Jan. 1   Unwmk.   Typo.

M1	M1	multi	3.50	3.50

OFFICIAL STAMPS

Catalogue values for unused stamps in this section are for Never Hinged items.

Ivory Coast Coat of Arms — O1

1974, Jan. 1   Photo.   Perf. 12

O1	O1	(35fr) green & multi	.75	.25
O2	O1	(75fr) orange & multi	1.20	.45
O3	O1	(100fr) lil rose & multi	1.50	.80
O4	O1	(250fr) violet & multi	4.00	1.50
		Nos. O1-O4 (4)	7.45	3.00

PARCEL POST STAMPS

Postage Due Stamps of French Colonies Overprinted

Overprinted In Black

1903   Unwmk.   Imperf.

Q1	D1	50c lilac	42.50	40.00
Q2	D1	1fr rose, buff	42.50	40.00

Overprinted In Black

Q3	D1	50c lilac	3,300.	3,400.
Q4	D1	1fr rose, buff	3,300.	3,400.

Accents on "O" of "COTE"
Nos. Q7-Q8, Q11-Q12, Q15, Q17-Q18, Q21-Q22, Q24-Q25 exist with or without accent.

Overprinted In Red and Black

Red Overprint

Q5	D1	50c lilac	120.00	120.00
a.		Inverted overprint	425.00	425.00

Blue Black Overprint

Q6	D1	1fr rose, buff	87.50	87.50
a.		Inverted overprint	350.00	350.00

Surcharged in Black

a

b

c

d

e

f

g

h

1903

Q7	D1	50c on 15c pale grn	16.00	16.00
a.		Inverted surcharge	225.00	225.00
Q8	D1	50c on 60c brn, buff	35.00	35.00
a.		Inverted surcharge	225.00	225.00
Q9		(a)1fr on 5c blue	4,400.	3,600.
Q10		(b)1fr on 5c blue	4,400.	2,800.
Q11		(c)1fr on 5c blue	18.00	16.00
a.		Inverted surcharge	950.00	950.00
Q12		(d)1fr on 5c blue	27.50	24.00
Q13		(e)1fr on 5c blue	4,800.	4,000.
Q14		(f) 1fr on 5c blue	12,000.	9,500.
Q15		(g)1fr on 5c blue	110.00	110.00
Q16		(h)1fr on 5c blue	3,750.	3,850.
Q17		(c) 1fr on 10c gray brn	27.50	24.00
a.		Inverted surcharge	325.00	325.00
Q18		(d) 1fr on 10c gray brn	47.50	45.00
a.		Inverted surcharge	475.00	475.00
Q19		(g)1fr on 10c gray brn	4,000.	3,850.
Q20		(h) 1fr on 10c gray brn	46,000.	

Some authorities regard Nos. Q9 and Q10 as essays. A sub-type of type "a" has smaller, bold "XX" without serifs.

Surcharged in Black

j   k

l

Q21		(j) 4fr on 60c brn, buff	140.00	140.00
a.		Double surcharge		5,600.
Q22		(k) 4fr on 60c brn, buff	375.00	375.00
Q23		(l) 4fr on 60c brn, buff	1,200.	1,000.

Surcharged in Black

Q24	D1	4fr on 15c green	130.00	130.00
a.		One large star	525.00	525.00
b.		Two large stars	300.00	300.00
Q25		4fr on 30c rose	130.00	130.00
a.		One large star	525.00	525.00
b.		Two large stars	300.00	300.00

Overprinted in Black

1904

Q26	D1	50c lilac	45.00	45.00
a.		Inverted overprint		
Q27	D1	1fr rose, buff	45.00	45.00
a.		Inverted overprint		

Overprinted in Black

Q28	D1	50c lilac	42.50	42.50
a.		Inverted overprint	225.00	225.00
Q29	D1	1fr rose, buff	42.50	42.50
a.		Inverted overprint	225.00	225.00

Surcharged in Black

Q30	D1	4fr on 5c blue	240.00	240.00
Q31	D1	8fr on 15c green	240.00	240.00

Overprinted in Black

1905

Q32	D1	50c lilac	92.50	92.50
Q33	D1	1fr rose, buff	92.50	92.50

Surcharged in Black

Q34	D1	2fr on 1fr rose, buff	240.00	240.00
Q35	D1	4fr on 1fr rose, buff	240.00	240.00
a.		Italic "4"	2,200.	2,200.
Q36	D1	8fr on 1fr rose, buff	700.00	700.00

INDEX AND IDENTIFIER

All page numbers shown are those in this Volume 3B.

Postage stamps that do not have English words on them are shown in the Illustrated Identifier.

A & T ovptd. on French Colonies .... **Vol. 1A**
Aberdeen, Miss. .... Vol. 1A
Abingdon, Va. .... Vol. 1A
Abu Dhabi .... Vol. 1A, Vol. 5A, Vol. 6B
Abyssinia (Ethiopia) .... Vol. 2B
A.C.C.P., A.D.C.P. .... Vol. 1B
A Certo ovptd. on stamps of Peru .... Vol. 5A
Acores .... Vol. 1B, Vol. 5B
Aden .... Vol. 1A
AEF .... Vol. 2B
Aegean Islands (Greek Occupation) .... Vol. 3A
Aegean Islands (Italian Occupation) ... 697
Aeroport International de Kandahar (Afghanistan #679) .... Vol. 1A
Afars and Issas .... Vol. 1A
AFF EXCEP .... Vol. 2B
Afghanistan, Afghan, Afghanes ... Vol. 1A
AFR .... Vol. 5B
Africa, British Offices .... Vol. 3A
Africa, German East .... Vol. 3A
Africa, German South-West .... Vol. 3A
Africa, Italian Offices 695
Africa Occidental Espanola .... Vol. 6A
Africa Orientale Italiana 586
Africa, Portuguese .... Vol. 5B
Afrique Equatoriale Francaise ... Vol. 2A, Vol. 2B, Vol. 4B, Vol. 6B
Afrique Francaise .... Vol. 2B
Afrique Occidentale Francaise ... Vol. 2B
Agion Oros Athoc (Greece) .... Vol. 3A
Aguera, La .... Vol. 6A
Aguinaldo .... Vol. 5A
AHA (Confed. #44X1) .... Vol. 1A
Aimeliik (Palau #686) .... Vol. 5A
Airai (Palau #686) .... Vol. 5A
Aitutaki .... Vol. 1A
Ajman .... Vol. 1A, Vol. 6B
Aland Islands .... Vol. 2B
Alaouites .... Vol. 1A
Albania .... Vol. 1A
Albania, Greek Occupation .... Vol. 3A
Albania, Italian Offices 696
Albany, Ga. .... Vol. 1A
Alderney .... Vol. 3A
Aleppo .... Vol. 6A
Alerta ovptd. on stamps of Peru ... Vol. 5A
Alexandretta, Alexandrette .... Vol. 1A
Alexandria, Alexandrie, French Offices .... Vol. 2B
Alexandria, Va. .... Vol. 1A
Alexandroupolis .... Vol. 3A
Algeria, Algerie .... Vol. 1A
Allemagne Duitschland .... Vol. 1B
Allenstein .... Vol. 1A
Allied Military Government (Austria) .... Vol. 1B
Allied Military Gov. (Germany) ... Vol. 3A
Allied Military Government (Italy) ... 692
Allied Military Government (Trieste) ... 701
Allied Occupation of Azerbaijan ... Vol. 1B
Allied Occupation of Thrace .... Vol. 6B
A L'Ocassion de la Journée Internationale de l'Alphabetisation (Afghan. #951) .... Vol. 1A
Alsace .... Vol. 2B
Alsace and Lorraine .... Vol. 2B
Alwar 313
A.M.G. .... 686, Vol. 1B, Vol. 3A
A.M.G./F.T.T. 701
A.M.G./V.G. 692
AM Post .... Vol. 3A
Anatolia .... Vol. 6B
Ancachs .... Vol. 5A
Andalusian Provinces .... Vol. 6A
Anderson Court House, S.C. ...... Vol. 1A
Andorra, Andorre .... Vol. 1A
Andorre .... Vol. 1A
Angaur (Palau #686) .... Vol. 5A
Angola .... Vol. 1A
Angra .... Vol. 1A
Anguilla .... Vol. 1A, Vol. 5B
Anhwei .... Vol. 2A
Anjouan .... Vol. 1A
Anna surcharged on France .... Vol. 2B
Anna surcharged on Great Britain ... Vol. 5A

Anna, Annas 221, 303
Annam 336
Annam and Tonkin .... Vol. 1A
Annapolis, Md. .... Vol. 1A
Ano do X Aniversario Comunidade dos Paises de Lingua Portugesa (Angola 1298-1300) .... Vol. 1A
Antigua .... Vol. 1A, Vol. 5B
Antigua & Barbuda .... Vol. 1A
Antioquia .... Vol. 2A
A.O. ovptd. on Congo .... Vol. 3A
AOF on France .... Vol. 2B
A.O.I. ovpt. on Italy 586
A Payer Te Betalen .... Vol. 1B
A percevoir (see France, French colonies, postage due) ... Vol. 2B, Vol. 3A
Apurimac .... Vol. 5A
A R .... Vol. 4B
A.R. ovptd. on stamps of Colombia .... Vol. 5A
Arabie Saoudite .... Vol. 6A
Arad 183
A receber (See Portuguese Colonies) .... Vol. 5A
Arequipa .... Vol. 5A
Argentina .... Vol. 1A
Argyrokastron .... Vol. 2B
Arica .... Vol. 5A
Armenia .... Vol. 1A, Vol. 6B
Armenian stamps ovptd. or surcharged .... Vol. 3A, Vol. 6B
Army of the North .... Vol. 5B
Army of the Northwest .... Vol. 5B
Aruba .... Vol. 1A
Arwad .... Vol. 5B
Ascension .... Vol. 1A
Assistencia Nacionalaos Tuberculosos .... Vol. 5B
Asturias Province .... Vol. 6A
Athens, Ga. .... Vol. 1A
Atlanta, Ga. .... Vol. 1A
Aunus, ovptd. on Finland .... Vol. 5B
Austin, Miss. .... Vol. 1A
Austin, Tex. .... Vol. 1A
Australia .... Vol. 1A
Australia, Occupation of Japan ... Vol. 1A
Australian Antarctic Territory .... Vol. 1A
Australian States .... Vol. 1A
Austria .... Vol. 1B
Austria, Allied Military Govt. ..... Vol. 1B
Austria, Adm. of Liechtenstein ... Vol. 4A
Austria, Lombardy-Venetia .... Vol. 1B
Austria-Hungary .... Vol. 1B
Austrian Occupation of Italy 692
Austrian Occupation of Montenegro .... Vol. 4B
Austrian Occupation of Romania ... Vol. 5B
Austrian Occupation of Serbia ... Vol. 6A
Austrian Offices Abroad .... Vol. 1B
Austrian stamps surcharged or overprinted .... 692, Vol. 1B, Vol. 5B, Vol. 6B
Autaugaville, Ala. .... Vol. 1A
Autopaketti, Autorahti .... Vol. 2B
Avisporto .... Vol. 5A
Ayacucho .... Vol. 5A
Aytonomoe .... Vol. 2B
Azerbaijan, Azerbaycan, Azerbaycan, Azerbaidjan .... 395, Vol. 1B, Vol. 6B
Azirbayedjan 395
Azores .... Vol. 1B, Vol. 5B

B .... **Vol. 1B, Vol. 5A, Vol. 6A**
B ovptd. on Straits Settlements ... Vol. 1B
Baden .... Vol. 3A
Baghdad .... Vol. 4B
Bahamas .... Vol. 1B
Bahawalpur .... Vol. 5A
Bahrain .... Vol. 1B, Vol. 5A
Baja Cal(ifornia) .... Vol. 4B
Bajar Porto 386
Baku .... Vol. 1A
Balcony Falls, Va. .... Vol. 1A
Baltimore, Md. .... Vol. 1A
Bamra 313
Banat, Bacska 186
Bangkok .... Vol. 1B
Bangladesh .... Vol. 1B
Bani ovptd. on Austria .... Vol. 5B
Bani ovptd. on Hungary 185
Baranya 185
Barbados .... Vol. 1B
Barbuda .... Vol. 1B
Barcelona .... Vol. 6A
Barnwell Court House, S.C. .... Vol. 1A
Barranquilla .... Vol. 2A
Barwani 313
Basel .... Vol. 6A

Bashahr 318
Basque Provinces .... Vol. 6A
Basutoland .... Vol. 1B
Batavia .... Vol. 5A
Baton Rouge, La. .... Vol. 1A
Batum, Batym (British Occupation) .... Vol. 1B
Bavaria .... Vol. 3A
Bayar Porto 386
Bayer., Bayern .... Vol. 3A
B.C.A. ovptd. on Rhodesia .... Vol. 1B
B.C.M. .... Vol. 4B
B.C.O.F. .... Vol. 1A
Beaufort, S.C. .... Vol. 1A
Beaumont, Tex. .... Vol. 1A
Bechuanaland .... Vol. 1B
Bechuanaland Protectorate .... Vol. 1B
Beckmann's City Post .... Vol. 1A
Behie .... Vol. 6B
Belarus .... Vol. 1B
Belgian (Belgisch) Congo .... Vol. 1B
Belgian East Africa .... Vol. 5B
Belgian Occ. of German East Africa .... Vol. 3A
Belgian Occupation of Germany ... Vol. 3A
Belgien .... Vol. 1B
Belgium, Belgique, Belgie .... Vol. 1B
Belgium (German Occupation) ... Vol. 1B
Belize .... Vol. 1B
Belize, Cayes of .... Vol. 1B
Benadir .... Vol. 6A
Bengasi 695
Beni .... Vol. 1B
Benin .... Vol. 1B
Benin, People's Republic of .... Vol. 1B
Bequia .... Vol. 5B
Bergedorf .... Vol. 3A
Berlin .... Vol. 3A
Berlin-Brandenburg .... Vol. 3A
Bermuda .... Vol. 1B
Besetztes Gebiet Nordfrankreich ... Vol. 2B
Besieged ovptd. on Cape of Good Hope .... Vol. 2A, Vol. 6B
Beyrouth, French Offices .... Vol. 2B
Beyrouth, Russian Offices .... Vol. 5B
B. Guiana .... Vol. 1B
B. Hneipoe .... Vol. 2B
Bhopal 313
Bhor 315
Bhutan .... Vol. 1B
Biafra .... Vol. 1B
Bijawar 316
B.I.O.T. ovptd. on Seychelles ..... Vol. 1B
Bishop's City Post .... Vol. 1A
Blagoveshchensk .... Vol. 2B
Bluefields .... Vol. 5A
Bluffton, S.C. .... Vol. 1A
B.M.A. Eritrea .... Vol. 3A
B.M.A. Malaya .... Vol. 6A
B.M.A. Somalia .... Vol. 6A
B.M.A. Tripolitania .... Vol. 3A
Bocas del Toro .... Vol. 5A
Boer Occupation .... Vol. 2A
Bogota .... Vol. 2A
Bohemia and Moravia .... Vol. 2B
Bohmen and Mahren .... Vol. 2B
Boletta, Bollettino ..... 692, 693, Vol. 6A
Bolivar .... Vol. 2A
Bolivia .... Vol. 2A
Bollo 692
Bollo Postale .... Vol. 6A
Bophuthatswana .... Vol. 2A
Borneo .... Vol. 5A
Boscawen, N.H. .... Vol. 1A
Bosna i Hercegovina ..... Vol. 1B, Vol. 6B
Bosnia and Herzegovina ... Vol. 1B, Vol. 6B
Bosnia, Muslim Gov. in Sarajevo ... Vol. 1B
Bosnia, Croat Administration, Mostar .... Vol. 1B
Bosnia, Serb Administration, Banja Luca .... Vol. 1B
Bosnia stamps overprinted or surcharged .... 692, Vol. 1B, Vol. 6B
Bosnien Herzegowina .... Vol. 1B
Boston, Mass. .... Vol. 1A
Botswana .... Vol. 1B
Boyaca .... Vol. 2A
Brattleboro, Vt. .... Vol. 1A
Braunschweig .... Vol. 3A
Brazil, Brasil .... Vol. 2A
Bremen .... Vol. 3A
Bridgeville, Ala. .... Vol. 1A
British Administration of Bahrain ... Vol. 1B
British Antarctic Territory .... Vol. 1B
British Bechuanaland .... Vol. 1B
British Central Africa .... Vol. 1B
British Colonies - Dies I & II ...... See table of contents

British Columbia & Vancouver Is. ... Vol. 2A
British Consular Mail .... Vol. 4B
British Dominion of Samoa .... Vol. 5B
British East Africa .... Vol. 1B
British Forces in Egypt .... Vol. 2B
British Guiana .... Vol. 1B
British Honduras .... Vol. 1B
British Indian Ocean Territory ..... Vol. 1B
British Mandate of Jordan .... Vol. 4A
British Levant .... Vol. 3A
British New Guinea .... Vol. 5A
British North Borneo .... Vol. 5A
British Occupation (of Batum) ... Vol. 1B
British Occupation of Bushire ..... Vol. 1B
British Occupation of Cameroun ... Vol. 2A
British Occupation of Crete .... Vol. 2A
British Occupation of Faroe Is. ... Vol. 2B
British Occ. of German East Africa .... Vol. 3A
British Occupation of Iraq ... 456, Vol. 4B
British Occupation of Mesopotamia .... Vol. 4B
British Occ. of Orange River Colony .... Vol. 5A
British Occupation overprint ...... Vol. 1B
British Occupation of Palestine ... Vol. 5A
British Occupation of Persia ...... Vol. 5A
British Occupation of Togo .... Vol. 6B
British Occ. of Transvaal .... Vol. 6B
British Offices in Africa .... Vol. 3A
British Offices in China .... Vol. 3A
British Offices in Morocco .... Vol. 3A
British Offices in Tangier .... Vol. 3A
British Off. in the Turkish Empire ... Vol. 3A
British Protectorate of Egypt ...... Vol. 2B
British Samoa .... Vol. 5B
British Solomon Islands .... Vol. 6A
British Somaliland (Somaliland Protectorate) .... Vol. 6A
British South Africa (Rhodesia) ... Vol. 5B
British stamps surcharged .... Vol. 5A
British Vice-Consulate .... Vol. 4B
British Virgin Islands .... Vol. 6B
British Zone (Germany) .... Vol. 3A
Brown & McGill's U.S.P.O. Despatch .... Vol. 1A
Brunei .... Vol. 1B
Brunei (Japanese Occupation) ... Vol. 1B
Brunswick .... Vol. 3A
Buchanan .... Vol. 1A, Vol. 4A
Buenos Aires .... Vol. 1A
Bulgaria, Bulgarie .... Vol. 1B
Bulgarian Occupation of Romania .... Vol. 5B
Bulgarian stamps overprinted or surcharged ..... Vol. 3A, Vol. 5B, Vol. 6B
Bundi 316
Bundi stamps overprinted 329
Bureau International .... Vol. 6A
Burgenland .... Vol. 1B
Burgos .... Vol. 6A
Burkina Faso .... Vol. 1B
Burma .... Vol. 1B
Burma (Japanese Occupation) ... Vol. 1B
Burundi .... Vol. 1B
Bushire .... Vol. 1B
Bussahir 318
Buu-Chinh .... Vol. 6B
Buu-Bien .... Vol. 6B
Byelorussia .... Vol. 1B

Cabo, Cabo Gracias a Dios ...... **Vol. 5A**
Cabo Juby, Jubi .... Vol. 2A
Cabo Verde .... Vol. 2A
Cadiz .... Vol. 6A
Caicos .... Vol. 6B
Calchi 699
Cali .... Vol. 2A
Calino, Calimno 699
Callao .... Vol. 5A
Camb. Aust. Sigillum Nov. .... Vol. 1A
Cambodia, (Int. Com., India) 303
Cambodia, Cambodge ... 303, 335, Vol. 2A
Camden, S.C. .... Vol. 1A
Cameroons (U.K.T.T.) .... Vol. 2A
Cameroun (Republique Federale) ... Vol. 2A
Campeche .... Vol. 4B
Canada .... Vol. 2A
Canadian Provinces .... Vol. 2A
Canal Zone .... Vol. 1A
Canary Islands, Canarias .... Vol. 6A
Candia .... Vol. 1B
Canouan .... Vol. 5B
Canton, French Offices .... Vol. 2B
Canton, Miss. .... Vol. 1A

INDEX AND IDENTIFIER

Cape Juby .... Vol. 2A
Cape of Good Hope .... Vol. 2A
Cape of Good Hope stamps
  surchd. (see Griqualand West) ... Vol. 3A
Cape Verde .... Vol. 2A
Carchi 699
Caribbean Netherlands .... Vol. 2A
Caribisch Nederland .... Vol. 2A
Carinthia .... Vol. 1B, Vol. 6B
Carlist .... Vol. 6A
Carolina City, N.C. .... Vol. 1A
Caroline Islands .... Vol. 1A
Carpatho-Ukraine .... Vol. 2B
Carriacou & Petite Martinique ... Vol. 3A
Carriers Stamps .... Vol. 1A
Cartagena .... Vol. 2A
Cartersville, Ga. .... Vol. 1A
Carupano .... Vol. 6B
Caso 699
Castellorizo, Castelrosso .... Vol. 2A
Catalonia .... Vol. 6A
Cauca .... Vol. 2A
Cavalla (Greek) .... Vol. 3A
Cavalle, Cavalla (French) .... Vol. 2B
Cayes of Belize .... Vol. 1B
Cayman Islands .... Vol. 2A
CCCP .... Vol. 5B
C.CH. on French Colonies ..... Vol. 2A
C.E.F. ovptd. on Cameroun ... Vol. 2A
C.E.F. ovptd. on India 302
Cefalonia ovptd. on Greece 389
Celebes .... Vol. 5A
Cent, cents ..... Vol. 1A, Vol. 2B, Vol. 4B, Vol. 5A
Centenaire Algerie RF
  (France No. 255) .... Vol. 2B
Centenary-1st Postage Stamp
  (Pakistan #63-64) .... Vol. 5A
Centesimi overprinted on Austria
  or Bosnia 692
Centesimi di corona ..... Vol. 1B, Vol. 2B
Centimes .... Vol. 2B
Centimes ovptd. on Austria .... Vol. 1B
Centimes ovptd. on Germany ... Vol. 3A
Centimos (no country name) ... Vol. 6A
Centimos ovptd. on France ... Vol. 2B
Central Africa (Centrafricaine) ... Vol. 2A
Central African Republic .... Vol. 2A
Central China .... Vol. 2A
Central Lithuania .... Vol. 2A
Cephalonia 389
Cerigo .... 389, Vol. 3A
Cervantes .... Vol. 6A
Ceska Republica .... Vol. 2B
Ceskoslovenska,
  Ceskoslovensko .... Vol. 2B
Ceylon .... Vol. 2B
CF .... Vol. 2B
CFA .... Vol. 2B
C.G.H.S. .... Vol. 6B
Ch .... 455, Vol. 4A
Chachapoyas .... Vol. 5A
Chad .... Vol. 2A
Chahar .... Vol. 2A
Chala .... Vol. 5A
Chamba 305
Channel Islands .... Vol. 3A
Chapel Hill, N.C. .... Vol. 1A
Charkhari 318
Charleston, S.C. .... Vol. 1A
Charlotte, N.C. .... Vol. 1A
Charlottesville, Va. .... Vol. 1A
Chateau de Beggen
  (Luxembourg #1466) .... Vol. 4A
Chateau de Dommeldange
  (Luxembourg #1467) .... Vol. 4A
Chattanooga, Tenn. .... Vol. 1A
Chekiang .... Vol. 2A
Chemins des Fer .... Vol. 2B
Cherifien Posts .... Vol. 2B
Chiapas .... Vol. 4B
Chiclayo .... Vol. 5A
Chiffre .... See France and French
  colonies, postage due
Chihuahua .... Vol. 4B
Chile .... Vol. 2A
Chilean Occupation of Peru ... Vol. 5A
Chimarra .... Vol. 2B
China, Chinese .... Vol. 2A
China (Japanese Occupation) ... Vol. 2A
China Expeditionary Force (India) ... 302
China, British Offices .... Vol. 3A
China, Formosa .... Vol. 2A, Vol. 4A
China, French Offices .... Vol. 2B
China, German Offices .... Vol. 3A
China, Italian Offices 694
China, Japanese Offices .... Vol. 4A
China, Northeastern Provinces ... Vol. 2A

China, Offices in Manchuria ... Vol. 2A
China, Offices in Tibet .... Vol. 2A
China, People's Republic ...... Vol. 2A
China, People's Republic Regional
  Issues .... Vol. 2A
China, People's Republic
  Hong Kong .... Vol. 2A
China, People's Republic Macao ... Vol. 4B
China, Republic of .... Vol. 2A
China, Russian Offices .... Vol. 5B
China, United States Offices ... Vol. 2A
Chine .... Vol. 2B
Chios .... Vol. 3A
Chita .... Vol. 2B
Chosen .... Vol. 4A
Christiansburg, Va. .... Vol. 1A
Christmas Island .... Vol. 2A
Chungking .... Vol. 2B
C.I.H.S. .... Vol. 6B
Cilicia, Cilicie ... Vol. 2A, Vol. 5A, Vol. 6A
Cincinnati, O. .... Vol. 1A
Cinquan Tenaire .... Vol. 5A
Cirenaica .... Vol. 2B
Ciskei .... Vol. 6A
City Despatch Post .... Vol. 1A
City Post .... Vol. 1A
Cleveland, O. .... Vol. 1A
Cluj 185
c/m .... Vol. 2B
C.M.T. .... Vol. 6B
Coamo .... Vol. 1A, Vol. 5B
Cochin 319
Cochin China .... Vol. 2A
Cochin, Travancore 333
Co. Ci. ovptd. on Yugoslavia ... Vol. 6B
Cocos Islands .... Vol. 2A
Colaparchee, Ga. .... Vol. 1A
Colis Postaux .... 839, Vol. 1B, Vol. 2B
Colombia .... Vol. 2A, Vol. 5A
Colombian Dominion of Panama ... Vol. 5A
Colombian States .... Vol. 5A
Colon .... Vol. 5A
Colonie (Coloniali) Italiane 585
Colonies de l'Empire Francaise ... Vol. 2B
Columbia, S.C. .... Vol. 1A
Columbia, Tenn. .... Vol. 1A
Columbus Archipelago .... Vol. 2B
Columbus, Ga. .... Vol. 1A
Comayagua 21
Commando Brief .... Vol. 5A
Common Designs .... See table of contents
Commissioning of Maryan
  Babangida (Nigeria #607) ... Vol. 5A
Communicaciones .... Vol. 6A
Communist China .... Vol. 2A
Comores, Archipel des .... Vol. 2A
Comoro Islands (Comores,
  Comorien) .... Vol. 2A, Vol. 4B
Compania Colombiana .... Vol. 2A
Confederate States .... Vol. 1A
Congo .... Vol. 1B, Vol. 2A
Congo Democratic Republic ... Vol. 2A, Vol. 6B
Congo People's Republic
  (ex-French) .... Vol. 2A
Congo, Belgian (Belge) .... Vol. 1B
Congo Francais .... Vol. 2B
Congo, Indian U.N. Force 303
Congo, Portuguese .... Vol. 5B
Congreso .... Vol. 6A
Conseil de l'Europe .... Vol. 2B
Constantinople, Georgian Offices ... Vol. 3A
Constantinople, Polish Offices ... Vol. 5B
Constantinople, Italian Offices ... 696
Constantinople, Romanian
  Offices .... Vol. 5B
Constantinople, Russian Offices ... Vol. 5B
Constantinople, Turkey .... Vol. 6B
Contribucao Industrial (Macao A14,
  P. Guinea WT1) .... Vol. 4B, Vol. 5B
Convention States (India) 305
Coo 699
Cook Islands .... Vol. 2A
Cook Islands, Niue .... Vol. 5A
Cordoba .... Vol. 1A
Corea, Coree .... Vol. 4A
Corfu .... 389, Vol. 2A
Corona .... Vol. 1B, Vol. 2B
Correio, Correios e Telegraphos ... Vol. 5B
Correo Submarino .... Vol. 6A
Correo, Correos (no name) ... Vol. 1A, Vol. 2A, Vol. 5A, Vol. 6A
Corrientes .... Vol. 1A
Cos 699
Costa Atlantica .... Vol. 5B
Costa Rica .... Vol. 2A
Costantinopoli 696
Cote d'Ivoire 705
Cote des Somalis .... Vol. 6A

Council of Europe .... Vol. 2B
Cour Permanente de Justice
  Internationale .... Vol. 5A
Courtland, Ala. .... Vol. 1A
Cpbnja .... Vol. 6A
Cracow .... Vol. 5B
Crete .... 695, Vol. 2A
Crete, Austrian Offices .... Vol. 1B
Crete, French Offices .... Vol. 2B
Crete, Italian Offices 695
Crimea .... Vol. 5B, Vol. 6A
Croat Administration of Bosnia,
  Mostar .... Vol. 1B
Croatia .... Vol. 2A
Croatia-Slavonia .... Vol. 6B
Croissant Rouge Turc. .... Vol. 6B
C.S.A. Postage .... Vol. 1A
CTOT .... Vol. 1B
Cuautla .... Vol. 4B
Cuthbert, GA .... Vol. 1A
Cuba .... Vol. 1A, Vol. 2A
Cuba stamps overprinted ...... Vol. 5B
Cuba, U.S. Administration ... Vol. 1A, Vol. 2A
Cucuta .... Vol. 2A
Cuernavaca .... Vol. 4B
Cundinamarca .... Vol. 2A
Curacao .... Vol. 2A, Vol. 5A
Cuzco .... Vol. 5A
C.X.C. on Bosnia and
  Herzegovina .... Vol. 6B
Cyprus .... Vol. 2B
Cyprus, Turkish Republic of
  Northern .... Vol. 2B
Cyrenaica ..... Vol. 2B, Vol. 3A, Vol. 4A
Czechoslovakia .... Vol. 2B
Czechoslovak Legion Post .... Vol. 2B
Czech Rep. .... Vol. 2B

D 398
Dahomey .... Vol. 1B, Vol. 2B
Dakar-Abidjan .... Vol. 2B
Dalmatia .... Vol. 2B
Dalton, Ga. .... Vol. 1A
Danish West Indies ..... Vol. 1A, Vol. 2B
Danmark .... Vol. 2B
Dansk-Vestindien .... Vol. 1A, Vol. 2B
Dansk-Vestindiske ..... Vol. 1A, Vol. 2B
Danville, Va. .... Vol. 1A
Danzig .... Vol. 2B
Danzig, Polish Offices .... Vol. 5B
Dardanelles .... Vol. 5B
Darlington C.H., S.C. .... Vol. 1A
Datia (Duttia) 322
D.B.L. ovptd. on Siberia
  and Russia .... Vol. 2B
D.B.P. (Dalni Vostochini
  Respoublika) .... Vol. 2B
D. de A. .... Vol. 2A
DDR .... Vol. 3A
Debrecen 184
Deccan (Hyderabad) 322
Dedeagatch (Greek) .... Vol. 3A
Dedeagh, Dedeagatch (French) ... Vol. 2B
Deficit .... Vol. 2B
Demopolis, Ala. .... Vol. 1A
Denikin .... Vol. 6A
Denmark .... Vol. 2B
Denmark stamps surcharged ... Vol. 2B
Denver Issue, Mexico .... Vol. 4B
Den Waisen ovptd. on Italy ... Vol. 6B
Despatch (US 1LB, 5LB) ...... Vol. 1A
Deutsch-Neu-Guinea .... Vol. 3A
Deutsch-Ostafrika .... Vol. 3A
Deutsch-Sudwest Afrika .... Vol. 3A
Deutsche Bundespost .... Vol. 3A
Deutsche Demokratische
  Republik .... Vol. 3A
Deutsche Nationalversammlung ... Vol. 3A
Deutsche Post .... Vol. 3A
Deutsche Post Berlin .... Vol. 3A
Deutsche(s) Reich .... Vol. 3A
Deutsche Reich, Nr.21, Nr.16 ... Vol. 3A
Deutschland .... Vol. 3A
Deutschosterreich .... Vol. 1B
Dhar 321
Diego-Suarez .... Vol. 2B
Diego-Suarez stamps surcharged ... Vol. 4B
Dienftmarke (Dienstmarke) ... Vol. 3A
Dies I & II, British Colonies ..... See table
  of contents
Diligencia .... Vol. 6B
Dinar .... Vol. 6B
Dire-Dawa .... Vol. 2B
Dispatch (US 1LB) .... Vol. 1A
Distrito ovptd. on Arequipa ... Vol. 5A
DJ ovptd. on Obock .... Vol. 6A
Djibouti (Somali Coast) ..... Vol. 2B, Vol. 6A
Dobruja District .... Vol. 5B

Dodecanese Islands .... 697, Vol. 3A
Dollar, ovptd. on Russia .... Vol. 5B
Dominica .... Vol. 2B
Dominican Republic, Dominicana ... Vol. 2B
Don Government .... Vol. 6A
Dorpat .... Vol. 6A
Drzava SHS .... Vol. 6B
Dubai .... Vol. 2B, Vol. 5A, Vol. 6B
Duck Stamps (Hunting Permit) ... Vol. 1A
Duitsch Oost Afrika overprinted
  on Congo .... Vol. 3A
Duke de la Torre Regency ..... Vol. 6A
Dulce et Decorum est Pro Patria
  Mori (Nepal O1) .... Vol. 5A
Dungarpur 321
Durazzo 696
Dutch Guiana (Surinam) .... Vol. 6A
Dutch Indies .... Vol. 2B
Dutch New Guinea .... Vol. 5A
Duttia 321

EA .... Vol. 1A
E.A.F. overprinted on stamps
  of Great Britain .... Vol. 3A
East Africa (British) .... Vol. 1B
East Africa (German) .... Vol. 3A
East Africa (Italian) 586
East Africa and Uganda
  Protectorates .... Vol. 2B, Vol. 4A
East Africa Forces .... Vol. 3A
East China .... Vol. 2A
Eastern Rumelia .... Vol. 2B
Eastern Rumelia stamps
  overprinted .... Vol. 6B
Eastern Silesia .... Vol. 2B
Eastern Szechwan .... Vol. 2A
Eastern Thrace .... Vol. 6B
East India 221
East Saxony .... Vol. 3A
East Timor .... Vol. 1A, Vol. 6B
Eatonton, Ga. .... Vol. 1A
Ecuador .... Vol. 2B
E.E.F. .... Vol. 5A
Eesti .... Vol. 2B
Egeo 698
Egiziane (Egypt types A9-A10) ... Vol. 2B
Egypt, Egypte, Egyptiennes ... Vol. 2B, Vol. 5A
Egypt, French Offices .... Vol. 2B
Eire, Eireann (Ireland) 491
Ekaterinodar .... Vol. 6A
Elobey, Annobon and Corisco ... Vol. 3A
El Salvador .... Vol. 5B
Elsas, Elfas .... Vol. 2B
Elua Keneta .... Vol. 1A
Emory, Va. .... Vol. 1A
Empire, Franc, Francais .... Vol. 2B
En .... Vol. 4A
England .... Vol. 3A
Epirus .... Vol. 2B
Equateur (Ecuador #19-21) ... Vol. 2B
Equatorial Guinea .... Vol. 2B
Eritrea .... Vol. 2B
Eritrea (British Military
  Administration) .... Vol. 3A
Escuelas .... Vol. 6B
Espana, Espanola .... Vol. 6A
Estado da India .... Vol. 5B
Est Africain Allemand overprinted
  on Congo .... Vol. 3A
Estensi 587
Estero 694
Estland .... Vol. 2B, Vol. 5B
Estonia .... Vol. 2B, Vol. 5B
Etablissments Francais
  dans l'Inde .... Vol. 2B
Ethiopia, Etiopia, Ethiopie,
  Ethiopiennes .... Vol. 2B, Vol. 3A
Eupen .... Vol. 3A
Europe .... Vol. 3A
Express Letter .... Vol. 2A

15 August 1947 (Pakistan #23) .... Vol. 5A
500 anos, viaje del descubrimiento
  de istmo (Panama #897) .... Vol. 5A
F .... Vol. 2B
F. A. F. L. .... Vol. 6A
Falkland Dependencies .... Vol. 2B
Falkland Islands .... Vol. 2B
Far Eastern Republic .... Vol. 2B
Far Eastern Republic surcharged
  or ovptd. .... Vol. 6A
Faridkot 306, 322
Faroe Islands .... Vol. 2B
FCFA ovptd. on France .... Vol. 6B
Federacion .... Vol. 6B
Federal Republic (Germany) ... Vol. 3A
Federated Malay States .... Vol. 4B
Fen, Fn. (Manchukuo) .... Vol. 4B

INDEX AND IDENTIFIER

Fernando Po, Fdo. Poo .... Vol. 2B
Feudatory States 313
Fezzan, Fezzan-Ghadames ..... Vol. 4A
Fiera Campionaria Tripoli .... Vol. 4A
Fiji .... Vol. 2B
Fiji overprinted or surcharged ..... Vol. 5A
Filipinas, Filipas. .... Vol. 5A
Fincastle, Va. .... Vol. 1A
Finland .... Vol. 2B
Finnish Occupation of Karelia ..... Vol. 4A
Finnish Occupation of Russia ... Vol. 4A, Vol. 5B
Fiume .... Vol. 2B
Fiume-Kupa Zone (Fiumano Kupa) .... Vol. 6B
Five Cents (Confed. #53X) .... Vol. 1A
Florida .... Vol. 6B
F. M. .... Vol. 2B
Foochow, Chinese .... Vol. 2A
Foochow, German .... Vol. 3A
Formosa .... Vol. 2A, Vol. 4A
Foroyar .... Vol. 2B
Forsyth, Ga. .... Vol. 1A
Fort Valley, Ga. .... Vol. 1A
Franc .... Vol. 2B
Franc ovptd. on Austria .... Vol. 1B
Franca ovptd. on stamps of Peru ... Vol. 5A
Francais, Francaise ...... See France and French colonies
France .... Vol. 2B
France (German occupation) ..... Vol. 2B
France D'Outre Mer .... Vol. 2B
Franco Bollo 587, 588, 691
Franco Marke .... Vol. 3A
Franco Scrisorei .... Vol. 5B
Franklin, N.C. .... Vol. 1A
Franqueo .... Vol. 5A
Franquicia .... Vol. 6A
Fraziersville, S.C. .... Vol. 1A
Fredericksburg, Va. .... Vol. 1A
Free .... Vol. 1A
Frei Durch Ablosung .... Vol. 3A
Freimarke (No Country Name) ..... Vol. 3A
French Administration of Andorra ..... Vol. 1A
French Administration of Saar ..... Vol. 5B
French Colonies .... Vol. 2B
French Colonies surcharged or overprinted ..... 335, Vol. 1A, Vol. 2B, Vol. 3A, Vol. 4B, Vol. 5A, Vol. 6A
French Commemoratives Index ..... Vol. 2B
French Congo .... Vol. 2B
French Equatorial Africa .... Vol. 2A, Vol. 2B, Vol. 4B, Vol. 6B
French Guiana .... Vol. 2B
French Guinea .... Vol. 2B
French India .... Vol. 2B
French Levant .... Vol. 2B, Vol. 6A
French Mandate of Alaouites ..... Vol. 1A
French Mandate of Lebanon ..... Vol. 4A
French Morocco .... Vol. 2B
French Occupation of Cameroun ..... Vol. 2A
French Occupation of Castellorizo ..... Vol. 2A
French Occupation of Crete ..... Vol. 2A
French Occupation of Germany ..... Vol. 3A
French Occupation of Hungary 183
French Occupation of Libya ..... Vol. 4A
French Occupation of Syria ..... Vol. 6A
French Occupation of Togo ..... Vol. 6B
French Oceania .... Vol. 2B
French Offices Abroad .... Vol. 2B
French Offices in China .... Vol. 2B
French Offices in Crete .... Vol. 2B
French Offices in Egypt .... Vol. 2B
French Offices in Madagascar ..... Vol. 4B
French Offices in Morocco .... Vol. 2B
French Offices in Tangier .... Vol. 2B
French Offices in Turkish Empire ..... Vol. 6A
French Offices in Turkish Empire surcharged .... Vol. 6A
French Offices in Zanzibar .... Vol. 2B
French Polynesia .... Vol. 2B
French Saar .... Vol. 5B
French Southern and Antarctic Territories .... Vol. 2B
French stamps inscribed CFA ..... Vol. 2B
French stamps surcharged ...... Vol. 2B, Vol. 4B, Vol. 6A
French Sudan .... Vol. 2B
French West Africa .... Vol. 2B
French Zone (Germany) .... Vol. 3A
Frimarke, Frmrk (No Country Name) .... Vol. 2B, Vol. 5A, Vol. 6A
Fujeira .... Vol. 2B, Vol. 6B
Fukien .... Vol. 2A
Funafuti .... Vol. 6B
Funchal .... Vol. 2B

G or GW overprinted on Cape of Good Hope .... Vol. 3A
GAB on French Colonies .... Vol. 3A
Gabon, Gabonaise .... Vol. 3A
Gainesville, Ala. .... Vol. 1A
Galapagos Islands .... Vol. 2B
Galveston, Tex. .... Vol. 1A
Gambia .... Vol. 3A
Gaston, N.C. .... Vol. 1A
Gaza 303
G & (et) D overprinted on French Colonies .... Vol. 3A
G.E.A. ovptd. .... Vol. 3A, Vol. 6A
General Gouvernement (Poland) ..... Vol. 5B
Geneva, Geneve .... Vol. 6A
Georgetown, S.C. .... Vol. 1A
Georgia .... Vol. 3A, Vol. 6B
Georgia, Offices in Turkey .... Vol. 3A
Georgienne, Republique .... Vol. 3A
German Administration of Albania .... Vol. 1A
German Administration of Danzig .... Vol. 2B
German Administration of Saar ..... Vol. 5B
German Democratic Republic ..... Vol. 3A
German Dominion of Cameroun ..... Vol. 2A
German Dominion of Caroline Islands .... Vol. 2A
German Dominion of Mariana Is. ..... Vol. 4B
German Dominion of Marshall Is. ..... Vol. 4B
German Dominion of Samoa ..... Vol. 5B
German Dominion of Togo .... Vol. 6B
German East Africa .... Vol. 3A
German East Africa (Belgian occ.) .... Vol. 3A
German East Africa (British occ.) ..... Vol. 3A
German New Guinea .... Vol. 3A
German New Guinea (New Britain) .... Vol. 5A
German Occupation of Belgium ..... Vol. 1B
German Occupation of Estonia ..... Vol. 2B
German Occupation of France ..... Vol. 2B
German Occupation of Guernsey ..... Vol. 3A
German Occupation of Ionian Is. 389
German Occupation of Jersey ..... Vol. 3A
German Occupation of Latvia ..... Vol. 4A
German Occupation of Lithuania ..... Vol. 5B
German Occupation of Ljubljana ..... Vol. 6B
German Occupation of Luxembourg .... Vol. 4A
German Occupation of Macedonia .... Vol. 4B
German Occupation of Montenegro .... Vol. 4B
German Occupation of Poland ..... Vol. 5B
German Occupation of Romania ..... Vol. 5B
German Occupation of Russia ..... Vol. 5B
German Occupation of Serbia ..... Vol. 6A
German Occupation of Ukraine ..... Vol. 5B
German Occupation of Yugoslavia .... Vol. 6B
German Occupation of Zante 389
German Offices in China .... Vol. 3A
German Offices in China surcharged .... Vol. 4A
German Offices in Morocco ...... Vol. 3A
German Offices in Turkish Empire .... Vol. 3A
German Protectorate of Bohemia and Moravia .... Vol. 2B
German South-West Africa .... Vol. 3A
German stamps surchd. or ovptd. .... Vol. 3A, Vol. 5B, Vol. 6A
German States .... Vol. 3A
Germany .... Vol. 3A
Germany (Allied Military Govt.) ..... Vol. 3A
Gerusalemme 697
Ghadames .... Vol. 4A
Ghana .... Vol. 3A
Gibraltar .... Vol. 3A
Gilbert and Ellice Islands .... Vol. 3A
Gilbert Islands .... Vol. 3A
Giumulzina District .... Vol. 6B
Gniezno .... Vol. 5B
Gold Coast .... Vol. 3A
Golfo del Guinea .... Vol. 6A
Goliad, Tex. .... Vol. 1A
Gonzales, Tex. .... Vol. 1A
Gorny Slask .... Vol. 6B
Government (U.S. 1LB) .... Vol. 1A
Governo Militare Alleato 692
G.P.E. ovptd. on French Colonies ..... Vol. 3A
Graham Land .... Vol. 2B
Granada .... Vol. 3A
Granadine Confederation, Granadina .... Vol. 2A
Grand Comoro, Grande Comore ..... Vol. 3A
Grand Liban, Gd Liban .... Vol. 4A

Great Britain (see also British) .... Vol. 3A
Great Britain, Gaelic ovpt. 491
Great Britain, Offices in Africa ..... Vol. 3A
Great Britain, Offices in China ..... Vol. 3A
Great Britain, Offices in Morocco ..... Vol. 3A
Great Britain, Offices in Turkish Empire .... Vol. 3A
Greater Rajasthan Union 329
Greece .... Vol. 3A
Greek Occupation of Albania, North Epirus, Dodecanese Islands ..... Vol. 3A
Greek Occupation of Epirus ..... Vol. 2B, Vol. 3A
Greek Occ. of the Aegean Islands ..... Vol. 3A
Greek Occupation of Thrace ..... Vol. 6B
Greek Occupation of Turkey ..... Vol. 3A, Vol. 6B
Greek stamps overprinted .... Vol. 2B, Vol. 6B
Greenland .... Vol. 3A
Greensboro, Ala. .... Vol. 1A
Greensboro, N.C. .... Vol. 1A
Greenville .... Vol. 4A
Greenville, Ala. .... Vol. 1A
Greenville, Tenn. .... Vol. 1A
Greenville Court House, S.C. ..... Vol. 1A
Greenwood Depot, Va. .... Vol. 1A
Grenada .... Vol. 3A
Grenadines of Grenada .... Vol. 3A
Grenadines of St. Vincent .... Vol. 5B
Grenville .... Vol. 4A
G.R.I. overprinted on German New Guinea .... Vol. 5A
G.R.I. overprinted on German Samoa .... Vol. 5B
G.R.I. overprinted on Marshall Is. ..... Vol. 5A
Griffin, Ga. .... Vol. 1A
Griqualand West .... Vol. 3A
Grodno District .... Vol. 4A
Gronland .... Vol. 3A
Grossdeutsches Reich (Germany #529) .... Vol. 3A
Groszy .... Vol. 5B
Grove Hill, Ala. .... Vol. 1A
Gruzija (Georgia) .... Vol. 3A
Guadalajara .... Vol. 4B
Guadeloupe .... Vol. 3A
Guam .... Vol. 1A
Guanacaste .... Vol. 2A
Guatemala .... Vol. 3A
Guayana .... Vol. 6B
Guernsey .... Vol. 3A
Guernsey, German Occupation ..... Vol. 3A
Guiana, British .... Vol. 1B
Guiana, Dutch .... Vol. 6A
Guiana, French .... Vol. 2B
Guine .... Vol. 3A, Vol. 5B
Guinea .... Vol. 3A, Vol. 6A
Guinea Ecuatorial .... Vol. 2B
Guinea, French .... Vol. 2B
Guinea, Portuguese .... Vol. 5B
Guinea, Spanish .... Vol. 6A
Guinea-Bissau, Guine-Bissau ..... Vol. 3A
Guinee .... Vol. 2B, Vol. 3A
Guipuzcoa Province .... Vol. 6A
Gultig 9, Armee .... Vol. 5B
Guyana .... Vol. 3A
Guyane, Guy. Franc. .... Vol. 2B
G.W. ovptd. on Cape of Good Hope .... Vol. 3A
Gwalior 307

Habilitado-1/2 (Tlacotalpan #1) ... Vol. 4B
Habilitado on Stamps of Cuba ... Vol. 1A, Vol. 2A, Vol. 5A
Habilitado on Telegrafos or revenues .... Vol. 5A, Vol. 6A
Hadhramaut .... Vol. 1A
Hainan Island .... Vol. 2A
Haiti 1
Hall, A. D. (Confed. #27XU1) ..... Vol. 1A
Hallettsville, Tex. .... Vol. 1A
Hamburg .... Vol. 3A
Hamburgh, S.C. .... Vol. 1A
Hamilton, Bermuda .... Vol. 1B
Hanover, Hannover .... Vol. 3A
Harar .... Vol. 2B
Harper .... Vol. 4A
Harrisburgh, Tex. .... Vol. 1A
Hatay 20
Hatirasi (Turkey Design PT44) ..... Vol. 6B
Hatohobei (Palau #686) .... Vol. 5A
Haute Silesie .... Vol. 6B
Haute Volta .... Vol. 1B
Haut Senegal-Niger .... Vol. 6B
Hawaii, Hawaiian .... Vol. 3A
H B A ovptd. on Russia .... Vol. 6A
Hebrew inscriptions 534

H.E.H. The Nizam's (Hyderabad) 322
Heilungkiang .... Vol. 2A
Hejaz .... Vol. 6A
Hejaz-Nejd .... Vol. 6A
Hejaz overprinted .... Vol. 4A, Vol. 6A
Helena, Tex. .... Vol. 1A
Heligoland, Helgoland 21
Hellas .... Vol. 3A
Helsinki (Helsingfors) .... Vol. 2B
Helvetia, Helvetica (Switzerland) ... Vol. 6A
Heraklion .... Vol. 2A
Herceg Bosna .... Vol. 1B
Herzegovina .... Vol. 1B
Herzogth .... Vol. 3A
H.H. Nawabshah Jahanbegam 313
H.I. Postage .... Vol. 1A
Hillsboro, N.C. .... Vol. 1A
Hoi Hao, French Offices .... Vol. 2B
Holkar (Indore) 323
Holland (Netherlands) .... Vol. 5A
Hollandale, Tex. .... Vol. 1A
Holstein .... Vol. 3A
Honan .... Vol. 2A
Honda .... Vol. 2A
Honduras 21
Honduras, British .... Vol. 1B
Hong Kong .... 47, Vol. 3A
Hong Kong (Japanese Occupation) 78
Hong Kong Special Admin. Region 56
Hong Kong ovptd. China .... Vol. 3A
Honour's (Hondur's) City .... Vol. 1A
Hopeh .... Vol. 2A
Hopei .... Vol. 2A
Horta 78
Houston, Tex. .... Vol. 1A
Hrvatska .... Vol. 1B, Vol. 2A, Vol. 6B
Hrzgl. .... Vol. 3A
Huacho .... Vol. 5A
Hunan .... Vol. 2A
Hungary .... 79, Vol. 1B
Hungary (French Occupation) 183
Hungary (Romanian Occupation) 184
Hungary (Serbian Occupation) 185
Huntsville, Tex. .... Vol. 1A
Hupeh .... Vol. 2A
Hyderabad (Deccan) 322

I.B. (West Irian) 389
Icaria .... Vol. 3A
ICC ovptd. on India 303
Iceland 187
Idar 323
I.E.F. ovptd. on India 303
I.E.F. 'D' ovptd. on Turkey ...... Vol. 4B
Ierusalem .... Vol. 5B
Ifni 218
Ile Rouad .... Vol. 5B
Imperio Colonial Portugues ..... Vol. 5B
Imposto de Selo .... Vol. 5B
Impuesto (Impto) de Guerra ..... Vol. 6A
Inde. Fcaise .... Vol. 2B
Independence, Tex. .... Vol. 1A
Index of U.S. Issues .... Vol. 1A
India .... 221, Vol. 5B
India, China Expeditionary Force 302
India, Convention States 305
India, Feudatory States 313
India, French .... Vol. 2B
India, Portuguese .... Vol. 5B
India stamps overprinted .... 305, Vol. 4A, Vol. 5A
India, surcharge and crown ..... Vol. 6A
Indian Custodial Unit, Korea 303
Indian Expeditionary Force 303
Indian U.N. Force, Congo 303
Indian U.N. Force, Gaza 303
Indian Postal Administration of Bahrain .... Vol. 1B
Indo-China, Indo-chine 335
Indo-China stamps surcharged ..... Vol. 6B
Indo-China, Int. Commission 303
Indonesia .... 338, Vol. 5A
Indore 323
Industrielle Kriegswirschaft 389
Inhambane 389
Inini 388
Inland (Liberia #21) .... Vol. 4A
Inner Mongolia (Meng Chiang) ..... Vol. 2A
Insufficiently prepaid .... Vol. 6B
Instrucao .... Vol. 6B
Instruccion .... Vol. 6B
International Bureau of Education .... Vol. 6A
International Commission in Indo-China 303
International Court of Justice ..... Vol. 5A
International Labor Bureau ..... Vol. 6A

INDEX AND IDENTIFIER

International Olympic Committee ... Vol. 6A
International Refugee
  Organization .... Vol. 6A
International Telecommunication
  Union .... Vol. 6A
Ionian Islands, IONIKON KPATOE ... 389
I.O.V.R. .... Vol. 5B
Iran, Iraniennes 390
Iran (Bushire) .... Vol. 1B
Iran, Turkish Occupation 395
Iran with Rs. 10 denomination
  (Pakistan #1101) .... Vol. 5A
Iraq 456
Iraq (British Occupation) .... 456, Vol. 4B
Ireland 491
Ireland, Northern .... Vol. 3A
Irian Barat 389
Isabella, Ga. .... Vol. 1A
Island 187
Isle of Man .... Vol. 3A
Isole Italiane dell'Egeo 698
Isole Jonie 389
Israel 534
Istria .... Vol. 6B
Itaca ovptd. on Greece 389
Ita-Karjala .... Vol. 4A
Italia, Italiano, Italiane 590
Italian Colonies 585
Italian Dominion of Albania .... Vol. 1A
Italian Dominion of Castellorizo ... Vol. 2A
Italian East Africa 586
Italian Jubaland .... Vol. 5A
Italian Occ. of Aegean Islands 697
Italian Occupation of Austria ...... Vol. 1B
Italian Occupation of Corfu .... Vol. 2A
Italian Occupation of Crete .... Vol. 2A
Italian Occupation of Dalmatia ..... Vol. 2A
Italian Occupation of Ethiopia ..... Vol. 2B
Italian Occupation of
  Fiume-Kupa .... Vol. 6B
Italian Occupation of Ionian Islands ... 389
Italian Occupation of Ljubljana .... Vol. 6B
Italian Occupation of Montenegro ... Vol. 4B
Italian Occupation of Yugoslavia ... Vol. 6B
Italian Offices Abroad 694
Italian Offices in Africa 695
Italian Offices in Albania 697
Italian Offices in China 694
Italian Offices in Constantinople ... 696
Italian Offices in Crete 695
Italian Offices in the Turkish Empire ... 695
Italian Social Republic 693
Italian Somaliland .... Vol. 6A
Italian Somaliland (E.A.F.) .... Vol. 3A
Italian stamps surcharged 694,
  Vol. 1B, Vol. 2B
Italian States 587
Italy (Allied Military Govt.) 692
Italy (Austrian Occupation) 692
Italy 590
Ithaca 389
Iuka, Miss. .... Vol. 1A
Ivory Coast 705

J. ovptd. on stamps of Peru .... Vol. 5A
Jackson, Miss. .... Vol. 1A
Jacksonville, Ala. .... Vol. 1A
Jacksonville, Fla. .... Vol. 1A
Jaffa .... Vol. 5B
Jaipur 324
Jamaica .... Vol. 4A
Jamhuri .... Vol. 6B
Jammu 325
Jammu and Kashmir 325
Janina 697
Japan, Japanese .... Vol. 1A
Japan (Australian Occ.) .... Vol. 1A
Japan (Taiwan) .... Vol. 2A, Vol. 4A
Japanese Offices Abroad .... Vol. 1A
Japan Occupation of Brunei .... Vol. 1B
Japan Occupation of Burma .... Vol. 1B
Japan Occupation of China .... Vol. 2A
Japan Occupation of Dutch
  Indies .... Vol. 5A
Japan Occupation of Hong Kong 78
Japan Occupation of Johore .... Vol. 4B
Japan Occupation of Kedah .... Vol. 4B
Japan Occupation of Kelantan ...... Vol. 4B
Japan Occupation of Malacca .... Vol. 4B
Japan Occupation of Malaya .... Vol. 4B
Japan Occupation of Negri
  Sembilan .... Vol. 4B
Japan Occupation of Netherlands
  Indies .... Vol. 5A
Japan Occupation of North
  Borneo .... Vol. 1A
Japan Occupation of Pahang .... Vol. 4B
Japan Occupation of Penang .... Vol. 4B
Japan Occupation of Perak .... Vol. 4B

Japan Occupation of
  Philippines .... Vol. 1A, Vol. 5A
Japan Occupation of Sarawak .... Vol. 6A
Japan Occupation of Selangor ...... Vol. 4B
Japan Occupation of
  Sts. Settlements .... Vol. 6A
Japan Occ. of Trengganu .... Vol. 4B
Other Japanese Stamps
  Overprinted .... Vol. 1B, Vol. 2A,
  Vol. 4A, Vol. 5A
Jasdan 326
Java .... 338, Vol. 5A
Jedda .... Vol. 6A
Jeend 308
Jehol .... Vol. 2A
Jersey .... Vol. 3A
Jersey, German Occupation .... Vol. 3A
Jerusalem, Italian Offices 697
Jerusalem, Russian Offices .... Vol. 5B
Jetersville, Va. .... Vol. 1A
Jhalawar 326
Jhind, Jind 308, 326
Johore, Johor .... Vol. 4B
Jonesboro, Tenn. .... Vol. 1A
J. P. Johnson (Confed. #66X1) ... Vol. 1A
Jordan .... Vol. 4A
Jordan (Palestine Occ.) .... Vol. 4A
Journaux .... Vol. 2B
Juan Fernandez Islands (Chile) ... Vol. 2A
Jubile de l'Union Postale Universelle
  (Switzerland #98) .... Vol. 6A
Jugoslavia, Jugoslavija .... Vol. 6B
Junagarh 330

K .... Vol. 1A
КАЗАКСТАН .... Vol. 4A
Kabul .... Vol. 1A
Kalaallit Nunaat, Kalatdlit Nunat ... Vol. 3A
Kamerun .... Vol. 2A
Kampuchea .... Vol. 2A
Kansu .... Vol. 2A
Karelia, Karjala .... Vol. 4A
Karema ovptd. on Belgian Congo ... Vol. 3A
Karki 699
Karolinen .... Vol. 2A
Kashmir 326
Katanga .... Vol. 4A
Kathiri State of Seiyun .... Vol. 1A
Kaunas .... Vol. 4A, Vol. 5B
Kayangel (Palau #686) .... Vol. 5A
Kazakhstan, Kazakhstan,
  Kazakstan .... Vol. 4A
Kedah .... Vol. 4B
Keeling Islands .... Vol. 2A
Kelantan .... Vol. 4B
Kentta Postia .... Vol. 2B
Kenya .... Vol. 4A
Kenya and Uganda .... Vol. 4A
Kenya, Uganda, Tanzania .... Vol. 4A
Kenya, Uganda, Tanganyika .... Vol. 4A
Kenya, Uganda, Tanganyika,
  Zanzibar .... Vol. 4A
Kerassunde .... Vol. 5B
Kermanshah 395
K.G.C.A. ovptd. on Yugoslavia ... Vol. 6B
K.G.L. .... Vol. 1A, Vol. 2B
Kharkiv .... Vol. 6B
Khmer Republic .... Vol. 2A
Khor Fakkan .... Vol. 6A
Kiangsi .... Vol. 2A
Kiangsu .... Vol. 2A
Kiauchau, Kiautschou .... Vol. 4A
Kibris .... Vol. 6B
Kibris Cumhuriyeti
  (Cyprus #198-200) .... Vol. 2B
Kigoma ovptd. on Belgian Congo ... Vol. 3A
Kilis .... Vol. 6A
King Edward VII Land
  (New Zealand #121a) .... Vol. 5A
Kingman's City Post .... Vol. 1A
Kingston, Ga. .... Vol. 1A
Kionga .... Vol. 4A
Kirghizia .... Vol. 4A
Kiribati .... Vol. 4A
Kirin .... Vol. 2A
Kishangarh, Kishengarh 327
Kithyra .... 389, Vol. 3A
K.K. Post Stempel (or Stampel) ... Vol. 1B
K.K.T.C. (Turk. Rep. N. Cyprus
  #RA1) .... Vol. 6B
Klaipeda .... Vol. 4B
Knoxville, Tenn. .... Vol. 1A
Kolomyia .... Vol. 6B
Kolozsvar 185
Kon .... Vol. 1B, Vol. 2B, Vol. 4A,
  Vol. 5B, Vol. 6A
Kongeligt .... Vol. 2B
Kop Koh .... Vol. 2B
Korca, Korce (Albania) .... Vol. 1A

Korea .... Vol. 4A
Korea, Democratic People's
  Republic .... Vol. 4A
Korea (Japanese Offices) .... Vol. 4A
Korea, Indian Custodial Unit 303
Korea, North .... Vol. 4A
Korea, Soviet occupation .... Vol. 4A
Korea, U.S. Military Govt. .... Vol. 4A
Koritsa .... Vol. 2B
Koror (Palau #686) .... Vol. 5A
Korytsa (Albania #81) .... Vol. 1A
Kos 699
Kosova .... Vol. 6A
Kosovo .... Vol. 1A, Vol. 4A
Kotah 328
Kouang Tcheou-Wan .... Vol. 2B
KPHTH (Crete) .... Vol. 2A
Kr., Kreuzer .... 79, Vol. 1B
Kraljevstvo, Kraljevina .... Vol. 6B
K.S.A. .... Vol. 6A
Kuban Government .... Vol. 6A
K.U.K., K. und K. ..... 686, Vol. 1B, Vol. 5B
Kunming .... Vol. 2B
Kupa Zone .... Vol. 6B
Kurdistan 395
Kurland, Kurzeme .... Vol. 4A, Vol. 5B
Kurus .... Vol. 6B
Kuwait, Koweit .... Vol. 4A, Vol. 5A
Kwangchowan .... Vol. 2B
Kwangsi .... Vol. 2A
Kwangtung .... Vol. 2A
Kweichow .... Vol. 2A
K. Wurtt. Post .... Vol. 3A
Kyiv .... Vol. 6B
Kyrgyz Express Post .... Vol. 4A
Kyrgyzstan .... Vol. 4A

La Aguera .... Vol. 1A
Labuan .... Vol. 4A
La Canea 695
Lady McLeod .... Vol. 6B
La Georgie .... Vol. 3A
Lagos .... Vol. 4A
La Grange, Tex. .... Vol. 1A
Laibach .... Vol. 6B
Lake City, Fla. .... Vol. 1A
Lanchow .... Vol. 2A
Land Post .... Vol. 3A
Lao, Laos .... Vol. 4A
Laos (Int. Com., India) 303
L.A.R. .... Vol. 4A
Las Bela 328
Latakia, Lattaquie .... Vol. 4A
Latvia, Latvija .... Vol. 4A, Vol. 5B
Laurens Court House, S.C. .... Vol. 1A
Lavaca .... Vol. 1A
League of Nations .... Vol. 6A
Lebanon .... Vol. 4A, Vol. 5A, Vol. 6A
Leeward Islands .... Vol. 4A
Lefkas .... 389, Vol. 3A
Lei ovptd. on Austria .... Vol. 5B
Lemnos .... Vol. 3A
Lenoir, N.C. .... Vol. 1A
Lero, Leros 699
Lesbos .... Vol. 3A
Lesotho .... Vol. 4A
Lesser Sundas .... Vol. 5A
Lettland, Lettonia .... Vol. 4A
Letzeburg .... Vol. 4A
Levant, British .... Vol. 3A
Levant, French .... Vol. 2B, Vol. 6A
Levant, Italian 695
Levant, Polish .... Vol. 5B
Levant, Romanian .... Vol. 5B
Levant, Russian .... Vol. 5B
Levant, Syrian (on Lebanon) ...... Vol. 6A
Lexington, Miss. .... Vol. 1A
Lexington, Va. .... Vol. 1A
Liaoning .... Vol. 2A
Liban, Libanaise .... Vol. 4A
Libau ovptd. on German .... Vol. 4A
Liberia .... Vol. 4A
Liberty, Va. .... Vol. 1A
Libya, Libia, Libye .... Vol. 4A
Libyan Arab Republic .... Vol. 4A
Liechtenstein .... Vol. 4A
Lietuva, Lietuvos .... Vol. 4A
Lifland .... Vol. 5B
Ligne Aeriennes de la France
  Libre (Syria #MC5) .... Vol. 6A
Lima .... Vol. 5A
Limestone Springs, S.C. .... Vol. 1A
L'Inde .... Vol. 2B
Linja-Autorahti Bussfrakt .... Vol. 2B
Lipso, Lisso 699
Lithuania .... Vol. 4A, Vol. 5B
Lithuania, Central .... Vol. 2A

Lithuanian Occupation of Memel ... Vol. 4B
Litwa Srodkowa, Litwy
  Srodkowej .... Vol. 2A
Livingston, Ala. .... Vol. 1A
Livonia .... Vol. 5B
Ljubljana .... Vol. 6A
Llanes .... Vol. 6A
L McL .... Vol. 6B
Local .... Vol. 6B
Local Post .... Vol. 2A
Lockport, N.Y. .... Vol. 1A
Lombardy-Venetia .... Vol. 1B
Lorraine .... Vol. 2B
Losen .... Vol. 6A
Lothringen .... Vol. 2B
Louisville, Ky. .... Vol. 1A
Lourenco Marques, L. Marques .... Vol. 4A
Lower Austria .... Vol. 1B
L P overprinted on Russian
  stamps .... Vol. 4A
LTSR on Lithuania .... Vol. 4A
Lubeck, Luebeck .... Vol. 3A
Lubiana .... Vol. 6B
Lublin .... Vol. 5B
Luminescence .... Vol. 1A
Luxembourg .... Vol. 4A
Lviv .... Vol. 6B
Lydenburg .... Vol. 6B
Lynchburg, Va. .... Vol. 1A

Macao, Macau .... Vol. 4B
Macedonia .... Vol. 4A
Machin Head definitives .... Vol. 3A
Macon, Ga. .... Vol. 1A
Madagascar, Madagasikara .... Vol. 4B
Madagascar (British) .... Vol. 4B
Madeira .... Vol. 4B, Vol. 5B
Madero Issue (Mexico) .... Vol. 4B
Madison, Ga. .... Vol. 1A
Madison Court House, Fla. .... Vol. 1A
Madrid .... Vol. 6A
Madura .... Vol. 5A
Mafeking .... Vol. 2A
Magdalena .... Vol. 2A
Magyar, Magyarorszag 79
Magy. Kir. 183
Majunga .... Vol. 4B
Makedonija .... Vol. 4B
Malacca .... Vol. 4B
Malaga .... Vol. 6A
Malagasy Republic .... Vol. 4B
Malawi .... Vol. 4B
Malaya .... Vol. 4B
Malaya (Japanese Occ.) .... Vol. 4B, Vol. 5A
Malaya (Thai Occ.) .... Vol. 4B
Malaya, Federation of .... Vol. 4B
Malaysia .... Vol. 4B
Malay States .... Vol. 4B
Maldive Islands, Maldives .... Vol. 4B
Malgache Republique .... Vol. 4B
Mali .... Vol. 4B
Malmedy .... Vol. 3A
Malta .... Vol. 4B
Maluku Selatan (So. Moluccas) ... Vol. 6A
Man, Isle of .... Vol. 3A
Manchukuo .... Vol. 4B
Manchukuo stamps overprinted ... Vol. 2A
Manchuria .... Vol. 2A
Manizales .... Vol. 2A
Mapka, Mapok .... Vol. 2B, Vol. 5B
Mariana Islands, Marianen .... Vol. 4B
Marienwerder .... Vol. 4B
Marietta, Ga. .... Vol. 1A
Marion, Va. .... Vol. 1A
Markka, Markkaa .... Vol. 2B
Maroc, Marocco, Marokko ..... Vol. 2B,
  Vol. 3A, Vol. 4B
Marruecos .... Vol. 4B, Vol. 6A
Mars Bluff, S.C. .... Vol. 1A
Marshall Islands, Marschall-Inseln,
  Marshall-Inseln .... Vol. 4B
Marshall Islands (G.R.I. surch.) ... Vol. 5A
Martinique .... Vol. 4B
Martin's City Post .... Vol. 1A
Mauritania, Mauritanie .... Vol. 4B
Mauritania stamps surcharged ... Vol. 2B
Mauritius .... Vol. 4B
Mayotte .... Vol. 4B
Mayreau .... Vol. 5B

INDEX AND IDENTIFIER

M.B.D. overprinted 328
McNeel, A.W. .... Vol. 1A
Mecca .... Vol. 6A
Mecklenburg-Schwerin .... Vol. 3A
Mecklenburg-Strelitz .... Vol. 3A
Mecklenburg-Vorpomm .... Vol. 3A
Mecklenburg-Vorpommern .... Vol. 3A
Medellin .... Vol. 2A
Medina .... Vol. 6A
Medio Real .... Vol. 2B
M.E.F. ovptd on Great Britain ..... Vol. 3A
Mejico .... Vol. 4B
Melaka .... Vol. 4B
Melekeor (Palau #686) .... Vol. 5A
Memel, Memelgebiet .... Vol. 4B
Memphis, Tenn. .... Vol. 1A
Meng Chiang .... Vol. 2A
Menge .... Vol. 4B
Mengtsz .... Vol. 2B
Merida .... Vol. 4B
Meched 392
Mesopotamia (British
  Occupation) .... Vol. 4B
Metelin .... Vol. 5B
Mexico, Mexicano .... Vol. 4B
Micanopy, Fla. .... Vol. 1A
Micronesia .... Vol. 4B
Middle Congo .... Vol. 4B
Middle East Forces .... Vol. 3A
Mihon .... Vol. 4A
Mil .... Vol. 4B
Militarpost (Milit. Post) .... Vol. 1B
Millbury, Mass. .... Vol. 1A
Milledgeville, Ga. .... Vol. 1A
Miller, Gen. .... Vol. 5B
Milliemes surch. on French
  Off. in Turkey .... Vol. 2B
Mitau .... Vol. 4A
Milton, N.C. .... Vol. 1A
M. Kir. 81
Mn. .... Vol. 4A
Mobile, Ala. .... Vol. 1A
Mocambique .... Vol. 4B
Modena, Modones 587
Moheli .... Vol. 4B
Moldavia .... Vol. 4B, Vol. 5B
Moldova .... Vol. 4B
Moluccas .... Vol. 5A
Monaco .... Vol. 4B
Monastir .... Vol. 6B
Mongolia .... Vol. 4B
Mongtseu, Mongtze .... Vol. 2B
Monrovia .... Vol. 4A
Mont Athos .... Vol. 5B
Montenegro .... Vol. 4B
Monterrey .... Vol. 4B
Montevideo .... Vol. 6B
Montgomery, Ala. .... Vol. 1A
Montserrat .... Vol. 5A
Moquea, Moquegua .... Vol. 5A
Morelia .... Vol. 4B
Morocco .... Vol. 4B
Morocco (British Offices) .... Vol. 3A
Morocco (German Offices) .... Vol. 3A
Morocco, French .... Vol. 4B
Morocco, Spanish .... Vol. 6A
Morvi 328
Moschopolis .... Vol. 2B
Mosul .... Vol. 4B
Mount Athos (Greece) .... Vol. 3A
Mount Athos (Turkey) .... Vol. 6B
Mount Athos, Russian Offices ..... Vol. 5B
Mount Lebanon, La. .... Vol. 1A
Mount Pleasant, NC .... Vol. 1A
Moyen-Congo .... Vol. 4B
Mozambique .... Vol. 4B
Mozambique Co. .... Vol. 4B
MQE ovptd. on French Colonies ... Vol. 4B
Muscat and Oman .... Vol. 5A
Mustique .... Vol. 5B
M.V.iR .... Vol. 5B
Myanmar (Burma) .... Vol. 1B
Mytilene .... Vol. 3A

Nabha 309
Naciones Unidas .... Vol. 1A
Nagyvarad 185
Namibia .... Vol. 5A, Vol. 6A
Nandgaon 328
Nanking .... Vol. 2A
Nanumaga .... Vol. 6B
Nanumea .... Vol. 6B
Naples, Napoletana 589
Nashville, Tenn. .... Vol. 1A
Natal .... Vol. 5A
Nations Unies .... Vol. 1A, Vol. 6A
Native Feudatory States, India 313

Nauru .... Vol. 5A
Navanagar 328
Navarra .... Vol. 6A
N.C.E. ovptd. on French
  Colonies .... Vol. 5A
Neapolitan Provinces 590
Ned. (Nederlandse) Antillen ..... Vol. 5A
Ned. (Nederl, Nederlandse) Indie .. Vol. 5A
Nederland .... Vol. 5A
Nederlands Nieuw Guinea .... Vol. 5A
Negeri Sembilan .... Vol. 4B
Negri Sembilan .... Vol. 4B
Nejd .... Vol. 6A
Nejd Administration of Hejaz ..... Vol. 6A
Nepal .... Vol. 5A
Netherlands .... Vol. 5A
Netherlands Antilles .... Vol. 5A
Netherlands Indies .... Vol. 5A
Netherlands New Guinea .... Vol. 5A
Nevis .... Vol. 5A
New Britain .... Vol. 5A
New Brunswick .... Vol. 2A
New Caledonia .... Vol. 5A
New Caledonia stamps
  overprinted .... Vol. 5A
Newfoundland .... Vol. 2A
New Granada .... Vol. 2A
New Greece .... Vol. 3A
New Guinea .... Vol. 5A
New Guinea, British .... Vol. 3A
New Guinea, German .... Vol. 3A
New Haven, Conn. .... Vol. 1A
New Hebrides (British) .... Vol. 5A
New Hebrides (French) .... Vol. 5A
New Orleans, La. .... Vol. 1A
New Republic .... Vol. 5A
New Smyrna, Fla. .... Vol. 1A
New South Wales .... Vol. 1A
New York, N.Y. .... Vol. 1A
New Zealand .... Vol. 5A
Nezavisna .... Vol. 2A
N.F. overprinted on
  Nyasaland Pro. .... Vol. 3A
Ngaraard (Palau #686) .... Vol. 5A
Ngardman (Palau #686) .... Vol. 5A
Ngaremlengui (Palau #686) ...... Vol. 5A
Ngchesar (Palau #686) .... Vol. 5A
Ngiwal (Palau #686) .... Vol. 5A
Nicaragua .... Vol. 5A
Nicaria .... Vol. 3A
Nieuwe Republiek .... Vol. 5A
Nieuw Guinea .... Vol. 5A
Niger .... Vol. 5A
Niger and Senegambia .... Vol. 6A
Niger and Upper Senegal .... Vol. 6B
Niger Coast Protectorate .... Vol. 5A
Nigeria .... Vol. 5A
Nikolaevsk .... Vol. 6A
Ningsia .... Vol. 2A
Nippon .... Vol. 4A
Nisiro, Nisiros 699
Niuafo'ou .... Vol. 6B
Niue .... Vol. 5A
Niutao .... Vol. 6B
Nlle. Caledonie .... Vol. 5A
No Hay Estampillas .... Vol. 2A
N. O. P. O. (Confed. #62XU1) ..... Vol. 1A
Norddeutscher Postbezirk .... Vol. 3A
Noreg (1st stamp #318) .... Vol. 1A
Norfolk, Va. .... Vol. 1A
Norfolk Island .... Vol. 5A
Norge .... Vol. 5A
North Borneo .... Vol. 5A
North China .... Vol. 2A
Northeast China .... Vol. 2A
Northeast Postal Service .... Vol. 2A
Northeastern Provinces (China) .. Vol. 2A
North Epirus (Greek Occupation) .. Vol. 3A
Northern Cook Islands .... Vol. 5A
Northern Cyprus, Turkish Rep. of .. Vol. 6B
Northern Ireland .... Vol. 3A
Northern Kiangsu .... Vol. 2A
Northern Nigeria .... Vol. 5A
Northern Poland .... Vol. 5B
Northern Rhodesia .... Vol. 5A
Northern Zone, Morocco .... Vol. 4B
North German Confederation ..... Vol. 3A
North Ingermanland .... Vol. 5B
North Viet Nam .... Vol. 6B
Northwest China .... Vol. 2A
North West (N. W.) Pacific
  Islands .... Vol. 5A
Norway .... Vol. 5A
Nossi-Be .... Vol. 5A
Notopher .... Vol. 3A
Nouvelle Caledonie .... Vol. 5A
Nouvelle Hebrides .... Vol. 5A
Nova Scotia .... Vol. 2A

Novocherkassk .... Vol. 6A
Nowa .... Vol. 5B
Nowa Bb ovptd. on Bulgaria ..... Vol. 5B
Nowanuggur 328
Nowta .... Vol. 6A
Nowte .... Vol. 4B
Noyta .... Vol. 1B, Vol. 3A, Vol. 4A,
                              Vol. 5B, Vol. 6B
NP surcharged on Great Britain ... Vol. 5A
Nr. 21, Nr. 16 .... Vol. 3A
N S B ovptd. on French Colonies ... Vol. 4B
N. Sembilan .... Vol. 4B
N.S.W. .... Vol. 1A
Nueva Granada .... Vol. 2A
Nui .... Vol. 6B
Nukufetau .... Vol. 6B
Nukulaelae .... Vol. 6B
Nyasaland (Protectorate) .... Vol. 5A
Nyasaland and Rhodesia .... Vol. 5B
Nyasaland, overprinted .... Vol. 3A
Nyassa .... Vol. 5A
N.Z. .... Vol. 5A

Oakway, S.C. .... **Vol. 1A**
Oaxaca .... Vol. 4B
Obock .... Vol. 5A
Ob. Ost ovptd. on Germany
  (Lithuania) .... Vol. 5B
Occupation Francaise 183
Oceania, Oceanie .... Vol. 2B
Oesterr. Post, Ofterreich .... Vol. 1B
Offentlig Sak, Off. Sak .... Vol. 5A
Oil Rivers .... Vol. 5A
O K C A (Russia) .... Vol. 5B
Oldenburg .... Vol. 3A
Olonets .... Vol. 5B
Oltre Giuba .... Vol. 5A
Oman, Sultanate of .... Vol. 5A
ONU (UN Offices in
  Geneva #384) .... Vol. 1A
Oradea 185
Orange River Colony .... Vol. 5A
Oranje Vrij Staat .... Vol. 5A
Orchha, Orcha 329
Ore surcharged on Denmark ..... Vol. 2B
Orense .... Vol. 6A
Organisation Mondiale
  de la Sante .... Vol. 6A
Oriental .... Vol. 6B
Orts-Post .... Vol. 6A
O.S. .... Vol. 5A
Osten .... Vol. 5B
Osterreich .... Vol. 1B
Ostland .... Vol. 5B
Ottoman, Ottomanes ..... Vol. 2B, Vol. 6B
Oubangi Chari .... Vol. 6B
Outer Mongolia .... Vol. 4B
Oviedo .... Vol. 6A
O.V.S. .... Vol. 5A
Oxford, N.C. .... Vol. 1A
O'zbekiston .... Vol. 6B

P .... **Vol. 2A, Vol. 2B, Vol. 4A, Vol. 6A**
P on Straits Settlements .... Vol. 4B
Pacchi Postali .... 694, Vol. 6A
Pacific Steam Navigation Co. .... Vol. 5A
Packhoi, Pakhoi .... Vol. 2B
Pahang .... Vol. 4B
Paid (Confed. #35X, etc.) .... Vol. 1A
Paid 5 (US #4X1, 7X1, many
  Confed.) .... Vol. 1A
Paid 10 (Confed. #76XU, 101XU,
  80XU) .... Vol. 1A
Paid 2 Cents (Confed. #2XU) .... Vol. 1A
Paid 3 Cents (Confed. #2AXU) ... Vol. 1A
Paita .... Vol. 5A
Pakistan .... Vol. 5A
Pakke-porto .... Vol. 5A
Palau .... Vol. 5A
Palestine .... Vol. 2B, Vol. 5A
Palestine (British Administration) ... Vol. 5A
Palestine (Jordan Occ.) .... Vol. 4A
Palestine overprinted .... Vol. 4A
Palestinian Authority .... Vol. 5A
Panama .... Vol. 5A
Panama (Colombian Dom.) ...... Vol. 2A,
                                    Vol. 5A
Panama Canal Zone .... Vol. 1A
Papua .... Vol. 5A
Papua New Guinea .... Vol. 5A
Para .... Vol. 2B, Vol. 6B
Para ovptd. on Austria .... Vol. 1B
Para ovptd. on France .... Vol. 5A
Para ovptd. on Germany .... Vol. 3A
Para ovptd. on Italy 695
Paraguay .... Vol. 5A
Paras .... Vol. 2B, Vol. 6B
Paras ovpt. on Great Britain ..... Vol. 3A

Paras ovpt. on Romania .... Vol. 5B
Paras ovpt. on Russia .... Vol. 5B
Parma, Parm., Parmensi 587
Pasco .... Vol. 5A
Patiala 310
Patmo, Patmos 700
Patterson, N.C. .... Vol. 1A
Patton, N.B. (Confed. #138XU1) ... Vol. 1A
Patzcuaro .... Vol. 4B
Paxos .... 389, Vol. 2A, Vol. 3A
PC CP .... Vol. 5B
PD .... Vol. 5B
P.E. (Egypt #4, etc.) .... Vol. 2B
Pechino, Peking 694
Peleliu (Palau #686) .... Vol. 5A
Pen, Penna .... Vol. 2B
Penang .... Vol. 4B
Penny Post (US 3LB, 8LB) .... Vol. 1A
Penrhyn Island .... Vol. 5A
Pensacola, Fla. .... Vol. 1A
Penybnnka Cpncka .... Vol. 1B
People's Republic of China .... Vol. 2A
Perak .... Vol. 4B
Perlis .... Vol. 4B
Persekutuan Tanah Melayu
  (Malaya #91) .... Vol. 4B
Persia (British Occupation) ...... Vol. 1B
Persia, Persanes 390
Peru, Peruana .... Vol. 5A
Pesa ovpt. on Germany .... Vol. 3A
Petersburg, Va. .... Vol. 1A
Pfennig, Pfg., Pf. ..... Vol. 2B, Vol. 3A, Vol. 4A
P.G.S. (Perak) .... Vol. 4B
Philadelphia, Pa. .... Vol. 1A
Philippines .... Vol. 2A, Vol. 5A
Philippines (US Admin.) .... Vol. 1A, Vol. 5A
Philippines (Japanese Occ.) ..... Vol. 1A,
                                    Vol. 5A
Piast., Piaster ovptd. on Austria ... Vol. 1B
Piaster ovptd. on Germany .... Vol. 3A
Piaster ovptd. on Romania .... Vol. 5B
Piastre, Piastra ovptd. on Italy 697
Piastre .... Vol. 2B, Vol. 4B, Vol. 6B
Piastre ovptd. on France .... Vol. 2B
Piastres ovpt. on Great Britain ... Vol. 3A
Piastres ovpt. on Russia .... Vol. 5B
Pies .... 322, Vol. 2A
Pietersburg .... Vol. 6B
Pilgrim Tercentenary (US #548) ... Vol. 1A
Pilipinas .... Vol. 1A, Vol. 5A
Pisco .... Vol. 5A
Piscopi 700
Pitcairn Islands .... Vol. 5B
Pittsylvania C.H., Va. .... Vol. 1A
Piura .... Vol. 5A
Plains of Dura, Ga. .... Vol. 1A
Pleasant Shade, Va. .... Vol. 1A
Plum Creek, Tex. .... Vol. 1A
P.O. Paid .... Vol. 1A
Pobres (Spain #RA11) .... Vol. 6A
РОССІЯ, РОССИЯ .... Vol. 5B
Poczta, Polska .... Vol. 2B, Vol. 5B
Pohjois Inkeri .... Vol. 5B
Pokutia .... Vol. 6B
Poland .... Vol. 5B
Poland, exile government in
  Great Britain .... Vol. 5B
Polish Levant .... Vol. 5B
Polish Offices in Danzig .... Vol. 5B
Polish Offices in Turkish Empire ... Vol. 5B
Polska .... Vol. 5B
Polynesia, French (Polynesie) .... Vol. 2B
Ponce .... Vol. 1A, Vol. 5B
Ponta Delgada .... Vol. 5B
Р.О.П.иТ. .... Vol. 5B
Poonch 329
Popayan .... Vol. 2A
Port Arthur and Dairen .... Vol. 2A
Porteado .... Vol. 5B
Porte de Conduccion .... Vol. 5A
Porte de Mar .... Vol. 4B
Porte Franco .... Vol. 5A
Port Gibson, Miss. .... Vol. 1A
Port Gdansk .... Vol. 5B
Port Hood, Nova Scotia .... Vol. 2A
Port Lagos .... Vol. 2B
Port Lavaca, Tex. .... Vol. 1A
Porto .... Vol. 1A, Vol. 1B, Vol. 6B
Porto Gazetei .... Vol. 5B
Porto Pflichtige .... Vol. 3A
Porto Rico .... Vol. 1A, Vol. 2A, Vol. 5B
Port Said, French Offices .... Vol. 2B
Portugal, Portuguesa .... Vol. 5B
Portuguese Africa .... Vol. 5B
Portuguese Congo .... Vol. 5B
Portuguese East Africa
  (Mozambique) .... Vol. 4B
Portuguese Guinea .... Vol. 5B

INDEX AND IDENTIFIER

Portuguese India .... Vol. 5B
Portuguese India overpinted ..... Vol. 6B
Posen (Poznan) .... Vol. 5B
Post .... 322, Vol. 3A
Post (Postage) & Receipt 322
Posta .... Vol. 1A, Vol. 6A
Postage(s) .... 221, 318, Vol. 1A, Vol. 3A, Vol. 4B, Vol. 5B
Postage Due .... Vol. 1A, Vol. 3A
Postas le hioc 534
Poste Locale .... Vol. 6A
Postes .... Vol. 1B, Vol. 2B, Vol. 4A
Postes Serbes ovptd. on France ... Vol. 6A
Postgebiet Ob. Ost. .... Vol. 5B
Postmarke .... Vol. 3A
Post Office (US #7X, 9X) .... Vol. 1A
Post Stamp 322
Postzegel .... Vol. 5A
P.P. ovptd. on French postage
  dues .... Vol. 2B
P.P.C. ovptd. on Poland .... Vol. 5B
Pre .... Vol. 6B
Prefecture issues .... Vol. 4A
Preussen .... Vol. 3A
Priamur .... Vol. 6A
Prince Edward Island .... Vol. 2A
Pristina .... Vol. 6B
Province of Canada .... Vol. 2A
Providence (Prov.), R.I. .... Vol. 1A
Prussia .... Vol. 3A
PS .... 318, Vol. 2A
P.S.N.C. (Peru) .... Vol. 5A
Puerto Principe .... Vol. 1A, Vol. 2A
Puerto Rico, Pto. Rico .... Vol. 1A, Vol. 2A, Vol. 5B
Puerto Rico (US Admin.) ... Vol. 1A, Vol. 5B
Pul .... Vol. 1A
Pulau Pinang .... Vol. 4B
Puno .... Vol. 5A
Puttialla State 310

Qatar .... **Vol. 5B**
Qu'aiti State in Hadhramaut .... Vol. 1A
Qu'aiti State of Shihr and
  Mukalla .... Vol. 1A
Queensland .... Vol. 1A
Quelimane .... Vol. 5B

R (Armenia) .... **Vol. 1A**
R (Jind, Iran) 326, 392, 455
R ovptd. on French Colonies ..... Vol. 2B
Rajasthan 329
Rajpeepla, Rajpipla 330
Raleigh, N.C. .... Vol. 1A
Rappen .... Vol. 6A
Rarotonga .... Vol. 2A
Ras al Khaima .... Vol. 5B, Vol. 6B
R.A.U. .... Vol. 6A
Rayon .... Vol. 6A
Recargo .... Vol. 6A
Redonda (Antigua) .... Vol. 1B
Refugee Relief 305
Regatul 184
Reichspost .... Vol. 3A
Reis (Portugal) .... Vol. 5B
Repubblica Sociale Italiana 693
Republic of China .... Vol. 2A
Republique Arab Unie .... Vol. 6A
Republique Democratique
  du Congo .... Vol. 6B
Reseau d'Etat .... Vol. 2B
Resistance overprinted on Syria ... Vol. 6A
Rethymnon, Retymno .... Vol. 6A
Reunion .... Vol. 2B
R.F. ...... See France or French Colonies
RF - Solidarite Francaise .... Vol. 2B
R H 21
Rheatown, Tenn. .... Vol. 1A
Rheinland-Pfalz .... Vol. 3A
Rhine Palatinate .... Vol. 3A
Rhodes 700
Rhodesia .... Vol. 5B
Rhodesia (formerly So. Rhodesia) .... Vol. 5B
Rhodesia and Nyasaland .... Vol. 5B
Rialtar 491
Riau, Riouw Archipelago 389
Ricevuta .... 686, 694, 692, Vol. 6A
Richmond, Tex. .... Vol. 1A
Rigsbank Skilling .... Vol. 2B
Ringgold, Ga. .... Vol. 1A
Rio de Oro .... Vol. 5B
Rio Muni .... Vol. 5B
RIS on Netherlands Indies 342
Rizeh .... Vol. 1A
Rn. .... Vol. 4A
RNS 318
R. O. ovptd. on Turkey .... Vol. 1A
Robertsport .... Vol. 4A
Rodi 700

Roepiah .... Vol. 5A
Romagna, Romagne 588
Romana .... 185, Vol. 5B
Romania, Roumania .... Vol. 5B
Romania, Occupation, Offices ..... Vol. 5B
Romanian Occupation of Hungary ... 185
Romanian Occupation of Western
  Ukraine .... Vol. 6B
Romania, Offices in the Turkish
  Empire .... Vol. 5B
Roman States 588
Ross Dependency .... Vol. 5A
Rossija .... Vol. 6A
Rostov .... Vol. 6A
Rouad, Ile .... Vol. 5B
Roumelie Orientale .... Vol. 2B
Rpf overprinted on Luxembourg .... Vol. 4A
RSA .... Vol. 6A
R S M (San Marino) .... Vol. 6A
Ruanda ovptd. on Congo .... Vol. 3A
Ruanda-Urundi .... Vol. 5B
Ruffifch-Polen ovptd. on
  Germany .... Vol. 5B
Rumania, Roumania .... Vol. 5B
Rumanien on Germany .... Vol. 5B
Rupee on Great Britain .... Vol. 5A
Russia .... Vol. 5B
Russia (Finnish Occupation) ...... Vol. 4A, Vol. 5B
Russia (German Occupation) ..... Vol. 5B
Russian Company of Navigation
  & Trade .... Vol. 5B
Russian Dominion of Poland ...... Vol. 5B
Russian Empire, Finland .... Vol. 2B
Russian Occupation of Crete ...... Vol. 2A
Russian Occupation of Germany ... Vol. 3A
Russian Occupation of Korea ..... Vol. 4A
Russian Occupation of Latvia ..... Vol. 4A
Russian Occupation of Lithuania ... Vol. 4A
Russian Offices .... Vol. 5B
Russian Offices in China .... Vol. 5B
Russian Offices in Turkish
  Empire .... Vol. 5B
Russian stamps surch. or ovptd. ... Vol. 1A, Vol. 2B, Vol. 3A, Vol. 4A, Vol. 5B, Vol. 6A
Russian Turkestan .... Vol. 5B
Rustenburg .... Vol. 6B
Rutherfordton, N.C. .... Vol. 1A
Rwanda, Rwandaise .... Vol. 6A
Ryukyu Islands .... Vol. 1A

S on Straits Settlements .... **Vol. 4B**
S A, S.A.K. (Saudi Arabia) .... Vol. 6A
Saar, Saargebiet, Saar Land ...... Vol. 5B
Saba (Caribbean Netherlands
  #111) .... Vol. 2A
Sabah .... Vol. 4B
Sachsen .... Vol. 3A
Sahara Occidental (Espanol) ...... Vol. 6A
St. Christopher .... Vol. 5B
St. Christopher-Nevis-Anguilla ... Vol. 5B
St. Eustatius (Caribbean
  Netherlands #112) .... Vol. 2A
Ste. Marie de Madagascar .... Vol. 5B
St. Georges, Bermuda .... Vol. 1B
St. Helena .... Vol. 5B
S. Thome (Tome) E Principe ..... Vol. 5B
St. Kitts .... Vol. 5B
St. Kitts-Nevis .... Vol. 5B
St. Louis, Mo. .... Vol. 1A
St. Lucia .... Vol. 5B
St. Martin .... Vol. 5B
St. Pierre and Miquelon .... Vol. 5B
St. Thomas and Prince Islands ... Vol. 5B
St. Vincent .... Vol. 5B
St. Vincent and the Grenadines ... Vol. 5B
St. Vincent Grenadines .... Vol. 5B
Salamanca Province .... Vol. 6A
Salem, N.C. .... Vol. 1A
Salem, Va. .... Vol. 1A
Salisbury, N.C. .... Vol. 1A
Salonicco, Salonika 697
Salonika (Turkish) .... Vol. 5B
Salonique .... Vol. 5B, Vol. 6B
Salvador, El .... Vol. 5B
Salzburg .... Vol. 1B
Samoa .... Vol. 5B
Samos .... Vol. 2B, Vol. 3A
San Antonio, Tex. .... Vol. 1A
San Marino .... Vol. 6A
San Sebastian .... Vol. 6A
Santa Cruz de Tenerife .... Vol. 6A
Santa Maura .... 389, Vol. 3A
Santander .... Vol. 6A
Sao Paulo .... Vol. 1B
Sao Tome and Principe .... Vol. 5B
Saorstat 491
Sarawak .... Vol. 4B, Vol. 6A
Sardinia 589

Sarre overprinted on Germany
  and Bavaria .... Vol. 5B
Saseno .... Vol. 6A
Saudi Arabia .... Vol. 6A
Saudi Arabia overprinted .... Vol. 4A
Saurashtra 330
Savannah, Ga. .... Vol. 1A
Saxony .... Vol. 3A
SCADTA .... Vol. 2A
Scarpanto 701
Schleswig .... Vol. 3A, Vol. 5B
Schleswig-Holstein .... Vol. 3A
Schweizer Reneke .... Vol. 6B
Scinde 221
Scotland .... Vol. 3A
Scutari, Italian Offices 697
Segel Porto (on Neth. Indies) ... 340
Segnatasse, Segna Tassa 691
Seiyun .... Vol. 1A
Selangor .... Vol. 4B
Selma, Ala. .... Vol. 1A
Semenov .... Vol. 6A
Sen, Sn. .... Vol. 1A, Vol. 4A, Vol. 5A
Senegal .... Vol. 6A
Senegal stamps surcharged ...... Vol. 6A
Senegambia and Niger .... Vol. 6A
Serb Administration of Bosnia,
  Banja Luca .... Vol. 1B
Serbia, Serbien .... Vol. 6A
Serbia & Montenegro .... Vol. 4B, Vol. 6A
Serbian Occupation of Hungary .. 185
Service .... 303, Vol. 5A
Sevastopol .... Vol. 6A
Seville, Sevilla .... Vol. 6A
Seychelles .... Vol. 6A
S.H. .... Vol. 3A
Shanghai .... Vol. 2A, Vol. 6A
Shanghai (U.S. Offices) .... Vol. 1A
Shanghai and Nanking .... Vol. 2A
Shansi .... Vol. 2A
Shantung .... Vol. 2A
Sharjah .... Vol. 6A
Shensi .... Vol. 2A
Shihr and Mukalla .... Vol. 1A
Shqipenia, Shqiptare, Shqiperija,
  Shqiperise (Albania) .... Vol. 1A
S.H.S. on Bosnia and
  Herzegovina .... Vol. 6B
S.H.S. on Hungary .... Vol. 6B
Siam (Thailand) .... Vol. 6B
Siberia .... Vol. 6A
Siberian stamps overprinted
  or surcharged .... Vol. 2B
Sicily, Sicilia 590
Siege de la Ligue Arabe
  (Morocco #44) .... Vol. 4B
Sierra Leone .... Vol. 6A
Sikang .... Vol. 2A
Silesia, Eastern .... Vol. 2B
Silesia, Upper .... Vol. 6B
Simi 701
Sinaloa .... Vol. 4B
Singapore .... Vol. 6A
Sinkiang .... Vol. 2A
Sint Maarten .... Vol. 5B
Sirmoor, Sirmur 330
Six Cents .... Vol. 1A
Sld. .... Vol. 1B
Slesvig .... Vol. 6A
Slovakia .... Vol. 2B, Vol. 6A
Slovene Coast .... Vol. 6B
Slovenia, Slovenija .... Vol. 6A
Slovenia, Italian .... Vol. 6B
Slovensko, Slovenska,
  Slovensky .... Vol. 2B, Vol. 6A
S. Marino .... Vol. 6A
Smirne, Smyrna 697
Smyrne .... Vol. 5B
S O ovptd. on Czechoslovakia,
  Poland .... Vol. 2B
Sobreporte .... Vol. 2A
Sociedad Colombo-Alemana ..... Vol. 2A
Sociedade de Geographia
  de Lisboa .... Vol. 5B
Societe des Nations .... Vol. 6A
Soldi .... Vol. 1B
Solomon Islands .... Vol. 6A
Somali, Somalia, Somaliya ...... Vol. 6A
Somalia, B.M.A. .... Vol. 3A
Somalia, E.A.F. .... Vol. 3A
Somali Coast (Djibouti) .... Vol. 6A
Somaliland Protectorate .... Vol. 6A
Sonora .... Vol. 4B
Sonsorol (Palau #686) .... Vol. 5A
Soomaaliya, Sooomaaliyeed ..... Vol. 6A
Soruth, Sorath 37
Soudan .... Vol. 2B, Vol. 6A
South Africa .... Vol. 6A

South African Republic
  (Transvaal) .... Vol. 6B
South Arabia .... Vol. 6A
South Australia .... Vol. 1A
South Bulgaria .... Vol. 2B
South Borneo .... Vol. 5A
South China .... Vol. 2A
Southern Nigeria .... Vol. 6A
Southern Poland .... Vol. 5B
Southern Rhodesia .... Vol. 6A
Southern Yemen .... Vol. 6B
South Georgia .... Vol. 2B, Vol. 6A
South Georgia and South
  Sandwich Islands .... Vol. 6A
South Kasai .... Vol. 6A
South Korea .... Vol. 4A
South Lithuania .... Vol. 4A
South Moluccas .... Vol. 6A
South Orkneys .... Vol. 2B
South Russia .... Vol. 6A
South Russian stamps
  surcharged .... Vol. 5B
South Shetlands .... Vol. 2B
South Sudan .... Vol. 6A
South Viet Nam .... Vol. 6B
South West Africa .... Vol. 6A
Southwest China .... Vol. 2A
Soviet Union (Russia) .... Vol. 5B
Sowjetische Besatzungs Zone ... Vol. 3A
Spain .... Vol. 6A
Spanish Administration of
  Andorra .... Vol. 1A
Spanish Dominion of Cuba ..... Vol. 2A
Spanish Dominion of Mariana
  Islands .... Vol. 4B
Spanish Dominion of Philippines ... Vol. 5A
Spanish Dominion of Puerto Rico ... Vol. 5B
Spanish Guinea .... Vol. 6A
Spanish Morocco .... Vol. 6A
Spanish Sahara .... Vol. 6A
Spanish West Africa .... Vol. 6A
Spanish Western Sahara .... Vol. 6A
Sparta, Ga. .... Vol. 1A
Spartanburg, S.C. .... Vol. 1A
SPM ovptd. on French Cols. ..... Vol. 5B
Srbija I Crna Gora .... Vol. 6A
Sri Lanka .... Vol. 6A
Srodkowa Litwa .... Vol. 2A
Stadt Berlin .... Vol. 3A
Stamp (Tibet #O1) .... Vol. 6B
Stampalia 701
Stanyslaviv .... Vol. 6B
Statesville, N.C. .... Vol. 1A
Steinmeyer's City Post .... Vol. 1A
Stellaland .... Vol. 6A
Stempel .... Vol. 1B
Straits Settlements .... Vol. 6A
Straits Settlements overprinted ... Vol. 6A
Strombus gigas Linne
  (Neth. Antilles #1193) .... Vol. 5A
STT Vuja, STT Vujna .... Vol. 6B
Styria .... Vol. 1B
S.U. on Straits Settlements ..... Vol. 4B
Submarine mail (Correo
  Submarino) .... Vol. 6A
Sudan .... Vol. 6A
Sudan, French .... Vol. 2B
Suid Afrika .... Vol. 6A
Suidwes-Afrika .... Vol. 6A
Suiyuan .... Vol. 2A
S. Ujong .... Vol. 4B
Sultanate of Oman .... Vol. 5A
Sumatra .... 340, Vol. 5A
Sumter, S.C. .... Vol. 1A
Sungei Ujong .... Vol. 4B
Suomi (Finland) .... Vol. 2B
Supeh .... Vol. 2A
Surakarta 340
Surinam, Suriname, Surinaamse ... Vol. 6A
Suvalki .... Vol. 5B
Sverige .... Vol. 6A
S.W.A. .... Vol. 6A
Swaziland, Swazieland .... Vol. 6A
Sweden .... Vol. 6A
Switzerland .... Vol. 6A
Switzerland, Administration
  of Liechtenstein .... Vol. 4A
Syria, Syrie, Syrienne .... Vol. 5A, Vol. 6A
Syria (Arabian Government) ... Vol. 6A
Syrie .... Vol. 6A
Syrie-Grand Liban .... Vol. 6A
Szechwan .... Vol. 2A
Szeged 186

T .... **Vol. 1B, Vol. 2B**
T ovptd. on stamps of Peru ..... Vol. 5A
Tabora ovptd. on Belgian Congo ... Vol. 3A
Tacna .... Vol. 5A
Tadjikistan, Tadzikistan .... Vol. 6A

INDEX AND IDENTIFIER

Tae Han (Korea) .... Vol. 4A
Tahiti .... Vol. 6A
Taiwan (Republic of China) .... Vol. 2A
Taiwan (Formosa) .... Vol. 6A
Taiwan, Japanese .... Vol. 2A, 4A
Tajikistan .... Vol. 6A
Takca .... Vol. 1B
Takse .... Vol. 1A
Talbotton, Ga. .... Vol. 1A
Talca .... Vol. 1A
Talladega, Ala. .... Vol. 1A
Tallinn .... Vol. 2B
Tanganyika .... Vol. 6A
Tanganyika and Zanzibar .... Vol. 6A
Tanganyika (Tanzania), Kenya,
  Uganda .... Vol. 4A
Tanger .... Vol. 2B, 6A
Tangier, British Offices .... Vol. 3A
Tangier, French Offices .... Vol. 2B
Tangier, Spanish Offices .... Vol. 6A
Tannu Tuva .... Vol. 6A
Tanzania .... Vol. 6A
Tanzania-Zanzibar .... Vol. 6B
Tartu .... Vol. 2B
Tasmania .... Vol. 1A
Tassa Gazzette 587
Taxa de Guerra .... Vol. 4B, Vol. 5B
Taxyapom .... Vol. 2B
Tchad .... Vol. 2A
Tchongking .... Vol. 2B
T.C. overprinted on Cochin 334
T.C., Postalari .... Vol. 6B
Te Betalen .... Vol. 1B, Vol. 5A, Vol. 6A
Tegucigalpa 21
Teheran 392
Tellico Plains, Tenn. .... Vol. 1A
Temesvar 186
Ten Cents .... Vol. 1A
T.E.O. ovptd. on Turkey or
  France .... Vol. 2A, 6A
Terres Australes et Antarctiques
  Francaises .... Vol. 2B
Territorio Insular Chileno
  (Chile #1061) .... Vol. 2A
Teruel Province .... Vol. 6A
Tete .... Vol. 6A
Tetuan .... Vol. 6A
Thailand, Thai .... Vol. 6B
Thailand (Occupation of Kedah) ... Vol. 4B
Thailand (Occupation of
  Kelantan) .... Vol. 4B
Thailand (Occupation of Malaya) ... Vol. 4B
Thailand (Occupation of Perlis) ... Vol. 4B
Thailand (Occupation of
  Trengganu) .... Vol. 4B
Thessaly .... Vol. 6B
Thomasville, Ga. .... Vol. 1A
Thrace .... Vol. 6B
Three Cents .... Vol. 1A
Thuringia, Thuringen .... Vol. 3A
Thurn and Taxis .... Vol. 3A
Tibet .... Vol. 6B
Tibet (Chinese province) .... Vol. 2A
Tibet, Chinese Offices .... Vol. 2A
Tical .... Vol. 6B
Tientsin (Chinese) .... Vol. 2A
Tientsin (German) .... Vol. 3A
Tientsin (Italian) 695
Tiflis .... Vol. 3A
Timbre ovptd. on France .... Vol. 2B
Timor .... Vol. 6B
Timor-Leste .... Vol. 6B
Timor Lorosae .... Vol. 1A, Vol. 6B
Tin Can Island .... Vol. 6B
Tjedan Solidarnosti
  (Yugoslavia #RA82) .... Vol. 6B
Tjenestefrimerke .... Vol. 2B, 5A
Tlacotalpan .... Vol. 4B
Tobago .... Vol. 6B
Toga .... Vol. 6B
Togo, Togolaise .... Vol. 6B
Tokelau Islands .... Vol. 6B
Tolima .... Vol. 2A
Tonga .... Vol. 6B
Tongareva .... Vol. 5A
Tonk 331
To Pay .... Vol. 3A
Toscano 589
Tou 455
Touva, Tovva .... Vol. 6A
Transcaucasian Federated
  Republics .... Vol. 6B
Trans-Jordan .... Vol. 4A, Vol. 5A
Trans-Jordan (Palestine Occ.) ... Vol. 4A
Transkei .... Vol. 6A
Transvaal .... Vol. 6B
Transylvania 185
Trasporto Pacchi 691
Travancore 331

Travancore-Cochin, State of 333
Trebizonde .... Vol. 5B
Trengganu .... Vol. 4B
Trentino .... Vol. 6B
Trieste .... 701, Vol. 1B, Vol. 6B
Trinidad .... Vol. 6B
Trinidad and Tobago .... Vol. 6B
Trinidad Society (Trinidad &
  Tobago #B1) .... Vol. 6B
Tripoli di Barberia (Tripoli) 789
Tripoli, Fiera Campionaria .... Vol. 4A
Tripolitania .... Vol. 4A, Vol. 6B
Tripolitania (B.M.A.) .... Vol. 3A
Tristan da Cunha .... Vol. 6B
Trucial States .... Vol. 6B
Tsinghai .... Vol. 2A
Tsingtau .... Vol. 2A, 4A
T. Ta. C .... Vol. 6B
Tullahoma, Tenn. .... Vol. 1A
Tumbes (Peru #129-133) .... Vol. 5A
Tunisia, Tunisie, Tunis, Tunisienne ... Vol. 6B
Turkestan, Russian .... Vol. 5B
Turkey, Turkiye, Turk .... Vol. 6B
Turkey (Greek Occupation) .... Vol. 3A,
  Vol. 6B
Turkey in Asia .... Vol. 6B
Turk Federe Devleti .... Vol. 6B
Turkish Empire, Austrian Offices ... Vol. 1B
Turkish Empire, British Offices ... Vol. 3A
Turkish Empire, French Offices ... Vol. 2B
Turkish Empire, Georgian Offices ... Vol. 3A
Turkish Empire, German Offices ... Vol. 3A
Turkish Empire, Italian Offices ... 695
Turkish Empire, Polish Offices ... Vol. 5B
Turkish Empire, Romanian
  Offices .... Vol. 5B
Turkish Empire, Russian Offices ... Vol. 5B
Turkish Occupation of Iran 395
Turkish Republic of Northern
  Cyprus .... Vol. 6B
Turkish stamps surcharged or
  overprinted ..... Vol. 2B, Vol. 3A, Vol. 6A
Turkish Suzerainty of Egypt ...... Vol. 2B
Turkmenistan, Turkmenpocta .... Vol. 6A
Turks and Caicos Islands .... Vol. 6B
Turks Islands .... Vol. 6B
Tuscaloosa, Ala. .... Vol. 1A
Tuscany 589
Tuscumbia, Ala. .... Vol. 1A
Tuva Autonomous Region .... Vol. 6A
Tuvalu .... Vol. 6B
Two Cents (Confed. #53X5) ...... Vol. 1B
Two Pence .... Vol. 1A
Two Sicilies 590
Tyosen (Korea) .... Vol. 4A
Tyrol .... Vol. 1B

UAE ovptd. on Abu Dhabi .... Vol. 6B
U.A.R. .... Vol. 2B, Vol. 6A, Vol. 6B
Ubangi, Ubangi-Shari .... Vol. 6B
Uganda, U.G. .... Vol. 6B
Uganda, and Kenya .... Vol. 4A
Uganda, Tanganyika, Kenya ..... Vol. 4A
Ukraine, Ukraina .... Vol. 6B
Ukraine (German Occupation) ... Vol. 5B
Ukraine stamps surcharged ...... Vol. 5B
Ukrainian Soviet Socialist
  Republic .... Vol. 6B
Ukraine, Western .... Vol. 6B
Uku Leta .... Vol. 1A
Ultramar .... Vol. 2A
Umm al Qiwain .... Vol. 6B
UNEF ovptd. on India 303
UNESCO .... Vol. 2B
U.N. Force in Congo or Gaza (India) 303
Union Island, St. Vincent .... Vol. 5B
Union Islands .... Vol. 6B
Union of South Africa .... Vol. 6A
Union of Soviet Socialist
  Republics .... Vol. 5B
Uniontown, Ala. .... Vol. 1A
Unionville, S.C. .... Vol. 1A
United Arab Emirates .... Vol. 6B
United Arab Republic (UAR) ...... Vol. 2B,
  Vol. 6A, Vol. 6B
United Arab Republic, Egypt .... Vol. 2B
United Arab Republic Issues
  for Syria .... Vol. 6A
United Kingdom .... Vol. 3A
United Nations .... Vol. 1A
United Nations European
  Office .... Vol. 1A, 6A
United Nations Offices in Geneva ... Vol. 1A
United Nations Offices in Vienna ... Vol. 1A
United Nations - Kosovo ... Vol. 1A, Vol. 4A
United Nations - West New
  Guinea Vol.1A
United State of Saurashtra 330

United States Adm. of Canal
  Zone .... Vol. 1A
United States Adm. of Cuba ..... Vol. 1A,
  Vol. 2A
United States Adm. of Guam ..... Vol. 1A
U. S. Adm. of Philippines .... Vol. 1A, Vol. 5A
U. S. Adm. of Puerto Rico .... Vol. 1A,
  Vol. 5B
U. S. Military Rule of Korea .... Vol. 4A
United States of America .... Vol. 1A
United States of Indonesia 342
United States of New Granada .... Vol. 2A
United States, Offices in China ... Vol. 1A
Un Real .... Vol. 2B
U.S. Zone (Germany) .... Vol. 3A
Universal Postal Union, Intl.
  Bureau .... Vol. 6A
UNTEA ovptd. on Netherlands
  New Guinea .... 389, Vol. 1A
UNTEAT .... Vol. 6B
UPHA ROPA .... Vol. 4B
Upper Austria .... Vol. 1B
Upper Senegal and Niger .... Vol. 6B
Upper Silesia .... Vol. 6B
Upper Volta .... Vol. 1B
Urgente .... Vol. 6A
U.R.I. ovptd. on Yugoslavia ...... Vol. 6B
Uruguay .... Vol. 6B
Urundi ovptd. on Congo .... Vol. 3A
Uskub .... Vol. 6B
U.S. Mail .... Vol. 1A
U.S.P.O. .... Vol. 1A
U.S.P.O. Despatch .... Vol. 1A
U.S.S.R. .... Vol. 6B
U. S. T.C. overprinted on Cochin 334
Uzbekistan .... Vol. 6B

Vaitupu .... Vol. 6B
Valdosta, Ga. .... Vol. 1A
Valencia .... Vol. 6A
Valladolid Province .... Vol. 6A
Valona 697
Valparaiso .... Vol. 2A
Vancouver Island .... Vol. 2A
Van Diemen's Land (Tasmania) ... Vol. 1A
Vanuatu .... Vol. 6B
Varldspost Kongress
  (Sweden #197) .... Vol. 6A
Vasa .... Vol. 2B
Vathy .... Vol. 2B
Vatican City, Vaticane, Vaticano .... Vol. 6B
Venda .... Vol. 6A
Venezia Giulia .... 692, Vol. 1B
Venezia Tridentina .... Vol. 1B
Venezuela, Veneza., Venezolana ... Vol. 6B
Venizelist Government .... Vol. 3A
Vereinte Nationen .... Vol. 1A
Vetekeverria .... Vol. 1A
Victoria .... Vol. 1A
Victoria, Tex. .... Vol. 1A
Victoria Land .... Vol. 5A
Vienna .... Vol. 1A, Vol. 1B
Vienna Issues 341
Viet Minh .... Vol. 6B
Viet Nam .... Vol. 6B
Viet Nam Buu Chinh .... Vol. 6B
Viet Nam Buu Dien .... Vol. 6B
Viet Nam Cong-Hoa .... Vol. 6B
Viet Nam Dan-Chu Cong-Hoa ... Vol. 6B
Viet Nam, Democratic Republic ... Vol. 6B
Viet Nam Doc-Lap .... Vol. 6B
Viet Nam, (Int. Com., India) 303
Viet Nam, North .... Vol. 6B
Viet Nam, Republic .... Vol. 6B
Viet Nam, South .... Vol. 6B
Villa Bella (Bolivia #97) .... Vol. 1B
Vilnius .... Vol. 4A, Vol. 5B
Vineta .... Vol. 3A
Virgin Islands .... Vol. 6B
Vladivostok .... Vol. 2B
Vojna Uprava .... Vol. 6B
Volksrust .... Vol. 6B
Vom Empfanger .... Vol. 2B, Vol. 3A
Vorarlberg .... Vol. 1B
V.R. ovptd. on Transvaal Vol. 2A, Vol. 6B
Vryburg .... Vol. 2A
Vuja-STT, Vujna-STT .... Vol. 6B

Wadhwan 334
Walachia .... Vol. 5B
Wales & Monmouthshire .... Vol. 3A
Wallis and Futuna Islands .... Vol. 6B
Walterborough, S.C. .... Vol. 1A
War Board of Trade .... Vol. 6A
Warrenton, Ga. .... Vol. 1A
Warsaw, Warszawa .... Vol. 5B
Washington, Ga. .... Vol. 1A
Watermarks (British Colonies) .... See
  table of contents

Weatherford, Tex. .... Vol. 1A
Weihnachten Joos van Cleve-Geburt
  Christi (Austria 2479) .... Vol. 1B
Wenden, Wendensche .... Vol. 5B
Western Army .... Vol. 4A
Western Australia .... Vol. 1A
Western Samoa .... Vol. 5B
Western Szechwan .... Vol. 2A
Western Thrace (Greek
  Occupation) .... Vol. 6B
Western Turkey .... Vol. 3A
Western Ukraine .... Vol. 6B
West Irian 389
West New Guinea .... 389, Vol. 1A
West Saxony .... Vol. 3A
Wet and dry printings .... Vol. 1A
Wharton's U.S. P.O. Despatch Vol.1A
White Russia .... Vol. 1B
Wiederaufbauspende .... Vol. 3A
Wilayah Persekutuan .... Vol. 4B
Wilkesboro, N.C. .... Vol. 1A
Williams City Post
Winnsborough, S.C. .... Vol. 1A
Wir sind frei .... Vol. 2B
Wn. .... Vol. 4A
Wohnungsbau .... Vol. 3A
Wolmaransstad .... Vol. 6B
World Health Organization .... Vol. 6A
World Intellectual Property
  Organization .... Vol. 6A
World Meteorological
  Organization .... Vol. 6A
Worldwide .... Vol. 3A
Wrangel issues .... Vol. 5B
Wurttemberg .... Vol. 3A
Wytheville, Va. .... Vol. 1A

Xeimappa .... Vol. 2B

Yambo .... Vol. 6A
Y.A.R. .... Vol. 6B
Yca .... Vol. 5A
Yemen .... Vol. 6B
Yemen Arab Republic .... Vol. 6B
Yemen People's Republic .... Vol. 6B
Yemen, People's Democratic
  Rep. .... Vol. 6B
Yen, Yn. .... Vol. 1A, Vol. 4A
Укр. Н.Р., Укрaiна .... Vol. 6B
Yksi Markka .... Vol. 2B
Yuan .... Vol. 2A
Yucatan .... Vol. 4B
Yudenich, Gen. .... Vol. 5B
Yugoslavia .... Vol. 6B
Yugoslavia (German Occupation) ... Vol. 6B
Yugoslavia (Italian Occupation) ... Vol. 6B
Yugoslavia (Trieste) .... Vol. 6B
Yugoslavia (Zone B) .... Vol. 6B
Yugoslavia Offices Abroad .... Vol. 6B
Yugoslavia stamps overprinted
  and surcharged .... Vol. 1B
Yunnan (China) .... Vol. 2A
Yunnan Fou, Yunnansen .... Vol. 2B

Za Crveni Krst (Yugoslavia
  #RA2) .... Vol. 6B
Z. Afr. Republiek, Z.A.R. .... Vol. 6B
Zaire .... Vol. 6B
Zambezia .... Vol. 6B
Zambia .... Vol. 6B
Zante 389
Zanzibar .... Vol. 6B
Zanzibar, French Offices .... Vol. 2B
Zanzibar (Kenya, Uganda,
  Tanganyika) .... Vol. 4A
Zanzibar-Tanzania .... Vol. 6B
Z.A.R. ovptd. on Cape of
  Good Hope .... Vol. 2A
Zelaya .... Vol. 5A
Zentraler Kurierdienst .... Vol. 3A
Zil Eloigne Sesel .... Vol. 6A
Zil Elwagne Sesel .... Vol. 6A
Zil Elwannyen Sesel .... Vol. 6A
Zimbabwe .... Vol. 6B
Zimska Pomoc ovptd. on Italy ... Vol. 6B
Zone A (Trieste) 701
Zone B (Istria) .... Vol. 6B
Zone B (Trieste) .... Vol. 6B
Zone Francaise .... Vol. 3A
Zuid Afrika .... Vol. 5A, Vol. 6B
Zuidafrikaansche Republiek ..... Vol. 6B
Zuidwest Afrika .... Vol. 6A
Zululand .... Vol. 6B
Zurich .... Vol. 6A

INDEX TO ADVERTISERS
2025 VOLUME 3B

ADVERTISER	PAGE
– A –	
Almaz Stamps	81
– G –	
Henry Gitner Philatelists, Inc.	535, 687
– H –	
Hungaria Stamp Exchange	83
– I –	
India and States LLC	317
Israelstamps.net	583
Indonesia Halim Stamp	339

ADVERTISER	PAGE
– K –	
Daniel F. Kelleher Auctions LLC	Inside Front Cover
– M –	
Mystic Stamp Co.	Back Cover
– P –	
Persiphila	391
Philasearch.com	47, 187, 225, 587, 591
– S –	
Stampbay.com	223

2025
VOLUME 3B
DEALER DIRECTORY
YELLOW PAGE LISTINGS

This section of your Scott Catalogue contains advertisements to help you conveniently find what you need, when you need it...!

Appraisals....................744	Collections...................744	Topicals - Columbus 744	Wanted Worldwide
Auctions 744	Ducks 744	United States................744	Collections 744
British	Hong Kong 744	U.S. - Classics/	Websites......................744
Commonwealth..........744	Korea 744	Moderns....................744	Worldwide....................744
Buying 744	New Issues..................744	U.S.-Collections	Worldwide -
Canada.......................744	Stamp Stores 744	Wanted 744	Collections 744
China..........................744	Supplies......................744		

Dealer Directory and Yellow Pages

Appraisals

DR. ROBERT FRIEDMAN & SONS STAMP & COIN BUYING CENTER
2029 W. 75th St.
Woodridge, IL 60517
PH: 800-588-8100
FAX: 630-985-1588
stampcollections@drbobstamps.com
www.drbobfriedmanstamps.com

Auctions

DUTCH COUNTRY AUCTIONS
The Stamp Center
4115 Concord Pike
Wilmington, DE 19803
PH: 302-478-8740
FAX: 302-478-8779
auctions@dutchcountryauctions.com
www.dutchcountryauctions.com

British Commonwealth

ARON R. HALBERSTAM PHILATELISTS, LTD.
PO Box 150168
Van Brunt Station
Brooklyn, NY 11215-0168
PH: 718-788-3978
arh@arhstamps.com
www.arhstamps.com

ROY'S STAMPS
PO Box 28001
600 Ontario Street
St. Catharines, ON
CANADA L2N 7P8
Phone: 905-934-8377
Email: roystamp@cogeco.ca
www.roysstamps.com

THE STAMP ACT
PO Box 1136
Belmont, CA 94002
PH: 650-703-2342
thestampact@sbcglobal.net

Buying

DR. ROBERT FRIEDMAN & SONS STAMP & COIN BUYING CENTER
2029 W. 75th St.
Woodridge, IL 60517
PH: 800-588-8100
FAX: 630-985-1588
stampcollections@drbobstamps.com
www.drbobfriedmanstamps.com

Canada

ROY'S STAMPS
PO Box 28001
600 Ontario Street
St. Catharines, ON
CANADA L2N 7P8
Phone: 905-934-8377
Email: roystamp@cogeco.ca
www.roysstamps.com

China

THE STAMP ACT
PO Box 1136
Belmont, CA 94002
PH: 650-703-2342
thestampact@sbcglobal.net

Collections

DR. ROBERT FRIEDMAN & SONS STAMP & COIN BUYING CENTER
2029 W. 75th St.
Woodridge, IL 60517
PH: 800-588-8100
FAX: 630-985-1588
stampcollections@drbobstamps.com
www.drbobfriedmanstamps.com

Ducks

MICHAEL JAFFE
PO Box 61484
Vancouver, WA 98666
PH: 360-695-6161
PH: 800-782-6770
FAX: 360-695-1616
mjaffe@brookmanstamps.com
www.brookmanstamps.com

Hong Kong

THE STAMP ACT
PO Box 1136
Belmont, CA 94002
PH: 650-703-2342
thestampact@sbcglobal.net

Korea

THE STAMP ACT
PO Box 1136
Belmont, CA 94002
PH: 650-703-2342
thestampact@sbcglobal.net

New Issues

DAVIDSON'S STAMP SERVICE
Personalized Service since 1970
PO Box 36355
Indianapolis, IN 46236-0355
PH: 317-826-2620
ed-davidson@earthlink.net
www.newstampissues.com

Stamp Stores

Delaware

DUTCH COUNTRY AUCTIONS
The Stamp Center
4115 Concord Pike
Wilmington, DE 19803
PH: 302-478-8740
FAX: 302-478-8779
auctions@dutchcountryauctions.com
www.dutchcountryauctions.com

Florida

DR. ROBERT FRIEDMAN & SONS STAMP & COIN BUYING CENTER
PH: 800-588-8100
FAX: 630-985-1588
stampcollections@drbobstamps.com
www.drbobfriedmanstamps.com

ROBERT M. SAZAMA
The Villages, FL 32163
PH: 931-561-7167
Email: bob@bobsazama.com
www.floridastampbuyer.com

Illinois

DR. ROBERT FRIEDMAN & SONS STAMP & COIN BUYING CENTER
2029 W. 75th St.
Woodridge, IL 60517
PH: 800-588-8100
FAX: 630-985-1588
stampcollections@drbobstamps.com
www.drbobfriedmanstamps.com

Indiana

KNIGHT STAMP & COIN CO.
237 Main St.
Hobart, IN 46342
PH: 219-942-4341
PH: 800-634-2646
knight@knightcoin.com
www.knightcoin.com

New Jersey

TRENTON STAMP & COIN
Thomas DeLuca
Store: Forest Glen Plaza
1800 Highway #33, Suite 103
Hamilton Square, NJ 08690
Mail: PO Box 8574
Trenton, NJ 08650
PH: 609-584-8100
FAX: 609-587-8664
TOMD4TSC@aol.com
www.trentonstampandcoin.com

Ohio

HILLTOP STAMP SERVICE
Richard A. Peterson
PO Box 626
Wooster, OH 44691
PH: 330-262-8907 (O)
PH: 330-201-1377 (C)
hilltop@bright.net
hilltopstamps@sssnet.com
www.hilltopstamps.com

Supplies

BROOKLYN GALLERY COIN & STAMP, INC.
8725 4th Ave.
Brooklyn, NY 11209
PH: 718-745-5701
FAX: 718-745-2775
info@brooklyngallery.com
www.brooklyngallery.com

Topicals - Columbus

MR. COLUMBUS
PO Box 1492
Fennville, MI 49408
PH: 269-543-4755
David@MrColumbus1492.com
www.MrColumbus1492.com

United States

ACS STAMP COMPANY
2914 W 135th Ave
Broomfield, Colorado 80020
303-841-8666
www.ACSstamp.com

BROOKMAN STAMP CO.
PO Box 90
Vancouver, WA 98666
PH: 360-695-1391
PH: 800-545-4871
FAX: 360-695-1616
info@brookmanstamps.com
www.brookmanstamps.com

U.S. Classics/Moderns

BARDO STAMPS
PO Box 7437
Buffalo Grove, IL 60089
PH: 847-634-2676
jfb7437@aol.com
www.bardostamps.com

U.S.-Collections Wanted

DUTCH COUNTRY AUCTIONS
The Stamp Center
4115 Concord Pike
Wilmington, DE 19803
PH: 302-478-8740
FAX: 302-478-8779
auctions@dutchcountryauctions.com
www.dutchcountryauctions.com

DR. ROBERT FRIEDMAN & SONS STAMP & COIN BUYING CENTER
2029 W. 75th St.
Woodridge, IL 60517
PH: 800-588-8100
FAX: 630-985-1588
stampcollections@drbobstamps.com
www.drbobfriedmanstamps.com

Wanted - Worldwide Collections

DUTCH COUNTRY AUCTIONS
The Stamp Center
4115 Concord Pike
Wilmington, DE 19803
PH: 302-478-8740
FAX: 302-478-8779
auctions@dutchcountryauctions.com
www.dutchcountryauctions.com

Websites

ACS STAMP COMPANY
2914 W 135th Ave
Broomfield, Colorado 80020
303-841-8666
www.ACSstamp.com

Worldwide

GUILLERMO JALIL
Maipu 466, local 4
1006 Buenos Aires
Argentina
guillermo@jalilstamps.com
philatino@philatino.com
www.philatino.com (worldwide stamp auctions)
www.jalilstamps.com (direct sale, worldwide stamps)

Worldwide-Collections

DR. ROBERT FRIEDMAN & SONS STAMP & COIN BUYING CENTER
2029 W. 75th St.
Woodridge, IL 60517
PH: 800-588-8100
FAX: 630-985-1588
stampcollections@drbobstamps.com
www.drbobfriedmanstamps.com